THE JOURNAL

OF

IMMUNOLOGY

VOLUME 105
NUMBERS 1 TO 3

BALTIMORE, MD. 21202
1970

JOIMA3

THE JOURNAL

OF

IMMUNOLOGY

VOLUME 105
NUMBERS 4 TO 6

BALTIMORE, MD. 21202
1970

JOIMA3

THE JOURNAL OF IMMUNOLOGY
Vol. 105, No. 6, December 1970

CONTENTS

NUMBER 1, JULY 1970

IMMUNOCHEMISTRY

Half-Lives, Body Distribution and Lack of Interconversion of Serum 19S and 7S IgM of Sharks. PARKER A. SMALL, JR., DAVID G. KLAPPER AND L. WILLIAM CLEM 29
Secretory IgA in Human Serum. R. H. WALDMAN, J. P. MACH, M. M. STELLA AND D. S. ROWE .. 43
The Subunit Structure of Mouse IgA. HOWARD M. GRAY, ALAN SHER AND NURIT SHALITIN 75
Physicochemical and Antigenic Studies on Human γE in Respiratory Fluid. RICHARD W. NEWCOMB AND KIMISHIGE ISHIZAKA 85
Studies on IgA. II. Isolation of IgA from Small Volumes of Human Serum by Immunoabsorption. TRUMAN O. ANDERSON, RAINER H. ZSCHOCKE AND GERHARD L. BACH 146
A Method for Preparing Monospecific Antisera to C1 Esterase (C1s): Microheterogeneity of Purified C1s. K. NAGAKI AND R. M. STROUD 162
Immunochemical Quantitation of Human C1 Esterase (C1s): Concentration in Normal Serum and Purification Yields. K. NAGAKI AND R. M. STROUD 170
The Relationship between Antibody Affinity and the Efficiency of Complement Fixation. ANTHONY S. FAUCI, MICHAEL M. FRANK AND JOHN S. JOHNSON 215
Studies on Human IgD. II. Physicochemical Characterization of Human IgD. ANIL SAHA, PARIMAL CHOWDHURY, SHELDON SAMBURY, YOUSSEF BEHELAK, DOUGLAS C. HEINER AND BRAM ROSE 238

IMMUNOGENETICS

Genetic and Cellular Factors in the Immune Response. I. Genetic Control of the Antibody Response to Poly Glu^{52} Lys^{33} Tyr^{15} in the Inbred Rat Strains ACI and F344. THOMAS J. GILL, III, HEINZ W. KUNZ, DANIEL J. STECHSCHULTE AND K. FRANK AUSTEN 14
Presence of Allotypic Specificities of Three Loci, *a*, *b* and *f*, on Individual Molecules of Rabbit Colostral γA Immunoglobulin. EDWARD A. LICHTER, THOMAS P. CONWAY, ALICE GILMAN-SACHS AND SHELDON DRAY 70
Genetic Control of the Antibody Response to Simple Haptens in Congenic Strains of Mice. W. E. RATHBUN AND W. H. HILDEMANN 98
γG Erythrocyte Autoantibodies: Comparison of *in Vivo* Complement Coating and *in Vitro* "Rh" Specificity. M. ELAINE EYSTER AND DAVID E. JENKINS, JR. 221

CELLULAR IMMUNOLOGY

Cytostasis of Mouse and Human Monolayer Cell Cultures by Normal, Unstimulated Lymphocytes. CRAWFORD W. JAMIESON AND JOHN H. WALLACE 7
Tonsillar Tissue Implants in Neonatally Thymectomized Mice. I. Effect on the Spleen. BETTINA HALL HARRISON 38
Inhibition of Target Cell Proliferation by Supernatants from Cultures of Human Peripheral Lymphocytes. J. A. GREEN, S. R. COOPERBAND, J. A. RUTSTEIN AND S. KIBRICK 48
Transformation of Mouse Lymphocytes to Allogeneic Lymphocytes and Phytohemagglutinin. RICHARD J. MANGI AND MICHAEL R. MARDINEY, JR. 90
The Effect of Heterologous Antilymphocyte Serum (ALS) on the Humoral Antibody Response to *Salmonella typhi* "H" Antigen and Bovine Serum Albumin. EUGENE M. LANCE 108
The Immune Response to Heterologous Red Cells in Mice. V. The Effect of Cyclophosphamide and Cortisone on Antigenic Competition. PETER DUKOR AND FELIX M. DIETRICH 118
Identification of Two Cell Populations Required for Mouse Immunocompetence. THOMAS BRODY 126
Ontogeny of Cell Populations Required for Immunocompetence. THOMAS BRODY AND BEN W. PAPERMASTER 139
Immunoglobulin Classes of Antibody-Forming Cells in Mice. IV. The Incorporation of Tritiated Thymidine into IgM and γ_1 Plaque-Forming Cells during the Primary Immune Response. ALBERT A. NORDIN, HUMBERTO COSENZA AND STEWART SELL 154
Delayed Hypersensitivity to *Trichinella spiralis*. III. Effect of Repeated Sensitizations in Donors and Recipients. C. W. KIM, M. J. JAMUAR AND L. D. HAMILTON 175

Early Mast Cell Responses in Mouse Popliteal Lymph Nodes to Localized Primary Antigenic Stimuli. AUDREY N. ROBERTS 187
The Immune Response of Mice to *Serratia marcescens* LPS or Intact Bacteria. CHARLES FIELD, JERRY L. ALLEN AND HERMAN FRIEDMAN 193
Characteristics of the *in Vitro* Response of Guinea Pig Blood Lymphocytes to PHA and Antigen. S. MICHAEL PHILLIPS AND BURTON ZWEIMAN 204
Migratory Response of Granulomatous Alveolar Cells from BCG-Sensitized Rabbits. BENITO GALINDO AND QUENTIN N. MYRVIK 227

IMMUNOPATHOLOGY

Metabolism of γG and γM Immunoglobulins in Normal and Hypogammaglobulinemic Chickens. D. FROMMEL, D. Y. E. PEREY AND R. A. GOOD 1
Depletion of Plasma Complement *in Vivo* by a Protein of Cobra Venom: Its Effect on Various Immunologic Reactions. CHARLES G. COCHRANE, HANS J. MÜLLER-EBERHARD AND BARBARA S. AIKIN 55
The Assessment by Immunofluorescence Methods of Humoral Anti-Myelin Antibodies in Man. THOMAS S. EDGINGTON AND DONALD J. DALESSIO 248

COMMUNICATIONS

L-Asparaginase in Experimental Auto-Immune Disease: Inhibition of Allergic Encephalomyelitis. AMANULLAH KHAN, JOSEPH M. HILL AND MITSUO ADACHI 256
Cells Involved in the Immune Response. XVII. The Elution of Antigen-Reactive Cells from Antigen-Sensitized Glass Bead Columns. The High Affinity of These Cells for the Glass Bead-Adsorbed Antigen. MAXWELL RICHTER 259
Some Characteristics of Anti-Dinitrophenyl Antibody of the Gray Snapper. WARREN J. RUSSELL, EDWARD W. VOSS, JR. AND M. MICHAEL SIGEL 262
An Immunogenic Polysaccharide-Protein Conjugate. R. J. FIELDER, C. T. BISHOP, S. F. GRAPPEL AND F. BLANK 265
Consumption of Hamster Complement by Bacterial Endotoxin. WILLIAM A. HOOK, RALPH SNYDERMAN AND STEPHAN E. MERGENHAGEN 268
Glycosyl Transferases for Mouse IgG. ISAAC SCHENKEIN AND JONATHAN W. UHR 271
Evidence for Synthesis of Human Colostral γA as 11S Dimer. JOHN BIENENSTOCK AND HANS STRAUSS 274

NUMBER 2, AUGUST 1970

IMMUNOCHEMISTRY

A Specific Method for Purification of the Second Component of Guinea Pig Complement and a Chemical Evaluation of the One-Hit Theory. MANFRED M. MAYER, JIMMIE A. MILLER AND HYUN S. SHIN 327
Streptococcal Group A Polysaccharide Haptens: Susceptibility to Degradation by β-N-Acetyl-glucosaminidases and Antibody-Combining Capacity of Haptens. ELIA M. AYOUB AND WILLARD C. SCHMIDT 342
Synthesis of the Ninth Component of Complement by a Clonal Strain of Rat Hepatoma Cells. FRED A. ROMMEL, MARVIN B. GOLDLUST, FRANK C. BANCROFT, MANFRED M. MAYER AND ARMEN H. TASHJIAN, JR. 396
Antigenic Analysis of Human Heart Tissue. Antigens with Restricted Organ Distribution in Acid Extracts of Human Myocardium. ENRIQUE ESPINOSA AND MELVIN H. KAPLAN 416
Dissociation of a Small Proportion of a Human IgM Population into Fc_μ, Fab_μ, and Free Light Chains Following Reduction. JAMES E. MORRIS AND F. P. INMAN 451
Variation in the Size of Antibody Sites for the Poly-L-Aspartate Hapten during the Immune Response. P. DIANNE MURPHY AND HARVEY J. SAGE 460
Immunochemical Studies of Phospholipids. VI. Haptenic Activity of Phosphatidylinositol and the Role of Lecithin as an Auxiliary Lipid. TATESHI KATAOKA AND SHOSHICHI NOJIMA 502
Studies on Brain Antigens. IV. Isolation and Partial Characterization of a Rat Species-Restricted Antigen of Nervous Tissue (SRANT). ATHANASIA LIAKOPOULOU AND CATHERINE F. C. MACPHERSON 512

IMMUNOGENETICS

The Antigenic Specificity of Blood Groups Which Differentiate Populations of Fresh Water Catfish. William J. Kuhns, Joseph V. Chuba and Ross F. Nigrelli 299
Genetic Control of the Specificity of Anti-DNP Antibodies. I. Differences in the Specificity of Anti-DNP Antibody Produced by Mammalian Species. Takeshi Yoshida, William E. Paul and Baruj Benacerraf 306
Genetic Control of the Specificity of Anti-DNP Antibodies. II. Differences in the Specificity of Anti-DNP Antibody Produced by Several Inbred Strains of Mice. William E. Paul, Takeshi Yoshida and Baruj Benacerraf 314

CELLULAR IMMUNOLOGY

Role of the Thymus in Tolerance. IX. Inhibition of Experimental Autoallergic Encephalomyelitis by Intrathymic Injection of Encephalitogen. George W. Ellison and Byron H. Waksman. 322
Antigen Binding and the Immune Response. I. The Early Primary Response to a Protein Antigen. Farrokh Modabber and Eli Sercarz 355
The Cytophilic Activity of Human Immunoglobulins. Christopher Inchley, Howard M. Grey and Jonathan W. Uhr 362
Interrelationships of Tolerance and Immunity. I. Induction of Immunology Tolerance in Adult Mice to Bovine γ-Globulin Purified *in Vitro*. Yi-Chi M. Kong and Donna L. Wiger 370
The Effects of a Blockading Agent on the Primary Immune Response. J. Gabriel Michael and Caroline Murray 441
Immunosuppressive Effect of Serum from CBA Mice Made Tolerant by the Supernatant from Ultracentrifuged Bovine γ-Globulin. James L. Tong and Dorothy Boose 426
Development of Antibody-Forming Cells in Neonatal Mice: Stimulation and Inhibition by Calf Thymus Fractions. Terry L. Hand, Walter S. Ceglowski, Damri Damrongsak and Herman Friedman 442
Delayed Hypersensitivity. IV. Hapten-Specific Delayed Reactions; Interaction of Immune Serum and Sensitized Cells. John P. Phair and Fred S. Kantor 471

IMMUNOPATHOLOGY

Antigen Quantitation in Experimental Immune Complex Glomerulonephritis. I. Acute Serum Sickness. Curtis B. Wilson and Frank J. Dixon 279
Complement and Conglutinin in the Serum of Germ-Free and Conventional Piglets. O. Barta, Vera Barta, O. P. Miniats and D. G. Ingram 350
Mechanisms of Release of Constituents from Rabbit Platelets by Antigen-Antibody Complexes and Complement. I. Lytic and Nonlytic Reactions. Peter M. Henson 476
Mechanisms of Release of Constituents from Rabbit Platelets by Antigen-Antibody Complexes and Complement. II. Interaction of Platelets with Neutrophils. Peter M. Henson 490

MICROBIAL AND VIRAL IMMUNOLOGY

Antigenic and Immunogenic Properties of Components Contained in Rabies Virus-Infected Tissue Culture Fluids. H. Dieter Schlumberger, Tadeusz J. Wiktor and Hilary Koprowski .. 291
Quantitative and Qualitative Studies of Antibody to Streptococcal M-Protein. Bascom F. Anthony 379
Immunochemical Analysis of a Uronic Acid Polymer of *Staphylococcus epidermidis* Strain 53. Hugh C. McDonald and Walter W. Karakawa 389
Heterogeneity of Immune Response to the Somatic (O) Antigens of *Proteus mirabilis*. James W. Smith, Jack A. Barnett and Jay P. Sanford 404
Characteristics of the Serum Vibriocidal and Agglutinating Antibodies in Cholera Cases and in Normal Residents of the Endemic and Non-Endemic Cholera Areas. Ansaruddin Ahmed, A. K. Bhattacharjee and Wiley H. Mosley 431

COMMUNICATIONS

Reaction of Serum from Pregnant Hamsters with Surface of Cells Transformed by SV40. Ronald Duff and Fred Rapp 521
Fetal Antigen Capable of Inducing Transplantation Immunity against SV40 Hamster Tumor Cells. J. H. Coggin, K. R. Ambrose and N. G. Anderson 524

Cellular Reactivity to Tuberculin in Immune and Serologically-Unresponsive Guinea Pigs. BERNARD W. JANICKI, GERALDINE P. SCHECHTER AND KAREN E. SCHULTZ 527
Recpirocal Neutralizing Cross-Reaction between Rhinovirus Types 9 and 32. MARION K. COONEY AND GEORGE E. KENNY 531
The Unblocked N-Terminal Sequence of Chicken IgG λ-like Light Chains. RALPH T. KUBO, IRWIN Y. ROSENBLUM AND ALBERT A. BENEDICT 534

NUMBER 3, SEPTEMBER 1970

IMMUNOCHEMISTRY

Antigenicity of Polypeptides (Poly α Amino Acids): Calcium-Dependent and Independent Antibodies. PAUL H. MAURER, L. G. CLARK AND P. A. LIBERTI 567
Independence of Allotypic Determinants and Antibody Specificity. SUSAN B. SPRING, ALFRED NISONOFF AND SHELDON DRAY 653
Rabbit IgA, IgM and IgG Antihapten Responses Assayed by C1a Fixation and Transfer. JOHN D. CLOUGH, JUNE ZACCARI AND WARREN STROBER 687
Quantitation of Canine Immunoglobulins. HERBERT Y. REYNOLDS AND JOHN S. JOHNSON 698
The Evolution of the Immune Response. VII. Antibody to Human "O" Cells and Properties of the Immunoglobulin in Lamprey. BERNARD POLLARA, GARY W. LITMAN, JOANNE FINSTAD, JOHN HOWELL AND ROBERT A. GOOD 738

IMMUNOGENETICS

Conversion of Non-Immune Rabbit Spleen Cells by Ribonucleic Acid of Lymphoid Cells from an Immunized Rabbit to Produce IgG Antibody of Foreign Light Chain Allotype. CLARA BELL AND SHELDON DRAY 541

CELLULAR IMMUNOLOGY

Frequency of Single Spleen Cells from Hyperimmune Rabbits Producing Antibody of Two Different Specificities. DAVID C. BENJAMIN AND WILLIAM O. WEIGLE 537
Ribonucleic Acid Synthesis in Rabbit Lymph Node Cells. HELAINE A. DONAHUE, VIRGINIA G. MOORE AND J. RUSSELL LITTLE 592
The Effect of Prior Transfusion on Marrow Grafts between Histocompatible Canine Siblings. RAINER STORB, ROBERT B. EPSTEIN, ROBERT H. RUDOLPH AND E. DONNALL THOMAS 627
Staircase Rise in the Antibody-Forming Cell Population in Secondary Response. TOSHIHIKO SADO, E. H. PERKINS AND T. MAKINODAN 642
Interaction of Lymphocytes and a Radioresistant Cell in PPD-Stimulated Human Leukocyte Cultures. GERALDINE P. SCHECHTER AND WILLIAM MCFARLAND 661
Receptor Sites for Complement on Certain Human Peripheral Blood Lymphocytes. GERHARD MICHLMAYR AND HEINZ HUBER 670
Detection of Immune Response against Synthetic Polymers of Amino Acids Employing the Plaque-Forming Cell System. III. Cross-Reaction Patterns of Antibody Secreted *in Vitro* against Immunochemically Related Synthetic Polypeptides. MARIANNE EGAN AND PAUL H. MAURER 704
Detection of Immune Response against Synthetic Polymers of Amino Acids Employing the Plaque-Forming Cell System. IV. Effect of Incorporation of Soluble Polypeptides into the Plaque Assay Medium. MARIANNE EGAN AND PAUL H. MAURER 710
Differentiation of Rosette-Forming Cells from Myeloid Stem Cells. G. E. EDWARDS, R. G. MILLER AND R. A. PHILLIPS 719
Initiation of Antibody Responses by Different Classes of Lymphocytes. II. Differences in the Tissue Distribution of Lymphocytes Involved in Primary and Secondary Antibody Responses. SAMUEL STROBER 730
Initiation of Antibody Responses by Different Classes of Lymphocytes. III. Differences in the Proliferative Rates of Thoracic Duct Lymphocytes Involved in Primary and Secondary Responses. SAMUEL STROBER 734
An *in Vitro* Correlative Assay for the Immunosuppressive Activity of Horse Anti-Rat Lymphocyte Sera: Estimation of Lymphocytophilic Antibody Activity Using ^{51}Cr-Labeled Thymocytes. MICHAEL K. BACH, JOHN R. BRASHLER AND ROBERT J. PERPER 746
The Induction of Bacteriophage-Neutralizing Antibody by Mouse Spleen Immunogenic RNA. I. Preparation and Properties of Immunogenic RNA. HERBERT B. HERSCOWITZ AND PETER STELOS 771

The Induction of Bacteriophage-Neutralizing Antibody by Mouse Spleen Immunogenic RNA. II. Evidence for the Presence of Phage Antigen in Immunogenic RNA. HERBERT B. HERSCOWITZ AND PETER STELOS 779

IMMUNOPATHOLOGY

Delayed Hypersensitivity to Insulin and Its Component Polypeptide Chains. CONNIE CLARK AND J. MUNOZ 574
The Effect of Cyclophosphamide on the Ontogeny of the Humoral Immune Response in Chickens. S. P. LERMAN AND W. P. WEIDANZ 614
Mechanism of Reticuloendothelial System Blockade Produced by Antilymphocyte Serum. JOHN SHEAGREN, ROLF F. BARTH, JOSEPH B. EDELIN AND RICHARD A. MALMGREN 634
Patterns of Serologic Specificity of Human γG Erythrocyte Autoantibodies. Correlation of Antibody Specificity with Complement-Fixing Behavior. JOHN P. LEDDY, PHYLLIS PETERSON, MARILYN A. YEAW AND RICHARD F. BAKEMEIER 677
Studies on the Cytotoxic Immune Reaction. I. The Action of Antibodies on Normal and Regenerating Corneal Tissues. W. MANSKI, G. EHRLICH AND F. M. POLACK 755
Studies on the Cytotoxic Immune Reaction. II. The Action of Antibodies on Normal and Metabolically Inhibited Tissue Cultures. W. MANSKI AND G. EHRLICH 764

MICROBIAL AND VIRAL IMMUNOLOGY

Immunochemical Studies of Foot-and-Mouth Disease. VIII. Detection and Quantitation of Antibodies by Radial Immunodiffusion. K. M. COWAN AND G. G. WAGNER 557
Changes in IgA and IgG Concentrations in Nasal Secretions Prior to the Appearance of Antibody during Viral Respiratory Infection in Man. WILLIAM T. BUTLER, THOMAS A. WALDMANN, ROGER D. ROSSEN, R. GORDAN DOUGLAS, JR. AND ROBERT B. COUCH 584
Complement Fixation and Immunodiffusion Tests for Assay of Hepatitis-Associated "Australia" Antigen and Antibodies. NATHALIE J. SCHMIDT AND EDWIN H. LENNETTE 604
Neuraminidase- and Hemagglutinin-Inhibiting Antibodies in Serum and Nasal Secretions of Volunteers Immunized with Attenuated and Inactivated Influenza B/Eng/13/65 Virus Vaccines. JEAN C. DOWNIE 620

COMMUNICATIONS

Structural Studies of Immunoglobulin E. II. Amino Terminal Sequence of the Heavy Chain. WILLIAM D. TERRY, MAKIO OGAWA AND SHAUL KOCHWA 783
Measurement of IgA Levels in Human Cord Serum by a New Radioimmunoassay. W. FAULKNER AND L. BORELLA 786
Appendix and γM-Antibody Formation. IV. Synergism of Appendix and Bone Marrow Cells in Early Antibody Response to Sheep Erythrocytes. H. OZER AND B. H. WAKSMAN 791
Relationship of Epstein-Barr Virus-Induced Membrane Antigens in Lymphoid Cells to Viral Envelop Antigens. PAUL GERBER AND GERALD GOLDSTEIN 793

NUMBER 4, OCTOBER 1970

IMMUNOCHEMISTRY

Passive Hemagglutination. II. Titration of Antibody against Determinants Unique for Aggregated Denatured Bovine Serum Albumin and Further Studies on Gelatin. GERALD WOLBERG, CHI TAN LIU AND FRANK L. ADLER 797
A Pre-Albumin Activator of Prekallikrein. ALLEN P. KAPLAN AND K. FRANK AUSTEN 802
Biologic Properties of a Mouse IgG2a Myeloma Protein with Anti-Dinitrophenyl Activity. NOEL L. WARNER AND ZOLTAN OVARY 812
Studies of Maleylated Chains of Human IgM. A. F. S. A. HABEEB, RALPH E. SCHROHENLOHER AND J. CLAUDE BENNETT 846
The Effect of Selective Modification of Tryptophan, Lysine and Arginine Residues of Basic Brain Protein on Encephalitogenic Activity. ROBERT H. SWANBORG 865
Degradation of Immunoglobulins by Intracellular Proteases in the Range of Neutral pH. JOSEPH J. LOSPALLUTO, KURT FEHR AND MORRIS ZIFF 886
Immunologic Responses of Pacific Hagfish. III. Serum Antibodies to Cellular Antigens. D. SCOTT LINTHICUM AND W. H. HILDEMANN 912

Hidden Rheumatoid Factors Reacting with "Non a" and Other Antigens of Native Autologous IgG. PER IVAR GAARDER AND JACOB B. NATVIG 928
Protein A from *Staphylococcus aureus*. X. Complement-Fixing Activity of Complexes between Protein A and Myeloma IgG or Papain Fragments of IgG. G. STÅLENHEIM AND J. SJÖQUIST .. 944
Characterization of a Monoclonal Canine Macroglobulin. J. DONALD CAPRA AND ARTHUR I. HURVITZ 949
Degradation of Immunoglobulin G by Lysosomal Acid Proteases. KURT FEHR, JOSEPH LOSPALLUTO AND MORRIS ZIFF 973
Biologic Activities of Peromyscus $7S\gamma_1$ and $7S\gamma_2$ Globulins. J. COE, L. PEEL AND R. F. SMITH 1006
Antigenicity of Polypeptides (Poly α Amino Acids): Immunogenicity of a Homopolymer Derivative PAUL H. MAURER 1011
Complement Fixation: The Effects of IgG and IgM Antibody Concentration on C1-Binding Affinity. WILLIAM D. LINSCOTT 1013
Studies of the Mechanism of Heat Aggregation of Human γG. WIPRECHT AUGENER AND HOWARD M. GREY 1024

IMMUNOGENETICS

Identification and Genetic Control of the Mt-3 and Mt-4 Allotypes of Rabbit Serum α_2-Macroglobulin. BERNARD H. BERNE, SHELDON DRAY AND KATHERINE L. KNIGHT 856
Genetic Control of the Immune Response in Mice. II. A Two-Way Selection Experiment for Specific Immunologic Competence. DAVID L. GASSER 908

CELLULAR IMMUNOLOGY

Natural and Antibody-Induced Adherence of Guinea Pig Phagocytic Cells to Autologous and Heterologous Thymocytes. ISRAEL SIEGEL 879
A Cytolytic System for the *in Vitro* Detection of Cell Mediated Immunity to Soluble Antigen. CHRISTOPHER S. HENNEY 919
The Kinetics of *in Vivo* Tolerance Introduction in Mice. SAROJ DAS AND SIDNEY LESKOWITZ .. 938
Antibody Production by Host Cells in X-Irradiated Recipients of Allogeneic Spleen Cells. U. STORB AND R. S. WEISER 957
Cellular Recognition by Mouse Lymphocytes *in Vitro*. II. Specific Stimulation by Histocompatibility Antigens in Mixed Cell Culture. W. H. ADLER, T. TAKIGUCHI, B. MARSH AND R. T. SMITH 984
Immunologic Tolerance to *Escherichia coli* Somatic Antigen Assessed by Bacteriolytic and Hemolytic Plaque Assays. JERRY L. ALLEN AND HERMAN FRIEDMAN 1001

IMMUNOPATHOLOGY

Persistent Lymphocytic Choriomeningitis Viral Infection. II. Virus-Anti-Viral Antibody Complexes and Associated Chronic Disease Following Transplacental Infection. MICHAEL B. A. OLDSTONE AND FRANK J. DIXON 829
The Effect of Aging on Human Serum Immunoglobulin Concentration. C. E. BUCKLEY, III AND F. C. DORSEY 964

MICROBIAL AND VIRAL IMMUNOLOGY

An Immunologic Marker Technique for the Cendehill Vaccine Strain of Rubella Virus. J. S. OXFORD AND C. W. POTTER 818
Immunologic Detection of Single-Stranded DNA in Adeno-Associated Satellite Virions. E. V. BARNETT, K. TORIKAI AND H. D. MAYOR 824
Immunoprecipitation Analysis of Soluble Complement-Fixing Antigens of Dengue Viruses. PHILIP K. RUSSELL, DUMRONG CHIEWSILP AND WALTER E. BRANDT 838
Studies on the Immune Capabilities of Chiroptera. I. Quantitative and Qualitative Nature of the Immune Responses in Bats to Bacteriophage ϕX174. BETTY A. HATTEN, RAE ALLEN AND S. EDWARD SULKIN 872
Cellular and Antibody Reactions to Streptococcal M Protein Types 1, 3, 6 and 12. LAUREN M. PACHMAN AND EUGENE N. FOX 898

COMMUNICATIONS

Streptococcal M Protein Vaccines, Rheumatic Fever and Human Histocompatibility Antigens. EUGENE N. FOX AND RAYMOND D. A. PETERSON 1031

Subgroup-Specific Antigenic Marker on Immunoglobulin λ Chains: Identification of Three Subtypes of the Variable Region. FRANK W. TISCHENDORF, MARGRIT M. TISCHENDORF AND ELLIOTT F. OSSERMAN 1033
Serologic Evidence That Infectious Canine Hepatitis Virus Commonly Infects Humans and Is Related to Human Adenovirus Type 8. KENDALL O. SMITH, WARREN D. GEHLE AND WILLIAM T. KNIKER 1036
Herpes-Like Virus (EB Virus) in Continuous Lymphoblastoid Cell Lines from Patients with Viral Hepatitis. DAVID P. STEVENS, LEWELLYS F. BARKER, HOPE E. HOPPS AND HARRY M. MEYER, JR. 1040
Enhancement by Reducing Agents of the Transformation of Human and Rabbit Peripheral Lymphocytes. MICHAEL W. FANGER, DAVID A. HART, J. VIVIAN WELLS AND ALFRED NISONOFF .. 1043
A Method for Typing Rabbit Sera for the A14 and A15 Allotypes with Cross-Linked Antisera S. LANDUCCI TOSI AND R. G. MAGE 1046
Predominant Contribution of IgA Antibody-Forming Cells to an Immune Response Detected in Extraintestinal Lymphoid Tissues of Germ-free Mice Exposed to Antigen by the Oral Route. H. BAZIN, G. LEVI AND G. DORIA 1049
Experience with a Mixed Lymphocyte-Tumor Reaction as a Method of Detecting Antigenic Differences between Normal and Neoplastic Cells. STEVEN P. KANNER, MICHAEL R. MARDINEY, JR. AND RICHARD J. MANGI 1052

NUMBER 5, NOVEMBER 1970

IMMUNOCHEMISTRY

Further Studies on Guinea Pig Skin Sensitizing Activities of Human Myeloma Proteins. ZOLTAN OVARY, HENRY G. KUNKEL AND FENNEKE G. JOSLIN 1103
Protein A Reactivity with Mouse Immunoglobulins: Structural Relationship between Some Mouse and Human Immunoglobulins. GÖRAN KRONVALL, HOWARD M. GREY AND RALPH C. WILLIAMS, JR. 1116
Antigenic Properties of Chemically Modified Collagen. R. TIMPL, I. WOLFF, W. MEIGEL, B. PONTZ, C. STEFFEN AND K. KÜHN 1131
A Method for Preparing Specific Fluorescein-Conjugated Antibody Reagents Using Bentonite Immunoadsorbents. MARGARET A. REISBERG, ROGER D. ROSSEN AND WILLIAM T. BUTLER .. 1151
Conversion of Soluble Immune Complex into Complement-Fixing Aggregates by IgM-Rheumatoid Factor. JOSEPH T. TEZAR AND FRANK R. SCHMID 1206
Structural and Antigenic Relationships between Avian Immunoglobulins. III. Antigenic Relationships of the Immunoglobulins of the Chicken, Pheasant and Japanese Quail. GERRIE A. LESLIE AND ALBERT A. BENEDICT 1215
Studies on Equine Immunoglobulins. II. Antigenic Interrelationships among Horse IgG, IgG(T) and Antipneumococcal γ_1-Component. CHARLES M. HELMS AND PETER Z. ALLEN 1253
Hypersensitivity to Ascaris Antigens. V. Production of Homocytotropic Antibodies in the Rabbit. GILL STREJAND AND DAN H. CAMPBELL 1264
The Evolution of the Immune Response. VIII. Structural Studies of the Lamprey Immunoglobulin. G. W. LITMAN, D. FROMMEL, J. FINSTAD, J. HOWELL, B. W. POLARA AND R. A. GOOD 1278

IMMUNOGENETICS

Antibody Responses to Two Synthetic Polypeptides: The Role of the Thymic Epithelial Reticulum. MARVIN L. TYAN AND HUGH O. MCDEVITT 1190

CELLULAR IMMUNOLOGY

Release of Virus Inhibitor from Tuberculin-Sensitized Peritoneal Cells Stimulated by Antigen. LEONARD N. MILSTONE AND BYRON H. WAKSMAN 1068
Abrogation of Immunologic Unresponsiveness by Whole Molecules and Fragments of Cross-Reacting. R. W. SCALES AND J. M. CRUSE 1072
Roles of Lymphoid Cells in Passive Transfer with Plasma of Delyed Hypersensitivity in Guinea Pigs. J. M. DUPUY AND R. A. GOOD 1111
Activation of Normal Rabbit Macrophage Monolayers by Supernatants of Antigen-Stimulated Lymphocytes. JOHN J. MOONEY AND BYRON H. WAKSMAN 1138
Hydrocortisone Resistance of Graft *vs* Host Activity in Mouse Thymus, Spleen and Bone Marrow. J. JOHN COHEN, MICHAEL FISCHBACH AND HENRY N. CLAMAN 1146

Heterogeneity of Blastogenic Factors Produced *in Vitro* by Antigenically Stimulated and Unstimulated Leukocytes. SHINPEI KASAKURA 1162
The Termination of Immunologic Unresponsiveness to BSA in Rabbits. II. Response to a Subsequent Injection of BSA. DAVID C. BENJAMIN AND WILLIAM O. WEIGLE 1231
In Vitro Induction of Sulfanilic Acid-Specific Antibodies by RNA Extracted from Rat Spleen. D. S. JURAS AND P. ABRAMOFF 1244
Procarbazine as an Immunosuppressant in Animals. P. BRIAN STEWART AND ROSALIND BELL 1271

IMMUNOPATHOLOGY

Biochemical Demonstration of the Activatable Esterase of the Rabbit Neutrophil Involved in the Chemotactic Response. PETER A. WARD AND ELMER L. BECKER 1057
Immunochemical and Biologic Properties of Rat IgE. I. Immunochemical Identification of Rat IgE. DANIEL J. STECHSCHULTE, ROBERT P. ORANGE AND K. FRANK AUSTEN 1082
Immunochemical and Biologic Properties of Rat IgE. II. Capacity to Mediate the Immunologic Release of Histamine and Slow-Reacting Substance of Anaphylaxis (SRS-A). ROBERT P. ORANGE, DANIEL J. STECHSCHULTE AND K. FRANK AUSTEN 1087
Immunochemical and Biologic Properties of Rat IgE. III. Modulation of the IgE-Mediated Release of Slow-Reacting Substance of Anaphylaxis by Agents Influencing the Level of Cyclic 3′, 5′-Adenosine Monophosphate. WILLIAM J. KOOPMAN, ROBERT P. ORANGE AND K. FRANK AUSTEN 1096
Apparent False-Positive Reactions in a Serologic Test for Syphilis and Presence of Antinuclear Factor in Hybrids of NZB and A/J Mice. LESLIE C. NORINS, LESLIE C. LOGAN AND MARJORIE A. LANTZ 1108
Physical Separation of Hemopoietic Stem Cells from Cells Causing Graft-*vs*-Host Disease. I. Sedimentation Properties of Cells Causing Graft-*vs*-Host Disease. R. A. PHILLIPS AND R. G. MILLER 1168
Production of Congenital Malformations Using Tissue Antisera. VIII. Effectiveness of Reduced, Alkylated and Digested Anti-Kidney Antibodies. J. ROBERT BRAGONIER, MICHAEL M. FRANK AND ROBERT L. BRENT 1175
The Prevention of Autoimmunity to the Thyroid and Allergic Thyroiditis by Antigenic Competition. PHILIP R. B. MCMASTER AND MICHAEL KYRIAKOS 1201
Immunologic Properties of the Main Encephalitogenic Peptide from the Basic Protein of Human Myelin. VANDA A. LENNON, ANN V. WILKS AND PATRICK R. CARNEGIE 1223

MICROBIAL AND VIRAL IMMUNOLOGY

Cross-Reactions among Group A Streptococci. III. The M and R Antigens of Type 43 and Serologically Related Streptococci. GROVE G. WILEY AND PAULINE N. BRUNO 1124
Characterization of Surface Antigen on Cells Infected by Fibroma Virus. WAYNE A. F. TOMPKINS, NORMAN A. CROUCH, S. S. TEVETHIA AND WILLIAM E. RAWLS 1181
A Type-Specific Immunodiffusion Technique for the California Encephalitis Virus Group. F. M. WELLINGS, G. E. SATHER AND W. MCD. HAMMON 1194

COMMUNICATIONS

Heterogeneity of Carbohydrate Content of Human Iga Myeloma Proteins. AN-CHUAN WANG AND H. HUGH FUDENBERG 1286
Inhibition of Guinea Pig Complement by Aromatic Amidine aud Guanidine Compounds. DAVID H. BING 1289
Use of Immunoadsorption Techniques in the Preparation of Chemical Agammaglobulinemia. D. FROMMEL, J. M. DUPUY, G. W. LITMAN AND R. A. GOOD 1292
Pepsin Digestion of Mouse Antibody. FRANCIS B. CASEY AND SEI TOKUDA 1294
Homologous Serum Passive Cutaneous Anaphylaxis in Guinea Pigs Mediated by Two $\gamma 1$ or $\gamma 1$-Type Heat-Stable Globulins and a Non-$\gamma 1$ Heat-Labile Reagin W. E. PARISH 1296
Ultrastructural Analysis of Hemolysin-Forming Cell Clusters. I. Preliminary Observations. GEORGE C. SAUNDERS AND WILLIAM S. HAMMOND 1299
Lymphocytes and Yellow Fever. I. Transient Virus Refractory State following Vaccination of Man with 17-D Strain. E. FREDERICK WHEELOCK, STEPHEN T. TOY AND RUNE L. STJERNHOLM 1304
Plasma Kinin System: Proenzyme Components. KIRK D. WUEPPER, ERNEST S. TUCKER, III AND CHARLES G. COCHRANE 1307

NUMBER 6, DECEMBER 1970

IMMUNOCHEMISTRY

Canine Secretory Immunoglobulins: Identification of Secretory Component. JOHN RICKS, MARY ROBERTS AND ROY PATTERSON 1327
Biological and Chemical Properties of Natural Antibodies in the Nurse Shark. STUART RUDIKOFF, EDWARD W. VOSS AND M. MICHAEL SIGEL 1344
Immunochemical Studies on the Interaction between Staphylococcal Protein A and γG Globulin. GÖRAN KRONVALL, RONALD P. MESSNER AND RALPH C. WILLIAMS, JR. 1353
Immune Hemolysis and the Functional Properties of the Second (C2) and Fourth (C4) Components of Complement. I. Functional Differences among C4 Sites on Cell Surfaces. TIBOR BORSOS, HERBERT J. RAPP AND HARVEY R. COLTEN 1439
Reactivity of Normal Shark Immunoglobulins with Nitrophenyl Ligands. GERRIE A. LESLIE AND L. WILLIAM CLEM 1547

CELLULAR IMMUNOLOGY

Transfer of the Delayed Hypersensitivity Skin Reaction in the Guinea Pig Using RNA-Treated Lymphoid Cells. R. E. JUREZIZ, D. E. THOR AND S. DRAY 1313
Specific Inhibition of an Anti-Hapten Immune Response by Chemical Modification of Cells. DAVID NAOR, ROBERT I. MISHELL AND LEON WOFSY 1322
Interspecies "Transfer" of Delayed Hypersensitivity *in Vitro* with RNA Extracts. RONALD E. PAQUE AND SHELDON DRAY 1334
Thymus Dependency of the Immune Response to Hemocyanin: An Evaluation of the Role of Macrophages in Thymectomized Mice. EMIL R. UNANUE 1339
Electron Microscopic Study of Inhibition of Macrophage Migration in Delayed Hypersensitivity. A. COLLIER SMYTH AND LEON WEISS 1360
Primary Rejection of Homologous Intraperitoneal Fibroblasts: An Electron Microscopic Study. LEON WEISS AND PRUDENCE SMYTH 1375
An *in Vitro* Model of the Anamnestic Response of Rabbit Lymph Node Cell Suspensions to Keyhole Limpet Hemocyanin. HERBERT B. HERSCOWITZ AND ABRAM B. STAVITSKY 1389
Studies on Rabbit Lymphocytes *in Vitro*. XIII. The Induction of Blast Transformation with the $F(ab')^2$ and Fab Fragments of Anti-Lymphocytic Anti-IgG and Anti-Allotypic Globulins. STEWART SELL, RUTH A. MASCARI AND STEPHANIE J. HUGHES 1400
Immunosuppression by Leukemia Viruses. IV. Effect of Friend Leukemia Virus on Antibody-Precursors as Assessed by Cell Transfer Studies. WALTER S. CEGLOWSKI AND HERMAN FRIEDMAN 1406
Human Immunologic Response to Soluble Antigens. Hypersensitivity Induced by a Hapten-Altered Native Protein. MICHAEL W. BRANDRISS AND WARD E. BULLOCK, JR. 1416
Inhibition of Leukocyte Migration: An Evaluation of This *in Vitro* Assay of Delayed Hypersensitivity in Man to a Soluble Antigen. STEVEN A. ROSENBERG AND JOHN R. DAVID 1447
The Mitogenic Effects of Endotoxin and Staphylococcal Enterotoxin B on Mouse Spleen Cells and Human Peripheral Lymphocytes. DUANE L. PEAVY, WILLIAM H. ADLER AND RICHARD T. SMITH 1453
Requirement for Cross-Linkage in the Stimulation of Transformation of Rabbit Peripheral Lymphocytes by Antiglobulin Reagents. MICHAEL W. FANGER, DAVID A. HART, J. VIVIAN WELLS AND ALFRED NISONOFF 1484
Rosette Formation in Relation to Active Synthesis of Antibody. NEOMI MOAV AND T. N. HARRIS 1501
Biologic Activities of Lymph Node Cells Fractionated on Bovine Plasma Albumin. NEOMI MOAV AND T. N. HARRIS 1512
Precursor Cells in Density Fractions of Lymph Node Cells: Relation to Antibody-Producing CELLS. NEOMI MOAV AND T. N. HARRIS 1522
Ultrastructural Localization of Horseradish Peroxidase and Endogenous Peroxidase Activity in Guinea Pig Peritoneal Macrophages. RAMZI S. COTRAN AND MORTIMER LITT 1436

IMMUNOPATHOLOGY

Lymphocytotoxic Antibody Response to Cardiac Allotransplantation in Man. I. Correlation with Post-Transplantation Clinical Course. KAMAL K. MITTAL, ROGER D. ROSSEN, WILLIAM T. BUTLER, ARMEAD H. JOHNSON, ROBERT D. LEACHMAN, JAMES J. NORA, DONALD G. ROCHELLE AND DAVID K. BROOKS 1427

Lymphocytotoxic Antibody Response to Cardiac Allotransplantation in Man. II. Characterization of Antigenic Specificities and Immunoglobulin Class. ARMEAD H. JOHNSON, WILLIAM T. BUTLER, ROGER D. ROSSEN AND KAMAL K. MITTAL........ 1432
Mechanisms of Passive Sensitization. I. Presence of IgE and IgG Molecules on Human Leukocytes. KIMISHIGE ISHIZAKA, HISAO TOMIOKA AND TERUKO ISHIZAKA........ 1459
Mechanisms of Endotoxin Tolerance. VII. The Role of the Liver. SHELDON E. GREISMAN AND CELESTE L. WOODWARD........ 1468
Properties of Soluble Immune Complexes. ROBERT W. LIGHTFOOT, JR., RONALD E. DRUSIN AND CHARLES L. CHRISTIAN........ 1493
Carbonyl Iron: A New Adjuvant for Experimental Autoimmune Diseases. SEYMOUR LEVINE AND RICHARD SOWINSKI........ 1530

MICROBIAL AND VIRAL IMMUNOLOGY

Specificity of Respiratory Secretion Antibody against Influenza Virus. R. H. WALDMAN, F. M. WIGLEY AND P. A. SMALL, JR........ 1477
Production of Interferon in Primary Chick Embryonic Cells Infected with *Rickettsia mooseri*. SEIYA KOHNO, MASAYOSHI KOHASE, HIROKO SAKATA, YUKIKO SHIMIZU, MICHIKO HIKITA AND AKIRA SHISHIDO........ 1553

COMMUNICATIONS

Immunoglobulin Elevations in the Serum of Patients with Chronic Bronchitis and Emphysema. GEORGE A. FALK, GREGORY W. SISKIND AND JAMES P. SMITH, JR........ 1559
Temporal Dissociation of Experimental Allergic Encephalomyelitis Transfer Activity and γ Globulin Staining of Lymphoid Cells from Sensitized Lewis Rats. WALTER P. RICHARDSON AND PHILIP Y. PATERSON........ 1563
Partial Purification and Characterization of a Dengue Virus Soluble Complement-Fixing Antigen. WALTER E. BRANDT, DUMRONG CHIEWSILP, DONALD L. HARRIS AND PHILIP K. RUSSELL........ 1565
The *in Vitro* Effects of Goat Antisera to Rabbit Thymocyte Subcellular Fractions. STEWART SELL, RUTH ANN MASCARI AND PETER J. GOLDBLATT........ 1569
Cells Involved in the Immune Response. XX. The "All or None" Nature of the Primary Immune Response (19S Antibody) by Individual Antibody-Forming Cells in the Rabbit. MAXWELL RICHTER, YOUSSEF BEHELAK, ROBERT HAASZ AND NABIH I. ABDOU........ 1575
C3 in High Molecular Weight Complexes: Separation from Plasma of Nephritic Patients and Normal Subjects by a Method That Avoids *in Vitro* Artifacts. PHILIP W. ASKENASE AND EDWARD J. LEONARD........ 1578
Evidence for the Existence of Two Functionally Distinct Types of Cells Which Regulate the Antibody Response to Type III Pneumococcal Polysaccharide. PHILLIP J. BAKER, PHILIP W. STASHAK, DIANA F. AMSBAUGH, BENJAMIN PRESCOTT AND ROLF F. BARTH........ 1581
Plaque-Forming Cells of Two Different Origins in Single Hemolytic Foci. D. C. VANN AND P. A. CAMPBELL........ 1584

THE JOURNAL OF IMMUNOLOGY
Vol. 105, No. 1, July 1970
Printed in U.S.A.

METABOLISM OF γG AND γM IMMUNOGLOBULINS IN NORMAL AND HYPOGAMMAGLOBULINEMIC CHICKENS[1]

D. FROMMEL,[2] D. Y. E. PEREY[3] AND R. A. GOOD[4]

From the Pediatric Research Laboratories of the Variety Club Heart Hospital, University of Minnesota, Minneapolis, Minnesota 55455

Received for publication March 9, 1970

The half-lives of immunoglobulins G and M were studied in normal chickens, in chickens rendered hypogammaglobulinemic by early bursectomy and x-irradiation, and in dysgammaglobulinemic chickens that had been subjected to bursectomy only. The catabolic rate of labeled IgM was found to be independent of serum levels whereas the disappearance curve of labeled IgG was related to the serum concentration of this immunoglobulin. These findings parallel prior observations in humans having inherited or acquired immune deficiencies. In the chicken, the relationship of the half-lives of IgM and IgG was found to be 1:1.5 in contrast to that observed for mammals, in which a ratio of about 1:4 is characteristic. It can thus be concluded that the metabolic properties of the 7S immunoglobulins in chickens differ markedly from those of mammals.

The physiologic factors regulating metabolism of immunoglobulins are related to the functional capacity of the antibody-forming system, the intensity of antigenic stimulation and the mechanisms of transport and catabolism of the immunoglobulins.

Experimental models and spontaneous human disease have delineated a variety of factors that affect antibody formation: genetic background, age, state of development of the lymphoid organs, the feedback mechanisms and hormonal influences (1). Furthermore, studies of animals in axenic conditions have established the requirement of antigenic stimulation for proliferation of immunoglobulin-producing cells and for antibody formation (2).

In the avian species, the immunologic status can be manipulated with relative ease by early removal of one or the other of the two central lymphoid organs, and this model has been used for studying immunologic deficiencies of humoral or cellular type (3). It seemed pertinent to determine whether the immunoglobulin metabolism of hypogammaglobulinemic chickens showed variations similar to those observed in hypogammaglobulinemic humans in whom the half-life of IgG is prolonged (4, 5).

MATERIALS AND METHODS

Chickens. Non-inbred, white Leghorn roosters, 4 to 5 months old, were obtained from a single local supplier (Ghostley Hatchery, Anoka, Minn.) and immunized by intraperitoneal injection of 1×10^6 sheep red blood cells. The animals were exsanguinated 1 week later. Their serum was used for preparation of purified immunoglobulins. Fertile eggs, obtained from the same hatchery, were incubated as reported previously (6).

Preparation of immunoglobulins. Non-hemolyzed chicken serum was subjected to repeated precipitation with sodium sulfate according to Benedict (7). The final precipitates obtained at 9% and 14%, respectively, were subjected to chromatography on agarose columns (Bio-Gel A 1.5 m, 200 to 400 mesh, Bio-Rad Laboratories, Richmond, Calif.) 2.4 x 120 cm calibrated with proteins of known molecular weight, human

[1] This work was aided by grants from The National Foundation-March of Dimes, American Heart Association, National Tuberculosis Association, the United States Public Health Service (AI-08677, NB-02042, HE-05222), the Minnesota Division of the American Cancer Society, and the Minnesota Chapter of the Arthritis Foundation.

[2] Assistant Professor, Department of Pediatrics.

[3] Advanced Research Fellow, American Heart Association. Present address: The Montreal Children's Hospital, Montreal, Canada.

[4] American Legion Memorial Research Professor, Regents' Professor of Pediatrics and Microbiology.

myeloma IgM and IgG. The 19S pools were purified by ion exchange chromatography on DEAE-cellulose (DE 52 microgranular Whatman, H. Reeve Angel and Co., Clifton, N. J.) equilibrated with 0.05 M sodium phosphate buffer, pH 6.4. A continuous gradient was established with 0.05 M sodium phosphate buffer containing 0.25 M NaCl, pH 6.0. The protein eluted at an ionic strength equivalent to 0.12 to 0.15 M was found to be pure IgM by immunoelectrophoresis, double diffusion in gel and electrophoresis in acrylamide gel (8–10) (Fig. 1*B*).

The 7S pool was recycled on DEAE-Sephadex A-50 (Pharmacia, Uppsala, Sweden) using the same system of buffers. Only the first portion of the eluted proteins was found to be pure IgG by the same criteria as above (Fig. 1*C*). IgG at a concentration of 20 mg/ml, was reduced with dithiothreitol (Cleland's reagent, Calbiochem, Los Angeles, Calif.) at a molar ratio DTT:IgG = 100:1 in 0.15 M Tris-HCl, 0.15 M NaCl, 0.002 M EDTA, pH 8.0 (11). Following alkylation with recrystallized iodoacetamide and dialysis against 1 M propionic acid, the reduced and alkylated IgG solution was applied to a Sephadex G-100 column (2.4 x 90 cm) equilibrated with 1 M propionic acid. The descending limb of the first peak was pooled, recycled under the same conditions and used for immunization.

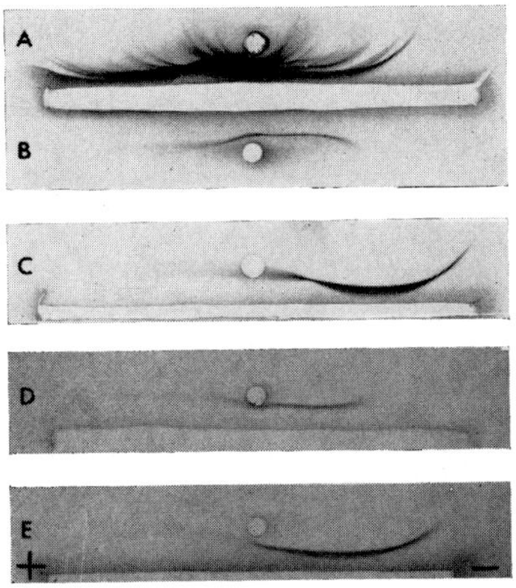

Figure 1. Immunoelectrophoretic patterns of the immunoglobulin preparations and antiglobulin sera. Antigens: Normal chicken serum in *A*, *D* and *E*; IgM preparation in *B*; IgG preparation in *C*. Antisera: *A*, *B* and *C* revealed by a goat anti-chicken serum, *D* by a goat anti-chicken IgM and *E* by a goat anti-chicken IgG.

Preparation of labeled immunoglobulins. Radioiodination with either ^{125}I or ^{131}I (New England Nuclear, Boston, Mass.) was performed according to a modification of the chloramine T method (12) using 20 μg of chloramine T/mg of protein and a reaction period of 5 min at 2°C. Following the addition of sodium metabisulfite, chicken serum albumin (Fraction V, Pentex Inc., Kankakee, Ill.) was added to the immunoglobulin solutions at a final concentration of 25 mg/ml. After removal of the free iodine, 98% of the radioactivity was precipitable by the addition of an equal volume of 20% of trichloroacetic acid. An average of 1.2 atoms of iodine was introduced per molecule of IgG and 2.0 atoms/molecule of IgM (assuming molecular weights of 165,000 and 900,000) (13, 14, and unpublished). Gel filtration on agarose of both labeled proteins in normal chicken serum showed minimal formation of polymeric aggregates; the radioimmunoelectrophoretic patterns (15) of the labeled proteins were identical with those of native immunoglobulins. The labeled proteins were injected within 72 hr after radioiodination.

Quantitation of immunoglobulins. Antisera to whole chicken serum, chicken IgM and IgG were obtained in goats. The antiserum to IgM was absorbed with plasma from newly hatched chickens in order to eliminate cross-reactivity with IgG. Antiserum to slow migrating IgG, obtained by injection of heavy chains, did not require absorption.

Immunoglobulin standards were determined by Kjeldhal analysis and quantitative IgM and IgG determinations were performed by single radial diffusion (16).

Experimental protocol. Newly hatched chickens of both sexes were divided into three groups. Those of group I were bursectomized surgically at hatching (17) and not further treated. Chickens in group II were subjected to bursectomy on the day of hatching and received near lethal x-irradiation on the following day. Group III chickens were x-irradiated on the day after hatching but not bursectomized. The conditions of x-irradiation were as follows: 220 kv, 15 mA, dose rate 21.6 R/min in air delivered by a General Electric Maximar 220 machine. The total skin surface dose of 725 R was delivered to chickens restrained in a Lucite box. This dosage approximates the LD_{50} at 30 days for 1-day-old chickens maintained in standard animal quarters.

The birds were provided with food and water *ad libitum*.

At 5 weeks of age, chickens from each of the three groups established at hatching were weighed and bled to determine their immunoglobulin levels and hematocrit values. By excluding birds with abnormally low hematocrit values or insufficient body weight and selecting chickens whose serum immunoglobulin levels were alike, it was possible to study immunoglobulin metabolism in relatively homogeneous groups of birds.

At the 5th week, Lugol's solution was added to the drinking water to give a 0.1% final concentration. At 6 weeks, birds representative of the different groups were injected in a wing vein with a mixture of the two immunoglobulins in an amount of 5 mg of ^{125}I IgG and 0.6 mg of ^{131}I IgM/100 g of body weight.

Blood samples were collected 5, 24, 48, 72, 96 and 144 hr following injection of the labeled immunoglobulins. The blood samples were obtained by puncturing a wing vein; after discarding the first drop of blood, 100 μl of blood were aspirated into calibrated micropipettes and transferred to micropolyethylene tubes (Coleman Instruments, Inc., Maywood, Ill.). The micropipettes were washed twice with physiologic saline containing 0.01 M EDTA. The wash was added to the blood sample to be counted. Eight days following the injection of tagged immunoglobulins, the birds were weighed again and bled for immunoglobulin and hematocrit determinations.

Determination of radioactivity. The radioactivity of all the samples was determined at the same time, with a dual channel scintillation counter (Nuclear Chicago Corp., model 4230, Chicago, Ill.). The ^{131}I activity was counted in all samples upon collecting the last samples at 7 days, whereas the ^{125}I activity was counted after a delay of 25 days in order to minimize interference with ^{131}I to less than 1%. The radioactivity was measured in whole blood and washing samples of fluid; 97% of the radioactivity present in the samples was precipitable by trichloroacetic acid. Duplicate samples yield counts which agreed within 5%.

Calculation of half-life of labeled immunoglobulins. To allow clearance of the injected immunoglobulins, denatured by the purification or labeling procedures, samples collected at 5 hr were taken to represent 100% of the initial radioactivity in the circulation. Radioactivity in subsequent samples was expressed as the percentage of radioactivity at 5 hr, plotted against time on semilogarithmic paper, and the half-lives of labeled immunoglobulins G and M were determined from the slope of elimination curves (18).

RESULTS

As anticipated from previous studies (3, 19, 20) immunoglobulin levels were distinctly different in each of the three groups. At 5 weeks of age unoperated, irradiated control birds had normal levels of IgG (4.8 ± 1.8 mg/ml) and IgM (1.1 ± 0.17 mg/ml). Bursectomized-irradiated birds of the same age had immunoglobulin levels which did not allow detection by immunoelectrophoresis and single radial diffusion in gel, even when attempts to detect the immunoglobulins employed numerous dilutions of antiserum. (Lowest sensitivity of detection: 0.05 mg/ml for IgG, 0.03 mg/ml for IgM.)

Bursectomized, non-irradiated chickens of group I had on the whole decreased levels of IgG (0.94 ± 0.34 mg/ml) but increased levels of IgM (2.4 ± 1.05 mg/ml) although nearly normal levels of this immunoglobulin were found in some birds. Group I chickens were on the average heavier than birds of the two other groups, which reflected the lack of exposure to x-irradiation. These data are summarized in Table I.

TABLE I

Characteristics of the three groups of chickens under study

Groups	No. of Birds	Weight	Hematocrit	Serum IgM	Serum IgG
		g	*%*	*mg/ml*	*mg/ml*
I (Bursectomy only)	7	405 ± 35[a]	32	2.4 ± 1.05[a]	0.9 ± 0.34[a]
II (Bursectomy + x-irradiation)	8	270 ± 25	34	0.03	0.07 ± 0.03
III (X-irradiation only)	10	330 ± 20	33	1.11 ± 0.17	4.8 ± 1.8

[a] Mean and standard deviation.

The elimination rates of each immunoglobulin of the birds of the three groups are plotted in Figure 2. Chickens within any particular group eliminated the circulating labeled immunoglobulins in a uniform fashion as reflected in the relatively small deviations at each sampling. Calculation of the half-life of injected immunoglobulins from the slope of their disappearance curves revealed that the half-life for IgM was similar in all groups, whereas distinct prolongation of the half-life for IgG was observed in group II, markedly hypogammaglobulinemic birds, and

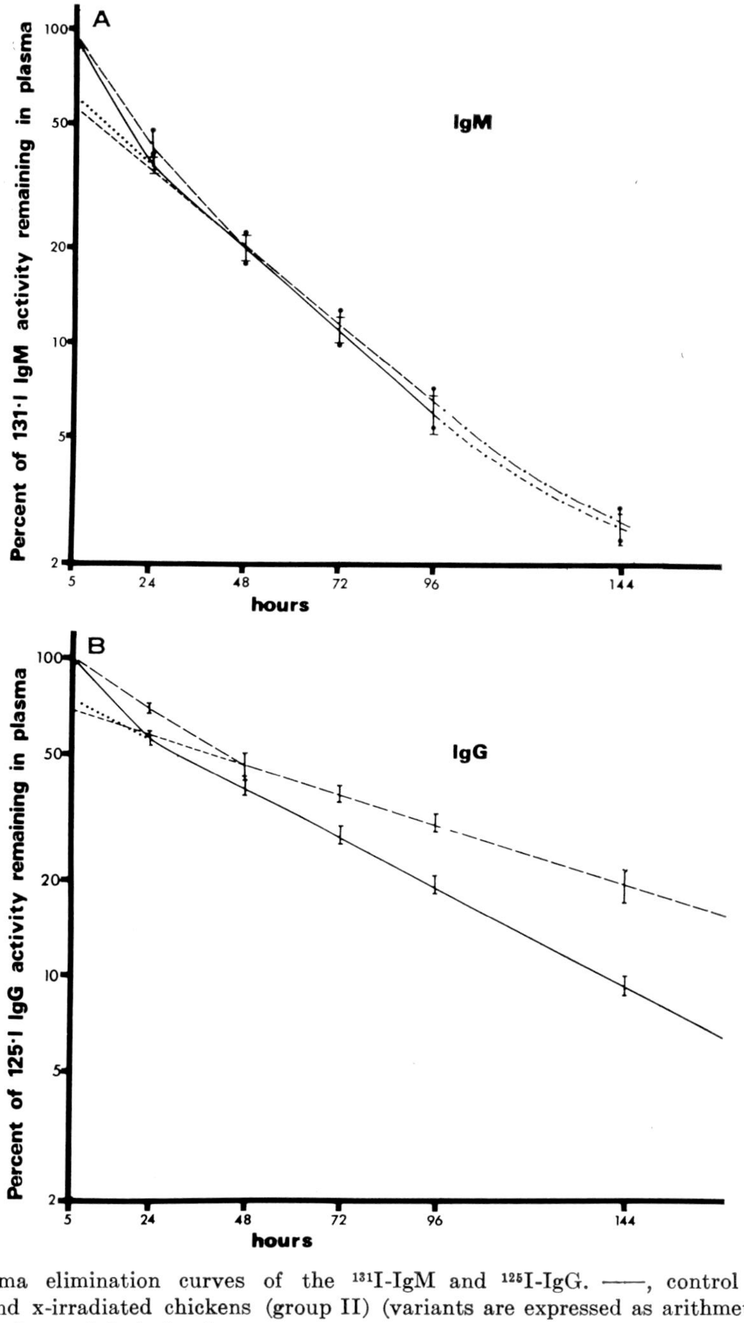

Figure 2. Plasma elimination curves of the ^{131}I-IgM and ^{125}I-IgG. ——, control group; -----, bursectomized and x-irradiated chickens (group II) (variants are expressed as arithmetical mean of the squares of the observed deviations).

TABLE II

Average half-lives of IgM and IgG in normal, hypogammaglobulinemic and "dysgammaglobulinemic" chickens[a]

Group	IgM	IgG
I	37.5	83
II	36.0	90
III	34.6	51

[a] Half-lives given in hours.

in group I, dysgammaglobulinemic birds, which had elevated IgM and decreased IgG levels. Table II summarizes the half-life data for immunoglobulins G and M calculated for each group.

DISCUSSION

In the studies reported here we have again illustrated the effects of surgical bursectomy combined with nearly lethal x-irradiation at hatching upon the development of the humoral immune system of chickens.

Using newly prepared antisera, different from those used in our laboratories previously, we demonstrated that bursectomized and irradiated chickens have, as a group, less than 5 mg/100 ml of IgG and less than 3 mg/100 ml of IgM in their serum. As observed earlier, bursectomy without x-irradiation induced a dysgammaglobulinemic state characterized by elevation of serum IgM and decrease in serum IgG. In this respect these experimental models provide a striking parallel to the immunoglobulin distribution in certain genetically determined immunologic deficiencies of man (21).

A further parallel is also noted between man and the chicken model with respect to the catabolism of the immunoglobulins. The catabolic rate of chicken IgM was shown to be independent of circulating levels of this immunoglobulin, while the catabolic rate of IgG was markedly decreased in the hypogammaglobulinemic chickens (groups I and II). Indeed, although the catabolism of IgM was studied in face of normal, elevated or almost complete absence of this immunoglobulin in the circulation, no significant differences between the groups could be demonstrated. The catabolism of IgG of chickens obeys different control mechanisms and a direct relation between rate of catabolism and the serum concentration was found (18). These results are in agreement with those described in immune deficiencies of man. In deficiencies affecting γG immunoglobulin, the disappearance rate of IgG is markedly prolonged and its catabolic rate is clearly dependent on the serum concentration. Koblet *et al.* (22) corrected the serum IgG level of a hypogammaglobulinemic patient by exogenous administration of IgG after which they observed a normal half-life for IgG. The catabolic rate of IgM, analyzed in various pathologic conditions remained of the order of 3 to 7 days (23).

Of interest was the observation of the relationship between the half-lives of the immunoglobulins γM and γG. Metabolism of the immunoglobulins being related to the body weight, the half-lives for IgM are 0.2 to 0.6 day in the mouse (24), 1 day in guinea pigs (25), 3 days in the rabbit (26), and 4 to 6 days in man (23); the value observed in this study for the 300-g chicken, 1.5 months old, fits well on this scale. Whereas the ratio of half-life IgM:IgG in mammals is of the order of 1:3 to 1:8, in chickens we found the ratio to be 1:1.5. The value of the half-life of chicken IgG agrees with that obtained by other investigators; using different methods the half-life in their studies varied from 1.5 to 4 days (27–29), as compared with 2 ⅛ days in our control animals. Therefore, it appears that we can eliminate the effects of x-irradiation as a cause of increased loss as was previously shown for mice by Bazin and Mallet (30).

Two alternative explanations for these findings can be proposed. The relatively short half-life of chicken IgG could reflect a higher percentage of intravascular distribution with a reduced extravascular pool, as compared with the IgG repartition in mammals; indeed, it has been shown that tissue-binding of chicken IgG was less effective than that observed with mammalian IgG (31). Nonetheless, transport to the conceptus occurs from the hen to the egg through the yolk (32).

On the other hand, chicken IgG, which differs physicochemically from the mammalian type of IgG by having a larger molecular weight, a higher carbohydrate content and unusual heavy-light chains interactions (14, and unpublished), could be considered biologically different from the major mammalian 7S immunoglobulin population and related to the short-lived IgG (33, 34) of man or other 7S immunoglobulins, IgA, IgD, which show higher catabolic rate than does IgG (35, 36).

It further appears clear from these studies that catabolism of the two major immunoglobulins of the chicken is not directly correlated with the integrity of the bursa itself but rather with the consequences of its early removal.

Acknowledgment. We gratefully acknowledge the assistance of Miss Connie L. Finstad in the preparation of certain portions of this manuscript.

REFERENCES

1. Šterzl, J. and Silverstein, A. M., Advances Immun., *6:* 337, 1967.
2. Sell, S. and Fahey, J. L., J. Immun., *93:* 81, 1964.
3. Cooper, M. D., Peterson, R. D. A., South, M. A. and Good, R. A., J. Exp. Med., *123:* 75, 1966.
4. Zak, S. J. and Good, R. A., J. Clin. Invest., *38:* 579, 1959.
5. Waldmann, T. A. and Schwab, P. J., J. Clin. Invest., *44:* 1523, 1965.
6. Papermaster, B. W., Bradley, S. G., Watson, D. W. and Good, R. A., J. Exp. Med., *115:* 1191, 1962.
7. Benedict, A. A., in *Methods in Immunology and Immunochemistry*, Edited by C. A. Williams and M. W. Chase, Vol. 1, p. 229, Academic Press, New York, 1967.
8. Scheidegger, J. J., Int. Arch. Allerg., *7:* 103, 1955.
9. Ouchterlony, Ö., Acta Path. Microbiol. Scand., *32:* 231, 1952.
10. Davis, B. J., Ann. N. Y. Acad. Sci., *121:* 404, 1964.
11. Edelman, G. M., Gall, W. E., Waxdal, M. J. and Konigsberg, W. H., Biochemistry, *7:* 1950, 1968.
12. McConahey, P. J. and Dixon, F. J., Int. Arch. Allerg., *29:* 185, 1966.
13. Orlans, E., Immunology, *14:* 61, 1968.
14. Leslie, G. E. and Clem. L. W., J. Exp. Med., *130:* 1337, 1969.
15. Messier, B. and Leblond, C. P., Proc. Soc. Exp. Biol. Med., *96:* 7, 1957.
16. Mancini, G., Carbonara, A. O. and Heremans, J. F., Immunochemistry, *2:* 235, 1965.
17. Peterson, R. D. A., Burmester, B. R., Frederikson, T. N., Purchase, H. G. and Good, R. A., J. Nat. Cancer Inst., *32:* 1343, 1964.
18. Andersen, S. B., in *Metabolism of Human Gamma Globulin*, Blackwell Scientific Publications, Oxford, 1964.
19. Cooper, M. D., Cain, W. A., Van Alten, P. J. and Good, R. A., Int. Arch. Allerg., *35:* 242, 1969.
20. Van Meter, R., Good, R. A. and Cooper, M.D., J. Immun., *102:* 370, 1969.
21. Seligmann, M., Fudenberg, H. H. and Good, R. A., Amer. J. Med., *45:* 817, 1968.
22. Koblet, H., Diggelmann, H., Barandun, S., Käser, S. and Riva, G., Helv. Med. Acta, *31:* 618, 1964.
23. Barth, W. F., Wochner, R. D., Waldmann, T. A. and Fahey, J. L., J. Clin. Invest., *43:* 1036, 1964.
24. Fahey, J. L. and Sell, S., J. Exp. Med., *122:* 41, 1965.
25. Taliaferro, W. H. and Talmage, D. W., J. Infect. Dis., *99:* 21, 1956.
26. Uhr, J. W. and Finkelstein, M. S., J. Exp. Med., *117:* 457, 1963.
27. Patterson, R., Younger, J. S., Weigle, W. O. and Dixon, F. J., J. Gen. Physiol., *45:* 501, 1962.
28. Wostmann, B. S. and Olson, G. B., J. Immun., *92:* 41, 1964.
29. Iványi, J., Hraba, T. and Černý, J., Folia Biol., *10:* 275, 1964.
30. Bazin, H. and Mallet, F., Immunology, *17:* 345, 1969.
31. Conway, A. M., Van Alten, P. J. and Hirata, A. A., Proc., Soc. Exp. Biol. Med., *129:* 694, 1968.
32. Patterson, R., Younger, J. S., Weigle, W. O. and Dixon, F. J., J. Immun., *89:* 272, 1962.
33. Spiegelberg, H. L., Fishkin, B. G. and Grey, H. M., J. Clin. Invest., *47:* 2323, 1968.
34. Ein, D. and Waldmann, T. J., J. Immun., *103:* 345, 1969.
35. Strober, W., Wochner, R. D., Barlow, M. H., McFarlin, D. E. and Waldmann, T. A., J. Clin. Invest., *47:* 1905, 1968.
36. Rogentine, J. N., Jr., Rowe, D. S., Bradley, J., Waldmann, T. A. and Fahey, J. L., J. Clin. Invest., *45:* 1467, 1966.

THE JOURNAL OF IMMUNOLOGY
Vol. 105, No. 1, July 1970

CYTOSTASIS OF MOUSE AND HUMAN MONOLAYER CELL CULTURES BY NORMAL, UNSTIMULATED LYMPHOCYTES[1]

CRAWFORD W. JAMIESON[2] AND JOHN H. WALLACE

From the Department of Surgery and the Department of Microbiology and Immunology, Tulane University School of Medicine, New Orleans, Louisiana 70112

Received for publication February 27, 1970

The effect of increasing concentrations of mouse and human lymphocytes on the growth of tumor cells, *in vitro*, has been studied by three independent methods. Growth was measured by sequential counts of the cells sheeted in predetermined microscopic fields of the culture flasks, by electronic counts of harvested cells and by thymidine uptake studies. All assay methods used indicate that inhibition of target cell growth is proportional to the ratio of lymphocytes to target cells. Control studies demonstrated that the effect is not due to exhaustion of the medium, the release of toxic breakdown products or elaboration of humoral antibody by the lymphocytes. Cell contact between the two cell types is essential, but there is no evidence that a cytotoxic factor is released as a result of this contact. No evidence for the accidental inclusion of a mitogenic agent was found.

The inhibitory capability is reduced by prior irradiation of the lymphocytes and is lost following their disruption. It is possessed, to a significantly lesser degree, by thymocytes but not by peritoneal macrophages. This cytostatic ability appears to represent a genuine capacity of apparently normal lymphocytes.

It is now well established that lymphocytes are capable of causing target cell lysis, *in vitro.* The studies of Covaerts (1) and of Rosenau and Moon (2), amply confirmed by subsequent investigators, prove that lymphocytes are capable of exerting a marked toxic effect on target cells carrying antigens to which the lymphocytes have been sensitized. Wilson (3) was able to demonstrate, by elegant quantitative studies, that the effect is directly proportional to the ratio of lymphocytes to target cells and of an exponential nature. The possibility that the mechanism of destruction is due to a soluble factor, liberated during antigen-sensitized cell contact, is suggested by the findings of Granger and Kolb (4). Holm, Perlmann and Werner (5) first reported similar cytotoxic effects when unsensitized lymphocytes, in the presence of phytohemagglutinin (PHA), were added to the system. This phenomenon has been extensively investigated by the Hellstroms (6) and the Mollers (7), and has been termed allogeneic inhibition. It appears to be at least partly distinct from the effect obtained with sensitized lymphocytes since allogeneic inhibition can be initiated by intact immunologically competent cells either before or after irradiation and by the subcellular fragments recovered following sonication of such cells. In addition, close contact of allogeneic cells which are not immunologically competent, in the generally accepted sense, results in allogeneic inhibition.

In the course of such investigations several investigators have reported mild cytotoxic effects of the control, normal lymphocytes (2, 6–8). Others have found that such lymphocytes had no effect on the growth of target cells or that they even produced enhanced growth (9). In a study concerned with the effect of human lymphocytes on fibroblast cultures, the Mollers (7) observed lysis in the absence of PHA. Similarly, in a qualitative experiment, Stuart (10) noted lysis of human monolayer cultures by xenogeneic lymphocytes. The methods employed by most investigators in this field have been designed to detect lysis only, and more subtle effects on target cell populations usually have not been sought.

Initial studies in this laboratory, repeating

[1] This investigation was supported by Grant PO2CA05837 from the National Cancer Institute and by the United Health Foundation.

[2] Wellcome Research Fellow. Present address: St. Mary's Hospital Medical School, London W2.

previously published experiments on the effect of lymphocytes on target cells in the presence of PHA, indicated that the control lymphocytes, while having no cytotoxic effect, did produce profound and consistent cytostasis of mouse melanoma cells (11). In the present study, this phenomenon has been examined in order to elucidate the mechanisms involved.

MATERIALS AND METHODS

The methods used have been published in detail (11) and are summarized here. The two mouse-cell lines employed were B16 mouse melanoma (of C57BL/6 origin) and clone 929 L cells (C3H3He). Both of these lines maintain the alloantigenic characteristics of the strain of origin but they also possess antigens different from normal C57BL/6(B6) and C3H3He (C3H) cells as evidenced by their ability to immunize the strains of origin against subsequent homologous tumor challenge (12, 13). The human cell line, designated "H" cells, was derived from the pigmented primary tumor of a patient with melanoma. It had been established and maintained in serial monolayer culture in the Norman William Blackwell Laboratory of Tulane University for 1 year prior to this study. These cells retained their ability to synthesize melanin. All cells were maintained at 37°C in an atmosphere of 5% CO_2 and air, in medium consisting of medium 199 to which 15% fetal calf serum, 50 units of penicillin, 50 μg of streptomycin and 10 μg/ml of L-glutamine were added.

Target tumor cells were harvested from 24-hr cultures by a mixture of 1 part 0.25% trypsin and 2 parts 0.002% Versene at 37°C. As soon as the monolayer had detached, the trypsin was neutralized by the addition of an excess of cold, complete medium, and, after washing by centrifugation at 500 × G for 5 min, cell viability was determined and suspensions were prepared with a final concentration of 10×10^4 cells/ml.

Mouse lymphocytes were obtained from 4- to 6-week-old male mice. Spleens and mesenteric nodes were removed aseptically and gently teased apart in cold medium 199. The cell suspensions obtained were centrifugated at 500 × G for 5 min, and contaminating erythrocytes were reduced by the addition of 1 ml of distilled water to the cell pellet for 30 sec before resuspension. Over 90% of the cells obtained in this manner were small lymphocytes and viability was always over 90%. Human lymphocytes were harvested from peripheral venous blood by the method of DeWitt (14). These cells were obtained from the patient from whom the H cells were established and from two allogeneic donors.

Assay of the effect on target cell growth of the addition of normal lymphocytes. The combination of lymphocytes with target cell cultures was performed as has been described previously (11). When growth was measured by set microscopic field counts of the target cell population, 10×10^4 tumor cells were seeded in plastic T flasks (Falcon Plastics Co., Los Angeles) in 6 ml of complete medium 199. After 24 hr the number of cells sheeted in each of 12 predetermined microscopic fields of the floor of each flask was determined using a Nikon model M inverted microscope and a warm stage. Groups of flasks were then composed, each containing the same mean number of cells in 12 set fields, and the medium was discarded. It was replaced with medium containing either no lymphocytes or from 20 to 100 lymphocytes/target cell seeded; cultures were refed 48 hr later. Results were determined by repeat counts of the same set fields of the floor of each flask 72 hr after addition of the lymphocytes.

Alternatively, 10×10^4 tumor cells were seeded in 4 ml of complete medium containing either no lymphocytes or up to 100 lymphocytes/target cell. The cultures were refed after 48 hr and 24 hr later, 72 hr after seeding, 3 ml of trypsin-Versene at 37°C were added after decanting the medium. When the monolayer had detached, 7 ml of cold complete medium were added, and the number of tumor cells present was determined from the mean of three counts with a model F Coulter counter appropriately set to exclude the lymphocyte population.

Other cultures were established in exactly the same way but were given a 24-hr pulse of 0.5 μCi/ml of tritiated thymidine 48 hr after seeding, at the time of refeeding. These were harvested after 72 hr in mixed culture, and the intracellular radioactivity was measured with a Packard Tri-Carb scintillation spectrometer.

RESULTS

Previously published concurrent studies have shown that the results obtained by the three assay methods were very similar and that B6 lymphocytes produced marked inhibition of

TABLE I

The relative effect of C3HHe and C57BL/6 lymphocytes on the growth of L cells at concentrations of 20, 50 and 100 lymphocytes/target cell,[a] in four series of experiments

Test	Series 1	Series 2	Series 3	Series 4
Control	817 ± 37	168 ± 7	366 ± 4	708 ± 46
C3H 20/1	300 ± 28		256 ± 33	562 ± 14
C3H 50/1	212 ± 17	130 ± 2	163 ± 11	260 ± 23
C3H 100/1	192 ± 14	88 ± 8	127 ± 4	154 ± 6
B6 20/1	341 ± 24	105 ± 10	147 ± 11	294 ± 21
B6 50/1	258 ± 12	80 ± 8	131 ± 9	164 ± 10
B6 100/1	259 ± 17	68 ± 4	110 ± 4	108 ± 16

[a] Each figure represents the mean $\times$ 1000 of 10 similar cultures obtained by electronic cell counts 72 hr after seeding 10×10^4 L cells.

TABLE II

The relative cytostatic effect of human peripheral lymphocytes and mouse lymphocytes on human melanoma cells[a]

Lymphocytes	Control[b]	50/1[c]	100/1[c]
C57BL/6	100 ± 11[a]		109 ± 18
Allogeneic human	100 ± 15	44 ± 6	6 ± 4
Autologous human	100 ± 17	78 ± 21	3 ± 5

[a] Results obtained from set field counts of one experiment, except the autologous human lymphocyte results which are derived from one experiment in which each group consisted of five cultures.

[b] Control growth expressed as 100% and standard error.

[c] Growth expressed as % of control and standard error.

growth of B16 mouse melanoma. This effect was proportional to the ratio of lymphocytes to target cells and exponential in nature (11). Table I demonstrates the effect of B6 and C3H lymphocytes on the growth of clone 929 L cells. Each reading represents the mean of 10 similar cultures. Marked inhibition of growth was produced by both lymphocyte types on this cell line. The effect of B6 lymphocytes was more marked than that of C3H in all but one experiment, and the possible significance of this difference will be discussed in a subsequent report.

The relative growth of H (human melanoma) cells in the presence of xenogeneic (B6 mouse) or allogeneic or autologous lymphocytes is contained in Table II. No inhibitory effect was exerted by the mouse lymphocytes but profound cytostasis was observed in the cultures containing either allogeneic or autologous human lymphocytes. The apparent differences in the effect at a ratio of 50:1 are not significant. It is interesting to compare the effect of autologous and homologous lymphocytes as the autologous cells were obtained from the donor after immunization. The patient received a course of intradermal administration of his own *in vitro* cultured and irradiated (30,000 R) tumor cells in an attempt to increase tumor resistance. His serum showed a weakly positive response, by hemadsorption, following this course which occurred 1 year prior to the test described here. The patient remained clinically tumor-free during this interval.

In general, the morphologic changes observed were identical to those previously reported in mixed cultures of target cells and normal lymphocytes. Slight clumping of the lymphocytes onto the cells was observed after 18 hr, becoming maximal around 36 hr and then decreasing. This effect was patchy, some tumor cells appearing to be markedly attacked while the majority were spared. Generally little evidence of target cell damage was seen.

Table III indicates the relative cytostatic effect of a ratio of 100 B6 and A strain lymphocytes on B16 melanoma with and without prior irradiation of the lymphocytes with 1500 R. Significant reduction in the cytostatic effect was observed. These results were obtained from the mean of eight experiments. Table IV indicates the effect of B6 peritoneal macrophages, obtained 48 hr after intraperitoneal administration of 1 ml of brain-heart infusion broth, and of the soluble and particulate fraction prepared from the

TABLE III

Effect of irradiation (1500 R) on the cytostatic effect of C57BL/6 and A/Jax (A) strain lymphocytes on B16 melanoma[a]

Strain	Growth of Controls[b]	Growth of Target Cells Plus 100:1 Lymphocytes
B6 normal	100 ± 5.4(242)	20.6 ± 3.9
B6 irradiated	100 ± 5.0(240)	37.6 ± 3.9
A normal	100 ± 6.5(248)	23.0 ± 4.5
A irradiated	100 ± 7.9(247)	51.6 ± 6.9

[a] Results obtained from set field counts of 74 cultures in seven series of experiments.

[b] Control growth expressed as 100% and standard error. Actual mean growth of control cultures during the 72 hr of the test in parentheses as percentage of cells seeded.

TABLE IV

The effect of a ratio of 50 peritoneal macrophages and the particulate and soluble product of the equivalent of 100 freeze-thaw disintegrated C57BL/6 lymphocytes on the growth of B16 melanoma cells

Cells or Product Tested	% Growth of Control[a] Cultures	% Growth of Test Cultures
Macrophages	100 ± 13	109 ± 16
Lymphocyte debris	100 ± 6	104 ± 8
Lymphocyte supernatant	100 ± 6	82 ± 10

[a] Controls expressed as 100% and the mean increase in cells over the 72-hr period of the test was 240%. Results obtained from set field counts of 50 cultures in seven experiments.

equivalent of 100 B6 lymphocytes/target cell on B16 melanoma cell growth. The lymphocytes were disrupted by repeated freezing and thawing. No significant impairment of the growth of these cultures was found when their growth rate was compared with simultaneously seeded control cultures. The apparent reduction in the case of the soluble product of frozen and thawed lymphocytes was not significant ($p > 0.2$).

Preliminary studies had shown no qualitative evidence of impaired tumor cell growth when 100 lymphocytes/target cell were separated from a B16 culture by an HA Millipore filter of large area (pore size 0.45 μ). Accurate counts of the tumor cells had not been possible. Double T flasks were therefore constructed, and compartments were separated by an HA Millipore filter. A culture of L cells alone, lymphocytes alone or L cells plus lymphocytes was seeded in one side, and 10×10^4 L cells were placed in the other side. The total cell concentration in medium was the same as that used in other experiments. Table V indicates the results of these experiments. In no case were any fewer cells recovered from test cultures after 72 hr than from the control cultures in which no lymphocytes were present in one side of the chamber. These results strongly indicate that exhaustion of medium components, release of toxic products by metabolizing or dead cells, or synthesis of a soluble factor of the molecular weight proposed by Granger and Kolb (4) by lymphocytes, did not account for the inhibition of target cell growth observed in previous experiments. In order to investigate further the possible release of toxic factors, medium was collected from mixed cultures of L cells and lymphocytes at a

TABLE V

Tumor cells recovered[a] *48 hr after seeding in one side of a double chamber, separated by an HA millipore filter from a mixed L cell and lymphocyte culture, lymphocytes alone or L cells alone*

Left Side	Right Side: Series 1	Right Side: Series 2	Right Side: Series 3
10×10^4 L cells	455 452	206 208 236 174	498 447 344 386
20×10^6 C3H lymphocytes	430 460	235 200	453 360
Lymphocytes plus L cells	456 405 448	210 212	456 352

[a] Results × 1000 obtained by electronic counts of L cells harvested from the right side of the various chambers.

TABLE VI

The effect of the medium from mixed L cell and lymphocyte cultures on the growth of a second L cell culture[a] in four series of experiments

Series	Lymphocyte Donor	Control	Medium of Mixed Cultures	Medium of L cells
1	C3H	516 ± 23[b]	432 ± 21	
2	C57	516 ± 23	476 ± 36	
3	C3H	260 ± 7	240 ± 9	265 ± 11
4	C3H	594 ± 37	278 ± 19	

[a] Each figure represents the mean of the count × 1000 of 10 similar L cell cultures.

[b] Counts × 1000.

ratio of 100 lymphocytes/target cell and at three times the total cell concentration used in the other experiments. This medium was subjected to ultrafiltration and then diluted with an equal volume of fresh complete medium. The concentration of any soluble toxin should have been greater than in other experiments. (A culture of 10 × 10⁴ L cells was then seeded in this medium, and growth was compared to that of identical cultures seeded in fresh medium.) Table VI indicates the results of these experiments. In only one experiment was any inhibition of growth observed in the test cultures, and this inhibition was much less than the profound inhibition observed in all other experiments in which this ratio of target cells to lymphocytes was used. These experiments, therefore, also failed to support the possibility that a soluble growth-inhibiting factor was released by the lymphocytes after contact with target cells.

Table VII compares the growth inhibition of L cells produced by a ratio of 20 B6 lymphocytes/target cell in experiments in which either fresh or heat-inactivated fetal calf serum was used in the medium. In two of the three experiments there was reduction in the cytostatic effect in the cultures containing heat-inactivated serum but in the third experiment no reduction was noted.

Table VIII compares the effect of a ratio of 50 thymocytes and 20 lymphocytes of C3H origin on the growth of L cells. The thymocytes were obtained by suspension of the whole thymus, and it is known that this method of harvest does result in accidental contamination of the thymic cells with lymphocytes from mediastinal nodes (15). In spite of this, significantly less cytostasis was observed in the cultures containing thymo-

TABLE VII

Comparative growth of L cells[a] in media containing fresh or heat-inactivated fetal calf serum, in the presence of 20 C57BL/6 lymphocytes per target cell

Cultures	Series 1	Series 2	Series 3
CM[b]	788 ± 11	666 ± 20	414 ± 5.6
CM + lymphocytes	604 ± 10.8	274 ± 4.6	182 ± 5.6
HI[c] serum	760 ± 15	566 ± 13.4	410 ± 7.2
HI serum + lymphocytes	670 ± 15.6	220 ± 5.4	302 ± 6.6

[a] Each figure represents the mean count × 1000 of 10 L cell cultures, by electronic cell counts, 72 hr after 10 × 10⁴ cells were seeded.

[b] CM, complete medium.

[c] HI, heat inactivated.

TABLE VIII

The relative cytostatic effect of C3H lymphocytes, at a ratio of 20/target cell, and C3HHe thymocytes, at a ratio of 50/target cell, on L cells

Aggressor Cells	Series 1	Series 2	Series 3	Series 4
None	410 ± 10[a]	588 ± 22	684 ± 9.2	562 ± 14.8
C3H lymphocytes	162 ± 8.8	322 ± 4.6	384 ± 8.0	446 ± 6.6
C3H thymocytes	220 ± 7.4	406 ± 6.8	446 ± 8.0	510 ± 5.8

[a] Cell counts × 1000.

cytes than in those containing the lesser number of lymphocytes.

DISCUSSION

This study has evaluated further the growth inhibitory effect of lymphocytes on target cells *in vitro* in the absence of a mitogenic agent. It would appear, from the control studies, that the effect is not an artifact of the culture conditions. No inhibitory effect was produced on potential target cells when they were separated from lymphocytes or from lymphocyte-target cell mixtures by a semi-permeable membrane. The reconstituted medium from mixed cultures was also without an inhibitory effect. It is highly unlikely that exhaustion of the medium, release of toxic metabolites or cell breakdown products or a production of a soluble factor, as described in other systems (1), is responsible. It is also unlikely that the growth inhibitory effect is due to the release of humoral antibody by the lymphocytes, although the rate of diffusion of macromolecules through such a filter is known to be slow (16). As no cytostasis was produced by the particulate product of disrupted lymphocytes, such fragments, too large to negotiate the filter, could not be a factor.

The accidental inclusion of a mitogenic agent is more difficult to exclude. There was evidence of a low level of hemagglutinin for mouse and human red cells in the fetal calf serum used but leukocyte agglutination studies were completely negative. No significant transformation occurred in lymphocyte cultures maintained in the complete medium employed in these experiments, and, had a mitogenic agent been present, some would have been expected. In mixed cultures, containing 100 lymphocytes/target cell, total thymidine uptake was not significantly elevated over control levels. The cytostatic effect was lessened in some of the experiments in which heat-inactivated serum was used in the culture medium. This might imply that complement is a co-factor but other thermolabile substances could also be lost, among them the lymphocyte stimulating factor of Metcalf (17); other investigators of similar effects of lymphocytes, *in vitro,* have been convinced that complement is not involved. Further indirect evidence against the inadvertant inclusion of a mitogenic agent here is the loss of the effect after disruption of the lymphocytes and its impairment following irradiation. Published data of experiments in which agents such as PHA were intentionally included in the system to stimulate target cell lysis by unsensitized lymphocytes suggest that this phenomenon is not impaired in either of these experimental conditions (6, 7). Other recently reported studies, however, do not fully support these conclusions (4).

It would appear that the cytostatic effect of unsensitized lymphocytes is dependent, at least in part, on the active metabolism of the lymphocytes as it is impaired by irradiation and lost following cell disruption; also, cell contact between the lymphocytes and target cells is an essential prerequisite. The mechanism most likely involves some very local phenomenon such as membrane-membrane interaction or the interchange of intracellular material. Cytoplasmic bridges containing DNA can be identified between normal lymphocytes and target cells in experimental conditions similar to those used in these experiments (18, 19). Whatever the mechanism, it would appear not to be a function of macrophages but to be possessed by lymphocytes, and to a significantly lesser extent, by thymocytes. It is thought that thymocytes do possess some immune competence (20) but there is also good evidence that the methods employed in their harvest usually result in contamination of the thymocyte population with lymphocytes (15). Thus, it is not certain that the effects observed in the experiments in which thymocytes were used were not caused by small numbers of contaminating lymphocytes.

The specificity of the reaction has not been proven. It is not possible, therefore, to categorically define the reaction as an "immune response." It is, however, a function of immunologically competent cells. Two possible explanations of the data are that the effect is a manifestation of *in vitro* or of prior *in vivo* sensitization of the lymphocytes. The former possibility seems less likely, although such sensitization has been claimed in long-term cultures (21). The magnitude of the response bears no relationship to the histocompatibility differences between the lymphocytes and the target cell donors. Little or no effect is seen in the xenogeneic system. Furthermore, the investigators who did obtain evidence of *in vitro* sensitization could not obtain this effect in mouse systems (21). The second possibility, that of prior sensitization, is complex. Many mouse tumor cell lines carry viral contaminants and prior sensitization of the lymphocyte donor to such viral antigens could result in cytotoxic effects on the target cells. There is also known cross-reactivity between bacterial and histocompatibility antigens and this might explain the phenomenon (22). Lastly, it is conceivable that prior sensitization to tumor antigens, as a result of neoplastic transformation of cells *in vivo*, without their multiplication to form recognizable tumors, could have sensitized the donors of lymphocytes to this minor degree. To explore this last intriguing possibility, an obviously profitable experiment would involve the incubation of lymphocytes with truly benign cells. If no cytostasis occurred, strong evidence in favor of sensitization to tumor antigens would have been obtained. Unfortunately, it has not proved possible, in our laboratory, to obtain sufficiently consistent growth from primary fetal cell cultures to permit this experiment and attempts with adult cells have been even less rewarding. There is, moreover, considerable doubt whether any cells, established in exponential growth *in vitro*, can ever be considered "benign" (23). Furthermore, fetal cells may well share antigenicity with tumor cells (24) and such a test would be of value only if no growth inhibition were to take place. The opposite result would neither invalidate nor support the hypothesis.

The results reported here have demonstrated that mouse and human lymphocytes are capable of causing inhibition of growth of homologous target cells *in vitro*, in the absence of a mitogenic agent and in the apparent absence of prior sensitization. While these effects are more subtle than those reported in previous studies concerned with the effect of sensitized or stimulated lymphocytes on target cells, they could be more closely related to cell-bound tumor specific resistance mechanisms than previously reported phenomena.

Acknowledgments. We wish to thank Dr. Charles W. DeWitt for his helpful discussions. Mr. Edmund N. Benes, Miss Julia E. Blazek and Miss Sharon Wilchar provided excellent technical assistance which we gratefully acknowledge.

REFERENCES

1. Covaerts, A., J. Immun., *85:* 516, 1960.
2. Rosenau, W. and Moon, H. D., J. Nat. Cancer Inst. *27:* 471, 1961.
3. Wilson, D. B., J. Exp. Med., *122:* 143, 1965.
4. Granger, G. A. and Kolb, W. P., J. Immun., *101:* 111, 1968.
5. Holm, G., Perlmann, P. and Werner, B., Nature, *203:* 841, 1964.
6. Hellstrom, K. E. and Hellstrom, I., Fed. Proc., *27:* 39, 1968.
7. Moller, E. and Moller, G., Cancer, *20:* 871, 1967.
8. Holm, G. and Perlmann, P., Immunology, *12:* 525, 1967.
9. Taylor, H. E. and Culling, C. F. A., Lab. Invest., *12:* 884, 1963.
10. Stuart, A. E., Lancet, *2:* 180, 1962.
11. Jamieson, C. W., Russin, D., Benes, E., DeWitt, C. W. and Wallace, J. H., Nature, *222:* 284, 1969.
12. Barlett, P. C., Bull. Tulane Med. Fac., *26:* 199, 1967.
13. Sanford, K. K., Hobbs, G. L. and Earle, W. R., Cancer Res., *16:* 162, 1956.
14. DeWitt, C. W., In *Histocompatibility Testing Series*. Haematology, *11:* 125, Ejnar Munksgaard, Copenhagen, 1965.
15. Blau, J. N. and Gaugas, J. M., Immunology, *14:* 763, 1968.
16. Amos, D. B. and Wakefield, J. D., J. Nat. Cancer Inst., *21:* 657, 1968.
17. Metcalf, D., Brit. J. Cancer, *10:* 442, 1956.
18. Robinson, S. H. and Brecher, G., Science, *142:* 392, 1963.
19. Svet-Moldavsky, G. J. and Chernakhovskaya, I. J., Nature, *215:* 1299, 1967.
20. Vos, O., Devries, M. J., Collenteur, J. C. and VanBekkum, D. W., J. Nat. Cancer Inst., *23:* 53, 1959.
21. Ginsburg, H., Jsachs, L., J. Cell. Comp. Physiol., *66:* 199, 1965.
22. Rapaport, F. T. and Chase, R. M., Science, *145:* 407, 1964.
23. Woodruff, M. F. A. and Symes, M. O., Brit. J. Cancer, *16:* 484, 1962.
24. Gold, P. and Freedman, S. O., J. Exp. Med., *122:* 467, 1965.

THE JOURNAL OF IMMUNOLOGY
Vol. 105, No. 1, July 1970

Printed in U.S.A.

GENETIC AND CELLULAR FACTORS IN THE IMMUNE RESPONSE

I. Genetic Control of the Antibody Response to Poly Glu^{52} Lys^{33} Tyr^{15} in the Inbred Rat Strains ACI and F344[1]

THOMAS J. GILL, III,[2] HEINZ W. KUNZ, DANIEL J. STECHSCHULTE[3] AND K. FRANK AUSTEN

From the Department of Pathology, Harvard Medical School and Department of Medicine, Robert B. Brigham Hospital and Harvard Medical School, Boston, Massachusetts 02115

Received for publication February 4, 1970

The antibody response to poly $Glu^{52}Lys^{32}Tyr^{15}$ was studied in two inbred strains of rats, the highly responding ACI strain and the poorly responding F344 strain. The amounts of antibody formed by the parental strains, the F_1 and F_2 generations and the backcrosses into the parental strains were assayed by a quantitative immunoadsorbent micro-method. Radio-immunoelectrophoretic studies showed that the antibody response was distributed among the IgM, γ_1 and IgG immunoglobulin classes in both males and females. There was no correlation between the quantity of antibody made and the immunoglobulin class. The results of the experiments are consistent with a model in which the genetic control of the antibody response is exercised by at least two independently segregating genes—one for recognition of antigen (R-gene) and one for quantitative control of the amount of antibody formed (Q-gene). In addition, there is a sex influence, which is most clearly seen in the highly responding ACI parental strain and in backcrosses to that strain; it is progressively diminished by increased cross-breeding. The functioning of the sex factor is associated with a higher and more heterogeneous antibody response in females. The effect of antigen dose was studied systematically over a range of 10^4. The ACI strain made more antibody as the dose of antigen was increased, and the response reached a plateau following immunization with 1.5 mg of antigen. On the other hand, the response in the F344 strain was low and erratic up to a dose of 1.5 mg of antigen; thereafter, the antibody response slowly increased, and all animals made antibody. At very low doses of antigen, the ACI strain made predominantly IgM antibody, and, as the antigen dose increased, all classes of immunoglobulin contained antibody. In contrast, the F344 strain always formed predominantly IgG antibody and very little, if any, IgM antibody. Aggregation of the antigen with methylated bovine serum albumin had different effects on the antibody response in the two strains of rats. The amount of antibody formed by the highly responding ACI strain was decreased or unchanged. The amount of antibody formed by the poorly responding F344 strain was either increased or unaltered. The antibody formed by the F344 strain was almost exclusively in the IgG class, whereas the ACI strain formed antibody in all immunoglobulin classes. The various hybrids of the ACI and F344 strains responded predominantly in the IgG class, in contrast to the findings following immunization with the unaggregated antigen, in which case the antibody response was distributed among all of the immunoglobulin classes. These findings suggest

---

[1] This research was supported by grants from the National Science Foundation (GB-8379) and the National Institutes of Health (HE-01771 and AI-07722).

[2] Recipient of a Research Career Development Award (K3-AM-5242) from the National Institutes of Health.

[3] Postdoctoral Fellow of the National Arthritis Foundation.

that an inability to make IgM antibody to poly $Glu^{52}Lys^{33}Tyr^{15}$ may be a factor in the poor response of the F344 strain to immunization with that antigen. The heterogeneity in the magnitude of the antibody response in the ACI strain was greatly restricted, and all animals in the F344 strain responded. Finally, the sex difference in the antibody response was unaltered or enhanced.

Studies on the genetic control of the antibody response using chemically defined, synthetic polypeptide antigens have been carried out mainly in guinea pigs, mice and rats. Many of these studies have been reviewed recently (1, 2). The work of Benacerraf and his colleagues in random bred guinea pigs (3) indicated that the ability to respond to a given antigen was transmitted as a dominant Mendelian (unigenic) trait. The same conclusion was reached by Maurer and his collaborators (4) using strain 2 and strain 13 guinea pigs. However, studies in guinea pigs with insulin as the antigen indicated that the genetic control of the antibody response was complex and that it was probably polygenic (5).

On the basis of studies with graft polymers composed of a backbone of lysine and alanine and carrying sidechains of tyrosine-glutamic acid, histidine-glutamic acid or phenylalanine-glutamic acid, McDevitt and his colleagues (2, 6, 7) concluded that the genetic control of the antibody response in the mouse was specific to the determinant site and that it appeared to act as a single autosomal dominant trait. Further studies (8) with graft polypeptides containing lysine and proline in the backbone and with the polypeptides mentioned above showed that: a) a portion of the sidechain, as well as the terminal residues, participated in the antigenic determinant; b) different inbred strains of mice made antibodies specific for different parts of the same polypeptide; and c) the immune response to the same amino acid determinant on different polypeptide backbones appeared to be under separate genetic control. Breeding studies demonstrated that the ability to make antibody specific for these polypeptides was linked to the H-2 histocompatibility locus, but not to the immunoglobulin class or to the allotype. These particular antibody specificities were designated the Ir-1 locus—a single autosomal locus—which localized to the IXth mouse linkage group. The ability to respond to an antigen could be transferred from a responder strain to a lethally irradiated non-responder strain by splenic cells in the mouse (9) and by bone marrow or by lymph node and spleen cells in the guinea pig (10). Therefore, the genetic control of the antibody response was exerted directly on the antibody-forming cells, and it was not due to some type of non-immunological mechanism. Pinchuck and Maurer (11, 12) studied the antibody response in the mouse to polypeptides containing glutamic acid, lysine and alanine, and they found that the antibody response to polymers containing different percentages of alanine was different within each strain of mice. The ability to respond was transferred as a dominant trait to the F_1 and F_2 generations.

Gasser (13) studied the production of agglutinating antibodies to the Ea-1 erythrocyte antigens of the mouse, and he concluded that their production appeared to be under the control of a single Mendelian recessive factor. The locus controlling the response, which he called the Ir-2 locus, was linked to the agouti locus in the Vth mouse linkage group, which, in turn, was linked to several histocompatibility loci. Playfair's studies (14) suggested that the antibody response in inbred mice to red blood cells from a variety of species was controlled by several genes.

Gill and his colleagues (15) investigated the antibody response in inbred rats and showed that the effects on the antibody response of the various structural aspects of an antigen, i.e., primary, secondary and tertiary structure, were under separate genetic control. Limited breeding studies indicated that the ability to make antibody was transmitted as a complex genetic control mechanism. The only other studies suggesting a polygenic control of the antibody response used the complex natural antigens insulin (5) and red blood cells (14); therefore, the conclusions drawn from these studies are complicated by the presence of many potentially different immunogenic determinants on the antigens. One way of reconciling all the different data would be to postulate that the control mechanisms are different in different species. A second and more likely possibility is that the control mechanism behaves as a dominant unigenic trait, but that it is governed by several genes which act essentially as one unit.

In conjunction with studies on the genetic control of the antibody response, a unique observation has been exploited to probe the antigen recognition process: aggregation of a poorly immunogenic macromolecule with an oppositely charged macromolecule enhanced the immunogenicity of the former (16–18). Most of the antibody was produced against the antigen (17), but when antibody was produced against the carrier, it was produced by different cells (19). The induction of tolerance to the carrier decreased or abolished the antibody response to the antigen (20). The genetic differences in the primary and secondary antibody responses to synthetic polypeptides in C57 and CBA mice were obliterated by complexing the antigens with methylated bovine serum albumin (21). In inbred rats (15) aggregation of a synthetic polypeptide[4] with methylated bovine serum albumin elicited an increased antibody response in those strains which produced a low titer to the polypeptide alone and reduced interstrain differences in the response.

The present study on the genetic control mechanisms regulating the antibody response in the rat was undertaken primarily to define more clearly the number of genes controlling the response and to explore some of the factors influencing the amount of antibody formed. The approach was to use a quantitative method for assaying antibody in order to obtain data that could be analyzed statistically. The experiments described provide evidence for the involvement of at least two genes in the control of the antibody response. In addition, the antibody response is sex-influenced; the biological basis of this effect is, as yet, unclear.

MATERIALS AND METHODS

Rats. The original breeding stock of inbred ACI and F344 rats and approximately one-third of the F_1 generation were obtained from Microbiological Associates Incorporated, Walkersville, Md.[5] The ACI strain was inbred for 83 generations, and the F344 strain for more than 97 generations. Subsequently we established our own breeding colony, which provided the remaining two-thirds of the F_1 generation and all the other progeny used in this study. All rats were numbered so that pedigree analyses could eventually be carried out. The rats were housed in group cages and fed Purina Laboratory Chow *ad libitum.* They were 2 months of age when immunized or mated.

TABLE I

Physical and chemical properties of different preparations of poly $Glu^{52}Lys^{33}Tyr^{15}$[a]

Preparation	Amino Acid Analysis: Glu	Lys	Tyr	Molecular Weight	Sedimentation Constant ($S^0_{20,w}$)
	mol %				
13-3	51.3	32.9	15.8	23,000[b]	1.67
13-4	48.9	35.6	15.8	29,000[c]	1.49
13-6	50.3	35.2	14.5	37,000	1.44
13-7	49.9	35.2	14.9	21,000	1.11
13-8	50.9	35.2	13.9	25,000	1.34

[a] There was no alteration in any of the amino acid residues or aggregation of the polymers over the course of 5 years.

[b] Intrinsic viscosity = 0.43

[c] Intrinsic viscosity = 0.62

Antigens. The synthetic polypeptide antigens were synthesized as described previously (22), and their properties are summarized in Table I. The molecular weights were determined using the high speed sedimentation equilibrium method (23). The chemical properties of these antigens were reproducible from one preparation to another, and the antibody response to the different preparations was consistently the same. The antigens were stable for at least 5 years when stored in amber bottles in a desiccator cabinet at 4°C, as determined by the constancy of the hydrodynamic properties and amino acid composition. More recently, the polypeptides were stored at −60° in 1-g amounts in amber bottles and under nitrogen.

Immunization schedule. All studies were carried

[4] The nomenclature of the synthetic polypeptides is defined according to the Tentative Rules on Abbreviated Nomenclature of Synthetic Polypeptides (J. Biol. Chem., *243:* 2451, 1968). The other abbreviations used are: S.D., standard deviation; S.E., standard error of the mean; Ab, antibody; N, number of animals; NS, not significant.

[5] In designating the various strain combinations, A is used for the ACI strain, and F, for the F344 strain. The first symbol in a hybrid denotes the maternal strain, e.g., FA is the F_1 generation resulting from an intercross between an F344 female and an ACI male. The symbol preceding the slash in the backcrosses also denotes the mother, e.g., FA/A is the backcross resulting from an FA female of the F_1 generation and a male of the ACI parental strain.

out with preparations 13-4 or 13-6 of poly Glu^{52}-$Lys^{33}Tyr^{15}$. The optimal method of immunization utilized 0.75 mg of antigen dissolved in 0.25 ml of 0.14 M NaCl-0.01 M phosphate, pH 7.2, (buffered saline) and emulsified with an equal volume of Difco Freund's complete adjuvant, to which additional tubercle bacilli (3 mg/ml final concentration) had been added. The first injection was distributed subcutaneously into the footpads and into the back of the neck, and it was followed 3 weeks later by an identical dose of antigen in 0.5 ml buffered saline injected intraperitoneally. The rats were bled from the heart on the 10th day after the second injection of antigen. The studies on the effect of dose on the magnitude of the antibody response were carried out with the same immunization schedule, and the total dose of antigen was evenly divided between the first and second injections. The time course of the antibody response showed that the antibody concentration reached approximately one-third of the maximal response 3 weeks after immunization; the highest antibody concentration was obtained 10 days after the second dose of antigen, and 3 weeks later the antibody concentration fell to approximately one-third of the maximum.

Aggregates were prepared by mixing 0.75 mg of antigen dissolved in water and 0.75 mg of methylated bovine serum albumin in water. The mixture was emulsified with Freund's complete adjuvant containing additional tubercle bacilli. The methylated bovine serum albumin was prepared by the method of Plescia *et al.* (16). The second dose of antigen was given intraperitoneally as an aggregate suspended in water.

Assay methods. The antibody concentration in each rat antiserum was determined by a quantitative micro-method utilizing the bromoacetyl cellulose immunoadsorbent (24). The assays were done in duplicate using 0.20 ml of serum for each determination, and the amount of antibody was calculated from the empirically determined extinction coefficient at 278 nm, $E^{1\%}_{1cm} = 14.6$. The minimal amount of antibody that could be detected was 20 μg/ml. The rat antiserum standards gave a value of 168 ± 27 (standard deviation) μg of antibody/ml (54 determinations), and the rabbit antiserum standards gave a value of 497 ± 42 μg/ml (57 determinations). In order to determine the effect of multiple assays and of storage on the antibody concentration in the serum, a freeze-thaw experiment was done with a specimen of rat antiserum. There was no change in the amount of antibody measured over at least a 3-month period with three episodes of freezing and thawing. Finally, the reactivity of antibody elicited by a given antigen preparation was tested with several other antigen preparations in order to determine whether the bromoacetyl cellulose immunoadsorbent could be prepared with an antigen preparation different from the one used for immunization. Antisera against preparations 13-4 and 13-6 were assayed with immunoadsorbents prepared with preparations 13-3 through 13-8, and there were no differences in the amount of antibody detected.

The classes of rat immunoglobulin (IgM, γ_1, and IgG) containing antibody were identified by radio-immunoelectrophoretic techniques as previously described (25, 26). This method could always detect antibody in the various immunoglobulin classes at a level of 100 μg of antibody/ml of serum; the lowest limit of detection was 50 μg of antibody/ml. Only the data from sera in which antibody in the immunoglobulin classes could be clearly detected were used. The amount of antibody in each class was scored visually as none, low and high, and the data are presented as histograms. In the dose response study the relative frequencies of the antibody classes are given for each dose level. In the studies on the antibody responses of the parental strains and their progeny, the relative frequency of the antibody response within each class is presented separately for males and for females.

Analyses of data. The data on the antibody responses were treated in several different ways. First, the frequency of the response was plotted against the magnitude of the response, using increments of 50 μg of antibody/ml in each category. Second, the mean antibody responses of the parental strains and their various crosses and the quantitative differences in the responses between males and females were compared using a *t* test. Third, the antibody responses elicited by the antigen aggregated with methylated bovine serum albumin were compared with the responses to the unaggregated antigen using a *t* test. Finally, the quantitative data were used in two ways to construct a theoretical model: a) the frequency data were calculated from the experimental populations and compared to the theoretical model using a chi square test, and b) the putative genotypes were assigned different ranges of antibody concentrations which were then graphically com-

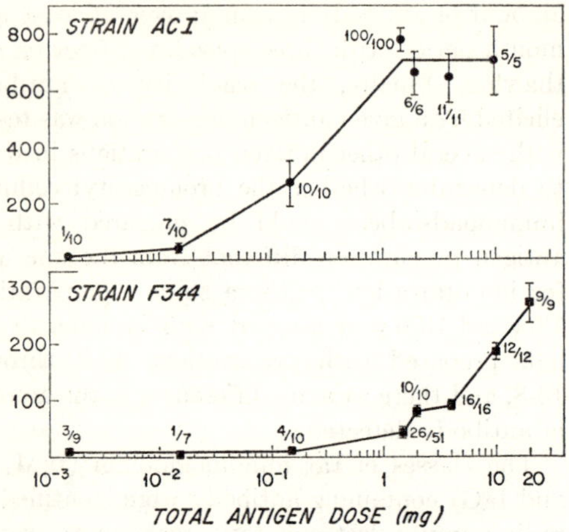

Figure 1. The effect of total antigen dose on the amount of antibody formed. In all cases the immunization schedule was the same, and it is described in the text. Each group of animals contained a mixed population of males and females. The fraction of rats making antibody at each antigen dose level is indicated near the point for that level.

pared with the experimental distributions of genotypes.

RESULTS

Dose response. The effects of immunization with different amounts of antigen in the ACI and F344 strains are shown in Figure 1. At the dose of antigen used for immunization (1.5 mg), the ACI rats were at their maximal response level and the F344 rats were just beginning to respond consistently.

The distribution of antibody among the different immunoglobulin classes varied with the amount of antigen and with the strain (Fig. 2). The F344 strain was much less capable of forming IgM and γ_1 immunoglobulin, and most of the response was in the IgG class. In contrast, the ACI strain responded well in all three immunoglobulin classes at the same antigen doses. At the lowest dose tested (0.15 mg), the ACI strain showed a high IgM response with low to absent γ_1 and IgG responses.

Effect of breeding on the antibody response. The data for the antibody responses are plotted as frequency histograms in Figures 3 and 4, and the mean antibody responses are summarized in Table II. The magnitudes of the antibody responses in females were always more heterogeneous than those of males, except in the parental F344 strain where the heterogeneity in the antibody responses of the males and of the females was approximately the same. The antibody response in the F_1 generation was intermediate between the responses of the parental strains, and all of the animals made antibody. The amounts of antibody formed were the same in reciprocal matings, i.e., in the AF and FA strain combinations. The F_2 generation showed a broader distribution in the magnitudes of the antibody responses than did the F_1 generation; in particular there were more low responders and a few nonresponders. In addition, there was a suggestion of segregation into populations of low, moderate and high responders. The antibody responses were essentially the same in reciprocal matings (AF/AF and FA/FA). The backcrosses showed segregation into three distinct populations of low,

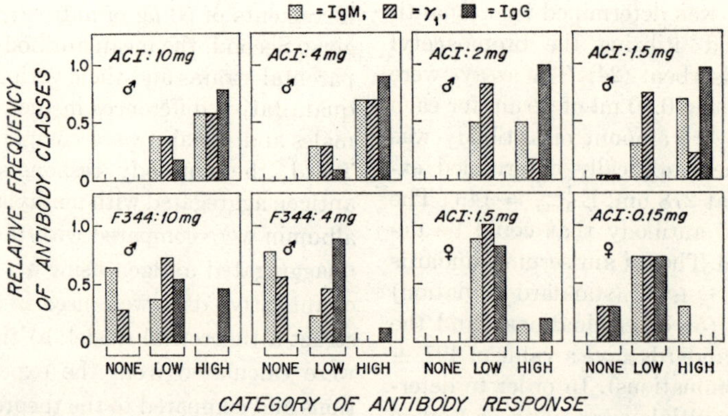

Figure 2. The distribution of antibody among the various immunoglobulin classes following immunization with different amounts of antigen. The immunization schedule is the same as in Figure 1. The numbers of rats in each group are, respectively: *top row*, 5, 10, 6, 32; and *bottom row*, 11, 9, 16, 7.

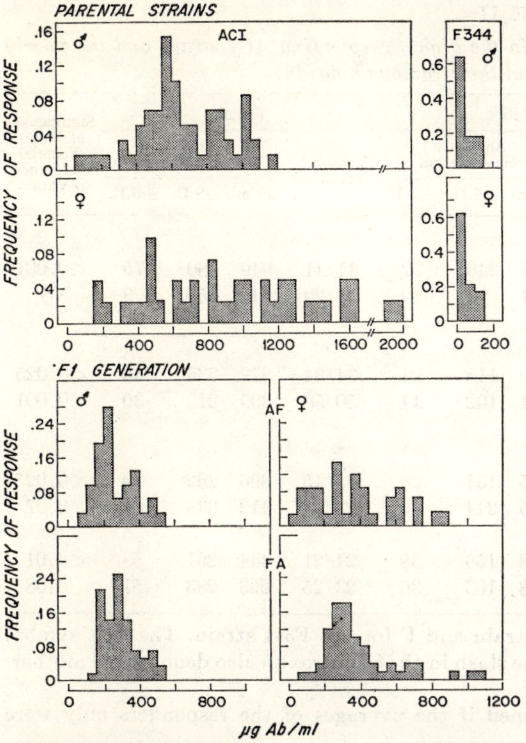

Figure 3. The antibody response to poly Glu^{52}-$Lys^{33}Tyr^{15}$ in the parental strains and in the F_1 generation. The abbreviation A is used for the ACI strain, and F for the F344 strain. The maternal strain is the first symbol and the paternal strain, the second. The mean antibody responses and the number of rats in each group are summarized in Table II.

moderate and high responders (Fig. 4). The FA/A backcross showed mainly moderate or high responders, and the FA/F backcross showed a large number of low responders. The numerical data for these three groups of responders are summarized in Table III.

In addition to the genetic factors shown above, the antibody response was sex-influenced (Table II). There were generally more high responders among the females and more low responders among the males, and the magnitudes of antibody response were more heterogeneous in the females of all generations, except for the poorly responding parental F344 strain. The sex influence was statistically significant in the highly responding ACI parental strain and in the backcrosses to that strain, but it was not seen in the F344 parental strain or in the backcrosses to that train. Progressive cross-breeding (F_1 and F_2 generations) decreased or abolished the higher antibody response in females.

The ACI parental strain and all of the various hybrids made antibody in each immunoglobulin class. The radio-immunoelectrophoretic data are summarized in Figure 5. There was no apparent linkage between the immunoglobulin class and the magnitude of the antibody response; a similar finding has been reported in mice (21). There was no significant sex difference in the distribution of the antibody response among the immunoglobulin classes.

Effect of aggregating the antigen. Aggregating the antigen with methylated bovine serum albumin had profound effects on the antibody response. The antibody responses are plotted as frequency histograms in Figure 6, and the data on the mean antibody responses are shown in

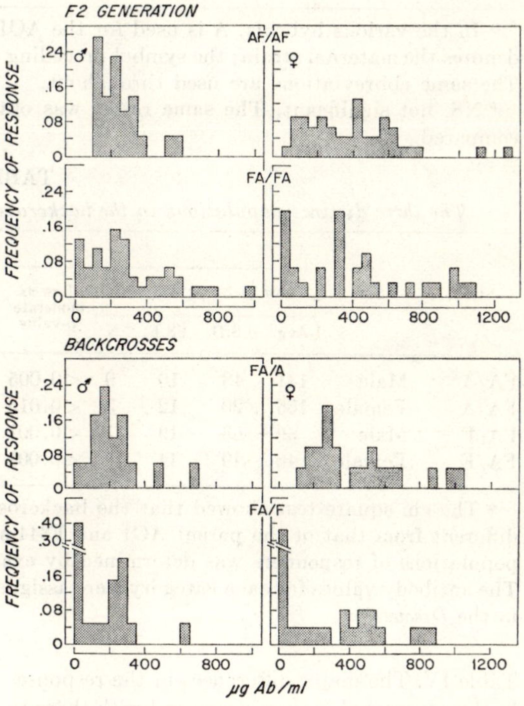

Figure 4. The antibody response to poly Glu^{52}-$Lys^{33}Tyr^{15}$ in the F_2 generation and in the backcrosses. The symbols have the same meaning as in Figure 3; the symbol to the left of the slash is the maternal strain and that to the right of the slash, the paternal strain. The mean antibody responses and the number of rats in each group are summarized in Table II.

TABLE II

The mean antibody response to poly $Glu^{52}Lys^{33}Tyr^{15}$ in the highly responding ACI strain and the poorly responding F344 strain and their various hybrids

Strain[a]	Total Population: Respond-ers/total	Total Population: Antibody concentration µg/ml	±S.D.	±S.E.	Male: Respond-ers/total	Male: Antibody concentration µg/ml	±S.D.	±S.E.	Female: Respond-ers/total	Female: Antibody concentration µg/ml	±S.D.	±S.E.	Significance of Male-Female Difference (p-Value)
Parental													
ACI	100/100	776	388	39	59/59	655	246	32	41/41	949	480	75	<0.001
F344	26/51	42	48	7	13/22	44	46	10	13/29	40	50	9	NS[b]
F_1 generation													
AF	65/65	319	420	52	31/31	260	115	21	34/34	372	236	40	<0.025
FA	106/106	339	170	16	56/56	284	102	14	50/50	399	212	30	<0.001
F_2 generation													
AF/AF	67/67	346	238	29	22/22	245	131	28	45/45	396	262	39	<0.025
FA/FA	72/77	342	279	32	44/46	295	244	33	28/31	412	338	61	0.07
Backcrosses													
FA/A	38/38	347	246	40	17/17	228	156	38	21/21	444	267	58	<0.01
FA/F	37/45	233	245	36	14/20	158	163	36	23/25	293	283	57	0.08

[a] In the various hybrids, A is used for the ACI strain and F for the F344 strain. The first symbol denotes the maternal strain; the symbol preceding the slash in the backcrosses also denotes the mother. The same abbreviations are used throughout.

[b] NS, not significant. The same result was obtained if the averages of the responders only were compared.

TABLE III

The three distinct populations in the backcrosses which produce different amounts of antibody[a]

Strain	Sex	Low (0–200 µg Ab/ml) Avg.	±S.D.	±S.E.	N	Low *vs* moderate p-value	Moderate (201–800 µg Ab/ml) Avg.	±S.D.	±S.E.	N	Moderate *vs* high p-value	High (>800 µg Ab/ml) Avg.	±S.D.	±S.E.	N
FA/A	Male	131	48	16	9	<0.005	339	164	58	8		None			
FA/A	Female	156	20	12	3	<0.015	425	159	44	13	<0.001	983	35	20	3
FA/F	Male	39	63	19	11	<0.001	304	123	41	9		None			
FA/F	Female	46	49	14	12	<0.001	462	154	46	11	<0.008	845	166	118	2

[a] The chi square test showed that the backcrosses form a population of animals that is distinctly different from that of the parent ACI and F344 strains ($p < 0.005$). The existence of three separate populations of responders was determined by examining the patterns of response shown in Figure 4. The antibody values for each category were assigned in accordance with the theoretical model proposed in the *Discussion*.

Table IV. The major differences in the responses to the aggregated antigen compared with those to the unaggregated antigen (Figs. 3 and 4, and Table II) were: a) every rat in each strain and strain combination made antibody; b) the heterogeneity of the antibody response was greatly restricted; c) the antibody response in the females, but not the males, of the poorly responding F344 strain was enhanced; d) in contrast, there was either a decrease or there was no change in the amount of antibody formed by the highly responding ACI strain and by the various hybrids of the ACI and F344 strains; and e) the sex difference in the antibody response (female > male) was unaltered or enhanced.

The effect of aggregation on the distribution of the antibody response among the different immunoglobulin classes was also quite striking, and

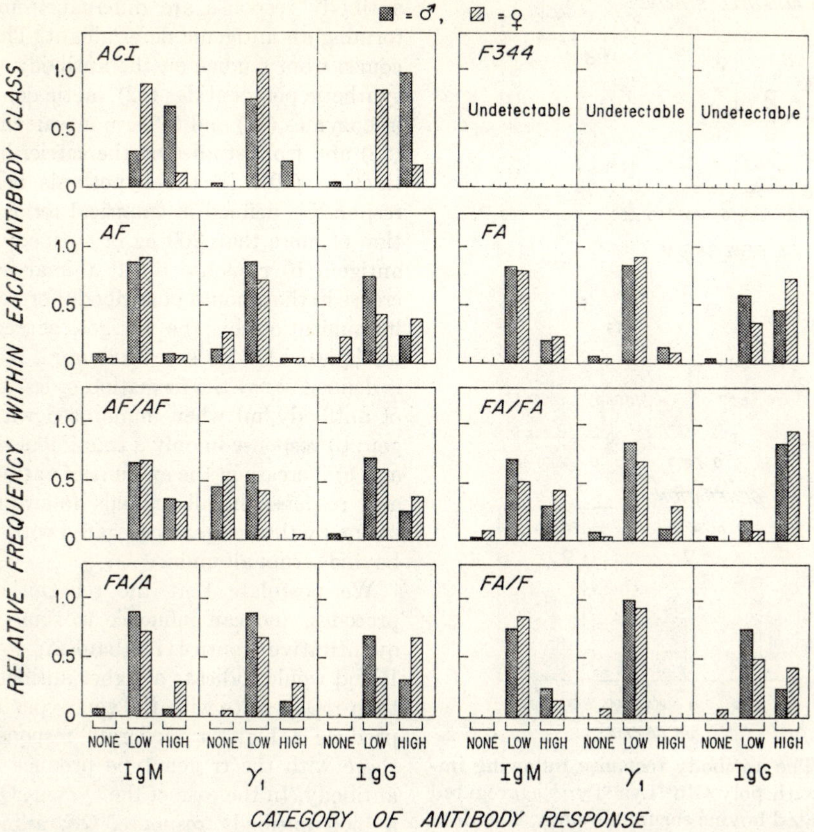

Figure 5. The distribution of the antibody response among the different immunoglobulin classes for the parental strains and their hybrids following immunization with poly $Glu^{52}Lys^{33}Tyr^{15}$. The relative frequency of response within each antibody class is given for each category of the antibody response. This method of presentation shows: a) the proportion of animals making a particular type of immunoglobulin; b) the relative magnitude of each immunoglobulin response; and c) a comparison of the responses between males and females. These comparisons can be made within a given strain or between strains. The numbers of males and females, respectively, in each group are: ACI, 32, 16; F344, 12, 20; AF, 26, 27; FA, 38, 37; AF/AF, 20, 43; FA/FA, 41, 24; FA/A, 16, 21; and FA/F, 12, 24.

the radio-immunoelectrophoretic data are plotted in Figure 7. The F344 parental strain, which either did not respond or responded at a level too low to measure when immunized with unaggregated antigen, formed antibody almost exclusively in the IgG class. The highly responding ACI parental strain formed antibody in all immunoglobulin classes, as in the case of immunization with the unaggregated antigen. The various hybrids of the parental strains responded predominantly in the IgG class, in contrast to the findings following immunization with the unaggregated antigen, in which case the antibody response was distributed among all of the immunoglobulin classes. There were no significant sex differences in the amounts of antibody in the various immunoglobulin classes.

DISCUSSION

The results of these genetic studies are consistent with the hypothesis that the antibody response is controlled by at least two independently segregating genes; no model involving only one gene will fit the data. Three approaches were taken in testing the hypothesis. In the first method, the antibody responses were assigned to low, moderate and high categories, and the experimental ratios for the various hybrids were compared to the theoretical predictions using a chi square test. Secondly, the fraction of the popu-

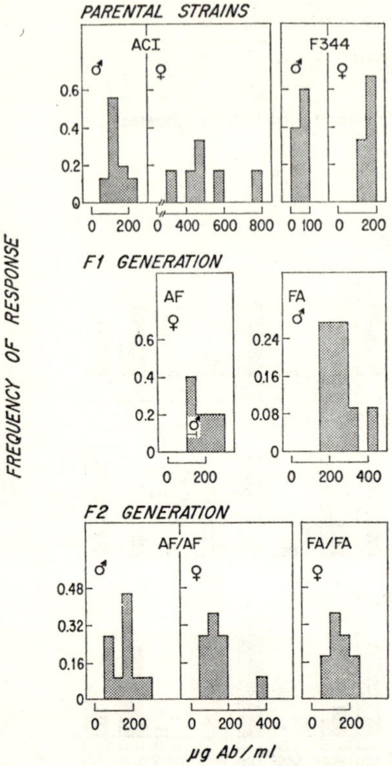

Figure 6. The antibody response following immunization with poly $Glu^{52}Lys^{33}Tyr^{15}$ aggregated with methylated bovine serum albumin. The data for the response in the males of the AF strain combination of the F_1 generation were inadequate for a histogram; therefore, only the range of the responses is given. The mean antibody responses and the number of rats in each group are given in Table IV.

lation making very large or very small amounts of antibody was compared to the theoretically predicted values for a system controlled by two genes. The third approach was to assign an antibody range to all of the putative genotypes and then to compare graphically the theoretical distribution of genotypes with the distribution obtained for the experimental data.

The hypothesis proposes that one of the two independently segregating genes is involved with antigen recognition and that the other gene is concerned with the quantitative regulation of the antibody response. These genes have been called the R-gene and the Q-gene, respectively. There is experimental evidence from several sources that immunogenicity is a distinct process and that the structural requirements for eliciting an antibody response are different from those for forming an antigenic determinant. This evidence comes from studies on the antibody response to synthetic polypeptides (22), lactic dehydrogenase isoenzymes (27) and tobacco mosaic virus protein (28) and from studies on the carrier-hapten relationship (20). In the hypothesis being tested, response is defined in empirical terms: a) elicitation of more than 200 μg of antibody/ml by the antigen; b) response in all animals; and c) decrease in the amount of antibody formed following immunization by the antigen aggregated with methylated bovine serum albumin. Non-response is defined as: a) the formation of less than 200 μg of antibody/ml when immunized with the antigen; b) response in only a fraction of the animals; and c) increase in the amount of antibody formed and response in all animals following immunization by the antigen aggregated with methylated bovine serum albumin.

We postulate that the recognition function precedes, and can influence to some extent, the quantitative control mechanism; for example, RRqq would indicate a higher antibody response than rrQQ. Rats with the genotypes RR and Rr produce a high or moderate response, whereas those with the rr genotype produce little or no antibody. In the case of the Q-gene, QQ indicates a high antibody response, Qq, a moderate response and qq, a low response. The categories of low, moderate and high response were chosen in accordance with the following experimental criteria. The low response includes all of the antibody responses in the parental F344 generation when these rats were immunized with the antigen alone or aggregated with methylated bovine serum albumin ($\leq$200 μg Ab/ml). The moderate category encompasses the antibody responses ranging from the low category to the mean of the female F_1 generation plus two standard deviations (201 to 800 μg Ab/ml). All other responses are in the high category (>800 μg Ab/ml). The designations of these categories are consistent with those used in most types of genetic analyses.

In the first approach to testing this model, the parental ACI strain was assigned the genotype RRQq, and the parental F344 strain was assigned the genotype rrQq. Thus, the highly responding parent was homozygous for response (RR), and the poorly responding parent was homozygous for non-response (rr). Since there is a broad distribution in the antibody response in the ACI strain, especially among the females, the gene for

TABLE IV

The effect on the antibody response of aggregating the antigen poly $Glu^{52}Lys^{33}Tyr^{15}$ with methylated bovine serum albumin

Strain	Total Population				Male				Female				Significance of Male-Female Differences (p-Value)	Comparison with Unaggregated Antigen			
	Responders/total	Antibody concentration			Responders/total	Antibody concentration			Responders/total	Antibody concentration				Male		Female	
		μg/ml	±S.D.	±S.E.		μg/ml	±S.D.	±S.E.		μg/ml	±S.D.	±S.E.		Effect	p-Value	Effect	p-Value
Parental																	
ACI	22/22	242	190	40	16/16	140	37	9	6/6	513	163	66	<0.001	Decrease	<0.001	Decrease	<0.040
F344	21/21	86	53	12	15/15	55	17	4	6/6	162	20	8	<0.001	None[a]		Increase[b]	<0.001
F_1 generation																	
AF	8/8	159	50	18	3/3	139	11	6	5/5	170	62	28	NS	None		None	
FA					11/11	250	70	21						None			
F_2 generation																	
AF/AF	22/22	153	65	14	11/11	160	58	18	11/11	147	74	22	NS	Decrease	<0.050	Decrease	<0.005
FA/FA									11/11	148	47	14				Decrease	<0.025

[a] If only the averages of responders are compared (74 ± 6 μg Ab/ml with the unaggregated antigen), aggregation with MeBSA increases the antibody response in males (p = 0.015).

[b] The difference is still significant at this level if only the averages of responders are compared.

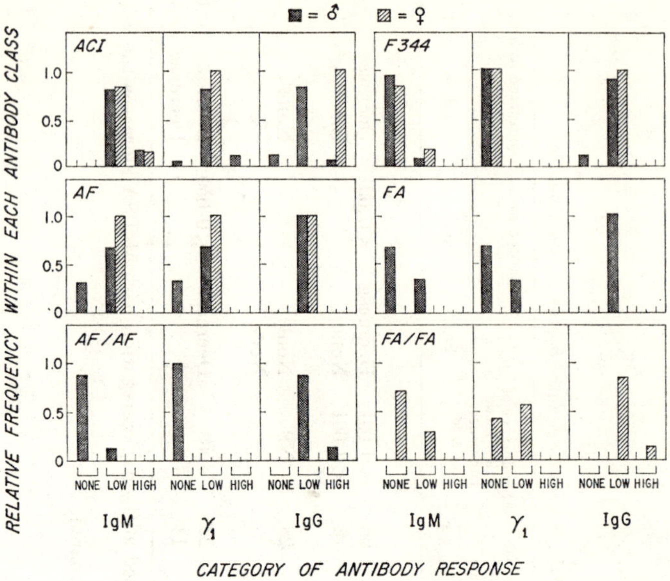

Figure 7. The distribution of the antibody response among the different immunoglobulin classes for the parental strains and their hybrids following immunization with poly $Glu^{52}Lys^{33}Tyr^{15}$ aggregated with methylated bovine serum albumin. The method of presentation is the same as in Figure 5. The number of males and females, respectively, in each group are: ACI, 16, 6; F344, 15, 6; AF, 3, 3; FA (male), 6; AF/AF (male), 8; and FA/FA (female), 7.

quantitative control was assumed to be heterozygous (Qq); the same assumption was made for the F344 strain. The assumption of heterozygosity at this locus is necessary to construct a model which will explain the quantitative data with a minimum of complexity—it is a first approximation and has some heuristic value. In biological terms, the basis for such behavior in an inbred animal could be explained by one of four possibilities: a) two or more genes at the locus which together affect the quantity of antibody produced; b) true residual heterozygosity at the locus, which is probably a rare event; c) homozygosity at the locus, but with variable penetrance of the gene, which would give the phenotypic appearance of heterozygosity; d) rapid mutation or recombination at the locus, which would mimic heterozygosity in the population.

Using these genotypes and the classification of the antibody response given above, the theoretically determined ratios among the three categories of responses were calculated. The experimentally obtained ratios and the theoretically calculated ones are given in Table V. The correspondence between the experimentally determined and theoretically predicted values was tested by the chi square analysis, and the results are shown in Table VI. The experimental model fits the data well with the exception of two cases: the females of the FA/FA strain combination of the F_2 generation contain too many high responders, and the males of the FA/A backcross contain too many low responders. In addition, there may be too many high responders in the females of the FA strain combination of the F_1 generation, but the magnitude of the difference is of questionable significance. Thus, in fitting the experimental values to the theoretical model, the only deviations are those due to a sex influence: a higher response among females and a lower response among males.

The second method of analysis involves the calculation of the population manifesting an extreme expression of a quantitative character—in this case, the quantity of antibody produced—under conditions in which independently segregating allelic pairs have cumulative effects (29). The theoretical value for the probability of the occurrence of such a character in the F_2 generation is $(1/2)^n$, where n is the number of segregating alleles. For control by two allelic pairs of genes, $n = 4$ and 1/16 of the population should show the extreme characteristic. In the genetic model proposed, the extreme expression would be

TABLE V

Comparison of experimental results and theoretical calculations for the hypothesis that two independently segregating genes control the antibody response to poly $Glu^{52}Lys^{33}Tyr^{15}$.

Putative genotype of the ACI strain is RRQq and that of the F344 strain is rrQq (see text). The frequencies are given to the base 16 in order to facilitate comparison with other types of genetic data for segregation of traits through different breeding schedules.

Strain	Category of Response								
	Low (≤200 μg Ab/ml)			Moderate (201–800 μg Ab/ml)			High (>800 μg Ab/ml)		
	Male	Female	Theoretical	Male	Female	Theoretical	Male	Female	Theoretical
Parental									
ACI	0.8	0.8		10.1	5.4		5.2	9.7	
F344	16.0	16.0		0	0		0	0	
F_1 generation									
FA	3.7	1.3		12.4	13.7		0	1.0	
AF	5.0	4.6	4	11.1	10.5	12	0	1.0	0
F_2 generation									
FA/FA	5.9	4.6		9.8	8.3		0.4	3.1	
AF/AF	6.6	4.3	6	9.4	11.0	9	0	0.7	1
Backcrosses									
FA/A	8.5	2.3	2	7.5	11.4	12	0	2.3	2
FA/F	8.8	7.7	10	7.2	7.0	6	0	1.3	0

TABLE VI

Chi square analysis of theoretical model for gene segregation

The p-values are the probabilities that the difference between the theoretical model and the experimental values occurred by chance. Values greater than 0.05 clearly indicate no significant differences from the model, and values between 0.05 and 0.01 are of questionable significance.[a]

Generation	Strain Combination	p-Values	
		Males	Females
F_1	AF	0.75	0.55
	FA	0.95	0.025[b]
F_2	AF/AF	0.45	0.25
	FA/FA	0.55	<0.01[b]
Backcrosses	FA/A	<0.001[c]	0.90
	FA/F	0.80	0.35

[a] Calculated from the data in Tables II and V.
[b] Too many high responders (>800 μg Ab/ml).
[c] Too many low responders (≤200 μg Ab/ml).

either a very small quantity of antibody (⩽50 μg/ml, genotype rrqq) or a very large quantity (>800 μg/ml, genotype RRQQ). In the total F_2 population, there are 144 rats of which 13 make ⩽50 μg Ab/ml and 9 make >800 μg Ab/ml. Therefore, the fraction of the population showing an extreme value for the quantity of antibody formed is 1/11 and 1/16, respectively. These ratios are compatible with control by two allelic pairs of genes, but not by only one pair.

The third approach to evaluating the theoretical model was to assign a given range of antibody responses to each of the putative genotypes and then to compare the theoretical and experimental distributions of the various genotypes. The antibody ranges chosen for each genotype are listed in Table VII. The high responders are postulated to be homozygous in both the R- and Q-gene. The moderate responders, which can be either homozygous or heterozygous in the R-gene, are then ranked according to their Q-genotypes; where both have the same Q-genotype, the one that is homozygous in R is ranked higher. In the low category, the genotype that is heterozygous in R is ranked above all the genotypes that are homozygous in r, and then the three groups in the latter category are ranked according to their Q-genotypes. The genotype that is heterozygous in both the R- and the Q-gene is assigned the broadest range of antibody because of its double heterozygosity. Of all the genotype assignments, the two most arbitrary ones are the assignment of RrQQ as the highest group in the moderate category and the assignment of Rrqq as the highest group in the low category. The theoretical and experimental data for the gene frequencies are plotted in Figure 8; the experimental data for the parental

TABLE VII

Putative genotypes of various hybrids of a cross between RRQq × rrQq (ACI × F344) parents where the R- and Q-genes segregate independently (see Fig. 8)

Category of Response	Putative Genotype	Antibody Range	Theoretical Frequency			
			F_1 generation	F_2 generation	FA/A backcross	FA/F backcross
		µg/ml				
High	RRQQ[a]	⩾801	0	1	2	0
Moderate	RrQQ	800–601	4	2	2	2
	RRQq	600–501	0	2	4	0
	RrQq[b]	500–251	8	4	4	4
	RRqq	250–201	0	1	2	0
Low	Rrqq	200–151	4	2	2	2
	rrQQ	150–101	0	1	0	2
	rrQq	100–51	0	2	0	4
	rrqq	⩽50	0	1	0	2

[a] Homozygous for recognition and high quantity of antibody production.

[b] Broadest range of antibody response because of heterozygosity for recognition and quantity of antibody.

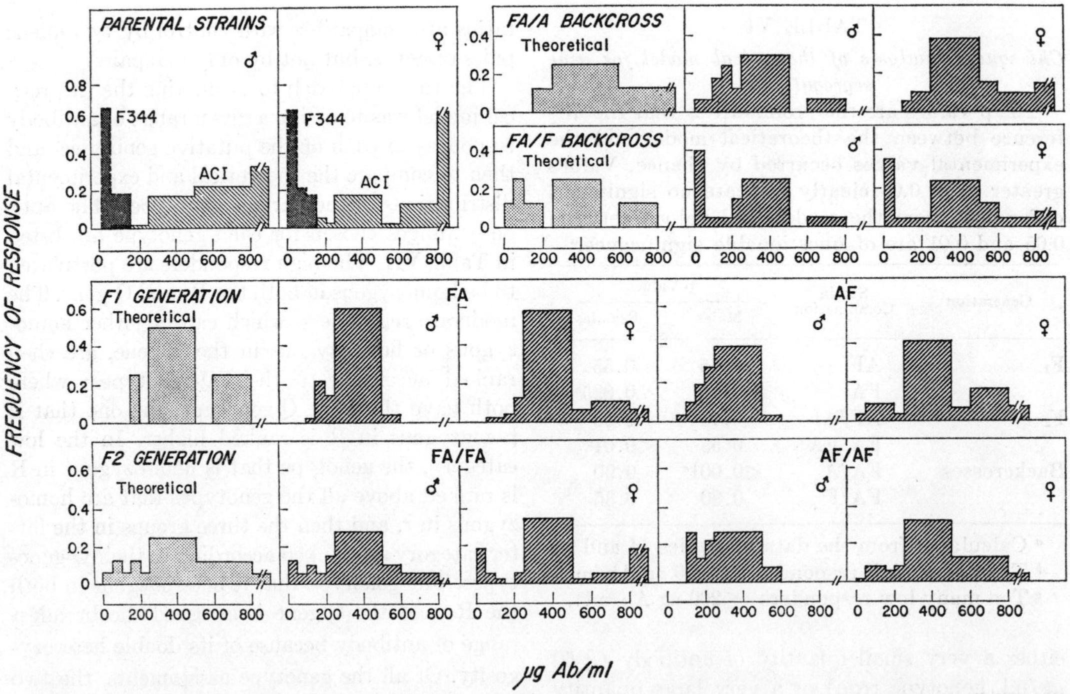

Figure 8. A comparison of the distribution of genotypes in the F_1 and F_2 generations and in the backcrosses compared to the theoretical distributions. The latter were predicted on the basis of the antibody response's being controlled by two independently segregating genes (see text). Each putative genotype was assigned an antibody range, and then the frequency of each genotype was plotted. The experimental data were plotted using the same antibody ranges. The data upon which these choices were made are shown in Table VII.

strains are given for comparison. In general, the experimentally determined distribution of genotypes follows the theoretical predictions reasonably well. The deviations are generally those that might be expected from the sex influence on the immune response: there are too few high responders among the males, for example, in the F_1 generation and in the FA/A backcross, and there are too many high responders among the females, for example, in the FA/FA strain combination of the F_2 generation. As the model is refined and the nature of the sex influence is better understood, the genotypes can be predicted with greater accuracy.

The factors responsible for the sex influence cannot be ascertained at present, but there are some salient features which should be noted.[6] Firstly, the higher antibody response in females is seen only in the highly responding ACI parental strain and in backcrosses to that strain, but not in the F344 strain or in backcrosses to the F344 strain. It appears to be diluted out with progressive cross-breeding: there were no clearly significant differences between females and males in the AF strain combination of the F_1 generation and in both strain combinations of the F_2 generation (Table II). Secondly, there is greater heterogeneity in the antibody response in the females of both parental strains and in their various hybrids. This finding could be explained by random selection of the X-chromosome (lyonization), so that in some cells the X-chromosome of the father is active, whereas in others, the X-chromosome of the mother is active. If the Q-gene were associated with, or influenced by, the X-chromosome, the random selection of the latter would increase the heterogeneity in the amount of antibody formed. Thirdly, immunization with the antigen aggregated with methylated bovine serum albumin did not change the sex difference in the response of the ACI strain; it caused the females of the F344 strain to respond with a larger amount of antibody than the males; and it did not significantly alter the male-female differences in the magnitude of the antibody responses in the F_1 and F_2 generations. These findings indicate that aggregation of the antigen with methylated bovine serum albumin enhanced already existing, or potential, sex differences in the parental strains, but it did not induce any sex difference in the antibody response in the F_1 and F_2 generations, where there was extensive mixing of the gene pools. Thus, the aggregate appears to act through an existing regulatory mechanism. Finally, if the difference in the magnitude of the antibody response were due to environmental factors, it should be seen in all generations. However, it was consistently active only in the highly responding ACI strain or in backcrosses to that strain. In conclusion, then, there may be some other factor involved in the control of the antibody response, or there may be a restriction on the segregation of the R- and Q-genes in females such that these genes are partially constrained to segregate together in the highly responding strains.

[6] Experiments in progress provide some further information about the sex influence. Backcrossing reciprocally mated F_1 hybrids and inbreeding within the F_2 and backcross generations gave different ratios of low, moderate and high responders. The hybrids whose maternal strain was ACI showed higher responses than those whose maternal strain was F344.

The changes in the antibody responses caused by immunization with the antigen aggregated with methylated bovine serum albumen are consistent with a dosage effect. Firstly, if aggregation protected the antigen from degradation, the amount of antigen available and the duration for which it was present would be greatly increased. The increased amount of antigen could then cause partial paralysis in the highly responding parental ACI strain and lead to a decrease in the amount of antibody formed. On the other hand, it could cause an enhanced antibody response in the parental F344 strain similar to that seen with high doses of antigen (Fig. 1). In both of these cases, the antibody response was primarily in the IgG class. This finding suggests that an inability to make adequate amounts of IgM antibody to poly $Glu^{52}Lys^{33}Tyr^{15}$ may be a factor in the poor response of the F344 strain to immunization with that antigen. Secondly, this mechanism could also explain the restricted heterogeneity in the amount of antibody formed. When the antibody response became partially paralyzed (e.g., in the ACI strain) or a large amount of antigen was needed to force the formation of antibody (e.g., in the F344 strain), only a relatively restricted population of cells may be stimulated. Finally, if the effect of aggregation is one of increasing the effective antigen dosage, it would not alter the normal sex difference seen in the antibody response—such is the case.

The better antibody response of the F344 strain

with increasing doses of poly $Glu^{52}Lys^{33}Tyr^{15}$ or with the aggregated antigen can be explained in one of two ways. Firstly, the cells capable of interacting with the antigen may have cellular receptors with a low binding affinity for the antigen. Therefore, large amounts of antigen are needed to cause binding and the subsequent initiation of the antibody response, in accord with the principles of the mass action law. Secondly, there may be only relatively few cells[7] capable of interacting with poly $Glu^{52}Lys^{33}Tyr^{15}$, so that the larger the amount of antigen given, the greater the probability of an antigen-immunocompetent cell interaction. The probability of such an encounter is directly dependent upon the amount of antigen available, which is determined by the dose administered and the degradation of the antigen. Again, this mechanism is in accord with the principles of the mass action law.

Acknowledgments. We wish to thank Colette F. Bernard, Ilene D. Kievman, Agnes H. Heafey and Adele Morse for their excellent technical assistance.

REFERENCES

1. McDevitt, H. O. and Benacerraf, B., Advances Immun., *11:* 31, 1969.
2. Herzenberg, L. A., McDevitt, H. O. and Herzenberg, L. A., Ann. Rev. Genet., *2:* 209, 1968.
3. Levine, B. B., Ojeda, A. and Benacerraf, B., J. Exp. Med., *118:* 953, 1963.
4. Ben-Efraim, S. and Maurer, P. H., J. Immun., *97:* 577, 1966.
5. Arquilla, E. R. and Finn, J., J. Exp. Med. *122:* 771, 1965.
6. McDevitt, H. O. and Sela, M., J. Exp. Med., *122:* 517, 1965.
7. McDevitt, H. O. and Sela, M., J. Exp. Med., *126:* 969, 1967.
8. Mozes, E., McDevitt, H. O., Jaton, J.-C. and Sela, M., J. Exp. Med., *130:* 493, 1969.
9. McDevitt, H. O. and Tyan, M. L., J. Exp. Med., *128:* 1, 1968.
10. Foerster, J., Green, I., Lamelin, J.-P. and Benacerraf, B., J. Exp. Med., *130:* 1107, 1969.
11. Pinchuck, P. and Maurer, P. H., J. Exp. Med., *122:* 673, 1965.
12. Pinchuck, P. and Maurer, P. H., in *Regulation of the Antibody Response*, Edited by Bernard Cinader, p. 97, Charles C Thomas, Springfield, Ill., 1968.
13. Gasser, D. L., J. Immun., *103:* 66, 1969.
14. Playfair, J. H. L., Immunology, *15:* 35, 1968.
15. Simonian, S. J., Gill, T. J., III and Gershoff, S. N., J. Immun., *101:* 730, 1968.
16. Plescia, O. J., Braun, W. and Palczuk, N. C., Proc. Nat. Acad. Sci., *52:* 279, 1964.
17. Gill, T. J., III and Kunz, H. W., Biochim. Biophys. Acta, *124:* 374, 1966.
18. Green, I., Paul, W. E. and Benacerraf, B., J. Exp. Med., *126:* 959, 1967.
19. Green, I., Vassalli, P. and Benacerraf, B., J. Exp. Med., *125:* 527, 1967.
20. Green, I., Paul, W. E. and Benacerraf, B., J. Exp. Med., *127:* 43, 1968.
21. McDevitt, H. O., J. Immun., *100:* 485, 1968.
22. Gill, T. J., III, Kunz, H. W. and Papermaster, D. S., J. Biol. Chem., *242:* 3308, 1967.
23. Yphantis, D. A., Biochemistry, *3:* 297, 1964.
24. Gill, T. J., III and Bernard, C. F., Immunochemistry, *6:* 567, 1969.
25. Stechschulte, D. J. and Austen, K. F. J. Immun., In press.
26. Bloch, K. J., Morse, H. C. and Austen, K. F., J. Immun., *101:* 650, 1968.
27. Rajewsky, K. and Rottlander, E., Cold Spring Harbor Symp. Quant. Biol., *32:* 547, 1967.
28. Spitler, L., Benjamini, E., Young, J. D., Kaplan, H. and Fudenberg, H. H., J. Exp. Med., *131:* 133, 1970.
29. Srb, A. M., Owen, R. D. and Edgar, R. S., *General Genetics*, 2nd Ed., p. 458, Freeman and Co., San Francisco, 1965.
30. Janeway, C. A., Jr., Immunology, *17:* 715, 1969.
31. Paul, W. E., Siskind, G. W., Benacerraf, B. and Ovary, Z., J. Immun., *99:* 760, 1967.
32. Paul, W. E., Benacerraf, B., Siskind, G. W., Goidl, E. A. and Reisfeld, R. A., J. Exp. Med., *130:* 77, 1969.

[7] Some preliminary experiments bearing on this point have been performed. Giving a third dose of antigen 2 months after the maximal antibody response greatly enhanced the amount of antibody made by the F344 rats that had previously received small amounts of antigen. In the groups that received three doses of 0.075 mg or 0.00075 mg, the antibody response increased 5- to 6-fold after the third dose as compared to the amount formed after the usual immunization (two doses) and bleeding schedule. This finding suggests that more cells responsive to stimulation by poly $Glu^{52}Lys^{33}Tyr^{15}$ can be progressively recruited by multiple injections of small amounts of antigen over a period of time; hence, the amount of antibody formed can be progressively increased. Similar phenomena have been reported with D-amino acid polymers (30) and with pneumococcal polysaccharides (31, 32).

THE JOURNAL OF IMMUNOLOGY
Copyright © 1970 by The Williams & Wilkins Co.

Vol. 105, No. 1, July 1970
Printed in U.S.A.

HALF-LIVES, BODY DISTRIBUTION AND LACK OF INTERCONVERSION OF SERUM 19S AND 7S IgM OF SHARKS[1]

PARKER A. SMALL, JR., DAVID G. KLAPPER AND L. WILLIAM CLEM

From the Department of Microbiology, University of Florida, College of Medicine, Gainesville, Florida, and Lerner Marine Laboratory, Bimini, Bahamas

Received for publication January 31, 1970

Passive administration of radiolabeled purified proteins derived from nurse and lemon shark serum to the homologous species revealed that the serum 7S IgM is neither a precursor nor a degradation product of the 19S IgM. The studies also showed that the 19S IgM is predominantly intravascular, as is the IgM of higher vertebrates, whereas the 7S IgM is distributed both extracellularly and intravascularly, as is the IgG in higher species. The half-lives of the 7S and 19S IgM depend on the species of shark, but the half-life of 19S IgM is comparable to that of man. In order to maintain the relatively high serum concentrations of 7S and 19S IgM in the shark, the rate of synthesis of both of these molecules exceeds that of higher vertebrates and totals 100 to 150 mg/kg/day.

The immunoglobulins of all mammalian species studied to date seem to consist of a basic 4-chain structure (sedimentation coefficient ~7S) containing 2H and 2L chains; immunoglobulin class distinctions (IgG, IgA, IgM) are based primarily upon differences in the H-chains (1). The predominant immunoglobulin (IgG) of most mammals is thought to occur only in this monomeric 7S form, although several reports indicate that newborn piglet serum (2) and cow's milk (3) contain a 19S (presumably pentameric) form of IgG. IgA consists predominantly of 7S monomers in serum but occurs as 11S dimers in colostrum (4, 5). IgM in mammals most commonly occurs as a polymer of five such 7S subunits, although in man a 7S (presumably monomeric) form of IgM has been detected in serum during the neonatal period (6, 7) and in certain disease states (7–11). This basic 4-chain (7S) subunit structure of immunoglobulins is also found in the most primitive vertebrates studied in this context, namely, sharks. At least four species of sharks have now been demonstrated to have a 19S pentameric immunoglobulin which physicochemically resembles the IgM of higher animals (12–16). These sharks also have as their predominant immunoglobulin a 7S form, which is of the same class as the 19S molecule and thus is referred to as 7S IgM. The relationship of the monomeric form of immunoglobulins to the polymeric form during the synthetic process is not clear in any of the above cases.

[1] This work was reported at the Federation Meeting in Atlantic City, April, 1969 (Fed. Proc., *28:* 819, 1969), and was supported by National Institutes of Health Grants AI 07713-03 and 5TI AI 0128-10 and Contract Nonr-552(07) between the Office of Naval Research and Lerner Marine Laboratory.

The finding that sharks possess rather high serum concentrations of both 19S and 7S IgM suggests that such animals are suitable for studying whether serum 7S IgM is a precursor or degradation product of 19S IgM. It was felt that such information might help to explain some of the dilemmas relating to valency and structure of the IgM molecule such as: a) the observations in sharks of polyvalent (presumably divalent) 7S IgM molecules but univalent 7S reductive subunits from this same species (14 15), and b) the observation in man of both kappa and lambda light chain types in individual IgM molecules (17). While attempting to answer the question of the relationship between the 19S and 7S IgM it was also possible to measure half-lives, rates of synthesis and the distribution of these molecules within the various body spaces in sharks.

MATERIALS AND METHODS

Preparation of proteins. 7S and 19S IgM were prepared from nurse (*Ginglymostoma cirratum*) and lemon (*Negaprion brevirostris*) shark sera as previously described in detail (14, 15). In brief, the preparation of these homologous (but not isologous) proteins consisted of DEAE-cellulose column chromatography followed by G-200 gel filtration. Shark transferrin was prepared as previously described (15) by DEAE-cellulose chromatography. These shark proteins were shown to be pure by analytic ultracentrifugation and immunoelectrophoresis at concentrations of 8 to 10 mg/ml. Bovine serum albumin was obtained commercially from the Armour Pharmaceutical Co., Kankakee, Ill. Sucrose gradient ultracentrifugation was also performed as described elsewhere (14).

Radiolabeling and counting. The proteins were radiolabeled with either ^{125}I or ^{131}I by the chloramine T method (18). The radioisotopes were detected using a gamma well counter (Baird-Atomic, Inc.) and all samples from an individual animal were counted within a 5-hr period so that corrections for isotope decay were deemed unnecessary.

Animals. Adult nurse (3 to 5 kg) and lemon (1.5 to 3 kg) sharks were kept in pens in free flowing ocean water (temperature ~28°C) at the Lerner Marine Laboratory, Bimini, Bahamas. They were removed from the pens and anesthetized by being placed in a tub of sea water containing MS-222 (Sandoz, Switzerland) until all swimming motions ceased. They were then withdrawn from the anesthetic solution and bled from the hemal arch just anterior to the caudal fin. Injections were made into this same vascular complex and blood was withdrawn both before and after the injection to insure that the sample was given intravascularly.

RESULTS

Determination of the half-life and equilibrium spaces of proteins. Homologous radioiodinated transferrin, 7S IgM, 19S IgM or bovine serum albumin were injected into nurse sharks and lemon sharks, designated as original recipients. Blood samples (4 ml) were subsequently drawn at appropriate times and portions of the serum were analyzed for radioactivity. More than 99% of the bovine serum albumin was eliminated in less than 16 hr and the decay never achieved first-order kinetics. Further studies using this protein were therefore abandoned. Turning to the homologous shark proteins, it can be seen (Fig. 1) that in the original recipients there was an initial rapid decrease followed by a slow first-order decrease in radioactivity. Since it was impossible to determine whether the initial rapid loss of serum radioactivity was due to equilibration of the injected protein within the various body spaces or to elimination of a denatured or otherwise altered fraction of the initial dose, the original recipient animals were bled of ~30 ml of blood and within 2 hr the serum from this blood was injected into other samples of the same species designated as second recipients. Samples were saved to determine the radioactive content of this injected serum. As can be seen in Figure 1, there was still a rapid decay when the transferrin or 7S IgM was administered to a second recipient animal, but with 19S IgM the rapid decay phase was largely eliminated. These data indicate that lemon shark 7S IgM and transferrin equilibrated over approximately a 10-hr period, whereas 19S IgM equlibrated rapidly (less than 2 hr) with its eventual pool. Equilibration in the nurse shark took slightly longer. In the nurse shark 19S IgM experiment, the donated sample was obtained somewhat prematurely, and this may account for the initial rapid drop in the second recipient. Once the initial rapid decrease period had passed and the decay approximated that of first-order kinetics, it was possible to calculate a half-life for the respective proteins in their homologous animals. These calculations are summarized in Table I. By knowing the amount of radioactivity injected and the concentration of radioactivity in the serum initially (after allowing time for mixing) and at equilibrium (defined by extrapolating the linear portion to zero time), it was possible to calculate the volume of fluid containing the protein after equilibration. These volumes, expressed as percentage of body weight, are shown in Table II. The 47% and 35% 19S IgM equilibration values for the original recipient lemon and nurse sharks are artifactually high due to the rapid elimination of a large portion of the 19S IgM administered. The 12% value for the second recipient nurse shark 19S IgM is perhaps high for similar reasons. Thorson (19) has studied plasma volume spaces, blood volume spaces and extracellular fluid spaces in lemon and nurse sharks and has found that the plasma volume makes up ~5.5%, and the extracellular fluid ~21%, of the body weight. Compar-

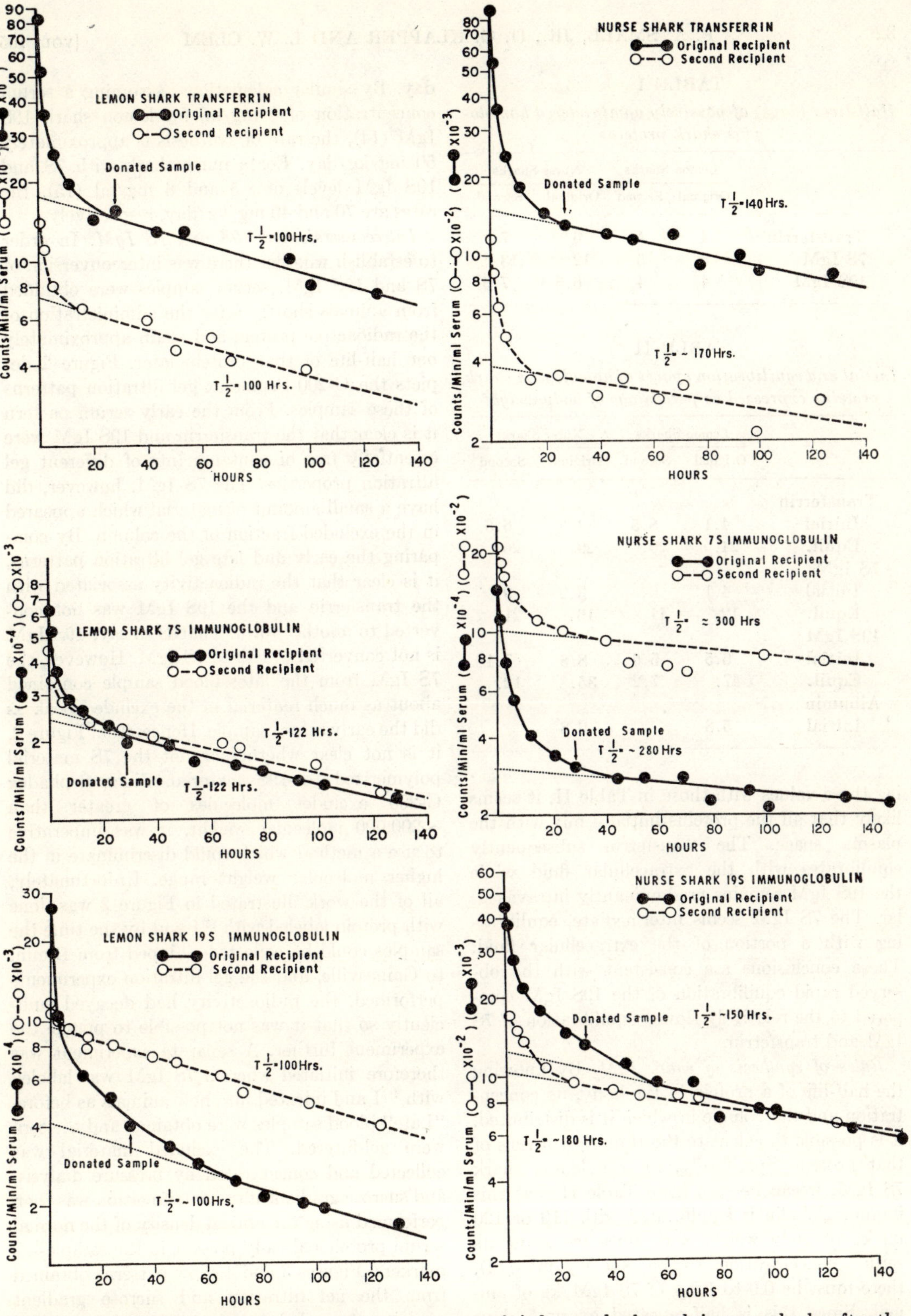

Figure 1. Disappearance of radioactivity from serum of six lemon sharks and six nurse sharks after the administration of ^{131}I-labeled homologous transferrin, 7S IgM or 19S IgM. Original recipients (●——●) refer to animals that originally received the above protein, and second recipients (○——○) refer to animals that received "biologically purified" protein in the form of serum drawn from the original recipient at the time designated as "donated sample."

TABLE I

Half-lives (days) of passively administered homologous shark proteins

	Lemon Sharks		Nurse Sharks	
	Original	Second	Original	Second
Transferrin	4	4	6	7
7S IgM	5	5	12	13
19S IgM	4	4	6.5	7.5

TABLE II

Initial and equilibration spaces of homologous shark proteins expressed as percentage of body weight

	Lemon Sharks		Nurse Sharks	
	Original	Second	Original	Second
Transferrin				
Initial	4.1	8.5	4.3	6.5
Equil.	24.	20.	29.	26.
7S IgM				
Initial	4.1	6.	3.2	9.
Equil.	12.	11.	16.	21.
19S IgM				
Initial	6.5	5.6	8.8	7.1
Equil.	47.	7.2	35.	12.
Albumin				
Initial	5.8		6.8	

ing these values with those in Table II, it seems likely that all the proteins initially mix with the plasma space. The transferrin subsequently equilibrates with the extracellular fluid while the 19S IgM remains predominantly intravascular. The 7S IgM seems intermediate, equlibrating with a portion of the extracellular fluid. These conclusions are consistent with the observed rapid equilibration of the 19S IgM compared to the relatively slower equilibration of 7S IgM and transferrin.

Rates of synthesis of shark IgM. By knowing the half-life of a protein in the body, its concentration and the volume in which it is distributed, it is possible to calculate the rate of synthesis of that protein. Specifically, for the lemon shark 7S IgM, it can be seen from Table II that this immunoglobulin is equilibrated with 110 or 120 ml/kg of body weight and, since we know its serum concentration to be 8.5 mg/ml (14), there must be 0.9 to 1.0 g of 7S IgM/kg of animal. Since this is half-repeated every 5 days (Table I), the animal must synthesize approximately 100 mg of 7S IgM/kg of body weight/day. By similar calculations, assuming a serum concentration of 6 mg/ml for lemon shark 19S IgM (14), the rate of synthesis is approximately 50 mg/kg/day. For a nurse shark with 7S and 19S IgM levels of 8.5 and 6 mg/ml (15), the rates are 70 and 40 mg/kg/day, respectively.

Interconversion of 19S and 7S IgM. In order to establish whether there was interconversion of 7S and 19S IgM, serum samples were obtained from animals shortly after the administration of the radioactive protein and again approximately one half-life of that protein later. Figure 2 depicts the G-200 Sephadex gel filtration patterns of these samples. From the early serum pattern it is clear that the transferrin and 19S IgM were essentially free of contaminants of different gel filtration properties. The 7S IgM, however, did have a small amount of material which appeared in the excluded fraction of the column. By comparing the early and late gel filtration patterns, it is clear that the radioactivity associated with the transferrin and the 19S IgM was not converted to another form. That is to say, 19S IgM is not converted *in vivo* to 7S IgM. However, the 7S IgM from the later blood sample contained about as much material in the excluded peak as did the early serum sample. Hence, from Figure 2, it is not clear whether or not the 7S material polymerized to 19S material. Since Sephadex G-200 excludes molecules of greater than ~200,000 molecular weight, it was imperative to use a method which could discriminate in the higher molecular weight range. Unfortunately, all of the work illustrated in Figure 2 was done with protein labeled with ^{131}I and by the time the samples could be collected, shipped from Bimini to Gainesville, and the gel filtration experiments performed, the radioactivity had decayed sufficiently so that it was not possible to pursue the experiment further. A separate experiment was therefore initiated wherein 7S IgM was labeled with ^{125}I and injected into new animals as before. "Late" blood samples were obtained and the sera were gel-filtered. The excluded material was collected and concentrated by pressure dialysis, and sucrose gradient ultracentrifugation was then performed using the optical density of the normal serum proteins already present in the samples as markers. Figures 3 and 4 show patterns obtained from the gel filtration and sucrose gradient experiments and demonstrate that the excluded radioactive material from the G-200 Sephadex gel filtration experiments was probably not a 19S

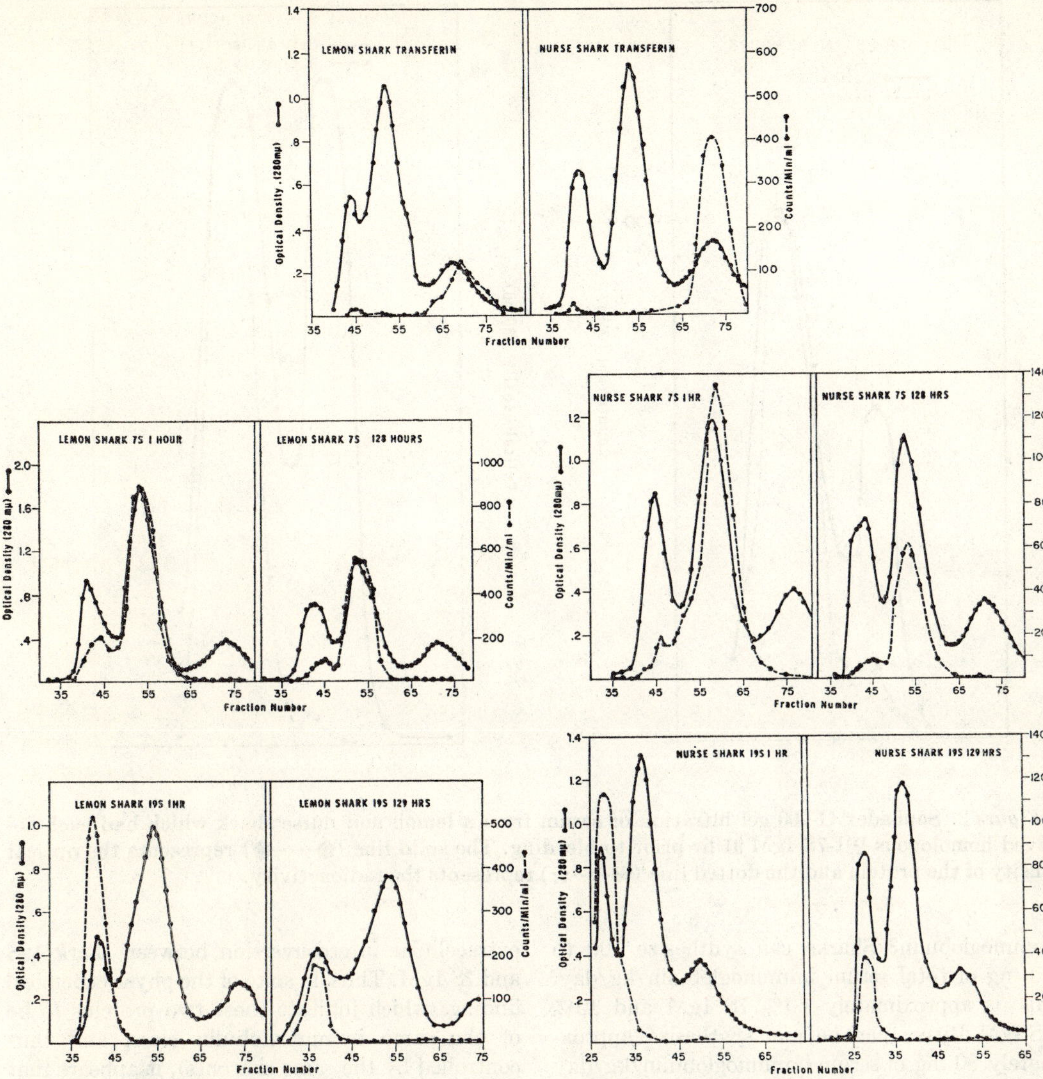

Figure 2. Sephadex G-200 gel filtration of serum samples obtained either 1 hr or 5 days after the administration of ^{131}I-labeled transferrin, 7S IgM or 19S IgM derived from the homologous species of shark. The 1-hr transferrin patterns are omitted. The solid lines denote the optical density of the serum proteins and the dotted lines denote the radioactivity of the passively administered protein. The first protein peak contains excluded material including 19S IgM, the second peak contains 7S IgM and the third peak contains smaller molecules including transferrin.

pentameric IgM molecule but rather consisted of dimers and/or trimers of the 7S IgM molecule. Since such entities have not been found in normal shark serum, it seems likely that they are artifacts resulting from the various chemical manipulations of the 7S IgM, and we therefore conclude that there is no evidence from these studies that serum 7S IgM is an extracellular precursor of the 19S IgM *in vivo*.

DISCUSSION

As one descends the vertebrate phylogenetic tree, the question arises as to whether there exists a lessening of immunologic capabilities. Clearly, the number of immunoglobulin classes is less for lower than for higher vertebrates, but the ability to respond to a diversity of antigenic stimuli is not apparently decreased (reviewed in 20). What about the ability to synthesize

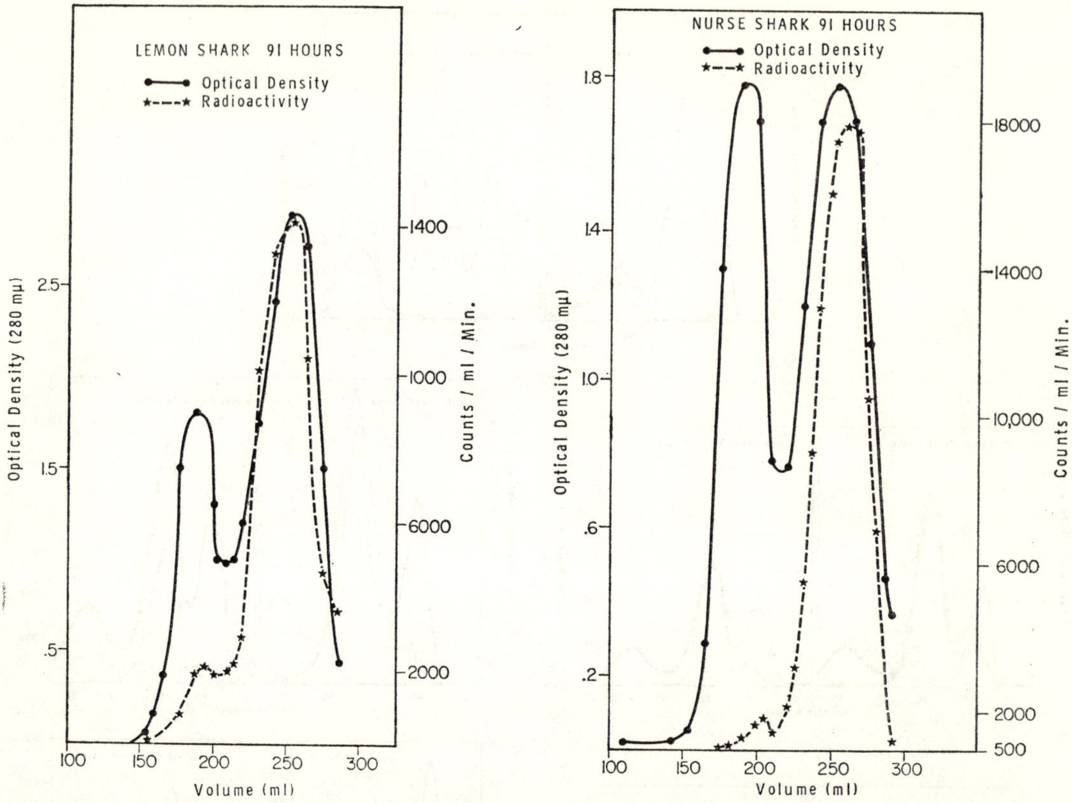

Figure 3. Sephadex G-200 gel filtration of serum from a lemon and nurse shark which had each received homologous ^{125}I-7S IgM 91 hr prior to bleeding. The solid line (●——●) represents the optical density of the protein and the dotted line (★-----★) represents the radioactivity.

immunoglobulin? Sharks can synthesize 100 to 150 mg of total serum immunoglobulin/kg/day. This is approximately 60% 7S IgM and 40% 19S IgM. By comparison, man synthesizes approximately 80 mg of serum immunoglobulin/kg/day of which only 6 mg/kg/day is IgM (21). Thus the ability of these two phylogenetically distant animals to synthesize immunoglobulin is comparable. The shark, however, synthesizes considerably more IgM than any other species thus far studied. It is also tempting to compare half-lives of IgM in sharks and man since each is in the range of 1 week. However, the greater differences exhibited by other mammals (e.g., mouse IgM $T_{1/2}$ = 0.5 days (21)) makes such comparisons of questionable value. An additional complication is that of comparing such factors in poikilotherms and homotherms, not to mention the unexplained differences between nurse and lemon sharks observed here.

The data indicate that there is no discernible extracellular interconversion between shark 19S and 7S IgM. Thus, in spite of the physicochemical findings which indicate these two proteins to be of the same immunoglobulin class, and thus controlled by the same cistron(s), it appears that they are distributed and therefore may function as if they were of different classes. The independence of the two molecules reported here is also illustrated by other studies. For example, at birth nurse sharks have no detectable 7S IgM and only low levels of 19S IgM, but as the animal matures the ratio of 19S to 7S IgM reverses (22). Similarly, antibodies produced in response to antigenic stimulation are detected first in 19S fractions and later in 7S fractions (14, 15). Although these later studies were conducted with antibody assays which may be biased in favor of greater sensitivity for 19S as opposed to 7S antibodies, it should be mentioned that specifically isolated "early" antibodies to Salmonella somatic antigens were exclusively of the

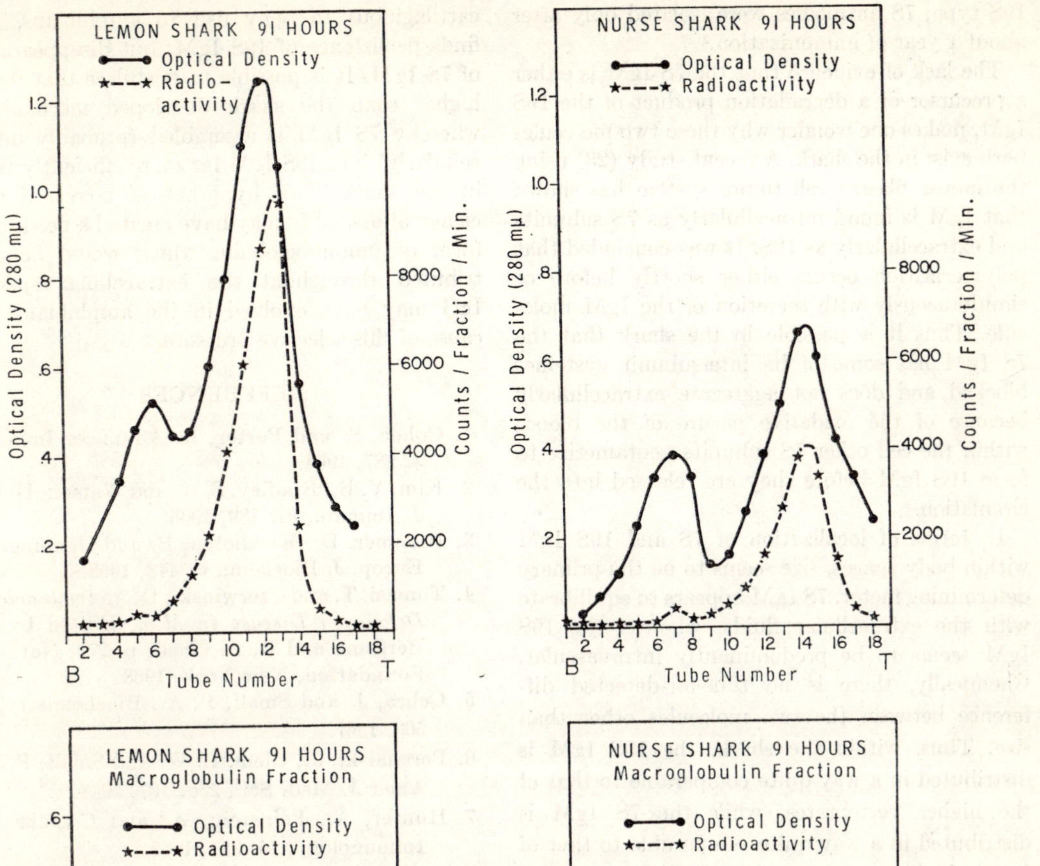

Figure 4. Sucrose density gradient ultracentrifugation of serum (*upper two patterns*) or the serum fraction eluting from Sephadex G-200 in the excluded peak (*lower two patterns*) derived from a lemon and nurse shark which had each received homologous ^{125}I-labeled 7S IgM 91 hr prior to bleeding. The solid line (●——●) represents the optical density and the dotted line (★-----★) represents the radioactivity. The bottom of the gradient is designated by B and the top by T. The optical density peak near the gradient bottom (~fractions 5 to 7) represents predominantly 19S IgM.

19S type; 7S antibodies were isolated only after about 1 year of immunization.[2]

The lack of evidence that the 7S IgM is either a precursor or a degradation product of the 19S IgM, makes one wonder why these two molecules both exist in the shark. A recent study (23) using the mouse plasma cell tumor system has shown that IgM is found intracellularly as 7S subunits and extracellularly as 19S. It was concluded that polymerization occurs either shortly before or simultaneously with secretion of the IgM molecule. Thus it is possible in the shark that the 7S IgM has some of its intersubunit cysteines blocked and does not aggregate extracellularly because of the oxidative nature of the blood; within the cell other 7S subunits pentamerize to form 19S IgM before they are released into the circulation.

In terms of localization of 7S and 19S IgM within body spaces, size seems to be the primary determining factor. 7S IgM appears to equilibrate with the extracellular fluids, whereas the 19S IgM seems to be predominantly intravascular. Chemically, there is no thus-far-detected difference between the two molecules other than size. Thus, within the shark, the 19S IgM is distributed in a way quite comparable to that of the higher vertebrates, while the 7S IgM is distributed in a way quite comparable to that of IgG in higher vertebrates. Since shark 7S IgM is presumably divalent (14, 15) and is distributed in the same general areas as IgG, one cannot help but wonder what advantages IgG has over 7S IgM. Stated differently, these data raise the question of why higher vertebrates "evolved" IgG when 7S IgM seems to be able to perform so many of its functions. There are at least two possible answers to this question: a) It may be that 7S IgM lacks the control mechanism function which seems to be associated with IgG. That is to say that IgG antibody has the ability to shut off the synthesis of 19S IgM antibody (reviewed in 24), and further work is required to show whether this type of control function can be attributed to 7S IgM. b) As one "goes" from cartilaginous to bony fish to amphibians, one finds persistence of 19S IgM, but disappearance of 7S IgM. It is possible to postulate that forms higher than the shark developed mechanisms whereby 7S IgM is assembled (probably intracellularly) into 19S IgM far more efficiently than in the shark. This hypothetical increased efficiency of assembly may have created a need for a form of immunoglobulin which would be distributed throughout the extracellular spaces. IgG may have evolved in the amphibians because of this selective pressure.

[2] Schulkind, M., Robbins, J., and Clem, L. W., Biological properties of specifically purified 19S and 7S IgM nurse shark antibodies to Salmonella somatic antigens, In preparation.

REFERENCES

1. Cohen, S. and Porter, R. Advances Immun., *4:* 287, 1964.
2. Kim, Y. B., Bradley, S. G. and Watson, D. W., J. Immun., *97:* 189, 1966.
3. Hammer, D., Kickhofeu, B. and Henning, G. Europ. J. Biochem., *6:* 443, 1968.
4. Tomasi, T. and Czerwinski, D., in *Immunologic Deficiency Disease in Man*, Edited by D. Bergsma and R. A. Good, p. 270, National Foundation, New York, 1968.
5. Cebra, J. and Small, P. A., Biochemistry, *6:* 503, 1967.
6. Perchalski, J., Clem, L. W. and Small, P. A., Amer J. Med. Sci., *256:* 107, 1968.
7. Hunter, A., Feinstein, A. and Coombs R., Immunology, *15:* 381, 1968.
8. Rothfield, N. F., Fragione, B. and Franklin, E. C., J. Clin. Invest., *44:* 62, 1965.
9. Stobo, J. D. and Tomasi, T. B., Arthritis Rheum. *9:* 543, 1966.
10. Bush, S. T., Swedlund, H. A. and Gleich, G. J., Fed. Proc., *26:* 529, 1967.
11. Solomon, A., Fed. Proc., *26:* 529, 1967.
12. Marchalonis, J. and Edelman G., J. Exp. Med., *122:* 601, 1965.
13. Marchalonis, J. and Edelman G., Science, *154:* 1567, 1966.
14. Clem, L. W. and Small, P. A., J. Exp. Med., *125:* 893, 1967.
15. Clem, L. W., DeBoutaud, F. and Sigel, M. M., J. Immun., *99:* 1226, 1967.
16. Suran, A., Tarail, M. and Papermaster, B., J. Immun., *99:* 679, 1967.
17. Costea, N., Yakulis, V. and Heller, P., Science, *152:* 1520, 1966.
18. MacConahey, P. and Dixon, F., Int. Arch. Allerg., *29:* 185, 1966.
19. Thorson, T. B., Science, *138:* 688, 1962.

20. Clem, L. W. and Leslie, G. A., in *Developmental Immunology*, Edited by M. Adinolfi, p. 62, Spastics International Medical Publications, London, 1969.
21. Schwartz, R. S., Med. Clin. N. Amer., *50:* 1487, 1966.
22. Fidler, J., Clem, L. W. and Small, P. A., Comp. Biochem. Physiol., *31:* 365, 1969.
23. Parkhouse, R. M. E. and Askonas, B. A., Biochem. J., *115:* 163, 1969.
24. Uhr, J. W. and Moller, G., Advances Immun., *8:* 81, 1968.

THE JOURNAL OF IMMUNOLOGY
Vol. 105, No. 1, July 1970

TONSILLAR TISSUE IMPLANTS IN NEONATALLY THYMECTOMIZED MICE

I. Effect on the Spleen[1]

BETTINA HALL HARRISON

From the Department of Biology, University of Massachusetts/Boston, Boston, Massachusetts 02116

Received for publication January 30, 1970

Palatine tonsils from 28- and 29-day fetal rabbits, and from 1-day-old rabbits were implanted into the abdominal cavities of 1-day-old mice thymectomized at birth. After 4 or 6 weeks the spleens of these mice showed restoration of follicular organization and repopulation by lymphocytes of thymus-dependent and perifollicular areas, as compared with thymectomized, non-implanted controls. These results clearly indicate functional similarities between palatine tonsillar tissue and thymic tissue.

Thymectomy of newborn animals affects both the morphologic and the physiologic aspects of the immune system (1–7). In the spleen the follicles develop poorly, with areas of lymphocyte depletion around the central arterioles, the so-called "thymus-dependent areas" (8, 9). If neonatally thymectomized mice are treated within a week by grafting newborn thymic tissue, or by injecting spleen or thymus cells, the splenic follicles develop normally (10–14).

Recent studies on the fetal development of the palatine tonsil of rabbits (15, 16) indicate that lymphopoiesis in the tonsil is similar to that in the thymus and suggest that the two organs may have a similar function. The purpose of this investigation was to see whether tonsillar tissue implants would have the same effect as thymus implants in restoring normal follicular development in the spleens of neonatally thymectomized mice.

MATERIALS AND METHODS

New Zealand White rabbits of 28 and 29 days gestation were killed with chloroform; the fetuses were rapidly removed and chilled to 8°C. One-day-old rabbits were also killed with chloroform and chilled. Using sterile equipment and solutions, the palatine tonsils were dissected free of the pharyngeal tissue, placed in Petri plates on filter paper moistened with physiologic saline and held for a short time at 8°C.

White mice of the Charles River strain were thymectomized at birth and maintained under clean but not sterile conditions. At 1 day of age half of each litter were implanted with tonsillar tissue by making a small slit in the lower abdominal wall, inserting a single tonsil into the abdominal cavity, and closing the incision with a nylon suture. During this procedure the animals were anesthetized by chilling (17) and sterile equipment and solutions were used. The animals were returned to their cages as soon as breathing and body temperature were normal.

All animals were killed at either 4 weeks or 6 weeks of age, the spleens were removed, fixed in Stieve's reagent (18), embedded in paraffin, sectioned at 4 μ and stained with hematoxylin and eosin. During preparation the spleens were positioned carefully in the paraffin blocks and sections were cut to the same depth in control and implanted specimens so that comparisons could be made on equivalent areas of splenic tissue. Every animal was checked for completeness of thymectomy by post-mortem examination and histologic sections. Animals with any sign of thymic tissue were eliminated from the experiment with the single exception mentioned subsequently in the text.

RESULTS

Spleens taken from normal 4-week-old mice showed incomplete development of the follicles;

[1] This work was supported by Faculty Research Grant FR-C53-69 from the University of Massachusetts.

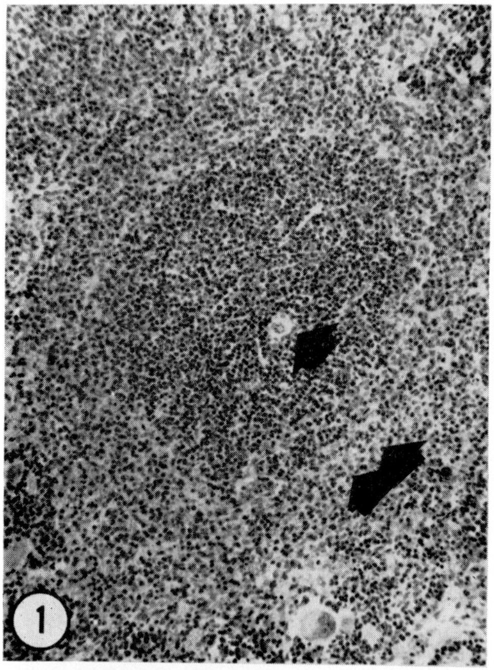

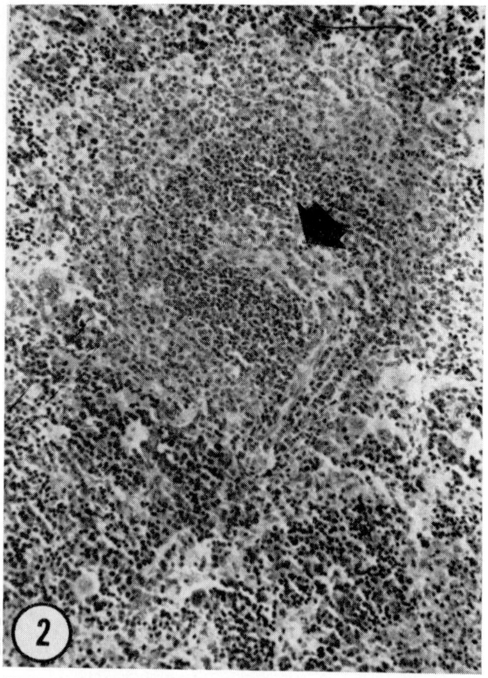

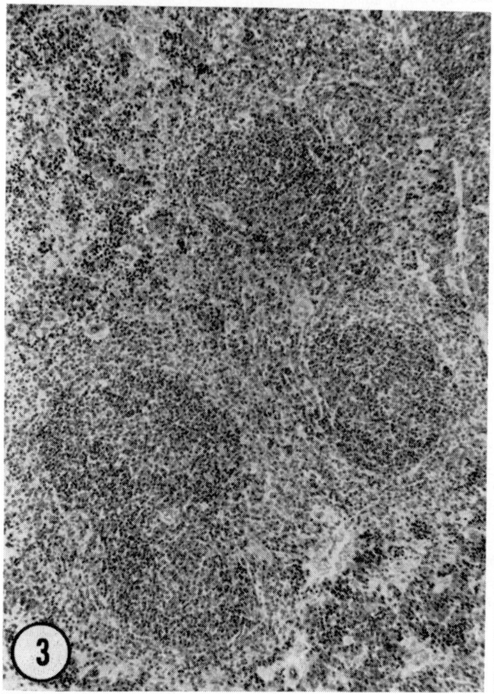

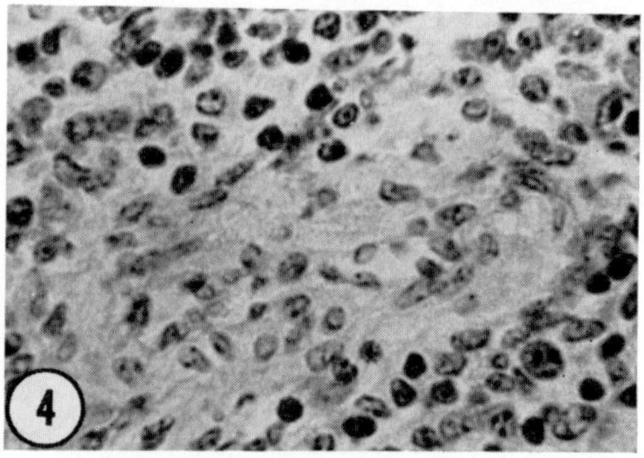

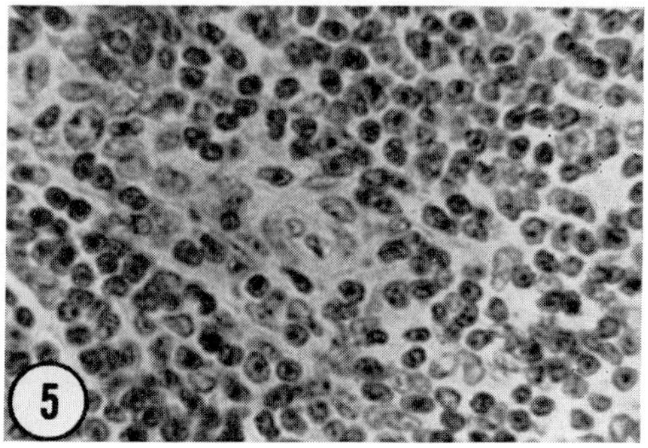

Figure 1. A follicle in the spleen of a normal 4-week-old mouse. The follicle has lymphocytes packed around the central arteriole (*arrow*), and the perifollicular border is well defined (*double arrow*) (× 140).

Figure 2. A follicle in the spleen of a 4-week-old mouse thymectomized at birth. The entire center of the follicle around the arteriole is depleted of lymphocytes (*arrow*) (× 140).

Figure 3. Follicles in the spleen of a 4-week-old mouse thymectomized at birth and implanted with tonsillar tissue from a 29-day rabbit fetus. The area around the arterioles is normal in appearance (× 100).

Figure 4. Detail of the central area of a follicle from the spleen of a 4-week-old mouse thymectomized at birth. Most of the cells are reticular cells (× 550).

Figure 5. Detail of the central area of a follicle from a 4-week-old mouse thymectomized at birth and implanted with tonsillar tissue from a 28-day rabbit fetus. The follicle is packed with lymphocytes (× 550).

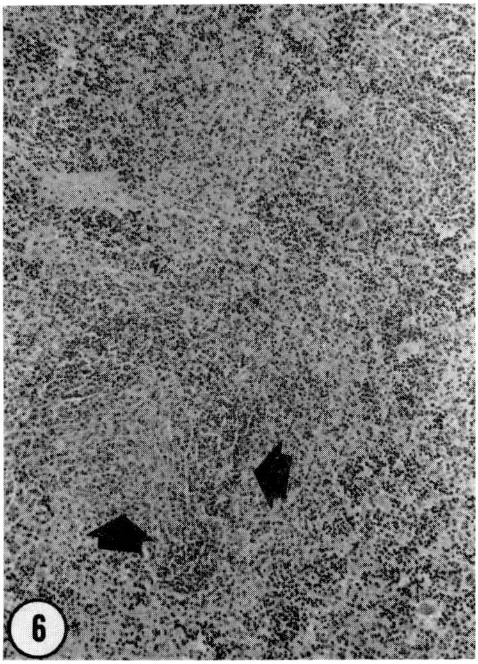

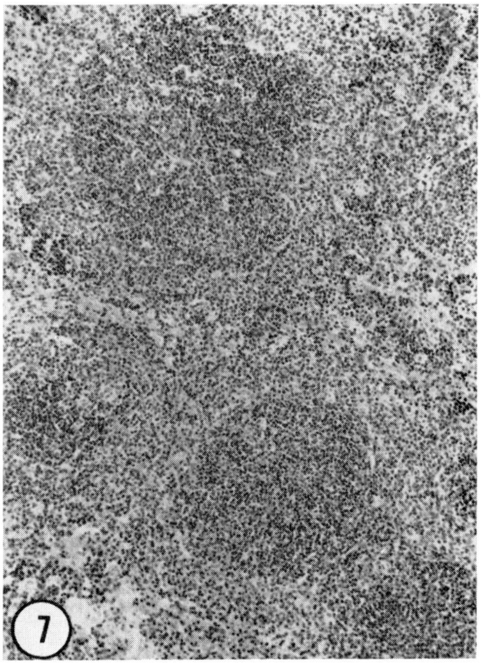

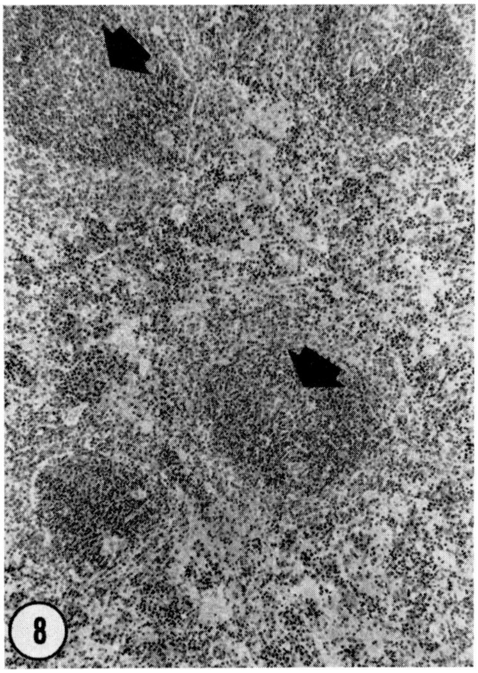

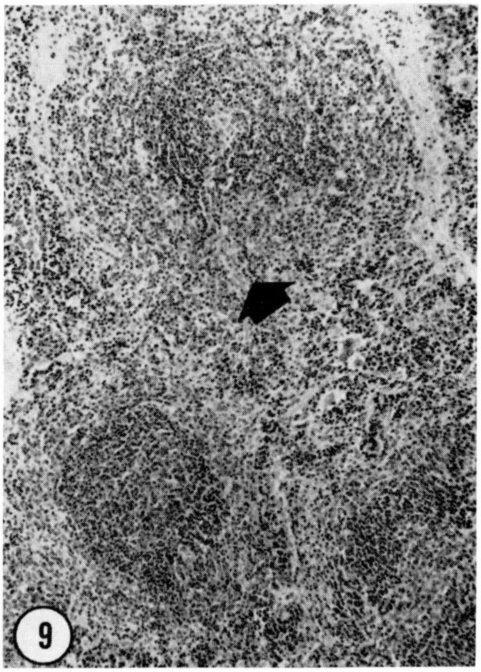

Figure 6. A follicle in the spleen of a 6-week-old mouse thymectomized at birth (*arrows*). Note the extreme depletion and disorganization (× 100).

Figure 7. Follicles in the spleen of a 6-week-old mouse thymectomized at birth, but with a large regenerated thymic mass. Lymphocytes fill the follicles, and the perifollicular border has become more cellular (× 100).

Figure 8. Follicles in the spleen of a 6-week-old mouse thymectomized at birth and implanted with tonsillar tissue from a 28-day rabbit fetus. The follicles are nearly normal in appearance and some have organized germinal centers (*arrows*) (× 100).

Figure 9. Follicles in the spleen of a 6-week-old mouse thymectomized at birth and implanted with tonsillar tissue from a 1-day-old rabbit. Lymphocytes fill the central areas, but the perifollicular border of one of them is still quite acellular (*arrow*) (× 100).

wide perifollicular areas were relatively free of lymphocytes, and the follicles were small. However, the areas around the central arterioles, the "thymus-dependent areas," were well populated with lymphocytes (Fig. 1). Spleens from thymectomized controls 4 weeks old showed a considerable change from normal (Figs. 2 and 4). The perifollicular areas were very large, and follicles were disorganized in appearance with pronounced areas of lymphocyte depletion around the central arterioles. This picture corresponded with that described by others for neonatally thymectomized animals (1, 2, 7, 8, 13). In the animals which had received tonsillar implants, however, over half the follicles were normal, or nearly normal in appearance. The perifollicular areas were reduced in size and the "thymus-dependent areas" were again populated with lymphocytes (Figs. 3 and 5).

Normal 6-week-old animals had spleens with well developed follicles; lymphocytes were packed around the central arterioles, germinal centers could be identified, and the perifollicular areas were no longer sharply defined. Thymectomized controls of the same age had abnormal spleens identical to those described in 4-week-old animals (Fig. 6). One control animals was found to have a regenerated thymic mass about half the size of a normal thymus. The spleen of this animal was not quite normal, but both the thymus-dependent and perifollicular areas in most follicles were well populated with lymphocytes (Fig. 7). The pattern of restoration resembled that seen in the spleens of 6-week-old animals implanted with tonsils from 28-day fetal rabbits or 1-day-old rabbits (Figs. 8 and 9). In these latter two cases, the thymus-dependent and perifollicular areas were also well populated with lymphocytes in more than half the follicles.

DISCUSSION

The role of the palatine tonsils in immunity is poorly understood. Their embryonic origin and life history are similar to those of the thymus (19, 20), and the results of this experiment indicate that when they are implanted into a thymectomized animal they function like thymus tissue implanted in the same manner. The results also show that spleens from species which do not normally have tonsils will react to the addition of tonsillar tissue. The inter-species effect suggests some general function for the tonsil. Either the lymphocytes of rabbits are enough like the lymphocytes of mice so that the former can migrate through the splenic tissue of mice to repopulate the thymus-dependent area, or rabbit tonsils produce some agent which induces mouse cells to repopulate those areas. The reduction in size of the depleted perifollicular area may be a secondary effect due to repopulation around the central arteriole, or the route of cell migration may cross this zone, as suggested by Parrott *et al.* (9).

Several lines of investigation to better define the action of the tonsils are currently underway and will be reported on at a later date.

REFERENCES

1. Good, R. A., Dalmasso, A. P., Martinez, C., Archer, O. K., Pierce, J. C. and Papermaster, B. W., J. Exp. Med., *116:* 773, 1962.
2. Grundmann, E. and Hobik, H. P., in *Germinal Centers in Immune Responses,* Edited by H. Cottier, N. Odartchenko, R. Schindler and C. C. Congdon, p. 349, Springer-Verlag, Berlin, 1967.
3. Miller, J. F. A. P., Proc. Roy. Soc. Ser. B, *156:* 415, 1962.
4. Miller, J. F. A. P. and Osoba, D., in *Ciba Foundation Study No. 16, The Immunologically Competent Cell: Its Nature and Origin,* Edited by G. E. W. Wolstenholme and J. Knight, p. 62, Little, Brown, Boston, 1963.
5. Osoba, D., Proc. Soc. Exp. Biol. Med., *127:* 418, 1968.
6. Rogister, G., in *Germinal Centers in Immune Responses,* Edited by H. Cottier, N. Odartchenko, R. Schindler and C. C. Congdon, p. 356, Springer-Verlag, Berlin, 1967.
7. Waksman, B. H., Arnason, B. G. and Janković, B. D., J. Exp. Med., *116:* 187, 1962.
8. Parrott, D. M. V., in *Germinal Centers in Immune Responses,* Edited by H. Cottier, N. Odartchenko, R. Schindler and C. C. Congdon, p. 168, Springer-Verlag, Berlin, 1967.
9. Parrott, D. M. V., de Sousa, M. A. B. and East, J., J. Exp. Med., *123:* 191, 1966.
10. Dalmasso, A. P., Martinez, C., Sjodin, K. and Good, R. A., J. Exp. Med., *118:* 1089, 1963.
11. East, J. and Parrott, D. M. V., J. Nat. Cancer Inst., *33:* 363, 1964.
12. Hays, E. F., in *Germinal Centers in Immune Responses,* Edited by H. Cottier, N. Odartchenko, R. Schindler and C. C. Congdon, p. 371, Springer-Verlag, Berlin, 1967.

13. Hilgard, H. R., Yunis, E. J., Sjodin, K., Martinez, C. and Good, R. A., Nature, *202:* 668, 1964.
14. Wong, F. M., Taub, R. N., Sherman, J. D. and Dameshek, W., Blood, *28:* 40, 1966.
15. Harrison, B. H. and Patt, D. I., Amer. Zool., *6:* 116, 1966.
16. Harrison, B. H., Patt, D. I. and Albright, J. T., Tissue and Cell, *2:* 33, 1970.
17. East, J. and Parrott, D. M. V., J. Endocrinol., *24:* 249, 1962.
18. Humason, G. L., *Animal Tissue Techniques*, p. 15, W. H. Freeman and Co., San Francisco, 1962.
19. Barnes, H. A., *The Tonsils*, C. V. Mosby Co., St. Louis, 1923.
20. Hammar, J. A., Anat. Anz., *27:* 23 and 41, 1905.

THE JOURNAL OF IMMUNOLOGY
Vol. 105, No. 1, July 1970

SECRETORY IgA IN HUMAN SERUM

R. H. WALDMAN, J. P. MACH, M. M. STELLA AND D. S. ROWE

From the World Health Organization Research and Training Centre for Immunology, the Institut de Biochimie, Université de Lausanne, and the University of Florida College of Medicine, Gainesville, Florida

Received for publication January 29, 1970

Secretory component (SC) was detected by the radioactive single radial diffusion technique in nearly all sera examined. The SC was shown to be associated with polymeric serum IgA. The mean level of secretory IgA (SIgA) in normal sera from India, Africa and Europe was about 0.03 to 0.04 mg/ml. The mean level was elevated in patients with a variety of disorders involving secretory surfaces (e.g., acute bacterial enterocolitis or respiratory tract carcinoma), but also in disorders with no known involvement of secretory surfaces. The highest levels were seen in lactating women, with a mean level five times higher than that in the general population. SIgA was also found at lower levels in cord serum, serum from breast-fed newborns and serum from children 3 to 10 years old.

Secretory IgA (SIgA), the predominant immunoglobulin found in external secretions, has unique properties, i.e., it exists as a IgA dimer and contains the additional non-immunoglobulin glycoprotein termed secretory component[1] (SC).

Thompson *et al.* recently reported the finding of SIgA in the serum of 9 of 101 normal individuals, 21 of 52 patients with untreated adult celiac disease, 5 of 38 patients with regional enteritis and 5 of 23 patients with ulcerative colitis (1). The serum SIgA was detected by a non-quantitative double diffusion immunoprecipitation technique. The present study was undertaken to quantitate the level of SIgA in the serum of normal individuals and patients with a variety of disorders, using the highly sensitive radioactive single radial diffusion technique (2).

MATERIALS AND METHODS

Serum specimens. These were obtained from a) Indian patients with cholera within 24 hr of the onset of the illness, and 2 to 4 weeks later,[2] b) Indian patients with non-choleric diarrhea[2] (predominantly bacillary dysentery), c) adult blood donors at Lausanne, Switzerland, d) Swiss patients with a variety of disorders whose sera had been sent to a clinical laboratory for immunoelectrophoresis, e) African (Gambian) villagers (3), and f) miscellaneous sera from the W.H.O. Research and Training Centre for Immunology and the hospitals of the University of Lausanne.

Antiserum to secretory component. SIgA was isolated from human colostrum. After centrifugation to remove lipid and casein the colostrum was brought to 40% saturation with ammonium sulphate. The precipitate was dissolved in 0.001 M PO_4, pH 7.4, and applied to a column of DEAE-cellulose equilibrated with the same buffer. Following the elution of IgG the buffer was changed to 0.005 M PO_4, pH 7.0. SIgA-rich fractions were then passed through a column of Sephadex G-200, the SIgA appearing as a peak at the void column. The pooled fractions from the descending limb of this protein peak were passed again through the same column to yield purified SIgA. Rabbit antiserum prepared to SIgA isolated in this way was absorbed with serum containing an IgA myeloma protein, with purified IgG and with lactoferrin (prepared from colostrum).

Free secretory component. This was prepared from an ammonium sulfate precipitate from colostrum by chromatography on Sephadex G-200. It contained a trace of lactoferrin.

[1] The term "secretory component" will be used in place of "transport piece," "T-piece" or "secretory piece." This is following W.H.O. recommendations for the extention of the nomenclature of immunoglobulins (Bull. W.H.O., *41:* 975, 1969).

[2] These samples were obtained courtesy of the joint W.H.O.-Indian Council of Medical Research-West Bengal government co-operative program for cholera research.

Quantitation of secretory IgA. This was carried out by radioactive single radial diffusion (RSRD) (2). This is a modification of the single radial diffusion technique (4) in which very low concentrations of antiserum are used in the agar. In this way, larger zones of precipitate are produced by lower concentrations of antigen. These zones are invisible but can be demonstrated by the use of ^{125}I- or ^{131}I-labeled antiserum to the immunoglobulin of the animal in which the original

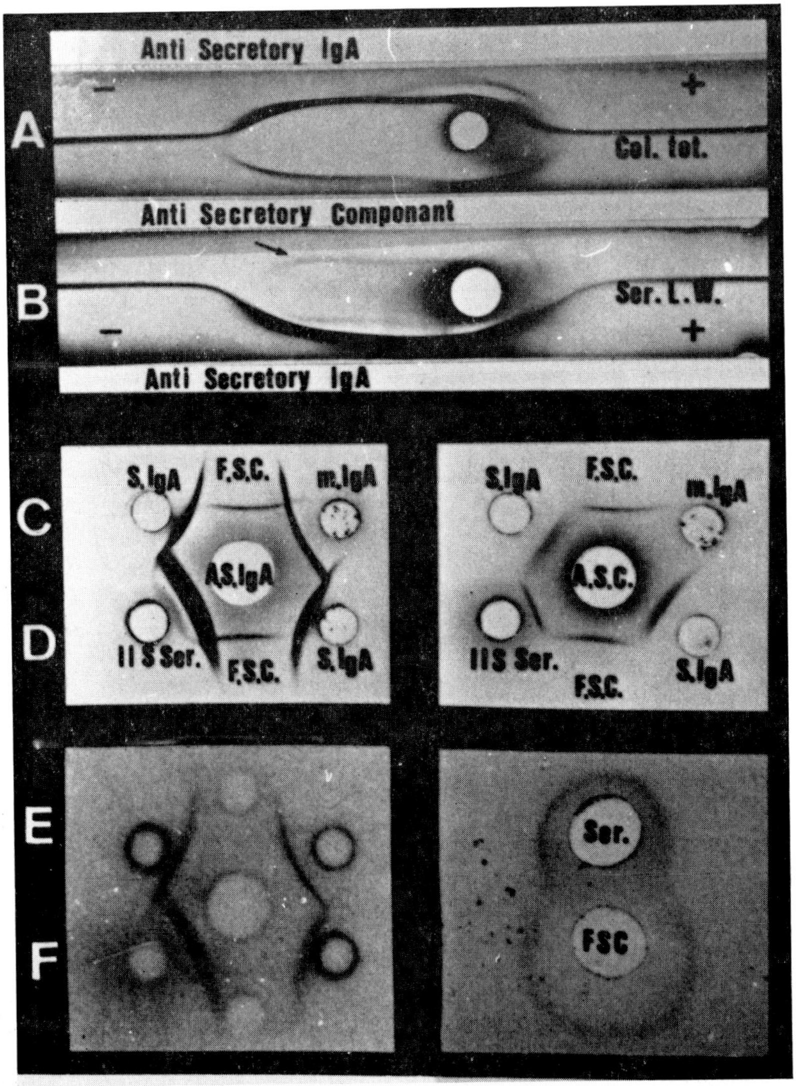

Figure 1. A and B, immunoelectrophoresis of colostrum and serum against anti-secretory IgA and anti-secretory component. The horizontal lines between the troughs are due to the absorption of the anti-secretory component with an excess of IgA which reacts with the anti-secretory IgA antiserum. *Col. tot.*, total human colostrum protein after removal of lipids and casein. *Ser. L.W.*, serum from lactating woman. *C and D*, double diffusion immunoprecipitation in agar. *A.S. IgA*, anti-secretory IgA. *A.S.C.*, anti-secretory component. *S.IgA*, secretory IgA. *F.S.C.*, free secretory component. *M.IgA*, myeloma IgA. *11S Ser.*, fraction from Sephadex G-200 filtration of positive serum, taken from the descending limb of the excluded peak. *E*, radioimmunodiffusion. Autoradiograph from the stained slide shown in *C*, reacted with ^{125}I-labeled anti-α-chain. *F*, single radial immunodiffusion. Anti-secretory component in agar, free secretory component in one well, positive serum in the other.

antiserum was made, i.e., sheep anti-rabbit immunoglobulin in this case. A series of dilutions of a standard of SIgA was included in each plate. This standard was the material used for immunization which appeared pure by immunoelectrophoresis using an antiserum to whole colostrum. Its concentration was adjusted to 1 mg/ml as determined by absorption at 280 nm assuming an extinction co-efficient of 13.4 (5). The limit of detectability of the technique as used in this study was 0.005 mg/ml.

RESULTS

Specificity of anti-SC antiserum. The antiserum was shown to be specific by the following tests. a) Immunoelectrophoresis: when whole colostrum was reacted against the unabsorbed anti-secretory IgA antiserum, a characteristic double line, fused at the cathodal end, was obtained, representing reaction with both secretory IgA and free SC. When whole colostrum was reacted with the antiserum absorbed so as to react only with SC only one line was obtained (*A* in Fig. 1). b) Single radial diffusion analysis using the anti-SC antiserum showed rings of identity (6) between serum samples and SC (*F* in Fig. 1). c) Ring formation in RSRD plates was completely abolished when the antiserum was previously absorbed with SC.

Nature of the material in serum which reacted with the antiserum to SC. Sera from one healthy individual, from pooled cord blood and from a lactating woman were fractionated on a Sephadex G-200 column. Following concentration the fractions were tested for SC by double diffusion immuno-precipitation in agar. Only fractions from the excluded peak gave a positive reaction (*D* in Fig. 1). When these fractions were tested against anti-SC and anti-α-chain antisera by double diffusion immunoprecipitation in agar, a single line of identity resulted, indicating that both SC and α-chain determinants were present

TABLE I

Levels of secretory IgA in serum

Source of Serum	No.	No. with Detectable Serum Secretory IgA	Mean Level of Secretory IgA in Serum	Mean Serum IgA
				mg/ml
Indian adult males	94	93	0.039 (±0.003)[a]	3.41
Acute diarrhea	32	32	0.054 (±0.006)	3.18
Cholera	22	22	0.055 (±0.008)	3.32
Non-choleric diarrhea	10	10	0.051 (±0.006)	2.90
Convalescent diarrhea	62	61	0.032 (±0.003)	3.52
African adults	16	15	0.034 (±0.007)	3.46
Swiss				
Blood donors	50	48	0.040 (±0.005)	2.98
Patients				
Cancer of epithelial surface	12	12	0.086 (±0.004)	4.10
Myeloma IgA	6	6	0.103 (±0.005)	>6.00
IgG	8	8	0.073 (±0.010)	2.29
Fever of unknown origin	5	5	0.102 (±0.025)	4.24
Osteomyelitis	2	2	0.055 (0.020–0.090)	4.16
Chronic dermatitis	5	5	0.048 (±0.024)	3.14
Chronic renal disease	3	3	0.037 (0.020–0.070)	2.24
Chronic respiratory tract disease	5	5	0.035 (±0.016)	2.79
Cord serum	3 pools	3	0.015	0.04
Newborns (breast-fed)	10	8	0.010 (±0.001)	0.19
Children aged 3–10	5	5	0.018 (±0.002)	0.40
Lactating women	11	11	0.194 (±0.012)	3.16

[a] mg/ml (± standard error of the mean).

on the same molecule. This was also demonstrated by reacting the immune precipitates formed between anti-SIgA and SC, SIgA, myeloma IgA and a positive serum pool, with an ^{125}I-labeled anti-α-chain antiserum. Two lines form between the anti-SIgA and the positive serum pool (*C* in Fig. 1). Both lines are continuous with SIgA lines, but only one is continuous with SC. Both lines contain radioactivity (*E* in Fig. 1). The line between anti-SIgA and SC did not contain radioactivity. Thus on the basis of molecular size and antigenic analysis we conclude that the material in serum reacting with anti-SC is SIgA.

Secretory IgA in serum. As shown in Table I, 239 of 245 sera tested contained detectable SIgA. The level was the same in Indian hospitalized acute diarrhea patients whether the cause of the diarrhea was cholera or not. The diarrhea patients, however, had a statistically significantly higher mean SIgA level than did the same patients during convalescence (Student's *t* test, $p < 0.01$). The level of SIgA in the African sera was not different from that of the convalescent Indian sera. Mean SIgA levels did not differ significantly between the Swiss blood donors and the African and Indian convalescent sera. Mean SIgA levels were frequently elevated among the groups of hospitalized patients. However, the numbers of individuals in each group were small, and only groups with epithelial cancers, IgA myeloma and fever of unknown origin had significantly elevated levels ($p < 0.01$).

SIgA levels also showed changes relative to age. SIgA was detectable in pooled serum from cord blood and in the serum of breast-fed infants obtained during the first 3 days of life. The mean levels in these groups were significantly lower than in adults ($p < 0.01$), but the ratio of SIgA to total serum IgA was higher than in adults. Children aged 3 to 10 years showed SIgA levels and a serum SIgA to total IgA ratio intermediate between those of newborns and adults.

Lactating women (3 to 5 days post-partum) had the highest SIgA levels of any groups examined.

DISCUSSION

By employing a sensitive immunochemical technique we found SC in the sera of nearly all the healthy and diseased individuals whom we studied. Further examination of some of the sera showed that the SC was in the form of SIgA. Thompson *et al.* (1) had previously reported the presence of SC in some human sera and evidence suggesting that it was in the form of SIgA. The findings presented here confirm the fact that SC and α-chain determinants are on the same molecule of greater than 200,000 molecular weight, and extend their observations concerning the presence of SIgA in sera from normal and diseased individuals.

Prior to the report of Thompson *et al.* there had been few reported studies on SIgA and serum. Tomasi *et al.* originally reported the absence of SIgA from serum (7). However, Tomasi *et al.* recently reported finding SC in some patients with chronic diseases of the alimentary tract and in concentrated normal sera (8). Havez *et al.* reported the presence of antigenic determinants which were possibly those of SC in certain pathologic sera (9). Ballieux *et al.* in studies of sera containing 10S IgA myeloma protein found that 4 of 16 sera showed a weak reaction of antiserum to secretory component, but they felt that the reaction was due to some component other than SC (10).

Following established practice we have referred to the protein that incorporated SC and IgA as secretory IgA. The major site of synthesis of SC and of the formation of SIgA is likely to be the mucosa of the gastrointestinal and respiratory tracts, as well as the mucosa of the lactating mammary gland. It has recently been reported, however, that SC is present in epithelial cells of tissues not normally considered to possess secretory surfaces, such Hassall's corpuscles and parathyroid follicles, and also in other sites such as the amniotic membrane and renal tubular epithelium, where SC may be found in the absence of IgA (8). SC from such sites might gain access to serum but it is not known whether SC in this form would combine with serum IgA. Thus, SIgA in serum could be a result of a) SC originating elsewhere than mucosal epithelium and subsequently becoming associated with two or more serum 7S IgA molecules; b) SC originating from mucosal epithelial cells, passing into the circulation, and then becoming associated with IgA; c) SIgA passing intact into the circulation from mucosal surfaces; or d) a combination of these. It is noteworthy, however, that we were unable to detect free SC in any serum.

The finding of Thompson *et al.* (1) and Tomasi *et al.* (8) that a higher percentage of persons with bowel disease had secretory IgA in their serum than did normals led them to conclude that a local phenomenon (b and/or c, above) was responsible for the presence of SIgA in serum. However, they presented no data on patients with chronic illness with no involvement of secretory surfaces. We found elevated levels in a variety of disorders involving epithelial surfaces, but we also found high levels in patients with no evidence of bowel or respiratory tract disease. Serum from patients with diseases involving other tissues which make SC, i.e., chronic respiratory tract disease and chronic renal disease, showed no significant increase over normal of the level of SIgA in the serum. The finding of increased SIgA levels in the serum of lactating women could reflect increased synthesis by the mammary gland; but other profound metabolic changes also occur around parturition, and these might be responsible for the elevated serum SIgA levels.

Using a double diffusion technique, Thompson *et al.* (1) observed SIgA in the serum of 9% of normal individuals. Using a more sensitive technique—radioactive single radial immunodiffusion—we found SIgA in the serum of 97% of normal individuals. No significant difference was found between Indians, Africans and Europeans. The mean level of serum SIgA was similar in the three populations.

SIgA levels also varied among different age groups. SIgA was detectable at low levels in cord blood and at a similar level in breast-fed newborns (days 3 to 5). This finding suggests that little if any SIgA is transferred to the circulation of the newborn by way of the colostrum and milk. Children aged 3 to 10 years showed levels of SIgA intermediate between those of newborns and adults.

SIgA appeared to comprise approximately 1% of the total IgA in normal adults, but in some patients, e.g., those with cholera or bronchogenic carcinoma, up to 6% of the serum IgA was in the form SIgA. In lactating women the mean SIgA content was also 6% of the total serum IgA. Although the level of SIgA in cord blood serum was lower than that in adults, it comprised 40% of the total IgA.

These findings show that SIgA is a normal component of serum. Whether SIgA has any specific function in the serum must remain doubtful since the protein may well arise from spillover of SIgA or possibly SC which is present in high concentrations in certain sites. Further studies appear warranted in patients with a variety of diseases, especially those with carcinoma and with immune deficiency states, to define the possible diagnostic significance of SIgA levels.

Acknowledgments. We thank Dr. R. Seematter, Dr. P. Frey, Dr. H. Bosshard and Professor S. Prod'hom, from the Departments of Biochemistry, Medicine, Obstetrics and Pediatrics, Université de Lausanne, for their help in collecting various sera.

REFERENCES

1. Thompson, R. A., Asquith, P. and Cooke, W. T., Lancet, *2:* 517, 1969.
2. Rowe, D. S., Bull. W.H.O., *40:* 613, 1969.
3. Rowe, D. S., McGregor, I. A., Smith, S. J., Hall, P. and Williams, K., Clin. Exp. Immun., *3:* 63, 1968.
4. Mancini, G., Carbonara, A. O. and Heremans, J. F., Immunochemistry, *2:* 235, 1965.
5. Schultze, H. E. and Heremans, J. F., *Molecular Biology of Human Proteins*. Vol. 1, p. 226, Elsevier Publishing, Amsterdam, 1966.
7. Tomasi, T. B., Tan, E. M., Solomon, A. and Prendergast, R. A., J. Exp. Med., *121:* 101, 1965.
8. Tomasi, T. B., Bull, D., Tourville, D. and Yurchak, A., *Concept of Local Immunity and The Secretory System*, Symposium of the Secretory Immunologic System, Vero Beach, Florida, December, 1969, In press.
9. Havez, R., Muh, J. P., Bonte, M. and Biserte, G., Clin. Chem. Acta, *15:* 7, 1967.
10. Ballieux, R. E., Stoop, J. W. and Zegers, B. J. M., Scand. J. Haemat., *5:* 179, 1968.

THE JOURNAL OF IMMUNOLOGY
Copyright © 1970 by The Williams & Wilkins Co.

Vol. 105, No. 1, July 1970
Printed in U.S.A.

INHIBITION OF TARGET CELL PROLIFERATION BY SUPERNATANTS FROM CULTURES OF HUMAN PERIPHERAL LYMPHOCYTES[1]

J. A. GREEN, S. R. COOPERBAND,[2] J. A. RUTSTEIN AND S. KIBRICK

From the Departments of Microbiology and Medicine, Boston University School of Medicine, Boston, Massachusetts

Received for publication January 22, 1970

Supernatants from cultures of phytohemagglutinin (PHA)-stimulated human lymphocytes inhibit the division of certain cells in tissue culture. This effect of lymphocyte culture supernatant was routinely estimated by the rate of tritiated thymidine incorporation into DNA. In this system dilutions of 1:20 of the proliferation inhibitory factor (PIF) reduced DNA synthesis to 10% to 20% of that in control cultures. At dilutions of less than 1:640, PIF generally inhibited DNA synthesis by greater than 50%. Consistent with the decrease in DNA synthesis, cell cultures growing in the presence of PIF had fewer mitotic figures and lower total cell density than did control cultures. Supernatants from cultures established with dead leucocytes and PHA, extracts of fresh leucocytes, or PHA alone failed to produce this effect. A lesser degree of inhibitory activity also was present in supernatants from "unstimulated" lymphocyte cultures. Inhibition of proliferation in susceptible cultures was not accompanied by loss of viability; and cells from treated cultures excluded trypan blue, retained the ability to re-attach to glass, were capable of division and formed microcolonies when cloned. In addition to HeLa cells, susceptible cell cultures included human amnion, HEp 2, and KB cells. PIF was not effective in cultures of mouse L cells or in cultures of chick embryo fibroblasts. Preliminary data suggest that PIF is heat stable at 85°C for one-half hr, nondialyzable, nonsedimentable at 90,000 × G and is destroyed by trypsin.

Stimulation of human lymphocyte cultures by antigens or by mitogens results in the production of a number of soluble substances which modify the *in vitro* behavior of other cells. The supernatants of appropriately stimulated lymphocyte cultures have been reported to: have interferon-like activity (1–3), stimulate normal lymphocytes to divide and transform (4), control macrophage mobility (5), direct mononuclear leucocyte migration (6), render non-immune lymphocytes sensitive to antigens (7) and cause a morphological transformation of epithelial cells to fibroblasts (8, 9). In addition, it has recently been demonstrated that stimulated lymphocytes produce a "cytotoxic" factor which, in high concentrations, lyses other types of cells (10–12). In this report we describe the production by lymphocytes of a substance or substances which inhibit the proliferation of susceptible cells without compromising their viability. To facilitate discussion, this property of the supernatant has been given the abbreviation "PIF" for proliferation inhibitory factor.

MATERIALS AND METHODS

Cultures of human blood leucocytes were prepared according to previously described techniques (13). Cultures were established with 1.0×10^6 lymphocytes/ml and initially contained a variable number of neutrophiles (20% to 40%) and monocytes (<2%). Maintenance medium consisted of medium 199 with Earle's salts, 20% inactivated fetal calf serum (FCS), and 100 units of penicillin and 100 μg of streptomycin/ml. Phytohemagglutinin M, Difco (PHA), was used at concentrations predetermined to produce maximal DNA synthesis in these cultures. PHA was added at the time the cultures were prepared,

[1] This work was supported in part by United States Public Health Service Grants AI 08579 and AI 04305, American Cancer Grant 6RO and Massachusetts Heart Grant 869.

[2] Recipient of Public Health Service Research Career Development Award AI 39096.

and the cells were then maintained at 36°C in a humidified atmosphere containing 5% CO_2. Four days after initiation, the leucocyte cultures were centrifuged at 300 × G to sediment cells and coarse debris, and the supernatants were decanted and stored at −20°C until examined for their ability to inhibit proliferation in susceptible cell cultures (hereafter referred to as "target cells").

The effect of lymphocyte culture supernatants on cell proliferation was routinely measured in HeLa cell cultures nourished with Eagle's minimal essential medium (MEM-Hanks') with 10% inactivated fetal calf serum, 50 units of penicillin, 5 μg of amphotericin and 50 μg of streptomycin/ml. Twofold serial dilutions of leucocyte culture supernatant were prepared in MEM-Hanks' solution and added in 0.1-ml quantities to duplicate confluent HeLa cell cultures in 16- x 150-mm tubes containing 0.9 ml of nutrient media. These target cell cultures which contained approximately 8 × 10^5 cells, were then incubated in stationary racks at 36°C for 2 to 4 days. Proliferation in the target cell cultures was routinely estimated by the rate of tritiated thymidine (^{3}HT) incorporation into DNA. In this procedure, 1 μCi of ^{3}HT in 0.01 ml of MEM was added to the cultures for the last 6 hr of the incubation period. DNA synthesis was terminated when the cultures were frozen at −20°C. A modification of the Schmidt-Thannhauser procedure (14) was used for separating newly synthesized DNA from the radioactive nucleotide. Cell cultures were thawed at 4°C, scraped from the glass and 5 ml of cold (4°C) 10% trichloracetic acid (TCA) were added. The reaction mixture was held at 4°C for 15 min and the cells were then centrifuged for 15 min at 600 × G in a refrigerated centrifuge. The acid insoluble material was twice resuspended in 10% TCA at 4°C, and then repelleted by centrifugation. The precipitate from the last centrifugation was finally suspended in 2 ml of 5% TCA and heated at 90°C for 30 min. Floccular material present in the hot acid extract was sedimented by centrifugation at 600 × G and 1 ml of the clarified supernatant was counted by liquid scintillation spectrometry, using a dioxane-naphthalene 2,5-diphenyloxazole (PPO) mixture. Two types of control cultures were included in all experiments. These consisted of a) untreated HeLa cell cultures and b) HeLa cell cultures which had received 0.1 ml of medium 199 with 10% fetal calf serum. The lymphocyte culture supernatants were also examined for PIF in Earle's L cells (strain 929), primary human amnion cells, HEp 2 cells, KB (CALT) cells and primary chicken embryo fibroblasts. These cultures were prepared and maintained according to standard methods (15).

Cell proliferation was also determined by direct microscopic count of dividing (mitotic) cells present in the stationary target cell cultures. The number of dividing cells in 10 microscopic fields was counted at a final magnification of 150 ×. Comparable fields were examined in all cultures in order to minimize the differences in cell density characteristic of tube cultures in general (16). Field size was maintained constant by use of a 1-mm^2 ocular micrometer.

Further quantitation of cell division was made by counting the total numbers of cells present in the target cell cultures. In this procedure, the supernatants from leucocyte cultures were added to 1 to 2.5 × 10^6 target cells in 4.5- x 11-cm milk dilution bottles. After 4 days incubation at 36°C, the medium was decanted, and the cell layer was treated with 0.25% trypsin and vigorously pipetted to disperse single cells. Cells were then pelleted in the centrifuge at 200 × G and resuspended in fresh medium. Five-tenths milliliter was removed, mixed with 0.1 ml of a 0.4% solution of trypan blue and total viable cells were then determined in a hemocytometer.

Viability was also determined by the ability of the treated cells to give rise to clonal microcolonies when subcultured. For these experiments, a portion of the cells used for the trypan blue counts (see above) was diluted so that approximately 100 viable cells were present in a final volume of 10 ml. These cells were then added to an 8-cm glass Petri dish. Quadruplicate cultures were routinely established. Petri dishes were maintained at 36°C in a humidified atmosphere containing 5% CO_2. After 7 days the supernatants were discarded, the cells stained *in situ* with Wright's Giemsa stain and the numbers of colonies counted. Cell viability was thus established by three methods: a) microscopic appearance of living cell cultures *in situ*, b) vital staining with trypan blue and c) demonstration that the target cells were capable of giving clones when subcultured in the absence of leucocyte culture supernatants.

RESULTS

The effect of the lymphocyte culture supernatants on DNA synthesis in HeLa cell cultures is seen in Figure 1. Marked inhibition of DNA synthesis occurred when the target cells were treated with supernatants from PHA-stimulated lymphocyte cultures. In target cell cultures containing the highest concentrations of PIF, DNA synthesis was often 10% to 20% of the DNA synthesis in control cultures. DNA synthesis in target cell cultures increased as the concentrations of PIF were diminished by further dilution of the lymphocyte supernatant. Nevertheless, even at dilutions of 1:640 or more, DNA synthesis was inhibited by greater than 50%. The inhibitory activity of "unstimulated" supernatants was also diminished by dilution, and activity was virtually abolished when unstimulated supernatants were diluted to 640 times their initial concentrations.

The titer of PIF in leucocyte culture supernatants was proportional to the number of lymphocytes and was independent of the numbers of neutrophiles that were present at the time the cultures were initiated (Table I). Leucocytes killed by repeated freezing and thawing were used to prepare "stimulated" (containing PHA) and unstimulated cultures. Supernatants removed at 4 days from these dead cell preparations did not inhibit HeLa cell DNA synthesis. Several concentrations of PHA added directly to HeLa cell cultures had no effect on DNA synthesis. Finally, the addition of stimulatory concentrations of PHA to the supernatants of unstimulated cultures did not enhance inhibitory activity.

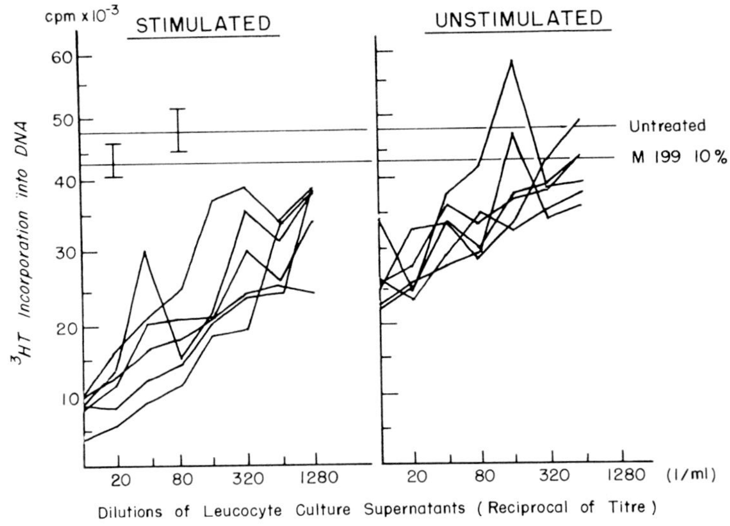

Figure 1. Figure 1 presents the results of six successive experiments which examine ^{3}HT incorporation into DNA by HeLa cells exposed to increasing dilutions of supernatant from "stimulated" and "unstimulated" leucocyte cultures.

TABLE I

Contribution of neutrophiles and lymphocytes to PIF production

No. of Lymphocytes/ml	No. of Neutrophiles/ml	^{3}HT Incorporation into DNA by HeLa Cell Cultures[a]	
		PIF cultures	Unstimulated cultures
1×10^6	0.18×10^6	6619 ± 285	15,100 ± 1800
1×10^6	0.92×10^6	7420 ± 182	12,734 ± 889
1×10^6	3.30×10^6	7488 ± 401	11,857 ± 2523

[a] HeLa cell cultures containing leucocyte culture supernatants at a final dilution of 1:80. DNA synthesis in untreated HeLa cell cultures was 27,568 ± 2006.

Consistent with the decrease in DNA synthesis, target cell cultures growing in the presence of PIF had fewer mitotic figures and lower total cell density than did control cultures (Fig. 2). In addition, individual cells in affected cultures appeared larger and occupied a greater surface area than cells in control cultures. Although morphologically distinct, cultures in which cell division was depressed appeared viable and were not stained by trypan blue. Similar morphologic changes have also been observed in primary cultures of human amnion and human kidney in response to these supernatants (9).

The marked microscopic difference between dividing and nondividing HeLa cells permitted a direct visual quantitation of cells undergoing mitosis in these target cultures. Calculations were made on the basis of the total numbers of mitotic figures present in 10 separate, representative areas of each pair of replicate target cultures. The results of such experiments (Table II) were similar to those obtained for the incorporation of ^{3}HT into DNA. Thus, the number of mitotic cells was inversely proportional to the quantity of PIF present in target cell cultures. Mitosis in target cell cultures containing unstimulated supernatants was only slightly less than that occurring in the appropriate controls.

Previous assays of PIF activity included direct determination of DNA synthesis over a 6-hr interval, and microscopic enumeration of dividing cells at a single point in time (on day 4). To supplement these time-limited data, experiments were also performed in which the cumulative effects of PIF inhibition could be examined. After 3 days' exposure to PIF, HeLa cell cultures were dispersed by trypsinization and the number of live cells determined by counting in the presence of trypan blue (Table III). The treated target cells were also examined for their ability to form clonal colonies. Control cultures were treated in a similar fashion. Cell suspensions prepared from both treated and untreated HeLa cell cultures excluded trypan blue, retained the ability to re-attach to glass, were capable of cell division and formed micro-colonies when cloned. Colonies formed by cells which had been exposed to either PIF or unstimulated supernatants,

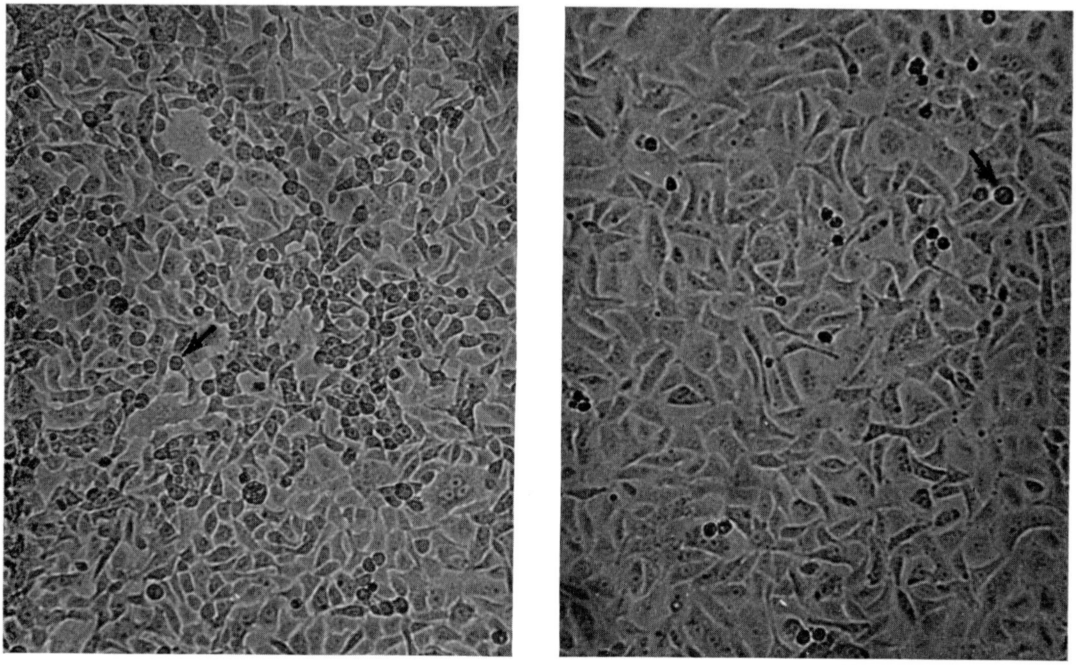

Figure 2. Microscopic appearance of HeLa cell cultures 4 days after the addition of 1:80 dilutions of supernatant from stimulated leucocyte cultures (*right*). Cells treated with medium 199 (*left*). Arrows point to mitotic figures. Both cultures were photographed *in situ*, unstained at a magnification of approximately 150 ×.

TABLE II

Effect of PIF on cell division. Microscopic enumeration of dividing cells (mitotic figures) in HeLa cell cultures

Treatment	Dilution	Average No. of Mitotic Figures	% Mitosis			
			Ia/II[a]	Ib/II[a]	Ia/III[b]	Ib/III[b]
I. Addition of leucocyte culture supernatants						
a. PHA-stimulated	1:20	24	22		15	
	1:80	68	62		42	
	1:320	105	96		64	
b. Unstimulated	1:20	115		104		70
	1:80	124		113		76
	1:320	161		146		99
II. Addition of M199 with 10% 10% FCS	1:20	163				
III. None		110				

[a] Comparison of mitosis in target cells containing leucocyte culture supernatants (either treated-Ia, or untreated-Ib) with mitosis in control cultures containing an equal volume of medium 199 (II).
[b] Comparison of mitosis in target cells containing leucocyte culture supernatants (either treated-Ia, or untreated-Ib) with mitosis in control cultures containing no new additive (III).

TABLE III

Total viable HeLa cells present after a 3-day exposure to supernatants from stimulated and unstimulated leucocyte cultures

Treatment	Dilution	Total No. of Live Cells × 10^6 [a,b]	Average No. of Colonies Formed on Passage of 100 Cells (range)	
Addition of leucocyte culture supernatants				
PHA-stimulated	1:20	5.0	73	(57–106)
		4.9		
	1:80	6.1	76	(70–88)
		6.3		
Unstimulated	1:20	9.7	54	(49–70)
		9.9		
	1:80	8.1	56	(49–70)
		10.6		
Addition of M199 with 10% FCS	1:20	7.5	115	(103–128)
		8.1		
None		7.8	105	(88–125)

[a] Initially, cultures contained 0.86×10^6 cells.
[b] Cell counts were performed in a hemocytometer in the presence of trypan blue in order to determine the total nubers of live and dead cells. There were <1% trypan blue stained cells in any culture.

however, differed from those derived from control cultures in several respects: a) slightly fewer colonies were formed by cells from HeLa cell cultures treated with leucocyte supernatants, b) the inhibition of cell proliferation persisted even though the cells were cloned in fresh medium without PIF, and, in general, c) the micro-colonies derived from PIF-treated cultures were small and contained fewer cells.

PIF and supernatants from unstimulated leucocyte cultures also inhibited cell proliferation in cultures of primary human amnion, human epidermoid carcinoma (HEp 2), and KB cells. When these additional target cell cultures were examined microscopically for periods of several days to several weeks, they appeared healthy and were not stained by trypan blue. Cells from cultures in which proliferation was inhibited maintained the capacity to re-attach to glass, and formed micro-colonies when cloned in the absence of leucocyte culture supernatants. As with the HeLa cells, growth of clones from PIF-treated cultures was slower than that in untreated controls. No inhibition of cell proliferation was evident in cultures of primary chicken embryo fibroblasts or mouse L cells.

Preliminary studies indicate that PIF is a) nondialyzable (there was no loss of activity upon extensive dialysis of the lymphocyte supernatants against fresh culture medium); b) not deposited by centrifugation for 2 hr at 90,000 × G; c) stable at 85°C for 30 min but not for 24 hr; and d) inactivated upon incubation with the proteolytic enzyme trypsin. The inhibitory activity of supernatants from unstimulated leucocyte cultures had similar characteristics to the PIF induced by PHA.

DISCUSSION

The proliferation inhibitory factor (PIF) described in this paper is present in high concentrations in supernatants obtained from PHA-stimulated cultures of human leucocytes. Our data indicate that PIF is produced primarily by the lymphocyte component of these cultures rather than by other cells. Thus, in cultures containing varying percentages of lymphocytes and neutrophiles, the titer of this substance was proportional to the number of lymphocytes. This finding is consistent with various previous observations indicating that the mitogenic action of PHA is selective for small lymphocytes (17).

PIF in lower concentrations was also demonstrable in supernatants from control cultures which contained no PHA. It is possible that this represents a lymphocyte response analogous to that obtained with PHA but induced by some component of the medium. In support of this hypothesis is the observation that lymphocyte transformation and proliferation have been noted in presumably unstimulated cultures (17). Thus, fetal calf serum has been shown to induce blastogenesis in such cultures (18). In addition, interferon production which occurs in response to PHA and antigen stimulation has occasionally been observed in the apparent absence of known inducers (2).

PIF inhibits cell division by mechanisms which are as yet unknown. Depletion of a medium constituent by activated lymphocytes does not explain this effect, since the target cell cultures which are inhibited by PIF contain a large excess of fresh medium. Enzymatic degradation of the target cell medium is also unlikely since the proliferation of cloned cells derived from PIF-treated cultures remains inhibited in the absence of PIF. PIF is not removed from solution at ultracentrifugal speeds known to deposit small viruses. This suggests that the inhibitory activity of the lymphocyte supernatants is not due to fragmented leucocyte debris or to infectious agents.

Many of the factors present in supernatants from cultures of activated lymphocytes have been correlated with *in vivo* phenomena. Thus, interferons have been demonstrated to be significant in recovery from primary viral infection (19) and may be involved in protection of the host against specific reinfection (20). The macrophage immobilization factor is accepted as an essential part of delayed type hypersensitivity (5) and lymphotoxin is currently believed to be the specific chemical mediator of the tissue damage which accompanies this response (10, 11). Unlike lymphotoxin, PIF does not produce cell death, and does not inhibit the division of mouse L cells when added at concentrations which markedly reduce the replication of sensitive target cells. There is as yet no ready association between PIF and lymphocyte function *in vivo*. We would hypothesize, however, that PIF may function to limit the growth of "foreign" cells present in such diverse situations as grafted organs and neoplasms.

REFERENCES

1. Wheelock, E. F., Science, *149:* 310, 1965.
2. Green, J. A., Cooperband, S. R. and Kibrick, S., Science, *164:* 1415, 1969.
3. Freidman, R. M. and Cooper, H. L., Proc. Soc. Exp. Biol. Med., *125:* 901, 1967.
4. Kasakura, S. and Lowenstein, L., Nature, *208:* 794, 1965.
5. Bloom, B. R. and Bennet, B., Science, *153:* 80, 1966.
6. Ward, P. A., Remold, H. G. and David, J. R., Science, *163:* 1079, 1969.
7. Valentine, F. T. and Lawrence, H. S., Science, *165:* 1014, 1969.
8. Green, J. A., Cooperband, S. R., Rabinowitz, L., Nahmias, A. J. and Kibrick, S., Fed. Proc., *26:* 702, 1967.

9. Nahmias, A. J., Cooperband, S. R., Green, J. A. and Kibrick, S., Nature, *216:* 1349, 1967.
10. Ruddle, N. H. and Waksman, B. H., J. Exp. Med., *128:* 1237, 1968.
11. Granger, G. A. and Kolb, W. P., J. Immun., *101:* 111, 1968.
12. Lebowitz, A. and Lawrence, H. S., Fed. Proc., *28:* 630, 1969.
13. Cooperband, S. R., Rosen, F. S. and Kibrick, S., J. Clin. Invest., *47:* 836, 1968.
14. Schmidt, G. and Thannhauser, S. J., J. Biol. Chem., *161:* 83, 1945.
15. Lennette, E. H. and Schmidt, N. J., *Diagnostic Procedures for Viral and Rickettsial Diseases*, American Public Health Association, 1964.
16. Chang, R. S., J. Nat. Cancer Inst., *40:* 491, 1968.
17. Ling, N. R., *Lymphocyte Stimulation*, John Wiley and Sons, New York, 1968.
18. Johnson, G. J. and Russell, P. S., Nature, *208:* 343, 1965.
19. Baron, S., *Modern Trends in Medical Virology*, Edited by A. P. Waterson and R. B. Heath, p. 77, Butterworth and Co., Ltd., London, 1966.
20. Glascow, L. A., J. Bact., *91:* 2185, 1966.

THE JOURNAL OF IMMUNOLOGY
Vol. 105, No. 1, July 1970

Printed in U.S.A.

DEPLETION OF PLASMA COMPLEMENT *IN VIVO* BY A PROTEIN OF COBRA VENOM: ITS EFFECT ON VARIOUS IMMUNOLOGIC REACTIONS[1]

CHARLES G. COCHRANE, HANS J. MÜLLER-EBERHARD AND BARBARA S. AIKIN

From the Department of Experimental Pathology, Scripps Clinic and Research Foundation, La Jolla, California 92037

Received for publication January 15, 1970

The purified low molecular weight anticomplementary factor (CoF) in the venom of the cobra *Naja naja* was tested for its behavior in vivo and for its effect on various components of complement in several species of animals and the development of several immunologic reactions. CoF complexed with a plasma protein immediately after injection, the sedimentation rate of the complex being about 9S. The complex which inactivated purified C3 circulated with a half-life of 32 hr in rabbits. High blood levels of the CoF complex and minimal side effects were obtained using multiple injections of CoF over a 24-hr period. Under these conditions hemolytic complement levels fell to less than 10% of normal values in rabbits, rats and guinea pigs. C3 was markedly diminished in these species, and in guinea pigs C3 levels, as revealed in immune adherence, fell to less than 1% of normal. C3 and hemolytic complement levels remained low for 4 to 6 days. In two species tested, C5 protein was also lost during CoF treatment and in rabbits C6 activity diminished about half to one third of normal. The effect of CoF treatment in several immunologic diseases was assayed. Lesions depending upon neutrophil participation for full development were markedly inhibited. In acute nephrotoxic nephritis neutrophil accumulation in glomeruli and proteinuria were diminished. Arthus reactions, especially in the rat, were also inhibited. By contrast, immunologic reactions not requiring neutrophils, i.e., homologous cutaneous anaphylactic reactions in guinea pigs and contact (delayed) sensitivity were not affected by CoF treatment. Other possible effects of CoF *in vivo* were studied. The numbers of formed elements of the blood were not markedly altered. The most consistent finding was a modest elevation in neutrophils. Hemolysis was avoided by treatment of animals with multiple small doses of CoF. Neutrophils responded normally to immune adherence and chemotactic stimuli. Kininogen levels and clotting tests were unchanged.

Since the beginning of the present century, an anticomplementary action of certain snake venoms has been recognized (1, 2). More recently, the major anticomplementary factor in cobra venom has been found to act upon the third (3–6) and, in certain species, the terminal components of complement (7–9). A second anticomplementary factor of larger molecular weight has recently been isolated from cobra venom that acts upon one or more of the first three components, but does not affect C3 (10). The anticomplementary activity of cobra venom has acquired greater significance with the recognition of the importance of plasma complement in immunologic disease. It may yield insight into the mechanism of complement action and open promising leads into our ability to block the development of immunologic disease.

These studies were therefore undertaken to gain information into the fate of purified cobra venom factor (CoF) *in vivo*, its mechanism of action,

[1] Publication 393 of the Department of Experimental Pathology, Scripps Clinic and Research Foundation. The work was supported by United States Public Health Service Grant AI-07007, National Multiple Sclerosis Society Grant 459, a Grant-in-Aid of the American Heart Association (and the Long Beach Heart Association) and Atomic Energy Commission Contract AT (04-3)-730.

duration of effectiveness and some of its side effects. The most effective means of administration were also tested. With this information at hand, the effect of treatment with the anticomplementary factor on the development of certain immunologic reactions was analyzed. The results, presented previously in part (8, 11, 12), indicate that depletion of C3 and more terminal components leads to an inhibition of neutrophil accumulation and thereby to inhibition of several immunologic reactions.

MATERIALS AND METHODS

Preparation of the anticomplementary factor in cobra venom. The CoF was prepared from the venom of the cobra *Naja naja* by separation in preparative block electrophoresis followed by gel filtration chromatography (6). Alternatively, 2 g of lyophilized cobra venom (Ross Allen Reptile Institute, Silver Springs, Fla.) was solubilized in 100 ml 0.01 M sodium phosphate, pH 8.0, and added to 40 g DEAE-cellulose in a 2.3- x 70-cm column. The neurotoxin was entirely eluted in the first excluded peak at pH 7.5 in 0.01 M sodium phosphate buffer. A linear gradient of NaCl was then started and the anticomplementary factor appeared in the eluates with a conductance of 0.015 to 0.020 mhos/cm, corresponding to the final (third) protein peak as described previously (5). The anticomplementary factor was pooled, concentrated by ultrafiltration and placed on a column of Sephadex G-200 (5.0 x 60 cm). Active material eluting in the molecular weight range of 130,000 to 150,000 was collected. Subsequent analyses have revealed a high molecular weight anticomplementary factor eluting in the excluded volume of G-200 Sephadex (10). The present report will deal only with the low molecular weight fraction. The anticomplementary factor, given the symbol CoF, was concentrated, sterilized by filtration through a micropore membrane and stored at 0°C. Tests for purity were performed in analytical polyacrylamide, showing at all times a single band when purification by either method was employed.

Tests for complement inhibition activity of the CoF were performed by adding 0.1 ml of twofold dilutions of the CoF to 0.4 ml of 1:20 dilutions of normal human serum. The serum was kept frozen at −70°C in portions, a tube being thawed once only for the test. Dilutions were made with Veronal buffer to which Ca^{++} (0.00015 M) and Mg^{++} (0.0005 M) were added (VB^{++}). Incubation of the dilutions of CoF with 1:20 normal human serum (NHS) was carried out at 37°C 20 min prior to addition of 2×10^8 sensitized sheep erythrocytes (EA). The tubes were further incubated in an automatic shaking device for 60 min; then 2 ml cold VB^{++} were added and the unlysed cells were removed by centrifugation. The optical densities of the supernatants were then measured at 541 nm.

A unit of CoF was defined as the quantity of CoF in 0.1 ml that reduces the hemolytic capacity of a 1:20 dilution of normal human serum by 50% (incubation of CoF and NHS at 37°C 20 min; 5×10^8 EA). In general, this amounted to 4 to 5 μg of the highly purified material.

Antibodies and antigens. Antibodies to mouse C3 and C5, rat, rabbit and guinea pig C3 were prepared as described previously (13). Antibodies to human C3, C5 and C4 were prepared by immunizing rabbits with the purified homologous component (14). Antibodies to bovine serum albumin (BSA) were prepared by repeated immunization of rabbits with saline solutions of the antigen. Antigens employed included five times crystallized BSA, obtained from Armour Pharmaceutical Co., Kankakee, Ill. and DNP poly-*l*-lysine, kindly given by Dr. Zoltan Ovary.

Fluorescent antibody techniques. Fluorescent antibodies were prepared by conjugating IgG preparations of antisera (isolated from DEAE-cellulose in a buffer medium of 0.01 M sodium phosphate, pH 8.0) with fluorescein isothiocyanate (Sigma Chemical Co., St. Louis, Mo.). Conjugation was performed by dialyzing the fluorescein into a 1% preparation of IgG antibody. Controls for specificity included those previously described (15).

Complement assays. Hemolytic assays (CH_{50}) of complement activity were performed according to the method of Osler *et al.* (16). Immune adherence (IA) tests were performed with sheep erythrocytes (Colorado Serum Co., Denver, Colo.) sensitized with antibody (Colorado Serum Co.) and alexinated with guinea pig C1,4 and limiting quantities of purified guinea pig C2 (17). Dilutions of the C3 source were made in Veronal buffer with added BSA to 0.1%. C1,4 activity on sensitized erythrocytes was evaluated by the T_{max} test according to previously described methods (18).

C2 in fresh serum was assayed by exposing dilutions of the C2 source in VB to EAC1,4 for the T_{max} time (usually 7 to 8 min) at 32°C. A 1:33 dilution of fresh guinea pig serum was then added in VB with neutral EDTA added to 0.01 M (19).

C5 was measured employing precipitation agar gel with specific antimouse C5 or antihuman C5. The antimouse C5 was obtained from B10 D2 old line mice immunized with B10 D2 new line serum.

C6 activity was evaluated by first mixing EA (1.4 ml of 5 × 10^8 cells) with C6-deficient rabbit serum (5.6 ml of 1:10 dilution) for 10 min at 32°C. The cells were then washed and resuspended in 2.8 ml of 1:40 diluted C6-deficient serum in EDTA (0.01 M). Four-tenths milliliter of this mixture was then added to 0.1-ml samples of material being tested for C6 activity and diluted in twofold steps. After incubation at 32°C for 60 min, the amount of lysis was determined spectrophotometrically. The titer of C6 is the reciprocal of the dilution yielding 50% hemolysis.

Chemotaxis of neutrophils. The technique for studying chemotaxis of neutrophils was the same as that described previously (20). C3a was used as chemotactic stimulus, and was prepared by trypsin treatment of purified human C3 followed by isolation of C3a on gel filtration (21).

Immune adherence of neutrophils and platelets. Peripheral rabbit neutrophils were prepared according to the method of Henson (22). Briefly, peripheral blood in EDTA (0.01 M) was centrifuged to obtain platelet-rich plasma and packed red cell mass which contains abundant neutrophils. The red cell mass was sedimented by gravity at room temperature in four volumes of 2% gelatin. The supernatant neutrophils were then cleared of residual erythrocytes by lysis in 0.83% NH_4Cl, washed and resuspended in Tyrode's solution with 0.1% gelatin (TG). The platelets from the platelet-rich plasma were washed three times and resuspended in TG. Neither neutrophils nor platelets were clumped by these procedures. For testing for their ability to react to the stimulus of C3 immune adherence, the cells were mixed with zymosan particles with C3 bound to their surfaces. The zymosan was previously boiled for 30 min, washed and suspended in Tyrode's solution. The particles were then exposed to fresh rabbit serum or rabbit serum in 0.01 M EDTA (10 mg zymosan/ml serum) for 30 min at 37°C, washed five times in TG and resuspended in TG at 2.5 mg/ml. The reaction between cells and zymosan was carried out in an aggregometer (Chrono-Log Corp., Broomall, Pa.) (23). Neutrophils (0.5 × 10^7 in 0.2 ml) or platelets (2.5 × 10^8 in 0.25 ml) were first added to the chamber with 2.5 ml TG at 37°C through which a beam of light passed. The cells were stirred at 1100 rpm. The recorder was adjusted to give a reading of maximal transmission of light and zymosan (0.25 mg in 0.1 ml) was then added. Light transmission fell immediately and rose only if clumping of cells and zymosan occurred, allowing greater passage of light.

Radioiodine labeling. Radioiodine labeling was performed by the chloramine T method (24).

Density gradient ultracentrifugation was carried out in 10% to 37% linear sucrose gradients using a Beckman Spinco 50,000 rpm swinging bucket rotor. The time of centrifugation at 50,000 rpm was generally 6 hr.

Immunoelectrophoresis was performed by the Scheidegger adaptation (25) of the technique of Grabar and Williams (26).

Coagulation. The partial thromboplastin time and the plasma prothrombin time (Quick, one-stage) were performed according to standard methods (27). A 1:10 dilution of plasma was required to obtain readily measurable values.

Tests of the kinin-forming system. Rabbits treated with CoF as indicated in the text were bled from the ear artery with siliconized needles into plastic tubes containing hexadimethrine bromide (Polybrene, generously donated by Mr. E. A. Pritchett, Abbott Laboratories, Chicago, Ill.) and ethylenediaminetetraacetate (EDTA) with final concentrations in the plasma of 50 μg/ml and 0.01 M, respectively. The plasmas were obtained by rapid sedimentation of the cells and frozen immediately. Plasmas treated in this manner have been found in this laboratory to have no activity of the clot-promoting contact factors, the prokininogenase activator and prokininogenase. Kininogen levels of the plasma were measured after first heating at 100°C for 5 min to inactivate kininases and plasma kininogenase inhibitors by a method similar to that of Diniz and Carvalho (28). Kinin was then liberated from kininogen by treatment with 50 μg trypsin/0.1 ml plasma in a total volume of 0.5 ml at 37°C for 2 hr. Soya bean trypsin inhibitor, 100 μg, was then added. Kinin released by this method was measured on the isolated uterus of an estrus virgin rat of 200 g. Quantities of kinin were compared with known amounts of synthetic kallidin (Sandoz Pharmaceuticals, Hanover, N. J.). Free kinin in the plasma was measured by adding portions of the treated, protected plasma to the uterine segment.

Animals. Rabbits weighing 1.2 to 1.5 kg, Hartley guinea pigs of 300 g, Sprague-Dawley rats of 150 to 200 g and Swiss mice of 25 g were used.

Immunologic reactions in vivo. Nephrotoxic nephritis was induced in rats with rabbit antirat glomerular basement membrane (GBM) and in rabbits with sheep antirabbit GBM as described previously (29). Reversed passive Arthus reactions (RPA) were induced according to published procedures (30). All antibodies were fractionated with ammonium sulfate at 50% saturation. Passive cutaneous anaphylaxis (PCA) reactions were induced in guinea pigs by injecting γ_1 guinea pig anti-DNP antibody (kindly provided by Dr. Zoltan Ovary) intradermally 6 hr before an i.v. injection of 0.5 ml 1% Evan's blue and 300 μg DNP_{13} ovalbumin. Reactions were recorded after 30 min. Delayed (contact) sensitivity to *o*-chlorobenzoyl chloride (OCBC) was induced by injection of OCBC in complete Freund's adjuvant in guinea pigs. After 10 days all guinea pigs were tested on the flank by topical application of 2% OCBC in olive oil according to methods outlined by Benacerraf (personal communication). Ninety per cent of guinea pigs so treated developed a large erythematous plaque after 15 to 24 hr. In order to assay the increased permeability developing in these reaction sites, ^{131}I BSA was injected intravenously 20 min before the animals were killed. The skin was removed by wide incision, laid flat on aluminum foil and rapidly frozen. A sharpened steel cylinder was then used to punch out perfect circles of skin with the center of the reaction site at the center of the cylindrical punch and the margin of the reaction extending more than 5 mm beyond the edge of the cylinder. The removed sites were then placed in glass tubes for isotope-counting.

Neutrophil depletion was performed as outlined previously (8) using specific antineutrophil antibody in all species except rabbits and nitrogen mustard (1.75 mg/kg) in rabbits.

RESULTS

The fate of cobra venom factor (CoF) after injection into rabbits. In order to examine the fate of CoF in vivo, 175 units of ^{125}I-labeled CoF were administered in a single injection i.v. in 1.2-kg rabbits. Blood samples were taken at intervals thereafter to test the following: rate of elimination of the CoF, possible binding of the CoF with proinactivator globulin, the duration of anticomplementary activity *in vivo*, and the formation of immunity to the CoF.

The elimination of ^{125}I CoF from the circulation as a function of time in three of the five rabbits injected is shown in Figure 1. After a phase of rapid loss occurring in the 1st day, the ^{125}I CoF was eliminated from the circulation with a half disappearance time of 32 hr. This constant rate of elimination continued until about day 5, at which time a far more rapid rate of loss from the circulation was observed, leading to complete elimination of ^{125}I activity by day 7 or 8. Since this third, rapid phase of loss suggested immune elimination, ^{125}I CoF was injected again intravenously 8 days after the initial exposure and its rate of elimination followed in each of three rabbits. Ninety-eight to 99% of the ^{125}I CoF was removed from the circulation in 24 hr. The same ^{125}I CoF, when injected into two additional normal control rabbits, equilibrated at the same concentration as previously in the normal rabbits, and was eliminated with a half-life of 32 hr. More rapid loss after the second injection could therefore not be attributed to denaturation of ^{125}I CoF.

Formation of a CoF-plasma protein complex following in vivo administration. Samples of serum from two rabbits treated with ^{125}I CoF as above

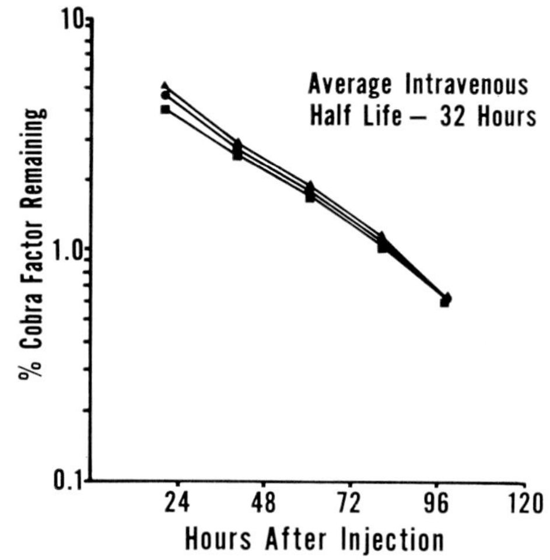

Figure 1. Elimination of ^{125}I CoF from the circulation in three rabbits following a single injection intravenously.

were obtained 18, 42 and 60 hr after injection. The freshly obtained serum was immediately submitted to ultracentrifugation in a sucrose density gradient. The sedimentation pattern was compared with that of 10 units of ^{125}I CoF alone and ^{125}I CoF combined and incubated 20 min at 37°C with 0.2 ml fresh rabbit serum *in vitro*. A typical sedimentation pattern is shown in Figure 2. The ^{125}I CoF in the serum of the injected rabbits sedimented more rapidly at each of the time intervals than ^{125}I CoF alone and at the same rate as the main peak of ^{125}I CoF incubated with fresh rabbit serum. Comparison of the sedimentation rate of the CoF in plasma with proteins of known sedimentation rates indicated a value of approximately 9S. To find if the rapid sedimentation rate of the ^{125}I CoF after injection was due to binding to the plasma C3 proinactivator, 0.1-ml samples of the ultracentrifuged fractions were added to 40 μg of purified human C3 and incubated at 37°C for 15 min. Immunoelectrophoresis of the incubated samples revealed conversion of the C3 to the more rapidly migrating inactive form by fractions containing the 9S material. Conversion to the inactive form was not complete in sera taken at 42 and 60 hr, presumably because of the lowered circulating amounts of ^{125}I CoF. Ultracentrifuged fractions of ^{125}I CoF alone were without effect on the purified C3.

The effect in vivo of cobra venom factor on the complement system. In order to determine the optimal dose of CoF required to maintain high levels of CoF and to deplete C3 *in vivo*, varying doses and injection schedules were tested. Three 1.0-kg rabbits were injected with a total of 150 units of ^{125}I CoF i.v., and the elimination of ^{125}I CoF was followed in the blood. Rabbit 3 received the 150 units CoF as a single injection, rabbit 2 received a divided dose of 75 units at 0 and 24 hr and rabbit 1 a divided dose of 50 units at 0, 4 and 24 hr. A fourth rabbit received 250 units in a single injection at 0 hr. ^{125}I activity remaining in the sera at 48 hr is shown in Table I. It is apparent that with the same total dose multiple injections of the CoF induced higher levels than a single injection. Twenty-four hours after administration of the accumulated dose of 150 units CoF, the total hemolytic complement activity fell to 12% to 15% of normal in each rabbit. The circulating level of CoF (in the inactivator complex form) was 0.1 at the lowest to 0.18 units/ml at the highest at that time, and C3 protein, by double diffusion precipitation in agar, was not completely eliminated. We therefore adopted a schedule of injections consisting of four equal doses at 0, 4, 10 and 24 hr, given i.p. using a total dose of 250 to 300 units/kg. Using this regimen, CH_{50} levels fell to less than 10% to 15% of pretreatment levels at the end of the injection period and C3 protein in agar diffusion precipitation was greatly reduced or absent. The effect of the injection of 250 units CoF given in four divided doses intraperitoneally upon levels of hemolytic complement activity is shown in Table II. The loss of C3 protein as demonstrated in immunoelectrophoresis is shown in Figure 3. Continuing injections of the CoF may be given intravenously (100 units/kg/day) in order to ensure nearly complete removal of C3 from the circulation as detected by agar diffusion techniques, although depletion after the initial treatment persists through 5 days. At

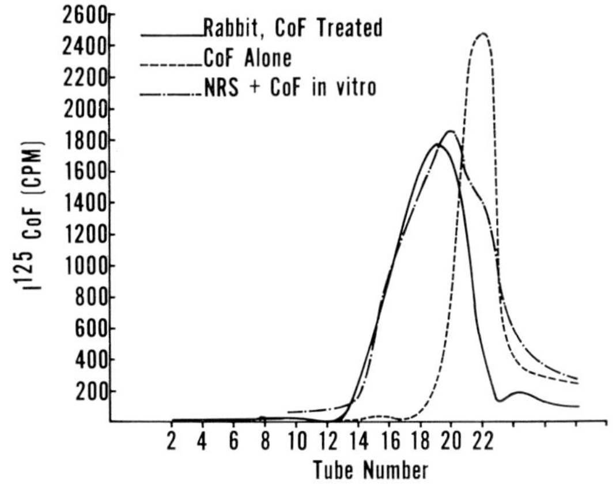

Figure 2. Sedimentation pattern of rabbit serum following an injection of ^{125}I CoF in sucrose gradient ultracentrifugation. The sedimentation pattern is compared with those of ^{125}I CoF alone and ^{125}I CoF after addition to normal rabbit serum *in vitro*.

TABLE I

The effect of multiple injections on the circulating levels of ^{125}I cobra factor in rabbits

Rabbit	Dosage Schedule (Units Injected at hr) 0	4	24	Total Dose	^{25}I CoF at 48 hr
				units	*counts/min/m*
1	50	50	50	150	8792
2	75		75	150	6555
3	150			150	4419
4	250			250	6650

TABLE II

The effect of cobra factor on hemolytic complement levels in rabbits

Rabbit	CH_{50} at hr				
	0	24	60	120	137
2	75	<10	<10	40	60
15	68	<10	<10	<10	30
16	102	<10	14.3		
17	72	10.4	18		
18	70	<10	10.2		

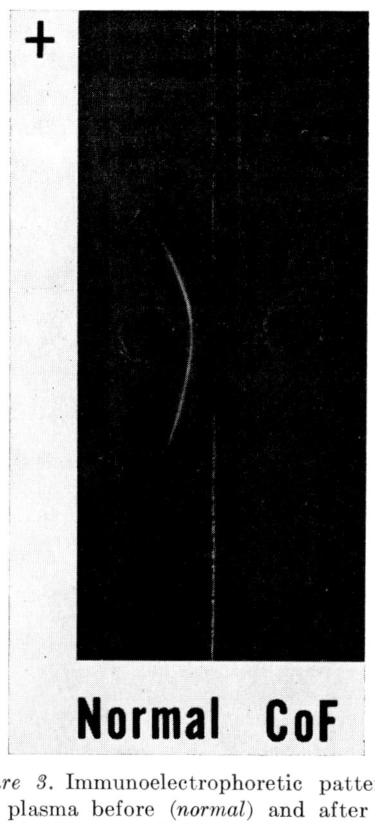

Figure 3. Immunoelectrophoretic patterns of rabbit plasma before (*normal*) and after (*CoF*) treatment of the rabbit with CoF. Antirabbit C3 was added to the trough.

4 and 16 hr after the initial injection a marked decrease of C3 protein was noted and in immunoelectrophoresis C3 protein migrated slightly more cathodally than unaltered C3. This alteration in migration was also seen when C3 reappeared in the circulation on the 5th to 6th day of CoF injection.

The effect of CoF on complement levels in rat, guinea pig and mouse. CoF at a dose of 250 units/kg was injected intravenously in four equally divided doses spaced over a 24-hr period into rats, guinea pigs and mice. Serum was obtained from the animals at 24 hr and up to 8 days after injection. The effects on hemolytic activity of the serum and C3 are shown in Table III. As noted, the hemolytic activity was markedly diminished and C3 protein detected antigenically in immunoelectrophoresis was reduced in amount below levels of detection. Double diffusion precipitation in agar often showed a trace of C3 protein, evidenced by the bending of a known C3-anti-C3 precipitin band in the vicinity of a well containing CoF-treated serum. In guinea pigs, serum of CoF-treated animals showed greater than 99.9% of C3 immune adherence activity to be depleted. As in the rabbit, these species remained depleted in C3 until 5 to 6 days after the initial injection.

The effect of cobra venom factor on other components of complement. C1,4 and 2. In a previous report (5) it was shown that the 140,000 molecular weight CoF does not affect isolated human C1,4 or 2. It was important, however, to find out if these components were affected after the standard intravenous injection course of CoF. Serum was obtained from three guinea pigs before and 48 hr after the series of CoF injections was begun. C1,4 activity was unchanged after the CoF treatment, as indicated by the T_{max} test (31), and C2 levels were also unaffected. In human serum treated with CoF (10 units/ml) the migration of C4 in immunoelectrophoresis was unchanged.

C5. The plasmas of the BALB/c mice (see Table III) obtained 4 to 120 hr after the initial injection of CoF were assayed for their content of C5 protein. Figure 4 demonstrates that C5 was depleted beyond detection until 96 hr. Similarly, incubation of 1.0 ml fresh normal human serum with 10 units CoF at 37°C for 30 min led to loss of C5 protein in double diffusion precipitation in agar. This loss did not occur in the presence of 0.03 M EDTA.

C6. Four 1.2-kg rabbits were given 250 units CoF/kg in a single injection and their serum was assayed at 16, 65 and 120 hr for hemolytic values (CH_{50}) and C6 levels. The results are shown in Table IV. As noted, the C6 values fell to less than half normal values by 16 hr, remaining low through 120 hr.

Effect of cobra factor on other systems. The blood clotting system. Blood was obtained using siliconized needles in ACD anticoagulant from the artery of the ear of two rabbits injected with 250

TABLE III

Effect of cobra venom factor in rat, guinea pig and mouse

Species	No. of Animals	CH_{50} (Average)	C3		Immune Adherence (Average)[a]
			IEP	Double diffusion	
Rat					
CoF[b]	6	<5 to 10	−	− to trace	ND[c]
Normal	5	60	+	+	ND
Guinea pig					
CoF	6	<15 to 22	−	− to trace	<50
Normal	5	206	+	+	640,000
Mouse[d]					
CoF	14	ND	−	− to trace	ND
Normal	7	ND	+	+	ND

[a] Immune adherence values represent reciprocal of greatest twofold dilution giving a 2+ test.

[b] CoF injected in a total dose of 250 units/kg given in divided doses over a 24-hr period. Serum values are those obtained 48 hr after initial injection.

[c] ND, not done.

[d] BALB/c males and females equally divided. Mice were bled into EDTA (approximately 0.01 M final concentration) and plasma was obtained.

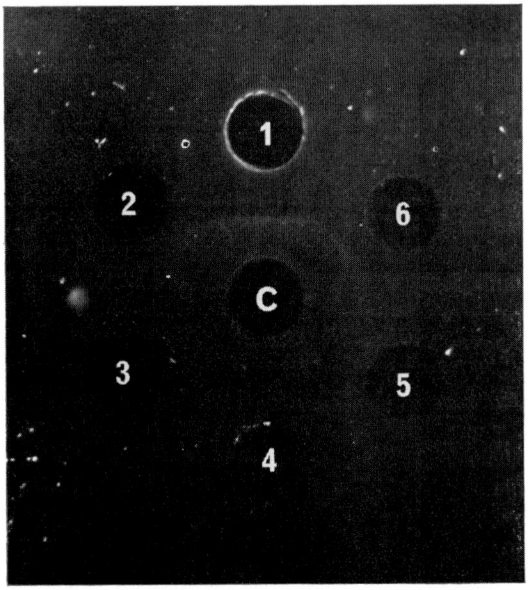

Figure 4. Agar precipitation of mouse C5 before and at various times after treatment of the mouse with CoF. *Center well*, B10 D2 old line mouse anti-mouse C5. *Well 1*, pretreatment serum. *Wells 2, 3, 4, 5 and 6*, serum taken 4, 16, 24, 48 and 96 hr after CoF treatment.

units/kg of CoF. Siliconized glassware was used throughout. Clotting tests were performed immediately on the plasma. As shown in Table V, both Quick times and partial thromboplastin times were within normal limits, as compared with normal rabbits tested simultaneously. Fibrinogen levels in the plasma before treatment and 24, 48 and 96 hr after treatment were tested by quantitative immune diffusion. There was no decrease in fibrinogen following treatment, and in one of the rabbits a slight increase was noted. In four guinea pigs, however, injection of 250 units of cobra factor/kg intravenously resulted in a diminution in levels of circulating fibrinogen to about half normal by quantitative agar diffusion precipitation.

Kininogen levels. Rabbits were tested before and 24 and 96 hr after a series of four CoF injections totaling 250 units/kg. The blood was collected in EDTA (0.01 M) and hexadimethrine bromide (50 μg/ml plasma) in plastic to prevent spontaneous activation of the kinin-forming system. The quantity of kininogen measured before and after treatment with CoF is given in Table VI in terms of kallidin equivalents. The levels were either unchanged or slightly elevated following treatment with CoF. The free kinin content of the same samples of plasma was examined using plasmas obtained as in the case of kininogen analyses, but that were brought to 100°C for 5 min to destroy kininase. No free kinin was found in the treated plasmas.

The formed elements of the blood. The formed elements of the blood were examined in rabbits, guinea pigs and rats injected with cobra factor.

TABLE IV

The effect of cobra venom factor on the levels of C6 in rabbits[a]

Rabbit	Hours after CoF Injection							
	0		16		65		120	
	C6	CH_{50}	C6	CH_{50}	C6	CH_{50}	C6	CH_{50}
1	300	105	118	<10	135	10.2	ND	ND[b]
2	330	64	100	<10	120	22.7	ND	ND
14	343	85	172	<10	196	10.2	204	20.8
15	333	77	139	<10	192	14.3	238	ND

[a] See *Materials and Methods* for assay procedure. CoF 250 units given intravenously in a single injection.

[b] ND, not done.

TABLE V

The effect of CoF on clotting tests

	Rabbit No.	Quick Time (Sec)			Partial Thromboplastin Time		
		Tube 1	Tube 2	Average	Tube 1	Tube 2	Average
CoF	64–16	19.6	18.2	18.9	27.0	27.0	27.0
	64–18	17.4	17.0	17.2	30.0	28.0	29.0
Control	64–19	17.2	18.6	17.9	27.0	27.0	27.0
	64–20	23.2	24.0	23.6	36.0	36.0	36.0

TABLE VI

Effect of cobra factor treatment on kininogen levels in rabbits

Time Plasma Obtained[a]	Kininogen Levels[b] for Rabbit No.			
	1	2	3	4
hr				
0	7.5	8.0	8.7	8.7
24	7.5	8.8	11.2	8.7
96	8.8	10.0	8.7	8.7

[a] Plasma samples obtained in EDTA (0.01 M) and hexadimethrine bromide (50 μg/ml) before and at times noted following the first of four injections of CoF. Final injection of CoF given i.p. at 20 hr.

[b] Kininogen levels given in terms of kallidin equivalents/ml plasma.

As shown in Table VII, a moderate increase in neutrophilic leukocytes was found in rats and rabbits 24 hr after the injection of cobra factor. In rats, an increase in mononuclear cells was also noticed. Platelet levels were not significantly reduced.

In preliminary studies large doses of cobra factor in the range of 300 to 400 units/kg administered intravenously at a single initial injection resulted in lysis of red cells *in vivo* and in blood obtained from injected animals *in vitro*. Hemolysis could be significantly reduced or completely eliminated by injecting less than 300 units/kg in the first 24-hr period and administering the CoF in four or more equally divided doses intraperitoneally as reflected in normal hematocrit values shown in Table VII.

Chemotaxis of neutrophils. Tests were performed on the capacity of neutrophils from CoF-treated rabbits to respond to a chemotactic stimulus. Two rabbits received CoF (250 units/kg in four divided doses intravenously) with two normal rabbits serving as controls. Twenty-four hours after the final injection, at a time when CH_{50} levels were less than 10 in treated rabbits, sterile 0.1% glycogen was instilled in the peritoneal cavity of all four rabbits (25). After 4 hr neutrophils were collected, washed three times in saline and tested in chemotaxis chambers (20) using purified human C3a as chemotactic stimulus. Counts of 10 microscopic fields revealed values of 429 and 325 for the neutrophils from CoF-treated rabbits (with counts of 6 and 8 as background) and 265 and 463 for neutrophils from normals (with background levels of 5 and 50, respectively). Thus neutrophils from CoF-

TABLE VII

Effect of CoF on formed elements of the blood

Species	No. of Animals	CH_{50}	Circulating Formed Elements (Average/mm³)[a]							
			WBC	N	L	M	B	E	Platelets	Hct
Rabbit										
CoF[b]	9	<10–18	10,400	71	24	2	3		666,000	31
Normal	6	107	9,500	50	37	9	4		689,000	36
Rat										
CoF[b]	6	<5–10	24,300	31	63	4		2	885,000	40
Normal	5	60	8,825	23	74	1		2	842,000	42
Guinea pig										
CoF[b]	10	<20	6,450	48	44	5	2	1	398,000	40
Normal	7	206	12,300	44	52	2	1	1	306,000	39

[a] Circulating formed elements tested in three guinea pigs and rats in each group.

[b] CoF injected i.p. 250 units/kg in five divided doses in 24 hr. Blood obtained for testing 48 hr following initial injection.

treated rabbits responded fully to a chemotactic stimulus.

Immune adherence of neutrophils from CoF-treated rabbits to bound C3. Two rabbits were treated with 250 units CoF in divided doses as in the preceding section and neutrophils and platelets were obtained from peripheral blood. These cells were then exposed in the aggregomator to zymosan particles treated previously with serum or serum containing EDTA (0.01 M). The cells from two normal rabbits served as controls. No difference was observed in the rate or total amount of clumping of neutrophils or platelets from CoF-treated or control rabbits (Fig. 5). Zymosan exposed to serum containing EDTA failed to induce immune adherence clumping of neutrophils and platelets from CoF-treated or normal rabbits. Microscopic examination of neutrophils and platelets revealed greater than 90% of these cells clumped with zymosan particles that had been treated with serum. Phagocytosis of the zymosan by neutrophils was abundant, and no differences were noted between cells from normal or CoF-treated rabbits. No adherence was observed with zymosan treated with serum containing EDTA.

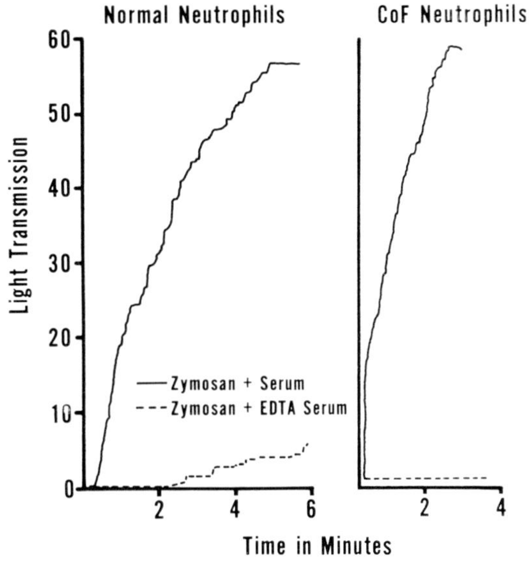

Figure 5. Aggregometer tracings of the clumping of rabbit peripheral neutrophils with zymosan and complement (zymosan serum). The increase in clumping of the neutrophils and zymosan is accompanied by an increase in transmission of light.

The effect of cobra factor treatment on immunologic disease. Nephrotoxic nephritis. Acute nephrotoxic glomerulonephritis was induced in three groups of rats: cobra factor-treated, neutrophil-depleted and rats receiving no pretreatment. The quantity of urinary protein was tested every 24 hr for 4 days. The results, shown in Table VIII, indicate that a marked reduction in the proteinuria in the first 24 hr occurred in rats pretreated with cobra factor or depleted of neutrophils. During the subsequent 3 days the proteinuria values fell in all three groups. In similar groups of pretreated rats, ^{131}I nephrotoxic globulin was injected to induce identical lesions. These rats, however, were killed 4 hr after injection of the nephrotoxic globulin in order to examine the glomeruli histologically for neutrophil accumulation and to measure the amount of nephrotoxic

TABLE VIII

The effect of CoF treatment on nephrotoxic glomerulonephritis in rats[a]

Pretreatment	No. Rats	CH_{50} (Average)[b]	Proteinuria	No. Rats[c]	Neutrophils/ Glomerular Section (Average)[c]	^{131}I Nephrotoxic Globulin in Glomeruli (Average)[c]
			mg/24 hr			
CoF	7	<5	24	3	1.2	0.44%
None	6	66	129	3	20.6	0.43%
Neutrophil-depleted[d]	5	48	55	3	0.2	ND[e]

[a] CoF 300 units/kg i.p. in five divided doses in 24 hr.
[b] Average CH_{50} value in rats obtained at the end of CoF treatment just prior to injection of nephrotoxic serum.
[c] Rats killed 4 hr after injection of ^{131}I nephrotoxic globulin in a dose equal to that in the 24-hr experiment shown in the left of the table. A thin slice of renal cortex was removed for determination of neutrophil accumulation in glomeruli and the remainder of the kidney was homogenized and washed to determine bound ^{131}I nephrotoxic globulin.
[d] PMN neutrophils depleted by injection of specific rabbit antirat neutrophil globulin i.p. 18 hr before injection of nephrotoxic serum.
[e] ND, not done.

globulin bound in glomeruli in the cobra factor and untreated groups. Sections of over 40 glomeruli were counted in each case and the results, presented in Table VIII, indicate that treatment with cobra factor prevented accumulation of neutrophils in the glomeruli. An average of 1.2 neutrophils was found per glomerular section, while 20.6 neutrophils were found per section in glomeruli of controls. Swelling and proliferation of glomerular cells were not apparent. Fluorescent antibody studies indicated strong binding of nephrotoxic globulin in all three groups, but rat C3-binding was markedly inhibited in the glomeruli of the cobra factor-treated group. The inhibition of neutrophil accumulation and proteinuria in the cobra factor-treated group could not be explained by decreased binding of nephrotoxic globulin, since equal amounts of the radioactive globulin were found bound in kidneys of cobra factor-treated rats (Table VIII). Previous work has shown that the radioactive nephrotoxic globulin binds equally well in neutrophil-depleted rats (35).

In rabbits, a similar observation was made. In Table IX are shown the results of experiments in which two doses of sheep antirabbit glomerular basement membrane were employed. The sheep antiserum used was known to produce a glomerulitis that was only partially dependent upon neutrophil accumulation in glomeruli for its injurious effect. As noted in Table IX, injection of a large amount of the sheep antibody induced injury yielding 1682 mg of protein in the urine in the first 24 hr. This was inhibited in the cobra factor-treated group, so that only 368 mg of protein appeared in the urine in the first 24 hr. When a smaller amount of this same antibody was injected so that 571 mg of protein appeared in the first 24 hr in untreated controls, cobra factor treatment almost entirely prevented the proteinuria from developing. Similar results have been produced in at least 30 other rabbits, in studies that will be reported separately.

TABLE IX

The effect of CoF treatment on nephrotoxic nephritis in rabbits

Pretreatment	No. of Rabbits	Anti-GBM	CH_{50}	Proteinuria
		ml		*avg. mg/24 hr*
CoF[a]	3	1.7	12–15	368
None	3	1.7	111–160	1682
CoF[a]	3	1.1	<8–18	50
None	8	1.1	100–120	571

[a] Quantity of CoF and times of testing for complement activity were the same as those reported in Table VII.

Cobra factor alone (300 units/kg in divided doses) failed to induce proteinuria in three rabbits in the initial 48-hr test period.

The effect of cobra factor treatment on the development of reverse passive Arthus reactions (RPA). Reversed passive Arthus reactions were induced in cobra factor-treated, untreated and neutrophil-depleted rats and rabbits, as shown in Table X. To produce the RPA reactions, 75 μg of rabbit anti-BSA N were injected intradermally followed immediately by 1 mg of BSA N intravenously. In the rats, Arthus reactions developed in controls with edema scores of 2.7 and an average diameter of hemorrhage of 8 mm at the height of reaction, 4 hr. In the cobra factor-treated and neutrophil-depleted groups, hemorrhage was prevented and development of edema was greatly inhibited. RPA reactions in normal and cobra factor-treated rats are shown in Figure 6.

Similar results were observed in rabbits, but the effect of the cobra factor was not as striking as in the rats. Edema was present in Arthus reactions of all cobra factor-treated rabbits, although to a lesser extent than in untreated controls, and a trace amount of hemorrhage was present in the Arthus reactions of three of five of the rabbits treated with cobra factor. In contrast, neutrophil-depleted rabbits showed neither edema nor hemorrhage.

Histologic sections of treated and control Arthus reactions in both rats and rabbits revealed

TABLE X

Effect of CoF on reversed passive Arthus (RPA) reactions in rats and rabbits

Pretreatment	No. of Animals	CH_{50}	RPA Reactions: Hemorrhage (diameter mm)	RPA Reactions: Edema[a]
Rats				
CoF[b]	8	<5	0	1.6
None	6	66	8	2.7
Neutrophil-depleted	5	48	0	1.2
Rabbits				
CoF[b]	5	<8–18	0–trace	1.0
None	7	60–110	7	2.9
Neutrophil-depleted	8	45–90	0	±

[a] Average value of palpable edema. 1, mild; 2, moderate; 3, moderate to marked; 4, marked.

[b] Three hundred units CoF/kg in divided doses for 24 hr followed by 50 units/kg from 24 to 48 hr. RPA reactions initiated 48 hr: 75 μg N anti-BSA i.d. + 1 mg N BSA i.v. Reactions in rats read at 4 hr and rabbits at 6 hr.

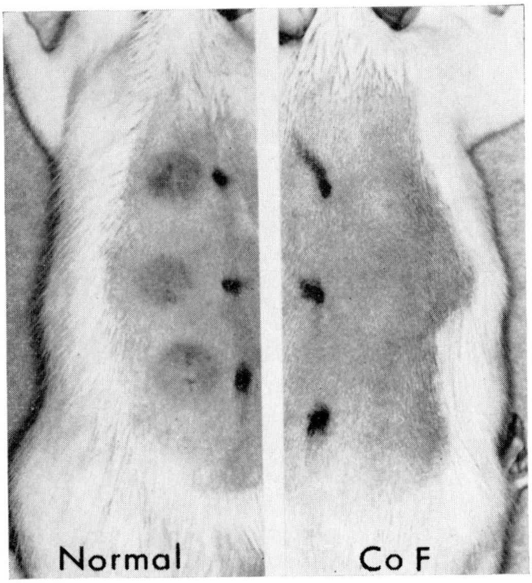

Figure 6. Three reversed passive Arthus reactions in a normal and CoF-treated rat. The black ink dots were placed approximately 1 cm medial to the point of antibody injection. Seventy-five micrograms of Ab N were used in each site.

the typical neutrophil accumulation in venule walls in the normal animals, with hemorrhage and edema fluid in the surrounding interstitial spaces of the skin. In the cobra factor-pretreated groups of rats and rabbits, neutrophil accumulation in the blood vessel walls was noted to a variable extent. While considerably less neutrophil accumulation was present in the reactions of most rats, histologic sections of rabbit Arthus reactions showed significant numbers of neutrophils in affected vessels. Fluorescent antibodies to BSA antigen, rabbit IgG and homologous C3 showed equal deposition of BSA and IgG in the vessel walls in the treated and untreated groups and a diminished but definite presence of C3 in the CoF-treated rabbits and rats. C3 was demonstrable in apparently greater amounts in the cutaneous vessels than in glomeruli of CoF-treated rats and rabbits receiving anti-GBM.

The effect of cobra factor treatment on the development of delayed (contact) sensitivity in guinea pigs. The effect of CoF treatment of guinea pigs on the development of contact sensitivity lesions is shown in Table XI. As noted, there was no difference in the size of erythematous reactions developing at 7 and 24 hr between the cobra factor-

TABLE XI

Delayed (contact) sensitivity in cobra factor-treated guinea pigs

Treatment	No. of Guinea Pigs	CH_{50} (Average)	Contact Reactions to OCBC[a] (mm Erythema)		No. of Guinea Pigs	Average ^{131}I BSA in OCBC Site (counts/min)		Histamine Site
			7 hr	24 hr		7 hr	24 hr	24 hr
CoF[b] OCBC-sensitized	11	<20	10	17.1	5	311	1343	3340
— OCBC-sensitized	13	257>	6	16.5	3	218	938	2600
— —	2	Not done	0	0	2	68	150	3260

[a] O-chlorobenzoyl chloride. Two drops of 2% OCBC in acetone-olive oil applied to skin surface.
[b] One hundred and fifty to two hundred units CoF/300 g guinea pig injected in divided doses 24 to 48 hr before cutaneous application of OCBC.

TABLE XII

Passive cutaneous anaphylaxis (PCA) in CoF-treated guinea pigs

Pretreated	No. of Guinea Pigs	PCA Reaction[a] (Average mm Blueing/Reciprocal Dilution of Ab)				
		500	1000	2000	4000	8000
CoF[b]	4	17.0	12.7	11	9.5	8.7
Normal	4	15.7	11.7	10	8.5	7.0

[a] γ_1 guinea pig anti-DNP antibody (courtesy of Dr. Zoltan Ovary) injected i.d. at the dilution shown 6 hr prior to i.v. injection of 300 μg DNP_{13} ovalbumin and 0.5 ml 1% Evans blue. Reactions recorded 30 min later.
[b] Two hundred and twenty units CoF in divided doses in 24 hr.

treated and the normal, sensitized groups. In order to assess the development of increased vascular permeability in the OCBC sites, ^{131}I BSA was injected intravenously 20 min before the animals were killed. The sites were then removed for counting (see *Materials and Methods*). An injection of 2 μg of histamine was given intradermally in each guinea pig at the time of ^{131}I BSA injection for comparison. As noted in Table XI, the leakage of the radioactive BSA into the skin sites at 7 and 24 hr was comparable in the cobra factor-treated and untreated sensitized groups, especially when the leakage of ^{131}I BSA into the histamine site was taken into account. In the third, unsensitized group reactions failed to develop at the site of application of OCBC and only small amounts of ^{131}I BSA were counted in the sites of removed skin.

Passive cutaneous anaphylaxis (PCA) in cobra factor-treated guinea pigs. The development of PCA reactions in CoF and normal guinea pigs is shown in Table XII. CoF depletion of C3 had no inhibitory effect on the reactions.

DISCUSSION

An anticomplementary agent in the venom of the cobra *Naja naja* has been purified and tested *in vivo* for its action on the complement system and on several antigen-antibody-induced lesions. The anticomplementary agent employed was the smaller in molecular size of the two so far identified in cobra venom (10), representing over 97% of the activity.

1. The effect of cobra venom factor (CoF) on the complement system following injection in vivo. Following injection of CoF into rabbits, this protein complexed with a constituent of the plasma, leading to the inactivation of C3. By 4 hr after injection of CoF, hemolytic complement activity was markedly diminished and C3 protein was present in only small amounts. By 24 to 48 hr, CH_{50} values were often less than 10% of normal and plasma C3 levels, measured in guinea pigs by immune adherence, were more than 99% depleted. While it was not possible to identify precisely the plasma constituent complexing with CoF, the sedimentation rate in density gradient ultracentrifugation of the inactivator complex formed *in vivo* (9S) was similar to that formed *in vitro*. It would thus appear that a similar if not identical inactivator complex is formed after injection of the CoF. In addition, the circulating inactivator remained capable of attacking C3.

Multiple injections of CoF resulted in higher circulating levels of the C3 inactivator complex. The blood level attained by a single injection of 150 units was about half that when three divided doses of 50 units were given in a 24-hr period. In terms of maintaining rabbits in a state of C3 depletion, it was found that levels of 0.2 units/ml plasma were required. Levels of inactivator complex were maintained by the relatively long half-disappearance time of 32 hr. Other complement-inhibiting agents given to experimental animals, such as heat-aggregated γ globulin of zymosan (19) were effective for only a few hours. The prolonged life-span of the inactivator complex allowed it to act up to 5 to 6 days. In addition, when levels of the complex dropped below 0.2 unit CoF/ml plasma, further administration of CoF resulted in an elevation of the level and further depletion of C3. This indicated that the proinactivator had not been exhausted. On about day 6 after initial injection of the CoF, rabbits and rats eliminated the inactivator complex rapidly, suggesting an immune response to the CoF. CoF injected in the next several days was eliminated from the circulation within 24 hr.

The effect of CoF on other complement components. The inactivator complex affects not only C3, but also C5 in mouse and human serum and C6 in the rabbit (the only species tested). C5 was detected by immune precipitation in agar and after CoF treatment of mice or of human serum *in vitro*, a complete loss of C5 protein was observed. In normal mouse serum C5 could be detected through a 1:4 dilution, suggesting that a reduction of 75% had occurred in the C5 concentration in the mice. Previously Klein and Willensiek found a fall in a guinea pig component similar in its properties to C5 after administration of CoF (3). Jensen also found CoF capable of cleaving guinea pig C5 (7). In rabbits, C6 levels fell from titers of 300 to 343 (average 321) to 100 to 172 (average 140) within 16 hr, indicating a profound effect (8). Recently Shin, Gewurz and Pickering (9) have found that addition of CoF to guinea pig serum inactivates more than 90% of C3 and considerable quantities of C5, 6, 7, 8 and 9 activities. Of interest, a chemotactic factor for rabbit neutrophils was generated having a molecular weight of about 15,000.

The mechanism by which C5 and the terminal components are depleted is not certain, but since no direct action by the inactivator complex has been detected on isolated human C5 and C6 (6), the possibility must be considered that during enzymatic cleavage of C3, C5 and C6 and the terminal components may be sequentially activated in a process akin to that initiated by C3 convertase ($C\overline{4,2}$).

Of the various complement-depleting agents available for studies *in vivo* (15), CoF has numerous advantages. Its action appears directed almost exclusively to the complement system and, in particular, to C3. Its action is prolonged and animals may be maintained 5 to 6 days in a C3-depleted state. Injections are well-tolerated when given according to the schedules reported here: 250 to 300 units/kg injected over a 24- to 36-hr period in divided doses, starting with 50 units/kg i.p., repeated every 4 to 6 hr for a total of four injections. A final intravenous injection of 50 units/kg may be given 10 to 20 hr after the final i.p. injection. Another 50 to 100 units/kg may be injected i.v. each day to maintain sufficiently high levels of inactivator complex to maintain C3 depletion.

One of the most undesirable effects *in vivo* of CoF administration is hemolysis. This has been noted in all species studied and follows injection of a large dose. Studies into the nature of the hemolytic effect (10, 32) have indicated that the complement system is involved in the lysis of red cells by CoF and that a proinactivator also is required for complement activation. These studies provided further rationale for the injection of small amounts of CoF at the beginning. Presumably the gradual removal of C3 from the circulation prevented lysis of the red cells so that high levels of inactivator complex could be attained safely. Circulating levels of kininogen in rabbits did not fall and no free kinin was measurable after administration of CoF.

2. The effect of cobra venom factor treatment on various experimental immunologic lesions. The principal effect of the treatment of animals with CoF is in inhibiting the accumulation of neutrophils at the site of antigen-antibody reactions. This was most clearly demonstrated in acute nephrotoxic nephritis where neutrophil accumulation in glomeruli was abolished and proteinuria in great part averted. In these experiments care was taken to ensure that the predicted quantity of antibody had reacted with glomerular basement membrane and that normal numbers of neutrophils were circulating. The neutrophils were also found to be fully responsive to a chemotactic stimulus and to C3 immune adherence. Thus, during the time that known amounts of antibody were reacting in glomeruli in the animal, neutrophils were circulating in abundant numbers and possessed full capacity to respond to the two complement-dependent stimuli known to affect neutrophil movement and adherence.

In two other neutrophil-dependent immunologic reactions, CoF treatment has been shown to block development of the lesion. In the polyarteritis of acute immune complex disease (serum sickness) neutrophil accumulation and structural injury were prevented by treatment with CoF, as will be reported separately (P. M. Henson and C. G. Cochrane, to be published). In addition, a PCA reaction in rabbits has recently been found that requires neutrophils and platelets. CoF treatment prevents development of this reaction (33). The present results parallel closely the inhibition produced by neutrophil depletion (34, 35) and substantiate previous results from this laboratory showing a correlation between the binding of C3 at the site of antigen-antibody reaction, the accumulation of neutrophils and the development of injury (19, 35).

In Arthus reactions the CoF treatment was not completely effective in preventing neutrophil accumulation and C3 could still be detected in limited but perhaps sufficient quantities in the affected blood vessels. This presence of small amounts of bound C3 could be explained by a reserve of C3 in interstitial spaces that escaped CoF degradation and reacted with bound C1,4 and 2 in the venular walls. On the other hand, additional factors could play a role in bringing about neutrophil accumulation in cutaneous lesions. Similar observations have been made independently by Maillard and Zarco (36). Guinea pigs depleted of hemolytic complement activity showed a decrease in edema and hemorrhage failed to appear. Restoration of hemorrhage and edema occurred when serum or isolated C3 were injected locally with the antigen.

The exact means by which complement components mediate the accumulation are not yet certain, but among the possibilities are C3 immune adherence, and chemotaxis by activated $\overline{C5\text{-}6\text{-}7}$ complex (20, 37), C3a (38), C5a (39, 40) and a plasmin-degraded fragment of C3 (41, 42). Treatment with CoF, with the resulting depletion of C3 prior to interaction of antigen and antibody, would abrogate each of these complement-dependent mechanisms.

Those reactions not having neutrophils as an essential intermediate in their development were not inhibited by CoF and C3 depletion. This included passive cutaneous anaphylactic reactions (PCA) in guinea pigs induced by a guinea pig γ_1 anti-DNP, and delayed (contact) sensitivity induced by *o*-chloromercuribenzoate in guinea pigs. Similar results have been reported by Maillard and Zarco (36). These data underscore previous findings (43) indicating that homocytotropic antibody-induced PCA reactions develop independently of the complement system. In rabbits, a second homocytotropic antibody PCA reaction develops in spite of neutrophil depletion. This reaction is also unaffected by C3 depletion (33). As noted above, this neutrophil-independent homocytotropic antibody PCA reaction has been contrasted recently with a neutrophil and platelet requiring PCA reaction in rabbits in which CoF depletion of C3 prevented development of the vascular permeability (33). The results do not substantiate the data of Neveu and Biozzi (44), or Willoughby *et al.* (45) in which a fall in complement levels was associated with an inhibition of reactions of delayed sensitivity.

REFERENCES

1. Flexner, S. and Noguchi, H., J. Exp. Med., *6:* 277, 1903.
2. Ritz, H., Z. Immunitätsforsch, *13:* 62, 1912.
3. Klein, P. G. and Wellensiek, H. J., Immunology, *8:* 590, 1965.
4. Carpenter, C. B. and Gill, J. J., III, Immunology, *10:* 355, 1966.
5. Nelson, R. A., Survey Ophthal., *11:* 498, 1966.
6. Müller-Eberhard, H. J., Fed. Proc., *26:* 744, 1967.
7. Jensen, J., Science, *155:* 1122, 1967.
8. Cochrane, C. G., Advances Immun., *9:* 97, 1968.
9. Shin, H. S., Gewurz, H. and Snyderman, R., Proc. Soc. Exp. Biol. Med., *131:* 203, 1969.
10. Ballow, M. and Cochrane, C. G., J. Immun., *103:* 944, 1969.
11. Cochrane, C. G. and Müller-Eberhard, H. J., Fed. Proc., *26:* 362, 1967.
12. Cochrane, C. G., Müller-Eberhard, H. J. and Fjellström, K. E., J. Clin. Invest., *47:* 21a, 1968.
13. Linscott, W. D. and Cochrane, C. G., J. Immun., *93:* 972, 1964.
14. Müller-Eberhard, H. J., Advances Immun., *8:* 2, 1968.
15. Cochrane, C. G., J. Exp. Med., *118:* 489, 1963.
16. Osler, A. G., Strauss, J. H. and Mayer, M. M., Amer. J. Syph. Gonorrhea Vener. Dis., *36:* 140, 1952.
17. Nishioka, K. and Linscott, W. D., J. Exp. Med., *118:* 767, 1963.

18. Mayer, M. M., in *Kabat and Mayer's Experimental Immunochemistry*, 2nd Ed., p. 133, Charles C Thomas, Springfield, Ill., 1961.
19. Ward, P. A. and Cochrane, C. G., J. Exp. Med., *121:* 215, 1966.
20. Ward, P. A., Cochrane, C. G. and Müller-Eberhard, H. J., J. Exp. Med., *122:* 327, 1965.
21. Bokisch, V. A., Müller-Eberhard, H. J. and Cochrane, C. G., J. Exp. Med., *129:* 1109, 1969.
22. Henson, P. M., J. Immun., In press.
23. Henson, P. M., J. Immun., In press.
24. McConahey, P. J. and Dixon, F. J., Int. Arch. Allerg., *29:* 185, 1966.
25. Scheidegger, J. J., Int. Arch. Allerg., *7:* 103, 1955.
26. Williams, C. A. and Grabar, P., J. Immun., *74:* 158, 1955.
27. Wintrobe, M. M., *Clinical Hematology*, 4th Ed., Lea and Febiger, Philadelphia, 1956.
28. Diniz, C. R. and Carvalho, I. F., Ann. N. Y. Acad. Sci., *104:* 77, 1963.
29. Unanue, E. R. and Dixon, F. J., Advances Immun., *6:* 1, 1967.
30. Cochrane, C. G., in *The Inflammatory Process*, Edited by B. Zweifach, L. Grant and R. McCluskey, Academic Press, New York, 1965.
31. Kabat, E. A., *Kabat and Mayer's Experimental Immunochemistry*, 2nd Ed., p. 200, Charles C Thomas, Springfield, Ill., 1961.
32. Pickering, M. R., Wolfson, M. R., Good, R. A. and Gewurz, H., Fed. Proc., *28:* 818, 1969.
33. Henson, P. M. and Cochrane, C. G., J. Exp. Med., *129:* 153, 1969.
34. Kniker, W. T. and Cochrane, C. G., J. Exp. Med., *122:* 83, 1965.
35. Cochrane, C. G., Unanue, E. R. and Dixon, F. J., J. Exp. Med., *122:* 91, 1965.
36. Maillard, J. L. and Zarco, R. M., Ann. Inst. Pasteur, *114:* 766, 1968.
37. Ward, P. A., Cochrane, C. G. and Müller-Eberhard, H. J., Immunology, *11:* 141, 1966.
38. Bokisch, V. A., Müller-Eberhard, H. J. and Cochrane, C. G., J. Exp. Med., *129:* 1109, 1969.
39. Shin, H. S., Snyderman, R., Friedman, E., Mellors, A. and Mayer, M. M., Science, *162:* 361, 1968.
40. Ward, P. A., J. Immun., *101:* 818, 1968.
41. Taylor, F. B., Jr. and Ward, P. A., J. Exp. Med., *126:* 149, 1967.
42. Ward, P. A., J. Exp. Med., *126:* 189, 1967.
43. Bloch, K. J., Kourilsky, F. M., Ovary, Z. and Benacerraf, B., J. Exp. Med., *117:* 965, 1963.
44. Neveu, T. and Biozzi, G., Immunology, *9:* 303, 1965.
45. Willoughby, D. A., Coote, E. and Turk, J. L., J. Path. Bact., *97:* 296, 1969.

THE JOURNAL OF IMMUNOLOGY
Vol. 105, No. 1, July 1970
Printed in U.S.A.

PRESENCE OF ALLOTYPIC SPECIFICITIES OF THREE LOCI, *a*, *b* AND *f*, ON INDIVIDUAL MOLECULES OF RABBIT COLOSTRAL γA IMMUNOGLOBULIN[1]

EDWARD A. LICHTER, THOMAS P. CONWAY,[2] ALICE GILMAN-SACHS AND SHELDON DRAY

From the Department of Preventive Medicine and Community Health and the Department of Microbiology, University of Illinois at the Medical Center, Chicago, Illinois 60680

Received for publication December 29, 1969

Colostral γA isolated from 12 rabbits of different genotypes were analyzed individually by quantitative radioprecipitation for the number of molecules bearing allotypic specificities of the *a*, *b* and *f* loci. In these experiments, the minimum percentage of molecules bearing allotypic specificities of all three loci ranged from 38% to 78% with the median sample at 69% as calculated from the percentage of molecules precipitable by each antiserum.

Cross-immunization of rabbits with purified colostral γA immunoglobulin resulted in the production of precipitating antibodies which identified five γA immunoglobulin allotypic specificities designated f71, f72, f73, f74 and f75.[3] That these antibodies were specific for γA immunoglobulin was indicated by the similar precipitin arcs observed in the α2-β region on immunoelectrophoresis when the anti-allotype antisera and goat anti-γA reacted with serum, whey or a highly purified colostral γA fraction (1, 2). The five allotypic specificities are on separate molecules of colostral γA as indicated by Ouchterlony analysis. Thus far, only six phenotypic combinations have been observed in our rabbit population: f71,75; f71,72,74,75; f71,73,74,75; f72,74; f73,74; and f72,73,74. Progeny data indicate that the five allotypic specificities are inherited as phenogroups in three combinations: f71,75; f72,74 and f73,74. The alleles for these phenogroups are designated $f^{71,75}$, $f^{72,74}$ and $f^{73,74}$. This complex *f* locus is not closely linked to the *a* heavy chain and *b* light chain loci of immunoglobulins. The *f* locus, unlike the *a* and *b* loci, does not appear to be involved in the control of γG and γM immunoglobulins. However, the three loci, *a*, *b* and *f*, are involved in the genetic control of serum and secretory γA immunoglobulins. The purpose of this study is to determine whether all three loci, *a*, *b* and *f*, control allotypic specificities on the same colostral γA molecule.

[1] This investigation was supported in part by United States Public Health Service Grants AI 07043-04 and AM 11914-02.

[2] Supported by United States Public Health Service Training Grant T01-AI-00335 from the National Institute of Allergy and Infectious Diseases.

[3] Investigators at a rabbit allotype workshop in Brussels, Belgium, May 5–7, 1969, agreed upon using unique numbers for allotypic specificities associated with immunoglobulins even when under genetic control at independent loci. Our previously published notation for the γA allotypes was f1, f2, f3, f4 and f5 (1, 2). However, in conformance with the agreement, the allotypic specificities are now designated Af71, Af72, Af73, Af74 and Af75. The three alleles at the *Af* locus are called $Af^{71,75}$, $Af^{72,74}$ and $Af^{73,74}$. For simplicity, the notation is abbreviated in this paper by deleting the "A."

MATERIALS AND METHODS

Isolation of colostral γA. The colostral γA was obtained from rabbit milk by the method of Cebra and Robbins (3) as modified by Conway *et al.* (1). By radioprecipitin analysis with goat anti-γA, more than 90% of the protein was precipitable from each γA preparation. Contamination with γG was minimal in that goat anti-Fc fragment of γG immunoglobulin precipitated less than 2% of the radioactivity.

Antisera. Antisera to the antigenic specificities of the *f* locus were obtained from rabbits that were cross-immunized with colostral γA as described previously (1, 2). Goat antiserum to rabbit Fc fragment of γG was obtained from Dr. A. Nisonoff, who prepared it by immunizing a goat with purified Fc fragment of γG immunoglobulin. This goat antiserum precipitated 98% of ^{125}I-labeled, purified γG and less than 1% of purified light chains. A second goat antiserum, specific for γA, was obtained from an animal immunized with a fragment of isolated γA obtained by pepsin digestion. The goat anti-γA antiserum precipitated 98% of ^{125}I-labeled, highly purified, colostral γA and less than 2% of ^{125}I-labeled purified γG. By immunoelectrophoresis, the goat anti-γA antiserum elicited a single precipitin arc in the α2-β region with whole rabbit serum or colostrum.

Radioprecipitin analysis. The precipitin analysis was based on the method of Gilman *et al.* (4). Briefly, the procedure was as follows. The γA was labeled with 1 to 3 atoms ^{125}I/molecule by the method of MacFarlane (5), assuming a molecular weight of 330,000. For the direct precipitation, 20 μg to 50 μg labeled antigen was added to 0.3 ml of anti-allotype antiserum. The amount of antigen added was such that the precipitation occurred in antibody excess. After 48 hr, the precipitate was washed and along with a weighed portion of the supernatant fluid was monitored for radioactivity in a well-type gamma counter. For the indirect precipitation, 5 μl of the supernatant fluid were added to 0.3 ml of goat anti-Fc fragment of γG which precipitated the immune complexes of labeled γA bound to γG antibody molecules. After 24 hr, the radioactivity in the washed precipitate and a weighed portion of the supernatant fluid was monitored.

The data presented here are the sum of the labeled protein brought down by direct precipitation with anti-allotype antiserum plus the indirect precipitation with goat anti-Fc γG performed on a weighed portion of the supernatant fluid of the first precipitation. No further counts could be precipitated from the supernatant fluid of the indirect precipitation. Mixing experiments which would determine variations in the extent of labeling of the different allotypes were not done.

RESULTS

The percentages of colostral 10S γA immunoglobulin molecules bearing the allotypic markers of the *a*, *b* and *f* loci are shown in Figure 1 for three rabbits. The solid bars indicate the amount of precipitable γA obtained by direct precipitation with anti-allotype antisera; the hatched bars indicate the amount obtained in the supernatant fluid by indirect precipitation with goat anti-FcγG antiserum. The sum of the percentage of precipitable labeled protein by direct plus indirect precipitation is shown in the column at the right.

Rabbits E106-1 and E208-6 are homozygous at all three loci. For rabbit E106-1 ($a^1a^1b^5b^5f^{71,75}f^{71,75}$) at least 86% of the molecules bear the a1 specificity; 89%, the b5 specificity; and 94%, the f71 or f75 specificities. This means that at least 69% (100 − (14 + 11 + 6)) of the molecules bear allotypic specificities of all three loci. The purity of the colostral γA preparation is indicated by its complete precipitability (98%) with monospecific goat anti-γA antiserum. Contamination of the colostral γA with γG was negligible (less than 1%). Colostral γA from rabbit E208-6 ($a^2a^2b^4b^4f^{71,75}f^{71,75}$) gave similar results, i.e., at least 65% (100 − (16 + 9 + 10)) of the molecules bear allotypic specificities of all three loci. In Figure 1, rabbit F164-5 ($a^1a^2b^4b^5f^{71,75}f^{72,74}$) is heterozygous at all three loci and in this animal 77% (63 + 14) of the molecules are calculated to have allotypic specificities of the *a* locus; 82% (61 + 21) of the *b* locus; and 104% (34 + 70) of the *f* locus. Thus, most of the molecules bear an allotypic specificity of all three loci. Since the number of a1 plus a2 or b4 plus b5 molecules does not exceed 100%, the results obtained cannot be attributed to significant amounts of nonspecific aggregation of γA colostral molecules.

Quantiative allotype analyses of the colostral γA isolated from 12 rabbits (including the three in Figure 1) of various phenotypes at the *a*, *b* and *f* loci are presented in Table I. The value presented for each locus is the sum of the precipitable protein obtained by direct plus indirect precipitation. For heterozygotes, the value at each locus is the sum of values obtained for each of the allelic allotypes. At the *a* locus, the reagents used were anti-a1, anti-a2 or anti-a3; at the *b* locus, anti-b4 or anti-b5. At the *f* locus, the analysis was complicated by the fact that the five allotypic specificities are inherited as phenogroups in three combinations as if controlled by three alleles, $f^{71,75}$, $f^{72,74}$, and $f^{73,74}$ (2). Based on agar-gel double diffusion experiments (1), the five allotypic specificities appear to be on separate molecules. For rabbits C5-2, F164-4 and F164-5, the percentage of *f* locus molecules precipitable was obtained as the sum of the molecules precipitable by anti-f71,75 and anti-f72,74 as follows: for rabbit F164-4, 25% by anti-f71,75 plus 61% by anti-f72,74 equals 86%

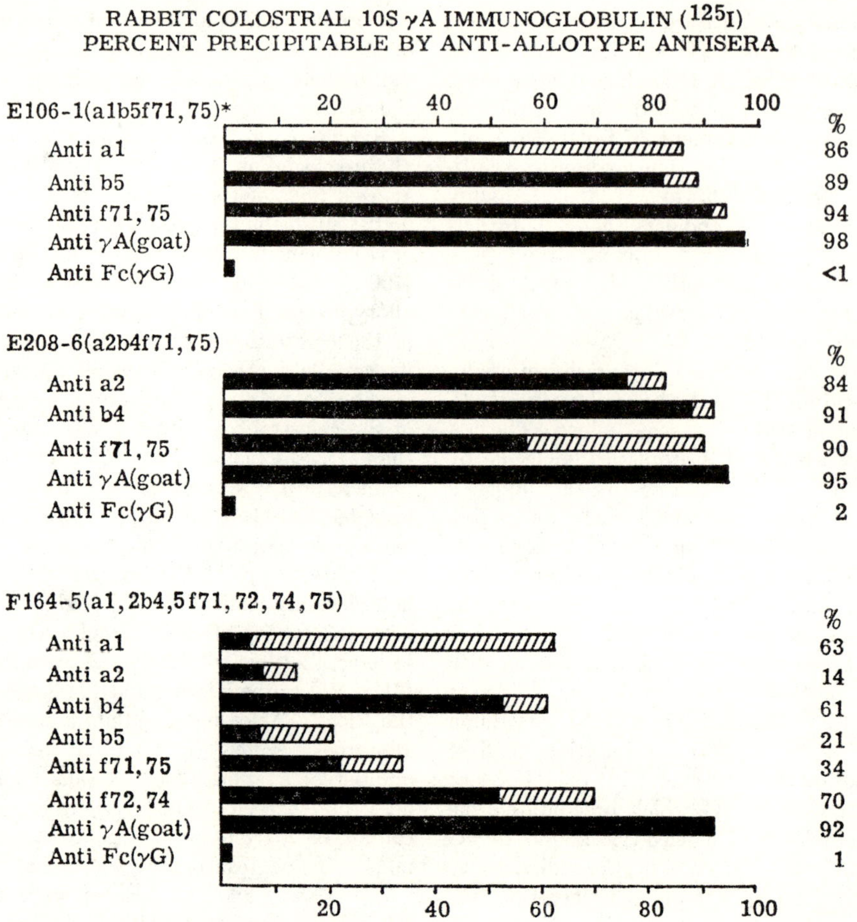

Figure 1. * The rabbit and its immunoglobulin phenotype: ■, direct precipitation by antiallotype antiserum or specific heterologous antiserum; ▨, indirect precipitation of soluble immune complexes in the supernatant fluid by goat antiserum to rabbit Fc fragment of γG immunoglobulin.

TABLE I

Distribution of allotypic specificities controlled by the a, b and f loci among the colostral 10S γA immunoglobulin molecules

Rabbit	Phenotype			Immunoglobulins Precipitated by Anti-allotype Antisera Specific for *a*, *b* and *f* Loci and Goat Anti-γA Antiserum			
	a locus	*b* locus	*f* locus	*a*	*b*	*f*	Total γA
E106-1	a1	b5	f71,75	86	89	94	98
D55-8	a1	b5	f71,75	86	92	96	96
E208-6	a2	b4	f71,75	84	91	90	95
D104-3	a2	b4	f71,75	85	91	93	92
D355-2	a1	b4,5	f71,75	81	95	62	96
D253-5	a2,3	b4	f71,75	104	90	87	93
E34-1	a1,2	b4	f71,75	91	97	90	98
C5-2	a1,2	b4	f71,72,74,75	68	82	107	90
F164-4	a1,2	b4,5	f71,72,74,75	78	84	86	92
F164-5	a1,2	b4,5	f71,72,74,75	77	82	104	91
D153-6	a2	b5	f71,73,74,75	76	84	101	92
CQ665-4	a1	b4,5	f72,73,74	79	98	106	94

f locus molecules; for F164-5, 34% by anti-f71,75 plus 70% by anti-f72,74 equals 104% *f* locus molecules (Table I).

DISCUSSION

Three loci, *a*, *b* and *f*, have been found to control the allotypic specificities of both serum and secretory γA immunoglobulin. Serum γA is thought to be composed of two heavy chains and two light chains held together by noncovalent interactions and disulfide bonding (6, 7). Rabbit colostral γA is a dimer of two serum γA units with an additional stabilizing transport or secretory protein (8). With this structure as a model and with the knowledge that the *a* and *b* loci are each associated with only one polypeptide chain, assignment of the *f* locus specificities to a polypeptide chain not under the control of another locus becomes difficult. Since the *b* locus specificities are associated with specific amino acid sequences in the light chains of γG immunoglobulin (9) and are found in all three classes of immunoglobulins (10–12), it is doubtful that the *f* locus specificities are associated with light chains because anti-*f* locus antisera do not react with γG or γM immunoglobulins. The *f* locus specificities are probably not associated with the secretory piece since the anti-*f* locus antisera react with serum γA, which presumably does not contain this polypeptide as is the case for human serum γA immunoglobulin (6).

Assuming that the *a* locus allotypes are associated with the amino acid sequences of the heavy chain, presumably in the Fd portion (13, 14), a number of possibilities exist for the location of the *f* locus specificities. Both the *a* and *f* locus specificities could be located on the same heavy chain. This would be in accord with a multigene hypothesis (15, 16) for the synthesis of the heavy chain, but would require gene interaction at the DNA or RNA level since biosynthetic experiments indicate that both the heavy and light chain polypeptides are synthesized continuously from the amino to the carboxy terminal end (17). Secondly, the *a* locus might control the synthesis of heavy chains of one subclass, while the *f* locus might control the synthesis of another subclass of γA heavy chains. Thus, in 10S γA molecules, one subunit could have *a* locus heavy chains whereas the other subunit could have the *f* locus heavy chains. In agar diffusion experiments, we have seen multiple banding phenomena with specific γA antisera which may be indicative of subclasses. Thirdly, the *f* locus might control the addition of a specific prosthetic group, either carbohydrate or peptide, that is attached to the γA molecule. Finally, the possibility also remains that our concept of the structure of rabbit γA may not be correct and that the *f* locus specificities may be located on a third polypeptide chain. Quantitative immunochemical analysis of the allotypes present on the rabbit γA immunoglobulin fragments and subunits will be necessary to clarify the relationship of the *f* locus to the structure and synthesis of the γA molecule.

Acknowledgment. We wish to acknowledge the excellent technical assistance of Mrs. B. Sturm.

Added in Proof. Recently an allotypic determinant, specific for γA immunoglobulin, was described by Masuda, Kuribayashi and Hanaoka (18) which may be identical to one of the five which we have reported (1, 2). Masuda *et al.* infer that the antigenic determinant is present on the Fc fragment of the α chain because they could not detect it on the Fab-like fragment resulting from treatment with papain. They were unable to isolate the Fc fragment in order to establish positive identification of the allotype and, therefore, the localization of the antigenic determinant remains in doubt.

REFERENCES

1. Conway, T. P., Dray, S. and Lichter, E. A., J. Immun., *102:* 544, 1969.
2. Conway, T. P., Dray, S. and Lichter, E. A., J. Immun., *103:* 662, 1969.
3. Cebra, J. J. and Robbins, J. B., J. Immun., *97:* 12, 1966.
4. Gilman, A. M., Nisonoff, A. and Dray, S., Immunochemistry, *1:* 109, 1964.
5. McFarlane, A. S., Nature, *183:* 1657, 1959.
6. Tomasi, T. B., Jr., Tan, E. M., Solomon, A. and Prendergast, R. A., J. Exp. Med., *123:* 615, 1965.
7. Abel, C. A. and Grey, H. M., Biochemistry, *7:* 2682, 1968.
8. Cebra, J. J. and Small, P. A., Biochemistry, *6:* 503, 1967.
9. Reisfeld, R. A., Dray, S. and Nisonoff, A., Immunochemistry, *2:* 155, 1965.
10. Todd, C. W., Biochem. Biophys. Res. Commun., *11:* 170, 1963.

11. Feinstein, A., Nature, *199:* 1197, 1963.
12. Lichter, E. A., J. Immun., *98:* 139, 1967.
13. Koshland, M. E., Reisfeld, R. A. and Dray, S., Immunochemistry, *5:* 471, 1968.
14. Inman, J. K. and Reisfeld, R. A., Immunochemistry, *5:* 415, 1968.
15. Dreyer, W. J. and Bennett, J. C., Proc. Nat. Acad. Sci., *54:* 864, 1965.
16. Koshland, M. E., Davis, J. J. and Fujita, N. J., Proc. Nat. Acad. Sci. *63:* 1274, 1969.
17. Fleischman, J. B., Biochemistry, *6:* 1311, 1967.
18. Matsuda, T., Kuribayashi, K. and Hanaoka, M., J. Immun., *102:* 1156, 1969.

THE JOURNAL OF IMMUNOLOGY
Vol. 105, No. 1, July 1970
Printed in U.S.A.

THE SUBUNIT STRUCTURE OF MOUSE IgA[1]

HOWARD M. GREY,[2,3] ALAN SHER[4] AND NURIT SHALITIN

From the Department of Experimental Pathology, Scripps Clinic and Research Foundation, and the Salk Institute for Biological Studies, La Jolla, California 92037

Received for publication December 22, 1969

Mouse IgA myeloma proteins have been studied for the structure of their polypeptide chains and papain fragments. Heavy and light chains, Fab and Fc fragments were shown to have molecular weights closely corresponding to their IgG equivalents and the mass ratio of Fab and Fc fragments indicate the presence of two Fab and one Fc fragment per IgA monomer. The results, taken together with the available hapten-binding data, suggest that a single light-heavy chain pair constitute a hapten-binding site in IgA. In addition, structural studies performed on normal mouse IgA indicate the presence in their structure of dimerized light chain as had been previously reported for IgA myeloma proteins.

Mouse IgA myeloma proteins have unique structural and antigen-binding properties. Although their unit structure (monomer) consists of two light (L) and two heavy (H) polypeptide chains like IgG and IgM, many IgA proteins lack the L-H interchain disulfide bonds present in immunoglobulins of the other classes (1, 2). Furthermore, while the monomer of IgG as well as selected IgM antibodies express two antigen-binding sites (3–5), the monomer and the Fab fragment of a mouse IgA myeloma protein with anti-DNP activity have a single combining site (6).

[1] This is publication 387 from the Department of Experimental Pathology, Scripps Clinic and Research Foundation, La Jolla, California. This investigation was supported by United States Public Health Service Grants from the National Institutes of Health, A1-07007, A1-05875 and Training Grant 5213 to Dr. Melvin H. Cohn, Atomic Energy Commission Contract AT(04-3)-410 and American Heart Association Grant 67-795.

[2] Established Investigator of the American Heart Association. Current address: Division of Allergy and Clinical Immunology, National Jewish Hospital and Respiratory Center, Denver, Colorado 80206.

[3] All reprint inquiries should be addressed to Dr. H. M. Grey, Division of Allergy and Clinical Immunology, National Jewish Hospital and Respiratory Center, 3800 East Colfax Avenue, Denver, Colorado 80206.

[4] Recipient of a United States Public Health Service Training Grant GM-00702.

In the present study the structure of mouse IgA proteins is further characterized. Molecular wieghts of the monomer, light chain, heavy chain subunits and papain fragments of IgA are very close to those reported for their IgG homologues. Furthermore, the absence of L-H interchain disulfide bonds described for IgA myeloma proteins is shown to characterize also the IgA of normal serum. The interpretation of these findings in terms of the IgA antigen-binding site is discussed.

MATERIALS AND METHODS

Myeloma proteins. IgA-secreting mouse myelomas S23, S63, S116, S121 and S129 from the collection of Dr. Melvin Cohn were used in this study. Serum or serum and sarcoma 180-provoked ascites fluid (7) were collected from BALB/c mice carrying the tumors and the myeloma protein was isolated by 50% ammonium sulfate precipitation followed by starch block electrophoresis at pH 8.6 (8) or DEAE-cellulose chromatography in phosphate buffer (pH 8.0, 0.03 to 0.3 M linear gradient). As a final purification step, IgA polymer and monomer were separated by gel filtration on Sephadex G-200 (column size 2.5 x 100 cm) in phosphate-buffered saline (pH 7.2). In some instances, proteins or fragments were labeled with ^{125}I or ^{131}I by a modification of the chloramine T method (9).

Papain digestion. IgA monomer or mixtures of polymer and monomer were digested with papain (Worthington, 1% to 3% w/w) in 0.1 M 2-mercaptoethanol, 2×10^{-3} M EDTA, at pH 7.5.

After 45 min at 37°C digestion was terminated by adding a one-molar excess of iodoacetamide and the mixture was allowed to stand for 1 hr at 0°C before dialysis. In preparation for peptide mapping ^{14}C iodoacentamide was used for alkylation. When subjected to immunoelectrophoresis against rabbit anti-mouse IgA myeloma sera, the digest consisted of two non-cross-reacting components (Fab and Fc) indicating that digestion was complete. Fab and Fc fragments were separated by either starch block electrophoresis or DEAE-cellulose chromatography in phosphate buffer (pH 8.0, 0.03 M and 0.3 M steps). Zone electrophoresis yielded Fab and Fc fragments that were pure as judged by immunoelectrophoresis, whereas the Fc fraction isolated by DEAE was contaminated with a small amount of Fab.

Starch gel electrophoresis. Vertical starch gel electrophoresis (10) was performed in an 8 M urea formate buffer (pH 3) (11). Gels were electrophoresed for 16 hr at 170 V at room temperature.

Separation of heavy and light chains. The isolated myeloma proteins were partially reduced with 0.2 M 2-mercaptoethanol in 0.55 M Tris buffer (pH 8.2) for 1 hr at room temperature and alkylated for 1 hr at 4°C by adding a 50% molar excess of recrystallized iodoacetamide. The partially reduced and alkylated proteins were separated into heavy and light chains by gel filtration through Sephadex G-200 in 8 M urea, 0.05 M propionic acid. In preparation for tryptic digestion the heavy and light chains were alkylated with ^{14}C iodoacetamide.

Peptide maps. These were done on tryptic digests (TPCK - trypsin, Worthington Biochemical Corp., Freehold, N. J.) of completely reduced and alkylated material as previously described (12). Peptide maps were stained with 0.2% ninhydrin in acetone and when ^{14}C iodoacetamide was used for alkylation, autoradiography was done using No-Screen medical X-ray film (NS-54t Eastman Kodak). ^{14}C-labeled peptides and glycopeptides were eluted from maps stained with 0.02% ninhydrin and analyzed for their amino acid composition.

Amino acid and carbohydrate analysis. Amino acid analysis was done with a Beckman 120C amino acid analyzer following hydrolysis of the proteins or peptides with double distilled 6 N HCl under 0.1 mm of vacuum at 105°C for 24 hr. Hexosamines were also determined with an amino acid analyzer using an 11-cm "short" column (at pH 5.28, which clearly differentiated glucosamine from galactosamine), following partial hydrolysis of the α chains or fragments in 4 N HCl for 6 hr at 105°C. Fucose, hexose and sialic acid were determined colorimetrically as previously described (13).

Molecular weights. Weight-average molecular weight values for the native IgA monomer, Fab and Fc fragments were determined by sedimentation equilibrium (14) in a Spinco model E ultracentrifuge equipped with Rayleigh interference optics. (Schlieren optics were employed in one determination on an Fab fragment.) Before loading, each protein sample (5 to 10 mg/ml) was tested for homogeneity in a separate sedimentation velocity experiment. All protein solutions were in phosphate-buffered saline, pH 7. Partial specific volumes ($\bar{v}$) for the 7S monomer, Fab fragment and heavy and light chains were determined from combined amino acid and carbohydrate composition data obtained from these proteins (15). As an additional molecular weight determination, Fab and Fc fragments were sized on a Sephadex G-100 column (dimensions 3 x 70 cm) equilibrated in phosphate-buffered saline and calibrated with chymotrypsin, β lactoglobulin, bovine serum albumin and blue dextran as void volume marker. Both Fab and Fc preparations gave symmetrical elution profiles with 100% recovery in the included volume of the column. The molecular weight of completely reduced and alkylated mouse α chains was determined by gel filtration on a Sephadex G-200 column equilibrated in 8 M urea—0.05 M propionic acid. Dextran blue, human γ and light chains were used as markers.

Structural analysis of IgA Fab. In order to estimate the size of the Fd and light chain subunits of the IgA Fab fragments, a ^{125}I-labeled preparation of Fab was analyzed by gel filtration through Sephadex G-100 (column dimensions 2.5 x 90 cm) in 1 M acetic acid. Actual separation of Fd and L components of Fab was performed by chromatography on a urea column (16). IgA Fab protein was absorbed to a DEAE-cellulose column equilibrated in 7 M deionized urea. Two buffer changes (0.01 M and 0.1 M phosphate buffer, pH 8.0, both in 7 M deionized urea) eluted two separate A280-absorbing peaks from the column. Application of higher ionic strength buffers caused no further protein elution from the DEAE. After dialysis against distilled water and concentration by lyophilization, the two peaks were analyzed

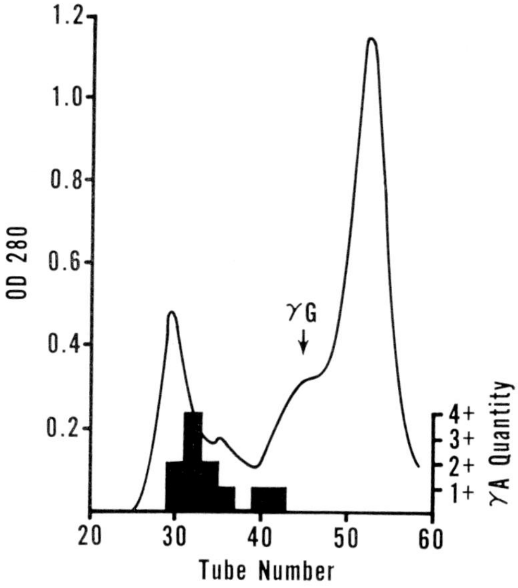

Figure 1. G-200 gel filtration of electrophoretically isolated IgA from normal BALB/c serum. The IgA-containing fractions obtained from zone electrophoresis were placed on G-200 and the IgA levels estimated by immunodiffusion. Arrow indicates peak of IgG activity.

for heavy and light chain antigenic determinants by immunodiffusion against specific rabbit antisera.

RESULTS

Normal mouse IgA. Because of the unique interchain disulfide bonds found in mouse IgA myeloma proteins it was considered of interest to characterize normal IgA with respect to the presence or absence of L-H disulfide bonds. At the same time it was possible to determine whether normal mouse IgA was present in serum predominantly as a polymer or monomer protein. By a combination of starch block electrophoresis, DEAE chromatography and G-200 gel filtration, 5 mg of IgA were isolated from 100 ml of BALB/c mouse serum. The relative amount of monomer and polymer present in the serum pool was estimated by immunodiffusion analysis of fractions obtained after gel filtration of the IgA-containing region from a starch block or by sucrose density gradient ultracentrifugation of whole mouse serum. Both methods clearly indicated that, unlike the situation in human serum (17), mouse serum IgA was present predominantly in polymeric form as is illustrated in Figure 1. Figure 2 illustrates an acid urea starch gel pattern of the isolated unreduced IgA polymer. A comparison with the pattern obtained from a polymeric IgA myeloma protein shows that a band is present where light chain dimers are usually found. This test system is a qualitative one, so that it can only be concluded that at least some normal serum IgA molecules lack L-H disulfide bridges and have L-L disulfide-linked dimers. Whether this type of molecule represents the major portion of IgA or only a minor fraction is not known.

Molecular weights. Molecular weight data for the monomer, Fab and Fc fragments are summarized in Table I. Values from separate sedimentation equilibrium determinations were in close agreement and no concentration dependence was observed in any of the samples analyzed. The molecular weights of the mouse α and light chains were determined by gel filtration of the completely reduced and alkylated chains on a G-200 column equilibrated in 8 M urea and 0.05 M propionic acid. The markers used were human γ and light chains whose molecular weights were taken to be 50,000 and 23,000, respectively (18). Under these conditions the mouse α chain had a molecular weight of 53,500 and the light

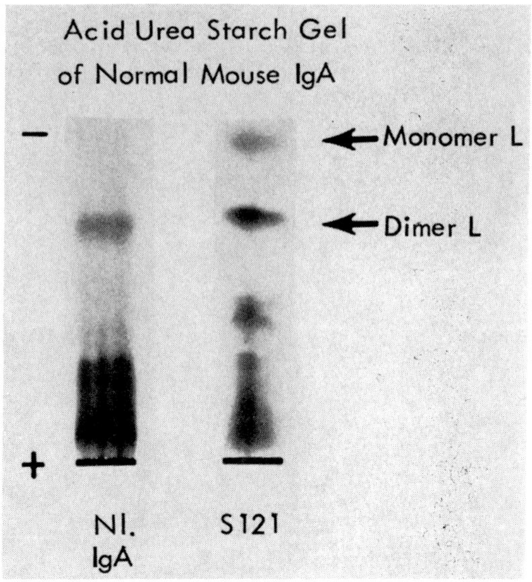

Figure 2. Starch gel electrophoresis (pH 3.0, 8 M urea) of polymer IgA from normal BALB/c mouse serum. The pattern of an IgA myeloma protein (S121) is shown for comparison. Arrows indicate positions of monomer and dimer light chains.

TABLE I

Summary of equilibrium sedimentation data for mouse IgA monomer and papain fragments[a]

Protein	Total No. of Determinations	Protein Concentrations	$\bar{v}$	RPM	Weight-Averaged Molecular Weights
		mg/ml			
S121 monomer	2	0.25–0.5	0.720 (calculated)	16,200	156,000 (154,000–158,000)
S121 Fab	4	0.25–1.0	0.724 (calculated)	24,630	53,000 (52,000–54,000)
S129 Fab (schlieren optics)	1	0.7	0.724 (assumed)	25,980	49,000
S121 Fc	4	0.1–0.4	0.726 (calculated from data obtained with H chain, L chain and Fab fragment)	23,160	51,000 (49,000–52,000)

[a] Samples in phosphate-buffered saline (pH 7.2) were run at a controlled temperature of 20°C in a Spinco model E ultracentrifuge equipped with Rayleigh interference optics. Molecular weights were calculated from the graphically averaged plot of ln C *vs* r^2 (14) and are presented as the average of the indicated number of determinations. The range of values is indicated in parentheses. (Partial specific volumes calculated for S121 heavy and light chain were 0.723 and 0.728, respectively.) Solvent density (ρ) was taken as 1.0 for all calculations.

TABLE II

Molecular weights of IgA papain fragments and polypeptide chains as estimated from elution position on Sephadex

Protein	$\frac{Vx}{Vo}$	Molecular Weight (Literature Value)	Calculated Molecular Weight
BSA	1.60[a]	65,000	
Chymotrypsin	2.60	21,600	
β Lactoglobulin	1.89	36,500	
S63 Fab	1.76		48,000
S63 Fc	1.76		48,000
γ Chain (human)	1.32[b]	50,000	
Light chain (human)	1.71	23,000	
S116 α chain	1.31		53,500
S124 α chain	1.31		53,500
S124 light chain	1.71		23,000

[a] Gel filtration done on Sephadex G-100 equilibrated with phosphate-buffered saline.

[b] Gel filtration done on completely reduced and alkylated light and heavy chains on Sephadex G-200 equilibrated in 8 M urea and 0.05 M propionic acid.

chain of 23,000. On the basis of there being two H and two L chains in the monomer, these data would indicate a molecular weight of 153,000 for the monomer, in close agreement with the figure of 156,000 determined by sedimentation equilibrium. Papain cleaved the IgA into Fab and Fc fragments, each of approximately 50,000 molecular weight as measured by sedimentation equilibrium (Table I) and gel filtration (Table II). The mass ratio of Fab to Fc was estimated by measuring the yields of the two fragments isolated by starch block electrophoresis. Of the total material assayed by OD280 in the dialyzed digest, 69% was recovered in the Fab fraction, and 31% in the Fc fragment; 18% of the digestion protein was lost in the dialysis step. Approximately the same yields were obtained with both starch block and DEAE separation techniques. From the mass ratio of Fab to Fc of 2.2:1, it can be concluded that an IgA monomer is made up of two Fab fragments and one Fc.

Antigen and structural characterization of Fab fragment. Since the functional and structural uniqueness of the IgA (i.e., univalency and L-L dimer formation) were characteristics of the Fab fragment, particular attention was focused on studying the structure of this fragment.

By chromatography on DEAE-cellulose, 7 M urea, it was possible to obtain two fractions from the IgA Fab, one carrying heavy and one light chain antigenic determinants. The first fraction, eluted with 7 M urea containing 0.01 M phosphate buffer pH 8.0, reacted by immunodiffusion with light chain specific antiserum only, whereas the second fraction, eluted with 7 M urea containing 0.1 M phosphate buffer pH 8.0, reacted with heavy chain specific antiserum only. These two fractions were present in approximately equal amounts as measured by OD280.

Analysis of IgA Fab by acid-urea starch gel electrophoresis confirmed the existence of two major subunits in the Fab fragment. As shown in Figure 3, IgA Fab (*slot 2*) was resolved into a component co-electrophoresing with monomer light chains, plus a series of components banding between the light chain dimer and heavy chain positions of the gel. In order to estimate the molecular weight of these two fractions obtained from the IgA Fab fragment, ^{125}I-labeled Fab was analyzed by gel filtration on G-100 in 1 M acetic

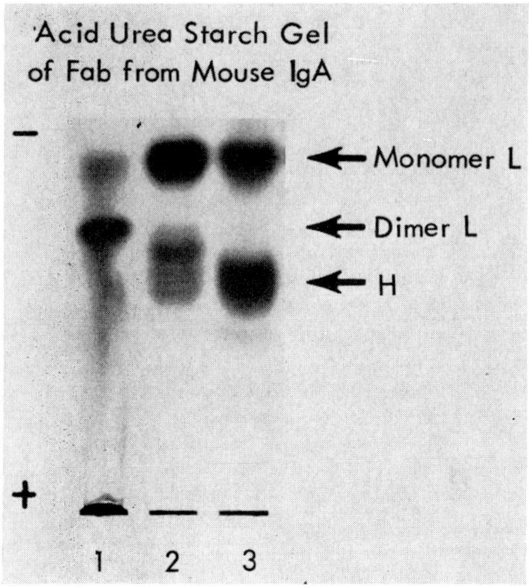

Figure 3. Starch gel electrophoresis (pH 3.0, 8 M urea) of S121 Fab (*slot 2*) compared with undigested polymer (*slot 1*) and reduced and alkylated polymer (*slot 3*). Arrows indicate the positions of L, H and L_2.

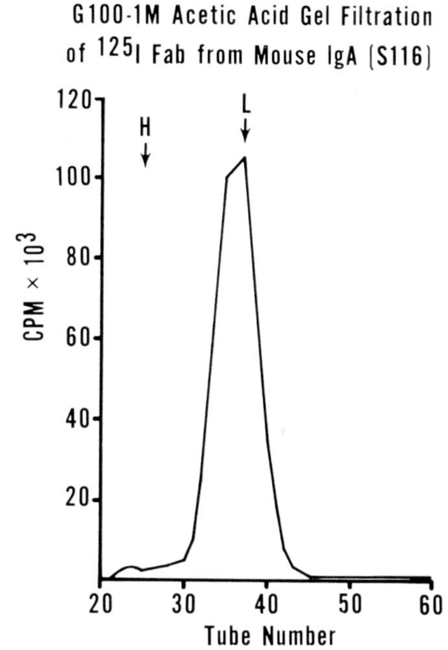

Figure 4. Sephadex G-100 gel filtration of IgA (S116) Fab. ^{125}I Fab was applied to the column together with reduced and alkylated ^{131}I HGG; (——) ^{125}I IgA Fab (counts/min). Arrows indicate the position of the heavy and light chain peaks of HGG.

acid. As shown in Figure 4, the Fab material was eluted from the column as a single symmetrical peak in the same position as the monomer light chains of human γ globulin.

These results indicate the presence of monomer L chains and an Fd fragment in the IgA Fab both of which have a molecular weight of approximately 23,000. As the Fd was shown to contain carbohydrate the heterogeneity of the fragment which was observed on starch gel electrophoresis may be due to variable amounts of sialic acid.

Peptide analysis. Peptide mapping of the tryptic peptides from heavy and light chains and Fab fragments was performed as was amino acid composition of partially and completely reduced and alkylated chains and fragment. Insufficient amounts of Fc fragment were available to obtain similar data on this fragment. These studies were performed: a) to obtain data for calculation of the partial specific volume; b) to determine the number and distribution of labile and stable disulfide bonds; c) to determine the distribution of carbohydrate; and d) to investigate whether the

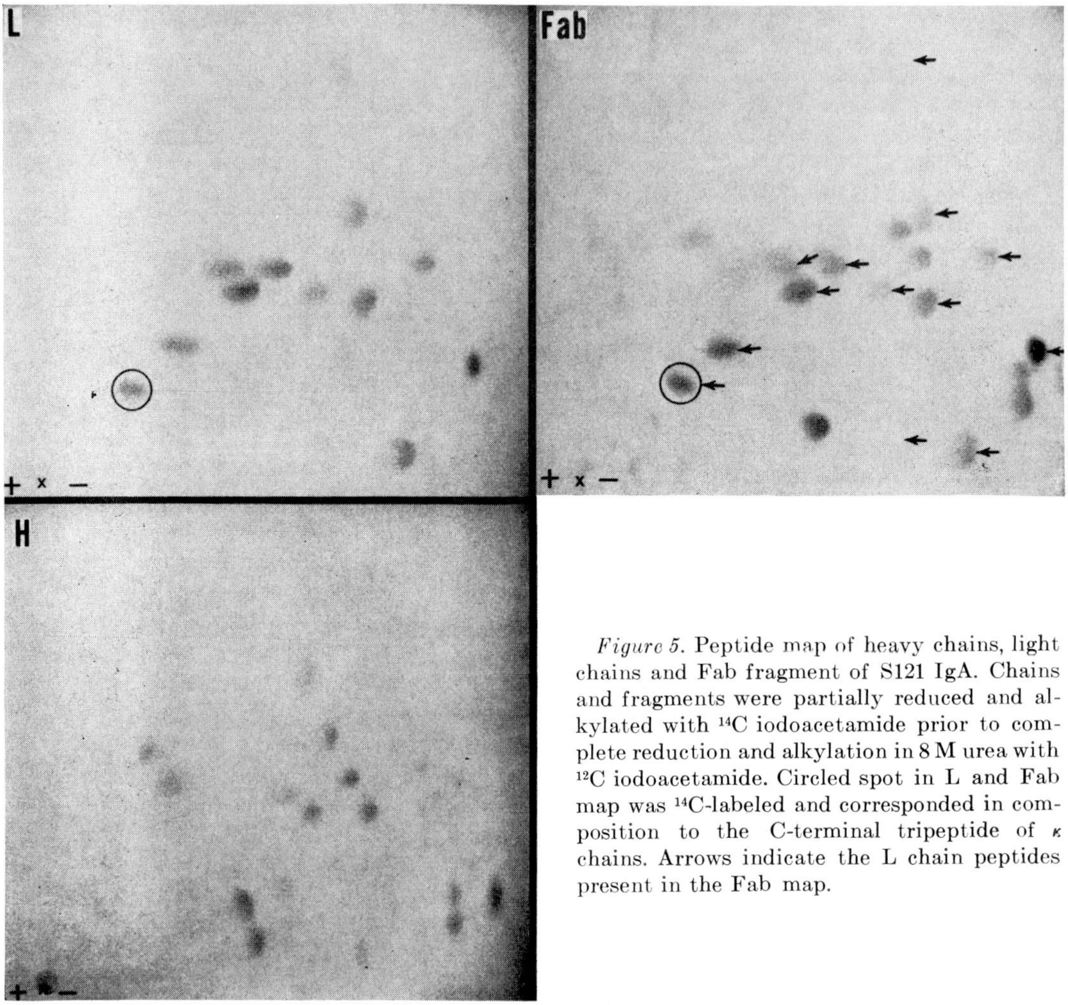

Figure 5. Peptide map of heavy chains, light chains and Fab fragment of S121 IgA. Chains and fragments were partially reduced and alkylated with ^{14}C iodoacetamide prior to complete reduction and alkylation in 8 M urea with ^{12}C iodoacetamide. Circled spot in L and Fab map was ^{14}C-labeled and corresponded in composition to the C-terminal tripeptide of κ chains. Arrows indicate the L chain peptides present in the Fab map.

Fab fragment contained intact light chains, or whether papain cleavage resulted in detectable proteolysis of this fragment. Peptide maps were performed on polypeptide chains and fragments that had been partially reduced and alkylated with ^{14}C iodoacetamide prior to complete reduction and alkylation. The peptide maps are shown in Figure 5. The ^{14}C-labeled peptides of L chains and Fab fragment were identified by autoradiography and are circled. The light chain contained a single radioactive spot which when analyzed for amino acid composition contained: CM Cys 1.0, Asp 1.0, Glu 1.3. This composition is the same as the carboxy-terminal tryptic peptide of mouse κ chains (19). The Fab fragment also had a single well-labeled peptide with the same composition. There were 14 easily recognizable ninhydrin positive peptides seen on the L chain map. All of these could be identified on the Fab map as well. Likewise, seven heavy chain spots were identified on the Fab map.

Analysis for CM Cys in the isolated chains and Fab fragment are shown in Table III. The partially reduced and alkylated light chains contained 0.9 to 1.5 mols of CM Cys which is very similar to the 0.9 to 1.4 mols obtained from the partially reduced and alkylated Fab fragment. These data together with those from the peptide maps indicate there were no labile disulfide bonds present in the Fd fragment of the heavy chain. The heavy chain contained a total of 13 or 14 CM Cys, 5 of which were labile. The positioning of the disulfide bonds is schematically represented in Figure 6. The Fab fragment with a total of nine CM Cys is assumed to have a similar arrangement of disulfides as are present in IgG with the exception of the absence of the H-L and the presence of the L-L bridge. By comparing the heavy chain with the Fab fragment, it is calculated that a single peptide chain of the Fc fragment has nine SH groups, five of which are involved in forming labile disulfide bonds. However, we have shown three rather than two intrachain disulfide bridges since there is evidence to suggest that the cysteine penultimate to the C-terminus may be involved in a labile intrachain bridge rather than an interchain disulfide bond (J. W. Prahl and H. M. Grey, to be published). The presence of carbohydrate on both Fd and Fc fragments was established by analyzing for fucose, hexosamine (glucosamine was the only amino sugar present), sialic acid and neutral hexoses in these fragments and in the case of the Fab fragment a tryptic glycopeptide was isolated. On a molar basis the Fd contained approximately twice the carbohydrate as the Fc. The exact number of glycopeptides is not known, but the data indicate the presence of at least two per heavy chain.

Three radiolabeled peptides were isolated from the H chain maps, two contained one labile CM Cys each and one contained two labile CM Cys, presumably one labile CM Cys was present in the insoluble core material. None of these peptides contained a high proline content or a carbohydrate moiety, which is of interest since the so-called "hinge" region of IgG which is the site of several interchain disulfides is proline rich and

TABLE III

Half cystine content of S121 IgA

Material	Half Cystine Content[a]		
	Total	Labile	Stable[b]
Fab	9	1 (0.9–1.4)	8
H	13–14	5	8–9
L	5	1 (0.9–1.5)	4
Fd[c]	4	0	4
Fc[c]	9–10	5	4–5

[a] Determined as carboxymethyl derivative.

[b] Stable half cystine calculated on the basis of the difference between the total and labile half cystine content.

[c] Half cystine content of Fd calculated from the difference between values for Fab and light chain. Half cystine content of Fc calculated from the difference between values for heavy chain and Fd piece.

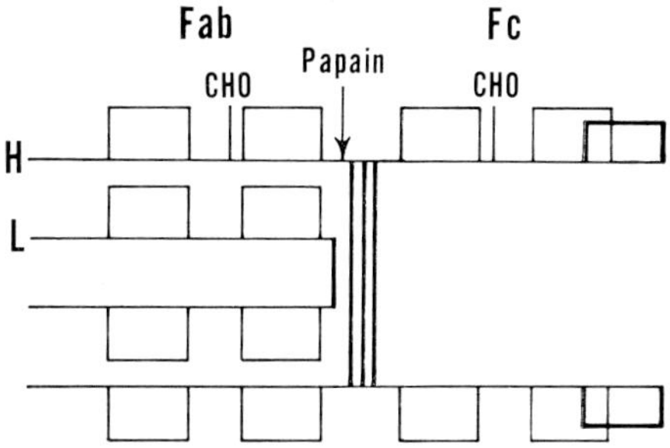

Figure 6. Schematic model of mouse IgA. The labile disulfide bonds are indicated by bold lines. The distribution of the interchain and intrachain bonds as well as carbohydrate (CHO) is known only with regard to their location in the Fab and Fc fragments and H and L chains. Their exact position within the subunit is not known, but they are placed, where possible, in homology to the disulfides of IgG.

may have carbohydrate associated with it (20, 21).

DISCUSSION

IgA myeloma proteins exhibit properties unusual for immunoglobulin molecules. Unlike proteins of the IgG and IgM classes, many IgA proteins have disulfide dimerized light chain as part of their polypeptide chain structure (1, 2). Furthermore, in the case of several mouse IgA antibody myeloma proteins, equilbrium dialysis studies indicate that the monomer expresses only one hapten-binding site (6; A. Sher and M.Cohn, to be published), a situation contrasted to the well-known bivalency of IgG antibodies.

Despite these apparently unique binding properties associated with IgA antibodies our data indicate that with the exception of the presence of L-L dimers the subunit structure of mouse IgA is very similar to that of IgG. The points of similarity are as follows: a) Both have similar molecular weights for the monomer as well as for their individual heavy and light chains. The slightly greater values obtained for the IgA (156,000 *vs* 150,000 for the intact molecule and 53,500 *vs* 50,000 for the heavy chains) are probably due to the greater carbohydrate content of the IgA, the α chain containing 12% carbohydrate compared with 4.5% for the γ chain. b) Papain cleaves both IgG and IgA into Fab and Fc fragments. The molecular weights and mass ratios of the fragments indicate the presence of two Fab and one Fc fragment/IgA monomer.

Certain differences between the structure of the IgA and IgG were also observed. Whereas most IgG proteins contain a single carbohydrate moiety in the Fc fragment, IgA proteins possess at least two glycopeptides since carbohydrate was localized to the Fc fragment as well as the Fd piece. Besides the absence of the L-H disulfide bridge and the presence of the L-L dimer in the IgA, there appear to be other distinctions between IgG and IgA which involve disulfide bonds. Most human IgG1 proteins have 11 SH groups/heavy chain, eight of which are involved in the formation of four intrachain disulfide bonds (two in the Fd and two in the Fc fragment), and the remaining three form interchain bonds—one with the light chain and two with the heavy chain. In the S121 IgA there are two to three more SH groups/heavy chain. The Fd fragment has 4 involved in intrachain disulfides and the Fc fragment has the remaining 9 or 10. We postulate the presence of three interchain bonds (at least one of which must be involved in IgA polymer formation), two stable intrachain bonds, and one labile intrachain bond that involves the penultimate cysteine to the C-terminus (22). This hypothesis comes from work with human IgA (Prahl, J. W. and Grey, H. M., to be published). Cyanogen bromide cleavage of partially reduced and alkylated α chains results in the release of a C-terminal fragment of eight amino acids including the penultimate cysteine. However, cyanogen bromide cleavage of intact IgA monomer or polymer does not release the C-terminal octapeptide or a dimer thereof, as would be expected if this cysteine were involved in a symmetrical interchain or intersubunit disulfide bridge. Therefore, this SH group must form either a labile intrachain bond or an asymmetrical interchain bond with a relatively large cyanogen bromide fragment. At present the former possibility is favored.

There are certain differences between some of the data reported above and those previously published. Studies on the MOPC 315 IgA protein indicated a molecular weight of 120,000 for the monomer and 56,000 for the Fab fragment (6). Whereas the latter value agrees quite well with the 53,000 obtained in this study, the value of 120,000 is considerably less than our value of 156,000. The reason for this discrepancy is at present not clear although since different myeloma proteins were used in the two studies it is possible that one or even both of the proteins represent variant forms of IgA. Molecular weight studies on other IgA proteins should resolve this point. The molecular weights of the heavy chain obtained by gel filtration in the present study are in agreement with the data of Seki *et al.* (23) and support the view that mouse IgA monomer has a molecular weight of approximately 155,000. In a previous study of the elution characteristics of mouse α chains on Sephadex G-100 equilibrated in 1 M acetic acid, it was found that the α chains eluted considerably later than human γ chains (1). This led to the erroneous impression that the mouse α chains had a molecular weight less than that of human γ chains. The reason for this atypical behavior of the mouse α chains is uncertain but it is possible that it was unduly retarded by the column due to some degree of binding to the Sephadex, or alternatively, the shape of the mouse α chain in 1 M acetic acid may have been considerably more globular than that of the human γ chains used for comparison resulting in their being eluted later.

Another point of discrepancy between the present study and that conducted on MOPC 315 regards the peptide mapping of the Fab fragment. It was found that the Fab fragment of MOPC 315 lacked many of the peptides present in the intact light chain including some of the constant region peptides. Since this would imply extensive proteolysis of the light chain portion of the Fab fragment and thereby render any molecular weight data of this fragment of dubious significance, we attempted to evaluate this problem in the present study. All the recognizable light chain peptides were present in the Fab fragment including the C-terminal peptide. We therefore found no evidence of light chain proteolysis by papain. Again, the differences between the findings in the two studies may reflect structural differences between the two myeloma proteins studied or minor, but significant, differences in the procedure of papain digestion.[5]

Studies on the anti-DNP antibody activity of mouse myeloma protein MOPC 315 have suggested unique structural properties for the univalent binding site of IgA. When affinity-labeled and separated into heavy and light chain sub-

[5] N and C-terminal analyses on MOPC 315 light chains (H. Metzger, personal communication) suggest that significant structural differences do exist between these light chains and others that have been previously characterized.

units, MOPC 315 showed labeling which was limited entirely to the light chain fraction (24). In another study (6) with MOPC 315 protein, digestion with papain in the presence of cysteine produced an active univalent fraction of 55,000 molecular weight constituting approximately 45% of the 7S monomer. These two sets of data were compatible with the hypothesis that the binding site, rather than being shared between a light and heavy chain pair as is thought to be the case with IgG, is in the case of IgA antibody located within the light chain dimer part of the IgA structure[6] (or possibly shared between two light and two heavy chains). This model would account for the univalency of the IgA on the one hand as well as the exclusive affinity-labeling of light chain on the other. Furthermore, it would predict that the active Fab fragment would be made up of two light chains (and two Fd fragments), i.e., it would be a dimer Fab_2 rather than an Fab fragment.

The results of the present study show that this hypothesis for explaining the univalent site of IgA is ruled out since we have been able to define the Fab fragment produced by papain digestion in the presence of reducing agent as a two chain (one light chain and one Fd piece) rather than a four chain structure. Several lines of evidence support this conclusion: a) the molecular weight and recovery data are consistent with papain cleaving IgA monomer (156,000) into two Fab fragments (m.w. = 50,000) and one Fc fragment (m.w. = 50,000); b) gel filtration in 1 M acetic acid indicates that the Fab fragment is composed of polypeptides of light chain size; and c) fingerprinting of the Fab fragment demonstrated that it contains the full complement of light chain peptides in addition to several heavy chain peptides.

Since these structural studies indicate that the IgA Fab is very similar to the Fab isolated from IgG and since functional studies indicate that both Fab fragments isolated from a univalent IgA monomer are capable of binding hapten (A. Sher and M. Cohn, to be published), an explanation must be sought for the observed univalency of IgA which can be treated to reveal its two potentially active combining sites. The situation is further complicated by the finding that not all IgA monomer antibodies are univalent since a recent report describes a bivalent protein (25). A model which would explain the expression of univalency in some IgA proteins and bivalency in others despite the presence of two potentially active Fab fragments in all IgA proteins is based on two assumptions: a) that the binding of hapten at one combining site places a steric restriction on the binding of hapten to another site, and b) that the position of the antibody-combining site within the three dimensional structure of an antibody molecule is variant from one molecule to another. One myeloma antibody (A) might have its combining region in a position on the Fab fragment, where the two Fab fragments are in close apposition to one another, whereas the combining site of myeloma antibody (B) may be located in a region of the Fab where the distance between the two Fab fragments is relatively great. Binding of antigen to one of the combining sites on antibody (A) would lead to steric inhibition of binding to the second site, whereas no such inhibition would be observed upon binding of antigen to a combining site on antibody (B).

As an alternative mechanism to steric inhibition being the cause of the lack of expression of the second combining site it could be postulated that the binding of hapten by one Fab fragment leads to a conformational change on the other Fab fragment which results in an inactive site.

As is the case with human IgA (26) it appears that the absence of the L-H disulfide bond may not be a feature of all mouse γA but rather an expression of a particular IgA subclass or allotype. It has recently been found that, whereas BALB/c-derived IgA almost uniformly lack the L-H disulfide bond, myeloma proteins produced in NZB mice possess the L-H disulfide bond (N. Warner, personal communication). In analogy with the situation found in the human, this difference may represent two allelic forms within the IgA2 subclass in which one allele lacks the L-H disulfide bond and the other has it. Since BALB/c and NZB are of different IgA allotypes this explanation is quite possible (27). Alternatively, however, the NZB strain may produce a greater incidence of IgA tumors which make proteins homologous to the human IgA1 subclass, the subclass which apparently uniformly possesses the L-H disulfide bond. More detailed structural studies should help in choosing between these alternatives.

[6] Urea starch gel electrophoresis of the MOPC 315 protein (kindly supplied by Dr. H. Eisen) indicated the presence of light chain dimers in this protein.

Note added in proof. Reexamination of the molecular weight of MOPC-315 protein has indicated a molecular weight of 150–155,000 rather than the 120,000 previously reported. Also, binding data at concentrations higher than those used in a previous study indicate that two binding sites per γ A monomer can be expressed (H. Eisen, personal communication, 1970).

Acknowledgments. The authors thank Dr. Mel Cohn for his generous supply of γA-producing tumors and for his generous advice during the course of this work. We also thank Mrs. Sharon Spears, Patricia Flanagan and Miss Sherry Humphreys for their excellent technical assistance.

REFERENCES

1. Abel, C. A. and Grey, H. M., Biochemistry, *7:* 2682, 1968.
2. Grey, H. M., Abel, C. A., Yount, W. J. and Kunkel, H. G., J. Exp. Med., *128:* 1223, 1968.
3. Eisen, W. and Karush, F., J. Amer. Chem. Soc., *71:* 363, 1949.
4. Merler, E., Karlin, L. and Matsumoto, S., J. Biol. Chem., *243:* 386, 1968.
5. Onoue, K., Grossberg, A. L., Yagi, Y. and Pressman, D., Science, *162:* 574, 1968.
6. Eisen, H. N., Simms, E. S. and Potter, M., Biochemistry, *7:* 4126, 1968.
7. Sartorelli, A. C., Fischer, D. S. and Downs W. G., J. Immun., *96:* 676, 1966.
8. Kunkel, H. G., Meth. Biochem. Anal., *1:* 141, 1954.
9. McConahey, P. J. and Dixon, F. J., Int. Arch. Allerg., *29:* 185, 1966.
10. Smithies, O., Advances Protein Chem., *14:* 65, 1959.
11. Poulik, M. D., Biochim. Biophys. Acta, *44:* 390, 1960.
12. Grey, H. M. and Kunkel, H. G., Biochemistry, *6:* 2326, 1967.
13. Abel, C. A., Spiegelberg, H. L. and Grey, H. M., Biochemistry, *7:* 1271, 1968.
14. Yphantis, D. A., Biochemistry, *3:* 297, 1964.
15. Cohn, E. J. and Edsall, J. T., in *Proteins, Amino Acids, and Peptides*, p. 372, Reinhold Publishing Corp., New York, 1943.
16. Knopf, P. J., Parkhouse, R. M. E. and Lennox, E. S., Proc. Nat. Acad. Sci., *58:* 2288, 1967.
17. Vaerman, J. P., Fudenberg, H. H., Vaerman, C. and Mandy, W. J., Immunochemistry, *2:* 263, 1965.
18. Edelman, G. M., Cunningham, B. A., Gall, W. E., Gottlieb, P. D., Rutishauser, U. and Waxdal, M. J., Proc. Nat. Acad. Sci., *63:* 78, 1969.
19. Apella, E. and Perham, R. N., Cold Spring Harbor Symp. Quant. Biol., *32:* 37, 1967.
20. Smyth, D. S. and Utsumi, S., Nature, *216:* 332, 1967.
21. Abel, C. A. and Grey, H. M., Fed. Proc., *28* (2): 495, 1969.
22. Abel, C. A. and Grey, H. M., Science, *156:* 1609, 1967.
23. Seki, T., Apella, E. and Itano, H. A., Proc. Nat. Acad. Sci., *61:* 1071, 1968.
24. Metzger, H. and Potter, M., Science, *162:* 1398, 1968.
25. Jaffe, B. M., Eisen, H. N., Simms, E. S. and Potter, M., J. Immun., *103:* 872, 1969.
26. Jerry, L. M., Kunkel, H. G., Grey, H. M. and Osserman, E. F., In press.
27. Herzenberg, L. A., Cold Spring Harbor Symp. Quant. Biol., *29:* 455, 1964.

THE JOURNAL OF IMMUNOLOGY
Vol. 105, No. 1, July 1970

PHYSICOCHEMICAL AND ANTIGENIC STUDIES ON HUMAN γE IN RESPIRATORY FLUID[1]

RICHARD W. NEWCOMB AND KIMISHIGE ISHIZAKA

From the Children's Asthma Research Institute and Hospital, Denver, Colorado 80204

Received for publication December 22, 1969

The γE in sputum and nasal fluid specimens from asthmatic children behaves like the γE in serum on ion-exchange chromatography, gel filtration and ultracentrifugation. No secretory piece antigen was demonstrable on the γE in respiratory exocrine fluids. Like the γE in serum, sputum γE sensitized monkey skin for passive cutaneous anaphylaxis.

The human immunoglobulin class responsible for the reaginic antibody activity of serum has been shown to be γE (1), an 8S protein comprising two heavy (ε) and two light immunoglobulin chains (2). The presence of γE in respiratory exocrine fluids (3) suggested the possibility that structural or antigenic differences may occur between the γE in serum and that in exocrine fluids, as have been shown in the case of γA (4). The present investigations were undertaken to test this possibility. The results indicated no differences between the γE in exocrine fluids and serum γE, as tested by gel filtration, anion exchange chromatography, or ultracentrifugation. Attempts to demonstrate the presence on exocrine γE of secretory piece, the protein that is linked to the exocrine form of γA, were unsuccessful. Moreover, high titers of the same reaginic antibody activity were found in sera and sputa from two patients.

MATERIALS AND METHODS

Serum and exocrine fluids. Specimens of serum, nasal washings, and sputum were collected during the course of a previous study (3) from three boys with asthma at the Children's Asthma Research Institute and Hospital. Specimens were stored at −20°C.

Antisera and antigens. Rabbit antibody preparations specific for the heavy chain determinants of human γA (anti-γA) (5), γE (anti-γE) (6) and human secretory piece (anti-SP) (7) were the same as those used in studies previously reported. Goat antiserum to rabbit γ globulin (anti-RGG) was purchased from Antibodies, Inc., Davis, Calif., and absorbed with human γG before use.

Exocrine γA was isolated from pooled, normal human colostrum by ion-exchange chromatography and gel filtration, as reported (7). E myeloma protein was isolated from the serum of patient PS (8) by DEAE-cellulose column chromatography and gel filtration (6). No serum protein other than γE was detected in the preparation by immunoelectrophoresis. The sedimentation coefficient ($s^0_{20,w}$) of the isolated E myeloma protein was 8.0S. An extract of timothy grass pollen was purchased from Center Laboratories, Port Washington, N. Y.

Methods of fractionation. Ion exchange chromatography was performed using diethylaminoethyl (DEAE)-cellulose (Mannex, Mann Research Laboratories, New York, N. Y.) packed under pressure into 23- x 3.2- (i.d.) cm columns. Serum or sputum specimens were applied after extensive dialysis against 0.005 M phosphate buffer, pH 8.0. To counteract the plugging caused by sputum, homogenized specimens were first freed of insoluble gel by centrifugation, dialyzed, recentrifuged, and applied to the column as a thick slurry in DEAE-cellulose (9). Proteins were eluted in the cold by the stepwise addition of phosphate buffers, pH 8.0, of molarities increasing from 0.005 to 0.025, 0.035, 0.08 and 0.3 M. Fractions were concentrated by vacuum dialysis at 4°C.

Gel filtration on a 100- x 3.5- (i.d.) cm column of Sephadex G-200 (Pharmacia, Uppsala, Sweden) at 4°C was effected by an upward flow of borate-buffered, 0.15 M saline (BBS) containing 0.001 M ethylenediaminetetracetate (EDTA)

[1] This work was supported by United States Public Health Service Grants AI-08500 and AI-04985.

at pH 8.0. Protein fractions were concentrated on finely ground sucrose, then dialyzed against cold BBS.

Ultracentrifugation was performed on 4.5 ml linear sucrose density gradients, from 5% to 20% sucrose in BBS, overlaid with 0.2 to 0.3 ml of protein solution. After centrifugation at 35,000 rpm for 15 hr in the swinging bucket rotor of a Beckman model L machine, fractions were collected through a needle piercing the bottom of the tubes.

Anti-γE immunoadsorbent. The γ globulin fraction of the rabbit anti-γE antiserum was aggregated with glutaraldehyde by the method of Avrames and Ternynck (10) with slight modifications (6). The immunoadsorbent prepared from 200 mg protein was suspended in 20 ml of borate-buffered saline, pH 8.0. Preliminary experiments showed that 1 ml of the suspension removed 8 μg of normal γE present in an atopic patient's serum.

Radioiodination. Both the anti-RGG and anti-SP antibody preparations were applied to columns of Sephadex G-200, and the γG fractions were recovered and concentrated. Each preparation was then labeled with ^{131}I (Abbott Laboratories, North Chicago, Ill.) by the method of McConahey and Dixon (11).

Immunological methods. Concentrations of immunoglobulins were determined by radial immunodiffusion in antibody-containing agar exactly as described (5). The sensitivity of the method was increased for measuring γE by adding a step using radioiodinated anti-RGG (3).

Passive cutaneous anaphylaxis (PCA) in *Macaca irus* monkeys was performed by injecting 0.05 ml of antibody dilutions into the shaved skin of the abdomen (12). In 24 hr the sites were challenged with 0.02 ml of grass extract diluted to 500 protein nitrogen units/ml. Intravenous Evans blue dye was used to visualize reactions.

RESULTS

Chromatography. Samples of serum or sputum from asthmatic children were applied to columns of DEAE-cellulose equilibrated with 0.005 M phosphate buffer, pH 8.0, and protein fractions were eluted in the cold by the stepwise addition of pH 8.0 phosphate buffers of 0.005 M, 0.025 M, 0.035 M, 0.08 M, and 0.3 M. Immunodiffusion measurements revealed that the bulk of γE from each source was eluted in 0.025 M buffer, although lesser amounts were found in other fractions (Table I).

TABLE I

γE in fractions of serum and sputum from DEAE-cellulose

Buffer[a]	Serum	Sputum
0.005 M	0.48[b]	—[c]
0.025 M	5.84	2.07
0.035 M	0.48	0.69
0.08 M	0.50	0.42
0.30 M	—	—

[a] Specimens of serum (4 ml) or sputum (60 ml) were applied to columns of DEAE-cellulose and eluted in phosphate buffers, pH 8.0, of the indicated molarities.

[b] Numbers refer to total micrograms of γE recovered in each fraction.

[c] —, undetectable.

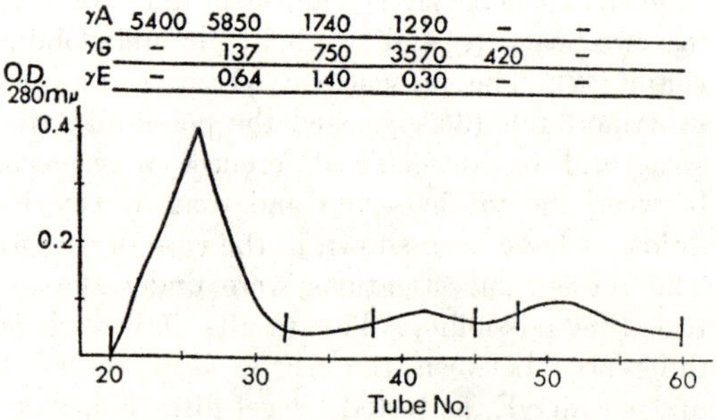

Figure 1. Gel fitration of sputum on Sephadex G-200. Fractions were pooled as indicated, concentrated, and tested by immunodiffusion. Figures refer to total μg protein of γA, γG, or γE in each fraction (—unmeasureable).

Gel filtration of a separate sample of sputum on a column of Sephadex G-200 (Fig. 1) yielded six fractions that were pooled as indicated, concentrated and tested for γE, γA and γG by immunodiffusion. Most of the γE was found in the fraction eluted after the peak containing exocrine γA but before the γG peak, as is the case for serum γE (1).

Immunoadsorbent purification. A 140-ml pool of sputum from two patients was stirred for 1 hr at 4°C with an equal volume of DEAE-cellulose made into a thick slurry in 0.3 M phosphate buffer, pH 8.0. The supernatant fluid recovered after centrifugation, thus freed of much of its mucinous material, was then concentrated to 60 ml by vacuum dialysis against BBS. A small amount of insoluble material was then removed by centrifugation. The concentration of γE in the supernatant was 145 ng/ml. The preparation was further concentrated to 30 ml and mixed with anti-γE immunoadsorbent which had the capacity to absorb 8 μg γE and the mixture was stirred overnight. After centrifugation and four washings with cold BBS, protein was eluted from the immunoadsorbent in three changes of 0.1 M glycine buffer, pH 3.0, containing 0.1% human serum albumin. The pH of the pooled eluates was rapidly adjusted to 7.5 by the dropwise addition of M Tris, pH 11.0, then dialyzed against BBS. By immunodiffusion only γE, 4 μg total, and a trace of γG could be detected.

Ultracentrifugation. Samples in 0.2 to 0.3 ml were ultracentrifuged on 4.5 ml linear density gradients composed of 5% to 20% sucrose solutions in borate-buffered saline, pH 8.0. Specimens of sputum or nasal fluids (sol phase) and of γE-rich preparations from DEAE-cellulose or γE-immunoadsorbent fractionation of sputum were examined. In each case, the γE migrated between the 11.7 S γA and the γG peaks, as did a separate specimen of E myeloma protein whose sedimentation coefficient ($s^0_{20,w}$) is 8.0. Assuming γG to have an $s^0_{20,w}$ value of 6.8, the γE of sputum was calculated to be 8.2 S, close to the values of 8.0 to 8.2 S found for serum γE (1) and E myeloma (2).

Tests for SP antigen. The question whether antibody to secretory piece (SP) of exocrine γA might react with the γE in sputum was investigated in two ways. A preparation of rabbit antiserum to exocrine γA was absorbed with excess serum γA (7). The antibody to SP in this preparation (anti-SP) was sufficient to precipitate completely the exocrine γA from an equal volume containing 30 μg/ml. Equal volumes of anti-SP were mixed with 2.0 μg/ml of γE purified from sputum using an immunoadsorbent. After incubation overnight, the mixtures were centrifuged (though no precipitate was visible) and the γE content of the supernatants was measured by immunodiffusion. The γE concentration was not measurably decreased by anti-SP.

In a second set of experiments, specimens of serum, sputum, or nasal fluids were placed in wells cut in agar containing antibody to γE. After 48 hr at room temperature, the agar plates were washed for 2 days and overlaid with radioiodinated antibody to either SP (anti-SP) or rabbit γ globulin (anti-RGG). One day later the plates were put to wash for 2 days, dried and placed in contact with x-ray film. Plates on which ^{131}I-labeled anti-RGG had been placed showed radioactive rings, but none were seen on the plates receiving ^{131}I-labeled anti-SP. When equal concentrations of exocrine γA were similarly tested using agar plates containing antibody to γA, plates treated with ^{131}I-labeled anti-SP showed definite radioactive rings (Fig. 2).

PCA in monkey skin. The ability of γE in sputum to sensitize monkey skin for passive cutaneous anaphylaxis was tested using γE purified from sputum by an immunoadsorbant. The sputum donors were twin boys with strong direct skin reactions to timothy grass pollen extract. Serum from each boy was tested at the same time. The results (Fig. 3) indicated that

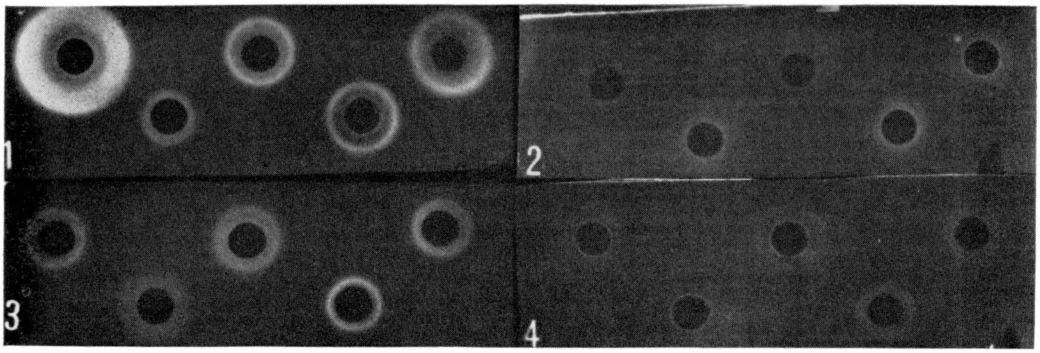

Figure 2. Specimens of respiratory fluids containing γE, in agar with anti-γE (*upper*) formed rings reacting with radioiodinated anti-RGG (*1*) but not anti-SP (*2*). Exocrine γA (*lower*) at the same concentrations, in agar with anti-γA, reacted with both radioactive anti-RGG (*3*) and anti-SP (*4*) but serum γA reacted only with anti-RGG.

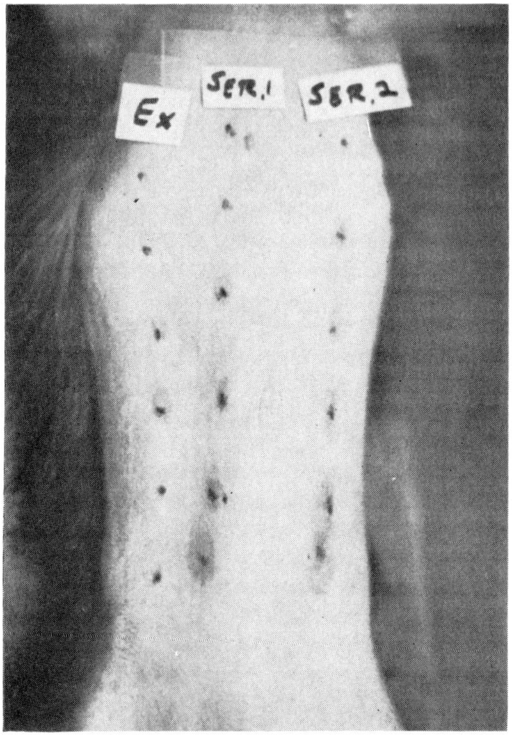

Figure 3. PCA reactions in monkey skin sensitized with γE purified from sputum (*Ex*) or sera from the sputum donors (*Ser 1* and *2*) and elicited by grass pollen extract. The amount of sputum γE needed to give a positive reaction was 12.5 ng, but only 3.1 and 2.2 ng γE in sera 1 and 2 respectively.

both the sputum γE preparation and sera were effective in sensitizing for a PCA reaction, but that about five times as much sputum γE was needed as serum γE.

DISCUSSION

The results reported here indicate that the γE in respiratory exocrine fluids shares several characteristics with γE in serum. Its affinity for DEAE-cellulose is such that it elutes in the same buffer as serum γE. Its size characteristics, as shown by gel filtration and sucrose-density ultracentrifugation, are similar to those of the protein in serum (1, 2). Moreover, monkey skin was sensitized for the PCA reaction to the same grass antigen extract both by patients' sera and by the γE isolated from their sputa. The requirement for about five times as much exocrine γE as serum γE to sensitize monkey skin could reflect a lower proportion of antibody to grass in the sputum γE, or a partial inactivation of exocrine γE antibody by the procedures used for isolation.

The present experiments were undertaken to test the extent of analogies between γE and γA. Studies using immunofluorescence techniques (13) have revealed that the proportion of γE-forming cells in lymphoid tissues is more than 100 times higher in the respiratory and gastrointestinal tracts than in spleen or subcutaneous lymph nodes. Subsequent work (3) has demonstrated that γE is present in exocrine fluids of the respiratory tract, and that the ratio of γE to γG concentration therein is too high to be explained by unselective transudation of serum proteins. The same findings have been reported for γA, whose structure in exocrine fluids consists of an 11.7S dimer of 7S γA subunits bound to a non-immunoglobulin protein, the secretory piece (SP) (7, 14).

It was therefore of interest to find that the γE in sputum and nasal fluids had approximately the same size as the serum protein, and that antibody to SP did not react with exocrine γE. The sensitivity of the method that we used to measure γE was not great enough to exclude the possibility that a minor portion of γE may be heavier or lighter than 8S, but was sufficient to limit such material to less than 5% to 10% of the total. Previous work (3) showed that incubation of sputum at 37°C did not change the γE values, as measured by this method, suggesting that depolymerization or proteolytic digestion of γE had not occurred. Although some of the γE examined in the present study had been treated with acid prior to ultracentrifugation, raising the possibility that an acid-labile γE-SP may have been split, other γE-rich respiratory fluids that had not been so treated sedimented similarly. Furthermore the SP attached to human exocrine γA is not dissociated at pH 2.5 (7). Even if SP were bound to monomer γE in such a way as to prevent reaction with antibody to SP, our results should have revealed a larger molecular size, since the molecular weight of SP is at least 55,000 (14). It is clear from data presented here that the structural differences that distinguish exocrine from serum γA do not find an analogue in γE. Despite these differences there are several similarities between γA and γE. The bulk of cells forming γA as well as γE are found near mucosal surfaces (13, 14) and in the overlying exocrine fluids the ratios of γA to γG and of γE to γG are higher than in serum (3, 14). It has been shown that nasal exocrine γA is produced and secreted locally in response to local antigenic stimulation (15). Experiments on atopic patients have suggested, moreover, that antigens given by inhalation are effective in producing reaginic antibody (16).

Since γE-forming plasma cells are present in the mucosa of the respiratory tract, it is possible to speculate that at least a portion of γE antibody may be formed locally in response to antigens encountered by mucosal tissues, and that its concentration in such tissues may be higher than in serum or in the overlying exocrine fluids. Recent data (J. Soothill, personal communication) have indicated that high γE levels may be found in some nasal polyps. Moreover, the observation has been made in our laboratories that large numbers of γE-forming cells may be found in nasal polyps from atopic patients (unpublished data). If γE antibody were locally formed, its concentration in respiratory tissues might not be adequately represented in serum γE, and γE antibody could be present in some mucosal tissues and not in others. Quantitative measurement of γE antibodies should be useful in examining these possibilities. In view of the fact that γE can sensitize primate lung tissue and mediate the release of histamine and slow reacting substance of anaphylaxis (SRS-A) (6), it appears clear that γE antibody concentrated in the mucosa of the respiratory tract would be strategically placed to mediate allergic reactions to inhaled antigens.

Finally it may be noted that attempts to sensitize monkey skin using human exocrine γA antibodies have given negative results (17, 18). Arbesman *et al.*, however, using a highly sensitive Schultz-Dale technique (18) reported that parotid γA from ragweed-sensitive humans sensitized monkey ileum. The data reported in the present paper suggest that such sensitization was not mediated by γE antibody.

Acknowledgment. We thank Mrs. B. L. DeVald and Mrs. M. M. Hornbrook for expert technical assistance.

REFERENCES

1. Ishizaka, K., Ishizaka, T. and Hornbrook, M. M., J. Immun., *97:* 840, 1966.
2. Bennich, H. and Johansson, S. G. O., Nobel Symposium, *3:* 199, 1967.
3. Ishizaka, K. and Newcomb, R. W., J. Allergy, In press.
4. Tomasi, T. B., Jr., Tan, E. M., Solomon, A. and Prendergast, R. A., J. Exp. Med., *121:* 101, 1965
5. Newcomb, R. W. and DeVald, B. L., J. Lab. Clin. Med., *73:* 734, 1969.
6. Ishizaka, T., Ishizaka, K., Orange, R. P. and Austen, K. F., J. Immun., *104:* 335, 1970.
7. Newcomb, R. W., Normansell, D. and Stanworth, D. R., J. Immun., *101:* 905, 1968.
8. Ogawa, M., Kochwa, S., Smith, C., Ishizaka, K. and McIntyre, O. R., New England J. Med., *281:* 1217, 1969.
9. Masson, P., Heremans, J. F. and Vaerman, C., Biochim. Biophys. Acta., *111:* 466, 1965.
10. Avrameas, S. and Ternynck, T., Immunochemistry, *6:* 53, 1969.
11. McConahey, P. J. and Dixon, F. J., Int. Arch. Allerg., *29:* 185, 1966.
12. Ishizaka, K., Ishizaka, T. and Arbesman, C. E., J. Allerg., *39:* 254, 1967.
13. Tada, T. and Ishizaka, K., J. Immun., *104:* 377, 1970.
14. Tomasi, T. B., Jr. and Bienenstock, J., Adv. Immunl., *9:* 2, 1968.
15. Newcomb, R. W., Ishizaka, K. and DeVald, B. L., J. Immun., *103:* 215, 1969.
16. Salvaggio, J., Kayman, H. and Leskowitz, S., J. Allerg., *38:* 31, 1966.
17. Newcomb, R. W. and Devald, B. L., Fed. Proc., *28:* 765, 1969.
18. Arbesman, C. E., Dolovich, J., Wicher, K., Dushenski, L. A., Reisman, R. E. and Tomasi, T. B., *Allergology: Proceedings of the Sixth Congress of the International Association of Allergology,* Edited by B. Rose, p. 287, Exerpta Medica Foundation, New York, 1968.

THE JOURNAL OF IMMUNOLOGY
Vol. 105, No. 1, July 1970
Printed in U.S.A.

TRANSFORMATION OF MOUSE LYMPHOCYTES TO ALLOGENEIC LYMPHOCYTES AND PHYTOHEMAGGLUTININ

RICHARD J. MANGI AND MICHAEL R. MARDINEY, JR.[1]

From the Section of Immunology and Cell Biology, The Baltimore Cancer Research Center, The National Cancer Institute, Baltimore, Maryland

Received for publication December 18, 1969

The inbred laboratory mouse may offer the best opportunity to investigate the sensitivity of the mixed lymphocyte reaction (MLR). Although previous investigators have reported transformation of mouse cells, they have not delineated the entire time sequence of the reaction. We have separated mouse lymphocytes from spleen by centrifugation and have successfully incubated them in 20% mule serum for up to 9 days. The one-way and the two-way MLR exhibited peak activity at 5 to 6 days. The response to phytohemagglutinin was maximal on the 3rd to 4th day. Histocompatibility differences at the H-2 locus were detected by both the one-way and the two-way MLR, whereas differences at non-H-2 loci were consistently detected by only the two-way MLR. There was significantly increased activity in the parent *vs* F_1 one-way irradiated MLR, but not in the F_1 *vs* parent irradiated.

The mixed lymphocyte culture test (MLR) is one of the three major matching tests currently being used for histocompatibility testing (1, 2). There has naturally been much interest in the limits of the sensitivity and specificity of the reaction. The extensively studied inbred laboratory mouse probably offers the best opportunity to investigate the subtleties of this reaction.

Mixed lymphocyte transformation of mouse cells was described by Dutton (3, 4) in 1965 and by Huemer (5) in 1968. These investigators assayed the reaction at 24 to 48 hr and at 88 hr, respectively.

In order to completely evaluate the sensitivity of the reaction it is necessary to know the time of peak activity of the system. Peak transformation activity of human lymphocytes occurs in 150 to 170 hr in the MLR and from 72 to 96 hr with phytohemagglutinin (PHA) stimulation. Human lymphocyte experiments are thus assayed at these times.

Although investigations of mouse cell transformation have been reported, there have been no complete studies of the time sequence of this reaction. Data gathered by different investigators at different times during a response curve may be conflicting and confusing for an evaluation of the reaction.

Modifications of cell preparation and culture techniques have enabled us to investigate the transformation of mouse cells in the two-way and one-way MLR and in response to PHA for a period of 9 days. We have evaluated the sequence of response and investigated certain factors that affect these reactions.

METHODS AND MATERIALS

Mice. The mice selected for study were the C57BL/6, the Balb/c, the DBA/2 and the F_1 hybrid of C57BL/6 and Balb/c (CBF_1). All animals were obtained from the Chemotherapy Research Colony of the National Cancer Institute.

Preparation of cell suspensions. The spleens of 60- to 90-day old male mice were aseptically removed, strained through wire mesh, poured through a nylon filter, and suspended in Roswell Park Memorial Institute (RPMI) 1630 medium with 50% mule serum (Grand Island Biological Co., Grand Island, N. Y.). The suspension was centrifuged in 40-ml test tubes at 400 rpm (50 × G) at 10°C for 7.5 min. The supernatant was carefully removed with a pipette and the red cell pellet was discarded. RPMI medium 1630 and

[1] Please address all requests for reprints to: Michael R. Mardiney, Jr., M.D., Section of Immunology and Cell Biology, Baltimore Cancer Research Center, 3100 Wyman Park Drive, Baltimore, Maryland 21211.

mule serum were added to the suspension to adjust the concentration to 2.5×10^6 cells/ml in 20% serum with 50 units/ml of penicillin, 50 μg/ml of streptomycin and 300 μg/ml of glutamine.

Cell culture system. One milliliter of cells was pipetted into quadruplicate sets of 16- x 150-mm sterile test tubes with Morton stainless steel caps. The tubes were incubated at 5° from the horizontal in a 1.5% CO_2, 98.5% air humidified atmosphere at 37°C.

Assay procedures. After the appropriate culture period had elapsed, 0.5 ml of RPMI 1630 medium containing 2 μCi of tritiated thymidine (specific activity 1.9 Ci/mmol (Schwarz Bioresearch, Inc., Orangeburg, N. Y.) was added to each tube. After 4 additional hr of culture, 8 ml of ice-cold saline were added to three tubes of each set. These tubes were then centrifuged at 1500 rpm at 5°C for 15 min. The supernatant was decanted and the pellets were frozen until they could be assayed for radioactivity.

A cell count using Centrimide diluent (Fisher Scientific, Pittsburgh, Pa.) in a model B Coulter counter and a trypan blue viability (6) assay were performed on the cells of the fourth tube of each set. The remaining cells were then washed twice, and resuspended in 1 ml of RPMI 1630 medium with 15% fetal calf serum. Slide preparations for radioautography of these suspensions were made using the Shandon Cytocentrifuge.

The triplicate specimens were later defrosted, washed twice with 5 ml of 5% trichloroacetic acid, washed twice with 5 ml of absolute methanol and dissolved in 1 ml of Hyamine (Packard Instrument Co., Donner's Grove, Ill.). Fourteen milliliters of scintillation fluid (Liquifluor, New England Nuclear Corp., Boston, Mass.) were added to each tube and the radioactivity was assayed in a model 4233 Packard Tricarb scintillation counter. A quench calibration curve derived from external standardization was used to convert counts/min to disintegrations/min. A background count/min was subtracted from each sample. All of the triplicated samples were averaged and the standard error of the means was computed. Any two means greater than three average standard errors apart are significantly different at the 95% confidence level.

The results are reported as disintegrations/min (DPM) ± standard error and as ratio of incorporation (13) $\frac{2 \times \text{cell mix}}{\text{Sum of cells cultured alone}} \pm$ standard deviation. Any ratio of incorporation increased more than three standard deviations above 1.00 is statistically significant at the 99% level of confidence.

Radioautographs. The slide preparations were fixed in absolute methanol, then rehydrated in water, dipped in photographic emulsion (Kodak NTB2), and stored in the dark for either 1 or 2 days. The slides were then developed and stained with Wright-Giemsa stain (Fisher Scientific). The number of labeled cells (more than five grains/nucleus) and cell differentials were performed on 700 cells of each sample. All mitoses, blast-like cells and plasmoid cells were classified as transformed cells. The 95% confidence limit of a differential count of 700 cells is 1.00% to 3.34% for as low as 2% of transformed cells.

RESULTS

Cell preparation. The initial centrifugation step yielded a relatively pure population of mouse lymphocytes. The mean lymphocyte count was 88.6% ± 4.4, with less variation within each strain (Table I). The cell yield was approximately 1×10^8 cells/spleen. The trypan blue viability of the preparation was greater than 90%.

Culture system factors

Cell number. Single cell mixes were prepared at different concentrations to determine the optimum number of cells for the system. Activity was maximal at 1.5 to 2.5×10^6 cells/ml (Fig. 1). Trypan blue viability decreased below 2×10^6 or above 3×10^6/ml. On the basis of these data, a cell concentration of 2.5×10^6/ml was used in subsequent experiments.

Radiation dosage for the one-way MLR. Ionizing radiation was used to prevent the irradiated cells from responding to non-irradiated cells in the one-way MLR. Radiation was delivered with a Theratron 80, cobalt 60 therapy unit, with a half value layer of 10.2 mm of lead, and an air exposure rate of 240 R/min at a treatment distance of 52 cm from the source. A constant volume (50 ml) and concentration (2.5×10^6/ml) of cells was placed in standardized 4-oz glass bottles that were then irradiated. Cell mixes with varying doses of radiation to one of the two cell populations are shown in Figure 2. As the dosage of radiation was increased, the activity of the irradiated cells and the activity of the cell mix (irradiated plus non-irradiated cells) fell to reach

TABLE I

Differential count and standard deviation of cell suspensions before and after centrifugation at 50 × G (400 rpm) for 7.5 min

	Lymphocytes	Neutrophiles	Monocytes	Nucleated Erythrocytes
Pre-centrifugation				
All strains	56.5 ± 5.2	3.5 ± 0.8	1.0 ± 1.3	39.0 ± 5.7
Post-centrifugation				
C57BL/6	93 ± 2.4	4.3 ± 2.3	2.0 ± 1.0	0.5 ± 0.5
Balb/c	90.5 ± 0.8	3.8 ± 1.0	1.0 ± 0.8	5.2 ± 1.3
DBA/2	82.7 ± 0.5	3.3 ± 0.9	1.0 ± 0.7	11.3 ± 4.1
All strains	88.6 ± 4.4	3.8 ± 1.4	1.5 ± 0.9	5.8 ± 4.8

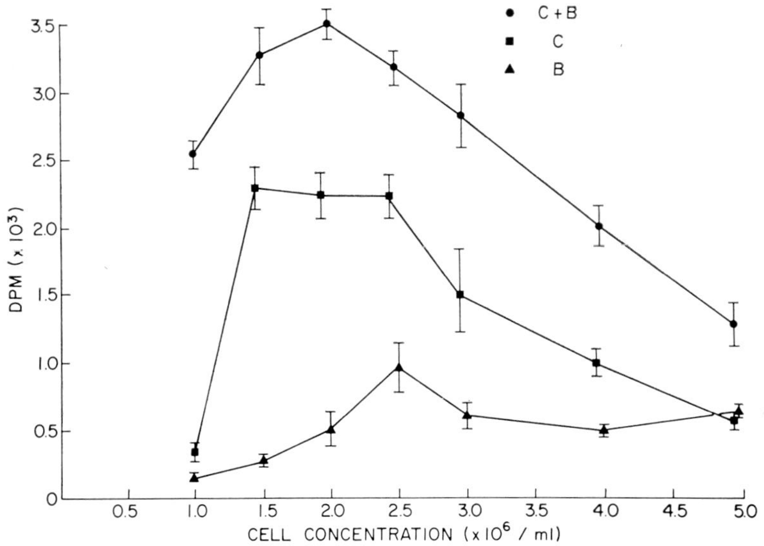

Figure 1. Two-way MLR at increasing concentrations of cells. C is C57BL/6, B is Balb/c. All mixes were assayed on day 6. Maximum activity occurs at 1.5 to 2.5 × 10^6 cells/ml.

a plateau at about 450 R. We found that in some experiments higher doses of the radiation inhibited the response of the non-irradiated cells. The best dosage of radiation would thus be that dose which inhibits all of the irradiated cells, but which inhibits as few of the responder cells as possible. A dosage of 450 R was noted to best fit these conditions in our system. At this dosage there was no significant transformation of the F_1 *vs* parent irradiated one-way MLR, but there was significant increased activity in the parent *vs* F_1 irradiated (Table II).

Cell response curve. Nine-day daily plots of the activity of cells cultured simultaneously in the two-way and one-way MLR and in response to PHA are depicted in Figures 3, 4 and 5, respectively. Lymphocytes cultured with homologous lymphocytes and with PHA were transformed into immature blastlike cells. Frequent mitosis and labeled nuclei were seen in the radioautograph preparations (Fig. 3).

The peak activity of the two-way MLR in Figure 4 occurred on day 5 when 57% of the cells were transformed and the percentage of labeled cells was 17. In 15 two-way MLR the day of peak activity was the 5th in 7, 6th in 5, and 7th in 2. The peak activity of the one-way MLR in Figure 5 occurred on the 6th day when 23% of the cells were transformed and 4% of the nuclei were labeled. In 26 one-way MLR the day of peak activity was the 5th in 14, 6th in 9, and 7th in 2. Peak response to PHA occurred on day 4 (Fig. 6). The percentage of transformed cells was 40 and the percentage of labeled nuclei was 15.5. In

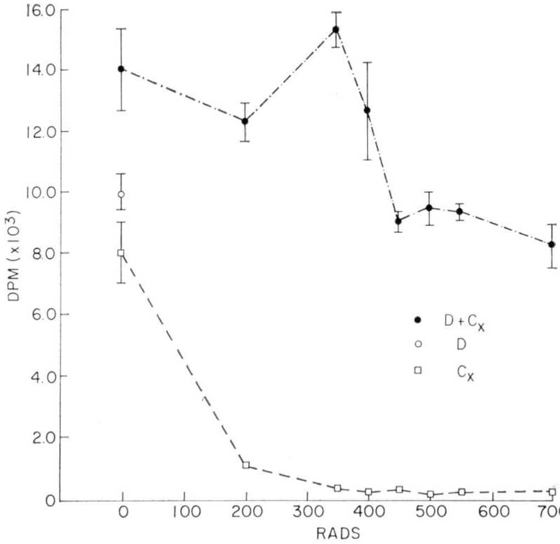

Figure 2. One-way MLR with increasing doses of irradiation to the cells. D is DBA/2, Cx is C57BL/6 irradiated. All mixes were assayed on day 6. As the radiation dose is increased the activity of the cell mix falls to a plateau at about 450 R.

nine PHA experiments the day of peak activity was the 2nd in 1, 3rd in 3, and 4th in 5. The trypan blue viabilities on the day of peak activity were: cells alone, 22.3% (range 7 to 60); cells irradiated, 21.8% (range 9 to 40); two-way MLR, 41.7% (range 17 to 69); one-way MLR, 32.7% (range 17 to 72); PHA, 66% (range 47 to 95).

Sensitivity of the reaction. The peak activity of lymphocytes in the one-way and two-way MLR in three experiments with C57BL/6, DBA/2, and Balb/c mice is shown in Tables III and IV.

The C57BL/6 differs from Balb/c and DBA/2 at both the H-2 and other minor histocompatibility loci. C57BL/6 possesses H-2 locus b (alloantigenic specificity 2, 5, 6, 14, 22, 27, 28, 29, 33). The DBA/2 and the Balb/c possess H-2 locus d (alloantigenic specificity 3, 4, 6, 8, 10, 13, 14, 27, 28, 29, 31) (7), but differ at at least three minor loci (H-1, H-6, H-7) (7, 8).

In these experiments, two-way or one-way MLR that cross the H-2 locus (C57 BL/6 *vs* Balb/c or DBA/2) were always of greater magnitude than mixes of cells that differ only at minor loci (DBA/2 *vs* Balb/c). It is also noted that the magnitude of the H-2 response overshadows any response due to minor loci and thus C57BL/6 *vs* DBA/2 is approximately the same as C57BL/6 *vs* Balb/c.

The ratios of response of mixes within the same H-2 locus are depicted in Table IV. The one-way MLR does not appear to be sensitive enough to consistently detect the variation of these minor loci, but the two-way MLR does.

Further studies with congenic resistant strains of mice that vary at just one locus should further delineate the ability of the MLR to sensitively detect histocompatibility differences between two populations of cells.

DISCUSSION

The sensitivity of the MLR and its role in histocompatibility testing have been frequently discussed and debated in recent years (1, 9–14). The inbred laboratory mouse, with greater versatility of known genetic variation, offers a unique opportunity to explore the limits of the reaction.

TABLE II

One-way MLR between F_1 and parents and between F_1 and unrelated strain

Control: DPM ± SE Cells Alone 2.5 × 10⁶ [a, b]	One-Way MLR	
	DPM ± S.E. 2.5 × 10⁶ cells [a, b]	Ratio of [c] increased activity ± S.D.
C 3153 ± 278	F_1Cx 515 ± 81	0.87 ± 0.09
B 1026 ± 267	F_1Bx 667 ± 318	1.19 ± 0.27
D 4538 ± 295	F_1Dx 1032 ± 302	2.13 ± 0.13
F_1 790 ± 126	CF_1x 3073 ± 877	1.84 ± 0.11
Cx 393 ± 87	BF_1x 2411 ± 665	3.99 ± 0.26
Bx 408 ± 12	DF_1x 7349 ± 180	3.11 ± 0.02
Dx 177 ± 18		
F_1x 183 ± 32		

[a] F_1 is CBF_1, C is C57BL/6, B is Balb/c, D is DBA/2.

[b] x, Irradiated cells.

[c] Ratio of increased activity $= \dfrac{2 \times \text{cell mix}}{\text{Sum of cells cultured alone}}$.

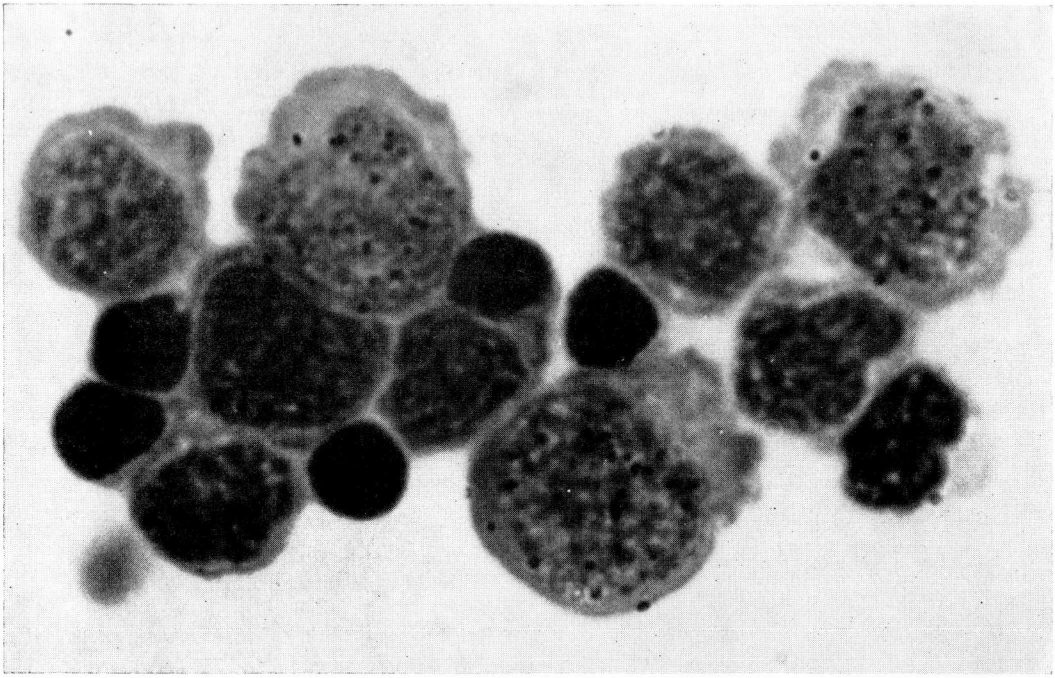

Figure 3. Radioautograph of one-way MLR (C57BL/6 + Balb/cx), after 6 days of culture, showing blast-like cells with labeled nuclei, blast-like cells without labeled nuclei, and several untransformed lymphocytes.

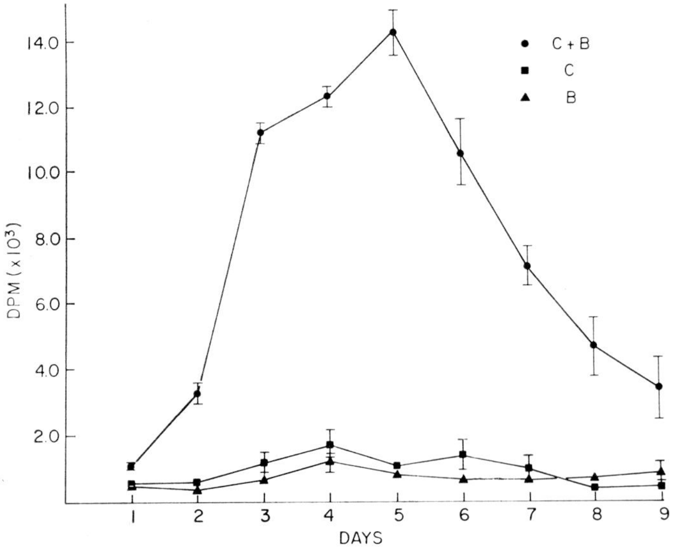

Figure 4. Nine-day plot of daily activity of two-way MLR. C is C57BL/6, B is Balb/c. Note maximal activity at 5 days.

Unfortunately, it has been extremely difficult to culture mouse cells (15, 16) and to develop a reliable system to study lymphocyte transformation. In order to assess the practical value of such a system, it must be shown that the reaction truly represents transformation, that the complete time course of the reaction is known, and that the data reported were collected at the sensitive peak activity of the reaction.

The first difficulty encountered in the mouse

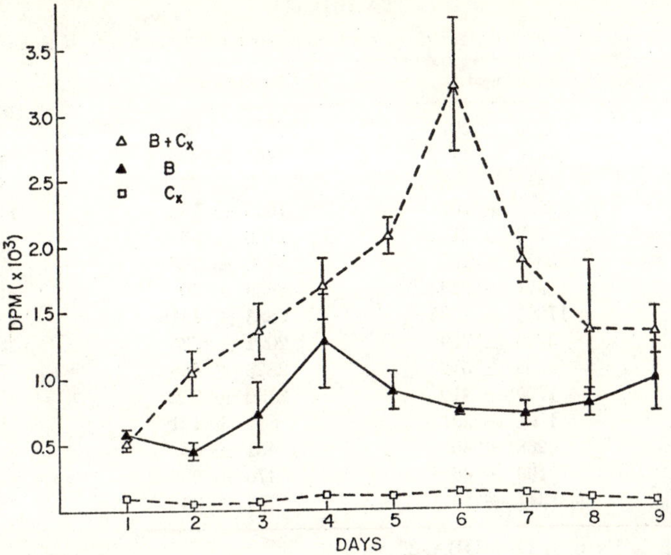

Figure 5. Nine-day plot of daily activity of one-way MLR. B is Balb/c, Cx is C57BL/6 irradiated. Note maximal activity at 6 days.

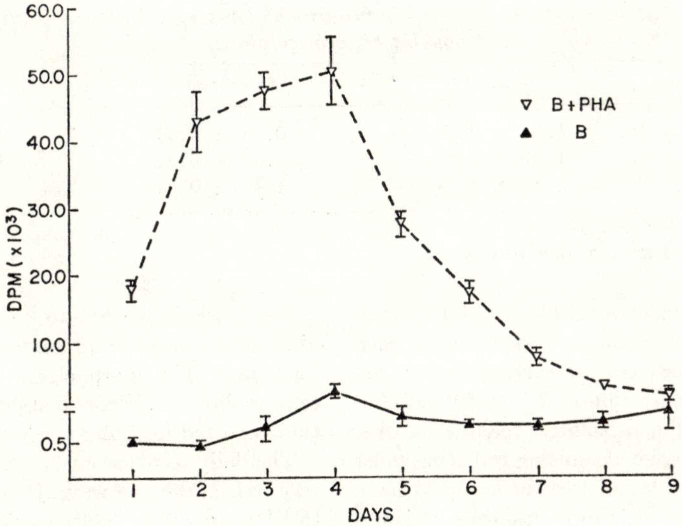

Figure 6. Nine-day plot of daily activity of PHA stimulated lymphocytes. B is Balb/c. Note maximal activity at 3 to 4 days.

cell culture technique is to obtain a large enough number of viable cells. Spleens offer a greater number of cells than peripheral blood, but they contain leukocytic elements, nucleated erythrocytes, and red blood cells known to be inhibitory to cell cultures (17, 18).

Red blood cell removal by lysis with distilled water or sedimentation with dextran was too toxic to the cells. The centrifugation process that we have developed has the threefold advantage of removing red blood cells, of leaving the lymphocytes in a hardy state, and of yielding a fairly standard cell differential each time.

Stimulation by heterologous plasma is another problem previously encountered in mouse cell culture work (3). Since homologous plasma is very expensive, it is fortunate that we found that 20% mule serum allowed good lymphocyte transformation to occur with little or no direct cell stimulation.

TABLE III

Two-way and one-way MLR between three strains of mice (DPM ± S.E.)

	Experiment 1	Experiment 2	Experiment 3
CBx[a, b]	3393 ± 207	2570 ± 262	3871 ± 240
CDx	3274 ± 1419	1705 ± 178	4202 ± 2402
DBx	1615 ± 263	923 ± 94	3233 ± 346
DCx	2060 ± 207	1653 ± 182	11341 ± 1136
BDx	793 ± 21	1106 ± 53	1123 ± 168
BCx	2891 ± 255	1406 ± 225	2455 ± 125
CB	10971 ± 2233	8639 ± 70	21260 ± 1700
CD	17291 ± 1385	3883 ± 1418	24681 ± 358
BD	3226 ± 720	2091 ± 235	13556 ± 1308
C	2305 ± 512	2826 ± 458	7646 ± 750
D	1729 ± 410	2130 ± 332	5864 ± 22
B	1121 ± 331	846 ± 121	1285 ± 710
Cx	268 ± 40	431 ± 80	415 ± 44
Dx	193 ± 68	470 ± 53	132 ± 62
Bx	347 ± 16	209 ± 33	638 ± 143

[a] C is C57BL/6; B is Balb/c; D is DBA/2.
[b] x, Irradiated partner in one-way MLR.

TABLE IV

Ratio of increased activity (±S.D.) in two-way and one-way MLR of cells differing at non-H2 histocompatibility

	Experiment 1	Experiment 2	Experiment 3
DBx[a, b]	1.55 ± 0.07	0.79 ± 0.03	0.99 ± 0.02
BDx	1.04 ± 0.11	1.68 ± 0.02	1.59 ± 0.32
BD	2.26 ± 0.15	1.41 ± 0.03	3.79 ± 0.02

[a] D is DBA/2; B is Balb/c.
[b] x, Irradiated partner in one-way MLR.

An optimum number of cells is crucial for maximum sensitivity and must be worked out for each different type of cell culture system. In our experiments, a concentration of 2.5×10^6 cells/ml yielded the most consistently reliable results.

Choosing the dosage of ionizing radiation must be done with the utmost care in order to have successful one-way MLR of mouse cells. It is obvious that too low a dose of radiation will not inhibit all of the irradiated cells and the reaction will be a semi-two-way MLR. We have further observed that too high a dose of radiation will not only inhibit the irradiated cells, but also inhibits the response of the non-irradiated responder cells. The best dose must thus be between these two extremes and must inhibit all of the irradiated cells with minimal effect on the responder cells. This dose must be derived for each system as explained above.

For the evaluation of the significance of the system, it is important to know that the thymidine incorporation represents lymphocyte transformation. The morphologic appearance of the cells as shown in Figure 3 appears to be similar to that reported for human cells (19).

The daily response curves reported for the two-way MLR, the one-way MLR, and the response to PHA are quite similar to those reported in the human cell culture system. For maximum sensitivity of the reaction it would be best to assay the systems at 5 to 6 days for the MLR and at 3 or 4 days in the PHA system. Previous investigations of mouse MLR have been assayed on the 2nd and 3rd (7) or the 3rd and 4th (13) days.

Both the two-way and the one-way MLR are helpful for the assessment of the sensitivity of the reaction. While the one-way MLR was sensitive enough to detect a difference at the H-2 locus, it was not consistently sensitive to differences at minor loci. The two-way MLR was sensitive enough to detect a difference at three or more minor loci. The larger response to the H-2 incompatibility masked the response of the minor loci.

We have presented a reliable model of lymphocyte transformation of mouse cells and have discussed some of the parameters pertinent to the system. Further investigation with inbred mice may be quite helpful in determining the sensitivity of the MLR and its role in histocompatibility testing.

REFERENCES

1. Bach, F. H., Prog. Med. Genet., *6:* 201, 1969.
2. Russell, P. S., Nelson, S. D. and Johnson, G. J., Ann. N. Y. Acad. Sci., *87:* 217, 1966.
3. Dutton, R. W., J. Exp. Med., *122:* 759, 1965.
4. Dutton, R. W., J. Exp. Med., *123:* 665, 1966.
5. Heumer, R. P., Keller, L. S. and Lee, K., Transplantation, *6:* 706, 1968.
6. Boyse, E. A., Old, L. T. and Thomas, G., Transplant. Bull., *29:* 63, 1962.
7. Snell, G. D. and Stimpfling, J. H., in *The Biology of the Laboratory Mouse*, Edited by E. L. Green, p. 457, McGraw-Hill Inc., New York, 1966.
8. Green, E. L., *Handbook on Genetically Standardized Jax Mice*, The Jackson Laboratory, Bar Harbor, Maine, 1968.
9. Bach, F. H. and Hirschhorn, K., Science, *143:* 813, 1964.
10. Bach, F. H. and Amos, D. B., Science, *156:* 1506, 1967.
11. Billingham, R. F. and Barker, C. F., Plast. Reconstr. Surg., *44:* 20, 1969.
12. Editorial, Lancet, *2:* 835, 1965.
13. Silvers, W. K. and Wilson, D. B., Science, *155:* 703, 1966.
14. Silvers, W. K., Wilson, D. B. and Palm, J., Transplantation, *5:* 1053, 1967.
15. Trowell, O. A., Exp. Cell Res., *16:* 118, 1959.
16. Willard, H. G., Hoppe, I. B. H. and Netteshein, P., Proc. Exp. Biol. Med., *118:* 993, 1965.
17. Earle, W. R., J. Exp. Med., *48:* 667, 1928.
18. Earle, W. R., J. Exp. Med., *48:* 683, 1928.
19. Bain, B., Magdelene, R. V. and Lowenstein, L., Blood, *23:* 108, 1964.

THE JOURNAL OF IMMUNOLOGY
Copyright © 1970 by The Williams & Wilkins Co.

Vol. 105, No. 1, July 1970
Printed in U.S.A

GENETIC CONTROL OF THE ANTIBODY RESPONSE TO SIMPLE HAPTENS IN CONGENIC STRAINS OF MICE[1]

W. E. RATHBUN AND W. H. HILDEMANN

From the Department of Medical Microbiology and Immunology, School of Medicine, University of California, Los Angeles, California 90024

Received for publication December 15, 1969

The antibody response to the 2,4,6-trinitrophenyl hapten (TNP) conjugated to mouse serum albumin (MSA) was found to be substantially regulated by products of alleles of the *H-2* locus. Mice from each of five strains representing congenic pairs differing at the *H-2* and *H-3* loci and their F_1 and F_2 progenies were tested. These mice were immunized with a variety of haptens coupled to MSA and their antibody responses were determined after individual serial bleedings by a sensitive test for antigen-binding capacity. The A/Jax and B10.A ($H\text{-}2^a$) strains regularly showed a low antibody response whereas their congenic partners, A.BY and C57BL/10 ($H\text{-}2^b$) gave a markedly higher response to TNP at all times tested. F_1 hybrid progeny gave a low response similar to the $H\text{-}2^a$ parent strain. The antibody responses of F_2 mice were consistent with the segregation of the histocompatability alleles as determined by skin transplants. These results support the hypothesis that low antibody responsiveness to the TNP hapten is determined by the $H\text{-}2^a$ allele as a dominant trait, whereas homozygosity for the $H\text{-}2^b$ allele leads to high responsiveness even on diverse strain backgrounds.

Considerable evidence from a variety of sources indicates that the immune response is under genetic control (1). Early studies, using complex antigenic systems and a variety of experimental animals, have shown a positive correlation between the responses of parent and offspring but in most instances have failed to show a simple or Mendelian basis for this heritability (2).

Several recent studies have shown various immune responses to be governed decisively by single genes in both mice and guinea pigs (2–6). These studies employed inbred strains of animals and immunogens presumed to possess a rather limited range of antigenic determinants. McDevitt and coworkers have shown that the immune response of mice to a branched, multichain synthetic polypeptide antigen, poly (tyr, glu)-poly-DL-ala--polylys (T, G)-A--L) is genetically controlled. The responsible locus now designated *Ir-1* is closely linked to the *H-2* locus on the ninth chromosome of mice (3). Gasser has shown that the response of mice to Ea-1 erythrocytic alloantigens is controlled by a recessive gene associated with a locus designated *Ir-2* which is linked to the *agouti* locus in the fifth linkage group (4). In guinea pigs the ability of poly-L-lysine to function as a macromolecular carrier for the 2,4-dinitrophenyl (DNP) group as a hapten also appears to depend upon a single gene, but with unknown linkage (5).

In the present experiments the immunogenicity of several haptens coupled to presumptively isogeneic mouse serum albumin (MSA) as a carrier protein has been studied in several congenic strain pairs of mice. Congenic strains represent imperfect but useful approximation of theoretically ideal coisogenic strains which are genetically identical except for a difference at a single genetic locus. Mice that were either homozygous or heterozygous for the $H\text{-}2^a$ allele were found to be low responders to 2,4,6-trinitrophenyl-MSA. By contrast, mice homozygous for the $H\text{-}2^b$ allele were high responders even on diverse strain backgrounds. The operational terms "high responder" and "low responder" indicate significant quantitative differences in the antigen-binding capacity of whole antiserum samples and do not

[1] This work was supported by United States Public Health Service Research Grants DE-00090 and AI-07970.

TABLE I

Congenic strains of mice used

Congenic Pair	Differential Genotype
No. 1	
A/J	*H-2*^{a}
A. BY	*H-2*^{b}
Nos. 2 and 3	
B10. A	*H-2*^{a}
C57Bl/10	*H-2*^{b},*H-3*^{a}
B10. LP-*a*	*H-2*^{b}, *H-3*^{b}

necessarily reflect each component or constituent immune response which may constitute the total immune response capability of the tested mice.

METHODS AND MATERIALS

Animals. The congenic strains of mice tested were: pair 1, A/Jax (*H-2*^{a}) and A.BY (*H-2*^{b}); pair 2, B10.A (*H-2*^{a}) and C57BL/10 (*H-2*^{b}); and pair 3, C57BL/10 (*H-3*^{a}) and B10.Lp-*a* (*H-3*^{b}). Additionally, F_1 and F_2 progeny of (C57BL/10 × B10.A) and (A.BY × A/Jax) hybrid crosses were extensively tested. The C57BL/10 and B10. LP-*a* strains were obtained from the Jackson Memorial Laboratory, Bar Harbor, Maine. The other strains and hybrid progeny were produced in our mouse colony from stock originally obtained from the Jackson Laboratory and maintained by brother-sister matings.

Antigens. Most of the studies were performed with the antigen 2,4,6-trinitrophenyl (TNP)-MSA prepared by coupling the haptenic component, 2,4,6-trinitrobenzene sulfonic acid (TNBS) to mouse serum albumin (MSA). Conjugation was effected by the technique of Rittenberg and Amkraut (7), which was modified as follows. Two hundred milligrams of mouse serum albumin was added to 5 ml of 0.1 M phosphate buffer containing 48 mg TNBS at a pH of 7.1. After stirring for 1 hr on ice, the conjugated protein, free TNBS and albumin were separated by twice filtering through a Sephadex[2] G-25 column (2.0 cm × 70 cm) equilibrated with buffered saline at pH 7.1. The purified hapten-protein conjugate was then passed through a 0.20 μ Nalgene[3] plain membrane filter and stored in the dark at 4°C until used. The albumin used was derived from the sera of the mouse strains tested by the technique of Korner and Debro (8), which uses the precipitation of protein by trichloracetic acid and subsequent solubilization in absolute alcohol. Although the MSA was derived from pooled sera of the strains tested, there is no evidence for the existence of albumin differences among laboratory mice (D. C. Shreffler, personal communication). The albumin was then tested to assure freedom from contaminants by agar gel immunoelectrophoresis with rabbit anti-mouse serum. The extent of the TNP substitution was estimated from the light absorption at 350 nm on the basis of a molar extinction coefficient of Σ-amino caproic acid of $\epsilon = 15{,}400$ (9). The average number of hapten groups/mole of protein is indicated by subscript (e.g., TNP_{11}), assuming a molecular weight of 7×10^4 for the mouse albumin. The protein concentration was estimated either by micro-Kjeldahl nitrogen analysis (10) or by a modification of the phenol-protein assay using the Folin-Ciocalteu reagent (11). Other antigens employed in these investigations were 2,4-dinitrophenyl (DNP)-MSA, arsanilate-azo(ARS) MSA, sheep erythrocytes, and dissociated spleen cells derived from F_1 hybrid mice. The DNP was coupled to MSA by techniques similar to those used for TNP (12). The degree of DNP substitution was estimated spectrophotometrically at 360 nm on the basis of the molar extinction coefficient $\epsilon = 17{,}400$ of E-amino-L-lysine (13). Protein concentration was determined by micro-Kjeldahl analysis. Arsanilic acid was coupled to MSA by diazotization (14). Fresh sheep erythrocytes[4] were washed three times in normal saline prior to injection. The antigen preparations used in the serum antibody determinations involved haptens coupled to a heterologous carrier, namely crystalline bovine serum albumin;[5] the same techniques for coupling the MSA were used.

Immunizations. Mice between 6 and 24 weeks of age were injected i.p. with 0.25 ml of emulsion containing 50 μg TNP_{11}-MSA (or DNP- or ARS-) in complete Freund's adjuvant containing 125 μg *Mycobacterium tuberculosis* H37Ra (Difco).[6] Five weeks after primary immunization the mice

[2] Sephadex G-25, Pharmacia, Uppsala, Sweden.

[3] Nalgene membrane filter, Nalg. D. V., Ritter Pfaudler Corp., Rochester, N. Y.

[4] Mission Laboratory Supply, Rosemead, Calif.

[5] Pentex Inc., Kankakee, Ill. 60901.

[6] Difco Laboratories, Detroit, Mich.

received a second injection of 50 μg antigen i.p. in 0.25 ml saline. Mice immunized with allogeneic spleen cells received three weekly i.p. injections of 10×10^6 cells from the appropriate F_1 hybrid.

Sera. At 7, 14 and 28 days after primary and 7 and 14 days after secondary immunizations blood samples were collected from the retro-orbital sinus in plain capillary blood collecting tubes.[7] After standing for 30 min at room temperature, the tubes were "ringed" with a 0.010 stainless steel wire and the serum was allowed to separate at 4°C. The serum samples were collected by breaking the tubes at the cell-serum interface after centrifugation at 1500 × G for 20 min in the cold. Anti-F_1 spleen cell sera were obtained from mice exsanguinated by the intracardiac route at 10 days after the third weekly injection.

Antibody determinations. Sera from at least 15 mice of each sex from both parental and F_1 hybrid combinations and from 60 to 100 F_2 mice of each sex were individually titered for antibody activity. *Anti-TNP:* 100 μl of the serum sample and 0.4 ml borate buffer were incubated overnight in the cold with 1.25 μg TNP_5-BSA (0.5 ml) which was trace labeled with ^{125}I[8] by the technique of McConahey and Dixon (15). The antibody and bound antigen were precipitated by adding 1 ml of saturated ammonium sulfate to each tube (13 × 100 mm). After 30 min the tubes were centrifuged in the cold for 30 min at 1500 × G, the precipitate was washed once with 2.0 ml half-saturated ammonium sulfate and then was counted in a well-scintillation detector, model DS-202V, Nuclear Chicago.[9] The anti-TNP results are expressed as "per cent antigen bound" at a fixed value of antigen added. This requires less serum than the alternative method of comparing antiserums at a fixed value of per cent antigen bound, such as 33%. The amount of antigen bound by normal serum was determined during each test and varied from 1% to 5%. The per cent antigen bound by normal serum was then subtracted for each sample before further computations. *Anti-DNP:* Similar techniques were employed for anti-DNP determinations and the values are expressed as "μg antibody/ml of serum" which is relative to a standard antiserum. *Anti-sheep erythrocyte responses:* The localized hemolysis-in-gel technique of Hildemann and Pinkerton (16) utilizing Ionagar 2[10] was employed to detect direct plaque-forming cells and the results are expressed as plaques/10×10^6 spleen cells at 4 days after immunization. *Anti-F_1 spleen cell antibodies:* To check for alloantigenic determinants or self-antigens similar to any of the haptens utilized, these alloimmune sera were also tested for possible increased binding of TNP_5-BSA by the techniques listed above.

Buffers. The phosphate buffer used was prepared from the formula of Gomori (17) and was 0.1 M, pH 7.1. Phosphate saline is this same buffer diluted 1:10 in 0.15 M NaCl. The borate buffer used in these experiments had a pH of 8.3 and an ionic strength of 0.1[11] (18).

Skin grafting. (A.BY × A/Jax) F_2 males and A.BY, A/Jax, and F_1 hybrid control males each received two 10-mm orthotopic skin grafts: an A/Jax graft was placed superiorly and an A.BY graft inferiorly by the technique of Thoenes (19). Similarly, (C57BL/10 × B10.A) F_2 females and C57BL/10, B10.A and F_1 hybrid female controls each received a B10.A and a C57BL/10 graft. The grafts were scored for acute rejection within 16 days as evidence of *H-2* disparities.

Statistical comparisons. The anti-hapten binding capacity values obtained from the various tested strains were compared by using Student's t distribution assuming unequal variances. The anti-sheep erythrocyte responses were compared using the Mann-Whitney test, and $p = 0.05$ was considered a significant difference.

RESULTS

Preliminary experiments using 10 animals each of the A/Jax A.BY, C57BL/10, B10.A, and B10.LP-*a* strains indicated substantial differences in response to TNP-MSA, which appeared to be determined by the *H-2* locus. Further experiments using at least 15 mice of each sex for the parent and F_1 strains, and 60 to 100 of each sex for the F_2's are reported here.

Anti-TNP results. The results of immunizing

[7] Sherwood Medical Industries, a division of American Hospital Supply Co., Evanston, Ill. 60201. Distributed by Scientific Products.

[8] 125-Iodine, CN 5352, Iso/Serve Division, Cambridge Nuclear Corp., Cambridge, Mass. 02139.

[9] DS-202V, Nuclear Chicago Corp., Des Plaines, Ill. 60018.

[10] Ionagar #2, Oxoid, Oxo Ltd., London, England.

[11] Borate buffer: 6.184 g boric acid; 9.356 g borax (sodium tetraborate); 4.384 g sodium chloride; make up to 1 liter, pH 8.3.

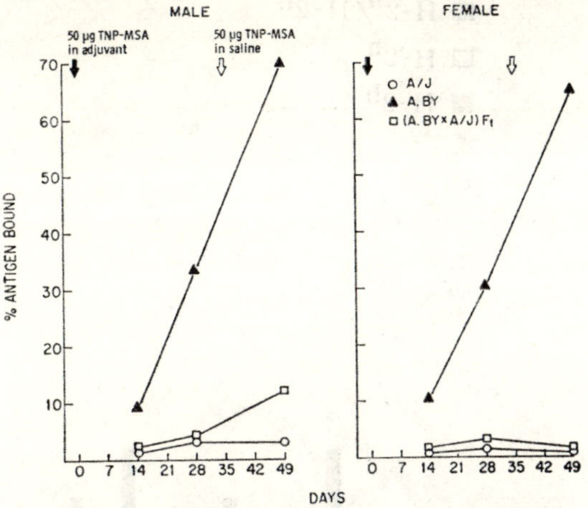

Figure 1. Comparative antigen-binding capacity (ABC) assays of individual sera from A/J, A.BY and (A.BY × A/J) F_1 mice as a function of per cent of antigen (TNP-BSA) bound and the time after immunization.

A/Jax, A.BY, and (A.BY × A/Jax) F_1 with 50 µg TNP_{11}-MSA in complete Freund's adjuvant followed 5 weeks later by 50 µg in saline are shown in Figure 1. Both sexes of the A.BY (H-2^b) strain gave significantly higher antibody responses to TNP-MSA than did either its H-2 disparate congenic partner A/Jax (H-2^a) or their (A.BY × A/Jax) F_1 progeny. A striking feature of these immune responses was the complete lack of overlap between the two parent strains and the considerable overlap of the low responder parent (A/Jax) with the F_1. Moreover, Figure 2 shows that strain C57BL/10, which also carries the H-2^b allele, gave a much

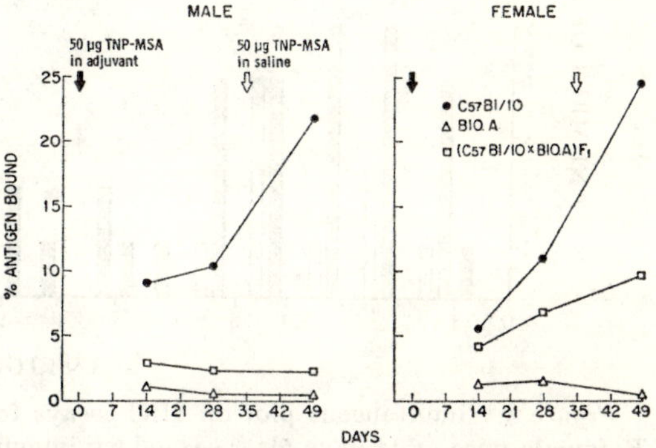

Figure 2. Comparative ABC assays on sera from B10.A, C57BL/10 and (C57BL/10 × B10.A) F_1 mice as a function of per cent of antigen (TNP-BSA) bound and the time after immunization.

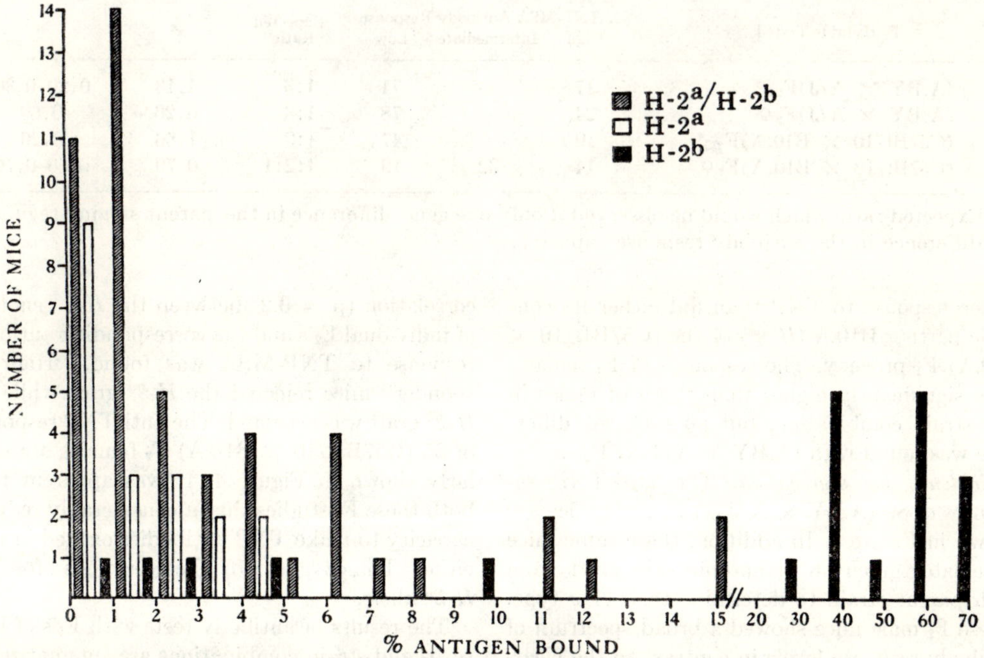

Figure 3. Simultaneous plot of ABC assays for anti-TNP-BSA produced by (A.BY × A/J) F_2 males at 14 days after secondary immunization in relation to H-2 type determined by skin grafting.

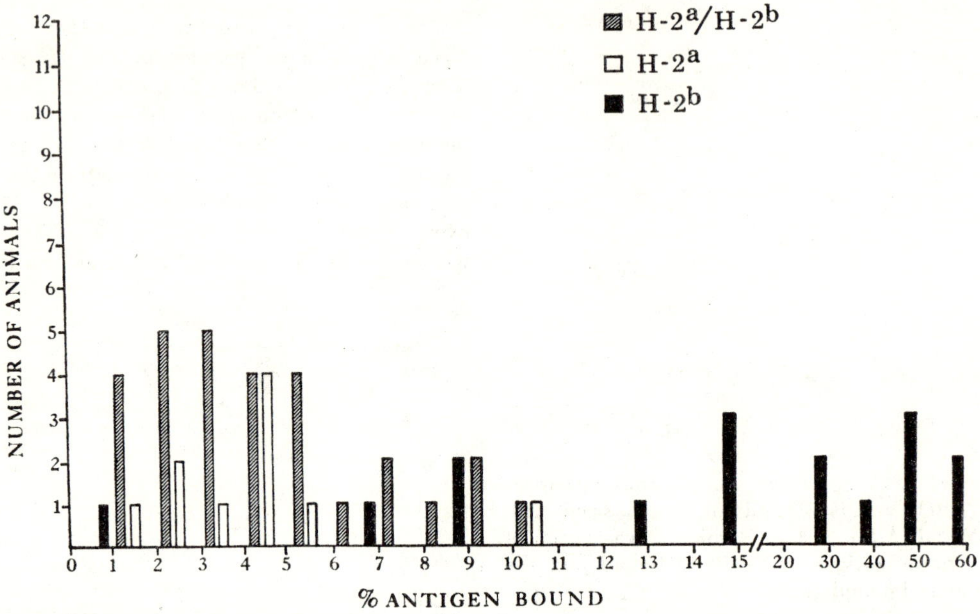

Figure 4. Simultaneous plot of ABC assays for anti-TNP-BSA produced by (C57BL/10 × B10.A) F_2 female mice at 14 days after secondary immunization in relation to *H-2* types.

TABLE II

Comparative ABC assays for anti-TNP antibodies produced by four groups of F_2 mice as "high," "intermediate," or "low responders"

F_2 Hybrids Tested	X-TNP-MSA Antibody Response High	Intermediate	Low	Expected Ratio[a]	χ^2	p
(A.BY × A/J)F_2♂	17		71	1:3	1.13	0.20–0.30
(A.BY × A/J)F_2♀	24		78	1:3	0.26	0.60
(C57Bl/10 × B10.A)F_2♂	19		47	1:3	1.66	0.20
(C57Bl/10 × B10.A)F_2♀	14	32	19	1:2:1	0.79	0.60–0.70

[a] Expected ratio which would be observed if only one gene difference in the parent strains regulated the difference in the antibody response capacity.

better response to TNP than did either its congenic partner B10.A (*H-2*^{a}) or the (C57BL/10 × B10.A) F_1 progeny. The responses of F_1 females were significantly higher than those of males in this strain combination, but no such sex difference was found with (A.BY × A/Jax) F_1's.

Evidence for segregation. The anti-TNP responses of 89 (A.BY × A/Jax) F_2 male mice are shown in Figure 3. In addition, these same mice were later given an orthotopic skin graft from each parent strain to determine their *H-2* type. These F_2 male mice showed a broad spectrum of antibody response levels in contrast to the clear-cut differences characteristic of the parent strains. However, an obvious and statistically significant correlation (p = 0.2) between the *H-2* genotype of individual F_2's and the corresponding antibody response to TNP-MSA was found. "High responder" mice rejected the *H-2*^{a} graft while the *H-2*^{b} graft was accepted. The anti-TNP responses of 55 (C57BL/10 × B10.A) F_2 females are similarly shown in Figure 4. It was apparent from both these F_2 studies that a considerably reduced capacity to make TNP antibodies existed in mice either homozygous or heterozygous for the *H-2*^{a} allele.

The results of antibody tests with F_2's of both sexes and strain combinations are summarized in Table II. The observed ratio of F_2's found to be high responders was compared to the ratio ex-

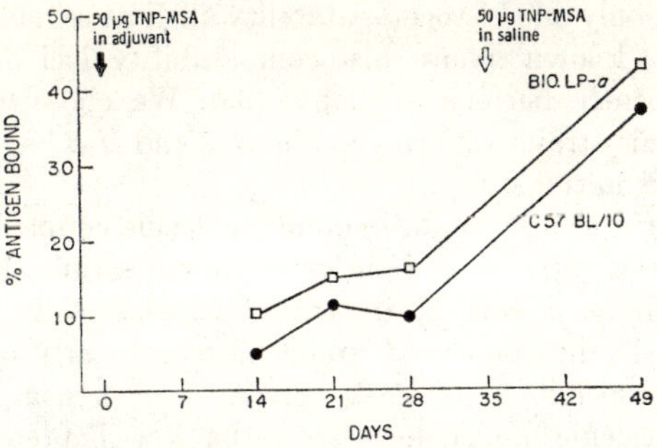

Figure 5. Comparative ABC assays done on individual sera from C57BL/10 (H-3^a) and B10.LP-*a* (H-3^b) mice as a function of TNP-BSA binding and time after immunizations.

pected if only one gene locus determined the difference in antibody response. The anti-TNP response of each F_2 mouse was ranked within its group and then compared with the parental and F_1 responses. When a few individual F_2 responses were found to be intermediate between those of the parental strains, an equal number of these responses were added to each "high" or "low" responder group. The strains of mice that were low responders to TNP did exhibit a measurable increase in the TNP-BSA binding capacity of their serums when compared to the pre-immunization levels. The observed ratios of the F_2 mice which are classified as "high" or "low" responders as shown in Table II are consistent with the hypothesis that the single autosomal gene difference between the parent strains is responsible for the distinctive immune responses of the F_2's to TNP-MSA.

A comparison of the anti-TNP response of C57BL/10 (H-2^b, H-3^a) and its H-3 disparate congenic partner, B10. LP-*a* (H-2^b, H-3^b), is shown in Figure 5. We observed no significant differences in the responses of these strains to TNP-MSA.

Other haptens. All strains immunized with 50 µg DNP-MSA responded similarly to DNP except C57BL/10 as shown in Figure 6. The C57BL/10 mice showed higher antibody levels than B10.A and B10.LP-*a* at all times tested. These congenic interstrain differences presumably reflect a synergistic superiority of the differential H-2^b, H-3^a genotype of C57BL/10 mice. Upon immunization with arsanilate-azo MSA, as illustrated in Figure 7, there were no significant differences in the anti-ARS responses of the strains tested.

Sheep erythrocyte antigens. Both A/Jax (H-2^a) and B10.A (H-2^a) mice gave a significantly higher response at the peak period of 4 days after immunization with 5×10^6 sheep red cells than

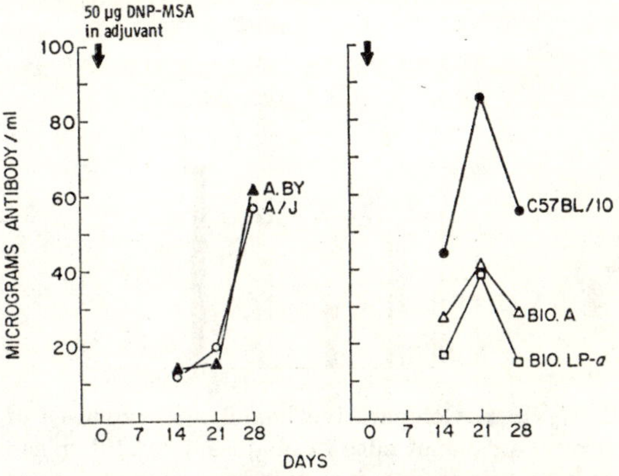

Figure 6. Comparative ABC assays done on sera from the listed strains as a function of µg anti-DNP-BSA/ml of serum and the time after immunization.

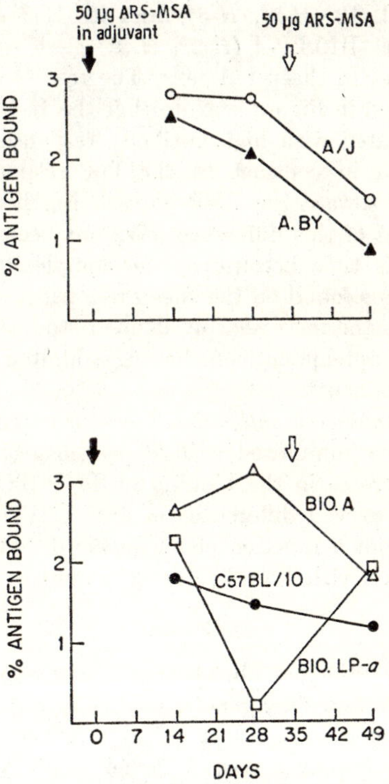

Figure 7. ABC capacity of serum from A/J, A.BY, C57BL/10, B10.A, and B10. LP-*a* comparing the per cent Ars-MSA bound and the time after immunizations.

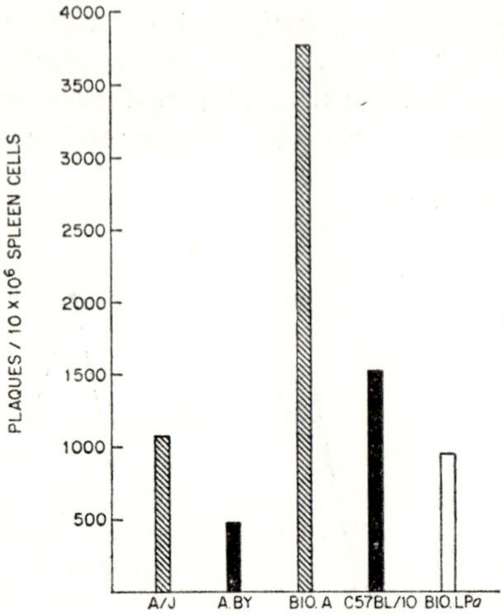

Figure 8. **Comparative hemolysin responses of several strains of mice in plaques/10 $\times$ 10⁶ spleen cells at 4 days after immunization with sheep red cells.**

did their respective H-2 disparate congenic partners A.BY (H-2^b) and C57BL/10 (H-2^b). Strain C57BL/10 (H-2^b, H-3^a) and its H-3 disparate partner B10.LP-*a* (H-2^b, H-3^b) gave similar responses to sheep red cells. The results are summarized in Figure 8. Note that the H-2^a allele is associated with high antibody responses in this system in contrast to the low responsiveness found toward the TNP hapten. Further genetic studies of this difference have not been pursued at this time because of the complexity of the antigens found on the sheep red cell in comparison to the more sharply defined studies possible with haptenic antigens having a limited range of determinants.

F_1 spleen cell antibodies. The four parent strains of mice immunized with F_1 spleen cells showed no increase in the binding of TNP-BSA. Thus, the observed differences in anti-TNP responses were not a function of allogeneic differences associated with TNP-like determinants.

DISCUSSION

The principal objective of these experiments was to study the genetic control of antibody responses in mice to chemically-defined antigens which display a narrow range of determinants. To obtain maximum definition of the genetic basis of an immune response it is desirable to compare inbred strains of animals which have single genetic differences. Animals which differ by only one histocompatability allele at several of the known mouse histocompatability loci have recently become available (20). We chose congenic strains differing at the *H-2* and *H-3* loci for this initial study.

By using a small haptenic molecule coupled to presumptively non-antigenic mouse serum albumin as a carrier, it was anticipated that the antibodies produced would be more nearly hapten-specific than if the carrier were a complex antigenic molecule. Given the low hapten-to-protein molar ratios in the present experiments, the albumin molecule should have undergone less conformational change than if it were highly substituted. Albumin molecules which have undergone considerable stereochemical changes might be potentially antigenic even in the strain of origin.

The assay system measured the total antigen-binding capacity of whole antiserum. However, this sensitive assay may not reveal all of the antibody present or even the full spectrum of antibodies produced. Several investigators have compared the antigen-binding capacity assay with other quantitative tests of antibody production (18, 21). Tests that measure the primary interaction between antigen and antibody were compared with those, such as agglutination or precipitation, which depend on secondary or tertiary reactions. In experiments dependent upon the presence or absence of detectable antibody, the protocol should ideally include at least one primary test, such as the antigen-binding assay used in these experiments (21). In studies of the type reported here, tests of antigen-binding capacity have the distinct advantage of being adaptable to albumin antigens and to small quantities of serum as obtained by individual serial bleedings of mice. The results are expressed as "per cent antigen bound" at a fixed level of antigen added; this uses less serum than methods which compare the antigen bound relative to a fixed per cent antigen bound. In antigen systems using branched synthetic polypeptide antigens, such as (T,G)-A--L (22), adding a fixed amount of antigen tended only to minimize differences among the sera tested relative to the 30% obtained using a fixed per cent antigen bound.

The results indicate that the immune response of mice to TNP-MSA is substantially influenced by the H-2 locus. Homozygosity for the H-2^b allele leads to high responsiveness even on diverse strain backgrounds. However, either homozygosity or heterozygosity for the *H-2^a^* allele leads to low responsiveness. Surprisingly there were no overlaps in the individual responses of the two pairs of parent strains to TNP-MSA. The homozygous $H\text{-}2^b$ animals gave a clearly superior immune response compared to the $H\text{-}2^a$ congenic partner in all strains tested.

Immunization of (A.BY × A/Jax) F_1 mice with TNP-MSA yielded significantly lower antibody responses than those obtained in the A.BY parent strain, but similar to those of the low responding A/Jax parent. F_1 male antibody production reached a level higher than was found in F_1 females only upon secondary immunization, i.e., at 49 days (Fig. 1). However, individual F_1 male sera showed considerable overlap with the low responding parent. By contrast, the responses of (C57BL/10 × B10.A) F_1 hybrid females were significantly higher than those of F_1 males over the entire testing period of 14 to 49 days. Also, the F_1 female antibody levels were clearly intermediate between those of the "low" and "high" responder parent strain females. Thus, the $H\text{-}2^a/H\text{-}2^b$ heterozygote on a C57BL/10 genetic background reveals a substantial deviation, especially in the females, from the dominant *vs* recessive behavior of these same alleles on the A/Jax genetic background. The quantitative anti-TNP response then must involve gene-product interactions and physiologic differences which go beyond the control of the *H-2* locus. One or more non-*H-2* alleles distinguishing these two pairs of congenic strains could of course affect the anti-TNP biosynthesis. Whether the molecular composition or classes of antibodies produced by F_1's are the same as that of the parent strains remains to be determined.

Considerable evidence has accumulated from studies of rodents that females often give more vigorous immune responses than do males (23). Since sex-influenced differences in alloimmune reactivity of mice were recently found to disappear after adrenalectomy or combined adrenalectomy-gonadectomy (24), corticosteroid hormonal regulation of certain immune responses may regularly occur. However, no significant sex differences in responsiveness to TNP-MSA were found in the present study within any of the parent strains tested. In the past, a clearly intermediate response like that found in (C57BL/10 × B10.A) F_1 female mice might simply have been attributed to "imperfect or incomplete penetrance" of the "dominant" $H\text{-}2^a$ allele. Many quite different mechanisms could come under the umbrella of variable penetrance, so nothing is really explained by invoking this concept. Certainly $H\text{-}2^a/H\text{-}2^b$ heterozygosity or allelic interaction *per se* was not the basis of the intermediate responses. Shifts in minor and obscure environmental factors may modify the activity of many genes and their products, but the present experiments were designed to minimize all non-genetic variables.

Whenever dominant unresponsiveness is found it becomes important to rule out the possibility that the hapten is found among the normal self-constitutents of the low responder host. To test for such "antigen sharing," we hyperimmunized the four parent strains with F_1 spleen cells. The resulting alloantiserum was then tested to determine if there was an increase in the binding of TNP-BSA over the normal background levels. The binding actually obtained with each such alloimmune serum was equal to or less than that of normal serum from unimmunized animals of the same sex and age.

The results of testing the four groups of F_2 mice for their respective anti-TNP-MSA responses were consistent with the hypothesis that a single gene difference is responsible for the observed interstrain dichotomy in antibody production. Homozygosity for the $H\text{-}2^b$ allele led to high responsiveness, whereas either heterozygosity or homozygosity for $H\text{-}2^a$ led to low responsiveness irrespective of strain background. Two of the four groups of F_2 mice, i.e., (A.BY × A/Jax) F_2 males and (C57BL/10 × B10.A) F_2 females, were tested by orthotopic skin grafting to determine their H-2 genotype for correlation with their previously determined levels of antibody production. There was a significant positive correlation in both F_2 groups between the H-2 type and the anti-TNP level as predicted by the responses of the parental and F_1 hybrid strains. In the (A.BY × A/Jax) F_2 group of 89 mice there were only 5 whose antibody responses were lower than would have been predicted from their possession of the $H\text{-}2^b$ allele. Among the 55 (C57BL/10 × B10.A) F_2 females, 5 gave similarly exceptional antibody responses. Thus the exceptional animals comprised about 5% to 8% of the total F_2's in each group. It is noteworthy that none of the exceptional animals produced an antibody response higher than expected. The possibility that some of these animals represent crossovers within the *H-2* region is being studied by testing the immune response and histocompatability type of the progeny from matings with the high responder parent strains. If a crossover occurred, the location of the sub-locus responsible for the difference in anti-TNP synthesis could be determined by use of antisera specific for several H-2 antigens and known crossovers within the H-2 region. However, it is quite unlikely that so many crossovers could have occurred within the *H-2* locus. These exceptions probably respresent the additive effects of very few crossovers plus animals that received merely improper immunizations or were adversely affected by environmental and physiologic factors at the time of testing.

Genetic linkage studies of this interstrain difference in antibody responsiveness would be of considerable interest. Perhaps the difference reported here is, in fact, controlled by the *Ir-1* locus. This locus has been mapped in the middle of the *H-2* locus on the basis of results with nine recombinant strains. The results indicate that *Ir-1* lies to the right of *Ss* between the *Ss* gene and the genes coding for the H-2 specificities 11 and 31 (H. O. McDevitt, D. C. Shreffler and J. H. Stimpfling, to be published). It is surprising to find that this single region of the ninth chromosome of the mouse controls numerous cell surface antigenic specificities, a serum protein and the ability to make specific antibodies to several unrelated antigens (25, 26).

The present study does not indicate which step in the overall sequence of events leading to specific serum antibody production to TNP is controlled by the *H-2* or a closely linked locus. A difference at the level of recognition of specific foreignness or ability to synthesize anti-TNP antibody is ruled out because all tested strains produced measurable concentrations of antibodies to all of the antigens inoculated. Further insights may be forthcoming in some systems by adoptive transfer of antibody-producing cells into irradiated recipients. By this approach Tyan *et al.* (26) have tentatively concluded that the *Ir-1* locus controls the immune response to the branched multichain, synthetic polypeptide antigen (T,G)-A--L, at the stage of antibody formation.

The mechanism of action of the genes associated with the complex *H-2* locus which govern the immune response to TNP-MSA invites further investigation. The linkage of this "antibody locus" to known regions of the *H-2* locus also invites study. A better understanding of specific gene action in relation to well-defined immune responses should also illuminate the basis of inherited differences in susceptibility to a variety of infectious diseases.

Acknowledgments. The authors acknowledge the expert technical assistance of Mrs. Lynda Frautnick. We also thank Dr. G. N. Trump, Department of Genetics, University of Hawaii, Honolulu, Hawaii, for supplying the standard anti-DNP serum. Computing assistance was obtained from the Health Science Computing Facility, University of California at Los Angeles, sponsored by National Institutes of Health Grant FR-3.

REFERENCES

1. Herzenberg, L. A., McDevitt, H. O. and Herzenberg, L. A., Ann. Rev. Genet., *2:* 209, 1968.
2. Hildemann, W. H., in *Immunogenetics*, Chapter 2 Holden-Day, San Francisco, 1969.
3. McDevitt, H. O. and Chintz, A., Science, *163:* 1207, 1969.
4. Gasser, D. L., J. Immun., *103:* 66, 1969.
5. Green, I., Paul, W. E. and Benacerraf, B., J. Exp. Med., *128:* 1, 1967.
6. Pinchuck, P. and Maurer, P. H., J. Exp. Med., *122:* 673, 1965.
7. Rittenberg, M. B. and Amkraut, A. A., J. Immun., *97:* 421, 1966.
8. Korner, A. and Debro, J. R., Nature, *178:* 1067, 1956.
9. Benacerraf., B. and Levine, B. B., J. Exp. Med., *115:* 1023, 1962.
10. Kabat, E. A., in *Kabat and Mayer's Experimental Immunochemistry*, 2nd Ed., pp. 476–482, Charles C Thomas, Springfield, Ill., 1961.
11. Kabat, E. A., in Kabat and Mayer's Experimental Immunochemistry, 2nd Ed., pp. 556–558, Charles C Thomas, Springfield, Ill., 1961.
12. Amkraut, A. A., Garvey, J. S. and Campbell, D. H., J. Exp. Med., *124:* 293, 1966.
13. Carsten, M. E. and Eisen, H. N., J. Amer. Chem. Soc., *75:* 4451, 1953.
14. Campbell, D. H., Garvey, J. S., Cremer, N. E. and Sussdorf, D. H., in *Methods in Immunology*, pp. 79–82, W. A. Benjamin, Inc., New York, 1964.
15. McConahay, P. J. and Dixon, F. J., J. Infect. Dis., *103:* 239, 1958.

16. Hildemann, W. H. and Pinkerton, W., J. Exp. Med., *124:* 885, 1966.
17. Gomori, G., in *Methods in Enzymology*, Edited by S. P. Colowick and N. O. Kaplan, Vol. 1, p. 138, Academic Press, Inc., N. Y., 1955.
18. Farr, R. S., J. Infect. Dis., *103:* 239, 1958.
19. Thoenes, G. H., Proc. Soc. Exp. Biol. Med., *138:* 68, 1969.
20. Snell, G. D. and Stimpfling, J. H., in *Biology of the Laboratory Mouse*, Edited by E. L. Green, Chap. 24, pp. 457–491, McGraw-Hill, New York, 1966.
21. Minden, P., Bascome, F. A. and Farr, R. S., J.Immun., *102:* 832, 1969.
22. McDevitt, H. O. and Sela, M., J. Exp. Med., *122:* 517, 1965.
23. Hildemann, W. H. and Cohen, N., in *Histocompatibility Testing*, Edited by E. S. Curtoni, P. L. Mattiuz and R. M. Tosi, p. 13, E. Munksgaard, Copenhagen, 1967.
24. Graff, R. J., Lappé, M. A. and Snell, G. D., Transplanation, *7:* 105, 1969.
25. Snell, G. D. and Stimpfling, J. H., in *Biology of the Laboratory Mouse*, Edited by E. L. Green, Chap. 8, pp. 87–150, McGraw-Hill, New York, 1966.
26. Tyan, M. L., McDevitt, H. O. and Herzenberg, L. A., Transplant. Proc., *1:* 548, 1969.

THE JOURNAL OF IMMUNOLOGY
Vol. 105, No. 1, July 1970

Printed in U.S.A.

THE EFFECT OF HETEROLOGOUS ANTILYMPHOCYTE SERUM (ALS) ON THE HUMORAL ANTIBODY RESPONSE TO *SALMONELLA TYPHI* "H" ANTIGEN AND BOVINE SERUM ALBUMIN[1]

EUGENE M. LANCE[2]

From the National Institute for Medical Research, Mill Hill, London, England, and The Hospital for Special Surgery-Cornell University Medical Center, New York, N. Y.

Received for publication December 8, 1969

The immunosuppressive effects of heterologous ALS were studied in mice immunized with a bacterial (*Salmonella typhi* "H") and a protein (BSA) antigen. The principal conclusions are that depression of the primary response depends upon the administration of ALS prior to antigen, the magnitude of depression varies directly with ALS dose and inversely with antigen dose, the secondary response is little affected, and ALS pretreatment may set the stage for the induction of tolerance. These results are discussed in relation to current knowledge of the humoral immune response and the mode of action of ALS.

The marked efficiency with which ALS opposes immune reactions of the cell-mediated type has been repeatedly documented (1–4). Humoral responses appear to be less effectively suppressed although relatively fewer studies have been devoted solely to this area (5–9).

In this report we investigate the effect in mice of heterologous antilymphocyte serum on the humoral antibody response to a bacterial and protein antigen. Attention is focused on the kinetics and magnitude of response, the effect of antigen dosage, the use of ALS to abet tolerance induction and the differential effect in virgin and primed animals.

MATERIALS AND METHODS

Mice. Adult CBA mice, 3 to 4 months old, were obtained from the breeding colony at the National Institute for Medical Research.

Antisera. ALS was raised in rabbits by the intravenous injection of mouse thymocytes according to a previously published method (10, 11). Gamma G (γG) fractions of ALS and normal rabbit serum (NRS) were prepared by passing a 50% ammonium sulphate insoluble cut of the serum through a column of DEAE-cellulose after both protein and column were equilibrated with 0.02 M phosphate buffer (pH 7.4). The protein eluted at 0.02 M phosphate was shown to be γG by immunoelectrophoresis. The whole antiserum or γG fractions were always administered subcutaneously.

Antigens. Salmonella. Animals were immunized by the intraperitoneal injection of 0.2 ml of a standard suspension of *Salmonella typhi* "H" antigen (Burroughs Wellcome and Co., Tuckahoe, N. Y.). Challenge was usually effected with the same dose but occasionally more dilute suspensions were used. The assay measured agglutinating antibody and was carried out on sera obtained from the median tail artery of mice by preparing serial twofold dilutions in 0.25 ml of phosphate-buffered saline (PBS), pH 7.2. To these dilutions, 0.2 ml of the "H" antigen suspension was added, mixed by vigorous shaking, incubated in a 37°C water bath for 30 min, and then stored overnight at 4°C. The titer for each sample was taken as the highest dilution that caused grossly visible agglutination and is expressed as the $\log_2$ of the reciprocal of that dilution.

Bovine serum albumin (BSA). The antigen was prepared from crystalline BSA (Armour Laboratories, Chicago, Ill.) and was used either as the saline solution (BSA-saline) or in a form precipi-

[1] This work was supported by Graduate Training Grant TI-AM 5414 from The National Institute for Arthritis and Metabolism, and by Grant AI-08750-01 from the National Institute of Allergy and Infectious Diseases, National Institutes of Health.

[2] Present address: The Hospital for Special Surgery, 535 East 70th Street, New York, N. Y. 10021.

TABLE I

The effect of ALS on the response to "H" antigen

	No. of Animals	Geometric Mean Titer (log_2 units)	Range
Normal primary response			
Females	10	12.2	11–13
Males	10	13.0	11–15
Normal secondary response			
Females	10	17.7	16–19
Males	10	17.6	15–19
Effect of 1.5 ml of ALS			
Primary response	10	5.8	4–7
Reimmunization (secondary response)	10	12.5	8–17
Effect of 2.0 ml of ALS on the secondary response			
Primary response (no treatment)	12	9.4	8–11
Secondary response after			
NRS	6	12.8	10–14
ALS	6	10.0	9–11
Challenge delayed 1 month after			
NRS	10	15.2	13–18
ALS	10	16.6	14–19

tated with potassium alum (BSA-alum) (12). In some instances *Bordetella pertussis* was incorporated in the immunizing injection (13). Antigen was always given intraperitoneally and antiserum always by the subcutaneous route. The antibody assay was performed on sera obtained by bleeding mice from the median tail artery at intervals, and was carried out by the Mitchison modification (14) of the Farr technique (15). The results are expressed as the log_{10} of the antigen-binding capacity. CBA female mice were used in all these experiments.

RESULTS

Salmonella typhi "H" antigen. The dimensions of the normal primary and secondary response were determined in 10 male and 10 female CBA mice. Antigen was injected intraperitoneally on day 0 and again on day 28, and serum was collected 10 days following each antigen injection. The results are given in Table I, which summarizes the studies with this antigen. No difference in response was discerned between the sexes. The titer after the second antigen exposure is clearly greater than that observed after primary exposure.

The effect of ALS on the primary response. Ten female CBA mice received "H" antigen on day 0 and ALS 0.5 ml on day −1, followed by four injections of 0.25 ml on days +3, +5, +7, and +9. Three days after the last ALS injection, serum samples were obtained. A reduction in titer was found in all animals and the geometric mean score for the group was only 5.8. On day 26 a second injection of "H" antigen was given and the response was measured on day 36. There was an increased response in all animals, the group mean of 12.5 was still depressed compared to that of untreated controls. Thus ALS given just before and during the developing primary response caused a reduction in the amount of agglutinating antibody and impaired, albeit to a lesser extent, the response of animals so treated to a second contact with antigen.

The effect of ALS on the secondary response. Two groups of CBA male mice were primed with "H" antigen, and the mean titer at 10 days was 9.4. Four days later one group received ALS and the other NRS, 0.5 ml every 3rd day × 4. Three days after the last serum injection a second injection of "H" antigen was given, and the serum samples used to evaluate the secondary response were obtained 10 days thereafter. The titer in the ALS-treated group was approximately eightfold lower than that in the NRS-treated animals. A repetition on a larger scale would be necessary to establish this difference beyond question.

In a second experiment a longer interval was

TABLE II

The effect of ALS IgG (5.0 mg) on the primary response: timing (mean log ABC-μg/ml)

Day	Day 6	Day 11	Day 15	Day 20	Day 32	Day 49
ALS IgG 5.0 mg (5 animals/group)						
−3	−1.00	−0.25	0.69	0.72	1.01	1.09
	(0.00)[a]	(0.54)	(0.29)	(0.37)	(0.24)	(0.34)
−1	−1.00	−0.75	1.16	1.20	1.32	1.36
	(0.00)	(0.31)	(0.25)	(0.21)	(0.08)	(0.29)
0	−1.00	1.23	1.17	1.63	1.80	1.70
	(0.00)	(0.28)	(0.23)	(0.16)	(0.14)	(0.13)
1	−1.00	1.38	1.31	1.58	1.34	1.51
	(0.00)	(0.06)	(0.35)	(0.11)	(0.07)	(0.33)
3	−1.00	1.00	1.01	1.32	1.24	1.53
	(0.00)	(0.06)	(0.26)	(0.22)	(0.08)	(0.30)
NRS IgG 5.0 mg (5 animals/group)						
−3	−0.97	1.23	1.24	1.66	1.45	1.73
	(0.07)	(0.22)	(0.36)	(0.16)	(0.66)	(0.17)
−1	−0.95	1.25	1.34	1.71	1.45	1.54
	(0.08)	(0.05)	(0.31)	(0.09)	(0.08)	(0.26)
0	−0.84	1.04	1.43	1.61	1.67	1.64
	(0.23)	(0.15)	(0.22)	(0.05)	(0.02)	(0.27)
1	−0.94	1.38	1.17	1.49	1.43	1.47
	(0.08)	(0.19)	(0.33)	(0.09)	(0.03)	(0.28)
3	−1.00	1.13	1.18	1.30	1.45	1.41
	(0.00)	(0.10)	(0.14)	(0.06)	(0.13)	(0.26)

[a] Standard error.

allowed to elapse, and the second injection of "H" antigen was delayed until 1 month after the last serum injection. The titers of "H" agglutinins were determined 10 days after challenge. In this instance the response of ALS-treated animals was equal to, or slightly in excess of, NRS-treated controls.

Bovine serum albumin. The effect of ALS on the primary response was studied with regard to several variables.

Timing. Ten groups of mice were immunized with 5 mg BSA-alum on day 0, and parallel group pairs received 5.0 mg of either ALS IgG or NRS IgG on days −3, −1, 0, +1 and +3. Serum samples were collected on days +6, +10, +15, +20, +32 and +49. The results are presented in Table II and Figure 1. The kinetics and magnitude of the primary response in all groups receiving NRS IgG was comparable to that observed for untreated controls (data not given). ALS caused a reduction in the magnitude of response and a delay in the appearance of antibody only when given prior to antigen. The greatest suppression was found in animals that received ALS 3 days before immunization. Therefore, while ALS can significantly reduce the primary response to BSA, the timing is critical.

Dosage (*Fig. 2*). Eight groups of mice were immunized with 1 mg BSA-alum plus 2×10^9 *B. pertussis* organisms on day 0. On day −3, one group each received either 10 mg, 1 mg, or 0.1 mg of ALS IgG. Controls received the equivalent amount of NRS IgG. An additional group pair received 10 mg of either ALS IgG or NRS IgG on day 0. The degree of suppression was clearly a function of ALS dosage. The greatest suppression occurred with the 10-mg dose while the 0.1-mg dose produced only a transient delay in the elaboration of peak titers equivalent to controls. The influence of timing is again shown in this experiment. The degree of suppression achieved by 10 mg of ALS IgG given with antigen (day 0) was equivalent to that found by one-tenth as much ALS IgG given 3 days before antigen (data not given).

Antigen dosage. Eight groups of mice received

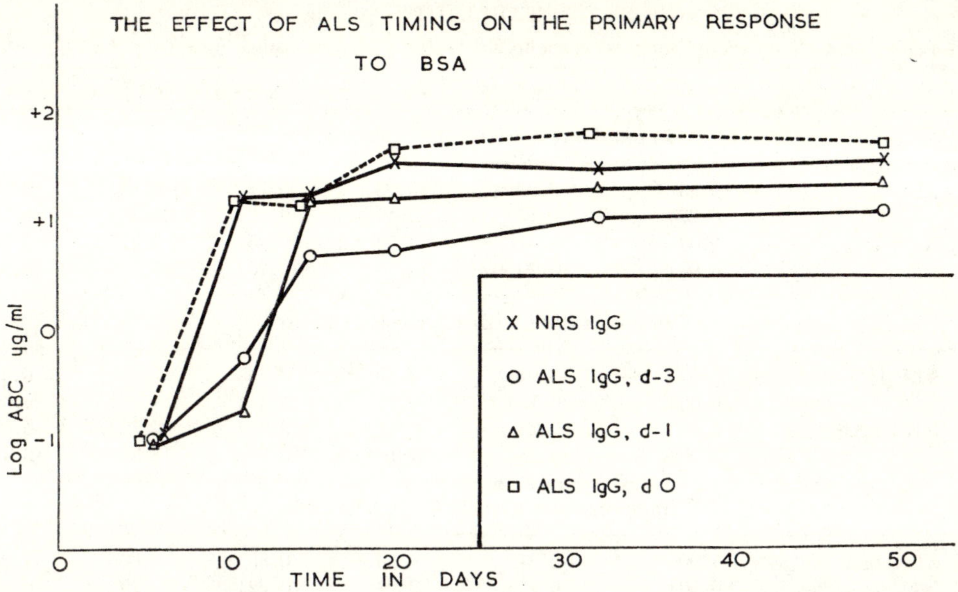

Figure 1. See text and Table III for details. The results for all groups receiving NRS IgG have been pooled and plotted as a single control line.

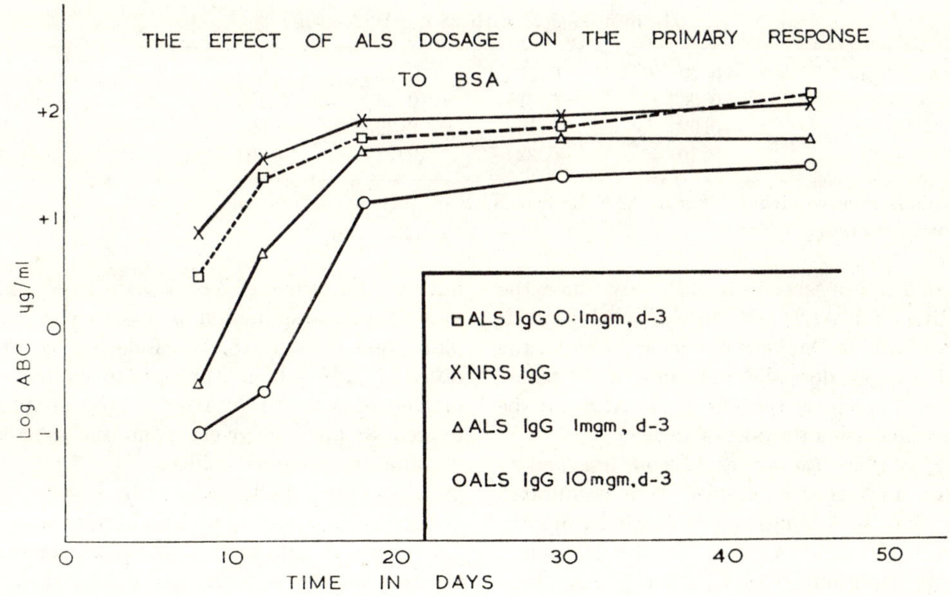

Figure 2. See text for details. The values for all groups receiving NRS IgG are once again pooled and plotted as a single control line.

increasing amounts of BSA-alum. Two groups each received 25 mg, 10 mg, 1 mg, or 0.1 mg of the precipitated protein. One of each group pair also received 5 mg of ALS IgG 3 days before immunization while controls received an equal amount of NRS IgG. Serum samples were collected 6, 10, 14, 20, 30 and 42 days after immunization. The overall responses for control animals in this experiment seemed lower than expected, but suppression was induced by ALS in the animals receiving 0.1, 1 and 10 mg of antigen (Table III). This took the form primarily of a

TABLE III

The effect of ALS on the primary response to BSA-alum: antigen dosage (mean log ABC-μg/ml)[a]

	Day 6	Day 10	Day 14	Day 20	Day 30	Day 42
Immunization with 0.1 mg BSA-alum						
ALS IgG	−0.83	0.00	0.29	0.77	0.34	0.77
	(0.27)[b]	(0.75)	(0.43)	(0.22)	(0.37)	(0.23)
NRS IgG	−1.00	0.41	0.70	0.85	0.42	0.85
	(0.00)	(0.20)	(0.10)	(0.20)	(0.15)	(0.25)
Immunization with 1.0 mg BSA-alum						
ALS IgG	−1.00	−0.02	0.37	0.96	0.66	0.98
	(0.00)	(0.18)	(0.16)	(0.34)	(0.20)	(0.02)
NRS IgG	−1.00	0.25	0.94	0.95	0.72	0.60
	(0.00)	(0.23)	(0.16)	(0.14)	(0.08)	(0.35)
Immunization with 10.0 mg BSA-alum						
ALA IgG	−1.00	−0.31	0.36	0.85	0.66	1.04
	(0.00)	(0.24)	(0.23)	(0.22)	(0.26)	(0.12)
NRS IgG	−1.00	0.15	0.49	0.83	0.52	—
	(0.00)	(0.37)	(0.73)	(0.36)	(0.35)	—
Immunization with 25 mg BSA-alum						
ALS IgG	−0.77	0.27	0.61	0.85	0.37	0.87
	(0.26)	(0.21)	(0.24)	(0.15)	(0.16)	(0.19)
NRS IgG	−0.92	0.19	0.39	0.69	0.35	0.57
	(0.15)	(0.22)	(0.28)	(0.26)	(0.21)	(0.20)

[a] Animals receive either 5 mg of ALS IgG or NRS on day −3 (6 animals/group).
[b] Standard error.

delay in the appearance of antibody since the peak titers for ALS and NRS-treated animals were comparable. Animals receiving ALS and the highest antigen dose did not show a depressed response. Therefore, the effects of ALS can be offset by increasing the dose of antigen.

The effect of a single dose of ALS on the secondary response. Two groups of mice were immunized with 5 mg of BSA-alum, and challenged 2 months later with 500 μg BSA-saline. On the day before challenge one group received 5 mg of ALS IgG. Serum samples for antibody titration were collected on days 0, 6, 10, 14, 20, 30 and 42 after challenge. A secondary response of equal magnitude and kinetics occurred in both groups, i.e., no suppression of the secondary response was observed (Table IV).

The use of ALS to abet the induction of tolerance to BSA. The general plan of the two experiments bearing on this point involved pretreatment of mice with a course of ALS known to be effective in abetting the induction of tolerance in a transplantation system (16, 17), followed by varying doses of BSA-saline. Appropriate controls were pretreated with NRS. After a lapse of time (intended to allow recovery from the generalized immunosuppression induced by ALS), both groups were challenged with either specific antigen (BSA-alum) or with an indifferent antigen (*S. typhi* "H" antigen). Again, an interval was allowed to elapse after which the mice were tested by a second injection of specific and indifferent antigen. The demonstration of the induction of tolerance to specific antigen would depend upon an inhibited response to BSA, but a normal response to "H" antigen in the ALS-treated group.

In the first experiment, 16 groups of mice received a total of 1.6 ml of either ALS or NRS in a decreasing dosage series over a 9-day interval.

TABLE IV

The effect of ALS on the secondary response to BSA-alum (mean log titer ABC μg/ml)

Day 6	Day 10	Day 14	Day 20	Day 30	Day 42
ALS IgG 5.0 mg on day −1 (10 animals/group)					
1.58 (0.10)[a]	2.05 (0.20)	2.01 (0.24)	1.76 (0.35)	1.48 (0.16)	1.45 (0.13)
Untreated controls					
1.66 (0.19)	1.79 (0.16)	1.70 (0.41)	1.82 (0.28)	1.46 (0.16)	1.61 (0.29)

[a] Standard error.

TABLE V

The use of ALS to abet tolerance induction to BSA

6 Animals/Group	Response to Test Dose of BSA (ABC μg/ml, Mean Log)	Response to Test Dose of *S. typhi* "H" Antigen (Mean Log_2 Reciprocal Dilution)
Priming with 0.1 mg BSA-saline × 3		
ALS	−0.72 (0.04)[a]	15.5 (15–16)[b]
NRS	Anaphylaxis 4 animals 0.74 (0.35)	15.8 (14–17)
Priming with 1.0 mg BSA-saline × 3		
ALS	−0.41 (0.62)	15.6 (14–17)
NRS	Anaphylaxis 5 animals 1.64 (0.00)	16.4 (13–17)
Priming with 10.0 mg BSA-saline × 3		
ALS	−0.35 (0.60)	15.5 (15–16)
NRS	Anaphylaxis all animals	15.0 (14–16)
Priming with 50.0 mg BSA-saline × 3		
ALS	−0.68 (0.27)	16.2 (15–17)
NRS	Anaphylaxis 4 animals 0.66 (0.58)	16.0 (15–17)

[a] Standard error.
[b] Range.

On days 10, 12 and 14 ALS- and NRS-treated animals received varying doses of BSA-saline: 0.1, 1, and 10 and 50 mg, respectively. On day 35, one pair of ALS- or NRS-treated animals at each BSA dose level received a challenge injection of BSA-alum plus 1 × 10^9 *B. pertussis*, while another pair received 0.2 ml of *S. typhi* "H" suspension. Three weeks later these animals received the test dose of antigen: 500 μg BSA-saline or 0.1 ml "H" antigen. Within 45 min of receiving the test dose of BSA, 85% of the mice that had been initially treated with NRS and BSA were dead. Only one mouse in the groups pretreated with ALS succumbed. At autopsy, the heart was empty of blood and the lungs and gut were congested and suffused with blood: findings that were compatible with anaphylactic shock. Ten days after the test dose of antigen, titrations for anti-BSA and anti-"H" antigen were performed (Table V). The response to "H" antigen was comparable in all groups regardless of the prior BSA-saline dosage, or pretreatment with ALS or NRS. However, those animals pretreated with NRS had titers of anti-BSA antibodies one

TABLE VI

The use of ALS to abet the induction of tolerance to BSA

10 Animals/ Group	Response to Challenge Dose of BSA-Alum (Mean Log ABC μg/ml)		Response to Test Dose BSA (Mean Log ABC μg/ml) (Day 11)	Response to "H" Antigen (Mean $\log_2$ Reciprocal Dilution)
	Day 6	Day 17		
	Priming with 0.25 mg BSA-saline × 3			
ALS	−0.68 (0.16)[a]	−0.04 (0.32)	0.69 (0.42)	14.8 (13–16)[b]
NRS	−0.03 (0.38)	0.95 (0.14)	1.34 (0.17)	15.4 (12–17)
	Priming with 2.5 mg BSA–saline × 3			
ALS	−0.75 (0.24)	−0.30 (0.50)	0.08 (0.45)	16.3 (14–18)
NRS	1.44 (0.42)	1.77 (0.29)	1.51 (0.24)	16.2 (15–18)
	Priming with 25.0 mg BSA–saline × 3			
ALS	−0.78 (0.17)	−0.57 (0.25)	−0.88 (0.38)	15.1 (12–18)
NRS	0.98 (0.19)	1.12 (0.22)	1.13 (0.11)	14.5 (11–17)

[a] Standard error.
[b] Range.

or two logs above the response of the ALS-treated animals. Because of the high attrition rate among the NRS-treated controls, this comparison is based upon an inadequate number, unless the differential susceptibility to anaphylaxis is accepted as an index of the greater antibody response to BSA in the NRS-pretreated animals.

In the second experiment, the priming doses of BSA-saline were 0.25, 2.5 and 25 mg, and the test doses of BSA and "H" were reduced: BSA-saline, 100 μg; "H", 0.01 ml. Antibody titrations were performed 6 and 17 days after challenge antigen, and 11 days after the test dose of antigen.

The response to "H" antigen both after challenge and test doses was comparable in all groups (Table VI). After both challenge and test doses of BSA, NRS-treated animals showed high titers of antibody to BSA (Fig. 3). To some extent, this response had been influenced by the amount of antigen used in priming, 2.5 mg × 3 giving the highest titers. All groups which had been pretreated with ALS showed a markedly diminished response in comparison to the appropriate controls. An inverse relationship between the degree of suppression and the primary dose of BSA-saline was readily apparent.

DISCUSSION

The principal findings that emerge from these studies may be summarized as follows. ALS inhibits the primary humoral response in mice to a variety of antigens. The degree of inhibition depends upon several factors, i.e., the amount of ALS, the timing between ALS and antigen and the amount of antigen. The relative timing between antigen and ALS is critical, for whereas ALS given prior to antigen is highly effective, ALS given with or after antigen is largely ineffective. Increasing doses of ALS exert greater inhibition upon the primary response, but, at least for "strong" immunogens, even massive doses of ALS do not completely abort this response. The effect of ALS can be countered to some extent by increasing the dose of antigen.

The effect of ALS upon the secondary response is far less than upon the primary response. In some examples slight immunosuppression was observed to follow massive treatment with ALS, but in others no suppression was found. Finally, ALS pretreatment appears to render animals susceptible to the induction of tolerance with a relatively weak antigen such as BSA. These findings (with the exception of the studies on antigen dosage and tolerance which have not been previously reported) are in substantial agreement with the observations of others on the effect of ALS on humoral antibody formation. Studies in mice (18), rats (7), and dogs (19) record suppression of the primary response to a variety of antigens. Therefore, this would appear to reflect a general property of ALS. The critical importance

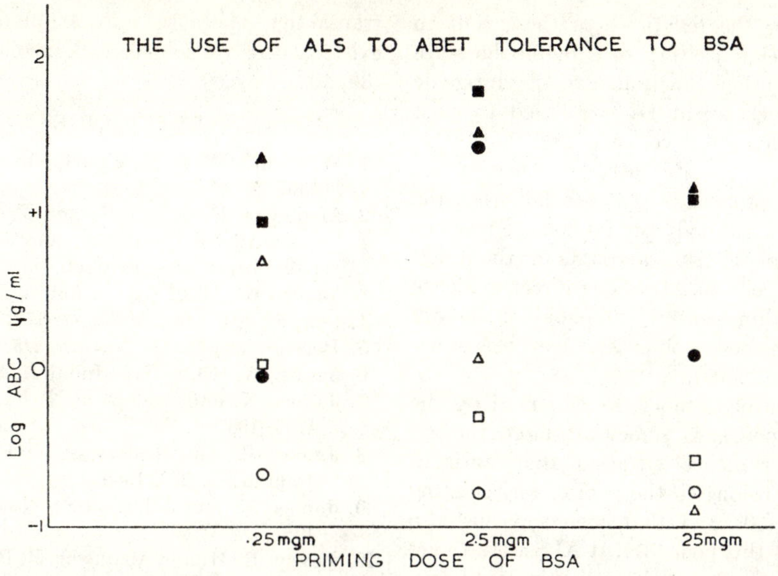

Figure 3. Diagrammatic representation of second BSA tolerance experiment. Solid symbols represent the mean response of NRS pretreated groups and open symbols represent the corresponding ALS pretreated groups. Circles denote the mean response at day 6, squares the response at day 17 and triangles the response 11 days after challenge. See text and Table VI for details.

of timing has been documented using BSA as antigen in rats, by James (6), and using SRBC as antigen in mice, by Berenbaum (5) and by Anderson, Dresser and Wortis (personal communication). The fact that ALS is much less effective in inhibition of the secondary response has also been widely reported (9, 18, 20, 21), and can be taken as an established fact.

Dresser and Mitchison (22) have recently reviewed the subject of tolerance and have pointed out that one class of antigens (including BSA) is immunogenic only within a certain dosage range. The doses used for priming in the current experiments would be expected to immunize, and did so in control animals. Pretreatment with ALS resulted in a failure of this same amount of BSA to immunize, and led to a subsequent inability to respond to this antigen at a time when normal responsiveness to an unrelated antigen could be demonstrated. Thus, the requirements for the demonstration of tolerance are fulfilled.

The success in this instance was achieved using an antigen known to be only feebly immunogenic, but recently Shellam achieved similar results with flagellin (23). The fact that ALS renders animals conducive to the induction of tolerance in both cell-mediated (16, 17) and humoral antibody systems is of interest for it suggests that the cell targets in both cases share common features.

ALS would appear to affect primarily the antigen-sensitive cell. The crucial importance of timing of ALS injection upon the primary response and the insensitivity of the secondary response provide the chief evidence for believing that this must be so, for it would appear that once the chain of events launched by antigen recognition is under way, ALS exerts little, or a greatly reduced, effect. The studies of Martin and Miller (24) strongly support this conclusion.

The fact that the immunosuppressive effect of ALS can be overcome by increasing the dose of antigen is extremely interesting and reminiscent of the similar observation of Sinclair and Elliott (25) after neonatal thymectomy. If, as Mitchison (26) proposes, the thymus-derived (antigen sensitive) cell cooperates by effecting a local concentration of antigen, then a rational explanation of the effect of antigen dosage in these two situations is readily available.

When antigen is administered parenterally the stage of antibody production appears to be subserved by cells which are resident in central lymphoid tissue (lymph nodes and spleen), or which take up residence in these sites after the recognition state (27). It is doubtful that the explanation for the resistance of these cells to ALS can be related either to a metabolic state attendant upon their function or to any antigenic differences which might be postulated to exist between antigen-sensitive cells and antibody-producing cells. An alternative explanation we should like to propose is that the fact that the cells engaged in antibody production are resident in central lymphoid tissue accounts for the resistance of these cells to ALS. The direct evidence that cells within central lymphoid tissue are protected from the action of ALS has been previously reported (28, 29).

The problem of memory, as measured by the secondary response, is somewhat more thorny. Considerable evidence suggests that antigen-sensitive cells belong to the pool of recirculating lymphocytes (30) and that memory cells also form a part of this pool (31). If ALS were to act specifically, or preferentially, on this population of cells, and if all the cells engaged in immunological memory were to belong to this pool, then ALS should be highly effective in suppressing the secondary humoral antibody response. The fact that this is not observed required explanation. Either cells subserving the function of memory are in themselves resistant to the effect of ALS or a substantial reservoir of memory cells must be held in addition to those which undoubtedly may be found in the mobilizable pool. Two lines of evidence suggest that some of the function of memory in humoral antibody transactions is subserved by units which do not belong to the mobilizible lymphocyte pool. The germinal center systems in both lymph nodes and spleen which are generated after initial contact with antigen are structures which participate heavily in the secondary response (32–34), and these areas are left intact following procedures which deplete the mobilizable pool, e.g., extracorporeal irradiation (35) and thoracic duct drainage (31). They are also spared after treatment with ALS (36–37) and, therefore, would remain to inaugurate a secondary response. The complementary evidence is that thoracic duct drainage has relatively little effect on the secondary humoral response (38) and if ALS were to act on the cells which would be drained away by a thoracic duct fistula, it too should not have a pronounced effect on the anamnestic response. These remarks concerning the effects of ALS on immunologic memory are strictly confined to humoral antibody transactions, because quite a different situation exists with relation to cell-mediated systems (39, 40).

REFERENCES

1. Woodruff, M. F. A., Transplantation, *5:* 1127, 1967.
2. Medawar, P. B., in *Human Transplantation*, Edited by F. Rapaport and J. Dausset, p. 501, Grune and Stratton Inc., N. Y., 1968.
3. James, K., Clin. Exp. Immun., *2:* 615, 1968.
4. Sell, S., Ann. Int. Med., *71:* 177, 1969.
5. Berenbaum, M. C., Nature, *215:* 1481, 1967.
6. James, K., Clin. Exp. Immun., *2:* 685, 1967.
7. James, K. and Anderson, N. F., Nature, *213:* 1195, 1967.
8. James, K. and Anderson, N. F., Clin. Exp. Immun., *3:* 227, 1968.
9. James, K. and Jubb, V. S., Nature, *215:* 367, 1967.
10. Levey, R. H. and Medawar, P. B., Ann. N. Y. Acad. Sci., *129:* 164, 1966.
11. Jooste, S. V., Lance, E. M., Levey, R. H., Medawar, P. B., Ruszkiewicz, M., Sharman, R. and Taub, R. N., Immunology, *15:* 697, 1968.
12. Proom, H., J. Path. Bact., *55:* 419, 1943.
13. Dresser, D. W., Immunology, *9:* 261, 1965.
14. Mitchison, N. A., Proc. Roy. Soc. Ser. B, *161:* 275, 1964.
15. Farr, R. S., J. Infect. Dis., *103:* 239, 1958.
16. Lance, E. M. and Medawar, P. B., Transplant. Proc., *1:* 429, 1968.
17. Lance, E. M. and Medawar, P. B., Proc. Roy. Soc. Ser. B, *173:* 447, 1969.
18. Gray, J. G., Monaco, A. P. and Russell, P. S., Surg. Forum, *15:* 142, 1964.
19. Atai, M. and Kelly, W., Surg. Gynec. Obstet., *125:* 13, 1967.
20. Monaco, A. P., Wood, M. L., Gray, J. G. and Russell, P. S., J. Immun., *96:* 229, 1966.
21. Lance, E. M., In *Cell-bound Immunity with Special Reference to Anti-lymphocyte Serum and the Immunotherapy of Cancer*, Les Congres et Colloques de l'Universite de Liege, *43:* 103, 1967.
22. Dresser, D. W. and Mitchison, N. A., Advances Immun., *8:* 129, 1968.
23. Shellam, G. R., Immunology, *17:* 267, 1969.
24. Martin, W. J. and Miller, J. F. A. P., Lancet, *2:* 1285, 1967.
25. Sinclair, N. R. and Elliot, E. V., Immunology, *15:* 325, 1968.
26. Mitchison, N. A., Fed. Proc., *29:* 222, 1970.
27. Ford, W. L. and Gowans, J. L., Proc. Roy. Soc. Ser. B, *168:* 244, 1967.
28. Taub, R. N. and Lance, E. M., Immunology, *15:* 633, 1968.

29. Lance, E. M., J. Exp. Med., *130:* 49, 1969.
30. Gowans, J. L. and McGregor, D. D., Prog. Allerg., *9:* 1, 1965.
31. Gowans, J. L. and McGregor, D. D., in *Immunopathology, IIIrd International Symposium*, Schwabe, Basel, p. 89, 1963.
32. White, R. G., in *Mechanisms of Antibody Formation*, Czechoslovak Academy of Sciences, Prague, p. 25, 1960.
33. Thorbecke, G. J., Asofsky, R. M., Hochwald, G. M. and Siskind, G. W., J. Exp. Med., *116:* 295, 1962. (See also Wakefield, J. D. and Thorbecke, G. J., J. Exp. Med., *128:* 153, 171.)
34. Cottier, H., Odartchenko, N., Keiser, G., Hess, M. and Stoner, R. D., Ann. N. Y. Acad. Sci., *113:* 612, 1964.
35. Cronkite, E. P., Jansen, C. R., Cottier, H., Rai, K. and Sipe, C. R., Ann. N. Y. Acad. Sci., *113:* 566, 1964.
36. Lance, E. M., in *Advances in Transplantation*, Edited by J. Dausset, J. Hamburger and G. Mathe, p. 107, Einar Munksgaard, Copenhagen, 1968.
37. Taub, R. N. and Lance, E. M., J. Exp. Med., *128:* 1281, 1968.
38. McGregor, D. D. and Gowans, J. L., J. Exp. Med., *117:* 303, 1963.
39. Levey, R. H. and Medawar, P. B., Proc. Nat. Acad. Sci., *58:* 470, 1967.
40. Lance, E. M., Nature, *217:* 557, 1968.

THE JOURNAL OF IMMUNOLOGY
Vol. 105, No. 1, July 1970
Printed in U.S.A.

THE IMMUNE RESPONSE TO HETEROLOGOUS RED CELLS IN MICE

V. The Effect of Cyclophosphamide and Cortisone on Antigenic Competition

PETER DUKOR[1] AND FELIX M. DIETRICH

From the Research Laboratories of the Pharmaceutical Department, CIBA Limited, Basle, Switzerland

Received for publication December 3, 1969

The effects of cyclophosphamide and cortisone acetate were examined in a model of antigenic competition between sequentially administered non-cross-reacting red cells from different species. In control mice receiving no drug, the relative immunogenic potency of heterologous red cells given with the first injection failed to determine the degree of unresponsiveness to subsequently injected unrelated cells. However, susceptibility to the suppressive action of previously administered erythrocytes was inversely related to the immunogenicity of the second antigen. Cyclophosphamide given 1 day after the initial red cell injection completely blocked competitive inhibition. On the other hand, impaired reactivity to the second of two sequentially administered antigens was further depressed by cortisone. The results are discussed in terms of targets of drug action and possible sites of antigenic interference.

Antigenic competition (1) is an operational term which refers to the mutual inhibition of immune responses directed against simultaneously or sequentially administered antigens (2). Conceptually, it implies that different epitopes compete for common limiting factors in the afferent, central, or efferent parts of the immune complex. Although the site of antigenic interference remains largely unknown, two major mechanisms could be operative in many experimental systems. Overloading at the level of the phagocytic and processing cells may be associated with a temporary impairment of immunologic reactivity (3–13). On the other hand, the lympho-proliferative events triggered by a first antigen may lead within a cellular compartment to spatial crowding (14), exhaustion of nutritional constituents (2, 15), humoral feed-back inhibition (16), or preemption of the antibody-synthesizing apparatus (17–19), and hence curtailed responsiveness to a second antigen. If this were true, immunosuppressive agents with distinct modes of action should have predictable effects in a model of antigenic competition.

Eearlier studies on drug-induced suppression of antibody formation to heterologous red cells in mice (20, 21) suggested that the impairment of immune responses by alkylating agents may be accounted for by their anti-proliferative properties, while immunosuppressive corticosteroids were thought to interfere mainly with antigen-handling. It would be expected, therefore, that appropriately timed administration of a cytostatic compound should inhibit cellular proliferation in response to a first of two sequentially injected antigens and thus abolish its competitive effect on antibody formation to the second antigen. Steroids, by contrast, should further enhance antigen-induced blockade of the afferent limb of the immune response.

The following communication deals with experiments which were undertaken in order to test these predictions. In the first part of this study conditions for antigenic competition in mice between non-cross-reacting heterologous red cells of differing immunogenicity were delineated. Later, the effects of cyclophosphamide and cortisone acetate on antigen interference were considered. Finally, attempts were made to induce specific tolerance by combining antigenic competition with drug-induced suppression of antibody formation.

MATERIALS AND METHODS

Animals. Six-week-old specific pathogen-free colony bred male Swiss Albino mice (Charles River CD1) weighing 18 to 22 g were purchased

[1] Present address: Department of Medicine, New York University School of Medicine, New York, N. Y. 10016.

from Charles River France SA and kept on commercial cubed feed and water *ad libitum*. Golden hamsters and gerbils (*Meriones shaui*) were obtained from Tierfarm AG, Sisseln.

Antigens and immunization. Washed erythrocyte suspensions from sheep (SRBC), hamsters (HRBC) and gerbils (GRBC) were prepared in a standard fashion. Cell counts were determined using a Coulter electronic particle counter, model B. Computation of the total erythrocyte surface administered with a given number of red cells, as well as the choice of optimal immunizing erythrocyte doses sufficient for the induction of a maximum antibody response were based on earlier experiments (22). Groups of 10 to 12 mice were injected intraperitoneally (i.p.) with graded amounts of cells as stated below. Absence of cross-reactivity between the erythrocyte types employed is shown in Table I.

Serologic procedures. Mice were bled repeatedly by retroorbital puncture. Hemagglutinin (HA) titers were assessed by serial twofold dilutions of individual inactivated sera using a Takatsy microtitration apparatus (23). If necessary, spontaneous agglutination of HRBC and GRBC was prevented by the addition of absorbed homologous serum to the diluent. Titers are expressed as logarithms to the base 2 of the reciprocal of the final dilution showing distinct agglutinates. Titer 0 was assigned to sera producing no hemagglutination at the initial dilution of 1:2. Mean titers were based on the arithmetic mean of the individual titers from a group of 10 to 12 mice.

Drugs. Solutions of cyclophosphamide (Endoxan, Asta) were made up in phosphate-buffered saline (0.15 M, pH 7.2–7.4) (PBS) and injected immediately. Cortisone acetate was suspended in PBS containing 0.5% carboxymethylcellulose. Both drugs were administered in weight-adjusted doses by the subcutaneous (s.c.) route as specified below.

Experimental schedule. The experimental outline is schematically depicted in Figure 1. Groups of mice were injected on day 0 with either 9.4×10^6, 4.7×10^7, 2.4×10^8, 1.1×10^9 and 5.9×10^9 SRBC, or 5.7×10^6, 2.9×10^7, 1.4×10^8, 7.1×10^8 and 3.6×10^9 HRBC, corresponding in both cases to 8×10^8, 4×10^9, 2×10^{10}, 1×10^{11} and 5×10^{11} μ^2 total erythrocyte surface/dose. One day later, mice received 20 or 100 mg/kg cyclophosphamide, or 100 or 500 mg/kg cortisone acetate, respectively. On day 2, the animals were challenged with an optimal immunizing dose of non-cross-reacting erythrocytes, i.e., 6.3×10^8 SRBC, 1.6×10^9 HRBC, or 1.3×10^9 GRBC. Mice were then bled for HA determinations on days 9, 15 and 29, reinjected on day 30 with the same dose and type of red cells as on day 2, as well as with an immunizing dose of cells to which they had not been exposed before, and bled again on day 39.

Suppressive index. In order to allow an assessment of the effect of the initial antigen load on day 0, results are expressed in terms of a suppressive index. It was defined as mean HA titer of an experimental group over mean titer from controls receiving no cells on day 0.

RESULTS

In the first series of experiments (Fig. 1), the effect of graded doses of erythrocytes on antibody formation to subsequently administered non-cross-reacting red cells was established. The chosen interval of 48 hr between the two antigen injections represents the previously determined condition for maximum suppression of the immune response to the second of the two antigens. In Figures 2–8 suppressive indices are plotted as

TABLE I

Absence of cross-reactivity between heterologous erythrocytes in mice

Antisera[a] to	No. of Sera with Agglutinins to: SRBC	HRBC	GRBC
SRBC	20/20	0/27	0/37
HRBC	0/20	20/20	1/20[b]
GRBC	0/9	0/10	9/9

[a] Sera obtained 5 to 6 days after i.p. injection of optimal immunizing erythrocyte doses.

[b] One serum exhibiting ± agglutination at initial dilution of 1:2.

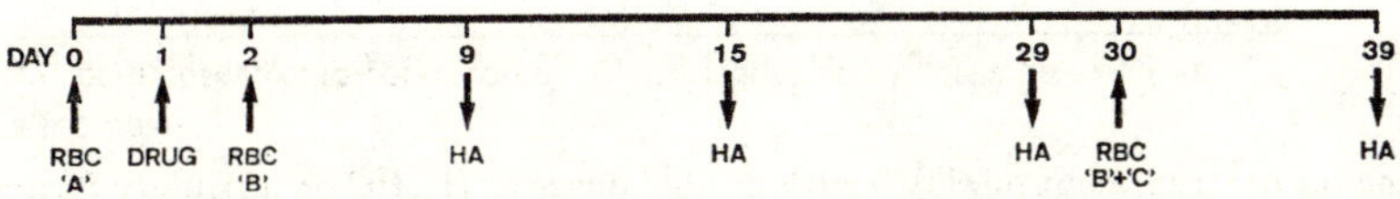

Figure 1. Experimental design (see text)

a function of the cell dose injected at the beginning of the experiment.

As can be seen from Figure 2, there was a dose-dependent inhibition of HA production to GRBC following previous administration of increasing doses of both the strongly immunogenic SRBC and the weakly immunogenic HRBC. Impaired antibody formation was noted throughout the period of observation (day 9 to day 29). The relative immunogenicity of the cells injected on day 0 had apparently no consistent effect on the degree of unresponsiveness to the second antigen.

Next, the importance of immunogenicity for the susceptibility to the suppressive action of a prior injection of red cells was examined. Figure 3 demonstrates that HA production to SRBC was consistently much less affected by previously administered HRBC than was the case for antibody formation against the very weakly immunogenic GRBC.

The effects of cyclophosphamide on antigenic competition are illustrated by Figures 4 and 5. Injection of 20 mg/kg of the cytotoxic drug on day 1 barely altered the marked inhibition of the

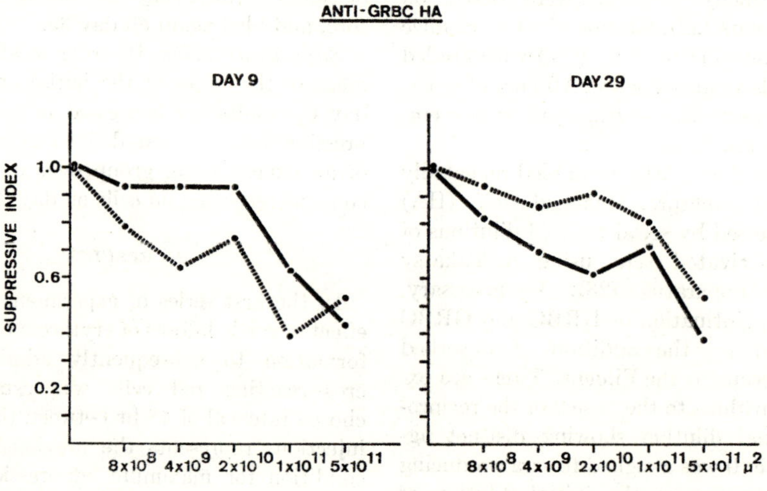

Figure 2. Effect of pretreatment on day 0 with graded doses of SRBC (●——●) or HRBC (●····●) on antibody formation to GRBC injected 2 days later. *Ordinate*, suppressive index; *abscissa*, total injected erythrocyte surface in μ^2. Each point represents the ratio of the mean HA titer of 10 to 12 experimental mice over the mean titer of 10 to 12 control mice receiving no cells on day 0.

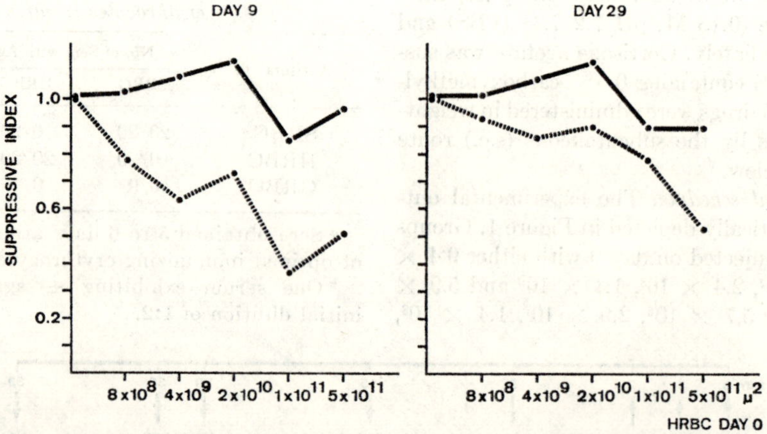

Figure 3. Effect of pretreatment on day 0 with graded doses of HRBC on antibody formation to SRBC (●——●) or GRBC (●····●) injected 2 days later. Ordinate and abscissa as in Figure 2.

immune response against HRBC by prior administration of SRBC. One hundred milligrams per kilogram of cyclophosphamide, however, completely abolished this competitive event (Fig. 4). On the other hand, if HRBC were given first and SRBC 2 days later (Fig. 5), HA formation against SRBC was not impaired. Under these conditions, cyclophosphamide failed to alter the pattern of antibody production against the second antigen.

Unlike cyclophosphamide, cortisone acetate injected on day 1 in doses of 100 or 500 mg/kg greatly enhanced the blocking action of SRBC on reactivity to HRBC (Fig. 6). Even when the order of antigen injections was reversed, cortisone markedly curtailed antibody production to the second antigen (Fig. 7). While administration of HRBC alone had little or no effect on HA formation to the subsequently injected strongly immunogenic SRBC, a cell dose-dependent inhibi-

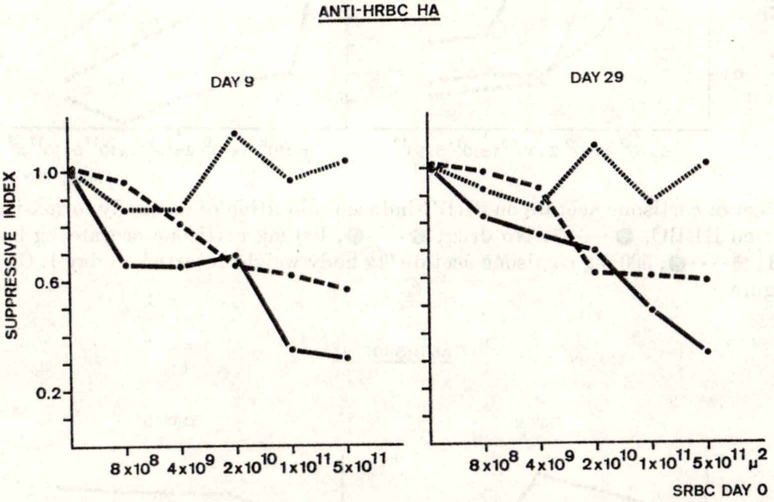

Figure 4. Effect of cyclophosphamide on SRBC-induced inhibition of antibody formation against subsequently injected HRBC. ●——●, No drug; ●-----●, 20 mg cyclophosphamide/kg body weight injected on day 1; ●····●, 100 mg cyclophosphamide/kg body weight injected on day 1. Ordinate and abscissa as in Figure 2.

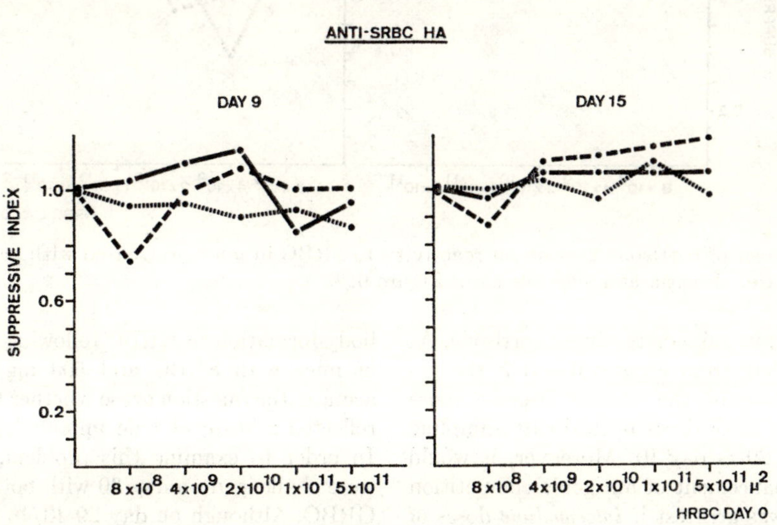

Figure 5. Effect of cyclophosphamide on reactivity to SRBC in mice pretreated with graded doses of HRBC. Ordinate, abscissa and symbols as in Figure 4.

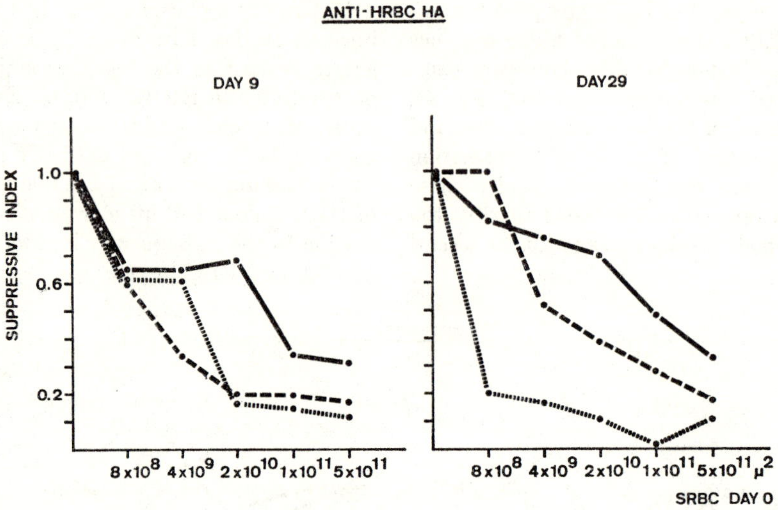

Figure 6. Effect of cortisone acetate on SRBC-induced inhibition of antibody formation against subsequently injected HRBC. ●——●, No drug; ●-----●, 100 mg cortisone acetate/kg body weight injected on day 1; ●····●, 500 mg cortisone acetate/kg body weight injected on day 1. Ordinate and abscissa as in Figure 2.

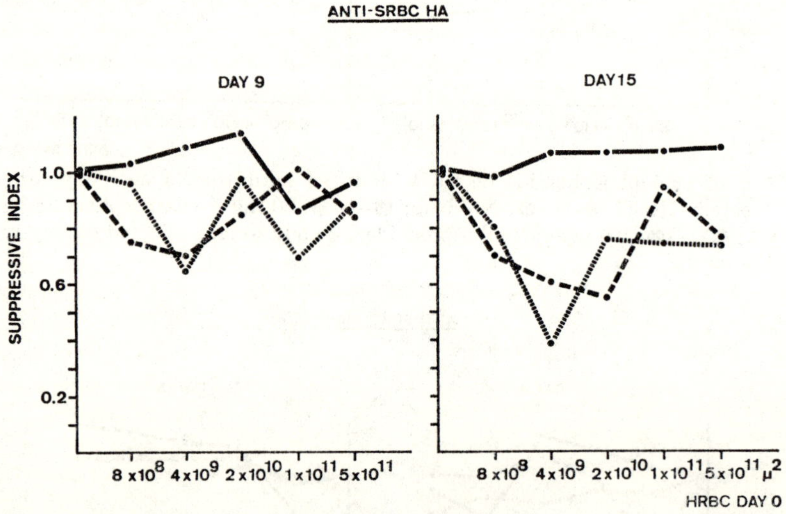

Figure 7. Effect of cortisone acetate on reactivity to SRBC in mice pretreated with graded doses of HRBC. Ordinate, abscissa and symbols as in Figure 6.

tion was noted in animals receiving cortisone. As is further evident from Figures 6 and 7, the potentiating action of the steroid became more marked at the later times of antibody sampling (days 15 and 29 *vs* day 9). Moreover, it would seem that enhancement of antigenic competition by cortisone was greatest if *intermediate* doses of the blocking antigen were given on day 0.

In view of the profound impairment of antibody formation to HRBC following pretreatment of mice with SRBC and 500 mg/kg cortisone acetate, the question arose whether this condition reflected a state of true immunologic tolerance. In order to examine this problem, the animals were challenged on day 30 with both HRBC and GRBC. Although on day 29 40/46 of these mice had failed to produce any demonstrable antibody to HRBC, 41/46 sera contained anti-HRBC

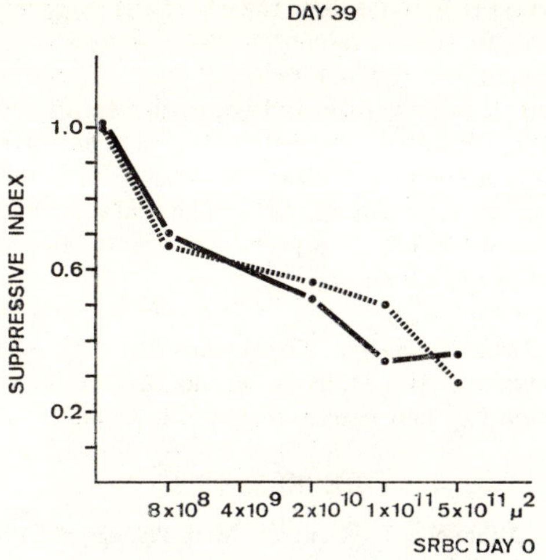

Figure 8. Effect of cortisone acetate and graded doses of SRBC on reactivity to HRBC and GRBC. Treatment schedule: Day 0, SRBC; day 1, cortisone acetate 500 mg/kg; day 2, HRBC; day 30, HRBC + GRBC. ●——●, Anti-HRBC hemagglutinins; ●····●, anti-GRBC hemagglutinins. Ordinate and abscissa as in Figure 2.

agglutinins 9 days after the challenge on day 30. Nevertheless, as can be seen from Figure 8, there was still a considerable SRBC dose-dependent depression of anti-HRBC reactivity. It is also evident, however, that as a consequence of the initial antigen injections responsiveness to GRBC was equally diminished.

DISCUSSION

Several facts emerge from the data reported in this communication.

1. The relative immunogenicity of heterologous red cells injected at the beginning of the experiment had apparently no consistent effect on the degree of unresponsiveness induced to subsequently injected non-cross-reacting erythrocytes. This is in agreement with earlier experiments in which equal doses of erythrocytes from sheep, guinea pigs and gerbils all caused an identical suppression of reactivity to unrelated red cells (24). This finding would militate against the idea that proliferative events play the only part in this model of antigenic competition. Rather would it seem that mere physical blockade of the afferent limb of the immune response was the main contributing factor. Indeed, overloading of the reticulo-endothelial system by non-antigenic agents, such as thorotrast (5), polyvinyl pyrrolidone (6), fatty acid esters (7–9) or colloidal carbon (12, 13), has been reported to markedly impair immunologic reactivity to subsequent antigenic stimulation.

2. Susceptibility to the suppressive effect of previously administered erythrocytes was determined by reference to the relative immunogenic potency of the second of the two antigens given in sequence. Antibody formation to a weak immunogen (HRBC) was more profoundly depressed than that against SRBC. Similar results were obtained by earlier workers who found that SRBC inhibited the response to rat erythrocytes (25, 26), whereas the reciprocal sequence of injections failed to reveal a competitive event (26). The findings are compatible with both an "overloading" and a "competitive proliferation" theory of antigenic competition. The relative immunogenicity of erythrocytes from different species is thought to reflect the numbers of opsonizing antibodies and/or antigen-reactive cells which are present in a host. These two factors may in turn determine the efficiency of antigen localization, of recruitment of antigen-reactive cells, and of their subsequent interaction with the precursors of antibody-producing cells (27–30). The immune response to weakly immunogenic erythrocytes could thus be expected to show an increased sensitivity both to reticulo-endothelial blockade and to the proliferation of a competing clone of immunologically committed cells.

3. A single dose of cyclophosphamide given 1 day after the initial antigen injection completely blocked the competitive effect on responsiveness to the subsequently administered unrelated erythrocytes. As cyclophosphamide is clearly most suppressive when injected 1 to 2 days after immunization (20, 31), it is possible to explain this seemingly paradoxical phenomenon in terms of a drug-induced inhibition of the cellular proliferation triggered by the first of the two sequentially administered antigens. Similar effects on antigenic competition between erythrocytes were reported with actinomycin D (26). It would follow that an important limiting factor in the response to the second erythrocyte is probably located within the central part of the immune complex. Proliferation of immunologically committed cells may exhaust humoral constituents, generate an inhibitor of antibody synthesis, or interfere with spatial requirements of competing clones. Alternatively, competitive proliferation may temporarily consume a cellular component.

Recent studies on the cooperation between thymus-derived and bone marrow-derived lymphocytes in antibody production to heterologous erythrocytes (27–29) and BSA (30) suggest that initial antigen recognition and immunoglobulin formation may reside in two distinct cell lineages. Preemption of conceivably multipotential bone marrow-derived precursors of antibody-producing cells by interaction with antigenically stimulated thymus-derived cells could provide a hypothetical basis for antigenic competition beyond the level of the phagocytic cells.

4. Impaired reactivity to the second of two sequentially administered antigens was further depressed by an injection of cortisone. Since steroids are much more efficient in reducing antibody formation to heterologous erythrocytes if given before rather than after immunization (20, 32), and as their suppressive activity increases with decreasing antigen doses (20, 33, 34), it is safe to assume that cortisone exerted its effects mainly with respect to the second of the two antigens. That potentiation of antigenic competition by cortisone became more marked at later times of antibody sampling, and that it was most pronounced when a weak immunogen (HRBC) was used also fits into the previously established characteristic pattern of steroid-induced immunosuppression (20, 21). Although the data do not permit a definite identification of the mode of cortisone action in this model of antigenic competition, a tentative interpretation seems possible. Steroids are known to interfere mainly with short-lived follicular lymphocytes which are probably identical with the bone marrow-derived precursors of antibody-forming cells, while they are much less cytotoxic for the recirculating, long-lived pool of thymus-derived lymphocytes (35–37). On the other hand, observations from this laboratory have also shown that clearance of weakly immunogenic erythrocytes from the circulation is delayed by cortisone in much the same way as by previous overloading with non-cross-reacting erythrocytes or by administration of RES-blocking fatty acid esters (38). It would thus seem that two main targets of the cortisone effect are at the very sites at which antigenic competition is thought to operate in the present experimental system.

5. Combination of antigen-overloading and cortisone administration was associated with a long-lasting depression of antibody formation to unrelated erythrocytes. Challenge with appropriate types of red cells at the end of the experiment revealed that unresponsiveness was clearly nonspecific and did not reflect a state of true immunologic tolerance. Indeed, earlier experiments have indicated that steroids may effectively block a common pathway leading to both tolerance and immunity (39). The data are thus compatible with the presumed steroid effect on antigen handling.

Acknowledgments. Thanks are due to Miss U. Petzoldt, Miss D. Nitsche and Mrs. T. Glanzmann for their careful technical assistance.

REFERENCES

1. Michaelis, L., Deutsch. Med. Wschr., *30:* 1240, 1904.
2. Adler, F. L., Progr. Allerg., *8:* 41, 1964.
3. Freund, J., J. Immun., *11:* 383, 1926.
4. Jaffe, R. H., Physiol. Rev., *11:* 277, 1931.
5. Lewis, L. A., Amer. J. Physiol., *179:* 285, 1954.
6. Stern, K., Spencer, K. and Farquar, M., Proc. Soc. Exp. Biol. Med., *89:* 126, 1955.
7. Wooles, W. R. and Di Luzio, N. R., Science, *142:* 1078, 1963.
8. Stuart, A. E. and Davidson, A. E., J. Path. Bact., *87:* 305, 1964.
9. Di Luzio, N. R. and Wooles, W. R., Amer. J. Physiol., *206:* 939, 1964.
10. Brody, N. I., Walker, J. G. and Siskind, G. W., J. Exp. Med., *126:* 81, 1967.
11. Eidinger, D., Khan, S. A. and Millar, K. G., J. Exp. Med., *128:* 1183, 1968.
12. Sabet, T., Newlin, C. and Friedman, H., Immunology, *16:* 433, 1969.
13. Sabet, T. and Friedman, H., Proc. Soc. Exp. Biol. Med., *131:* 1317, 1969.
14. Glenny, A. T., Hopkins, B. E. and Waddington, H., J. Path. Bact., *28:* 305, 1925.
15. Cremer, N. E., J. Immun., *90:* 685, 1963.
16. Radovich, J. and Talmage, D. W., Science, *158:* 512, 1967.
17. Schechter, I., Biochim. Biophys. Acta, *104:* 303, 1965.
18. Schechter, I., J. Exp. Med., *127:* 237, 1968.
19. Makinodan, T. and Albright, J. F., Progr. Allerg., *10:* 1, 1966.
20. Dukor, P. and Dietrich, F. M., Int. Arch. Allerg., *34:* 32, 1968.
21. Dukor, P. and Dietrich, F. M., in *Organtransplantation*, Edited by A. Heymer and D. Ricken, p. 255, Schattauer Verlag, Stuttgart-New York, 1969.
22. Dietrich, F. M. and Dukor, P., Immunology, *13:* 585, 1967.
23. Dietrich, F. M., Immunology, *10:* 365, 1966.

24. Dietrich, F. M. and Dukor, P., Int. Arch. Allerg., *36:* 91, 1969.
25. Albright, J. F., and Makinodan, T., in *Molecular and Cellular Basis of Antibody Formation*, Edited by J. Šterzl, p. 427, Czechoslovak Academy of Science Press, Prague, 1965.
26. Wust, C. J. and Hanna, M. G., J. Reticuloendothel. Soc., *3:* 415, 1966.
27. Miller, J. F. A. P. and Mitchell, G. F., Transplant. Rev., *1:* 3, 1969.
28. Davies, A. J. S., Transplant. Rev., *1:* 43, 1969.
29. Claman, H. N. and Chaperon, E. A., Transplant. Rev., *1:* 92, 1969.
30. Taylor, R. B., Transplant. Rev., *1:* 114, 1969.
31. Santos, G. W. and Owens, A. H., Bull. Johns Hopkins Hosp., *114:* 384, 1964.
32. Berglund, K., Acta Path. Microbiol. Scand., *38:* 311, 1956.
33. Newsom, S. E. and Darrach, M., Canad. J. Biochem., Physiol., *32:* 372, 1954.
34. Berglund, K., Acta Path. Microbiol. Scand., *38:* 329, 1956.
35. Miller, J. J., III and Cole, L. J., J. Exp. Med., *126:* 109, 1967.
36. Craddock, C. G., Winkelstein, A., Matsuyuki, Y. and Lawrence, J. S., J. Exp. Med., *125:* 1149, 1967.
37. Dukor, P. and Dietrich, F. M., in *Lymphatic Tissue and Germinal Centers in Immune Response*, Edited by L. Fiore-Donati and M. G. Hanna, p. 387, Plenum Publishing Corp., New York, 1969.
38. Dukor, P. and Dietrich, F. M., In preparation.
39. Dukor, P. and Dietrich, F. M., Proc. Soc. Exp. Biol. Med., *133:* 280, 1970.

THE JOURNAL OF IMMUNOLOGY
Vol. 105, No. 1, July 1970

IDENTIFICATION OF TWO CELL POPULATIONS REQUIRED FOR MOUSE IMMUNOCOMPETENCE[1, 2]

THOMAS BRODY[3,4]

From the Department of Immunology, University of California, Berkeley, California, and Roswell Park Memorial Institute, Buffalo, New York

Received for publication November 26, 1969

Two cell populations participating in the mouse immune response to sheep erythrocytes (SRBC) are identified. Cells of one population can attach SRBC by means of surface receptors. These cells are present in bone marrow and spleen. Bone marrow receptor-bearing cells show synergism with thymus in response to SRBC in a cell transfer assay. Cells with receptors for antigen act as the direct cellular precursors of antibody-producing cells. Receptor-bearing cells may be fractionated from hematopoietic colony-forming units. The second cell population required for an immune response to SRBC acts in conjunction with receptor-bearing cells. This population is present in the peripheral lymphoid organs and can be fractionated from the receptor-bearing cells of these organs. This cell population is called the peripheral thymic population because its role in the immune response can be carried out by thymocytes.

Two cell populations participating in immunocompetence of spleen cells to sheep erythrocytes (SRBC) can be detected in cell transfer assays. Kennedy (1) found that spleen cell suspensions lose reactivity to SRBC upon removal of cells with receptors for this antigen. The cells to which SRBC can adhere are called rosette- or cluster-forming cells (2, 3). Rosette-forming cells (RFC) can be fractionated from cells without receptors or with receptors of different specificity after spleen cells have been incubated with SRBC to form rosettes, since the rosettes have a higher sedimentation velocity than do free cells. Rosettes are not able to respond alone in a cell transfer assay to SRBC. Reactivity to SRBC can be regained only when rosettes are mixed with the rosette-depleted spleen population. This experiment suggests that although cells with receptors for SRBC are necessary for the response of spleen cells to antigen, there is at least one other cell population among the receptor-cell-depleted spleen population that is also essential for response of spleen cells to SRBC.

That at least two cell populations participate in the immune response to SRBC may also be inferred from the work of Claman *et al.* (4). They found that neither mouse bone marrow cells nor thymus cells are able to respond alone in a cell transfer system to SRBC by producing hemolytic plaque-forming cells (PFC). However, when these two cell populations are mixed and tested together for response to antigen, they are immunocompetent. This phenomenon is known as bone marrow-thymus synergism. A principal goal of this work was to discover which cell population in bone marrow shows synergism with thymus. The multipotent stem cell population (CFU) defined by Till and McCulloch (5) was one candidate, but it seems more likely that cells that have already lost the characteristics of multipotent stem cells and have begun to differentiate into an antigen-reactive population take part in syner-

[1] This work was supported by General Research Support Grant FR-05648 from the Division of Research Facilities and Resources, and Grant AI-08899, National Institute of Allergy and Infectious Diseases, National Institutes of Health.

[2] This paper and the subsequent one were taken from a thesis submitted in partial fulfillment of the requirements for a Doctor of Philosophy Degree in Immunology, University of California, Berkeley.

[3] Predoctoral fellow National Science Foundation, on leave from the Department of Bacteriology and Immunology, University of California, Berkeley, at the Roswell Park Memorial Institute, Buffalo, New York.

[4] Present Address: Department of Biochemistry, Stanford University, Stanford, Calif.

gism. The finding of Kennedy (1) and R. G. Miller and R. A. Phillips (personal communication) that cells with receptors for SRBC are among the cells responsible for immunocompetence of spleen suggested that these cells which are present in bone marrow but nearly absent from thymus (6) are the cells in bone marrow which show synergism with thymus.

The two cell populations that are needed for the response of splenic cells to SRBC may have the same role in the immune response as do the cell populations participating in bone marrow-thymus synergism. That is, there may be a cell population among receptor-cell-depleted spleen cells that acts as a peripheral thymic system required for the immune response to SRBC of receptor cells. This peripheral thymic system would act in synergism with splenic RFC just as thymocytes act in synergism with bone marrow RFC. The existence of such a peripheral thymic system participating in response to SRBC has already been suggested. Thymus-derived cells show a mitotic response to SRBC when this antigen is injected into mice grafted with chromosomally marked thymus (7). When thymocytes are primed with antigen in a lethally irradiated primary recipient, these cells display a marked increase in activity when tested for synergism with bone marrow in lethally irradiated secondary recipients (8). Thus the mitotic response of thymus-derived cells is functionally related to immunocompetence to SRBC. In spite of this demonstrated role of thymus-derived cells in the immune response to SRBC, thymus-derived cells are not the direct precursors of antibody-producing cells (9, 10). In this paper and the one that follows, the cell population that participates in the immune response in conjunction with cells with receptors for SRBC will be shown to have the properties of a peripheral thymic population. These properties include the ability to show synergism with rosettes and dependence for its differentiation on thymic function. It will be shown that thymocytes can functionally substitute for the cell population in receptor-cell-depleted spleen cells that is required for the immune response to SRBC.

MATERIALS AND METHODS

Mice. The F1 hybrid mice used in these experiments were either 6- to 12-week-old male CBF1 (C_3H/St♀ × $C_{57}Bl/6Ha$♂) mice obtained from the mouse production facilities at Roswell Park Laboratories in West Seneca, New York, or 6- to 12-week-old male BDF1 ($C_{57}Bl/6J$♀ × DBA/2J♂) mice obtained from Jackson Memorial Laboratory, Bar Harbor, Maine.

Preparation of cell suspensions. Cell suspensions were made in medium 199 (medium 199 minus bicarbonate (Grand Island Biological Co., Grand Island, N. Y.), 5% fetal calf serum (Armour Pharmaceutical Co., Chicago, Ill.), 0.005 M Tris, pH 7.4). Spleen cell suspensions were made by milking cells out of the splenic capsule and passing the undispersed cells through 18-gauge, 22-gauge, and finally 26-gauge needles. Bone marrow cell suspensions were made by removing bone marrow from the femurs and tibias of mice by aspiration and passing the undispersed cells through a 22-gauge needle. Thymus cell suspensions were made by teasing the organ and passing the cells successively through 16-, 18-, 22- and 26-gauge needles. Fibrous material was removed by allowing it to settle. All cell suspensions were washed in medium 199 by centrifugation at 800 × G for 5 min at least once before injection. The number of nucleated cells was determined after lysis of erythrocytes with 2% acetic acid and counting at least a total of 300 cells in at least two hemocytometer grids.

Formation of rosettes and fractionation of cells. Cell suspensions to be fractionated were prepared in TC-EDTA (tissue culture medium 199 minus bicarbonate, 5% fetal calf serum, 0.005 M EDTA, 0.005 M Tris, pH 7.4) which was used throughout the procedure. EDTA was used to diminish cell aggregation. Unless otherwise noted, the fractionation was carried out at 4°C. Cells were washed twice by sedimentation and incubated at 37°C for 15 min at a concentration of 1×10^8 cells/ml. Fibrous material and cell aggregates were removed by zone sedimentation at 36 × G for 10 min in a 30-ml linear bovine serum albumin (BSA) density gradient with a density range 1.03 to 1.06 g/cm^3. BSA solutions for this sedimentation as well as those described below were prepared by dissolving 200 g BSA (Armour) in 400 ml H_2O and dialyzing against 0.1 M Tris-Cl, pH 7.0, adjusted with NaCl to an osmolarity of 295 milliosmols/liter as measured by freezing point depression using a Fiske osmometer. The density of the BSA solution was measured in capillary tubes, and the BSA solutions were diluted to the proper density with TC-EDTA. Fractions were collected by downward flow. Those fractions containing single cells were washed free of BSA by sedimentation in TC-EDTA. This first incubation and sedimentation procedure freed the cell preparation of cell aggregates which interfere with subsequent steps in the purification.

Single cells were adjusted to a concentration of 1×10^7 cells/ml and incubated at 37°C for 85 min with a 2% suspension of washed SRBC in order to form rosettes (11). Rosettes were concentrated and partially freed of single cells and SRBC by sedimentation at $36 \times G$ for 10 min. Rosette-depleted supernatants were saved. The concentrated rosettes, in 5 ml, were separated from remaining single cells by zone sedimentation at $18 \times G$ for 13 min in a 24-ml linear BSA density gradient with density range 1.035 to 1.06 g/cm^3. Some streaming (12) occurred in this sedimentation procedure. For this reason, the fractions containing rosettes (including the pellet) were washed and concentrated by sedimentation at $36 \times G$ for 10 min and sedimented in a second $18 \times G$ zone sedimentation. The cell fraction in the first sedimentation step which contained non-rosettes was pooled with the fraction obtained earlier. Rosettes obtained from the second zone sedimentation were completely separated from the single cell distribution. However, some contamination of rosette fractions with cell clumps occurred because of streaming and cell aggregation during the experiment. The degree of contamination of the rosette fraction with non-rosettes was variable and will be noted in the results of each experiment. Rosette fractions and rosette-depleted single cell fractions were sedimented and resuspended in medium 199 lacking EDTA. After an additional wash by sedimentation in this medium, the cells were resuspended for counting and injection.

Irradiation procedure. Mice that were to be recipients of cells were exposed to 900 R total body x-irradiation. The x-ray machine operated under conditions of 250 kv, 25 mA, 0.025 mm Cu and 1 mm Al filtration, and a focal skin distance of 50 cm. The dose rate, which was 190 R/min, was measured with a Victoreen model 570 R-meter.

Cell transfers. After anesthetising the recipients with ether, cells were injected intravenously through the retroorbital plexus in a volume of 0.4 to 0.5 ml. Sheep, pig, or chicken erythrocytes obtained from Colorado Serum Company and washed three times in PBS (8 g NaCl, 0.2 g KCl, 1.145 g Na_2HPO_4, 0.2 g KH_2PO_4, 0.1 g $MgCl_2 \cdot 6H_2O$, 1000 ml distilled water) were injected along with the cells at a dose of 4×10^8 cells. Prior to injection of cells the recipients were given a single i.p. injection of 10 units heparin, 2 mg streptomycin sulfate, and 100 units procaine penicillin in 0.25 ml saline.

Housing of mice. Mice that had been used as recipients of cells after lethal irradiation were housed no more than three to a cage. The bedding was changed 4 or 5 days after irradiation.

Assay for PFC. The number of hemolytic PFC in spleens of recipient mice 8 days after transfer of cells was determined by the method of Jerne *et al.* (13).

Recording of results. Usually five or six recipients were used for determining the PFC-response of a donor cell suspension. The PFC-response in each spleen was determined from three samples of an appropriate dilution of cells and the geometric mean PFC was then calculated. The geometric mean is used because the PFC-response in the cell transfer system falls in a log normal distribution (R. A. Phillips, personal communication). The standard deviation from the geometric mean of logarithmic values of PFC-response was calculated as an index of dispersion of the experimental results.

The criteria for synergism can be expressed as follows. Three groups of mice are compared in a synergism experiment. Group A receives an injection of cell population 1. Group B receives an injection of cell population 2. Group C, in which synergism is tested, receives a mixture of cell populations 1 and 2. To calculate whether group C is significantly different from the sum of A and B, Student's t distribution (14) is applied to compare the sum of groups A and B with group C. The standard deviations of groups A and B are pooled (14) to approximate the standard deviation of the sum of these groups. P is the probability of the degree of certainty that no synergism was observed.

Assay for CFU. The assay for CFU was performed by the procedure of Till and McCulloch (5).

RESULTS

Synergism between bone marrow rosettes and thymus. An experiment was carried out to test whether the cells of bone marrow that show synergism with thymus are cells that have receptors for sheep erythrocytes. Bone marrow was incubated with SRBC, and rosettes were separated from single cells by zone sedimentation as described in the section on *Materials and Methods.* The yield of rosettes from bone marrow was usually 1 rosette/2000 nucleated cells. RFC and rosette-depleted single cells were mixed with thymocytes and tested for PFC-response in the cell transfer assay. In Table I it can be seen that the PFC-response in mice receiving only RFC or the rosette-depleted single cells was low. RFC, when tested for immunocompetence in the presence of thymus, showed synergism with thymus ($0.1 > p > 0.05$). Similar results were obtained in two other experiments. Conversely, the ability of the rosette-depleted single cells to show synergism with thymus ($p > 0.25$) has been diminished in comparison to unfractionated bone marrow ($p \sim 0.1$). Depletion of immunocompetence of single cells in combination with thymus by removal of rosettes was as variable as the results obtained with spleen (see below). The synergism between unfractionated bone marrow and thymus is relatively low in this experiment compared with that in Table VII (see below). Bone marrow cells that have been subjected to the treatment necessary for the formation and fractionation of rosettes typically have lost 50% of their ability to show synergism.

Are bone marrow RFC able to act as CFU? To prove that CFU are not the cells which show synergism with thymus, it is necessary to show that RFC—the cells in bone marrow which show synergism—do not act as CFU. Bone marrow cells were incubated with SRBC and rosettes were again separated from single cells by zone sedimentation. Rosettes and rosette-depleted single cells were assayed for their content of CFU as described in *Materials and Methods.* Unfractionated cells were also assayed for their content of CFU.

In Figure 1 the frequency of nucleated cells, CFU, and rosettes in the control unfractionated bone marrow, the rosette-depleted single cell fraction and the rosette fraction are shown. It can be seen that the rosettes appear to be completely fractionated from CFU. The number of rosettes in the rosette-depleted single cell fraction is hard to estimate because this number depends both on the yield of rosettes in the fractionation procedure and on knowledge of the absolute number of RFC in unfractionated bone marrow. The yield of rosettes in this experiment was 1 rosette/1500 nucleated cells.

From this experiment the minimum number of rosettes that could be CFU can be estimated. The number of rosettes in the rosette fraction was 5.5×10^4. It can be estimated that 15% of these rosettes (8300) were seeded in the spleens of the recipient mice. This estimate is based on data which show that approximately 15% of antigen-reactive-cells localize in the spleens of lethally irradiated mice (15). The number of colonies

TABLE I

Plaque-forming cell responses of fractionated bone marrow cells: test for synergism with thymus

Cell Inoculum	No. of Mice Assayed	Cell Dose	PFC in Spleens of Recipients (Geometric Mean)	Log Geometric Mean (± S.D.)
Bone marrow + Thymus	6	1.7×10^7 7×10^7	635	2.80 ± 0.19
Rosettes[a]	6	1.2×10^4 (8×10^5)[b]	40	1.60 ± 0.15
Rosettes + Thymus	6	1.2×10^4 (8×10^5)[b] 7×10^7	1060	3.03 ± 0.23
Non-rosettes	6	1.7×10^7	69	1.84 ± 0.24
Non-rosettes + Thymus	6	1.7×10^7 7×10^7	150	2.18 ± 0.33
Thymus	6	7×10^7	75	1.88 ± 0.31

[a] The yield of rosettes in this experiment was 1 rosette/1500 bone marrow cells.

[b] The number of rosettes transferred. In parentheses is the number of contaminating non-rosettes transferred along with the rosettes.

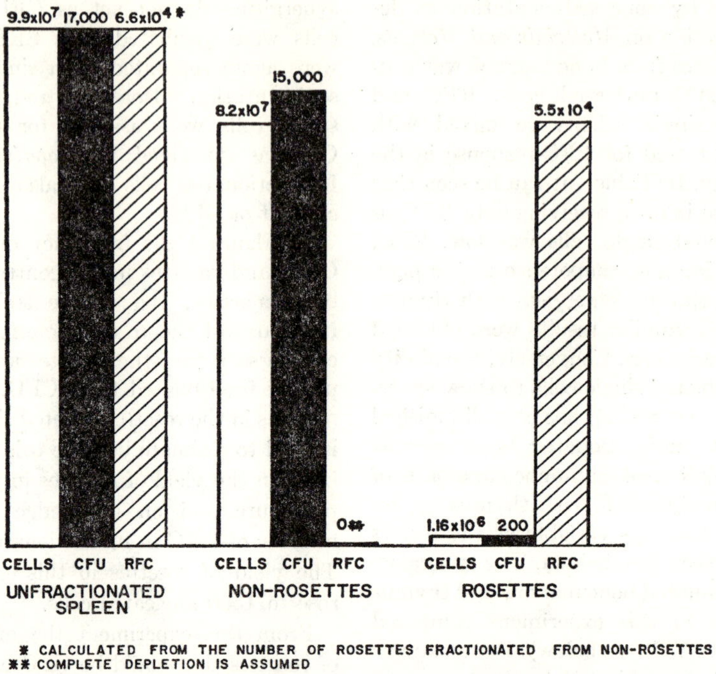

Figure 1. Fractionation of cells which act as colony-forming units from cells which form rosettes with SRBC. (* Calculated from the number of rosettes fractionated from non-rosettes; ** complete depletion is assumed.)

present in mice that received rosettes was 200. Thus, 200/8300 or approximately 2.5% of RFC could be CFU. This result has been verified in another experiment which showed that the frequency was less than 5%. Since the rosette fraction was contaminated by 1.16×10^6 single non-rosette-forming cells, the calculated frequency of RFC that could be CFU is a maximum estimate.

Synergism between spleen rosettes and thymus. The demonstration that RFC from bone marrow show synergism with thymus suggests that possibly RFC from spleen may similarly show synergism. This would imply that spleen RFC require a cell system, already present in immunocompetent organs, that can be replaced by thymus in fulfilling its role in the immune response to SRBC. Also, if this second cell system can be replaced by thymus, it must be functionally similar to thymus. Thus this second cell system should show synergism with bone marrow as does thymus.

The yield of rosettes from spleen cells was usually 1 rosette/2000 spleen cells. To test whether RFC of spleen show synergism with thymus, spleen cells were incubated with SRBC, and RFC were separated by zone sedimentation from cells not forming rosettes. Rosettes and rosette-depleted single cells were tested for PFC-response in the cell transfer system in combination with thymus. In Table II it may be seen that neither rosettes ($0.05 > p > 0.01$) nor non-rosettes ($0.25 > p > 0.1$) are as responsive to SRBC alone as are unfractionated spleen cells. This confirms experiments by Kennedy (1). In addition only RFC show synergism with thymus ($0.1 > p > 0.05$) when tested for immunocompetence in combination with thymus. This result has been verified in five different experiments. Therefore spleen RFC are similar to bone marrow RFC in showing synergism with thymus. Non-rosettes show a slightly increased responsiveness in this experiment when tested for immunocompetence in combination with thymus, but this is not statistically significant ($p > 0.25$).

Synergism between spleen non-rosettes and bone marrow and between spleen rosettes and non-rosettes. Synergism between the rosette-depleted single cell fraction and bone marrow has been demonstrated with less certainty. To test for synergism of rosette-depleted single cells with bone marrow, spleen cells were incubated with

SRBC, rosettes were separated by zone sedimentation from cells not forming rosettes and rosettes and rosette-depleted single cells were tested for their immunocompetence in combination with bone marrow. The results of this experiment are given in Table III. Also included in this experiment is a measurement of the immunocompetence of mixed rosettes and rosette-depleted single cells in order to compare this immunocompetence with unfractionated spleen.

As shown before, neither the immunocompetence of rosettes ($0.05 > p > 0.01$) nor of rosette-

TABLE II

Plaque-forming cell response of fractionated spleen cells: test for synergism with thymus

Cell Inoculum	No. of Mice Assayed	Cell Dose	PFC in Spleens of Recipients (Geometric Mean)	Log Geometric Mean (±S.D.)
Unfractionated spleen	6	2.5×10^7	3480	3.54 ± 0.34
Rosettes[a]	4	1.8×10^4 (1.3×10^6)[b]	20	1.30 ± 0.06
Rosettes + Thymus	6	1.8×10^4 (1.3×10^6)[b] 7.5×10^7	974	2.99 ± 0.29
Non-rosettes	6	2.5×10^7	520	2.72 ± 0.26
Non-rosettes + Thymus	4	2.5×10^7 7.5×10^7	875	2.94 ± 0.14
Thymus	3	7.5×10^7	40	1.60 ± 0.15

[a] The yield of rosettes in this experiment was 1 rosette/1900 spleen cells.

[b] The number of rosettes transferred. In parentheses is the number of contaminating non-rosettes transferred along with the rosettes.

TABLE III

Plaque-forming cell response of fractionated spleen cells: test for synergism with bone marrow

Cell Inoculum	No. of Mice Assayed	Cell Dose	PFC in Spleens of Recipients (Geometric Mean)	Log Geometric Mean (± S.D.)
Unfractionated spleen	5	2×10^7	6380	3.80 ± 0.49
Rosettes[a]	4	1.5×10^4 (2×10^5)[b]	8	0.9 ± 0.6
Rosettes + Bone marrow	6	1.5×10^4 (2×10^5)[b] 2.5×10^7	120	2.08 ± 0.39
Non-rosettes	5	2×10^7	1080	3.03 ± 0.26
Non-rosettes + Bone marrow	6	2×10^7 2.5×10^7	2870	3.46 ± 0.27
Rosettes + Non-rosettes	6	1.5×10^4 (2×10^5)[b] 2×10^7	5700	3.76 ± 0.18
Bone marrow	5	2.5×10^7	137	2.14 ± 0.20

[a] The yield of rosettes in this experiment was 1 rosette/1700 spleen cells.

[b] The number of rosettes transferred. In parentheses is the number of contaminating non-rosettes transferred along with the rosettes.

depleted single cells ($0.25 > p > 0.1$) is as great as is the immunocompetence of unfractionated spleen. The immunocompetence of mixed rosettes and non-rosettes approaches that of unfractionated spleen ($p > 0.25$). There is a threefold increase in immunocompetence of non-rosettes when they are tested for immunocompetence in the presence of bone marrow. Because of the large standard deviation in the experimental results, this increase is not significant ($p > 0.25$). Rosettes show no synergism with bone marrow ($p > 0.25$).

Whenever this kind of experiment was tried, the extent of depletion of immunocompetence of rosette-depleted single cells was often not sufficient to detect synergism with bone marrow. That is, the residual immunocompetence of non-rosettes was too high for the detection, at a statistically significant level, of increased immunocompetence from bone marrow. In most experiments the extent of depletion of immunocompetence of spleen by removal of rosettes was of the order of two- or threefold relative to the immunocompetence of unfractionated spleen. In each case, however, when rosettes were added back to rosette-depleted single cells, the immunocompetence returned to that of unfractionated spleen.

Sedimentation analysis of cells showing synergism with thymus. Cells which form rosettes with SRBC may not be the cells which show synergism with thymus. A large cell with a high sedimentation velocity may contaminate the rosette fraction and may be responsible for the synergism with thymus of this fraction. In order to test this possibility, spleen cells were incubated with pig erythrocytes (PRBC) in order to form rosettes, which were fractionated by zone sedimentation from single cells not forming rosettes. The pig rosettes were used as a marker so that cells which normally sediment in the rosette region could be tested for immunocompetence to SRBC in the presence of thymus. The results of this experiment are shown in Table IV.

It can be seen that, unlike sheep rosettes, the cells in the pig rosette fraction fail to show synergism with thymus in response to SRBC. Although there is some difference between the group receiving rosettes alone and the group receiving rosettes in combination with thymus, this difference is not enough to qualify as synergism ($p > 0.25$) It can be concluded that the cells that show synergism with thymus in response to SRBC do not co-sediment with pig rosettes. In fact, cells which show synergism with thymus are medium lymphocytes, and large cells fail to show synergism (R. G. Miller and R. A. Phillips, personal communication).

The degree of commitment of RFC. Are cells which have receptors for an antigen committed to respond only to this antigen? Two approaches to this question were taken. The first was a study of the ability of cells which form rosettes to attach two non-cross-reacting antigens to their surface. In the second, the capacity of rosettes formed with one antigen to react to a second antigen by production of PFC in a cell transfer assay was measured. A partial answer to the second approach may already be given. In the experiment in Table IV, the capacity of cells which form rosettes with PRBC to react to SRBC in synergism with thymus in the cell

TABLE IV

The ability of cells in the fraction containing rosettes formed with PRBC to respond to SRBC in synergism with thymus

Cell Inoculum	No. of Mice Assayed	Cell Dose	PFC in Spleens of Recipients (Geometric Mean)	Log Geometric Mean (± S.D.)
Pig rosettes[a]	6	5×10^3 (3×10^6)[b]	30	1.48 ± 0.30
Pig rosettes + Thymus	5	5×10^3 (3×10^6)[b] 6.5×10^7	101	2.01 ± 0.35
Thymus	5	6.5×10^7	6	0.8 ± 0.5

[a] The yield of pig rosettes in this experiment was 1 rosette/13,000 cells. This figure is typical for incubation of spleen cells with PRBC.

[b] The number of rosettes transferred. In parentheses is the number of contaminating non-rosettes transferred alone with the rosettes.

transfer assay was found to be minimal. Very few cells which form rosettes with chicken erythrocytes (CRBC) can also form rosettes with SRBC (6).

Since PRBC and SRBC are similar in appearance, it is more difficult to find out whether the same cells form rosettes with both of them. After incubation of spleen cells with SRBC, cells forming rosettes with SRBC were separated by zone sedimentation from cells not forming rosettes with SRBC. The rosette-depleted population was then passed through a 27-gauge needle in order to destroy any rosettes that had not been removed. This step is important because the fractionation procedure does not guarantee 100% depletion, and the levels of remaining rosettes would seriously interfere with the counting procedure. It is unlikely that rosettes re-form after they are destroyed (11). In fact only 3% of the original number of SRBC rosettes could be detected after the procedure described above and a second incubation with SRBC. On the other hand, the frequency of PRBC rosettes that formed upon incubation of the SRBC rosette-depleted cells with PRBC was not diminished from the frequency of PRBC rosette-forming cells present in a non-depleted spleen suspension. However, since it is very difficult to count rosettes accurately, a small depletion of PRBC rosettes could occur without being detected. Therefore, most cells that form rosettes with SRBC do not form rosettes with PRBC, although it cannot be stated that no cells that form cells with SRBC can form rosettes with PRBC.

An experiment was carried out to ascertain whether cells that form rosettes with SRBC show synergism with thymus in response to PRBC, and whether cells which fail to form rosettes with SRBC remain competent to respond to PRBC after the removal of sheep rosettes. Spleen cells were incubated with SRBC, and rosettes were separated from single cells by zone sedimentation. RFC and rosette-depleted single cells were assayed for immunocompetence to SRBC and PRBC. The results of this experiment are given in Table V. Sheep rosettes show synergism with thymus in response to SRBC ($0.05 > p > 0.01$). Sheep rosette-depleted single cells show almost a fourfold depletion in immunocompetence in comparison to unfractionated spleen ($0.25 > p > 0.1$). The response of sheep rosette-depleted single cells to PRBC is twofold less than the response of unfractionated spleen cells to PRBC. This result is suggestive of de-

TABLE V

Commitment to respond to SRBC and PRBC of splenic SRBC rosettes and SRBC rosette-depleted single cells

Cell Inoculum	Antigen Used to Stimulate Recipients	No. of Mice Assayed	Cell Dose	PFC in Spleens of Recipients (Geometric Mean)	Log Geometric Mean (± S.D.)
SRBC-rosettes[a] + Thymus	SRBC	6	1.8×10^4 (7×10^5)[b] 8×10^7	1950	3.29 ± 0.9
SRBC-rosettes + Thymus	PRBC	6	1.8×10^4 (7×10^5)[b] 8×10^7	17	1.24 ± 1.14
SRBC-non-rosettes	SRBC	6	3×10^7	1650	3.22 ± 0.18
SRBC-non-rosettes	PRBC	6	3×10^7	420	2.62 ± 0.31
Unfractionated spleen	SRBC	6	3×10^7	5930	3.77 ± 0.28
Unfractionated spleen	PRBC	6	3×10^7	789	2.90 ± 0.24
Thymus	SRBC	4	8×10^7	4	0.6 ± 0.3
Thymus	PRBC	4	8×10^7	2	0.3 ± 0.1

[a] The yield of rosettes in this experiment was 1 rosette/2800 spleen cells.

[b] The number of rosettes transferred. In parentheses is the number of contaminating non-rosettes transferred along with the rosettes.

creased responsiveness upon removal of sheep RFC, but the decrease is not statistically significant ($p > 0.25$). The response of sheep rosettes is low but the standard deviation is large because two of six mice responded with 600 PFC/spleen. Synergism between bone marrow and thymus in response to PRBC gives a large standard deviation (see below, Table VI). It is therefore possible that some cells in the sheep rosette fraction show synergism with thymus in response to PRBC. Almost identical results were obtained in the second experiment.

Test for bone marrow-thymus synergism with three antigens. The immunocompetence of mouse bone marrow and thymus cells and the synergism that occurs between these two cell populations in response to three antigens is shown in Table VI. For comparison, the PFC-response to these three antigens of spleen cells is shown. Neither bone marrow cells nor thymocytes alone are responsive to any of the antigens. Bone marrow cells and thymocytes show synergism in response to all three antigens as shown by the PFC-response when a mixture of bone marrow and thymus is tested for immunocompetence. The response of a mixture of bone marrow and thymus is usually lower than a comparable number of spleen cells. It will be noted that the variance in the response to PRBC and CRBC by bone marrow-thymus combinations is high, indicating the great variability in the response. The synergism between bone marrow and thymus to PRBC

TABLE VI

Plaque-forming cell response of bone marrow, thymus and spleen cells to three antigens: Test for synergism between bone marrow and thymus

Cell Inoculum	No. of Mice Assayed	Cell Dose	PFC in Spleens of Recipients (Geometric Mean)	Log Geometric Mean (±S.D.)
A. Response to sheep erythrocytes				
Thymus	6	7×10^7	272	2.43 ± 0.31
Bone marrow	5	2.5×10^7	339	2.53 ± 0.12
Thymus + Bone marrow	6	7×10^7 2.5×10^7	4,920	3.69 ± 0.21
Spleen	6	4×10^7	7,650	3.88 ± 0.21
B. Response to pig erythrocytes				
Thymus	8	1×10^8	11	1.04 ± 0.07
Bone marrow	8	2.5×10^7	24	1.38 ± 0.36
Thymus + Bone marrow	8	1×10^8 2.5×10^7	226	2.35 ± 0.52
Spleen	5	3×10^7	1,030	3.01 ± 0.16
C. Response to chicken erythrocytes				
Thymus	6	7×10^7	240	2.38 ± 0.37
Bone marrow	6	2.5×10^7	326	2.51 ± 0.27
Thymus + Bone marrow	6	7×10^7 2.5×10^7	2,610	3.41 ± 0.38
Spleen	6	3.2×10^7	11,100	4.04 ± 0.18

TABLE VII

Cross-reactions among three red cell antigens

Red Cell Injected	No.[a] of Spleen PFC against:		
	Sheep	Pig	Chcben
None	150	40	78
Sheep	275,000	8	1,780
Pig	1,050	138,000	1,480
Chicken	250	24	11,500

[a] Geometric mean.

is less significant ($0.25 > p > 0.1$) than is the synergism to CRBC ($p \sim 0.1$), or SRBC ($p \sim 0.05$).

In order to establish that the three antigens used to test for synergism are quantitatively different, the degree of cross-reaction was measured. This experiment is similar to that of Radovich and Talmadge (16). Groups of three adult mice were immunized with sheep, pig, or chicken erythrocytes and the spleen of each mouse was assayed on day 4 for the frequency of cells forming hemolytic antibody to each of the three antigens. A control group was unimmunized. The results of this experiment are shown in Table VII. In no case was there greater than 15% cross-reaction.

DISCUSSION

Function of cells with receptors for antigen in the expression of immunocompetence. The studies reported here demonstrate that cells which form rosettes with SRBC are important in the expression of immunocompetence to this antigen. Since bone marrow is the source of antibody-producing cells in a bone marrow-thymus synergism experiment (8, 9), it may be concluded that RFC, which are the cells in bone marrow responsible for synergism, are the cellular precursors of cells which produce antibodies to SRBC. By extention of this argument, it is probably true that RFC are the direct precursors of PFC *in situ* in the response to SRBC of immunocompetent organs such as spleen.

A minimal hypothesis for the function of RFC may be stated as follows. A cell population committed to respond to SRBC antigens has receptors for one of these antigens on its surface. When SRBC interact with these surface receptors, the antigen target cells proliferate and give rise to clones of cells actively producing antibody specific to the stimulating antigen.

The fact that RFC have receptors for antigen does not *a priori* mean that these receptors interact directly with the antigen in the form it is given to the animal. Possibly the peripheral thymic system or else a macrophage system influences the immunogenicity of the SRBC antigens by gathering and concentrating antigen or processing the antigen and then delivering it to the cell system with receptors for antigen.

Armstrong *et al.* (17) have shown that bone marrow cells alone are responsive to flagellar antigens and that no synergism can be found to occur between thymus and bone marrow in response to this antigen. Stuttman and Good (18) showed that no synergism could be detected between thymus and bone marrow in the graft *vs* host reaction. These observations place doubt on generalizations that the same cell systems are necessary for the immune response to all antigens. Since most of the experiments described in this paper have been performed with SRBC, the statements that are made implicating multiple cell systems in response to antigen are always qualified by stating that SRBC is the antigen being investigated.

Numerical difficulties resulting from the high frequency of RFC. The frequency of cells forming rosettes with SRBC in spleens of unimmunized mice is approximately 1 RFC/ 2000 cells. The number of cells which form rosettes with CRBC is threefold the number which form rosettes with SRBC (6), whereas the number which form rosettes with PRBC is less than one-third the number which form rosettes with SRBC. Miller and Phillips (personal communication) have shown that the size distribution of cells forming rosettes with SRBC is homogeneous, suggesting a unique function. On the other hand, the estimated frequency of cells reactive to SRBC antigens in the spleen is 1 antigen-reactive cell/10^5 nucleated spleen cells (15, 19). Thus there are about 50-fold more RFC in spleens of unimmunized mice than there are antigen-sensitive units.

It is possible that there are so many RFC because the mouse has already mounted an immune response to some of the red cell antigens. In fact, it is known that there are serum hemolytic antibodies to CRBC in mice (6). Animals exposed to SRBC show a marked increase in RFC (2, 3, 20). RFC from immunized mice are larger than RFC from unimmunized mice and form a heterogeneous cell population consisting of dividing antibody-producing cells and some macrophages. RFC similar to those of unimmunized mice are present in immunized mice, but cells characteristic of RFC produced as a result of immunization with SRBC are completely absent from unimmunized mice. These observations appear to rule out the possibility that the high frequency of cells forming rosettes with SRBC could be due to previous exposure to this antigen.

The high frequency of RFC may be due to rosette formation by cells that have absorbed cytophilic antibody (21) onto their surfaces. It is known that macrophages from mice stimulated with more than one red cell antigen can form mixed rosettes (2). RFC have the size of medium lymphocytes (6) and are too small to be classified as macrophages. Because non-macrophage cells cannot form rosettes with red cells from more than one species, it is unlikely that the high frequency of RFC may be due to cytophilic antibody.

Nossal *et al.* (22) showed that when flagellar antigens are injected into rats, the antigens localize on the surface of specialized macrophages with long, dendritic arms. The relationship of these cells to the class of cells forming rosettes with SRBC is uncertain although these cells are probably not fulfilling the critical role in the immune response ascribed to RFC because these reticular macrophages are larger than RFC from unimmunized mice and they have probably absorbed their receptors for antigen (23).

The high frequency of RFC, relative to the number of cells which give rise to foci of PFC in lethally irradiated mice, could also be understood if cells had receptors for more than one antigen and could respond to several antigens. This theory would predict that a low frequency of cells with receptors for SRBC respond to this antigen and become committed to produce antibody of a single specificity after interaction with antigen has taken place.

The experiments which attempted to show the precommitment of RFC to respond to one antigen were done in order to exclude this possibility. It can be said that most if not all of the cells forming rosettes with SRBC do not form rosettes with PRBC. Less than 1.5% of cells forming rosettes with CRBC form rosettes with SRBC as well (6). Therefore very few cells form rosettes with more than one antigen. This is strong evidence for the precommitment of the RFC. The partial reactivity of sheep RFC to PRBC and the partial depletion of the reactivity to PRBC of SRBC non-rosettes by removal of sheep RFC may, however, be cited as evidence against commitment.

The difficulty encountered in the depletion of immunocompetence to SRBC of the SRBC non-rosettes most likely arose from the low stability of rosettes once they are formed (11). It is also possible that new cells with receptors for antigen could differentiate from stem cells in the non-rosette fraction leading to immunocompetence in this fraction (Miller and Phillips, personal communication).

The role of the peripheral thymic system in response to antigen. The cell system with receptors for SRBC is not competent to respond to antigen but requires another cell population for immunocompetence. Two different synergistic phenomena involving RFC have been observed. RFC from spleen and bone marrow can show synergism with thymus (Tables I and II). RFC from spleen and bone marrow show synergism with the rosette-depleted single cell fraction of spleen (Table III). These two synergistic phenomena may not occur by exactly the same mechanism. The fact that the cellular components of synergism are interchangeable argues that similar cell systems are involved. That cells of the central and peripheral thymic system appear to have the same size distribution (Miller and Phillips, personal communication) is evidence for their identity. Further evidence comes from the fact that bone marrow-thymus combinations give rise to the clonal distribution of antibody-producing cells (24) as do unfractionated spleen cells (15, 20).

The responsiveness of rosettes when tested for immunocompetence in combination with thymus is not equal to that of unfractionated spleen (Table III). This may be due to loss of activity in the rosette fraction, or may be due to the potency of the thymocytes in promoting synergism relative to the potency of the peripheral thymic system. The former possibility seems unlikely because a mixture of rosettes and non-rosettes is as immunocompetent as unfractionated spleen (Table III). The latter possibility is made more likely by an observation of Miller and Mitchell (25) that thoracic duct lymphocytes, which probably contain the peripheral thymic system, are much more potent in restoring immunocompetence of thymectomized mice than is thymus. This is evidence that there may be some difference between the peripheral thymic system and thymocytes. The relative abilities of thymocytes and of the peripheral thymic system to proliferate in response to antigen are not known. This experiment would be important in establishing whether the central and peripheral thymic systems are made up of the same cellular constituents.

The exact mechanism of action of the thymic system is not known. The finding that cells derived from thymocytes proliferate under antigenic stimulation (7) and the finding that this proliferation enhances the immunocompetence of thymocytes when they are tested for immunocompetence in combination with bone marrow (10) are the only clues we have at present of the role of the thymic system in the immune response.

The possibility that thymocytes may be committed to respond to single antigens or may have some apparatus for the recognition of antigen must be considered. The experiments of R. B. Taylor (personal communication) show that induction of tolerance in the thymic system may occur. This unpublished result would favor the hypothesis that the thymus system has specific interaction with antigen. The frequency of RFC among thymocytes (6) is 2% that of spleen, bone marrow and Peyer's patches, making it unlikely that these thymocyte RFC are responsible for the interaction of thymus with antigen. This could be tested, however, by removing rosettes from thymus and seeing if rosette-depleted thymus could be stimulated by antigen in primary recipients as successfully as unfractionated thymocytes. This would not exclude the possibility that the interaction of thymus with antigen is receptor-mediated. The surface concentration of receptors on thymocytes may be too low to allow for the formation of rosettes.

Possibly immunogenicity is conferred upon antigen by an interaction with the thymic system which is not receptor-mediated. Under these circumstances, the antigen would be immunogenic when a direct interaction of the cell system with receptors for antigen with a thymus system-antigen complex would occur. This hypothesis could be tested by treating thymocytes that have been exposed to antigens with antibody specific to the antigens to find out if this diminished the activity of thymus in showing synergism with bone marrow.

Comparison of in vitro studies of multiple cell system with results obtained in vivo. The evidence obtained *in vivo* that there are multiple cell systems in mice participating in the immune response to SRBC is supportive of studies *in vitro* of the cell systems participating in the immune response to SRBC. Interactions of three cell populations in the *in vitro* response to SRBC have been demonstrated by Mosier and Coppleson (26) who fractionated spleen cells into adherent and non-adherent fractions on the basis of their ability to attach to plastic. They found that neither adherent nor non-adherent spleen cells were responsive in culture to SRBC. The response of mixtures of adherent and non-adherent cells of spleen was not related linearly to the dose of non-adherent cells but to the log of the dose. This indicated that more than one cell population in the non-adherent fraction was needed for response to SRBC. The adherent population is heterogeneous, but the cell type in it that functions in the immune response to SRBC is probably the macrophage population. The adherent population would not be detected in cell transfer assays *in vivo* because its function appears to be radiation resistant (27). The other two cell populations, which do not adhere to plastic, may be the populations which Kennedy (1) has detected in *in vivo* cell transfer assays and which are described in this paper. At least one of the cell populations among the non-adherent cells has been identified as a thymus-derived population (28).

Acknowledgments. I would like to thank Dr. B. W. Papermaster for his support and encouragement and Drs. M. Saifer and H. Miller for their thoughtful evaluation of my work. I am indebted to R. A. Phillips for a discussion for his unpublished experiments. Technical assistance was provided by C. Abendschein and K. Kaufman.

REFERENCES

1. Kennedy, J. C., Unpublished data.
2. Biozzi, G., Stiffel, C., Mouton, D., Liacopoulos-Briot, M. Decreusefond, C. and Bouthillier, Y., Ann. Inst. Pasteur, *110:* 7, 1966.
3. Zaalberg, O. B., Van Der Meul, V. A. and Van Twisk, J. M., Nature, *210:* 544, 1966.

4. Claman H. N., Chaperon, E. A. and Triplett, R. F., J. Immun., *97:* 828, 1966.
5. Till, J. E. and McCulloch, E. A., Radiat. Res., *14:* 213, 1961.
6. Laskov, R., Nature, *219:* 973, 1968.
7. Davies, A. J. S., Leuchars, E., Wallis, V. and Kohler, P. C., Transplantation, *4:* 438, 1966.
8. Miller, J. F. A. P. and Mitchell, G. F., Nature, *216:* 659, 1967.
9. Davies, A. J. S., Leuchars, E., Wallis, V., Marchant, R. and Elliott, E. V., Transplantation, *5:* 222, 1967.
10. Mitchell, G. F. and Miller, J. F. A. P., J. Exp. Med., *128:* 821, 1968.
11. Shearer, G. M. and Cudkovicz, G., J. Immun., *101:* 1264, 1968.
12. Miller, R. G. and Phillips, R. A., J. Cell. Physiol., *73:* 191, 1969.
13. Jerne, N. K., Nordin, A. A. and Henry, C., in *Cell Bound Antibodies*, Edited by B. Amos and H. Koprowski, p. 109, Wistar Institute Press, Philadelphia, 1963.
14. Wine, R. L., *Statistics for Scientists and Engineers*, Prentice-Hall, Inc., Englewood Cliffs, N. J., 1964.
15. Kennedy, J. C., Till, J. E., Siminovitch, L. and McCulloch, E. A., J. Immun., *96:* 973, 1966.
16. Radovitch, J. and Talmage, D. W., Science, *158:* 512, 1967.
17. Armstrong, W. D., Diener, E. and Shellam, G. R., J. Exp. Med., *129:* 393, 1969.
18. Stuttman, O. and Good, R. A., Proc. Soc. Exp. Biol. Med., *130:* 848, 1969.
19. Playfair, J. H. L., Papermaster, B. W. and Cole, L. J., Science, *149:* 998, 1965.
20. Shearer, G. M., Cudkowicz, G., Connell, M. S. J. and Priore, R. L., J. Exp. Med., *128:* 437, 1968.
21. Boyden, S. V. and Sorkin, E., Immunology, *3:* 272, 1960.
22. Nossal, G. J. V., Ada, G. L. and Austin, C. M., Aust. J. Exp. Biol. Med. Sci., *42:* 311, 1964.
23. McDevitt, H. O., Askonas, B. A., Humphrey, J. H., Schechter, I. and Sela, M., Immunology, *11:* 337, 1966.
24. Shearer, G. M., Cudkovicz, G. and Priore, R. L., J. Exp. Med., *130:* 467, 1969.
25. Miller, J. F. A. P. and Mitchell, G. F., J. Exp. Med., *128:* 801, 1968.
26. Mosier, D. E. and Coppleson, L. W., Proc. Nat. Acad. Sci., *61:* 542, 1968.
27. Roseman, J. M., Science, *165:* 1125, 1969.
28. Mosier, D. E., Fitch, F. W., Rowley, D. A. and Davies, A. J. S., Fed. Proc., *28:* 375, 1969.

THE JOURNAL OF IMMUNOLOGY
Vol. 105, No. 1, July 1970
Printed in U.S.A.

ONTOGENY OF CELL POPULATIONS REQUIRED FOR IMMUNOCOMPETENCE[1]

THOMAS BRODY[2] AND BEN W. PAPERMASTER[3]

From the Department of Immunology, University of California, Berkeley, California and the Roswell Park Memorial Institute, Buffalo, New York

Received for publication November 26, 1969

Differentiation from cellular progenitors of two cell populations required for the immune response to sheep erythrocyte antigens was studied. The receptor-bearing population differentiates from bone marrow progenitors much more rapidly than the peripheral thymic population. The differentiation from bone marrow progenitors of the cells with receptors for antigen is completely independent of thymus, while the differentiation of the peripheral thymic population is dependent upon thymus function. Peyer's patches may not be considered solely as primary lymphoid organs. Peyer's patches in adults have all the cell populations required for immunocompetence. In addition, Peyer's patches cannot be considered the initial source in the neonatal period of the cells with receptors for antigen, because these cells are present in the prenatal period in fetal liver.

Stem cell colony-forming units (CFU) are present in mouse bone marrow which are unable to respond to antigen but are able to restore the immunocompetence to sheep erythrocytes (SRBC) of lethally irradiated mice in a period of about 30 days (1). In experiments in which chromosome markers were induced in cells by irradiation, it was shown that these multipotent stem cells are able to differentiate into erythrocytes and granulocytes as well as lymphocytes and also are capable of restoring the cellularity of the thymus of lethally irradiated mice (2). From this evidence, there seems little doubt that the bone marrow stem cells for the immune system can differentiate into the cell systems that participate in the immune response: the cell population with receptors for antigen and the peripheral thymic system.

The thymus participates in the differentiation of immunocompetent cells from stem cell progenitors. This has been shown in studies of neonatally thymectomized animals (3–6) and mice that have been thymectomized as adults and then lethally irradiated and reconstituted with bone marrow (7). These mice are immunologically impaired. The immune deficiency of these mice may be compensated for by grafting of thymus (4, 8, 9) or by injecting thymocytes or thoracic duct cells into thymectomized recipients (6).

These experiments failed to show whether the grafted thymocytes act as a cellular system participating directly with mature immunocompetent cells in response to antigen or whether the thymus acts in the differentiation of immunocompetent cells from stem cells. The latter has appeared to be most likely because simply removing the thymus from an adult animal which possessed fully developed immunocompetence does not immediately impair its immunocompetence (10–13). Even this consideration does not lead to a clarification of what cell population participating in immunocompetence is dependent on thymus function for differentiation. In this paper it will be shown that the defective immunocompetence of thymectomized mice to SRBC is caused by a deficiency in a cell system which in fully immunocompetent organs functions as the peripheral thymic system. This system is called the peripheral thymic system because its role in the immune response may be carried out by thymocytes themselves.

[1] This work was supported by General Research Support Grant FR-05648 from the Division of Research Facilities and Resources, and Grant AI-08899, National Institute of Allergy and Infectious Diseases, National Institutes of Health.

[2] Present address: Department of Biochemistry, Stanford University, Palo Alto, California.

[3] Present address: Associated Biomedic Systems, Inc., Buffalo, New York.

Cooper *et al.* (14) have been concerned with the ultimate cellular origins of "the antibody producing system of lymphocytes" in mammals. The avian bursa of Fabricius has been implicated as the organ in birds which acts as the *anlage* of "the antibody producing system of lymphocytes" during a critical neonatal period (15–17). Cooper *et al.* (14) have suggested that Peyer's patches, which are nodular concentrations of lymphoid cells in the gut tract of mammals, are lymphoid organs having the same function as the avian bursa of Fabricius. Since the progenitors of antibody-producing cells are the cells with receptors for antigen (18), the finding of a bursal system in mammals would indicate the organ source of the cell system with receptors for antigen.

Experimental evidence for the role of gut tract-associated lymphatic tissue in the differentiation of immunocompetent cell populations of mammals has been arrived at by use of neonatal extirpation of Peyer's patch type lymphoepithelial tissues in rabbits (19) and extirpation of such tissues in adults followed by lethal irradiation and reconstitution with fetal liver (20). Rabbits that have undergone these drastic treatments are immunologically impaired. This evidence, which is not altogether compelling because of the radical nature of the surgical procedure, suggests that lymphoepithelial tissues in the gut tract of mammals may be the origin in differentiation of the cell system with receptors for antigen. Contradicting this evidence, Armstrong *et al.* (21) and Cooper and Turner (22) have shown that Peyer's patch cells are fully immunocompetent, and thus have thrown doubt on their supposed function as primary lymphoid organs. In this paper is reported an analysis of the cell populations present in Peyer's patches. This analysis supports the belief that Peyer's patches are simply peripheral lymphoid organs containing all the cell populations participating in the immune response to SRBC antigens. The preliminary results of this experiment have been published (23).

MATERIALS AND METHODS

The source of mice, preparation of cell suspensions, formation of rosettes, fractionating of cells, irradiation procedure, cell transfer, housing of mice, assay for plaque-forming cells and recording of results have been described in the preceding paper (18).

Preparation of thymectomized and irradiated (TIR) mice. Adult mice, five or six weeks of age, were thymectomized by the method of Kaplan (24) except that the incision was sealed with wound clips (Tomac O11). After 1 or 2 weeks, thymectomized mice were lethally irradiated (900 R) and reconstituted with 2×10^6 bone marrow cells. Donor TIR mice were always checked for thymic remnants before use.

Preparation of Peyer's patch cells. Peyer's patches were removed from the intestinal wall simply by cutting them off with a fine pair of scissors. A single cell suspension in medium 199 was prepared by passing teased Peyer's patches successively through 16, 18, 22, and 26 gauge needles. Fibrous material was removed by allowing it to settle. All cell suspensions were washed in medium 199 by centrifugation at $800 \times G$ for 5 min at least once before injection. Injections of streptomycin and penicillin into recipients of Peyer's patch cells are particularly important for the expression of immunocompetence of Peyer's patch cells because of the likelihood of contamination of cell suspensions with intestinal bacteria.

RESULTS

Restoration of immunocompetence with bone marrow injections. The restoration of immunocompetence in lethally irradiated mice from transferred bone marrow proceeds with a doubling time of approximately 1.5 days after a 10-day lag time (1, 25). Twenty days after transplantation of 2×10^6 bone marrow cells into lethally irradiated mice, only 2% of the normal immunocompetence has been achieved. After 30 days the restoration is complete (1, 25). Since a cell population with receptors for antigen and another cell population for which thymus can substitute both participate in the immune response to SRBC, it would be interesting to know the length of time required for the maturation of each system and thus which cellular system is limiting in the restoration of immunocompetence from bone marrow.

If the cell population with receptors for antigen were to mature faster than the peripheral thymic population, there would be a time during the restoration of immunocompetence from bone marrow when rosette-forming cells (RFC), which are the cells with receptors, would be detectable and the peripheral thymic system would be lacking resulting in impaired immunocompetence. Groups of mice were given from 7×10^4 to 2×10^7 bone marrow cells after lethal irradiation. Fourteen days after reconstitution the spleens of these mice were removed and assayed for frequency of RFC, immunocompetence in secondary irradiated recipients and finally immunocompetence in secondary recipients in combination with thymus.

Figure 1 shows the frequency of cells forming rosettes with SRBC in the spleens of mice 14 days after irradiation and reconstitution with varying doses of bone marrow. Also shown is the immunocompetence of these spleen cells in secondary recipients and immunocompetence of the spleen cells when tested for immunocompetence in combination with thymus. There is no detectable immunocompetence of spleen cells alone in any of the groups, however, the frequency of RFC approximately parallels the PFC-response of spleen when tested for immunocompetence in combination with thymus.

The effect of thymectomy on the maturation from bone marrow of cells participating in immunocompetence. The maturation of full immunocompetence from bone marrow seems to be limited by the maturation of the peripheral thymic system. It would be interesting to know whether the nonresponsiveness resulting from thymectomy is also due to the absence of the peripheral thymic system. In Table I, the immunocompetence of spleen cells of adult thymectomized mice 66 days after lethal irradiation and reconstitution with bone marrow (TIR mice) is demonstrated. Also shown is the immunocompetence of spleen and bone marrow of such mice when tested for PFC-response in combination with thymus. As a control for decreased immunocompetence as a result of thymectomy, the spleens of mice that were not thymectomized but were lethally irradiated and reconstituted with bone marrow (IR mice) were also tested. It can be seen that spleen cells of TIR mice show little detectable immunocompetence ($p \sim 0.05$) but that these spleen cells show marked synergism with thymus ($0.25 > p > 0.1$). Spleen cells from IR mice demonstrate normal immunocompetence and no synergism with thymus ($p > 0.25$). It thus appears that there is no peripheral thymic system in TIR mice.

In order to substantiate this conclusion, spleen

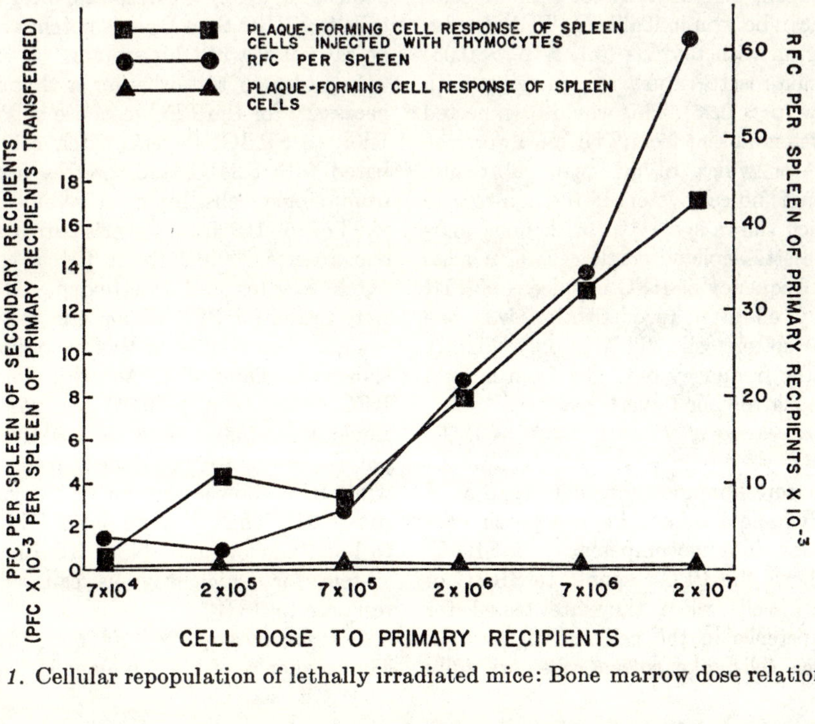

Figure 1. Cellular repopulation of lethally irradiated mice: Bone marrow dose relationship.

TABLE I

Plaque-forming cell response of cells from TIR mice

Cell Inoculum	No. of Mice Assayed	Cell Dose	PFC in Spleens of Recipients (Geometric Mean)	Log Geometric Mean (±S.D.)
TIR bone marrow	5	1.9×10^7	63	1.80 ± 0.22
TIR bone marrow + Thymus	5	1.9×10^7 5.0×10^7	1,068	3.03 ± 0.23
TIR spleen	5	4.3×10^7	747	2.87 ± 0.34
TIR spleen + Thymus	5	4.3×10^7 5.0×10^7	6,940	3.84 ± 0.14
IR spleen	5	4.3×10^7	15,900	4.20 ± 0.04
IR spleen + Thymus	5	4.3×10^7 5.0×10^7	13,350	4.13 ± 0.16
Thymus	2	5.0×10^7	204	2.31 ± 0.03

cells from TIR mice 55 days after bone marrow reconstitution were fractionated into rosettes and rosette-depleted single cells and the ability of the rosettes to show synergism with thymus and of the rosette-depleted single cells to show synergism with bone marrow was measured. IR spleen was again also assayed for immunocompetence. As can be seen in Table II, TIR rosettes show synergism with thymus ($0.1 > p > 0.05$) while TIR non-rosettes show no synergism with bone marrow ($p > 0.25$). This would be expected if the cell system absent from TIR mice were the cell system for which thymus can substitute. That is, there is no cell system in the non-rosette fraction which shows synergism with bone marrow as do rosette-depleted single cells of normal spleen. The frequency of RFC in spleens of TIR mice on day 40 after reconstitution was one rosette/3600 spleen cells. This is only slightly lower than the frequency obtained from normal spleen, bone marrow, or Peyer's patches.

Immunocompetence of Peyer's patch cells. To test whether Peyer's patches have the characteristics of a mature immunocompetent organ or of a primary lymphoid organ, Peyer's patch cells are tested for immunocompetence to SRBC. Table III shows the PFC-response to SRBC of Peyer's patch cells when they are tested for immunocompetence in the cell-transfer system. Peyer's patch cells, like spleen cells, are fully competent to respond to SRBC. This confirms the findings that Peyer's patch cells are immunocompetent (21, 22). When Peyer's patch cells are tested for immunocompetence in the presence of thymocytes, no increase response is observed ($p > 0.25$). This suggests that if a thymic system is necessary for the response of Peyer's patch cells to SRBC then Peyer's patches must already be saturated with this system.

In order to test whether a thymic system is necessary for the PFC-response of Peyer's patch RFC to SRBC, Peyer's patch cells were incubated with SRBC, and rosettes were separated from single cells by zone sedimentation. The yield of rosettes from Peyer's patches was usually one rosette/2000 Peyer's patch cells. Peyer's patch rosettes and rosette-depleted single cells were tested for PFC response in the cell transfer system. The results of this experiment are also shown in Table III. As with spleen, neither RFC ($0.05 > p > 0.01$) nor rosette-depleted single cells ($0.05 > p > 0.01$) from Peyer's patches are competent alone to respond to SRBC, while RFC show synergism with thymus ($0.05 > p > 0.01$). Thus, Peyer's patch RFC are similar to bone marrow and spleen RFC in requiring a system for which thymus can substitute for response to SRBC.

The presence of RFC in the prenatal period. The frequency of RFC present in fetal liver was

TABLE II

Plaque-forming cell response of fractionated rosettes and rosette-depleted single cells from spleens of TIR mice

Cell Inoculum	No. of Mice Assayed	Cell Dose	PFC in Spleens of Recipients (Geometric Mean)	Log Geometric Mean (±S.D.)
TIR spleen + Bone marrow	5	2.5×10^7 2.3×10^7	32	1.50 ± 0.24
TIR spleen + Thymus	5	2.5×10^7 6.8×10^7	883	2.95 ± 0.52
TIR rosettes[a]	4	8×10^3 (4×10^4)[b]	5	0.7 ± 0.4
TIR rosettes + Thymus	4	8×10^3 (4×10^4) 6.8×10^7	795	2.90 ± 0.34
TIR non-rosettes		2.5×10^7	12	1.1 ± 0.3
TIR non-rosettes + Bone marrow	5	2.5×10^7 2.3×10^7	20	1.30 ± 0.50
IR spleen	5	2.5×10^7	2090	3.32 ± 0.28
Bone marrow	5	2.3×10^7	18	1.26 ± 0.58
Thymus	4	6.8×10^7	42	1.62 ± 0.27

[a] The yield of rosettes in this experiment was one rosette/5900 spleen cells.

[b] The number of rosettes transferred. In parentheses is the number of contaminating non-rosettes transferred along with the rosettes.

TABLE III

Plaque-forming cell response of Peyer's patch cells

Cell Inoculum	No. of Mice Assayed	Cell Dose	PFC in Spleens of Recipients (Geometric Mean)	Log Geometric Mean (±S.D.)
Peyer's patch	6	1.0×10^7	7490	3.87 ± 0.40
Peyer's patch + Thymus	5	1.0×10^7 5×10^7	6700	3.83 ± 0.24
Rosettes[a]	6	5×10^3 (2×10^5)[b]	33	1.52 ± 0.40
Rosettes + Thymus	6	5×10^3 (2×10^5) 7.5×10^7	2157	3.34 ± 0.24
Non-rosettes	6	1.5×10^7	100	2.00 ± 0.18
Thymus	6	7.5×10^7	68	1.84 ± 0.21

[a] The yield of rosettes in this experiment was one rosette/3000 Peyer's patch cells.

[b] The number of rosettes transferred. In parentheses is the number of contaminating non-rosettes transferred along with the rosettes.

measured. There was one rosette/30,000 nucleated cells in mice that had 17 ± 2 days of fetal development. The frequency of CFU in fetal liver is one-fifth that of adult bone marrow (26). Thus, the ratio of RFC to CFU in fetal liver is one-third the ratio of RFC to CFU in adult bone marrow, and is greater than the ratio of RFC to CFU in adult spleen.

DISCUSSION

The cell system lacking from the spleens of thymectomized mice and whose absence accounts for the immune deficiencies of these mice is the peripheral thymic system which acts synergistically with cells with receptors for antigen. It is clear from the work of Davies *et al.* (27) that the peripheral thymic system can be generated from thymocytes and thus it is accurate to call the peripheral thymic system the thymus-derived system.

In Figure 1 is shown the dose relationship for the restoration of the cell system with receptors for antigen from bone marrow. The frequency of RFC and the ability to show synergism with thymus are not linearly related to bone marrow dose but are related approximately to the square root of the bone marrow dose. Similar results were obtained by Shearer and Cudkowicz (25) for the restoration of full immunocompetence at a later time in the restoration process.

In the group receiving the highest dose of bone marrow, the number of spleen rosettes and the immunocompetence of spleen cells in combination with thymus is approximately that to be expected of mice whose receptor cell population has been fully reconstituted.

The important aspect of this experiment is that the maturation of the cell system with receptors for antigen is rapid and is not limiting in the restoration of full immunocompetence. However, thymus can substitute for the cell system that is limiting. The peripheral thymic system probably appears after the restoration of the cellularity of the thymus. There is evidence that there is a constant outpouring of thymocytes into the peripheral lymphoid organs (28). This outpouring probably results in the maintenance of the peripheral thymic system.

It seems likely from experiments of Wu *et al.* (2) that the bone marrow colony-forming units (CFU) are the source of cells with receptors for antigen. In experiments involving thymectomy, reported here, it was shown that the development of the cell system with receptors for antigens is independent of thymic function, while the development of the peripheral thymic system is fully dependent on thymus function. The existence of the cell system with receptors for antigen in the prenatal period in fetal liver is also evidence for the dissociation of the thymic system's development from the development of the receptor cell system since work of Archer and Pierce (3), Miller (4), Martinez *et al.* (5) and Miller and Mitchell (6) shows that the thymus does not influence the development of the peripheral thymic system until after birth.

Peyer's patches may be the intial source of the cell system with receptors for antigen but adult Peyer's patches are fully immunocompetent. All the cell populations required for response to antigens are present in adult Peyer's patches. Peyer's patches contain RFC and are fully immunocompetent while bursal cells are not immunocompetent and do not contain RFC (29). These facts are strong evidence against the functional equivalence of the two organs. It is still conceivable that Peyer's patches are bifunctional lymphoid organs having all cell populations participating in immunocompetence as well as the capacity in the neonatal period to act as a source of the cells with receptors for antigen. However, the existence of the cell system with receptors for antigen in the prenatal period is evidence against a unique involvement of Peyer's patches in the generation of this system in the neonatal period.

REFERENCES

1. Till, J. E., McCulloch, E. A., Phillips, R. A. and Siminovitch, L., Cold Spring Harbor Symp. Quant. Biol., *32:* 461, 1967.
2. Wu, A. M., Till, J. E., Siminovitch, L. and McCulloch, E. A., J. Exp. Med., *127:* 454, 1968.
3. Archer, O. K. and Pierce, J. C., Fed. Proc., *20:* 26, 1961.
4. Miller, J. F. A. P., Lancet, *2:* 748, 1961.
5. Martinez, C., Kersey, J., Papermaster, B. W. and Good, R. A., Proc. Soc. Exp. Biol. Med., *109:* 193, 1962.
6. Miller, J. F. A. P. and Mitchell, G. F., J. Exp. Med. *128:* 801, 1968.
7. Miller, J. F. A. P., Doak, S. M. A. and Cross, A. M., Proc. Soc. Exp. Biol. Med., *112:* 785, 1963.
8. Dalmasso, A. P., Martinez, C., Sjodin, K.

and Good, R. A., J. Exp. Med., *118:* 1089, 1963.

9. Leuchars, E., Cross, A. M. and Dukor, P., Transplantation, *3:* 28, 1965.
10. Aisenberg, A. C. and Wilkes, B., J. Immun., *93:* 75, 1964.
11. Taylor, R. B., Nature, *208:* 1334, 1965.
12. Metcalf, D., Nature, *208:* 1336, 1965.
13. Miller, J. F. A. P., Nature, *208:* 1337, 1965.
14. Cooper, M. D., Perey, D. V., McKneally, M. G., Gabrielson, A. E., Sutherland, D. E. R. and Good, R. A., Lancet, *1:* 1388, 1966.
15. Glick, B., Ghang, T. S. and Jaap, R. G., Poult. Sci., *35:* 224, 1956.
16. Warner, N. L., Szenberg, A. and Burnet, F. M., Aust. J. Exp. Biol., *40:* 373, 1962.
17. Cooper, M. D., Schwartz, M. L. and Good, R. A., Science, *151:* 471, 1966.
18. Brody, T., J. Immun., *105:* 126, 1970.
19. Perey, D. Y., Cooper, M. D. and Good, R. A., Science, *161:* 265, 1968.
20. Perey, D. Y., Cooper, M. D. and Good, R. A., Surgery, *64:* 614, 1968.
21. Armstrong, W. D., Diener, E. and Shellam, G. R., J. Exp. Med., *129:* 393, 1969.
22. Cooper, G. N. and Turner, K., Aust. J. Exp. Biol. Med. Sci., *45:* 363, 1967.
23. Brody, T. and Hencin, R., Fed. Proc., *28:* 309, 1969.
24. Kaplan, H. S., J. Nat. Cancer Inst., *11:* 83, 1950.
25. Shearer, G. M. and Cudkowicz, B., J. Exp. Med., *129:* 935, 1969.
26. Thompson, M. W., McCulloch, E. A., Siminovitch, L. and Till, J. E., Brit. J. Haemat., *12:* 153, 1966.
27. Davies, A. J. S., Leuchars, E., Wallis, V. and Kohler, P. C., Transplantation, *4:* 438, 1966.
28. Murray, R. G. and Woods, P. A., Anat. Rec., *150:* 113, 1964.
29. Dent, P. D. and Good, R. A., Nature, *207:* 491, 1965.

THE JOURNAL OF IMMUNOLOGY
Vol. 105, No. 1, July 1970

STUDIES ON IgA

II. Isolation of IgA from Small Volumes of Human Serum by Immunoabsorption[1]

TRUMAN O. ANDERSON, RAINER H. ZSCHOCKE[2] AND GERHARD L. BACH

From the Clinical Immunology Section, Hektoen Institute of Medical Research of the Cook County Hospital, and the Department of Medicine, University of Illinois College of Medicine, Chicago, Illinois

Received for publication November 20, 1969

Bromoacetyl cellulose was used to prepare a monospecific anti-IgA immunoabsorbent for the one-step isolation of IgA from small volumes of human serum. Two features were essential to this procedure. a) Anti-IgA globulin was freed of inert γ globulin by immunoabsorption and was used for coupling to bromoacetyl cellulose. The binding capacity of this immunoabsorbent was 15 mg IgA/g absorbent (using whole human serum). b) 3 M urea wash solution was used to minimize contamination of the eluted IgA by nonspecifically absorbed serum proteins. The IgA obtained by this method was 98.5% pure; it retained biologic activity and showed the electrophoretic pattern of IgA in serum.

Among the immunoglobulins, those of the IgA class have proven particularly difficult to isolate in the pure state in any quantity. Recently, our laboratory has reported a new fractionation method for this purpose (1) which employs the technique of immunoabsorption to achieve final purification. The yield from this procedure approximates 9% of the IgA in the starting plasma pool. In terms of electrophoretic mobility, the end product appears to be broadly representative of the IgA in native, unfractionated serum. Based on this experience, the present work was undertaken to adapt the principle of immunoabsorption to the isolation of IgA from small volume specimens of serum. The basic method employed was patterned after the pioneering work of Jagendorf *et al.* (2) and the subsequent studies of Robbins *et al.* (3) using stable immunoabsorbents prepared with bromoacetyl cellulose according to Patchornik (4).

Ordinarily, immunoabsorbents are prepared by coupling antigen to an insoluble carrier and derive much of their efficiency from the ability of most antigens to combine with amounts of antibody many times their own weight. This advantage is lost if the immunoabsorbent is to be used to isolate antigen, in which case the insoluble carrier is coupled with antibody. It is possible, however, to develop useful immunoabsorbents of this latter type if the covalently linked antibody is comprised solely of antibody specific for a given antigen, an approach originally demonstrated by the work of Williams and Stone (5). The present study describes the preparation of such an immunoabsorbent which was developed to permit isolation of IgA from small amounts of human serum. The efficiency of this reagent expressed as percentage of total input recovered varied as a function of IgA load/unit weight of immunoabsorbent. This ranged from 50% at low IgA input to 20% at an IgA input which saturated available binding sites on the reagent.

MATERIALS AND METHODS

Antigen. To accomplish a preliminary purification of anti-IgA antibody for subsequent coupling to bromoacetyl cellulose, a myeloma protein of the IgA type was isolated by precipitation with a final concentration of 9% Na_2SO_4 at room temperature. This precipitate was dialyzed at pH 6.0 against 0.02 M PO_4 buffer again at room

[1] These studies were supported by Research Contract NIH 69-2092 (Principal Investigator, Truman O. Anderson), Vaccine Development Branch, National Institute of Allergy and Infectious Diseases, National Institutes of Health.

[2] Present address: Department of Biochemistry, Presbyterian-St. Luke's Hospital, Chicago, Illinois 60612.

temperature. The proteins soluble under these conditions (supernatant) yielded a secondary precipitate upon standing for 48 hr at 4°C in the same buffer. This latter precipitate was comprised mainly of IgA myeloma protein and was dissolved and brought to a concentration of 1% at pH 7.0. It was then dialyzed against distilled water at 4°C. The material precipitating under these conditions was discarded and after concentration the cold water-soluble proteins contained in the supernatant were subjected to batch elution on DEAE-Sephadex. The effluents obtained with 0.075 and 0.2 M PO_4 buffer at pH 8.0 were highly purified IgA.

The purified material showed a single precipitation arc on immunoelectrophoresis when tested at 20 mg/ml against anti-whole human serum. On ultracentrifugal analysis it showed three distinct peaks with sedimentation constants from 7S to 13S. The preparation was used a) to immunize sheep for the production of an anti-IgA antiserum, and b) for coupling to bromoacetyl cellulose to remove anti-IgA antibody protein from the sheep antiserum previously rendered monospecific for IgA.

Antiserum. Two adult female sheep were immunized with the antigen in Freund's adjuvant, with the use of the myeloma protein described above. The animals received an initial intramuscular injection of 50 mg of the myeloma globulin and 4 weeks later another dose of 50 mg i.m. This was followed at weekly intervals by two more doses administered subcutaneously. The animals were bled 10 days after the final injection. Five hundred milliliters of this antiserum were made monospecific for IgA by absorption with IgG purified by a) precipitation twice with 12% and 10% Na_2SO_4, respectively, at room temperature, and b) absorption and batch elution from DEAE-cellulose previously brought to pH 8.0 and equilibrated with 0.01 M PO_4 buffer. The eluate was collected with the equilibration buffer.

Preparation of bromoacetyl cellulose conjugates. The bromoacetyle cellulose (BAC) carrier was made according to the method of Patchornik (4) as modified by Robbins *et al.* (3) and was stored at 4°C in distilled water until used.

a) BAC-IgA (myeloma) conjugate. For the production of the BAC-IgA (myeloma) conjugate, 1.0 g of BAC (dry weight) and 200 to 400 mg of the purified myeloma protein, predialyzed at pH 5.2, were suspended in citrate-phosphate buffer to a final volume of 7.5 ml. Physical adsorption and chemical binding of the protein to the BAC was accomplished under the conditions described by Robbins *et al.* (3) and Zschocke *et al.* (1). This BAC-IgA (myeloma) immunoabsorbent was employed to obtain pure anti-IgA antibodies from the monospecific sheep anti-IgA antiserum as follows. In a typical experiment, 200 to 300 ml of monospecific anti-IgA antiserum were absorbed by adding 2 g (dry weight) of BAC-IgA absorbent and incubating for 60 min at 37°C and overnight at 4°C with gentle stirring. The suspended BAC-IgA particles with the now absorbed anti-IgA antibodies were centrifuged at 10,000 × G and the supernatant was saved for reabsorption. The cellulose was then washed three times with a total of 300 ml of PO_4-buffered saline at pH 7.4 followed by extracting twice with 30 ml of 0.1 N HOAc for 30 min at 37°C. After centrifugation at 10,000 × G at 10°C for 20 min, the two HOAc extracts were pooled and titrated to pH 7.0 with approximately 15 ml of 0.5 M PO_4 buffer, pH 8.0. The neutralized solutions were then dialyzed against 0.15 M PO_4 buffer pH 7.5 and were subsequently concentrated to 20 mg protein/ml by negative pressure dialysis.

b) BAC-anti-IgA (myeloma) immunoabsorbent. The immunoabsorbent for isolation of IgA from small volumes of human serum was then prepared by essentially the same method and under conditions similar to those described for producing the BAC-IgA conjugate. Briefly, in a typical experiment, 300 mg of purified monospecific anti-IgA antibody was adsorbed to 2 g of BAC (dry weight) in a total reaction volume of 15 ml at pH 3.9 and was further processed as described above. The characteristics of the BAC-anti-IgA immunoabsorbents are described under the section on results. Figure 1 presents a flow sheet of the general reaction sequences employed in this study.

Use of BAC-anti-IgA conjugate for the isolation of IgA from small volumes of human serum. The immunoabsorbent (0.2 to 0.5 g dry weight) was equilibrated with 0.05 PO_4 buffer, pH 8.0, containing 2% glycine, and was packed by centrifugation at 1465 × G for 10 min. It was then suspended in 5 ml of serum which was previously dialyzed against 1 liter of the same phosphate-glycine buffer for 24 hr. The suspension was incubated for 60 min at 37°C with occasional stirring. It was subsequently sedimented at 10,000 × G for 10 min at 4°C. Ordinarily the supernatant was preserved for later analysis. At this point the immunoabsorbent was washed four times with 20 ml of 3 M urea solution, pH 8.0, containing 1% glycine and 0.05 M PO_4. For each washing, the absorbent was suspended in the wash solution, stirred vigorously for 5 min and then centrifuged at 10,000 × G for 10 min at 4°C. After the fourth wash the absorbent was washed a final time with 20 ml of distilled water.

Step I

(Preparation of BAC)

10 g cellulose powder are first washed in acetone followed by washing in dioxane. Cellulose dried *in vacuo* over P_2O_5 → suspended in solution of 100 g bromoacetic acid in 30 ml absolute dioxane, stirred for 20 hr at 25°C under exclusion of moisture, addition of

↓ 75 ml bromoacetyl bromide (ρ = 2.317 g/ml)

Rapid stirring for 15–18 hr at 25°C with NaOH trap for evolved HBr, oily mixture is poured slowly into 3–4 liters of ice water (distilled) under

↓ stirring.

Stirred for 15 min, supernatant decanted from flocculated cellulose and discarded, cellulose washed extensively with distilled water, followed by 4 liters 0.1 M $NaHCO_3$ and 4 liters distilled water, pH should be neutral.

↓ BAC stored at 4°C in distilled water.

Step II

(BAC-protein conjugates)

a) Adsorption of protein to BAC

1.0 g BAC in 0.15 M citrate-phosphate buffer pH 3.9–5.2 + 200–400 mg predialyzed protein at pH 3.9–5.2, citrate-phosphate buffer, total volume 7.5 ml, stirred for 30 hr at 25°C, centrifuged at 10,000 × G for 10 min.

Supernatant: non-adsorbed protein ← | → Sediment ↓

b) Chemical binding of protein

Cellulose resuspended in 30 ml 0.1 M $NaHCO_3/Na_2CO_3$ buffer, pH 8.9, suspension adjusted to pH 8.9, occasional stirring for 24 hr at 4°C, periodic readjustment of pH necessary, centrifuged at 10,000 × G for 10 min.

Supernatant: non-bound protein ← | → Sediment ↓

c) Blockage of non-reacted bromoacetyl groups

Cellulose resuspended in 30 ml 0.1 M $NaHCO_3/Na_2CO_3$ buffer, pH 8.9, containing 0.05 M ethanolamine, suspension adjusted to pH 8.9. Stirred for 24 hr at 4°C, centrifuged at 10,000 × G for 10 min, washed twice with phosphate-buffered saline, pH 7.4.

Supernatant: non-bound protein ← | → Sediment ↓

d) Final removal of non-bound protein

Cellulose resuspended in 30 ml 8 M urea, stirred for 24 hr at 4°C, centrifuged at 10,000 × G for 20 min, washed with 30 ml 8 M urea.

Supernatant: non-bound protein ← | → Sediment ↓

Cellulose resuspended in 30 ml phosphate-glycine buffer of pH 8.0, repeated washing with the same buffer (3–4 times). Storage of the absorbent—ready for use—in phosphate-glycine buffer at 4°C.

Figure 1. Flow sheet; preparation of bromoacetyl cellulose (BAC)-protein conjugates; modified from Robbins *et al.* (3). The cellulose powder used in step 1 was Whatman CF-12 cellulose powder.

To dissociate the IgA from the BAC-anti-IgA immunoabsorbent, each 0.5 g (dry weight) of absorbent was suspended in 10 ml of 0.1 N HOAc and was immediately sedimented at 10,000 × G for 10 min. The supernatant was saved, and the sedimented absorbent was resuspended in 20 ml of 0.1 HOAc and incubated at 37°C with continuous stirring for 30 min. The acetic acid eluate was recovered by removing the cellulose by centrifugation at 10,000 × G for 10 min. This eluate was combined with the supernatant from the previous acetic acid treatment. The pooled supernatants were then dialyzed against 2 liters of 0.15 M PO_4 buffer at pH 7.5 for 24 hr at 4°C. Traces of insoluble denatured protein and fine residual cellulose particles were removed by a final high speed centrifugation. The neutralized, eluted IgA was concentrated by negative pressure dialysis to a final volume of 1 ml.

Regeneration of the immunoabsorbent. After the acetic acid extraction to dissociate bound antigen (IgA), the immunoabsorbent was washed once with 30 ml of 0.15 M PO_4 buffer at pH 7.5. This was followed by washing with 30 ml of 8 M urea solution with stirring for 10 min at room temperature. The absorbent was recovered by centrifugation and was washed two or three times with phosphate-glycine buffer. The immunoabsorbent was stored in the same buffer at 4°C until reuse.

RESULTS

Table I illustrates the maximum antibody-binding capacity of the BAC-IgA (myeloma) conjugate. It can be seen that with 2 g of the immunoabsorbent containing about 230 mg of chemically bound IgA, it is possible to recover a maximum of 187 mg of anti-IgA antibody protein. Nearly doubling the volume of antiserum does not increase the yield.

TABLE I

Composition and efficiency of BAC-γA conjugate

Absorption	BAC-γ_1A Used	Antiserum Absorbed	Yield Purified Anti-IgA
	g[a]	*ml*	*mg*
1	2	170	187
2	2	325	174
3[b]	2	495	81

[a] Two grams of the conjugate (dry weight) contained 115 mg/g of chemically bound IgA.

[b] Combined supernatants from the first and second absorptions were reabsorbed.

The immunoelectrophoretic patterns of the isolated anti-IgA globulin and of the whole sheep antiserum are shown in Figure 2.

Table II shows selected data which define the optimum pH for physical adsorption of the isolated monospecific anti-IgA antibodies to the BAC cellulose carrier. While the differences in protein nitrogen adsorbed are relatively small between pH 4.4 and 3.4, a distinct maximum can be noted at pH 3.9. While similar pH manipulation was attempted to determine the optimum pH for adsorption of the myeloma protein to the insoluble carrier, the selection of pH was limited by the tendency of the protein to gel below pH 5.2.

On initial use, the BAC-anti-IgA immunoabsorbent, which contained approximately 70 mg of anti-IgA globulin/g of cellulose, was able to bind from serum 15 mg of IgA antigen/g of absorbent. This represented a maximum binding ratio of antibody to antigen of 4.65 to 1. Although this ratio was calculated on the basis of protein nitrogen, it can be taken as the molecular binding ratio in view of the similarity in molecular weights between the antibody and antigen involved. These data are representative of the binding capacity of two separate preparations of

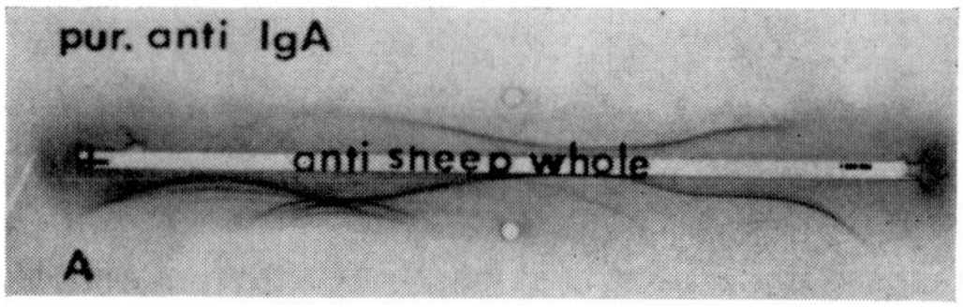

Figure 2. Immunoelectrophoresis: *pur. anti-IgA*, purified anti-IgA globulin (see *Results*) *A*, whole sheep anti-IgA antiserum (see *Materials and Methods*).

TABLE II

Optimum pH for anti-IgA adsorption[a]

pH	BAC Nitrogen after Adsorption (Kjeldahl)
	mg
4.4	1.04
3.9	1.27
3.4	1.11

[a] Adsorption time = 30 hr, amount anti-IgA added = 10 mg, amount of BAC carrier used = 0.08 g (dry weight).

BAC-anti-IgA immunoabsorbent. On successive reuse, the binding capacity for IgA antigen dropped progressively, until after five absorptions 1 g of the conjugate had a binding capacity of 11 mg/g as compared to the initial capacity of 15 mg/g.

Figure 3 illustrates the recovery efficiency of the BAC-anti-IgA immunoabsorbent as a function of IgA input. It can be seen from this curve that by increasing the IgA input/g of absorbent, the yield of IgA/g of absorbent increases to reach a maximum capacity of about 15 mg/g. Based on these data, it is clear that the recovery efficiency of this difficult-to-prepare reagent (BAC-anti-IgA) is maximum at lower IgA input levels. On the other hand, in order to recover maximum amounts of IgA, the input level must reach 15 mg/0.2 g of immunoabsorbent, at which point all available binding sites are apparently saturated. At this input level the recovery efficiency of the absorbent is reduced to about 20% (expressed as IgA recovered/IgA input × 100). These stoichiometric considerations should be borne in mind and used to dictate how much immunoabsorbent is employed in the recovery of IgA from a given serum sample. Preliminary measurement of IgA concentration in the specimen to be absorbed is of help in this regard.

Table III shows the effectiveness of various wash solutions in ridding the BAC-anti-IgA-IgA complex of extraneous, nonspecifically adsorbed protein. The superiority of the 3 M urea is apparent from these data. Preliminary experiments with 2 M guanidine-HCl wash, a concentration which is equivalent in its effect to 3 M urea, showed appreciable denaturation of the isolated IgA as noted on immunoelectrophoresis (see bottom pattern, Fig. 3). Ethylamino and ethanolamino acetyl cellulose prepared according to Step II c, Figure 1, were found to absorb nonspecifically IgA and IgG in approximately equivalent ratios. This absorption amounted to 250 to 350 μg of protein/g (dry weight) of cellulose

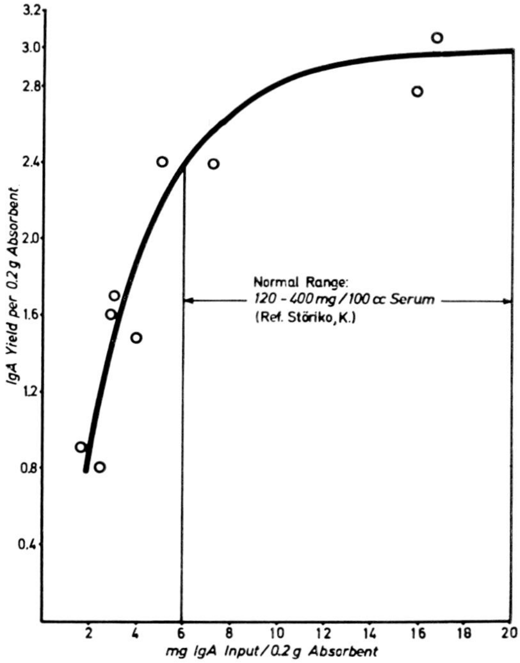

Figure 3. Recovery efficiency of BAC-anti-IgA conjugate as a function of IgA concentration (input).

TABLE III

Contamination of IgA isolated from small volumes of human serum as a function of the wash solution used

Wash Solution	Total Contamination	Total Contamination Due to		Total Contamination mg Protein/g Absorbent
		IgG[a]	IgM[a]	
	%	%		
0.15 M NaCl/PO_4 pH 6.5	8–14	60–80	20–40	0.5–0.87
0.15 M to 1.0 M NaCl/PO_4 pH 7.0	7–13	50–80	20–50	0.4–0.7
0.15 M to 1.0 M NaCl/PO_4 pH 8.0	4–6	90	10	0.3–0.5
3 M urea, 1% glycine pH 8.0	1.5	50	50	0.07

[a] Determined by radial diffusion using Immunoplates, Hyland Laboratories, Los Angeles, Calif. and Partigen immunodiffusion plates, Behringwerke Diagnostics, Woodbury, N.Y. Partigen plates proved to be advantageous when measuring low concentrations of IgG and IgM.

(the amount of IgM could not be determined with certainty, but as can be seen from Table III, was always considerably less than IgG, except for the values given in the last row of the table). This total nonspecific absorption corresponds well with the observed 0.3 to 0.5 mg/g found for the anti-IgA cellulose conjugate when washing was performed at pH 8.0 with the washing buffer as indicated in Table II.

The IgA isolated from small volumes of human serum by use of the BAC-anti-IgA immunoabsorbent is characterized by immunoelectrophoretic analysis in Figure 4. The top slide shows the isolated IgA compared to the starting whole serum with the patterns developed against rabbit anti-whole human serum. It should be noted that the electrophoretic heterogeneity of the isolated product is essentially the same as that of the IgA in the starting material. This analysis was done at an isolated IgA concentration of about 20 mg/ml and shows only a single precipitin arc. The lower slide compares IgA isolated after washing with 3 M urea (*upper pattern*) and 2 M guanidine-HCl (*lower pattern*). The antiserum used was a rabbit anti-human F II. The slightly altered electrophoretic mobility of the guanidine-treated material and the central distortion of the precipitin arc suggest some degree of denaturation; the latter, however, may also be an artifact.

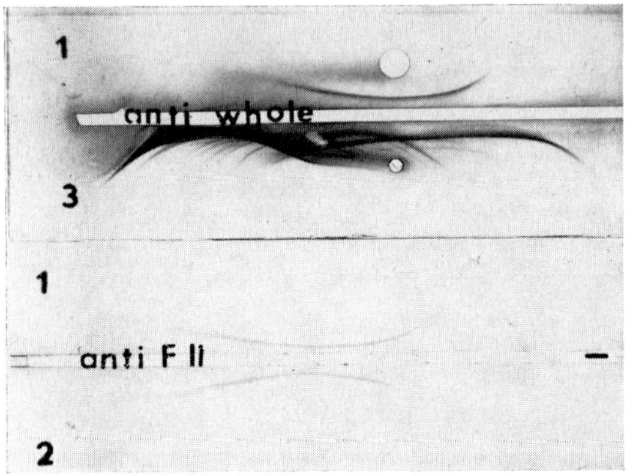

Figure 4. Immunoelectrophoresis. *Upper: 1,* IgA isolated with BAC-anti-IgA immunoabsorbent, approximately 20 mg IgA/ml; *3,* whole human serum. *Lower: 1,* IgA as in *upper; 2,* IgA isolated with BAC-anti-IgA immunoabsorbent, using 2 M guanidine/HCl, pH 8.0, as wash solution, approximately 20 mg/ml.

DISCUSSION

The development of effective immunoabsorbents for isolation of a variety of biologically active substances (4, 6–10) has marked a major methodologic advance in protein chemistry. As previously noted, these techniques have been subject to certain limitations. From the earlier work of Jagendorf and his associates (2) on an antibody-containing conjugate (anti-ovalbumin bromo acetyl-cellulose) it became apparent that a) such preparations were relatively inefficient compared to antigen-carrier absorbents, and b) the problem of nonspecific absorption of extraneous proteins was substantial wherever critical measurements of biologic activity were involved.

The first of these dilemmas was partially overcome by Williams and Stone (5), who achieved a significant increase in binding efficiency of an antibody-carrier conjugate by attaching only antibody of given specificity. In the present study the same tack was used by prefractionating an anti-IgA serum from sheep to isolate the anti-IgA antibody and eliminate the bulk of inert γ globulins. This was a particularly critical step in view of the limited capacity of the BAC preparation to bind protein. To illustrate this, in previous work in our laboratory, a crude, whole γ globulin preparation with a high anti-IgG antibody content (1 to 2 mg Ab protein/ml) was bound to BAC. This absorbent had only one-fourth the binding capacity of the anti-IgA absorbent described in the present study.

Even with the use of this preliminary isolation of pure anti-IgA antibodies and their subsequent coupling to the BAC carrier, the binding efficiency of the resultant conjugate was below the theoretical maximum which might be anticipated from quantitative precipitin curve data. Similar findings have been described by previous workers. Jagendorf *et al.* (2) working with an ovalbumin-anti-ovalbumin system attained an Ab:Ag ratio of 2.4. The lowest figure we were able to reach in extracting IgA from whole serum was 4.65. In our laboratory the R value at equivalence of the normal IgA-anti-IgA system was found to be 3.2 by the conventional precipitin test. As is pointed out below, using prepurified IgA for absorption, an R value of 3.2 was obtained. It is not known whether these findings are fortuitous but Jagendorf also observed that the limiting ratio is that of the combining ratio at equivalence. Such observations suggest that the chemical coupling and resultant surface configuration of the bound antibody restrict the availability of active sites for combination with antigen.

Optimally, it might have been better to develop the anti-IgA antibody against normal IgA rather than against a myeloma protein. This has not been practicable, however, until recently (1) since normal serum IgA has been so difficult to isolate in a state of relative purity and in some quantity.

The data in Figure 2 which relate bound (recovered) IgA to IgA input/unit weight of immunoabsorbent may reflect the law of mass action on the Ag + Ab⇆Ag-Ab reaction. In order to drive the reaction to the right, substantial concentrations of free antigen are required. The interesting consequences of this situation relating to the recovery efficiency of the immunoabsorbent have been referred to previously.

With respect to the maximum binding capacity of the immunoabsorbent, we have conducted a preliminary experiment with purified IgA and have found that this same immunoabsorbent can carry as much as 22 mg IgA/g at saturation. This increase from 15 mg/g absorbent which is extractable from whole serum to 22 mg/g absorbent using pure IgA probably reflects interferences by extraneous proteins.

Unfortunately, we have no definitive data on the influence of the time of incubation on either the rate of binding or its completeness. This deserves study since any factor which might drive the reaction to the right would improve the overall effectiveness of the absorbent and consequently the total economy of the procedure.

With regard to nonspecific absorption of extraneous proteins, it was found that the main contaminants, IgG and IgM, could be removed by use of a 3 M urea PO_4 wash at pH 8.0. As nonspecific adsorption of IgG and IgM appeared to be pH dependent (Table III) an increase of pH beyond the isoelectric point minimized this contamination. On the other hand, this approach is of limited value since above pH 8.0 there is a marked tendency of the antigen-Ab complex to dissociate with resultant Ag loss. Urea as a wash solution did not suffer from this disadvantage. At a 3 M urea concentration, pH 8.0, we were unable to detect any dissociation of the complex while there was a marked reduction in the nonspecific adsorption of the contaminating proteins. Guanidine-HCl accomplished a similar result. However, the IgA obtained appeared to have suffered some degree of denaturation. The work with ethylamino and ethanolamino acetylcellulose which occluded the active bromine groups suggests that this nonspecific adsorption may be an inherent property of the carrier cellulose used. Admittedly, this is at variance from the explanation and the findings of Jagendorf, Patchornik and Sela (2). These authors reported a marked variation in nonspecific binding which appeared to be a property of the individual proteins concerned. Our preoccupation with this problem of minimizing nonspecific adsorption stems from the requirement that the isolated IgA have a high degree of purity in order that biologic activity measurements be reliable.

It is unfortunate that Jagendorf, Patchornik and Sela chose to work with the non-acid dissociable ovalbumin-anti-ovalbumin system. This prevented them from recovering the antigen by acid dissociation of the complex. Our system does not suffer from this defect. Preliminary data indicate that the IgA removed from the carrier retains biologic activity and shows no physico-chemical evidence of denaturation.

There is a disparity between our data relative to the total protein-binding capacity of the BAC in our test system (70 to 127 mg protein/1 g (dry weight) BAC) as compared to the findings of other authors. For example, Robbins *et al.* (3) reported binding of up to 400 mg protein to BAC working with diphtheria toxoid. Such discrepancies may be traceable as has been suggested to inherent properties of the protein or may alternatively be a function of the number of active bromine groups available and the physical state of the cellulose preparation.

The immunoabsorbent described in the current study is difficult to prepare. In spite of this, the effort required is justified for a number of reasons: a) the reagent once manufactured is stable for a long time and can be easily stored; b) the immunoabsorbent can be regenerated and reused as many as five times with minimal loss of binding efficiency; c) in practice the method for extracting antigen from whole serum is technically very simple and very rapid once the immunoabsorbent has been prepared; d) the reagent as used in the present study can remove IgA from very small amounts of human serum and other biologic fluids and in this sense is vastly superior to any known physico-chemical fractionation procedure; e) the isolated product as previously noted appears to be minimally denatured on elution from the carrier; and finally f) in the light of current intense interest in the biologic role and reaction characteristics of IgA antibody, this method of isolation seems to hold considerable promise and wide applicability, which has also been pointed out recently by Ito *et al.* (9) and Davis *et al.* (10).

Acknowledgment. We thank Mrs. Dorothea Zschocke for the preparation of the purified myeloma IgA protein.

REFERENCES

1. Zschocke, R. H., Grieble, H. G., Bach, G. L. and Anderson, T. O., J. Immun., *102:* 625, 1969.
2. Jagendorf, A. T., Patchornik, A. and Sela, M., Biochim. Biophys. Acta, *78:* 516, 1963.
3. Robbins, I. B., Haimovich, I. and Sela, M., Immunochemistry, *4:* 11, 1967.
4. Patchornik, A., Israel Patent Application No. 18207, 1962.
5. Williams, R. R. and Stone, S. S., Arch. Biochem., *71:* 377, 1957.
6. Silman, I. and Katchalski, E., Ann. Rev. Biochem., *35:* 873, 1966.
7. Gill, T. J. and Bernard, C. I., Immunochemistry, *6:* 567, 1969.
8. Cuatrecasas, P., Biochem. Biophys. Res. Commun., *35:* 531, 1969.
9. Ito, K., Wicher, K. and Arbesman, C. E., J. Immun., *103:* 622, 1969.
10. Davis, R. V., Blanken, R. M. and Beagle, R. J., Biochemistry, *8:* 2706, 1969.

THE JOURNAL OF IMMUNOLOGY
Vol. 105, No. 1, July 1970
Printed in U.S.A.

IMMUNOGLOBULIN CLASSES OF ANTIBODY-FORMING CELLS IN MICE

IV. The Incorporation of Tritiated Thymidine into IgM and γ_1 Plaque-Forming Cells during the Primary Immune Response[1]

ALBERT A. NORDIN,[2] HUMBERTO COSENZA AND STEWART SELL[3]

From the Department of Microbiology, Lobund Laboratory, University of Notre Dame, Notre Dame, Indiana 46556, and the Department of Pathology, University of Pittsburgh, School of Medicine, Pittsburgh, Pennsylvania 15213

Received for publication November 20, 1969

The incorporation of tritiated thymidine (^{3}HT) into hemolysin-in-agar plaque-forming cells (PFC) was determined for direct (IgM) and indirect (γ_1) PFC following a single optimal injection of sheep red blood cells (SRC) into mice. After immunization with SRC, ^{3}HT was injected into mice at various time intervals. The PFC of all mice tested were assayed at 5.5 days after immunization because γ_1 PFC are not detectable in significant numbers until this time. The percentage of PFC labeled and the number of grains/labeled cell indicated that the onset, duration and extent of incorporation of ^{3}HT were the same for both types of PFC. The potential γ_1 PFC appear to be formed at the same time as the IgM PFC, but γ_1 PFC do not synthesize or release γ_1 antibody until 5 to 6 days after immunization, when proliferation of PFC has essentially stopped. IgM PFC appear 2 days after immunization and appear to synthesize DNA, divide and produce antibody simultaneously.

The autoradiographic detection of tritiated thymidine incorporation into DNA has been used by numerous investigators as an index of cellular proliferation in a variety of tissues (1). Baney *et al.* (2) combined autoradiographic and fluorescent antibody techniques to show that newly formed antibody-containing cells arise by mitotic division during the secondary immune response. More recently, autoradiographic studies of single antibody-producing cells, as detected by the plaque technique (3), have been used to determine whether these cells arise by a process of proliferation and/or differentiation during the primary immune response. Some investigators maintain that the early appearance and rapid increase of plaque-forming cells (PFC) are largely due to cellular proliferation (4–6) while others suggest that cell differentiation plays a very important role during the onset of the primary immune response (7, 8). *In vitro* stimulation of normal mouse spleen cell suspensions with heterologous erythrocytes (9) has indicated that DNA synthesis is required but does not begin until approximately 24 hr after the addition of antigen. All of these observations have been confined to IgM PFC which apparently are able to divide and produce antibody while differentiating (6, 10, 11).

The present studies provide evidence that IgG (γ_1) PFC, which are detected 5 to 6 days after the primary injection of sheep erythrocytes, incorporate tritiated thymidine at the same time and to the same extent as the IgM PFC. These results demonstrate that the potential γ_1 antibody-producing cells proliferate at the same rate as the IgM PFC but do not synthesize and/or secrete antibody until 5 days after immunization, a time at which the number of PFC synthesizing IgM hemolysin is already decreasing.

MATERIALS AND METHODS

Experimental animals. CFW virgin female mice between 8 to 12 weeks of age were provided by the Lobund Laboratory animal production unit. Each experimental group of mice was kept in disposable plastic cages and maintained on L-485 diet (12) and water *ad libitum.*

[1] This work was supported by USPHS Grants AI-07659 and AI-07712.

[2] Recipient of Career Development Award 1K 2-AI-37562.

[3] Recipient of Career Development Award 1K 3-AI-23308.

Immunization. The sheep red cells (SRC) were obtained in sterile Alsever's solution and prior to injection were washed in phosphate-buffered saline (PBS), pH 7.2, and finally resuspended in PBS to a 20% suspension. All mice were given 0.1 ml intravenously (approximately 5×10^8 SRC).

Injection of mice with tritiated thymidine. A single lot of 10 mCi of tritiated thymidine (^{3}HT, New England Nuclear Corp., Boston, Mass.) was obtained in 5-ml amounts in 70% ethanol. Each 5 ml contained 0.075 mg of ^{3}HT and the specific activity was 16.1 Ci/mM. Prior to injection, each 5 ml of the ^{3}HT stock solution was evaporated to approximately 1.5 ml by vacuum at room temperature, and PBS was added to give a total of 2.0 ml. The concentrated solution of ^{3}HT now contained 2500 μCi/ml and 0.1 ml was injected intravenously at the time indicated for each experiment.

Preparation of antiserum. Mouse myeloma γ_1 globulin was isolated from the ascitic fluid of BALB/c mice carrying the MOPC-70A transplantable tumor. A specific anti-γ_1 serum was obtained by injecting the Fc fragment into sheep. Detailed description of the isolating procedures and the specificity of the antiserum has been reported elsewhere (13).

Preparation of single cell suspension. At the time of assay, each animal was anesthetized with ether, the spleen aseptically removed and placed into a 60- x 15-mm sterile plastic Petri dish containing 5 ml of cold Eagle's tissue culture medium supplemented with non-essential amino acids. The spleens were disrupted by gently rubbing them against a stainless steel wire mesh. The resulting cell suspensions were filtered through two layers of sterile gauze and washed twice with cold Eagle's medium to remove soluble radioactive materials.

Agar plaque technique adapted to microscope slides. Clean microscope slides, 75 x 50 mm, were placed on a warming table set at 52°C and coated with a thin layer of 0.5% agarose in 0.3% NaCl. About 0.5 ml of this solution was added onto each warm slide and spread with a glass rod. The excess agarose-NaCl solution was drained off the slide by touching one of its long edges onto absorbent paper towels. The coated slides were replaced on the warming table until they were completely dried. This first agarose coat was necessary to assure the adherence of the SRC-spleen cell-agarose layer.

On the day of the experiment, the coated slides were warmed on a heated slide table (52°C). Disposable glass tubes containing 0.45 ml of 0.5% agarose in Eagle's medium were kept in a 48°C water bath. Into each test tube was added 0.03 ml of the 20% SRC suspension and 0.03 ml of the spleen cell suspension. The contents of each tube were thoroughly mixed, quickly poured onto a warm precoated slide and carefully spread with a clean glass rod. To obtain a very thin layer, the excess was then drained off as previously described and the slide gently tilted from side to side to spread the mixture uniformly. All slides were placed on a level surface at room temperature until the agar solidified. The slides were then placed into specially designed Plexiglas trays (14) and incubated for 1 to 1.5 hr at 37°C in a 5% CO_2 environment at 100% humidity.

After the initial 1 to 1.5 hr incubation, all slides were washed in 0.85% NaCl for 15 min. Slides to be assayed for IgM PFC were immediately incubated with a 1:30 dilution of fresh guinea pig serum (complement source) for 30 min. Those slides to be assayed only for γ_1 PFC were first incubated for 1 hr with a 0.4 mg/ml solution of concanavalin A dissolved in PBS, pH 7.2. Concanavalin A, which combines with the carbohydrate moiety of IgM, inhibits the expression of the IgM PFC without affecting the γ_1 PFC or the morphology of the cells as determined by light microscopy (15). Following incubation, the concanavalin A-treated slides were thoroughly washed in three changes of 0.85% NaCl over a 30-min interval. The slides were then incubated with a 1:350 dilution of sheep anti-mouse γ_1 serum for 1 hr and washed in 0.85% NaCl for 15 min before being developed for PFC by the addition of complement for 30 min (16, 17). In preliminary studies, a 1:350 dilution of the anti-γ_1 serum gave optimal enhancement using the slide technique.

After development of all IgM and γ_1 plaques, the slides were washed in 0.85% NaCl for 15 min before fixation in absolute acetone (10 min) and 95% ethanol (20 min). All slides were then rapidly air dried under a fan at room temperature.

Autoradiographic techniques. NTB 3 nuclear track emulsion was warmed in a 40°C water bath for 45 min. Two plastic containers were placed in the water bath; distilled water was placed in one and the emulsion in the other. The slides were placed on a warming table set at 45°C. The warm slides were first dipped into distilled water to facilitate spreading the emulsion. The excess water was shaken off before the slides were dipped into the emulsion. The backs of the slides were wiped clean with a paper towel and the excess emulsion was drained off by standing the slides upright in a rack on wet paper towels. The slides were air dried for 1 hr in the dark room. All slides were then placed into light tight boxes containing Drierite. The boxes were sealed with black tape and stored at 4°C for 10 days.

The emulsion-coated slides were developed in D-19 developer for 2 min, rinsed in distilled water and placed in acid fixer for 5 min. All slides were then washed for 20 min in running tap water, rinsed in distilled water and air dried. All solutions used in the developing process were contained in Coplin jars and kept at 18°C ± 2°C.

Microscopic examination of autoradiographic slides. After the emulsion was developed, the slides were stained with Wright's stain. All plaques were circled under × 30 magnification and the circles were joined by arrows so that the same PFC would not be counted twice. The PFC were located at × 100 magnification and the grain counts were performed at × 1000 magnification.

RESULTS

Efficiency of detecting labeled PFC. Experiments were conducted to determine the efficiency of detecting labeled PFC by the present autoradio-

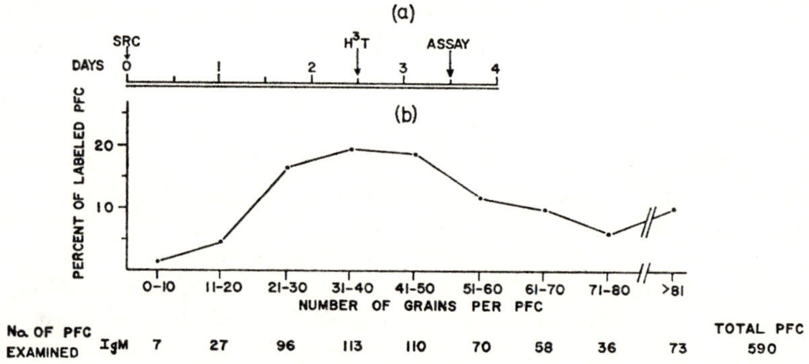

Figure 1. a, Mice were injected intravenously with sheep erythrocytes (SRC) on day 0 and tritiated thymidine (^{3}HT) on day 2.5 and the spleens were assayed on day 3.5. *b,* The labeling pattern of the IgM PFC from the spleens of mice treated and assayed according to the schedule shown in Figure 1*a*.

TABLE I

The distribution of labeled IgM plaque-forming cells in mice injected with tritiated thymidine at various times after immunization

Group[a]	No. of Grains/PFC								
	0–10	11–20	21–30	31–40	41–50	51–60	61–70	71–80	>80
A[b]									
No. of PFC	242	18	3			1			
% PFC	92	7	1			0.4			
B[c]									
No. of PFC	35	127	148	91	57	27	16	6	23
% PFC	7	24	28	17	11	5	3	1	4
C[d]									
No. of PFC	30	126	111	56	23	21	7	3	7
% PFC	8	33	30	15	6	6	2	0.8	2

[a] All mice assayed 3 days after SRC.
[b] ^{3}HT injected 24 hr after SRC.
[c] ^{3}HT injected 48 hr after SRC.
[d] ^{3}HT injected 24 hr and 48 hr after SRC.

graphic techniques. Three mice were injected with 250 μCi of ^{3}HT at day 2.5 and the spleens assayed for IgM PFC at 3.5 days after immunization. This period of labeling was chosen because it has been reported (4, 5, 8) that the great majority of the IgM PFC observed during the exponential phase of the primary response are able to incorporate ^{3}HT. The results presented in Figure 1 confirm this observation and demonstrate that the procedures used in the experiments to be reported were able to detect labeled PFC with high efficiency. Only 7 PFC (1.2%) out of a total of 580 cells examined had less than 10 grains/cell. This observation also indicated that the thin, dried agarose layer, in which the IgM PFC were embedded, did not interfere with the detection of the β particles emitted by the tritium since 98.8% of the IgM PFC were labeled with at least 11 grains/cell.

In each experiment, several slides prepared from the spleens of mice which had been immunized but not injected with ^{3}HT were coated with emulsion and stored in the same container with the experimental slides. The majority (48%) of the PFC examined had no grains, 37% had 1 grain, 12% had 2 grains and only 3% of the PFC had 3 to 5 grains/cell. Therefore, PFC which showed more than 10 grains were considered labeled. Furthermore, it was found that the amount of ^{3}HT used to label the PFC did not interfere with the total number of PFC, since the number of PFC in mice injected with one or two doses of ^{3}HT was not significantly different from the number of PFC found in the spleens of mice injected with unlabeled thymidine.

Labeling of IgM PFC. To determine the time after SRC injection when ^{3}HT was incorporated in detectable amounts, three groups of mice (three mice/group) were injected with ^{3}HT at various time intervals following immunization and assayed 3 days after the SRC injection. The results are presented in Table I. In group A, which was injected with ^{3}HT 24 hr after immunization, only 8% of the PFC were labeled. However, if the ^{3}HT was given 48 hr after the SRC (group B), 93% of the PFC were labeled. Because it could be argued that the PFC from group A did incorporate ^{3}HT but lost the label as a result of proliferation, a group of mice was injected with ^{3}HT at 24 and 48 hr (group C). The PFC of group C mice were labeled to the same extent as those in group B (92%). This indicates that the ^{3}HT given at 48 hr was responsible for labeling the PFC. This result agrees well with the results of others (9, 11, 18). In all subsequent experiments the first injection of ^{3}HT was not given until 36 hr after antigenic stimulation.

Labeling patterns of IgM and IgG PFC. By means of the plaque technique, it is possible to detect a significant increase in the number of cells actively synthesizing IgM hemolysin at day 2, while IgG PFC are not detected until 4.5 days after immunization (13, 14, 19). The question is whether IgM and potential γ_1 antibody-producing cells start to synthesize DNA simultaneously or in a sequential manner as suggested by the respective lag phases.

This problem was approached by injecting four different groups of mice (four to six mice/group) with ^{3}HT from 1.5 to 4.5 days after immunization. If there was complete inactivity in both

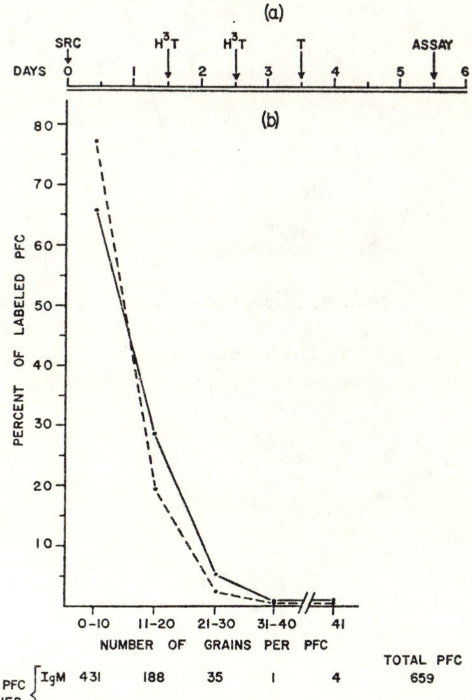

		0-10	11-20	21-30	31-40	41	TOTAL PFC
No. OF PFC EXAMINED	IgM	431	188	35	1	4	659
	γ_1	348	85	11	3	2	449

Figure 2. a, Mice were injected intravenously with sheep erythrocytes (SRC) on day 0, tritiated thymidine (^{3}HT) on days 1.5 and 2.5 and unlabeled thymidine (T) on day 3.5 and the spleens were assayed on day 5.5. *b,* The labeling patterns of IgM PFC (——) and γ_1 PFC (-----) from the spleens of mice treated and assayed according to the schedule shown in Figure 2*a*.

DNA synthesis and proliferation of the γ_1 PFC during the 4.5 day lag phase, these cells would not be labeled when the ^{3}HT was given. However, IgM PFC should be labeled since these cells would be actively synthesizing DNA and proliferating at the time ^{3}HT was given.

The first group of mice was injected with ^{3}HT at 1.5 and 2.5 days and the spleens were assayed at 5.5 days after immunization (Fig. 2). An injection of unlabeled thymidine was given at 3.5 days to retard any further incorporation of the labeled thymidine. Figure 2*b* gives the labeling patterns of both IgM and γ_1 PFC. The distribution curves of both classes of labeled PFC are almost identical and the majority of the cells are grouped in the low part of the curve. A total of 659 IgM PFC were examined and 431 cells (65%) contained 0 to 10 grains and were considered as non-labeled PFC. The remaining 228 IgM PFC (35%) were labeled with more than 10 grains/cell. Among the γ_1 PFC, 348 cells (77%) were not labeled and 91 PFC (23%) were labeled with more

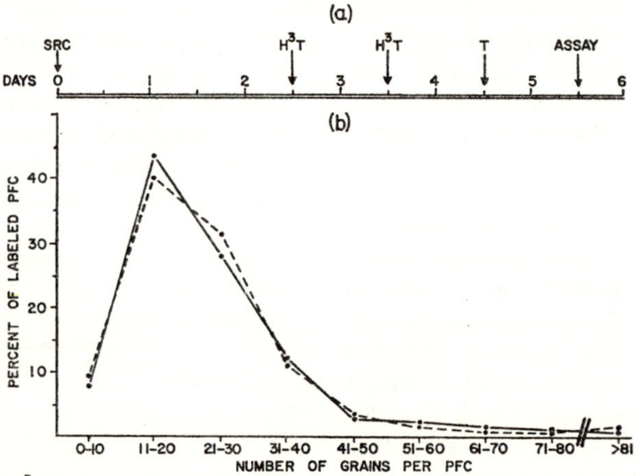

No. OF PFC EXAMINED	0-10	11-20	21-30	31-40	41-50	51-60	61-70	71-80	>81	TOTAL PFC
IgM	54	293	190	81	18	14	10	6	6	672
γ_1	42	179	141	49	14	8	3	2	6	444

Figure 3. a, Mice were injected intravenously with sheep erythrocytes (SRC) on day 0, tritiated thymidine (^{3}HT) on days 2.5 and 3.5 and unlabeled thymidine (T) on day 4.5 and the spleens were assayed on day 5.5. *b,* The labeling patterns of IgM PFC (——) and γ_1 PFC (-----) from the spleens of mice treated and assayed according to the schedule shown in Figure 3*a*.

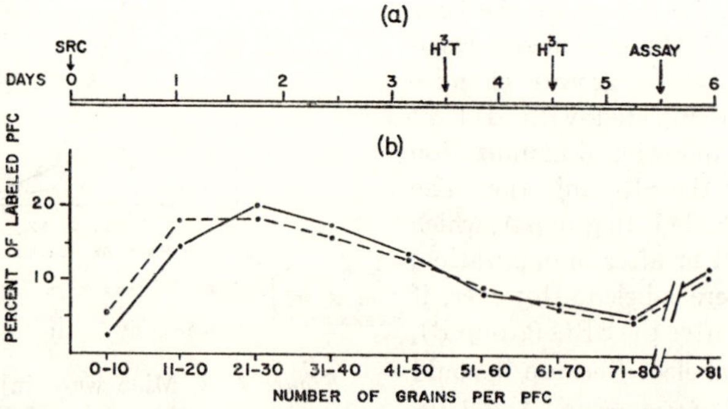

No. OF PFC EXAMINED	0-10	11-20	21-30	31-40	41-50	51-60	61-70	71-80	>81	TOTAL PFC
IgM	18	119	165	144	112	68	56	42	91	817
γ_1	43	144	144	125	103	72	50	34	82	797

Figure 4. a, Mice were injected intravenously with sheep erythrocytes (SRC) on day 0 and tritiated thymidine (^{3}HT) on days 3.5 and 4.5 and the spleens were assayed on day 5.5. *b,* The labeling patterns of IgM PFC (——) and γ_1 PFC (-----) from the spleens of mice treated and assayed according to the schedule shown in Figure 4*a*.

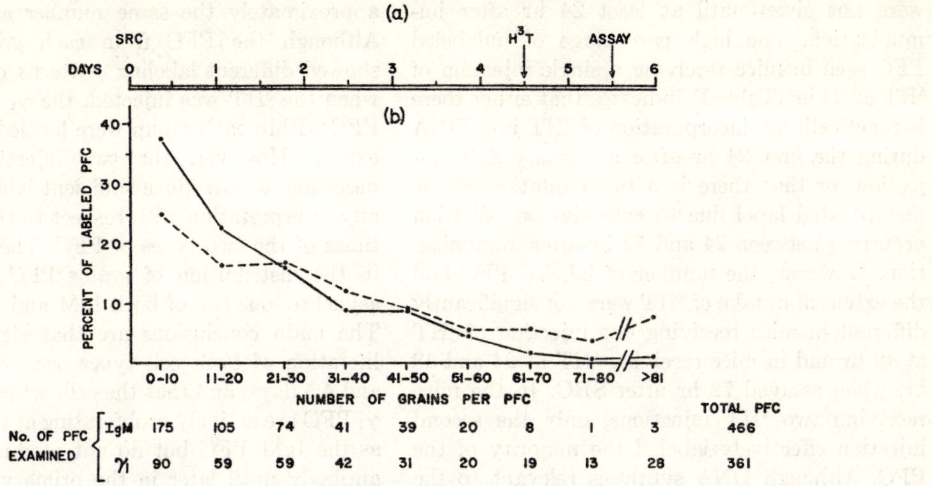

Figure 5. a, Mice were injected intravenously with sheep erythrocytes (SRC) on day 0 and tritiated thymidine (^{3}HT) on day 4.5 and the spleens assayed on day 5.5. *b*, The labeling patterns of IgM PFC (——) and γ_1 PFC (-----) from the spleens of mice treated and assayed according to the schedule shown in Figure 5*a*.

than 10 grains/cell. Very few PFC contained more than 40 grains and therefore were grouped together.

The second group of mice was injected with ^{3}HT at 2.5 and 3.5 days, unlabeled thymidine was given at 4.5 days, and the spleens were assayed at 5.5 days after immunization. Figure 3 shows the strikingly similar labeling patterns of both IgM and γ_1 PFC. Out of a total of 672 IgM PFC counted, only 54 cells (8%) could be considered not labeled. Among the 444 γ_1 PFC examined, 90% were labeled while only 42 PFC (10%) were not labeled.

The third group of mice was injected with ^{3}HT at 3.5 and 4.5 days and assayed at 5.5 days after immunization. The distribution of both IgM and γ_1 PFC (Fig. 4) was almost identical, most of the PFC examined being heavily labeled. Out of 817 IgM PFC examined only 18 cells were not labeled, and out of a total of 797 γ_1 PFC only 43 cells were not labeled. PFC labeled with more than 80 grains/cell were grouped together because high grain counts could not be scored with any degree of accuracy.

The fourth group of mice was injected with ^{3}HT at 4.5 days and assayed 5.5 days after immunization. Only one injection of ^{3}HT was given because of the short period of time between the labeling and assay time. There was, however, a large number of unlabeled PFC. Out of 466 IgM PFC, 175 were not labeled; 90 of 361 γ_1 PFC were not labeled. The labeling patterns of IgM and γ_1 PFC were still remarkably similar (Fig. 5).

DISCUSSION

The cellular events leading to the formation of a large number of antibody-producing cells have been extensively examined by the hemolysis-in-agar technique (3–11). The importance of DNA synthesis as an indication of the role of cell division in the production of IgM PFC has been demonstrated. IgM PFC that are detected in significant numbers 2 days after immunization incorporate ^{3}HT *in vivo* and *in vitro* (4, 7–9, 11). There are, on the other hand, no comparable studies reported on the uptake of ^{3}HT by IgG PFC which are first detectable when the number of IgM PFC has started to decline (13, 14, 19). The results of the experiments reported herein show that the cells which give rise to the IgG-γ_1 PFC incorporate ^{3}HT at the same time as the IgM PFC even though no synthesis or release of γ_1 antibody is detected until later in the primary immune response.

Although the exact duration of the lag phase is not conclusively established and depends largely on the sensitivity of the methods used for antibody detection, there is agreement that DNA synthesis and cell division do not occur during the first 24 hr after exposure to heterologous red cells (9, 11). In the present studies, ^{3}HT injections were not given until at least 24 hr after immunization. The high percentage of unlabeled PFC seen in mice receiving a single injection of ^{3}HT at 24 hr (Table I) indicates that either there is practically no incorporation of ^{3}HT into DNA during the first 24 hr after a primary SRC injection, or that there is a rapid dilution of the incorporated label due to extensive cell division occurring between 24 and 72 hr after immunization. However, the number of labeled PFC and the extent of uptake of ^{3}HT were not significantly different in mice receiving one injection of ^{3}HT at 48 hr and in mice receiving ^{3}HT at 24 and 48 hr, when assayed 72 hr after SRC. In the mice receiving two ^{3}HT injections, only the second injection effectively labeled the majority of the PFC. Although DNA synthesis relevant to the immune response has been reported to begin 18 hr after antigenic stimulation (20), the onset of DNA synthesis as determined by these experimental conditions occurs later than 24 hr after immunization.

Because of the long lag period before γ_1 PFC are detectable in significant numbers (5 to 6 days following immunization (13)), the possibility of dilution of label by cellular proliferation must be considered in evaluating labeled IgM and γ_1 PFC at this time. For example, a single injection of ^{3}HT containing 250 μCi given 3.5 days after immunization did not label the majority of either class of PFC when assayed at day 5.5. To minimize a possible dilution effect, two injections of ^{3}HT were given at 24-hr intervals, on the assumption that the proliferating lymphoid cells would be able to incorporate the label from both injections. A single injection of 500 μg of unlabeled thymidine was given to eliminate any further incorporation of ^{3}HT. This was done only as a precautionary measure because it is known that the great majority (98%) of the labeled thymidine is incorporated within 2 hr after injection (21, 22). Mice injected with these amounts of thymidine or ^{3}HT showed no significant increase or decrease in the number of IgM or γ_1 PFC when compared with mice injected with only SRC.

The labeling patterns obtained after injecting ^{3}HT at different times following immunization demonstrate that both γ_1 PFC and IgM PFC incorporate ^{3}HT at the same time. In all experiments done to compare the uptake of ^{3}HT by IgM and IgG PFC, the mice were assayed at 5.5 days when γ_1 PFC were consistently detected in approximately the same number as IgM PFC. Although the PFC from each group of mice showed different labeling patterns depending on when the ^{3}HT was injected, the γ_1 and the IgM PFC within each group were labeled to the same extent. However, the two injections of ^{3}HT necessary to introduce sufficient label complicate any interpretation with respect to the generation times of the two types of PFC. The broad range in the distribution of grains/PFC indicates an asynchronous rise of both IgM and γ_1 PFC (23). The main conclusions are that significant proliferation of both cell types occurs between 1.5 and 4.5 days, and that the cells which give rise to γ_1 PFC are actively proliferating at the same time as the IgM PFC but do not produce detectable antibody until later in the primary immune response.

The mechanism of the early appearance of IgM PFC and the later appearance of IgG PFC remains unexplained. It seems evident that the IgM PFC are able to synthesize DNA, divide and produce antibody simultaneously (6, 10). The large number of IgG PFC that appears between 4.5 and 5.5 days is too great to be explained by proliferation, and the incorporation of ^{3}HT given at different days following immunization indicates that significant proliferation of PFC is ended by 4.5 days after SRC injection. Therefore the large number of IgG PFC observed on or about 5 days after immunization must arise from potential γ_1 PFC which have proliferated and formed numerous cells which are synchronously activated to produce antibody. The mechanism of this activation is unknown.

REFERENCES

1. Hughes, W. L., Bond, V. P., Brecher, G., Cronkite, E. P., Painter, R. B., Quastler, H. and Sherman, F. G., Proc. Nat. Acad. Sci., *44:* 476, 1958.
2. Baney, R. N., Vasquez, J. J. and Dixon, F. J., Proc. Soc. Exp. Biol. Med., *109:* 1, 1962.
3. Jerne, N. K. and Nordin, A. A., Science, *140:* 405, 1963.
4. Szenberg, A. and Cunningham, A. J., Nature, *217:* 747, 1968.
5. Koros, A. M. C., Mazur, J. M. and Mowery, M. J., J. Exp. Med., *128:* 235, 1968.
6. Rowley, A. A., Fitch, F. W., Mosier, D. E., Solliday, S., Coppleson, L. W. and Brown, B. W., J. Exp. Med., *127:* 983, 1968.
7. Sterzl, J., Vesely, J., Jilek, M. and Mandel, L., *Molecular and Cellular Basis of Antibody*

Formation, Edited by J. Sterzl, Publishing House of the Czechoslovak Academy of Science, Prague, Czechoslovakia, 1965.
8. Tannenberg, W. J. K. and Malaviya, A. N., J. Exp. Med., *128:* 895, 1968.
9. Dutton, R. W. and Mishell, R. I., J. Exp. Med., *126:* 443, 1967.
10. Claflin, A. J. and Smithies, O., Science, *157:* 1561, 1967.
11. Dutton, R. W. and Mishell, R. I., in *The Control of Nuclear Activity*, Edited by L. Goldstein, Prentice-Hall, Inc., Englewood Cliffs, N. J., 1967.
12. Kellogg, T. F. and Wostman, B. S., Gnotobiotic Newsletter *3:* 3, 1967.
13. Sell, S., Park, A. B. and Nordin, A. A., J. Immun., *104:* 483, 1970.
14. Plotz, P. H., Talal, N. and Asofsky, R., J. Immun., *100:* 744, 1968.
15. Nordin, A. A., Cosenza, H. and Hopkins, W., J. Immun., *103:* 859, 1969.
16. Sterzl, J. and Riha, I., Nature, *208:* 858, 1965.
17. Dresser, D. W. and Wortis, H. H., Nature, *208:* 859, 1965.
18. Cohen, E. P. and Talmadge, D. W., J. Exp. Med., *121:* 125, 1965.
19. Eidinger, D. and Pross, H. F., J. Exp. Med., *126:* 15, 1967.
20. Holterman, O. and Nordin, A. A., Proc. Soc. Exp. Biol. Med., *132:* 1003, 1969.
21. Rubini, J. R., Cronkite, E. P., Bond, V. P. and Fiedner, T. M., J. Clin. Invest., *39:* 909, 1960.
22. Staroscik, R. N., Jenkins, W. H. and Mendelsohn, M. L., Nature, *202:* 456, 1964.
23. Cleaver, J. E., *Thymidine Metabolism and Cell Kinetics*, John Wiley & Sons, Inc., New York, 1967.

THE JOURNAL OF IMMUNOLOGY
Vol. 105, No. 1, July 1970
Printed in U.S.A.

A METHOD FOR PREPARING MONOSPECIFIC ANTISERA TO C1 ESTERASE (C1s): MICROHETEROGENEITY OF PURIFIED C1s[1]

K. NAGAKI AND R. M. STROUD

From the Division of Clinical Immunology and Rheumatology, Department of Medicine, Birmingham Veterans Administration Hospital, University of Alabama in Birmingham, 1919 Seventh Avenue South, Birmingham, Alabama 35233

Received for publication October 30, 1969

Highly purified C1s has been obtained by immunization of rabbits using popliteal node injections of highly purified C1s followed by booster injections with gel segments containing C1s after disc-acrylamide gel electrophoresis. The antisera are monospecific and unexpectedly reveal electrophoretic microheterogeneity in highly purified C1s preparations. We have studied this electrophoretic heterogeneity in highly purified and in crude C1s preparations and hypothesize that it is due to two factors: 1) The partial proteolysis of C1s produced either by other serum enzymes or perhaps by autocatalysis. This can be demonstrated in highly purified C1s preparations. 2) The presence in crude preparations of another serum protein(s) which appears to influence the migration of C1s. These antisera are useful for quantitating C1s by single radial diffusion. We consider the heterogeneity of C1s to be an important feature of this molecule and future quantitative studies should take account of it.

Previous studies of human C1 esterase (C1s), a subunit of the first complement component, C1, by Lepow and Haines (1) and Nagaki and Stroud (2) demonstrated that this serum enzyme cannot be quantitatively assayed in whole serum or in any biologic fluid that contains other complement components and varying amounts of the other subunits of C1 (C1q and C1r (3)) by current hemolytic and esterase assays. The specificity of C1s, either for synthetic esters such as N-acetyl-*l*-tyrosine ethyl ester or *p*-tosyl-*l*-arginine methyl ester, is not sufficient for a specific synthetic substrate assay. Furthermore, other enzymes react with the natural substrates, C2 (4) and C4 (5), causing a destructive loss of activity of these substrates. The distinguishing feature of C1s is that it is capable of specifically attacking C2 and C4 to create a biologically active complex, $C\overline{42}$ convertase (6). It is possible to assay highly purified C1s by measuring the rate of formation of this complex. However, the rate and extent of formation is markedly dependent on the concentration of other subunits in macromolecular C1 (2, 7) and on the C2 concentration when the $C\overline{42}$ complex is formed on sensitized erythrocytes (2). Presumably the same will be true for fluid phase $C\overline{42}$ formation by C1s. Consequently, in accordance with the significant advantages of practical immunochemical methods, as outlined by Kohler and Müller-Eberhard (8), we have developed monospecific antibody to C1s. The method of preparation of the antigen and antisera will be described here. In an accompanying publication (9) we describe the use of these antisera to quantitate C1s in whole serum by single radial immunodiffusion. These antisera have been used to quantitate C1s in various diseases (R. M. Stroud and K. Nagaki, to be published).

In the process of obtaining a highly purified antigen for these studies we noted significant electrophoretic and functional heterogeneity of C1s. A preliminary communication has described this and also described a more gross electrophoretic alteration depending on whether EDTA and other C1 subunits are present (10). Further description of the electrophoretic microheterogeneity of purified preparations of C1s will be presented here because this knowledge should facilitate understanding of the molecular structure of this enzyme.

[1] This work was supported by grants from the National Institutes of Health (AI 08422), the American Cancer Society and the Veterans Administration.

MATERIALS AND METHODS

Whole human serum was separated from fresh or outdated blood by centrifugation at 720 × G for 20 min followed by repeat centrifugation at 10,000 × G for 35 min. Diethylaminoethyl cellulose and CM-cellulose (Brown Co., Berlin, N. H.) were prepared for chromatography as previously described (2). Analytical and preparative acrylamide gel electrophoresis were performed as described by Davis (11). Immunoelectrophoresis was carried out on 1.0% agarose or 1.2% Special Agar Noble (lot no. 462512) in 0.026 M Veronal, 0.032 M acetate buffer at pH 8.6, containing 0.01 M EDTA, for 120 min at 3 volts/cm. Horse anti-whole human serum was obtained from the Osaka Microbiological Diseases Research Foundation, Osaka University, Japan. The purification of C1s has been described (2) and only if new steps were introduced will details be given. TAMe esterase activity and hemolytic activity of C1s were titrated as described previously (2). The electrical resistance of buffer solutions was measured at 0°C and is related to NaCl solutions yielding an equivalent resistance (relative salt concentration, RSC).

RESULTS

Purification of antigen. With conventional methods of immunization and using the previously described highly purified C1s preparations (2), it was not possible to obtain monospecific antisera; the rabbits consistently made antibody

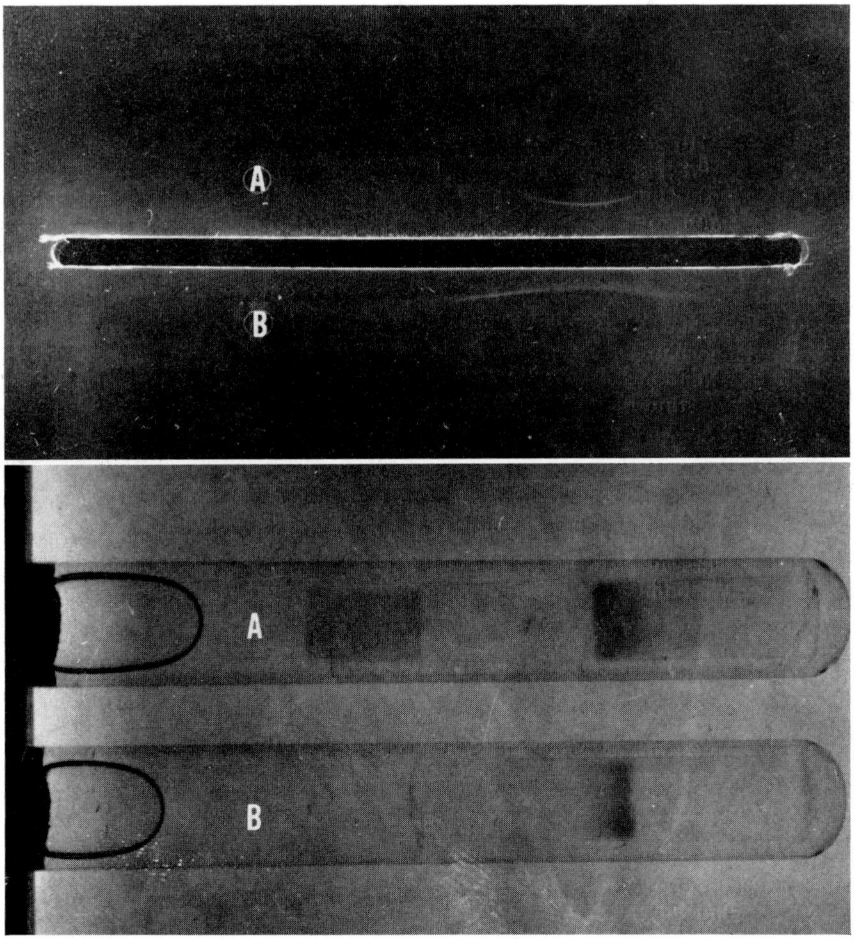

Figure 1. Immunoelectrophoretic pattern of highly purified C1s on agarose and acrylamide gel electrophoresis pattern. Anode is to the right. Trough contains horse anti-whole human serum.

to C1s and albumin. As albumin has a tendency to trail into the α globulin region on Pevikon electrophoresis, preparatory acrylamide electrophoresis was substituted for this last step in the previously described purification process. A 10- x 15-cm vertical 7.5% acrylamide slab and a discontinuous buffer system at pH 8.6 were used. The fractions containing C1s from DEAE-cellulose chromatography were pooled, concentrated and layered on the stacking gel generally in a volume of 5 to 15 ml. The duration of the run was 3 to 5 hr and the migration distance of C1s was approximately 6 to 9 cm. The gel segments were cut into 0.5-cm segments eluted by stirring with several volumes of Tris buffer (0.1 M, pH 7.4) for 5 to 7 days at 0.4°C. The fractions containing C1s, as detected by hemolytic activity, were pooled and concentrated by vacuum ultrafiltration. C1s obtained by this method showed a single band on immunoelectrophoresis against anti-whole human serum and a single heterogeneous band on discontinuous analytical acrylamide electrophoresis. Electrophoretic microheterogeneity of varying degrees was detected in these preparations, as shown by the comparison of two separate C1s preparations in Figure 1.

Immunization of rabbits. Monospecific antibody to C1s was obtained by immunizing rabbits with highly purified C1s. Each rabbit was injected with 60 μg of C1s emulsified in Freund's com-

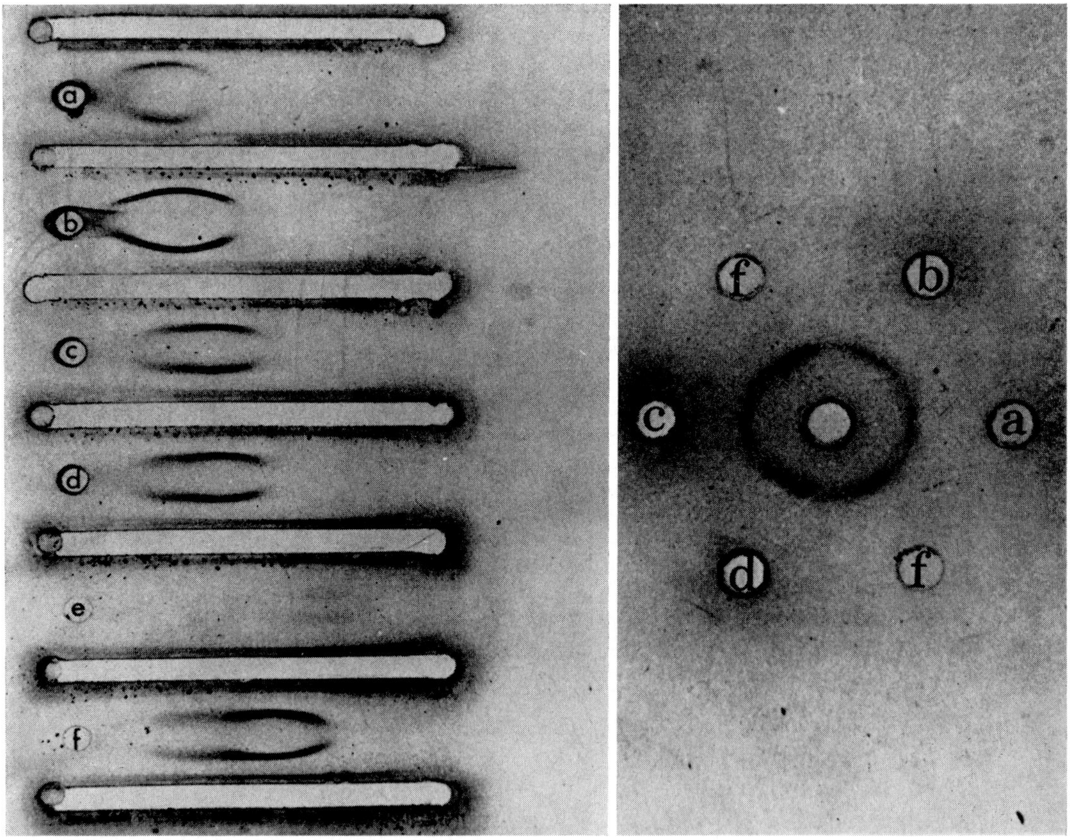

Figure 2. Immunoelectrophoresis on Special Agar Noble (*left*) and Ouchterlony analysis (*right*). Immunoelectrophoresis troughs and the center well of the Ouchterlony plate have rabbit anti-C1s. *Well a*, 3 × concentrated normal human serum; *well b*, acid euglobulin; *well c*, acid euglobulin, incubated at 30°C for 30 min in the presence of 0.01 M EDTA at ionic strength 0.15; *well d*, acid euglobulin incubated with C1s no. 7 at 30°C for 30 min; *well e*, C1s no. 7 diluted with buffer to the same concentration used in well d and incubated at 30°C for 30 min; *well f*, C1s no. 7. Note the gradual shift of the electrophoretic position which is also accompanied by increased esterase activity. All samples show a reaction of identity.

plete adjuvant. The injections were made directly into the popliteal nodes. Three weeks later the same amount of C1s with Freund's complete adjuvant was given i.m., and the rabbits were bled 1 week after the second injection. Booster injections increased the antibody content and were given at 6- to 8-week intervals by locating the single 2-mm segment from an analytical acrylamide gel electrophoresis run to which 30 μg of highly purified C1s were applied and which contained the greatest C1s activity as judged by hemolytic assay. The hemolytic activity of C1s in this segment was located after 2 hr of elution with 0.2 ml of buffer. The segment was then homogenized and injected i.m. Antisera were harvested 1 week after a booster injection.

Monospecificity of antibody. As shown in the left side of Figure 2, well a, the antisera obtained were monospecific, yielding one precipitin arc after immunoelectrophoresis of whole human serum concentrated threefold. Also on Ouchterlony analysis only one band was seen when diffused against concentrated whole human serum (right side of Fig. 2, well a). Similar results were found with acid euglobulin precipitates (made by the method described by Lepow (7)) concentrated 10-fold over the original serum volume (Fig. 2, well b). Also, the same euglobulin preparation, which had increased TAMe esterase activity after incubation at 37°C for 30 min (Fig. 2, well c) or after a similar incubation with a small amount of active C1s (Fig. 2, well d), gave a single line on immunoelectrophoresis and showed a reaction of identity with normal human serum or C1s on Ouchterlony analysis.

The heterogeneity of highly purified C1s as shown by immunoelectrophoresis on agar (note the long tail toward the cathode, Fig. 2, well f) was previously described (10). The heterogeneity is not as apparent when agarose is used as a supporting medium but is emphasized by using selected lots of Special Agar Noble. Acrylamide immunoelectrophoresis was also used to check the antisera for contaminating antibody. Purified C1s or whole human serum was electrophoresed on acrylamide cylinders and the antiserum was

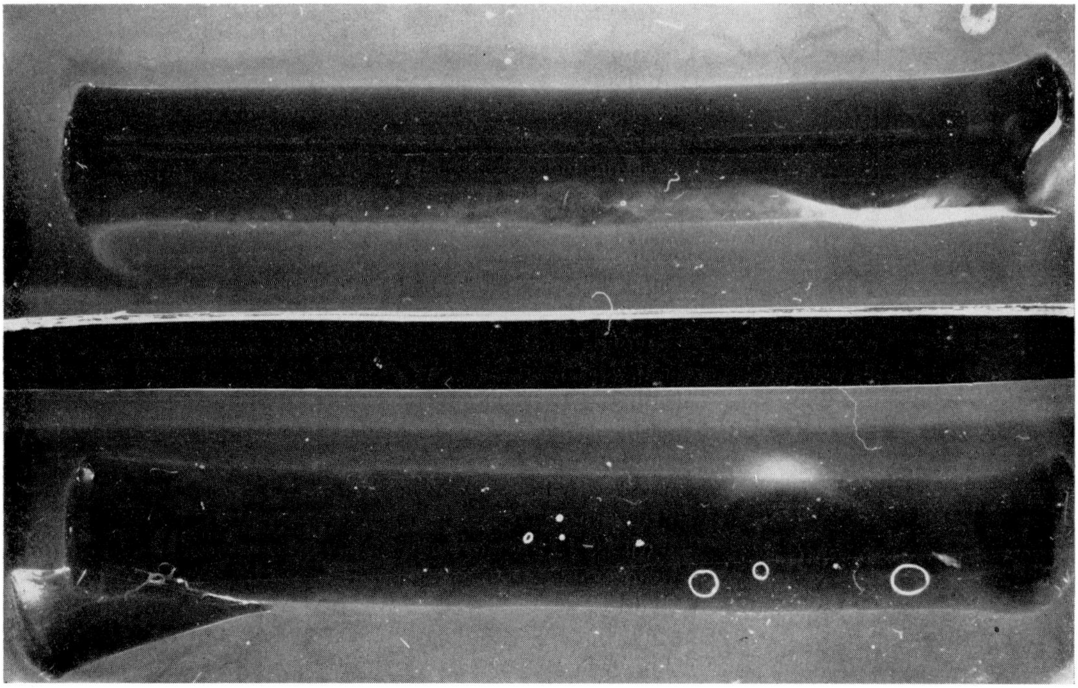

Figure 3. Immunodiffusion after acrylamide gel electrophoresis. Anode is to the right. Top gel received 22 μg of C1s no. 8 and bottom gel received 0.1 ml of fresh human serum pretreated with 0.01 M EDTA for 30 min at room temperature. Trough contains anti-C1s antiserum. Note that highly purified C1s migrates faster than C1s in serum and is more heterogeneous.

then allowed to diffuse toward the cylinders from a trough cut in agar. As shown in Figure 3 one precipitin arc formed for each acrylamide gel cylinder. The location of C1s with these antisera corresponds to the hemolytic and esterase activity of C1s in these bands. The migration position of the C1s in fresh human serum is more cathodal than is highly purified C1s. This is also seen after immunoelectrophoresis on agar on agarose. On close inspection, it can be noted that the position of the long tail toward the cathode on agar immunoelectrophoresis of C1s corresponds to the slower moving arc in whole human serum (Fig. 2, wells a and f), and after acrylamide electrophoresis the heterogeneous band, as shown in Figure 1, probably corresponds to these two arcs. The leading edge is more dense than the trailing edge but the reverse situation has also been seen. The entire heterogeneous band on acrylamide contains the hemolytic and esterase activity of C1s and reacts with antisera to C1s. Antisera prepared and checked for monospecificity to C1s in this fashion have been used for radial immunodiffusion to quantitate C1s immunochemically, as described in the accompanying publication (9).

The ability of these antisera to neutralize the hemolytic activity of C1s was also demonstrated in tests similar to those described by Haines and Lepow (12), who studied the neutralization of the destructive reaction with C4. The experiments were designed according to principles outlined by Mayer and Miller (13). The neutralization assay of antisera (no. 23) revealed that one site-forming unit of C1s was neutralized by a 1:25,000 dilution of antisera.

Heterogeneity of C1s. The electrophoretic heterogeneity of C1s was noted on Pevikon electrophoresis when two protein peaks with hemolytic and esterase activity were sometimes noted in the α globulin region. An example of this is shown in Figure 4. The starting material for this 5- x 50-cm Pevikon block was 2 ml of C1s obtained from human serum euglobulin that had been chromotographed on CM- and DEAE-cellulose as previously described (2). The two peaks were pooled separately, concentrated, and the specific activities of C1s as measured by hemolytic and esterase measurements were identical, as shown in the data accompanying Figure 4. Electrophoresis on agarose immunoelectrophoresis

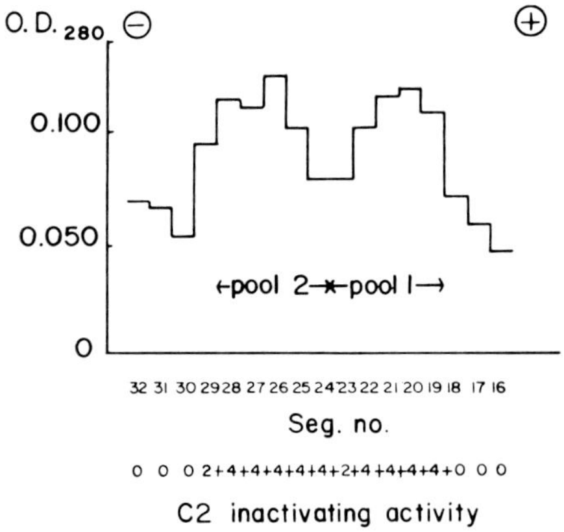

After Concentration	O.D.$_{280}$	Hemolytic Activity S.F.U./ml	Esterase Activity U/ml
pool I	0.880	21,200	567
pool 2	0.790	17,400	480

Figure 4. Diagram of Pevikon block electrophoresis of C1s eluted from DEAE-cellulose column. Anode is to the right. C2 inactivating activity was tested by incubating an equal volume of sample and C2 for 30 min at 37°C, followed by addition of EAC14 and C-EDTA. 4+ indicates complete inactivation and 2+ 50% inactivation of the offered amount of C2. After concentration of each pool, hemolytic and esterase activities were measured. The entire block was sectioned but only a portion of the block is illustrated. The origin is at segment 39 and each segment is 1.0 cm in width.

showed identical positions of each pool. At the time that this experiment was done the utility of agar in revealing electrophoretic heterogeneity of C1s had not been discovered. After recognizing that agar clearly separated purified C1s preparations into two forms, as shown in Figure 2, well f, other experiments were carried out to obtain the slow form free of the fast migrating form and to convert one into the other. To date it has not been possible to obtain the slow form in a highly purified state, free of the fast form. Our working hypothesis has been that C1s is activated from its proesterase form by proteolysis as suggested by Naff and Ratnoff (14). Proteolysis may be autocatalytic or produced by traces of proteolytic enzymes. Such proteolysis would be expected to produce electrophoretic alterations of C1s. In order to prevent the electrophoretic conversion we have used siliconized glassware, since Donaldson (15) suggested that C1s is activated by active Hageman factor. The use of siliconized glassware should tend to prevent its activation. We have also kept purification temperatures at 4°C and worked rapidly. All of this has been partially successful. In Figure 5 a characteristic experiment is shown. Blood was obtained in siliconized glassware, clotted, separated and then subjected to the acid euglobulin precipitation method described by Lepow *et al.* (7). The CM-cellulose step in our purification procedure (2) was not used but the dissolved euglobulin was applied to a DEAE-cellulose column at pH 7.4 and RSC 0.175 M NaCl. The column was washed with this same buffer and then C1s was eluted with buffer at a RSC of 0.37 M NaCl. This C1s was free of C1s inhibitor but contained several other proteins.

As shown in Figure 5 the starting material, euglobulin and DEAE fractions containing C1s are all slow moving on agar immunoelectrophoresis developed with anti-C1s. After acrylamide electrophoresis there are two characteristic arcs of C1s. The specific activity of the final product is the same as that obtained by the usual purification process. Only one preparation (not shown) has been eluted from acrylamide in the predominantly slow moving form, free of other proteins, as judged by immunoelectrophoresis. Its specific activity was the same as the predominantly fast moving form suggesting that if it is proesterase, activation occurs during assay. We have also seen more extensive heterogeneity of C1s after acrylamide electrophoresis with a distinct band moving to the far albumin region. This band reacted with monospecific anti-C1s but did not have hemolytic or esterase activity. Acrylamide electrophoresis has been reported to inactivate several biologically active proteins. As acrylamide is very useful in obtaining C1s free of albumin we hope to modify the procedure so that this type of artifactural heterogeneity will not be introduced. To date pre-washing the gel with buffer has not eliminated the microheterogeneity or the conversion of slow moving forms to faster forms, although heterogeneity may be slightly less.

Other approaches to this problem have been used. As shown in Figure 2, well b, the C1s in an acid euglobulin is slow-migrating. After incubation at pH 7.4 and a relative salt concentration of 0.15 M NaCl at 37°C for 30 min, a method of

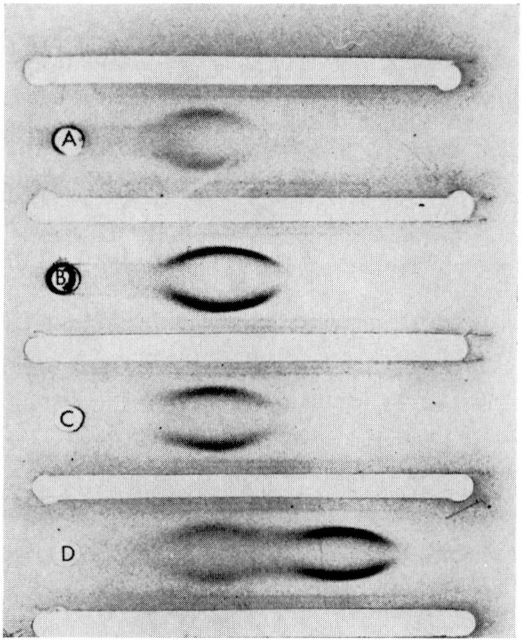

Figure 5. Immunoelectrophoretic pattern of C1s at each stage of purification. Anode is to the right. Supporting medium is 1.2% Special Agar Noble. *Well A*, starting material (fresh human serum) for C1s no. 10. *Well B*, euglobulin precipitated at acid pH. *Well C*, C1s after DEAE chromatography. *Well D*, C1s no. 10 after acrylamide electrophoresis. Troughs received anti-C1s antiserum. Samples in wells A, B, and C showed a homogeneous slowly migrating pattern. After acrylamide gel electrophoresis, heterogeneity in C1s is evident as shown by two continuous arcs.

activation suggested by Haines and Lepow (1), a slight shift in electrophoretic position is noted (Fig. 2, well c). If incubated with purified C1s predominantly in the fast moving form, a greater shift occurs (well d) and if C1s is incubated alone it also shifts its electrophoretic position anodaly (well e). Incubation of a similar euglobulin preparation with sensitized erythrocytes or trypsin or incubation of whole serum with EA or trypsin produces a similar electrophoretic shift of the C1s arc. In the experiment in which euglobulin was incubated alone or with C1s a markedly significant increase in esterase activity was noted. This procedure has been shown to increase hemolytic activity as well. These experiments are compatible with the proteolytic activation hypothesis of Naff and Ratnoff (14); however, precise quantitative correlation of specific activity with the electrophoretic forms is under investigation. We feel that this approach will lead to a detailed knowledge of activation, and correlation of structure and function should then be possible.

DISCUSSION

Monospecific antisera to highly purified C1s can be readily obtained by the method of purification and immunization described. These antisera have already proven useful in further purification and immunochemical analysis of the activation mechanism. Activation of C1s may be one of the important initial events in a variety of inflammatory reactions, not all of which are mediated by antibody, and thus these antisera should find widespread application. The clinical use of these antisera has already been demonstrated and will be published shortly. They add an important dimension to the practical assessment of the complement system, and antibodies to C1q, C4, C3 and C5 are now in clinical use (16).

Unexpectedly these antisera reveal heterogeneity of highly purified C1s as shown after acrylamide gel and agar electrophoresis (Figs. 1 and 2). Not shown is that the migratory position of C1s can be similarly affected by trypsin. Also on one occasion a hemolytically inactive degradatory product which migrated to the far albumin region but reacted with anti-C1s was noted to appear after acrylamide electrophoresis. This was considered to be a degradation produced by a gel ingredient. It is possible that the heterogeneity of highly purified C1s is in part due to degradation occuring during purification, particularly during the acrylamide step (17). However, C1s is susceptible to proteolysis and proteolytic enzyme treatment leads to activation (14). Furthermore when specific activities were measured on slow and fast moving forms after Pevikon electrophoresis, the slow moving form had a similar specific activity. We postulate that it activates autocatalytically before or during the assay. In fact this has been shown during esterase measurements which are recorded continuously. Alternatively, the electrophoretic positions may indicate structural changes unrelated to activation. We favor the concept that structural alteration is inherent in the activation process. In results to be published, increased esterase and hemolytic activity occur after incubation of crude C1s preparations at 37°C. Another type of electrophoretic heterogeneity has been discussed in previous experiments (10) which show that whole serum and other crude serum factions influence the migration of fast moving highly purified active C1s when mixed, converting it to slow moving C1s. Therefore, it is known that at least one serum protein influences the electrophoretic migratory position of fast moving C1s. This type of protein-protein interaction does *not* account for the heterogeneity of highly purified preparations illustrated in Figures 1 and 2. As Gigli and Austen (18) suggest that C4 has an allosteric effect on C1s, we are investigating the influence of C4 on highly purified C1s. Other strong possibilities for proteins which may interact with C1s are C1r and C1q. Our preliminary studies indicate that C1q does not influence C1s in the presence of EDTA. C1r is under investigation. Our studies also show that the C1 esterase inhibitor, which is known to complex stochiometrically with C1 esterase (19), is not responsible for the slowing effect on migration by crude serum fractions, although it is possible that the inhibitor could influence C1s when conditions are right. The protein that affects C1s is found in the pseudoglobulin fraction. Our current efforts are designed to purify C1 proesterase and this unknown protein. Antisera produced against the proesterase may show immunochemical differences correlating with these structural and functional changes. If spontaneous conversion to faster moving active forms can be controlled it should be possible to prepare such antisera as well as to quantitatively measure each form.

Acknowledgment. The technical assistance of Miss Sue Williamson is gratefully acknowledged.

REFERENCES

1. Haines, A. L. and Lepow, I. H., J. Immun., *92:* 468, 1964.
2. Nagaki, K. and Stroud, R. M., J. Immun., *102:* 421, 1969.
3. Naff, G. B., Pensky, J. and Lepow, I. H., J. Exp. Med., *119:* 593, 1964.
4. Stroud, R. M., Austen, K. F. and Mayer, M. M., Immunochemistry, *2:* 219, 1965.
5. Müller-Eberhard, H. J. and Lepow, I. H., J. Exp. Med., *121:* 819, 1965.
6. Müller-Eberhard, H. J., Polley, M. J. and Calcott, M. A., J. Exp. Med., *125:* 359, 1967.
7. Lepow, I. H., Naff, G. B., Todd, E. W., Pensky, J. and Hinz, C. F., Jr., J. Exp. Med., *117:* 983, 1963.
8. Kohler, P. F. and Müller-Eberhard, H. J., J. Immun., *99:* 1211, 1967.
9. Nagaki, K. and Stroud, R. M., J. Immun., *105:* 170, 1970.
10. Nagaki, K. and Stroud, R. M., J. Immun., *103:* 141, 1969.
11. Davis, B. J., Ann. N. Y. Acad. Sci., *121:* 404, 1964.
12. Haines, A. L. and Lepow, I. H., J. Immun., *92:* 479, 1964.
13. Mayer, M. M. and Miller, J. A., Immunochemistry, *2:* 71, 1965.
14. Naff, G. B. and Ratnoff, O. D., J. Exp. Med., *128:* 571, 1968.
15. Donaldson, V. H., J. Exp. Med., *127:* 411, 1968.
16. Kohler, P. F. and Bensel, R. T., Clin. Exp. Immun., *4:* 191, 1969.
17. Mitchell, W. M., Biochim. Biophys. Acta, *147:* 171, 1967.
18. Gigli, I. and Austen, K. F., J. Exp. Med., *129:* 679, 1969.
19. Lepow, I. H. and Leon, M. A., Immunology, *5:* 222, 1962.

THE JOURNAL OF IMMUNOLOGY
Vol. 105, No. 1, July 1970
Printed in U.S.A.

IMMUNOCHEMICAL QUANTITATION OF HUMAN C1 ESTERASE (C1s): CONCENTRATION IN NORMAL SERUM AND PURIFICATION YIELDS[1]

K. NAGAKI AND R. M. STROUD

From the Division of Clinical Immunology and Rheumatology, Department of Medicine, Birmingham Veterans Administration Hospital, University of Alabama in Birmingham, 1919 Seventh Avenue South, Birmingham, Alabama 35233

Received for publication October 30, 1969

Immunochemical quantitation of C1s is possible with the single radial immunodiffusion technique. C1s is the complement component with the lowest concentration for which this technique has been used. The normal adult concentration is 32.8 ± 6.2 μg/ml (1 S.D.). The C1s concentration in normal human serum is relatively insensitive to the method of storing and collecting blood samples. Sera or EDTA plasma can be kept at 0°C, −20°C or −70°C, so this should be a practical method for clinical laboratories. Clinical studies in various disease states are in progress. Using this method, the recovery and overall yield at each stage of purification as well as the specific hemolytic and esterase activities were calculated. The overall yield of C1s averaged 3% to 4% with specific hemolytic activities of 150,000 to 350,000 site-forming units/mg, and specific esterase activities ranging from 1500 to 2500 units/mg. These figures are the best obtained to date, but with increasing knowledge of this important serum enzyme more rigid criteria of purification are being determined with the goal of achieving high constant specific activity. The yields at various steps should be helpful in redesigning the methods of purification.

Using monospecific antisera, the immunochemical determination of serum proteins has proven to be clinically practical for immunoglobulin and various complement components, notably C1q, C4, C3 and C5. As the complement system consists of 11 proteins, 3 of which are complexed in macromolecular C1 (C1q, C1r, C1s), and as hemolytic assays require supplies of functionally purified components some of which are unstable (1), the use of radial immunodiffusion to quantitate these proteins has already proven clinically rewarding (2, 3). This method has begun to provide new knowledge of the biochemistry and pathophysiology of this important serum enzyme system, and it is likely that all of the complement components will be assayed in a similar manner. The advantages of this method have been stated recently (3), but certain difficulties exist that make interpretation hazardous. Potential problems may occur as complement components rapidly change their structure and function in response to activation, primarily by enzymatic attack. Consequently, it should be kept in mind that the amount of protein assayed by an immunochemical method may not be related to the degree of functional activity. In this communication, a method to quantitate human C1 esterase is described. Subsequent publications will illustrate the use of this method for assaying the esterase in various disease states (4) and in hypogammaglobulinemic syndromes (R. M. Stroud *et al.*, to be published). The use of this method to quantitate recovery of C1s during its purification will be described, since the technique represents an improvement of the methods of purification described previously (5).

MATERIALS AND METHODS

Blood samples from randomly selected healthy adults were allowed to clot for 1 to 2 hr at room temperature. The serum was separated by centrifugation and stored at −20°C or −70°C. Highly purified C1s and its monospecific antibody were obtained as described in the preceding

[1] This work was supported by grants from the National Institutes of Health (AI 08422), the American Cancer Society and the Veterans Administration.

publication (6) and as in (5, 7). The purity of C1s was established by acrylamide gel electrophoresis, Ouchterlony double diffusion and immunoelectrophoretic analysis employing potent antibody to whole serum. Electrophoretic microheterogeneity of this purified protein occurs as described by Nagaki and Stroud (6). The principle of radial immunodiffusion was modified from the method of Mancini *et al.* (8). The buffer used was 0.02 M potassium phosphate buffer, pH 8.0, containing 0.07 M NaCl, 0.01 M EDTA and 0.01% sodium azide. This buffer has the same electrical resistance as 0.14 M NaCl. One volume of diluted anti-C1s antiserum was mixed with an equal volume of 2.5% molten agarose at 56°C, and 16 ml of antibody containing agarose were poured on glass slides measuring 3.5 x 4 inches. After the antibody-agarose mixture had solidified, 3.0-mm diameter circular antigen wells were cut. 0.012 ml of reference standards and test samples were placed in antigen wells in duplicate, and the plate was kept at 4°C for 18 to 21 hr. At the end of this period, two crossed diameters of the precipitin rings formed by the interaction of C1s and its antibody were measured using a hand magnifying lens. The concentrations of C1s in the test samples were determined from a standard curve relating the mean diameter of the reference standards to their C1s concentrations. Five dilutions were determined on each plate, and a linear relationship from 23 to 72 μg/ml was obtained. As a reference standard, highly purified C1s was used originally, but subsequently we have used a 33% to 45% ammonium sulfate fraction of fresh normal human serum. This fraction contains 60% to 80% of the total C1s and does not contain C1q. In this buffer system varying concentrations of C1q had no effect on the C1s precipitin ring. If EDTA is not present the specifically precipitated ring is markedly decreased in size, presumably because C1s is complexed to C1q and C1r. It is not necessary to add EDTA to the serum sample as the result is the same whether or not this is done. Hemolytic and TAMe esterase activities were determined as described before (5).

RESULTS

Determination of protein concentrations in reference C1s. The protein concentration of highly purified C1s (C1s No. 6, Table I) was determined using the method described by Mayer and Miller (9) with minor modification. The optical density of C1s No. 6 was determined at 195 nm using a Beckman DU-2 spectrophotometer and 1.0-cm light path cuvettes. Because of the high absorbance of chloride ions at 195 nm, all samples were dialyzed against 0.15 M NaF (9). The nitrogen concentrations of solutions of human serum albumin (× 4 crystallized, Nutritional Biochemicals Corp., Cleveland, lot no. 5865) and of human Cohn fraction II (F-II, 98% pure, Mann Research Laboratories, New York, N. Y., lot no. 53451) in 0.15 M NaF were determined by Kjeldahl analysis and multiplied by 6.25 to estimate protein concentration. The albumin solution and F-II solution at a concentration of 1.0 mg/ml gave an optical density of 0.718 and 1.875, respectively, at 280 nm in a 1.0-cm light path. However, the optical density of the same solutions when determined at 195 nm was essentially the same, 0.750 for albumin and 0.756 for F-II at a concentration of 10 μg/ml. The absorbance was linear up to about 0.7. We have compared these values to those obtained by Mayer and Miller (9) for a variety of serum proteins and the agreement is quite good. Therefore, assuming that purified C1s would have the same optical density (0.75) at 195 nm for a 10 μg/ml solution, the protein concentration can be calculated from its absorbance at 195 nm. C1s No. 6 used to standardize the radial immunodiffusion assay had an $O.D._{195}$ of 8.53 (absorbancy times dilution factor) after extensive dialysis against NaF buffer. As eluates from acrylamide gels may have a slowly dialyzable substance which absorbs at 195 nm, the magnitude of this nonspecific absorbance was determined in blank control runs. The percentage of the O.D. at 195 nm due to the acrylamide was less than 3%. This error is acceptable for the radial immunodiffusion analysis. Using the average absorbancy of 0.75 for albumin and F-II solutions at a concentration of 10 μg/ml, C1s No. 6 has 113.7 μg of protein/ml. As a more convenient reference point, the optical density at 280 nm was determined. The same solution of C1s No. 6 measured 0.192 at 280 nm. Therefore the extinction coefficient at 280 nm is calculated to be 16.9 for a solution containing 1 g in 100 ml similar to IgG but higher than albumin. Another preparation of highly purified C1s (C1s No. 7) which had an $O.D._{280}$ of 0.460 should have 272 μg/ml of C1s protein calculated from the above determined absorbancy coefficient of 16.9. This was confirmed by radial immunodiffusion using C1s No. 6 as a reference standard. All of our highly purified preparations, i.e., one band on acrylamide electrophoresis, have shown that the protein concentration as calculated from the $O.D._{280}$ correlates with the C1s concentration determined by radial immunodiffusion.

Normal values of C1s in human serum using radial immunodiffusion. The C1s concentration in normal human serum was measured. The mean value of C1s in normal adult human serum (13 males and 18 females) was 32.8 μg/ml serum with a standard deviation of 6.2 μg. C1s in males was 34.9 ± 6 μg/ml and in females 31.3 ± 5.2 μg/ml. Rapidly freezing and thawing serum six times did not have any effect on the C1s measurement. Repeated measurements of the same serum sample kept at −70°C or at −20°C for 8 months did not show any change of the C1s concentration. The content of C1s in normal human serum is about 20% of the C1q concentration.

Radial immunodiffusion to study the purification process. Using this radial immunodiffusion method, we determined the concentration of C1s and the total C1s yield in euglobulin precipitates prepared by classical methods. C1 has been considered to be a euglobulin for many years, but Tamura and Nelson (10) recently have shown that on reprecipitation C1 activity is lost. Using Tamura and Nelson's neutral precipitation method at pH 7.5, ionic strength 0.04, we found that only 20% of the total C1s was in the final precipitate and the rest could be accounted for in the supernatant fractions. All of the C1q was in the precipitate. As C1s without C1q is at least 20 times less efficient hemolytically than C1, there is relatively little first component activity in the supernatant by the usual titration methods. When the acid euglobulin precipitation method described by Lepow *et al.* (11) was used about 60% to 80% of the total C1s was precipitated. However, we found that it was difficult to obtain highly purified C1s preparations from this acid euglobulin material as it contained more contaminating proteins than the precipitate obtained at pH 7.5 and ionic strength 0.04. This was pointed out by Tamura, who described their precipitate as functionally pure with a high degree of chemical purity. By modifying Nelson's method and incubating for 12 to 16 hr at 0 to 4°C instead of 30 min, about 50% of the C1s in whole serum was precipitated. The next step in our purification scheme was DEAE-cellulose chromatography. Recovery from this column has averaged 28% to 47%. The final step is acrylamide gel disc electrophoresis on a 10- x 15-cm slab as described in the accompanying publication (6), and recoveries have ranged from 10% to 36%. More complete data on percentage recovery at various stages for our preparations are shown in Table I.

Specific activity of C1s. As described in a previous publication (5), hemolytic assay methods are not exceptionally reproducible and vary from 20% to 50% for the same batch of C1s. For example, the hemolytic activity of C1s No. 11 and 12 after acrylamide electrophoresis was 397,000 site-forming units (SFU)/mg C1s, the highest value we have seen. After 12 days at 0°C in 0.1 M Tris buffer, pH 7.4, the activity decreased to 238,700 SFU/mg C1s using the same lot of EAC4 cells, C2 and C-EDTA. Simultaneous parallel titrations of C1s No. 10 which was also stored at 0°C remained the same and have been stable for 2 months. Because of persistent uncertainty regarding the reasons for these variations, we have not yet defined a standard hemolytic unit of C1s. When methods to maintain stability are known and when we are certain that we have obtained reproducibly high constant specific activities from one preparation to another, this will be done. Several technical factors already have been determined to be the cause of some of the hemolytic variations. Certain lots of EAC14 cells, although the T_{max} (12) is the same, do not produce as many $SAC14\overline{2}$ sites. As previously pointed out (13), this may relate to incompetent SAC4 sites. We note that C1s titers are also low when this occurs. The C1s titer is sensitive to the C2 concentration and conditions must be precisely controlled. C1s has some instability and, although it is well preserved at 0°C for 2 or 3 months, it loses activity at −70°C after 6 to 12 months. When very dilute it is lost on the surface of glassware. We have avoided this problem by using 0.1% gelatin or 2% lysine in various buffers when possible. Even though designation of a proper C1s activity standard has not been accomplished, we would like to illustrate how hemolytic and esterase activities measured by previously described methods correlate with the C1s protein concentration measured by radial immunodiffusion at various stages of purification and in the final product. These figures represent most of our preparations and should afford other investigators values which will be helpful in purification.

TABLE I

Characteristics of C1s esterase preparations

Preparation No.	5	6	7	9	10	11 + 12[a]	13
	Yield (%)	Yield (%)	Yield (%)	Yield (%)	Yield (%)	Yield (%)	Yield (%)
Starting material (human serum)	100	100	100	100	100	100	100
Euglobulin	NC[b]	NC	NC	78[c]	72[c]	52[d]	59.9[d]
CM column	NC	NC	NC	ND[e]	ND	ND	ND
DEAE column	NC	NC	NC	35	2[f]	14	28.4
Acrylamide electrophoresis	4.4	4.8	4.4	6	0.63	2.8	3.2
Analytical acrylamide electrophoresis	Single Band	Single Band	Single Band	4 Bands	5 Bands	Single Band	2 Bands
C1s μg/O.D.$_{280}$	591	591	591	276	NC	(425)[g]	316
Hemolytic activity (SFU)/mg after DEAE	ND	ND	ND	ND	16,700	61,180	ND
Hemolytic activity (SFU)/mg after acrylamide	86,100	93,400	135,000	157,600	350,000	397,000 (239,000)[g]	115,100
Esterase activity (units)/mg after DEAE	ND	ND	ND	ND	672	1,598	ND
Esterase activity (units)/mg after acrylamide	1,766	2,670	1,984	2,674	2,060	1,524	1,524

[a] Preparations 11 and 12 were mixed after DEAE chromatography.
[b] NC not calculated.
[c] Precipitated by the method of Lepow *et al.* (11).
[d] Precipitated by Tamura and Nelson's method (10) for 18 hr.
[e] ND not done.
[f] A major portion of the C1s passed through this DEAE column.
[g] Assays were performed after dialysis against 0.15 M NaF at a low concentration.

As shown in Table I the variable specific hemolytic activities are compared to the relatively stable specific esterase activities. By the method reported previously using Pevikon electrophoresis (5), we usually obtained C1s preparations with lower and more constant specific hemolytic activities. Since using acrylamide gel electrophoresis instead of Pevikon, the specific hemolytic activity is generally higher (for example C1s No. 10) and more variable. Aside from the technical factors in the actual C1s hemolytic titration discussed above, another reason for this variation in specific hemolytic activity may be a variable degree of degradation during acrylamide gel electrophoresis. The latter has been demonstrated with C1s No. 9 obtained after a single acrylamide gel slab electrophoresis. Two bands were formed, both of which reacted with specific anti-C1s antisera. The slower band had high specific hemolytic and esterase activities and was more homogeneous. The other band was heterogeneous, migrated to the far albumin region and had very low specific hemolytic and esterase activities—90% lower than any reported in Table I. This inactive form of C1s was discarded from the final preparation. We suspect that the more limited variation seen in Table I is in part due to the varying degrees of microheterogeneity of C1s reported before (7) and in the accompanying publication (6). The biologic significance of this heterogeneity is still under study. As mentioned we are in the process of defining an activity standard that will have more stability, but an approximate useful figure is that 0.003 μg to 0.01 μg of C1s protein corresponds to one site-forming unit, and 0.4 μg to 0.6 μg of C1s corresponds to one esterase unit by these methods.

DISCUSSION

The determination of C1s in whole human serum by radial immunodiffusion reveals that C1s has an average concentration of 32.8 ± 6.2 μg/ml. The variations in normal human serum are wide and undoubtedly reflect several types of physiologic influences on this protein. Other complement components also have relatively large standard deviations (3) as do immunoglobulin levels using similar methods. The mechanism of synthesis of C1s and its control has not been studied, but it has been suggested that C1q concentrations correlate with IgG levels (14). We are measuring C1s concentrations in hypogammaglobulinemic patients and will report these values soon (to be published). The studies of Colten *et al.* (15) showing that C1 activity is synthesized by the human colon are interesting. As C1s is an α globulin with a molecular weight of 108,000 and has biologic functions independent of C1q and C1r, there is no obvious reason why its serum concentration should correlate with the serum C1q concentration. Exploration of the *in vivo* structure and function of C1 subunits is limited. Preliminary results show that some patients have widely scattered values of C1q and C1s and that hemolytic activity may not correlate with either protein. These results are being collected for publication (4).

The specific activities of highly purified preparations can now be determined with this technique and are variable. Most of the technical problems causing some of this variation have been discussed above. Also, as described in the accompanying publication the final product has various degrees of electrophoretic microheterogeneity (6). As the specific activity of the proesterase might be lower than active C1s by the method of hemolytic assay, we would expect variation if varying ratios of proesterase to active esterase were present in different preparations. The esterase measurement may not be as susceptible to variation as activation may occur more readily in that assay. It is possible to show that electrophoretically slow-migrating forms of C1s activate during the esterase assay as activity can be continuously recorded. The optimal conditions of activation are under study, and we hope to eliminate variation in hemolytic specific activity by complete conversion to the active form before assay. These studies are in progress.

Acknowledgment. The technical assistance of Miss Sue Williamson is gratefully acknowledged.

REFERENCES

1. Mayer, M. M., in *Kabat and Mayer's Experimental Immunochemistry*, Chapter 4, 2nd Ed., Charles C Thomas, Springfield, Ill., 1961.
2. Hanauer, L. B. and Christian, C. L., Amer. J. Med., *42:* 882, 1967.
3. Kohler, P. F. and Müller-Eberhard, H. J., J. Immun., *99:* 1211, 1967.
4. Stroud, R. M. and Nagaki, K., C1s Concentrations in SLE, Rheumatoid Arthritis and Other Syndromes. Presented at the meeting of the American Rheumatism Association, Boston, June, 1969.
5. Nagaki, K. and Stroud, R. M., J. Immun., *102:* 421, 1969.
6. Nagaki, K. and Stroud, R. M., J. Immun., *105:* 162, 1970.
7. Nagaki, K. and Stroud, R. M., J. Immun., *103:* 141, 1969.
8. Mancini, G., Carbonara, A. O. and Heremans, J. F., Immunochemistry, *2:* 235, 1965.
9. Mayer, M. M. and Miller, J., Anal. Biochem., In press.
10. Tamura, N. and Nelson, R. A., Jr., J. Immun., *101:* 1333, 1968.
11. Lepow, I. H., Naff, G. B., Todd, E. W., Pensky, J. and Hinz, C. F., J. Exp. Med., *117:* 983, 1963.
12. Borsos, T., Rapp, H. J. and Mayer, M. M., J. Immun., *87:* 310, 1961.
13. Borsos, T. and Rapp, H. J., J. Immun., *99:* 263, 1967.
14. Kohler, P. F. and Müller-Eberhard, H. J., Science, *163:* 474, 1969.
15. Colten, H. R., Gordon, J. M., Borsos, T. and Rapp, H. J., J. Exp. Med., *128:* 595, 1968.

THE JOURNAL OF IMMUNOLOGY
Vol. 105, No. 1, July 1970
Printed in U.S.A.

DELAYED HYPERSENSITIVITY TO *TRICHINELLA SPIRALIS*

III. Effect of Repeated Sensitizations in Donors and Recipients[1,2]

C. W. KIM, M. P. JAMUAR AND L. D. HAMILTON

From the Division of Microbiology, Medical Research Center, Brookhaven National Laboratory, Upton, Long Island, New York 11973

Received for publication October 20, 1969

Guinea pigs were sensitized four times at 1-, 2- or 3-week intervals with crude saline extract of *Trichinella spiralis* larvae emulsified in Freund's complete adjuvant, then skin-tested 28, 56 or 84 days after the initial sensitization. The skin-test reaction was not typical of delayed hypersensitivity but was somewhat like the Arthus reaction. Electron microscopic examination of the lymphocytes from these animals showed structural changes that are generally associated with synthetic functions. In addition, passive cutaneous anaphylaxis (PCA) and precipitating antibodies were detected in their sera. The 2-week interval between sensitizations proved optimal for synthetic activity and for antibody production of both γ_1 and γ_2 classes. Correlation was noted between the degree of antigenic stimulus and proliferation of cellular organelles associated with protein synthesis in lymphocytes. Indeed, with the largest dose and optimal interval of antigenic stimulation, fine-structure studies indicated the production of lymphocytes very much like plasma cells. Lymph node cells from repeatedly sensitized donor animals transferred to normal recipients elicited negligible skin reactions, somewhat like the Arthus rather than the delayed hypersensitivity type. Even on day 1 after transfer of cells from repeatedly sensitized donors, antibody was detected by PCA in recipients, especially when the donors had been sensitized at 2-week intervals. Since PCA antibody was detected within 24 hr after transfer, it seems likely that the lymphocytes themselves produce antibody in recipients, at least until the lymphocytes possibly can develop into another type. Precipitating antibody was not detected in any of the recipients by either micro-immunoelectrophoresis or the ring test. In contrast, the transfer of delayed hypersensitivity was successful with lymphocytes from donors sensitized only once irrespective of dosage. The present findings suggest that animals repeatedly sensitized by the antigen apparently "lose" delayed hypersensitivity.

The optimal latent period for inducing delayed hypersensitivity in guinea pigs to crude saline extract of *Trichinella spiralis* is 7 days after initial intradermal sensitization with antigen emulsified in complete adjuvant (2). However at 14 days after sensitization the skin test showed a mixed, delayed-Arthus type, and at 21 and 28 days after sensitization more of the Arthus type.

When lymph node cells from guinea pigs sensitized only once with *T. spiralis* antigen and skin-tested 7 days later were transferred to normal guinea pigs, transfer of delayed hypersensitivity response to recipient animals ensued but was unaccompanied by transfer of the secondary antibody response (3). Furthermore, cells from sensitized donors skin-tested still later—at 14, 21 and 28 days—did not transfer either delayed hypersensitivity or secondary antibody response in recipient animals, although the cells were presumed to be more committed to antibody production.

The ability of lymph node cells to transfer a secondary antibody response has been repeatedly reported (4–13). Furthermore, cells transferring delayed hypersensitivity and cells giving rise to circulating antibody were obtained from the same

[1] This work was supported by the United States Atomic Energy Commission.

[2] A preliminary report was presented at the 1968 FASEB Annual Meeting (1).

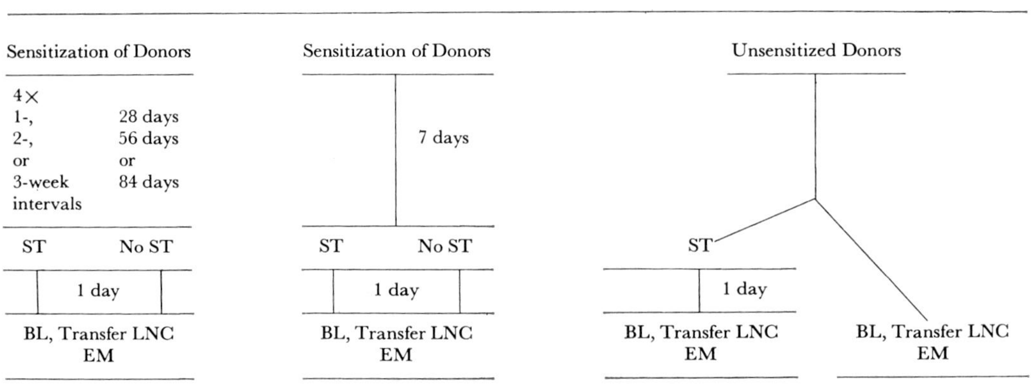

Figure 1. Experimental design. ST, skin test; BL, bleed for PCA, micro-immunoelectrophoresis, ring test; LNC, lymph node cells; EM, electron microscopy of cells.

source—lymph nodes (14–17). The question remained: did the same cells mediate both reactions?

The present study was undertaken to determine the effect of repeated sensitizations on a) the development and duration of delayed hypersensitivity and antibody response in guinea pigs, and b) the ability of lymph node cells from these donors, primarily small lymphocytes (~90%), to produce antibody in recipients and to relate the findings to ability to transfer delayed hypersensitivity.

MATERIALS AND METHODS

Procedures for sensitization, skin test, antibody detection, transfer of lymph node cells (2, 3, 18), and electron microscopy (19) have been given in detail; only modifications will be cited. Figure 1 diagrams the experimental design for donors and Figure 2 that for recipients.

Preparation of antigen. T. spiralis larvae from rats infected for 6 weeks to 6 months were obtained by artificial gastric digestion (1% v/v HCl-0.7% w/v pepsin-Merck in distilled water) and washed with normal saline until the biuret test was negative. After the final washing they were suspended in normal saline and homogenized in a Potter-Elvehjem homogenizer at 5°C until microscopic examination revealed no intact larvae. The mixture, brought to a final dilution of 1:20 by volume with saline, was extracted for 3 hr at room temperature and overnight at 5°C. The mixture was then centrifuged at 27,000 × G for 1 hr at 5°C and the sediment discarded. The supernatant solution was incubated at 56°C

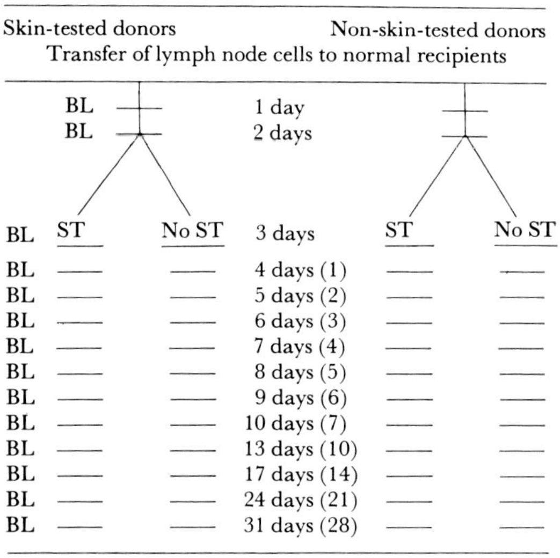

Figure 2. Experimental design. BL, bleed for PCA, micro-immunoelectrophoresis, ring test; ST, skin test. Numbers in parentheses indicate days after skin test.

(water bath) for 1 hr and recentrifuged at 27,000 × G for 1 hr at 5°C. The supernatant solution was removed, filtered through a fritted disc filter (F) and used as a 1:20 stock antigen.

Sensitization and skin-testing of donors. Albino, pen-inbred 460-g average weight guinea pigs were injected intradermally into the digital spaces in the footpads with the sensitizing antigen which contained 0.1 ml of crude saline extract of *T. spiralis* larvae emulsified in 0.1 ml of Freund's complete adjuvant (Difco Laboratories, Detroit, Mich.). One group of animals was sensitized once with 76 μg or 380 μg of total protein; half the animals in each group were skin-tested 7 days later. Three groups of animals were sensitized four times at 1-, 2- or 3-week intervals (1.5 mg protein); half in each group were skin-tested 28, 56 or 84 days after initial sensitization. In all instances the skin-test dose contained 76 μg protein.

Unsensitized skin-tested or unsensitized non-skin-tested donors were included in each experiment. The skin reactions were observed from 30 min to 24 hr later at specified intervals.

Detection of antibody in donors. At the peak of the skin reaction and just before removal of the lymph nodes, animals were bled and the serum was obtained. Passive cutaneous anaphylaxis (PCA), agar micro-immunoelectrophoresis and the precipitin ring test were used to detect antibody in the serum.

For PCA, serum samples from animals sensitized only once, as well as from unsensitized control animals, were diluted 1:5; serum samples from animals repeatedly sensitized were diluted 1:20. Normal guinea pig serum served as a control. Antigen (1.9 mg protein) was injected from 16 to 17 hr after the serum injections. Reactions were examined at ½, 1 and 4 hr after the challenging injection of antigen.

For micro-immunoelectrophoresis, undiluted serum samples were used with 1:20 antigen. Normal and known anti-*Trichinella* guinea pig serum were included as controls. Slides were left at room temperature for 4 days before being washed in saline. All readings were made after staining with buffalo black NBR (naphthol blue black).

For the ring test, 0.05 ml of undiluted serum samples was overlayered with 0.05 ml of antigen dilutions: 1:100 (38 μg protein), 1:200 (19 μg), 1:400 (9.5 μg), 1:800 (4.75 μg), 1:1600 (2.38 μg) and 1:3200 (1.19 μg). Normal and known immune sera served as controls. The optimal reaction was with a 1:200 dilution of antigen against a known positive serum. Therefore for the control serum samples a 1:200 dilution of antigen was used. In addition, serum samples were diluted twofold (1:2, 1:4, 1:8, 1:16, 1:32 and 1:64) and overlayered with 1:200 antigen. All tests were read 15, 30 and 60 min after overlaying the serum with antigen.

Lymph node cell transfer. At the peak of the skin reaction to *T. spiralis* antigen in the donors, the lymph nodes (cervical, axillary, and inguinal) were removed and prepared for transfer. The cells came from donor animals sensitized once and those sensitized four times at 1-, 2- or 3-week intervals and skin-tested or not skin-tested, as well as from unsensitized skin-tested and non-skin-tested control animals. Then 1×10^8 cells were injected intraperitoneally into normal recipient animals, except one group of animals sensitized at 3-week intervals in which 5×10^8 cells were injected. Half of each group of recipient animals were skin-tested with *T. spiralis* antigen (76 μg protein) 3 days after transfer of cells and the reactions were observed as in the donor animals.

Electron-microscope preparation of donor cells. The lymph node cells remaining after transfer were processed for electron microscopy.

Detection of antibody in recipients. Recipient animals were bled daily from day 1 after transfer through day 10 and at days 13, 17, 24 and 31. Passive cutaneous anaphylaxis (PCA), agar micro-immunoelectrophoresis and the precipitin ring test were used to detect antibody in the serum. Serum samples were used undiluted for all three tests. The procedures for PCA, micro-immunoelectrophoresis and the ring test in recipients were identical to those used for donors.

RESULTS

Skin test reactions in donors. Delayed skin reactions were observed in animals skin-tested 7 days after one sensitization with 76 μg protein (Table I). The reaction began to appear 4 hr after the skin test, and the peak reaction (17 x 25 mm) occurred between 18 and 24 hr (group A). The area was erythematous and indurated, and in some animals there was a blanched or necrotic center. When the sensitizing dose was increased fivefold to 380 μg protein (group B), the reaction began somewhat sooner—at 2 hr—but also reached its peak (16 x 18 mm) between 18 and 24 hr.

When the donor animals were repeatedly sensitized (four times), the skin test reaction was accelerated; it started very early—within 1 hr—as small hemorrhagic spots, reached a maximal reaction of only 8 x 8 to 8 x 10 mm at 6 to 12 hr, and decreased in size and intensity thereafter. The reaction was Arthus-like: diffused, slightly hemorrhagic and circumscribed by pale edema. This was expected since our previous findings showed that when 14 days or more had elapsed after sensitization an Arthus-like reaction predominated (2, 3). There was no apparent difference attributable to the different time intervals between sensitizations (groups C–E).

Skin tests of control animals not sensitized previously were always negative.

Detection of antibody in donors. In animals skin-tested 7 days after sensitization with 76 μg protein, antibody in some animals was detected by PCA and in more animals that were skin-tested than in those that were not (Table II, group A). When the initial dose was increased fivefold to 380 μg protein (group B), antibody was detected in all the animals whether or not they were skin-tested. Indeed the size of the reaction was slightly larger in those not skin-tested (11 x 22 mm). In animals sensitized repeatedly, antibody was detected by PCA in all animals, whatever the different intervals between sensitizations and the skin test (groups C–E). The PCA reactions from these serum samples were too extensive when the serum was diluted only 1:5; hence the serum samples were diluted 1:20.

Precipitating antibody was not detected by agar micro-immunoelectrophoresis (Table II) or the ring test (Table III) in animals sensitized only once, irrespective of dosage (groups A and B). Nor was antibody detectable by the ring test when antigen or antiserum was diluted. However, in repeatedly sensitized donors, $7S\gamma_1$ and γ_2 fractions were detected by micro-immunoelectrophoresis (groups C–E). The anti-*Trichinella* pre-

TABLE I

Skin test reaction to Trichinella spiralis antigen in sensitized donor animals[a]

Group	No. Sensitization(s) (Intervals)	No. Animals	Sensitizing Antigen (Total Protein)	Days between Sensitization and Skin Test	First Appearance	Average Peak Reaction
					hr	*mm (hr)*
A	1	6	76 μg	7	4	17 x 25 (20)
B	1	6	380 μg	7	2	16 x 18 (22)
C	4 (1-week)	11	1.5 mg	28	1	8 x 8[b] (6–12)
D	4 (2-week)	8	1.5 mg	56	1	8 x 10[b] (6–12)
E	4 (3-week)	12	1.5 mg	84	1	8 x 10[b] (6–12)

[a] Skin test dose = 76 μg protein.
[b] Arthus-like reaction.

TABLE II

Detection of antibody by passive cutaneous anaphylaxis (PCA) and micro-immunoelectrophoresis in donor animals

Group	Amount Skin Test Antigen (Protein)	PCA: Dilution of antiserum	PCA: Positive/samples	PCA: Average reaction	Micro-immunoelectrophoresis[a]: Positive/samples	Micro-immunoelectrophoresis[a]: Type of antibody 7S
	μg		*no.*	*mm*	*no.*	
A	76	1:5	5/6	14 x 34	0/6	
	No ST	1:5	2/6	13 x 29	0/6	
B	76	1:5	6/6	8 x 18	0/6	
	No ST	1:5	6/6	11 x 22	0/6	
C	76	1:20	12/12	23 x 80	12/12	γ_1, γ_2
	No ST	1:20	6/6	22 x 74	6/6	γ_1, γ_2
D	76	1:20	8/8	19 x 67	8/8	γ_1, γ_2
	No ST	1:20	8/8	21 x 70	8/8	γ_1, γ_2
E	76	1:20	12/12	26 x 79	12/12	γ_1, γ_2
	No ST	1:20	6/6	19 x 62	6/6	γ_1, γ_2

[a] Antiserum for micro-immunoelectrophoresis was undiluted.

cipitin arc had the typical bat-wing aspect, indicating γ_1 and γ_2 type antibodies. Anti-*Nippostrongylus* serum used as a control gave negative results. In addition, anti-*Trichinella* serum with *Ascaris* antigen also was negative. Similarly, in the ring test (Table III), the sera of all the repeatedly sensitized animals contained precipitating antibody (groups C–E). In general more animals sensitized at 2-week (group D) intervals gave positive ring tests with the highest dilution of antigen, as well as with the highest dilution of antiserum, than in the 1-week (group C) or 3-week (group E) interval donors.

None of the serum samples from unsensitized animals, skin-tested or non-skin-tested, contained any precipitating antibody as judged by both micro-immunoelectrophoresis and the ring test.

Electron microscopy of donor cells. Lymphocytes from animals which had been sensitized once with antigen plus complete adjuvant, and were then skin-tested, were usually larger and had a greater nucleo-cytoplasmic ratio than unstimulated lymphocytes. This type of reaction has been reported (19). The nucleus was eccentric with patches of compact peripheral chromatin; some were also scattered in the nucleoplasm. The cytoplasm was greatly increased, packed with ribosomal particles, and contained few scattered channels of endoplasmic reticulum. Several mitochrondria, Golgi bodies, few dark granules, and vesicles were seen.

Lymphocytes from animals repeatedly sensitized were distinct in many ways. In lymphocytes from animals sensitized four times at 1-week intervals there were definitely more of the structures generally associated with synthetic function: channels of endoplasmic reticulum, mitochondria, vesicles and Golgi bodies. The nucleolus was quite distinct (Fig. 3). Lymphocytes from animals sensitized four times at 2-week intervals were more advanced than those sensitized at 1-week intervals and the cells appeared to be less spherical (Fig. 4). More cells in this group had a more eccentric nucleus and well-developed endoplasmic reticulum filled with electron-opaque material so that they more nearly resembled antibody-producing plasma cells. Lymphocytes from animals sensitized at 3-week intervals showed less development of distinct structural units as seen in the two previous groups, e.g., fewer distinct channels. Also there seemed to be fewer lymphocytes that displayed the structural changes just described.

Skin test reactions in recipients. Maximal skin reactions occurred in animals skin-tested 3 days after intraperitoneal transfer of lymph node cells (1×10^8) from donors skin-tested 7 days after a single sensitization (Table IV). The reactions were typically delayed: they appeared at 3 to 4 hr and reached a peak at 24 hr with erythema and induration. When the animals that received cells from donors (group B) sensitized with a higher single dose (380 μg protein) were skin-tested, the reactions were of the delayed type but appeared somewhat later (at 6 hr), reached their peak slightly earlier at 12 hr, and waned sooner.

TABLE III

Detection of antibody by the ring test in donor animals sensitized to Trichinella spiralis antigen

Group	Days between Sensitization and Skin Test	No. Positive/No. of Samples						
		Antigen dilutions[a]			Antiserum dilutions[b]			
		1:400	1:800	1:1600	1:4	1:8	1:16	1:32
A	7							
	No ST							
B	7							
	No ST							
C	28	5/12	6/12	1/12		1/12	7/12	4/12
	No ST	3/6	3/6			2/6	4/6	
D	56	1/7	2/7	4/7	2/8	3/8	2/8	1/8
	No ST	3/8	2/8	3/8		3/8	4/8	1/8
E	84	1/12	11/12			10/12	2/12	
	No ST		6/6			2/6	4/6	

[a] Antiserum undiluted.
[b] Antigen 1:200.

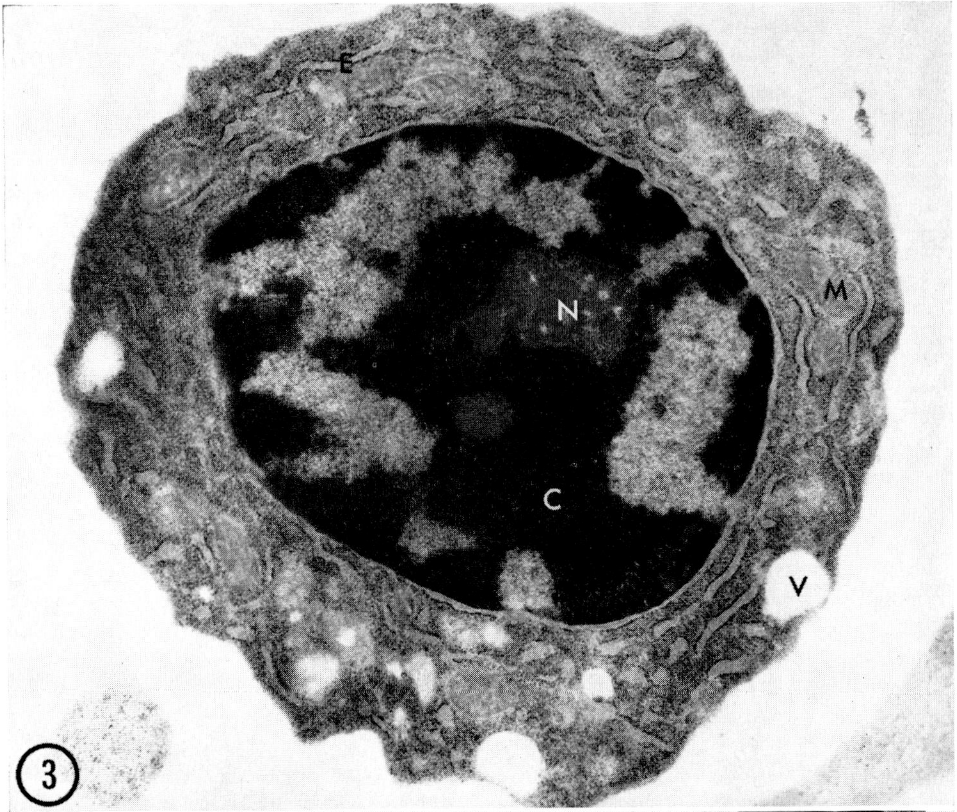

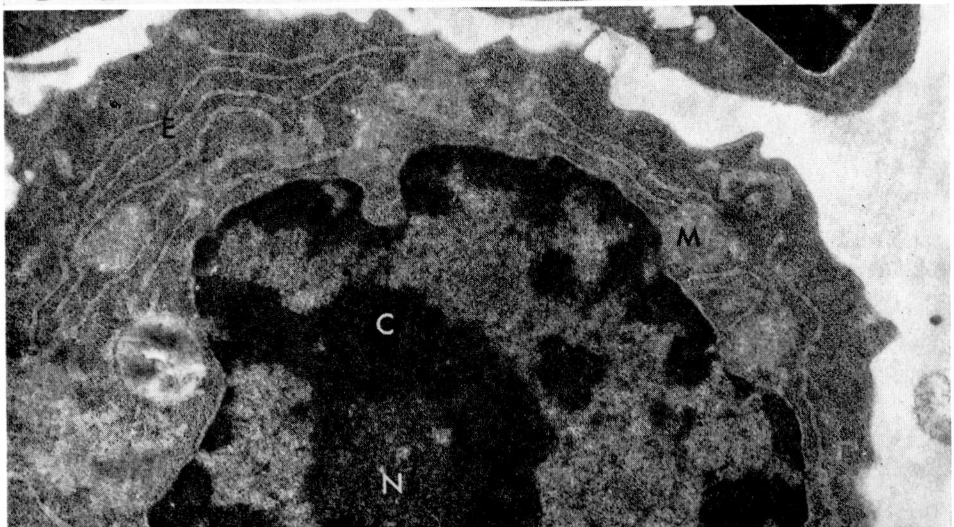

Figures 3–4

The skin reactions were negative in many animals that received cells from repeatedly sensitized donors (groups C–E). When present they began as very small hemorrhagic spots, later circumscribed by pale edema. However, even at their peak the spots were small (3 x 4 mm). This was expected since we had shown that cells from donors skin-tested after 14 days or more failed to transfer the delayed response and the negligible reactions were Arthus-like (2, 3). The skin test reactions in animals that received cells from donors repeatedly sensitized at 1- (group C) or 2-week (group D) intervals began to appear at 1½ hr but never reached any appreciable size (Table IV). Animals receiving cells from donors sensitized at 3-week (group E) intervals did not react to the skin test until 6 hr and then in only one instance. However, after transfer of 5 × 10^8 cells, the reaction appeared at 1½ hr as in the other groups, but the average size was still small (6 x 6 mm). The character of the reaction was identical with those in animals receiving 1- (group C) and 2-week (group D) interval donor cells. As expected, the reactions were negative in animals receiving cells from unsensitized skin-tested or non-skin-tested donors.

TABLE IV

Skin reaction in recipients after transfer of lymph node cells (1 × 10^8) from sensitized donors

Donors		Recipients		
Group	Amount skin test antigen (protein)	Positive/ samples	First appearance	Average peak reaction
	μg	*no.*	*hr*	*mm (hr)*
A	76	20/20	3	8 x 13 (24)
	No ST	6/6	4	8 x 10 (24)
B	76	6/6	6–12	8 x 12 (12)
	No ST	4/5	6–12	7 x 9 (12)
C	76	2/11	1½	3 x 4[a] (6)
	No ST	0/2		
D	76	6/8	2	3 x 4[a] (5–6)
	No ST	5/7	1½	3 x 5[a] (5–6)
E	76	1/10	6	3 x 3[a] (6)
	No ST	0/4		

[a] Arthus-like reaction.

Detection of antibody in recipients. Antibody was detected by PCA in skin-tested recipients 24 days after transfer of cells from donors sensitized once (76 μg protein) and skin-tested, or 17 days after transfer from non-skin-tested donors (Table V). However, when recipients were not skin-tested antibody was not detected, whether the donors had or had not been skin-tested so that the skin-test dose acted as a booster. Antibody was detected earlier (10 days) after transfer of cells from donors that received a higher dosage of a single sensitization (380 μg protein). Even with the higher dosage of sensitization antibody was first detected in non-skin-tested recipients as late as 31 days after transfer of cells from sensitized non-skin-tested donors.

In animals that received cells from repeatedly sensitized donors, antibody was detected by PCA as soon as day 1 after transfer (Table VI). The interval between sensitization in donors had some effect on the production of antibody in recipients in respect to time of appearance and number of positive reactions. Antibody was detected on day 1 in more animals receiving cells from donors sensitized at 2-week intervals than in those receiving cells from donors sensitized at 1- and 3-week intervals. Indeed, antibody was detected in all animals that received cells from donors sensitized at 2-week intervals and skin-tested from day 6 after transfer through day 31. However, in animals that received more cells (5 × 10^8) from donors sensitized at 3-week intervals, antibody was detected on day 1 after transfer in all animals.

Antibody was detected by PCA only in skin-tested recipients 13 days after transfer of cells from unsensitized skin-tested or non-skin-tested donors (Table VI—continued).

Precipitating antibody was not detected by either agar micro-immunoelectrophoresis or the ring test in any of the recipients throughout the 31-day period after transfer.

DISCUSSION

As reported with the *Trichinella* system (2, 3), periods of more than 7 days between initial sen-

Figure 3. Lymph node lymphocyte from guinea pig sensitized four times at 1-week intervals. The cytoplasm shows well-developed, rough endoplasmic reticulum (E), several mitochondria (M) and vesicles (V). The nucleus has large aggregations of chromatin (C) and a distinct nucleolus (N) (× 19,000).

Figure 4. Lymph node lymphocyte from guinea pig sensitized four times at 2-week intervals showing well-developed channels of endoplasmic reticulum (E), Golgi body (G), and mitochondria (M). The nucleus is somewhat eccentric with patches of compact chromatin (C) and a distinct nucleolus (N) (× 13,000).

TABLE VI

Detection of antibody by passive cutaneous anaphylaxis (PCA) in recipients after transfer of lymph node cells (1 x 10⁸) from repeatedly sensitized donors

Donors			Days after Transfer (after Skin Test) 1: Positive/Sample	1: Avg. (mm)	2: Positive/Sample	2: Avg. (mm)	3: Positive/Sample	3: Avg. (mm)	4(1): Positive/Sample	4(1): Avg (mm)	5(2): Positive/Sample	5(2): Avg. (mm)	6(3): Positive/Sample	6(3): Avg. (mm)	7(4): Positive/Sample	7(4): Avg. (mm)
4 × (1.5 mg) 1-week intervals 28 days	ST	ST	0/12		5/12	15 x 33	3/11	14 x 27	3/7	11 x 18	4/7	15 x 31	2/7	15 x 31	3/6	19 x 47
		No ST							2/7	10 x 24	4/6	11 x 21	3/6	11 x 20	6/6	19 x 37
	No ST	ST	1/2	10 x 19	0/2		1/2	17 x 39	1/2	27 x 60	1/2	20 x 49	1/2	25 x 65	1/2	19 x 50
		No ST							1/2	25 x 50	2/2	11 x 24	2/2	14 x 30	2/2	12 x 31
4 × (1.5 mg) 2-week intervals 56 days	ST	ST	6/11	14 x 31	7/11	16 x 39	8/10	14 x 33	4/5	12 x 32	4/5	15 x 35	4/5	18 x 41	4/5	18 x 38
		No ST							4/5	14 x 32	3/4	12 x 27	4/5	15 x 34	4/5	15 x 28
	No ST	ST	5/8	18 x 41	8/8	20 x 51	7/8	17 x 29	4/5	21 x 37	3/5	14 x 31	3/4	20 x 55	4/4	19 x 48
		No ST							5/5	14 x 31	5/5	16 x 37	5/5	15 x 29	5/5	16 x 32
4 x (1.5 mg) 3-week intervals 84 days	ST	ST	2/11	16 x 48	4/11	16 x 34	6/11	13 x 29	6/7	14 x 29	7/7	13 x 28	6/7	14 x 38	6/7	13 x 34
		No ST							3/7	15 x 32	2/7	20 x 68	3/7	17 x 40	3/7	16 x 43
	No ST	ST	1/3	6 x 12	0/3		1/3	7 x 14	0/3		1/3	15 x 30	2/3	16 x 35	1/3	15 x 50
		No ST							1/3	10 x 16	1/3	10 x 20	1/3	15 x 20	1/3	20 x 35
Unsensitized	ST	ST	0/8		0/8		0/8		0/6		0/6		0/6		0/6	
		No ST							0/6		0/6		0/6		0/5	
Controls	No ST	ST	0/14		0/13		0/11		0/9		0/7		0/7		0/7	
		No ST							0/7		0/7		0/6		0/6	

			Days after Transfer (after Skin Test)													
			8(5)		9(6)		10(7)		13(10)		17(14)		24(21)		31(28)	
4 × (1.5 mg) 1 week intervals 28 days	ST	ST	3/6	14 x 35	4/6	19 x 43	4/6	16 x 46	4/5	25 x 66	4/6	20 x 53	6/6	19 x 57	7/7	24 x 72
		No ST	6/6	14 x 33	6/6	18 x 49	6/6	17 x 50	6/6	19 x 48	7/7	24 x 55	7/7	19 x 54	8/8	22 x 67
	No ST	ST	1/2	17 x 35	1/2	22 x 58	1/2	25 x 65	1/2	20 x 60	1/2	25 x 70	2/2	20 x 58	1/1	20 x 60
		No ST	2/2	15 x 35	2/2	21 x 49	2/2	15 x 38	2/2	15 x 48	2/2	18 x 48	2/2	18 x 55	2/2	21 x 60
4 × (1.5 mg) 2-week intervals 56 days	ST	ST	5/5	21 x 55	5/5	20 x 59	5/5	25 x 71	5/5	27 x 74	5/5	23 x 70	4/4	29 x 69	4/4	28 x 85
		No ST	5/5	22 x 47	5/5	17 x 59	4/4	22 x 62	4/4	28 x 65	4/4	27 x 74	3/3	27 x 78	4/4	26 x 80
	No ST	ST	4/5	19 x 43	3/4	19 x 55	3/4	18 x 57	4/5	28 x 74	5/5	23 x 61	5/5	27 x 69	5/5	27 x 83
		No ST	5/5	14 x 33	5/5	18 x 51	4/4	17 x 46	5/5	22 x 59	5/5	21 x 61	5/5	23 x 64	4/4	22 x 74
4 × (1.5 mg) 3-week intervals 84 days	ST	ST	7/7	20 x 66	7/7	17 x 40	7/7	21 x 55	7/7	24 x 62	7/7	24 x 67	8/8	23 x 69	8/8	23 x 81
		No ST	5/7	20 x 48	2/6	16 x 38	4/6	23 x 50	3/5	20 x 53	4/6	20 x 50	5/5	21 x 64	7/7	21 x 69
	No ST	ST	1/3	13 x 22	2/3	15 x 43	3/3	14 x 32	2/3	18 x 40	3/3	16 x 42	3/3	25 x 73	3/3	28 x 78
		No ST	1/3	22 x 40	1/3	18 x 55	1/3	15 x 35	1/3	15 x 30	2/3	15 x 40	1/2	23 x 55	0/1	
Unsensitized	ST	ST	0/6		0/6		0/6		1/6	15 x 20	2/6	16 x 40	3/6	20 x 43	7/9	19 x 49
		No ST	0/5		0/5		0/5		0/5		0/5		0/5		0/5	
Controls	No ST	ST	0/6		0/5		0/5		3/5	21 x 45	3/5	21 x 53	4/5	21 x 50	3/4	27 x 77
		No ST	0/6		0/6		0/6		0/6		0/5		0/5		0/5	

TABLE V

Detection of antibody by passive cutaneous anaphylaxis (PCA) in recipients after transfer of lymph node cells (1 × 10^8) from sensitized donors

Donors			Days after Transfer (after Skin Test)											
			1–9(6)		10(7)		13(10)		17(14)		24(21)		31(28)	
			Positive/Samples	Avg. (mm)	Positive/Samples	Avg. (mm)	Positive/Samples	Avg. (mm)	Positive/Samples	Avg. (mm)	Positive/Samples	Avg. (mm)	Positive/Samples	Avg. (mm)
1X (76 μg) 7 days	ST	ST	0/3		0/3		0/3		0/3		2/2	14 x 30	1/2	15 x 25
		No ST	0/1		0/1		0/1		0/2		0/1		0/1	
	No ST	ST	0/2		0/2		0/3		2/2	18 x 35	1/3	15 x 30	1/1	15 x 25
		No ST	0/2		0/3		0/3		0/4		0/2		0/3	
1X (380 μg) 7 days	ST	ST	0/3		0/3		3/3	20 x 57	3/3	20 x 68	3/3	26 x 68	4/4	26 x 79
		No ST	0/3		0/3		0/3		0/3		0/3		0/4	
	No ST	ST	0/3		1/3	12 x 35	1/3	15 x 40	3/3	16 x 40	3/3	27 x 68	3/3	22 x 65
		No ST	0/3		0/3		0/3		0/3		0/3		2/4	21 x 45

sitization and the skin test led to the typical delayed response being replaced by an Arthus-like reaction. The apparent "loss" of delayed hypersensitivity seems due to circulating antibody, particularly precipitating antibody. The present findings with repeatedly sensitized donors confirm our earlier findings, i.e., as the animals became immunized and produced precipitating antibody, the skin reaction to the homologous antigen appeared and waned sooner, more like the Arthus-type reaction than the typical delayed response. Therefore, our results with *Trichinella* are like those with diphtheria toxoid and ovalbumin (20).

The detection of $7S\gamma_1$ and γ_2 antibodies in all donors repeatedly sensitized has been reported (21–24). Furthermore, the anti-*Trichinella* precipitin arc had the typical bat-wing aspect (γ_1 and γ_2 types of antibodies) described by Strejan and Campbell (23) for the anti-*Ascaris* precipitin arc. According to Ovary *et al.* (25) only the $7S\gamma_1$ antibody fraction can attach to guinea-pig tissues. On the other hand, Strejan and Campbell (24) reported that $7S\gamma_2$ could also elicit skin anaphylactic reactions. In the present study, positive PCA reactions were obtained when neither $7S\gamma_1$ nor γ_2 was detectable by means of micro-immunoelectrophoresis, as in the serum of donors sensitized only once.

Circulat ng antibody was detected by PCA in some of the guinea pigs at about 1 week after initial sensitization when the animals manifested skin reactions of the delayed type as reported earlier (2, 3). With increase in dosage from 76 μg to 380 μg, antibody was detected in more animals. However, with a larger single dose or with repeated doses of antigen, the booster effect of the skin test was obscured. Apparently, once antibody production has begun and reached a certain level, addition of antigen has no effect. In fact, more of the animals that were not skin-tested had precipitins than did those that were skin-tested. The parallel results of antigen dilution ring tests with those of antiserum dilution showed that antibody concentration can be determined both ways although the ring test is only qualitative. Although quantitative studies were not done, the highest titers obtained by the ring test with the 2-week-interval donors accord with the electron-microscope studies, which showed that this group also had the most highly developed structures indicative of synthetic activity in their lymphocytes.

Detection of antibody by PCA in animals 24 hr after transfer of lymph node cells from repeatedly sensitized donors suggests that the transferred cells themselves elicited a secondary antibody response in the recipients. Yet in animals that received cells from repeatedly sensitized donors the delayed response was absent in both donors and recipients. The dose of antigen given to donors has been known to affect the serum titers in the recipients so that if the dose were drastically reduced no antibody appeared at all (26). In the present study, antibody was detected much later after transfer of lymph node cells from donors sensitized only once, which is about one-ninth of the total dose of antigen that the repeatedly sensitized donors received, than after transfer of cells from donors repeatedly sensitized. The interval of 2 weeks between sensitizations in the donors appears optimal for antibody production in the recipients, since antibody was detected in more recipients on day 1 and generally throughout the 31-day period after transfer of the 2-week donor cells than with donor cells having other intervals of stimulation. This corresponds well with our electron-microscope observation of the 2-week-interval donor lymphocytes; these showed the most cytologic changes that are generally associated with protein synthesis. The number of cells transferred also affected the secondary antibody response in recipients as shown by the 3-week donors. When 5×10^8 cells of the 3-week donors were transferred, antibody was detected in all animals on day 1 after transfer, whereas when the usual number of cells (1×10^8) was transferred, antibody was detected in only a few recipients on day 1. Usually, whether or not the donors were skin-tested after sensitization, there was no additive effect on the antibody response in the recipients. However, the skin test exerted a booster effect on antibody synthesis by recipients, but only in animals that received cells from donors that were either sensitized once or unsensitized. A skin-test dose in the recipient does not have a booster effect on antibody response once the cells in the donors have reached a threshold synthetic activity, as in those repeatedly sensitized. This effect is dose dependent: the effect of sensitization alone on the antibody response in recipients was observed (31 days after transfer) in recipients not skin-tested themselves which had received cells from sensitized (380 μg), non-skin-tested donors and not in those receiving cells from donors sensitized with a smaller dosage (76 μg). Failure to detect $7S\gamma_1$ and/or $7S\gamma_2$ by micro-immunoelectrophoresis in any of the recipients throughout the 31-day period after transfer is obviously quantitative. The failure to detect any precipitating antibody by the ring test may be quantitative or qualitative, i.e., the fraction of antibody responsible for the two tests may be different.

The present findings suggest that animals repeatedly sensitized by the antigen apparently "lose" delayed hypersensitivity. Some specific changes, e.g., production of precipitating antibody as well as morphologic changes within lymphocytes, suggest that lymphocytes are primary sites of antibody production. Whether the lymphocytes themselves from lymph nodes act as a primary source of antibody production (27–35) or as antigen-sensitive precursors to antibody-forming cells (36–38) is uncertain. The changes seen by electron microscopy suggest that antigen not only mobilizes lymphocytes to produce antibodies but that with increasing antigenic dose synthetic structures of individual lymphocytes increase. Indeed with the largest dose and optimal interval of antigenic stimulation fine-structure studies indicate the production of lymphocytes that are similar to plasma cells.

It is tempting to attribute the secondary antibody response in recipients to the lymphocytes. Probably the transferred lymphocytes themselves produce antibody in recipients, since circulating antibody was detected within 24 hr after transfer; it seems unlikely that the transferred but not further stimulated lymphocytes would have been transformed into another cell type able to produce antibody so quickly. Later the secondary response may be due to cells other than lymphocytes, such as plasma cells, which may possibly develop from the lymphocytes since the number of plasma cells which appear at the transfer site has been correlated with the amount of antibody synthesized (8).

Acknowledgment. We wish to thank Mr. John P. Shanley for his technical assistance.

REFERENCES

1. Kim, C. W., Jamuar, M. P. and Hamilton, L. D., Fed. Proc., *27:* 543, 1968.
2. Kim, C. W., Savel, H. and Hamilton, L. D., J. Immun., *99:* 1150, 1967.
3. Kim, C. W., Jamuar, M. P. and Hamilton, L. D., J. Immun., *99:* 1156, 1967.
4. Harris, S. and Harris, T. N., Fed. Proc., *10:* 409, 1951.
5. Harris, S., Harris, T. N. and Farber, M. B., J. Immun., *72:* 148, 1954.

6. Roberts, J. C., Jr. and Dixon, F. J., J. Exp. Med., *102:* 379, 1955.
7. Dixon, F. J., Weigle, W. O. and Roberts, J. C., J. Immun., *78:* 56, 1957.
8. Dixon, F. J., Roberts, J. C. and Weigle, W. O., Fed. Proc., *16:* 649, 1957.
9. Stavitsky, A. B., Fed. Proc., *16:* 652, 1957.
10. Neil, A. L. and Dixon, F. J., Arch. Pathol., *67:* 643, 1959.
11. Vazquez, J. J., Lab. Invest., *10:* 1110, 1961.
12. Taliaferro, W. H. and Taliaferro, L. G., J. Infect. Dis., *110:* 165, 1962.
13. Zlotnick, A., Vazquez, J. J. and Dixon, F. J., Lab. Invest., *11:* 493, 1962.
14. Chase, M. W., Fed. Proc., *10:* 404, 1951.
15. Wager, O. A. and Chase, M. W., Fed. Proc., *11:* 485, 1952.
16. Chase, M. W., Immunological Reactions Mediated Through Cells, in *The Nature and Significance of the Antibody Response*, Edited by A. M. Pappenheimer, Jr., p. 156, Columbia University Press, New York, 1953.
17. Chase, M. W. and Wager, O. A., Fed. Proc., *16:* 639, 1957.
18. Kim, C. W., J. Infect. Dis., *116:* 208, 1966.
19. Jamuar, M. P., Kim, C. W. and Hamilton, L. D., J. Immun., *100:* 329, 1968.
20. Salvin, S. B., J. Exp. Med., *107:* 109, 1958.
21. Benacerraf, B., Ovary, Z., Bloch, K. J. and Franklin, E. C., J. Exp. Med., *117:* 937, 1963.
22. Weigle, W. O., Int. Arch. Allerg., *29:* 254, 1966.
23. Strejan, G. and Campbell, D. H., J. Immun., *98:* 893, 1967.
24. Strejan, G. and Campbell, D. H., J. Immun., *99:* 347, 1967.
25. Ovary, Z., Benacerraf, B. and Bloch, K. J., J. Exp. Med., *117:* 951, 1963.
26. Harris, T. N., Harris, S. and Farber, M. B., J. Immun., *72:* 161, 1954.
27. Dougherty, T. F., Chase, J. H. and White, A., Proc. Soc. Exp. Biol. Med., *57:* 295, 1944.
28. Harris, T. N., Grimm, E., Mertens, E. and Ehrich, W. E., J. Exp. Med., *81:* 73, 1945.
29. Harris, S. and Harris, T. N., J. Immun., *61:* 193, 1949.
30. Helmreich, E., Kern, M. and Eisen, H. N., J. Biol. Chem., *236:* 464, 1961.
31. Attardi, G., Cohn, M., Horibata, K. and Lennox, E. S., J. Immun., *92:* 346, 1964.
32. Harris, T. N., Hummeler, K. and Harris, S., J. Exp. Med., *123:* 161, 1966.
33. Hummeler, K., Harris, T. N., Tomassini, N., Hechtel, M. and Farber, M. B., J. Exp. Med., *124:* 255, 1966.
34. Hummeler, K., Harris, S. and Harris, T. N., Fed. Proc., *25:* 1734, 1966.
35. Sundaram, K., Phondke, G. P. and Sundaresan, P., Immunology, *13:* 433, 1967.
36. Gowans, J. L. and McGregor, D. D., The Origin of Antibody-forming Cells, in *Immunopathology IIIrd International Symposium*, Edited by P. Grabar and P. A. Miescher, Schwabe and Co., Basel, Switzerland, 1963.
37. McGregor, D. D. and Gowans, J. L., J. Exp. Med., *117:* 303, 1963.
38. McGregor, D. D., McCullagh, P. J. and Gowans, J. L., Proc. Roy. Soc. Ser. B, *168:* 229, 1967.

THE JOURNAL OF IMMUNOLOGY
Vol. 105, No. 1, July 1970
Printed in U.S.A.

EARLY MAST CELL RESPONSES IN MOUSE POPLITEAL LYMPH NODES TO LOCALIZED PRIMARY ANTIGENIC STIMULI[1]

AUDREY N. ROBERTS[2]

From the Department of Microbiology, University of Tennessee Medical Units, Memphis, Tennessee 38103

Received for publication October 17, 1969

Mast cell responses were quantitated in the regional draining lymph nodes of mice during the first 24 hr after primary footpad stimulation with three concentrations each of three soluble protein antigens. The time and intensity of response varied with the type and dosage of antigen. Immunization with 50 μg of bovine serum albumin (BSA) and ferritin induced the highest mast cell responses, with peak counts five times the normal mean at 5 and 3 hr, respectively. A low antigenic dose (10 μg) of BSA or ferritin stimulated peak responses at 16 hr, and the greatest response to 7.5 μg of sulfanilazo porcine γ globulin was observed at 3 hr. At doses of 100 to 150 μg, the three antigens yielded variable results and established no definite response patterns. During peak responses the mast cells accumulated in large clusters in the interfollicular cortex and medullary regions of the nodes. No degranulation or disruption of mast cells was observed, indicating the absence of "cytophilic antibodies" on the cell surfaces. Autoradiography was employed to study the incorporation of tritiated thymidine by responding mast cells at hourly intervals through the first 24 hr after immunization. No tritium was observed in mast cell nuclei, suggesting that the mast cell responses were not due to rapid cell proliferation.

Investigations on the origin, replication and functions of mast cells have demonstrated their participation in numerous important physiologic reactions. A localized increase in mast cells has been demonstrated in tissue sites of hyperplasia or precancerous proliferation (1). Evidence has been presented that mast cells neutralize certain polysaccharides necessary for tumor growth (2). Studies also have demonstrated a localized increase in mast cell numbers in the process of wound healing (3) and have implicated mast cells as possible "buffer cells" in maintaining the homeostatic pH of connective tissue (4). Of principle importance are the functions of mast cells in inflammatory reactions and hypersensitivity in various animal species (5–7). During inflammation mast cells quickly respond by release of "bound" histamine, which may or may not be accompanied by cell disruption. The more severe immunologic trauma that occurs in anaphylaxis results in the early release of histamine, followed by mast cell disruption or degranulation and heparin release (7–11). These physiologically active products function in the vasodilation and increased vascular permeability characteristic of the inflammatory response. Mast cells possess numerous other biochemical constituents, which include approximately 20 different enzymes whose functions have yet to be elucidated (7, 12–15).

Several investigations have demonstrated the direct involvement of mast cells in antigen-antibody interaction. The localized injection of homologous antigen into sensitized animals results in the immediate degranulation of mast cells in tissue surrounding the injection site (7–11, 16, 17). It has been proposed that such reaction is due to the presence of "mast cell-sensitizing" or "cytophilic" antibodies adsorbed to the cell surface (7, 9, 18). On contact with specific antigen *in vivo*, these "sensitized" mast cells respond by vasodilation, disturbance of the molecular equilibrium of surface membranes and release of granules (19). Normal mast cells can be passively sensitized *in vitro* with immune serum.

[1] This study was supported by United States Public Health Service Research Grant AI-04217 from the National Institute of Allergy and Infectious Diseases.

[2] Research Career Development Awardee 5-K3-AI-21,517 of the National Institute of Allergy and Infectious Diseases.

This adsorption of sensitizing antibodies has been demonstrated directly by the immunofluorescence method which revealed the fixation of immunoglobulin G and heavy (γ) chains to mast cell surface membranes (20). Subsequent *in vitro* contact of these passively sensitized cells with specific antigen induces cell damage and histamine release. The fixation of specific radioactive antigen to passively sensitized mast cells also has been reported (21). Several investigations have indicated that the sensitizing immunoglobulin is a non-precipitating, reagin-like antibody which usually is produced early after antigenic stimulation (9, 22).

We recently described an early intensive mast cell accumulation in regional lymph nodes of mice after localized primary immunization with a tritiated soluble protein antigen (23). Autoradiographs of these lymph nodes revealed heavy incorporation of labeled antigen by the responding mast cells. Active proliferation of mast cells also has been shown in rat lymph nodes after a primary or secondary stimulus with *Salmonella adelaide* flagella (24). In light of these results, the present investigation was designed to further characterize the early mast cell response to primary immunization, to quantitate the dose-response relationship and to determine whether mast cells are actively proliferating in the sensitized tissue.

MATERIALS AND METHODS

Mice. Random bred male Swiss Webster mice (Pel-Freez Bio-Animals, Inc., Rogers, Ark.) were used. At the time of immunization, the mice were approximately 6 to 8 months of age and weighed 25 to 30 g.

Immunization procedures. For mast cell response studies, nine groups of mice, 24 mice/group, were injected subcutaneously in the right hind footpad with a primary antigenic stimulus. Three concentrations each of three sterile aqueous antigen solutions were administered, one concentration/mouse group: 10, 50 and 100 μg of bovine serum albumin (BSA, crystallized, Pentex Biochemicals, Kankakee, Ill.), 10, 50 and 100 μg of ferritin (6 $\times$ crystallized, horse spleen, Pentex Biochemicals, Kankakee, Ill.), and 7.5, 75 and 150 μg of sulfanilazo porcine γ globulin (S-PGG) (25). Four mice from each group were killed at 1, 3, 5, 8, 16 and 24 hr after injection. The right draining popliteal node and the contralateral unstimulated control popliteal node were removed from each mouse.

For studies on the replication of mast cells in stimulated and unstimulated lymph nodes, each of 96 mice was injected subcutaneously with 50 μg of BSA in the right hind footpad. Four mice were killed at hourly intervals from 1 through 24 hr after injection. Each mouse was injected intraperitoneally with 100 μCi of thymidine-methyl-^{3}H (^{3}HT, 6.7 Ci/mM, New England Nuclear Corp., Boston, Mass.) 3 hr before death. The right draining popliteal node and the contralateral unstimulated control popliteal node were removed from each mouse and prepared for autoradiography.

Histology and mast cell quantitation. All lymph nodes were fixed in Carnoy's solution (26) for 18 to 24 hr and embedded in Paraplast. Five micron sections were cut completely through each node, retaining every 10th section for mast cell counts. The tissue sections were deparaffinized and stained by the following modified methyl green-pyronin technique: The stain was prepared by combining 1.62 ml of 5% aqueous pyronin Y, 18.0 ml of 2% aqueous methyl green (chloroform extracted), 108.0 ml of deionized water and 126.0 ml of 0.2 M acetate buffer, pH 4.8. The tissue sections were stained for 15 min, flushed with deionized water and passed through two changes of acetone, acetone-xylene (1:2), acetone-xylene (1:10), cleared in xylene and mounted with Permount. With this technique, the mast cell granules stain a brilliant red and their nuclei stain blue.

The total number of mast cells per section was counted microscopically at $\times$ 1200 magnification in every 10th section prepared from each node. The average number of sections counted per node was 20 $\pm$ 2. The normal (unstimulated) mean mast cell count/section of 66 $\pm$ 12 was determined from counts on 20 sections from each of the 216 contralateral control popliteal nodes. For statistical analysis, the mean index of mast cell responses in draining popliteal nodes at each time interval was expressed as the ratio of the mean mast cell count/section/node: the mean normal mast cell count and the standard deviations were calculated from these ratios.

Autoradiography. After fixation, the popliteal lymph node sections prepared from the ^{3}HT-injected mice were coated with Kodak NTB3 liquid emulsion and exposed for 18 days. The slides were developed in Dektol (1:2 dilution) and stained for 1 hr in the above methyl green-pyronin solution. All sections were observed microscopically at × 1200 magnification for the presence of grains over nuclei of mast cells and other lymphoid cell types.

RESULTS

Mast cell response to primary antigenic stimuli. The resulting data show that mast cells actively respond in lymph nodes draining the site of a localized primary antigenic stimulus (Fig. 1). The time and intensity of response appear to differ with each antigen and are at least partly dependent on dosage of the stimulus. A low antigenic dose (10 μg) of BSA or ferritin stimulated peak mast cell responses at 16 hr, which were preceded and followed by normal or subnormal means throughout the 24-hr interval. Variation of this pattern was observed with 7.5 μg of S-PGG, which stimulated a peak response at 3 hr. The 50-μg doses of BSA and ferritin induced highest mast cell responses, with peak levels five times the normal mean at 5 and 3 hr, respectively. This response to BSA was especially pronounced, with mean indices three to five times the normal mean from 1 through 16 hr post-injection. The response to 75 μg of S-PGG was less striking with only low level responses at 8 and 16 hr. The highest dose of each of the three antigens yielded variable results and established no definite response patterns. With the exception of BSA, however, two- to threefold increases in the mean indices were observed between 8 and 24 hr. During this interval, the high mast cell responses persisted in animals receiving 150 μg of S-PGG, but peaked sharply at 8 hr, then fell to sub-normal levels in animals injected with 100 μg of ferritin.

In the responding popliteal nodes, mast cells first accumulated in the medullary areas and were dispersed among heavy populations of macrophages and reticular cells (Fig. 2). These phagocytic cell types were shown in previous studies to incorporate high concentrations of the sensitizing antigen (23). As the mast cell responses intensified, the cells clustered in large numbers in both the interfollicular cortex and medullary regions of the nodes (Fig. 3). These mast cells remained intact, with no degranulation or disruption occurring. In unstimulated control nodes, the mast cells remained lightly distributed in the medullary and hilar areas, and no clusters were observed.

The proliferation of mast cells in responding popliteal nodes. Autoradiographs of the responding and control popliteal nodes were observed for the incorporation of ^{3}HT into mast cell nuclei to establish the presence and rate of mast cell replication. In stimulated lymph nodes, heavy concentrations of grains were localized over nuclei of germinal center blast cells and other lymphoblasts lightly distributed throughout the medullary areas within 1 hr after antigen injection. By 2 hr a tremendous increase was noted in labeled sinus-lining cells, germinal center cells and immature medullary cells. After 4 hr numerous medium and small lymphocytes in the inter-

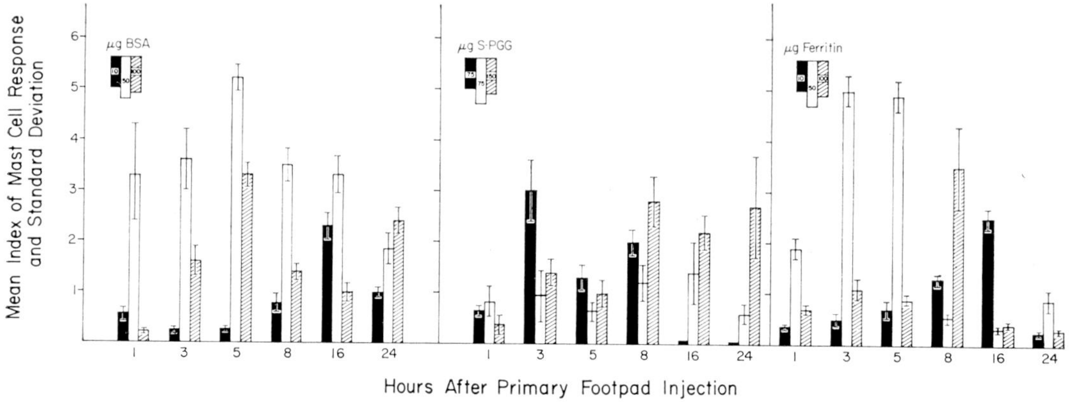

Figure 1. Quantitation of mast cell responses in draining popliteal lymph nodes of mice after primary footpad stimulation with soluble protein antigens. Each bar is the mean index calculated from the total counts of four nodes. The normal mean index = 1.

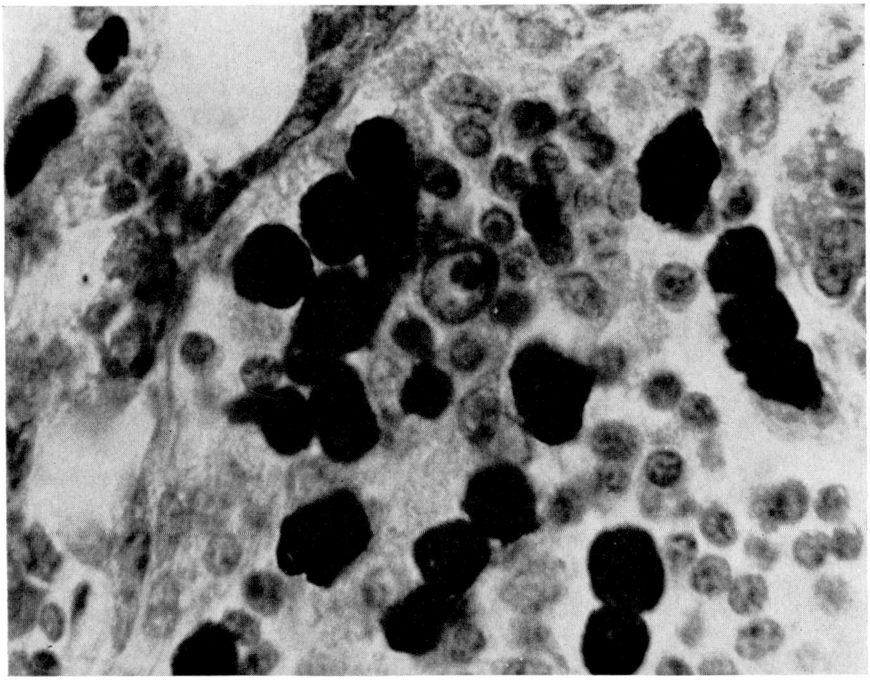

Figure 2. Clustered mast cells in draining mouse popliteal lymph node 5 hr after primary footpad stimulation with 50 μg of BSA. The mast cells are surrounded by macrophages, reticular cells and a few lymphocytes (× 1000).

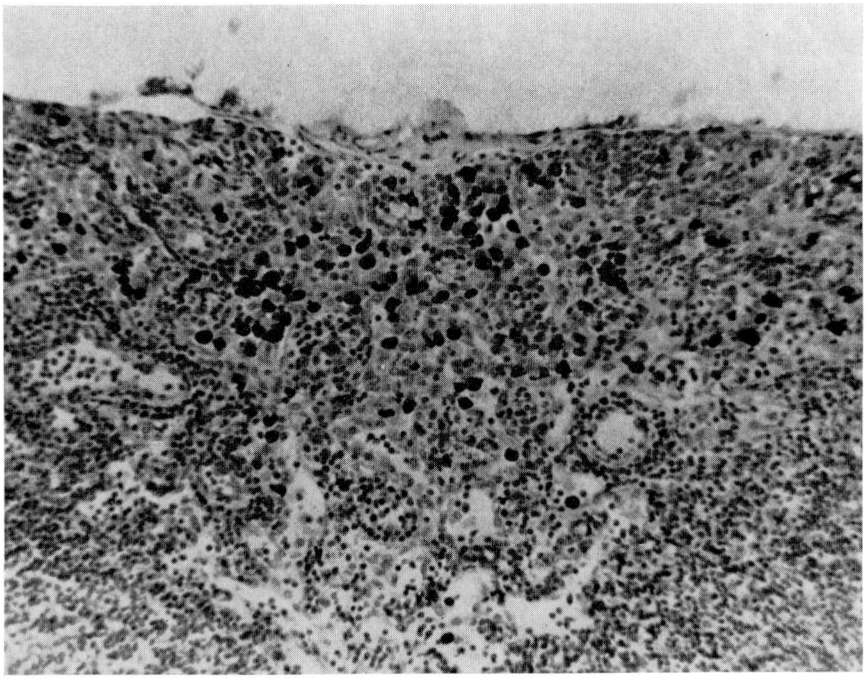

Figure 3. Mast cells clustered in the interfollicular cortex of draining mouse popliteal lymph node 5 hr after primary footpad stimulation with 50 μg of BSA (× 400).

follicular cortex demonstrated nuclear ^{3}H localization with further increases in labeled medullary cells. This pattern of ^{3}H incorporation persisted throughout the 24-hr study. Peak mast cell responses occurred at 5 and 6 hr post-injection. These mast cells accumulated in clusters of 20 to 30 cells in the interfollicular cortex and medullary regions of the nodes, but autoradiography detected no localization of ^{3}HT in the mast cell nuclei. No labeled mast cells were observed in stimulated or control popliteal node autoradiographs throughout the study period. These results indicated that the intensive mast cell responses did not develop by proliferation of mast cells in the stimulated nodes.

DISCUSSION

These results support and expand previous observations that mast cells rapidly respond in lymph nodes regional to the site of a localized primary antigenic stimulus (23). The intensive mast cell increases suggest a possible function in the early sequence of cellular events which characterize the primary immune response. The role of mast cells in mild to acute inflammatory reactions has been described repeatedly (5–11, 16–19). It is possible that their localized accumulation was due to the release of inflammatory metabolic substances by the adjacent, highly phagocytic macrophages and reticular cells which have been shown in earlier investigations to incorporate heavy concentrations of sensitizing antigen (23). These previous studies also demonstrated the localization of relatively large quantities of labeled antigen in the responding mast cells, but the role, if any, of mast cells in antibody synthesis is unknown.

Studies which have demonstrated the adsorption of early synthesized cytophilic antibodies by mast cells and the subsequent localization of specific sensitizing antigen on mast cell surfaces (7, 9, 18–21) would suggest that this was perhaps occurring in the responding lymphatic tissues. However, it is unlikely that such cytophilic antibodies were associated with these cells, since the degranulation or disruption which often accompanies antigen-antibody interaction at the cell surface was not observed (7–11, 17, 18). Also, it is improbable that cytophilic antibodies had been synthesized and released at the early time periods of these mast cell responses, since studies have indicated that delayed hypersensitivity (immune cell development) precedes the formation of mast cell-sensitizing antibodies (18, 22). However, the possible presence of minute amounts of cytophilic antibodies, undetectable by available techniques, can not be ignored. These minute amounts could contribute to the mast cell responses, and yet be insufficient to effect disruption on contact with the sensitizing antigen.

Small (10 μg) and large (100 μg) doses of BSA and ferritin did not stimulate as great a response as did the intermediate dose (50 μg), indicating a possible correlation between the antigenic dose and the resulting mast cell activities, as shown by other investigators (24).

Failure to demonstrate the incorporation of ^{3}HT by responding mast cells indicated that antigenic stimulation did not initiate an enhanced rate of mast cell proliferation. The early appearance of the mast cell responses also would not favor their accumulation due to proliferation, since other studies have shown lengthy mast cell generation times (24, 27–29). Such slow mast cell replication was described recently by Miller and Cole (24) in regional rat lymph nodes following footpad stimulation with typhoid-paratyphoid A and B vaccine and *Salmonella adelaide* flagella. The present studies indicate, therefore, that the the mast cells either migrated rapidly into the responding nodes from the circulation and surrounding connective tissues or possibly were formed by transformation of lymphatic "precursor" cells immediately following penetration of sensitizing antigens into the regional draining nodes. The latter would correlate with reports suggesting numerous origins of mast cells, including lymphocytes (4, 29), fibroblasts (30) and precursor or "stem" cells (31, 32).

Acknowledgment. The author expresses grateful appreciation to Mrs. Janelle S. Hunt for excellent technical assistance.

REFERENCES

1. Simpson, W. L., Ann. N. Y. Acad. Sci., *103:* 4, 1963.
2. Csaba, G., Acs, T., Horvath, C. and Mold, K., Brit. J. Cancer, *15:* 327, 1961.
3. Wichmann, B.-E., Acta Path. Microbiol. Scand. (Suppl.), *108:* 1, 1955.
4. Chu, C. H. U., Anat. Rec., *145:* 217, 1963.
5. Asboe-Hansen, G., Int. Rev. Cytol., *3:* 399, 1954.

6. Benditt, E P., and Lagunoff, D., Progr. Allerg., *8:* 195, 1954.
7. Keller, R., *Tissue Mast Cells in Immune Reactions*, Monographs in Allergy, Vol. 2, p. 40, American Elsevier, New York, 1966.
8. Briggs, N. T., J. Infect. Dis., *113:* 22, 1963.
9. Mota, I., Immunology, *7:* 681, 1964.
10. Lima, A. Q., Vaz, N. M., Netto, M. B. and Janini, J. B., Int. Arch. Allerg., *25:* 65, 1964.
11. Riley, J. F., Ann. N. Y. Acad. Sci., *103:* 151, 1963.
12. Riley, J. F. and Drennan, J. M., J. Path. Bact., *61:* 245, 1949.
13. Lagunoff, D. and Benditt, E. P., Ann. N. Y. Acad. Sci., *103:* 185, 1963.
14. Smith, D. E., Int. Rev. Cytol., *14:* 327, 1963.
15. Ende, N., Katayama, Y. and Auditore, J. V., Nature, *201:* 1197, 1964.
16. Goldgraber, M. B. and Lewert, R. M., J. Parasit., *51:* 169, 1965.
17. Carter, P. B., Higginbotham, R. D. and Dougherty, T. F., J. Immun., *79:* 259, 1957.
18. Mota, I., Immunology, *7:* 700, 1964.
19. Mota, I. and Dias da Silva, W., Nature, *186:* 245, 1960.
20. Todorov, D. M., Wilkinson, P. C. and White, R. G., Immunology, *15:* 51, 1968.
21. Keller, R. and Sorkin, E., Nature, *199:* 709, 1963.
22. Prouvost-Danon, A., Peixoto, J. M. and Javierre, M. Q., Immunology, *15:* 271, 1968.
23. Roberts, A. N., Amer. J. Path., *49:* 889, 1966.
24. Miller, J. J., III and Cole, L. J., Nature, *217:* 263, 1968.
25. Roberts, A. N., Nature, *210:* 266, 1966.
26. Pearse, A. G. E., *Histochemistry, Theoretical and Applied*, p. 788, Little, Brown and Co., Boston, 1960.
27. Asboe-Hansen, G. and Levi, H., Acta Path. Microbiol. Scand., *56:* 241, 1962.
28. Coombs, J. W., Lagunoff, D. and Benditt, E. P., J. Cell Biol., *25:* 577, 1965.
29. Burnet, F. M., J. Path. Bact., *89:* 271, 1965.
30. Hissard, R., Moncourier, E. and Jacquet, J., Presse Méd., *59:* 1765, 1951.
31. Watson, W. C. and Kennedy, J. S., Brit. J. Exp. Path., *41:* 385, 1960.
32. Padawer, J., Angiology, *12:* 538, 1961.

THE JOURNAL OF IMMUNOLOGY
Vol. 105, No. 1, July 1970

THE IMMUNE RESPONSE OF MICE TO *SERRATIA MARCESCENS* LPS OR INTACT BACTERIA[1]

CHARLES FIELD,[2] JERRY L. ALLEN AND HERMAN FRIEDMAN

From the Departments of Microbiology, Temple University School of Medicine, and Albert Einstein Medical Center, Philadelphia, Pennsylvania

Received for publication October 13, 1969

Injection of adult mice with lipopolysaccharide (LPS) somatic antigen, or a heat-killed vaccine of *Serratia marcescens* resulted in rapid appearance of specific antibody-forming cells in the spleen, as well as other lymphoid tissues such as the mesenteric nodes and the thymus. Either immunogen in a dose of 50 μg resulted in a maximum cellular antibody response 3 to 5 days later; higher or lower doses resulted in a lesser response. Injection of 500 or 750 μg antigen gave the least response. In mice injected with the high doses of antigen, there was no compensatory increase in the number of antibody-forming cells in lymphoid organs other than the spleen. Regardless of antigen dose used or the time period after immunization antiglobulin facilitation yielded no evidence for additional plaque-forming cells. All concentrations of antigen gave a rapid increase in hemagglutinin and bacterial agglutinin titers, the vaccine giving the highest titers. Mice injected with 500 or 750 μg of either form of antigen had lower serum titers. Mice given the higher doses of either LPS or vaccine displayed a marked increase in the number of nonspecific antibody-forming cells to sheep erythrocytes. These results are viewed as evidence for development of immunologic tolerance to large doses of Serratia antigens, either vaccine or LPS. The toxicity of the antigenic preparations did not appear to be involved in the immunodepression. Both the antigenic state and dose markedly influenced the number of antibody-forming cells appearing after immunization.

Gram-negative microorganisms are ubiquitous, are markedly immunogenic and readily stimulate rapid appearance of specific antibody (1–5). It is generally accepted that bacterial antigens play an important role in nonspecific resistance, induce "natural" antibodies, and serve as an adjuvant in the immune response to unrelated antigens (6–10). Most investigations on Gram-negative bacteria and their associated somatic antigens have been concerned primarily with their physiologic and endotoxic properties.

The development of immunoplaque techniques (11, 12) has provided an objective means for studying the immune response at the cellular level to antigens of Gram-negative bacteria (13–18). A number of investigations attest to the marked effect of antibody dose on appearance of both humoral and cellular antibody to a variety of Gram-negative organisms, such as *Salmonella enteritidis*, *Escherichia coli* and *Shigella paradysenteriae* (16, 19–26). Most of the serum antibody appearing after a single immunizing injection of these bacterial antigens consists of 19S IgM globulins (4, 20, 27, 28). Accordingly, antibody-forming cells involved in this response are readily detected by the passive hemolytic plaque technique in agar gel, using sheep or other erythrocytes sensitized with the specific bacterial somatic extract.

[1] This work was supported in part by Research Grants from the National Science Foundation (GB 3278 and GB 6251), a Training Grant from the United States Public Health Service (A-1233-04) and Fellowship No. 1-F2-AI-38,012-01 from the National Institute of Allergy and Infectious Diseases to J. L. A.

[2] The data in this report were taken in part from a thesis submitted by C. F. for the M. S. degree. Present address: Department of Bacteriology and Public Health, Utah State University, Logan, Utah.

Most studies using immunoplaque procedures have been made in rabbits, which are markedly responsive to the pyrogenic effects of somatic antigens, but less susceptible to their lethal effects. Rabbits respond with many antibody-forming cells to nanogram quantities of lipopolysaccharide antigen from Salmonella (20, 21). A thousand-fold or greater antigen dose also results in appearance of many plaque-forming cells, in both the regional lymph nodes and the spleen. Lesser doses evoke correspondingly fewer antibody-forming cells. In contrast, the results of the present work, using mice and a somatic antigen and whole cell vaccine derived from *Serratia marcescens*, indicate that larger doses of antigen may cause a marked immunosuppression. An antigen concentration approximately 100-fold greater than that needed for an optimum response yielded far fewer antibody-forming cells. A number of factors influencing this response have been determined, as well as the effect of graded doses of the antigen—both lipopolysaccharide and whole cell vaccine—on the production of antibody-forming cells to sheep erythrocytes.

METHODS AND MATERIALS

Animals. NIH albino A and Swiss-Webster mice were used. They were generally 6 to 8 weeks old and were obtained from a local dealer in the Philadelphia area (16). The animals were housed in groups of five or six in plastic cages and fed Purina mouse pellets and water *ad libitum*.

Antigen. A lipopolysaccharide (LPS) somatic antigen derived from *Serratia marcescens* was used. The antigen was extracted by the TCA precipitation method, and was prepared at Difco Laboratories, Detroit, Mich. The killed vaccine was prepared by washing overnight broth cultures with sterile saline by centrifugation and resuspending to a concentration of 10% (v/v) with sterile saline. The organisms were killed by heating for 1 hr at 80°C. Sterility was assessed by appropriate bacteriologic tests and the suspension of microorganisms was freeze-dried and lyophilized. For injection, varying quantities were resuspended in appropriate volumes of sterile saline.

Immunization. Mice were injected intraperitoneally (i.p.) with 0.5 ml of graded doses of either the LPS or the vaccine, generally ranging from 0.1 μg to 500 or 750 μg. Control animals were injected with saline only.

Serology. Blood was collected from the retroorbital venous plexus of individual animals in each group before and at various times after immunization (16). The blood samples were allowed to clot at room temperature and the serum was separated by centrifugation. Antibody titers were determined by either the direct bacterial agglutination technique or by passive hemagglutination (PHA). For either procedure, two-fold serial dilutions were prepared with individual serum specimens, using microtiter plates and 0.025-ml volumes of saline (16). For bacterial agglutination, 0.025 ml of an 0.05% suspension of the heat-killed Serratia was added to each cup, followed by incubation for 2 hr at 37°C and overnight in the cold. The titer was recorded as the highest dilution of serum resulting in complete agglutination of the added bacteria.

For passive hemagglutination, sheep erythrocytes were sensitized with previously boiled LPS at a concentration of 1 mg/ml (24). Washed, packed sheep erythrocytes were treated with the LPS, at a ratio of 1 part RBC to 9 parts antigen in 0.15 M PO4-buffered saline, pH 7.2. The red cell-LPS mixture was incubated for 1 hr at 37°C, and then washed three times by serial centrifugation in the cold, using sterile buffer. The cells were resuspended to a 10% concentration with Veronal-buffered saline. For hemagglutination, the cells were further diluted to a concentration of 0.5% and 0.025 ml was added to each dilution cup. The plates were incubated for 2 hr at 37°C and then overnight in the cold. The titer was recorded as the reciprocal of the highest dilution of serum that completely agglutinated the LPS sensitized red cells.

As controls, duplicate serum dilutions were treated with 0.025 ml of a similar concentration of unsensitized red cells. In addition, inhibition experiments were performed in which 10 or 100 μg of LPS from *Serratia marcescens*, or from other organisms, were added, in 0.025-ml volumes, to individual serum dilutions before adding the sensitized red cells or bacteria.

The sensitivity of the serum antibody activity to inactivation with 2-mercaptoethanol (2-ME) was used as an indicator of 7S and 19S antibody. For this purpose duplicate samples of sera were incubated for 1 hr at 37°C with an equal volume of 0.2 M 2-ME before dilution. The sera were then treated exactly as above. The serum titer remaining after such treatment was considered to be due to 7S antibody.

Immunoplaque assay. Five or more mice from each experimental or control group were killed on a given day and the spleen, lymph nodes and thymus were excised and placed in cold, sterile Hank's solution. Dispersed cell suspensions were prepared in Hank's solution, as described previously, using the "teasing" procedure with needles and forceps (16). The cells were washed several times in the cold and the number of viable leukocytes was determined by hemocytometer count, using trypan blue stain. The number of antibody plaque-forming cells (PFC) was then determined. For this purpose, 0.1 ml of individual cell suspensions was added to 2 ml of warm, melted 0.7% Noble agar containing 0.1 ml of a 15% suspension of LPS-sensitized sheep red cells, or, as a control, unsensitized red cells. The agar also contained 1 mg DEAE-dextran to inhibit the anti-complementary activity of the agar. The agar-leukocyte-RBC mixture was then carefully poured onto a previously prepared base layer consisting of 10 to 15 ml 1.4% Noble agar in a 100-mm diameter Petri plate.

When the upper layer had solidified, the plates were incubated for 1 hr at 37°C and then treated with approximately 5 ml of a 1:15 dilution of sterile guinea pig serum as a source of complement. Following further incubation for 30 min to 1 hr, discrete zones of hemolysis (plaques) appearing against the background of unlysed red cells were considered to be due to individual antibody-forming cells. The number of plaques on three or more plates containing similar concentrations of splenocytes was determined with the aid of a Quebec colony counter, and the numbers of PFC per whole spleen and per million leukocytes plated were calculated. The numbers of PFC observed on plates containing spleen cells from control mice or with unsensitized red cells were subtracted from those occurring with plates containing cells from experimental animals and LPS-treated erythrocytes. The additional numbers of PFC appearing on plates with unsensitized RBC and spleen cells from mice immunized with LPS and/or Serratia vaccine were considered to be due to increased "background" PFC nonspecifically stimulated by the antigen (see below).

Inhibition experiments. Specificity of the PFC was determined by a number of inhibition experiments. Various quantities of LPS were incorporated directly into the 2-ml agar samples before plating in order to specifically inhibit plaque formation to Serratia. In addition, rabbit anti-mouse polyvalent γ globulin serum was used as an inhibitor in the agar plates to demonstrate the globulin nature of the antibody plaques (16, 24). In other experiments, higher dilutions of anti-γ globulin serum were used in an effort to facilitate or enhance detection of 7S IgG plaque-forming cells (28). However, as described below, no facilitation occurred.

Experimental design. Groups of mice were injected with graded doses of either LPS or killed vaccine (Figure 1). The numbers of PFC specific for Serratia appearing in the spleen, deep and superficial lymph nodes and the thymus were determined at specified intervals after immunization, using the immunoplaque assay with LPS-sensitized sheep red blood cells. In addition, the effect of immunization on appearance of antibody-forming cells to unsensitized sheep RBCs was also determined. The responses were determined as a function of antigen dose and time after immunization. The serum antibody titers to Serratia antigen, as determined both by bacterial agglutination and passive hemagglutination with LPS-sensitized RBCs, were determined and correlated with the dose and form of antigen used. The molecular nature of the serum antibody was studied by inactivation treatment with mercaptoethanol. Low-efficiency antibody-forming cells to Serratia were sought by means of the enhancement plaque procedure. Inhibition experiments were performed to demonstrate specificity of the anti-Serratia plaques, as well as the "nonspecific" plaques to sheep red cells.

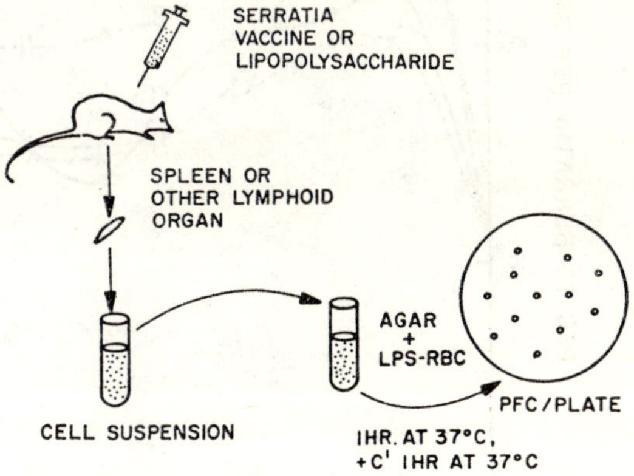

Figure 1. Schematic representation of the experimental procedures used to enumerate antibody-forming cells to Serratia antigen in the spleen and other lymphoid organs of mice immunized with graded doses of Serratia vaccine or lipopolysaccharide.

RESULTS

Cytokinetics of the immune response to graded doses of LPS. Groups of mice were injected with either 0.5, 5, 50, or 500 μg LPS. Five or more animals were killed at varying intervals thereafter over a period of a month. As can be seen from Figures 2 and 3, there was a rapid rise in the number of splenic PFC during the first few days after immunization. A "background" of 100 to 300 PFC/spleen existed before immunization. By 3 to 5 days after immunization there was a 10- to 80-fold increase. Mice injected with the 5- or 50-μg dose had the greatest response. There was a peak of over 8500 PFC/spleen, representing nearly 700 to 800 PFC/10 million leukocytes (Figs. 1 and 2). Mice that received a lower concentration of LPS also had a rapid rise in the number of PFC, but the peak was less than one-half to one-fourth of that occurring in the other two groups. Mice injected with the 500-μg dose also had a lower plaque response, with a peak of less than 1500 PFC/spleen or 100/10 million leukocytes. The number of PFC rapidly declined between days 8 and 15 in spleens of all mice, regardless of antigen dose. However, the most rapid decline occurred in the mice injected with the 5- or 50-μg dose. The lowest rate of PFC decline during this time occurred in spleens of the mice injected with the 500-μg antigen dose. Mice injected with 5 or 50 μg LPS appeared to have a secondary rise in PFC on day 28. Further studies (unpublished observations) suggest that this secondary rise reflects a second peak occurring about 5 to 6 weeks after immunization.

Cytokinetics of the immune response to graded doses of vaccine. Other groups of mice were injected with similar concentrations of a vaccine prepared from the heat-killed Serratia. As can be seen from Figures 2 and 3, there was a similar rapid rise in the number of PFC. The number of splenic PFC at the peak of the response was higher in mice injected with the 5- and 50-μg dose of antigen, as compared to those injected with higher or lower concentrations (Figs. 2 and 3).

The number of PFC rapidly decreased in the spleens of mice injected with 0.5 or 50 μg vaccine (Figs. 2 and 3). Mice injected with the lowest dose had the sharpest decline. The number of PFC declined much less rapidly in spleens of mice injected with 500 μg of the vaccine. By day 28

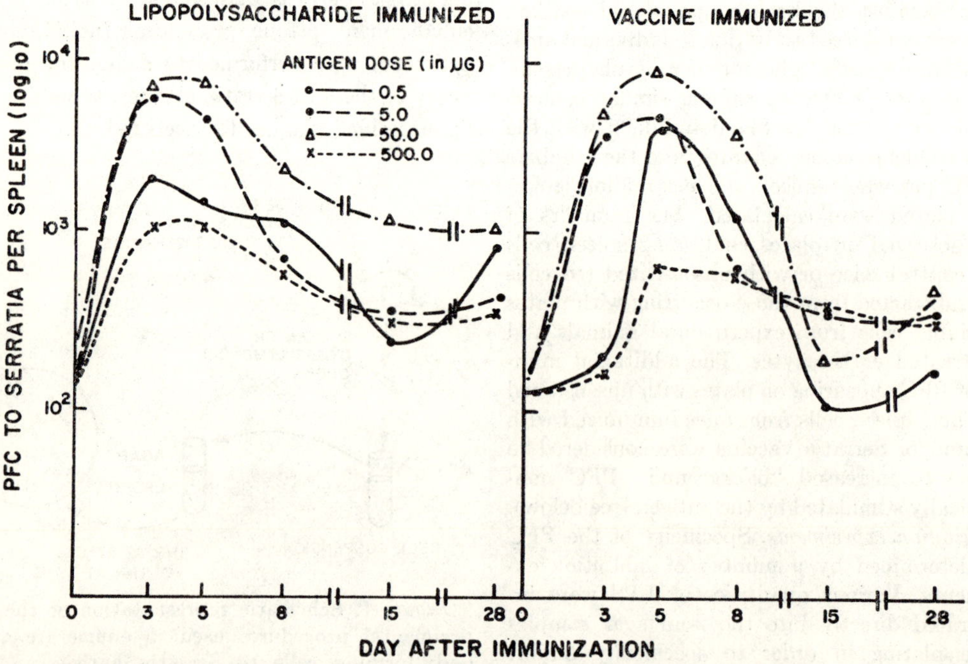

Figure 2. The cytokinetics of Serratia antigen PFC in the spleens of mice injected i.p. with graded doses of either Serratia LPS or heat-killed vaccine. Each point represents the average number of PFC/spleen for groups of five or more mice.

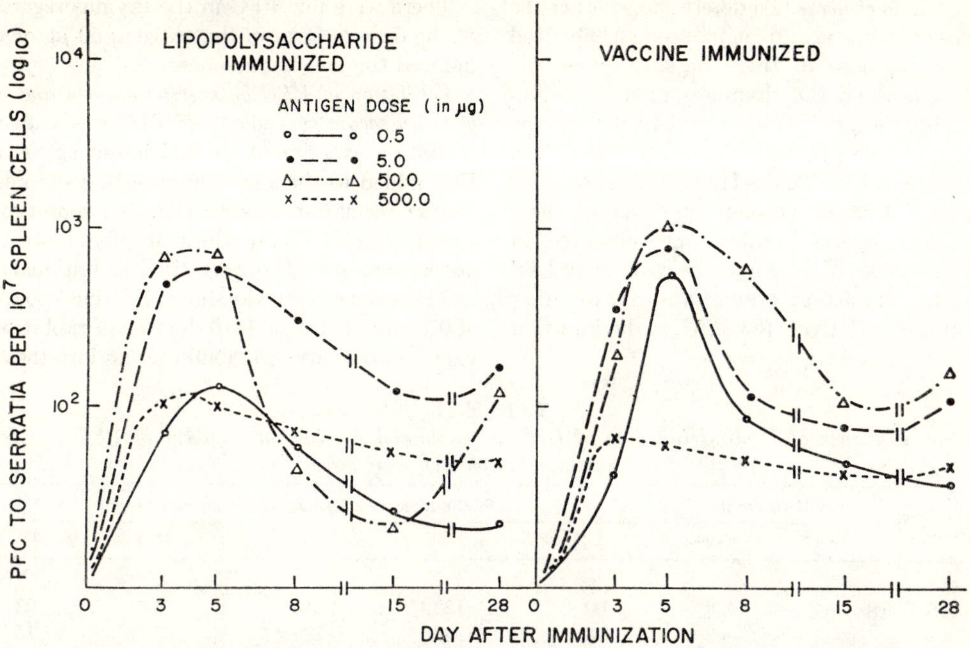

Figure 3. The cytokinetics of Serratia PFC in spleens of mice injected i.p. with graded doses of either Serratia LPS or heat-killed vaccine. Each point represents the average number of PFC/10 million splenocytes for groups of five or more mice.

there was a consistent increase in the number of PFC in spleens of all mice, regardless of the antigen dose.

Effect of anti-globulin serum on facilitation of PFC to Serratia. Since the number of PFC was markedly depressed in mice that received the 500-μg dose of antigen, evidence was sought for a rapid IgG antibody plaque response, since this would be less readily detected in the complement-mediated hemolytic reaction with LPS-treated RBC. Accordingly, polyvalent rabbit anti-globulin serum was used in facilitation experiments. Plates containing spleen cells from mice immunized 3 to 28 days previously with either 50 or 500 μg LPS were treated in duplicate with a 1:50 dilution of the enhancing rabbit antiserum (Table I). There was no significant increase in the number of PFC detected in such plates. There was no difference observed when the antiserum was overlaid onto the plates, after initial incubation with complement or when incorporated directly into the 2-ml agar pours.

TABLE I

Direct and facilitated PFC in spleens of mice immunized with a high and low dose of Serratia lipopolysaccharide

Day after Immunization[a]	Dose of LPS Injected			
	50 μg		500 μg	
	Direct PFC	Plus anti-γG[b]	Direct PFC	Plus anti-γG
3	420	423	11	18
5	443	458	83	84
8	161	176	52	71
15	136	152	60	60
28	101	111	54	55

[a] Groups of mice injected i.p. with indicated dose of antigen; three to five mice killed on day indicated and average number of PFC/10^7 spleen cells determined/group.

[b] Duplicate test plates treated with 1:50 dilution of rabbit anti-mouse globulin serum which facilitates appearance of 7S IgG PFC to sheep erythrocytes.

Appearance of antibody-forming cells in mesenteric lymph nodes and thymus. Although the spleen is regarded as the principal organ for antibody formation to sheep erythrocytes, a number of studies have shown that other lymphoid organs, including the superficial and deep lymph nodes, and also the thymus, may contain antibody-forming cells to antigens such as *Salmonella*, *E.*

coli, or *Vibrio cholerae*. To determine whether the high dose of Serratia antigen induced an enhanced antibody response in these organs, mesenteric lymph nodes and the thymuses of mice immunized with the graded doses of LPS or vaccine were assayed for PFC at various times thereafter. As can be seen from Tables II and III, many PFC to Serratia LPS or vaccine appeared in these organs. The largest number were observed in mesenteric nodes of mice injected with 50 μg LPS or vaccine. The 0.5-μg dose of antigen, in either form, induced relatively few PFC, as did injection of the 500-μg dose.

There were few PFC in the thymus regardless of the dose or form of the antigen; 50 μg of LPS induced the greatest response.

Inhibition of PFC by specific antigen and antiglobulin serum. Specificity of PFC was shown by inhibition experiments in which 100 μg Serratia LPS added to the agar before testing suppressed plaque formation (Table IV). Incorporation of 100 μg *E. coli* LPS into the agar did not affect the appearance of PFC to Serratia. In additional control experiments, it was shown that incorporation of 0.1 ml of a 1:5 or 1:10 dilution of rabbit polyvalent anti-mouse γ globulin serum into the agar

TABLE II

Influence of immunizing dose of LPS or whole cell vaccine on numbers of PFC in mesenteric lymph nodes of mice

Antigen Dose Injected[a]	Antigen Form		PFC/10^7 Mesenteric Lymph Node Cells on Day				
	LPS	Vaccine	3	5	8	15	28
μg							
0.5	+		90	122	45	13	93
		+	<5	62	139	165	15
5.0	+		31	138	110	22	
		+	45	169	138	69	98
50.0	+		135	1860	615	18	565
		+	865	651	47	52	753
500.0	+		110	38	46	28	389
		+	96	25	950	12	565

[a] Groups of mice injected i.p. with indicated concentration of Serratia antigen, either LPS or vaccine; three to five mice/group killed on day indicated.

TABLE III

Influence of immunizing dose of LPS or whole cell vaccine on numbers of PFC in thymus of mice

Antigen Dose Injected[a]	Antigen Form		PFC/10^7 Thymus Cells on Day				
	LPS	Vaccine	3	5	8	15	28
μg							
0.5	+		<5	11	53	21	36
		+	<5	<5	<5	<5	29
5.0	+		9	5	36	15	21
		+	41	11	<5	<5	38
50.0	+		5	168	12	83	341
		+	45	16	<5	<5	16
500.0	+		65	11	<5	23	16
		+	<5	<5	52	12	27

[a] Groups of mice immunized i.p. with indicated dose of antigen, either LPS or vaccine; three to five mice/group killed on day indicated.

completely abolished PFC, regardless of the dose of antigen used for immunization.

Effect of antigen concentration on serum antibody titers. All mice used for plaque assay were tested for serum antibody to Serratia. As can be seen from Figure 4, there was a rapid rise in titer following immunization with either form of antigen, as detected by either the PHA or bacterial ag-

TABLE IV

Specificity of PFC; suppression of plaque formation by specific LPS and anti-globulin serum in vitro

LPS Dose for Immunization[a]	No Addition	Serratia LPS 1.0	Serratia LPS 10	Serratia LPS 100	*E. coli* LPS (100 μg)	Anti-mouse γG Serum (0.1 ml of 1:10 Dilution)
μg		μg				
0.5	32	31	5	2	36	1
5.0	176	165	29	8	169	3
50.0	289	293	41	5	301	4
500.0	29	20	11	3	33	1

[a] Groups of five mice immunized with indicated dose of LPS and killed 5 days later; 2×10^6 spleen cells tested in agar with or without indicated inhibitor.

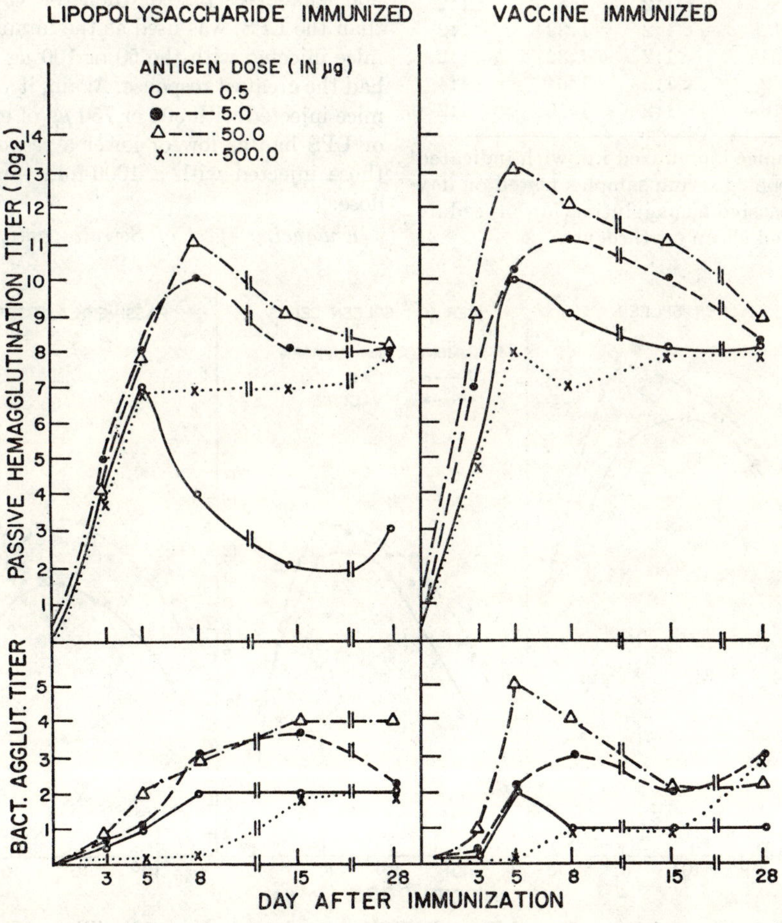

Figure 4. Serum antibody levels in mice immunized with graded doses of either Serratia LPS or heat-killed vaccine. Each point represents the mean serum agglutinin or hemagglutinin titer of groups of five mice each.

glutination method. However, the hemagglutinin titers were generally much higher. The peak titers occurred 5 to 8 days after immunization, with the vaccine inducing higher responses than the LPS (Fig. 4). Mice injected with 5 or 50 μg of either LPS or vaccine generally had the highest titers. There was a lesser response in mice injected with 500 μg antigen. However, the titer remained relatively stabile for a period of at least 28 days.

TABLE V

Effect of 2-ME treatment on serum antibody developed in mice injected with small or large doses of Serratia LPS

Day after Immunization[a]	Dose of LPS Injected			
	50 μg		500 μg	
	Untreated	+2-ME	Untreated	+2-ME
3	1:8	<1:2	1:8	<1:2
5	1:128	<1:2	1:32	<1:2
8	1:64	<1:2	1:32	<1:2
15	1:32	<1:2	1:64	1:4
28	1:16	1:2	1:16	1:2

[a] Groups of mice immunized i.p. with indicated dose of LPS; pooled serum samples tested on day indicated by passive hemagglutination procedure with LPS-coated sheep erythrocytes.

Nearly all of the serum activity throughout the 28-day observation period was susceptible to inactivation by 2-ME (Table V). There was a slight indication of 2-ME resistant antibody 15 days after immunization with 500 μg LPS (titer 1:4), but this did not seem significant.

Effect of antigen dose and form on peak antibody response. In an additional comparative experiment, eight groups of five mice each were simultaneously injected with antigen doses ranging from 0.5 to 750 μg (Fig. 5). Five days later all of the mice were killed and their spleens assayed for specific PFC to Serratia. Their sera were titrated for hemagglutinating antibody. As can be seen from Figure 5, there was a marked dose response effect regardless of the form of antigen used. As found in the individual cytokinetic studies, there were more PFC/spleen or/10 million leukocytes plated when the vaccine, rather than the LPS, was used as the immunogen. Also, mice injected with the 50 or 100 μg antigen dose had the greatest response. Again, it was clear that mice injected with 500 or 750 μg of either vaccine or LPS had as low or lower a response than did those injected with a 1000-fold smaller antigen dose.

Enhancing effect of Serratia antigen on "non-

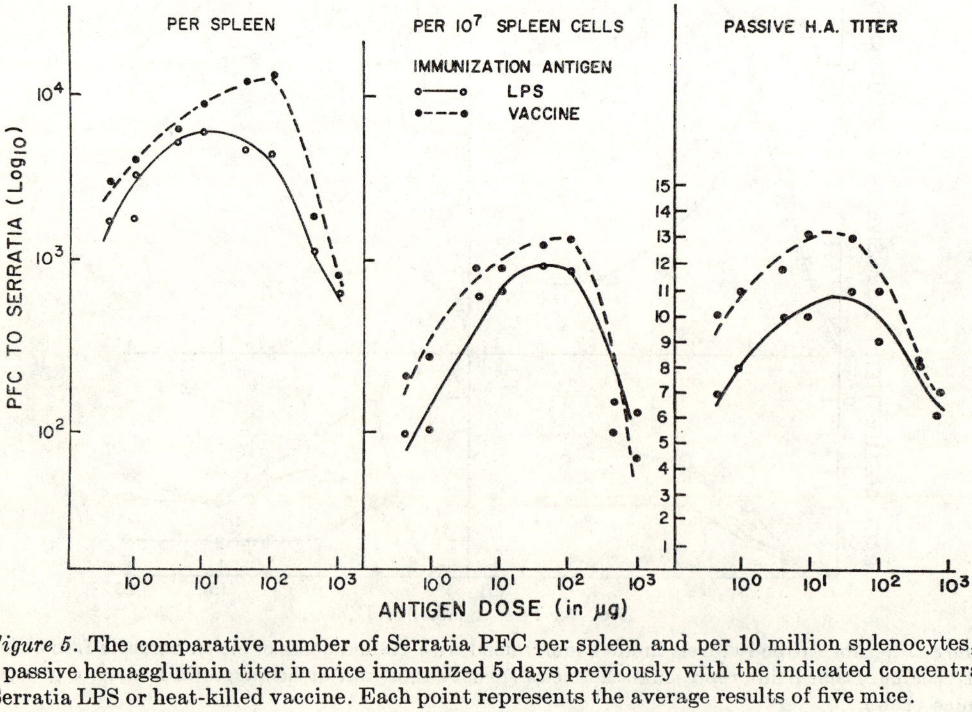

Figure 5. The comparative number of Serratia PFC per spleen and per 10 million splenocytes, and the passive hemagglutinin titer in mice immunized 5 days previously with the indicated concentration of Serratia LPS or heat-killed vaccine. Each point represents the average results of five mice.

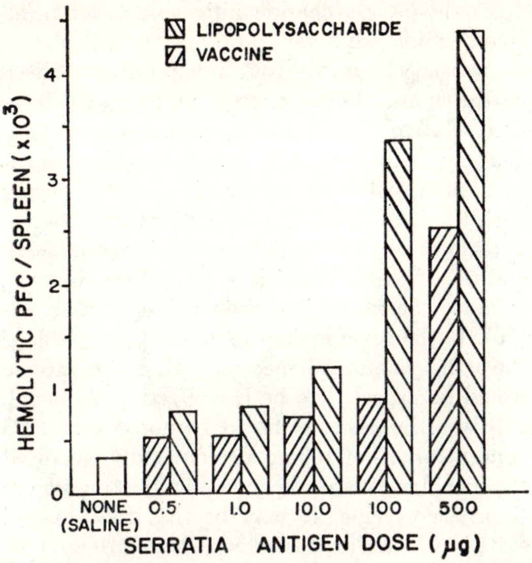

Figure 6. The number of S-RBC PFC in spleens of mice immunized 5 days previously with the indicated concentration of either Serratia lipopolysaccharide or heat-killed vaccine. Each bar represents the average results of five or more mice.

specific" PFC to sheep erythrocytes. In all plaque assays non-sensitized erythrocytes were also used for control plates. The "background" of 100 or fewer PFC to sheep erythrocytes in spleens of non-immunized mice increased markedly after the injection of either LPS or vaccine. As can be seen from Figure 6, the greatest increase occurred in spleens of mice injected with the largest dose of LPS. There were more than 4000 PFC to sheep RBC in spleens of mice injected with 500 μg LPS when assayed 5 days later. There was a lesser enhancement of this "background" when lower doses were used.

Detection of antigen in sera of immunized animals. There was no inhibition of agglutination of LPS-coated RBC and immune rabbit serum, except in instances where sera were obtained 1 or 2 days after injection with 500 or 750 μg LPS; these inhibition titers did not exceed 1:2 or 1:4.

DISCUSSION

It is now generally appreciated that among the many factors that influence the magnitude and character of the immune response the dose of antigens is probably the most important. A number of recent studies, using the immunoplaque assay with sheep erythrocytes, have shown that the magnitude of the response and the rate at which individual antibody-forming cells appear in lymphoid organs of immunized animals are dependent upon the concentration of antigen used for immunization. A plateau is generally reached when the concentration of erythrocytes is 4×10^9 RBC or higher (29–34). Only passing mention has been made of the findings that fewer PFC are developed when much larger RBC doses are used for challenge immunization.

In studies on antigen dose effects on the immune response to *Salmonella enteritidis* lipopolysaccharide, Landy and associates reported that many antibody-forming cells appeared in the regional lymph nodes and the spleen of rabbits immunized with antigen concentration ranging from 10^{-1} to 10^{-9} μg (20–21). Higher doses of this toxic product were not used. However, within this range the maximum response occurred when the rabbits were injected with the largest dose.

The results of the present studies indicate that both the whole cell vaccine and LPS antigen of *Serratia marcescens* induce a rapid appearance of specific antibody plaque-forming cells. The maximum response occurred when 50 μg of the antigen was used for immunization. Tenfold increases in this dose resulted in approximately a 10-fold decrease in the response. This suppression did not appear to be due to the toxic properties of the antigen. The LD_{50} of the LPS used in this study was greater than 850 μg/mouse. The 500-μg dose resulted in few, if any, deaths and most of the animals appeared to be as healthy as those injected with the lower concentrations. Moreover, an LD_{50} dose of LPS induced rapid mortality or *illness* in most of the mice within 48 to 72 hr after injection, whereas the immune responses of the mice injected with the 500-μg dose was determined for a period of 28 days, long beyond the time period involved in toxic manifestations. Finally, mice injected with the 100-μg dose, which caused no deaths, had a moderately suppressed PFC response as compared to mice injected with 50 μg.

Relatively similar events appear to occur in adult mice injected with a toleragenic dose of a serum protein or a bacterial polysaccharide. In this situation there is either no response or only a poor one to the large dose of antigen, followed by a prolonged period of unresponsiveness as assessed by a subsequent challenge injection with the same antigen. The present experiments did not reveal whether mice injected with the larger doses of Serratia antigen had indeed become "tolerant" or unresponsive to the antigen. Tests for tolerance are in progress. Similar studies, using *E. coli* lipopolysaccharide and a direct bacteriolytic plaque assay, suggest that partial tolerance may be induced in mice to such an antigen (23).

It was recognized that a large dose of Serratia antigen could have induced the rapid appearance of low-efficiency IgG antibody-forming cells, rather than the more usual IgM PFC, which are readily detected by the complement-dependent plaque assay with LPS-sensitized erythrocytes. However, facilitation experiments with antiglobulin serum did not provide evidence that this occurred. Nor did the serologic results indicate that any significant amount of 2-ME-resistant antibody appeared in the sera of mice injected with antigen at any dose level studied. There has been a report of rapid appearance of 2-ME-resistant antibody to Serratia in the serum of rabbits injected with antigens from this organism (35), but there is an extensive literature indicating that Gram-negative somatic antigens generally elicit 19S antibody only, particularly after a single injection of antigen. Serologic analysis also failed to disclose the other possibility of any compensatory increase in antibody formation in lymphoid organs other than the spleen, since there was a depressed titer in mice treated with high doses of antigen. Further information on this point came from the examination of antibody formation in the mesenteric lymph nodes and the thymus. There was no significant increase in the number of PFC in these tissues, regardless of antigen dose or form used for immunization.

The depressed responses observed in high-dose-treated mice may be attributable to large concentrations of antigen which, while not lethal, may nevertheless have resulted in physiologic stresses or damage to the mouse and the immune system in general. However, it should be noted that high doses of *both* the bacterial vaccine and LPS suppressed the PFC response. It seems apparent that there would be less endotoxin/unit weight in the whole cell vaccine than in the LPS. The calculated LD_{50} of the vaccine was over 2 mg/mouse. Nevertheless, 500 μg of this material resulted in as great or greater suppression than did the more toxic LPS. Moreover, it seems unlikely that there would be a marked increase in the number of "nonspecific" PFC to sheep erythrocytes in animals succumbing to the physiologic effects of an endotoxin.

The lipopolysaccharide antigens of Gram-negative bacteria are known to be potent stimulators of nonspecific antibody-forming cells to sheep erythrocytes. However, most investigators have used relatively small concentrations of these antigens to stimulate RBC plaques. In this study it was found that even greater stimulation occurred with the high doses. It may well be that the endotoxin moiety of the LPS results in tissue death and the release of nucleic acids, which, in turn, enhance the formation of anti-sheep hemolysins (36). If the toxic moiety of the antigen induced the RBC plaque enhancement, then the vaccine would be expected to be less effective. Although this was the case, it should be noted that LPS concentrations of 100 μg also markedly enhanced the hemolytic response, generally five times more than the vaccine. It may be that the physical state in which the antigen is presented to the host is an important factor for the nonspecific enhancement of the PFC response to sheep red cells. There may also be an antigenic relationship between Serratia LPS and red blood cells, but the results of the inhibition experiments with LPS in agar plates containing unsensitized RBC did not provide support for this possibility. Nor did immunization of mice with sheep red cells elicit an immune response to the Serratia. Finally, agglutinins to Serratia could not be removed from serum samples by exhaustive absorption with sheep erythrocytes.

Recently, Liacopoulos and associates (37, 38) reported that a number of antigens, when injected at a relatively high concentration, could "nonspecifically" suppress the immune response to a variety of other antigens. For example, bacterial antigens, administered in a relatively large dose, prolonged skin allografts and suppressed other immune responses. In a related observation, Franzl and McMaster (7) recently observed that a bacterial lipopolysaccharide antigen not only stimulated the immune response to sheep RBC, but also suppressed antibody formation when administered 1 or 2 days *before* the red blood cells. In those experiments a relatively small amount of LPS was used and it seems unlikely that competitive inhibition between antigens occurred. It would be of interest to determine whether mice injected with the relatively large or small dose of the Serratia antigen, either LPS or whole bacteria, also develop a marked nonspecific unresponsiveness to other antigens, including serum proteins and allografts. Such studies are in progress and may yet provide relevant information on the mechanism of the immunosuppression obtained with large doses of a bacterial antigen.

Acknowledgements. The excellent technical assistance of Mrs. Leoney Mills, Mr. Jerry Rosenzweig, Miss Nancy Uszko and Miss Maryse Israel is acknowledged.

REFERENCES

1. Britton, S. and Möller, G., J. Immun., *100:* 1326, 1968.
2. Cooper, M. L., Keller, H. M. and Hart, A. M., J. Immun., *63:* 465.
3. Doak, B. W., Halbert, P., Smolens, J. and Madel, S., J. Immun., *52:* 113, 1946.
4. Kenney, K. and Hertzberg, M., J. Bact., *93:* 773, 1967.
5. Smith, R. T. and Ertzmon, D. V., Pediatrics, *33:* 163, 1963.
6. Condie, R., Zak, S. and Good, R., Proc. Soc. Exp. Biol. Med., *90:* 355, 1955.
7. Franzl, R. and McMaster, P., J. Exp. Med., *127:* 1109, 1968.
8. Howard, J. C., Rowley, D. and Wardlow, A. C., Immunology *1:* 181, 1958.
9. Ward, P. A., Johnson, A. G. and Abelb, D. R., J. Exp. Med., *109:* 463, 1959.
10. Landy, M. and Braun, W., *Bacterial Endotoxins*, Rutgers University Press, New Brunswick, N. J., 1964.
11. Jerne, N. K. and Nordin, A. A., Science, *140: 45*, 1963.
12. Ingraham, J. S. and Bussard, A., J. Exp. Med., *119:* 667, 1964.
13. Landy, M., Sanderson, P. P., Bernstein, M. T. and Jackson, A. C., Nature, *204:* 1320, 1964.
14. Landy, M., Sanderson, P. P., Bernstein, M. T. and Lerner, E. M., Science, *147:* 1591, 1965.
15. Halliday, W. S. and Webb, A., Aust. J. Exp. Biol. Med. Sci., *43:* 163, 1965.
16. Friedman, H., J. Bact., *92:* 820, 1966.
17. Dominque, G. and Neter, E., Immunology, *13:* 539, 1967.
18. Medlin, J., Folia Microbiol., *12:* 562, 1967.
19. Sorkin, E. and Landy, M., Experientia, *21:* 673, 1965.
20. Landy, M., Sanderson, R. P. and Jackson, A. L., J. Exp. Med., *122:* 483, 1965.
21. Landy, M., Ann. Med. Exp. Fenn., *44:* 201, 1966.
22. Landy, M. and Baker, P. J., J. Immun., *97:* 620, 1966.
23. Allen, J. and Friedman, H., Fed. Proc., *28:* 767, 1969.
24. Allen, J., Young, I. and Friedman, H., Proc. Soc. Exp. Biol. Med., *130:* 615, 1969.
25. Britton, S., Immunology, *16:* 527, 1968.
26. Pike, R. M. and Schulze, M. L., Proc. Soc. Exp. Biol. Med., *115:* 829, 1964.
27. Pike, R. M., Schulze, M. L. and Chandler, C. H., J. Bact., *92:* 880, 1966.
28. Robbins, J. D., Kenny, K. and Sutes, E., J. Exp. Med., *122:* 385, 1965.
29. Dresser, E. W. and Wortis, H. H., Nature, *208:* 859, 1965.
30. Koros, A. M. C., Mazor, J. M. and Mowery, M. J., J. Exp. Med., *128:* 235, 1968.
31. Henry, C. and Jerne, N. K., J. Exp. Med., *128:* 33, 1968.
32. Sercarz, E. and Beyers, V. S., J. Immun., *98:* 836, 1967.
33. Sterzl, J., Cold Spring Harbor Symp. Quant. Biol., *32:* 453, 1967.
34. Friedman, H., in *Immunological Tolerance*, Edited by M. Landy and W. Braun, Academic Press, Inc., N. Y., 1969.
35. Nowotny, A., Proc. Soc. Exp. Biol. Med., *127:* 745, 1968.
36. Braun, W. and Nakono, M., Proc. Soc. Exp. Biol. Med., *119:* 701, 1965.
37. Liacopoulos, P., Halpern, B. N. and Perramant, F., Nature, *195:* 112, 1962.
38. Liacopoulos, P. and Neveu, T., Immunology, *7:* 26, 1964.

THE JOURNAL OF IMMUNOLOGY
Vol. 105, No. 1, July 1970

Printed in U.S.A.

CHARACTERISTICS OF THE *IN VITRO* RESPONSE OF GUINEA PIG BLOOD LYMPHOCYTES TO PHA AND ANTIGEN[1]

S. MICHAEL PHILLIPS AND BURTON ZWEIMAN

From the Department of Medicine, University of Pennsylvania School of Medicine, Philadelphia, Pennsylvania

Received for publication September 30, 1969

The *in vitro* response of guinea pig lymphocytes to phytohemagglutinin and tuberculin in tuberculin-sensitive and non-sensitive animals was studied. Measurements of tritiated thymidine incorporation, mitotic activity, and blast cell transformation were used to establish optimal conditions of culture and to investigate the mechanisms of *in vitro* interactions of antigen and cells. The pattern of response to phytohemagglutin (PHA) was found to be similar to that reported with human lymphocytes. Tuberculin-induced proliferative responses were limited to cells from sensitized animals, with a fairly consistent antigen dose-response and period of optimal incubation. Evidence was found to suggest a considerable dependence of the degree of *in vitro* responses to PHA or antigen upon the source of serum used in the culture medium. A high degree of correlation was found between isotope uptake and mitotic division in both PHA- and tuberculin-induced proliferative responses, with a less impressive correlation of these findings with the degree of blast cell transformation. When high concentrations of antigen were employed, there was an apparent dissociation of the blast cell transformation from DNA synthesis and mitotic activity in the lymphocytes of sensitized animals.

The *in vitro* proliferative response of human peripheral blood lymphocytes to specific antigens has been the subject of much recent interest (1, 2). The *in vitro* response has been shown to be antigen-specific (3) and probably dependent on multiple subpopulations of cells in the peripheral blood (4).

Early attempts to demonstrate antigen-induced *in vitro* proliferation using peripheral blood lymphocytes of the guinea pig met with little success (5, 6). However, more recent studies including those reported from this laboratory (7–11) showed that peripheral blood lymphocytes from tuberculin-sensitive guinea pigs would proliferate when cultured *in vitro* in the presence of tuberculin or a nonspecific mitogen such as phytohemagglutinin (PHA). The guinea pig is an ideal experimental animal for the study of delated hypersensitivity. It is easily sensitized to antigens such as tuberculin, exhibits excellent skin reactivity, is available in inbred strains and can be sampled repeatedly for sizeable volumes of peripheral blood. For these reasons, it would be important to learn more about the *in vitro* responses of guinea pig lymphocytes. The object of this study was to further characterize the *in vitro* proliferative response of these cells to PHA and to specific antigens with comparative measurements of isotope uptake into DNA (12), incidence of mitotic division (13) and morphologic changes (14). The effects of PHA and antigen concentration, duration and conditions of culture on the proliferative response were studied. Experimental factors have been detected which may help to explain the negative results reported by some groups (5, 6) looking for antigen-induced proliferation of guinea pig lymphocytes.

[1] This work was supported by Grant 5 T01 AI 00319 from the National Institutes of Health, and by the Ship 'n Shore Fund, Philadelphia, Pa.

MATERIALS AND METHODS

Sensitization techniques. Outbred albino male guinea pigs weighing 750 to 950 g were sensitized by injecting a total of 1.0 ml complete Freund's adjuvant (CFA with 1.0 mg of heat-killed *Mycobacterium tuberculosis*, strain H-37 Ra/ml, Difco Laboratories, Detroit, Mich.), into the footpads and subcutaneously 5 to 7 weeks prior to *in vitro* study of their lymphocytes. Intradermal testing was performed using 0.1 ml of PDD-S (0.0001 mg, 5 T.U.) from stocks kindly supplied by Dr. Lydia Edwards (Medical Director, Research Section, TB Program, Washington Office NCDC, United States Public Health Service). Skin tests were read at 24 hr and expressed as perpendicular diameters (mm) of induration. Sensitized animals exhibited strongly positive reactions (10 x 10 mm or greater). Unsensitized animals showed reactions of 2 x 2 mm or less. Selected PPD-positive animals skin-tested with histoplasmin (Parke, Davis and Co., Detroit, Mich.) and coccidioidin (Cutter Laboratories, Berkeley, Calif.) showed reactions of less than 2 x 2 mm induration at 24 hr.

Cell culture techniques. Cardiac blood specimens collected in heparinized syringes at the time of skin-testing were layered over an equal volume of a mixture of methyl-cellulose (Dow Chemical Co., Midland, Mich.) and sodium diatrizoate (Hypaque), using a modification of the method of Hulliger and Bleskovec (15). After sedimentation at 37°C for approximately 30 min, the leukocyte-rich plasma (containing an average of 20 million leukocytes per 20 ml original blood specimen, composed of about 75% lymphocytes) was collected and centrifuged at 220 G for 5 min. The cell button was washed in chilled Hank's solution, recentrifuged and resuspended in Eagle's minimal essential media modified for suspension culture (MEM-S, Grand Island Biological Co., Grand Island, New York), supplemented with 20% sterile unfiltered pre-colostrum calf serum (Colorado Serum Co., Denver, Colo.), glutamine (2 μM/ml), pencillin (100 units/ml) and streptomycin (100 μg/ml). In selected studies noted below, normal guinea pig serum obtained from individual animal bleedings or from pooled normal guinea pig serum sources (Grand Island) was used. Cell cultures were set up consisting of 1×10^6 mononuclear cells in a total volume of 0.9 ml in a 13- x 125-mm disposable glass tube (RTU tubes, Becton Dickinson Co., Rutherford, N. J.). To replicate vials was added either 0.1 ml of tuberculin, phytohemagglutinin or additional culture medium. Various concentrations (described in *Results*) were prepared from stock solutions of old tuberculin (Koch's Old Tuberculin, 250 mg/ml, Jensen-Salesbury) and phytohemagglutinin (PHA-P, 1 mg/ml Difco Laboratories). To selected vials was added 0.1 ml of a 1:10 dilution of histoplasmin (a supernatant fraction of lot HCK-5, kindly supplied by Dr. Charles Kirkpatrick, National Institutes of Health, United States Public Health Service) or 0.1 ml of a 1:4 dilution of coccidioidin (stock solution of 1.65 mg/ml NDS kindly supplied by Dr. D. Pappagianis, University of California School of Medicine, Davis). Control cultures received 0.1 ml of additional culture media instead of one of the additives noted above. The cultures were incubated for varying times (see *Results*) at 37°C in a 5% CO_2-air atmosphere. Replicate vials from each group were assayed for cellular proliferative responses as measured by either isotope incorporation or cytologic findings.

Isotope incorporation studies. Eighteen hours before termination of the cultures, 1.0 μCi of tritiated thymidine (New England Nuclear Co., Boston, Mass., specific activity 6.7 Ci/mM) was added to each vial. Uptake of the isotope into DNA was assayed as previously reported (16). The proliferative response was expressed as an isotope incorporation index (I.I.I.), representing the ratio of the mean counts/min of replicate culture vials containing either PHA or antigen divided by mean counts/min of replicate control culture vials in the same experiment.

Cytologic study techniques. Twelve to fourteen hours before termination of the culture, 0.5 μg Colcemide (Ciba) was added to each culture. Cell cultures with replicate vials containing either PHA, tuberculin or control media were terminated by a method modified from that of Moorhead and Nowell (13) as previously described (8). One thousand cells were counted on each slide in a coded fashion with determination of a) the percentage of blast cells using the usual cytologic criteria (14) and b) the number of cells found arrested in a metaphase stage of mitotic division (called the mitotic index—M.I.) per 1000 cells counted.

RESULTS

The effect of PHA and OT concentration in vitro on isotope incorporation by guinea pig lymphocytes

Phytohemagglutinin (PHA). Lymphocytes from 17 guinea pigs were each studied on several occasions for the effect of PHA upon the *in vitro* incorporation of tritiated thymidine (t^3H). Figure 1 shows the effect of increasing PHA concentration upon the incorporation of tritiated thymidine by cultures harvested after 72 hr of incubation. Isotope incorporation increased with higher concentrations of PHA to a maximum at 0.5 to 1.0 μl/ml. Concentrations of PHA greater than 1.0 μl/ml in the culture media caused decreasing total isotope incorporation; at very high concentrations of PHA (100 μl/ml) there was suppression of the isotope uptake as compared with control cultures (I.I.I. < 1.0). There was no difference in the pattern of response

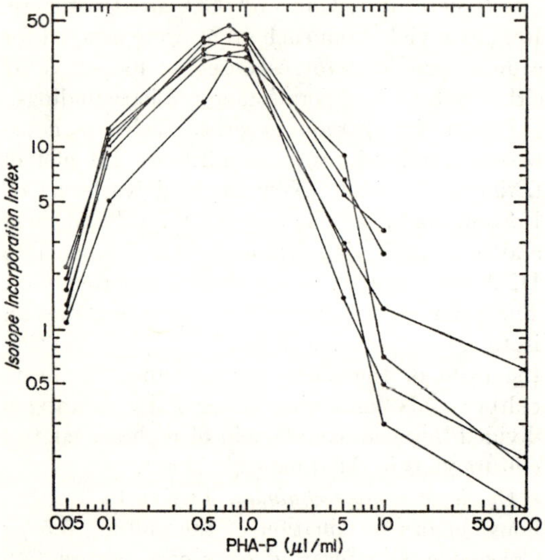

Figure 1. The effect of PHA concentration on isotope uptake into guinea pig lymphocytes.

to PHA between lymphocytes obtained from tuberculin-sensitized or unsensitized animals.

Tuberculin (OT). Cultures of lymphocytes from 16 tuberculin-sensitive and 9 unsensitized animals were terminated on the 5th day to study the effect of the concentration of tuberculin on the *in vitro* cellular proliferative response. (Fig. 2).

a) *Lymphocytes from sensitized animals.* At low OT concentrations (0.05 mg/ml) very little stimulation of isotope incorporation was noted. Isotope incorporation increased with use of increasing concentrations OT with maximum stimulation at a final concentration of 0.25 to 2.5 mg OT/ml. Use of concentrations higher than 2.5 mg/ml of OT resulted in decreased total isotope incorporation. At even higher concentrations of OT, there was suppression of the isotope incorporation as compared to control cultures (I.I.I. < 1.0). Lymphocytes failed to demonstrate increased isotope incorporation in the presence of histoplasmin or coccidioidin.

b) *Lymphocytes from unsensitized animals.* At low concentrations of OT, no effect on isotope incorporation was noted. Use of increasing concentrations of OT resulted in a suppression of spontaneous isotope incorporation (I.I.I. < 1.0). It is of note that the latter occurred at concentrations of OT which stimulated isotope incorporation by lymphocytes from sensitized animals.

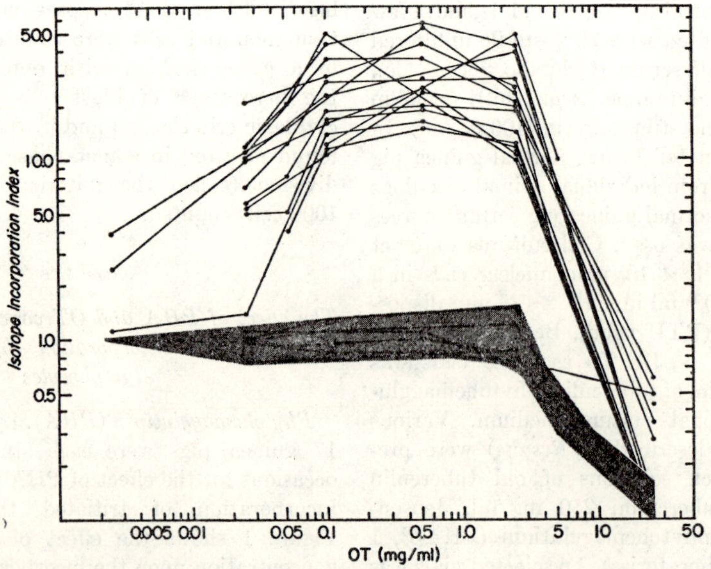

Figure 2. The effect of tuberculin concentration on isotope uptake into lymphocytes of sensitized and unsensitized (*points in shaded area*) guinea pigs.

The effect of duration of culture upon isotope incorporation of cells incubated in the presence of PHA or OT

Lymphocytes from each animal were cultured in vials containing either PHA (final concentration, 0.75 μl/ml) or control culture medium. Starting on the 2nd day, replicate vials were terminated at 24-hr intervals (Fig. 3). Maximum isotope incorporation occurred on the 3rd day of culture. No difference in the pattern of response to PHA between lymphocytes of tuberculin-sensitized or unsensitized guinea pigs was found.

Lymphocytes from 13 tuberculin-sensitized and 6 unsensitized animals were cultured with OT (final concentration, 0.5 mg/ml) or control culture medium. Replicate vials were terminated at 24-hr intervals. Maximum isotope incorporation by lymphocytes from sensitized animals occurred on the 5th and 6th day of culture (Fig. 4). Cultures of lymphocytes obtained from unsensitized animals did not show increased isotope uptake at any time in response to antigen *in vitro.*

Comparison of Morphologic Blast Cell Transformation, Isotope Incorporation and Mitotic Response by Guinea Pig Lymphocyte Cultures In Vitro

Phytohemagglutinin (PHA). Twelve lymphocyte culture experiments terminated after 72 hr of incubation were performed to compare isotope uptake and cytologic events at various concentrations of PHA. Six representative responses are are shown in Table I. Control cultures (without PHA) showed moderate numbers of blast forms (14.2 ± 4%) but very low levels of isotope incorporation (116 ± 93 cpm) and only occasional mitotic figures (0.41 ± 0.59 mitoses/1000 cells). Low concentrations (0.1 μl/ml) of PHA resulted in the stimulation of blast cell transformation, isotope incorporation (I.I.I.) and mitotic division (M.I.). At higher concentrations of PHA (0.75 μl/ml) there was an increase in both I.I.I. and M.I. with a very high degree of overall correlation between these two phenomena (correlation coefficient 0.95). The percentage of blast cells also increased but the correlation between this finding and the mitotic index was of much lower degree (correlation coefficient ± 0.46). At progressively higher concentrations of PHA (10.0 μl/ml) there was a progressive decrease in the I.I.I. and M.I. Cell lysis, vacuolization, bizarre distortion and loss of viability were seen. Many cells indistinguishable from blast forms morphologically were present under

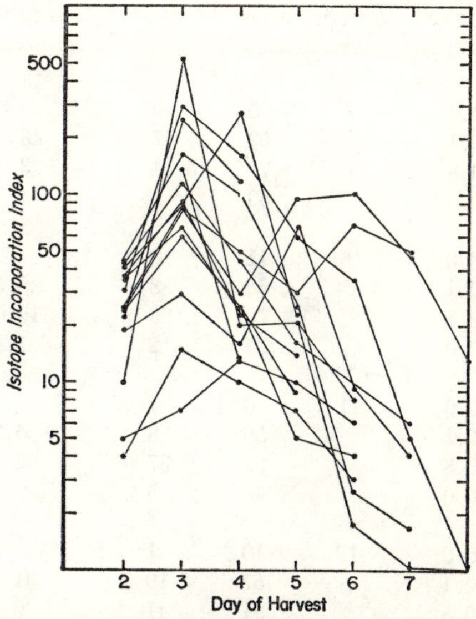

Figure 3. The effect of duration of culture with PHA on isotope uptake into guinea pig lymphocytes.

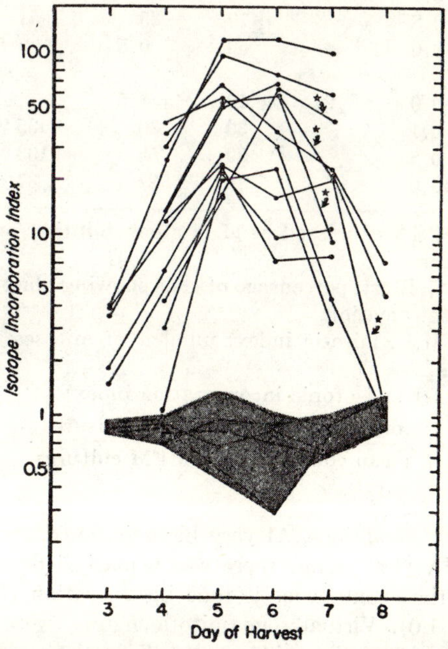

Figure 4. The effect of duration of culture with tuberculin on isotope uptake into lymphocytes of sensitized and unsensitized (*points in shaded area*) guinea pigs.

TABLE I

Comparison of blast cell transformation, mitotic index and isotope uptake of guinea pig lymphocytes at variable concentrations of PHA

Final PHA[a]	Guinea Pig. No.	Blast[b]	M.I.[c]	I.I.I.[d]
		%		
0.0	4	5	0	
0.1		53	47	43
0.8		71	54	73
10.0		59	2	4
0.0	8	11	0	
0.1		55	8	8.5
0.8		79	20	19
10.0		34	2	1.4
0.0	11	6	1	
0.1		56	8	5.7
0.8		82	37	52
10.0		43	5	2
0.0	12	10	1	
0.1		57	19	31
0.8		91	41	69
10.0		55	1.6	3.5
0.0	16	21	2	
0.1		41	21	29
0.8		79	35	51
10.0		69	9.5	9.5
0.0	24	19	1.5	
0.1		30	30	35
0.8		89	58	103
10.0		46	22	37

[a] PHA expressed as μl of stock solution/ml of culture.

[b] % Blast, percentage of cells showing blast cell transformation.

[c] M.I., mitotic index: number of mitoses/1000 cells.

[d] I.I.I., isotopic incorporation index:

$$\frac{\text{mean counts/min in PHA cultures}}{\text{mean counts/min in MEM cultures}}.$$

these conditions. At very high concentrations of PHA (100 μl/ml) there was a marked decrease in the spontaneous isotope incorporation (I.I.I. < 1.0). Virtually no mitotic figures were observed and the evidence of cell death was more prominent. However, even at this very high PHA concentration, apparent transformation of the residual cell population was very prominent (47 ± 14%). As noted in Figure 3, peak isotope incorporation was most commonly seen in cultures terminated at 72 hr. Maximum mitotic division activity occurred in the same 24-hr period as peak isotope incorporation, with maximum blast cell transformation generally occurring 24 hr earlier.

Tuberculin. Lymphocytes from a total of 16 sensitized and 12 unsensitized animals were studied to compare isotope uptake and cytologic events in response to incubation with various concentrations of OT. Cultures were terminated on the 5th day. Results of representative experiments are shown in Table II. In control cultures (without OT) there were numbers of blast forms (23 ± 3.1%) but only occasional mitotic figures (0.75 ± 0.61 mitoses/1000 cells) and very low levels of isotope incorporation (69 ± 84 cpm).

a) *Lymphocytes from sensitized animals* cultured with low concentrations of OT (0.01 mg/ml) showed minimal increases in isotope incorporation, cell division and morphologic transformation as compared with control cultures. With increasing concentrations of OT a progressive increase in both I.I.I. and M.I. was noted with excellent correlation between these two findings (correlation coefficient 0.94). Blast cell transformation also became more prominent, but the correlation between the blast cell and mitotic figure changes was not nearly as impressive (correlation coefficient 0.69). At a higher concentration of OT (5.0 mg/ml), I.I.I. and M.I. were less prominent. Use of very high concentrations of OT (25 mg/ml) led to marked morphologic evidence of cell death and a decrease in numbers of viable cells. There was depression of the spontaneous isotope incorporation (I.I.I. < 1.0) and very few mitotic figures were seen. The proportion of the residual cells showing morphologic changes of blast cell transformation (31 ± 14%) was not significantly different than seen in control cultures. In lymphocyte cultures containing OT (final concentration 0.5 mg/ml) terminated at daily intervals, mitotic division was seen to closely parallel isotope incorporation with the maximum activity occurring on the 5th and 6th days. Peak blast cell transformation generally occurred 24 hr earlier.

b) *Lymphocytes from unsentized animals* cultured in the absence of OT did not differ in the degree of blast cell transformation, I.I.I., and M.I. from similar control cultures of lymphocytes from sensitized animals. However, the lympho-

TABLE II

Comparison of blast cell transformation, mitotic index and isotope uptake in lymphocytes cultured with several concentrations of OT

Final OT[a]	Guinea Pig No.	Blast[b]	M.I.[c]	I.I.I.[d]	Guinea Pig No.	Blast	M.I.	I.I.I.
Sensitized Animals								
		%				%		
0.0	5	12	1.0		16	19	0.5	
0.1		51	18	14		33	24	22
0.5		41	27	22		51	60	58
5.0		47	14	9		50	17	15
25.0		33.0	1.0	0.7		24	1.5	0.5
0.0	22	18	0		11	24	1.5	
0.1		55	12	5.5		40	33	22
0.5		44	42	26		73	89	83
5.0		45	37	21		78	68	60
25.0		39	0.5	0.6				
0.0	23	27	1.0		12	35	0	
0.1		29	34	27		32	20	16.0
0.5		72	42	39		32	29	19.0
5.0		58	27	19		49	15	7.9
Unsensitized Animals								
0.0	17	19	0.5		33	21	1.0	
0.1		17	1.0	1.2		19	0.5	1.0
0.5		18	1.0	0.9		14	0.5	1.0
5.0		24	1.5	0.7		29	1.0	0.7
25.0		29	0.0	0.2		38	0.0	0.2
0.0	4	27	0.5		11	28	1.0	
0.1		28	0.0	0.9		27	0.5	1.1
0.5		22	0.5	0.9		21	1.0	1.9
5.0		16	0.5	0.4		29	0.0	0.3
25.0		41	0.0	0.3				

[a] OT expressed as mg of OT/ml of culture.
[b] % Blast, percentage of cells showing blast cell transformation.
[c] M.I., mitotic index = number of mitoses/1000 cells.
[d] I.I.I., isotopic incorporation index: $\frac{\text{mean counts/min in OT cultures}}{\text{mean counts/min in MEM cultures}}$.

cytes of the unsensitized animals differed from those of the sensitized subjects in that addition of tuberculin to the culture medium led to no increase in isotope incorporation or mitotic division, regardless of the concentration of OT employed. In fact, at a concentration of OT (5.0 mg/ml) which led to stimulation of proliferative changes in lymphocytes from sensitized animals, there was suppression of the spontaneous isotope incorporation (I.I.I. < 1.0) in cells from unsensitized animals. Use of even higher concentrations of tuberculin in culture with cells from unsensitized animals led to an even greater suppression of I.I.I. and more bizarre morphologic changes. Some blast cell transformation was seen only at high concentrations of OT (25 mg/ml). The lack of stimulation of cells from unsensitized guinea pigs was observed at cultures terminated at intervals between 48 and 192 hr of incubation.

The effect of conditions of culture

Temperature. Selected cultures of lymphocytes from sensitized animals were incubated with OT at 35.5°C instead of at the usual 37°C. These cultures (the results of which are shown marked with an asterisk in Fig. 4) showed a more variable maximum ^3H thymidine incorporation with the peak most commonly appearing about 24 hr later than cultures incubated at 37°C. At temperatures in excess of 38.5°C, loss of cell viability was observed.

pH. CO_2 flow into the incubator was adjusted to maintain the pH between 6.9 and 7.2, as monitored by observing the color of the phenol red indicator in the culture media and confirmed by direct measurements with a pH meter. Conditions of marked acidosis (pH $<$ 6.8) and alkalosis (pH $>$ 7.4) resulted in decreased proliferative responses at the 3rd day for PHA and at the 5th day for OT.

Nature of the serum used in culture. The effects of autologous serum (fresh or frozen at −20°C), homologous guinea pig sera (obtained from individual unsensitized animals, indicated by numbers, or from commercially available pools indicated as NGPS), and heterologous sera (calf serum obtained from several distributors in various lots, indicated as FCS) were studied. Lymphocyte suspensions in culture medium were prepared in the usual manner and divided into portions. To each portion was added either autologous, homologous or heterologous serum to make a final serum concentration of 20% in the culture vial. To replicate cultures containing a given serum was added PHA (0.75 μl/ml), OT (0.5 mg/ml), or additional culture medium. Cultures containing PHA and selected control cultures were terminated on the 3rd day; cultures containing OT and other control cultures were terminated on the 5th day. Cells were observed for isotope incorporation, mitotic activity and blast cell transformation. A total of 23 sensitized animals and 18 sources of serum were used for this portion of the study.

There was considerable variation in the PHA- or tuberculin-induced proliferative responses between lymphocytes from the same tuberculin-sensitive animals, as a function of the serum source used in the culture media. Several patterns were seen, as illustrated in representative studies listed in Table III. The use of serum from certain individual guinea pigs in the culture medium was associated with a prominent *in vitro* proliferative response by all guinea pig lymphocytes to PHA or OT (e.g., guinea pig 12). Similar use of serum from other guinea pigs was associated with little or no proliferative response (e.g., guinea pig 18). A similar variation was noted between lots of pooled normal guinea pig serum.

TABLE III

Effect of the source of serum used in the culture medium on isotope uptake by lymphocytes incubated with PHA or OT

Serum	Animal No.			
	4	5	8	11
GP 12[a]	27/7[b]	55/48	33/22	39/16
GP 18[a]	1.9/1.2	0.6/1.2	7.2/6.6	7/2.3
$NGPS_1$[c]	36/23	28/10	27/11	83/20
$NGPS_2$	1.3/4.2	3/2.5	2.8/2.5	9/4
$PFCS_1$[d]	27/16.6	71/60	65/20	105/26
$PFCS_2$	3.2/3.9	4.6/13.5	7.1/2.7	19/7.3

[a] GP, homologous serum from guinea pig 12 or 18.

[b] Isotope incorporation index for PHA/OT incubated cultures.

[c] NGPS, normal guinea pig pooled serum (two lots).

[d] PFCS, pre-colostrum fetal calf serum (two lots).

Autologous sera were not consistently superior to homologous (pooled or individual sera) in "supporting" the proliferative response. It was generally observed that if the serum from an individual animal was associated with a good *in vitro* proliferative response, then this good response was seen in both autologous and homologous cell populations. Freshly obtained serum did not differ significantly from serum obtained from the same animal and stored up to 6 weeks at −20°C in its capacity to support a proliferative response.

The ability of a given serum to support an *in vitro* response to PHA was closely correlated with its ability to support a response to OT by lymphocytes from sensitized animals.

Pools of fetal calf serum also showed marked variation in their ability to support proliferative responses (e.g., $PFCS_1$ *vs* $PFCS_2$ in Table III).

The isotope incorporation induced by PHA or OT was relatively more prominent in lymphocytes cultured in medium containing FCS than those containing NGPS. As a result, the isotope incorporation index was generally slightly higher in cultures containing the heterologous serum.

The effect of the serum source in the culture media on the spontaneous isotope incorporation

TABLE IV

Blast cell transformation, isotope uptake and mitotic division in control cultures of lymphocytes using medium containing either homologous or heterologous serum

Key

A	B
C	D

A = 3-day culture in heterologous serum medium
B = 3-day culture in homologous serum medium.
C = 5-day culture in heterologous serum medium.
D = 5-day culture in homologous serum medium.

% Blast Cell Transformation

14.2 ± 4.4	7.8 ± 2.8	P < 0.0005 (A *vs* B)
23 ± 3.1	12.5 ± 3.5	P < 0.0005 (C *vs* D)
P < 0.0005 (A *vs* C)	P < 0.001 (B *vs* D)	

Absolute CPM/Culture[a]

116 ± 93	57 ± 37	P – N.S. (A *vs* B)
69 ± 84	58 ± 59	P – N.S. (C *vs* D)
P[b] – N.S.[c] (A *vs* C)	P – N.S. (B *vs* D)	

Mitotic Figures/1000 Cells[a]

0.41 ± 0.59	0.4 ± 0.55	P – N.S. (A *vs* B)
0.75 ± 0.61	0.5 ± 0.52	P – N.S. (C *vs* D)
P – N.S. (A *vs* C)	P – N.S. (B *vs* D)	

[a] Non-Gaussian distribution.

[b] $P = \text{determined as } t = \dfrac{\text{difference of means}}{\text{standard error of difference.}}$

[c] N.S., not significant.

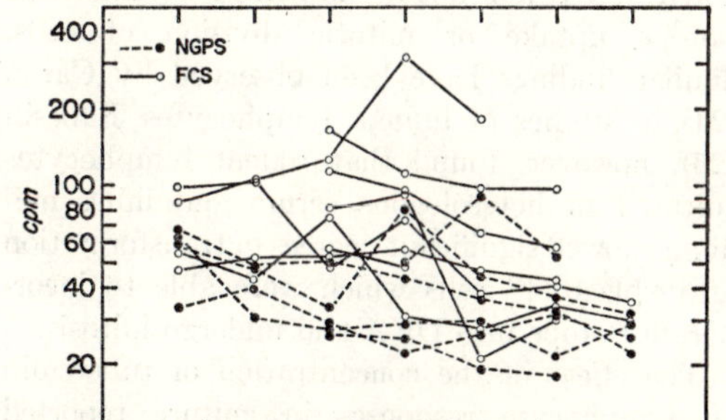

Figure 5. Comparison of spontaneous isotope uptake by lymphocytes cultured in medium containing normal guinea pig serum (NGPS) (●-----●) or fetal calf serum (FCS) (○——○).

by cells in the control vials was also evaluated using cells cultured in homologous or heterologous serum for varying periods of time. Control cultures in media containing FCS showed slightly higher rates of spontaneous isotope incorporation when compared to control cultures containing NGPS. However, this difference in spontaneous activity was not statistically significant and was not accompanied by an increase in the number of mitotic figures observed (Table IV). There was no significant progressive increase in spontaneous isotope incorporation in lymphocytes cultured over a period of time, regardless of whether the culture medium contained homologous or heterologous serum (Fig. 5). There was, however, a greater degree of spontaneous blast cell transformation in lymphocytes cultured in medium containing heterologous serum as compared to cells cultured in homologous serum-containing medium. This increased spontaneous blast cell transformation increased significantly with increased time duration of culture.

DISCUSSION

The results of this study amplify previous findings in this laboratory (7, 8) and those by Oppenheim *et al.* (9, 10) and Loewi *et al.* (11) that peripheral blood lymphocytes from tuberculin-sensitive guinea pigs can proliferate when incubated *in vitro* with tuberculin as well as a "nonspecific" mitogen (PHA).

The pattern of PHA-induced replication of guinea pig blood lymphocytes is generally similar to that observed by Sabesin (17). A large majority of the residual lymphocyte population after 3 days of culture with PHA show characteristic blast cell transformation. Under suitable culture conditions the isotope incorporation indices for these cultures are quite comparable to the results obtained with PHA-incubated human lymphocyte cultures in this laboratory.

On the basis of evidence listed below, it is likely that an *in vitro* response to tuberculin represents antigen-specific cellular reactivity: a) tuberculin-induced lymphocyte proliferation in this study was limited to cells of tuberculin-sensitive animals, with no cell replication (and sometimes even toxic effects) resulting from incubation of lymphocytes of non-sensitive animals with tuberculin in the same concentrations; b) the lymphocytes of sensitized animals were no more responsive to a nonspecific mitogen (PHA) than were cells of non-sensitive animals; c) lymphocytes from guinea pigs sensitized to tuberculin did not respond *in vitro* to two other test antigens to which these animals had not been previously sensitized *in vivo* (histoplasmin and coccidioidin); d) tuberculin-induced lymphocyte proliferation followed a consistent pattern for dose response and optimal incubation period; and e) it was again observed, as reported previously from this laboratory (8), that in the *in vitro* tuberculin-induced lymphocyte responsiveness and tuberculin delayed skin test reactivity developed at about the same time after sensitization with complete Freund's adjuvant, and that *in vitro* and *in vivo* phenomena correlated grossly in intensity.

Several factors may explain the relatively vigorous tuberculin-induced proliferative response of guinea pig blood lymphocytes reported here as compared to negative results reported by Aspergren and Rorsman (5) and Knight *et al.* (6) and relatively modest and inconsistent proliferation observed by Oppenheim *et al.* (9) and Loewi *et al.* (11). In the present study, maximum *in vitro* lymphocyte responses were found in cells obtained 5 to 7 weeks after sensitization of the donor; in other studies lymphocytes were commonly studied less than 21 days after sensitization. Guinea pig lymphocytes appear to require more stringent control of culture conditions than do human cells (18) with reference to factors such as pH and temperature. The particular serum used as a component of the culture medium exerted a considerable effect on the degree of PHA- or tuberculin-induced proliferative responses by lymphocytes of a particular animal. This variation in response was observed with use of autologous serum or different pools of both normal homologous and normal heterologous (newborn calf) serum. Other studies have also shown variation in primary *in vitro* response to antigen of rodent lymphocytes and responses to PHA of lymphocytes from human donors (19–21) depending upon the source of the serum used in the culture medium. In those studies variations were found not only among the species but also among lots of sera from the same species.

In the present study the control cultures (without PHA or tuberculin) showed higher degrees of blast cell transformation when cells were cultured in the calf serum-containing medium than in similar control cultures using medium containing homologous or autologous serum. Similar findings with cells of a variety of species had prompted Dutton (22) and Johnson and Russell (23) among others to raise the question whether use of heterologous serum led to a possible heterophile antigen-induced response in cells of another species. However, in the present study, the higher "spontaneous" blast cell transformation noted above was not accompanied by increased isotope uptake or mitotic division of cells. Similar findings have been observed by Caron (24) in studies of human lymphocytes. Sabesin (25), however, found that rodent lymphocytes cultured in heterologous serum-containing medium showed significant degrees of transformation into "blastoid" cells which were able to incorporate isotope into DNA and undergo mitosis.

The effect of the concentration of tuberculin on lymphocyte responses in culture reported here may cast light on at least two concurrent events resulting from the interaction of tuberculin with these cells. A definite dose-response by lymphocytes of sensitized animals to tuberculin concentration was noted, with a progressive decrease in total isotope incorporation and mitotic division as the dose of tuberculin in culture was progressively increased past the optimal concentration; at very high concentrations, isotope incorporation was was suppressed below levels observed in control cultures and few if any mitoses were seen. However, there was no significant suppression of the percentage of blast cells below control values. In comparable dose-response studies using cells of unsensitized animals, no proliferation as measured by isotope incorporation or mitotic index was seen at any concentration of tuberculin. In addition, isotope incorporation was suppressed below control culture values at concentrations of tuberculin which stimulated proliferation in cells of sensitized animals.

These observations concerning the disparity between the prevalence of blast cell transformation on the one hand, and the degree of isotope incorporation and mitotic division on the other, might be interpreted in a number of ways, several of which are discussed here for consideration. 1) A finite proportion of the blood leukocyte sample, of monocyte origin, can transform under the conditions of culture into cells which may resemble blast cells by the usual criteria for light microscopy, but which do not synthesize DNA (26) or divide (27). 2) Blast cell transformation may reflect more sensitively than does either isotope incorporation or mitotic division weak antigenic stimulation of lymphocyte proliferation. This could explain the higher degrees of blast cell transformation (without associated significant increases in isotope incorporation or mitotic division) in control cultures of the guinea pig lymphocytes incubated in medium containing heterologous serum as compared with the cells cultured in a similar fashion using medium containing homologous serum. 3) Studies in a number of laboratories have shown that the interaction of antigen with lymphocytes obtained from animals sensitized to that antigen may, under varying conditions of culture, stimulate cellular proliferation, or on the other hand, may inhibit such proliferation or exert cytotoxic acitivity (28). Therefore, it is certainly conceivable that the end-result of lymphocytes cultured in the presence of antigen may reflect a number of concomitant processes, some leading to cell proliferation and others retarding. One of the factors which could affect the end-result of such responses in culture could be the concentration of antigen employed. Here it was seen that lymphocytes from sensitized animals showed an overall proliferative response, as measured by all three parameters noted above, of increasing degrees with the use of increasing antigen concentrations up to a point. With use of progressively higher antigen concentrations above this point, the degree of isotope incorporation and mitotic division decreased progressively to levels below those in the control cultures, while levels of blast cell transformation remained unchanged or even increased. It is possible that the use of such high antigen concentrations in culture might result in both antigenically-specific and nonspecific morphologic changes in the lymphocytes but at the same time either directly or indirectly inhibit the subsequent incorporation of isotope into DNA and mitotic division. Walker and Lucas (29) have shown that alteration of another conditions of lymphocyte culture (use of a serum-free medium) will result in significant morphologic transformation without subsequent isotope incorporation. These transformed cells would then incorporate thymidine rapidly into DNA upon additions of even small amounts of serum to the medium.

Additional studies will be necessary to help clarify whether these or other interpretations are partially or completely valid in explaining the complex inter-relationships leading to the end-result of lymphocyte proliferation.

REFERENCES

1. Pearmain, G., Lycette, R. R. and Fitzgerald, P. H., Lancet, *1:* 637, 1963.
2. Marshall, W. H. and Roberts, K. B., Lancet, *1:* 773, 1963.
3. Ling, N. R. and Husband, E. M., Lancet, *1:* 363, 1963.
4. Talmage, D. W., Radovich, J. and Hemmingsen, H., J. Allerg., *43:* 323, 1969.
5. Aspergren, N. and Rorsman, H., Int. Arch. Allerg., *24:* 119, 1964.
6. Knight, S., Ling, N. R., Sell, S. and Oxnard, C. E., Immunology, *9:* 565, 1965.
7. Zweiman, B., Besdine, R. W. and Hildreth, E. A., Nature, *212:* 422, 1966.
8. Zweiman, B., Immunology, *13:* 315, 1967.
9. Oppenheim, J. J., Wolstencroft, R. A. and Gell, P. G. H., Immunology, *12:* 89, 1967.
10. Oppenheim, J. J., Fed. Proc., *27:* 21, 1968.
11. Loewi, G., Temple, A. and Vischer, T. L., Immunology, *14:* 257, 1968.
12. Dutton, R. W. and Eady, J. D., Immunology, *7:* 40, 1964.
13. Moorehead, D. S. and Nowell, P. C., Meth. Med. Res., *10:* 310, 1964.
14. Robbins, J. H., Science, *146:* 1648, 1964.
15. Hulliger, L. and Blazkovec, A. A., Lancet, *1:* 1304, 1967.
16. Zweiman, B., Pappagianis, D., Maibach, H. and Hildreth, E. A., J. Immun, *102:* 1284, 1969.

17. Sabesin, S. M., Proc. Soc. Exp. Biol. Med., *122:* 551, 1966.
18. Nowell, P. C., Cancer Res., *20:* 462, 1960.
19. Mishell, R. I. and Dutton, R. W., J. Exp. Med., *126:* 423, 1967.
20. Mellman, W. J., Personal communication.
21. Holt, P. J. L., *The Biological Effects of Phytohemagglutinin*, Edited by M. W. Elves, Hunt Orthopaedic Hospital Management Committee, Oscwestry, England, 1966.
22. Dutton, R. W., Advances Immun., *6:* 253, 1967.
23. Johnson, G. J. and Russel, P. S., Nature, *208:* 343, 1965.
24. Caron, G. A., Brit. J. Haemat., *13:* 68, 1967.
25. Sabesin, S. M., Science, *149:* 1385, 1965.
26. Jones, A. L., Transplantation, *4:* 337, 1966.
27. Oppenheim, J. J. and Wolff, S. M., Nature, *211:* 767, 1966.
28. Burnet, F. M., *The Clonal Selection Theory of Acquired Immunity*, Cambridge University Press, London, 1959.
29. Walker, S. and Lucas, Z., Fourth Leukocyte Culture Conference, 1969, In press.

THE JOURNAL OF IMMUNOLOGY
Vol. 105, No. 1, July 1970

THE RELATIONSHIP BETWEEN ANTIBODY AFFINITY AND THE EFFICIENCY OF COMPLEMENT FIXATION

ANTHONY S. FAUCI, MICHAEL M. FRANK AND JOHN S. JOHNSON

From the Laboratory of Clinical Investigation, National Institute of Allergy and Infectious Diseases, National Institutes of Health, Bethesda, Maryland 20014

Received for publication September 25, 1969

The efficiency of complement fixation by antigen-antibody complexes is shown for the first time to be directly related to the affinity of IgG antibody for its antigenic determinant. Decreased complement fixation by IgG antibody at 37°C is independent of antibody affinity. The biologic activity of the complexes in terms of complement fixation parallels their activity in the passive cutaneous anaphylaxis reaction. The implications of these observations with respect to the mechanisms of complement fixation by immune complexes formed with IgG antibody are discussed.

A variety of studies have established that antisera produced against a haptenic determinant represent a heterogeneous population of antibodies that differ greatly in their affinity for the determinant. In addition, it is known that affinities may vary within individual sera (1). The antibody-hapten association constant is influenced significantly by differences in the dose of antigen as well as the time at which the antibody populations are isolated after immunization (2–7). Recently, there has been considerable interest in the correlation between the affinities of antibodies and their biologic activities (1, 8, 9). Antibodies specific for the 2,4-dinitrophenyl group (DNP) are used widely in studies of the relationship between antibody affinity and certain biologic factors (e.g., passive cutaneous anaphylaxis, hemagglutination assays) since simple and precise methods are available for the preparation of purified antibody and the measurement of antibody affinities (2, 10, 11). The direct relationship between the increasing affinities of anti-DNP antibodies and the greater strength of allergic skin responses with these antibodies has been studied (1, 8). The sensitivity of a hemagglutination assay method for dinitrophenol specific antibodies has been shown to be dependent upon antibody affinity (9).

In the present work, the relationship of variation in the antibody-hapten association constant to the efficiency of these complexes in fixing complement and the relationship to passive cutaneous anaphylaxis were studied. The efficiency of the antibody-hapten complex in fixing complement was found to vary directly with the association constant of the given antibody. The significance of these findings in understanding the precise mechanisms involved in the fixation of complement by immune complexes is discussed.

MATERIALS AND METHODS

Immunization. Fifteen adult New Zealand albino rabbits (allotype 1144, mixed sexes) were immunized with 0.05 mg to 5.0 mg of dinitrophenylated rabbit γ globulin (DNP_{17}-RGG) prepared and analyzed according to Eisen (12). An emulsion containing the antigen in complete Freund's adjuvant was injected in a volume of 0.25 ml into each footpad and into one subcutaneous site on the back. The animals were exsanguinated on the 25th day following immunization and the sera were pooled.

Preparation of immunoabsorbents. Bovine γ globulin was coupled to Sepharose 2B by the Rejnek *et al.* (13) modification of the method described by Axen *et al.* (14), employing cyanogen halide coupling. The derivative was then prepared with trinitrobenzene sulfonic acid according to Eisen (12). Polyacrylamide beads (Bio-Gel P 300+) were amino-ethylated by the method of Inman and Dintzis (15) to produce a specific capacity of approximately 1 mM/g. The material was then reacted with unrecrystallized dinitrobenzene sulfonic acid at pH 10.0 (12).

Purification of antibodies. Purified antibody was prepared as follows: EDTA was added to 300 ml of pooled rabbit antisera to give a final concentration of 0.001 M and the material was passed over trinitrophenylated bovine γ globulin (TNP-BGG) Sepharose immunoabsorbent. The serum containing unbound anti-DNP antibody was then set aside for isolation and purification of "low affinity" antibody. The "high affinity" anti-DNP antibody which adhered to the TNP-BGG Sepharose was eluted with three washes of 25 ml of 0.1 M dinitrophenolate. The first 25 ml of eluent was designated fraction A, high affinity antibody. The remaining eluent was pooled as fraction B. The column was washed with borate saline, pH 8.0, after the elution with dinitrophenolate. Collection was terminated when the wash eluent gave a reading of 0.005 optical density units at 280 nm in a Beckman DU spectrophotometer. This eluent was then pooled as part of fraction B. The two pools were then dialyzed extensively, first against running tap water and then against 0.15 M NaCl, passed through a Dowex 1-X4 column,[1] followed by separation of IgG and IgM components by passage through a G-200 Sephadex gel column. The specifically purified rabbit IgG anti-DNP was used in all the subsequent work.

The serum pool containing "low affinity" antibody which had been through the TNP-BGG Sepharose was then passed over a dinitrophenylated aminoethyl polyacrylamide immunoabsorbent. The column was eluted with 150 ml of 0.1 M dinitrophenolate. The eluent (fraction C) was dialyzed and purified as described above. All three specifically purified antibody fractions were capable of 87% to 95% binding to the DNP immunoabsorbent.

Measurement of antibody-hapten equilibrium constant. Association constants were measured by fluorescence quenching (2, 11, 16). Purified anti-DNP antibody at concentrations ranging from 52 μg/ml to 70 μg/ml in 1 ml of 0.1 M Tris-HCl, pH 7.5, were titrated with 0.025-ml increments of a 2.9 mM/ml solution of ϵ-DNP-L-lysine until a total added volume of 0.2 ml was reached, and then 0.05-ml increments until a total added volume of 0.4 ml was attained. Fluorescence was measured in an Aminco-Bowman spectrophotofluorometer with incident exciting light of about 290 nm and recording emission of about 350 nm. The average intrinsic association constants (K_0) were calculated as described by Eisen (16), using a digital computer.

Passive cutaneous anaphylaxis. Passive cutaneous anaphylaxis (PCA) was performed according to Ovary (17). Hartley strain guinea pigs weighing about 250 g received 0.1 ml intradermally of varying dilutions of purified antibody in borate-buffered saline, pH 8.0. Individual guinea pigs received multiple injections consisting of varying dilutions of the same antibody as well as equivalent concentrations of antibodies of different average intrinsic association constants (K_0). Three and one-half to four hours later each animal was injected intravenously with 0.5 ml of a 1% solution of Evans blue containing 10 μg of dinitrophenylated bovine γ globulin (DNP_{32}-BGG) prepared according to Eisen (12). The animals were killed 20 to 25 min later and skinned. Reactions were scored on a 0 to 4+ scale according to the extent and intensity of blueing as observed from the flesh side of the pelt.

Complement fixation. Complement fixation tests were performed in two dimensional blocks as described by Kabat (18) with volumes scaled down by a factor of 60. The titration was performed in Microtiter (Cooke) trays. Guinea pig complement was obtained from Suburban Serum Laboratories, Silver Spring, Md. It was absorbed twice with one-twentieth volume of packed washed sheep erythrocytes at 0°C, which were obtained from sheep raised on the National Institutes of Health farm. Veronal-buffered saline (VBS) containing gelatin and appropriate amounts of Ca^{++} and Mg^{++}, optimally sensitized cells and guinea pig complement were employed as described (18). All solutions were kept at 4°C except where indicated. Titrations were carried out as twofold serial dilutions of antibody over the concentration range of 1.333 to 0.1 μg/ml and threefold serial dilutions of antigen (DNP_{32}-BGG) over the range of 0.243 to 0.001 μg/ml. To 50 μl of antibody solution were added 50 μl of antigen. Exactly 3 CH_{50} units of guinea pig complement contained in 25 μl of solution were added to the mixtures and the trays were incubated at 4°C for 18 hr. At the end of the period of incubation, 25 μl containing 3.2×10^8 optimally sensitized sheep erythrocytes were added. The trays were covered with Mystic tape and frequently mixed for 1 hr at 37°C. After incubation the cells were allowed to settle for 1 hr at room temperature and the end point was determined visually on scoring the reaction from 4+

[1] Spectral analysis indicated that less than 6% of the combining sites were occupied by hapten. This calculation was based on comparison of absorbance at 278 and 360 nm (11).

(complete hemolysis) to 0 (no hemolysis). The results were expressed as the antibody dilution which, in the presence of a minimum antigen concentration, fixed 2 units of CH_{50}, thus leaving residual complement activity to give 2+ hemolysis. In a parallel series of experiments, the antigen, antibody and complement mixture was incubated at 37°C for 1 hr, instead of at 4°C for 18 hr. The remainder of the procedure was then carried out exactly as described.

Controls included tests done with complement alone and complement with either antigen or antibody. No anticomplementary activity was encountered in any of the control preparations.

RESULTS

Relationship of affinity and the concentration of antibody required for PCA response. The minimum concentration of antibody needed to elicit a positive PCA reaction was determined for each of three preparations of antibodies of varying dilutions (see *Materials and Methods*). Each

TABLE I

Relationship of affinity and the concentration of antibody required for passive cutaneous anaphylaxis[a]

Antibody Preparation	K_0[b]	Minimum Antibody Concentration Giving Positive Reaction
	liters/mol × 10⁻⁶	*μg/ml*
A	900	31.3, 31.3, 7.8, 31.3
B	10	62.5, 62.5, 31.3
C	1.1	>500, 500, 500

[a] Reaction obtained with 10 μg of DNP_{32}-BGG.
[b] K_0, association constant.

TABLE II

Two dimensional complement fixation tests with purified rabbit anti-DNP and dinitrophenylated bovine γ globulin[a]

DNP_{32}-BGG (μg/ml)	Antibody Dilution (μg/ml)											
	133	66.5	33.3	16.6	8.3	4.2	2.1	1.0	0.5	0.3	0.1	0
Fraction A												
0.243	0[a]	0	0	0	0	0	3	4	4	4	4	4
0.081	0	0	0	0	0	0	1	2	3	4	4	4
0.027	0	0	0	0	0	0	1.5	3	4	4	4	4
0.009	3	3.5	4	4	4	4	4	4	4	4	4	4
0.003	4	4	4	4	4	4	4	4	4	4	4	4
0.001	4	4	4	4	4	4	4	4	4	4	4	4
0.000	4	4	4	4	4	4	4	4	4	4	4	4
Fraction B												
0.243	0	0	0	0	0	0	1	4	4	4	4	4
0.081	0	0	0	0	0	0	0.5	1.5	4	4	4	4
0.027	0	0	0	0	0	0	2	2	4	4	4	4
0.009	3.5	3.5	3.5	3.5	3	3.5	3.5	4	4	4	4	4
0.003	4	4	4	4	4	4	4	4	4	4	4	4
0.001	4	4	4	4	4	4	4	4	4	4	4	4
0.000	4	4	4	4	4	4	4	4	4	4	4	4
Fraction C												
0.243	0	0	0	0	1	4	4	4	4	4	4	4
0.081	0	0	0	0	1	3.5	4	4	4	4	4	4
0.027	1	1	2	3	4	4	4	4	4	4	4	4
0.009	4	4	4	4	4	4	4	4	4	4	4	4
0.003	4	4	4	4	4	4	4	4	4	4	4	4
0.001	4	4	4	4	4	4	4	4	4	4	4	4
0.000	4	4	4	4	4	4	4	4	4	4	4	4

[a] 0, no lysis; 4, complete lysis.

preparation was titrated in three or four guinea pigs. The animals were injected intradermally with varying dilutions of two purified antibodies of different association constants so that results might be contrasted in the same animal. As seen in Table I, the minimum eliciting dose for a PCA response varied directly with the antibody-hapten association constant. Antibody preparations with highest affinity gave positive reactions at concentrations of 7.8 to 31.3 μg/ml, whereas preparations of low affinity required 500 μg/ml or more.

Effect of affinity on the efficiency of complement fixation. Efficiency of complete fixation is taken in this study to represent the minimum concentration of antibody (reacting with the minimum amount of antigen) needed to fix a given amount of complement. This was determined for each antibody preparation. As seen in Table II, the efficiency of complement fixation varied directly with the association constants of the antibodies. Both fraction A and fraction B required a minimum concentration of 0.027 μg/ml of antigen and 2.1 μg/ml of antibody to fix 2 of 3 CH_{50} units. Optimal fixation by fraction C required an antigen concentration of 0.081 μg/ml and an antibody concentration of 8.3 μg/ml. Since the antibody in question is IgG, altering the incubation conditions of the hapten, antibody and complement mixture (37°C for 1 hr, instead of 4°C for 18 hr) leads to decreased complement fixation (19, 20), and therefore to an increase in the minimum concentration of antigen and antibody necessary to fix a given amount of complement. Table III shows that the decreased complement fixation associated with incubation

TABLE III

Two dimensional complement fixation test with purified rabbit anti-DNP and dinitrophenylated bovine γ globulin under altered conditions of incubation

DNP_{32}-BGG (μg/ml)	Antibody Dilution (μg/ml)											
	133	66.5	33.3	16.6	8.3	4.2	2.1	1.0	0.5	0.3	0.1	0
Fraction A												
0.243	0[a]	0	0	1	2	4	4	4	4	4	4	4
0.081	0	0	0	1	2	3	3.5	4	4	4	4	4
0.027	1	2	2	2	3	3.5	4	4	4	4	4	4
0.009	3.5	3.5	3.5	3.5	3.5	3.5	4	4	4	4	4	4
0.003	4	4	3.5	4	4	3.5	4	4	4	4	4	4
0.001	3.5	4	4	4	4	4	4	4	4	4	4	4
0.000	3.5	4	4	4	4	4	4	4	4	4	4	4
Fraction B												
0.243	0	0	0	1	3	4	4	4	4	4	4	4
0.081	0	0	0	1	2	3.5	4	4	4	4	4	4
0.027	1.5	2	2	2.5	3	3.5	4	4	4	4	4	4
0.009	4	4	4	4	4	4	4	4	4	4	4	4
0.003	4	4	4	4	4	4	4	4	4	4	4	4
0.001	4	4	4	4	4	4	4	4	4	4	4	4
0.000	4	4	4	4	4	4	4	4	4	4	4	4
Fraction C												
0.243	2	3	4	4	4	4	4	4	4	4	4	4
0.081	2.5	2.5	4	4	4	4	4	4	4	4	4	4
0.027	3.5	4	4	4	4	4	4	4	4	4	4	4
0.009	4	4	4	4	4	4	4	4	4	4	4	4
0.003	4	4	4	4	4	4	4	4	4	4	4	4
0.001	4	4	4	4	4	4	4	4	4	4	4	4
0.000	3.5	3.5	4	4	4	4	4	4	4	4	4	4

[a] 0, no lysis; 4, complete lysis.

at 37°C was noted to about the same degree in all three preparations.

DISCUSSION

Recent studies correlating the avidity of antibody for its antigenic determinant with its role in biologic reactions (1, 8, 9) raise the possibility that antibody affinity is directly related to the complement-fixing efficiency of the immune complex. The work of Siskind and Eisen (1) and others (8) indicates that high affinity antibody is more efficient in eliciting allergic skin responses. Our findings with PCA confirm these data. Levine (9) has found that increasing affinities of dinitrophenyl specific antibodies parallel the increasing sensitivity of a hemagglutination assay method for the antibody. However, it has been suggested (21) that low affinity antibody may wander from site to site on an antigenic surface activating complement components at each site and thus increasing the damaging effects of the antibody. It has recently been shown (22) that "Forssman shock" induced by injecting rabbit anti-Forssman antibody intravenously into guinea pigs is produced inefficiently, if at all, by IgM antibody prepared by a method which yields high affinity antibody, but is regularly produced by IgG anti-Forssman antibody with known low affinity.

We have attempted to evaluate systematically the effect of variation of antibody affinity for its antigenic determinant upon its efficiency of complement fixation. Our studies indicate that when the same antigen is allowed to complex with antibodies of varying affinity under the same conditions, low affinity antibody does not fix complement as efficiently as does high affinity antibody. Moreover, the previously described phenomenon (19, 20) of greater fixation at 4°C as compared with fixation at 37°C by IgG antibody is qualitatively independent of the affinity of the antibody. These studies give further support to the concept of differing mechanisms of complement fixation between IgM and IgG antibodies as the cause of their different biologic effectiveness.

Complement fixation by an IgG antibody-antigen system requires the presence of complexes with lattice formation (23). The smallest complex that will fix complement has been shown to be Ag_2Ab_3 (23). In order for complement to react with immune complexes, aggregation of antibody appears necessary (24), and it has further been shown (24) that the initiation of complement fixation in the fluid phase requires two IgG molecules side by side (doublet formation). In our experiments, the same antigen (DNP-BGG) with a known DNP/BGG molar ratio of 32 was used throughout. In such a system in which all other features are constant, the frequency of doublet formation must be a function of antibody affinity. It seems reasonable to suggest that a smaller proportion of low affinity antibody is complexed with the soluble antigen during the period of fixation and, therefore, less complement is fixed. Whether similar results can be obtained with antibodies directed at cell surface antigens has yet to be established.

REFERENCES

1. Siskind, G. W. and Eisen, H. N., J. Immun., *95:* 436, 1965.
2. Eisen, H. N. and Siskind, G. W., Biochemistry, *3:* 996, 1967.
3. Fujio, H. and Karush, F., Biochemistry, *5:* 1856, 1966.
4. Nussenzweig, V. and Benacerraf, B., J. Exp. Med., *126:* 727, 1967.
5. Paul, W. E., Siskind, G. W., Benacerraf, B. and Ovary, Z., J. Immun., *99:* 760, 1967.
6. Paul, W. E., Siskind, G. W. and Benacerraf, B., J. Exp. Med., *127:* 25, 1968.
7. Goidl, E. A., Paul, W. E., Siskind, G. W. and Benacerraf, B., J. Immun., *100:* 371, 1968.
8. Parker, C. W., Kern, M. and Eisen, H. N., J. Exp. Med., *115:* 789, 1962.
9. Levine, B. B. and Levytska, V., J. Immun., *98:* 648, 1967.
10. Farah, F. S., Kern, M. and Eisen, H. N., J. Exp. Med., *122:* 1195, 1960.
11. Velick, S. F., Parker, C. W. and Eisen, H. N., Proc. Nat. Acad. Sci., *46:* 1470, 1960.
12. Eisen, H. N., in *Methods in Medical Research*, Vol. 10, p. 94, Yearbook Medical Publishers, Inc., Chicago, 1964.
13. Rejnek, J., Mage, R. G. and Reisfeld, R. A., J. Immun., *102:* 638, 1969.
14. Axen, R., Porath, J. and Ernack, J., Nature, *214:* 1302, 1967.
15. Inman, J. K. and Dintzis, H. M., Biochemistry, *8:* 4074, 1969.
16. Eisen, H. N., in *Methods in Medical Research*, Vol. 10, p. 115, Yearbook Medical Publishers, Inc., Chicago, Ill., 1964.
17. Ovary, Z., Progr. Allerg., *5:* 459, 1958.
18. Kabat, E. A., *Kabat and Mayer's Experimental*

Immunochemistry, 2nd Ed., Charles C Thomas, Springfield, Ill., 1961.
19. Sandberg, A. L. and Stollar, B. D., J. Immun., *96:* 764, 1966.
20. Cunniff, R. V. and Stollar, B. D., J. Immun., *100:* 7, 1968.
21. Humphrey, J. H. and Dourmashkin, R. R., Advances Immun., In press.
22. Bauman, N. and Elliott, W. J., Fed. Proc., *28:* 502, 1969.
23. Ishizaka, K., Progr. Allerg., *7:* 32, 1963.
24. Cohen, S., J. Immun., *100:* 407, 1968.

THE JOURNAL OF IMMUNOLOGY
Vol. 105, No. 1, July 1970
Printed in U.S.A.

γG ERYTHROCYTE AUTOANTIBODIES: COMPARISON OF *IN VIVO* COMPLEMENT COATING AND *IN VITRO* "Rh" SPECIFICITY[1]

M. ELAINE EYSTER AND DAVID E. JENKINS, JR.

From the Hematology Services, Departments of Medicine, The New York Hospital-Cornell Medical Center, New York, and the Veterans Administration Hospital and Vanderbilt University School of Medicine, Nashville, Tennessee

Received for publication September 23, 1969

Panreacting γG antibodies were eluted from the red cells of 35 patients with positive direct Coombs' tests. Twelve patients had γG coated cells and 23 had γG + C coated cells. Six of 12 γG and 6 of 23 γG + C eluates showed "Rh" specificity by their failure to react with the Rh_{null} blood. After absorption with Rh_{null} cells, an additional γG eluate and seven γG + C eluates showed "Rh" specificity. In these eluates specificity was obscured by the presence of additional antibodies of other specificities and was not apparent until antibodies lacking "Rh" specificity were removed by absorption with Rh_{null} cells. These findings suggest that the γG antibodies from γG and γG + C coated cells are similar and provide additional support for the concept that surface configuration of red cells as well as the characteristics of antibodies involved may be important in determining whether γG autoantibodies coat erythrocytes with C.

The erythrocytes from patients with positive direct Coombs' tests may be coated with γG globulin (γG) alone, with complement (C) alone, or with both γG and C (1–3). Coating with only γG appears to be produced by non-agglutinating, non-complement binding "warm" antibodies (4). Coating with γG and complement (γG + C) is produced at least in some instances by γG antibodies which also bind C (5, 6). Antibodies eluted from both γG and γG + C coated cells have been shown to have specificity within the Rh system ("Rh" specificity) by their ability to react with erythrocytes of all phenotypes tested except the rare Rh_{null} blood which lacks all serologically detectable Rh antigens (7, 8). Antibodies eluted from cells coated with only γG have been reported to show a higher incidence of "Rh" specificity than antibodies eluted from γG + C coated cells (7), suggesting that the γG antibodies in the two groups differ.

In order to define further the characteristics of the γG antibodies involved in these two separate groups of patients, panreacting[2] antibodies eluted from γG and γG + C coated cells were tested with Rh_{null} cells for their ability to coat Rh_{null} cells with γG globulin. Eluates which gave a positive reaction with Rh_{null} cells were absorbed with these cells and retested with standard (control) cells of common Rh phenotype. The results showed a high incidence of antibodies with "Rh" specificity in both groups. Antibodies of other specificities were frequently found in the γG + C group. When antibodies of other specificities were present, antibodies with "Rh" specificity could not be detected. After the eluate was absorbed with Rh_{null} cells to remove antibodies with other specificities, antibodies with "Rh" specificity could be detected by their ability to react with control cells of common Rh phenotype.

[1] This work was supported by Grant PRA-35 from the American Cancer Society, by the Kreizel Fund, and by Grants AM-10545 and AM-5129 from the United States Public Health Service.

[2] The term panreacting refers to eluted γG autoantibodies which sensitize all red cells on a commercial panel at temperatures above 25°C, usually maximally at 37°C, to agglutination by antiglobulin serum. An eight cell panel was employed containing the following Rh antigen combinations, expressed as the most probable phenotypes: CDe/cDE (R_1R_2), CDe/CDe (R_1R_1), cDE/cDE (R_2R_2), cDe/cde (R_0r), Cde/cde (r′r), cdE/cde (r″r), and two samples of cde/cde (rr). The test cells were also grouped in the Kell-Cellano, Duffy, Kidd, Lutheran, Lewis, MNSs and P blood group systems.

METHODS

Red cells of phenotypes A_1 Rh_{null} (L.M.), O -D-/-D- (L.H.), A_1 -D-/-D- (E.V.), O cD-/cD- (Spectra Tencell), B R_1r LW negative (Mc), and A LW negative (M.B.) were kindly provided by Dr. F. H. Allen, Jr. of the New York Blood Center. A second sample of A_1 Rh_{null} cells (H.H.) was supplied by Spectra Biologicals.

Blood from patients with γG and $\gamma G + C$ coated cells was defibrinated at 37°C or collected in EDTA. The cells were washed four times with large volumes of saline and eluates were prepared by the method of Kochwa and Rosenfield (9). Eluates were initially tested with a commercial panel of eight reagent cells plus two additional samples of cells of common phenotypes. When sufficient quantities of eluate were available, 10 additional samples of group O cells, 5 Rh positive and 5 Rh negative, were used. Eluates that reacted with all cells were tested with each of two different Rh_{null} cells. Eluates that reacted with Rh_{null} cells were absorbed with Rh_{null} cells at 37°C for 1 hr prior to retesting with group O R_1R_2 (CDc/cDE) cells designated control cells.

Indirect antiglobulin tests were performed with native and absorbed eluates as follows. One drop of 5% suspension of cells of appropriate phenotype was incubated with 3 drops of eluate for 30 min at 37°C. The mixture was centrifuged and examined grossly to make certain there was no agglutination before washing the cells three times and adding the γG antiglobulin reagent. Antiglobulin agglutination readings were graded on a 0 to 4+ scale, with a 2+ reaction only being visible microscopically.

Antisera to γG globulin and to complement were prepared as previously described (10, 11).

The probability (p) that as large a deviation from the expected distribution would have occurred by chance was calculated from the Fisher Exact Probability Test using 2 x 2 contingency tables. A low p value enables one to conclude that eluates were unreactive with Rh_{null} cells because of "Rh" specificity rather than by chance. An eluate that reacted with each of 20 samples of cells of common Rh phenotypes tested and failed to react with each of two samples of Rh_{null} cells tested had a p value of <0.005. An eluate that reacted with each of 10 samples of cells of common Rh phenotypes tested and failed to react with each of 2 samples of Rh_{null} cells tested had a p value of <0.02. An eluate that reacted with each of 10 samples of cells of common Rh phenotype and failed to react with the single sample of Rh_{null} cells tested had a p value of <0.1.

RESULTS

A total of 37 eluates were studied. One showed showed anti-e specificity; another failed to react with some cells tested, but no definite specificity was apparent. The remaining 35 eluates were panreacting.

Twelve eluates were from cells coated with γG alone (γG eluates). Six of these failed to react with each of two samples of Rh_{null} cells, indicating anti- "Rh" specificity (Table I). One of these (No. 1) failed to react with -D- and cD- cells, indicating anti-Hr_0 specificity (12). Four (Nos. 2, 3, 4 and 5) reacted with -D- and cD- cells as well as LW negative cells, suggesting anti-"total Rh" (Rh 29) specificity. One (No. 6) reacted with -D- and cD- but not with LW negative cells, indicating anti-LW specificity.

Six γG eluates reacted with Rh_{null} cells (Table II). After absorption with Rh_{null} cells, one (No. 7) retained activity for the control cells, indicating the presence of at least two populations of antibodies, one of which was "Rh" specific and the other was not. The population with "Rh" specificity remained after absorption and was detected by the reaction with the control cells. ("Rh" specific antibodies could not be removed by absorption with cells lacking all detectable Rh antigens.) The population of other specificity was removed by absorption with Rh_{null} cells. (These antibodies were reacting with antigens other than the known antigens of the Rh system.) Two absorbed eluates (Nos. 8 and 9) lost all activity, indicating a lack of "Rh" specificity. (These antibodies were reacting with antigens outside the Rh system and were removed by absorption with the Rh_{null} cells.)

Twenty-three eluates were from cells coated with $\gamma G + C$ ($\gamma G + C$ eluates). Six of these failed to react or reacted only weakly with Rh_{null} cells, indicating anti- "Rh" specificity (Table III). Four (Nos. 13, 14, 15 and 16) did not react with -D- cells but did react with cD- cells. This specificity is unexplained but could be due to the presence of anti-c or anti-f plus anti-Hr_0. Two of them (Nos. 15 and 16) did not react with LW negative cells. This specificity is also unexplained since the -D- blood is LW positive. Two (Nos. 17 and 18) reacted with -D- as well as LW negative cells, suggesting anti-"total Rh" (Rh29) specificity.

Seventeen γG + C eluates reacted with Rh_{null} cells (Table IV). After absorption with Rh_{null} cells, seven (Nos. 19–25) retained activity for the control cells indicating the presence of at least two populations of antibodies, one of which was "Rh" specific, and one of which was not. The "Rh" specific antibodies remained after absorption with Rh_{null} cells and were detected by their reaction with control cells. The antibodies of other specificities were removed by absorption with Rh_{null} cells. Nine absorbed eluates (Nos.

TABLE I

γG eluates which failed to react with Rh_{null} cells

Test Cells	Eluate					
	1 (A)[a]	2 (A)	3 (O)	4 (O)	5 (B)	6
Rh_{null}						
L.M. (A_1)[b]	0	0	0	0	0	0
H.H. (A_1)	0	0	0	0	0	0
-D-						
E.V. (A_1)	0	3+	3+	4+	4+	
L.H. (O)						2+
cD-						
Tencell (O)	0	4+	4+	4+	3+	3+
LW negative						
M.B. (A)	4+	3+	3+	4+	4+	
Mc (B)						0
Control (O)	4+	3+	4+	4+	3+	3+
p[c]	<0.005	<0.005	<0.005	<0.005	<0.005	<0.02

[a] Denotes ABO group of coated cell from which eluate was obtained.
[b] Denotes ABO group of test cell.
[c] A small value for p indicates a high likelihood of "Rh" specificity.

TABLE II

γG eluates which reacted with Rh_{null} cells

Test Cells	Native Eluate					
	7 (A)[a]	8 (O)	9 (A)	10 (A)	11 (A)	12 (A)
Rh_{null}						
L.M. (A_1)[b]	4+	3+	3+	4+	3+	3+
H.H. (A_1)	4+	3+	3+	4+		
Control (O)	3+	3+	4+	4+	3+	3+
	Eluate Absorbed with Rh_{null} Cell					
Rh_{null}	0					
Control	3	0	0	NT[c]	NT	NT

[a] Denotes ABO group of coated cell from which eluate was obtained.
[b] Denotes ABO group of test cell.
[c] NT, not tested.

26–34) lost all activity indicating a lack of "Rh" specificity.

One absorbed $\gamma G + C$ eluate which retained activity (No. 23) gave weaker reactions with R_2R_2 (e negative) cells than with cells of other common phenotypes (Table V). After subsequent absorption with e negative cells, the eluate reacted with all cells on the panel except the e negative cells, indicating the presence of an additional antibody with anti-e specificity. Thus, two

TABLE III

$\gamma G + C$ eluates which failed to react with Rh_{null} cells

Test Cells	Eluates 13 (O)[a]	14 (A)	15 (A)	16 (O)	17 (A)	18
Rh_{null}						
L.M. (A_1)[b]	0	0	0	0	+	0
H.H. (A_1)	0	0			±	
-D-						
E.V. (A_1)	0	0			2+	
L.H. (O)			0	0		3+
cD-						
Tencell (O)	2+	1+	3+	2+		3+
LW negative						
M.B. (A)	4+				3+	
Mc (B)			0	0		3+
Control (O)	4+	2+	3+	2+	3+	3+
p[c]	<0.005	<0.005	<0.1	<0.1	<0.005	<0.1

[a] Denotes ABO group of coated cell from which eluate was obtained.
[b] Denotes ABO group of test cell.
[c] A small value for p indicates a high likelihood of "Rh" specificity.

TABLE IV

$\gamma G + C$ eluates which reacted with Rh_{null} cells

Test Cells	Native Eluate 19 (O)[a]	20 (A)	21 (A)	22 (O)	23 (O)	24 (A)	25 (O)	26 (A)	27 (A)	28 (O)	29 (O)	30 (O)	31 (O)	32 (B)	33 (O)	34 (O)	35 (A)
Rh_{null}																	
L.M. (A_1)[b]	4+	4+	3+	4+	4+	4+	2+	3+	4+	3+	4+	4+	4+	3+	3+	3+	3+
H.H. (A_1)	3+	3+	2+	3+	3+	3+			3+		2+	2+	3+	3+	3+	3+	3+
Control (O)	4+	4+	4+	4+	4+	3+	3+	3+	4+	4+	4+	4+	4+	3+	3+	1+	4+
	Eluate Absorbed with Rh_{null} Cell 19	20	21	22	23[c]	24	25	26	27	28	29	30	31	32	33	34	35
Rh_{null}	0	0	0	0	0	0	0										
Control	3+	2+	3+	2+	3+	3+	2+	0	0	0	0	0	0	0	0	0	NT[d]

[a] Denotes ABO group of coated cell from which eluate was obtained.
[b] Denotes ABO group of test cell.
[c] This eluate is further characterized in Table V.
[d] NT, not tested.

TABLE V

Successive absorption of one eluate (23) which appeared to be non-specific

Test Cells	Native Eluate	Eluate after Absorption with Rh_{null} Cells	Eluate after Absorption with Rh_{null} + e Negative Cells
1. R_1R_2	4+	3+	1+
2. R_1R_1	4+	3+	1+
3. R_2R_2	4+	2+	0
4. R_0r	4+	3+	2+
5. r'r	4+	3+	2+
6. r''r	4+	3+	1+
7. rrK+	4+	3+	2+
8. rrV+	4+	3+	1+
9. Rh_{null}	4+	0	NT[a]
Specificity	None detected	Anti-"Rh"	Anti-e

[a] NT, not tested.

specific antibodies (anti-e and anti-"Rh") were detected in this eluate which appeared to be nonspecific prior to absorption.

Therefore, 7 of 12 γG eluates and 13 of 23 γG + C eluates showed anti-"Rh" specificity. However, in one of the γG eluates and seven of the γG + C eluates, the "Rh" specificity was masked by the presence of antibody populations of other specificities and was not apparent until the population lacking "Rh" specificity was removed by absorption with Rh_{null} cells.

DISCUSSION

γG antibodies eluted from the red cells of patients with positive direct Coombs' tests can frequently be shown to have blood group specificity by their failure to react with the rare Rh_{null} blood which lacks all serologically detectable Rh antigens (13). This "Rh" specificity is presumably directed against the entire Rh complex or against a reactive site always exposed on the Rh complex (14). Sometimes distinct blood group specificity to one of the Rh antigens such as e (hr″) or c (hr′) is found (4, 5). Occasionally, specificity for the phenotypically related, but genetically independent, LW antigen can be demonstrated by the failure of these antibodies to react with LW negative blood (15).

The red cells of patients with autoimmune hemolytic anemia (AIHA) may be coated with complement as well as γG antibodies (1–3). C components have been eluted with γG antibodies from these cells, suggesting that C is directly attached to the γG molecule (6, 16). It is thought that C can be bound only when two γG molecules are fixed close enough at the surface of the red cell to become aggregated and, in *in vitro* systems, at least two molecules of γG are required to fix one molecule of C (17).

γG isoantibodies with Rh specificity are seldom C-fixing because the Rh antigenic determinants are too far apart for the antibodies to aggregate (18), but γG Rh isoantibodies can fix C when three different antibodies react with three different Rh antigens (19). Therefore it would seem reasonable to assume that C could be fixed by γG autoantibodies with "Rh" specificity if multiple antibodies reacted with different red cell antigens in close proximity. In support of this proposal we have presented data elsewhere which show that the ability of γG autoantibodies to coat normal cells with C may depend not only upon properties of the antibody but also upon properties of the test cells employed (6).

In the present study, seven of 12 γG eluates and 13 of 23 γG + C eluates showed "Rh" specificity. "Anti-total Rh," corresponding to anti-pdl of Weiner (13) was the "Rh" antibody most often demonstrated, but anti-Hr_0, anti-e, and anti-LW were also seen. One γG and seven γG + C eluates contained more than one population of antibodies. "Rh" antibodies could be detected in eluates with multiple antibody populations only after antibodies lacking "Rh" specificity were removed by absorption with Rh_{null} cells.

These data suggest that the antibodies from γG coated cells are similar to those from γG + C coated cells but that multiple populations of antibodies are more frequently found in the latter group. Leddy and Bakemeier found that 12 of 13 γG eluates showed "Rh" specificity compared to only 5 of 18 γG + C eluates (7). However, absorptions with Rh_{null} cells were performed in only two instances. Therefore "Rh" antibodies in the γG + C groups would not have been detected.

We cannot be certain that all the γG antibodies detected in these eluates were autoantibodies. Some may have been transfusion-induced isoantibodies which were adherent to erythrocyte antigen-antibody complexes and were eluted with them (the Matuhasi-Ogata phenomenon) (20). This phenomenon could have accounted for positive reactions of eluates containing anti-A (from group O or group B cells) with group A_1 Rh_{null} cells. However, it is unlikely that the Matuhasi-Ogata phenomenon was responsible for the findings reported herein, since the specificities described are distinctly unusual for transfusion-induced isoantibodies. Moreover many of our patients had never received transfusions.

We have previously shown that γG antibodies in AIHA are a heterogeneous group, composed of both κ and λ light chains (10). The γG antibodies in AIHA are remarkably similar to those associated with α-methyl dopa therapy (21). Bakemeier and Leddy demonstrated a heterogeneous group of antibodies comprised of both κ and λ light chains as well as γG_1, γG_2 and γG_3 heavy chain subclasses in a patient receiving α-methyl dopa (22). At least four serologically distinct antibodies were present: anti-c, anti-e, and two antibodies reacting with two defined antigens or groups of antigens absent from Rh_{null} cells. This patient and all other reported patients with positive Coombs' tests associated with α-methyl dopa therapy have had cells coated with γG alone. However, coating with γG + C may occur with both α-methyl dopa and L-dopa therapy (23, D. E. Jenkins, Jr. and M. E. Eyster, unpublished). This might be expected to occur when the Rh antigenic determinants were of proper configuration on the red cell and a sufficient number of antibodies with different "Rh" specificities were present.

Acknowledgments. The authors are extremely grateful to René Solow, Olga Mychajliw, W. Hugh Moore, and Dean Birdwell for technical assistance, and to Dr. F. H. Allen, Jr. for his critical review of these data.

REFERENCES

1. Leddy J. P., Hill, R. W., Swisher, S. N. and Vaughan, J. H., in *Immunopathology, Third International Symposium*, Edited by P. Grabar and P. A. Miescher, Grune and Stratton, New York, 1963.
2. Swisher, S. N., Trabold, N., Leddy, J. P. and Vaughan, J. H., Ann. N. Y. Acad. Sci., *124:* 441, 1965.
3. Eyster, M. E. and Jenkins, D. E., Jr., Amer. Med., *46:* 360, 1969.
4. Dacie, J. V., *The Hemolytic Anemias, Congenital and Acquired*, Vol. II, Grune and Stratton, New York, 1962.
5. Leddy, J. P., Sem. Hematol., *3:* 48, 1966.
6. Jenkins, D. E., Jr. and Eyster, M. E., J. Lab. Clin. Med., *72:* 886, 1968 (abstract).
7. Leddy, J. P. and Bakemeier, R. F., Proc. Soc. Exp. Biol. Med., *125:* 808, 1967.
8. Eyster, E. and Jenkins, D., Jr., Clin. Res., *16:* 320, 1968 (abstract).
9. Kochwa, S. and Rosenfield, R. E., J. Immun., *92:* 682, 1964.
10. Eyster, M. E., Nachman, R. L., Christenson, W. N. and Engle, R. L., Jr., J. Immun., *96:* 107, 1966.
11. Jenkins, D. E., Jr., Christenson, W. N. and Engle, R. L., Jr., J. Clin. Invest., *45:* 796, 1966.
12. Rosenfield, R. E., Allen, F. H., Jr., Swisher, S. N. and Kochwa, S., Transfusion, *2:* 287, 1962.
13. Weiner, W. and Vos, G. H., Blood, *22:* 606, 1963.
14. Pirofsky, B., Ann. N. Y. Acad. Sci., *124:* 448, 1965.
15. Celano, M. J. and Levine, P., Transfusion, *7:* 265, 1967.
16. Leddy, J. P., Bakemeier, R. F. and Vaughan, J. H., J. Clin. Invest., *44:* 1066, 1965 (abstract).
17. Borsos, T. and Rapp, H., Science, *150:* 505, 1965.
18. Miescher, P. A., in *Immunopathology*, Grune and Stratton, New York, 1969.
19. Rosse, W. F., J. Clin. Invest., *47:* 2430, 1968.
20. Ogata, T. and Matuhasi, T., Proceedings 8th Congress International Society for Blood Transfusion, Tokyo, 1960.
21. Worlledge, S. M., Brit. J. Haemat., *16:* 5, 1969.
22. Bakemeier, R. F. and Leddy, J. P., Blood, *32:* 1, 1968.
23. LoBuglio, A. F., Masouredis, S. P., Pisciotta, A. V., Papavasiliou, P. S. and Cotzias, G. C., Clin. Res. *17:* 333, 1969 (abstract).

THE JOURNAL OF IMMUNOLOGY
Vol. 105, No. 1, July 1970
Printed in U.S.A.

MIGRATORY RESPONSE OF GRANULOMATOUS ALVEOLAR CELLS FROM BCG-SENSITIZED RABBITS[1]

BENITO GALINDO[2] AND QUENTIN N. MYRVIK[3]

From the Department of Microbiology, The Bowman Gray School of Medicine of Wake Forest University, Winston-Salem, North Carolina 27103

Received for publication August 22, 1969

Rabbits sensitized subcutaneously with bacillus Calmette Guérin (BCG) in oil routinely developed dermal tuberculin sensitivity but failed to develop pulmonary granulomas. Alveolar cells procured from such animals were not always inhibited by purified protein derivative (PPD) in the migration-inhibition test. In contrast, the majority of rabbits sensitized with the same dose of BCG by the intravenous route developed a pulmonary granulomatous response reflected by increased lung weight/body weight ratios and increased numbers of alveolar cells. The majority of such animals did not develop dermal tuberculin sensitivity. However, the granulomatous alveolar cells obtained from rabbits sensitized by the i.v. route were consistently inhibited by PPD in the migration-inhibition test. Alveolar cells procured from rabbits with extensive pulmonary granulomas exhibited inhibition of migration (auto-inhibition) in the absence of PPD. Granulomatous cells exhibiting auto-inhibition showed a tendency to escape both auto-inhibition and PPD-induced inhibition. Some BCG-immune sera potentiated PPD-induced inhibition, whereas other BCG-immune sera exhibited a tendency to relieve the auto-inhibitory response of granulomatous cells. Supernatant fluids obtained from granulomatous cells incubated with PPD inhibited the migration of normal alveolar cells. The possible role of the migration-inhibition response in granuloma formation is discussed.

The inhibition of migration of sensitive cells in the presence of antigen has generally been accepted as the *in vitro* counterpart of delayed sensitivity (1–8). The capillary migration technique originally described by George and Vaughan (3) and extended by other investigators (4, 5, 8) has become the prototype of the *in vitro* assay. It now appears certain that at least two cell types are concerned in delayed sensitivity reactions *in vitro*, i.e., lymphocytes and macrophages. Lymphocytes function as primary reacting cells which under the effect of specific antigenic stimulation produce a soluble factor, probably a protein, which inhibits the migration of macrophages. In this regard, the macrophages appear to function as indicator cells. Most of the above investigations have employed exudate cells induced by the injection of mineral oil into the peritoneal cavity of guinea pigs. Under these circumstances the macrophages in the exudate probably represent a random population of cells not all necessarily engaged in an antigen-induced granulomatous response.

To our knowledge, the migratory behavior of alveolar cells from the lungs of rabbits undergoing a granulomatous type reaction has not been reported. The studies to be presented are concerned with the migratory behavior of cells that have actively participated in an allergic granuloma.

MATERIALS AND METHODS

Animals. Rabbits of the New Zealand strain weighing between 2 and 3 kg were used. A considerable number of rabbits from the stock of

[1] This study was supported in part by Grants AI 05667 and AI 07888 from the National Institutes of Health, United States Public Health Service, and a grant from the North Carolina Tuberculosis Association.

[2] Visiting Research Associate from Instituto Venezolano de Investigaciones Cientificas, Caracas, Venzuela.

[3] Reprint requests should be sent to: Dr. Quentin N. Myrvik, Bowman Gray School of Medicine, Department of Microbiology, Winston-Salem, North Carolina 27103.

animals used in the present experiments were found to have pulmonary infection due to *Bordetella bronchiseptica*. In order to control pulmonary infections most animals received intramuscular injections of 50 mg of tetracycline on 2 consecutive days. Throughout the sensitization period the animals were maintained on water containing tetracycline (10 mg/day/kg body weight). The animals received their sensitizing dose of antigen approximately 1 week after the beginning of treatment. This antibiotic treatment did not influence results because nontreated Bordetella-free companion rabbits yielded cells that gave equivalent results. The presence of *Bordetella bronchiseptica* was monitored using nasal swab cultures on a Casman's medium containing penicillin (900 units/ml), mycostatin (1800 units/ml) and neutral red (0.005%).

Sensitization. Rabbits were sensitized with a single injection of 100 μg of heat-killed BCG suspended in 0.1 ml of Bayol F either subcutaneously in the base of the ear or intravenously. The challenge dose of BCG given vaccinated animals consisted of 5 mg of BCG suspended in 1 ml of saline.

Skin tests. The tuberculin skin tests were conducted, using 10 μg of PPD[4] in 0.1 ml of saline, 2, 3, 4 and 5 weeks following sensitization. The diameter of the erythema and the degree of induration were measured in millimeters. Induration was measured using calipers[5] by comparing the thickness of a fold of the skin at the test site before injection and the same fold 24 and 48 hr after the injection. The values for induration represent the difference of the thickness of the fold of the tuberculin skin reaction and the fold of normal skin divided by two.

Migration-inhibition tests. The alveolar cells were procured by flushing the lungs of rabbits according to a technique previously described (9). The viability of the cell populations was estimated using the trypan blue exclusion technique (10).

The cells were washed twice in medium 199 without serum and recovered by centrifugation at 500 × G for 5 min. The migration-inhibition test was similar to that described by others (3, 11), and employed medium 199 containing 33% normal rabbit serum.

The areas of migration were estimated by projecting the migration patterns at 10 × magnification. The silhouettes of migration areas were traced on paper having a constant weight/unit area. The silhouettes were cut out and weighed. The weight of the paper representing the areas of migration was reconverted to the actual area of migration and expressed in square millimeters. Photographs were made of the migration areas by projecting the migration patterns onto standard 2- × 10-in Kodak projector slide plates (as used for electron microscopy).

The following formula was used to express the percentage of migration of alveolar cells in the presence of PPD (migration index) (12):

$$\frac{\text{Average area of migration with PPD}}{\text{Average area of migration without PPD}} \times 100.$$

The average area was calculated with at least four capillary tubes. The migration index (M. I.) was determined at 24 and 48 hr of incubation. In many instances the 48-hr interval proved to be a more sensitive test period for granulomatous cells.

RESULTS

Migration of normal rabbit alveolar cells. Alveolar cell populations were procured from lungs of nonsensitized rabbits lacking macroscopic evidence of pulmonary lesions. The animals selected for use in these experiments had normal lung weight/body weight ratios (LW/BW $< 0.45 \times 10^{-2}$) and their alveolar cell suspensions exhibited the following characteristics: a) no bacterial growth at 5 days when cultured on blood-agar plates; b) cell yield/rabbit was less than 0.3 ml of packed cells; c) viability exceeded 95%; and d) less than 10% of lymphoid cells and polymorphonuclear leukocytes were present.

Migration without PPD. Such normal cell populations exhibited an area of migration ranging from 13 to 18 mm²/capillary tube during the first 24 hr of incubation in the absence of PPD (Table I). At 24 hr the migration pattern of cells assumed a lacy fan-like shape with smooth borders and without clumps (Fig. 1). At 48 hr the area of migration varied from 24 to 41 mm²/capillary tube (Table I) and showed morphology similar to that seen at 24 hr. The results indicate

[4] The PPD used in this investigation was generously supplied by Dr. Myron Fisher, Parke, Davis and Company.

[5] Schnelltaster, H. C. Kröplin (Germany).

TABLE I

Migration of alveolar cells from normal rabbits

Animal No.	LW/BW[b] (× 10^{-2})	PPD	Average Area of Migration[a]				Migration Index[c]	
			24 hr		48 hr			
			No PPD	PPD	No PPD	PPD	24 hr	48 hr
		μg/ml			*mm²*			
N-25	0.41	35	14	14	40	39	100	98
N-26	0.38	35	18	17	41	42	94	102
N-27	0.41	35	16	14	38	38	88	100
N-4	0.40	35	16	16	34	34	100	100
N-1	0.42	35	17	17	35	35	100	100
N-29	0.45	20	14	14	24	24	100	100
N-23	0.33	10	13	13	24	24	100	100
N-24	0.36	10	13	13	32	35	100	109
N-21	0.33	5	15	16	30	30	107	100
N-40	0.39	5	15	16	30	31	107	103
N-33	0.44	5	17	17	34	45	100	132
N-20	0.44	2.5	15	15	32	33	100	103

[a] Average area of migration of four capillary tubes.

[b] Lung weight/body weight ratio.

[c] $\text{Migration index} = \dfrac{\text{Average area of migration with PPD}}{\text{Average area of migration without PPD}} \times 100.$

that the rate of expansion of the area of migration appeared to be constant over a 48-hr incubation period.

Migration with PPD. Tuberculin PPD in doses of 2.5, 5, 10, 20 and 35 μg/ml did not affect the migratory patterns of normal alveolar cells (Fig. 1). The M.I. of normal cells ranged from 88 to 132 (Table I).

Migration of alveolar cells from animals sensitized subcutaneously with BCG. Eighteen rabbits sensitized subcutaneously showed strong dermal reactivity to 10 μg of PPD. The lungs of these animals showed no macroscopic evidence of granulomas. The cell yield and the percentage of lymphocytes obtained from these animals were similar to those obtained from normal rabbits. The migration of these cell populations in chambers lacking PPD was essentially identical to that of cells from nonsensitized animals. The alveolar cell populations obtained from rabbits sensitized subcutaneously with BCG were not uniformly inhibited by 30 μg/ml of PPD (Table II). Alveolar cells procured from three animals exhibiting very strong dermal sensitivity to PPD were not inhibited by PPD *in vitro*.

Migration of alveolar cells from animals sensitized intravenously with BCG. Less than one-third of 37 rabbits sensitized intravenously showed detectable dermal reactivity to 10 μg of PPD. Animals in this group developed a strong pulmonary granulomatous response 2 weeks following sensitization as indicated by the LW/BW ratio which reached a peak about 3 to 4 weeks after sensitization (Table III). The lungs of these animals showed extensive consolidation and the cell yields always exceeded 0.6 ml of packed cells. Many animals yielded 1 to 2 ml of alveolar cells. The cell populations were composed of 60% to 80% macrophages, epithelioid cells and giant cells; 5% to 15% lymphocytes; and 5% to 10% polymorphonuclear leukocytes. Viability always exceeded 95%.

Migration without PPD. Cells procured from strongly granulomatous animals (LW/BW > 0.8×10^{-2}) and incubated in chambers without PPD showed an inhibitory pattern of migration during the first 24 hr of incubation when compared with the migration pattern of cells obtained from normal rabbits or rabbits sensitized subcutaneously with BCG in oil. The average area of migration in this case was approximately 50% of that exhibited by normal cells (Table III). Characteristically, this auto-inhibitory pattern showed an irregular border and numerous cell clumps (Fig. 1).

Migration studies of alveolar cells obtained at

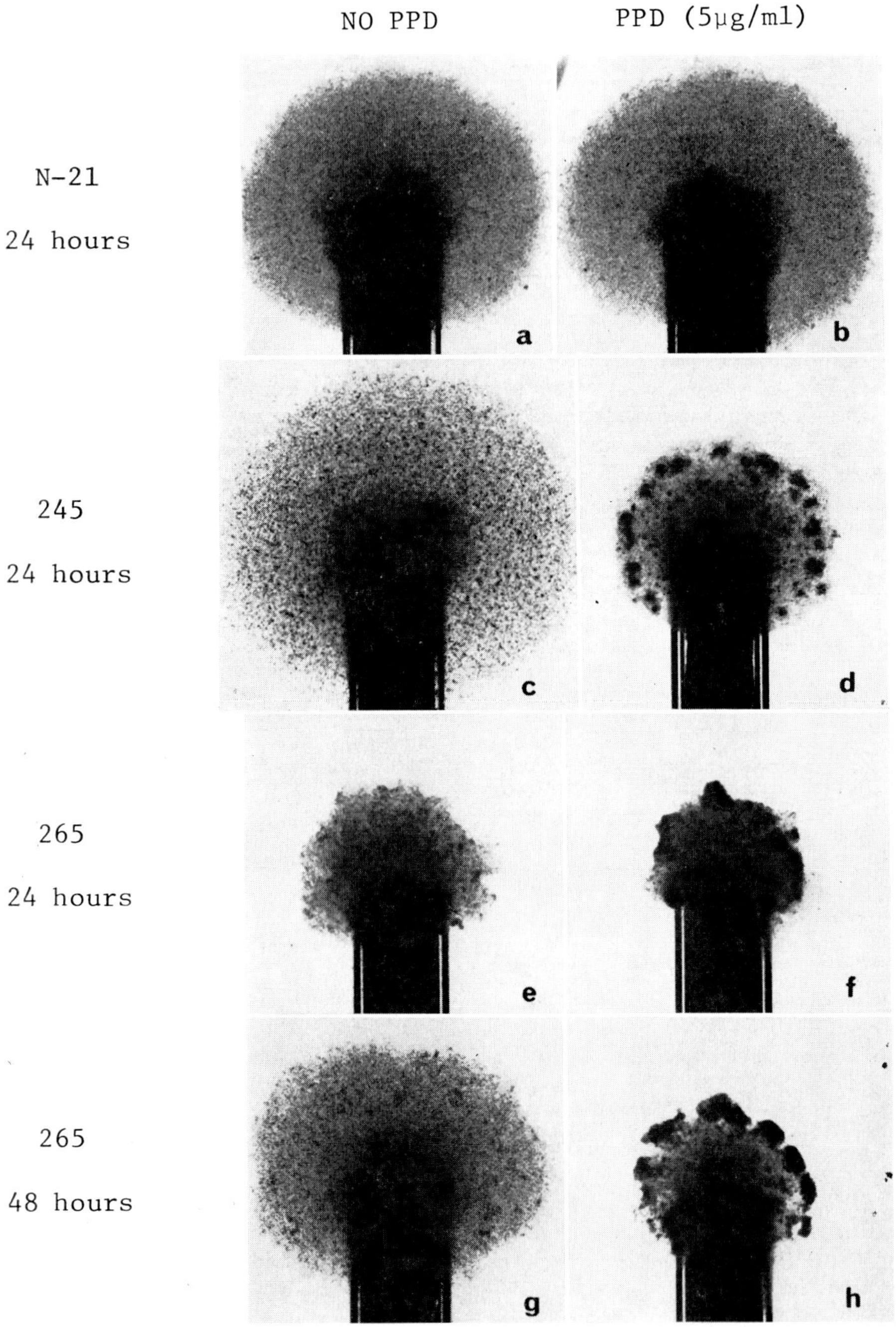

Figure 1. Migration of alveolar cells from normal and intravenously sensitized (BCG) rabbits: *a*, Normal cells without PPD. *b*, Normal cells in the presence of PPD. Note the absence of clumps in both cases. *c*, Alveolar cells from a rabbit with a mild granulomatous response (LW/BW = 0.54×10^{-2}). The migratory pattern in the absence of PPD is similar to that of normal cells. *d*, Migration is markedly inhibited in the presence of PPD and cell clumps are evident. *e*, Alveolar cells from a rabbit with a strong granulomatous response (LW/BW = 0.86×10^{-2}) incubated without PPD. An auto-inhibitory pattern of migration is evident. Note small cell clumps and irregular borders. *f*, The presence of PPD accentuates inhibition and clumping. *g*, After 48 hr of incubation without PPD the auto-inhibitory pattern is no longer evident. The migration pattern resembles that of normal cells at 24 hr. *h*, In the presence of PPD the migration area is slightly larger than at 24 hr. The clumps are larger and are more evident. Animal 245 was not skin tested. Animal 265 exhibited no dermal reactivity when skin tested 5 days before death with 10 μg of PPD.

various intervals following sensitization indicated that auto-inhibition was most evident with cells procured from animals 4 weeks after sensitization. In addition, cells procured from sensitized (3 weeks) animals 4 days after an i.v. challenge dose of BCG showed marked auto-inhibition (Fig. 2).

Cells taken from animals with LW/BW ratios

TABLE II

Migration of alveolar cells from rabbits sensitized subcutaneously with 100 μg BCG in Bayol F[a]

Animal No.	Days following Sensitization	LW/BW[b] (× 10⁻²)	Skin Reaction: Erythema	Skin Reaction: Induration	Migration Index[b] (48 hr)
			mm		
1466	30	0.48	20 × 25	1.25	57
1467	29	0.50	23 × 18	2.60	65
1311	35	0.40	24 × 24	3.70	55
1491	30	0.47	20 × 20	1.65	119
1482	32	0.40	24 × 24	2.00	118
1485	30	0.47	20 × 21	1.00	119

[a] Media contained 30 μg/ml of PPD.
[b] See footnote *c* in Table I.

TABLE III

Migration of alveolar cells from rabbits sensitized intravenously with 100 μg BCG in Bayol F

Animal No.	Days following Sensitization	LW/BW[a] (× 10⁻²)	PPD	Average Area of Migration[a]: 24 hr, No PPD	24 hr, PPD	48 hr, No PPD	48 hr, PPD	Migration Index[a]: 24 hr	48 hr
			μg/ml			*mm²*			
255	10	0.55	2.5	10	10	16	17	100	106
254	10	0.59	2.5	16	12	31	25	75	81
245	11	0.54	15	14	8	24	10	57	42
258	12	0.80	2.5	6	5	18	14	83	78
86	17	0.71	10	16	10	33	20	62	61
93	18	0.94	1	8	6	21	14	75	67
79	19	0.76	5	17	10	26	16	59	62
248	21	1.10	5	10	6	15	9	60	60
83	21	0.94	10	6	4	11	6	67	55
249	21	0.60	5	11	6	26	14	55	54
176	22	0.86	2.5	15	6	26	13	40	50
97	22	1.10	1	6	5	17	8	83	47
96	23	1.00	1	8	4			50	
85	25	0.68	2.5	11	8	25	15	73	60
89	25	1.20	2.5	8	5	26	12	62	46
88	25	0.93	2.5	6	4	12	9	67	75
177	25	0.90	0.5	8	5	31	22	62	71
84	27	0.79	5	9	5	26	12	57	46
264	28	0.68	5	11	6	31	10	55	32
265	28	0.85	5	6	4	13	6	67	46
99	29	0.76	1	7	6	34	16	86	47
95	29	0.75	1	10	7	30	23	70	77
86	39	0.77	2.5	10	6			60	
233	39	0.70	15	6	3	13	4	50	31
230	40	0.63	15	11	6			55	
241	45	0.76	15			22	10		45
235	46	0.86	15	4	3	8	4	75	50

[a] See footnote *c* in Table I.

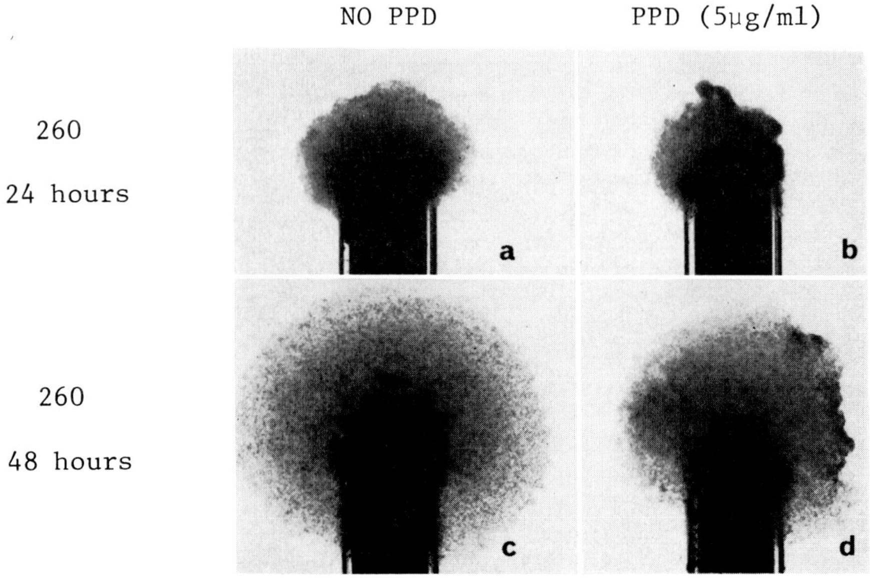

Figure 2. Migration of alveolar cells from intravenously sensitized and challenged rabbits: *a*, Granulomatous cells without PPD exhibiting an auto-inhibitory pattern of migration after 24 hr of incubation. *b*, Granulomatous cells showing further inhibition in the presence of PPD. *c*, Granulomatous cells after 48 hr of incubation without PPD. The auto-inhibitory pattern of migration is no longer evident. The cells show a migratory pattern similar to that of normal cells after 24 hr of incubation. *d*, Granulomatous cells after 48 hr of incubation with PPD. The cells show a tendency to escape PPD-induced inhibition.

less than 0.80×10^{-2} showed wide variations in the extension and morphology of the area of migration during the first 24 hr of incubation (Table III). In some cases, the migratory pattern and the extension of the area of migration were similar to the area of migration exhibited by normal cells (Fig. 1). In other instances, however, an auto-inhibitory pattern was evident.

The initial results obtained in these experiments suggested a possible inverse relationship between the granulomatous index (LW/BW) and the area of migration in the absence of PPD. Correlation analysis of the areas of migration during the first 24 hr of incubation and the LW/BW ratios of animals sensitized i.v., including challenged animals, gave a correlation coefficient of −0.73 (27 observations).

To evaluate the possibility that auto-inhibition was caused by variations in the media, which contained serum from different normal rabbits, a group of 10 rabbits was arranged in pairs. Each pair was composed of one animal with a large LW/BW ratio and either an experimental animal with a low LW/BW ratio or a normal animal. Each pair was killed on the same day and cells were incubated in chambers with the same medium. It was evident that after 24 hr of incubation the area of migration of cells obtained from animals with high LW/BW ratios was appreciably smaller than that of normal cells or of cells from animals exhibiting a weak pulmonary granulomatous response (low LW/BW ratio).

Migration with PPD. The migration of alveolar cells obtained 10 to 12 days after sensitization was not consistently inhibited by PPD, whereas cells obtained 12 to 46 days after sensitization were inhibited (Table III). This inhibition was observed with cells even though they were procured from animals without dermal reactivity to 10 μg of PPD (Fig. 1).

The degree of inhibition of migration was not directly proportional to the intensity of the granulomatous response. Cells taken from animals bearing a weak granulomatous response were inhibited to the same degree as those obtained from animals with extensive granulomas (Fig. 1). When cells exhibited an auto-inhibitory pattern of migration, the addition of PPD effected a significant increment of inhibition as well as a marked increase in the number and size of cell clumps. Furthermore, PPD-induced clumps tended to become more evident during the second 24-hr period of incubation (Fig. 1).

The possibility that "BCG-immune" sera could potentiate the sensitivity of rabbit granulomatous cells to PPD as measured by the migration-inhibition test was investigated. The BCG-immune serum was substituted for the normal rabbit serum in the tissue culture medium. A potentiating effect on migration inhibition was observed with some but not all BCG-immune sera. On the contrary, a few sera reversed the auto-inhibition response and one serum reversed both the auto-inhibitory response and the PPD-induced inhibition (Fig. 3).

Migration-inhibition factor(s) produced by granulomatous cells. Normal and BCG-sensitized alveolar cells were incubated separately at a concentration of 4 × 10^6 cells/ml in medium 199 containing 20% normal rabbit serum and 5 μg of PPD/ml. Samples of the same cell populations were incubated in the same medium but without PPD. After 18 to 24 hr of incubation the cells were removed by centrifugation and the supernatant fluids were filtered through Millipore filters (0.45 μ). Normal alveolar cells were incubated in migration chambers containing the respective undiluted supernatant fluids without the inclusion of additional PPD. Table IV summarizes the results of six experiments. It is evident that only supernatant fluids obtained from BCG-sensitized cells incubated with PPD inhibited the migration of normal alveolar cells and induced clumps which appeared a few hours after incubation (Fig. 4).

Migration of cells from intravenously sensitized and challenged rabbits. Animals which received an intravenous sensitizing dose of BCG in Bayol F followed 3 weeks later by an intravenous challenge dose of 5 mg of BCG in saline showed very strong pulmonary granulomatous responses 4 days after challenge. The LW/BW ratios varied from 1.03 to 1.92 × 10^{-2} (Table V). Cell yields usually exceeded 3 ml of packed cells. The cell populations in this case were composed of 60% to 70% macrophages, epithelioid cells and giant

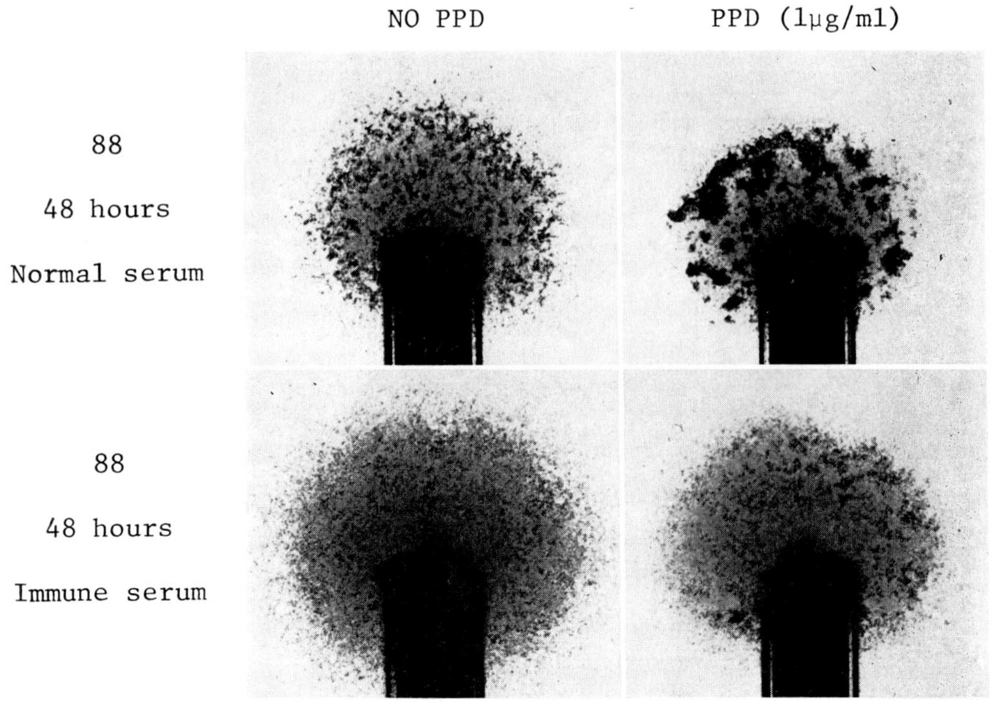

Figure 3. Reversal of auto-inhibition by BCG-immune serum. The serum was obtained from a rabbit sensitized with 100 μg of BCG in Bayol F by the intravenous route. It is evident that cells incubated in media containing BCG-immune serum migrate more extensively than in the media containing normal serum. In addition, a marked reduction of the clumping of cells is evident.

cells, 18% to 25% lymphoid cells, and the remainder polymorphonuclear leukocytes. About 70% of the lymphoid cells would be classified as medium-size or large lymphocytes.

Migration without PPD. In the absence of PPD, granulomatous cells procured from sensitized-challenged animals exhibited a very strong auto-inhibition during the first 24 hr of incubation. The average area of migration of cells from sensitized-challenged animals ranged from 2 to 9 mm^2 per capillary tube (Table V).

The average rate of migration of alveolar cells from sensitized-challenged animals during the second 24-hr period of incubation was greater than the rate of migration during the first 24-hr interval ($p < 0.005$). In addition, cell clumps tended to disappear and the migration pattern at 48 hr resembled the migration pattern of normal cells at 24 hr (Fig. 2).

Migration with PPD. A concentration of 5 μg of PPD/ml in the medium produced additional inhibition of migration and an increase in clumps during the first 24-hr incubation interval (Table V; Fig. 2). However, the rate of migration (in the presence of PPD) during the second 24-hr period was greater than the rate of migration during the first 24-hr period ($p < 0.005$).

Cells from sensitized-challenged rabbits showed a consistent tendency to overcome both auto-inhibition and PPD-induced inhibition during the second 24-hr period of incubation, whereas cells from sensitized (non-challenged) animals exhibited a tendency to overcome auto-inhibition but not PPD-induced inhibition. The M.I. of cells obtained from sensitized-challenged animals was higher than that of cells from sensitized (non-challenged) animals. This was probably due to different degrees of auto-inhibition of these cells and their differing abilities to overcome both auto-inhibition and PPD-induced inhibition.

Even though granulomatous cells procured from intravenously sensitized rabbits exhibited auto-inhibition, they were in addition highly

TABLE IV

Effect of supernatant fluids from BCG-sensitized granulomatous cells incubated with PPD on the migration of normal alveolar cells

Normal Cell Donor for Test	Supernatant Fluid from Cells Incubated 24 hr with PPD[a]	Migration Index[b] 24 hr	48 hr
N-29	Normal N-28	98	98
	Sensitized 264	73	55
	Sensitized 265	58	45
N-30	Normal N-28	110	102
	Sensitized 264	70	51
	Sensitized 265	47	34
N-33	Normal N-32	103	130
	Sensitized 263	35	21
	Sensitized 275	40	22

[a] Animals 263, 264, 265 and 275 were sensitized with 100 μg BCG in 0.1 ml Bayol F. Cell free supernatant fluids obtained from the sensitized cells (263, 264, 265 and 275) incubated without PPD failed to produce inhibition of normal alveolar cells.

[b] See footnote *c* in Table I.

TABLE V

Migration of alveolar cells from rabbits intravenously sensitized and challenged[a]

Animal No.	Days following Sensitization	LW/BW[b] (× 10^{-2})	Average Area of Migration[b] 24 hr No PPD	24 hr PPD[c]	48 hr No PPD	48 hr PPD[c]	Migration Index[b] 24 hr	48 hr
				mm^2				
256	21	1.03	6	5	16	14	83	88
257	21	1.41	4	3	14	10	75	71
260	21	1.55	4	2	15	10	50	73
261	21	1.92	5	4	15	11	80	73
100	21	1.76	2	1	13	4	50	31
272	34	1.40	9	4	39	14	44	36

[a] Animals sensitized intravenously with 100 μg BCG in 0.1 ml Bayol F. Challenged by the same route with 5 mg BCG in 1.0 ml saline 4 days before death.

[b] See footnote *c* in Table I.

[c] Media contained 5 μg/ml of PPD.

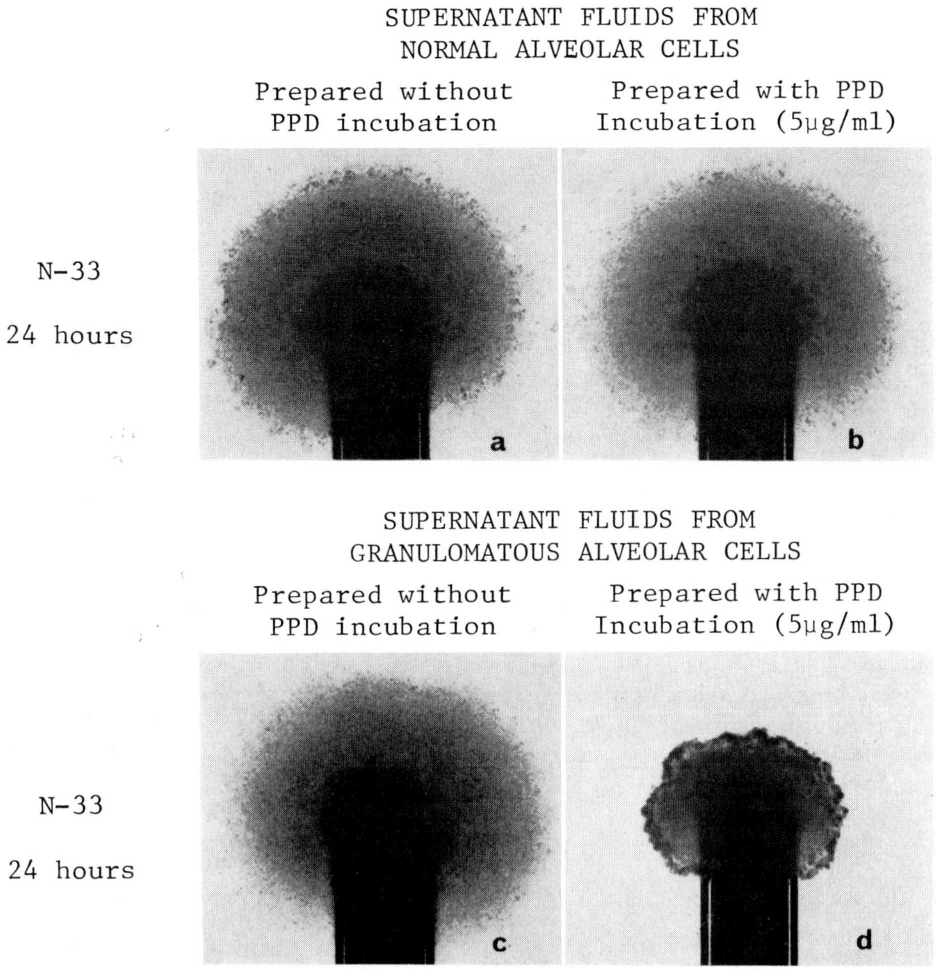

Figure 4. Effect of supernatant fluids from BCG-sensitized granulomatous cells on the migration of normal alveolar cells: *a*, Migration of normal cells in supernatant fluid from normal cells incubated without PPD. *b*, Migration of normal cells in supernatant fluid from normal cells incubated with PPD. *c*, Migration of normal cells in supernatant fluid from granulomatous cells incubated without PPD. *d*, Migration of normal cells in supernatant fluid from granulomatous cells incubated with PPD.

sensitive to PPD. Concentrations of PPD as low as 0.5 μg/ml produced additional inhibition of migration and extensive clumping of the cells.

DISCUSSION

The BCG-induced granulomatous lung provides a source of cells that are actively participating in a cellular immune response. This model may be useful in analyzing the mechanisms that are responsible for various cellular immune reactions associated with delayed sensitivity, antibacterial immunity, anti-tissue immunity and allergic granuloma formation.

Our studies with this model have revealed a dissociation between delayed dermal sensitivity and migration inhibition of rabbit alveolar cells. Rabbits which were sensitized with BCG in Bayol F by the intravenous route failed to develop significant dermal reactivity to PPD. However, they yielded alveolar cells which were markedly inhibited by PPD *in vitro*. In contrast, animals that received equivalent doses of BCG in Bayol F by the subcutaneous route developed moderate to strong dermal sensitivity but did not yield alveolar cells that were consistently inhibited by PPD *in vitro*.

These observations raise questions with regard to what constitutes a tuberculin-positive animal. Based on present information, it is likely that dermal sensitivity to tuberculin requires a critical number of circulating sensitive lymphoid cells. The circumstance by which alveolar cells from tuberculin-positive rabbits, sensitized by the subcutaneous route, were not inhibited by PPD suggests that insufficient numbers of sensitive cells were present in the alveolar cell population. In contrast, BCG-induced granulomatous alveolar cells were invariably sensitive to PPD. Collectively, these observations indicate that an animal may be PPD-negative by the skin test but may possess focal collections of granulomatous cells that are sensitive to PPD as measured by the migration-inhibition test.

The results obtained by mixing small numbers of sensitive alveolar cells with nonsensitive cells indicated that as few as 0.5% "sensitive" lymphocytes can effect the inhibition of migration of the total cell population by PPD (unpublished observations). These results are in agreement with those reported by David (13) who employed oil-induced peritoneal cells from normal and BCG-sensitized guinea pigs. In the guinea pig model it appears that macrophages function only as indicator cells in the migration-inhibition test. However, it is possible that macrophages may have a more direct involvement in this reaction if they are procured from an allergic granuloma. In this regard, a migration-inhibition factor(s) has been reported to be secreted by macrophages (14, 15). Alternatively, if macrophages could react directly with antigen (16), inhibition of migration would not be solely dependent on a nonspecific migration-inhibition factor.

In a series of experiments designed to evaluate the effect of BCG-immune sera on the migration-inhibition response of granulomatous cells, divergent effects of some sera were observed. Two BCG-immune sera obtained from tuberculin-positive rabbits, sensitized by the subcutaneous route, clearly potentiated the inhibition response of granulomatous cells to PPD. In contrast, a few sera from intravenously sensitized rabbits relieved the auto-inhibitory response of granulomatous cells. In one case, a serum obtained from a rabbit sensitized by the intravenous route markedly relieved the auto-inhibitory response as well as the PPD-induced inhibition of migration. The potentiating effects of BCG-immune sera on the migration inhibition response to PPD may be mediated by some form of cytophilic antibody (16). The nature of the serum factor(s) that can relieve both the auto-inhibitory response and the PPD-induced inhibition is unknown. It is possible that this factor is represented by another type of immunoglobulin analogous to enhancing antibodies (17).

The migratory response of granulomatous cells obtained from rabbits sensitized with BCG in oil by the intravenous route appears to be unique in that an auto-inhibitory pattern of migration (in the absence of PPD) was observed. The degree of auto-inhibition tended to parallel the intensity of the granulomatous response as measured by the lung weight/body weight ratio (LW/BW). In contrast, rabbits sensitized by the subcutaneous route had essentially normal LW/BW ratios and their alveolar cells did not exhibit the auto-inhibitory pattern of migration. The auto-inhibition phenomenon observed *in vitro* may also occur *in vivo* and could be responsible for the focal accumulation of cells during the development of the allergic granuloma. It is possible that granulomatous cells contain antigenic fragments remaining from the sensitizing injection of BCG and that auto-inhibition results from the secretion of MIF by these cells. However, preliminary experiments have shown that the supernatant fluids obtained from granulomatous cells exhibiting auto-inhibition (without PPD) failed to inhibit the migration of normal alveolar cells. This could be explained if inadequate amounts of MIF were secreted or released into the medium. Alternatively, complexes of antigen with macrophage cytophilic antibody could be responsible for auto-inhibition.

REFERENCES

1. Bloom, B. R. and Chase, M. W., Prog. Allerg., *10:* 151, 1967.
2. Rich, A. R. and Lewis, M. R., Bull. Hopkins Hosp., *50:* 115, 1932.
3. George, M. and Vaughan, J. H., Proc. Soc. Exp. Biol. Med., *111:* 514, 1962.
4. David, J. R., Fed. Proc., *27:* 6, 1968.
5. Bloom, B. R. and Bennett, B., Fed. Proc., *27:* 13, 1968.
6. Carpenter, R. R. and Brandriss, M. W., J. Exp. Med., *120:* 1231, 1964.
7. Švejcar, J. and Johanovský, J., Z. Immunitätsforsch., *122:* 398, 1961.
8. Thor, D. E. and Dray, S., J. Immun., *101:* 469, 1968.

9. Myrvik, Q. N., Leake, E. S. and Fariss, B., J. Immun., *86:* 128, 1961.
10. McLimans, W. F., Davis, E. V., Glover, F. L. and Rake, G. W., J. Immun., *79:* 428, 1957.
11. David, J. R., J. Exp. Med., *122:* 1125, 1965.
12. Carpenter, R. R., J. Immun., *91:* 803, 1963.
13. David, J. R., Lawrence, H. S. and Thomas, L., J. Immun., *93:* 274, 1964.
14. Pincus, W. B., J. Reticuloendothel. Soc., *4:* 122, 1967.
15. Pincus, W. B., J. Reticuloendothel. Soc., *4:* 140, 1967.
16. Heise, E. R., Han, S. and Weiser, R. S., J. Immun., *101:* 1004, 1968.
17. Kaliss, N., Ann. N. Y. Acad. Sci., *129:* 155, 1966.

THE JOURNAL OF IMMUNOLOGY
Vol. 105, No. 1, July 1970

Printed in U.S.A.

STUDIES ON HUMAN IgD

II. Physicochemical Characterization of Human IgD

ANIL SAHA,[1] PARIMAL CHOWDHURY,[1] SHELDON SAMBURY, YOUSSEF BEHELAK, DOUGLAS C. HEINER AND BRAM ROSE

From the Harry Webster Thorp Laboratories, Royal Victoria Hospital, McGill University, Montreal, Canada

Received for publication August 15, 1969

Physicochemical studies were undertaken on two human IgD (Δ:λ) myeloma proteins. Sedimentation equilibrium analyses using a photoelectric ultraviolet scanner showed that the apparent weight-average molecular weight of IgD is 200,000 ± 2000. On the basis of carbohydrate content, IgD is a high carbohydrate immunoglobulin, the ratio of the oligosaccharide moieties being quite distinct from other high carbohydrate immunoglobulins, IgA, IgM and IgE. One IgD molecule differs considerably from another with regard to several amino acid residues, e.g., asp, glu, ser, ile, gly, ala and val. The proline content of IgD was low in comparison with the other immunoglobulins. One IgD myeloma patient excreted λ-type Bence Jones protein which contained 12 oligosaccharide moieties. Fluorescence emission maxima of IgD occurred at 326 nm and 330 nm, the excitation wavelengths being 278 nm and 295 nm, respectively. Temperature-dependent fluorescence emission spectra showed an absence of a definite transition temperature in the case of IgD, whereas both IgA and IgM showed a definite transition temperature of 60°C.

Human immunoglobulins, IgG, IgA, IgM, IgD and IgE are glycoproteins and may be divided into two categories: low carbohydrate glycoproteins such as IgG, and high carbohydrate glycoproteins such as IgA and IgM (1–5). It is often difficult to procure a sufficient quantity of IgD (2, 3) and IgE (4, 5) in monoclonal form to evaluate their molecular features. However, we were fortunate to have access to two patients (M and P) with IgD myeloma, and studies were undertaken to obtain a better knowledge of the physicochemical and chemical characteristics of their myeloma proteins. In this communication we report the results of studies that were carried out to establish the molecular features of human IgD, as compared with other immunoglobulins representative of the IgG, IgA and IgM classes.

MATERIALS AND METHODS

IgD was isolated from the serum of IgD myeloma patients by a combined procedure of ammonium sulfate fractional precipitation, gel filtration on Sephadex G-200, DEAE-cellulose chromatography, and removal of the contaminating proteins by specific immunoadsorbents (D. C. Heiner, A. Saha and B. Rose, to be published). Monoclonal IgG, IgA and IgM myeloma proteins were isolated from the serum by a combined procedure of ammonium sulfate (18% to 35% saturation) fractional precipitation, Sephadex G-200 gel filtration, and column chromatography on DEAE-cellulose (0.6 mEq/g dry wt, Bio-Rad Laboratories, Richmond, Calif.) and CM-cellulose (0.7 mEq/g, dry wt, Bio-Rad Laboratories). The homogeneity was established by immunodiffusion and immunoelectrophoretic analysis employing specific rabbit antisera (6, 7). For the isolation of Bence Jones proteins, the urine of the patients with Bence Jones proteinuria was collected with 0.01% sodium azide, dialyzed against cold water, and lyophilized. The lyophilized material was reconstituted in 0.025 M sodium phosphate buffer, pH 8.0, and chromatographed on a DEAE-cellulose column 3.5 × 36 cm, with a one-step development technique, using as initial developer 0.025 M sodium phosphate buffer, pH 8.0. Antigenic homogeneity of Bence Jones proteins was established by employing λ-

[1] Present address: New Jersey College of Medicine and Dentistry, Newark, New Jersey 07103.

and κ-type L chain specific rabbit antisera, and immunodiffusion and immunoelectrophoretic analysis (7). Immunoadsorbents were used to remove the trace amount of undesirable protein components in the chromatographic fractions. Rabbit antisera to various clsses of immunoglobulins were fractionated at 18% to 35% ammonium sulfate saturation, and then made specific for the γ, α or μ chains by absorbing with λ- and κ-type Bence Jones proteins, followed by conjugation to bromoacetyl-cellulose (8, 9). A suspension of cellulose-antibody conjugate was added to the protein solution, incubated at 37°C for 1 hr, and centrifuged at 3°C. The entire process was repeated until the undesirable proteins were no longer detectable by immunodiffusion analysis (10).

The apparent weight-average molecular weight was determined according to Yphantis (11). A short liquid column, 0.115 ml, protein solution of A_{280nm} −0.25 was layered to the bottom of a double sector cell with filled-Epon center pieces, 12 mm and 2.5° (12). The sedimentation equilibrium runs were conducted with a 4-cell An-F rotor with standard controls, with or without the bottom layer of fluorocarbon oil FC 43 (Beckman Instruments, Inc., Fullerton, Calif.). The sedimentation equilibrium analyses were carried out in a Beckman/Spinco analytical ultracentrifuge model E fitted with ultraviolet monochromator, double beam automatic photoelectric scanner (13–15), and multiple cell scanning accessories (16). Weight-average apparent molecular weight of the proteins was calculated according to the equation (17, 18):

$$M_{w,app} = \frac{2RT}{(1 - \bar{v}\rho)\omega^2} \frac{d \ln c}{dr^2}$$

where R is the gas constant, T the absolute temperature, ω the rotor speed in radians/sec, r the radial distance from the axis of the rotation for which c is protein concentration, ρ density, and $\bar{v}$ the partial specific volume. Casassa and Eisenberg's definition of a two-component system was satisfied, since the protein solutions were dialyzed and the scanner circuit automatically deducted the contribution of the buffer salts present in the protein solutions (19). The initial protein concentration, C_0, was determined at 280 nm, 15 min after the rotor attained the speed of 9000 rpm. At each calibration, the absorbance at 280 nm recorded by the photoelectric scanner was related to the protein solution, the absorbance of which was determined simultaneously at 280 nm by a Cary recording spectrophotometer model 14. The term, $d \ln c$ *vs* dr^2 was obtained from the raw scanner density data by the method of least squares curve fitting, using orthogonal polynomials of the first order. An IBM 360 computer with Fortran IV language was used for computing the scanner data (7, 12). The conservation of mass in a sectorial ultracentrifuge cell during the ultracentrifugal run was assumed and the theoretical slope was obtained from the basic equilibrium equation as suggested by Yphantis (11).

Fluorescence emission spectra were determined with an MPF-2A Hitachi-Perkin Elmer fluorescence spectrophotometer fitted with a recorder and thermostated cell assembly. Temperature was maintained by a water circulator coupled with heater and cooler, the temperature fluctuation being ±0.1°C. Fluorimetric studies were carried out using a 4-cell assembly and in the presence of other myeloma proteins. Since a concentration-dependent quenching was noticed at an A_{280nm} − 0.4 and above, the fluorimetric studies were conducted with protein solutions of A_{280}nm below the concentration-dependent quenching range.

Amino acid composition was determined with a Beckman/Spinco amino acid analyzer model 120 B fitted with an Integrator model 125, high sensitivity cuvette, and range expander. An accelerated procedure at 55°C was used with a developer flow rate of 70 ml/hr and ninhydrin flow rate of 35 ml/hr (7, 20, 21). An IBM 360 computer with Fortran IV language was used to extrapolate the values of amino acid residues to zero hour hydrolysis and to calculate the number of amino acid residues/mol of protein (7). Tryptophan content was determined by hydrolyzing 3 to 5 mg protein in 2 M $Ba(OH)_2$ at 108°C for 70 hr in Vycor tubes (Corning Glass, Corning, N.Y.) in a nitrogen atmosphere (22). CO_2 gas was bubbled through the solution and $BaCO_3$ formed was centrifuged off at 1°C. The precipitate was washed with distilled water and the combined supernatant was evaporated to dryness under vacuum on a rotary evaporator. The dry residue was dissolved in 10 ml of distilled water and filtered through a sintered glass funnel. The solution was lyophilized and dissolved in 5 ml of 0.2 N sodium citrate buffer, pH 2.2. 0.025 ml of 0.2 M Na_2SO_4

solution was added to ensure complete precipitation of Ba. The precipitate was spun down and the solution adjusted to pH 2.2 with a few drops of concentrated HCl. Tryptophan content was determined by the amino acid analyzer on a Beckman PA 35 (7.5% cross-linking) column, 0.9 x 16 cm, at 55°C and developed with 0.38 M sodium citrate buffer, pH 5.1, which contained organic alcohols (21).

Total hexoses (mannose and galactose) were measured according to Dische and Popper (23) with a mixture of mannose and galactose (5:3) as reference (24). Duplicate analyses were carried out with the mannose:galactose ratio in the reference solution identical to that obtained with each class of immunoglobulins. Fucose content was measured according to Dische and Shettles (25). Sialic acid was determined according to the thiobarbituric acid reaction of Warren (26). For the determination of glucosamine and galactosamine a sample (4 to 5 mg of protein solution in 0.2 M ammonium bicarbonate buffer, pH 8.6) was dried overnight at 100°C and then hydrolyzed in glass-distilled 4 N HCl for 4, 6 and 8 hr at 100°C under nitrogen in sealed tubes (27). HCl was removed under vacuum in a rotary evaporator and the dry residue was dissolved in 0.2 M sodium citrate buffer, pH 2.2. The amino-sugars were determined by the amino acid analyzer employing a short column, 0.9 x 16 cm (Beckman resin PA 35, 7.5% cross-linking), and a duplicate run on long columns, 0.9 x 57 cm (Beckman resin PA 28). The short column was developed with 0.38 M sodium citrate buffer, pH 5.1, and the long column with amino acid analyzer buffers, under usual amino acid analysis conditions (47).

RESULTS

The $s_{20,w}$ values of IgD myeloma proteins are higher than those of IgG myeloma proteins according to Rowe and Fahey (2, 3) and as observed in our laboratory (28). This observation on the $s_{20,w}$ values prompted the use of comparative sedimentation equilibrium analyses employing multiple cell scanning accessories. The scans obtained during the progress of sedimentation equilibrium runs revealed that the cell meniscus clearance of IgD was faster than that of IgG for a given rotor speed, the initial protein concentration being nearly equal. Figure 1 shows the mass distribution of IgD (M) myeloma protein as revealed by the photoelectric scanner 15 hr after the rotor attained full speed of 14,000 rpm. The weight-average apparent molecular weight of IgD (M) myeloma protein was found to be 200,000 ± 2000. The apparent partial specific volume, $\bar{v}_{app}$, was assumed to be 0.72 ml/g, since the IgD protein contained a large amount of oligosaccharide. Figure 1 also includes the plot, ln *c vs* r^2, for IgG ($\gamma 1:\lambda$, Gm 4) obtained at 16,000 rpm. The theoretical mass distribution of IgG was obtained on the basis of its molecular weight being 150,000. $\bar{v}_{app}$ for IgG was determined as 0.73 ml/g in 0.1 M Tris-HCl buffer, pH 8.6, at 20°C, according to the equation (29), where

$$\bar{v}_{app} = \frac{1}{\rho_0} - \frac{1}{c}\frac{\rho - \rho_0}{\rho_0},$$

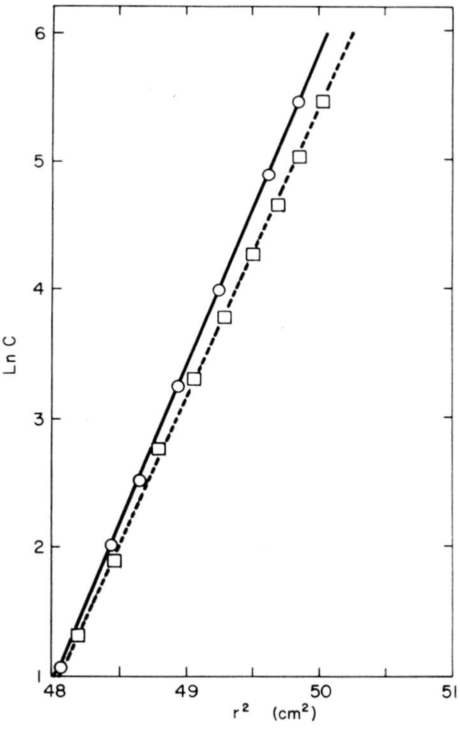

Figure 1. Sedimentation equilibrium plots of human IgG and IgD myeloma proteins. □-----□, IgG, C_0—0.25 (A_{280} nm); rotor speed—16,000 rpm; $\bar{v}$—0.73; and ○——○, IgD, C_0—0.25 (A_{280} nm); rotor speed—14,000 rpm; $\bar{v}$—0.72. The plots represent the logarithm of concentration as a function of the square of the radial distance. The initial protein concentration (C_0) has been reported as absorbance at 280 nm. The theoretical mass distribution of the proteins has been calculated according to Yphantis (11) and presented as —— for IgD and ----- for IgG.

ρ_0 and ρ were densities of solvent and solution, respectively, and c was the concentration of protein in g/ml solution. During the sedimentation equilibrium runs, no molecular aggregation of IgD myeloma proteins was observed at the bottom of the ultracentrifuge cells with or without the layer of fluorocarbon oil FC 43.

Chemical characterization of the IgD proteins was carried out by determining the amino acid composition of the two available IgD myeloma proteins (M and P) and comparing them with those of monoclonal myeloma proteins representing different classes of immunoglobulins. Both IgD myeloma proteins possessed λ-type L chains. Table I presents the amino acid composition of the representative immunoglobulins of various classes. The mol amino acid residues/mol of protein were computed according to the oligosaccharide content. The number of amino acid residues of IgD (m. w. 200,000) was computed on the basis of the carbohydrate content being 14%. Differences between IgG and IgA may be noted with lys, ser, val and leu residues. IgG contains more lys residues than IgA and also more val and ser residues. The α chains are smaller and contain fewer amino acid residues since a large part of the IgA molecules was constituted by the oligosaccharide moieties. IgA contains more leu residues. IgD molecules contain fewer residues of lys and more acidic amino acid residues (asp and glu). Leu content was also fairly high in IgD. One IgD molecule differs considerably from another in regard to several amino acid residues, e.g., asp, glu, ser, ile, gly, ala and val. Pro content of IgD was unusually low in comparison with the other immunoglobulins.

One of the two IgD myeloma patients excreted λ-type Bence Jones protein and we compared the amino acid composition of this particular protein (P) with other λ-type Bence Jones proteins available in our laboratory. Table II presents the amino acid composition of the λ-type Bence Jones proteins. The presence of three met residues appeared to be the unusual feature of Bence Jones

TABLE I

Amino acid composition of IgG, IgA, IgM and IgD[a]

	IgG		IgA			IgM			IgD	
	I	II	I	II	III	I	II	III	M	P
Lys	86	75	53	48	59	64	70	80	48	44
His	23	19	24	22	22	26	28	42	15	23
Arg	45	38	54	56	41	69	56	60	55	53
Asp	111	93	81	88	92	121	126	129	123	170
Thr	103	115	113	108	120	131	147	144	146	142
Ser	156	152	137	135	138	131	163	154	186	166
Glu	122	141	120	117	118	146	170	148	205	162
Pro	103	104	99	101	104	131	134	113	55	62
Gly	96	93	91	90	91	107	103	114	125	144
Ala	81	82	81	89	82	101	103	116	125	144
Cys/2	24	26	24	24	24	24	22	24	24	24
Val	128	127	87	94	84	144	134	120	123	133
Met	12	16	14	12	17	30	20	20	20	20
Ile	26	28	35	38	32	42	54	59	38	28
Leu	99	93	113	115	106	106	126	112	169	162
Tyr	63	49	50	41	40	52	56	51	67	75
Phe	43	52	43	49	41	66	67	60	73	65
Trp	20	22	22	18	20	24	20	24	22	22
Molecular weight	150,000	150,000	150,000	150,000	150,000	185,000	185,000	185,000	200,000	200,000
Carbohydrate molecular weight	4,635	4,746	12,810	12,315	15,000	21,275	21,275	21,275	28,000	28,000

[a] The values represent average of duplicate analyses after 22, 48 and 70 hr of hydrolysis with 6 N HCl, at 108°, and corrected for the hydrolysis loss. Computations were made after the correction for the contribution of the carbohydrate moiety present in each molecular species. The data represent mole amino acid residues present/mol of protein (for apparent molecular weight, see 1, 48).

TABLE II

Amino acid composition of λ Bence Jones proteins[a]

	P	I	II	III	IV	V
Lys	11	13	12	14	11	11
His	3	3	3	4	4	4
Arg	6	6	9	4	7	8
Asp	17	14	18	17	15	14
Thr	25	18	19	22	19	19
Ser	31	25	25	27	28	32
Glu	24	20	21	20	22	19
Pro	16	19	16	15	14	16
Gly	16	20	16	17	17	17
Ala	19	20	16	17	20	18
Cys/2	5	5	5	5	5	5
Val	17	17	17	17	15	17
Met	3					
Ile	5	5	5	6	5	4
Leu	15	15	15	14	15	15
Tyr	12	7	12	12	9	10
Phe	6	6	5	6	4	4
Trp	3	3	4	3	3	4

[a] The values represent duplicate analyses of 22, 48 and 70 hr of hydrolysis corrected for the hydrolysis loss and extrapolated to zero hour hydrolysis. The data represent mole amino acid residues/mol of protein.

protein (P). Besides the met residues, the other amino acid residues appeared to be within the normal range. The amino acid sequence of three human λ-type Bence Jones proteins, SH, HA and Bo (30) revealed an absence of met residues. However, Edmundson *et al.* (31) reported the presence of one met residue in the carbohydrate-containing human λ-type Bence Jones protein (Hul) obtained from an IgG myeloma patient. Whether this met residue belongs to the integral polypeptide chain or is a member of a peptide strongly adsorbed onto the polypeptide chain has not yet been established (A.B. Edmundson, personal communication).

Table III presents the molar ratios of oligosaccharide moieties as they occur in various immunoglobulins. Based on its carbohydrate content, IgD may be categorized as a high carbohydrate glycoprotein. IgD (M) contained an unusually large number of glucosamine residues (56 residues) in comparison to IgD (P). The combined glucosamine and galactosamine residues in IgD are higher than those of any other class of immunoglobulins. The hexose content of IgD appeared to be similar to that of IgM and IgE. The fucose content appeared to be similar to that of IgM but differed from that of IgE. IgG molecules contained fewer oligosaccharides. Table III also presents a summary of carbohydrate analysis of a dozen Bence Jones proteins available in our labortory. Bence Jones protein (P) possessed 12 residues of oligosaccharide moieties based on molecular weight of 25,000. Since other Bence Jones proteins (Table III, 31) contained sialic acid, a cleavage of the sialic acid residue of protein (P) in all probability occurred at some stage during the isolation procedure. Alternatively, it may be surmised that sialic acid, a terminal residue, was not incorporated in the carbohydrate chain. This confusing phenomenon needs further study in the near future. Bence Jones protein (P) contained more galactosamine residues as compared to Hul Bence Jones protein (31).

A study of the fluorescence emission spectra of proteins provides a sensitive means of evaluating the environmental conditions of tyr and trp residues (32–34). Studies of fluorescence emission spectra excited at wavelengths beyond 290 nm preclude the contribution of tyr residues in the trp emission spectra while those at 278 nm as the excitation wavelength include the contribution of both tyr and trp residues. Fluorescence emission spectra of IgD (M) obtained at two different temperatures showed that the maxima appeared at 326 nm and 330 nm at 25°C, and, at 10°C, 328 nm and 331 nm, with respect to the excitation wavelengths of 278 and 295 nm (Fig. 2). Figure 3 presents the fluorescence emission characteristics of other representative immunoglobulins. The fluorescence emission maxima occurred at 335 nm (IgG, $\gamma 1:\lambda$), 338 nm (IgA, $\alpha 1:\kappa$), and 339 nm (IgM, $\mu:\lambda$) at 25°C and 0.1 M Tris-HCl buffer, pH 8.6:0.15 M NaC1. A comparative study of the fluorescence emission characteristics of eight monoclonal IgG proteins revealed that the emission maxima occurred within the range of 329 to 335 nm. Of these IgG proteins, three possessed λ-type L chains and the remaining five κ-type. Five of these IgG proteins had $\gamma 1$ type H chains and the rest $\gamma 2$ type. The fluorescence emission maxima of the λ-type Bence Jones protein (P) obtained from the IgD myeloma patient (P) occurred at 345 nm, the range of emission maxima being 340 to 351 nm for other λ-type Bence Jones proteins (Fig. 4). Two κ-type Bence Jones proteins showed 340 and 348 nm as their fluorescence emission maxima. Gally and Edelman (35) have reported that the maximum fluorescence oc-

TABLE III

Molar ratio of oligosaccharides to immunoglobulins

		Molecular Weight	Mannose + Galactose	Fucose	Glucosamine	Galactosamine	Sialic Acid
IgD (M)	δ:λ	200,000	66.5	8.55	56	9.42	23[b]
(P)	δ:λ	200,000	56.4	8.27	30	20	23[b]
IgA	α1:κ	150,000	26.6	2.56	12.6	12.0	10.36
	α1:κ	150,000	26.5	3.19	14.8	8.1	9.5
	α1:κ	150,000	25.8	2.20	15.3	7.8	11.15
(IgM)₅	μ:λ	185,000	63.4	7.89	30.5	2.43	8.3
	μ:κ	185,000	62.6		28.5	3.65	8.0
IgE[c]		196,000	60.0	6.17	——39.8——		6.3
IgG	γ1:λ	150,000	12.6	2.38	7.53	0.15	2.0
	γ2:λ	150,000	12.4	2.36	7.5	0.0	2.23
		150,000	9.9	1.65	9.5	1.0	1.80
Bence Jones protein	P λ	50,000	12.86	1.7	1.5	5.6	0
	H λ	50,000	0	0	0.34	0.34	0
	L λ	50,000	0	0.36	1.5	2.4	1.0
	B λ	50,000	2.5	0.91	1.0	1.0	1.0
	M κ	50,000	0	0	1.0	1.0	1.1
	I[d] λ	50,000	10	4	4	4	4

[a] The oligosaccharide moieties were reported on the basis of the molecular weight of the individual proteins. Bence Jones proteins were obtained from the patients with following clinical syndromes: P, IgD myeloma; H, IgG (γ1:λ) myeloma; L and B, Bence Jones proteinuria; M, IgA (α1:κ) myeloma, and I, IgG myeloma (31).

[b] Obtained from Spiegelberg *et al.* (42).

[c] Johansson and Bennich (4).

[d] Edmundson *et al.* (31).

curred between 330 and 350 nm for 13 Bence Jones proteins.

Since the fluorescence emission characteristics depend on the solvent properties and the ground state energy, temperature plays an important role in the energy transfer (35–37). Fluorescence measurements of IgD at two different temperatures, 25°C and 10°C, showed an increase in the relative fluorescence intensity and also a shift in the emission maxima (Fig. 2). Between 25°C and 10°C, a 2-nm red shift in the emission maxima was observed with IgD (M), and a blue shift, 337 nm to 336 nm for IgM and 334 nm to 333 nm for IgA was noted, the excitation wavelength being 278 nm. This shift in the emission maxima, however small, reflects a conformational change due to the decrease in solution temperature. The effect of temperature on the fluorescence emission characteristics of three classes of high carbohydrate immunoglobulins, IgA, IgM and IgD, is shown in Figure 5. Between 25° and 68°C the fluorescence emission maxima shifted from 334 to 339 nm for IgA, from 326 to 333 nm for IgD and from 337 to 339 nm for IgM. The relative fluorescence intensity decreased with increase in temperature until the transition temperature was reached. The transition temperature as obtained from the slope of the plot, relative fluorescence intensity *vs* temperature, was 60°C for both IgA and IgM. A definite transition temperature could not be attained with IgD, and furthermore the protein coagulated above 72°C. While IgA and IgM behaved similarly, IgD showed certain dissimilarities (Fig. 5). In the case of IgD, the rate of decrease in the relative fluorescence intensity was slow between 8° to 20°C, followed by a sharp decrease between 20° and 50°C and a slower one between 50° and 68°C. Correspondingly, the rate of decrease in relative fluorescence intensity of IgA and IgM with respect to temperature is of the following order: 8° to 20° > 20° to 50° > 50° to 60°C (Fig. 5). An increase in the relative fluorescence intensity beyond the transition temperature was observed with both IgA and IgM, the maximal point being reached at 68°C for both (Fig. 5). The relative fluorescence intensity at 68°

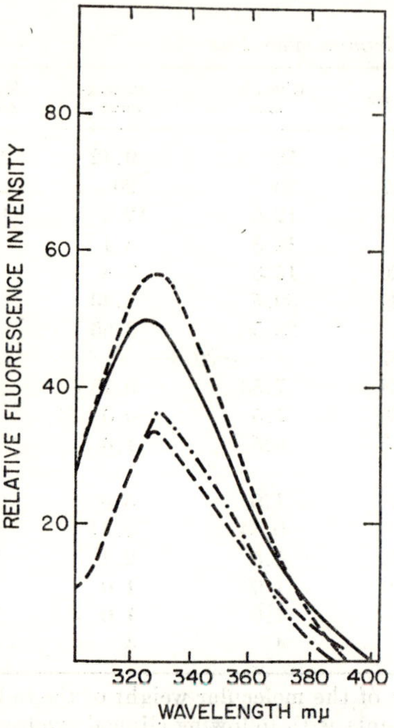

Figure 2. Fluorescence emission spectra of IgD molecule at 10° and 25°C. The spectra were obtained employing an excitation wavelength of 278 nm at 25°C—— and at 10°C-----; and at excitation wavelength of 295 nm at 25°C----- and at 10°C-·-·-·-·-·.

was higher than that at 25°C for IgA and lower than that at 25°C for IgM. The relative fluorescence intensities at 68°C were 84.1% and 84.6% of the values obtained at 8°C for IgA and those for IgM, 68.3% and 66.0%, the excitation wavelengths being 278 and 295 nm, respectively.

DISCUSSION

The presence of L chains, λ- and κ-types, common to all immunoglobulins is one of the distinctive features in their covalent structure. Amino acid sequence studies of κ- and λ-type human L chains showed the presence of 213 to 221 amino acid residues, the range being 214 to 221 for κ-, and 213 to 217 for λ-type chains (30). Thus, the molecular weight of the L chain varies from 22,500 to 24,500. Since all major immunoglobulins possess a basic tetra-chain structure and there are two L chains and two H chains with or without S-S bridges, the molecular weight of the individual H chain may be estimated indirectly from that of the whole molecule. If the molecular weight of IgG were considered as 150,000, and the carbohydrate content as 3%, the molecular weight of the protein moiety of the γ chain would amount to 48,000 to 50,000. Recently, Edelman *et al.* (38) reported the complete amino acid sequence of a human IgG (γ1:κ), with 214 and 446 amino acid residues constituting the κ- and γ1 chains, respectively. The α-chain protein moiety would show an approximate molecular weight of 43,000 to 45,000 considering the carbohydrate content of 10%. Likewise, the protein moieties of the μ- and ϵ-chains would have approximate molecular weight of 57,000 to 59,000 and 63,000 to 65,000, the carbohydrate content being 12% and 10.7%, respectively. A similar consideration would entitle the protein moiety of the δ-chain to have an approximate molecular weight of 61,500 to 63,500. These considerations point out the existence of a variation in both the number of oligosaccharide moieties and constituent amino acid residues in a given immunoglobulin mole-

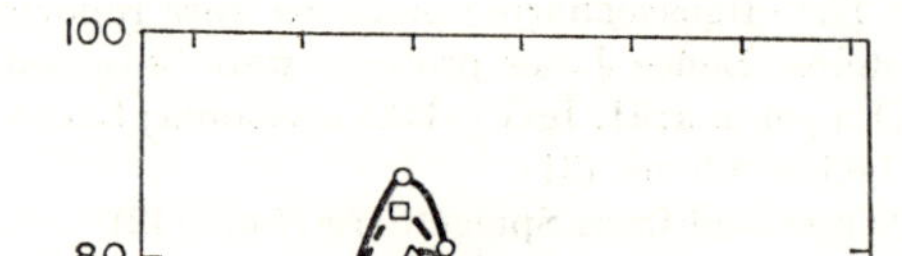

Figure 3. Fluorescence emission spectra of human immunoglobulins. The fluorescence emission spectra were obtained with an excitation wavelength of 278 nm with a cutoff filter of 310 nm, and in 0.1 M Tris-HCl buffer, pH 8.6, and at 25°C. IgM was in 0.1 M Tris-HCl buffer, pH 8.6:0.1 M NaCl. ●, IgG (γ1:λ); ○, IgA (α1:η); □, IgM (μ:λ); △, IgD (P) (Δ:λ); and ▲, IgD (M) (Δ:λ).

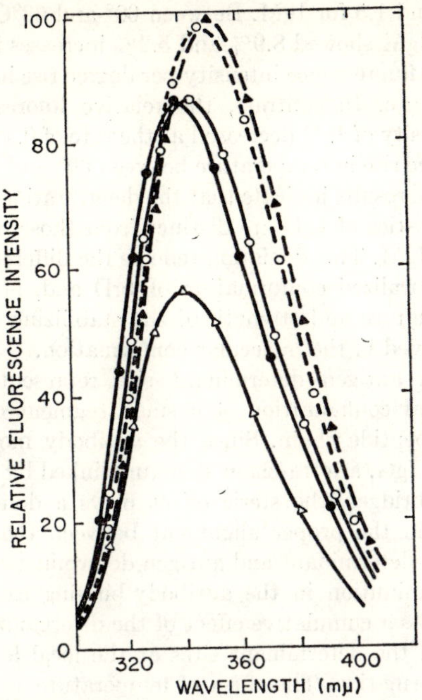

Figure 4. Fluorescence emission spectra of Bence Jones proteins. The fluorescence emission spectra were obtained with an excitation wavelength of 278 nm and a cutoff filter of 310 nm at 25°C and in 0.1 M Tris-HCl buffer, pH 8.6. ○——, λ(P); ●——, λ(H); △——, λ(B); ○-----, κ(F); and ▲- - -, κ(M).

cule. There is considerable variation between the different classes of immunoglobulins in the number of oligosaccharide moieties, although a certain range may be noticed with respect to a single class (Table III). The survey by Abel *et al.* (39) into the carbohydrate content of IgG (76 IgG myeloma proteins) revealed that although the median range of carbohydrate content of 54 IgG is 2.8% to 3.3%, the remaining 22 IgG myeloma proteins contain as much as 5% to 6%.

That the carbohydrate moiety is located on the Fc fragment of IgG was reported by Porter (40) and subsequently confirmed by several investigators (for review, see 41). The Fab fragment of IgG molecules does not contain carbohydrate except in those IgG molecules with a high carbohydrate content of 5% to 6% (42). Proportionately, the Fc fragments contain more carbohydrate than the Fab fragments. During the studies on the enzymic fragmentation of IgG and IgA myeloma proteins we have detected carbohydrate in the Fab fragments of some IgG proteins and also in IgA proteins. Neither the L chains obtained by the reductive cleavage of human immunoglobulins nor the Bence Jones proteins, under normal conditions, contain oligosaccharide moieties. However, the presence of 13 oligosaccharide moieties in the variable region of the Bence Jones proteins (Hul and Nev) has been reported by Edmundson *et al.* (31). The L chains

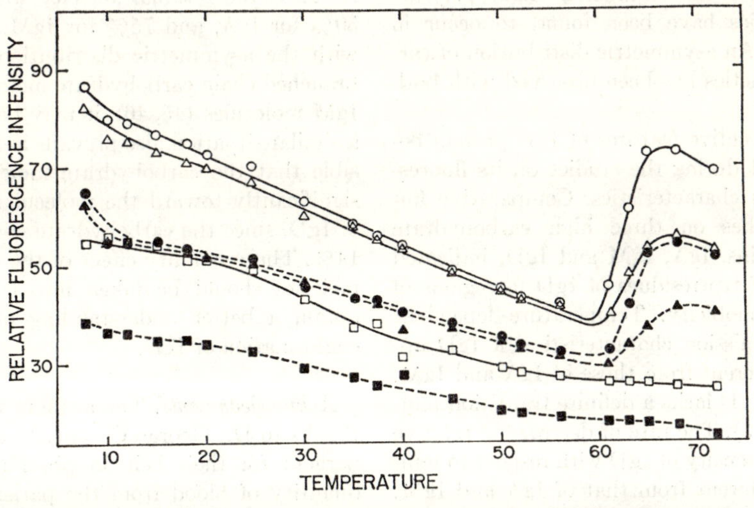

Figure 5. Temperature-dependent fluorescence characteristics of immunoglobulins. The emission spectra of the immunoglobulins as the function of temperature were obtained by employing excitation wavelengths of 278 and 295 nm, respectively: ○——○, ●——●, IgA; △——△ ▲-----▲, IgM; □——□, ■-----■, IgD (M).

from Nev myeloma IgG did not contain carbohydrate moieties. Table III shows that although Bence Jones protein (P) contain 12 oligosaccharide residues, direct correlation between the distribution of different oligosaccharide moieties present in the IgD myeloma protein and that in the Bence Jones protein (P) could not be established. A similar situation was demonstrated by the comparative study of the myeloma and Bence Jones proteins obtained from the same patient, irrespective of the class of myeloma (IgG, IgA and IgM). A similarity exists between the ratio of mannose and galactose:fucose in IgD (P), 6.8:1, and in the Bence Jones protein (P), 7.5:1. A distinct deviation was noted with glucosamine: galactosamine ratio. While IgD (P) contained more glucosamine than galactosamine (30:20), the reverse was true with Bence Jones protein (P), the ratio being 1.5:5.6. The ratio of glucosamine:galactosamine in the Hul Bence Jones protein was found to be 1:1 (31). Carbohydrate-protein linkages in immunoglobulins have been found to be of two kinds: 2-acetamido-2-deoxy-D-glucose linked as a glycosylamide to the 4-carboxyl group of aspartic acid, and O-glycosidic linkage between 2-acetamido-2-deoxy-D-galactose and hydroxy amino acids, serine and threonine (for review, see 43). While the former type is associated with IgG, both the types have been found in IgA and IgM (44–46). While both linear and branched chain polysaccharide moieties are present in IgA, only branched chain polysaccharide moieties have been found to occur in IgM (45, 46). An asymmetric distribution of carbohydrate moieties has been observed with both IgA and IgM.

Several distinctive features of IgD protein became apparent during the studies on its fluorescence emission characteristics. Comparative fluorimetric studies on three high carbohydrate immunoglobulins, IgA, IgM and IgD, indicated the location of trp residues of IgD in regions of higher hydrophobicity. Temperature-dependent fluorescence emission characteristics of IgD appear to be different from those of IgA and IgM. For example, IgD lacks a definite transition temperature (Fig. 5). The rate of decrease in relative fluorescence intensity of IgD with respect to temperature is different from that of IgA and IgM. The percentage decrease in relative fluorescence intensity per degree rise in temperature between 8° to 20°, 20° to 50° and 50° to 60°C was 1.15, 2.4 and 0.76 for IgD, 2.4, 1.9 and 1.3 for IgA and 2.4, 1.9 and 1.5 for IgM. Between 60° and 68°C, IgA and IgM showed 8.9% and 5.2% increases in relative fluorescence intensity per degree rise in temperature. In contrast, the relative fluorescence intensity of IgD decreased at the rate of 0.4% per degree rise in temperature between 60° and 68°C. These results indicate that the denaturation characteristics of IgD are distinct from those of IgA and IgM. This deviation reflects the difference in the localized conformation of IgD and, in turn, the nature and strength of the stabilizing forces involved in the molecular conformation.

An antigen determinant site represents the spatial configuration of a small segment of the polypeptide chain. Since the antibody molecule is an IgG, a tetra-chain structure linked by disulfide bridges, the steric effect plays a dominant role in the proper alignment between the antibody-determinant and antigen-determinant sites. A diminution in the antibody-binding capacity reflects a cumulative effect of the disorganization of all the determinant sites at the local level of conformation. The effect of temperature on these myeloma proteins was investigated by employing antigen-antibody reactions. Irreversible disorganization of the antigenic determinant sites of IgD occurred at 61°C for 4 hr (28). Prior to the transition temperature, no loss in the antigen-antibody reaction was observed with IgA and IgM. With further increase in temperature the rate of loss was higher in IgG followed by IgA and IgM. At 72°C the residual activity was 8% for IgG, 50% for IgA, and 75% for IgM. In accordance with the asymmetric distribution of linear and branched chain carbohydrate moieties in IgA and IgM molecules (45, 46), it may be surmised that a similar situation also prevails in IgD. It is plausible that the carbohydrate moieties contribute significantly toward the molecular conformation of IgD, since the carbohydrate content of IgD is 14%. The proximity effect of the oligosaccharide moieties should be taken into consideration to obtain a better understanding of the localized conformation of IgD.

Acknowledgments. The authors wish to express thanks to Dr. George Cartwright and Dr. Austin Sargent for their help in providing a sufficient quantity of blood from the patients, M and P. Thanks are due to Miss Vijay Luxmi Sawh and Mr. Anthony B. Chen for sedimentation equilibrium analyses and to Mr. W. Rankowicz for sedimentation velocity analyses.

This work was supported by the National Cancer Institute of Canada and the Medical Research Council of Canada.

REFERENCES

1. Putnam, F. W., in *The Proteins*, Edited by H. Neurath, Vol. 3, p. 153, Academic Press, New York, 1965.
2. Rowe, D. S. and Fahey, J. L., J. Exp. Med., *121:* 171, 1965.
3. Rowe, D. S. and Fahey, J. L., J. Exp. Med., *121:* 185, 1965.
4. Johansson, S. G. O. and Bennich, H., Immunology, *13:* 381, 1967.
5. Bennich, H., Ishizaka, K., Johansson, S. G. O., Rowe, D. S., Stanworth, D. R. and Terry, W. D., Immunology, *15:* 323, 1968.
6. Saha, A., Edwards, M. A., Sargent, A. U. and Rose, B., Immunochemistry, *5:* 341, 1968.
7. Saha, A., Sambury, S., Smart, K., Heiner, D. C., Sargent, A. U. and Rose, B., J. Immun., *102:* 476, 1969.
8. Jagendorf, A. T., Patchornik, A. and Sela, M., Biochim. Biophys. Acta, *78:* 516, 1963.
9. Robbins, J. B., Haimovich, J. and Sela, M., Immunochemistry, *4:* 11, 1966.
10. Campbell, D. H., Garvey, J. S., Cramer, N. and Sussdorf, D. H., in *Methods in Immunology*, W. A. Benjamin, Inc., New York, 1964.
11. Yphantis, D. A., Biochemistry, *3:* 297, 1964.
12. Saha, A., Sawh, V. and Chen, A. B., Arch. Biochem., *133:* 178, 1969.
13. Hanlon, S., Lamers, K., Lauterbatch, G., Johnson, R. and Schachman, H. K., Arch. Biochem., *99:* 157, 1962.
14. Schachman, H. K., Gropper, L., Hanlon, S. and Putney, F., Arch. Biochem., *99:* 175, 1962.
15. Lamers, K., Putney, F., Steinberg, I. Z. and Schachman, H. K., Arch. Biochem., *103:* 379, 1963.
16. Beckman Instruments Inc., Tech. Bull. ETD-024, March, 1967.
17. Svedberg, T. and Pedersen, K. O., in *The Ultracentrifuge*, Oxford University Press, London, 1940.
18. Schachman, H. K., in *Ultracentrifugation in Biochemistry*, Academic Press, New York, 1959.
19. Casassa, E. F. and Eisenberg, H., Advances Protein Chem., *19:* 287, 1964.
20. Spackman, D. H., Stein, W. H. and Moore, S., Anal. Chem., *30:* 1190, 1958.
21. Hubbard, R. W., Biochem. Biophys. Res. Commun., *19:* 679, 1965.
22. Noltman, E. A., Mahowald, T. A. and Kuby, S. A., J. Biol. Chem., *237:* 1146, 1962.
23. Dische, Z. and Popper, H., Biochem. Z., *175:* 371, 1926.
24. Clamp, J. R. and Putnam, F. W., J. Biol. Chem., *239:* 3233, 1964.
25. Dische, Z. and Shettles, L. B., J. Biol. Chem., *175:* 595, 1948.
26. Warren, L., J. Biol. Chem., *234:* 1971, 1959.
27. Spiro, R. G., J. Biol. Chem., *237:* 646, 1962.
28. Heiner, D. C., Saha, A. and Rose, B., Fed. Proc., *27:* 484, 1968.
29. Schachman, H. K., in Meth. Enzymol., *4:* 32, 1957.
30. Putnam, F. W., Titani, K., Wikler, M. and Shinoda, T., Cold Spring Harbor Symp. Quant. Biol., *32:* 9, 1967.
31. Edmundson, A. B., Sheber, F. A., Ely, K. R., Simonds, N. B., Hutson, N. K. and Rossiter, J. L., Arch. Biochem., *127:* 725, 1968.
32. Chen, R. F., in *Fluorescence*, Edited by G. G. Guilbault, p: 443, Marcel Dekker, Inc., New York, 1967.
33. Chen, R. F., Edelhoch, H. and Steiner, R. F., in *Physical Principles and Techniques of Protein Chemistry*, p. 171, Academic Press, New York, 1969.
34. Brand, L. and Witholt, B., Meth. Enzymol., *9:* 776, 1967.
35. Gally, J. A. and Edelman, G. M., Biopolymer Symp., *1:* 367, 1964.
36. Steiner, R. F. and Edelhoch, H., J. Amer. Chem. Soc., *84:* 2139, 1962.
37. Kronman, M. J., Biochim. Biophys. Acta, *133:* 19, 1967.
38. Edelman, G. M., Cunningham, B. A., Gall, W. E., Gottlieb, P. D., Rutishauer, U. and Waxdal, M. J., Proc. Nat. Acad. Sci., *69:* 78, 1969.
39. Abel, C. A., Spiegelberg, H. L. and Grey, H. M., Biochemistry, *7:* 127, 1968.
40. Porter, R. R., Biochem. J., *73:* 119, 1959.
41. Fleischman, J. B., Ann. Rev. Biochem., *35:* 835, 1966.
42. Spiegelberg, H. L., Prahl, J. and Grey, H. M., Fed. Proc., *28:* 495, 1969.
43. Spiro, R. G., New England J. Med., *281:* 991, 1969.
44. Rosevear, F. W. and Smith, E. L., J. Biol. Chem., *236:* 425, 1961.
45. Dawson, G. and Clamp, J. R., Biochem. J., *107:* 341, 1968.
46. Spragg, B. P. and Clamp, J. R., Biochem. J., *114:* 57, 1969.
47. Saha, A., Chowdhury, P., Sambury, S., Smart, K. and Rose, B., J. Biol. Chem., *245:* 2730, 1970.
48. Edelman, G. M. and Gall, W. E., Ann. Rev. Biochem., *38:* 415, 1969.

THE JOURNAL OF IMMUNOLOGY Vol. 105, No. 1, July 1970

THE ASSESSMENT BY IMMUNOFLUORESCENCE METHODS OF HUMORAL ANTI-MYELIN ANTIBODIES IN MAN[1]

THOMAS S. EDGINGTON AND DONALD J. DALESSIO

From the Division of Clinical Pathology of the Department of Experimental Pathology and the Division of Neurology, Scripps Clinic and Research Foundation, La Jolla, California 92037

Received for publication August 4, 1969

The indirect immunofluorescence assay provides an immunologically specific primary binding test for the measurement and characterization of anti-myelin antibodies in man. Anti-myelin antibodies of the IgG class are found in 88% of normal individuals and appear to be acquired between 1 and 4 years of age, a period associated with active myelination of the central nervous system. A slightly higher titer of these antibodies is observed in the sera of patients with amyotrophic lateral sclerosis than in the sera of normal individuals and of patients with certain other diseases. Anti-myelin antibodies of the IgA and IgM classes are relatively infrequently detected in sera of normal individuals, although they appear with considerable frequency in sera of patients with amyotrophic lateral sclerosis and multiple sclerosis. No significant *in vivo* fixation of these antibodies could be detected by radioimmunochemical means, and it would appear that anti-myelin antibodies may reflect release of myelin immunogen rather than serve a primary role in the mediation of disease.

The presence and some of the structural characteristics of antibody to a number of antigens of the central and peripheral nervous system have been established in certain experimental and clinical diseases. Antibodies (7S) to myelin sheaths and the surface of glial cells capable of inducing complement-dependent (1) dissolution of myelin sheaths and cytotoxic effects on glial cells were demonstrated in experimental allergic encephalomyelitis and in the sera of patients with certain demyelinating diseases by Bornstein and Appel (2, 3). Humoral antibodies to glial cells were demonstrated by Berg and Källén (4) using a cytotoxic assay, and Koprowski and Fernandez (5) employed a lymphocyte-target cell agglutination system to demonstrate sensitized lymphocytes in experimental allergic encephalomyelitis. A number of apparently distinct complement-fixing antibodies have been described. Some of them, which are reactive with ethanolic extracts of nervous tissue, appear to react with lipids (6) rather than with encephalitogenic protein (7). Wilkinson (8) has shown the presence of complement-fixing antibodies reactive with central nervous system antigens in carcinomatous neuropathy, and subsequent studies (9, 10) have demonstrated the apparent neuronal localization of the target antigen. Complement-fixing antibodies to undefined antigenic determinants of the central nervous system were found in sera from subjects with Guillain-Barré syndrome by Melnick (11).

In an attempt to assay anti-myelin antibodies by the indirect immunofluorescence method, Allerand and Yahr (12) reported that normal human IgG reacted uniformly with glial cells and myelin sheaths of the nervous system. It was suggested that this phenomenon might be related to an immunologically nonspecific molecular interaction between IgG and myelin. However, Wilkinson and Zeranski (9) and Croft *et al.* (10), in studying antineuronal antibodies, did not describe the reaction of IgG with myelin.

In the present study we have assessed the immunofluorescence method as a primary binding test for anti-myelin antibodies, and have explored the characteristics of this immune response in man. Pair-labeled radioimmunochemical methods have also been used to assess tissue fixation

[1] This is publication 350 from the Department of Experimental Pathology, Scripps Clinic and Research Foundation. This work was supported in part by United States Public Health Service Research Grants AI-07007 and AM-12920 and by Atomic Energy Commission Contract AT (04-3)-410.

and the potential pathogenetic role of these antibodies *in vivo*.

MATERIALS AND METHODS

Sera and fractions. Sera were collected from normal random individuals with no evidence of neurologic disease and from subjects with clinically established neurologic diseases. IgG fractions of these sera were prepared by precipitation of the γ globulins at 50% ammonium sulfate saturation followed by ion exchange chromatography on DEAE-cellulose according to Levy and Sober (13). Fab fragments of IgG were prepared by papain digestion and isolation on DEAE-cellulose as described by Franklin (14). All sera and their fractions were stored at $-35°C$.

Antisera. Antisera to specific human serum proteins were prepared in rabbits by repeated immunization with 50 to 100 μg of highly purified antigen in incomplete Freund's adjuvant. Anti-IgM and anti-IgA were repeatedly absorbed with IgG to render the antisera specific for the μ and α chains respectively; the specificity was confirmed by Ouchterlony and immunoelectrophoretic techniques. Specificity for the Fc fragment was produced by repeated absorption of anti-IgG with $F(ab')_2$ fragments derived from pepsin digestion of IgG (15). Rabbit antisera to human albumin, transferrin and γ globulin absorbed with human IgG were employed in controls. Sheep antiserum to rabbit γ globulin was prepared in a similar fashion. The IgG fractions of each antiserum were isolated chromatographically (13). Rabbit anti-myelin sera were prepared by repeated immunization of rabbits with 5 mg of purified rat or rabbit myelin incorporated into incomplete Freund's adjuvant.

Fluoresceinated antibodies. The IgG fractions of antisera were fluoresceinated by dialysis according to the method of Clark and Shepard (16), and the fluoresceinated IgG was then fractionated on DEAE-cellulose (17). Following elution of poorly fluoresceinated IgG at 0.01 M phosphate, pH 7.4, an optimally fluoresceinated fraction was eluted with 0.07 M NaCl–0.01 M phosphate pH 7.4 and concentrated to approximately 2 mg protein/ml for use in the immunohistochemical procedures.

Tissue. Fresh human, monkey, rabbit and rat spinal cord blocks were snap-frozen in liquid nitrogen and retained in isopentane at $-35°C$. All tissues were used within 3 months as antigenic reactivity was reduced beyond this period. Recently tissues have been stored at $-76°C$ with somewhat improved antigenic stability.

Immunohistochemical techniques. Unfixed 4-micron sections of human spinal cord were regularly used as the tissue substrate in the indirect immunofluorescence technique (18). Slides were washed 5 min in phosphate-buffered saline (PBS) prior to application of the first layer test serum or serum dilution for 30 min. The titer of the anti-myelin reaction was expressed as the reciprocal of the dilution of test serum. Following three PBS washes, the fluoresceinated anti-human γ globulin or other fluoresceinated antibody was applied for 30 min. Blocking experiments employed a 30-min incubation of the tissue section with the competitive antisera and washing with PBS prior to application of a known human serum containing anti-myelin antibody. In specific experiments to assess the effects of organic solvent fixation on spinal cord, fixation was with acetone for 10 min, or 1:1 ether–ethanol for 10 min followed by 95% ethanol for 20 min.

Myelin. Myelin was isolated from fresh rabbit and rat spinal cord according to the method of Autilio *et al.* (19), and was lyophilized and sorted at $-35°C$.

Tissue absorptions. Selected sera and their IgG fractions were absorbed for 18 to 24 hr at 4°C with 10 mg myelin, 200 mg whole spinal cord, or 200 mg tissue/ml. Following centrifugation the supernatant was employed in the immunofluorescence assay.

Paired label in vivo experiments. The capacity for *in vivo* tissue fixation of anti-myelin antibodies was evaluated using the paired label method of Pressman *et al.* (20) as performed in our laboratory (21). Selected sera or IgG containing anti-myelin antibodies were trace labeled with ^{131}I and matched control serum or IgG devoid of these antibodies were labeled with ^{125}I according to the method of McConahey and Dixon (22). In duplicate experiments the radioiodine labels were reversed. The anti-myelin ^{131}I and control ^{125}I were mixed, absorbed three times with washed rat erythrocytes, and from 2.5 to 6 $\times 10^6$ cpm (approximately 360 μg serum protein or 100 μg IgG) were administered intravenously to three Lewis strain rats. The animals were killed 1 hr later, and specific quantitative fixation of the experimental sera or IgG to spinal cord, peripheral nerve (sciatic), cerebellum, medulla, cerebral cortex, heart, liver, kidney, skeletal muscle, stomach, spleen and erythrocytes was calculated as the percentage of the dose/g of tissue.

Quantitative immunoglobulin assays. Immunoglobulins were quantitated in sera by the radial diffusion method of Mancini *et al.* (23).

RESULTS

The immuunhistochemical reaction with myelin. Eighty-eight per cent of normal sera contained γ globulin reactive with myelin of human spinal cord in the indirect immunofluorescence assay. This was expressed by specific fluorescence of the myelin sheaths of large and small myelinated nerve fibers throughout the spinal cord (Fig. 1). There was no reaction with neurons, but distinct reactions with the cytoplasm and processes of astrocytes were observed with some sera (Fig. 2). On occasion weak reactions with the cytoplasm of oligodendroglia were also observed. Appropriate controls confirmed the immunologic specificity of the anti-myelin reactions (Table I). The IgG fractions of sera with titers of 1:4 were positive at concentrations of 1.4 to 1.8 mg/ml, and specific fluoresceinated antibodies to Fc fragment confirmed that these antibodies belonged to the IgG class.

Anti-myelin antibodies reactive with small myelin sheaths, as in the dorsal columns of the spinal cord, were observed in 80% of the random normal sera with a mean titer of 1.14 for the group (Table II). Eighty-eight per cent of the sera reacted with large myelin sheaths with a mean titer of 1.56. Four of the 50 sera reacted only with large myelin sheaths, suggesting an additional antigenic determinant or a greater concentration of antigen in the myelin of large nerve fibers. Twenty-four per cent of sera reacted independently with the cytoplasm and processes of astrocytes. This latter reaction was not consistently associated with a positive reaction for anti-myelin antibodies, and was not abolished by absorption of the test serum with myelin.

Myelin antigen. The identity of myelin as the target antigen was confirmed using rabbit antisera to purified myelin (Table I). These antisera reacted with myelin sheaths in a fashion indistinguishable from that of the human antibodies, and when incubated with spinal cord prior to application of positive human sera the reaction of human γ globulin with myelin was inhibited. There was no inhibition by sera obtained from these rabbits prior to immunization. No species specificity was apparent, for the anti-myelin reaction was observed with rabbit, rat, monkey and human spinal cord sections. The lability of the myelin antigen(s) was indicated by gradual loss of antigenic reactivity of frozen spinal cord and by marked attenuation following exposure to organic solvents.

Anti-myelin antibodies in neurologic diseases. Anti-myelin antibodies were demonstrated at

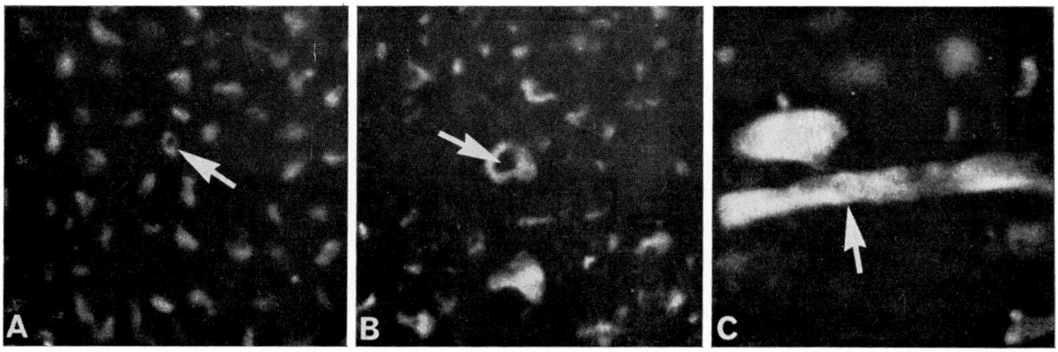

Figure 1. Positive anti-myelin reactions of human sera. Fluoresceinated anti-human γ globulin was used to develop these reactions. *A*, the myelin sheaths of small nerve fibers of the dorsal columns of the spinal cord are shown on cross-section. Minute central non-reactive axon spaces are observed when precise orientation of the fiber is achieved (*arrow*) (× 600). *B*, the morphology of myelin sheaths of the lateral corticospinal tract of human spinal cord is demonstrated. The axon (*arrow*) of the large fiber shown in cross-section does not react (× 1000). *C*, the myelin sheath of a large fiber (*arrow*) of the spinal cord in longitudinal section (× 1000).

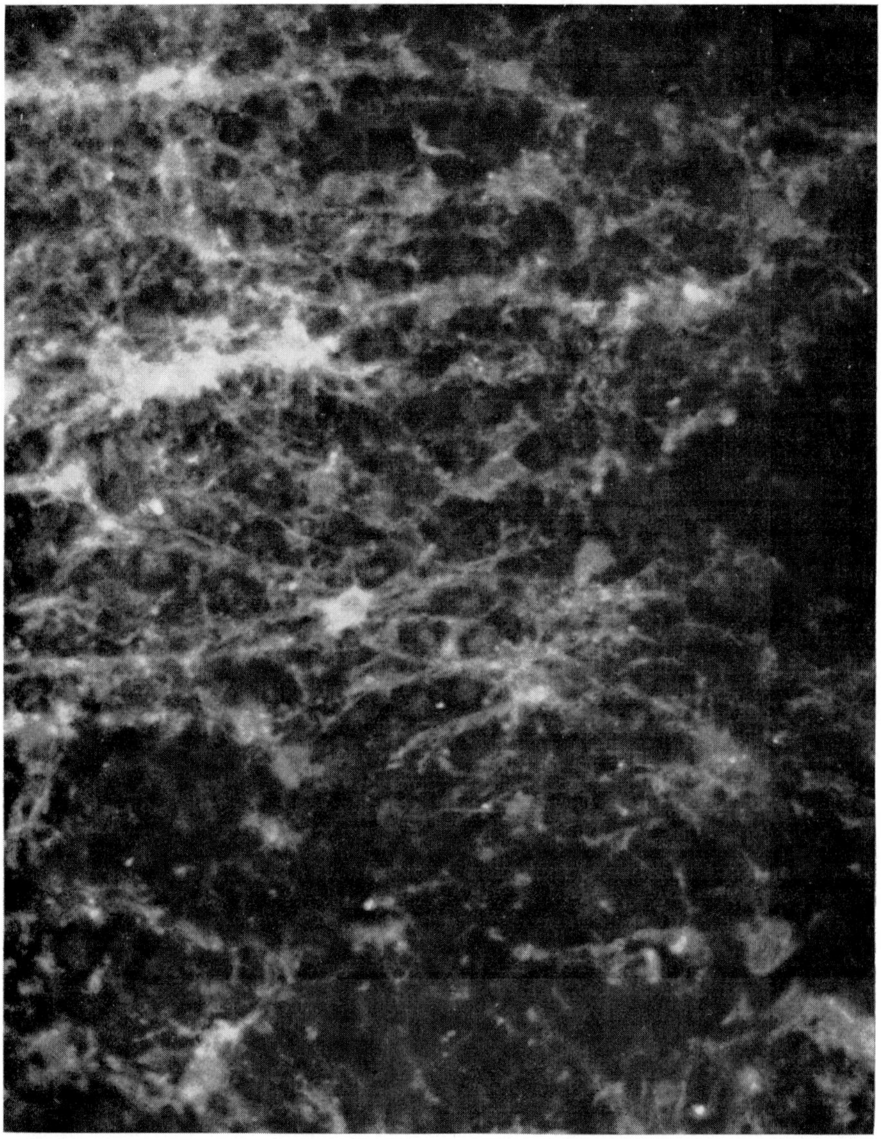

Figure 2. A positive reaction of a test serum with the cytoplasm and processes of fibrillary astrocytes of human spinal cord. There is no reaction with myelin. This was developed with anti-γ globulin, but similar reactions were observed with anti-Fc and anti-IgA.

somewhat higher titer in sera from subjects with amyotrophic lateral sclerosis and multiple sclerosis (Table III), and the highest individual and mean titers observed have been found in these sera. Sequential sera gave relatively consistent titers, although a decrease in titer late in the clinical course has been observed in a few cases. Anti-myelin antibodies were observed in slightly higher titer in a small number of subjects with miscellaneous neurologic diseases whereas normal titers were found in patients with lupus erythematosus. A distinctively lower incidence (38%) and mean titer (0.75) of anti-myelin antibodies were observed in children under 3 years of age (Table III). This period is limited to the first 3 or 4 years of life as is shown in Table IV, and suggests that these antibodies are acquired at this time. There was no correlation

TABLE I

Control reactions for immunologic specificity

Site of Control	Method	Immunofluorescent Reaction with Myelin
Tissue antigen[a]	Incubate with saline	+
	Incubate with rabbit anti-myelin	0
	Incubate with rabbit anti-kidney	+
Test serum with anti-myelin antibodies	Absorb with erythrocytes	+
	Absorb with spinal cord	0
	Absorb with kidney	+
Fluoresceinated anti-γ globulin	Absorb with human IgG	0
	Absorb with human albumin	+

[a] Cryostat sections of human spinal cord.

TABLE II

Incidence and titer of antibodies to central nervous system antigens in 50 random normal sera

Target Antigen[a]	Positive	Titer[b]	Range
	%		
Small myelin	80	1.14 ± 0.81	0–4
Large myelin	88	1.56 ± 0.99	0–4
Astrocytes	24	1.42 ± 0.88	0–2

[a] Human spinal cord.

[b] Precision of the method was ±0.21.

between reactivity in the immunofluorescence assay and the concentration of serum IgG in children, thus lending little support to the concept of a nonspecific concentration-dependent interaction between IgG and myelin.

Anti-myelin antibodies belonging to the IgA and IgM classes were observed in 71% to 73% of sera from patients with amyotrophic lateral sclerosis and multiple sclerosis, whereas only 20% of normal sera contained such antibodies and none was observed in cord sera or sera from young children (Table V). The increased incidence was relatively greater for IgM than for IgA antibodies and was far more distinctive than the mild increase in IgG anti-myelin titer. There was no apparent relationship between clinical activity, onset, or duration of disease except for the occasional terminal decline in antibody titer. Although the pathogenetic relationship is not known, remarkably little demyelination was observed histologically at postmortem examination in the two patients with amyotrophic lateral sclerosis who produced no detectable anti-myelin antibodies.

Fab binding of anti-myelin antibodies. The possibility that the observed reactions might be the result of immunologically nonspecific molecular interactions between myelin and the Fc portion of the IgG molecule was explored with Fab fragments of IgG prepared from eight positive and two negative sera. The IgG fractions, at 10 mg/ml, and the Fab fragments, at 6 to 8 mg/ml, gave equivalent immunofluorescence reactions with myelin.

In vivo binding of anti-myelin antibodies. The capacity of anti-myelin antibodies to localize to myelin or other tissues *in vivo* was assessed by the paired label method. Both sera and IgG from individuals with amyotrophic lateral sclerosis and multiple sclerosis were evaluated. These radiolabeled proteins exhibited no significant specific fixation (±0.005%/g tissue) to spleen, stomach, skeletal muscle, kidney, liver, heart and five regions of the nervous system, spinal cord, cerebral cortex, cerebellum, medulla oblongata and peripheral nerve of normal rats.

DISCUSSION

Antibodies to a variety of tissue antigens of the nervous system previously have been assayed in the sera of experimental animals by indirect immunofluorescence (24–27); however, the nearly uniform reaction of human IgG with myelin has been interpreted as evidence for an immunologically nonspecific interaction between this protein and myelin (12). An interaction of IgG in most normal human sera with myelin is confirmed in this study, but we would contend that this is an immunologically specific reaction based upon: a) the binding of Fab fragments to myelin; b) the lack of correlation between absolute IgG concentration and the titer of anti-

TABLE III

Anti-myelin antibodies in normal sera and in sera from subjects with selected diseases

Titer	Normal		SLE[b]	ALS[c]	Multiple Sclerosis	Other Neurologic Diseases[d]
	Adults	Children[a]				
16				1		
8				4	3	1
4	4	1	1	4	4	5
2	22		4	4	6	5
1	18	2	4	2	2	3
0	5	5	3	2		2
Mean titer	1.56	0.75	1.30	4.35	3.60	2.56
Positive	88%	38%	78%	88%	100%	88%

[a] Sixteen to 36 months of age.
[b] Systemic lupus erythematosus.
[c] Amyotrophic lateral sclerosis.
[d] Parkinson's disease, peripheral neuropathy, carcinomatous neuropathy and cerebrovascular accidents.

TABLE IV

Humoral IgG anti-myelin antibodies in normal individuals

Age	No. Tested	Positive	Titer	
			Mean	Range
years		%		
1–3	8	38	0.75	0–4
3–8	10	90	2.20	0–4
8–12	8	88	3.00	0–4
12–16	9	78	1.40	0–4
16–65	50	88	1.56	0–4

TABLE V

Occurrence of IgA and IgM anti-myelin antibodies

Group	No. of Sera	Anti-Myelin Antibody		
		IgA	IgM	IgA and/ or IgM
Normal				
Adult	50	10	2	10 (20%)
Children[a]	8	0	0	0
Cord[b]	12	0	0	0
Neurologic disease				
Amyotrophic lateral sclerosis	17	9	5	12 (71%)
Multiple sclerosis	15	8	6	11 (73%)
Miscellaneous[c]	16	3	2	5 (32%)

[a] Sixteen to 36 months of age.
[b] Serum from umbilical cord at birth.
[c] Parkinson's disease, peripheral neuropathy, carcinomatous neuropathy and cerebrovascular accident.

myelin reactivity; c) the non-reactivity of IgG from the sera of some individuals; d) the absorption of anti-myelin reactivity by myelin; and e) the appearance of IgA and IgM anti-myelin reactivity in some sera.

The inordinately high incidence of anti-myelin autoantibodies is distinctive but not unique. Issitt and Jackson (28) have demonstrated the presence of cold agglutinins in all of a series of normal individuals. Apparently autoantibody responses may be sustained under circumstances of immunogen availability and tolerated when coupled with functional masking or anatomic isolation of the antigen.

Anti-myelin antibodies have been previously reported in normal individuals but are apparently infrequent in non-immunized animals (24–27). We observed anti-myelin antibodies in 88% of normal human sera, Hughes and Field (29) found 24% of such sera to contain myelotoxic antibodies, Raskin (30) found anti-brain antibodies in 42.6% of normal sera by complement fixation, and Field *et al.* (31) found a 20.4% incidence of antibodies to encephalitogenic protein, a constituent of myelin (26).

Anti-myelin antibodies were first observed in the first 3 to 4 years of life, during a period of active myelination of the nervous system. It may be that release of myelin immunogen during this period may be responsible for the initiation of the anti-myelin response, and additional release of myelin immunogen during life may serve to sustain this immune response. Field and co-workers have suggested that the anti-myelin antibodies observed in association with certain neurologic diseases may be stimulated by injury to the nervous system and constitute a secondary rather than primary immunologic phenomenon (29, 31, 32). The observed chemical differences between normal myelin and that isolated from patients with multiple sclerosis (33) is consistent with, but not proof of, such an hypothesis.

The anti-myelin reaction was not species-specific. The presence of an additional antigenic determinant on large myelinated fibers was suggested. This may be similar to the recognized serologic difference between the myelin of rabbit peripheral nerve and spinal cord (27). Wolfgram and Kotorii (34) have demonstrated differences in amino acid composition and physicochemical properties between myelin of the central nervous system and that of the peripheral nervous system of man.

The inordinately high incidence of IgG anti-myelin antibodies in normal individuals detracts from consideration of a primary pathogenetic role in demyelination, and the mildly increased titers associated with amyotrophic lateral sclerosis and multiple sclerosis are not sufficiently elevated above normal to constitute a distinctive feature of these diseases. IgA and IgM anti-myelin antibodies were observed more frequently in both multiple sclerosis and amyotrophic lateral sclerosis, although the former is a primary demyelinating disease and the latter a primary neuronal disease with secondary demyelination. The presence of IgA or IgM antimyelin antibodies may provide an ancillary laboratory aid in the recognition of these diseases.

Although described in some studies, the pathogenetic significance of IgM anti-myelin antibodies has not been proven. Induction of experimental allergic encephalomyelitis in the rat is associated with the appearance of an antibody, probably IgM, which is capable of suppressing induction of this disease (35), and is not necessarily found in association with successful induction of disease (36). Complement-fixing myelotoxic antibodies have been described in experimental allergic encephalomyelitis (2) as well as multiple sclerosis (3) and some of these antibodies appear in both IgG and IgM classes (37). The complement-fixing capacity of various anti-myelin antibodies observed in our study is a subject of current investigation. No previous information is available concerning the significance of IgA anti-myelin antibodies. Although experimental allergic encephalomyelitis is reputedly mediated by cellular immunity, and the same is hypothesized for some of the demyelinating diseases in man, anti-myelin antibodies may play an ancillary role in the pathogenesis of myelin injury as well as in suppressing or modifying the immune response.

In vivo pairedlabel experiments provided no evidence for localization of anti-myelin antibodies in normal test animals, and the work of Vulpe *et al.* (38) and Broman (39) suggests that the blood-brain barrier would normally preclude passage and localization of antibodies in the central nervous system, whereas increased permeability across the blood-brain barrier has been demonstrated in experimental allergic encephalomyelitis (30) and multiple sclerosis (39). If some anti-myelin antibodies should prove pathogenetically functional, relatively increased permeability of the blood-brain barrier would appear to be a necessary prerequisite. The observations of Oldstone and Dixon (40) and Cutler and Barlow (41), indicating an early increase in vascular permeability of blood vessels in the central nervous system prior to appearance of cellular infiltrates, suggest poorly understood mechanisms by which certain types of humoral antibodies might contribute to the pathogenesis of immunologically mediated demyelination.

Acknowledgments. Support of the initial studies by Dr. Frank J. Dixon is gratefully acknowledged. We are pleased to acknowledge the diligent and skillful assistance of Mrs. Shirley Gourdine and Mrs. Inez Wright, and typing of the manuscript by Mrs. Cleo-Mae Mrozek.

REFERENCES

1. Appel, S. H. and Bornstein, M. B., J. Exp. Med., *119:* 303, 1964.
2. Bornstein, M. B. and Appel, S. H., J. Neuropath. Exp. Neurol., *20:* 141, 1961.
3. Bornstein, M. B., Nat. Cancer Inst. Monogr., *11:* 197, 1963.
4. Berg, O. and Källén, B., Acta Path. Microbiol. Scand., *58:* 72, 1962.
5. Koprowski, H. and Fernandes, M. V., J. Exp. Med., *116:*467, 1962.
6. Harwin, S. M., Paterson, P. Y. and Didakow, N. C., Nature, *189:* 322, 1961.
7. Paterson, P. Y., J. Immun., *78:* 472, 1957.

8. Wilkinson, P. C., Lancet, *1:* 1301, 1964.
9. Wilkinson, P. C. and Zeranski, J., Brain, *88:* 529, 1965.
10. Croft, P. B., Henson, R. A., Urich, H. and Wilkinson, P. C., Brain, *88:* 501, 1965.
11. Melnick, S. C., Brit. Med. J., *1:* 368, 1963.
12. Allerand, C. D. and Yahr, M. D., Science, *144:* 1141, 1964.
13. Levy, H. B. and Sober, H. A., Proc. Soc. Exp. Biol. Med., *103:* 250, 1960.
14. Franklin, E. C., J. Clin. Invest., *39:* 1933, 1960.
15. Nisonoff, A., Wissler, F. C. and Woernley, D. L., Biochem. Biophys. Res. Commun., *1:* 318, 1959.
16. Clark, H. F. and Shepard, C. C., Virology, *20:* 642, 1963.
17. Cebra, J. J. and Goldstein, G., J. Immun., *95:* 230, 1965.
18. Coons, A. H., Leduc, E. H. and Connelly, J. M., J. Exp. Med., *102:* 49, 1955.
19. Autilio, L. A., Norton, W. T. and Terry, R. D., J. Neurochem., *11:* 17, 1964.
20. Pressman, D., Day, E. D. and Blau, M., Cancer Res., *17:* 845, 1957.
21. Edgington, T S., Glassock, R. J., Watson, J. I. and Dixon, F. J., J. Immun., *99:* 1199, 1967.
22. McConahey, P. J. and Dixon, F. J., Int. Arch. Allerg., *29:* 185, 1966.
23. Mancini, G., Carbonara, A. O. and Heremans, J. F., Immunochemistry, *2:* 235, 1965.
24. Beutner, E. H., Witebsky, E., Rose, N. R. and Gerbasi, J. R., Proc. Soc. Exp. Biol Med., *97:* 712, 1958.
25. Sherwin, A. L., Richter, M., Cosgrove, J. B. R. and Rose, B., Science, *134:* 1370, 1961.
26. Rauch, H. C. and Raffel, S., Ann. N. Y. Acad. Sci., *122:* 297, 1965.
27. Field, E. J., Ridley, A. R. and Caspary, E. A., Brit. J. Exp. Path., *44:* 631, 1963.
28. Issitt, P. D. and Jackson, V. A., Vox Sang., *15:* 152, 1968.
29. Hughes, D. and Field, E. J., Clin. Exp. Immun., *2:* 295, 1967.
30. Raskin, N., Arch. Neurol., *73:* 645, 1955.
31. Field, E. J., Caspary, E. A. and Ball, E. J., Lancet, *2:* 11, 1963.
32. Field, E. J. and Hughes, D., Brit. Med. J., *2:* 1399, 1965.
33. Cumings, J. N. and Goodwin, H., Lancet, *1:* 664, 1968.
34. Wolfgram, F. and Kotorii, K., J. Neurochem., *15:* 1291, 1965.
35. Paterson, P. Y. and Harwin, S. M., J. Exp. Med., *117:* 755, 1963.
36. Harwin, S. M., Paterson, P. Y. and Didakow, N. C., Nature, *189:* 322, 1961.
37. Dowling, P. C., Kim, S. U., Murray, M. R. and Cook, S. D., J. Immun., *101:* 1101, 1968.
38. Vulpe, M., Hawkins, A. and Rozdilsky, B., Neurology, *10:* 171, 1960.
39. Broman, T., Acta Neurol. Scand., *40* (Suppl. 10): 21, 1964.
40. Oldstone, M. B. A. and Dixon, F. J., Amer. J. Path., *52:* 251, 1968.
41. Cutler, R. W. P. and Barlow, C. F., J. Neuropath. Exp. Neurol., *26:* 558, 1967.

THE JOURNAL OF IMMUNOLOGY
Vol. 105, No. 1, July 1970

COMMUNICATIONS

L-Asparaginase in Experimental Auto-Immune Disease: Inhibition of Allergic Encephalomyelitis

AMANULLAH KHAN, JOSEPH M. HILL AND MITSUO ADACHI

From the Department of Hematology, Wadley Institutes of Molecular Medicine, 9000 Harry Hines Blvd., Dallas, Texas 75235

Various immunosuppressive drugs have proved to be effective in auto-immune diseases (1). Experimental allergic encephalomyelitis (EAE) has been used to study the effectiveness of various drugs in auto-immune disease in general. Nitrogen mustard, 6-mercaptopurine, chlorambucil, cyclophosphamide and methotrexate have been shown to suppress EAE in animals (2–7).

L-Asparaginase (L-asparagine amido hydrolase), a new antileukemic agent (8), has been shown to be immunosuppressive (9–11). The effectiveness of L-asparaginase in suppressing EAE was studied in Lewis rats as a preliminary to its possible use in auto-immune disease in man. The Lewis strain was chosen for this study because these rats develop a more severe form of the disease (12).

The present report describes the inhibition of EAE in rats by L-asparaginase. This drug, being an enzyme, belongs to an entirely new class of therapeutic agents. It has an advantage over the previously described cytotoxic drugs of being non-myelosuppressive.

MATERIALS AND METHODS

Animals. Male Lewis rats[1] weighing between 150 and 240 g were used. The animals were given commercial food and water daily. Total and differential peripheral leukocyte counts were done at weekly intervals by standard methods.

L-Asparaginase. Escherichia coli L-asparaginase, prepared at the Wadley Institutes of Molecular Medicine, was given intraperitoneally (i.p.) in a varying dosage schedule starting on the day of sensitization (Table I). The enzyme preparation had a specific activity of 354 international units (IU)/mg of protein.

Sensitization of rats. The rats were sensitized by intracutaneous (i.c.) injections of Hartley guinea pig spinal cord emulsified in complete Freund's adjuvant (13). They were observed daily for weakness, ataxia, incontinence, paralysis, convulsions, coma and death.

Histologic studies. Autopsies were done on all the animals that died during the experiment. The surviving animals were exsanguinated under ether anesthesia on the 29th day. Bone marrow smears were made from the femurs and stained with Wright's stain. Brain, spinal cord, liver, spleen, pancreas, kidneys, heart, lungs and skin sites of i.c. injections were removed from each animal and fixed in 10% formalin. The sections were examined after staining with hematoxylin and eosin.

RESULTS

The results of L-asparaginase administration on EAE are summarized in Table I. The same experiment was repeated at 2 months' interval with similar results. All the control animals developed clinical or histologic evidence of EAE in 2 to 3 weeks. One of the control animals, after developing paraplegia and incontinence, died on the 17th day. Autopsy revealed lesions of EAE (13). All the rats that received L-asparaginase 50 IU/kg/day showed clinical signs and lesions of EAE. Further increase in the dose of asparaginase led to a decline in the incidence of EAE. Three of five animals that received 500 IU/kg and two of five that were given 1000 IU/kg developed signs or lesions of EAE. The latter group had histologic evidence of EAE but exhibited no clinical signs of the disease. Complete inhibition of EAE was observed in the rats that received L-asparaginase 2500 IU/kg and 10,000 IU/kg for 28 days.

There was no statistically significant difference in the absolute lymphocyte and neutrophil counts when control and treated animals were compared weekly for 4 weeks. The bone marrows of the treated and control rats showed no differences in

[1] Lewis rats were obtained from Simonsen Laboratories, Inc., Gilroy, Calif.

TABLE I

Inhibition of EAE by L-asparaginase

L-Asparaginase Administered i.p.	No. of Rats	Incidence of EAE		
		Lesions only	Clinical signs and lesions	Total incidence
	5	1	4	5
50 IU/kg daily × 28	5		5	5
500 IU/kg daily × 28	5		3	3
1000 IU/kg daily × 28	5	2		2
2500 IU/kg daily × 28	5			0
10,000 IU/kg daily × 28	5			0

cellularity. No pathologic changes were seen in the sections of liver, spleen, kidneys, lungs, heart, and pancreas. The sites of i.c. inoculation showed chronic granulomatous inflammation interspersed with clear spaces of various sizes, representing dissolved lipid material. There was no difference in the inflammatory reaction in the animals treated with L-asparaginase and the controls.

A group of six rats was treated with L-asparaginase 2500 IU/kg/day for 28 days after sensitization. These animals were observed for 6 weeks after asparaginase therapy was stopped and at the end of this period autopsies were performed. No clinical evidence of EAE was seen during or after therapy. Brain and spinal cord sections failed to reveal lesions of EAE. In a control group of six rats, five developed EAE.

DISCUSSION

L-Asparaginase has been shown to suppress delayed hypersensitivity and antibody formation (11). Immunosuppressive agents have been used to treat auto-immune disease with success. The present study indicates that L-asparaginase inhibits EAE, an experimental auto-immune disease, when given i.p. in doses of 2500 IU/kg or more for 28 days.

Skin lesions resulting from the sensitizing inoculum were studied histologically to see whether the enzyme has an anti-inflammatory effect. The lesions in the control and treated animals showed comparable inflammatory reactions, and therefore the effect of asparaginase is not merely anti-inflammatory.

Suppression of EAE with other immunosuppressive agents is usually temporary and the disease appears within 9 to 20 days after stopping the drug (14). The suppression is prolonged, if not made permanent, by L-asparaginase treatment. It is not clear whether this difference is due to a prolonged immunosuppressive effect of L-asparaginase as compared to other agents, or to permanent inhibition of EAE. Work is currently in progress on these lines.

Most of the cytotoxic drugs that suppress EAE also carry the added risk of myelosuppression. There was no leukopenia or myelosuppression in the treated animals with the doses employed. It is suggested that L-asparaginase may become an important agent in the management of auto-immune disease in man, especially in view of the absence of observable myelosuppression in these experiments.

Acknowledgment. We thank Mr. Salvador Comparini for his assistance in handling the animals.

SUMMARY

EAE was induced in Lewis rats by intracutaneous injections of guinea pig spinal cord in Freund's adjuvant. Clinical or histologic evidence of EAE developed in all the control rats. The experimental animals were treated with L-asparaginase in varying doses. The enzyme was given intraperitoneally starting on the day of inoculation and was continued for 28 days. Doses of 2500 IU/kg/day or higher inhibited EAE in all the animals. EAE did not develop in a group of treated animals during 6 weeks after the cessation of therapy. L-Asparaginase did not produce myelosuppression or an anti-inflammatory effect. It is suggested that L-asparaginase may prove to be useful in the management of auto-immune disease in man.

REFERENCES

1. Paterson, P. Y., Advances Immun., *5:* 131, 1966.
2. Kolb, L. C., Karlson, A. G. and Sayre, G. P., Trans. Amer. Neurol. Ass., *77:* 117, 1952.
3. Hoyer, L. W., Condie, R. M. and Good, R. A., Proc. Soc. Exp. Biol. Med., *103:* 205, 1960.
4. Hoyer, L. W., Good, R. A. and Condie, R. M., J. Exp. Med., *116:* 311, 1962.
5. Thompson, J. D., Austin, R. W. and Streetman, R. P., Neurology, *13:* 505, 1963.
6. Calne, D. B. and Leibowitz, S. N., Nature, *197:* 1309, 1963.
7. Brandriss, M. W., Science, *140:* 186, 1963.
8. Hill, J. M., Roberts, J., Loeb, E., Khan, A.,

MacLellan, A. and Hill, R. W., J.A.M.A., *202:* 882, 1967.

9. Schwartz, R. S., Nature, *224:* 275, 1969.
10. Berenbaum, M. C., Nature, *225:* 550, 1970.
11. Khan, A. and Hill, J. M., J. Immun., *104:* 679, 1970.
12. Paterson, P. Y., Drobish, D. G., Hanson, M. A. and Jacobs, A. F., Int. Arch. Allerg., *37:* 26, 1970.
13. Paterson, P. Y. and Bell, J., J. Immun., *89:* 72, 1962.
14. Paterson, P. Y., Hanson, M. A. and Gerner, E. W., Proc. Soc. Exp. Biol. Med., *124:* 928, 1967.

THE JOURNAL OF IMMUNOLOGY
Vol. 105, No. 1, July 1970
Printed in U.S.A.

Cells Involved in the Immune Response. XVII. The Elution of Antigen by Antigen-Reactive Cells from Antigen-Sensitized Glass Bead Columns. The High Affinity of these Cells for the Glass Bead-Adsorbed Antigen[1]

MAXWELL RICHTER[2]

From the Harry Webster Thorp Laboratories, Division of Immunochemistry and Allergy, McGill University Clinic, Royal Victoria Hospital, Montreal, Quebec, Canada

It was recently reported that antigen-reactive cells (ARC) of specific antigenic specificity in the bone marrow of *normal* rabbits (1–3) and antibody-forming cells (AFC) in the spleens of immune mice (4) can be isolated by the passage of these cells through an antigen-sensitized glass bead column. The cells which traverse the column possess no reactivity with respect to the antigen coating the glass beads; however, the cells which are eluted from the glass beads by vigorous shaking for several minutes react only with the antigen coating the beads and not with any other antigen (1, 2, 4). This highly specific antigenic reactivity of the eluted as compared with the effluent cells can be demonstrated by both *in vitro* incubation of the cells with the antigen (2, 3) or by transfer of the cells to irradiated immunoincompetent (800 R) rabbits (1) or mice (4). In the former case the reactivity of the cells can be demonstrated by the mitotic and blastogenic response of the cells with uptake of tritiated thymidine only in the presence of the specific antigen, while in the latter case it can be shown that the eluted cells reconstitute immunologic responsiveness only with respect to the antigen used to coat the glass beads. The normal rabbit bone marrow lymphoid cells are ARC and not AFC, since the AFC in the bone marrow-reconstituted irradiated recipient are of recipient, and not donor, origin (5). Although the antigenic specificity of the immune response in the recipient rabbit is determined by the antigen used to coat the beads (1), it is interesting that very few of the eluted cells (2 to 10 $\times 10^6$) are required to reconstitute the immune response to the same extent as a much larger number of unfractionated bone marrow cells (500 $\times 10^6$). The interpretation previously offered for these results is that only a small number of the whole bone marrow cell suspension is committed to any specific antigen and that only these cells are activated once they are challenged with the specific antigen (1). However, this interpretation has recently been questioned (3) in the sense that it would not appear possible that such few eluted cells could wholly reconstitute the immune response. Recent findings in this laboratory (6) shed further light on this matter. It was demonstrated that normal bone marrow ARC cells could be activated by *in vitro* incubation with the specific antigen in a much lower concentration than that required by intravenous injection to induce an immune response in the irradiated recipient rabbit. Thus, it would appear that increasing the number of possible collisions between the antigen and the ARC by confining both components in a small volume for 24 hr at 37°C might result in a marked increase in the specific reactivity (number of activated ARC/number of total specific ARC) of the ARC population. It would therefore be expected that ARC which are eluted from an antigen-sensitized glass bead column would be maximally activated since all would have been in direct contact with the antigen. As will be seen below, antigen is in fact eluted with the lymphoid ARC from the antigen-sensitized glass bead column.

The antigens used were human serum albumin (HSA) (Hyland Laboratories, Los Angeles, Calif.) and bovine γ globulin (BGG) (Pentex Incorp., Kankakee, Ill.). HSA-^{125}I was obtained from the Charles C. Frosst Co., Montreal (^{125}I to HSA = 1:1). These two antigens, HSA and BGG, were found to have no, or undetectable, cross-reactivity in our hands. The antigen-sensitized glass bead column was prepared as previously described (1, 3) except that nitric acid was used instead of aqua regia. In the first series of three experiments HSA was combined with HSA-^{125}I to contain 10^8 cpm/100 mg HSA as measured in a

[1] Supported by a grant from the Medical Research Council, Canada.

[2] Medical Research Associate, Medical Research Council, Canada.

TABLE I

The elution of "fixed" antigen (HSA) from HSA-sensitized glass bead columns by shaking the beads with or without specifically adsorbed bone marrow cells.

Material Analyzed for ^{125}I Content	Radioactive Content of Preparation	
	Total radioactivity	No. of HSA mol/10^6 cells
	cpm	
Original HSA-^{125}I preparation (100 mg) incubated with beads	100×10^6	
Recovered HSA-^{125}I not fixed to beads	95×10^6	
3rd wash of beads (600 ml medium)	35	
Glass beads following 3rd wash	225,000	
Effluent cells (150×10^6 cells)	2,644	
3rd wash of effluent cells	32	
Effluent cells after 3rd wash	2,224	1.3×10^5
Eluted cells (20×10^6 cells)	44,385	
3rd wash of eluted cells	41	
Eluted cells after 3rd wash	38,208	2×10^7
HSA-^{125}I sensitized glass beads after 5th wash (500 ml)	216,000	
5th wash	52	
Supernatant of HSA-sensitized glass beads shaken for 5 min with medium (5 ml)	46,055	
Supernatant of HSA-sensitized glass beads shaken for a further 5 min with medium (5 ml)	4,655	

Packard gamma counter. This preparation was used to sensitize the glass beads. The beads were then washed with medium 199 (Microbiological Associates, Bethesda, Md.) to the point where no further radioactivity could be detected in the wash solution (600 ml). The glass beads were then washed with a further 200 ml of medium. A suspension of normal bone marrow cells (400 to 500×10^6) prepared as previously described (1) was then passed through the glass bead column. The cells which passed through (effluent cells) were then washed three times with 4 ml of medium 199 and each of the washes and the final cell preparation were analyzed for radioactive content. The glass beads with their retained cells were shaken in a flask with 5 ml of medium for 5 min. The cells which came off the beads (eluted cells) were also washed five times with medium 199 and the washes and the cell preparation were analyzed for their content of ^{125}I. As can be seen in Table I, 95% of the HSA was recovered following incubation with the glass beads. Following the passage of 600 ml of medium through the column, 225,000 cpm HSA could still be detected on the glass beads. The effluent cells managed to dislodge a further amount of HSA (1.3×10^5 molecules HSA/10^6 cells) while the eluted cells carried with them 200×10^5 molecules HSA/10^6 cells. It must be emphasized that this HSA could not be eluted by the simple passage of medium through the column. However, it is interesting to note (Table I) that the HSA-adsorbed glass beads could be made to liberate HSA simply by shaking them in the absence of cells. Moreover, the amount of HSA eluted was as great as the amount eluted in the presence of specifically-adsorbed ARC. Similar results were obtained in the two other experiments.

TABLE II

The uptake of HSA-^{125}I by bone marrow cells eluted from HSA- and BGG-sensitized glass bead columns

Cell Preparation Incubated with HSA (10^6 cpm)	Uptake of HSA-^{125}I by the Cell Preparation (No. of HSA mol/10^6 Cells)
Cells eluted from HSA-sensitized glass bead column	
Exp. I (20×10^6 cells)	4.5×10^6
Exp. II (1.5×10^6 cells)	6.2×10^6
Exp. III (8.5×10^6 cells)	13×10^6
Average	8×10^6
Cells eluted from BGG-sensitized glass bead column	
Exp. I (0.9×10^6 cells)	10^6
Exp. II (9×10^6 cells)	2×10^6
Exp. III (18×10^6 cells)	2.5×10^6
Average	1.8×10^6

In a second series of six experiments, bone marrow cells were passed through either an HSA- or BGG-sensitized glass bead column. The eluted cells (HSA-ARC and BGG-ARC) were then incubated overnight at 4°C with HSA-^{125}I (10^6 cpm equivalent to 10^{15} molecules HSA), then washed five times with medium 199 and counted in a Packard gamma counter. As can be seen in Table II, the number of HSA molecules taken up by 10^6 HSA-ARC was consistently three to four times greater than that taken up by the BGG-ARC cells. Furthermore, since the eluted cells already possessed 20×10^6 molecules HSA/cell (Table I), the number of HSA molecules adsorbed/eluted cell, as presented in Table II, is actually much greater (20×10^6 plus 8×10^6). The results could have been anticipated as it would be expected that HSA-ARC would have a greater affinity for HSA than would BGG-ARC. In fact, it might be asked why BGG-ARC took up any HSA at all. The answer probably lies in the fact that a large number of the cells eluted from the glass beads on shaking (eluted cells) are not antigen-specific ARC, but rather uncommitted ARC or nonspecifically adsorbed immunoincompetent lymphoid cells (1, 3). Such cells would interact with any antigen nonspecifically and, because of their relatively large number, would tend to mask the very high uptake of the antigen by the specific ARC.

The finding that glass bead-adsorbed antigen can be eluted with the cells from the glass beads to the extent of 20×10^6 molecules/cell might facilitate an understanding of the greater efficacy of these cells, on a numerical basis, as compared to the whole bone marrow cell preparation, in transferring immunocompetence to ARC-depleted irradiated rabbits. These eluted cells would already have adsorbed a large number of antigen molecules, probably sufficient in number to activate the majority of them. On the other hand, the intravenous administration of the whole bone marrow cell preparation followed by the antigen would not result in a sufficient number of collisions of ARC and antigen to activate all of the specific ARC. Furthermore, a large number of the antigen molecules would probably be taken up by host cells, which are largely immunoincompetent. Thus, it is not surprising that a relatively few eluted ARC could transfer immunocompetence to the same extent as does a whole bone marrow cell suspension (1). The finding that much less antigen is required to activate the ARC following *in vitro* incubation of the cells prior to their transfer (6) would also support the interpretation offered above, that the greater number of collisions between the ARC and antigen incubated *in vitro* prior to transfer more than offsets the administration of a much larger number of unincubated cells.

In summary, it has been demonstrated that antigen supposedly "fixed" to glass beads can be eluted by shaking of these beads in culture medium following the adsorption of specifically-committed bone marrow ARC. A similar amount of antigen can be eluted from the beads by shaking them in the absence of adsorbed cells. It has also been demonstrated that cells eluted from the antigen-sensitized glass beads have a much higher affinity for this antigen than for a heterologous, non-cross-reacting antigen.

REFERENCES

1. Abdou, N. I. and Richter, M., J. Exp. Med., *130:* 141, 1969.
2. Singhal, S. K. and Wigzell, H., Fed. Proc., *28:* 309, 1969.
3. Singhal, S. K. and Wigzell, H., J. Exp. Med., *131:* 149, 1970.
4. Wigzell, H. and Andersson, B., J. Exp. Med., *129:* 23, 1969.
5. Richter, M. and Abdou, N. I., J. Exp. Med., *129:* 1261, 1969.
6. Abdou, N. I. and Richter, M., J. Immun., *104:* 1009, 1970.

THE JOURNAL OF IMMUNOLOGY
Vol. 105, No. 1, July 1970

Printed in U.S.A.

Some Characteristics of Anti-Dinitrophenyl Antibody of the Gray Snapper[1]

WARREN J. RUSSELL, EDWARD W. VOSS JR. AND M. MICHAEL SIGEL

From the Department of Microbiology, University of Miami School of Medicine, Miami, Florida 33152, the Variety Children's Research Foundation, Miami, Florida, the Lerner Marine Laboratory, Bimini, Bahamas, and the Department of Microbiology, University of Illinois, Urbana, Illinois 61801

The primary structure of marine teleost and elasmobranch antibody molecules resembles that of mammals. Shark (1) and grouper (W. J. Russell and L. W. Clem, unpublished) possess heavy and light chains similar in molecular weight to those found in higher animals. However, in contrast with mammals, only γ M immunoglobulin appears to be synthesized, and may exist in 19S and 7S forms (1, 2), both of which are electrophoretically and antigenically indistinguishable. The gray snapper, *Lutjanus griseus*, is of particular interest since a 7S molecular species has not been observed. More significantly, however, Clem and Sigel (3) found that a substantial amount of snapper macroglobulin was relatively insensitive to reduction with mercaptoethanol, suggesting the existence of a modified configuration or linkage of peptide chains. As a prelude to structural analysis, we have evaluated some functional capabilities of snapper antibody and explored the possible existence of 7S antibody. These experiments were facilitated by using purified antibody against a haptenic determinant (2,4-dinitrophenol).

Gray snappers were maintained in marine tidal waters and immunized intramuscularly with dinitrophenylated hemocyanin (4) in complete Freund's adjuvant. The hemocyanin was derived from the keyhole limpet (Pacific Bio-Marine Supply Co.) and substituted with approximately 200 dinitrophenyl (DNP) groups/mol of hemocyanin. Animals were anesthetized with Tricaine (Sigma Chemical Co., St. Louis, Mo.) prior to immunization and bleeding. Sera from each animal were monitored by passive hemagglutination (5) using sheep erythrocytes coated with DNP-hemocyanin and DNP-bovine γ globulin. From two separate serum pools (day 14 and days 98 to 172 after primary stimulation) anti-DNP antibodies were purified by immune adsorption on to DNP human serum albumin bromoacetyl cellulose and eluted with an excess of DNP-glycine according to the method of Robbins *et al.* (2, 6). However, Dowex 1-X8 could not be used to separate DNP-glycine from antibody because the protein adsorbed to the resin. Thus, the complex was dialyzed against 0.072 M phosphate, pH 8.0, at 4°C until its optical density (360 nm) was <0.05. To improve antibody yields the material was then subjected to variations in pH by means of a 3-hr dialysis against 0.2 M NaCl during which the pH was gradually adjusted from 8.0 to 3.2 to 8.0 to 11.0 to 8.0. Each antibody preparation recovered in this manner was found to be 80% to 85% active when submitted to readsorption onto the adsorbent.

TABLE I

Density gradient centrifugation of purified snapper anti-DNP antibody[a]

Fraction	Snapper Antibody				Controls	
	Day 14		Days 98–172		IgG	19S IgM
	OD_{280}	Titer	OD_{280}	Titer	Titer	Titer
1	<0.05	<1:2	<0.05	<1:2	<1:20	<1:20
2	<0.05	<1:2	<0.05	<1:2	1:40	<1:20
3	<0.05	<1:2	<0.05	<1:2	1:320	<1:20
4	0.08	<1:2	<0.05	<1:2	1:2560	<1:20
5	0.08	<1:2	0.09	1:4	1:1280	1:20
6	0.10	1:8	0.11	1:16	1:320	1:80
7	0.12	1:32	0.12	1:32	1:40	1:320
8	0.14	1:64	0.13	1:64	<1:20	1:1280
9	0.10	1:32	0.13	1:64	<1:20	1:640
10	0.10	1:16	0.10	1:32	<1:20	1:40

[a] Undiluted samples were applied to an equilibrated gradient (six concentrations of sucrose ranging from 10% to 37%) and spun at 100,000 × G for 16 hr. Each of the 10 fractions collected was diluted in phosphate-buffered saline, pH 7.2, the OD_{280} was determined (corrected for 37% sucrose (OD_{280} = 0.059), and the antibody titer was measured by passive hemagglutination.

Purified antibody obtained by immune adsorption passively agglutinated erythrocytes coated with either DNP-hemocyanin or DNP-bovine γ globulin and precipitated both of these antigens

[1] This work was supported by Public Health Service Research Grants AI-05758 and AI-08288 from the National Institute of Allergy and Infectious Diseases.

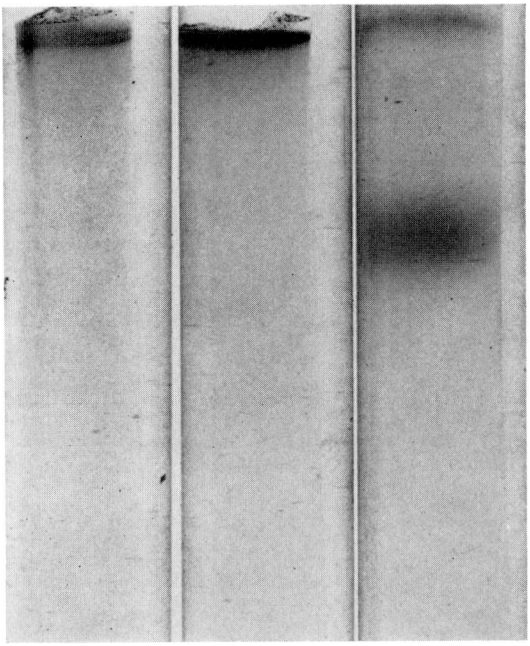

Figure 1. Polyacrylamide gel electrophoresis. Purified snapper antibody (150 μg) was applied to 7.5% gels and electrophoresed at 4 mg/tube for 1 hr at room temperature. *Left,* 14 days; *middle,* 98 to 172 days; *right,* mixture of 75 μg each of shark 19S and 7S IgM.

in gel diffusion. Reactions could be inhibited with 10^{-4} M ε-DNP-L-lysine but not with concentrations of hemocyanin up to 1%.

The molecular form(s) of purified γ M anti-DNP in each isolation was determined by density gradient centrifugation (7) and polyacrylamide disc electrophoresis (8). Table I depicts the location of known 7S and 19S molecules within the gradient. These controls consisted of rabbit 7S IgG anti-DNP and shark 19S IgM anti-bovine γ globulin, the purities of which were predetermined by gel diffusion and disc gel electrophoresis. Both snapper antibody preparations appeared to contain only molecules with sedimentation properties similar to the 19S control. No serologic test was made for the presence of univalent antibody fractions 4 and 5, but disc gel electrophoresis (Fig. 1) failed to disclose a protein that would correspond to 7S antibody. The antibody diffused only slightly into the gel, typical of 19S γ M under these conditions, with no traces of other materials entering the gel. Each antibody sample contained 6 M urea to avoid misinterpretation due to noncovalent aggregation.

Ligand-binding properties were studied by equilibrium dialysis as previously described (2). Prior to binding studies it was determined by optical density readings at 278 and 360 nm that

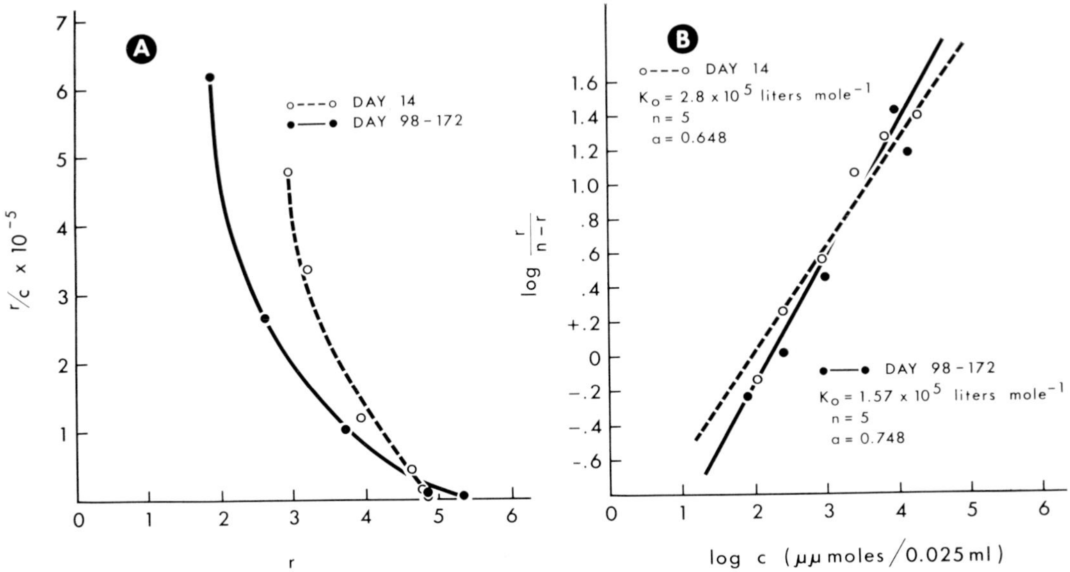

Figure 2. Equilibrium dialysis. Purified snapper antibody (1.06 and 1.32 mg/ml) was equilibrated at 4°C for 22 hr against various concentrations of ^{3}H-ε-DNP-aminocaproic acid. Samples were placed in Bray's scintillation fluid and counted in a Packard Tri-Carb spectrometer. The regression lines (Fig. 2*B*) were calculated by the least squares method. r = Mols hapten bound/mol of antibody (assuming m.w. = 900,000 and $E^{1\%}_{280}$ = 13.7). The value for antibody concentration was adjusted to correspond to 100% activity. c = Free hapten concentration (mols/liter); K_0 = average intrinsic association constant; n = valence; a = heterogeneity index.

less than 2% of the sites contained bound DNP-glycine from the purification procedure. Figure 2*A* shows the binding curves of each preparation using ^{3}H-ε-DNP-aminocaproic acid as ligand (9). A valence of 5 was measured for both preparations. A Sips plot (10) of the data (Fig. 2*B*) shows the antibody to have a relatively low affinity for the ligand with an average intrinsic association constant (K_0) of 1.6 to 2.8 × 10^5 liters/mol. The slope (a) of the Sips plots indicated a heterogeneity index of 0.65 to 0.75.

The techniques employed in this study demonstrated the presence of only heavy (19S) antibody having a valence of 5. In this respect, the present findings differ from those made from the sera of the nurse shark (2) and grouper (11) in which substantial amounts of both heavy and light IgM anti-DNP antibody were found. The association constants determined for the early and late snapper antibodies denote low affinity with no observed increase in magnitude with time, unlike mammalian IgG antibody in which 1000-fold or greater increases in association constants with time have been reported (12). The observed valence of 5, as compared with the theoretical value of 10, is probably a reflection of the low association constant and the sensitivity of the measuring technique.

SUMMARY

Gray snappers were immunized with dinitrophenylated hemocyanin and purified antibodies to the haptenic determinant (2,4-dinitrophenol) were obtained from two serum pools by by immune absorption. Examination of these antibodies revealed a single high molecular weight protein with an apparent valence of 5 and a relatively low binding constant.

REFERENCES

1. Clem, L. W. and Small, P. A., J. Exp. Med., *125:* 893, 1967.
2. Voss, E. W., Russell, W. J. and Sigel, M. M., Biochemistry, *8:* 4866, 1969.
3. Clem, L. W. and Sigel, M. M., *Phylogeny of Immunity*, p. 209, University of Florida Press, 1966.
4. Eisen, H. N., Meth. Med. Res., *10:* 115, 1964.
5. Stavitsky, A. B., J. Immun., *72:* 360, 1954.
6. Robbins, J. B., Haemovich, J. and Sela, M., Immunochemistry, *4:* 11, 1967.
7. Edelman, G. M., Kunkel, H. G. and Franklin, E. C., J. Exp. Med., *108:* 105, 1958.
8. Ornstein, L., Ann. N. Y. Acad. Sci., *121:* 321, 1964.
9. Green, I., Paul, W. E. and Benacerraf, B., J. Exp. Med., *123:* 859, 1966.
10. Sips, R., J. Chem. Phys., *16:* 490, 1948.
11. Clem, L. W. and Small, P. A., Fed. Proc., *27* (No. 2, Abst.): 684, 1968.
12. Eisen, H. N. and Siskind, G. W., Biochemistry, *3:* 996, 1964.

THE JOURNAL OF IMMUNOLOGY
Vol. 105, No. 1, July 1970
Printed in U.S.A.

An Immunogenic Polysaccharide-Protein Conjugate[1]

R. J. FIELDER,[2] C. T. BISHOP,[2] S. F. GRAPPEL[3] AND F. BLANK[3]

From the Biochemistry Laboratory, National Research Council of Canada, Ottawa, Canada, and the Skin and Cancer Hospital, Temple University Health Sciences Center, Philadelphia, Pennsylvania 19140

As part of a continuing program to relate structure to specificity in polysaccharide antigens it was desirable to obtain antisera against well-defined polysaccharides. Polysaccharides are known to be antigenic in mice (1) and man (2), but usually are not antigenic in rabbits (1). Mice provide only small quantities of antisera, and clinical facilities and suitable volunteers are needed if man is the donor. It would therefore be convenient if a method could be found to induce antibodies to polysaccharides in rabbits.

Low molecular weight carbohydrates can be linked to an antigenic protein carrier by diazo-coupling of their *p*-aminophenylglycosides to histidyl, lysyl, and tyrosyl side chains (3–5). An analogous approach has been used to couple an acidic polysaccharide to serum globulin (6). However, the procedure involved successive *p*-nitrobenzylation of the polysaccharide, reduction to the *p*-aminobenzyl ether, diazotization, coupling, and a number of purification steps. The present communication describes a new, simple and practical method for preparing antigenic polysaccharide-protein conjugates.

It is known that replacement of one chlorine atom in 2,4,6-trichloro-*s*-triazine (cyanuric chloride) deactivates the remaining two so that stepwise reactions can be obtained by temperature control (7, 8). Advantage of this property was taken to covalently link a polysaccharide to a protein as follows:

The polysaccharide (162 mg of galactomannan I from *Epidermophyton floccosum*) was dissolved in water (2 ml) and cooled to 4°C. To the cooled, stirred solution was added a solution of 2,4,6-trichloro-*s*-triazine (9.3 mg) in dimethylformamide (0.5 ml). The reaction was stirred at 4°C for 1 hr before addition of a solution of bovine γ globulin (162 mg) in physiologic saline (2 ml). The solution was then stirred at 25°C for 1 hr, diluted with an equal volume of water, and kept at 5°C for 18 hr. Low molecular weight products were removed by dialysis against distilled water for 30 hr and the non-dialysable material was recovered by freeze-drying; yield, 294 mg.

Evidence of a cross-linked product was obtained by disc electrophoresis that revealed a component having a mobility that was intermediate between the unreacted polysaccharide and γ globulin and giving a positive reaction with both amido black and periodate-Schiff reagents (9).

The conjugate, in Freund's complete adjuvant, was injected into white male rabbits (New Zealand strain); rabbits 1 and 2 received a total of 20 mg each and rabbits 3 and 4 a total of 40 mg each. Two sets of injections, subcutaneous and intramuscular, were made with an interval of 3 weeks. Figure 1 shows the curves for the complement fixation reaction with the galactomannan of sera obtained from these rabbits 12 days after the final injections. Rabbits 1 and 2 gave the best responses to the galactomannan. The rabbits were subsequently given two injections of the galactomannan (5 mg) in sterile saline 1 month and 3 months later. Precipitins to the polysaccharide, the conjugate and the γ globulin were then detectable by gel diffusion analysis.

The best antiserum, that from rabbit 2, was absorbed with bovine γ globulin until no further precipitate was detectable. The absorbed antiserum still gave precipitins with the polysaccharide and with the conjugate in gel diffusion (Fig. 2); it contained 51 μg of precipitating antibody nitrogen/ml to the galactomannan I. The minor, secondary precipitin bands were shown by gel diffusion analysis to be due to small amounts of a glucan and a galactomannan II that were present, together with galactomannan I, in *E. floccosum*. It is clear that the chemical procedure

[1] This investigation was supported in part by Public Health Service Research Grant 1R01 AI07705 from the National Institute of Allergy and Infectious Diseases, and by a grant from the John A. Hartford Foundation, Inc., New York, N. Y.

[2] Biochemistry Laboratory, National Research Council of Canada.

[3] Skin and Cancer Hospital, Temple University Health Sciences Center.

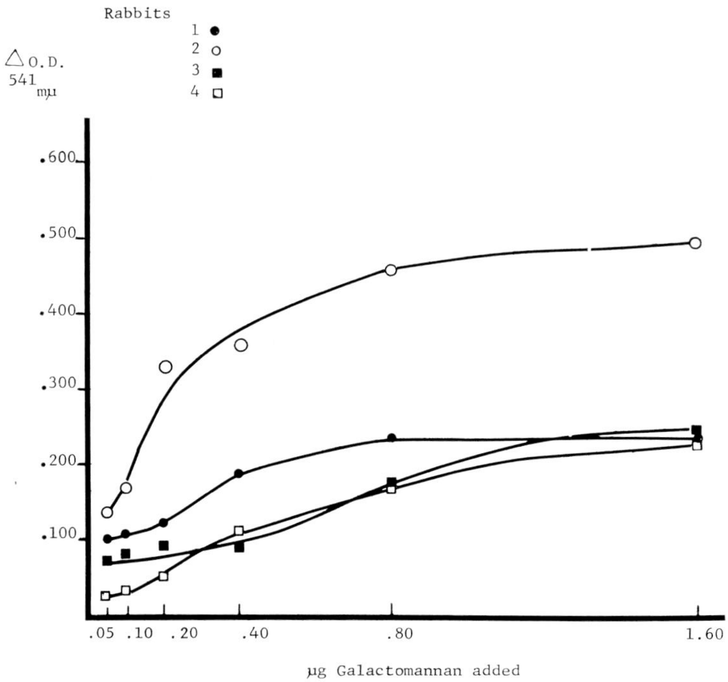

Figure 1. Complement fixation analysis of the reactivity of galactomannan I of *E. floccosum* with 0.2 ml of rabbit antiserum against the polysaccharide-protein conjugate diluted 1:100. Δ O.D. 541 nm is the difference between the optical density of the antiserum blank and the reaction mixture at 541 nm.

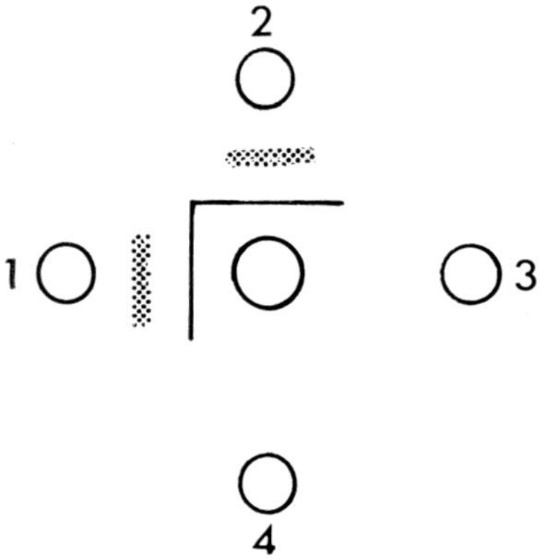

Figure 2. Diagrammatic representation of immunodiffusion analysis of rabbit antiserum to the conjugate absorbed with bovine γ globulin. *Peripheral wells: 1,* galactomannan I, 100 μg/ml; *2,* galactomannan-bovine γ globulin complex, 500 μg/ml; *3,* bovine γ globulin, 100 μg/ml; *4,* saline. *Central well:* rabbit antiserum to galactomannan-bovine γ globulin conjugate absorbed with bovine γ globulin.

used to separate these three polysaccharides (10) was not sufficiently sensitive to detect or prevent this minor cross-contamination.

As a check on the specificity of the antiserum, the following polysaccharides were tested for cross-reactivity by gel diffusion, complement fixation and precipitin ring tests: dextran, baker's yeast mannan, larch arabinogalactan, guar galactomannan, and λ carrageenin. None of these polysaccharides cross-reacted with this antiserum when tested by gel diffusion and complement fixation tests. Only the λ carrageenin gave a faint precipitin ring, possibly due to precipitation of globulin by the sulfate groups in this polysaccharide. The galactomannan, when injected alone, elicited no antibody response.

Rabbit 2 was tested for cutaneous hypersensitivity reactions 5 weeks following the last injection with galactomannan-globulin conjugate. Delayed-type reactions were obtained with the galactomannan, the whole conjugate and the bovine γ globulin. Reactions with the polysaccharide and the conjugate started to appear after 6 hr, reached a peak at 24 hr and were still strong at 48 hr. Injection sites were raised and the average diameter of erythema was 15 mm for both antigens. The reaction with the bovine γ globulin appeared after 24 hr. The site of injection was hemorrhagic. The average diameter of erythema was 18 mm and decreased at 48 hr.

These results show that neutral polysaccharides can be convalently linked to proteins by reaction with cyanuric chloride and that such conjugates will induce antibodies to the polysaccharide in the rabbit. Variations on the method of cross-linking and the specificity of the response are being investigated and will be reported elsewhere.

SUMMARY

A galactomannan isolated from the dermatophyte *Epidermophyton floccosum* was covalently linked to bovine γ globulin by reaction with 2, 4,6-trichloro-*s*-triazine (cyanuric chloride). This polysaccharide-protein conjugate induced humoral antibody formation in the rabbit. The antibodies gave precipitin reactions with the polysaccharide, with the conjugate and with the γ globulin. Absorption of the antiserum with γ globulin left a preparation of antibodies that were specific for the polysaccharide. Hyperimmunized rabbits also developed cutaneous hypersensitivity to the polysaccharide.

REFERENCES

1. Avery, O. T. and Goebel, W. F., J. Exp. Med., *58:* 730, 1933.
2. Francis, T., Jr. and Tillett, W. S., J. Exp. Med., *52:* 573, 1930.
3. Landsteiner, K., *The Specificity of Serological Reactions*, Harvard University Press, Cambridge, Mass., 1945.
4. Goebel, W. F. and Avery, O. T., J. Exp. Med., *50:* 521, 1929.
5. Allen, P. Z., Goldstein, I. J. and Iyer, R. N., Biochemistry, *6:* 3029, 1967.
6. Goebel, W. F. and Avery, O. T., J. Exp. Med., *54:* 431, 1931.
7. Thurston, J. T., Dudley, J. R., Kaiser, D. W., Hechenbleikner, I., Schaefer, F. C. and Holm-Hansen, D., J. Amer. Chem. Soc., *23:* 2981, 1951.
8. Beech, W. F., J. Chem. Soc. (C), 466, 1967.
9. Ornstein, L., Ann. N. Y. Acad. Sci., *121:* 321, 1964.
10. Bishop, C. T., Perry, M. B. and Blank, F., Canad. J. Chem., *44:* 2291, 1966.

THE JOURNAL OF IMMUNOLOGY

Vol. 105, No. 1, July 1970
Printed in U.S.A.

Consumption of Hamster Complement by Bacterial Endotoxin

WILLIAM A. HOOK, RALPH SNYDERMAN AND STEPHAN E. MERGENHAGEN

From the Immunology Section, Laboratory of Microbiology, National Institute of Dental Research, National Institutes of Health, Bethesda, Maryland 20014

While studying the interaction of normal hamster serum incubated with endotoxin (LPS) to form a substance capable of releasing histamine from mast cells, it was observed that a concomitant loss of total hemolytic complement (C) activity occurred (1). Gewurz *et al.* have studied reaction mixtures containing guinea pig serum incubated with LPS and found that there was a preferential consumption of the terminal C components C3 through C9 (2). In contrast, we have found that LPS incubated in normal hamster serum under similar conditions caused a marked consumption of C1, C4 and C2 in addition to classical C EDTA (C3–C9). Accordingly, experiments were performed to compare C consumption by LPS with hamster and guinea pig serum under varying experimental conditions.

Blood was collected from female golden hamsters 5 to 10 weeks of age obtained from the Animal Production Unit, National Institutes of Health. Animals were anesthetized by carbon dioxide inhalation, blood collected by cardiac puncture was allowed to clot in individual tubes and the sera from 20 to 30 animals were pooled. Pooled serum from guinea pigs was purchased as ether-free, fresh frozen complement (Texas Biological Laboratories, Fort Worth, Texas). Consumption of C activity in 1 ml serum diluted 1:2 was measured by incubation with 100 μg LPS contained in 0.1 ml for 20 min at 37°C unless specified otherwise. The diluent used was gelatin-Veronal-buffered saline (GVB) at pH 7.3 containing calcium and magnesium in concentrations optimal for immune hemolysis by human and guinea pig C (3). Residual total C activity was measured by hemolysis of antibody-sensitized sheep erythrocytes (EA) as previously described (4). C components were quantitated using intermediates prepared from guinea pig serum and sheep erythrocytes (3, 5). Residual C3–C9 was assayed by diluting serum in 0.01 M EDTA-GVB without added calcium and magnesium and titrating with EAC$\overline{1}$, $\overline{4}$,$\overline{2}$. LPS was extracted from *Veillonella alcalescens* by the method of Westphal and Lüderitz (6). LPS for *Salmonella typhosa* strain 0901 was purchased from Difco Laboratories, Detroit, Mich. Normal hamster serum was adsorbed twice at 1°C for 20 min with 2 mg/ml heat-killed (100°C, 30 min) washed *V. alcalescens* or *S. typhosa* cells. After adsorption, cells were removed by centrifugation at 1°C for 20 min at 10,000 × G.

Table I indicates that the percentage of total C activity consumed at 37°C for 20 min by equal amounts of *V. alcalescens* was greater with hamster serum than that observed with guinea pig serum (97% *vs* 30%). The reaction between LPS and hamster serum yielded a profile of complement consumption resembling that of a typical antigen-antibody reaction exhibiting significant fixation of C1, C4 and C2 as well as C3–C9 (2). Although only 9% of hamster C1 was consumed, this amounted to 8000 units since titration of untreated hamster serum revealed an exceptionally high content of C1. In contrast, the reaction between guinea pig serum and LPS indicated less than 2% consumption of C1, C4 and C2, while a consumption of 73% of the available C3–C9 occurred (Table I). It was also found in another experiment that a mixture containing equal volumes of hamster serum and guinea pig serum incubated for 20 min at 37°C had a total C titer that was nearly identical to the sum of the individual sera tested alone. This suggested that hamster serum components were not anticomplementary toward guinea pig C.

Figure 1 reveals that marked differences in C consumption were also evident when varying amounts of LPS were reacted with hamster or guinea pig serum at 0°C or 37°C. No fixation of C in serum from either species was detected after incubation of 0°C for 20 min, but after 18 hr at 0°C hamster serum demonstrated greater than 90% consumption of C with an optimum concentration of 25 to 50 μg LPS. At most, 5% of the guinea pig C activity was lost following incubation of 12.5 to 200 μg LPS at 0°C for 18 hr. In hamster serum LPS in 100-μg or 200-μg amounts showed decreased fixation of C activity at 0°C, an effect resembling inhibition of complement fixation by excess antigen. Thus, the greatest difference in C comsumption between the two species was observed after an incubation of 18 hr at 0°C with 25 to 50 μg LPS.

To learn if the consumption of hamster C by LPS could be ascribed to natural antibody, an adsorption experiment was performed. Table II shows that the consumption of whole hamster C at 0°C was lessened by two adsorptions of serum with homologous bacterial cells prior to the addition of LPS. This suggested that a natural antibody reactive with LPS at 0°C was removed and that the adsorption was specific for the bacterial genera tested. However, adsorbed serum

TABLE I

Consumption of hamster or guinea pig complement components in normal serum by 100 μg V. alcalescens endotoxin (LPS)

Component Titrated[a]	Hamster Serum			Guinea Pig Serum		
	Units available	Units fixed by LPS[b]	Complement fixed	Units available	Units fixed by LPS	Complement fixed
			%			%
Total C	217	210	97	760	230	30
C1	89,000	8000	9	16,500	10	<1
C4	3,500	3490	99	78,000	1000	1
C2	310	270	87	25,000	<10	<3
C3–C9[c]	20	17	85	450	330	73

[a] Titers expressed in 50% hemolytic units/ml serum.

[b] Residual activity after incubation with LPS at 37°C for 20 min.

[c] C3 through C9 measured as C EDTA.

incubated with both homologous and heterologous LPS at 37°C for 20 min exhibited marked C consumption. This implied that the consumption of hamster C by LPS at 37°C was not dependent upon an antibody which could be adsorbed at 0°C. It was noteworthy that two 20-min adsorptions of serum with bacterial cells at 0°C resulted in less than a 5% loss of total hemolytic C activity. These results suggest that C consumption by LPS at 37°C may result by a pathway in addition to that known to occur with conventional antibody at 0°C. This concept is consistent with the finding that C is consumed by LPS in immunoglobulin-deficient serum (7). Stollar and Sandberg (8) have found using DNA antigens that 7S immunoglobulin fixed C more efficiently at low temperature (4°C) than did the 19S fraction, which was shown to react more efficiently at 37°C. If this observation can be extended to natural antibody toward LPS it is possible that the hamster possesses sizeable amounts of naturally-occurring 7S and 19S immunoglobulins that can react at low temperature and body temperature, respectively. It is interesting to speculate that low temperature reactivity may be of particular use to a hibernating animal such as the hamster

The serum of immunized guinea pigs contains γ1 and γ2 classes of 7S immunoglobulins, which exhibit differing abilities to activate the complement sequence. Osler *et al.* have recently shown that γ1 and γ2 antibody subclasses can react with homologous C components whereas earlier work had indicated that only γ2 antibody could react

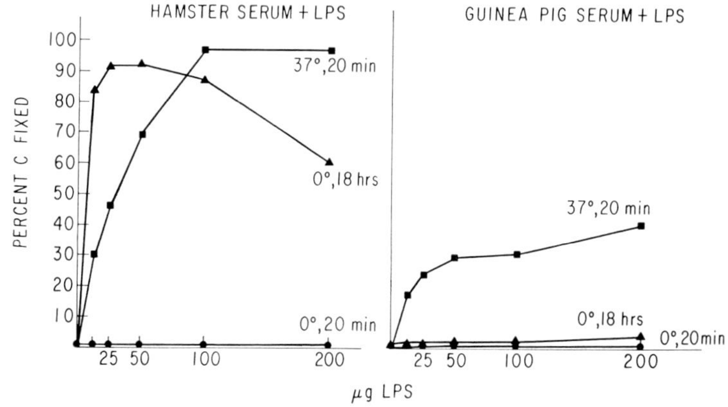

Figure 1. Consumption of total hemolytic complement activity of hamster and guinea pig serum by endotoxin (LPS) from *Veillonella alcalescens* following incubation at 0°C and 37°C.

TABLE II

Complement consumption by endotoxin (LPS) incubated with adsorbed hamster serum at 0°C or 37°C.

Adsorption[a] of Serum with Cells of:	Incubation[b] of Serum with LPS from:	Complement Activity Remaining[c] after Incubation at: 0°C, 18 hr		37°C, 20 min	
		CH_{50}/ml	Loss[d]	CH_{50}/ml	Loss
			%		%
Not adsorbed	None	173		164	
Not adsorbed	*V. alcalescens*	74	57	8.7	95
Not adsorbed	*S. typhosa*	54	69	4.2	97
V. alcalescens	None	170	2	158	4
V. alcalescens	*V. alcalescens*	160	6	5.4	97
V. alcalescens	*S. typhosa*	27	84	3.9	98
S. typhosa	None	172	1	158	4
S. typhosa	*V. alcalescens*	87	50	5.4	97
S. typhosa	*S. typhosa*	143	17	6.3	96

[a] Normal hamster serum adsorbed twice with heat-killed *V. alcalescens* or *S. typhosa* cells at 1°C for 20 min.

[b] Incubation with LPS at 37°C for 20 min.

[c] Residual activity after incubation with LPS at specified temperature. Titers expressed in 50% hemolytic units/ml serum.

[d] Percentage loss compared to nonadsorbed serum in absence of LPS.

with C (9). They speculated that $\gamma 1$ antibody may bypass the early C components and enter the sequence at the C3 stage (9). The present work suggests that natural antibody in hamster serum which is reactive with LPS at 0°C (possibly 7S antibody) can be removed by adsorption, thus leaving nearly intact the C titer and other serum components capable of interacting with LPS at 37°C. The present findings show that the hamster differs from the guinea pig with regard to preferential consumption by LPS of the terminal C components. Whereas guinea pig serum reacted with LPS at 37°C shows significant consumption of only C3–C9, normal hamster serum in the presence of LPS exhibits consumption of C1, C4 and C2 as well. The dog may be similar to the hamster in this respect since a recent report has described a decrease in the level of total C and its four classical components following intravenous injection of LPS, or after incubation *in vitro* of dog serum with LPS (10).

REFERENCES

1. Hook, W. A. and Mergenhagen, S. E., Fed. Proc. *29* (No. 2, Abst.): 638, 1970.
2. Gewurz, H., Shin, H. S. and Mergenhagen, S. E., J. Exp. Med., *128:* 1049, 1968.
3. Mayer, M. M., in *Kabat and Mayer's Experimental Immunochemistry*, 2nd Ed., p. 133, Charles C Thomas, Springfield, Ill., 1961.
4. Hook, W. A. and Muschel, L. H., Proc. Soc. Exp. Biol. Med., *117:* 292, 1964.
5. Nelson, R. A., Jr., Jensen, J., Gigli, I. and Tamura, N., Immunochemistry, *3:* 111, 1966.
6. Westphal, O. and Lüderitz, O., Angew. Chem., *66:* 407, 1954.
7. Gewurz, H., Pickering, R. J., Snyderman, R., Lichtenstein, L. M., Good, R. A. and Mergenhagen, S. E., J. Exp. Med., *131:* 817, 1970.
8. Stollar, B. D. and Sandberg, A. L., J. Immun., *96:* 755, 1966.
9. Osler, A. G., Oliveira, B., Shin, H. S. and Sandberg, A. L., J. Immun., *102:* 269, 1969.
10. Füst, G. and Keresztes, M., Acta Microbiol. Acad. Sci. Hung., *16:* 135, 1969.

THE JOURNAL OF IMMUNOLOGY
Vol. 105 No. 1, July 1970

Glycosyl Transferases for Mouse IgG[1]

ISAAC SCHENKEIN AND JONATHAN W. UHR

From the Irvington House Institute and Department of Medicine, New York University School of Medicine, New York 10016

Cell-free fractions from a variety of mammalian tissues can catalyze the addition of carbohydrate to polypeptide (1–5). One of these reports describes the transfer of uridine diphosphate (UDP)-galactose to endogenously present IgG, mediated by the microsomal fraction of rabbit lymph node cells (6). The enzymatic activity appears membrane bound in all cases, and use of detergents (such as Triton X-100) has been necessary for its demonstration.

This paper describes initial studies on three distinct glycosyl transferases from a murine myeloma tumor and the partial purification of two of them: a galactosyl and an N-acetyl-glucosaminyl (NAG) transferase. In contrast to some reports by others, these latter two enzymes have been obtained in water-soluble form. An important aspect of our experiments was the use as substrate of mouse IgG from which a substantial portion of the carbohydrate had been removed by enzymatic digestion.

MATERIALS AND METHODS

Mouse IgG (Pentex Inc., Kankakee, Ill.) was purified to immunoelectrophoretic purity by passage through a column of DEAE-Sephadex using 0.01 M Tris buffer (pH 8.0) as equilibrating solution and eluant. Sugars were removed by digestion with neuraminidase, beta-glucosidase, beta-galactosidase, and beta-N-acetyl-glucosaminidase at the appropriate pH's (7). After lyophilization, the mixture was subjected to molecular sieving on a column of Sephadex G-200 (8). Loss of carbohydrate of the IgG was determined by comparison of neuraminic acid, hexose, and hexosamine content before and after the above procedure (9). The percentage of carbohydrate removed in different experiments varied from 40% to 60%.

Enzymes were prepared from solid LPC_1 tumors (from Dr. John Fahey, National Institutes of Health) carried in BALB/c mice. The material was homogenized in Tris buffer which was 1% (v/v) with respect to Triton X-100. The homogenate was stirred in the cold for 16 hr, and the supernatant obtained after centrifugation for 15 min at 10,000 × G was brought to 50% saturation with ammonium sulfate. The resulting precipitate was pelleted by centrifugation, taken up in H_2O and desalted on a column of Sephadex G-25 medium. The glycosyl transferase activity (mostly galactosyl and N-acetyl-glucosaminyl) emerged in the V_0 of the column. This material was lyophilized and stored in the cold. Activity was lost upon standing in solution (in the cold) in 2 to 3 weeks.

The assay system consisted of indicated quantities (see Tables I and II) of 1.0 M Tris buffer (pH 7.2), 0.25 M $MnCl_2$, radioactive sugar, enzyme fraction and substrate (carbohydrate-poor mouse IgG). Incubation was for 2 hr at 37°C. Goat antiserum to mouse IgG was added in excess and the tubes were incubated at 37°C for 30 min followed by standing in an ice-H_2O bath for 1 hr. The precipitate was washed four times in phosphate-buffered saline, pH 7.4 (PBS). The pellet was solubilized in 1 ml of the PBS and a few drops of a solution of 20% sodium dodecyl sulfate. It was then transferred to vials containing 10 ml of cocktail D (Beckman) and counted in a Beckman LS-250 liquid scintillation counter.

Incorporation of radioactive carbohydrate into substrate was shown by the following observations. a) Exhaustive dialysis did not remove a portion of radioactivity from substrate. b) Specific precipitates were radioactive after thorough washing. c) Reduction and alkylation of the radioactive IgG (10) and separation of the resulting alkyl H and L chains on a column of Sephadex G-200 showed coincidence of radioactivity with optical density at 280 nm. d) Radio-

[1] This work was done under the sponsorship of the Commission on Immunization of the Armed Forces Epidemiological Board and was supported in part by the U. S. Army Medical Research and Development Command, Department of the Army, under Research Contract DADA 17-69-C 9177, and in part by U. S. Public Health Service Grants AI-08034 and HE-09239, and by National Science Foundation Grant GB-74-73-X.

TABLE I

Incorporation experiment using the crude and the dialyzed $(NH_4)_2SO_4$ fraction[a]

Test Tube No.	Sugar	Substrate	Enzyme	IgG	Enzyme Protein
				cpm	*cpm/mg*
1	^{3}H-UDP-galactose	−	AS	131	
2		+	crude	1,735	230
3		+	AS	1,071	842
4		+		60	
5	^{14}C-UDP N-acetyl	−	AS	27	
6	glucosamine	+	crude	4,755	634
7		+	AS	595	464
8		+		55	
9	^{3}H-galactose	−	AS	700	
10		+	crude	14,500	1930
11		+	AS	1,280	1000
12		+		28	
13	^{14}C-N-acetyl glucosamine	−	AS	95	
14		+	crude	641	80
15		+	AS	224	175
16		+		22	
17	^{3}H-fucose	−	AS	487	
18		+	crude	27,000	3600
19		+	AS	1,980	1546
20		+		495	

[a] Assay system: 20 µl 0.25 M $MnCl_2$; 50 µl 1 M Tris (pH 7.2); 10 µl 1% Triton X-100; 10 µl radioactive sugar (1.5–10 mCi/mM, 1 to 3.5 × 10^7 cpm/tube); 50 µl enzyme fraction (crude = 7.54 mg/ml; $(NH_4)_2SO_4$ fraction = 1.28 mg/ml); 50 µl substrate (10 mg/ml). Incubation for 2 hr at 37°C.

TABLE II

Incorporation experiment using the Sephadex fraction[a]

Test Tube No.	Sugar	Substrate[b]	Enzyme[b]	IgG
		µg	*µg*	*cpm*
1	^{14}C-UDP-NAG	400	0	132
2		0	40	79
3		200	40	475
4		400	40	803
5		600	40	1409
6		800	40	1870
7	^{3}H-UDP-galactose	400	0	147
8		0	40	87
9		200	40	359
10		400	40	624
11		600	40	954
12		800	40	1011

[a] Assay system as in Table I, but no Triton X-100 added. Incubation 1 hr at 37°C.

[b] µg = Protein estimated by the method of Layne (12).

active sugars incorporated into the H chains were identified by the method of Boas (11), which involves mild acid hydrolysis, exchange of peptides and free carbohydrate on Dowex-50 (H+) followed by paper chromatography with standard sugars as markers.

RESULTS AND DISCUSSION

Tables I and II show the results of two representative experiments in which incorporation of sugars was mediated by either the crude homogenate, the dialyzed 50% ammonium sulfate fraction, or the material from the Sephadex G-25 column. The last fraction was soluble and, in contrast to the first two, did not require Triton X-100 for activity. It can be seen that the crude fraction was active in the transfer to substrate of galactose, NAG (or their UDP derivatives) and fucose. The ammonium sulfate fraction showed a relative enrichment of the incorporation of UDP-galactose. Table II shows that the Sephadex fraction was active in the incorporation of UDP-galactose and UDP-NAG into IgG. It can also be seen that a rough proportionality exists between radioactivity of the washed specific precipitate and quantity of substrate used. There was an absolute requirement for manganese chloride, consistent with earlier reports on transferases in other systems. However, the Sephadex material had lost most of the fucose transferase activity as well as activity for galactose and NAG themselves. Analytical acrylamide gel electrophoresis of this fraction indicated considerable heterogeneity. Further purification steps and attempts at localization of the enzymatic activity in terms of intracellular organelles are in progress.

REFERENCES

1. Hagopian, A. and Eylar, E. H., Arch. Biochem., *129:* 447, 1969.
2. Caccan, J. F. and Eylar, E. H., Arch. Biochem., *137:* 315, 1970.
3. Morre, J., Merlin, L. M. and Keenan, T. W., Biochem. Biophys. Res. Commun., *37:* 813, 1969.
4. Bouchiloux, S., Ferrano, M., Gregoire, J. and Chabaud, O., Biochem. Biophys. Res. Commun., *37:* 538, 1969.
5. Tuppy, H. and Schenkel-Brunner, H., Europ. J. Biochem., *10:* 152, 1969.
6. D'Amico, R. P. and Kern, M., J. Biol. Chem., *243:* 3425, 1968.
7. Neuraminidase and the gluco- and galactosidases were obtained from Worthington. The beta-N-acetyl-glucosaminidase was prepared by the method of Eylar and Murakami, described in *Methods in Enzymology*, Vol. 8, 1957 (Colowick, Kaplan, Neufeld and Ginsburg, Eds.). Conditions used for hydrolysis are also described in this volume, p. 40.
8. Manual for Preparation of Sephadex Columns, Pharmacia Inc., 1967.
9. *Methods in Enzymology*, Edited by Colowick, Kaplan, Neufeld and V. Ginsburg, Vol. 8, pp. 16, 58 and 93, Academic Press, New York, 1957.
10. Fleischman, J. B., Pain, R. and Porter, R. R., Arch. Biochem., *16* (Suppl. 1): 174, 1961.
11. Boas, N. F., J. Biol. Chem., *204:* 553, 1953.
12. Layne, E., in *Methods in Enzymology*, Edited by S. P. Colowick and N. O. Kaplan, Vol. 3, p. 447, Academic Press, New York, 1957.

THE JOURNAL OF IMMUNOLOGY
Vol. 105, No. 1, July 1970

Printed in U.S.A.

Evidence for Synthesis of Human Colostral γA as 11S Dimer[1]

JOHN BIENENSTOCK[2] AND HANS STRAUSS[3]

From the Department of Medicine, Division of Immunology, McMaster University, School of Medicine, Hamilton, Ontario, Canada

It is generally accepted that the secretory γA molecule in both rabbit and man is constituted by a serum type γA dimer plus an additional protein now termed secretory component (SC). It was first proposed by Tomasi *et al.* (1) that the secretory γA molecule was formed in plasma cells adjacent to the mucous surface and that combination with the secretory component, synthesized by glandular epithelial cells, occurred somewhere in transit of the γA molecule to the luminal surface. Examination of human colostral secretory γA isoagglutinin with anti-blood group A activity by Costea *et al.* (2) suggested to these investigators that the majority of the colostral secretory γA population was made up of molecules containing both κ and λ light chains. Thus, secretory γA appeared to be a hybrid molecule, implying random rather than specific combination of γA molecules. On the other hand, Lawton and Mage (3) obtained evidence in the rabbit, using animals heterozygous for the b^4/b^5 loci, that in this species colostral γA was synthesized as an 11S dimer, since γA molecules had either b^4 or b^5 light chains, but not both.

The present study was therefore undertaken in an attempt to shed some light on the mechanism of synthesis of human colostral γA. Advantage was taken of the method described by Moreno and Kabat (4) to isolate pure secretory γA and serum γG anti-blood group A isoaglutinin from colostrum and serum, respectively. The method, as slightly modified by us, is outlined below. Blood group A substance was obtained through the generosity of the Canadian Red Cross Society. Insoluble polyleucyl blood group A was prepared by cross-linking with N-carboxyleucyl anhydride as described by Kaplan and Kabat (5). The washed, insolubilized A substance was suspended in an equal volume of P6 (BioRad Laboratories, Richmond, Calif.) and packed into a 1- x 15-cm column. Serum was collected from blood donors, or colostrum from nursing mothers within 3 days of parturition. Samples were used in this study only if hemagglutination titers, tested on A_1 red cells, were greater than 1:256. The serum or centrifuged colostrum was applied to the bottom of the column and eluted upward at a constant flow rate of 15 ml/hr at 4°C. The eluant fractions were tested by agglutination every 20 ml. When the titers of the eluate exceeded 1:8 the column was washed with phosphate-buffered saline pH 7.2 (PBS). When the eluate read less than 0.05 at 280 nm in a Zeiss PMQ II spectrophotometer, 6 ml of 10% N-acetyl-D-galactosamine (GalNAc) were applied to the column and incubated for 1 hr at 37°C. The column was eluted for a second time with 10% GalNAc and the two eluates were pooled. Further washing was now performed with PBS, and then 2 M potassium thiocyanate (KCNS) was applied to the column to remove all adherent protein. The column was now extensively washed in PBS and the whole cycle repeated. Only the GalNAc eluates were utilized in this study. The GalNAc eluates were concentrated and passed over a P6 column. The first protein peak emerging from the column was placed in dialysis membranes (previously boiled for 15 min in distilled water) and dialyzed against PBS for 2 days. The protein was then concentrated with Aquicide II (Calbiochem, Los Angeles Calif.) and tested. The specific anti-A antibody was subjected to 10% to 40% sucrose density gradient ultracentrifugation at 37,000 rpm in a SB 405 rotor, B 60 International ultracentrifuge. The protein corresponding to the distribution of purified 11S γA and 7S γG, run as markers in parallel gradients, was pooled, dialyzed against PBS for 2 days, and concentrated with Aquicide II. These preparations will be referred to subsequently as 11S γA anti-A and 7S γG anti-A. The colostral anti-A antibody before centrifugation was usually contaminated with less than 5% γM. After density gradient separation the preparations were pure within the limits of sensitivity of the method of detection (3%). The serum anti-

1 This work was supported by the Medical Research Council of Canada.

2 Medical Research Council Scholar.

3 Fourth year medical student, University of Toronto.

body preparation contained usually more γM than γG. Intermediate portions of the gradient usually contained some γA but this was always contaminated by γG. The final 7S γG anti-A antibody was less than 1% contaminated by γG.

Pure 7S γG was obtained from pooled normal human serum by elution from DE 52 (Whatman, Reeve Angel, Clifton, N. J.) with 0.005 M, pH 7.5, phosphate buffer. The 11S γA preparation was obtained from a pool of normal colostrum, and also from colostrum after passage over the cross-linked blood group A substance column, having an anti-A_1 isoagglutinin titer of less than 1:4.

Either 50 or 100 μg of protein were labeled with ^{125}I according to the modified chloramine T method of McConahey and Dixon (6) with either 0.5 of 1 mCi respectively. This 11S γA anti-A was the only protein labeled with 0.5 mCi. Two different preparations of 11S γA anti-A were labeled. In both cases less than 40% of the label was incorporated into the protein; only one preparation was used in this study. When 100 μg of normal secretory γA were labeled with 1 mCi, better than 80% incorporation was obtained. Similar efficiency of labeling was achieved with either 7S γG or 7S γG anti-A when using 100 μg protein. The labeled protein was immediately transferred to a 2-g G-50 Sephadex column (Pharmacia (Canada) Ltd., Montreal, P. Q.) previously eluted with 2 ml of 20 mg/ml bovine serum albumin. The first radioactive peak to emerge from this column was pooled and dialyzed against PBS for 2 days with several changes of buffer.

The immune precipitation technique employed was as follows. The appropriate antiserum in a volume that varied between 0.1 and 0.3 ml according to potency was added to 0.1 ml of labeled protein,[4] incubated at 37°C with agitation for 30 min and centrifuged at 15,000 rpm for 20 min. The supernatant was decanted and kept at 4°C. The precipitate was washed three times in cold PBS, and then dissolved in 0.5 ml 1 N NaOH. To the supernatant was added 0.3 ml of goat anti-rabbit γG antiserum, and the procedure was repeated as before. Three-tenths milliliter of anti-rabbit γG antiserum was again added to the final supernatant in order to insure that all counts capable of being precipitated by this coprecipitation technique had been removed. The three dissolved precipitates were counted separately in a Packard gamma counter, and the total radioactivity of the precipitates was combined and expressed as counts/min minus background. This indirect coprecipitation technique was found to be essential in order to precipitate all labeled immunoglobulin, particularly in the experiments employing anti-κ and anti-λ antisera. Similar problems have been recently encountered by other investigators with these antisera (7).

The H chain antisera employed in this study directed against α, γ, and μ chains have been previously described (8). The secretory component antiserum was prepared as described elsewhere (9) except that the rabbit was used for immunization. The anti-κ and anti-λ antisera were obtained from Cappel Laboratories, Dowington, Pa., and were demonstrated to be pure in immunodiffusion experiments employing light chains of κ and λ antigenic specificity. The antilactoferrin antiserum was obtained by immunizing rabbits with colostral lactoferrin prepared according to the methods of Montreuil *et al.* (10). The resulting antiserum reacted with serum γA and was made specific for lactoferrin by absorption with normal human serum.

The results of the experiments can be seen in Table I expressed as the percentage of counts/min precipitated by the appropriate anti-heavy chain antiserum. Less than 6% of the total number of counts/min precipitated by the relevant anti-heavy chain antisera were precipitated by irrelevant antisera including anti-lactoferrin and secretory component.

No evidence was obtained in this study to support the contention that human colostral secretory γA, with or without anti-A substance isoagglutinin activity, is predominantly constituted by molecules containing both κ and λ determinants. The data shed no light on the actual percentage of secretory γA molecules with both κ and λ determinants, but suggest that if these exist in colostrum, the actual amounts are likely to be very small. The data further suggest that the human secretory γA molecules are synthesized as 11S dimers, as has already been suggested for the rabbit by Lawton and Mage (3). Similar conclusions have recently been reached by Curry and Small (7) in experiments with human secretory γA without specific isoagglutinin activity obtained from both saliva and colostrum.

Although it might have been expected from the

[4] Fifty micrograms of unlabeled protein were added in all experiments at this stage.

TABLE I

¹²⁵I-Labeled Immunoglobulin	No. of Counts Precipitated[a]				
	Rabbit anti-κ	Anti-λ	Anti-α	Anti-γ	Anti-SC[b]
11S γA anti-A	44%[c] 4,856	54% 5,545	10,240	383	10,823
11S γA	57% 23,288	42% 17,440	41,161	1,615	42,064
7S γG anti-A	58% 29,718	42% 22,708	1,583	51,161	1,712
7S γG	64% 40,050	39% 24,355	1,678	62,228	ND[d]

[a] Includes all counts coprecipitated by anti-rabbit γG.
[b] SC, secretory component.
[c] Percentage of counts/min precipitated by relevant anti-heavy chain antiserum.
[d] ND, not determined.

hapten elution technique used to prepare the pure antibody that a highly restricted homogeneous antibody population would be obtained, heterogeneity, at least with respect to light chain classes, was observed. This finding is in keeping with the observations of Moreno and Kabat (4).

One possible explanation for the discrepancy between our results and those of Costea *et al.* (2), referred to previously, might be the relatively insignificant amounts of polymeric secretory γA in our preparations. Polymeric serum γA isoagglutinins are known to have enhanced hemagglutinating activity relative to the monomeric forms (11, 12), and it may well be that such polymers occur by random association in serum. In secretions where such polymeric association of multiples of 11S γA molecules also occurs (1), it would not be surprising to find evidence for enhanced agglutinin activity with hybrid κ and λ polymers. In this regard it is pertinent to note that reduction of serum γA polymers to monomers occurs on treatment with mercaptoethanol (12), and that similar treatment of polymeric γA isoagglutinins results in a decrease of hemagglutinating activity (13). Mercaptoethanol destroyed the agglutinating potency of the G-200 pool used by Costea and associates as secretory γA, whereas 11S secretory γA, with and without antibody activity, is resistant to the effects of such mild reductive procedures (1, 14).

Although it is widely assumed that locally synthesized γA in large part gains access to the mucous surfaces, recent evidence obtained by Vaerman and Heremans in the dog (15) suggests at least in this species that the gastrointestinal tract is responsible for maintaining the serum γA pool. Similar conclusions as to the contribution of the gastrointestinal tract to serum γA have been drawn from experiments involving *in vitro* perfused human colon (16). Although the balance of evidence in man is against the transport of γA from serum to secretions (17), it is possible that the 11S serum-type γA molecule might have some transport advantage in crossing the mucous epithelium. Thus, the demonstration in the present study that the majority of the colostral secretory γA contains only one type of L chain does not shed light on the percentage of the γA molecules that were locally synthesized, and the percentage of colostral γA which might have been synthesized as 11S molecules elsewhere and transported by an as yet undefined mechanism into the colostrum.

Acknowledgments. We thank Mrs. V. Wawrzyniak for her invaluable help, and Miss Spiak and the Canadian Red Cross for generous assistance throughout the course of this study.

REFERENCES

1. Tomasi, T. B., Jr., Tan, E. M., Solomon, A. and Prendergast, R. A., J. Exp. Med., *121:* 101, 1965.
2. Costea, N., Yakulis, V., Schmale, J. and Heller, P., J. Immun., *101:* 1248, 1968.
3. Lawton, A. R., III and Mage, R. G., J. Immun., *102:* 693, 1969.

4. Moreno, C. and Kabat, E. A., J. Exp. Med., *129:* 871, 1969.
5. Kaplan, M. E. and Kabat, E. A., J. Exp. Med., *123:* 1061, 1966.
6. McConahey, P. J. and Dixon, F. J., Int. Arch. Allerg., *29:* 185, 1966.
7. Curry, J. H. and Small, P. A., Fed. Proc., *29:* 642, 1970.
8. Bienenstock, J. and Poortmans, J., J. Lab. Clin. Med., *75:* 295, 1970.
9. Bienenstock, J. and Poortmans, J., Proc. Soc. Exp. Biol. Med., In press.
10. Montreuil, J., Tonnelat, J. and Mullet, S., Biochim. Biophys. Acta, *45:* 413, 1960.
11. Ishizaka, K., Ishizaka, T., Lee, E. H. and Fudenberg, H. H., J. Immun., *95:* 197, 1965.
12. Franklin, E. C., Nature, *195:* 394, 1962.
13. Ishizaka, K., Ishizaka, T. and Lee, E. H., J. Immun., *95:* 771, 1965.
14. Bienenstock, J., Goldstein, J. and Tomasi, T. B., Jr., J. Lab. Clin. Med., *73:* 389, 1969.
15. Vaerman, J. P. and Heremans, J. F., Immunology, In press.
16. Bull, D. B., Bienenstock, J. and Tomasi, T. B., Jr., Fed. Proc., *28:* 324, 1969.
17. Tomasi, T. B., Jr., and Bienenstock, J., Advances Immun., *9:* 1, 1968.

THE JOURNAL OF IMMUNOLOGY
Vol. 105, No. 2, August 1970
Printed in U.S.A.

ANTIGEN QUANTITATION IN EXPERIMENTAL IMMUNE COMPLEX GLOMERULONEPHRITIS

I. Acute Serum Sickness[1]

CURTIS B. WILSON AND FRANK J. DIXON

From the Department of Experimental Pathology, Scripps Clinic and Research Foundation, 476 Prospect Street, La Jolla, California 92037

Received for publication May 14, 1970

Acute serum sickness glomerulonephritis was induced in rabbits with radiolabeled bovine serum albumin (I*BSA) 250 mg/kg. The kidneys of these rabbits contained 1 to 35 μg of I*BSA following >99% elimination of I*BSA from the circulation. The I*BSA disappeared from the kidneys with a half time of about 10 days. The severity of glomerulonephritis in these rabbits was related to the rapidity of of immune elimination and the amount of I*BSA deposited. As little as 0.25 μg/g of kidney of I*BSA could be detected by immunofluorescence. During the 8-day period following immune elimination the BSA detectable by immunofluorescence decreased rapidly while host immunoglobulin and complement increased. The continued presence of I*BSA in these kidneys shown by isotopic studies suggested that this BSA was being covered by host anti-BSA antibody and complement from the circulation. These immunofluorescence findings occurred during the time of resolution of the glomerulonephritis by histologic and functional criteria. This suggested that the immune complexes formed initially in antigen excess were nephritogenic while immune complexes deposited in an extravascular site were less phlogogenic in spite of continued interaction with antibody and complement.

The production of glomerular injury by the deposition of circulating immune complexes has been demonstrated in acute (1, 2) and chronic (3) serum sickness and in lupus erythematosus (4–6). Presumptive evidence has been presented that streptococcal antigen(s) in the form of immune complexes (7, 8) is deposited in glomeruli in acute poststreptococcal glomerulonephritis, and a similar situation exists for malarial antigen(s) in the nephrosis associated with the quartan malaria (9) and for thyroglobulin in the occasional nephritis accompanying thyroiditis.[2, 3] Viral, antigens have been identified in circulating immune complexes and in glomeruli where persistent viral infections exist in animals (10–12). Despite these advances in the detection of etiologic agents in a few immune complex glomerulonephritides, the etiologic antigens in the majority of cases of human immune complex glomerulonephritis have not been identified.

The present studies were undertaken in order to quantitate some of the immunologic parameters of experimental glomerulonephritis induced by the deposition of circulating immune complexes. This information will provide guidelines for attempts to identify the antigens involved in human immune complex nephritis. The amount of radioiodinated bovine serum albumin (I*BSA) deposited in the kidneys of rabbits with acute serum sickness was found to be 1 to 35 μg. By combining the radiolabeled study with immunofluorescence detection of the antigen, the sensitivity of the immunofluorescent staining technique in immune complex glomerulonephritis was determined. For the 1st week following elimination of circulating complexes, I*BSA in the kidneys decreased with a half life of approximately

[1] This is publication 396 from the Department of Experimental Pathology, Scripps Clinic and Research Foundation, La Jolla, California. This research was supported by United States Public Health Service Contract PH-43-68-621, United States Public Health Service Grant A1-07007, and Atomic Energy Commission Contract AT (04-3)-410.

[2] R. S. Schwartz, personal communication.

[3] D. Koffler, personal communication.

10 days while amounts of IgG and complement detectable by immunofluorescence increased. During this period of apparent IgG and complement accumulation in the glomeruli, there was histologic and functional improvement in the glomerular disease. The accumulation of IgG and complement in the glomeruli appeared to block the immunofluorescence detection of antigen. The possibility of urinary excretion of immune complexes from the glomeruli was also evaluated.

MATERIAL AND METHODS

General. Quantitative studies were done in 68, 3-kg male New Zealand White rabbits procured from a local breeder. The rabbits were maintained on Purina rabbit chow with KI in their drinking water. Acute serum sickness was produced by the intravenous administration of crystallized BSA (Armour Pharmaceutical, Kankakee, Ill.) labeled with ^{131}I or ^{125}I (13) in a dose of 250 mg/kg. To increase the incidence and uniformity of the serum sickness, 2.5 mg of rabbit anti-BSA N/kg were administered 18 hr prior to I*BSA administration (14). To prevent passive anaphylaxis and binding of the I*BSA to the passively administered antibody the first 80 mg of BSA were administered in divided, unlabeled doses. In 45 rabbits ^{131}I rabbit serum albumin (I*RSA) was administered at least 48 hr prior to the onset of immune elimination of ^{125}I BSA as a paired label control (15). The amount of I*RSA given was calculated to equal the I*BSA remaining in the circulation. The RSA was prepared by a modification (16) of the method of Schwert (17). In an additional 23 rabbits ^{131}I BSA alone was used.

The rabbits were housed in metabolic cages, and 24-hr, unrefrigerated urine samples were obtained for the measurement of proteinuria by comparing the turbidity produced by 3% sulfosalicylic acid with a standard curve at 595 nm in a Coleman Jr. spectrophotometer. Hematuria was detected by the use of Hemastix (Ames Company, Elkhart, Ind.). Serum creatinine was determined as a measure of renal function (18).

*The elimination of circulating I*BSA and quantitation of circulating immune complexes.* The rate of elimination of the injected I*BSA from the circulation was determined in a well-type, dual channel, NaI scintillation counter of duplicate plasma precipitates prepared at a final concentration of 10% trichloracetic acid (TCA). Amounts of I*BSA present in the circulation in the form of immune complexes were quantitated in duplicate washed precipitates formed in a final concentration of 50% ammonium sulfate (19). In the 45 rabbits used for determination of circulating immune complexes, the presence of a paired label I*RSA allowed individual correction of each sample for nonspecific entrapment of I*BSA in the precipitates.

*Renal bound I*BSA determination.* The renal bound I*BSA was determined in Waring Blendor homogenates (4°C) of the kidneys washed three times in cold 0.01 M sodium phosphate-buffered 0.15 M NaCl, pH 7.0 (PBS). The specimens were obtained either by nephrectomy[4] using a clean, but not sterile, technique under local anesthesia or at autopsy after an overdose of sodium pentobarbital when over 99% of the injected I*BSA had been cleared from the circulation. The specific I*BSA present in the kidney in the paired label studies was calculated as follows:

$$\text{Specific renal } ^{125}\text{I BSA} = \text{Renal } ^{125}\text{I BSA} - \left[\frac{\text{Renal } ^{131}\text{I RSA} \times \text{serum } ^{125}\text{I BSA}}{\text{Serum } ^{131}\text{I RSA}}\right]$$

No correction was used in the single label experiments.

The total recovery of radioactivity in the washed sediment, supernatant and washes was usually greater than 90% of that originally detected in the intact kidney. The radioactivity present in the washed sediment was 95% precipitable with TCA. Less than 10% of the radioactivity present in the sediment after three washes could be removed by multiple additional washings. Some of the I*BSA which appeared in the supernatant from the Waring Blendor homogenate was precipitable by ammonium sulfate indicating its presence as immune complexes. However, these immune complexes were not in excess of the amount expected to be in the blood contained within the kidney, suggesting that immune complexes were not being dislodged from the kidney during homogenization.

Control injections of five different paired label mixtures of I*BSA and I*RSA were made in normal rabbits and the I*BSA in the kidney was determined at 24 hr. No I*BSA was found bound in the kidneys of these control rabbits.

[4] Hereafter referred to as the nephrectomy kidney.

*Disappearance of I*BSA from the kidney.* The disappearance rate of I*BSA from the kidney in 24 rabbits was determined by comparing I*BSA in kidneys surgically removed after over 99% of the injected I*BSA had been cleared from the circulation with kidneys taken at autopsy[5] following an overdose of sodium pentobarbital 4 to 8 days later. In seven additional rabbits kidneys were removed 3 or 4 days following elimination of >99% of the circulating I*BSA and compared to kidneys taken at autopsy 6 to 8 days later.

Histology. Renal tissue at nephrectomy and portions of kidney, heart, lung, spleen and liver taken at autopsy were fixed in Bouin's solution and post-fixed in 50% ethyl alcohol. Hematoxylin-eosin and periodic acid-Schiff (PAS) stained sections of the kidney were examined for increased cellularity and other abnormalities of the glomeruli. Hypercellularity was graded 1 to 3+, and when accompanied by focal necrosis of a portion of the glomerular tuft was graded 4+. The other tissues were examined for evidence of arteritis.

Immunofluorescence. Blocks of renal cortex 5 mm in greatest diameter were snap-frozen in liquid nitrogen. Sections 4μ thick were cut in a Harris cryostat, air dried, washed in PBS and fixed in ether-ethyl alcohol (1:1) and ethyl alcohol (absolute). The fixed sections were stained for immunofluorescence microscopy (20) with fluoresceinated (21) sheep IgG (22) specific for rabbit IgG and C3 and rabbit IgG specific for BSA as shown by immunoelectrophoresis and double diffusion in 1% agarose. Appropriate controls included known positive and negative sections, absorption of the fluoresceinated antisera with the specific antigen and prior blocking with the specific reagent unconjugated. The sections were examined with a Zeiss fluorescence microscope using an Osram HBO 200 W light source with KG 1 heat absorption filter, UG 1 (1.5 mm) excitation filter and GG 4 barrier filter.

The amount of immunofluorescence was graded 0 to 4+. Trace amounts indicated only focal glomerular granularity. The immunofluorescent staining was graded 1+ when a minimal amount of granularity involved portions of most glomerular capillaries. The staining was 2+ when all capillaries in all glomeruli were involved and 3+ when the granular staining along capillary walls became nearly confluent. The staining was 4+ when the glomeruli were filled with immunofluorescent deposits. The immunofluorescence pattern was further defined as being finely granular, coarsely granular and globular on the basis of the size of the individual deposits.

*Urinary excretion of I*BSA, I*RSA and I*BSA-anti-BSA immune complexes.* The urine of 20 rabbits in the paired label group was studied for the presence of I*RSA, I*BSA and I*BSA-anti-BSA immune complexes. The I*RSA and I*BSA were determined in duplicate washed precipitates of the urine formed at a final concentration of 10% TCA. Normal rabbit serum was added as a carrier protein to urines from nonproteinuric rabbits. The values were corrected for nonspecific entrapment of nonprotein bound I* in the precipitates formed in urines of comparable protein concentrations. The clearance of I*RSA and I*BSA was calculated using the standard clearance formula

$C_x = \frac{U_x V}{P_x}$ in which U_x = the concentration of x in the urine, P_x = the concentration of x in the plasma and V = urine volume.

The I*BSA-anti-BSA immune complexes were determined in duplicate washed precipitates of the urine formed at a final concentration of 50% ammonium sulfate. Again, carrier protein was added to the urine from nonproteinuric rabbits. Each sample was corrected individually for nonspecific entrapment by the presence of I*RSA. Control studies demonstrated that 80% of I*BSA-anti-BSA immune complexes formed *in vitro* in threefold antigen excess could be precipitated with ammonium sulfate after standing in normal rabbit urine for 24 hr at room temperature. Likewise, I*BSA-anti-BSA immune complexes were found to form with equal efficiency in normal rabbit urine and PBS.

RESULTS

General. Elimination of >99% of the circulating I*BSA occurred between 10 and 15 days following injection in 36 of the 45 rabbits used in the paired label studies. Although all the rabbits that eliminated had histologic evidence of glomerulonephritis, only 26 had proteinuria of greater than 20 mg/day for 2 consecutive days. The maximum proteinuria was 1.9 g/24 hr with a

[5] Hereafter referred to as the autopsy kidney.

mean of 337 mg/24 hr. The 23 rabbits studied quantitatively in the single label experiments had >99% elimination of the injected I*BSA between 10 and 15 days following injection. All 23 had histologic evidence of glomerulonephritis, and 19 had proteinuria averaging 772 mg/24 hr with the maximum being 2.9 g. Occult hematuria was present in all proteinuric rabbits.

Renal function was monitored in the 45 paired label rabbits by serum creatinine. The normal serum creatinine level was 1.3 ± 0.3 (S.D.) mg/100 ml, and only three rabbits had elevations of serum creatinine to 2.0 (2710), 2.3 (2704) and 8.2 (3123) mg/100 ml.

*Rate of elimination of I*BSA from the circulation and quantitation of circulating immune complexes.* The amounts of I*BSA in the kidneys of 38 paired label rabbits on the day of >99% elimination of I*BSA from the circulation are given in Table I. The data are divided according to the day of elimination of circulating I*BSA. Twenty rabbits eliminated >99% of the injected dose betwen days 10 and 12, nine between days 13 and 15, and nine had not eliminated by day 14 or 15 at time of autopsy. The rapidity of elimination of the I*BSA from the circulation was directly related to the severity of glomerulonephritis as manifested by the magnitude of the histologic change and evidence of proteinuria. Of the nine rabbits that failed to eliminate, five had histologically normal kidneys and four showed only focal hypercellularity of the glomeruli. Only one showed minimal proteinuria. The elimination curves from these nine rabbits are presented in

TABLE I

*Renal bound I*BSA in acute serum sickness*

Elimination Day	Mean I*BSA μg/TKW[a]	Glomerulonephritis Hypercellularity	Proteinuria Mean mg/24 hr	Immunofluorescence α-BSA
10	21	2-4[b] (5/5)[c]	239 (5/5)[c]	5/5[c]
11	18	1-4 (5/5)	1024 (2/5)	5/5
12	17	1-4 (10/10)	320 (9/10)	10/10
13	13	1-3 (5/5)	58 (3/5)	3/4
14	5	1-3 (2/2)	125 (1/2)	1/2
15	12	1-2 (2/2)	— (0/2)	0/2
15+	3	Trace (4/9)	42 (1/9)	0/9

[a] TKW, total weight both kidneys (estimated as twice weight of nephrectomy kidney).

[b] Degree of hypercellularity graded 1 to 4 plus.

[c] Number of rabbits affected/total number of rabbits studied.

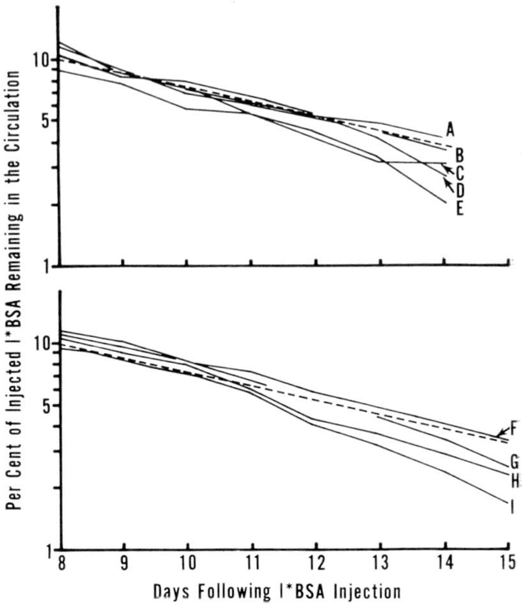

Figure 1. Elimination rate of I*BSA from the circulation. Nonimmune catabolism rate of I*BSA (-----) (23). Rabbits C (3118), D (3116), E (3112) and I (2714) had focal glomerulitis. Rabbits A (3125), D, E, G (2715) and I had coronary arteritis, endocarditis or valvulitis. Rabbits B (3115), F (2722) and H (2709) had no histologic alterations.

Figure 1 and are similar to the non-immune catabolism rate of BSA in rabbits of 4.3 days (23). The 23 rabbits studied in the single label experiments had eliminated >99% of the injected I*BSA from the circulation between days 10 and 15. Again a direct relationship was evident between the rate of elimination and evidence of glomerulonephritis.

The amount of I*BSA precipitable at 50% ammonium sulfate, when corrected for nonspecific entrapment of I*BSA, was assumed to represent I*BSA-anti-BSA immune complexes. The total amount of I*BSA present as immune complexes in the circulation each day could then be calculated. The mean amounts of I*BSA in such immune complexes for rabbits having >99% elimination of the circulating I*BSA on various days are presented in Figure 2 for days 7 through 15 following injection. Rabbits eliminating on day 10 had large amounts of complexes in the circulation when first examined on day 7 followed by a precipitous decline corresponding to immune elimination. The rabbits eliminating on days 11,

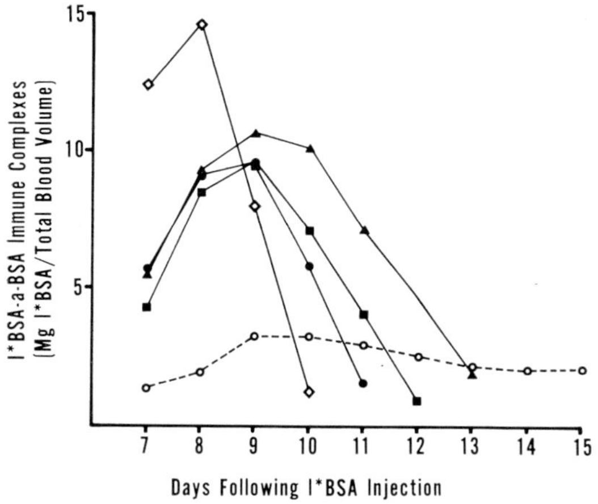

Figure 2. The mean amount of I*BSA present as circulating immune complexes in rabbits having immune elimination on day 10 (◇), day 11 (●), day 12 (■) and day 13 (▲). The mean amount of I*BSA as circulating immune complexes in nine rabbits failing to exhibit immune elimination by days 14 or 15 is shown for comparison (○).

12 and 13 had very similar levels of complexes on day 7 with an increase and slower rate of decrease corresponding to more gradual elimination. The total exposure to circulating immune complexes would thus be larger in rabbits eliminating on day 13 than those on day 11. Yet the glomerulonephritis found in the day 13 rabbits, as manifest histologically and by proteinuria, was less than in rabbits eliminating on day 11 or 12.

A lower, but definite, level of I*BSA in the form of immune complexes was seen in animals not experiencing elimination of >99% of the circulating I*BSA prior to day 14 or 15 (Fig. 2). The four rabbits which eliminated on days 14 and 15 had an amount of complexed I*BSA between that of the day 13 rabbits and the rabbits not demonstrating immune elimination.

*Quantitation of I*BSA in the kidney.* The amount of I*BSA in the kidneys is presented in Table I. The greatest amount of I*BSA was found in the 20 rabbits eliminating on the 10th, 11th and 12th days with a mean of 18 μg/total kidney weight (range 9 to 35 μg). In the nine rabbits eliminating on days 13, 14 and 15, the mean I*BSA in the kidneys was 11 μg (range 4 to 23 μg). In the nine rabbits which did not eliminate by day 14 or 15, a mean of only 3 μg (range 1 to 4 μg) was found. Although elimination of >99% of circulating I*BSA did not occur, in the latter group, small amounts of I*BSA were present as immune complexes in the circulation.

In the group of 23 rabbits studied following the administration of I*BSA without a paired label control a mean of 10 μg of I*BSA/total kidney weight (range 4 to 20 μg) was found. A similar relationship of the amount of I*BSA found in the kidney to the rapidity of immune elimination was noted in this group.

The calculated specific I*BSA found in the washed Waring Blendor sediment was felt to represent I*BSA most likely in the form of immune complexes. Most of the I*BSA was in the cortical portion of the kidneys. Other studies of rabbits with chronic serum sickness showing much larger amounts of I*BSA in the kidneys have indicated that most of this I*BSA in the cortex was actually in glomeruli isolated by the method of Krakower and Greenspon (24). The I*BSA could be eluted at pH 3.2 from the renal sediment of these chronic serum sickness kidneys indicating that it was present as an immune complex (C. B. Wilson and F. J. Dixon, to be published). In addition, the results of immunofluorescence studies to be discussed also have shown the BSA to be glomerular in location associated with rabbit IgG and complement.

*Disappearance rate of I*BSA from the kidney.* Preliminary experiments in nine rabbits demonstrated no mean difference in the amounts of I*BSA in kidneys obtained at nephrectomy when >99% of the circulating I*BSA had been eliminated and at autopsy 4 days later. This suggested continued renal deposition of the 1.2 to 2.3 mg of I*BSA-anti-BSA immune complexes remaining in the circulation at the time of nephrectomy. Indeed, complete clearance of circulating immune complexes did not occur until 2 days following the time of 99% elimination.

To determine the disappearance rate of the I*BSA in the kidneys, seven rabbits that eliminated >99% of the circulating I*BSA between days 10 and 13 were studied by allowing an additional 3 to 4 days to elapse prior to nephrectomy. The determinations at autopsy were made 6 to 8 days following nephrectomy. The mean I*BSA in the kidneys obtained at nephrectomy was 12 μg/total kidney weight. The disappearance rate (T_{50}) of this I*BSA was 9.4 ± 1.3 (S.E.) days. This value was confirmed by calculating the disappearance rate of I*BSA in the kidneys of 15 rabbits nephrectomized on the day of >99% elimination of the circulating I*BSA and killed 5 to 8 days later. By assuming, as had been previously shown, that there was no mean change in the I*BSA in the kidney during the first 4 days following >99% elimination, the calculated disappearance time of the I*BSA in these kidneys was 10.5 days (T_{50}).

Histology. The histologic alterations in the renal specimens obtained at the time of immune elimination corresponded, in general, to their I*BSA content. The kidneys of 15 rabbits used for the paired label studies with 3 and 4+ glomerular changes were found to contain a mean of 20 μg of I*BSA/total kidney weight. In the kidneys of 14 paired label rabbits with 1 and 2+ changes there was a mean of only 12 μg of I*BSA.

Partial to almost complete resolution of glomerular hypercellularity and cellular swelling was seen in 38 rabbits studied with both nephrectomy, on the day of >99% elimination, and specimens taken at autopsy 4 to 8 days later. The histologic changes were paralleled by diminishing proteinuria. In only one rabbit (3123) did the glomerulonephritis progress after elimination of circulating I*BSA, accompanied by continued proteinuria and a measurable decrease in renal function with a serum creatinine elevation to 8 mg/100 ml. Figure 3 presents photomicrographs of representative glomeruli from the kidney of this rabbit obtained by nephrectomy compared to glomeruli from the kidney taken at autopsy 7 days later. In the specimen taken at autopsy a good deal of interstitial and tubular injury, probably secondary to the glomerular change, was also present. This rabbit had 9.5 μg of I*BSA in the kidney obtained by nephrectomy (19 μg/total kidney weight) and 8 μg in the kidney taken at autopsy 7 days later. The immunofluorescence staining of these kidneys revealed an accumulation of rabbit C3 during this interval (Fig. 3).

The examination of the other organs of the 45 paired-label rabbits 4 to 12 days after I*BSA elimination revealed frequent carditis. Nineteen out of the 36 rabbits eliminating by day 15 had residual evidence of coronary vasculitis. In addition 29 of the 36 had evidence of endocarditis, valvulitis or both. Of the nine rabbits not eliminating by day 14 or 15, two (2714, 3112) had focal coronary vasculitis and five focal endocarditis or valvulitis. Rabbit 2714 also had focal glomerulitis, mild proteinuria and 4 μg of I*BSA/total kidney weight. Rabbit 3112 had minimal focal glomerulitis without proteinuria and also had 4 μg of I*BSA/total kidney weight. The elimination curves of circulating I*BSA were lower in these two rabbits than in the other seven rabbits not eliminating prior to day 14 or 15 (Fig. 1). Rabbit 2714 had 6.6 mg of I*BSA present in immune complex form in the circulation on the 9th day and 2.8 mg on the 15th day following injection. Rabbit 3112 had 7.7 mg of circulating immune complex I*BSA on the 8th day and 3.0 mg on the 14th day following injection.

Immunofluorescent staining. Sections of kidneys taken at nephrectomy and/or autopsy in 37 rabbits used in the paired-label experiments were examined for BSA, rabbit IgG and C3 by the immunofluorescence technique. The incidence of detectable BSA deposition is shown in Table I. All rabbits eliminating between days 10 and 12 had BSA in a granular pattern in the glomeruli by immunofluorescence, whereas only four of eight of the rabbits eliminating between days 13 and 15 had BSA in the glomeruli that could be detected by immunofluorescence. None of the rabbits that failed to eliminate had detectable BSA by immunofluorescence. The amount of BSA detected by immunofluorescence also decreased as immune elimination was delayed.

No BSA could be detected in any kidney containing less than 5 μg of renal bound I*BSA/total kidney weight (20 g). It was calculated that the lower level of sensitivity of the immunofluorescence technique was 0.25 μg of BSA/g of kidney in these immune complex kidneys. At this level the immunofluorescent deposits were minimal, being focal in nature and involving only a portion of the glomerulus and, in instances, only parts of the glomerular capillary walls.

The immunofluorescence in the kidneys removed at autopsy from 24 rabbits 4 to 8 days following immune elimination was compared to that in the kidneys obtained by nephrectomy (Table II). The BSA detectable by immunofluorescence remained constant at a low level in eight kidneys removed at autopsy and decreased or disappeared in 14. Two rabbits had an increase in BSA detected by immunofluorescence corresponding to increased I*BSA at autopsy 4 days following immune elimination. In contrast to BSA the amount of IgG detected by immunofluorescence remained constant in 13 rabbits and increased in 11 of the 24 autopsy specimens. Increases in C3 were found in 20 kidneys taken at autopsy, and remained constant in only four. The

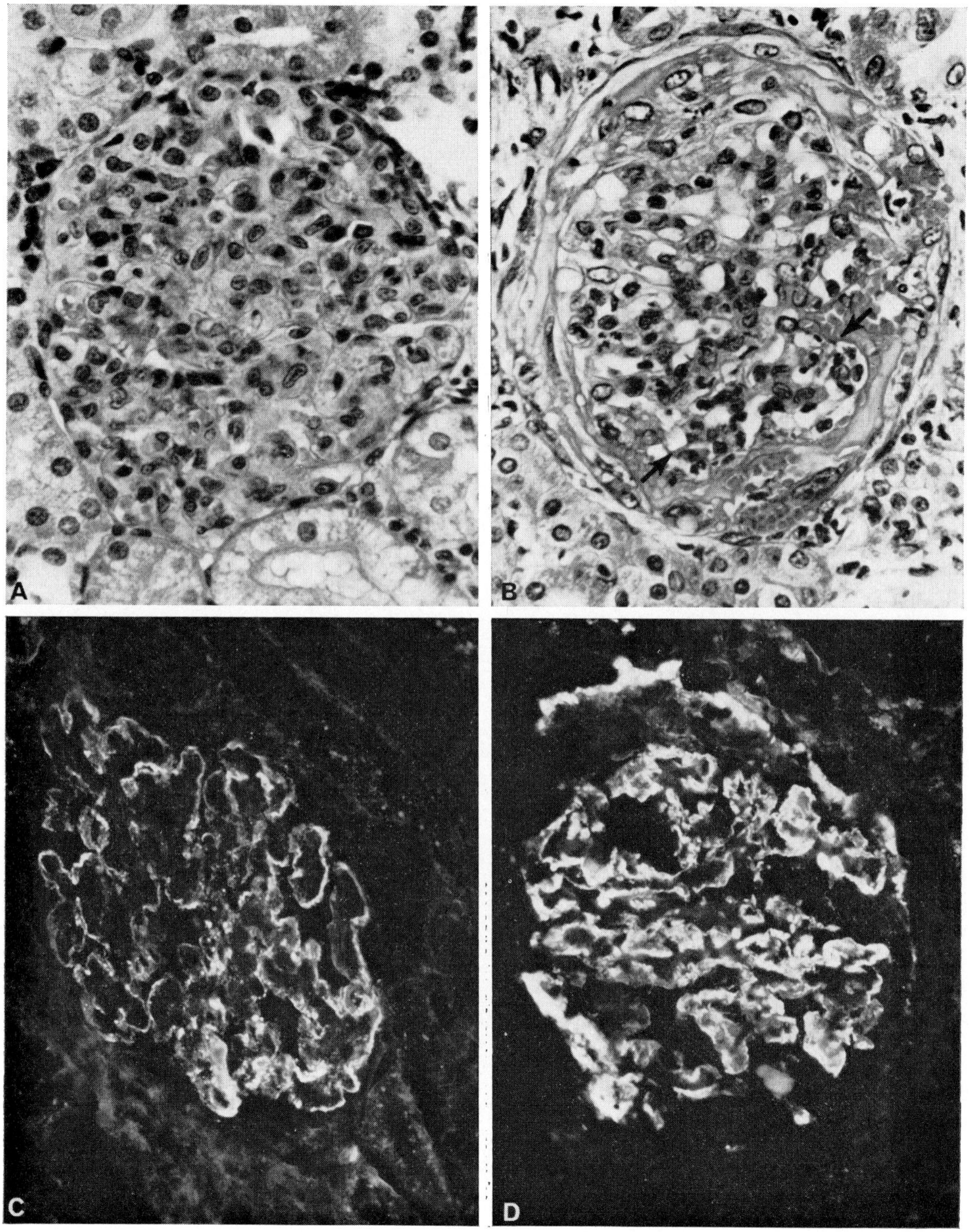

Figure 3. Rabbit 3123 with progressive glomerulonephritis. A section of the nephrectomy kidney (*A*) shows glomerular hypercellularity and cellular swelling. A section of the kidney obtained at autopsy 7 days later (*B*) shows hyperplasia of cells of Bowman's capsule and early crescent formation. The glomerular tuft is less cellular and foci (*arrows*) of polymorphonuclear cells are evident. (Hematoxylin-eosin stain; original magnification, ×400). A section of the nephrectomy kidney stained with fluoresceinated anti-rabbit C3 antisera (*C*) shows light granular deposits nearly confluent in areas along the glomerular capillary walls. A section of kidney removed at autopsy (*D*) shows increased granular deposits of C3 in a nearly confluent distribution along the glomerular capillary wall and in an area of crescent formation (original magnification, ×400).

TABLE II

Comparison by immunofluorescence of kidneys obtained by nephrectomy and at autopsy

Rabbit No.	Day of Elimination	I*BSA at Death[a]	Immunofluorescent Staining					
			BSA		IgG		C3	
			Nephrectomy	Autopsy	Nephrectomy	Autopsy	Nephrectomy	Autopsy
4-day interval between nephrectomy and autopsy								
2704	11	40	1+	2+	2+	2+ G[b]	1+	2+ G[b]
2706	11	10	tr	tr	tr	tr	tr	1+
2707	13	8	tr	0	tr	tr	tr	tr
2710	11	12	1+	0	tr	tr	tr	1+ G
2711	12	8	1+	0	tr	tr	tr	tr
2712	12	40	1+	2+	tr	2+ G	tr	2+ G
2716	13	6	tr	tr	tr	tr	tr	tr
2717	13	6	tr	tr	tr	2+ G	tr	2+ G
2719	12	20	1+	1+	1+	1+ G	tr	1+ G
5-day interval between nephrectomy and autopsy								
2705	10	22	tr	tr	1+	1+	tr	1+ G
2718	10	20	tr	tr	tr	1+	tr	1+ G
3122	13	14	tr	0	tr	1+	tr	1+ G
6-day interval between nephrectomy and autopsy								
3109	12	8	tr	tr	1+	1+ G	1+	2+ G
3110	12	16	tr	0	tr	1+ G	tr	1+ G
3111	12	8	tr	tr	tr	1+ G	tr	1+ G
3114	12	12	tr	0	tr	tr	tr	tr G
3120	12	8	tr	0	tr	1+ G	tr	1+ G
3127	12	14	1+	tr	2+	3+ G	1+	3+ G
3128	12	8	tr	0	tr	1+	tr	1+ G
7-day interval between nephrectomy and autopsy								
3121	11	14	1+	tr	1+	1+ G	1+	2+ G
3123	11	16	1+	tr	2+	3+	1+	3+
8-day interval between nephrectomy and autopsy								
3119	10	16	1+	tr	1+	1+ G	tr	1+ G
3124	10	10	1+	0	1+	1+ G	1+	2+ G
3126	10	30	1+	0	1+	2+ G	tr	3+ G

[a] Micrograms/total kidney weight.
[b] Globular glomerular deposits (G).

deposits of both rabbit IgG and C3 were finely granular at nephrectomy corresponding to the pattern seen for BSA. At autopsy, however, the finely granular pattern was replaced by globular deposits of IgG in 13 of the 24 kidneys and of C3 in 19 of the 24 kidneys.

Figure 4 shows the fine focal granular deposits of C3 and BSA in a glomerulus from rabbit 3124 taken at nephrectomy on day 10 together with the hematoxylin and eosin histologic appearance of the kidney. Globular C3 deposits are seen in the glomeruli of this rabbit at autopsy 8 days later together with some resolution of the histologic lesion (Fig. 5). During the same interval the BSA detectable by immunofluorescence disappeared while the 14 μg of I*BSA/total kidney weight found at nephrectomy had decreased only 20% during the same interval.

*Urinary excretion of I*RSA, I*BSA and I*BSA-anti-BSA immune complexes.* In the paired-label urines both I*RSA and I*BSA were present only in microgram quantities/24 hr prior to immune elimination in the 20 rabbits studied. Excretion of these two albumins became significant with the onset of proteinuria. When the urinary concentration was related to the plasma levels by the clearance formula $C_x = \frac{U_x V}{P_x}$, the clearance of BSA was routinely greater than that of RSA.

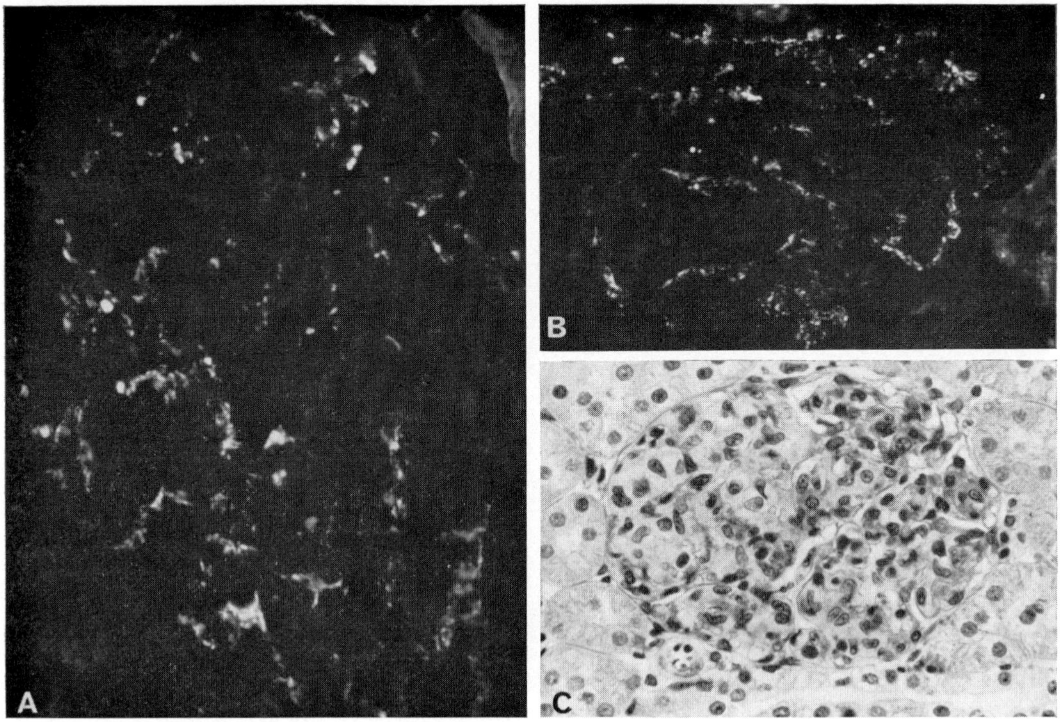

Figure 4. Sections from the kidney of rabbit 3124 obtained at nephrectomy. *A*, a glomerulus stained with fluoresceinated anti-rabbit C3 showing a fine granular pattern of deposits along the glomerular capillary walls. *B*, the same pattern of fluorescence is seen with fluorescein-conjugated anti-BSA antiserum. *C*, histologic sections of this kidney show hypercellularity and cellular swelling (original magnification, ×400).

The amount of I*BSA in the urine precipitable by ammonium sulfate after individual correction for nonspecific entrapment was very small. Concentrations greater than 1 μg/ml were reached in only two heavily proteinuric rabbits (3119 and 3123) on the day of >99% elimination. In the 12 rabbits of this group that developed proteinuria a mean maximum excretion of I*BSA as immune complexes of 54 μg/24 hr (range 0 to 241) was noted between day 9 and the day following >99% elimination from the circulation. In the eight nonproteinuric rabbits the mean maximum excretion was 28 μg/24 hr (range 0 to 82). The urinary excretion of complexes fell below the sensitivity of the technique 48 hr following >99% elimination.

DISCUSSION

This study was designed to quantitate the amount of I*BSA deposited in the kidneys in acute serum sickness, to determine its disappearance rate, to follow its interaction with host IgG and complement and to relate these data to the degree of associated glomerulonephritis. The incidence and severity of the glomerulonephritis produced in the rabbits studied were similar to those in previous enhanced acute serum sickness experiments (14, 25–27).

The results of this study provide the first quantitation of antigen in the form of antigen-antibody complexes involved in the production of glomerulonephritis. An average of 10 μg of I*BSA was deposited/rabbit kidney in acute serum sickness. Since each kidney contained 200,000 glomeruli (28), it could be calculated[6] that the deposition of 4.4×10^8 molecules of BSA/glomerulus was associated with the development of acute nephritis. No values were available for the amounts of antibody and complement that

[6] Using a molecular weight of 68,000 for BSA and Avogadro's number 6.02×10^{23} molecules/g mol.

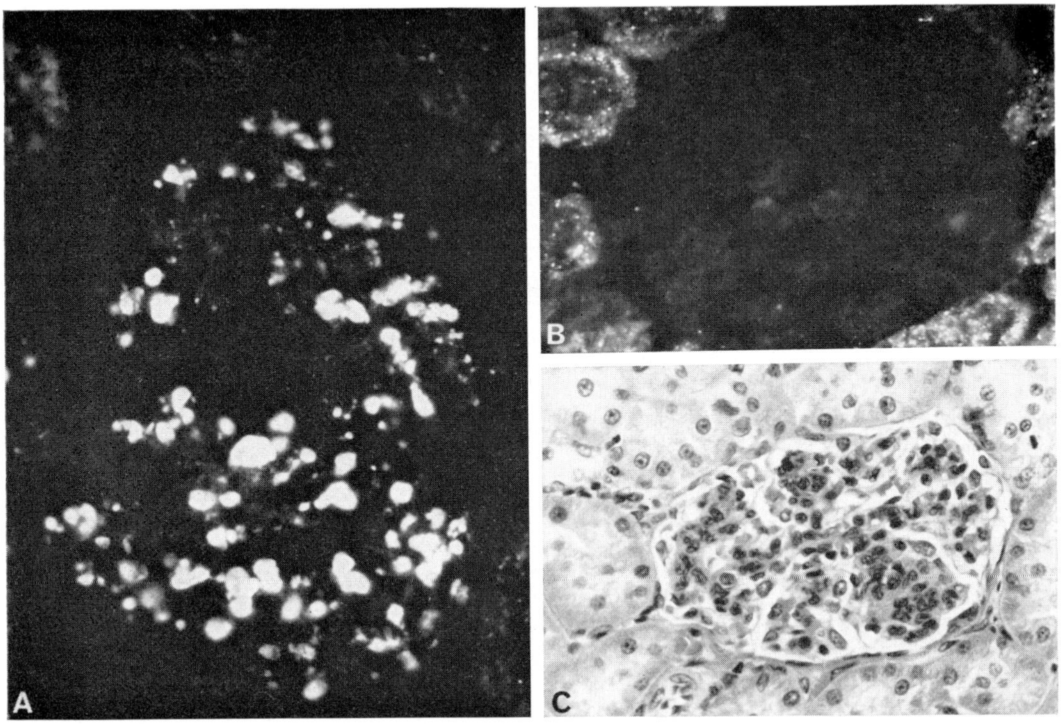

Figure 5. Sections from the kidney of rabbit 3124 obtained at autopsy 8 days following nephrectomy. *A*, a glomerulus stained with fluoresceinated anti-rabbit C3. Large globular deposits of C3 have replaced the fine granular deposition seen in the nephrectomy specimen. *B*, no deposits of BSA were detectable in this kidney when stained with fluoresceinated anti-BSA antiserum. *C*, histologic sections of this kidney show a decrease in cellular swelling, however, some focal hypercellularity remains (original magnification, ×400).

were present in these complexes. However, since complexes initially were formed at a time of antigen excess, a ratio of less than 5 antibody molecules/antigen molecule would be expected. If the ratio of 3 antibody molecules/antigen molecule were assumed, this would increase the combined amount of antigen and antibody to 1.8×10^9 molecules/glomerulus. The deposition of the complexes in the kidneys was in random aggregates along the glomerular capillary basement membrane. Therefore, extremely high concentrations of immunologic reactants would be in small anatomic foci with uninvolved regions intervening. This suggestion was supported by the observation of focal glomerulitis in the rabbits with small amounts of I*BSA in the glomeruli.

The disappearance of I*BSA from the kidneys after elimination of all circulating complexes had a half time of about 10 days. Extensive studies on chronic serum sickness glomerulonephritis have shown a half time disappearance of I*BSA from the kidneys of about 5 days, twice as rapid as in acute serum sickness (C. B. Wilson and F. J. Dixon, to be published). The mechanism of loss of the BSA from the glomeruli is still unknown. It is possible that the BSA could be excreted in the urine in the form of BSA-anti-BSA complexes but the present techniques were not sensitive enough to establish this point.

The interaction of I*BSA with rabbit IgG and complement was studied by immunofluorescence. During the 8-day period following immune elimination of circulating complexes, increasing amounts of rabbit IgG and, more strikingly, complement were observed in the glomeruli while the amount of detectable BSA decreased sharply. Fish *et al.* (29) have previously described this finding. The present isotope data indicated that the actual amount of BSA in the kidneys during this period decreased quite slowly. This suggested that following elimination of circulating I*BSA, the BSA deposited in the glomeruli was being covered by host anti-BSA antibody and complement from the circulation rendering it undetectable by the immunofluorescent technique. The increase in IgG and complement occurred while evidence of glomerulonephritis was decreasing both histologically and as manifested by proteinuria. This suggests that the circulating complexes formed initially in antigen excess were nephritogenic while the subsequent accumulation of antibody and complement did not continue to produce glomerular injury. It may be that the circulating complexes produced their greatest injury during transit through the capillary wall or via release of mediators while they were still circulating. Once deposited in an extravascular site, they appeared to be less phlogogenic in spite of continued interaction with antibody and complement.

In only one rabbit (3123) did progressive renal disease occur during the 7 days after elimination of circulating complexes. This rabbit had the greatest proteinuria and also the heaviest deposits of complement at autopsy. The complement deposits were present along the glomerular capillary wall and were not globular. This unusual progression of acute serum sickness to "chronic" renal disease may be analogous to the unusual progression of acute poststreptococcal glomerulonephritis in man. However, the nature of the continuing phlogogenic stimulus in either instance is unknown.

The severity but not the incidence of glomerulonephritis in this study related directly to the rate of immune elimination of the injected I*BSA from the circulation. The rabbits with the most rapid elimination had the greatest amounts of I*BSA in their glomeruli and the most severe glomerulonephritis. The total exposure to circulating I*BSA-anti-BSA complexes was greatest in rabbits with slower rates of elimination although they had less severe nephritis. In the paired label studies 9 of 45 rabbits had no detectable immune elimination and yet had evidence of antibody production as indicated by circulating immune complexes. Focal renal and/or cardiac histologic alterations were present in five of these rabbits associated with deposition of small amounts of I*BSA in the kidneys. Weigle and Dixon (30) have previously reported similar histologic observations.

It was possible to get some rough comparison of the phlogogenic capacity of antigen-antibody complexes deposited irregularly along the glomerular capillary walls and in the mesangia and of anti-glomerular basement membrane (GBM) antibody fixed rather uniformly along the inner aspect of the GBM. The deposition of 4.4×10^8 molecules of BSA/glomerulus, or an assumed 1.3×10^9 molecules of anti-BSA antibody, was associated with the development of acute glomerulonephritis in these rabbits. In anti-GBM antibody induced acute nephritis in rabbits approximately 3×10^9 molecules of antibody were fixed per glomerulus (31).

Acknowledgments. We wish to thank Mrs. Sharon Reck and Miss Susan Hillson for their excellent technical assistance.

REFERENCES

1. Germuth, F. G., J. Exp. Med., *97:* 257, 1953.
2. Dixon, F. J., Vazquez, J. J., Weigle, W. O. and Cochrane, C. G., Arch. Path., *65:* 18, 1958.
3. Dixon, F. J., Feldman, J. D. and Vazquez, J. J., J. Exp. Med., *113:* 899, 1961.
4. Tan, E. M., Schur, H. G. and Kunkel, H. G., J. Clin. Invest., *44:* 1104, 1965.
5. Krishnan, C. and Kaplan, M. H., J. Clin. Invest., *46:* 569, 1967.
6. Koffler, D., Schur, P. and Kunkel, H. G., J. Exp. Med., *126:* 607, 1967.
7. Andres, G. A., Accinni, L., Hsu, K. C., Zabriskie, J. B. and Seegal, B. C., J. Exp. Med., *123:* 399, 1966.
8. Treser, G., Semar, M., Ty, A., Sagel, I., Franklin, M. A. and Lange, K., J. Clin. Invest., *49:* 762, 1970.
9. Ward, P. A. and Kibukamusoke, J. W., Lancet, *1:* 283, 1969.
10. Oldstone, M. B. A. and Dixon, F. J., J. Exp. Med., *129:* 483, 1969.
11. Porter, D. D., Larsen, A. E. and Porter, H. G. J. Exp. Med., *130:* 575, 1969.
12. Banks, K. L. and Henson, J. B., Fed. Proc., *28:* 752, 1969.
13. McConahey, P. J. and Dixon, F. J., Int. Arch. Allerg., *29:* 185, 1966.
14. Kniker, W. T. and Cochrane, C. G., J. Exp. Med., *122:* 83, 1965.
15. Pressman, D., Day, E. D. and Blau, M., Cancer Res., *17:* 845, 1957.
16. Weigle, W. O., J. Immun., *87:* 599, 1961.
17. Schwert, G. W., Amer. Chem. Soc., *79:* 139, 1957.
18. MacFate, R. P., Cohn, C., Eichelberger, L. and Cooper, J. A. D., Amer. J. Clin. Path., *24:* 511, 1954.

19. Farr, R. S., J. Infect. Dis., *103:* 239, 1958.
20. Coons, A. H. and Kaplan, M. H., J. Exp. Med., *91:* 1, 1950.
21. Clark, H. F. and Shepard, C. C., Virology, *20:* 642, 1963.
22. Wood, B. T., Thompson, S. H. and Goldstein, G., J. Immun., *95:* 225, 1965.
23. Weigle, W. O., Proc. Soc. Exp. Biol. Med., *94:* 306, 1957.
24. Krakower, C. A. and Greenspon, S. A., Arch. Path., *51:* 629, 1951.
25. Germuth, F. G., Pace, M. G. and Tippett, J. C., J. Exp. Med., *101:* 135, 1955.
26. West, C. D., Hinkle, N. H. and Landing, B. H., J. Lab. Clin. Med., *55:* 439, 1960.
27. Rhyne, M. B. and Germuth, F. G., J. Exp. Med., *114:* 633, 1961.
28. Smith, H. W., in *The Kidney. Structure and Function in Health and Disease,* Oxford University Press, Inc., New York, 1951.
29. Fish, A. J., Michael, A. F., Vernier, R. L. and Good, R. A., Amer. J. Path., *49:* 997, 1966.
30. Weigle, W. O. and Dixon, F. J., Proc. Soc. Exp. Biol. Med., *99:* 226, 1958.
31. Unanue, E. R., Dixon, F. J. and Feldman, J. D., J. Exp. Med., *125:* 163, 1967.

THE JOURNAL OF IMMUNOLOGY
Vol. 105, No. 2, August 1970
Printed in U.S.A.

ANTIGENIC AND IMMUNOGENIC PROPERTIES OF COMPONENTS CONTAINED IN RABIES VIRUS-INFECTED TISSUE CULTURE FLUIDS

H. DIETER SCHLUMBERGER,[1] TADEUSZ J. WIKTOR AND HILARY KOPROWSKI[2]

From The Wistar Institute of Anatomy and Biology, 36th and Spruce Streets, Philadelphia, Pennsylvania 19104

Received for publication April 17, 1970

Following differential centrifugation or zinc acetate precipitation, it was possible to fractionate rabies-infected tissue culture fluids into components which exhibited different complement-fixing, protective and immunogenic activities. The virion-depleted fraction showed higher complement-fixing activity than the fraction which contained essentially all the virions. The virion-depleted fraction obtained after precipitation of the virus with zinc acetate showed, in addition to complement-fixing activity, good protective activity. Thus, it is possible to produce material which contains a minimum quantity of infectious virus, is immunogenic and induces protection against challenge with virulent virus.

Our laboratory reported previously that the protective activity of inactivated rabies vaccines of tissue culture origin (1) is enhanced by concentration of rabies virions using zinc acetate precipitation (2). We found also, however, that supernatant fluids obtained after precipitation of the virus by zinc acetate show appreciable protective activity. Other investigators also reported recently that rabies-specific antigens from brains of infected mice, freed of the bulk of infectious virus by high speed centrifugation, were able to induce the formation of virus-neutralizing antibody (3).

This communication describes a further investigation of the distribution of infectivity, complement-fixing (CF), protective and immunogenic activities in various fractions of rabies-infected tissue culture fluids obtained by differential centrifugation or by zinc acetate precipitation. Such information is a prerequisite for determining the possible feasibility of developing an effective vaccine composed of subviral components.

MATERIALS AND METHODS

Virus

Tissue culture-adapted PM and Flury HEP strains of rabies virus (4) were purified by cloning using a plaque technique employing agarose-suspended BHK-13 S cells (5). The cloned virus was propagated in monolayer cultures of BHK-21 cells according to methods described previously (2) except that the medium contained only 0.1% bovine serum albumin (BSA).

Virus infectivity levels in the original tissue culture fluids and in different fractions obtained during concentration and purification procedures were determined by the plaque assay technique (5). Titers are expressed as plaque-forming units (PFU)/ml.

Fractionation and concentration procedures

A. Concentration by ultrafiltration. Rabies-infected tissue culture fluid was clarified by centrifugation at 750 × G for 30 min at 4°C to remove cellular debris. The supernatant fluid was subsequently concentrated by ultrafiltration at 4°C, employing nitrocellulose membranes with a porosity of 10 to 20 nm (Filter SM 12 133, Membranfiltergesellschaft mbH, Göttingen, Germany) in a specially-designed filtration apparatus (6) in which fluid is recirculated from a supply vessel and passed tangentially over the surface of the membrane at a constant speed. This procedure eliminates the problem of membrane clogging encountered during conventional filtration. Prior to use, the filtration apparatus and filters were sterilized by circulation of 5% formaldehyde in distilled water for 24 hr, followed by exhaustive rinsing with sterile distilled water and sterile 0.13 M NaCl, 0.05 M tris(hydroxy-

[1] Fellow of The Wistar Institute from the Max Planck Institut für Virusforschung, Tübingen, Germany.

[2] Requests for reprints should be addressed to Dr. H. Koprowski at The Wistar Institute.

methyl)aminomethane (Tris)-chloride buffer pH 7.8 (NT buffer). A series of four membranes was used with an effective filtration area of 1100 cm^2. At a filtration speed of 360 to 440 ml/hr, a fluid volume of 2 liters was concentrated 15- to 20-fold in 4 to 5 hr. Concentration by ultrafiltration resulted always in quantitative recovery of infectivity, CF and protective activity.

B. Fractionation by differential centrifugation. The tissue culture fluid, concentrated by ultrafiltration, was again clarified by centrifugation at 750 × G for 30 min at 4°C and then fractionated by successive high speed centrifugations at increasing speed in the No. 30 rotor of a Spinco centrifuge. The content of the tubes (20 ml) was centrifuged at given speeds for 60 min. Under these conditions, more than 95% of the infectious virus sedimented at 12,500 rpm (13,600 × G). The 13,600 × G supernatant fluid was sequentially recentrifuged at 16,000 rpm (22,300 × G), 20,000 rpm (34,900 × G) and finally at 28,000 rpm (68,000 × G). The sediment obtained at each centrifugation was dissolved in NT buffer for assay of biologic activities.

Precipitation with zinc acetate. Infected tissue culture fluid or 13,600 × G supernatant fluid (see above) was treated with zinc acetate as described previously (2). The precipitate was collected by centrifugation at 750 × G for 20 min and resuspended in a saturated solution of disodium EDTA adjusted to pH 7.8 by addition of Tris. Some resuspended precipitates were desalted by filtration through a Sephadex G-25 column equilibrated with NT buffer. The desalted preparations were then fractionated by centrifugation at 13,600 × G.

The supernatant fluid remaining after zinc acetate precipitation was concentrated by ultrafiltration and fractionated by centrifugation at 17,100 × G.

Inactivation of virus. Beta propiolactone (BPL) was added to the fractions to give a final concentration of 0.025% and maintained at 4°C for 20 hr, followed by 2 hr at 37°C. The absence of residual infectious virus was determined by intracerebral inoculation of adult and newborn mice.

Immunologic and protective activity

A. CF test. A previously described (2) microtechnique was used for titrations of CF activity. The reciprocal of the highest dilution of antigen showing partial reaction was taken as the titer, i.e., as the number of CF units (CFU)/milliliter.

Immune sera for CF antigen assay were prepared in adult New Zealand rabbits injected with PM or HEP rabies virus prepared by concentration of infectious tissue culture fluids by ultrafiltration, followed by two cycles of high speed centrifugation at 13,600 × G. The final sediment was resuspended in NT buffer containing 0.1% human serum albumin (Hyland Laboratories, Los Angeles, Calif.).

Rabbits immunized with HEP virus were given four intravenous inoculations of 3 × 10^9 PFU of infectious virus at weekly intervals and bled 7 days after the last inoculation. To prepare immune serum against the PM strain, animals were given two intramuscular inoculations at a week's interval with 4 × 10^9 PFU of virus inactivated by ultraviolet radiation (1) and emulsified in equal parts of incomplete Freund's adjuvant. The animals then received two intravenous inoculations of 1 × 10^9 PFU of live virus, and were bled 7 days after the last inoculation. Serum was absorbed with BHK cells according to methods described previously (7) as well as with calf serum and with human serum albumin.

B. Virus neutralization test. The level of virus neutralizing antibody in sera of immunized animals was determined by a plaque assay technique (5, 8). Neutralizing antibody titer was expressed as the reciprocal of the highest dilution of immune serum causing a 50% reduction in plaques.

C. Protective activity (NIH mouse potency test). The test was performed as described before (1). The antigenic values (AV) of experimental vaccines were obtained by dividing the effective dose (ED_{50}) dilution endpoints of the test preparations by that of the reference vaccine.

D. Immunogenic activity. The preparations were administered subcutaneously in 1-ml doses to groups of four rabbits each. Fourteen days after the initial inoculation, selected animals were given a booster dose. All animals were bled before the first inoculation and on the 3rd, 7th and 14th day after both primary and booster inoculations. Ninety-eight days after the first inoculation, all rabbits were challenged by intramuscular inoculation with $10^{5.7}$ mouse LD_{50} of a DR street rabies virus of vampire bat origin obtained through the courtesy of Dr. Boris Szyfres, Director of the Centro Panamericano de Zoonosis (Buenos Aires,

Argentina). Two unvaccinated control animals were challenged simultaneously.

RESULTS

Biologic activity of tissue culture fluid fractions obtained by differential centrifugation. The biologic properties of fractions obtained by differential centrifugation of infectious tissue culture fluids of two rabies virus strains, concentrated by ultrafiltration, are shown in Tables I and II. Because previous experiments had demonstrated that the maintenance of infectivity and protective activity requires the presence of stabilizing proteins, BSA at a concentration of 0.1% was incorporated in all suspending media.

The initial centrifugation of the concentrated PM rabies tissue culture fluid at 13,600 × G gave a quantitative recovery of infectivity in the sediment, whereas only one-fourth of the CF activity was sedimented under these conditions. After inactivation with BPL, this fraction contained 70% of the original protective activity. Recentrifugation of the virus-depleted supernatant fluid at 22,300 × G yielded a sediment which contained 3.5% of the initial infectivity, 6.8% of the CF activity and 12.1% of the protective activity. After further centrifugation of the preceding supernatant fluid at 34,900 × G and at 68,400 × G, respectively, the sediments exhibited extremely low infectivity, as well as protective and CF activities. The final 68,400 × G supernatant fluid showed, however, a high CF activity, very little infectivity and only 2.4% of the protective activity.

The 13,600 × G sediment, which contained the bulk of infective virions, had high protective activity, with an AV of 52.5, whereas the 22,300 × G sediment showed an AV of 18. The latter protective activity could not be accounted for by the presence of infective virions.

Similar results were obtained with fractions of concentrated HEP rabies virus infected tissue culture fluid (Table II). The 13,600 × G sediment contained 98.5% of the infectivity of the original concentrate, 91% of the protective activity and 33% of CF activity. In the 64,400 × G supernatant fluid, 50% of the CF activity but only 3.8% of the protective activity were recovered.

Results similar to those shown in Tables I and II were obtained with several different batches of PM and HEP Flury virus-infected tissue culture fluids.

Biologic activities of tissue culture fluid fractions obtained by the zinc acetate precipitation method. Infectious tissue culture fluids depleted of virus by treatment with zinc acetate exhibited mark-

TABLE I

Biologic activities of fractions obtained after differential centrifugation of infectious tissue culture fluid (strain PM)

Fraction	Infectivity (PFU × 10^{-7})			CF Activity			Protective Activity: ED_{50}			Protective Activity: AV
	Per ml	Total	% recovery	Per ml	Total	% recovery	Per ml	Total	% recovery	Per ml
Tissue culture fluid concentrated by ultrafiltration (× 14.5[a])	20	3,400	100	64	10,900	100	370	62,900	100	9.2
13,600 × G sediment (× 117)	190	4,000	117	128	2,700	24.8	2,100	44,000	70.0	52.5
23,300 × G sediment (× 223)	11	120	3.5	64	680	6.2	720	7,600	12.1	18.0
34,900 × G sediment (× 223)	0.4	4.2	0.12	32	340	3.1	109	1,150	1.8	2.7
64,400 × G sediment (× 223)	0.00002	0.0001	0.001	32	340	3.1	74	790	1.3	1.85
64,400 × G supernatant (× 14.5)	0.0003	0.05	0.0014	64	10,900	100	9	1,530	2.4	0.23

[a] Concentration factor: Ratio of the original tissue culture fluid to the fraction volume.

TABLE II

Biologic activities of fractions obtained after differential centrifugation of infectious tissue culture fluid (strain HEP Flury)

Fraction	Infectivity (PFU × 10^{-7})			CF Activity			Protective Activity			
							ED_{50}			AV
	Per ml	Total	% recovery	Per ml	Total	% recovery	Per ml	Total	% recovery	Per ml
Tissue culture fluid concentrated by ultrafiltration (× 19[a])	60	7,200	100	128	15,400	100	260	31,200	100	6.5
13,600 × G sediment (× 236)	710	7,100	98.5	512	5,120	33.2	2,840	28,400	91	71.0
23,300 × G sediment (× 236)	6	60	0.8	64	640	4.2	234	2,340	7.5	5.9
34,900 × G sediment (× 236)	0.01	0.1	0.0014	32	320	2.1	56	560	1.8	1.4
54,400 × G sediment (× 236)	0.03	0.3	0.0042	64	640	4.2	14	140	0.4	0.35
54,400 × G supernatant fluid (× 19)	0.0001	0.012	0.0002	64	7,680	49.8	10	1,200	3.8	0.25

[a] Concentration factor: for explanation see Table I.

TABLE III

Protective activity of infective tissue culture fluid component obtained by fractionation with zinc acetate

Fraction	Protective Activity (ED_{50})		
	Per ml	Total	% recovery
Unconcentrated tissue culture fluid [a]	9.5	5,700	100
Sediment after zinc acetate precipitation, resuspended in EDTA solution (× 133 [b])	260	11,700	205
Supernatant fluid after zinc acetate precipitation, concentrated by ultrafiltration (× 6.3)	93	8,930	157
17,100 × G sediment of the virus-depleted preparation (× 11)	154	8,383	148
17,100 × G supernatant fluid of the virion-depleted preparation (× 6.3)	5	538	10

[a] The unconcentrated tissue culture fluid contained 7 × 10^7 PFU of rabies virus/ml.

[b] Concentration factor: for explanation see Table I.

edly higher protective activity (1) than those freed of the bulk of the virus by high speed centrifugation (Tables I and II). Both procedures were equally efficient, however, in removing infectious virus from the preparations, since less than 4% of the original infectivity was recovered in both types of supernatant fluids. In order to confirm the enhancing effect of zinc acetate on the protective activity of rabies virus preparations, infectious tissue culture fluids were treated with zinc acetate (Table III) and the resulting supernatant fluid, after concentration by ultrafiltration, was sedimented by centrifugation at 17,100 × G. The results (Table III) show that substantially more protective activity was recovered both in the precipitate and in the supernatant fluid obtained after treatment with zinc acetate than was originally contained in the untreated tissue culture fluid, and that the bulk of protective components present in the supernatant fluid could be sedimented at 17,100 × G. This finding indicates that aggregation of rabies-specific antigens by zinc acetate was probably responsible for the enhanced protective activity of the virus-depleted preparations.

As we observed before (2), in addition to the bulk of the virus, zinc acetate precipitates other proteins, including rabies-specific antigens, that are present in the infectious tissue culture fluid. We have designed an experiment in which (Table IV) infectious tissue culture fluid is first treated directly with zinc acetate; the resulting precipitate is then resuspended in EDTA solution and subsequently fractionated by centrifugation at 13,600 × G after desalting on a Sephadex G-25 column. The results (Table IV) indicate that the zinc acetate-precipitated material, which could be separated from the virions by differential centrifugation, exhibited appreciable protective activity.

In view of the apparent discrepancy between the protective activity of preparations freed of virions by high speed centrifugation and that of preparations depleted of virions by precipitation with zinc acetate, an investigation of the effect of Zn^{+2} ions on tissue culture fluid from which the bulk of infectious virus was removed by centrifugation at 13,600 × G was carried out. This study showed that (Table V), indeed, the protective activity of the virion-depleted preparation was enhanced because 44.7% of the original protective activity was recovered in the precipitate, as compared with 13.2% recovered in the untreated preparation.

TABLE IV

Fractionation of protective and infectious components present in the precipitate obtained by treatment of tissue culture fluid with zinc acetate

Fraction	Infectivity (PFU × 10^{-7})			Protective Activity (ED_{50})		
	Per ml	Total	% recovery	Per ml	Total	% recovery
Unconcentrated tissue culture fluid (strain PM)	2	1,280	100	18	11,520	100
Sediment precipitated with zinc acetate resuspended in EDTA solution (× 23)[a]	80	2,240	175	416	11,648	101
Sephadex G-25 filtrate (× 12)	19.5	1,053	82	178	9,612	83
13,600 × G sediment (× 28)	47	592	46.5	285	3,613	31
13,600 × G supernatant fluid (× 12)	0.35	20.8	1.6	76	4,911	42

[a] Concentration factors: for explanation see Table I.

TABLE V

Effect of zinc acetate on the protective activity of tissue culture fluid depleted of virions by high speed centrifugation

Fraction	Infectivity (PFU × 10^{-7})			Protective Activity (ED_{50})		
	Per ml	Total	% recovery	Per ml	Total	% recovery
Tissue culture fluid concentrated by ultrafiltration (× 10.7)[a]	17	1,024	100	182	10,920	100
13,600 × G sediment (× 42.6)	60	900	87.5	575	8,652	78.9
Precipitate from the zinc acetate treated 13,600 × G supernatant fluid, filtered through Sephadex G-25 (× 12.8)	0.60	30	2.9	98	4,900	44.7
13,600 × G supernatant fluid (× 10.7)	0.45	27	2.6	24	1,440	13.2
Supernatant fluid after zinc acetate precipitation (× 10.7)	0.008	0.036	0.1	5	230	2.1

[a] Concentration factor: for explanation see Table I.

The results of each of these experiments have shown that treatment with zinc acetate markedly enhanced the protective activity of virus-depleted preparations and indicated that aggregation of rabies-specific antigens might be responsible for their increased activity.

Immunogenicity of infectious tissue culture fluid fractions in rabbits. The immunogenicity of the virion-depleted fraction of tissue culture fluid (strain PM), prepared by differential ultracentrifugation, was compared with that of a virion-rich fraction by immunization of rabbits. The concentrated virion fraction (comparable to 13,600 × G sediment, Table I) contained 4.5 × 10^9 PFU and 128 CFU/ml, while the virion-depleted fraction contained 4.0 × 10^4 PFU and 256 CFU/ml (comparable to 64,400 × G supernatant fluid, Table I). A mixture containing as much infectious virus (4 × 10^4 PFU/ml and BSA (80 mg/ml) as the virion-depleted preparation was used as control inoculum.

The results (Fig. 1) indicate that the concentrated virion and the virion-depleted preparations induced the formation of virus neutralizing antibodies after a single inoculation. Although the level of antibodies induced by the virion-depleted preparation was approximately 10 times lower than that elicited by the preparation containing a high concentration of virions, the virion-depleted preparation gave a much more pronounced booster effect. Two doses of the virion-depleted preparation produced an antibody response similar to that obtained with two inoculations of the concentrated virion vaccine

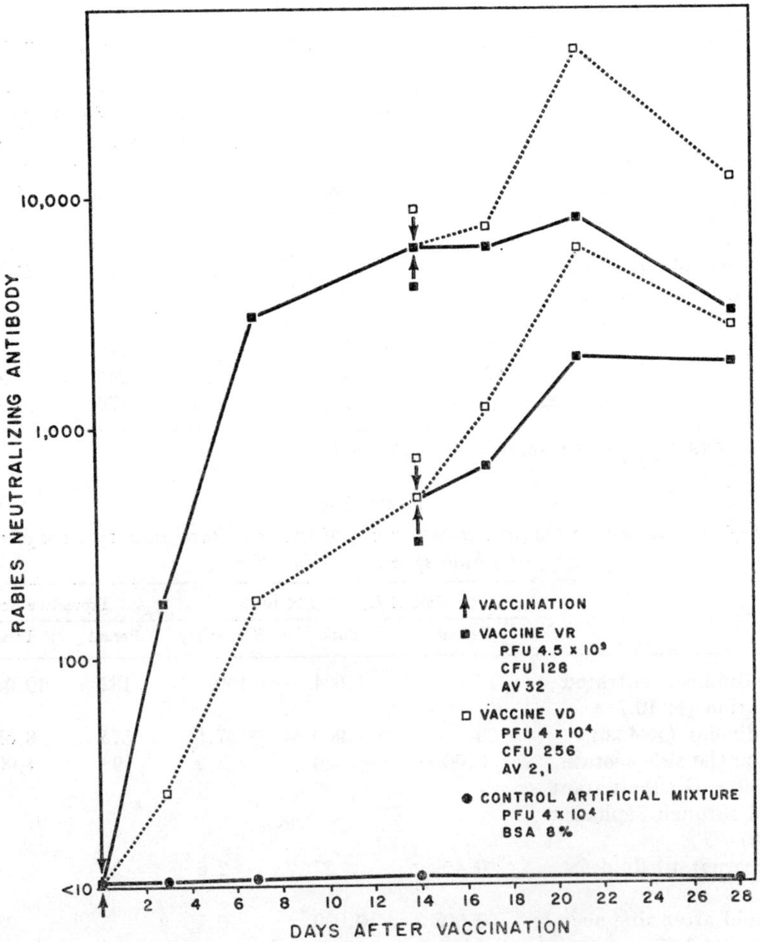

Figure 1. Dynamics of virus-neutralizing antibody formation in rabbits inoculated with virion vaccine and vaccine prepared from rabies-specific antigens depleted of virions.

The highest level of virus neutralizing antibodies (neutralization titer of 1:40,000) was obtained when an initial inoculation with the virion-rich fraction was followed by a second inoculation with the virion-depleted preparation. No neutralizing antibodies were detected in animals vaccinated with the control inoculum.

All animals vaccinated with virion-depleted and virion-rich preparations survived the challenge with virulent virus. All untreated control rabbits, as well as three out of four rabbits inoculated with the control inoculum containing 4 × 10^4 PFU of virus, died from rabies infection following similar incubation periods.

DISCUSSION

Although the existence of virion-free proteins occurring as soluble antigens in infected cells has been described for a variety of viruses, immunogenicity of these preparations has been studied extensively only in the case of poxviruses and some of the myxoviruses. A protein with a molecular weight of 100,000 to 200,000 daltons extracted from rabbit pox-infected cells induced formation of virus-neutralizing antibodies in rabbits (9) and behaved as serum-blocking antigen in the presence of such antibody (10).

The non-infectious hemagglutinin of fowl plague virus showed as good protective activity in the chicken protection test as did the virion-containing fraction. The CF activity of this preparation was, however, considerably lower than that of the virion-containing fraction (11).

The results obtained in this study showed that the terminal supernatant fluid (64,400 × G) obtained after sequential differential high speed centrifugation of the concentrate derived from ultrafiltration of rabies virus-infected tissue culture fluids, was essentially virion-free and contained most of the CF activity of the original preparation. The 13,600 × G fraction (Tables I and II), which contained essentially all the virions, showed lesser CF activity; and fractions obtained from material centrifuged at rates calculated to sediment viral components successively smaller in size than the virions and showing sharply reduced infectivity, had little CF activity.

In spite of high CF activity, the virion-depleted 64,400 × G supernatant fluid of the rabies preparation showed poor protective activity in the mouse potency test. Conversely, in rabbits, the same fractions elicited formation of significant level of virus neutralizing antibody. Moreover, a booster injection of these preparations caused a much greater rise in antibody level than did a booster injection of a virion-rich fraction (Fig. 1). The apparent discrepancy between the results obtained in mouse protection tests and those obtained in immunized rabbits may reflect either the fact that the two tests measured different properties of the preparations or that the virion-depleted fraction was destroyed in the body of the mouse before it could effectively elicit an antibody response. The latter possibility may merit consideration in the light of results obtained by replacing high speed centrifugation with zinc acetate treatment as the method for concentration of the virion-depleted fraction.

In contrast to preparations obtained from high speed centrifugation, preparations obtained after treatment with zinc acetate showed good protective activity, although their residual infectivity was as low as that of the other preparations. Of particular interest were the results indicating that the virion-depleted supernatant fluid obtained after concentration of the virus by precipitation with zinc acetate showed no loss in protective activity after sedimentation following centrifugation at 13,600 × G (Table IV).

It is possible that, following zinc acetate precipitation, large aggregates of the virus-depleted fraction are formed which retain their protective activity in mice longer than do the unaggregated antigens. The enhancement of the protective activity of rabies-specific antigens by treatment with zinc acetate preparations may be comparable to the enhancement of the protective activity previously demonstrated by addition of aluminum phosphate (12).

Whether the immunogenic virion-depleted protein represents a true "soluble antigen" produced in the infected cells or a product of spontaneous degradation of disrupted virus particles is impossible to state at present. Further studies of proteins associated with the virus itself and of their relationship with proteins isolated from virus-infected cells may throw some light on this problem.

What we have shown in the present study is that material which contains minimum quantities of infectious virus is immunogenic, and, when properly handled, induces protection against challenge with virulent virus. Thus, it may constitute a good material for the production of a safe and effective rabies vaccine.

Acknowledgments. This investigation was supported in part by Public Health Service Research Grant No. RO1-AI 02954 from the National Institute of Allergy and Infectious Diseases; Grant No. R22-AI 07988 SSS of the United States-Japan Cooperative Medical Science Program, administered by the National Institute of Allergy and Infectious Diseases; Public Health Service Research Grant No. R01-CA 10028 from the National Cancer Institute; and funds from the World Health Organization.

We are grateful to Dr. Frantisek Sokol for his councel and helpful criticism in this work.

REFERENCES

1. Wiktor, T. J., Sokol, F., Kuwert, E. and Koprowski, H., Proc. Soc. Exp. Biol. Med., *131:* 799, 1969.
2. Sokol, F., Kuwert, E., Wiktor, T. J., Hummeler, K. and Koprowski, H., J. Virol., *2:* 836, 1968.
3. Crick, J. and Brown, F., Nature, *222:* 92, 1969.
4. Wiktor, T. J., Fernandes, M. V. and Koprowski, H., J. Immun., *93:* 353, 1964.
5. Sedvick, W. D. and Wiktor, T. J., J. Virol., *1:* 1224, 1967.
6. Strohmaier, K., in *Methods in Virology*, Vol. 2, Academic Press, New York, 1967.
7. Hummeler, K., Tomassini, N., Sokol, F., Kuwert, E. and Koprowski, H., J. Virol., *2:* 1191, 1968.
8. Wiktor, T. J., Kuwert, E. and Koprowski, H., J. Immun., *101:* 1271, 1969.
9. Appleyard, G. and Westwood, J. C. N., Brit. J. Exp. Path., *45:* 162, 1964.
10. Appleyard, G., Zwartouw, H. T. and Westwood, J. C. N., Brit. J. Exp. Path., *45:* 150, 1964.
11. Schäffer, W., In *Ciba Foundation Symposium, The Nature of Viruses*, Edited by G. E. W. Wolstenholme and E. C. P. Millar, p. 91, 1957.
12. Fenje, Paul and Pinteric, L., Amer. J. Public Health, *56:* 2106, 1966.

THE JOURNAL OF IMMUNOLOGY
Vol. 105, No. 2, August 1970
Printed in U.S.A.

THE ANTIGENIC SPECIFICITY OF BLOOD GROUPS WHICH DIFFERENTIATE POPULATIONS OF FRESH WATER CATFISH

WILLIAM J. KUHNS,[1] JOSEPH V. CHUBA[1] AND ROSS F. NIGRELLI[2]

From the Immunohematology Laboratory, Bellevue Hospital Center, New York University School of Medicine, Department of Pathology, and the Osborne Laboratories of Marine Biology, New York Aquarium, New York, N. Y.

Received for publication April 10, 1970

Erythrocytes derived from fresh water catfish, *Ictalurus nebulosus* (Le Sueur) and *Ictalurus catus* (Linneaus), referred to as groups I and II, were capable of eliciting specific immune responses as demonstrated by cross-immunization, stimulation of goats and rabbits, and absorption studies of immune antisera. Two forms of immune response were elicited in goats and rabbits, one against an antigen common to erythrocytes from individuals of groups I and II, and the other against a Forssman-like antigenic substance present on group I, but not group II, erythrocytes. The presence of two classes of immunoglobulins formed during immune responses was suggested on the basis of differences in sensitivity of agglutinins to mercaptoethanol before and after antigenic stimulation. Members of group I possessed a soluble blood group substance in serum and mucus, as demonstrated by agglutination-inhibition tests in the presence of human anti-A antiserum, lima bean lectin, and hemagglutinins in serum from group II individuals.

In earlier experiments, it was shown that fresh water catfish maintained under laboratory conditions possessed cross-reacting hemagglutinins which permitted a classification into two distinct blood groups, I and II. A further distinction was provided by using an extract of *Phaseolus limensis*, the lima bean, and human anti-A antiserum These reagents indicated that the agglutinogen on erythrocytes from group I individuals was A-like, and contained Forssman-like activity judged by absorption studies with guinea pig kidney. Group II erythrocytes were distinguished by a lack of reactivity in the presence of the corresponding reagents (1). The anatomic features of fish possessing group I and II erythrocytes were those of *Ictalurus nebulosus* (Le Sueur) and *Ictalurus catus* (Linneaus), respectively.

The advantages of piscine species for blood group studies are particularly great in the area of blood group genesis during early differentiation because development is not accompanied by placentation. Genetic studies are enhanced in view of the ease with which fish can be experimentally hybridized; in addition single matings yield large numbers of offspring. If blood group antigens are capable of providing discrete markers for hybrids, the differences may prove to be of practical use provided that correlations with certain forms of hybrid vigor (i.e., weight increase and size) can be demonstrated.

The original studies did not present comprehensive evidence for the antigenic nature or specificity of agglutinogens I and II. The experiments to be reported indicate the existence of discrete specificity for the erythrocytic factors in groups I and II catfish by cross-immunization and by stimulation of rabbits and goats. The presence of a soluble factor in mucosal secretions, which is similar in reactivity to an agglutinogen possessed by group I erythrocytes, was also demonstrated by agglutination-inhibition tests.

MATERIALS AND METHODS

Fish populations. A reference population of catfish maintained at the New York Aquarium contained individuals deemed suitable for immunization experiments based upon size and weight and general state of health. Individuals weighing from 300 to 400 g were selected for this purpose. They had been obtained originally from

[1] Immunohematology Laboratory, Bellevue Hospital Center.

[2] Osborne Laboratories of Marine Biology.

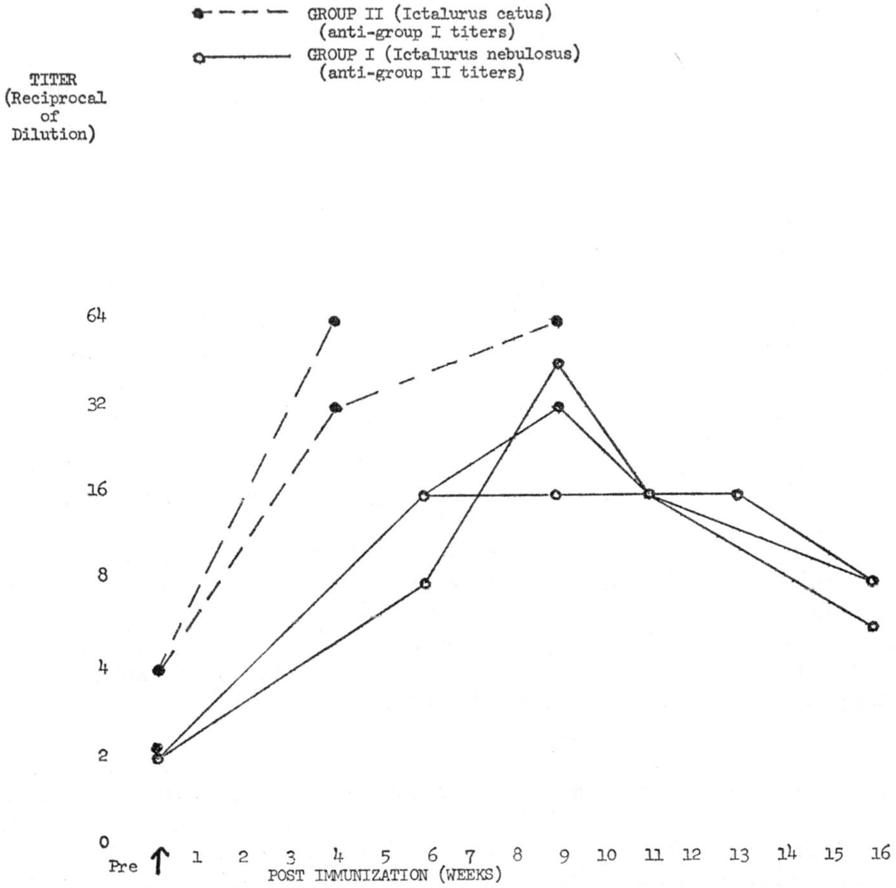

Figure 1. Immune response of five fresh water catfish groups I and II following injection of erythrocytes of the reciprocal group.

lake areas in southern New Jersey and Long Island, and had been maintained in captivity over a period of months with occasional bleedings.

Immunization. Cross-immunization of individual fish in groups I and II with erythrocytes from the reciprocal groups was carried out in accordance with schedules published elsewhere (2). Intramuscular immunizations of rabbits and goats with groups I and II erythrocytes were carried out as described by Kabat (3). Immune sera were obtained at intervals up to 16 weeks following injections.

Soluble blood group substances. Mucus was procured for soluble blood group activity from alimentary tract mucosa using cotton-tipped swabs from which secretory material was removed and placed in a small volume of phosphate buffer, pH 7.2. Secretions were collected by placing fish in a water-filled plastic container for several hours; the contents were then lyophilized, reconstituted in small volume, and dialyzed against phosphate buffer, pH 7.2.

Serologic tests. Methods of blood collection, preservation, storage, and agglutination testing using reagents from groups I and II fish are described in detail elsewhere (1, 2, 4). Inhibition studies were carried out using these reagents in combination with mucuous secretions or controls as described by Kabat (3). In cases where hemolyins interfered with agglutination tests, sera were heated at 56°C for 30 min prior to use. Screening studies were carried out using mercaptoethanol (5) to determine the classification of blood group immunoglobulins on samples obtained before and after immunization. Sheep erythrocytes and rabbit anti-sheep serum used in

TABLE I

Mercaptoethanol resistance of hemagglutinins produced following immunization with groups I and II catfish erythrocytes

Animal Immunized	Erythrocytes Used for Immunologic Testing		Agglutinin Titer Pre-Immunization	Post-Immunization	
	Immunization	Agglutination studies		6 weeks	9 weeks
Goat	I	I	32 (0)[a]	4096 (2048)	1024 (1024)
		II	2 (0)	32 (32)	64 (64)
Goat	II	I	16 (0)	512 (128)	
		II	2 (0)	128 (64)	
Catfish I	II	II	2 (0)	16 (8)	32 (16)
Catfish II	I	I	4 (0)		64 (16)

[a] Figures in parentheses refer to residual titer following mercaptoethanol treatment.

studies of groups I and II catfish antigens were obtained from commercial sources.[3]

RESULTS

Cross-immunization. Figure 1 depicts hemagglutinin titers carried out on serial blood samples collected over a 6- to 16-week period. Three catfish were members of group I injected with group II erythrocytes, and two were members of group II immunized with cells from the reciprocal group. Rises in agglutinin titers to 1:32 to 1:64 were demonstrated in all instances beginning at the 4th to 6th week, and in three cases followed for a relatively prolonged period of time, extending to the 16th week. Treatment of sera with mercaptoethanol (5) indicated sensitivity of agglutinins to this reagent prior to immunization, but mercaptoethanol resistance as immunization proceeded (Table I). It was possible to remove detectable agglutinins in all instances by absorption with erythrocytes from members possessing the reciprocal blood group (Table II).

Immunization of goats and rabbits. Three goats were immunized with erythrocytes from group I and group II individuals; two goats received group I erythrocytes and one goat received group II erythrocytes. Species-specific mercaptoethanol-sensitive antibodies in low titer could be demonstrated in blood samples collected prior to injection. Following injection, high titers of agglutinins were stimulated (Fig. 2), a portion of which proved resistant to mercaptoethanol (Table I).

[3] Sheep erythrocytes and rabbit anti-sheep sera were obtained from Sylvana Company, Millburn N. J.

TABLE II

Effects of absorption by erythrocytes of reciprocal group upon immune hemagglutinin titers in serum from fresh water catfish groups I and II[a]

Material Used to Absorb	Titer of Antiserum[b]	
	Group I (*I. nebulosus*) (anti-*catus*)	Group II (*I. catus*) (anti-*nebulosus*)
None	32	64
Group I (*I. nebulosus* erythrocytes)	32	0
Group II (*I. catus* erythrocytes)	0	64

[a] Serum to be absorbed was added to two times its volume of washed packed red blood cells. Tests were carried out on centrifuged supernatant after 1 hr during which time mixture was mildly agitated.

[b] Reciprocal of dilution.

Absorption of immune sera with groups I and II cells indicated the existance of a species factor contained on cells from group I which was lacking on those derived from group II (Table III), and also a generic factor possessed in common by members of groups I and II. Immunization of four rabbits with groups I and II erythrocytes (two animals used for erythrocytes of each group) yielded an immune response which possessed the characteristics of that observed in goats (Fig. 3). Absorption of rabbit antisera with catfish erythrocytes indicated differences between cells derived from groups I and II individuals similar to the properties defined by absorbed goat antisera, i.e., an agglutinin common to both groups and a

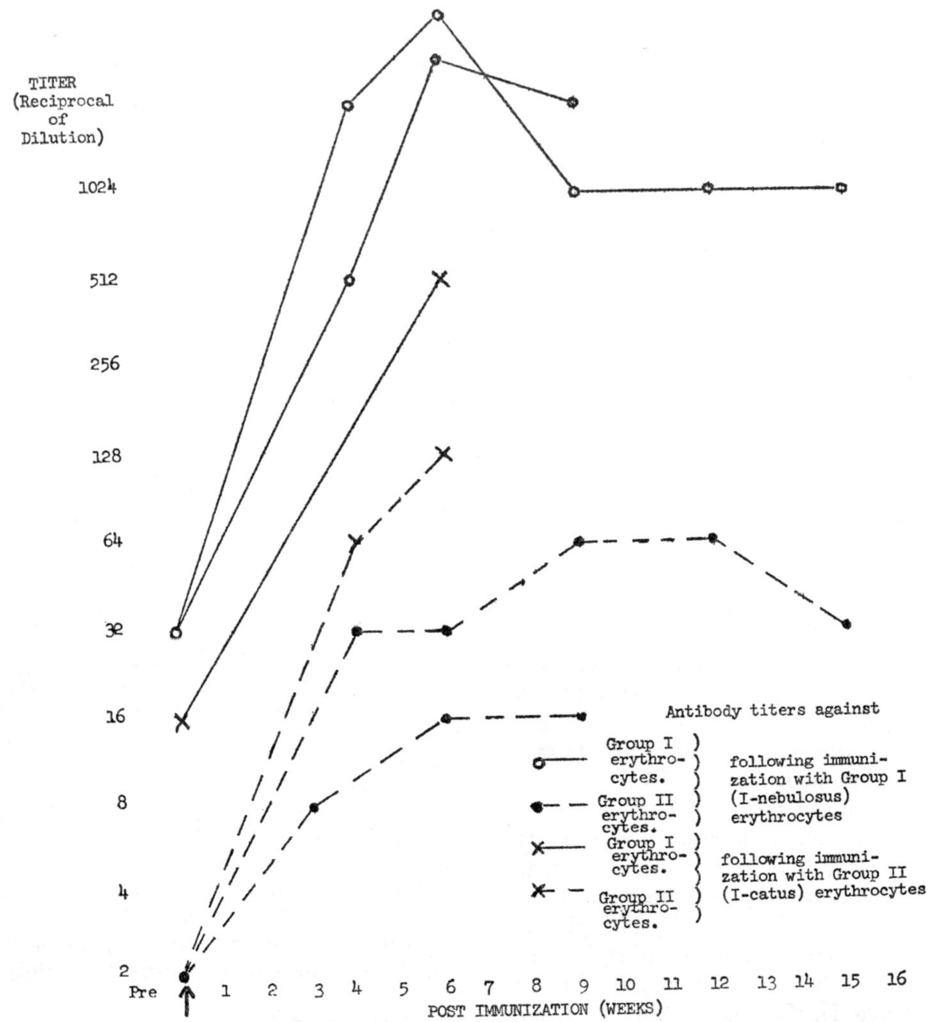

Figure 2. Immune responses of three goats following injection of erythrocytes from fresh water catfish.

TABLE III

Effects of absorption upon immune titers in serum from goats by erythrocytes from fresh water catfish

Material Used to Absorb	Titer of Antiserum			
	Goat anti-group I (*I. nebulosus*)		Goat anti-group II (*I. catus*)	
	Group I cells	Group II cells	Group I cells	Group II cells
None	4096	128	512	64
Group I (*I. nebulosus* erythrocytes)	0	0	0	0
Group II (*I. catus* erythrocytes)	256	0	0	0

TABLE IV

Effects of absorption upon immune titers in serum from rabbits by erythrocytes from fresh water catfish

Material Used to Absorb	Titer of Antiserum			
	Rabbit anti-group I (*I. nebulosus*)		Rabbit anti-group II (*I. catus*)	
	Group I cells	Group II cells	Group I cells	Group II cells
None	1024	64	512	128
Group I (*I. nebulosus* erythrocytes)	0	0	0	0
Group II (*I. catus* erythrocytes)	64	0	0	0

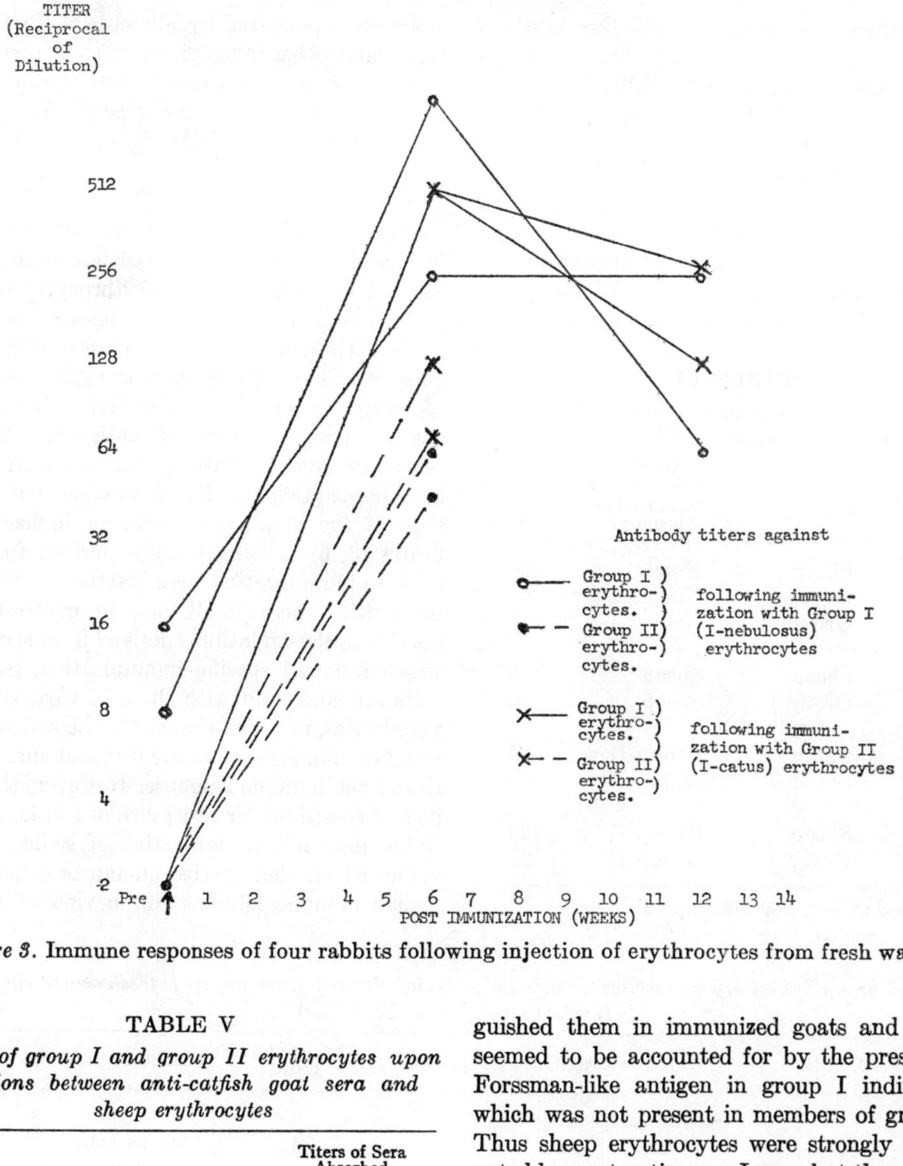

Figure 3. **Immune responses of four rabbits following injection of erythrocytes from fresh water catfish.**

TABLE V

Effects of group I and group II erythrocytes upon reactions between anti-catfish goat sera and sheep erythrocytes

Reagent	Unabsorbed	Titers of Sera Absorbed	
		Group I erythrocytes (*I. nebulosus*)	Group II erythrocytes (*I. catus*)
Goat anti-group I serum (*I. nebulosus*)	4096	16	2048
Goat anti-group II serum (*I. catus*)	16	8	8

species agglutinin which distinguished group I from group II catfish (Table IV). The basis for differences in cross-reactivity between groups I and II cells or between the factor which distinguished them in immunized goats and rabbits seemed to be accounted for by the presence of Forssman-like antigen in group I individuals, which was not present in members of group II. Thus sheep erythrocytes were strongly agglutinated by goat anti-group I sera, but they reacted only to a relatively slight extent in mixture with anti-group II sera. Cross-absorption studies showed that group I erythrocytes could remove a large proportion of the goat anti-group I agglutinin, in contrast to the negative behavior of group II erythrocytes (Table V).

In other experiments it was demonstrated that group I erythrocytes, but not group II erythrocytes, were reactive against rabbit anti-sheep serum. The reaction with group I erythrocytes could be eliminated by absorption with sheep erythrocytes. In addition the reaction between sheep erythrocytes and rabbit anti-sheep erythrocyte serum could be partially absorbed using catfish group I red blood cells (Table VI).

Tests for soluble blood group substance. Soluble blood group substances were demonstrated in secretions derived from individuals in group I. Serum from group I catfish possessed such activity as judged by the ability, even in dilution, to eliminate cross-reactions between human anti-A serum, lima bean lectin and group II anti-group I serum, and group I erythrocytes. Similar properties were possessed by alimentary tract secretions, and other mucosal secretory material derived from individual catfish, but the inhibitory properties were of lesser degree than those observed in sera (Table VII).

TABLE VI

Agglutination reactions of group I and group II erythrocytes against rabbit anti-sheep erythrocyte serum (RAS)[a]

Reagent	Testing Cells	Cells Used for Absorption	Titer
RAS	Sheep	None	256
	Group I	None	48
	Group II	None	0
RAS	Sheep	Sheep	0
	Group I	Sheep	0
RAS	Sheep	Group I	24
	Group I	Group I	0
RAS	Sheep	Group II	128
	Group I	Group II	32

[a] Heated at 56°C for 30 min prior to use.

DISCUSSION

Two populations of fresh water catfish differing in regard to species and serologic characteristics were observed to react to erythrocytic antigens derived from the reciprocal species by increases in circulating antibody titer. Thus the agglutinogens which caused reciprocal agglutination of blood from groups I and II individuals exhibited the behavior expected of antigens. Antibody responses were essentially those which might have been anticipated based upon current knowledge of the immune response in higher vertebrates (3, 6). The agglutinins derived from fish prior to immunization were inactivated by treatment with mercaptoethanol, in contrast to a portion of the agglutinins derived from specimens which followed specific immunization. Such results are consistent with those in various higher vertebrates, in which changes in the ratio of IgM to IgG immunoglobulins are frequent characteristics of the immune response. However, the findings of sensitivity or resistance of fish hemagglutinins may not be indicative of sedimentation values which characterize human or other mammalian immunoglobulins (6) in view of variant

TABLE VII

Blood group inhibitory properties of soluble material derived from group I fresh water catfish (Ictalurus nebulosus, Le Sueur)

Source of Material	Erythrocyte-Agglutinin Test System	No. of Fish Tested	Inhibition Potency	Control
Serum	Group I erythrocytes			
	Human anti-A	4	1:4 to 1:16[a]	0
	Lima bean lectin	2	1:8	0
	Group II anti-group I	2	1:4 and 1:8	0
Secretions	Group I erythrocytes			
	Human anti-A	6	1:2	0
	Lima bean lectin	6	Undiluted	0
	Group II anti-group I	6	Undiluted	0
Alimentary mucus	Group I erythrocytes			
	Human anti-A	3	1:2	0
	Lima bean lectin	3	1:2	0
	Group II catfish anti-group I	3	1:2	0

[a] The end point of titers was the dilution which caused total inhibition of agglutination in system characterized by strong ++++ agglutination reactions.

forms of immunoglobulins and variant behavior observed in globulin fractions derived from teleosts and other marine animals (7). Further studies of the characteristics of fish immunoglobulins are in progress.

It was of interest that the goat and rabbit, upon immunization with these antigens, were able to distinguish between erythrocytes from group I and group II individuals based upon the nature of the agglutinin responses and upon cross-absorption studies. Thus group I and II erythrocytes evoked a common form of generic response in goats and rabbits. However, a separate response caused only by group I erythrocytes could also be distinguished. This appeared to correspond to the group I agglutinins, described earlier (1), which exhibited Forssman-like behavior.

The presence of soluble blood group substance in group I individuals is important since it permits further biochemical approaches to the development of blood groups which are not possible in the case of erythrocyte or structural antigens. Despite the A-like nature of the antigen-antibody reaction which was inhibited by group I secretions, it was of interest that in six individuals, analyses of this material by Dr. Maxwell Schubert failed to reveal evidence of hexosamines. This result requires confirmation using larger amounts of material from additional individuals, but if confirmed would be of interest in view of findings by others that N-acetylgalactosamine comprises the major immunodeterminant amino sugar from human blood group A (8).

The occurrence of soluble antigenic material in *Ictalurus nebulosus* (Le Sueur) might also be of importance as a stimulator of antibody responses in other animal species. Fluctuations in antibody titers and various forms of cross-reactions might be explained in part on the presence of soluble antigenic material produced by fish in a natural environment, assuming the existence in other exposed animals of immunocompetence and conditions of temperature which allow antibody formation to occur (7, 9–11).

In view of these findings and experimental results of others (11), the potential of fish for immunization studies merits further exploration, as do the opportunities for basic study into the biochemical development of blood groups, and studies of the significance of such material related to health and disease within natural systems. The discrete nature of these antigens in two different species of catfish also suggests their use as markers in hybridization studies, particularly if correlations with hybrid vigor can be demonstrated (H. Dupree and O. Green, personal communication).

REFERENCES

1. Kuhns, W. J., Nigrelli, R. and Chuba, J. V., J. Immun., *103:* 454, 1969.
2. Chuba, J. V., Kuhns, W. J. and Nigrelli, R., J. Immun., *101:* 1, 1968.
3. Kabat, E., *Kabat and Mayer's Experimental Immunochemistry, 2nd Ed., Charles C Thomas, Springfield, Ill., 1961.*
4. Wiener, A. S., Chuba, J. V., Gordon, E. B. and Kuhns, W. J., Transfusion, *8:* 226, 1968.
5. Grubb, R. and Swahn, B., Acta Path. Microbiol. Scand., *43:* 305, 1958.
6. Boyd, W., *Fundamentals of Immunology*, 4th Ed., Interscience, New York, 1966.
7. Smith, R., Miescher, P. and Good, R. *Phylogeny of Immunity*, University of Florida Press, Gainesville, 1966.
8. Watkins, W. M., Science, *152:* 172, 1966.
9. Kuhns, W. J., Nigrelli, R. and Chuba, J. V., J. Immun., *103:* 62, 1969.
10. Rowland, D. T., *Immunity to Parasitic Animals*, Edited by G. Jackson and I. Singer, Appleton-Century-Crofts, New York, 1968.
11. Cushing, J. E., Advances Marine Biol., *2:* 85, 1964.

THE JOURNAL OF IMMUNOLOGY
Vol. 105, No. 2, August 1970
Printed in U.S.A.

GENETIC CONTROL OF THE SPECIFICITY OF ANTI-DNP ANTIBODIES

I. Differences in the Specificity of Anti-DNP Antibody Produced by Mammalian Species

TAKESHI YOSHIDA,[1] WILLIAM E. PAUL AND BARUJ BENACERRAF

From the Laboratory of Immunology, National Institute of Allergy and Infectious Diseases, National Institutes of Health, Bethesda, Maryland 20014

Received for publication March 10, 1970

The fine specificity of anti-hapten antibodies was quantitatively characterized in terms of the capacity of a series of nitrophenyl ligands to inhibit the binding of ^{3}H-2,4-dinitrophenyl-ε-aminocaproic acid (^{3}H-DNP-EACA) by anti-DNP antibody. Applying this assay to antisera produced by mice, rats, guinea pigs and rabbits in response to immunization with DNP keyhole limpet hemocyanin (DNP-KLH), species-specific binding characteristics were noted. These differences involve the relative affinity and relative slopes of inhibition for dinitrophenol, trinitrophenyl ε-aminocaproic acid and dinitroaniline. Anti-DNP antibodies produced by rabbits and guinea pigs in response to immunization with DNP-bovine γ globulin resemble those produced by these species in response to DNP-KLH immunization. Thus, different mammalian species produce antibody populations with different patterns of cross-reactivity in response to the same antigenic stimulus.

The analysis of the genetic mechanisms which control antibody synthesis and the generation of diversity has been severely complicated by the heterogeneity of antibody populations. This heterogeneity, which includes differences in immunoglobulin class (1), intrinsic association constant (2) and range of cross-reactivity (3, 4), has had the effect of obscuring underlying similarities which might exist in the specificity of antibody produced by animals of a given species or by a given inbred strain of a single species.

In the work described in this paper we used a simple, quantitative method to characterize the patterns of cross-reactivity of anti-2,4-dinitrophenyl (DNP) antibodies produced by different mammalian species. Thus, we compared the capacity of a series of nitrophenyl ligands to inhibit the binding of ^{3}H-DNP-ε-aminocaproic acid (^{3}H-DNP-EACA) by anti-DNP antibodies. The results, expressed in quantitative terms, can be viewed as illustrating the fine specificity of such antibodies. Anti-DNP antibodies produced by rabbits, guinea pigs, rats and mice in response to immunization with DNP-keyhold limpet hemocyanin (DNP-KLH) show species-specific cross-reactivity patterns. Furthermore, anti-DNP-bovine γ globulin (DNP-BGG) antibodies produced by rabbits and guinea pigs resemble the anti-DNP-KLH antibodies produced by those species. In a companion paper (5), similar data for anti-DNP antibody produced by various inbred strains of mice are presented. The analysis of differences in the fine specificity of antibody populations may offer important insights into the genetic control of antibody structure.

[1] Present address: Department of Tuberculosis, The National Institute of Health, Tokyo, Japan.

MATERIALS AND METHODS

Keyhole limpet hemocyanin (KLH) was obtained from Pacific Bio-Marine Supply Company, Venice, Calif. Bovine γ globulin (BGG) and bovine fibrinogen (BF) were purchased from Armour Pharmaceutical Company, Kankakee, Ill. 1-Fluoro-2-nitrobenzene (oNFB), 1-fluoro-4-nitrobenzene (pNFB), 1-fluoro-2,4-dinitrobenzene (DNFB), 2,4-dinitrobenzene sulfonic acid, sodium salt (DNBS), 2,4-dinitrophenol (DNPOH), 2,4-dinitroaniline ($DNPNH_2$) and 1-chloro-2,4,6-trinitrobenzene (picryl Cl) were purchased from Eastman Organic Chemicals, Rochester, N. Y. DNPOH was crystallized from hot water prior to use. N^ε-2,4-dinitrophenyl-L-lysine (DNP-LYS) was obtained from Schwarz

Bio-Research Co., Orangeburg, N. Y. ϵ-Aminocaproic acid (EACA) was obtained from Mann Research Laboratories, New York. ^{3}H-DNFB, specific activity 1.6 Ci/mM, was purchased from Amersham-Searle, Des Plaines, Ill.

DNP-KLH was prepared by the reaction of 1 g of DNBS, in 10 ml of water, with 1 g of KLH in 60 ml of 2% K_2CO_3. The reaction mixture was stirred overnight at room temperature; the product was extensively dialyzed against 0.01 M sodium phosphate buffer, pH 7.6 (6). DNP-BGG and DNP-BF were prepared by reacting DNFB with protein under alkaline conditions, essentially as previously described (7). The degree of substitution (mols of DNP/mol of protein, or per 100,000 g of KLH) was determined by absorbance at 360 nm (ϵ = 17,400 for DNP-LYS) (8) and by micro-Kjeldahl nitrogen analysis (molecular weights for BGG and BF taken as 150,000 and 330,000, respectively). The compounds had a degree of substitution of 23, 42 and 109 for KLH, BGG and BF, respectively.

DNP-EACA, *o*-nitrophenyl-EACA (o-NO_2-ϕ-EACA), *p*-nitrophenyl-EACA (p-NO_2-ϕ-EACA) and picryl-EACA were prepared by the reaction of EACA with DNFB, oNFB, pNFB and picryl Cl, respectively. The syntheses were performed essentially as previously described (7) and the products were purified by repeated acid precipitation. Purity was demonstrated by thin layer chromatography on silica gel, using n-butanol to develop the chromatograms.

^{3}H-DNP-EACA was prepared by the reaction of ^{3}H-DNFB with a 100-fold molar excess of EACA. The reaction was performed in 5% Na_2CO_3. The mixture was chromatographed on a thin layer of silica with n-butanol and the material which migrated with an R_F equivalent to non-radioactive DNP-EACA was eluted from the silica with water.

Complete Freund's adjuvant was obtained from Difco Laboratories, Detroit, Mich., and contained 0.5 mg of killed *Mycobacterium butyricum*/ml of oil. Hartley guinea pigs, 300 to 400 g in weight, were immunized with 100 μg of DNP-KLH, as a complete Freund's adjuvant emulsion. Guinea pigs were injected either in the four footpads or subcutaneously. Animals which received footpad injections were bled 2 weeks after immunization, whereas those which received subcutaneous injections were bled 4 weeks after immunization. A pool of serum was collected from guinea pigs which had been immunized with 50 μg DNP-BGG emulsified in complete Freund's adjuvant 3 to 4 weeks earlier.

New Zealand White rabbits were immunized subcutaneously with 500 μg of DNP-KLH, as a complete Freund's adjuvant emulsion. They were bled 4 weeks later. Purified rabbit anti-DNP antibody, prepared from the sera of rabbits immunized with DNP-BGG, was the gift of Dr. Ira Green.

Lewis strain rats were obtained from Microbiological Associates, Bethesda, Maryland. They received subcutaneous immunizations of 1 mg of DNP-KLH in complete Freund's adjuvant and were bled 4 weeks later.

General purpose Swiss mice obtained from the Animal Production Section, National Institutes of Health, were immunized subcutaneously with either 0.1 mg or 1.0 mg of DNP-KLH, emulsified in complete Freund's adjuvant. Groups of 10 or more mice were bled 2, 4 or 8 weeks after immunization and sera from mice in a given group were pooled.

Serum concentrations of anti-DNP antibody were measured by quantitative precipitin analysis with DNP-BF (9). Serum (0.2 ml) was mixed with varying concentrations of DNP-BF in 0.1 ml of phosphate-buffered saline (PBS: 0.15 M NaCl, 0.01 M potassium phosphate, pH 7.6). After incubation at 37°C for 1 hr and at 4°C for 24 to 48 hr, the precipitates were collected by centrifugation, washed twice in cold PBS, dried and dissolved in 0.02 M sodium lauryl sulfate. The absorbancy of the dissolved specific precipitates were determined at 278 and 360 nm and the anti-DNP antibody concentrations calculated as previously described (10). In each case, the results were corrected on the basis of the amount of precipitate obtained when DNP-BF was mixed with normal, non-immune serum.

Average association constants of antibody and DNP-ligands were calculated from data obtained by an ammonium sulfate precipitation technique and are termed K_F. We have recently described this technique (11), which represents an extension of the Farr technique (12). It should be noted that K_F calculated by this method is in satisfactory agreement with the average intrinsic association constant (K_0) obtained by equilibrium dialysis when ^{3}H-DNP-L-lysine is used and the antibody is diluted in either serum or globulin. When ^{3}H-DNP-EACA is used as ligand, as was the case in these studies, the use of antibody in undiluted serum yields values for K_F which are low compared to K_0 obtained by equilibrium dialysis of purified antibody. This is presumably due to the relatively high affinity of albumin for ^{3}H-DNP-EACA (13). The results can be improved considerably by using the globulin fraction of serum or, alternatively, a 1:5 dilution of serum. In the studies reported here, DNP-LYS appeared to bind to anti-DNP antibody with a relative association constant approximately three times greater than that for DNP-EACA (see Table II). In view of the published observations (2) that purified anti-DNP antibody binds the two ligands equally well, this difference illustrates the magnitude of the serum effect in these studies.

In brief, the technique used here consisted of mixing 50 μl of diluted serum or, if necessary, undiluted serum with 50 μl of ^{3}H-DNP-EACA at varying concentrations. After incubation for 1 hr or more at room temperature, 200 μl of 75% cold saturated ammonium sulfate was added. One hour later the mixture was centrifuged at 2500 rpm, 4°C for 20 min; a 100-μl sample of supernatant was added to 10 ml of a solution consisting of 25 parts of toluene, 5 parts of Bio-Solv 3 (Beckman Instrument Co., Fullerton, Calif.) and 1 part of Liquifluor (New England Nuclear Corp., Boston, Mass.). Radioactivity was then measured in a liquid scintillation spectrometer.

Supernatant hapten concentration is equivalent to free hapten concentration (c). The difference between the values of c when normal and immune sera are compared is equivalent to the bound hapten concentration for the immune sera. Total antibody is determined by quantitative precipitin analysis, but may also be measured by extrapolation of curves of binding. K_F is calculated on the basis of the Sips equation:

$$\text{Log}\, r/n - r = a \log K_F + a \log c \qquad (13, 14)$$

where r is the concentration of bound hapten divided by the concentration of antibody molecules, n is the number of antigen-binding sites/antibody molecule (assumed to be 2) and a is the Sips heterogeneity index.

The specificity of anti-DNP antibody for a series of nitrophenyl ligands was measured on the basis of hapten inhibition of the binding of ^{3}H-DNP-EACA to anti-DNP antibody. Thus, 50 μl of antisera (or diluted antisera) was mixed with 25 μl of ^{3}H-DNP-EACA and with 25 μl of nitrophenyl ligand, at initial concentrations up to 2×10^{-3} M. In each case, concentrations of antibody and of ^{3}H-DNP-EACA were selected so that approximately 50% of the antigen-binding sites of antibody were occupied when no inhibitor was present. The percentage inhibition by added ligand was calculated as follows:

$$\frac{[\text{Free } ^3\text{H-DNP-EACA in presence of inhibitor}] - [\text{Free } ^3\text{H-DNP-EACA in absence of inhibitor}]}{\text{Bound } ^3\text{H-DNP-EACA in absence of inhibitor}} \times 100$$

The free concentration of non-radioactive ligand was determined by subtracting the numerator of the above expression from the total concentration of that ligand. The percentage inhibition was plotted against free concentration of inhibiting ligand on semi-logarithmic paper. The relative affinity of antibody for a given ligand is expressed in terms of the ratio of the free concentration of that ligand required for 50% inhibition of the reaction of ^{3}H-DNP-EACA with anti-DNP antibody to the free concentration of non-radioactive DNP-EACA required for equivalent inhibition. Numerically large values thus signify low relative affinities and numerically small values, high relative affinities. The highest concentration of DNPOH (5×10^{-4} M) often failed to inhibit 50% of the binding of ^{3}H-DNP-EACA by antibody. Thus, for this ligand, relative affinities were calculated on the basis of 25% inhibition by DNPOH and DNP-EACA. In the statistical comparison of relative affinities, the values were transformed to logarithms, the means and variances were calculated and Student's t test was performed. The means were expressed in terms of antilogarithms. In those cases in which p values of less than 0.05 were obtained, the data were also treated without logarithmic transformation. In each case, p values remained less than 0.05.

The relative slope of inhibition is the ratio of slope of inhibition (%/log) for the given ligand to the slope of inhibition for DNP-EACA. Means and variances were calculated directly.

RESULTS

Immunization resulted in the production of significant amounts of anti-DNP antibody by each of the species tested. Thus, among the sera employed in this study, concentrations of anti-

TABLE I

Amount and affinity of anti-DNP antibody produced by different species after immunization with DNP-KLH

Species	Animal No.	Ab. Conc[a]	K_F L/M × 10^6 [b]
		mg/ml	
Guinea pig	1	1.2	0.59
	2	1.6	0.27
	3	1.7	0.72
	4	1.45	1.6
	5	0.75	2.6
Rat	13	0.45	0.28
	14	0.42	1.2
	16	0.18	1.9
	17	0.35	1.6
	18	0.60	0.63
	19	1.20	0.43
Rabbit	6	0.62	1.5
	7	0.63	1.6
	8	0.20	1.6
	9	1.1	2.2
	10	0.65	2.0
Mouse (pools)	2-4	0.52	0.60
	4-3	0.46	1.7
	8	1.31	1.7

[a] Antibody concentration determined by quantitative precipitin analysis with DNP-BF.

[b] Average association constant of anti-DNP antibody for ^{3}H-DNP-EACA determined by an ammonium sulfate precipitation technique, as described in the text.

DNP antibody ranged from 0.75 to 1.7 mg/ml in guinea pigs, 0.18 to 1.2 mg/ml in rats, 0.20 to 1.1 mg/ml in rabbits, and 0.46 to 1.3 mg/ml in serum pools from mice (Table I). Furthermore, the affinities of these anti-DNP antibodies were quite comparable. Thus, K_F, as measured by the modified Farr technique, for reaction with ^{3}H-DNP-EACA ranged from 0.27 to 2.6 × 10^6 L/M for guinea pig antibody, from 0.28 to 1.9 × 10^6 L/M for rat antibody, from 1.5 to 2.2 × 10^6 L/M for rabbit antibody, and from 0.60 to 1.7 × 10^6 L/M for mouse antibody (Table I).

Clear differences in the quantitative cross-reactions of anti-DNP antibody produced by different species existed in the face of the comparable affinity for ^{3}H-DNP-EACA. In Figure 1, representative sets of inhibition curves are presented. Inspection of these curves reveals that guinea pig anti-DNP antibodies have a high relative affinity for picryl-EACA, and a steep slope of inhibition with DNPOH. Mouse antibodies have a high relative affinity for DNPOH, especially as compared with rat and rabbit antibodies.

Quantitative comparison on the basis of relative affinity (concentration ratios for 50% or 25% inhibition) and relative slope confirm these differences and reveal some additional ones (Tables II and III). Thus, the ratio of inhibitory concentrations in the case of picryl-EACA is significantly lower ($p < 0.01$) for guinea pig antibodies than for rabbit, rat or mouse antibodies. Furthermore, the comparison of ratios of inhibitory concentrations for picryl-EACA and p-NO_2-ϕ-EACA in sera of individual animals shows that inhibitory ratio for picryl-EACA/inhibitory ratio for p-NO_2-ϕ-EACA is significantly lower for guinea pig antibodies (0.22) than for rabbit (1.52), rat (0.89) or mouse (1.07) antibodies. All these differences are significant at < 0.02. Thus, guinea pig antibodies bind picryl-EACA with greater affinity than they bind p-NO_2-ϕ-EACA whereas antibodies of the other species bind the two ligands equally well, or prefer p-NO_2-ϕ-EACA.

Mouse antibodies have significantly lower inhibitory ratios for DNPOH than do either rabbit or rat antibodies ($p < 0.02$ and < 0.05, respectively). No statistically significant differences in the relative affinity for DNP-LYS exist among the anti-DNP antibodies of these species.

In addition to these differences in inhibitory ratios, certain statistically significant differences in the relative slopes of inhibition exist (Table III). Thus, the relative slope of inhibition by DNPOH for guinea pig antibody (0.70) is greater than that for rabbit (0.26), mouse (0.35) or rat (0.29) antibody. The p values are < 0.01, <0.01 and <0.05, respectively.

Finally $DNPNH_2$ inhibits rabbit antibody with a relative slope of 0.46, which is significantly lower than is the case with guinea pig (0.98) or rat (0.74) antibody. The p values are <0.01 and <0.02, respectively.

Thus, several differences in fine specificity of anti-DNP antibody produced in response to immunization with DNP-KLH by different species can be demonstrated. In order to determine whether these differences are characteristic of

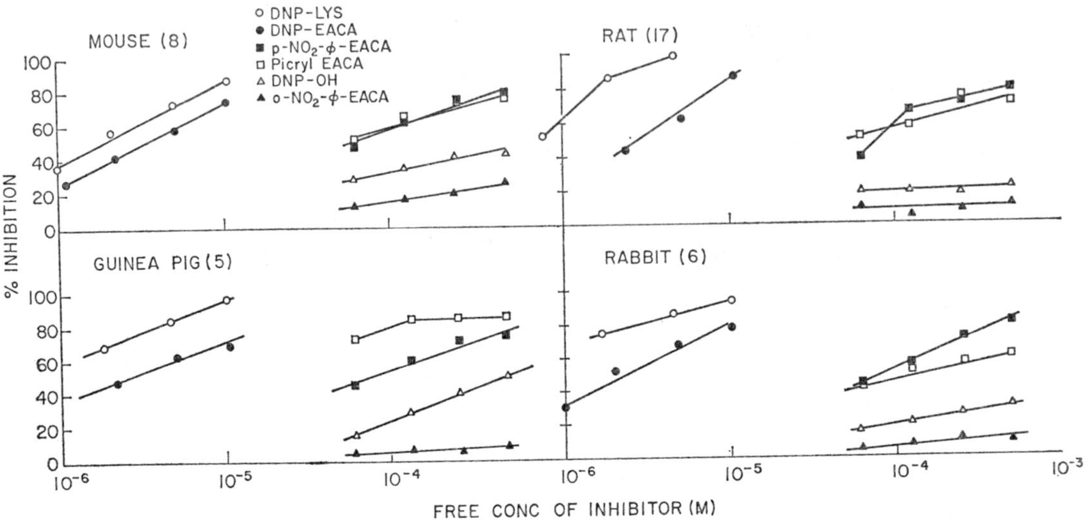

Figure 1. Inhibition by nitrophenyl ligands of the binding of ³H-DNP-EACA by anti-DNP-KLH antibodies produced by an individual rat, guinea pig and rabbit and by a group of mice. The number next to the species refers to the number of the individual serum or of the serum pool which is illustrated.

TABLE II

Relative affinity for nitrophenyl ligands of anti-DNP antibodies produced by different species

Species and No.[b]	Ligand[a] DNP-LYS	DNP-OH	Picryl-EACA	p-NO$_2$-ϕ EACA	DNP-NH$_2$
Rabbit (5)	0.24[c]	340	22.4	16.4	3.2
Guinea pig (5)	0.36	151	5.6	27.4	5.9
Rat (6)	0.29	428	25.3	30.3	3.9
Mouse (3) (pools)	0.43	48.9	18.5	24.5	n.d.[d]
	p values <0.05[e]				
	None	Rabbit-mouse (<0.01) Rat-mouse (<0.05)	Rabbit-guinea pig (<0.01) Rat-guinea pig (<0.01) Mouse-guinea pig (<0.01)	None	None

[a] Nitrophenyl ligand used to inhibit the interaction of anti-DNP-antibodies with ³H-DNP-EACA.

[b] Number refers to the number of sera tested. These were obtained from individual animals except in the case of mice where serum pools, each prepared from the serum of 10 or more individuals, were used.

[c] Geometric mean of the ratio of the free concentration of the given ligand required for 50% inhibition to the free concentration of DNP-EACA required for 50% inhibition. In the case of DNP-OH, the ratios were calculated for 25% inhibition.

[d] n.d., not done.

[e] p values were calculated for the six possible combinations in a given column. All those pairs in which p values of less than 0.05 were obtained are shown.

the anti-DNP antibody response of a given species, or a function of immunization with a given hapten-carrier conjugate, anti-DNP antibody produced as a result of immunization with DNP conjugated to BGG was also studied. A comparison of the data obtained from a pool of guinea pig anti-DNP-BGG sera and a pool of purified rabbit anti-DNP-BGG antibody with

TABLE III

Relative slope of inhibition, by nitrophenyl ligands, of the binding of ^{3}H-DNP-EACA by anti-DNP antibodies produced by different species

Species and No.[b]	Ligand[a]				
	DNP-LYS	DNP-OH	Picryl-EACA	p-NO_2-ϕ EACA	DNP-NH_2
Rabbit (5)	0.96[c]	0.26	0.43	0.75	0.46
Guinea pig (5)	1.35	0.70	0.70	1.09	0.98
Rat (6)	1.12	0.29	0.72	0.78	0.74
Mouse (3) (pools)	0.92	0.35	0.61	0.84	n.d.[d]
	p values <0.05[e]				
	None	Rabbit-guinea pig (<0.01) Rat-guinea pig (<0.01) Mouse-guinea pig (<0.05)	None	None	Rabbit-guinea pig (<0.02) Rabbit-rat (<0.01)

[a] Nitrophenyl ligand used to inhibit the interaction of anti-DNP-antibodies with ^{3}H-DNP-EACA.

[b] Number refers to the number of sera tested. These were obtained from individual animals except in the case of mice where serum pools, each prepared from the serum of 10 or more mice, were used.

[c] Mean of the ratio of slope of inhibition obtained with the given ligand to that obtained with DNP-EACA.

[d] n.d., not done.

[e] p values were calculated for the six possible combinations in a given column. All those pairs in which p values of less than 0.05 were obtained are shown.

TABLE IV

Relative affinity and slope of inhibition of guinea pig and rabbit anti-DNP-KLH and anti-DNP-BGG for several ligands

Species	Carrier	DNP-LYS	DNP-OH	Picryl-EACA	p-NO_2-ϕ EACA
Guinea pig	KLH	0.36[a] (1.35)[b]	151 (0.70)	5.6 (0.70)	27.4 (1.09)
	BGG	0.56 (1.02)	104 (0.59)	9.2 (0.71)	21.7 (1.02)
Rabbit	KLH	0.24 (0.96)	340 (0.26)	22.4 (0.43)	16.4 (0.75)
	BGG	0.73 (0.98)	400 (0.33)	136. (0.28)	25.7 (0.90)

[a] Relative affinity in terms of the ratio of the free concentration of the given ligand required for 50% inhibition to the free concentration of DNP-EACA required for 50% inhibition. In the case of DNP-OH, the ratios were calculated for 25% inhibition. The data for anti-DNP-KLH antibodies is the mean data shown in Table II; that for anti-DNP-BCG is from a single analysis of a pool of antibody in the case of both rabbits and guinea pigs.

[b] Relative slope of inhibition in terms of the ratio of the slope of inhibition obtained with the given ligand to that obtained with DNP-EACA. The data for anti-DNP-KLH antibodies is the mean data shown in Table III; that for anti-DNP-BGG is from a single analysis of a pool of antibody in the case of both rabbits and guinea pigs.

the mean data of guinea pig and rabbit anti-DNP-KLH antisera is presented in Table IV. The differences between guinea pig and rabbit anti-DNP KLH antibodies also exist between guinea pig and rabbit anti-DNP-BGG antibodies (Fig. 2). Thus, the ratios of inhibitory concentrations for DNPOH are 151 for guinea pig anti-DNP KLH and 104 for guinea pig anti-DNP BGG, whereas they are 340 for rabbit anti-DNP KLH and 400 for rabbit anti-DNP-BGG. Similarly, for picryl-EACA, the ratios of inhibitory concentration for guinea pig anti-DNP-KLH and anti-DNP-BGG are 5.6 and 9.2, respectively, whereas for rabbit anti-DNP antibodies they are

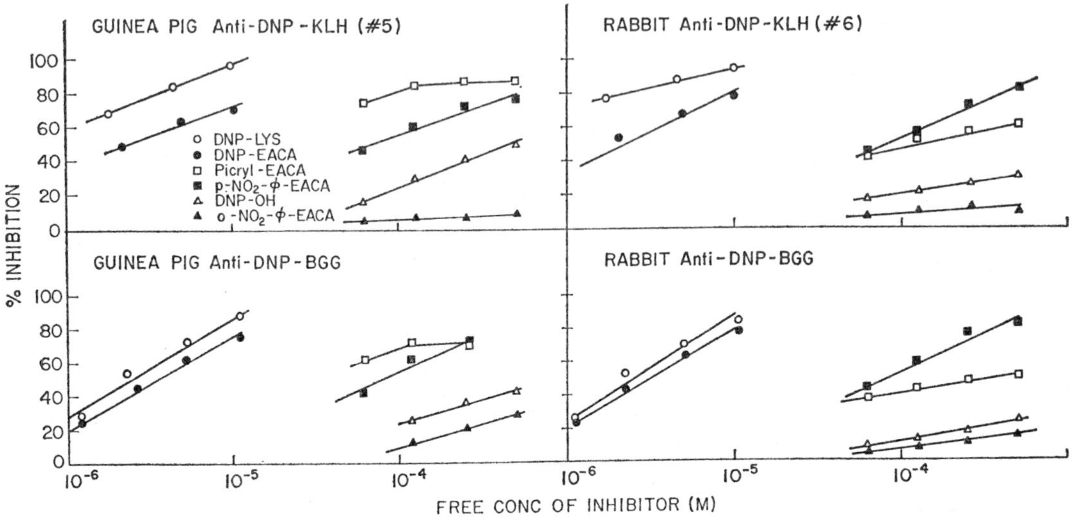

Figure 2. Inhibition by nitrophenyl ligands of the binding of guinea pig and rabbit anti-DNP-KLH and anti-DNP-BGG antibodies to ^{3}H-DNP-EACA. The anti-DNP-KLH antibodies were obtained from individual animals (the number of the individual is shown in parentheses) and the anti-DNP-BGG antibodies were obtained from groups of animals.

22.4 and 136. Finally, the relative slopes of inhibition by DNPOH are 0.70 and 0.59 for guinea pig anti-DNP-KLH and anti-DNP-BGG, respectively, whereas they are 0.26 and 0.33 for rabbit antibody. Thus the observed differences seem to be more a feature of the species studied than of the carrier used in immunization.

DISCUSSION

We have described the use of ligand inhibition of the binding of ^{3}H-DNP-EACA by anti-DNP antibody to describe the fine specificity, in quantitative terms, of such antibodies produced by four different mammalian species. Individual members of a species produce anti-DNP antibodies in response to DNP-KLH immunization which more closely resemble antibodies produced by other members of the same species than antibodies produced by members of different species.

These species-specific features of anti-DNP antibodies are characteristics of major fractions of the anti-DNP antibody population since the inhibition studies were performed under conditions in which 50% of the antigen-binding sites of the anti-DNP antibody were occupied. These differences cannot be accounted for by either the amount or the affinity of these antibodies, since the serum concentration and K_F were comparable in each species. In addition, KLH is a potent immunogen and thus a large fraction of the cells that are potentially reactive to the DNP group can be expected to have been stimulated by DNP-KLH immunization. Finally, the specificity analysis of anti-DNP-KLH and anti-DNP-BGG antibodies produced by guinea pigs and rabbits shows that the characteristic species-specific patterns of anti-DNP antibodies are relatively carrier-independent.

It is of interest that the difference between rabbit and guinea pig anti-DNP antibodies in their relative specificity for DNPOH appears to be correlated with a previously observed difference in the capacity of DNPOH to dissociate immune complexes formed by DNP-BF and either rabbit or guinea pig anti-DNP antibody. Thus, yields of approximately 30% are obtained for the specific purification of rabbit anti-DNP antibodies by the Farah, Kern and Eisen (15) method whereas yields for the purification of guinea pig antibodies are of the order of 70% (16).

The differences observed in the fine specificity of anti-hapten antibody might be due either to qualitative differences in the specificity of all the anti-DNP antibody molecules synthesized by a given species as compared to another or, alternatively, by a different relative representation in the population of similar antibody molecules.

Studies aimed at resolving this problem are now in progress.

Recent observations of Wofsy *et al.* (L. Wofsy, D. C. Parker, I. Corneil and B. Burr, personal communication) on the affinity labeling characteristics of anti-*p*-nitrophenyl lactoside antibodies have also shown species-specific differences. This suggests that the observations reported here will prove to be true in a wide range of situations.

In the subsequent paper (5) we demonstrate that inbred strains of mice also produce anti-DNP antibodies that are characteristic, in their fine specificity, of that strain. This affords an opportunity to examine the genetic control of antibody specificity to simple haptens.

REFERENCES

1. Cohen, S. and Porter, R. R., Advances Immun., *4:* 287, 1964.
2. Eisen, H. N. and Siskind, G. W., Biochemistry, *3:* 996, 1964.
3. Kitagawa, M., Yagi, Y. and Pressman, D., J. Immun., *95:* 991, 1966.
4. Fazekas de St. Groth, S. Cold Spring Harbor Symp. Quant. Biol., *32:* 525, 1967.
5. Paul, W. E., Yoshida, T. and Benacerraf, B., J. Immun., *105:* 314, 1970.
6. Ovary, Z. and Benacerraf, B., Proc. Soc. Exp. Biol. Med., *114:* 72, 1963.
7. Benacerraf, B. and Levine, B. B., J. Exp. Med., *115:* 1023, 1962.
8. Carsten, M. E. and Eisen, H. N., J. Amer. Chem. Soc., *75:* 4451, 1953.
9. Eisen, H. N., Carsten, M. E. and Belman, B., J. Immun., *73:* 296, 1954.
10. Siskind, G. W., Paul, W. E. and Benacerraf, B., J. Exp. Med., *123:* 673, 1966.
11. Stupp, Y., Yoshida, T. and Paul, W. E., J. Immun., *103:* 625, 1969.
12. Farr, R. S., J. Infect. Dis., *103:* 239, 1958.
13. Sips, R., J. Chem. Phys., *16:* 490, 1948.
14. Karush, F., Advances Immun., *2:* 1, 1962.
15. Farah, F. S., Kern, M. and Eisen, H. N., J. Exp. Med., *112:* 1195, 1960.
16. Nussenzweig, V. and Benacerraf, B., J. Exp. Med., *124:* 805, 1966.

THE JOURNAL OF IMMUNOLOGY
Vol. 105, No. 2, Aug. 1970

Printed in U.S.A.

GENETIC CONTROL OF THE SPECIFICITY OF ANTI-DNP ANTIBODIES

II. Differences in the Specificity of Anti-DNP Antibody Produced by Several Inbred Strains of Mice

WILLIAM E. PAUL, TAKESHI YOSHIDA[1] AND BARUJ BENACERRAF

From the Laboratory of Immunology, National Institute of Allergy and Infectious Diseases, National Institutes of Health, Bethesda, Maryland 20014

Received for publication March 10, 1970

Differences in the fine specificity of anti-2,4-dinitrophenyl (DNP) antibodies produced by different inbred mouse strains were demonstrated. These differences are expressed in terms of the relative capacity of a given nitrophenyl ligand to inhibit the binding of ^{3}H-DNP-ϵ-aminocaproic acid (^{3}H-DNP-EACA) by anti-DNP antibodies. The most prominent differences concerned the relative affinity of AKR and of BALB/c anti-DNP antibodies for 2,4-dinitrophenol and 2,4-dinitroaniline and the relative affinity of AL/N and C57BL/6 anti-DNP antibodies for picryl-ϵ-aminocaproic acid. These strain-specific fine specificity patterns could not be explained by systematic differences in average association constant for ^{3}H-DNP-EACA. The specificity patterns of anti-DNP keyhole limpet hemocycanin and anti-DNP bovine γ globulin antibodies produced by a given strain were generally similar. The differences in fine specificity pattern between AKR and BALB/c anti-DNP antibodies were noted in antisera collected at various times in the course of the immune response. Strain-determined variation in the fine specificity of anti-DNP antibodies may present a model system for studying the genetic control of antibody specificity.

The mode of generation of antibody diversity and the mechanisms controlling the expression of one or another of the specific antibodies which an organism can synthesize are key issues in both genetics and immunology (1, 2). In the previous paper (3) we described the use of an inhibition of binding assay to obtain a quantitative expression of the range of cross-reactivity of anti-2,4-dinitrophenyl (DNP) antibodies. Using this technique we observed species-specific fine specificity patterns for such antibodies. This method would therefore seem applicable to the study of genetic control of antibody specificity.

In this paper we described the existence of strain-specific differences in the fine specificity of anti-DNP antibodies produced by inbred mice in response to immunization with DNP conjugated to a potent immunogen, keyhole limpet hemocyanin (KLH). The differences observed are not explicable by the amount of antibody produced, the average association constant of that antibody for hapten, or the protein carrier used in immunization. The differences rather appear to be characteristic of the mouse strain and thus offer the possibility of genetic analysis.

MATERIALS AND METHODS

In general, the materials and techniques utilized in this study are identical to those of the previous paper (3).

The additional materials employed were α-tertiary butyloxycarbonyl-L-lysine acetate (α-tboc-lysine, Cyclo Chemical Corp., Los Angeles, Calif.); ^{3}H-dinitrofluorobenzene (^{3}H-DNFB, 10 Ci/mmol, Amersham-Searle, Des Plaines, Ill.) and protein 315 B, as ascitic fluid. This protein, which was the gift of Dr. Michael Potter, is the product of the BALB/c2 myeloma MOPC 315 B and is known to bind nitrophenyl ligands with a high energy of interaction (4).

^{3}H-DNP-L-lysine (^{3}H-DNP-LYS) was prepared by the reaction of 10^{-4} mmol of ^{3}H-DNFB

[1] Present address: Department of Tuberculosis, The National Institute of Health, Tokyo, Japan.

(10 Ci/mmol) with 10^{-2} mmol of α-tboc-lysine in 0.1 ml of 5% Na_2CO_3. After the reaction mixture had stirred for 1 hr, 0.1 ml of 12 N HCl was added to remove the tertiary butyloxycarbonyl group. One hour later the reaction mixture was applied to silica gel thin layer chromatography plates (250 μ thickness) and developed with a solvent consisting of N-butanol:acetic acid:water (4:1:1). The area of the gel containing ^{3}H-DNP LYS was scraped from the plate and the compound was eluted with phosphate-buffered saline (PBS:0.15 M NaCl, 0.01 M potassium phosphate, pH 7.6).

The mice used in this study were all females and were obtained either from the Animal Production Section, National Institutes of Health, or from the Jackson Laboratories, Bar Harbor, Maine. The following strains were obtained from NIH: general purpose Swiss mice, AL/N, BALB/cAnN, C57BL/6N, DBA/2N and the F_1 hybrid produced by the mating of AL/N males with BALB/cAnN females. The latter mice are here termed C-AL-F_1. From the Jackson Laboratories were obtained: A/HeJ, AKR/J, C3H/HeJ, C57BL/6J, DBA/2J and BALB/cJ.

The amount and the affinity of anti-DNP antibodies were measured as described in the preceding communication (3). Similarly, the relative affinity and relative slope of inhibition for a series of nitrophenyl ligands were measured in terms of their capacity to inhibit the binding of ^{3}H-DNP-ϵ-aminocaproic acid (^{3}H-DNP-EACA) by anti-DNP antibodies, under conditions in which approximately half of the added antibody sites were bound in the absence of inhibitor.

RESULTS

Selection of immunization schedule. In order to obtain a standard immunization technique which would result in significant serum anti-DNP antibody concentrations, a comparison of several doses of DNP-KLH and several bleeding times was carried out in Swiss mice. Groups of 10 mice were immunized intramuscularly with 0.001, 0.01, 0.1 or 1 mg of DNP-KLH, emulsified in complete Freund's adjuvant, and were bled at either 2, 4 or 8 weeks after immunization. Anti-DNP antibody concentrations of pools of serum collected from these mice were measured by quantitative precipitin analysis and are presented in Table I. An immunizing dose of 1 mg and a bleeding time of 4 weeks after immunization were selected as standard procedure, except for certain experiments to be described later.

TABLE I

Anti-DNP antibody concentration in Swiss mice after DNP-KLH immunization

Immunizing Dose	Time after Immunization		
	2 weeks	4 weeks	8 weeks
mg			
0.001	<0.05[a]	<0.05	<0.05
0.01	<0.05	<0.05	0.08
0.1	0.45	0.46	0.09
1.0	0.52	0.51	0.32

[a] Anti-DNP antibody concentration in serum (mg/ml) as determined by quantitative precipitin analysis with DNP-bovine fibrinogen.

TABLE II

Serum concentration and affinity of anti-DNP antibody in several mouse strains 4 weeks after immunization with 1 mg of DNP-KLH

Strain	Age at Immunization	Antibody Concentration	K_F[a] (DNP-EACA) L/M × 10^6
	weeks	*mg/ml*	
A/He	11	1.01	1.0
AKR	4	0.88	0.71
AKR	11	1.02	0.76
AL/N	4	1.40	1.59
AL/N	11	1.32	0.78
BALB/c	4	0.26	0.79
BALB/c	11	0.33	0.44
C3H	4	0.42	0.91
C3H	11	1.18	0.52
C57BL/6	4	0.24	1.2
C57BL/6	11	0.34	0.79
DBA/2	4	0.03	
DBA/2	11	0.15	0.76
C-AL-F_1	11	0.60	0.56
Swiss	~4	0.51	1.38
Swiss	10	1.31	1.7

[a] Average association constant for ^{3}H-DNP-EACA determined by an ammonium sulfate precipitation method.

Amount and affinity of anti-DNP antibody produced by various strains. The strains of mice showed considerable variability in their serum concentrations of anti-DNP antibodies in response to DNP-KLH immunization (Table II). Thus AL/N mice had concentrations of 1.40 and 1.32 mg/ml in groups which had been 4 and 11 weeks old at the time of immunization; at the other extreme, DBA/2 mice had concentrations of 0.03 and 0.15 mg/ml in the 4 and 11 week groups, respectively. The remaining strains displayed intermediate concentrations. In most instances, little difference was observed in the serum concentration of anti-DNP antibody between the 4 and 11 week groups. However, the 11-week C3H and DBA/2 mice had considerably higher serum concentrations than did the 4-week groups. Average association constants were calculated, as previously described (3, 5), from data obtained by an ammonium sulfate precipitation technique and are referred to as K_F. The anti-DNP antibodies produced by the various groups of inbred mice had K_F's for DNP-EACA ranging from 0.44 to 1.59 $\times 10^6$ L/M (Table II). No reproducible strain differences were noted.

Relative specificity for nitrophenyl ligands of anti-DNP antibody produced by different strains. The relative specificity of anti-DNP antibody produced by different strains in response to DNP-KLH immunization was analyzed by using various nitrophenyl ligands to inhibit the binding of ^{3}H-DNP-EACA by anti-DNP antibody. The relative affinity of antibody for a given nitrophenyl ligand is the ratio of the free concentration of that ligand required to cause 50% inhibition of the binding of ^{3}H-DNP-EACA by anti-DNP-antibody to the free concentration of non-radioactive DNP-EACA required for the same inhibition. In the case of dinitrophenol (DNPOH), concentrations yielding 25% inhibition were compared because 50% inhibition was frequently not achieved. A large numerical value for this ratio indicates a low relative affinity and a small numerical value, a high relative affinity. The relative slope of inhibition is the ratio of slope of inhibition (%/log) for a given nitrophenyl ligand to the slope of inhibition for DNP-EACA. Table III presents relative affinities of anti-DNP antibodies produced by each strain of mouse for DNPOH, 2,4,6-trinitrophenyl-ε-aminocaproic acid (picryl-EACA), *p*-nitrophenyl-ε-aminocaproic acid (p-NO_2-φ-EACA) and 2,4-dinitroaniline ($DNPNH_2$).

The most striking difference noted is that of the relative affinities of AKR and of BALB/c anti-DNP antibodies for DNPOH. Ratios of 25% inhibitory concentrations were 2.7 and 4.6 for the two pools of AKR antibody whereas the ratios were 1250 and 1670 for the two pools of BALB/c antibody. The large numerical differences are partially due to the low slopes for this inhibition (Fig. 1). The data may also be compared in terms of the absolute inhibition of binding of ^{3}H-DNP-EACA at the highest final concentration of DNPOH (5×10^{-4} M) used in these experiments. These values were 62% and 50% for AKR anti-DNP antibody and 19% and 25% for BALB/c antibody. Figure 1 presents semilogarithmic plots of inhibition data for the two pools of AKR antisera and of BALB/c antisera, respectively. There is definite similarity in the intrastrain comparison and definite difference in the interstrain comparison. The pattern of inhibition of the binding of ^{3}H-DNP-EACA by antisera from individual members of a given strain is very similar to the pattern observed for antiserum pools from that strain. This is illustrated in Figure 2, where data for four individual AKR antisera are presented.

In addition to the difference between AKR and BALB/c antisera in their relative affinity for DNPOH, other differences may also be noted. Thus, an AKR antiserum has a greater relative affinity for $DNPNH_2$ (1.4) than does a BALB/c

TABLE III

Relative affinity of anti-DNP antibody from several mouse strains for nitrophenyl ligands

Strain	Ligand			
	DNPOH	Picryl-EACA	p-NO_2-φ EACA	$DNPNH_2$
A/He	; 29[a]	; 12	; 39	; 3.4
AKR	2.7; 4.6	15; 16	22; 23	; 1.4
AL/N	18; 16	8; 8	19; 17	; 3.4
BALB/c	1250; 1670	23; 24	24; 33	; 27
C3H	54; 45	19; 31	17; 28	; 4.6
C57BL/6	77; 40	39; 62	32; 42	; 5.3
DBA/2	; 108	; 19	; 13	; 4.0
C-AL-F_1	; 157	; 15	; 17	; 4.8
Swiss	47; 30	25; 12	26; 19	

[a] Relative affinity is the ratio of the free concentration of a given ligand required to cause 50% inhibition of the reaction of antisera with ^{3}H-DNP-EACA to the free concentration of DNP-EACA required for similar inhibition. In the case of DNPOH, 25% inhibition was used. Thus, the *greater* the numerical value, the *lower* the relative affinity. The value before the semicolon was obtained with antisera from mice immunized at the age of 4 weeks; the value after the semicolon was obtained with sera of mice immunized at 11 weeks of age.

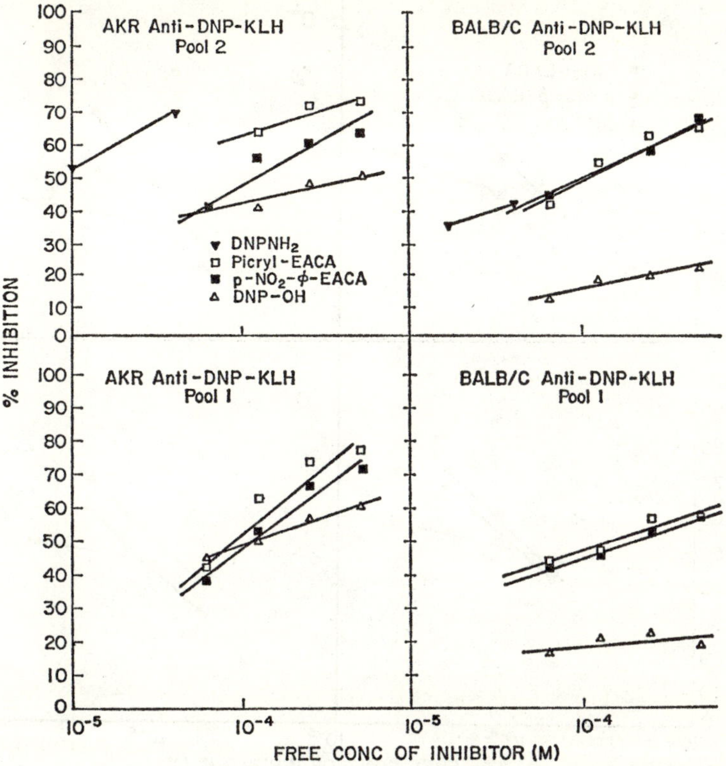

Figure 1. Inhibition, by nitrophenyl ligands, of the binding of ^{3}H-DNP-EACA by anti-DNP-antisera. Pool 1 is a pool of antisera collected from AKR and from BALB/c mice which were 4 weeks old at time of immunization. Pool 2 was collected from mice 11 weeks old at time of immunization.

antiserum (27). AL/N antisera have greater relative affinity for picryl-EACA (8 and 8) than do C57BL/6 antisera (39 and 62). Furthermore, AL/N anti-DNP antisera have higher relative affinities for picryl-EACA (8 and 8) than for *p*-NO_2-ϕ-EACA (19 and 17) whereas C57BL/6 antisera bind picryl-EACA (39 and 62) less well than they bind p-NO_2-ϕ-EACA (32 and 42). Antisera from the A/He strain of mice have a pattern of inhibition similar to that of antisera from the closely related AL/N strain.

The only F_1 hybrid strain studied thus far is the C-AL-F_1 (the F_1 of AL/N males and BALB/c females). The antiserum of these mice has a relative affinity for DNPOH (157) intermediate between that of AL/N antisera (18 and 16) and of BALB/c antisera (1250 and 1670). A comparison of relative affinities for picryl-EACA shows a similar tendency. AL/N sera have a 50% inhibitory ratio for picryl-EACA of 8 and 8; C-AL-F_1-15; and BALB/c-23 and 24. Figure 3 presents plots of absolute inhibition by these ligands for the binding of parental and F_1 strain antisera to ^{3}H-DNP-EACA. Here the effect of picryl-EACA on the binding of ^{3}H-DNP-EACA by C-AL-F_1 sera cannot be distinguished from its effect on binding by AL/N sera. The difference in absolute and relative inhibitory data in this instance is due to difference in inhibition by the reference ligand, DNP-EACA. The relative affinity for $DNPNH_2$ of C-AL-F_1 antisera (4.8) is similar to the AL/N (3.4) antiserum and different from BALB/c antiserum (27).

The relative slopes of inhibition are quite similar for sera from each of the strains studied for each of the ligands tested.

Relative specificity for nitrophenyl ligands of protein 315B. Protein 315B is the product of the BALB/c 2 myeloma MOPC-315B. It binds DNP-LYS with an average intrinsic association constant of approximately 1.5×10^7 L/M (4). An analysis of the fine specificity of this protein

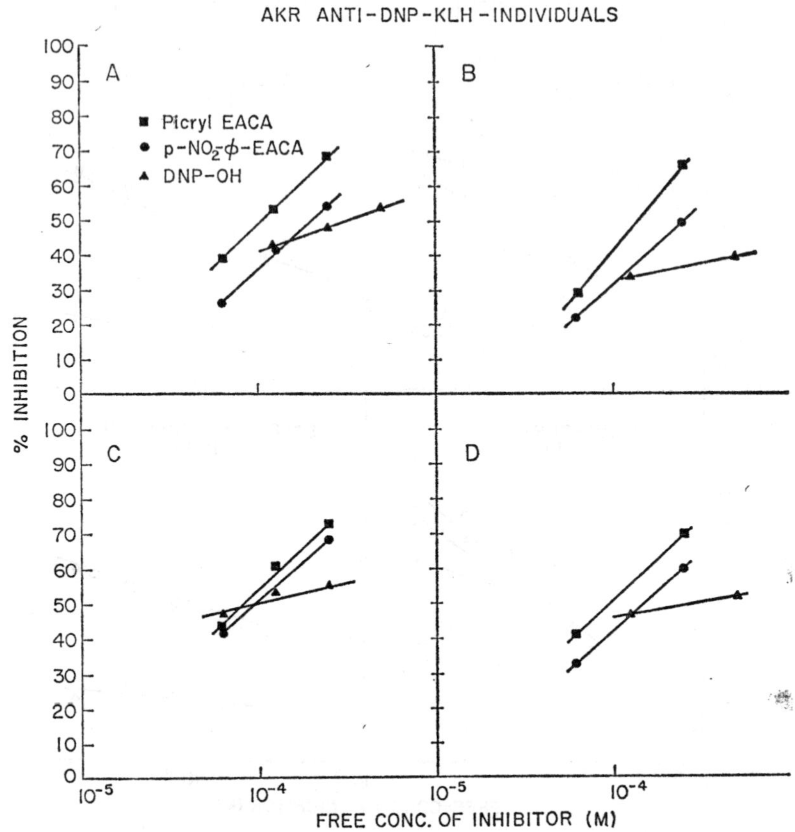

Figure 2. Inhibition by nitrophenyl ligands of the binding of ³H-DNP-EACA by anti-DNP antisera produced by four individual AKR mice.

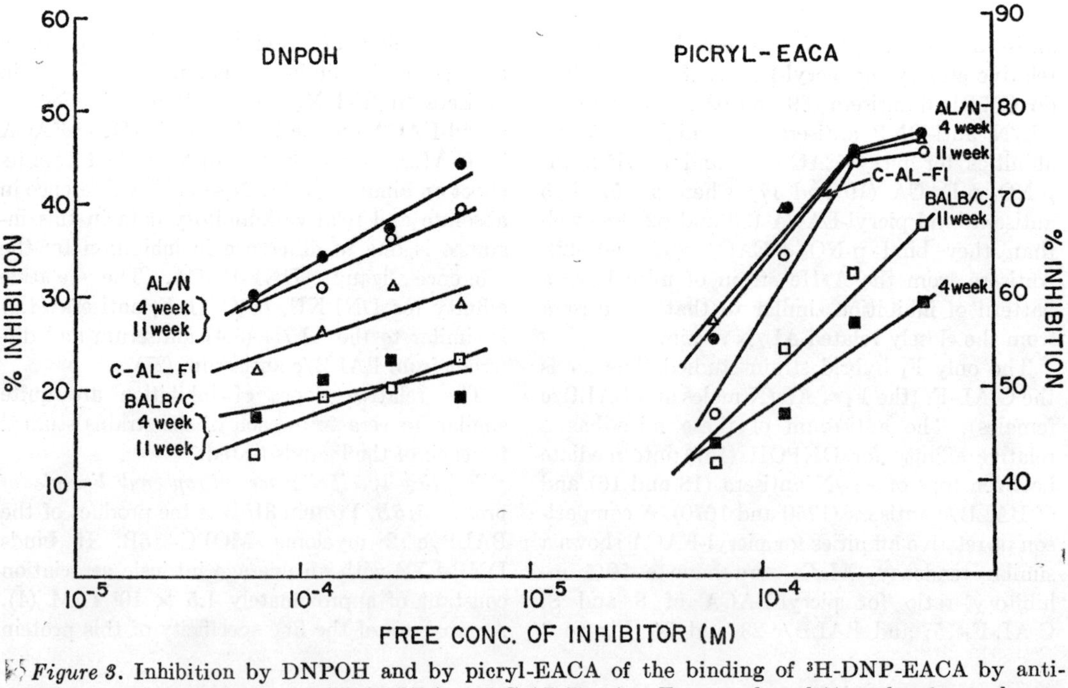

Figure 3. Inhibition by DNPOH and by picryl-EACA of the binding of ³H-DNP-EACA by anti-DNP antisera produced by AL/N, BALB/c and C-AL-F₁ mice. Four week and 11 week refer to the age of AL/N and BALB/c mice at time of immunization. The C-AL-F₁ mice were 11 weeks old at time of immunization.

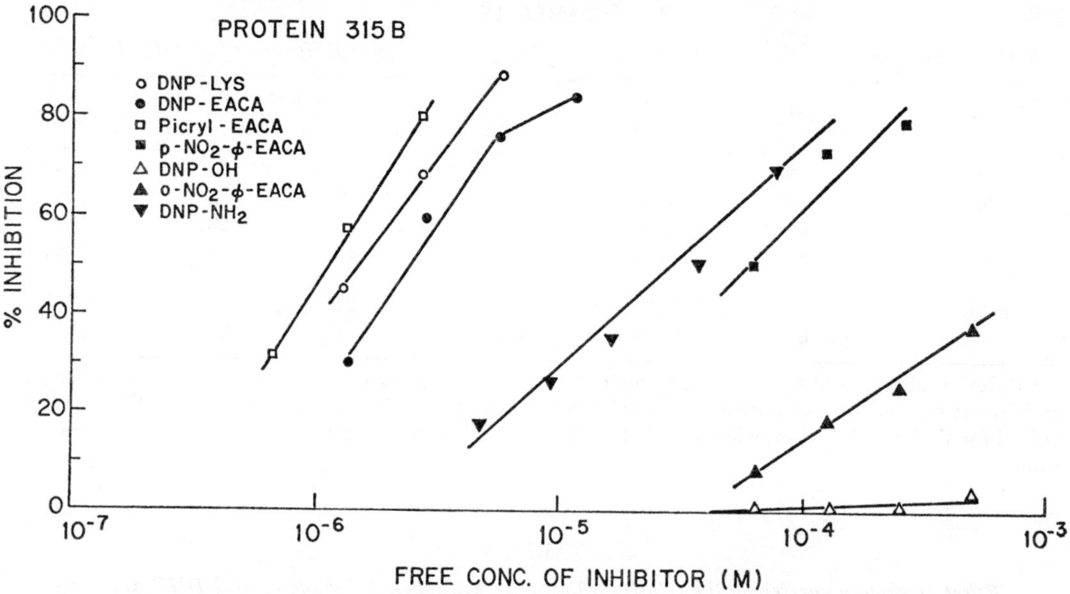

Figure 4. Inhibition, by nitrophenyl ligands, of the binding of ³H-DNP-EACA by Protein 315 B

was performed in the hope that it might provide a standard reagent against which induced anti-DNP antibodies could be compared. Figure 4 presents the pattern of inhibition by nitrophenyl ligands of the binding of this protein to ³H-DNP-EACA; it binds picryl-EACA more avidly than either DNP-LYS or DNP-EACA, as previously reported by Eisen *et al.* (4), and thus is quite unlike a typical anti-DNP antibody. Furthermore, DNP-OH is not appreciably bound and *o*-nitrophenyl-EACA (*o*-NO_2-ϕ-EACA) causes considerable inhibition of binding. Both of these characteristics are also unusual for anti-DNP-antibodies (3). The slopes of inhibition observed here are similar to that of the reference ligand, DNP-EACA. This is what would be expected from a homogeneous class of binding sites and is quite different from what is observed with induced anti-DNP antibodies.

The effect of time after immunization on relative affinity. It is well known that the average intrinsic association constants of anti-DNP antibody for DNP-LYS and for DNP-EACA are higher in sera collected late in the course of immunization than they are in early sera (6). In order to determine whether this phenomenon was contributing to the interstrain differences observed in relative affinities, sera were collected from AKR and BALB/c mice at various times after immunization. The relative affinities for DNPOH, picryl-EACA and $DNPNH_2$ for AKR sera (2, 4 and 8 weeks after immunization) and BALB/c sera (4 and 8 weeks after immunization) are presented in Table IV. There is an increase in association constant for ³H-DNP-EACA, as expected. The relative affinity for nitrophenyl ligands is very similar for each serum of a given strain, with one exception. The earliest AKR serum, which has the lowest K_F, has an inhibitory ratio for DNPOH of 32 as compared to 4.6 and 3.3 for the later sera. This difference is small, however, when compared to the interstrain difference.

The effect of protein carrier used in immunization on relative affinity. Carrier proteins affect the absolute K_0 of anti-DNP antibody produced after DNP-carrier immunization (7). In order to determine whether the carrier also affected fine specificity, a comparison of the relative affinity of anti-DNP antibodies produced by AL/N and A/He mice in response to DNP-KLH and DNP-BGG immunization was performed (Table V). The K_F for ³H-DNP-EACA was lower in sera collected from mice immunized with DNP-BGG than with DNP-KLH. The relative affinity for DNPOH was also lower in the anti-DNP-BGG sera, as the relative affinity for DNPOH had been lower in the early, low affinity AKR anti-DNP antibody. No significant differences in regard to the relative affinities for the other ligands were noted.

TABLE IV

Effect of time after immunization on the relative affinity for nitrophenyl ligands of anti-DNP antibody

Strain	Time after Immunization	K_F DNP-EACA L/M × 10^6	Ligand			
			DNPOH	Picryl-EACA	p-NO_2-ϕ EACA	$DNPNH_2$
	weeks					
AKR	2	0.28	32[a]	19	22	2.8
	4	0.76	4.6	16	23	1.4
	8	1.18	3.3	23	26	1.7
BALB/c	4	0.44	1670	24	33	27
	8	2.40	1650	51	22	20

[a] Relative affinity is the ratio of the free concentration of a given ligand required to cause 50% inhibition of the reaction of antisera with ^{3}H-DNP-EACA to the free concentration of DNP-EACA required for similar inhibition; when DNPOH is the inhibiting ligand, 25% inhibition is used for calculation.

TABLE V

Effect of protein carrier on the relative affinity for nitrophenyl ligands of anti-DNP antibody

Strain	Carrier	K_F DNP-EACA L/M × 10^6	Ligand			
			DNPOH	Picryl-EACA	p-NO_2-ϕ EACA	$DNPNH_2$
AL/N	KLH	0.78	16[a]	8	17	3.4
AL/N	BGG	0.20	273	9	33	4.5
A/He	KLH	1.0	29	12	39	3.4
A/He	BGG	0.26	311	14	24	3.9

[a] Relative affinity is the ratio of the free concentration of a given ligand required to cause 50% inhibition of the reaction of antisera with ^{3}H-DNP-EACA to the free concentration of DNP-EACA required for similar inhibition; when DNPOH is the inhibiting ligand, 25% inhibition is used for calculation.

The effect of the diluent used in the measurement of relative affinity on interstrain differences. In order to rule out the possibility that the differences in relative affinity of AKR and of BALB/c anti-DNP antibody might be due to interactions of ligand with proteins other than specific antibody, the relative affinity for DNPOH and for $DNPNH_2$ of AKR antisera was measured using antibody either in the form of diluted serum or as a globulin fraction dissolved in pooled globulin prepared from sera of either non-immunized Swiss mice or non-immunized BALB/c mice. In this case ^{3}H-DNP-LYS was used in the binding assay, and non-radioactive DNP-LYS was the reference ligand in the calculation of relative affinity.

Because DNP-LYS has no appreciable affinity for albumin in contrast to DNP-EACA (8), the

TABLE VI

Role of serum or globulin diluent on relative affinity of AKR and BALB/c anti-DNP antibodies

Strain Producing Antibody	Diluent	Relative Affinity[a]	
		DNPOH	$DNPNH_2$
AKR	Serum	89	
	Swiss globulin	73	3.8
	BALB/c globulin	86	5.7
BALB/c	Serum	1525	
	Swiss globulin	1077	18.4

[a] Relative affinity is the ratio of the free concentration of the indicated ligand required to cause 50% inhibition of the binding of ^{3}H-DNP-LYS to the free concentration of DNP-LYS required for the same degree of inhibition.

K_F of anti-DNP antibody is higher for DNP-LYS than for DNP-EACA when whole serum is employed in the assay (this, however, is not the case when globulin fractions are used). Since the K_F for DNP-LYS is higher, 50% binding of antibody in the absence of inhibitor could be achieved with considerably lower concentrations of both hapten and antibody than when ^{3}H-DNP-EACA was used. In turn, the concentration of DNPOH employed was sufficient to cause 50% (or more) inhibition of binding and thus relative affinities could be calculated for this ligand at 50% inhibition.

Table VI reveals that the relative affinity of AKR anti-DNP antibody for DNPOH, as compared with DNP-LYS, is essentially the same whether the diluent is serum, Swiss globulin or BALB/c globulin. Similarly, BALB/c anti-DNP antibody has a comparable relative affinity for DNPOH when it is diluted in either serum or Swiss globulin. Furthermore, the differences in relative affinity for both DNPOH and $DNPNH_2$ between AKR and BALB/c antisera are preserved under this new set of binding conditions.

DISCUSSION

Clear and reproducible differences in the fine specificity of anti-DNP antibodies produced by several mouse strains exist. These differences exist in the face of similar association constants for the interaction of antibody with DNP-EACA and persist throughout the course of immunization. Furthermore, the binding characteristics of antibody produced by a given strain are generally similar when either DNP-KLH or DNP-BGG are used for immunization.

The differences observed consist of differences in the capacity of several nitrophenyl ligands to inhibit the binding of ^{3}H-DNP-EACA by anti-DNP antibody. The largest differences observed are between the relative affinity of AKR and BALB/c antisera for DNPOH and for $DNPNH_2$, and between the relative affinity of AL/N and C57BL/6 antisera for picryl-EACA. The single F_1 hybrid studied had binding characteristics intermediate between those of the parental strains (AL/N and BALB/c) for two ligands and similar to one of the two parents for a third ligand.

Wofsy and his colleagues (L. Wofsy, D. C. Parker, I. Corneil and B. Burr, personal communication) have described differences in affinity labeling characteristics of anti-*p*-nitrophenyl lactoside antibodies produced by different inbred mouse strains. This observation may well be closely related to the fine specificity differences reported here. Genetically controlled specificity differences in the antibodies produced by guinea pigs in response to insulin (9, 10) and by mice in response to a branch chain polymer of tyrosine, glutamic acid, proline and lysine (11, 12) have been reported. These differences appear to concern the nature of the antigenic determinant to which the animal makes its most vigorous response rather than to fine specificity differences of antibodies with the same general specificity.

The phenotypic differences observed in this study may reflect genetic control of the complex process whereby antigenic determinants are recognized and cause the stimulation of the production of antibodies of given fine specificity. Alternatively, the differences may be secondary to heritable differences in structural genes for variable regions of immunoglobulin polypeptide chains.

The level of genetic complexity represented by these phenotypic differences is not yet known. Crosses of AKR and BALB/c mice to produce F_1, F_2 and backcross generations are now in progress and antisera produced by individual animals will be analyzed.

REFERENCES

1. Herzenberg, L. A., McDevitt, H. O. and Herzenberg, L. A., Advances Genet., *2:* 209, 1968.
2. McDevitt, H. O. and Benacerraf, B., Advances Immun., *11:* 31, 1969.
3. Yoshida, T., Paul, W. E. and Benacerraf, B., J. Immun., *105:* 306, 1970.
4. Eisen, H. N., Simms, E. S. and Potter, M., Biochemistry, *7:* 4126, 1968.
5. Stupp, Y., Yoshida, T. and Paul, W. E., J. Immun., *103:* 625, 1968.
6. Eisen, H. N. and Siskind, G. W., Biochemistry, *3:* 996, 1964.
7. Siskind, G. W., Paul, W. E. and Benacerraf, B., J. Exp. Med., *123:* 673, 1966.
8. Carsten, M. E. and Eisen, H. N., J. Amer. Chem. Soc., *75:* 4451, 1953.
9. Arquilla, E. R. and Finn, J., J. Exp. Med., *122:* 771, 1965.
10. Arquilla, E. R., Miles, P., Knapp, S., Hamlin, J. and Bromer, W., Vox Sang., *13:* 32, 1967.
11. Mozes, E., McDevitt, H. O., Jaton, J.-C. and Sela, M., J. Exp. Med., *130:* 493, 1969.
12. Mozes, E., McDevitt, H. O., Jaton, J.-C. and Sela, M., J. Exp. Med., *130:* 1263, 1969.

THE JOURNAL OF IMMUNOLOGY

Vol. 105, No. 2, Aug. 1970
Printed in U.S.A.

ROLE OF THE THYMUS IN TOLERANCE

IX. Inhibition of Experimental Autoallergic Encephalomyelitis by Intrathymic Injection of Encephalitogen[1]

GEORGE W. ELLISON[2] AND BYRON H. WAKSMAN

From the Department of Microbiology, Yale University, New Haven, Connecticut 06510

Received for publication March 5, 1970

Adult rats received 750 or 800 R of whole body x-irradiation with simultaneous thymic or splenic shielding and immediately thereafter were given intrathymic, intrasplenic, or intraperitoneal injections of suspensions of rat spinal cord or acid-extracted rat cord encephalitogen. Three weeks later the animals were challenged with the corresponding antigen in Freund's adjuvant. Animals receiving intrathymic encephalitogenic material showed a slight but definite decrease in the severity of experimental autoallergic encephalomyelitis (EAE). The acid-extracted encephalitogen showed four components after filtration through Sephadex G-200. Electrophoresis on 5% acrylamide gel in the presence of 8 M urea revealed at least four cathodally migrating and four anodally migrating bands.

Experiments from this laboratory (1, 2) have demonstrated that intrathymic injection of bovine γ globulin in normal or irradiated rats is more effective than intrasplenic or intraperitoneal injection in inducing specific tolerance. In the present study, an attempt was made to induce specific tolerance for the antigen(s) of experimental autoallergic encephalomyelitis (EAE) by the use of this technique. Intrathymic injection of suspensions of spinal cord or basic protein encephalitogen in rats following x-irradiation was found to induce partial tolerance, as judged by decreased severity of EAE when the rats were challenged 3 weeks later with adjuvant mixtures containing cord or encephalitogen.

MATERIALS AND METHODS

Animals. Male Lewis rats (Microbiological Associates, Bethesda, Md.), 8 to 9 weeks old, were used in experiments in which suspensions of spinal cord were given. Male Sprague-Dawley rats (Camm Research Institute, Inc., Wayne, N. J.), 7 to 8 weeks old, were used in experiments with the encephalitogen. Groups of four to five animals were kept in plastic cages and maintained on standard laboratory chow. Lewis rats were given tetracycline (1.8 g/liter) and Sprague-Dawley rats neomycin and polymyxin B (Daribiotic liquid, S. E. Massengill Co., Bristol, Tenn.) in concentrations of 3 mg and 750 units/liter, respectively, in their drinking water beginning the day following irradiation. Antibiotics were stopped at the time of challenge.

Antigen preparations. Freshly prepared 20% and 5% w/v saline suspensions of rat spinal cord and kidney were used in one experiment. For the second, a basic protein "encephalitogen" (BP) was prepared from rat spinal cord by a modification of the method of Kies (3). Spinal cord, cleaned of meninges and blood and stored at −20°C for not over 2 months, was homogenized in chloroform:methanol 2:1 (v/v) (20 ml/g wet weight) in a Waring Blendor cooled by Dry Ice. Subsequent manipulations were carried out at 4°C. The homogenate was stirred 10 min, then filtered with suction on Whatman 541 filter paper. The cake was resuspended in cold acetone (10 ml/g of original cord), stirred 60 min, filtered by suction, dried, and weighed. After two washes in distilled water (10 ml/g), the solids were extracted with 10 volumes of cold 0.1 N acetic acid for 30 min. The acidic suspension was partially clarified by centrifugation, filtered through Whatman No. 1 paper by gravity, and finally filtered through a 0.45 μ

[1] This work was supported by Grants AI-06112 and AI-06455 from the National Institutes of Health.

[2] Special National Institutes of Health Fellowship NB-1548.

filter (Millipore Corp., Bedford, Mass.) at room temperature, lyophilized, and stored at −20°C. The resulting light tan material was suspended in 5% dextrose in water, or dissolved in 8 M urea for emulsification in adjuvant or injection into animals.

Antigen characterization. The protein was determined by the method of Lowry *et al.* (4) using bovine serum albumin as a standard. A K9/30 column charged with Sephadex G-200 (Pharmacia Fine Chemicals, Inc., Piscataway, N. J.) of 25-cm bed height was used for analytic fractionation of the BP obtained by this procedure. Twenty milligrams, dissolved in 0.5 ml 8 M urea, were passed through the column at a flow rate of 4.4 ml/hr at 4°C and the optical density of the effluent was measured.

The encephalitogen also was separated by electrophoresis on 5% polyacrylamide gel in 8 M urea at pH 10.6, using the method of Martenson and Gaitonde (5) (chemicals from Canal Industries, Rockville, Md.). Ammonium persulfate was used as the catalyst. The sample, dissolved in 8 M urea, was mixed with 0.1 ml 20% sucrose and layered on the gel. Gels were fixed in 5% trichloracetic acid-5% sulfosalicylic acid and stained for 4 to 5 hr with Coomassie blue (Colab Laboratories, Inc., Chicago Heights, Ill.) (6).

The immunogenicity of the BP preparation was evaluated by mixing various amounts, suspended in 5% dextrose, with an equal volume of complete Freund's adjuvant and injecting into a hind footpad of Sprague-Dawley rats (see below). A similar bioassay of the encephalitogen, in solution in 8 M urea, was carried out in Lewis rats.

Treatment groups. The procedure followed closely that used in our earlier studies (1, 2). Animals were matched for weight, assigned at random to the various experimental groups, and anesthetized with chloral hydrate supplemented with ether. After irradiation with 800 R central axis dose (250 kv, 2.0 mm Al filtration, 0.8 mm Cu half-value layer, 14.5 mA and 69 cm FSD) and lead shielding of either the thymus region or the spleen (1, 2), injections of whole spinal cord or kidney suspensions were carried out, some rats receiving intrathymic (i.t.) and others intraperitoneal (i.p.) or intrasplenic (i.s.) suspensions of whole tissue.

In a second experiment, animals received 750 R rather than 800 R (to reduce mortality from the x-irradiation) and were similarly injected with 10, 1, 0.1, or 0.01 mg BP, in 0.2 ml 5% dextrose in water, or with bovine serum albumin (BSA) as a control.

Three weeks after irradiation, animals pretreated with tissue suspensions were challenged with 0.05 ml of an emulsion containing equal parts of spinal cord and adjuvant (3 mg/ml heat-killed tubercle bacilli in mineral oil) in a single hind footpad. Those pretreated with BP were challenged with 500 μg BP in 5% dextrose and water emulsified with an equal volume of complete Freund's adjuvant (6 mg/ml tubercle bacilli in oil, with added Arlacel A (Atlas Chemical Industries, Inc., Wilmington, Del.)). All were killed shortly after onset of neurologic impairment, usually within 2 to 3 days. Those showing no signs were dispatched 26 and 21 days after challenge, respectively, in the first and second experiments.

Quantitation of the EAE response was based on day of clinical onset, clinical severity (on a 0–+++, scale), histologic severity (0–+++), and a composite graded score between 0 and 6 (7–9). The rats were bled at the times of irradiation and challenge, 10 and 20 days after challenge, and at the time of autopsy. The sera were examined for antibody by quantitative complement fixation, with 0.05% spinal cord in saline as antigen (10), or by the use of the BP preparation in a passive hemagglutination test with tanned formalinized erythrocytes (11).

RESULTS

Characterization of encephalitogen. One microgram of the acid lyophilizate was obtained from approximately 228 μg (wet weight) of fresh spinal cord. The material was completely soluble in 8 M urea, partially soluble in distilled water, and insoluble in physiologic saline. In the effluent from a Sephadex G-200 column, there were two major and two minor peaks (Fig. 1). An additional peak at 19 to 20 ml was seen with the continuous flow monitor (280 nm) but was not detected in the collected fractions. Electrophoresis in polyacrylamide gel revealed four components migrating toward the cathode and four migrating toward the anode (Fig. 2). Our material was similar to that prepared from rat myelin by Martenson *et al.* (12).

For the production of EAE of maximal in-

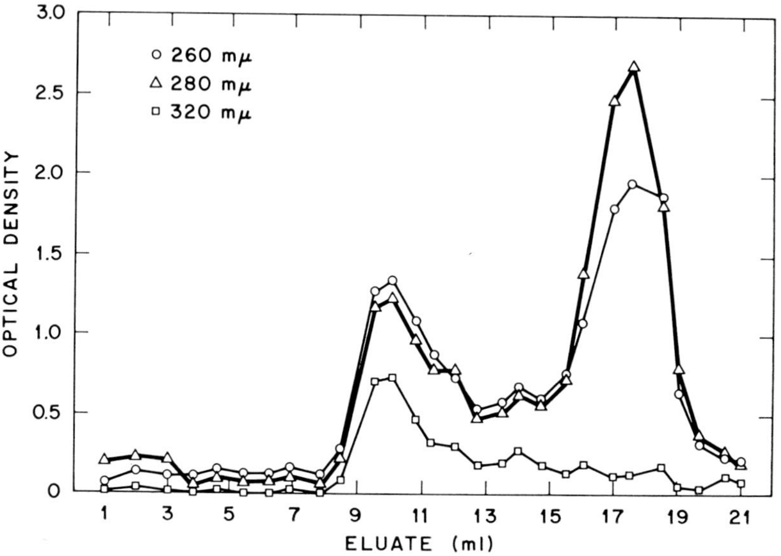

Figure 1. Elution profile of acid-extracted material from rat spinal cord after passage through Sephadex G-200. Void volume 4.8 ml (estimated).

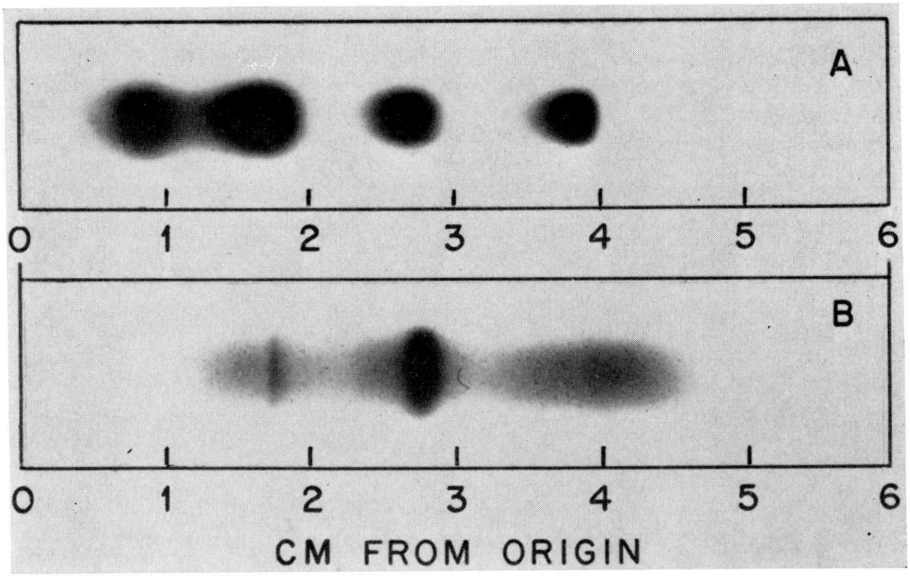

Figure 2. Electrophoresis of acid-extracted material from rat spinal cord. Migration time is 8 hr in 5% acrylamide gel, pH 10.6 in 8 M urea with current constant at 2.5 mA/gel. The upper pattern (*A*) is the migration of 500 μg protein toward the cathode; the lower pattern (*B*), 200 μg protein toward the anode.

tensity in Sprague-Dawley rats, a challenge dose of 500 μg BP in 0.05 ml adjuvant mixture was required. In Lewis rats, challenge with 5 μg BP yielded a 100% incidence with average onset at day 14, an average clinical severity of 2, histologic severity of 2, and a graded score of approximately 3. A dose of 50 μg was maximally effective (day of onset 11.5, clinical and histologic severity 2, and average graded score of 4.7).

EAE in animals pretreated with whole tissue suspensions. Irradiated rats pretreated by injection of a 20% suspension of spinal cord into the

TABLE I

Effect of pretreatment with tissue suspensions upon EAE

Treatment Group					Factors of Disease Severity				
800 R	Shielded organ	Antigen	Antigen concen- tration (in 0.2 ml)	Injection route	Incidence	Day of onset	Clinical severity (0–3)	Histologic severity (0–3)	Graded score (0–6)
			%						
0					9/9	12.5[a]	2.0[a]	1.7[a]	2.6[a]
+					8/8	14.5	1.6	1.3	2.1
+	T	Saline		i.t.	8/8	12.7	2.3	1.2	2.0
+	S	Saline		i.s.	8/8	12.9	1.9	1.9	4.2
+	T	Kidney	20	i.t.	7/7	12.3	2.3	1.6	4.1
+	T	Kidney	5	i.t.	8/8	12.3	2.3	1.4	2.4
+	T	Spinal cord	20	i.t.	7/8	15.6	1.0	1.1	1.4
+	T	Spinal cord	5	i.t.	6/7	15.2	1.4	1.9	2.7
+	T	Spinal cord	20	i.p.	7/8	15.4	1.1	1.8	2.6
+	T	Spinal cord	5	i.p.	7/7	13.0	2.1	1.3	2.3
+	S	Spinal cord	20	i.s.	9/9	12.8	1.1	2.6	2.0
+	S	Spinal cord	5	i.s.	8/8	14.4	1.5	1.8	2.0

[a] Average values.

TABLE II

Effect of pretreatment with encephalitogen (BP) upon EAE

Treatment Group					Factors of Disease Severity				
750 R	Shielded organ	Antigen	Antigen dose (in 0.2 ml)	Injection route	Incidence	Day of onset	Clinical severity (0–3)	Histologic severity (0–3)	Graded score (0–6)
			mg						
0					9/9	15.9[a]	1.3[a]	2.3[a]	3.7[a]
+					8/8	15.5	1.1	1.6	2.4
+	T				7/8	13.7	1.5	1.4	3.0
+	S				8/10	13.7	1.2	1.4	3.1
+	T	BSA	10	i.t.	8/8	14.5	1.7	2.4	4.3
+	T	BP	10	i.t.	7/8	17.9	0.8	1.1	1.6
+	T	BP	1	i.t.	4/7	18.4	0.8	1.0	1.7
+	T	BP	0.1	i.t.	9/10	15.6	1.3	1.5	2.9
+	T	BP	0.01	i.t.	8/8	12.1	2.3	2.0	4.3
+	T	BP	10	i.p.	5/7	15.9	1.3	1.7	3.0
+	T	BP	1	i.p.	6/8	15.6	1.1	1.2	2.6
+	T	BP	0.1	i.p.	6/8	16.3	1.2	1.1	2.1
+	T	BP	0.01	i.p.	7/7	14.8	1.5	2.1	2.3
+	S	BP	10	i.s.	8/9	17.3	1.2	1.6	2.6
+	S	BP	1	i.s.	8/9	14.4	1.4	1.8	3.3
+	S	BP	0.1	i.s.	8/9	17.6	0.7	1.3	2.4
+	S	BP	0.01	i.s.	5/6	18.5	0.5	1.7	2.2

[a] Average values.

shielded thymus showed, when challenged, a slight delay in onset of EAE, as well as a decrease in the clinical and histologic severity and in the graded score in which these factors are combined (Table I). Injection of a comparable dose of kidney homogenate by the same route did not influence the subsequent production of EAE. Injection of a lower dose of spinal cord suspension by the intrathymic route or of a high dose by other routes resulted in inconstant reduction of individual factors of the later EAE response. No complement-fixing antibodies were found in the sera at any time.

EAE in animals receiving encephalitogen. Intrathymic injection of 1.0 or 10.0 mg BP produced a subsequent delay in EAE onset and diminution in the clinical and histologic severity and in the graded score, whereas 10 mg BSA given by the same route had no effect (Table II). Statistically these changes were of borderline significance. However the disease response in the test rats was well below the level observed in the group irradiated in the absence of lymphoid tissue shielding. An inconstant reduction of some features of the response but not of others followed pretreatment with BP by the intraperitoneal or intrasplenic routes. Hemagglutinating antibody titers in the sera followed no pattern related to the experimental treatment. Most sera had titers less than 1:8.

DISCUSSION

A slight but definite reduction in the severity of EAE was induced in rats of two strains, differing in susceptibility to the disease, by pretreatment with whole spinal cord or BP following whole body irradiation. The effect was considerably more marked when the antigen was introduced directly into the shielded thymus. It was specific since no reduction in the disease response followed similar injections of kidney homogenate or BSA, and it appeared comparable to the specific "tolerance" obtained in earlier experiments by intrathymic injection of bovine γ globulin (1, 2). That the tolerance seen in the present experiment was not more complete may be attributable to our use of insoluble tissue suspensions or a partially soluble encephalitogen, which could not diffuse freely throughout the organ into which they were injected.

The apparently superior effectiveness of intrathymic injection over pretreatment with antigen by other routes in the induction of tolerance to central nervous system antigen is in agreement with our earlier experiments with protein and transplantation antigens and with a substantial body of evidence suggesting that the thymus is the actual source of a cell population participating in cell-mediated immune responses (13). Nevertheless, a slight inhibition of the EAE response also resulted from intrasplenic or indeed intraperitoneal injection of antigen. This agrees with earlier work from other laboratories, showing the inhibitory effect of systemic doses of encephalitogen (14–16) and an extensive series of studies on tolerance to protein antigens produced by this means (17).

Acknowledgments. We are grateful to Mrs. Francine Burrows, Mrs. Ann Shapiro and Mr. Rod Hugueley for expert technical assistance.

REFERENCES

1. Staples, P. J., Gery, I. and Waksman, B. H., J. Exp. Med., *124:* 127, 1966.
2. Horiuchi, A. and Waksman, B. H., J. Immun., *101:* 1322, 1968.
3. Kies, M. W., Ann. N. Y. Acad. Sci., *122:* 161, 1965.
4. Lowry, O., Rosebrough, N. J., Farr, A. L. and Randall, R. J., J. Biol. Chem., *193:* 265, 1951.
5. Martenson, R. E. and Gaitonde, M. J., J. Neurochem., *16:* 333, 1969.
6. Chambrack, A., Reisfeld, R. A., Wyckoff, M. and Zaccari, J., Anal. Biochem., *20:* 150, 1967.
7. Ferraro, A. and Cazullo, C. L., J. Neuropath. Exp. Neurol., *7:* 235, 1948.
8. Waksman, B. H., Porter, H., Lees, M. D., Adams, R. D. and Folch, J., J. Exp. Med., *100:* 451, 1954.
9. Kosunen, T. U., Waksman, B. H. and Samuelsson, I. K., J. Neuropath. Exp. Neurol., *22:* 367, 1963.
10. Osler, A. G., Strauss, J. H. and Mayer, M. M., Amer. J. Syph. Gonor. Ven. Dis., *36:* 140, 1952.
11. Csizmas, L., Proc. Soc. Exp. Biol. Med., *103:* 157, 1960.
12. Martenson, R. E., Diebler, G. E. and Kies, M. W., J. Biol. Chem., *244:* 4268, 1969.
13. Miller, J. F. A. P. and Osoba, D., Physiol. Rev., *47:* 437, 1967.
14. Alvord, E. J., Jr., Shaw, C. M., Hruby, S. and Kies, M. W., Ann. N. Y. Acad. Sci., *122:* 333, 1965.
15. Cunningham, V. R. and Field, E. J., Ann. N. Y. Acad. Sci., *122:* 346, 1965.
16. Einstein, E. R., Csejtey, J., Davis, W. J. and Rauch, H. C., Immunochemistry, *5:* 567, 1968.
17. Dresser, D. W. and Mitchison, N. A., Advances Immun., *6:* 129, 1969.

THE JOURNAL OF IMMUNOLOGY

Vol. 105, No. 2, Aug. 1970
Printed in U.S.A.

A SPECIFIC METHOD FOR PURIFICATION OF THE SECOND COMPONENT OF GUINEA PIG COMPLEMENT AND A CHEMICAL EVALUATION OF THE ONE-HIT THEORY[1, 2]

MANFRED M. MAYER, JIMMIE A. MILLER AND HYUN S. SHIN

From the Department of Microbiology, The Johns Hopkins University School of Medicine, Baltimore, Maryland 21205

Received for publication March 2, 1970

The second component of guinea pig complement (C2) may be isolated in good yield and in highly purified form by a specific method involving adsorption on EAC4 (sheep erythrocytes carrying rabbit anti-Forssman and guinea pig C4) at ionic strength 0.0686, pH 8.5 and 25° to 30°C, in the presence of 0.002 M $MgCl_2$, 0.0003 M $CaCl_2$ and 0.1% gelatin, followed by elution at ionic strength 0.147, pH 6.5 and 0°C, in the presence of 0.05% gelatin. The product is stable and does not contain guinea pig serum proteins other than C2, but there is heavy contamination with sheep erythrocyte proteins, mostly hemoglobin, which may be removed by two successive electrophoretic fractionations on polyacrylamide gel. The number of C2 molecules required for lysis of one cell was 1.1.

Studies of the nature of the complement (C) system[3] and its mechanism of action are now at a stage of biochemical exploration for which highly purified C components are required. The customary techniques of purification by chromatographic and electrophoretic procedures usually involve substantial losses of material at each step of the isolation process and this poses a problem which is especially difficult with C2 because of its low concentration in serum. Therefore we explored an alternative approach, namely, purification by a specific method, with EAC4 as adsorbent.

As shown by Sitomer *et al.* (2), EAC4 adsorb C2 to form the complex EAC4,2, provided Mg^{++} is present. Cleavage of C2 does not occur in this reaction since $C\overline{1}$ is lacking. The adsorption of C2 on EAC4 is specific in the sense that E or EA do not adsorb C2. Adsorption is favored by high temperature, high pH and low ionic strength. Reversal of these environmental conditions leads to dissociation of the EAC4,2 complex, and the released C2 can be recovered in good yield from the fluid phase. On the basis of these observations, we have now developed a simple and practical method for specific isolation of guinea pig C2 in a high state of purity from the partially purified C2 preparation described by Borsos *et al.* (3). The product so obtained has substantially higher specific activity than the C2 isolated from human serum by chromatographic and electrophoretic fractionation (4). On a molecular basis, our product comes close to satisfying the one-hit theory, since only 1.1 molecules of C2 are needed for lysis of one cell.

MATERIALS AND METHODS

Buffer A. pH 7.3 to 7.4, ionic strength 0.147, Veronal-NaCl buffer was prepared daily from

[1] A preliminary report was presented at the Complement Workshop held in Boston, Mass., June 3–5, 1968 (1).

[2] This work was supported in part by United States Public Health Service Training Grant (5TO1-AI-00282-06), United States Public Health Service Research Grant (5-RO1-AI-02566-10), National Science Foundation Grant (GB-7406X) and a contract with the Office of Naval Research, ONR 248(60).

[3] The symbols E, EA and C represent, respectively, a sheep erythrocyte, one molecule of IgM or two molecules of IgG antibody, and complement molecules, the individual complement components being designated by number, i.e., C1, C2, etc. The letters a and b are used to designate fragments of the complement molecules. The symbol S represents a site on the cell membrane, and S* stands for a lesion in the cell membrane. E* designates an erythrocyte with at least one S*. The bar over certain complement components indicates enzymic activity.

fivefold concentrated stock, as described in (5). Gelatin, 0.1%, was added.

Buffer B. pH 7.3 to 7.4, ionic strength 0.150, Veronal-NaCl buffer was prepared like buffer A, except for addition of optimal concentrations of $CaCl_2$ and $MgCl_2$ (0.15 mM and 1 mM, respectively).

Buffer C. pH 7.3 to 7.4, isotonic Veronal-NaCl buffer containing 0.01 M EDTA (ethylenediaminetetraacetate) was prepared by 10-fold dilution of 0.10 M trisodium ethylenediaminetetraacetate (adjusted to pH 7.3 to 7.4) with buffer A.

Buffer D. pH 8.5, ionic strength 0.0544, buffer contained 0.199 M sucrose, 0.00494 M sodium barbital, 0.0426 M NaCl, 0.002 M $MgCl_2$, 0.0003 M $CaCl_2$ and 0.1% gelatin; HCl was used to adjust pH.

Buffer E. pH 8.5, ionic strength 0.0686, buffer contained 0.17 M sucrose, 0.00494 M sodium barbital, 0.0568 M NaCl, 0.002 M $MgCl_2$, 0.0003 M $CaCl_2$ and 0.1% gelatin; pH was adjusted with HCl.

Buffer F. pH 6.5, ionic strength 0.147, buffer was prepared like buffer A except that pH was adjusted to 6.5 with HCl, and the gelatin concentration was reduced to 0.05%.

Buffer G. pH 7.0 Tris-phosphate buffer containing 0.0587 M(tris[hydroxymethyl]aminomethane) and 0.032 M H_3PO_4.

Buffer H. pH 7.3 to 7.4, Veronal-NaCl buffer was prepared like buffer A, except that the gelatin concentration was reduced to 0.01%, and NaF was incorporated to a final concentration of 0.075 M.

Dialysis and ultrafiltration. The equipment supplied by Carl Schleicher and Schuell Co., Keene, N. H., was used.

Erythrocytes, antibody and complement. Pooled guinea pig serum as a source of the C components, partially purified guinea pig C2, rabbit antisera to boiled sheep erythrocyte stromata, standardized suspensions of sheep erythrocytes and $EAC\overline{1},4$ were obtained and used as described by Borsos *et al.* (3, 6). EAC4 were made by treatment of $EAC\overline{1},4$ with EDTA, according to a modification of Becker's technique described in (7), followed by four washings with buffer C and two washings with buffer B. Before use, the cells were given a final wash with buffer E. Analyses for $C\overline{1}$ were done according to Borsos and Rapp (8), C2 according to (6), except for minor modifications (2, 9, 10), C3 according to Shin and Mayer (11), C4 according to Hoffman *et al.* (12), and C5, C6, C7, C8 and C9 according to Nelson *et al.* (13).

Preparative electrophoresis in polyacrylamide gel. The vertical gel chamber from EC Corporation (Philadelphia, Pa.) was modified by removing the cylindrical gasket of black porous sponge rubber from each side and cementing into its place a Plexiglas spacer, 3 mm thick x 8 mm wide x 200 mm long. Pure gum rubber strips, 3 mm thick x 8 mm wide x 200 mm long, were then placed on top of each spacer to serve as a gasket, thereby making a gel chamber approximately 6 mm thick. The entire 120-mm width of the chamber was used for preparative electrophoresis. The separating gel and the buffer for the electrode chambers were prepared as described by Davis (14). The stacking gel was also prepared according to Davis (14), except for addition of 0.1 ml of TEMED (N, N, N′, N′-tetra-ethyl-ethylenediamine) and 40 g of sucrose/400 ml of solution.

Analytic electrophoresis in polyacrylamide gel. This was performed at 3° to 6°C, according to Davis (14), with samples of 5 to 10 μg of C2 protein. The protein solution was mixed with an equal volume of 10% sucrose and a volume not exceeding 50 μl was layered on the large-pore gel. The remaining space in the tube was filled with the Tris-buffer used in the electrode compartments. The upper electrode compartment was filled carefully so as not to disturb the sample layer. Analyses were set up in pairs, and one gel of each pair was used for staining with amido black, while the other was used for sectioning, followed by elution of the segments at 3°C in buffer H, for a period of at least 30 hr. Electrophoresis was terminated when the tracking dye, bromphenol blue, emerged from the anodal end of the small-pore gel.

Immunoelectrophoresis. Electrophoresis was carried out for 1 to 2 hr at 3 V/cm according to the method of Scheidegger (15), on a supporting medium of 1% agarose (Marine Colloid, Inc.). Precipitation lines were allowed to develop for 48 hr and stained with amido black before pictures were taken. The antiserum to purified C2 was raised in rabbits by four weekly intramuscular inoculations, each of 11 μg of purified C2 in complete Freund's adjuvant. Blood was drawn 7 to 10 days after the last injection. Rabbit antiserum to whole guinea pig plasma was kindly given us by Dr. Robert L. Marcus, Department of Medicine of this school.

Protein analysis. Analyses for protein nitrogen by the micro-Kjeldahl method could not be performed because a single set of duplicate analyses would have consumed the entire yield usually obtained in a batch of specificially purified C2 (approximately 300 μg protein at stage IV of the purification process, see below). Furthermore, the final product is contaminated with soluble acrylamide polymers which would interfere with nitrogen analysis. Therefore, protein concentration was determined by photometric absorption measurement at 280 nm. The specific absorbance ($A_{1cm}^{1\%}$) of highly purified C2 at 280 nm is 13.9, a value which was obtained as described in the next section.

Specific absorbance of C2 at 280 nm. For the purpose of these measurements, the protein concentration was determined by a photometric method recently described by Mayer and Miller (16), in which light absorption is measured in the 191 to 194 nm region where peptide bonds exhibit a strong absorption band. This method has two advantages over photometry at 280 nm, namely, greater sensitivity and less variation in the specific absorbance of different proteins. Since all commonly used anions, except fluoride, absorb strongly near 190 nm, aqueous solutions of sodium fluoride were used as solvent. A complication arises from the fact that stage IV C2 is contaminated with soluble acrylamide polymers. While the concentration of this contaminant is low, it interferes significantly in photometric measurements at 191 to 194 nm, but not at 280 nm. In order to remove the contaminating polyacrylamide, stage IV C2 was passed through a small DEAE-cellulose column equilibrated with 0.015 M NaF solution. After washing with the solvent to remove the acrylamide polymers, the C2 was eluted with 0.25 M NaF solution and the eluate was concentrated about 25-fold by ultrafiltration. While the recovery of C2 from the DEAE column is fairly good, most of the material comes off in inactive form and, therefore, it is not possible to use it for measurements of specific hemolytic activity. For this reason, we used the C2 recovered from the DEAE column for determining the specific absorbance at 280 nm (A_{280}). Lots 13 and 14 were processed in this fashion and yielded $A_{191-194}$ values of 0.260 and 0.312, respectively, at a dilution of 1/20. By use of the specific absorbance value ($A_{1cm}^{1\%}$) of 686 (16), the protein concentration of lots 13 and 14 was then calculated to be 76 and 91 μg/ml, respectively. Measurements of the undiluted preparations yielded A_{280} values of 0.094 and 0.140, respectively. Both of these readings were checked carefully on two different Beckman DU spectrophotometers, as well as a Beckman DBG for the sake of maximal precision. From these measurements, the $A_{1cm}^{1\%}$ values of lots 13 and 14 were calculated to be 12.4 and 15.4, respectively, yielding an average of $A_{1cm}^{1\%} = 13.9$ at 280 nm.

Since this value was established on C2 that was largely inactive in hemolytic tests, it was necessary to ascertain whether it had suffered chemical degradation, because if this were the case the specific absorbance at 280 nm might be affected. For this purpose, the electrophoretic mobility of the inactive C2 on 7.5% polyacrylamide gel was compared with that of native C2. Since this type of analysis is markedly dependent on molecular weight and/or shape, it would reveal any major degradation of the C2 molecule. Since we observed no difference between inactive and native C2, it is believed that the treatment with DEAE-cellulose does not produce major fragmentation and, therefore, it is reasonable to use the value 13.9 for the specific absorbance of native, hemolytically active C2 at 280 nm.

Procedure for isolation of C2

As starting material we have used the partially purified preparation of C2 described by Borsos, Rapp and Cook (3), which is designated "stage I C2" for the purposes of the present work. This material is converted to stage II C2 by adsorption and elution with EAC4 under appropriate experimental conditions. The product so obtained is essentially free of guinea pig serum proteins other than C2, but contaminating erythrocyte proteins are present. For most purposes these do not interfere. However, for experiments requiring highly purified C2 these contaminating proteins are removed by two successive electrophoretic separations on polyacrylamide gel, yielding stage III and stage IV C2, respectively.

Preparation of stage II C2 by adsorption and elution (refer to Table I for summary of experimental conditions). Each of six 250-ml centrifuge bottles is filled with 235 ml of EAC4 (1×10^9 cells/ml, high C4/cell), the cells are sedimented by centrifugation, the supernatant fluid is removed and the sedimented cells (ca. 12 ml) are warmed to 30°C. A 1/5 dilution of stage I C2 is prepared by mixing 250 ml of stage I C2 (approximately 1000 to 1500 arbitrary units/ml) with

TABLE I

Conditions for adsorption and elution of C2

	Temp.	Ionic Strength	pH	Mg^{++}	Ca^{++}	Gelatin
	°C			M	M	%
Adsorption and two washes	25–30	0.0686	8.5	0.002	0.0003	0.1
Elution	0	0.147	6.5	NA[a]	NA[a]	0.05

[a] NA, none added.

1000 ml of buffer D. After equilibration at 30°C, 208 ml of the 1/5 dilution of stage I C2 are added to each of the centrifuge bottles, the contents are mixed and the adsorption reaction is allowed to proceed at 30°C for 10 min. The resulting EAC4,2 are then sedimented by centrifugation at room temperature and washed twice with 1250 ml of buffer E at room temperature, or slightly above (ca. 25° to 30°C). After removal of the second wash fluid, the C2 is eluted from the cells with 450 ml of buffer F at 0°C. After 10 min in the cold, the EAC4 are removed by centrifugation at 0°C.

This adsorption and elution procedure is repeated with the same EAC4 cells and another batch of 250 ml of stage I C2. The two 450-ml eluates are combined, centrifuged again to remove any remaining cells, one-tenth volume of 0.75 M NaF is added to retard microbial growth and the material is concentrated at 5°C by ultrafiltration to approximately 10 ml, with simultaneous dialysis against buffer G during the terminal stages of concentration. Due to the high gelatin concentration, the contents of the collodion bags will solidify. Therefore, the collodion bags are immersed in buffer G at 37°C to liquify the solution for transfer to a suitable container and for storage at about −20° to −30°C. The bags are rinsed with buffer G to remove all of the C2, making a final volume of 15 ml.

Preparation of stage III by disc electrophoresis on a rectangular slab of polyacrylamide gel. Fifteen milliliters of stage II material, warmed to 37°C, are placed on the stacking gel in the modified vertical electrophoresis chamber and this is followed by a carefully applied overlay of Tris-buffer to fill the remaining space at the top of the chamber. Coolant at 5° to 8°C is circulated around the chamber. A current of 30 to 40 mA (200 to 250 V) is applied until the sample has become stacked at the top of the separating gel. At this time, the current is increased to 70 to 80 mA (400 to 450 V) and kept at this value until the separation is complete (6 to 7 hr). At the end of the run, the separating gel (12 cm wide x 10 cm high x 0.6 cm thick) is removed from the chamber and placed on a piece of glass. One-quarter centimeter is trimmed from each edge and the gel is cut into strips, 0.5 cm x 12 cm, beginning at the top and working toward the hemoglobin boundary. Each of these segments is then chopped into as many small pieces as possible, collected in a 40-ml tube and eluted as a separate fraction with 5 ml of buffer H. Each fraction is eluted four times at 3° to 5°C, for 2 days each. The four eluates of each fraction are combined, checked for C2 activity, and a pool is made of the active fractions. This material is designated stage III. It still contains some contaminating erythrocyte proteins. In preparation for processing to stage IV by disc electrophoresis on a cylindrical gel of polyacrylamide, it is concentrated to approximately 0.5 to 1.0 ml and dialyzed against buffer G.

Preparation of stage IV by disc electrophoresis on a cylindrical gel of polyacrylamide. The concentrated stage III material is placed on the stacking gel, 25 μl of buffer G containing 50% sucrose and 2 μl of 0.1% aqueous bromphenol blue are admixed and this is followed by an overlay of the Tris buffer used in the electrode chamber to fill the remaining space. Electrophoretic stacking is carried out with a field of 100 V and a current of 1 mA/tube. When the sample enters the small-pore gel, the field is increased to 400 V and a current of 3 mA/tube is maintained until the bromphenol blue tracking dye migrates to the bottom of the separating gel. In some cases, electrophoresis was continued for 1 hr after emergence of the dye. At the end of the run, each of the 4, 5 or 6 separating gels (40 mm length, 5 mm diameter) is cut into 1.25-mm segments and

TABLE II

Yield of C2 at each of the four purification stages

Stage	Lot No.	Volume	C2 Concentration (Arbitrary Units/Ml)[a]	Total C2 (Arbitrary Units)[a]	C2 Yield[b]
		ml			%
I (DEAE- and CM-cellulose chromatography)	13	500	1,520	760,000	100
	14	500	1,520	760,000	100
	15	500	1,520	760,000	100
	16	450	1,520	684,000	100
II (EAC4 adsorption and elution)	13	970	560	543,000	71
	14	930	587	546,000	72
	15	990	619	613,000	81
	16	1,010	587	593,000	87
III (1st Electrophoresis on polyacrylamide gel)[c]	13	126	2,206	278,000	37
	14	144	1,590	229,000	30
	15	179	1,782	319,000	42
	16	126	2,255	284,000	42
IV (2nd Electrophoresis on polyacrylamide gel)[c]	13	1.25	121,000	151,000	20
	14	1.05	118,000	124,000	16
	15	1.00	165,000	165,000	22
	16	1.10	136,000	150,000	22

[a] See reference (9) for explanation.

[b] Referred to stage I starting material. Corrected for loss resulting from removal of analytical samples.

[c] The approximate 100-fold concentration by ultrafiltration before the stage III and IV electrophoreses entails loss of about 5% to 10%. For calculation, this loss has been combined with that suffered in the stage III and IV electrophoreses.

eluted in 4 ml of buffer H for 24 hr at 3° to 5°C.[4] Corresponding segments from each of the four gels are eluted together and considered as one fraction. The gel segments are eluted a second time with 1.5 ml of buffer H for 18 hr and the first and second eluates of each fraction are pooled and checked for C2 activity. The active fractions are combined (volume approximately 50 ml) and concentrated to about 0.5 to 1 ml and stored at −20° to −30°C.

RESULTS

The essential data of four typical purification runs are summarized in Table II. The starting material (stage I) contained about 6.8×10^5 to 7.6×10^5 arbitrary units of C2, which represents approximately 1700 to 1900 μg C2 protein (specific activity = 391 arbitrary units/μg; see Table IV). The stage I C2 was converted to stage II by adsorption on EAC4 and elution. The recovery in this operation ranged from 71% to 87%. The stage II product is essentially free of the other eight complement components (see next section), but there is heavy contamination with sheep erythrocyte proteins, largely hemoglobin (Fig. 1). We have used stage II C2 in many experiments where the contaminating erythrocyte proteins would not cause difficulties.

The subsequent two purification steps to stages III and IV, involving electrophoretic fractionation, serve the purpose of removing the contaminating erythrocyte proteins. The final yield ranged from 16% to 22%, which represents about 300 μg C2 protein.

Physical, chemical and immunologic tests for purity

Since each batch of stage IV C2 contained only about 300 μg of protein, examination for purity

[4] If a preparation is to be analyzed photometrically, the gelatin in buffer H should be replaced by 2% L-lysine. Prior to the photometric analysis, the lysine is removed by dialysis. In all other cases, gelatin is used because its protective action is somewhat better than that of L-lysine.

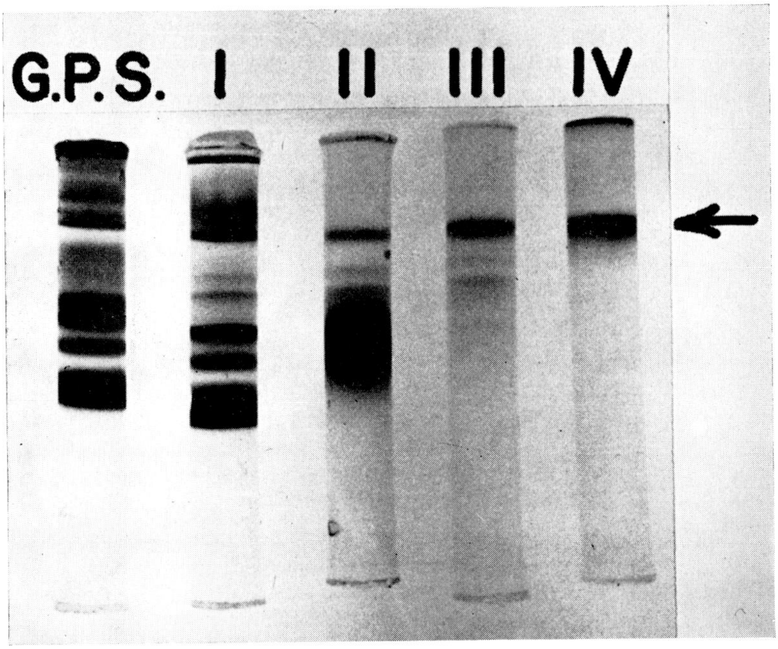

Figure 1. Purification of guinea pig C2 as judged by electrophoresis on 7.5% polyacrylamide gel. GPS refers to guinea pig serum, and the roman numbers designate the successive stages of the purification process. The *arrow* marks the C2 band. Gels stained with amido black.

TABLE III

Functional purity of C2 preparations

	Complement Components Titrated								
	C1	C2	C3	C4	C5	C6	C7	C8	C9
Guinea pig serum	60,000	10,000	15,000	10,000	50,000	10,000	40,000	250,000	270,000
Stage I (lot 9)	nil	966	0.6	0.3	0.2	14.3	169	7.6	20.7
Stage II (lot 9)	nil	28,000	2.0	0.9	2.6	26	3.8	1.5	3.2
Stage IV (lot 5)	<0.35	10,000	<0.45	<0.05	<0.15	<0.2	<0.04	<0.1	<0.2
Stage IV (lot 6)	<0.50	23,000	<0.40	<0.07	<0.20	<0.2	<0.10	<0.2	<0.7

was limited to hemolytic tests for the other eight C components, analyses by disc electrophoresis and immunoelectrophoresis, photometric assay for hemoglobin, absorption analysis on EAC4 and estimates of the degree of contamination with hemolytically inactive C2 derivatives.

Functional purity. Data indicating the degree of functional purity at stages I, II and IV are summarized in Table III. As is well known, stage I is heavily contaminated with the late-acting C components, notably C6, C7, C8 and C9. At stage II this contamination was much reduced, and at stage IV none of the other eight components were present in measurable quantity. For comparison, the titers of the nine components usually observed in guinea pig serum are also shown in Table III.

Electrophoresis on polyacrylamide gel. Disc electrophoretic analyses, assembled in Figure 1, show that stage I contains many different contaminating proteins, while in stage II the major contaminant is hemoglobin from the sheep erythrocytes. The quantity of C2 protein at stage II can be estimated by visual comparison of the staining intensity of the C2 band with that of reference standards of known protein concentration (see next paragraph).

Figure 2 shows the result of electrophoretic analysis on polyacrylamide gel of stage IV C2 in which one of two gels was stained, while the other was sectioned and eluted for C2 analysis. It is evident that the protein stain is in the same region of the gel as the C2 activity, which would support the view that the stained protein represents C2. Furthermore, we have made estimates of C2 protein on the gel by visual comparison with standards of human serum albumin subjected to the same staining procedure. With nine different lots of purified C2 this procedure yielded estimates of C2 concentration which were in satisfactory agreement (ca. twofold) with estimates derived from hemolytic activity by application of the factor 391 for the specific activity of C2 (see Table IV and text below). This lends further support to the view that the stained protein actually represents C2.

Immunoelectrophoresis. Immunoelectrophoretic analyses with rabbit antiserum 828_1 (raised by inoculation with stage IV C2) were set up with stage III (Fig. 3) and with stage IV C2 (Fig. 4). As a control test for ascertaining the purity of antiserum 828_1, whole guinea pig serum was also run as antigen against this antiserum. In Figure 3, this control test yielded no visible arc of precipitation, while in Figure 4 a very faint arc is seen in the C2 region. As a further test of purity, shown in Figure 5, stage IV C2 was set up against rabbit antiserum to guinea pig blood plasma. Again, only a single, very faint, arc appeared in the C2 region. These results indicate that stage III and stage IV C2 are essentially free of guinea pig proteins other than C2.

Photometric tests for hemoglobin. From the electrophoretic analyses on polyacrylamide gel, shown in Figure 1, it is evident that stage II is heavily contaminated with sheep hemoglobin while stage III contains only a small amount of this contaminant. No hemoglobin band can be seen in stained gels of stage IV C2. However, photometric scans of stage IV material showed a small absorption peak near 412 nm which indicates the presence of hemoglobin. From the absorbance at 412 nm the extent of hemoglobin contamination of stage IV was estimated at approximately 2%.

Adsorption analysis with EAC4. Since Sitomer *et al.* (2) have shown that the adsorption of C2 on EAC4 is highly specific, a further test for purity was performed by comparing adsorption of stage II C2 on EAC4 by measurement of hemolytic activity and by assay of protein. In one experiment, 22,000 units of C2 were allowed to react with EAC4 at 30°C, pH 8.5 and ionic strength 0.0686. After equilibration for 30 min, the fluid phase containing 1360 units of C2 was separated, concentrated by ultrafiltration and analyzed by disc electrophoresis. The adsorbed C2 was eluted at 0°C, pH 6.5 and ionic strength 0.147 and the eluate, containing 17,450 units of C2, was analyzed by disc electrophoresis. Pictures of the stained gels, shown in Figure 6, indicate that the stained protein band corresponding to C2 disappeared following adsorption on EAC4 and was recovered on elution. In another experiment of this type, conditions were adjusted for partial adsorption of C2 on EAC4. The supernatant fluid, the eluted C2, as well as the starting material were analyzed by disc electrophoresis, as shown in Figure 7. In each case, a visible band appeared on staining and the intensity of the stain was

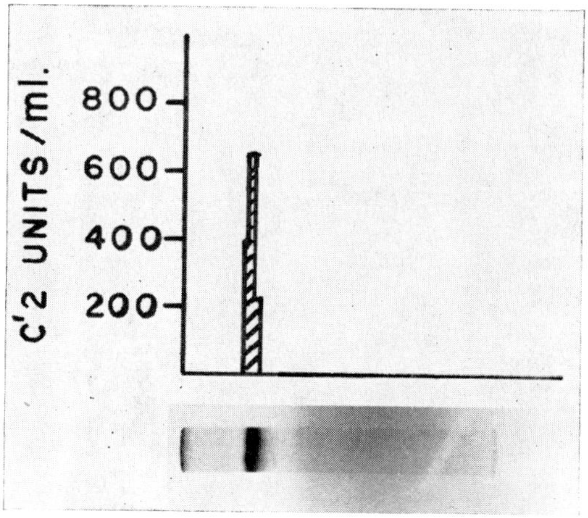

Figure 2. Electrophoresis of stage IV C2 (lot 6) on 7.5% polyacrylamide gel. Correlation of stained band with elutable hemolytic C2 activity. Results corrected for the swelling of the stained gel (ca. 15%).

TABLE IV

Specific activity and molecular efficiency of purified C2

	Lot No.			
	13_{IV}	14_{IV}	15_{IV}	16_{IV}
C2, arbitrary units/ml[a]	1.21×10^5	1.18×10^5	1.65×10^5	1.36×10^5
C2, actual units/ml (corrected)[b]	2.19×10^5	2.13×10^5	2.98×10^5	2.44×10^5
Absorbance at 280 nm	0.430	0.433	0.545	0.510
Protein, μg/ml	309	311	392	367
Specific activity, arbitrary units/μg	392	378	421	371
Molecules protein/ml	1.43×10^{15}	1.46×10^{15}	1.82×10^{15}	1.70×10^{15}
SFU from arbitrary titer[c]	0.87×10^{15}	0.84×10^{15}	1.18×10^{15}	0.97×10^{15}
SFU from actual titer[d]	0.82×10^{15}	0.80×10^{15}	1.11×10^{15}	0.91×10^{15}
Molecules protein/SFU (arbitrary titer)	1.64	1.74	1.54	1.75
Molecules protein/SFU (actual titer)	1.74	1.83	1.64	1.87
Percentage inactive C2	17	17	15	19
Molecules C2 protein/SFU (arbitrary titer)[e]	1.36	1.44	1.31	1.42
Molecules C2 protein/SFU (actual titer)[e]	1.44	1.52	1.39	1.52

[a] Arbitrary titer is obtained by comparative titration with a standard lot of C2 (see reference 9).
[b] Corrected for curvature of dose-response curve by linear extrapolation from its initial slope.
[c] Site-forming units = arbitrary titer $\times$ 7.14 $\times$ 10^9.
[d] Site-forming units = actual titer $\times$ 3.08 $\times$ 10^9 $\times$ t_{max} correction.
[e] Corrected for percentage of inactive C2.

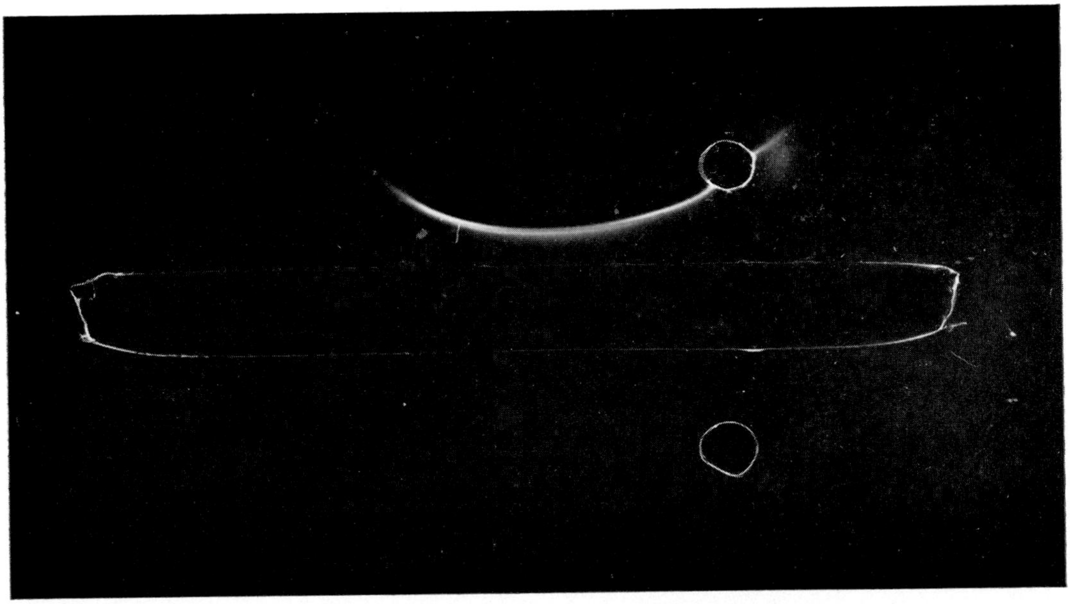

Figure 3. Immunoelectrophoresis with rabbit antiserum to stage IV C2. The upper well was charged with ca. 1800 arbitrary units (ca. 5 μg) of stage III C2, lot 9. The lower well contained 8 μl of guinea pig serum pool 512.

approximately proportional to the number of C2 units. These tests indicate a rough correlation between adsorption of hemolytic activity and adsorption of protein and this is interpreted as further evidence indicating that C2 eluted from EAC4,2 approaches a high degree of purity, except for the contamination with hemoglobin.

Further tests by adsorption on EAC4 were

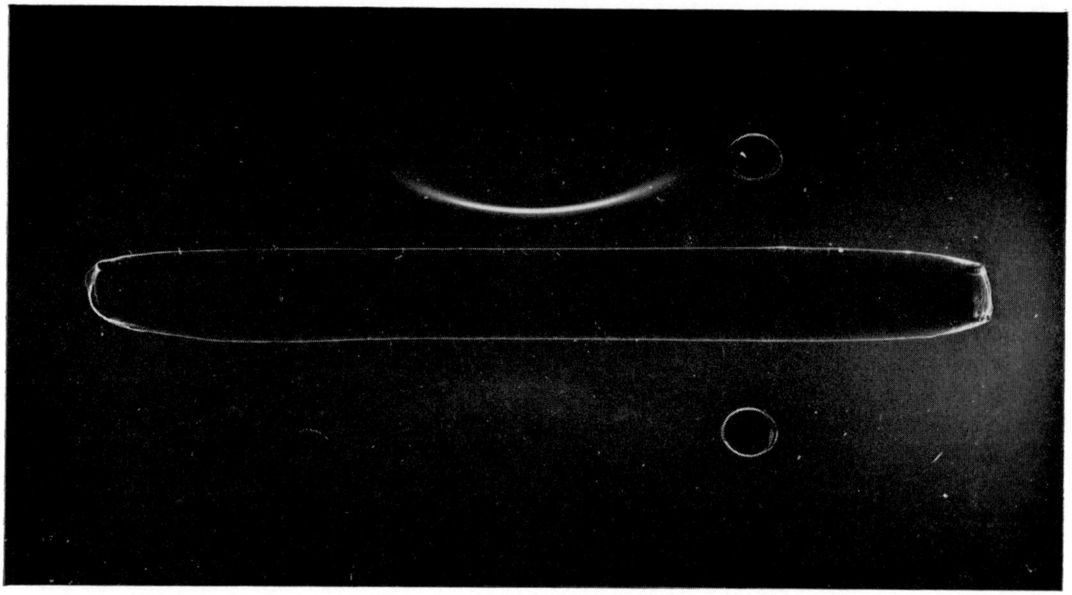

Figure 4. Immunoelectrophoresis with rabbit antiserum to stage IV C2. The upper well was charged with ca. 1300 arbitrary units (ca. 3.3 μg) of stage IV C2, lot 9. The lower well contained 8 μl of guinea pig serum pool 514.

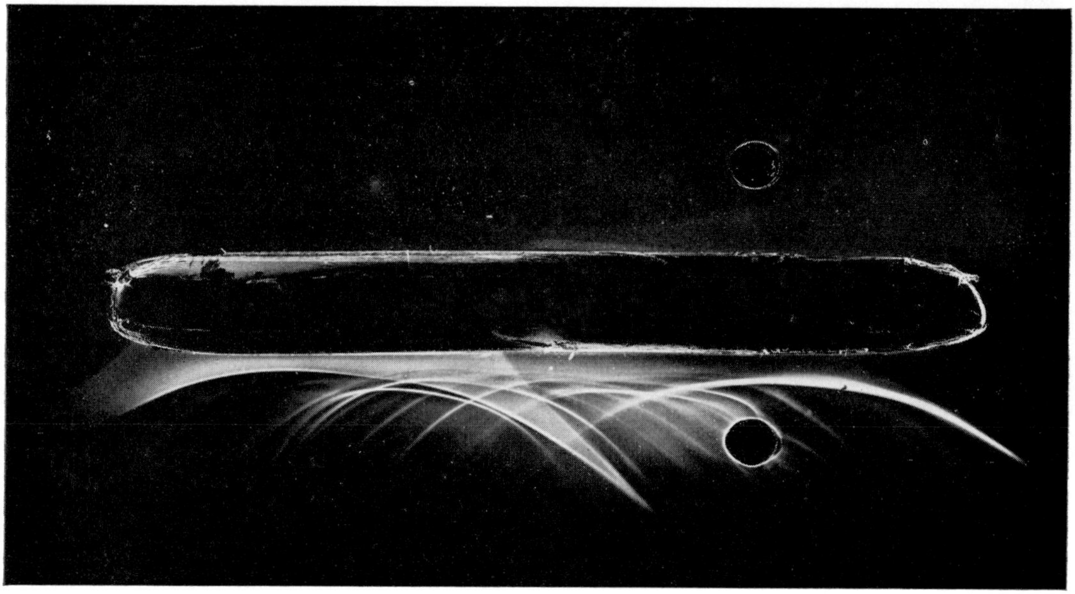

Figure 5. Immunoelectrophoretic analysis of stage IV C2, lot 9, with a rabbit antiserum *vs* guinea pig plasma. The upper well contained ca. 1300 arbitrary units (ca. 3.3 μg) of stage IV C2. The lower well was charged with 8 μl of guinea pig serum pool 514.

conducted so as to ascertain whether the purified preparations of C2 contain any material which is antigenically related to C2, but which does not adsorb on EAC4. These tests were performed in a quantitative manner in order to obtain estimates of contamination with inactive C2 derivatives, as described in the next section.

Analysis for contamination by hemolytically in-

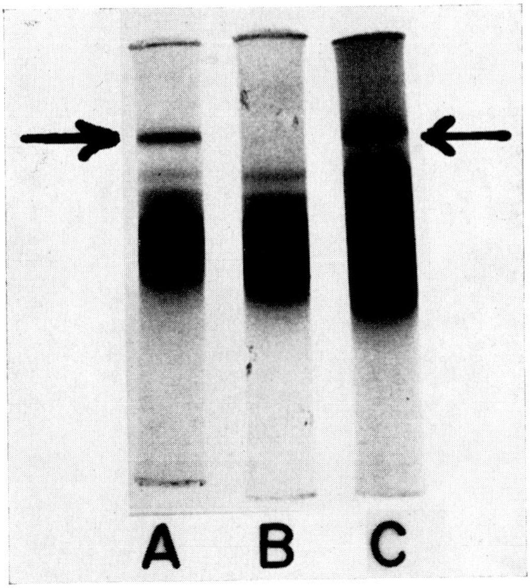

Figure 6. Adsorption of C2 on EAC4 as judged by electrophoresis on 7.5% polyacrylamide gel. Gel A shows the stained pattern of 2450 arbitrary units of stage II C2, lot 5. Gel B shows the stained pattern of the fluid phase following adsorption of most of the C2 on EAC4 (130 arbitrary units applied to the gel). Gel C shows the stained pattern of the eluate from the EAC4,2 (2100 arbitrary C2 units applied to gel). The *arrows* indicate position of C2 band.

active derivatives of C2. Two milliliters each of stage I, II, III and IV C2 14 (1100, 908, 827 and 1035 units/ml, respectively) were treated four times with 7 × 10⁹ packed EAC4 for about 5 min at 30°C in order to remove C2. After these four absorptions, the stage I, II, III and IV preparations contained 2.24, 1.67, 3.64 and 2.06 units of C2/ml, respectively. Each of these absorbed preparations was diluted 1/6 and adjusted to contain 10 units of C2/ml by addition of stage I C2. Analyses for inactive C2 derivative were then performed by the competition-inhibition method (9). The results were expressed relative to C2 concentration by assuming immunologic equivalence between C2 and inactive C2 derivative. It was found that stages I, II, III and IV contained approximately 8%, 6%, 23% and 18% inactive C2 derivative, respectively. It is evident from this that some inactive C2 is generated during disc electrophoresis on acrylamide gel. Therefore, part of the loss of C2 which occurs during disc electrophoresis is due to conversion of C2 to hemolytically inactive, but antigenically active material.

Specific activity and molecular efficiency of C2

As shown in Table IV, four lots of C2 were used for determination of specific activity. Hemolytic activity was measured in terms of arbitrary units, which are obtained by comparative titration with a standard lot of C2, as explained in (9). Protein concentration was calculated from absorbance measurements at 280 nm by use of the specific absorbance value ($A^{1\%}_{1cm}$) of 13.9 which was determined as explained in an earlier section. The specific activity values, expressed in arbitrary units/μg of protein, varied from 371 to 421, with the average of the four lots being 391.

For estimating the molecular efficiency of C2 in the hemolytic reaction, the number of protein molecules/ml of each of the four lots was calculated from the protein concentration by use of Avogadro's number, 6.06×10^{23}, and of a molecular weight value of 130,000 (17). The number of "effective C2 molecules" or "site-forming units" (SFU) was calculated from the arbitrary C2 titer

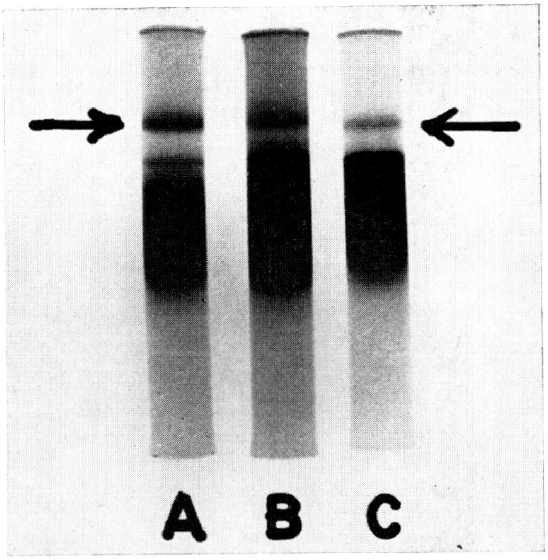

Figure 7. Adsorption of C2 on EAC4 as judged by electrophoresis on 7.5% polyacrylamide gel. Gel A shows the stained pattern of 3755 arbitrary units of stage II C2 lot 6. Gel B shows the stained pattern of the fluid phase after partial adsorption of the C2 on EAC4 (2286 arbitrary units applied to the gel). Gel C shows the stained pattern of the eluate from the EAC4,2 (1300 arbitrary units applied to gel). The *arrows* indicate C2 bands.

by multiplication with the factor 7.14×10^9. This conversion factor is derived from the old conversion factor of 5×10^8 (9) by taking into account the work of Miyakawa (18), who showed that rat C-EDTA is 17.2 to 21.6 times more efficient than guinea pig C-EDTA for conversion of $EAC\overline{4,2a}$ to E*. (We have fully confirmed this observation.) By taking an approximate gain factor of 20 from the data of Miyakawa, and from the old assumption that the conversion of $EAC\overline{4,2a}$ to E* by guinea pig C-EDTA is 70% complete (which forms part of the old factor of 5×10^8), one obtains the new factor of 7.14×10^9.

As shown in Table IV, the ratio of protein molecules to SFU, calculated in this way, ranged from 1.54 to 1.75. Since each of the four preparations of purified C2 contained some inactive C2, the data have been further corrected to take account of this contamination, yielding ratios of molecules of C2 protein to SFU ranging from 1.31 to 1.44, the average being 1.38. When further corrected for the known extent of C2 waste at ionic strength 0.15 (see below), the number of C2 molecules required for one membrane lesion becomes 1.08.

In view of the theoretical importance of these estimates of molecular efficiency, we have repeated the evaluation of the data by use of a different route of calculation, namely, instead of "arbitrary units" of C2 we used "actual units." Since the dose-response curve of C2 titration is slightly concave to the abscissa, the "actual units" shown in Table IV were corrected for this curvature by linear extrapolation from the initial slope of the dose-response curve. In order to obtain SFU, we multiplied the actual titer units by the factor 3.08×10^9, which incorporates the number of cells, 1.54×10^8, in the assay, as well as the conversion gain of 20 from Miyakawa's data (18). The result is then corrected further by application of the usual correction for decay of $SAC\overline{4,2a}$ prior to t_{max} (6). As shown in Table IV, the data on molecular efficiency obtained by this route of calculation are in good agreement with those based on arbitrary titer units. They are slightly higher because the conversion factor, 7.14×10^9, applicable to arbitrary titer units, incorporates a slightly better correction for the curvature of the dose-response curve than that which we used in the present treatment of actual titer units. For this reason, we consider that the molecular efficiency values based on the arbitrary titer are more accurate.

TABLE V
Stability of purified C2 at 37°C

Time at 37°C	Arbitrary Units/ml	
	Lot 5	Lot 6
hr		
0	974	549
3	956	542
20	945	519

Correction for ionic strength effect. In the present C2 titrations, the reaction between $EAC\overline{1},4$ and C2 was performed at ionic strength 0.15. Under these conditions, 22% fewer SFU are obtained than at ionic strength 0.06, presumably due to cleavage of C2 without fixation of the C2a fragment. By correcting our data for this waste of C2, one obtains an average value of 1.08 for the ratio of molecules of C2 protein to SFU. This should be rounded off to 1.1 C2 molecules per SFU.

Significance and probable error limits. The principal sources of error are the values for the molecular weight and for specific photometric absorbance at 280 nm. Collectively, these could cause a large error in the final result, perhaps ±30%. Hence, the true ratio of C2/ SFU could be as high as 1.4. In addition, as explained in the *Discussion*, it would go as high as 2 or 3 if the data were based on "actual units" obtained with $EAC\overline{1},4$ of low lytic susceptibility. It should also be emphasized that the efficiency of conversion with rat C-EDTA might be less than 100%. If this were so, the true value for the ratio of C2 molecules to SFU would be lower than 1.1 ± 30%. Since the one-hit theory (19) imposes a lower limit of 1.0, the efficiency of conversion of $EAC\overline{4,2a}$ by rat C-EDTA is probably not less than 70%.

Stability of purified C2. C2 lots 5 and 6 were checked for stability at 37°C over a period of 20 hr. As shown in Table V, the loss of activity was very small. After storage for 3 months at −32°C, the hemolytic activity of lot 5 decreased from 992 to 895. This 10% loss in activity might be prevented by storing the purified C2 in a more concentrated state, ca. 50,000 units/ml.

DISCUSSION

The preparation of partially purified C2 (now designated stage I C2) by Borsos *et al.* (3) more than 8 years ago made available a reagent of great utility for investigations of the reaction mechanism of the complement system. With its aid much information has been gained about the reactions among C1, C4 and C2, especially the cleavage of the C2 molecule and the union of the C2a fragment with cell-bound C4 to form $\overline{C4,2a}$, an enzyme which cleaves the C3 molecule. However, chemical studies of these reaction steps have been handicapped by the crude nature of stage I C2, and this was the motivation for a concerted effort at isolation of C2 in a high state of purity. Initially, we explored purification by chromatographic and electrophoretic techniques, but serious technical difficulties were encountered and this led us to consider the present method of specific purification. In exploratory experiments a clean product was obtained, as judged by immunoelectrophoresis, and this success encouraged us to study the method of specific purification systematically.

One of the greatest difficulties in the purification of most C components derives from their low concentration in blood serum. This is especially serious in the case of C2 since guinea pig serum contains only about 20 μg of C2/ml. Each batch of purified C2 is derived from 160 ml of guinea pig serum, i.e., the purification process starts with about 3000 μg of C2. The final yield is roughly 10%, or approximately 300 μg. Thus, 90% of the C2 is lost in only four purification steps. This is a fairly typical experience in the purification of C components from guinea pig serum, and it indicates that the success or failure of a purification program depends on reaching a satisfactory state of purity in five, or at most, six successive purification steps. Otherwise, the loss of material becomes prohibitive. The success of the present procedure is directly attributable to the remarkable efficiency of the second purification step, *viz.*, adsorption and elution with EAC4, in which practically all guinea pig serum proteins, other than C2, are eliminated, at a cost of only about 15% to 30% C2 loss. For many immunologic purposes the stage II product is entirely satisfactory since its degree of functional purity is very high. On the other hand, in chemical experiments the contaminating sheep erythrocyte proteins may interfere, in which case the purification process must be carried to stage IV.

Purity of isolated C2. The purity of the stage IV product has been evaluated by chemical, immunologic and functional tests. Due to the severe limitation of material, chemical tests were limited to photometry at 412 nm, which indicated 2% contamination with hemoglobin, and to electrophoretic analyses on polyacrylamide gel. As shown in Figure 1, the stage IV material yielded only a single stainable band after electrophoresis on polyacrylamide gel. Furthermore, as shown in Figure 2, hemolytic C2 activity migrated at precisely the same rate as the stainable protein. In addition, the staining intensity was in satisfactory agreement with the number of hemolytic units used in the electrophoretic analysis. Hence, it is reasonable to conclude that the protein revealed by the stain is, indeed, C2 and that the preparation is free of proteins differing from C2 with respect to migration rate on polyacrylamide gel. (The 2% contamination with hemoglobin is too low for detection by staining.)

Immunologic tests for purity also yielded satisfactory results. As shown in Figure 3, stage III C2 gave a single symmetrical arc of precipitation in its reaction with rabbit antibody against stage IV C2. Furthermore, as shown also in Figure 3, no precipitation arcs were seen in tests of this antiserum against guinea pig serum as antigen. A similar set of immunoelectrophoretic tests is shown in Figure 4, except that in this case stage IV C2 was used in the upper well and the guinea pig serum run in the lower well differed from the one used in Figure 3. In this case, the guinea pig serum yielded a very faint precipitation arc in the same position as the precipitation arc produced by the C2 in the upper well. It should also be noted that in this test the C2 arc in the upper half showed a very faint converging arc near its anodic end. An additional electrophoretic test, shown in Figure 5, was performed with a rabbit antiserum to guinea pig plasma. This yielded a very faint arc in the reaction with stage IV C2. Altogether, these immunoelectrophoretic tests indicate that stage III and stage IV preparations are essentially free of guinea pig serum proteins other than C2.

Functional tests for purity, shown in Table III, were also satisfactory. In no case could we detect more than 1 part of any of the other eight complement components in 20,000 parts of C2. This is a matter of considerable practical importance because it is often necessary to use an excess of C2 in hemolytic studies of the late-acting C components. For example, if 200 units of stage IV C2 were used in such tests, maximal contamination with any of the other complement components would be less than 0.01 unit. Hence, the possibility of formation of contaminating intermediate sites on the erythrocytes would be held well below significant levels.

A different kind of functional purity test, which is highly specific for C2, was performed by measuring the degree of correlation between adsorption of hemolytic C2 activity and adsorption of protein on EAC4. The results of these tests, shown in Figures 6 and 7, indicate that most or all of the protein in stage IV material is adsorbed by EAC4 and, hence, behaves like C2. Of course, this result does not come as a surprise because adsorption on EAC4 was used in the purification procedure. Indeed, if it were assumed, for the sake of argument, that stage I C2 contains two kinds of C2 molecules, namely, some that adsorb to EAC4 and others that do not, the procedure of purification would select those molecules that possess the capacity to be adsorbed on EAC4. However, there is no experimental basis for assuming that such selection actually takes place. Indeed, comparative tests with stage I and stage II indicate that there is no difference with respect to the proportion of hemolytic C2 activity adsorbed by EAC4.

With respect to various conceivable types of contamination of purified C2, consideration had to be given to the possible presence of inactive derivatives of C2, i.e., altered forms which lack hemolytic activity but can be detected by reactivity with anti-C2. For checking such contamination, we subjected purified C2 to three or four successive absorptions with EAC4, which removed practically all of the hemolytic activity. The supernatant fluid from these absorptions was then analyzed for inactive C2 by the competitive inhibition test (9). Analyses of this type on stage I and stage II C2 showed only 8% and 6% contamination with inactive C2 analog, respectively, but stage III and IV contained 23% and 18% of C2 analog, respectively. The low extent of contamination of stage II C2 confirms the finding, presented in Figure 6, that absorption with EAC4 removes the C2 band on polyacrylamide gel, as detected by staining. The observation that stage III and IV material contains a substantial amount of inactive C2 derivative suggests that some of the loss of hemolytic C2 during electrophoresis on polyacrylamide gel involves conversion from native C2 to a form which is hemolytically inactive, though reactive with anti-C2.

Molecular efficiency of C2. The most interesting phase of the present study concerns the data presented in Table IV, dealing with specific activity and molecular efficiency of purified C2. In discussing these results it is necessary to stress that hemolytic measurements of C2 are subject to considerable variation depending on the source of the EAC$\bar{1}$,4. Most batches of EAC$\bar{1}$,4 do not deviate more than ±25% from the norm, but a few (ca. 10%) are likely to be two- to threefold lower. We will discuss the interpretation of these variations in a later section and for the purposes of the present part of the discussion the problem of cell variability will be dealt with by use of the "arbitrary titer." As the term implies, the arbitrary titer has no absolute significance. It is arrived at by comparative titration of an unknown batch of C2 with a lot of known arbitrary titer. The known arbitrary titer of this lot, in turn, has been measured by comparison with another known lot of C2, and so on, the first batch of C2 in this process of comparative titration having been assigned a titer of 1000 arbitrarily (9).

The specific activity values, expressed in arbitrary units of C2/μg of protein, shown in Table IV, range from 371 to 421, with an average value of 391. These values are not corrected for inactive C2. If one accepts an average contamination with 17% inactive C2, the corrected average specific activity value would be 471 arbitrary units/μg of C2 protein. Several other preparations of C2, analyzed for protein by the method of staining the C2 band after electrophoresis on polyacrylamide gel, have yielded specific activity values in the same range, within a factor of twofold, which is the extent of variation to be expected in estimates of protein concentration by staining.

In evaluating the molecular efficiency of C2 we have used two methods of calculation, one of which involves use of the arbitrary titer, while the other is based on the actual titer. The number of site-forming units has been calculated from the arbitary titer by multiplication with the factor 7.14×10^9, which was derived as explained in an earlier section. It should be noted that the different batches of EAC$\bar{1}$,4 used in evaluating this factor exhibited lytic susceptibilities in the "normal" range.

The other method of calculation based on the

actual titer involves application of the curvature correction, the correction for decay prior to t_{max} and the correction for conversion efficiency of $EAC\overline{4,2a}$ to E*, based on the data in (18). It is evident from Table IV that both methods of calculation yielded results that are in good agreement. This is a direct consequence of the fact that the $EAC\overline{1},4$ which we used for titration in the present work also exhibited lytic susceptibility in the "normal" range. Obviously, if we had used a lot of $EAC\overline{1},4$ of markedly sub-normal susceptibility, we would have obtained very different results. Thus, the molecular efficiency values are directly dependent on the choice of the lot of $EAC\overline{1},4$, unless arbitrary titers are used.

For interpretation of the meaning of the molecular efficiency value we shall use the average, 1.38, of the values derived from the arbitrary titers, which becomes 1.1 when corrected for the ionic strength effect and rounded off. As explained in the *Results*, this value is subject to considerable uncertainty, perhaps as much as ±30%. The one-hit theory, which is based on a statistical interpretation of titration data (19), predicts that one membrane lesion is sufficient for lysis of an erythrocyte. A single molecule of C2 should suffice to generate one lesion *provided* that the over-all efficiency be 100%, i.e., that there be no waste due to side reactions or other interfering processes. Since the present chemical analysis yields a ratio of 1.1 ± 0.3 molecule of C2/SFU, it is evident that waste of C2 would not be expected to exceed 0.4 molecule per SFU.

Causes of C2 waste. Among the various possibilities of C2 waste, the first to be considered is that of C2 cleavage by $C\overline{1}$ without fixation of the C2a fragment. As pointed out in the *Results*, C2 titrations conducted at ionic strength 0.15 yield 22% less sites than those done at ionic strength 0.06. Since our C2 titrations were performed at ionic strength 0.15, the molecular efficiency data have been corrected for the waste of 22% of C2 under these conditions. We do not know whether unfruitful cleavage causes any C2 waste at ionic strength 0.06.

The second kind of loss to be considered is incomplete conversion of $EAC\overline{4,2a}$ to E*. We do not know how to estimate to what extent the data of Miyakawa with rat C-EDTA deviate from 100% conversion. If we assume that at ionic strength 0.06 no C2 is wasted by cleavage without fixation, conversion of $EAC\overline{4,2a}$ by rat C-EDTA could be as low as 70%. Conversely, if we assume that the conversion efficiency is 100%, cleavage of C2 without fixation at ionic strength 0.06 could be as high as 0.4 molecule/SFU. Most likely, both pathways are responsible for some waste of C2, but the total waste by both routes should not be greater than 0.4 molecule/SFU.

Variation of cell susceptibility. Experimental fluctuations due to variation of the lytic susceptibility of different batches of erythrocytes have been eliminated in the present experiments by use of the "arbitrary unit" system. Nonetheless, this vexing problem needs to be discussed and this can best be done by describing what would have happened if "actual units" had been used instead of "arbitrary units." Indeed, this is precisely what we did in the alternative method of calculation shown in Table IV. The final values so obtained were approximately the same as those derived from arbitrary units only because cells of normal lytic susceptibility had been used. If we had employed cells of low lytic susceptibility, the final result derived from actual units would have been that 2 or 3, and not 1.1, molecules of C2 are required to produce one membrane lesion.

We have no information which would explain why sheep erythrocytes vary in lytic susceptibility, but we regard the variation as a reflection of variable waste of complement components. Possibly this might be due to presence of interfering or destructive factors on some batches of cells. Alternatively, stabilizing substances on or in the cell membrane, or changes in membrane structure, might affect the lytic response.

REFERENCES

1. Mayer, M. M., Miller, J. A. and Shin, H. S., J. Immun., *101:* 813, 1968.
2. Sitomer, G., Stroud, R. M. and Mayer, M. M., Immunochemistry, *3:* 57, 1966.
3. Borsos, T., Rapp, H. J. and Cook, C. T., J. Immun., *87:* 330, 1961.
4. Polley, M. J. and Müller-Eberhard, H. J., J. Exp. Med., *128:* 533, 1968.
5. Mayer, M. M., in *Kabat and Mayer's Experimental Immunochemistry*, 2nd Ed., Chapter 4, Charles C Thomas, Springfield, Ill, 1961.
6. Borsos, T., Rapp, H. J. and Mayer, M. M., J. Immun., *87:* 310, 1961.
7. Borsos, T. and Cooper, M., Proc. Soc. Exp. Biol. Med., *107:* 227, 1961.

8. Borsos, T. and Rapp, H. J., J. Immun., *91:* 851, 1963.
9. Mayer, M. M. and Miller, J. A., Immunochemistry, *2:* 71, 1965.
10. Stroud, R. M., Austen, K. F. and Mayer, M. M., Immunochemistry, *2:* 219, 1965.
11. Shin, H. S. and Mayer, M. M., Biochemistry, *7:* 2991, 2997, 3003, 1968.
12. Hoffmann, L. G., McKenzie, A. T. and Mayer, M. M., Immunochemistry, *2:* 13, 1965.
13. Nelson, R. A., Jr., Jensen, J., Gigli, I. and Tamura, N., Immunochemistry, *3:* 111, 1966.
14. Davis, B. J., Ann. N. Y. Acad. Sci., *121:* 404, 1964.
15. Scheidegger, J. J., Intern. Arch. Allerg., *7:* 103, 1955.
16. Mayer, M. M. and Miller, J. A., Anal. Biochem., In press.
17. Stroud, R. M., Mayer, M. M., Miller, J. A. and McKenzie, A. T., Immunochemistry, *3:* 163, 1966.
18. Miyakawa, Y., Sekine, T., Shimada, K. and Nishioka, K., J. Immun., *103:* 374, 1969.
19. Mayer, M. M., in *Immunochemical Approaches to Problems in Microbiology*, Edited by M. Heidelberger and O. J. Plescia, p. 268, Rutgers University Press, New Brunswick, N. J., 1960.

THE JOURNAL OF IMMUNOLOGY
Copyright © 1970 by The Williams & Wilkins Co.

Vol. 105, No. 2, Aug. 1970
Printed in U.S.A.

STREPTOCOCCAL GROUP A POLYSACCHARIDE HAPTENS: SUSCEPTIBILITY TO DEGRADATION BY β-N-ACETYLGLUCOSAMINIDASES AND ANTIBODY-COMBINING CAPACITY OF HAPTENS[1]

ELIA M. AYOUB[2] AND WILLARD C. SCHMIDT

From the Departments of Pediatrics, University of Minnesota School of Medicine, Minneapolis, Minnesota and the Cleveland Metropolitan General Hospital, Cleveland, Ohio

Received for publication February 28, 1970

Oligosaccharides of different sizes were prepared by acid hydrolysis of group A streptococcal carbohydrate. Separation of the oligosaccharides was performed by dialysis and chromatography on G-25 Sephadex. The activity of β-N-acetylglucosaminidase enzymes derived from the soil bacillus and from macrophage cells was assessed on the various haptens. The soil bacillus enzyme was equally active on the various sized haptens. However, the activity of the macrophage enzyme was strictly related to the size of the oligosaccharide, with hydrolytic activity increasing with decreasing size of the substrate. The capacity of the oligosaccharide fragments to inhibit the reaction between the group A polysaccharide and its antibody was studied using a radioimmune precipitation technique. The capacity of the haptens to inhibit antibody was directly related to the molecular weight of the oligosaccharides. Both the soil bacillus and macrophage β-N-acetylglucosaminidases were effective in eliminating most of the antibody inhibitory activity of the haptens, although this was achieved at lower concentrations of the soil bacillus enzyme. The amount of macrophage enzyme required to achieve a similar decrease in the antibody inhibitory activity of the haptens increased proportionately to the size of the haptens.

The occurrence of a β-N-acetylglucosaminidase in phagocytic cells was reported in a previous study (1). The activity of this enzyme on the streptococcal group A polysaccharide was compared with the activity of the soil bacillus enzyme. While both enzymes were equally active when tested with a low molecular weight substrate, *p*-nitrophenyl-β-N-acetylglucosaminide, the phagocytic enzyme exhibited a much lower affinity for the polysaccharide substrate. The possibility that steric hinderance might be a factor in the lower affinity of the phagocytic enzyme to the more complex polysaccharide substrate was suggested by chromatographic studies which showed that the phagocytic enzyme had a considerably larger molecular size than the soil bacillus enzyme.

In the present report, data are presented on the relationship of the activity of the β-N-acetylglucosaminidases to the molecular size of the substrate. Group A polysaccharide was hydrolyzed chemically, haptenic fragments of varying sizes were separated by column chromatography and the hydrolytic activity of the macrophage and soil bacillus enzymes on these fragments was compared. The activity of the fragments produced by enzymatic hydrolysis as inhibitors of the reaction between the group A polysaccharide and its antibody is also reported.

MATERIALS AND METHODS

Hydrolysis of group A carbohydrate. Cell walls of group A streptococcal cells (strain C203S) were prepared by the method of Bleiweis *et al.* (2). The cell wall carbohydrate was solubilized by hot formamide extraction (3). Acid hydrolysis of carbohydrate was performed by a modification

[1] This study was supported by Research Grant AI 08539-02 from the National Institutes of Health, United States Public Health Service; American Heart Association Grant 68-621; Developmental Physiology Training Grant NIH T1-HD0054; and National Institutes of Health Undergraduate Training Grant NIH 2T1-HE5108.

[2] Present address: Department of Pediatrics, University of Florida College of Medicine, Gainesville, Florida 32601.

of the method described by McCarty (4); 100 mg of lyophilized carbohydrate were dissolved in 10 ml of 0.1 N H_2SO_4 and hydrolysis was carried out in a sealed ampule at 100°C for 5 hr. After cooling, the solution was titrated back to neutrality using 1 N to 0.1 NaOH with constant monitoring on a pH meter. Because chemical analysis of the hydrolysate indicated the presence of unacetylated glucosamine, reacetylation of the hydrolysate was carried out with acetic anhydride (5). The reacetylated preparation was dialyzed against 1 liter of distilled water and the dialysate, which contained the haptens (dialyzable low molecular weight fragments), was concentrated by evaporation under vacuum to a final volume of 1 ml. The concentrate was centrifuged to remove non-soluble residues and the clear supernatant used for column chromatography.

Column chromatography of the carbohydrate hydrolysates was performed on G-25 and G-15 Sephadex using a 1- x 100-cm column. The columns were equilibrated and elution was carried out with 0.005 M citrate buffer, pH 5.2. Specimens of the eluates were tested for rhamnose and free N-acetylglucosamine.

Analytical methods. Rhamnose was determined by the method of Dische and Shettles (6), hexosamine by the method of Rondle and Morgan (7) and free N-acetylglucosamine by the method of Reissig *et al.* (8).

Preparation of β-N-acetylglucosaminidases. Phagocytic β-N-acetylglucosaminidase from rabbit lung macrophages was prepared and partially purified as previously described (1). β-N-acetylglucosaminidase from soil bacillus was prepared as described by McCarty (4). The unit of enzyme used is as defined previously (1).

Immunologic studies. Hyperimmune rabbit antisera to group A or A-variant polysaccharides were prepared as described previously (9). Adsorption of the sera with group A and A-variant streptococcal cell walls was performed when required to eliminate most of the cross-reactivity encountered; 1 ml of antiserum was adsorbed with 1 mg (dry weight) of cell walls.

Radioimmune precipitin technique. Initial studies using the immune precipitin technique demonstrated that reliable results were obtained at the expense of large amounts of the fragments. The radioimmune precipitin technique (10) offered a better approach for this study because of the small amount of antigen used in the test.

The method used consists of incubating varying amounts of the "inhibitor" with 0.5 to 1 μg of ^{14}C-labeled formamide-extracted group A or A-variant polysaccharide (10) and an appropriate dilution of a group A or A-variant rabbit antiserum previously titrated to precipitate 80% to 90% of the amount of radioactive antigen being used in the test. Diluents were either phosphate-buffered saline, 0.01 M phosphate, or 0.1 M phosphate buffer, pH 7.4. The final volume of the incubation mixture was 1.0 ml. Following incubation for 2 hr at 37°C and overnight at 4°C, 0.1 ml of normal rabbit serum was added as carrier protein. An equal volume of saturated ammonium sulfate was then added to the reaction mixture and mixed. After 1 hr at 4°C, the tubes were centrifuged at 5000 × G for 15 min at 4°C. The supernatant was suctioned off and discarded and the pellet washed with 2 ml of half saturated ammonium sulfate. The pellet was dissolved in 1 ml of alkaline solubilizer (NCS solubilizer: 0.6 N in toluene, Amersham/Searle Corp., Des Plaines, Ill.). The clear solution was taken up in 5 ml of scintillation fluid (2,5-diphenyloxazole (PPO) 0.4% in toluene) and transferred to a counting vial. The tube was rinsed with another 5 ml of scintillation fluid and added to the fluid in the vial. Counting was performed in a Beckman liquid scintillation counter at room temperature; all samples were counted for 50 min or to a 3% error, with a background of 18 cmp.

RESULTS

The elution pattern of the carbohydrate hydrolysis products from G-25 Sephadex was followed by rhamnose determinations. A gradual rise in the amount of rhamnose eluted occurred directly after the void volume, then leveled off to a plateau and declined shortly before the end of the elution volume. Finally, separate sharp peaks of rhamnose and free N-acetylglucosamine were obtained at the end of the carbohydrate elution, representing the free monosaccharides obtained during hydrolysis. Separation of the monosaccharides from the small sized oligosaccharide was achieved by further chromatography of the concentrated eluates on G-15 Sephadex.

Finer separation of the fragments was attempted by rechromatography of monosaccharide-free eluates on G-25 Sephadex with elution of 0.5-ml sample volumes. This resulted in the appearance of three small peaks at intervals of

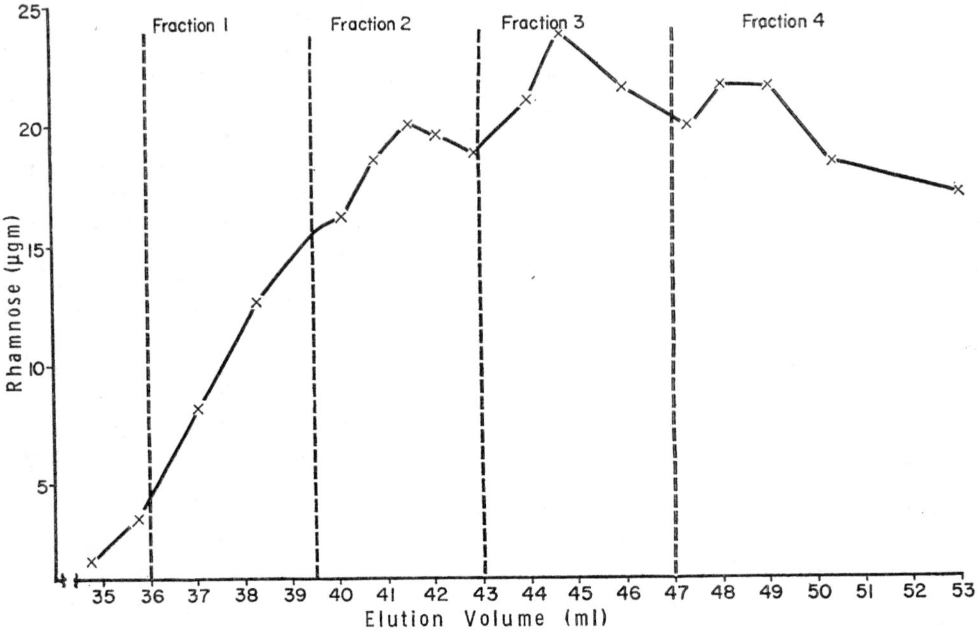

Figure 1. Elution pattern of the group A streptococcal carbohydrate oligosaccharides on G-25 Sephadex. The broken lines delineate the division of the eluate into the fractions used in the study.

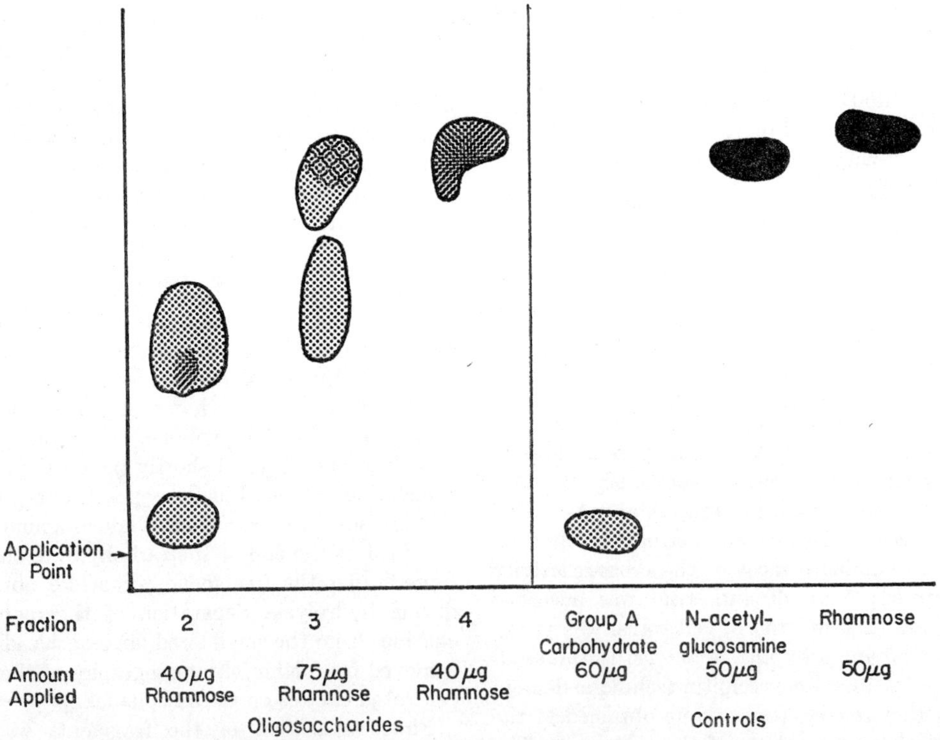

Figure. 2. Diagram of the silica-gel thin layer chromatography of group A streptococcal carbohydrate oligosaccharide fractions and of formamide-extracted carbohydrate, N-acetylglucosamine and rhamnose monosaccharides. Solvent system: butanol/pyridine/water (68/54/29—v/v/v); spray: Dichromate-sulfuric acid. (The separation was performed in the laboratory of Dr. Jim Berry.)

TABLE I

Chemical analysis of G-25 Sephadex eluate fractions of the streptococcal group A carbohydrate hydrolysates

Fraction	Rhamnose		Glucosamine[a]		Molar Ratio (Rhamnose: Glucosamine)
	μg/ml	*μmoles*	*μg/ml*	*μmoles*	
1	590	3.6	150	0.84	4.3:1
2	1270	7.8	250	1.40	5.6:1
3	1090	6.7	170	0.95	7.0:1
4	700	4.3	130	0.73	5.9:1

[a] Determined as glucosamine base after hydrolysis in 2 N HCl for 4 hr. Free glucosamine found in fraction 4 at 35 μg/ml not included.

4 to 5 ml (Fig. 1). The eluates were pooled into four fractions, as designated in Figure 1, consisting of three consecutive 4.5-ml volumes and a fourth comprising the following 9 ml of eluate after the void volume. While definitive separation of homogeneous peaks for the varying sized haptenic fragments could not be achieved, it was considered that the first fraction would contain the larger oligosaccharides and that the small oligosaccharides would be concentrated in the last fraction. This distribution was confirmed by thin layer chromatography of the fractions as shown in Figure 2.

The chemical analysis of the four fractions is shown in Table I. The data indicate a higher proportionality of rhamnose to N-acetylglucosamine than that of the group A polysaccharide, suggesting that there is some degree of selective destruction of the N-acetylglucosamine linkage under these conditions of hydrolysis with H_2SO_4. This is supported by the amounts of free N-acetylglucosamine eluted by chromatography. The changing ratio of rhamnose to glucosamine found in the four fractions indicates that hydrolysis leaves residues of either pure rhamnose oligosaccharides or oligosaccharides with preponderance of rhamnose similar to the A-variant carbohydrate.

Activity of the β-N-acetylglucosaminidases on the fragments. The activity of β-N-acetylglucosaminidase derived from the soil bacillus or macrophages on the haptenic fragments was studied. The results in Table II show that 50 units of the soil bacillus enzyme effected relatively complete hydrolysis of oligosaccharides with release of 75% to 100% of the N-acetylglucosamine in the four fractions within 20 hr of incubation. After hydrolysis with 1000 units of enzyme from rabbit lung macrophages, 14% to 55% of the glucosamine appeared as free hexosamine. These values represent only a fraction of the N-acetylglucosamine that was released by 50 units of the soil bacillus enzyme.

The data show also that the activity of the rabbit lung macrophage enzyme, determined by the percentage release of the total N-acetylglucosamine from the substrate, increases with decreasing size of the substrate. This is evidenced by the finding that an equal amount of enzyme released only 12% of the available N-acetylglucosamine in fraction 1 and 72% of the N-acetylglucosamine in fraction 4. The critical relationship of substrate size to macrophage β-N-acetylglucosaminidase activity was shown by rechromatography of fraction 4 on G-15 Sephadex, then subjecting to enzymatic hydrolysis the haptens eluted early after the void volume and those eluted at the end of the elution volume. It was found that 80% of the N-acetylglucosamine in the early eluates was released by hydrolysis with the macrophage enzyme, while 100% of the N-acetylglucosamine in the terminal eluates was released by the same amount of the enzyme over the same incubation period.

Effect of enzyme concentration on hydrolytic activity. The amount of macrophage enzyme required to completely hydrolyze fraction 1 was determined. Equal portions of fraction 1 were incubated with 1500, 3000 and 6000 units of the enzyme. The percentages of the total glucosamine released following 20 hr of incubation were 74%, 83% and 100%, respectively. These results show that fragments in fraction 1 required 100-fold higher amounts of the macrophage enzyme than soil bacillus enzyme to effect total hydrolysis of this carbohydrate fragment. This finding contrasts with the 50,000-fold requirement of the macrophage over the soil bacillus enzyme required to hydrolyze completely the intact group A polysaccharide (1).

The relative susceptibility of the haptens in the four fractions to hydrolysis by the macrophage enzyme was studied at varying concentrations of the enzyme. Equal amounts of the fractions containing 5 to 6 μg of N-acetylglucosamine were incubated with 1000 and 2000 units of macrophage enzyme. Free N-acetylglucosamine was assayed at 0 hr and after incubation at 37°C

TABLE II

Hydrolysis of N-acetylglucosamine from streptococcal group A carbohydrate haptenic fraction by β-N-acetylglucosaminidases from soil bacillus and rabbit lung macrophage

Enzyme Source	Enzyme Units	N-Acetylglucosamine Released[a]							
		Fraction 1		Fraction 2		Fraction 3		Fraction 4	
		μg/ml	*% total*	*μg/ml*	*% total*	*μg/ml*	*% total*	*μg/ml*	*% total*
Soil bacillus	50	220	100	264	86	204	96	122	75
Macrophages	1000	26	14	76	25	98	47	88	55
			(12)[b]		(29)		(48)		(72)

[a] Incubation at 37°C for 20 hr in final volume of 0.5 ml.

[b] Values in parentheses represent percentage of N-acetylglucosamine that was released by the macrophage enzyme compared to total N-acetylglucosamine released by soil bacillus enzyme.

TABLE III

Hydrolysis of N-acetylglucosamine from haptenic fractions by rabbit lung macrophage enzyme

Enzyme Units	Percentage of Total N-Acetylglucosamine Released[a b]			
	Fraction 1	Fraction 2	Fraction 3	Fraction 4
1000	35	53	82	93
2000	558	91	94	96

[a] Incubation at 37°C for 6 hr in a final volume of 0.1 ml.

[b] Total N-acetylglucosamine in fractions used: 1, 130 μg/ml; 2, 130 μg/ml; 3, 100 μg/ml; 4, 94 μg/ml.

TABLE IV

Comparative amounts of macrophage enzyme for release of approximately 50% of the total N-acetylglucosamine in fractions (incubation at 37°C for 6 hr in final volume of 0.1 ml)

Fraction	Enzyme Units	Percentage of Total Glucosamine Released
1	2000	52
2	1000	50
3	800	60
4	500	52

for 6 hr. The results of Table III show that under these conditions, hydrolytic activity of the enzyme increased with the higher enzyme concentration for each fraction as well as with decreasing size of the oligosaccharides. The latter relationship was also illustrated by determining the amount of enzyme necessary to hydrolyze about 50% of the glucosamine in the different fractions. A step-wise decrease in the amount of enzyme required to hydrolyze half the glucosamine in fractions 1 to 4 is evident (Table IV).

To test whether the hydrolytic activity of the macrophage enzyme can approach that of the soil bacillus enzyme on the smallest sized carbohydrate fragments obtained, equal amounts of both enzymes were used on the late eluates of fraction 4 that had been rechromatographed on G-15 Sephadex. Fifty units of enzyme were incubated with equal amounts of the subfraction and the amount of N-acetylglucosamine released was assayed. The data obtained showed that 50% of the total N-acetylglucosamine was released after 1 hr and 100% after 3 hr by the soil bacillus enzyme. In the sample incubated with 50 units of the macrophage enzyme, no appreciable N-acetylglucosamine was released at 1 hr, 20% was released after 3 hr and 60% after 20 hr incubation.

Inhibition of the A carbohydrate-A antibody reaction. Studies on the precipitin inhibition capacity of the fractions were performed using group A antiserum and ^{14}C-labeled group A carbohydrate in the radioimmune precipitin technique. Inhibition of antigen-antibody combination by group A and A-variant polysaccharide, *p*-nitrophenyl-β-N-acetylglucosaminide, N-acetylglucosamine monosaccharide and the hapten fractions were tested. The results obtained (Table V) show that inhibition in the A carbohydrate-antibody systems decreased with diminishing concentrations of the specific inhibitor, N-acetylglucosamine, in each preparation. Although the inhibition by fractions 1 and 2 was similar at the estimated equivalent concentrations of N-acetylglucosamine, the capacity of the other oligosaccharides to inhibit decreased with decreasing size of the hapten. Thus, while an amount of the group A polysaccharide containing 5 μg of the specific inhibitor, N-acetylglucosa-

TABLE V

Inhibition of group A antigen-antibody radioimmune precipitin reaction by group A polysaccharide haptenic fractions, p-nitrophenyl-β-N-acetylglucosamine and N-acetylglucosamine

N-Acetylglucosamine Content of Inhibitor	Percentage Inhibition[a]						
	A-CHO[b]	Fractions				p-np-GlcNAc[c]	GlcNAc[d]
		1	2	3	4		
μg							
50	97	86	84	70	43	8	1
25	95	74	73		31		
12.5	90	60	57		15		
5	82						
2.5	69						

[a] Decrease in percentage of labeled antigen precipitated in the absence and presence of inhibitor.
[b] A-CHO, group A polysaccharide.
[c] p-np-GlcNAc, p-nitrophenyl-β-N-acetylglucosamine.
[d] GlcNAc, N-acetylglucosamine.

TABLE VI

Inhibition of group A-variant antigen-antibody precipitation by the haptenic fraction and rhamnose monosaccharide

Inhibitor	Rhamnose Content	N-Acetylglucosamine Content	Percentage Inhibition[a]
	μg	μg	
A-CHO	100	50	47
A-variant	100	15	97
1	200	50	78
2	250	50	79
3	320	50	78
4	270	50	80
Rhamnose	200		19

[a] Decrease in percentage of labeled antigen precipitated in the absence and presence of inhibitor.

mine, produced 82% blocking of the antibody, 10 times that amount, 50 μg of either fraction 1 or 2, were required to achieve this degree of blocking.

The blocking capacity of these preparations was also tested in a similar system using unadsorbed A-variant antibody and labeled ^{14}C A-variant antigen (Table VI). The inhibition by the "A" carbohydrate preparation used indicates that a minority of side-chains without terminal N-acetylglucosamine residues is present in this preparation. However, the higher degree of inhibition obtained with the hapten fractions at concentrations of N-acetylglucosamine equivalent to that of the group A polysaccharide is attributed to the high proportion of rhamnose to N-acetylglucosamine found in these fractions. This marked inhibitory action by the fractions is best explained by the presence in these fractions of rhamnose oligosaccharides which closely resemble A-variant polysaccharide subunits described by McCarty (4).

Effect of enzymatic digestion on the antibody-blocking capacity of the fractions. The effect of the enzymatic removal of N-acetylglucosamine from the polysaccharides and the haptenic fractions on their antibody-blocking capacity in the radioimmune precipitin technique was tested. Portions of the group A carbohydrate and of the fractions that would block 70% to 80% of the antibody were dried under vacuum from the frozen state. Soil bacillus or macrophage enzymes were added in appropriate buffers. Controls included the carbohydrate preparations without enzyme. Samples were taken after incubation at 37°C, diluted in 0.1 M phosphate buffer, pH 7.4, and placed in boiling water bath for 10 min to destroy enzyme activity. Portions were then used to assay for free N-acetylglucosamine, and the rest was used in precipitin inhibition tests. The data presented in Table VII show the decrease in antibody-blocking capacity with prolonged incubation of the polysaccharide and haptens with the β-N-acetylglucosaminidases.

Assays for free N-acetylglucosamine revealed that the loss of inhibitory capacity of the fractions correlated with the percentage of N-acetylglucosamine released, although this varied somewhat with each fraction. While 100% of the estimated total N-acetylglucosamine was released from fractions 1 and 2 and 80% to 90% of the

TABLE VII

Decrease in antibody inhibition by haptenic fragments following digestion by β-N-acetylglucosaminidases

Enzyme	Incubation Period	Percentage Decrease of Inhibition[a]				
		A-CHO	Fractions			
			1	2	3	4
	hr					
Macrophages:	8	8	62	56	58	54
8000 units	18	61	85	81	70	62
Soil bacillus:	2	68		16		
3000 units	4	87		35		
	18	87		68		

[a] Decrease of percentage inhibition obtained with inhibitors not subjected to enzymatic digestion.

total N-acetylglucosamine was released from fractions 3 and 4, in no instance was there complete loss of antibody-blocking capacity. Studies with the soil bacillus, limited to fraction 2 only because other haptens were not available, yielded results similar to those obtained with the macrophage enzyme. The lack of complete removal of inhibiting activity after complete release of acetylglucosamine by the enzymes may be explained by the presence of A-variant antibody in the unadsorbed group A antisera. Studies of this group A antiserum showed that equal amounts (0.7 μg) of labeled A and A-variant antigen precipitated 81% and 22% of the antibody, respectively, in the radioimmune precipitin technique. Adsorption of the A-antiserum with A-variant cell walls resulted in a decrease of the A-variant precipitation to approximately 10%. It is likely that this residual percentage of antibody had A-variant specificity which was inhibited by the A-variant antigen resulting from the enzymatic removal of the N-acetylglucosamine determinant from the A specific oligosaccharides.

DISCUSSION

Previous studies on the activity of β-N-acetylglucosaminidases from the soil bacillus and phagocytic cells showed a considerably lower capacity of the phagocytic enzyme to hydrolyze the streptococcal polysaccharide (1). The present studies were undertaken to explore the possibility that this decreased activity was related to the molecular size of the substrate as well as the alternative explanation that the link in the *p*-nitrophenyl-β-N-acetylglucosaminide substrate was more susceptible to hydrolysis by this enzyme than the rhamnosyl-β-N-acetylglucosamine linkage of the streptococcal polysaccharide. The description by McCarty of a method for hydrolysis of the group A carbohydrate into fragments that had group A specificity (4), together with the report by Heymann and his co-workers of the preparation of group A biose and triose of rhamnose-β-N-acetylglucosamine (5), suggested that these fragments could be used in clarifying the basis for the difference in enzyme activity. The use of the sulfuric acid hydrolysis technique was resorted to because of the heterogeneity in the products, which would enable the testing of enzymes on fragments of various sizes. The use of the dialyzable products limited the size of such fragments to haptens, while chromatography on Sephadex allowed gross separation of the fragments into groups of various sized haptens. Evidence for this separation is provided by the results of thin layer chromatography and the studies of the blocking capacity of these fractions for the group A antibody.

The data obtained on the enzymatic hydrolysis of the fractions show that activity of the macrophage enzyme is related to the size of the substrate. Of note is the fact that even with fraction 4, which eluted prior to the appearance of the monosaccharides, approximately 10 times more of the macrophage than soil bacillus enzyme was required to effect complete hydrolysis. This can be attributed to the possibility that this fraction consists of a heterogeneous mixture of disaccharides and larger oligosaccharides, with the latter being less susceptible to enzymatic digestion. That this is the case is suggested both by the higher antibody-blocking capacity of this fraction as compared to that of *p*-nitrophenyl-β-N-acetylglucosamine biose. The increased hydrolytic activity of the macrophage enzyme on the slower eluting components obtained by rechromatography of fraction 4 on G-15 Sephadex also corroborates the occurrence of varying sized fragments in this fraction.

It is also interesting to note the relative correlation between susceptibility to degradation by the macrophage enzyme and capacity of the A polysaccharide and its fragments to block the group A antibody precipitation with A antigen. A calculation of the percentage of unhydrolyzed glucosamine for fractions 1 to 4 (macrophage enzyme) in Table II shows values of 86%, 75%, 53% and 45%, respectively. These values correlate with those obtained for the percentage inhibition obtained using the fractions at concentrations corresponding to a content of 50 μg N-acetylglucosamine. A similar correlation can be extended to the *p*-nitrophenyl-glucosamine, which is the most susceptible to enzymatic hydrolysis and shows the least inhibitory capacity for the A antibody.

The specificity of β-N-acetylglucosamine linked to rhamnose as the immunologic determinant of the group A polysaccharide was clearly demonstrated by McCarty (4). The studies presented here are in accord with those findings, both for the polymer as well as for the haptens. The capacity of the antigen and haptens to combine with antibody seems related directly to the N-acetylglucosamine content in oligosaccharides of equal molecular size, and to the molecular weight of the carrier molecule. The specific action of both the soil bacillus and macrophage enzyme on the antigenic determinant is illustrated by the release of the N-acetylglucosamine and the corresponding alteration in antigenicity of the compounds tested.

Studies on the degradation of streptococcal organisms by phagocytic cells *in vitro* (11) have revealed that the intraphagocytic degradative process results in the release of dialyzable as well as non-dialyzable products. This raises the possibility that some of these products of degradation might include group A polysaccharide haptens similar to those obtained by acid hydrolysis. The formation of such haptens *in vivo*, their degradation by the β-N-acetylglucosaminidases from patients with various complications of group A streptococcal infections and their possible role in the persistence of the group A antibody in certain individuals (10) is the subject of further investigation.

Acknowledgments. The authors would like to acknowledge the technical assistance of Sami Karayusuf, Carol Dahl and Barbara Riviere.

REFERENCES

1. Ayoub, E. M. and McCarty, M., J. Exp. Med., *127:* 130, 1968.
2. Bleiweis, A. S., Karakawa, W. W. and Krause, R. M., J. Bact., *88:* 1198, 1964.
3. Fuller, A. T., Brit. J. Exp. Path., *19:* 130, 1938.
4. McCarty, M., J. Exp. Med., *104:* 629, 1956.
5. Heymann, H., Manniello, J. M., Zeleznick, L. D. and Barkulis, S. S., J. Biol. Chem., *239:* 1656, 1964.
6. Dische, Z. and Shettles, L. B., J. Biol. Chem., *175:* 595, 1948.
7. Rondle, C. J. M. and Morgan, W. T. J., Biochem. J., *61:* 586, 1955.
8. Reissig, J. L., Strominger, J. L. and Leloir, L. F., J. Biol. Chem., *217:* 959, 1955.
9. McCarty, M. and Lancefield, R. C., J. Exp. Med., *102:* 11, 1955.
10. Dudding, B. A and Ayoub, E. M., J. Exp. Med., *128:* 1081, 1968.
11. Ayoub, E. M. and Wannamaker, L. W., J. Immun., *90:*1099, 1967.

The Journal of Immunology
Copyright © 1970 by The Williams & Wilkins Co.

Vol. 105, No. 2, August 1970
Printed in U.S.A.

COMPLEMENT AND CONGLUTININ IN THE SERUM OF GERM-FREE AND CONVENTIONAL PIGLETS

O. BARTA,[1] VERA BARTA,[1] O. P. MINIATS and D. G. INGRAM

From the Departments of Veterinary Microbiology and Immunology and of Clinical Studies, University of Guelph, Guelph, Ontario, Canada

Received for publication February 25, 1970

The sera of piglets raised as germ-free and colostrum-deprived or as conventional colostrum-fed animals were examined for their levels of complement and conglutinin. The level of hemolytic complement was higher in germ-free animals in the first 3 days of life and again from days 20 to 56. The data indicate that natural contact with bacteria after birth or monoinfection of 56-day-old germ-free piglets caused an increased complement activity in the serum. Feeding of colostrum may stimulate increased serum complement levels but direct absorption of complement components from the colostrum is considered to be unlikely.

Conglutinin levels were higher in the serum of germ-free pigs from 10 to 42 days of age. A decrease in conglutinin activity of the serum and significant variations in conglutinin titers followed exposure of the newborn to a conventional environment or monoinfection of 56-day-old germ-free animals with a strain of *Escherichia coli*.

The serum complement system has attracted the attention of many research workers in the past few years because of its participation in various biologic activities. The biologic effects of complement are primarily directed against the cell membrane and may be classified as altered functional state of certain cells, alterations of the cell membrane surface and damage to the cell membrane (1). Although few reports on the complement in pig serum have been published, it has been shown that porcine complement components can be titrated with the classical R reagents prepared from guinea pig serum (2). The serum from suckling piglets has been reported to have higher titers of hemolytic complement than serum from colostrum-deprived piglets (3). The complement level in serum of porcine fetuses was detectable as early as the 40th day of gestation (3). In newborn piglets the level of conglutinating complement was about five times higher than that of hemolytic complement (3).

Conglutinin is a naturally occurring serum protein of Bovidae (4). Lachmann (4) suggested that in non-ruminants, only immunoconglutinin is present. However, Tlaskalova and Barta (5) reported conglutinating activity in serum from newborn piglets obtained prior to the feeding of colostrum. The conglutinin from newborn piglets was similar to bovine conglutinin in that it required the presence of Ca^{++} for its activity and was not inactivated by treatment with 2-mercaptoethanol. In some other respects it resembled immunoconglutinin (6). The present experiments trace the level of complement activity and of conglutinin in conventional and in germ-free colostrum-deprived piglets during the first 8 to 10 weeks after birth.

[1] Present address: Department of Microbiology, Oklahoma State University, Stillwater, Oklahoma 74074.

MATERIALS AND METHODS

Serum from conventional piglets was obtained from blood samples collected from the anterior vena cava of nine piglets belonging to one healthy litter. The piglets were raised on the sow under conventional conditions of housing and feeding. All sera were stored at $-20°C$ and all serum samples from one piglet were tested at the same time.

Serum from germ-free piglets was obtained from blood samples collected from the anterior vena cava of four piglets of one litter derived by hysterectomy and raised under germ-free conditions as described by Alexander *et al.* (7). The environment (incubator) and feces of the piglets were examined for sterility once weekly. One of the piglets died at 12 days of age following an injury caused by bleeding but the other three were maintained germ-free until 56 days of age.

Monoinfection of piglets was accomplished by feeding each of the 56-day-old germ-free animals 5 ml of an 18-hr broth culture of *Escherichia coli* strain 1787, serotype 0137:K79. This strain is highly virulent for colostrum-deprived calves (8). Two of the three piglets died 30 to 48 hr after infection.

Sheep red blood cells were obtained from one ram which was bled weekly into a flask containing glass beads (9). The washed erythrocytes were used at a concentration of 1×10^8 cells/ml.

Antiserum to sheep red blood cells was obtained from one rabbit and was used at a dilution of 1:6000.

Conglutinin was supplied by the serum obtained from one cow. The serum was heat-inactivated (56°C for 30 min), absorbed with sheep red blood cells, and used at a dilution of 1:300.

Complement was fresh serum from one horse. It was stored at −20°C and was used at a dilution of 1:40.

Diluent was isotonic Vernonal buffer (pH 7.3) containing 1.5×10^{-4} M Ca^{++} and 1×10^{-3} M Mg^{++}. Purified bovine serum albumin (Difco Laboratories, Detroit, Mich.) was added to the diluent to a final concentration of 0.5%.

The plate conglutination test was used for the titrations of conglutinating complement and conglutinin (10) using microtiter plates with V-shaped wells. Each serum was tested in a two-fold dilution series. When conglutinating complement was titrated each well contained 0.025 ml of piglet serum or its dilution, and 0.075 ml of a mixture of equal parts a) 2 units of rabbit antibody to sheep erythrocytes, b) 2 units of bovine conglutinin and c) a suspension of sheep erythrocytes (1×10^8 cells/ml). When conglutinin was titrated each well contained 0.025 ml piglet serum or its dilution and 0.075 ml of a mixture of equal parts a) 2 units of horse complement, b) 2 units of antibody to sheep erythrocytes and c) a suspension of sheep erythrocytes (1×10^8 cells/ml).

The plates were shaken to insure thorough mixing of the reagents in each well and were incubated at 37°C for 75 min and then at 4°C for 18 hr. The dilution of serum causing 50% conglutination of erythrocytes was taken as the end-point.

Titration of hemolytic complement was carried out in microtiter plates using 0.025 ml of piglet serum or its dilution and 0.075 ml of a mixture of equal parts a) 2 units of rabbit hemolysin, b) diluent and c) a suspension of sheep red blood cells (1×10^8 cells/ml). The procedure was the same as that for the conglutination test. The dilution of serum giving 50% hemolysis was considered to be the end-point.

RESULTS

The titer of conglutinating complement in the sera of the piglets was very rarely higher than the titer of hemolytic complement. Hemolysis of the red blood cells occurred in the tests for the titration of conglutinating complement and, in most sera, conglutination was not observed beyond the end-point of hemolysis. Thus, the hemolytic activity of the complement masked the end-point of conglutinating activity and no valid observations were possible on the titer of conglutinating complement.

In conventional piglets the titer of hemolytic complement was at its lowest during the first 3-days of life (Table I). A sharp increase in titer occurred by 7 days and reached a peak at 10 days of age. Between 10 and 21 days of age, a declining level of complement activity was recorded. From 21 to 69 days of age, a gradual but consistent rise in the level of hemolytic complement was demonstrated.

TABLE I

The hemolytic complement level in the serum of conventional piglets

Age	Mean[a]	Standard Deviation	Coefficient of Variation	No. of Sera Tested
days	*ml*			
0	0.0287	0.0105	0.37	9
3	0.0315	0.0086	0.27	9
7	0.0155	0.0083	0.54	8
10	0.0037	0.0014	0.38	5
14	0.0135	0.0066	0.49	8
21	0.0178	0.0059	0.33	8
28	0.0152	0.0098	0.64	7
35	0.0112	0.0035	0.31	8
42	0.0105	0.0031	0.30	8
49	0.0088	0.0041	0.47	7
56	0.0081	0.0054	0.66	5
63	0.0058	0.0027	0.46	4
69	0.0028	0.0020	0.73	4

[a] Milliliters of serum necessary to produce 50% hemolysis.

In germ-free piglets the level of complement activity was twice as high as it was in conventional piglets during the 1st day of life (Table II). During the first 10 days of life the complement titer did not change significantly in the germ-free animals. The level of complement activity in the serum of the germ-free piglets showed an uninterrupted rise between day 10 and day 42 when a plateau was reached which lasted until day 56 when the animals were infected.

The hemolytic complement levels in conventional and germ-free piglets are compared in Figure 1 and the points showing significant differences are shown. There was a significantly higher level of hemolytic complement in the serum of

TABLE II

The hemolytic complement level in the serum of germ-free piglets

Age	Mean[a]	Standard Deviation	Coefficient of Variation	No. of Sera Tested
days	*ml*			
0	0.0141	0.0065	0.46	4
3	0.0156	0.0059	0.38	4
7	0.0161	0.0072	0.45	4
10	0.0143	0.0070	0.49	4
14	0.0073	0.0033	0.45	3
21	0.0052	0.0030	0.58	3
28	0.0037	0.0019	0.51	3
35	0.0025	0.0016	0.65	3
42	0.0021	0.0008	0.40	3
49	0.0019	0.0013	0.69	3
56	0.0021	0.0008	0.40	3

[a] Milliliters of serum necessary to produce 50% hemolysis.

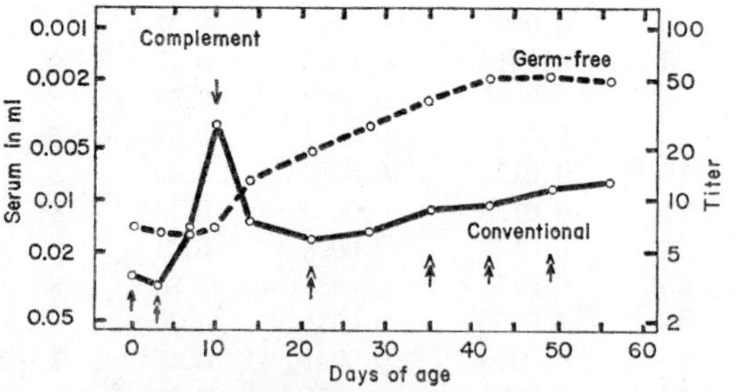

Figure 1. Comparison of mean levels of hemolytic complement in conventional and germ-free piglets. ↑ Significant difference at 5% level of probability. ↟ Significant difference at 2% level of probability.

TABLE III

The level of conglutinin in the serum of conventional piglets

Age	Mean[a]	Standard Deviation	Coefficient of Variation	No. of Sera Tested
days	*ml*			
0	0.0037	0.0015	0.41	9
3	0.0059	0.0029	0.49	9
7	0.0072	0.0033	0.46	8
10	0.0200	0.0041	0.20	5
14	0.0154	0.0047	0.31	8
21	0.0219	0.0110	0.50	8
28	0.0140	0.0053	0.38	7
35	0.0047	0.0028	0.60	8
42	0.0201	0.0091	0.45	8
49	0.0020	0.0006	0.30	7
56	0.0025	0.0007	0.28	5
63	0.0019	0.0007	0.34	4
69	0.0016	0.0006	0.36	4

[a] Milliliters of serum necessary to produce 50% conglutination.

TABLE IV

The level of conglutinin in the serum of germ-free piglets

Age	Mean[a]	Standard Deviation	Coefficient of Variation	No. of Sera Tested
days	*ml*			
0	0.0078	0.0058	0.74	4
3	0.0042	0.0030	0.73	4
7	0.0034	0.0019	0.57	4
10	0.0033	0.0017	0.51	4
14	0.0024	0.0005	0.21	3
21	0.0024	0.0005	0.21	3
28	0.0020	0.0008	0.40	3
35	0.0019	0.0001	0.05	3
42	0.0033	0.0023	0.70	3
49	0.0023	0.0012	0.52	3
56	0.0026	0.0015	0.58	3

[a] Milliliters of serum necessary to produce 50% conglutination.

germ-free piglets as compared to the level in conventional piglets from 21 to 56 days of age. The peak of activity at 10 days of age in conventional piglets was not seen in germ-free animals.

Table III presents the data on the level of conglutinin in the serum of conventional pigs. On day 1, the level of conglutinin was relatively high but it dropped significantly during the first 10 days of life. In these conventional pigs, the level of conglutinin varied in an irregular manner from 10 to 42 days of age. Then a rapid rise occurred to a relatively constant level between 49 and 69 days of age.

The data on the level of conglutinin in germ-free pigs is shown in Table IV. On the 1st day of life, the level of conglutinin in the serum of germ-free piglets was about one-half that in conventional piglets. During the first 2 weeks of life, there was a relatively rapid increase in titer of conglutinin in the serum of germ-free piglets. From day 14 to day 56 a stable, high level of conglutinin was maintained.

The levels of conglutinin in germ-free and conventional piglets are compared in Figure 2 and the points of significant difference are designated. From 10 to 35 days of age and again at 42 days significantly higher levels of conglutinin occurred in germ-free piglets. On days 49 and 56, the level of conglutinin was very similar in the two groups of animals.

After infection of the three germ-free piglets at 56 days of age with *E. coli*, two animals died within 48 hr. The third piglet survived and the levels of conglutinin and hemolytic complement in this animal were followed until it was 69 days of age. Figure 3 shows the variations in the level of conglutinin and complement in the serum of this piglet.

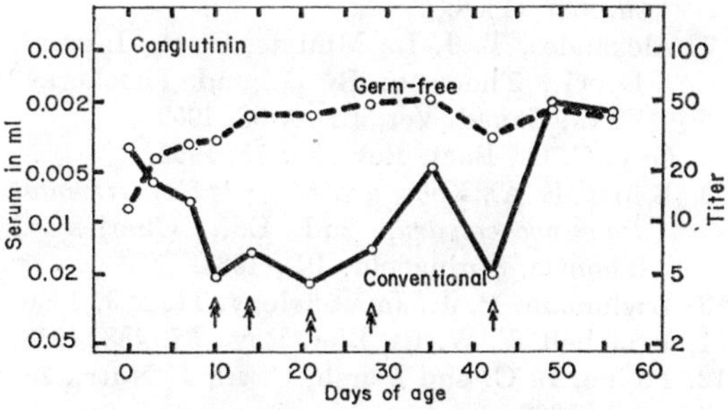

Figure 2. Comparison of mean levels of conglutinin in conventional and germ-free piglets. ↑, Significant difference at 2% level of probability.

DISCUSSION

In many serum samples the level of conglutinating complement was the same as, or lower than, the level of hemolytic complement. Day et al. (3) have reported that conglutinating complement activity was five times higher than hemolytic activity in newborn piglets but our data failed to confirm their findings. The hemolytic complement levels in newborn piglets were comparable to those published by Day *et al.* (3). However, the post-natal changes in complement level did not support the suggestion (3) that direct passive absorption of complement components occurred in newborn piglets. If active complement components were passively absorbed from colostrum, the first peak of complement activity would be expected to coincide with the peak of colostral derived immunoglobuins in the serum. The time of direct absorption of colostral antibody is 12 to 35 hr after birth (11, 12). The peak level of hemolytic complement at 10 days of age in conventional piglets suggests that colostrum does not supply the complement components directly. Colostrum may supply a stimulating factor which leads to the release of complement components into the blood stream. Similar results have been reported on complement levels in colostrum-fed and colostrum-deprived calves (13). Newton

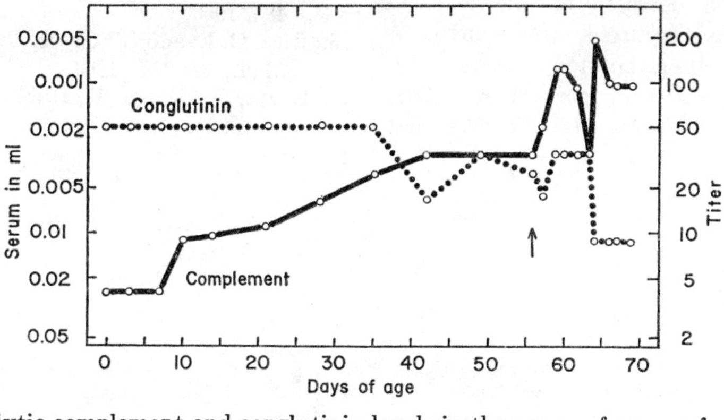

Figure 3. Hemolytic complement and conglutinin levels in the serum of a germ-free piglet which was infected orally with *Escherichia coli* strain RVC 1787 at 56 days of age. ↑, Day of infection.

et al. (14) reported no significant differences in the level of complement in conventional and germ-free guinea pigs. Higher levels of hemolytic complement in colostrum-fed piglets than in colostrum-deprived piglets between 1 and 22 days of age have been reported (15). These discrepancies may be due to the different strains of animals tested or to differences in the experimental techniques used by the various investigators.

The complement level increased markedly within 3 days after oral infection of a germ-free, 56-day-old pig with a strain of *E. coli*. The level dropped to the original level during the 2nd week post-infection and then increased to another high during the 3rd week and was maintained at this high level for at least 6 days. These data indicate that the microflora of the intestine constitute one of the stimuli for increasing the level of complement activity of the serum. It is suggested that the production and release of complement components are stimulated by live bacteria colonizing the intestine in the early post-natal period and that the feeding of colostrum may also be a stimulus. The decrease in the level of complement activity after this first peak may reflect a degree of exhaustion of the production system. In germ-free piglets, the complement level could be influenced by neither microflora nor colostrum and the gradual increase was a continuation of the increase in complement activity which occurs during fetal life (3).

Conglutinin is apparently produced during fetal life in the porcine species as it is in the bovine (16). The level of conglutinin in the serum of germ-free piglets increased continuously throughout the first few weeks of life. In conventional piglets, a decrease in the level of conglutinin activity occurred after birth. A similar decrease has been reported in calves (13). Following monoinfection of germ-free piglets, the conglutinin level decreased indicating that the conglutinin takes part in some *in vivo* reactions with the bacterial flora.

Acknowledgments. This investigation was supported in part by Grants MT873 and MA2082 from the Medical Research Council of Canada and by the Ontario Department of Agriculture and Food.

REFERENCES

1. Müller-Eberhard, H. J., Bokisch, V. A. and Budzko, D. B., *Allergology*, Edited by B. Rose, M. Richter, A. Sehon and A. W. Frankland, p. 379, Excerpta Medica Foundation, Amsterdam, 1968.
2. Rice, C. E., J. Immun., *65:* 201, 1950.
3. Day, N. K. B., Pickering, R. J., Gewurz, H. and Good, R. A., Immunology, *16:* 319, 1969.
4. Lachmann, P. J., Advances Immun., *6:* 479, 1967.
5. Tlaskalova, H. and Barta, O., Folia Microbiol. (Prague), *13:* 450, 1968.
6. Bienenstock, J. and Block, K. J., J. Immun., *96:* 637, 1966.
7. Alexander, T. J. L., Miniats, O. P., Ingram, D. G., Thomson, R. G. and Thackeray, E. L., Canad. Vet. J., *10:* 98, 1969.
8. Gay, C. C., Bact. Rev., *29:* 75, 1965.
9. Kabat, E. A., *Kabat and Mayer's Experimental Immunochemistry*, 2nd Ed., Charles C Thomas, Springfield, Ill., 1961.
10. Lachmann, P. J., Immunology, *11:* 263, 1966.
11. Brambell, F. W. R., Biol. Rev., *33:* 488, 1958.
12. Payne, L. C. and Marsh, C. L., J. Nutr., *76:* 151, 1962.
13. Barta, O., Ph.D. Dissertation, University of Guelph, 1969.
14. Newton, W. L., Pennington, R. M. and Lieberman, J., Proc. Soc. Exp. Biol. Med., *104:* 486, 1960.
15. Rice, C. E. and L'Ecuyer, C., Canad. J. Comp. Med., *27:* 157, 1963.
16. Barta, O., Barta, V., Hubbert, W. T. and Ingram, D. G., J. Immun., In press.

THE JOURNAL OF IMMUNOLOGY

Vol. 105, No. 2, August 1970
Printed in U.S.A.

ANTIGEN BINDING AND THE IMMUNE RESPONSE

I. The Early Primary Response to a Protein Antigen[1]

FARROKH MODABBER[2] AND ELI SERCARZ

From the Department of Bacteriology, University of California at Los Angeles, Los Angeles, California 90024

Received for publication February 20, 1970

The cellular, immune response in the A/J mouse spleen to β-galactosidase (βGz) was examined by the A–H assay, which very sensitively measures the amount of antigen bound to cells. The early primary response can be subdivided into three phases: 1) a rise in activity which is completed by 12 hr, 2) a plateau from 12 to 48 hr, during which no substantial change can be discerned, and 3) a rapid increase from this time to the peak activity on days 4 to 6. There was no comparable latency in the secondary response. The existence of phase 2 supports the concept of a "true" preparative or latent period, not owing to difficulties in detection. The argument was favored that this first 48 hr represents splenic recruitment, cell-finding and interaction, followed by biochemical preparation for antibody synthesis.

The period between the administration of antigen and the first appearance of antibody is often called the "lag," "latent" or "inductive" phase. Several schools of thought exist concerning the nature of the latent period. One view is that the biochemical events preceding specific protein synthesis, and lasting several hours, are the only causes contributing to the lapse of time between antigen injection and antibody production. Hence, the apparent lag of 1 or more days in most systems must be a quantitative phenomenon, accounted for by the lack of sufficiently sensitive methods for early detection of antibody (1–3). On the other hand, the latent period may represent a stage of variable duration, on the order of days, during which intracellular differentiation or vital cellular interactions must occur preparatory to antibody synthesis (4–8). Another notion is that the early latent period may be due to a temporary, reversible state of immune paralysis (9–11).

The argument for the existence of a "true" latent period is supported by reports of qualitative differences which exist between cells in early as compared with later phases of the immune response. For example, x-ray sensitivity (12–14) and sensitivity to inhibitors of nucleic acid synthesis (15, 16) certainly are different in the "inductive" and the "productive" phases of the *in vivo* response. Likewise, in the secondary response elicited *in vitro*, studies indicate a difference between inductive and productive phases in their susceptibility to inhibition by a number of drugs (11, 17–19). A distinct difference between the early latent period and the latter productive period in vulnerability to agents interfering with cell division can be shown in the sheep red cell system (20, 21). These data seem to exclude the simplest explanations of the latent period as a completely quantitative phenomenon, since on such a basis there would be little reason to suspect a difference in susceptibility to drugs during the latency.

To directly examine this problem, however, a highly sensitive method is required for detecting antibody at a molecular level. Most of the available techniques have the limitation that a large number of molecules are required to bind a sufficient amount of antigen to render antibody-producing cells detectable. To approach a resolution, we have developed a technique with the potential sensitivity of detecting 1 antigen-binding unit, presumably a single antibody molecule (22). In this method, β-galactosidase of *Escherichia coli* (βGz) is used as antigen. Since the hydrolytic

[1] This work was supported by grants from the National Science Foundation (GB-5410) and the Academic Senate of University of California at Los Angeles (2044).

[2] Present address: Department of Bacteriology and Immunology, Harvard Medical School, Boston, Massachusetts 02115.

activity of this enzyme is unaffected by its antibody (23), βGz attached to cells containing anti-βGz can be assayed by Rotman's technique in which the activity of single molecules of the enzyme is measurable (24). Repeated action of specifically bound enzyme molecules on a fluorogenic substrate, fluorescein di-β-galactopyranoside (FDβG) (25), produces increasing amounts of fluorescent products which accumulate and can be accurately measured by microfluorometry. This large amplification factor residing in the repeated use of βGz makes available a powerful tool to detect anti-βGz. This method was later called the A–H assay for *A*ntigen *B*inding to *C*ells *D*etermined by *E*nzymatic *F*luorogenic *G*roup *H*ydrolysis (26). Employing this method, we have been able to show a latent period in the primary response to βGz in mice which is not due to difficulties in detecting antibody.

MATERIALS AND METHODS

Antigens. Keyhold limpet hemocyanin (KLH) and catalase were purchased from Calbiochem, Los Angeles, Calif. Beta-galactosidase of *Escherichia coli* ML 308 was kindly supplied by Dr. I. Zabin, Department of Biological Chemistry, University of California at Los Angeles.

Animals and immunization. Male and female, 4- to 8-month-old mice of the A/Jax strain, maintained in this laboratory, were used in these experiments. All injections were performed with 100 μg of antigen in saline, intraperitoneally.

Substrates. Ortho-nitrophenyl-β-D-galactopyranoside (ONPG) was purchased from Calbiochem, Los Angeles, Calif. The enzyme was assayed by the method of Horiuchi *et al.* (27). The weight of active enzyme was calculated from ONPG assay assuming a specific activity of 400,000 ONPG units/mg of enzyme at 29°C.

Fluorescein–di–β–galactopyranoside (FDβG) (25) was a generous gift of Dr. Boris Rotman, Department of Biochemistry, Brown University, Providence, R. I., early in these studies, and later was purchased from Mann Research Laboratories, Inc., New York.

Preparation of cell suspension. Hanks' balanced salt solution (Hyland Laboratories, Los Angeles) supplemented by the addition of 50 mg streptomycin, 60,000 units of penicillin and 10,000 units of heparin/liter was used for preparation and washing of the cells.

Spleens of at least three identically treated mice were removed and teased into single-cell suspensions by using fine forceps. The suspensions were filtered through 250-gauge stainless steel gauze (Industrial Wire Company, Los Angeles). The cells were washed once and resuspended in the same medium. Portions were removed for the following treatments:

1) *Determination of "intrinsic" βGz activity.* Intrinsic activity of normal mice represents the amount of mouse βGz present in the cells. The intrinsic activity of immunized animals may also include the activity of residual antigen injected. These values are subtracted from total measurements to calculate binding activities.

2) *Fixation.* A cell suspension was centrifuged at 2000 RPM (600 × G) in an International centrifuge at 4°C, the supernatant was removed and the cells were incubated in 10 ml 95% ethanol for 10 min at room temperature. After this period, the cells, referred to as "fixed cells," were centrifuged, washed twice and tested for antigen-binding ability as in 3 below.

3) *Unfixed antigen-binding activity.* Fifty micrograms of active βGz contained in 0.1 ml of Hanks' solution were added to approximately 1 ml of a 10% suspension of fixed or unfixed washed cells. Cells were then incubated at 37°C for 1 hr and at 4°C for an additional 12 hr. Unbound enzyme was removed by washing the cells four times with 40 ml of Hanks' solution. Finally, the washed cells were suspended in Hanks' solution and nucleated cells were counted with a hemocytometer. To 0.1 ml of the final cell suspension, 0.1 ml of 4.8×10^{-5} M FDβG was added and droplets of 2×10^{-4} ml were placed in oil chambers using a 10-μl Hamilton syringe. The oil chambers were made from 5- x 7.5-cm microscope slides (Scientific Products) and contained silicone fluid SF 96(200) purchased from General Electric Company. Fluorescence of each droplet was measured by a Zeiss fluorescence microscope equipped with darkfield condenser, 10× objective and 12.5× eyepiece. The microscope was attached to an Aminco photmultiplier-microphotometer unit (Model 10–213, American Instrument Company, Silver Springs, Md). with a 931-A RCA photomultiplier tube, in the same manner that was reported by Rotman (24). The light source was a tungsten lamp (12 volt, 100 watt) purchased from Zeiss. A BG-12 filter (2 mm) was employed as a primary filter and the Zeiss 500 + 410 barrier filters of the microscope were used together as

the secondary filters. The fluorescence of each droplet was measured at least three times in the course of 5 to 16 hr incubation of oil chambers at room temperature. The average linear increase of fluorescence of at least 15 droplets, expressed as microphotometer units/hr, was calculated for a given cell suspension. Extremely active droplets as well as droplets containing clumps were excluded from the calculations.

Inactivation of βGz. A solution of 5 to 10 mg/ml βGz in saline was inactivated at 56°C for 10 min. The coagulated material cross-reacted with antibody to native βGz but lacked enzyme activity. To avoid reactivation, the heated enzyme was kept at room temperature in the absence of Mg^{++}, Mn^{++}, and 2-mercaptoethanol.

Antibody unit. Antigen-binding activity equivalent to 1 unit of antibody was arbitrarily defined as that amount of antibody which will bind sufficient enzyme molecules to hydrolyze the fluorogenic substrate and increase the intensity on the microphotometer, 1×10^{-11} amperes in 1 hr at room temperature.

RESULTS

Early detection of antigen-binding activity. By conventional techniques, detectable antibody to soluble protein antigens does not appear for at least several days (28–30). In contrast, with the A–H method it was possible to detect higher than normal antigen binding 12 hr after a primary intraperitoneal injection of soluble βGz (Fig. 1). In these experiments, mice were injected with 100

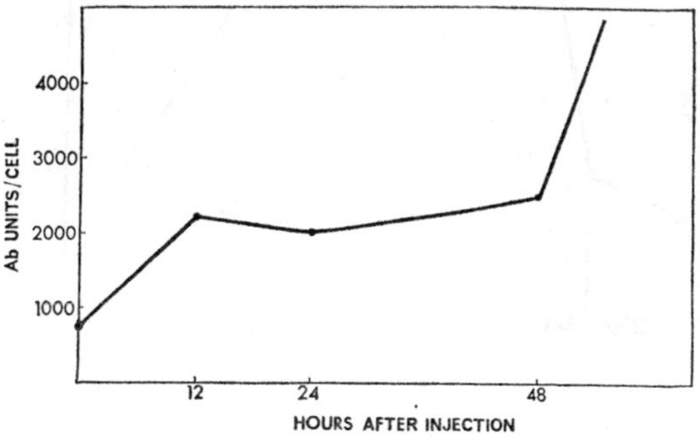

Figure 1. The antigen binding activity (antibody unit/cell) of ethanol-treated spleen cells of A/J mice after a primary intraperitoneal injection of 100 μg of βGz. The value at 0 time indicates the A–H activity of normal mice. Each point represents the average of at least five experiments with three pooled spleens/experiment.

TABLE I

Nonspecific and specific stimulation of A–H activity[a]

Antigen Used	Intrinsic Activity[b]	Unfixed Activity	Fixed Activity
KLH	210	2650	900
Catalase	270	1860	890
βGz	300	1160	2180
None	210	470	850

[a] Activity is expressed as antibody units/cell in cell suspensions removed 12 hr after injection of the antigens in question.

[b] Intrinsic activity, no *E. coli* βGz added *in vitro*.

μg soluble βGz intraperitoneally and their spleen cells were fixed and assayed for antigen-binding activity. In every experiment the spleen cells from at least three mice were pooled for each point. Three findings are noteworthy: a) higher than normal activity at 12 hr; b) no further increase between 12 and 48 hr; c) peak of response at 4 to 6 days.

1) *"Twelve hour" activity.* Although we did not examine at earlier times, we invariably (approximately 25 occasions) observed a clear increase in spleen-binding activity by the 12th to 14th hr after injection. The possibility was entertained of nonimmunologic stimulation of adsorption of βGz by cells, 12 hr after injection. In the first set of experiments, mice were injected with 10 μg or 100 μg of high molecular weight, non-cross-reactive proteins such as KLH and catalase, respectively. Spleen cells were prepared 12 hr after injection and the cells were assayed unfixed or after ethanol fixation. The results in Table I indicate, first, that there is nonspecific stimulation in uptake of βGz by unfixed cells induced by KLH or catalase injection. This nonspecific stimulation can be attributed to enhancement of phagocytosis, because as can also be seen from Table I, upon fixation the nonspecific adsorption of βGz in KLH or catalase-injected animals is reduced to normal levels. Secondly, Table I shows that the A–H activity in βGz-injected mice was enhanced by fixation, rather than being reduced to the normal level.

In the second set of experiments, the specificity of the 12-hr rise was tested by the ability of cross-reacting material to specifically inhibit βGz uptake by cells. Mice were injected with 100 μg βGz intraperitoneally. After 12 hr their spleen cells were incubated for 1 hr at 37°C with 0.5 mg heat-inactivated βGz/ml prior to the A–H assay. The heated enzyme lacks enzymatic activity but cross-reacts with antibody to native enzyme and hence can be used as a specific inhibitor of the A–H activity. As a control, a portion of the same cell suspension was incubated with 50 mg/ml human serum albumin (HSA) prior to incubation with active βGz. The results are presented in Table II. Whereas preincubation with HSA has little or no effect on the βGz binding, heat-inactivated enzyme completely inhibits the usual 12-hr activity. It is noteworthy that such treatment under these conditions does not influence antigen-binding by normal spleen cells, an indication that normal cells bind βGz nonspecifically rather than because of preformed anti-βGz.

TABLE II

Inhibition of A–H activity by heated βGz

Primary Injection	Preincubation[a]		
	None	HSA	Heated βGz
0 time (before antigen)	690	620	660
12 hr	2200	2150	780
3 days	8900	8680	900

[a] After fixation, the cells were incubated with the inhibitors for 1 hr at 37°C prior to incubation with native enzyme for an additional hour at 37°C. Overnight incubation at 4°C was omitted in these experiments to overcome complications due to reactivation of heat-inactivated βGz. Hence, after the incubation with the native enzyme, the cells were washed and assayed immediately. Noninbred Swiss mice were used in this experiment.

2) *The latent period of 12 to 48 hr.* The apparent average antigen-binding activity/spleen cell as measured by the A–H assay does not increase over a period of 36 hr starting from 12 hr after injection and extending to 48 hr, at which time the rise begins and is continuous until the first peak (Figs. 1 and 2).

3) *Peak at 4 to 6 days.* As can be seen in Figure 2, the primary response of mice to an intra-

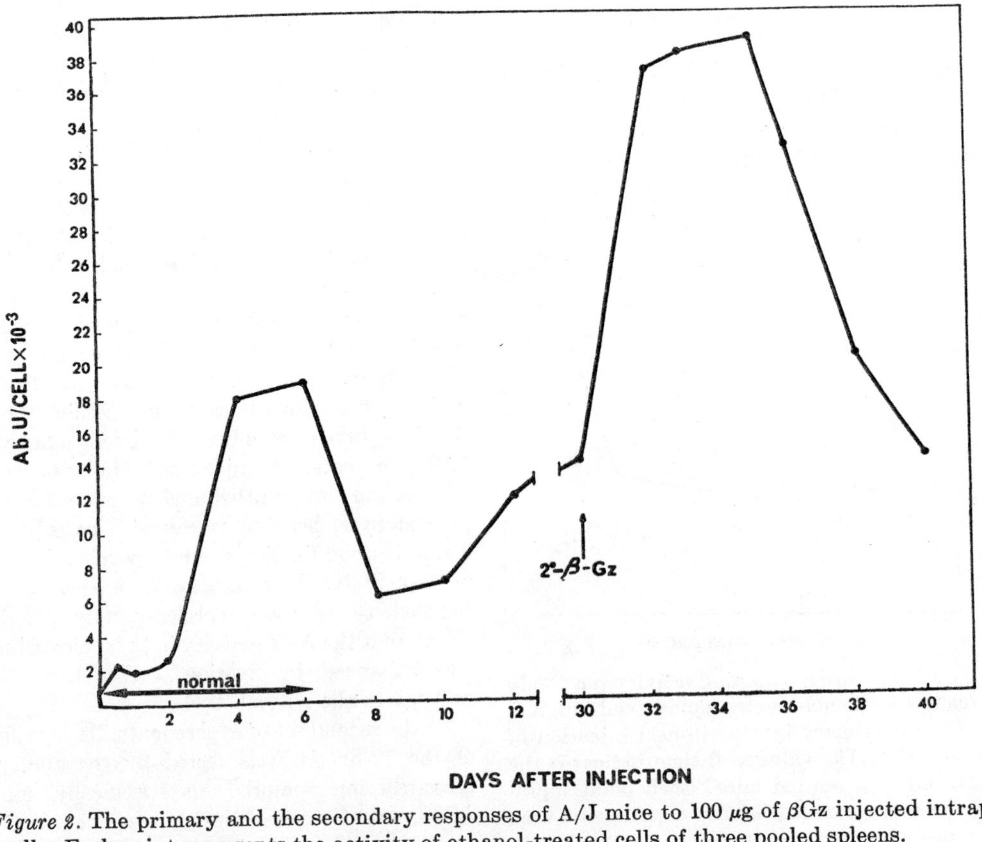

Figure 2. The primary and the secondary responses of A/J mice to 100 μg of βGz injected intraperitoneally. Each point represents the activity of ethanol-treated cells of three pooled spleens.

peritoneal injection of 100 μg βGz, as measured by the A–H assay, peaked at 4 to 6 days. The activity dropped very sharply thereafter. Without a second injection of βGz, another increase in the A–H activity was observed which started after the 2nd week; this activity reached a plateau around day 20.

The secondary response. To ascertain that the response to the first injection of βGz was indeed a "primary" response to the antigen, the A–H activity was measured after a secondary stimulus. Groups of primed mice were reinjected with 100 μg βGz and their spleens were assayed at intervals thereafter. When a second injection was given a month after the primary injection, a typical booster response was observed, as shown in Figure 2. The "net secondary response," presented in Figure 3, is calculated by subtracting binding values for the primary response on a particular day from values obtained on the same day of the secondary response. It is of importance that the net secondary response in the primed animal shows no lag after the booster injection.

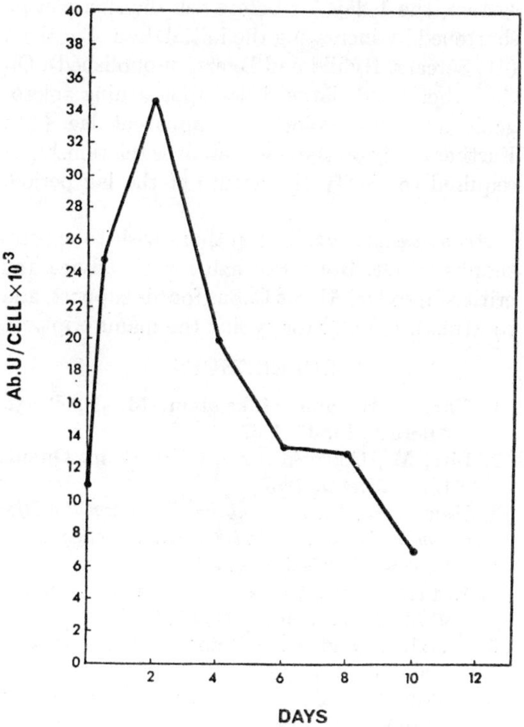

Figure 3. The "net secondary response" of A/J mice to a second intraperitoneal injection of 100 μg βGz, 1 month after priming. Calculation of these points was made by subtracting the primary A–H value from the secondary A–H value on the day in question.

DISCUSSION

We have studied the kinetics of the cellular response in the A/J mouse spleen to β-galactosidase, during its first several days. An intensive study was especially in order with a sensitive system of assay; it seemed possible to distinguish a true latent period in the immune response from an artifactual one, due to insensitivity of detection. Whereas other investigators have studied the response to viral (31) and carbohydrate (32) antigens within the 1st day, there is no report available in which the quantitative activity *vs* protein antigens has been described within such an early time.

The A–H assay, a cellular antigen-binding method employed in these studies, exploits the continuous enzymatic hydrolysis of fluorogenic substrate by a few molecules of antibody-bound β-galactosidase until enough fluorescent molecules are produced to be detected. The time amplification factor inherent in the method makes it sensitive enough to obviate the argument of technical inability to detect antibody.

Our results show a rise in antigen-binding activity by the spleen at 12 hr after β-galactosidase injection (first rise) followed by a 36-hr plateau. This is succeeded by a second rise in activity towards a peak on the 4th to 6th day. The length of the latent period may be a function of dose and remains to be studied in detail.

It has repeatedly been shown that the 12-hr rise is specific; heat-inactivated βGz inhibits this activity. The experiments on the nonspecific stimulation of βGz uptake, occurring after injection of high molecular weight antigens such as hemocyanin and catalase, affirm that this effect depends upon an enhancement of active uptake of βGz by phagocytosis and pinocytosis. When phagocytosis is prevented by fixation of such cells in 95% ethanol, prior to *in vitro* incubation with βGz, uptake of this enzyme is inhibited, as expected. However, the binding of βGz by immune cells is greatly enhanced after treatment by ethanol, and the enhancement varies in cells at different stages of immunity.

The plateau following the initial rise demands explanation. We have considered the following possibilities to explain the early rise and the 12- to 48-hr plateau:

True early biosynthesis. a) Some active cells

start to leave the spleen during the 12 to 48 hr following antigen injection, balancing out a continuous intrasplenic rise in activity due to antibody or receptor biosynthesis. The presence of antibody-binding cells migrating from the draining lymph node of rabbits 18 hr after antigen introduction has been shown in preliminary experiments by Morikawa, Modabber and Coons (unpublished). b) A true increase in antigen binding by the total spleen is underestimated by the method of expressing A–H activity (antibody units/cell). Hence, a concomitant rise in spleen cell number renders the A–H activity apparently constant. c) It is possible that some antibody is synthesized immediately, conceivably from stored messenger (33), but soon the necessary ingredients for additional synthesis are exhausted; the time needed for subsequent formation of precursors accounts for the latent period.

Recruitment of antigen reactive cells. Alternatively, the initial rise in spleen activity may *not* reflect antibody synthesis but rather the accumulation of actively binding cells from other parts of the body. Antigen-reactive cells with specific receptors may be recruited from the thymus and/or bone marrow (34, 35) and this *net* accumulation may cease at 12 hr, being succeeded by a steady state. Macrophage-associated antigen might then act as a rallying point at which cell types bearing specific receptors can congregate. Thus, the latent period would be comprised of sequential recruitment, "finding-time," cellular interaction, followed by necessary biochemical preparatory reactions.

The origin of receptors on antigen-reactive cells is unknown but their existence certainly precedes antigen injection. Naor and Sulitzeanu (36) have demonstrated the presence of lymph node cells capable of binding ^{125}I-BSA specifically in normal mice. Byrt and Ada (37) and Humphrey (38) also have evidence for binding of antigens by normal spleen and lymph node cells. Although incubation of large numbers of normal spleen cells with heat-inactivated βGz did not decrease the subsequent binding of active enzyme by these cells, our results are not contradictory to these reports. As mentioned earlier, the droplets with extreme activity were excluded from the calculations. Thus, the rare βGz-reactive cells, binding relatively large numbers of molecules (39, 40) would not be included in our analysis.

It is often argued that the response to complex antigens such as erythrocytes is not truly primary in nature. This argument may certainly be relevant for βGz of *E. coli* since the organism producing this enzyme is ubiquitous, and the βGz's produced by various *E. coli* strains are cross-reactive. Hence, preexposure of conventional mice to this enzme cannot be ruled out. However, the dramatic difference between the response to the first antigen injection and that after the secondary stimulation (in spite of the fact that the organisms are present in the gut of these animals constantly) detracts from the significance of such an argument.

It may actually be that the cell finding and association events occurring during our lag period are not only essential for the establishment of the primary response, but also underlie the establishment of delayed hypersensitivity and immune memory. Further antigen contacts by intrinsic antigen following cellular interaction might be required to initiate the second rise in activity at 48 hr. This period may be shorter if sufficient antigen is present. In the sheep erythrocyte system, the 1-day lag before cell division can be shortened by increasing the initial dose of antigen (41; Sercarz, Byfiild and Byers, unpublished). On the other hand, large doses approaching tolerogenic amounts prolong the apparent lag (42). Further study on the dose-response relationship is required to clarify the nature of the lag period.

Acknolwedgments. The authors wish to express thanks to Dr. Boris Rotman for his advice and criticism, to Dr. Albert Coons for his support, and to Mrs. S. Lavidor for typing the manuscript.

REFERENCES

1. Uhr, J. W. and Finkelstein, M. S., Progr. Allergy., *10:* 37, 1967.
2. Litt, M., Cold Spring Harbor Symp. Quant. Biol., *32:* 447, 1967.
3. Haurowitz, F., *Immunochemistry and the Biosynthesis of Antibodies*, Interscience Publishers, New York, 1968.
4. Leduc, E. H., Coons, A. H. and Connolly, J. M., J. Exp. Med., *102:* 61, 1955.
5. Šterzl, J. and Silverstein, A. M., Advances Immun., *6:* 337, 1967.
6. Makinodan, T. and Albright, J. F., Progr. Allerg., *10:* 1, 1967.
7. Miller, J. F. A. P. and Mitchell, G. F., Transplant. Rev., *1:* 3, 1969.
8. Claman, H. N. and Chaperon, E. A., Transplant. Rev., *1:* 92, 1969.
9. Sercarz, E. E., Ph.D. Dissertation, Harvard University, 1960.

10. Siskind, G. W. and Benacerraf, B., Advances Immun., *10:* 1, 1969.
11. Byers, V. and Sercarz, E., Submitted to J. Exp. Med., 1970.
12. Dixon, F. J., Talmage, D. W. and Maurer, P. H., J. Immun., *68:* 693, 1952.
13. Taliaferro, W. H., Taliaferro, L. G. and Janssen, E. F., J. Infect. Dis., *91:* 105, 1952.
14. Taliaferro, W. H. and Taliaferro, L. G., J. Immun., *103:* 559, 1969.
15. Šterzl, J. in *Mechanisms of Antibody Formation*, Czech. Acad. Sci. Symp., p. 107, 1960.
16. Ivanyi, J. M., Maler, M., Wudl, L. and Sercarz, E., J. Exp. Med., *127:* 1149, 1968.
17. Ambrose, C. T., Bact. Rev., *30:* 408, 1966.
18. Ambrose, C. T., J. Exp. Med., *124:* 461, 1966.
19. Ambrose, C. T., J. Exp. Med., *130:* 1003, 1969.
20. Dutton, R. W. and Mishell, R. I., in *The Control of Nuclear Activity*, Symp. Soc. Gen. Physiol., Edited by L. Goldstein, p. 19, Prentice-Hall, Englewood Cliffs, N. J., 1967.
21. Byfield, P. and Sercarz, E., J. Exp. Med., *129:* 897, 1969.
22. Modabber, F. and Sercarz, E., Bact. Proc., *67:* 90, 1967.
23. Cohn, M. and Torriani, A. M., J. Immun., *69:* 471, 1952.
24. Rotman, B., Proc. Nat. Acad. Sci., *47:* 1981, 1961.
25. Rotman, B., Zderic, J. A. and Edelstein, M., Proc. Nat. Acad. Sci., *50:* 1, 1963.
26. Sercarz, E. and Modabber, F., Science, *159:* 884, 1968.
27. Horiuchi, T., Tomizawa, J. and Novick, A., Biochim. Biophys. Acta, *55:* 152, 1962.
28. Weigle, W. O., Proc. Soc. Exp. Biol. Med., *94:* 306, 1957.
29. Vischer, T. L. and Stastny, P., Immunology, *12:* 675, 1967.
30. Daniels, J. C. and Weigle, W. O., J. Immun., *101:* 1230, 1968.
31. Svehag, S. E. and Mandel, B., J. Exp. Med., *119:* 1, 1964.
32. Baker, P. B., Bernstein, M., Pasanen, V. and Landy, M., J. Immun., *97:* 767, 1966.
33. Spirin, A. S., Current Topics in Developmental Biology, *1:* 1, 1966.
34. Miller, J. F. A. P. and Mitchell, G. F., J. Exp. Med., *128:* 801, 1968.
35. Abdou, N. I. and Richter, M., J. Exp. Med., *130:* 141, 1969.
36. Naor, D. and Sulitzeanu, D., Israel J. Med. Sci., *5:* 217, 1969.
37. Byrt, P. and Ada, G. L. Immunology, *17:* 503, 1969.
38. Humphrey, J., in *Symposium on Developmental Aspects of Antibody Formation and Structure*, Czech. Acad. Sci., Prague, In press.
39. Modabber, F. and Coons, A. H., Fed. Proc., *29:* 697 Abstract, 1970.
40. DeLuca, D., Decker, J. and Sercarz, E., Fed. Proc., *29:* 697 Abstract, 1970.
41. Perkins, E. H., Sado, T. and Makinodan, T., J. Immun., *103:* 668, 1969.
42. Sercarz, E., in *Immunological Tolerance* Edited by M. Landy and W. Braun., p. 237, Academic Press, New York, 1969.

THE JOURNAL OF IMMUNOLOGY
Vol. 105, No. 2, August 1970
Printed in U.S.A.

THE CYTOPHILIC ACTIVITY OF HUMAN IMMUNOGLOBULINS[1]

CHRISTOPHER INCHLEY,[2] HOWARD M. GREY[3] AND JONATHAN W. UHR

From Irvington House Institute and the Department of Medicine, New York University School of Medicine, New York, 10016, and the Department of Experimental Pathology, Scripps Clinic and Research Foundation, La Jolla, California 92037

Received for publication February 19, 1970

The ability of human myeloma immunoglobulins of different subclasses to bind to the surface of guinea pig macrophages was investigated. Using ^{125}I-labeled proteins, it was found that those belonging to the subclass IgG_1 generally bound to a greater extent than did those in other subclasses, and that the cell-associated radioactivity remained largely on the cell surface during the short periods of observation employed. The Fc fragment of one such IgG_1 protein was shown to contain virtually all of the cytophilic property of the parent molecule. Pre-incubation of guinea pig macrophages with IgG_1 proteins, but not with representatives of other groups, resulted in a pronounced inhibition of the binding of cytophilic antibody, suggesting that the inhibiting proteins occupied the same site on the macrophage membrane involved in cytophilic binding.

Certain classes of immunoglobulins bind to the membrane of reticuloendothelial (RE) cells. Such antibodies have been termed "cytophilic" (1–7). The binding activity may be highest when sera and phagocytes from the same species are used, but cross-species sensitization is widespread (4). The cytophilic property of such antibodies is lost when the Fc fragment is removed by pepsin digestion (3, 4, 7).

The objective of the present studies was to localize the property of cytophilia within the immunoglobulin molecule as well as to determine the distribution of cytophilia among classes and subclasses of human immunoglobulins since certain of the biologic properties of the different immunoglobulins are known to differ (8–10). Our results, using human myeloma proteins and guinea pig macrophages, indicated that some of the proteins, particularly those belonging to the γG_1 subclass, became attached to the membrane of macrophages and markedly inhibited the binding of guinea pig cytophilic antibody. It was also demonstrated that the Fc fragment of one such IgG_1 protein accounted for virtually all of the cytophilic property of the parent molecule.

MATERIALS AND METHODS

Myeloma proteins. These were obtained from the sera of patients with multiple myeloma; they were purified and subsequetly iodinated as previously described (11, 12), and were stored in phosphate buffer, pH 7.2, at −20°C. Dilutions for assay of binding activity were made in phosphate-buffered saline, pH 7.4 (PBS), at protein concentrations between 0.2 and 2.0 mg/ml and maintained at 4°C. The proteins used in this study included seven IgG_1, three each of IgG_2, IgG_3, and IgG_4 as well as one IgA and one IgM. Proteins were typed by immunodiffusion using subclass and class specific antisera and are identified in the test by three-letter abbreviations of the patient's name.

Preparation of enzymatic fragments. Fragments resulting from papain and pepsin digestion of

[1] This work was done under the sponsorship of the Commission on Immunization of the Armed Forces Epidemiological Board, and was supported in part by the United States Army Medical Research and Development Command, Department of the Army, under Research Contract DADA 17-69-C-9177, in part by United States Public Health Service Grants AI-0834 and AI-07007, National Science Foundation Grant GB-7473-X, Atomic Energy Commission Contract AT(04-3)-410, and American Heart Association Grant 67-795, and is Publication 385 from the Department of Experimental Pathology.

[2] Present address: Department of Zoology, University of Edinburgh, Edinburgh, Scotland.

[3] Established Investigator of the American Heart Association.

human IgG were prepared and isolated as described previously (11).

Peritoneal exudate cell suspensions. Adult male Hartley albino guinea pigs, weighing 500 to 600 g were injected intraperitoneally with 20 ml of heavy mineral oil. Four or 5 days later, the peritoneal cavity was washed twice with 20 ml PBS. The cells so obtained were washed four times in PBS and suspended at 10^7/ml in medium 1066 (Grand Island Biological Company) buffered at pH 7.4 with 0.01 M Tris and HCl. Approximately 80% of all cells were macrophages as indicated by the uptake of neutral red (13). Viability was greater than 92%.

Assay for the binding of ^{125}I-labeled proteins. One-milliliter amounts of cell suspensions containing 10^7 peritoneal exudate cells (PE) were equilibrated in an ice bath. ^{125}I-labeled myeloma proteins of different classes were added in a volume of 0.05 ml PBS at 4°C, the cells were gently mixed, and the mixture was transferred to a 37°C water bath for 20 min. Following incubation the cells were cooled to 4°C and washed four times in 2.5 ml of Tris-1066 prior to final suspension in 1.0 ml medium for assay in a well-type scintillation counter. In some experiments, the binding of labeled protein was measured in the presence of an excess of unlabeled protein from another source. On these occasions, the inhibiting protein was added to the cells in a volume of 0.05 ml PBS at 4°C immediately prior to addition of the labeled immunoglobulin.

Preparation of guinea pig cytophilic antiserum. A pooled cytophilic antiserum against sheep red blood cells (SRBC) was obtained from guinea pigs according to the method of Boyden (2). The passive direct titer of this serum (4) was 128, the passive indirect titer, 8000. The serum was heated at 56°C for 30 min before use in the assay.

Cytophilic antibody against H antigen of *Salmonella paratyphi* B was prepared by injecting 100 μg *Salmonella* flagella (14) in complete Freund's adjuvant intramuscularly into guinea pigs. Thirty weeks later, the animals were given a further 100 μg in saline intraperitoneally, and bled out 7 days later. The pooled serum was shown to have cytophilic activity by the passive direct assay as follows: 3×10^6 PE cells were incubated with antiserum at a final dilution of 1:160 for 30 min at 37°C, washed twice and then assayed for bacterial adherence by the method described for antibody-producing cells (14).

Inhibition of binding of anti-SRBC cytophilic antibody by myeloma proteins. The passive indirect cytophilic assay was used for these experiments and SRBC were sensitized with cytophilic antibody as follows: Freshly supplied sheep blood in Alsever's solution was washed four times in isotonic saline and made up in Tris-buffered medium 199 (Grand Island Biological Company) at pH 7.4 at a 2% concentration; 0.5-ml amounts were incubated for 45 min with an equal volume of appropriately diluted antibody. After washing twice in Tris-199 at room temperature, the sensitized cells were suspended in 1.0 ml of this medium to give a final concentration of 1.0%. Assays were carried out by a modification of the technique of Boyden (2). PE cells were made up in Tris-199 at a concentration of 10^6 cells/ml. One-tenth-milliliter amounts were dispensed into wells formed by 1.0 cm i.d. Lucite rings (Millipore Company) attached to coverslips on one side only with silicone grease. The cells stood at room temperature for 30 min to allow macrophages to become attached to the coverslip. The supernatant fluid was then removed together with unattached cells and replaced with fresh Tris-199. One hundred- to 500-μg amounts of myeloma protein in 0.05 ml PBS were added to duplicate wells, and the mixture was incubated for 30 min at 37°C. Following washing with three to four changes of Tris-199, 0.1 ml of the 1.0% suspension of antibody-sensitized SRBC was added to the cells which were then allowed to stand at room temperature for 1 hr. After this period, excess medium and red cells were removed from the wells and replaced with Tris-199 containing 0.02% neutral red dye. The wells were sealed with a glass slide, inverted, and the binding of SRBC to PE cells was scored under a low power light microscope as follows. Macrophages were identified by uptake of neutral red. Each macrophage which passed under a fixed point in the eye piece during three or four straight traverses of each well was scored for the number of SRBC attached, up to 9 red cells; where 10 or more SRBC were bound they were counted in a single category. Ten or more were sufficient to surround most peritoneal macrophages and are designated "rosettes" in this paper. Between 150 and 300 macrophages were scored in this manner in each pair of duplicate wells.

RESULTS

The uptake of human immunoglobulins by PE cells. Twelve ^{125}I-labeled myeloma proteins representative of the four subclasses of human IgG and one IgA protein were tested for their ability to bind to PE cells. Ten micrograms of each protein were added to 10^7 cells for incubation as described under *Materials and Methods.* In Table I the mean data from a series of experiments are given as the percentage of added radioactivity that became bound to the cells.

It was found that two of the labeled IgG_1 proteins invariably bound better than the third IgG_1 or those of the other three subclasses ($p < 0.05$). There was no significant variation in the binding of IgG_{2-4}. The single IgA tested, BRO, showed poor binding to PE cells at a level similar to that of BSA, about 1% of the dose.

The effect of protein concentration on uptake by PE cells. The results for one such experiment are presented in Figure 1. One-, 10- and 100-μg amounts of two proteins which bound well, GRE and FIS, and one which bound relatively poorly, DAH, were used, together with a labeled preparation of purified guinea pig $\gamma 2$. It can be seen that whereas the abolute amount of protein

TABLE I

Percentage of ^{125}I-myeloma proteins bound to macrophages[a]

Class	Individual Proteins[b]	Number of Experiments	Activity Bound: Mean ± S.D.
			%
IgG_1	GRE	19	6.1 ± 1.5
	FIS	8	4.2 ± 0.7
	BOU	6	1.5 ± 0.5
IgG_2	DAH	4	1.1 ± 0.5
	SAW	4	0.8 ± 0.4
	TSC	4	1.4 ± 0.5
IgG_3	RIC	4	0.9 ± 0.5
	SHE	4	2.4 ± 0.9
	VIC	4	1.7 ± 1.0
IgG_4	GER	5	1.5 ± 0.5
	HEB	5	2.0 ± 0.8
	REY	5	1.7 ± 0.9
IgA	BRO	6	1.1 ± 0.5
BSA		5	1.3 ± 0.4

[a] 10^7 cells incubated with 10 μg ^{125}I-protein for 20 min at 37°C.

[b] Proteins are identified by abbreviation of patient's name.

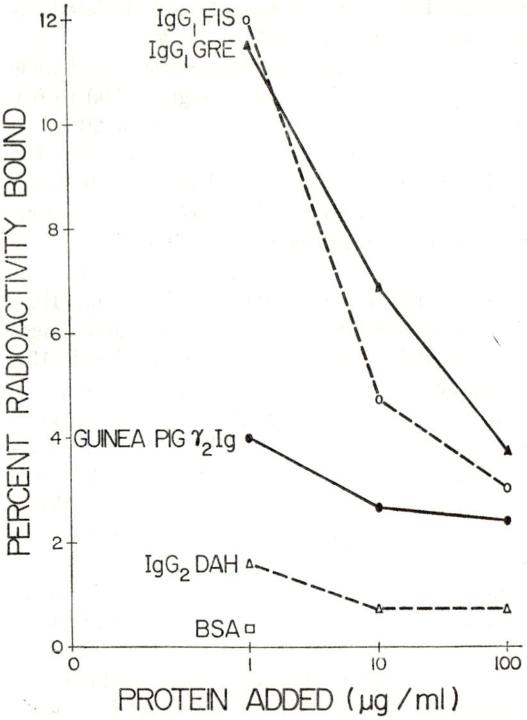

Figure 1. The effect of protein concentration on the uptake of ^{125}I-proteins by macrophages.

fixed by the cells increased with increasing dose, there was a decrease in the percentage of added protein that was bound. BSA, tested at only the lowest level, showed little affinity for the cells compared with GRE and FIS. These two proteins showed a generally similar pattern of binding at all three doses. Guinea pig $\gamma 2$—the cytophilic class of guinea pig immunoglobulin—bound less well than the two IgG_1 proteins, but better than IgG_2 DAH. The distinction between the binding of IgG_1 and IgG_2 was more evident at the 1.0-μg dose level than at the 10-μg level, and this dosage might have given a better picture of the differences between the four IgG subclasses. The level of incorporation of ^{125}I on some of the labeled proteins, however, dictated a choice of the 10-μg dose for most of this work. The steepness of the saturation curve between 1 and 10 μg is somewhat surprising and raises the possibility that monolayering of the protein in the most dilute solution may have resulted in denaturation which favored binding.

The effect of inhibiting glycolysis on the uptake of IgG. The possibility that phagocytosis of protein might account in part for the uptake of cell-bound radioactivity was considered. A number of agents such as sodium fluoride (NaF) have been shown to depress the level of glycolysis in macrophages and consequently to bring about a drastic reduction in phagocytic activity (15).

Table II shows the effect of pre-incubation with NaF on the ability of guinea pig PE cells to take up labeled proteins. Two series of tubes containing 10^7 cells in 1.0 ml Tris-1066 were incubated at 37°C for 30 min, one with NaF at a final concentration of 2×10^{-2} M and the other without any addition. Without washing the cells, myeloma proteins (10 μg in 0.05 ml) were added and incubation was continued for a further 20 min, after which the cells were washed and counted. All proteins tested showed some reduction in binding as a result of treatment with NaF. However, while the uptake of GRE and FIS was inhibited by 7% and 18%, respectively, that of other IgG subclasses, with the exception of IgG_3 VIC, was reduced by at least 47%. The surprisingly large uptake of BSA on this occasion, 2.4% of the dose, was reduced 70% by NaF, suggesting that the BSA may have become aggregated and thus was easily phagocytosed. The IgA protein, BRO, was inhibited to a somewhat lesser extent than most human IgG.

TABLE II

The effect of treatment with NaF on the binding of ^{125}I-proteins to macrophages

Class	Individual Proteins	Radioactivity Bound: Normal cells	Radioactivity Bound: Treated cells	Reduction in Binding
		%	%	%
IgG_1	GRE	5.8	5.5	7
	FIS	3.6	3.0	18
IgG_2	DAH	0.7	0.4	47
	SAW	1.6	0.7	55
	TSC	1.7	0.6	64
IgG_3	RIC	1.7	0.4	74
	SHE	2.9	1.1	64
	VIC	1.8	1.5	16
IgG_4	GER	2.1	0.9	57
	HEB	1.6	0.6	61
	REY	2.0	0.7	63
IgA	BRO	1.3	0.9	35
BSA (control)		2.4	0.7	70

That FIS and GRE remained bound to the surface of macrophages was also indicated by elution studies. When the washed cells were incubated for a second period of 20 min at 37°C, 35% to 45% of the bound counts were lost into the supernatant. This observation is similar to that reported for guinea pig cytophilic antibody (4).

Inhibition of binding of ^{125}I-GRE with unlabeled IgG. In order to screen larger numbers of proteins and to determine whether or not there is competition between cytophilic proteins for membrane sites, inhibition studies were performed. Ten-microgram amounts of ^{125}I-GRE were incubated with PE cells in the presence of an excess (100 μg) of unlabeled myeloma proteins from other sources. These were mainly of the IgG_1 subclass and could be further divided into proteins with a normal or high content of carbohydrate (11). Also included in these experiments was IgG_2 DAH as a known example of a low binding protein. Incubation tubes were set up in duplicate and the binding of ^{125}I-GRE in control tubes in the absence of unlabeled protein was equated to 100%. The combined results for a series of experiments are given in Figure 2. As can be seen, BSA had little or no effect on the binding of ^{125}I-GRE for PE cells. In contrast, addition of 100 μg unlabeled GRE reduced the binding of labeled protein by 86%. Other unlabeled IgG_1 proteins caused inhibition of binding of ^{125}I-GRE to varying degrees. There was no clearcut relationship of carbohydrate content to inhibition although there was a tendency for the proteins with normal carbohydrate content to inhibit better than the high carbohydrate proteins. The poor affinity of DAH for PE cells was confirmed. It is of interest that the one IgM protein tested did not significantly inhibit the binding of ^{125}I-GRE to PE cells.

Inhibition of binding with fragments of IgG. To determine whether affinity of human IgG for macrophages could be attributed to a particular portion of the molecule, duplicate incubations were set up with ^{125}I-GRE in the presence of 50 μg of FIS-Fab, $-F(ab')_2$ and $-Fc$, or 100 μg of intact FIS. The combined results for two separate experiments are shown in Figure 3. Neither the Fab nor $F(ab')_2$ fragments of FIS were able to alter the binding of GRE by more than 15%,

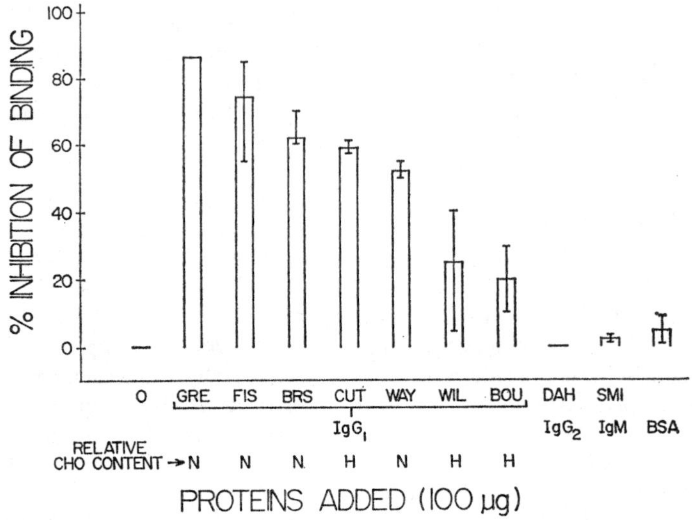

Figure 2. Inhibition of binding of ^{125}I-GRE in the presence of 10-fold excess of unlabeled proteins. Columns represent the mean and vertical lines the range of four to six observations made in three separate experiments. N, normal carbohydrate (CHO) constant; H, high CHO.

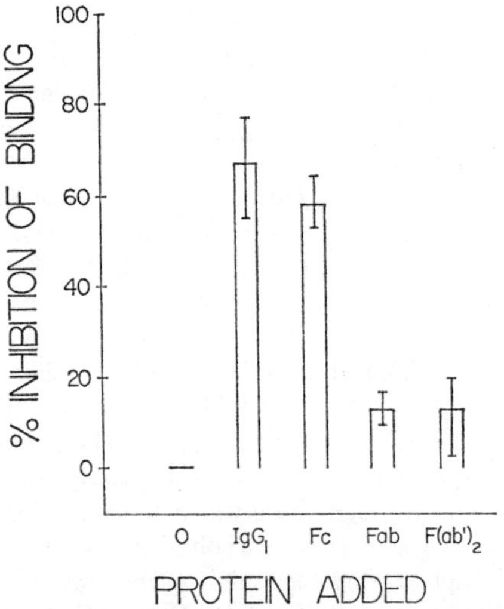

Figure 3. Inhibition of binding of ^{125}I-GRE in the presence of FIS or fragments of FIS. The height of the columns represents the mean and vertical lines the range of four observations made in two separate experiments.

TABLE III

Inhibition of cytophilic antibody to S. paratyphi B flagella by myeloma proteins

Protein		Inhibition of Rosette Formation: Experiment 1[a]	Inhibition of Rosette Formation: Experiment 2
		%	%
IgG_1	GRE	77	67
IgG_1	FIS	92	77
IgG_2	DAH	23	0
IgA	BRO	9	0
IgM	SMI	7	0

[a] Ten-minute incubation of cells with protein. Experiment 2, 20 min.

whereas incubation of GRE with FIS-Fc had an effect almost equal to that of intact FIS.

Inhibition of cytophilic antibody by myeloma proteins. Is the ability of certain human IgG myeloma proteins, particularly of the IgG_1 subclass, to bind to guinea pig PE cells similar to that demonstrated for cytophilic antibody? To investigate this question some of the same unlabeled IgG proteins that were used in the above experiments were also tested for their ability to inhibit the binding of guinea pig cytophilic antibody.

The ability of five human myeloma proteins to inhibit the binding of guinea pig anti-H cytophilic antibody is recorded in Table III. Fifty-microgram amounts of protein were added to 5 $\times 10^6$ PE cells immediately prior to addition of antibody as described above, and the mixture was incubated at 37°C for 10 or 20 min. Fifty micrograms BSA were added to control cells, and in the presence of this protein 65% to 80% of all cells scored showed rosette formation. The results obtained in the presence of the myeloma proteins are expressed as the percentage inhibition relative to the BSA controls. It was found that IgG_1 proteins, GRE and FIS, were able to effect a pronounced decrease in the number of rosettes, to a level one-third or less that of the controls. The IgG_2 protein DAH was less effective, producing at best a 25% decrease, while IgA BRO and IgM SMI had little or no effect.

In a second series of experiments, the effect of prior incubation with protein on the uptake by macrophages of antibody-coated SRBC was investigated. Red cells were incubated with anti-SRBC cytophilic antibody, diluted 1:2000 or 1:4000, washed and added to macrophages previously incubated with 100 or 500 μg of inhibiting protein. The results are shown in Figure 4. Macrophages were scored for the quantity of SRBC bound to their surface. For each pair of duplicate wells the numbers of macrophages bearing 0, 1, 2 to 5, 6 to 9 or ≧ 10 SRBC (rosettes) are expressed as a percentage of the total cells scored, the value for each group being represented by the height of the corresponding vertical column. PE cells bearing single red cells were placed in a

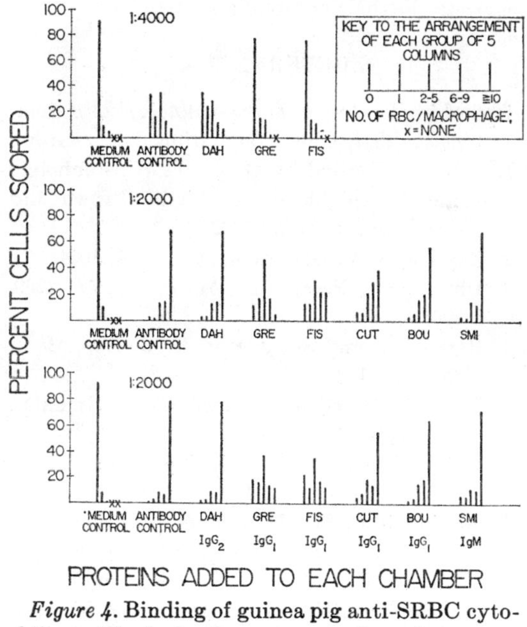

Figure 4. Binding of guinea pig anti-SRBC cytophilic antibody in the presence of myeloma proteins. The distribution of macrophages with respect to the number of SRBC adhering is given. The five columns represent the proportion of cells bearing 0, 1, 2 to 5, 6 to 9, ≧ 10 SRBC/macrophage.

separate category as there was a low background level of nonspecific adherence in untreated controls.

It was found in untreated controls that 90% of macrophages were free of SRBC, whereas previous incubation of SRBC with 1:2000 antibody resulted in 70% to 80% rosettes. At the higher dilution of 1:4000, binding of sensitized SRBC to macrophages was still evident in the antibody control, but was considerably reduced. About 50% of all cells counted had two or more bound SRBC, but only 6% showed rosettes.

Prior incubation of macrophages with GRE and FIS produced a striking shift in the distribution of bound red cells toward that found in the medium control. At the higher dilution of antibody the presence of rosettes was abolished and the number of macrophages bearing no SRBC was increased from 30% to nearly 80%. With 1:2000 antibody the number of rosettes was decreased to 10% or less by GRE and 20% or less by FIS in both experiments, compared with the high level of rosettes in the controls. In contrast to these results, treatment of PE cells with IgG_2 DAH or IgM SMI had little or no effect on the binding of SRBC. Treatment with the two IgG_1 proteins CUT and BOU had an intermediate effect which closely paralleled their inhibition of binding of ^{125}I-GRE (see Fig. 2). CUT protein was able to inhibit attachment of SRBC to some extent, but not to the level of GRE and FIS, whereas BOU had very little effect on the distribution of bound SRBC.

DISCUSSION

The experiments reported here indicate, in general, that human myeloma proteins of the IgG_1 subclass are better able to bind to guinea pig peritoneal exudate cells than are proteins of the three other subclasses. Thus, of 12 ^{125}I-labeled IgG proteins examined, the two that bound to the greatest extent were both members of the IgG_1 subclass. In contrast, other labeled proteins showed little or no binding above background. Although IgG_1 proteins as a group showed the greatest affinity for macrophages, inhibition studies revealed a heterogeneity in binding within this subclass; a similar heterogeneity within subclasses has been observed in the catabolism of IgG proteins (11).

The differences that were observed between IgG_1 and the other IgG subclasses were not due to greater phagocytosis of this group. Prevention of phagocytosis by use of a glycolytic inhibitor had only a small effect on the binding of IgG_1 proteins. It was therefore evident that members of this group were fixed to the cell surface and not ingested. This deduction was confirmed by experiments which showed that such proteins were easily eluted from the surface. On the other hand, treatment with the glycolytic inhibitor resulted in a pronounced reduction in the uptake of proteins with low affinity for cells, suggesting that this much of the background level of uptake was caused by phagocytosis.

Our results are in only partial agreement with those of Huber and Fudenberg (16). Using inhibition of phagocytosis in an homologous system with human antibody and monocytes, they found both IgG_3 and IgG_1 myelomas to be active. The differences in methodology between the two studies may account for the differences in results with IgG_3.

We equate the binding of IgG_1 human myeloma proteins to phagocytes to that of cytophilic antibody for the following reasons: (a) The heterogeneity of binding both within and between subclasses of immunoglobulin suggests that this is not a nonspecific affinity between protein and cell surface but rather a selective binding. (b) Myeloma proteins that bind are able to inhibit the binding of guinea pig cytophilic antibody for cells. (c) The bound proteins remain almost entirely on the cell surface and are not phagocytized during the short periods of observation employed in our experiments. (d) The Fab and $F(ab')_2$ fragments of one such protein that bound well showed no binding activity whereas the Fc fragment did.

The only reported study of the direct binding capacity of Fc fragment is that of LoBuglio *et al.* (17), who state that it inhibited cytophilic binding far more efficiently than Fab; no further data are presented. Also of interest is the observation by Herd and Ada (18) that injection of Fc fragments into the footpads of rabbits results in its retention by the follicles of the regional lymph nodes whereas the Fab fragment is not retained. Our studies indicate that with one IgG_1 protein, virtually all cytophilia can be accounted for by the Fc fragment. This finding appears at variance with the observed heterogeneity of binding within the IgG_1 subclass because the Fc fragments within a subclass are thought to be identical except for minor allotypic differences. If the binding site is entirely restricted within the Fc fragment, then either (a) minor structural differences with the Fc fragment (carbohydrate sequence or allotypic variation) are important for the binding site, or (b) the variable region of the Fab fragment in some manner modulates the binding site located on the Fc fragment thereby resulting in the differences observed. There were differences in the carbohydrate content of the IgG_1 proteins used. In general the proteins with normal carbohydrate content bound to a greater extent than the high carbohydrate proteins, but the correlation was not absolute so that more detailed studies will have to be done to evaluate the possible significance of the extra carbohydrate moiety on the PE cell binding.

Of the four subclasses of human IgG_1 the greatest structural similarity is between classes 1 and 2. Peptide mapping has revealed only four peptides which differentiate the Fc fragments of these two subclasses (19) and the currently available sequence data substantiate this observation (20). It is of particular interest, therefore, that members of these two groups differ so markedly in their cytophilic properties.

REFERENCES

1. Sorkin, E. A., in *The Immunologically Competent Cell*, Ciba Foundation Study Group No. 16, Edited by G. E. W. Wolstenholme and J. Knight, p. 38, Little, Brown and Company, Boston, 1963.
2. Boyden, S. V., Immunology, *7:* 474, 1964.
3. Uhr, J. W., Proc. Nat. Acad. Sci., *54:* 1599, 1965.
4. Berken, A. and Benacerraf, B., J. Exp. Med., *123:* 119, 1966.
5. Lay, W. H. and Nussenzweig, V., J. Immun., *102:* 1172, 1969.
6. Phillips-Quagliata, J., Levine, B. and Uhr, J. W., Nature, *220:* 1290, 1969.
7. Rabinovitch, M., J. Immun., *99:* 1115, 1967.
8. Terry, W. D., J. Immun., *95:* 1041, 1965.
9. Ishizaka, T., Ishizaka, K., Salmon, S. and Fudenberg, H. H., J. Immun., *99:* 82, 1967.
10. Spiegelberg, H. L., Fishkin, B. G. and Grey, H. M., J. Clin. Invest., *47:* 2323, 1968.
11. Abel, C. A., Spiegelberg, H. L. and Grey, H. M., Biochemistry, *7:* 1271, 1968.

12. McConahey, P. J. and Dixon, F. J., Int. Arch. Allerg., *29:* 185, 1966.
13. Gesner, B. M. and Howard, J. G., in *Handbook of Experimental Immunology*, Edited by D. M. Weir, p. 1009, Blackwell, Oxford, 1967.
14. Mäkelä, O. and Nossal, G. J. V., J. Immun., *87:* 457, 1961.
15. Karnovsky, M. L., in *Biological Activity of the Leucocyte*, Ciba Foundation Study Group No. 10, Edited by G. E. W. Wolstenholme and M. O'Connor, Churchill, London, 1961.
16. Huber, H. and Fudenberg, H. H., Int. Arch. Allerg., *34:* 18, 1968.
17. LoBuglio, A. F., Cotran, R. S. and Jandl, J. H., Science, *158:* 1582, 1967.
18. Herd, Z. L. and Ada, G. L., Austral. J. Exp. Biol. Med. Sci., *47:* 63, 73, 1969.
19. Grey, H. M. and Kunkel, H. G., Biochemistry, *6:* 2326, 1967.
20. Milstein, C., Frangione, B. and Pink, J. R. L., Cold Spring Harbor Symp. Quant. Biol., *32:* 31, 1967.

THE JOURNAL OF IMMUNOLOGY
Vol. 105, No. 2, August 1970
Printed in U.S.A.

INTERRELATIONSHIPS OF TOLERANCE AND IMMUNITY

I. Induction of Immunologic Tolerance in Adult Mice to Bovine γ Globulin Purified *in Vivo*[1,2]

YI-CHI M. KONG AND DONNA L. WIGER

From the Department of Microbiology, Wayne State University School of Medicine, Detroit, Michigan 48207

Received for publication February 6, 1970

Passage of Armour bovine γ globulin (A-BGG) through the circulation of donor mice for 24 hr resulted in a preparation, P-BGG, which was essentially nonimmunogenic in recipient mice at a dose of 0.3 mg except when given in adjuvant. Immunoelectrophoresis of P-BGG against hyperimmune antiserum to A-BGG showed the presence of the major γ component but a lack of the minor fast γ component. P-BGG induced tolerance readily to the major component in adult mice; all mice challenged with P-BGG in Freund's adjuvant showed nonimmune elimination of labeled BGG and most showed either no hemagglutinins or 2-mercaptoethanol (ME)-sensitive antibodies with titers of 1:40 or below. When A-BGG was used for challenge, the hemagglutinins formed were primarily against the contaminant and were mainly ME-sensitive. In contrast, control mice given A-BGG in adjuvant and challenged with either antigen form showed immune elimination and ME-resistant antibodies with titers up to 1:2560. Attempts to prevent the removal of the phagocytizable components in A-BGG by blockade of the reticuloendothelial system with a suppressive dose of Thorotrast were unsuccessful. Pretreatment of donor mice with Thorotrast also did not affect the capacity of P-BGG to induce tolerance in the recipients.

The capacity of a single dose of a protein antigen to induce immunologic tolerance in adult animals may be enhanced markedly by the prior removal of aggregated materials. Among the methods used are ultracentrifugation (1) first reported by Dresser (2), heat-aggregation followed by ultracentrifugation (3), gel-filtration (4) and salt-fractionation (5). Additionally, passage of the antigen through the reticuloendothelial system (RES) of donor animals has been employed (5–8), and this method has aided our understanding of the mechanisms of immunity and tolerance. Frei *et al.* (6) hypothesized that phagocytosis was essential in the induction of the immune response, since the tolerogenicity of bovine serum albumin for rabbits was augmented by passage through the circulation of another rabbit for 48 hr. Recently, Mergenhagen *et al.* (7) also induced tolerance in mice to human γ globulin after *in vivo* processing but others (5) found it necessary to combine ultracentrifugation and *in vivo* passage for certain strains.

Whereas many commercially prepared proteins are relatively pure, certain preparations of bovine γ globulin (BGG), however, are contaminated with a component which is highly antigenic and is thus a complicating factor in the induction and assay of tolerance (3, 8). This paper describes the induction of tolerance in adult mice with a preparation of BGG which is simultaneously cleared of aggregates and freed of contaminants by *in vivo* passage. The attempt to blockade the filtering capacity of the RES of donor mice with Thorotrast (Fellows-Testagar, Detroit, Mich.) is also reported.

MATERIALS AND METHODS

Mice. Female inbred mice of the BALB/c strain were obtained from Cumberland View Farms, Clinton, Tenn., and used at 6 to 8 weeks

[1] This investigation was supported by the United States Public Health Service Grant AI-08076.

[2] Presented, in part, at the 69th Annual Meeting of the American Society of Microbiology, Miami Beach, Florida (Bact. Proc., p. 90, 1969).

of age (17 to 19 g). Potassium iodide (0.1%) was added to their drinking water 48 hr before the injection of a tracer dose of ^{131}I-labeled antigen and was present throughout the assay.

Thorotrast. To produce a blockade of the RES, Thorotrast (lots 14222 and 14882), 24% to 26% thorium dioxide, was given in doses of 25 or 50 mg, i.v or i.v. and i.p., at 6 to 48 hr before the injection of antigen.

Antigen and immune sera. BGG (fraction II of bovine plasma, lot A 30702) was purchased from Armour Pharmaceutical Co., Kankakee, Ill., and was designated A-BGG. For the production of immune sera, A-BGG was dissolved in 0.15 M NaCl (saline) and injected without purification into New Zealand albino rabbits of both sexes. Sera from rabbits given a dose of 30 to 50 mg of A-BGG were pooled and used as a positive serum control in the hemagglutination test. For immunoelectrophoresis and the hemagglutination-inhibition test, hyperimmune sera were obtained 7 days after three more weekly, subcutaneous injections of 10 mg of A-BGG emulsified in complete Freund's adjuvant (Difco Laboratories, Detroit, Mich.) (volume ratio 1:1) and pooled. All normal and immune sera were inactivated at 56°C for 30 min and absorbed with packed sheep erythrocytes at a volume ratio of 3:1 at room temperature for 15 min.

Antigen preparations. All antigens destined for injection into mice were prepared in nonpyrogenic saline (Sherman Laboratories, Detroit, Mich.). A-BGG was passaged *in vivo* essentially according to the method of Frei *et al.* (6). Each of 18 to 23 donor mice was given i.v. 10 mg of A-BGG in 0.2 ml of saline. After 24 hr, blood was collected by decapitation and the sera were harvested within 3 hr and pooled. The antigen remaining in the serum was designated "passaged-BGG" (P-BGG) and 0.1 ml was injected i.v. into recipient mice on the same day. To establish the concentration of P-BGG in this system, a group of 10 mice was given 10 mg of ^{131}I-labeled A-BGG (see below), with a specific activity of 7 to 8 μCi/mg. Individual sera were harvested 24 hr later and their ^{131}I content was determined in a well-type scintillation counter (Nuclear Chicago, model no. 8725). The concentration of P-BGG in the serum was calculated from the amount of radioactivity present and averaged 3 mg/ml. This concentration was compared with the hemagglutination-inhibition test (see below), which consistently gave a somewhat lower value. P-BGG used for the induction of tolerance was not labeled. Its concentration was checked by the hemagglutination-inhibition procedure and its purity by immunoelectrophoresis (9) against a standard hyperimmune serum to A-BGG. To ascertain the antigenicity of P-BGG, a control group of at least five mice was included for each preparation. These mice received the same dose (0.3 mg) of P-BGG emulsified in complete Freund's adjuvant and their antibody responses were measured individually by antigen clearance and/or passive hemagglutination procedures.

A-BGG was purified also *in vitro* with DEAE-cellulose (Carl Schleicher and Schuell Co., Keene, N. H.) by the batch method of Stansworth (10). The last traces of DEAE-cellulose were removed by glass wool filtration. The optical density at 280 nm was determined with a Beckman DB-G spectrophotometer and the protein content was calculated from a standard curve. The purity of this preparation was also checked by immunoelectrophoresis against a standard hyperimmune serum to A-BGG. The purified BGG was dialysed against distilled water at 4°C, lyophilized and stored at −20°C.

A-BGG was labeled with Na^{131}I (Tracerlab, Waltham, Mass.) according to the method of Banerjee and Ekins (11). Inorganic ^{131}I was removed by passage through a Sephadex G-25 column. Radioactivity was determined with a well-type scintillation counter and the protein concentration calculated from a standard curve at 225 nm. Tracer ^{131}I-BGG had a specific activity of 18 to 21 μCi/mg and was diluted in 1% normal mouse serum for injection within 24 hr.

Induction and assay of tolerance. Mice were injected i.v. with 0.3 mg of P-BGG and bled from the ventral artery of the tail on day 12. Depending on the experiment, the challenge was either an i.v. dose of fluid A-BGG or a subcutaneous dose of emulsified A-BGG or P-BGG given on day 12 or 13. Two days after challenge, a tracer dose (5 to 7 $\times 10^5$ CPM) was administered i.v. Blood was collected from the tail vein into preweighed capillary tubes at 1 hr and at 1, 3, 5 and 7 days. The tubes were reweighed and the radioactivity was determined as CPM/g blood. The concentrations of antigen retained in the circulation were expressed as percentages of the 1-hr value, corrected for decay, and were plotted on a semilogarithmic scale against time in days. Control groups given A-BGG or P-BGG in adjuvant and then challenged were treated similarly. Seven days after the tracer dose, mice were decapitated and their sera harvested for titration by passive hemagglutination. In some experiments, only the hemagglutinin response was used to assay the tolerant state.

Passive hemagglutination. A modification of Boyden's method by Stavitsky (12) was adapted to the Microtiter apparatus (Cooke Engineering, Alexandria, Va.). All sera were kept at 4°C and tested within 48 hr of bleeding (the sera of our BALB/c mice contain no Forssman antibody). Antibody sensitivity to 2-mercaptoethanol (ME) (Eastman Kodak Co., Rochester, N. Y.) was carried out in parallel at a serum dilution of 1:5. After 2 hr of incubation at room temperature in a humidified chamber, all ME-treated and untreated serum samples were serially diluted. Sheep erythrocytes, coated with A-BGG or BGG purified *in vitro,* were then added and the endpoints determined 2 hr later. To simplify the tabulation of hemagglutinin titers, the negative sera in each group were presented in one column and the positive sera in the animals remaining in the groups were placed in columns showing ranges of titers from 1:10 to 1:80 up to ⩾1:1280. Although the exact titer of each serum is not shown by this method, differences in response to antigen among various groups are readily discernible.

The hemagglutination-inhibition test was used to verify the concentration of P-BGG calculated from the ^{131}I content. Duplicate series of standard hyperimmune rabbit antiserum to A-BGG (hemagglutinin titer of 20,000) were prepared in dilutions of 1:640 to 1:10,000 in phosphate buffer saline (pH 7.2) containing 1:100 normal rabbit serum. To one series of dilution, 8 to 60 μg of BGG purified *in vitro* were added; to the other, dilutions of P-BGG were added. After 30 min of incubation at room temperature, erythrocytes sensitized with purified BGG were added and the tubes were incubated for another 2 hr. The concentration of P-BGG was determined by comparing its inhibition patterns with those of known concentrations of purified BGG.

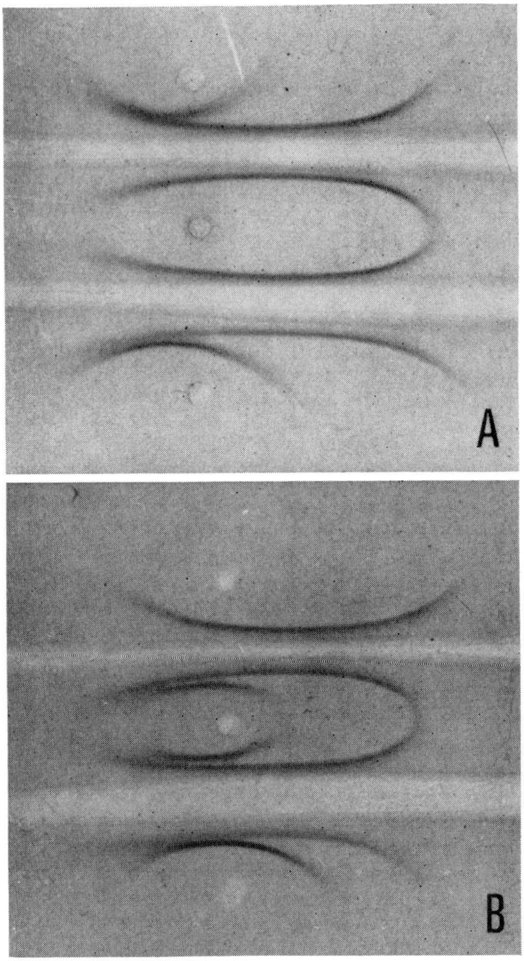

Figure 1. Immunoelectrophoresis of BGG purfied *in vivo* and *in vitro* against hypermmune rabbit antiserum to A(Armour)-BGG, showing the absence of the fast γ component in both purified preparations. *A, center well,* BGG passaged *in vivo* at 3 mg/ml; *top and bottom wells,* A-BGG at 3 and 10 mg/ml, respectively. *B, top well,* BGG purified with DEAE-cellulose; *center well,* A-BGG; *bottom well,* BGG eluted from DEAE-cellulose (1 M NaCl); all at a concentration of 8 mg/ml.

RESULTS

Antigenicity of P-BGG. As seen in Figure 1*A*, after passage of 10 mg of A-BGG *in vivo* for 24 hr, the resultant preparation, P-BGG, showed the presence of the major γG component but not the minor fast γ component readily detectable in A-BGG by immunoelectrophoresis. Thus, passage of A-BGG through the RES resulted in the loss of the contaminating globulin; this contaminant resembled the γA component (1) or the β component (3) described by other workers. P-BGG was comparable to the BGG purified *in vitro* with DEAE-cellulose (Fig. 1*B*); the fast γ component had been removed by the absorbent

TABLE I

Antigenicity of P-BGG[a] for mice

Antigen Dose	No. Positive/Total Hemagglutinin titer (day 12) <10	 20–80	 160–640
A-BGG 1 mg i.v.	1/12	3/12	8/12
P-BGG in complete Freund's adjuvant s.c.		2/12	10/12
A-BGG 0.3 mg i.v.	5/11	6/11	
P-BGG i.v.	18/20	2/20	

[a] Concentration, 0.3 mg in 0.1 ml serum pooled from mice which had received 10 mg of A(Armour)-BGG i.v. 24 hr previously.

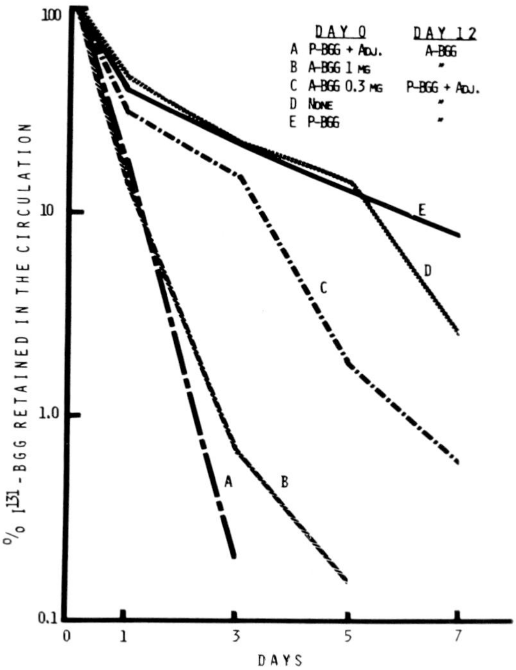

Figure 2. Effect of an i.v. dose of 0.3 mg of P-BGG on the elimination of ^{131}I-BGG from the circulation of mice challenged with 0.3 mg of P-BGG in complete Freund's adjuvant. The tracer dose was given 2 days after challenge and the median values for individual groups were plotted (see Table II for other details).

but could be eluted in a buffer containing 1 M NaCl.

The antigenicity of P-BGG for BALB/c mice was next determined. Compared to A-BGG which induced hemagglutinin titers of 1:160 to 1:640 and 1:20 to 1:80 in doses of 1 mg and 0.3 mg, respectively (Table I), P-BGG, at a concentration of 0.3 mg, was essentially nonimmunogenic; the sera from 18 of 20 mice were negative at a dilution of 1:10. P-BGG was antigenic when given in complete Freund's adjuvant, however; 10 of 12 mice showed titers of 1:160 to 1:640. In other trials, the antigenicity of P-BGG was not increased by doubling the dose to 0.6 mg (0.2 ml).

Induction of tolerance with P-BGG. The capacity of P-BGG to induce tolerance is shown in Figure 2 and Table II. In Figure 2, the median values from some groups of animals are plotted to illustrate that the type of antigen elimination observed depended upon the treatment. A 0.3-mg dose of P-BGG emulsified in adjuvant (group A) was as immunogenic as 1 mg of A-BGG (group B); both groups showed an immune elimination rate typical of a secondary response after reexposure to antigen. The use of adjuvant in the challenge was unnecessary. On the other hand, a single dose of emulsified P-BGG without challenge (group D) induced in mice an antigen clearance rate typical of a primary response. In contrast, 0.3 mg of P-BGG without adjuvant rendered the animals in group E tolerant to a challenge dose of P-BGG in adjuvant. Neither a primary nor a secondary response was observed and the nonimmune elimination rate was identical to that in mice given the tracer dose alone (not presented). Furthermore, 0.3 mg of A-BGG (group C), less immunogenic than 1 mg of A-BGG or emulsified P-BGG, was evidently less tolerogenic than the same dose of P-BGG. As seen in Table II, only 7 of 15 mice in the two groups which had received 0.3 mg of A-BGG and were challenged with A-BGG or P-BGG in adjuvant showed nonimmune elimination, whereas all of 9 mice in the P-BGG-treated group were tolerant.

Presented in Table II also are the hemagglutinin titers of individual mice. In general, the hemagglutinin response corresponded to the animal's immune status as reflected by antigen elimination, and, in most control mice, the antibodies were ME-resistant. However, low hemagglutinin titers (1:10 to 1:80) were observed in many animals treated with P-BGG and challenged with P-BGG in adjuvant. Thus, mice considered tolerant by the criterion of antigen clearance may show low levels of hemagglutinins.

TABLE II

Induction of tolerance with P-BGG[a] in mice

Antigen Dose		No. Positive/Total					^{131}I-BGG Elimination[b]	
		2-Mercaptoethanol treatment	Hemagglutinin titer (day 21)					
Day 0	Day 12		<10	10–80	160–640	≥1280	Non-immune	Immune
A-BGG 1 mg i.v.	A-BGG 1 mg i.v.	−			8/12	4/12		2/12
		+		4/12	7/12	1/12		
P-BGG in complete Freund's adjuvant s.c.	A-BGG 1 mg i.v.	−		1/10	5/10	4/10		10/10
		+	1/10		7/10	2/10		
A-BGG 0.3 mg i.v.	A-BGG 1 mg i.v.	−		6/10	4/10		6/9	3/9
		+	4/10	3/10	3/10			
A-BGG 0.3 mg i.v.	P-BGG in complete Freund's adjuvant s.c.	−		2/7	5/7		1/6	5/6
		+	1/7	3/7	3/7			
P-BGG i.v.	P-BGG in complete Freund's adjuvant s.c.	−		7/9	2/9		9/9	
		+	6/9	1/9	2/9			

[a] Concentration, 0.3 mg in 0.1 ml serum pooled from mice which had received 10 mg of A(Armour)-BGG i.v. 24 hr previously.

[b] Tracer dose was given i.v. on day 14.

However, in contrast to mice primed with A-BGG and challenged similarly, most of the antibodies were ME-sensitive.

Effect of challenge with A-BGG on tolerance to P-BGG. In Table III, a comparison of challenge with A-BGG or P-BGG was made in mice treated with P-BGG. As shown above, low hemagglutinin titers (usually 1:40 or below) were obtained in 6 of 12 mice after challenge with emulsified P-BGG (Experiments 1 and 2), and 5 of the 6 had ME-sensitive antibodies. When emulsified A-BGG (Experiment 1) or fluid A-BGG (Experiment 2) was used for challenge, hemagglutinins were detected in all 12 animals and the titers were relatively high. However, 9 of 11 mice tested also had ME-sensitive antibodies. Thus, compared to P-BGG-challenged mice, a sizable portion of the antibodies in the A-BGG-challenged mice was attributable to the fast γ component in the A-BGG. Indeed, in experiments not presented here, the hemagglutinin titers in mice challenged with A-BGG were reduced markedly when titrated with erythrocytes coated with BGG lacking the fast γ component (Fig. 1*B*) instead of with A-BGG.

Induction of tolerance with P-BGG from Thorotrast-treated mice. Since filtering an immunogenic preparation of A-BGG through the RES for only 24 hr resulted in a highly tolerogenic preparation, the participation of macrophages was indirectly implicated in the initiation of an immune response, as has been suggested by Frie *et al.* (6) and others (see 13). We therefore attempted to interfere with the removal of the phagocytizable substances in A-BGG by blockade of the RES with Thorotrast, using the fast γ component as an indicator of the effectiveness of the blockade.

To determine initially whether Thorotrast was capable of suppressing the hemagglutinin response in mice to A-BGG, 25 or 50 mg of Thorotrast were given i.v. or i.v. and i.p. 6 to 48 hr before an intravenous dose of 1.5 mg of A-BGG. The animals were bled on days 7 and 10 and their hemagglutinin titers were determined. Antibody formation was actually enhanced when Thorotrast was given 6 hr before antigen. However,

TABLE III

Effect of challenge with A-BGG on the response of mice made tolerant with P-BGG[a]

Exp. No.	Antigen Dose (day 0)	No. Positive/Total: 2-Mercaptoethanol treatment	Hemagglutinin titer (day 12): <10	Hemagglutinin titer (day 12): 10–80	Hemagglutinin titer (day 12): 160	Antigen Dose (day 13)	No. Positive/Total: 2-Mercaptoethanol treatment	Hemagglutinin titer (day 23): <10	Hemagglutinin titer (day 23): 10–80	Hemagglutinin titer (day 23): 160–320
1	P-BGG i.v.	−	3/6	3/6		A-BGG 1 mg in complete Freund's adjuvant s.c.	−		1/6	5/6
		+	6/6				+	4/5	1/5	
	P-BGG i.v.	−		6/6		P-BGG in complete Freund's adjuvant s.c.	−	1/6	5/6	
		+	6/6				+	5/6	1/6	
	P-BGG in complete Freund's adjuvant s.c.	−		5/6	1/6					
		+	6/6							
						P-BGG in complete Freund's adjuvant s.c.	−		1/5	4/5
							+		5/5	
2	P-BGG i.v.	−	5/6	1/6		A-BGG 1 mg i.v.	−		6/6	
		+	6/6				+	5/6	1/6	
	P-BGG i.v.	−	6/6			P-BGG in complete Freund's adjuvant s.c.	−	5/6	1/6	
		+	6/6				+	6/6		
	P-BGG in complete Freund's adjuvant s.c.	−		5/6	1/6					
		+	1/6	4/6	1/6					
						P-BGG i.v.	−	5/6	1/6	
							+	6/6		

[a] Concentration, 0.3 mg in 0.1 ml serum pooled from mice given 10 mg of A(Armour)-BGG i.v. 24 hr previously.

suppression was frequently observed when Thorotrast was given 9 to 18 hr before antigen and, most consistently, when 50 mg was administered 15 or 18 hr before antigen (Table IV). The 15- and 18-hr intervals were therefore chosen to attempt a blockade of the RES in donor mice of P-BGG.

Donor mice were given 50 mg of Thorotrast 15 or 18 hr before 10 mg of A-BGG and bled 24 hr after antigen administration. The P-BGG thus obtained was assayed for purity by immunoelectrophoresis and for tolerogenicity by injection into recipient mice. As shown in a representative sample in Figure 3, no difference between the P-BGG from Thorotrast-treated mice and that from untreated mice was detected by immunoelectrophoresis. Thus, Thorotrast given 15 or 18 hr before A-BGG did not prevent the removal of the fast γ component by the RES within 24 hr.

Thorotrast treatment also did not affect the capacity of P-BGG to induce tolerance. Table V shows that both P-BGG from untreated and Thorotrast-treated mice were very weakly antigenic, as primary hemagglutinins were few or absent. After challenge with P-BGG in adjuvant, antibodies were still low or absent in recipients of either preparation of P-BGG and, as noted before, these antibodies were ME-sensitive. When the animals were challenged with A-BGG in adjuvant, antibody titers of 1:160 to 1:640 were again observed in most of the animals. As noted earlier in Table III, these hemagglutinins were

TABLE IV

Effect of Thorotrast on the hemagglutinin response to A-BGG in mice

Thorotrast[a] Treatment	Antibody Titer (Day 7)	
	Experiment 1	Experiment 2
None	40	80
	40	80
	160	160
	160	160
	320	160
	320	320
15 hr before antigen	20	40
	20	80
	20	80
	20	80
	20	160
	80	
18 hr before antigen	<10	10
	40	20
	40	40
	40	40
	40	40
	40	80

[a] Thorotrast was given in two doses of 25 mg i.v. and i.p. prior to an i.v. injection of 1.5 mg of A(Armour)-BGG.

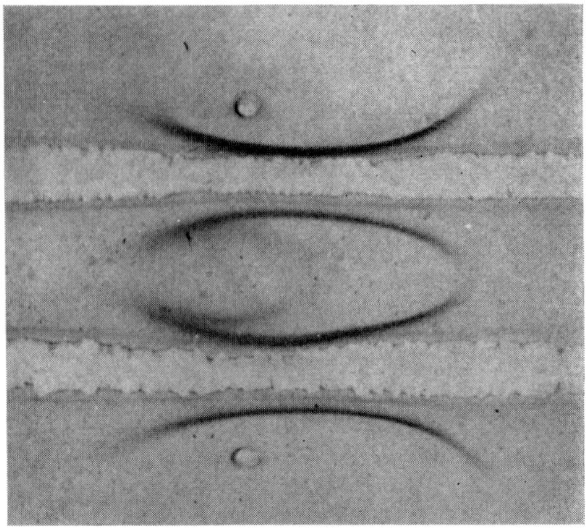

Figure 3. Immunoelectrophoresis of P-BGG passaged in Thorotrast-treated or untreated mice against hyperimmune rabbit antiserum to Armour-BGG, showing the absence of the fast γ component in both preparations (3 mg/ml). *Center well,* Armour-BGG; *top and bottom wells,* respectively, P-BGG from mice given two 25-mg doses of Thorotrast i.v. and i.p. 15 hr earlier and P-BGG from untreated mice.

ME-sensitive and were directed primarily against the fast γ component, since their titers could be reduced markedly by coating erythrocytes with BGG purified *in vitro*.

DISCUSSION

The above studies showed that P-BGG, purified by *in vivo* passage of A-BGG through the circulation of donor mice for 24 hr, no longer contained the fast γ component normally detectable in A-BGG (Fig. 1) and that it readily induced tolerance to the γG component in BALB/c mice (Fig. 2, Table II). The fast γ contaminant was also removed by *in vitro* fractionation with DEAE-cellulose (Fig. 1) as shown by others (1, 3), but not by passage through Sephadex G-200 or centrifugation at 100,000 × G for 60 min (unpublished data). The ineffectiveness of ultracentrifugation in removing the fast γ component may be reflected by the inability of others (14) to induce tolerance in certain mouse strains with centrifuged A-BGG unless high doses (9 or 24 mg) were used, particularly since this minor component interfered with the induction and/or assay of tolerance in BALB/c mice (Tables III and V) as well as in CBA mice (1) and rats (3). An additional explanation had been offered earlier by Golub and Weigle (5) that the BALB/c strain might have a higher capacity than other strains to "handle" antigens containing small amounts of aggregates.

Since P-BGG and similarly prepared HGG (7) were highly tolerogenic in BALB/c mice, and since the fast γ component, removed by the RES within 24 hr, was relatively antigenic, our findings support the hypothesis of Frei *et al.* (6) that phagocytosis is a primary step in the induction of an immune response. The rapid uptake of antigenic HGG aggregates within 4 hr by the spleen of rabbits has also been shown recently (15). On the other hand, as summarized by Leskowitz (13), a soluble antigen is tolerogenic since it is not easily phagocytized and presumably can reach the antigen-sensitive cells without processing by the macrophages. At present, there is some evidence pointing to the importance of the macrophages in the immune responses (16) and, although the induction of tolerance requires approximately 4 days for completion (2, 17), evi-

TABLE V

Induction of tolerance with P-BGG[a] from Thorotrast-treated mice

Treatment of P-BGG Donor	Antigen Dose (day 0)	Average Hemagglutinin Titer (day 12)	Antigen Dose (day 13)	No. Positive/Total: 2-Mercaptoethanol treatment	Hemagglutinin titer (day 23): <10	10–80	160–640
None	P-BGG i.v.	<30	A-BGG 1 mg in complete Freund's adjuvant s.c.	−			6/6
				+	6/6		
None	P-BGG i.v.	<20	P-BGG in complete Freund's adjuvant s.c.	−	2/6	4/6	
				+	6/6		
None	P-BGG in complete Freund's adjuvant s.c.	110					
Thorotrast[b]	P-BGG i.v.	10	A-BGG 1 mg in complete Freund's adjuvant s.c.	−	1/6	1/6	4/6
				+	6/6		
Thorotrast	P-BGG i.v.	10	P-BGG in complete Freund's adjuvant s.c.	−	1/6	5/6	
				+	6/6		
Thorotrast	P-BGG in complete Freund's adjuvant s.c.	145					

[a] P-BGG, 0.3 mg, was obtained from mice given 10 mg of A(Armour)-BGG 24 hr previously.

[b] Thorotrast was given in two doses of 25 mg i.v. and i.p. 15 hr before the i.v. injection of 10 mg of A-BGG.

dence pointing to the direct involvement of lymphocytes in the induction is lacking.

To determine whether passage of BGG in donor mice with an inpaired macrophage function would render it immunogenic rather than tolerogenic, we used Thorotrast to interfere with the removal of phagocytizable substances in A-BGG and the fast γ contaminat as an indicator of the effectiveness of the blockade. Although suppression of the immune response to the nonparticulate antigen was observed by giving Thorotrast 15 or 18 hr before A-BGG (Table IV), P-BGG prepared in Thorotrast-treated mice also did not contain detectable contaminant (Fig. 3) and was as tolerogenic as the P-BGG from untreated donors (Table V). It is possible that interference with the clearance of a 10-mg dose of antigen by Thorotrast requires a shorter time interval than the 15 hr used, but we have repeatedly found that an interval of less than 12 hr enhanced the immune response even to lower doses of A-BGG. It is likely, however, that a single dose of Thorotrast was insufficient to saturate the RES and that small amounts of the contaminant and aggregates were still removed by the unoccupied macrophages in preference to the soluble antigen. As reported recently by Cruchaud (18), overloading of the RES to suppress antibody formation to protein antigens was dificult and required multiple and near-toxic doses of various blockading agents.

The procedures used in the assay of tolerance require some comment because they may vary in sensitivity. As seen in Table II, seven of nine mice considered tolerant by the criterion of non-immune elimination showed low hemagglutinin levels (1:10 to 1:80). Most of the antibodies and those presented subsequently (Tables III and V) were ME-sensitive. However, in two of the nine animals (Table II), the hemagglutinins were ME-resistant. These results indicate the relative sensitivity of the hemagglutination test and the possibility that an undetectable trace amount of the fast γ contaminant was present in both the first and second P-BGG preparations. In this and other experiments (Tables III and V), the ME-sensitive titers were markedly reduced by using BGG, purified with DEAE-cellulose (Fig. 1), to sensitize the sheep erythrocytes. Thus, the ME-sensitive antibodies observed also after challenge with emulsified P-BGG could be due to a primary antibody response to the fast γ component (3). Alternatively, some of the hemagglutinins might be directed toward the γG component; the soluble BGG might have selectively inhibited 7S antibody formation as suggested by Borel *et al.* (19). However, our findings and theirs are not directly comparable, since they employed centrifuged A-BGG which might have contained the antigenic contaminat and three daily doses were given to rabbits in contrast to the single dose used here. At present, it is not known whether the low levels of ME-sensitive antibodies reflected incomplete tolerance in these animals.

Acknowledgment. The authors are indebted to Mrs. Susan Van Hoeck for her competent technical assistance.

REFERENCES

1. Dresser, D. W. and Mitchison, N. A., in *Advances in Immunology*, Edited by F. J. Dixon and H. G. Kunkel, Vol. 8, p. 129, Academic Press, New York, 1968.
2. Dresser, D. W., Immunology, *5:* 378, 1962.
3. Gery, I. and Waksman, B. H., J. Immun., *98:* 446, 1967.
4. Frei, P. C., Cruchaud, S., Arnaudo, L. and Vannotti, A., J. Immun., *101:* 605, 1968.
5. Golub, E. S. and Weigle, W. O., J. Immun., *102:* 389, 1969.
6. Frei, P. C., Benacerraf, B. and Thorbecke, G. J., Proc. Nat. Acad. Sci., *53:* 20, 1965.
7. Mergenhagen, S. E., Notkins, A. L. and Dougherty, S. F., J. Immun., *99:* 576, 1967.
8. Dresser, D. W., Immunology, *6:* 345, 1963.
9. Scheidegger, J. J., Int. Arch. Allerg., *7:* 103, 1955.
10. Stansworth, D. R., Nature, *188:* 156, 1960.
11. Banerjee, R. N. and Ekins, R. P., Nature, *192:* 746, 1961.
12. Stavitsky, A. B., J. Immun., *72:* 360, 1954.
13. Leskowitz, S., Ann. Rev. Microbiol., *21:* 157, 1967.
14. Staples, P. J. and Talal, N., J. Exp. Med., *129:* 123, 1969.
15. Biro, C. E. and Garcia, G., Immunology, *8:* 411, 1965.
16. Pinchuck, P., Fishman, M., Adler, F. L. and Maurer, P. H., Science, *160:* 194, 1968.
17. Golub, E. S. and Weigle, W. O., J. Immun., *99:* 624, 1967.
18. Cruchaud, A., Lab. Invest., *19:* 15, 1968.
19. Borel, Y., Franklin, E. C. and Miescher, P. A., Immunology, *14:* 899, 1968.

THE JOURNAL OF IMMUNOLOGY

Vol. 105, No. 2, Aug. 1970
Printed in U.S.A.

QUANTITATIVE AND QUALITATIVE STUDIES OF ANTIBODY TO STREPTOCOCCAL M-PROTEIN[1]

BASCOM F. ANTHONY[2]

From the Division of Allergy and Immunology, Scripps Clinic and Research Foundation, La Jolla, California, and the Department of Pediatrics, University of Minnesota Medical School, Minneapolis, Minnesota

Received for publication January 31, 1970

Rabbit antibody to group A streptococcal M-protein was measured by incubating dilutions of unabsorbed serum with partially purified and ^{131}I-labeled M-protein from a type 12 strain (^{131}I-M12) and coprecipitating the resulting complexes with anti-rabbit γ globulin. The method was found to be sensitive, quantitative and reproducible, but no antigen preparations, all of which were purified from acid extracts of cell walls, were found to be free of significant reaction with heterologous, unabsorbed antisera. This limitation was overcome by preincubating serum with an excess of unlabeled type 6 antigen; heterologous sera so treated subsequently reacted with ^{131}I-M12 in a manner indistinguishable from normal rabbit serum (NRS). The specificity of the homologous reaction was indicated by its complete inhibition when serum was preincubated with unlabeled type 12 antigen and lack of inhibition with type 6 antigen. Significant binding of ^{131}I-M12 was measurable with all type 12 sera examined and was present in early sera (20 days) which lacked detectable precipitating antibody and also in sera with insignificant or equivocal bactericidal activity. There was generally a linear relationship between the antigen-binding and precipitating capacity of different sera but a definite correlation between antigen-binding capacity and bactericidal activity of individual sera was not apparent. On indirect radio-immunoelectrophoresis, binding of ^{131}I-M12 was observed only with IgG.

The existing state of knowledge concerning immunity to the M-proteins of group A streptococci has been reviewed (1). Despite the practical usefulness of artificially induced rabbit precipitins in the serotyping of group A streptococcal isolates and the significant protective function of naturally induced human antibody, little detailed knowledge of antibody to M-protein is available for either species, primarily because of difficulties in measuring and studying type-specific streptococcal antibody.

The present investigation was undertaken in an attempt to develop techniques which might be useful in the quantitative and qualitative study of antibody to M-protein. This report describes studies of the interaction between partially purified and ^{131}I-labeled M-protein of type 12 and unabsorbed rabbit anti-streptococcal serum.

MATERIALS AND METHODS

Streptococcal strains. Group A streptococci used are listed in Table I. Most strains were fresh clinical isolates from the University of Minnesota or were from the collection of Dr. Rebecca Lancefield. All were maintained in the lyophilized state. One of each type was used in vaccine preparation, including strain 18341 (type 12). During the course of these studies, however, this strain no longer reacted strongly in precipitin tests against type 12 serum from the National Communicable Disease Center and strain 8533 was used for most preparations of

[1] This work was supported by Research Grant AI-2E-214 from the National Institutes of Health, United States Public Health Service.

[2] Recipient of a Research Career Development Award from the National Institute of Allergy and Infectious Diseases. Present address: Department of Pediatrics, University of California at Los Angeles School of Medicine, Harbor General Hospital, Torrance, California 90509.

TABLE I

Group A streptococci used in this investigation

Designation	M-Type	Source
18357	6	Minnesota
18341	12	Minnesota
8533	12	Minnesota
41448	12	Colindale
3185	49	Minnesota
B930/34/5	3	Rockefeller
T5B/90/3	5	Rockefeller
T13/51/6	13	Rockefeller
T14/46/4	14	Rockefeller
C107/24/6	33	Rockefeller
C101/2/5	41	Rockefeller

type 12 M-protein. Strain 41448, provided by Mr. W. R. Maxted, was superior to the other type 12 streptococci with respect to growth in human blood and was used in the indirect bactericidal test. All other strains were kindly provided by Dr. S. S. Chapman.

Preparation of antiserum. New Zealand rabbits were immunized intravenously by Lancefield's method as described by Moody (2) with heat-killed streptococci of type 6, 12 or 49. Serum was collected at 20-day intervals and stored at −10°C in sterile lots, which were thawed at the time of testing. After the collection of all serum to be tested, several animals immunized with type 12 received three additional injections and were bled 1 week later; these hyperimmune sera were combined to provide a sufficient pool of type 12 serum to standardize the quantitative tests.

Several rabbits received a pooled vaccine of types 3, 5, 13, 14, 33 and 41 streptococci, each grown, washed and heat-killed separately. The suspensions were combined to provide the usual concentration of streptococci for immunization (2). Sera were set up in capillary tubes against acid extracts of all six vaccine strains. These extracts had been precipitated four times with ethanol to remove group A carbohydrate (3). Two months of injections were required before sera from these animals gave strong precipitin reactions with all six extracts refined by alcohol precipitation.

Normal rabbit serum (NRS), unless specified otherwise, consisted of pooled serum from adult animals obtained commercially (Pel-Freez Biologicals, Inc., Rogers, Ark.).

Preparation of M-protein. Partially purified M-protein was prepared by modifications of the methods of Lancefield and Perlmann (4) and of Fox and Wittner (5). A lyophilized culture was inoculated into 10 ml of Todd-Hewitt broth (Difco Laboratories, Inc., Detroit, Mich.). After incubation overnight at 37°C, this was transferred to 500 ml of the same medium for overnight growth. The sediment of this culture was used to inoculated 40 liters of Todd-Hewitt broth supplemented with glucose, $NaHCO_3$ and Na_2HPO_4 (6). After 18 hr of growth, streptococci were harvested with an RC-2B refrigerated centrifuge and continuous-flow apparatus (Ivan Sorvall, Inc., Norwalk, Conn.). The cells were washed three times in phosphate-buffered saline (PBS, consisting of 0.15 M NaCl and 0.1 M K_2HPO_4/KH_2PO_4 pH 7.0) and lysed in 40-ml lots by shaking with glass beads in a Braun homogenizer (Bronwill Scientific, Inc., Rochester, N. Y.) cooled by liquid CO_2. Cell breakage was monitored by phase microscopy. Glass beads were removed by coarse sintered-glass filtration and the cell walls were isolated by differential centrifugation (7). A 10% suspension (w/v) of cell walls in PBS was treated with 22.5 units/ml of RNAse-T_1 (Worthington Biochemical Corporation, Freehold, N. J.) for 4 hr at 37°C and RNAse was removed by centrifugation and washing (three times). To a 25% suspension of cell walls, 1 N HCl was added until the pH reached 2.0. This was immediately placed in a boiling water bath and held at 90° to 95°C for 10 min. The suspension was cooled in ice and the pH adjusted to 7.0 with 1 N NaOH. The cell walls were separated by centrifugation and again boiled in acid and the two acid extracts combined. Subsequent procedures were performed at 4°C. At pH 7.0, $(NH_4)_2SO_4$ was added slowly with stirring to 33% saturation and, after 30 min, the scanty precipitate was removed. The pH was readjusted to 8.0 and more $(NH_4)_2SO_4$ was added to 60% saturation. After 2 hr, the resulting precipitate was separated, taken up in 5 ml distilled water, dialyzed for 36 hr against three changes of distilled water and lyophilized.

The $(NH_4)_2SO_4$ preparation was further fractionated at room temperature by ultramembrane filtration (Amicon Corporation, Lexington, Mass.). PBS (usually 50 ml) containing 1 mg/ml was filtered through an XM-50 membrane until the latter was almost dry. The membrane was washed in place in the filtration cell with PBS (usually 20 ml) and the retained material (m.w.

> 50,000) designated "50 R." In early experiments, the filtrate was subsequently put through a UM-10 membrane, which was similarly washed for the "10R" fraction (m.w. > 10,000), and the second filtrate was designated "10F."

Alternatively, the $(NH_4)_2SO_4$ preparation was fractionated on carboxymethylcellulose (CMC) as described by Fox and Wittner (5). The protein peak eluted around pH 6.0 with phosphate buffer was saved for further study.

Isotopic labeling and nitrogen determinations. "50R" preparations of M-protein were trace-labeled with ^{131}I by a previously described method (8). For preliminary evaluation of antigenicity, $(NH_4)_2SO_4$ and CMC preparations were also labeled. Nitrogen determinations were performed by a micro-Kjeldahl technique (9).

Preparation of anti-rabbit γ globulin (anti-RGG). Adult female sheep were immunized with rabbit IgG, prepared from NRS by diethylaminoethyl (DEAE)-cellulose chromatography (10, 11). Approximately 12 mg of the first eluted protein peak (DEAE-1) was mixed with complete Freund's adjuvant and injected subcutaneously monthly for 6 to 8 months. The amount of serum required to precipitate all radioactivity in 0.5 ml of 1:10 NRS containing trace amounts of ^{131}I-DEAE-1 was determined (12).

Quantitative measurement of antigen-binding by rabbit serum. Because of the insolubility in 50% saturated $(NH_4)_2SO_4$ of all M-protein preparations examined, this reagent could not be used to precipitate immune complexes, but serum and antigen protein diluents and dilution schemes were similar to those used in the Farr technique (13). Rather, a coprecipitation technique similar to that described by Feinberg (14) was used. Unabsorbed immune rabbit serum was diluted 1:10 in PBS containing 0.005 N KI (PBS-KI) and further 1:5 dilutions were made in 1:10 NRS in PBS-KI. For inhibition studies, 0.5 ml of unlabeled streptococcal antigen diluted in 1% NRS (in PBS-KI) was added to 0.5 ml of serum dilutions in duplicate 10- x 75-mm tubes. Corresponding control tubes of serum received 0.5 ml of 1% NRS. After overnight incubation at 4°C, 0.5 ml of labeled antigen in 1% NRS in PBS-KI (0.02 γN, unless otherwise stated) was added to the serum tubes. The following day, 0.3 to 0.5 ml of anti-RGG, a volume in excess of that required to precipitate all IgG in 0.5 ml of 1:10 NRS, was added and the tubes were mixed and incubated at 4°C for 2 hr. The tubes were centrifuged at 1000 × G for 30 min, the precipitates washed once with cold PBS-KI, recentrifuged and counted for radioactivity. The percentage of added radioactive counts contained in immune precipitates was determined.

Quantitative measurement of precipitating antibody. The technique of Talmage and Maurer (15), as adapted by Farr for anti-bovine serum albumin (13), was modified slightly. Serum dilutions with unlabeled and subsequently labeled antigens were set up identically and simultaneously with the antigen-binding determinations. Anti-RGG was omitted and the tubes were incubated for 6 days at 4°C and centrifuged. Radioactivity in the unwashed precipitates was determined.

Immunoelectrophoresis and indirect radio-immunoelectrophoresis. These were done by the method of Scheidegger (16) and of Yagi *et al.* (17), respectively. Microscope slides were coated with 2% Ionagar No. 2 (Colab Laboratories, Inc., Chicago Heights, Ill.) and rabbit serum was placed in the center well for electrophoresis at 40 V for 45 min. Goat antiserum to rabbit whole serum or to rabbit γ globulin (Hyland Laboratories, Los Angeles, Calif.) was applied to both troughs for diffusion for 24 hr. For immunoelectrophoresis, the slides were next washed with saline, dried and stained with azocarmine G. For radio-immunoelectrophoresis, the slides were washed in saline-KI for 48 hr and the troughs filled with radioactive antigen for 24 hr. The slides were washed another 48 hr, dried and overlaid with x-ray film (RS Pan, Eastman Kodak Co., Rochester, N. Y.).

Indirect bactericidal tests. Bactericidal antibody to type 12 streptococci was assayed by the method of Lancefield, using normal human blood as a source of phagocytes (18). The full set of sera from a single rabbit was examined simultaneously and each set was tested at least twice. The results of a test were accepted only when the type 12 strain in the presence of heterologous serum (type 6) and a heterologous strain (type 6) in the presence of test serum (type 12) increased in colonies 64-fold or greater over the inoculum. A serum with known significant bactericidal activity for type 12 was also included as a positive control. For the sake of brevity in presenting these results, the "bactericidal index" was computed according to Stollerman *et al.* (19).

RESULTS

Selection of M-protein preparation for use in quantitative antibody tests. To determine the suitability of various M-protein preparations, appropriate amounts of ^{131}I-labeled antigens were incubated with 1:10 dilutions (antibody excess) of homologous, heterologous and normal rabbit serum (NRS) for coprecipitation with sheep anti-rabbit γ globulin (anti-RGG). In numerous experiments, the radioactivity of $(NH_4)_2SO_4$ preparations was partially bound (25% to 40%) by homologous immune serum, slightly bound (<10%) by RNS and bound to an intermediate degree by heterologous serum. These findings with a type 12 antigen are illustrated in Table II. Ultrafiltration of the $(NH_4)_2SO_4$ preparation removed considerable material (molecular weight < 50,000) which did not combine with immune serum and left a fraction (m.w. > 50,000) which was bound to a significantly greater degree (53%). The XM-50 filtrate (both the fractions retained and filtered by the UM-10 membrane) combined to a minor extent (16% and 7%) with homologous serum.

Several $(NH_4)_2SO_4$ preparations from both type 6 and type 12 were fractionated on carboxymethylcellulose (5) and the protein eluted with phosphate buffer around pH 6.0 was labeled with ^{131}I. When incubated with 1:10 dilutions of type 12 serum, these antigens, like the "50R" fractions from membrane ultrafiltration (Table II), combined to a larger extent than the $(NH_4)_2SO_4$ preparations. However, intermediate reactions with heterologous unabsorbed sera also occurred. Some of these findings are summarized in Table III.

Because membrane ultrafiltration was a simpler technique and a good yield (40% by nitrogen determination) of the starting material was recovered in the "50R" fraction, in the results which follow, ^{131}I-labeled type 12 M-protein (^{131}I-M12) was prepared by membrane ultrafiltration of $(NH_4)_2SO_4$ preparations and subsequent labeling of the "50R" fractions.

Preincubation of unlabeled antigens with homologous serum. To evaluate the specificity of the reaction between unabsorbed type 12 serum and ^{131}I-M12, dilutions of the type 12 standard serum were incubated with 0.02 γN of ^{131}I-M12 to determine antigen binding by coprecipitation (Fig. 1). From these data, a 1:1000 dilution was selected for preincubation with different amounts of unlabeled type 6 and type 12 antigens prior to the addition of ^{131}I-M12. As shown in Figure 2, type 6 antigen even in great excess (>100-fold) over ^{131}I-M12 inhibited the reaction only slightly (<5%), while increasing amounts of type 12 antigen abolished the homologous reaction or at least reduced it to the level of NRS. This indicated that the combination of unabsorbed type 12 serum with ^{131}I-M12 was largely type-specific,

TABLE II

Percentage of radioactivity of different preparations of type 12 M-protein bound by unabsorbed immune and normal rabbit serum (NRS)[a]

Serum	Type 12 Antigen Preparation			
	(NH)$_2$SO$_4$	50R	10R	10F
NRS	6.3	8.0	2.1	1.0
Type 12	26.4	53.2	15.7	6.6
Type 6	13.1	18.7	5.8	2.9

[a] A 33% to 60% $(NH_4)_2SO_4$ precipitate labeled with ^{131}I was fractionated with XM-50 and UM-10 membranes. The unfractionated antigen [$(NH_4)_2SO_4$] and the fractions retained by XM-50(50R) and by UM-10 (10R) and the final filtrate (10F) were all diluted in 1% NRS/PBS-KI to the same approximate N concentration (0.1 γ) and incubated with 1:10 serum dilutions for coprecipitation. (See *Materials and Methods*.)

TABLE III

Percentage of radioactivity of different lots of M-protein prepared by carboxymethylcellulose chromatography bound by unabsorbed immune and normal rabbit serum (NRS)[a]

Serum	Type of M-protein				
	6	12	12	12	12
NRS	16.3	14.0	8.7	7.1	6.1
Type 12[b]	25.7	60.0	65.8	59.4	60.5
Type 12[b]		60.2	63.7		62.7
Type 6	36.5	32.4	39.4	31.7	26.2
Anti-pool[c]					37.1

[a] ^{131}I-labeled antigens were incubated in amounts of 0.02 to 0.1 γN with 1:10 serum dilutions for coprecipitation. (See *Materials and Methods*.)

[b] These sera were from different animals.

[c] This serum was prepared against a mixture of types 3, 5, 13, 14, 33 and 41.

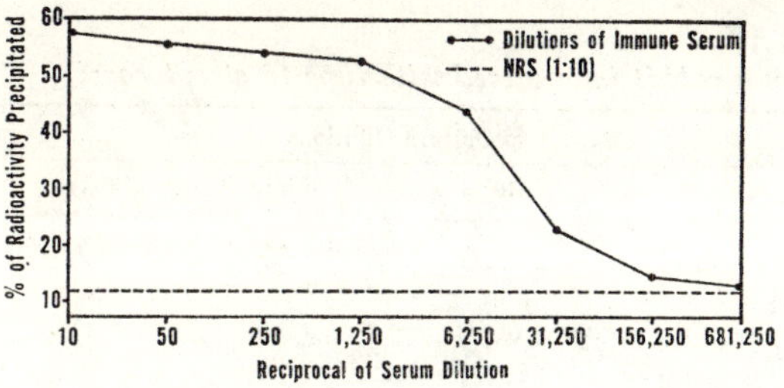

Figure 1. Binding of 0.02 γN of ^{131}I-M12 by dilutions of type 12 standard serum as determined by coprecipitation.

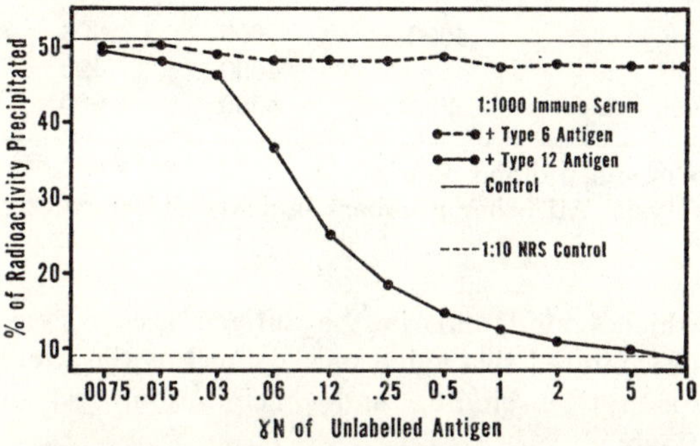

Figure 2. Inhibition of binding of ^{131}I-M12 by 1:1000 dilution of standard serum when latter was preincubated with unlabeled crude type 6 and type 12 antigens ($(NH_4)_2SO_4$ preparations) in 0.5 ml of 1% NRS in PBS-KI. Control sera (1:1000 immune serum and 1:10 NRS) were preincubated with 0.5 ml of 1% NRS.

but the cross-reaction between ^{131}I-M12 and unabsorbed heterologous serum (Table II) and the slight inhibition of the homologous reaction by unlabeled type 6 antigen (Fig. 2) suggested that some homologous binding was nonspecific and related to antigenic groups shared by other streptococcal types.

Preincubation of unlabeled antigen with heterologous sera and NRS. Before the addition of ^{131}I-M12 to several unabsorbed sera against other streptococcal types than 12, these sera were first incubated with unlabeled type 6 antigen. If the cross-reactions with ^{131}I-M12 could be thus eliminated, cross-reacting antibodies in unabsorbed type 12 serum might be similarly inhibited and the binding of ^{131}I-M12 thus rendered more highly specific. As shown in Figure 3, although 1:10 dilutions of heterologous sera in control experiments bound significant amounts of ^{131}I-M12, after preincubation with sufficient type 6 antigen the reaction was indistinguishable from that of NRS. As a result of these experiments, in the measurements of antibody to type 12 M-protein which follow, 10 γN of unlabeled type 6 antigen was added to *all* serum dilutions 1 day before the addition of ^{131}I-M12.

The percentage of radioactivity bound by 1:10 dilutions of NRS was unaffected by preincubation with large amounts of type 6 and type 12 antigen. In addition, while the extent of reaction with 1:10 NRS varied slightly for different "50R" preparations and considerably for antigens prepared by other methods (Tables II and III), it was identical with pooled NRS from adult (>1 year) and from immature animals (8 to 12 weeks) and with individual pre-immune sera. These data

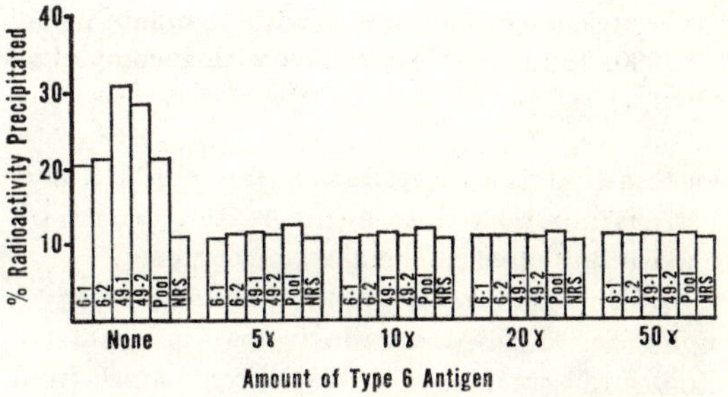

Figure 3. Inhibition of ^{131}I-M12 binding when different amounts (expressed as γN) of crude type 6 antigen were preincubated with 1:10 dilutions of the following unabsorbed heterologous antisera: type 6 (1 and 2), type 49 (1 and 2), anti-pool (types 3, 5, 13, 14, 33 and 41) and NRS.

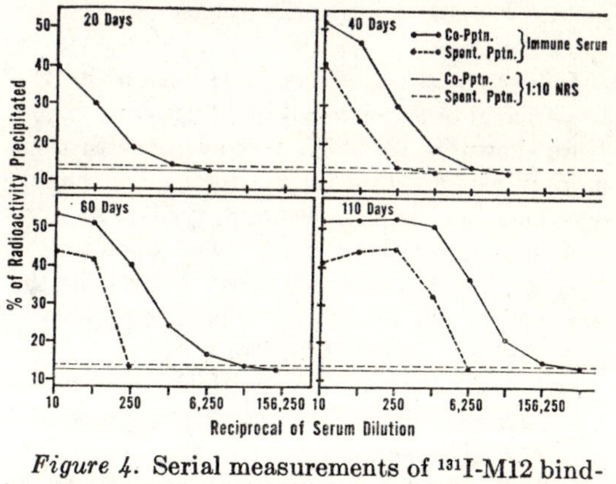

Figure 4. Serial measurements of ^{131}I-M12 binding (by coprecipitation) and precipitins (by spontaneous precipitation) in rabbit 1. All serum dilutions were preincubated with 10 γN of crude type 6 antigen before addition of 0.02 γN of ^{131}I-M12. 1:10 dilutions of pre-immune serum bound essentially the same percentage as 1:10 NRS.

TABLE IV

Indirect bactericidal tests with serial bleedings from a rabbit immunized with type 12 streptococci

Streptococcal Type		Culture Dilutions			
		10^5	$10^5/4$	$10^5/16$	$10^5/64$
12	No. of chains inoculated	159	26	8	2
	No. after incubation with human blood and:				
	Day 40 serum	20	15	10	0
	Day 60 serum	33	3	1	1
	Day 110 serum	77	9	5	2
	Type 6 serum	∞[a]	4000[b]	976	201
6	No. of chains inoculated	195	64	18	11
	No. after incubation with human blood and:				
	Day 40 serum	∞	4000	600	203
	Day 60 serum	∞	∞	4000	490
	Day 110 serum	∞	4000	4000	960

[a] ∞, Innumerable colonies with complete hemolysis of sheep blood pour-plates.

[b] 4000, Innumerable colonies with incomplete hemolysis. All other numbers indicate direct colony counts.

suggest that the reaction between ^{131}I-M12 and NRS is not related to antibody but occurs by some other physico-chemical mechanism.

Serial measurements of antigen-binding and precipitation. Figure 4 illustrates quantitative studies of sera collected at different times from a single animal (rabbit 1). These findings are typical of all serial studies in that no precipitating antibody was demonstrable at 20 days, although measurable amounts of antigen-binding were. Thereafter, precipitins were detectable in quantities roughly parallel to, but in lesser quantity than, total antibody as detected by coprecipitation.

Indirect bactericidal test. The results of the bactericidal test with serial bleedings from rabbit 1 are shown in Table IV. In contrast with their uninhibited growth (>2 log increase in chains over inoculum) in type 6 serum, type 12 streptococci were significantly inhibited or killed by the 40-, 60- and 110-day sera when rotated in the presence of human blood. Type 6 streptococci grew normally in the same sera.

Standardization and reproducibility of quantitative antibody determinations. To express the capacity of a serum to bind and precipitate ^{131}I-M12, an arbitrary endpoint was chosen as the percentage of radioactivity midway between the maximum bound by lower dilutions of the type 12 standard serum (and other hyperimmune sera) and the percentage coprecipitated with NRS. The reciprocal values of serum dilutions which bound and, in the antigen excess zone, precipitated this value were defined as the titers for antigen-binding and precipitation, respectively.

All sera from a single animal were examined simultaneously and each determination included dilutions of the standard serum. As defined above, on repeated testing the endpoint determined with the standard serum varied between 30.7% and 32.9% and the antigen-binding titer of the standard serum between 7000 and 8500. In every instance, a 1:10 dilution of pre-immune serum from the test animal was included and this consistently bound within 1% of the NRS value.

Correlation of antigen-binding, precipitating capacity and indirect bactericidal tests. Titers of ^{131}I-M12 binding and precipitins and bactericidal indices of consecutive sera from four rabbits are summarized in Table V. The bactericidal index of Stollerman *et al.* (19) is used to represent bactericidal activity. This is the ratio between growth in normal or heterologous serum and that in test serum and it has been suggested that an index of less than 25 represents insignificant bactericidal activity (19).

As shown in Table V, levels of antibody to M-protein, as reflected in all three measurements, were greater in rabbits 1 and 2 than in rabbits 3 and 4. This is probably explained in part by additional courses of vaccine given in the 10th and 12th weeks to the first two animals.

When the precipitin and antigen-binding titers

TABLE V

Quantitative measurements of antigen-binding, precipitating and bactericidal antibodies

Rabbit	Day Serum Collected	Antigen-binding Titer[a]	Precipitin Titer[a]	Bactericidal Index[b]
1	20	35	0	Not done
	40	200	25	320 (3+)
	60	500	75	390 (3+)
	110	9,500	1,250	160 (2+)
2	20	<10	0	4 (0)
	60	300	55	20 (0)
	80	15,000	2,100	29 (±)
	110	6,000	1,250	128 (2+)
3	20	35	0	9 (0)
	40	140	152	6 (0)
	60	70	14	12 (0)
	110	40	10	2 (0)
4	20	30	<10	8 (0)
	40	300	27	15 (0)
	60	170	19	12 (0)
	110	65	<10	6 (0)

[a] Derivation of antigen-binding and precipitating titers is explained in text. (See *Results*.)

[b] Bactericidal indices were computed and graded 0 to 4+ as suggested by Stollerman *et al.* (19).

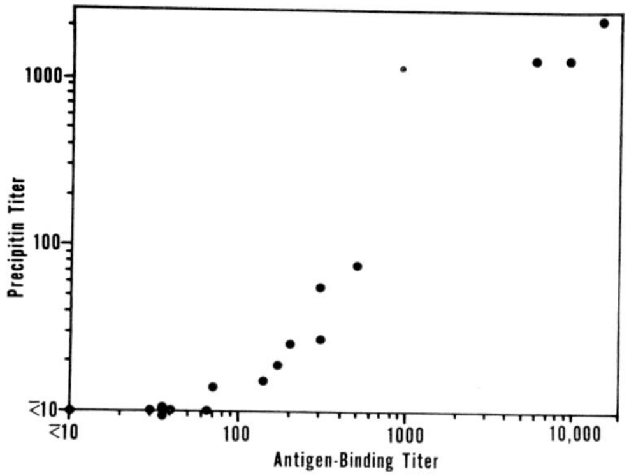

Figure 5. Correlation of individual serum titers for antigen-binding (*horizontal scale*) and precipitation (*vertical scale*) of ^{131}I-M12.

for each serum were plotted on logarithmic scales, there appeared to be a linear relationship between the two values (Fig. 5). Antigen-binding titers below 1:60 were not accompanied by detectable precipitins, while higher values were generally associated with a proportionate precipitating capacity.

Such a linear relationship between antigen-binding and bactericidal indices of individual sera was not as clear. However, the animals developing the highest levels of ^{131}I-M12-binding (rabbits 1 and 2) also gave the most impressive bactericidal results. Also, four of the six sera with antigen-binding titers of 300 or greater had indices of 25 or more, while only one of nine sera with titers below 300 had a bactericidal index this high. Although bactericidal activity was often unimpressive, it should be noted that all type 12 sera examined permitted less growth (bactericidal index of 2 or more) than did the heterologous control serum.

Immunoelectrophoresis and indirect radio-immunoelectrophoresis (*Fig. 6*). When rabbit serum was subjected to electrophoresis and precipitin lines were developed with anti-rabbit serum and anti-rabbit γ globulin, ^{131}I-M12 was bound to the IgG line of immune serum but not to lines developed against pre-immune serum from the same animal (Fig. 6, *A* and *B*). Figure 6*C* confirms the inhibition of binding between immune serum and ^{131}I-M12 by homologous but not by heterologous antigen: preincubation with excess unlabeled type 12 antigen blocked the fixation of radioactivity to the IgG line, whereas preincubation with type 6 did not.

DISCUSSION

Although the significance of the M-antigens of group A streptococci in human disease is clearly established, available methods for measuring type-specific antibodies to M-protein are not fully satisfactory. Biologic manifestations of the combination of antibody with M-protein, as expressed in the indirect bactericidal test (20), mouse-protection (21) and the long-chain reaction (22), are sufficiently specific to be used in the study of unabsorbed serum. None of these tests, however, can be easily quantitated and all are complicated by various technical difficulties. Even the most widely accepted assay of M-protein antibody, the indirect bactericidal technique, is laborious and is subject to both known and unknown variables (19, 23–25). On the other hand, some serologic determinations, such as passive hemagglutination, can be readily quantitated, but careful studies of this technique (26, 27) suggest that it requires prior absorption of

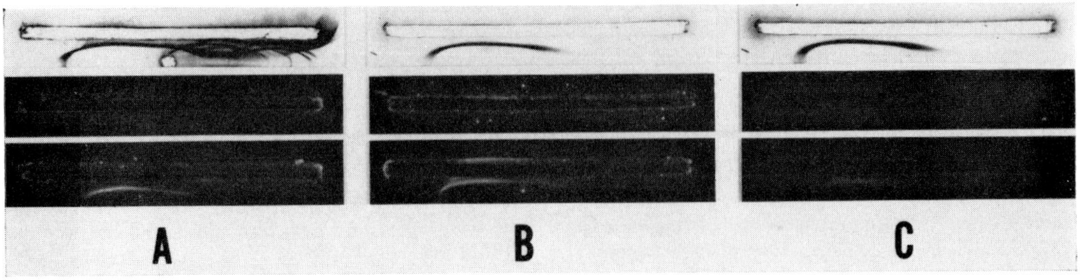

Figure 6. Immunoelectrophoresis (*top*) and radio-immunoelectrophoresis (*center, bottom*) of serum from rabbit 3. *A*, after electrophoresis of immune serum in well, lines were developed with anti-rabbit serum in trough (*top*). Lines were similarly developed with pre-immune serum (*center*) and immune serum (*bottom*) and ^{131}I-M12 was then added to trough for diffusion. *B*, identical to *A*, except lines were developed with anti-rabbit γ globulin. *C*, electrophoresis of immune serum and development of lines as in *B*. In *center*, unlabeled crude type 12 antigen was added before ^{131}I-M12. In *bottom*, type 6 antigen was added before ^{131}I-M12. (See *Materials and Methods*).

test serum, inhibition with soluble heterologous antigen, or the use of highly purified M-protein preparations that are free of measurable cross-reacting antigens.

The above procedures also share the feature that they detect secondary manifestations of the reaction between antigen and antibody. Grey has shown the feasibility of directly measuring this reaction by precipitating complexes formed between absorbed serum and ^{131}I-labeled M-protein with 40% saturated ammonium sulfate (28), a concentration selected because of diminishing solubility of M-protein at the higher concentrations required to precipitate all antibody in rabbit serum (13). The binding of M-protein by rabbit antiserum was found to be accompanied by lower levels of precipitating antibodies, while a human serum which bound ^{131}I-labeled type 12 antigen contained no detectable precipitins (28). The present study of rabbit serum confirms and extends the observations of Grey, but differs in that anti-γ globulin was used to precipitate immune complexes and serum was not absorbed but was preincubated with unlabeled heterologous antigen to inhibit non-type-specific reactions. Conventional adsorption of human serum with whole streptococci has been reported to remove M-antibody, in part or in full (29), and it is hoped that information gained in this study may be useful in the study of human antibody to M-protein.

In sensitive, quantitative measurements of M-antibody, the most serious limitation appears to be the state of purity of antigen preparations. This was evidenced in this study by the 40% to 45% of radioactivity in antigen preparations which could not be coprecipitated with immune serum, and by the reaction between ^{131}I-M12 and heterologous unabsorbed serum. M-proteins isolated and purified by procedures similar to those used here have been reported free of cross-reactions with heterologous unabsorbed sera when tested by double diffusion in agar (5, 6). In the present study, however, all labeled M-preparations cross-reacted with heterologous sera when examined by coprecipitation. Johnson and Vosti have suggested that cross-reactions between similar M-protein preparations and heterologous serum may be demonstrated by hemagglutination when undetected by less sensitive serologic techniques (30). Although true cross-reactions, apparently on the basis of similar or identical groups in the M-protein molecules *per se,* have been reported and confirmed with the indirect bactericidal test (31, 32), the reactions between antigen and heterologous serum described here more likely result from contamination of M-protein by other cell wall constituents and may be unavoidable with hot acid extraction, which presumably disrupts covalent bonds (33, 34). It is conceivable that further purification of M-protein released from cell walls by enzymatic hydrolysis (35–38) might provide alternative and more satisfactory antigen preparations for more sensitive studies of antibody.

Despite these limitations, the technique described here offers a sensitive, quantitative and reproducible measurement of type-specific antibody. The specificity of the coprecipitation determinations was indicated by the identical behavior of normal rabbit serum, pre-immune serum and antiserum to other streptococcal types (when preincubated with unlabeled heterologous antigen) toward ^{131}I-M12 and by specific inhibition with unlabeled homologous antigen. Additional evidence for immunologic specificity was provided by indirect radio-immunoelectrophoresis, in which ^{131}I-M12 was bound only to the IgG line. (Antiserum to rabbit IgA and IgM could not be obtained or successfully prepared.)

An obvious advantage of this technique is the opportunity of determining certain serologic and biologic capacities of antibody to M-protein. Although measurable antigen-binding but no precipitins could be detected in the earliest sera examined (20 days), it was not clear if this was the result of a qualitative peculiarity of early antibody or of a quantitative phenomenon, since later sera demonstrated greater antigen-binding capacities usually associated with detectable and roughly proportionate precipitating antibodies. The relationship of quantitative antigen-binding to bactericidal activity was less striking than to the precipitating capacity. In part, this may reflect difficulties in quantitating the bactericidal test, as described by others (19). The bactericidal index of a particular serum varied rather widely on different occasions, but repeated values of a given serum were consistently above or below 25. Moreover, in general, the animals with the highest antigen-binding levels also demonstrated the most impressive bactericidal effect and the higher titers of ^{131}I-binding were more consistently accompanied by significant bactericidal activity (bactericidal index ≥ 25).

Since most observations on streptococcal type-specific antibody have been based upon serologic and biologic manifestations of the antigen-antibody reaction, it is unknown whether antibody to M-protein may vary in its capacity to express these manifestations. Continued study should indicate whether such variations occur and, if so, some of the practical and biologic consequences.

Acknowledgments. The author wishes to thank Drs. R. S. Farr, R. T. Reid and L. W. Wannamaker for their support and advice, and Dr. U. J. Lewis for his helpful suggestions. Dr. E. N. Fox and Mrs. M. K. Wittner graciously permitted the author to spend a week in their laboratory, learning some of the preparative techniques used in this study. Technical assistance was provided by Mrs. Marjorie Young. Isotopic labeling of antigens was done by Miss Patricia McConahey and nitrogen determinations were performed in the laboratory by Dr. W. O. Weigle.

REFERENCES

1. Lancefield, R. C., J. Immun., *89:* 307, 1962.
2. Moody, M. D., Padula, J., Lizana, D. and Hall, C. T., Health Lab. Sci., *2:* 149, 1965.
3. Lancefield, R. C., J. Exp. Med., *47:* 469, 1928.
4. Lancefield, R. C. and Perlmann, G. E., J. Exp. Med., *96:* 71, 1952.
5. Fox, E. N. and Wittner, M. K., Proc. Nat. Acad. Sci., *54:* 1118, 1965.
6. Fox, E. N., J. Immun., *93:* 826, 1964.
7. Salton, M. R. J. and Horne, R. W., Biochim. Biophys. Acta, *7:* 177, 1951.
8. McConahey, P. J. and Dixon, F. J., Int. Arch. Allerg., *29:* 185, 1966.
9. Ferrari, A., Ann. N. Y. Acad. Sci., *87:* 792, 1960.
10. Sober, H. A., Gutter, F. J., Wyckoff, M. M. and Peterson, E. A., J. Amer. Chem. Soc., *78:* 756, 1956.
11. Reid, R. T., Minden, P. and Farr, R. S., J. Exp. Med., *123:* 845, 1966.
12. Minden, P., Anthony, B. F. and Farr, R. S., J. Immun., *102:* 832, 1969.
13. Farr, R. S., J. Infect. Dis., *103:* 239, 1958.
14. Feinberg, R., Fed. Proc., *13:* 493, 1954.
15. Talmage, D. W. and Maurer, P. H., J. Infect. Dis., *92:* 288, 1953.
16. Scheidegger, J. J., Int. Arch. Allerg., *7:* 103, 1955.
17. Yagi, Y., Maier, P., Pressman, D., Arbesman, C. E. and Reisman, R. E., J. Immun., *91:* 83, 1963.
18. Lancefield, R. C., J. Exp. Med., *106:* 525, 1957.
19. Stollerman, G. H., Kantor, F. S. and Gordon, B. D., J. Exp. Med., *108:* 475, 1958.
20. Rothbard, S., J. Exp. Med., *82:* 93, 1945.
21. Hirst, G. K. and Lancefield, R. C., J. Exp. Med.. *69:* 425, 1939.
22. Stollerman, G. H., Siegel, A. C. and Johnson, E. E., J. Exp. Med., *110:* 887, 1959.
23. Maxted, W. R. Brit. J. Exp. Path., *37:* 415, 1956.
24. Lancefield, R. C., J. Exp. Med., *110:* 271, 1959.
25. Stollerman, G. H., Rytel, M. and Ortiz, J., J. Exp. Med., *117:* 1, 1963.
26. Denny, F. W. and Thomas, L., J. Clin. Invest., *32:* 1085, 1953.
27. Vosti, K. L. and Rantz, L. A., J. Immun., *92:* 185, 1964.

28. Grey, H. M., J. Exp. Med., *115:* 671, 1962.
29. Stollerman, G. H., Arthritis Rheum., *10:* 245, 1967.
30. Johnson, R. H. and Vosti, K. L., J. Immun., *101:* 381, 1968.
31. Wiley, G. G. and Bruno, P. N., J. Exp. Med., *128:* 959, 1968.
32. Wiley, G. G. and Bruno, P. N., J. Immun., *103:* 149, 1969.
33. McCarty, M., *The Streptococcus, Rheumatic Fever and Glomerulonephritis,* Edited by J. W. Uhr, p. 3, Williams and Wilkins Co., Baltimore, 1964.
34. McCarty, M. and Morse, S. I., Advances Immun., *4:* 249, 1964.
35. Maxted, W. R., J. Gen. Microbiol., *16:* 584, 1957.
36. Krause, R. M., J. Exp. Med., *108:* 803, 1958.
37. Kantor, F. S. and Cole, R. M., J. Exp. Med., *112:* 77, 1960.
38. Schmidt, W. C., J. Exp. Med., 121: 771, 1965.

THE JOURNAL OF IMMUNOLOGY
Vol. 105, No. 2, Aug. 1970

IMMUNOCHEMICAL ANALYSIS OF A URONIC ACID POLYMER OF *STAPHYLOCOCCUS EPIDERMIDIS*, STRAIN 53[1,2]

HUGH C. McDONALD AND WALTER W. KARAKAWA

From the Department of Microbiology, The Pennsylvania State University, University Park, Pennsylvania

Received for publication January 15, 1970

An acidic polysaccharide was isolated from the culture filtrate of a strain of *Staphylococcus epidermidis* by a combination of cetavlon precipitation, ion-exchange chromatography and gel-filtration. Chemical analyses of the acidic polysaccharide indicate that it is an equimolar polymer of D-glucuronic acid and glucosamine. Immunologic studies revealed that the material is antigenic, but hapten-inhibition studies did not disclose any structural features of the antigenic determinants.

Morse (1) isolated a capsular polysaccharide from the Smith strain of *Staphylococcus aureus* which was shown to be, in part, the virulence factor of this organism. Subsequent chemical studies by Haskell and Hanessian (2) clearly demonstrated that the capsular material of the Smith strain consisted of repeating units of 2-amino-2-deoxy-D-glucuronic acid. However, since the Smith strain until recently was considered to be only a virulent laboratory strain, the significance of its capsular material was not considered to be a vital factor in the existing host-parasite relationship involving staphylococci and man. Recently, Yoshida and Ekstedt (3) were able to show a direct relationship between the virulence in mice of staphylococci and their ability to produce slime material when grown under appropriate growth conditions. Maverakis and Wiley (4) isolated at least four type-specific capsular polysaccharides from mouse strains of staphylococci, one of which was immunologically related to the Smith capsular material. These findings indicate that the production of slime materials may be a common feature of many clinical isolates of staphylococci. There is, however, as yet little definitive data on the chemical composition of these materials.

This report describes the isolation, partial purification and immunochemical properties of an acidic polysaccharide isolated from the culture filtrate of *Staphylococcus epidermidis*.

MATERIALS AND METHODS

Organisms. Strain 53 was obtained from the Department of Microbiology, The Pennsylvania State University. This organism was classified as a *S. epidermidis* on the basis of the species-specific glycerol teichoic acid which was isolated from the cell wall. *S. aureus* Smith strain was kindly supplied by Dr. R. Ekstedt, Northwestern University, Chicago, Ill. *Diplococcus pneumoniae*, type III, strain A66, was obtained from Dr. M. McCarty, Rockefeller University, New York.

Preparation of culture filtrates of strain 53. Large batches of cells were grown in a MicroFerm Laboratory fermentor (New Brunswick Scientific Co., New Brunswick, N. J.) in a medium of brain heart infusion broth supplemented with 3.5% sucrose. Cells were grown with low aeration and mild agitation (250 rpm) at 35°C. Antifoam (Antifoam-60, General Electric Co., Waterford, N. Y.) was adjusted automatically and a pH of approximately 6.5 was maintained by the addition of a 30% solution of NaOH. After 18 hr, cells were removed from the fermentor and treated with formalin (13 ml/liter). The formalized cells were kept at 4°C for 2 days and harvested in a Sorvall RC-2B centrifuge (Ivan Sorvall Co., Norwich, Conn.) at 20,000 × G at 4°C. Yields from fermentor-grown cells were

[1] This study was supported in part by NIH Research Grant AI 08015 and was conducted in part under the sponsorship of the Commission on Streptococcal and Staphylococcal Disease, Armed Forces Epidemiological Board, with support from the Office of the Surgeon General, Department of the Army, Washington, D. C.

[2] Submitted by Hugh C. McDonald in partial fulfillment of the requirement for the Ph.D. degree.

approximately 6 g wet weight/liter. The supernatant fraction was collected and stored at 4°C for future use.

Analytical methods. Analysis for hexosamines and amino acids was performed by the method of Moore, Spackman and Stein (5) as described by Karakawa and Krause (6). Analysis of glucose and hexoses was previously described (7). Total phosphorus was determined by the method of Chen *et al.* (8).

Chemicals. The lactone of D-glucuronic acid was prepared by dissolving 36 mg of D-glucuronic acid in 6 ml of 2 N HCl and heating at 105°C for 4 hr. After drying, the sample was reconstituted in 5 ml of distilled water, filtered, and employed as a chromatographic standard.

Sodium borohydride reduction. After esterification, hexuronic acid polymers were reduced with sodium borohydride. Esterification was accomplished using methanolic HCl as described by Smith (9). Sodium borohydride reduction of the esterified polymer was performed in 20% glycerol solution according to the modified method described by Park (J. T. Park, personal communication).

Paper chromatography. Descending paper chromatography was performed using Whatman No. 1 and Whatman No. 4 filter papers and two solvent systems: solvent system A was *n*-butanol, pyridine, water (6:4:3) and solvent system B was *n*-butanol, acetic acid, water (2:1:1).

Sugars were detected with the alkaline silver nitrate reagent of Partridge (10). Amino acids were detected by a solution of 0.6% ninhydrin in *n*-butanol (11). Sugar phosphates were detected by a dipping reagent described by Burrows *et al.* (12).

Staphylococcal vaccine. The vaccine was prepared from strain 53 according to the method described by McCarty and Lancefield (13). The bacteria was grown in 500 ml of brain heart infusion broth supplemented with 3.5% sucrose for 6 hr at 37°C and collected by centrifugation. The bacterial sediment was resuspended in 30 ml of 0.2% formalized saline and stored at 4°C.

Serologic methods. Methods for qualitative and quantitative precipitin tests have been previously described by McCarty and Lancefield (13). Double diffusion studies in agar and immunoelectrophoresis procedures were performed according to the method described by Osterland *et al.* (14).

Sephadex gel-filtration and ion-exchange chromatography. Gel-filtration and DEAE-cellulose (diethylaminoethyl cellulose, Gallard-Schlesinger Corp., New York, N. Y., 0.68 mEq/g) chromatography were performed by the methods described by Young (15).

RESULTS

Isolation of crude acidic polysaccharide. Depicted in Figure 1 is a schematic diagram for the isolation of crude acidic polysaccharide from the culture filtrates of strain 53. In this procedure, the supernatant fraction was concentrated 10-fold by dialysis against polyethylene glycol (PEG) and treated with 10% trichloroacetic (TCA) acid. After the removal of protein and nucleic acid precipitates by centrifugation, the TCA soluble fraction was dialyzed against distilled water, concentrated by flash evaporation and precipitated with three volumes of ethanol.

When the ethanol precipitate was subjected to DEAE-cellulose chromatography and eluted with varying concentrations of $(NH_4)_2CO_3$, a fraction with immunologic activity was eluted from the column with 0.3 M $(NH_4)_2CO_4$. This immunologically active polysaccharide fraction was also isolated from the crude ethanol fraction by precipitation with cetavlon (CTAB) according to the method described by Gotschlich *et al.* (16).

The schematic diagram for the isolation of

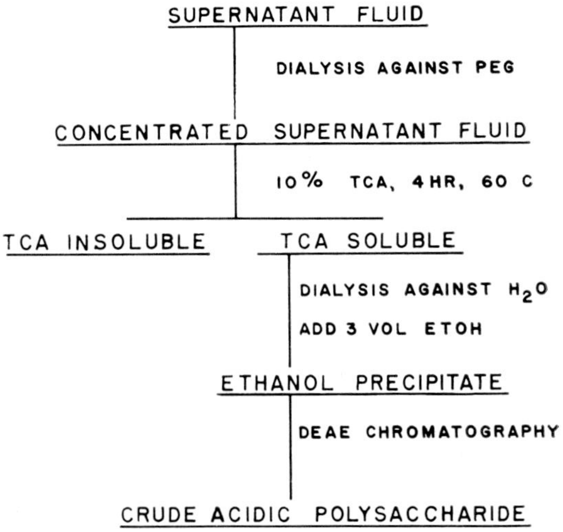

Figure 1. Schematic diagram for the isolation of crude acid polysaccharide from culture filtrate of strain 53.

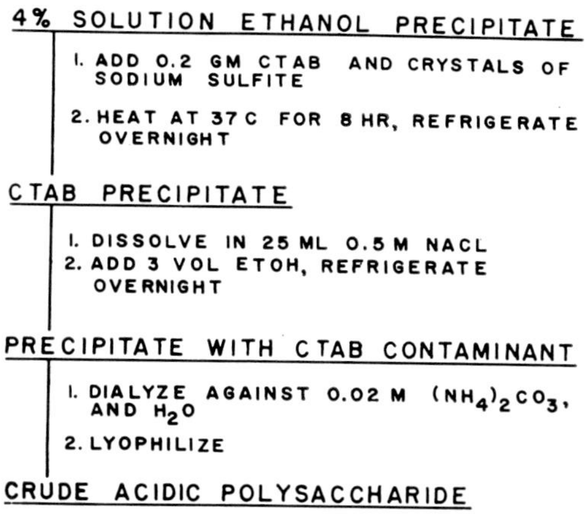

Figure 2. Schematic diagram for the isolation of an immunologically active polysaccharide by the cetavlon (CTAB) precipitation method.

immunologically active material from the ethanol precipitate by cetavlon is depicted in Figure 2. From 20 liters of culture filtrate, approximately 1 g of crude acidic polysaccharide was recovered. It should be noted that the polysaccharide isolated by this method gave precipitin reactions with anti-53 serum; analysis of the double diffusion studies in agar clearly indicated that this polysaccharide was immunologically identical to the fraction isolated by ion-exchange chromatography.

In view of the fact that the CTAB precipitation method for the isolation of acidic polysaccharide is a more convenient method than ion-exchange chromatography, this procedure was used throughout the work described in this report.

Purification of crude acidic polysaccharide. The crude acidic polysaccharide was subjected to Sephadex gel-filtration. Illustrated in Figure 3 is the elution pattern of the polysaccharide preparation on a Sephadex G-75 column eluted with saline. An immunologically active peak designated fraction 1 and an immunologically inert peak designated fraction 2 were isolated. Double diffusion studies in agar employing fraction 1 and anti-53 serum demonstrated that fraction 1 formed two distinct precipitin bands with the antiserum. These results indicated that fraction 1 contained at least two immunologically distinct polymers. In an attempt to separate these polymers, pooled material of fraction 1 was treated with 10% TCA for 4 days at 4°C After removal of the TCA by dialysis against distilled water, the material was subjected to Sephadex G-75 gel-filtration. Illustrated in Figure 4 is the elution pattern of the TCA treated material of fraction 1. Three fractions, designated *a*, *b* and *c* were obtained. Precipitin analysis employing the capillary precipitin technique demonstrated that fractions *a* and *b* were immu-

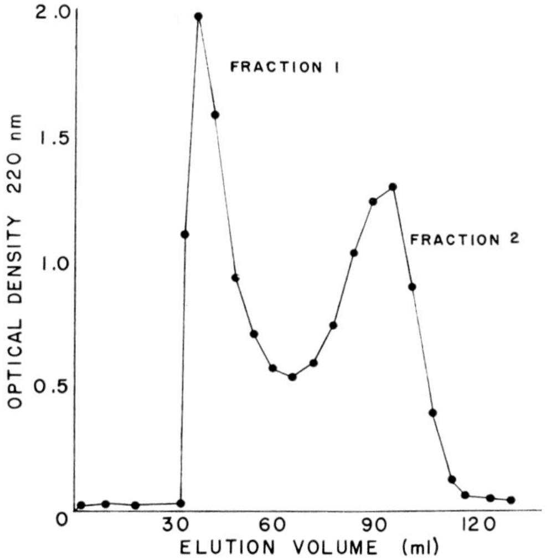

Figure 3. Gel-filtration on Sephadex G-75 of the crude CTAB-extracted polysaccharide. Column dimensions: 900 x 15 mm.

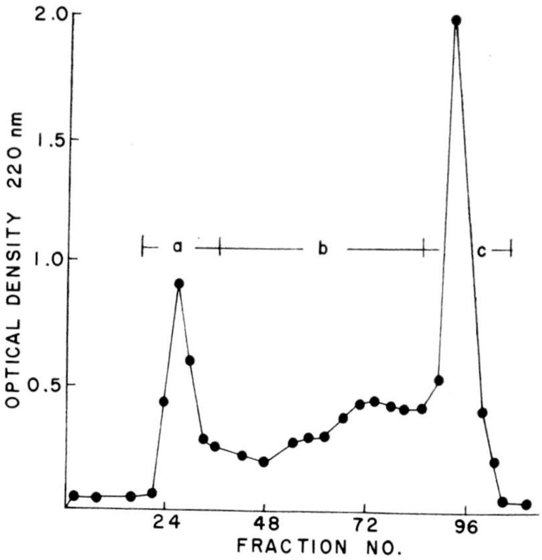

Figure 4. Gel-filtration on Sephadex G-75 column of the TCA-treated fraction 1 eluted from G-75 column depicted in Figure 3. Column dimensions: 900 x 15 mm.

TABLE I

Chemical composition of fraction a isolated from strain 53 culture filtrate

Component	Crude Fraction	Fraction *a*
	μmol/mg	
Hexuronic acid	0.763	1.212[a]
Hexosamine	1.208	1.237[a]
D-Glucose	0.446[a]	0.01
Muramic acid		[b]
Glucosamine		1.140[c]
Amino acids		[b]

[a] Hydrolyzed with 2 N HCl at 100°C for 2 hr.

[b] The concentrations of individual amino acids were 0.01 μmol/mg or less.

[c] Hydrolyzed with 4 N HCl at 100°C for 16 hr. The microgram/milligram values for the amino sugars have not been calculated to include the acetylation of these sugars in the native state.

nologically active, whereas fraction *c* was inactive.

In an extension of these observations, double diffusion studies in agar indicated that fraction *a* represented an immunologically homogeneous polymer, since it formed only a single precipitin band with anti-53 serum. Fraction *b*, however, formed a double diffusion precipitin band with anti-53 serum. The following experiments will emphasize the immunochemical properties of fraction *a*.

Chemical properties of fraction a. A sample of fraction *a* (1 mg/ml) that was hydrolyzed in 2 N HCl for 2 hr at 100°C was applied to Whatman No. 2 filter paper and subjected to descending paper chromatography in solvent system A. Analysis of the chromatogram stained with alkaline silver nitrate indicated that fraction *a* contained glucose, galactose, glucosamine, galactosamine, and an unidentified sugar migrating in the region of a pentose, and components that migrated in the region of glucuronic acid and its lactone. When ninhydrin was used as a detection reagent, glucosamine, galactosamine, trace amounts of amino acids, and several slower moving components were observed. When hydrolysates were subjected to decending chromatography in solvent system B and stained with ammonium molybdate reagent, no sugar phosphates were observed.

The composition of fraction *a* as indicated by paper chromatography was confirmed and substantiated by quantitative chemical analysis. The results of the chemical analysis of fraction *a* are illustrated in Table I. Note that the crude acidic polysaccharide consists of a relatively high concentration of D-glucose. On the other hand, the purified fraction *a* consists of reduced amounts of glucose and elevated amounts of hexuronic acid. These results suggest that fraction *a* is composed of equimoles of hexuronic acid and glucosamine.

Identification of hexuronic acid. Previous results indicated that fraction *a* was composed in part of hexuronic acid. Paper chromatography of fraction *a* hydrolysates suggested that the hexuronic acid was probably glucuronic acid. Chemical analysis of fraction *a* reduced with sodium borohydride supported this view. These results are illustrated in Table II. Note that after two cycles of reduction, the concentration of hexuronic acid in fraction *a* decreased approximately 6% whereas the concentration of D-glucose, as measured by D-glucose oxidase, increased 4%. This suggested that a portion of the hexuronic acid originally present in the untreated fraction *a* was in fact D-glucuronic acid. To evaluate the efficiency of the reduction process which was employed to reduce fraction *a*, a known sample of hyaluronic acid was treated with sodium borohydride and analyzed simultaneously with fraction *a*. These results are also depicted in Table II. In one reduction cycle, the concentration of hexuronic acid was decreased 8.5% whereas the concentration of D-glucose was increased from 0 to 5.5%. These results indicate that the reduction procedure employed in these experiments was effective.

Immunologic analysis of fraction a. Illustrated in Figure 5 are the precipitin reactions in agar between fraction *a*, fraction *b*, the crude ma-

TABLE II

Chemical composition of fraction a before and after sodium borohydride reduction

Component	Fraction *a*	Reduced[a] Fraction *a*	Hyaluronic Acid	Reduced[b] Hyaluronic Acid
	%	%	%	%
Hexuronic acid	19.8	13.8	37.5	29.0
Glucosamine	26.1	27.3	25.5	27.7
D-Glucose	2.8	6.8	0.0	5.5

[a] Two reduction cycles.

[b] One reduction cycle.

terial and antiserum 53. Note that the precipitin band formed between fraction *a* (*1*) and its homologous antiserum merged with the minor precipitin band which formed between the crude preparation and antiserum, whereas, the precipitin band formed between fraction *b* (*2*) and its antiserum merged with the major precipitin band formed between the crude material (*3*, *4*) and antiserum. The immunologic homogeneity of fraction *a* is in agreement with the chemical analyses of this substance.

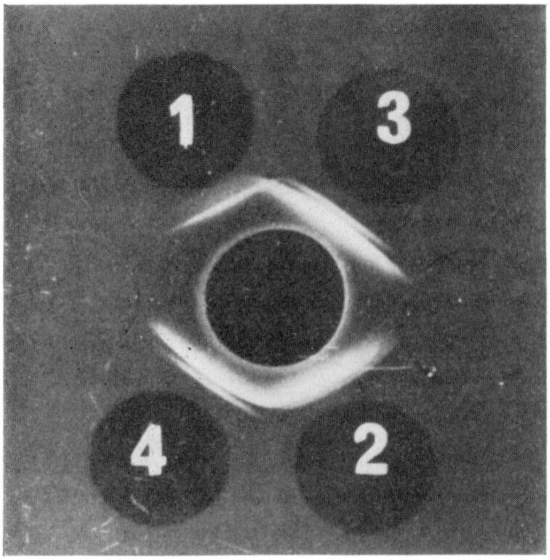

Figure 5. Immunodiffusion reaction in agar gel between crude acidic polysaccharide (*3*, *4*), fraction *a* (*1*), fraction *b* (*2*) and antiserum.

Immunoelectrophoretic studies employing purified fraction *a* and anti-53 serum, which are depicted in Figure 6, clearly support the view that this polymer is acidic in nature. It should be noted that fraction *a* was negatively charged and appeared to be immunochemically similar to the minor precipitin arc formed between the crude material and antiserum.

In view of the fact that fraction *a* was immunologically homogeneous, quantitative precipitin analyses were attempted to elucidate the immunochemical basis for the antigenic specificity of the polysaccharide. Figure 7 shows the results of the quantitative precipitin tests obtained between fraction *a* and antiserum derived from two different rabbits immunized with strain 53. Note that both antisera contain significant amounts of antibody which are directed against the fraction *a* antigen.

In an effort to determine the antigenic basis for the precipitin reaction between fraction *a* and anti-53 serum, quantitative precipitin-inhibition tests were performed with D-glucose, D-glucuronic acid, N-acetylglucosamine, cellobiose and maltose. None of these substances inhibited the reaction between fraction *a* and anti-53 serum. The inability of D-glucuronic acid and glucosamine, which are structural components of fraction *a*,

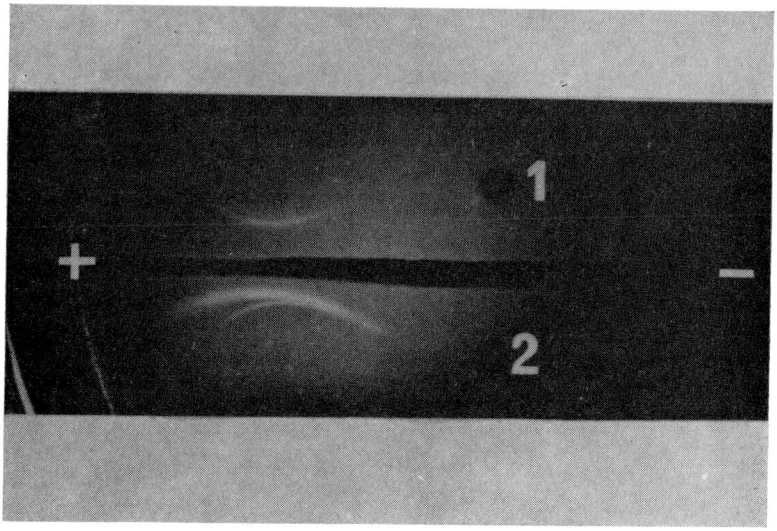

Figure 6. Immunoelectrophoresis of fraction *a* and crude acidic polysaccharide. *Well 1*, fraction *a*; *well 2*, crude extract; *lateral trough*, anti-53 serum.

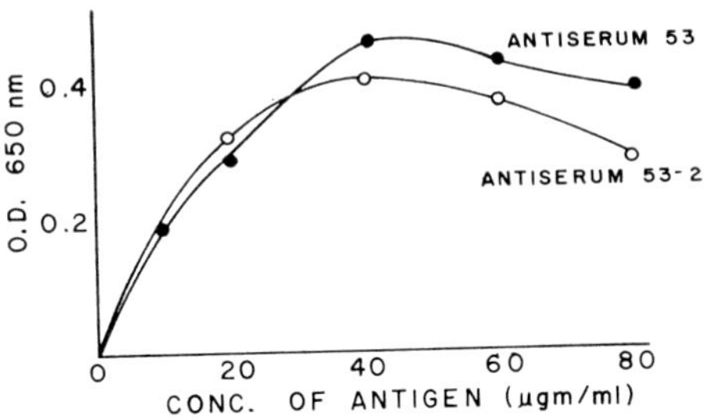

Figure 7. Quantitative precipitin reaction between fraction *a* and anti-53 serum.

to inhibit the precipitin reaction between fraction *a* and anti-53 serum could indicate that the antigenic specificity depends upon the linkage of the two sugar residues and is not dependent on the individual components.

DISCUSSION

Hunt and Moses (17) observed that the Smith strain of *S. aureus* produced two colonial variants in serum-soft agar which differed markedly in their virulence for mice. The diffuse variant consistently killed mice when injected intraperitoneally whereas the same number of cells from the compact colonial variant failed to do so. Later, Wiley and Maverakis (18) demonstrated a specific capsular reaction with the Smith strain, and chemical studies by Haskell and Hanessian (2) indicated that the Smith antigen was in part composed of 2-amino-2-deoxy-D-glucuronic acid. Recent studies have focused attention on the fact that appropriate cultural conditions can stimulate the production of slime material by many strains of *S. aureus* (3).

At present very little is known about the surface antigens of *S. epidermidis*. This study presents evidence of the existence of an acidic polysaccharide associated with *S. epidermidis*, strain 53. Chemical analysis of fraction *a* that was isolated from the culture filtrate of strain 53 indicated that it was composed in part of D-glucuronic and glucosamine. Immunologic studies showed that fraction *a* gave a strong precipitin reaction with antiserum obtained from rabbits which were immunized with whole cells of strain 53. However, after borohydride reduction the fraction exhibited an increase in D-glucose concentration and enhancement of the immunologic reaction with antiserum. Since some D-glucuronic acid residues of the antigen are reduced to D-glucose in the reduction process, the increased immunologic reactivity of the reduced polymer could be attributed to the increased availability of D-glucose determinants, which could react with antibodies with glucose specificity present in anti-53 serum. This notion is consistent with the observation that anti-*Staphylococcus epidermidis* serum, in most cases, contains antibodies that are directed against the D-glucose residue of the species-specific glycerol teichoic acid, and these antibodies could be responsible for the increased reactivity of the reduced antigen.

A polysaccharide designated fraction *b*, which was isolated simultaneously with the uronic acid polymer of strain 53, could prove to be an interesting antigen. Chemical analysis indicates that fraction *b* could be a macromolecular structure consisting of glucose, phosphate, and fragments of the uronic acid polymer. Attempts to detect glycerol in fraction *b* hydrolysates were unsuccessful, thus suggesting that this polymer is not the typical glycerol teichoic acid of cell walls. Quantitative inhibition studies employing mono- and disaccharides have shown that cellobiose, β-glucoside and glucose-6-PO_4 were able to inhibit approximately 50% of the precipitin reaction between fraction *b* and its homologous antiserum. These results tend to indicate that this polysaccharide could be composed of glucose-phosphate polymer, but further studies are needed to elucidate its structure.

Polymers containing D-glucuronic acid have been isolated from *Pneumococcus*, *Streptococcus*, *Bacillus* and *Aerobacter* spp. In the case of pneumococci and streptococci, these polymers have been shown to be important factors involved in the invasiveness of these organisms *in vivo* (19, 20). Although *S. epidermidis* is not considered to be highly virulent in man, it is conceivable that under certain clinical conditions the production of uronic acid polymer by *S. epidermidis* might have some immunologic importance. This possibility merits attention because the strain 53 uronic acid polymer contains essentially the same chemical constituents as does the hyaluronic acid of mammalian tissue. This chemical similarity between hyaluronic acid and strain 53 uronic acid polymer suggests that an immunochemical relationship could exist between these two polymers which are composed of D-glucuronic acid and glucosamine. However, immunologic experiments with bovine hyaluronic acid and anti-53 serum have failed to show any immunologic cross-reactivity between hyaluronic acid and strain 53 antigen. These results indicate that the linkage bridging D-glucuronic acid and glucosamine of strain 53 antigen is not $\beta1,2:\beta1,4$, as is the case in hyaluronic acid. This view is supported by the fact that pneumococcal capsular polysaccharide, type III, which consists of D-glucuronic acid and glucose linked $\beta1,3:\beta1,4$ also failed to cross-react with anti-53 serum. Hyaluronidase had little or no effect upon the immunologic reactivity of strain 53 antigen. These findings clearly suggest that the strain 53 antigen and mammalian hyaluronic acid, although similar in chemical composition, differ immunochemically: this could reflect the differences in the chemical linkages between the individual sugar residues.

The difference in sugar linkage between strain 53 antigen and hyaluronic acid could account for the fact that strain 53 antigen is immunogenic in animals whereas hyaluronic acid is not. The reason for the immunogenic nature of strain 53 antigen on one hand and the non-immunogenic nature of hyaluronic acid on the other should be the object of further studies.

In addition, in view of the possible presence of slimelike polysaccharides in *S. epidermidis,* one may assume that in the future these polymers could be of taxonomic value in devising a more useful scheme for the classification of staphylococci.

REFERENCES

1. Morse, S. I., J. Exp. Med., *115:* 195, 1962.
2. Haskell, T. and Hanessian, R., Nature, *199:* 1075, 1963.
3. Yoshida, K. and Ekstedt, R. D., J. Bact., *96:* 902, 1968.
4. Maverakis, N. H. and Wiley, B. B., J. Bact., *99:* 4727, 1969.
5. Moore, S., Spackman, D. H. and Stein, W. H., Anal. Chem., *30:* 1185, 1958.
6. Karakawa, W. W. and Krause, R. M., J. Exp. Med., *124:* 155, 1966.
7. Curtis, S. N. and Krause, R. M., J. Exp. Med., *119:* 997, 1964.
8. Chen, P. S., Jr., Toribara, T. Y. and Warner, H., Anal. Chem., *28:* 1756, 1956.
9. Smith, E., J. Biol. Chem., *243:* 5139, 1968.
10. Partridge, S. N., Biochem. J., *42:* 238, 1948.
11. McCarty, M., J. Exp. Med., *96:* 569, 1952.
12. Burrows, S., Grylls, F. S. M. and Harris, J. S., Nature, *170:* 800, 1952.
13. McCarty, M. and Lancefield, R. C., J. Exp. Med., *102:* 11, 1955.
14. Osterland, C. K., Miller, E. J., Karakawa, W. W. and Krause, R. M., J. Exp. Med., *123:* 599, 1966.
15. Young, F. E., J. Bact., *92:* 839, 1966.
16. Gotschlich, E. C., Liu, T. Y. and Artenstein, M. S., J. Exp. Med., *129:* 1349, 1969.
17. Hunt, G. A. and Moses, A. J., Science, *128:* 1574, 1958.
18. Wiley, B. B. and Maverakis, N. H., J. Bact., *95:* 998, 1968.
19. Avery, O. T. and Dubos, R., Science, *72:* 151, 1930.
20. Lancefield, R. C., J. Immun., *89:* 307, 1962.

THE JOURNAL OF IMMUNOLOGY
Vol. 105, No. 2, Aug. 1970
Printed in U.S.A.

SYNTHESIS OF THE NINTH COMPONENT OF COMPLEMENT BY A CLONAL STRAIN OF RAT HEPATOMA CELLS[1]

FRED A. ROMMEL, MARVIN B. GOLDLUST, FRANK C. BANCROFT, MANFRED M. MAYER AND ARMEN H. TASHJIAN, JR.

From the Department of Microbiology, the Johns Hopkins University School of Medicine, Baltimore, Maryland 21205, the Pharmacology Department, Harvard School of Dental Medicine and the Department of Pharmacology, Harvard Medical School, Boston, Massachusetts 02115

Received for publication January 12, 1970

The MH_1C_1 strain of rat hepatoma cells was found to produce the ninth component of complement (C9). Most of the C9 produced by the cells was secreted into the culture medium. The production of C9 by MH_1C_1 cells was temperature sensitive with a Q_{10} of 2.2. Cycloheximide completely inhibited the production of C9 within 6 hr. Removal of cycloheximide at 24 hr resulted in a rapid return of C9 production. The production of C9 was also inhibited by treatment of the cells with actinomycin D. Hydrocortisone (3×10^{-6} M), which stimulates the production of serum albumin by MH_1C_1 cells 4- to 5-fold, did not increase C9 production. C9 produced by MH_1C_1 cells in culture was similar to guinea pig and rat serum C9 when comparisons were made by density gradient ultracentrifugation, by inhibition of hemolytic activity by antrypol, and by kinetic analysis of the reaction between C9 and EAC14235678. The results of these studies show that MH_1C_1 hepatoma cells synthesize C9 and secrete this complement component into the culture medium by processes that require both protein and RNA synthesis.

Previous investigations have implicated a variety of tissues and cell types in the synthesis of complement (C) components (1–8). The present studies are concerned with the investigation of C synthesis by a recently established clonal strain (MH_1C_1) of rat hepatoma cells (9) which are of different origin from those used previously for studies of C synthesis (2, 3). The MH_1C_1 cell strain exhibits several functions characteristic of normal liver, including the synthesis of serum albumin and tyrosine aminotransferase and the conjugation of testosterone with glucuronic acid (9, 10). In this report evidence is presented for the synthesis by this cell line of the ninth component of C (C9). The results of experiments on the production of albumin under the same conditions are given for comparison. The C9 activity found in medium from MH_1C_1 cells was compared with the C9 activity in rat serum and in a preparation of guinea pig C9. The physical and hemolytic properties of C9 from all three sources were similar.

[1] This work was supported in part by research grants from the United States Public Health Service (AM 11011), the American Cancer Society, Massachusetts Division (P-374). A. H. T. is a U.S.P.H.S. Career Development Awardee (AM 13,561), F. C. B. is a U.S.P.H.S. postdoctoral research fellow (GM 21,175), and F. R. and M. B. G. are supported by U.S.P.H.S. Training Grant (2TO1-AI-00282-06), National Science Foundation Grant (GB-7406X), U.S.P.H.S. Grant (AI-02566-10), and a contract with the Office of Naval Research O.N.R. 248 (60).

MATERIALS AND METHODS

Cycloheximide was purchased from the Nutritional Biochemicals Corp., Cleveland, Ohio. Actinomycin D was a gift from Merck Sharp & Dohme Research Laboratories, Rahway, N. J. Antrypol was obtained from Imperial Chemical Industries, Ltd., Cheshire, England. Hydrocortisone hemisuccinate was purchased from the Upjohn Co., Kalamazoo, Mich.

Cell culture methods. The methods of establishment, cloning and culture of MH_1C_1 hepatoma cells have previously been described in detail (9). In brief, cells were grown at 37°C in a humidified atmosphere of 5% CO_2 and 95% air, in plastic tissue culture dishes or bottles (Falcon Plastics,

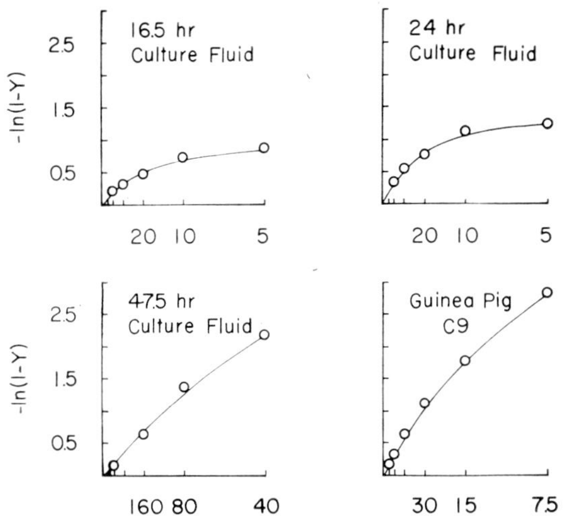

Figure 1. Representative dose-response curves obtained for the hemolytic assay of C9 in culture fluids of MH_1C_1 cells grown in F 10− compared with a functionally purified guinea pig serum C9 preparation. Assays were performed as described in *Materials and Methods.*

Oxnard, Calif.) or in glass bottles in a roller-bottle cell production apparatus (Bellco Glass Co., Vineland, N. J.). For use in the C detection studies, the cells were grown to the desired density in Ham's F 10 medium (11) supplemented with 15% (v/v) horse serum and 2.5% (v/v) fetal calf serum (F 10+). The cells were then washed three times with saline or serum-free medium (F 10−) and F 10− was added to each vessel. Albumin production was observed to decrease gradually when the cells were incubated in F 10−, reaching a value 50% of that observed in F 10+ by about 90 hr.

For characterization of C9 and for kinetic measurements, culture medium (F 10−) from a 24-hr roller-bottle culture was concentrated, dialyzed and frozen as described in Table I. Gelatin (final concentration of 0.1%) was usually added to experimental samples collected for assay of C9. This concentration of gelatin protected C9 against the effects of freezing to the same extent as a concentration of 1%, while freezing in the absence of gelatin led to a 23% loss in C9 activity.

Couplement components and methods of assay. Functionally purified C components for use in assay reagents were prepared from guinea pig serum as described previously (12–14) with the following modifications. C5 was prepared as described by Shin and Mayer (manuscript in preparation). C6 and C9 were further fractionated on hydroxyapatite and Sephadex G-200, respectively. Erythrocyte-antibody-complement intermediates were prepared with functionally purified components or guinea pig C as described in (12, 15, 16). Hemolytic assays were performed as described earlier (12, 14–18), except that for components C5, C6 and C7 a single incubation for 60 min at 37°C was used.

TABLE I

Synthesis of complement by hepatoma cell line MH_1C_1

C component	CH_{63} Units/ml[a]				
	24-hr culture[b]	Control[c] F 10− medium	Pooled guinea pig serum	Rat serum[d]	
				Buffalo	Holtzman
1	0	0	14,100	23,600	23,600
2	0.12	0.21	18,000	450	160
3	0.23	0	3,050	10,400	10,700
4	0	0	14,900	634	590
5	1.15	0.005	127,000	20,200	23,200
6	0[e]	0	51,800	41,700	28,600
7	0.38	0.016	65,600	98,000	180,000
8	0.51	0.007	247,000	274,000	154,000
9	42.0	0	150,000	140,000	129,000

[a] All component assays were performed using guinea pig component reagents.

[b] Ten milliliters of culture medium harvested after 24 hr from a roller-bottle containing 25 ml of F 10− and approximately 10^7 cells were dialyzed at 4°C against 1 liter of isotonic glucose-Veronal, $\mu = 0.074$, pH 7.3. The culture fluid was concentrated 10-fold by negative pressure in a collodion bag (Schleicher and Schuell). Gelatin was added to a final concentration of 1% (w/v) before freezing. Hemolytic activity is expressed in terms of the original volume of culture medium.

[c] Five milliliters of culture medium without serum (F 10−) were dialyzed as indicated under (*b*). The medium was not concentrated, but gelatin was added to a final concentration of 1% before freezing.

[d] Values are the average of two individual male rats of the Buffalo and Holtzman strains.

[e] Heat labile (56°C, 10 min) inhibitory material in culture medium interfered with detection of guinea pig C6 in the assay system. Absence of C6 in culture medium is, therefore, not conclusive. The effect, if any, of this material on other component assays was not determined.

When culture fluids were assayed for hemolytic C9, the dose-response curves were not linear, as shown in Figure 1. This effect was most marked in fluid samples taken from short incubation periods, since low amounts of C9 were present and consequently low dilutions of culture medium were used for assay. Presumably, this deviation is due to inhibitory material. Moderate deviation from linearity was also observed with guinea pig C9.

The unit of hemolytic activity chosen for these studies was the dilution of sample giving 63% lysis [$-\ln(1\text{-}y) = 1.0$ and $y = 0.63$] of 3.85×10^7 cells and was expressed as the number of CH_{63}/ml (15, 19). Initial slopes of dose-response curves were obtained by a plot of $1/-\ln(1\text{-}y)$ *vs* 1/concentration, as described by Stroud *et al.* (20) and Hoffmann *et al.* (18). Calculations were made from $-\ln(1\text{-}y)$ values of 0.5 or lower, and the results extrapolated to the CH_{63} unit.

Albumin assays. Rat serum albumin was measured by the semi-micro complement fixation method of Wasserman and Levine (21) employing an antiserum against purified rat albumin, as described previously (9).

Disruption of cells. Cells were scraped from Petri dishes in 6 ml of F 10−, and the suspension was subjected to sonic oscillation in a Raytheon model DF 101 sonic oscillator for 5 min at 5°C. In control experiments, this procedure decreased C9 activity in MH_1C_1 culture medium by 23%.

Protein determination. Cell protein was measured by the method of Lowry *et al.* (22).

Production of C9 by MH_1C_1. All cultures of MH_1C_1 cells were originally grown in medium containing serum. Since such medium contained all nine complement components, synthesis of complement by the cells would have been obscured. In order to eliminate C9 contamination from F 10+, the cell cultures were washed three times with saline or with F 10−. This reduced the C9 in the final wash fluid to below the limit of detection. F 10− medium was then added and the cells were incubated at 37°C. Titrations of all nine complement components in a sample of medium collected after 24 hr incubation are shown in Table I, along with assays of the F 10− medium, and guinea pig and rat sera. The results indicate substantial production of C9 as well as the presence of small quantities of several of the other complement components. The negative results obtained in the case of C6 are not considered significant because of the presence of a heat-labile inhibitory material of unknown nature. Therefore, these results with respect to C6

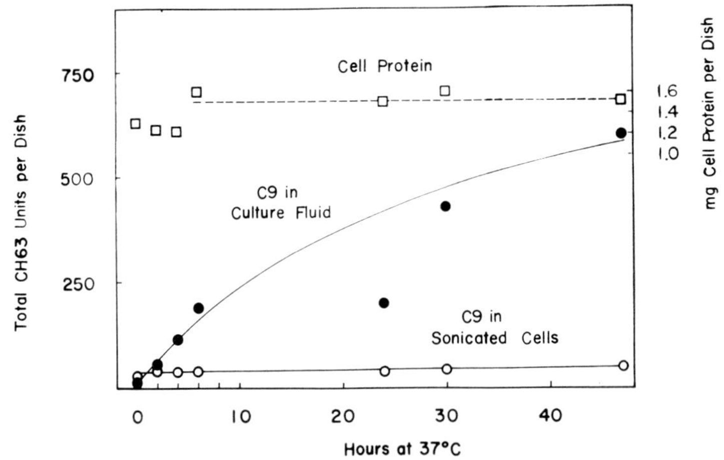

Figure 2. The accumulation of C9 in the medium of MH_1C_1 cells in culture. Replicate cultures grown in supplemented F 10 medium were washed three times with F 10−. Each culture was then incubated with 6 ml F 10−. A culture was harvested at zero time and after 2, 4, 6, 24, 30 and 47.5 hr of incubation. Gelatin was added to the medium to a final concentration of 0.1% and the samples were frozen at −20°C. After medium was collected, the cells from that plate were washed three times with F 10−, suspended in 6 ml of fresh F 10−, and disrupted by sonic oscillation. A portion of the cell sonicate was assayed for protein, correcting for the small blank given by the F 10− medium. Gelatin was added to a final concentration of 0.1%, and the cell sonicates were kept frozen until C9 was assayed. C9 assays were performed in duplicate: mean values are given.

are not necessarily in conflict with those described in a preliminary report of C6 synthesis by another rat hepatoma (2).

Kinetics of C9 production. In these experiments, separate dishes were used for each time point so that cell protein and C9 in the sonicated cells could be measured in addition to the C9 secreted into the medium. As shown in Figure 2, C9 concentration in the culture fluids increased with time. By contrast, the low levels of C9 in disrupted cells, as well as the amounts of cell protein, remained nearly constant throughout the experiment. C9 activity in culture medium harvested at 24 hr was stable for at least 50 hr at 37°C, and therefore it seemed reasonable to assume that no significant loss of C9 occurred during incubation in these kinetic experiments.

In order to measure intracellular C9, and in order to ascertain whether intact cells are required for C9 synthesis, cells collected after 24-hr incubation in F 10 − were sonicated in fresh medium. The resulting sonicate was reincubated for an additional 48 hr at 37°C. No increase in C9 activity was found.

From these data it was concluded that the increasing amount of C9 in culture medium was not due to release of preformed intracellular C9 or C9 adsorbed from the F 10+, and that vital intact cells were required for the appearance of C9 hemolytic activity.

Influence of temperature on C9 production. Appearance of C9 in the culture medium was markedly dependent on the temperature of incubation of MH_1C_1 cells. After 24 hr, three replicate cultures which were incubated at 4°, 25° and 37°C were found to contain 2.5, 15 and 34 CH_{63} units/ml, respectively. The Q_{10} for this temperature range was 2.2.

Effects of inhibitors of protein and RNA synthesis. To obtain further evidence of C9 synthesis by MH_1C_1 cells, C9 production was investigated in medium containing cycloheximide, a specific inhibitor of protein synthesis (23). In separate experiments, cycloheximide (10 μg/ml) was found to inhibit the incorporation by MH_1C_1 cells of ^{14}C-amino acids into acid-insoluble material by 90%, within 3 hr.

Four replicate culture dishes were washed as usual. Two of them then received F 10 − and two received F 10 − containing cycloheximide (10 μg/ml). At intervals, medium was removed and assayed for C9. The presence of cycloheximide did not have any effect on the stability of C9 from cultures incubated in F 10 − for as long as 124 hr, nor did its presence interfere with the assay of either guinea pig or hepatoma C9. Figure 3 shows

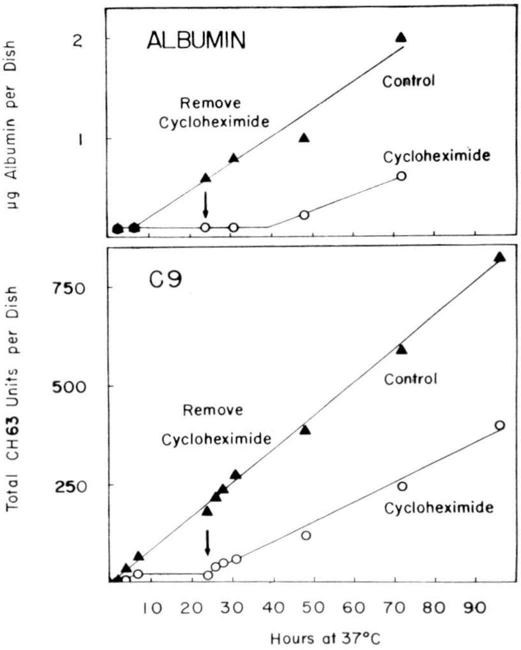

Figure 3. Effect of cycloheximide on albumin and C9 synthesis. Two series of replicate cultures, one for C9 and one for albumin, were grown in F 10+ medium and then washed three times with F 10− at zero time. One set was then incubated in 8 ml F 10− medium alone (control) and another in 8 ml of F 10− medium containing 10 μg cycloheximide/ml (cycloheximide). Five-tenths-milliliter amounts were removed at 0, 2, 4 and 7 hr and frozen for assay. At 24 hr all the remaining medium was removed and frozen. The cells were washed three times with F 10− lacking cycloheximide and then incubated for an additional 24 hr in 8 ml F 10− medium during which time samples were removed at 26, 28 and 31 hr after the experiment was started. The remaining medium was again removed, the cells were washed, and fresh medium was added at 48 and 72 hr. Samples for albumin and C9 assay were collected at 72 and 98 hr. All samples received gelatin at a final concentration of 0.1% before freezing. The mean total cell protein values at the end of the experiment for the control cells and cells treated with cycloheximide for 24 hr were 1.0 and 0.77 mg protein, respectively. The values for C9 and albumin were corrected for changes in volume of medium during the experiment.

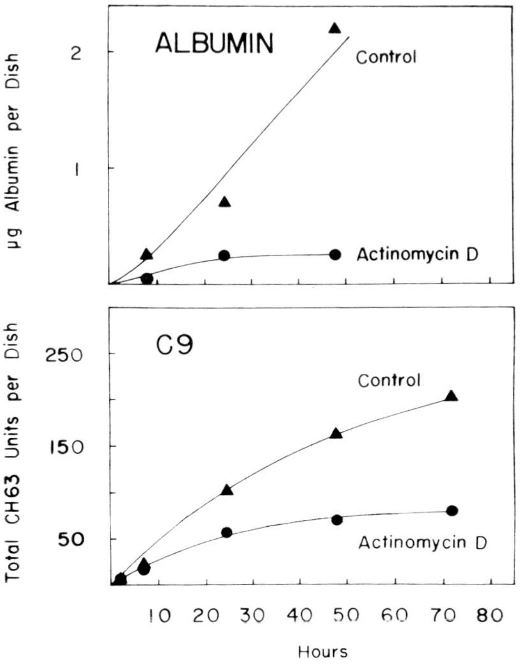

Figure 4. Effect of actinomycin D on C9 and albumin synthesis. Replicate cultures, one for C9 and one for albumin, grown in F 10+ medium were washed three times with F 10− at zero time. One set was then incubated in 8 ml F 10− medium alone (control) and another in 8 ml F 10− containing 1 µg actinomycin D/ml (actinomycin). Five-tenths-milliliter amounts were removed at 0, 2, 7, 24, 48 and 72 hr and frozen for assay. All samples received gelatin at a final concentration of 0.1%. The mean total cell protein values at the end of the experiment for the control cells and for cells treated with actinomycin D throughout the experiment were 0.74 and 0.52 mg protein, respectively. The values for C9 and albumin were corrected for changes in the volume of medium during the experiment.

that within 6 hr after the addition of cycloheximide, C9 production was completely blocked. Removal of the inhibitor at 24 hr resulted in a rapid return of C9 production. Similar results were obtained for albumin production. Protein synthesis is required for the continued production of C9 by MH_1C_1 cells.

The effect of C9 production of actinomycin D, an inhibitor of DNA-dependent RNA synthesis (24) was also investigated. In separate experiments, actinomycin D (1 µg/ml) was found to inhibit the incorporation by MH_1C_1 cells of ^{3}H-uridine into acid-insoluble material by 87% within 1.5 hr.

Four replicate culture dishes were washed as usual. Two then received F 10− and two received F 10− containing actinomycin D (1 µg/ml). Medium was periodically removed and assayed for C9. The presence of actinomycin D had only a slight effect (5% loss) on the stability of C9 in culture medium incubated at 37°C for as long as 124 hr, and it did not interfere with the assay of either guinea pig or hepatoma C9. Figure 4 shows that inhibition of C9 production was almost complete by 24 hr. Similar results were observed for albumin production. At 72 hr the dishes receiving actinomycin D were found to contain 30% less total cell protein than the control dishes, indicating that long-term exposure to this metabolic inhibitor has a toxic effect on the MH_1C_1 cells. These data suggest that RNA synthesis is required for the continued production of C9 by MH_1C_1 cells.

Effect of hydrocortisone. Although C9 production and albumin synthesis appeared to be affected similarly by metabolic inhibitors, the effect of hydrocortisone on these two cell products was quite different (Fig. 5). There was a clear

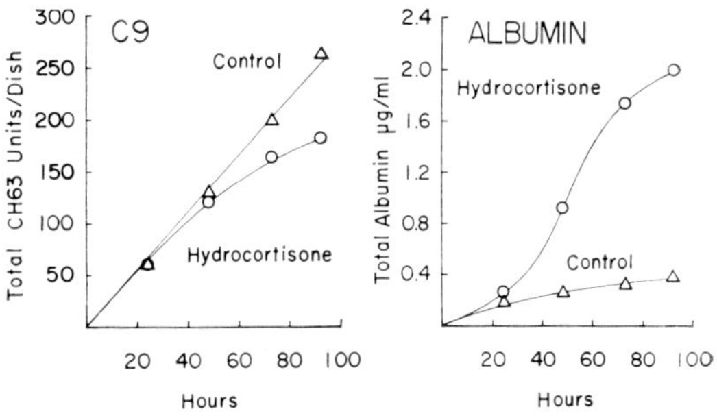

Figure 5. The effect of hydrocortisone on production of C9 and albumin by MH_1C_1 cells. Four replicate cultures were washed and 3 ml of F 10− were added to two of them (control). Three milliliters of F 10− containing 3×10^{-6} M hydrocortisone were added to each of the other two cultures (hydrocortisone) and all dishes were placed at 37°C. Culture medium was collected at 24, 48, 73 and 92 hr and 3 ml of either F10− or F 10− containing hydrocortisone were added to the appropriate cultures. Fluids collected from one culture grown in F 10− and one culture grown in the presence of the steroid were assayed for albumin. Media collected from the remaining two cultures were frozen after addition of gelatin to a final concentration of 0.1% for assay of C9.

stimulation of albumin production with no increase, or even possibly a decrease, in C9 production. After 92 hr in cultures containing 3×10^{-6} M hydrocortisone, the total amount of albumin synthesized was fivefold higher than in control cultures. In contrast, C9 production appeared to be depressed. This decrease of C9 production has not been investigated in detail, but no interference by the steroid of the assay for C9 was detected. In another experiment in which 24 hr culture medium was reincubated at 37°C for 80 hr under sterile conditions in the absence or in the resence of 3×10^{-5} M hydrocortisone, a 27% decrease in C9 activity was observed with steroid present. Instability of C9 in the presence of hydrocortisone may account in part for the apparent decrease of C9 production during culture in the presence of this compound.

Characterization of C9 from MH_1C_1 culture media. a. Sedimentation rate. Linear sucrose gradients (5% to 20%) in isotonic Veronal buffer, pH 7.3, were prepared (25). One-tenth milliliter of either concentrated, dialyzed hepatoma C9, rat serum diluted 1:50 or guinea pig C9, each containing ^{125}I-human serum albumin (HSA) as a marker, was applied to the top of three separate gradients of 4.5 ml each. Each tube was centrifuged at 29,000 rpm for 22 hr at 4°C in the SW 39 swinging bucket rotor using a Beckman Spinco model L centrifuge. Thirty to 34 fractions were collected from each gradient. C9 hemolytic activity coincided in all gradients with HSA, which sediments as a 4.6S molecule.

b. Inhibition by antrypol. Antrypol was previously found to inhibit the reaction between EAC1423567 and C8 (16). It was also found to block the reaction between EAC14235678 and C9. The sensitivity to inhibition by antrypol of hepatoma C9, rat serum C9, and guinea pig C9 was compared. Fifty per cent inhibition of 1 CH_{63} hemolytic unit was observed at 1.3×10^{-4} M for guinea pig, 0.5×10^{-4} M for rat serum C9, and 0.8×10^{-4} M for hepatoma C9.

c. Kinetic behavior. A characteristic of the reaction between C9 and EAC14235678 is the occurrence of a lag of about 10 to 15 min at 37°C before lysis can be detected. Guinea pig and hepatoma C9 were compared in this respect. Equal volumes of EAC14235678 at 1.5×10^8/ml and guinea pig or hepatoma C9 or buffer were mixed at 37°C. Samples were diluted 1:8 with 0.1 M EDTA, pH 7.4, at 0°C to prevent further lysis and immediately centrifuged in the cold. Percentage lysis was calculated from OD_{412}. A lag of 15 min before lysis was observed occurred in reaction mixtures containing C9 from both sources.

Hepatoma C9 was also compared with guinea pig C9 with respect to depletion from the fluid phase by EAC14235678 and generation of C9 sites. In separate tubes EAC14235678 (1×10^9/ml) were mixed at 0°C with an equal volume of buffer or with C9 containing about 1 CH_{63} unit/ml. Controls consisted of EAC1423567 + C9 or buffer, and C9 mixed with buffer. After 8 min the tubes were centrifuged at 0°C. Supernatant fluids were saved for assay of residual C9. The cells were rapidly washed twice at 0°C and were then placed at 37°C for 90 min. Consumption of hepatoma C9 was only 17% compared to 54% for guinea pig C9. However, the number of sites generated by hepatoma C9 was about threefold less. These results suggest that rat hepatoma C9 did not react as rapidly at 0°C as did guinea pig C9.

DISCUSSION

In investigations of the production of complement by various tissues and cell types, Stecher *et al.* (4) and Stecher and Thorbecke (3, 5) found incorporation of ^{14}C-amino acids into C protein, *viz.* C3, C4 and C1q, which could be detected by the combined use of radioautography and anticomplement antibodies. Fractions of peritoneal exudates that were rich in macrophages were most active. Established fibroblast cell lines also synthesized C3 and C4 (5) and a hepatoma cell line was observed to produce C3 (3). However, it is not known whether any of these cell products possessed hemolytic activity. Evidence has been obtained by Jensen (8) that guinea pig liver produces hemolytic C4. Rother *et al.* (1) reported increases in C6 activity during incubation of rabbit liver and obtained preliminary evidence that a rat hepatoma cell line may synthesize hemolytically active C6 and C9 (2), but actual synthesis of these components was not unequivocally demonstrated. Colten *et al.* (6, 7) examined a variety of organs for the ability to synthesize Cl and found *in vitro* incorporation of ^{14}C-amino acids into a hemolytically active form of this component only by fragments of small intestine. In additional experiments it was found that columnar epithelial cells were particularly active in producing Cl.

In the present studies the following evidence

has been obtained for synthesis of the ninth component of complement by rat liver. Serum-free culture medium from an established strain of rat hepatoma cells, which were previously grown on serum-containing medium but washed free of detectable C9, was shown to contain increasing amounts of C9 hemolytic activity for periods of at least 96 hr. Levels of cell protein and C9 found inside cells disrupted by treatment with sonic oscillation remained constant during this time. In addition, culture medium containing sonicated cells reincubated at 37°C for 48 hr showed no increase in C9 activity. Production of C9 was markedly influenced by temperature and had a Q_{10} of 2.2 in the range of 4° to 37°C. Both C9 and albumin production by MH_1C_1 cells were blocked by inhibitors of protein and RNA synthesis. The experiments with actinomycin D were somewhat difficult to interpret, due to the possibility of effects other than those on DNA-directed RNA synthesis (26–28) and to the possibility of toxic effects arising from long-term inhibition of cellular RNA synthesis (26). However, the results obtained with actinomycin D suggest that the RNA messenger(s) involved in C9 synthesis may be rather long-lived. The C9 obtained from MH_1C_1 culture media was found to be similar to C9 in rat serum and in partially purified guinea pig serum preparations by sucrose density sedimentation rate studies, by sensitivity to inhibition by antrypol, and by the capacity to interact with EAC14235678.

Culture medium from MH_1C_1 cells was also assayed for the other components of complement and low level of C2, C3, C5, C7 and C8 were found. Whether these small amounts represent *de novo* synthesis has not yet been determined. In contrast to the results of Rother *et al.* (2), C6 was not detected in our experiments. It is unlikely that the difference in results was due to insensitivity of the C6 assay used in the present study (G. J. Thorbecke and U. Rother, personal communication). Medium from MH_1C_1 cells, but not fresh medium, was inhibitory in assays of guinea pig C6. Except for its heat lability (56°C, 10 min), the inhibitory material was not characterized and its relationship to other complement inhibitors (29) has not been investigated. Inhibition was also found in culture media (kindly supplied by Dr. G. J. Thorbecke) from another rat hepatoma cell line (H4-II-EC3). Lack of detection of C6 activity may be due to a difference in the cell line investigated or the use of different reagents and assay methods, in addition to the presence of inhibitory material in culture fluids.

To characterize further the MH_1C_1 cell strain, production of C9 was compared with another differentiated function exhibited by these cells, namely, the production of serum albumin. The effects of metabolic inhibitors and hydrocortisone on albumin production by MH_1C_1 cells have been described elsewhere (10, 30). As is the case with albumin, C9 production was blocked by metabolic inhibitors (Fig. 3 and 4). However, in contrast to albumin, the production of C9 was not enhanced by hydrocortisone (Fig. 5). As the extent of the characterization of the MH_1C_1 cell strain increases, valuable information can be obtained concerning the integration of multiple differentiated organ-specific functions *in vitro*, and the regulatory mechanisms which control these functions both in culture and *in vivo*. Whether C9 production is a normal liver-specific function or represents a unique feature of the MH_1C_1 cell strain must await the results of further experiments.

Acknowledgments. The authors wish to thank Mrs. Adele K. Gallucci, Miss Norma J. Barowsky, Mrs. Lethia S. Gilliard, Miss Frances N. Atwell and Mr. Michael L. Hayden for expert assistance.

REFERENCES

1. Rother, U., Thorbecke, G. J., Stecher-Levin, V. J., Hurlimann, J. and Rother, K., Immunology, *14:* 649, 1968.
2. Rother, K. O., Rother, U. A., Philips, M. E., Goetze, O. and Thorbecke, G. J., Abstracts of the Third International Complement Workshop, June 1968, Boston, Mass., J. Immun., *101:* 814, 1968.
3. Stecher, V. J. and Thorbecke, G. J., J. Immun., *99:* 660, 1967.
4. Stecher, V. J., Morse, J. H. and Thorbecke, G. J., Proc. Soc. Exp. Biol. Med., *124:* 433, 1967.
5. Stecher, V. J. and Thorbecke, G. J., J. Immun., *99:* 643, 1967.
6. Colten, H. R., Borsos, T. and Rapp, H. J., Proc. Nat. Acad, Sci., *56:* 1158, 1966.
7. Colten, H. R., Gordon, J. M., Rapp, H. J. and Borsos, T., J. Immun., *100:* 788, 1968.
8. Jensen, J. A., J. Exp. Med., *130:* 217, 1969.
9. Richardson, U. I., Tashjian, A. H., Jr. and Levine L., J. Cell Biol., *40:* 236, 1969.

10. Tashjian, A. H., Jr., Bancroft, F. C., Richardson, U. I., Goldlust, M. B., Rommel, F. A. and Ofner, P., *In Vitro*, In press.
11. Ham, R. G., Exp. Cell Res., *29:* 515, 1963.
12. Nelson, R. A., Jr., Jensen, J., Gigli, I. and Tamura, N., Immunochemistry, *3:* 111, 1966.
13. Borsos, T., Rapp, H. J. and Mayer, M. M., J. Immun., *87:* 330, 1961.
14. Shin, H. S. and Mayer, M. M., Biochemistry, *7:* 2991, 1968.
15. Borsos, T., Rapp, H. J. and Mayer, M. M., J. Immun., *87:* 310, 1961.
16. Rommel, F. and Stolfi, R., Immunology, *15:* 469, 1968.
17. Borsos, T. and Rapp, H. J., J. Immun., *91:* 851, 1963.
18. Hoffmann, L. G., McKenzie, A. T. and Mayer, M. M., Immunochemistry, *2:* 13, 1965.
19. Mayer, M. M., in *Kabat and Mayer's Experimental Immunochemistry*, 2nd Ed., Chapter 4, Charles C Thomas, Springfield, Ill., 1961.
20. Stroud, R. M., Austen, K. F. and Mayer, M. M., Immunochemistry, *2:* 219, 1965.
21. Wasserman, E. and Levine, L., J. Immun., *87:* 290, 1961.
22. Lowry, O. H., Rosebrough, N. F., Farr, A. L. and Randall, R. J., J. Biol. Chem., *193:* 265, 1951.
23. Wettstein, F. O., Nell, H. and Penman, S., Biochim. Biophys. Acta, *87:* 525, 1964.
24. Reich, E., Franklin, R. M., Shatkin, A. J. and Tatum, E. L., Proc. Nat. Acad. Sci., *48:* 1238, 1962.
25. Martin, R. G. and Ames, B. N., J. Biol. Chem., *236:* 1372, 1961.
26. Wiesner, R., Acs, G., Reich, E. and Shafig, A., J. Cell Biol., *27:* 47, 1965.
27. Revel, M., Hiatt, H. H. and Revel, J., Science, *146:* 1311, 1964.
28. Lazlo, J., Miller, D. S., McCarty, K. S. and Hochstein, P., Science, *151:* 1007, 1966.
29. Tamura, N. and Nelson, R. A., Jr., J. Immun., *99:* 582, 1967.
30. Bancroft, F. C., Levine, L. and Tashjian, A. H., Biochem. Biophys. Res. Commun., *37:* 1028, 1969.

THE JOURNAL OF IMMUNOLOGY
Vol. 105, No. 2 Aug. 1970
Printed in U.S.A.

HETEROGENEITY OF IMMUNE RESPONSE TO THE SOMATIC (O) ANTIGENS OF *PROTEUS MIRABILIS*[1]

JAMES W. SMITH,[2] JACK A. BARNETT AND JAY P. SANFORD

From the Department of Internal Medicine, The University of Texas (Southwestern) Medical School at Dallas, and The Veterans Administration Hospital, Dallas, Texas 75235

Received for publication January 12, 1970

A variation in the antibody response to antigenically differing somatic antigens (O) *Proteus mirabilis* was noted in rats. Certain strains induced the synthesis of 2-mercaptoethanol sensitive (2-MES), or IgM, antibody, whereas other strains led to the rapid appearance of 2-mercaptoethanol resistant (2-MER), or IgG, antibody. The varying response was not due to the differences in the quantity of lipopolysaccharide administered and was demonstrated when animals were challenged either separately or simultaneously with two strains. These differences in antibody response were not solely dependent upon antigenic mass administered as demonstrated by the failure of a 100-fold increase in antigenic mass to convert a 2-MES response to that of 2-MER, although a 100-fold diminution in antigenic mass converted the 2-MER response to 2-MES. No difference in the carbohydrate composition of the lipopolysaccharides obtained from these strains was apparent from gas chromatographic analysis. Thus, these studies demonstrate that the immune response of a given host can be determined not only by the quantity of antigen but also by differing characteristics of lipopolysaccharides from a single bacterial species.

The sequential developement of IgM and IgG antibody to antigenic challenge with most soluble proteins, viral and flagellar antigens has been demonstrated in various animal species (1–7). With these antigens, the latent period before appearance of IgG is characteristically short. In contrast, somatic antigens (O) of some Gram-negative organisms, e.g., *Salmonella typhosa*, evoke an IgM antibody response but induce little IgG antibody except with hyperimmunization (1–4, 8, 9). Even when IgG antibody activity is elicited by somatic antigen, the latent period may be as long as several months after primary challenge (1–9).

In the course of studies on experimental pyelonephritis in rats, a variation in antibody response to antigenically differing somatic antigen (O) of organisms within the same bacterial species was noted. Certain strains of *Proteus mirabilis* induced the synthesis of 2-mercaptoethanol sensitive, or IgM, antibody, whereas challenge with other strains led to the rapid appearance of 2-mercaptoethanol resistant, or IgG, antibody. The following studies were designed to determine whether the difference in immunoglobulin response was the result of differences in antigenic mass, cell wall structure or host factors.

[1] This study was supported by United States Public Health Service Grant 5-R01-HD-00851 from the National Institute of Child Health and Human Development.

[2] Veterans Administration Clinical Investigator and supported in part by a Public Health Service Research Career Development Award (1 K04 AI-05097-01) from the National Institute of Allergy and Infectious Diseases.

MATERIAL AND METHODS

Preparation of antigen. Twelve isolates of *Proteus mirabilis* were obtained from the bacteriology laboratory. These strains differed from each other by the Dienes effect, and their antigenic differences were confirmed by tube agglutination tests involving homologous and heterologous antisera (10). Antigen for injection was prepared by growing the bacteria in trypticase soy broth[3] for 6 hr at 37°C. The cultures were boiled for 2 hr, sedimented by centrifugation, washed with normal saline, and resuspended in a volume equal

[3] Baltimore Biological Laboratories, Cockeysville, Md.

to the original volume. Preparation of antigen in this manner consistently yielded 1 × 10^9 killed organisms/ml.

Immunization. Sprague-Dawley rats[4] weighing 200 to 250 g were injected subcutaneously at four sites with a total volume of 1 ml (1 × 10^9 organisms). Sequential bleedings were made from the retrobulbar venous plexus. The blood was held for 1 hr at room temperature and overnight at 4°C, then the serum was separated by centrifugation, placed in sterile tubes, and stored at −20°C.

Preparation of lipopolysaccharide (endotoxin). Ethanol-precipitated aqueous ether extracts of two Proteus strains designated G and F were prepared by the method of Ribi *et al.* (11). The concentration of organisms in cultures of both strains had been adjusted to the same optical density before extraction and nearly equal quantities of the purified lipopolysaccharide were obtained after extraction. Ten rats were each given 0.1 mg subcutaneously of either Proteus F or G purified lipopolysaccharide suspended in 1 ml of normal saline.

Bacterial agglutination. Serum antibody levels were determined using an agglutination technique. The somatic antigen of each of the 12 Proteus strains (designated A to L) was prepared by boiling an 18-hr trypticase soy broth culture for 2 hr. The antigen was sedimented, washed in normal saline, and resuspended in normal saline containing formalin at a final concentration of 0.5%. This antigen contained 2 × 10^9 organisms/ml. Agglutination titers were performed on duplicate twofold serial dilutions of sera using microtiter equipment.[5] Antigen (50 μl containing 1 × 10^8 organisms) was added to one set of sera and an equal amount of antigen containing 2-mercaptoethanol (2-ME) to a final concentration of 0.1 M was added to the second set. The plates were incubated for 2 hr at 50°C and held overnight at 4°C. The titers are expressed as the $\log_2$ of the last dilution exhibiting gross agglutination. The antibody titers reported are the mean of at least 10 animals in each group.

Characterization of antibodies. Centrifugation was performed in a Spinco model L ultracentrifuge at 100,000 × G. One-half milliliter of serum was layered on 4.5 ml of a 10% to 40% sucrose gradient and centrifuged for 15 hr in a SW 39 swinging bucket rotor. Fractions were collected by puncturing the bottom of cellulose nitrate centrifuge tubes. Protein content was estimated by absorbance at 280 nm. Antibody activity in fractions was assessed as described above.

Immunoelectrophoresis was done by the microtechnique of Scheidegger, using goat anti-rat globulin as antiserum[6] (12).

Gas chromatographic analysis of carbohydrates in the somatic antigens. The carbohydrates in the somatic antigens were analyzed by gas-liquid chromatography of *o*-trimethylsilyl derivatives by the method of Sweeley *et al.* as adapted by Davis *et al.* (13, 14). Boivin extracts (endotoxins) of the 12 proteus strains were prepared by the method of Webster *et al.* (15). One to two milligrams of the lyophilized Boivin extracted endotoxin was weighed into a screwcap test tube provided with a Teflon liner and treated with 4 ml of 0.5 N methanolic HCl for 24 hr at 75 to 80°C. The reaction mixture was cooled to room temperature, an equal volume of hexane was added, and the upper layer was discarded. The preparation was then placed over a column containing 3 ml of Amberlite CG4B and 8 to 10 ml of Amberlite IR-120. The sample was eluted with 40 to 50 ml of anhydrous methanol.

The eluted material was evaporated to dryness with a vacuum evaporator. The dry carbohydrates were washed out of the tube with methanol into a small screwcap test tube and taken to dryness under a stream of nitrogen. Trimethylsilyl (TMS) derivatives were prepared by the addition of 0.2 ml of Tri-Sil[7] to the dry endotoxin extract. The mixture was allowed to react overnight at ambient temperature, taken to dryness with a stream of nitrogen and then dissolved in 25 μl of acetone. Three to five microliters of the mixture were injected into the injection port of a Hewlett-Packard 5750 gas chromatograph which was equipped with a hydrogen flame ionization detector. The column consisted of SE-52 coated on a chromasorb W support in ⅛ in. by 24 ft. coiled silanized stainless steel column.[8] All determinations were performed at 180°C.

RESULTS

Response of rats to somatic antigen of Proteus mirabilis. Two patterns of immune response were observed following primary challenge. Nine of 12

[4] Ferguson Rabbit Farm, Lewisville, Texas.
[5] Cooke Engineering Co., Alexandria, Va.
[6] Hyland Laboratories, Los Angeles, Calif.
[7] Pierce Chemical Co., Rockford, Ill.
[8] Hewlett-Packard, Avondale, Pa.

TABLE I

Antibody response to somatic antigen of Proteus mirabilis strains which evoked synthesis of predominantly 2-ME sensitive antibody

Strain	Day	Agglutination Titer ($\log_2$) ± 1 SD	
		Total	2-MER[a]
A	6	8.7 ± 1.4	1.0
B	6	6.4 ± 1.6	0.9
	14	5.6 ± 2.2	1.9 ± 2.1
	21	4.8 ± 1.1	1.4 ± 2.0
D	6	8.1 ± 1.2	0
E	6	5.6 ± 1.4	0
G	6	7.4 ± 1.4	0
	14	3.9 ± 0.9	2.3 ± 1.0
	21	3.2 ± 1.2	2.4 ± 0.8
H	6	6.9 ± 1.2	1.5 ± 1.1
I	6	7.5 ± 0.7	1.9
	12	6.9 ± 1.3	0
K	6	7.5 ± 0.9	0.6
	12	5.0 ± 1.0	0
L	6	8.4 ± 1.5	1.4 ± 1.0
	12	5.1 ± 1.2	1.0 ± 1.2

[a] Abbreviation for titer performed in the presence of 0.1 M 2-mercaptoethanol.

TABLE II

Antibody response to the somatic antigens of Proteus mirabilis strains which led to the synthesis of 2-ME resistant antibody

Strain	Day	Agglutination Titer ($\log_2$) ± 1 SD	
		Total	2-MER
C	6	8.4 ± 0.7	4.7 ± 0.6
	14	8.8 ± 3.0	5.6 ± 3.0
	29	5.4 ± 3.3	3.8 ± 2.3
F	6	7.1 ± 0.9	5.4 ± 1.8
	14	6.4 ± 3.1	5.0 ± 2.6
	20	4.2 ± 1.7	4.2 ± 2.8
J	6	9.4 ± 0.9	3.8 ± 1.4
	12	7.2 ± 0.4	4.9 ± 1.4
	19	9.1 ± 3.5	5.0 ± 2.4

strains induced the synthesis of antibody which was predominantly 2-ME sensitive (2-MES) (Table I). The peak antibody response was present 6 days after challenge and was almost completely reduced by 2-mercaptoethanol (2-MES). As the total antibody declined by day 12 to 14, small quantities of 2-ME resistant (2-MER) antibody were noted with strains B, G and L. No significant increase in 2-MER antibody occurred in the animals receiving the two strains (B and G) evaluated at 21 days.

Three other strains which had been designated C, F and J evoked the synthesis predominantly of 2-MER antibody (Table II). In these studies 2-MER antibody was present at the initial day of study (day 6), although total antibody levels at this time were not significantly different from levels seen in response to the other nine strains. Both total and 2-MER antibody persisted at high levels through day 14. As the total antibody level declined, 2-MER antibody persisted in significant titer.

The antibody response to two strains (G and F) selected to represent both patterns of antibody response was compared over a period of time in different animals (Table III). Again, strain G evoked the synthesis of 2-MES antibody, this immunoglobulin being present on days 14 and 20.

TABLE III

Sequential antibody response to Proteus mirabilis strains G and F in different animals

Strain	Day	Agglutination Titer ($\log_2$) ± 1 SD	
		Total	2-MER
G	4	5.4 ± 1.0	0
	6	7.0 ± 1.3	0
	14	3.9 ± 0.9	2.3 ± 0.5
	20	3.2 ± 1.2	2.4 ± 0.8
F	4	8.3 ± 1.2	3.8 ± 0.8
	6	8.2 ± 1.8	5.3 ± 0.8
	14	6.4 ± 3.1	5.0 ± 2.6
	20	4.2 ± 1.7	4.3 ± 2.8

TABLE IV

Sequential antibody response to the somatic antigen of Proteus mirabilis strains G and F given simultaneously to the same animals

Strain	Day	Agglutination Titer ($\log_2$) ± 1 SD	
		Total	2-MER
G	3	2.2 ± 0.5	0
	5	4.2 ± 0.9	0
	8	5.2 ± 1.9	0
	11	4.2 ± 1.3	1.4 ± 2.0
	18	2.8 ± 2.2	2.5 ± 1.1
F	3	6.4 ± 1.1	0.6 ± 1.0
	5	7.5 ± 1.5	3.5 ± 1.4
	8	7.2 ± 0.9	6.0 ± 1.6
	11	6.5 ± 0.7	4.2 ± 0.4
	18	4.2 ± 0.4	3.8 ± 1.4

TABLE V

The effect of antigenic mass on antibody response to somatic antigen of Proteus mirabilis strain G

No. of Organisms Injected	Day	Agglutination Titer (log_2) ± 1 SD	
		Total	2-MER
10^9	6	7.4 ± 1.4	0
	14	3.9 ± 1.5	2.3 ± 1.0
	29	3.2 ± 1.2	2.4 ± 0.8
10^{10}	5	3.7 ± 0.9	1.4 ± 1.0
	9	6.9 ± 0.4	0.6 ± 1.0
	19	3.0 ± 0.6	2.6 ± 0.5
10^{11}	4	3.6 ± 0.6	0
	7	6.4 ± 1.5	1.8 ± 0.4
	10	7.4 ± 0.9	1.2 ± 1.1
	17	2.8 ± 2.7	2.2 ± 2.0

TABLE VI

The effect of antigenic mass on antibody response to somatic antigen of Proteus mirabilis strain F

No. of Organisms Injected	Day	Agglutination Titer (log_2) ± 1 SD	
		Total	2-MER
10^9	4	8.3 ± 0.8	2.2 ± 3.0
	7	10.3 ± 0.8	5.5 ± 1.8
	14	8.8 ± 1.0	5.6 ± 2.2
	29	5.4 ± 0.5	3.8 ± 1.4
	51	5.3 ± 0.5	3.5 ± 0.8
10^8	7	8.1 ± 0.9	3.2 ± 1.6
	14	6.9 ± 0.9	3.3 ± 1.4
	29	4.1 ± 1.3	2.7 ± 1.2
	51	3.4 ± 0.5	2.0 ± 1.4
10^7	4	6.8 ± 1.2	0
	7	8.0 ± 0.8	1.3 ± 1.0
	14	5.9 ± 1.9	0
	29	0	0
10^5	7	3.0 ± 2.2	0
	14	2.0 ± 0	0

In contrast, strain F led to the synthesis of 2-MER antibody which was present even by day 4.

To determine whether this difference in immune response was dependent upon variations in the immunologic capabilities of the host, individual animals were challenged simultaneously with the same two representative strains studied previously (G and F) (Table IV). The patterns of immune responses were similar to those observed in animals receiving a challenge with a single organism. In response to proteus G, the total antibody, which reached a peak by day 8, was 2-MES. As noted before, as the total antibody level declined, very small quantities of 2-MER antibody appeared. A sequence of classes of antibody occurred with strain F. At day 3 the antibody was 2-MES, but 2-MER antibody appeared by day 5 and remained present in significant titer throughout the period of study.

Further studies were done to determine whether these differences in the pattern of immune response might be due to differences in antigenic mass. Heat-killed organisms from strain G, concentrated 10-fold and 100-fold, were used to challenge animals (Table V). No significant difference in either the total antibody response or in the quantity of 2-MER antibody was noted in animals which received increased quantities of antigen compared with those which received the standard challenge of 10^9 organisms.

The immune responses following challenge with decreasing quantities of somatic antigen from proteus F were compared (Table VI). As previously noted, 10^9 organisms induced the synthesis of 2-MER antibody which persisted through day 51. Reduction in dose to 10^8 organisms resulted in slightly lower total and 2-MER antibody levels. However, when the challenge dose had been reduced to 10^7 organisms, only 2-MES antibody was produced and none was detectable at 29 days.

Antibody response to purified lipopolysaccharide (endotoxin). Challenge with the lipopolysaccharide from proteus G resulted in a very low titer of 2-MES antibody (Table VII). In contrast, challenge with an equal amount of lipopolysaccharide from proteus F elicited good 2-MER antibody response which was detectable by day 4 and persisted through day 39.

Characterization of antibody by sucrose gradient ultracentrifugation. Sucrose gradient ultracentrifugation of a number of sera was performed to

TABLE VII

Antibody response to purified lipopolysaccharides of Proteus mirabilis strains G and F

Strain	Day	Agglutination Titer (log_2) ± 1 SD	
		Total	2-MER
G	4	2.0 ± 1.0	0
	6	1.5 ± 1.2	0
	9	0	0
F	4	7.4 ± 1.1	4.2 ± 1.9
	6	8.3 ± 0.9	5.5 ± 2.6
	9	8.4 ± 1.4	4.8 ± 3.2
	39	4.4 ± 1.7	3.4 ± 1.0

confirm the data obtained by reductive cleavage as to the class of antibody synthesized. Titers were performed on fractions collected from sucrose gradients of sera obtained from animals given proteus G or F. Analysis of representative sera having 2-MES but no 2-MER antibody demonstrated the antibody activity to be present in the early sedimenting fractions (Fig. 1). Ultracentrifugation of representative sera from animals challenged with proteus F which contained 2-MER antibody revealed that 2-MES antibody was also present in the early sedimenting fractions (Fig. 2). Later sedimenting fractions (tubes 4 to 7) contained antibody which was 2-MER. Immunoelectrophoresis with goat anti-rat serum demonstrated IgG in fractions 4 to 7.

Gas chromatographic analysis of carbohydrates of purified lipopolysaccharides. A large number of peaks (10 to 18) were present when gas chromatography was performed on the extracted endotoxins of the proteus strains (Table VIII). In general, the same peaks were present in a similar distribution in the proteus strains eliciting a 2-MES response as in the strains eliciting 2-MER responses. No separate peak or numbers of peaks were present or absent in proteus strains C, F and J which were not similarly present or absent in at least some of the other nine strains. Of the standard sugars studied, only a few were possibly present in these endotoxins, rhamnose, D-ribose and the second peak of α-D-glucose. No peaks with the retention times of galactose, β-D-glucose or the major peak of α-D-glucose were discernible. As a control of the method, endotoxins of a Salmonella species and *Escherichia coli* 075 were prepared by the same method and chromatographed. Both galactose and the major peak of α-D-glucose were present in chromatographs of the lipopolysaccharides of both organisms.

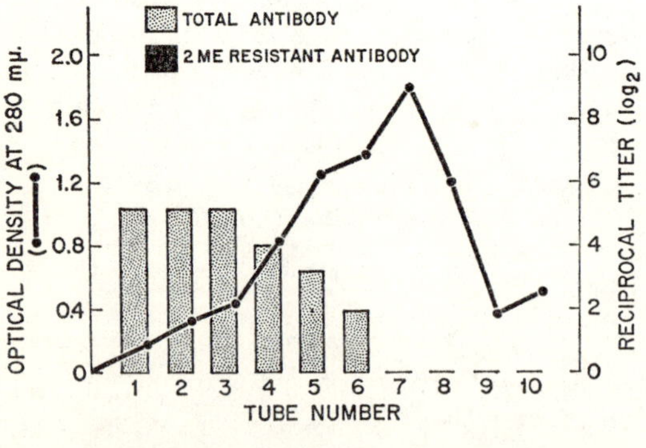

Figure 1. Total reciprocal serum antibody titer was 8 (log_2) and 2-MER was zero on serum obtained from animal given proteus G. Tubes were obtained from bottom of cellulose nitrate tube following ultracentrifugation in sucrose gradient.

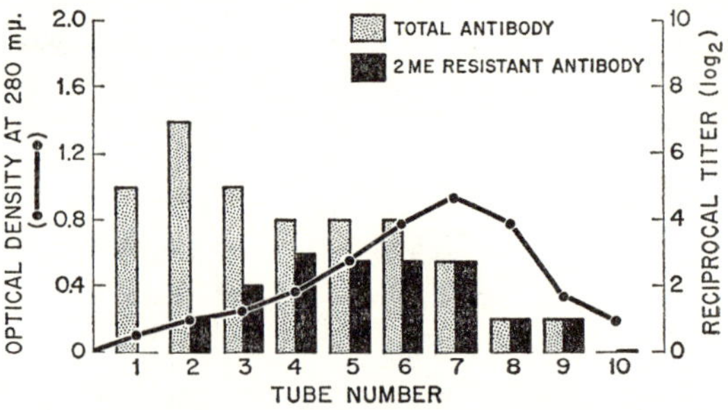

Figure 2. Total reciprocal serum antibody titer was 8 (log_2) and 2-MER was 7 on serum obtained from animal given proteus F. Tubes were obtained from bottom of cellulose nitrate tube following ultracentrifugation in sucrose gradient.

DISCUSSION

Earlier studies have demonstrated that antigens administered intravenously to rats elicit an antibody response which is predominantly IgM or 2-mercaptoethanol sensitive (2-MES) (16). Yet the capability of the rat to produce IgG or 2-mercaptoethanol resistant (2-MER) antibody has been demonstrated following hyperimmunization with antigen injected in Freund's adjuvant or antigen given as viable organisms which lead to an infection (16, 17). The character of the host response to an antigen may be of major importance in protection against the consequences of infection. While IgM antibody has been demonstrated to surpass IgG quantitatively in agglutination reactions, IgG is more effective in the neutralization of toxins and in the opsonization of bacteria (18–21).

The present studies demonstrate a remarkable difference in the immunologic response of the rat to primary challenge with different antigenic strains of *Proteus mirabilis*. The response to the majority of the strains of *Proteus mirabilis* is similar to that evoked by most other somatic antigens of Gram-negative organisms in that they induce the synthesis of only 2-MES antibody with primary challenge (1–4). In contrast, one-quarter of the strains of *Proteus mirabilis* studied induced the rapid appearance of 2-MER antibody upon primary challenge. With these latter strains

TABLE VIII

Gas chromatographic analysis of carbohydrates of purified lipopolysaccharides from Proteus strains[a]

Retention Time[b] of Separate Peaks	Proteus Strains Eliciting:											
	2-MES response									2-MER response		
	A	B	D	E	G	H	I	K	L	C	F	J
0.115	+	+	+	0	+	+	0	+	+	+	+	+
0.176	+	+	+	+	+	+	+	+	+	+	+	+
0.195	+	+	0	+	+	+	+	+	+	+	0	+
0.221	+	0	0	+	+	0	+	0	+	0	+	0
0.260	+	+	+	+	+	+	+	+	+	+	0	+
0.290	0	0	0	+	+	0	+	0	+	0	0	0
0.310	+	0	0	+	0	+	0	+	+	0	+	+
0.350	+	0	0	+	0	0	+	+	+	0	+	0
0.380	+	0	0	0	+	+	+	+	+	0	0	+
0.400	0	+	+	0	0	0	0	0	0	+	+	+
0.440	+	0	+	+	+	+	+	+	+	+	0	+
0.466	+	+	0	0	0	+	+	+	0	0	0	0
0.527	+	0	+	+	0	0	+	+	0	+	0	0
0.565	+	0	0	0	+	+	+	0	+	0	+	+
0.600	+	+	+	+	+	0	0	0	0	+	0	0
0.650	+	0	0	0	0	0	0	0	0	+	+	0
0.750	0	+	+	+	0	+	0	0	0	+	0	0
0.860	+	0	0	0	+	0	0	0	+	+	0	+
0.915	0	0	0	0	+	+	+	0	0	0	+	0
0.960	0	+	0	0	0	0	0	0	0	+	0	0
1.05	0	0	+	+	+	+	+	0	+	+	0	+
1.15	+	+	+	+	0	+	0	0	0	0	0	0
1.22	+	0	0	+	+	0	0	0	+	0	+	+
1.34	+	0	0	+	0	0	+	0	0	0	+	0
1.42	0	0	0	+	0	+	0	0	0	0	0	0

[a] *Standards Sugars*	*Retention Time*
L-Arabinose	0.298
D-Ribose	0.351
Rhamnose	0.371
Xylose	0.449
D-Mannose	0.699
β-D-Fructose	0.736
Galactose	0.887
α-D-Glucose I	1.0
α-D-Glucose II	1.05
β-D-Glucose	1.48

[b] Retention times are calculated on the basis of α-D-glucose having a retention time of 1.0 on a SE-52 column at 180°C.

the sequential appearance of IgM, then IgG was noted. Also, the class of antibody produced was dependent upon antigenic mass administered (4–7). This 2-MER antibody response was not due to hyperimmunization, since none of the animals tested before immunization had serum antibody and only a single dose of antigen was administered.

One possible explanation for the failure of certain strains to elicit a 2-MER antibody response might have been that less somatic antigen was present per volume of heat-killed organisms injected. The demonstration that a 100-fold increase in the quantity of antigen injected failed to stimulate a 2-MER antibody response militates against this explanation. Also, injection of nearly equal quantities of purified lipopolysaccharides prepared from representative strains led to the same antibody response as did the injection of heat-killed organisms.

Antigenic differences between somatic antigens within the Salmonella species are dependent upon different immunodominant sugars (22, 23). Previous workers have demonstrated that the absence of a single sugar from a strain of *E. coli* 013 correlated with a significant alteration in the antigenic characteristics of this bacterium (24). For this reason, gas chromatography of the purified lipopolysaccharides was performed to determine whether these differences in character of antibody response i.e., 2-MES and 2-MER, might be correlated with differences in sugar content within the bacterial cell walls of *Proteus mirabilis*. The analysis failed to uncover differences in sugar composition that correlated with the induction of 2-MES or 2-MER antibody, but the studies did demonstrate that these 12 Proteus strains differ markedly from Salmonella species in that neither galactose nor the major peak of α-D-glucose is a component of the proteus cell wall (22).

Thus, these studies demonstrate that the immune response of a given host can be determined not only by quantity of antigen but also by differing characteristics of lipopolysaccharides obtained from a single bacterial species. No difference in the carbohydrate composition of the lipopolysaccharides was obvious from gas chromatographic studies. However it is possible that alterations in the sequence of immunodominant sugars or configurational differences could have been responsible for the variation in immune response.

Acknowledgment. The authors wish to express their appreciation to Miss Martha Jane Adkins for her excellent technical assistance and to Mr- George Crowley of Analytical Consultants, Inc., Dallas, Texas, who performed the gas chromatography. The excellent support of Carolyn Wickwire in preparation of the manuscript is gratefully acknowledged.

REFERENCES

1. Bauer, D. C. and Stavitsky, A. B., Proc. Nat. Acad. Sci., *47:* 1667, 1961.
2. LoSpalluto, J., Miller, W., Jr., Dorward, B. and Fink, C. W., J. Clin. Invest., *41:* 1415, 1962.
3. Fink, C. W., Miller, W. E., Jr., Dorward, B. and LoSpalluto, J., J. Clin. Invest., *41:* 1422, 1962.
4. Bauer, D. C., Mathies, M. J. and Stavitsky, A. B., J. Exp. Med., *117:* 889, 1963.
5. Uhr, J. W. and Finkelstein, M. S., J. Exp. Med., *117:* 457, 1963.
6. Svehag, S.-E. and Mandel, B., J. Exp. Med., *119:* 1, 1964.
7. Uhr, J. W. and Finkelstein, M. S., Progr. Allerg., *10:* 37, 1967.
8. Pike, R. M. and Schulze, M. L., Proc. Soc. Exp. Biol. Med., *115:* 829, 1964.
9. Mulholland, J. H., Wolff, S. M., Jackson, A. L. and Landy, M., J. Clin. Invest., *44:* 920, 1965.
10. Dienes, L., Proc. Soc. Exp. Biol. Med., *63:* 265, 1946.
11. Ribi, E., Haskins, W. T., Landy, M. and Milner, K. C., J. Exp. Med., *114:* 647, 1961.
12. Scheidegger, J. J., Int. Arch. Allerg., *7:* 103, 1955.
13. Sweeley, C. C., Bentley, R., Makita, M. and Wells, W. W., J. Amer. Chem. Soc., *85:* 2497, 1963.
14. Davis, C. E., Freedman, S. D., Douglas, H. and Braude, A. I., Anal. Biochem., *28:* 243, 1969.
15. Webster, M. E., Sagin, J. F., Landy, M. and Johnson, A. G., J. Immun., *74:* 455, 1955.
16. Dixon, F. J., Jacot-Guillarmod, H. and McConahey, P. J., J. Immun., *97:* 350, 1966.
17. Pazin, G. J. and Braude, A. I., J. Immun., *102:* 1454, 1969.
18. Robbins, J. B., Kenny, K. and Suter, E., J. Exp. Med., *122:* 385, 1965.
19. Robbins, J. B., in *Molecular and Cellular Basis of Antibody Formation*, Edited by J. Sterzl, p. 241, Academic Press, Inc., New York, 1965.
20. Smith, J. W., Barnett, J. A., May, R. P. and Sanford, J. P., J. Immun., *98:* 336, 1967.
21. Laxdal, T., Messner, R. P., Williams, R. C., Jr. and Quie, P. G., J. Lab. Clin. Med., *71:* 638, 1968.
22. Lüderitz, O., Staub, A. M. and Westphal, O., Bact. Rev., *30:* 192, 1966.
23. Kim, Y. B. and Watson, D. W., Ann. N. Y. Acad. Sci., *133:* 727, 1966.
24. Tate, W. J., III, Douglas, H. and Braude, A. I., Ann. N. Y. Acad. Sci., *133:* 746, 1966.

THE JOURNAL OF IMMUNOLOGY

Vol. 105, No. 2, August 1970
Printed in U.S.A.

THE EFFECTS OF A BLOCKADING AGENT ON THE PRIMARY IMMUNE RESPONSE[1]

J. GABRIEL MICHAEL[2] AND CAROLINE MURRAY

From the Department of Microbiology, University of Cincinnati College of Medicine, Cincinnati, Ohio

Received for publication January 12, 1970

The effects of the blockading agent Thorotrast on the uptake of Escherichia coli O127:B8 by the cells of the reticuloendothelial system (RES) in the mouse and on the immune response to the bacterial antigen were investigated. It was found that Thorotrast given both intraperitoneally and intravenously suppressed the immune response to the bacterial antigen. Reduction in the immune response was not directly related to blockade of the RES. Thorotrast in addition to blocking selectively phagocytic cells of certain organs of RES was found to affect lymphoid cells involved in the process of antibody formation.

Agents that blockade the reticuloendothelial system (RES) have been reported to suppress the primary immune response to various antigens. Since they are known to interfere with the phagocytic activity of cells in RES, it was suggested that the inhibition of antibody formation results from inability of the antigen to enter phagocytic cells (1–3). These observations were considered as evidence that the phagocytosis of antigen is an essential step in initiation of the immune response. Some investigators noted, however, that a blockading agent can act as an adjuvant and enhance antibody formation (4, 5). To resolve this controversy we re-examined the role of a blockading agent in the immune response. We followed the fate of the antigen in blockaded animals, and we investigated the effect of the blockading agent on the mouse peritoneal macrophages and on the lymphoid cells of the spleen during the process of antibody formation.

MATERIALS AND METHODS

Animals. Six-week-old female CF_1 mice, supplied by Carworth Farms, Kalamazoo, Mich., were used throughout the studies.

Bacteria. Escherichia coli O127:B8 susceptible to antibody-complement bactericidal activity was employed, and the bacteria were heat-killed when they were used for immunization. The cells were internally labeled by growing them in a synthetic medium containing $Na_2{}^{32}SO_4$. External label was removed from the bacteria by repeated washing, and their radioactivity was determined in a gas-flow window counter (Nuclear Chicago Corp., Des Plaines, Ill.). When investigating the distribution of microorganisms in mouse organs, 0.2 ml of a heat-killed suspension containing 2×10^8 cells was used. This quantity of radioactive bacteria provided 3×10^5 counts/min in the gas-flow window counter.

Blockading agent. Thorotrast, a colloidal thorium dioxide preparation provided by Testagar Co., Detroit, Mich., was used to blockade the mouse RES. Two-tenths milliliter of the suspension contained about 50 mg of thorium dioxide and was found to be safely tolerated by mice. Thorotrast was injected i.p. or i.v.

Determination of the immune response. Antibody formation to the somatic antigen of *E. coli* O127: B8 was measured by Jerne's plaque-assay method, by counting the number of clear plaques in agar gel that appeared around bactericidal antibody-forming cells from mouse spleen. The technique has been described in detail elsewhere (6). The circulating bactericidal antibodies were measured by a complement-dependent system, using human cord serum as a source of complement. The details of the bactericidal antibody assay have been published (7).

Immunization. The immunizing dose of bacteria consisted of 5×10^8 heat-killed cells suspended

[1] This work was supported by United States Public Health Service Research Grant AI-08344, and by a grant from the Heart Association of Southwestern Ohio, Inc.

[2] United States Public Health Service Career Development Awardee.

in 0.5 ml of saline and injected i.v. or i.p. into the mice.

Carbon clearance and determination of K values. A technique described by Biozzi, Benacerraf and Halpern was followed (8). Commercial India ink, Pelican, prepared by Gunther Wagner, Hanover, Germany, was injected into mice i.v. in a dose of 0.2 ml. Samples of blood were removed by a capillary from the retro-orbital plexus at various time intervals and the concentration of carbon in the blood was determined spectrophotometrically. The rate of clearance followed an experimental function of the time $K = (\log C_1 - \log C_2)T$.

Collection of macrophages and preparation of spleen cell suspensions. An increase in the number of macrophages in the mouse peritoneal cavity was stimulated by the i.p. injection of 3 ml of Difco nutrient broth 3 days before the cells were collected. Ninety-five per cent of the peritoneal cells were shown to be macrophages capable of ingesting thorium dioxide particles. These cells were washed and suspended in culture medium 199. Suspensions of single spleen cells were prepared by gently probing the organ through a stainless steel sieve (mesh no. 80) into culture medium 199.

Irradiation. To suppress the immune mechanism, mice were given 850 R of total body irradiation, using a Westinghouse 250 kilovolt x-ray machine with a half layer value of 1.4 mm of copper, a focal distance of 60 cm (source to midpoint), and 0.5 mm copper plus 1 mm aluminum filter. The machine delivered about 85 R/min. The antigen was injected into mice about 6 hr after irradiation.

RESULTS

Suppression of the primary immune response. Thorotrast was administered i.v. or i.p. to mice at various times from 1 hr to 7 days before injection of the antigen. The antigen, i.e., heat-killed *E. coli* O127:B8, was also administered i.v. or i.p. Table I shows the results of experiments in which the immune response was measured by counts of the bactericidal plaque-forming cells in the spleen (*A*) and by the titers of bactericidal antibodies in the serum (*B*). The tests were performed 4 days after injecting the antigen. As shown by both the numbers of plaque-forming cells and the antibody titers, an interval of 24 hr was needed between the intravenous injections of the two substances to obtain a significant reduction of the immune response. Seven days after injecting Thorotrast the immune response had returned to normal. Injection of Thorotrast followed by intraperitoneal injection of the bacteria had a more immediate effect. The experimental data show that after an interval of only 1 hr between i.p. injections of the two substances, there was a marked reduction in the immune response. The suppressive effect of Thorotrast was still evident after 3 days. Thus, although Thorotrast suppressed the immune response when injected by both routes, it was more effective sooner and for a longer time when injected by the i.p. route.

Blockade of RES by Thorotrast. The blockading activity of Thorotrast was investigated by measuring the *K* values of carbon clearance in the blood as described in *Materials and Methods.* Samples of mouse blood were obtained at 2, 5, 10 and 20 min after the injection of India ink. Table

TABLE I

Effect of Thorotrast on the immune response to the somatic antigen of E. coli

Time Interval between Thorotrast and *E. coli* Injections	A		B	
	i.v. injections plaque-forming cells/spleen × 10^3	Bacteridical antibody titer[a]	i.p. injections plaque-forming cells/spleen × 10^3	Bactericidal antibody titer[a]
1 hr	67.7 ± 4.4	1:4000	6.3 ± 0.3	1:360
3 hr	72.3 ± 5.2	1:3600	5.1 ± 0.5	1:300
6 hr	21.8 ± 2.7	1:2200	3.3 ± 0.2	1:240
1 day	4.9 ± 0.7	1:320	8.3 ± 0.4	1:600
3 days	32.5 ± 3.6	1:1200	25.6 ± 3.0	1:3000
7 days	89.4 ± 6.5	1:5200	77.5 ± 4.6	1:6000
Control	82.6 ± 5.2	1:4500	91.4 ± 6.4	1:7500

[a] Antibody determinations were made 4 days after injection of the bacteria.

TABLE II

Carbon blood clearance following Thorotrast treatment

Thorotrast Treatment	K value[a]
i.v. 1 hr before carbon	0.002
i.v. 6 hr before carbon	0.004
i.v. 24 hr before carbon	0.011
i.p. 1 hr before carbon	0.023
i.p. 6 hr before carbon	0.043
i.p. 24 hr before carbon	0.023
Controls (untreated animals)	0.031

[a] Each K value expresses an average from a group of three to five mice.

II shows the average K values from groups of three to five mice after i.v. or i.p. administration of Thorotrast. RES blockade occurred when Thorotrast was injected i.v. 1 hr before India ink and was still present after 24 hr; it failed to occur when Thorotrast was injected i.p. at similar intervals before India ink. These results provided the first indication that blockade of the RES was not necessarily related directly to suppression of the immune response by Thorotrast.

To further investigate the relationship between blockade of the RES and antibody formation radiolabeled antigen was used. Table III shows the results of experiments in which Thorotrast was administered i.v. (*A*) and i.p. (*B*) 24 hr before the labeled bacteria. Groups of three mice were exsanguinated at varying times from 1 to 24 hr after i.v. injection of bacteria and the amounts of radioactivity in the blood, spleen and liver were determined (Table III*A*). As expected, the blood of blockaded animals contained more labeled antigen than did that of control animals. As compared to the corresponding tissues in control mice, the spleen also contained more labeled antigen, but the liver substantially less. In a similar experiment in which Thorotrast was injected i.p., the amounts of radioactivity in the peritoneum, blood, spleen and liver were distributed in a different pattern (Table III*B*). In comparison with the corresponding tissues of control mice, the peritoneum retained more labeled antigen, but none of the organs contained excess label.

It could be postulated that the bacteria were retained in the peritoneum because the Thorotrast-filled macrophages were unable to phagocytize and remove them. For this reason we examined these macrophages for their viability and ability to take up bacteria at various times after the injection of Thorotrast. In a short time (less than 1 hr) all macrophages were filled with the thorium dioxide particles and remained viable for several hours as ascertained by vital staining. These macrophages after contact with the labeled bacteria acquired radioactivity, but it was impossible to determine whether the bacteria had actually been phagocytized or were merely adherent to the leucocytes.

TABLE III

Effect of Thorotrast on the organ distribution of E. coli labeled with ^{35}S in normal mice as determined by the percentage of total radioactivity in various sites

Time after Injection of *E. coli*	A Intravenous[a]			B Intraperitoneal[b]			
	Blood	Spleen	Liver	Peritoneum	Blood	Spleen	Liver
hr							
	Treated						
1	4.4	7.0	26	85	2.0	1.1	4.0
2	3.7	6.6	18	72	4.7	2.3	13.0
6	3.6	6.7	15	46	4.0	3.3	21.0
24	2.4	2.2	8	20	2.6	1.8	10.2
	Controls: no Thorotrast						
1	2.2	1.6	70	70	1.8	1.2	4.5
2	2.6	1.8	54	47	5.0	2.0	15.0
6	2.8	2.0	37	21	3.6	3.1	22.0
24	2.1	1.0	12	1.5	2.2	1.6	12.0

[a] Thorotrast injected i.v. 24 hr before *E. coli*.
[b] Thorotrast injected i.p. 24 hr before *E. coli*.

Effect of immunization on the blockade. Several suggestions have been made to explain the mechanism of the RES blockade. One is that blockading agents act by loading the phagocytic cells to their utmost capacity; alternatively it has been proposed that blockading agents combine with factors in the circulation that are essential for phagocytosis. To determine which mechanism was operative in the production of blockade by Thorotrast, the following experiments were performed. Mice were immunized with *E. coli* O127: B8 or with *Salmonella typhosa* and 8 days later were injected i.v. with Thorotrast and labeled *E. coli*. As shown in Table IV, mice immunized

TABLE IV

Effect of Thorotrast on the organ distribution of an i.v. injection of E. coli labeled with ^{35}S into immunized mice as determined by the percentage of total radioactivity in various sites

Treatment	1 hr after i.v. Injection of *E. coli*		
	Blood	Spleen	Liver
Immunized with *E. coli*	2.6	2.1	58
Injected with *E. coli* antiserum	4.5	7.2	26
Immunized with *S. typhosa*	4.2	6.2	29
Untreated mice (controls)	3.9	6.6	31

with the homologous strain of bacteria did not develop the anticipated blockade of the liver. Abolition of the blockade was not observed in mice immunized with *S. typhosa* or given serum from other mice immunized with *E. coli*. It seemed that removal of the blockade involved some immunologically specific factors that were not circulating antibodies, since they were not transferred by serum.

Restoration of immune response in irradiated mice. Since the results did not indicate a correlation between Thorotrast blockade of the RES and suppression of the immune response, it was decided to determine whether cells other than macrophages were affected by Thorotrast. Syngeneic lymphoid spleen cells are known to restore the immune response in lethally irradiated mice. As shown in Table V a partial recovery of immune response to the somatic antigen of *E. coli* was obtained when 5×10^7 normal spleen cells were injected i.p. into heavily irradiated (850 R) mice. Spleen cells and the antigen were injected 6 hr after irradiation. Injection of the spleen cells from Thorotrast-treated animals into irradiated mice did not lead to the recovery of the immune system. In order to determine whether macrophages were the effective cells in the spleen, normal untreated peritoneal macrophages (10^6 cells) were injected together with the spleen cells from Thorotrast-treated animals. The addition of the normal peritoneal macrophages did not restore the immune response. It is therefore apparent that Thorotrast also affected the lymphoid cells of the spleen.

Induction of antibody formation by macrophage-associated antigen. It has been demonstrated that some antigens become more immunogenic when they are associated with macrophages (9). We wished to determine whether Thorotrast-filled peritoneal macrophages were capable of taking up bacterial antigen and, consequently, of inducing antibody formation. Mice were injected i.p. with Thorotrast and 1 hr later with labeled bacteria (2×10^8 cells). Controls were not given Thorotrast. Thirty minutes after injection of *E. coli* the mice in the two groups were exsanguinated, and their peritoneal cells were collected, washed and suspended in medium 199. Peritoneal cells (10^7 cells) from the Thorotrast-treated or control mice were then injected i.p. into untreated mice. The immune response to macrophage-associated bacterial antigens in mice is shown in Table VI. It is evident that Thorotrast did not alter the ability of the macrophage-linked antigen to initiate antibody formation.

TABLE V

Effect of Thorotrast-treated spleen cells on restoration of the immune response in irradiated (850 R) mice

Treatment of Mice Irradiated with 850 R Prior to *E. coli*[a]	Plaque-forming Cells/Spleen $\times 10^3$	Bactericidal Antibody Titer[b]
Thorotrast-spleen cells	0.09 ± 0.02	<1:5
Thorotrast-spleen cells + peritoneal macrophages	0.12 ± 0.01	<1:5
Control: normal spleen cells	3.65 ± 0.26	1:300
Control: no cells	0.03 ± 0.005	<1:5

[a] Cells and *E. coli* were injected i.p. simultaneously.

[b] Antibody response was tested 6 days after injection of *E. coli*.

TABLE VI

The effect of Thorotrast-filled macrophages exposed 30 min to E. coli in vivo when injected i.p. into normal mice

Treatment of Macrophages	Plaque-forming Cells/Spleen $\times 10^3$	Bactericidal Antibody Titer[a]
Thorotrast + *E. coli*	18.6 ± 2.1	1:2200
No Thorotrast + *E. coli*	22.4 ± 2.8	1:2400
Thorotrast-filled but no *E. coli*	0.02 ± 0.002	1:5
No Thorotrast and no *E. coli*	0.04 ± 0.004	1:5

[a] Antibody determinations were made 4 days after injection of the bacteria.

DISCUSSION

In this study we confirmed observations made by other investigators that agents that blockade the RES suppress the primary immune response (1–3). We limited our study to a single blockading agent, Thorotrast, and to a single antigen, *E. coli*. Although some of our results coincided with those of other investigators we did not reach the conclusion that blockade of the RES is the basis of the immunosuppressive activity of Thorotrast. Blockade was not observed in all organs rich in RES cells; the spleens of Thorotrast-treated animals showed a substantial increase in the uptake of labeled bacteria over that seen in normal animals. Stimulation of splenic uptake of erythrocyte stroma in mice injected by various blockading agents was also reported by Fisher (5). The injection of Thorotrast i.p. did not cause major blockade of the RES organs, as witnessed by the carbon clearance and labeling experiments, but antibody formation was suppressed. Using carbon as the blockading agent and sheep erythocytes as the antigen, Sabet *et al.* also reported immunosuppression by intraperitoneal injection (2, 3). The blockading agent affected cells other than the phagocytes, as is evident from the experiments in which irradiated mice were given spleen cells from syngeneic animals in an attempt to restore their immunologic competence. Neither spleen cells alone from Thorotrast-treated animals nor spleen cells combined with normal peritoneal macrophages were able to restore immunologic competence to the irradiated animals.

It has been reported that Thorotrast is toxic to peritoneal macrophages and ultimately destroys them (4). Under our experimental conditions this toxicity was not apparent. Thorotrast-filled macrophages remained viable and were capable of taking up labeled antigen. It was not determined, however, whether the antigen entered the macrophage or merely adhered to the cell surface, although the antigen induced the formation of antibacterial antibodies. The spleens of Thorotrast-treated mice were also examined histologically, and our findings were similar to those reported by Jenkin *et al.* (4), who showed that i.v. injection of Thorotrast caused depletion of cells from the germinal centers. Thorotrast-filled macrophages concentrated in the follicles and the red pulp became devoid of lymphocytes. These changes in spleen were evident for several days and could be correlated with decreased ability of the animal to respond to an antigenic stimulus.

Macrophages have been found by many investigators to be essential for initiating the immune response. Fishman and Adler (10) reported isolation of an immunogenic RNA from macrophages which ingested the antigen prior to RNA extraction. Askonas and Rhodes (11) suggested that the antigen forms a complex with macrophage RNA and that this complex is highly immunogenic. Mitchison showed that macrophage-associated antigen is more immunogenic than free antigen (9). Unanue and Cerrotini (12) suggested that antigen does not enter the macrophage but remains attached to its surface. Galily and Feldman (13) claimed that irradiated macrophages are incapable of processing antigen and that immune response in sublethally irradiated mice could be restored by administration of normal peritoneal macrophages. The present study does not deny the possible role of macrophages in antibody formation, but it shows that the suppressive effect of a blockading agent of the RES on the immune response cannot be used as evidence for the function of macrophages in antibody formation. Our results demonstrate that the damaging effect of Thorotrast extends to a wider spectrum of cell types involved in antibody formation.

REFERENCES

1. DiLuzio, N. R. and Wooles, W. R., Amer. J. Physiol., *206:* 939, 1967.
2. Sabet, T., Newlin, C. and Friedman, H., Proc. Soc. Exp. Biol. Med., *128:* 274, 1968.
3. Sabet, T., Newlin, C. and Friedman, H., Immunology, *16:* 433, 1969.
4. Jenkin, C. R., Auzins, I. and Reade, P. C., Austral. J. Exp. Biol. Med. Sci., *53:* 607, 1965.
5. Fisher, S., Immunology, *11:* 127, 1966.
6. Michael, J. G., J. Exp. Med., *123:* 205, 1966.
7. Landy, M., Michael, J. G. and Whitby, J., J. Bact., *83:* 631, 1962.
8. Biozzi, G., Benacerraf, B. and Halpern, B. N., Brit. J. Exp. Path., *34:* 441, 1953.
9. Mitchison, N. A., Immunology, *16:* 1, 1969.
10. Fishman, M. and Adler, F. L., J. Exp. Med., *117:* 595, 1963.
11. Askonas, B. A. and Rhodes, J. M., Nature, *205:* 470, 1965.
12. Unanue, E. R. and Cerrotini, J. C., Nature, *222:* 1193, 1969.
13. Galily, R. and Feldman, M., Immunology, *12:* 197, 1967.

THE JOURNAL OF IMMUNOLOGY
Vol. 105, No. 2, August 1970
Printed in U.S.A.

ANTIGENIC ANALYSIS OF HUMAN HEART TISSUE. ANTIGENS WITH RESTRICTED ORGAN DISTRIBUTION IN ACID EXTRACTS OF HUMAN MYOCARDIUM[1,2]

ENRIQUE ESPINOSA AND MELVIN H. KAPLAN[3]

From the Department of Medicine, Metropolitan General Hospital, Case Western Reserve University School of Medicine, Cleveland, Ohio

Received for publication January 9, 1970

Antigens of human myocardium solbuilized by acid extraction at pH 2.5 were submitted to further analysis by double diffusion and immunoelectrophoresis using rabbit antisera to fractions of human heart acid extract obtained by DEAE-cellulose chromatography. Combined immunodiffusion and specific absorption tests demonstrated at least six antigens common to cardiac and skeletal muscle in acid extracts of myocardium. An additional heart-specific antigen was demonstrated in such acid extracts as well as in saline washes of myocardium. Of the antigens common to cardiac and skeletal muscle, four were found present in the different mammalian species tested, and two showed specificity for primates. The heart-specific antigen exhibited both species-specific and species-cross-reactive antigenic properties. Rabbit antisera to human heart fractions were reactive also with rabbit antigen common to heart and skeletal muscle and with rabbit heart-specific antigen. The antigens common to cardiac and skeletal muscle varied in susceptibility to proteolytic digestion by Pronase, trypsin and pepsin. The heart-specific antigen was susceptible to all three enzymes.

It has been shown previously that antigens of human heart associated with sarcolemma of cardiac myofibers may be solubilized by acid extraction (1). With rabbit antisera to such acid extract preparations, two protein antigens restricted in organ distribution to heart and skeletal muscle were demonstrated by immunodiffusion and immunofluorescence. One of these antigens was found only in primate species while the other was found widely distributed among mammalian species. Ion-exchange chromatography on DEAE-cellulose permitted partial separation of these antigens in fractions which contained the antigen of wide species distribution only and fractions which contained both cardiac antigens.

In the present study, potent rabbit antisera were prepared against these separate chromatographic fractions of human heart acid extract. Whole acid extract and chromatographic fractions were subjected to immunodiffusion analysis with these antisera. Antisera to the fraction previously shown to contain only the antigen of wide species distribution now permitted differentiation of at least four heart antigens which were common to both heart and skeletal muscle and present in all species tested. Antisera to the fraction previously shown to contain both the antigen restricted to primates and the antigen of wide species distribution now revealed several of the foregoing antigens and three additional antigens: two of these latter antigens were common to heart and skeletal muscle and were restricted to primates, and one antigen exhibited organ specificity for heart and species-cross-reactive properties.

MATERIALS AND METHODS

Preparation of acid extracts of heart and other organs. Human post-mortem tissues or tissues from recently killed animals, stored in the frozen state, were thawed and homogenized in cold saline, and soluble constituents were extracted by three washes with saline and two washes with distilled water, as described (1). The washed tis-

[1] Presented in part at the 52nd Annual Meeting of the Federation of American Societies for Experimental Biology, April 1968, Atlantic City, New Jersey.

[2] Supported by Grant H-3726 from the National Heart Institute, United States Public Health Service.

[3] Research Career Awardee, United States Public Health Service (K-HE-4576).

sue homogenate was then extracted twice for 1 hr with 0.05 M citric acid, at a final pH of 2.5. In an alternative procedure, the homogenate was first dried with cold acetone, and the resultant powder was used for acid extraction. Both preparations gave identical immunodiffusion results. The acid extract was dialyzed for 24 hr in the cold against 0.01 M Na_2HPO_4 and then dialyzed for 3 to 4 days against frequent changes of distilled water until free of salt. Material rendered insoluble following dialysis was removed by high speed centrifugation, (16,000 rpm, 30 min) and the supernatant clear solution was lyophilized.

Preparation and properties of DEAE-cellulose chromatographic fractions I and II. Fractions of human heart acid extract were obtained by chromatography on DEAE-cellulose equilibrated with 0.005 M phosphate buffer, pH 8.0, as previously described (1). Twenty milliliters of acid extract at a concentration of 25 mg protein/ml were applied to a column 2 cm in diameter packed with DEAE-cellulose to a height of 28 cm. Fractions I and II were the protein peaks at 280 nm obtained by elution at pH 8.0 with 0.005 M phosphate and 0.3 M phosphate, respectively. The former peak was shown previously to contain antigen of wide species distribution, and the latter peak contained in addition antigen restricted to primates (1). The fractions were dialyzed against distilled water and lyophilized.

Fractions I and II contained respectively 13.3% and 13.1% nitrogen as determined by micro-Kjeldahl and nesslerization procedures (2) and 85.6% and 82.0% protein estimated by the biuret method of Dittenbrandt (3). The ultraviolet absorption spectrum of both fractions showed a maximum peak at 275 nm with a ratio of 280/260 = 1.27 for fraction I and 1.13 for fraction II. Fraction I showed four bands moving to the cathode and two to the anode on acrylamide gel electrophoresis (1). Fraction II showed three bands with anodal electrophoretic mobility.

Preparation of antisera. Chromatographic fractions I and II were dissolved in saline in a concentration of 10 mg/ml and emulsified in an equal volume of Freund's complete adjuvant (Difco Laboratories, Detroit, Mich.). Penicillin 100 units/ml and streptomycin 0.1 mg/ml were incorporated in the mixture. Four albino rabbits were immunized with each chromatographic fraction. The antigens were injected weekly as follows: first injection: 0.4 ml adjuvant mixture in the four footpads intradermally; second and third injection: 1 ml adjuvant mixture, intramuscularly, divided between two sites; fourth injection: 2 ml of antigen solution without adjuvant, 10 mg/ml, intraperitoneally. One week after the last injection blood was obtained from the marginal ear artery or by cardiac puncture. After a 2-month rest period, the above course of injection was repeated. Serum samples were stored in the frozen state.

Reaction of these immune sera with human plasma constituents was eliminated by absorption with 40 mg of lyophilized pooled normal human plasma/ml antiserum. Additional absorption with acid extracts of kidney or other tissue extracts was carried out with 40 mg lyophilized acid or saline extract/ml antiserum, unless otherwise stated.

Saline extracts of human and animal tissues. Human tissues considered to be normal grossly at post-mortem were selected from random autopsies within a few hours after death. Normal animal tissues were obtained immediately after they were killed. The tissues were dissected free of connective tissue, fat, and larger blood vessels and stored in the frozen state. They were thawed and minced with scissors in cold saline sufficient to remove most of the blood, and homogenized in five volumes of cold 0.85% NaCl in a Waring Blendor for 5 min. After centrifugation at 16,000 rpm for 30 min, the supernatant fluid containing the saline soluble extract was dialyzed against distilled water until free of salt. The slight flocculent material resulting after dialysis was removed by high speed centrifugation, and the supernatant was then lyophilized.

Homogenates of human myocardium treated as above were washed twice more with saline and twice with distilled water and the homogenate was then lyophilized. The saline and water washes of myocardium were dialyzed against distilled water until free of salt and material rendered insoluble following dialysis was removed by centrifugation. They were then lyophilized and their weights recorded. Acid extracts of the washed heart homogenates were prepared as described above.

Immunodiffusion. Double diffusion was carried out in 0.5% agarose (Marine Colloid, Inc., Springfield, N. J.) in 0.01 M phosphate-buffered saline, pH 7.2 containing 0.1% sodium azide. Circular wells 2 mm in diameter at 2 mm distance were generally used, and in some cases 5-mm wells at 5 mm distance. Immunoelectrophoretic analysis was performed according to the microtechnique of Scheidegger (4), using 1.5% agar in 0.025 M Veronal buffer at pH 8.2 on 1- x 3-inch slides. Electrophoresis was carried out at 5 V/cm for 40 min. Ouchterlony and immunoelectrophoresis plates were incubated at room temperature from 3 to 5 days and stained with amido black 10B.

Enzymatic treatment. Trypsin, pepsin and Pronase at a final concentration of 0.5 mg/ml were added to appropriately buffered heart extract preparations, at a concentration of the latter of 25 or 100 mg/ml, and the mixture was incubated at 37°C for 24 hr. Trypsin (twice crystallized, Worthington Biochemical Corp., Freehold, N.J.) was used in 0.1 M phosphate buffer, pH 8.0; pepsin (twice crystallized, Worthington) in 0.25 M citrate buffer, pH 3.0 and Pronase (Calbiochem, Los Angeles, Calif.) in 0.01 M phosphate-buffered saline, pH 7.2. Trypsin action was blocked by adding soy bean inhibitor; pepsin action was stopped by neutralization. Buffer alone was used in the control mixtures.

RESULTS

Antigens restricted in distribution to heart and skeletal muscle. Absorption of antisera with lyophilized human plasma and with kidney acid extract abolished all reactivity with acid extracts of organs other than heart and skeletal muscle. Antisera absorbed in this manner were used routinely in this work except as otherwise indicated.

With absorbed antisera to fraction I, up to four lines or bands of precipitation were obtained in double diffusion with whole acid extract preparations of human heart and skeletal muscle. These lines of precipitation were common to both organs; no evidence of an organ-specific antigen was obtained. No precipitation was obtained with acid extracts of kidney, lungs, spleen and liver (Fig. 1). After absorption of antisera with acid extracts of heart or of skeletal muscle, all lines of precipitation were abolished. Antisera to fraction I gave the same number of identical lines with fraction I, fraction II and the original acid extract. These lines could be completely abolished following absorption with either fraction. Absorption with washed homogenate of human heart, 100 mg/ml antiserum, also abolished precipitation with both heart and skeletal muscle extracts. Thus the antigens were present in reactive form in the homogenate. In contrast, absorption with saline soluble extract of heart was ineffective. In immunoelectrophoresis, four strong arcs of precipitation were obtained with whole acid extract of heart (Fig. 2). These antigens all moved toward the cathode during electrophoresis.

With absorbed antisera to chromatographic fraction II, from four to six lines of precipitation were obtained with whole acid extract of heart, as shown by immunoelectrophoresis (Fig. 3). The electrophoretic mobilities of these antigens were in some cases similar to and in other cases more anodal than the antigens defined with antisera to chromatographic fraction I. At least two of these antigens were present only in chromatographic fraction II since absorption with fraction I failed to remove these two lines of precipitation, while absorption with fraction II abolished these reactions completely.

In double diffusion tests with acid extracts of the various organs, these lines of precipitation were observed with heart and skeletal muscle extracts, but not with extracts of other organs (Fig. 4). Absorption of the antisera with heart acid extract or with washed homogenate of human heart, 100 mg/ml antiserum, abolished all lines of precipitation. Absorption of the antisera with acid extracts of skeletal muscle left a single line of precipitation with heart acid extract (Fig. 5). This line was not affected by an additional absorption of these latter antisera with acid extracts of lung, spleen, or liver. Thus this line of precipitation was related to an antigen with strict organ specificity for heart. Direct tests of fractions I and II with the antiserum to fraction II indicated that this antigen was present in both fractions.

Presence of heart specific antigen in both saline and acid extracts of heart. It was subsequently observed with antisera to fraction II that saline soluble extracts of heart also contained heart-specific antigen which gave a reaction of identity with that in acid extracts (Fig. 6). Organ specificity was confirmed by failure of saline or acid extracts of organs other than heart to abolish this reaction in absorption tests. However, it was abolished after absorption with saline or acid extracts of heart.

Successive saline and water washes of heart tissue and the acid extract prepared from this washed human heart tissue were tested for the

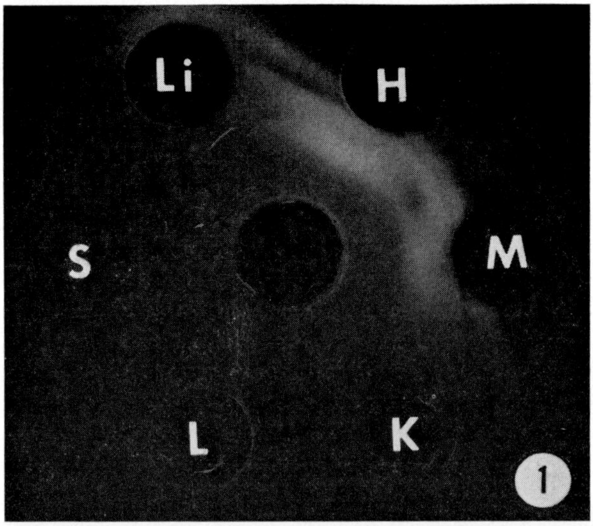

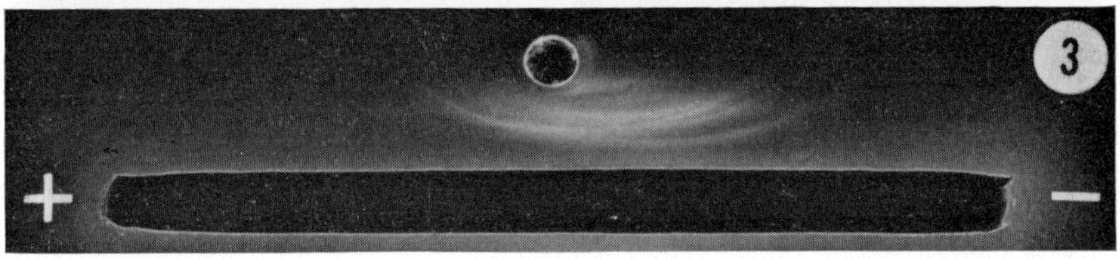

Figure 1. Central well contains antiserum 193D to fraction I. In this and in succeeding figures, antiserum is absorbed with human plasma and kidney acid extract, except as otherwise noted. Peripheral wells contain acid extracts of human organs at 1% concentration: *H*, heart; *M*, skeletal muscle; *K*, kidney; *L*, lungs; *S*, spleen; and *Li*, liver.

Figure 2. Trough contains antiserum 193D to fraction I. Well was filled with heart acid extract at 10% concentration.

Figure 3. Trough contains antiserum 902D to fraction II. Well was filled with heart acid extract at 10% concentration.

presence of heart-specific antigen using antiserum absorbed with acid extracts of kidney and muscle. The saline and water washes and acid extract were reconstituted from the lyophilized powders to their original concentration. As shown in Figure 6, the heart-specific antigen was present in the first two saline washes, was not detected in the third saline wash or in the subsequent two water washes, but was again found in the acid extract.

Estimates of the relative content of heart-specific antigen in saline and acid extracts were made based on dilution titers of antigenic activity in relation to weight of extracted material. As shown in Table I from a representative experiment, at equivalent concentration, the dilution titer of precipitating activity was approximately fourfold greater in acid extracts than in the first or subsequent saline washes. The sequential saline washes extracted diminishing amounts of solid material, which exhibited antigenic activity at the same concentration. Fourth and fifth saline washes extracted only small amounts, 5 to 10 mg of additional material, which were not tested.

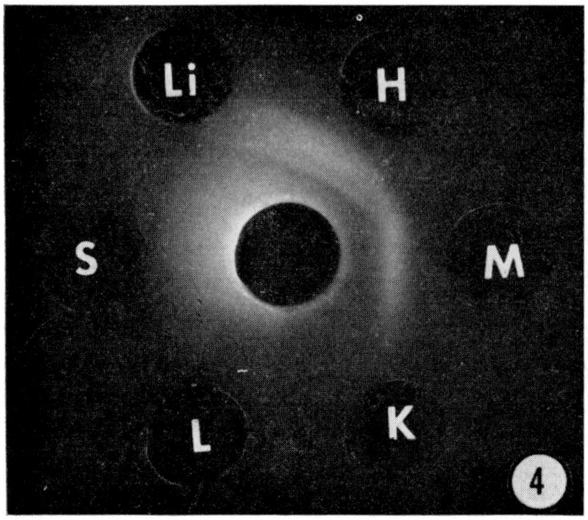

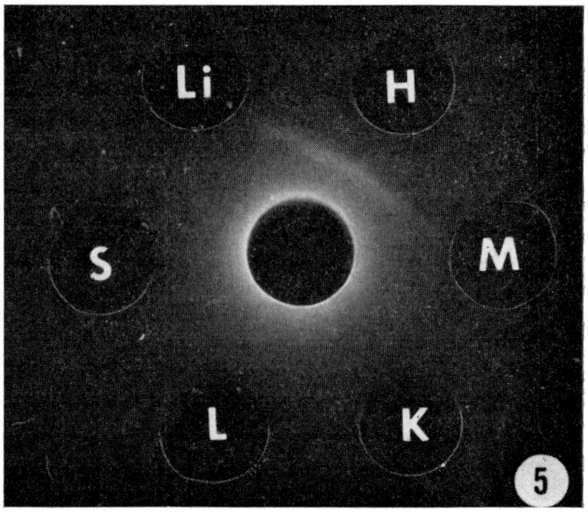

Figure 4. Central well contains antiserum 902D to fraction II. Peripheral wells as in Figure 1.
Figure 5. Central well contains antiserum 902D to fraction II, additionally absorbed with acid extract of skeletal muscle. Peripheral wells as in Figure 1.

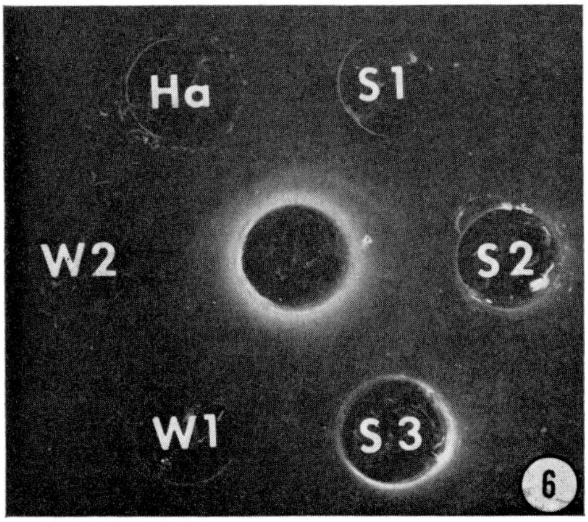

Figure 6. Central well contains antiserum 902D to fraction II, additionally absorbed with acid extract of skeletal muscle. Peripheral wells contain successive saline washes, *S1*, *S2* and *S3*; water washes, *W1* and *W2*; and acid extract, *Ha*, of human heart. The concentration in each case was adjusted to that of the original extract.

TABLE I

Organ-specific antigen of heart in saline and acid extracts

Preparation Tested	Weight Solid Extracted from 30 g (Wet Weight) Heart Tissue	Minimal Concentration Giving Precipitin Line with Absorbed Antiserum to Fraction II
	g	*mg/ml*
Saline wash 1	0.453	0.62
Saline wash 2	0.085	0.62
Saline wash 3	0.025	0.62
H_2O wash 1	0.014	>10.0[a]
H_2O wash 2	0.005	>10.0[a]
Acid extract	0.190	0.16

[a] Not reactive at 10 mg/ml, the highest concentration tested.

Distilled water washes contained little or no active antigen. A selective concentration of antigen in acid extract as compared with saline extracts was thus indicated by the data.

It was of interest that the line of precipitation related to the heart-specific antigen in both saline and acid extracts of heart often appeared split, particularly at lower concentration (Fig. 7), consistent with some degree of antigenic heterogeneity of the heart-related determinants.

As indicated by crossing of their precipitin lines, as well as by absorption tests, the heart-specific antigen was unrelated to any of the antigens of skeletal muscle (Fig. 8).

Species cross-reactivity of antigens in acid and saline extracts of heart. Immunodiffusion analysis of acid extracts of hearts of man, rhesus monkey, dog, rabbit, rat and beef were carried out in the present study. With antisera to fraction I, three or four lines of precipitation were observed with heart extracts of man, monkey, and dog, which showed reactions of complete identity (Fig. 9).

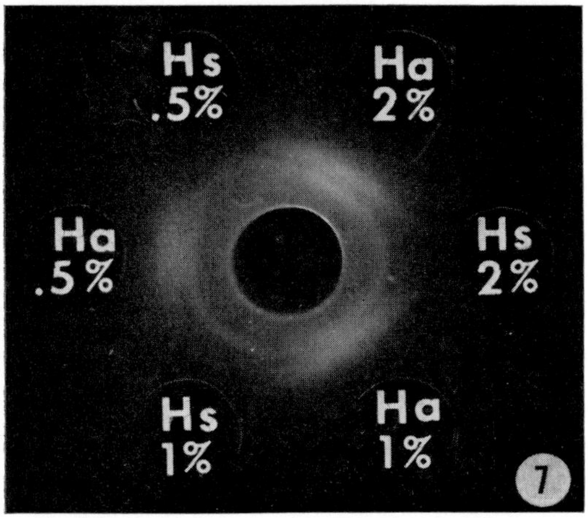

Figure 7. Central well contains antiserum 902D to fraction II. Peripheral wells contain heart acid extract, *Ha*, and saline extract of heart, *Hs*, at indicated concentrations.

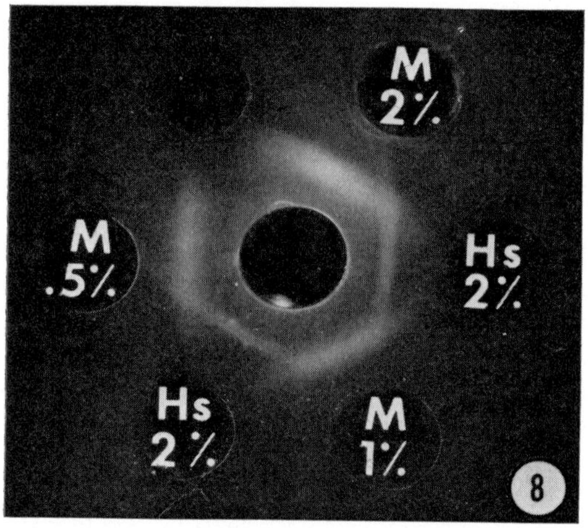

Figure 8. Central well contains antiserum 902D to fraction II. Peripheral wells contain acid extract of skeletal muscle, *M*, and saline extract of heart, *Hs*, at indicated concentrations.

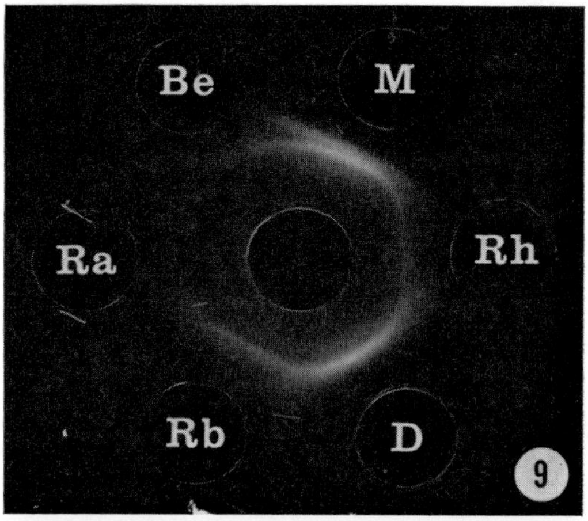

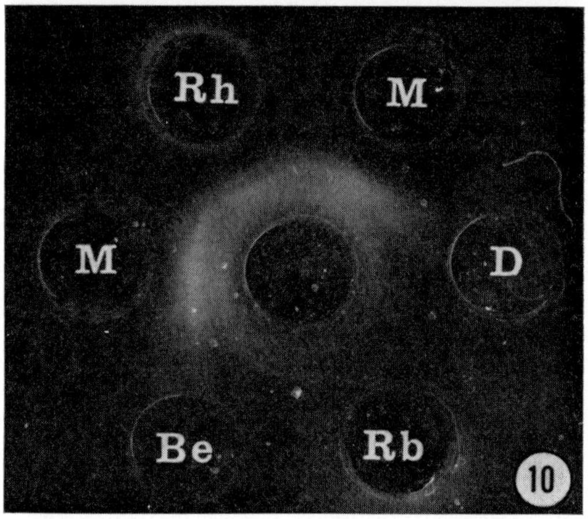

Figure 9. Central well contains antiserum 193E to fraction I. Peripheral wells contain 2% heart acid extract of man, *M*; rhesus monkey, *Rh*; dog, *D*; rabbit, *Rb*; rat, *Ra*; beef, *Be*.

Figure 10. Central well contains antiserum 902E to fraction II. Peripheral wells as in Figure 9.

With heart extracts of rabbit, rat, and beef, two lines of precipitation were observed which were common to all species tested. All of these lines were eliminated following absorption of antiserum with acid extracts of either human or dog heart. Thus, these lines were common to both primate and non-primate species. These lines were also eliminated following absorption of antiserum with either fraction I or fraction II thus indicating presence of these antigens in both chromatographic fractions.

In contrast, tests performed with antisera to fraction II gave at least one line or band of precipitation which was common to the heart extracts of all the various species tested and an additional two lines with extracts of human and monkey heart (Fig. 10). Absorption of antisera with dog heart extract abolished only the single line or band common to the various species. Absorption with human heart acid extract abolished all lines of precipitation.

Analogous results were obtained following absorption with chromatographic fractions I and II. Absorption with fraction I abolished the line related to the antigen of wide species distribution. Fraction II, on the other hand, abolished all lines of precipitation, and therefore contained both types of species-related antigen.

Species-related antigenic properties of organ-specific antigen of heart. The antigen in both saline and acid extracts of heart, which exhibited strict organ specificity for heart, demonstrated species-cross-reactive properties. Saline extracts of hearts of several non-primate species including rabbit, rat and beef were examined for reaction with antiserum to fraction II. With saline extracts of each of these species, a single faint line was observed which was completely abolished following absorption of antiserum with saline extract of heart of these species, and by saline extract of human heart, but not by saline extracts of other organs. In contrast with these observations, the strong reaction of this antiserum with saline extract of human heart appeared unaffected by absorption of antiserum with saline extracts of hearts of non-primate species. However, immunodiffusion patterns comparing reactions of human and non-primate heart extracts showed faint lines of fusion with spur consistent with their partial identity or cross-reactive relation.

Reaction of rabbit antisera with homologous rabbit organ extracts. The reaction of rabbit antisera with acid extract of pooled rabbit hearts was examined in further detail as an example of reactivity with homologous species antigens and presumptively of autoimmune reaction, although autologous heart extracts were not available for testing in this work. Reaction of antiserum to fraction I with rabbit heart acid extract revealed two lines of precipitation, related antigenically to two lines given also with rabbit muscle acid extract (Fig. 11). No lines were obtained with acid extracts of rabbit kidney and liver. Absorption tests confirmed the specificity of these antisera for two antigens common to rabbit heart and skeletal muscle. Antisera to fraction II gave only very weak lines of precipitation with acid extract of rabbit heart, and this system was therefore not further studied.

Effect of Pronase, trypsin and pepsin on heart-related antigens. Enzyme-treated and control mixtures of heart extract were examined by double diffusion and immunoelectrophoresis. A concentration of extract of 10 mg/ml was used for the former and 100 mg/ml for the latter procedure. These were tested with antisera to fractions I and II.

As demonstrated with antiserum to fraction I,

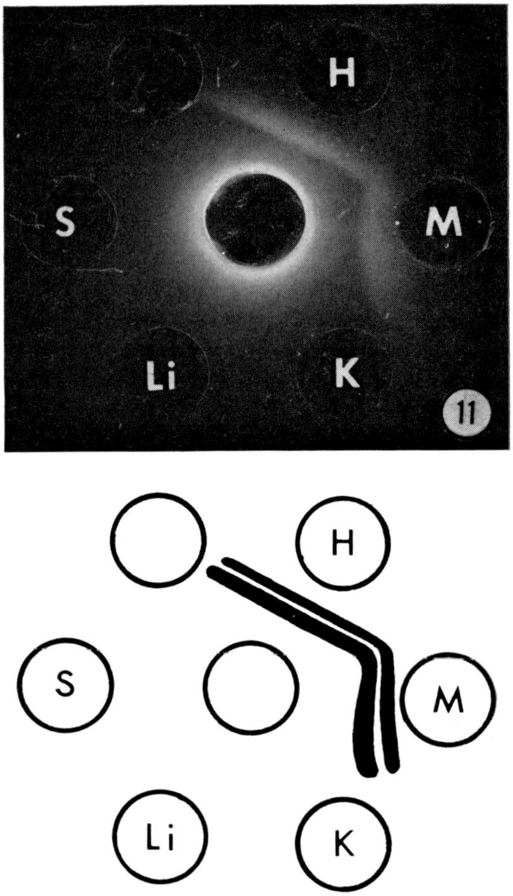

Figure 11. Reaction of rabbit antiserum with rabbit organ extracts. Central well contains antiserum 193D to fraction I. Peripheral wells contain 1% acid extracts of rabbit heart, *H*; skeletal muscle, *M*; kidney, *K*; liver, *Li*; and serum, *S*.

Pronase destroyed reactivity of all but one of the antigens common to cardiac and skeletal muscle, and trypsin abolished reactivity of all but three of these antigens (Fig. 12). In similar experiments with pepsin, prolonged exposure at 37°C of the extract at pH 3.0 in the control buffer in the absence of enzyme resulted in loss or weakening of several of the precipitating antigens, indicating their instability under these conditions. It was possible to conclude from this latter experiment only that at least one antigen related to both heart and skeletal muscle was unaffected by pepsin or the conditions of digestion.

Treatment with Pronase and trypsin abolished reactivity of the two antigens restricted in dis-

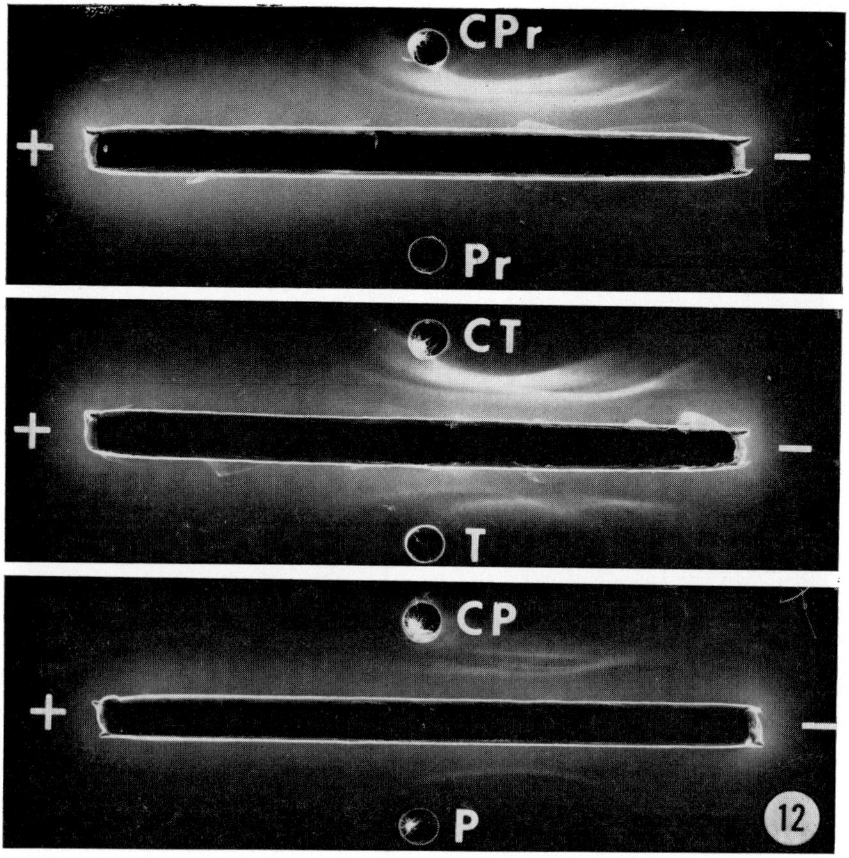

Figure 12. Wells contain 10% solutions of human heart acid extract treated with (*top*) pronase, *Pr*; (*middle*) trypsin, *T*; and (*bottom*) pepsin, *P*. Buffer controls for pronase, *CPr*; trypsin, *CT*; and pepsin, *CP*.

tribution to primates, differentiated by antiserum to fraction II.

In the case of the heart-specific antigen present in acid and saline soluble extracts of human heart, treatment with Pronase, pepsin and trypsin resulted in all cases in loss of this antigen.

DISCUSSION

The present data have indicated presence of at least six antigens in heart acid extracts, which are restricted in organ distribution to heart and skeletal muscle only, and an additional antigen which exhibits strict organ specificity for heart. Of the former six antigens, four antigens were common to all species tested, while two antigens were present only in primate species. The organ-specific antigen of heart gave evidence of both species-specific antigenic determinants and species-cross-reactive determinants, as indicated by immunodiffusion patterns and absorption tests.

Multiplicity of the antigenic components of acid extracts of heart tissue was not fully revealed in previous immunodiffusion studies which had employed antisera prepared against whole acid extracts of human heart (1). Nevertheless, the complexity of such extracts was suggested in these previous studies by acrylamide gel electrophoresis of individual fractions of heart acid extract separated by DEAE-cellulose chromatography. At least six protein-stained bands were demonstrated in peak 1, corresponding to fraction I in the present work, and at least two additional bands of more rapid electrophoretic mobility were noted in peaks 2 and 3, corresponding to fraction II in this work. Immunoelectrophoretic and immunodiffusion analysis of fraction I, in fact, indicated a minimum of four antigens strongly reactive with the test antisera, as well as suggesting evidence of additional weakly reactive components. Fraction II contained from four to six antigens, of which two antigens could be differentiated by absorption tests from the antigens of fraction I.

It was further established, in support of the previous work, that two of the antigens of fraction II were limited to primate species while the remaining antigens of fraction II and all of the antigens of fraction I exhibited wide species distribution.

Both acid extracts and saline extracts of human myocardium contained heart-specific antigen with identical antigenic properties. After the presumed removal of this antigen by repeated and sequential washing in saline and distilled water, the antigen was again detected on acid extraction. These findings are consistent either with presence of a single antigenic component which was bound or became bound to heart tissue components, or, alternatively, with occurrence of two closely similar antigens with quite different tissue binding or solubility properties. In contrast to the above, it should be pointed out that all of the antigens with organ distribution limited to heart and skeletal muscle described in this work could not be detected in saline or distilled water extracts, but were detected only after solubilization resulting from acid treatment.

Thus far, other workers have largely confined themselves to the study of heart antigens that are extractable in saline solution. Such studies have permitted differentiation of several cardiac antigens, some of which were restricted in distribution to heart alone, whereas others were distributed in heart and skeletal muscle, or in heart and other organs. Antigens with strict organ specificity for heart have been described in high speed sedimentable fractions of saline extracts of mammalian heart by Henle *et al.* (5) and Kaplan and Meyeserian (6) and in saline soluble extracts by Gery *et al.* (7, 8) and more recently by Halbert *et al.* (9). These last investigators have demonstrated the presence of at least three cardiac-specific autoimmune precipitating systems in sera of rabbits hyperimmunized with homologous heart. Antigens shared by heart and skeletal muscle have been described by several authors in saline soluble extracts or infusions (10, 11) and in insoluble fractions (1, 12). Antigen related to the latter group has been shown reactive with sera of patients with rheumatic fever (13) and has been shown related to the cross-reaction of group A streptococci with heart, skeletal and smooth muscle (14). This antigen has been localized by immunofluorescence to sarcolemmal and subsarcolemmal sites in cardiac myofibers and has been solubilized by acid treatment of human heart (15). Since antisera to acid extracts of myocardium have also been found reactive with sarcolemmal-subsarcolemmal sites of myofibers (1), the question may be properly posed whether any of the antigens differentiated in the present work are concerned with this streptococcal-related component. The further definition of the streptococcal cross-reactive system is essential to this undertaking, inasmuch as the possible heterogeneity or multiplicity of this system has become evident from current studies, as recently summarized (16). Various aspects of this problem have been reviewed by Kaplan (17) and Zabriskie (18). The relation of the streptococcal cross-reactive system to cardiac antigens has been considered in a recent brief review of the antigenic composition of heart tissue (19).

Acknowledgments. The technical assistance of Sigmar Massengeil and Elsa Clemente is acknowledged.

REFERENCES

1. Espinosa, E. and Kaplan, M. H., J. Immun., *100:* 1020, 1968.
2. Koch, F. C. and McMeekin, T. L., J. Amer. Chem. Soc., *46:* 2066, 1924.
3. Dittebrandt, M., Amer. J. Clin. Path., *18:* 439, 1948.
4. Scheidegger, J. J., Int. Arch. Allerg., *7:* 103, 1955.
5. Henle, W., Chambers, L. A. and Groupé, W., J. Exp. Med., *75:* 495, 1941.
6. Kaplan, M. H. and Meyeserian, M. J., J. Immun., *88:* 450, 1962.
7. Gery, I. and Davies, A. M., J. Immun., *87:* 351, 1961.
8. Gery, I., Davies, A. M. and Lazarov, E., Immunology, *7:* 192, 1964.
9. Halbert, S. P., Holm, S. E. and Thompson, A., J. Exp. Med., *127:* 613, 1968.
10. Bailey, G. H. and Raffel, S., J. Exp. Med., *73:* 617, 1941.
11. Kushner, I. and Kaplan, M. H., J. Immun., *99:* 526, 1967.

12. Kaplan, M. H. and Meyeserian, M., J. Immun., *88:* 450, 1962.
13. Kaplan, M. H., Meyeserian, M. and Kushner, I., J. Exp. Med., *113:* 16, 1961.
14. Kaplan, M. H., J. Immun., *90:* 595, 1963.
15. Kaplan, M. H., Espinosa, E. and Frengley, J. D., Fed. Proc., *26:* 701, 1967.
16. Kaplan, M. H.,, Transplantation Proc., *1:* 976, 1969.
17. Kaplan, M. H., Progr. Allerg., *13:* 408, 1969.
18. Zabriskie, J. B., Advances Immun., *7:* 147, 1967.
19. Espinosa, E., Kushner, I. and Kaplan, M. H., Amer. J. Cardiol., *24:* 508, 1969.

THE JOURNAL OF IMMUNOLOGY
Vol. 105, No. 2, August 1970

IMMUNOSUPPRESSIVE EFFECT OF SERUM FROM CBA MICE MADE TOLERANT BY THE SUPERNATANT FROM ULTRACENTRIFUGED BOVINE γ GLOBULIN

JAMES L. TONG AND DOROTHY BOOSE

From the Department of Medical Research, Veterans Administration Hospital, Denver, Colorado 80220

Received for publication January 9, 1970

In studies on tolerance to bovine γ globulin (BGG) induced in CBA mice by injection of the supernatant fraction of ultracentrifuged BGG, tolerance was not terminated by adoptive transfer of 10^8 spleen cells from normal or immune mice. Moreover, the serum of tolerant mice passively transferred to normal mice inhibited the immune response to BGG. This inhibition was attributed to the presence of specific antibody in the serum of tolerant mice.

An expedient model for the experimental study of tolerance was introduced by Dresser (1) when he reported the induction of specific tolerance in adult mice by injection of a small amount of supernatant from an ultracentrifuged solution of bovine γ globulin (BGG). This work was confirmed and extended in several laboratories (reviewed in 2, 3). In some unpublished studies, we compared tolerance induced by supernatant BGG (S-BGG) to the tolerance that is present because of x-irradiation. We found as others have (4) that spleen cells from normal mice restored immunocompetence to x-irradiated mice. However, our results indicated that normal spleen cells did not restore immunocompetence to mice made tolerant by pretreatment with S-BGG. The present report describes our confirmation and additional studies of this finding.

MATERIALS AND METHODS

Materials. Female CBA mice (Jackson Laboratories) approximately 10 weeks old at the beginning of the experiments were used. The BGG was bovine fraction II (Hyland Laboratories, Los Angeles, Calif.). Carrier-free ^{131}I was purchased from IsoServe, Inc., Cambridge, Mass.

Method for inducing tolerance. A saline solution containing 25 mg/ml of BGG was centrifuged for 30 min at 40,000 × G in a Beckman model L2 ultracentrifuge equipped with a swinging bucket rotor. After centrifugation, the top third of the solution was carefully aspirated with a Pasteur pipette and used as S-BGG. For tolerance induction, 1.0 mg of S-BGG was injected intraperitoneally (i.p.) into each mouse.

Method for inducing immunity. Mice were immunized by i.p. injection of 0.1 mg BGG contained in 0.1 ml of an emulsion of BGG and Freund's complete adjuvant (Difco).

Irradiation. Mice were given 630 R whole body x-irradiation with a GE Maxitron: 100 kv, 30 ma, 1.0 mm Al, at a distance of 50 cm.

Cell transfers. The method used for cell processing was based on one in use at Dr. William Weigle's laboratory. Donor mice were killed by cervical dislocation; their spleens were removed and pooled in cold Hanks' balanced salt solution (BSS). The spleens were placed on a square of 80-mesh stainless steel screen in cold BSS in a Petri dish and mashed with a pestle. The suspension of dispersed spleen cells was then filtered through nylon gauze into a centrifuge tube containing a small amount of BSS. The cell suspension war then centrifuged at 800 rpm for 8 min, the supernatant was discarded, and the cells were resuspended in BSS and again filtered through nylon gauze. A cell count was done and the suspension was then diluted to contain 10^8 cells in 0.5 ml or lesser volume. Each cell recipient was inoculated i.p. with 10^8 cells. For experiments in which both spleen cells and serum were taken from the donor, mice were anesthetized with ether, their chest cavities were opened, and blood was obtained by exsanguination after severing the aorta. The spleens were then removed for processing.

Method for tracer studies. Tracer studies were made with ^{131}I-labeled BGG (I*BGG). Details and procedures for these studies were unchanged from those described in a previous paper (5). Whether 24-hr or 48-hr counts were used to assess the tolerant or immune status of the mice was determined by the percentage antigen disappearance (%AD) of the immunization control: if the %AD was 90 or better by 24 hr we used the 24-hr results, otherwise the 48-hr results were used.

EXPERIMENTS AND RESULTS

Effect of normal or immune cells on BGG-tolerant mice. Preliminary data (unpublished) indicated that normal spleen cells adoptively transferred to BGG-tolerant mice did not respond to immunologic challenge with BGG. The purposes of this experiment were to confirm the inital finding and to determine whether spleen cells from BGG-immunized mice would restore competence to BGG-tolerant animals. There were seven groups of six mice each: groups A, B and C were respectively the tolerance, irradiation, and immunization controls; groups D and F were x-irradiated cell recipients to serve as controls to show that the transferred cells were viable and responsive. Groups E and G were mice that were made tolerant with S-BGG: 12 days after tolerance induction, group E received 10^8 spleen cells from normal mice and group G received 10^8 spleen cells from mice immunized with BGG 7 days previously. In all cell transfer studies, cells from the same cell pool were used to inoculate the corresponding control group. Six hours after cell transfer, each mouse in every group received an i.p. inoculation of BGG in Freund's complete adjuvant. Seven days later all mice were given I*BGG i.p. for tracer studies. The radioactivity, expressed in counts/minute, was determined for each mouse in a total body counter at the 3rd, 27th and 51st hr after injection of the tracer.

RESULTS

The results expressed as the means of the %AD between the 3rd and 51st hr for each group are recorded in Table I. The %AD for the irradiation control (group C), for the BGG-tolerant mice that received normal cells (group E), and for the BGG-tolerant mice that received immune cells (group G) were not significantly different at p = 0.01 from the BGG-tolerance control group (group A).[1] The cell transfer control groups (D and F) clearly were making an immune response and thus the cells were viable and responsive. These results indicate that neither normal nor immune cells terminated BGG-tolerance. We gave two possible explanations to these findings: tolerant mice lack something that is required for the immune response, or tolerant mice have something that inhibits the immune response. For the first explanation, we considered the possibility that tolerant mice lack natural antibody. We found, however, that the injection of 1 to 2 ml of serum from normal mice together with 10^8 normal spleen cells into BGG-tolerant mice did not restore immunocompetence (unpublished data). Our studies pertaining to the second explanation are described in the following experiment.

Effect of serum and spleen cells from BGG-tolerant mice on immune response of normal mice. Tolerance was induced in 50 mice by i.p. injection of S-BGG 11 days before the cell and serum transfer studies. Subsequently six of these mice were used as tolerance controls (group A) and six others were used to show again the inability of normal spleen cells to terminate BGG tolerance (group B). The remaining 38 tolerant mice were used on day 11 as serum and spleen cell donors for normal mice.

The sera from tolerant mice were pooled and 1 ml was given on day 11 to each of six normal mice (group D); the spleen cells from these same donors were also pooled and 10^8 cells were inoculated i.p. into each of six normal mice (group F). Group E were normal mice that were inoculated with 1.0 ml of serum from normal mice and served as a control for group D. Group G were normal mice that received 10^8 normal cells and served as a control for group F. Group C was the immunization control. The results (Table II) indicate that spleen cells from tolerant mice did not interfere with the immune response of normal mice to BGG challenge (group F). However, the serum from tolerant mice caused significant inhibition of the immune response of normal mice to immunologic challenge (group D).

DISCUSSION

The results of the first experiment indicated that neither normal nor immune spleen cells cor-

[1] Tests of statistical significance were done by analysis of variance with Duncan's multiple range test and arc sine square root transformation of the %AD data.

TABLE I

Effect of adoptively transferred syngeneic normal and immune spleen cells on adult CBA mice previously made tolerant to bovine γ globulin (BGG)

Experimental Groups of Six Mice Each	Day 0	Day 11	Day 12	6 Hr Later	Mean 48-Hr AD[a] ± S.E. of ^{131}I-BGG Given on Day 19
					%
A	Supernatant BGG (1.0 mg i.p.)			BGG-Freund's complete adjuvant (0.1 mg i.p.)	47 ± 1.3
B				BGG-Freund's complete adjuvant (0.1 mg i.p.)	95 ± 0.4
C		630 R (whole body x-irradiation)		BGG-Freund's complete adjuvant (0.1 mg i.p.)	44 ± 1.3
D[b]		630 R (whole body x-irradiation)	10^8 normal spleen cells (i.p.)	BGG-Freund's complete adjuvant (0.1 mg i.p.)	89 ± 6.5
E	Supernatant BGG (1.0 mg i.p.)		10^8 normal spleen cells (i.p.)	BGG-Freund's complete adjuvant (0.1 mg i.p.)	50 ± 1.0
F		630 R (whole body x-irradiation)	10^8 immune spleen cells[c] (i.p.)	BGG-Freund's complete adjuvant (0.1 mg i.p.)	81 ± 2.4
G	Supernatant BGG (1.0 mg i.p.)		10^8 immune spleen cells (i.p.)	BGG-Freund's complete adjuvant (0.1 mg i.p.)	54 ± 3.7

[a] The mean of the percentage of antigen disappearance (AD) was calculated from the means of the cpm taken at the 3rd and 51st hr after the intraperitoneal (i.p.) injection of ^{131}I-BGG.

[b] One mouse dead from x-irradiation.

[c] Spleen cells from CBA mice 7 days after i.p. challenge with 0.1 mg BGG-complete Freund's adjuvant.

rected BGG tolerance; we interpreted this to mean that tolerance, in our experimental system, was not due solely to the absence of responsive cells. The results of the second experiment indicated that tolerance was due to the presence of an inhibitor in the serum of tolerant animals. A third alternative—that tolerance was due both to the absence of responsive cells and to the presence of an inhibitor—was not ruled out.

Conceivably the inability of transferred normal or immune spleen cells to respond to BGG challenge could be due to tolerance induced in these cells by residual S-BGG in the tolerant host. We consider this unlikely because others (1, 6) have

TABLE II

Effect of spleen cells or serum from BGG-tolerant CBA mice on the response of syngeneic normal mice to immunologic challenge with bovine γ globulin (BGG)

Groups of Six Mice Each	Day 0	Day 11	Day 12	Mean 24-Hr AD[a] ± S.E. of ^{131}I-BGG Given on Day 19
				%
A	Supernatant BGG (2.0 mg i.p.)		BGG-Freund's complete adjuvant (0.1 mg i.p.)	37 ± 2.8
B	Supernatant BGG (2.0 mg i.p.)	10^8 normal spleen cells (i.p.)	BGG-Freund's complete adjuvant (0.1 mg i.p.)	37 ± 1.6
C			BGG-Freund's complete adjuvant (0.1 mg i.p.)	96 ± 0.7
D		1 ml tolerant serum[b] (i.p.)	BGG-Freund's complete adjuvant (0.1 mg i.p.)	57 ± 5.1
E		1 ml normal serum (i.p.)	BGG-Freund's complete adjuvant (0.1 mg i.p.)	93 ± 1.2
F		10^8 tolerant spleen cells[b]	BGG-Freund's complete adjuvant (0.1 mg i.p.)	93 ± 1.2
G		10^8 normal cells (i.p.)	BGG-Freund's complete adjuvant (0.1 mg i.p.)	94 ± 1.0

[a] The mean of the percentage of antigen disappearance (% AD) was calculated from the means of the cpm taken at the 3rd and 27th hr after the intraperitoneal (i.p.) injection of ^{131}I-BGG.
[b] Serum and cells from same group of mice made tolerant 11 days previously.

shown that there is a 3- to 4-day induction period before tolerance is established by the S-BGG method—in our experiment, tolerant mice were given immunologic challenge 6 hr after having received cells. Additionally, it is unlikely that residual S-BGG could render immune cells tolerant. Our findings that adoptively transferred lymphoid cells did not abrogate tolerance is contrary to the results of others. Abrogation of neonatally induced tolerance by adoptively transferred syngeneic lymphoid cells was obtained for cellular antigens by several groups of investigators (7–9). Weigle and Dixon (10) found that adoptively transferred homologous lymph node cells broke tolerance in 8 of 15 rabbits made tolerant neonatally to BGG. Mitchison (11) found that adoptively transferred syngeneic lymphoid cells led to antibody production in adult mice made tolerant by high doses of bovine serum albumin. However, Chase (12) found that transferred syngeneic lymph node cells did not break tolerance to 2:4 dinitrochlorobenzene in guinea pigs. We have not found any reference to the effect of adoptively transferred lymphoid cells on mice made tolerant by S-BGG.

We attributed the inability of normal spleen cells to break BGG tolerance in our experiments to the presence of an inhibitor in the serum of BGG-tolerant mice. Since tolerance phenomena are antigen-specific and since there is no other known substance that can recognize antigen specifically, the inhibitor is probably antibody. It is known that antibody may have an immunosuppressive effect (reviewed in 13). In certain experimental systems, antibody-induced suppression of the immune response appears to require very small quantities of antibody (14). Rowley and Fitch (15) theorized that antibody actively produced in small quantities may be responsible for maintaining unresponsiveness. Crowle and Hu (16) recently found that antibody produced in hyperimmunized mice and injected into normal mice prevented the development of delayed hypersensitivity; the antibody also suppressed induction of Arthus hypersensitivity, although to a lesser extent.

It would appear from our experiments that the observed immunosuppressive effect of the serum of tolerant mice could be accounted for on the basis of specific antibody. The question is: what is the source of these antibodies in the tolerant mice? One possibility is that our mice were not rendered completely tolerant and were thus partially immune. However, in the first experiment, the tolerant mice did not give a response that was significantly different from the response given by x-irradiated mice (group A *vs* group C, Table I). Another possible explanation for the presence of specific antibody in the serum of BGG-tolerant mice is that the S-BGG method of inducing tolerance led to the production of trace amounts of antibody and that these antibodies were responsible for the tolerant state. If this is true and if we accept unequivocally that tolerance represents a central failure of the immune response and thus that there should not be antibody present, then tolerance induced by S-BGG must not be regarded as true tolerance. Directly pertinent to these questions is the recent finding by Habicht *et al.* (17) that lymphoid cells from mice made tolerant to deaggregated human γ globulin yielded no plaque-forming cells when tested against antigen covalently coupled to erythrocytes. A key experiment would be to determine whether the serum from a tolerant mouse that showed no plaques would inhibit the immune response of normal mice to human γ globulin as measured by immune elimination. Also of interest would be experiments to determine whether the serum from mice made tolerant by neonatal or high dosage induction would have inhibitory effects on the immune response of normal mice. Still another possible explanation for the presence of specific antibody in the serum of tolerant animals would be that specific antibody was formed as a consequence of the terminal exhaustive differentiation postulated by Sterzl (18) to be the mechanism of tolerance.

Although the serum from tolerant animals inhibited the immune response in normal mice, adoptively transferred spleen cells from the same tolerant animals into normal mice did not cause detectable inhibition. This could be due to: a) an insufficient number of transferred cells, b) cessation of antibody formation by spleen cells, or c) insufficient time between transfer and challenge.

Acknowledgment. We thank Dr. David W. Talmage for his interest and advice in this study. We also thank Mr. Gary Zerbe for help with the statistical analyses.

REFERENCES

1. Dresser, D. W., Immunology, *5:* 378, 1962.
2. Weigle, W. O., *Natural and Acquired Immunologic Unresponsiveness*, World Publishing Co., Cleveland, 1967.
3. Dresser, D. W. and Mitchison, N. A., in *Advances Immun.*, *8:* 129, 1968.
4. Dietrich, F. M. and Weigle, W. O., J. Immun., *92:* 167, 1964.
5. Gadgett, B. and Tong, J. L., J. Immun., *99:* 1017, 1967.
6. Golub, E. S. and Weigle, W. O., J. Immun., *99:* 624, 1967.
7. Billingham, R. E., Brent, L. and Medawar, P. B., Phila. Trans. B, *239:* 357, 1956.
8. Gowans, J. L., in *The Immunologically Competent Cell*, p. 23, Little, Brown and Co., Boston, 1963.
9. Denman, A. M., Vischer, T. L. and Stasny, P., J. Immun., *98:* 442, 1967.
10. Weigle, W. O. and Dixon, F. J., J. Immun., *82:* 516, 1959.
11. Mitchison, N. A., in *Mechanisms of Immunologic Tolerance*, Academic Press, New York, 1962.
12. Chase, M., in *La Tolērance Acquise et La Tolērance Naturale à L'ėgard de Substances Antigėniques Dėfinies*, p. 160, Centre National de la Recherche Scientifique, Paris, 1963.
13. Uhr, J. W. and Möller, G., *Advances Immun.*, *8:* 81, 1968.
14. Möller, G. and Wigzell, H., J. Exp. Med., *121:* 969, 1965.
15. Rowley, D. A. and Fitch, F. W., J. Exp. Med., *120:* 987, 1964.
16. Crowle, A. J. and Hu, C. C., J. Allerg., *43:* 209, 1969.
17. Habicht, G. S., Chiller, J. M. and Weigle, W. O., In press.
18. Sterzl, A. J., Nature, *209:* 416, 1966.

THE JOURNAL OF IMMUNOLOGY
Vol. 105, No. 2, August 1970

Printed in U.S.A.

CHARACTERISTICS OF THE SERUM VIBRIOCIDAL AND AGGLUTINATING ANTIBODIES IN CHOLERA CASES AND IN NORMAL RESIDENTS OF THE ENDEMIC AND NON-ENDEMIC CHOLERA AREAS[1]

ANSARUDDIN AHMED, A. K. BHATTACHARJEE AND WILEY H. MOSLEY

From the Pakistan-SEATO Cholera Research Laboratory, Dacca, G.P.O. Box 128, East Pakistan[2]

Received for publication December 31, 1969

Vibriocidal and agglutinating antibodies in sera from acute cholera cases, normal residents of endemic and non-endemic cholera areas and maternal and cord blood were characterized by 2-mercaptoethanol (2-ME) sensitivity and density gradient fractionation. In acute cholera there was a rapid and parallel rise in whole serum and 2-ME-resistant vibriocidal and agglutinating antibodies, peaking in 7 to 10 days, and then a parallel fall in titers in whole serum and 2-ME-resistant antibodies. Density gradient studies confirmed this pattern, demonstrating the rise and fall of vibriocidal and agglutinating titers in both the IgM and IgG-IgA fractions. The apparent independence of the vibriocidal and agglutinating activity in the IgG-IgA fractions suggested that IgA as well as IgG might be contributing to the agglutinating titers. The presence of vibriocidal and agglutinating titers on admission in many adult cholera cases, coupled with a rapid rise in IgG antibody, indicates that this is a secondary response in individuals already primed by natural infection or cholera vaccine. Most residents of the endemic cholera area (East Pakistan) had high vibriocidal and agglutinating titers with activity in both IgM and IgG, in contrast to sera from residents of non-endemic areas (U. S. A. and Czechoslovakia) who had non-detectable or low titers with vibriocidal activity in most cases exclusively in IgM. Transplacental transfer of IgG vibriocidal antibody was demonstrated.

Cholera in man is characterized serologically by a prompt response in agglutinating and vibriocidal antibodies (1–4). The vibriocidal test, which is more sensitive than the agglutinating test, shows in some patients a detectable titer rise as early as the 2nd day of disease (4). Peak titers of agglutinating and vibriocidal antibodies are usually reached between the 7th and 10th days following onset of the disease. This is followed by a rapid fall in titer such that within 60 days more than half of the patients will no longer have agglutinating or vibriocidal titers significantly higher than they were on admission to the hospital (4).

Serologic surveys of residents of the endemic cholera area in East Pakistan reveal that the great majority of the population acquire vibriocidal antibodies with increasing age (5). Epidemiologic field studies have shown an inverse correlation between the cholera case rate and the presence of vibriocidal antibody titers in the population (5, 6). Vaccine field trials in rural East Pakistan have also shown a direct relationship between the level of vibriocidal antibody produced by whole cell cholera vaccines and the degree of protection induced (7, 8). In the 1968 field trial a purified antigen prepared from cell walls of the Inaba serotype of *Vibrio cholerae* was tested (9, 10). This antigen, which represents the major bacterial component that reacts with

[1] These studies were supported in part by Research Agreement 196802 between the National Institutes of Health, and the Pakistan-SEATO Cholera Research Laboratory, Dacca, East Pakistan.

[2] The Pakistan-SEATO Cholera Research Laboratory is a part of the SEATO Cholera Research Program and is supported by the United States Agency for International Development, Department of State; the National Institutes of Health and the National Communicable Disease Center of the Department of Health, Education and Welfare; and by the Governments of Pakistan, United Kingdom and other SEATO nations. The National Institutes of Health Cholera Advisory Committee co-ordinates the research program.

vibriocidal antibody, was highly protective against Inaba cholera.

Because of the close association between serum antibody titer and protection from cholera, it was of interest to study in more detail the characteristics of the antibodies reacting in the agglutinating and vibriocidal tests. This paper reports the immunoglobulin characteristics of the vibriocidal and agglutinating antibodies based on treatment of the sera with 2-mercaptoethanol and fractionation by density gradient centrifugation. These studies were carried out on sera from cholera cases during the course of acute disease, and on sera from normal adult residents of the endemic cholera area (East Pakistan) and of non-endemic areas (U. S. A. and Czechoslovakia). Transplacental transfer of vibriocidal and agglutinating antibody was also studied.

METHODS

All cholera patients in this study had the typical severe diarrheal syndrome and were treated at the Pakistan-SEATO Cholera Research Laboratory (PSCRL) hospital in Dacca or the PSCRL field hospital in Matlab Bazar, East Pakistan. The cases received only intravenous fluids, without antibiotics unless otherwise specified in the report. The diagnosis was confirmed by the repeated isolation of *V. cholerae* from stool cultures. Sera from normal residents of the endemic cholera area were obtained by random sample serologic surveys of participants in the cholera vaccine field trials in Comilla District, rural East Pakistan.

Sera from normal residents of non-endemic areas were obtained from two sources. Dr. Karel Zacek of the Institute of Epidemiology and Microbiology, Prague, provided sera from the WHO Serum Reference Board taken from a random sample survey in Czechoslovakia. Drs. Thomas Vernon, Robert Armstrong and Eugene Gangarosa, Epidemiology Program, National Communicable Disease Center, Atlanta, Georgia, provided sera from normal Americans with no history of vaccination against cholera or of foreign travel.

Maternal and cord blood was obtained from the maternity ward of the Sir Salimullah Medical College Hospital in Dacca, East Pakistan, with the co-operation of Professor N. Islam. Expectant mothers without complications and not on antibiotics were selected. At the time of delivery, approximately 5 ml of cord blood were collected and the following day a venous blood specimen was obtained from the mother. All serum specimens were frozen until titrations were performed.

Reduction with 2-mercaptoethanol. Sera were treated with 2-mercaptoethanol (2-ME) at a final concentration of 0.1 molar for 90 min at room temperature. Subsequent alkylation was carried out for 30 min at room temperature by adding iodoacetamide in a final concentration of 10% excess molarity to that of 2-mercaptoethanol. The mixture was then dialyzed at 4°C with constant stirring against a large quantity of repeatedly changed phosphate-buffered saline, pH 7.2. As a control, a duplicate sample of each serum was handled in the same way as the treated serum, except that initially saline was added instead of 2-ME. Titrations were performed simultaneously on the reduced and control sera.

Density gradient ultracentrifugation. Density gradient fractionation was carried out according to the method of Kunkel (11) on a Beckman model L-2 preparative ultracentrifuge using a swinging bucket rotor type SW-50L. Four solutions of sucrose containing 40, 30, 20 and 10 g/100 ml were successively layered in three 5-ml cellulose nitrate tubes in 1-ml amounts. The tubes were placed under refrigeration for 24 hr. Afterwards 0.5-ml serum samples (diluted 1/2 with normal saline) were than layered on top of each tube and the top was gently stirred. Centrifugation was performed at 35,000 rpm for 18 hr at 5°C. At the end of the run, holes were pierced in the bottom of the tubes and approximately 20 fractions were collected from each tube. The protein content of each fraction was estimated by the method of Lowry *et al.* (12) and protein curves were drawn by plotting O. D. at 660 nm. The presence of immunoglobulins in the fractions was determined by the Ouchterlony double diffusion test (13) using specific goat anti-IgG, anti-IgM and anti-IgA antisera (Hyland Laboratories, Inc., Los Angeles, Calif.) and each fraction was titered for vibriocidal and agglutinating antibodies.

Titration for agglutinating and vibriocidal antibodies. The agglutinating and vibriocidal antibody titrations were carried out on the serum specimens and fractions utilizing the microtechniques described by Benenson *et al.* (2, 3) and microtiter equipment (Cooke Engineering Co., Alexandria, Va.). For the agglutination test, serial twofold dilutions of the specimen to be tested were prepared in normal saline in the microtiter plates in a volume of 0.025 ml. To each dilution was added a suspension containing 6.3×10^5 viable *Vibrio cholerae* organisms in a total volume of 0.025 ml. Fresh bacterial suspensions were prepared daily from an 18-hr harvest of *Vibrio cholerae* grown in 1% tripticase broth with 1% sodium chloride and standardized photometrically. Titrations against Ogawa and Inaba serotypes of *Vibrio cholerae* were performed in parallel. After addition of antigen, the plates were incubated at 40°C in a water bath for 1 hr and kept overnight under refrigeration. The titer was the highest dilution showing agglutination of the organisms as evidence by no "button" formation at the bottom of the cup.

For the vibriocidal antibody test, serial two-fold dilutions of the serum or fraction were made in a 0.025-ml volume as described above. To each dilution was added 2.5×10^6 viable *Vibrio cholerae* suspended in an excess of guinea pig complement in a total volume of 0.025 ml. The antigen was prepared fresh daily from a saline harvest of 3-hr heart infusion agar cultures of *Vibrio cholerae* and the suspension was standardized photometrically. Titrations with the Ogawa and Inaba strains were determined in parallel. Following the addition of the bacteria-complement mixture, the plates were incubated for 1 hr at 37°C in a waterbath and then 0.15 ml of heart infusion broth was added to each cup and the plates again were incubated for about 2 hr until a reference control inoculum reached the proper turbidity as measured photometrically. The test was then read and the plates were refrigerated and read again the following morning. The endpoint was the highest dilution at which there was complete lysis as evidence by a clear cup with no turbidity and no "button" formation at the bottom of the cup.

RESULTS

Vibriocidal and agglutinating antibodies in acute cholera. Serial serum specimens were obtained from eight cholera cases on the day of onset and on the 3rd, 7th, 10th, 14th and 21st days follow-

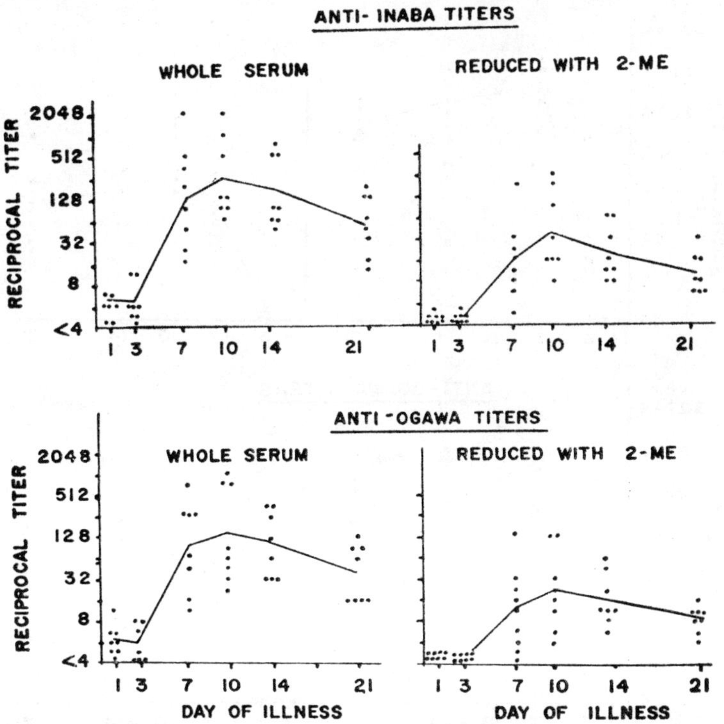

Figure 1. Serum agglutinating titers against Inaba and Ogawa organisms before and after reduction with 2-mercaptoethanol in eight cholera cases, by day of illness (the line indicates the geometric mean titers).

ing onset. These patients ranged from 8 to 45 years of age, and all were infected with the Inaba serotype of *Vibrio cholerae*. Figure 1 illustrates the agglutination antibody response against both the Inaba and Ogawa organisms in these cholera patients before and after treatment of the sera with 2-ME. There was a rapid rise in the agglutinating titers during the course of the disease, both in the whole serum and following reduction with 2-ME. A significant rise in titer was detectable in essentially all specimens on the 7th day and peak titers were reached by the 10th day. This was followed by a rapid and parallel decline in the agglutinating titers in both the whole serum and the 2-ME-resistant antibody by the 21st day.

Figure 2 illustrates the vibriocidal titers in these patients. In the whole serum, a detectable rise was seen against the Inaba organisms on the 3rd day with a peak response by the 7th day. The vibriocidal response to Ogawa organisms was somewhat slower in rising, with the peak being reached by the 10th day. The vibriocidal response of the 2-ME-resistant antibodies also showed a significant rise by the 7th day, the geometric mean titer reaching a peak on the 10th day. As seen with the agglutinating titers, there was a significant decline in the vibriocidal titers both in the whole serum and in the 2-ME-resistant antibodies between the 10th and the 21st day.

These eight cases demonstrated the parallel response in the vibriocidal and agglutinating antibody titers generally seen during the course of cholera. In the whole sera, as well as following 2-mercaptoethanol treatment, the vibriocidal titers were consistently higher than the agglutinating titers with the differences ranging from two- to eightfold.

Figure 3 presents the results of density gradient

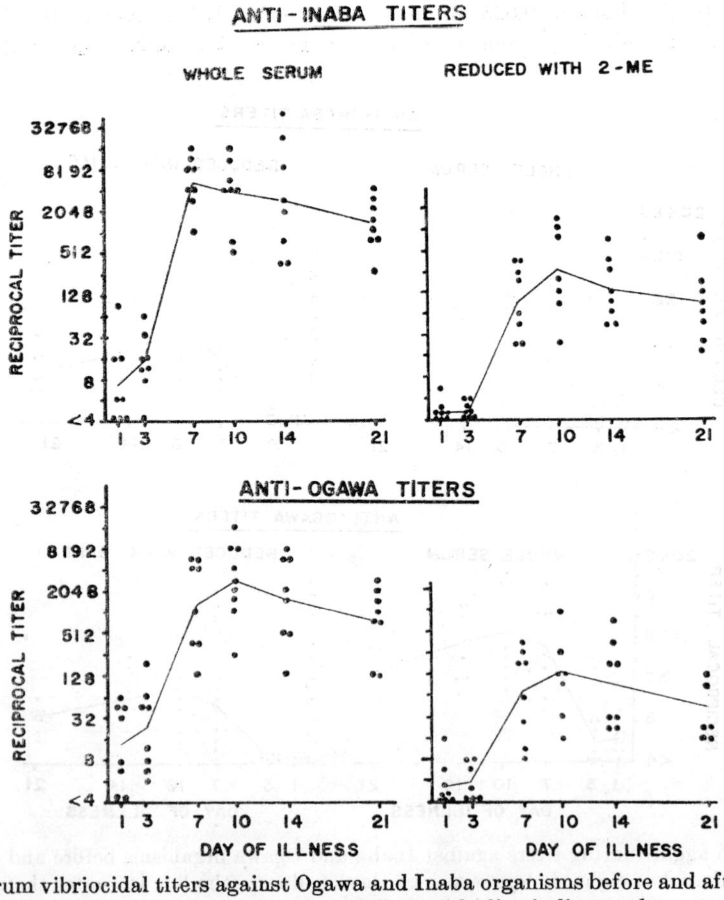

Figure 2. Serum vibriocidal titers against Ogawa and Inaba organisms before and after reduction with 2-mercaptoethanol in eight cholera cases, by day of illness (the line indicates the geometric mean titers).

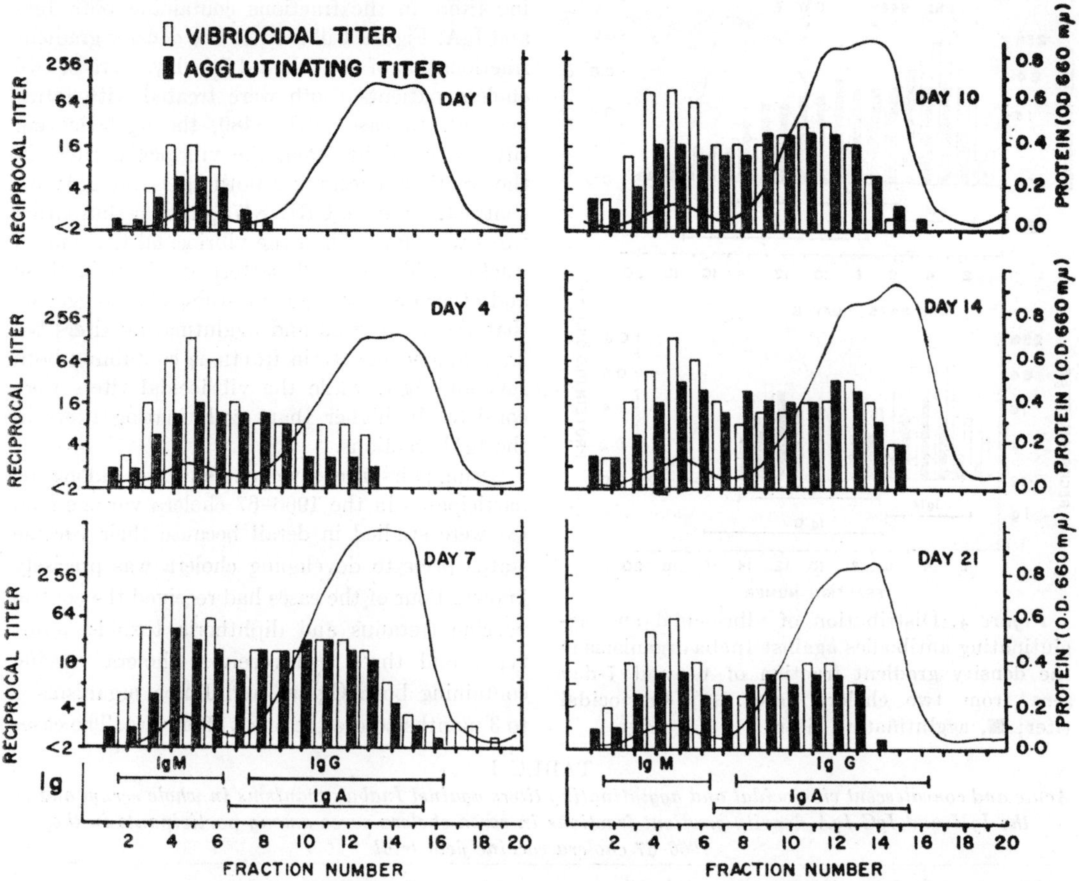

Figure 3. **Distribution of vibriocidal and agglutinating antibodies against Inaba organisms in density gradient fractions of the sera from an Inaba cholera case on days 1, 4, 10, 14 and 21 following onset.**

ultracentrifugation of sera collected on days 1, 4, 7, 10, 14 and 21 from one cholera patient. This patient had both vibriocidal and agglutinating antibodies on admission. The density gradient pattern indicates that these antibodies were limited to the fractions containing IgM. By day 4, there was a rise in the titers detectable in the IgM fractions as well as the appearance of both vibriocidal and agglutinating activity in the fractions containing IgG and IgA. A further rise in titers in all fractions was detectable on the 7th day. This was followed by a gradual decline in titers in all fractions on days 10, 14 and 21.

The ratio of vibriocidal to agglutinating titers in these fractions showed considerable variation, in contrast to the consistently higher vibriocidal titers seen in the whole serum or with 2-ME-resistant antibodies. In the IgM fractions, the vibriocidal titers were higher than the agglutinating titers with the differences ranging from four- to eightfold. In the fractions containing both IgG and IgA, however, there was no consistent relationship in the ratio of the vibriocidal to the agglutinating titers. As illustrated in Figure 3, in the day 4 serum the fractions immediately following IgM have agglutinating titers equal to or higher than the vibriocidal titers, while in subsequent fractions the vibriocidal titers were higher than the agglutinating titers. On days 7 through 21 there was a close parallel in the vibriocidal and agglutinating titers in the IgG/IgA fractions, although occassionally, as illustrated on day 14, the agglutinating titers were higher than the vibriocidal titers in the zone immediately following IgM.

Fractionation of sera from additional convalescent cholera patients has confirmed this varying ratio in the vibriocidal and agglutinat-

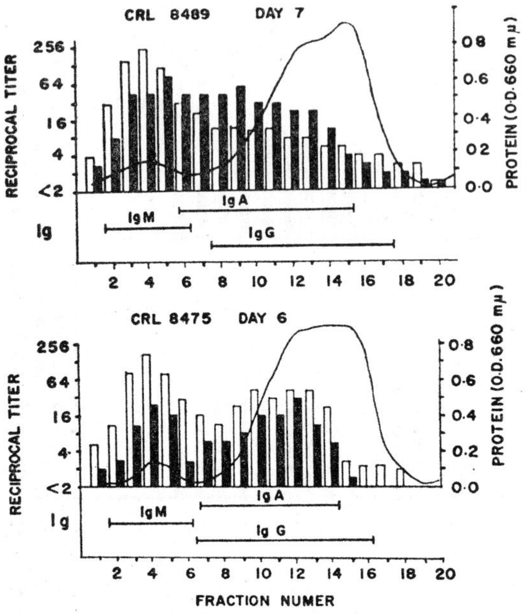

Figure 4. Distribution of vibriocidal and agglutinating antibodies against Inaba organisms in the density gradient fraction of 6- and 7-day sera from two cholera cases. □, Vibriocidal titer; ■, agglutinating titer.

ing titers in the fractions containing both IgG and IgA. Figure 4 illustrates the density gradient fractionation of the 6th and 7th days' sera of two cholera patients (both were treated with tetracycline). In case CRL 8489, the agglutinating titers were higher than the vibriocidal titers in the fractions containing both IgG and IgA. By contrast, in case CRL 8475, the agglutinating titers were lower than the vibriocidal titers in all fractions. The overall pattern of titers in these and other density gradient studies has suggested that the vibriocidal and agglutinating titers behave independently in fractions containing both IgG and IgA, while the vibriocidal titers were consistently higher than agglutinating titers in the IgM fractions.

Serum pairs from seven cholera cases among the participants in the 1966–67 cholera vaccine field (8) were studied in detail because their vaccine status prior to developing cholera was precisely known. Four of the cases had received the control vaccine (tetanus and diphtheria toxoids, adult type) and three had received cholera vaccine containing both Ogawa and Inaba organisms 1 to 3 months before the onset of cholera. The cases

TABLE I

Acute and convalescent vibriocidal and agglutinating titers against Inaba organisms in whole serum and in the IgM and IgG-IgA density gradient fractions in seven cholera cases among participants in the 1966–67 cholera vaccine field trial

Case No.	Age/Sex	Vaccine	Time	Reciprocal Titers					
				Vibriocidal			Agglutinating		
				Whole serum	IgM[a]	IgG-IgA[a]	Whole serum	IgM[a]	IgG-IgA[a]
M 2878	1/F	Control	Acute[b]	<10	NT[d]	NT	<10	NT	NT
			Conv.[c]	160	112	<2	10	10	<2
M 2764	4/F	Control	Acute	<10	NT	NT	<10	NT	NT
			Conv.	1280	358	154	320	62	146
M 2563	4/M	Control	Acute	40	20	<2	10	10	<2
			Conv.	640	362	56	160	80	12
M 3123	6/F	Control	Acute	80	4	6	10	2	<2
			Conv.	640	320	200	80	30	46
M 2754	5/F	Cholera	Acute	20	2	<2	10	4	<2
		(1 dose)	Conv.	640	124	62	160	70	146
M 2968	8/M	Cholera	Acute	80	12	16	20	2	2
		(1 dose)	Conv.	160	140	32	80	26	24
M 2823	1/F	Cholera	Acute	160	80	2	80	30	2
		(2 doses)	Conv.	160	100	62	160	32	74

[a] IgM and IgG-IgA titers represent the arithmetic sum of titers in the individual fractions containing the respective immunoglobulins.

[b] Day of onset of diarrhea.

[c] Nine or 10 days following onset.

[d] NT, not tested.

TABLE II

Distribution of vibriocidal antibody titers against Ogawa and Inaba organisms in sera from normal adult residents of East Pakistan, U.S.A. and Czechoslovakia

Antigen	Reciprocal Titer							Total	% ⩾ 1:20
	<20	20	40	80	160	320	640		
East Pakistanis									
Ogawa	12	10	17	14	12	3		68	82.3
Inaba	12	13	11	14	13	5		68	82.3
Americans									
Ogawa	70	2	2	2	1			77	9.1
Inaba	72	1	4					77	6.5
Czechoslovakians									
Ogawa	35	4	2	1				42	16.6
Inaba	41		1					42	2.4

were hospitalized between 2 and 21 hr following the onset of diarrhea. The results of density gradient fractionation of the acute and convalescent serum pairs from these 7 cases are summarized in Table I. Among the four cases receiving the control vaccine three, ages 4 to 6 years, showed a good vibriocidal and agglutinating response in both the IgM and IgG-IgA fractions. The youngest case, age 1 year, showed only an IgM vibriocidal antibody response.

Among the three vaccinated children, there was considerable variation in the response. Case M2754 had a significant rise in vibriocidal and agglutinating titers in the whole serum, and the IgM and IgG-IgA fractions. Case M2986, who had relatively high IgG vibriocidal activity on admission, showed only a twofold rise in the whole serum titer with most of the increase in activity in the IgM fractions. Case M2823, a 1-year-old who had received two injections of cholera vaccine, had a high IgM vibriocidal titer on admission, and only showed a significant increase in vibriocidal activity in the IgG-IgA fractions. This case also had essentially no response in the IgM agglutinins.

In all seven of these cases the vibriocidal titers were greater than the agglutinating titers in the IgM fractions; however, in the IgG-IgA fractions the vibriocidal titers were lower than the agglutinating titers in one case, and were approximately equal to the agglutinating titers in three cases.

Characteristics of vibriocidal and agglutinating antibodies in the sera of residents of an endemic cholera area, and of non-endemic areas. Serologic surveys have revealed that over 80% of adult East Pakistanis who deny having ever received cholera vaccine have naturally acquired vibriocidal antibodies detectable at a titer of 1:20 or greater, by the microtechnique (5). Table II summarizes the distribution of vibriocidal titers in unvaccinated (by history) East Pakistani adults, and also shows, for comparison, the distribution of titers found in unvaccinated Czechoslovakian and American adults who have never traveled to cholera-affected areas. Natural vibriocidal antibodies were detected at a titer of 1:20 or greater in only 9% of the Czechoslovakian adults and 17% of American adults as compared to 83% of East Pakistani adults, when tested by the microtechnique.

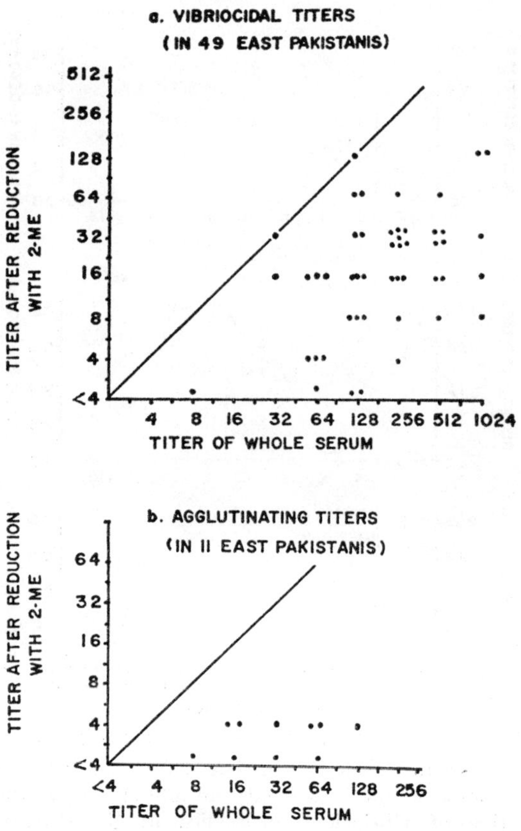

Figure 5. Relationship of vibriocidal and agglutinating titers against Inaba organisms in the sera of normal East Pakistanis before and after reduction with 2-mercaptoethanol. (The line represents points with no reduction in titer.)

Sera from 49 normal East Pakistanis who had been shown to have sustained high titers over a 4-month period were titered before and after treatment with 2-ME. All sera were tested for vibriocidal titer and 11 were examined for agglutination titers. As shown in Figure 5, 45 of the 49 sera had 2-mercaptoethanol-resistant vibriocidal antibody titers, although there was on the average an 8- to 16-fold reduction in the vibriocidal titers. The agglutination titers were quite low in those sera with detectable titers; treatment with 2-ME produced an average fall in agglutination of eightfold. Although 36 of these individuals had received cholera vaccine 1 to 2 years previously as a part of the field trials, while 13 had received the control injection, there was no significant difference in the 2-ME-resistant antibody titers related to this different vaccine history.

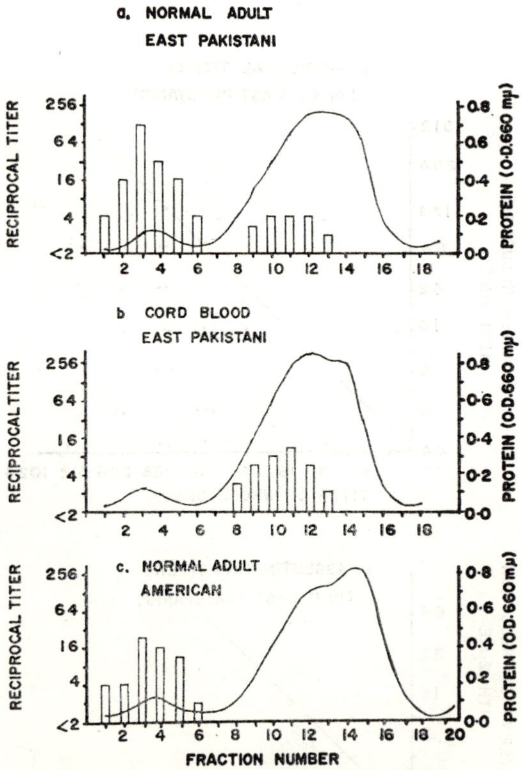

Figure 6. a, Distribution of vibriocidal antibodies in the density gradient fractions of sera from a normal East Pakistani adult; *b,* distribution of vibriocidal antibodies in the density gradient fractions of sera from cord blood of an East Pakistani newborn; *c,* distribution of vibriocidal antibodies in the density gradient fractions of sera from a normal American adult.

TABLE III

Vibriocidal titers against Ogawa and Inaba organisms in whole serum and density gradient fractions from six normal East Pakistanis

	Age/Sex	Reciprocal Vibriocidal Titers					
		Inaba			Ogawa		
		Whole serum	IgM[a]	IgG-IgA[a]	Whole serum	IgM	IgG-IgA
1	6/M	64	44	0	256	60	0
2	45/F	32	32	8	64	32	14
3	50/F	128	60	2	256	60	6
4	30/F	512	200	36	128	46	8
5–6	Pool[b]	256	146	28	512	208	28

[a] IgM and IgG-IgA titers represent the arithmetic sum of titers in individual fractions continuing the respective immunoglobulins.

[b] Sera from a 40-year-old male and a 40-year-old female.

Density gradient studies confirmed the findings with 2-ME. Figure 6*a* illustrates the typical pattern obtained with adult East Pakistani sera and Table III summarizes the results of density gradient studies of six of those sera (including one pool of two sera). The five sera from adults had vibriocidal activity in both the IgM and IgG-IgA fractions, with most of the activity in the IgM fractions. The one child had activity only in the IgM fractions.

Density gradient centrifugation of six American and 10 Czechoslovakian sera with natural vibriocidal antibody revealed vibriocidal activity detectable only in the IgM fractions in 15 sera (Fig. 6*c*) and in both IgM and IgG-IgA in one.

Transplacental transfer of vibriocidal and agglutinating antibodies. Figure 7 summarizes the results of titration of maternal and cord serum pairs by the vibriocidal and agglutination tests. The cord blood titers of both vibriocidal and agglutinating antibodies were approximately eightfold lower than the maternal titers. Table IV illustrates the vibriocidal titers in 10 of these maternal and cord blood specimens before and after reduction with 2-ME. (Because of the low titers in the cord blood, the sensitivity of the vibriocidal test was increased by reducing the number of organisms inoculated into each dilution from 2.5×10^6 to 2.5×10^2. This change in procedure increases the sensitivity of the vibriocidal test approximately 1000-fold.) There was a marked fall in the titer of the maternal blood

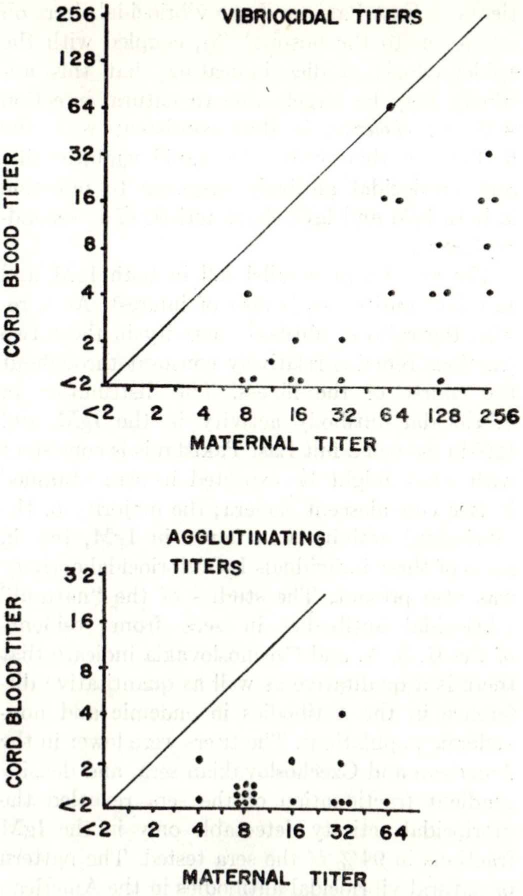

Figure 7. Relationship of vibriocidal and agglutinating titers against Inaba organisms in paired maternal and cord sera from normal East Pakistanis. (The line represents equal maternal and cord blood titers.)

following treatment with 2-ME. The cord blood titer corresponded closely to the 2-ME-resistant titer of the maternal blood. In addition, the vibriocidal titer in the cord blood in 7 out of 10 cases showed no change or no more than a two-fold fall following treatment with 2-ME. Density gradient centrifugation of three cord sera specimens revealed vibriocidal activity only in fractions containing IgG; a typical pattern is shown in Figure 6*b*.

DISCUSSION

These studies indicate that both IgM and IgG contribute to the vibriocidal and agglutinating antibody response in cholera. The activity of IgA is not precisely defined by these studies,

TABLE IV

Vibriocidal titers against Inaba organisms in paired maternal and cord sera before and after reduction with 2-mercaptoethanol

Case No.	Maternal		Cord	
	Whole serum	2-ME	Whole serum	2-ME
1	512	32	16	16
2	1,024	32	64	32
3	>16,000	32	32	8
4	>16,000	256	256	256
5	>16,000	256	64	4
6	128	32	16	<4
7	1,024	16	8	8
8	>16,000	64	64	32
9	8,192	256	32	32
10	128	<4	32	32

but several observations can be made. It is unlikely that IgA is contributing to the vibriocidal response, since this is a complement-dependent reaction and a number of studies have indicated that IgA does not fix complement or cause bacteriolysis (14–16). The pattern of agglutinating titers on the density gradient studies suggests that IgA may contribute to the agglutinating response, since there is an apparent independence of the vibriocidal and agglutinating titers in fractions containing both IgG and IgA with agglutinating titers being higher than the vibriocidal titers in some cases. IgA agglutinating activity in cholera would be consistent with the findings of Heremans *et al.* (16) who demonstrated *Brucella* agglutination with human serum IgA. It is interesting that *Brucella* and *Vibrio cholerae* are antigenically closely related and cross-react in the bacteriocidal and agglutinating tests (17; Gangarosa, personal communication; Ahmed, unpublished observation).

In the cholera patients, as well as in the normal adult East Pakistani, IgM accounts for the major part of the whole serum agglutinating and vibriocidal activity. This does not indicate the relative amounts of antibody since both the agglutination and vibriocidal tests usually favor the detection of IgM. Studies of the bacterial agglutinating test have suggested that over 10 times as much IgG as IgM antibody is required for agglutination (18, 19). In the complement-dependent bactericidal test a quantitative comparison by Robbins *et al.* showed that on a weight basis 18 times as much IgG as IgM was required to kill 50% of a standard suspension of *Salmonella typhimurium* (18).

A striking finding of the antibody response in cholera has been the rapid and almost simultaneous appearance of both IgM and IgG antibodies in the majority of cases, reaching a peak by the 7th to 10th day following the onset of symptoms. For all practical purposes, this can be considered as the interval from the period of effective exposure to the antigen since in most cases the incubation period of cholera is generally short, ranging from 24 to 48 hr. The rapidity of the antibody rise, particularly in IgG, suggests that this is a secondary response in an already primed individual. Only the 1-year-old child shown in Table I had exclusively an IgM antibody response in the day 10 convalescent blood.

Epidemiologic and serologic studies support the thesis that many (if not most) cholera cases in older children and adults in East Pakistan occur in persons who have had previous infections with *V. cholerae*. Serologic surveys have indicated that East Pakistanis rapidly acquire vibriocidal and agglutinating antibodies with increasing age; 50% of the children with no history of receiving cholera vaccine have detectable vibriocidal antibodies by the age of 5 to 6 years (5). Assuming that one infection produced a sustained vibriocidal titer in children, this would require an infection rate of 10% per year. McCormack has shown, however, that more than half the children under age 5 with clinical cholera no longer had detectable vibriocidal titers after 6 months (4). Thus, he postulated that in order for the East Pakistani children to acquire *sustained* vibriocidal titers at a rate of 10% per year, the annual infection rate must be two to three times higher, and reinfections must occur (4). Direct evidence for a higher inapparent infection rate with *V. cholera* in rural East Pakistan comes from an intensive bacteriologic and serologic study of one village of 1600 persons (20). During the 1966–67 cholera season there were no clinical cases of cholera; however, 27 mild diarrheas and inapparent infections due to *V. cholerae* were detected either bacteriologically or serologically. The infection rate in children under age 5 was 5%. In the 1968–69 cholera season there were 12 hospitalized cholera cases, and 104 mild diarrheas or inapparent infections due to *V. cholerae* were detected. The infection rate that year in children under age 5 was 25% (Woodward, in preparation).

The observation that 70% of all cholera patients in East Pakistan have vibriocidal titers on admission to the hospital (3), coupled with the epidemiologic studies indicating that this antibody may be largely due to natural infection with *V. cholerae*, is thus consistent with the findings in this study of a rapid agglutinating and vibriocidal antibody response to infection in both IgM and IgG, characteristic of a "secondary" response.

The rapid and parallel fall in both IgM and IgA-IgG antibodies is also of interest. As a result, the ratio of antibody activity in these two fractions remains relatively constant throughout the course of the illness. The distribution of vibriocidal antibody activity in the IgM and IgG in normal adult East Pakistanis is consistent with what might be expected in sera obtained in late convalescent cholera; the majority of the vibriocidal activity was found in IgM, but in most of these individuals IgG vibriocidal activity was also present. The studies of the "natural" vibriocidal antibodies in sera from residents of the U. S. A. and Czechoslovakia indicate that there is a qualitative as well as quantitative difference in the antibodies in endemic and nonendemic populations. The titers were lower in the American and Czechoslovakian sera, and density gradient fractionation of the sera revealed the vibriocidal activity detectable only in the IgM fractions in 94% of the sera tested. The pattern of natural vibriocidal antibodies in the American and Czechoslovakian sera is consistent with other studies that indicate that natural antibodies to Gram-negative bacteria reside almost exclusively in IgM (21, 22). The higher vibriocidal titers seen in adult East Pakistanis with activity detectable in IgG as well as IgM in most cases are indicative of specific (and repeated) antigenic stimulation by natural infection with *V. cholerae* and/or by cholera vaccine.

Since the IgG antibody titers parallel the whole serum titers closely throughout the course of the disease as well as in the normal East Pakistani adult, it is not possible in this endemic cholera area to define a distinctive vibriocidal or agglutinating antibody pattern that could distinguish the individual recently infected with *Vibrio cholerae* in the manner that the IgG antibodies have been used so effectively to identify active cases of brucellosis (23). Chronic *active* infection with *V. cholerae* has been excluded by purging studies of adults in the endemic area with sustained high titers (unpublished data). The presence of IgG vibriocidal antibody may be useful in the retrospective diagnosis of suspect cholera in an individual outside the endemic cholera area since the natural vibriocidal antibody in these persons appears in most cases to be IgM.

The studies on the transplacental transfer of vibriocidal and agglutinating antibodies revealed a pattern consistent with the findings in the normal East Pakistani adult. The major portion of the vibriocidal and agglutinating activity of the maternal serum did not cross the placenta. Confirmation that the transplacentally-transferred vibriocidal antibody was IgG was obtained by the studies with 2-ME and density gradient ultracentrifugation.

It is not possible from these studies to relate any class of antibody to protection against cholera. Although the majority of patients admitted with vibriocidal titers had activity primarily in the IgM fractions, a significant number of patients on admission show vibriocidal activity in both IgM and IgG globulins. All three classes of immunoglobulin have been found in jejunal aspirates of convalescent cholera patients (Ahmed, unpublished data). Since the vibriocidal activities of IgG and IgM are complement-dependent, it is questionable whether this reaction occurs within the intestinal lumen as a mechanism of protection from *V. cholerae*. It is quite possible that intestinal immunity against cholera may be due to secretory IgA and that the serum vibriocidal antibody levels correlate with protection against cholera only because they reflect the presence of intestinal IgA antibodies. There is a report to suggest that secretory IgA may be bacteriolytic in the presence of lysozyme and complement (24).

REFERENCES

1. Sack, R. B., Barua, D., Saxena, R. and Carpenter, C. C. J., J. Infect. Dis., *116:* 630, 1966.
2. Benenson, A. S., Saad, A. and Paul, M., Bull. WHO, *38:* 267, 1968.
3. Benenson, A. S., Saad, A. and Mosley, W. H., Bull. WHO, *38:* 277, 1968.
4. McCormack, W. M., Chakraborty, J., Rahman, A. S. M. M. and Mosley, W. H., J. Infect. Dis., *120:* 192, 1969.
5. Mosley, W. H., Benenson, A. S. and Barui, R., Bull. WHO, *38:* 327, 1968.
6. Mosley, W. H., Ahmad, S., Benenson, A. S. and Ahmed, A., Bull. WHO, *38:* 777, 1968.
7. Mosley, W. H., Benenson, A. S. and Barui, R., Bull. WHO, *38:* 335, 1968.
8. Mosley, W. H., McCormack, W. M., Ahmed, A., Chowdhury, A. K. M. A. and Barui, R., Bull. WHO, *40:* 177, 1969.
9. Verwey, W. F., Watanabe, Y., Phillips, P. E. and Williams, H. R., Proceedings of the Cholera Research Symposium, Hawaii, p. 259, U. S. Government Printing Office, 1965.
10. Mosley, W. H., Woodward, W. E., Aziz, K. M. A., Chowdhury, A. K. M. A., Rahman, A. S. M. M., Ahmed, A. and Feeley, J. C., J. Infect. Dis., 121 (Suppl.) May, 1970.
11. Kunkel, H. G., in *The Plasma Proteins*, Vol. 1, p. 294, Academic Press, New York and London, 1960.
12. Lowry, O. H., Rosebrough, N. J., Farr, A. L. and Randall, R. J., J. Biol. Chem., *193:* 265, 1951.
13. Ouchterlony, O., Acta Path. Microbiol. Scand., *25:* 186, 1948.
14. Ishizaka, K., Ishizaka, R., Borsos, T. and Rapp, H., J. Immun., *97:* 716, 1966.
15. Ishizaka, K., Ishizaka, T., Lee, E. H. and Fudenberg, H. H., J. Immun., *95:* 197, 1965.
16. Heremans, J. F., Vaerman, J. P. and Vaerman, C., J. Immun., *91:* 11, 1963.
17. Pollitzer, R., *Cholera,* p. 267–269, World Health Organization, Geneva, 1959.
18. Robbins, J. P., Kenney, K. and Suter, E., J. Exp. Med., *122:* 385, 1965.
19. Pike, R. U., Schulze, M. L. and Chandler, C. H., J. Bact., *92:* 880, 1966.
20. McCormack, W. M., Islam, M. S., Fahimuddin, M. and Mosley, W. H., Amer. J. Epidem., *89:* 658, 1969.
21. Michael, J. G. and Rosen, F. S., J. Exp. Med., *118:* 619, 1963.
22. Evans, R. T., Spaeth, S. and Mergenhagen, S. E., J. Immun., *97:* 112, 1966.
23. Reddin, J. L., Anderson, R. K., Jenness, R. and Spink, W. W., New England J. Med., *272:* 24, 1965.
24. Adinolfe, M., Glynn, A. A., Lindsay, M. and Milne, C. M., Immunology, *10:* 517, 1966.

THE JOURNAL OF IMMUNOLOGY
Vol. 105, No. 2, Aug. 1970

DEVELOPMENT OF ANTIBODY-FORMING CELLS IN NEONATAL MICE: STIMULATION AND INHIBITION BY CALF THYMUS FRACTIONS[1]

TERRY L. HAND, WALTER S. CEGLOWSKI, DAMRI DAMRONGSAK AND HERMAN FRIEDMAN

From the Departments of Microbiology, Temple University School of Medicine and Albert Einstein Medical Center, Philadelphia, Pennsylvania

Received for publication December 29, 1969

Crude and purified saline extracts prepared from calf thymus glands, as well as two fractions prepared by disc electrophoresis from the purified fractions, were studied as to their effects on development of antibody-forming cells in neonatal mice. Mice injected at birth with microgram quantities of the purified extract or a stimulatory fraction, prepared by disc electrophoresis, had a 10- to 40-fold enhancement in the number of plaque-forming cells when challenged at 1 or 2 weeks of life, as compared with normal animals. There was also an enhancement of spleen size and weight. Another purified fraction, also prepared by disc electrophoresis and previously found to inhibit lymphocytopoesis, markedly suppressed development of antibody plaque-forming cells in the neonatal mice. The effect was relatively temporary, since older mice injected at birth with this fraction responded normally when challenged with the sheep red cells.

The study of antibody formation on the cellular level has been facilitated in recent years by development of a number of immunoplaque assays in semi-solid gel (1–4). Most studies have been concerned with immune responses of normal adult animals. It is recognized, however, that neonatal animals do not develop the capacity to produce antibody-forming cells to sheep erythrocytes or bacterial antigens until 1 to 2 weeks of age, or longer, after birth (5–11).

Development of the capacity of newborn rodents to form specific immunocompetent cells is related to a number of important factors, one of which appears to be an intact thymus gland (12–15). It has been shown by a number of workers that thymectomy of mice at birth, or shortly thereafter, markedly interferes with immunocompetence to sheep erythrocytes, as assessed on either the cellular or humoral level (16–20). As time progresses, however, the surviving animals generally acquire the capacity to form antibody to the red blood cells.

[1] This study was supported in part by research grants from the Damon Runyon Cancer Research Fund (DRG-1037), the American Cancer Society, Inc. (T-382D), the National Science Foundation (GB-7719) and a summer research scholarship from the Allergy Foundation of America to T. L. H.

A number of studies of this type have established an important role for the thymus in the development of immunologic responsiveness. In this regard, several studies have implicated a thymus "hormone" or other extracellular product as an immunologic enhancing agent in the development of immunologic competence (21–28). Evaluation of these reports have been complicated by the fact that a) thymus extraction procedures differ greatly between investigators, b) methods used to detect immunologic competence vary markedly, and c) the dose and frequency of administration of thymus products are often quite different. Despite these reservations, it appears that extracts from calf thymus glands may, under appropriate conditions, restore or enhance some, if not all, immunologic responses of neonatally thymectomized mice. Effects in normal animals have been variable.

In general, such "restoration" studies have been concerned with the effects of thymus extracts on lymphocytopoesis, increased lymphoid tissue size and weight (12, 13, 21–25). Other studies have shown that calf thymus extracts may prevent "wasting disease" and fatal virus infections in thymectomized mice (26–29). In 1966, Goldstein, Slater and White (30) reported that a partially purified calf thymus extract could be further processed to obtain a protein material, termed "thymosin," capable of stimulating lymphocytopoesis, lymphoid tissue hyperplasia and increased DNA, RNA and protein synthesis. Several milligrams of this material were necessary for demonstrable effects in newborn mice. In 1967, Hand, Caster and Luckey (31) fractionated saline extracts of calf thymus glands and prepared protein capable of stimulating lymphocytopoesis and lymphoid cell hyperplasia. This material was characterized as a basic protein of approximately 17,000 molecular weight. Recently, Law and Agnew (32) and Law, Goldstein and White (33) reported that this partially purified extract could restore the immune capacity of spleen cells from thymectomized mice as assessed by a graft *vs* host reaction in recipient animals. Moreover, Trainin, Small and Globerson (34) demonstrated in an *in vitro* assay system that a thymus extract could restore immunocompetence to spleen cells obtained from thymectomized mice. In a preliminary study it was reported from this laboratory that extremely small amounts of partially purified calf thymus extract could stimulate development of antibody plaque-forming cells to sheep erythrocytes in neonatal mice (35, 36). The present report extends these observations and describes the biologic effects of whole calf thymus extracts, as well as two purified fractions, derived by electrophoresis, which either enhance or suppress development of immune responsiveness of neonatal mice.

METHODS AND MATERIALS

Animals. ICR and NIH random-bred albino mice were obtained from Rockland Farms, Gilbertsville, Pa. The pregnant mice were received 5 to 7 days before parturition and were housed individually in plastic cages. They were fed commercial mouse pellets and water *ad libitum.* The animals were observed at approximately 8-hr intervals and the time of litter delivery and number recorded.

Preparation of extracts and fractions. Fresh calf thymus glands, obtained from Cross Brothers Meat Packer Co., Philadelphia, Pa., were extracted and fractions prepared as described previously (31). In brief, fresh thymuses were extracted in 0.85% saline at 4°C (Fig. 1). Following centrifugation, the cellular debris was discarded and the crude saline extract (CSE) precipitated with 20% crystallized ammonium sulfate. The resulting precipitate was dissolved in a small amount of distilled water and clarified by centrifugation at 10,000 × G in the cold. Three parts supernatant were added to one part absolute alcohol. The resulting precipitate was recovered and dissolved in distilled water. This material was clarified by centrifugation in the cold at 10,000 × G and the supernatant dialyzed for 12 to 18 hr in the cold, using distilled water. The dialyzed material was then freeze-dried and stored at −20°C until used further. As required, the material was dissolved in distilled water and the resulting suspension clarified by centrifugation in the cold. The supernatant was referred to as the partially purified extract (PPE) and was used as the starting material for polyacrylamide disc electrophoresis (31). Following electrophoresis, two of the fractions (Fig. 2) were used for the biologic studies. The first, designated fraction B-C, was previously found to contain a lymphoid cell stimulator (31). The second fraction, with less rapid mobility in the electrophoretic field, was designated fraction D-E and had been previously found to contain an inhibitory material for lymphocytopoesis (31). The protein content of each preparation or fraction was determined, using the Folin reagent and bovine serum albumin as a standard.

Administration of extracts and fractions. Mice were injected within 12 hr of birth with 0.05 ml of a saline solution of either CSE, PPE, or fractions B-C or D-E (Fig. 3). In general, the material was diluted so that each animal received either 3 or 15 μg of protein.

Immunization. Control non-treated animals, and those treated at birth with one of the test substances, were challenged by i.p. injection of 0.1 ml of a 50% suspension of washed sheep red blood cells (RBC) either on the day of birth (immediately after injection of the test material) or at 1, 2, 3, 4 or 6 weeks of life (Fig. 3).

Serology. Individual mice 2 weeks of age or older were bled from the retro-orbital venous plexus. Younger animals were decapitated and blood was pooled from mice within a group. Serum was separated from all blood specimens after clotting at room temperature and stored at −20°C until used. For serologic assay, 0.025-ml dilutions of each serum sample were prepared in microtiter plates, using calibrated wire loops and 0.025-ml volumes physiologic saline, pH 7.2. To each dilution cup was added 0.025 ml of an 0.5% suspension of washed sheep erythrocytes. The

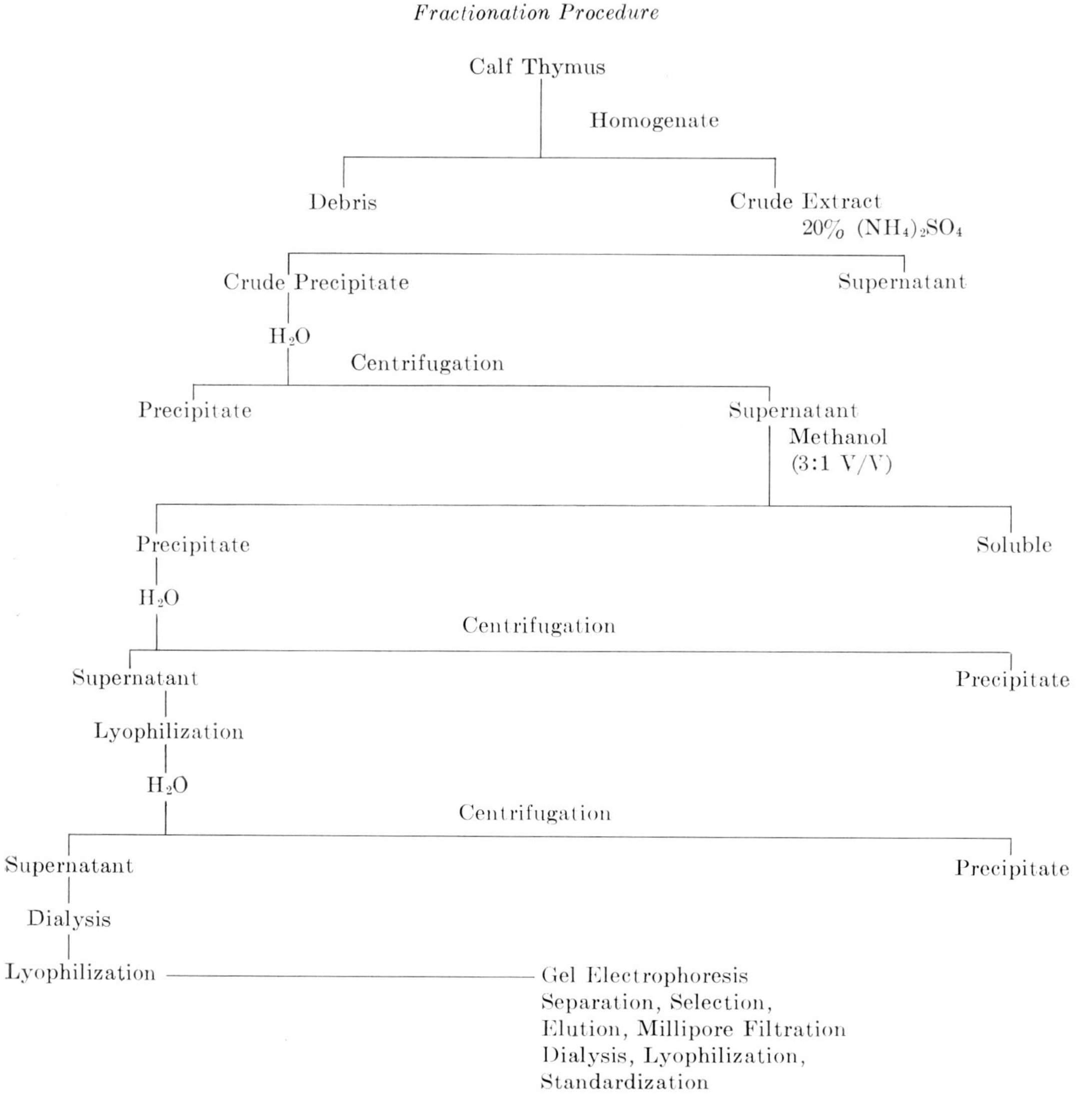

Figure 1. Schematic representation of the procedure used to prepare the calf thymus extracts.

plates were agitated and incubated for 2 hr at 37°C and overnight in the cold. Serum titers were recorded as the reciprocal of the highest dilution resulting in complete hemagglutination of the added erythrocytes. All sera were tested in duplicate on at least two occasions.

Antibody plaque procedure. The number of antibody plaque-forming cells (PFC) was enumerated in the spleens of control and treated animals using the immunoplaque assay as described elsewhere (4, 16). Only the direct procedure with one complement incubation was used, so that all plaques were considered to be due to high-efficiency 19S IgM antibody.

RESULTS

Development of antibody-forming cells in immunized meonatal mice. As can be seen from Figures 4 and 5, and Table I, control mice injected with RBC alone had the anticipated progressive increase in the number of PFC with age, as well as a rapid increase in spleen weight (Fig. 6). No PFC could be detected in spleens of animals immunized at birth with sheep erythrocytes and tested 4 days later. However, mice immunized the 2nd or 3rd week of life developed several hundred to several thousand PFC/spleen (Fig. 4). This corresponded to one or two hundred PFC/million splenocytes (Fig. 5). The peak number generally occurred on day 4 after immunization. Four- to 6-week-old animals generally responded with 10 to 30 thousand PFC/spleen, representing about 300 to 400 PFC/million spleen cells.

The apparent discrepancy between the faster rate of appearance of maximum numbers of PFC/whole spleen (Fig. 4) as compared to the slower rate of development of PFC/million splenocytes (Fig. 5) in 2- to 4-week-old animals seemed to be due to the marked increase in spleen size with age (Fig. 6). Although the spleens were much smaller in the younger animals, the total

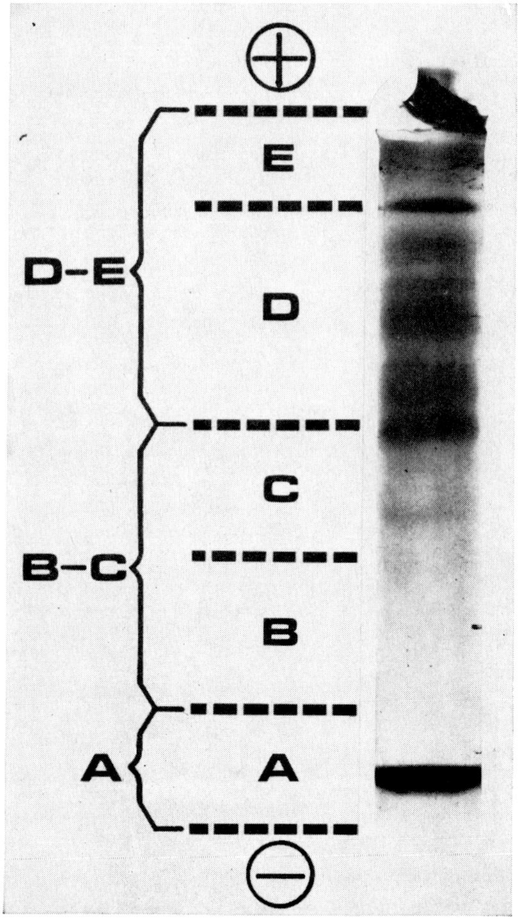

Figure 2. Polyacrylamide gel electrophoresis pattern of partially purified calf thymus extract.

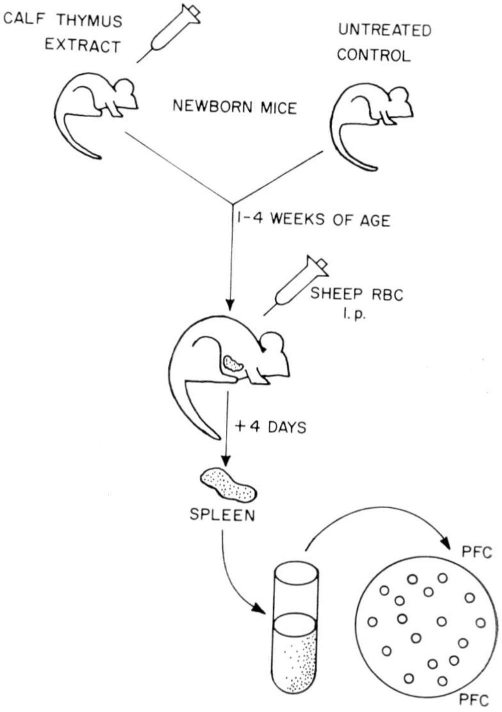

Figure 3. Experimental scheme to study the effect of calf thymus extracts on the immune competence of neonatal mice.

number of nucleated cells was also low. Thus, there appeared to be less of a difference in the number of PFC/10^6 spleen cells between younger and older animals, as compared to the total number of PFC/whole spleen. Furthermore, the cytokinetics of the immune response in 2-, 3-, 4- and 6-week-old mice was previously found to be relatively similar, with a peak response on day 4 to 5, except that the magnitude of the response was markedly lower in the younger animals.

Development of "background" antibody-forming cells to sheep erythrocytes was also dependent upon the age of the animals (Table I). Mice younger than 1 week of age had no detectable PFC in their spleens. A few PFC appeared between 1 and 2 weeks of age. About a dozen PFC appeared in the spleens of untreated animals by 3 weeks of age. Mice 4 to 6 weeks of age had the same number as adults, which averaged about 40 to 70/spleen.

Development of the immune response to sheep cells could be enhanced by high doses of antigen. As can be seen from Figure 7, spleens of mice

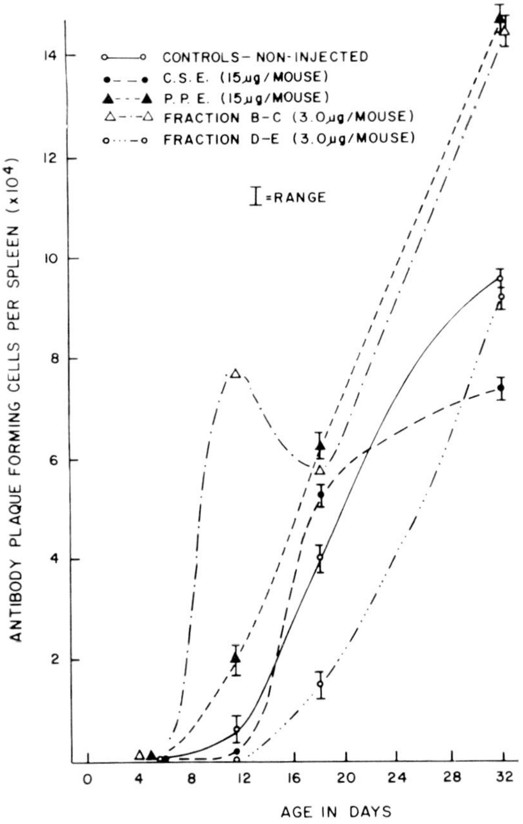

Figure 4. Effect of calf thymus fractions on the number of PFC/spleen observed 4 days after immunization at 0, 7, 14, or 28 days of age. Each point represents the average of at least five mice.

injected at 1 day of life with either a 0.5% or a 5.0% suspension of sheep erythrocytes had very few, if any, PFC when tested 7 to 14 days later. However, inoculation of a similar quantity of a 50% suspension of sheep cells resulted in appearance of about 600 to 800 PFC 7 to 12 days later, without further stimulation (Fig. 7). Thus, a relatively large quantity of RBC injected at birth appeared to stimulate larger numbers of antibody-forming cells.

Effects of crude and purified thymus extracts. Inoculation of mice at birth with 15 μg CSE had little if any effect on the development of the immune response to sheep erythrocytes (Figs. 4 and 5). The only difference seemed to be a moderate enhancement of the number of PFC/spleen in treated animals when challenged during the 1st or 2nd week of life. However, this enhancement, although consistent, was generally less than the 50% variation considered significant in most studies utilizing the immunoplaque assay.

Inoculation of 15 μg PPE into newborn mice resulted in a marked stimulation of the number of PFC (Figs. 4 and 5), as well as spleen weight (Fig. 6), after subsequent challenge immunization. Injection of these mice with sheep erythrocytes at 1 week of age resulted in more than twice as many PFC in their spleens as compared with controls. There was a moderate enhancement of the PFC response at 2 weeks of life. Furthermore, at 4 weeks of age there were 12 to 15 times as many PFC in the spleens of these neonatally treated mice as compared with controls (Figs. 4 and 5). The spleen weights were also stimulated throughout the first month of life in these animals, as compared with nontreated control mice (Fig. 6).

There was little if any effect on the number of "background" antibody-forming cells in the

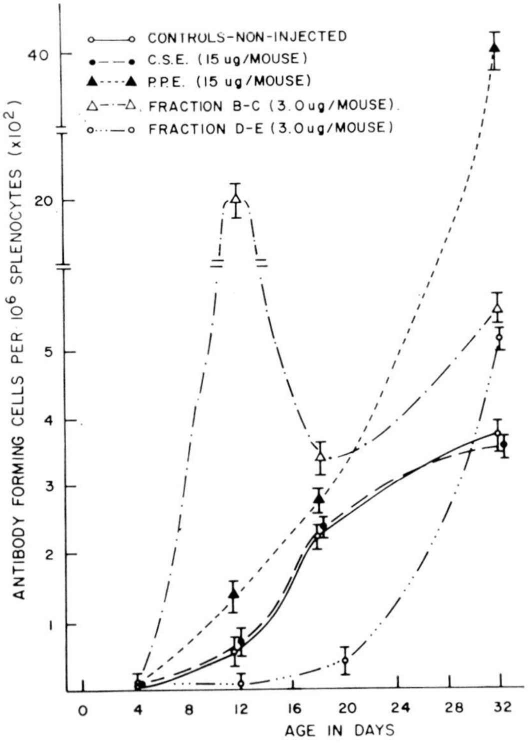

Figure 5. Effect of calf thymus fractions injected at birth on the number of PFC/million splenocytes in mice immunized at 0, 1, 2, or 4 weeks of age. Each point represents the average number of PFC observed 4 days postimmunization of at least five mice/group.

spleens of mice injected at birth with either CSE or PPE, when compared with the controls. Also, the serum antibody titers were not significantly different between control and treated mice after challenge immunization during the first 4 weeks of life, or thereafter. In most instances, peak serum titers were generally 1:4 to 1:16 or lower for all groups tested during the first 4 weeks of life.

Effect of purified fractions on the antibody response. Injection of mice at birth with 3 μg of the purified gel fraction B-C resulted in a marked enhancement of development of PFC during the first 2 weeks of life (Figs. 4 and 5). The PFC response was enhanced when calculated both per million splenocytes and per whole spleen. Animals

TABLE I

Appearance of "background" PFC to S-RBC in spleens of normal mice at various ages

Age	No. of Mice Tested	PFC/Spleen	
		Range	Average No.
days			
1	17	0	0
7	38	0–3	0.5
14	24	0–8	2.6
21	18	0–15	2.4
28	49	0–39	19.6
35	26	12–122	48.3
>60	130	15–149	73.1

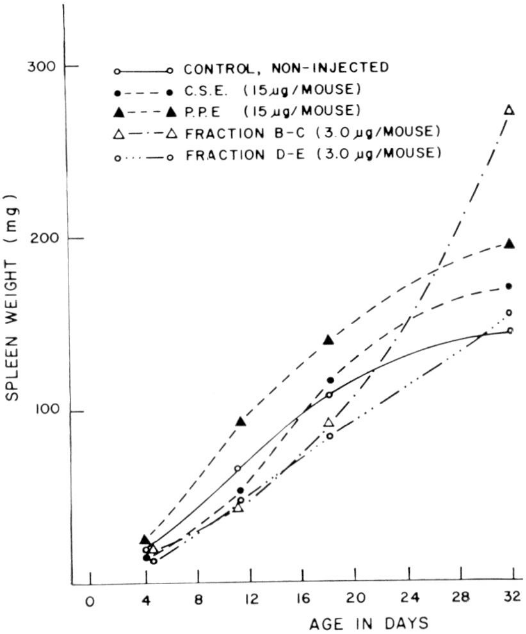

Figure. 6 Spleen weight of control and calf thymus extract treated mice. Each point represents the average of 5 to 10 mice on day indicated.

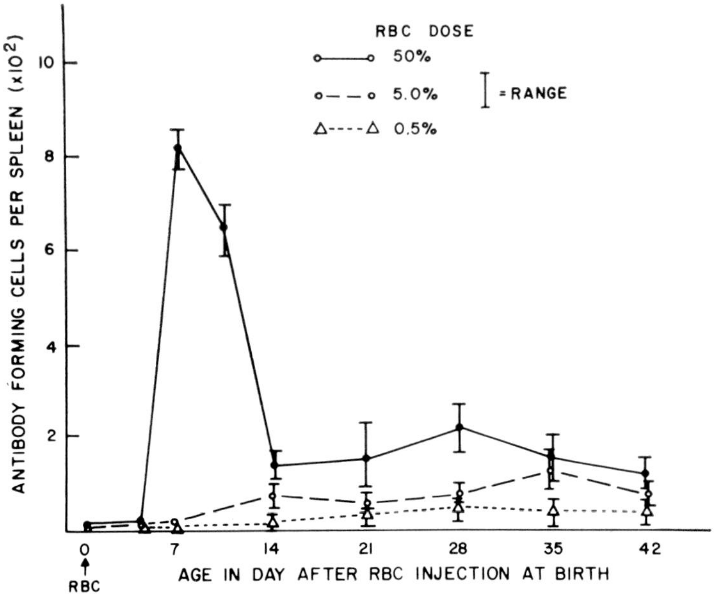

Figure 7. PFC response to three different doses of S-RBC in spleens of mice immunized in birth; each point represents the average of 5 to 10 mice/day and treatment indicated.

injected with this material at birth had 10 to 15 times more PFC/spleen and 30 to 40 times more PFC/10^6 splenocytes when challenged at 1 week of life, as compared with control animals. Neonatally treated mice had approximately 50% to 60% more PFC when challenged at 2 weeks of age than did controls. There was only a moderate enhancement when challenge immunization occurred at the 4th week of life. Spleen size was not significantly different for the treated mice except at 4 weeks of age, when there was a two- to threefold increase (Fig. 4).

In contrast to the stimulatory effects of fraction B-C, injection of fraction D-E at birth markedly suppressed appearance of PFC during the first weeks of life (Figs. 4 and 5). This fraction had previously been found to inhibit lymphocytopoesis (31). Injection of 3 μg at birth resulted in an 80% to 95% depression of the expected number of PFC appearing in spleens of mice challenged with RBC at 1 or 2 weeks of age. The greatest percentage of suppression occurred in the youngest mice. Spleen size and weight were only moderately suppressed during this time, with the least suppression occurring in the older age group (Fig. 6).

Neither fraction, at the dosage used, had any significant effect on development of "background" antibody-forming cells in spleens of the young mice. There were similar numbers of PFC in spleens of nonimmunized mice, regardless of treatment at birth, with the fewest in the spleens of the youngest mice.

DISCUSSION

The results of a number of recent studies have demonstrated that calf thymus extracts contain factors which may influence lymphoid cell number and type in neonatal or adult mice (12, 13, 20–25). Furthermore, other studies have shown that some extracts may restore immunocompetence of thymectomized animals as assayed by a graft *vs* host procedure (26, 27). A preliminary report has also described a slight to moderate enhancement of the number of PFC in thymectomized mice injected with extracts during the first 4 weeks of life (29). Milligram amounts of the various thymus preparations have been used in these studies. In contrast, the results presented in this report indicate that very small quantities, on the microgram level, may markedly influence development of immunocompetence in normal mice, as determined by the cellular antibody plaque procedure. For this study the effect of thymus extracts on development of immunocompetence was considered only in relation to the number of antibody-forming cells appearing in spleens of control, non-treated mice challenged at the same age with sheep erythrocytes.

Several studies, including those reported here, have shown that neonatal animals slowly develop the capacity to form PFC to sheep erythrocytes during the first weeks of life. Full immunologic maturation, as assessed by PFC responsiveness, generally does not occur until about the 4th to 6th week of life. The calf thymus extracts and fractions used in this study markedly influenced the development of such immunocompetence. However, the effects did not seem to be due to a direct action on antibody-forming cells *per se*. In other studies it was found that adult mice injected with these materials, including the purified enhancing factor B-C, responded similarly to control mice, regardless of antigen dose or quantity of thymus extract.

The mechanism whereby the stimulating fraction B-C enhances development of immune competence is not known. It is possible that this preparation either stimulates a pool of precursor stem cells, which may already be present in neonatal mice, or may provide a factor(s) necessary for the more rapid maturation and proliferation of cells involved in immunogenesis. It is also possible that this fraction provides, in a nonspecific manner, metabolites necessary for more rapid immunologic maturation. This seems unlikely since results of preliminary experiments, in progress, have suggested that similar extracts prepared from organs other than the thymus do not significantly affect immunocompetence. Nevertheless, more extensive studies should be performed to rule out the nonspecific nature of the effect.

It also may be possible, though unlikely, that the purified material from the calf thymus extract is a "cross-reacting" antigen shared by sheep erythrocytes. It has already been shown that bovine serum, including fetal calf serum, will stimulate antibody plaque formation to sheep RBC *in vitro*. This is thought to be due to a "shared" antigen. The same may be true in this study. In that case, the factor, or factors, if functioning as an antigen, should merely "prime" the mice to respond anamnestically to a subsequent injection of RBC. However, this does not seem very likely, since *both* stimulation and inhibition occurred, using different fractions. Nevertheless, serologic analysis of the extracts, and of their fractions, in comparison to sheep RBC extracts, would be of value. Also, the effect of the extracts on development of immune responsiveness to antigens other than sheep RBC should be determined.

The immunologic inhibition induced by fraction C-D could be due to induction of a temporary but specific immunologic tolerance to an antigen shared by RBC and this fraction. This also seems unlikely, since this material did not stimulate a PFC response when injected into nonimmunized mice. The presence of a shared antigen should have "primed" adult mice, if present in a sufficiently high concentration capable of "paralyzing" newborn animals. Antigenic competition is also a possible explanation for the suppressive properties of fraction C-D. Injection of this material into newborn mice could conceivably stimulate a limited number of antigen-sensitive cells, and thus prevent a subsequent response to challenge injection of sheep RBC. This possibility also seems remote, expecially since extremely small quantities of this fraction are effective. In addition, even larger quantities had no effect in older animals.

Since very small amounts of the extracts stimulated enhanced appearance of antibody-forming cells, it is possible that the effects were due to a "hormonal" factor. It should be noted that the crude thymus extract contains at least seven to eight proteins detectable by disc electrophoresis (31). The partially purified extract contains five to six proteins. The purified fraction B-C contains one major protein band, and three minor ones, while fraction D-E has one major band and two minor ones. These are distinguishable by electrophoresis (31). Thus, these preparations, even the electrophoretic fractions, are not "pure" and their effects on the PFC response may be due to any one of the proteins, not necessarily the major one, or even to substances which have not been detected.

Studies concerning the effects of proteolytic enzymes on the biologic activity of the fractions may provide information as to the chemical nature of the inhibitory and stimulatory factors. Furthermore, it seems apparent that both factors are present in the crude extract, and the effect of one may be neutralized by the other. It also seems apparent that the purified fractions used in this investigation may be related to the active materials present in extracts studied by other investigators. The presence of an inhibitory factor in the extracts used by others could account for the relatively large quantities of material needed for stimulatory activity. The effectiveness of very small amounts of the fraction B-C in this study may be due to its relative purity.

Acknowledgments. The capable technical assistance of Mrs. Vivian Simmons, Mrs. Leony Mills and Miss Elaine Forsch is acknowledged.

REFERENCES

1. Ingraham, J. S., Compt. Rend. Acad. Sci., *256:* 5005, 1963.
2. Ingraham, J. S. and Bussard, A. E., J. Exp. Med., *119:* 667, 1964.
3. Jerne, N. K. and Nordin, A. A., Science, *140:* 405, 1963.
4. Jerne, N. K., Nordin, A. A. and Henry C., *The Cell-Bound Antibodies*, Edited by B. Amos and H. Koprowski, p. 109, Wistar Institute Press, Philadelphia, 1963.
5. Rowley, D. A. and Fitch, F. W., J. Exp. Med., *121:* 671, 1965.
6. J. Sterzl, Cold Spring Harbor Symp. Quant. Biol., *32:* 445, 1967.
7. Friedman, H., J. Bact., *92:* 820, 1966.
8. Hechtel, M., Dishon, T. and Braun, W., Proc. Soc. Exp. Biol. Med., *120:* 728, 1965.
9. Hechtel, M., Dishon, T. and Braun, W., Proc. Soc. Exp. Biol. Med., *119:* 991, 1965.
10. Cheng, V. and Trentin, J. J., Proc. Soc. Exp. Biol. Med. *126:* 467, 1967.
11. Nordin, A. A., Proc. Soc. Exp. Biol. Med., *129:* 57, 1968.
12. Miller, J. F. A. P. and Osoba, D., Physiol. Rev., *47:* 937, 1967.
13. Metcalf, D., *Recent Results in Cancer Research*, Vol. 5, Springer-Verlag, New York, 1966.
14. Hess, M. W., *Experimental Thymectomy*, Springer-Verlag, New York, 1968.
15. Good, R. A. and Papermaster, B. W., Advances Immun., *4:* 1, 1964.
16. Friedman, H., Proc. Soc. Exp. Biol. Med., *118:* 1176, 1965.
17. Miller, J. F. A. P., deBurgh, P. M. and Grant, G. A., Nature, *208:* 1332, 1965.
18. Metcalf, D., Nature, *208:* 1336, 1965.
19. Miller, J. F. A. P., Nature, *208:* 1337, 1965.
20. Claman, H. N., Chapman, E. A. and Triplett, R., Proc. Soc. Exp. Biol. Med., *122:* 1167, 1966.

21. Roberts, S. and White, A., Biol. Chem., *178:* 151, 1949.
22. Gregoire, G. and Duchateau, G., Arch. Biol. (Liege), *67:* 269, 1956.
23. Metcalf, D., Brit. J. Cancer, *10:* 442, 1956.
24. Metcalf, D., Ann. N. Y. Acad. Sci., *73:* 113, 1958.
25. Duplan, J. F., Foschi, G. V. and Manson, L. A., Proc. Soc. Exp. Biol. Med., *110:* 426, 1962.
26. DeSomer, Dewys and Leyton, R., Life Sci., *11:* 810, 1963.
27. Trainin, N., Bejerano, A., Strakilevitch, M., Goldring, D. and Small, M., Israel J. Med. Sci., *2:* 549, 1966.
28. Trainin, N. and Linker-Israel, M., Cancer Res., *27:* 309, 1967.
29. Small, M. and Trainin, N., Nature, *216:* 377, 1967.
30. Goldstein, A. L., Slater, F. D. and White, A., Proc. Nat. Acad. Sci., *56:* 1010, 1966.
31. Hand, T., Caster, P. and Luckey, T. D., Biochem. Biophys. Res. Comm., *26:* 18, 1967.
32. Law, L. W. and Agnew, H. D., Proc. Soc. Exp. Biol. Med., *127:* 953, 1968.
33. Law, L. W., Goldstein, A. L. and White, A., Nature, *219:* 1391, 1968.
34. Trainin, N., Small, M. and Globerson, A., J. Exp. Med., *130:* 765, 1969.
35. Hand, T., Ceglowski, W. S., Damrongsak, D. and Friedman, H., J. Reticuloendothel. Soc., *5:* 403, 1968 (abstract).
36. Hand, T., Ceglowski, W. S. and Friedman, H., Sumbitted for publication, Experientia, 1969.

THE JOURNAL OF IMMUNOLOGY
Vol. 105, No. 2, Aug. 1970

DISSOCIATION OF A SMALL PROPORTION OF A HUMAN IgM POPULATION INTO Fc_μ, Fab_μ, AND FREE LIGHT CHAINS FOLLOWING REDUCTION[1]

JAMES E. MORRIS AND F. P. INMAN[2]

From the Department of Microbiology, University of Georgia, Athens, Georgia 30601

Received for publication December 22, 1969

Preparations of human IgM were treated with 0.1 M 2-mercaptoethanol and the reaction was terminated after 1 hr by adding neutralized iodoacetic acid. Dissociation into subunits, IgM_s, was complete, but more slowly sedimenting material also was evident in the schlieren patterns. After gel filtration on Bio-Gel P-150 using a neutral salt buffer for solvent, several fractions were isolated in addition to the IgM_s. The composition of the fractions was determined by ultracentrifugation, immunoelectrophoresis, and analysis of polypeptide chain contents. It was demonstrated that three fractions consisted primarily of IgM_s, but that Fc_μ and Fab_μ also were present. One fraction comprised only Fc_μ and Fab_μ, and a fifth fraction consisted largely of free light chains.

The basic structure of the human IgM molecule seems to be similar to that of IgG in its polypeptide chain composition. Although it has not been accepted without challenge (1), most investigators have concluded that IgM comprises two μ chains and two light chains for each of its five subunits, IgM_s (2–5).

Several investigators have studied the structure of IgM and IgM_s by the use of disulfide bond-reducing agents. With very low concentrations of mercaptoethylamine (5) or cysteine (3), IgM_s molecules can be obtained with their interchain disulfide bonds intact. Treatment of IgM with higher concentrations of certain reducing agents, or even a low concentration of dithiothreitol (3), causes disruption of intrasubunit interchain disulfide bonds.

Suzuki and Deutsch (1) reported that free light chains were released under non-dissociating conditions from human IgM reduced with 2-mercaptoethanol. A similar observation was made with reduced chicken IgM (6).

Dominguez *et al.* (7) reported that upon sufficient reduction with mercaptans, the IgM molecules were extensively degraded to slowly sedimenting material. In addition, they concluded that there were at least two antigenically distinct classes of IgM_s on the individual IgM molecule.

The fact that on several occasions we have noted in schlieren patterns the presence of a small amount of material which sedimented more slowly than IgM prompted the work now reported. It is concerned with the degradation of human IgM following moderate reduction with 2-ME. The IgM we studied was incompletely fragmented subsequent to reduction. A small amount of light chain material dissociated from the reduced and alkylated IgM under neutral conditions.

MATERIALS AND METHODS

Preparation of IgM. Plasma from patient Dau., who was suffering from Waldenström's macroglobulinemia, was defatted by adjusting the density to 1.2 with saturated NaBr solution. IgM was prepared as previously described (5). Essentially, crude IgM was precipitated in water, and then purified by filtration through Bio-Gel P-200 equilibrated with 0.32 SB.[3] Each preparation of IgM was tested for purity by immunoelectrophoresis and double diffusion in agarose using anti-IgM, anti-IgG and anti-whole human serum

[1] This research was supported by a grant from the National Science Foundation (GB-5551). F.P.I. also received partial support from the Institute of Comparative Medicine of the University of Georgia.

[2] To whom inquiries should be directed.

[3] Abbreviations used: 0.32 SB, 0.32 M NaCl solution made 10^{-3} M in sodium borate, pH 8; 2-ME, 2-mercaptoethanol (redistilled); Tris, tris(hydroxymethyl)aminomethane.

antisera (Hyland Laboratories, Los Angeles, Calif.). IgM (Dau.) was a kappa type paraprotein. Some work was done with IgM (Aug.), which was prepared similarly.

Reduction and alkylation of IgM. The protein was dialyzed overnight at room temperature (to negate cryoprecipitation) in 0.2 M Tris[3] buffer, pH 8.0. Under these conditions, a variable amount of protein (5% to 10%) precipitated and was discarded. The IgM was reduced with 0.1 M 2-ME[3] for 1 hr at 30°C, and subsequently was alkylated with 0.15 M neutralized iodoacetic acid for 1 hr at 4°C. The reduced and alkylated protein was dialyzed at least 10 hr at 4°C against 0.32 SB.

In some experiments, IgM_s with its interchain disulfide bonds intact was used. The subunits were prepared as previously described (5) by reduction of IgM with 0. 015 M mercaptoethylamine followed by alkylation with neutralized iodoacetic acid.

Ultracentrifugation. Protein samples were centrifuged at 68,000 rpm in a Spinco model E analytical ultracentrifuge equipped with electronic speed control and a schlieren optic system. Rotor temperature was maintained at 20°C, and sedimentation values were corrected for viscosity and density according to Schachman (8) except where noted.

Immunologic analyses. An antiserum (anti-Aug.) was prepared by injecting rabbits with IgM (Aug.) (9). It was absorbed with light chains from IgM (Dau.), and Fab_μ (Ov) and Fab_μ (Aug.) prepared as described previously (9). The absorbed antiserum, referred to as anti-Aug. (abs.), did not react with normal human IgG, light chains (Dau.), Fab_μ (Dau.), Fab_μ (Aug.), or Fab_μ (Ov). It did react with IgM (Dau.), IgM (Aug.) and with Dau. μ chains at a concentration at least as low as 88 μg/ml. Consequently, it was considered specific for Fc_μ.

Double diffusion in gel was done with 1% agarose in 0.05 M barbital, pH 8.2. The depth of the gel was about 1 to 2 mm. Immunoelectrophoresis was carried out in the same gel. Samples were electrophoresed for 90 min at 160 V, and 6 to 7 mA/plate. Double diffusion and immunoelectrophoresis plates were incubated at room temperature in a water-saturated atmosphere.

Gel filtration. Some samples were filtered through columns of Bio-Gel P-150 equilibrated with 0.32 SB. Others were filtered through the same gel, but equilibrated with 1 M propionic acid, or 4 M guanidine-HCl solution adjusted to pH 7. The ratio of packed column volume to mg weight of protein was about 4:1, and the flow rate was adjusted to approximately 4 ml/hr.

Protein fractionated by filtration in the presence of propionic acid or guanidine solution was renatured for immunologic analysis by dialysis against two changes of water during 2 days. It was then dialyzed overnight in 0.16 M NaCl solution containing 10^{-3} M sodium borate, pH 8. $E^{1\%}_{1\,cm}$ for μ chains was considered to be 13.7 and for light chains 11.8 (10).

Prealkylation of IgM. IgM was treated with 0.15 M iodoacetic acid in the presence of 4 M guanidine-HCl solution, pH 7.2. Alkylation was allowed to proceed overnight at room temperature. The protein then was dialyzed against 0.2 M Tris buffer, pH 8, for further study.

RESULTS

Sedimentation characteristics of reduced IgM. IgM (Dau.) (Fig. 1*A*) was reduced with 0.1 M 2-ME and alkylated. After dialysis for 1 day or 1 week, portions were examined in the ultracentrifuge. The photographs of representative schlieren patterns shown in Figure 1 indicated that reduction to subunits was complete. The main component (Fig. 1*B*) appeared to be IgM_s (6.4S); in addition, a more slowly sedimenting peak of material was evident. The increase in the amount of the latter component was not striking after the reduced IgM "aged" for a week (Fig. 1*C*). However, the results of several experiments led one to conclude that dissociation of reduced IgM progressed slightly over a period of 1 week, and the more slowly sedimenting material manifested itself as a sharper schlieren peak with age. Similar results were noted for IgM_s treated in a manner like that of IgM.

Immunoelectrophoretic analysis of reduced and alkylated IgM. The reduced and alkylated IgM was analyzed by immunoelectrophoresis. When the developing antiserum was anti-Aug., two precipitating components were evident (Fig. 2). The more rapidly migrating one showed partial identity with the slower. Complete identity of the two components was noted when anti-Aug. (abs.) was used to develop the plate. Only the more slowly migrating component appeared to contain light (kappa) chains.

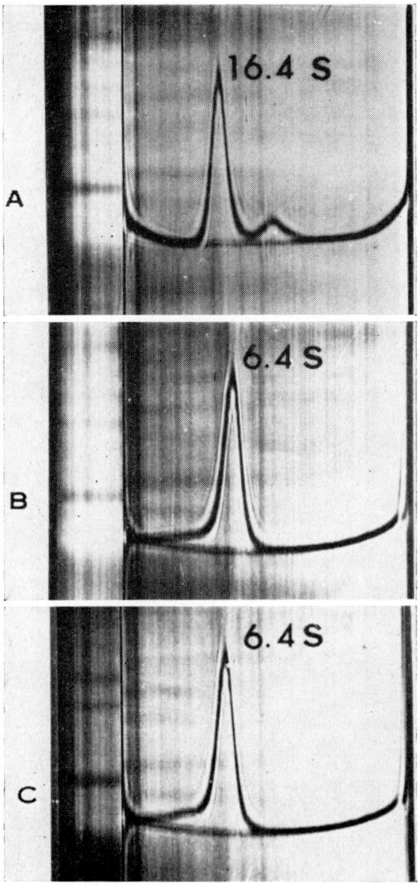

Figure 1. Schlieren patterns of IgM (Dau.) and the products of its reduction. IgM suspended in 0.2 M Tris, pH 8, was treated with 0.2 M 2-ME for 1 hr at 30°. The reaction was terminated by addition of neutralized iodoacetic acid. *A*, native IgM (Dau.). *B*, IgM reduced, alkylated, and dialyzed in Tris buffer for 1 day. *C*, IgM reduced, alkylated, and dialyzed in Tris. Sample was centrifuged 1 week after reduction. All samples were analyzed at 6 mg/ml. Sedimentation values are not corrected for the buffer, and sedimentation is from left to right. Sample *A* was photographed 12 min after speed was attained, and samples *B* and *C* were photographed after 32 min.

Gel filtration of reduced IgM. IgM was reduced with 0.1 M 2-ME, alkylated, and dialyzed overnight. The components of the mixture were resolved by filtration of 110 mg through a column (2.5 cm x 95 cm) of Bio-Gel P-150 equilibrated with 0.32 SB (Fig. 3). Several components, which were not perceptible in the schlieren patterns (Fig. 1 *B* and *C*), were discerned upon filtration. It is noteworthy that the peaks observed on the elution profiles were obtained using a neutral salt buffer. It appeared that filtration separated components present, but not observed, during ultracentrifugation, or that dissociation occurred on the column.

The protein collected in the tubes during filtration was pooled as indicated in the elution profile (Fig. 3). Pools c and d were shown by ultracentrifugation to contain much material sedimenting at the same rate as pool b. Therefore, pools c and d were refiltered to diminish the quantity of faster sedimenting material. After appropriate concentration, each of the pools was centrifuged, and the schlieren pattern composite is given in Figure 4.

Pools a and b, which comprised 13.8% and 55.4%, respectively, of the total eluted optical density units, were very similar (Fig. 4, *A* and *B*), except that a small amount of a faster sedimenting constituent preceded the sedimentation of the major component of pool a. The apparently homogeneous protein of pool b had a sedimentation coefficient of 6.4S.

The protein constituting pool c (Fig. 3) comprised 18.2% of the optical density units eluted. The major component probably was the same as that in pool b, as indicated by the similar sedimentation value (6.4S). After refiltration, the major component sedimented at 4.6S (Fig. 4*C*).

The protein of pool d (Fig. 3) accounted for 3.6% of the eluted optical density. After refiltration, the sedimentation coefficient of its major component was 3.5S (Fig. 4*D*).

The schlieren pattern of pool e (Fig. 4*E*) was only slightly asymmetrical. Its sedimentation coefficient was 2.0S, and it comprised 3.7% of the eluted, absorbing material.

Immunologic analysis of protein pools. In addition to pools c and d, pools a, b and e were refiltered through P-150 and the major component of each was isolated. These fractions then were examined by immunoelectrophoresis. The specificity of the various antisera for μ or light chains is shown in Figure 5*A*. With the exception of pool e, each of the pools (a to d) was electrophoretically heterogeneous when developed with anti-Aug. antiserum (Fig. 5*B*). Pools a and b contained a small amount of an anodally migrating component in addition to the main component which migrated cathodally.

Pool c comprised three components. One,

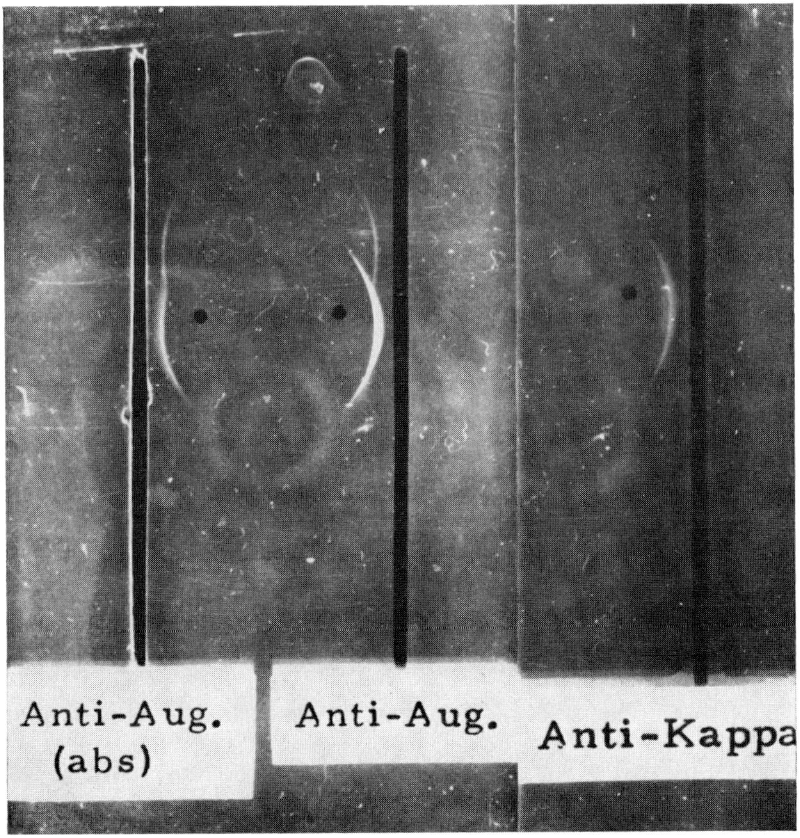

Figure 2. Immunoelectrophoretic analyses of reduced and alkylated IgM (Dau.). Reduced and alkylated IgM was placed in the wells after dialysis against 0.32 SB. The anode is at the top of the picture. Anti-Aug. antiserum and anti-Aug. (abs.) antiserum were prepared as described in *Materials and Methods*. Anti-kappa antiserum was a commercially prepared antiserum specific for light chains.

which migrated rapidly, identified with another cathodally migrating constituent (Fig. 5*B*). A third antigenically distinct substance migrated slowly.

Pool d consisted of two antigenically distinct proteins (Fig. 5*B*). One migrated rapidly and the other somewhat more slowly.

Pool e had one constituent which migrated cathodally (Fig. 5*B*). However when the developing antiserum was anti-Aug. (abs.), no precipitin line appeared (Fig. 5*C*). That this pool consisted of light chain material was made evident when a precipitin line formed with anti-kappa antiserum (Fig. 5*D*).

When pools a and b were analyzed with anti-Aug. (abs.), they still appeared to contain two components which joined in a line of identity (Fig. 5*C*). In addition, pool a may have contained a third constituent which migrated slightly cathodally.

The more rapidly migrating component of pool c (Fig. 5*C*) antigenically identified with the major cathodally migrating component. A minor third component, which migrated cathodally, also was observed.

Only one protein in pool d precipitated with anti-Aug. (abs.) (Fig. 5*C*). The second constituent, noted in Figure 5*B*, apparently contained light chain antigenic sites (Fig. 5*D*). Some of the material in pools a, b and c which migrated slightly cathodally also contained light chains (Fig. 5*D*).

Mu and light (*kappa*) *chain composition.* Additional attempts were made to characterize the proteins. IgM was reduced and the pools were prepared as described above. Pools c, d and e

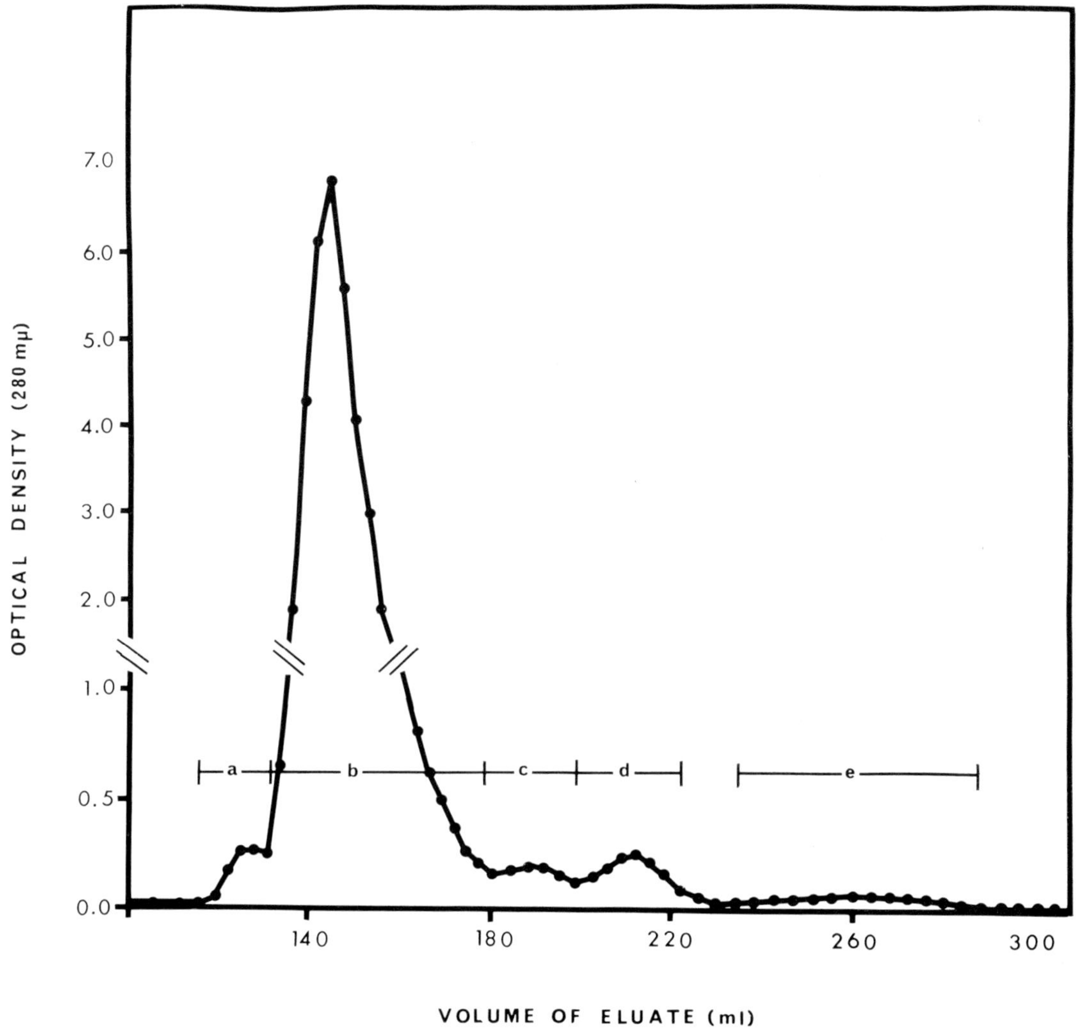

Figure 3. Elution profile of reduced and alkylated IgM (Dau.). The IgM was treated with 0.1 M 2-ME as described, and alkylated. After dialysis against 0.32 SB the protein was filtered through a column of Bio-Gel P-150 equilibrated with 0.32 SB. Protein pools were taken from the areas denoted by horizontal bars and lower case letters.

were refiltered through P-150 using 0.32 SB as the dispersal phase. The protein in the fractions comprising the main peak of optical density in each instance was pooled, concentrated, and examined by ultracentrifugation. The pooled proteins then were dissociated into their constituent polypeptide chains by gel filtration in the presence of 1 M propionic acid. The results are summarized in Table I.

Of the absorbing protein in pool b 73% reacted antigenically as μ chains and 26% as light chains (Table I). The protein of undissociated pool b had a sedimentation coefficient of 6.4S, and upon immunoelectrophoresis it migrated in the position expected of IgM_s (Fig. 5).

The main component of the undissociated pool c sedimented at 4.6S. After gel filtration in the presence of propionic acid 69% of the eluted protein reacted with anti-Aug. (abs.) antiserum, and 31% reacted with anti-kappa chain antiserum.

Approximately 58% of the protein of pool d

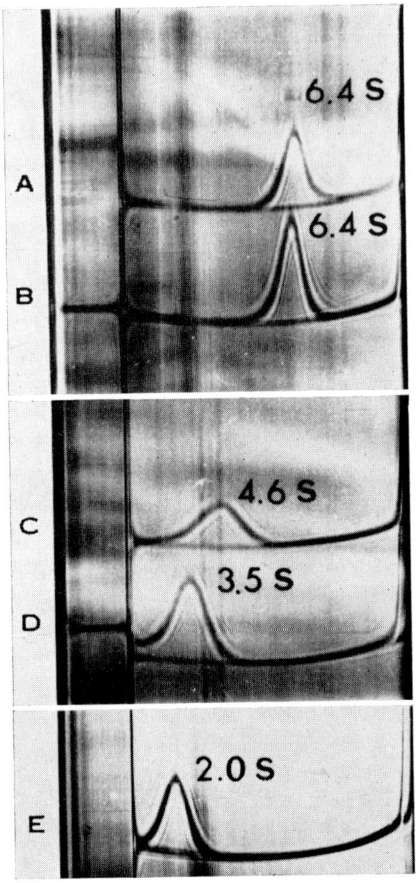

Figure 4. Schlieren patterns of the protein pools denoted in Figure 3. *A*, pool a; *B*, pool b; *C*, pool c after refiltration through Bio-Gel P-150; *D*, pool d after refiltration through Bio-Gel P-150; *E*, pool e. Samples were centrifuged in 0.32 SB, and photographs were made 56 min after reaching rotor speed of 68,000 rpm. Sedimentation is left to right.

reacted with anti-Aug. (abs.) antiserum after filtration in propionic acid (Table I). Light chain materials accounted for 42% of the eluted protein. The sedimentation coefficient of the protein before filtration in propionic acid was 3.5S.

Light chains evidently comprised the main part of pool e (Table I). The sedimentation coefficient of this material was 2.0S.

Reduction of prealkylated IgM. The data to this point indicated that fragmentation of part of the IgM population is prompted by reduction with 2-ME. Since treatment of the molecules with 4 M guanidine-HCl solution, pH 7.2, did not result in fragmentation, the 2-ME seemed to be directly responsible for dissociation.

IgM was prealkylated with iodoacetic acid in the presence of guanidine-HCl solution. Then the protein was dispersed in Tris buffer and subsequently treated with 0.1 M 2-ME and alkylated. Upon centrifugation, dissociation similar to that depicted in Figure 1, *B* and *C* was observed. The amount of dissociation of the reduced prealkylated IgM was the same as that of reduced IgM which had not been subjected to the prealkylation procedure. Immunoelectrophoresis patterns of the IgM from the two experiments also were identical.

Dissociation subsequent to reduction was not restricted to IgM (Dau.). Similar results were obtained with IgM (Aug.), the other IgM preparation tested.

DISCUSSION

After reduction and alkylation, the schlieren patterns of the IgM clearly demonstrated the presence of material sedimenting at a rate less than that of IgM_s. It appeared that the quantity of this slowly sedimenting material might have increased slightly with time. Similar schlieren patterns have been published previously (1, 7, 11), but in only one instance was the nature of the slowly sedimenting material investigated (1). In the latter case, light chains were reported to detach themselves in small quantities from reduced and alkylated human IgM at pH 8. Benedict (6) has reported the release of light chains from reduced chicken IgM. In the present report also, we noted that light chain material was released from reduced and alkylated IgM at pH 8. However, much of it was associated with μ chains or μ chain fragments bearing Fc_μ determinant sites.

Following reduction, part of the IgM population was fragmented. The fragments could be partially purified by gel filtration under non-dissociating-solvent conditions. They had sedimentation coefficients of 4.3S to 4.6S, 3.5S and 2.0S. Evidently, strong non-covalent bonds were not involved in holding these fragments to the main body of the IgM_s molecules. The amount of material which dissociated after reduction was not extensive. It was variable and usually accounted for about 7% to 15% of the optical density units from the elution profiles.

The composition of the pooled protein fractions was determined by immunoelectrophoresis. Pools

Figure 5. Immunoelectrophoretic analyses of the protein pools denoted in Figure 3 after subsequent filtration through Bio-Gel P-150. The anode is at the top of the picture. Anti-Aug. and anti-Aug. (abs.) antisera were prepared as described in *Materials and Methods*. Anti-kappa antiserum was a commercial antiserum specific for light chains. Lower case letters represent the pools pointed out on Figure 3 except in *A* where *a* denotes μ chains and *b* denotes light chains.

a and b consisted primarily of IgM_s (Fig. 5, *B* and *C*). The ratio of μ to light chains as a function of eluted optical density units (Table I) also was consistent with this conclusion. We (5) reported earlier that IgM_s (Dau.) comprised 77% μ chains and 23% light chains when measured similarly. In addition, a very small amount of Fc_μ was detected. The presence of Fab_μ was difficult to ascertain, but it is likely that it was responsible for the spur noted when the immunoelectrophoresis plate of pool a was developed with anti-Aug. (abs.) antiserum (Fig. 5*C*). The reason anti-Aug. (abs.) antiserum, which is specific for a large part of the μ chain in the direction of the C-terminus (Fig. 5*A*), could react with Fab_μ probably has to do with the method of absorption of the antiserum. The Fab_μ with which the anti-Aug. antiserum was absorbed (see *Materials and Methods*) was prepared by prolonged digestion of IgM with papain (9). Under the conditions used, it was considered likely that the Fab_μ fragment is a little smaller, as regards the C-terminal portion of the μ chain fragment, than Fab_μ produced under other conditions. Hence, the specificity of the antiserum for Fc_μ may include an antigenic site located high on the C-terminal portion of some Fab_μ fragments, but which has been enzymati-

TABLE I

Polypeptide chain composition of the proteins comprising each of the pools denoted in Figure 3 after subsequent refiltration through Bio-Gel P-150 equilibrated with 0.32 SB; the pooled protein then was suspended in 1 M propionic acid and filtered through Bio-Gel P-150 equilibrated with propionic acid

Pool	$s_{20,w}$	%[a] μ Chains or μ Chain Fragments[b]	%[a] Light Chains[c]
a	6.4	ND[d]	ND[d]
b	6.4	73	26
c	4.6	69	31
d	3.5	58	42
e	2.0	0	100

[a] Refers to that fraction of the total area in the elution profile attributable to μ chains or μ chain fragments, or to light chains.

[b] Since the antiserum used for testing was anti-Aug. (abs.), the antigenic sites detected were in the Fc_μ region. Hence, one could not distinguish intact μ chains from Fc_μ fragments.

[c] Anti-kappa chain antiserum was used for testing.

[d] ND, not done.

cally degraded on the type Fab_μ fragments used to absorb the antiserum. It was clearly evident that light chains (Fig. 5*D*) as well as μ chains bearing Fc_μ sites composed the more slowly migrating major constituent of pools a and b, ostensibly IgM_S.

Pool c, which was heterogeneous by ultracentrifugation, consisted of three components. Some unfragmented IgM_s was present, but of more interest was the presence of easily detectable Fc_μ and Fab_μ fragments (Fig. 5, *B* and *C*), which according to the schlieren pattern (Fig. 4*C*) were present in a considerable amount.

Pool d apparently consisted of Fc_μ and Fab_μ (Fig. 5, *B* and *C*). These two fragments were clearly evident when the immunoelectrophoresis plate was developed with anti-Aug. antiserum. Only one component, Fc_μ, precipitated when the plate was developed with anti-Aug. (abs.) antiserum. The light chain constituent of Fab_μ (and perhaps of some residual IgM_S) was demonstrated by development of the plate with anti-kappa chain antiserum (Fig. 5*D*).

Dissociation of IgM (Dau.) and of IgM (Aug.) was related to the presence of 2-ME. The IgM did not fragment in the presence of 4 M guanidine-HCl solution. The two most likely explanations for these observations were that 2-ME activated a sulfhydryl-requiring serum enzyme that was adsorbed to the IgM, or that a small percentage of the IgM molecules had been hydrolyzed by a serum enzyme prior to isolation.

The experiments with prealkylated IgM tended to rule out the presence of an adsorbed enzyme which required reducing conditions for its activation. Furthermore, treatment with guanidine solution had no effect in dissociating or denaturing an adsorbed enzyme; prealkylated IgM dissociated just as much as untreated IgM subsequent to reduction.

We feel, then, that the 2-ME was reducing intrachain disulfide bonds which were holding together a pre-cleaved region of the μ chains. In the case of rabbit IgG, Utsumi (12) has described *in vitro* conditions where the γ chain can be pre-split so that upon subsequent reduction intrachain disulfide bonds apparently are reduced resulting in the liberation of Fc_γ and Fab_γ fragments. Furthermore, similar results with regard to human IgM have been noted recently in this laboratory. The enzyme responsible for the presently reported observations could be one involved in normal catabolism of serum IgM. However, it is also possible that another type of proteolytic enzyme was slightly active in the stored plasma.

It was interesting to note that some free light chains were released at neutral pH. Most likely this was the result of reduction by 2-ME of μ-light chain disulfide bonds. The release of light chains from reduced IgM has been reported by several other investigators (1, 6, 7). Since apparently only a small amount of the total available light chains dissociated, it would appear that the non-covalent bonds between certain μ-light chain pairs may be considerably weaker than most of these associations.

Acknowledgments. We wish to thank Dr. Claude Bennett for plasma Dau. and Dr. Hugh Fudenberg for plasma Aug.

REFERENCES

1. Suzuki, T. and Deutsch, H. F., J. Biol. Chem., *242:* 2725, 1967.
2. Miller, F. and Metzger, H., J. Biol. Chem., *240:* 3325, 1965.

3. Miller, F. and Metzger, H., J. Biol. Chem., *240:* 4740, 1965.
4. Lamm, M. E. and Small, P. A., Biochemistry, *5:* 267, 1966.
5. Morris, J. E. and Inman, F. P., Biochemistry, *7:* 2851, 1968.
6. Benedict, A. A., *7th International Congress of Biochemistry, Abst:* 979, 1967.
7. Dominguez, C. J., Caggiano, V., Kochwa, S. and Wasserman, L. R., J. Immun., *101:* 1159, 1968.
8. Schachman, H. K., in *Methods in Enzymology,* Edited by S. P. Colowick and N. O. Kaplan, Vol. 4, p. 32, Academic Press, New York, 1957.
9. Goodman, A., and Inman, F. P., J. Immun., *102:* 1032, 1969.
10. Haber, E. and Stone, M., Biochemistry, *6:* 1974, 1967.
11. Schrohenloher, R. E. and Barry, Carolyn B., J. Immun., *100:* 1006, 1968.
12. Utsumi, S., Biochem. J., *112:* 343, 1969.

THE JOURNAL OF IMMUNOLOGY
Vol. 105, No. 2, Aug. 1970

VARIATION IN THE SIZE OF ANTIBODY SITES FOR THE POLY-L-ASPARTATE HAPTEN DURING THE IMMUNE RESPONSE[1]

P. DIANNE MURPHY[2] AND HARVEY J. SAGE[3]

From the Biochemistry Department, Duke University Medical Center, and the Veterans Administration Hospital, Durham, North Carolina 27706

Received for publication December 18, 1969

Rabbit antisera specific for poly-L-aspartate were prepared by immunization with poly-L-aspartyl-bovine serum albumin. Homogeneous L-aspartate oligopeptides were isolated from partially acid hydrolyzed commercial poly-L-aspartic acid by DEAE-cellulose chromatography. Hapten inhibition of the anti-poly-L-aspartyl-bovine serum albumin-poly-L-aspartyl-rabbit serum albumin reaction by L-aspartate oligomers was studied in a single rabbit with sera isolated after the first and second immunizations. The ability of oligopeptides to inhibit the poly-L-aspartate immune system increased with the size of the oligopeptide. With first course antisera an upper limit was reached with the triaspartate. With second course antisera the upper size limit of antibody-combining sites appeared to be larger than that found early in immunization.

The strength of binding or "avidity" of antibodies directed toward an antigenic determinant is affected by a number of factors. Two such factors are the type of immunization procedure and the time at which antisera are collected. In animals repeatedly immunized with well-characterized immunogens it has been commonly observed that the avidity increases (1, 2). Eisen and Siskind (3) showed that animals given a single injection of a dinitrophenyl-carrier protein complex produced anti-hapten sera, which, with increasing time, contained antibodies with a progressively wider spectrum of specificities and binding affinities for the hapten together with an increasing average association constant. Several workers have suggested that an increase in the avidity of antisera could be explained by an increasing proportion of antibodies with larger binding sites (see 4). In contrast, Little and Counts (5) have presented evidence that high affinity antibodies to the DNP hapten can have smaller combining sites than do lower affinity antibodies.

Richards *et al.* (6) showed that animals immunized with a dinitrophenyl hapten attached to a defined sequence polymer produced antisera whose association constant for ε-dinitrophenyl lysine did not change with time. These authors suggested that the change in association constant noted by Eisen and Siskind (3) is related to heterogeneity in the environment of the individual haptenic groups and a shifting population of antibody molecules with a combined hapten-carrier specificity. Major problems associated with the use of the DNP as a probe of the size and specificity of antibody combining sites are its small size compared to most estimates of the size of antibody-combining sites and its hydrophobic nature.

We have studied the specificity of antisera prepared against a large hydrophilic hapten, poly-aspartic acid. This hapten was chosen because it should be less affected by the carrier protein than most of the reported haptens used to study variations in hapten binding at various stages of the immune response. The present paper describes studies on the size of antibody sites specific for poly-L-aspartate in a single rabbit. Data are presented which indicate that the upper size limit of the antibody-combining site after a second course

[1] This work was supported in part by Grant AI-06710 from the National Institutes of Health.

[2] This report is from a portion of a thesis submitted by P. Dianne Murphy in partial fulfillment of the requirements for a Ph.D. degree in Biochemistry, Duke University, Durham, North Carolina. United States Public Health Service Predoctoral Fellow.

[3] Research Career Development Awardee of the National Institutes of Health.

of immunization was larger than it was after the initial course of immunization.

MATERIALS AND METHODS

Preparation of poly-L-aspartyl-protein antigens. Poly-L-aspartyl-proteins were prepared by reacting carrier proteins, bovine serum albumin (BSA,[4] Armour lot X69508) or rabbit serum albumin (RSA, Pentex fraction V lot 7503), with β-benzyl-L-aspartate-N-carboxyanhydride (Pilot Chemical Co., Watertown, Mass.) by modified published procedures (7), followed by removal of the benzyl groups with mild base.

The two preparations used in the studies reported below were prepared with a ratio of anhydride to initiator of 15, assuming 60 lysine residues/molecule of BSA (8) or RSA. Samples (225 mg) of BSA and RSA were dissolved in 60 ml of 0.15 M $NaHCO_3$, and to each sample was added rapidly 2.5 g of β-benzyl-L-aspartate-N-carboxyanhydride in 10 ml of peroxide-free freshly distilled dioxane. After reaction at room temperature for 1 hr the flocculent suspensions were stored overnight at 4°C. Debenzylation of the poly-β-benzyl-L-aspartyl-protein suspensions was achieved by raising the pH to 11.25 at 25°C and maintaining that pH with 0.15 N NaOH for 2 hr in a CO_2-free environment. The completely solubilized products were acidified to pH 3.0 with 0.15 N HCl to precipitate the poly-L-aspartyl-proteins. The precipitates were centrifuged at 10,000 rpm for 20 min, the supernatants (containing benzyl alcohol) discarded and the solids dissolved in 0.05 N $NaHCO_3$. The pH 11.25 incubation was repeated until the pH was steady for 30 min without addition of base. After acidification and centrifugation as above the poly-aspartyl proteins were dissolved in 0.05 N $NaHCO_3$, dialyzed against H_2O and lyophilized. A UV spectrum done on the poly-aspartyl-proteins in 0.05 N $NaHCO_3$ showed that 99% of the benzyl groups had been removed. The number of added aspartyl residues was calculated by amino acid analysis (9) of the carrier proteins and the poly-aspartyl conjugates. The number of added poly-L-aspartyl chains was determined by amino acid analysis of the carrier proteins and poly-L-aspartyl-proteins before and after deamination with nitrous acid according to published procedures (10). Both preparations had approximately 36 added chains with an average of 15 aspartate residues/chain.

Immunization. Adult male New Zealand White rabbits were immunized with poly-L-aspartyl-BSA in Freund's complete adjuvant (Difco Laboratories, Detroit, Mich.) every 4 weeks. The first course of 10 mg was given half in the toepads and half subcutaneously. Two subsequent booster injections of 5 mg each were given subcutaneously. Bleedings were made 14 days after each injection.

All antisera were tested for reaction with the carrier protein (BSA), the immunogen (poly-L-aspartyl-BSA), and the homologous antigen (poly-L-aspartyl-RSA) by Ouchterlony analysis. Antisera were further characterized by quantitative precipitin analysis with the above antigens and selected antisera were examined by micro complement fixation (11) and inhibition of micro complement fixation. Selected antisera were analyzed for charge heterogeneity of anti-poly-L-aspartate by the DEAE-Sephadex method of Sela and Mozes (12).

Preparation of L-aspartate oligomers. Oligopeptides of L-aspartate were separated from partial acid hydrolysates of poly-L-aspartate (Pilot Chemical Co., lot A-38, m.w. 20,000) by DEAE-cellulose chromatography.

Poly-L-aspartate (50 mg) was dissolved in 5 ml of 0.15 N NaOH, rapidly neutralized to pH 8.0 with 0.15 N HCl, and dialyzed against distilled H_2O to remove low m.w. components. An equal volume of concentrated HCl was added and hydrolysis was carried out in a 105°C oil bath for 9 to 17 min. Hydrolysis was terminated by chilling in an ice bath, diluting 40-fold with deionized H_2O, and neutralizing with 0.15 N NaOH. The material was lyophilized, taken up in a minimal amount of deionized H_2O, and desalted on a 90- x 1.5-cm column of Sephadex G-15 (Pharmacia) using ninhydrin (13) to locate the peptides. The average chain length was determined by trinitrobenzene sulfonate end group analysis (14).

Using CO_2-free solutions, a 42- x 1.5-cm column of DEAE-cellulose (Whatman DE-32) was packed in 0.01 M potassium phosphate buffer, pH 8.0. The column was equilibrated at room temperature with 0.001 M phosphate-0.03 M NaCl buffer, pH 8.0, and attached to a Spinco automatic amino acid analyzer equipped with a

[4] Abbreviations: Bovine plasma albumin (BSA), rabbit serum albumin (RSA), pH 7.4 Tris-buffered isotonic NaCl containing 0.00015 M Ca^{++}, 0.0005 M Mg^{++}, and 0.1% gelatin (Iso-Gel-Tris).

stream divider and fraction collector. The desalted partial acid hydrolysate was dissolved in 5 ml of 0.001 M phosphate-0.03 M NaCl buffer and a marker consisting of 1 μmol of L-aspartic acid (Mann) and 0.1 μCi of uniformly ^{14}C-labeled L-aspartic acid (Nuclear-Chicago) in the same solvent added to the sample. After the sample was applied to the column and washed in with the equilibrium buffer a linear salt gradient of 1.35×10^{-4} M/min in the equilibrium buffer was applied to the column at a flow rate of 30 ml/hr. The stream divider delivered 90% of the column effluent to a fraction collector collecting 3-min samples and 10% to the amino acid analyzer for analysis. Samples from the first peak (L-aspartic acid) were counted for ^{14}C using a Packard Tri-Carb liquid scintillation spectrometer and a correction was made for the lag time between the delivery of the sample to the fraction collector and delivery of the analytical sample to the colorimeter. Portions of each peak coming off the column were pooled and analyzed for peptide length as described below.

Several L-aspartate oligomers were also prepared from t-BOC β-benzyl-L-aspartate (Schwarz) by the solid phase peptide synthesis method of Merrifield (15) and were characterized by the methods described below.

The chain length of aspartate oligomers was determined by measuring free amino groups before and after complete hydrolysis with ninhydrin according to the method of Goodman and Nitecki (16). The accuracy of this method was examined by analyzing several partial acid hydrolysates and a suspected $(L\text{-asp})_2$ preparation by the trinitrobenzene sulfonate method (14) and the above method. Results obtained by both methods always agreed within experimental error. Hydrolysis in 6 N HCl at 110°C for 24 hr *in vacuo* gave complete hydrolysis of the oligoaspartates and amino acid analysis (9) showed no other components than aspartic acid, an indication of non-contamination and/or interconversion of aspartate at any step in the preparation of these oligopeptides. Hydrolysis of the oligomers gave optical rotations which were identical to a similarly treated sample of L-aspartic acid and to L-aspartic acid not subjected to hydrolytic conditions.

Studies of the immunologic specificity of rabbit anti-poly-L-aspartate. Various antisera prepared against poly-L-aspartyl-BSA were analyzed by quantitative precipitin (17) and micro complement (C) fixation (11) using BSA, poly-L-aspartyl-BSA and poly-L-aspartyl-RSA as test antigens. One animal, rabbit 76, was chosen for further studies. This animal gave antisera which had appreciable amounts of antibodies directed against the poly-L-aspartate hapten. C fixation analysis was performed on the reaction of poly-L-aspartyl-RSA with first and second course bleedings of rabbit 76 (Ra $76b_1$ and Ra $76b_2$) by the micro-modification of the technique of Wasserman and Levine (11). Studies were performed in Iso-Gel-Tris buffer with 0.2-ml volumes of antigen, 1:225 guinea pig complement (Baltimore Biological Laboratory, Baltimore, Md.) and heated antiserum dilutions (1:400 Ra $76b_1$ and 1:3000 Ra $76b_2$) in a total volume of 1.2 ml.

It is important to point out that most studies using this technique have reported results in terms of *added* complement, antiserum, antigen and (where applicable) inhibitor (11, 18, 19). Because of the nature of the assay the concentrations of added materials were actually sixfold greater than in the incubation mixture before addition of sensitized red cells and sevenfold greater than in the final assay mixture. To avoid confusion we have chosen to continue this convention and report concentrations of added materials except where noted.

Studies were then performed on inhibition of the reaction of Ra 76 antisera and poly-L-aspartyl-RSA by poly-L-aspartate, the partial acid hydrolysate, the separated L-aspartate oligomers, the stepwise synthesized aspartate oligomers, L-aspartic acid, D-aspartic acid (Mann Research Laboratories, New York) and poly-L-glutamate (m.w. 5,400, Miles Laboratories, Elkhart, Ind.). The ionic strength of solutions of the various test inhibitors was adjusted conductimetrically to that of the Iso-Gel-Tris by either dilution with distilled H_2O or addition of solid NaCl, and the pH was adjusted to pH 7.4. The concentrations of the various inhibitors were measured with ninhydrin and dilutions were made with Iso-Gel-Tris. Hapten inhibition of C fixation was performed as described above for C fixation except that 0.2-ml samples of test inhibitor were added to the antiserum-complement-antigen mixtures with the same final volume.

To determine whether the assay procedure itself had any non-immunologic effect on oligoaspartates (such as hydrolysis or chemical alteration) control studies were performed on partially hydrolyzed poly-L-aspartate (5.5 residues/molecule) and ^{14}C uniformly labeled L-aspartate (Nuclear-Chicago). Solutions of poly-L-aspartate (40 μM) and L-aspartic acid (60 μM) were incubated at 4°C for 18 hr and 50 min at 37°C with the same concentrations of guinea pig and heated normal rabbit serum as used in the assay and with double those concentrations. Portions were removed and analyzed for NH_2 with ninhydrin. Appearance or disappearance of free NH_2 was determined by comparison with similarly treated controls containing the test hapten or the sera alone. Specimens of the ^{14}C L-aspartic acid control and the ^{14}C L-aspartic acid-double sera incubation mixture were spotted on chromatography papers and analyzed by one-dimensional chromatography in two separate solvent mixtures, butanol:acetic acid:H_2O (50:12:50) and methanol:H_2O:pyridine (80:20:5), according to published procedures (20). Individual sample strips were then sprayed with ninhydrin to locate L-aspartic acid. Other strips were analyzed for ^{14}C activity associated with L-aspartic acid and other possible ^{14}C-containing materials by cutting the strips into multiple widthwise sections and counting the sections with a Packard Tri-Carb liquid scintillation spectrometer.

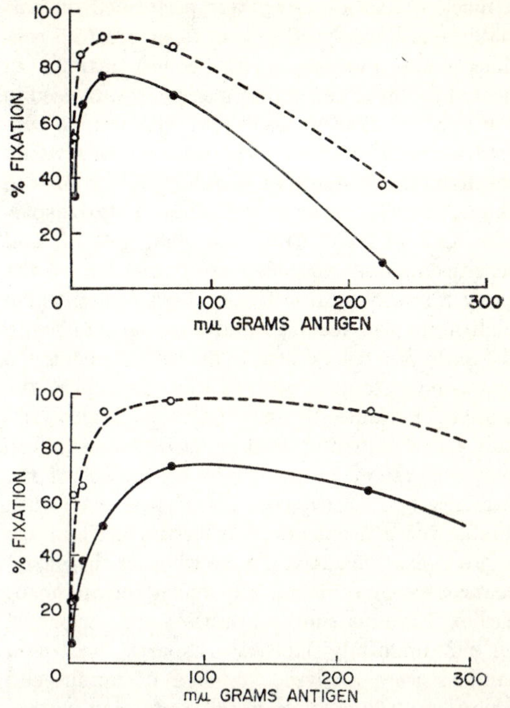

Figure 1. Micro complement fixation analysis of Ra 76b$_1$ and Ra 76b$_2$. Percentage C fixation *vs* nanograms antigen added. *Top*, Ra 76b$_1$ (1:400); *bottom*, Ra 76b$_2$ (1:3000). O-----O, Poly-L-aspartyl BSA; ●——●, poly-L-aspartyl RSA.

RESULTS

Ouchterlony, precipitin, and C fixation analyses of Ra 76 antisera. First and second course bleedings of Ra 76 were analyzed by Ouchterlony agar gel diffusion with BSA, poly-L-aspartyl-BSA and poly-L-aspartyl-RSA. Both antisera gave single precipitin lines with the poly-L-aspartyl-proteins but not with the carrier. The precipitin lines obtained with Ra 76b$_1$ were much fainter than with Ra 76b$_2$. Quantitative precipitin analysis of Ra 76b$_2$ showed a total of 0.4 mg Ab protein/ml of which 65% of the antibodies in the sera were anti-poly-L-aspartate. Although no precipitin lines were seen with BSA by Ouchterlony analysis, 30% of the antibodies in the sera were directed against the carrier. Anti-poly-L-aspartate in this serum was of the IgG type and, by the DEAE-Sephadex method of Sela and Mozes (12), was located exclusively in the more positively charged IgG class peak I. The amounts of antibody in Ra 76b$_1$ were just barely detectable (less than 0.02 mg Ab protein/ml) and further studies of antibody class were not done because of limited amounts of this antiserum. Quantitative precipitin and C fixation analysis of the third course immunization antiserum (Ra 76b$_3$) were indistinguishable from Ra 76b$_2$. Figure 1 shows typical micro C fixation curves for Ra 76b$_1$ and Ra 76b$_2$. The reaction of Ra 76b$_2$ with poly-L-aspartyl-RSA gave about 70% of the C fixation observed with the reaction of Ra 76b$_2$ with poly-L-aspartyl-BSA, in agreement with the quantitative precipitin analysis. By C fixation analysis Ra 76b$_1$ appeared to have a somewhat higher proportion (about 85%) of antibodies specific for the poly-L-aspartate hapten. The antisera of several other rabbits gave similar Ouchterlony patterns and quantitative precipitin analyses.

Studies on the effects of guinea pig and rabbit sera on partially acid-hydrolyzed poly-L-aspartate and L-aspartic acid. A major concern was whether enzymes were present in the rabbit serum and/or guinea pig complement which might alter oligoaspartates under the conditions of the micro C fixation assay. To determine whether any hydrolysis of oligoaspartates occurred during the assay, a mock C fixation assay was performed on partially acid-hydrolyzed poly-L-aspartate (5.5 residues/chain average) with concentrations of heated rabbit serum and guinea pig serum used in the micro C fixation assay and with double concentrations. Hydrolysis of poly-L-aspartate would result in the appearance of more NH_2 groups in the test solution than in the sum of poly-L-aspartate and serum controls. Antigen, gelatin, and sensitized sheep red cells were omitted from the assay mixture because their presence might give high ninhydrin readings and obscure changes in the ninhydrin color due to hydrolysis of oligomers. It was consistently observed that the sum of the ninhydrin values for the partially hydrolyzed poly-L-aspartate and serum controls was equal to the test system, indicating no hydrolysis of the partially hydrolyzed poly-L-aspartate even with double the concentrations of serum used in the micro C fixation assay. To see whether these concentrations of sera had any effect on amino or carboxyl groups similar studies were performed on ^{14}C uniformly labeled L-aspartic acid and samples were analyzed for loss of amino end groups and the presence of ^{14}C containing materials other than aspartic acid. Labeled aspartic acid was chosen as a model for the oligopeptides because radiolabeled oligoaspartates and/or radiolabeled polyaspartic acid are not commercially available nor is ^{14}C-labeled poly-L-aspartate easily prepared. It is assumed that any alterations in the end groups of oligopeptides by enzymes in serum would also alter these same groups in aspartic acid itself. This non-uniqueness of the end groups is borne out by the end group analyses of purified oligoaspartates (see below). No significant change in the amino end group content was observed. On paper chromatography all of the ^{14}C label in the L-aspartic acid (^{14}C)-double serum incubation mixture was associated with aspartic acid. At double the levels of sera used in the C fixation assay, there were apparently no materials present which altered the oligoaspartate molecules.

Isolation and characterization of L-aspartate oligomers. Figure 2 shows an analyzer tracing of a typical DEAE-cellulose chromatographic run performed on a partially acid-hydrolyzed poly-L-aspartate preparation (average chain length 5.5). Several easily separable peaks were eluted from the column by the salt gradient. Analysis of each peak for chain length is given in Table I. The oligomers were eluted in order of their increasing charge and length and 10 oligomers were readily separated. The amounts of the various oligomers varied from experiment to experiment and were particularly a function of the hydrolytic conditions used in the preparation of partial acid hydrolysates. However, each peak came off at a characteristic salt concentration. A triaspartate oligomer, (L-asp)$_3$, was prepared by stepwise solid phase synthesis. Table I shows that analysis of its length gave the same value as the third eluted peak, the suspected triaspartate.

Inhibition of the anti-poly-L-aspartyl-BSA-poly-L-aspartyl-RSA reaction by high and low molecular weight poly-amino acids and partial hydrolysates. Table II shows the effectiveness of various test

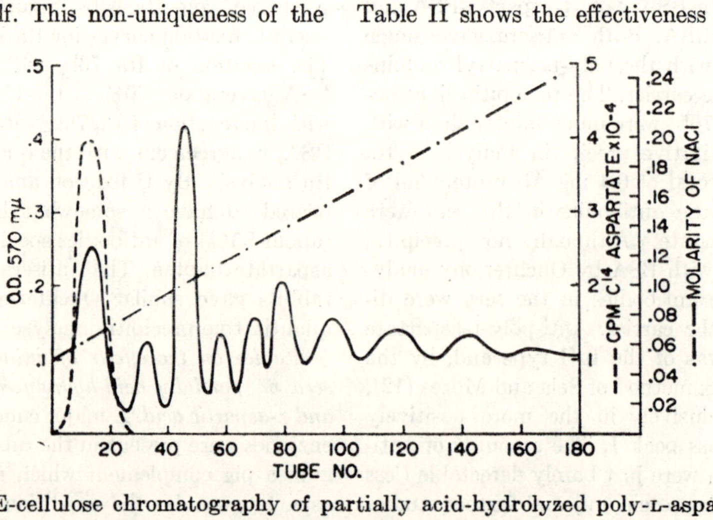

Figure 2. DEAE-cellulose chromatography of partially acid-hydrolyzed poly-L-aspartate. -----, ^{14}C L-aspartate marker; –·–·, NaCl concentration; —— ninhydrin color of eluted peptides (chart reading). Actual ninhydrin color was one-tenth of the recorded readings.

TABLE I

Analysis of aspartate oligopeptides

Chromatographic Peak	Corrected Ninhydrin Color (O.D. 570)		Calculated Average Length[b]
	Non-hydrolyzed	Hydrolyzed	
1	0.606		1.0
2	0.806	1.646[a]	2.04
3	0.310	0.956[a]	3.08
4	0.224	0.862	3.85
5	0.152	0.744	5.03
6	0.206	1.206	5.85
7	0.200	1.380	6.90
8	0.181	1.433	7.90
9	0.163	1.456	8.9
Synthetic tripeptide	0.029	0.085	2.95

[a] Carefully measured volumes of oligoaspartate were analyzed by the ninhydrin reaction. Samples of the same solution (usually the same volume) were totally hydrolyzed before ninhydrin analysis. Where the volumes of the unhydrolyzed and hydrolyzed oligopeptide were different the reported O.D. 570 has been corrected for the difference by the formula O.D. 570 (cor)

$$= \text{O.D. 570 (measured)} \times \frac{\text{Vol. unhydrolyzed}}{\text{Vol. hydrolyzed}}.$$

[b] $\text{Average length} = \frac{\text{O.D. 570 hydrolyzed}}{\text{O.D. 570 unhydrolyzed}}.$

TABLE II

Test of amino acid and stereospecificity of Ra 76b$_2$: Ability of various poly-L-aspartates, poly-L-glutamate, and amino acids to inhibit the complement fixation reaction of the poly-L-aspartate immune system

Test Inhibitor	Maximum Concentration Tested	Maximum Inhibition
	nmol/0.2 ml	%
L-glutamic acid	5000	0
L-aspartic acid	5000	25
D-aspartic acid	5000	0
Poly-L-aspartic acid	220	19
Poly-L-glutamic acid	240	0
Poly-L-aspartic acid (hydrolysate—aver. size: 4.8 residues)	10.4	56

materials in inhibiting the reaction of the immune poly-L-aspartyl system. All poly-L-aspartates tested inhibited the reaction including unhydrolyzed poly-L-aspartic acid (m.w. ~ 20,000). In contrast to poly-L-aspartic acid, poly-L-glutamic acid (m.w. ~ 5400) was not an effective inhibitor at the same concentration. L-Aspartic acid was an inhibitor of the immune poly-L-aspartyl system but an identical concentration of D-aspartic acid was not. These studies indicated an amino acid-specific and stereospecific activity for anti-poly-L-aspartate.

Inhibition of the poly-L-aspartyl immune system by oligomers. Figure 3 shows the effect of four different concentrations of the heptamer (L-asp)$_7$ on the Ra 76b$_2$ poly-L-aspartyl immune system. As can be seen this oligomer was an effective inhibitor at added amounts above 2.25 mμmol. Figure 4 shows the inhibition of the Ra 76b$_2$ poly-L-aspartyl immune system by oligomers from the dimer through the hexamer. The effectiveness of the oligomers as inhibitors increased progressively with size from the monomer to the pentamer. The hexamer was not distinguishable from the pentamer, nor were the heptamer, octomer and nonomer (not shown). Figure 5 shows the same type of study done on Ra 76b$_1$. The effectiveness of the oligomers as inhibitors increased from the monomer through the trimer. Oligomers of 4 to 9 residues were as effective as the trimer in inhibiting the Ra 76b$_1$ poly-L-aspartyl immune system. Also shown in Figure 5 is the inhibition with (L-asp)$_3$ prepared by stepwise solid phase synthesis. Its inhibition characteristics were not distinguishable from (L-asp)$_3$ separated by DEAE-cellulose chromatography. Figure 6 shows the added amount of each oligomer required for 50% inhibition of the Ra 76b$_1$ and Ra 76b$_2$ poly-L-aspartyl immune systems. The curve for the Ra

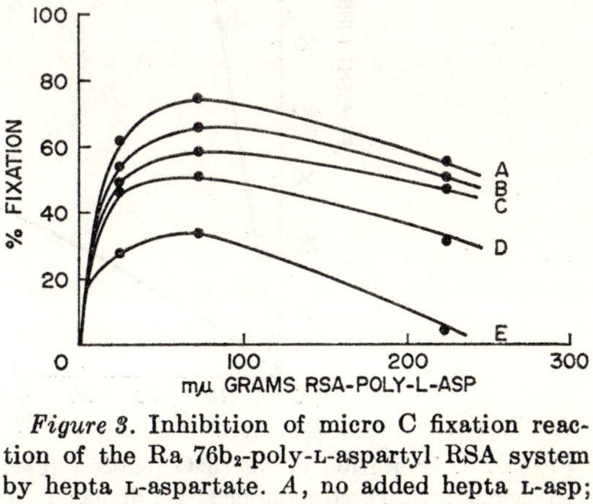

Figure 3. Inhibition of micro C fixation reaction of the Ra 76b$_2$-poly-L-aspartyl RSA system by hepta L-aspartate. *A*, no added hepta L-asp; *B*, 2.25 nmol added; *C*, 4.5 nmol added; *D*, 9.0 nmol added; *E*, 18 nmol added.

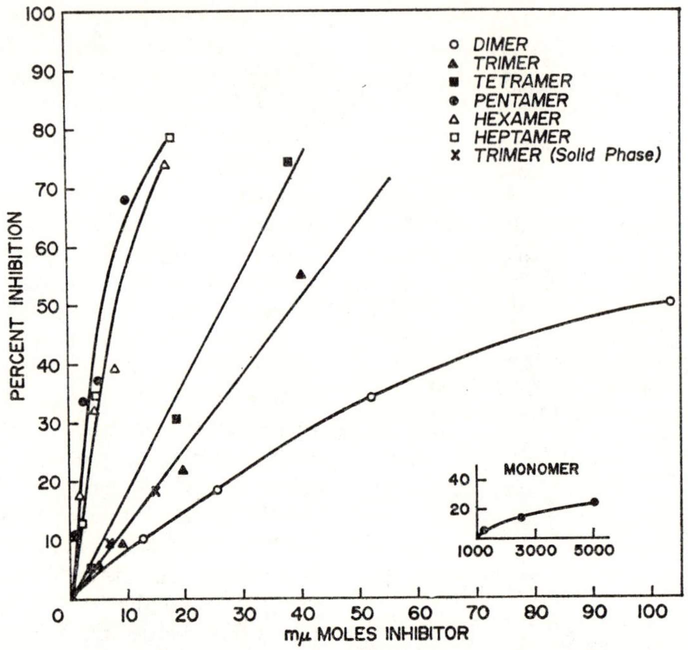

Figure 4. Inhibition of micro C fixation reaction of the Ra 76b$_2$-poly-L-aspartyl RSA system by oligoaspartates. *Inset*, monomer; ○, dimer; ▲, trimer; ■, tetramer; ●, pentamer; △, hexamer; □, heptamer; ×, solid phase synthesized trimer.

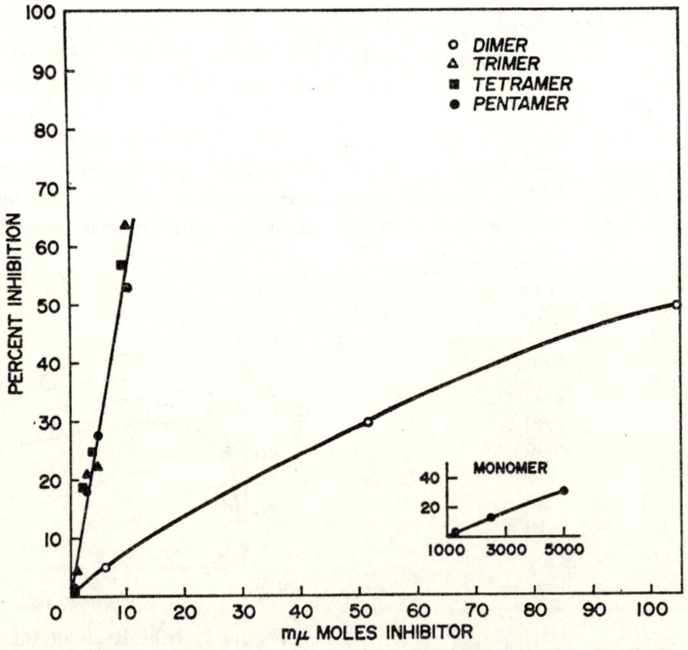

Figure 5. Inhibition of micro C fixation reaction of the Ra 76b$_1$-poly-L-aspartyl RSA system by oligoaspartates. *Inset*, monomer; ○, dimer; △, trimer; ■, tetramer; ●, pentamer.

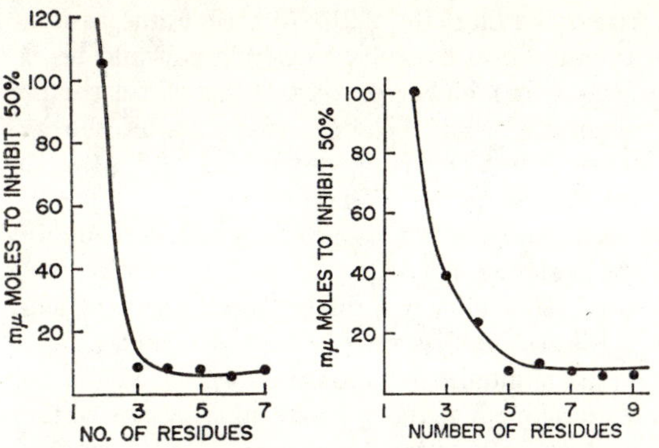

Figure 6. Inhibition of micro C fixation reaction of the poly-L-aspartyl immune systems. Nanomols of oligomers added to inhibit C fixation by 50% *vs* size of oligomer. *Left*, Ra $76b_1$; *right*, Ra $76b_2$.

$76b_1$ system levels off with the trimer and for the Ra $76b_2$ system with the pentamer. These results are consistent with the upper size limit of Ra $76b_1$ and Ra $76b_2$ combining sites being such as to accommodate 3 and 5 aspartate residues, respectively. With molecular models this corresponds to molecular dimensions of 16 x 9 x 7Å and 22 x 9 x 7Å in the most extended form.

DISCUSSION

Studies of the interactions of antibodies prepared against antigenic determinants composed of small repeating subunits with oligomeric fragments of these determinants have been valuable in estimating the size of antibody-combining sites. Following the elegant studies of Kabat and his co-workers (21, 22) on human antidextrans a number of workers have examined the size of rabbit antibodies to antigenic determinants composed of synthetic poly-α-amino acids containing a single amino acid. Estimates have been made of the upper size limit of antibodies to poly-L- and D-alanine (18, 23), poly-L- and D-lysine (19, 24) and the naturally occurring poly-D-γ-glutamate determinant of *Bacillus anthracis* (25). The upper size limit in the majority of reported cases for both dextrans and poly-amino acid determinants has ranged from 3 to 6 oligomer residues/antibody site. However, most of the reported studies have been performed on sera obtained after repeated courses of the immunogen.

The early antiserum of rabbit 76, Ra $76b_1$, contained just barely detectable amounts of antibodies as measured by Ouchterlony and quantitative precipitin analysis. By micro C fixation analysis a large proportion of these antibodies was directed against the poly-L-aspartate hapten. The ability of oligoaspartates to inhibit the poly-L-aspartate-specific immune system leveled off at the trimer; an indication that the upper size limit of anti-poly-L-aspartate was such as to include 3 aspartate residues. The early immune response of animals to certain immunogens has frequently been reported to consist mainly of the IgM class (see 26). No data on the nature of the antibodies in Ra $76b_1$ have been obtained in this laboratory because the amounts of antibody were just barely detectable by quantitative precipitation. However, Haimovich *et al.* (27) have reported that the upper size limit of anti-poly-D-alanine of the IgM class was such as to accommodate 4 alanine residues, a number in agreement with the upper size limit of anti-poly-D-alanine of the IgG class.

Anti-poly-L-aspartate isolated after two courses of poly-L-aspartyl-BSA reacted progressively better with oligomers of increasing size from the monomer to the pentamer. Larger oligomers were indistinguishable from the pentamer. These results are consistent with an upper size limit of Ra $76b_2$ being such as to include 5 aspartate residues, which is in agreement with other reported systems. Amino acid specificity of this antiserum was demonstrated by its non-reactivity with L-glutamic acid and stereospecificity by its non-reactivity with D-aspartic acid as compared to its reaction with L-aspartic acid. These antibodies were of the IgG type and were of higher positive charge than the average IgG population. Sela and Mozes (12) have shown that the charge type of antibodies elicited by a hapten-carrier complex is determined by the charge of the complex. Poly-aspartyl-BSA is highly negatively charged. It is important to point out that antisera from a single animal were examined and that the results reported may not be representative of the average rabbit population. Slight variations in the upper size limit of human antidextrans have been noted in individuals (21, 22) and the variation of individual responses to immunogens is, of course, a well-known phenomenon. However, the upper size limit of 5 residues for Ra $76b_2$ is consistent with most reported values for anti-poly-amino acids. Ouchterlony analysis of first and second course bleedings of several other rabbits in this study yielded results which were qualitatively similar to those obtained with rabbit 76. In addition, quantitative precipitin analysis of second course bleedings of several animals gave amounts and specificity distributions of antibodies which were very similar to Ra $76b_2$, suggesting that the immune response of rabbit 76 was not unusual.

Schechter *et al.* (23) have demonstrated a proteolytic activity in normal and immune rabbit serum which caused appreciable hydrolysis of oligomers of L-alanine but no hydrolysis of D-alanine oligomers. Using DEAE-cellulose purified anti-poly-L-alanine, these authors found that the upper size limits of both the anti-poly-L-alanine- and anti-poly-D-alanine-combining sites were such as to include 3 to 4 alanine residues, and they suggested that the estimate of 5 residues made by Sage *et al.* (18) for the poly-L-alanine system could be erroneous due to serum proteolytic activity on test L-alanine oligomers. The studies of Sage *et al.* (18) and those reported in this paper were done by micro C fixation analysis. The final concentrations of serum and oligopeptide inhibitors were about one-thousandth as much as those used in quantitative precipitin analysis. The maximum rate of hydrolysis of the oligopeptides will be one-thousandth that observed in the quantitative precipitin assay. The actual rate could be several orders of magnitude smaller than this depending upon the K_m of hydrolysis. In the studies of Sage *et al.* (18) it was found that low molecular weight poly-L-alanine (4 to 5 alanines/molecule) and a similar preparation of poly-D-alanine inhibited their homologous anti-L- and anti-poly-D-alanine systems at about the same concentration. This is similar to the findings of Schechter *et al.* (23) for the inhibition of the homologous anti-poly-D-alanine system (using whole serum) and anti-poly-L-alanine system (using purified antibodies devoid of measurable hydrolytic activity). This indicates that with the micro C fixation assay the concentrations of hydrolytic enzyme(s) and oligopeptide were not large enough to result in appreciable hydrolysis. At double the maximum concentrations of serum used in the micro C fixation assay and a 2- to 20-fold higher level of oligoaspartate no detectable hydrolysis of oligoaspartate was observed. This could be due to the low levels of serum used in the assay or to the absence of serum enzymes with hydrolytic activity toward asp-asp bonds. If the larger binding site of Ra $76b_2$ were due to large amounts of a hydrolytic enzyme it would be expected that higher concentrations of L-aspartate oligomers would be required to inhibit the immune poly-L-aspartate system in Ra $76b_2$ than in the Ra $76b_1$ system. The concentrations of penta-, hexa-, and hepta-L-aspartate required to inhibit the immune poly-L-aspartate reaction by 50% were not significantly different in the two systems.

Eisen and Siskind (3) observed that after a single immunization of rabbits with DNP-bovine γ globulin, K_A, the average intrinsic association constant of hapten binding for DNP-lysine increased continuously with time. These authors observed a larger difference in the K_A values of hapten binding for DNP-lysine and smaller DNP-lysine analogues in later (high affinity) antisera than in early antisera. It was suggested that later serum antibodies had sites directed against a somewhat larger portion of the DNP-lysine hapten than did sites in the early antisera. Concurrent with the increasing K_A there was a greater heterogeneity of binding constants in the antibody population and a greater participation of the residues to which the DNP groups were attached on the carrier molecule to the specificity of the antisera. Other authors have noted increasing K_A of hapten binding with time after a single immunization (28) and with multiple immunizations (29, 30). Fujio and Karush (30) also noted an apparent increase in the binding site size. Atsumi *et al.* (31) noted a greater percentage of antibodies with larger binding sites in late antisera than in early antisera after a single hapten-protein immunization. The appearance of antibody with sites accommodating progressively larger portions of a hapten as an explanation of increasing K_A and "avidity" is an attractive hypothesis.

Recent experiments by Little and Counts (5) and by Richards *et al.* (6) call into question such a hypothesis. Little and Counts (5) immunized guinea pigs with a preparation of DNP-insulin in which the DNP group was attached to the single lysine residue of bovine insulin. Although an increase in K_A of hapten binding was noted with time, a comparison of K_A for various DNP-derivatives indicated that the later antisera were specific for a smaller haptenic determinant than the early antisera. Richards *et al.* (6) showed that rabbits immunized with the DNP hapten attached at regular intervals to a copolymer consisting of a repeating sequence of an oligopeptide gave early antibodies with a high K_A for DNP-lysine and that this K_A value did not change with time. With a random DNP-copolymer of the same composition as the repeating DNP-oligopeptide an increase in K_A was noted with time. However, the increase was not nearly as large as that observed by Eisen and Siskind (3) and others for DNP-protein immunogens. These authors suggest that some portion of early antisera prepared against a DNP-protein conjugate is composed of high avidity antibodies directed against a heterogeneous mixture of hybrid determinants containing both the hapten and groups from the carrier protein. These antibodies would appear to be of low avidity because the test hapten (DNP-lysine) is only a portion of the determinant. The shift in the *apparent* K_A could result from selective pressures for cells producing high affinity antibodies to the hapten. This interpretation certainly questions the relationship between K_A and the size of antibody-combining sites.

The DNP hapten is very small compared to most estimates of the size of antibody-combining sites. If there are changes in the size and specificity of antibody sites during the immune response the nature of these changes is not likely to be revealed by studies of this hapten. Studies of haptens which are complementary to their antibody-combining site and with which contributions of the carrier to antibody specificity are minimal appear to be more useful. Studies of the kind that are relevant to those reported in this paper are those of Schlossman and Kabat (32), who found that the size distribution of human anti-dextrans did not change over a period of 10 years. Measurements of the K_A of hapten binding have not been done in the antidextran system and in the present studies.

Clearly further studies on several rabbits are needed to determine whether the observed increase in the size of anti-poly-L-aspartate sites is a common phenomenon. In addition it must be determined whether further increases in the binding site size occur after multiple immunizations. For this hapten inhibition studies on third and subsequent immunization bleedings are necessary. It would also be interesting to see whether there is a change in the size of the combining site with time after a single immunization. The procedures outlined above for separating and characterizing oligoaspartates gave only milligram quantities of such peptides. Studies on more than one animal and on the third course serum of Ra 76 have been precluded by the difficulty in obtaining larger amounts of oligoaspartates. Modifications of this method are presently under investigation. It is also contemplated that radiolabeled oligoaspartates will be prepared to perform direct binding studies. In this way it may be possible to relate a change in hapten binding with the size of the antibody-combining site.

REFERENCES

1. Talmage, D. W. and Maurer, P. H., J. Infect. Dis., *92:* 288, 1953.
2. Farr, R. S., J. Infect. Dis., *103:* 239, 1958.
3. Eisen, H. N. and Siskind, G. W., Biochemistry, *3:* 996, 1964.
4. Hooker, S. B., Ann. Allerg., *4:* 425, 1946.
5. Little, J. R. and Counts, R. B., Biochemistry, *8:* 2729, 1969.
6. Richards, F. F., Pincus, J. H., Bloch, K. J., Barnes, W. T. and Haber, E., Biochemistry, *8:* 1377, 1969.
7. Katchalski, E. and Sela, M., Advances Protein Chem., *13:* 243, 1958.
8. Rideal, E. K. and Roberts, R., Proc. Roy. Soc., Series A., *205:* 391, 1951.
9. Spackman, D. H., Stein, W. H. and Moore, S., Anal. Chem., *30:* 1190, 1958.
10. Anfinsen, C. B., Sela, M. and Cooke, J. P., J. Biol. Chem., *237:* 1825, 1962.
11. Wasserman, E. and Levine, L., J. Immun., *87:* 290, 1961.
12. Sela, M. and Mozes, E., Proc. Nat. Acad. Sci., *55:* 445, 1966.
13. Greenstein, J. P. and Winitz, M., *Chemistry of the Amino Acids*, p. 1309, John Wiley & Sons, New York, 1961.
14. Sataki, K., Okuyama, T., Ohashi, M. and Shinoda, T., J. Biochem., *47:* 654, 1960.
15. Merrifield, R. B., Biochemistry, *3:* 1385, 1964.
16. Goodman, J. W. and Nitecki, D. E., Biochemistry, *5:* 657, 1966.
17. Campbell, D. H., Garvey, J. S., Cremer, N. E. and Sussdorf, D. H., *Methods in Immunology*, W. A. Benjamin Co., New York, 1963.
18. Sage, H. J., Deutsch, G. F., Fasman, G. D. and Levine, L., Immunochemistry, *1:* 133, 1964.
19. Van Vunakis, H., Kaplan, J., Lehrer, H. and Levine, L., Immunochemistry, *3:* 393, 1966.
20. Gordon, A. H. and Eastoe, J. E., *Practical Chromatographic Techniques*, George Newnes Ltd., London, 1964.
21. Kabat, E. A., J. Immun., *97:* 1, 1966.

22. Kabat, E. A. and Berg, D., J. Immun., *70:* 514, 1953.
23. Schechter, I., Schechter, B. and Sela, M., Biochim. Biophys. Acta, *127:* 438, 1966.
24. Arnon, R., Sela, M., Yaron, A. and Sober, H. A., Biochemistry, *4:* 948, 1965.
25. Goodman, J. W., Nitecki, D. E. and Stoltenberg, I. M., Biochemistry, *7:* 706, 1968.
26. Bauer, D. C. and Stavitsky, A. B., Proc. Soc. Nat. Acad. Sci., *47:* 1667, 1961.
27. Haimovich, J., Schechter, I. and Sela, M., Europ. J. Biochem., *7:* 537, 1969.
28. Parker, C. W., Godt, S. M. and Johnson, M. C., Biochemistry, *6:* 3417, 1967.
29. Klinman, N. R., Rocky, J. H., Frauenberger, G. and Karush, F., J. Immun., *96:* 587, 1966.
30. Fujio, H. and Karush, F., Biochemistry, *5:* 1856, 1966.
31. Atsumi, T., Adache, M., Kimoshita, Y., Kawasaki, M. and Horiuchi, Y., J. Immun., *101:* 1016, 1968.
32. Schlossman, S. F. and Kabat, E. A., J. Exp. Med., *116:* 535, 1962.

THE JOURNAL OF IMMUNOLOGY
Vol. 105, No. 2, Aug. 1970

Printed in U.S.A.

DELAYED HYPERSENSITIVITY

IV. Hapten-Specific Delayed Reactions; Interaction of Immune Serum and Sensitized Cells[1]

JOHN P. PHAIR[2] AND FRED S. KANTOR[3]

From the Infectious Disease Division, Department of Medicine, University of Cincinnati College of Medicine, Cincinnati, Ohio, and Department of Medicine, Yale University, New Haven, Connecticut

Received for publication December 17, 1969

Delayed hypersensitivity reactions to hapten-protein antigens are largely conjugate specific. Concurrent elicitation of related or unrelated immediate reactions at challenge sites, however, resulted in hapten-specific 24-hr reactions in passively and actively immunized guinea pigs. Challenge with a 10-fold increase in the concentration of antigen also resulted in hapten-specific 24-hr transfer reactions. Hapten-specific reactions were elicited at sites prepared by injection of normal guinea pig serum. Increased antigen concentration and nonspecific infiltration of mononuclear cells at prepared skin sites are possible mechanisms underlying these hapten-specific delayed reactions.

Delayed hypersensitivity reactions to hapten protein antigens are largely conjugate or carrier specific (1). However, previous studies of the specificity requirements of delayed reactions have demonstrated a hapten-specific component of this cell-mediated response in the skin of actively sensitized hyperimmune guinea pigs (1, 2). Normal recipients of sensitized hyperimmune cells manifest only conjugate-specific delayed reactions upon suitable challenge (2). Administration of immune serum plus sensitized cells produced larger delayed transfer reactions (3). This enhancement was thought to be due to increased retention of antigen at the challenge site and nonspecific inflammatory effects (4). The present studies were undertaken to determine whether these two factors also influence the specificity requirements of delayed reactions.

The interaction of the concentration of challenge antigen, immune serum and sensitized cells upon the specificity requirements of delayed reactions was investigated in passively and actively immunized guinea pigs. Hapten-specific delayed reactions were produced in recipients of cells by challenge with a high concentration of hapten-heterologous carrier protein. Recipients of cells and hyperimmune serum also manifested hapten-specific delayed reactions. Challenge of recipients of sensitized cells at the site of an unrelated immediate reaction also resulted in hapten-specific delayed reactions.

Preparation of challenge sites in the skin of actively immunized guinea pigs by injection of antihaptenic antibody and normal serum, and elicitation of an unrelated immediate reaction also resulted in hapten-specific reactions.

[1] This investigation was supported in part by National Science Foundation Grant GB 4190 and a grant from the National Tuberculosis and Respiratory Disease Association and American Thoracic Society.

[2] Supported in part by United States Public Health Service Grant TI A 187.

[3] Research Career Development Awardee, United States Public Health Service, National Institute of Allergy and Infectious Diseases, National Institutes of Health.

MATERIALS AND METHODS

Animals. Hartley strain albino male guinea pigs weighing between 400 and 500 g were immunized and used as donors of cells and serum. Guinea pigs of the same breeding stock weighing approximately 250 g served as recipients.

Antigens. Conjugates of picryl guinea pig albumin (Pic-GPA) and picryl human serum albumin (Pic-HSA) were prepared by modification of methods previously described (5). Appropriate concentrations of picryl chloride (Eastman Organic Chemicals, Rochester, N. Y.) were dissolved in volumes of 1,4-dioxane calculated not to exceed 5% of the total volume of the protein solution. The pH of the protein solution was maintained between 8.5 and 9 by the addition of 5% Na_2CO_3. Hapten solutions were added slowly to the protein with constant stirring for 2 hr at room temperature. Separation of hapten-protein conjugates from unreacted hapten was accomplished by gel filtration with Sephadex G-25. Protein concentrations were determined by the micro-Kjeldahl technique. The number of haptenic groups/mol of protein was determined by spectrophotometric analysis using the molar extinction coefficient of 15,400 for picryl groups at a wave length of 347 nm. Both conjugates had approximately 20 haptenic groups/mol of protein. Ovalbumin (OVA) was obtained from General Biochemicals, Inc., Chagrin Falls, Ohio.

Immunization. Guinea pigs were immunized by footpad injection with a total of 100 μg of Pic-GPA or OVA emulsified in complete Freund's adjuvant (Difco Laboratories).

Preparation of cell suspension. Sterile peritoneal exudates in donor animals were provoked by the i.p. injection of brain-heart infusion broth containing 10% proteose peptone (Difco) 8 days after immunization. Forty-eight hours later the animals were anesthesized and exsanguinated by cardiac puncture. The peritoneum was rinsed with 50 ml of 199 tissue culture medium (Baltimore Biological Laboratory). The suspension of cells was centrifuged at 1200 rpm for 15 min at 4°C. Following removal of the supernatant, cells were washed in medium 199. The volume of the cell suspension was adjusted so that each recipient received approximately 2.0×10^8 cells. Differential counts of the smears stained with Wright's stain revealed exudates consisting of approximately 60% mononuclear cells, 30% polymorphonuclear cells and 10% small round cells. All suspensions were given intravenously to recipients within 2 hr of harvest.

Preparation of antiserum and determination of antibody activity. Sera were obtained by cardiac puncture from sensitized guinea pigs 7 to 10 days and 21 to 28 days after immunization. Antihaptenic antibody titers were determined by passive cutaneous anaphlyaxis (PCA) (6). Serum obtained at 7 to 10 days produced PCA reactions upon challenge with Pic-HSA when diluted 1:50 and that harvested 21 to 28 days following immunization gave PCA reactions at a dilution of 1:800.

Titers of hemagglutination antibody were determined by the chromic chloride coupling method (7). Fresh O Rh-positive red cells were utilized throughout. Pic-GPA 5 mg/ml was mixed with an equal volume of a 0.1% $CrCl_3$ in 0.9% NaCl solution. An equal volume of washed erythrocytes was added and left at room temperature for 4 min. The red cells were washed three times in 20 volumes of saline. The final volume of saline and red cells was adjusted to provide a 2% suspension. Sera absorbed with the O Rh-positive red cells were diluted serially in twofold steps using equal volumes (0.25 ml) of EDTA buffer pH 7.5 in RB-96 Disposo trays (Linbro Chemical Co., New Haven, Conn.). To each dilution an equal volume of the red cell suspension was added. Titers of hemagglutinating antibody were 1:160 and 1:5120 of early and late antisera respectively.

Fractionation of antisera. Guinea pig γ 1 and γ 2 were prepared from the serum of animals immunized with Pic-GPA emulsified in complete Freund's adjuvant 21 days prior to harvest. The γ 1 and γ 2 antipicryl antibody was separated from $(NH_4)_2SO_4$-precipitated γ globulin by starch block electrophoresis. The γ 1 antibody was identified as a fast moving fraction of γ globulin by immunoelectrophoresis which did not cause lysis of red cells tagged with Pic-GPA in the presence of guinea pig complement. The fraction selected for these experiments produced PCA reactions at a dilution of 1:50 when reactions were elicited with Pic-HSA. The γ 2 antibody did not cause PCA reactions at a dilution of 1:10 but did cause lysis of red cells tagged with Pic-GPA in the presence of complement (8). Guinea pig γ 1 and γ 2 anti-OVA were prepared and identified in a similar fashion.

Skin tests. Animals were injected intradermally on their shaved flanks with 30 μg of the challenge antigen in 0.1 ml saline within 1 hr of being passively sensitized. Reactions were read at 4 and 24 hr following challenge. Two perpendicular diameters of the reaction site were measured and averaged. Reactions were recorded as positive when an area of erythema was larger than 4 x 4 mm and indurated at 24 hr. Reactions elicited at the site of immediate reactions were recorded as positive if there was an increase in size of the area and induration during the interval between 4 and 24 hr.

RESULTS

Skin reactions in recipients of serum. Antisera harvested 7 to 10 days after immunization of donor animals with Pic-GPA were injected intravenously into six recipients. The recipients received approximately 20% of their blood volume or 5 ml of antisera. Challenge with 30 μg of Pic-GPA or Pic-HSA resulted in no discernible delayed reactions. Pic-GPA and Pic-HSA challenge of recipients of antisera harvested 21 to 28 days after immunization with Pic-GPA elicited the expected immediate reactions. At 24 hr, however, reactions elicited with either the sensitizing conjugate or the hapten-heterologous carrier protein were negligible (less than 4 x 4 ml) (Table I).

Effect of increasing concentration of challenge with homologous hapten-heterologous carrier protein. Recipients of cells harvested 10 days after immunization with Pic-GPA were challenged with an increased concentration of hapten-heterologous protein conjugate to determine the effect upon the specificity requirements of the transfer reaction. Twenty-one recipients of cells obtained from donors immunized with Pic-GPA were challenged with 30 μg of Pic-GPA and the expected positive delayed responses were elicited. Nine of these animals were challenged with 30 μg of Pic-HSA and none demonstrated a positive 24-hr reaction. The remaining 12 recipients were challenged with 300 μg of Pic-HSA and 9 of these animals demonstrated a hapten-specific 24-hr response which averaged 6.6 mm in diameter (Table II). Six unimmunized animals demonstrated no irritative skin reactions following injection with this concentration of Pic-HSA at 4 or 24 hr.

Specificity of delayed reactions in recipients of immune serum and sensitized cells. Nine recipients were given cells harvested 10 days after immunization of donors with Pic-GPA and 5 ml of antisera harvested 7 to 10 days after similar immunization. The reactions at 24 hr elicited by Pic-GPA (30 μg) averaged 8.5 mm in diameter. Of these nine recipients only two had small hapten-specific reactions elicited by Pic-HSA (30 μg). These two reactions averaged 5.8 mm in diameter. Recipients of 5 ml of serum harvested 21 to 28 days after immunization with Pic-GPA and cells harvested 10 days after such immunization produced the expected delayed reactions when challenged with Pic-GPA (30 μg). These conjugate-specific reactions averaged 9.6 mm in diameter. Challenge with Pic-HSA (30 μg) produced hapten-specific reactions in 12 of these 18 recipients with an average diameter of 8.5 mm (Table III).

Biopsies of reaction sites were examined without prior awareness of the experimental group from which the skin sections were obtained. The histopathology of the 24-hr skin reactions paral-

TABLE I

24-hour transfer reactions in recipients of serum

Serum[a] (Day of Harvest)	No. Recipients	Challenge: Pic-GPA: 30 μg avg. diameter	Challenge: Pic-HSA: 30 μg avg. diameter
		mm	mm
7–10	6	0	0
21–28	21	3.8	3.5

[a] Donors immunized with 100 μg Pic-GPA in complete Freund's adjuvant.

TABLE II

Specificity of 24-hour transfer reactions: effect of increasing concentration of challenge with heterologous conjugate[a]

Challenge: Pic-GPA (30 μg) No. positive/no. tested	Pic-GPA (30 μg) Avg. diameter	Pic-HSA 30 μg No. positive/no. tested	Pic-HSA 30 μg Avg. diameter	Pic-HSA 300 μg[b] No. positive/no. tested	Pic-HSA 300 μg[b] Avg. diameter
	mm		mm		mm
21/21	8.8	0/9		9/12	6.6

[a] Recipients were given cells obtained from donors immunized with 100 μg Pic-GPA in complete Freund's adjuvant.

[b] Six control animals manifested no skin irritation to challenge with 300 μg of Pic-HSA.

TABLE III

Specificity of 24-hour transfer reactions in recipients of immune serum and sensitized cells

Serum[a] (Day of Harvest)	Cells[a] (Day of Harvest)	Challenge: Pic-GPA: 30 μg No. positive/no. recipients	Pic-GPA: 30 μg Avg. diameter	Pic-HSA: 30 μg No. positive/no. recipients	Pic-HSA: 30 μg Avg. diameter
			mm		mm
7–10	10	9/9	8.5	2/9	5.8
21–28	10	18/18	9.6	12/18	8.5

[a] Donors were immunized with 100 μg Pic-GPA in complete Freund's adjuvant.

leled the macroscopic appearance of the lesions. Hapten-specific reactions occurring in recipients of 21 to 28 day serum and sensitized cells demonstrated mononuclear infiltration and perivascular "cuffing" equal to that seen in sections of conjugate-specific reactions elicited with the sensitizing antigen.

Effect of unrelated immediate reactions upon the specificity of the 24-hour transfer reaction (Table IV). Unrelated antigen-antibody reactions were produced in the skin of recipient guinea pigs to determine if nonspecific inflammatory effects also influenced the specificity of delayed reactions. One group of animals, passively sensitized with cells from donors immunized with Pic-GPA, was given serum obtained from guinea pigs immunized with OVA. These recipients were challenged with a mixture of Pic-GPA (30 μg) and OVA (30 μg) on the right flank and Pic-HSA (30 μg) plus OVA (30 μg) on the opposite flank. The recipients of the cells alone produced the expected conjugate-specific 24-hr reaction at the site of the challenge with Pic-GPA:OVA in five animals. The mixture of Pic-HSA and OVA produced two small hapten-specific reactions at 24 hr in these animals. Challenge of the six recipients of cells and anti-OVA serum produced both conjugate and smaller but consistent (5/6) hapten-specific 24-hr reactions.

Specificity of delayed reactions at prepared skin sites. To determine whether the effects of either specific or nonspecific antisera were the property of a single antibody class the following experiments were undertaken. Animals were immunized with 100 μg of Pic-GPA emulsified in complete

TABLE IV

Effect of unrelated immediate hypersensitivity reactions upon specificity of 24-hour transfer reaction

Immunization	Challenge: Pic-GPA: OVA (30 μg:30 μg)		Challenge: Pic-HSA:OVA (30 μg:30 μg)	
	No. positive/ no. recipients	Avg. diameter	No. positive/ no. recipients	Avg. diameter
		mm		*mm*
Cells[a]	5/5	7.5	2/5	5.7
Cells[a] + anti-OVA serum[b]	6/6	8.5	5/6	6.0

[a] Cells were obtained from donors immunized with 100 μg Pic-GPA 10 days before harvest.

[b] Serum obtained from donors immunized with 100 μg OVA 21 days before harvest.

TABLE V

Specificity of delayed reactions: effect of skin preparation upon reactions in actively immunized animals[a]

Skin Preparation	Challenge: Pic-GPA:OVA (30 μg:30μg)		Challenge: Pic-HSA:OVA (30 μg:30 μg)	
	No. positive/ no. tested	Avg. diameter	No. positive/ no. tested	Avg. diameter
		mm		*mm*
None	13/13	12.8	3/13	6.6
Anti-Pic-GPA				
γ1	13/13	13.0	14/17	7.1
γ2	13/13	13.0	16/22	7.7
Anti-OVA				
γ1	11/11	12.8	12/13	8.0
γ2	11/11	11.9	13/14	6.5
Normal guinea pig serum	18/19	16.6	11/12	5.8

[a] Immunized with 100 μg Pic-GPA in complete Freund's adjuvant 5 days before challenge.

Freund's adjuvant. Five days later skin sites were injected intradermally with either γ 1 anti-Pic-GPA, γ 2 anti-Pic-GPA, γ 1 anti-OVA, and, as a control, normal guinea pig serum. Four hours later these sites were challenged with 30 μg of Pic-GPA or Pic-HSA mixed with 30 μg of OVA (Table V). Animals were immunized and challenged in three different experiments. The number and pattern of skin sites prepared varied in each experiment. Results of all the challenges are combined in Table V. The expected conjugate-specific reactions were elicited with the Pic-GPA:OVA combinations. Hapten-specific reactions were consistently produced by challenge with the combination of Pic-HSA:OVA at prepared skin sites. Specific antigen-antibody reactions, unrelated immediate reactions and injection of normal serum all were effective in facilitating elicitation of hapten specific reactions.

DISCUSSION

The response of immune cells to antigen has been demonstrated to be heterogeneous; lymphocytes obtained from animals immunized with hapten-protein conjugates respond *in vitro* in a hapten-specific manner to critical concentrations of conjugates (1, 9) and production of a secondary response of antihaptenic antibody *in vivo* can occur following challenge with hapten coupled to a new carrier protein (10, 11). These hapten-specific cellular responses have been explained by the development of cells which have a high affinity for antigen and consequently are capable of stimulation by the haptenic group coupled to a differing carrier protein (9, 10). Passive transfer of sensitized cells, however, has failed to produce hapten-specific reactions in recipients (2). In the present studies hapten-specific reactions were elicited in recipients of sensitized cells and hyperimmune serum. Hapten-specific transfer reactions were also elicited in recipients of cells alone by increasing the concentration of hapten-heterologous protein used in challenge 10-fold. Asherson (4) has demonstrated a specific increase in the retention of radiolabeled antigen in the skin of recipients passively sensitized with hyperimmune serum and cells. The implication of the present studies taken in conjunction with those of Asherson is that a sufficient concentration of hapten heterologous protein conjugate is retained at the site of the reaction of hyperimmune serum and antigen to stimulate cells capable of responding to the hapten group alone. Antisera harvested 7 to 10 days after immunization did not influence the specificity of requirements of delayed reactions in the present experiments.

An unrelated antigen-antibody reaction has been shown to enhance the 24-hr transfer reaction but not to increase retention of antigen in the skin of guinea pigs (4). The small but consistently produced hapten-specific delayed reactions in recipients of cells at the sites of irrelevant immediate reactions demonstrated in the present studies implies that local inflammatory effects are also important in the production of hapten-specific reactions. Small hapten-specific reactions were also produced in actively immunized guinea pigs by varied preparation of skin sites before challenge. Elicitation of related or unrelated immediate reactions at the site of injection of γ 1 and γ 2 antibodies and injection of normal serum were equally effective in influencing the specificity of delayed reactions. These hapten-specific reactions were elicited at a time when only conjugate-specific delayed reactions are consistently demonstrable in the unprepared skin of actively immunized animals. Hill has demonstrated that the temporal course and intensity of delayed reactions are altered by induction of a mononuclear infiltrate with injection of guinea pig globulin (12). Cells capable of responding to the haptenic group possibly are present in increased numbers at the site of such an induced mononuclear infiltrate and could be responsible for the haptenic-specific reactions. The hapten-specific reactions elicited in guinea pigs immunized with arsanilic acid conjugates have been explained by postulating that this haptenic group, independent of the carrier molecule, provides sufficient energy to interact with the cells responsible for delayed reactions (13). Alternate explanations may be that this haptenic group elicits a more intense cellular infiltration thus increasing the number of cells at the site capable of responding to the haptenic group alone, or that local retention of arsanilic acid results in concentrations high enough to allow interaction with hapten-specific cells.

The results of the present studies of the effect of hyperimmune serum upon the specificity of cellular reactions imply that two mechanisms underlie production of hapten-specific reactions in highly sensitized animals. Hapten-specific delayed reactions may be due to a) increased retention of antigen at the skin site secondary to antigen-antibody interaction and consequent stimulation of those cells capable of responding to an increased concentration of hapten, and b) a nonspecific increase in the number of mononuclear cells at the reaction site, thereby increasing the probability of interaction of antigen and cells with a high affinity for the haptenic group.

REFERENCES

1. Paul, W. E., Siskind, G. W. and Benacerraf, B., J. Exp. Med., *127:* 25, 1968.
2. Phair, J. P. and Kantor, F. S., J. Immun., *100:* 302, 1968.
3. Asherson, G. L. and Loewi, G., Immunology, *11:* 277, 1966.
4. Asherson, G. L., Immunology, *13:* 441, 1967.
5. Eisen, H. N., Belman, S. and Carsten, M. E., J. Amer. Chem. Soc., *75:* 4583, 1953.
6. Ovary, Z., Prog. Allerg., *5:* 460, 1958.
7. Gold, E. R. and Fudenberg, H. H., J. Immun., *99:* 859, 1967.
8. Block, K. J., Kourilsky, F. M., Ovary, Z. and Benacerraf, B., J. Exp. Med., *117:* 965, 1963.
9. Steiner, L. A. and Eisen, H. N., J. Exp. Med., *126:* 1185, 1967.
10. Paul, W. E., Siskind, G. W., Benacerraf, B. and Ovary, Z., J. Immun., *99:* 760, 1967.
11. Rittenberg, M. B. and Campbell, D. H., J. Exp. Med., *127:* 717, 1968.
12. Hill, W. C., J. Exp. Med., *129:* 363, 1969.
13. Leskowitz, S., Jones, V. E. and Zak, J. J., J. Exp. Med., *123:* 229, 1966.

THE JOURNAL OF IMMUNOLOGY
Vol. 105, No. 2, August 1970

Printed in U.S.A.

MECHANISMS OF RELEASE OF CONSTITUENTS FROM RABBIT PLATELETS BY ANTIGEN-ANTIBODY COMPLEXES AND COMPLEMENT

I. Lytic and Nonlytic Reactions[1]

PETER M. HENSON[2]

From the Department of Experimental Pathology, Scripps Clinic and Research Foundation, La Jolla, California 92037

Received for publication November 17, 1969

Two mechanisms have been described by which antigen-antibody complexes in the presence of complement induce release of vasoactive amines from rabbit platelets. The reaction of soluble antigen, antibody in excess, normal rabbit plasma and platelets caused adherence of the platelets to the immune complexes (which required the action of C3) and lysis of the platelets (which required the action of C6). The lysis was observed microscopically and was accompanied by release of vasoactive amines, nucleotides and cytoplasmic and lysosomal enzymes. The release did not require active participation of the platelet and was postulated to result from cell lysis by complement components activated by the immune complexes in or on the platelet membrane. A nonlytic, complement-dependent release of vasoactive amines resulted from immune adherence of platelets to erythrocytes or zymosan that had fixed complement components through C3. Vasoactive amines and nucleotides were released by the reaction, but not intracellular enzymes or potassium (measured with rubidium 86). Platelet energy and activated platelet esterases were required for the release, which appeared to result from the C3-induced adherence of the platelets to the particulate antigens.

Mammalian platelets exhibit characteristic clumping and releasing reactions under the influence of a variety of stimuli. In at least two immunologic inflammatory reactions in rabbits, the release of histamine and serotonin from platelets has been pathogenetically implicated in the disease: the deposition of antigen-antibody complexes in experimental serum sickness (1) and the induction of increased vascular permeability in a complement-dependent passive cutaneous anaphylactic reaction (2).

Rabbit platelets have been shown previously to release their vasoactive amines following interaction with antigen and antibody *in vitro* (3–8). Recent examination of this phenomenon revealed two different processes (9). Both involved complement, but they could be differentiated by their requirement for C6. Soluble antigen, in combination with excess antibody, induced platelet clumping in the presence of plasma, and platelet histamine release. The histamine release was not seen if C6-deficient plasma was employed. It was suggested that this release might result from a cytolytic reaction brought about by the terminal complement components (10). The process has been termed complement-dependent (lytic) release. The second reaction was seen if particulate antigens such as sheep erythrocytes or zymosan were employed. Having fixed complement components up to C3 (or C5), such particles could be washed and would induce adherence of washed rabbit platelets and release of their histamine. Zymosan or sensitized sheep erythrocytes (EA) that had reacted with either normal or C6-deficient plasma were equally effective, after washing, in producing this release. The reaction will be called complement-dependent (nonlytic) release. If either of these reactions were performed in the presence of neutrophils, increased release of vaso-

[1] This is Publication 364 from the Department of Experimental Pathology, Scripps Clinic and Research Foundation. The work was supported by United States Public Health Service Grant AI-07007-04.

[2] Supported by United States Public Health Service Training Grant 5 T6 GM683.

active amines was observed (10, 11). This involvement of neutrophils in the platelet release reaction is discussed in the accompanying paper (12).

To elucidate further the mechanisms whereby the complement system induces the release of vasoactive amines from platelets, three approaches were adopted. First, the morphology of platelets undergoing the release reactions was examined by electron microscopy. Second, the platelets were studied to determine whether there was a specific release of vasoactive amines or release of other materials and enzymes as well. Third, the requirement for platelet energy processes and serine esterases and the role of platelet clumping were examined to determine the extent of platelet participation in the release reactions.

The two complement-dependent platelet release reactions were compared with a known cytolytic reaction as given by antiplatelet antibody in the presence of complement. Since antiplatelet antibody also induces histamine release from platelets in the absence of plasma (13), this latter reaction was used as an example of a noncytolytic process.

MATERIALS AND METHODS

Platelets. Siliconized glassware and needles were used for all handling of platelets. Rabbit blood was obtained from the ear artery of healthy adult New Zealand White rabbits and collected in one-sixth volume of acid citrate dextrose (ACD) (14). The platelet-rich plasma was separated and the platelets were washed essentially by the method of Ardlie (personal communication from Dr. Ardlie, McMaster University, Hamilton, Ontario). This involved one wash with a large volume of Tyrode's solution, pH 6.5, from which the $CaCl_2$ had been omitted but with 10^{-4} M ethylene glycol tetraacetic acid (EGTA) included. The second wash was with the same solution without the EGTA. The platelets were finally suspended to approximately 5×10^9/ml in this solution. The optical density of a dilution of this stock suspension was used to assess the platelet concentration. Before use the platelets were diluted with Tyrode's solution (pH 7.4). All of the Tyrode's solutions had 0.25% gelatin included and the washing procedures were carried out at either 4°C or at room temperature. For studies of energy requirements, the platelets were washed in Tyrode's solution from which the glucose was omitted and a 15-min incubation at 37°C was included after the first wash.

Plasma. Blood was obtained from rabbit ear arteries into one-fortieth volume of 0.2 M ethylene diamine tetraacetic acid (EDTA). The formed elements were removed by centrifugation and the plasma from a number of rabbits was pooled and frozen in small amounts at −70°C. For studies on energy requirements, plasma glucose was removed by dialysis in the cold against saline with 0.005 M EDTA. The effectiveness of this procedure has been described elsewhere (13). Before use the calcium and magnesium were restored by addition of one-twentieth volume of 2% $CaCl_2$ and $MgCl_2$. Heparin (10 units/ml) prevented coagulation. Plasma was depleted of C3 with purified cobra venom factor as described previously (9).

Antisera. Antiserum to rabbit platelets was raised in sheep and extensively absorbed with other formed elements (13). This material was purified by ammonium sulfate precipitation followed by diethylaminoethyl (DEAE)-cellulose column chromatography. The material not binding to the column in 0.01 M phosphate buffer (pH 8.1) was used. The properties and activity of these antibody preparations have been described elsewhere (13). The rabbit anti-bovine serum albumin (BSA) antiserum was that used previously (9) and was also an IgG fraction. Antibody nitrogen levels were determined by quantitative precipitation. Antiferritin antiserum was raised in rabbits by repeated intravenous injections of horse spleen ferritin (cadmium-free, Nutritional Biochemicals Corp., Cleveland, Ohio). An IgG fraction was obtained from DEAE-cellulose as described above.

Zymosan. Alexinated zymosan (ZC) was prepared by incubating zymosan (Nutritional Biochemicals Corp.) with rabbit plasma (36 mg/ml for 20 min at 37°C) in order to allow complement components (in particular, C3) to fix. The particles were then washed extensively. A control suspension of zymosan incubated in plasma containing 0.005 M EDTA (Z EDTA C) was also used. Zymosan-thrombin was prepared by incubating zymosan with bovine thrombin (Parke, Davis and Co., Detroit, Mich.) 5 IU/10^8 particles, for 20 min at 37°C. The zymosan-thrombin was washed three times and incubated with platelets (2.5×10^8 Z particles with 2.5×10^8 platelets).

Rubidium. ^{86}Rb was incorporated into the platelets according to the procedure described by Siraganian, Secchi and Osler (15). Two milliliters (2×10^{10}) platelets which had been centrifuged from the platelet-rich plasma were incubated with 0.5 mCi ^{86}Rb (New England Nuclear) for 1 hr at 37°C. The platelets were then washed as usual.

Test conditions. The reactions were performed in three different ways. a) With a final reaction volume of 2.5 ml, 2.5×10^8 washed platelets were incubated with the releasing stimuli for 30 min at 37°C with mild shaking. The *complement-dependent nonlytic reaction* was produced by incubating ZC (2.5×10^8 particles, 3.6 mg) with the washed platelets. The effect of antiplatelet antibody without plasma was achieved by the use of 0.1 ml of the IgG antibody preparation. As a control for these two reactions in which plasma (free complement components) was not present, washed platelets were incubated in Tyrode's solution alone. For the *complement-dependent lytic reaction*, 0.1 μg N BSA, 12 μg N anti-BSA (i.e., 25 times the amount required for equivalence), 10% plasma and platelets were incubated together. Antiplatelet antibody (0.05 ml) was also reacted with platelets in the presence of 10% plasma to provide an example of a cytolytic reaction. Finally, platelets were incubated with 10% plasma in Tyrode's solution as a control. b) For studies on release of enzymes and nucleotides from platelets and for electron microscopy, increased platelet concentrations (5×10^9 in a 5-ml reaction volume) were employed. The plasma concentration was kept at 10%, but the amounts of ZC, antiplatelet antibody, BSA and anti-BSA were increased proportionally. To allow easy visualization of the antigen-antibody complexes in the electron microscope, a ferritin (10 μg protein)—antiferritin (20 times antibody excess) system was also used. c) Examination of platelet aggregation was carried out in an aggregometer (Chromo-Log Corp., Broomall, Pa.). A 2.5-ml reaction volume with 5×10^8 or 10^9 platelets was used. The platelets were stirred at 1100 rpm at 37°C during the reaction and the increase in light transmission was recorded for 15 min. At the end of each incubation period the tubes were centrifuged and the materials released into the supernatant medium were assayed.

Histamine, serotonin and rubidium in the sedimented platelets were released by boiling for 2 min so that the percentage released could be determined. The cells were lysed for residual enzyme activity by either six freeze/thaw cycles or 1 mg/ml Triton ×100. Triton ×100 gave slightly higher total activities and was more generally used.

Assays. Histamine was assayed on the atropinized guinea pig ileum and serotonin was determined on the estrus rat uterus using appropriate standard solutions of synthetic amines.

Lactic dehydrogenase was assayed according to the method of Wroblewski and LaDue (16). Acid phosphatase was determined with *p*-nitrophenyl phosphate (17) and β glucuronidase with phenolphthalein glucuronide (18) as substrates. Two-tenths milliliter of material to be tested was employed in these reactions.

Adenosine triphosphate (ATP) (19) and adenosine diphosphate (ADP) and adenosine monophosphate (AMP) (20) were determined enzymatically following sample extraction with 4% perchloric acid. The enzymes for these assays were obtained from Calbiochem, Los Angeles, Calif.

The levels of materials found in the plasma pool were subtracted (where appropriate) from the values found in the supernatant. The total quantities found in 5×10^9 platelets in the experiment shown in Figure 5 are depicted in Table I.

Inhibitors. Diisopropyl fluorophosphate (DFP, Boots Pure Drug Co., Ltd., Nottingham, U. K.), 2-deoxyglucose (Nutritional Biochemicals Corp., Cleveland, Ohio), acetyl salicylate, sodium salicylate and adenosine were dissolved in saline (2×10^{-2} M or 10^{-2} M). Incorporation of one-tenth volume into the reaction mixture gave a final concentration of 10^{-3} M. Mg EGTA (ethylene glycol tetraacetate) was prepared by employing sodium EGTA with an excess of $MgCl_2$ (0.005 M EGTA and 0.01 M $MgCl_2$).

Electron microscopy. Platelets were prepared as usual with ACD as anticoagulant, but were washed at room temperature. The reactions were carried out as described above and after differing incubation periods 1 ml was added to 4 ml of 3% glutaraldehyde, pH 7.3, previously warmed to 37°C. After 20 min fixation at 37°C the platelets were centrifuged, fixed in osmic acid in the cold and embedded in Vestopal. Sections were cut, stained with uranyl acetate and lead citrate and examined in the Hitachi HU11 microscope.

RESULTS

Morphology of platelets undergoing complement-dependent release of vasoactive amines. In order to determine whether the two release processes (in particular that requiring C6) involved platelet lysis, platelets undergoing the reaction were examined in the electron microscope.

Figure 1 (*lower right*) depicts a platelet incubated in Tyrode's solution alone and is representative of platelets which had not released their vasoactive amines. Incubation of ZC (zymosan which had fixed rabbit complement components and was then washed) with such platelets produced the changes seen in Figure 1 (*upper left*). Close adherence of platelets to the zymosan occurred. These adherent platelets showed varying degrees of loss of internal organization. In most platelets, both types of granules could no longer be seen and the canalicular system became less apparent. Microtubules became disorganized and, due to the lack of other structures, mitochondria were prominent. No lysis of platelets was observed in this complement-dependent (nonlytic) reaction.

In contrast the reaction of antigen, antibody in excess, plasma and platelets resulted in the changes seen in Figure 2. Ferritin was employed as antigen to allow visualization of the antigen-antibody-complement complexes. Clumps of platelets and immune complexes were observed. Many platelets exhibited disappearance of granules and canaliculi as described for the reaction with ZC. Other platelets, however, were lysed, showing complete loss of internal constituents and breaks in the plasma membrane. Some platelets had large internal membrane-bound spaces (Fig. 2) containing a loose network of undetermined material. Occasionally immune complexes were found within such a space. The percentage of cells lysed increased with the time of incubation. This reaction has therefore been called the complement-dependent lytic release of vasoactive amines.

Incubation of antigen, antibody, platelets and C6-deficient plasma resulted in clumps of platelets and immune complexes (Fig. 3). Lysis of the platelets was not seen.

Release of vasoactive amines, enzymes, nucleotides and rubidium from platelets. The two complement-dependent mechanisms of platelet release were studied further by an examination of a number of platelet constituents in addition to histamine to see if they were also released. The materials measured were histamine, serotonin, the nucleotides ATP, ADP and AMP, the lysosomal enzymes β glucuronidase and acid phosphatase, the cytoplasmic enzyme lactic dehydrogenase and rubidium (Rb) 86. The ^{86}Rb was incorporated into the platelets before the reactions and behaves like potassium (15). Cathepsins and the platelet permeability factor (21) were not found in high enough concentration to study in this way, ATP, ADP and AMP have been considered together, since the ATP (in highest concentration in the platelets) may be converted to ADP and AMP, especially in plasma, and possibly during release. The quantities of materials released are expressed as a percentage of the material available in the platelets and the total quantities found are shown in Table I.

The results are shown in Figure 4. Platelets incubated in Tyrode's solution alone exhibited some release of nucleotides and of ^{86}Rb. ZC stimulated the release of histamine, serotonin and nucleotides (predominantly ATP). Rubidium levels were similar to those in the control, although very large amounts of ZC did induce the release of a little ^{86}Rb. Five per cent of the β glucuronidase activity was present in the supernatant but the other two enzymes were not released.

In contrast to this nonlytic reaction, incubation of platelets with BSA, anti-BSA and plasma (lytic reaction) resulted in release of each of the materials studied. Higher percentages of histamine, serotonin, nucleotides and ^{86}Rb appeared in the supernatant than of the three enzymes, but appreciable levels (20% to 30%) of these lysosomal and cytoplasmic enzymes were also released.

These results are from a single representative experiment with duplicate points. The experiment was repeated five times, but the percentages of substances released have not been compiled into a single diagram, since the platelet concentrations were varied. Nevertheless, the results of the different experiments were identical in pattern with that described. To confirm that the reactions were similar at lower concentration of platelets, the percentage histamine release was also compared with the ^{86}Rb release from 2.5×10^8 platelets (see *Materials and Methods*). Again, only the lytic reaction resulted in appreciable Rb release above the background levels.

Release of platelet constituents as a function of incubation time. Figure 5 depicts an experiment relating the release of selected materials to time of incubation. ^{86}Rb was released slowly over 45 min in both controls (platelets with Tyrode's and platelets with plasma). Incubation with ZC resulted in immediate release of histamine, but not of enzymes. In contrast, the lytic reaction of antigen, antibody, plasma and platelets resulted in a lag period of about 4 min before release of

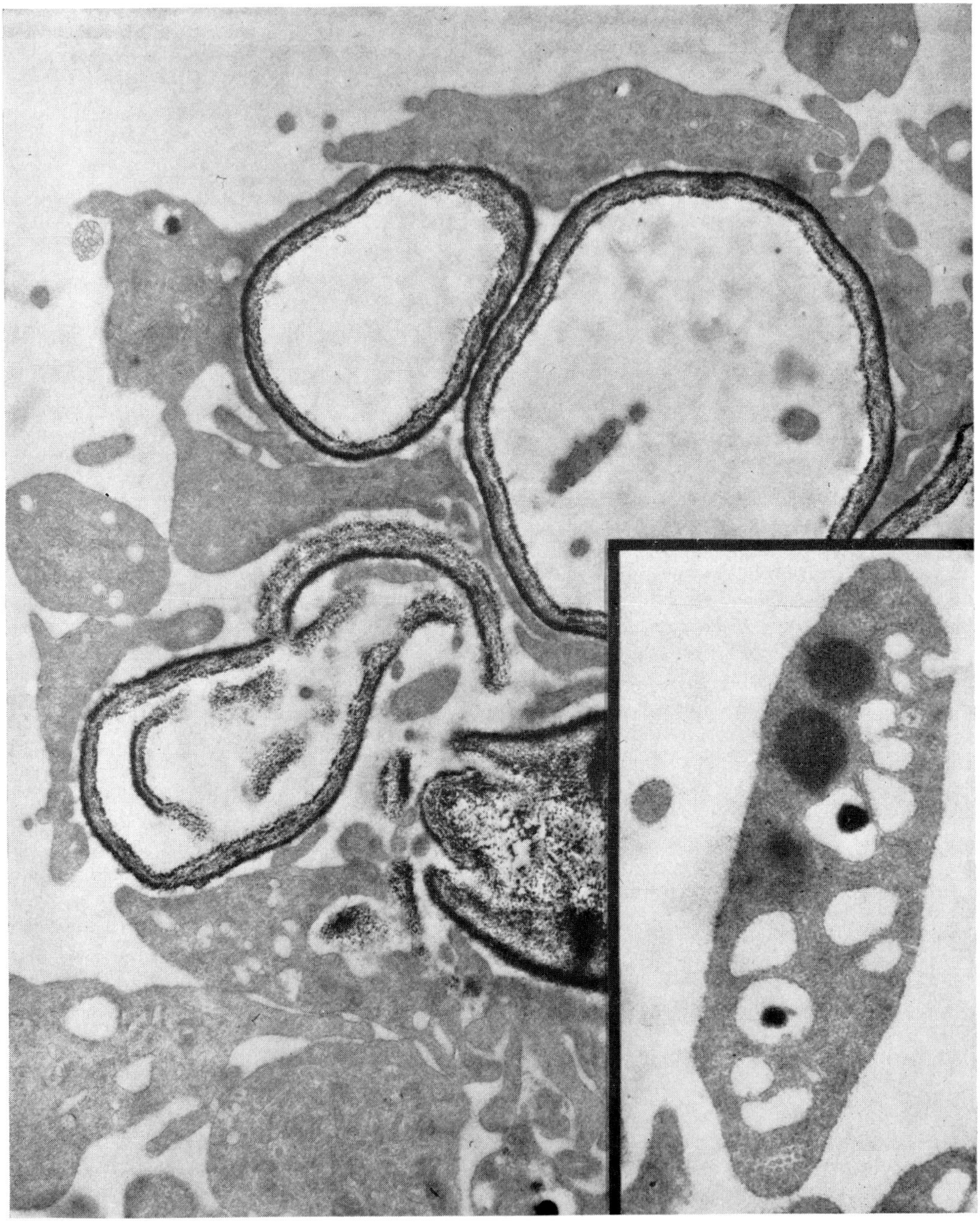

Figure 1. Lower right, control platelets. The platelets were prepared at room temperature and incubated for 15 min at 37°C in Tyrode's solution before fixation with glutaraldehyde at 37°C (× 40,000). *Upper left,* platelets reacting with alexinated zymosan (ZC). Washed platelets (5 × 10^9 were incubated for 15 min with ZC (2.5 × 10^9 particles of zymosan which had been incubated with rabbit plasma to fix complement and then washed). The platelets are closely adherent to the ZC. A disappearance of granules and canaliculi (but not of mitochondria) is apparent and where membranous intracellular stuctures can be seen *(bottom)* they appear somewhat disorganized. Lysis of platelets was not observed (×28,200).

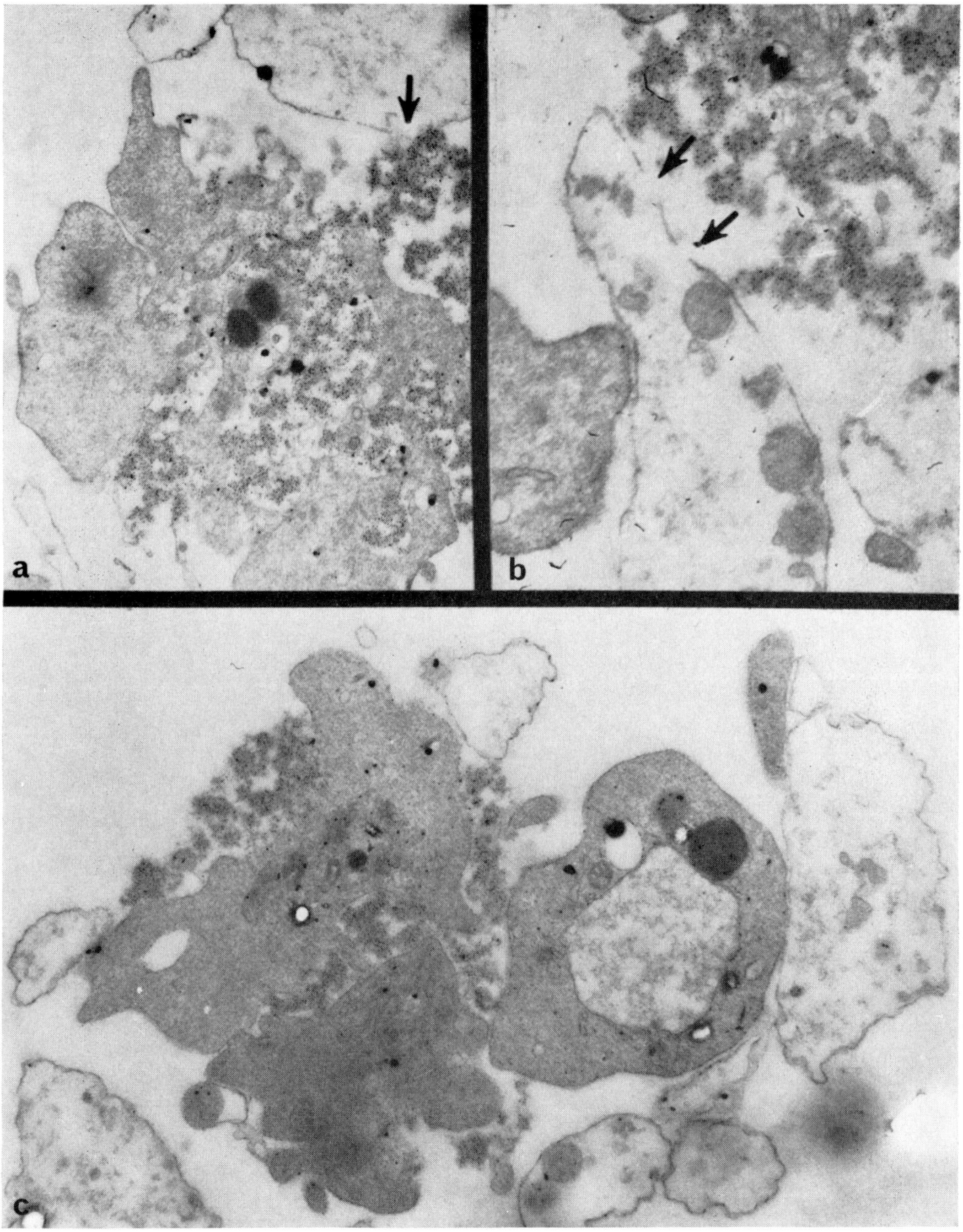

Figure 2. Platelets reacting with antigen, antibody and plasma. Ferritin, antiferritin, normal rabbit plasma and platelets (see *Materials and Methods*) were incubated together for 20 min at 37°C. Clumps of antigen-antibody-complement complexes and platelets may be seen. Disappearance of granules and canaliculi from platelets in such clumps is evident. A platelet with a large membrane-bounded space containing diffuse material may be seen (*c*). Other platelets exhibit lysis with breaks in the membrane (*arrows* in *a* and *b*) and loss of internal organization and constituents (*a*, × 24,100; *b*, × 41,200; *c*, × 31,000).

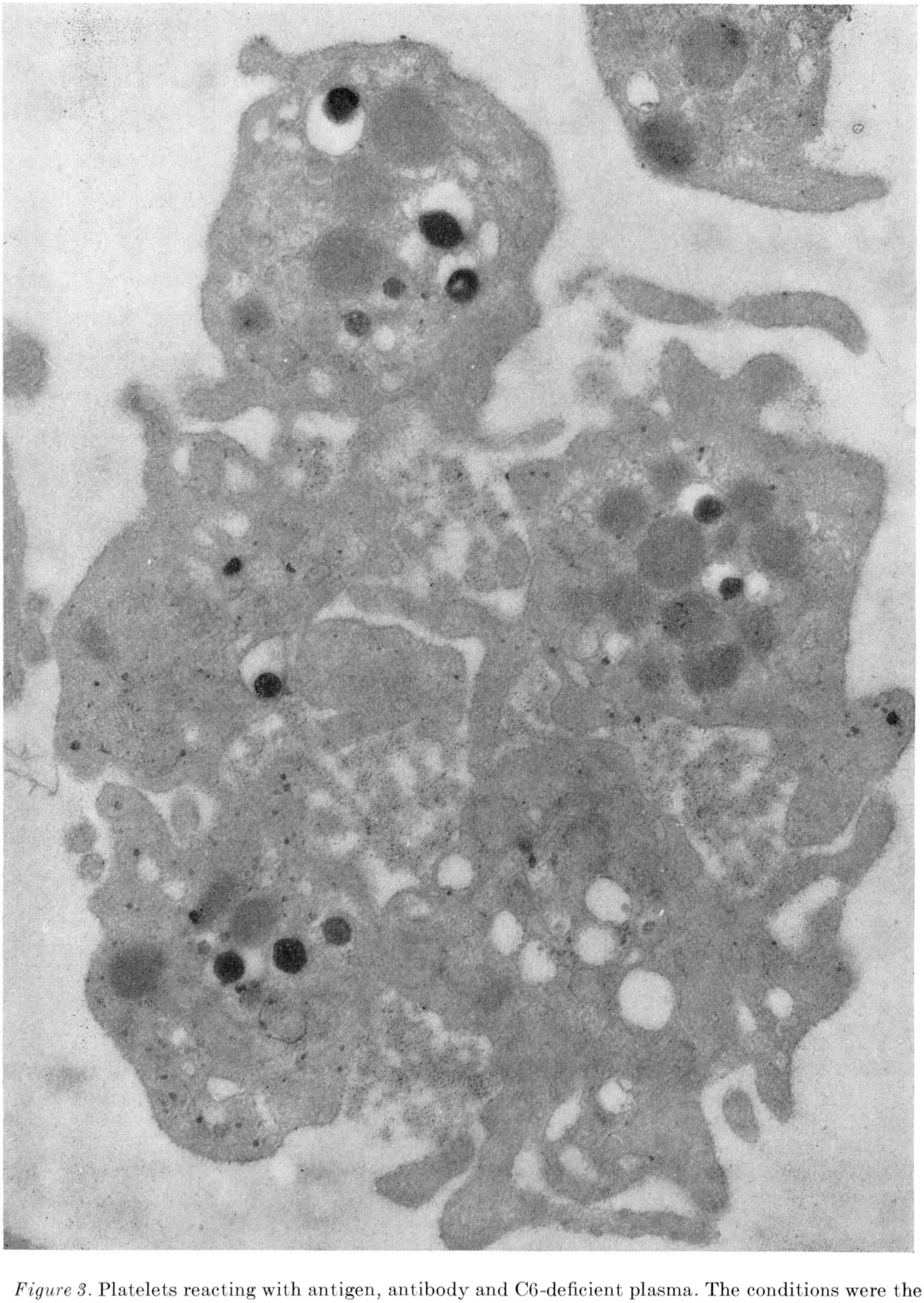

Figure 3. Platelets reacting with antigen, antibody and C6-deficient plasma. The conditions were the same as those for the platelets shown in Figure 2, except that C6-deficient plasma was used. Clumps of immune complexes and platelets may be seen and the platelets exhibit irregular shapes. There is some clustering of granules towards the center of the platelets but these structures have not disappeared. Lysis of platelets is not apparent (× 47,000).

TABLE I

Total quantities of vasoactive amines and enzymes in 5 × 10⁹ platelets in the experiment shown in Figure 5

Histamine	261 nM
Serotonin	180 nM
ATP + ADP + AMP	644 nM
Acid phosphatase	160 nM *p*-nitrophenol liberated/30 min
β glucuronidase	3.46 μmols phenolphthalein liberated/16 hr
Lactic dehydrogenase	14,300 units[a]

[a] Decrease in optical density at 340 nm of 0.001/min.

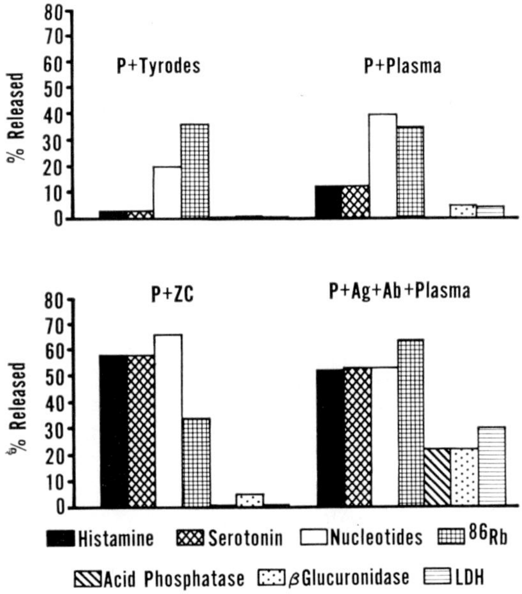

Figure 4. Release of intracellular constituents from platelets. P, 5 × 10⁹ washed platelets; ZC, 2.5 × 10⁹ zymosan particles incubated with plasma to fix complement and then washed; Ag, 1 μg N BSA; Ab, 120 μg N anti-BSA; plasma, 10%; LDH, lactic dehydrogenase. The amount of materials released from the platelets after 30 min at 37°C is expressed as a percentage of the total available.

rubidium and histamine occurred. The release of histamine proceeded over the whole 45-min incubation period. A further delay preceded the release of acid phosphatase and lactic dehydrogenase.

For comparison, Figure 6 shows the effect of antiplatelet antibody on platelets. In the absence of plasma, histamine release occurred immediately, reaching a maximum in 7 to 15 min. A cytolytic reaction involving antiplatelet antibody and plasma (complement) resulted in an early release of histamine and rubidium and slightly delayed release of acid phosphatase and lactic dehydrogenase just as in the complement-dependent lytic release shown in Figure 5.

Glucose requirements for complement-dependent histamine release from rabbit platelets. The requirement for glucose was studied by eliminating glucose from the reaction mixture. An incubation step during the washing procedure was introduced to allow some depletion of intracellular glucose levels. The effect of 2-deoxyglucose, an inhibitor of glucose metabolism, was also examined in this glucose-free situation as a further test of glucose requirement for platelet histamine release.

Figure 7 shows dose-response curves for C3-dependent (nonlytic) and C6-dependent (lytic) histamine release in the presence of glucose, in the

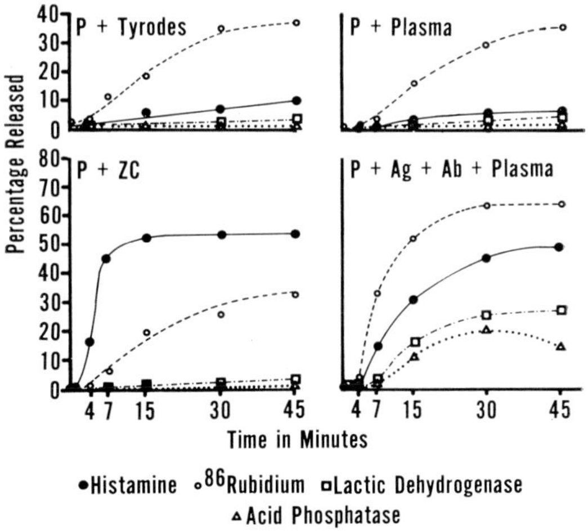

Figure 5. Release of platelet constituents with time. At intervals during the incubation at 37°C the reaction was stopped by cooling and addition of 0.01 M EDTA, the platelets were centrifuged and the supernatant fluid was assayed for released materials. The quantities were those described in Figure 4.

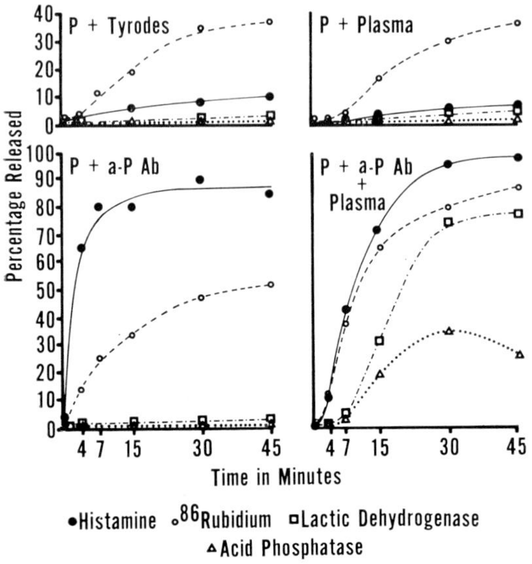

Figure 6. Release of platelet constituents by antiplatelet antibody. The reaction was performed as described for Figure 5. The antiplatelet antibody (a-P Ab) is described in reference 12. In the absence of plasma, 3.0 ml (3.3 mg IgG globulin N) of antiplatelet antibody preparation was used. With 10% plasma, 1.5 ml was employed.

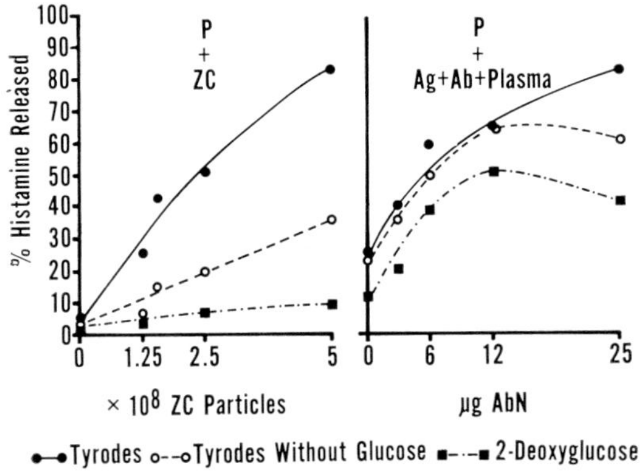

Figure 7. The effect of glucose on the complement-dependent release of histamine from platelets. P, 2.5 × 10⁹ platelets; ZC, alexinated zymosan; Ab, anti-BSA; Ag, BSA to give conditions of 25 times antibody excess; plasma, 10%. The plasma had been dialyzed to remove glucose. 2-Deoxyglucose was used (10^{-3} M final concentration) under gluose-free conditions.

absence of glucose and with the inclusion of 10^{-3} M 2-deoxyglucose. It may be seen that omission of glucose had a marked inhibitory effect on the histamine release produced by zymosan-complement (ZC), i.e., on the nonlytic release. The presence of 2-deoxyglucose increased this inhibition. Histamine release by BSA, anti-BSA and plasma (lytic reaction) was unaffected by absence of glucose, except at high levels of antigen and antibody. Some inhibition was seen if 2-deoxyglucose was included. The results indicate a glucose requirement for the nonlytic system.

Inhibition of histamine release by DFP. The two histamine-releasing systems were examined for the inhibitory action of 2×10^{-3} M DFP. Since C1 esterase is susceptible to this inhibition, the reactants (releasing stimuli and platelets) were allowed to interact for 7 min before adding DFP in order to allow reaction of C1 in the systems containing plasma. The results are shown in Figure 8. DFP inhibited the histamine release by ZC, but not that induced by antigen, antibody and plasma (lytic release).

Controls for this inhibition are shown in Table II. To show that DFP was effective in the presence of plasma, zymosan was reacted with platelets in the presence of plasma, i.e., *not* washed before addition to platelets. Only slight inhibition was observed with DFP. However, the use of C6-deficient plasma in this way showed that, in the absence of C6 (where only the nonlytic process was operative), DFP could be inhibitory even in the presence of 10% plasma.

Inhibition of the nonlytic release by DFP could be due to inhibition of complement components

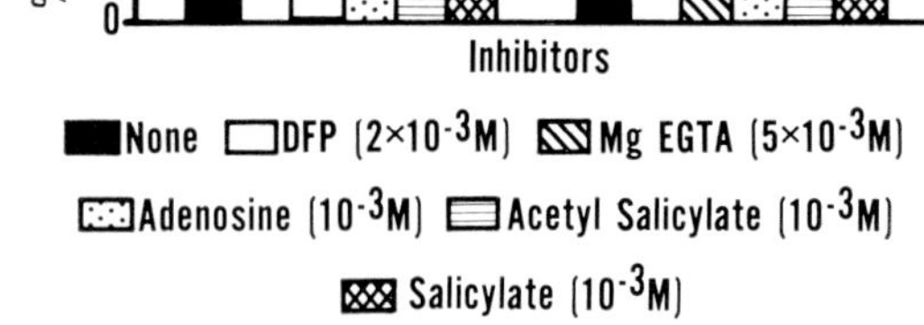

Figure 8. The effect of inhibitors on the complement-dependent reactions of platelets. P, 2.5×10^8 platelets; ZC, 2.5×10^8 particles of alexinated zymosan; Ag, 0.1 μg N BSA; Ab, 12 μg N anti-BSA. DFP and Mg EGTA were added to the reaction after 7 min incubation. The results are representative of six similar experiments.

TABLE II

The effect of DFP on platelet histamine release in the presence of plasma

Releasing Agent	Histamine Release	
	No DFP	10^{-3} M DFP
	%	%
None	10	<5
Z + normal plasma[a]	70	65
Z + C6-def. plasma	44	20

[a] The zymosan, plasma and platelets were allowed to react for 7 min before addition of DFP to permit C1 activation.

TABLE III

The effect of pretreatment of ZC on platelets with DFP[a]

	Histamine Release
	%
ZC + platelets	45
ZC (DFP-pretreated) + platelets	43
Z-thrombin + platelets	55
Z-thrombin (DFP-pretreated) + platelets	14
Platelets	10
DFP-pretreated platelets	<7
Platelets + ZC	43
DFP-pretreated platelets + ZC	46

[a] Pretreatment was with 2×10^{-3} M DFP for 30 min at 4°C followed by washing. The quantities of reagents used are described in *Materials and Methods*.

on the zymosan. This was examined by pretreatment of the ZC with DFP before reaction with platelets (Table III). No inhibition occurred. To show that such pretreatment was effective, zymosan which had been treated with bovine thrombin was used. Some thrombin is taken up by the zymosan and remains through several washes. Such preparations which normally release histamine from platelets were inhibited by pretreatment with DFP (Table III). Heparin and hirudin were also both inhibitory to the histamine-releasing effect of zymosan thrombin in contrast to their lack of effect on the complement-dependent processes (9).

Pretreatment of the platelets with DFP did not affect the nonlytic histamine release by ZC (Table III), suggesting activation of a platelet esterase as part of the release process.

Inhibition by chelating agents. A requirement of calcium for the complement-dependent, nonlytic release of histamine was demonstrated by the use of Mg EGTA. This chelating agent was inhibitory to the reaction with ZC (Fig. 8), but only partial inhibition of the lytic reaction was found if the Mg EGTA was added to the reaction mixture after 7 min of incubation to allow C1 activation.

Inhibition by adenosine and acetyl salicylate. Two other agents known to affect platelet function are aspirin and adenosine. Figure 8 shows the inhibitory activity of adenosine and acetyl salicylate on the nonlytic release reaction induced by ZC. Sodium salicylate was not inhibitory under these conditions. In contrast, the salicylates were without effect on the lytic release and adenosine had only a slight effect.

Platelet adherence and aggregation during the

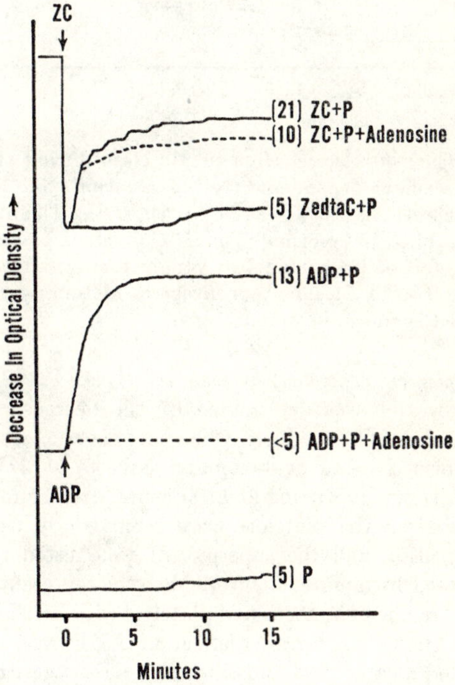

Figure 9. Aggregation of platelets during the complement-dependent (nonlytic) reaction. The decrease in optical density of the platelet suspension incubated at 37°C with stirring at 1100 rpm is shown. P, 10^9 platelets; ZC, 1.25×10^8 zymosan particles incubated with normal plasma and washed; Z EDTA C, zymosan incubated with EDTA plasma (no complement fixed); ADP, 10^{-5} M; adenosine, 2×10^{-4} M. The percentage of histamine released under these conditions is shown in parentheses.

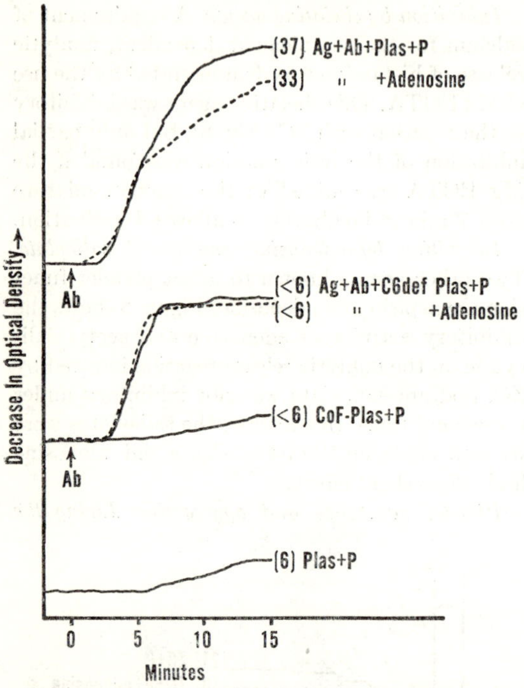

Figure 10. Aggregation of platelets during the complement-dependent (lytic) reaction. P, 10^9 platelets; Ag, 0.2 μg N BSA; Ab, 20 μg N anti-BSA; plas, 10% normal plasma; CoF-plas., plasma depleted of C3 with cobra venom factor; adenosine: 2×10^4 M. The percentage of histamine released is shown in parentheses.

complement-dependent release reactions. Platelet aggregation was determined by the decrease in optical density produced when the reactions were performed in an aggregometer cuvette at 37°C with constant stirring at 1100 rpm. After 15 min incubation the platelets were removed by centrifugation and the supernatant was tested for released histamine. Figure 9 shows a representative tracing of a reaction of platelets with ZC. The well-known aggregating effect of ADP was included as a control and since this ADP aggregation is inhibited by adenosine the effect of adenosine on the complement-dependent reactions was also studied.

Addition of ZC to the platelet suspension increased the optical density, but was followed immediately by clumping of the platelets and ZC, shown by a subsequent decrease in the optical density. Release of histamine occurred. The clumping and release were not observed if zymosan which had been incubated with EDTA plasma was used. Adenosine inhibited the release, but only slightly reduced the degree of clumping.

Figure 10 shows the platelet clumping and histamine release in the complement-dependent (lytic) reaction. Antigen, antibody and C3-depleted (with cobra venom factor) plasma did not induce platelet aggregation. Platelet clumping occurred with C6-deficient plasma, but did not result in histamine release. In contrast, if normal plasma containing all the later-acting complement components was used, increased clearing of the platelet suspension was seen. Some inhibition of this additional optical density decrease was produced by the addition of adenosine. In both cases, however, the optical density did not level off, but decreased gradually over the 15-min incubation period.

DISCUSSION

The reaction of rabbit platelets with components of complement fixed to antigen-antibody complexes results in a release of vasoactive amines by two mechanisms (9). Further examination has clarified the differences between the two reactions.

Complement-dependent (lytic) release. Release of histamine from rabbit platelets by antigen, antibody in excess and plasma has been well-documented (3–8, 15). Plasma factors are essential for this reaction and although some reports suggested that the complement system was required (3, 7), others have concluded that complement was not the plasma factor involved (4, 5, 8, 15). Recently, the possible action of thrombin in the reaction was excluded (9) and a clear role of complement was shown by the use of C6-deficient plasma and plasma depleted of C3 with cobra venom factor. Neither source of plasma supported the release.

Analysis of this complement-dependent release of vasoactive amines as reported herein has shown that the reaction results in lysis of the platelets and may therefore be termed a cytotoxic process. The first step in this reaction appears to be a clumping of the platelets. This requires the complement sequence through C3, since it is inhibited by treating the plasma with cobra venom factor. The use of the platelet aggregometer for this study confirms the findings reported earlier (9). The clumping is not inhibited by the use of C6-deficient plasma and commences after an initial 2- to 4-min lag period. It is suggested that the clumping is brought about by adherence of the platelets to the antigen-antibody complement complexes by the process of C3 immune adherence. The adherence proceeds after a time period during which the complexes are forming and fixing complement. This adherence was confirmed by light and electron microscopic examination. Since adenosine did not inhibit the clumping induced by antigen, antibody and C6-deficient plasma, ADP does not seem a likely cause of this aggregation.

When normal plasma was employed, however, increased clearing of the platelet suspension resulted. This increase was partly inhibited by adenosine and may in part be due to additional aggregation induced by release of ADP. However, the clearing is also partly caused by lysis of a proportion of the platelets and this proceeds gradually over a 30-min incubation period. This lysis can be seen by light microscopy and was confirmed in the electron microscope. Any effects of ADP on the platelets would be greatly enhanced under these particular incubation conditions, i.e., with vigorous stirring of the suspension. The percentage of release of vasoactive amines, however, was not appreciably increased in the aggregometer when compared with reactions performed in tubes with only mild shaking.

Electron microscopic examination confirmed the platelet cytolysis, showing breaks in the plasma membrane and loss of internal constituents. It was found that a proportion of all the platelet constituents examined (histamine, serotonin, ATP, ADP, AMP, β glucuronidase, acid phosphatase, lactic dehydrogenase and rubidium 86) were released by this reaction, including both lysosomal and cytoplasmic enzymes. Rubidium was released early and in large amount in confirmation of the findings of Siraganian, Secchi and Osler (15). Rubidium behaves like potassium and potassium loss has also been described as one of the first steps in complement cytolysis of nucleated cells (22). The three enzymes studied were released to a lesser extent and more slowly than the vasoactive amines or ^{86}Rb and after a longer lag period, suggesting a requirement for greater damage to the cells. Siraganian *et al.* (15) also demonstrated an earlier release of ^{86}Rb and histamine than of protein. In addition, some of the amine and nucleotide release may also result from a nonlytic process, as described below.

Further evidence that the reaction of soluble antigen, antibody and plasma with platelets resulted in complement-mediated cytolysis came from a study of the platelet energy requirements for the reaction. Since omission of glucose from the medium was not inhibitory, the cytolysis appears not to involve the platelet glycolytic pathway. This may be contrasted with the nonlytic release system. The lytic release reaction was not inhibited by DFP or chelating agents (after an initial period to allow C1 activation) or by aspirin. These combined findings serve to support the passive part played by the platelet in the release of its constituents by the lytic mechanism and contrast with the findings for the nonlytic reaction.

Antiplatelet antibody in the presence of the complete complement sequence also causes lysis of platelets. In nearly all respects, such cytolysis (13) is identical with the reaction described herein induced by a soluble antigen unrelated to the platelet membrane, antibody and plasma. Thus, the platelet morphology (13), time course of reaction, release of enzymes and rubidium (Fig. 6) and lack of active platelet participation are all very similar. In contrast, antiplatelet antibody in the absence of plasma (complement components) also induces a release of histamine, but this is an active and specific release (13) and more closely resembles the complement-dependent (nonlytic) release reaction.

It is suggested that the antigen-antibody complement complex is brought into close contact with the platelet surface by the C3 immune adherence process which thus causes platelet clumping. When C6-deficient plasma was employed some evidence of immune complexes within vacuoles or canaliculi was seen, but whether this involved active phagocytosis is not certain. In normal plasma the later-acting complement components reacting with the immune complex in close apposition to the platelet membrane may be able to act on this membrane to produce lysis. Evidence for the transfer of complement components from sensitized erythrocytes to nonsensitized cells has recently been reported (23). Moreover, the transfer was more effective with increased concentrations of reactants. In the platelet system, immune adherence would seem to bring the activation of C5–9 to a site right against the platelet membranes. If this activation of later-acting complement components has to occur at the site and occasion of transfer, as suggested by studies with erythrocytes (23), the apparent "decay" of antigen and antibody preincubated with plasma before addition of platelets (4, 6, 9) may be more fully explained.

Lysis of platelets by this process results in liberation of the platelet constituents. In addition to the materials examined, potentially harmful lysosomal enzymes and permeability factors (24) will also be released. In addition, platelet-clotting factors may be liberated, and occasionally experiments involving a high percentage of histamine release (lysis) did result in coagulation.

Complement-dependent (nonlytic) release. Adherence of platelets to a particulate antigen that has fixed complement components to C3 results in release of vasoactive amines (9). Components beyond C5 are not required. Additional study of this reaction has revealed clear differences between it and the lytic release reaction in addition to the lack of the requirement for C6.

The initial process is, in both cases, adherence of platelets induced by the C3. In the nonlytic reaction, when the complement was already fixed to the erythrocytes or zymosan, the platelet clumping was immediate. Following adherence there was a release of histamine, serotonin and nucleotides, a process which reached completion within 10 min. Very low levels of β glucuronidase were also released, as seen when the effect of thrombin on platelets was studied (25–27). Acid phosphatase, lactic dehydrogenase and rubidium were not released. In addition, platelets which had undergone such a reaction with ZC were still capable of incorporating rubidium. The reaction involving soluble antigen, antibody, plasma and platelets was shown by Siraganian *et al.* (14) to impair the rubidium uptake, which implied damage to the potassium pump mechanism.

Morphologic changes in the nonlytic reaction involved apparent disappearance of both α granules and dense bodies, and of the canalicular system, within the platelets that were adherent to the zymosan. Microtubules became disorganized. This type of change is common to the action of antiplatelet antibody in the absence of complement (13) and to the reactions involving neutrophils (12). There is a considerable amount of evidence that platelet serotonin is contained within the dense bodies (28–31). Since histamine and serotonin were released under identical conditions, to the same degree and following the same time course, it is likely that these granules contain both the histamine and the serotonin in the rabbit platelet. Consequently, release of these vasoactive amines might be expected to result in disappearance of the dense bodies. No evidence of extrusion of granules was obtained. Moreover, the α granules which are thought to contain lysosomal enzymes also disappeared (or lost the properties which made them visible) although in this reaction no significant release of lysosomal enzymes was detected.

The nonlytic reaction requires an active participation of the platelet in the release process. In the environment, glucose and calcium are necessary. Omission of glucose from the medium prevents other platelet activities (32) and its inhibitory effect suggests the need for platelet energy metabolism. The adherence process activates a proesterase on or in the platelet which can then be inhibited by DFP and which is involved in the release process. Aspirin, which is known to affect platelet aggregating and releasing reactions (33, 34), probably by interacting with and acetylating components of the cell membrane (35, 36), is also inhibitory to the complement-dependent, nonlytic release reaction. Adenosine inhibited the release of histamine by ZC, but only slightly inhibited the clumping. This suggested that the release of ADP in the reaction might (under conditions of vigorous stirring) augment the clumping effect of the C3 immune adherence. The initial stimulus, however, for release of histamine and for ADP probably arises from the adherence and may be another example of surface activation. The potent inhibitory effect of adenosine on the histamine release may indicate an action of this substance on the platelet additional to its activity in inhibiting ADP-induced aggregation.

In vivo, both lytic and nonlytic reactions may occur simultaneously. It appears that the adherence of platelets to a surface may be important in the active stimulation of the release of vasoactive amines and involvement of platelets with surfaces such as vascular basement membrane or endothelium *in vivo* might lead to this type of reaction. In man, C3 immune adherence of platelets does not occur, but adherence to fixed γ globulin does induce amine release, possibly by a similar process to that of the nonlytic reaction of the rabbit platelets.

Acknowledgments. The author thanks Dr. C. Cochrane for his help and advice, Mrs. D. Durham for preparing the sections for electron microscopy, Miss C. Brown for technical assistance and

Mrs. K. Prescott and Mr. G. Sandford for the illustrations.

REFERENCES

1. Henson, P. and Cochrane, C., Fed. Proc., *28:* 312, 1969.
2. Henson, P. M. and Cochrane, C. G., J. Exp. Med., *129:* 153, 1969.
3. Humphrey, J. H. and Jaques, R., J. Physiol., *128:* 9, 1955.
4. Barbaro, J. F., J. Immun., *86:* 369, 1961.
5. Barbaro, J. F., J. Immun., *86:* 377, 1961.
6. Gocke, D. J. and Osler, A. G., J. Immun., *94:* 236, 1965.
7. Gocke, D. J., J. Immun., *94:* 247, 1965.
8. Bryant, R. and DesPrez, R., Clin. Res., *16:* 318, 1968.
9. Henson, P. M. and Cochrane, C. G., J. Exp. Med., *129:* 167, 1969.
10. Henson, P. M., Fed. Proc., *28:* 1721, 1969.
11. Henson, P. M. and Cochrane, C. G., in *Cellular and Humoral Mechanisms of Anaphylaxis and Allergy*, Edited by H. Z. Movat, S. Karger, Basel, 1969.
12. Henson, P. M., J. Immun., *105:* 490, 1970.
13. Henson, P. M., J. Immun., *104:* 924, 1970.
14. Aster, R. H. and Jandl, J. H., J. Clin. Invest., *43:* 843, 1964.
15. Siraganian, R. P., Secchi, A. G. and Osler, A. G., J. Immun., *101:* 1130, 1140 and 1148, 1968.
16. Wroblewski, F. and LaDue, J. S., Proc. Soc. Exp. Biol. Med., *90:* 210, 1955.
17. Linhardt, K. and Walter, K., in *Methods of Enzymatic Analysis*, Edited by H. U. Bergmeyer, p. 779, Academic Press, New York, 1965.
18. Fishman, W. H., in *Methods of Enzymatic Analysis*, Edited by H. U. Bergmeyer, p. 869, Academic Press, New York, 1965.
19. Lamprecht, W. and Trautschold, I., in *Methods of Enzymatic Analysis*, Edited by H. U. Bergmeyer, p. 543, Academic Press, New York, 1965.
20. Adam, H., in *Methods of Enzymatic Analysis*, Edited by H. U. Bergmeyer, p. 573, Academic Press, New York, 1965.
21. Packham, M. A., Nishizawa, E. E. and Mustard, J. F., Biochem. Pharmacol., *17* (Suppl.): 171, 1968.
22. Green, H., Fleischer, R. A., Barrow, P. and Goldberg, B., J. Exp. Med., *109:* 511, 1959.
23. Götze, O. and Müller-Eberhard, H. J., Fed. Proc., *28:* 818, 1969.
24. Mustard, J. F., Movat, H. Z., Macmorine, D. R. L. and Senyi, A., Proc. Soc. Exp. Biol. Med., *119:* 988, 1965.
25. Holmsen, H. and Day, H. J., Nature, *219:* 760, 1968.
26. Davey, M. G. and Lüscher, E. F., Biochim. Biophys. Acta, *165:* 490, 1968.
27. Mills, D. C. B., Robb, I. A. and Roberts, G. C. K., J. Physiol., *195:* 715, 1968.
28. White, J. C., Amer. J. Path., *53:* 791, 1968.
29. Wurzel, M., Marcus, A. J. and Zweifach, B. W., Proc. Soc. Exp. Biol. Med., *118:* 468, 1965.
30. Wood, J. G., Texas Rep. Biol. Med., *23:* 828, 1965.
31. Tranzer, J. P., DaPrada, M. and Pletscher, A., Nature, *212:* 1574, 1966.
32. Kinlough, R. L., Packham, M. A. and Mustard, J. F., Fed. Proc., *28:* 509, 1969.
33. Weiss, H. J., Aledort, L. M. and Kochwa, S., J. Clin. Invest., *47:* 2169, 1968.
34. Evans, G., Packham, M. A., Nishizawa, E. E., Mustard, J. F. and Murphy, E. A., J. Exp. Med., *128:* 877, 1968.
35. Zucker, M. B., Peterson, J. and Grant, R., Fed. Proc., *28:* 576, 1969.
36. Al-Mondhiry, H., Marcus, A. and Spaet, T. H., Fed. Proc., *28:* 576, 1969.

THE JOURNAL OF IMMUNOLOGY
Vol. 105, No. 2, August 1970
Printed in U.S.A.

MECHANISMS OF RELEASE OF CONSTITUENTS FROM RABBIT PLATELETS BY ANTIGEN-ANTIBODY COMPLEXES AND COMPLEMENT

II. Interaction of Platelets with Neutrophils[1]

PETER M. HENSON[2]

From the Department of Experimental Pathology, Scripps Clinic and Research Foundation, La Jolla, California 92037

Received for publication November 17, 1969

The presence of neutrophils during the reaction of platelets with immune complexes increased the release of vasoactive amines. Two different neutrophil-dependent release mechanisms were involved, both requiring the complement system through C3, but not beyond C5. Soluble antigen, antibody in excess, C6-deficient plasma, platelets and neutrophils were used to demonstrate the first neutrophil-dependent mechanism. Release of vasoactive amines and nucleotides from the platelets followed the clumping together of the platelets, neutrophils and antigen-antibody-complement complexes. The release reaction required glucose and did not result from platelet lysis. Neutrophil procoagulant activity leading to thrombin activation in close proximity to the platelets in the clumps appeared to cause the vasoactive amine release. In the second process particulate antigens such as zymosan, which have fixed complement components, released increased histamine, serotonin and nucleotides from platelets when neutrophils were included in the reaction. The augmentation of release by neutrophils again required glucose and activated esterases and followed the aggregation of zymosan-complement, platelets and neutrophils.

Rabbit platelets release their content of the vasoactive amines histamine and serotonin upon reaction with antigen-antibody complexes (1–4). This release has been shown to result from two different processes, both requiring complement (5, 6). One involves lysis of the platelet and release of most of the platelet constituents (complement-dependent, lytic reaction) and the other involves an active release of vasoactive amines (complement-dependent, nonlytic release). Both reactions appear to follow an initial adherence of the complexes induced by fixed C3.

Platelets and neutrophils are often found together in inflammatory reactions *in vivo*. In addition, neutrophils, as well as rabbit platelets, undergo a C3 immune adherence reaction (7, 8). *In vivo* neutrophils and platelets have been implicated in such reactions as the generalized Shwartzman reaction (9) and a complement-dependent passive cutaneous anaphylactic reaction (10). For these reasons, the possible interaction of neutrophils with antigen-antibody-complement complexes and platelets was examined. Two processes whereby the presence of neutrophils augmented the release of constituents from platelets were found (11) and will be described.

MATERIALS AND METHODS

The methods of preparation of platelets, diluents, plasma and antisera have been described in the preceding paper (6).

Neutrophils. Neutrophils were washed from the peritoneal cavity of normal adult New Zealand White rabbits following an intraperitoneal injection of 200 ml of phosphate-buffered saline or 0.1% glycogen in saline 5 to 16 hr previously. The neutrophils were harvested into saline with 5 units/ml heparin or 0.005 M EDTA, washed three times and resuspended in Tyrode's solution with gelatin.

For some experiments peripheral neutrophils

[1] This is Publication 365 from the Department of Experimental Pathology, Scripps Clinic and Research Foundation. The work was supported by United States Public Health Service Grant AI-07007-04.

[2] Supported by United States Public Health Service Training Grant 5 T6 GM683.

were obtained following sedimentation of erythrocytes from blood (0.005 M EDTA as anticoagulant) with one-fourth volume 6% dextran. The leukocyte-rich supernatant was freed of platelets by repeated centrifugation for 5 min at 160 × G. Alternatively, EDTA anticoagulated blood was centrifuged for 20 min at 400 to 450 × G. The platelet-rich plasma and the buffy coat layer were removed and the remaining erythrocytes and leukocytes were resuspended with an equal volume of 2.5% gelatin in saline. The erythrocytes were sedimented at 1 × G and 37°C for 30 min and the leukocyte-rich supernatant was removed and washed. This technique gave neutrophil suspensions with some erythrocyte contamination but containing 15% (or less) mononuclear leukocytes.

Test conditions. These were identical to those described in the preceding paper (6), but with the addition of neutrophils. A 30-min incubation period was employed at the end of which the cells were sedimented and the supernatant examined for release of platelet constituents. With a reaction volume of 2.5 ml, 2.5 × 10^8 platelets were used with 10^8 particles of ZC (zymosan which had fixed complement components through C3 (6)) or 0.5 μg bovine serum albumin (BSA), 50 μg anti-BSA and 10% plasma. For study of release of enzymes or electron microscopy the quantities of ZC, antigen, antibody, platelets and neutrophils were increased 10-fold.

Assays. Histamine and serotonin were assayed on the atropinized guinea pig ileum and estrus rat uterus, respectively. Lactic dehydrogenase (12), β glucuronidase (13), acid phosphatase (14), adenosine triphosphate (ATP) (15), adeonsine diphosphate (ADP) and adenosine monophosphate (AMP) (16) were determined by standard procedures. Sedimented platelets and neutrophils were lysed with Triton × 100 or freeze-thawing so that total levels of each material could be determined and the percentage released calculated.

Platelet aggregation and morphology. Suspensions of platelets and neutrophils undergoing the reaction were examined for decrease in optical density in an aggregometer (Chronolog Corp., Broomall, Pa.) to determine the extent of aggregation. Cell morphology was studied by examination of ultrathin sections in the electron microcope. Both techniques are described in the preceding paper (6).

Inhibitors. The use of diisopropyl fluorophosphate (DFP), adenosine, acetyl salicylate and Mg EGTA has been described previously (6). 2-Deoxyglucose (10^{-3} M final concentration) was used under conditions in which the glucose had been omitted from the medium and dialyzed away from the plasma. The inhibitors were also tested against the release of histamine by 0.05 units of bovine thrombin (Parke, Davis Co., Detroit, Mich.).

RESULTS

In order to determine the effect of neutrophils on the complement-dependent release of histamine from platelets, increasing numbers of neutrophils were included in the two reactions (Fig. 1). Addition of neutrophils from the rabbit peritoneum to 2.5 × 10^8 platelets and washed zymosan-complement (ZC) (2.5 × 10^8 particles, 3.6 mg Z) resulted in an increased release of histamine. The effect of a control preparation of zymosan treated with EDTA complement was not appreciably altered by the presence of neutrophils.

In a similar way, neutrophils augmented the release of histamine induced by antigen, antibody in excess (12 μg N anti-BSA plus 0.1 μg N BSA), plasma and platelets (complement-dependent lytic release). In this case the control release without antigen was increased by high levels of neutrophils.

To more easily demonstrate the effect of neutrophils on antigen, antibody and platelets in the presence of plasma, C6-deficient plasma was used (Table I). BSA and anti-BSA did not release histamine from platelets in the presence of C6-deficient plasma (6), but when neutrophils were included massive clumping of platelets and neutrophils occurred and histamine was released. Under conditions of antigen excess the release did not occur. Table I shows, too, that the neutrophil-dependent release was inhibited in the cold. It may be noted that the ratio of neutrophils to platelets in either of these neutrophil-dependent reactions was of the order of 1:500.

Requirement for complement. When the zymosan-complement was prepared with plasma containing 0.005 EDTA to inhibit the uptake of complement, the neutrophil-platelet clumping and platelet histamine release did not occur (Fig. 1). Similarly, ZC prepared with cobra factor-treated (C3-depleted) plasma was also not effective.

Table II shows the inhibition of the reaction with soluble antigen, antibody and C6-deficient

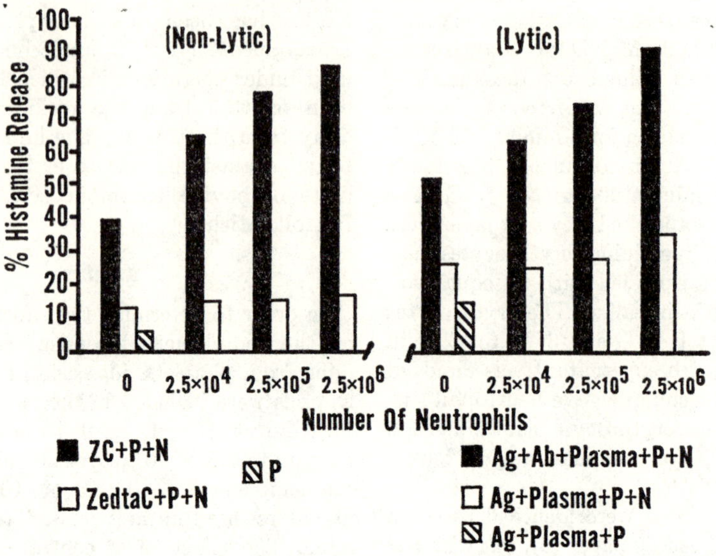

Figure 1. The augmentation by neutrophils of complement-dependent release of histamine from platelets. P, 2.5×10^8 platelets; ZC, 2.5×10^8 zymosan particles incubated with plasma to fix complement and then washed; Z EDTA C, zymosan incubated with EDTA-plasma (no complement fixed); Ag, 0.1 μg N BSA; Ab, 12 μg N anti-BSA; plasma, 10%. After 30 min at 37°C the percentage of released histamine was determined.

TABLE I

Release of histamine from platelets by antigen, antibody, neutrophils and C6-deficient plasma

BSA-anti-BSA	Plasma 10%	Incubation Temperature	Histamine Release: Without neutrophils	Histamine Release: With 5×10^6 neutrophils
			%	%
Antibody excess (20×)[a]	C6-def.	37°C	5	36
Antigen excess (5×)[b]	C6-def.	37°C	8	8
	C6-def.	37°C	4	9
Antibody excess	C6-def.	4°C	0	8

[a] BSA (0.1 μg N) + 12 μg Ab N.
[b] BSA (10 μg N) + 12 μg Ab N.

plasma when the plasma was depleted of C3 with cobra venom factor (5, 6), heated at 56°C for 30 min, or treated with EDTA. These results suggested the involvement of complement components through C3 in both types of reaction. That the neutrophils were not supplying C6 to the C6-deficient plasma was shown by unsuccessful attempts to restore the hemolytic activity of such plasma with the neutrophil preparations. Moreover, neither of the reactions with neutrophils resulted in platelet lysis (see below).

Morphology of platelets and neutrophils during the reactions. Samples of the reaction mixtures were removed after 15 and 30 min of incubation and the cells were examined by electron microscopy.

The reaction with zymosan-complement is shown in Figure 2*a*. Large clumps of platelets, neutrophils and ZC were seen, and many of the ZC particles were phagocytosed by the neutro-

TABLE II

Effect of inhibition of complement activity on the release of platelet histamine induced by antigen, antibody, plasma and neutrophils

BSA + Anti-BSA + Platelets + Neutrophils +:[a]	Histamnie Release
	%
C6-def. plasma	56
C3-depleted (CoF), C6-def. plasma	7
Heated (56°C, 30 min) C6-def. plasma	8
C6-def. plasma + EDTA	7
(0.01 M)	8

[a] The quantities of reagents were those shown in Table III.

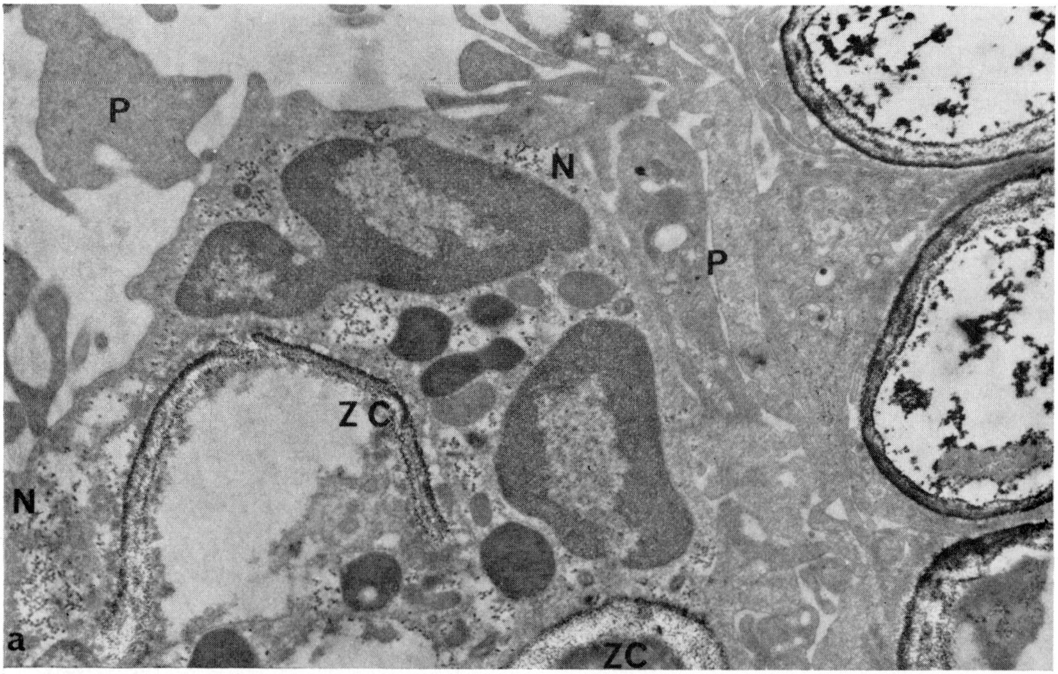

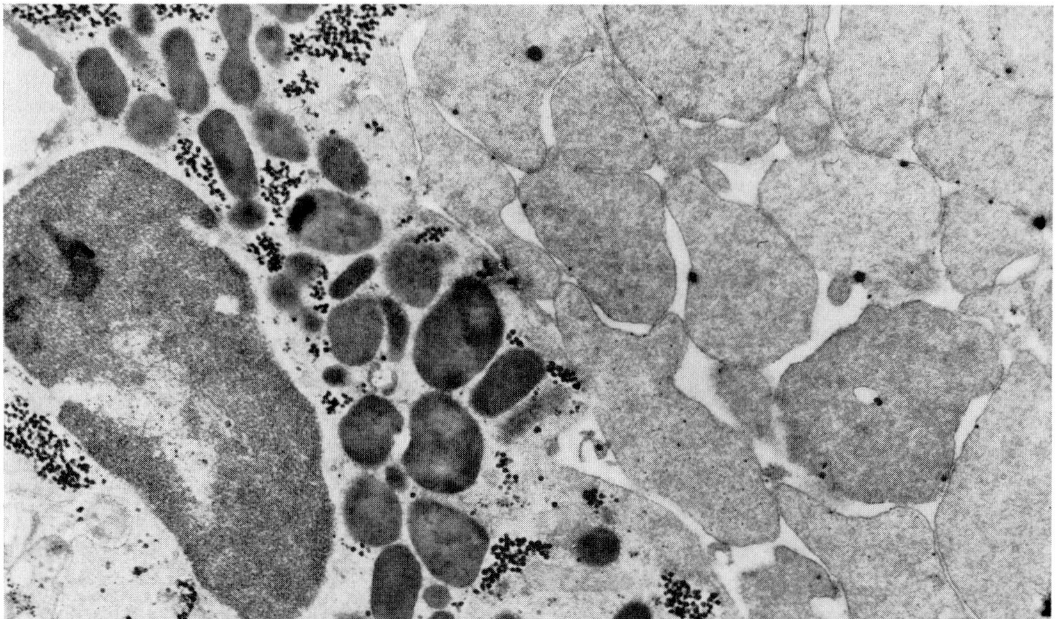

Figure 2. a, Platelets reacting with ZC and neutrophils. The quantities of materials used were those shown in Figure 3. Clumps of neutrophils (*N*), alexinated zymosan particles (*ZC*) and platelets (*P*) may be seen. The neutrophils have phagocytosed some of the ZC particles. Disappearance of granules and canaliculi from the platelets in the clump has occurred (× 18,250). *b*, Platelets reacting with antigen, antibody, complement and neutrophils. Ferritin, anti-ferritin (see reference 6) in antibody excess, normal plasma and platelets were incubated for 20 min at 37°C before fixation in glutaraldehyde at 37°C. Clumps of immune complexes, platelets and neutrophils occurred, and some of the complexes have been phagocytosed by the neutrophils (*arrows*). The platelets are closely packed in the clumps and also make close contact with the neutrophils. However, not all the platelets appear to be associated with immune complexes. The cytoplasm is homogeneous, and granules and canaliculi have disappeared (× 23,300).

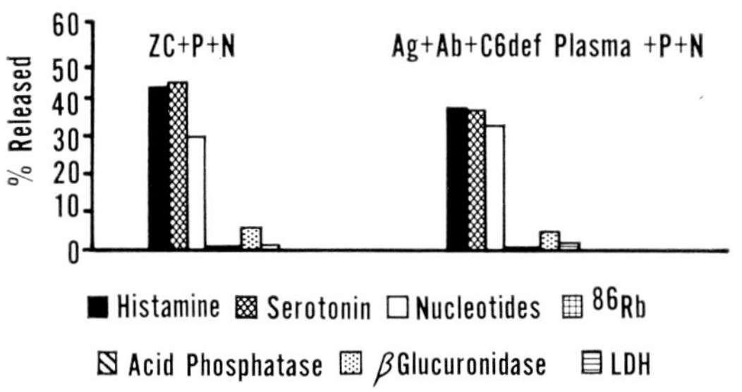

Figure 3. Release of intracellular constituents from platelets. P, 5×10^9 platelets; ZC, 2.5×10^9 particles of alexinated zymosan; N, 10^7 neutrophils; Ag, 2 μg N BSA; Ab, 200 μg N anti-BSA; C6-deficient plasma, 10%; LDH, lactic dehydrogenase; nucleotides, ATP, ADP and AMP. The amounts released after 30 min 37°C are expressed as a percentage of the total available. The results are representative of four similar experiments. As described in the text, control values have been subtracted so that the release shown is due to the presence of neutrophils.

phils. Interdigitation of platelet and neutrophil microvilli occurred. The platelets in the clumps exhibited changes similar to those seen when they were reacted with ZC without neutrophils (6), i.e., disappearance of granules and canaliculi from the platelets adherent to the ZC or neutrophils. Platelets on the outside of the clumps were less affected. Evidence of platelet lysis or of extensive phagocytosis of platelets by neutrophils was not seen.

To examine the reaction of antigen, antibody, C6-deficient plasma, platelets and neutrophils, ferritin was used as the antigen described previously (6). Again, large clumps of platelets, neutrophils and antigen-antibody-complement complexes were seen (Fig. 2*b*). Some phagocytosis of the immune complexes by the neutrophils was apparent. Many of the platelets in the clumps did not appear to be adherent to complexes, but showed an even, rounded profile. Complete disappearance of granules and canaliculi was observed but platelet lysis was not apparent.

Release of vasoactive amines, enzymes, nucleotides and rubidium from platelets. Both the neutrophil-dependent reactions (involving ZC or antigen, antibody and C6-deficient plasma) were examined for the release of a number of platelet constituents. Control reactions omitting platelets were included to determine the levels of materials released from the neutrophils. No histamine or serotonin was detected in the neutrophils, but low levels of nucleotides (5% to 12% of the amounts liberated by the platelets) were released by ZC. Any release from the neutrophils which was dependent upon the reaction with platelets, however, could not be determined. Other controls consisted of neutrophils and platelets incubated together without the releasing stimuli or platelets incubated with the stimuli in the absence of neutrophils. The relevant control values have been subtracted from the percentages given which thus represent the neutrophil-dependent release from the platelets.

Figure 3 depicts the results. In both reactions, a similar percentage of serotonin and the nucleotides ATP, ADP, and AMP were released. A small amount of β glucuronidase was also found in the supernatant after the reactions, but significant levels of rubidium 86, acid phosphatase and lactic dehydrogenase were not released. These findings suggest a similarity of the neutrophil-dependent reactions to the active release mechanisms attributed to the effect of ZC, antiplatelet antibody or thrombin on platelets (6, 7).

The inhibitory effect of hirudin. In order to determine whether thrombin was involved in the reactions, hirudin, a potent inhibitor of thrombin, was tested. The results are shown in Figure 4 and

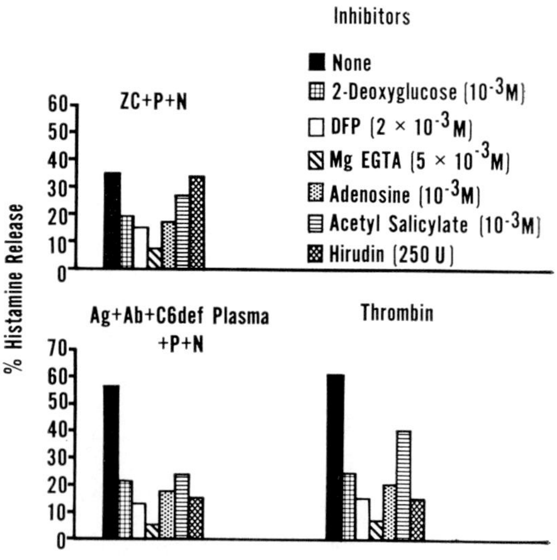

Figure 4. The effect of inhibitors on the neutrophil-dependent release of histamine from platelets. The quantities of materials used are shown in Table III and in *Materials and Methods*. DFP and Mg EGTA were added after 7 min of incubation. 2-Deoxyglucose was used in a glucose-free system (see reference 6).

TABLE III

The effect of hirudin on the neutrophil-dependent reactions in the presence and absence of plasma

Reaction	Histamine Release	
	Without hirudin	With 25 units hirudin
	%	%
BSA + anti-BSA + C6-def. plasma + P + N[a]	48	9
C6-def. plasma + P + N	17	9
ZC + P + N	43	46
ZC + C6-def. plasma + P + N	89	45

[a] BSA, 0.5 μg N; antibody, 25 μg N; plasma, 10%; platelets (P), 2.5×10^8; neutrophils (N), 10^6; ZC, 10^8 particles.

Table III. A clear difference between the neutrophil-dependent reaction with ZC and that with BSA, anti-BSA and C6-deficient plasma was found, since the former was not inhibited by 250 units of hirudin, whereas the reaction in plasma was inhibited, even by 2.5 units (not shown in the Table).

The inhibition by hirudin of the release of histamine from platelets by antigen, antibody, plasma and neutrophils suggested that thrombin or a thrombin-like enzyme was participating in the reaction. When the reaction with ZC was performed in the presence of plasma (Table III) it was seen that an increment of additional histamine release associated with the presence of plasma was again inhibited by hirudin, but that the effect of ZC itself was unaffected.

The ability of antigen, antibody, platelets and neutrophils to generate a thrombin-like activity in the presence of plasma was not confined to any one preparation of cells or plasma. In some experiments the effect was so strong that the heparin (10 units/ml) in the plasma was not sufficient to prevent clotting of the reaction mixture.

The requirement for glucose and the effect of inhibitors on the neutrophil-dependent reactions. Figure 4 shows that the combination of omission of glucose from the medium (the plasma glucose was dialyzed away) and 10^{-3} M 2-deoxyglucose on inhibition of glucose metabolism was markedly inhibitory to the two neutrophil-dependent release reactions. For comparison, the similar effect on the release of histamine from platelets by thrombin is also shown. The results indicated a requirement for glucose.

DFP and Mg EGTA were also inhibitory to the reactions. In the system with antigen, antibody and plasma these inhibitors were added after 7 min incubation to allow C1 activation. Even after this time period both agents were inhibitory. Other agents tested were adenosine and aspirin. They were inhibitory to both reactions, although under the conditions used (1 to 2 min preincubation with the platelets) aspirin was less effective than adenosine.

The inhibitory effect of DFP could be due to its action on existing esterases on the neutrophils, platelets or ZC. Pretreatment of ZC with DFP was shown to have no effect on its ability to release histamine from platelets, although the pretreatment was effective in inhibiting the action of thrombin fixed to zymosan (6). In a similar way, neutrophils and platelets were treated with DFP, washed and then tested for their ability to participate in the neutrophil-dependent reactions (Table IV). Pretreatment of the neutrophils with DFP did not affect either reaction and pretreatment of the platelets only slightly diminished the reaction in plasma and did not affect that with ZC.

The results indicate the requirement for calcium in the medium, and serine esterase activation and energy metabolism in the platelets or neutrophils.

Platelet aggregation in the neutrophil-dependent release reactions. Platelet aggregation was determined by observing the decrease in optical density in an aggregometer at 37°C with stirring at 1100 rpm. Figure 5 depicts the effect of addition of ZC to a suspension of platelets. Following an initial increase in light scattering due to the zymosan, the ZC and platelets clumped together by the process of C3 immune adherence (6). When neutrophils were also present an increased clearing of the suspension was observed. The clumping started immediately and was complete in 10 min. Increased release of histamine was also observed. No clumping or histamine release occurred if zymosan which had been incubated with EDTA-

TABLE IV

The effect of pretreating platelets or neutrophils with DFP on the histamine release from platelets

Reaction	Histamine Release
	%
Ag + Ab + C6-def. plasma + P + N[a]	80
Ag + Ab + C6-def. plasma + pretreated P[b] + N	60
Ag + Ab + C6-def. plasma + P + pretreated N	78
ZC + P + N	88
ZC + pretreated P + N	80
ZC + P + pretreated N	85

[a] The quantities of reagents are those shown in Table III.
[b] Platelets and neutrophils were pretreated for 30 min at 4°C with 2×10^{-3} M DFP.

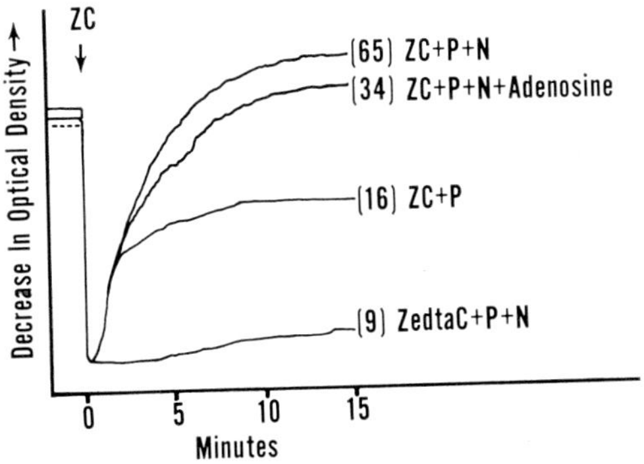

Figure 5. Aggregation of platelets by ZC and neutrophils. P, 1×10^9 platelets; ZC, 1.25×10^8 zymosan particles incubated with plasma to fix complement and then washed; Z EDTA C, zymosan incubated with EDTA-plasma; N, 1×10^6; adenosine, 2×10^{-4} M. The reaction was performed at 37°C with stirring at 1100 rpm and the decrease in optical density produced by cell aggregation is shown. The percentages of histamine released are shown in parentheses.

plasma was added. To try to ascertain the role of ADP aggregation in this neutrophil-augmented clumping, adenosine was included in the reaction. Inhibition of histamine release was seen and also some inhibition of the optical density decrease suggesting at least a partial role for ADP under these reactive conditions.

When the effect on platelets of BSA, anti-BSA, C6-deficient plasma and neutrophils was examined in this way (Fig. 6), again an additional clumping was seen, attributable to the presence of neutrophils. This was accompanied by an increased release of histamine. Although hirudin did inhibit the increased clumping and release to some extent, its effect under these conditions was not as great as when the reaction was performed with increased quantities of reagents (Table III) in test tubes shaken only mildly (compared with vigorous stirring). Adenosine was inhibitory to both the clumping and release. It may be noted that the inhibitory effect of adenosine on both the reactions was predominantly an effect on the neutrophil augmentation, since the reactions without neutrophils were but little affected by adenosine (6).

Peripheral neutrophils. Neutrophils obtained from the blood of normal rabbits were examined for their ability to give the neutrophil-dependent release reactions with platelets. Table V shows that both types of reaction were obtained and that the effect of BSA, anti-BSA, plasma and neutrophils on platelets was inhibited by hirudin. The reaction of peripheral neutrophils was there-

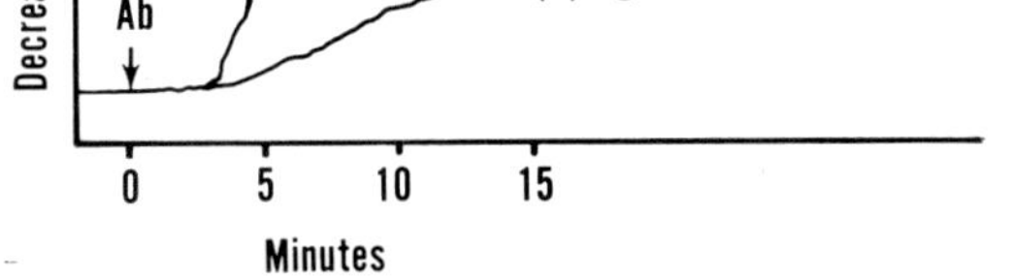

Figure 6. Aggregation of platelets by antigen, antibody plasma and neutrophils. P, 5×10^8 platelets; Ag, 0.2 μg N BSA; Ab, 20 μg N anti-BSA; C6-deficient plasma, 10%; neutrophils, 10^6; hirudin, 250 units; adenosine, 2×10^{-4} M. The reaction was performed at 37°C with stirring at 1100 rpm. The percentages of histamine released are shown in parentheses.

TABLE V

Neutrophil-dependent release of histamine by peripheral neutrophils

Reaction	Histamine Release	
	Without hirudin	With 25 units hirudin
	%	%
Ag + Ab + C6-def. plasma + P + N[a]	43	17
C6-def. plasma + P + N	19	14
ZC + P + N	34	30
ZC + P	17	17

[a] The quantities of reagents used were those shown in Table III. Neutrophils (N) (5×10^5/tube) were obtained from the blood.

TABLE VI

The release of material from neutrophils incubated with ZC and its effect on platelets

Platelets + Supernatant from:	Histamine Release		
	Tube[a]	Aggregometer[b]	Aggregometer + 2×10^{-4} M adenosine
	%	%	%
Neutrophils (5×10^6) + ZC (5×10^8)	17	19	6
Neutrophils + ZC EDTA C	6	7	
Neutrophils	6	6	
Neutrophils + Ag + Ab + C6-def. plasma	9		

[a] Incubated with mild shaking in a test tube.

[b] Incubated in an aggregometer cuvette with stirring at 1100 rpm.

fore similar to that of cells obtained from the peritoneum. However, the amount of histamine released from platelets by peripheral neutrophils, antigen, antibody and plasma was more variable and generally less than the amount released by peritoneal neutrophils.

Release of substances from neutrophils and the effect of neutrophil lysates. Since a ratio of 1 neutrophil to 500 platelets was capable of inducing neutrophil-dependent histamine release in the ZC system, the possibility of release of a soluble factor from the neutrophils was examined. It may be seen (Table VI) that the supernatant fluid from neutrophils incubated for 7.5 min at 37°C with ZC induced low levels of histamine release from platelets and caused transient platelet clumping. Both effects were inhibited by adenosine, suggesting that they were due to released ADP. Moreover, low levels (28 nanomols) of released ADP were detected by the enzymatic assay when 2×10^7 neutrophils were incubated with 5×10^9 ZC particles for 30 min at 37°C. The supernatant fluid from neutrophils incubated alone or with Z EDTA C did not cause histamine release. ADP release may therefore play some contributory role in the reaction.

Neutrophils apparently contain and/or release materials which can lead to active thrombin in plasma. To examine this effect further, neutrophils were lysed by cycles of freezing and thawing in distilled water. After restoration to isotonicity the lysates were examined for their effect on platelets (Table VII). It may be seen that histamine was released only when plasma was present and that this effect appeared to be due to thrombin, since it was inhibited by hirudin, and clotting occurred if the amount of lysate was increased so that the effect of the heparin in the plasma (10 units/ml) was overcome.

The effect of neutrophils on platelets brought together by nonimmunologic means. Platelets and neutrophils were centrifuged (650 × G for 10 min) together in the presence or absence of plasma and the hirudin-inhibitable histamine release was determined (Table VIII). In the presence of plasma only, platelets that had been brought mechanically into close contact with neutrophils released their histamine.

DISCUSSION

The presence of neutrophils during the reaction of rabbit platelets with antigen-antibody-comple-

TABLE VII

The effect of lysates of neutrophils on histamine release from platelets

Reaction	Neutrophil Lysate (Equivalent of 5×10^6 N)	Histamine Release	
		Without hirudin	With 25 units hirudin
		%	%
Ag + Ab + C6-def. plasma + P[a]	+	74	33
	−	17	20
C6-def. plasma + P	+	80	20
	−	15	16
ZC + P	+	30	44
	−	36	37
P	+	13	12
	−	10	11

[a] The quantities of reagents were those shown in Table III.

TABLE VIII

The effect of bringing platelets and neutrophils into close contact by centrifugation[a]

Reaction	Histamine Release	
	Without hirudin	With 25 units hirudin
	%	%
Platelets + C6-def. plasma + neutrophils	75	45
Platelets + neutrophils	9	5
Platelets + C6-def. plasma	13	
Platelets	20	

[a] Peritoneal neutrophils (10^6) were centrifuged with 2.5×10^8 platelets in a volume of 2.5 ml with 10% plasma. The tube was incubated at 37°C for 5 min and the pellet was resuspended and incubated for a further 15 min before final centrifugation and assay of released histamine.

ment complexes has been shown to result in increased release of vasoactive amines and nucleotides. Two systems were used for study. One consisted of a reaction of zymosan which had fixed complement components (ZC), platelets and neutrophils in a plasma-free medium. The second comprised BSA, anti-BSA in antibody excess, C6-deficient plasma, platelets and neutrophils. The use of limited amounts of ZC, or C6-deficient plasma instead of normal plasma, minimized the release of vasoactive amines from platelets alone and allowed study of the neutrophil effects. Although C6-deficient plasma was employed for many of the reactions, the augmentation of histamine release by neutrophils was also observed with normal plasma.

Platelet aggregation and the role of complement in neutrophil-dependent reactions. The ability of neutrophils to augment the release of vasoactive amines from platelets apparently depended upon clumping of the cells by C3 immune adherence. Thus, C6-deficient plasma could be used as a complement source in both reactions, but the histamine release and the accompanying platelet clumping were inhibited when the plasma C3 was depleted with cobra venom factor. A requirement for complement components through C3 is suggested and the initial platelet clumping appears to result from C3 immune adherence as seen in the reactions of platelets without neutrophils (6). During the incubation of ZC or antigen, antibody and plasma with platelets, additional aggregation was observed when neutrophils were included. Some of this neutrophil-dependent clumping may be due to released ADP acting on the platelets (see below), since adenosine gave partial inhibition. The clumping was measured by optical density decrease so that phagocytosis of zymosan particles by neutrophils might contribute to the additional decrease. However, studies with neutrophils and ZC alone have shown that this contribution is likely to be minimal. The optical density decrease was shown not to result from platelet lysis by electron microscopy. Finally, neutrophils also adhere to fixed C3 and are thus incorporated into the C3 immune adherence clumps, probably providing opportunities for more platelet-platelet or platelet-neutrophil contact. Evidence for the importance of this cell-cell contact was provided by centrifugation of neutrophils and platelets together. In the presence of plasma this procedure induced release of vasoactive amines from the platelets and thus mimicked the immune adherence effect of the immune complexes.

The mechanism of action of neutrophils on platelets. The effect of neutrophils on platelets induced by ZC in the absence of plasma resulted in release of vasoactive amines and nucleotides. The release process required the participation of esterases and energy metabolism in the platelets, since DFP and 2-deoxyglucose were inhibitory. Pretreatment of either the neutrophils or platelets with DFP was not inhibitory, suggesting that as with ZC and platelets alone a platelet esterase was activated by the reaction and was only then available for DFP inhibition. The reaction was also inhibited by aspirin and adenosine and required the presence of environmental calcium. These characteristics were similar to those of the reaction of ZC with platelets in the absence of neutrophils (6) and suggest an active, energy-requiring release of histamine, serotonin and nucleotides from the platelet, although in this case the inhibition might also have been on the neutrophil effect. The active nature of the release process was confirmed by finding no platelet lysis by electron microscopy and no acid phosphatase or lactic dehydrogenase released. Rubidium, too, was not liberated significantly when compared with the controls.

The low numbers of neutrophils required for the reaction suggested the release of an active material from the neutrophils. Since, in the absence of plasma, no effect of the thrombin-generating material in neutrophils could be found (suggesting an insufficiency of the necessary clotting factors and prothrombin on the surface of the washed platelets), thrombin did not appear to be involved. Moreover, hirudin was not inhibitory. A release of low levels (28 nanomols) of ADP from a large number of neutrophils (2×10^7) incubated with ZC was demonstrated and was able to induce clumping of a suspension of platelets stirred at 1100 rpm in the aggregometer. However, the ability of ZC and neutrophils to release vasoactive amines from platelets could be elicited with 5×10^5 neutrophils and was effective in a tube with only mild shaking, i.e., under conditions where the ADP effect is less. In addition, adenosine only partly inhibited the platelet clumping. It appeared, therefore, that although ADP might contribute to the platelet aggregation and release of histamine, it was unlikely to be the sole cause. Platelet-platelet, platelet-neutrophil and platelet-ZC contact induced by the C3 immune adherence may lead to the release of vasoactive amines by a similar contact activation process as for the reaction of ZC with platelets alone.

The role of thrombin generation in plasma by neutrophils in the release of vasoactive amines from platelets. In the presence of plasma, the reaction of immune complexes, platelets and neutrophils results in release of histamine which was inhibited by hirudin. With strong reactions, moreover, clotting of the plasma occurred even in the presence of the heparin used as an anticoagulant. This suggested that generation of thrombin might be participating in the reaction. While clumping of platelets and neutrophils by C3 immune adherence played a major role in this mechanism, it was found that merely centrifuging the cells together in the presence of plasma, i.e., without immune reactants, was also effective in bringing about release of histamine. This release was in great part inhibitable by hirudin, suggesting that thrombin had been activated.

Preliminary attempts have been made to characterize the activator of this thrombin-like activity. Neutrophils lysed by freezing and thawing in distilled water without the addition of plasma had no direct action on platelets or platelets reacting with ZC. This finding that the thrombin-like activity does not reside *per se* in the neutrophil was confirmed when it was found that pretreating the neutrophils with DFP did not affect their reactivity. Plasma was at all times required for the action of neutrophil lysates on platelets. Preliminary study has shown that peritoneal neutrophils will accelerate the coagulation of normal rabbit plasma. Moreover, Rapaport and Hjort (17) have shown that rabbit peritoneal neutrophils have tissue thromboplastic activity capable of initiating the extrinsic coagulation sequence. Such a neutrophil thromboplastin could therefore account for generation of thrombin in the experiments reported herein.

Whole neutrophils required antigen and antibody as well as plasma in the reaction mixture for maximal histamine release. The effect of the immune complexes could therefore be to induce release of thromboplastic material from the neutrophils. Attempts to detect this directly were unsuccessful. When the supernatant from the incubation of antigen, antibody, C6-deficient plasma and neutrophils was added to platelets, release of vasoactive amines failed to occur. This could have been because no such thromboplastic activity was released, or because it had already acted on the plasma factors and generated thrombin, which had then been inhibited by the heparin present. It appeared, therefore, that generation of thrombin activity by material present on the neutrophil or perhaps in part released or activated by phagocytosis of complexes then leads to thrombin-induced histamine release from the platelets. Platelets may also contribute to the thrombin-generating activity of the neutrophils, possibly through the action of platelet factor 4 which is known to inhibit heparin (18).

The use of inhibitors demonstrated that the effect of the antigen, antibody, C6-deficient plasma and neutrophils on the platelets was similar to the effect of thrombin. Thus the histamine release was prevented if the glucose in medium was replaced with 2-deoxyglucose, or if calcium was removed. DFP, adenosine and acetyl salicylate were also inhibitory. The pattern of inhibition with these agents was seen to be identical when the effects of thrombin and of the neutrophil-dependent reaction were compared. The results suggest a requirement for calcium and platelet energy metabolism for release. DFP probably inhibits the thrombin directly, and aspirin is known to prevent many platelet aggregation and release reactions (19–21). The morphology of the platelets undergoing the reaction was similar to those in other reactions leading to an active release of vasoactive amines (6, 8). Thus a homogeneous cytoplasm was seen with apparent disappearance of granules and canaliculi. Lysis was not observed and this was confirmed when the vasoactive amines and nucleotides were found to be the predominant materials released. Although low levels of β glucuronidase were detected, as has also been found with thrombin (22–24) and with other active release reactions (6, 8), the percentages released were not comparable to those of the vasoactive amines.

Immune complexes reacting with whole complement, platelets and neutrophils *in vivo* are likely to initiate to varying degrees all the reactions described in this and the preceding paper. Thus the complement-dependent nonlytic reaction may be augmented by the ubiquitous neutrophils and ADP release, and the presence of clotting factors can lead to thrombin generation. Moreover, since late-acting complement components are also present, platelet lysis and release of constituents including enzymes, would result. Possible release of platelet clotting factors could thus contribute to thrombin generation and fibrin formation.

Several experimental immunologic reactions display *in vivo* many of the features of the reactions analyzed *in vitro* in this and the preceding paper (6). A unique passive cutaneous anaphylactic reaction has been described in rabbits which was inhibited by depletion of platelets, neutrophils or C3 and was inhibited by antihistaminics (10). Such a reaction could in part result from interactions of antigen, antibody, complement, platelets and neutrophils. The finding that the vascular permeability associated with this reaction is also produced in C6-deficient rabbits would suggest that platelet lysis is not essential. Neutrophils and platelets have been found together in the lungs in systemic, aggregate anaphylaxis (25). The Shwartzman reaction (both local and generalized) is characterized by intravascular coagulation, clumps of neutrophils and platelets and fibrin deposition (9). Moreover, endotoxin has been shown to increase the "procoagulant" activity of neutrophils (26) and depletion of neutrophils (9) and reportedly in some instances removal of platelets (27) has diminished the severity of the reaction. It is possible, therefore, that neutrophil-platelet interactions of the type described above may contribute to the pathogenesis of the Shwartzman reaction and to other inflammatory processes in which neutrophils, platelets and fibrin deposition are common findings.

Acknowledgments. The author thanks Dr. C. Cochrane for his help and advice, Mrs. D. Durham for preparing the sections for electron microscopy. Miss C. Brown for technical assistance and Mrs. K. Prescott and Mr. G. Sandford for the illustrations.

REFERENCES

1. Humphrey, J. H. and Jaques, R., J. Physiol., *128:* 9, 1955.
2. Barbaro, J. F., J. Immun., *86:* 369, 1961.
3. Gocke, D. J., and Osler, A. G., J. Immun., *94:* 236, 1965.
4. Siraganian, R. P., Secchi, A. G. and Osler A. G., J. Immun., *101:* 1130, 1140 and 1148, 1968.
5. Henson, P. M. and Cochrane, C. G., J. Exp. Med., *129:* 167, 1969.
6. Henson, P. M., J. Immun., *105:* 490, 1970.
7. Nelson, D. S., in *CIBA Foundation Sym-*

posium: Complement, Edited by G. E. W. Wolstenholme and J. Knight, p. 22, Churchill, London, 1965.

8. Henson, P. M., Immunology, *16:* 107, 1969.
9. Lee, L. and Stetson, C. A., Jr., in *The Inflammatory Process*, Edited by B. W. Zweifach, L. Grant and R. T. McCluskey, p. 791, Academic Press, New York, 1965.
10. Henson, P. M. and Cochrane, C. G., J. Exp. Med., *129:* 153, 1969.
11. Henson, P. M. and Cochrane, C. G., in *Cellular and Humoral Mechanisms of Anaphylaxis and Allergy*, Edited by H. Z. Movat, S. Karger, Basel, 1969.
12. Wroblewski, F. and LaDue, J. S., Proc. Soc. Exp. Biol. Med., *90:* 210, 1955.
13. Fishman, W. H., in *Methods of Enzymatic Analysis*, Edited by H. U. Bergmeyer, p. 869, Academic Press, New York, 1965.
14. Linhardt, K. and Walter, K., in *Methods of Enzymatic Analysis*, Edited by H. U. Bergmeyer, p. 779, Academic Press, New York, 1965.
15. Lamprecht, W. and Trautschold, I., in *Methods of Enzymatic Analysis*, Edited by H. U. Bergmeyer, p. 543, Academic Press, New York, 1965.
16. Adam, H., in *Methods of Enzymatic Analysis*, Edited by H. U. Bergmeyer, p. 573, Academic Press, New York, 1965.
17. Rapaport, S. I. and Hjort, P. F., Thromb. Diath. Haemorrh., *17:* 222, 1967.
18. Niewiarowski, S. and Thomas, D. P., Nature *222:* 1269, 1969.
19. O'Brien, J. R., Lancet, *1:* 894, 1968.
20. Weiss, H. J., Aledort, L. M. and Kochwa, S., J. Clin. Invest., *47:* 2169, 1968.
21. Evans, G., Packham, M. A., Nishizawa, E. E., Mustard, J. F. and Murphy, E. A., J. Exp. Med., *128:* 877, 1968.
22. Holmsen, H. and Day, H. J., Nature, *219:* 760, 1968.
23. Davey, M. G. and Lüscher, E. F., Biochim. Biophys. Acta, *165:* 490, 1968.
24. Mills, D. C. B., Robb, I. A. and Roberts, G. C. K., J. Physiol., *195:* 715, 1968.
25. Movat, H. Z., Uriuhara, T., Taichman, N. S., Rowsell, H. C. and Mustard, J. F., Immunology, *14:* 637, 1968.
26. Niemetz, J., Fed. Proc., *28:* 442, 1969.
27. Margaretten, W., Fed. Proc., *28:* 510, 1969.

THE JOURNAL OF IMMUNOLOGY
Vol. 105, No. 2, August 1970

Printed in U.S.A.

IMMUNOCHEMICAL STUDIES OF PHOSPHOLIPIDS

VI. Haptenic Activity of Phosphatidylinositol and the Role of Lecithin as an Auxiliary Lipid

TATESHI KATAOKA AND SHOSHICHI NOJIMA

From the Faculty of Pharmaceutical Sciences, the University of Tokyo, Hongo, Tokyo, and the Department of Chemistry, the National Institute of Health, Shinagawa-ku, Tokyo, Japan

Received for publication October 27, 1969

Antiserum against the phosphatidylinositol hapten was obtained in rabbits by injecting a complex of the hapten and methylated bovine serum albumin. The specificity of the antiserum was concerned with the inositol moiety of phosphatidylinositol and was influenced by the ratio of phosphatidylinositol to lecithin. The role of lecithin as an auxiliary lipid in the phosphatidylinositol hapten as well as the cardiolipin hapten was partly explained from observations of the nature of the phospholipase C-treated phospholipid haptens. The lecithin molecule as a whole is indispensable in forming micellar structure of the hapten. However, once the micelle is prepared, the phosphorylcholine moiety of lecithin is no longer necessary, at least in the case of the phosphatidylinositol hapten, and the diglyceride portion of lecithin is important in preserving the micelle already formed. Chemical analysis, reactivity with antisera and binding ability with methylated bovine serum albumin of the enzyme-treated phospholipid hapten in comparison with the original hapten supported the above conclusions.

The haptenic activity of phospholipids has been investigated to a limited extent, although cardiolipin, phosphatidylinositol and phosphatidylinositol oligomannosides have been employed or proposed to be usable as haptens for serodiagnosis of some diseases (1–5). Fowler and Allen (6) obtained antisera against cardiolipin and phosphatidic acid haptens and investigated the effect of the nature of fatty acid residues on their serologic reactions. Recently Inoue and Nojima (7) clarified the reactive site of cardiolipin hapten using various synthetic analogues of cardiolipin. In the present report the haptenic activity of another phospholipid hapten, phosphatidylinositol hapten, was examined, and the role of lecithin in this phospholipid hapten and also in cardiolipin hapten was investigated. Lecithin is, in general, required for the serologic reactions of most of the glycolipid and phospholipid haptens as an auxiliary lipid (8). Cytolipin H hapten consists of ceramide lactoside and lecithin in the ratio of 1:50 ~ 100 (w/w) (9). Phosphatidic acid and cardiolipin haptens contain 10 times more lecithin than these phospholipids. Up to the present time, however, the role of lecithin as an auxiliary lipid in these haptens has remained obscure. The present paper describes some experimental evidence that helps to explain its function. The immunochemical results obtained are also discussed in relation to the formation and preservation of micellar structures of the lipid haptens.

MATERIALS AND METHODS

Haptens. Cardiolipin, lecithin and phosphatidylinositol were prepared from beef heart (10), egg yolk (11) and yeast (12), respectively. Each gave a single spot on a thin-layer chromatogram of silica gel G developed with chloroform-methanol-water (65:25:4, v/v). Their phosphorus contents were 4.0%, 4.0% and 3.3%, respectively. Alkaline hydrolysis gave di(glycerylphosphoryl)-glycerol, glycerylphosphorylcholine and glycerylphosphorylinositol, respectively. Cholesterol was purchased from Koso Chemical Co. Ltd., Tokyo.

Phosphatidylinositol hapten or cardiolipin hapten suspension was prepared by adding 0.5 ml of tetrahydrofuran solution of the lipid mixture containing 0.03% phosphatidylinositol or cardiolipin, 0.9% cholesterol and an appropriate amount of lecithin to 0.4 ml of phosphate-buffered saline consisting of 0.093 g of $Na_2HPO_4 \cdot 12H_2O$, 0.170 g of KH_2PO_4, 10.0 g of NaCl and 1000 ml of deionized water, and further by combining the resulting suspension with 4.0 ml of this buffered saline. This was well suspended by manual shaking. In the experiment using phospholipase C, Tris-HCl-buffered saline (0.005 M, pH 7.5) was employed instead of phosphate-buffered saline and the suspension formed by manual shaking was sonicated at 10 kc for 30 min.

Phosphatidic acid was prepared by hydrolyzing lecithin with phospholipase D (13). Phosphatidic acid hapten suspension was prepared like those of phosphatidylinositol and cardiolipin as described above. Diglyceride was prepared by hydrolyzing lecithin with phospholipase C.

Immunization. One and one-half milliliter of phospholipid hapten suspension was centrifuged at 700 × G for 30 min and the precipitate was well suspended in 1.0 ml of 0.1% methylated bovine serum albumin (MBSA) solution and stored at 5°C overnight. This was injected intravenously into a rabbit. Injections were made every other day for about 3 weeks (14).

Titration of antibody activity. A microflocculation test by the VDRL method (15) was employed with a modification in haptenic lipid composition described above. Measurements were carried out as follows: One drop ($\frac{1}{60}$ ml) of the hapten suspension was added to a series of twofold dilutions of serum (0.05 ml), placed on a glass slide in a paraffin ring and rotated for 5 min (120 rpm). The slide was then examined microscopically at × 100 magnification. Results of the test were evaluated as follows: no clumping of hapten particles, 0; very small but definite clumps, 1+; small clumps, 2+; medium sized clumps, 3+; large clumps, 4+.

Complement fixation tests (16) were carried out as follows: 0.4 ml of the diluted antisera was mixed with 0.4 ml of the diluted hapten suspension and further with 0.5 ml of guinea pig sera which was equivalent to $5CH_{50}$. After incubation at 4°C overnight and further at 37°C for 30 min, the mixture was combined with 0.2 ml of sheep erythrocyte suspension (5×10^8/ml) sensitized with an optimal amount of amboceptor. After incubation at 37°C for 60 min, the mixture was centrifuged at 1000 × G for 10 min and 50% hemolysis was measured by oxyhemoglobin in the supernatant fluid. Veronal buffer (0.01 M, pH 7.5) containing 0.1% gelatin, 0.15 mM $CaCl_2$ and 0.5 mM $MgCl_2$ was employed throughout this test.

Immunoelectrophoresis. Immunoelectrophoresis was carried out according to the method described previously (17).

Treatment with phospholipase C. A solution of phospholipase C purified from *Clostridium welchii* with 315 egg units/mg protein was kindly supplied by Dr. Ohsaka (Department of Bacteriology II, the National Institute of Health). Six milliliters of a hapten suspension prepared by sonication as described above were concentrated to 0.6 ml under reduced pressure and 0.2 ml of 3×10^{-2} M $CaCl_2$ solution and of the enzyme solution prepared by diluting the phospholipase C solution to an appropriate concentration with 0.1% bovine serum albumin were added successively to the hapten suspension. The final volume of the mixture was 1.0 ml. This was incubated at 37°C for 30 min. Haptenic activity was titrated after adding 5 ml of water and sonicating for 10 min. At the same time, the original 1-ml reaction mixture was extracted three times with 2 or 3 ml of ether and the combined ether extract and the remaining aqueous solution were analyzed. Phospholipase C hydrolyzes lecithin into diglyceride and phosphorylcholine. Diglyceride is extractable into the ether layer while phosphorylcholine is not. Under the experimental conditions employed, neither cardiolipin nor phosphatidylinositol was hydrolyzed because both were recovered quantitatively in the ether layer. Thus, water-soluble phosphorus was derived only from phosphorylcholine. From the ratio of phosphorus in the aqueous layer to that of lecithin in the original suspension, the percentage hydrolysis of lecithin was determined as follows. The phosphorus of lecithin in the original suspension was estimated by calculating the total phosphorus recovered in both the aqueous and ether layers, since a certain amount of the phospholipids was always lost during manipulation of the sonicator. Thus, for example, total phosphorus was calculated as 30.3 μg by combining 5.7 μg in the ether layer and 24.6 μg in the aqueous layer (third column in Table VI). The phosphorus ratio of phosphatidylinositol to lecithin in the original suspension is 3.3:16.0, considering their weight ratio (1:4) and their phosphorus contents (phosphatidylinositol, 3.3%; lecithin, 4.0%). Therefore, phosphorus of lecithin in the original suspension is $30.3\ \mu g \times 16.0/(3.3 + 16.0) =$

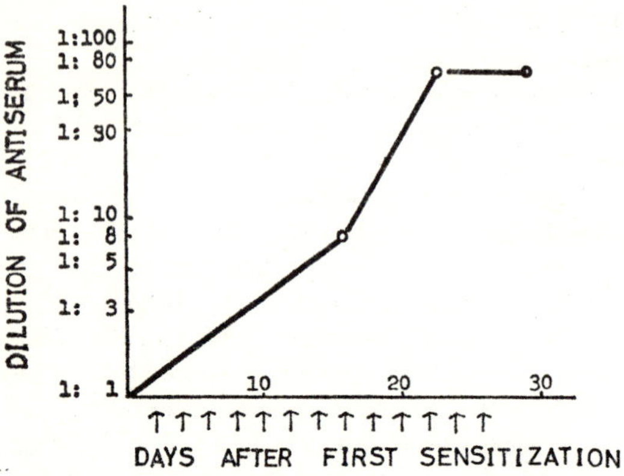

Figure 1. Antibody response to the phosphatidylinositol hapten. The immunogen was prepared by suspending the lipid mixture containing phosphatidylinositol, lecithin and cholesterol (1:4:30, w/w) in phosphate-buffered saline and binding with methylated bovine serum albumin as described in *Materials and Methods*. The immunogen (1.0 ml/rabbit/injection) was injected intravenously every other day for about 3 weeks as shown by arrows. Antiserum was titrated by the microflocculation test of modified VDRL method.

25.2 μg. The percentage of hydrolysis is 24.6 μg(aqueous layer)/25.2 μg(total lecithin) × 100 = 97.6%.

Binding with MBSA. The complex of hapten and MBSA prepared as described above was centrifuged at 700 × G for 30 min and the precipitate was washed three times with saline. This was analyzed for its content of phosphorus, cholesterol and protein (17).

RESULTS

Immunogenicity of the lipid haptens containing phosphatidylinositol, lecithin and cholesterol. The complexes of MBSA and the phosphatidylinositol haptens containing phosphatidylinositol, lecithin and cholesterol in various ratios were injected into rabbits and the antisera thus obtained were assayed by the microflocculation test using homologous haptens. As shown in Figure 1, maximal antibody production was generally observed after about 3 weeks from the first injection of the hapten. With the hapten containing phosphatidylinositol, lecithin and cholesterol (1:4:30, w/w), a secondary response was not observed, as was the case in cardiolipin antibody production (18). The antiserum with maximal titer in the primary response was used in the present experiments. The immunogenicity of phosphatidylinositol haptens with various ratios of phosphatidylinositol to lecithin is shown in Table I. High immunogenicity was always observed in the hapten consisting of phosphatidylinositol, lecithin and cholesterol (1:4:30). The amount of MBSA bound to the hapten is also shown in Table I. The hapten with phosphatidylinositol, lecithin and cholesterol (1:1:30) bound more MBSA than that of 1:4:30, but did not show higher immunogenicity. In addition, the hapten without lecithin containing phosphatidylinositol and cholesterol (1:30) did not show any immunogenicity in spite of binding three times more MBSA than the hapten containing phosphatidylinositol, lecithin and cholesterol (1:4:30). This result together with that of the previous experiment with the cardiolipin hapten (14) would show that no quantitative relation between immunogenicity and the amount of bound MBSA exists, although MBSA is necessary to render the lipid hapten immunogenic. This result also suggests that the ability to induce antibody production depends on the arrangement of the reactive sites of phosphatidylinositol in the presence of lecithin. The immunologic reac-

TABLE I

Immunogenicity of phosphatidylinositol haptens with various ratios of phosphatidylinositol to lecithin

Immunogens[a]	Titer of Antisera Measured by the Microflocculation Test[b]	MBSA Bound to Immunogen/Phosphatidylinositol in Immunogen
w/w		*w/w*
1:0:30	<1:4, <1:4, <1:4	7.3
1:1:30	<1:4, <1:4, <1:4, <1:4, 1:8, 1:128	3.0
1:4:30	1:16, 1:16, 1:16, 1:64, 1:64	2.4
1:10:30	<1:4, <1:4, 1:8, 1:16	0.78

[a] Phosphatidylinositol:lecithin:cholesterol.

[b] Antisera were titrated with their homologous haptens and the titers are the maximal dilutions that gave positive reactions.

TABLE II

Complement fixation test of antiserum against phosphatidylinositol hapten[a]

Reciprocal of Antiserum Dilution	Reciprocal of Hapten Dilution[b]											
	2.5	5	10	20	40	80	160	320	640	1280	$5CH_{50}$	$3CH_{50}$
20	ND[c]	ND	ND	0	0	0	0	0	0	0	0	0
40	ND	ND	ND	0	0	0	0	0	0	0	1	1
80	ND	ND	ND	0	0	0	0	0	0	1	3	2
160	0	0	0	0	0	0	0	0	1	2	4	3
320	0	0	0	0	0	0	0	0	2	3	4	3
640	0	0	0	0	0	0	0	1	3	4	4	4
1280	0	1	0	0	0	0	1	3	4	4	4	4
2560	0	2	3	3	3	4	4	ND	ND	ND	4	4
5120	0	2	3	4	4	4	4	ND	ND	ND	4	4
$5CH_{50}$	0	2	2	4	4	4	4	4	4	4	4	4
$3CH_{50}$	0	2	2	4	4	4	4	4	4	4	4	4

[a] Phosphatidylinositol:lecithin:cholesterol = 1:4:30 (w/w).
[b] Homologous hapten was employed.
[c] ND, not determined.

TABLE III

Reactivity of the antisera against phosphatidylinositol hapten with cardiolipin hapten

Antisera against Phosphatidylinositol Hapten[a]	Rabbit No.	Titer Measured by the Microflocculation Test Using	
		Cardiolipin hapten	Homologous phosphatidylinositol hapten
w/w			
1:1:30	1	<1:2	1:128
1:1:30	2	<1:2	1:8
1:4:30	3	<1:2	1:64
1:4:30	4	<1:2	1:64
1:10:30	5	<1:2	1:16

[a] Phosphatidylinositol:lecithin:cholesterol.

tion of phosphatidylinositol hapten with its immune serum was further confirmed by complement fixation tests. Table II shows the result of the titration of a sample of serum from a rabbit immunized with the above lipid hapten. Fifty per cent hemolysis was observed at the dilution of 1:1280 to 1:2560 of the antiserum employing the hapten at 1:40 dilution. This result is available because the antiserum and the hapten were not anticomplementary at dilutions above 1:160 and 1:20, respectively.

Specificity of antisera. The cross-reactivity of the antiserum against the phosphatidylinositol hapten with the cardiolipin hapten, which is composed of cardiolipin, lecithin and cholesterol (1:10:30), was examined. As shown in Table III, antisera that reacted with the phosphatidylinositol haptens of various ratios did not react with the cardiolipin hapten which contained cardiolipin instead of phosphatidylinositol in the lipid mixture. This result suggests that specificity of the antiserum is concerned with phosphatidylinositol rather than lecithin and/or cholesterol. This was also confirmed using the phosphatidic acid hapten containing phosphatidic acid, lecithin and cholesterol (1:4:30). The result is shown in Table IV. No cross-reaction was observed. These experiments indicate that the reactive site is concerned with *myo*-inositol primarily.

Inhibition tests were also carried out. The antiserum reacting with the phosphatidylinositol hapten (1:4:30) was used. After preincubation with *myo*-inositol, glycerylphosphoryl *myo*-inositol, which is the deacylated product of phosphatidylinositol or phosphatidylinositol itself, the anti-

TABLE IV

Reactivity of antisera against phosphatidylinositol hapten[a] *with phosphatidic acid*[b] *hapten*

Antiserum No.	Titer Measured by the Microflocculation Test Using the Hapten of	
	Phosphatidylinositol	Phosphatidic acid
3	1:64	<1:1
4	1:32	<1:1

[a] Phosphatidylinositol : lecithin : cholesterol = 1:4:30 (w/w).
[b] Phosphatidic acid:lecithin:cholesterol = 1:4:30 (w/w).

TABLE V

Inhibition test of antisera[a] against phosphatidylinositol hapten[b] measured by the microflocculation test

Compounds Tested	Ratios of Molar Concentration of the Compounds Tested to that of Phosphatidylinositol in the Hapten	Reciprocal of Antiserum Dilution				
		8	16	32	64	128
None		ND[c]	ND	+2	+1	−
Phosphatidylinositol	70	ND	ND	+2	+1	−
Cardiolipin	70	ND	ND	+2	+1	−
Lecithin	70	ND	ND	+2	+1	−
None		+3	+2	+1	−	−
myo-inositol	1000	+3	+2	+1	−	−
Glycerylphosphorylinositol	20	+3	+2	+1	−	−
Glycerylphosphorylinositol	200	+3	+2	+1	−	−

[a] Antisera from three rabbits, the titers of which were 1:32, 1:32 and 1:64, were pooled.
[b] Phosphatidylinositol:lecithin:cholesterol = 1:4:30 (w/w).
[c] ND, not determined.

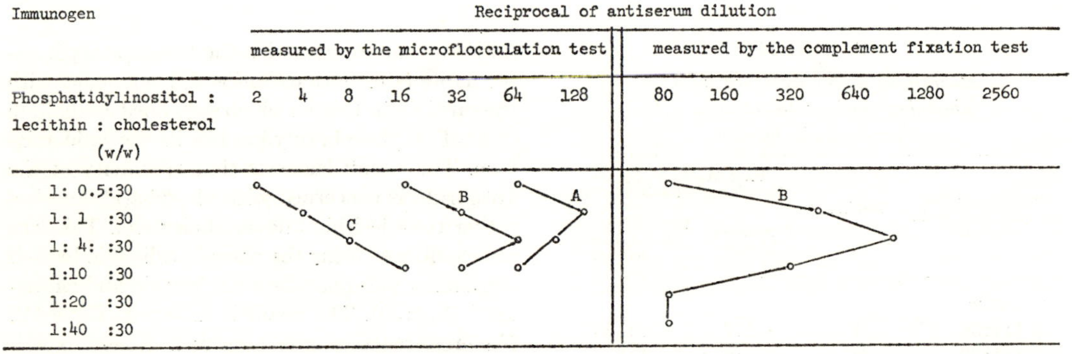

Figure 2. The ratio of phosphatidylinositol to lecithin in phosphatidylinositol hapten and its effect of haptenic specificity. *A*, *B* and *C*, antisera obtained from rabbits immunized with the lipid haptens containing phosphatidylinositol:lecithin:cholesterol in the weight ratio of 1:1:30, 1:4:30 and 1:10:30, respectively.

serum was titrated by the microflocculation test. None of them inhibited the reaction of the antiserum with the corresponding phosphatidylinositol hapten. The results are shown in Table V. The explanation of the discrepancy between *myo*-inositol as the main determinant group and the non-inhibitory action of *myo*-inositol, glycerylphosphoryl *myo*-inositol or phosphatidylinositol to the hapten-antibody reaction is very difficult. Faure (19) has observed and the authors also have confirmed that di(glycerylphosphoryl)-glycerol, which is the deacylated product of cardiolipin, does not inhibit the reaction of cardiolipin hapten with the Wassermann-positive human serum It seems to the authors that some kind of micellar structure might be necessary for the hapten to react with the antibody and that the reactive site including *myo*-inositol might possess some rigidity or configuration required to react with antibody.

The ratio of phosphatidylinositol to lecithin in the phosphatidylinositol hapten and its effect on the hapten-antibody reaction. Antisera were obtained from rabbits immunized with phosphatidylinositol haptens containing phosphatidylinositol, lecithin and cholesterol in the ratios of 1:1:30, 1:4:30 or 1:10:30. The reactivities of the antisera were analyzed with the phosphatidylinositol haptens of various ratios of phosphatidylinositol to lecithin. The results are shown in Figure 2. For example, the antiserum obtained from the rabbit immunized with hapten in the ratio of 1:4:30 gave the highest reactivity with the homologous hapten which was also confirmed using the complement fixation test. This was

TABLE VI

Effect of phospholipase C on phosphatidylinositol hapten

	Amount of Phospholipase C Used (μg)		
	0	46	46 + deoxycholate (1 mg)
Phosphorus (μg) recovered in			
Aqueous layer	2.0	24.6	26.3
Ethereal layer	26.8	5.7	6.9
Hydrolysis %[a]		97.6	95.0
Haptenic activity	+[b]	+	ND[c]
Complex formation of the hapten with MBSA			
Phosphorus (μg)	6.6[d]	1.1	
Cholesterol (μg)	1490	990	
Phosphatidylinositol:lecithin:cholesterol (w/w)	1:4:44	1:0:30	
MBSA (μg)	83	98	
MBSA/phosphatidylinositol (w/w)	2.5	3.3	

[a] Calculated as described in *Materials and Methods.*

[b] + is qualified by the reactivity with homologous antisera and the non-reactivity with either normal sera or antisera against the cardiolipin hapten.

[c] ND, not determined.

[d] Phosphorus of phosphatidylinositol (1.1 μg) + phosphorus of lecithin (5.5 μg).

verified with other antisera. The highest reactivity with the homologous hapten and the result described before that the reactive site of the three immunogens might include *myo*-inositol in common would indicate the existence of some molecular arrangement of phosphatidylinositol brought by lecithin around the reactive site of the lipid haptens. This contribution of lecithin was further investigated in the following experiment.

Contribution of lecithin to the reactive site in the hapten. The phosphatidylinositol hapten containing phosphatidylinositol, lecithin and cholesterol in the ratio of 1:4:30 was treated with phospholipase C and its residual haptenic reactivity to the homologous antisera was examined by microflocculation and complement fixation tests. The results are shown in Tables VI and VII. Forty-six micrograms of the enzyme hydrolyzed 97.6% of lecithin in the hapten after 30 min incubation. The thin-layer chromatogram of the hydrolyzed haptens is shown in Figure 3. Disappearance of lecithin and the concomitant appearance of diglyceride were observed. The treated hapten was reactive with the homologous antisera up to the same dilution (1:64) of the antisera by the microflocculation test, but not with normal sera (<1:4) or antisera against the cardiolipin hapten (<1:4). This result was also confirmed by the complement fixation test, showing that the treated hapten was reactive to the same dilution as the original hapten to the antisera at 1:160 dilution. There was no difference in their binding ability with MBSA (the ratio of MBSA to phosphatidylinositol (w/w); original hapten, 2.5 and treated hapten, 3.3). These data suggest that the original haptenic structure was retained after hydrolysis of 97.6% lecithin in the original phosphatidylinositol hapten. Further, substitution of lecithin by diglyceride was investigated. The hapten containing phosphatidylinositol, diglyceride and cholesterol in the same molar ratio as that in the original hapten was prepared and its haptenic activity was titrated using the antiserum against the hapten of phosphatidylinositol, lecithin and cholesterol in the ratio of 1:4:30. The diglyceride-substituted hapten did not react with the antiserum at 1:4 dilution, while the original homologous hapten reacted with the antiserum at 1:32 dilution. The complete preservation of the haptenic activity after hydrolysis by phospholipase C and the failure in making up hapten with diglyceride instead of lecithin may probably suggest the necessity for phosphorylcholine, the ionic group of lecithin, to bring phosphatidylinositol into the reactive arrangement. However, once the haptenic site was formed, the diglyceride part, the hydrophobic group of lecithin, alone is required to maintain the reactive site.

A similar result was obtained with the cardiolipin hapten as shown in Table VIII. The cardio-

TABLE VII

Haptenic activity of phosphatidylinositol hapten[a] treated with phospholipase C

Serum	Serum No.	Enzyme Treatment[b]	Reciprocal of Serum Dilution[c]					
			4	8	16	32	64	128
Antisera against phosphati- dylinositol hapten	3	−	+4	+4	+4	+3	+1	−
		+	+3	+3	+2	+2	+1	−
	6	−	+3	+3	+3	+2	+1	−
		+	+3	+3	+3	+2	+1	−
Antisera against cardiolipin hapten[d]		−	−	−	−	−	−	−
		+	−	−	−	−	−	−
Normal serum		−	−	−	−	−	−	−
		+	−	−	−	−	−	−
			Reciprocal of hapten dilution[e]					
			160	320	640	1280	2560	
Antisera against phosphati- dylinositol hapten	3	−	0	0	1	3	4	
		+	0	1	3	4	4	
	4	−	0	0	1	3	4	
		+	0	0	3	4	4	
	6	−	0	0	3	4	4	
		+	0	1	3	4	4	

[a] Phosphatidylinositol:lecithin:cholesterol = 1:4:30 (w/w).

[b] Forty-six micrograms of phospholipase C were used. See also *Materials and Methods*.

[c] Measured by the microflocculation method.

[d] Measured by the microflocculation method. The titer of this antiserum was 1:64 as measured by the cardiolipin antigen.

[e] Measured by the complement fixation test, employing antiserum of 1:160 dilution.

lipin hapten after up to 80 ~ 90% hydrolysis of lecithin by phospholipase C retained its reactivity with the homologous antiserum. Its specificity was proved by the low cross-reactivity with the antiserum against phosphatidylinositol hapten (<1:4 dilution) and no reactivity with the normal serum (<1:2 dilution). In addition, the cardiolipin hapten substituted by diglyceride consisting of cardiolipin, diglyceride and cholesterol in the same molar ratio as that in the original hapten did not react with the antiserum (1:4 dilution) against cardiolipin hapten, while the intact cardiolipin hapten was reactive with the antiserum up to 1:64 dilution. The residual haptenic activity after treatment with phospholipase C and no reactivity of the diglyceride-substituted cardiolipin hapten also supported the conclusion on the role of lecithin in the lipid hapten.

DISCUSSION

The present investigation demonstrated that the phosphatidylinositol haptens when combined with MBSA stimulated rabbits to produce the antibody specific for phosphatidylinositol, but not for lecithin or cholesterol. The specificity was proved by the following experiments: a) The assay system employed did not contain MBSA, although the immunogen contained MBSA. b) The antiserum did not cross-react with the cardiolipin hapten containing cardiolipin, lecithin and cholesterol (1:10:30) nor with the phosphatidic acid hapten containing phosphatidic acid, lecithin and cholesterol (1:4:30). This means that the antiserum reacted neither with lecithin nor with cholesterol. c) Further, the fact that the phosphatidylinositol hapten treated with phospholipase C to remove phosphorylcholine still retained the full haptenic activity proved definitely that the specificity resides in the phosphatidylinositol moiety itself, but not in lecithin.

The antiserum against the phosphatidylinositol hapten contained antibody of two distinct types. One was resistant and the other was susceptible to 0.2 M mercaptoethanol. The former appeared to be γ globulin by electrophoresis. The titer of

TABLE VIII

Haptenic activity of cardiolipin hapten treated with phospholipase C

Amount of Phospholipase C Used[a]	Hydrolysis % of Lecithin[a]	Reactivity with: Antisera against: Cardiolipin hapten: Microflocculation test[b]	Cardiolipin hapten: Complement-fixation test[c]	Cardiolipin hapten: Immunoelectrophoresis	Phosphatidylinositol hapten: microflocculation test[b]	Normal serum: microflocculation test[b]
μg						
0	0	1:32	1:2560	+	<1:4	<1:4
1.9	82	1:64	1:1280	+	<1:4	<1:2
2.2	91	1:8	1:1280	+	<1:4	ND[d]
4.2	100	1:4	1:240	−	ND	<1:2

[a] Calculated from phosphorus content in ether layer (see Table VI).
[b] The highest dilution of antiserum that gave a positive reaction is shown.
[c] The highest dilution of the hapten that gave 50% hemolysis, using antiserum at 1:160 dilution.
[d] ND, not determined.

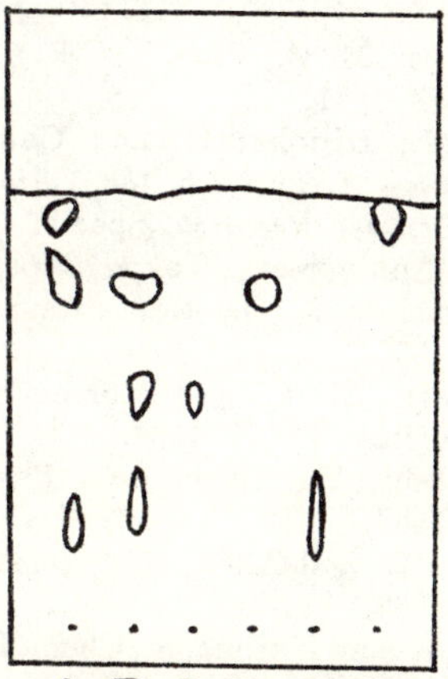

Figure 3. Thin-layer chromatogram of phosphatidylinositol hapten treated with phospholipase C. Developed on silica gel G plate with chloroform-methanol-water (65:25:4, v/v) and charred after spraying with dilute H_2SO_4. *A*, phosphatidylinositol hapten after treatment with phospholipase C (12.5 μg); *B*, original phosphatidylinositol hapten; *C*, lecithin; *D*, cholesterol; *E*, phosphatidylinositol; and *F*, diglyceride. In *A* disappearance of lecithin and appearance of diglyceride occurred concomitantly.

the antiserum did not increase remarkably after secondary stimulation (17). These characteristics are in good agreement with those of the cardiolipin hapten (18).

Certain functions of lecithin in the phosphatidylinositol or cardiolipin haptens were found in the present experiments: the entire lecithin molecule is required when the haptens are prepared by mixing their lipid components, and the diglyceride structure of lecithin rather than the phosphorylcholine moiety is important in preserving the haptenic structure. Treating phosphatidylinositol hapten with phospholipase C completely eliminated phosphorylcholine from the hapten. The treated hapten reacted with the homologous antiserum to the same degree as the original hapten but did not react with the normal serum or the antiserum against the cardiolipin hapten. Further, it bound MBSA to the same extent as did the original hapten. Thus, the haptenic activity was conserved completely by diglyceride of the lecithin molecule. However, diglyceride derived from egg yolk lecithin by elimination of phosphorylcholine could not substitute for lecithin in forming the phosphatidylinositol hapten. This is comparable with the finding that the mixed monolayer of cholesterol and dimyristin differs from that of cholesterol and dimyristoyllecithin in physical behavior (20). Phosphorylcholine might play a role in arranging phosphatidylinositol in a reactive configuration during the preparation of the hapten. This conclusion was also supported by the experiment using the cardiolipin hapten. In the cardiolipin hapten, however, complete elimination of phosphorylcholine seemed to cause degradation of the haptenic structure. This was confirmed by the fact that the cardiolipin hapten lost its haptenic activity when more than 80% of lecithin was hydrolyzed by phospholipase D (unpublished). It was clearly shown in the previous report (21) that the distance between two phosphate groups and the free hydroxyl group of glycerol between them in the cardiolipin molecule were concerned with the reactive site in the cardiolipin hapten. Therefore, these groups in the cardiolipin molecule should be highly rigid to be bound with the antibody. To preserve this rigidity, phosphorylcholine of the residual 10% lecithin after hydrolysis with phospholipase C might be necessary. In the original hapten, the weight ratio of cardiolipin to lecithin was 1:10 and the phospholipase-treated hapten contained cardiolipin and lecithin in a weight ratio of 1:1. The molar ratio was about 1:2 in the treated hapten. Therefore, it may be suggested that two phosphatidyl groups in cardiolipin are supported structurally by two molecules of lecithin directly or indirectly in the phospholipase-treated hapten.

A previous report (14) showed the ability of MBSA to immunogenize the cardiolipin haptens. Such was the case also with the phosphatidylinositol hapten. Binding of MBSA was a prerequisite for antibody production against the phospholipid haptens. The binding of MBSA, however, does not necessarily bring about antibody production. The cardiolipin hapten without lecithin, noted in the previous report, and the phosphatidylinositol hapten without lecithin in the present experiments bound MBSA to a considerable extent when compared with highly immunogenic haptens but failed to induce antibody. These results suggest that an appropriate amount of lecithin is necessary for the suitable configurational arrangement of cardiolipin or phosphatidylinositol in the immunogenic haptens in addition to the binding of MBSA. This configurational arrangement brought about by lecithin might be partly explained by the following. One is the arrangement of the phosphatidylinositol molecules in the micelle with appropriate distances among them, as the antiserum was most reactive with the hapten of the homologous lipid composition in the phosphatidylinositol hapten. The other is the rigidity of the reactive sites of haptens required for immunogens, as shown by the fact that the diglyceride moiety of lecithin can serve to preserve the micellar structure of haptens.

Lecithin appears to play an essential role in several biologic reactions. The D(-)β-hydroxybutyric dehydrogenase in mitochondria shows an absolute requirement for lecithin (22). The Rh antigen activity of the human erythrocyte membrane (23) and cytolipin H (8) also require lecithin as an auxiliary lipid. In these cases, lecithin appears to form the necessary sites which other phospholipids have not the ability to form. Recently Friedman and Pastan (24) showed that infectivity of Semliki Forest virus was almost completely destroyed when more than 60% of viral phospholipid was hydrolyzed with phospholipase C. Such a sudden decrease in biologic activity was observed also in the haptenic activity of cardiolipin when more than 80% to 90% of lecithin was hydrolyzed by the enzyme.

Acknowledgments. The authors are indebted to Professor D. Mizuno, University of Tokyo, for his encouragement and helpful suggestions throughout this work. They also wish to thank Dr. K. Nishioka, Department of Virology, National Cancer Center, Tokyo, who provided us facilities for performing complement fixation tests and gave us valuable suggestions.

REFERENCES

1. Pangborn, M. C., Proc. Soc. Exp. Biol. Med., *48:* 484, 1941.
2. Abe, M., Hijioka, H. and Chinone, S., in *Research Activities of the National Institute for Leprosy Research,* Special Issue for the 10th Anniversary, Tokyo, Japan, 1965.
3. de Almeida, J. O., Rev. Brasil. Lepr., *26:* 181, 1958.
4. Pangborn, M. C. and McKinney, J. A., J. Lipid Res., *7:* 627, 1966.
5. Takahashi, Y., Amer. Rev. Resp. Dis., *85:* 708, 1962.
6. Fowler, E. and Allen, R. H., J. Immun., *88:* 591, 1962.
7. Inoue, K. and Nojima, S., Chem. Phys. Lipids, *2:* 68, 1968.
8. Rapport, M. M., J. Lipid Res., *2:* 25, 1961.
9. Rapport, M. M., Graf, L., Skipski, V. P. and Alonzo, N. F., Cancer, *12:* 438, 1959.
10. Faure, M. and Morelec-Coulon, M. I., Ann. Inst. Pasteur, *95:* 180, 1958.
11. Faure, M., Bull. Soc. Chim. Biol., *32:* 503, 1950.
12. Trevelyan, W. E., J. Lipid Res., *7:* 445, 1966.
13. Kates, M., Canad. J. Biochem. Physiol., *33:* 575, 1955.
14. Inoue, K. and Nojima, S., Biochim. Biophys. Acta, *144:* 409, 1967.
15. Kwapinski, J. B., in *Methods of Serological Research,* p. 191, John Wiley and Sons, Inc., New York, 1965.
16. Mayer, M. M., in *Kabat and Mayer's Experimental Immunochemistry,* 2nd Ed., p. 133, Charles C Thomas, Springfield, Ill., 1961.
17. Kataoka, T. and Nojima, S., Jap. J. Exp. Med., *39:* 39, 1969.
18. Kataoka, T. and Nojima, S., Jap. J. Exp. Med., *38:* 251, 1968.

19. Faure, M. and Morelec-Coulon, M. I., Ann. Inst. Pasteur, *104:* 246, 1963.
20. Cadenhed, D. A. and Philips, M. C., in *Molecular Association in Biological and Related Systems*, p. 13, American Chemical Society Publications, Washington, D. C., 1968.
21. Inoue, K. and Nojima, S., Chem. Phys. Lipids, *1:* 360, 1967.
22. Jurtshuk, P., Jr., Sekuzu, I. and Green, D. E., J. Biol. Chem., *238:* 3595, 1963.
23. Green, F. A., J. Biol. Chem., *243:* 5519, 1968.
24. Friedman, R. M. and Pastan, I., J. Molec. Biol., *40:* 107, 1969.

THE JOURNAL OF IMMUNOLOGY
Vol. 105, No. 2, August 1970
Printed in U.S.A.

STUDIES ON BRAIN ANTIGENS

IV. Isolation and Partial Characterization of a Rat Species-Restricted Antigen of Nervous Tissue (SRANT)[1]

ATHANASIA LIAKOPOULOU AND CATHERINE F. C. MACPHERSON

From the Departments of Biochemistry and Psychiatry, Allan Memorial Institute, McGill University, Montreal, Quebec

Received for publication October 16, 1969

The major species-restricted antigen of rat nervous tissue (SRANT) exists in saline extracts of rat brain in two molecular forms that have the electrophoretic mobilities of an α_1 globulin and an albumin. The more acidic form of the protein predominates. This was obtained free from admixture with other brain proteins and serum proteins by the following steps: a) ammonium sulfate fractionation, b) preparative electrophoresis in starch gel, c) removal of rat serum albumin by specific precipitation, and d) preparative electrophoresis in 9% polyacrylamide gel. Although SRANT is electrophoretically heterogeneous it appears to be homogeneous in size and to have a molecular weight of about 70,000. SRANT was found in the cerebral cortex, hippocampus, cerebellum, spinal cord and sciatic nerve of adult rats. After the 1st week of life it becomes one of the major antigens of the soluble fraction of rat brain.

Increasing attention is being paid to the roles that brain proteins may play in various kinds of brain activity. Recently Hyden and Lange (1) found increased protein synthesis in pyramidal neurons of the hippocampus when rats were trained on the reversal of handedness. Other authors have reported that humoral antibodies to soluble brain proteins caused psychotic states in normal humans (2) and could have a deleterious effect on learned behavior in animals (3). Almost nothing is known of the nature or the number of the antigens involved in these activities.

Another way of ascertaining the functions of brain proteins would be to measure the concentrations of known proteins in various areas of the brain during normal development and to determine how these values might change after treatment with drugs, following training regimes, or after the induction of neurologic disease. This kind of approach to the study of brain proteins can be made now with those proteins that are antigenic provided they can be purified and used to produce the monospecific antisera needed to make quantitative immunochemical measurements.

The water soluble antigens of human, rat and bovine brain have been studied in several labotories (4–10). Although there are more than 200 proteins in aqueous extracts of brain, rarely have more than 15 been found to be antigenic, and of these only about 5 are specific for nervous tissue. In our survey of the antigens in rat brain extracts (RBE) (6) we observed that some of the brain-specific antigens could be detected only in rat brain extracts and not in the brain extracts of other mammalian species. Such antigens have specificities directed to both the organ and the species and were not previously known to exist in brain, although Witebsky had found one in the adrenal (11). The major antigen of this type existed in two molecular forms with electrophoretic mobilities corresponding to those of an α_1 globulin and an albumin; most of the antigen was in the more acidic form.

[1] This work was supported by grants from the Multiple Sclerosis Society of Canada and the Medical Research Council of Canada. It was presented in part at the meeting of the Federation of American Societies for Experimental Biology in Atlantic City, N. J., in April, 1967, and is from a thesis submitted by Athanasia Liakopoulou to the Faculty of Graduate Studies and Research of McGill University, in partial fulfillment of the requirements for the degree of Doctor of Philosophy.

It occurred to us that the functions of a protein with this dual specificity might be easier to discern than the functions of brain-specific antigens, for it would be likely to play a more critical role in the activities of the rat brain. For this reason we have attempted to purify the more acidic form of this species-restricted antigen of nervous tissue (SRANT) so that immunochemical methods could be used in the studies made to ascertain its function.

MATERIALS AND METHODS

Frozen brains from male and female rats were purchased from Pel-Freeze Biologicals, Rogers, Arkansas. Fresh rat brains, rat spinal cords and peripheral nerve were obtained from rats that had been anesthetized with Nembutal and perfused with saline through the inferior vena cava.

Cytochrome *c* (horse heart), ribonuclease (bovine pancreas), and α chymotrypsinogen (bovine pancreas) were products of Sigma Chemical Co., St. Louis, Mo. Ovalbumin, bovine serum albumin, fraction V, and bovine γ globulin, fraction II, were obtained from Nutritional Biochemicals Corp., Cleveland, Ohio. Sephadex G-100 and Blue Dextran 2000 were manufactured by A. B. Pharmacia, Uppsala, Sweden. Dimethyldichlorosilane was purchased from the California Corporation for Biochemical Research. Hydrolyzed starch was prepared by the Connaught Medical Research Laboratories, Toronto. N,N,N′,N′-tetramethylethylenediamine and 3-dimethylaminopropionitrile were from Distillation Products Industries, Division of Eastman Kodak Company. Cyanogum 41 was a product of American Cyanamid Co., Wayne, N. J., and is a mixture of two monomers, acrylamide and N,N-methylenebis acrylamide. Ammonium persulfate, reagent grade and glycine (ammonia free) were purchased from Fisher Scientific Co.

Starch gel electrophoresis. Hydrolyzed starch was used at a concentration of 10.4% and was prepared in a buffer composed of 0.076 M Tris and 0.005 M citric acid, pH 8.6. The electrode buffer was composed of 0.3 M boric acid and 0.05 M NaOH, pH 8.3 (12). Electrophoresis was carried out at 4°C using a voltage gradient of 6 to 7 V/cm until the buffer front had moved 10 cm across the gel. To locate the SRANT protein, a longitudinal section of the gel 0.5 cm in width was excised immediately after electrophoresis was stopped, placed in a shallow tray and surrounded with 1% melted agar. After the agar had gelled a trough was cut in the agar 0.5 cm from and parallel to the starch gel strip and filled with "completely absorbed" anti-rat brain serum. The mid-point of the precipitin arc that formed indicated the area in the starch gel to which the SRANT protein had migrated. The SRANT protein was eluted electrophoretically from the area of the gel slab according to Hoerman *et al.* (13).

Polyacrylamide gel electrophoresis. Polyacrylamide gel electrophoresis was performed according to Raymond and Wang (14) in gel slabs composed of 7% polyacrylamide. Cyanogum 41 was dissolved in 0.4 M Tris-HCl buffer, pH 8.9, containing 0.06 ml of N,N,N′,N′-tetramethylethylenediamine/100 ml. To 60 ml of polyacrylamide solution, approximately 0.03 ml of 3-dimethylaminopropionitrile and 0.04 g of ammonium persulfate were added. A mold (0.8 x 20 x 18 cm) was filled to the brim with the liquid gel, covered with a glass plate and the gel was allowed to set for 2 hr before being used.

Molecular weight determination by gel filtration. A column of 2 x 80 cm previously coated with dimethyldichlorosilane was packed with Sephadex G-100 and calibrated as described by Andrews (15), using the following proteins of known molecular weights as standards: cytochrome *c* (12,400), ribonuclease (13,700), α chymotrypsinogen (25,000), hen egg albumin (45,000), bovine serum albumin (67,000), bovine γ globulin (160,000). The protein concentration of the 2.5-ml effluent fractions was estimated spectrophotometrically at 280 nm except for that of cytochrome *c*, which was estimated at 408 nm. Elution volumes, Ve, corresponding to the maximum concentrations of the proteins (16) were estimated to the nearest 1 ml.

The protein concentration was determined by the method of Lowry *et al.* (17) with bovine serum albumin as the standard.

Immunologic methods. Antisera to RBE were prepared as previously described by MacPherson and Liakopoulou (6). Double diffusion analysis (18) and micro-immunoelectrophoresis (19) were carried out as described in reference (6).

Absorption of immune sera. All rabbit anti-rat brain sera were absorbed with normal rat serum to remove antibodies against the serum proteins that are always found in aqueous extracts of brain. In addition, samples of anti-rat brain sera were absorbed with lyophilized rat kidney extract (to remove antibodies directed against species-specific antigens) and lyophilized human brain extracts (to remove antibodies directed against rat brain antigens shared with other mammalian brains). This antiserum is designated as "completely absorbed" antiserum and can be used to detect antigens unique to rat brain. Details of the absorption procedures were given in an earlier paper (6).

Fractionation of brain tissue. One part of fresh adult brain was homogenized at 800 rpm for 3 min at 0°C with a Tri-R homogenizer in 3 parts of 0.32 M sucrose containing 0.02 M Tris buffer, pH 7.6, and 3×10^{-3} M $MgCl_2$. The nuclear, crude mitochondrial and microsomal fractions were collected after centrifugation of the homogenate first at 900 × G for 10 min, then at 11,500 × G for 20 min and finally at 100,000 × G for 1 hr. The supernatant of the microsomal precipitate was the soluble fraction (20).

Preparation of γ globulin fraction of rabbit anti-normal rat serum. The γ globulin fraction of the rabbit antiserum to normal rat serum was precipitated at 33% saturation with ammonium at room temperature. The mixture was centrifuged for 30 min at 12,000 × G, the supernatant discarded and the precipitate resuspended in 33% saturated ammonium sulfate. After stirring for 30 min the suspension was centrifuged as above and the supernatant was discarded. The washing procedure was repeated and then the precipitate was dissolved in 0.9% saline, dialyzed against several changes of saline for 24 hr and concentrated to half the original volume of antiserum by the method of Mies (21).

RESULTS

Purification of SRANT. The anti-rat brain serum used to detect the species-restricted antigen of nervous tissue (SRANT) in the course of purification was a "completely absorbed" antiserum from which antibodies directed against antigens common to other rat organs and antibodies directed against antigens found in the brain tissue of most species of mammals had been removed. When necessary, immunoelectrophoretic analyses were performed on the purified fractions to identify the antigen with certainty, as RBE contains two other more basic antigens that are both species- and tissue-restricted.

Step 1: Preparation of rat brain extract. Fresh or frozen rat brains were homogenized at 0° to 4°C at 800 rpm in a Tri-R homogenizer using 4 ml of saline/brain. The homogenates were centrifuged at 0° to 4°C at 50,000 × G for 1 hr and the supernatants concentrated by ultrafiltration to about 30 mg of protein/ml (22).

Step 2: Ammonium sulfate fractionation. A saturated solution of ammonium sulfate was added slowly to RBE, with stirring, to bring the concentration of ammonium sulfate to 44% saturation. The precipitate (fraction 2I) was collected by centrifugation and the supernatant was brought to 66% saturation by the dropwise addition of the required volume of saturated ammonium sulfate solution. The precipitate (fraction 2II) was removed by centrifugation. The supernatant was brought to 100% saturation with respect to ammonium sulfate by the addition of the solid salt. The precipitate (fraction 2III) was collected by centrifugation and the supernatant (fraction 2IV) was concentrated by pressure dialysis to the original volume of RBE. All precipitates were dissolved in 0.9% saline at a concentration of 20 mg of protein/ml and dialysed for 24 hr against saline. It can be seen (Fig. 1*B*) that only fraction 2I and fraction 2II contained the SRANT proteins. However, fraction 2I contained not only two SRANT proteins but also a larger number of other antigens than fraction 2II as evidenced by the greater number of precipitin lines opposite fraction 2I in Figure 1*A*. Immunoelectrophoretic analyses (Fig. 1*C*) of fraction 2I and fraction 2II developed with a "completely absorbed" antiserum showed that fraction 2I contained the slower electrophoretic form of the major SRANT protein as well as a second SRANT antigen that had an electrophoretic mobility similar to that of an α_2 or β_1 globulin. The two antigens were, however, immunologically non-identical as shown by the crossing of the precipitin arcs. Fraction 2II contained both molecular forms of the major SRANT antigen and the characteristic double arc of the antigen can be seen in the immunoelectrophoretic pattern.

Step 3: Starch gel electrophoresis. Fraction 2II, containing only the major SRANT protein, was next subjected to starch gel electrophoresis. Figure 2*A* shows that the patterns obtained with 2 mg of fraction 2II protein had about 15 bands. The SRANT was located in an area 8 to 10 cm from the origin directly behind the buffer front.

Beginning at the line of the buffer front two

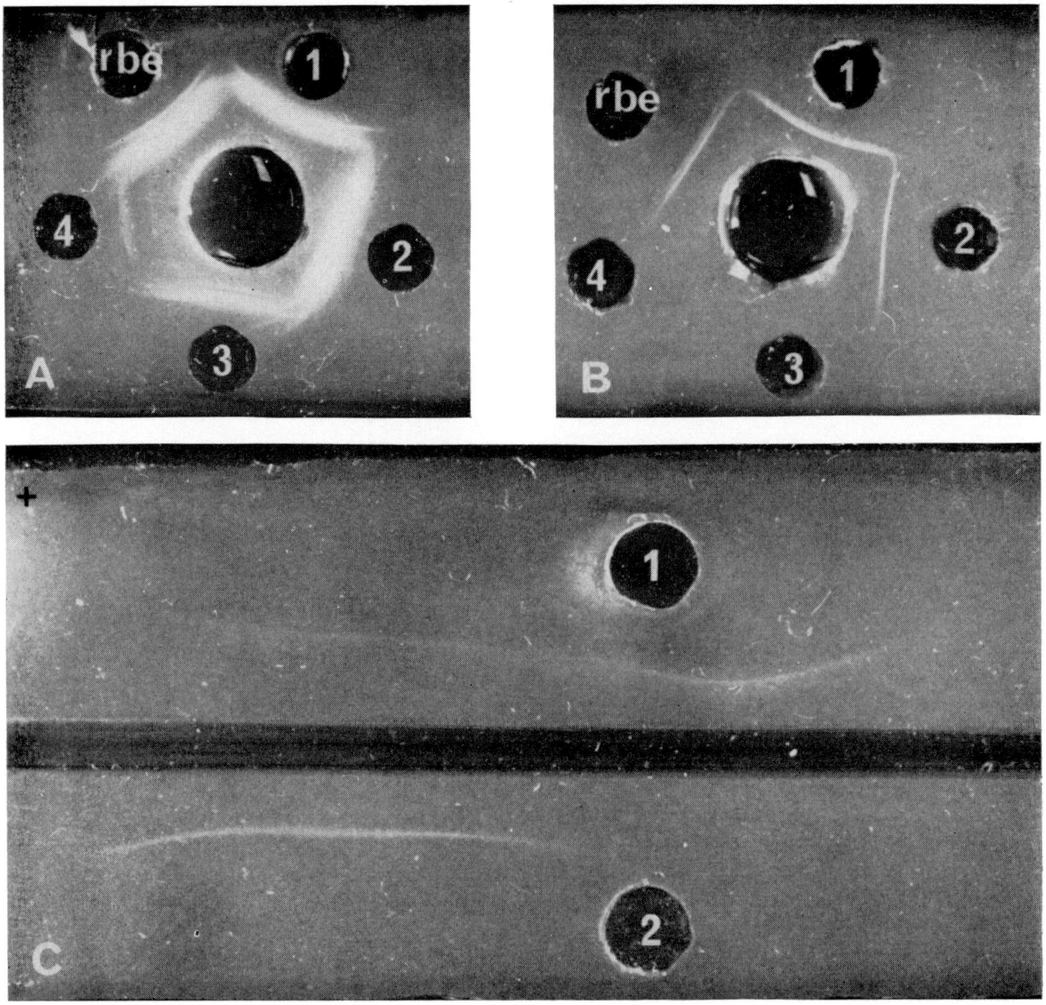

Figure 1. Immunodiffusion analyses of rat brain extract (RBE) and fractions obtained by ammonium sulfate precipitation with anti-RBE serum (*A*) and "completely absorbed" anti-RBE serum (*B*) in the center wells. The peripheral wells contained: *1*, fraction 2I; *2*, fraction 2II; *3*, fraction 2III; and *4*, fraction 2IV. All fractions were tested at a protein concentration of 20 mg/ml. *C*, immunoelectrophoretic patterns of fraction 2I (*1*) and fraction 2II (*2*) developed with "completely absorbed" anti-RBE serum.

gel blocks, 1 cm wide, were excised and the proteins in them were eluted electrophoretically (13). Figure 2*B* shows fraction 3I containing the faster moving molecular form of SRANT and fraction 3II containing the slower moving molecular form in a double diffusion experiment with "completely absorbed" anti-rat brain serum. Both fractions were found to be heavily contaminated with rat serum albumin (RSA) by immunodiffusion experiments using a rabbit antiserum to rat serum (Fig 2*C*).

Step 4: Removal of rat serum albumin from fraction 3I. There was too much serum albumin in fractions 3I and 3II to recover pure SRANT from them by electrophoretic procedures. Moreover, earlier experiments had shown that SRANT and rat serum albumin were about the same size so that they could not be separated by gel filtration. Since fraction 3II contained most of the serum albumin along with the slower moving form of SRANT, we decided to isolate only the acidic form of the protein from fraction 3I and to

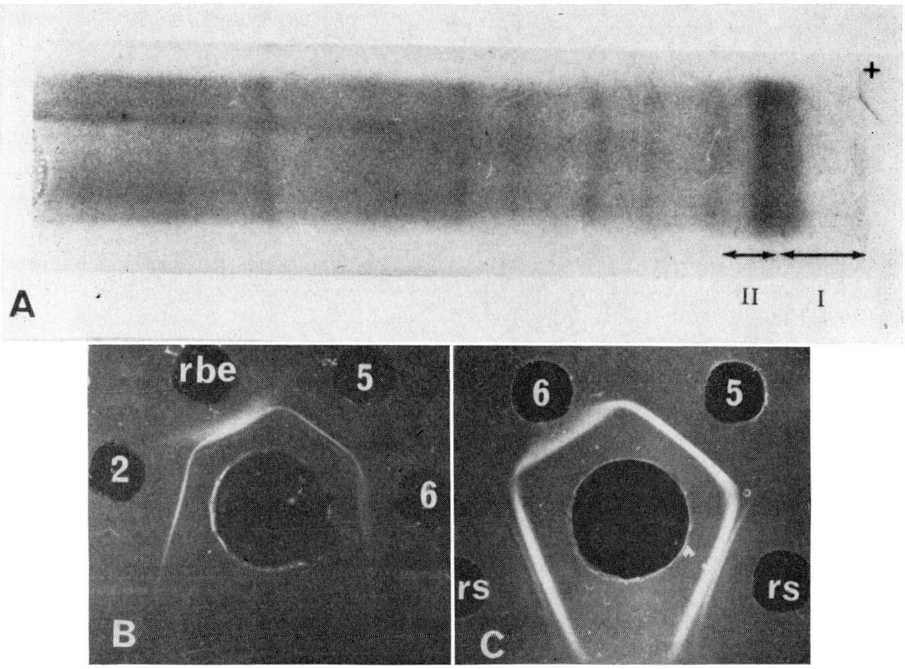

Figure 2. A, starch gel electrophoretic analysis of fraction 2II (2 mg protein). *B*, immunodiffusion analyses of RBE, fraction 2II (*2*), fraction 3I (*5*) and fraction 3II (*6*) with "completely absorbed" anti-RBE serum. RBE and fraction 2II were tested at a concentration of 20 mg protein/ml, and fraction 3I and 3II at a concentration of 4 mg/ml. *C*, immunodiffusion analysis of rat serum (RS) and fractions 3I (*5*) and 3II (*6*) with a rabbit anti-RS serum in the center well.

remove the contaminating serum albumin in the form of a specific precipitate. A predetermined amount of the purified γ globulin fraction of a rabbit antiserum to rat serum was added to fraction 3I to precipitate completely all the rat serum albumin present. The specific precipitate was removed by centrifugation and the supernatant, designated fraction 4, was subjected to polyacrylamide electrophoresis. The rabbit γ globulin remained at the cathodal end of the gel slab, several centimeters from the SRANT.

Step 5: Polyacrylamide gel electrophoresis. The electrophoretic profile of fraction 4 in 7% polyacrylamide showed three bands close together in the anodal section of the pattern. By increasing the polyacrylamide concentration to 9% the distances between the gel bands were increased so that there were clear areas between the bands (Fig. 3*Ab*). At the origin a few bands corresponding to the rabbit γ globulin contaminant are seen. The dotted lines in Figure 3*Ab* denote the points at which cuts were made in the 9% polyacrylamide gel and the roman numbers I, II and III indicate the polyacrylamide blocks from which protein was eluted. The material eluted from block III (fraction 5III) was found to be the major SRANT protein by immunodiffusion experiments with "completely absorbed" anti-rat brain serum. In Figure 3*B* it is shown that the precipitin lines formed opposite RBE, fraction 2II, fraction 3I and fraction 5III fused, indicating that an antigenically identical protein was present in all of these fractions. When RBE and fraction 5III were compared in a double diffusion experiment against anti-rat brain serum (Fig. 3*C*) only one precipitin line was formed opposite fraction 5III, whereas up to seven bands could be seen opposite the well containing RBE. The absence of rat serum albumin from fraction 5III was also demonstrated by immunodiffusion experiments (Fig. 3*D*).

Fraction 5III was also electrophoretically homogeneous, for when it was rerun on 9% polyacrylamide gel it was found to migrate as a single band (Fig. 3*Aa*).

Table I indicates the amount of protein re-

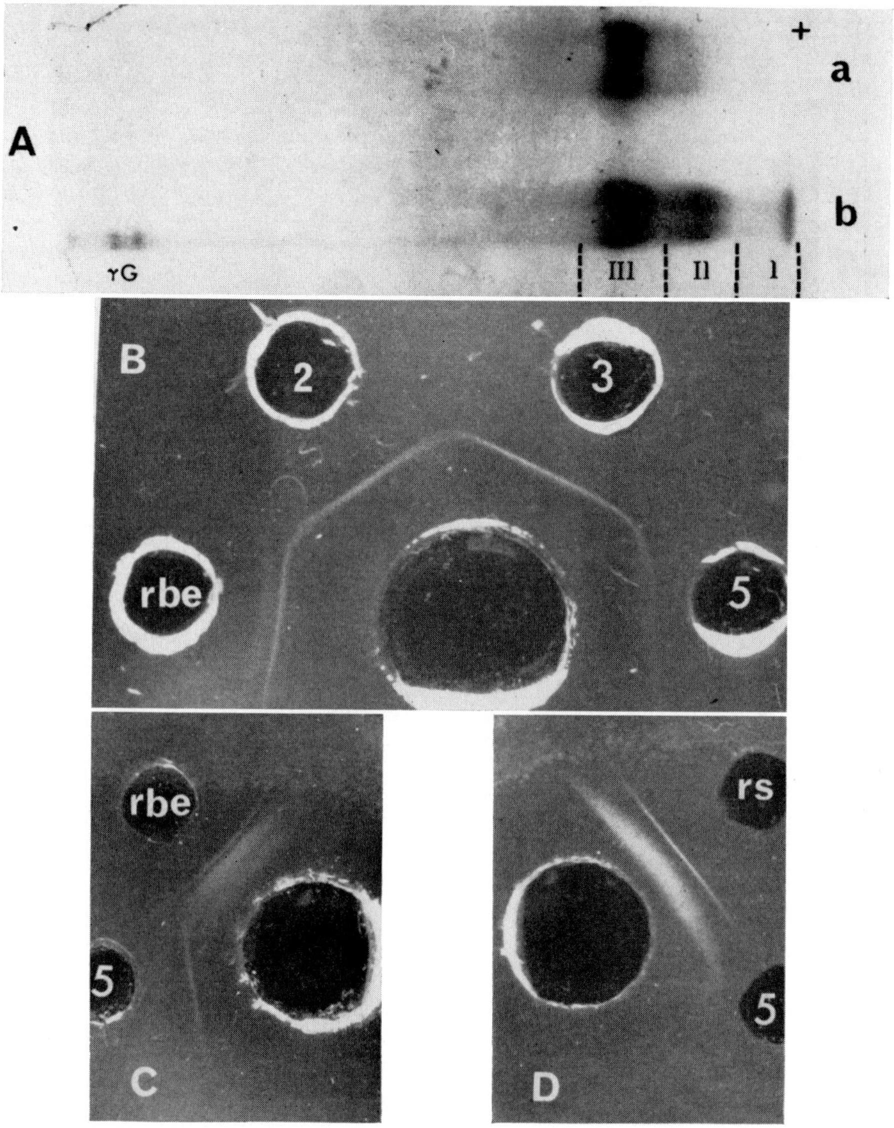

Figure 3. A, polyacrylamide gel electrophoretic patterns of fraction 4 (*b*) and fraction 5III (*a*). *B*, immunodiffusion analysis of RBE, fraction 2II (*2*), fraction 3I (*3*) and fraction 5III (*5*), with a "completely absorbed" anti-RBE serum in the center well. The protein concentration of the fractions tested was RBE, 20 mg/ml; fraction 2II, 20 mg/ml; fraction 3I, 4 mg/ml, and fraction 5III, 2 mg/ml. *C*, immunodiffusion analysis of RBE and fraction 5III with anti-RBE. *D*, immunodiffusion analysis of fraction 5III and RS with anti-RS antiserum.

covered at each step of the isolation procedure. The amount of purified SRANT obtained was 0.07% of the protein in the original sample of RBE.

Molecular weight of SRANT. The graph in Figure 4 shows that when the volumes, Ve, in which proteins of known molecular weight were eluted from a sephadex G-100 column, were plotted against the logarithms of the molecular weights of the proteins, the experimental points lay close to a straight line over the molecular weight range 12,000 to 70,000. A sample of partially purified RBE that contained both molecular forms of SRANT (fraction 2II) was

TABLE I

Amount of protein in fractions containing SRANT

Fraction	Amount of Protein at Each Step	Recovery[a]
	mg	%
RBE	8600	100
Fraction 2II	2300	25
Precipitated from RBE by 44% to 66% saturated ammonium sulfate		
Fraction 3I	258	3
Preparative electrophoresis of fraction 2II on starch		
Fraction 4	43	0.5
Removal of serum albumin from fraction 3I		
Fraction 5III	6	0.07
Preparative electrophoresis of fraction 4 on 9% polyacrylamide		

[a] The protein recovered in each step was calculated as a percentage of the original amount of protein.

used to determine the elution volume and the protein was detected in the effluent by immunodiffusion experiments using a "completely absorbed" anti-RBE antiserum. The elution volume of the immunologically active material corresponded to a molecular weight of 70,000.

SRANT antigens in the developing brain. Immunodiffusion experiments with extracts of adult rat brain cortex have indicated that at least three SRANT-type antigens can be detected by the use of "completely absorbed" antiserum to RBE. The major SRANT antigen of adult brain is present in the cerebral cortex of 1-day-old rats but at that stage it is the minor in respect to concentration of two such antigens. However, its concentration increases with maturation while the concentration of the other antigen decreases so that by the 8th day after birth the adult major SRANT antigen predominates. The third species-restricted antigen of nervous tissue appears about the 12th day after birth.

SRANT antigens in spinal cord, peripheral nerve and different regions of the rat brain. Extracts of rat spinal cord contain about as much SRANT as do brain extracts, judging from the heaviness of the precipitin lines formed in immunodiffusion analysis with a "completely absorbed" anti-RBE serum. It is of interest that the spinal cord extracts lack some of the brain-specific antigens of RBE. SRANT was also detected in extracts of rat sciatic nerve. When extracts prepared from the cerebral cortex, decorticated cerebrum,

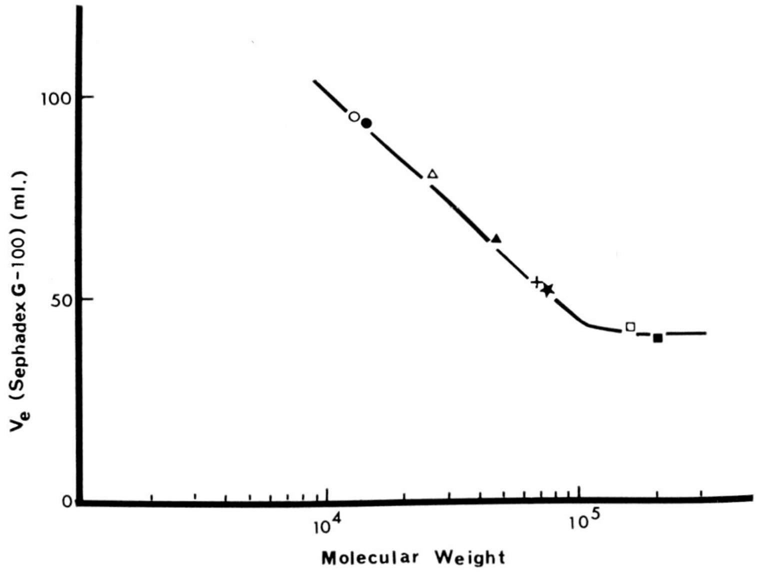

Figure 4. Plot of elution volume (Ve) against log (molecular weight) for proteins on a Sephadex G-100 column. ○, Cytochrome *c*; ● ribonuclease; △, chymotrypsinogen; ▲, ovalbumin; +, bovine serum albumin; ★, SRANT; □, bovine serum γ globulin; ■, blue dextran.

hippocampus, and cerebellum were examined by immunodiffusion analysis with an anti-RBE serum, it was noted that the cerebellum lacked at least four antigens that were present in the other regions; but the major SRANT antigen was present in all the brain areas tested. SRANT was detected only in the "soluble" fraction of rat brain homogenate, although species-specific antigens shared by other rat organs were found in the nuclear, crude mitochondrial and microsomal fractions.

DISCUSSION

The multiplicity of proteins present in aqueous extracts of brain (4, 9) and the fact that the major SRANT antigen existed in two forms having electrophoretic mobilities corresponding to those of an α_1 globulin and an albumin (6) made the purification of this antigen a tedious task and we concentrated our efforts on isolating the more acidic form of the antigen.

Rat serum albumin was always present in RBE even when rats had been thoroughly perfused prior to the removal of their brains. The amount of rat serum albumin could not be reduced below 0.5% of the total protein of RBE. Thus, while preparative electrophoresis, first in starch gel, and then in polyacrylamide gel, was an effective means of separating the antigen from other brain proteins, it was not an efficient method for separating rat serum albumin from the SRANT as the proteins were about the same size and migrated in adjacent bands that overlapped. Thus, the rat serum albumin was eliminated from the purified SRANT in the form of a specific precipitate. The unreactive rabbit γ globulin that remained did not move from the cathodal end of the gel strip during the final stage of preparative electrophoresis.

The purified SRANT gave only one band after it was subjected to electrophoresis in 9% polyacrylamide gel (Fig. 3*A*), indicating that it was electrophoretically homogeneous. It formed only one precipitin line when diffused against an unabsorbed anti-rat brain serum or a "completely absorbed" anti-rat brain serum (Fig. 3 *B* and *C*), indicating that no other antigenic brain proteins or serum proteins could be detected in the preparation.

The molecular weight of SRANT was determined by exclusion gel chromatography on a calibrated Sephadex G-100 column and found to be of the order of 70,000. The fraction of RBE precipitated at 44% saturation with ammonium sulfate was used for this determination and contained both molecular forms of SRANT (see Fig. 1*C*). Since all antigenic activity was eluted in a single peak, there was no evidence for heterogenity in size and one may conclude that the two molecular forms of the protein are characterized physically only by differences in electrical charge.

Three other antigens that also exist in rat brain and are specific for nervous tissue have been characterized. These are the S-100 protein (9), antigen α, purified by Bennett and Edelman (8) from rat brain extracts, and α-BASNT, isolated from bovine brain extracts by Hatcher and MacPherson (22), and found to be an antigen shared by several mammalian species, including the rat. The SRANT protein was discovered a few years ago (6), mainly because of its species-restricted nature; it is thus clearly different from these other brain proteins that are common to mammalian nervous tissue.

The function of the protein is not yet known. In earlier papers (6, 10) the antigen was referred to as an organ- and species-restricted (OSR) antigen. In view of the fact that it is now known to be a component of rat peripheral nerve, it can no longer be characterized accurately as an organ antigen. It is now referred to as a "species-restricted antigen of nervous tissue," abbreviated as SRANT. The antigen was found in the cerebral cortex, the hippocampus and the cerebellum of adult rats and it is the major brain antigen after the 1st week of life. It is restricted to the "soluble" fraction of nervous tissue cells, for it was not detected in the nuclear, crude mitochondrial or microsomal fractions of brain homogenate. Studies of the chemical and physical properties of the protein, of the type of brain cell in which it is localized and of its concentration in various anatomical areas of the brain are continuing in order that its function in nervous tissue may be elucidated.

REFERENCES

1. Hyden, H. and Lange, P. W., Science, *159:* 1370, 1968.
2. Heath, R. G. and Krupp, I., Arch. Gen. Psychiat., *16:* 1, 1967.
3. Mihailovic, L., Divac, I., Milrovic, K., Milosevic, D. and Jankovic, B. D., Exp. Neurol., *24:* 325, 1969.
4. Bogoch, S., Rajam, P. C. and Belval, P. C., Nature, *204:* 73, 1964.

5. Rajam, P. C., Gaudreau, C. J., Grady, A. and Rundlett, S. I., Immunology, *17:* 367, 1969.
6. MacPherson, C. F. C. and Liakopoulou, A., J. Immun., *97:* 450, 1966.
7. Kosinski, E. and Grabar, P., J. Neurochem., *14:* 273, 1967.
8. Bennett, G. S. and Edelman, G. M., J. Biol. Chem., *243:* 6234, 1968.
9. Moore, B. W. and McGregor, D., J. Biol. Chem., *240:* 1647, 1965.
10. Hatcher, V. and MacPherson, C. F. C., J. Immun., *102:* 877, 1969.
11. Witebsky, E., Ann. N. Y. Acad. Sci., *124:* 29, 1965.
12. Poulik, M. D., Nature, *180:* 1477, 1957.
13. Hoerman, K. C., Belekzian, A. Y. and Bersinskas, V. J., Anal. Biochem., *12:* 403, 1965.
14. Raymond, S. and Wang, Y., Anal. Biochem., *1:* 591, 1960.
15. Andrews, P., Biochem. J., *91:* 222, 1964.
16. Gelotte, B., J. Chromatogr., *3:* 330, 1960.
17. Lowry, O. H., Rosebrough, N. J., Farr, A. L. and Randall, R. S., J. Biol. Chem., *193:* 265, 1951.
18. Ouchterlony, O., Acta Path. Microbiol. Scand., *32:* 231, 1953.
19. Scheidegger, J. J., Int. Arch. Allerg., *7:* 103, 1955.
20. De Robertis, E., Pellegrino De Iraldi, A., De Lopes Arnaiz R. and Salfanicoff, L., J. Neurochem., *9:* 23, 1962.
21. Mies, J. H., Klin. Wschr., *31:* 159, 1953.
22. Hatcher, V. and MacPherson, C. F. C., J. Immun., *104:* 633, 1970.

THE JOURNAL OF IMMUNOLOGY

Vol. 105, No. 2, August 1970
Printed in U.S.A.

COMMUNICATIONS

Reaction of Serum from Pregnant Hamsters with Surface of Cells Transformed by SV40 [1]

RONALD DUFF AND FRED RAPP

From the Department of Microbiology, College of Medicine, The Milton S. Hershey Medical Center of The Pennsylvania State University, Hershey, Pennsylvania 17033

Human adenocarcinomas of the digestive tract contain common "tumor-specific" antigens (1). These antigens have also been found to cross-react with antigens found in embryonic and fetal tissue but not with normal tissue (2). Sera from pregnant women appear to contain antibodies directed against these antigens (Gold, personal communication). Hamster cells which have been transformed by simian virus 40 (SV40) have a surface (S) antigen which has been found to be specific for cells transformed by the virus (3). This report describes observations that suggest that the surface antigen on SV40-transformed Syrian hamster cells may be immunologically related to an antigen found during embryonic development.

MATERIALS AND METHODS

Immunofluorescence techniques for the detection of SV40 S antigen have been previously described (3, 4). Antisera reacting specifically with the S antigen were prepared by two methods. In the first method weanling hamsters (Con Olsen) were injected with 10^6 SV40-transformed marmoset monkey cells at weekly intervals for 4 weeks. Five weeks after the initial injection, the animals were bled by cardiac puncture and the sera were collected and pooled. The second method utilized SV40 virus which had been purified by density gradient centrifugation in cesium chloride. Weanling hamsters were injected five times at weekly intervals with 10^{10} viral particles and bled by cardiac puncture 7 weeks after the initial injection.

RESULTS

Sera from pregnant hamsters 14 or 15 days after onset of their second pregnancy were collected and reacted with cells transformed by SV40 or by PARA (defective SV40)-adenovirus 7 (Ad 7), or with spontaneously transformed hamster cells. As shown in Table I, the majority (greater than 80%) of the pregnant hamster sera reacted specifically with the surface of cells transformed by the SV40 genome. No reaction was observed with normal cells or with the spontaneously transformed cells.

The specificity of the pregnant sera for cells transformed by SV40 is also demonstrated in Table II. In this experiment, pregnant sera which reacted with SV40- and PARA-transformed cells did not react with hamster cells transformed by simian adenovirus 7 or by dimethylbenzanthracene (DMBA), or with either spontaneously transformed cells or normal hamster embryo fibroblasts. Furthermore, antisera specifically prepared against the SV40 S antigen reacted in an identical manner and served as the positive control. Serum from female hamsters known never to have been pregnant did not react with the surface of any of the cell types tested.

The correlation of the appearance of this S antibody with the gravid state of the animal is shown in Table III. Sera from weanling female hamsters which did not react with the surface of the SV40-transformed cells were a negative control. Sera from hamsters which were 3 to 5 days pregnant for the first time did not contain anti-S antibodies. The surface reaction occurred in only one of seven sera from initially gravid hamsters, 13 to 15 days after impregnation. The results with second pregnancy hamsters were in contrast to those obtained with first pregnancy hamsters. One of three sera collected 3 to 5 days after impregnation contained antibodies against the S antigen. However, five of six sera were positive when the hamsters were 13 to 15 days pregnant for the second time.

The persistence of the antibody in hamsters after the termination of pregnancy was found to be limited. It was not detectable 1 week after

[1] This work was supported by Contract NIH 70-2024 from the National Institutes of Health, Department of Health, Education and Welfare.

TABLE I

Surface reaction with sera from gravid hamsters against transformed hamster cells carrying the SV40 genome

Cell Type	Positive Sera	Negative Sera	Per Cent Positive	Per Cent Negative
SV40-transformed (H-50)[a]	22	4	85	15
PARA-Ad7 transformed (1e)[b]	25	5	83	17
PARA-Ad7 transformed (2cT-1)[c]	23	5	82	18
Hamster embryo[d] fibroblasts	0	31	0	100
BHK-21[e]	0	14	0	100

[a] The H-50 cells were from a tumor induced by the injection of SV40 into a newborn Syrian hamster. They have been carried for 28 to 35 passages in cell culture.

[b] The 1e cells were transformed by PARA-Ad7 *in vitro*. These cells have been shown to be oncogenic in weanling hamsters. The 1e cells were in tissue culture passage 35 to 45.

[c] The 2cT-1 cells were transformed by a variant of PARA-Ad7 which induces the SV40-tumor antigen in the cytoplasm. The 2cT-1 cells were in tissue culture passage 36 to 38.

[d] The hamster embryo fibroblasts were from 14-day hamster embryos and were used in tissue culture passage 1.

[e] A spontaneously transformed line of baby hamster kidney cells.

delivery and did not reappear during the ensuing 5 weeks in which the animals were tested. Dilution of the positive sera yielded negative results; therefore, slight loss in titer following termination of pregnancy may account for this rapid loss of activity.

DISCUSSION

The results presented in the paper show that sera from pregnant hamsters may contain antibodies which react with an antigen on the surface of hamster cells transformed by SV40. Preliminary results indicate that the reaction is specific for SV40-transformed cells and that normal hamster cells, as well as SA7, DMBA, and spontaneously transformed cells do not have this antigen on their surface. Neither a direct nor an indirect relationship of a fetal antigen to the previously described SV40 S antigen has been demonstrated. However, it has been shown by other investigators that the presence of the SV40 genome is not necessary for the presence of SV40 S antigen on transformed cells (5). The loss of the viral genome from the cell without loss of a specific antigen may indicate that the antigen

TABLE II

Specificity of the surface reaction of pregnant hamster sera for transformed cells containing the SV40 genome

Type of Serum	Cells Transformed by					
	SV40	PARA	SA7[a]	DMBA	Spont.	None[b]
Pg. hamster	+	+	−	−	−	−
Pg. hamster	+	+	−	−	−	−
Pg. hamster	+	+	−	−	−	−
Anti-SV40 S[c]	+	+	−	−	−	−
Anti-SV40 S[d]	+	+	−	−	−	−
Nor. hamster[e]	−	−	−	−	−	−
Nor. hamster	−	−	−	−	−	−

[a] SA7, simian adenovirus 7.

[b] None, hamster embryo fibroblasts.

[c] Antiserum prepared by injection of transformed marmoset cells, see *Materials and Methods*.

[d] Antiserum prepared by injection of purified SV40, see *Materials and Methods*.

[e] Nor. hamster: sera from 3-month-old female hamsters.

TABLE III

Correlation of the surface reaction with the gravid state of the hamster

Pregnant State of the Animal	Days after Impregnation	Cell Type		
		AHK[a]	H-5[b]	PARA-Ad7 (1e)[c]
Weanling female hamster	0	0/7[d]	0/7	0/7
First pregnancy	3–5	0/3	0/3	0/3
First pregnancy	13–15	0/7	1/7	1/7
Second pregnancy	3–5	0/3	1/3	1/3
Second pregnancy	13–15	0/6	5/6	5/6

[a] AHK: adult hamster kidney cells, tissue culture passage number 1.

[b] H-50: cells from a tumor induced by SV40 in a newborn Syrian hamster. Animal passage number 4 and tissue culture passage number 25.

[c] 1e: hamster cells transformed *in vitro* by the PARA-Ad7 hybrid, tissue culture passage number 30.

[d] Number sera positive/number sera tested.

represents the expression of a cellular gene, which might be normally expressed during embryonic development.

A second alternative is suggested by the possibility that the surface antigen detected with sera from pregnant hamsters is one of a mosaic of antigens found on the surface of a cell following transformation by SV40. Some of these antigens may represent the derepression of cellular genes, and other surface antigens may be the result of gene products from the SV40 genome itself.

REFERENCES

1. Gold, P. and Freedman, S. O., J. Exp. Med., *121:* 439, 1965.
2. Gold, P. and Freedman, S. O., J. Exp. Med., *122:* 467, 1965.
3. Tevethia, S. S., Katz, M. and Rapp, F., Proc. Soc. Exp. Biol. Med., *119:* 896, 1965.
4. Duff, R. and Rapp, F., J. Virol., In press.
5. Levin, M. J., Oxman, M. N., Diamandopoulos, G. T., Levine, A. S., Henry, P. H. and Enders, J. F., Proc. Nat. Acad. Sci., *62:* 589, 1969.

THE JOURNAL OF IMMUNOLOGY
Vol. 105, No. 2, August 1970

Fetal Antigen Capable of Inducing Transplantation Immunity against SV40 Hamster Tumor Cells[1]

J. H. COGGIN, K. R. AMBROSE AND N. G. ANDERSON

From the Molecular Anatomy (MAN) Program, Oak Ridge National Laboratory, Oak Ridge, Tennessee and the Department of Microbiology, University of Tennessee, Knoxville, Tennessee

Hamster, mouse and human cells transformed by simian virus 40 (SV40) share a common antigen capable of stimulating specific transplantation immunity against SV40-induced tumors in hamsters (1, 2). Cursory consideration of this observation might suggest that the viral genome must code for the common tumor-specific antigen in the different cell species. Knowledge acquired recently about the size of the SV40 genome limits the potential informational complement of this virus to seven to eight genes (3). Available data indicate that at least six genes are required for virus synthesis (3, 4), and radiation studies suggest that one or two different genes are required for transformation (5). It is becoming increasingly difficult to adhere to the concept that the virus codes directly for the tumor-specific transplantation antigen (TSTA) which is incorporated into the membrane of transformed cells unless the TSTA is a small protein and is a pleiotropic viral gene product.

An alternative hypothesis could be that the specificity of the transforming potential of the virus may be accomplished by the specific activation (repression or derepression) of cellular genes. Prehn reported that embryomas might possess antigens which are cross-reactive with antigens of certain methylcholanthrene-induced tumors (6). Ting concluded that mouse fetus injected into syngeneic adult mice did not promote transplantation immunity against polyoma-transformed mouse cells (7). In this and other similar studies (2) presentation of fetal tissue to the adult animal may result in the rapid maturation of the fetal cell under the humoral (hormonal) influence of the mature animal eliminating or masking fetal antigens comparable to those expressed as transplantation antigens in tumor cells. A preliminary examination of the role of fetal antigen in transplantation resistance indicates that irradiated hamster and mouse fetal tissues contain antigens which evoke immunity to SV40-induced tumors in syngeneic hamsters.

MATERIALS AND METHODS

The results reported here were obtained using the SV40 hamster tumor cell line, F5-1, produced in random-bred Syrian golden hamsters, and also an SV40-induced tumor cell line derived in the inbred LSH/LAK line of hamsters. The F5-1 line has never been observed to yield infectious virus whereas the inbred tumor cell line yields virus in low titer. No histoincompatability has ever been reported for the random-bred hamsters used. Irradiated tumor cell preparations as well as adult control tissue were prepared as previously described (8). Hamster cells were obtained from fetuses of 9, 12 and 14 days gestation. Fetuses at each age were harvested aseptically, rinsed several times in Hanks' balanced salt solution (HBSS) and aspirated gently through a 26-gauge needle. The dispersed cells were then pelleted at 25°C by centrifugation and resuspended in HBSS. The procedure was repeated once and the pellet resuspended in HBSS to contain 5×10^6 viable cells/ml. BALB/c mouse fetal tissue was obtained during the 10th to 14th day of gestation and treated in a similar fashion. All tissue used to immunize 4- to 6-week-old hamsters was subjected to 5000 R x-irradiation as described previously (9) and injected by the intraperitoneal route in volumes of 1 ml. Immunization was administered on three occasions at 1-week intervals with freshly prepared cells. SV40 tumor cells were sealed into diffusion chambers as previously described (9) and implanted into the peritoneal cavity of anesthetized hamsters 10 days following the last immunization. Chambers were left in place 5 days, removed and examined for viable cells by the trypan blue dye exclusion test.

[1] Research conducted under the joint NIH-AEC Molecular Anatomy (MAN) Program supported by the National Cancer Institute, the National Institute of General Medical Sciences, the National Institute of Allergy and Infectious Diseases, and the United States Atomic Energy Commission, under contract with the Union Carbide Corporation Nuclear Division.

TABLE I

Induction of transplantation immunity to SV40 hamster tumor cells employing hamster fetal tissues as immunogen

Antigen[a]	Average No. of Viable Cells/Chamber at 5 Days Post-Implant[b]	Percentage Inhibition of Target Cell Growth	Percentage Protection against SV40 Tumor Cell Challenge[c]
Unvaccinated controls	339,400		0
SV40 tumor cells	101,800	70	100
Adult syngeneic kidney cells	330,400	NSD[d]	
Hamster fetal cells			
9-day gestation	145,700	57	70
12-day gestation	163,200	53	60
14-day gestation	315,600	7	0
Mouse fetal cells			
12-day gestation	203,500	40	40

[a] All cells subjected to 5000 R of x-irradiation before intraperitoneal injection.

[b] Chambers originally inoculated with 15,000 viable SV40 tumor cells.

[c] Protective efficacy against cell challenge in animals receiving test preparations compared to tumor incidence in hamsters receiving adult hamster tissue as immunogen.

[d] NSD, not a statistically significant difference from unvaccinated control result as determined by the Wilcoxon test. All other differences significant at 1% confidence level.

Following removal of the chambers, the hamsters were subsequently challenged with 5×10^4 SV40 tumor cells in the right subscapular space. Animals were palpated weekly for tumors.

RESULTS AND DISCUSSION

SV40 tumor cells in diffusion chambers in adult hamsters immunized with 9- or 12-day irradiated hamster fetal cells failed to proliferate to the same extent as did the target cells in diffusion chambers of control animals. The degree of inhibition in a typical experiment is shown in Table I. Previous studies using the diffusion chamber assay indicate that the inhibition results from the binding of specific antibody at the plasma membrane of the target cell (8). Immunization with 14-day hamster fetal cells failed to induce cytostatic antibody. SV40 hamster tumor cells (F5-1) exhibited cytostatis in diffusion chambers in hamsters immunized against irradiated mouse fetal cells. Cell challenge studies from three experiments confirmed the existence of transplantation immunity in those animals which had exhibited cytostatic antibody. The degree of protection against challenge obtained with 9-day fetus from hamsters was 10% in one experiment, 30% in another and 70% in the experiment cited. Variation may result from either difference in fetus (number per mother or size) or in the cell challenge standardization. Similar results to those described in Table I using the random-bred hamster were obtained in the inbred hamster following immunization with 9- and 14-day irradiated hamster fetal cells.

The results reported here suggest that hamster and mouse fetal cells possess an equivalent or at least cross-reactive antigen to that present in SV40 hamster tumor cells as determined by the induction of cytostatic antibody and transplantation immunity. In the hamster fetus the antigen was no longer expressed by the 14th day of gestation. The negative results obtained by Ting (7), Kit *et al.* (2) and ourselves with non-irradiated fetal cells injected into adult animals can most plausibly be explained on the basis of rapid maturation of the fetal cell in the mature environment. These data clearly suggest that transplantation-like antigens are present in the hamster fetus during embryogenesis and are not expressed in the terminal stages of gestation. Duff and Rapp (10) have observed that normal pregnant hamsters develop antibody against SV40 hamster tumor cell S antigen, in agreement with our results. The observation that irradiated mouse fetal tissue was immunogenic against SV40-induced hamster tumors in hamsters is compatible with the fact that mouse and hamster tumor cells induced by SV40 share a common TSTA. It is important in future work that we establish whether the antigens expressed in embryogenesis are, in fact, identical to those present in the virus-transformed cell. Of equal importance is the need to establish the spectrum of tumor transplantation-like antigens present in fetal cells employing a variety of viral and chemically stimulated tumors. Finally, the relationship between human fetal antigens and human tumors must be examined in the light of this observation.

REFERENCES

1. Girardi, A. J., Proc. Nat. Acad. Sci., *54:* 445, 1965.

2. Kit, S., Kurimura, T. and Dubbs, D. R., Int. J. Cancer, *4:* 384, 1969.
3. Dulbecco, R., Science, *166:* 962, 1969.
4. Crawford, L., in *Molecular Basis of Virology*, Edited by H. Frankel-Conrat, p. 393, Reinhold Book Corporation, New York, 1968.
5. Defendi, V. and Jensen, F., Science, *157:* 703, 1967.
6. Prehn, R. T., in *Cross-reacting Antigens and Neoantigens*, Edited by J. J. Trentin, p. 105, The Williams & Wilkins Company, Baltimore, 1967.
7. Ting, R. C., Nature, *217:* 858, 1968.
8. Ambrose, K. R., Candler, E. L. and Coggin, J. H., Proc. Soc. Exp. Biol. Med., *132:* 1013, 1969.
9. Coggin, J. H. and Ambrose, K. R., Proc. Soc. Exp. Biol. Med., *130:* 246, 1969.
10. Duff, R. J. and Rapp, F., Bact. Proc., p. 172, 1970.

THE JOURNAL OF IMMUNOLOGY
Vol. 105, No. 2, August 1970
Printed in U.S.A.

Cellular Reactivity to Tuberculin in Immune and Serologically-Unresponsive Guinea Pigs[1,2]

BERNARD W. JANICKI, GERALDINE P. SCHECHTER AND KAREN E. SCHULTZ

From the Veterans Administration Hospital, Washington, D. C. 20422

We have reported that the serologic reactivity of young guinea pigs to mycobacterial antigens decreased proportionately as the sensitizing dose of heat-killed tubercle bacilli was increased (1). Using animals from 0 to 4 weeks old, we found that approximately 67% of those that received doses of 0.5 mg (dry weight) or less exhibited precipitating and complement-fixing antibodies against an unheated mycobacterial culture filtrate when tested 4 weeks after injection, whereas only 34% of the animals that received doses greater than 0.5 mg reacted serologically when similarly tested. Serologic unresponsiveness was induced quite effectively by injecting newborn animals with a 5-mg dose; only 1 of 14 animals sensitized in this manner exhibited anti-mycobacterial precipitins when tested 4 to 5 weeks later. Hypersensitivity to tuberculin purified protein derivative (PPD) in the serologically-unresponsive animals, however, appeared to be unaffected. Animals injected with the 5-mg dose at birth exhibited unequivocal skin reactivity to PPD 5 weeks later, but the reactions were smaller than those of adults that received the same sensitizing dose (1). Although it was likely that the lessened skin reactivity could be attributed to an incomplete recovery from the temporary inability (1–4) of sensitized young guinea pigs to express delayed-type hypersensitive skin reactions, it seemed pertinent for a more complete definition of serologic unresponsiveness to examine its influence on delayed hypersensitive reactivity more closely. For this reason, we performed a series of experiments in which the *in vitro* tuberculin reactivity of cells from serologically-unresponsive guinea pigs was measured and compared with that of responsive littermate animals using the macrophage migration-inhibition reaction and the lymphocyte blastogenic response. The purpose of this report is to provide evidence that serologically-unresponsive guinea pigs develop completely unimpaired delayed hypersensitivity to PPD, their cells reacting to the same degree as those of responsive animals.

As described previously (1), a suspension of autoclaved *Mycobacterium tuberculosis* (H37Rv strain) in incomplete Freund's adjuvant (Difco Laboratories, Detroit, Mich.) was prepared for sensitizing Hartley strain guinea pigs. Three littermate groups of newborn animals were used; those designated for the unresponsive group were injected intramuscularly in the upper part of the hind leg on the day of birth with 1 ml of the suspension which contained 5 mg (dry weight) of killed bacilli. Each animal of the immune young group similarly received 0.1 ml (0.5 mg) of the suspension and each of the normal young animals received 1 ml of incomplete adjuvant. As required, the mothers of the litters served as immune adult controls, and each received 1 ml of the sensitizing suspension on the day of parturition. The animals' reactivity to tuberculin was determined 6 weeks after injection.

Oil-induced peritoneal exudate cells were used for the migration-inhibition studies; the methods described by David *et al.* (5) were used for this purpose with only minor modifications. Animals were injected intraperitoneally with 30 ml of sterile paraffin oil (Fisher Scientific, Westford, Mass.) and killed 4 days later; the peritoneal exudates were collected in cold, sterile Hanks' balanced salt solution (Microbiological Associates, Bethesda, Md.). The cell suspension was kept at room temperature in a separatory funnel for 15 min after which the aqueous phase was withdrawn and centrifuged in the cold for 10 min at 200 × G. The sedimented cells were washed twice with Hanks' solution and adjusted to an approximately 10% concentration in Eagle's minimal essential medium (Microbiological Associates) which contained 15% guinea pig serum

[1] This investigation was supported in part by the United States-Japan Cooperative Medical Science Program administered by the National Institute of Allergy and Infectious Diseases of the National Institutes of Health, Departmnt of Health, Education and Welfare (Grant AI-07967).

[2] This material was presented at the annual meeting of the American Society for Microbiology in Boston, Mass., on April 29, 1970.

(Hyland Laboratories, Los Angeles, Calif.), 1% L-glutamine, penicillin G (100 units/ml) and streptomycin (0.1 mg/ml). Non-heparinized capillary tubes (1.3 to 1.5 mm diameter, 75 mm long) were filled with the suspension, sealed at one end with paraffin wax and centrifuged. The tubes were cut just below the cell-fluid interface and the sections containing the cells were placed in sterile silicone grease (Dow Corning) on the bottom of a plastic Cooper dish (Falcon Plastics). Each dish contained 4 to 6 capillary tubes and received 4 ml of culture medium as described above, with or without excipient-free tuberculin PPD (provided by Dr. M. W. Fisher, Parke, Davis and Company) at a final concentration of 10 μg/ml. The dishes were sealed with transparent tape and incubated at 37°C for 24 hr. Migration of cells from the capillary was recorded by tracing a 15.6 × projection of the area surrounding the capillary tip. The area of cell migration was measured by planimetry of the tracing. Cellular migration in the presence of PPD was expressed as a percentage of the migration area of the same animal's cells in medium without PPD. At least four capillaries in both control and PPD cultures were measured for each animal.

The uptake of tritiated thymidine by lymph node cells was used to measure the PPD-induced blastogenic response. For this purpose, the animal was killed and the aortic lymph nodes, as well as the inguinal nodes opposite the sensitization site, were excised, trimmed of extraneous tissue, minced and teased apart in a small volume of medium 199 (Grand Island Biological, Grand Island, N.Y.). The cell suspension was kept at room temperature for 15 min to allow the heavy particles to settle after which the supernatant cell suspension was removed and centrifuged at 200 × G for 10 min. The sedimented cells were washed once and resuspended in medium 199 and total and differential cell counts were performed on the suspension. The cells were cultured in 16- x 125-mm screw-capped plastic tubes (Falcon) in 3 ml of medium containing 80% medium 199, 20% guinea pig serum (Hyland Laboratories), penicillin G (100 units/ml), and streptomycin (0.1 mg/ml). Six tubes, each containing 2.5 to 5 × 10^6 lymphocytes, were prepared for each animal. Excipient-free PPD was added in a final concentration of 1 μg/ml, as suggested by Loewi *et al.* (6), to three tubes of each set; the remaining tubes served as unstimulated controls. The cultures were incubated in an upright position without agitation at 37°C. On the 4th day, tritiated thymidine (Amersham/Searle) was added at a final concentration of 0.1 μCi/ml of culture medium and the cultures were incubated for an additional 3 hr after which they were processed using the procedure described by Moorhead *et al.* (7). Trichloroacetic acid-precipitable radioactivity was measured in a scintillation counter with an efficiency of counting, as determined by a chloroform-quenched standard, in a range of 40% to 45%. The values of individual cultures generally were well within 30% of the mean. PPD-induced blastogenesis was expressed as a stimulated to control ratio (S/C) which was calculated by dividing the disintegrations/min of PPD cultures by that of their unstimulated controls. Blastogenesis also was confirmed morphologically by examination of Wright-stained smears made from selected cultures.

In some experiments the animals also were tuberculin-tested and serum specimens were obtained for serologic testing. In this case, 2 days before death the animals were injected intradermally with 5 μg of PPD (Merck, Sharp and Dohme). On the day of death the average diameter of induration at the skin test site was measured and 5 to 10 ml of blood were withdrawn by cardiac puncture. The sera were stored at −20°C until tested for the presence of anti-mycobacterial precipitins by diffusion in agar against an unheated culture filtrate of the H37Rv strain as described previously (1).

The first experiment was designed to provide a comparison of the dermal, cellular and humoral responses to the tubercle bacillus in immune and serologically unresponsive littermate animals using normal littermates as controls. The results obtained with six animals in each group are summarized in Table I; both immune and unresponsive animals exhibited unequivocal ($p < 0.01$) dermal and cellular hypersensitivity to tuberculin. No difference ($p > 0.10$) in dermal and cellular reactivity between immune and unresponsive littermates was noted although, as expected (1), the majority of the immune group exhibited precipitins against the H37Rv culture filtrate antigen and none of the unresponsive group was serologically reactive.

The blastogenic response to tuberculin was studied in a second experiment. In this case, sensitized adult animals served as positive controls for the immune and unresponsive young

TABLE I

Comparison of anti-mycobacterial responses in normal, immune and serologically-unresponsive young guinea pigs

Group	Immune response		
	Dermal[a]	Cellular[b]	Humoral[c]
Normal	0.0	77.2 ± 18.2	0/6
Immune	18.1 ± 2.9	35.6 ± 24.3	5/6
Unresponsive	17.4 ± 2.7	40.2 ± 19.3	0/6

[a] Values represent mean diameter of induration (mm) ± standard deviation.

[b] Values represent mean percentage of migration ± standard deviation.

[c] Values represent number of sera exhibiting anti-mycobacterial precipitins over number of sera tested.

TABLE II

Comparison of PPD-induced blastogenesis in normal, immune and serologically-unresponsive young guinea pigs and in immune adult animals

Group[a]	Blastogenic Response[b]
Normal young (4)	1.3 ± 0.4
Immune young (6)	7.0 ± 3.7
Unresponsive young (7)	4.9 ± 3.2
Immune adults (5)	7.1 ± 4.6

[a] Values in parentheses represent number of animals in the group.

[b] Values represent mean S/C ratio ± standard deviation.

and normal littermates were used as negative controls. The results, which are summarized in Table II, clearly demonstrated significant blastogenesis in cultures of lymph node cells from immune adults ($p < 0.02$), as well as with cells from immune and unresponsive young animals ($p < 0.01$). No difference ($p > 0.10$) was found between immune and unresponsive littermates or when either group of young animals was compared with the immune adult controls.

It also should be noted that matched littermates and adults in this experiment were selected for parallel measurements of PPD-induced migration inhibition and blastogenesis, the same animal's cells being tested by both methods. The results obtained with animals representative of each group are presented in Table III. All animals injected with tubercle bacilli showed marked inhibition of peritoneal cell migration by PPD. Similarly, but with the exception of one unresponsive animal, lymph node cells of sensitized animals exhibited PPD-induced blastogenesis. It was of interest that, although there appeared to be a general parallelism between these factors of cell reactivity, analysis of the data indicated no significant correlation ($p > 0.10$) between the degree of blastogenesis and the degree of migration inhibition. This finding is consistent with the recent demonstration by Bast and Dvorak (8) that the blastogenic response can be dissociated from delayed hypersensitivity in guinea pigs exhibiting cutaneous basophil (Jones-Mote) hypersensitivity. Thus, it may well be, as implied recently by Oppenheim and his associates (9), that the antigen-induced blastogenic response may represent a cellular reaction common to the secondary immune response rather than a reaction unique to the delayed hypersensitive state.

Taken collectively, the results of these experiments provide unequivocal evidence that the serologically-unresponsive animal develops delayed hypersensitivity to tuberculin to the same degree as its immunologically-unimpaired, sensitized littermate. It therefore appears reasonable to consider that serologic unresponsiveness is a form of partial immunologic paralysis in which the animal's humoral response to one or more mycobacterial antigens is suppressed while its hypersensitive responses to the same or other mycobacterial antigens are unaltered. Because the development of delayed hypersensitivity to tuberculin has been shown to be unimpaired, it

TABLE III

Summary of parallel measurements of PPD-induced migration inhibition and blastogenesis in littermate and adult animals

Litter	Cellular Reactivity[a]			
	Normal young	Immune young	Unresponsive young	Immune adults
A	87.2/1.6			26.7/3.6
B		42.2/5.1		45.1/3.4
C		31.1/5.7	27.7/4.5	41.0/9.5
		18.2/3.1		
D		15.5/5.4	28.2/1.6	9.5/14.0

[a] Values represent percentage of migration over S/C ratio.

is quite likely that the diminished dermal reactivity to tuberculin noted earler (1) for unresponsive animals can be attributed solely to an incomplete recovery from their temporary inability to effectively express delayed reactivity in the skin.

REFERENCES

1. Janicki, B. W. and Aron, S. A., J. Immun., *101:* 121, 1968.
2. Freund, J., J. Immun., *17:* 465, 1929.
3. Waksman, B. H. and Matoltsy, M., J. Immun., *81:* 235, 1958.
4. Salvin, S. B., Gregg, M. G. and Smith, R. F., J. Exp. Med., *115:* 707, 1962.
5. David, J. R., Al-Askari, S., Lawrence, H. S. and Thomas, L., J. Immun., *93:* 264, 1964.
6. Loewi, G., Temple, A. and Vischer, T. L., Immunology, *14:* 257, 1968.
7. Moorhead, J. F., Connolly, J. J. and McFarland, W., J. Immun., *99:* 413, 1967.
8. Bast, R. C., Jr. and Dvorak, H. F., Fed. Proc., *29:* 501, 1970.
9. Oppenheim, J. J., Blaese, R. M. and Waldmann, T. A., J. Immun., *104:* 835, 1970.

THE JOURNAL OF IMMUNOLOGY
Vol. 105, No. 2, August 1970

Reciprocal Neutralizing Cross-Reaction between Rhinovirus Types 9 and 32[1]

MARION K. COONEY AND GEORGE E. KENNY

From the Department of Preventive Medicine, School of Medicine, University of Washington, Seattle, Washington 98105

Rhinoviruses are a large group of small, acid-labile RNA viruses which presently are classified in 55 serotypes and one subtype (1). Some 30 additional types are being considered for admission as new serotypes.

Rabbit antisera to 25 rhinovirus types produced in our laboratories (2) were tested for neutralization against 30 to 300 tissue culture infectious doses (TCD_{50}) of the corresponding 24 heterologous rhinovirus types in HeLa cell tubes. Details of the method have been described elsewhere (2). Antisera were tested at a 1:20 dilution, which represented an antibody concentration of 50 to 500 times the 50% neutralization endpoint for the homologous virus. The rhinovirus serotypes tested are listed in Table I. Reciprocal neutralization was shown between rhinovirus types 9 and 32, and four possible one-way cross-reactions (not involving types 9 or 32) were seen, but are not shown in the table since they have not been verified to date. The previously described reaction between 1A and 1B is also shown in Table I.

The cross-reaction between types 9 and 32 was confirmed with reference antiserum to rhinovirus 32 (bovine) obtained from the Research Resources Branch of the National Institutes of Health. A 1:20 dilution of this antiserum (homologous titer 1:512) neutralized three field strains of rhinovirus type 9 (identified with polyvalent serum produced for the New York Virus Watch Program (3)) and the prototype strain of rhinovirus type 9. Reference antiserum to type 9 was not available.

In order to rule out the possibility that a mixture of viruses had been used as immunogens, rhinovirus type 9 (CV 13, strain 211) and type 32 (strain NIH 363) were triply plaque-purified and the progeny of a single plaque from the third successive plating were used as immunogens for rabbits (two for each immunogen). The resultant neutralizing antibody titers are shown in Table I.

Table II shows the neutralization rate constants (k values), calculated according to the formula given by Adams (4), for rabbit antisera produced to parental and plaque-purified rhinovirus 9 and 32 immunogens. The results obtained with the serum from only one rabbit are shown because the responses in pairs of rabbits were essentially identical. The results with rhinovirus types 1A and 1B (5) are shown for comparison. Rhinovirus types 9 and 32 cross-reacted strongly enough so that 20 antibody units of type 32 parental-strain antiserum just neutralized type 9, whereas 20 antibody units of antiserum to the plaque-purified strain of type 32 did not neutralize type 9. However, 20 antibody units of both type 9 antisera failed to neutralize type 32, indicating that the cross-reaction is stronger with the type 32 antiserum. This cross-reaction is similar to that between 1A and 1B, which was relatively stronger with 1B than with 1A serum (Table II). Antiserum to plaque-purified type 9 gave results similar to those obtained with the original type 9 immunogen. Although the neutralizing antibody titer and the k value of antiserum to plaque-purified rhinovirus 32 were lower than those of the original, the cross-reactivity of types 9 and 32 was still demonstrable.

Fairly extensive cross-reactions among rhinovirus serotypes have been reported by others (6), but Conant and Hamparian (7) showed that neutralizing activity for heterologous viruses could be removed by adsorption with human liver powder. Although our rabbit antisera did not produce observable cytotoxic effects in HeLa cell cultures, anticellular agglutinin titers of 1:80 to 1:160 could be demonstrated by the mixed cell agglutination test (2). After adsorption with HeLa cells, anticellular agglutination titers were <1:10, but the neutralizing antibody titers for rhinovirus types 9 and 32 were not reduced. Furthermore, the large final dilution factor (1:2000 minimum) in determining neutralization rate constants virtually removes the possibility that anticellular antibody could produce apparent neutralization.

[1] This work was supported by NIH Grant 5-R01-AI 07062 and Vaccine Development Branch Contract PH 43-63-562.

In view of these findings, we suggest that rhinovirus type 32 be considered as a subtype of rhinovirus type 9, since the latter has priority. However, individual antisera would be necessary for identification, as is the case with types 1A and 1B. Since the degree of antigenic heterogeneity among the rhinoviruses is presently unknown, we also suggest that reclassification be delayed until more data are available. Recently Schieble *et al.* (8) reported the isolation of variant (prime) strains of rhinovirus 22 in which the prototype strain is neutralized well by antiserum to the variant, but the variant is neutralized poorly by antiserum to the prototype. In addition, Stott and Walker (9) have shown the existence of serologically differentiated variants of rhinovirus 51.

TABLE I

Neutralizing antibody titers of 25 rhinoviruses vs homologous and heterologous antisera

Anti-Rhinovirus Rabbit Sera	Antibody Titer[a]	
	Homologous type	Heterologous type: titer
1A	5760	1B:50
1B	2048	1A:100
2	2048	
9	2882	32:40
11	1448	
14	2048	
29	2048	
30	1448	
31	2048	
32	1620	9:160
33	2882	
34	5760	
35	4096	
36	5760	
37	2882	
38	4096	
39	1620	
40	2576	
41	10000	
42	2048	
43	2200	
47	1024	
49	5760	
51	23000	
54	256	
9 plaque-purified	1024	32:16
32 plaque-purified	730	9:20

[a] Expressed as reciprocal of serum dilution which completely neutralized virus in 50% of tubes inoculated.

TABLE II

Comparison of neutralization constants of rhinovirus types 9, 32, 1A, 1B

Virus	Antibody					
	Parental strains		Plaque-purified strains			
	9	32	9	32	1A	1B
9	575[a]	5.8	460	4.1		
32	3.1	194	2.3	133		
9 plaque-purified			492	5.6	<0.7	
32 plaque-purified			2.8	86.5	<0.7	
1A			<0.7	<0.7	1012[b]	8.2
1B					4.6	110

[a] Neutralization rate constant calculated by the equation: $k = 2.3 \times (D/t) \times \log (V_o/V_t)$ where D = reciprocal of final serum dilution in virus-serum mixture, t = time (min), V_o = virus plaque-forming units (pfu) at time O, V_o = virus pfu at time t (4).

[b] Data reported in a previous publication (5).

We are unaware of any previous evidence that rhinovirus 9 and 32 have been directly compared. The titers of antibody to the heterologous type (9 or 32) are such that these viruses could easily be considered to be serologically unique when only 20 antibody units of either antibody are employed. The fact that potent rhinovirus antiserum without excessive anticellular antibody can be prepared in rabbits when sufficiently high-titered viral immunogens are administered (2) indicates that comparisons among the entire rhinovirus group could readily be made. Such comparisons would be facilitated by the use of combinatorial pools (5).

REFERENCES

1. Kapikian, A. Z., Conant, R. M., Hamparian, V. V., Chanock, R. M., Chapple, P. J., Dick, E. C., Fenters, J. D., Gwaltney, J. M., Hamre, D., Holper, J. C., Jordan, W. S., Lennette, E. H., Melnick, J. L., Mogabgab, W. J., Mufson, M. A., Phillips, C. A., Schieble, J. H. and Tyrrell, D. A. J., Nature, *213:* 761, 1967.

2. Cooney, M. K. and Kenny, G. E., Proc. Soc. Exp. Biol. Med., *133:* 645, 1970.
3. Fawzy, K. Y., Fox, J. P., Ketler, A., Brandt, C. D., Hall, C. E. and Haraway, A. W., Amer. J. Epidem., *86:* 653, 1967.
4. Adams, M. H., *Bacteriophages*, p. 110, Interscience Publishers, New York, 1969.
5. Kenny, G. E., Cooney, M. K. and Thompson, D. J., Amer. J. Epidem., *91:* 439, 1970.
6. Fenters, J. D., Gillum, S. S., Holper, J. C. and Marquis, G. S., Amer. J. Epidem., *84:* 10, 1966.
7. Conant, R. M. and Hamparian, V. V., J. Immun., *100:* 114, 1968.
8. Schieble, J. H., Lennette, E. H. and Fox, V. L., Proc. Soc. Exp. Biol. Med., *133:* 329, 1970.
9. Stott, E. J. and Walker, M., Nature, *224:* 1311, 1969.

THE JOURNAL OF IMMUNOLOGY
Vol. 105, No. 2, August 1970
Printed in U.S.A.

The Unblocked N-Terminal Sequence of Chicken IgG λ-Like Light Chains[1]

RALPH T. KUBO, IRWIN Y. ROSENBLUM AND ALBERT A. BENEDICT

From the Department of Microbiology and the Department of Biochemistry and Biophysics, University of Hawaii, Honolulu, Hawaii 96822

The light chains of human and mouse immunoglobulins belong to two antigenically and chemically distinct classes, κ and λ (1, 2). Hood *et al.* (3) have suggested that the light chains of the immunoglobulins of other animal species can be classified as homologues of the κ and/or λ classes and that the ratios of κ to λ are variable among the species. The κ class has a free (unblocked) N-terminal amino acid and a C-terminal cysteine residue, whereas light chains of the λ class generally have a blocked N-terminal position, usually pyrrolid-2-one-5-carboxylic acid (PCA), and a penultimate cysteine residue at the C-terminal end (3, 4).

Light chains of both κ and λ classes have a unique structural feature: a variable region of about 107 amino acid residues in the N-terminal half of the light chain, and a common region of approximately residues 108 to 215. In the variable half certain regions of conserved sequences can be detected (4–7). Based primarily on the 20 to 30 amino acid residues at the N-terminal end, both κ and λ chains have been placed into subgroups (8, 9). A significant degree of homology in structure exists between κ and λ light chains despite their antigenic distinctions.

Based on an unblocked N-terminal sequence of Ala-Leu and a C-terminal sequence of Ser-Glu-Cys, Hood *et al.* (3) suggested that at least 60% of the chicken light chains were of the κ type. In the present study we have confirmed the N-terminal sequence of Ala-Leu; however, the first 17 residues appear to fit the N-terminal sequence of human λ rather than κ chains.

Approximately 10 mg of chicken IgG light chains were subjected to 17 degradation cycles in the Beckman Protein Sequencer. The thiazolinones recovered from the Sequencer were converted to the phenylthiohydantoin (PTH) amino acid derivatives by treatment with 1 N HCl for 10 min at 80°C. The PTH amino acids were identified by gas chromatography (10) and thin layer chromatography on silica gel employing a solvent system of ethylene dichloride: acetic acid (30:7) (H. Niall, personal communication). The percentage yields of certain PTH amino acids were calculated from the nanomols of PTH amino acid detected by gas chromatography to the total nanomols of dry weight protein used for the degradation procedure. No corrections were made for procedural losses. Certain PTH amino acids (e.g., threonine and glutamine) were identified from the results of thin layer chromatography, and the yields of these PTH amino acids were not quantitated. For most positions, identifications were confirmed in a duplicate run.

The sequences are shown in Table I. In several positions the minor amino acids are listed; these may represent subgroup sequences. At position 5, "background" amino acids became noticeable and persisted at a low but slowly-rising level throughout the remainder of the analysis. This made it difficult to identify minor amino acids, which probably represent variable positions. Although the protein was actually carried through 23 degradation cycles, no major amino acid could be positively identified after position 17. Whether this was due to increasing levels of "noise" from the release of free N-terminal amino acids by nonselective degradation of the polypeptide chain or to increasing variability in amino acid sequence is not known at present.

Comparison of the major N-terminal sequences of the chicken light chain with the N-terminal sequences of 64 human light chains (11) revealed a marked homology between the sequence of the chicken light chains and human λ chains if a deletion of the first two N-terminal positions in chicken light chains is assumed. In human λ chains, PCA usually occurs at the N-terminal position, although in some λ Bence Jones proteins a deletion of the N-terminal PCA has been observed (12). Thus, assuming deletion of the first two amino acids and a deletion at position 9 (11), the chicken light chains are compared to the prototype N-terminal sequences of human λ sub-

[1] This investigation was supported in part by Research Grant AI-05660-06 and Training Grant AI-00243-07 from the National Institute of Allergy and Infectious Diseases.

TABLE I

Amino-terminal sequence of chicken light chains

Position	Major Amino Acids	Minor Amino Acids
1	Ala(25)[a]	
2	Leu(15)	Val(7.8)
3	Thr[b]	
4	Gln[b]	
5	Pro(6.3)	Ser(5.7), Ala(3.7)
6	Ala(10.3)	
7	Ala(8.3)	
8	Val(8.9)	Ala(4.7), Leu(3.5)
9	Gly(8.4)	Leu(7.1), Val(4.1), Thr[b]
10	Ala(9.5)	Ser(6.9)
11	Gln[b]	Ser(6.9), Ala(6.8)
12	Ile(4.4)	Val(3.1), Pro[b]
13[c]		
14	Ser[b]	Ala(4.5), Gly(3.3)
15	Thr[b]	
16	Val(4.3)	
17	Val(4.4)	

[a] Percentage yield of PTH amino acid calculated from the nanomols of PTH amino acid detected by gas chromatography/nanomol of dry weight protein.

[b] Identified by thin layer chromatography; no quantitation of yield was made.

[c] Sample was lost; no positive identification was made on first analysis.

groups (11) in Table II. The chicken light chains are homologous to $V_{\lambda I}$, $V_{\lambda III}$ and $V_{\lambda IV}$ subgroups in 6 positions; to $V_{\lambda II}$ subgroup in 7 positions; and to $V_{\lambda V}$ subgroup in 8 positions. On the other hand, when compared to the N-terminal sequences of V_κ subgroup prototypes (11), the chicken light chains show homology in only 4 positions at best (Table II). Thus, compared to 23 λ chains and to 41 κ chains given by Hood and Talmage (11), chicken light chains show homology in 12 of the 17 residues of λ chain sequences, but only 5 of 17 positions can be aligned with κ chains. It is remarkable that of the first 10 residues of the chicken light chains, 9 can be aligned with the various λ sequences. The Leu-Thr-Gln-Pro sequence (positions 4 through 7) appears to be characteristic for the λ chains. Based on the percentage yield of alanine at position 1 (Table I) at least 25% of our chicken light chain preparations belong to a λ-type class. The difference in yield of alanine at position 1 that Hood *et al.* (3) obtained (60%) and the yield that we obtained

TABLE II

Comparison of the amino-terminal sequences of chicken IgG light chains and human κ and λ chains[a]

Type	Protein	Position 1	2	3	4	5	6	7	8	9	10	11	12	13	14	15	16	17	18	19	20
Kappa	$V_{\kappa I}$	Asp	Ile	Gln	Met	Thr	Gln	Ser	Pro	Ser	Ser	Leu	Ser	Ala	Ser	Val	Gly	Asp	Arg	Val	Thr
Kappa	$V_{\kappa II}$	Glu	Ile	Val	Leu	Thr	Gln	Ser	Pro	Gly	Thr	Leu	Ser	Leu	Ser	Pro	Gly	Glu	Arg	Ala	Thr
	BJ Win	Asp								Ala											
Kappa	$V_{\kappa III}$	Asp	Ile	Val	Met	Thr	Gln	Ser	Pro	Leu	Ser	Leu	Pro	Val	Thr	Pro	Gly	Glu	Pro	Ala	Ser
Chicken	L chain	[ ]	[ ]	Ala	Leu	Thr	Gln	Pro	Ala	Ala	Val	Gly	Ala	Gln	Ile	—[b]	Ser	Thr	Val	Val	
Lambda	$V_{\lambda I}$	Glp	Ser	Val	Leu	Thr	Gln	Pro	Pro	[ ]	Ser	Val	Ser	Gly	Ala	Pro	Gly	Gln	Arg	Val	Thr
	BJ New	Glu												Ala					Lys		
Lambda	$V_{\lambda II}$	Glp	Ser	Ala	Leu	Thr	Gln	Pro	Ala	[ ]	Ser	Val	Ser	Gly	Ser	Pro	Gly	Gln	Ser	Ile	Thr
Lambda	$V_{\lambda III}$	[ ]	Tyr	Val	Leu	Thr	Gln	Pro	Pro	[ ]	Ser	Val	Ser	Val	Ser	Pro	Gly	Gln	Thr	Ala	Ser
	BJ Kern			Ala																	Val
Lambda	$V_{\lambda IV}$	Glp	Ser	Ala	Leu	Thr	Gln	Pro	Pro	[ ]	Ser	Ala	Ser	Gly	Ser	Pro	Gly	Gln	Ser	Val	Thr
Lambda	$V_{\lambda V}$	[ ]	Ser	Glu	Leu	Thr	Gln	Pro	Pro	[ ]	Ala	Val	Ser	Val	Ala	Leu	Gly	Gln	Thr	Val	Arg
Chicken	L chain	[ ]	[ ]	Ala	Leu	Thr	Gln	Pro	Ala	[ ]	Ala	Val	Gly	Ala	Gln	Ile	—[b]	Ser	Thr	Val	Val

[a] Prototype sequences for human κ and λ subgroups and the sequences of Bence Jones (BJ) proteins Win, New and Kern were taken from Hood and Talmage (11). Homologous positions between chicken light chains and the human κ and λ subgroups are *underlined*. Deletions of amino acids are marked by [ ]. Deletion at position 9 of the λ chains is according to Hood and Talmage (11).

[b] The amino acid residue at this position was not identified (see Table I).

(25%) might represent differences in strains of chickens. Work is in progress to search for chicken light chains which possess a blocked N-terminus.

The N- and C-terminal sequences of chicken heavy chains are being investigated. So far we have found that a large portion of the heavy chains has the N-terminal sequence of Ala- Val.

Acknowledgment. Grateful acknowledgment is given to Dr. C. H. Folsome for his assistance with the gas chromatographic analyses.

REFERENCES

1. Mannick, M. and Kunkel, H. G., J. Exp. Med., *117:* 213, 1962.
2. McIntire, K. R., Asofsky, R. M., Potter, M. and Kuff, E. L., Science, *150:* 361, 1965.
3. Hood, L., Gray, W. R., Sanders, B. G. and Dreyer, W. J., Cold Spring Harbor Symp. Quant. Biol., *32:* 133, 1965.
4. Putnam, F. S., Science, *163:* 633, 1969.
5. Putnam, F. W., Titani, K., Wikler, M. and Shinoda, T., Cold Spring Harbor Symp. Quant. Biol., *32:* 9, 1967.
6. Putnam, F. W., Brookhaven Symp. Biol., *21:* 306, 1969.
7. Edelman, G. M. and Gall, E., Ann. Rev. Biochem., *38:* 415, 1969.
8. Milstein, S., Nature, *216:* 330, 1967.
9. Langer, B., Steinmetz-Kayne, M. and Hilschmann, N., Z. Physiol. Chem., *349:* 945, 1968.
10. Pisano, J. J. and Bronzert, T. J., J. Biol. Chem., *244:* 5597, 1969.
11. Hood, L. and Talmage, D. W., Science, *168:* 325, 1970.
12. Putnam, F. W., Shinoda, T., Titani, K. and Wikler, M., Science, *157:* 1050, 1967.

THE JOURNAL OF IMMUNOLOGY
Vol. 105, No. 3, September 1970

FREQUENCY OF SINGLE SPLEEN CELLS FROM HYPERIMMUNE RABBITS PRODUCING ANTIBODY OF TWO DIFFERENT SPECIFICITIES[1]

DAVID C. BENJAMIN[2] AND WILLIAM O. WEIGLE[3]

From the Department of Experimental Pathology, Scripps Clinic and Research Foundation, La Jolla, California 92037

Received for publication May 27, 1970

Spleen cells from rabbits hyperimmune to bovine serum albumin (BSA) were assayed for their ability to produce hemolytically inefficient (7S) antibodies of two specificities by the hemolytic plaque assay. When assayed against a mixture of rabbit red cells conjugated with either of two cyanogen bromide fragments of BSA, only 1 of 37,568 antibody-producing cells could have been a double producer, suggesting that a given single cell can produce antibody of only a single specificity. These results were discussed in the light of previous studies with single cells and in relation to the two main theories of the origin of antibody diversity.

Few, if any, immunologists still seriously entertain the instructive theories of antibody formation. Most, however, accept the basic premise that the immunocompetent cell possesses the genetic information for synthesizing antibody. The question now is, does the cell possess the information necessary for coding for all the possible specificities (germ line theory) (1, 2) or does it possess the information for only one or at the most a few specificities (somatic variation theory) (3–6). Over the past decade a number of attempts have been made to show whether or not a single cell is capable of producing antibodies of more than one specificity in the hope of differentiating between the two possibilities above. These attempts have included studies with fluorescent antibody (7–9), fluorescent antibody coupled with autoradiography (10), phage neutralization (11), bacterial immobilization and agglutination (12, 13) and the hemolytic plaque assay (14, 15). In most cases, however, multiple antigens were used and when only a single antigen with multiple determinants was employed, there was doubt as to either the techniques or the suitability of the antigen. More recently, however, Gershon *et al.* (15) have shown that single cells from rabbits, immunized with a protein carrying two non-cross-reacting haptens, produced only a single specificity antibody. Their assay detected only cells producing hemolytically efficient (19S) antibodies and only two determinants were involved. The experiments reported here were designed to test whether a single cell from rabbits hyperimmune to bovine serum albumin (BSA) can produce hemolytically inefficient (7S) antibodies with specificities toward different areas of the BSA molecule. This was done by using the hemolytic plaque assay and two cyanogen bromide fragments of BSA each of which carries several determinants.

[1] Publication 416 from the Department of Experimental Pathology of Scripps Clinic and Research Foundation, supported by United States Public Health Service Grant AI 07007 and Atomic Energy Commission Contract AT (04-3)-410.

[2] This work was performed during the tenure of a United States Public Health Service predoctoral fellowship (5-F01-GM-29,481-04) from the National Institute of General Medical Science. Data taken, in part, from a dissertation submitted to the Department of Biology, University of California, San Diego, in partial fulfillment of requirements for the degree of Doctor of Philosophy. Present address: Department of Biology, The Johns Hopkins University, Baltimore, Maryland 21218.

[3] Recipient of United States Public Health Service Research Career Award 5-K6-GM-6936.

MATERIALS AND METHODS

Antigens. BSA was obtained from Armour and Co., Kankakee, Ill., lot D71209. Rabbit γ globulin (RγG) was prepared from whole serum by ammonium sulfate precipitation and chromatography on diethylaminoethyl (DEAE)-cellulose.

Preparation of the cyanogen bromide fragments of BSA. The procedure used was essentially that described by King (16, 17). Six grams of BSA were dissolved in 100 ml of 0.26 M Tris (trihydroxymethyl aminomethane) buffer, pH 7.4. L-Cystine (125.4 mg, a sixfold molar excess) was added and the mixture was stirred under aerobic conditions for 20 hr at 37°C. This solution was then dialyzed against distilled water and concentrated to 30 ml by vacuum dialysis. Eighty-eight per cent formic acid was then added to a final concentration of 75% followed by 590 mg cyanogen bromide (a 16-fold molar excess over the number of methionine residues). The solution was stirred at room temperature for 24 hr, dialyzed against several changes of 0.2 M ammonium formate, pH 2.5, and concentrated to 60 ml by vacuum dialysis. Twenty milliliters of this digest were then added to a reverse flow G-100 Sephadex column (5 x 100 cm) and the fragments were eluted with 0.2 M ammonium formate. The absorbancy of the fractions was measured at 280 nm and the fragments were concentrated by vacuum dialysis. Each of the fragments was then recycled through G-100 Sephadex until a single symmetrical absorbancy peak was obtained.

Immunization of rabbits with BSA. Five normal New Zealand White rabbits (3 kg body weight) were given four 1-week courses of immunization with soluble BSA totaling 680 mg and spaced 2 weeks apart. Each course consisted of four daily subcutaneous injections of 20 mg of BSA followed by 30 mg of BSA/kg body weight on day 5. These hyperimmune rabbits were rested 5 months and then given 20 mg BSA intravenously. Four days later they were killed by exsanguination and their spleens were removed and assayed for plaque-forming cells as described below.

Preparation of amplifying antibody. Squirrel monkeys were injected at 1-week intervals with 0.5, 1.0 and 1.5 mg of RγG (intramuscularly in the thigh) in 0.5 ml complete Freund's adjuvant containing 0.15 mg mycobacteria (*Mycobacterium tuberculosis* var. *hominis*). Three weeks later each monkey received 1.5 mg of heat-aggregated, alum-precipitated RγG intramuscularly. The animals were bled 4 weeks later and those sera showing a precipitin band in agar were pooled.

Hemolytic plaque assay. The plaque assay used was essentially that of Ingraham *et al.* (18) but modified for use with soluble protein antigens and is described elsewhere (19). Separate batches of rabbit red blood cells were conjugated with BSA and with each of the two cyanogen bromide fragments of BSA. The same molar concentration as for BSA was used in the conjugation of the fragments (19).

RESULTS

Properties of the cyanogen bromide fragments of BSA. Gross and Witkop (20) have shown that cyanogen bromide specifically cleaves peptide bonds to which methionine contributes the carboxyl group thereby converting methionine to homoserine lactone. King and Spencer (16) have shown that BSA is cleaved by this reagent into two fragments with molecular weights of 44,000 and 22,000, termed the C and N fragments respectively. Cleavage of BSA with cyanogen bromide and gel filtration of the digest through G-100 Sephadex results in solutions of pure C and N fragments. The chemical and immunochemical properties of these fragments are to be presented elsewhere and let it suffice to say here that these fragments do not cross-react (i.e., do not share determinants) and together seem to possess all the determinants of the native BSA, as determined by gel diffusion in agar and inhibition of ^{131}I-BSA-anti-BSA reactions. By cross-reaction analyses of these fragments, several heterologous albumins and a hyperimmune anti-BSA, it was seen that each fragment carried at least several of the determinants of intact BSA (unpublished data).

Criterion for double producers. The rabbit spleen cell suspensions were assayed against each of several red cell suspensions: 1) red cells conjugated with BSA; 2) red cells conjugated with the C fragment of BSA; 3) red cells conjugated with the N fragment of BSA; 4) a 1:1 (v/v) mixture of 2 and 3; and 5) red cells without conjugated antigen. Preparation 5 serves as a background control to detect those cells producing antibody to rabbit red cell membrane antigens (isoantibody). Any cell producing antibody of a single specificity would, when assayed against 1 and 2 or 3, give rise to a clear plaque (i.e., one in which all the red cells have been lysed) whereas the same cell, if assayed against the mixture 4, would give rise to a cloudy plaque (i.e., one in which only half of the red cells are lysed). However, if a cell was producing antibody of two different specificities (one towards C fragment and one towards N fragment) it would

TABLE I

Frequency of single spleen cells from hyperimmune rabbits producing antibody of two different specificities

Rabbit No.	Total Spleen Cells Plated × 10^5	Total Anti-C,[a] PFC	Total Anti-N,[b] PFC	Anti-RRBC PFC/10^6	Expected Anti-RRBC[c]	Double Plaques[d]
1	3.90	5,120	1,880	0.5	0.2	1
2	3.78	9,880	1,920	0	0	0
3	3.52	4,480	1,808	0	0	0
4	2.86	4,280	1,480	0	0	0
5	3.30	4,080	2,640	0	0	0
Total	17.36	27,840	9,728	0.5	0.2	1

[a] C = 44,000 molecular weight fragment of BSA.
[b] N = 22,000 molecular weight fragment of BSA.
[c] Calculated on the basis of 0.5 × 10^6 PFC to non-conjugated RRBC.
[d] Clear plaques containing only a single central nucleated cell.

give rise to a clear plaque when assayed against the mixture.

The difference in appearance of clear and cloudy plaques in the monolayer method used is quite striking and it is relatively easy to scan a large number of plates for double producers. Any double plaque found was examined under 100× magnification and only those plaques having a single nucleated cell at the center were regarded as double producers.

Assay. Several dilutions of each spleen cell suspension were assayed against each of the red cell suspensions 1, 2 and 3. The number of plaque-forming cells (PFC) against 2 plus 3 was always less than or equal to the number of PFC to BSA-coated cells (suspension 1). From the number of PFC to each of the fragments alone, the spleen cell suspension was diluted so that when tested against mixture 4 each plate would have between 75 and 100 PFC. Eighty plates were prepared per spleen, the plaques were examined and the results are shown in Table I. A sufficient number of plates was counted to insure that the number of PFC found in the mixture was the same as expected from the preliminary PFC found with the individual fragments. Of the 37,568 plaques observed, only 24 clear plaques were seen. When these clear plaques were examined at 100× magnification, 23 of 24 had two or more nucleated cells at their center. Thus only 1 of 37,568 PFC could be considered a possible double producer.

DISCUSSION

The results presented indicate that each antibody-forming cell from rabbits hyperimmune to BSA can produce antibody of only a single specificity. Only 1 of 37,568 PFC could possibly have been making two antibodies of different specificities. However, this single cell came from the only rabbit showing background activity to non-conjugated red cells. The methods used were chosen to enhance the possibility of detecting the rare cell which might produce two specificities. First of all, the chances of a single cell being stimulated by two different determinants would be greatly increased if these two determinants were carried on the same molecule. BSA was chosen for several reasons: a) it is a natural antigen; b) it can be split into two non-cross-reacting fragments by reaction with cyanogen bromide; c) the fragments can easily be obtained in pure form and each carries several determinants; and d) the two fragments together possess all the determinants of the native BSA molecule. Thus any cell producing antibody to a determinant on one fragment would be detected as a double producer if it also produced antibody to any one of the determinants on the other fragment. This multideterminant approach has been used by others but only a few cells were examined. Hiramoto and Hamlin (8) reported approximately 45% of the antibody-forming cells produced antibody to both the Fab and Fc portions of the human γ globulin molecule which was used as the immunogen. The results of Green *et al.* (10), however, suggest that the above may have been due to the impurity of the papain fragments used and that cells produce antibody of only one specificity. Secondly, the plaque assay method of Jerne (21) as modified by Ingraham (18) was used because it provided a simple, sensitive method of rapidly scanning a large number of antibody-forming cells for the possible double producer. The use of homologous red cells as carrier in this technique reduced the number of background plaques to essentially zero.

Observations of others also strongly suggest that PFC produce antibody of a single specificity. Friedman (14), using the plaque assay method, did not observe any mouse spleen cells of the 365 he studied which could produce antibody to both the chicken and sheep erythrocytes which were injected. Gershon *et al.* (15) examined over 44,000 PFC from animals immunized with sheep and camel red cells or with human serum albumin coupled with two non-cross-reacting haptens and did not observe any single cell producing antibodies of two specificities. Both of these studies, however, would have only detected those cells producing hemolytically efficient antibodies. The present study extends these latter observations by showing that a single cell does not produce hemolytically inefficient (7S) antibodies of two specificities. The possibility still exists, however, that a single cell may produce antibodies of two specificities, one of which is 19S and one which is 7S, or any cell producing very low quantities of the second antibody is undetectable by present methods. These cells would not have been observed as double producers in the previous studies or in the present experiments.

The present study and those of others show only that once antibody is produced by a given cell it is of a single specificity. They do not necessarily support either the germ line or the somatic variation theory of the origin of antibody diversity. The majority of the studies on single antibody-producing cells could be interpreted as suggesting that a given cell possesses the genetic information for only a single specificity. Recent data (22–25), however, suggest this may not be the case and that the same variable region (which presumably carries the antibody-combining site) may be associated with different constant regions of the heavy chain of antibody molecules. Wikler *et al.* (22) have proposed the existence of a pool of variable genes which can be translocated into juxtaposition to constant region genes on the chromosome. This translocated variable gene and the constant region gene would then be transcribed and translated as a single message. If at any time during differentiation (presumably before contact with antigen) a given variable gene is translocated and locked into position, then antibody of only a single specificity would result even though the cell possesses the genetic information for many specificities.

REFERENCES

1. Szilard, L., Proc. Nat. Acad. Sci., *46:* 293, 1960.
2. Dreyer, W. J. and Bennett, J. C., Proc. Nat. Acad. Sci., *54:* 864, 1965.
3. Burnet, F. M., *The Clonal Selection Theory of Acquired Immunity*, Vanderbilt University Press, Nashville, Tenn., 1959.
4. Cohen, S. and Milstein, C., Nature, *214:* 449, 1967.
5. Smithies, O., Science, *157:* 267, 1967.
6. Edelman, G. M. and Gally, J. A., Proc. Nat. Acad. Sci., *57:* 353, 1967.
7. Hiramoto, R. N. and Hamlin, M., J. Immun., *95:* 214, 1965.
8. Vasquez, J. J., Lab. Invest., *10:* 1110, 1961.
9. White, R. G., Nature, *182:* 1383, 1958.
10. Green, I., Vassal, P., Nussenzweig, V. and Benacerraf, B., J. Exp. Med., *125:* 571, 1967.
11. Attardi, G., Cohn, M., Horibata, K. and Lennox, E., J. Immun., *92:* 335, 1964.
12. Nossal, G. J. V. and Makela, O., J. Immun., *88:* 604, 1962.
13. Schwartzman, J. S., Nature, *213:* 925, 1967.
14. Friedman, H., Experientia, *20:* 564, 1964.
15. Gershon, H., Bauminger, S., Sela, M. and Feldman, M., J. Exp. Med., *128:* 223, 1968.
16. King, T. P. and Spencer, E. M., Fed. Proc., *27:* 391, 1968.
17. King, T. P., Personal communication.
18. Ingraham, J., Petersen, B. and Watanabe, M., Information Exchange Group No. 5, 1967.
19. Benjamin, D. C. and Weigle, W. O., J. Immun., In press.
20. Gross, E. and Witkop, B., J. Biol. Chem., *237:* 1856, 1962.
21. Jerne, N. K. and Nordin, A. A., Science, *140:* 405, 1963.
22. Wikler, M., Kohler, H., Shinoda, T. and Putnam, F. W., Science, *163:* 75, 1969.
23. Kohler, H., Shimizu, A., Paul, C., van Dalen, A. and Putnam, F. W., Fed. Proc., *29:* 257, 1970.
24. Penn, G. M., Kunkel, H. G. and Grey, H. M., Fed. Proc., *29:* 258, 1970.
25. Hopper, J. E., Wilson, S. K., Nisonoff, A., Wang, A. C. and Fudenberg, H. H., Fed. Proc., *29:* 258, 1970.

THE JOURNAL OF IMMUNOLOGY
Vol. 105, No. 3, September 1970

CONVERSION OF NON-IMMUNE RABBIT SPLEEN CELLS BY RIBONUCLEIC ACID OF LYMPHOID CELLS FROM AN IMMUNIZED RABBIT TO PRODUCE IgG ANTIBODY OF FOREIGN LIGHT CHAIN ALLOTYPE[1, 2]

CLARA BELL[3] AND SHELDON DRAY

From the Department of Microbiology, University of Illinois at the Medical Center, Chicago, Illinois 60680

Received for publication May 22, 1970

Spleen cells (SpC) from non-immunized rabbits were converted to antibody "indirect" plaque-forming cells (PFC) by incubating them with ribonucleic acid (RNA) extracts of lymph node cells (LNC) obtained from rabbits 18 to 24 days after they were immunized with several intravenous injections of 4 × 10⁸ sheep red blood cells (SRBC). The RNA extract was inactivated by ribonuclease (RNAse) but not by deoxyribonuclease (DNAse) or trypsin, indicating that the conversion required intact RNA. "Indirect" PFC were developed with optimal amounts of goat anti-IgG-Fc fragment and these were not inhibited by 2-mercaptoethanol (2-ME) or goat anti-IgM but were inhibited by excess anti-IgG-Fc fragment. This indicated that the antibodies produced by the PFC are of the IgG immunoglobulin class. The conversion was specific for the SRBC antigen injected. The light chain allotype of the IgG antibody produced by the PFC was identified by use of anti-b4 and anti-b5 to develop the "indirect" PFC, to visualize the PFC by radioautography and to inhibit plaque formation. Most of the "indirect" PFC of the converted SpC (64% to 84%) possessed IgG antibody with the allotype characteristic of the donor of the RNA extract; some of the "indirect" PFC (4% to 32%) possessed IgG antibody with the allotype characteristic of the donor of SpC. When the "RNA-converted" SpC were lysed by freezing and thawing, the anti-SRBC titer of the lysate, measured by the localized hemolysis in gel technique, was 4096 compared to 4 for lysates from the same number of lysed, non-immune SpC alone. Moreover, anti-SRBC antibody could not be detected in the RNA extracts. These results indicate that a component of the RNA extract, presumably RNA itself, is providing information for the synthesis of at least part of the IgG antibody molecule.

By use of the b4 and b5 light chain immunoglobulin allotypes as genetic markers and the plaque technique of localized hemolysis in gel to assess antibody formation by single cells, we reported previously (1) that ribonucleic acid (RNA) extracts of lymphoid cells from immunized homozygous rabbits with the b^4 or b^5 allele converts spleen cells (SpC) from non-immunized homozygous rabbits with the b^5 or b^4 allele, respectively, to produce IgM antibody of foreign light chain allotype. The RNA extracts were obtained from peritoneal exudate cells (PEC) or lymph node cells (LNC) of immunized rabbits 5 days after one intravenous injection of 4×10^8 sheep red blood cells (SRBC). Plaque formation was inhibited by 2-mercaptoethanol (2-ME) or goat anti-rabbit-IgM but not by goat anti-rabbit-IgG-Fc fragment indicating that the antibody produced by the PFC was of the IgM immunoglobulin class. The RNA extract was inactivated by ribonuclease (RNAse) but

[1] Presented in part at the 54th Annual Meeting of the Federation of American Societies for Experimental Biology, Atlantic City, New Jersey, April 12–17, 1970.

[2] This investigation was supported in part by a Research Grant from the National Institute of Allergy and Infectious Diseases, AI-07043.

[3] Supported in part by a Training Grant from the National Institute of Allergy and Infectious Diseases, AI-00335.

not by deoxyribonuclease (DNAse) or trypsin indicating that the conversion required intact RNA. Moreover, these results could not be explained by contamination of the RNA extracts with anti-SRBC, thus implying that the RNA itself was providing information for the synthesis of at least part of the IgM antibody molecule.

Our experiments (1) were an extension of the pioneering work of Fishman *et al.* (2–5) and later of Cohen *et al.* (6–8) and Friedman (9, 10) which suggested an informational role for RNA extracts of "immunized" lymphoid cells. However, because of the possibility that RNA extracts may be contaminated with antigen (11–15), studies with genetic markers were necessary to assess whether the antibody synthesized indeed reflected the genome of the cells from which the RNA was extracted. Thus, Adler *et al.* (5) reported that the initial IgM antibody produced *in vitro* possessed the genetic marker of the cell donor for the RNA whereas the subsequent IgG antibody produced possessed the genetic marker of the cells treated with the RNA. Our previous experiments (1) confirmed and extended those of Adler *et al.* (5) with respect to the production of IgM antibodies using a different antigen, i.e., SRBC instead of T_2 phage, and a different assay for the antibody produced, i.e., localized hemolysis in gel instead of phage neutralization.

The purpose of this investigation was to explore further the possible informational role of RNA extracts with respect to the synthesis of IgG antibodies. This was done by use of genetic markers at the *b* locus of immunoglobulins to identify the source of information and by use of a localized hemolysis in gel technique for enumerating the cells producing IgG antibodies and for assaying the anti-SRBC titer in lysed spleen cells. For this purpose, RNA was extracted from the LNC of rabbits 18 to 24 days after the first of several injections of SRBC at a time when the rabbit was synthesizing IgG antibodies to SRBC.

MATERIALS AND METHODS

Immunization of rabbits to produce IgM and IgG antibodies to sheep red blood cells (SRBC). Rabbits homozygous at the *b* light chain immunoglobulin locus (b^4b^4 or b^5b^5) were immunized by one intravenous injection of 4×10^8 SRBC to obtain IgM antibodies. Rabbits were given 6 to 10 intravenous injections of 4×10^8 SRBC at 2- to 3-day intervals over a period of 18 to 24 days to stimulate production of IgG antibodies.

Assay of IgM and IgG antibodies. Antibodies to SRBC in serum, spleen cell lysates, and RNA extracts were assayed by the localized hemolysis in gel technique as described by Uyeki and Klassen (16). Two- or 10-fold serial dilutions of the sample in Hanks' balanced salt solution (HBSS) were examined on dishes containing 100 µl of 10% SRBC suspension per 2 ml of agarose in HBSS. For the assay of hemolysin, presumably IgM antibodies, 2 ml of complement solution (1:10 dilution in HBSS of the reconstituted lyophilized preparation of guinea pig complement: Grand Island Biological Co., Grand Island, N. Y.) were added and the plate was incubated at 37°C for 30 min. For the assay of enhanced hemolysins, presumably IgG antibodies, "indirect" hemolysis was observed by adding, in another plate, 2 ml of an optimal dilution of goat antiserum to rabbit IgG-Fc fragment in HBSS and incubating at 37°C for 30 min before adding complement. The highest dilution giving a clear zone of hemolysis in duplicate plates was recorded as the titer.

In addition, hemolysin and hemagglutin titers were obtained by the usual tube methods (17): the results were comparable to the localized hemolysis in gel technique but the latter was usually more sensitive by one serial dilution.

Assay of "direct" and "indirect" plaque-forming cells (PFC). Antibody-producing cells were identified by the area of hemolysis (plaques) surrounding cells which release antibodies to SRBC. The "direct" hemolytic plaque test, which presumably detects cells releasing IgM antibody, was a modification of the procedure described by Jerne *et al.* (18) as described previously (1).

The assay of "indirect" PFC, which presumably detects cells releasing IgG antibody (19–21), was similar to the assay of "direct" PFC except that before adding complement, 2 ml of goat anti-IgG-Fc at a predetermined optimal dilution in HBSS were added and the plates were incubated at 37°C for 30 to 60 min and washed twice with 5 ml of HBSS. The "direct" and "indirect" plaques were counted under 2 to 3 × magnification; for closer scrutiny, 50 × to 100 × magnification was used. Plaque assays were performed in duplicate or triplicate. The average of all counts was expressed as the number of PFC/10^6 viable spleen cells. The total number of PFC observed in the plates to which goat anti-IgG-Fc was added represents the sum of both the "direct" and "indirect" PFC. The number of "direct" PFC obtained on a separate plate was subtracted from this total in order to obtain the number of the "indirect" PFC. The effect of various reagents on the appearance of "direct" or "indirect" PFC was assessed by procedures described previously (1); i.e., incorporation of the reagent in the agarose or by preincubation of the cells with the reagent, usually at 37°C for 30 min, with subsequent washing of the cells.

Incubation of "non-immune" lymphoid cells with RNA extracts of lymph nodes from immunized rabbits ("immune" RNA extracts). As a control, the incubation of "non-immune" SpC or LNC with "5 day immune" RNA extracts for conversion to "direct" PFC was done as reported previously (1).[4] For the conversion of "non-immune" SpC or LNC to "indirect" PFC the RNA was extracted as described previously (1) but from lymph nodes of rabbits obtained 18 to 24 days following the first and 3 days after the last of 6 to 10 intravenous injections of SRBC, i.e., "18 to 24 day immune" RNA. "Non-immune" SpC or LNC of individual rabbits (2×10^7 viable cells in 0.1 ml HBSS at pH 7.4) were incubated with various amounts of the RNA extracts (50 to 2000 μg RNA as estimated by the optical density at 260 nm) in 0.1 ml of HBSS at pH 7.4 for 15 min at 37°C with periodic shaking. The cells were washed once with 50 volumes of HBSS; the cell pellet was then resuspended in HBSS and assayed for "indirect" PFC. Plaques were counted 4 to 5 hr and again 18 to 24 hr after initial contact of the SpC or LNC with the "immune" RNA extract. In order to assess the nature of the active component in the RNA extracts, they were treated with various reagents (listed in Table I) for 15 to 30 min, at various temperatures as described previously (1) and as indicated explicitly for each experiment in *Results.*

TABLE I

Regeants used in three types of experiments to assess their effect on the release of antibody by the plaque-forming cells and on the activity of the RNA extracts prior to conversion of non-immunized cells to PFC

Reagents	Incorporated into the Agarose	Preincubation of Cells	Preincubation of RNA Extracts
Normal rabbit serum	+	+	+
IgG	−	−	+
Goat anti-IgM	+	+	+
Goat anti-IgG-Fc	+	+	−
Anti-b4	+	+	+
Anti-b5	+	+	+
IgG anti-b4	+	−	+
IgG anti-b5	+	−	+
2-Mercaptoethanol[a]	+	+	+
RNAse	−	+	+
DNAse	−	+	+
Trypsin	−	+	+

[a] Fisher Chemicals, Chicago Ill. (distilled and stored frozen at −20°C).

RESULTS

Optimal time after immunization for assay of "indirect" plaque-forming cells. Antibody formation in rabbits given single or multiple intravenous injections of sheep red blood cells was studied, at various time intervals after the initial injection, by assaying the spleen cells for "direct" and "indirect" hemolytic plaque-forming cells (Fig. 1) and also by assaying the serum for "direct" and enhanced "indirect" hemolytic activity (Fig. 2). The data in Figure 1 are expressed as the number of "direct" and "indirect" PFC/10^6 SpC. The number of "direct" PFC reached a peak of 275 to 345 at 5 to 7 days; by day 14, the number declined to about 25. At 18 to 24 days, the number of "indirect" PFC reached a peak of 490 to 750.

The rise in circulating "direct" IgM hemolysins in the serum (Fig. 2) parallels the "direct" PFC response curve in the SpC (Fig. 1) of the same animal. The rise in circulating IgG-enhanced "indirect" hemolysins in the serum parallels the "indirect" PFC response curve in the SpC of the same animal.

When 0.1 M 2-ME was incorporated into the agarose, the number of "direct" PFC was reduced to the background level of 0 to 10 PFC without detectably affecting the values of the "indirect" PFC (Fig. 1). Likewise, the incorporation of 2-ME, to a final concentration of 0.1 M in the agarose, resulted in a drop in the direct hemolytic

[4] In our previous paper the amount of polyvinyl sulfate used in the isolation of RNA was indicated in error to be 8 mg/ml instead of 8 μg/ml actually used.

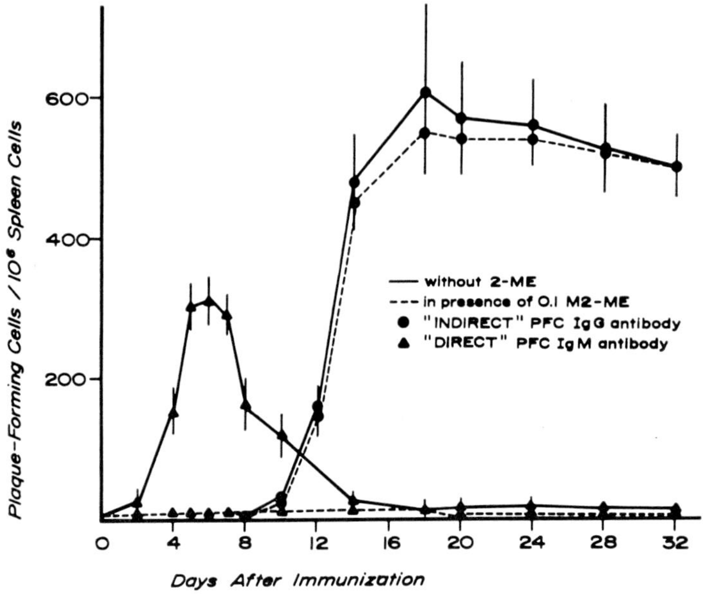

Figure 1. Plaque-forming cells (PFC) produced in spleens of rabbits at various times after one intravenous injection of 4×10^8 sheep red blood cells (SRBC), i.e., "direct" PFC (*first peak*) or several intravenous injections of 4×10^8 SRBC, i.e., "indirect" PFC (*second peak*). Each point at 0 to 4, 8 to 16 and 28 to 32 days represents the mean determination of PFC from spleens of 5 rabbits whereas each point at 5 to 7 days and 18 to 24 days represents the mean determination of PFC from spleens of 12 rabbits.

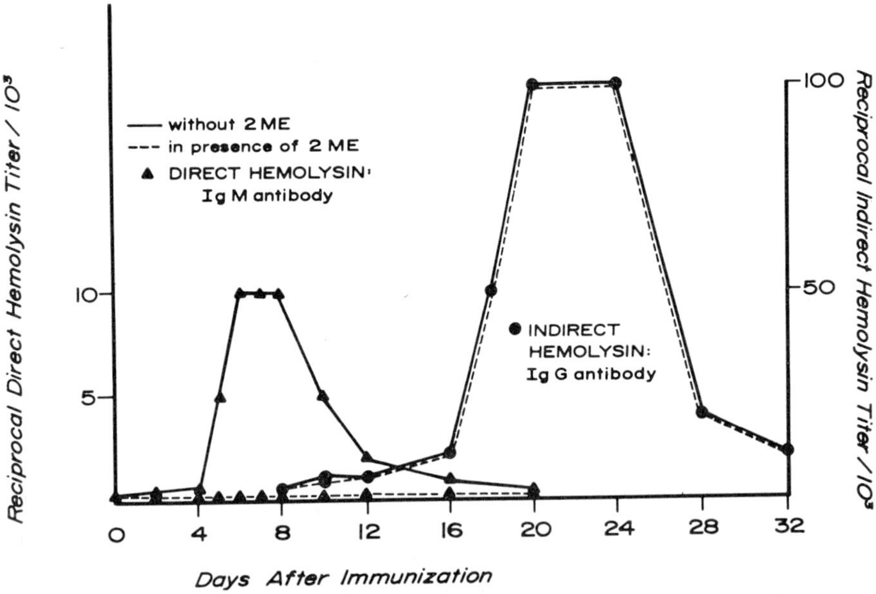

Figure 2. Hemolysin response curve in the serum of rabbits at various times after one intravenous injection of 4×10^8 sheep red blood cells (SRBC) "direct" IgM hemolysin (*first peak*) or several intravenous injections of 4×10^8 SRBC, enhanced "indirect" IgG hemolysin (*second peak*).

titer from 1/10,000 to 1/50 or less without significantly affecting the enhanced "indirect" hemolytic titer (Fig. 2).

Conversion of SpC derived from non-immunized rabbits to "indirect" PFC by incubation with "18 to 24 day immune" RNA extracts. SpC derived from non-immunized rabbits (2 × 10^7 SpC in 0.1 ml) were converted to "indirect" PFC by incubating then with "immune" RNA extracts (0.1 ml containing 750 to 1000 μg RNA) of LNC, taken from immunized rabbits at 18 to 24 days after the initial intravenous injection and 3 days following the last of 7 to 10 intravenous injections of SRBC. Using 10 different "immune" RNA preparations with SpC derived from 10 different non-immunized rabbits, we observed "indirect" PFC within a range of 180 to 420 "indirect" PFC/10^6 SpC, the average being about 300 PFC (Fig. 3, *first bar*). Only 0 to 3 "indirect" PFC were observed with SpC derived from non-immunized rabbits (Fig. 3, *second bar*) or from such "non-immune" SpC treated *in vitro* with RNA extracts obtained from the LNC of non-immunized rabbits (Fig. 3, *third bar*). The average number of "non-immune" SpC converted *in vitro* to "indirect" PFC by "immune" RNA extracts, however, is somewhat lower than the average of about 620 "indirect" PFC (with a range of 490 to 750) obtained with SpC derived from the RNA donor rabbits immunized *in vivo* (Fig. 3, *fourth bar*). No "indirect" plaques could be observed when the SpC treated with the "18 to 24 day immune" RNA were plated with rabbit RBC or mouse RBC.

Amount of "18 to 24 day immune" RNA required for conversion of spleen cells to "indirect" PFC. The number of SpC from non-immunized rabbits converted to "indirect" PFC by incubation *in vitro* with "18 to 24 day immune" RNA extracts containing different quantities of RNA is plotted in Figure 4. The SpC and the RNA were obtained from rabbits homozygous at the *b* locus, b^4b^4 or b^5b^5. As more RNA was added the number of PFC increased rapidly until a maximum was reached with 1000 to 1500 μg RNA; additional amounts of RNA caused little or no increase in the number of PFC. With 10 different RNA extracts, the maximum number of cells converted ranged from 148 to 420 "indirect" PFC/10^6 SpC. In the two control experiments with "non-immune" RNA, no "indirect" PFC were observed (Fig. 4).

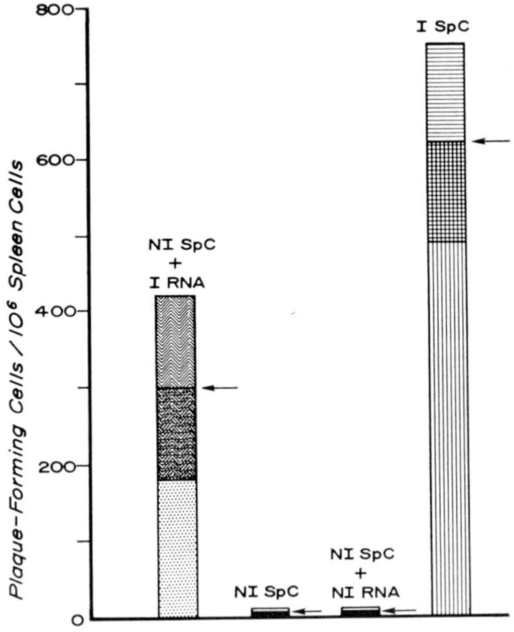

Figure 3. "Indirect" plaque forming cells (PFC/10^6 SpC) among spleen cells obtained as follows: a) from non-immunized rabbits (NI SpC); b) from immunized rabbits (I SpC); c) from non-immunized rabbits and treated with "18 to 24 day immune" RNA (NI SpC + I RNA) and d) from non-immunized rabbits and treated with "non-immune" RNA (NI SpC + NI RNA). The I RNA (extracted from lymph nodes) and the I SpC were obtained from rabbits 18 to 24 days after the initial intravenous injection and 3 days following the last of 7 to 10 injections of 4 × 10^8 SRBC. The SpC were incubated with RNA for 15 min at 37°C and washed prior to plating. Each vertical bar shows the results of 10 determinations; the arrow indicates the average number of "indirect" PFC and the shaded areas above and below each arrow represent the mean deviation. Experiments with LNC instead of SpC yielded similar data.

Characterization of "indirect" PFC as due to IgG antibodies to SRBC. The antibody in the plaques developed by both the "direct" and "indirect" method was identified as either IgM or IgG by observing the effects on plaque formation of 2-ME, anti-IgM, and anti-IgG-Fc. The incorporation of 0.05 M 2-ME into the agarose reduced the number of "direct" PFC to the background level (1 to 7 PFC) (Table II) of non-immunized rabbits. The number of "indirect"

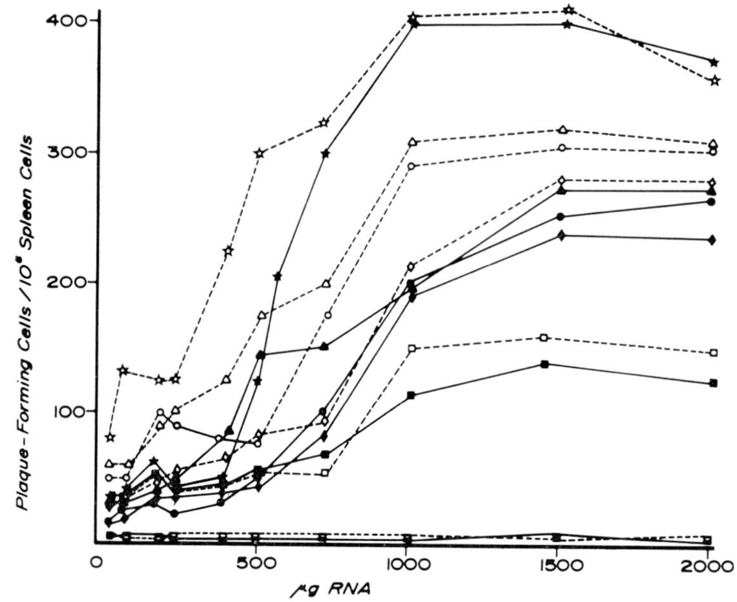

Figure 4. The number of "non-immune" spleen cells (SpC) converted by "18 to 24 day immune" RNA to "indirect" PFC as a function of the quantity of RNA. The experiments were done with SpC and RNA preparations from rabbits of different genotype as follows: ☆, △ And ○, "immune" b4 RNA + b5 SpC; ★, ▲ and ●, "immune" b4 RNA + b4 SpC; □ and ◇, "immune" b5 RNA + b4 SpC; ■ and ◆, "immune" b5 RNA + b5 SpC; ▭, "non-immune" b4 RNA + b4 SpC; ▬, "non-immune" b5 RNA + b5 SpC.

plaques was not significantly reduced by incorporation of as much as 0.1 M 2-ME (Table II) whether the SpC were from immunized rabbits (461 to 502 compared to 495 to 525) or whether the SpC were from non-immunized rabbits and incubated *in vitro* with "immune" RNA (compare 172 to 306 with 195 to 330).

The incorporation of 0.2 ml of goat anti-IgM antiserum into the agarose considerably reduced the average number of "direct" PFC from 375 to 41 (experiment 1) and 290 to 31 (experiment 2) for SpC from immunized rabbits (Table III) and from 301 to 28 (experiment 1) and 190 to 20 (experiment 2) for "non-immune" SpC converted with "5 day immune" RNA *in vitro* (Table III). On the other hand, with 0.2 ml anti-IgM, the average number of "indirect" PFC showed an increase: 560 to 615 (experiment 1) and 629 to 671 (experiment 2) for SpC of the immunized rabbit and 297 to 310 (experiment 1) and 150 to 178 (experiment 2) for "18 to 24 day immune, RNA-converted" SpC (Table III).

Incorporation of 0.2 ml anti-IgG-Fc into the agarose only slightly decreased the average number of "direct" PFC observed for SpC of immunized rabbits and for "5 day immune, RNA-converted" SpC. On the other hand, 0.2 ml of the goat anti-IgG-Fc decreased the average number of "indirect" PFC for SpC of immunized rabbits and for "18 to 24 day immune, RNA-converted" SpC. Smaller quantities of anti-IgG-Fc (0.05 ml) effected a slight increase in the number of "indirect" PFC for the SpC of immunized rabbits and for the "18 to 24 day immune, RNA-converted" SpC (Table III).

Effect of RNAse, DNAse and trypsin on the activity of "18 to 24 day immune" RNA extracts. The effect of enzymes on the conversion ability of "immune" RNA extracts was assessed by treating the RNA extracts with ribonuclease (RNAse), deoxyribonuclease (DNAse) and trypsin (Table IV). After the RNA extracts were incubated with 40 µg RNAse, the reextracted RNA had lost almost all of its ability to convert SpC to "indirect" PFC: 10 to 32 "indirect" PFC compared to the 247 to 392 PFC with untreated RNA (Table IV). A similar loss of activity occurred when the "immune" RNA extract and

TABLE II

Effect of 2-mercaptoethanol (2-ME) present in the agarose on the appearance of "direct"[a, b] and "indirect"[c, d] plaque-forming cells (PFC)[a, b]. Number of PFC/10⁶ spleen cells (SpC) derived from immunized rabbits or from non-immunized rabbits after incubation with different "immune" RNA extracts

Concentration of 2-ME in the Agarose Mixture	Exp. No.[e]	"Direct" IgM Plaques[a, b]		"Indirect" IgG Plaques[c, d]	
		SpC from imimunized rabbit[a]	SpC from non-immunized rabbit incubated with RNA extracts[b]	SpC from immunized rabbit[c]	SpC from non-immunized rabbit incubated with RNA Extracts[d]
None	1	315	202	515	195
	2	260	275	495	215
	3	342	329	525	330
0.005 M	1	300	190	501	182
	2	250	265	470	201
	3	334	331	518	321
0.01 M	1	203	101	482	170
	2	160	200	463	192
	3	257	245	510	315
0.05 M	1	2	1	470	168
	2	6	2	450	180
	3	10	7	505	309
0.1 M	1	1	0	480	172
	2	2	1	461	195
	3	0	0	502	306

[a] "Direct" PFC of SpC obtained from a rabbit 5 days after a single intravenous injection of 4×10^8 SRBC.

[b] Non-immunized SpC (2×10^7 SpC in 0.1 ml HBSS) were incubated for 15 min at 37°C with "immune" RNA extracts (500 μg in 0.1 ml HBSS) of peritoneal exudate cells or lymph node cells obtained from a rabbit 5 days after one intravenous injection of 4×10^8 SRBC. The cells were washed with HBSS.

[c] "Indirect" PFC of SpC obtained from rabbits 18 to 24 days after the initial intravenous injection and 3 days after the last of 7 to 10 intravenous injections of 4×10^8 SRBC.

[d] Non-immunized SpC (2×10^7 SpC in 0.1 ml HBSS) were incubated for 15 min at 37°C with "immune" RNA extracts (1000 μg in 0.1 ml HBSS) of LNC obtained from immunized rabbits 18 to 24 days after the initial intravenous injection and 3 days after the last of 7 to 10 intravenous injections of 4×10^8 SRBC. The cells were washed with HBSS.

[e] Three rabbits were used in each experiment; one rabbit was used as a source for non-immune SpC, one rabbit was a source for "5 day immune" RNA and one rabbit was a source for "18 to 24 day immune" RNA.

the SpC were incubated together with 40 μg RNAse; 12 to 69 "indirect" PFC were observed (Table IV). The addition of either DNAse or trypsin to the "immune" RNA had no detectable effect on the number of cells converted to "indirect" PFC. A range of 236 to 388 "indirect" PFC was observed with DNAse and 220 to 376 "indirect" PFC was observed with trypsin (Table IV). When SpC from immunized rabbits were similarly treated with each enzyme in the same manner and washed prior to plating, no reduction in the "indirect" PFC was observed (Table IV). Incubation of RNAse with SpC derived from non-immunized rabbits followed by washing of the cells with HBSS did not alter the subsequent conversion of the SpC to "indirect" PFC with "immune" RNA extracts indicating that the RNAse does not have a direct deleterious effect on the cells. Thus, these experiments indicate that the activity of the RNA extracts requires intact RNA.

Identification of the allotypic specificity of the IgG antibody in the "indirect" plaques of "18 to 24 day immune, RNA-converted" spleen cells

TABLE III

Effect of goat anti-rabbit-IgM antisera and of goat anti-rabbit-IgG-Fc fragment present in the agarose on appearance of "direct"[a] and "indirect"[b] plaque-forming cells (PFC). Number of PFC/10⁶ spleen cells (SpC) derived from immunized rabbits or from non-immunized rabbits after incubation with different "immune" RNA extracts

Amount of Antiserum in the Agarose Mixture	Exp. No.[c]	"Direct" IgM Plaques[a]		"Indirect" IgG Plaques[b]	
		SpC from immunized rabbit	SpC from non-immunized rabbit incubated with RNA extracts[d]	SpC from immunized rabbit	SpC from non-immunized rabbit incubated with RNA extracts[e]
ml					
None	1	375	301	560	297
	2	290	190	629	150
Goat anti-rabbit-IgM					
0.05	1	300	295	551	305
	2	291	130	595	160
0.1	1	102	82	587	285
	2	80	51	602	165
0.2	1	41	28	615	310
	2	31	20	671	178
Goat anti-rabbit-IgG-Fc					
0.05	1	382	290	652	328
	2	275	182	691	178
0.1	1	361	295	430	203
	2	280	162	415	101
0.2	1	300	281	200	105
	2	241	173	182	62

[a] "Direct" PFC of SpC obtained from a rabbit 5 days after a single intravenous injection of 4×10^8 SRBC.

[b] "Indirect" PFC of SpC obtained from rabbits 18 to 24 days after the initial intravenous injection and 3 days after the last of 7 to 10 intravenous injections of 4×10^8 SRBC.

[c] Three rabbits were used in each experiment; one rabbit was used as a source for non-immune SpC, one rabbit was a source for "5 day immune" RNA and one rabbit was a source for "18 to 24 day immune" RNA.

[d] Non-immunized SpC (2×10^7 SpC in 0.1 ml HBSS) were incubated for 15 min at 37°C with "immune" RNA extracts (500 μg in 0.1 ml HBSS) of PEC or LNC obtained from a rabbit 5 days after one intravenous injection of 4×10^8 SRBC. The cells were washed with HBSS.

[e] Non-immunized SpC (2×10^7 SpC in 0.1 ml HBSS) were incubated for 15 min at 37°C with "immune" RNA extracts (1000 μg in 0.1 ml HBSS) of LNC obtained from immunized rabbits 18 to 24 days after the initial intravenous injection and 3 days after the last of 7 to 10 intravenous injections of 4×10^8 SRBC. The cells were washed with HBSS.

(SpC) by developing the "indirect" plaques with anti-b4 or anti-b5. To assess whether the "indirect" plaques possessed the b4 or b5 allotype, the "indirect" plaque-forming cells were developed with optimal amounts of anti-b4 or anti-b5. The "indirect" PFC were also developed with goat anti-IgG-Fc as a measure of the total number of "indirect" PFC. In the four experiments shown in Table V, four different rabbits homozygous at the *b* locus served as a source of "non-immune" SpC and four other homozygous rabbits served as donors of "18 to 24 day immune" RNA. When b5 RNA was used to convert b4 SpC, 73% to 84% of the "indirect" PFC were developed with anti-b5 and 8% to 9% of the PFC were developed with anti-b4. On the other hand, when b4 RNA was used to convert b5 SpC, 74% to 79% of the "indirect" PFC were developed with anti-b4 and 7% to 14% of the PFC were developed with anti-b5. The number of "indirect" PFC developed by anti-b4 and anti-b5 in each experiment was slightly less than the total number developed by goat anti-IgG-Fc. Thus, most of the "indirect" PFC (73% to 84%) were developed with the antibody directed against the *b* locus allotype of the RNA donor rabbit.

TABLE IV

Effect of RNAse, DNAse and trypsin on the conversion of spleen cells (SpC) derived from non-immunized rabbits to "indirect" PFC by "immune" RNA extracts obtained from lymph node cells (LNC) of immunized rabbits 18 to 24 days after the initial intravenous injection and 3 days after the last of 7 to 10 intravenous injections of 4 × 10⁸ sheep red blood cells (SRBC)[a]

SpC Assayed	Exp. No.[b]	No Enzyme Added (Control)	40 μg RNAse		10 μg DNAse		10 μg Trypsin	
			+RNA[c]	+RNA +cells[d]	+RNA	+RNA +cells[d]	+RNA[c]	+RNA +cells
Non-immune SpC	1	1	3	2	0	1	2	0
	2	2	0	0	1	0	0	3
	3	0	0	1	1	2	1	1
Non-immune SpC+ "immune" RNA of LNC	1	359	32	69	340	335	342	320
	2	392	10	21	388	382	376	370
	3	247	18	12	240	236	231	220
SpC of immunized rabbits (control)	4	515		506[e]		510[e]		502[e]
	5	420		402[e]		407[e]		412[e]
	6	637		622[e]		629[e]		630[e]

[a] Data are expressed as "indirect" PFC/10^6 SpC.

[b] One rabbit was used as a source of SpC in each experiment.

[c] The <enzymes (in 0.1 ml HBSS) were incubated with 750 to 1000 μ9 of "18 to 24 day immune" RNA (in 0.1 ml HBSS); RNAse for 10 min at 26°C, DNAse for 30 min at 37°C and trypsin for 30 to 60 min at 37°C. The RNA was reextracted with phenol and reprecipitated with alcohol. Then 2 × 10^7 SpC derived from non-immunized rabbits (in 0.1 ml HBSS) were added to the enzyme treated RNA preparations (750 to 1000 μg in 0.1 ml HBSS) and incubated for an additional 15 min at 37°C. The supernatant fluid was removed and the cells were washed with HBSS before assaying for "indirect" PFC.

[d] As above but the RNA, enzymes and SpC derived from non-immunized rabbits were incubated together for the periods of time mentioned above.

[e] No RNA extract present.

TABLE V

Identification of the allotypic specificity of the IgG antibodies in the plaques of "non-immune" spleen cells (SpC) converted with "18 to 24 day immune" RNA by developing the indirect plaques with anti-b4 or anti-b5. Data are expressed as the number of indirect PFC/10⁶ SpC and as the percentage (in parentheses) of the total indirect PFC/10⁶ SpC developed by goat anti-IgG-Fc

Exp. No.[a]	Genotype of the "Non-Immune" SpC Donor	Genotype of the "Immune" RNA[b] Donor	Indirect Plaques Developed with		
			Anti-b4[c]	Anti-b5[d]	Anti-IgG-Fc[e]
1	b^4b^4	b^5b^5	41 (8)	450 (84)	537
2	b^4b^4	b^5b^5	31 (9)	240 (73)	329
3	b^5b^5	b^4b^4	284 (74)	26 (7)	382
4	b^5b^5	b^4b^4	375 (79)	69 (14)	476

[a] In each experiment different rabbits were used as a source of SpC and "immune" RNA. LNC as well as SpC of the same rabbit were used for assay of PFC and similar results were obtained.

[b] As stated in *Materials and Methods*, 0.1 ml of RNA in HBSS was added to 0.1 ml of 2 × 10^7 SpC. The concentration of RNA (mg/ml) used for each experiment was as follows: 1) 9.2, 2) 10, 3) 8.7 and 4) 11.1.

[c] Seven and five-tenths micrograms of IgG anti-b4 in 2 ml HBSS were layered onto the agarose.

[d] Ten micrograms of IgG anti-b5 in 2 ml HBSS were layered onto the agarose.

[e] Two milliliters of a 1:50 dilution of goat anti-IgG-Fc were layered onto the agarose.

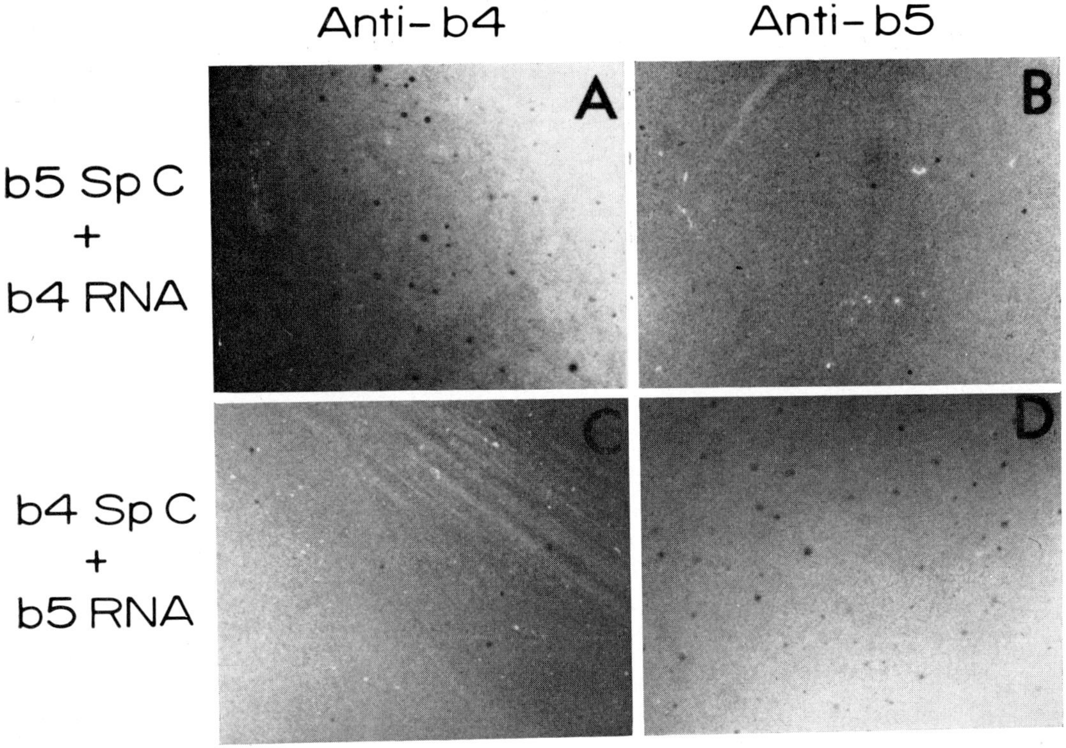

Figure 5. The allotype of the IgG antibodies in the "indirect" plaques identified by radioautography with ^{125}I-IgG-anti-b4 and ^{125}I-IgG-anti-b5.

For controls, the "non-immune" SpC and the SpC obtained from the "immune" RNA donor were also assayed for "indirect" PFC. The "non-immune" SpC used in these experiments yielded only 0 to 3 "indirect" PFC with each of the three antibody reagents. For the "immune" b4 SpC, the numbers of indirect PFC were as follows: 751 and 820 with anti-b4; 18 and 15 with anti-b5; and 733 and 873 with anti-IgG-Fc. For the "immune" b5 SpC, the numbers of "indirect" PFC were as follows: 19 and 22 with anti-b4; 630 and 549 with anti-b5; and 692 and 610 with anti-IgG-Fc.

In order to obtain more direct evidence about the allotypic specificity of the IgG antibody in the "indirect" plaques, ^{125}I-IgG-anti-b4 and ^{125}I-IgG-anti-b5 were used to develop the "indirect" plaques and the radiolabel in the plaques was then visualized by radioautography (1). When "non-immune" b5 SpC were converted to "indirect" PFC with "21 day immune" b4 RNA, 309 "indirect" PFC were observed with anti-b4 (Fig. 5*A*) and 46 PFC were observed with anti-b5 (Fig. 5*B*). Alternatively, when "non-immune" b4 SpC were converted to "indirect" PFC with "21 day immune" b5 RNA, 95 "indirect" PFC were observed with anti-b4 (Fig. 5*C*) and 351 PFC were observed with anti-b5 (Fig. 5*D*). Thus, again, most of the "indirect" PFC (69% to 83%) were developed with the antibody directed against the *b* locus allotype of the RNA donor rabbit.

Identification of the allotypic specificity of the IgG antibodies in the "indirect" plaques by inhibition of the appearance of the "indirect" plaques with anti-allotype antibodies. "Immune" RNA extracts from LNC of immunized b^4b^4 homozygous rabbits were used to convert SpC from non-immunized b^4b^4 or b^5b^5 rabbits to "indirect" PFC. Likewise, RNA extracts from LNC of immunized b^5b^5 rabbits were used to convert SpC from non-immunized b^4b^4 or b^5b^5 rabbits to "indirect" PFC. To identify the b4 or b5 allotypic specificity of the IgG antibodies in the "indirect" PFC, anti-b4 or anti-b5 antibodies (antisera or their isolated IgG immunoglobulins) were incorporated into the agarose plate so that

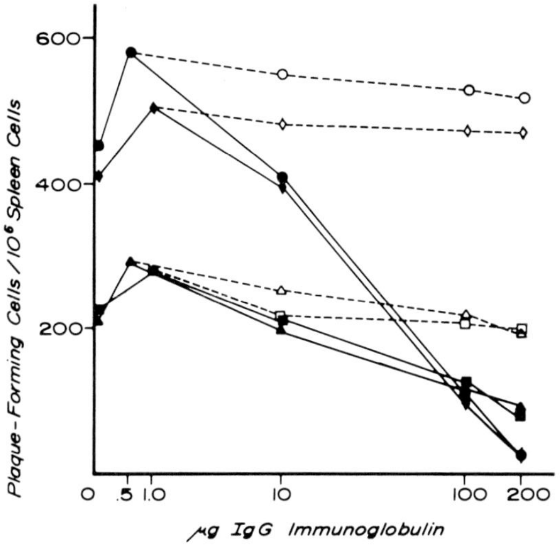

Figure 6. The effect of anti-b4 and anti-b5 (isolated IgG immunoglobulins) on the number of "indirect" PFC among "immune" SpC and "non-immune" SpC treated with "18 to 24 day immune" RNA as follows: ●, "Immune" b4 SpC + anti-b4; ○, "immune" b4 SpC + anti-b5; ◆, "immune" b5 SpC + anti-b5; ◇, "immune" b5 SpC + anti-b4; ▲, "non-immune" b5 SpC + "immune" b4 RNA + anti-b4; △, "non-immune" b5 SpC + "immune" b4 RNA + anti-b5; ■, "non-immune" b4 SpC + "immune" b5 RNA + anti-b5; □, "non-immune" b4 SpC + "immune" b5 RNA + anti-b4.

the anti-allotype antibodies were present during the release of IgG antibodies by "indirect" PFC (Fig. 6 and Table VI).

The effect of various amounts of anti-allotype antibodies on the appearance of "indirect" PFC is plotted in Figure 6. Small amounts of IgG antibodies (0.5 μg IgG anti-b4 in 2 ml agarose) enhanced the appearance of "indirect" PFC to a maximum of 580 "indirect" PFC for SpC derived from an immunized b^4b^4 rabbit and 295 "indirect" PFC for SpC derived from a non-immunized b^5b^5 rabbit and incubated *in vitro* with "immune" b4 RNA extracts (Fig. 6). Further increase in the amounts of IgG antibody led to reduction in the number of "indirect" PFC, so that with 200 μg IgG anti-b4, 28 "indirect" PFC were observed for SpC derived from an immunized b^4b^4 rabbit and 98 "indirect" PFC were observed for the b^5b^5 SpC incubated *in vitro* with "immune" b4 RNA (Fig. 6). Similarly, 1.0 μg IgG-anti-b5 enhanced the appearance of "indirect" PFC to a maximum of 505 "indirect" PFC for SpC derived from an immunized b^5b^5 rabbit and 280 "indirect" PFC for SpC derived from a non-immunized b^4b^4 rabbit incubated *in vitro* with "immune" b5 RNA extracts (Fig. 6). The presence of 200 μg IgG-anti-b5 significantly reduced the number of "indirect" PFC to 26 "indirect" PFC for SpC derived from an immunized b^5b^5 rabbit and to 81 "indirect" PFC for b^4b^4 SpC incubated *in vitro* with "immune" b5 RNA (Fig. 6).

The effectiveness of excess anti-allotype antibodies in inhibiting the appearance of "indirect" plaques is shown in Table VI. The first four experiments were performed with SpC from immunized rabbits, i.e., SpC not treated with RNA. The number of "indirect" PFC in immunized rabbits was found to be 490 to 629 "indirect" PFC (Table VI, experiments 1 to 4, column 3). When anti-b4 (antiserum or IgG-immunoglobulin) was present in the agarose, the number of "indirect" PFC from SpC of immunized b^4b^4 rabbits was reduced to 28 to 89 "indirect" PFC (Table VI, experiments 1 and 2, columns 5 and 7). The number of "indirect" PFC from b^5b^5 SpC was not affected by anti-b4; 458 to 484 "indirect" PFC were observed (Table VI, experiments 3 and 4, columns 5 and 7). Alternatively, when anti-b5 was incorporated into the agarose, the number of "indirect" PFC from b^5b^5 SpC was reduced whereas the number of "indirect" PFC from b^4b^4 SpC was not affected. Thus, the anti-allotype antibodies directed against the allotype of the immunized rabbit were effective in significantly reducing the number of "indirect" PFC. The percentage inhibition is indicated by the numbers in parentheses.

The last four experiments were performed with SpC derived from non-immunized b^4b^4 or b^5b^5 homozygous rabbits. When these SpC were converted to "indirect" PFC with "immune" b4 RNA extracts, anti-b4 antibodies incorporated into the agarose reduced the number of "indirect" PFC to 51 to 59 "indirect" PFC (Table VI, experiments 5 and 7, columns 5 and 7). Anti-b5 had much less effect. Alternatively, when "non-immune" SpC were incubated with "immune" b5 RNA extracts, anti-b5 antibodies incorporated into the agarose reduced the number of "indirect" PFC, while anti-b4 had much less effect. As a control, normal rabbit serum incorporated in the agarose did not significantly reduce the

TABLE VI

Identification of the allotypic specificity of the IgG antibodies in the "indirect" plaques by inhibition of the appearance of the plaques in the presence of anti-allotype antibodies incorporated into the agarose mixture[a]

Source of SpC[b, c]	Exp. No.	1. Genotype of the SpC Used for Plaque Assay	2. Genotype of Donor of "Immune" RNA	3. No Serum or Antibody Added	4. Normal Rabbit Serum 0.2 ml	Anti-Allotype Antisera 0.2 ml[d]		IgG Immunoglobulin 200 μg[e]	
						5. Anti-b4	6. Anti-b5	7. Anti-b4	8. Anti-b5
Immunized rabbits[b]	1	b^4b^4	None	550	525 (5)[a]	89 (84)	500 (9)	38 (93)	505 (8)
	2	b^4b^4	None	629	619 (2)	76 (88)	592 (6)	28 (96)	583 (7)
	3	b^5b^5	None	508	500 (2)	484 (5)	74 (85)	483 (5)	30 (94)
	4	b^5b^5	None	490	478 (2)	458 (6)	83 (83)	473 (4)	32 (94)
Non-immunized rabbits[c]	5	b^4b^4	b^4b^4	335	307 (8)	57 (83)	283 (16)	56 (83)	279 (17)
	6	b^4b^4	b^5b^5	310	300 (3)	233 (25)	60 (81)	211 (32)	86 (72)
	7	b^5b^5	b^4b^4	285	273 (1)	59 (79)	220 (23)	51 (82)	211 (26)
	8	b^5b^5	b^5b^5	297	280 (6)	251 (16)	58 (80)	247 (17)	53 (82)

[a] Data are expressed as "indirect" PFC/10^6 SpC and in parentheses as percentage inhibition. Percentage inhibition is calculated by the following formula:

$$\frac{\text{No. of PFC in standard agarose mixture (column 3)} - \text{No. of PFC with reagent added to agarose}}{\text{No. of PFC in standard agarose mixture}}.$$

[b] SpC obtained from immunized rabbits 18 to 24 days after the initial intravenous injection and 3 days after the last of 6 to 10 intravenous injections of 4 × 10^8 SRBC.

[c] SpC obtained from non-immunized rabbits converted to "indirect" PFC *in vitro* by incubation with "immune" RNA extracts of LNC, obtained from immunized rabbits 18 to 24 days after the initial intravenous injection and 3 days after the last of 6 to 10 intravenous injections of 4 × 10^8 SRBC.

[d] Amount of anti-allotype antisera incorporated into the agarose mixture (2.2 ml total volume).

[e] Amount of IgG-immunoglobulin in the agarose mixture (2.2 ml total volume).

TABLE VII

Identification of the allotypic specificity of the IgG antibodies in the "indirect" plaques by inhibition of appearance of the plaques by incubation of the SpC with anti-allotype antibodies prior to plating[a]

Source of SpC[b, c]	Exp. No.	1. Genotype of the SpC Used for Plaque Assay	2. Genotype of Donor of "Immune" RNA	3. No Serum or Antibody Added	4. Normal Rabbit Serum 0.2 ml[d]	Anti-Allotype Antisera 0.2 ml[d]	
						5. Anti-b4	6. Anti-b5
Immunized rabbits[b]	1	b^4b^4	None	605	595 (2)[a]	121 (80)	582 (4)
	2	b^4b^4	None	549	530 (2)	111 (79)	533 (3)
	3	b^5b^5	None	510	491 (4)	490 (5)	148 (71)
	4	b^5b^5	None	482	473 (2)	463 (4)	105 (79)
Non-immunized rabbits[c]	5	b^4b^4	b^4b^4	341	334 (2)	82 (76)	329 (4)
	6	b^4b^4	b^5b^5	289	275 (5)	251 (14)	99 (67)
	7	b^5b^5	b^4b^4	319	309 (3)	115 (64)	249 (22)
	8	b^5b^5	b^5b^5	272	263 (2)	259 (5)	91 (67)

[a] Data are expressed as "indirect" PFC/10^6 SpC and in parentheses as percentage inhibition. Percentage inhibition is calculated by the following formula:

$$\frac{\text{No. of PFC in standard SpC-HBSS incubation mixture (column 3)} - \text{No. of PFC with reagent added to SpC}}{\text{No. of PFC in standard SpC-HBSS incubation mixture}}.$$

[b] SpC obtained from immunized rabbits 18 to 24 days after the initial intravenous injection and 3 days after the last of 7 to 10 intravenous injections of 4 × 10^8 SRBC.

[c] SpC obtained from non-immunized rabbits incubated *in vitro* with "immune" RNA extracts of LNC, obtained from immunized rabbits 18 to 24 days after the initial intravenous injection and 3 days after the last of 7 to 10 intravenous injections of 4 × 10^8 SRBC.

[d] SpC[b] and SpC[c] (in 0.1 ml HBSS) were incubated with 0.2 ml undiluted normal rabbit sera (NRS) or anti-allotype antisera for 30 min at 37°C, then washed with HBSS prior to plating.

TABLE VIII

Anti-SRBC titer[a] in serum and number of PFC in spleen cells (SpC) of donor rabbits for RNA extracts and SpC used in experiment shown in Table IX

Rabbit	Donor	Serum Titer				No. of PFC per 10^6 SpC			
		Without 2-ME		With 2-ME		Without 2-ME		With 2-ME	
		Direct	Indirect	Direct	Indirect	Direct	Indirect	Direct	Indirect
CB1:	"5 day immune" RNA[b]	8,192	8,192	0	0	495	0	0	0
CB2:	"24 day immune" RNA[c]	4,096	65,536	128	32,768	380	820	20	750
CB3:	"Non-immune" RNA[d]	8	8	0	2	0	0	0	1
CB4:	SpC[e]	4	4	0	2	0	0	0	0
CB5:	SpC[f]	8	8	0	0	2	1	0	0
CB6:	SpC[g]	4	4	0	0	5	1	1	0

[a] Anti-SRBC titer determined by the method of "direct" and enhanced "indirect" localized hemolysis in gel as described in *Materials and Methods*.

[b] "Five day immune" RNA was extracted 5 days after a single intravenous injection of 4×10^8 SRBC.

[c] "Twenty-four day immune" RNA was extracted 24 days after the first and 3 days after the last of eight intravenous injections of 4×10^8 SRBC.

[d] "Non-immune" RNA was extracted from a non-immunized rabbit.

[e, f, g] CB4, CB5, CB6 are spleen cell suspensions from three different non-immune rabbits.

number of "indirect" PFC (Table VI, column 4). Thus, the anti-allotype antibodies directed against the allotype of the immunized rabbit serving as a donor of the "immune" RNA caused a 72% to 83% inhibition in the number of "indirect" PFC.

As an alternate method of inhibition for allotype identification of "indirect" plaques, SpC from immunized or non-immunized b^4b^4 or b^5b^5 rabbits after incubation *in vitro* with "immune" b4 or b5 RNA were incubated with anti-allotype antisera for 30 min at 37°C (Table VII). The cells were washed once, resuspended to a volume of 0.1 ml HBSS and plated to assess the number of "indirect" PFC. Anti-b4 reduced the number of "indirect" PFC in b^4b^4 SpC obtained from b^4b^4 immunized rabbits and anti-b5 reduced the number of b5 "indirect" PFC in SpC obtained from immunized b^5b^5 rabbits. Similarly, anti-b4 reduced the number of "indirect" PFC for SpC from either b^4b^4 or b^5b^5 non-immunized rabbits and incubated *in vitro* with "immune" b4 RNA, and anti-b5 reduced the number of "indirect" PFC in SpC obtained from either b^4b^4 or b^5b^5 non-immunized rabbits and treated *in vitro* with "immune" b5 RNA. As a control, incubation of cells with normal rabbit serum did not significantly reduce the number of "indirect" PFC (Table VII, column 4). Thus, the anti-allotype antibodies directed against the allotype of the immunized rabbit serving as a donor of the "immune" RNA caused a 64 to 76 per cent inhibition of the number of "indirect" PFC.

Experiments to assess the possibility that the activity of the "immune" RNA extract is a result of contamination with antibody (anti-SRBC) extracted with the RNA from the "immune" LNC. The protein content of the RNA extracts was assessed by the biuret reaction; the amount of biuret positive material was approximately 3% of the total weight. If IgG or IgM antibody to SRBC were present in the RNA extract, it might be inhibited by antibody directed against IgG or IgM determinants; i.e., goat anti-IgM, rabbit anti-b4 and rabbit anti-b5. Incubation of RNA extracts (550 μg to 1500 μg in 0.1 to 0.15 ml HBSS) with goat antiserum to IgM, rabbit antiserum to b4 and rabbit antiserum to b5 (0.1 ml) or the isolated IgG immunoglobulins (200 μg in 0.1 ml HBSS) did not inhibit the activity of the RNA extract. Moreover, in similar experiments with 2-ME, the activity of "5 day" or of "18 to 24 day immune" RNA was not inhibited. The possibility that preformed antibody was present in the RNA extracts was evaluated by determining the anti-SRBC titer in "5 day" or "18 to 24 day immune" RNA extracts. No anti-SRBC titer was detected in these

TABLE IX

Anti-SRBC titer[a] of lysed spleen cell suspensions obtained from non-immune rabbits before and after incubation with "immune" and "non-immune" RNA extracts

	Hanks' Soln.	1.8×10^8/ml "Non-Immune" SpC of Rabbit CB4	2.3×10^8/ml "Non-Immune" SpC of Rabbit CB5	2.0×10^8/ml "Non-Immune" SpC of Rabbit CB6
Hanks' solution	0	4	4	2
"5 day immune" RNA; 6.4 mg/ml	0	1024	1024	512
"24 day immune" RNA; 8.5 mg/ml	0	4096	4096	4096
"Non-immune" RNA; 10.7 mg/ml	0	32	32	8
"5 day immune" RNA (6.4 mg/ml) + RNAse (1 mg/ml)	4	8	4	8
"24 day immune" RNA (8.5 mg/ml) + RNAse (1 mg/ml)	16	4	0	8
'Non-immune" RNA (10.7 mg/ml) + RNAse (1 mg/ml)	4	4	8	4
RNAse (1 mg/ml)	8			

[a] The reagents listed in the top row were mixed with equal volumes (0.1 ml) of the reagents listed in the left column. All mixtures were subject to the same experimental conditions of incubation and freezing and thawing.

RNA preparations when tested by both the localized "direct" and enhanced "indirect" hemolysin technique in 10% SRBC agarose plates.

Active synthesis of anti-SRBC immunoglobulins by SpC from non-immunized rabbits after incubation with "immune" RNA extracts. The origin of the anti-SRBC antibodies was further evaluated by assaying the anti-SRBC titer in RNA extracts, lysed preparations of "non-immune" SpC and lysed preparations of the same number of "non-immune" SpC preincubated with the same amount of the RNA. The anti-SRBC titer in serum and the number of PFC in SpC of donor rabbits for the three RNA preparations and the three "non-immune" SpC populations are shown in Table VIII. The hemolytic activity of the serum was determined by the localized hemolysis in gel technique using both the "direct" and the enhanced "indirect" methods. The total anti-SRBC titer was obtained by the enhanced "indirect" technique using goat anti-IgG-Fc.

Three RNA preparations from lymph nodes were used. The "5 day immune" RNA was extracted 5 days after one intravenous injection of 4×10^8 SRBC. At this time, the serum anti-SRBC titer was 8192 and the spleen had 495 "direct" PFC/10^6 SpC. When 0.1 M 2-ME was present in the agarose no anti-SRBC titer in the serum or "direct" PFC of the SpC could be detected. The "24 day immune" RNA was extracted 24 days after the first and 3 days after the last of eight intravenous injections of 4×10^8 SRBC. At this time, the serum anti-SRBC titer was 65,536 and the spleen had 820 PFC/10^6 SpC. The presence of 2-ME reduced the "direct" anti-SRBC titer in the serum (compare 128 with 4096) and the number of "direct" PFC in the spleen (compare 20 with 380) without significantly affecting the "indirect" hemolytic titer of the serum (compare 32,768 with 65,536) or the number of "indirect" PFC in the spleen (compare 750 with 820). The "non-immune" RNA was extracted from a non-immunized rabbit, showing a background anti-SRBC titer of 8 and no "indirect" PFC. The three rabbits used as donors of "non-immunized" SpC had a background anti-SRBC titer in their serum of 4 to 8 and a background of 0 to 5 "direct" and 0 to 1 "indirect" PFC/10^6 SpC.

Each RNA preparation was mixed with an equal volume (0.1 ml) of each "non-immune" SpC suspension. The mixtures were incubated for 95 min at 37°C, 0.3 ml HBSS was added and then the cells were lysed by freezing and thawing. The anti-SRBC titers of the lysates in each tube are presented in Table IX. Control experiments were performed with the same number of cells without RNA and with the same amount of RNA without cells. The anti-SRBC titers obtained when "non-immune" SpC were incubated with "5 day immune" RNA (512 to 1024) or with

"24 day immune" RNA (4096) were substantially higher than that obtained with "non-immune" RNA (8 to 32) or untreated cells (2 to 4). Furthermore, no anti-SRBC activity was detected in the RNA extracts.

To assess the unlikely possibility that preformed anti-SRBC antibody may be present but in an undetectable combination with the RNA, each RNA preparation was pretreated with RNAse and the above experiments were repeated. Background titers of 4 to 16 were obtained. The RNAse preparation apparently had some nonspecific hemolytic activity.

DISCUSSION

SpC from non-immunized rabbits were converted to "indirect" PFC possessing IgG antibody of foreign allotype by incubation of the SpC with RNA extracts obtained from LNC of rabbits 18 to 24 days after 7 to 10 intravenous injections of 4×10^8 SRBC. The RNA conversion of SpC to PFC did not occur with RNA extracts of non-immunized animals. The "immune" RNA extracts were inactivated by RNAse but were unaffected by DNAse or trypsin suggesting that intact RNA itself was essential for the conversion. The conversion was specific for the SRBC antigen; plaques did not form with rabbit or mouse red blood cells.

The dose response curve with "18 to 24 day immune" RNA was similar in shape to that obtained previously by us for "5 day immune" RNA (1) except that approximately twice the amount of RNA (1000 μg) than formerly (500 μg) was necessary for maximum conversion. The fact that a maximum is reached may mean that only a limited number of SpC in any population may be converted under the conditions of our experiments to produce antibody specific for SRBC. Moreover, the amount of RNA pertinent for the specific antibody could represent only a small percentage of the total RNA extracted; RNA for other antibodies may be converting SpC to produce antibodies which are not being tested.

Anti-SRBC antibodies were detected in the SpC population by plating SpC suspensions in SRBC-agarose plates and counting the number of "direct" PFC and the added number of "indirect" PFC developed with goat anti-IgG-Fc and complement. That the "indirect" PFC contained anti-SRBC antibody of the IgG immunoglobulin class was indicated by inhibition of plaque formation with excess goat anti-IgG-Fc and by lack of such inhibition with goat anti-IgM or with 2-mercaptoethanol, both known to inhibit the appearance of IgM plaques (1).

The appearance of IgG plaques (4% to 32%) bearing the allotype of the SpC donor may be attributable to an immunogenic effect of antigen or an RNA-antigen complex probably present in the RNA extracts (5, 14–17). These results are not inconsistent with the findings of Adler, *et al.* (5) who have shown in a different experimental system, in which the RNA was extracted from peritoneal exudate cells stimulated *in vitro* with T_2 phage as the antigen, that the IgG antibody produced in the "RNA treated" lymph node fragments cultured for 10 to 14 days had the allotypic specificity of the host cells. They attributed their results to an immunogenic role of RNA-antigen complexes in the RNA extracts. However, IgG antibody bearing the allotype of the RNA donor (64% to 84% of the plaques in our present work) was not found by Adler *et al.* (5). The antibodies of foreign allotype found in the present experiments are unlikely to be explained by a mechanism whereby antigen could transform a cell to produce antibody of foreign allotype.

Plaques of foreign allotype could be attributed to contamination of the RNA extracts with preformed anti-SRBC antibody present in the lymph nodes of the immunized rabbit. However, anti-SRBC antibody could not be detected in any of our RNA extracts when tested by enhanced "indirect" hemolysis in SRBC-agarose gel. Furthermore, preincubation of RNA extracts with anti-IgG-Fc, anti-b4 or anti-b5 failed to impair the activity of the RNA extracts. Nevertheless, the argument might be made that these experiments were not sensitive enough to eliminate the possibility that a sufficient number of preformed anti-SRBC antibody molecules may in some way be complexed to the RNA.

To demonstrate active synthesis of anti-SRBC antibodies by the "RNA-converted" SpC, a quantitative experiment was designed to assay the presence of anti-SRBC antibodies in and produced by the same number of SpC with or without incubation with RNA extracts (which had no anti-SRBC titer). The anti-SRBC titer was determined after lysis of the SpC by freezing and thawing. Without incubation with RNA, the lysed SpC gave a titer of 2 to 4; after incubation with "5 day immune" RNA, the same number of lysed SpC gave a titer of 512 to 1024 for IgM anti-SRBC antibodies; after incubation with "24 day immune" RNA, the same number of lysed SpC gave a titer of 4096 for IgG anti-SRBC antibodies. The background titer using "non-immune" RNA ranged from 8 to 32. The possibility that anti-SRBC antibody molecules were complexed to the RNA in the extracts, in an undetectable form, was tested in the experiment designed to see if anti-SRBC antibodies would be detected after fragmenting the RNA with RNAse. In these experiments, background titers of 4 to 16 were obtained which were probably nonspecific since the RNAse itself in a 1:8 dilution caused hemolysis of SRBC.

The active synthesis of IgM and IgG antibody with foreign allotype by "RNA-converted" cells in our experiments is most readily explained by attributing a messenger role for the RNA. However, this interpretation must be guarded until an active RNA component of appropriate base composition is isolated and characterized. Alternatively, an insertion mechanism for transfer of information could be conceived which may require relatively small units of RNA. However, the possibility must also be considered that the DNA for b4 and b5 polypeptide chains is indeed present in all rabbits and that the allelic genes controlling the synthesis of these polypeptide chains are control, rather than structural genes. If this were so, the RNA extracts might act by having its effect on the control genes.

Acknowledgments. We are grateful to Judith Newman and Margaretha Bergman for technical assistance and to Alice Gilman-Sachs for characterization of the anti-allotype sera. We thank Dr. Leon LeBeau for taking the photographs of the plaques and Dr. A. Nisonoff for a generous supply of goat anti-rabbit-IgG-Fc.

REFERENCES

1. Bell, C. and Dray, S., J. Immun., *103:* 1196, 1969.
2. Fishman, M., J. Exp. Med., *114:* 837, 1961.
3. Fishman, M. and Adler, F. L., J. Exp. Med., *117:* 595, 1963.
4. Fishman, M. and Adler, F. L., *Third International Immunopathology Symposium, La Jolla, Calif., 1963*, Edited by P. Grabar and P. Miescher, p. 79, Grune and Stratton, N. Y., 1963.
5. Adler, F. L., Fishman, M. and Dray, S., J. Immun., *97:* 554, 1966.
6. Cohen, E. P. and Parks, J. J., Science, *144:* 1012, 1964.
7. Cohen, E. P., Newcomb, R. W. and Crosby, L. K., J. Immun., *94:* 416, 1965.
8. Cohen, E. P., Nature, *213:* 462, 1967.
9. Friedman, H., Science, *146:* 934, 1964.
10. Friedman, H., Nature, *199:* 502, 1963.
11. Friedman, H. P., Stavitsky, A. B. and Solomon, J. M., Science, *149:* 1106, 1965.
12. Askonas, B. A. and Rhodes, J. M., Nature, *205:* 470, 1965.
13. Gottlieb, A. A., in *Nucleic Acids in Immunology*, Edited by O. J. Plescia and W. Braun, p. 471, Springer-Verlag, New York, 1968.
14. Gottlieb, A. A., J. Reticuloendothel. Soc., *5:* 270, 1968.
15. Askonas, B. A. and Rhodes, J. M., *Molecular and Cellular Basis of Antibody Formation*, Edited by J. Sterzl, p. 503, Academic Press, New York, 1965.
16. Uyeki, E. M. and Klassen, R. S., J. Immun., *101:* 271, 1968.
17. Kabat, E. A., *Kabat and Mayer's Experimental Immunochemistry*, 2nd Ed. pp. 114, 153 and 154, Charles C Thomas, Springfield, Ill., 1961.
18. Jerne, N. K., Nordin, A. A. and Henry, C., in *Conference on Cell Bound Antibodies, Washington, D. C., 1963*, Edited by B. Amos and H. Koprowski, p. 109, Wistar Institute Press, Philadelphia, 1963.
19. Sterzl, J. and Riha, I., Nature, *208:* 858, 1965.
20. Dresser, D. W. and Wortis, H. H., Nature, *208:* 859, 1965.
21. Wortis, H. H., Taylor, R. B. and Dresser, D. W., Immunology, *11:* 603, 1966.

THE JOURNAL OF IMMUNOLOGY
Vol. 105, No. 3, September 1970
Printed in U.S.A.

IMMUMOCHEMICAL STUDIES OF FOOT-AND-MOUTH DISEASE

VIII. Detection and Quantitation of Antibodies by Radial Immunodiffusion

K. M. COWAN AND G. G. WAGNER[1]

From the Plum Island Animal Disease Laboratory, Animal Disease and Parasite Research Division, Agricultural Research Service, United States Department of Agriculture, Greenport, New York 11944

Received for publication April 20, 1970

Guinea pig antiserum containing known quantities of antibody to foot-and-mouth disease virus (140S antigen) and virus protein subunit (12S antigen) was used as a standard in radial immunodiffusion (RID) analyses for determining the antibody content of other antisera. The antibody contents estimated by RID for the unknown sera were in close agreement with those subsequently established by quantitative precipitin analyses. Relatively small amounts of reagents are required and the procedure is simple to perform. Consequently, it provides a feasible procedure for the quantitative estimation of the antibody content of many antisera to the different antigenic components occurring in foot-and-mouth disease. The RID techniques used were approximately 10 times more sensitive for detecting either antibody or virus (140S antigen) than the Ouchterlony double diffusion method. The sensitivity of the procedure used was such that it approached that of complement fixation for the detection of 7S antibody. The greatest sensitivity for detecting either 140S antigen or antibody was obtained when the reactant sought was incorporated into the agar layer. Antibody was detected at a concentration of 1 μg/ml in agar, and 140S antigen was detected at a concentration of 1.25 μg/ml in agar by 19S antibody, and at 2.5 μg/ml by 7S antibody.

Immunodiffusion analyses of the Ouchterlony double-diffusion type have been used extensively to examine foot-and-mouth disease virus (FMDV) immune systems (1–9). Although valuable qualitative information on the antigenic components and physical-chemical classes of antibodies involved was obtained, the double-diffusion technique is not readily amenable to quantitation. The radial immunodiffusion (RID) technique of Mancini *et al.* (10, 11) has been widely used for the quantitative estimation of soluble antigens, particularly the immunoglobulins (12). Although it was shown that the area of the precipitin rings produced was inversely related to the concentration of antibody (11), relatively few reports on the application of this finding for the measurement of antibody are available (13, 14).

Investigations in our laboratory involve attempts to examine FMDV immune systems by quantitative immunochemical techniques. The measurement of antibody by quantitative precipitin analysis utilizes relatively large amounts of purified viral antigens, and the procedures are laborious and time-consuming. These factors have obviously limited the number of assays that have been performed. Therefore, it was of interest to examine RID procedures and determine their potential as alternative techniques for antibody measurement. This report presents observations on the sensitivity of RID techniques for detecting viral antigens and antibodies, and the potential of the procedures for antibody quantitation.

MATERIALS AND METHODS

Virus. The two different antigenic variants of FMDV, type A, subtype 12, strain 119 (FMDV, A-119) used in these studies were described previously (8). Briefly, the 140S-Lo-pass virus was from infectious bovine tongue

[1] This work was conducted during Dr. Wagner's tenure as a Postdoctoral Resident Research Associate of the Agricultural Research Service and the National Academy of Sciences, National Research Council.

epithelium and was passaged seven times in primary calf kidney cell cultures. It was then grown in quantity in baby hamster kidney cell (BHK-21, clone 13) cultures, concentrated by precipitation with polyethylene glycol (Carbowax 20-M, Union Carbide Co., Chicago, Illinois), and purified by two cycles of ultracentrifugation into isodense CsCl (1.43 g/ml) (15). The 140-S-Lo-pass virus contains both the a- and b-subdeterminant antigenic groupings (8), and will be referred to as 140S-ab virus. The other variant was the 140S-b virus which was isolated from tissue culture high passage virus by serologic and plaquing techniques and possesses only the b-subdeterminant grouping (8). It was concentrated and purified as above.

Virus concentration was determined spectrophotometrically using the virus extinction $E_{259}^{1\%}$ nm of 77.7 (16) and by quantitative complement-fixation (CF) assays (17). The purified preparations contained 2 to 6 mg of virus/ml.

Virus protein (12S) and infection-associated (VIA) antigens. Purified high passage tissue culture FMDV, A-119 was degraded by treatment at pH 4.5 and the 12S antigen purified by column chromatography on diethylaminoethyl cellulose (17). The concentration of 12S antigen was determined spectrophotometrically using the virus protein extinction $E_{278}^{1\%}$ nm of 11.1 (18).

The preparation of VIA antigen has been described (7). This antigen has not been purified, but the preparations were free of detectable 140S and 12S antigenic components.

Antisera. Guinea pigs were infected by intradermal inoculation of the plantar pads with a guinea pig vesicular fluid source of FMDV, A-119. Blood collected 7 days postinfection (DPI) provided serum containing antibodies of the 19S class (3–5). Serum having antibodies of the 7S class was prepared by infecting guinea pigs as above, but they were given an additional inoculation of guinea pig adapted virus 10 to 12 weeks later (3–5). Blood samples were obtained 10 days later and the collected serum was pooled and termed "hyperimmune" serum. Analyses were also done on pooled serum from guinea pigs immunized with 25 μg of purified FMDV, A-119 inactivated with acetylethyleneimine (AEI) and incorporated in incomplete Freund's adjuvant. The animals were bled 85 days (DPIm) after a single inoculation of the vaccine (17).

All sera studied were heated for 30 min at 56°C and then centrifuged at 4°C for 1 hr at approximately 27,000 × G in an angle-head rotor (No. SS-34 in the RC2-B centrifuge, Ivan Sorvall Inc., Norwalk, Conn.). Lipid material was carefully aspirated from the surface and the clear serum poured off the slight pellet that was evident.

Quantitative precipitin analyses were performed on hyperimmune sera with both 140S-ab antigen and 12S antigen as described previously (17), except that the precipitates were sedimented initially and in subsequent washing steps by centrifuging at 5000 rpm (approximately 3000 × G). Folin-Ciocalteu analyses were used to determine the protein content of the precipitates (19). Purified guinea pig γ globulin that had been standardized by Kjeldahl analysis for nitrogen served as the protein standard.

Radial immunodiffusion analyses. Thoroughly washed agar was melted in distilled water to give a 2% solution, filtered, and stored at 4°C. Diluent for the agar was 1.0 M glycine, 0.05 M sodium barbital and 1% NaN_3, adjusted to pH 7.7 to 7.8 by addition of HCl.

The usual procedure for preparing plates for RID analyses was as follows:

1. Four parts of buffer warmed to 50°C were added to 5 parts of 2% melted agar. Nine milliliters of the buffer-agar mixture were pipetted into screw-cap vials and held at 50°C.

2. One milliliter of serum or antigen suitably diluted in agar gel buffer was added to 9.0 ml of buffer-agar mixture giving a 10-fold dilution of the incorporated reagent.

3. Duplicate plates of the mixtures were prepared by pipetting 4.0 ml into level 60-mm plastic tissue culture dishes (Model 3002, Falcon Plastics, Los Angeles, Calif.) or 2.0 ml into 35-mm diameter cups of 6-cup disposable plastic trays (Linbro Chemical Co., Inc., New Haven, Conn.). After the agar had solidified, the plates were held overnight at 4°C.

4. Wells of either 3 mm or 3.6 mm in diameter were cut and the plugs were removed by aspiration. Antigen or serum preparations were placed in the wells using microliter syringes; 5 μl into 3-mm wells, or 10 μl when 3.6-mm wells were used.

5. The plates were incubated at room temperature in a humidified chamber. The diameter of the precipitin rings formed around the wells

TABLE I

Diameter of precipitin rings obtained in reversed radial immunodiffusion[a] with varying amounts of FMDV (140S-ab) and varying concentrations of 7S and 19S antibodies

Antiserum[b]			Virus Concentration in Agar (μg/ml)					
Dilution	Antibody class	Antibody/ml	40	20	10	5	2.5	1.25
		μg						
1:1	7S	160	4.6[c]	6.1	8.2	11.0	+[d]	—
1:2	7S	80	<4[e]	4.5	6.0	8.5[f]	10.0[f]	—
1:4	7S	40	—[g]	<4[e]	4.0[f]	7.0[f]	8.0[f]	—
1:8	7S	20	—	—	—	—	—	—
1:16	7S	10	—	—	—	—	—	—
1:1	19S	87	4.2	5.7	7.5	10.1	11.0[f]	+[d]
1:2	19S	44	<4[e]	<4[e]	5.6	7.4	9.8[f]	12.0[f]
1:4	19S	22	—	<4[e]	4.0	5.2	7.1	9.0[f]
1:8	19S	11	—	—	—	<4[e]	6.0[f]	7.0[f]
1:16	19S	5.5	—	—	—	—	—	—

[a] Virus (140S-ab) incorporated in the agar layer and 5 μl of antisera placed in wells.
[b] Hyperimmune serum 1-9-68 contained 7S antibody and 7-DPI serum contained 19S antibody.
[c] Mean ring diameter in mm.
[d] Evident reaction but diameter not measurable.
[e] Precipitation evident at rim of well.
[f] Approximation due to indistinct edge of precipitin ring.
[g] No evident reaction.

was determined with a measuring magnifier. Plates were photographed unstained.

RESULTS

Antigen and antibody detection by reversed and conventional RID techniques. The applicability of the conventional (11, 13) and reversed (20) RID techniques to FMDV systems was examined when differing amounts of both antibody and antigen were used. Only virus (140S-ab) was examined as antigen in these preliminary screening tests.

In the reversed system experiment, twofold dilutions of 140S-ab antigen were prepared and incorporated into agar to give from 1.25 μg to 40 μg of virus/ml of agar-virus mixture. Two 3.0-mm diameter wells were cut in each plate to permit the testing of both hyperimmune (1-9-68) and 7-DPI sera so that the reactions of 7S and 19S antibodies could be compared. Quantitative precipitin analyses indicated serum 1-9-68 contained 160 μg antibody protein/ml (AbP/ml) for 140S-ab virus, and 137 μg of AbP/ml for 12S antigen. A value of 87 μg AbP/ml was obtained for the 7-DPI serum using 140S-ab virus as antigen. Twofold dilutions of each serum were added in 5-μl amounts to their respective wells. Diameters were measured periodically and no changes were noted after about 10 days of incubation (Table I). Since determinations of the antibody content of the hyperimmune and 7-DPI sera had been obtained, the table includes antibody protein concentration values as well as the dilution factor of the sera.

The results obtained were as anticipated, i.e., the diameters of the precipitin rings were directly related to the amount of antibody added to the wells, and inversely related to the virus content of the agar. There was an apparent difference in the sensitivity of 7S and 19S antibodies for detecting 140S antigen. The serum containing 7S antibody gave a reaction with virus at a concentration of 2.5 μg virus/ml, whereas the 19S antibody could detect as little as 1.25 μg virus/ml. Similarly, 19S antibody at a concentration of 11 μg AbP/ml (0.055 μg in 5 μl) gave positive reactions, whereas approximately four times as much 7S antibody was required to give evident precipitin rings.

Although these initial results were encouraging, several features of the reversed procedure were undesirable. One factor of concern was the

TABLE II

Diameter of precipitin rings obtained in conventional radial immunodiffusion[a] with varying concentrations of 7S antibody and virus (140S-ab) antigen

Virus	Final Dilution of Serum[b] in Agar				
	1:10	1:20	1:40	1:80	1:160
	µg antibody/ml of serum-agar mixture				
	16	8	4	2	1
	Mean ring diameter				
µg/ml	*mm*				
400	<4[c]	4.6	6.4	8.2	11.5[d]
300	<4	<4	5.1	7.0	10.0[d]
200	<4	<4	4.2	6.3	9.0
100	<4	<4	<4	4.3	6.0
50	—[e]	<4	<4	<4	<4
25	—	—	—	<4	—

[a] Serum incorporated in agar and 5 µl of virus (140S-ab) placed in wells.
[b] Hyperimmune serum 1-9-68.
[c] Precipitation evident at rim of the well.
[d] Approximation due to weak reaction and indistinct edge of precipitin rings.
[e] No evident reaction.

recognized heat lability of FMDV. The addition of virus to heated agar could degrade the virus to an extent which would be difficult to control. Another point of concern was that the edges of the precipitin rings tended to be more diffuse than those obtained by the conventional method (cf. 20). Finally, reactions were obtained only with relatively high concentrations of antibody which, as will be shown, were contrary to results obtained by the conventional procedure.

The conventional RID method was examined where varying dilutions of hyperimmune serum 1-9-68 were incorporated into the agar. In this instance, 2.0-ml volumes of serum-agar mixture were placed in 35-mm diameter cups of disposable trays. A single 3.0-mm diameter well was cut in each plate, and 5 µl of 140S-ab antigen at concentrations ranging from 25 µg to 400 µg/ml were placed in the wells. The results of this experiment are summarized (Table II). The precipitin reactions obtained were similar to those shown in Figures 2 and 4.

This experiment demonstrated that the conventional RID procedure was extremely sensitive for detecting antibody, i.e., a concentration as low as 1 µg AbP/ml of serum-agar mixture gave measurable precipitin rings when lower concentrations of virus (100 µg or 200 µg/ml) were used. In comparison to the reversed RID procedure, much higher concentrations of virus (25 µg/ml) were required to give an evident reaction.

In view of this sensitivity for antibody and antigen detection, the RID methods were compared with Ouchterlony and CF procedures. Varying dilutions of hyperimmune serum 1-9-68 were tested against different concentrations of 140S-ab antigen by the Ouchterlony method (Fig. 1). The pattern used had wells 4 mm in diameter, outer wells were 6 mm from the central well, and the wells were filled flush with the surface of the agar. The serum sample was placed in the central well, and the surrounding wells received various concentrations of 140S-ab virus. Weak positive reactions were obtained with serum diluted 1:16 (10 µg AbP/ml), but no reactions were evident at a 1:32 dilution. Thus, the conventional RID method appears to be approximately 10 times more sensitive

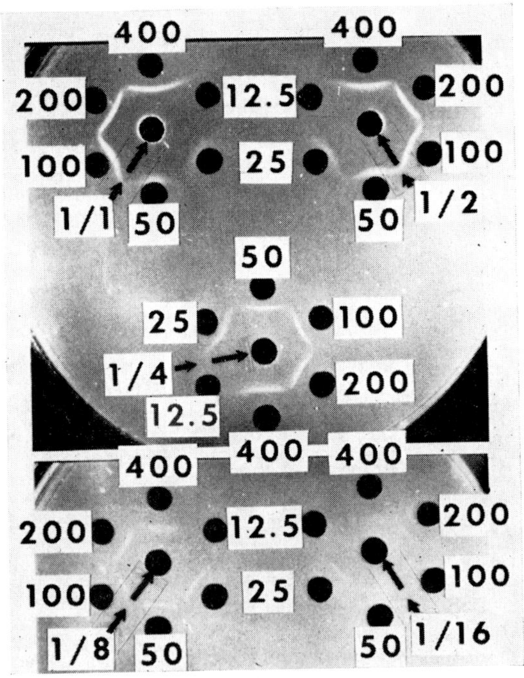

Figure 1. Immunodiffusion precipitin reactions with varying dilutions of guinea pig anti-FMDV, A-119 hyperimmune serum 1-9-68 and varying concentrations of purified 140S-ab FMDV, A-119. Undiluted (1:1) serum and dilutions from 1:2 up to 1:16 were tested against 140S-ab antigen at concentrations ranging from 400 µg/ml to 12.5 µg/ml.

TABLE III

Diameter of precipitin rings obtained in radial immunodiffusion analyses of guinea pig anti-FMDV hyperimmune sera 1-9-68 and 10-31-69 tested against FMDV, A-119 140S-ab, 12S and VIA antigens

Serum Dilution	Antigen	Serum	
		10-31-69 Diameter	1-9-68 Diameter
		mm	*mm*
1:10	140S-ab	5.6, 5.6	6.1, 6.5
1:15	140S-ab	6.0, 6.1	7.7, 7.8
1:20	140S-ab	6.9, 6.8	8.2, 8.6
1:30	140S-ab	7.8, 8.0	10.0, 10.0
1:40	140S-ab	8.9, 9.0	11.5, 11.1
1:60	140S-ab	9.8, 10.4	12.9, 12.3
1:10	12S	7.5, 7.5	8.3, 8.8
1:15	12S	8.3, 8.7	9.8, 9.8
1:20	12S	9.5, 9.7	11.4, 11.1
1:30	12S	11.8, 11.2	13.3, 13.2
1:40	12S	13.1, 13.2	15.0, 15.0
1:60	12S	15.9, 16.7	
1:10	VIA	8.0, 8.1	10.0, 10.0
1:15	VIA	9.8, 9.6	11.9, 11.5
1:20	VIA	11.2, 10.5	N.M.[a]
1:30	VIA	13.1, 13.1	N.M.

[a] Not readily measurable due to indistinct edge.

for detecting 7S antibody to FMDV than the double diffusion method used here. With respect to virus detection, approximately 25 μg/ml were required to give a reaction. As indicated previously, the reversed RID method detected virus at a concentration of approximately 2.5 μg/ml when 7S antibody was used, and even lower concentrations of virus were detected with 19S antibody.

Complement-fixation tests were performed with hyperimmune serum 1-9-68 and 140S-ab antigen using a 20-hr fixation period at 4°C (17). This serum titered 1:240 (0.67 μg AbP/ml) indicating that the conventional RID procedure approached the sensitivity of the CF test for detecting 7S antibody to FMDV. Antibody of the 19S class fails to fix complement with 140S antigen (5, 6) which is an important advantage of RID techniques. An antigen endpoint was obtained with approximately 0.15 μg of 140S-ab/ml; thus, CF was more sensitive for detecting virus than RID procedures.

Estimation of the antibody content of antisera to multiple antigenic components. The conventional RID data in Table II demonstrated an inverse relationship between the diameter of the precipitin rings and the concentration of antibody when a constant amount of antigen was used. Therefore, analyses of several sera at various dilutions tested with a constant amount of antigen should provide relative values of the antibody content of these sera. This possibility was explored using hyperimmune sera 1-9-68 and 10-31-69. Since each serum contained antibody to three different antigenic components, i.e., 140S, 12S and VIA antigens, this experiment was also performed to determine if estimations of antibody content for the different antigens could be made in a single experiment.

Duplicate 60-mm plates were prepared for each serum where the final dilutions of serum in agar were 1:10, 1:15, 1:20, 1:30, 1:40 and 1:60. Three reservoirs 3.6 mm in diameter were cut in each plate. In one well of each plate were placed 10 μl of 140S-ab antigen at a concentration of 500 μg/ml; in another well, 10 μl of 12S antigen at a concentration of 200 μg/ml; and in the remaining well, 10 μl of a stock VIA antigen preparation diluted 1:6. Preliminary experiments with 12S and VIA antigens had indicated the concentration of each giving satisfactory reactions. Final readings of ring diameters were made at 10 days (Table III) at which time the plates were photographed (Fig. 2). Only one plate of each duplicate set is shown.

Various methods of plotting mean precipitin ring dimensions *vs* antibody concentrations were explored. Although other plotting methods could be satisfactorily applied, a plot of ring diameter *vs* the reciprocal of the serum dilution on log-log graph paper proved most convenient (Fig. 3). It was then assumed that precipitin rings of the same diameter would be produced by equal concentrations of antibody when a constant amount of antigen was used. The plots shown in Figure 3 could be used to determine the dilution of each serum required to give a precipitin ring of a given diameter, e.g., rings of 7.0 mm diameter for 140S-ab would be obtained with serum 10-31-69 diluted 1:20.5 and serum 1-9-68 diluted 1:12.5. Thus, serum 10-31-69 was estimated to contain $\frac{20.5}{12.5} = 1.64$ times more antibody to 140S-ab than serum 1-9-68. Quantitative precipitin tests indicated serum 1-9-68 contained 160 μg AbP/ml for 140S-ab; therefore, the

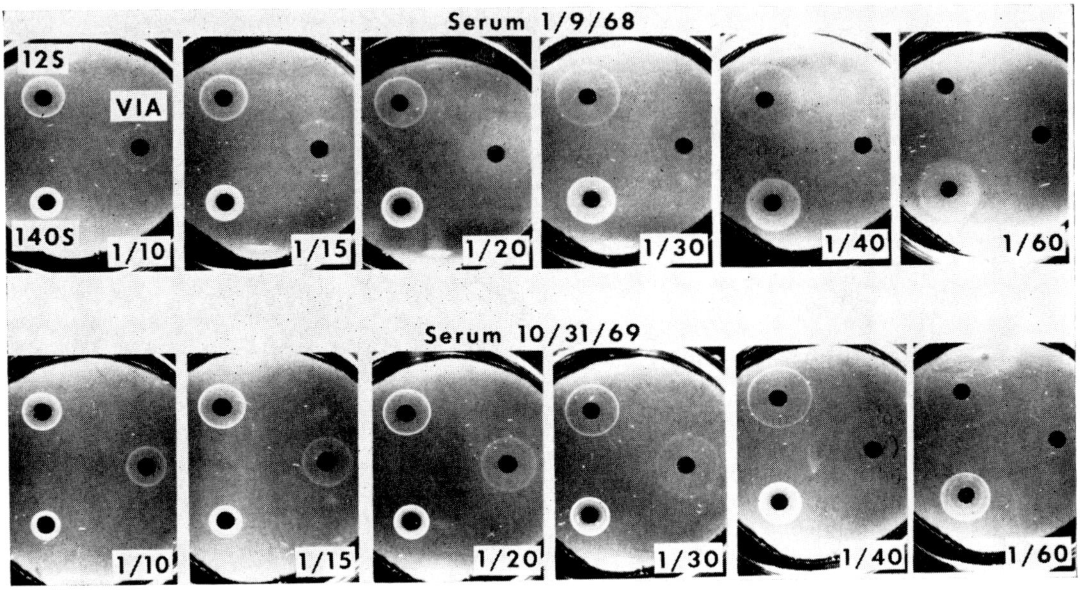

Figure 2. Conventional radial immunodiffusion reactions of varying dilutions of guinea pig anti-FMDV, A-119 hyperimmune sera 1-9-68 and 10-31-69 tested against FMDV, A-119 140S-ab, 12S and VIA antigens. The position of the antigens in all plates was as indicated in the upper left-hand photograph.

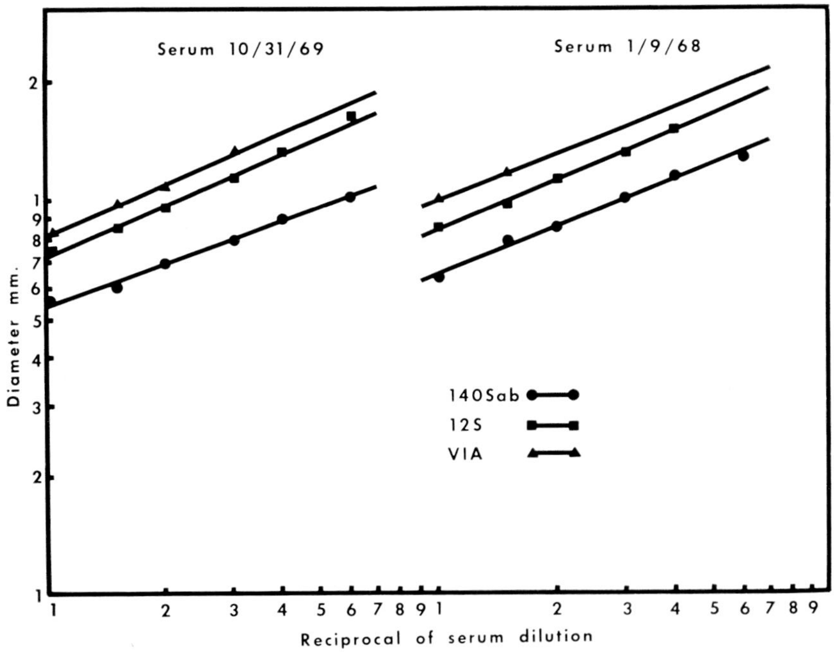

Figure 3. Log-log scale plots of precipitin ring diameters *vs* reciprocal of serum dilutions. Sera tested were guinea pig anti-FMDV, A-119 hyperimmune sera 1-9-68 and 10-31-69 tested against FMDV, A-119 140S-ab, 12S and VIA antigens. The data are from Table III.

TABLE IV

Calculation of antibody content of guinea pig anti-FMDV hyperimmune serum 10-31-69 using serum 1-9-68 as the standard serum

Ring Diameter	Antigen	Reciprocal of Serum Dilution Required[a]		Antibody Content of Serum 10-31-69 Relative to Serum 1-9-68[b]	Calculated Antibody Content of Serum 10-31-69	Mean Antibody Content of Serum 10-31-69
		10-31-69	1-9-68			
mm					*μg/ml*	*μg/ml*
6	140S-ab	13.3	8.3	1.60	256[c]	273.2
7	140S-ab	20.5	12.5	1.64	262	
8	140S-ab	29.5	17.5	1.68	269	
9	140S-ab	42.0	24.0	1.75	280	
10	140S-ab	57.0	30.5	1.87	299	
8	12S	12.2	9.0	1.36	186[d]	189.4
9	12S	16.2	11.7	1.39	190	
10	12S	20.7	15.0	1.38	189	
12	12S	32.0	23.0	1.39	190	
15	12S	56.0	40.0	1.40	192	
10	VIA	16.0	10.0	1.60		
12	VIA	25.0	16.0	1.56		
15	VIA	42.0	28.0	1.50		

[a] Determined from Figure 3.

[b] $\frac{\text{Reciprocal of dilution of serum 10-31-69}}{\text{Reciprocal of dilution of serum 1-9-68}}$.

[c] Antibody content of 10-31-69 relative to 1-9-68 × 160 μg AbP/ml.

[d] Antibody content of 10-31-69 relative to 1-9-68 × 137 μg AbP/ml.

antibody content of serum 10-31-69 would be estimated at 160 × 1.64 = 262 μg AbP/ml. It was in this way that the values shown in Table IV were calculated. The failure to obtain the same anti-140S-ab antibody values for the different ring diameters is due to slope differences of the serum 10-31-69 and 1-9-68 plots (Fig. 3). The slope of the 10-31-69 serum plot was calculated to be 0.346 (S.E. = 0.017), and that of 1-9-68 was 0.388 (S.E. = 0.017). In view of the differing antibody values thus calculated, a mean value of 273 μg AbP/ml for serum 10-31-69 was taken to be the anti-140S content. In the same manner, the antibody to 12S antigen was estimated at 189 μg AbP/ml. With respect to antibody to VIA antigen, it is possible to express this in only relative terms; thus, serum 10-31-69 was estimated to contain 1.55 times more antibody than serum 1-9-68. Quantitative precipitin analyses subsequently performed with serum 10-31-69 were in remarkably close agreement with the RID values. Antibody protein precipitated by 140S-ab and 12S antigens was determined to be 265 μg/ml and 184 μg/ml, respectively.

A consideration of the nature of the RID procedure indicates that the method used in this study should provide accurate estimates of the antibody content of antisera. What is actually determined in these assays is the volume of antibody-agar required to complex all of the introduced antigen. As reasonably suggested by Mancini *et al.* (11), when the precipitin ring ceases growing, the precipitate is similar to one formed at antibody-antigen equivalence, i.e., no uncomplexed antibody or antigen is present within the precipitin cylinder. Consequently, the volume of antibody-agar mixture required to achieve antibody-antigen equivalence with a given amount of antigen might be expected to be inversely proportional to the antibody concentration. Recognizing the fact that the volume of a cylinder varies as the square of the diameter, a log-log plot of precipitin ring diameters *vs* the reciprocal of the serum dilutions should give a straight line with a slope of 0.5. This slope

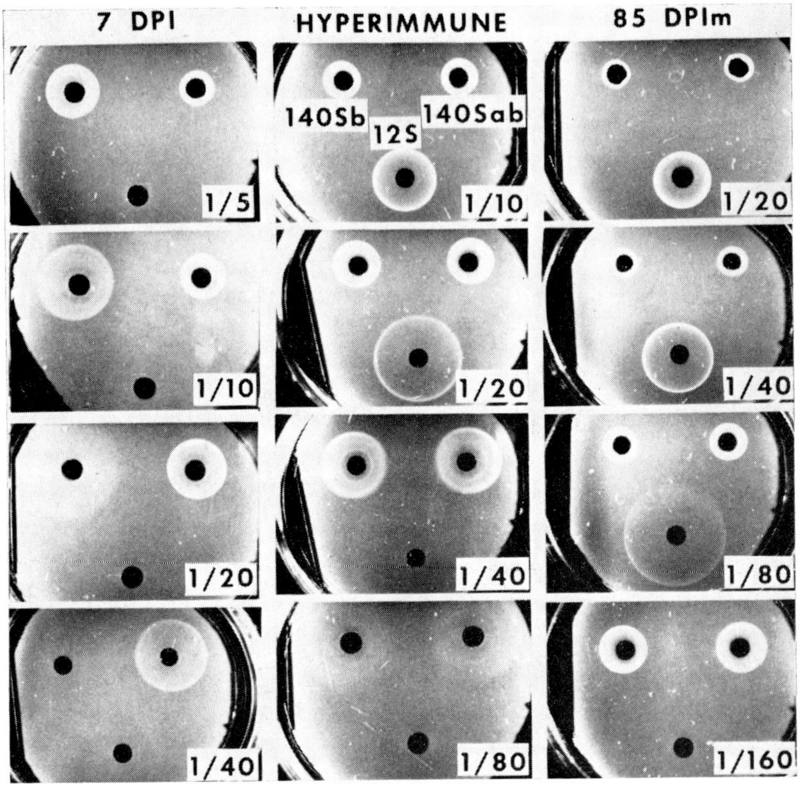

Figure 4. Conventional radial immunodiffusion reactions of varying dilutions of guinea pig anti-FMDV, A-119 sera tested against FMDV, A-119 140S-ab, 140S-b and 12S antigens. 7 DPI = 7 day post-infection serum; hyperimmune = serum 1-9-68; 85 DPIm = serum obtained 85 days after inoculation with inactivated virus. The position of the antigens for all plates was as indicated in the top middle photograph.

value was not obtained because the volume of the precipitin cylinder had been altered by the removal of a plug of agar to provide the antigen reservoir. However, slope values of approximately 0.5 may be obtained if ring diameters corrected for well diameter

$$(D \text{ corrected} = \sqrt{D^2 \text{ ring} - D^2 \text{ well}})$$

are used for plotting.

Influence of virus variants on RID analyses with 7S and 19S antibodies. It was reported that guinea pig 19S antibody was able to distinguish between 140S-ab and 104S-b virus variants of FMDV, A-119 in Ouchterlony analyses, while 7S antibody was unable to do so (8, 9). It was suggested that 19S antibodies have distinct anti-a or anti-b subdeterminant specificities, and that anti-a antibody was at a higher concentration than anti-b antibody in 7-DPI sera. The 7S antibody was considered to have anti-ab activity and, as such, could not distinguish between 140S-ab and 140S-b viruses (9). Thus, RID results could be influenced by the variant selected for the assays, particularly when 19S antibody was being tested. This was examined by testing the following: a) hyperimmune serum 1-9-68: b) serum collected from guinea pigs 85 DPIm with purified inactivated virus emulsified in incomplete Freund's adjuvant; and c) 7-DPI guinea pig serum. Antibody in the 85 DPIm serum was of the 7S class. Twofold dilutions of each serum were prepared, combined with agar, and added to 60-mm plates. Three 3.6-mm diameter wells were cut in each plate. Ten microliters of 140S-ab at a concentration of 500 μg/ml were added to one well, 10 μl of 140S-b at 500 μg/ml to another, and 10 μl of 12S antigen at 400 μg/ml to the remaining well. Photographs of the reactions obtained are shown (Fig. 4).

The precipitin rings produced by 140S-ab and 140S-b viruses had essentially the same diameter for a given serum dilution for both serum 1-9-68 and 85 DPIm serum. However, it is evident from Figure 4 that the 85 DPIm serum had a considerably higher antibody content than serum 1-9-68. Using the procedures described previously, the 85 DPIm serum was estimated to contain about 1100 μg AbP/ml to 140S antigens, and 400 μg AbP/ml to 12S antigen. A preliminary quantitative precipitin analysis of this serum indicated it contained approximately 950 μg AbP/ml to 140S-ab; however, it was not certain that antibody-antigen equivalence had been achieved in this test. Therefore, the value merely confirms the relatively high anti-140S activity demonstrated by RID.

The results with 7-DPI serum were considerably different than those obtained with serum 1-9-68 and 85 DPIm serum. For a given serum dilution, the 140S-b ring was considerably larger than the 140S-ab ring which confirms an earlier proposal that antibody to the a-subdeterminant is at a higher concentration than the anti-b antibody (8, 9). This 7-DPI serum had been examined by quantitative precipitin analysis with 140S-ab virus and was determined to contain 87 μg AbP/ml. It might be assumed that this value of 87 μg represented the total anti-a and anti-b antibody when 140S-ab virus is used as antigen. If it is also assumed that the RID test with 140S-ab virus is a measure of total antibody, a plot of the 7-DPI serum-140S-ab values could be considered as the assay standard. Based on these assumptions, it was calculated that the 140S-b reaction accounted for 30 μg AbP/ml. Thus, the serum may be estimated to contain 57 μg/ml of anti-a antibody and 30 μg/ml of anti-b antibody.

It was of interest that even at a 1:5 dilution, the 7-DPI serum gave no reaction with 12S antigen. Ouchterlony analyses of 7-DPI guinea pig sera also fail to give reactions with this antigen. In view of the high sensitivity of the RID procedure for detecting antibody, it is evident that 7-DPI guinea pig sera contain very low levels of antibody to 12S antigen. Also, treatment of 7-DPI serum with 2-mercaptoethanol (2-ME) resulted in complete loss of precipitation at a 1:5 dilution indicating that it contained less than 5 μg/ml of 7S or 2-ME stable antibody.

DISCUSSION

Although the RID procedures are being used extensively for the quantitation of immunoglobulins and other soluble antigens (11, 12, 21), the potential of the technique for the detection and quantitation of antibody has apparently not been exploited. The reports we are aware of on antibody measurement have expressed antibody content in relative terms, and have not indicated the extreme sensitivity of the technique for antibody detection (13, 14, 20). However, a report by Feinberg *et al.* (22) has demonstrated the greater sensitivity of the RID procedure for detecting autoprecipitins to thyroglobulin as compared to Ouchterlony methods. The present studies have attempted to establish the antibody content of antisera in absolute weight units. As a consequence, this permitted a more definitive evaluation of the relative sensitivity of RID for antibody and antigen detection as compared to other routine serologic procedures.

The greatest sensitivity for the detection of either antibody or antigen was obtained when the reactant being tested was incorporated into the agar. The reversed RID procedure was the most sensitive for detecting virus where 2.5 μg virus/ml of agar-virus mixture was detected with 7S antibody, and as little as 1.25 μg virus/ml by 19S antibody. However, this procedure did not approach the sensitivity of CF for virus detection. For antibody detection, the conventional RID procedure proved most sensitive. As little as 1 μg AbP/ml of antibody-agar mixture could be detected with virus as antigen. To obtain a precipitin line by the Ouchterlony double diffusion method that was used, approximately 10 times the concentration of antibody or virus was required. The sensitivity of the conventional RID procedure was such that it approached that of CF for the detection of 7S antibody.

The conventional RID procedure applied here is of particular interest in that quantitative estimates of the antibody content of the sera may be possible where suitably calibrated sera are available to serve as standards. Although the data are limited, the quantity of antibody to FMDV 140S and 12S antigens as determined by RID was in close agreement with that established by quantitative precipitin analyses. In comparison to quantitative precipitin tests, the RID procedure was exceedingly simple to perform and utilized relatively small quantities of reagents.

Acknowledgments. The excellent technical assistance of Messrs. Nicholas Shuot and Jay Card, and the assistance of Dr. Rodes Trautman on plotting methods and calculations are acknowledged.

REFERENCES

1. Brown, F. and Crick, J., Virology, *5:* 133, 1958.
2. Brown, F. and Crick, J., J. Immun., *82:* 444, 1959.
3. Brown, F., Cartwright, B. and Newman, J., J. Immun., *93:* 397, 1964.
4. Graves, J. H., Cowan, K. M. and Trautman, R., J. Immun., *92:* 501, 1964.
5. Cowan, K. M. and Trautman, R., J. Immun., *94:* 858, 1965.
6. Cowan, K. M., Amer. J. Vet. Res., *27:* 1217, 1966.
7. Cowan, K. M. and Graves, J. H., Virology, *30:* 528, 1966.
8. Cowan, K. M., J. Exp. Med., *129:* 333, 1969.
9. Cowan, K. M., J. Immun., *104:* 423, 1970.
10. Mancini, G., Vaerman, J. P., Carbonara, A. O. and Heremans, J. F., Protides Biol. Fluids, *11:* 370, 1964.
11. Mancini, G., Carbonara, A. O. and Heremans, J. F., Immunochemistry, *2:* 235, 1965.
12. Fahey, J. L. and McKelvey, E. M., J. Immun., *94:* 84, 1965.
13. Vaerman, J. P., Lebacq-Verheyden, A. M., Scolari, L. and Heremans, J. F., Immunochemistry, *6:* 279, 1969.
14. Becker, W., Immunochemistry, *6:* 539, 1969.
15. Wagner, G. G., Card, J. L. and Cowan, K. M., Arch. Ges. Virusforsch., In press, 1970.
16. Bachrach, H. L., Trautman, R. and Breese, S. S., Jr., Amer. J. Vet. Res., *25:* 333, 1964.
17. Cowan, K. M., J. Immun., *101:* 1183, 1968.
18. Bachrach, H. L. and Vande Woude, G. F., Virology, *34:* 282, 1968.
19. Kabat, E. A., in *Kabat and Mayer's Experimental Immunochemistry,* 2nd Ed., p. 22 and p. 556, Charles C Thomas, Springfield, Ill., 1961.
20. Vaerman, J. P., Lebacq-Verheyden, A. M., Scolari, L. and Heremans, J. F., Immunochemistry, *6:* 287, 1969.
21. Ryan, C. A., Anal. Biochem., *19:* 434, 1967.
22. Feinberg, J. G., Hill, C. W., Doniach, D. and Roitt, I. M., Int. Arch. Allerg., *35:* 335, 1969

THE JOURNAL OF IMMUNOLOGY
Vol. 105, No. 3, September 1970
Printed in U.S.A.

ANTIGENICITY OF POLYPEPTIDES (POLYαAMINO ACIDS): CALCIUM-DEPENDENT AND INDEPENDENT ANTIBODIES

PAUL H. MAURER, L. G. CLARK AND P. A. LIBERTI[1]

From the Department of Biochemistry, Thomas Jefferson University, Jefferson Medical College, Philadelphia, Pennsylvania

Received for publication April 10, 1970

It has been shown that sheep antisera against negatively charged synthetic polymers of amino acids such as poly (L-glu^{60}-L-ala^{30}-L-tyr^{10})$_n$ of high glutamic acid content contain two populations of antibodies one of which requires calcium ("Ca^{++} dependent") for reaction to occur. The Ca^{++}-dependent antibodies are directed against immunogenic determinants created by the reaction of Ca^{++} with glutamyl residues which changes the conformation of the polymer and thereby creates the new determinants. The reaction of the specific polymer with this antibody is maximal at 0.008 M Ca^{++}. Dissociation of the polymer-Ca^{++}-antibody complex can be accomplished by removal of Ca^{++} with EDTA, citrate or oxalate or by washing the antigen-antibody precipitate with phosphate-buffered saline. Dilution of the antiserum in non-Ca^{++}-containing diluents, which in effect lowers the Ca^{++} concentration, reduces precipitation of the antibody. This loss can be reversed by addition of Ca^{++} to the diluting buffer. The amounts of these two populations of antibodies vary from animal to animal within any species. No Ca^{++}-dependent antibody was found with the polymers of slight negative or neutral charge or against several protein antigens. Peptide maps (finger prints) of these two kinds of purified antibody (both 7S IgG) revealed no significant differences.

While studying the effects of complement on the precipitin reaction of sheep antibodies to the synthetic random polymer poly (L-glu^{60}-L-ala^{30}-L-tyr^{10})$_n$, it was observed that the use of the chelating agent, ethylenediaminetetraacetate (EDTA), to prevent complement in serum from adding to specific precipitates resulted in an unexpectedly large decrease in the amount of the precipitate formed. In addition, during the washing of some of the specific precipitates with 0.15 M saline-phosphate buffer, a notable decrease in size of the precipitate was also observed. Another initially perplexing finding was that significantly different concentrations of antibody were found in the original serum, if undiluted or diluted sera were analyzed. A possible explanation for these observations appeared to be related to the effect of calcium removal on unique antigen-antibody systems. The present report will explain the above findings and show that the precipitation of some antibodies was independent of the presence or absence of calcium and others required calcium for precipitation. The major effect of Ca^{++}, which is due to the formation of antigenic determinants in glutamic acid containing polymers, will be mentioned in this report and the complete experimental proof and discussion constitute another report. A preliminary report of these findings has been presented (1).

[1] Supported by Grant AI 07825 and TIAI 334 from the National Institute of Allergy and Infectious Diseases and American Cancer Society Grant T-452.

MATERIALS AND METHODS

Polymers. Table I gives the mol ratio of the amino acids and molecular weights of polymers used in this report. The preparation and properties of these polymers have been reported previously (2, 3).

Immunization. The antisera were prepared in sheep (4), rabbits (5) and mice (6) by methods reported previously. The polymers and proteins were injected repeatedly in the respective species in complete adjuvants. The numbers ascribed to the sheep sera are described in (4). The sheep number (e.g., 5) is followed by the specific bleeding pool analyzed (e.g., II). All of the sera em-

TABLE I

Polymers of amino acids used in this investigation

Nomenclature of Polymer[a]	Nomenclature Employed in Text	Molecular Weight
$(Glu^{60}Ala^{30}Tyr^{10})_n$	GAT	45,000
$(Glu^{60}Ala^{40})_n$	GA	45,000
$(Glu^{90}Tyr^{10})_n$	GT	70,000
$(Glu^{54}Ala^{36}Lys^{10})_n$	GAL^{10}	40,000
$(Glu^{42}Lys^{28}Ala^{30})_n$	GLA^{30}	62,000
Poly (γN-3 hydroxypropylglutamide^{60}-L-ala^{40})$_n$	GA amide	50,000
Poly (γN-3 hydroxypropylglutamide^{60}-L-ala^{30}-tyr^{10})$_n$	GAT amide	22,000

[a] Superscript is the mol ratio of amino acid in the polymer.

ployed in this study are from hyperimmunized animals. They were stored at −20°C until analysis.

Decomplementation of sera. Sera were initially "decomplemented" by making the serum concentration of EDTA 0.008 M (7). Because of the unexpected reduced amounts of antibody precipitated after the above treatment relative to values obtained with undecomplemented sera, decomplementation was also performed with specific antigen-antibody precipitate, i.e., 100 μg N/ml serum (8). Rabbit antisera against bovine serum albumin or ovalbumin were used to prepare the precipitates.

Sera were analyzed for antibody by the procedure referred to previously (9). Varying conditions were studied: a) undiluted non-decomplemented sera; b) undiluted sera "decomplemented" by EDTA or another specific antigen-antibody precipitate; c) dilutions of decomplemented sera. Different diluents were employed such as 0.15 M saline pH 7.5, normal sheep sera, "decalcified" sheep sera, dialyzed sheep sera plus 0.01 M Ca^{++}.

Ordinarily, dilutions of antigen were added in volumes less than 20% of the volume of the undiluted antisera. Reaction mixtures were incubated at 0 to 5°C for 48 to 72 hr and the precipitates centrifuged and washed twice with small volumes of either phosphate-buffered saline (PBS) or borate- (0.01 N) buffered pH 7.5 saline (BBS) containing 0.005 M calcium chloride. Precipitates were analyzed by the micro-Kjeldahl or Folin-Ciocalteu method.

The effects of the different conditions on the amount of antibody precipitable were determined by the first establishing the precipitin curve and equivalence point of each undiluted antiserum. Thereafter comparisons were made by setting up a few points near equivalence to obtain the maximum precipitable antibody and antigen. These precipitates were analyzed by either dissolving the precipitate in 0.1 N NaOH and reading the absorption at 280 mμ or by the Folin-Ciocalteu method.

The dependence of some of the cross-reactions on calcium concentration was studied similarly. When studying dilution effects, equivalent amounts of antigen were added to undiluted sera.

The final volumes of reaction mixture were adjusted with PBS or BBS to the dilution of serum desired.

Ca^{++} independent and dependent antibodies

Determination of distribution in serum. The total amount of antibody, Ca^{++} independent and Ca^{++} dependent, was determined by adding the specific polymer in a small volume to undiluted sera. The specific precipitates were washed with Ca^{++}-containing BBS and analyzed accordingly. Identical antigen-antibody reactions were also set up in the presence of 0.008 M EDTA. These specific precipitates were washed with BBS before analysis. This latter antibody is termed "Ca^{++} independent"; and the "Ca^{++}-dependent" antibody is determined by subtracting the Ca^{++}-independent from the total antibody obtained above. The percentage distribution of these two kinds of antibodies was calculated accordingly.

Isolation of specific anti-GAT antibody. a) Sheep calcium independent antibodies (anti-GAT) were precipitated in the presence of 0.008 M EDTA. After washing the precipitates with BBS, they were dissolved in 8 M urea (10) and the antigen separated from the antibody by passage through a DEAE-cellulose column equilibrated with 8 M urea in BBS (pH 7.5). The negatively charged antigen was retained by the column. The eluted antibodies were dialyzed against saline until free of urea and then concentrated by pervaporation to the volume of serum originally employed.

b) To the above supernatants (containing GAT and Ca^{++} complexed with EDTA) excess calcium chloride was added (0.02 M) to allow the GAT to react with and precipitate the "Ca^{++}-dependent" antibodies. The washed precipitates were dissolved in a solution made 0.1 M EDTA (to complex the Ca^{++}), 0.01 M borate, pH 7.5, and 0.15 M NaCl, employing volumes less than the original volume of serum. The antigen was removed by passage through a DEAE-cellulose column equilibrated with BBS, pH 7.5. The column retained the antigen and EDTA. The eluted antibodies were dialyzed against borate buffer and concentrated by pervaporation to the original volume of serum.

The concentration of Ca^{++} needed for precipitation of GAT and purified Ca^{++}-dependent antibody (sheep 5-II) was studied from 0.04×10^{-3} to 9×10^{-3} M. The following divalent cations (0.008 N) were added in place of Ca^{++}; Mg^{++}, Sr^{++} and Ba^{++}. In addition, the concentration of Na^{+}, up to 1 M was studied.

Immunoelectrophoretic analysis. Immunoelectrophoresis was done by the method of Scheidegger (11). The antisera against whole sheep sera and against purified sheep γ globulin were prepared in rabbits. The concentration of GAT polymer was 20 μg N/ml and the Ca^{++} concentration employed was 0.1 M.

Analytical ultracentrifugation. Sedimentation analysis was done at 20°C, with a Spinco model E ultracentrifuge.

Peptide mapping.[2] The purified antibodies were extensively reduced with 0.3 M β mercaptoethanol in 7 M guanidine HCl at pH 8.2 and acetylated with iodoacetamide. Tryptic digests were mapped by the method of Katz *et al.* (12).

RESULTS

Table II compares the effect of decomplementation of several anti-polymer and anti-protein sera by EDTA and specific antigen-antibody precipitates. It is apparent that the decrease of antibody precipitated from anti-GAT, anti-GA, and anti-GAL^{10} in the presence of EDTA is greater than that observed after treatment with specific precipitates. Table II also shows that both methods of decomplementation yield similar values for antibody when antisera against a neutral, or slightly negatively charged polymer, and protein antigens were analyzed.

The effect of dilution of sheep serum on the precipitation of anti-GAT sera is shown in Table III. The most marked effect occurs at a 1:4 dilution of the serum, where about 70% of the antibody is precipitated. Much of the dilution effect (although not all) can be reversed by the addition of 0.01 M Ca^{++} to the diluent. Although the data are not shown, normal sheep sera that had been treated with EDTA and then dialyzed exhaustively against 0.15 M NaCl when used as the diluent behaved as did saline in causing a

TABLE II

Comparison between effects of decomplementation by EDTA and specific antigen-antibody precipitate on precipitable sheep antibody

Immunogen	Method of Decomplementation	
	EDTA	Specific precipitate
	μg N antibody/ml serum	
DNP-BSA	340.5	329.8
Mouse γ globulin	275.6	270.6
GLA^{30}	150.8	147.6
GAT amide	55.4	54.3
GAT	205.1	406.0
GA	75.2	125.5
GAL^{10}	160.5	201.0

TABLE III

Effect of dilution of sheep serum 5 (anti-GAT) on precipitable antibody

Sheep Serum	Dilution	Percentage of Antibody in Undiluted Serum Precipitable after Dilution with		
		0.15 M saline	Normal sheep serum	0.15 M saline, 0.01 M Ca^{++}
5-II	1:2	95	95	90
	1:4	77	89	85
	1:8	59	93	91
	1:16	50	79	82
5-VI	1:2	80	85	88
	1:4	67	89	90
	1:8	43	85	83
Mouse γ globulin	1:4	94		99
	1:16	83		85

[2] These experiments were kindly performed by Doctor C. Merryman.

TABLE IV

Effect of removal of calcium on cross-reactions with sheep anti-GAT serum

Cross-Reacting Polymer[a]	Percentage of Original Cross-Reaction	
	Diluent	
	0.15 M NaCl, 0.01 M EDTA	0.15 M NaCl, 0.01 M Ca^{++}
GA(23)	18	100
GT(54)	65	100
GAT^4 (100)	60	100

[a] Values in parentheses indicate the percentage cross-reactions.

TABLE V

Effect of dilution (1:16) with 0.15 M NaCl and 0.15 M NaCl, 0.01 M, Ca^{++} on precipitation of several anti-polymer systems

Polymer	Antibody/ml Serum (Undiluted)	Percentage Antibody Precipitated (Undiluted Serum Value)	
		Diluent	
		0.15 M NaCl	0.15 M NaCl, 0.01 N Ca^2
	μg N		
$G^{60}A^{40}$	102.4	22	83
$G^{60}A^{30}T^{10}$	218.8	35	82
$G^{54}A^{36}L^{10}$	201.0	26	60
$G^{42}L^{28}A^{30}$	104.2	45	38

marked decrease in the precipitation of anti-GAT. Adding Ca^{++} again to the above dialyzed sheep serum reversed this effect. A similar action of EDTA and the reversal by Ca^{++} was also noted with the cross-reactions with the anti-GAT sera. Typical data are presented in Table IV.

Table V presents the effect of dilution at a single dilution (1:16) on the antibody precipitated from several sheep antisera and the partial reversal of the indicated loss by incorporating 0.01 N $CaCl_2$ in the diluting buffer. The order of the extent of reversal by Ca^{++} varied with the polymer studied. The order decreases from top $(G^{60}A^{40})_n$ to bottom $(G^{42}L^{28}A^{30})_n$, of the table. Similarly, as listed in the table, the net negative charge of the polymers decreases in the same order.

Figure 1 shows typical precipitin reactions of undiluted sheep anti-GAT in the presence (Ca^{++}-independent antibody) and absence (Ca^{++}-dependent and independent antibody) of 0.008 M EDTA. With sheep 5-II about 50% of the total anti-GAT required Ca^{++} for precipitation.

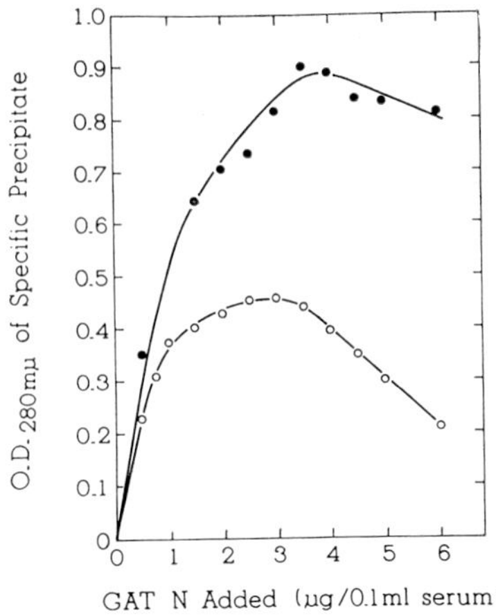

Figure 1. Precipitin reactions of undiluted sheep anti-GAT serum (sheep 5-II) in the presence (●) and absence (○) of 0.008 M EDTA.

TABLE VI

Distribution among different species of calcium-dependent and -independent anti-GAT antibodies

Serum	Antibody/ml Serum	Percentage Distribution	
		Calcium-dependent antibody	Calcium-independent antibody
	μg N		
Sheep 2-II	118	15	85
Sheep 5-II	968	50	50
Sheep 6-III	268	90	10
Rabbits 754–800	150–200	20–50	80–50
Mouse (2 pools)	350, 380	0	100

The distribution of Ca^{++}-independent and dependent anti-GAT antibodies among sheep, rabbit and mouse sera is shown in Table VI. With the three sheep sera shown, the distribution of the two kinds of antibodies ranged from 15:85 to 90:10. A similar variation from animal to animal was noted with the rabbit sera but the two mouse pools studied showed no Ca^{++}-dependent antibodies. In addition, no calcium dependency was found with the following systems: sheep anti-mouse γ globulin, sheep anti-DNP-BSA, sheep anti-$(G^{42}L^{28}A^{30})_n$ and GAT amide, and rabbit anti-GA amide. All of these systems have antigens of slight negative or neutral charge.

Figure 2 shows data obtained with sheep 5-II

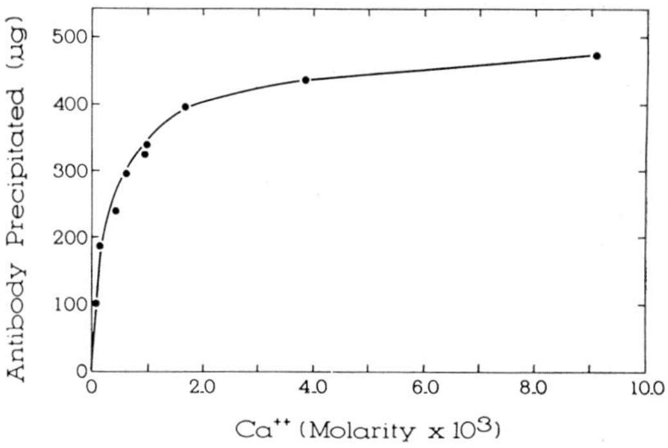

Figure 2. Effect of increasing concentrations of calcium on the specific precipitation of purified calcium-dependent antibody, (sheep 5-II).

purified Ca++-dependent antibody and GAT illustrating the effect of increasing Ca++ concentration on the precipitation of the purified anti-GAT antibody. Above 0.002 M the curve begins to plateau and approaches the maximum precipitation of antibody. The optimal concentration is 0.005 M Ca++ which is close to the concentration of Ca++ in normal sera.

A comparison of the effects of calcium and other divalent cations is shown in Table VII. The amount of precipitate formed is expressed relative to the amount precipitated by Ca++, which precipitated the most antibody. The effectiveness of precipitation of the divalent cations is presented in decreasing order, relative to Ca++. This same order follows the approximate difference in ionic radii of the various cations with respect to calcium. 1 M Na^+ had no effect on precipitation of calcium-dependent antibody.

In the isolation procedures the recovery of Ca++-independent antibody (sheep 5-II) was 75%. This purified antibody was 90% precipitable by GAT. The presence or absence of EDTA or Ca++ had no effect on the precipitation behavior of this antibody. The recovery of calcium-dependent antibody (sheep 5-II) was 90%, but 95% was precipitable only in the presence of GAT and calcium. This is also shown in Figure 3 where the immunoelectrophoretic patterns on whole sheep serum, and isolated antibodies in the presence and absence of Ca++ are shown. Both Ca++-dependent and independent antibodies had similar electrophoretic mobilities. The Ca++-dependent antibodies again require Ca++ for precipitation with GAT. Ultracentrifugal analysis of both antibodies gave an $s_{20,w}$ value of 6.5.

TABLE VII

Effect of 0.008 N cations on precipitation of Ca++ dependent antibodies

Ion	% Precipitation	Anhydrous Ionic Radius of Cation, Å	($R_{Ca^{++}}$-$R_{M^{++}}$) Å
Ca^{2+}	100	0.99	0
Sr^{2+}	66	1.12	−0.13
Mn^{2+}	26	0.80	+0.19
Ba^{2+}	22	1.34	−0.35
Mg^{2+}	4	0.66	+0.33

The peptide maps obtained with purified independent and dependent antibodies (sheep 5-V) indicated slight differences in the patterns of the two antibodies in about four peptides. Relative to the independent antibody, the dependent antibody had one additional peptide and was missing three that were present in the independent antibody.

DISCUSSION

The observations related to the effects of EDTA, and dilution of antisera on the amounts of antibody precipitated by antisera against different synthetic polymers of amino acids and proteins can best be explained by assigning a specific role to Ca++ in the specific antigen-antibody reaction.

Over and above the problem of the high solubility of sheep antigen-antibody complexes (13) one is dealing with here, the role of Ca++ in maintaining conformationally dependent antigenic determinants in the glutamic acid containing polymers. EDTA, through chelation with the Ca++, and dilution through reduction of the concentration of Ca++, show the most marked effects on the GAT and GA systems and the least effects when neutral polymers or proteins are the specific immunogens. When Ca++ is removed from these systems, the appropriate antigenic determinant (conformation) no longer exists and therefore no reaction with the specific antibody site takes place. The ability of the other divalent cations to replace Ca++ is somehow related not only to the charge but also to the ionic radius. These observations will be reported in a future publication.

The large losses in precipitates observed when washings were done in saline-phosphate buffer were related to the removal of the Ca++ from the

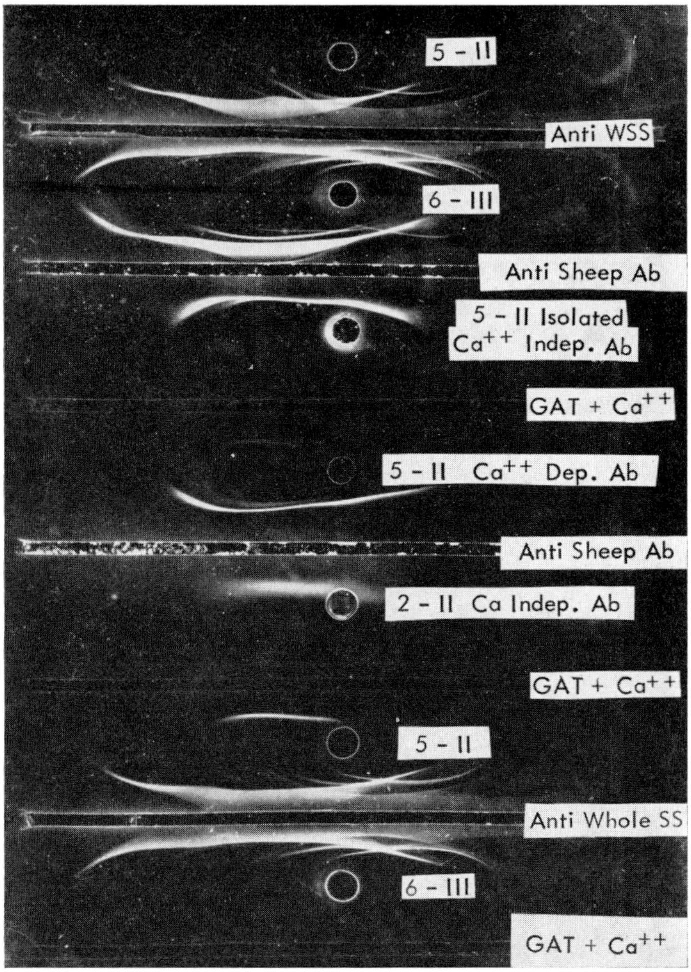

Figure. 3. Immunoelectrophoretic patterns of whole sheep sera and isolated specific antibodies to GAT from sheep 2-II, 5-II and 6-III. Anti-WSS—rabbit anti-whole sheep sera; anti-sheep Ab—rabbit anti-sheep antibodies to GA prepared as in reference 4.

GAT-antibody complex, which then led to its dissociation from the precipitate. In other words, the several and repeated washings with phosphate buffer were analogous to suspending the precipitate in EDTA. This effect of phosphate in reducing the amount of the precipitate formed was enhanced greatly when citrate or oxalate were added to the specific serum or diluent. Oxalate was about as effective as EDTA whereas citrate required a slightly higher concentration to produce the same effect. The addition of Ca^{++} to either 0.15 M NaCl or decalcified serum reverses the above by reforming the determinants in the glutamic acid containing polymers.

The amount of Ca^{++}-dependent and Ca^{++}-independent antibody varied significantly from animal to animal within any species. A plausible explanation for these findings is that *in vivo*, the glutamic acid-containing immunogens can react with the physiologic divalent cation which is present in the highest concentration, i.e., Ca^{++}, and by changing the conformation of the polymer create another immunogenic determinant. The factors governing the extent of the response of any animal against the Ca^{++}-dependent or Ca^{++}-independent immunogenic determinants are the same as against any other determinant. It is interesting that no Ca^{++}-dependent antibody was found in the two mouse anti-GAT sera studied.

Whether one can ascribe any real significance

to the slight differences in the peptide maps of the calcium-dependent and independent antibodies (both γ_1 immunoglobulins) must be investigated further especially as these differences were studied only with purified whole antibodies. Experiments planned with purified Fab$'_2$ fragments might be more revealing.

Several recent reports have shown that antibodies that are specific for a protein ligand conformation do not react with the apo protein. Examples are transferrin (14), iron conalbumin (15), horse oxy-(16) and deoxyhemoglobin (17). Whereas the above systems related totally to *in vitro* findings, our data point out the importance of the *in vivo* "handling" of the immunogen by the specific host. Although the immunogen was prepared in a saline-phosphate buffer we do not know whether any changes occurred during incorporation in the adjuvant emulsion to create another determinant (Ca^{++}-dependent), or whether this alteration was dependent upon the presence *in vivo* of physiologic concentrations of Ca^{++} in the local environment of the polymer. Recent experiments involving immunization of rabbits with GAT-methylated bovine serum albumin complexes and the production of some Ca^{++}-dependent antibody against this aggregated complex would tend to exclude the former explanation (P. Liberti and P. H. Maurer, unpublished).

Acknowledgments. The authors wish to acknowledge the technical assistance of Mrs. B. Berardinelli and Miss M. Filinska.

REFERENCES

1. Clark, L. G., Maurer, P. H. and Liberti, P., *Fed. Proc.*, *27:* 259, 1968.
2. Blout, E. R. and Idelson, M., J. Amer. Chem. Soc., *78:* 497, 1956.
3. Katchalski, E. and Sela, M., Advances Prot. Chem., *13:* 243, 1958.
4. Clark, L. G. and Maurer, P. H., Int. Arch. Allerg., *35:* 58, 1969.
5. Maurer, P. H., Gerulat, B. F. and Pinchuck, P., J. Immun., *90:* 388, 1963.
6. Pinchuck, P. and Maurer, P. H., J. Exp. Med., *122:* 1965.
7. Levine, L., Cowan, K. M., Osler, A. G. and Mayer, M. M., J. Immun., *71:* 367, 1953.
8. Maurer, P. H. and Talmage, D. W., J. Immun., *70:* 135, 1953.
9. Maurer, P. H., Gerulat, B. F. and Pinchuck, P., J. Biol. Chem., *239:* 922, 1964.
10. Slobin, L. J. and Sela, M., Biochem. Biophys. Acta, *107:* 593, 1965.
11. Scheidegger, J. J., Int. Arch. Allerg., *7:* 103, 1955.
12. Katz, A. M., Dreyer, W. J. and Anfinsen, C. B., J. Biol. Chem., *234:* 2897, 1959.
13. Zimmering, P. E., Beiser, S. M. and Erlanger, B. F., J. Immun., *95:* 262, 1965.
14. Kourilsky, F. M. and Burtin, P., Nature, *218:* 375, 1968.
15. Tengerdy, C., Azari, P. R. and Tengerdy, R. P., Nature, *211:* 203, 1966.
16. Reichlin, M., Bucci, E., Antonini, E., Wyman, J. and Rossi-Fanelli, A., J. Molec. Biol., *9:* 785, 1964.
17. Reichlin, M., Bucci, E., Wyman, J., Antonini, E. and Rossi-Fanelli, A., J. Molec. Biol., *11:* 775, 1965.

THE JOURNAL OF IMMUNOLOGY
Vol. 105, No. 3, September 1970
Printed in U.S.A.

DELAYED HYPERSENSITIVITY TO INSULIN AND ITS COMPONENT POLYPEPTIDE CHAINS

CONNIE CLARK AND J. MUNOZ

From the United States Department of Health, Education, and Welfare, Public Health Service, National Institutes of Health, National Institute of Allergy and Infectious Diseases, Rocky Mountain Laboratory, Hamilton, Montana 59840

Received for publication April 9, 1970

Bovine insulin produces a state of pure delayed hypersensitivity in guinea pigs from the 7th to the 13th days after sensitization with 10 μg of insulin in Freund's complete adjuvant. A delayed response in insulin-sensitized animals was readily elicited with insulin and with the isolated B-chain of insulin, while the A-chain, at equivalent doses, elicited only marginal reactions. Desensitization experiments wherein guinea pigs were immunized with insulin, B-chain or A-chain showed that each of these molecules contains determinants capable of inducing and eliciting a delayed response, and that at least one locus on the isolated B-chain produces delayed reactivity which can be elicited with the intact insulin molecule. Guinea pig anti-insulin serum was not reactive with isolated A- or B-chain. The use of insulin as a model protein for analysis of the relative contribution of stereochemical configuration in producing the immediate as opposed to the delayed immune response is discussed.

The possibility that different structural features of protein antigens are important in antigen recognition in the immediate, as opposed to the delayed response, has been suggested by previous studies. The work of Sela *et al.* (1) showed that circulating antibodies are directed toward conformational dependent determinants on the surface of the antigen molecule. The abrogation of the requirement for conformational integrity of the antigen in the delayed response was demonstrated by Gell and Benacerraf (2): sensitized guinea pigs gave an immediate response to the intact antigen only but a delayed response was elicited with denatured antigen as well. Recent work by Henney (3) has also shown that while early antibody reacted only with the intact sensitizing antigen, a delayed response was readily elicited with fragments derived from the antigen. These data (1–3) demonstrate that the delayed hypersensitive animal responds to conformational antigenic determinants which elicit the immediate response and to determinants in the molecule which do not react with circulating antibody.

Evidence that essentially the same antigenic determinant can elicit a delayed response and also bind antibody has been obtained with a variety of haptens conjugated to natural or synthetic carriers (4–7). These studies have led to a proposal that the major difference between immediate and delayed immune reactions is due to the requirement in delayed hypersensitivity for a greater part of the antigen molecule to be present (7–11). Although the data of Gell and Benacerraf (2) and Henney (3) are not in disagreement with this hypothesis, the important and as yet unanswered question is whether immunologic mechanisms in delayed hypersensitivity provide for recognition of determinants which are not recognized by circulating antibody. Synthetic antigens might well be used to provide information on this question, but the desirability of using a structurally complex, natural protein antigen to define the specificity of the immune responses has been pointed out by Sela (12).

There are many protein antigens which possess some, but, in most cases, not all of the characteristics which would facilitate comparative analysis of the structural specificity of immune responses. Those molecules whose stereochemical structures have been determined include hemoglobin, carboxypeptidase A, α-chymotrypsin, papain, myoglobin, lysozyme, ribonuclease (13) and insulin (14, 15). The latter three are comparatively small, with molecular weights (m.w.) of approximately 14,600, 14,000 (16) and 6000

(17), respectively, and yet possess the structural complexity of higher m.w. proteins, as evidenced by their alpha helical content (16, 18).

Insulin was selected for the present investigation because of its lower m.w. and because it has been extensively studied both immunologically (19–23) and chemically. The complete chemical synthesis of insulin has been accomplished (24, 25) and interactions between insulin molecules have received considerable attention (26–29). In addition, biologically active derivatives (30–33) and hybrids (25, 34) have been prepared and methods for rigorous evaluation of purity (35) and biologic activity (36, 37) are available. All of these characteristics facilitate analysis of the role of molecular structure in the specificity of the immune responses.

Despite the fact that the humoral response to insulin has been studied extensively, only brief attention has been paid to the delayed response in animals (38, 39) and man (40, 41) to this molecule. The present study was undertaken to evaluate the effectiveness of insulin in producing delayed hypersensitivity in guinea pigs. Our findings are in agreement with previous reports (34, 42–47), which indicate that the immunologic specificity of the humoral response to insulin is directed to the intact molecule and not to the isolated chains. In addition, the results show that insulin produces a state of delayed hypersensitivity in guinea pigs, which can be demonstrated by challenge with either intact insulin or isolated B-chain but not by A-chain. Thus, the evidence supports the contention that insulin may constitute a useful system for comparing and contrasting the specificity of immediate and delayed immune reactions.

MATERIALS AND METHODS

Animals. Hartley guinea pigs weighing 300 to 600 g were used in all experiments

Antigens. Beef insulin, beef insulin-carboxymethylated chain B-reduced and beef insulin-carboxymethylated chain A-reduced were purchased from Mann Research Laboratories, Orangeburg, N. Y.

Sensitization. Ten milligrams of antigen were dissolved in 5.0 ml of 0.01 N NaOH, followed by addition of an equal volume of 0.15 M phosphate-buffered saline (PBS), pH 7.3 to 7.5. Appropriate antigen concentrations were obtained with a diluent composed of one part 0.01 N NaOH to one part PBS (NaOH-PBS). Antigen-containing emulsions were prepared by thorough mixing of equal volumes of antigen solution and Freund's complete adjuvant (Difco Laboratories, Detroit, Mich.). Guinea pigs were sensitized by injecting 0.1 ml emulsion into each hind footpad. Control groups, which consisted of non-injected or saline-adjuvant injected guinea pigs, did not produce positive skin-test reactions to the antigens.

Skin tests. Intradermal (i.d.) injections of 0.1 ml of the appropriate antigen solutions were given on the shaved flanks of the animals. Immediately before the 4-hr readings the flanks were depilated with Nair (Carter Products, New York, N. Y.).

Evaluation of immediate and delayed skin reactions. The immediate response was considered positive if erythema or edema was present 4 hr after skin test. The delayed response was measured at 24 hr and, in several experiments, at 48 and 72 hr. Delayed reactions were evaluated by intensity and diameter of erythema (reactions greater than 5 mm in diameter were considered positive), and by degree of induration, thickness in millimeters (skin test site minus control site) measured with special calipers (Schnelltaster, H. C. Kroplin GMBH, 649 Schluchtern Postfach, Deutschland). Histologic examinations of 4-, 24-, 48- and 72-hr skin lesions were also performed. Tissue sections were prepared by Histology Service, Philadelphia, Pa.

Desensitization experiments. Desensitization was accomplished by two to four subcutaneous (s.c.) injections of the appropriate antigen given 24 to 3 hr before skin tests. Two doses of 2.5 mg each, one given 24 hr and the other 3 hr before testing completely desensitized guinea pigs to insulin or B-chain. In some experiments, animals were desensitized with four doses of B-chain (total dose 4.5 mg) at 24 (0.25 mg), 20 (0.5 mg), 16 (1.25 mg) and 3 hr (2.50 mg) before skin test, or with three doses of insulin (total dose of 2 mg) given at 24 (0.25 mg), 20 (0.50 mg) and 16 hr (1.25 mg) before testing. Animals desensitized to insulin also received 10 ml of 50% glucose SC; additional glucose was administered as needed to avoid insulin shock. In several experiments, control groups of guinea pigs, which were not desensitized, received equivalent quantities of glucose.

Antibody determinations. Sera were obtained immediately before skin testing and the presence of antibody was determined by passive cutaneous anaphylaxis (PCA) (48) and by passive hemagglutination (HA) (49) with pooled or individual sera. The PCA antigen challenge was done intravenously 24 hr after i.d. injection of the sera.

Production of anti-insulin serum. Adult guinea pigs were immunized and bled, essentially according to the method of Robinson and Wright (50). Antigen emulsions were prepared with Freund's incomplete adjuvant (Difco Laboratories, Detroit, Mich.). The titers of 15 animals measured by HA ranged from 1:32 to 1:2048.

Purity of antigen preparations. Availability of insulin preparations of a high degree of purity has essentially eliminated the possibility that unrelated antigens are major participants in immunologic reactions attributed to insulin. Although recent studies (51, 52) in which definitive assays for insulin were employed clearly support this observation, we verified the purity of the antigen preparations used in this study to establish the immunologic specificity of the phenomena observed. The methods used included microgranular diethylaminoethyl (DEAE)-cellulose chromatography, gel filtration with Sephadex G-25 fine (Pharmacia Fine Chemicals, Inc., Piscataway, N. J.), DEAE-Sephadex G-25 fine chromatography, cationic polyacrylamide disc electrophoresis and amino acid analysis.

When samples of commercial insulin, A-chain and B-chain were chromatographed on DEAE Sephadex G-25 fine columns with a linear gradient of ammonium formate, 0.01 to 1.0 M, pH 9.4 to 9.5, only the chain preparations were found to contain minor components with absorbence at 280 nm. The gradient range of elution of the peaks indicated that, while the A-chain preparation contained both insulin and B-chain, the B-chain contained neither insulin nor A-chain. Larger samples of commercial insulin and B-chain were then eluted from DEAE-cellulose columns with a linear gradient of ammonium formate 0.05 M to 1.5 M, pH 9.4 to 9.5, and the peak fractions thus obtained were pooled and lyophilized to remove residual ammonium formate. The purified preparations were designated insulin-DE and B-chain-DE. Since sufficient quantities of A-chain were not available to permit similar purifications, the commercial preparation of A-chain was employed and the immunologic data were interpreted accordingly.

Insulin, insulin-DE, B-chain and B-chain-DE were next subjected to Sephadex G-25 fine gel filtration. While the elution patterns of insulin and insulin-DE were the same, the B-chain and B-chain-DE profiles differed in that the former contained a minor component. Subsequent examination of commercial and purified samples by cationic polyacrylamide disc electrophoresis (pH 2.7) showed that insulin and insulin-DE gave only one band, while both B-chain preparations gave two bands. The minor component did not migrate as far toward the cathode as either insulin or the major component of B-chain preparations and was considered to be insulin or B-chain with altered charge. Accordingly, an amino acid analysis was carried out on B-chain-DE samples to determine whether the minor component observed was insulin. Samples of 5 to 7 mg were hydrolyzed in 1.0 ml of 6 N HCl, under N_2, at 110°C for 24 hr. Hydrolysates were evaporated to remove the acid and then analyzed on the Beckman model 120 B automatic amino acid analyzer. Of primary concern was the detection of isoleucine as this amino acid is not present in the isolated B-chain of insulin. The analyses indicated that B-chain-DE preparations had a purity of approximately 98.4% whereas commercial B-chain samples were 96% to 97% pure. In both cases (B-chain and B-chain-DE) the degree of purity was sufficient to exclude insulin from consideration in accounting for the most anodal band observed on cationic polyacrylamide disc electrophoresis of B-chain preparations. It was most probable that the minor component present in B-chain samples was in fact B-chain with altered charge.

Immunologic evidence of the purity of insulin and B-chain preparations was obtained by PCA, HA and skin tests. Anti-insulin serum (1:200 titer by PCA with a 1000-μg insulin challenge) at a 1:10 dilution gave positive PCA reactions with a 1-μg insulin challenge but not with a 200-μg B-chain-DE challenge. This indicated that the B-chain-DE sample had a purity of 99.5%. While 0.1 μg of insulin completely inhibited passive HA, a 1000-fold greater concentration of B-chain had no effect. Furthermore, 0.5 μg, but not 0.1 μg, insulin elicited delayed skin reactions in sensitized guinea pigs. Ten micrograms of B-chain-DE, which were shown to contain less than 0.5 μg of insulin, elicited positive responses in insulin-sensitized animals. This chemical and biologic evidence obtained with respect to the high de-

TABLE I

Delayed skin reactions of guinea pigs sensitized with insulin or insulin-DE[a]

Sensitizing Antigen	Insulin				Insulin-DE			
Skin Test Antigen	Insulin		Insulin-DE		Insulin		Insulin-DE	
	10 μg	1 μg	10 μg	1 μg	10 μg	1 μg	10 μg	1 μg
Erythema[b]	15.1	10.3	15	9.8	13.3	8.2	13.0	8.6
Induration[c]	0.8	0.5	0.9	0.4	0.8	0.3	0.6	0.3
Reactors/total tested[d]	9/9	9/9	9/9	9/9	10/10	7/10	9/10	8/10

[a] Animals were sensitized via the footpads with 10 μg of antigen in complete Freund's adjuvant and 10 days later skin tested with the antigen indicated.

[b] Average diameter of reactions in millimeters.

[c] Average thickness of all reactions in millimeters.

[d] Number of animals with erythema >5 mm diameter/total number tested.

gree of purity of the commercial and purified preparations of insulin and B-chain established to our satisfaction the immunologic specificity of the reactions reported.

RESULTS

Delayed response to insulin. The results of preliminary experiments indicated that insulin was an effective antigen for producing delayed hypersensitivity in guinea pigs. We then compared insulin and insulin-DE with respect to their efficiency in producing and eliciting a delayed immune response. The results shown in Table I demonstrated that the compounds tested were equally effective in both respects.

A number of experiments were designed to further evaluate the delayed response to insulin; the combined results are shown in Table II. The sensitizing dose of insulin was 10 μg, except for day 10 when additional groups used had been sensitized with 5 or 1 μg of insulin. Strong delayed responses were obtained in animals that had been sensitized with 10 μg: those receiving 5 μg gave a good response on day 10, while the reactions of those receiving 1 μg were not as consistent. Maximum induration and erythema were observed from day 9 on. Although 4-hr reactions were recorded for some animals, they typically consisted of extremely faint and diffuse areas of erythema with no edema. All sera were negative when assayed for antibody by PCA and HA, indicating that a state of delayed hypersensitivity was produced in these animals.

Since optimal delayed reactions were evident on day 10, experiments (data not shown) were next carried out to examine the sensitivity of the skin test and define conditions of sensitization

TABLE II

Delayed skin reactions to insulin[a]

Skin Test Day	Sensitizing Dose	Insulin (10 μg)		
		4 hr	24 hr	
		ery[b]	ery	ind[c]
	μg			
7	10	—[d]	9.4 (10/13)	—
9	10	—	13.0 (13/13)	0.6
10	10	— (1/22)	14.2 (22/22)	0.8
	5	— (5/13)	13.0 (13/13)	0.9
	1	— (3/13)	8.5 (9/13)	0.5
11	10	—	14.6 (14/14)	0.6
13	10	—	14.8 (4/4)	0.8
15	10	10.5 (4/4)	13.0 (4/4)	0.7
17	10	8.5 (3/4)	13.0 (4/4)	0.6

[a] All controls were negative.

[b] Average diameter erythema of all reactions in millimeters. Parentheses: number of animals with reactions >5 mm diameter/total tested.

[c] Average thickness of all reactions in millimeters.

[d] No reaction.

which would induce detectable circulating antibody. When 100 μg insulin were used for sensitization, the 4-hr reactions on day 9 were weak while those on days 10 and 11 were decidedly stronger. The presence of erythema accompanied by edema, which typifies the immediate response, precluded evaluation of the 24-hr skin reactions as a manifestation of delayed hypersensitivity. Individual sera contained detectable circulating antibody on days 10 and 11 only; four of six were positive by HA on day 10 and four of seven were positive by both PCA and HA on day 11. The absence of detectable circulating antibody on day 9 indicated that the immediate response was marginal even at a 10-fold higher sensitizing dose than that which was routinely used in these experiments.

A successively diminished response was obtained when decreasing quantities of insulin were used for skin testing. Eleven of 17 animals gave positive responses to 0.1 μg insulin, while 17 of 18 reacted to a 0.5 μg dose. Guinea pigs sensitized with 10 μg insulin routinely responded to 10-, 1- and 0.5-μg but not to 0.1-μg challenges. Sensitization with 1 and 0.1 μg gave inconsistent results, while 0.01 and 0.001 μg produced few responders up to 31 days postsensitization.

Delayed response to the component chains of insulin. The results of a series of experiments in which the A- and B-chains of insulin were used to elicit the delayed response in insulin sensitized animals are shown in Table III. Except for experiment "L" all skin tests were done on day 10 postimmunization. The delayed response elicited with the B-chain paralleled that of insulin in intensity of the erythema, although the diameter of the reaction and the induration were somewhat diminished. In these groups, 38 of 46 animals (83%) gave a positive response to B-chain challenge. By contrast, only 10 of 31 animals (32%) produced positive reactions to skin test with A-chain. Responders to A-chain challenge were most likely reacting to the insulin present in this preparation. These results indicated that a delayed response was readily elicited by the B-chain. Essentially the same results were obtained when B-chain-DE was used as the skin-test antigen (Table IV). The delayed response elicited with 10 μg insulin was stronger than that elicited with 1 and 0.5 μg, but all doses caused positive reactions in all animals. In these same animals, the 24-hr reactions obtained with B-chain-DE were essentially equivalent at 20 and 10 μg, with 21 and 17 responders, respectively, out of 23 animals tested. Most reactions consisted of intense erythema, the others were medium to weak. At 1 μg of B-chain-DE skin test, 3 of 15 animals gave positive responses, and none responded to 0.5 μg.

Desensitization experiments. To obtain information on the antigenic determinants eliciting delayed responses, desensitization experiments were conducted. The following combinations for immunization/desensitization were used: 1) insulin/B-chain-DE; 2) B-chain-DE/insulin, and 3) A-chain/insulin plus B-chain. All skin tests were done on day 10 after immunization (Table V).

When animals were sensitized with insulin and desensitized with B-chain-DE, the delayed response to insulin obtained was essentially equivalent to that in the non-desensitized control group. The absence of reactivity to B-chain-DE among desensitized guinea pigs clearly shows that determinants which elicit the delayed response to insulin are not all shared with the B-chain.

TABLE III

Delayed skin reactions to A- and B-chains of insulin in guinea pigs sensitized with 10 μg insulin

Experiment Skin Test Day	B-Chain 20 μg					A-Chain 20 μg				
	4 hr	24 hr		Positive/total[c]	Range[d]	4 hr	24 hr		Positive/total	Range
		ery[a]	ind[b]				ery	ind		
M-10	—[e]	5.6	0.2	8/15	6–11	—	<5	—	4/15	6–10
J-10	—	11.4	0.8	7/7	8–14	—	—	—	0/7	—
L-9	—	6.7	0.2	8/9	6–9	—	5.7	—	6/9	6–12
N-10	—	7.7	0.6	15/15	6–10	ND[f]	ND	ND	ND	ND

[a] Average diameter reactions of all animals tested.
[b] Average thickness of all reactions in millimeters.
[c] Number of animals with reactions >5 mm diameter/total tested.
[d] Range of reaction size among responders in millimeters.
[e] No response.
[f] Not done.

TABLE IV

Delayed response to insulin and B-chain-DE[a]

Skin Test Antigen Dose	Response to the Skin Test			
	4 hr	24 hr		Positive/total[d]
	ery[b]	ery	ind[c]	
μg				
Insulin				
10	—[e]	13.3	1.1	15/15
1	—	10.3	0.7	15/15
0.5	—	8.9	0.8	15/15
B-chain-DE				
20	—	7.6	0.6	21/23
10	—	6.6	0.6	17/23
1	—	4.3	—	3/15
0.5	—	—	—	0/15

[a] Sensitized with 10 μg insulin.

[b] Average diameter reactions of all animals tested in millimeters.

[c] Average thickness of all reactions in millimeters.

[d] Number of animals with reactions >5 mm diameter/total tested.

[e] No response.

Conversely, when animals were immunized with B-chain-DE and subsequently desensitized with insulin, reactivity to B-chain-DE was maintained in the absence of a response to insulin. These reciprocal experiments suggest that both insulin and B-chain contain a minimum of two antigenic determinants capable of eliciting a delayed response: desensitization to one determinant did not alter the reactivity to the "second" determinant.

To obtain information on the delayed response to A-chain, three groups of guinea pigs were sensitized with 50, 20 and 10 μg A-chain, respectively. Half of the animals in each group were desensitized with both insulin and B-chain prior to skin testing. Delayed responses were observed only at the highest sensitizing dose of A-chain. The results in Table V shown for the control group cannot be attributed to A-chain, since insulin was known to be present in this preparation. In the desensitized groups, delayed reactivity to insulin and B-chain was absent, as expected, although 100 and 50 μg of A-chain elicited a marginal response. The 24-hr skin reactions to A-chain were typically pale, which is in marked contrast to the intense erythema produced by insulin and B-chain challenge in either insulin- or B-chain-sensitized guinea pigs. Experiments with pure preparations of A-chain are necessary before definitive characterization of the response to this peptide is possible.

Histology of skin lesions. Histologic examinations of the skin-test sites were conducted to determine if cellular infiltrates produced by insulin and B-chain were typical of delayed reactions. Guinea pigs were sensitized with 10 μg insulin in complete Freund's adjuvant and on day 10 were skin tested with 10 and 20 μg insulin and B-chain, respectively. At 4, 24, 48 and 72 hr, two or three animals were killed and skin-test sites were removed and fixed in 10% neutral buffered formalin. Mounted sections were stained with hematoxylin-eosin.

At 4 hr, both insulin and B-chain skin-test sites showed a degree of cellular infiltration comparable to that observed in sites injected with diluent only. The 24-, 48- and 72-hr reactions showed a marked monocytic infiltration most pronounced at 48 hr (Fig. 1). Insulin generally induced greater cellular infiltration than did B-chain. These results confirmed our observations on the delayed nature of the skin reactions and are in agreement with the capacity of lymph-node cell suspensions to passively transfer the delayed response to insulin.

For passive transfer each of 15 guinea pigs was sensitized with 100 μg insulin and the lymph nodes were harvested on day 7. Cell suspensions were prepared from the lymph nodes of 6, 4, 3 and 2 sensitized animals, respectively. Each cell suspension was injected intraperitoneally into a normal animal that was subsequently challenged, 24 hr later, with 50 μg insulin i.d. All 24-hr post-challenge reactions were 6 mm in diameter and showed intense erythema.

DISCUSSION

Our results demonstrated that bovine insulin induced in guinea pigs delayed hypersensitivity which occurred in the absence of detectable circulating antibody and could be passively transferred with lymphoid cells. A 10-μg sensitizing dose of insulin produced a state of delayed hypersensitivity without demonstrable circulating antibodies from the 7th through the 13th days. Sensitization with 10 μg insulin routinely induced a delayed immune response in nearly all guinea pigs, whereas 0.01 μg of insulin produced few responders. This delayed response was specific for insulin.

TABLE V

Effect of desensitization on skin reactivity of guinea pigs to insulin and A- and B-chain

Sensitized with (μg): Desensitized with	Dose of Antigen Used for Skin Testing per Site																				
	Insulin									B-chain						A-chain					
	50 μg			20 μg			10 μg			50 μg			20 μg			100 μg			50 μg		
	ery[a]	ind[b]	P/T[c]	ery	ind	P/T	ery	ind	P/T	ery	ind	P/T	ery	ind	P/T	ery	ind	P/T	ery	ind	P/T
Insulin (10 μg):																					
B-chain-DE	11.2	0.9	8/8	9.0	0.6	8/8	7.6	0.6	7/8	ND[d]	ND	ND	—[e]	—	1/8	ND	ND	ND	ND	ND	ND
Insulin sensitized controls	13.5	0.9	8/8	10.8	0.7	8/8	9.2	0.6	7/8	ND	ND	ND	7.5	0.7	6/8	ND	ND	ND	ND	ND	ND
B-chain-DE (20 μg):																					
Insulin	—	—	1/8	—	—	1/8	ND	ND	ND	8.1	0.9	7/8	5.8	0.5	6/8	ND	ND	ND	ND	ND	ND
B-chain sensitized controls	8.5	0.5	7/8	7.2	0.5	6/8	ND	ND	ND	10.4	1.0	8/8	7.0	0.4	6/8	ND	ND	ND	ND	ND	ND
A-chain (50 μg):																					
Insulin and B-chain	—	—	—	—	—	—	ND	ND	ND	—	—	—	—	—	—	7.7	0.3	3/4	7.3	0.4	3/4
A-chain sensitized controls	7.1	0.4	6/8	6.4	0.2	6/8	ND	ND	ND	3.6	0	3/8	3.0	0.2	3/8	6.2	0.4	6/8	4.3	0.3	5/8

[a] Average diameter erythema of all reactions in millimeters.
[b] Average thickness of all reactions in millimeters.
[c] Number of positive responders (erythema >5 mm diameter)/total tested.
[d] Not done.
[e] No response.

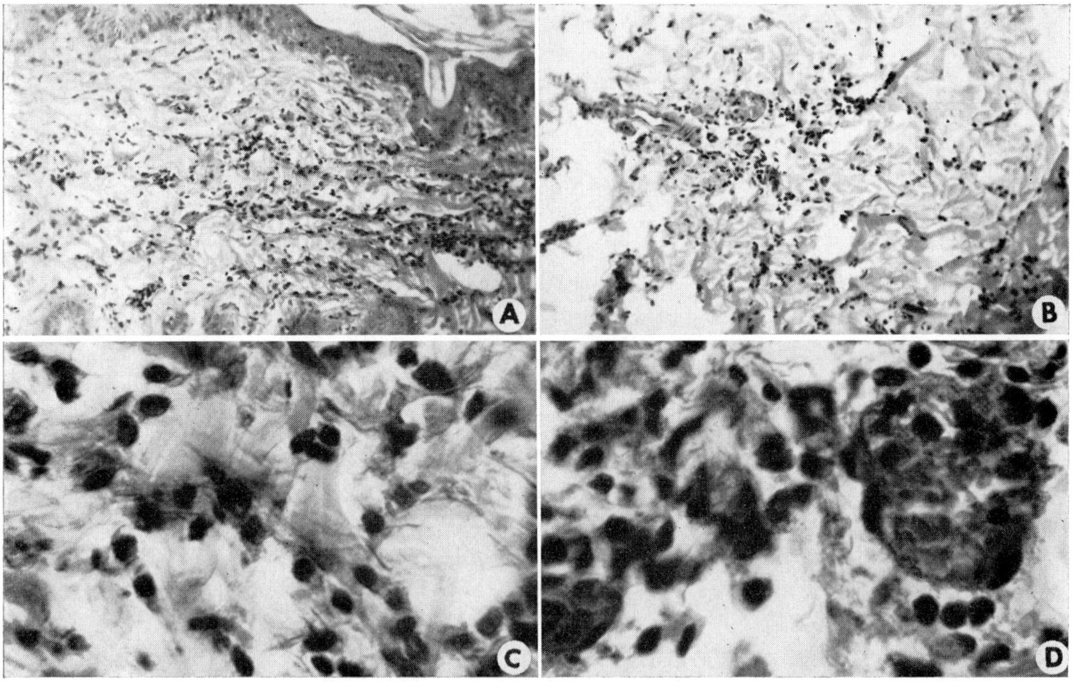

Figure 1. Histologic sections from skin taken 48 hr after intradermal injection of 10 μg of insulin (*A* and *C*) and 20 μg of B-chain (*B* and *D*). Low power, × 80; high power, × 560 (hematoxylin-eosin stain). Guinea pigs were sensitized with 10 μg of insulin in Freund's complete adjuvant and skin tested on day 10.

Animals with delayed sensitivity to insulin also responded immunospecifically to B-chain challenge, while the A-chain at the concentrations employed produced only insignificant reactions, which might have been due to insulin shown to be present in the preparations.

Desensitization experiments showed that both insulin and B-chain have determinants capable of inducing and eliciting delayed reactions in guinea pigs. When insulin-sensitized animals were desensitized with B-chain, a delayed response could still be elicited with insulin; in the reciprocal experiment wherein B-chain-sensitized animals were desensitized with insulin, a response could still be elicited with B-chain. These experiments established that there are at least two antigenic determinants in the insulin and B-chain molecules; at least one B-chain determinant was common to both molecules.

Early studies on the specificity of antibody to insulin (34, 43) indicated that the A-chain contained the determinants reacting with antibodies to insulin hybrids. A hybrid composed of ox A-chain and cod B-chain retained the immunologic specificity of ox insulin, while cod A-chain-ox B-chain behaved like cod insulin. More recent experiments (44, 46, 47) demonstrated that insulin antibodies did not cross-react with isolated A-chain and only to a minor extent with isolated B-chain. Similarly, anti-A-chain sera showed no reactivity with insulin, while anti-B-chain sera showed insignificant reactivity with insulin. These data (44, 46, 47, 53) are in agreement with the observations of Arquilla and Bromer (42) that interaction between the A- and the B-chain is necessary for spatial configuration of the molecule and for the integrity of most antigenic determinants of insulin. Recent work by Patterson *et al.* (45) with reaginic antibody against insulin also indicated an absence of reactivity with isolated A- and B-chain, whereas submolecular units of intact insulin maintained demonstrable reactivity.

We obtained similar evidence from PCA tests, which is relevant to the requirement of an intact insulin molecule for reactivity with circulating antibody, since as much as 200 μg B-chain failed to elicit PCA, while as little as 1 μg insulin gave positive reactions. Our results agree with the data of Corcos and Ovary (53) and were confirmed by passive HA inhibition tests.

The evidence clearly demonstrated that although conformational integrity of the molecule is necessary for interaction with circulating antibody, this requirement is abrogated in the cell-mediated immune response. The basis for this apparent difference in specificity was considered by Gell and Benacerraf (2): they suggested that the delayed response could be an early stage in immunity, which precedes antibody production and is directed against the same determinants on the molecule against which antibodies are subsequently formed, or that the delayed response may be a qualitatively different response, not directed against the same antigenic groupings as those which react with antibody.

Determinants which are reactive in delayed hypersensitivity may not be strictly conformational dependent surface loci, but may involve regions of the molecule which are exposed only during or after antigen processing. It is apparent from the cross-reactivity between insulin and B-chain, which was observed in delayed sensitive animals, that at least one locus on the B-chain is recognized by cells rendered sensitive to either molecule. In further work with insulin we will attempt to define these delayed reactive loci and similarly determine antibody reactivity with these loci as they exist in the intact insulin molecule.

The present report indicates that insulin may well constitute a useful protein model for comparing and contrasting immediate and delayed responses in terms of the type of antigenic determinants involved. These studies could provide the basis for a clearer interpretation of similarities and differences in the mechanisms which are involved in inducing immediate and delayed immunologic responses.

Acknowledgments. The authors are grateful to Dr. E. L. Schmidt, University of Minnesota, Minneapolis, Minnesota for the amino acid analyses, and to Adelbert E. Reynolds for technical assistance.

REFERENCES

1. Sela, M., Schechter, B., Schechter, I. and Borek, F., Cold Spring Harbor Symp. Quant. Biol., *32:* 537, 1967.
2. Gell, P. G. H. and Benacerraf, B., *Immunopathology Symposium*, Vol. 1, Benno Schwabe and Co., Basel, Switzerland, 1959.
3. Henney, C. S., J. Immun., *103:* 519, 1969.
4. Benacerraf, B. and Gell, P. G. H., Immunology, *2:* 53, 1959.
5. Borek, F. and Silverstein, A. M., Nature, *205:* 299, 1965.
6. Gell, P. G. H. and Silverstein, A. M., J. Exp. Med., *115:* 1037, 1962.
7. Schlossman, S. F., Ben-Efraim, S., Yaron, A. and Sober, H. A., J. Exp. Med., *123:* 1083, 1966.
8. Benacerraf, B. and Gell, P. G. H., Immunology, *2:* 219, 1959.
9. Salvin, S. B. and Smith, R. F., J. Exp. Med., *113:* 935, 1961.
10. Schlossman, S. F. and Levine, H., J. Immun., *98:* 211, 1967.
11. Silverstein, A. M. and Gell, P. G. H., J. Exp. Med., *115:* 1053, 1962.
12. Sela, M., Advances Immun., *5:* 29, 1966.
13. Venkatachalam, C. M. and Ramachandean, G. N., Ann. Rev. Biochem., *38:* 45, 1969.
14. Adams, M. J., Blundell, T. L., Dodson, E. J., Dodson, G. G., Vijayan, M., Baker, E. N., Harding, M. M., Hodgkin, D. C., Rimmer, B. and Sheat, S., Nature, *224:* 491, 1969.
15. Dodson, G., New Scientist, *43:* 370, 1969.
16. Stryer, L., Ann. Rev. Biochem., *37:* 25, 1968.
17. Sanger, F., Brit. Med. Bull., *16:* 183, 1960.
18. Mercola, D. A., Morris, J. W. S., Arquilla, E. R. and Bromer, W. W., Biochim. Biophys. Acta, *133:* 224, 1967.
19. Miles, L. E. M. and Hales, C. N., Biochem. J., *108:* 611, 1968.
20. Pope, C. G., Advances Immun., *5:* 209, 1966.
21. Prout, T. E., J. Chron. Dis., *15:* 879, 1962.
22. Prout, T. E., Metabolism, *12:* 673, 1963.
23. Wilson, S., *Antibodies to Biologically Active Molecules*, Pergamon Press, N. Y., 1967.
24. Katsoyannis, P. G., Tometsko, A. M., Zalut, C. and Fukuda, K., J. Amer. Chem. Soc., *88:* 5625, 1966.
25. Katsoyannis, P. G., Trakatellis, A. C., Zalut, C., Johnson, S., Tometsko, A. M., Schwartz, G. and Ginos, J., Biochemistry, *6:* 2656, 1967.
26. Craig, L. C., King, T. P. and Konigsberg, W., Ann. N. Y. Acad. Sci., *88:* 571, 1960.
27. Doty, P., Gellert, M. and Rabinovitch, B., J. Amer. Chem. Soc., *74:* 2065, 1952.
28. Jeffrey, P. D. and Coates, J. H., Biochemistry, *5:* 489, 1966.
29. Jeffrey, P. D. and Coates, J. H., Biochemistry, *5:* 3820, 1966.
30. Arquilla, E. R., Ooms, H. and Mercola, K., J. Clin. Invest., *47:* 474, 1968.
31. Bromer, W. W., Sheehan, S. K., Berns, A. W.

and Arquilla, E. R., Biochemistry, *6:* 2378, 1967.
32. Evans, R. L. and Saroff, H. A., J. Biol. Chem., *228:* 295, 1957.
33. Tietze, F., Mortimore, G. E. and Lomax, N. R., Biochim. Biophys. Acta, *59:* 536, 1962.
34. Wilson, S., Dixon, C. H. and Wardlaw, A. C., Biochim. Biophys. Acta, *62:* 483, 1962.
35. Mirsky, A. and Kawamura, K., Endocrinology, *78:* 1115, 1966.
36. Brien, T. G. and Devlin, J. G., Irish J. Med. Sci., *6:* 103, 1966.
37. Samols, E. and Bilkus, D., Proc. Soc. Exp. Biol. Med., *115:* 79, 1964.
38. Grodsky, G. M., Feldman, R., Toreson, W. E. and Lee, J. C., Diabetes, *15:* 579, 1966.
39. Toreson, W. E., Feldman, R., Lee, J. C. and Grodsky, G. M., Amer. J. Clin. Path., *42:* 531, 1964.
40. Devlin, J. G., *Clinical Aspects of Immunology*, F. A. Davis Co., Philadelphia, 1968.
41. Renold, A. E., Steinke, J., Soeldner, J. S., Gonet, A. and LeCompte, P. M., *Immunopathology Symposium, 4:* Grune and Stratton, Inc., New York, 1965.
42. Arquilla, E. R. and Bromer, W. W., Särtr. Nord. Med., *78:* 932, 1967.
43. Berson, S. A., and Yalow, R. W., J. Clin. Invest., *38:* 2017, 1959.
44. Meek, J. C. and Bolinger, R. E., Biochemistry, *5:* 3198, 1966.
45. Patterson, R., Lucena, G., Metz, R. and Roberts, M., J. Immun., *103:* 1061, 1969.
46. Varandani, P. T., Biochemistry, *6:* 100, 1967.
47. Yagi, Y., Maier, P. and Pressman, D., Science, *147:* 617, 1965.
48. Ovary, Z., Progr. Allerg., *5:* 459, 1958.
49. Arquilla, E. R., Alexander, J. D., Ptacek, E. D. and Loosli, E. S., Diabetes, *11:* 412, 1962.
50. Robinson, B. H. B. and Wright, P. H., J. Physiol., *155:* 302, 1961.
51. Patterson, R., Colwell, J. A., Gregor, W. H. and Cary, E., J. Lab. Clin. Med., *64:* 399, 1964.
52. von Fellenberg, R. and Rose, N. R., Int. Arch. Allerg., *33:* 454, 1968.
53. Corcos, J. M. and Ovary, Z., Proc. Soc. Exp. Biol. Med., *119:* 142, 1965.

THE JOURNAL OF IMMUNOLOGY
Vol. 105, No. 3, September 1970
Printed in U.S.A.

CHANGES IN IgA AND IgG CONCENTRATIONS IN NASAL SECRETIONS PRIOR TO THE APPEARANCE OF ANTIBODY DURING VIRAL RESPIRATORY INFECTION IN MAN[1]

WILLIAM T. BUTLER,[2] THOMAS A. WALDMANN, ROGER D. ROSSEN, R. GORDON DOUGLAS, JR. AND ROBERT B. COUCH

From the Departments of Microbiology and Medicine, Baylor College of Medicine, Houston, Texas 77025; the Laboratory of Clinical Investigations, National Institute of Allergy and Infectious Diseases and the Metabolism Branch, National Cancer Institute, National Institutes of Health, Bethesda, Maryland 20014; and the Veterans Administration Hospital, Houston, Texas 77031

Received for publication April 4, 1970

To investigate the mechanisms of appearance of locally synthesized and plasma-derived proteins at the nasal membrane surface during upper respiratory viral infection, nasal secretions and sera from six volunteers experimentally infected with coxsackievirus A type 21 or rhinovirus type 15 were analyzed for their content of viral neutralizing antibodies, immunoglobulin and albumin. Nasal IgA increased significantly 24 hr after viral inoculation and before transudation started. In coxsackievirus infection, nasal secretion IgA concentrations continued to rise for 2 weeks to nearly twice baseline levels, whereas in rhinovirus infection a sustained rise in IgA began only after illness had subsided. Significant amounts of specific antibody did not appear in the nasal secretions during the same period. Marked transudation of albumin and IgG from plasma occurred during respiratory illness. Before illness half of the IgG in nasal secretions was synthesized locally; the remainder came from plasma as indicated by the quantity of isotopically labeled IgG which entered nasal secretions from the circulation. Viral infection inhibited local IgG synthesis; therefore, after illness subsided, nearly all IgG in nasal secretions came from the plasma. These results are consistent with the hypothesis that immunoglobulins are delivered to the nasal membrane surfaces by three different mechanisms: release of pre-formed secretory IgA during the incubation period of viral infection, transudation from the plasma before and after illness but particularly during the rhinorrhea phase of illness, and local synthesis of IgA and IgG. After illness subsides, local IgG synthesis is inhibited, but there is a marked stimulation of IgA synthesis, which, after a further period, develops specificity for the infecting virus.

A prominent feature of the common cold is rhinorrhea. Considerable effort in treatment of the common cold is directed at suppressing the rhinorrhea, although it is not known whether the rhinorrhea represents a nonspecific inflammatory response to viral infection or whether it is an adaptive response which facilitates the delivery of substances to the mucous membrane surface which may modify or prevent the spread of the viral infection.

Previous work has suggested that there may be a prominent increase in proteins of the nasal secretion during acute viral infection of the upper respiratory tract (1–3). Part of this protein comes from the plasma, but there is also a considerable increase in immunoglobulin A (IgA) which has many of the physical characteristics of secretory IgA, a protein known to be wholly synthesized within the respiratory mucous membranes (4–5). Nasal secretions also contain other poorly characterized proteins, some of which may be locally

[1] This work was supported in part by The Veterans Administration Hospital, Houston, Texas, and by Grant HE-05435 from the National Heart Institute and Grant RR-00350 from the General Clinical Research Center Branch, National Institutes of Health, Bethesda, Maryland.

[2] Address reprint requests to William T. Butler, M.D., Director, Immunology Research Laboratory, Veterans Administration Hospital, Houston, Texas 77031.

synthesized (5–6). Which of these substances, then, predominates in nasal secretions during the rhinorrhea of acute upper respiratory viral infection? Does rhinorrhea facilitate the delivery of antibody or other anti-viral substances to the respiratory mucous membranes from the plasma or from local sources? Is the rise seen in secretory IgA during acute infection due to release of stored IgA or due to newly synthesized IgA? Finally, what portion, if any, of newly synthesized IgA is specific for the infecting virus?

The present experiments were designed to investigate some of these questions by measuring quantitatively the concentrations of albumin and immunoglobulins A and G in nasal secretions before, during, and immediately after experimentally induced viral respiratory illness. Nasal secretions and sera were also analyzed for the presence of antibody to the inoculated virus in an attempt to relate changes in nasal secretion protein to the emergence of specific virus-neutralizing activity.

MATERIALS AND METHODS

Volunteers. The subjects were six normal adult males from federal correctional institutions admitted to the Clinical Center, National Institute of Allergy and Infectious Diseases. They were examined daily for signs and symptoms of respiratory illness by physicians uninformed as to the timing and nature of the virus inoculum (7).

Study protocol. Serum and nasal secretion specimens were collected daily from the six volunteers, processed as described below, and examined quantitatively for immunoglobulin and antibody content before and after inoculation with known respiratory viruses. Three of these volunteers were also given 50 μCi of ^{131}I-labeled IgG intravenously on two occasions: 14 days and 2 days before virus inoculation. The second dose was given to assure adequate levels of radioactivity in the nasal secretions for measurement during the period of recovery from viral illness. Each volunteer received 10 drops of Lugol's solution three times daily, starting 48 hr before isotope administration, to block thyroidal uptake.

Collection and processing of specimens. Nasal secretions were collected daily by rinsing each nostril with 10 ml of sterile lactated Ringer's solution as previously described (4). Immediately after homogenization and centrifugation of the nasal washes (4), the supernatants from each specimen were placed in separate cellulose dialysis casings and concentrated to between 1.3 and 1.7 ml by packing the casings in dry Sephadex G-200. This caused approximately a 10-fold concentration of the nasal wash, since the original volume of all except two supernatants varied from 12 to 18 ml, with an average of 15 ml. The volume of nasal wash fluid recovered from an individual volunteer remained remarkably constant from day to day, confirming a previous study (6). After concentration of the remaining specimens the casings were dialyzed against phosphate-buffered saline, pH 7.0, for 24 hr at 4°C, opened, and the exact volume of the concentrated nasal secretions was recorded. All further measurements were done directly on these specimens, and for comparative purposes the results of quantitative protein assays were corrected to 10-fold concentration of the original specimen.

Laboratory procedures. Immunoglobulin concentrations were measured by radial single diffusion in agar, employing antisera specific for immunoglobulin heavy chains (4). Total protein was measured by the biuret reaction (8). Techniques for immunoelectrophoresis, sucrose density gradient ultracentrifugation, and radioactivity measurement have been described (4).

Preparation of labeled proteins. Human IgG was prepared from recently drawn serum as described previously (4). The protein was labeled with ^{131}I by the iodine monochloride technique of McFarlane (9). Normal human serum albumin was added to the preparation to a final concentration of 35 mg/ml to prevent protein damage by self-irradiation. The mixture was sterilized by passage through a Millipore filter and tested for sterility and for lack of pyrogenicity in rabbits before administration to the volunteers.

Virus inoculation. Virus inoculation was performed by inhalation of a small particle aerosol (mean diameter 1.5 μ) as previously described (10). Three volunteers (S, M and G) received an inhaled dose of 119 50% tissue culture infectious doses ($TCID_{50}$) of rhinovirus type 15. The calculated dose which will infect 50% of exposed individuals (HID_{50}) is 0.68 $TCID_{50}$. The other three men (R, H and K) were given 890 $TCID_{50}$ of coxsackievirus A type 21 (HID_{50} = 34 $TCID_{50}$).

Virus isolation and antibody measurement. Nasal secretions were examined periodically throughout the study for the presence of infectious virus by techniques described previously (10). All volunteers shed the virus with which they were inoculated. Nasal secretion and serum virus-neutralizing activity was determined by neutralization tests (11), and all volunteers developed a significant rise in titer in convalescent specimens.

RESULTS

Immunoglobulin, albumin and total protein concentrations in nasal washings before and after viral respiratory illness

Changes after infection with rhinovirus type 15 (*Fig. 1*). The mean albumin concentration of three volunteers increased nearly fourfold during illness, indicating a significant increase in plasma transudation based on the fact that all albumin in nasal secretions has been shown to originate from the plasma (4). IgA concentration increased transiently the day after virus inoculation, but sustained increases in IgA and total protein concentrations occurred only after illness subsided. While IgA and total protein changes appeared to fluctuate together, changes in the concentration of IgG tended to follow those of albumin, suggesting that at least part of the IgG may be derived from the plasma (see below).

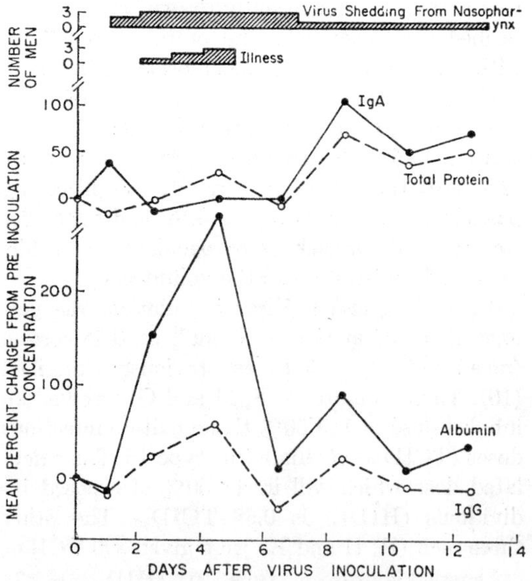

Figure 1. Mean percentage change from preinoculation concentrations of IgA, IgG, albumin and total protein in nasal secretions from three volunteers after inoculation with rhinovirus type 15.

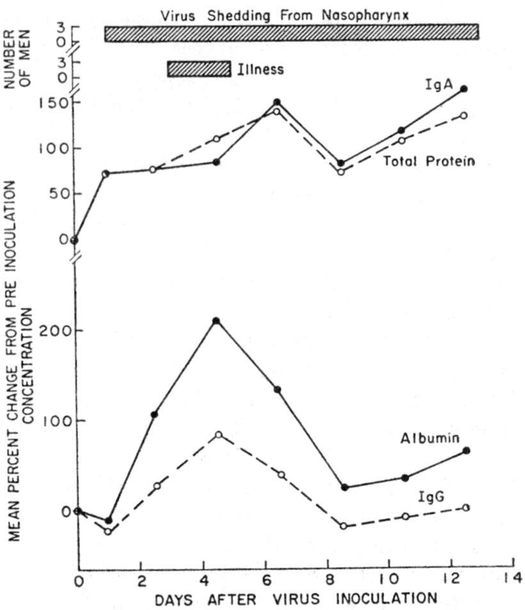

Figure 2. Mean percentage change from preinoculation concentrations of IgA, IgG, albumin and total protein in nasal secretions from three volunteers after inoculation with coxsackievirus A type 21.

Changes after infection with coxsackievirus A type 21 (*Fig. 2*). In contrast to what was seen in rhinovirus infection, there was an immediate, sustained rise in nasal IgA which was evident within 24 hr in two and in 48 hr following inoculation in all three men infected with this virus. Again, the changes in nasal wash IgA levels were closely paralleled by the changes in the total protein concentrations. Just as in rhinovirus infection, the rise in nasal albumin was brisk and limited to a 6-day period during and immediately following illness. Changes in nasal IgG followed those of nasal albumin concentration as seen previously in rhinovirus infection. Mean increases on days 12 and 13 in all components studied were greater for volunteers infected with coxsackievirus than for volunteers infected with rhinovirus (Fig. 3). This finding correlated with earlier and more persistent virus shedding from the nasopharynx in the coxsackievirus group. In contrast to the net increases in IgA and total and unidentified protein, IgG concentrations fell on days 12 and 13 in volunteers inoculated with both viruses.

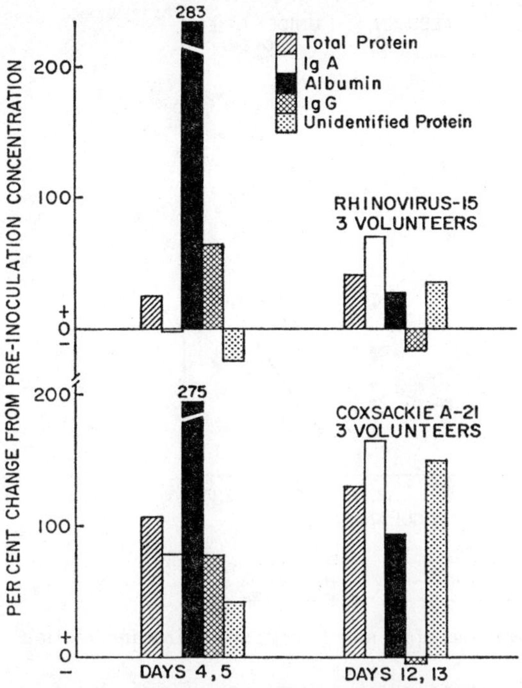

Figure 3. Net changes from preinoculation values of protein components in nasal secretions during height of illness and after illness had subsided.

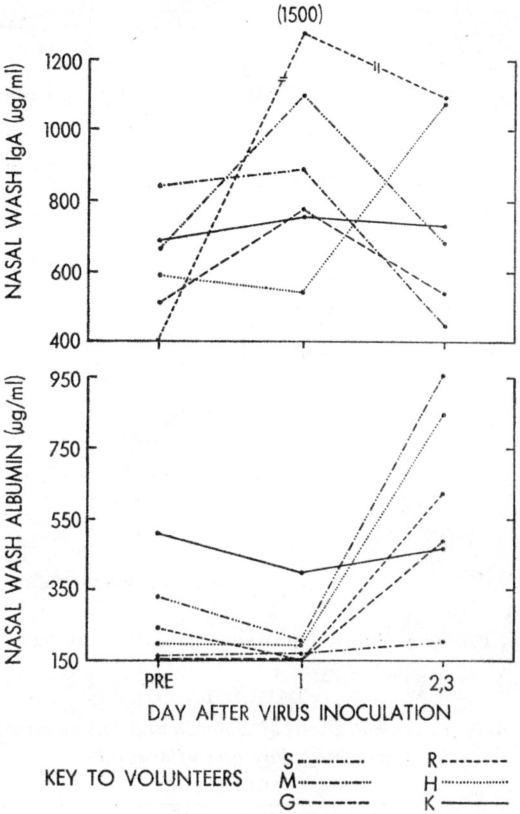

Figure 4. Changes in albumin and IgA concentrations in nasal secretions after virus inoculation but prior to onset of illness.

Early IgA changes after virus inoculation. Twenty-four hours after virus inoculations five of the six volunteers showed a rise in nasal wash IgA concentration (Fig. 4). By the next day, however, IgA levels in each of these men had decreased from the peak reached at 24 hr. Note that albumin transudation first appeared at least 1 day after the peak IgA concentration. Therefore, the early rise in IgA concentration was independent of the transudative process.

Relative protein composition of nasal secretions before and 2 weeks after virus inoculation. The net changes in the relative contributions of the measured components in the nasal secretion are shown in Figure 5. In all six volunteers the relative contribution of IgG decreased after infection. Similarly, the relative contribution of albumin fell in five of the six volunteers. In contrast, the relative contribution of IgA increased substantially in three volunteers, remained essentially unchanged in two, and decreased slightly in only one volunteer. In the latter three men the failure to see an increase in the relative contribution of IgA despite the observed absolute increase in IgA concentration was due to the large increase in the contribution of unidentified protein. Despite this there was relatively more IgA than albumin in the nasal secretions 2 weeks after infection than there was before in all six men leading to a decrease in the ratio of albumin to IgA after illness (Table I). This result suggests that increased nasal secretion IgA concentrations after illness were due to net increases in IgA synthesis.

Source of IgG in nasal secretions during upper respiratory viral infection

Two of the volunteers inoculated with coxsackievirus and one man who experienced a rhinovirus infection were given ^{131}I-labeled human IgG intravenously prior to virus inoculation to determine what proportion of the IgG found in nasal washings during viral infection came from the plasma (Fig. 6). Prior to virus inoculation, the specific activities of IgG in 11 nasal secretion specimens from the three volunteers ranged be-

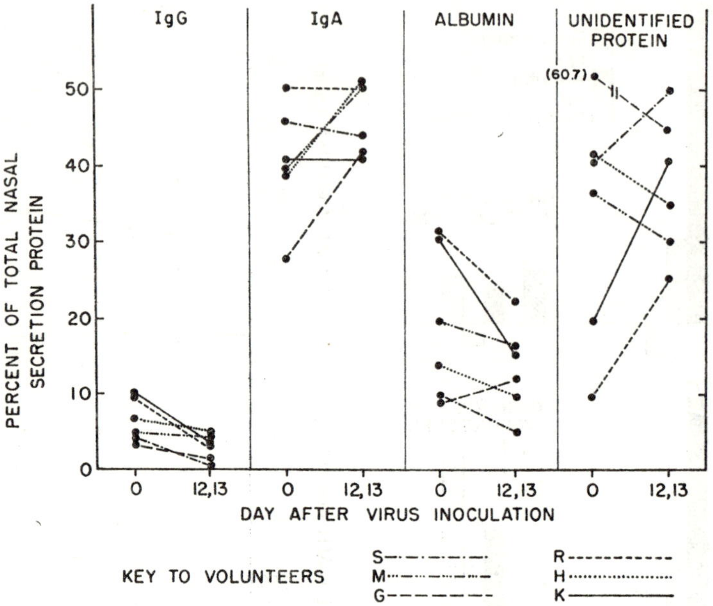

Figure 5. Relative protein composition of nasal secretions before and 2 weeks after virus inoculation

TABLE I

Relative concentrations of albumin and IgA in nasal secretions before and after viral respiratory infection*

Volunteer	Albumin/IgA	
	Before viral illness	After viral illness (days 12, 13)
S	0.20	0.10
M	0.49	0.32
G	0.30	0.29
R	0.62	0.44
H	0.35	0.19
K	0.75	0.35

tween 38% and 73% (mean 56%) of those in the corresponding serum samples. During and after illness, the specific activities of IgG in nasal secretions and sera tended to approach unity. This finding suggested that local IgG synthesis was severely impaired and in some cases completely inhibited during acute viral respiratory illness.

To determine whether IgG from plasma accumulates selectively in nasal secretions, we calculated how much of the IgG in each nasal secretion specimen came from the plasma by measuring the quantity of IgG in that specimen and its specific activity relative to serum IgG. Changes in the concentration of plasma-derived IgG paralleled the changes in albumin concentration in the same nasal wash specimens, suggesting that IgG, like albumin, may be transferred from plasma to nasal secretion by transudation (Table II).

Virus neutralizing activity and virus shedding

All six inoculated volunteers became infected as evidenced by the pattern of virus shedding and by the late rise (day 42) in serum-neutralizing titers against the infecting virus. However, during the 2-week period immediately after virus inoculation, no consistent change in neutralizing activity was detected in nasal secretions or sera of the volunteers despite the marked increases in IgA concentrations which had occurred (Table III). Fluctuations in titers were seen in both nasal secretions and serum. Such fluctuations have been seen in previous studies although no consistent increases occur prior to 14 days after inoculation (12). One of the volunteers (G) had low levels of neutralizing activity (1:4) in nasal secretions before virus inoculation. On day 12 his titer had increased slightly (1:8) and serum-neutralizing activity was first detected. All three of the men infected with coxsackievirus continued to shed virus for up to 2 weeks following inoculation, and one of the men infected with rhinovirus 15 behaved similarly; however, all six men were

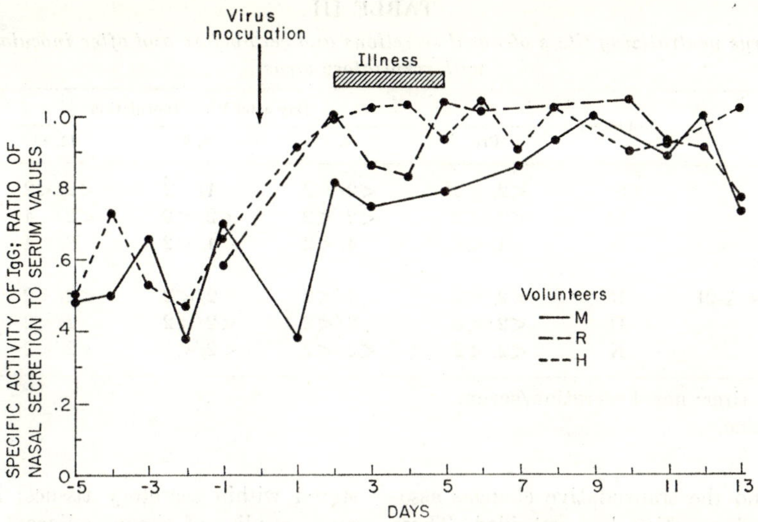

Figure 6. Source of IgG in nasal secretions during upper respiratory viral infection in three volunteers

TABLE II

Changes in concentrations of plasma-derived albumin and IgG in nasal secretions

Time after Virus Inoculation	Percentage Change from Pre-Inoculation Concentration	
	Albumin	IgG[a]
days		
Pre	0	0
1	−15.5	−12.0
2, 3	+221.6	+190.6
4, 5	+269.0	+231.0
6, 7	+293.0	+289.0
8, 9	+56.5	+66.5
10, 11	+81.6	+128.3
12, 13	+102.0	+112.0

[a] Calculations based only on plasma-derived portion of IgG.

symptom-free by the 5th day post-inoculation (Figs. 1 and 2).

DISCUSSION

The changes observed in the nasal secretion proteins of six men following infection with respiratory viruses known to cause acute, self-limited upper respiratory infection suggest that at least two processes may participate in the local humoral response to such infections: transudation of plasma proteins, and local synthesis of immunoglobulins. The transudative phase of illness results presumably from a defect in vascular permeability, which in turn may be a consequence of the release of vasoactive substances from inflammatory cells attracted to the site of infection. This is reflected by the substantial increase in nasal wash albumin and to a lesser extent in the rise in nasal IgG during the middle of the 1st week following virus inoculation (Fig. 3). This corresponds to the period of maximum virus shedding and illness (13). Interestingly, the transudation decreased abruptly after the clinical illness had subsided although virus shedding persisted. Therefore, transudation cannot be due to viral infection *per se*. Previous quantitative studies on virus shedding with these same viral inocula have shown that there is a 100- to 1000-fold reduction in the virus concentration of nasal washings after the clinical signs and symptoms of illness subside in either rhinovirus (13) or coxsackievirus illness (Couch, R. B., Douglas, R. G., Jr., Cate, T. R. and Knight, V., unpublished). This fall in virus concentration coincides temporally with an abrupt decrease in transudation. Whether this reduction of virus shedding reflects a decrease in the number of infected cells or that a different cell type becomes infected, and whether this reduction is causally related to ability of the host to maintain an inflammatory response have not yet been determined.

IgA levels in nasal secretions increased initially during the first 24 hr after virus inoculation. A second rise occurred 6 to 9 days after inoculation and reached a peak during the 2nd week, well

TABLE III

Virus neutralizing titers of nasal secretions and sera before and after inoculation with respiratory virus

Virus	Volunteer	Day after Virus Inoculation				
		Pre	4, 5	8, 9	12, 13	42
Rhinovirus-15	S	<2/<2[a]	<2/ 2	4/ 2	<2/<2	ND[b]/64
	M	<2/<2	<2/<2	<2/<2	<2/ 4	ND/64
	G	4/<2	4/<2	4/<2	8/ 4	ND/4
Coxsackievirus A-21	R	<2/<2	4/<2	2/<2	<2/<2	ND/64
	H	<2/<2	2/<2	<2/<2	2/<2	ND/64
	K	<2/<2	<2/<2	<2/<2	<2/<2	ND/128

[a] Reciprocal titer: nasal secretion/serum.
[b] ND, not done.

after illness and the transudative changes associated with inflammation had subsided. These later changes in nasal wash IgA were most likely caused by a stimulation of local synthesis of secretory IgA and were accompanied by a rise in concentration of other unidentified nasal proteins which presumably were also synthesized by cells within the upper respiratory mucous membranes (Figs. 3 and 5). An alternative that must be considered is that the increased protein concentrations represent an increased efficiency of capturing the proteins of nasal secretions in the nasal wash. It is unlikely that this happened, however, since after illness IgA constituted a relatively larger portion of the nasal wash protein than before illness in three volunteers (Fig. 5), the mean percentage increase from baseline values was greater for IgA than for any of the other components (Fig. 3), and the relative amount of albumin in the secretions decreased significantly in five of the six volunteers (Fig. 5). If the nasal wash procedure had simply rinsed out more protein after illness than before, and if no changes in the relative contribution of the protein components had occurred, we should have seen a proportional increase in all measured components. In order to explain the relative decrease in albumin concentration observed, one would otherwise have to postulate that transudation of albumin into the nasal passages was inhibited after illness, an unlikely occurrence.

A rather striking finding was the increase in IgA concentration observed 24 hr after virus inoculation (Fig. 4). It is unlikely that the rate of IgA synthesis would increase this rapidly. This early rise in IgA may represent the release of IgA stored within secretory tissues; immunofluorescence studies of tissues adjacent to respiratory and other mucous membrane surfaces have revealed that the apical portions of the cytoplasm of glandular epithelial cells contain IgA which presumably has been taken up by these cells from the interstitial plasma cells (14–15). It is conceivable that the viral respiratory infection stimulates release of this epithelial cell-associated IgA possibly as part of the same mechanism which provokes rhinorrhea. If this hypothesis is valid, one would expect that the IgA released into nasal secretions immediately following viral infection would possess antibody specificity for antigens previously encountered by the individual, rather than for the agent causing the current infection. We believe that this possibility deserves further exploration for it would help to explain the heterologous reacting antibodies to influenza viruses that are seen in respiratory secretions during the first 7 to 10 days after infection and before antibodies to the infecting strain are detectable (16).

Normally, about 50% of the IgG present in nasal secretions is synthesized locally (17). During respiratory illness, however, local synthesis was shown to be significantly inhibited. The defect in IgG synthesis persisted throughout 2 weeks of observation although some recovery appeared to begin just prior to the end of the study. Whether the delay in recovery was due to continued low grade viral infection or to the time necessary to replenish lymphoid cells destroyed during the height of illness, or to some other mechanism remains to be determined. The delay in recovery of local IgG synthesis does explain, however, the net and relative decreases in nasal wash IgG after illness (Figs. 3 and 5).

Since these changes in nasal immunoglobulins were not associated with detectable increases in either nasal or serum antibodies during the first 2 weeks following viral infection, one may postulate that the increase in nasal wash IgA represents newly synthesized secretory IgA which is either not specific for the infecting virus or its specificity is not measureable by virus neutralization tests or that the antibody has a relatively weak affinity for virus antigens. We may have failed to detect antibody in secretions because it was already combined with excess viral antigens during the first 2 weeks after inoculation. This is unlikely, however, since in one volunteer (G) there was no diminution in pre-existing nasal wash antibody during the height of virus shedding and in two volunteers antibody was not detected for a full week after virus shedding had stopped.

These studies have provided quantitative data on immunoglobulins in nasal secretions that now suggest three different mechanisms whereby viral infection of the respiratory tract might be prevented or modified: 1) release of pre-formed IgA antibody into secretions during the incubation period of a viral infection which if of appropriate specificity might prevent the perpetuation of this infection and any subsequent illness; 2) transudation during the rhinorrhea-phase of upper respiratory illness might result in increased quantities of serum IgG antibody bathing infected tissues and thus serve to limit spread of infection and ameliorate illness; and 3) local synthesis of IgA antibody, which may serve to limit spread of the infection and prevent subsequent illness. Since IgA-associated antibody only appears after illness has subsided, the latter mechanism probably does not usually influence recovery from primary illness except possibly during influenza infection (18). The ability to synthesize IgA, however, may vary from person to person. It has been shown previously that the quantity of IgA in nasal secretions varies among different individuals (6) and that those with high baseline IgA values mobilize an antibody response quicker and appear less likely to develop illness with influenza viral infection than those with low baseline values (18). Each of these protective mechanisms would apply to individuals experiencing reinfection but mechanisms for recovery from primary infection have yet to be fully elucidated, and may involve cellular immune mechanisms more than humoral antibody.

REFERENCES

1. Anderson, T. O., Riff, J. M. and Jackson, G. G., J. Immun., *89:* 691, 1962.
2. Artenstein, M. S., Bellanti, J. A. and Buescher, E. L., Proc. Soc. Exp. Biol. Med., *117:* 558, 1964.
3. Rossen, R. D., Butler, W. T., Cate, T. R., Szwed, C. F. and Couch, R. B., Proc. Soc. Exp. Biol. Med., *119:* 1169, 1965.
4. Butler, W. T., Rossen, R. D. and Waldmann, T. A., J. Clin. Invest., *46:* 1883, 1967.
5. Tomasi, T. B., Jr. and Bienenstock, J., Advances Immun., *9:* 1, 1968.
6. Rossen, R. D., Schade, A. L., Butler, W. T. and Kasel, J. A., J. Clin. Invest., *45:* 768, 1966.
7. Knight, V., Progr. Med. Virol., *6:* 1, 1964.
8. Kabat, E. A., *Kabat and Mayer's Experimental Immunochemistry,* 2nd Ed., Charles C Thomas, Springfield, Ill., 1961.
9. McFarlane, A. S., Nature, *182:* 53, 1958.
10. Couch, R. B., Cate, T. R., Douglas, R. G., Jr., Gerone, P. J. and Knight, V., Bact. Rev., *30:* 517, 1966.
11. Douglas, R. G., Jr., Fleet, W. F., Cate, T. R. and Couch, R. B., Proc. Soc. Exp. Biol. Med., *127:* 497, 1968.
12. Douglas, R. G., Jr., Rossen, R. D., Butler, W. T. and Couch, R. B., J. Immun., *99:* 297, 1967.
13. Douglas, R. G., Jr., Cate, T. R., Gerone, P. J. and Couch, R. B., Amer. Rev. Resp. Dis., *94:* 159, 1966.
14. Rossen, R. D., Morgan, C., Hsu, K. C., Butler, W. T., and Rose, H. M., J. Immun., *100:* 706, 1968.
15. Tourville, D. R., Adler, R. H., Bienenstock, J. and Tomasi, T. B., Jr., J. Exp. Med., *129:* 411, 1969.
16. Fulk, R. V., Fedson, D. S., Huber, M. A., Fitzpatrick, J. R. and Kasel, J. A., J. Immun., *104:* 8, 1970.
17. Butler, W. T., Rossen, R. D. and Waldmann, T. A., XVI Colloquium: Protides of the Biologic Fluids, Edited by Hub Peeters, p. 331, Pergamon Press, Oxford, 1969.
18. Rossen, R. D., Butler, W. T., Waldman, R. H., Alford, R. H., Hornick, R. B. Togo, Y. and Kasel, J. A., J. A. M. A., *211:* 1157, 1970.

THE JOURNAL OF IMMUNOLOGY
Vol. 105, No. 3, September 1970

Printed in U.S.A.

RIBONUCLEIC ACID SYNTHESIS IN RABBIT LYMPH NODE CELLS[1]

HELAINE A. DONAHUE,[2] VIRGINIA G. MOORE AND J. RUSSELL LITTLE[3]

From the Department of Microbiology, Washington University School of Medicine and the Department of Medicine, The Jewish Hospital, St. Louis, Missouri 63110

Received for publication March 20, 1970

Suspensions of lymph node cells were prepared from immunized and from unimmunized rabbits. In a totally synthetic medium at 37°C, these cells incorporated ^{3}H-uridine into RNA at an initially rapid linear rate without lag. After 60 to 90 min of incubation, the rate of uridine incorporation changed to a second linear rate which was about 9% of the initial rate. Maximal initial rates of ^{3}H-uridine incorporation were observed 5 days after immunization, though differences were small between cells from immunized and nonimmune animals. Sucrose gradient analyses of whole cell RNA revealed that the major classes of cellular RNA contained significant radioactivity and antigen-stimulated cells revealed predominant labeling in a 12 to 13S fraction. These experiments provide a reasonable approach to the preparation and isolation of high specific activity RNA for use in the RNA-DNA hybridization studies or in the functional characterization of various classes of RNA implicated in immune responses.

Work done in other laboratories has suggested that antibody biosynthesis may involve RNA species that function in several different metabolic roles. For example, two rapidly labeled RNA species from rabbit popliteal lymph nodes had properties consistent with those expected for monocistronic messenger RNA coding for immunoglobulin H and L chains (1). Gottlieb and co-workers (2, 3) have studied a unique association of antigenic fragments with a particular ribonucleoprotein fraction of the macrophage and Roelants and Goodman (4, 5) have extended these observations. Earlier observations by Halac *et al.* indicated changes in the RNA base composition of peritoneal exudate cells exposed to antigen *in vitro* (6). An informational role for peritoneal exudate and lymphoid cell RNA in the immune response was supported by the detection of antibodies bearing the allotype of the RNA donor which were synthesized in lymphoid cells from recipients with a different allotype (7, 8). RNA:DNA hybridization studies have revealed the presence of antigen-induced changes in mouse spleen cell RNA (9) and an increased diversity and antigen-directed specificity of RNA molecules synthesized in the mouse spleen and peritoneal lymphocytes (10, 11). Experiments with molecular hybridization of RNA from mouse myeloma tumor cells have also furnished evidence for the presence of cytoplasmic messenger RNA coding for immunoglobulins (12–14). There is also evidence from studies with human lymphocytes (15, 16) and rat spleen cells (17, 18) indicating a stimulation by antigen or phytohemagglutinin of ribosomal RNA synthesis.

In view of the broad range of experiments suggesting that newly synthesized RNA may function in the determination of the primary structure of antibody molecules, we have undertaken the development of techniques for the labeling and isolation of RNA from rabbit lymph node cells. We have patterned our experiments

[1] This work was supported, in part, by Research Grants AI-03231 and 52742 and Training Grant 5TI-AI-257 from the National Institute of Allergy and Infectious Diseases, and by Contract DA-49-193-MD-2330, with the Research and Development Command, Department of the Army, recommended by the Commission on Immunization of the Armed Forces Epidemiology Board.

[2] Most of this work was performed in partial fulfillment of the requirements for an M.A. degree awarded by the Committee on Molecular Biology (and was supported by NIH Traineeship 5 TI GM 00714) of the Graduate School of Arts and Science of Washington University, St. Louis, Missouri.

[3] Recipient of a Research Career Program Award (1-K3-AM-38,620) from the National Institute of Arthritis and Metabolic Diseases.

on earlier studies of immunoglobulin production in suspensions of rabbit lymph node cells *in vitro* (19–21) in an effort to relate events of protein and nucleic acid synthesis. A major purpose of this study was to determine the feasibility of experiments with RNA:DNA hybridization during the immune response (22).

MATERIALS AND METHODS

Preparation of lymph node cells for incubation. Randomly bred mature male and female albino rabbits were used for all experiments. Experiments with immunized animals were performed after each animal was injected with either 2 mg of egg albumin or 1 mg of heavily substituted 2,4,6-trinitrophenylated bovine γ globulin (TNP-BγG[4]) or 2,4-dinitrophenylated bovine γ globulin (DNP-BγG) in complete Freund's adjuvant (23). The total dose of antigen for each animal was divided such that equal amounts were injected in all four footpads.

The cells used in these studies were obtained from the popliteal and axillary lymph nodes of immunized and nonimmunized rabbits. Immediately after these animals were killed by a sharp blow to their heads their nodes were removed and placed in a supportive medium (T.M.) of salts and vitamins at 4°C (19). Cells from immunized rabbits were never combined with lymph node cells from nonimmunized animals, but in some experiments teased cells from two or three nonimmunized animals were added to a common pool of cells. All preparative manipulations of the nodes and lymph node cells were performed at 0 to 4°C. Excess fat was removed from the nodes and they were then individually teased apart with a stroking motion on a fine mesh screen of stainless steel with stainless steel rakes. The cells falling through the screen were collected in a small glass Petri dish containing T.M. The cells and capsular material were filtered through a double layer of four-ply gauze into a glass centrifuge tube. After centrifugation for 10 min at 800 rpm, the supernatant fluid was removed and the cells were resuspended with gentle agitation in 0.5 ml of ice-cold incubation medium (19). This synthetic medium contained salts, vitamins, and an amino acid mixture which was sometimes lacking leucine but was free of nucleosides. When the cells were suspended, an additional 4.5 ml of incubation medium were added and the cell number was determined by sampling 0.5 ml of the cell suspension into a McNaught tube. After 10 min at 2000 rpm, the packed cell volume in the McNaught tube was determined and related to cell number (20). The cell concentration was adjusted to 1.5 to 3.0 $\times$ 10^8 cells/ml. Microscopic examination of the concentrated cell suspension in a hemocytometer revealed that greater than 90% of the cells were isolated single cells and the remaining 10% occurred in aggregates of two to five cells.

Incubation conditions with ^{3}H-uridine. A portion of the concentrated cell suspension was diluted such that there were 10 μl of packed cells per ml or 2.56 $\times$ 10^7 cells/ml in 15 ml of incubation medium. At zero time, ^{3}H-uridine (New England Nuclear, Boston, Mass., 4.4 to 25.7 Ci/mmol generally labeled[5] or C-5 labeled) was pipetted into the ice-cold cell suspension in siliconized 500-ml wide-mouth Erlenmeyer flasks. The cell suspension was then immediately transferred to a covered water bath at 37°C with a water-saturated atmosphere of 95% O_2, 5% CO_2. The cell suspension was not agitated during the incubation period except when necessary for the removal of aliquots.

Kinetics of macromolecular incorporation of ^{3}H-uridine. Immediately after the addition of ^{3}H-uridine and after 15, 30, 60, 90, 180 and 360 min, 0.1 ml of the incubation mixture was added to ice-cold 10% trichloracetic acid (TCA). After a minimum of 2 hr at 4°C, the TCA precipitates were collected on glass fiber filters (type AP20, Millipore Corp., Bedford, Mass.) supported on an ice-cold stainless steel filter apparatus (Tracerlab, Waltham, Mass., model E-8b). In experiments done with generally labeled ^{3}H-uridine, the filtered precipitates were washed with organic

[4] Abbreviations used in this work: SSC, standard saline citrate is 0.15 M NaCl, 0.015 M sodium citrate; TNP, the 2,4,6-trinitrophenyl group; DNP, the 2,4-dinitrophenyl group; BγG, bovine γ-globulin; HSA, human serum albumin; TCA, trichloracetic acid; SDS, sodium dodecyl sulfate; ϵ-DNPI, bovine insulin bearing a single ϵ-2,4-DNP group on the sole lysine residue.

[5] This designation is used by New England Nuclear for tritium-labeled compounds prepared by exchange. They state, "Compounds are designated as generally labeled when there is reason to believe that there is a random (i.e., nonuniform) distribution of radioactivity on the various labeled positions."

solvents as described by Kennell (24), but when 5-^{3}H-uridine was employed, precipitates were washed three times with 10% TCA, once with 0.1 N HCl, and then dried for liquid scintillation counting in toluene solution containing a phosphor (25), in a Packard scintillation spectrometer. Counting efficiency in toluene was found to be 16%.

To determine the fraction of TCA precipitable ^{3}H-uridine which was incorporated into deoxyribonucleic acid (DNA), the total TCA precipitable material was subjected to alkaline hydrolysis (24).

Extraction of ^{3}H-RNA from lymph node cells. After incubation with ^{3}H-uridine, flasks were removed from the 37°C bath, chilled on ice and adjusted to 0.1 M in Tris-acetate buffer, pH 5.0. Cells were lysed at 60°C by adding sodium dodecyl sulfate (SDS) (Matheson Coleman and Bell, Cincinnati, Ohio) to a final concentration of 2%. When the solution was clear of suspended cellular aggregates, self-digested pronase (Calbiochem, Los Angeles, Calif.; predigested in 0.1 M Tris-acetate, pH 5.0 at 37°C for 2 hr) was added to a concentration of 1 mg/ml and the solution was gently shaken for 10 min. An equal volume of phenol at 60°C was then poured into the cell lysate and the miscible phases were vigorously shaken for 6 min at 60°C. The flask was plunged into an alcohol-ice bath at −10°C (26) for 2 min and then the contents were transferred into conical glass tubes. Phases were separated by centrifugation at 15 to 20°C. The aqueous phase and interface were re-extracted 6 to 8 times with fresh phenol to which was added ⅕ volume of 0.1 M Tris-acetate, pH 5.0 containing 0.5% SDS. The aqueous phase was then extracted with chloroform-isoamyl alcohol (24:1 by volume) (27) until no interfacial precipitate remained. The RNA was precipitated in 0.1 M NaCl by the addition of two volumes of 95% ethyl alcohol and allowed to stand overnight at 0 to 4°C for maximal precipitation. The precipitate was collected by centrifugation, washed once with 70% ethyl alcohol and dissolved in the desired aqueous solvent.

Rabbit liver RNA (unlabeled) was prepared by the same method but in addition the RNA precipitated with ethyl alcohol was dissolved in ⅒ volume of SSC (standard saline citrate, SSC = 0.15 M sodium chloride, 0.015 sodium citrate). Electrophoretically pure DNase (Worthington Biochemical Corp., Freehold, N. J.) was then added at 20 μg/ml and the solution was incubated for 15 min at 37°C. α-Amylase (Worthington Biochemical Corp.) was then added at 20 μg/ml and incubation continued until the solution was transparent (approximately 10 min). Self-digested pronase was added and the solution was incubated for 1 hr at 37°C and then extracted two or three times with chloroform-isoamyl alcohol. The RNA was then reprecipitated with NaCl and ethyl alcohol as before.

Autoradiography. Isolated rabbit lymph node cells prepared as described above were suspended in 1.5% bovine serum albumin. Smears made on glass slides were air dried and fixed in absolute acetone for 10 min. Kodak AR-10 stripping film was applied, exposed, developed, and stained with Giemsa as described by Bond *et al.* (28). For the cell-binding experiments with ^{125}I-labeled ε-2,4-dinitrophenylinsulin (^{125}I-ε-DNPI), acetone-fixed smears were incubated for 30 min at 4°C in a moist chamber with an overlay of ^{125}I-ε-DNPI. The slides were then washed three times with 2 to 3 liters of buffered saline at 4°C for 24 hr each and then dried in order to prepare them for film stripping as described above. Hapten incubation experiments with unlabeled ε-DNPI, bovine insulin and ε-DNP-L-lysine were always performed on the same slide with the uninhibited incubation. The film was exposed at −10°C in dark, desiccated slide boxes (14 days for ^{3}H and 25 hr for ^{125}I), and then developed, rinsed, dried, and stained with Giemsa, pH 5.75.

Preparation of ^{125}I-ε-DNPI. ε-DNPI was prepared as described previously (29) and iodinated by the chloramine-T method of Hunter and Greenwood (30) using carrier free Na-^{125}I (Iso-serve division of Cambridge Nuclear Corp., Cambridge, Mass.). Five millicuries of isotope solution were used to iodinate 20 nmols of ε-DNPI (calculated from the concentration of ε-DNP groups determined spectrophotometrically). After iodination was complete, the entire reaction mixture was applied to a Sephadex G-25 column (53 × 1.2 cm) equilibrated with 0.05 M phosphate buffer pH 7.4. Radioactivity appearing at the void volume was pooled and aliquots were examined spectrophotometrically and by γ-counting on a Packard scintillation spectrometer. The product had 1.4 × 10^{8} CPM/nmol of DNP groups.

Sucrose gradient analysis of RNA. Zone sedimentation of lymph node cell ^{3}H-RNA was performed in 5 to 20% sucrose gradients containing 0.5% SDS in a Spinco SW-50 rotor. After 1.75 hr at 49,000 rpm at 20°C, each gradient was collected in fractions which were precipitated with 10% TCA and counted in a Packard liquid scintillation spectrometer. Each gradient contained purified *Aerobacter aerogenes* ^{14}C-RNA as a marker. Bacterial cell RNA was labeled with ^{14}C-uracil (New England Nuclear, Boston, Mass.) with a 5-min pulse of 35 mCi/mmol followed by a 30-min chase with unlabeled uracil (31).

RESULTS

Kinetics of incorporation of ^{3}H-uridine into RNA. The rate of incorporation of ^{3}H-uridine into RNA of rabbit lymph node cells is shown in Fig. 1. Each time point represents the average ^{3}H-uridine incorporated by 1.0 μl of packed cells from eight experiments. In several kinetic experiments, the incubation medium was lacking the amino acid leucine, but this deficiency resulted in no significant differences in the rate of incorporation when compared with incubations in complete medium. A comparison of uridine incorporation by lymph node cells from nonimmunized animals showed no detectable difference from cells obtained from animals 3 to 6 weeks after primary antigenic stimulation when serum antibody concentrations were generally at their peak levels during the primary response. The data shown in Fig. 1 are average values from three experiments with nonimmune and five experiments with immune animals killed between 3 and 6 weeks after a primary stimulus with 2 mg of TNP-BγG in complete adjuvant.

The initially linear incorporation of uridine suggests that there was rapid equilibration of exogenous uridine with the intracellular pools. Since the label used in most of these experiments was 5-^{3}H-uridine, various RNA species are believed to be the only macromolecular source of label. The rate of incorporation was linear for 60

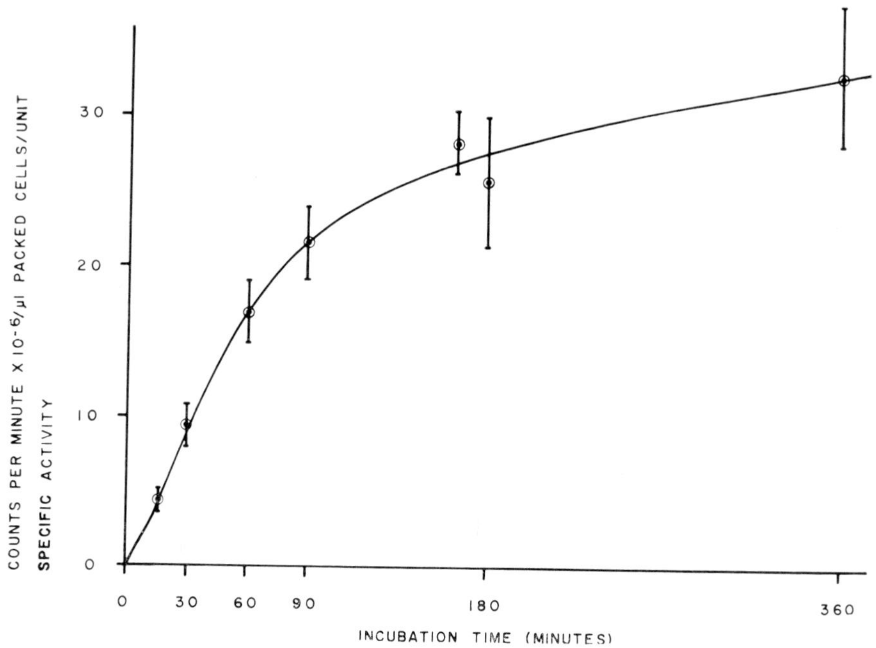

Figure 1. Kinetics of incorporation of ^{3}H-uridine into lymph node cell RNA. Rabbit lymph node cell suspensions were incubated at 37°C in culture medium containing ^{3}H-uridine labeled either in the 5 position or generally labeled throughout the nucleoside. At intervals, aliquots of cells were removed from the culture flask and precipitated with 10% TCA. Precipitates were washed on glass fiber filters and radioactivity was determined by liquid scintillation counting. Each time point is an average from eight separate experiments. The counts/minute in TCA precipitates were normalized to the same volume of packed cells sampled from the incubation medium and the same specific activity. The data are plotted with one standard deviation.

to 90 min and then declined to a second, slower, somewhat more variable rate. This change of rate was observed clearly in every experiment and in one incubation medium (supplemented with 10% fetal calf serum) the slower rate was essentially unchanged between 1.5 and 14 hr, and both the initial rate and the slower rate observed after 90 min were identical to a parallel incubation lacking fetal calf serum. Supplementation of the incubation medium with 3×10^{-5} M unlabeled uridine did not produce a qualitative change in the pattern observed in Fig. 1. Hemocytometer cell counts were regularly obtained at 0, 90 and 300 min of incubation (and often at other intervals). Loss of cells was directly proportional to the duration of incubation *in vitro* during the first 300 min and losses were much less thereafter. The cell concentration fell to 85 to 90% of the initial value after 90 min incubation at 37°C. The values plotted in Fig. 1 (and Fig. 6) have been corrected for cell losses during incubation and the change in incorporation rate of ^{3}H-uridine is therefore not attributable to this effect.

TABLE I

Incorporation of generally labeled *^{3}H-uridine into DNA*[a]

Incubation Time	Total TCA Precipitable Radioactivity	TCA Precipitable Radioactivity after Alkaline Hydrolysis	Percentage of Radioactivity in DNA
min	*cpm*	*cpm*	
0	177	0	0
15	2558	8	0.3
30	5541	54	0.9
60	9835	154	1.5
90	11397	318	2.8
180	16612	977	5.9
360	18456	1070	5.8

[a] Duplicate samples of 0.1 ml were withdrawn from the incubating cell suspension containing 6.67 μCi/ml at the intervals shown. Each sample was precipitated with 10% cold TCA, plated on glass fiber filters, washed, and dried. One filter at each time point was subjected to alkaline hydrolysis, reprecipitated with TCA, washed, and dried. The radioactivity of each filter was counted on a liquid scintillation counter. The radioactivity resistent to alkaline hydrolysis was considered to be present in DNA and was expressed as a percentage of the radioactivity on the duplicate filter which was not incubated in 0.5 M NaOH.

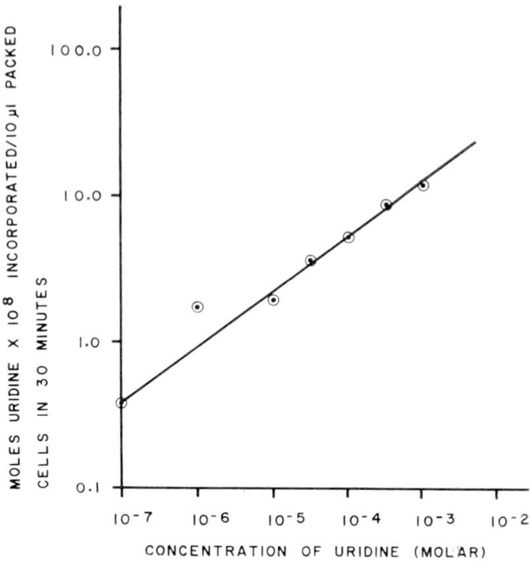

Figure 2. Dependence of uridine incorporation on the concentration of uridine in the culture medium. Rabbit lymph node cells were incubated, sampled and radioactivity was determined as in Fig. 1. Exogenous uridine incorporated was calculated from a series of lymph node cell cultures which differed only in the concentration of uridine in the medium. The specific activity of uridine varied from 8.1×10^{3} to 5.0 mCi/mmol with the changing ratio of ^{3}H- to ^{1}H-uridine. Aliquots of cells were removed from each flask at intervals to establish linearity of initial incorporation rate. The TCA precipitable radioactivity in the aliquots removed after 15 and 30 min incubation was used to obtain the values shown in this figure. Millimols of uridine incorporated into RNA were calculated from the ^{3}H-uridine specific activity in each culture assuming that cell radioactivity present in the TCA precipitates represented ^{3}H-uridine in RNA.

Since alkaline hydrolysis solubilizes the ^{3}H-labeled RNA, the percentage of total TCA precipitated radioactivity retained by the glass fiber filters after hydrolysis in 0.5 M NaOH provides a maximum estimate of the incorporation of the nucleoside label into DNA. Table I shows that even when generally labeled ^{3}H-uridine was used in the incubation medium, less than 6% of the label became incorporated into nonhydrolyzable material.

Concentration dependence of uridine incorporation. Fig. 2 shows the linear relationship between the concentration of uridine in the incubation medium and the initial rate of uridine incorporation into RNA. These data were obtained from a series of incubations containing the same concentrations of cells but different concentrations of uridine. ^{3}H-uridine incorporation was linear through 90 min at each uridine concentration and no lag or toxicity was observed. This relationship between incorporation rate and uridine concentration in the medium permitted the addition of large amounts of isotope with the incubating cells in order to obtain ^{3}H-RNA of high specific activity.

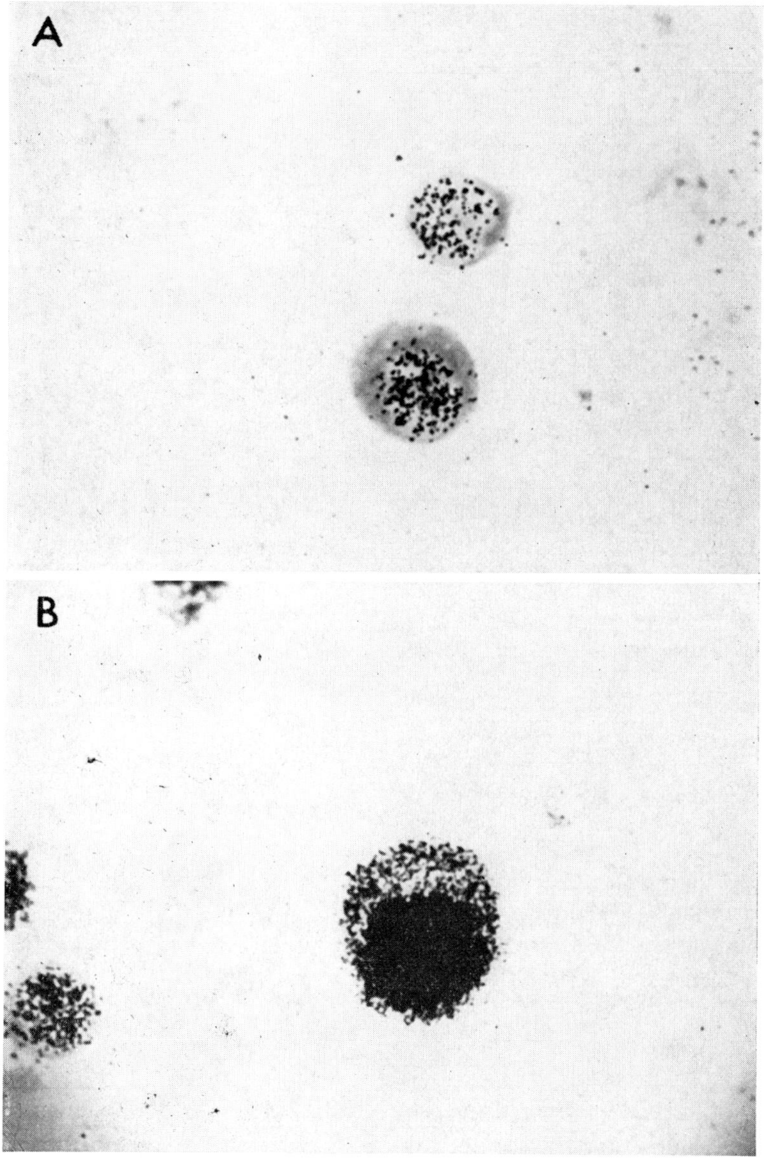

Figure 3. Autoradiograms of rabbit lymph node cells after incubation in ^{3}H-uridine. Panel A on the left was obtained with cell suspensions incubated at 37°C for 15 min in the presence of 1.5×10^{-6} M uridine (6.67 μCi/ml). Air dried smears were prepared from cell suspensions in 1.5% bovine serum albumin. The Kodak AR-10 stripping film around the microslides was exposed for 14 days at −10°C, then developed, and the cells were stained with Giemsa. These cells show the preponderance of nuclear incorporation of ^{3}H-uridine. The autoradiograms in panel B on the right show the density of nuclear labeling and the increased density of cytoplasmic labeling with longer incubation times (90 min).

TABLE II

Autoradiography of ^3H-uridine incorporation into antigen-stimulated lymph node cells[a]

Time of Incubation at 37°C	No. of Cells Counted	Percentage Cells Labeled	Percentage Small Lymphocytes
min			$\leq$10 μ *diameter*
0	226	14.6	96.4
15	201	97.5	96.5
30	216	96.3	92.6
60	199	96.5	95.9
90	232	98.7	95.3
180	200	100	94.5

[a] Lymph node cells were examined on stained films covered by autoradiographic stripping film, Kodak AR-10. Samples were obtained from incubation flasks containing 1.5×10^{-6} M ^{3}H-uridine, 6.67 μCi/ml. Each cell was scored as labeled (>3 grains/cell) or unlabeled and as smaller or larger than 10 μ in diameter. The number of silver grains present, but not lying directly over a cell, was less than 2/100 μ^2 (background).

Autoradiography following ^3H-uridine incorporation by rabbit lymph node cells. Autoradiography was employed to determine the fraction of cells capable of incorporating ^{3}H-uridine into RNA *in vitro* and as a check of cell viability. Representative autoradiograms are shown in Fig. 3*A* and 3*B*. Fig. 3*A* shows the preponderance of grains over the nuclei of cells sampled after a short incubation time. With longer periods of incubation, the intensity of tritium was heavier and there was an increase in cytoplasmic labeling as seen in Fig. 3*B*. Table II shows the proportion of labeled cells in a suspension made from lymph nodes stimulated with antigen. Labeled cells were present even when samples were obtained a few seconds after isotope addition, but this may be attributable to a slow but significant incorporation of uridine at 4°C during the sampling and centrifugation of cells used to prepare the smears.

In agreement with the rapid incorporation of isotope found in kinetic experiments, 97% of the total cells were labeled after 15 min of incubation in medium containing ^{3}H-uridine and no differences were detected between the morphology or frequency of labeled cells from antigen-stimulated or unstimulated lymph nodes. By 30 min, the nuclei were heavily labeled, with more than 50 grains per nucleus. At 180 min all cells were labeled, and although most were densely labeled, some had fewer grains, and appeared similar to those cells observed after 30 to 60 min of incubation.

Variation during the primary immune response in initial incorporation rate of ^3H-uridine. The failure to observe significant differences in rates of ^{3}H-uridine incorporation with immune and nonimmune cells prompted a systematic examination of changes in RNA biosynthesis during the early days after injection of a single dose of antigen in complete adjuvant. Fig. 4 shows the relationship between the duration of the primary response to DNP-BγG and the initial rate of ^{3}H-uridine incorporation into TCA precipitates in aliquots of rabbit lymph node cell suspensions. As indicated in Fig. 1, initial rates of uridine incorporation were always linear for 60 min and often for 90 min before the appearance of a

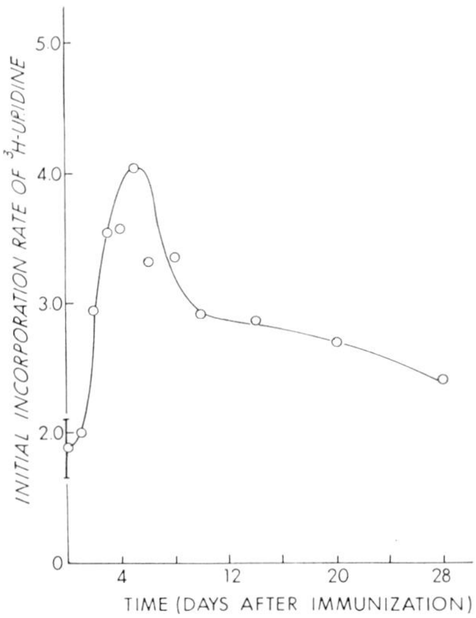

Figure 4. Variation in the initial rate of uridine incorporation by rabbit lymph node cells obtained at various times after primary immunization. Each animal was immunized with DNP-BγG by injecting 0.25 mg of antigen in complete Freund's adjuvant in each footpad. At intervals after immunization, animals were killed and cell suspensions prepared from the inguinal and popliteal lymph nodes. The cell density was adjusted to 2.56×10^7 cells/ml and the ^{3}H-uridine concentration was 1.5×10^{-6} M (6.67 μCi/ml) in each experiment. The initial rate of uridine incorporation was calculated from aliquots precipitated with TCA and plated after 15 and 30 min of incubation. The units for the ordinate scale are the same as those of Fig. 2. The zero time point (with one standard deviation) was calculated from the average of eight experiments shown in Fig. 1.

second slower incorporation rate. The values shown in Fig. 4 have been normalized to the same cell concentration, and the same concentration and specific activity of ^{3}H-uridine was used in each experiment. There was a sharp maximum in initial rate of uridine incorporation 5 days after antigen injection, but this quickly declined and by 10 days after immunization, there was less than a 50% increase in incorporation rate when compared with unstimulated cells (zero time point).

Antigen binding of cells from stimulated lymph nodes. Unincubated aliquots of each cell suspension used for obtaining the data in Fig. 4 were smeared on microscope slides, fixed briefly in acetone and exposed to an overlay solution of radioiodinated dinitrophenylated insulin bearing a single 2,4-DNP group (^{125}I-ε-DNP) on the sole lysine residue of bovine insulin (29). The labeled cells shown in Fig. 5 were obtained 14 days after immunization from regional lymph nodes. The figure clearly shows the difference between background and cell-bound grain density of these lymph node cells. Hapten inhibition of labeling by unlabeled ε-DNPI and ε-DNP-L-lysine was complete and bovine insulin failed to inhibit. Table III shows the proportion of labeled cells in each of the suspensions used to provide the data in Fig. 4.

Pulse-chase with ^{3}H-uridine in normal and antigen-stimulated lymph node cells. Fig. 6 illustrates the kinetics of ^{3}H-uridine incorporation between continuously labeled and pulse-labeled RNA and between normal and antigen-stimulated lymph node cells, and Fig. 7 shows sucrose gradient comparisons for RNA extracted from these same cells. Fig. 6 shows that after 60 min of linear incorporation of ^{3}H-uridine into RNA, the addition of excess unlabeled uridine (in 200-fold excess to the labeled species) results in a plateau in incorporation. Since equilibration of exogenous uridine with intracellular pools occurs promptly, this result suggests that the newly synthesized ^{3}H-RNA is stable for several hours in normal and antigen-stimulated cells. After 4 hr of incubation, the remaining cells in all four flasks were chilled rapidly, pelleted by centrifugation and the RNA was extracted. Linear sucrose gradients

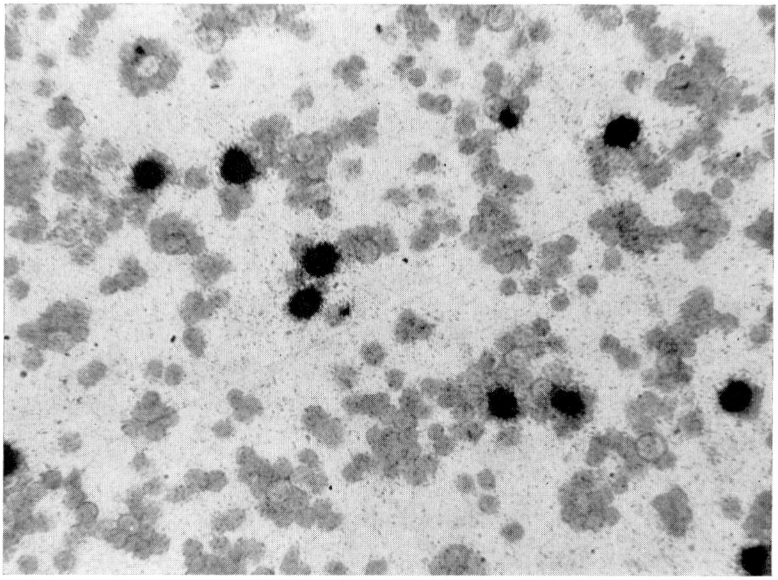

Figure 5. Autoradiogram of specific binding of ^{125}I-ε-dinitrophenylinsulin (^{125}I-ε-DNPI) by lymph node cells from rabbits immunized with DNP-BγG. Microslides were prepared from a separate unincubated aliquot of the lymph node cell suspensions used in the experiment described in Fig. 4 and Table III. Each dried and fixed slide was divided into four separate areas for incubation at 4°C with 2×10^{-6} M ^{125}I-ε-DNPI (shown above) or with the same ligand mixed with 5×10^{-4} M ε-DNP-L-lysine, unlabeled ε-DNPI, or bovine insulin. The proportion of labeled cells was calculated for each of the four test areas on each slide. Only the areas incubated with ^{125}I-ε-DNPI or with ^{125}I-ε-DNPI and bovine insulin showed significant binding of isotope.

TABLE III

Proportion of cells binding ^{125}I-ε-DNPI during the primary immune response to DNP-BγG[a]

Days after Immunization	No. of Cells Counted	Percentage of Total Cells Binding Antigen
0	524	
1	816	
2	600	0.2
3	662	
4	515	0.2
5	886	
6	724	0.5
8	615	0.2
10	210	1.2
14	518	2.8
20	592	2.3
28	624	2.9

[a] Aliquots of the lymph node cell suspensions isolated from the animals described in the legend to Figure 4 were used to make smears on miscroscope slides. Each slide was dried, fixed in acetone, and divided into four sectors. Each sector was incubated at 0 to 4°C 30 min with a solution of ^{125}I-ε-DNPI. In three sectors, the ^{125}I-ε-DNPI was first mixed with either unlabeled ε-DNPI, bovine insulin or ε-DNP-L-lysine and the fourth sector contained ^{125}I-ε-DNPI, but no potential inhibitor. After extensive washing of each slide, they were covered with Kodak AR-10 stripping film, exposed, developed, and stained through the stripping film with Giemsa. The labeled cells were scored only when they bore an almost uncountable number of grains as shown in Figure 5. The proportion of labeled cells was the same in the uninhibited and bovine insulin inhibited sectors. ε-DNP-L-lysine and unlabeled ε-DNPI completely blocked the specific binding of ^{125}I-ε-DNPI. The remaining portions of each cell suspension were used for the kinetic experiments described in Figure 4.

ranging from 5 to 20% in 0.5% SDS were then prepared from each preparation of isolated RNA to which ^{14}C-RNA from *Aerobacter aerogenes* had been added to serve as an internal marker of sedimentation rate. Assay of the radioactivity in each gradient fraction revealed clear differences between immune (Fig. 7*A* and 7*B*) and nonimmune cells (Fig. 7*C* and 7*D*) and between pulsed (Fig. 7*B* and 7*D*) and continuously labeled (Fig. 7*A* and 7*C*) cells. The three major classes of stable RNA (4S, 18S, and 28S) are identifiable in each gradient. The striking difference between pulse

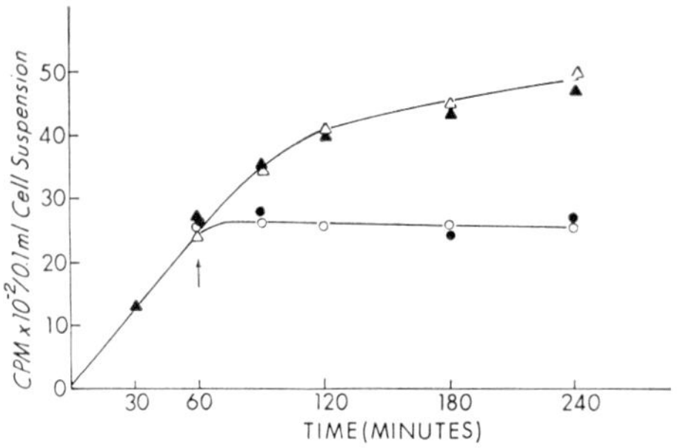

Figure 6. Comparison of kinetics of incorporation of ^{3}H-uridine into continuously labeled and pulse-chase labeled cell suspensions from immune and nonimmune rabbits. Lymph node cell suspensions were prepared and assayed as in Fig. 1 from one immunized rabbit (△ and ○) and from three nonimmune rabbits (● and ▲). Two separate flasks contained identical concentrations of ^{3}H-uridine (3×10^{-6} M) and aliquots of lymph node cells from the immunized rabbit. To one of these flasks (○) was added a 200-fold excess of unlabeled uridine after 60 min (*arrow*) and the incubation was continued and sampled at 90, 120, 180 and 240 min while the other flask (△) served as a continuously-labeled, control cell suspension. In a similar fashion, two flasks contained cell suspensions from the pool of nonimmune cells and the same ^{3}H-uridine concentration (3×10^{-6} M). To one of these (●), a 200-fold excess of unlabeled uridine was added after 60 min (*arrow*) and the other flask (▲) served as a continuously labeled control. After 240-min incubation all four flasks were chilled, the remaining cells were harvested by centrifugation, and the whole cell RNA was isolated for sucrose gradient analysis. The animal which served as the immune cell donor was killed 16 days after immunization with 1 mg TNP-BγG.

labeled and continuously labeled RNA from immune cells is in the amount of radioactivity in the 12 to 13S region of the gradient. In the gradient of RNA from continuously labeled nonimmune cells, the amount of ^{3}H-RNA in the 12 to 13S region is not nearly as great relative to the 28S peak. It seems likely that the leading and trailing edges of the 12 to 13S peak of ^{3}H-RNA from immune cells so overlap the 4S and 18S peaks that the latter appear to be greater than expected when compared with the magnitude of the 28S peak in the same gradient. In addition to the three major classes of stable RNA, three of the gradient profiles (7*A*, 7*C* and 7*D*) permit tentative identification of ^{3}H-RNA peaks attributable to precursors of ribosomal RNA.

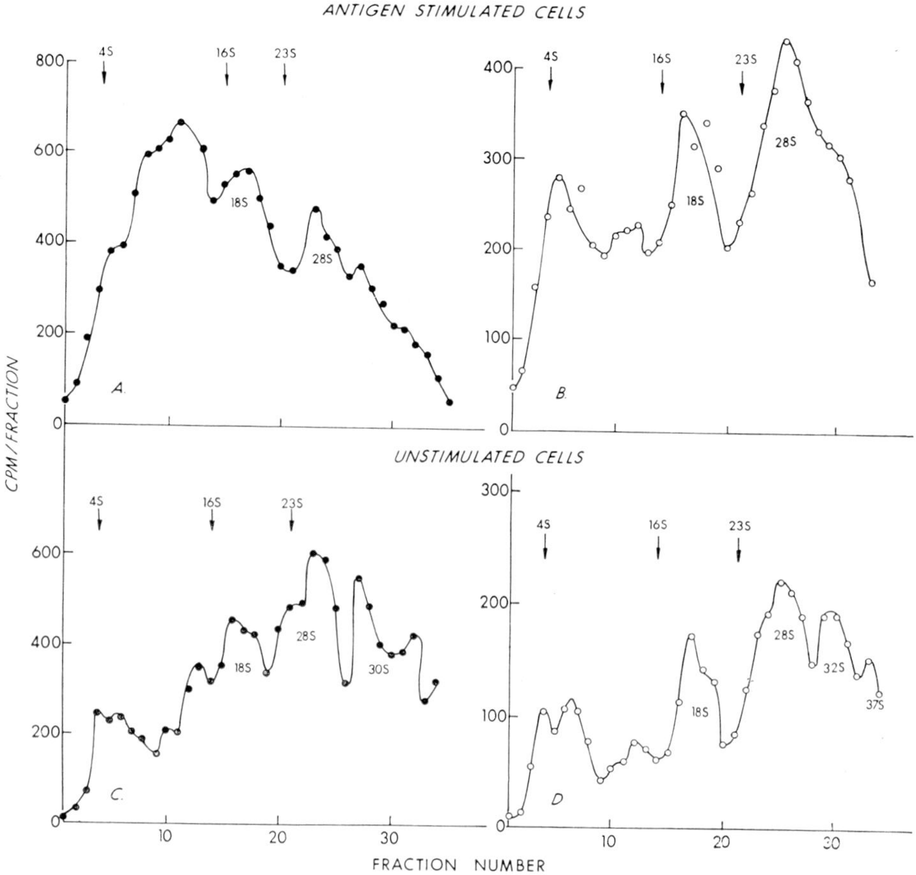

Figure 7. Sucrose gradient analyses of RNA from whole lymph node cells from antigen-stimulated and from unstimulated rabbits. The four sucrose gradient radioactivity profiles were obtained from the four incubation flasks described in the legend to Fig. 6. Gradient A was obtained with ^{3}H-RNA from continuously labeled and gradient B with pulse-chase labeled antigen-stimulated cells. Patterns *C* and *D* were obtained with ^{3}H-RNA from continuously labeled or pulse-chase labeled unstimulated cells respectively. Each gradient contained an internal marker of ^{14}C-uracil labeled *A. aerogenes* RNA containing 4S, 16S and 23S peaks (*see arrows*). Gradient fractions were precipitated with 10% TCA, plated on glass fiber filters and ^{14}C and ^{3}H radioactivity were determined simultaneously on each sample by liquid scintillation counting. Only the ^{3}H counts are plotted.

DISCUSSION

The foregoing results establish the feasibility of preparing highly labeled ^{3}H-RNA by short-term incubation of lymph node cells in a totally synthetic medium containing 5-^{3}H-uridine, a highly specific precursor of cellular RNA. Kinetic experiments indicated relatively minor differences between the rate of uridine incorporation into lymph node cells from antigen-stimulated and from nonimmune rabbits. There was a monophasic rise and fall in uridine incorporation rate per cell with a peak occurring at 5 days (Fig. 4). Many experiments showed no detectable difference in rates of uridine incorporation between unstimulated lymphoid cells and cells obtained several weeks after a single injection of antigen in Freund's adjuvant (Fig. 1). Although prolonged incubations can be performed *in vitro*, the rate of uridine incorporation was reduced to about 9% of the initial rate after 90 min of incubation at 37°C. This change in rate suggests that the medium becomes exhausted in some vital component. This rate change was unaltered by addition of 10% fetal calf serum, and did not appear to be related to limiting amounts of uridine or amino acids. Autoradiography showed that virtually all cells incorporated ^{3}H-uridine. Only 3% (Table III) of the cells from the regional lymph nodes of antigen-stimulated donors bound isotopically labeled antigen (ε-DNPI). This result corresponds to earlier observations made by Green *et al.* in the guinea pig immunized with DNP-BγG (32).

The sucrose gradient patterns of ^{3}H-RNA isolated from pulse-chase and continuously labeled lymph node cells (Fig. 7) revealed that antigen stimulation resulted in the rapid incorporation of ^{3}H-uridine into a major fraction of heterogeneous RNA distributed around 12 to 13S as well as peaks attributable to transfer RNA, ribosomal RNA, and ribosomal RNA precursors. The heavily labeled 12 to 13S fraction corresponds to similar findings of Mach and Vassalli (26), who examined whole spleen cell RNA and showed that pooled gradient fractions from this region had the highest template activity in a cell-free assay of polypeptide synthesis. Since this region of the gradient showed a marked decrease in radioactivity during the chase, the 12 to 13S region must represent a fraction subject to rapid turnover. However, it is uncertain whether it represents mainly messenger RNA molecules, heterogeneous rapidly labeled nuclear RNA (33) or ribosomal RNA precursors.

It should be noted that RNA labeling with ^{3}H-uridine did not achieve a steady state value in the intervals employed in these experiments (up to 14 hr). Since DNA synthesis and cell doubling did not occur to any significant extent, it must be assumed that the radioactivity of whole cell RNA continued to increase with a resulting increase in specific activity.

Identical conditions of immunization, preparation of cell suspensions, and incubation were employed in our studies and in earlier investigations (19–21) of the kinetics of antibody synthesis and secretion. We have confirmed the linear rate of amino acid incorporation into cell protein (unpublished) over a 5-hr period in the same cells in which ^{3}H-uridine incorporation into RNA showed the typical change in rate at 60 to 90 min as shown in Fig. 1. Further studies are in progress to elucidate the mechanism of this change in rate of uridine incorporation.

REFERENCES

1. Kuechler, E. and Rich, A., Proc. Nat. Acad. Sci., *63:* 520, 1969.
2. Gottlieb, A. A., Glisin, V. R. and Doty, P., Proc. Nat. Acad. Sci., *57:* 1849, 1967.
3. Gottlieb, A. A., Biochemistry, *8:* 2111, 1969.
4. Roelants, G. E. and Goodman, J. W., Biochemistry, *7:* 1432, 1968.
5. Roelants, G. E., and Goodman, J. W., J. Exp. Med., *130:* 557, 1969.
6. Halac, E., Rife, V. and Rinaldini, L. M., Nature, *202:* 558, 1964.
7. Adler, F. L., Fishman, M. and Dray, S., J. Immun., *97:* 554, 1966.
8. Bell, C. and Dray, S., J. Immun., *103:* 1196, 1969.
9. Church, R. B., Storb, U., McCarthy, B. J. and Weiser, R. S., J. Immun., *101:* 399, 1968.
10. Cohen, E. P., Proc. Nat. Acad. Sci., *57:* 673, 1967.
11. Raska, K. and Cohen, E. P., Nature, *217:* 720, 1968.
12. Greenberg, L. J. and Uhr, J. W., Proc. Nat. Acad. Sci., *58:* 1878, 1967.
13. Greenberg, L. J. and Uhr, J. W., Cold Spring Harbor Symp. Quant. Biol., *32:* 243, 1967.
14. Kimmel, C. B., Biochim. Biophys. Acta, *182:* 361, 1969.
15. Cooper, H. L., J. Biol. Chem., *243:* 34, 1968.
16. Cooper, H. L., J. Biol. Chem., *244:* 1946, 1968.
17. Lazda, V. A., Starr, J. L. and Rachmeler, M., J. Immun., *101:* 349, 1968.
18. Lazda, V. A., Starr, J. L. and Rachmeler, M., J. Immun., *101:* 359, 1968.
19. Helmreich, E., Kern, M. and Eisen, H. N. J. Biol. Chem., *236:* 464, 1961.
20. Kern, M. and Eisen, H. N., J. Exp. Med., *110:* 207, 1959.
21. Helmreich, E., Kern, M. and Eisen, H. N., J. Biol. Chem., *237:* 1925, 1962.
22. Little, J. R. and Donahue, H. A., Proc. Nat. Acad. Sci., In press.
23. Little, J. R. and Eisen, H. N., in *Methods in Immunology and Immunochemistry*, Edited by C. Williams and M. Chase, Vol. 1, p. 128, Academic Press, Inc., New York, 1967.
24. Kennell, D., in *Methods in Enzymology*, Edited by L. Grossman and K. Moldave, Vol. 12, p. 686, Academic Press, Inc., New York, 1967.
25. Davidson, J. D. and Feigelson, P., Int. J. Appl. Radiat., *2:* 1, 1957.
26. Mach, B. and Vassalli, P., Proc. Nat. Acad. Sci., *54:* 975, 1965.
27. Marmur, J., J. Molec. Biol., *3:* 208, 1961.
28. Bond, V. P., Fliedner, T. M., Cronkite, E. P.,

Rubini, J. R., Brecher, G. and Shork, P. K., Acta Haemat., *21:* 1, 1959.

29. Little, J. R. and Counts, R. B., Biochemistry, *8:* 2729, 1969.

30. Hunter, W. M. and Greenwood, F. C., Nature, *194:* 495, 1962.

31. Kennell, D. and Kotoulas, A., J. Bact., *93:* 334, 1967.

32. Green, I., Vassalli, P., Nussenzweig, V. and Benacerraf, B., J. Exp. Med., *125:* 511, 1967.

33. Church, R. and McCarthy, B. J., Proc. Nat. Acad. Sci., *58:* 1548, 1967.

The Journal of Immunology
Copyright © 1970 by The Williams & Wilkins Co.

Vol. 105, No. 3, September 1970
Printed in U.S.A.

COMPLEMENT FIXATION AND IMMUNODIFFUSION TESTS FOR ASSAY OF HEPATITIS-ASSOCIATED "AUSTRALIA" ANTIGEN AND ANTIBODIES[1]

NATHALIE J. SCHMIDT and EDWIN H. LENNETTE

From the Viral and Rickettsial Disease Laboratory, California State Department of Public Health, Berkeley, California 94704

Received for publication March 18, 1970

A serologic comparison was made of "Australia" (Au) antigens and antisera from different individuals using complement fixation (CF) and immunodiffusion tests. Titers of Au antigens varied widely in block CF titrations and in immunodiffusion tests against different antisera. CF titers of the antisera varied to a lesser extent in tests against different antigens. The importance of using optimal proportions of reagents for assay of Au antigen or antibody was demonstrated in both CF and immunodiffusion tests. In CF tests an excess of antigen produced an extensive "prozone" of inhibitory activity, and it was essential to examine a wide range of serum dilutions for antigen in order to avoid "false negative" results. An excess of either antigen or antibody was also shown to be inhibitory in immunodiffusion tests. The sensitivity of immunodiffusion assays for Au antigen or antibody could be enhanced by testing sera adjacent to wells containing positive reagents. Thus, of 204 sera from hepatitis patients which were positive for Au antigen by CF, 197 (approximately 98%) were positive by immunodiffusion; of 280 sera negative by CF, only 1 gave a positive immunodiffusion reaction. In contrast to findings reported by others, only a low proportion of sera from hepatitis patients in this study showed anti-complementary activity, and the activity was not reversed by an excess of Au antigen, although in some instances it was reduced by treatment with either antigen-containing or negative human sera. Sera from a few hepatitis patients in whom Au antigen had disappeared showed low titers of CF activity against their homologous antigens, which suggested that the convalescent-phase sera might contain very low levels of free Au antibody.

An antigen, first detected in the serum of an Australian aborigine and therefore termed "Australia antigen," has been shown to be present in the serum of a high proportion of patients with "serum hepatitis" (1, 2). There have been conflicting reports (3–7) as to the occurrence of the antigen in patients with so-called "infectious" hepatitis, characterized by a shorter incubation period. The "SH" antigen, reported by Prince (3) to appear during the incubation period of serum hepatitis, is identical to the Australia (Au) antigen (7, 8). Biophysical studies (5, 9–11) have shown the Au antigen to be a particle with a size and morphology resembling that of some of the smaller animal viruses, and it has been speculated that this particle might actually be the viral etiologic agent of hepatitis. This view has been strengthened by the findings that donor bloods containing Au antigen have produced hepatitis in recipients (4, 6, 12, 13), and also by the demonstration, through fluorescent antibody staining, that Au antigen was present in the liver cells of patients with viral hepatitis (14).

Free antibody to the Au antigen has not been conclusively demonstrated in the sera of individuals convalescent from viral hepatitis, but it is present in the sera of some persons who have received multiple blood transfusions, in which case it was presumably elicited by repeated exposure to antigen present in donor bloods. Antibody has also been produced by immuni-

[1] This study was supported by Grant AI-01475 from the National Institute of Allergy and Infectious Diseases, National Institutes of Health, United States Public Health Service.

zation of rabbits (15) and chimpanzees (16) with sera containing the antigen.

Assays for Au antigen are useful in detecting blood products which might produce hepatitis in recipients and also as an aid in the diagnosis of viral hepatitis infections, and there is increased interest on the part of blood bank and diagnostic laboratories in performing tests for this antigen. Au antigen and antibodies were first detected by immunodiffusion tests (1–3), which, although possessing the advantages of simplicity and economy, are relatively insensitive for detecting small quantities of antigen or antibodies. Recently, complement fixation (CF) tests have been described for assay of Au antigen and antibodies (17, 18), and CF tests were shown to detect lower concentrations of antigen and antibody than were demonstrable by immunodiffusion.

In the present study, a comparison was made of the relative sensitivity of immunodiffusion and CF tests for detection of Au antigen and antibodies. Factors affecting the sensitivity of the assays were studied and methods were explored for increasing the sensitivity of tests. An inquiry was made into possible differences in the reactivity of antigens and antisera from different individuals. The occurrence of anti-complementary activity in sera from hepatitis patients was studied, since it has been reported that sera from a high proportion of hepatitis patients are anticomplementary (17), and it has been suggested that this activity might be due to hepatitis antigen-antibody complexes. Also, the possibility was explored of demonstrating Au antibody in convalescent-phase sera from hepatitis patients.

MATERIALS AND METHODS

Sera examined. Reference sera containing Au antigen or antibody were provided by Dr. L. F. Barker of the Division of Biologics Standards, National Institutes of Health, Bethesda, Md. Sera from 25 patients who had received multiple transfusions were obtained from Dr. M. Silvija Hoag of the Hematology Research Laboratory, Children's Hospital, San Francisco, Calif. Sera from 3 of these patients contained Au antigen, 10 contained antibody, and 12 patients were negative for both. A total of 484 sera representing serial bleedings from 86 hepatitis patients from the San Francisco General Hospital were obtained from Drs. Moses Grossman and Austin Brewin.

Immunodiffusion tests. Tests were conducted in flat-bottom cups in plastic panels (Linbro Chemical Company, model FB-54). Each cup received 0.5 ml of molten gel consisting of 0.8% agarose, 0.45% NaCl and 0.1% sodium azide; this formed a layer approximately 3 mm in depth. Wells 3 mm in diameter were punched into the solidified gel; the center-to-center distance between the central and peripheral wells was 6 mm. Approximately 9 μl of antigen or antiserum were added to appropriate wells and tests were incubated in a humidified atmosphere at 37°C for 1 day followed by incubation at room temperature for 4 to 5 days. Sera were not heat-inactivated for use in immunodiffusion tests.

Complement fixation (CF) tests. The standard micro-CF-technique of this laboratory (19) was employed for the assay of Au antigen and antibody. Prior to examination in CF tests, sera were heated at 56°C for 30 min to inactivate native complement.

RESULTS

Differences in the reactivity of Au antigen and antibody from different individuals. Purcell *et al.* (18) reported that Au CF antibody titers varied in tests against different antigens when "straight line" titrations were employed in which varying dilutions of antiserum were tested against a constant dilution of each antigen. For the present studies, "block titrations" were employed for comparing the reactivity of different Au antigens and antisera.

Table I gives the titers of eight different antigens obtained in CF block titrations using varying dilutions of antigen against varying dilutions of 11 different antisera. The antigen titers are expressed in terms of the highest dilution giving 3-plus or 4-plus complement fixation with the highest dilution of antiserum. Each antigen showed widely different titers against the different antisera. CF titers of the 11 antisera against the eight antigens are shown in Table II; antibody titers showed less variation than antigen titers, differing by only two- to fourfold against the various antigens. The CF titer obtained for an antigen did not relate directly to the antibody titer of the serum against which it was tested. For example, antiserum DaFl, which had one of highest antibody titers, gave low antigen titers while antisera BrJo and RoPo, which had low antibody titers, gave high antigen endpoints.

TABLE I

CF titers of Au antigens obtained in tests against different antisera

Antiserum	Titer[a] of Antigen							
	BeZe	WmCo	Dan.	HaDu	FrGe	ArTh	SyHo	MaMc
1 DaFl	256[b]	64	64	256	32	512	64	64
2 KeKi	1024	256	128	512	128	2048	256	256
3 Ebe.	1024	128	64	1024	128	1024	256	64
4 LaHa	2048	512	128	1024	128	2048	512	256
5 RiCl	256	256	64	128	32	512	128	128
6 DoFl	1024	64	64	128	64	2048	128	128
7 DaGo	64	32	32	1024	128	2048	256	128
8 BrJo	1024	256	64	1024	128	2048	256	128
9 RoPo	2048	1024	64	1024	256	1024	128	64
10 JaCa	128	128	32	1024	32	1024	128	64
11 RoCo		64	32	128	128	1024	128	128
Range of antigen titers	64–2048	32–1024	32–128	128–1024	32–256	512–2048	64–512	64–256

[a] Highest dilution of antigen giving 3-plus or 4-plus complement fixation with the highest dilution of antiserum in block titration.

[b] Reciprocal of antigen titer.

TABLE II

CF titers of Au antisera when tested against different antigens

Antigen	Titer[a] of Antiserum										
	DaFl	KeKi	Ebe.	LaHa	RiCl	DoFl	DaGo	BrJo	RoPo	JaCa	RoCo
1 BeZe	64[b]	64	32	32	64	16	8	8	4	4	<2
2 WmCo	64	32	16	32	16	16	4	8	4	2	2
3 Dan.	32	64	32	32	8	8	4	8	2	4	2
4 HaDu	32	32	16	16	32	16	4	4	4	4	4
5 FrGe	32	32	16	16	16	8	8	4	4	4	2
6 ArTh	32	16	16	16	16	8	8	4	4	2	2
7 SyHo	32	32	16	16	16	16	8	4	2	2	2
8 MaMc	64	32	32	16	8	8	8	4	4	4	2
Range of	32–64	16–64	16–32	16–32	8–64	8–16	4–8	4–8	2–4	2–4	<2–4

[a] Highest dilution of antiserum giving 3-plus or 4-plus complement fixation in a block titration.

[b] Reciprocal of antibody titer.

Figure 1 illustrates the reactions, in block CF titrations, of antigen BeZe against the 10 antisera which fixed complement with this antigen. Each section of the figure compares the reactions of antisera with the same titers, and it is seen that the optimal dilutions of antigen (those giving the highest antibody titer) varied greatly, even against antisera with the same titers. For example, the optimal dilutions of antigen reacting with antiserum DaFl were 1:128 to 1:256 and the optimal dilutions reacting with antiserum KeKi were 1:256 to 1:1024, but both antisera showed antibody endpoints of 1:64 against the antigen. With low-titered antiserum JaCa the optimal dilutions of antigens were 1:64 to 1:128, while with antiserum RoPo, having the same antibody titer, the optimal antigens dilutions were 1:64 to 1:2048. In all block titrations with the eight antigens and 11 antisera, a marked CF inhibitory effect was seen in the region of excess antigen. This has also been noted by other investigators (17, 18).

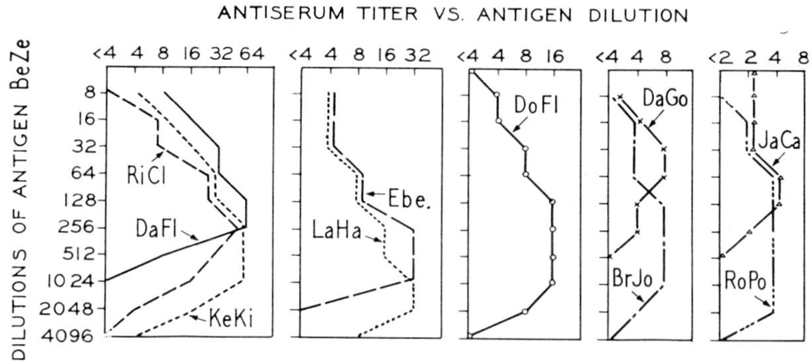

Figure 1. Reactions of Au antigen BeZe in block titrations against 10 different antisera

TABLE III

Immunodiffusion titers of Au antigens obtained against different antisera

Antiserum	Titer[a] of Antigen							
	BeZe	WmCo	Dan.	DaDu	FrGe	ArTh	SyHo	MaMc
1 DaFl	8[b]	4	0	16	2	32	2	4
2 KeKi	64	4	1	32	8	64	4	4
3 Ebe.	32	4	1	16	2	32	4	8
4 LaHa	64	4	1	32	8	128	8	4
5 RiCl	8	2	1	16	4	32	4	2
6 DoFl	16	4	1	8	4	16	4	2
7 DaGo	16	4	0	16	8	16	4	2
8 BrJo	8	4	1	4	1	1	1	0
9 RoPo	8	1	0	0	0	0	1	1
10 JaCa	8	0	0	8	2	8	4	2
11 RoCo	1	0	1	0	0	0	0	0
Range of antigen titers	1–64	0–4	0–1	0–32	0–8	0–128	0–8	0–8

[a] Highest dilution of antigen reacting with undiluted antiserum.
[b] Reciprocal of antigen titer.

Table III shows that immunodiffusion titers of the eight antigens also varied widely in tests against different antisera. There was a greater tendency in immunodiffusion tests than in CF tests for higher-titered antisera to give higher antigen titers, but there were a number of instances in which similar titers were obtained with low-titered (by CF) and high-titered antisera. Antigen titers given in Table III were obtained by testing dilutions of antigen against undiluted sera. None of the antisera gave clear-cut immunoprecipitation reactions when diluted beyond 1:2, and most of them reacted only when used undiluted.

An inhibitory effect of an excess of antigen was also noted in certain immunodiffusion tests, and this is illustrated in Table IV, which compares the intensity of immunodiffusion reactions of various dilutions of antigen BeZe against the different antisera. Against antisera LaHa, BrJo and RoPo concentrated antigen gave negative or minimal reactions, while more dilute antigen gave heavier precipitates. The inhibitory effect of high concentrations of antigen was also noted in titrations with the other antigens; inhibition was most marked with the higher-titered antigens, BeZe, HaDu and ArTh.

Comparative sensitivity of complement fixation and immunodiffusion tests for detection of Au antigen in sera of hepatitis patients. To assess the relative sensitivity of immunodiffusion and CF tests for detecting Au antigen in human sera, a total of 484 sera representing serial bleedings from 86 hepatitis patients from the San Francisco

TABLE IV

The effect of an excess of Au antigen in immunodiffusion tests

Antiserum[a]	Intensity of Immunodiffusion Reaction with BeZe Antigen Diluted							
	Undiluted	1:2	1:4	1:8	1:16	1:32	1:64	1:128
1 DaFl	++	++	+++	++++	±	0	0	0
2 KeKi	++++	+++	+++	+++	+	+	+	0
3 Ebe.	++	++	++	++++	++	+	0	0
4 LaHa	+	+	++	+++	+	0	0	0
5 RiCl	++	+++	++++	+	0	0	0	0
6 DoFl	+++	+++	+++	0	0	0	0	0
7 DaGo	++++	+++	++	+	+	0	0	0
8 BrJo	±	±	±	+++	+	0	0	0
9 RoPo	0	0	0	+	0	0	0	0
10 JaCa	++++	++	+	+	0	0	0	0
11 RoCo	+	0	0	0	0	0	0	0

[a] Antisera used undiluted.

General Hospital were examined by both procedures. In an effort to circumvent the possible inhibitory effect of an excess of antigen or antibody in immunodiffusion tests, all sera were tested against an antiserum showing a low titer by CF (DaGo) and against one showing a relatively high CF titer (RiCl).

In CF tests sera were assayed for antigen at dilutions ranging from 1:4 through 1:2048 in order to overcome possible "false negative" reactions which might be caused by an excess of antigen. The serum dilutions were tested against an antiserum diluted to contain 4 to 8 units of antibody, and all sera in this group were tested against the same antiserum (DaFl). Sera were also examined for possible anti-complementary (AC) activity and for ability to fix complement with a negative serum diluted to the same extent as the Au antiserum.

Forty-seven, or approximately 55%, of the 86 patients had Au antigen demonstrable in one or more of their serum specimens. Forty-five patients had antigen demonstrable by both CF and immunodiffusion tests, and two had antigen demonstrable only by CF. The relationship of Au antigen to the clinical diagnosis of hepatitis and to the time of onset of illness will be discussed in another communication.

Table V compares the results of CF and immunodiffusion tests on the patients' sera. Of the 204 sera positive for Au antigen by CF, 187 gave a positive immunodiffusion reaction with the low-titered antiserum and 173 gave a positive reaction with the higher-titered antiserum. Of the 280 sera negative by CF, only 1 gave a positive immunodiffusion reaction.

TABLE V

A comparison of the results of CF and immunodiffusion assays for Au antigen performed on 484 sera from 86 patients having a clinical diagnosis of viral hepatitis

Reaction of Sera in CF Test	No. of Sera	No. of Sera Positive by Immunodiffusion *vs* Antiserum		No. of Sera Negative by Immunodiffusion *vs* Antiserum	
		DaGo	RiCl	DaGo	RiCl
Positive ≥1:4	204	187	173	17	31
Negative <1:4	280	1	1	279	279
Total	484	188	174	296	310

Table VI relates CF antigen titers of the sera to their reactivity in immunodiffusion tests. Sera with Au antigen titers of 1:128 or higher by CF all gave positive immunodiffusion reactions with both antisera. However, a number of sera having low CF titers, and particularly titers of 1:8, were negative in immunodiffusion tests. Of the 117 sera with CF titers of 1:4 to 1:64, 31 gave negative immunodiffusion reactions with the higher-titered antiserum, while only 17 gave negative reactions with the low-titered antiserum. Apparently the low-titered antiserum contained a more optimal concentration of antibodies which preduced visible precipitates with the low-titered

TABLE VI

Relationship between CF titers of Au antigen and reactions of sera in immunodiffusion tests

CF Titer of Au Antigen	No. of Sera	No. of Sera Positive by Immunodiffusion *vs* Antiserum		No. of Sera Negative by Immunodiffusion *vs* Antiserum	
		DaGo	RiCl	DaGo	RiCl
<1:4	280	1	1	279	279
1:4	2	2	2	0	0
1:8	30	17	10	13	20
1:16	21	19	14	2	7
1:32	38	36	36	2	2
1:64	26	26	24	0	2
1:128	31	31	31	0	0
1:256	26	26	26	0	0
1:512	19	19	19	0	0
1:1024	5	5	5	0	0
≥1:2048	6	6	6	0	0

antigens, while the higher-titered antiserum produced soluble antigen-antibody complexes due to an excess of antibody. Although the low-titered antiserum gave a greater number of positive reactions in immunodiffusion tests, the higher-titered antiserum produced heavier precipitates with the antigens having higher CF titers, and thus it was considered desirable to use both a low- and a high-titered antiserum for detection of Au antigen.

Enhancement of the sensitivity of immunodiffusion tests for Au antigen and antibody. In addition to using a low-titered antiserum to provide an optimal concentration of antibodies for reactions with low-titered antigens, it was found that the sensitivity of immunodiffusion tests for Au antigen and antibody could also be increased in certain other ways.

The micro-method using small, flat-bottomed cups was found to give heavier lines of precipitates than those obtained in parallel tests conducted in larger plates with the same depth of gel and the same size and pattern of reaction chambers. It is possible that the smaller cups restrict diffusion of reagents away from the reaction area and thus heavier lines of precipitate are formed.

The reactivity of low-titered Au antisera and antigens could be greatly enhanced by testing them in wells adjacent to those containing positive reagents. Figure 2 shows that antiserum RoCo failed to give a visible precipitate with the antigen in the central well when tested adjacent to a negative serum, but a precipitate was formed when the serum was tested adjacent to a relatively high-titered antiserum (KeKi). All of the low-titered antisera shown in Table III to give negative immunodiffusion reactions with certain antigens gave positive reactions with the same antigen when tested adjacent to a positive antiserum.

Similarly, the reactivity of most of the low-titered antigens from hepatitis patients which were positive by CF but negative by immunodiffusion could be enhanced by testing the antigens adjacent to a moderately high-titered (1:256 by CF) antigen (MaFa). Of the 17 sera from hepatitis patients which were positive for Au antigen by CF but negative by immunodiffusion, 10 gave positive reactions when tested adjacent to antigen MaFa, and 7 gave negative reactions. Thus, by testing sera adjacent to a positive antigen, the sensitivity of the immunodiffusion test was increased to detect Au antigen in 197 of the 204 sera positive by CF.

Prozone reactions in CF tests for Au antigen. The inhibitory effect of an excess of antigen in CF tests for Au antigen has been noted by other investigators (17, 18), and it was observed in the

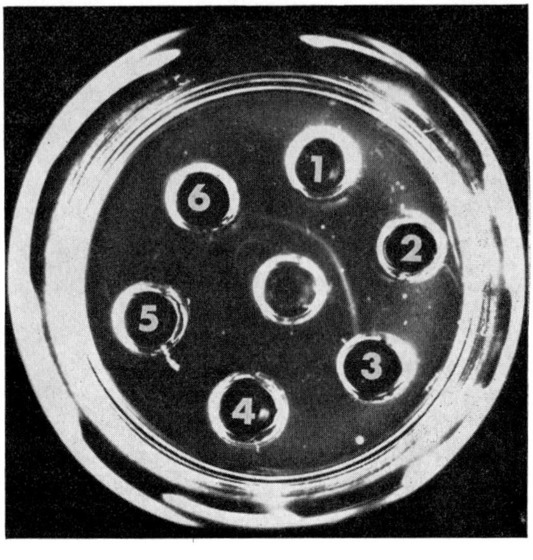

Figure 2. Enhancement of the reactivity of an Au antiserum by testing adjacent to a high-titered antiserum. *Central well,* Au antigen; *wells 1 and 5,* Au antiserum RoCo; *well 2,* Au antiserum KeKi; *wells 3, 4 and 6,* negative sera.

TABLE VII

Occurrence of prozones of inhibitory activity in CF assays for Au antigen. Relationship of antigen titer to extent of prozone

Prozone Endpoint	CF Antigen Endpoint									Total
	1:8	1:16	1:32	1:64	1:128	1:256	1:512	1:1024	≥1:2048	
<1:8	30[a]	19	21	9	9		4			92
1:8		2	17	15	10	9	3			56
1:16				2	12	12	7	1		34 }
1:32						5	5	3		13 } 27%
1:64								1	6	7 }
Total	30	21	38	26	31	26	19	5	6	202

[a] Number of sera.

block titrations conducted in this study. In one report on CF assays for Au antigen (17), sera were examined at dilutions ranging from 1:16 through 1:2048, and in another (18) they were screened at dilutions from 1:2 through 1:16. For our antigen assays on the 484 sera from hepatitis patients, sera were tested at dilutions of 1:4 through 1:2048, and an antiserum was used which was the least inhibited by an excess of antigen in block titrations. Nevertheless, extensive prozones were seen in the CF tests for Au antigen.

Table VII relates the extent of the prozone reaction (negative complement fixation) to the antigen titers of the sera. There was a tendency for the higher-titered sera to show the most extensive prozones, but fairly broad prozones were also seen with some lower-titered sera. Of particular significance is the fact that approximately 27% of the sera containing antigen gave prozone reactions extending through or beyond the 1:16 dilution; thus, over one-fourth of the antigen-containing sera would have been considered negative if the sera had been screened only at dilutions through 1:16.

Anti-complementary activity of sera from hepatitis patients. Shulman and Barker (17) reported that 95% of patients having hepatitis associated with blood products developed anti-complementary (AC) activity in their sera at some time during the course of hepatitis, with AC titers ranging from 1:4 to ≥1:512. They found that the AC activity could be reversed by preliminary incubation with excess Au antigen or antibody, and suggested that the activity might be due to complexes of hepatitis antigen and antibody in the sera. Purcell *et al.* (18) also observed AC activity in the sera of hepatitis patients, but in a lower proportion of patients (5 of 32) and at lower titers (1:2 to 1:16).

In this study, 5 of 39 hepatitis patients without Au antigen and 6 of 47 patients with antigen had one or more AC serum specimens. However, as shown in Table VIII, the AC titers of the sera were generally low, and only 5.5% of the total serum specimens on these patients showed AC activity at titers of 1:4 or greater.

Attempts were made to reverse the AC activity of these sera by treatment with an excess of Au antigen. Twenty-two AC sera from hepatitis patients and two from individuals without hepatitis were treated in parallel with a dilution of serum containing 128 units of Au antigen and with two negative sera diluted to the same extent. Treatment was conducted without incubation prior to the addition of complement and with a preliminary incubation period of 2 hr at 37°C. The results are shown in Table IX. The 1:4 AC titers of 13 sera from hepatitis patients and 1 serum from a non-hepatitis patient were unchanged by treatment with antigen or with negative sera. AC titers of 1:8 to 1:32 were reduced two- to fourfold by treatment with either antigen-containing or negative sera. Serum number 330, which had an AC titer of 1:128, was the only specimen for which the antigen-containing serum reduced the AC activity to a greater extent than did the negative sera. The 1:128 AC titer of hepatitis serum 70-433 was reduced to 1:4 by treatment with antigen-containing and negative sera, and the 1:64 titer of the non-hepatitis serum was reduced four- to eightfold by treatment with positive or negative sera. These results suggest that the AC activity of sera from this group of patients was not due to

TABLE VIII

Anti-complementary (AC) activity of sera from hepatitis patients

Patient Group	No. of Patients	No. of Sera	No. of Sera with AC Titers				
			<1:4	1:4	1:8	1:16	≥1:32
Au antigen present in 1 or more sera	47[a]	280	266	14		1	
Au antigen absent in all sera	39[b]	204	192	5	1	2	4
Total	86	484	458	19	1	3	4
				5.5% (1:4 through ≥1:32)			

[a] One patient had two specimens, two had three, and the remainder had four or more.
[b] Two patients had three specimens and the remainder had four or more.

TABLE IX

Effect of an excess of Au antigen and of negative serum on AC activity of sera from hepatitis patients

Serum Examined	Au Antigen Present	AC Titer of Serum	AC Titer of Serum: No preliminary incubation period			AC Titer of Serum: Incubated at 37°C 2 hr before complement added		
			Antigen excess[a]	Neg. serum 1[b]	Neg. serum 2	Antigen excess	Neg. serum 1	Neg. serum 2
4 Sera from hepatitis patients	0	4[c]	4	4	4	4	4	4
9 Sera from hepatitis patients	+	4	4	4	4	4	4	4
Hepatitis serum no.								
389	0	8	4	4	4	8	8	8
311	0	16	4	4	4	4	4	4
387	0	16	16	8	16	16	16	16
393	+	16	4	4	4	4	8	4
335	0	32	4	4	4	4	4	4
390	0	32	16	8	16	16	16	16
391	0	32	16	16	16	16	8	8
330	0	128	16	32	128	16	128	128
70–433	+	128	4	4	4	4	4	4
1 Serum from non-hepatitis patient	0	4	4	4	4	4	4	4
1 Serum from non-hepatitis patient	0	64	16	16	16	8	8	16

[a] Serum diluted 1:16 to contain 128 units of Au antigen.
[b] Negative serum diluted 1:16.
[c] Reciprocal of titer.

Au antigen-antibody complexes, or at least not to complexes which were dissociable by an excess of Au antigen. Instead the AC activity of these sera appeared to be due to another factor(s) which in some instances could be reduced by treatment with either negative or antigen-containing human sera.

Attempts to demonstrate Au antibody in sera of hepatitis patients. The possibility was explored of demonstrating free Au antibody in the sera of patients convalescent from hepatitis by using their own homologous antigen for CF and immunodiffusion tests. Antigen-containing serum collected early in the course of infection was used to test for antibodies in a later serum from the same patient, collected after antigen had disappeared. Sera from 22 hepatitis patients were examined for Au antibody against their homologous antigens. The sera were tested in CF block titrations at dilutions of 1:2 through 1:32 against varying dilutions of the homologous antigen. In immunodiffusion tests the sera were examined for antibody in wells adjacent to those containing a positive antiserum.

Sera from 14 of the 22 patients had CF antibody titers of <1:4 and gave negative reactions in immunodiffusion tests. Serum from one patient had a CF titer of 1:2 against the homologous antigen, and at this dilution it did not show AC activity or CF activity with a negative serum. Sera from seven patients had CF titers of 1:4 against their homologous antigens; all of these sera were AC at the 1:2 dilution, but at the 1:4 dilution they were not AC and did not react with negative serum. Thus, very low levels of CF activity, which might be attributable to antibody, were demonstrable for some of the patients' convalescent-phase sera, but the CF titers barely exceeded the AC activity of the sera.

In immunodiffusion tests, two of the sera with a 1:4 CF titer gave reactions suggesting that they might contain Au antibody; the arc of precipitate formed by the antigen and the positive antiserum was deviated by the test serum, which is characteristic of a reaction in which antibody is present in the test serum but at too low a concentration to form a precipitate (20). Sera from the 20 other patients gave negative reactions in immunodiffusion tests.

DISCUSSION

The block titrations on different antigens and antisera illustrated the importance of using optimal proportions of reagents in CF assays for Au antigen or antibody. Since the optimal dilutions of an antigen or antiserum may vary in tests against different reagents, it is preferable to test varying dilutions of antigen against varying dilutions of antiserum, or at least to test a number of dilutions past the expected zone of inhibition by an excess of antigen or antibody. In this laboratory sera are assayed for Au antibody in block titrations against varying concentrations of antigen, and they are assayed for antigen at dilutions of 1:4 through 1:2048 against 4 to 8 units of antibody. The block titrations also demonstrated the difficulty in assigning a CF titer to Au antigen preparations, since titers are dependent upon the antiserum used for assay.

Whether differences in the reactivity of Au antigens and antisera from different individuals are a reflection of antigenic variation can not be clearly established by tests using antisera from multiply transfused persons, since these individuals have probably been exposed to antigens from a number of different individuals. Antigenic variation in Au antigens might best be demonstrated by serologic comparisons using antisera from animals immunized with antigen from a single individual, and one who has not received multiple transfusions.

The importance of using optimal proportions of reagents was also demonstrated in immunodiffusion tests. An excess of antigen was shown to give negative or minimal reactions with low-titered antisera, and in some instances a low-titered antiserum formed visible precipitates with low-titered antigens which gave negative reactions with a higher-titered antiserum.

Although the CF test was somewhat more sensitive than immunodiffusion tests for detection of Au antigen, the latter is a simpler and more economical technique which can serve as a useful screening procedure for demonstrating the presence of antigen. Sera negative by immunodiffusion can then be tested by the more sensitive CF technique. The sensitivity of the immunodiffusion test for detecting Au antigen or antibody can be greatly enhanced by testing sera in wells adjacent to those containing positive reagents.

The marked CF inhibitory effect of an excess of antigen, which produces a "prozone" reaction, must be taken into consideration in performing assays for Au antigen, and sera should be tested at a number of dilutions extending beyond the expected prozone in order to avoid "false negative" results. In the present study over one-fourth of the sera containing Au antigen showed prozones extending through or beyond the 1:16 dilution of test serum. It is possible that higher-titered antisera would give less extensive prozones in CF antigen assays.

Our findings on the anti-complementary activity of sera from hepatitis patients are at variance with those reported by Shulman and Barker (17) who noted that AC activity was present in the sera of 95% of hepatitis patients and that this activity was reversible by an excess of Au antigen or antibody. Only a very low proportion of sera from the hepatitis patients in our study showed AC activity. In fact, the proportion of AC sera in this group was no higher than that generally seen in this laboratory for other blocks of sera which have been stored in the frozen state. For example, in one set of 240 sera from pregnant women, tested in this laboratory as a part of a perinatal study, 12% showed AC titers of 1:4 or greater. In contrast, only 5.5% of sera from the hepatitis patients had an AC titer of 1:4 or greater. (It is well-recognized that low dilutions of serum tend to fix complement nonspecifically, and many sera show AC activity at a dilution of 1:2; for this reason viral CF tests are generally performed on sera diluted 1:8, and in some instances 1:4.)

With a single exception, the AC activity of sera from hepatitis patients in our study could not be specifically reduced by treatment with an excess of Au antigen. Instead, the activity was either unchanged or reduced to an equal degree by antigen-containing serum or negative human serum. Thus, it would appear that the AC activity in most of the sera from our group of hepatitis patients was due to factors other than Au antigen-antibody complexes. These findings point up the difficulties which may be encountered in attempting to determine whether AC activity of hepatitis sera is specifically related to Au antigen-antibody reactions.

It has been suggested that inability to demonstrate Au antibody in the sera of patients convalescent from hepatitis might be attributable to the fact that the small quantities of antibody produced are bound to antigen (17). This concept has been strengthened by the electron microscopic studies of Almeida and Waterson (21) who observed complexes of Au antigen and antibody in the sera of a patient with chronic hepatitis and one with fatal hepatitis. In the latter case the immune complexes appeared to contain a low proportion of antigen and an excess of antibody, but no mention was made of the demonstration of free antibody by immunodiffusion or CF. In the present studies, convalescent-phase sera from 7 of 22 patients in whom Au antigen had disappeared showed low levels of CF activity against the patients' homologous Au antigen, but the specificity of these titers might be open to question, since they barely exceeded the AC activity of the sera. Thus, more sensitive techniques are required to demonstrate conclusively the presence of free Au antibody in sera of patients convalescent from hepatitis.

These studies have illustrated some of the pitfalls which may be encountered in performing CF or immunodiffusion assays for Au antigen or antibody, and they point up the need for production and standardization of high-titered antisera for use in antigen assays.

Acknowledgments. The authors are indebted to Drs. M. Silvija Hoag, Moses Grossman, Austin Brewin and L. F. Barker for providing the sera used in these studies, and to Dr. Ronald R. Roberto for making arrangements to obtain some of the sera.

REFERENCES

1. Blumberg, B. S., Sutnick, A. I. and London, W. T., Bull. N. Y. Acad. Med., *44:* 1566, 1968.
2. Blumberg, B. S., Sutnick, A. I. and London, W. T., J.A.M.A., *207:* 1895, 1969.
3. Prince, A. M., Proc. Nat. Acad. Sci., *60:* 814, 1968.
4. Gocke, D. J. and Kavey, N. B., Lancet, *1:* 1055, 1969.
5. Hirschman, R. J., Shulman, N. R., Barker, L. F. and Smith, K. O., J.A.M.A., *208:* 1667, 1969.
6. Giles, J. P., McCollum, R. W., Berndtson, I. W., Jr. and Krugman, S., New England J. Med., *281:* 119, 1969.
7. Wright, R., McCollum, R. W. and Klatskin, G., Lancet, *2:* 117, 1969.
8. Prince, A. M., Lancet, *2:* 462, 1968.
9. Bayer, M. E., Blumberg, B. S. and Werner, B., Nature, *218:* 1057, 1968.
10. Barker, L. F., Smith, K. O., Gehle, W. D. and Shulman, N. R., J. Immun., *102:* 1529, 1969.
11. Gerin, J. L., Purcell, R. H., Hoggan, M. D., Holland, P. V. and Chanock, R. M., J. Virol., *4:* 763, 1969.
12. Gocke, D. J., Greenberg, H. B. and Kavey, N. B., Lancet, *2:* 248, 1969.
13. Zuckerman, A. J. and Taylor, P. E., Nature, *223:* 81, 1969.
14. Millman, I., Zavatone, V., Gerstley, B. J. S. and Blumberg, B. S., Nature, *222:* 181, 1969.
15. Melartin, L. and Blumberg, B. S., Nature, *210:* 1340, 1966.
16. Lichter, E. A., Nature, *224:* 810, 1969.
17. Shulman, N. R. and Barker, L. F., Science, *165:* 304, 1969.
18. Purcell, R. H., Holland, P. V., Walsh, J. H., Wong, D. C., Morrow, A. G. and Chanock, R. M., J. Infect. Dis., *120:* 383, 1969.
19. Lennette, E. H., *Diagnostic Procedures for Viral and Rickettsial Infections*, 4th Ed., p. 52, American Public Health Association, Inc., New York, 1969.
20. Ouchterlony, Ö., *Handbook of Immunodiffusion and Immunoelectrophoresis*, Ann Arbor Science Publishers, Inc., Ann Arbor, Mich., 1968.
21. Almeida, J. D. and Waterson, A. P., Lancet, *2:* 983, 1969.

THE JOURNAL OF IMMUNOLOGY
Vol. 105, No. 3, September 1970
Printed in U.S.A.

THE EFFECT OF CYCLOPHOSPHAMIDE ON THE ONTOGENY OF THE HUMORAL IMMUNE RESPONSE IN CHICKENS[1]

S. P. LERMAN[2] AND W. P. WEIDANZ

From the Department of Microbiology, Hahnemann Medical College and Hospital, Philadelphia, Pennsylvania 19102

Received for publication March 17, 1970

Antibody formation and immunoglobulin synthesis were severely depressed in adolescent chickens treated daily with the alkylating agent, cyclophosphamide (Cy), for the first 3 days of extraembryonic life. Most birds failed to produce significant levels of antibodies to three test antigens injected at 7 and 11 weeks of age. Moreover, IgM and IgG levels in the sera of 5 out of 13 Cy-treated birds were less than 0.5% of the immunoglobulin levels found in untreated birds of the same age. The selective nature of Cy suppression on the ontogeny of the humoral immune response was evidenced by the intact graft-*vs*-host reactivity of peripheral blood cells derived from Cy-treated birds.

In chickens, immunoglobulin synthesis and antibody formation are dependent upon the bursa of Fabricius. Suppression of normal bursal development has been shown to cause severe defects in the ontogeny of the humoral immune response (1–4). Among the various procedures which have been employed to interfere with bursal development, bursectomy, achieved *in ovo* by either hormonal (5) or surgical means (6), has produced the most severe deficiency in immunologic capabilities. Birds so treated did not respond to antigenic stimulation and demonstrated severe hypogammaglobulinemia. Moreover, some of these chickens were agammaglobulinemic. The escape of bursal stem cells committed to the plasma cell line of differentiation prior to treatment was presumed to account for the lack of a more uniform agammaglobulinemia in treated birds (7). When near lethal total body x-irradiation was combined with surgical bursectomy in the early post-hatch period, a significant proportion of the treated birds were agammaglobulinemic (8). Apparently, the lymphoid cells, which had populated the peripheral lymphoid tissues prior to bursectomy, were destroyed by x-irradiation.

In search of other agents which could destroy immunocytes in both central and peripheral lymphoid organs we turned to the immunosuppressant, cyclophosphamide (Cy), a potent alkylating agent with known lymphocytotoxicity (9). A brief report from our laboratory (10) has indicated that Cy was indeed capable of interfering with the ontogeny of the humoral immune response in chickens. These findings have been extended in the present investigation by a characterization of the immunologic deficiency resulting from early treatment with Cy. Evidence will be presented to show that Cy is capable of producing severe hypogammaglobulinemia when administered to chicks in neonatal life.

MATERIALS AND METHODS

Cyclophosphamide treatment. On the first 3 days after hatching, groups of 12, 25 and 31 White Leghorn chickens, Cornell Randombred variety, purchased as embryonated eggs from the North Central Regional Poultry Breeding Laboratory, Purdue University, Lafayette, Ind., were injected daily by the intramuscular route with 4, 6 or 8 mg of Cy respectively. Ten birds served as controls and did not receive the drug. Cy was generously donated by Dr. P. A. Walter of the Mead-Johnson Research Center, Evansville, Ind.

Antigens. Bovine serum albumin (BSA), five times recrystallized, was purchased from Pentex Laboratories, Kankakee, Ill. Sheep erythrocytes (SRBC) in Alsever's solution were obtained from the School of Veterinary Medicine, University of Pennsylvania, Philadelphia, Pa. A formalinized

[1] This work was supported by American Cancer Society Institutional Grant IN-8-H.

[2] Supported by National Defense and Education Act, Title IV Graduate Fellowship 68-05-217.

suspension of *Salmonella typhimurium*, strain 76, MUTT, in saline was prepared according to the procedure of Campbell *et al.* (11).

Immunization. At 6 and 10 weeks of age surviving birds were injected intravenously with an antigenic mixture consisting of 0.1 ml of a 20% suspension of SRBC, 3×10^9 formalinized *Salmonella typhimurium*, and 40 mg of BSA, all contained in a total volume of 0.5 ml of saline. The birds were bled immediately before and 1 week after each immunization. All sera were stored at −20°C prior to assay.

Antibody determinations. Antibodies to BSA and SRBC were measured by microtitration techniques described previously (12). Agglutinins against *Salmonella typhimurium* were determined by a modification of a microagglutinin technique used for the measurement of antibody against *Escherichia coli* (12). In this instance, a suspension of formalin-killed bacteria in saline containing 0.02% Merthiolate was standardized to give a reading of 38 Klett units at 420 nm and employed as the test antigen.

Immunoglobulin measurements. To determine the effect of neonatal Cy treatment on production of γ globulin, serum samples from 11-week-old test and control birds were examined by immunoelectrophoresis (13). Precipitin arcs were developed with divalent rabbit anti-chicken γ globulin prepared by the absorption of rabbit anti-chicken serum with chicken plasma lacking immunoglobulins (8). This reagent was capable of detecting IgG in pooled sera from control birds when the sera were diluted 1:200 in saline prior to assay.

Since immunoelectrophoresis is a relatively insensitive technique for the measurement of IgM, test sera were examined by Ouchterlony analysis employing monovalent antiserum specific for chicken IgM. This reagent was prepared by absorbing 5 volumes of divalent anti-chicken globulin with 1 volume of serum obtained from newly hatched chickens (8). The monovalent antiserum was capable of detecting chicken IgM globulin at 0.5% of the concentration present in pooled control sera obtained from 11-week-old birds.

The specificity of the divalent antiserum was identical to that of a reference divalent anti-chicken globulin kindly provided by Dr. W. A. Cain, Department of Pediatrics, University of Minnesota. Proof that our antiserum was capable of precipitating chicken proteins having antibody activity was obtained by the demonstration of specific binding of radiolabeled BSA in autoradiographic studies employing serum from a chicken immunized with BSA.

Graft-vs-host reactions. Cellular immunity was assessed by testing the ability of peripheral blood cells obtained from 8-week-old normal and Cy-treated donors to induce splenomegalia in 15-day-old embryonic recipients (8). Each of six Regional Red Randombred embryos, purchased from the North Central Regional Poultry Breeding Laboratory, was injected intravenously with 0.1 ml of whole donor blood containing 1 unit of heparin. The embryos were then incubated at 39°C for 5 days. The spleen weight and body weight of each surviving embryo was used to calculate the mean relative spleen weight for each experimental group.

As controls, six untreated 15-day-old embryos were injected with 0.1 ml of heat-killed blood cells obtained from an untreated 8-week-old donor bird. Whole blood containing 10 units of heparin/ml was heated at 56°C for 30 min prior to use. The mean relative spleen weight of the control group was calculated from the relative spleen weights of the surviving embryos.

RESULTS

The relationship between the amount of Cy injected on each of the first 3 days of life and survival is shown in Figure 1. While all doses of Cy employed were toxic, the least number of deaths occurred in the group treated with multiple 4-mg doses of the drug. The majority of deaths in each of the groups occurred within 2 weeks following treatment. Relatively few birds died within the 14- to 40-day period. After 40 days birds began to die idiopathically. It should be noted that fecal plugs, a common problem encountered after surgical or hormonal bursectomy (2), did not occur as a consequence of treatment with Cy. At necropsy the bursas of Cy-treated birds were found to be reduced markedly in size when compared with those of untreated birds of the same age.

Early treatment with Cy caused a marked suppression of the primary antibody response to the three test antigens injected at 6 weeks of age (Fig. 2*A*). Ten of 16 treated birds failed to produce detectable levels of antibody. Of 12 Cy-treated birds that received a second immunization 3 weeks later, only one responded in a normal manner (Fig. 2*B*). This same bird had produced antibodies to all three test antigens

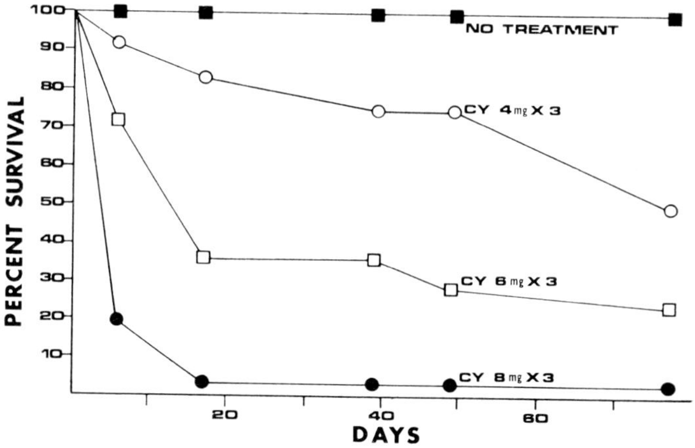

Figure 1. The effect of early treatment with Cy on host survival

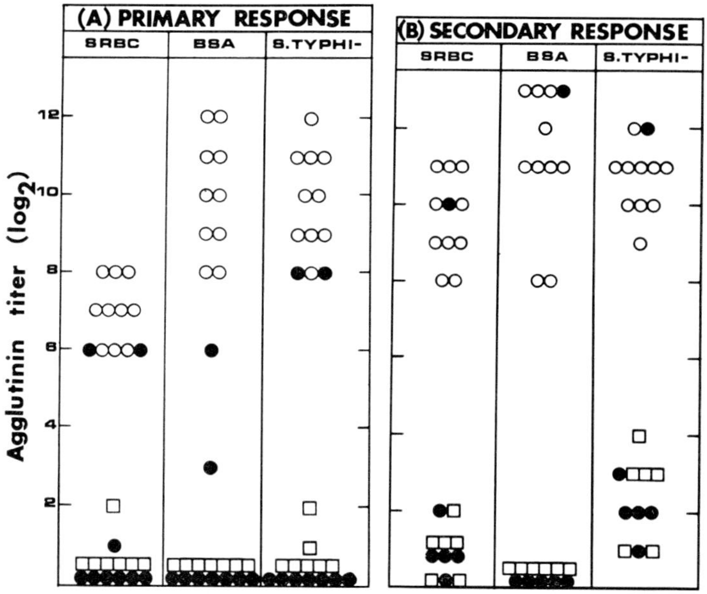

Figure 2. Antibody response of untreated and cyclophosphadmide-treated birds after primary (*A*) and secondary (*B*) antigenic stimulation: ○, no treatment; ●, (Cy) 4 mg × 3; □, (Cy) 6 mg × 3.

following the first immunization. The one chicken surviving the multiple 8-mg treatment schedule also failed to produce significant levels of antibody following both primary and secondary immunization.

Although the data might suggest that the birds injected with multiple 4-mg doses of Cy were less deficient as antibody producers than birds which had received multiple 6-mg doses, the relationship between the dose of Cy employed and the defect in antibody-synthesizing capability must await further investigation.

Early treatment with Cy also had a pronounced effect on immunoglobulin synthesis in later life. Immunoelectrophoresis of sera obtained from 13 Cy-treated birds at 11 weeks of age revealed that they were severely hypogammaglobulinemic with only one exception. The Cy-resistant bird also responded well to antigenic stimulation. Seven birds lacked detectable levels of both IgM and IgG. There was no evidence of a dose-response relationship between the amount of Cy employed and the severity of the resulting IgG deficiency. The concentration of IgG in the serum of normal

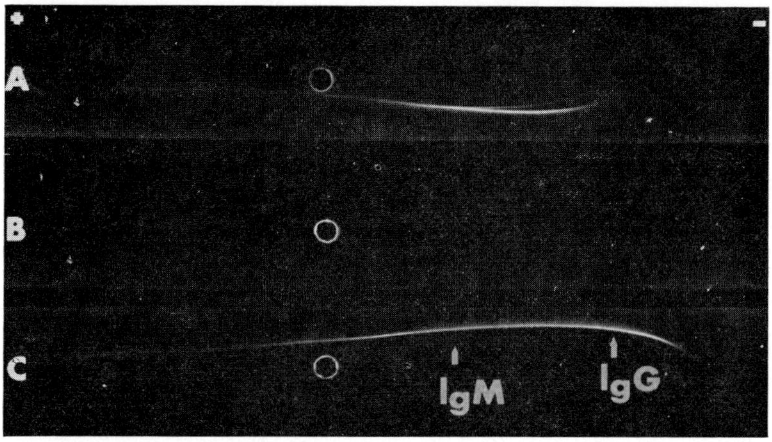

Figure 3. Immunoelectrophoretic patterns of selected sera from cyclophosphamide-treated (*A* and *B*) and untreated (*C*) chickens collected at 7 weeks of age.

chickens of this age is 6 to 12 mg/ml (5, 7). The data would indicate that the Cy-treated birds lacking detectable levels of IgG had less than 0.5% of the amount present in the sera of untreated birds. Immunoelectrophoretic patterns of selected sera are shown in Figure 3. Serum samples A and B were obtained from birds which had been treated with 4-mg doses of Cy. Sample C was taken from an untreated chicken of the same age. Note the absence of immunoglobulins in sample B. In contrast IgG and IgM were present in sample A, but were diminished in amount. Both of these Cy-treated birds failed to synthesize significant levels of antibody upon antigenic stimulation.

As demonstrated by gel diffusion analysis, the IgM levels of Cy-treated birds were markedly depressed. Of the seven birds treated with doses of Cy exceeding 4 mg, four had IgM concentrations less than 0.5% of the level present in pooled control sera. Only one of six birds receiving multiple 4-mg doses of Cy lacked detectable levels of IgM. The results suggest a dose-response relationship between the IgM deficiency and the amount of Cy injected in early life.

The results of the semiquantitative immunoglobulin studies have been summarized in Table I. The presence of IgG and IgM were detected by immunoelectrophoresis and gel diffusion studies, respectively. The results clearly show that a significant proportion of the birds lacked detectable levels of both immunoglobulins.

Cellular immunity, as evidenced by the graft-*vs*-host reactivity of peripheral blood cells, remained functional in Cy-treated birds. As shown in Table II, blood cells, derived from 8-week-old chickens which had received multiple 6-mg doses of Cy at the time of hatch, produced splenomegaly in recipient embryos. While the mean relative spleen weight of embryos injected with cells from Cy birds was less than that of embryos injected with blood cells from untreated donors ($p < 0.1$), an increase in spleen weight exceeding by fivefold the mean relative spleen weight of the control group was observed in one or more recipients in every group of embryos injected with peripheral blood cells obtained from Cy-treated donors.

TABLE I

Serum immunoglobulins in Cy-treated birds

Treatment	No. of Birds	Presence of Immunoglobulins[a]		
		Undetectable	Diminished	Normal
Cy 8 mg × 3	1	1	0	0
Cy 6 mg × 3	6	3	3	0
Cy 4 mg × 3	6	1	4[b]	1

[a] IgM and IgG immunoglobulins were detected by Ouchterlony analysis and immunoelectrophoresis, respectively. Birds with undetectable immunoglobulins had less than 0.5% of the level of IgG and IgM present in pooled sera from untreated birds of the same age. Sera that were scored as having diminished levels of immunoglobulins had significantly less globulin than the pooled control sera.

[b] IgG could not be detected in the sera of two birds within this group.

TABLE II

Graft-vs-host reactivity of peripheral blood cells from Cy-treated and untreated chickens

Donor Treatment	No. of Donors	No. of Survivors/ No. Injected	Mean Relative Spleen Weight
Cy[a]	7	35/42	24.0 ± 2.8[c]
None	6	32/36	36.0 ± 4.4
Control[b]	1	5/6	3.7 ± 1.3[d]

[a] Cyclophosphamide, 6 mg/day on first 3 days of extra-embryonic life.

[b] Heparinized whole blood heated at 56°C for 30 min.

[c] Mean relative spleen weight = mean spleen weight (g) × 10^4/mean body weight (g) ± standard error of the mean.

[d] Mean relative spleen weight = mean spleen weight (g) × 10^4/mean body weight (g) ± standard deviation.

Further analysis of these data revealed that relative spleen weights of individual embryos showed great variation within a group of recipients injected with blood cells derived from a single donor. In contrast, individual relative spleen weights of control embryos injected with heat-killed cells showed little variation from the mean value. The difference in the ability of blood cells derived from treated and untreated donors to induce splenomegaly in immunologically incompetent recipients may simply reflect the genetic disparity between individual donor birds as well as between individuals within the recipient group.

DISCUSSION

These results demonstrate that Cy is capable of selectively suppressing the ontogeny of the humoral immune response in chickens. The immunologic deficiencies resulting from treatment with this drug are similar to those resulting from bursectomy *in ovo* and bursectomy combined with x-irradiation in early neonatal life (5, 6, 8). A significant proportion of the Cy-treated chickens failed to synthesize detectable amounts of IgM and IgG while the remaining birds produced one or both of the immunoglobulins which have been found in the serum of normal birds (8). Furthermore, most chickens failed to make antibodies in response to antigenic stimulation. Cellular immune mechanisms as shown by the graft-*vs*-host reactivity of peripheral blood cells remained functional in Cy-treated birds.

While the overall effect of Cy on humoral immunity is essentially the same as that caused by other procedures interfering with the development of the immune response in chickens, the mechanism of action obviously is different. That is, stem cells committed to the plasma cell line of differentiation have, in all likelihood, reached the peripheral lymphoid tissues at the time of hatching (8, 14, 15). These cells were probably destroyed by the known cytotoxic action of the drug. In any event, evidence that differentiation did not occur after Cy treatment is supported by the absence of detectable immunoglobulins in the sera of treated birds. For the same reason, the repopulation of peripheral lymphoid tissues with competent cells apparently did not take place. This would indicate that Cy also acted directly upon the bursa of Fabricius to prevent the eventual migration of resident stem cells to peripheral lymphoid tissues during the post-treatment period. The destruction by Cy of the bursal microenvironment, the only site where the induction of the plasma cell line of differentiation occurs (16), could account for the prolonged duration of the resulting deficiency. Alternatively, the inductive environment of the bursa may remain unaffected by Cy treatment. Instead, the drug might destroy the primordial stem cells. Reconstitution studies involving progenitor lymphoid cells and bursal grafts should serve to delineate the mechanism of Cy action on the bursa of Fabricius.

When compared with other agents capable of causing severe hypogammaglobulinemia or agammaglobulinema, the use of Cy possesses certain advantages. For example, it is easily administered in measured doses requiring neither special techniques nor instruments. Since the animals do not develop fecal plugs, post-treatment care consists of providing feed and water *ad libitum*. Cy treatment can be accomplished in a minimal amount of time, which should prove particularly useful in preparing large numbers of deficient birds.

The observation that Cy can suppress the ontogeny of the humoral immune response in birds may be an important step in developing even more consistent models of avian agammaglobulinemia. It is possible that this goal could be achieved by changing the regimen of drug treatment or by employing other cytotoxic agents. In this regard, preliminary findings (10) and other data to be reported elsewhere in detail have demonstrated that hormonal bursectomy combined with neonatal treatment with Cy produced agammaglobulinemia in a higher percentage of treated birds than has been observed following Cy treatment alone (to be published).

Acknowledgment. We thank Dr. Peter Stelos for performing the autoradiographic studies with the divalent antiserum.

ADDENDUM

After this paper was submitted for publication, a communication by F. Seto and W. G. Henderson (J. Exp. Zool., *169:* 501, 1968) came to our attention. They demonstrated that the formation of both natural and immune antibodies against mouse erythrocytes was suppressed in chickens which had received a single dose of Cy in early life. In their study the immunologic deficient state was short lived.

REFERENCES

1. Glick, B., Chang, T. S. and Jaap, R. G., Poult. Sci., *35:* 224, 1956.
2. Meyer, R. K., Rao, M. A. and Aspinall, R. L., Endocrinology, *64:* 890, 1959.
3. Mueller, A. P., Wolfe, H. R. and Meyer, R. K., J. Immun., *85:* 172, 1960.
4. Szenberg, A. and Warner, N. L., Nature, *194:* 146, 1962.
5. Warner, N. L., Uhr, J. W., Thorbecke, G. J. and Ovary, Z., J. Immun., *103:* 1317, 1969.
6. Cooper, M. D., Cain, W. A., Van Alten, P. J. and Good, R. A., Int. Arch. Allerg., *35:* 242, 1969.
7. Van Meter, R., Good, R. A. and Cooper, M. D., J. Immun., *102:* 370, 1969.
8. Cooper, M. D., Peterson, R. D. A., South, M. A. and Good, R. A., J. Exp. Med., *123:* 75, 1966.
9. Aisenberg, A. C., J. Exp. Med., *125:* 833, 1967.
10. Lerman, S. P. and Weidanz, W. P., Bact. Proc., p. 91, 1969.
11. Campbell, D. H., Garvey, J. S., Cremer, N. E. and Sussdorf, D. H., *Methods in Immunology*, p. 163, W. A. Benjamin, Inc., New York, 1964.
12. Weber, W. T. and Weidanz, W. P., J. Immun., *103:* 537, 1969.
13. Scheidegger, J. J., Int. Arch. Allerg., *73:* 103, 1955.
14. Cooper, M. D., Schwartz, M. L. and Good, R. A., Science, *151:* 471, 1966.
15. Woods, R. and Linna, J., Acta Path. Microbiol., *64:* 470, 1965.
16. Moore, M. A. S. and Owen, J. J. T., Develop. Biol. *14:* 40, 1966.

THE JOURNAL OF IMMUNOLOGY
Vol. 105, No. 3, September 1970

NEURAMINIDASE- AND HEMAGGLUTININ-INHIBITING ANTIBODIES IN SERUM AND NASAL SECRETIONS OF VOLUNTEERS IMMUNIZED WITH ATTENUATED AND INACTIVATED INFLUENZA B/ENG/13/65 VIRUS VACCINES

JEAN C. DOWNIE

From the Virus Research Laboratory, Lodge Moor Hospital, University of Sheffield, Sheffield 10, England

Received for publication March 13, 1970

The antibody response to virus hemagglutinin and neuraminidase in serum and nasal secretions was studied in 19 volunteers immunized with attenuated or inactivated influenza B/Eng/13/65 virus vaccines. The live attenuated virus given intranasally produced high titers of neuraminidase- and hemagglutinin-inhibiting antibodies in nasal secretions and moderate titers in serum. High titers of hemagglutinin-inhibiting antibody were also present in nasal secretions and serum after subcutaneous immunization with inactivated influenza virus. However, the inactivated virus was found to produce little or no neuraminidase-inhibiting antibody in nasal secretion despite high titers of this antibody in the serum. Absorption studies indicated that the neuraminidase-inhibiting antibody in nasal secretion was associated with the IgA class of immunoglobin. These observations indicate that the intranasal administration of live virus was a better route for the stimulation of neuraminidase-inhibiting antibody in nasal secretion than a single subcutaneous dose of inactivated virus.

Influenza virus has at least two virus-coded, external antigenic components: the hemagglutinin and the enzyme neuraminidase. Antibody against the hemagglutinin is found in the serum after infection or immunization with influenza viruses and it is this antibody which has been thought to be principally responsible for virus neutralization. Moreover, the level of antibody produced to the virus hemagglutinin has been used for many years to indicate immunity (1). Less is known about the enzyme component of the virus. However, there is evidence that these two antigens are distinct structural entities of the virus envelope. Thus, recombinant viruses have been isolated which possess the hemagglutinin of one parent virus and the neuraminidase of the other (2). Furthermore, two morphologically distinct sub-units of the influenza virus particle have been isolated, one of which is associated with the enzyme activity, and the other with the hemagglutinin (3). Antibody directed against the neuraminidase inhibits the release of virus from infected cells but does not inhibit the virus hemagglutinin or neutralize its infectivity (4–6).

Schulman (7) has shown that specific immunization of mice against influenza virus neuraminidase reduced the severity of infection after subsequent challenge, and also reduced the ability of certain A2 influenza viruses to be transmitted from one mouse to another. Antibody against neuraminidase was also found in the serum and respiratory secretions of the immunized and infected mice. Although neuraminidase-inhibiting antibody has been found in the serum of persons infected or immunized with influenza viruses (8, 9), nothing has been published concerning its presence or absence in the nasal secretions of such people. In the present study, nasal secretions and sera from volunteers immunized with live or inactivated influenza virus were examined for the presence of virus neuraminidase-inhibiting and hemagglutinin-inhibiting antibody.

MATERIALS AND METHODS

Viruses. A live attenuated influenza B/Eng/13/65 virus vaccine (10) was kindly supplied by Dr. D. C. Breeze, Evans Medical Ltd., Speke. This virus had a titer of $10^{9.4}$ EID_{50}/ml. Formalin-inactivated vaccine was prepared from the same virus strain by Evans Medical Ltd. and contained 5.5 $\times$ 10^3 hemagglutinating units (HAU)/ml.

Volunteers. A group of 19 medical students (aged 21 to 23 years) volunteered to participate in this study. Eleven students were each given an intranasal dose of 1.0 ml of the live attenuated vaccine diluted in Hanks' saline to contain $10^{5.4}$ EID_{50}/ml. The second group of eight volunteers was inoculated by deep subcutaneous injection with 1.0 ml of inactivated virus vaccine. One month later, all the volunteers were given an intranasal dose of 1.0 ml of live attenuated virus vaccine diluted to contain $10^{6.4}$ EID_{50}/ml. The first inoculation of virus was designated as the immunizing dose and the second as the challenge dose of virus. Serial nasal secretions were obtained before and after immunization and after challenge during a total period of 53 days. Serum specimens were collected before immunization, 3 weeks after immunization, and 3 weeks after challenge, and were stored at -20°C.

Collection of nasal secretions. The method for collecting nasal secretions has been described elsewhere (11). Approximately 9 ml of secretion were obtained after multiple nasal washings with sterile phosphate-buffered saline pH 7.2 (PBS). The secretion was then shaken vigorously with glass beads and centrifuged at 500 $\times$ G for 15 min and the supernatant fluid was stored at -20°C. The specimens were tested for the presence of hemoglobin by the guaiac test for occult blood and positive specimens were discarded.

Neuraminidase-inhibition (NI) test. Influenza virus was partially purified and concentrated by absorption onto fowl erythrocytes at 4°C and elution at 37°C into PBS containing 0.8% sodium azide to one-tenth of the original volume.

The neuraminidase activity of the virus preparation was assayed by a modification of the method of Laver and Kilbourne (2). Equal volumes (0.05 ml) of virus, fetuin (2.4% w/v), 0.4 M sodium phosphate pH 5.9 and normal rabbit serum (10% v/v) in a final volume of 0.25 ml were incubated for either 1 hr or 18 hr at 37°C. Normal rabbit serum was incorporated into the test since it was found to enhance the activity of the enzyme (12). Liberated N-acetylneuraminic acid was assayed by a modification of the Warren method in which the color was extracted into n-butanol containing 5% (v/v) concentrated HCl.

In the NI test, the virus was used at a concentration which gave an optical density reading of 0.50 at 549 nm on a Unicam SP 500 spectrophotometer. It was found that the virus concentration required to give this reading after incubation for 18 hr at 37°C was one-tenth that needed after incubation for 1 hr. Because less virus could be used, incubation for 18 hr was found to be 10 times more sensitive for the detection of NI antibody than was incubation for 1 hr.

Serum and nasal secretions were heated at 56°C for 30 min before testing and 0.05 ml of fourfold dilutions were incubated for 1 hr at 4°C with an equal volume of virus. Serum-virus mixtures were incubated with fetuin for 1 hr at 37°C and nasal secretion-virus mixtures were incubated for 18 hr at 37°C. A normal rabbit serum, a normal nasal secretion, and an immune rabbit serum with a titer of 120 (1 hr incubation) and 1280 (18 hr incubation) to influenza B/Eng/13/65 virus were included as controls.

Virus treated with pronase (0.5% w/v) to destroy the hemagglutinin (13) was found to give the same results as untreated virus in the NI test—the untreated virus was used in all tests.

Hemagglutination-inhibition (HI) test. Assays for hemagglutinin and the inhibition of hemagglutination (HI) by serum and nasal secretions were performed according to the methods of Fazekas de St. Groth and Webster (14). Before testing, all specimens were treated with receptor-destroying enzyme (RDE) which was kindly supplied by Dr. G. C. Schild, Institute for Medical Research, Mill Hill. Normal rabbit serum, normal nasal secretion and immune rabbit serum with a titer of 12,800 to influenza B/Eng/13/65 virus were included as controls.

Neutralization test. Nasal secretion specimens in which the titer of HI antibody was less than 1:8 were tested for neutralizing antibody by hemadsorption-inhibition in Patas monkey kidney cell cultures as described elsewhere (11).

Complement fixation (CF) test. CF tests were carried out by standard methods using two exact units of complement and overnight fixation at 4°C.

Absorption of immunoglobins. The immunoglobins in nasal secretions were assayed by the radial diffusion precipitation method in agar

TABLE I

Hemagglutinin-inhibiting and neuraminidase-inhibiting antibody titers in serum of volunteers immunized and challenged with influenza B/Eng/13/65 virus

Immunization Procedure	Total No. in Group	Volunteers Showing Fourfold Rise in Serum HI Antibody	Serum Antibody Titers[a] Pre-trial: day 0 HI antibody	Pre-trial: day 0 NI antibody	Post-immunization: day 21 HI antibody	Post-immunization: day 21 NI antibody	Post-challenge:[b] day 21 HI antibody	Post-challenge:[b] day 21 NI antibody
Live influenza B/Eng/13/65 intranasal	11	SHM	<6	8	12	30	12	30
		RSC	<6	5	6	5	96	60
		JBB	12	10	12	15	48	20
Inactivated influenza B/Eng/13/65 subcutaneous	8	SDT	<6	<5	6,400	60	12,800	80
		FGS	36	5	3,200	20	3,200	30
		MEH	72	5	1,536	30	800	30
		MCT[c]	<6	2	36	2	48	10
		DNS	<6	2	18	2	18	10
		DFS	<6	5	48	5	72	5
		RMS	24	15	96	25	72	20

[a] Serum titers are the reciprocals of the highest dilution which produced 50% inhibition of enzyme activity. Sera were collected 3 weeks after immunization and challenge.

[b] Challenge virus was given intranasally.

[c] This volunteer showed a fourfold rise in serum CF antibody following challenge.

(15). IgA and IgG were specifically absorbed by mixing nasal secretion with an equal volume of goat serum containing anti-human immunoglobin at optimal precipitating concentration (16). After incubation overnight at 4°C, the mixture was centrifuged at 20,000 × G for 20 min. The supernatant was removed and tested by immunodiffusion for specific absorption of the nasal secretion immunoglobin. If the immunoglobin was still present, the above absorption procedure was repeated using small increments of anti-immunoglobin serum until no reaction was detected. Control specimens of immunoglobin and nasal secretion were treated in the same manner as those which were absorbed. Goat anti-human IgA serum was obtained from Hyland Laboratories, Los Angeles, Calif., and goat anti-human IgA and IgM sera were kindly supplied by Professor P. G. H. Gell, Department of Experimental Pathology, Birmingham University, England.

RESULTS

The serologic response of the 19 volunteers to immunization and challenge with virus is given in Table I. Three of the 11 volunteers immunized intranasally with live virus showed a fourfold rise in serum HI antibodies after either immunization or challenge with virus. Seven of the eight volunteers given inactivated virus subcutaneously responded serologically to immunization, and there was no further rise of serum HI antibody titer in this group after challenge with live virus. The 10 volunteers who responded serologically in the HI test to either immunization or challenge with virus were studied in detail.

Serum antibody after intranasal immunization with live virus. Of the three volunteers responding serologically to live virus, volunteer SHM showed a fourfold rise in serum HI and NI antibody titers after immunization and these titers remained unchanged after challenge (Table I). In contrast, volunteers RSC and JBB did not respond serologically to immunization but did show a fourfold or greater rise in serum HI and NI antibody after the challenge dose of live virus.

Serum antibody after subcutaneous immunization with inactivated virus. Of the eight volunteers given inactivated virus subcutaneously, seven (SDT, FGS, MEH, MCT, DNS, DFS and RMS) showed a fourfold or greater rise in serum HI antibody after immunization (Table I). Three of these (SDT, FGS and MEH) also showed a fourfold or greater rise in serum NI antibody after immunization (Table I). Two others (MCT

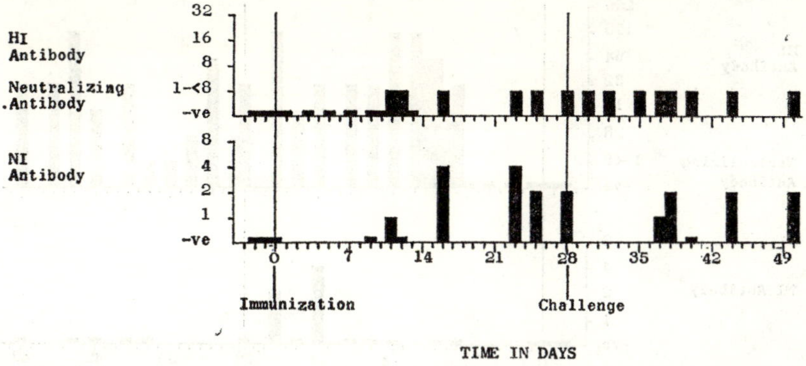

Figure 1. Antibody in nasal secretion after immunization with live influenza B/Eng/13/65 (volunteer SHM, Table I).

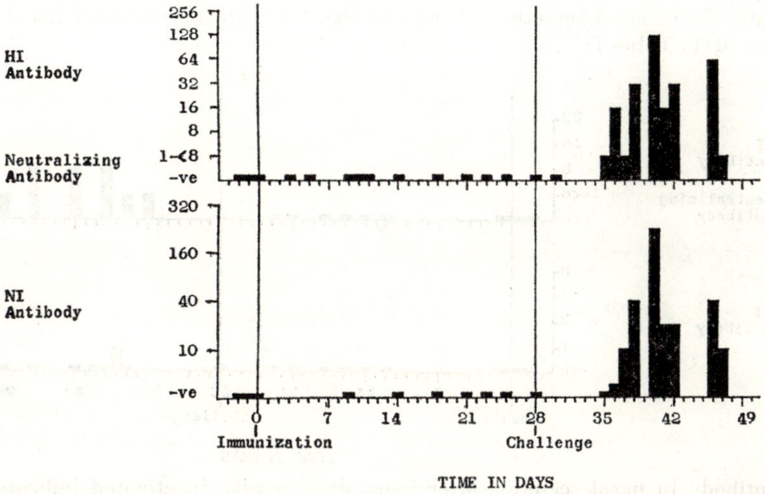

Figure 2. Antibody in nasal secretion after immunization with live influenza B/Eng/13/65 virus (volunteer RSC, Table I).

and DNS) showed no rise in serum NI antibody after immunization, but did show a fourfold rise after challenge with live virus. The remaining two volunteers in this group (DFS and RMS) showed no change in serum NI antibody titers after immunization or after challenge with live virus.

Nasal secretion antibody following intranasal immunization with live virus. There was a good correlation between HI and NI antibody titers in the nasal secretion of those volunteers given live virus intranasally. Antibody to both these antigens appeared in the nasal secretion during the 2nd week after virus was administered and rose to high titers (1:128 and 1:240).

Figure 1 shows the antibody response in nasal secretions of volunteer SHM to immunization with live virus. NI and neutralizing antibody were first detected 11 days after immunization and were consistently found thereafter in low levels of not greater than 1:8. Subsequent challenge with live virus produced no further rise in nasal secretion of either NI or HI antibody.

Figure 2 shows the results of antibody studies on serial nasal secretions of volunteer RSC who responded serologically to the challenge dose of virus but not to the immunizing dose. NI and HI antibody were not detected before immunization with the live attenuated virus or during the 4-week period after immunization. However, both NI and HI antibody were detected 8 days after challenge with live virus and reached peak titers of 1:240 and 1:128 respectively on day 12 after challenge. These results were consistent with those found in the serum in which there was a

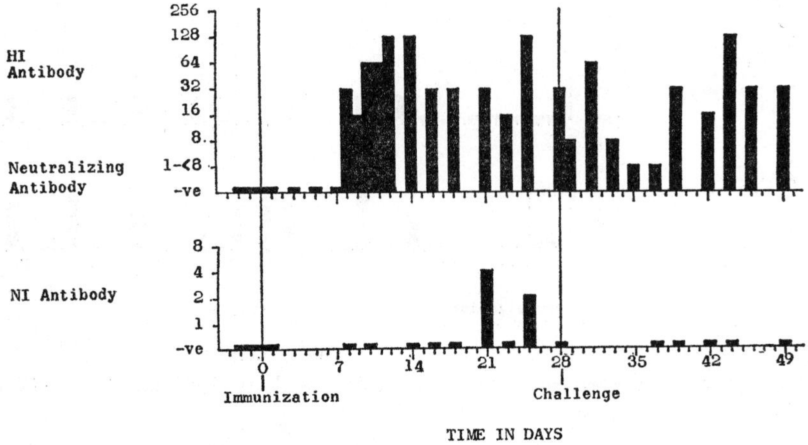

Figure 3. Antibody in nasal secretion after immunization with inactivated influenza B/Eng/13/65 virus (volunteer SDT, Table I).

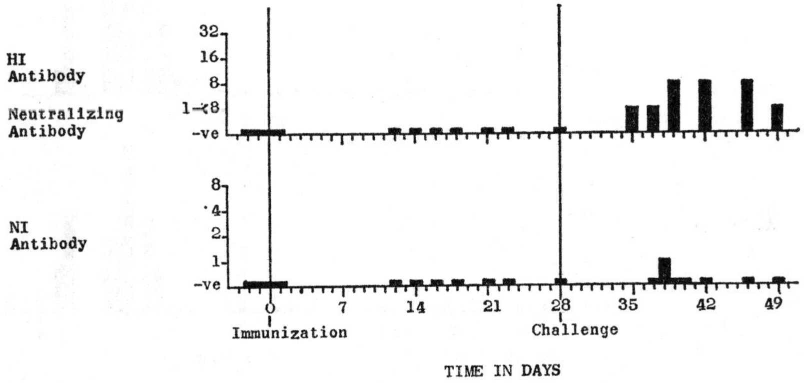

Figure 4. Antibody in nasal secretion after immunization with inactivated influenza B/Eng/13/65 virus (volunteer MCT, Table I).

greater than fourfold rise in both HI and NI antibody titers after challenge (Table I). The results obtained for the nasal secretions from JBB were similar to those found for volunteer RSC; both NI and HI antibody appeared in the nasal secretion 8 days after challenge and were still detectable up to day 21 after challenge. However, the NI and HI antibody titers did not exceed 1:8.

Nasal secretion antibody following subcutaneous immunization with inactivated virus. In contrast to the results with intranasally administered live virus, there was no correlation between the NI and HI antibody titers in nasal secretion after subcutaneous immunization with inactivated virus. Thus, high levels of NI antibody were not detected in those nasal secretions which had high (>1:32) HI antibody titers.

Figure 3 shows the titers of NI and HI antibody in serial nasal secretions from volunteer SDT, which were typical of the findings for those volunteers who showed a 20-fold or greater rise in serum HI antibody after subcutaneous immunization with inactivated virus vaccine (Table I). Relatively high titers of HI antibody (1:32 to 1:128) were present in nasal secretions taken 8 days after immunization and these titers persisted throughout the period of study. However, only two nasal secretions taken during the 4 weeks before challenge were found to contain detectable levels of NI antibody despite high titers of NI antibody in the serum.

The results of volunteer MCT, who showed a fourfold rise in both serum NI and CF antibody after challenge (Table I), are shown in Figure 4. HI and NI antibody were not detected in the

TABLE II

Presence of neuraminidase-inhibition (NI) antibody after the specific absorption of IgA and IgG from nasal secretions of a volunteer immunized and challenged with live influenza B/Eng/13/65 virus (volunteer RSC)

Nasal Secretion Specimen, Day after Challenge	Before Absorption			After Absorption			
	NI[a] antibody titer	Total IgA	Total IgG	Control	IgA absorbed	IgG absorbed	IgA and IgG absorbed
				NI[a] antibody titer			
		mg/100 ml	mg/100 ml				
12	240	20	14	120	<10	60	<10
18	40	8	6	15	<2	20	<2

[a] Titers are the reciprocals of the highest dilution which produced 50% inhibition of enzyme activity.

nasal secretions taken during the 4-week period before challenge. However, after challenge with live virus, both HI and NI antibody were present in low titers (1:8).

Specific absorption of immunoglobin in nasal secretion. IgA and IgG were specifically removed from two specimens of nasal secretion taken from volunteer RSC 12 and 18 days after challenge (Fig. 2) and these were then tested for the presence of NI antibody. IgM was not detected in either of these two specimens. The results of these absorption experiments are shown in Table II. In both instances, the specific removal of IgA also removed the NI activity of the nasal secretion, while the removal of IgG had little or no effect on the NI activity of the secretions when compared to that of the unabsorbed control specimens. These results indicate that the NI antibody is associated with the IgA immunoglobin fraction of nasal secretion.

DISCUSSION

The effectiveness of subcutaneous immunization with inactivated influenza vaccines to protect against infection has been difficult to assess and there is not always a direct correlation between immunity and the level of antibody in serum (17). Smith *et al.* (18) reported that the presence of neutralizing antibody in nasal secretion to parainfluenza type I virus was a better index of immunity than was the level of neutralizing antibody to this virus in the serum. It has since been shown that neutralizing antibody can be demonstrated in both nasal secretions and serum after infection with influenza virus or immunization with inactivated vaccines (19, 20).

Russian workers have developed, and have used for many years, live attenuated influenza virus vaccines which have given good protection in the face of influenza epidemics (21). In addition, Beare *et al.* (22) compared live and inactivated influenza virus vaccines and concluded that the attenuated vaccine given intranasally gave better protection against a challenge virus than did the inactivated vaccine given intramuscularly.

The present study compares the antibody production in serum and nasal secretion of volunteers receiving two immunization procedures commonly used against epidemic influenza. It was shown that live attenuated influenza B/Eng/13/65 virus vaccine given intranasally was capable of stimulating relatively large amounts of both neuraminidase- and hemagglutinin-inhibiting antibodies in nasal secretion as well as in serum. In contrast, subcutaneous immunization with formalin-inactivated vaccine, although producing comparable HI antibody titers in nasal secretions, produced little or no antibody against the virus neuraminidase even when serum levels of NI antibody were relatively high. Thus, the local application of live influenza virus can induce NI antibody in nasal secretions to a greater extent than a single subcutaneous inoculation of inactivated virus. However, one of the main difficulties in using live influenza vaccines at the present time is to attenuate the virus to an acceptable reaction level and yet to retain its infectivity and immunogenicity (22). In this study, only 3 of the 11 volunteers given two doses of live influenza B/Eng/13/65 virus (SHM, RSC and JBB) showed serologic evidence of infection.

Specific absorption tests indicated that the NI activity in nasal secretion was associated with the IgA immunoglobin fraction. Other studies have shown the IgA (11S) is the predominant immunoglobin in nasal secretion (23) and is associated with influenza virus neutralizing antibody (19, 20). In addition, there is evidence that this IgA is produced locally in the cells lining the respiratory tract (23, 24). Since serum neutralizing antibody to influenza is mainly associated with the IgG fraction (25), transudation of NI antibody from the serum into the nasal secretion seems unlikely. Furthermore, two volunteers in this study given inactivated vaccine (SDT and FGS) and who had relatively high levels of NI antibody in their sera (1:20 to 1:80) had little or no NI antibody in their nasal secretion. This suggests a local production of NI antibody.

Acknowledgments. The author would like to thank the medical students of Sheffield University who participated in this study and Professor C. H. Stuart-Harris for his help and criticism of the manuscript.

REFERENCES

1. Bell, J. A., Ward, T. G., Kapiklan, A. Z., Shelokov, A., Reichelderfer, T. E. and Huebner, R. J., J. A. M. A., *165:* 1366, 1957.
2. Laver, W. G. and Kilbourne, E. D., Virology, *30:* 493, 1966.
3. Laver, W. G. and Valentine, R. C., Virology, *38:* 105, 1969.
4. Seto, J. T. and Rott, R., Virology, *30:* 731, 1966.
5. Webster, R. G. and Laver, W. G., J. Immun., *99:* 49, 1967.
6. Kilbourne, E. D., Laver, W. G., Schulman, J. L. and Webster, R. G., J. Virol., *2:* 281, 1968.
7. Schulman, J. L., Bull. W.H.O., *41:* 647, 1969.
8. Kilbourne, E. D., Christenson, W. N. and Sande, M., J. Virol., *2:* 761, 1968.
9. Schild, G. C. and Newman, R. W., J. Hyg. (Camb.), *67:* 353, 1969.
10. Beare, A. S., Bynoe, M. L. and Tyrrell, D. A. J., Brit. Med. J., *2:* 482, 1968.
11. Downie, J. C. and Stuart-Harris, C. H., J. Hyg. (Camb.), *68:* 233, 1970.
12. Ada, G. L., Lind, P. E. and Laver, W. G., J. Gen. Microbiol., *32:* 225, 1963.
13. Easterday, B., Laver, W. G., Pereira, H. G. and Schild, G. C., J. Gen. Virol., *5:* 83, 1969.
14. Fazekas de St. Groth, S. and Webster, R. G., J. Exp. Med., *124:* 331, 1966.
15. Fahey, J. L. and Lawrence, M. E., J. Immun., *91:* 597, 1963.
16. Wright, S. T. C., Nature, *183:* 1282, 1959.
17. McDonald, J. C., Zuckerman, A. J., Beare, A. S. and Tyrrell, D. A. J., Brit. Med. J., *1:* 1036, 1962.
18. Smith, C. B., Purcell, R. H., Bellanti, J. A. and Chanock, R. M., New England J. Med., *275:* 1145, 1966.
19. Alford, R. H., Rossen, R. D., Butler, W. T. and Kasel, J. A., J. Immun., *98:* 724, 1967.
20. Mann, J. J., Waldman, R. H., Togo, Y., Heiner, G. G., Dawkins, A. T. and Kasel, J. A., J. Immun., *100:* 726, 1968.
21. Smorodincev, A. A., Bull. W.H.O., *41:* 585, 1969.
22. Beare, A. S., Tyrrell, D. A. J., Hobson, D., Howells, C. H. L., Pereira, M. S., Pollock, T. M. and Tyler, L. E., J. Hyg. (Camb.), *67:* 1, 1969.
23. Tomansi, T. B., Jr., Tan, E. M., Solomon, A. and Prendergrast, R. A., J. Exp. Med., *121:* 101, 1965.
24. Butler, W. T., Rossen, R. D. and Waldmann, T. A., J. Clin. Invest., *46:* 1883, 1967.
25. Waldman, R. H., Kasel, J. A., Alford, R. H. and Mann, J. J., Proc. Soc. Exp. Biol. Med., *125:* 316, 1967.

THE JOURNAL OF IMMUNOLOGY

Vol. 105, No. 3, September 1970
Printed in U.S.A.

THE EFFECT OF PRIOR TRANSFUSION ON MARROW GRAFTS BETWEEN HISTOCOMPATIBLE CANINE SIBLINGS[1]

RAINER STORB, ROBERT B. EPSTEIN, ROBERT H. RUDOLPH AND E. DONNALL THOMAS[2]

From the Department of Medicine, University of Washington, Seattle, Washington 98105 and the United States Public Health Service Hospital, Seattle, Washington 98144

Received for publication March 13, 1970

Twenty-three canine littermate donor-recipient pairs were matched on the basis of histocompatibility typing with four lymphocytotoxic isoantisera. Eighteen of the 23 pairs were also tested in a one-way mixed leukocyte culture (MLC). Recipient dogs were given 1580 R whole body irradiation followed within 4 hr by infusion of marrow from the donor. Group 1 consisted of 10 recipients not given a preceding blood transfusion. Group 2 was made up of 13 dogs given a single transfusion of 100 ml of blood from the donor 10 days before irradiation. Seven of the 10 recipients in group 1 showed prompt and sustained marrow engraftment and survived beyond 70 days. Three died within 22 days of transplantation, two of marrow graft rejection and one of graft-*vs*-host disease. These three were mismatched with their donors in MLC. Only one of the 13 pretransfused recipients in group 2 lived beyond 70 days. Twelve dogs died within 36 days including eight that were matched by MLC as well as by serologic test. In most of these animals there was evidence of successful marrow engraftment followed by rejection. The results show that, even in histocompatible donor-recipient pairs, a single prior blood transfusion from the donor to the recipient significantly diminishes the chance of long-term survival following the marrow graft ($p < 0.01$).

Transplantation of allogeneic bone marrow has been accomplished consistently in a number of animal species (1–3). However, marrow grafts in man have, in general, not been successful (4). Human marrow graft recipients have usually been given multiple transfusions in the management of their disease. Immunization against transplantation antigens by leukocytes and platelets in the transfused blood may account for the many unsuccessful human marrow grafts (5). Experiments in histoincompatible mice (6–8) and monkeys (9) support this hypothesis.

In the experiments reported here, marrow grafts between canine sibling donor-recipient pairs matched for histocompatibility antigens were undertaken with or without a prior blood transfusion from donor to recipient. The experiments were designed to determine whether or not blood transfusion from a compatible donor would diminish the chance of long-term survival following a marrow graft.

[1] This research was supported by Grant AI 09419 and Contract 43-67-1435, National Institute for Allergy and Infectious Diseases, and Grant CA 10895, National Cancer Institute, National Institutes of Health, United States Public Health Service.

[2] Supported by Research Career Program Award 1-K6-AI-2425 from the National Institutes of Allergy and Infectious Diseases.

MATERIALS AND METHODS

Twenty-three canine littermate pairs of various breeds, between 6 and 12 months of age and weighing 5 to 15 kg, were observed for disease for 3 weeks before use. They were typed for canine red cell antigen A, dewormed and immunized against distemper and hepatitis. Each pair of siblings was selected on the basis of histocompatibility matching with four canine lymphocytotoxic isoantisera. Details of the development of the antisera, the testing technique and data on the usefulness of the antisera in selecting compatible donor-recipient combinations for marrow grafting have been described (10–13). Cells of 18 of the 23 sibling pairs were tested in a one-way mixed

TABLE I

Survival of recipients in group 1 not given a preceding blood transfusion from the matched sibling marrow donor

Dog No.[a]		Sex	Red Cell Type	Lymphocyte Type[b]	MLC[c] "Match"	No. of Marrow Cells Infused × 10^9	Rise in WBC (>1000/mm³)	Rise in Platelet Count	Marrow Rejection	Survival	Bone Marrow Histology at Autopsy
										days	
807	D	M	A+	ABCD	No	29.5	Yes	No	Yes	10	Extremely hypocellular
808	R	F	A+	ABCD							
660	D	M	A+	AC	No	19.9	No	No	Yes	13	Extremely hypocellular
661	R	M	A+	AC							
A-17	D	F	A+	BD	No	9.7	Yes	Yes	No	21	Cellular
A-18	R	F	A+	BD							
870	D	M	A+	ABD	Yes	10.0	Yes	Yes	No	>70	—
886	R	F	A+	ABD							
865	D	F	A+	—	Yes	20.0	Yes	Yes	No	>70	—
868	R	F	A−	—							
888	D	F	A+	BD	Yes	10.2	Yes	Yes	No	>70	—
890	R	M	A+	BD							
731	D	F	A+	AC	—	7.1	Yes	Yes	No	>70	—
728	R	M	A+	AC							
765	D	F	A+	—	Yes	10.1	Yes	Yes	No	>70	—
766	R	F	A−	—							
772	D	M	A−	—	Yes	12.9	Yes	Yes	No	>70	—
773	R	M	A−	—							
718	D	F	A+	AC	Yes	30.4	Yes	Yes	No	>70	—
719	R	F	A+	AC							

[a] D, donor; R, recipient.

[b] Dashes indicate negative reaction with all four antisera.

[c] Mixed leukocyte culture. Dash indicates that MLC data are not available.

leukocyte culture (MLC) (14). One member of each sibling pair served as the marrow donor and the other as the marrow recipient.

Recipient dogs were prepared for transplantation by 1580 R of total body irradiation from two opposing ^{60}Co sources at an exposure rate of 5.3 R/min with a source-target distance of 200 cm. This corresponded to a midbody exposure of approximately 1200 to 1300 rads (15). Donor animals were killed with pentobarbital sodium, and marrow was removed under aseptic conditions from long bones and ribs and prepared for i.v. infusion (16). Donor marrow cells, 7.1 to 42.5 × 10^9, were infused within 4 hr of irradiation of the recipient.

Two groups of recipients were studied. Group 1 included 10 dogs not receiving a preceding blood transfusion. Group 2 consisted of 13 dogs given a single transfusion of 100 ml of fresh heparinized whole blood from the prospective marrow donor 10 days before irradiation and marrow transplantation.

All recipients were given sodium ampicillin, 250 mg twice daily, during periods of white blood cell counts below 1000/mm³. Parenteral fluid and electrolyte support were given twice daily for the first 7 days following irradiation. White cell counts, platelet counts and hematocrits were obtained at least three times weekly. Marrow engraftment was defined as a rise of the white blood cell count to above 1000/mm³ subsequent to the post-irradiation nadir. Cytogenetic analysis of recipient bone marrow cells for sex chromosome pattern was carried out in two dogs that received bone marrow from donors of opposite sex (17). Only cells with 78 chromosomes were evaluated. Gross autopsy and histologic examination were performed on all recipients that died.

RESULTS

Table I summarizes the data on the 10 recipients in group 1 not given a blood transfusion from the marrow donor before irradiation and transplantation. All 10 matched their sibling donors by

TABLE II

Survival of recipients in group 2 given a single blood transfusion from the matched marrow donor before irradiation and marrow transplantation

Dog No.[a]		Sex	Red Cell Type	Lymphocyte Type[b]	MLC[c] "Match"	No. of Marrow Cells Infused × 10^9	Rise in WBC (>1000/mm³)	Rise in Platelet Count	Marrow Rejection	Survival	Bone Marrow Histology at Autopsy
										days	
705	D	F	A+	—	—	11.7	Yes	No	No	9	Moderately cellular
706	R	F	A+	—							
692	D	F	A+	AB	—	26.7	Yes	No	No	10	Moderately cellular
695	R	M	A+	AB							
716	D	F	A+	AC	Yes	13.6	No	No	Yes	16	Extremely hypocellular
717[d]	R	F	A+	AC							
895	D	M	A+	BD	Yes	19.0	Yes	Yes	?	22	Moderately cellular
896[d]	R	M	A+	BD							
756	D	F	A+	B	Yes	42.5	Yes	Yes	Yes	24	Extremely hypocellular
757[d]	R	M	A+	B							
645	D	M	A−	AD	—	30.8	Yes	Yes	Yes	24	Extremely hypocellular
646[d]	R	M	A+	AD							
A-12	D	F	A+	BD	Yes	14.1	Yes	Yes	Yes	25	Extremely hypocellular
A-13[d]	R	F	A+	BD							
681	D	M	A−	—	—	26.2	Yes	Yes	Yes	25	Extremely hypocellular
683[d]	R	M	A−	—							
A-5	D	F	A+	AC	Yes	38.7	Yes	Yes	Yes	26	Extremely hypocellular
A-6[d]	R	F	A−	AC							
882	D	F	A+	BD	Yes	29.9	Yes	Yes	?	27	Moderately cellular
883	R	F	A+	BD							
780	D	F	A−	—	Yes	29.3	Yes	Yes	Yes	29	Extremely hypocellular
781	R	F	A−	—							
891	D	F	A+	BD	Yes	35.2	Yes	Yes	No	36	Moderately cellular
892	R	F	A+	BD							
658	D	F	A+	AC	Yes	18.0	Yes	Yes	No	>70	—
655[d]	R	M	A+	AC							

[a] D, donor; R, recipient.
[b] Dashes indicate negative reactions with all four antisera.
[c] Mixed leukocyte culture. Dash indicates that MLC data are not available.
[d] Recipient serum on the day of transplantation was tested for cytotoxic antibodies against donor cells.

serologic histocompatibility typing. Six of the 10 pairs were matched in MLC and three were mismatched. In one pair (728 and 731) MLC was not carried out. The three recipients that were mismatched with their donors in MLC died. Two (808 and 661) showed acute marrow graft rejection and died with hemorrhage and infection on days 10 and 13. Examination of the bone marrow at autopsy showed profound hypoplasia. One (A-18) showed successful and sustained marrow engraftment and died on day 21 with clinical and pathologic findings consistent with those described in graft-*vs*-host disease (18, 19). The autopsy bone marrow was cellular. The remaining seven recipients in group 1 also showed prompt marrow engraftment and survived for more than 70 days. The white blood cell and platelet changes in one of these dogs (728) are illustrated in Figure 1*A*.

Table II summarizes the data of 13 recipients in group 2 given a single blood transfusion from the prospective marrow donor 10 days before irradiation and marrow transplantation. All recipients matched their sibling donors by serologic histocompatibility typing. In addition, nine of the 13 pairs were matched in MLC. In four pairs the MLC reaction was not carried out. Sera of eight of the 13 recipients were tested for cytotoxic antibodies on the day of transplantation (10). All failed to show antibodies against cells

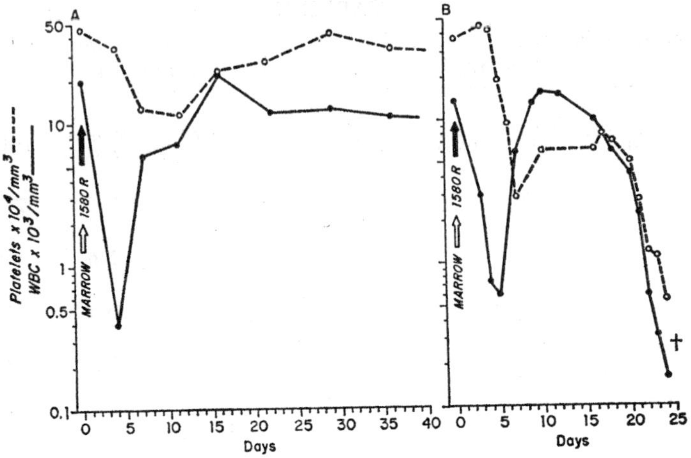

Figure 1. A, white blood cell and platelet changes in a recipient of group 1 (728); *B*, white blood cell and platelet changes in a recipient of group 2 (683).

of their donor. Twelve of the 13 recipients died between 9 and 36 days. Two (706 and 695) dying on days 9 and 10 with infection showed rises in white blood cell counts after the post-irradiation nadir. A rise in platelet counts did not occur in these two animals. Their autopsy bone marrow showed moderate cellularity. One dog (717) showed no rise in white blood cell or platelet counts. He appeared clinically well until day 15 when he developed hemorrhage and infection followed by death on day 16. The autopsy marrow was aplastic. The hematologic findings in this dog were consistent with acute marrow graft rejection. Nine showed prompt rises in white blood cell (5,100 to 15,000/mm³) and platelet counts (28,000 to 80,000/mm³) between days 12 and 19. Subsequently, six of the nine rejected the marrow graft with a resulting rapid decline in white blood cell counts to less than 1000/mm³ and platelet counts to less than 10,000/mm³. They died from hemorrhage and infection between days 24 and 29. Their bone marrow at autopsy was extremely hypocellular. Figure 1*B* illustrates the white blood cell and platelet changes in one of these dogs (683). Three of the nine died with pneumonia between days 22 and 36. Two of these (892 and 896) showed declining white blood cell counts prior to death, and two (883 and 896) showed falling platelet counts with values of 17,000 and 33,000/mm³ by the day of death. The bone marrow at autopsy in these three dogs showed decreased cellularity. Only one of the 13 recipients in group 2 survived more than 70 days with prompt and sustained allogeneic marrow engraftment (655).

Figure 2 summarizes the survival curves of all recipients in both groups. Statistical analysis of the data (two-sided Fisher's Exact Test (20, 21)) showed that the survival of the 10 recipients in group 1 not given a blood transfusion before transplantation was significantly greater than that of the 13 recipients in group 2 given a preceding transfusion of donor blood ($p < 0.01$). Figure 3 illustrates the survival curves in the 15 recipients in both groups that matched their donor both by serologic histocompatibility testing and in MLC. All six dogs in group 1 survived for more than 70 days. Eight of the nine animals

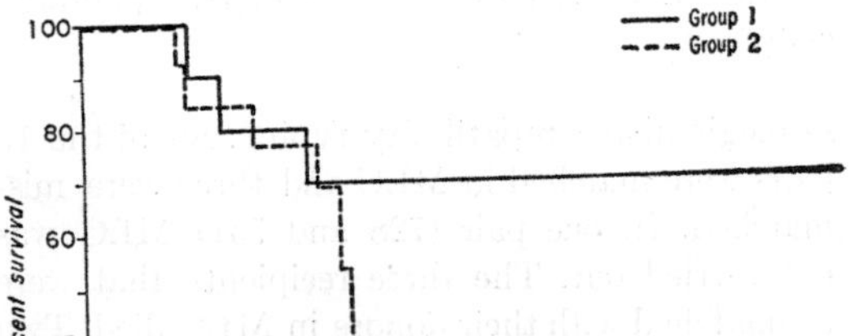

Figure 2. Survival of 10 recipients in group 1 and 13 recipients in group 2, all receiving bone marrow infusion from a sibling donor matched by serologic canine histocompatibility testing.

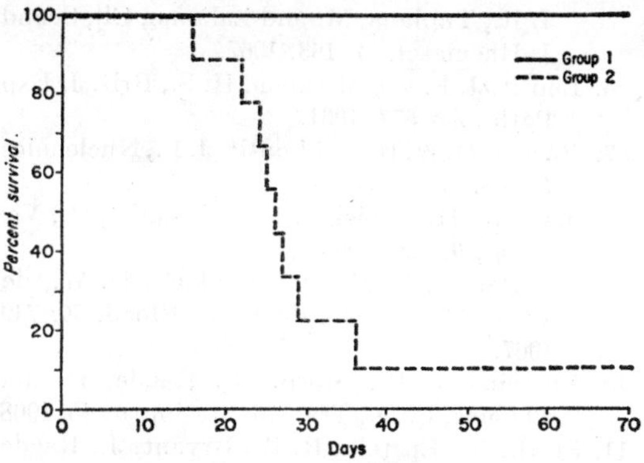

Figure 3. Survival of six recipients in group 1 and nine recipients in group 2, all matched with their marrow donors both by serologic histocompatibility testing and the mixed leukocyte culture reaction.

in group 2 died between days 16 and 36, and one animal survived for more than 70 days.

Dog 868 differed from its donor with regard to canine red cell antigen A. When tested more than 70 days after transplantation, the red cells were of donor type. Dogs 728 and 655 were infused with marrow from donors of the opposite sex. Cytogenetic analysis of bone marrow cells more than 70 days after transplantation showed all 20 cells analyzed in each dog to be of donor karyotype. In previous studies cytogenetic analysis of recipients of marrow grafts following 1200 to 1500 R have always shown only cells of donor karyotype (11–13, 17).

DISCUSSION

In recent years, rapid progress has been made in human histocompatibility typing (22). There is strong evidence that most of the major human histocompatibility antigens are located on a single chromosome pair. Typing by cytotoxic antisera and by the MLC test has made possible the selection of human siblings that have inherited the same histocompatibility chromosome from each parent (23). Several human marrow grafts have now been reported using a "matched" sibling as donor (24–27). Preliminary evidence also indicates that a matched sibling may be the best donor of platelets for the patient who has received multiple transfusions (28).

In this laboratory, a system of canine histocompatibility testing was developed using the cytotoxicity test (10). Prompt and sustained marrow grafts and long-term survival were observed in recipients that matched their sibling donors using this method of histocompatibility testing (10). In addition, good correlation between cytotoxicity testing and the results of the MLC reaction was found (14). Thus, canine sibling pairs matched for histocompatibility antigens and nonreactive in MLC make an excellent outbred animal model for experiments that may be applicable to HL-A matched human siblings.

In mice, allogeneic bone marrow engraftment was prevented when the recipients were given several blood transfusions from the prospective marrow donor before irradiation and transplantation (7, 8). Immunization against subsequent bone marrow transplants and failure of the infused marrow to take was observed in rhesus monkeys after transfusions with blood from the intended donor and after multiple transfusions from third party donors (9). These reports show clearly that blood transfusion may jeopardize a subsequent marrow graft, but the data so far reported refer to randomly selected donor-recipient pairs or pairs that were mismatched for H-2 histocompatibility antigens. Loutit and Micklem (6) showed that prior immunization by H-2 compatible donor spleen cell injections caused increased mortality in x-irradiated recipient mice following marrow grafting, thus suggesting that minor antigenic differences may also be important. In view of the importance of matched human siblings for platelet transfusions and for marrow grafting, the present study was undertaken to evaluate the effect of a preceding blood transfusion from the donor to the matched canine sibling recipient. The results show that, even in this compatible combination, a single blood transfusion significantly diminishes the chance of long-term survival following the marrow graft.

Garver and Cole (29) showed that anti-C_3H antisera raised in LAF_1 mice and given at the same time as C_3H bone marrow can prevent marrow grafting in x-irradiated LAF_1 recipients. Loutit and Micklem (6) also showed that marrow grafts could be prevented by serum antibodies when donor and recipient differed at the H-2 locus but not when they were H-2 compatible. In the present study, circulating antibodies did not appear to be responsible for the increased mortality since cytotoxic antibodies could not be demonstrated in the eight pretransfused recipients that were tested. In addition, it would be expected that antibodies would have an immediate toxic effect on the infused marrow. However, in 12 of 13 pretransfused recipients, successful marrow engraftment was observed only to be rejected later in the majority of cases. Apparently, rejection was due to immunity not destroyed by the irradiation exposure of 1580 R. Most investigators seem to agree that the secondary immune response is more radioresistant than the primary response (30–32). However, the effect of irradiation on established immunity, especially at supralethal exposures, is not well understood.

The four antisera used for cytotoxicity typing in these studies were developed by cross-immunization of littermates. In previous experiments they were found to be of value in selecting donor-recipient pairs for marrow grafting within litters and in unrelated dogs (10–13). Presumably there are many canine histocompatibility antigens not recognized by these sera. In the present experiments, the MLC test was employed in 17 littermate pairs that appeared to be matched by typing with the four cytotoxic antisera. In three instances, reactivity was observed in the MLC test. These three littermate pairs were all in the group not given the preceding blood transfusion and they account for the only three deaths in that group. Thus, these three animals appeared to be mismatched by the test of marrow grafting confirming the incompatibility predicted by the MLC test. Previous studies demonstrated uniform mortality in irradiated recipients given marrow from mismatched siblings when no immunosuppressive drug was given after grafting (10).

Acknowledgments. We wish to thank Mr. P. Wootton, Department of Radiology, for carrying out the radiation dosimetry studies. We are grateful to Mrs. V. Jacobsen, Mr. E. Mickelson and Mr. T. Graham for excellent technical assistance.

REFERENCES

1. Congdon, C. C., Blood, *12:* 746, 1957.
2. Thomas, E. D., Storb, R., Epstein, R. B. and Rudolph, R. H., Transplantation Proc., *1:* 31, 1969.
3. van Bekkum, D. W., Balner, H., Dicke, K. A. and van Putten, L. M., Transplantation Proc., *1:* 25, 1969.
4. Bortin, M. M., Transplantation, In press.
5. Mathé, G., Schwarzenberg, L., Amiel, J. L., Schneider, M., Cattan, A., Schlumberger, J. R., Tubiana, M. and Lalanne, Cl., Scand. J. Haematol., *4:* 193, 1967.
6. Loutit, J. F. and Micklem, H. S., Brit. J. Exp. Path., *42:* 577, 1961.
7. Barnes, D. W. H. and Loutit, J. F., Nucleonics, *12:* 68, 1954.
8. daCosta, H., Amiel, J. L. and Mathé, G., Vox Sang., *9:* 420, 1964.
9. van Putten, L. M., van Bekkum, D. W., deVries, M. J. and Balner, H., Blood, *30:* 749, 1967.
10. Epstein, R. B., Storb, R., Ragde, H. and Thomas, E. D., Transplantation, *6:* 45, 1968.
11. Storb, R., Epstein, R. B., Bryant, J., Ragde, H. and Thomas, E. D., Transplantation, *6:* 587, 1968.
12. Epstein, R. B., Storb, R., Clift, R. A. and Thomas, E. D., Transplantation, *8:* 496, 1969.
13. Storb, R., Epstein, R. B., Rudolph, R. H. and Thomas, E. D., Transplantation, *7:* 378, 1969.
14. Rudolph, R. H., Hered, B., Epstein, R. B. and Thomas, E. D., Transplantation, *8:* 141, 1969.
15. Thomas, E. D., LeBlond, R., Graham, T. and Storb, R., Rad. Res., *41:* 113, 1970.
16. Thomas, E. D., Ashley, C. A., Lochte, H. L., Jr., Jaretzki, A., Sahler, O. D. and Ferrebee, J. W., Blood, *14:* 720, 1959.
17. Epstein, R. B., Bryant, J. and Thomas, E. D., Transplantation, *5:* 267, 1967.
18. deVries, M. J. and Vos, O., J. Nat. Cancer Inst., *23:* 1403, 1959.
19. deVries, M. J., in *Proceedings of the International Symposium on Bone Marrow Therapy and Chemical Protection in Irradiated Primates*, p. 101, Radiobiological Institute TNO, Rijkswijk, The Netherlands, 1962.
20. Bliss, C. I., *Statistics in Biology*, Vol. 1, Chapter 4, McGraw-Hill Book Co., New York, 1967.
21. Finney, D. J., Latsuha, R., Bennet, B. M. and Hsu, P., *Tables for Testing Significance in a 2 × 2 Contingency Table*, Cambridge University Press, London, 1963.
22. *Histocompatibility Testing 1970*, Munksgaard, Copenhagen, In press.
23. Bach, F. H. and Amos, D. B., Science, *156:* 1506, 1967.
24. Meuwissen, H. J., Gatti, R. A., Terasaki, P. I., Hong, R. and Good, R. A., New England J. Med., *281:* 691, 1969.
25. deKooning, J., Dooren, L. J., van Bekkum, D. W., van Rood, J. J., Dicke, K. A. and Rádl, J., Lancet, *1:* 7608, 1969.
26. Graw, R. G., Brown, J. A., Yankee, R. A.,

Leventhal, B. G., Whang-Peng, J., Rogentine, G. N. and Henderson, E. S., Exp. Hematol., In press.
27. Bach, F., Albertini, R. J., Anderson, J. L., Joo, P. and Bortin, M. M., Lancet, *2:* 1364, 1968.
28. Yankee, R. A., Grumet, F. C. and Rogentine, G. N., New England J. Med., *281:* 1208, 1969.
29. Garver, R. M. and Cole, L. J., J. Immun., *86:* 307, 1961.
30. Dixon, F. J., Talmage, D. W. and Maurer, P. H., J. Immun., *68:* 693, 1952.
31. Hašek, M. and Lengerová, A., in *Mechanisms in Radiobiology*, Edited by M. Errera and A. Forssberg, Vol. II, p. 207, Academic Press, New York, 1960.
32. Taliaferro, W. H., Taliaferro, L. G. and Jaroslow, B. N., *Radiation and Immune Mechanisms*, Academic Press, New York, 1964.

THE JOURNAL OF IMMUNOLOGY
Vol. 105, No. 3, September 1970
Printed in U.S.A.

MECHANISM OF RETICULOENDOTHELIAL SYSTEM BLOCKADE PRODUCED BY ANTILYMPHOCYTE SERUM

JOHN N. SHEAGREN,[1] ROLF F. BARTH,[2] JOSEPH B. EDELIN[1] AND RICHARD A. MALMGREN[2]

From the Laboratory of Clinical Investigation, National Institute of Allergy and Infectious Diseases, and the Pathologic Anatomy Branch, National Cancer Institute, National Institutes of Health, Bethesda, Maryland 20014

Received for publication March 13, 1970

Mice treated with antilymphocyte serum (ALS) were found to have impaired blood clearance of aggregated human serum albumin (AA) and colloidal carbon. The clearance of AA was found to be immediately slowed by ALS with return to a normal rate by 24 hr. Clearance of a very small blood-flow dependent dose of AA was similarly affected, suggesting that the blockade of the AA clearing system could be related to altered perfusion of reticuloendothelial system organs (primarily decreased hepatic blood flow). Carbon clearance, in contrast, was found to be accelerated for a few hours prior to the development of blockade. Clearance of a very small blood flow-dependent dose of carbon also showed transient, immediate impairment, but then became and remained normal at a time when clearance of the larger dose of carbon was blocked. Impairment of carbon clearance appears, therefore, to be due to altered phagocytosis at the cellular level.

Antimacrophage serum has been shown to slow the rate of clearance of colloidal carbon in guinea pigs (1) and mice (2). We recently reported that antilymphocyte serum (ALS) markedly impairs the clearance of colloidal carbon and microaggregated human serum albumin (AA) from the blood of mice (3). The degree of reticuloendothelial system (RES) depression was most profound with intravenously administered ALS, and its effect on the clearance of carbon was more prolonged than on the clearance of AA. Using only AA as the test colloid, the onset of RES blockade after injection of ALS was found to be instantaneous.

This report describes various aspects of the effect of ALS on the clearance of both microaggregated albumin and colloidal carbon. ALS has a biphasic action on carbon clearance first accelerating and then slowing the clearance rate; the probable mechanism of blockade is inhibition of the uptake of carbon at the cellular level. Blockade of AA clearance is immediate, of short duration, and may be accomplished primarily through impairment of perfusion of the RES.

[1] National Institute of Allergy and Infectious Diseases.

[2] National Cancer Institute.

MATERIALS AND METHODS

Animals. The mice used throughout these studies were inbred BALB/c males weighing 18 to 22 g obtained from the Rodent and Rabbit Production Section, National Institutes of Health (NIH). New Zealand White rabbits (NIH animal colony) weighing 1.5 kg were used to test for pyrogenic contamination of the antiserum (3).

Antiserum. Burro anti-mouse lymphocyte serum (BAMLS) with potent immunosuppressive properties was prepared and tested as previously described (3), and normal burro serum (NBS) was obtained from unimmunized healthy animals. All sera were heat-inactivated at 56°C for 30 min and passed through a Millipore filter. The sera were administered intravenously in a dose of 0.01 ml/g weight unless indicated otherwise. For dose-response studies, various dilutions of ALS were given in the same volume, while increased doses were given by increasing the total volume of undiluted BAMLS.

Colloidal test particles. Colloidal carbon (Pelikan, Guenther-Wagner, lot C11-1431A) was diluted 2:1 with normal saline and injected in a dose of 0.01 ml/g weight of mouse. This dose was empirically determined as one which would give a half-time of disappearance (T-½) from the blood of approximately 10 min. The microaggregated human serum albumin (AA) was prepared as described by Briner (4). A solution containing 2.5 mg/ml of AA and 1.0 μCi/ml of ^{125}I was administered to each mouse in the amount 0.01 ml/g weight. To assess clearance of both carbon and AA simultaneously, equal volumes of the carbon and of the AA suspensions were mixed and administered in a dose of 0.02 ml/g weight of mouse.

Colloidal clearance tests. The rate of disappearance of either colloid was determined by obtaining 20-μl samples of blood from the retroorbital sinus at 3, 6, 9 and 12 min after injection of the test colloid. For determination of carbon concentration, the samples of blood were added to 3.0 ml of Na_2CO_3 solution and the optical density was read at 650 nm. For determination of AA concentration, the 20-μl samples were added to 2.0 ml of water and counts/unit time were determined in a gamma counter (Nuclear Chicago model 4223). Clearance rates for both colloids were expressed as half-times of clearance (T-½) in minutes as calculated by a computer from the sequential plasma concentrations of carbon or AA. Clearance of both carbon and AA simultaneously was determined after injection of the mixture of both colloids by obtaining two 20-μl samples from the same mouse at each 3-min interval, and then assaying one for carbon and the other for AA.

Estimation of liver blood flow. To assess perfusion of RES tissues, a blood flow-dependent dose of each colloid was determined as previously described by Dobson and Jones (5) and Benacerraf *et al.* (6). Essentially, the relationship between the dose of colloid and its rate of clearance was determined for both AA (as illustrated in Fig. 1) and carbon, and doses of each colloid below the "critical dose" (6) were determined. Any dose smaller than the "critical dose" in the normal animals gives a rate of clearance which is purely blood flow-dependent and is therefore at a constant maximal value. A 1:4 dilution of colloidal carbon was found to be at or below the "critical dose", and a 1:10 dilution of AA was found to be at or below the "critical dose" of AA. Studies of RES perfusion were actually carried out with the 1:4 dilution of carbon and 1:40 and 1:400 dilutions of AA, all given in a dose of 0.01 ml/g weight of mouse. Increased amounts of ^{125}I were added to the dilutions of AA in order

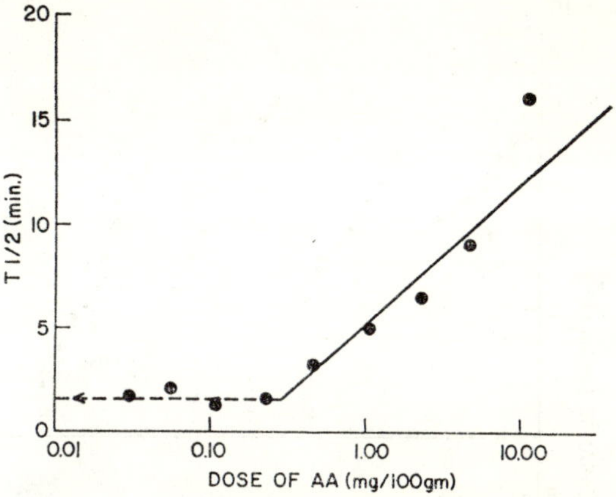

Figure 1. Relationship between the dose of microaggregated human serum albumin (AA) and the T-½ in mice. The rate of clearance is constant at approximately 1.5 min at doses of AA below 0.2 mg/100 g. Each point is the mean of at least four animals.

to obtain adequate numbers of counts. For the 1:4 dose of carbon, blood samples were obtained at 10, 20, 30 and 40 sec after injection and for the 1:40 and 1:400 doses of AA, blood samples were taken at 30, 60, 90 and 120 sec. More rapid sampling was required to obtain adequate points from which to calculate the T-½'s. Even under these conditions, the clearance rates at best only approximated minimum rates of hepatic blood flow: for both carbon and AA, the fastest T-½'s that could be obtained in normal mice were about 1 to 2 min. Calculation of hepatic blood flow for the normal mouse from that T-½ range yields a flow rate of approximately 0.5 ml of blood/g of liver/min, a rate below the published flow rates of 1 to 1.5 ml/g/min for the mouse (5, 6). The reasons for this discrepancy are not apparent, but may have resulted from difficulty in calculating the T-½'s (due to "tailing" of the curves) or from poor efficiency of extraction by the liver of our particular colloids (a factor not measured in our experiments). That these values do indeed reflect or parallel RES blood flow is indicated by the fact that the T-½'s remained constant at doses of colloid, even below those used in these studies to assess blood flow (Fig. 1).

Passive transfer studies. Passive transfer of freshly obtained normal BALB/c serum (NMS) to mice pretreated with BAMLS was carried out in several different ways. Up to 0.5 ml of NMS was administered during the clearance of one

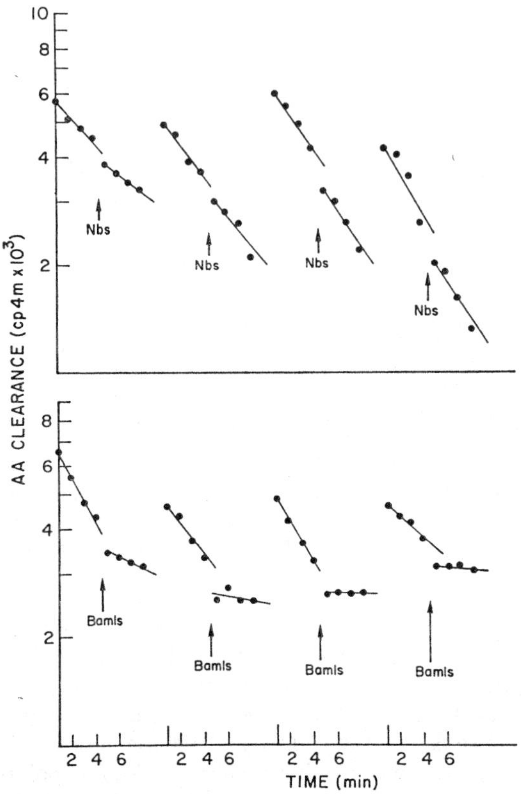

Figure 2. Minute by minute clearance of AA in individual mice. The top four mice were injected with normal burro serum (NBS); the bottom four with antilymphocyte serum (BAMLS) at 4.5 min (↑).

of the colloidal particles in the following manner. The colloid was injected and blood samples were taken at 1, 2, 3 and 4 min; the NMS was then given i.v. at 4.5 min and further blood samples were obtained at 5, 6, 7 and 8 min. Thus, the effect of the NMS on the clearance rate of the colloid in question could be ascertained by comparing the T-½ of colloid disappearance for the first 4 min with the T-½ of the last 4 min. Other experiments involved the administration of up to 1.0 ml of NMS i.v. 15 min before performance of the usual colloidal clearance test in mice injected earlier with BAMLS. The effect of transfer of 300×10^6 viable, non-erythroid spleen cells to BAMLS-blockaded mice was studied in a similar manner.

Absorption studies. Four milliliters of BAMLS were absorbed for 4 hr at 4°C with an equal volume of 300×10^6 viable non-erythroid spleen cells, and following centrifugation the supernatant antiserum was administered at a dose of 0.01 ml/g weight, as there appeared to be essentially no dilution of the antiserum during the absorption procedure.

RESULTS

Time of onset of the RES-blockading effect of BAMLS. Injection of BAMLS while clearance was in progress produced an immediate, marked impairment of further clearance of AA (Fig. 2), but had no effect on the clearance of colloidal carbon (Fig. 3). Experiments were therefore carried out to determine at what time after the i.v. injection of BAMLS the clearance of carbon would become impaired. It was found (Fig. 4) that an accelerated rate of clearance of carbon was seen for the first 2 hr following BAMLS administration. The clearance rate slowed to normal by about 4 hr, and impaired clearance was demonstrated from 8 hr on. Only minor fluctuations in mean rates of carbon clearance were seen in the NBS-treated control mice.

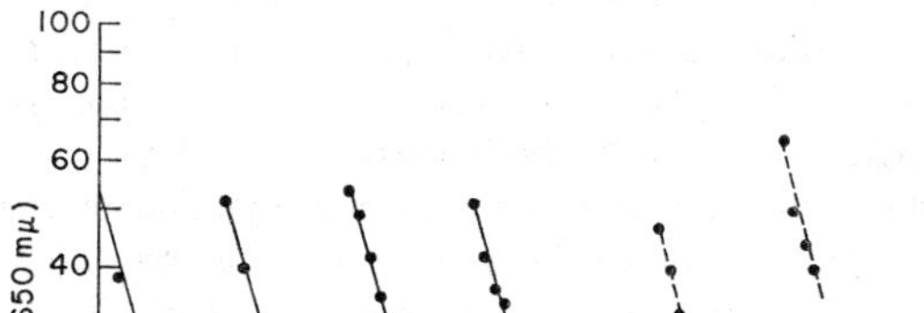

Figure 3. Minute by minute clearance of carbon in individual mice. No effect of either antilymphocyte serum (BAMLS) or normal burro serum (NBS), injected at 4.5 min (↑), is evident.

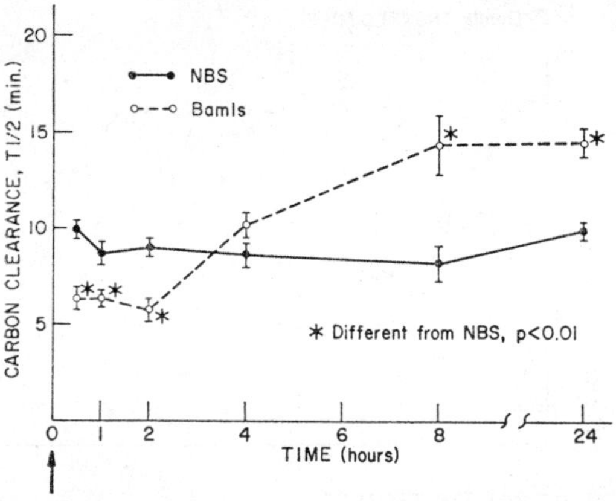

Figure 4. Rates of clearance of carbon over a 24-hr period after injection of either antilymphocyte serum (BAMLS) or normal burro serum (NBS) at time "0" (↑). Each point is the mean of four animals with bars indicating standard errors.

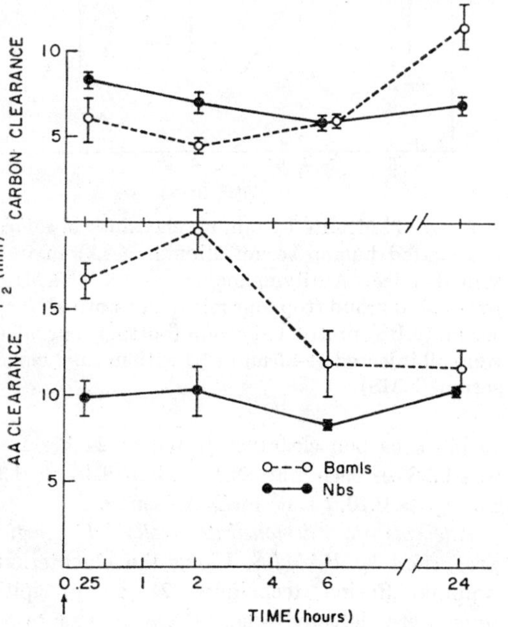

Figure 5. Rates of clearance of carbon (*top graph*) and microaggregated human serum albumin (AA) (*bottom graph*) in mice injected simultaneously with both colloids at various times after the injection of either antilymphocyte serum (BAMLS) or normal burro serum (NBS) at time "0" (↑).

The effect of a single i.v. dose of BAMLS on the clearance of both colloidal particles administered simultaneously is shown in Figure 5. Clearance of AA was impaired soon after a single BAMLS injection at the same time that clearance of carbon in the same mouse was found to be accelerated (Fig. 5). At 24 hr AA clearance had returned to normal while carbon clearance in the same mouse was impaired.

Effect of dose of BAMLS on impairment of colloid clearance. Varying doses of BAMLS were given to groups of four mice and AA clearance was determined at 6 hr and carbon clearance at 24 hr (Fig. 6). No effect was seen on either colloid at 50% of the usual antiserum dose or below, but more marked impairment was produced by increasing the size of the dose. A dose of BAMLS five times greater than normal was lethal within 30 min, while the same dose of NBS was well-tolerated and did not significantly alter the clearance of either colloid.

A dose-related response was also evident with regard to the "accelerated" phase of carbon clearance. Thirty minutes after injection the usual dose of BAMLS produced a T-½ of 4.55 ± 0.15 min (all data are expressed as means ± standard errors) in comparison with a mean of 7.45 ± 0.68 min in NBS controls, i.e., the expected degree of acceleration occurred. Animals given 250% of the usual dose had a clearance

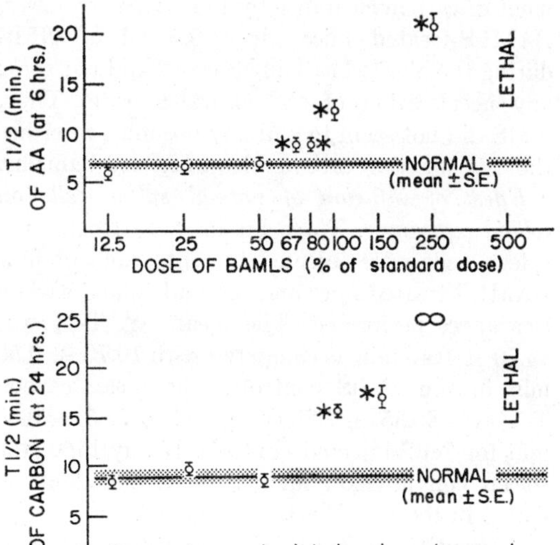

Figure 6. Degree of RES blockade (T-½ prolongation) as a function of dose of antilymphocyte serum (BAMLS). Each point is the mean of four animals with bars indicating standard errors. Starred means (*) are significantly ($p < 0.05$) different from normal.

rate so rapid that at the first bleeding (3 min after injection of carbon) the colloid had already been almost entirely cleared from the blood.

Effect of normal mouse serum (NMS) on BAMLS-induced RES blockade. NMS was given to mice pretreated with BAMLS to see if any serum factors (opsonins) might have been removed by the BAMLS. Mice were given BAMLS and 6 hr later received either 1.0 ml of NMS or 1.0 ml of saline i.v.; AA clearances were performed 15 to 30 min later. The mean T-½ of saline-injected mice was 10.15 ± 1.20 min and that of the NMS-injected group was 10.23 ± 0.54 min, indicating no restoration of normal clearance. Further experiments were performed to see whether NMS administered during the blocked clearance of AA would enhance particle removal (Fig. 7). Again, no enhancement of AA clearance was seen in either the NBS- or BAMLS-injected animals.

Similar experiments were performed using carbon as the test colloid. Again, animals were given BAMLS and at 24 hr were given either 1.0 ml i.v. of NMS or saline. The four NMS-treated animals had a mean T-½ of 14.58 ± 1.07 min in comparison with 14.03 ± 1.08 min for saline-injected controls, indicating no enhancement of carbon clearance by the NMS. Similarly, BAMLS-treated mice given 0.5 ml of NMS during the blocked carbon clearance did not show any acceleration of the clearance rate. Thus, NMS did not seem to add any opsonins to either the AA or the carbon clearance mechanisms.

Effect of infusion of normal spleen cells on colloid clearances. Three hundred × 10^6 normal spleen cells were injected i.v. into each of four BAMLS-treated mice and AA and colloid carbon clearances performed. The mean AA T-½ was 15.70 ± 0.40 min as compared with 10.70 ± 0.50 min in four NBS controls. The mean carbon T-½ was 40.35 ± 2.85 compared to 7.85 ± 0.85 min for NBS-injected controls. If anything, the spleen cell infusion further blocked colloid removal in the BAMLS-treated group.

Absorption of BAMLS with spleen cell suspensions. BAMLS absorbed with spleen cells retained its ability to block the clearance of AA. The mean T-½ of four mice given absorbed BAMLS was 8.63 ± 0.13 min compared with that of 6.98 ± 0.31 min ($p < 0.01$, t test) for animals given absorbed NBS. On the other hand, the same absorbed BAMLS no longer was able

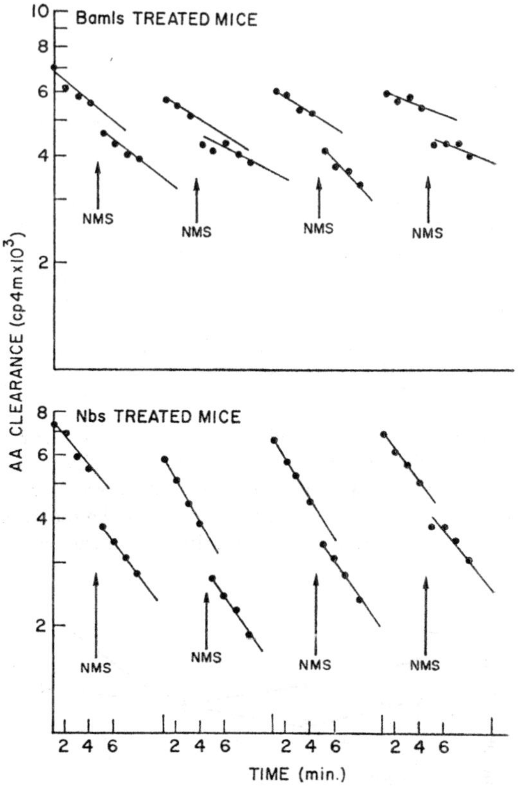

Figure 7. Minute by minute clearance of microaggregated human serum albumin (AA) in individual mice. Antilymphocyte serum (BAMLS) pretreated group (top four mice) and normal burro serum (NBS) pretreated group (bottom four mice) were all injected at 4.5 min (↑) with normal mouse serum (NMS).

to block carbon clearance tested at 24 hr. T-½ was 9.28 ± 0.41 min compared to 8.48 ± 0.31 min ($p > 0.10$, t test) for NBS controls.

Attempts to demonstrate colloidal particle production by BAMLS. Using the Ouchterlony immunodiffusion technique (7) no precipitin lines were detected when BAMLS was tested against normal serum, indicating the absence of demonstrable antigen-antibody complexes, particles which could, in theory, compete with AA or carbon. Passively transferred serum from BAMLS-treated mice failed to prolong the clearance rates of AA or carbon in normal mice, thus ruling out the production of other intravascular colloidal particles by BAMLS which might interfere with the clearance of the test colloids.

Evaluation of RES perfusion (liver blood flow)

after BAMLS treatment. Removal of the small, "trace dose" of AA (the 1:40 dilution of the usual AA dose) which reflected primarily liver blood, was markedly impaired by BAMLS: the mean T-½ of the "trace dose" of AA in 10 normal mice was 2.02 ± 0.21 min; that of 9 mice given NBS 30 min previously was not different at 1.94 ± 0.32 min, but that of 10 mice given BAMLS 30 min previously was 5.21 ± 0.70 min, a value significantly different from either the normal or NBS group ($p < 0.01$, *t* test). Studies done with an even smaller dose of AA (1:400 dilution of the usual AA dose) produced similar results: the mean T-½ in four mice given NBS was 1.58 ± 0.21 min and that in four mice given BAMLS was 4.93 ± 0.84 min ($p < 0.01$, *t* test).

The time course of impairment of the rate of clearance of the "trace dose" of AA is shown in Figure 8. Marked impairment was present immediately, less at 6 and 12 hr, and by 24 hr the clearance rate had almost returned to normal. These changes paralleled those seen with the large regular test dose of AA where marked impairment was seen immediately, less at 6 hr and none at 24 hr (3).

Studies were done using both the "trace dose" and the regular dose of carbon at various time intervals after BAMLS administration (Fig. 9). Fifteen minutes after BAMLS was given there was the expected acceleration in clearance of the

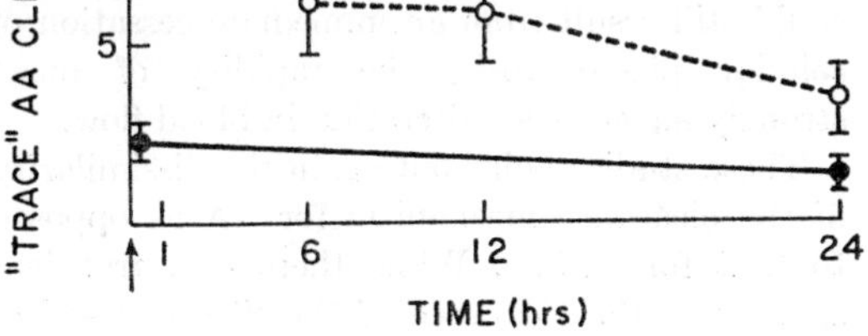

Figure 8. Rates of clearance (T-½) of the very small, "trace dose" of microaggregated human serum albumin (AA) at various intervals after injection of either antilymphocyte serum (BAMLS) or normal burro serum (NBS) at time "0" (↑). Each point is the mean of four animals with bars indicating standard errors.

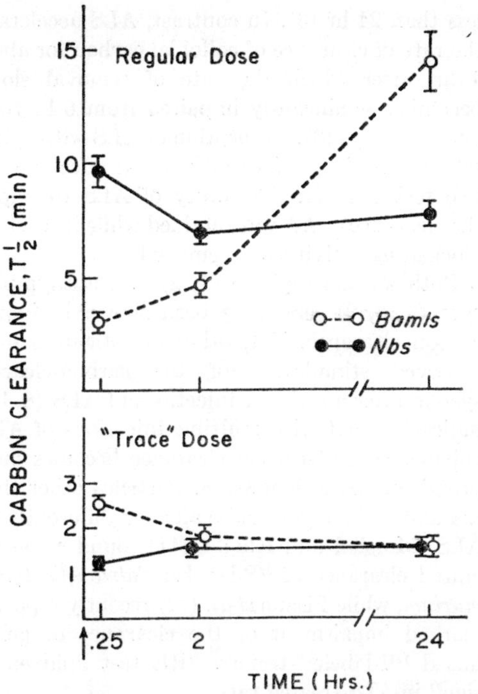

Figure 9. Rates of clearance of the regular (*top graph*) and "trace" (*bottom graph*) doses of carbon at various intervals after injection of either antilymphocyte serum (BAMLS) or normal burro serum (NBS) at time "0" (↑). Each point is the mean of four animals with bars indicating standard errors.

usual dose of carbon but impairment of the "trace dose" of carbon, implying decreased perfusion of RES tissues at a time when hyperphagocytic cellular activity must also have been present. Accelerated clearance of the usual carbon dose was still present at 2 hr, but clearance of the "trace dose" was not different from the control. At 24 hr, when there was marked impairment of the clearance of the usual dose of carbon, clearance of the "trace dose" of carbon was normal.

DISCUSSION

The present studies illustrate the profound and complex effects which ALS has on the clearance of colloidal particles from the blood. The degree, duration, and probably even the basic mechanisms of this effect seem to be dependent upon the type of colloid used to evaluate RES function. BAMLS immediately and profoundly impairs the clearance of AA from the blood; the degree of impairment is dose-dependent and the effect lasts less than 24 hr (3). In contrast, ALS accelerates the rate of clearance of colloidal carbon for about 4 hr, after which the rate of removal slows, becoming significantly impaired from 6 hr to as long as 3 days (3). Absorption of ALS with spleen cells results in another differential effect on the two test colloids: the ability of ALS to impair the clearance of AA was retained while its carbon-blockading activity was removed.

Both antimacrophage (1, 2) and antilymphocyte (3, 8, 9) sera have been shown to impair carbon clearance. Yet, other investigators have observed stimulation of the carbon-clearing system after a series of injections of ALS (8–10), indicating that with multiple injections of ALS, enhancement of carbon clearance becomes more prominent than depression. Particles other than AA and carbon seem to be affected differently by ALS. Marshal and Knight (11) found an accelerated clearance of ^{32}P-labeled *Salmonella typhimurium*, while Pisano *et al.* (12) recently reported marked impairment of the clearance of gelatinized ^{131}I-labeled triolein "RE test lipid emulsion" in ALS-treated rats.

Impaired phagocytosis of any colloidal particle could be explained by 1) direct injury of the macrophage responsible for phagocytosis, 2) removal or inactivation of serum factors (opsonins) which permit phagocytosis to occur, 3) production of other particles, such as other colloids or opsonized cells, which could compete with the test colloid at the cellular level or for opsonins, or 4) factors which might physically prevent interaction between the particle and the phagocytizing cell (e.g., decreased perfusion of the phagocytic cells). The exploration of each of these possibilities has been made much more difficult by the fact that ALS may affect the clearance of carbon and AA differently.

Pisano *et al.* (12) have studied the hepatic macrophages (Kupffer's cells) of rats and have found a direct injurious effect of their ALS preparation. They showed that *in vitro* phagocytosis of the gelatinized "RE test lipid emulsion" was impaired in liver slices from ALS-treated rats, and that the impairment was not due to a lack of opsonins. They further demonstrated the direct cytotoxicity of ALS on Kupffer cell suspensions. The gelatinized "RE test lipid emulsion" is handled quite similarly to carbon under other experimental conditions (13, 14).

Using carbon as the test colloid in ALS-treated rats, Grogan (8) found that the impaired clearance was corrected by the administration of non-heated normal rat serum. This is in contrast with our observation that even very large quantities of normal mouse serum failed to reverse the slowed carbon clearance, and with the finding of Pisano *et al.* (12) that normal rat serum failed to restore the phagocytic activity of ALS-treated Kupffer cells.

The intravascular production by ALS of colloidal particles or opsonized cells which could compete with either AA or carbon at the cellular level could be an important factor in the production of impaired RES phagocytosis. No particles were detectable either *in vitro* by the Ouchterlony technique or *in vivo* by passive transfer of ALS-treated mouse serum to normal mice. Everett *et al.* (15), however, have observed a massive accumulation of lymphocytes within macrophages of liver, spleen and lymph nodes of ALS-treated mice. This was seen as early as 2 hr after injection and was maximal at 8 hr. These findings suggest the possibility that opsonized cells could compete with colloidal particles, thereby producing an apparent RES blockade.

The major factor which might physically prevent interaction between the colloidal particle and the phagocytizing cell could be a decrease in perfusion of the RES organs, resulting in a decrease in clearance rate independent of actual cellular phagocytic activity. This was strongly suggested by the rapidity of onset of blockade when AA was used as the test colloid, and was supported by studies done with the "trace doses" of AA. These doses of AA clearly reflected RES (mainly hepatic) blood flow as shown by the constancy of the T-½ of doses below the "critical dose" (Fig. 1), and the clearance rates of these "trace doses" were immediately prolonged by ALS administration. While such alterations could still result from an immediate cessation of cellular phagocytosis, the rapidity of onset strongly suggests an alteration in blood flow.

These studies point out again the dissimilarity of the clearance mechanism for AA as opposed to that for carbon. While there is a transient slowing of the clearance of the "trace dose" of carbon immediately after ALS administration, as would be expected with altered blood flow, the "trace dose" carbon clearance rate becomes normal at a time when there is still marked blockade of the clearance of the "trace" AA dose. More importantly, it remains normal at a time when clearance of the large dose of carbon becomes markedly slowed, indicating that at least for the carbon-clearing mechanism, factors relating directly to cellular phagocytic function have been altered. Since there does not seem to be a decrease in opsonins, the most reasonable alternatives are a direct, injurious effect of ALS on phagocytizing cells *per se* (12) and/or blockade of particle uptake by masses of phagocytized lymphocytes (15).

RES blockade may be related to the immunosuppressive properties of ALS, since the uptake and processing of antigens constitute part of the inductive phase of the immune response (16). Although RES blockade by other means can diminish immunologic responsiveness (17), the effects of ALS must be more complex, since sera directed primarily against macrophages are only weakly immunosuppressive, if at all (18,19).

REFERENCES

1. Loewi, G., Temple, A., Nind, A. P. P. and Axelrad, M., Immunology, *16:* 99, 1969.
2. Hirsch, M. S., Gary, G. W., Jr. and Murphy, F. A., J. Immun., *102:* 656, 1969.
3. Sheagren, J. N., Barth, R. F., Edelin, J. B. and Malmgren, R. A., Lancet, *2:* 297, 1969.
4. Briner, W. H., J. Nucl. Med., *9:* 482, 1968.
5. Dobson, E. L. and Jones, H. B., Acta Med. Scand., *144* (Suppl.)*:* 273, 1952.
6. Benacerraf, B., Biozzi, G., Halpern, B. N., Stiffel, C. and Mouton, D., Brit. J. Exp. Path., *38:* 35, 1957.
7. Ouchterlony, O., Progr. Allerg., *5:* 1, 1958.
8. Grogan, J. B., J. Reticuloendothel. Soc., *6:* 411, 1969.
9. Gill, P. G. and Gotjamanos, T., Lancet, *2:* 645, 1969.
10. Kinnaert, P., Penneman, R. and Dirks, M., Lancet, *2:* 1250, 1969.
11. Marshall, V. R. and Knight, P. R., J. Immun., *102:* 1498, 1969.
12. Pisano, J. C., Patterson, J. T. and DiLuzio, N. R., Proc. Soc. Exp. Biol. Med., *132:* 517, 1969.
13. Filkins, J. P., Chase, R. E. and Smith, J. J., J. Reticuloendothel. Soc., *2:* 287, 1965.
14. Saba, T. M. and DiLuzio, N. R., J. Reticuloendothel. Soc., *2:* 437, 1965.
15. Everett, N. B., Schwarz, M. R., Tyler, R. W. and Perkins, W. D., Fed. Proc., *29:* 212, 1970.
16. Frei, P. C., Benacerraf, B. and Thorbecke, G. J., Proc. Nat. Acad. Sci., *53:* 20, 1965.
17. Wooles, W. R. and DiLuzio, N. R., Science, *142:* 1078, 1963.
18. Unanue, E. R., Nature, *218:* 36, 1968.
19. Barth, R. F., J. Immun., *103:* 648, 1969.

THE JOURNAL OF IMMUNOLOGY
Vol. 105, No. 3, September 1970

STAIRCASE RISE IN THE ANTIBODY-FORMING CELL POPULATION IN SECONDARY RESPONSE[1]

TOSHIHIKO SADO,[2] E. H. PERKINS AND T. MAKINODAN

From the Biology Division, Oak Ridge National Laboratory, Oak Ridge, Tennessee 37830

Received for publication March 9, 1970

Secondary anti-sheep RBC response by dispersed mouse spleen cells cultured in cell-impermeable diffusion chambers was assessed by the hemolytic plaque assay in combination with autoradiography and treatment with vinblastine. The results showed that, as in the spleen of mice undergoing a primary response, growth of the antibody-forming cell population occurred non-randomly in a staircase manner and recruitment of precursor cells into the antibody-forming cell population occurred repeatedly in a non-random manner. However, the size of the recruitment was significantly larger than that in the spleen of mice undergoing a primary response (i.e., a maximum of 40-fold *vs* 4-fold). Further studies on these precursor cells indicated that they transform into antibody-forming cells after a short but distinct lag following completion of mitosis. Another important observation was that the antigen-triggered proliferation of immunocompetent precursor cells could have occurred as early as 30 min after exposure of dispersed spleen cells to the test antigen, in contrast to a lag of more than 10 hr in the spleen of mice undergoing a primary response.

We have shown that in spleens of mice undergoing a primary antibody response to sheep red blood cells (RBC) the antibody-forming cell population increased non-randomly in a staircase manner (1, 2) due to transformation of antigen-triggered, proliferating precursor cells into antibody-forming cells (i.e., recruitment). The data indicated that the recruitment size increased exponentially with time after the initial recruitment of antibody-forming cells. Because the spleen is an "open" system, precursor cells, as well as antibody-forming cells, can migrate to and from the spleen. Thus, we do not know to what extent migration might contribute to the staircase pattern of growth. For a similar study in a closed system, we chose the cell-impermeable Millipore diffusion chamber culture system (3, 4). The secondary anti-sheep RBC response was assessed because earlier studies (5) indicated that this culture system supported the development of both indirect and direct hemolytic plaque-forming cells (PFC) extremely well when spleen cells from previously immunized (primed) mice were cultured together with the test antigen. In contrast, only direct PFC developed when non-primed cells were cultured with the test antigen. Additionally, kinetic data could be obtained not only for direct PFC but also for indirect PFC (the predominant cell type in a secondary response) in this closed system. Thus, the kinetics of development of indirect and direct PFC were studied by means of short interval sampling, on the one hand, and combined autoradiography and the hemolytic plaque procedure, on the other. A potent mitotic inhibitor, vinblastine, was also employed to analyse the role of cellular proliferation in relation to the time of appearance and recruitment of antibody-forming cells. Special attention was directed towards the question of whether the antibody-forming cell population increased in a non-random manner.

These studies strongly indicate that in the closed chamber, as well as in the spleen of antigen-stimulated mice (1, 2), growth of the antibody-forming cell population did not occur in a random manner. Another important observation was that transformation of precursor cells into antibody-forming cells occurred shortly after mitosis.

[1] Research sponsored by the United States Atomic Energy Commission under contract with the Union Carbide Corporation.

[2] Present address: Division of Physiology and Pathology, National Institute of Radiological Sciences, Chiba, Japan.

MATERIALS AND METHODS

In vivo diffusion chamber culture. This technique has been described in detail in earlier publications from this laboratory (3, 4). In the experiments reported here the cell-impermeable Millipore diffusion chambers (porosity of Millipore filters, 0.22 ± 0.02 μ), containing 2.4×10^7 dispersed, primed spleen cells from young adult (C3H × 101)F_1 mice and 2.4×10^6 sheep RBC, were implanted into the peritoneal cavities of syngeneic mice that had received 600 R of whole-body irradiation a few hours earlier. Control chambers contained identical numbers of primed spleen cells and syngeneic mouse RBC. Donors of spleen cells were immunized 6 to 10 weeks earlier with a single intraperitoneal injection of 2.5×10^8 sheep RBC.

Assessment of specific antibody-forming cells by the hemolytic plaque procedure. Spleen cells producing specific antibodies against sheep RBC were assayed by hemolytic plaque formation in agar gels. Indirect and direct PFC were assayed according to the method of Wortis *et al.* (6) and Jerne *et al.* (7), respectively. Details of harvesting cells from chambers for PFC assay have been described elsewhere (5).

Autoradiographic analysis of proliferation of PFC and their precursors. A combined autoradiographic and PFC assay method, described in detail previously (2), has been developed to study the proliferation of PFC. In the present study, however, Kodak NTB3 nuclear track emulsion was used exclusively for detecting ^{3}H- or ^{14}C-thymidine-labeled PFC; the exposure time was 14 days.

For an experiment employing the double labeling technique with ^{3}H- and ^{14}C-thymidine, the double dipping method of Wimber and Quastler (8) was adapted to the Petri-dish method used to detect individual PFC (2).

The ^{3}H-thymidine and the ^{14}C-thymidine (Schwarz BioResearch, Inc., Orangeburg, N. Y.) had a specific activity of 0.36 Ci/mmol and 100 mCi/mmol, respectively. The dose of injected isotope as well as the injection schedule will be described in each section of the experimental results.

Vinblastine. Vinblastine sulphate (Velban, Eli Lilly and Co.) was dissolved in sterile physiologic saline at concentrations of 25 μg/ml and was injected intraperitoneally in volumes of 1 ml/mouse.

Morphology of PFC. Morphologic analysis of PFC was carried out on plates prepared for autoradiographic analysis of individual PFC. As expected, cellular differential analysis of individual plaques was not easy by this method. Nevertheless, it allowed a rough classification of the plaques into the following six categories: a) typical plasma cells, b) typical small lymphocytes (cells with nearly naked nuclei), c) basophilic mononuclear cells (9), d) unidentifiable cells (in most cases, damaged cells), e) degenerative cells (cells with fragmented nuclei, lobulated nuclei or pycnotic nuclei, etc.), and f) plaques with no cells detected.

RESULTS

Kinetics of appearance and disappearance of indirect and direct PFC. The secondary anti-sheep RBC response profile of dispersed mouse spleen cells in diffusion chambers, in terms of number of indirect and direct PFC, is shown in Figure 1. It can be seen that after a lag period of about 2 days indirect and direct PFC began to increase with doubling times of ∼4 and ∼7 hr, respectively, between days 2 and 4, and doubling times of ∼22 and ∼48 hr, respectively, between days 4 and 6. During the next few weeks the number of indirect and direct PFC decreased with a half-time ($T_{1/2}$) of 5 and 4 days, respectively. At the time of peak response, 1 out of every 10 nucleated cells in each culture, or 10% of the cells, was a specific hemolysin-type antibody producer, confirming an earlier observation by one of us (5). Furthermore, at this time there were 10 times more indirect PFC than direct PFC. The difference was even larger after 8 weeks of culture; i.e., at this time the chambers yielded on an average 6690 indirect and 175 direct PFC.

Estimates of the cell cycle time. Three groups of mice, each consisting of three mice bearing 4-day cultures, were injected intraperitoneally with a single dose of either a) ^{3}H-thymidine (^{3}H-TdR, 10 μCi/mouse) (group A), b) ^{14}C-thymidine (^{14}C-TdR, 5 μCi/mouse) (group B), or c) both ^{3}H-TdR and ^{14}C-TdR successively with an interval of 45 min (group C). Chambers were harvested 30 min after injection of the isotope in groups A and B and, in the case of group C, 30 min after injection of the second isotope. The results are shown in Table I. It can be seen that the frequency of labeled PFC (labeling index) in groups A and B showed a fairly good agreement for

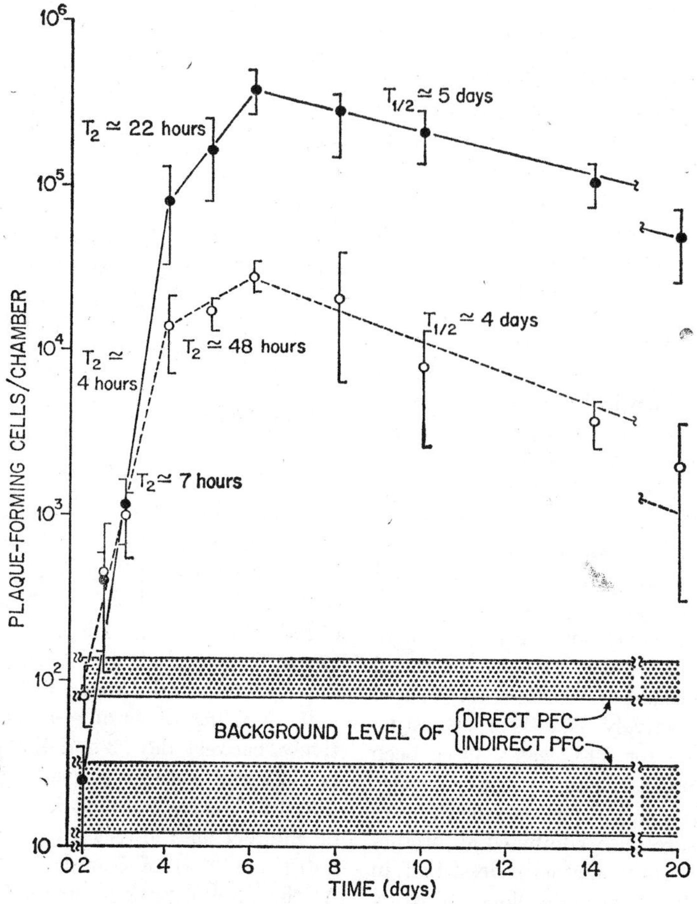

Figure 1. Kinetics of secondary anti-sheep RBC response in terms of number of indirect and direct PFC in diffusion chamber cultures of dispersed mouse spleen cells (2.4×10^7 primed spleen cells + 2.4×10^6 sheep RBC). Sample size, 4 to 10 chambers/point. ●, Indirect PFC; ○, direct PFC. *Vertical bar*, 2 standard errors. Background PFC level was determined from the negative control cultures (see *Materials and Methods*).

both indirect and direct PFC, indicating that our autoradiographic method was as sensitive with ^{3}H-TdR as with ^{14}C-TdR. Thus, in the later experiments only ^{3}H-TdR was used to label PFC. The frequency of labeled PFC in group C was a little lower than in the first two groups. This may have been due to a decrease in the fraction of PFC in the DNA synthesis phase caused by a time lag of ~1 hr for this assessment as compared to a lag of 30 min for groups A and B. This is expected if, as will be seen below, the growth of PFC population is not random.

From the results obtained from group C, the DNA synthesis time (T_s) of PFC may be estimated by using the generally accepted equation $(^3H)/(^{14}C) = t/T_s$, where (^{3}H) and (^{14}C) are the numbers of PFC labeled with ^{3}H-TdR and ^{14}C-TdR, respectively, and t the time between two injections (8, 10). As indicated in the next to last column of this table, the estimated T_s for indirect and direct PFC at this time of assessment were 2.2 and 4.5 hr, respectively. These estimates are considerably shorter than those reported previously for many other mammalian cell types (e.g., see 11). Nevertheless, if one accepts these estimates and further assumes that the PFC population is growing *exponentially* in a *random* manner, then the cell-cycle time of PFC can be estimated by use of the equation, labeling index $= 0.693 \times T_s/T_c$ (12), where T_c is the cell-cycle or generation time. The calculated cell-cycle times for indirect and direct PFC were

TABLE I

Analysis of proliferative indices of PFC during the log phase[a]

Group	Isotope	Type of PFC	Labeled with ^{3}H-TdR	Labeled with ^{14}C-TdR	Unlabeled	Total	Frequency of Labeled PFC[b]	(^{3}H)/(^{14}C)	T_s	T_c[c]
A	^{3}H-TdR	Indirect	154		210	364	0.423			
		Direct	96		103	198	0.485			
B	^{14}C-TdR	Indirect		407	393	800	0.509			
		Direct		126	135	261	0.483			
C	^{3}H-TdR + ^{14}C-TdR	Indirect	36	106	112	254	0.417	0.340	2.2	3.6
		Direct	25	149	205	379	0.393	0.168	4.5	7.9

[a] (^{3}H), number of PFC labeled with ^{3}H-TdR; (^{14}C), number of PFC labeled with ^{14}C-TdR; T_s, DNA synthesis time; T_c, cell cycle time.

[b] Determined 30 min after a single pulse exposure to radioactive thymidine, and therefore in group C only those cells labeled with ^{14}C-TdR were included here. When ^{3}H-TdR-labeled cells are deleted from the total number of cells counted, the frequency of labeled PFC is 0.486 rather than 0.417 for indirect PFC, and 0.421 rather than 0.393 for direct PFC.

[c] Calculated from the formula: labeling index = $0.693 \times T_s/T_c$ (12) on the assumption that the PFC population was growing exponentially and randomly at this time of examination.

3.6 and 7.9 hr, respectively. These values correspond fairly well with the doubling times of 4.0 and 7.2 hr estimated from Figure 1 during this same period of assessment. Thus, it is tempting to assume that the PFC population is growing exponentially *in a random manner during the log phase*. However, our earlier studies (1, 2) and studies to be discussed in the subsequent section show that growth of the antibody-forming cell population does not occur in a random manner. Hence, this restricts one from using kinetic equations applicable to systems where cells are growing randomly.

Stepwise expansion of PFC population during the log phase. To determine whether the exponential growth of PFC population during the log phase is entirely random (linear increase in a semilogarithmic plot) or non-random (stepwise increase), an experiment was conducted in which chambers were sampled every 2 hr for a 38-hr period starting at 48 hr after culture, the time when the number of PFC in the chambers is expected to increase exponentially. The data were then subjected to statistical analysis of the slope at varying time increments. Thus, the slope, which measures the rate of increase in the number of PFC in the chamber/unit time interval, was calculated for a 6-, 8-, 10-, and 12-hr increment beginning 48 hr after exposure to antigen and progressively at each 2-hr interval thereafter. Hence, the slopes were determined for the 6-hr increment at intervals of 48 to 54 hr, 50 to 56 hr, 52 to 58 hr, etc., and for the 8-hr increment at intervals of 48 to 56 hr, 50 to 58 hr, 52 to 60 hr, etc. The slopes were also determined for the 10- and 12-hr increments in a similar manner. If the number of PFC increases randomly, the slope for any time increment should not be a function of time, and it should not differ significantly from that estimated for the time increment of 48 to 86 hr (doubling time of 2.83 hr for indirect PFC and 3.42 hr for direct PFC). Thus, a horizontal line would be expected from plots of the calculated slopes of these time increments *vs* time after antigenic stimulation. If, on the other hand, the increase in the number of PFC were due to non-random growth, the slopes would vary drastically with time after stimulation. The results of such an analysis are presented in Figure 2. It can be seen that doubling times ranged from less than 1 hr to over 100 hr. Furthermore, the fact that the pattern of change in the slope as a function of time after antigenic stimulation is independent of the 6-, 8-, 10-, or 12-hr increment employed in the analysis indicates that the number of PFC in the chamber during the log phase is increasing non-randomly to a great extent.

These findings justified presentation of the data in the manner shown in Figure 3. In spite of the fairly large scatter of individual samples, the data strongly suggest a stepwise expansion of the PFC population. The results of both indirect and direct PFC strongly indicate that there were at least three stages of stepwise expansion between 60 hr and 86 hr. The expansions during the first

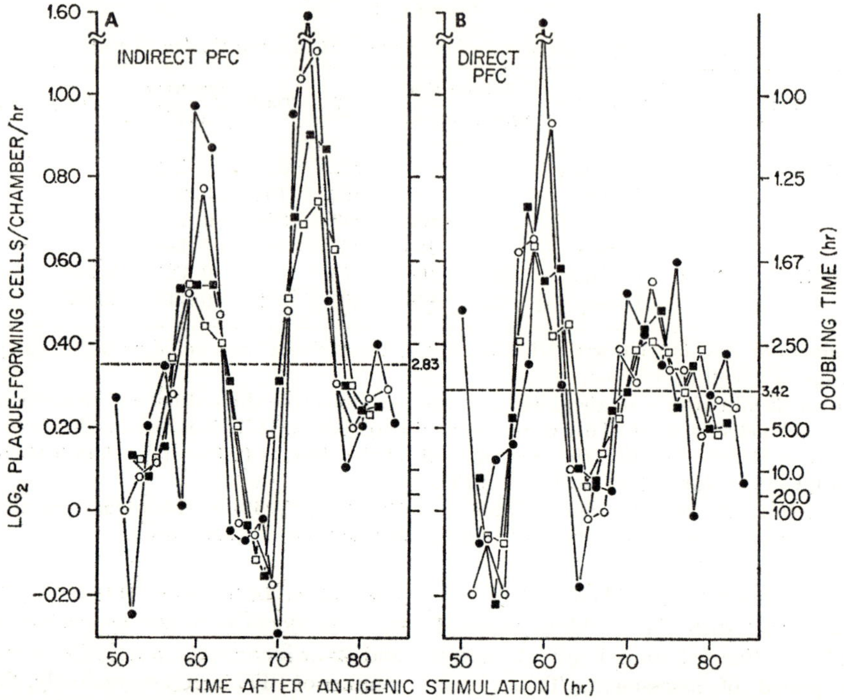

Figure 2. Estimates of the slopes for 6-, 8-, 10-, and 12-hr increments progressing at a 2-hr interval during the 48- to 84-hr portion of the log phase of secondary anti-sheep RBC response—evidence for a non-random increase in the number of PFC. ●, 6-Hr increment (48–54, 50–56, → 78–84); ○, 8-hr increment (48–56, 50–58, → 76–84); ■, 10-hr increment (48–58, 50–60, → 74–84); □, 12-hr increment (48–60, 50–62, → 72–84).

two steps were dramatic, showing an increase of 10- and 40-fold, respectively. If all PFC had arisen exclusively from the division of previously functional PFC this increase should have been only twofold at each step of expansion. Thus, these results indicate that massive numbers of precursor cells were transforming into functional PFC non-randomly. The data also show that the exact length of the lag phase for the appearance of both indirect and direct PFC in this culture system was 60 hr.

The phase of the cell cycle at which the transformation event takes place. In order to see if this massive transformation from precursor cells into antibody-forming cells involves mitosis, we studied the effect of vinblastine, a mitotic poison, on this process. Approximately 4, 2, and 0 hr before the expected time of the dramatic stepwise increase in the number of PFC, groups of chamber-bearing mice were injected intraperitoneally with 25 μg of vinblastine dissolved in 1 ml of saline. This dose was selected because preliminary experiments indicated that 25 μg of vinblastine, given 60 hr after culture, resulted in 99.9% suppression in the number of indirect and direct PFC harvested on day 6. Every 2 hr after injection of the drug, five chambers were harvested from each group and their contents were assessed for the number of PFC. Another group of mice, which had received an equal volume of saline, was used as a control. The results of this experiment are summarized in Table II. Increase in the PFC population at this time interval between 68 hr and 78 hr was not as great as that observed previously (cf. Fig. 2). Nevertheless, there was a significant fivefold increase in the number of indirect and direct PFC between 70 hr and 72 hr. When vinblastine was given at 68 hr, increase in the number of indirect PFC during the next 8 hr was completely suppressed, indicating a predominant role of cellular division for this transformation event. When vinblastine was administered at 70 hr, suppression was only partial, suggesting that significant numbers of transformable precursor cells were no longer susceptible to the effect of the drug. The drug was

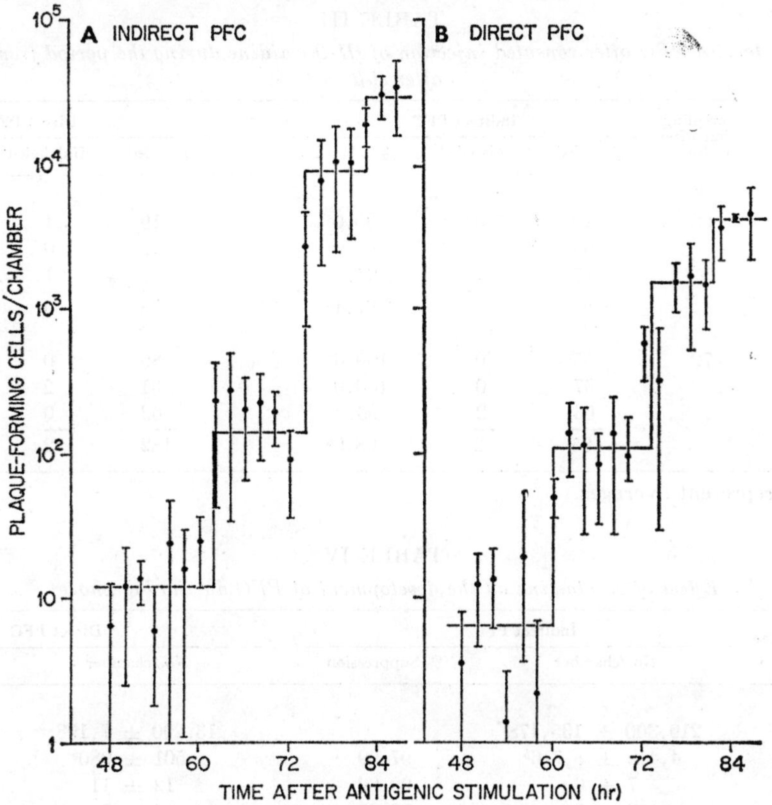

Figure 3. Staircase growth pattern of indirect (*A*) and direct (*B*) plaque-forming cell population in diffusion chamber cultures of dispersed mouse spleen cells undergoing secondary anti-sheep RBC response. Sample size, five chambers/point. *Vertical bar*, 2 standard errors.

TABLE II

Effect of vinblastine on the expansion of PFC population[a]

Type of PFC	Sampling Time after Culture	Control	Time (hr) of Administration of Vinblastine: 68	70	72
	hr				
Indirect	68	174 ± 76			
	70	431 ± 282	322 ± 256		
	72	2141 ± 1252	268 ± 154	1019 ± 896	
	74	2528 ± 1660	170 ± 242	599 ± 308	2021 ± 1998
	76	5460 ± 4118	415 ± 340	710 ± 320	1599 ± 1000
	78	7117 ± 3840	1382 ± 1122	3577 ± 3494	3222 ± 1376
Direct	68	466 ± 158			
	70	489 ± 240	673 ± 456		
	72	2509 ± 1112	1136 ± 480	519 ± 240	
	74	2774 ± 1636	186 ± 254	1188 ± 734	2303 ± 2600
	76	7853 ± 6648	364 ± 272	1451 ± 778	3279 ± 2524
	78	3585 ± 1720	1674 ± 1136	6381 ± 5092	3222 ± 1376

[a] Sample size, five chambers/group; values expressed as mean number of PFC ± 2 S.E.

TABLE III

Appearance of labeled PFC after repeated injection of ^3H-thymidine during the period from 24 hr to 48 hr after culture

Chamber No.	Sampling Time after Culture	Indirect PFC			Direct PFC		
		Labeled	Unlabeled	% Labeled	Labeled	Unlabeled	% Labeled
	hr						
1	60	19	0	100.0	19	1	95.0
2		63	2	96.9	12	0	100.0
3		17	1	94.4	7	1	87.5
Total		99	3	97.1[a]	38	2	95.0[a]
1	72	85	0	100.0	89	0	100.0
2		37	0	100.0	31	2	93.9
3		63	2	96.9	62	0	100.0
Total		185	2	98.9[a]	182	2	98.9[a]

[a] Numbers represent averages.

TABLE IV

Effect of vinblastine on the development of PFC during lag phase[a]

Time of Vinblastine Treatment	Indirect PFC		Direct PFC	
	No./chamber	% Suppression	No./chamber	% Suppression
hr				
Control	219,300 ± 135,178		13,290 ± 7,198	
0.5	4,410 ± 8,716[b]	97.99	501 ± 980[b]	96.23
6	7 ± 6	99.99	12 ± 11	99.91
12	3 ± 6	99.99	6 ± 7	99.96
24	6,013 ± 11,994[b]	97.26	1,434 ± 2,552[b]	89.21
36	26 ± 14	99.99	5 ± 4	99.97
48	74 ± 60	99.97	17 ± 10	99.98

[a] Sample size, four to six chambers/group; values expressed as mean number of PFC ± 2 S.E.

[b] One out of five chambers contained high PFC counts.

least effective when administered at the time of the transformation event. The results obtained with direct PFC were comparable but less clear-cut. Thus, these results strongly indicate that transformation of precursor cells into antibody-forming cells requires cellular division prior to this event, a notion which has been held by many investigators in the field of cellular differentiation (13, 14) but has never been tested in a comprehensive manner for the antibody-forming cell system. Finally, it should be noted that if the effect of the drug is almost instantaneous, the results further indicate that transformation of precursor cells occurs not immediately but a few hours after mitosis.

Role of proliferation during the lag phase on the development of PFC. In this study ^{3}H-TdR was injected five times between 24 hr and 48 hr after culture, and PFC were analyzed autoradiographically 12 hr and 24 hr after the last injection of the isotope. The results shown in Table III clearly indicate that practically all PFC were labeled. It is obvious from these results that precursors of antibody-forming cells were themselves proliferating before they transformed into functional antibody-forming cells.

These studies did not answer the question of when the antigen-triggered proliferation event essential for the development of PFC commenced in this culture system. In an attempt to provide this answer we carried out an experiment in which 25 μg of vinblastine were administered intraperitoneally 30 min and 12, 24, 36 and 48 hr after implantation of chambers, and the number of both indirect and direct PFC assayed on the 6th day of culture. The results, given in Table IV,

TABLE V

Morphology of PFC during time of peak secondary response

Type of PFC	Chamber No.	Cell Type in Plaque[a]: Basophilic mononuclear cells (i)	Typical plasma cells (ii)	Typical small lymphocytes[b]	Unidentified damaged cells	Degenerative cells (iii)[c]	Plaques with no cells	Sum	i + ii + iii / Total Identified Cells
Indirect	1	4 (11.4)	18 (51.4)	0 (0.0)	3 (8.6)	6 (17.4)	3 (8.6)	35 (100.0)	
	2	2 (4.8)	24 (57.1)	0 (0.0)	6 (14.3)	8 (19.0)	2 (4.8)	42 (100.0)	
	3	14 (17.1)	30 (36.6)	3 (3.7)	5 (6.1)	17 (20.7)	13 (15.9)	82 (100.0)	
	4	15 (27.8)	17 (31.5)	1 (1.9)	7 (13.0)	9 (16.7)	5 (9.3)	54 (100.0)	
	Total	35 (16.4)	89 (41.8)	4 (1.9)	21 (9.8)	40 (18.8)	23 (10.8)	212 (100.0)	164/168 (97.6)
Direct	1	5 (29.4)	9 (52.7)	0 (0.0)	1 (5.9)	2 (11.8)	0 (0.0)	17 (100.0)	
	2	5 (18.5)	17 (63.0)	0 (0.0)	3 (11.1)	1 (3.7)	1 (3.7)	27 (100.0)	
	3	12 (24.0)	26 (52.0)	1 (2.0)	1 (2.0)	10 (20.0)	0 (0.0)	50 (100.0)	
	4	9 (17.3)	24 (46.1)	1 (1.9)	0 (0.0)	14 (26.9)	4 (7.7)	52 (100.0)	
	Total	31 (21.2)	76 (52.1)	2 (1.4)	5 (3.4)	27 (18.5)	5 (4.1)	146 (100.0)	134/136 (98.5)

[a] Values in parentheses indicate percentages of total cells counted.
[b] Cells with nearly naked nuclei.
[c] Cells with fragmented nuclei, lobulated nuclei, pycnotic nuclei, etc.

show that vinblastine caused a nearly complete suppression of the development of PFC when injected even as early as 30 min after implantation of the chambers. This would suggest that the antigen-triggered proliferation essential for the development of PFC commenced immediately after the precursor cells of primed donors had been stimulated with the antigen.

Morphology of plaque-forming cells. Differential counts of PFC performed at the time of peak response (i.e., on day 6) are given in Table V. The proportion of cells with a typical plasma cell morphology constituted approximately 42% and 52% for indirect and direct PFC, respectively. It must be pointed out, however, that many of the cells classified as basophilic mononuclear cells (9) could be atypical plasma cells with larger nuclear-cytoplasmic ratios. Furthermore, cells classified as degenerative cells, which included binucleated cells and cells with lobulated or fragmented nuclei, frequently had characteristics of plasma cells. Thus, it is possible that as high as 98% of the total indirect or direct PFC may be typical and atypical plasma cells. Electron microscopic analysis of these individual PFC is now in progress.

The frequency of plaques not containing any identifiable cell was 11% for indirect and 4% for direct PFC. This means that plaques caused by cellular fragment or debris which may be peculiar to the present system do not constitute a significant fraction of the total plaques enumerated.

DISCUSSION

Information on the cytokinetics of antibody response has been accumulating at an expanding rate during the past few years (see, for example, Cold Spring Harbor Symposium on Quantitative Biology, Vol. XXXII, and references 15 and 16) and the hemolytic plaque procedure developed independently by Jerne *et al.* (7), Ingraham (17), and Ingraham and Bussard (18) and their modifications (6, 19, 20) have contributed enormously to the accelerated progress of this field. Thus, most of the recent investigators attempting to analyse the role of cellular proliferation during the exponential growth of the antibody-forming cell population have used the hemolytic plaque procedure in conjunction with autoradiographic analysis (1, 2, 21–26) or have used mitotic inhibitors (1, 2, 27, 28).

Two major conclusions were drawn from these studies: a) antibody-forming cells are derived from a single recruitment of precursor cells and are proliferating randomly (28) and b) antibody-forming cells are continuously recruited from precursor cells and proliferate in a random manner with steady-state kinetics (21). In both cases it was concluded that growth of the antibody-forming cell population is occurring in a random manner. However, it became apparent, in terms of model analysis (16), that data derived from sampling intervals longer than the estimated doubling time of the antibody-forming cell population were inadequate for critical analysis. Review of the literature (16) indicated that, with the exception of one published work performed *in vivo*, all the data accumulated in this area were based on a sampling interval equal to, or longer than, the estimated doubling time. The exception is that reported by Perkins *et al.* (1, 2)—who, as stated earlier, performed their sampling at intervals of 2 hr. They found that the number of direct PFC in the spleen of mice undergoing a primary response did not increase in a random manner, but in a staircase manner, suggesting a considerable degree of synchronous growth. They also noted that recruitment of precursor cells into the antibody-forming cell population was occurring discontinuously at about the time when the proliferating cells completed their mitosis. Furthermore, the size of each successive recruitment was noted to increase exponentially during the log phase of response, as deduced by Dutton and Mishell (29). Finally, they showed, in confirmation of the earlier studies of Syeklocha *et al.* (27), that the precursor cells do not undergo proliferation until at least 10 hr after antigenic stimulation. More recently, Saunders (30) reported that growth of the direct plaque-forming cell population during early log phase of the primary response initiated *in vitro* also proceeds synchronously in a staircase manner.

We have undertaken to extend these findings by assessing the secondary anti-sheep RBC reponse of dispersed spleen cells in cell-impermeable diffusion chamber cultures. The following questions were asked: 1) What is the growth pattern of the antibody-forming cell population in a secondary response? 2) Can recruitment of precursor cells into the antibody-forming cell population occur more than once after antigenic stimulation in a closed system? If so, is the pattern of recruitment distinct from that seen *in situ* in the spleen, which is an open system? 3) Must precursor cells undergo at least one cell cycle before they can transform into antibody-forming cells, as seen in the spleen, and, if so, how soon after antigenic stimulation do they undergo their first cell cycle?

The results reported here show that during the log phase of a secondary response in diffusion chambers, growth of the PFC population, particularly the indirect PFC, the predominant type of PFC, occurred non-randomly, as in the case of direct PFC population in the spleen of mice undergoing a primary response. Furthermore, recruitment of precursor cells into both the indirect and direct PFC population occurred more than once and non-randomly. However, the size of the recruitment was significantly larger than that in the spleen of mice undergoing a primary response for reasons not known. Thus, for example, the magnitude of increase in the PFC population at each of the first two staircase steps ranged from 10- to over 40-fold. In contrast, the maximum amplification between two staircase steps was fourfold during the primary response in the spleen. Thus, it is clear from these studies that non-random recruitment of precursor cells can also take place in a secondary response in a closed system where migration of precursor cells is not possible.

What, then, is the nature of precursor cells which are recruited discontinously into the PFC population? Experiments were designed using vinblastine to determine how soon after exposure to the test antigen precursor cells began to proliferate. The results indicated that proliferation may have commenced as early as 30 min after antigenic restimulation. It is also possible that the precursor cells of the spleen of primed donors may have entered the cell cycle immediately after they were dispersed mechanically by teasing. In contrast, it has been shown previously (1, 2) that in the spleen of unstimulated mice, precursor cells are normally in a "resting" stage and in a primary anti-sheep RBC response they do not undergo proliferation until at least 10 hr after antigenic stimulation. The difference in the proliferative property of precursor cells undergoing primary and secondary responses may reflect the existence of distinct types of precursor cells, differences in the availability of antigen, and/or differences in the catabolism of the drug between the primary responders and the 600 R-treated bearers of diffusion chamber cultures.

Again, experiments were carried out with vinblastine to determine how soon after mitosis the precursor cells transform into antibody-forming cells. The results indicated that this transformation takes place not immediately but 1 to 2 hr after division. It remains to be established if this is also characteristic of precursor cells involved in the staircase growth of the antibody-forming cell population in a primary response.

One of the common pitfalls in the analysis of the growth patterns of antibody-forming cell populations is to assume that growth is occurring randomly, as in the case of many nondifferentiating cell systems. As emphasized elsewhere (16), this assumption is based on data derived primarily from sampling of cells at intervals of 12 hr or more. With many of the nondifferentiating cell systems this would have been a satisfactory method because the generation time is $\geq$24 hr and the frequency of death is minimal. However, growth of the antibody-forming cell population is exceedingly complex, involving not only proliferation but also differentiation. Furthermore, the doubling time of the antibody-forming cell population, reflective of the growth rate, is not constant and can be less than 6 hr. The following information emphasizes the danger in assuming random growth of the antibody-forming cell population. Using data derived from the very sensitive (^{3}H- and ^{14}C-thymidine) double labeling method that has been used previously by others (21), and equations suitable for nondifferentiating cells growing randomly, generation times of indirect and direct PFC during the log phase were calculated to be 3.6 hr and 7.9 hr, respectively. These estimates were comparable to the estimated doubling time of the respective PFC population (i.e., 4 hr and 7.2 hr, respectively). Unpublished data of T. Sado revealed that at later times after antigenic stimulation the estimates of generation times can be extended beyond 24 hr, provided the frequency of nonproliferating, fully differentiated antibody-forming cells, which increases with time after the initiation of the growth phase, is not taken into consideration. Unfortunately, the double pulse labeling procedure does not permit us to distinguish these cells from those that are proliferating but are not in the DNA synthesis phase. Hopefully, this information may discourage others from taking this approach.

Finally, we wish to comment briefly on the morphology of indirect and direct PFC. Recent studies on isolated (direct) plaque-forming cells in a primary response showed that they are heterogeneous with respect to morphology (9, 31–35). Our present results on both indirect and direct PFC obtained during the peak of secondary response are consistent with these observations. An additional observation of interest was that a significant frequency of the PFC (18%) can be classified as degenerative cells, i.e., cells with fragmented nuclei, lobulated nuclei, pycnotic nuclei, etc. Whether or not these cells are reflective of an "end" stage in the differentiation vector of antibody-forming cells or of errors resulting from acceleration in differentiation and proliferation needs to be resolved.

Acknowledgments. We are grateful to Dr. William E. Lever of the Mathematics Division, Oak Ridge National Laboratory, for statistical treatment of the data, and to Mr. James M. Ellis for expert technical assistance.

REFERENCES

1. Perkins, E. H., Sado, T. and Makinodan, T., J. Reticuloendothel. Soc., *5:* 560, 1968.
2. Perkins, E. H., Sado, T. and Makinodan, T., J. Immun., *103:* 668, 1969.
3. Capalbo, E. E., Albright, J. F. and Bennett, W. E., J. Immun., *92:* 243, 1964.
4. Nettesheim, P., Makinodan, T. and Chadwick, C. J., Immunology, *11:* 427, 1966.
5. Sado, T., Int. J. Radiat. Biol. *15:* 1, 1969.
6. Wortis, H. H., Taylor, R. B. and Dresser, D. W., Immunology, *11:* 603, 1966.
7. Jerne, N. K., Nordin, A. A. and Henry, C., in *Cell-Bound Antibodies*, Edited by B. Amos and H. Koprowski, p. 109, Wistar Institute Press, Philadelphia, 1963.
8. Wimber, D. E. and Quastler, H., Exp. Cell Res., *30:* 8, 1963.
9. Cunningham, A. J., Austral. J. Exp. Biol. Med. Sci., *46:* 141, 1968.
10. Wimber, D. E., in *Cell Proliferation*, Edited by L. F. Lamerton and R. J. M. Fry, p. 1, Blackwell Scientific Publications, Oxford, 1963.
11. Defendi, V. and Manson, L. A., Nature, *198:* 359, 1963.
12. Steel, G. G. and Lamerton, L. F., Exp. Cell Res., *37:* 117, 1965.
13. Quastler, H., in *Cell Proliferation*, Edited by L. F. Lamerton and R. J. M. Fry, p. 18, Blackwell Scientific Publications, Oxford, 1963.
14. Thrasher, J. D., in *Methods in Cell Physiology*, Edited by D. M. Prescott, Vol. II, p. 323, Academic Press, New York and London, 1966.
15. Makinodan, T. and Albright, J. F., Progr. Allerg., *10:* 1, 1967.
16. Makinodan, T., Sado, T., Groves, D. L. and

Price, G., in Curr. Top. Microbiol. Immun., *49:* 80, 1969.
17. Ingraham, J. S., Compt. Rend. Acad. Sci., *256:* 5005, 1963.
18. Ingraham, J. S. and Bussard, A., J. Exp. Med., *119:* 667, 1964.
19. Sterzl, J. and Riha, I., Nature, *208:* 858, 1965.
20. Dresser, D. W. and Wortis, H. H., Nature, *208:* 859, 1965.
21. Tannenberg, W. J. K. and Malaviya, A. N., J. Exp. Med., *128:* 895, 1968.
22. Sterzl, J., Vesely, J., Jilek, M. and Mandel, L., in *Molecular and Cellular Basis of Antibody Formation*, Edited by J. Sterzl, p. 463, Czechoslovak Academy of Sciences, Prague, 1965.
23. Sterzl, J., Jilek, M., Vesely, J. and Mandel, L., in *Proceedings of the G. Mendel Memorial Symposium, Genetic Variations in Somatic Cells*, p. 233, Academia, Prague, 1966.
24. Harris, G., J. Exp. Med., *127:* 661, 1968.
25. Szenberg, A. and Cunningham, A. J., Nature, *214:* 747, 1968.
26. Krisch, R. E., Nature, *222:* 1295, 1969.
27. Syeklocha, D., Simminovitch, L., Till, J. E. and McCulloch, E. A., J. Immun., *96:* 472, 1966.
28. Rowley, D. A., Fitch, F. W., Mosier, D. E., Solliday, S., Coppelson, L. W. and Brown, B. W., J. Exp. Med., *127:* 983, 1968.
29. Dutton, R. W. and Mishell, R. I., Cold Spring Harbor Symp. Quant. Biol., *32:* 407, 1968.
30. Saunders, G. C., J. Exp. Med., *130:* 543, 1969.
31. Bussard, A. E. and Binet, J. L., in *Molecular and Cellular Basis of Antibody Formation*, Edited by J. Sterzl, p. 477, Czechoslovak Academy of Sciences, Prague, 1965.
32. Fitch, F. W., Rowley, D. A. and Coulthard, S., Nature, *207:* 994, 1965.
33. Harris, T. N., Hummeler, K. and Harris, S., J. Exp. Med., *123:* 161, 1966.
34. Hummeler, K., Harris, T. N., Tomassini, N., Hechtel, M. and Farber, M. B., J. Exp. Med., *124:* 255, 1966.
35. Irimajiri, K., Horiuchi, A., Okamoto, Y. and Amaki, I., Blood, *33:* 149, 1969.

THE JOURNAL OF IMMUNOLOGY
Vol. 105, No. 3, September 1970

Printed in U.S.A.

INDEPENDENCE OF ALLOTYPIC DETERMINANTS AND ANTIBODY SPECIFICITY[1]

SUSAN B. SPRING,[2] ALFRED NISONOFF[3] AND SHELDON DRAY

From the Departments of Biochemistry and Microbiology, University of Illinois at the Medical Center, Chicago, Illinois 60680

Received for publication March 7, 1970

Studies were carried out to ascertain whether the specificity of an IgG antibody molecule influences the expression of the full complement of determinants characteristic of a given allotype. The presence of determinants was measured by the capacity of a given IgG preparation to displace from anti-allotypic antibodies all of a reference ^{125}I-Fab fragment, possessing the same allotype, but derived from a different source. The results indicated that all IgG molecules studied, including specifically purified antibodies, possess a full complement of determinants (a1, a3, b4) and suggest that the portion of the surface of the molecule comprising the antibody-combining site is independent of the region of the surface which combines with anti-allotypic antibodies.

The work of Koshland (1) and Wilkinson (2) has provided strong evidence that the amino acids determining allotypic specificities a1 and a3 of the heavy chains of rabbit IgG are localized largely or entirely in the N-terminal quarter of the chain. This region has been shown to be variable with respect to amino acid sequence (3–5). By analogy with human IgG (5) the variable region probably comprises approximately the first 115 N-terminal residues. Most of the amino acid differences between heavy chains of allotypes a1 and a3 have been localized to the 34 residues of the heavy chain at the N-terminus (1, 2).

Since the variable region of the chain must also be responsible for antibody specificity it is likely that the surfaces of the molecule which comprise the allotypic determinants may be in close proximity to the antibody-combining site. Therefore, it was of interest to ascertain whether the expression of allotypic determinants on an antibody molecule is influenced by the specificity of its combining site. For example, the constraints necessary to provide a combining site specific for a given hapten might alter or eliminate one or more of the several antigenic regions (6) which characterize an allotypic specificity. Elimination of one such region should be reflected as a loss of capacity to interact with part of an anti-allotypic antibody population. The results of experiments to explore this possibility are presented here.

[1] This work was supported by grants from the National Science Foundation (GB-5424 and GB-5536) and the National Institutes of Health (AI-06281 and AI-07043).

[2] Recipient of a National Science Foundation Postdoctoral Fellowship.

[3] Recipient of a Research Career Award from the National Institutes of Health (K06-2947).

MATERIALS AND METHODS

IgG fractions of rabbit sera were prepared by two precipitations with sodium sulfate (18% and 14%) (7), followed by chromatography on DEAE-cellulose (8) in 0.02 M phosphate buffer, pH 6.8. Digestions of IgG with papain were carried out as described by Porter (9) for 4 hr. After dialysis against cold neutral buffer, which resulted in crystallization of fragment Fc, the supernatant was dialyzed against 0.02 M sodium acetate buffer, pH 6.0, and passed through carboxymethyl cellulose equilibrated with the same buffer. Under these conditions nearly all of fragment Fab passes through the column while any remaining fragment Fc and undigested IgG are retained. The absence of fragment Fc from each Fab preparation was demonstrated by immunoelectrophoresis.

Specifically purified anti-*p*-azobenzoate (10) and anti-2,4-dinitrophenyl (DNP) antibodies (11) were prepared from rabbit antisera of high titer. These were found by immunoelectrophoresis to be of the IgG class.

An antiserum specific for rabbit fragment Fc was prepared in goats by inoculation according to the following schedule: one intramuscular inoculation of 1.5 mg of the antigen incorporated in complete Freund's adjuvant followed by three inoculations of 1.5 mg each in incomplete Freund's adjuvant at 3-week intervals. Using this regimen, an antiserum of high titer against fragment Fc was obtained which also contained small amounts of antibody reactive with fragment Fab. The latter antibody was precipitated at equivalence with fragment Fab and an additional quantity of 100 μg Fab/ml was added to the supernatant serum. Monospecific antisera directed against allotypes a1, a3 and b4 were prepared as described elsewhere (12).

Proteins were labeled with ^{125}I by the method of McFarlane (13), incorporating less than one atom of iodine/molecule of protein. After exhaustive dialysis, more than 98% of the radioactivity in the labeled protein was precipitable by trichloroacetic acid at a final concentration of 5%.

The experimental procedure was designed to determine whether all immunoglobulin molecules possess the same spectrum of allotypic determinants. Varying amounts of an unlabeled immunoglobulin were added to a reference ^{125}I-labeled Fab fragment, in the presence of limiting amounts of anti-allotypic antiserum. The capacity of the unlabeled immunoglobulin to displace all the labeled reference preparation was taken as evidence of the presence of the same antigenic determinants on both the reference and test molecules. Absence of a determinant in the competitor population would be detected as the inability of these molecules to displace completely ^{125}I-labeled reference Fab.

The percentage of labeled molecules reactive with a given anti-allotypic antiserum was determined by indirect precipitation with the goat anti-rabbit Fc (14). A typical mixture comprised 25 μg bovine serum albumin (added to minimize the adherence of the radioactive material to glass); 0.5 μg ^{125}I-labeled Fab of the selected allotype (reference preparation); unlabeled competitor (varying amounts); anti-allotype antiserum (typically 5 μl of antiserum diluted with 3 volumes of normal rabbit serum of allotype differing at the *a* and *b* loci from the labeled reference Fab fragment). The labeled Fab and inhibitor were mixed prior to the addition of anti-allotype antiserum. The amount of anti-allotype antiserum used was that previously shown to be slightly less than equivalent to the amount of labeled Fab fragment present.

After incubation for 1 hr at 37°C, excess goat anti-Fc (typically 0.5 ml) was added to precipitate IgG and complexes containing labeled Fab fragments. After standing overnight at 4°C the mixture was centrifuged, the precipitate was washed three times and dissolved in 0.04 N NaOH. The radioactivities of the combined supernatants and redissolved precipitate were determined with a Nuclear Chicago gamma scintillation counter and the percentage of the radioactivity precipitated was calculated. More than 3000 counts were recorded for each supernatant-precipitate pair. Control experiments were always carried out using normal rabbit serum in place of the anti-allotype antiserum.

Preparations tested as inhibitors of the reaction included IgG or Fab fragments from nonimmunized rabbits and specifically purified anti-*p*-azobenzoate and anti-DNP antibodies. Each preparation was derived from an individual rabbit of the appropriate allotype. Concentrations of IgG and/or Fab fragments were estimated by utilizing the extinction coefficient, $E^{1\%}_{1cm} = 15$, at 280 nm.

The failure to observe differences in the displacement curves of the various competitors might be attributed to the fact that the anti-allotypic sera used in these studies were obtained from individual rabbits and that a particular rabbit's antibodies represented a response to some but not all of the determinants of a particular allotypic specificity. To minimize this possibility each experiment was performed with antisera from at least two rabbits.

In addition the specificity of the competition test was demonstrated for each system in preliminary experiments in which it was determined that a 30-fold excess of unlabeled Fab fragment of allotypic specificity different from that of the refence ^{125}I-Fab fragment was unable to displace an appreciable fraction of the bound radioactivity, while a 20-fold excess of unlabeled Fab fragment of the same allotype would displace nearly all the bound radioactivity.

Preliminary experiments also demonstrated that the order of addition of reagents to the reaction mixture was important. Unlabeled immunoglobulin molecules were ineffective as competitors when added 1 hr after mixing the reference labeled preparation and anti-allotypic serum at 37°C, followed by the addition of goat

TABLE I

Source and allotype of immunoglobulins used as reference or competitor molecules

Preparation[a]	Specificity of Antibody for Antigen	Rabbit	Allotype
^{125}I-Reference Fab			
Fab-1	*p*-Azobenzoate	AZ4	$a^3a^3b^4b^4$
Fab-5	Nonimmunized	R1	$a^1a^1b^4b^4$
Fab-11-Ab	*p*-Azobenzoate	Z3	$a^1a^1b^4b^4$
Fab-12	Nonimmunized	R12	$a^3a^3b^4b^4$
Unlabeled Competitors			
Fab-1	*p*-Azobenzoate	AZ4	$a^3a^3b^4b^4$
IgG-1[b]	*p*-Azobenzoate	AZ4	$a^3a^3b^4b^4$
IgG1-Ab	*p*-Azobenzoate	AZ4	$a^3a^3b^4b^4$
IgG2-Ab	2,4-DNP	5K	$a^3a^3b^4b^4$
Fab-3	*p*-Azobenzoate	AZ3	$a^1a^3b^4b^4$
IgG-3	*p*-Azobenzoate	AZ3	$a^1a^3b^4b^4$
IgG3-Ab	*p*-Azobenzoate	AZ3	$a^1a^3b^4b^4$
Fab-4	*p*-Azobenzoate	AZ1	$a^1a^3b^4b^4$
IgG-4	*p*-Azobenzoate	AZ1	$a^1a^3b^4b^4$
IgG4-Ab	*p*-Azobenzoate	AZ1	$a^1a^3b^4b^4$
Fab-5	Nonimmunized	R1	$a^1a^1b^4b^4$
IgG6-Ab	*p*-Azobenzoate	AZ8	$a^1a^3b^4b^4$
IgG7-Ab	*p*-Azobenzoate	AZ10	$a^3a^3b^4b^4$
Fab-8	Nonimmunized	RH	$a^1a^1b^4b^4$
IgG-8	Nonimmunized	RH	$a^1a^1b^4b^4$
IgG9-Ab	*p*-Azobenzoate	A9A	$a^1a^1b^4b^4$
Fab-10	Nonimmunized	R10	$a^3a^3b^4b^4$
IgG-10	Nonimmunized	R10	$a^3a^3b^4b^4$
Fab-11-Ab	*p*-Azobenzoate	Z3	$a^1a^1b^4b^4$
IgG-11-Ab	*p*-Azobenzoate	Z3	$a^1a^1b^4b^4$
Fab-12	Nonimmunized	R12	$a^3a^3b^4b^4$
IgG-12	Nonimmunized	R12	$a^3a^3b^4b^4$
IgG-13-Ab	*p*-Azobenzoate	IN	$a^1a^1b^4b^4$
IgG-14-Ab	*p*-Azobenzoate	IP	$a^1a^1b^4b^4$
IgG-15-Ab	*p*-Azobenzoate	AZ6	$a^3a^3b^4b^4$

[a] Preparation of IgG fractions, Fab fragments, and specifically purified antibodies (designated by "-Ab") are described in *Materials and Methods*.

[b] This is a designation number for the preparation; it does not refer to a subclass of IgG.

anti-Fc reagent. Thus the small excess of Fab fragment present in the absorbed goat-anti-rabbit Fc antiserum would not interfere with the reaction.

RESULTS

The main objective of these experiments was to determine whether IgG molecules and in particular specifically purified antibodies possess the same spectrum of allotypic determinants. This question was approached by ascertaining whether various IgG or Fab preparations had the capacity to displace from anti-allotypic antibodies all of a reference ^{125}I-labeled Fab fragment possessing the same allotype.

Four ^{125}I-labeled Fab preparations from individual rabbits (Table I, top) were used as references for inhibition studies at the *a* and *b* loci: Fab-5 and Fab-12 were derived from nonimmunized rabbits; Fab-1 was prepared from the whole IgG fraction of an immunized rabbit having a serum titer of 1.5 mg/ml of anti-*p*-azobenzoate antibody; Fab-11-Ab was prepared from specifically purified anti-*p*-azobenzoate antibody. All four rabbits were homozygous for *b*4; two were homozygous for *a*1 and two were homozygous for *a*3.

The capacity to displace these fragments from anti-*b*4 antibodies was tested utilizing various unlabeled immunoglobulin preparations. These competitors included IgG preparations from nonimmunized or immunized rabbits and specifically purified anti-*p*-azobenzoate or anti-DNP antibodies from individual rabbits homozygous for allotype *b*4 (Table I).

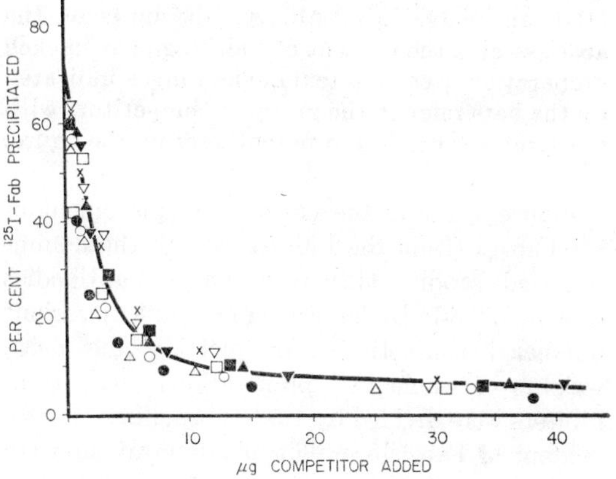

Figure 1. Inhibition of binding of reference ^{125}I-Fab-12 to anti-b4 antibody (serum E315-7) by varying amounts of unlabeled competitor immunoglobulin molecules from rabbits homozygous for the b4 allele. Fragment Fab-12 was prepared from the IgG fraction of a nonimmunized rabbit (R12) The unlabeled competitors were: nonspecific IgG fractions, IgG-3, △; IgG-10, ■; IgG-12, ▼; IgG-8, ▽; nonspecific Fab preparations, Fab-8, □; Fab-10, ●; and specifically purified anti-*p*-azobenzoate antibodies, IgG-13-Ab, ▲; IgG-14-Ab, ×; IgG-15-Ab, ○. The units on the abscissa give the content of Fab fragment in each preparation used (see text).

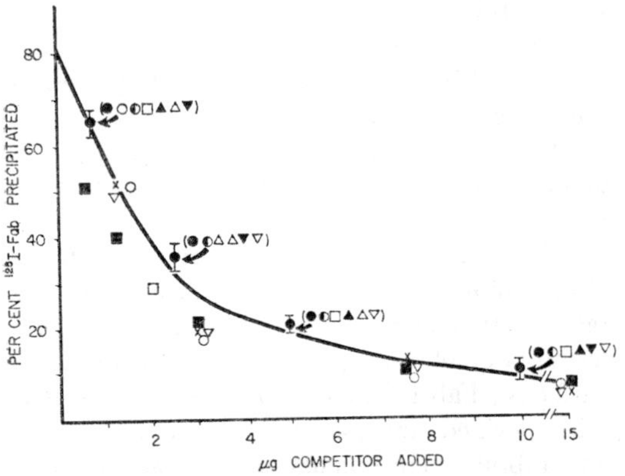

Figure 2. Inhibition of binding of reference ^{125}I-Fab-1 to anti-b4 antibody (serum E334-1) by varying amounts of unlabeled competitor immunoglobulins from rabbits homozygous for the b4 allele. Fragment Fab-1 was prepared from the IgG fraction of an immunized rabbit (AZ4) having a serum titer of 1.5 mg/ml of anti-*p*-azobenzoate antibody. The unlabeled competitors were: nonspecific IgG fractions; IgG-1, □; IgG-4, ▼; nonspecific Fab preparations, Fab-1, ■; Fab-3, ×; Fab-5, ○; Fab-4, ▽; specifically purified anti-*p*-azobenzoate antibodies, IgG-1-Ab, ●; IgG-3-Ab, ◐; IgG-6-Ab, △; and specifically purified anti-DNP antibody, IgG-2-Ab, ▲. The units on the abscissa give the content of Fab fragment in each preparation used (see text). The ranges indicated by the bars refer to the group of competitors with the symbols enclosed in parentheses on the figure.

Figure 1 shows the curve of displacement of ^{125}I-Fab-12 (from the IgG fraction of the nonimmunized rabbit R12) from anti-*b*4 antibodies (serum E315-7) by increasing amounts of various unlabeled competitors. In plotting the data, weights of whole IgG preparations used as inhibitors were divided by 1.5 to normalize for their content of Fab, since allotypic determinants are localized to the Fab fragment (15–18). The fact that all the experimental points fall approximately on the same curve indicated that all the preparations tested, including the specifically purified antibodies, were approximately equivalent with respect to capacity to displace reference ^{125}I-Fab fragments from anti-b4 antibodies.

The results of similar experiments with two other reference ^{125}I-Fab preparations (Fab-1 and Fab-11-Ab) from homozygous *b*4 rabbits are shown in Figures 2 and 3. In Figure 2, Fab-1 was derived from a rabbit hyperimmunized to the *p*-azobenzoate hapten. The anti-b4 serum was from rabbit E334-1. In Figure 3, the labeled Fab-11-Ab fragments were prepared from specifically purified anti-*p*-azobenzoate antibodies; the anti-b4 antiserum was obtained from rabbit E315-7. All unlabeled competitors tested were approximately equivalent quantitatively in their capacity to displace the labeled Fab fragments from anti-b4 antibodies. Also, essentially complete displacement could be attained with a large excess of any of the competitors tested.

Figures 4 to 7 show similar data with respect to the heavy chain (*a*) locus. Specificities tested were a1 (Figs. 4 and 5) and a3 (Figs. 6 and 7). Again all unlabeled competitors tested were essentially equivalent with respect to their capacity to displace the labeled Fab fragments from anti-a1 or anti-a3 antibodies.

The experiments in Figures 1, 2 and 6 were repeated by using different preparations of anti-allotypic antisera from rabbits E334-1, E315-7 and 141-CD, respectively, with virtually identical results.

The effect of the presence of specific hapten (*p*-nitrobenzoate or ε-2,4-DNP-lysine) on the capacity of the corresponding anti-hapten anti-

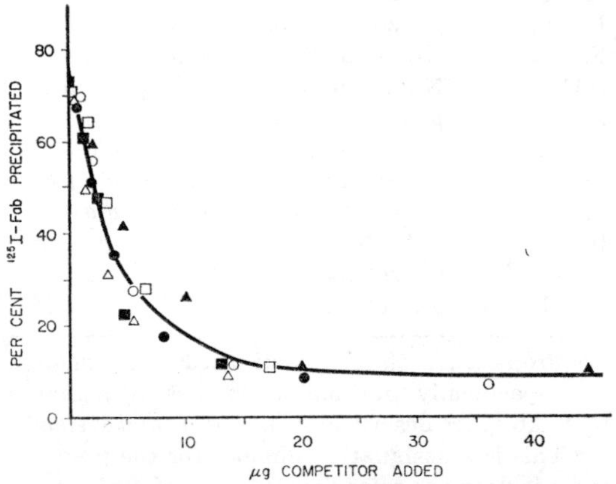

Figure 3. Inhibition of binding of reference ^{125}I-Fab-11 to anti-b4 antibody (serum E315-7) by varying amounts of unlabeled competitor immunoglobulin molecules from rabbits homozygous for the b4 allele. Fragment Fab-11 was prepared from specifically purified antiazobenzoate antibody of rabbit Z3. The unlabeled competitors were: nonspecific IgG fractions; IgG-1, △; IgG-10, □; IgG-12, ●; and specifically purified anti-*p*-azobenzoate antibody preparations, IgG-1-Ab, ▲; IgG-11-Ab, ○; IgG-15-Ab, ■. The units on the abscissa give the content of Fab fragment in each preparation used (see text).

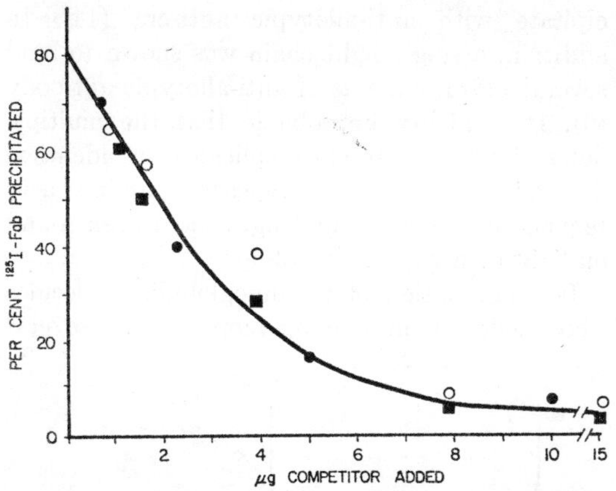

Figure 4. Inhibition of binding of reference ¹²⁵I-Fab-5 to anti-a1 antibody (serum D161-4) by varying amounts of unlabeled competitor immunoglobulin molecules from rabbits homozygous for the a1 allele. Fragment Fab-5 was prepared from the IgG fraction of a nonimmunized rabbit (R1). The unlabeled competitors were Fab preparations Fab-5, ■; Fab-8, ○; and specifically purified anti-*p*-azobenzoate antibody IgG-9-Ab, ●. The units on the abscissa give the content of Fab fragment in each preparation used (see text).

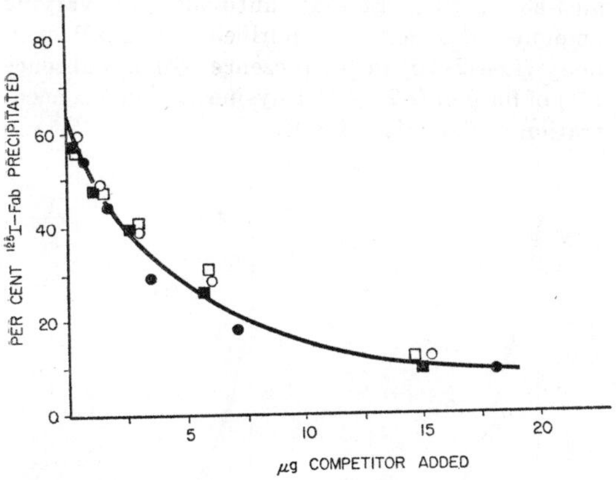

Figure 5. Inhibition of binding of reference ¹²⁵I-Fab-11-Ab to anti-a1 antibody (serum 53923) by varying amounts of unlabeled competitor immunoglobulin molecules from rabbits homozygous for the a1 allele. Fragment Fab-11 was prepared from specifically purified antibenzoate antibody of rabbit Z3. The unlabeled competitors were nonpecific IgG fraction IgG-8, □; and specifically purified antibody preparations IgG-11-Ab, ■; IgG-13-Ab, ●; and IgG-14-Ab, ○. The units on the abscissa give the content of Fab fragment in each preparation used (see text).

body to displace labeled Fab fragments was determined (Figs. 8, 9 and 10) for both the *a* and *b* loci. No changes in the shape of the displacement curves were noted.

DISCUSSION

The results indicate that anti-*p*-azobenzoate or anti-DNP antibodies purified from the serum of each individual rabbit investigated contain a complete complement of the antigenic determinants associated with an allotypic specificity, i.e., a1, a3, or b4. Other allotypic markers such as A8, A11-A12, and A14-A15 which are closely linked to Aa1 or Aa3 were not considered since their determinants presumably are not present on the Fab fragment (19–22). The contribution of "hidden" antigenic determinants (23–25), present on Fab fragments, to the reactions studied were not significant as shown by the equivalence of whole IgG and Fab fragments as competitors of the binding of ¹²⁵I-Fab. This suggests that the titers of antibodies to hidden determinants are low as compared to those of anti-allotype antibodies in the antisera used. Consistent results were obtained with different labeled Fab preparations and also with different preparations of

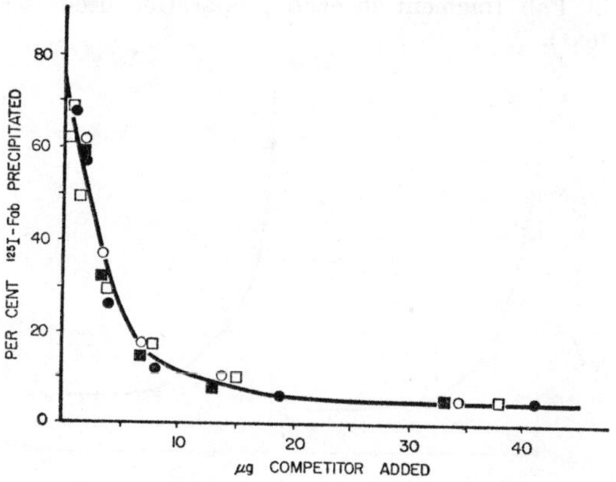

Figure 6. Inhibition of binding of reference ¹²⁵I-Fab-12 to anti-a3 antibody (serum D153-5) by varying amounts of unlabeled competitor molecules from rabbits homozygous for the a3 allele. Fragment Fab-12 was prepared from the IgG fraction of a nonimmunized rabbit (R12). The unlabeled competitors were: nonspecific IgG fractions, IgG-10, ○; IgG-12, ●; nonspecific Fab preparation Fab-10, □; and specifically purified anti-*p*-azobenzoate antibody IgG-15-Ab, ■. The units on the abscissa give the content of Fab fragment in each preparation used (see text).

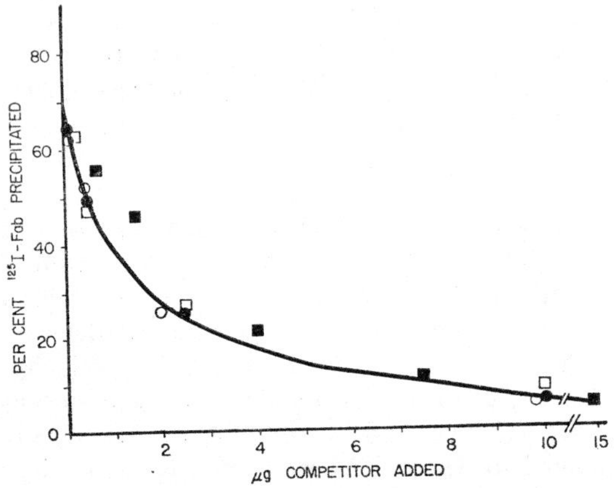

Figure 7. Inhibition of binding of reference ^{125}I-Fab-1 to anti-a3 antibody (serum D107-3) by varying amounts of unlabeled competitor immunoglobulin from rabbits homoyzgous for the a3 allele. Fragment Fab-1 was prepared from the IgG fraction of an immunized rabbit (AZ4) having a serum titer of 1.5 mg/ml of anti-*p*-azobenzoate antibody. The unlabeled competitors were nonspecific IgG fraction IgG-1, □; nonspecific Fab preparation, Fab-1, ■; specifically purified anti-*p*-azobenzoate antibody, IgG-7-Ab, ●; and specifically purified anti-DNP antibody, IgG-2-Ab, ○. The units on the abscissa give the content of Fab fragment in each preparation used (see text).

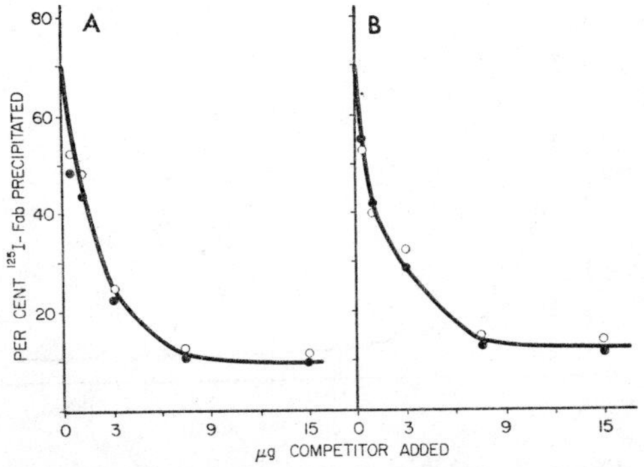

Figure 8. Inhibition of binding of reference ^{125}I-Fab-1 to (A) anti-b4 (serum E334-1) or (B) anti-a3 (serum D107-3) by varying amounts of specifically purified anti-*p*-azobenzoate antibody (IgG-1-Ab) in the presence (●) and absence (○) of hapten (*p*-nitrobenzoate at a final concentration of 0.075 M, pH 8.0).

anti-allotypic antisera. In interpreting these data it is relevant that each marker at the *a* or *b* locus evidently comprises more than one determinant since isolated Fab fragments precipitate with anti-allotypic antisera (14). In addition, a single light chain was shown to bind several Fab fragments of anti-allotypic antibody (6). It is highly improbable that the multiple determinants represent replicates of identical determinants since no repeating amino acid sequences of significant length have been found on light or heavy chains (3–5).

If a population of immunoglobulin molecules were deficient in one or more of the several

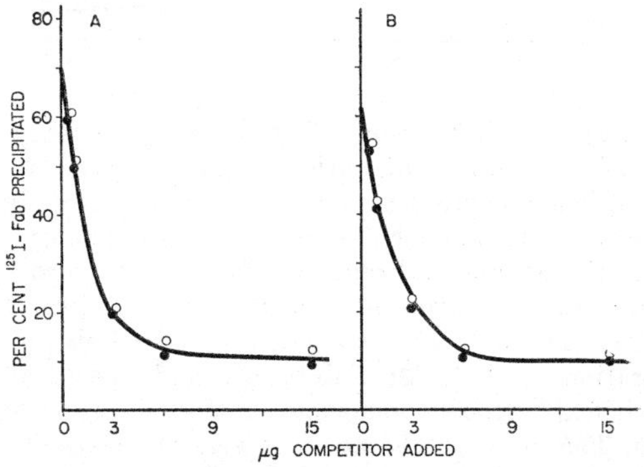

Figure 9. Inhibition of binding of reference ^{125}I-Fab-1 to (A), anti-b4 (serum D107-3) or (B) anti-a3 (serum E334-1) antibody by varying amounts of specifically purified anti-DNP antibody (IgG-2-Ab) in the presence (●) and absence (○) of hapten (ε-2,4-DNP-lysine at a final concentration of 0.01 M, pH 8.0).

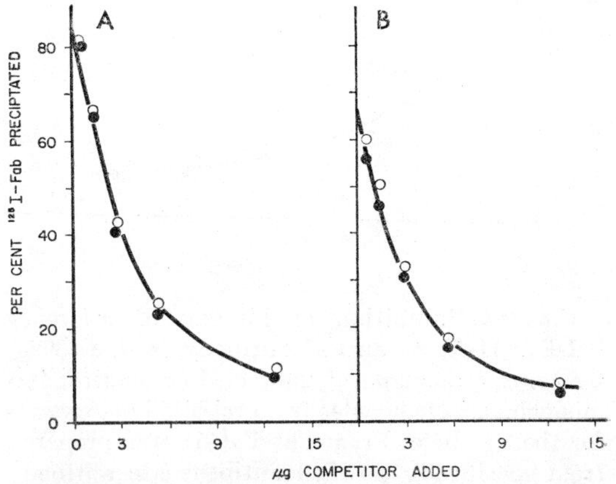

Figure 10. Inhibition of binding of reference ^{125}I-Fab-12 to (A) anti-b4 (serum E315-7), or (B) anti-a3 (serum D153-5) antibody by varying amounts of specifically purified anti-*p*-azobenzoate antibody (IgG-15-Ab) in the presence (●) and absence (○) of hapten (*p*-nitrobenzoate at a final concentration of 0.075 M, pH 8.0).

allotypic determinants, it should be unable to displace a corresponding fraction of the bound, labeled Fab fragment for each determinant it lacked, since slightly less than an equivalent amount of anti-allotypic antiserum was used in each experiment. The results show that the specifically purified antibodies (anti-*p*-azobenzoate or anti-DNP) express all of the allotypic determinants present on the Fab fragments derived from the IgG fraction of nonimmunized rabbits (Figs. 1, 2, 4, 6, 7). Conversely, Fab fragments of specifically purified anti-*p*-azobenzoate antibody from an individual rabbit, used as the labeled reference material, did not contain allotypic determinants absent from the other immunoglobulin preparations tested as competitors (Figs. 3 and 5). Unlabeled competitors included 4 nonspecific IgG preparations, 10 specifically purified anti-*p*-azobenzoate antibodies, and 1 purified anti-DNP antibody, all from individual rabbits. The presence of a full complement of determinants was shown by the capacity to displace all 4 of the reference labeled Fab fragments.

In addition to possessing all of the allotypic determinants of nonspecific IgG, it appears that purified antibodies express these determinants quantitatively in a manner indistinguishable from nonspecific IgG (Figs. 1–7). This is indicated by the similarity of the curves for displacement of labeled Fab fragments from anti-allotypic antibody by unlabeled nonspecific IgG or unlabeled purified antibodies. Although the precision of the data is not sufficient to permit the conclusion that the allotypic determinants are identical, they must be very similar.

These results indicate that the portion of the surface of the molecule comprising the antibody-combining site is independent of the region of the surface which combines with anti-allotypic antibody. This is of particular interest in the case of the heavy chain since it appears that amino acid residues responsible for both allotypic determinants and antibody specificity reside in the N-terminal quarter of the chain (approximately 115 residues) (1, 2, 5). It remains to be determined whether this applies also to the light chain. It is, of course, possible that the formation of the combining site involves juxtaposition of two or more segments of the heavy chain.

Since many of the amino acid substitutions associated with differences in allotypic specificities a1 and a3 are localized to the 34 residues at the N-terminus (1, 2) it seems possible that the N-terminus of the chain does not contribute significantly to the specificity of the antibody, despite the variability of certain residues in this segment. If so, specificity would be largely determined by the remaining residues in the variable segment. If the rabbit and human heavy chains are constructed on a similar principle, then by analogy with human IgG (5) this region would comprise about 75 amino acid residues. The importance to antibody specificity of the region around position 86 of both the heavy and light chain has been suggested by affinity labeling (26).

Our data also suggest the independence of allotypic and antibody specificity regions in the light chains of allotype b4. Interpretation of these findings must await the location of the particular amino acid residues responsible for allotypic specificities in light chains.

It may be relevant that the presence of hapten had no discernible effect on the capacity of specifically purified anti-*p*-azobenzoate antibody or anti-DNP antibody to displace nonspecific Fab fragments from anti-allotypic antibody (Figs. 8–10). This suggests that the combining site itself is not part of an allotypic determinant and that any conformational changes associated with the interaction with hapten do not drastically alter such determinants.

Our data are consistent with the findings of Koshland *et al.* (1, 27) that differences in amino acid composition associated with allotypic specificity occur independently of compositional changes associated with antibody specificity.

The correspondence in the shape of the curves of displacement from anti-b4 antibodies for the various unlabeled preparations (Figs. 1–3) suggests that the proportions of κ and λ chains present in the inhibitors used did not vary greatly since λ chains lack determinants controlled by the *b* locus. This was not unexpected since substantial proportions of λ chains have so far been noted only in rabbits suppressed at the *b* locus (28–30). Small variations in proportions of κ and λ chains would probably not be detected in our system.

Acknowledgments. The authors would like to thank Miss Cynthia J. Subach for her very competent technical assistance and Mrs. Alice Gilman-Sachs for the preparation of the anti-allotypic antisera.

REFERENCES

1. Koshland, M. E., Cold Spring Harbor Symp. Quant. Biol., *32:* 119, 1967.
2. Wilkinson, J. M., Biochem. J., *112:* 173, 1969.
3. Cohen, S. and Milstein, C., Advances Immun., *7:* 1, 1967.
4. Dayhoff, M. O., Editor, *Atlas of Protein Sequence and Structure*, Vol. 4, National Biomedical Research Foundation, Silver Spring, Md., 1969.
5. Edelman, G. M., Cunningham, B. A., Gall, W. E., Gottlieb, P. D., Rutishauser, U. and Waxdal, M. J., Proc. Nat. Acad. Sci., *63:* 78, 1969.
6. Mage, R., Reisfield, R. A. and Dray, S., Immunochemistry, *3:* 299, 1966.
7. Kekwick, R. A., Biochem. J., *34:* 1248, 1940.
8. Levy, H. B. and Sober, H. A., Proc. Soc. Exp. Biol. Med., *103:* 250, 1960.
9. Porter, R. R., Biochem. J., *73:* 119, 1959.
10. Daugharty, H., Hopper, J. E., MacDonald, A. B. and Nisonoff, A., J. Exp. Med., *130:* 1047, 1969.
11. Eisen, H., Meth. Med. Res., *10:* 94, 1964.
12. Dray, S., Young, G. O. and Gerald, L., J. Immun., *91:* 403, 1963.
13. McFarlane, A., Nature, *182:* 53, 1958.
14. Gilman, A., Nisonoff, A. and Dray, S., Immunochemistry, *1:* 109, 1964.
15. Dubiski, S., Dudziak, Z., Skalba, D. and Kelus, A., Immunology, *4:* 236, 1961.
16. Marrack, J. R., Richards, C. B. and Kelus, A., Protides Biol. Fluids, *9:* 200, 1961.
17. Leskowitz, S., J. Immun., *90:* 98, 1963.
18. Stemke, G. W., Thesis, University of Illinois, Urbana, 1963.
19. Hamers, R. and Hamers-Casterman, C., Cold Spring Harbor Symp. Quant. Biol., *32:* 129, 1967.
20. Dubiski, S. and Muller, P. J., Nature, *214:* 696, 1967.
21. Mandy, W. J. and Todd, C. W., Vox Sang., *14:* 264, 1968.
22. Mandy, W. J. and Todd, C. W., Immunochemistry, *6:* 811, 1969.
23. Osterland, C. K., Harboe, J. and Kunkel, H. Vox Sang., *8:* 133, 1963.
24. Mandy, W. J., Fudenberg, H. and Lewis, F. B., J. Immun., *95:* 501, 1966.
25. Waller, M. and Blaylock, K. J., J. Immun., *97:* 483, 1966.
26. Singer, S. J. and Thorpe, N. O., Proc. Nat. Acad. Sci., *60:* 1371, 1968.
27. Koshland, M. E., Reisfeld, R. A. and Dray, S., Immunochemistry, *5:* 471, 1968.
28. Dubiski, S., *Nature, 214:* 1365, 1967.
29. Vice, J. L., Hunt, W. L. and Dray, S., J. Immun., *103:* 629, 1969.
30. David, G. S. and Todd, G. W., Proc. Nat. Acad. Sci., *62:* 860, 1969.

THE JOURNAL OF IMMUNOLOGY
Vol. 105, No. 3, September 1970

INTERACTION OF LYMPHOCYTES AND A RADIORESISTANT CELL IN PPD-STIMULATED HUMAN LEUKOCYTE CULTURES

GERALDINE P. SCHECHTER AND WILLIAM McFARLAND

From the Veterans Administration Hospital, Hematology Research Section, Washington, D. C. 20422

Received for publication March 6, 1970

A 5- to 7-day incubation of heavily irradiated (2000 R) human leukocytes yielded a macrophage-rich population which was capable of markedly increasing blastogenic reactivity to PPD (purified protein derivative) of lymphocytes from sensitive donors as measured by incorporation of tritiated thymidine. These radioresistant cells were also demonstrated in some donors to be capable of initiating the blastogenic response after being only briefly exposed to antigen. This activity was demonstrable only when these cells were intact, viable, in direct contact with the lymphocytes and pulsed with antigen sometime within the preceding 72 hr. This ability to initiate blastogenesis in lymphocytes was inhibited if macrophage exposure to antigen occurred at low temperature or in the presence of actinomycin D or cyanide.

Evidence has increased in recent years that interactions between cells of diverse type and origin play an important role in immunologic phenomena and in their *in vitro* models (1, 2). The demonstration that an RNA species and an RNA-antigen complex, which were capable of initiating an immune response in lymphoid cells, could be extracted from macrophages which had been exposed to antigen (3–6) indicated that the macrophage may be involved in these phenomena at the antigen-processing level. Macrophages have also been shown to correct *in vivo* the immunologic deficit caused by sublethal irradiation (7), and adult macrophages transfused into immunologically immature animals allow these animals to respond normally to antigens (8). The transformation of peripheral blood lymphocytes to blast-like cells in response to specific antigens *in vitro* is decreased when lymphocytes are separated from phagocytic cells (9–13). Restitution of monocytes or macrophages to the cultures of separated lymphocytes causes an increased degree of transformation (9, 11–13).

In vitro radiation of leukocytes has been shown to yield a population of cells capable of stimulating allogeneic cells unilaterally (14) and of increasing the reactivity of separated lymphocytes in mixed leukocyte cultures (15). Using a modification of this technique, we have been able to obtain cell populations from the peripheral blood of PPD (purified protein derivative)-sensitive human donors that contain approximately 90% macrophages and less than 10% lymphocytes. This macrophage-rich population was incapable of responding to PPD. However, when these cells were added to syngeneic, column-separated lymphocytes, blastogenesis in response to PPD occurred at levels comparable to the reaction of the unseparated leukocytes. Furthermore, these irradiated macrophage suspensions were capable of inducing blastogenesis in lymphocytes after only a brief exposure to PPD and subsequent washing. The effects of variations in the amount of radiation, the ratio of macrophages to lymphocytes, the time of addition of antigen and inhibitors are reported.

MATERIALS AND METHODS

The preparation of the various cell suspensions is outlined below.

Unseparated leukocytes. Heparinized blood from PPD-sensitive human donors was allowed to stand for 1 to 2 hr (16). The leukocyte-rich plasma was then removed and centrifuged at 100 × G for 12 min, and the resulting cell pellet was resuspended in plasma that had been centrifuged at 1000 × G for 20 min. This cenrifugation decreased the platelet concentration of the leukocyte suspension by 50% and thereby reduced platelet aggregation, and consequent cell clumping, during the course of preparing the cultures.

Separated lymphocytes. Incubation of the leukocyte-rich plasma on a glass bead column, using a modification of the method of Rabinowitz (17), removed the glass-adherent cells and yielded relatively pure lymphocytes. The column was incubated at 37°C for 1 hr and then washed with medium 199 (Grand Island Biological Co., Grand Island, N. Y.). Approximately 60% of the lymphocytes were recovered from the column and generally the differential count of the effluent showed 95% to 99% lymphocytes, with less than 2% monocytes.

Macrophage-rich suspensions. The lympholytic effect of radiation and the natural early mortality of polymorphonuclear leukocytes allowed the production of macrophage-rich suspensions. The leukocyte-rich plasma, contained in a plastic tube and immersed in a water-bath to decrease the effect of backscatter, was exposed to a cobalt-60 γ source at 77 to 80 R/minute. Unless otherwise noted, the leukocytes were exposed to 2000 R and then divided into portions of 300,000 monocytes and cultured in 3 ml of medium containing 20% fresh autologous plasma and 80% medium 199 in 16- x 125-mm screw-capped plastic tubes (Falcon), in the upright position and without agitation. Differential counts from Wright-stained smears or by phase microscopy were unchanged immediately following irradiation; however, after 5 to 7 days of incubation at 37°C the percentage of lymphocytes decreased markedly and the predominant surviving cells were macrophages. The average differential count of leukocytes so cultured was 95% macrophages (89% to 98%), 4% lymphocytes (1% to 6%), and 1% other cells, usually eosinophils (0 to 5%). This macrophage-rich population derived from the incubation of irradiated leukocytes will hereafter be referred to as the irradiated macrophages. These macrophages were demonstrated to be capable of phagocytosis of carbon particles and were often noted to contain phagocytized platelets.

In some experiments albumin flotation was used to enrich the concentration of monocytes in the leukocyte-rich plasma by a modification of the method of Bennett and Cohn (18). Human albumin was used, but enrichment of the percentage of monocytes rarely reached 30% of the total leukocytes.

The general conditions of culture of the above cell suspensions or combinations thereof were as described previously (16) and are outlined under the preparation of the irradiated macrophages. No antibiotics were used, the conditions being kept sterile throughout. Excipient-free PPD (provided by Parke, Davis and Co.) in amounts of 0.5 μg or 1 μg/ml of culture was used.

After the antigen was added, cultures were incubated for 4 days at 37°C, except where noted, and then assayed by measuring the uptake of tritiated thymidine (3000 to 5000 mCi/mM) after 3 hr of incubation at a concentration of 0.1 μCi/ml of culture. The harvesting procedure has been described (19). Trichloracetic acid-precipitable radioactivity was assayed in a Beckman scintillation counter and expressed in disintegrations/sec (dps). Efficiency of counting, determined by a chloroform-quenched standard, was generally in the range of 40% to 45%. Cultures were done in triplicate and individual cultures were generally well within 25% of the mean. Direct smears were also made from selected cultures to quantitate blastogenesis morphologically.

RESULTS

Effect of time of antigen exposure on the response of irradiated leukocytes to PPD. The magnitude of the response of unseparated leukocytes was found to depend both on the amount of irradiation administered and on the time when antigen was added to the cultures. Unseparated leukocytes (10^6 lymphocytes/tube) were cultured after being exposed to varying amounts of irradiation. PPD was added to one group of cultures immediately post-irradiation and a second group was cultured without antigen. The medium of those cultured without antigen was renewed 7 days later and PPD then added. Cell cultures were assayed by measuring the uptake of tritiated thymidine and by examination of Wright-stained smears 4 days after the addition of antigen.

In the cultures to which PPD was added immediately following irradiation, there was a rapid decline in the uptake of tritiated thymidine with increasing radiation exposure. Cells exposed to 1000 R showed 1% of the uptake of tritiated thymidine obtained with cells not exposed to irradiation (Table I). However, despite this marked decrease in thymidine uptake, a significant number of blast forms were still seen in the smears made from cultures of lymphocytes which were exposed to as much as 2500 R and antigen on the same day.

When the irradiated leukocytes were placed in culture for 7 days before antigen was added, the

TABLE I

Effect of radiation dose on the uptake of ^3H-thymidine (DPS) by PPD-stimulated leukocyte cultures

Roentgen Exposure	Antigen Added Immediately Post-Radiation		Antigen Added 7 Days Post-Radiation	
	Exp. 1	Exp. 2	Exp. 1	Exp. 2
0	3316	2753	3125	2310
0 control[a]	13	4	33	60
500	186	211	89	12
1000	40		2	2
1500	31	62		2
2000	35		3	2
2500	22	33	2	2
2500 (PHA)[b]		143		2

[a] No antigen added.

[b] PHA-P (Difco) 0.06 ml/culture added instead of PPD.

decline in tritiated thymidine uptake was much steeper with increasing radiation exposure. There was >97% decrease in tritiated thymidine uptake at 500 R as compared to the non-irradiated cells (Table I). Furthermore, smears from these cultures showed no blast forms in the cultures receiving from 1500 R to 2500 R, in contrast to those cultures to which antigen was added immediately after irradiation. The experimental data cited in Table I were obtained with leukocytes from a donor with a very active response to PPD. A more moderate response to the antigen could be completely abolished with as little as 500 R. Phytohemagglutinin (PHA) stimulation of cells irradiated with 2500 R showed slight uptake if this mitogen was added at the time of irradiation and none if added 7 days later (Table I).

Effect of irradiated leukocytes and macrophage-rich suspensions on the reactivity of separated lymphocytes to PPD. Leukocytes processed on glass bead columns generally yielded a population of 95% to 99% lymphocytes, <2% monocytes and the rest polymorphonuclear leukocytes. These column-separated lymphocytes had a 50% to 90% decrease in reactivity to PPD, as compared to unseparated lymphocytes, in the four experiments whose results are shown in Table II. When freshly irradiated leukocytes were added to the separated lymphocytes to restore the number of monocytes of the original population of unseparated leukocytes, there was a partial restitution of uptake of tritiated thymidine at the end of the incubation period. The irradiated leukocytes by themselves reacted to PPD at the level of control cultures (cultures without antigen). When the concentration of irradiated leukocytes was increased, the uptake of tritiated thymidine decreased (Experiment 4, Table II), possibly due to the large number of total cells per culture.

Albumin flotation was used in one experiment in an attempt to decrease the number of polymorphonuclear leukocytes and lymphocytes relative to the monocytes in the freshly irradiated cell population; however, restitution of blastogenesis again was only partial (Experiment 3, Table II).

The effect of the irradiated macrophages on the PPD-reactivity of separated lymphocytes was much greater. The irradiated macrophages were derived from leukocytes which were treated with 2000 R and cultured, 300,000 monocytes/tube, without antigen for 5 to 7 days as described above. When separated lymphocytes, approximately 10^6/culture, and PPD were added to the irradiated macrophages, the level of tritiated thymidine uptake at the end of 4 days of further incubation was 3 to 11 times that of the separated lymphocytes cultured alone with PPD. Table III shows that the level of thymidine uptake in the restituted group (fourth column) was comparable to that of the unseparated lymphocytes with PPD and occasionally was significantly greater. Experiments in which both the percentage of blast transformation from Wright-stained smears and the uptake of tritiated thymidine were

TABLE II

Effect of freshly irradiated leukocytes on uptake of ^3H-thymidine (DPS) by separated lymphocytes in the presence of PPD

Experiment	Unseparated Leukocytes	Separated Lymphocytes	Irradiated Leukocytes	Separated Lymphocytes + Irradiated Leukocytes
1	640	230	7	485
2	2135	280	52	1245
3	1725	165	13[a]	590[a]
4a	1320	315	16	665
4b	1320	315	16	290[b]

[a] Irradiated leukocytes after albumin flotation to decrease polymorphonuclear leukocytes and lymphocytes.

[b] Concentration of irradiated cells was twice that in 4a.

TABLE III

Effect of irradiated macrophages on the uptake of ³H-thymidine (DPS) by separated lymphocytes in presence of PPD

Experiment	Unseparated Leukocytes	Separated Lymphocytes	Irradiated Macrophages	Separated Lymphocytes + Irradiated Macrophages
1	1030	150	27	1620
2	1840	270	24	1250
3	2690	770	26	2320
4	2970	660	2	2680
5	3180	510	4	3370

TABLE IV

Effect of irradiated macrophages and irradiated lymphocytes on the uptake of tritiated thymidine (DPS) of syngeneic lymphocytes in the presence of PPD

Experiment	Unseparated Leukocytes	Unseparated Leukocytes + Irradiated Macrophages	Separated Lymphocytes	Separated Lymphocytes + Irradiated Macrophages	Separated Lymphocytes + Irradiated Lymphocytes
1	530	1420	180	270	125
2	615	875	190	490	205
3	2790		430	2630	690
4	800	1500	210	370	

determined showed that both measures gave similar results.

Addition of irradiated separated lymphocytes, rather than irradiated macrophages, had little effect on the uptake of tritiated thymidine by the PPD-stimulated lymphocytes (Table IV). The freshly irradiated (2000 R) lymphocytes were added in sufficient numbers so that the total number of cells was approximately the same as in the unseparated leukocyte cultures.

In three experiments, the number of leukocytes initially placed in culture after irradiation was varied so that there were between 50,000 and 400,000 monocytes/culture. Between 5 and 7 days later, a constant number of separated lymphocytes, PPD and fresh plasma and medium were added to each culture. Figure 1 represents the combined results of these three experiments. The mean increase of the reactivity (as measured by tritiated thymidine uptake) of the combination of separated lymphocytes and irradiated macrophages over that of the separated lymphocytes alone is plotted against the initial concentration of monocytes. The optimal concentration appears to be 300,000 monocytes/culture, but the range of values at each concentration tested was broad. In one experiment, peak activity was reached when the irradiated macrophages derived from an initial concentration of 100,000 monocytes/culture were used.

The effect of varying the number of lymphocytes added to the cultures of irradiated macrophages was also determined. The macrophages were derived from a constant number of leukocytes, and the lymphocytes added to each culture varied between 300,000 and 1,200,000 cells. The results for both separated and unseparated lymphocytes are plotted in Figure 2. The combination of separated lymphocytes and irradiated macrophages had the same reactivity to PPD as did the unseparated leukocytes. At lower lymphocyte concentrations the macrophages also increased the reactivity of the unseparated leukocytes to PPD. In experiments with other PPD-sensitive donors a significant increase also was

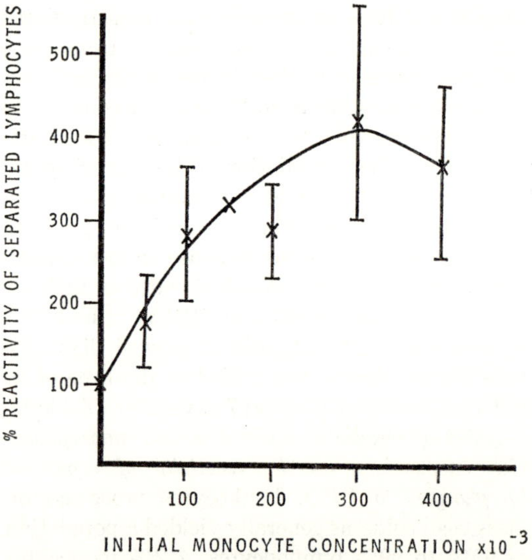

Figure 1. Effect of the initial number of monocytes from which the irradiated macrophages were derived on the ability of the latter cells to increase the reactivity of separated lymphocytes to PPD. The ordinate represents the ratio of reactivity (tritiated thymidine uptake) of the separated lymphocyte-irradiated macrophage combination to the reactivity of the separated lymphocytes alone × 100. The points and bars represent the mean increase and range found in three separate experiments.

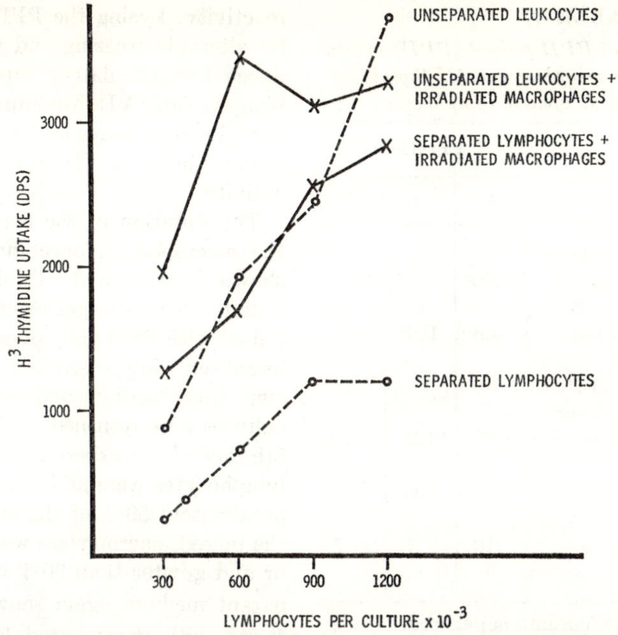

Figure 2. **Effect of irradiated macrophages on the uptake of tritiated thymidine of cultures of unseparated leukocytes and separated lymphocytes of varying concentration in the presence of PPD. The irradiated macrophages were derived from cultures initially containing 300,000 monocytes each.**

noted at higher lymphocyte concentrations (10^6 lymphocytes/culture) when macrophages were added to unseparated leukocytes (Table IV).

Effect of PPD-pulsed irradiated macrophages on separated lymphocytes. The blastogenic capabilities of irradiated macrophages after brief exposure to PPD and subsequent washing was examined. The cultures of irradiated macrophages were incubated with PPD (1 μg/ml culture) at 37°C for 2 hr after which they were washed extensively with medium 199 and transferred to new tubes before fresh syngeneic lymphocytes were added. Transfer was necessitated by the finding that the PPD adhered to the walls of the plastic culture tube and was not removed by simple changes of medium. In the transfer of the macrophages, a silicone plastic policeman was used to dislodge cells adherent to the bottom of the tube. Unseparated leukocytes added to macrophages which had been heat-killed at 56°C for 30 min and then pulsed, washed and transferred in the same manner served as a control to detect extracellular antigen. The cultures were assayed 4 days later. The results of five experiments using two different donors are presented in Table V. Pulsing the macrophages with PPD for as little as 2 hr rendered them capable of causing marked blastogenesis in

TABLE V

Effect of PPD-pulsed (PPD) irradiated macrophages on uptake of ^3H-thymidine (DPS) of separated lymphocytes

Experiment	(PPD) Irradiated Macrophages + Separated Lymphocytes	(PPD) Heat-Killed Macrophages + Unseparated Leukocytes	Unseparated Leukocytes + PPD	Separated Lymphocytes + PPD
1	1410	15	1770	225
2	2070	14	1640	170
3	1400	8		480
4	3020	55		
5	365	5	390	50

separated lymphocytes, sometimes greater than the effect of the continuous presence of PPD on the unseparated leukocytes from which the separated lymphocytes were derived. The uptake of tritiated thymidine by unseparated leukocytes added to PPD-pulsed, heat-killed macrophages was similar to cultures to which no antigen had been added. The induction of blastogenesis by the PPD-pulsed, irradiated macrophages was noted consistently in the donors cited, but it could not be demonstrated in a number of other PPD-sensitive donors.

TABLE VI

Effect of supernatant of PPD-pulsed (PPD) macrophages and of lysed macrophages on ³H-thymidine uptake (DPS) by syngeneic lymphocytes

Cells Cultured	Experiment		
	1	2	3
Syngeneic lymphocytes plus:			
(PPD) irradiated macrophages	3250[a]	3323[b]	1225
Lysed (PPD) irradiated macrophages	289[a]	160[b]	
Supernatant from (PPD) irradiated macrophages	40[b]		17[b]
Unseparated leukocytes + PPD	1900	3125	2010
Separated lymphocytes + PPD		506	563
Unseparated leukocytes without PPD	10	7	7

[a] Lymphocytes were column-separated.
[b] Lymphocytes were unseparated.

The cells of one donor whose pulsed macrophages were consistently capable of inducing blastogenesis were used to conduct a number of experiments to determine the requirements for the reactivity. Lysing the PPD-pulsed macrophages by alternate freezing and thawing markedly reduced the stimulatory capability of the macrophages (Table VI). Medium incubated with PPD-pulsed macrophages for 24 hr (designated "supernatant" in Table VI) also showed no stimulatory activity.

The duration of the blastogenic capability of the macrophages, once pulsed with antigen, is shown in Figure 3. Triplicate cultures of irradiated macrophages from the same donor were pulsed with PPD daily over a 5-day period, a different set being pulsed each day. After the pulsing step, fresh medium and plasma were added and cultures were returned to the incubator until the 5th day of the experiment when fresh syngeneic lymphocytes were added to all the cultures. Approximately 50% of the stimulatory activity of the pulsed macrophages was lost at the end of 24 hr and greater than 90% by 4 days. The supernatant medium again showed no activity when tested with unseparated leukocytes, suggesting that the gradual loss of blastogenic capabilities of the macrophages was not due to leakage of antigen into the surrounding medium.

The effect of various inhibitors added at the time of the antigen pulse on the subsequent

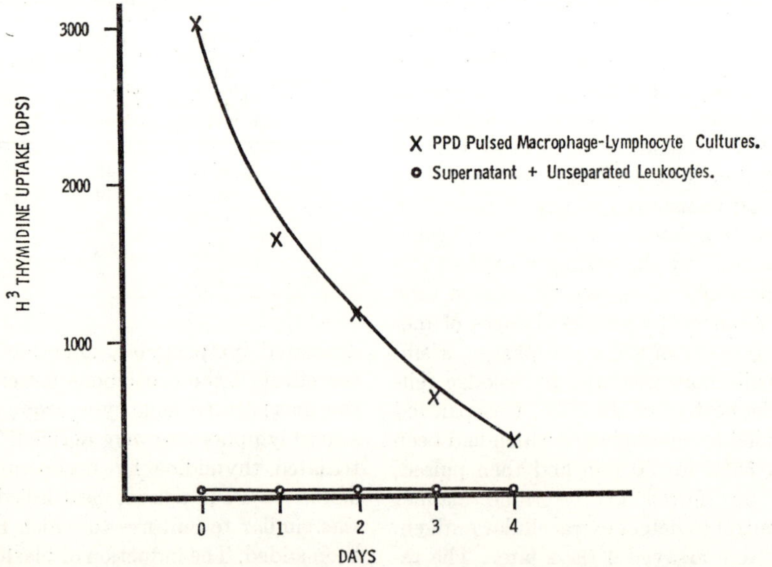

Figure 3. Effect of time on the ability of the PPD-pulsed macrophages to induce lymphocyte transformation. The abscissa refers to the period between the pulsing of the macrophages with antigen and the addition of separated lymphocytes to test the blastogenic capabilities of the pulsed macrophages. The supernatant medium removed from the pulsed macrophages at the time of the addition of lymphocytes was also tested with unseparated leukocytes.

TABLE VII

Effect of metabolic inhibitors on the induction of lymphocyte transformation by PPD-pulsed irradiated macrophages

Treatment of Macrophages Prior to Addition of Separated Lymphocytes	^{3}H-Thymidine Uptake (DPS)
Cold	
PPD 4°C (30 min)	9
PPD 37°C (30 min)	760
PPD 4°C (30 min, then PPD throughout culture period at 37°C)	1500
10^{-3} M NaCN	
PPD + CN^- (2 hr)	790
PPD (2 hr)	2070
PPD + CN^- (2 hr, wash, then PPD throughout culture period)	2400

TABLE VIII

Effect of actinomycin D (AcD)[a] on the induction of lymphocyte transformation by PPD-pulsed irradiated macrophages

Treatment of Macrophages Prior to Addition of Separated Lymphocytes	^{3}H-Thymidine Uptake (DPS) in Experiment:		
	1	2	3
PPD (2 hr)	3320	2810	1410
PPD and AcD (2 hr)	40	560	80
PPD (2 hr, followed by AcD)	2330[b]	2173[c]	
AcD (2 hr, wash, then PPD pulse)		1910	550

[a] AcD concentration 0.5 μg/ml of culture.
[b] AcD added just prior to washout of antigen.
[c] AcD added for 2 hr after incubation with PPD.

blastogenic capabilities of the macrophages is tabulated in Table VII. In each case suitable controls indicated that the cells were not injured by the particular treatment. Macrophages which had been exposed to PPD at 4°C were unable to stimulate blastogenesis in lymphocytes added subsequently. 10^{-3} M NaCN, an inhibitor of phagocytosis, decreased the macrophages' capability of inducing blastogenesis by 66% in this experiment.

Actinomycin D was found to be a potent inhibitor of the blastogenic capabilities of the macrophages. In three experiments, (Table VIII), there was an 80% to 99% inhibition of blastogenesis when actinomycin D (0.5 μg/ml culture) and PPD were incubated together with the macrophages for 2 hr and then washed out before the addition of lymphocytes. The macrophages were quite viable after this temporary incubation with actinomycin D and were capable of phagocytosis of carbon. When, however, the macrophages were pulsed with PPD first and the actinomycin D was added afterwards for up to 2 hr, there was only moderate diminution (25% to 36%) in the uptake of tritiated thymidine. Treatment of the macrophages with actinomycin D for 2 hr, followed by washing and subsequent incubation with PPD, also allowed significant blastogenesis to occur. Only when the macrophages were incubated simultaneously with PPD and actinomycin D was there a marked diminution in blastogenesis.

DISCUSSION

Blast transformation of lymphocytes in response to specific antigens is most intense in cultures in which leukocytes are in close approximation to one another (19). Whether this is due to increased opportunity for cell-to-cell contact, be it lymphocyte-lymphocyte or lymphocyte-macrophage, or to some other change in the micro-environment is not known. Previous attempts to obtain pure macrophages from human leukocytes in order to examine the role of lymphocyte-macrophage interactions have utilized large surfaces to form macrophage monolayers and therefore have not tested macrophages under optimal conditions of culture (11, 13).

We have used radiation to eliminate lymphocytes and yet maintain macrophages cultured on a small surface area. Smears of cultures of leukocytes exposed to 2000 R and then incubated without antigen for 5 to 7 days showed 89% to 98% macrophages with 1% to 6% lymphocytes. Although this small percentage of lymphocytes persisted, exposure to antigen 7 days post-irradiation resulted in blast transformation or uptake of tritiated thymidine comparable to cultures to which no antigen had been added. Whether these persistent lymphocytes had undergone functional but not morphologic damage, or whether they are members of a relatively radioresistant group in the heterogeneous population that are called lymphocytes, is not known. If the latter is the case, then these lymphocytes appear to be functionally different in terms of their response to antigen. In contrast, some blasts were noted when antigen was added immediately after radiation exposure, although the increase in uptake of tritiated thymidine was minimal. Apparently the immune stimulus was partially protective in this situation in that some lymphocytes were able to transform into relatively radioresistant blasts. The timing of an immune stimulus relative to radiation exposure has been shown to be important in determining the effect of radiation on antibody production *in vivo* in many systems (20).

In the studies reported here, the macrophage-rich population produced by radiation exposure has been shown to restore the PPD reactivity of separated lymphocytes to the level found in cultures of unseparated leukocytes. The macrophages were also capable of increasing still further the reactivity of unseparated leukocytes to PPD. Evidence that this restitution is dependent on the macrophage, rather than the few lymphocytes remaining after irradiation, includes the failure of separated lymphocytes or unseparated leukocytes to be as effective in increasing blast transformation as the lymphocyte-depleted macrophage populations. These findings, however, could have also been due to a depressant effect of the irradiated lymphocytes or to the increased number of cells per culture necessary to restore the number of monocytes to that present in the cultures of unseparated leukocytes.

After brief exposure to antigen, the irradiated macrophages of some donors were also noted to be able to induce transformation and uptake of tritiated thymidine by subsquently added separated lymphocytes. Incorporation of radioactivity was the same as that of unseparated leukocytes continuously exposed to PPD in the culture medium throughout the incubation period. The inability to demonstrate this capability of the pulsed macrophages in all donors tested is presently under investigation.

In order that the pulsed macrophages be capable of inducing lymphocyte transformation, they had to be intact, viable, in contact with the lymphocytes, and have relatively recent exposure to antigen. The stimulatory capabilities of the pulsed macrophages were gradually lost over a 4-day period without detectable leakage of the antigen into the supernatant. Apparently the antigen or immunogen had been metabolized during this period.

These observations confirm the work of Hersh and Harris (11), who found that macrophage monolayers derived from human leukocytes had a stimulatory effect on the response of separated lymphocytes to various antigens and extend these observations in that the stimulatory cell has been shown to be radioresistant. Cline and Swett (13) have also previously reported "indirect" transformation of lymphocytes by PPD-pulsed monocytes (separated by albumin flotation and monolayer formation). Our results differ from theirs in that they found no difference between the response of separated lymphocytes cultured continuously with antigen and lymphocytes exposed to PPD-pulsed monocytes. We noted a marked increase of blastogenesis in separated lymphocytes induced by the PPD-pulsed macrophages, comparable to that seen in unseparated leukocytes. The reason for this discrepancy may be due to the different methods of culture, or to a decreased efficiency of the monocyte compared to the mature macrophage or, less likely, to an enhancing effect of radiation. Gallily and Feldman (7) noted a depressant effect on the immunologic function of macrophages when irradiation was given *in vivo*. This was confirmed by Mitchison (21) who noted, however, that the ability itself to take up antigen was not impaired by irradiation. Another recent report using irradiated donors showed no deleterious effect on the macrophages when tested *in vitro* by the Jerne technique (22).

The nature of the stimulatory effect of the macrophage is not clear. Whether it is due to processing of antigen or merely to increasing the availability of antigen to the lymphoid cell has not been determined. There is evidence that the macrophage effect is nonspecific in that prior knowledge of antigen is not necessary (23, 24).

Studies in animals have also indicated that the adjuvant effect of macrophage-associated antigen is dependent on the antigen. Certain antigens have less potency after incubation with peritoneal macrophages (25). It would appear from our studies, and those quoted above, that PPD gains potency from its association with macrophages, at least as exhibited by *in vitro* blastogenesis.

The depressant effect of the metabolic inhibitors of phagocytosis and pinocytosis, particularly that of decreased temperature, observed in this and other studies (13, 24), would appear to indicate that uptake of antigen by the macrophage, and not merely surface attachment, occurs. Kasakura has recently reported the ability of freshly irradiated lymphocytes to take up antigen (26); however, the uptake was not inhibited by cold, suggesting that a simple surface attachment had occurred on the lymphocytes.

We were able to demonstrate inhibition by actinomycin D of the induction of blastogenesis by pulsed macrophages. However this inhibition was marked only when actinomycin D was added simultaneously with PPD. If the macrophages were pretreated with actinomycin D and then washed before the addition of PPD, only moderate inhibition was noted. Therefore it would appear that new RNA synthesis is not necessary under these experimental conditions. Gottlieb *et al.* (6) found that immunogenic RNA isolated from antigen-treated macrophages is indistinguishable by molecular hybridization from the RNA isolated from untreated macrophages. We also found that actinomycin D was less inhibitory once PPD was taken up by the cell or attached to the site from which its immunogenic potential can be manifest. Actinomycin D has been shown to inhibit macrophage pinocytosis by Cohn (27); however, this effect is a delayed one and probably cannot account for the inhibition of the immunogenic potential of the macrophages noted here. A possible explanation is that the actinomycin D is inhibiting the uptake of PPD through a more specific mechanism than a general depression of pinocytosis, possibly by interfering with attachment to the cell membrane.

Acknowledgments. We thank Dr. Robert Andrews and his staff for the use of the cobalt γ source and Miss Frances Soehnlein for her invaluable assistance.

REFERENCES

1. Miller, J. F. A. P. and Mitchell, G. F., J. Exp. Med., *128:* 801, 1968.
2. Mosier, D. E., Science, *158:* 1573, 1967.
3. Fishman, M. and Adler, F. L., J. Exp. Med., *117:* 595, 1963.
4. Askonas, B. A. and Rhodes, J. M., Nature, *205:* 470, 1965.
5. Friedman, H. P., Stavitsky, A. B. and Solomon, J. M., Science, *149:* 1106, 1965.
6. Gottlieb, A. A., Glisin, V. R. and Doty, P., Proc. Nat. Acad. Sci., *57:* 1849, 1967.
7. Gallily, R. and Feldman, M., Immunology *12:* 197, 1967.
8. Argyris, B. F., J. Exp. Med., *128:* 459, 1968.
9. McFarland, W., Proceedings of Third Annual Leukocyte Culture Conference, Edited by W. O. Rieke, Appleton-Century-Crofts, New York, 1969.
10. Heilman, D. H. and McFarland, W., Fed. Proc., *26:* 528, 1967.
11. Hersh, E. M. and Harris, J. E., J. Immun., *100:* 1184, 1968.
12. Oppenheim, J. J., Leventhal, B. G. and Hersh, E. M., J. Immun., *101:* 262, 1968.
13. Cline, M. J. and Swett, V. C., J. Exp. Med., *128:* 1309, 1968.
14. Kasakura, S. and Lowenstein, L., Proc. Soc. Exp. Biol. Med., *125:* 355, 1967.
15. Gordon, J., Proc. Soc. Exp. Biol. Med., *127:* 30, 1968.
16. McFarland, W. and Heilman, D. H., Amer. Rev. Resp. Dis., *93:* 742, 1966.
17. Rabinowitz, Y., Blood, *23:* 811, 1964.
18. Bennett, W. E. and Cohn, Z. A., J. Exp. Med., *123:* 145, 1966.
19. Moorhead, J. F., Connolly, J. J. and McFarland, W., J. Immun., *99:* 413, 1967.
20. Taliaferro, W. H., Taliaferro, L. G. and Jaroslow, B. N., Radiation and Immune Mechanisms, Academic Press, New York, 1964.
21. Mitchison, N. A., Immunology, *16:* 1, 1969.
22. Roseman, J., Science, *165:* 1125, 1969.
23. Seeger, R. C. and Oppenheim, J. J., Proceedings of Fourth Leukocyte Culture Conference, In press.
24. Hersh, E. M. and Harris, J. E., Proceedings of Fourth Leukocyte Culture Conference, In press.
25. Unanue, E. R., J. Immun., *102:* 893, 1969.
26. Kasakura, S., J. Immun., *103:* 1078, 1969.
27. Cohn, Z. A., J. Exp. Med., *124:* 557, 1966.

THE JOURNAL OF IMMUNOLOGY

Vol. 105, No. 3, September 1970
Printed in U.S.A.

RECEPTOR SITES FOR COMPLEMENT ON CERTAIN HUMAN PERIPHERAL BLOOD LYMPHOCYTES

GERHARD MICHLMAYR AND HEINZ HUBER[1]

From the Medizinische Universitätsklinik Innsbruck, Austria

Received for publication February 24, 1970

Receptor sites for complement (C) on human peripheral blood lymphocytes were assessed by their capacity to bind red cells coated with C. Rosette formation was observed around 20% (12 to 29%) of blood lymphocytes obtained from normal donors. The number of lymphocytes with rosettes was related to the amount of C bound to the red cells. Treatment of lymphocytes with trypsin or incubation with anti-lymphocyte globulin inhibited the receptor activity. In contrast to the inhibition of rosette formation resulting from adding EDTA to the incubation mixture of monocytes and C-coated red cells, there was no inhibitory effect by EDTA on lymphocytes and C-coated red cells. Rosettes were almost exclusively observed around small lymphocytes. When lymphocytes were separated in a discontinuous bovine serum albumin gradient, the highest percentage of lymphocytes with receptor activity was found in fractions of low density. In patients with chronic lymphocytic leukemia there was a significantly lower percentage of rosette-forming cells.

The demonstration and characterization of cell surface receptors for complement components, immunoglobulins and antigens on cells of the lymphoid and monocyte-macrophage series may give important clues to the functions of these cell types in the immune response. The attachment of antigen-antibody complexes to mononuclear leukocytes of unsensitized donors has been demonstrated (1–6). Using sensitized erythrocytes, independent receptors for γG and for complement (C) have been demonstrated on human and rabbit monocytes and macrophages. Receptor sites for C have been observed on certain lymphocyte populations (4, 7), and very recently Coombs *et al.* (2, 8) have shown that a very small percentage of human peripheral blood lymphocytes have surface determinants for γ, μ, κ and λ immunoglobulin chains. In order to further assess receptor sites on human peripheral blood lymphocyte populations, the reactivity of normal cells separated by sedimentation on a discontinuous density gradient and of cells from patients with chronic lymphocytic leukemia was tested with C-coated erythrocytes.

MATERIAL AND METHODS

Preparation of lymphocytes. Human lymphocytes were isolated from the peripheral blood of 19 normal donors and from 10 patients with chronic lymphocytic leukemia by standard methods using filtration through nylon wool (9). Five of the patients had received no treatment for at least 2 months prior to the study. Three others had been treated with low doses of prednisolone (up to 15 mg/day) and two with chlorambucil (Leukeran, Burroughs Wellcome) up to 6 mg/day. Of the total white cell counts which ranged from 13,500 and 114,000/mm^3, 51 to 97% were lymphocytes. The cell suspension, which after filtration through nylon wool contained at least 95% lymphocytes, was washed three times with culture medium TC 199 (Burroughs Wellcome) and finally diluted to 6×10^6 cells/ml in the same medium.

Preparation of C-coated erythrocytes. Equal volumes of a 5% suspension of washed sheep red cells and inactivated (56°C for 90 min) hyperimmune rabbit anti-Forssman antiserum (4 hemolytic units, Serotherapeutisches Institut, Vienna) were incubated at 37°C for 30 min. The cell suspension was brought to 5% and an equal volume of fresh human serum (as a source of C) serially diluted with phosphate buffered saline was added. Further details are given under *Results.* After 30 min of incubation at 37°C, the red cells were washed three times in TC 199 and finally diluted with the culture medium to a concentration of 1.25%.

[1] Please direct correspondence to: Dr. H. Huber, Medizin. Univ. Klinik, 6020 Innsbruck, Austria.

In one series of experiments performed at room temperature group O human red cells were sensitized with appropriate dilutions of a typical "monoclonal" γM cold agglutinin of high titer. The agglutinin titer against compatible normal adult red cells was 1:16,000 at 4°C. A dilution of 1:100 was used in these particular experiments. Fresh human serum was added at a dilution of 1:40.

Assay of C receptor. Equal volumes of C-coated red cells (EAC) and the lymphocyte suspension were mixed. The tubes were rotated in a 37°C water bath (along a horizontal axis at about 50 rpm) for 30 min and examined for rosettes. As controls, unsensitized (E) and sensitized red cells (EA) were also added to the lymphocyte preparations.

Evaluation of rosette-forming cells. The percentage of lymphocytes with rosettes was determined by counting at least 200 lymphocytes in wet preparations. Lymphocytes with at least three attached red cells were considered positive. Simultaneously, cells were also fixed and stained with May-Grünwald-Giemsa. In order to obtain preparations suitable for staining, about 20 drops of loosely packed cells were placed on a slide using a Pasteur pipette with a very small orifice. The extra fluid was quickly reaspirated. By this procedure white cells with and without rosettes were well preserved. The diameters of these cells were found to be comparable to those obtained on well spread smears. In smears, however, many rosettes were torn apart. Lymphocytes with diameters of up to 8 μ were classified as small, those with diameters more than 8 to 10 μ as medium, and those more than 10 μ in diameter as large lymphocytes.

Density fractionation of lymphocytes. Suspensions of purified blood lymphocytes were separated on a discontinuous bovine serum albumin gradient using a modification (10) of the method of Raidt *et al.* (11). The following dilutions of sterile, preservative-free bovine albumin (Pentex, Inc., Kankakee, Ill.) in Hanks' solution were prepared: 33, 29, 26, 23, 20, 17, 14 and 10%. Eight-tenths-milliliter aliquots of albumin in decreasing concentrations (33 to 23%) were carefully overlayered in a centrifuge tube (12 × 100 mm). The layers ranging from 20 to 10% albumin consisted of 0.4-ml volumes to which a spacing layer of 0.8 ml of Hanks' solution was added. Finally the tube was loaded with about 10^8 cells in 1 ml of Hanks' solution. The tube was then centrifuged at 22°C for 5 min at 1000 × G and for 25 min at 3000 × G. At the interfaces, discrete bands of cells became visible which were designated: A (at the interface 20 to 23% albumin), B (23 to 26%), C (26 to 29%), D (29 to 33%) and E (pellet). The cells were harvested with a Pasteur pipette, counted, washed in Hanks' solution, and further processed as described. The distribution of small, medium, and large lymphocytes in the various fractions is shown in Table I.

Inhibition experiments. A horse antiserum against human lymphocytes was prepared using thoracic duct lymphocytes. It was partially purified by precipitation with ammonium sulfate and provided by the Behringwerke, Marburg/Lahn, Germany (12). One-tenth milliliter of antilymphocyte globulin (ALG) dilutions, without C, was added to 3 × 10^5 lymphocytes (in 0.1 ml) and these were incubated for 90 min. The lymphocytes were washed three times, resuspended to the original volume, and the C-coated red cells were added. The results were evaluated as described previously. Cell viability, assessed by the exclusion of 0.5% trypan blue, was at least 85%. Trypsin (twice crystallized) was dissolved in PO_4-buffer (pH 7.2) and 0.1 ml of a 0.1% solution of this was added to the lymphocytes. After 30 min incubation at 37°C, the lymphocytes were washed three times with excess saline and subsequently tested for receptor activity.

In other experiments, sodium EDTA in various concentrations was added to the incubation medium together with the C-coated red cells.

Monocyte test system. The isolation of monocytes and the test system for demonstrating

TABLE I

Fractionation of blood lymphocytes by a bovine serum albumin gradient: Distribution of small, medium and large lymphocytes

Fraction/ % BSA	Distribution of Lymphocytes of Different Sizes within Each Fraction (%)		
	Small	Medium	Large
A/10–23	83 (78–90)[a]	10 (7–14)	6 (3–8)
B/23–26	73 (58–84)	11 (8–15)	16 (8–27)
C/26–29	62 (58–64)	16 (8–20)	23 (16–24)
D/29–33	47 (45–51)	25 (17–32)	28 (23–32)
E/pellet	34 (18–46)	16 (13–22)	50 (40–69)

[a] Each value gives the mean and range at three experiments.

TABLE II

Demonstration of complement (C) receptor sites on lymphocytes using C-coated human (4 experiments) or sheep red cells (19 experiments)

Type of Experiment	Red Cell Complexes	Incubation Temperature	Lymphocytes with Rosettes
			%
Human red cells sensitized with γ^M "monoclonal" cold agglutinin	E	r.t.[b]	0.25 (0–0.5)
	EA	r.t.	0.25 (0–0.5)
	EAC 1:40[a]	r.t.	12.0 ± 2.2[c]
Sheep red cells sensitized with an anti-Forssman antiserum	E	37°	0.1 (0–0.5)
	EA	37°	0.4 (0–1.5)
	EAC 1:40[a]	37°	20.0 ± 1.4[c]
	EAC 1:80	37°	14.3 ± 1.4
	EAC 1:160	37°	16.2 ± 1.5
	EAC 1:320	37°	9.7 ± 1.6
	EAC 1:640	37°	9.1 ± 1.0
	EAC 1:1280	37°	8.7 ± 1.4
	EAC 1:2560	37°	3.3 ± 0.7
	EAC 1:5120	37°	1.0 ± 1.0

[a] Dilutions of C (fresh human serum).
[b] Room temperature.
[c] Mean and standard error.

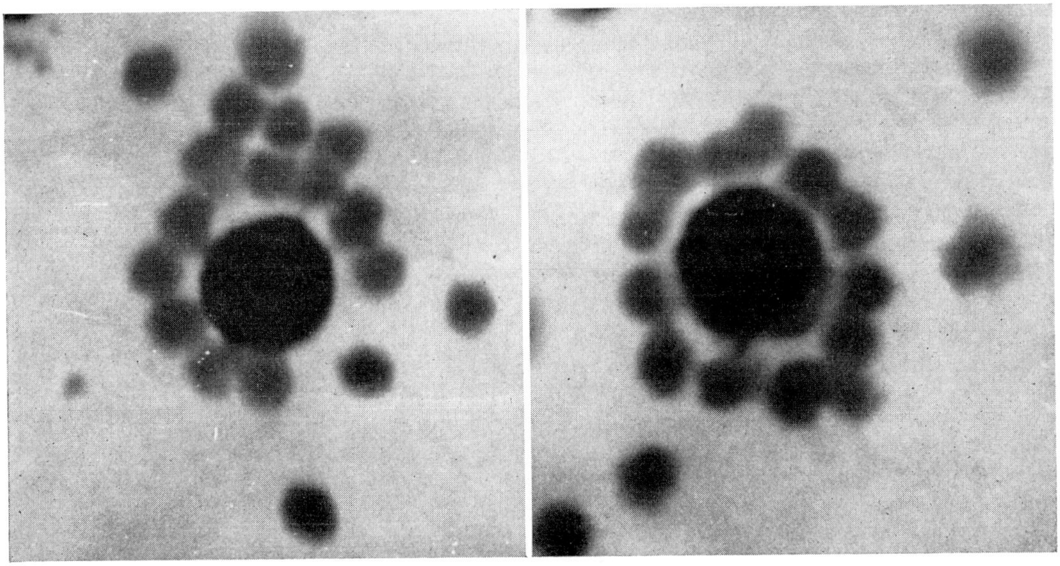

Figure 1. Rosettes formed by lymphocytes and EAC. Isolated blood lymphocytes were incubated with sheep red cells coated with an anti-Forssman-antiserum and complement.

C receptor sites on these cells has been described in detail previously (13–15).

RESULTS

Description of the test system. Red cells coated with human C formed rosettes around a significant percentage of blood lymphocytes obtained from normal donors (Table II, Fig. 1). This was first shown with red cells sensitized with a γM "monoclonal" cold agglutinin and C, which were tested at room temperature. The percentage of reactive lymphocytes averaged 12%. A higher

TABLE III

Effect of inhibitors on the C receptor activity of normal lymphocytes

Treatment of Lymphocytes	Concentration of Inhibitors	Degree of Inhibition[a]
ALG[b]	Undiluted	+++
	1:4	+++
	1:16	+++
	1:64	+++
	1:256	++
	1:512	+
	1:1024	+
	1:2048	—
	1:4096	—
	1:8192	—
Trypsin	0.1%	+++
EDTA	10 mM	—
	5 mM	—
	2.5 mM	—
	1.25 mM	—

[a] +++, rosette formation completely inhibited; ++, rosette formation reduced at least 50%; +, rosette formation reduced 25 to 50%; —, no inhibition or inhibition less than +.

[b] Cytotoxicity titer 1:256.

percentage of lymphocytes formed rosettes in experiments at 37°C, using sheep red cells coated with antibody and C. Under these conditions, 20% of the lymphocytes were positive. In fixed and stained preparations the percentage of lymphocytes with rosettes was slightly lower and averaged 17%. When lymphocytes were incubated with sheep red cells alone (E), rosette formation rarely occurred. In 4 out of 19 experiments a small number of rosettes was observed after adding sheep red cell-antibody complexes (EA) without C. Their number, however, did not exceed 1.5%.

Titration experiments indicated that the number of lymphocytes with rosettes was related to the amount of C bound to the red cells (Table II). In parallel experiments red cells coated with different dilutions of C were added to lymphocytes and monocytes. At optimal concentrations of C, the percentage of monocytes showing rosette formation was much higher than ever seen for lymphocytes. Rosettes were observed around more than 90% of the isolated monocytes. Reducing the amount of C, however, resulted in a comparable decrease in the number of reactive cells. The percentage of reactive lymphocytes (Table II) as well as monocytes decreased to about half of the optimal value at a C dilution of 1:320.

Sensitivity of the C receptor to various treatments. When lymphocytes were incubated with ALG, rosette formation was impaired (Table III). Treatment of lymphocytes with trypsin resulted in a loss of their receptor activity (Table III). This inhibition was comparable to that obtained with monocytes (15). In contrast to the results with monocytes, however, EDTA had no adverse effect on the receptor activity of lymphocytes.

Receptor activity of lymphocytes after fraction-

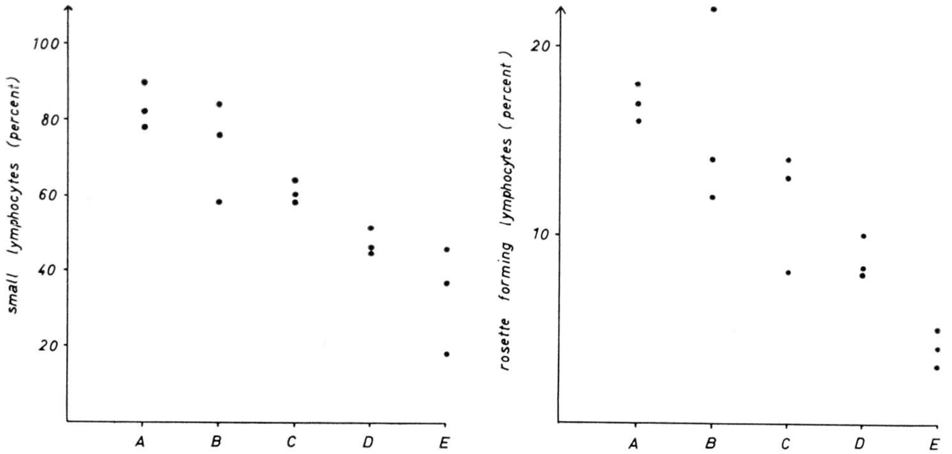

Figure 2. Distribution of small lymphocytes (*left*) and rosette-forming cells (*right*) in the various fractions after centrifugation in a discontinuous albumin gradient. The five fractions obtained are designated *A* to *E*.

TABLE IV

Presence of a C receptor as related to different sizes of lymphocytes

Size of Lymphocytes[a]	C Receptor Present[b]	Significance[c]
	mean and range	
Small (1204)[d]	19.4 (15.9–25.1)	
Medium (489)	3.9 (0.9–6.7)	<0.001
Large (601)	1.5 (0–4.5)	<0.001

[a] Small: $\leqq 8\mu$, medium: 8–10μ, large: $>10\mu$.

[b] Percentage of cells with rosettes.

[c] X^2 test (p values for comparison of the percentage of positive cells among small lymphocytes vs medium and large lymphocytes).

[d] Total number of cells evaluated in five experiments.

ation in an albumin density gradient. By centrifugation in a discontinous bovine serum albumin gradient, lymphocytes of normal donors were separated into fractions of different density. Five discrete bands of cells were obtained. The percentage of C-reactive lymphocytes differed markedly between these fractions. The cells of low density contained a higher percentage of lymphocytes with C receptor activity; whereas, those of high density were almost unreactive (Fig. 2).

Receptor activity of small, medium and large lymphocytes. In stained preparations lymphocytes were classified according to their size, and the percentage of reactive cells within these classes was evaluated (Table IV). The majority of cells with receptor activity were small lymphocytes. In five experiments, 91% of all rosettes counted were observed around small lymphocytes. Usually more than 95% of medium or large lymphocytes lacked the receptor. In the albumin gradient the upper fractions were enriched to some extent in small lymphocytes, whereas large lymphocytes predominated at the interface of the heavy layers (Table I). The relative frequency of the former cell type corresponded to the portion of rosette-forming cells (Fig. 2).

C receptors on lymphocytes from patients with chronic lymphocytic leukemia. Lymphocytes from ten patients with chronic lymphocytic leukemia were studied. The percentage of rosette-forming lymphocytes was reduced below the range of the normal controls for cells from nine of these patients (Fig. 3). Differences in the percentage of reactive small lymphocytes between cells from patients and controls were also significant. In these nine patients 4 to 13% of lymphocytes were positive, whereas in the controls the percentage was 16 to 25%.

DISCUSSION

In our test system about 20% of normal human peripheral blood lymphocytes exhibited receptor

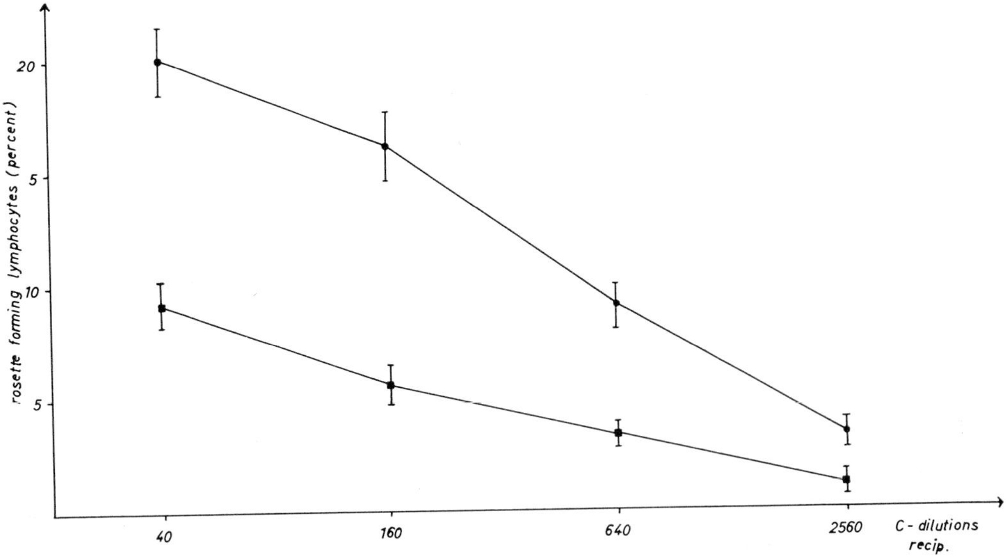

Figure 3. Percentage of rosette-forming lymphocytes obtained from normal donors and from patients with chronic lymphocytic leukemia. Means and standard errors obtained with lymphocytes from the patients (■——■) and from the normal controls (●——●) at various dilutions of C are given.

activity for C bound to red cells. In the absence of C, the majority of lymphocytes neither bound unsensitized red cells nor those coated with immunoglobulins. In contrast, monocytes contained distinct receptor sites for C as well as for immunoglobulin G. The latter receptor system appeared to be specific for macrophages and related cells (3). Lymphocytes and monocytes differed also in the percentage of reactive cells. Furthermore, C-coated red cells bound effectively to lymphocytes, but not to monocytes in the presence of EDTA (*cf.* 4). In this respect, their receptor resembled the immune adherence receptor present on primate red cells (4, 6). In earlier experiments the amount of C required for binding to monocytes or to primate red cells was compared (14). For both cell types a similar number of C 3 molecules was effective. In the present experiments labeled C 3 was not available, and only simple titrations were performed in parallel on both types of mononuclear cells. These experiments suggested that C receptor sites of comparable sensitivity were present on lymphocytes and monocytes. A more definitive answer, however, requires the use of purified and labeled components.

Circulating blood lymphocytes are a heterogenous population of cells involved in a variety of functions. When rosette-forming lymphocytes were classified according to their density in albumin, mainly those of low density exhibited receptor activity for C. When this property was related to cell size, cells classified as small lymphocytes were almost exclusively involved. In contrast, usually more than 95% of the medium and large lymphocytes lacked the receptor.

In comparison to normal lymphocytes those from patients with chronic lymphocytic leukemia appeared defective in several test systems (e.g., blast cell transformation (16), content of lysosomal enzymes (17)). In our experiments lymphocytes from the majority of these patients were less suitable for binding C-coated red cells. Perhaps, under these conditions, lymphocytes with receptor activity were "diluted" by those lacking the receptor. The absolute number of reactive cells, however, was not reduced.

By means of their C receptor, small lymphocytes, which have not been specifically sensitized, may acquire reactivity with antigen. In cultures of normal lymphocytes, blast cell transformation has been induced by antigen-antibody complexes, but the participation of C has not been conclusively demonstrated (18, 19). An intimate contact between aggressor and target cells might facilitate the cytotoxic potential of lymphoid cells. Under certain experimental conditions this effect required the presence of some components of complement (20), and receptor sites for C may well play a part in facilitating this interaction.

Acknowledgments. We thank Prof. Dr. H. Braunsteiner for interest and support, Dr. H. H. Fudenberg for many valuable discussions, Dr. G. Riethmüller for introducing us to the method of lymphocyte separation on a density gradient, Dr. S. D. Douglas for critically reading the manuscript and Mrs. A. Maneschg and Mrs. F. Oberwasserlechner for excellent technical assistance.

REFERENCES

1. Berken, A. and Benacerraf, B., J. Exp. Med., *123:* 119, 1966.
2. Coombs, R. R. A. and Franks, D., Progr. Allerg., *13:* 174, 1969.
3. Huber, H., Douglas, S. D. and Fudenberg, H. H., Immunology, *17:* 7, 1969.
4. Lay, H. W. and Nussenzweig, V., J. Exp. Med., *128:* 991, 1968.
5. Lobuglio, A. F., Cotran, R. S. and Jandl, J. H., Science, *158:* 1582, 1967.
6. Nelson, D. S., in *Complement*, Edited by G. E. W. Wolstenholme and J. Knight, p. 222, Churchill, London, 1965.
7. Nussenzweig, V., Lay, W. H. and Miescher, P. A., in *Cellular Recognition*, Edited by R. T. Smith and R. A. Good, Appleton-Century-Crofts, New York, 1969.
8. Coombs, R. R. A., Feinstein, A. and Wilson, A. B., Lancet, *2:* 1157, 1969.
9. Rabinowitz, Y., Blood, *23:* 811, 1964.
10. Rieber, H. P. and Riethmüller, G., Paper read at the first session of the German Society for Immunology, Freiburg/Brsg., Oct. 16–18, 1969.
11. Raidt, D. J., Mishell, R. I. and Dutton, R. W., J. Exp. Med., *1, 8:* 681, 1968.
12. Heide, K., Seiler, F. and Schwick, H. G., Paper read at the first session of the German Society for Immunology, Freiburg/Brsg., Oct. 16–18, 1969.
13. Huber, H. and Fudenberg, H. H., Int. Arch. Allerg., *34:* 18, 1968.
14. Huber, H., Polley, M. J., Linscott, W. D., Fudenberg, H. H. and Müller-Eberhard, H. J., Science, *162:* 1281, 1968.

15. Huber, H. and Douglas, S. D., Brit. J. Hemat., In press.
16. Oppenheim, J. J., Whang, J. and Frei, E., Blood, *26:* 121, 1965.
17. Brittinger, G., In preparation.
18. Bloch-Shtacher, N., Hirschhorn, K. and Uhr, J. W., Clin. Exp. Immun., *3:* 889, 1968.
19. Möller, G., Clin. Exp. Immun., *4:* 65, 1969.
20. Müller-Eberhard, H. J., Perlmann, P., Perlmann, H. and Manni, J. A., in *Current Problems in Immunology*, Edited by O. Westphal, H. E. Bock and E. Grundmann, p. 5, Springer, Berlin-Heidelberg-New York, 1969.

THE JOURNAL OF IMMUNOLOGY
Vol. 105, No. 3, September, 1970

Printed in U.S.A.

PATTERNS OF SEROLOGIC SPECIFICITY OF HUMAN γG ERYTHROCYTE AUTOANTIBODIES

Correlation of Antibody Specificity with Complement-Fixing Behavior

JOHN P. LEDDY,[1] PHYLLIS PETERSON, MARILYN A. YEAW AND RICHARD F. BAKEMEIER[2]

From the Department of Medicine, University of Rochester School of Medicine and Dentistry, Rochester, New York 14620

Received for publication February 18, 1970

The serologic specificity of warm-reacting γG autoantibodies eluted from the red blood cells (RBC) of 46 patients with acquired immune hemolytic anemia was systematically studied with a panel of rare human RBC including Rh_{null}, -D-/-D-, LW-negative, and K^oK^o cells as well as with several monkey RBC. Based on the patterns obtained, a tentative classification of autoantibody specificities into four major groups is proposed as a framework for further research. Autoantibody populations with anti-LW specificity or with specificity in the Kell blood group system could not be demonstrated in this series. These observations also provided evidence that autoantibody specificity is an important factor governing the presence or absence of complement fixation to RBC *in vivo*, as determined by direct antiglobulin (Coombs') tests with specific anti-complement (anti-C3) serum. Sixteen of 20 autoantibody eluates derived from patients whose RBC were coated with both γG globulin and complement exhibited strong reactions with Rh_{null} RBC. Conversely, 12 eluates displaying essentially no reactivity with Rh_{null} RBC, and strongly suspected to have specificities related to the Rh system, were from patients with only γG globulin detectable on their RBC.

The commonest form of acquired immune hemolytic anemia (AIHA) in man involves γG erythrocyte autoantibodies with optimal reactivity at 37°C ("warm-reacting" autoantibodies). Knowledge of the antigenic determinants on the human red blood cell (RBC) with which such antibodies react is very incomplete.

Historical background. Earlier studies established that these autoantibodies usually reacted with all of the common human RBC phenotypes but failed to react with the RBC of non-human species except certain primates (1, 2). Such antibodies have been termed "non-specific" (i.e., specificity undetermined). Since 1953 increasing numbers of cases have been recorded in which autoantibodies in the patient's serum or RBC eluate exhibited specificity for one or more antigens of the Rh system (1), often in the company of antibodies with undetermined specificity. Rare instances of apparent specificity for Kell, Kidd, or Xg^a blood group antigens were also described (1, 3). Subsequently it was found that a significant number of seemingly "non-specific" autoantibody populations showed selective non-reactivity (a) with rare human Rh_{null} RBC (4) which lack all known Rh antigens (5, 6), or less commonly, (b) with the rare -D-/-D- ($\overline{\overline{Rh_o}}$) RBC (4, 7) which lack any known expression of cC or eE determinants (8). These findings, confirmed by us in a small series in 1965 (9), have been interpreted as supporting the postulate (10) that many warm-reacting autoantibodies possess specificity for the "nucleus" or "core" substance(s) of the Rh complex common to all human RBC except Rh_{null} cells. Recently, autoantibodies with anti-LW specificity have been reported (11).

In general, these earlier investigators each em-

[1] Supported by a Senoir Investigator Award of the Arthritis Foundation and by United States Public Health Service Grant AM-09810.

[2] Supported by a United States Public Health Service Research Career Development Award and by United States Public Health Service Grant AI-04841.

ployed certain selected types of test erythrocytes. In the present study, all of the foregoing serologic criteria, and others, were applied systematically to 46 isolated autoantibody populations (eluates) in an effort to identify major patterns of serologic specificity and thereby provide a clearer basis for immunochemical study of the relevant membrane antigens.

MATERIALS AND METHODS

Red cells. Rare human red cells were obtained as follows: 1) Rh_{null} (donors L. M. (6) and H. H.) and -D-/-D- ($\overline{\overline{Rh_o}}$) (donors L. H. and J. C.) in liquid N_2 from Dr. F. H. Allen, New York Blood Center; 2) fresh Rh_{null} (donor L. M.) and R_zR_z (CDE/CDE) in liquid N_2 from Dr. Paul Schmidt, Bethesda; 3) fresh Rh_{null} (donor J. R. B. (12)) from Dr. R. E. Rosenfield, New York; 4) fresh LW-negative A CDe/ce (R_1r) (donor Mrs. B.) from Dr. L. L. DeVeber, London, Ont.; 5) fresh cells of phenotype K (−), k (−), Kp (a−) (b−), or K°K°, from the Canadian Red Cross Blood Transfusion Service, Winnipeg. The evidence for the LW-negative status of Mrs. B.'s red cells and for the anti-LW specificity of her serum antibody is being prepared for publication (G. Clark, M. Hunking, L. L. DeVeber and M. Stroup, in preparation). In our hands, her serum antibody (γG class), obtained from the same bleeding as the red cell sample, fulfilled the following criteria for anti-LW specificity: no reaction with Rh_{null} RBC, strong reactions with all six monkey RBC in our panel (see below), and stronger reactions with R_1R_1 and R_2R_2 cells than with several rr cells. Red cells were recovered from liquid N_2 as previously described (13). An additional sample of O cDE/cDE (R_2R_2) cells, stored concurrently in liquid N_2 throughout this study, displayed no demonstrable change in its serologic reactions. Panels of human red cells of known genotypes were obtained as the Selectogen and Identogen series from Ortho Diagnostics, Raritan, N. J., and as the Panocell series from Pfizer Diagnostics, New York, N. Y.

Red cells of four rhesus (*Macaca mulatta*) and two stump-tail (*Macaca speciosa*) monkeys were freshly obtained from our own stock. In preliminary studies no significant differences were observed in the reactions of the various monkey RBC. Therefore, most eluates were tested against two individual rhesus samples and a pool of the stump-tail RBC; some, however, were tested against the RBC of four to six individual monkeys.

Autoantibodies. All 46 autoantibody populations studied were eluates from the RBC of patients with AIHA. The only selection used was that direct Coombs' tests were positive with anti-γG serum, and eluates had to be serologically potent. The majority of patients had no recognizable underlying disease. Eleven had a lymphoproliferative disease. Five had systemic lupus erythematosus, two rheumatoid arthritis, and one polymyositis. Two cases were associated with α-methyldopa therapy.

For preparation of eluates, the patients' RBC were washed (20 vol/vol RBC) once in 0.15 M NaCl at room temperature, twice with cold (5°C) triethanolamine-buffered saline (pH 7.3), and three times with cold 0.15 M NaCl. Red cell stromata were prepared by the freeze-thaw method (14) in some earlier cases but mainly by digitonin lysis (15). Stromata were washed five or more times with cold saline and eluted in pH 3.0 citrate (14) or glycine-HCl (15) at room temperature. Eluates were immediately dialyzed against cold phosphate-buffered saline, pH 7.3. We have found that five to eight cycles of elution are required to dissociate all of the recoverable antibody (J. P. Leddy and R. F. Bakemeier, unpublished). The yields from the various cycles were pooled, concentrated by ultrafiltration, and stored at −20°C.

Antisera. Specific rabbit antisera to human γG, γA and γM globulins and to human complement (C) components were prepared and characterized as described elsewhere (16). By immunodiffusion and hemagglutination-inhibition studies with purified components supplied by Dr. H. Müller-Eberhard, the anti-C serum has its major specificity against C 3 and lesser reactivity with C 4.

Serologic procedures. Antiglobulin reactions (direct and indirect) were performed by standard tube technique, using unmodified red cells. Agglutination was read macroscopically on a 5-point scale from trace to 4+. Direct antiglobulin tests on patients' RBC utilized multiple dilutions of anti-γG and anti-C sera. In most cases the RBC were also tested with specific anti-γA or anti-γM sera, with uniformly negative results (16, 17).

To study the reactivity of autoantibody

eluates with the various special types of red cells, three kinds of serologic protocols were employed: a) a survey protocol applied to all eluates; b) block titrations of selected eluates in each major serologic group (see below); and c) absorption studies on selected eluates.

The first step in the *survey protocol* was to determine for each eluate the "critical dilution," i.e., the highest dilution which would sensitize normal human RBC of common phenotypes, e.g., group O CDe/ce (R_1r) or ce/ce (rr), to give a 3+ to 4+ antiglobulin reaction with optimally diluted anti-γG serum. Testing of eluates at this "critical dilution" was considered essential for making comparisons of the reactivity of various types of RBC because too large a dose of autoantibody was found in some instances to mask real differences and too little autoantibody led to weak antiglobulin reactions which were difficult to evaluate. The "critical" eluate dilution was then used to survey comparative strengths of reactions with various kinds of red cells. In all such studies, human RBC of common phenotype, (group O R_1r or rr), hereafter termed "normal" RBC, were retested in each experiment as a known standard. Except when frozen RBC were studied, every effort was made to employ "normal" RBC of the same *in vitro* age as that of the test RBC. A typical survey experiment would involve concurrent incubation of 0.1-ml amounts of the chosen dilution of an eluate with carefully standardized 2.5% saline suspensions of "normal" human RBC, Rh_{null} RBC and -D-/-D-RBC; or with comparable suspensions of "normal" human RBC and two or more different monkey RBC, and so forth. Incubations were at 37°C for 60 min with frequent mixing. After washing three times with cold 0.15 M saline, the RBC were tested for agglutination by an optimal (e.g., 1:40) dilution of anti-γG serum.

Block titrations were basically similar except that a range of doses of autoantibody were used to sensitize the RBC and the sensitized RBC were tested with a range of antiglobulin serum dilutions.

Absorption experiments were performed by exposing a given eluate to small volumes of washed, packed RBC of a given type at 37°C. Such additions were repeated until the absorbing red cells gave negative antiglobulin reactions. Absorption of another portion of the same eluate with similar volumes of washed, packed sheep RBC, which do not react with autoantibodies, served to control the effects of dilution and entrapment inherent in absorptions with red cells. Absorbed eluates were then tested against other types of RBC, as well as the absorbing cell, by the usual indirect antiglobulin procedure.

Statistical analysis of relevant portions of the data in Table I was carried out by the chi-square method using the Yates correction for small numbers of occurrences.

RESULTS

The autoantibody eluates, except for a few in short supply, had been found by the survey protocol to react strongly with all of the common human RBC phenotypes in one or more standard panels. Quantitative differences were, however, observed in a few cases which later proved to have subpopulations with identifiable specificities (see below).

Rh_{null} cells. Reactions of the autoantibody eluates with two different Rh_{null} cells (L. M.

TABLE I

Reactions of autoantibodies with Rh_{null} RBC related to pattern of direct Coombs' test

Direct Coombs' Test Pattern	No. of Patients Whose Red Cell Eluates Gave the Following Reactions[a] with:			
	Rh_{null} RBC[b]			"Normal" RBC[b]
	Essentially neg. (0 to trace)	Intermediate (+ to 2+)	Strong (3+ to 4+)	Strong (3+ to 4+)
γG alone (moderate to strong)	11	5	3	19
γG alone (weak)[c]	1	3	3	7
γG + C	0	4	16	20

[a] Reactions based on the survey protocol (see *Materials and Methods*).

[b] Two different Rh_{null} RBC and several "normal" human RBC of common phenotype were tested concurrently against each eluate. Each eluate was tested in this fashion at least twice, and usually three times, before assignment to one of the above categories.

[c] Weak but definitely positive direct Coombs' reactions with anti-γG, negative with anti-C. These cases are listed separately because quantitative relationships, i.e., fewer antibodies/cell rather than antibody specificity, might limit C binding to a level below threshold for anti-C Coombs' reactions (see *Discussion*).

TABLE II

Effect of absorption of selected eluates with Rh_{null} RBC

Patient	Direct Coombs' Test Pattern	Eluate Absorbed with	Reactions with RBC of Phenotype:	
			Rh_{null}	"Normal"
4 patients (Tr., Fr., Po., Re.)	γG + C	Sheep RBC[a]	3+ to 4+	3+ to 4+[b]
		Rh_{null} RBC	0 to tr.[c]	0 to tr.[d]
2 patients (Ad., Ba.)	γG	Sheep RBC	3+ to 4+	3+ to 4+[b]
		Rh_{null} RBC	0	0
We.	γG + C	Sheep RBC	4+	4+[b]
		Rh_{null} RBC	0	+[e]
2 patients (Co., Li.)	γG	Sheep RBC	2+	4+
		Rh_{null} RBC	0	3+
Bur.	γG + C	Sheep RBC	2+	4+
		Rh_{null} RBC	0	3+

[a] Sheep RBC do not react with the autoantibodies. See *Materials and Methods*.

[b] Titration revealed 1:8 to 1:32 titer against "normal" RBC.

[c] tr., trace.

[d] Trace reaction was observed with "normal" RBC only when trace reactivity with Rh_{null} RBC also persisted in the absorbed eluate.

[e] Positive reactions were observed with R_1R_1 (CDe/CDe), R_2R_2 (cDE/cDE), rr (ce/ce), r'r (Ce/ce), r″r (cE/ce) and R_zR_z (CDE/CDE) red cells but no reaction occurred with two different Rh_{null} cells (L. M. and H. H.).

and J. R. B.) were similar, so the results are grouped together in Table I. In agreement with Weiner and Vos (4), 12 eluates which had reacted strongly with various common human RBC phenotypes gave negative or only trace reactions with two different Rh_{null} cells. In contrast, 22 other eluates reacted with Rh_{null} cells just as strongly as with "normal" RBC[3] (Table I). Absorption of six eluates in this group with Rh_{null} RBC (L. M. or H. H.) left no detectable antibody reactive with "normal" RBC (Table II, upper section). A seventh eluate (We.), after repeated absorptions to remove a *major* population of antibodies reactive with Rh_{null} RBC, still exhibited some reactivity with "normal" RBC but this did not fit any particular specificity (Table II—footnote).

Twelve other eluates consistently gave reactions of "intermediate" strength with Rh_{null} cells, i.e., the reactions were definitely positive but distinctly weaker than those with "normal" RBC (Table I). Absorptions of three such eluates with Rh_{null} RBC (L. M.) removed only a portion of the total antibody, leaving potent antibody reactive with "normal" RBC (Table II, lower section: patients Co., Li., Bur.).

Five representative eluates which did not react detectably with Rh_{null} RBC in the survey protocol were selected for block titration (Tables III and IV). Two of these eluates, illustrated by eluate He. (Table III), failed to sensitize Rh_{null} RBC over a considerable range of autoantibody doses and antiglobulin serum dilutions. Eluate Me. (Table IV) and two other eluates did exhibit weak reactions with Rh_{null} RBC when tested at very high concentrations of autoantibody. This

[3] The term "normal" red cells is used to designate group O human RBC having common Rh phenotypes.

TABLE III

Block titration: He. autoantibody vs normal and Rh_{null} RBC

Red Cells	RBC Sensitized with He. Eluate	Dilution of Anti-γG Coombs' Serum			
		1:20	1:40	1:80	1:160
Normal	1:2	4+	4+	4+	4+
	1:8	4+	3+	3+	3+
	1:32	+	+	+	+
Rh_{null}	1:2	0	0	0	0
	1:8	0	0	0	0
	1:32	0	0	0	0

TABLE IV

Block titration: Me. autoantibody vs normal and Rh_{null} RBC

Red Cells	RBC Sensitized with Me. Eluate	Dilution of Anti-γG Coombs' Serum			
		1:20	1:40	1:80	1:160
Normal	1:4	4+	4+	4+	4+
	1:16	4+	4+	4+	4+
	1:64	4+	4+	3+	3+
Rh_{null} (L. M.)	1:4	tr.[a]	+	2+	2+
	1:16	0	0	0	0
	1:64	0	0	0	0
Rh_{null} (J. R. B.)	1:4	2+	2+	2+	2+
	1:16	tr.	tr.	+	+
	1:64	0	0	0	0

[a] tr., trace.

suggests that the latter eluates contained minor antibody populations with differing specificity.

Of interest was the correlation of these reactions with Rh_{null} cells with the pattern of *direct* Coombs' test given by the patients' RBC (Table I). This will be discussed below.

-D-/-D- cells. Studies with 33 eluates (not shown) confirmed earlier observations: a) that some seemingly "nonspecific" autoantibody eluates, seven in this series, exhibit negative or weak reactions with human -D-/-D- ($\overline{\overline{Rh}}_o$) cells (4, 7); b) that such eluates invariably give even weaker reactions with Rh_{null} RBC. All seven patients in the present series whose eluates gave weaker reactions with -D-/-D- RBC than with "normal" RBC had displayed direct Coombs' tests of the "γG-alone" type. In eluates giving negative reactions with Rh_{null} cells but positive reactions with -D-/-D- RBC, the latter reactivity does not appear to be anti-D (Rh_o) since, in several cases so studied, it could be absorbed by ce/ce (rr) cells.

Monkey cells. Only 13 of the 45 eluates tested reacted positively with monkey RBC. The 10 strongest reactions were observed with eluates which had shown strong reactions with Rh_{null} RBC; the other three were with eluates exhibiting "intermediate" reactions with Rh_{null} RBC (summarized in Table V; by X^2, $p < 0.05$). Positive reactions with monkey RBC were invariably weaker than with human, and absorption of these (monkey-reactive) eluates with monkey RBC invariably left potent antibody reactive with human RBC. Absorption with human RBC, however, removed all detectable antibody.

As will be developed in the discussion, the data accumulated to this point were the basis for a tentative classification set forth in Table V. Brief reference to this scheme will be made in the next three sections.

LW-negative (LW(−)) cells. In a search for possible anti-LW autoantibodies, survey tests were performed on 16 eluates selected because their reactions with Rh_{null} or monkey RBC would be compatible with anti-LW (see *Discussion*). None of the 16 gave weaker reactions with LW(−) R_1r cells (Mrs. B.) than with LW(+) R_1r cells of the same *in vitro* age. (The LW(+) status of the normal R_1r donor cells was supported by their strong reaction with anti-LW

TABLE V

Working classification of major specificities of γG autoantibodies

Proposed Serologic Group	No. of Cases in Present Series	Reactions with Human RBC[a]		Reactions with Monkey RBC	*In Vivo* C Fixation[b]
		Common phenotype	Rh_{null} phenotype	(No. pos./No. tested)	(No. pos./No. tested)
I	12	4+	Neg.	0/12	0/12
II	12	4+	2+[c]	3/11[c, d]	4/12
III	12	4+	4+[e]	0/12	8/12
IV	10	4+	4+[e]	10/10[c]	8/10

[a] For details, see text and Tables I to IV. For the purposes of illustration, "4+" means a full strength reaction, "2+" means a reaction of intermediate strength, and "neg." means a negative or trace reaction, as compared to concomitant strong reactions with RBC of common phenotype.

[b] As determined by direct Coombs' tests with anti-C serum.

[c] Absorption of representative eluates in this group with this type of RBC removed only *part* of total antibody.

[d] One eluate could not be tested. The three positive eluates gave reactions which were weak but consistently positive. There was no correlation of positive monkey reactions and *in vivo* C fixation in this group.

[e] Absorption of representative eluates in this group with this cell type removed *all* antibody, with exception of weak reactivity in one group III case (We., Table II).

TABLE VI

Effect of absorption of selected eluates with LW-negative RBC

Patient	Serologic Group[a]	Eluate Absorbed with	Reactions with RBC of Phenotype:[b]						
			LW(−)	R_1r	R_1R_1	R_2R_2	rr	r″r	Rhesus
Bo.	I	Sheep RBC[c]	3+	3+	4+	3+	4+	4+	0
		LW(−) RBC	0	0	0	0	0	0	0
He.	I	Sheep RBC	4+	4+	4+	4+	4+	4+	0
		LW(−) RBC	0	0	0	0	0	0	0
Fr.	III	Sheep RBC	3+	3+	3+	3+	3+	3+	0
		LW(−) RBC	0	0	0	0	0	0	0
Tr.	IV	Sheep RBC	3+	4+	4+	4+	4+	4+	3+
		LW(−) RBC	0	tr.[d]	tr.	0	tr.	tr.	0
Re.	IV	Sheep RBC	2+	2+	2+	2+	2+	2+	0
		LW(−) RBC	0	0	0	0	0	0	0
Me.	IV	Sheep RBC	3+	3+	3+	3+	3+	3+	3+
		LW(−) RBC	0	0	0	0	0	0	0

[a] See Table V and *Discussion.*

[b] LW(−) = LW-negative; R_1r = CDe/ce; R_2R_2 = cDE/cDE; r″r = cE/ce, etc.

[c] Concurrent absorption of a portion of each eluate with sheep RBC was carried out to control nonspecific loss of antibody during absorptions with LW(−) RBC (see *Materials and Methods*).

[d] tr., trace

antibody of Mrs. B.). Absorption of six of these eluates with LW(−) RBC left no antibody reactive with D(Rh_o)-positive or D-negative human RBC, or with rhesus RBC (Table VI).

K°K° cells. Because autoantibodies with apparent specificity in the Kell system had previously been reported (1), studies were made with the rare human red cells of phenotype K(−), k(−) Kp(a−)(b−), (K°K° cells) in the hope of elucidating the group III or IV specificities, as listed in Table V. Most of the eluates which had exhibited full reactivity with Rh_{null} RBC and representative eluates from the other serologic categories (Table V) were tested. All gave reactions of comparable strength with K°K° and "normal" RBC.

Isoantibodies and the Matuhasi-Ogata phenomenon. Several laboratories (e.g., 18) have confirmed the observation (19) that an anti-RBC antibody, lacking specificity for the RBC under study, may nevertheless bind to such RBC when the latter react with another (specific) antibody, and that the "wrong" antibody may subsequently appear in RBC eluates along with the "right" antibody. This phenomenon has now been documented for RBC eluates in warm-antibody AIHA (18). Therefore, the possibility had to be reckoned with that the differing serologic patterns just described could reflect, in part, nonspecific inclusion of serum *iso*-antibodies in certain autoantibody eluates. Our approach to this problem was based on two principles: a) If the more common isoantibodies could not be detected in the AIHA patient's undiluted serum from the same date as the eluate under study, it is unlikely that the eluate would contain a sufficient quantity of such isoantibodies to alter the results in Tables I to IV; b) if an isoantibody *is* present in the serum, absorption of the eluate with RBC of appropriate type should reveal the isoantibody if it is present in sufficient quantity to affect the major serologic patterns.

The extensive studies carried out are summarized in Table VII. Thirty of the 46 patients lacked demonstrable anti-RBC antibodies in their sera.[4] In seven cases (Table VII), low-titered serum antibodies, which were serologically indistinguishable from the autoantibodies eluted from the patient's RBC, appeared to be unbound ("free") autoantibodies rather than isoantibodies. Nine other patients exhibited serum antibodies with recognizable blood group specificity (Table VII). These appeared to be *auto*-antibodies in three cases, by virtue of the presence of the corresponding antigen on the patient's own RBC (cases Bo., Ha. and Mey.). The six re-

[4] Very few of the patients in this study had been transfused prior to obtaining blood for preparation of eluates. Naturally occurring serum anti-A or anti-B agglutinins were, course, of present.

TABLE VII

Summary: Evaluation of Matuhasi-Ogata phenomenon

Patients (Blood Groups)	Serologic Group of Eluate[a]	Serum Findings[b]	Eluate Findings
30 patients	All groups represented	No serum antibody demonstrated[c]	
7 patients	1—group I 5—group II 1—group III	Equal, low titer reactions with all test RBC; judged to be "free" autoantibody	Similar to serum
Bo. (0 ce/ce)	I	Anti-e (autoantibody)	Anti-e + undefined group I antibodies
Ha. (0 cCDEe)	I	Strong reactions with all common RBC but weaker with R_2R_2. Absorption studies revealed anti-e (auto) + undefined group I antibodies	Similar to serum
Mey. (A_1 cCDEe)	I	Probable weak anti-C (auto) plus trace of undefined group I antibodies	Similar to serum (but undefined antibodies much stronger)
Ed. (A_1 CCDee)	I	Iso-anti-E (1:16), probably weak iso-anti-c, + "free" autoantibody shown by reaction with autologous RBC[d]	Absorption with R_1R_1 RBC revealed anti-E and probably anti-c, i.e., isoantibodies
Bl. (0 ce/ce kk)	II	Iso-anti-D (1:4) and anti-K (1:64) Autologous RBC neg[d]	Absorption with rr kk cells or autologous RBC revealed trace iso-anti-K, no anti-D
We. (0 cCee)	III	Iso-anti-D (1:16) Autologous RBC neg[d]	Absorption with rr RBC removed all antibody
Mel. (B cCDEc kk)	III	Iso-anti-K (1:2) Autologous RBC neg.[d]	Equal titers *vs* Kk and kk cells
Ru. (A cCDee kk)	IV	Iso-anti-K (1:2) Autologous RBC neg[d]	Equal titers vs Kk and kk cells
Tr. (A_1 ce/ce)	IV	Iso-anti-D (1:320), + weak reactivity with all RBC	Absorption with Rh_{null} RBC removed all antibody[e]

[a] See Table V.

[b] Serum from same dates as eluates under study. Each serum was tested against at least two standard panels containing human RBC of various phenotypes (Ortho Identogen).

[c] By use of standard screening tests with Ortho Selectogen and Pfizer Hemantigen systems.

[d] Serum obtained at the time the eluate was made, i.e., during active disease, was tested against autologous Coombs'-negative RBC obtained during later remission.

[e] See Table II.

maining sera clearly contained *iso*antibodies; in only two of these cases (Ed. and Bl.) was evidence found for the presence of such *iso*antibody in that patient's *auto*antibody eluate (Table VII). These "wrong" antibodies, however, could not have affected the pattern of reaction of these eluates with Rh_{null} cells (Table I and V) because a) the isoantibodies (anti-E and anti-c) of Ed. would still fit group I reactivity, i.e., no reaction with Rh_{null} RBC; b) the weak anti-Kell in case Bl. (and in cases Mel. and Ru.) was circumvented by testing the eluate against Kell-negative RBC of both Rh_{null} (donor L. M., see ref. 6) and normal donors.

DISCUSSION

Autoantibody specificity. The tentative scheme in Table V is offered mainly as a framework for further research. Group I includes 12 eluates which had reacted strongly with all of the more common human RBC phenotypes but exhibited a selective inability to sensitize two different human Rh_{null} red cells (Table I). Since Rh_{null} RBC lack all known determinants of the Rh complex (5, 6, 20), this serologic behavior is consistent with, but does not prove, specificity for one or more antigenic determinants of the Rh system (4). On the other hand, these observations could be due to the absence from both Rh_{null} cells of some other high-incidence blood group antigen(s). The LW antigen has been proposed (11) and will be discussed below. These Rh_{null} RBC also demonstrate anomalous U and s antigens and may have some fundamental membrane defect (12, 21).

Nevertheless, the interpretation that the selective inability of these 12 eluates to sensitize Rh_{null} cells is attributable to the latter's lack of Rh system determinants is supported by: a) the much weaker reactivity of some of these same eluates with -D-/-D- ($\overline{\overline{Rh}}_o$) RBC than with "normal" RBC; b) the finding that each of five autoantibody populations in group I, when examined in detail (22, and unpublished), contained serologically separable subpopulations behaving as anti-e (hr″) in three cases, both anti-e and anti-c (hr′) in another, and probable weak anti-C (rh′) in the fifth. In each case the corresponding antigens were part of the patient's own phenotype. These identifiable Rh specificities were part of a mixture of specificities in each eluate, and were revealed by differential absorption, e.g., absorption with cDE/cDE cells to reveal "anti-e," and so on (see also 1, 7). The other specificities in these five eluates could not be defined but had in common the capacity to react with all available human RBC phenotypes except Rh_{null}. Thus, the proposed group I (Table V) would include autoantibodies with demonstrable specificity against one or more known Rh antigen(s) (defined by *iso*antibodies), and antibodies reactive with one or more determinants found on all human RBC except Rh_{null} and, in some instances, -D-/-D- RBC. The latter specificity may be very similar or identical to anti-"total Rh" (anti-Rh 29) produced as an isoantibody by an Rh_{null} subject after exposure to human RBC of common Rh phenotype (12). Neither type of group I autoantibodies displayed reactivity with monkey RBC.

The specificity of the 22 autoantibody populations in groups III and IV (Table V) is also undetermined but, in view of their strong reactivity with Rh_{null} cells, their specificity clearly differs from that of group I antibodies. Specificity for a "primitive" Rh-related precursor substance, present even on Rh_{null} cells, remains a possibility. Alternatively, these autoantibodies could be reactive with determinants entirely unrelated to the Rh system. Present studies with K^oK^o RBC failed to implicate the Kell system. Despite similarities, group III and IV antibodies have been tentatively separated in Table V because the differences in reactivity with monkey RBC could signify basically different specificities.

The 12 autoantibody populations giving reactions of intermediate strength with Rh_{null} RBC (Tables I and II) are more difficult to classify, but have been given a working designation as group II in Table V. Such antibodies could have affinity for antigens which are distinct from those involved in groups I, III and IV, and which, like U or s antigens (12, 21), are present on Rh_{null} cells but at reduced "strength" compared to "normal" RBC. Alternatively, such eluates could contain a mixture of group I and group III or IV specificities. The latter idea receives some support from the absorption data in Table II (lower section). If "intermediate" reactions with Rh_{null} RBC represented a distinct antigen system expressed in a qualitatively normal but quantitatively reduced manner on Rh_{null} RBC, then absorption with an excess of Rh_{null} should have removed all the antibody, but it did not. Indeed, the group II cases together with the observations on eluates We. (Table II) and Me. (Table IV) suggest the possibility that all of the autoantibody populations in this study represent varying mixtures of a spectrum of related specificities, although the relationship is far from clear at this time.

In a large series of autoantibody eluates reported in 1963, Weiner and Vos found no evidence for anti-LW ("D-like") specificity (4). More recently, Celano and Levine, utilizing absorptions with LW-negative human RBC which possess a normal Rh phenotype (LW(−) cells), concluded that autoantibody populations from six consecutive referred cases of AIHA contained anti-LW as a significant component among other undefined specificities (11). The LW antigen is exhibited by rhesus monkey RBC and by all human RBC except Rh_{null} cells and LW(−) cells (6, 20, 23). In the present study, therefore, the autoantibody eluates selected for study with the limited volume of LW(−) cells available were mainly those which had given a) positive reactions with rhesus RBC, or b) weaker reactions with Rh_{null} cells than with "normal" human RBC. In theory, an autoantibody eluate containing significant anti-LW ought to fulfill both criteria, but only one of our cases did so.[5] Perhaps the first criterion could be waived if the LW antigens in man and monkey are not identical (24) and the autoantibodies were narrowly specific for human LW. In any event, our studies with the LW(−) cells failed to reveal anti-LW in six eluates examined in detail (Table VI), and suggest that in 10 additional eluates anti-LW, if present, was not a major population. These findings seem difficult to reconcile with the high incidence of anti-LW implicit in the report of Celano and Levine. However, this subject is very complex (e.g., see 25) and merits further study.

The possibility exists that the factors initiating autoantibody formation to different red cell determinants may be fundamentally different. Drugs such as α-methyldopa appear to be associated with group I autoantibodies (26, 27). Our two cases were no exception. In the present series the autoantibodies of all five cases of systemic lupus erythematosus and two of three patients with other rheumatic disorders reacted strongly with Rh_{null} cells and were associated with *in vivo* C fixation (group III or IV).

Relation of specificity to complement-fixing behavior. It has long been recognized that among patients with AIHA associated with γG autoantibodies, some are found, by direct Coombs' test, to have bound complement components (mainly C3 and C4) to their RBC *in vivo* while other patients exhibit no detectable C on their RBC (17, 28).[6] This difference had never been explained and, in our experience, could not be attributed to a) differences in strength of anti-γG direct Coombs' reaction or quantity of autoantibody recoverable in eluates, b) primary C deficiency, as measured by CH_{50} titers, in cases lacking demonstrable cell-bound C, or c) γG subclasses with differing C-fixing capacities. The γG_1 subclass, which is active in C binding (30, 31), has predominated in virtually all of the autoantibody eluates (32).

In 1967, we reported a correlation of *in vivo* C fixation to autologous RBC with autoantibody specificity (13). This correlation, now extended to a larger series (Tables I and V), is as follows. The great majority of patients showing RBC autosensitization with both γG globulin and C, (Table I, row 3), presumably due to C-fixing γG autoantibodies, yielded eluates having equally strong reactions with Rh_{null} and "normal" RBC ($X^2 = 18.1$, $p < 0.001$), i.e., group III or IV specificity (Table V). On the other hand, autoantibody eluates which gave negative or merely trace reactions with Rh_{null} RBC, i.e., group I specificity, were found only in patients whose direct Coombs' tests had indicated RBC autosensitization by γG globulin alone (Table I, column 1) ($X^2 = 10.1$, $p \simeq 0.001$). If, however, one considers *all* cases with the "γG alone" pattern of direct Coombs' test (Table I, row 1 or rows 1 and 2), there is no significant correlation with the degree of reactivity with Rh_{null} cells. A generally similar relationship has very recently been reported by Dacie and Worlledge (33).

The effect of antibody specificity on the C-fixing potential of γG autoantibodies is likely to be related to the required interaction of at least two γG antibody molecules, closely placed on the cell membrane, to activate C (34–36). Fulfillment of this condition might depend upon a) a high density or clustered distribution of the relevant antigenic determinants, b) the presence of an optimal number or proportion of *related* but distinct antibody specificities when a multideterminant antigenic system, e.g., Rh (36), is involved, or c) the distance of an antigen site from C4 and C3 receptor sites (37) on the membrane. Immunoferritin localization of $D(Rh_o)$ sites on the human red cell seems consistent with a low density ("scattered") distribution, in contrast to the greater site density, apparently in clusters, of A antigens (38). Finally, further work is needed to assess the possibility that inhibitory serum factors, such as high titered rheumatoid factors (39) which are present in a few of our cases, may limit *in vivo* C-binding in certain

[5] Unfortunately, insufficient eluate from this case remained to carry out the absorption experiment (Table VI) but in the survey protocol this eluate gave equally strong reactions with LW(+) and LW(−) cells.

[6] The limitation of the anti-C Coombs' test as a means of detecting cell-bound C is recognized. For example, presently available data indicate that less than 200 to 500 molecules of bound C4/cell would not be detected by this method (ref. 29, p. 432). Nevertheless, the direct Coombs' test data do indicate significant quantitative differences in *in vivo* C fixation.

patients to a level below the sensitivity of the anti-C Coombs' reaction.

Acknowledgments. We wish to thank Drs. F. H., Allen, Paul Schmidt, R. E. Rosenfield and L. L. DeVeber for generous gifts of rare red cells, Dr. Bruce Chown for arranging the procurement of the K°K° red cells, Drs. John Vaughan and S. N. Swisher for helpful criticism, and Jo Ann Gifford for preparation of the manuscript. Finally, we thank the many physicians who made their patients available for study.

REFERENCES

1. Dacie, J. V., *The Haemolytic Anaemias, Congenital and Acquired. II. The Auto-Immune Haemolytic Anaemias*, 2nd Ed., pp. 443–449, Grune and Stratton, New York, 1962.
2. Pirofsky, B. and Pratt, K., Amer. J. Clin. Path., *45:* 75, 1966.
3. Yokoyama, M., Eith, D. T. and Bowman, M., Vox Sang., *12:* 138, 1967.
4. Weiner, W. and Vos, G. H., Blood, *22:* 606, 1963.
5. Vos, G. H., Vos. D., Kirk, R. L. and Sanger, R., Lancet, *1:* 14, 1961.
6. Levine, P., Celano, M. J., Falkowski, F., Chambers, J. W., Hunter, O. B., Jr. and English, C. T., Transfusion, *5:* 492, 1965.
7. Dacie, J. V. and Cutbush, M., J. Clin. Path., *7:* 18, 1954.
8. Race, R. R., Sanger, R. and Sewyln, J. G., Brit. J. Exp. Path., *32:* 124, 1951.
9. Leddy, J. P. and Bakemeier, R. F., J. Exp. Med., *121:* 1, 1965.
10. Wiener, A. S., Gordon, E. B. and Gallop, C., J. Immun., *71:* 58, 1953.
11. Celano, M. J. and Levine, P., Transfusion, *7:* 265, 1967.
12. a) Haber, G. V., Bastani, A., Arpen, P. D. and Rosenfield, R. E., Transfusion, *7:* 389 (abstract), 1967; b) Bar-Shany, S., Bastani, A., Cuttner, J. and Rosenfield, R. E., Transfusion, *7:* 389 (abstract), 1967.
13. Leddy, J. P. and Bakemeier, R. F., Proc. Soc. Exp. Biol. Med., *125:* 808, 1967.
14. Kidd, P., J. Clin. Path., *2:* 103, 1949.
15. Kochwa, S. and Rosenfield, R. E., J. Immun., *92:* 682, 1964.
16. Leddy, J. P., Hill, R. W., Swisher, S. N. and Vaughan, J. H., *Immunopathology, IIIrd International Symposium*, Edited by P. Grabar and P. A. Miescher, p. 318, Schwabe and Co., Basel, 1963.
17. Leddy, J. P., Seminars Hemat., *3:* 48, 1966.
18. Allen, F. H., Jr., Issitt, P. D., Degnan, T. J., Jackson, V. A., Reihart, J. K., Knowlin, R. J. and Adebahr, M. E., Vox Sang., *16:* 47, 1969.
19. Ogata, T. and Matuhasi, T., Proceedings of the Eighth Congress of the International Society of Blood Transfusion, p. 208, 1962; Proceedings of the Ninth Congress of the International Society of Blood Transfusion, p. 528, 1964, Karger, Basel/New York.
20. Race, R. R., Ann. N.Y. Acad. Sci., *127:* 884, 1965.
21. Schmidt, P. J., Lostumbo, M. M., English, C. T. and Hunter, O. B., Jr., Transfusion, *7:* 33, 1967.
22. Bakemeier, R. F. and Leddy, J. P., Blood, *32:* 1, 1968.
23. Levine, P., Celano, M., Fenichel, R., Pollack, W. and Singher, H., J. Immun., *87:* 747, 1961.
24. Levine, P. and Celano, M. J., Nature, *193:* 184, 1962.
25. Giles, C. M. and Lundsgaard, A., Vox Sang., *13:* 406, 1967.
26. Worlledge, S. M., Carstairs, K. C. and Dacie, J. V., Lancet, *2:* 135, 1966.
27. Lo Buglio, A. F. and Jandl, J. H., New England J. Med., *276:* 658, 1967.
28. Dacie, J. V., *The Haemolytic Anaemias, Congenital and Acquired. II. The Auto-Immune Haemolytic Anaemias*, 2nd Ed., pp. 429–432, Grune and Stratton, New York, 1962.
29. Mollison, P. L., *Blood Transfusion in Clinical Medicine*, F. A. Davis Co., Philadelphia, 4th Ed., p. 346–349, 1966.
30. Ishizaka, T., Ishizaka, K., Salmon, S. and Fudenberg, H., J. Immun., *99:* 82, 1967.
31. Müller-Eberhard, H. J., Advances Immun., *8:* 1, 1968.
32. Bakemeier, R. F. and Leddy, J. P., Blood, *30:* 869 (abstract), 1967.
33. Dacie, J. V. and Worlledge, S. M., Progr. Hemat., *6:* 82, 1969.
34. Borsos, T. and Rapp, H. J., Science, *150:* 505, 1965.
35. Ishizaka, T., Ishizaka, K., Borsos, T. and Rapp, H. J., J. Immun., *97:* 716, 1966.
36. Rosse, W. F., J. Clin. Invest., *47:* 2430, 1968.
37. Mardiney, M. R., Müller-Eberhard, H. J. and Feldman, J. D., Amer. J. Path., *53:* 253, 1968.
38. Lee, R. E. and Feldman, J. D., J. Cell Biol., *23:* 396, 1964.
39. Heimer, R., Levin, F. M. and Kahn, M. F., J. Immun., *91:* 866, 1963.

THE JOURNAL OF IMMUNOLOGY
Vol. 105, No. 3, September 1970

RABBIT IgA, IgM AND IgG ANTIHAPTEN RESPONSES ASSAYED BY C1a FIXATION AND TRANSFER

JOHN D. CLOUGH, JUNE ZACCARI AND WARREN STROBER

From the Metabolism Branch, National Cancer Institute, National Institutes of Health, Bethesda, Maryland 20014

Received for publication February 14, 1970

The present report describes an adaptation of the C1a fixation transfer test (C1a FTT) for measurement of rabbit antibody in three immunoglobulin classes—IgM, IgG and IgA—without serum fractionation. IgM antibody was measured directly and IgA and IgG antibodies were measured indirectly using specific antisera against rabbit IgG and IgA to permit complement fixation by antibodies in these immunoglobulin classes. The ability of the test to discriminate among antibodies in these classes was demonstrated by immunochemical examination of the anti-antisera and by use of the C1a FTT to show that 1) the effects of the enhancing anti-antisera could be summated, 2) the enhancing ability of the anti-antisera could be specifically inhibited by purified rabbit immunoglobulins, and 3) antibody activity in rabbit serum could be fractionated by DEAE-cellulose gradient chromatography into its immunoglobulin components. The ability of the test to quantitate antibody in each class was examined by assay of serial dilutions of rabbit antiserum by the C1a FTT; the amount of C1a fixed and quantitated was found to be directly proportional to the amount of antibody present. Primary and secondary humoral responses of rabbits to intravenously administered haptenic arsanilic acid were studied using the C1a FTT. In the primary response, IgA antibody reached an early peak together with IgM antibody. IgG antibody had a more gradual rise and peaked later than IgA or IgM; a small second peak of IgA antibody sometimes accompanied the IgG peak. In the secondary response IgA antibody showed an accelerated onset, rising to an earlier but lower peak than in the primary response. The secondary IgM antibody response was similar to that of IgA while IgG antibody reached an earlier, higher peak level than in the primary response.

It is well established that antibody activity occurs in several distinct immunoglobulin classes (1). However, precise data on the magnitude and pattern of antibody responses in the different immunoglobulin classes are difficult to obtain owing to the lack of assay methods capable of detecting antibody in all classes with equal efficiency. Data on factors controlling the immune response in the IgA class are especially incomplete because practical methods for separating this protein from other serum immunoglobulins are not available.

In the rabbit an antibody class analogous to human IgA was first recognized by Feinstein (2) in colostrum; later Onoue *et al.* (3) found beta-migrating serum antibody to *p*-azobenzene arsonate, and Cebra and Robbins (4) isolated and further characterized IgA from rabbit colostrum. This material was similar in molecular size and chemical characteristics (including "T-piece") to human secretory IgA (5). Antisera prepared against rabbit colostral IgA by Cebra and Robbins were used in quantitative precipitation studies to assay total serum IgA; relatively low values compared to those of other rabbit immunoglobulins and to those of human IgA were found (4). Studies of the distribution of IgA-producing cells in rabbit with fluorescent antibody (6) showed a predominance of these (80% to 90% of the immunoglobulin-containing cells) in the lamina propria of the gastrointestinal tract, but a relative paucity (2% to 10%) in other lymphoid tissues. This contrasts with the relatively high proportion of IgA-producing cells in human spleen tissue (45%) (7).

The present paper describes an adaptation of

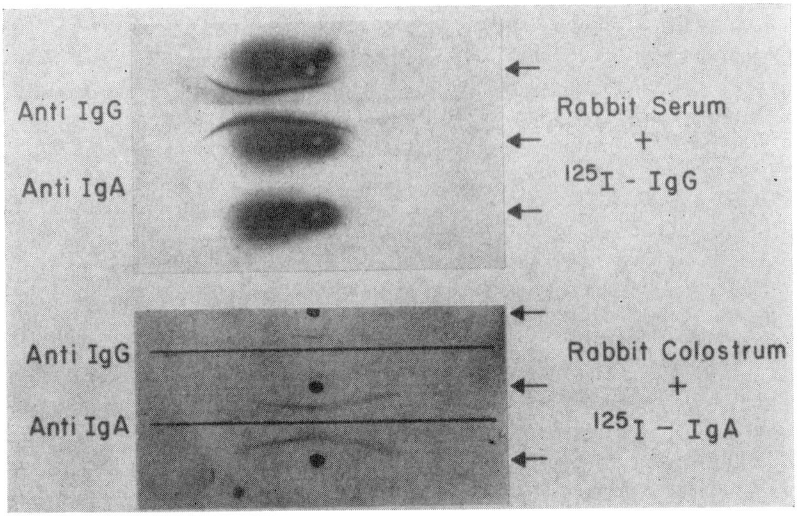

Figure 1. Radio-autographs of immunoelectrophoresis plates. Top three wells contain rabbit serum with radioiodinated rabbit IgG added. Lower three wells contain ultracentrifuged rabbit colostrum with radioiodinated rabbit IgA added. Anti-rabbit immunoglobulin antisera were placed in troughs. Radioiodinated IgG was precipitated only by anti-IgG and radioiodinated IgA was precipitated only by anti-IgA.

the C1a fixation-transfer test (C1a FTT) (8) for the simultaneous measurement of rabbit serum antibody IgM, IgA and IgG. This method was used to study rabbit primary and secondary humoral responses to a single intravenous administration of the haptenic antigen arsanilic acid, with the particular goal of clarifying the place of IgA in the circulating immune response.

MATERIALS AND METHODS

Animals. Female New Zealand White rabbits weighing 1.5 to 2.0 kg were obtained from the National Institutes of Health Animal Production Section and were maintained on NIH feed "A" and water *ad libitum.* All bleedings were by cardiac puncture, and sera were stored at $-20°C$ until tested.

Antigen. The antigen used in these studies, arsanilic acid-azobovine serum albumin (AABSA), was prepared by diazotization and coupling of *p*-arsanilic acid[1] with bovine serum albumin[2] by the method of Campbell *et al.* (9). This material contains about 20 atoms of arsenic/molecule of albumin. Animals were immunized intravenously with 2.5 ml of 1% AABSA (25 mg).

Reagents used in the C1a FTT. ES: Erythrocytes with antigenic sites (S) were prepared by diazotization of *p*-arsanilic acid with rabbit red blood cells according to the method of Ingraham (10). ES were used within 1 week of preparation, and erythrocytes were always obtained from the same rabbit.

C1a and C2a were prepared from fresh frozen guinea pig serum[3] by the methods of Borsos and Rapp (11, 12). C1a preparations were absorbed with ES to reduce background activity due to guinea pig antibody directed at rabbit red cells.

EAC4 was prepared at 0°C from sheep erythrocytes (SRBC) and guinea pig serum by the method of Borsos and Rapp (13). Anti-SRBC (amboceptor) used in this preparation was raised in rabbits using boiled SRBC stromata prepared by a standard method (14). The t_{max} (13) of EAC4 was always 3 to 8 min with peak lysis greater than 70%. EAC4 were used within 2 weeks of preparation.

Anti-rabbit-immunoglobulin antisera. Anti-IgG was raised in goats against rabbit Fc piece prepared from rabbit γ globulins[4] by papain digestion (15). Fc piece was purified by three recrystallizations. The specificity of the goat antiserum for rabbit IgG was demonstrated by double diffusion in agar and radioimmunoelectrophoresis (Fig. 1). In the latter the anti-IgG

[1] Eastman Organic Chemicals.
[2] Armour Pharmaceutical Company.
[3] Suburban Serum Company.
[4] Mann Research Laboratories.

was able to precipitate only IgG from normal rabbit serum to which radioiodinated rabbit IgG had been added; it could not precipitate radioactivity from colostrum containing radioiodinated IgA. For use in the C1a FTT, anti-IgG was absorbed with ES to reduce background activity due to goat antibody directed against rabbit erythrocytes. *Anti-IgA* was raised in goats against IgA prepared from rabbit colostrum by Sephadex gel filtration and DEAE-cellulose chromatography according to the method of Cebra and Robbins (4). This goat antiserum was absorbed with soluble rabbit IgG by successive precipitations, following which it produced a single precipitin line on double diffusion in agar against normal rabbit serum. By immunoelectrophoresis it could be shown that this line was neither IgM nor IgG. The anti-IgA could not precipitate radioactivity from rabbit serum containing radioiodinated IgG on radioimmunoelectrophoresis (Fig. 1), although it could precipitate radioactivity from rabbit colostrum containing radioiodinated IgA. In colostrum it reacted with two additional components on immunoelectrophoresis, neither of which was an immunoglobulin as shown by the difference in distribution between these proteins and those reacting with anti-rabbit-L-chain antiserum.[5] For use in the C1a FTT the anti-IgA was also absorbed with ES to reduce background activity due to goat antibody directed against rabbit erythrocytes. Optimal enhancing activity in the C1a FTT was obtained by use of an appropriate dilution of the second protein peak resulting from Sephadex G-200 fractionation of the anti-IgA-containing goat serum.

C1a FTT. The C1a FTT is a method of measuring antibody devised by Borsos and Rapp (8), which depends on the ability of the antibody in question to fix the first component of complement when it reacts with antigen in particulate form. The C1a thus fixed is then transferred quantitatively to a standard SRBC-amboceptor system where it is again fixed and can be measured in its active form by the degree of hemolysis produced on addition of subsequent complement components. Since IgM antibodies fix complement with much greater efficiency than IgG (which requires the formation of antibody doublets on the antigen (16)) or IgA (which does not fix complement at all (17)), it is possible to prepare dilutions of most antibody-containing sera which produce fixation of C1a only by the efficient IgM antibody. Addition to the system of complement-fixing antibodies directed against rabbit IgG or IgA before addition of C1a permits fixation of C1a at sites where these molecules are attached in addition to the IgM sites. Thus, it becomes possible to measure IgM, IgA and IgG antibodies without fractionating or otherwise pretreating the unknown serum.

[5] Supplied by Dr. Rose Mage.

In our system ES is the particulate antigen, the substrate for fixation of C1a. Three portions of ES are exposed to diluted unknown serum. After a 10-min incubation at 30°C and wash, anti-IgA is added to one tube, anti-IgG to a second tube, and the third tube receives nothing; these tubes are used to measure IgA, IgG and IgM antibody, respectively. The tubes are again incubated for 10 min at 30°, after which the cells are washed and excess C1a is added to each tube. Fixation of C1a is allowed to proceed for 10 min at 30°C. The cells are then washed and transferred to a new set of tubes because of nonspecific fixation of C1a to glass in the original set. After thorough washing with an isotonic buffered sucrose solution of low ionic strength (μ = 0.065), C1a previously fixed by antibody is released by raising the ionic strength to μ = 0.15 and is quantitatively transferred to EAC4. C2a is then introduced, and finally the remaining components of complement are added. Following a period of incubation at 37°C the amount of red cell lysis is determined spectrophotometrically.

Since only one C1a molecule is required to sensitize a single EAC4 for lysis, the average number of C1a/EAC4 (and hence per ES) can be calculated using an expression derived from the Poisson distribution (18). This value is directly proportional to the number of complement-fixing antibody molecules attached to ES in the first two steps of the test, and as such is a measure of the amount of antibody present. Since in the absence of enhancing anti-antisera only IgM fixes C1a, the value for IgM antibody is obtained directly from the tube to which anti-antiserum was not added. IgG and IgA values are calculated by subtraction of IgM from the appropriate anti-immunoglobulin-enhanced values. Each experimental value was obtained by assays for antibody at three dilutions, so that in effect the assays were carried out in triplicate.

RESULTS

Studies on the ability of the C1a FTT to detect antibody in individual immunoglobulin classes. In order to establish the ability of the C1a FTT to detect antibodies in individual immunoglobulin classes, it was essential to demonstrate monospecificity of each of the anti-immunoglobulin antisera. In addition to the immunochemical methods outlined in the previous section, several tests were devised in which the anti-antisera were used in the C1a FTT under conditions designed to detect significant affinity for rabbit immunoglobulins other than intended.

In the first study, a summation test, anti-IgG and anti-IgA were prepared as described above and titrated for maximal enhancement of C1a fixation. Then rabbit antisera raised against AABSA were assayed in the C1a FTT without anti-antisera, with each one individually, and with both simultaneously (Fig. 2). When the amount of antibody present in each class was determined and compared with the total amount of antibody present, the sum of the individual antibody class values was found to agree with total antibody determined by simultaneous addition of anti-IgG and anti-IgA. This indicated that anti-IgG and anti-IgA enhancing antisera were reacting with distinct, non-overlapping entities.

A further indication that the two anti-antisera were specific for different immunoglobulins was obtained using DEAE-cellulose gradient chromatography. A 0.5-ml sample of rabbit anti-arsanilic acid antiserum was placed on a 2.5- x 30-cm column containing Whatman microgranular DEAE-cellulose equilibrated at 0.5 mmho and pH 8 with phosphate-buffered NaCl solution. The concentration of NaCl was gradually increased as shown in Figure 3*A*, and 5-ml fractions were collected. Performance of the C1a FTT on those fractions yielded the results shown in Figure 3*A*. Separation of several peaks of IgG from IgM and IgA is seen. A second gradient with a more gradual slope at higher ionic strength combined with a gradual decrease in pH was able to separate IgA and IgM peaks of antibody activity (Fig. 3*B*). It is of interest that serum IgA antibody activity is eluted here under conditions similar to those for colostral IgA elution in Cebra and Robbins' work (4).

In a final test of the specificity of the C1a FTT purified IgG, obtained by DEAE-cellulose chromatography of normal rabbit serum, and purified IgA, obtained from rabbit colostrum as outlined above, were each incubated in various amounts with each of the enhancing anti-antisera. It was found that IgG was able to nullify only the enhancing ability of anti-IgG, and IgA was able to inhibit only the activity of anti-IgA (Fig. 4), and neither immunoglobulin could significantly affect the enhancing ability of the opposite anti-antiserum.

Relationship of antibody titer to antibody activity assayed in C1a FTT. Serial dilutions of anti-arsanilic acid serum from several immunized rabbits were tested for antibody in each class

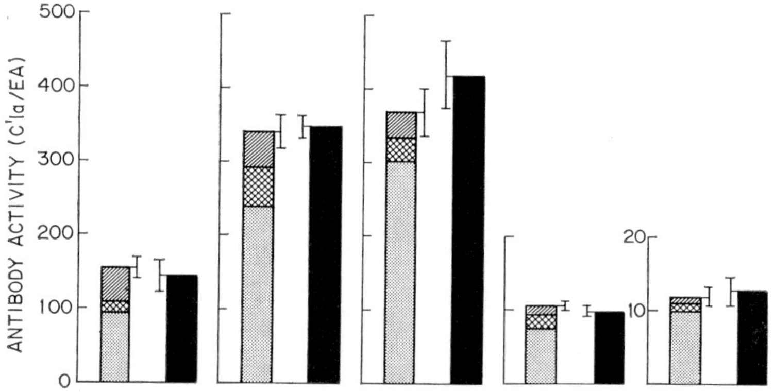

Figure 2. Summation study. Each pair of bars denotes anti-arsanilic acid activity in a single sample of rabbit serum. Solid bars represent total antibody activity; in divided bars, stippled areas represent IgM, cross-hatched areas represent IgG and diagonally hatched areas represent IgA. Standard deviations for quintuplicate determinations of each value are shown. In no case does the summated value (*left*) differ significantly from the total antibody value (*right*).

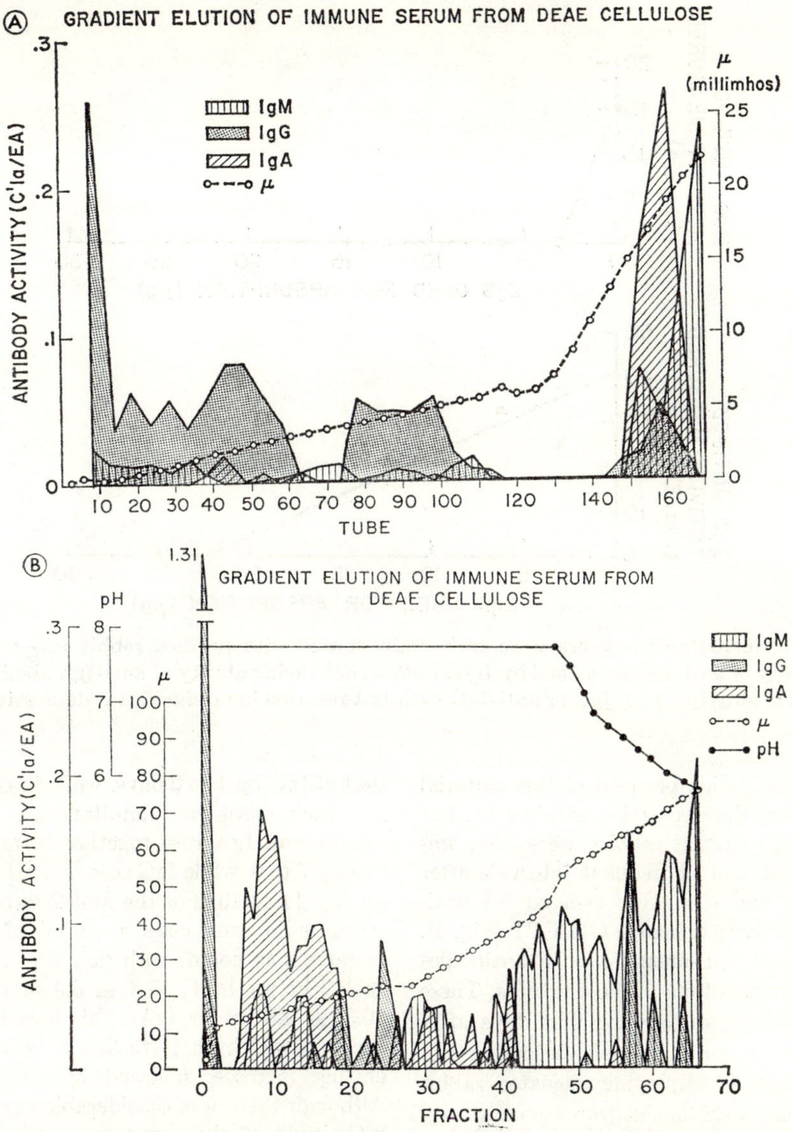

Figure 3. DEAE-cellulose gradient elutions of rabbit anti-arsanilic acid antiserum with gradual rise in ionic strength (*A and B*) coupled with decrease in pH (*B*) demonstrate separation of antibody activity into immunoglobulin components. Ionic strength is given in mmho.

and for total antibody (with simultaneous addition of anti-IgA and anti-IgG). Log-log plots of antibody concentration as determined by the C1a FTT ($-\ln (1 - y)$, where y = fraction of EAC4 lysed, is converted to C1a/EA by application of certain factors to correct for losses of C1a at the transfer step and for efficiency of lysis of EAC1,4 on addition of subsequent complement components (8)) *vs* dilution of serum were then constructed. In each instance a straight line with a slope of one was obtained (Fig. 5). This study indicates that within each class the value obtained for antibody activity is directly proportional to the amount of antibody actually present.

Primary response of rabbits to AABSA. Eleven rabbits were each given a single intravenous injection of a solution containing 25 mg of AABSA. Two of these rabbits received antigen that had been previously labeled with ^{131}I, and frequent samples were obtained from these rabbits in the

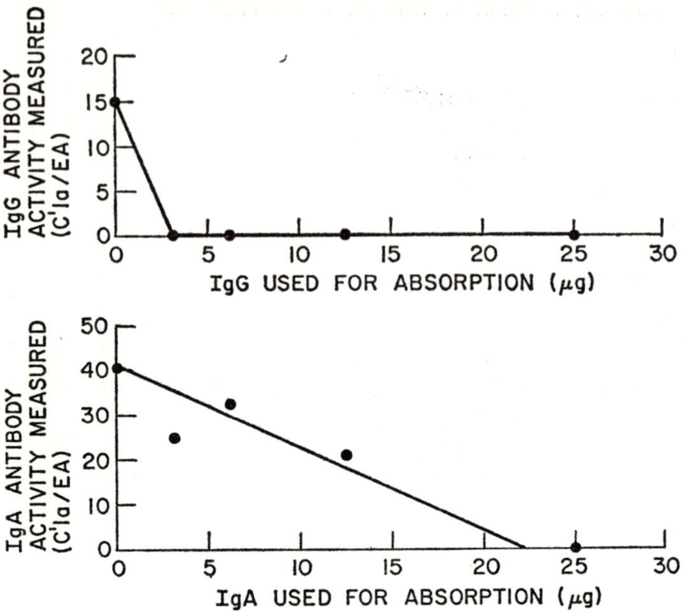

Figure 4. Enhancing anti-antisera were each preincubated with purified rabbit IgG and IgA. *Top*, enhancing ability of anti-IgG abolished by IgG. *Bottom*, enhancing ability of anti-IgA abolished by IgA. Preincubation of anti-IgA with IgG or anti-IgG with IgA resulted in no significant depression of enhancing ability.

first 24 hr. Ninety-nine per cent of this material was cleared from the circulation within 7 hr. For antibody assay, all the rabbits were bled immediately before and at frequent intervals after immunization, and sera were assayed for anti-arsanilic acid activity using the C1a FTT (Fig. 6).

Low levels of anti-arsanilic acid antibodies were present at zero time in most rabbits. These levels fell markedly during the first days after immunization, in some animals becoming undetectable. Controls employing uncoated rabbit red cells instead of ES demonstrated no antibody directed at rabbit erythrocyte antigens, so that these levels do, in fact, represent anti-arsanilic acid activity.

The onset of increase in IgM antibody was always noted from the 2nd to 3rd day after immunization, whereas IgG began to rise from as early as the 4th to as late as the 10th day after immunization. IgA was intermediate in appearance, being first noted between the 3rd and 7th day of the study. In each individual rabbit the onset of IgM response preceded that of IgA by 1 to 4 days and that of IgG by 1 to 8 days. In nine of the rabbits the IgA response preceded that of IgG by 1 to 2 days, while in the remaining two their onset was simultaneous.

IgM and IgA rose together to an early peak on day 7 to 9, while IgG rose more slowly peaking on day 11 to 13. For the first 2 to 3 days of the response in each class a period of logarithmic increase was noted, with doubling times of 12.4 $\pm$ 2.2 hr for IgM, 17.8 $\pm$ 3.9 hr for IgG, and 10.3 $\pm$ 4.8 hr for IgA. This logarithmic phase was followed by a 1- to 3-day period of decelerating increase, followed by declining levels. Although there was considerable variation in the magnitude of the response in all three classes from rabbit to rabbit, it was apparent in all cases that IgM dominated the primary response. By the 30th day after immunization antibody activity had returned to less than 5% of its peak level in each class.

Secondary response of rabbits to AABSA. Approximately 1 month after primary immunization, four of the rabbits were secondarily immunized with the same dose of antigen by the intravenous route (Fig. 7). As before, the early fall in activity was noted in all classes, but this time the increase in IgM was detected 24 hr earlier in each rabbit than had been the case in

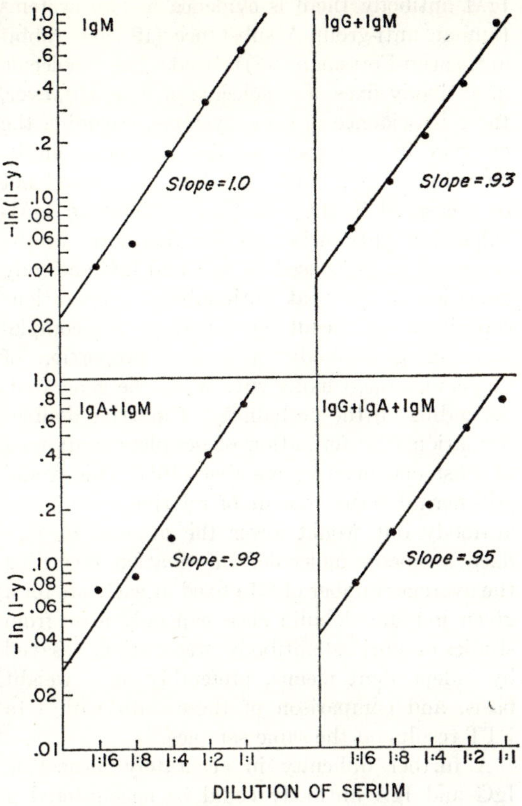

Figure 5. Serial dilutions of rabbit serum containing anti-arsanilic acid activity assayed with the C1a FTT yielded straight line plots of antibody activity (represented by —ln (1−y), see text) against serum dilution without anti-antiserum (*upper left*), with each anti-antiserum alone (*upper right, lower left*), and with both anti-antisera together (*lower right*).

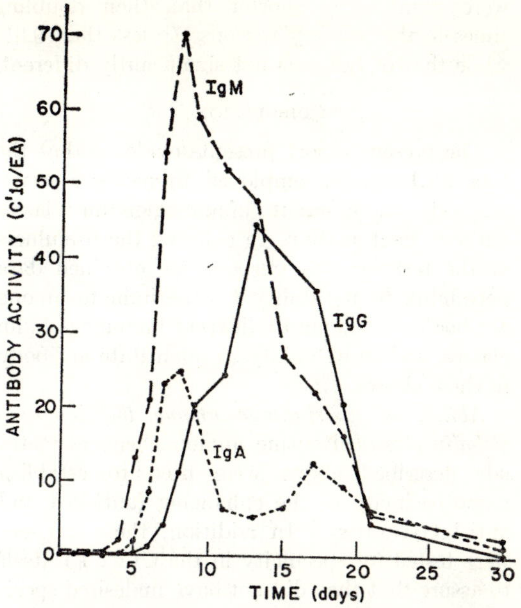

Figure 6. Primary serum response of rabbits to single intravenous injection of 25 mg AABSA. Each point represents average value for 11 rabbits.

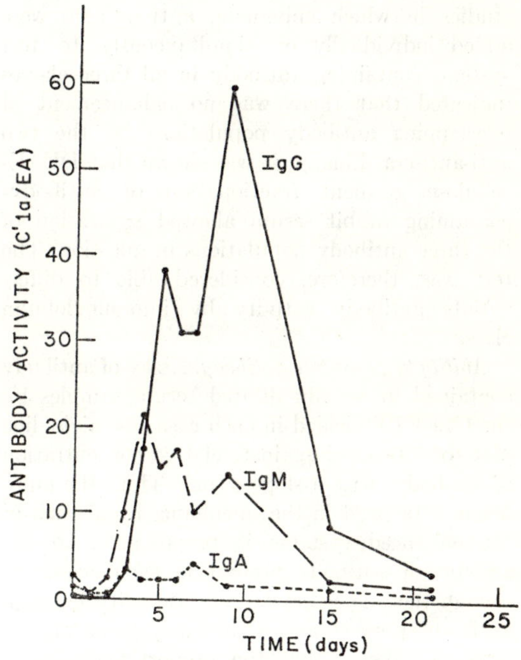

Figure 7. Secondary serum response of rabbits to intravenous injection of 25 mg AABSA 30 days after initial immunization. Each point represents average value for four rabbits.

the primary response. Increase in IgG was noted from 1 to 6 days earlier than in the primary response, now occurring at 48 to 72 hr, while IgA began to rise 2 to 5 days earlier than in the primary response, also at 48 to 72 hr after immunization. In two of the rabbits, IgM, IgA and IgG began to rise simultaneously; in a third, IgG lagged a day behind; and in the last, both IgG and IgA appeared a day after IgM. The greatest response was in the IgG class, with IgM and IgA present, but to a lesser extent than in the primary response. Again antibody levels increased logarithmically for the first 2 days of the response with doubling times of 9.3 ± .99 hr for IgM, 10.2 ± 2.0 hr for IgG, and 14.4 ± 2.4 hr for IgA. The doubling times of IgM and IgG were significantly shorter than their doubling times in the primary response (p less than 0.01) while that of IgA was not significantly different.

DISCUSSION

The present report presents evidence that the C1a FTT can be employed to measure serum antibody in different immunoglobulin classes without fractionation. In defining the usefulness of the test for this purpose, we obtained data pertaining to its ability to discriminate among antibodies belonging to different immunoglobulin classes, and to its ability to quantitate antibody in these classes.

Ability to discriminate among the immunoglobulin classes. Routine immunochemical methods described above were used to establish monospecificity of the enhancing (anti-IgA and anti-IgG) antisera. In addition, these antisera were tested for specificity in the C1a FTT itself to assure that they did not have undesired specificities missed with the less sensitive techniques of precipitation in gel. Thus, absorption with the appropriate immunoglobulin completely abolished the ability of each of the anti-antisera to enhance C1a fixation. Moreover, summation studies in which enhancing anti-antisera were added individually or simultaneously to test systems containing antibody in all three classes indicated that there was no enhancement of overlapping antibody populations by the two anti-antisera. Finally, it was shown that DEAE-cellulose gradient fractionation of antibody-containing rabbit serum allowed separation of the three antibody populations in question. The test was, therefore, considered able to differentiate antibody activity by immunoglobulin class.

Ability to quantitate antibody. Assay of antibody contained in serially diluted serum samples by the C1a FTT yielded in each case a straight line plot (of C1a fixed against relative concentration of antibody) with a slope of one. Thus, the number of C1a fixed in the unenhanced and each of the enhanced systems is proportional to the amount of antibody present in each class. Although there is a direct proportionality between antibody present and C1a fixed, there are no data to indicate that the proportionality constants (which would depend on the number of C1a fixed at each site) are the same in all the classes; this makes comparison of amounts of antibody in the various classes uncertain. For IgM antibody there is evidence in two systems (human anti-group-A substance (19) and rabbit anti-sheep-Forssman (8)) that one molecule of antibody fixes one molecule of C1a. However, there is evidence in some systems, including the one used in the present studies, that non-complement-fixing IgM exists (20, 21); this would not be measured in the C1a FTT without an IgM-enhancing anti-antiserum. Furthermore, in the enhanced systems used for IgA and IgG antibody detection if the goat anti-globulin preparations contained significant amounts of non-complement-fixing antibody, a certain proportion of non-complement-fixing sites would be generated, depending on the probability of inactive doublet formation (the formation of doublets containing at least one inactive member (16)). This would still permit measurement of relative amounts of antibody but would lower the amount of C1a fixed/antibody molecule. Information regarding the average number of C1a fixed at each site for a given immunoglobulin class can only arise from studies on purified antibody preparations assayed by independent means, preferably on a weight basis, and comparison of these data with C1a FTT results on the same samples.

A further difficulty in accurately measuring IgG and IgA antibody could be encountered if relatively low levels of IgG and/or IgA antibody existed in the presence of high levels of IgM antibody. This circumstance would require the determination of a small value (IgG or IgA antibody activity) by subtraction of one large value (unenhanced IgM antibody activity) from another slightly larger value (antibody activity enhanced with either anti-IgG or anti-IgA), resulting in possible inaccurate estimation of the small value. This situation occurred only in determining the earliest points in the IgG response; it was not ordinarily a problem in evaluating the IgA response, since IgA and IgM antibody activity paralleled each other following intravenous immunization.

Other obstacles standing in the way of absolute quantitation of antibody molecules by the C1a FTT arise from technical difficulties inherent in the test. Losses of antibody and/or C1a could occur during washing. These losses would relate to antibody-antigen affinity, a property of antibody that may change during the course of an immune response (22); thus, the assay procedure can only detect antibody molecules with a certain minimum affinity and could miss early, low-affinity molecules. Linscott (23) has defined the conditions of temperature and ionic strength in the washing procedure that give the highest values for antibody activity in IgM and unenhanced IgG in heat-treated rabbit anti-Forssman serum. These conditions differ considerably from those, originally described by Borsos and Rapp (8), which were used in the present study. In the few assays we have performed using Linscott's conditions we have obtained results essentially similar to his, in effect revealing fixation of greater amounts of C1a in the presence of the same amount of antibody. Whether this actually represents detection of increased amounts of antibody or merely fixation of increased numbers of C1a molecules/antibody site, however, has not yet been determined, and can only be determined by reference to a known standard antibody preparation assayed by an unimpeachable method.

These various technical difficulties may give rise to different ratios of C1a fixed to antibody present, depending on the exact conditions under which the test is done. It should be reiterated, however, that the straight line plots with slopes of unity assure us that, within each immunoglobulin class, the ratio of C1a fixed to antibody present will be constant regardless of antibody concentration. Thus the C1aFTT can provide a relative value for the magnitude of response in each immunoglobulin class. The test is most reliable in comparing antibody responses within a given immunoglobulin class under various experimental conditions. Comparisons of the magnitude and order of the responses among the immunoglobulin classes using data derived from the C1aFFT are less reliable.

Primary and secondary responses. The C1a FTT was used to study rabbit primary and secondary responses to haptenic arsanilic acid. This antigen was selected because, as a simple chemical hapten, it presents to the animal a minimum diversity of antigenic determinants. It has the additional advantages of being easily attached to red cells and to protein carriers through diazotization reactions. The antigen was administered intravenously to provide as brief an antigenic stimulus as possible and to minimize the likelihood of interference with the assay by persistent antigen in serum samples; that this played little role is evident from the antigen clearance studies, which showed virtually total elimination of antigen from the circulation in less than a day.

Low levels of anti-arsanilic acid antibody were found in nearly all preimmunization sera, and this activity was distributed through all three immunoglobulin classes. This probably represents cross-reaction with antibody formed against something in the animals' environment; it is well known that continuing immunization leads to production of antibody with "broadened specificity" including reactivity with chemical dissimilar haptens (24).

Our data agree with those of most others (25–27) in that IgM antibody production was always detected before IgG antibody production, but there is considerable danger in drawing conclusions regarding the lengths of "latent periods" for the individual antibody classes from a study in which only serum is examined. It should be noted, for instance, that application of the Jerne plaque technique to the measurement of anti-sheep erythrocyte responses allows detection of antibody at least a day earlier than in serum studies (28), probably due to the lack of circulatory dilution *in vitro*. Cellular activity can be detected even earlier using the adherence technique of Baker and Landy (29): antigen reactive cells capable of binding antigen-coated bentonite particles can be found as early as 1 to 6 hr after stimulation with pneumococcal polysaccharide or *Escherichia coli* Vi antigen. Thus, it seems likely that cellular events leading to an eventual rise in serum levels of antibody are in progress quite early; the first measurable increases in serum levels occur so remotely from the initiation of these cellular events that data on sequential appearance of these increases in serum may bear little relationship to actual sequential onset of antibody production by cells in the different classes. In the primary response IgA antibody appeared early and rose to a peak simultaneously with IgM antibody in all the rabbits. A few animals (4/11) had, in addition, a second maximum which coincided with the IgG peak. First detection of an increase in IgA antibody followed that of IgM antibody by at least a day, occurring either before or simultaneously with that of IgG antibody. Thus, since IgA antibody appears early in the primary immune responses of rabbit immunized intravenously, the possibility that IgA-producing cells arise from IgG-producing cells appears unlikely.

Immunologic memory in each of the classes

was examined by inducing secondary responses with the same dose and route of administration of antigen as used for primary immunization. Possible criteria indicating anamnesis would be earlier appearance, faster production rate and higher peak values than in the primary response. Although the IgM response fulfilled the first two of the criteria, it had a lower peak value than in the primary response. The IgG response fulfilled all three of the criteria and, therefore, showed anamnesis very clearly. The IgA response fulfilled only the first of these criteria, having a doubling time that did not differ significantly from that seen in the primary response, and an earlier but lower peak. Thus, the only evidence supporting IgA memory in this study is its earlier appearance, which could also be explained by a more rapid elimination of antigen in the secondary response due to the persistence of circulating antibody.

The lower, earlier peaks of IgA and IgM antibody in the secondary response might be the result of a "feedback mechanism" as suggested by Möller and Wigzell (30) and by Sahiar and Schwartz (31), in which IgM antibody production can be curtailed by the presence of high levels of IgG antibody, which occur much earlier in the secondary than in the primary response. If this is the explanation, it is of considerable interest that IgA seems to be subject to the same kind of suppression by IgG. Whether IgA antibody in secretions (secretory IgA) can be similarly suppressed by high levels of serum IgG antibody remains to be examined.

In rabbits serum IgA antibody responses have not previously been studied, probably because of the very low concentration of this immunoglobulin in serum; Cebra and Robbins (4) have reported average IgA levels of 200 μg/ml in rabbit serum and we have confirmed this finding using radial immunodiffusion. In rabbit colostrum, however, IgA is the predominant immunoglobulin and colostral IgA responses evoked by direct injection of antigen to mammary tissue have been demonstrated; no such response followed footpad injection (32). In rats, serum responses to dinitrophenol-bovine γ globulin emulsified in Freund's adjuvant were estimated in four immunoglobulin classes (including IgA) by Bloch *et al.* (33) who employed radioimmunoelectrophoresis with anti-immunoglobulin antisera; an early response in IgM followed by prolonged IgA, IgG_a and IgG_b responses was found.

In humans the evaluation of the IgA response has so far been accomplished by using immune precipitation techniques with specific anti-immunoglobulin antibodies. In one study (34) using diphtheria toxoid, the primary response consisted solely of IgG, with IgG and small amounts of IgA participating in the secondary response; at no time was IgM antibody found. In another study (35) using *Limulus polyphemus* hemocyanin, IgM and IgA antibodies were found early and IgG antibody late in the primary response; all three were found early in the secondary response. In this study both primary and secondary IgA responses were quite large relative to the other immunoglobulins. The differences in these human responses could be due to the dissimilar antigens used, or they could be due to methodologic difficulties. Other methods, such as the C1a FTT, may be helpful in deciding such issues.

REFERENCES

1. Cohen, S. and Porter, R. R., Advances Immun., *4:* 287, 1964.
2. Feinstein, A., Nature, *199:* 1197, 1963.
3. Onoue, K., Yagi, Y. and Pressman, D., J. Immun., *92:* 173, 1964.
4. Cebra, J. J. and Robbins, J. B., J. Immun., *97:* 12, 1966.
5. Cebra, J. J. and Small, P. A., Biochemistry, *6:* 503, 1967.
6. Crandall, R. B., Cebra, J. J. and Crandall, C. A., Immunology, *12:* 147, 1967.
7. Bernier, G. M. and Cebra, J. J., J. Immun., *95:* 246, 1965.
8. Borsos, T. and Rapp, H. J., J. Immun., *95:* 559, 1965.
9. Campbell, D. H., Garvey, J. S., Cremer, N. E. and Sussdorf, D. H., *Methods in Immunology*, p. 79, W. A. Benjamin, Inc., New York, 1964.
10. Ingraham, J. S., J. Infect. Dis., *91:* 268, 1952.
11. Borsos, T. and Rapp, H. J., J. Immun., *91:* 851, 1963.
12. Borsos, T., Rapp, H. J. and Cook, C. T., J. Immun., *87:* 330, 1961.
13. Borsos, T. and Rapp, H. J., J. Immun., *99:* 263, 1967.
14. Mayer, M. M., in *Kabat and Mayer's Experimental Immunochemistry*, p. 150, Charles C Thomas, Springfield, Ill., 1961.
15. Putnam, F. W., Tan, M., Lynn, L. T., Easley, C. W. and Migita, S., J. Biol. Chem., *237:* 717, 1962.

16. Cohen, S., J. Immun., *100:* 407, 1968.
17. Ishizaka, T., Iskizaka, K., Borsos, T. and Rapp, H. J., J. Immun., *97:* 716, 1966.
18. Borsos, T., Rapp, H. J. and Mayer, M. M., J. Immun., *87:* 310, 1961.
19. Ishizaka, T., Tada, T. and Ishizaka, K., J. Immun., *100:* 1145, 1968.
20. Hoyer, L. W., Borsos, T., Rapp, H. J. and Vannier, W. E., J. Exp. Med., *127:* 589, 1968.
21. Plotz, P. H., Colten, H. and Talal, N., J. Immun., *100:* 752, 1968.
22. Eisen, P. H. and Siskind, G. W., Biochemistry, *3:* 996, 1964.
23. Linscott, W. D., J. Immun., *102:* 993, 1969.
24. Hooker, S. B. and Boyd, W. C., Proc. Soc. Exp. Biol. Med., *47:* 187, 1941.
25. Altemeier, W. A., III, Robbins, J. B. and Smith, R. T., J. Exp. Med., *124:* 443, 1966.
26. Bauer, D. C. and Stavitsky, A. B., Proc. Nat. Acad. Sci., *47:* 1667, 1961.
27. Uhr, J. W. and Finkelstein, M. S., J. Exp. Med., *117:* 457, 1963.
28. Jerne, N. K., Nordin, A. A. and Henry, C., in *Cell-Bound Antibodies*, Edited by B. Amos and H. Koprowski, p. 109, Wistar Institute Press, Philadelphia, 1963.
29. Baker, P. J. and Landy, M., J. Immun., *99:* 687, 1967.
30. Möller, G. and Wigzell, H., J. Exp. Med., *121:* 969, 1965.
31. Sahiar, K. and Schwartz, R. S., J. Immun., *95:* 345, 1965.
32. Gence, R. J. and Taubman, M. A., Nature, *221:* 679, 1969.
33. Bloch, K. J., Morse, H. C., III and Austen, K. F., J. Immun., *101:* 650, 1968.
34. Newcomb, R. W. and Ishizaka, K., J. Immun., *99:* 40, 1967.
35. Bandilla, K. K. and McDuffie, F. C., Fed. Proc., *27:* 563, 1968.

THE JOURNAL OF IMMUNOLOGY
Vol. 105, No. 3, September 1970
Printed in U.S.A.

QUANTITATION OF CANINE IMMUNOGLOBULINS

HERBERT Y. REYNOLDS AND JOHN S. JOHNSON

From the Laboratory of Clinical Investigation, National Institute of Allergy and Infectious Diseases, National Institutes of Health, Bethesda, Maryland

Received for publication February 10, 1970

Quantitative immunoglobulins were measured in canine serum, colostrum, milk and intestinal secretions, and normal mean values were established. Two groups of dogs, pure bred and mongrel, were used because of significantly different serum levels of IgG subclasses $IgG_{a,b}$ and IgG_d. The immunoglobulin content of breast secretions diminished during the 1st week post-partum and only IgA persisted in appreciable amounts until weaning. Intestinal fluid was immunoglobulin-poor except for high levels of IgA, which reaffirms the secretory origin of the molecule.

The relative concentrations of canine immunoglobulins in external secretions and serum have been estimated (1–3), but no information has appeared which defines the normal levels of immunoglobulins in canine serum, except in a preliminary report (4). The present article attempts to establish normal values for the concentrations of the major canine immunoglobulins in sera from mongrel and pure bred dogs and in two canine external fluids, colostrum and intestinal secretions. The single radial immunodiffusion test was the quantitative method used. This method has been well described by several authors (5–7).

MATERIALS AND METHODS

Preparation of immunodiffusion plates and experimental method. From a stock supply of 2.5% agarose (L'Industrie Biologique Francaise) dissolved in 1X borate-saline buffer, pH 8.0 (8), an agarose aliquot was melted and cooled to 56°C in a water bath. Seven milliliters of the agarose solution were mixed with 1 ml of antiserum, previously heated to 56°, and applied evenly to a preheated 3- x 4-in. glass slide. The final concentration of agarose was approximately 2.2%. The antibody-containing agarose diffusion plates were stored at 4°C until used. From a paper grid pattern, 60 antigen wells 1.5-mm diameter and 1 cm apart were punched on each plate. The antigen wells, which held about 2 μl volume, were filled with a micropipet. The immunodiffusion plates were incubated in moist Petri dishes at room temperature. The plates were photographed, and the diameter of the precipitin rings was measured from the photograph with calipers to 0.1 mm accuracy. All samples were run in duplicate or triplicate and the average measurement from the several determinations was used. For each plate a calibration curve was constructed, using a purified canine immunoglobulin protein as a standard antigen, and several control canine sera were included. The calibration curves were plotted on three-cycle semi-log paper as protein concentration (mg/ml) *vs* precipitin ring diameter.

Sources of canine sera and other body fluids. Serum samples were obtained from normal adult mongrel dogs, quartered at the National Institutes of Health animal facilities, without consideration of size or sex of the animals. Additional sera were obtained from several groups of adult pure bred dogs (16 American foxhounds, 10 English foxhounds, and 11 collies). The samples of canine colostrum and milk, and fecal extracts taken from the terminal ileum and proximal colon of autopsied dogs, were obtained as described (2, 9). Four post-partum American foxhounds had colostral and milk samples taken at intervals up to 30 days, when their pups are customarily weaned, with concomitant blood specimens to study the persistence of immunoglobulins in the breast secretions. The colostral specimens were centrifuged twice at 20,000 rpm for 1 hr, and whey (clarified colostrum) was removed between the floating fat layer and casein precipitate.

Canine immunoglobulin reference proteins. The methods for isolating the various canine immunoglobulin classes have been described recently (9). In brief, serum IgM was isolated chromatographically from a lipoprotein-depleted serum euglobulin precipitate; IgA was obtained from canine colostrum and from normal canine serum (10). Subclass $IgG_{a,b}$ was separated chromatographically from Pentex canine fraction II. Subclass IgG_d ($7S\gamma_1$) was prepared from a canine myeloma serum (11). γ_{2c}, which is probably an IgG subclass and will be designated IgG_c in this study was purified from a canine myeloma serum (1). Serial dilutions of the protein standard were made with 1× borate buffer, pH 8.0. The protein concentrations (mg/ml) were determined by converting optical density units obtained spectrophotometrically at 280 nm to milligrams. Extinction coefficients for the IgG subclasses, using human IgG as a reference (12), were found by refractometric boundary analysis with a synthetic boundary ultracentrifuge cell. The $E_{1cm, 280}^{0.1\%}$ for $IgG_{a,b}$ and IgG_d was 1.43 and for IgG_c was 1.50. The value for colostral IgA was 1.22 (9). The published value for human IgM $E_{1cm,280}^{1\%}$ of 11.85 (12) was assumed for canine IgM.

Antisera. Antisera to the canine immunoglobulins were raised in New Zealand White rabbits. The rabbit anti-canine antisera were purified by using protein-specific Sepharose 2-B (Pharmacia) immunoabsorbents (13), followed by an additional absorption with canine IgG F_{ab} fragments to remove light chain cross-reactivity. The antisera were specific by immunoelectrophoresis for heavy chain determinants of the respective immunoglobulin classes. The preparation and specificity of the antisera have been described (2, 9). Antiserum to IgG_c (1) was not purified with an immunoabsorbent, but was made specific for this IgG subclass in canine serum by absorbing it with appropriate fractions obtained from DEAE chromatography of canine serum.

The antiserum concentration in the agarose medium which gave a sharp and easily measurable precipitin ring with a standard reference protein in a concentration range that included the average canine serum level was considered to be optimal for antigen-antibody precipitation. The ratio of antiserum to 2.5% agarose was routinely 1:7. All of the rabbit antisera were IgG antibody, and an extinction coefficient of 1.36 (14) was used to convert optical density units of purified antiserum to milligram quantities, with the exception of the IgG_c antiserum.

RESULTS

For the quantitative determination of canine immunoglobulins in serum and other body fluids, a single radial immunodiffusion method was used in which the antiserum was mixed into an agarose-borate saline supporting medium. The availability of specific and purified antigen and antibody reagents allowed us to try a number of antibody concentrations and to select those that seemed optimal for precipitation of the immunoglobulins. Table I indicates the antibody concentration range tested and gives the concentration selected for the antiserum-agarose mixture. The sensitivity of the immunoprecipitation re-

TABLE I

Antibody concentration and sensitivity of immunodiffusion plates

Antiserum	Optimal Concentration[a]	Concentration Range	Sensitivity[b]
	mg/ml	*mg/ml*	*mg/ml*
IgM	4.1	1.5–5.0	0.32
IgA	6.5	2.2–10.7	0.11
$IgG_{a,b}$	2.8	2.0–3.7	0.31
IgG_d ($7S\gamma_1$)	5.5	3.7–8.8	0.17
IgG_c			0.20

[a] Antiserum concentration which mixed 1:7 with agarose gives good precipitation ring at average serum immunoglobulin levels.

[b] Minimal amount of protein standard detected at optimal antibody concentration.

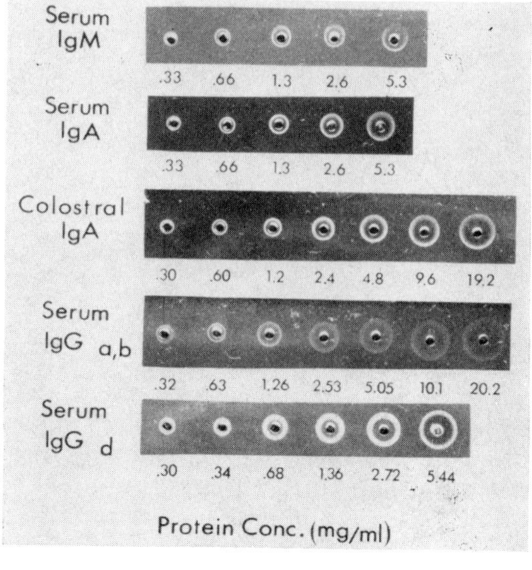

Figure 1. Precipitation of reference immunoglobulin proteins on antibody specific agarose immunoplates are the basis of calibration curves. IgG_c is not shown.

TABLE II

Mean values for canine immunoglobulins (mg/ml)

Immunoglobulin Class	Serum: Pure bred[a]	Serum: Mongrel	Colostrum: Mongrel	Fecal Extract: Mongrel
	mg/ml		*mg/ml*	*mg/ml*
IgM	1.56 (37)[b] (0.7–3.0)[c]	1.45 (35) (0.8–2.1)	2.17 (10) (0.7–3.7)	0.91 (9) (0.5–1.6)
IgA	0.83 (37) (0.4–2.4)	0.79 (33) (0.3–2.4)	3.13 (12) (1.7–5.2)	3.02 (10) (0.8–5.4)
$IgG_{a,b}$	5.12 (37) (2.6–10.2)	7.71 (35) (1.2–14.0)	6.70 (10) (2.6–10.1)	0.56 (10) (0.3–1.4)
IgG_d	3.00 (37) (0.9–6.2)	5.62 (28) (1.0–13.0)	6.94 (7) (4.0–9.0)	3.48 (5)[d] (0.3–8.4)
IgG_c	1.13 (21) (0.6–2.7)	1.12 (20) (0.3–3.0)	0.89 (7) (0.5–1.4)	0.48 (7) (0.3–.9)

[a] Pure bred dogs (foxhounds and collies).
[b] Number of animals tested.
[c] Concentration range observed.
[d] Detected in 5 of 10 samples.

action was gauged by the least concentration of the immunoglobulin standard protein detected that remained on the linear part of the calibration curve. These values for individual immunoglobulins varied from 0.1 to 0.3 mg/ml. Figure 1 shows a sample of the precipitation reactions of the standard immunoglobulin proteins at various dilutions from which a group of calibration curves were constructed. The $IgG_{a,b}$ precipitin rings were photographed 6 hr after the plate was set up; the other IgG subclasses, IgM and IgA, required 18 to 24 hr for optimal development of their precipitin rings, and these plates were photographed during this interval.

Canine sera obtained from adult pure bred and mongrel dogs, colostrum, and fecal extracts were measured for their content of five immunoglobulin classes and subclasses. Table II lists the mean values obtained and the concentration range observed. Figure 2 depicts the grouping of these data. The probable error in the measurement from 10 different immunoplates was found for each immunoglobulin class or subclass using a normal reference serum. For $IgG_{a,b}$ the probable error was about 5%, and for the other immunoglobulins it varied from 7% to 10%. These variations agree with those in another report (7). The error in size and measurement of the precipitin ring for five or more separate determinations of a reference serum on the same plate was less than 2%.

The IgM and IgA serum concentrations were grouped closely about the mean value, but the IgG subclasses showed considerable dispersion, particularly in the mongrel group of dogs. The IgM, IgA and IgG_c levels were generally the same for the two groups, pure bred and mongrel, but $IgG_{a,b}$ and IgG_d values were lower[1] in the pure bred animals. Although there was considerable variation in the individual serum concentrations of $IgG_{a,b}$ and IgG_d subclasses, mongrel dogs with a lower $IgG_{a,b}$ level also have a lower value of IgG_d,[2] so that the lower or higher serum concentrations of both IgG subclass immunoglobulins were a consistent finding within individual animals. The same correlation could not be made ($p>0.20$) for the pure bred dogs, but the IgG subclass values were more uniform in this group so that the IgG_d concentration was generally about 60% of the corresponding $IgG_{a,b}$ level.

[1] $p < 0.01$, Student's $t = 3.7$ for $IgG_{a,b}$; $t = 3.01$ for IgG_d.

[2] $p < 0.05$, Spearman's rank correlation $r = 0.375$, $t = 2.06$.

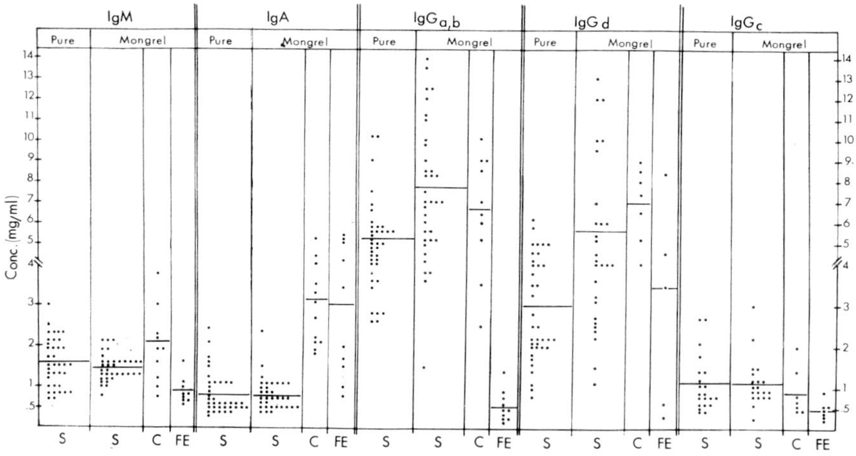

Figure. 2. Individual immunoglobulin values in serum (*S*) from pure bred and mongrel dogs, and colostrum (*C*) and fecal extract (*FE*) from mongrel dogs are shown with mean values (*horizontal bar*).

The immunoglobulin concentrations in colostrum and fecal extracts from mongrel dogs only are given in Table II and Figure 2. Although the mean value for colostral IgM was about 25% greater than serum, the variable concentration of this immunoglobulin in the colostral samples does not make this value significantly greater than the serum concentration. The mean IgM concentration in colostrum from four pure bred foxhounds (Fig. 3) was less than the serum IgM mean. It seems that colostral IgM is present in approximately its serum concentration and an appreciably higher concentration is unusual. Colostral IgA levels were consistently greater than the corresponding serum concentrations in mongrel and pure bred animals. Mean values in colostrum and serum showed a 3- to 6-fold excess of secretory to serum IgA in mongrel and pure bred dogs, but the wide concentration range of colostral IgA makes a fixed ratio for secretory to serum IgA meaningless. The IgG class of colostral immunoglobulins, likewise, showed considerable variation in individual samples. In general, the first day colostral IgG levels were equal to corresponding mean serum values. Of note, the colostral IgG_d values did not greatly exceed serum values in mongrel or pure bred dogs.

Immunoglobulin levels in fecal extracts are given for mongrel dogs only, since autopsy specimens from the groups of pure bred dogs were unavailable. The fecal extract represents natural

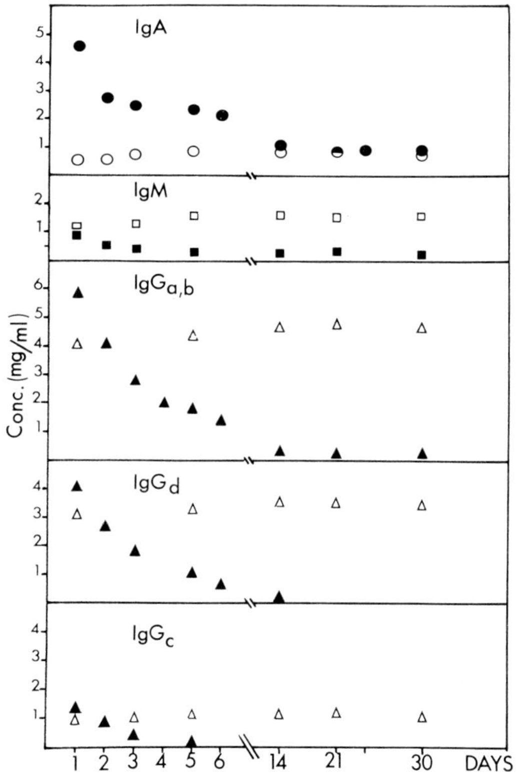

Figure 3. Mean immunoglobulin values in colostrum and milk (*solid figures*) with serum values (*open figures*) from four American foxhounds are given for the corresponding post-partum day.

intestinal fluid altered only by the separation of particulate matter from the specimens and the addition of preservatives (2) to prevent bacterial growth. The intestinal fluid was somewhat immunoglobulin poor when mean or individual values were compared with corresponding serum concentrations, except for IgA. In all of the dogs studied, the fecal IgA level was greater than the animal's serum level. The presence of IgG_d in the fecal extracts was unpredictable, being detected in only 5 of 10 specimens tested and quite variable in its concentration when present. The fecal specimens were not contaminated with blood.

Figure 3 depicts the immunoglobulin pattern in canine colostrum and milk for 1 month following parturition. Mean values for colostrum or milk and serum were calculated for a group of four American foxhounds. Although mean values are plotted, the individual values follow the general pattern well. In the first post-partum day, colostral immunoglobulins approximated serum values, except for IgA which was in considerable excess; during the succeeding 5 to 6 days immunoglobulin levels diminished, particularly the IgM and IgG subclasses. The yellowish-green whey visibly becomes milk between the 3rd and 5th post-partum days. During the last 3 weeks of lactation, minimal amounts of IgM and $IgG_{a,b}$ in 0.1 to 0.3 mg/ml concentrations were present. In contrast, colostral IgA was present in a 2- or 3-fold excess of the serum IgA concentration during the first 2 weeks of lactation; thereafter, IgA persisted in the milk at serum levels until weaning.

DISCUSSION

Some of the technical problems in the measurement of quantitative immunoglobulins, particularly in secretory fluids (15), have been eliminated in this study by the use of specific and purified standard protein antigen and antibody preparations. This permitted the immunoprecipitation reactions to be balanced optimally and avoided the nonspecific precipitation lines frequently seen with colostral or intestinal secretion samples. The single radial immunodiffusion system used had an acceptable reproducibility of 10% or better.

Mean immunoglobulin values for IgM and IgA classes and the IgG subclasses in normal canine serum, colostrum and fecal extract were determined. Two groups of dogs, pure bred and mongrel, were used for the quantitation of serum immunoglobulin levels because of variations in the levels of the IgG subclasses $_{a,b}$ and $_d$. The significantly lower concentration of IgG globulin in the pure bred group is unexplained except for the speculation that the more restricted environment of the kennel bred and housed dogs might reduce the variety or frequency of immunologic challenges, and therefore be reflected in lower levels of 7S antibodies belonging to the $IgG_{a,b}$ and $_d$ subclasses. Furthermore, the restricted breeding of the pure bred dogs resulted in more predictable concentrations of these IgG subclasses (Fig. 2) than were found in the randomly outbred or mongrel group of animals. The IgM and IgA levels did not vary significantly between the groups.

IgA is one of the principal immunoglobulins in colostrum and the predominant one in the fecal extract (2), so that its presence in greater than serum concentration was consistent with its secretory origin. Although first day colostral fluid contained all of the immunoglobulins in amounts comparable to serum concentrations, the immunoglobulin levels in breast secretions diminished rapidly during the 1st week of lactation. IgA is the only immunoglobulin that persisted in milk in apparently significant amounts. IgM and $IgG_{a,b}$ could be detected in minimal amounts in some milk samples throughout lactation, but their presence was inconstant. It is probable that breast-derived secretory IgA has some important immunologic function in the gastrointestinal tract of suckling pups. As with human neonates (16), canine pups do not have detectable serum IgA levels at 2 or 6 weeks of age (unpublished observation).

IgA used for protein standards (Fig. 1) was isolated from canine colostrum (9) and from normal canine serum (10). Canine serum IgA is unusual in that it exists almost exclusively as a dimer in serum and it was isolated in this form. The serum molecule has a sedimentation coefficient of about $10s^0_{20,w}$. The quantitative IgA immunoglobulin levels were calculated using the respective IgA standard isolated from the serum or colostrum; however, use of either IgA standard made very minimal changes in the quantitative value since the calibration curves were virtually the same and could have been used interchangeably.

The concentrations of IgG immunoglobulin

subclasses found in 1st-day colostrum from pure bred and mongrel dogs approximated the serum levels. Previously IgG_d ($7S\gamma_1$) was reported (1) to be present in colostrum well in excess of its serum concentration. Recently, Vaerman and Heremans (3) were unable to confirm this finding in a single animal. We found after examining a number of colostral specimens that the IgG_d levels were variable, but the mean value was only slightly greater than that of serum. The calculation of a meaningful fixed ratio between serum and colostral IgG_d was impossible because of the wide concentration ranges found. In general, the respective concentrations of serum and colostral immunoglobulins immediately post-partum may be distorted slightly in favor of a colostral excess because of a relative reduction in serum immunoglobulin levels (Fig. 3). Serum immunoglobulins did not return to pre-delivery levels until 3 to 5 days post-partum for reasons that were unclear.

Immunoglobulin levels were low in the fecal specimens, except for IgA. The $IgG_{a,b}$ subclass was found in fecal extracts in less than 10% of its serum concentration. As discussed previously (2), the IgG molecule is more susceptible to degradation from bacterial and proteolytic enzymes in the gastrointestinal tract than is secretory IgA, and this may account for the low levels of $IgG_{a,b}$ in fecal extracts. IgG_d, which was detected in only 50% of the fecal specimens measured, may be degraded also, or possibly it is inconstant in its secretion into the intestinal fluids.

Since the antisera used in the immunodiffusion plates were specific for heavy chain determinants of the immunoglobulins, there was no overlap in the quantitative measurements of the IgG subclasses. The individual subclass values can be added to give an approximation of the total IgG concentration. The mean values for canine serum immunoglobulins, using the total IgG globulin concentration, did not differ appreciably from the profile values of human serum immunoglobulins (7, 17), except for canine serum IgA which was about one-third of the human level. Since the mechanisms maintaining serum IgA levels are not understood, we have no certain explanation for the disparity in the serum IgA concentrations in these two species. However, if the antibody activity of IgA is a factor influencing the serum concentration, then the reduced level of serum IgA could be explained by the finding that serum IgA is a dimer and may have more efficient antibody properties.

Acknowledgments. The authors appreciate the help of Drs. Chester W. Anderson and Terry Pitts, Division of Research Sciences, NIH Animal Center, and Dr. David C. Dale, Laboratory of Clinical Investigation, NIAID, in collecting colostral and blood specimens. Also, we wish to thank Mrs. Louise E. Johnson, Silcrest Kennels, Brandywine, Maryland, for blood samples from her collies.

REFERENCES

1. Johnson, J. S. and Vaughan, J. H., J. Immun., *98:* 923, 1967.
2. Reynolds, H. Y. and Johnson, J. S., J. Immun., *104:* 888, 1970.
3. Vaerman, J. and Heremans, J. F., Immunochemistry, *6:* 779, 1969.
4. Reynolds, H. Y. and Johnson, J. S., J. Infect. Dis., In press.
5. Feinberg, J. G., Int. Arch. Allerg., *11:* 129, 1957.
6. Mancini, G., Vaerman, J. P., Carbonara, A. O. and Heremans, J. F., *XI Colloquim on Protides of the Biological Fluids*, Edited by H. Peeters, p. 370, Elsevier Publishing Co., Amsterdam, 1964.
7. Fahey, J. L. and McKelvey, E. M., J. Immun., *94:* 84, 1965.
8. Helmkamp, R. W., Goodland, R. L., Bale, W. F., Spar I. L. and Mutschler, L. E., Cancer Res., *20:* 1495, 1960.
9. Reynolds, H. Y. and Johnson, J.S., J. Immun., *104:* 1000, 1970.
10. Reynolds, H. Y. and Johnson, J. S., Fed. Proc., *29* (No. 2, Abst.): 641, 1970.
11. Johnson, J. S. and Reynolds, H. Y., Immunochemistry, In press.
12. Miller, F. and Metzger, H., J. Biol. Chem., *240:* 3325, 1965.
13. Rejnek, J., Mage, R. G. and Reisfeld, R. A., J. Immun., *102:* 638, 1969.
14. Small, P. A., Jr. and Lamm, M. E., Biochemistry, *5:* 259, 1966.
15. Tomasi, T. B., Jr. and Bienenstock, J., Advances Immun., *9:* 1, 1968.
16. Haworth, J. C. and Dilling, L., J. Lab. Clin. Med., *67:* 922, 1966.
17. Waldmann, T. A., New England J. Med., *281:* 1170, 1969.

THE JOURNAL OF IMMUNOLOGY
Vol. 105, No. 3, September 1970

DETECTION OF IMMUNE RESPONSE AGAINST SYNTHETIC POLYMERS OF AMINO ACIDS EMPLOYING THE PLAQUE-FORMING CELL SYSTEM

III. Cross-Reaction Patterns of Antibody Secreted *in Vitro* against Immunochemically Related Synthetic Polypepides[1]

MARIANNE EGAN[2] AND PAUL H. MAURER

From the Department of Biochemistry, Jefferson Medical College, Thomas Jefferson University, Philadelphia, Pennsylvania 19107

Received for publication February 2, 1970

The secretion of anti-polypeptide immunoglobulins by popliteal lymph node cells from rabbits immunized with synthetic polymers of α-L and α-D amino acids was detected with the localized hemolysis in gel (LHG) assay employing polypeptide-coated tanned sheep erythrocytes. Plaque-forming cells (PFC) were detected 5 to 7 days following primary immunization of rabbits with poly(L-glu^{42}-L-lys^{28}-L-ala^{30})$_n$, or poly (L-glu^{36}-L-lys^{24}-L-ala^{35}-L-tyr^{5})$_n$, and with poly (L-glu^{60}-L-lys^{40})$_n$, and poly (D-glu^{42}-D-lys^{28}-D-ala^{30})$_n$, when complexed with methylated bovine serum albumin (MBSA). No PFC were detected 5 days after immunization with poly (L-glu^{42}-L-lys^{28}-D-ala^{30})$_n$, poly (D-glu^{42}-L-lys^{28}-L-ala^{30})$_n$ or poly (D-glu^{42}-D-lys^{28}-D-ala^{30})$_n$. Cross-reacting antibody was detected at the cellular level. The PFC were due to immunoglobulin secretion since they were inhibited by sheep anti-rabbit globulin and specific anti-allotype serum.

Synthetic polymers composed of a limited combination of amino acids are useful tools for investigating the minimum requirements for immunogenicity and serologic specificity. Studies on the immunogenicity of these polypeptides have contributed to ideas about the importance of ionic charge, optical configuration, amino acid content, conformation, and size of a molecule necessary to stimulate an immune response (1–5). The importance of various factors in the response against synthetic polypeptides has been learned from studies of cross-reaction patterns of serum immunoglobulins against polypeptides which have been slightly modified from the original homologous immunogen.

An adaption of the localized hemolysis in gel (LHG) technique of Jerne and Nordin (6) and Ingraham and Bussard (7) to the anti-polypeptide system has made possible the study of the response to synthetic polypeptides at the cellular level (8, 9). The antibody produced by single cells as measured by this technique is probably of a restricted specificity and immunoglobulin class, whereas that found in the serum represents a heterogeneous population (10–12). It therefore was of interest to determine whether the anti-polypeptide antibody produced by single cells as measured in the LHG technique displayed the same cross-reaction patterns as those observed previously by the measurement of serum antibody (1).

MATERIALS AND METHODS

Polypeptides. Poly-α-amino acid polymers were prepared by polymerization of N-carboxy-α-amino acid anhydrides using sodium methoxide as the initiator and the general method outlined in (13). Optical configuration, lot number, average molecular weight, and abbreviated

[1] This work was supported by Grants A1-07825 and T1A1-334 from the National Institute of Allergy and Infectious Diseases and Public Health Service Predoctoral Fellowship 1-F1-GM-38,458-01. Paper 33 in a series of "Antigenicity of Polypeptides (Poly-α-Amino Acids)."

[2] Public Health Service Predoctoral Fellow. Taken from a thesis submitted in partial fulfillment of the requirements for the Doctor of Philosophy Degree in Biochemistry.

TABLE I

Properties of synthetic polymers of α-L and α-D amino acids employed in this study

Composition and Nomenclature of Polymer	Abbreviation Used in Text	Lot No.	Average Molecular Weight[a]
Poly (L-glu^{42}-L-lys^{28}-L-ala^{30})$_n$[b]	GLA^{30} (LLL)	M-21-D	32,000
Poly (L-glu^{57}-L-lys^{38}-L-ala^{5})$_n$	GLA^{5} (LLL)	M-22	50,000
Poly (L-glu^{36}-L-lys^{24}-L-ala^{40})$_n$	GLA^{40} (LLL)	M-11B	50,000
Poly (L-glu^{42}-L-lys^{28}-D-ala^{30})$_n$	GLA^{30} (LLD)	M-52B	12,000
Poly (D-glu^{42}-L-lys^{28}-L-ala^{30})$_n$	GLA^{30} (DLL)	M-50-B	6,000
Poly (D-glu^{42}-D-lys^{28}-D-ala^{30})$_n$	GLA^{30} (DDD)	M-54B[c]	50,000
Poly (L-glu^{60}-L-lys^{40})$_n$	GL (LL)	C-35	90,000
Poly (L-glu^{100})$_n$	Poly G (L)	G-12	85,140
Poly (L-glu^{36}-L-lys^{24}-L-ala^{35}-L-tyr^{5})$_n$	GLAT	M-17-G	30,000

[a] Molecular weights estimated by viscosometric and ultracentrifugal measurements.

[b] Nomenclature based on recommendation of IUPAC-IUB Commission on Biochemical Nomenclature, October, 1967. Biochem. J., *106:* 577, 1968.

[c] Employed in GLA^{30} (DDD)·MBSA studies.

nomenclature of synthetic polypeptides are presented in Table I.

Preparation of methylated bovine serum albumin polymer complexes. Methylated bovine serum albumin (MBSA) was prepared according to (14) and was lyophilized after dialysis until chloride free. Aggregates were formed between the polymers GLA^{30} (DDD) and GL (LL) by the addition of 2% aqueous solution of MBSA (pH 8.5) to 2% polymer solution (pH 8.5) until no precipitate occurred on addition of MBSA. The final ratio of MBSA to polymer varied between 3:1 to 4:1.

Immunization of rabbits. New Zealand White rabbits (2.5 to 3.5 kg) were injected in each rear footpad with 1 ml polymer or polymer·MBSA aggregate (10 mg polymer/ml) in complete Freund's adjuvant (CFA). The animals were killed 5 to 7 days after injection unless otherwise noted.

Plaque assay. Plaque-forming cells (PFC) against synthetic polypeptides were detected by employing polypeptide-coated tanned erythrocytes (15) in the plaque assay as previously reported (8, 9). Data are reported as the average of PFC/10^6 lymph node cells from triplicate plates. A random sample of plaques was checked under high power magnification (× 450) for the presence of a lymphoid cell in the center of each plaque. To study the effect of sheep anti-rabbit globulin, assay plates were incubated for 1 hr at 37°C followed by the addition of 2 ml of the appropriate dilution of sheep anti-rabbit globulin (Pentex) in Eagle's medium, and incubated for an additional hour at 37°C. After addition of 2 ml of a 1:10 dilution of guinea pig complement in Eagle's medium, the plates were incubated for another 2.5 hr at 37°C and stored at 4°C overnight.

The effect of anti-allotype serum was determined by incorporating 0.1 ml of the appropriate dilutions of anti-allotype serum in PBS, pH 7.4, into the plaquing medium. The anti-allotype serum was kindly supplied by Dr. Charles W. Todd, City of Hope, Duarte, California. Incubation and addition of guinea pig complement followed the original protocol.

Hemagglutination titers on microtiter plates. On the day of death the hemagglutination titers of individual rabbits' sera were determined by the Takatsy microtiter method (16). The same batch of polymer-coated cells was used both for the plaquing and hemagglutination assays. Proper coating of the cells was checked at this time with an anti-polymer serum of standard titer.

Passive cutaneous anaphylaxis (PCA) titers. The PCA test was performed in guinea pigs (200 to 250 g) as described by Ovary (17).

RESULTS

Induction of cells producing antibody against the synthetic polypeptides GLA^{30} (LLL) and GLAT. Immunization of rabbits with GLA^{30} (LLL) stimulated an average of 99 to 230 PFC/10^6 lymph node cells 5 to 7 days after injection. Serum obtained on the same day as lymph node harvest had hemagglutination titers ranging from 4 to 64. Immunization with GLAT generally stimulated a slightly greater average number of PFC (195 to 257 PFC/10^6 lymph node cells); the hemagglutination titers in the sera of these animals ranged from 8 to 128. PFC against normal sheep erythrocytes or tanned erythrocytes ranged from 0.1 to 10 PFC/10^6 lymph node cells. Unfractionated sheep anti-rabbit globulin diluted 1:50, 1:100, or 1:1,000 inhibited the primary PFC against polymer-coated erythrocytes. With the exception of one (no. 326) of the 10 rabbits tested, a 1:10,000 dilution of antiglobulin serum did not affect the number of PFC. With rabbit 326 this dilution of sheep anti-rabbit globulin increased the PFC only by 33%. Parallel results were obtained with anti-allotype serum. In general, the addition of a 1:10 dilution of specific anti-allotype serum suppressed the primary PFC. The inhibition was reduced at higher dilutions of antiserum.

Comparison of cross-reactions of anti-GLA^{30} (LLL) and anti-GLAT antibody measured at the cellular level and in the serum. To determine the percentage of cells producing antibody that cross-reacted with polymers related to GLA^{30} (LLL), in addition to the homologous GLA^{30} (LLL) and GLAT plaque assay plates, plates were made with tannic acid-treated sheep erythrocytes coated with GL (LL), GLA^{30} (LLD), GLA^{30} (DLL), GLA^{30} (DDD), GLA^{5} (LLL) and GLA^{40} (LLL). Table II summarizes the percentages of cells that formed cross-reacting antibody 5 to 7 days following primary immunization with GLA^{30} (LLL) or GLAT. In most rabbits the number of cells which secreted antibody against the homologous antigen was greater than those which secreted antibody against an immunochemically or structurally related (cross-reacting) one. However, in several rabbits more PFC were detected against the heterologous than against the homologous "antigen-coated" erythrocytes. The specificity of the antibody produced against the same antigen varied among these random bred rabbits (Table II).

In most experiments (13/16), reactions against GLA^{30} (LLD)-coated cells were greater than or equal to the reaction against GLA^{30} (DLL)-coated cells. An unexpected result was that in many experiments (8/15), the number of PFC reacting against GLA^{30} (DDD) polymer-coated cells was greater than the number of PFC reacting against cells coated with either GLA^{30} (LLD) or (DLL).

TABLE II

PFC and HA titers of rabbit anti-GLA^{30} and GLAT 5 to 7 days after immunization

Range of PFC/10^6 Lymph Node Cells against Homologous Coated Erythrocytes ± S.E.	Immunogen	
	GLA^{30} (LLL) 19 ± 0–558 ± 30 (4–64)[a]	GLAT 123 ± 6–436 ± 95 (8–42)
Range of % cross reaction[b]		
GLA^{30} (LLL)	100	27–201
	(4–64)	(3–32)
GLAT	13–197	100
	(2–8)	(8–42)
GLA^{30} (LLD)	2–59	7–34
	(2–8)	(2–6)
GLA^{30} (DLL)	1–86	1–13
	(1–4)	(0–3)
GLA^{30} (DDD)	3–60	4–54
	(0–4)	(1–3)
GL (LL)	7–113	26–116
	(0–4)	(2–6)
GLA^{40} (LLL)	1–111	ND[c]
GLA^{5} (LLL)	1–124	ND

[a] Values in parentheses indicate hemagglutination titers.

[b] The percentage of cells forming cross-reacting antibody is calculated by the equation:

$$\frac{\text{No. PFC against heterologous antigen}}{\text{No. PFC against homologous antigen}} \times 100.$$

[c] ND, not done.

The Takatsy microhemagglutination titers included in Table II indicate that it is difficult to detect substantial differences in cross-reactions in serum hemagglutinating antibody in the early stages of the immune response against synthetic polypeptides.

Table III compares the results of analysis by hemagglutination, LHG and PCA techniques of early primary response anti-GLAT sera produced 5 to 7 days after a primary immunization. Although these sera were from rabbits which produced antibody detectable by LHG assay against the homologous and cross-reacting antigens, little or no homologous or cross-reacting antibody in these early immune sera could be detected by PCA performed in guinea pigs.

Induction of PFC after immunization with polymers chemically related to GLA^{30} (LLL). Rabbits were immunized according to the origi-

TABLE III

Detection of antibody production 5 to 7 days after immunization with GLAT: Comparison of results obtained with the localized hemolysis in gel, hemagglutination, and passive cutaneous anaphylaxis analytical techniques[a]

Rabbit No.	Antigen Tested														
	GLAT			GLA^{30} (LLL)			GLA^{30} (LLD)			GLA^{30} (DLL)			GLA^{30} (DDD)		
	PFC	HA	PCA	PFC	HA	PCA	PFC	HA	PCA	PFC	HA	PCA	PFC	HA	PCA
326	314	16	18	177	8	18	21	2	0	18	0	0	12	0	0
390	166	16	0	105	16	0	53	3	0	13	0	0	86	3	0
408	198	42	0	53	32	0	49	4	0	2	0	0	88	3	0
437	123	21	13	66	16	10	11	6	0	16	2	0	12	2	0
442	400	8	0	180	3	0	93	2	0	15	0	0	110	2	0

[a] The numbers of PFC against homologous and heterologous antigens were measured on LHG plates and compared with the amount of homologous antibody present in the serum on the day of death as determined by hemagglutination and passive cutaneous anaphylaxis techniques. PFC are reported/10^{6} lymph node cells. HA titers are the reciprocal of the highest dilution of antiserum which agglutinated antigen-coated sheep erythrocytes. PCA reactions are reported as millimeters of bluing produced by intravenous injection of the antigens into guinea pigs whose skin was sensitized with 0.1 ml of undiluted serum. Appropriate positive controls were included in the hemagglutination and PCA tests. Serum from one hyperimmune anti-GLAT rabbit had antibody which cross-reacted with GLA^{30} (LLL), GLA^{30} (LLD), and GLA^{30} (DDD) (data not shown).

nal protocol with GLA^{30} (LLD), GLA^{30} (DLL), GA (LL), or GL (LL), the latter complexed in a 1:2.7 weight ratio with MBSA.

No PFC were detected early after immunization with GLA^{30} (LLD), (DLL), or GA. In one of the two rabbits injected with GL·MBSA a response was detected. The cross-reacting pattern indicated that glutamyl residues were an important part of the antigenic determinant since the numbers of PFC were approximately equal against GL-, GLA^{30} (LLL)-, and GLA^{30} (LLD)-coated erythrocytes (80, 83 and 73 PFC/10^{6} lymph node cells, respectively) but low against GLA^{30} (DLL)- (7 PFC/10^{6} lymph node cells) coated erythrocytes.

GLA^{30} (DDD) (at 20 mg immunization levels) stimulated PFC against GLA^{30} (DDD)-coated erythrocytes only when this polymer was complexed to an immunogenic carrier, MBSA (Table IV). Immunization with GLA^{30} (DDD) or MBSA separately at the above high concentrations did not result in PFC against polymer-coated cells. Immunization with the GLA^{30} (DDD)·MBSA complex led to detectable PFC after the second and third injection of antigen. The number of PFC that was stimulated by GLA^{30} (DDD)·MBSA was an order of magnitude lower than the number stimulated by GLA^{30}

TABLE IV

Comparison of the number of plaque-forming cells against GLA^{30} (DDD) and GLA^{30} (LLL) detected after a primary, secondary and tertiary injection of GLA^{30} (DDD)·MBSA aggregate

Course[a]	Day of Test	PFC/10^{6} Lymph Node Cells against Erythrocytes Coated with:[b]	
		GLA^{30} (DDD)	GLA^{30} (LLL)
1	4	0.6– 1.4 (2)[c]	0.3–0.7 (2)[c]
1	5	4.1–11.3 (8)	0.3–3.1 (8)
1	6	14.6–30 (3)	1.3–3.0 (3)
2	3	0.3–43 (3)	0.2–14 (3)
2	4	2.1–13 (2)	1.0–8 (2)
2	6	0.4– 2 (3)	0.4–0.5 (3)
3	4	2 –22 (4)	2 –14 (4)

[a] Primary 1, secondary 2, or tertiary 3, injection of the complex GLA^{30} (DDD)·MBSA (in complete Freund's adjuvant, 10 mg polymer/footpad).

[b] Lymph node cells from rabbits immunized with GLA^{30} (DDD)·MBSA, GLA^{30} (DDD), or MBSA (10 mg/footpad, one, two, or three injections) were measured for their ability to form plaques against GLA^{30} (DDD) and GLA^{30} (LLL)-coated erythrocytes. No antipolymer plaques were produced by cells immunized with MBSA or DDD alone.

[c] (Number) of animals tested.

(LLL). The anti-GLA^{30} (DDD) PFC were specific for the polymer in the D configuration as evidenced by the higher number of PFC against GLA^{30} (DDD)-coated erythrocytes than against GLA^{30} (LLL)-coated erythrocytes.

DISCUSSION

The number of PFC detected against synthetic polypeptides is in qualitative agreement with the reported serum antibody responses in rabbits and other species against these polymers (1, 2). Thus, GLAT, which stimulated a slightly higher average PFC response than GLA^{30} (LLL), is also a more potent immunogen when measured by serum assays. Previous results on the non-immunogenicity of high doses of polypeptides composed only of α-D-amino acids were confirmed (18), i.e., high doses (20 mg) of GLA^{30} (DDD) could not induce antibody-producing cells unless the polymer was complexed to an immunogenic carrier (MBSA); even then only a weak response was obtained.

Inhibition of PFC by sheep anti-rabbit γ globulin or by specific anti-allotype serum indicated that PFC produced 5 to 7 days after primary immunization with synthetic polypeptides were due to IgM antibody (19, 20).

We have never been able to detect either direct or indirect PFC in the lymph node of rabbits producing a secondary response to polypeptides in the L configuration. A "secondary" and even "tertiary" PFC response could be detected in the regional lymph node when a polymer of α-D-amino acids was complexed to an immunogenic carrier and employed for immunization. The plaques observed in the secondary and tertiary responses to the polypeptide of amino acids in the D configuration resembled those detected in the primary response against either α-L or α-D amino acid polymers and probably were due to IgM antibody, since no anti-globulin was necessary to detect them.

Although many studies have been performed on the cross-reactions of antibodies found in the serum of animals stimulated with synthetic polypeptides (18, 21), none have previously been tested for cross-reactions at the *cellular level*. The present studies indicate that cross-reacting anti-polymer antibody can be measured at the cellular level and that antibody so detected in the early immune response has cross-reaction patterns which differ from those observed when hyperimmune serum containing a heterogeneous population of antibodies is tested. Thus analysis by hemagglutination and precipitation reactions has shown that antibody from *hyperimmune* rabbits directed against the polymer GLA^{30} (LLL) will cross-react with the GLA^{30} polymers in which the configuration of one or all of the amino acids is changed. The amount of cross-reaction is greatest with the GLA^{30} (LLD) polymer, is less with GLA^{30} (DLL) and is very slight with GLA^{30} (DDD). However, in the plaquing system, where *early primary* immune antibody (IgM) was studied, the number of cells producing antibody which cross-reacted with GLA^{30} (DDD) was often greater than those which produced antibody which cross-reacted with the GLA^{30} (LLD)- or (DLL)-coated erythrocytes. Whether this was due to the difference in sensitivity of the methods (LHG *vs* hemagglutination and precipitation) or to a true difference in the type of specificity of early antibody secreted by single cells *vs* hyperimmune serum antibody cannot be determined by the present experiments. The serum hemolysin titers at the time of testing for PFC were low and precluded any direct comparison of the two assay methods. Also no precipitating antibody could be detected in the sera tested. These results are in agreement with the observations of Makëlä who found that single cells displayed marked differences in cross-reactions with chemically related haptens compared to the "average" values of cross-reaction found in serum antibodies (12, 22).

It has been demonstrated that hyperimmune antibody against the polymers of α-L amino acids cross-reacted weakly with polymers of amino acids in the D configuration. This cross-reaction was not detected by the precipitin reaction, which requires high levels of antibody and a relatively stable association of antigen with antibody, but was detected by passive cutaneous anaphylaxis (PCA), which requires only a momentary interaction of antigen with antibody (21). The LHG assay also detects a weak antigen-antibody reaction since it requires only a brief association of antigen with antibody to fix complement to the erythrocyte and initiate the lytic reaction. Therefore, although both reactions (LHG and PCA) measure different kinds of antibody, they can detect weakly cross-reacting systems more readily than the hemagglutination or precipitin reactions.

Although the PCA reaction of rabbit antibody in the guinea pig will detect as little as 0.2 μg of IgG antibody, this method did not detect antibody in the immune serum at the time of optimal PFC production, since antibody at this time is presumably IgM. Later in the immune response against synthetic polypeptides in the L configuration antibody was detected by PCA but not by LHG, indicating a switch to IgG production. The fact that direct PFC stimulated by polypeptides in the D configuration can be detected after a second and third injection of these polymers suggests that the production of IgM continues for a longer time than after the injection of the corresponding L configuration polymers.

Since the LHG technique could detect small numbers of antibody-producing cells early in the immune response, an attempt was made to detect antibody stimulated by GLA^{30} (LLD), (DLL), and GA (LL) which ordinarily are weaker immunogens in the rabbit than GLA^{30} (LLL). However, even the sensitive technique of LHG could not detect antibody synthesis 5 to 6 days after rabbits had been immunized with these polymers. Thus the LHG technique has confirmed previous experiments which demonstrated that introduction of a D-amino acid into a copolymer containing L-amino acids will reduce considerably the immunogenicity of this polymer (18).

The cross-reaction patterns of GLA^{30} (LLL) immune lymph node cells against GLA^{5} and GLA^{40} demonstrate that in a random bred population of rabbits, the specificity of the antibody from individual rabbits can be directed against different determinants in the same antigenic molecule. Thus the data from PFC experiments showed that some rabbits produced antibody which cross-reacted significantly with GLA^{5}, while most of the antibody produced by other rabbits cross-reacted with GLA^{40} and others produced antibody which cross-reacted equally with both GLA^{40} and GLA^{5}.

Several laboratories have offered proof that both the ability to respond to a given antigenic determinant and the specificity of the antibody produced is genetically determined (23–25). Thus the different patterns of cross-reacting antibodies observed early in the immune response may be due to differences in the genetic background of rabbits in the random bred population.

Acknowledgment. The authors wish to acknowledge the many fruitful discussions and the contributions to this work made by the late Dr. Paul Pinchuck.

REFERENCES

1. Maurer, P. H., *Progress in Allergy*, Vol. 8, p. 1, S. Karger, Basel, 1964.
2. Sela, M., Advances Immun., *5:* 1, 1966.
3. Maurer, P. H. and Pinchuck, P., *Nucleic Acids in Immunology*, p. 301, Springer-Verlag, Berlin, 1969.
4. Borek, F., Stupp, Y. and Sela, M., Biochim. Biophys. Acta, *140:* 360, 1967.
5. Arnon, R. and Sela, M., Proc. Nat. Acad. Sci., *62:* 163, 1969.
6. Jerne, N. K. and Nordin, A. A., Science, *140:* 405, 1963.
7. Ingraham, J. S. and Bussard, A. J., J. Exp. Med., *121:* 667, 1964.
8. Walsh, P., Maurer, P. H. and Egan, M., J. Immun., *98:* 344, 1967.
9. Walsh, P., Maurer, P. H. and Egan, M., J. Immun., *100:* 266, 1968.
10. Bernier, G. and Cebra, J. J., J. Immun., *95:* 246, 1965.
11. Pernis, B., Chippino, G., Kelus, D. S. and Gell, P. G. H., J. Exp. Med., *122:* 853, 1965.
12. Mäkelä, O. J., J. Exp. Med., *126:* 159, 1967.
13. Sela, M. and Fuchs, S., *Methods in Immunology*, Vol. 1, p. 167, Academic Press, New York, 1967.
14. Fraenkel-Conrat, H. A. and Olcott, H. S., J. Biol. Chem., *161:* 259, 1945.
15. Maurer, P. H., Gerulat, B. F. and Pinchuck, P., J. Exp. Med., *116:* 521, 1962.
16. Takatsy, G., Acta Microbiol. Acad. Sci. Hung., *4:* 365, 1955.
17. Ovary, Z., *Progress in Allergy*, Vol. 5, p. 459, S. Karger, Basel/New York, 1964.
18. Maurer, P. H., J. Exp. Med., *121:* 339, 1965.
19. Daniels, J. C. and Weigle, W. O., J. Immun., *101:* 1230, 1968.
20. Ingraham, J. S., Biegel, A. A., Watanabe, M. R. and Todd, C. W., J. Immun., *99:* 1023, 1967.
21. Maurer, P. H., Gerulat, B. F. and Pinchuck, P., J. Biol. Chem., *239:* 922, 1964.
22. Makëlä, O. J., J. Immun., *95:* 378, 1965.
23. McDevitt, H. O., J. Immun., *100:* 485, 1968.
24. Pinchuck, P. and Maurer, P. H., J. Exp. Med., *122:* 673, 1965.
25. McDevitt, H. O. and Benacerraf, B., Advances Immun., In press.

THE JOURNAL OF IMMUNOLOGY
Vol. 105, No. 3, September 1970

DETECTION OF IMMUNE RESPONSE AGAINST SYNTHETIC POLYMERS OF AMINO ACIDS EMPLOYING THE PLAQUE-FORMING CELL SYSTEM

IV. Effect of Incorporation of Soluble Polypeptides into the Plaque Assay Medium[1, 2]

MARIANNE EGAN[3] AND PAUL H. MAURER

From the Department of Biochemistry, Jefferson Medical College, Thomas Jefferson University, Philadelphia, Pennsylvania 19107

Received for publication February 2, 1970

Incorporation of homologous polypeptide (10^{-5} M) into plaque assay plates containing anti-GLA[30] (LLL) immune lymph node cells specifically inhibited these PFC. However, at lower levels of antigen incorporation an enhancement of PFC was noted. The enhancement was complement-dependent, did not occur with non-immune lymph node cells and was inhibited by specific anti-allotype serum. Cross-reaction studies suggested that the polypeptide did not enhance by merely optimally coating the erythrocytes. Serum titers were measured on modified localized hemolysis-in-gel plates. Titers were increased when certain concentrations of antigen were incorporated into these plates, thereby implicating the increased hemolytic efficiency of complement or antibody in the presence of excess antigen. Puromycin (5 to 25 μg/ml) did not inhibit the production of unenhanced plaques, but prevented the optimal enhancement of plaques by antigen. These same concentrations of puromycin inhibited (40% to 96%, respectively) the incorporation of ^{14}C-L-leucine into trichloroacetic acid precipitable protein. The inclusion of polypeptide in the incubation medium increased the above incorporation by 20% to 170%; puromycin in addition to polypeptide prevented this increase, although the radioactivity was above that obtained when puromycin alone was present. A similar effect was noted with chloramphenicol. The results suggest that enhancement of anti-polypeptide plaques by incorporation of polymer in the medium is a complex phenomenon and is probably due to at least two factors: the increased hemolytic efficiency of immunoglobulin or complement in the presence of excess antigen, and the stimulation of protein synthesis in immune lymph node cells in the presence of excess antigen.

Inhibition of immunologic reactions by excess homologous antigen or fragments of antigen is a useful tool for examining the serologic specificity of a reaction. This principle has been applied to the "*in vitro*" localized hemolysis-in-gel technique in attempts to prove the immunologic nature of the "plaques" detected. Plaques against penicillin, ovalbumin, DNP-lysine, and immunoglobulins have been inhibited by incorporation of soluble antigen into the plaquing medium (1–5).

The present report deals with proving the antigenic specificity of plaque-forming cells (PFC) directed against synthetic polypeptides (6) by incorporating these antigens into the assay medium. Although certain concentrations of polypeptides inhibited PFC, enhanced numbers of PFC were observed when concentrations slightly below the "inhibiting" level were included in the plaquing plates.

The possibilities that incorporation of excess

[1] This work was supported by Grants A1-07825 and T1A1-334 from the National Institute of Allergy and Infectious Diseases and Public Health Service Predoctoral Fellowship 1-F1-GM-38,458-01. Paper 34 in a series of "Antigenicity of Polypeptides (Poly-α-Amino Acids)."

[2] This paper was presented in part at the 53rd Annual Meeting of the Federation of American Societies for Experimental Biology, Atlantic City, New Jersey, April, 1969.

[3] Public Health Service Predoctoral Fellow. Taken from a thesis submitted in partial fulfillment of the requirements for the Doctor of Philosophy Degree in Biochemistry.

polypeptide into the plaquing plates increased PFC by either optimally coating the tanned erythrocytes with antigen, increasing lytic efficiency of immunoglobulin by the formation of antigen-antibody complexes, increasing cell viability or permeability, or stimulating secretion and/or synthesis of immunoglobulins are considered and discussed in this report.

MATERIALS AND METHODS

Immunization with polypeptides. All lymph nodes tested for plaque-forming cells were from rabbits immunized 5 to 7 days previously with 20 mg of poly-α-(L-glu^{42}-L-lys^{28}-L-ala^{30}) in complete Freund's adjuvant, except for three rabbits (522, 525, 538) which were immunized with poly-α-(L-glu^{57}-L-lys^{38}-L-ala^{5}). Polymers examined for their *in vitro* effect on PFC were poly-α-(L-glu^{42}-L-lys^{28}-L-ala^{30}), poly-α-(D-glu^{42}-D-lys^{28}-D-ala^{30}), poly-α-(L-glu^{57}-L-lys^{38}-L-ala^{5}), poly-α-(L-glu^{36}-L-lys^{24}-L-ala^{40}), poly-α-(L-glu^{60}-L-lys^{40}), and poly-α-(L-glu^{100}).[4] The molecular weights of the polymers varied from 36,000 to 90,000.

Plaque assay plates. Plaque assay plates were prepared with polypeptide-coated tanned erythrocytes as in the previous paper (6). To study the effect of incorporation of additional soluble antigen in the medium (in addition to the polypeptide on the erythrocytes), 0.1 ml of polymers (0.7 μg to 2700 μg/ml) was incorporated into the plaquing medium at the time when lymph node cells and erythrocytes were added.

Viability studies. To study the effect of polypeptides on the viability of immune and nonimmune lymph node cells, popliteal lymph nodes were removed from immune or from normal rabbits. Cell suspensions were made (20 $\times$ 10^6 lymph node cells/ml in Eagle's medium) and incubated with or without antigen (740 μg/ml). Viable cell counts were determined by the trypan blue dye exclusion test 1 to 5 hr after incubation (37°) under 5% CO_2.

Hemolytic titers on localized hemolysis-in-gel (LHG) plates. The use of LHG assay plates to determine hemolysin titers in serum was similar to the method reported by Uyeki and Klassen (7). The usual plaque assay plates were made with the omission of lymph node cells. Serial dilutions of sera were made in Eagle's medium and 0.025 ml of each dilution was spotted on duplicate LHG plates. After the plates were incubated for 1 hr (37°) in an atmosphere of 5% CO_2, 2 ml of a 1:10 dilution of guinea pig serum in Eagle's medium were added and the plates were incubated for an additional 30 min. Hemolytic titers are reported as the reciprocal of the highest dilution which led to a visible spot of lysis on the antigen-coated sheep erythrocyte layer. To detect the effect of excess soluble antigen on the hemolytic titers, soluble antigen was incorporated into the upper layer of some of these plates.

^{14}C-L-leucine incorporation into TCA-precipitable protein. Cell suspensions were made in Eagle's medium 5 to 7 days after a primary immunization with GLA^{30} (LLL) and incubated in a rotating incubator under 5% CO_2 for 30 min (37°) in the presence or absence of puromycin (5, 20, or 25 μg/ml) or chloramphenicol (50 μg/ml).[5] After this preincubation, 2 μCi of ^{14}C-L-leucine were added to each flask. At this time, GLA^{30} (LLL) or GLA^{30} (DDD) (final concentration, 740 μg/ml) was also added to some flasks. Incubation was continued for 2 hr; then the reaction was stopped and the cells were lysed by rapid freezing and thawing. To exclude possible nonspecific adsorption of ^{14}C-leucine by polymer present in the experimental tubes and also to provide a protein carrier, the concentration of polymer in all tubes was adjusted to 2 mg/ml immediately before freezing. Protein was then precipitated by adding an equal volume of 10% cold trichloracetic acid (TCA). The precipitate that formed after 5 hr at 0° was washed three times with 5% cold TCA, once in 5% TCA at 90° for 15 min to hydrolyze nucleic acids, once in ether:ethanol (1:3) to remove lipids, and finally in ether. The dry precipitate was solubilized in Nuclear Chicago Solubilizer (NCS) and washed into a scintillation vial with 10 ml of scintillation fluid (2,5-diphenyloxazole) 4.0 g; 1,4 bis [2-(5 phenyloxazolyl)] benzene, 100 mg; toluene, 1000 ml). Radioactivity was determined in a Nuclear Chicago liquid scintillation counter. The radioactivity present in the total TCA precipitable protein was corrected for nonspecific counts by subtraction of a zero time control.

[4] Nonmenclature based on recommendation of IUPAC-IUB Commission on Biochemical Nomenclature, October, 1967, Biochem. J., *106:* 577 (1968). Abbreviations used in the text for the above polymers are respectively: GLA^{30} (LLL), GLA^{30} (DDD), GLA^{5}, GLA^{40}, GL, poly-G.

[5] Chloramphenicol was a kind gift of Dr. Fisher, Parke, Davis, and Co., Detroit, Michigan.

RESULTS

Effect of incorporation of antigen into the plaque assay medium. The original reason for incorporating excess soluble polymer into the plaque assay plates containing anti-polypeptide immunocytes was to prove the specificity of the anti-polymer plaques by inhibiting the appearance of plaques on these plates. Although inhibition of GLA^{30} (LLL) PFC was always observed on plates containing more than 740 μg/ml (2.3×10^{-5} M) of homologous antigen (GLA^{30} LLL), in many experiments the number of PFC on plates containing 74 or 740 μg/ml of GLA^{30} (LLL) was increased from 5 to 10 times above those detected on plates without excess antigen (Fig. 1). The weakly cross-reacting antigen GLA^{30} (DDD) also enhanced the number of PFC produced against GLA^{30} (LLL) (Fig. 2). With increase in interval after immunization, lower concentrations of homologous polymer inhibited PFC and no enhancement was observed; heterologous polymer continued to enhance.

Immunologic nature and specificity of the enhancement phenomenon. No PFC were observed on plates prepared with or without the addition of excess polymer which contained a) non-immune lymph node cells, b) immune lymph node cells and heat-inactivated complement, or c) an inhibiting concentration of anti-allotype serum. Incubation of immune and non-immune lymph node cells with antigen did not affect the viability of the total cell population. Incorporation of 5% agammaglobulin horse serum into the plaquing medium did not significantly change the number of PFC.

The incorporation of the cross-reacting polymers GLA^{30} (DDD), GLA^{5}, GLA^{40}, GL and poly-G into the plaquing medium also increased to a variable extent the number of PFC detected with GLA^{30} (LLL)-coated erythrocytes (Table I). For example, with lymph node cells from rabbit 505, a significant amount of glutamyl specificity appeared to be involved in the enhancement phenomenon since GLA^{5}, GL, and poly-G en-

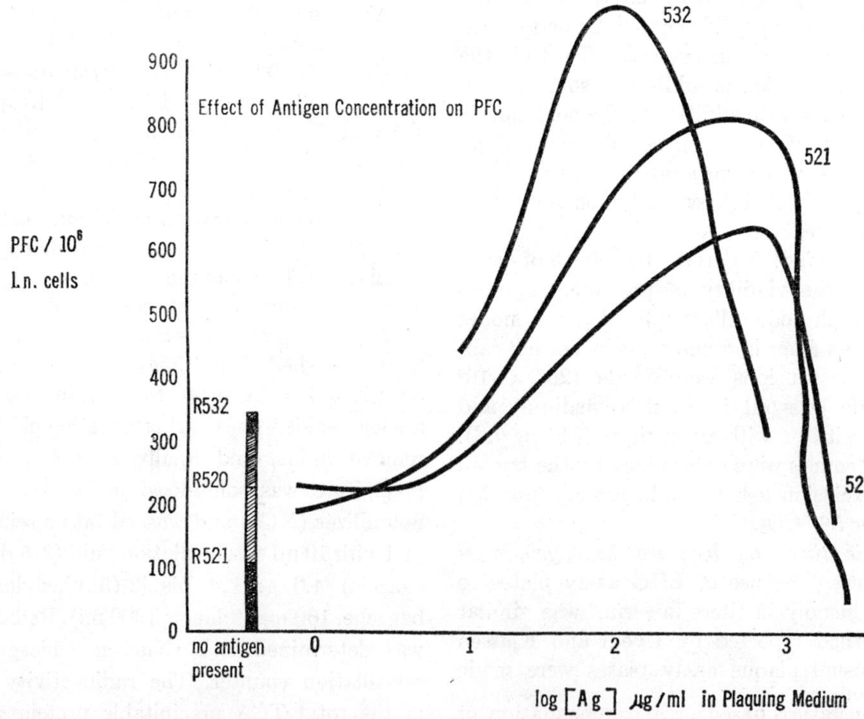

Figure 1. Effect of incorporation of additional homologous polypeptide in assay medium on primary response PFC against synthetic polypeptides. GLA^{30} (LLL) was incorporated in the plaque assay system with anti-GLA^{30} (LLL) immune lymph node cells. The numbers of PFC observed without addition of the antigen are indicated by the bar to the left of the curves.

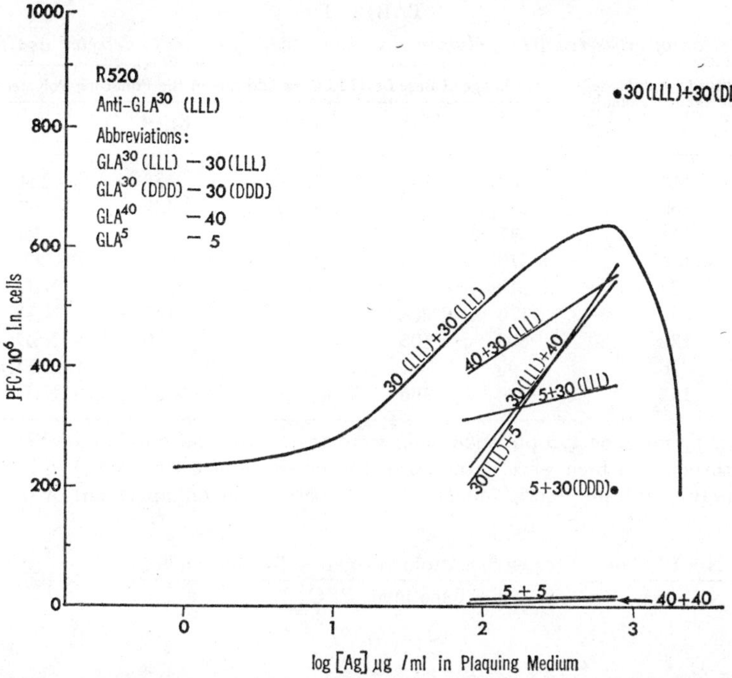

Figure 2. Effect of incorporation of immunochemically related polymers into the medium of assay plates or onto the erythrocytes on *anti-GLA*^{30} (*LLL*) *PFC*. The first number on each curve indicates the type of coated erythrocyte present in the medium; the second indicates the antigen incorporated into the medium. Unenhanced PFC/10^6 lymph node cells against erythrocytes coated with: GLA^{30} (LLL), 232; GLA^{40}, 67; GLA^5, 46; GLA^{30} (DDD), 3.

hanced 70%, 154%, and 108%, respectively. In contrast, PFC from rabbit 507 were enhanced to a greater extent by GLA^{40} (139%) than by polymers such as GL containing a higher proportion of glutamyl residues (53%). The polymer with 100% glutamyl residues, poly-G, inhibited these PFC (−33%).

Lymph node cells from rabbits immunized with GLA^{30} (LLL) or GLA^5 were tested for antibody production against cross-reacting antigens as described in the previous paper (6). The effect of incorporation of homologous and heterologous antigens in the plaquing medium was tested on these plates containing erythrocytes coated with homologous and heterologous antigens. Enhancement by the various polymers was specific since maximum enhancement of PFC by homologous polymers occurred only on those plates where the tanned erythrocytes were first coated with the antigen employed for immunization (Figs. 2 and 3).

Serum "titers" on LHG plates. Serum titrations were performed under conditions which duplicated those used in the LHG assay for immune lymph node cells. Although *inhibition* of serum "titers" occurred on those plates with 740 µg/ml of homologous polymer, an increase in "titer" was generally observed on those plates which contained lower concentrations of antigen (74, 7.4, or 0.74 µg/ml) (Table II). An increase in serum "titer" also occurred on those plates containing the heterologous antigen, GLA^{30} (DDD), although a higher concentration of this polymer was required for optimal enhancement of serum "titers."

Effect of puromycin on PFC. The effect of puromycin on PFC depended on the concentration of puromycin and the length of preincubation period. The normal levels of PFC were not affected if cells were preincubated for 30 min in 5 to 20 µg puromycin/ml or if these concentrations were incorporated directly onto the LHG plates. Preincubation in higher levels of puromycin (50 to 472 µg/ml, 30 min) caused a 20% and 54% inhibition of base level PFC, respectively, while 2 hr preincubation in 5 µg and 50 µg pu-

TABLE I

Effect of incorporation of cross-reacting polymers in assay medium on PFC detected against GLA³⁰ (LLL)

Rabbit No.	PFC/10^6 Lymph Node Cells Against Homologous GLA³⁰ (LLL)-Coated Erythrocytes	% Change of Base Level PFC by Addition of the Following Polymers to the Medium[a]					
		GLA³⁰ (LLL)	GLA³⁰ (DDD)	GLA⁵	GLA⁴⁰	GL	poly-G
505	13	463	100	70	−86	154	108
507	59	239	80	−25	139	53	−33
508	141	241	90	45	14	95	52
512	108	370	180	140	−36	360	280
518	139	219	226	N.D.[b]	N.D.	N.D.	N.D.
520	232	176	268	147	137	N.D.	N.D.
521	132	503	605	655	170	N.D.	N.D.
526	376	−99	51	−18	−51	N.D.	N.D.
527	152	−86	165	61	−85	N.D.	N.D.

[a] Anti-GLA³⁰ (LLL) immune lymph node cells were tested for the number of PFC against GLA³⁰ (LLL)-coated erythrocytes which were detected in the presence of GLA³⁰ (LLL), GLA³⁰ (DDD), GLA⁵, GLA⁴⁰, GL, and poly-G (all polymers, 740 μg/ml). The percentage enhancement or inhibition is calculated by:

$$\frac{\text{No. PFC on plates with soluble antigen} - \text{No. base level PFC}}{\text{No. base level PFC}} \times 100.$$

[b] N.D., not done.

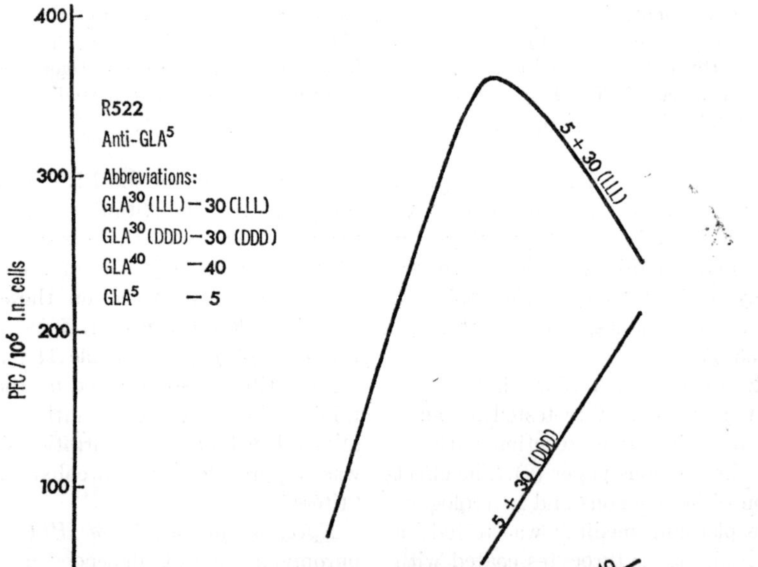

Figure 3. Effect of incorporation of immunochemically related polymers in the medium or onto the erythrocytes on *anti-GLA⁵ PFC*. The first number on each curve indicates the type of coated erythrocytes present in the medium; the second indicates the antigen incorporated into the medium. Unenhanced PFC/10^6 lymph node cells against erythrocytes coated with: GLA⁵, 9.9; GLA³⁰ (LLL), 1.0; GLA³⁰ (DDD), 0.1; GLA⁴⁰, 0.6.

TABLE II

Determination of serum "titers" on LHG plates in the presence and absence of polymer incorporated in the plaquing medium

Concentration of Polypeptide in Medium (μg/ml)	Hemolytic "Titer" for Rabbit No.			
	507	508	512	527
None	256	512	128	128
GLA^{30} (LLL), 740	128	128	128	64
GLA^{30} (LLL), 74	512	1024	4096	512
GLA^{30} (LLL), 7.4	2048	4096	512	4096
GLA^{30} (LLL), 0.74	4096	1024	256	
GLA^{30} (LLL), 0.074	256	512	128	
GLA^{30} (DDD), 740	128	512	512	256
GLA^{30} (DDD), 74	256	4096	256	256
GLA^{30} (DDD), 7.4	128	4096	256	256
GLA^{30} (DDD), 0.74	512	2048	256	

TABLE III

Effect of puromycin on enhancement phenomenon of PFC by polypeptide in the medium

Assay Medium	Rabbit No.				
	527	528	531	532	
	PFC/10^{6} lymph node cells				
Normal	164	20	536	353	
+ GLA^{30} (LLL)[a]	21	3	218	959	
+ GLA^{30} (DDD)	306	83	1120	1298	
Puromycin	160[b]	21[b]	660[c]	375[b]	370[c]
+ GLA^{30} (LLL)	12	3	67	697	551
+ GLA^{30} (DDD)	239	42	800	1111	766

[a] Rabbits 527, 528, 531 GLA^{30} (LLL) and GLA^{30} (DDD), 740 μg/ml; 532, GLA^{30} (LLL), 74 μg/ml; GLA^{30} (DDD), 740 μg/ml.

[b] Puromycin, 5 μg/ml.

[c] Puromycin, 20 μg/ml.

romycin/ml inhibited PFC 66% and 94%, respectively.

When concentrations of puromycin which did not affect the base level of PFC were incorporated into the LHG plates containing antigen, maximal enhancement by the antigen was not obtained (Table III). The degree of inhibition of enhancement was dependent on the concentration of puromycin.

Figure 4 illustrates the effect of two concentrations of puromycin on the relative enhancement of anti-GLA^{30} (LLL) PFC by various concentrations of GLA^{30} (DDD). Over the entire range of enhancement by polymer, preincubation in 5 μg/ml puromycin for 30 min inhibited the maximal enhancement of PFC. Preincubation in 50 μg/ml puromycin was more efficient in preventing enhancement by polymer, although at this concentration base level PFC were also inhibited. Preincubation in either concentration of puromycin for 2 hr completely prevented enhancement of PFC by polypeptide.

Effect of puromycin on ^{14}C-L-leucine incorporation into TCA-precipitable protein in the presence and absence of polypeptide. Lymph node cells removed 5 to 7 days after primary immunization with GLA^{30} (LLL) incorporated approximately 1800 to 1900 cpm/10^{6} lymph node cells into TCA precipitable protein when incubated for 2 hr in Eagle's medium containing 2 μCi ^{14}C-L-leucine (Table IV). Preincubation in puromycin, 20 μg/ml, for 30 min reduced this incorporation by 86% to 96%, while 5 μg/ml caused a 40% reduction in the radioactivity incorporated. Addition of the polymers GLA^{30} (LLL) or GLA^{30} (DDD) to the medium increased the incorporation by 20% to 670%, depending on the polymer and lymph node preparation. The increased ^{14}C-L-leucine incorporation in the presence of polymer was partially inhibited by puromycin, but the presence of the polymer partially overcame the inhibitory effect of puromycin. Although chloramphenicol (50 μg/ml) prevented the optimal enhancement of ^{14}C-L-leucine incorporation stimulated by the GLA^{30} (LLL) polymer, its effect was not as dramatic as that of puromycin and it had no effect on the stimulation of incorporation observed with GLA^{30} (DDD).

DISCUSSION

The results presented indicate that anti-polypeptide plaques are inhibited by incorporation into the assay medium of specific concentrations of polymer, a method which has shown the specificity of PFC formation in anti-hapten and anti-protein systems (1–5). However, to our knowledge the *enhancement* of PFC when certain concentrations of antigen are incorporated into the assay medium has not been observed heretofore.

In agreement with classical inhibition systems, anti-GLA^{30} (LLL) PFC were inhibited more efficiently by homologous antigen, GLA^{30} (LLL),

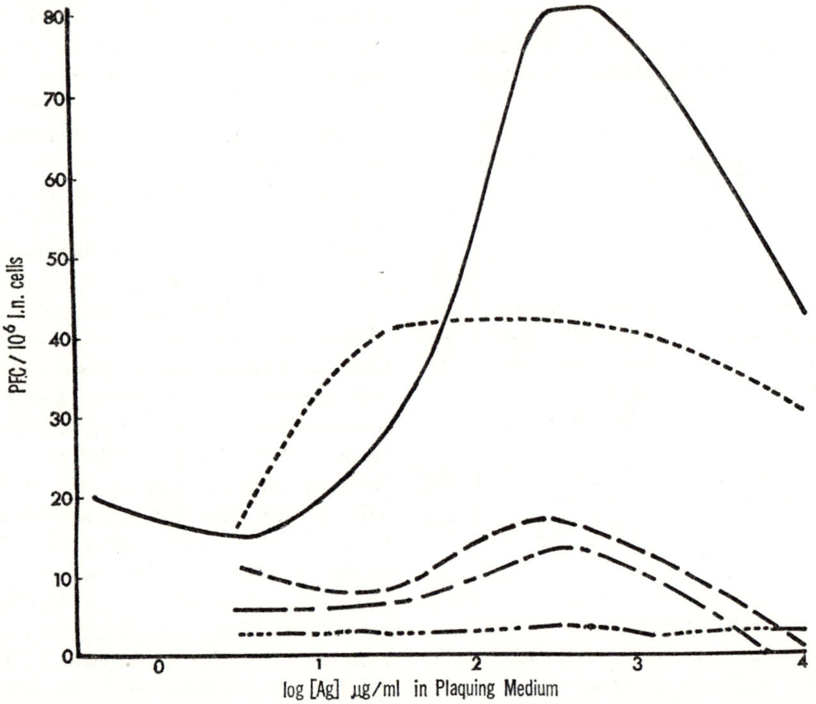

Figure 4. Effect of puromycin on enhancement by GLA^{30} (DDD) of anti-GLA^{30} (LLL) PFC by preincubation in puromycin and incorporation of puromycin and various polypeptide concentrations on assay plates. Eighteen PFC/10^{6} lymph node cells were present on plates without excess antigen. Legend: ——, PFC on control plates; -----, preincubation in puromycin, 5 µg/ml, 30 min; – – –, preincubation in puromycin, 50 µg/ml, 30 min; – - – -, preincubation in puromycin, 5 µg/ml, 2 hr; – · · · · –, preincubation in puromycin, 50 µg/ml, 2 hr.

TABLE IV

^{14}*C-L-Leucine incorporation into trichloroacetic acid precipitable protein by GLA*^{30} (LLL) *immune lymph node cells in the presence or absence of puromycin and/or polypeptide*

Assay Medium	Exp. 1	Exp. 2	Exp. 3
	cpm/10^{6} *lymph node cells*		
Eagle's medium	752[a], 1836	1937	1942
+ GLA^{30} (LLL)[b]		3049	2274
+ GLA^{30} (DDD)	5082	1685	2337
Puromycin	450[a], 592[c]	112[d]	299[d]
+ GLA^{30} (LLL)		1055	523
+ GLA^{30} (DDD)		492	431
Chloramphenicol		1126[e]	
+ GLA^{30} (LLL)		2479	
+ GLA^{30} (DDD)		2607	

[a] Incubation for 60 min after addition of isotope. All other incubations were for 120 min.
[b] Polypeptide, 740 µg/ml.
[c] Puromycin, 5 µg/ml.
[d] Puromycin, 20 µg/ml.
[e] Chloramphenicol, 50 µg/ml.

rather than by the heterologous polymers GLA^{30} (DDD), GLA^{40}, and GLA^{5}. In contrast to the behavior with classical inhibition reactions, certain concentrations of polypeptide in the plaque assay medium (74 to 740 µg/ml) resulted in increased rather than decreased PFC. However, often a heterologous polymer enhanced more efficiently than did the homologous polymer. At least two factors might determine the degree of enhancement observed with a given concentration of the polymer in this system: 1) an inhibition reaction which occurs according to classical mechanisms, and which is greater with the homologous antigen; and 2) a stimulation which is due to some other mechanism, and which is also greater with the homologous polymer. However, since the finally observed degree of enhancement is determined by the true enhancement minus the inhibition, the more efficient inhibitor, i.e., the homologous polymer, will apparently produce a lower degree of enhancement under some circumstances since it also inhibits better, while the heterologous polymer, which only enhances and has little inhibitory power, will *appear* to enhance more than the homologous polymer.

The following observations indicate that the enhancement by antigen is a true immunologic phenomenon: 1) the plaques are complement-dependent and appear only on plates containing specific immune lymph node cells; 2) enhanced plaques are inhibited by specific anti-allotype serum; and 3) the phenomenon has all the specificities one would expect from an immunologic reaction, that is, enhancement will occur with polypeptides immunochemically related to the immunizing antigen and will not occur with a non-related protein such as agammaglobulin horse serum. The specificity of the enhancement for the polypeptide system was also shown by the absence of any effect on the number of PFC directed against the arsanilate and dinitrophenyl groups when these polypeptides were incorporated into the respective assay plates. (These experiments were kindly performed by Drs. J. Ingraham and T. Hraba, respectively.)

The enhancement of PFC by polymer may be due to one or more of the following factors.

1. Excess polymer in the medium may have increased the efficiency of coating the tanned erythrocytes with antigen and thus made them more susceptible to immune lysis. This is not a likely mechanism for enhancement since cross-reacting polymers occasionally enhanced to a greater extent than the immunizing antigen, but only when the immunizing antigen was previously coated on the tanned erythrocytes. The results obtained with puromycin also do not favor this hypothesis, since a concentration of puromycin which did not inhibit the base level of PFC prevented the optimal enhancement of PFC by antigen.

2. Since incorporation of serum is necessary to maintain the viability of cells producing IgA antibody (8), it was considered possible that excess polypeptide might have functioned by a similar mechanism. The viability studies suggested that this was not the case. Nevertheless the possibility that the polypeptide affected the viability of a certain small population of immune lymph node cells still cannot be excluded.

3. Some highly charged polymers, such as polynucleotides (10), and other compounds, such as endotoxin and chlorpromazine (11, 12), are known to nonspecifically increase cell permeability. The polymer used in these experiments, composed of 42% glutamic acid and 28% lysine, and which has a net negative charge similar to serum albumin, might possibly have exerted such an effect. However, this possibility can be excluded since synthetic polypeptides did not increase anti-DNP or anti-arsanilate PFC.

4. IgG immunoglobulins must be complexed with anti-immunoglobulin for efficient lysis of antigen coated erythrocytes. By analogy with this situation, it was considered possible that a certain ratio of antigen complexed with antibody in the LHG assay increased the lytic efficiency of the antibody rather than inhibited it. Part of the enhancement phenomenon may indeed be due to increased lytic efficiency of antibody in the presence of excess antigen since serum titers on LHG plates were higher on those assay plates which contained certain concentrations of soluble antigen in addition to the polymer-coated erythrocytes. These results could also be interpreted as being due to increased efficiency of coating the tanned erythrocytes by soluble polypeptides. However the previously mentioned cross-reaction experiments tend to rule out this possibility.

5. It has been reported that the concentrations of Ca^{++} (1.27×10^{-3} M) and Mg^{++} (8.9×10^{-4} M) present in the assay medium (Eagle's basal medium) are too high for the optimal activity of guinea pig complement (13). Therefore, the possibility that some of the glutamyl residues of the polypeptide antigen might have chelated some of the Ca^{++} and established optimal conditions for complement activity was considered. This mechanism is eliminated by the fact that polymers with the same percentage of glutamyl residues but with the amino acids in different configurations, GLA^{30} (LLL) and (DDD), enhanced to different extents in the assay of individual rabbit PFC.

6. Excess antigen may have exerted its effect directly on the lymph node cells by causing increased secretion of antibody, increased synthesis of antibody, or differentiation of primed cells into antibody-producing cells. The results presented here suggest that some enhancement was due to stimulation of protein synthesis. Puromycin (5 μg/ml to 25 μg/ml) did not inhibit the base level of PFC, indicating that most of the PFC detected during the 4.5-hr incubation period were due to preformed antibody which was released during the incubation period. This is in agreement with the observations of Helm-

reich *et al.* (14, 15), who showed that most antibody-secreting cells contain enough preformed antibodies to continue secretion up to 2 hr after incubation in puromycin (47.2 μg/ml). Fitch *et al.* (9) and Strander (16) also found no inhibition of PFC at these concentrations of puromycin. The same concentration of puromycin which did not inhibit the base level of PFC prevented the maximal enhancement of PFC by excess antigen, indicating that protein synthesis is necessary in this enhancement phenomenon.

The concentrations of puromycin employed in the plaquing medium (5 to 25 μg/ml) were sufficient to inhibit protein synthesis as evidenced by 40% to 96% inhibition of ^{14}C-L-leucine incorporation into TCA precipitable protein. This correlates with the 14% to 49% reduction of enhancement observed when these concentrations of puromycin were included in the plaque assay plates.

An additional observation which suggested that polypeptide stimulated protein synthesis was that incubation with polypeptide increased the amount of ^{14}C-L-leucine incorporated into TCA precipitable protein by immune lymph node cells. This increased incorporation was inhibited by puromycin or chloramphenicol. Therefore, an analogous situation was observed in both types of experiments, i.e., specific antigen enhanced PFC and stimulated increased ^{14}C-L-leucine incorporation into protein, while puromycin inhibited the enhancing effect of polypeptide in both systems. This has been interpreted as circumstantial evidence that the increased radioactivity was due to specific antibody. Experiments are currently in progress to definitely prove this, by isolating the labeled antibody and demonstrating an increase in its specific activity.

Acknowledgments. The authors wish to acknowledge the valuable contributions of the late Dr. Paul Pinchuck and the helpful suggestions of Dr. George Kalf. We wish to thank Drs. J. Ingraham and T. Hraba for testing the synthetic polypeptides in the anti-arsanilate and anti-DNP systems.

REFERENCES

1. Harrell, B. E., Wright, W. and Merchant, B., Int. Arch. Allerg., *32:* 21, 1967.
2. Segre, M. and Segre, D., J. Immun., *99:* 867, 1967.
3. Layson, M. N. and Sehon, A. H., Canad. J. Biochem., *45:* 1773, 1967.
4. Hraba, T. and Havas, H. F., Fed. Proc., *28:* 814, 1969.
5. Segre, M., Segre, D. and Inman, F. P., J. Immun., *102:* 1368, 1969.
6. Egan, M. and Maurer, P. H., J. Immun., *105:* 704, 1970.
7. Uyeki, E. M. and Klassen, R. S., J. Immun., *101:* 271, 1968.
8. Walters, C. S. and Jackson, A. L., J. Immun., *101:* 541, 1968.
9. Fitch, F. W., Roseman, J. M. and Rowley, D. A., Nature, *218:* 972, 1968.
10. Brown, W., Nakano, M., Jaraskova, L., Yajima, Y. and Jiminez, L., in *Nucleic Acids in Immunology*, p. 347, Springer-Verlag, New York, 1968.
11. Becker, G. A. and Pisciotta, A. V., Proc. Soc. Exp. Biol. Med., *124:* 764, 1967.
12. Friedman, H. H., Fox, A. E. and Willis, R. S., Proc. Soc. Exp. Biol. Med., *129:* 796, 1968.
13. Hubner, K. F. and Gengozian, N., J. Immun., *102:* 155, 1969.
14. Helmreich, E., Kern, M. and Eisen, H. N., J. Biol. Chem., *236:* 464, 1961.
15. Helmreich, E., Kern, M. and Eisen, H. N., J. Biol. Chem., *237:* 1925, 1962.
16. Strander, H., Immunology, *10:* 45, 1966.

THE JOURNAL OF IMMUNOLOGY
Vol. 105, No. 3, September 1970

DIFFERENTIATION OF ROSETTE-FORMING CELLS FROM MYELOID STEM CELLS[1]

G. E. EDWARDS,[2] R. G. MILLER AND R. A. PHILLIPS

From the Ontario Cancer Institute and the Department of Medical Biophysics, University of Toronto, Toronto, Ontario, Canada

Received for publication January 26, 1970

Evidence is presented that the myeloid and lymphoid systems of the adult mouse are derived from a common stem cell. Ionizing radiation was used to induce unique chromosome markers in individual stem cells of the myeloid system. This marked stem cell was injected into genetically anemic mice of genotype W/W^v and repopulated their myeloid systems with chromosomally marked cells. To determine whether or not cells of the lymphoid system also contained the chromosome marker, we purified rosette-forming cells from the spleens of mice bearing a marker.

Mice were immunized with sheep erythrocytes (SRBC), and at the peak of the secondary immune response a spleen cell suspension was prepared. Cells in this suspension were allowed to bind SRBC and form rosettes, and the rosette-forming cells (RFC) were purified by velocity sedimentation. The RFC population appears to include all antibody-producing cells, but the converse may not be true. Karyotype analysis of the purified rosettes showed a high frequency of chromosomally marked cells, indicating that some RFC can be derived from stem cells that can also differentiate into myeloid cells.

These stem cells are probably pluripotent and able to give rise to RFC of many specificities. RFC specific for SRBC were found among the progeny of all the clones examined. It is highly unlikely that stem cells with restricted specificity would give such a result. The simplest interpretation is that there exist in bone marrow of adult mice pluripotent stem cells able to differentiate into functional cells of both the myeloid and lymphoid systems.

It is well established that different cells of the myeloid system are derived from a single stem cell, the spleen colony-forming cell (1), the most convincing evidence being that of Wu *et al.* (2). There is, however, only indirect evidence to suggest that these stem cells also produce lymphoid progeny[3] (3–6). A direct demonstration of this hypothesis would be to show that functional cells of the lymphoid system are derived from the same cell that repopulates the myeloid system (3). This paper contains such a demonstration.

We proceeded on the hypothesis that the lymphoid and myeloid systems do have a common precursor. The method of Wu *et al.* (2) was used to obtain clones of cells derived from a single stem cell bearing a unique radiation-induced chromosome marker. The advantage of the method is that the presence of this marker is unequivocal proof that this cell is derived from the marked stem cell. Presence of the marker in cells of a spleen colony was taken as evidence of myeloid function. The test for lymphoid function was more difficult.

The functional cells of the immune system that we chose to investigate were the rosette-forming cells (RFC). RFC are produced in large numbers during an immune response to foreign erythrocytes and are distinguished by their ability to

[1] This investigation was supported by the National Cancer Institute of Canada and the Donner Canadian Foundation.

[2] Recipient of a Studentship from the Medical Research Council.

[3] The word *lymphoid* is used here to refer to the class of cells involved in the immune response, and *myeloid* refers to erythrocytes, granulocytes and megakaryocytes, i.e., cells found in spleen colonies.

bind heterologous erthrocytes to their surfaces. A particular RFC appears to bind only one kind of foreign erythrocyte. It is generally assumed that RFC produced during an immune response are antibody-producing cells. RFC and antibody-producing cells have similar specificities and kinetics of production (7).

An unambiguous demonstration of the chromosome marker in lymphoid tissue required cell populations highly enriched in the lymphoid cell chosen. To accomplish this we used velocity sedimentation, a procedure which separates cells primarily on the basis of size (8). Since the cluster of cells forming a rosette is much larger than most single cells (only megakaryocytes and a few granulocytes are as large), a highly enriched population of rosettes can be easily obtained.

MATERIALS AND METHODS

Mice. Control experiments were done using F1 hybrids between C57Bl/6JOci and C3H/HeOci (C3B6F1) obtained from the animal colony at the Ontario Cancer Institute. The mice were housed three to four to a cage. Chromosome marker experiments were done with mice of genotype W/W^v and littermate controls were obtained from the Jackson Laboratory, Bar Harbor, Maine, or from the Ontario Cancer Institute. The mice were housed one or two to a cage. All mice were allowed free access to food and water.

Irradiation of mice. Mice were irradiated in a ^{137}Cs irradiator (9) at a dose rate of 106 rads/min.

Immunization. Sheep erythrocytes (SRBC) were used as antigens throughout. Citrated sheep blood obtained from Woodland Farms Limited, Guelph, Ontario, was stored at 4°C. Before use, SRBC were washed three times in cold phosphate-buffered saline (PBS) (10).

Mice were immunized with two intravenous injections of 4×10^8 red cells 4 weeks apart except in one case when the mice received three immunizations at 4-week intervals. In all cases the mice were killed 4 days after the final immunization.

Cell preparation and cell counting. Suspensions of spleen cells were made by placing the spleens in 1 ml of cold PBS and repeatedly forcing the spleen tissue through a 1-ml plastic syringe. Large clumps were allowed to settle and were removed. The cells were centrifuged at $220 \times G$ for 10 min, resuspended in 5% fetal calf serum (FCS) in PBS and then filtered through a 37-μ capillary array filter (Mosaic Fabrications, Sturbridge, Mass.) to remove any remaining cell clumps. A portion of this suspension was used to form rosettes and was then refiltered through the capillary array filter. The final filtration did not disrupt the rosettes. Suspensions of bone marrow cells were obtained by flushing cold PBS through the femur. This cell suspension was used without further washing or filtration.

Cell counts of marrow and spleen were made with a hemocytometer. Fractions obtained after cell separation were counted with an electronic cell counter.

Chromosomal analysis. Mice to be analyzed were injected intraperitoneally with 67.5 μg of colchicine 1 hr before sacrifice. The small number of cells available after purification of RFC required that a new method of karyotype analysis be developed to mimimize loss of cells.

The cells, suspended in PBS, were diluted 20-fold in 1% sodium citrate to a final cell concentration not to exceed 10^6 cells/ml. The suspension was incubated in a water bath at 37°C for 15 min. After incubation 1 drop of fresh fixative (glacial acetic acid:methanol, 1:3) per milliliter of hypotonic solution was immediately added. Six or more drops of this suspension were put on a clean, breath-moistened slide and allowed to sit for 15 min while the cells attached to the slide. The slide was then very carefully immersed into fresh fixative, as cells at this stage are fragile and easily broken, making them unsuitable for karyotype analysis. The best procedure was to tilt the container of fixative at a 45° angle and slowly lower the slide into the fixative, holding the slide as close to horizontal as possible. The slide was transferred to fresh fixative after 15 sec. During this transfer, the slide could be held vertically. After 5 min in the second fixative, the slide was again transferred to fresh fixative. After 5 min in the third fixative, the slide was removed, the excess fixative wiped off the back of the slide, and the remaining fixative ignited. When the slides were completely dry, they were stained with Giemsa stain or with 0.6% toluidine blue.

If the starting cell suspension was in a medium containing serum, it was necessary to remove the serum by centrifugation (10 min at $135 \times G$), resuspension in PBS and a second centrifugation. All but 0.1 ml of the final supernatant was removed, and 0.9 ml of 0.8% sodium citrate was added. After a 15-min incubation at 37°C, the standard procedure for chromosome preparation on slides as just described was followed.

All metaphases were examined under oil immersion at 1100 × magnification. Only chromosome spreads with 40 clearly discernible chromosomes were included in the data.

Rosette formation. Published methods for rosette formation require long periods of incubation (2 to 16 hr) (7, 11–15); unfortunately, these methods destroy chromosome morphology. To avoid this difficulty, we developed a centrifugation technique that allows rapid formation of rosettes: 2×10^7 washed spleen cells were mixed with 1.4 to 2.0×10^8 red blood cells in 5% FCS. This suspension was centrifuged at 220 × G for 10 min at 4°C and the pellet was incubated an additional 15 min at 4°C. Control experiments showed that the rosettes formed by centrifugation are identical to rosettes formed by other methods (16).

RFC were scored using a specially designed, large hemocytometer. Any cell with three or more erythrocytes bound to its surface was scored as a rosette. In the separation experiments, rosettes containing only three SRBC were found only near the top of the gradient. Those in the region of interest near the bottom of the gradient contained 10 and usually more SRBC.

Detection of rosettes and granulocytes on filters. Cell suspensions in which rosettes had been preformed were collected on Millipore filters and stained by the method of Fowler *et al.* (17). This histochemical test detects granulocytes because of their high content of peroxidase enzyme, and, in addition, allows rosettes to be scored since the stain colors erythrocytes a light yellow. Mitotic cells can also be recognized. However, two minor modifications of this method were required to permit the observation of rosettes. First, instead of pulling the cells onto the filters by suction, a process which appeared to tear rosettes apart, the cells were allowed to settle onto the filter under the force of gravity. Secondly, 1 ml of 0.5% of glutaraldehyde (w/v) in PBS was passed through the filter before it was placed in the fixative and the standard procedure for peroxidase staining was followed.

Assay for antibody-producing cells. Hemolysin-producing cells were detected by the technique of Jerne *et al.* (18). Indirect or 7S globulin-producing cells were detected by the method of Dresser and Wortis (19) as previously described (20).

Cell separation. The sedimentation chamber (Fig. 1) is constructed from two circular sheets of Lucite separated by a Lucite ring 1.8 cm high and 30 cm in diameter: the chamber has a volume of 1270 ml. The bottom sheet is glued to the Lucite ring; to facilitate cleaning the upper sheet is bolted to the Lucite ring with 12 bolts. A large O-ring provides a seal between the top sheet and the Lucite ring. On the outer edges are two stainless steel outlets (0.64 cm o.d.), one on the upper surface and the other 180° from it on the lower surface. Ninety degrees from each opening a short stainless steel rod is inserted in the Lucite ring and clamped to a stand. This allows the chamber to be rotated on its axis during the loading and unloading procedures.

The separation procedure (Fig. 2) consists of these steps: a) The chamber is filled with PBS and all air bubbles are removed. It is then rotated 30° from the horizontal plane and filled through the lower inlet with a linear gradient of 15 to 30% FCS (or 1 to 2% bovine serum albumin (BSA)) while PBS is displaced through the upper outlet. This procedure takes approximately 1 hr. The protein gradients prevent mixing during the mechanical manipulations, and help maintain cell viability. b) A cell suspension of 280 ml with 4×10^6 cells/ml in 5% FCS (or 0.5% BSA) is siphoned through the upper inlet with the chamber still in the tilted position. Introduction of cells into the chamber takes 11 to 12 min. c) The chamber is carefully returned to the horizontal position; the suspension flows over the upper gradient surface forming a sharp band 4 mm thick. The difference in density between the cell layer and the top of the gradient provides the stability necessary to prevent the cell suspension from mixing with the gradient. The cells are allowed to sediment for 40 to 60 min; with longer sedimentation times, some rosettes fall to the bottom of the chamber and are difficult to collect. d) After sedimentation the chamber is tilted to 30° and six fractions of 200 ml each are collected from the lower outlet while PBS is run into the upper outlet. Collection of fractions requires 30 to 35 min. Each fraction is concentrated to 17 ml by centrifugation, and aliquots of these concentrated suspensions are used for various assays.

Production of chromosomally marked stem cells. Mice with abnormal karyotypes were generated as described by Wu *et al.* (2). Two methods for obtaining marked spleen cells were used (Fig. 3).

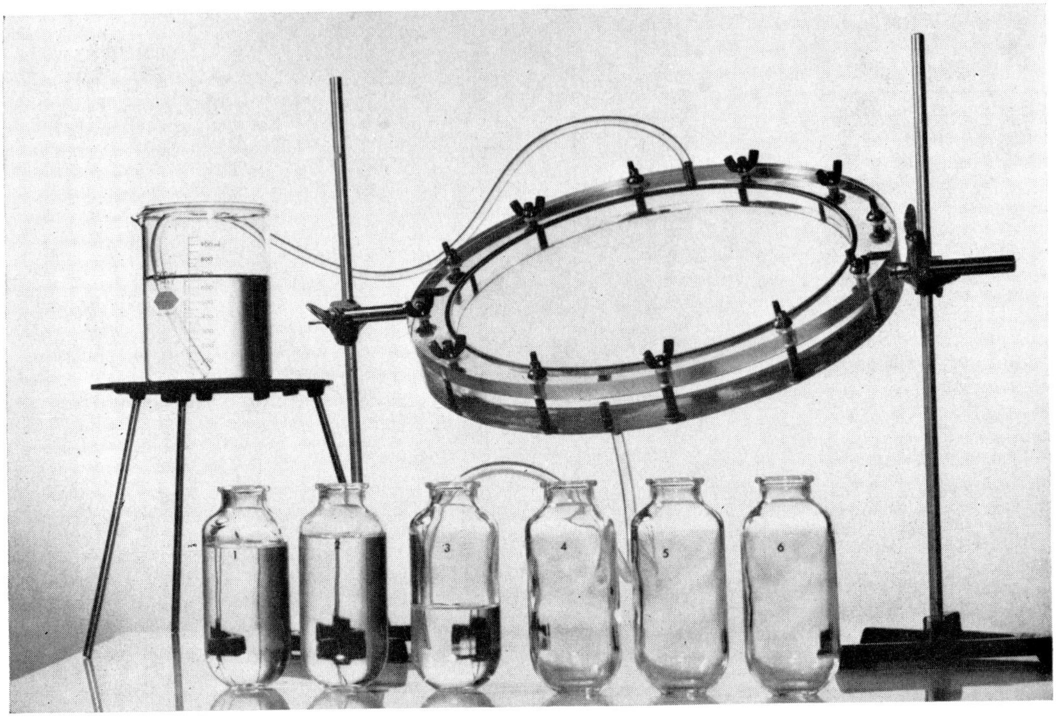

Figure 1. Photograph of separation chamber. The chamber is shown in the tilted position used to collect fractions after sedimentation (see Figure 2).

Chromosome aberrations were induced in stem cells by irradiation of the donor mice which were normal female mice coisogenic with W/W^v. In early experiments, donors were exposed to two doses of 425 rads 5 hr apart. In later experiments, we found that a single dose of 700 rads was sufficient. In either case, 10 to 30% of the stem cells surviving irradiation contained unique chromosome aberrations that do not appear to alter cellular function (2, 6, 21, 22). The irradiated donor bone marrow was injected into W/W^v recipients that had received 200 rads whole body irradiation. (The advantages of using W/W^v recipients at this stage have been discussed in detail by Wu *et al.* (2).) The number of bone marrow cells transplanted, 1×10^7, was calculated (2) to give only a few surviving stem cells since the goal was to produce W/W^v recipients whose entire myeloid system was repopulated with progeny from a single, chromosomally marked stem cell. Two to 6 months after transplantation the W/W^v recipients were immunized with SRBC and were examined individually for the presence of an abnormal karyotype in their bone marrow cells. We used the criterion of 50% abnormal karyotypes in bone marrow to select the mice that were likely to be repopulated by a single, marked clone of myeloid stem cells (2).

The abnormal karyotypes observed in this series of experiments were similar to those described previously by Wu *et al.* (2, 6). The most common aberration was a translocation producing a long chromosome and a minute chromosome. In one mouse the translocation gave rise to a metacentric chromosome and a minute chromosome. Since all normal chromosomes in the mouse are telocentric, this aberration provides a unique clonal marker.

After selecting a marked W/W^v mouse two different experimental protocols were used to obtain RFC for karyotype analysis. In the first design (type I, Fig. 3) spleen cells from the selected W/W^v mouse were used to form rosettes. The advantage of this method is that the immune response of the mice is normal in magnitude, but there are several disadvantages. The frequency of chromosomally marked W/W^v recipients is low, and in general only 1 out of 10 mice examined can

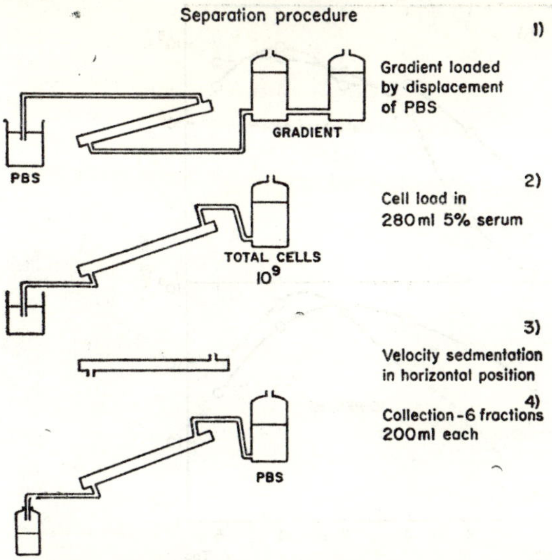

Figure 2. Outline of the procedure for cell separation.

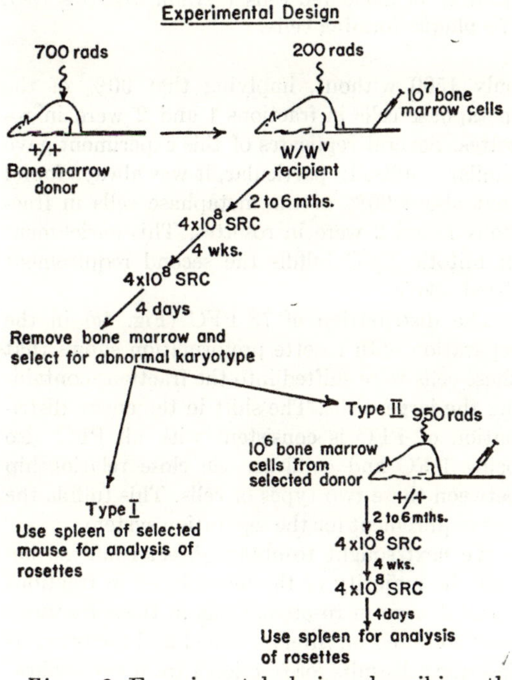

Figure 3. Experimental design describing the procedure for obtaining chromosomally marked spleen cells. In some type II design experiments, the selected W/W^v donors were not immunized.

be used for marker experiments. In addition, only one spleen is available for cell separation and analysis and one spleen does not provide enough cells to do all of the controls that are needed in the separation experiments. Finally, W/W^v recipients, even 6 months after transplantation, still have many host cells in their spleens and bone marrow. The high frequency of normal karyotypes (up to 60%) makes it difficult to interpret some of the results of the separation experiments described below.

To overcome these problems a second method of obtaining marked spleen cells was used (type II, Fig. 3): 10^6 bone marrow cells from a W/W^v mouse having marked bone marrow were injected into heavily irradiated (950 rads) mice that were coisogenic with W/W^v. After 2 to 6 months had elapsed to allow the hemopoietic and immune systems to recover, recipients were immunized and their spleens were used as a source of RFC. This design has the advantage that spleens from several mice repopulated with the same clone can be pooled to produce the large number of cells required for the separations and karyotype analyses. Mice in this group did not always contain the original marker even under conditions where 100% of the spleen colonies at 10 days after transplantation contained the marker chromosome. Presumably, in some mice, surviving endogenous stem cells overgrow the marked stem cells in the graft and repopulate the animal with chromosomally normal cells. Nevertheless, there is a high proportion of marked mice after transplantation of marrow from the selected donor. The major disadvantage to the type II design is a low immune response in the irradiated recipients. The reason for the defective immune response in these mice is not known. It may be related to the declining proliferative potential of stem cells that accompanies serial transplantation of bone marrow (23).

RESULTS

Separation of RFC. This section presents control experiments done to establish that the separation procedure fulfills three requirements: 1) a highly purified population of RFC is obtained, 2) mitotic RFC are present in the purified population, and 3) enrichment of antibody-producing cells occurs in the fractions enriched for RFC.

Spleens were taken from mice immunized with SRBC and sacrificed on day 4 of the secondary response. Two cell suspensions, each containing 1.2×10^9 SRBC and 1.8×10^8 nucleated spleen cells in 10 ml of 10% FCS, were prepared. One

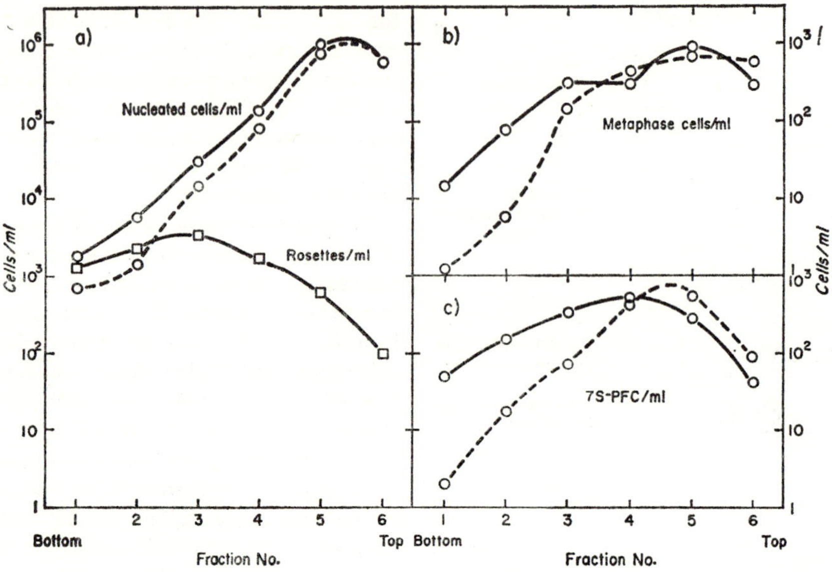

Figure 4. Number of cells plotted against the fraction number for separations of sample with (——) and without (-----) preformation of rosettes. *a*, Distribution of nucleated cells (○) and rosettes (□). *b*, Distribution of metaphase cells. *c*, Distribution of 7S plaque-forming cells.

suspension was centrifuged to form rosettes, diluted to 350 ml and separated by sedimentation as described. The second suspension was immediately diluted to 350 ml and also separated by sedimentation, care being taken to ensure that separation of the cells occurred before rosettes formed. Each fraction in both separations was assayed for its content of nucleated cells, rosettes, and 7S-PFC.

Maximum rosette enrichment was obtained in fraction 1 where 70% of the objects (cells, rosettes and cell clumps) are rosettes (Fig. 4*a*). No rosettes were seen in the separation done without preformation. The broad distribution of rosettes (with peak number in fraction 3) reflects variations in the size of rosettes. Some RFC bind a large number of red cells and thus sediment quickly, whereas other RFC bind as few as three red cells and sediment more slowly. Nevertheless, the high concentration of rosettes at the bottom of the gradient fulfills the first requirement for the separation procedure.

The distribution of the metaphase cells with and without preformation of rosettes is shown in Figure 4*b*. Clearly, some of the metaphase cells were shifted to a higher sedimentation velocity after preformation of rosettes. In particular, in fractions 1 and 2 there were approximately 19,000 metaphase cells with rosette preformation and only 1500 without, implying that 90% of the metaphase cells in fractions 1 and 2 were in rosettes. Several replicates of this experiment gave similar results. In particular, it was always found that about 90% of the metaphase cells in fractions 1 and 2 were in rosettes. This enrichment in mitotic RFC fulfills the second requirement listed above.

The distribution of 7S-PFC (Fig. 4*c*) in the separation with rosette preformation shows that these cells were shifted into the fractions containing the larger cells. The shift in the entire distribution of PFC is consistent with all PFC also being RFC and confirms the close relationship between these two types of cells. This fulfills the last requirement for the separation system.

We next sought to obtain direct confirmation that the majority of the metaphases in fractions 1 and 2 were in rosettes. Cells in these fractions were collected on filters, stained and analyzed as described. Results for fraction 1 from two separations are given in Table I. The frequency of mitotic RFC on the filters was 65% to 70%. This value is considerably lower than the frequency of 90% estimated from the separation data shown in Figure 4. The lower frequency of mitotic RFC on the filters is an experimental artifact resulting from the disruption of rosettes during fixation before filtering (compare columns

TABLE I

Microscopic analysis of rosettes in fraction 1

Rosette Frequency		Mitotic Frequency		Mitotic RFC/Total Mitoses[b]
Original[a] suspension	On filter[b]	Slide[c]	Filter[b]	
%	%	%	%	
60	40	1.3	0.75	17/26 (65%)
57	30	0.73	0.52	18/26 (70%)

[a] Frequency measured by hemocytometer counts of fraction 1.

[b] Frequency measured after collection of cells on Millipore filter.

[c] Frequency measured on slide prepared for karyotype analysis.

1 and 2), and the difficulties encountered in scoring metaphase cells on the filters (compare columns 3 and 4). The correct value for the percentage of metaphases in rosettes is closer to 90% than the 70% measured by direct observation of cells on the filters.

Granulocytes are known to be progeny of hemopoietic stem cells (2). Thus, it was important to show that metaphase granulocytes were not present and that the granulocytes did not form rosettes. Analysis of the filters showed that 15% of the cells in fraction 1 and 30% of the cells in fraction 2 were peroxidase positive, i.e., granulocytes. However, in two separate experiments, no mitotic granulocytes were observed in these fractions. In addition, the frequency of rosettes formed by peroxidase positive cells was less than 2%: 57 peroxidase-positive rosettes out of 3422 rosettes scored.

Karyotype analysis of RFC. In this section we present data to show that RFC from mice whose myeloid system has been repopulated by chromosomally marked cells also contain the marker. In the first experiments spleens were used from several mice all of which had been restored after irradiation with marked bone marrow from a single donor (type II design, Fig. 3). Chromosomally marked mice were sacrificed on day 4 of a secondary immune response to SRBC. Separations with and without preformation of rosettes were done as described in the preceding section and each fraction was assayed for rosettes, 7S-PFC and mitoses. In addition, a karyotype analysis was made on all fractions, on the initial spleen cell suspension and on the bone marrow of the donors.

The cell distributions observed (Fig. 5) are similar to those obtained with normal mice (Fig. 4). The high numbers of rosettes in fractions from the top of the gradient may be attributed to suboptimal rosette formation in the initial suspension and subsequent formation during the centrifugation procedures after the separation. As discussed previously, the number of PFC is less than 10% of the number found in normal mice, but the sedimentation distribution is normal. Most importantly, the sedimentation profiles of metaphase cells indicates that 99% of the metaphases in fractions 1 and 2 in the separation with preformed rosettes were in rosettes; in fractions 1 and 2 there were 6000 metaphase cells in the rosette separation and only 60 in the control experiment.

Table II shows the results of the karyotype analysis. The bone marrow of one of the two donor mice had a normal karyotype indicating that it was probably repopulated with nonmarked cells derived from endogenous stem cells that survived irradiation. Eighty-seven per cent of the metaphases in the bone marrow of the other mouse were marked. In the pooled, unfractionated spleen cell suspension five out of eight or 63% of the metaphases examined contained the marker. In fractions 1 and 2, where 99% of the metaphases were in rosettes, chromosome analysis showed that 36 out of 80 or 45% of the metaphase cells in these fractions had the abnormal karyotype. Since the percentage of metaphase cells with marker (45%) is greater than the percentage of metaphase cells not in rosettes (1%) some of the rosettes must contain the chromosome marker.

A second series of four experiments was done using single spleens each repopulated by a different clone of marked cells. Both the type I and type II design were used for induction of the marker. Each spleen contained enough cells for only the preformed rosette separation. Only marked spleens were used. As usual, spleen cell suspensions were prepared on day 4 of the secondary response. In all four experiments the distributions of nucleated cells, rosettes, metaphases and 7S-PFC were determined and found to be very similar to the distributions shown in Figures 4 and 5 (Table III).

In fraction 1 the percentage of rosette-forming cells was about 50% in all cases except experiment 2. The frequency of the marker in metaphase cells ranged from 40 to 80% in fraction 1 and from 28 to 70% in fraction 2. Assuming that at least 90% of the metaphase cells are in rosettes,

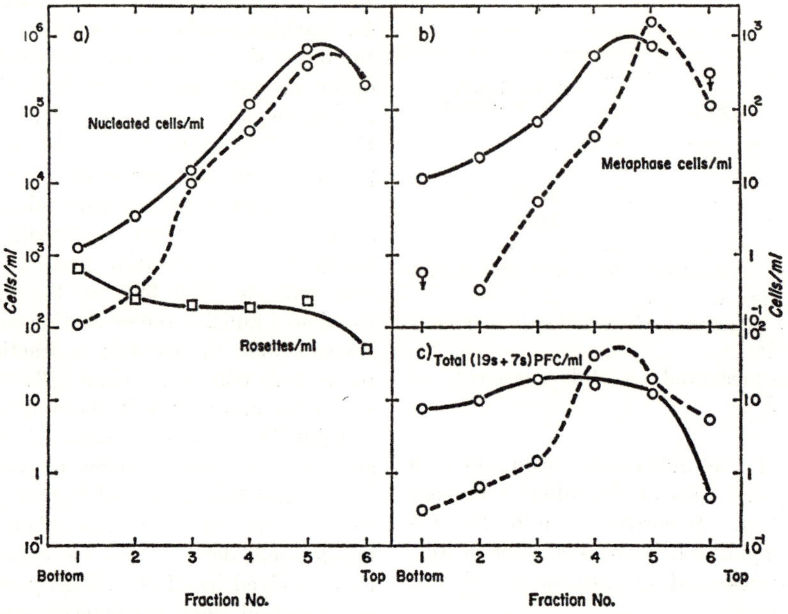

Figure 5. Number of cells plotted against the fraction number for separations with (——) and without (-----) preformation of rosettes. Type II design was used to obtain marked mice. *a*, Distribution of nucleated cells (○) and rosettes (□). The presence of rosettes in all fractions may be attributed to suboptimal rosette formation and subsequent formation during the centrifugation procedures after the separation. *b*, Distribution of metaphase cells. The circles with downward arrows indicate upper limits for the mitotic index; no mitoses were seen in the 5000 cells scored. *c*, Distribution of PFC. Because of the low immune response in these mice, the total of both 7S and 19S PFC is shown. 19S PFC are about 10% of the 7S PFC.

as was shown above, we conclude that each of the four independent clones examined contained marked cells capable of forming rosettes with SRBC.

The alternative interpretation of the data in Table III is that all of the abnormal karyotypes in fractions 1 and 2 came from the mitotic cells that were not in rosettes. This hypothesis can be tested statistically. We first assumed that 10% of the mitotic cells in fractions 1 and 2 are not in rosettes. We then used the binomial distribution to calculate the probability that, if only the non-rosette mitotic cells were marked, they could account for all the abnormal karyotypes observed in fractions 1 and 2. The results of these calculations are given in Table IV. For example, the first line of the table shows that, if the frequency of non-rosettes is 10%, the probability of observing 36 or more cells of this kind in a sample of 80 cells is less than one in a million. This test

TABLE II

Karyotype analysis of rosette separation and control

Fraction No.	No. Marked Metaphases/Total Metaphases[a]	
	Rosettes preformed	Rosettes not preformed
1	14/44 (32%)	0/2 (0%)
2	22/36 (61%)	4/11 (36%)
3	6/16 (37%)	12/28 (43%)
4	14/31 (45%)	20/38 (53%)
5	4/9 (44%)	0/7 (0%)
6	0/0[b]	0/2 (0%)

[a] The separations were done using pooled spleens from two mice treated according to type II design (Fig. 2). The frequency of the marker in the bone marrow of one mouse was 13/15 (87%); in the bone marrow of the other mouse, 0/14; in the pooled unfractionated spleen cell suspension, 5/8 (63%).

[b] One slide was scanned and no well spread mitoses were seen.

TABLE III

Karyotype analysis of populations enriched in rosettes

Experiment No.	Experimental Design	Type of Marker	Marked Colonies/ Total Colonies[b]	Percent RFC in Fraction 1	No. of Marked Cells/Total Metaphases[a]				
					Unfractionated spleen	Fraction 1	Fraction 2	Fraction 3	Fraction 4
				%					
1	II	Long + minute[c]	N.A.[d]	45	11/14 (79%)	4/5 (80%)	4/6 (67%)	17/24 (71%)	26/34 (76%)
2	II	Minute	8/15	15[e]	5/8 (63%)	5/7 (71%)	7/10 (70%)	30/36 (83%)	38/41 (93%)
3	I	Long + minute	7/8	60	16/25 (64%)	5/7 (71%)	17/30 (57%)	26/50 (52%)	17/31 (55%)
4	I	Metacentric + minute	10/12	57	14/27 (52%)	4/10 (40%)	8/29 (28%)	14/36 (39%)	16/50 (32%)

[a] Parentheses contain the percentage of abnormal karyotypes.

[b] Fraction of spleen colonies containing the chromosome marker when bone marrow from the spleen cell donors was assayed for CFU by transplantation (1).

[c] This is the same marker used for the experiment shown in Figure 5 and Table II, but obtained from other mice of the group repopulated by marrow from the selected donor.

[d] Data not available.

[e] This low percentage of RFC was due to a disturbance of the gradient which caused a mixing of the cells.

TABLE IV

Statistical analysis of karyotype data to test the hypothesis that all marked cells come from cells unable to form rosettes

Source of Data	Frequency of Non-Rosettes	No. of Mitoses Analyzed[a]	No. of Abnormal Karyotypes	p[b]
Table II	0.1	80	36	$<10^{-6}$
Table III, Exp. 1	0.1	11	8	$\sim10^{-6}$
Table III, Exp. 2	0.1	17	12	$<10^{-6}$
Table III, Exp. 3	0.1	37	22	$<10^{-6}$
Table III, Exp. 4	0.1	39	12	0.0003

[a] For this test we pooled the data from fractions 1 and 2. See relevant tables for the values obtained in individual fractions.

[b] The values in this column give the probability of obtaining the observed number (or greater) of abnormal karyotypes assuming that all such karyotypes come from cells unable to form rosettes. The probability was calculated using the binomial distribution (BITEST*** program, Polycom-Time-Sharing Computer, Toronto).

showed that for all five experiments it was highly unlikely that the abnormal karyotypes were derived only from cells unable to form rosettes. Even in the last experiment, where the frequency of abnormal karyotypes was lowest (31%), it was improbable that all of the abnormal chromosomes came from the non-rosettes. We conclude that some RFC contain the chromosome marker and are therefore progeny of myeloid stem cells.

DISCUSSION

The data presented in this paper lead to two conclusions concerning differentiation in the immune system. The first is that a single stem cell can give rise to progeny in both the myeloid and lymphoid systems (24). Other workers in studies with chromosome markers have arrived at a similar conclusion. Wu *et al.* (6) showed that chromosome markers induced in single myeloid stem cells were eventually found in lymph nodes and thymus, but they were not able to demonstrate that the marker was present in a functional cell of the immune system. A similar criticism can be made of the work of Trentin *et al.* (5). They used bone marrow from mice with the T6 chromosome marker to make spleen colonies and then transplanted these colonies into lethally irradiated recipients. They observed the T6 marker in the lymph nodes of long-term survivors that had been immunized and concluded that antibody-producing cells were probably derived from colony-forming cells. This conclusion depended on several assumptions about their experimental system. It was essential that the spleen colonies be pure clones. The experiments of Wu *et al.* (6) and of Becker *et al.* (25) show that at least 5% of the cells in a spleen colony do not belong to that clone. Even with colonies made with T6-marked bone marrow, the contaminating cells might be marked, and it is conceivable that some of these contaminants could be marked lymphoid cells. In addition to the problem of being unable to detect contamination in their spleen colonies, they did not give proof that the marker was in functional cells of the immune system. Because of the low antibody response in the irradiated recipients, the presence of a few lymph node cells with the T6 marker cannot be taken as evidence that the marker is in antibody-producing cells.

Our experimental design overcomes most of the difficulties encountered in these earlier experiments. The uniqueness of the radiation-induced markers ensured that only a single clone of cells was being examined and made it possible to identify cells in the clone regardless of their location in the mouse. In addition, the use of populations enriched in RFC allowed us to examine directly the karyotypes of functional cells of the immune system. Our data show that RFC contain chromosome markers also present in the myeloid stem cells that form spleen colonies. This finding indicates that the myeloid and lymphoid systems are derived from a common stem cell in the adult mouse.

The data of Figure 4*b* indicate the necessity of separating rosettes before doing a karyotype analysis. While 90 per cent of the metaphases in fractions 1 and 2 are probably in rosettes, only 5 per cent of the total metaphases in the initial suspension are in fractions 1 and 2. Thus, it is obvious that an analysis of karyotypes in the initial suspension would be meaningless for studies on the origin of RFC since mitotic RFC represent a minority of the total mitotic cells in the spleen.

The second conclusion is that the stem cells are pluripotent with respect to their ability to generate RFC of different specificity. Four different clones were examined in this study and all were found to contain RFC specific for sheep erythrocytes, the only antigen tested. If stem cells were restricted in the number of different specificities they could generate, we should have observed some clones that could not produce RFC specific for SRBC since the probability is small of selecting four restricted clones, all of which by chance make RFC specific for the same antigen.

Unfortunately, our data do not indicate precisely which cells of the immune system are derived from myeloid stem cells. That RFC are specific cells functioning in an immune response has been shown by many workers. It is generally assumed that RFC are antibody-producing cells (7), and many cells actively synthesizing antibody certainly form rosettes (15, 26). It is also obvious from our data (Figs. 4 and 5) that most RFC do not synthesize sufficient antibody to form a plaque in the Jerne assay. The reasons for this discrepancy between the numbers of RFC and PFC are not known; many explanations are possible. Nevertheless, this discrepancy prevents us from concluding that antibody-producing cells are derived from stem cells of the myeloid system.

REFERENCES

1. Till, J. E. and McCulloch, E. A., Radiat. Res., *14:* 213, 1961.
2. Wu, A. M., Till, J. E., Siminovitch, L. and McCulloch, E. A., J. Cell. Physiol., *69:* 177, 1967.
3. Ford, C. E., Micklem, H. S., Evans, E. P., Gray, J. G. and Ogden, D. A., Ann. N. Y. Acad. Sci., *129:* 283, 1966.
4. Micklem, H. S., Ford, C. E., Evans, E. P. and Gray, J., Proc. Roy. Soc. Ser. B., *165:* 78, 1966.
5. Trentin, J., Wolf, N., Cheng, V., Fahlberg, W., Weiss, D. and Bonhag, R., J. Immun., *98:* 1326, 1967.
6. Wu, A. M., Till, J. E., Siminovitch, L. and McCulloch, E. A., J. Exp. Med., *127:* 455, 1968.
7. Biozzi, G., Stiffel, C. and Mouton, D., *Immunity, Cancer and Chemotherapy*, Edited by E. Mihich, p. 103, Academic Press Inc., New York, 1966.
8. Miller, R. G. and Phillips, R. A., J. Cell. Physiol., *73:* 191, 1969.
9. Cunningham, J. R., Bruce, W. R. and Webb, H. P., Phys. Med. Biol., *10:* 381, 1965.
10. Dulbecco, R. and Vogt, M., J. Exp. Med., *99:* 167, 1954.

11. Laskov, R., Nature, *219:* 973, 1968.
12. Nota, N. R., Liacopoulos-Briot, M., Stiffel, C. and Biozzi, G., Compt. Rend. Acad. Sci., *259:* 1277, 1964.
13. Shearer, G. M. and Cudkowicz, G., J. Immun., *101:* 1264, 1968.
14. Zaalberg, O. B., Nature, *202:* 1231, 1964.
15. Zaalberg, O. B., Van Der Meul, V. A. and Van Twisk, M. J., J. Immun., *100:* 451, 1968.
16. Edwards, G. E., Master of Science Thesis, University of Toronto, 1969.
17. Fowler, J. H., Wu, A. M., Till, J. E., McCulloch, E. A. and Siminovitch, L., J. Cell. Comp. Physiol., *69:* 65, 1967.
18. Jerne, N. K., Nordin, A. A. and Henry, C., *Cell-Bound Antibodies*, Edited by B. Amos and H. Koprowski, p. 109, Wistar Institute Press, Philadelphia, 1963.
19. Dresser, D. W. and Wortis, H. H., Nature, *208:* 859, 1965.
20. Phillips, R. A. and Miller, R. G., J. Cell and Tissue Kinet., *3:* 263, 1970.
21. Barnes, D. W. H., Ford, C. E., Gray, S. M. and Loutit, J. F., *Progress in Nuclear Energy*, Series VI, Edited by J. G. Bugher, J. Coursaget and J. F. Loutit, Vol. 2, p. 1, Pergamon Press, London, 1959.
22. Barnes, D. W. H., Evans, E. P., Ford, C. E. and West, B. J., Nature, *219:* 518, 1968.
23. Siminovitch, L., Till, J. E. and McCulloch, E. A., J. Cell. Comp. Physiol., *64:* 23, 1964.
24. Trentin, J. J. and Fahlberg, W. J., *Conceptual Advances in Immunology and Oncology*. Sixteenth Annual Symposium on Fundamental Cancer Research, Houston, Texas, p. 66, Harper and Row, New York, 1962.
25. Becker, A. J., McCulloch, E. A. and Till, J. E., Nature, *197:* 452, 1963.
26. Cunningham, A. J., Smith, J. B. and Mercer, E. H., J. Exp. Med., *124:* 701, 1966.

THE JOURNAL OF IMMUNOLOGY
Vol. 105, No. 3, September 1970

Printed in U.S.A.

INITIATION OF ANTIBODY RESPONSES BY DIFFERENT CLASSES OF LYMPHOCYTES

II. Differences in the Tissue Distribution of Lymphocytes Involved in Primary and Secondary Antibody Responses

SAMUEL STROBER

From the National Cancer Institute, Bethesda, Maryland 20014

Received for publication January 22, 1970

Thoracic duct cells and spleen cells from normal and immunized Lewis rats were injected into syngeneic recipients which had received 500 R x-irradiation 2 hr earlier. Tetanus and diphtheria toxoids were injected 24 hr after irradiation and the antibody response was measured for 2 to 3 weeks thereafter. Immunologically competent units were detected in normal spleen cells but not in normal thoracic duct cells. Immunization of the cell donors produced at least a 10^3- to 10^4-fold increase in units in the thoracic duct lymph and a much smaller increase in units in the spleen resulting in a change in the distribution (relative concentrations) of units in these lymphoid tissues.

Recent studies in our laboratory show that lymphocytes which are involved in initiating the antibody response to tetanus and diphtheria toxoids are found in high concentrations in the spleen and in very low concentrations in the thoracic duct lymph of normal rats (1–3). Experiments by Ellis *et al.* (4, 5) indicate that there is a considerable increase in the concentration of these cells in the lymph after immunization, since thoracic duct cells from immunized donors restore a vigorous response to tetanus toxoid in x-irradiated rats.

The object of the present investigation was to a) determine the magnitude of the increase of these cells in the thoracic duct lymph after immunization and b) determine if a change in the relative concentrations (i.e., distribution) of these cells in different lymphoid tissues is associated with this increase. Accordingly, we compared the relative abilities of spleen cells and thoracic duct cells from normal and immunized rats to restore the antibody response of x-irradiated hosts to diphtheria and tetanus toxoids.

MATERIALS AND METHODS

Animals. Adult male Lewis rats (Microbiological Associates, Inc., Walkersville, Md.) weighing 150 to 200 g were used throughout.

X-irradiation. Rats were placed in Lucite containers and received 500 R whole body x-irradiation (15 ma; 200 kv; 54 cm SAD; 0.25 mm Cu + 0.55 mm Al filtration; dose rate 130 R/min) from two Westinghouse Quadrocondex units.

Collection of thoracic duct cells and spleen cells. The thoracic duct of 175- to 200-g rats was cannulated by a modification of the technique of Bollman *et al.* (6). All lymph collections were made within 24 hr after cannulation of the thoracic duct. Collection of lymph and preparation of thoracic duct cells for intravenous injection have been described elsewhere (7). Spleen cell suspensions were made in medium 199 according to the method of Billingham (8). Cell suspensions were injected into the lateral tail vein of prospective recipients.

Incubation of thoracic duct cells in vitro. Thoracic duct cells were incubated *in vitro* for 24 hr at 37°C according to the technique of Gowans and Uhr (9). At the end of the incubation period, the cells were harvested by centrifugation at 150 × G for 10 min and resuspended in medium 199 for intravenous injection. Approximately 50 to 85% of thoracic duct cells were recovered after incubation. Incubated cells were arbitrarily discarded when the recovery of cells was less than 75% and when cell survival was less than 90% as judged by trypan blue exclusion. The incubation procedure reduced the number of large lymphocytes (cells greater than 8 μ in diameter) present in the thoracic duct lymph from 34 to 79/1000 cells to 0 to 5/1000 cells.

Immunization procedures. Rats were immunized

to tetanus toxoid adsorbed to alum (Eli Lilly Co., Indianapolis, Ind.) or to diphtheria toxoid adsorbed to aluminum phosphate (Parke Davis Co., Detroit, Mich.) by a single subcutaneous (7.5 Lf) and intraperitoneal (7.5 Lf) injection of 15 Lf toxoid. The same procedures were used to immunize donors and hosts. Donors were immunized 3 to 4 months prior to collection of thoracic duct cells or spleen cells.

Antibody titrations. Titrations of antibodies to tetanus and diphtheria toxoids were performed in microtiter agglutination plates (Cooke Engineering Co., Alexandria, Va.) by a previously described modification (1, 3) of the tanned red cell hemagglutination technique of Stavitsky (10). For these titrations, about 0.2 to 0.3 ml of blood was collected from the tail vein of the rat either once or twice a week for 2 to 3 weeks.

RESULTS

Restoration of antibody responses with lymphoid cells from normal donors. Lewis rats received 500 R whole body x-irradiation, and an intravenous injection of thoracic duct cells or spleen cells 2 hr later. Antigen was injected 24 hr after irradiation. Antibody determinations were made until the onset of the plateau phase of the response. Figures 1*A* and 2*A* show that 100 × 10⁶ spleen cells from normal donors restored a measureable primary antibody response to tetanus and diphtheria toxoids, but 250 × 10⁶ or even 1 × 10⁹ thoracic duct cells did not. Antibody titers were detected during the 3rd week after immunization of irradiated hosts reconstituted with spleen cells.

Restoration of antibody responses with lymphoid cells from immunized donors. As few as 2 × 10⁶ thoracic duct cells from donors immunized 3 to 4 months prior to cell transfer restored a vigorous antibody response to both toxoids (Figs. 1*B* and 2*B*). Antibody titers were detected within the 1st week after immunization of the reconstituted hosts. On the other hand, irradiated hosts reconstituted with 2 × 10⁶ spleen cells from immunized donors showed no antibody titers for at least 2 wk (Figs. 1*B* and 2*B*).

In further experiments, "immune" thoracic duct cells were incubated *in vitro* at 37°C for 24

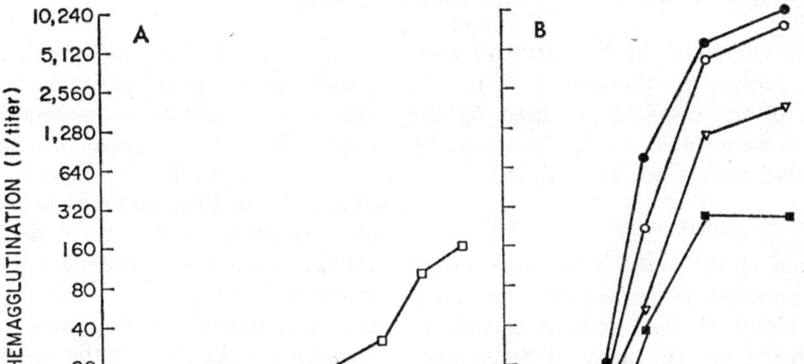

Figure 1. Mean hemagglutinin titers in groups of rats irradiated with 500 R that received 2 hr after irradiation an intravenous injection of thoracic duct cells or spleen cells, and 24 hr after irradiation an intraperitoneal and subcutaneous injection of 15 Lf of tetanus toxoid. In Figure 1*A* normal cells were given, and in Figure 1*B*, "immune" cells. Note in Figure 1*A* the restorative action of 100 × 10⁶ normal spleen cells (□—□); and the absence of this effect with 1 × 10⁹ (▼—▼) or 250 × 10⁶ (■—■) normal thoracic duct cells. The control group given antigen but no cells (▲—▲) gave a negative response. In these 4 groups, there were 11, 3, 18 and 9 rats, respectively. Note in Figure 1*B* the marked restorative action of 10 × 10⁶ "immune" thoracic duct cells either untreated (●—●) or incubated *in vitro* (○—○) and that of 2 × 10⁶ untreated "immune" thoracic duct cells (▽—▽). Note, however, the lesser restorative action of 10 × 10⁶ (■—■) and 2 × 10⁶ (□—□) "immune" untreated spleen cells. A negative response was obtained with the control group given 10 × 10⁶ "immune" untreated thoracic duct cells but no antigen (▲—▲). In these 6 groups, there were 12, 8, 7, 6, 6 and 4 rats, respectively.

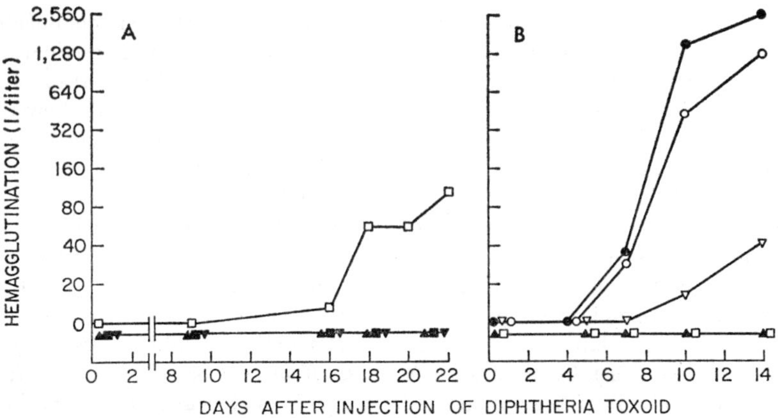

Figure 2. Mean hemagglutinin titers in groups of rats irradiated with 500 R that received 2 hr after irradiation an intravenous injection of thoracic duct cells or spleen cells, and 24 hr after irradiation an intraperitoneal and subcutaneous injection of 15 Lf diphtheria toxoid. In Figure 2*A* normal cells were given, and in Figure 1*B*, "immune" cells. Note in Figure 2*A* the restorative action of 100 × 10⁶ normal spleen cells (□—□); and the absence of the effect with 1 × 10⁹ (▼—▼) or 250 × 10⁶ (■—■) normal thoracic duct cells. The control group given antigen but no cells (▲—▲) gave a negative response. In the 4 groups, there were 11, 3, 13 and 8 rats, respectively. Note in Figure 2*B* the marked restorative action of 10 × 10⁶ "immune" thoracic duct cells, either untreated (●—●) or incubated *in vitro* (○—○) as compared to the lesser action of 2 × 10⁶ "immune" untreated thoracic duct cells (▽—▽) and the negative effect of the same number (2 × 10⁶) of untreated "immune" spleen cells (□—□). A negative response was obtained with a control group given 10 × 10⁶ "immune" untreated thoracic duct cells but no antigen (▲—▲). In these 5 groups, there were 12, 8, 7, 6 and 4 rats, respectively.

hr in order to eliminate the 5 to 10% of large lymphocytes present in thoracic duct lymph. The kinetics of the response produced by the incubated cells were similar to that produced by the unincubated cells (Figs. 1*B* and 2*B*).

DISCUSSION

An inoculum of 10^8 spleen cells from normal Lewis rats restored a measureable antibody response to diphtheria and tetanus toxoids in x-irradiated hosts, but 10^9 normal thoracic duct cells did not (1, 3). Thoracic duct cells from donors immunized 3 to 4 months prior to cell transfer showed at least a 500-fold increase in their restorative ability, since 2×10^6 "immune" cells restored a vigorous response to the toxoids. The kinetics of the adoptive immune responses were similar to those in unirradiated controls in that the latent period and exponential phase were followed by a prolonged plateau phase. The plateau antibody titers restored by the highest cell doses used in the present experiments were similar to those of unirradiated rats; however, the latent period of the adoptive responses was prolonged by about 3 to 7 days (1, 3, 4).

If the regression lines for the responses restored by normal and "immune" thoracic duct cells are parallel on a double logarithmic plot of antibody titer at the onset of the plateau phase and cell dose, then the increase in immunologically competent units[1] in the thoracic duct lymph is at least 10^3 or 10^4. This figure is one to two orders of magnitude greater than that reported by Perkins *et al.* (11) for the increase of units in the spleen of immunized mice using sheep red blood cells as antigen. The difference in these figures may be due in part to the more heterogenous populations of cells found in the spleen as compared to the thoracic duct lymph (12). That is, some restricted populations of cells may show a greater increase in units after immunization than the composite populations of cells present in the spleen. Differences in the antigens and species used in the present study and that of Perkins *et al.* (11) almost certainly play a part in the discrepancies noted above (1–3).

Elimination of the large, dividing thoracic

[1] An immunologically competent unit can be defined as a single cell or minimum combination of different cells which can restore the ability of an immunologically inert host to produce an immune response to a given immunogen.

duct lymphocytes by *in vitro* incubation for 24 hr at 37°C did not reduce the responses restored by "immune" thoracic duct cells. This finding confirms reports of the carriage of immunologic memory by circulating small lymphocytes (9).

A change in the distribution of immunologically competent units in the lymphoid tissues was associated with the marked increase in competent units in the thoracic duct lymph of immunized rats, so that "immune" thoracic duct cells were more efficient than an equal number of "immune" spleen cells in restoring the antibody response to the toxoids. Similar distributional changes in competent units have been reported in the lymphoid tissues of normal and immunized rabbits using sheep red blood cells as antigen (13, 14).

Several explanations of the present experimental findings can be proposed. The simplest explanation is that competent units in the immunized rat are formed only from circulating cells. These circulating cells are derived from relatively fixed cells which form the units in the normal rat. An alternative explanation is that units found in immunized rats are formed from both fixed and circulating cells. However, the circulating cells may have a longer life span than the fixed cells (15, 16), so that the majority of units found 3 to 4 months after immunization will be circulating. This is not an unlikely possibility in view of the report by Celada (17) that two lines of "memory" cells are established in the mouse after immunization with human serum albumin, one with a calculated half life of 26 days and the other with a half life of 100 days.

REFERENCES

1. Strober, S., Nature, *219:* 649, 1968.
2. Strober, S. and Mandel, M. A., Proc. Soc. Exp. Biol. Med., *130:* 336, 1969.
3. Strober, S. and Law, L. W., Proc. Nat. Acad. Sci., *62:* 1023, 1969.
4. Ellis, S. T., Gowans, J. L. and Howard, J. C., Cold Spring Harbor Symp. Quant. Biol., *32:* 395, 1967.
5. Ellis, S. T., Gowans, J. L. and Howard, J. C., Antibiot. Chemother., *15:* 40, 1969.
6. Bollman, J. L., Cain, J. C. and Grindlay, J. H., J. Lab. Clin. Med., *33:* 1349, 1948.
7. Strober, S., J. Exp. Med., *130:* 895, 1969.
8. Billingham, R. C., in *Transplantation of Tissues and Cells*, Edited by R. C. Billingham and W. K. Silvers, p. 96, The Wistar Institute Press, Philadelphia, 1961.
9. Gowans, J. L. and Uhr, J. W., J. Exp. Med., *124:* 1017, 1966.
10. Stavitsky, A. B., J. Immun., *72:* 360, 1954.
11. Perkins, E. H., Robinson, M. A. and Makinodan, T., J. Immun., *86:* 553, 1961.
12. Haskill, J. S., J. Exp. Med., *130:* 877, 1969.
13. Singhal, S. K. and Richter, M., J. Exp. Med., *128:* 1099, 1968.
14. Richter, M. and Abdou, N. I., J. Exp. Med., *129:* 1261, 1969.
15. Caffrey, R. W., Rieke, W. O. and Everett, N. B., Acta Haemat., *28:* 145, 1962.
16. Ottesen, J., Acta Physiol. Scand., *32:* 75, 1954.
17. Celada, F., J. Exp. Med., *125:* 199, 1967.

THE JOURNAL OF IMMUNOLOGY
Vol. 105, No. 3, September 1970

INITIATION OF ANTIBODY RESPONSES BY DIFFERENT CLASSES OF LYMPHOCYTES

III. Differences in the Proliferative Rates of Thoracic Duct Lymphocytes Involved in Primary and Secondary Responses

SAMUEL STROBER

From the National Cancer Institute, Bethesda, Maryland 20014

Received for publication January 22, 1970

Thoracic duct cells from normal and immunized Lewis rats restored the antibody response of x-irradiated hosts to *Salmonella typhi* flagella and horse spleen ferritin. Elimination of the large dividing lymphocytes by treatment of the cell donors with the mitotic inhibitor, vinblastine, or by *in vitro* incubation of the thoracic duct cells markedly reduced the responses restored by cells from normal donors. On the other hand, the responses restored by thoracic duct cells from immunized donors were not reduced by elimination of dividing cells and were dramatically enhanced in the case of horse spleen ferritin. These findings suggest that rapidly dividing thoracic duct cells play an important part in the immunologically competent unit for *S. typhi* flagella and horse spleen ferritin in normal rats but not in immunized rats.

Thoracic duct cells from normal rats can restore the primary antibody response of x-irradiated hosts to *Salmonella typhi* flagella and horse spleen ferritin (1). These responses are markedly reduced by treatment of the cell donors with the mitototic inhibitor, vinblastine, or by *in vitro* incubation of the thoracic duct cells (1). Both procedures eliminate the large, rapidly dividing lymphocytes found in thoracic duct lymph. These findings suggest that rapidly dividing lymphocytes play an important role in the initiation of the primary antibody response to these protein antigens.

The present investigation was carried out to determine if dividing thoracic duct lymphocytes from immunized rats play a similar role in the initiation of the secondary antibody response. "Immune" thoracic duct cells with and without large dividing lymphocytes were, therefore, tested for their ability to restore the antibody response of irradiated hosts to *S. typhi* flagella and horse spleen ferritin.

MATERIALS AND METHODS

Animals. Adult male Lewis rats weighing 150 to 200 g were used exclusively.

X-irradiation. Rats were given 500 R whole body x-irradiation, as described previously (2).

Collection and incubation of thoracic duct cells. Thoracic duct cells were harvested and incubated *in vitro* as before (2).

Treatment of thoracic duct cell donors with vinblastine. A single intraperitoneal injection (0.3 mg in 1 ml of saline) of the mitotic inhibitor, vinblastine sulfate (Eli Lilly & Co., Indianapolis, Ind.), was administered to several cell donors 24 hr before their thoracic ducts were cannulated. Thoracic duct cells from these donors showed 0 to 12 large lymphocytes (>8 μ in diameter) present per 1000 cells. Untreated donors showed 34 to 79 large lymphocytes present per 1000 cells.

Immunization procedures. Immunization to *S. typhi* flagella[1] was achieved by a single intravenous injection of 5 μg of flagella in 1 ml of saline. Flagella were prepared by a modification of the method of Kobayashi *et al.* (3). Rats were immunized to horse spleen ferritin (Pentex, Inc., Kankakee, Ill.) in complete Freund's adjuvant (Difco Laboratories, Inc., Detroit, Mich.) by the injection of 0.1 mg of emulsion into each hind footpad to give a total dose of 2 mg of protein per animal. Several thoracic duct cell donors were immunized to flagella or ferritin 2 to 3 months before cannulation of the thoracic duct.

Antibody titrations. Titrations of antibody to

[1] Kindly supplied by Dr. R. Hunter, National Institute of Infectious Diseases, Bethesda, Md. 20014.

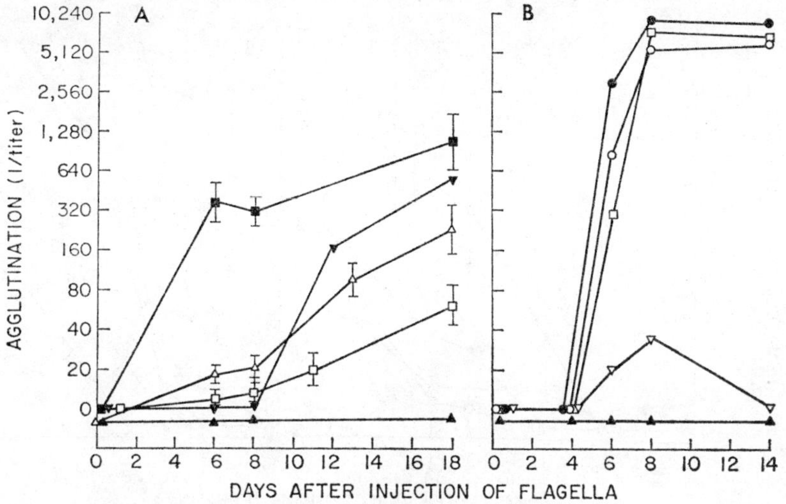

Figure 1. Mean hemagglutinin titers in groups of rats irradiated with 500 R that received intravenous injections of thoracic duct cells 2 hr after irradiation and 5 μg of *S. typhi* flagella 24 hr after irradiation. In Figure 1*A* normal cells were given and in Figure 1*B*, "immune" cells. Note in Figure 1*A* the restorative ability of 250 × 10⁶ normal thoracic duct cells (■—■). This ability is less with 50 × 10⁶ normal cells (▼—▼), 250 × 10⁶ thoracic duct cells incubated *in vitro* (□—□), and 250 × 10⁶ thoracic duct cells from donors treated with vinblastine (△—△). The control group given antigen but no cells (▲—▲) gave a negative response. In these 5 groups there were 6, 6, 6, 6 and 7 rats, respectively. Brackets show the standard error of the mean. Note in Figure 1*B* the marked restorative ability of 50 × 10⁶ "immune" thoracic duct cells either untreated (●—●), incubated *in vitro* (○—○), or treated *in vivo* with vinblastine (□—□), and that of 10 × 10⁶ untreated "immune" thoracic duct cells (▽—▽). A negative response was obtained with the control group given 50 × 10⁶ untreated "immune" thoracic duct cells but no antigen (▲—▲). In these 5 groups, there were 8, 7, 6, 7 and 4 rats, respectively.

horse spleen ferritin were performed in microtiter agglutination plates (Cooke Engineering Co., Alexandria, Va.) by the tanned red cell hemagglutination technique of Stavitsky (4). Titration of agglutinins to *S. typhi* flagella has been described elsewhere (1). Bleedings were performed as before (2).

RESULTS

Restoration of antibody responses with thoracic duct cells from normal donors. Lewis rats were irradiated and injected intravenously with 250 × 10^6 or 50 × 10^6 thoracic duct cells from unimmunized donors 2 hr later. *S. typhi* flagella or horse spleen ferritin was injected 24 hr after irradiation. Antibody determinations were made until the onset of the plateau phase of the response. The responses restored by 250 × 10^6 thoracic duct cells from normal rats rose more rapidly and achieved a higher plateau titer than those restored by 50 × 10^6 cells (Fig. 1*A* and 2*A*). Elimination of the large dividing lymphocytes by treatment of cell donors with vinblastine or by *in vitro* incubation of thoracic duct cells for 24 hr at 37°C markedly reduced the responses restored by 250 × 10^6 cells. The latter responses were slightly lower than those restored by 50 × 10^6 untreated thoracic duct cells.

Restoration of antibody responses with thoracic duct cells from immunized donors. Injection of 50 × 10^6 thoracic duct cells from donors immunized 2 to 3 months before restored a vigorous response to both *S. typhi* flagella and horse spleen ferritin (Figs. 1*B* and 2*B*). The responses restored by 10 × 10^6 "immune" thoracic duct cells were considerably less than those restored by 50 × 10^6 "immune" cells. Elimination of large dividing lymphocytes did not reduce the response to *S. typhi* flagella and produced a dramatic enhancement of the response to horse spleen ferritin. Indeed, thoracic duct cells from donors treated with vinblastine produced antibody titers at days 6, 8 and 14 which were approximately seven $\log_2$ units higher than that produced by cells from untreated donors.

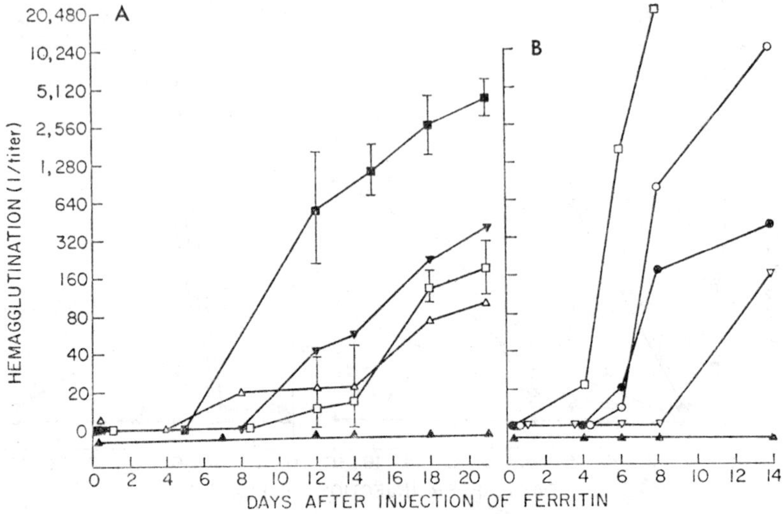

Figure 2. Mean hemagglutinin titers in groups of rats irradiated with 500 R that received an intravenous injection of thoracic duct cells 2 hr after irradiation and a subcutaneous injection of 2 mg of horse spleen ferritin in complete Freund's adjuvant 24 hr after irradiation. In Figure 2*A* normal cells were given and in Figure 2*B*, "immune" cells. Note in Figure 2*A* the restorative ability of 250 × 10⁶ normal thoracic duct cells (■—■). This ability is less with 50 × 10⁶ normal cells (▼—▼), 250 × 10⁶ thoracic duct cells incubated *in vitro* (□—□), and 250 × 10⁶ thoracic duct cells from donors treated with vinblastine (△—△).The control group given antigen but no cells (▲—▲) gave a negative response. In these 5 groups there were 6, 6, 6, 6 and 7 rats, respectively. Brackets show the standard error of the mean. Note in Figure 2*B* the marked restorative ability of 50 × 10⁶ "immune" thoracic duct cells either untreated (●—●), incubated *in vitro* (○—○), or treated *in vivo* with vinblastine (□—□), and that of 10 × 10⁶ untreated "immune" thoracic duct cells (▽—▽). A negative response was obtained with the control group given 50 × 10⁶ untreated "immune" thoracic duct cells but no antigen (▲—▲). In these 5 groups, there were 8, 8, 7, 8 and 4 rats, respectively.

DISCUSSION

Thoracic duct cells from normal and immunized Lewis rats restored the antibody response of x-irradiated hosts to *S. typhi* flagella and horse spleen ferritin. The plateau antibody titers restored by the highest cell doses used in the present experiments were similar to those of normal unirradiated controls (1). The adoptive responses lagged the normal responses by about 2 to 4 days (1). As reported previously, elimination of the large, rapidly dividing lymphocytes by *in vitro* incubation or by treatment of the cell donors with vinblastine markedly reduced the responses restored by thoracic duct cells from normal donors (1). This finding suggests that large, rapidly dividing lymphocytes are part of the immunologically competent unit (2) for these protein antigens in the normal rat.

The importance of large dividing lymphocytes in the initiation of primary antibody responses in rodents has been reported by several investigators. Naor and Sulitzeanu (5) showed that the majority of cells in the normal mouse spleen and lymph nodes which bind ^{125}I-labeled bovine serum albumin *in vitro* and *in vivo* are large and medium lymphocytes. Similarly, Ada and Byrt (6, 7) showed that normal mouse lymphoid cells up to 12 μ in diameter (presumably medium or large lymphocytes) are able to bind ^{125}I-labeled *Salmonella adelaide* flagella *in vitro*. These studies suggest that large lymphocytes have receptors on their surface which can recognize protein antigens. Density gradient studies with albumin by Haskill (8) indicate that some populations of cells in the rat spleen which initiate the primary antibody response to sheep red blood cells are rapidly proliferating as judged by their sensitivity to vinblastine *in vivo*. In addition, Nossal *et al.* (9) showed that elimination of large thoracic duct lymphocytes by passage through a column of glass beads reduces the ability of the thoracic duct cells to restore the primary response of irradiated mice to *S. adelaide* flagella.

The present experiments show that although the responses restored by thoracic duct cells from normal donors are reduced by elimination of the large dividing lymphocytes, the responses restored by thoracic duct cells from immunized donors are not. Indeed, elimination of dividing lymphocytes by treatment of cell donors with vinblastine produced a dramatic increase in the ability of "immune" thoracic duct cells to restore the response to horse spleen ferritin. These findings indicate that the dividing cells are not a necessary part of the immunologically competent unit in immunized animals, and in fact, can inhibit the full expression of the secondary antibody response by thoracic duct cells. Similar findings have been reported by Gowans and Uhr (10) in the rat using bacteriophage ϕX174 as antigen. However, Nossal *et al.* (9) reported a slight decrease in the ability of "immune" thoracic duct cells to restore the response to *S. adelaide* flagella in irradiated mice after large lymphocytes were eliminated by means of a column of glass beads. Perhaps differences in the techniques of cell separation and in the species of animals studied may account for the different results.

The initiation of the primary antibody response by short-lived dividing lymphocytes is consistent with the view that the precursor cells of the primary response form a self-renewal system which does not require antigen for continuous cell cycling (11). The studies of Nettesheim *et al.* (12, 13) indicate that cells which initiate the secondary antibody response in the mouse ("memory" cells) do not form a self-renewal system, and that antigen is required for their continued proliferation. This suggests that immunologic memory must be carried by long-lived cells after the antigen used for primary immunization has disappeared. The non-dividing lymphocytes in the thoracic duct lymph would be well suited to carry immunologic memory, since some of these cells have life spans in excess of 100 days in the rat (14).

Although the present study indicates that some of the lymphocytes involved in the initiation of the primary response to *S. typhi* flagella and horse spleen ferritin are dividing rapidly, previous studies show that lymphocytes involved in the primary response to other antigens are not dividing or are dividing very slowly (1). For example, thoracic duct cells or spleen cells from unimmunized donors treated with vinblastine show no reduction in the ability to restore the antibody responses to sheep red blood cells and bovine serum albumin (1) or to diphtheria and tetanus toxoids, respectively (16). The different proliferative rates of cells which initiate the primary response to different antigens may reflect changes in the functional or maturational state of cells derived from the same precursor. Indeed, it is tempting to speculate that short-lived lymphocytes which are derived from a common bone marrow precursor and participate in a self-renewal system are part of the immunologically competent unit for all primary responses. As suggested in the previous paper (2), these lymphocytes may give rise to long and short-lived cells which are part of the competent unit in the secondary response, but do not participate in a self-renewal system.

REFERENCES

1. Strober, S., J. Exp. Med., *130:* 895, 1969.
2. Strober, S., J. Immun., *105:* 730, 1970.
3. Kobayashi, R., Rinker, T. N. and Koffler, M., Arch. Biochem., *84:* 342, 1959.
4. Stravitsky, A. B., J. Immun., *72:* 360, 1954.
5. Naor, D. and Sulitzeanu, D., Nature, *214:* 687, 1967.
6. Ada, G. L. and Byrt, P., Nature, *222:* 1291, 1969.
7. Byrt, P. and Ada, G. L., Immunology, *17:* 503, 1969.
8. Haskill, J. S., J. Exp. Med., *130:* 877, 1969.
9. Nossal, G. J. V., Shortman, K. D., Miller, J. F. A. P., Mitchell, G. F. and Haskill, J. S., Cold Spring Harbor Symp. Quant. Biol., *32:* 369, 1967.
10. Gowans, J. L. and Uhr, J. W., J. Exp. Med., *124:* 1017, 1966.
11. Nettesheim, P., Williams, M. L. and Hammons, A. S., J. Immun., *103:* 505, 1969.
12. Nettesheim, P., Makinodan, T. and Williams, M. L., J. Immun., *99:* 150, 1967.
13. Nettesheim, P. and Williams, M. L., J. Immun., *100:* 760, 1968.
14. Little, J. R., Brecher, G., Bradley, T. R. and Rose, S., Blood, *19:* 236, 1962.
15. Strober, S., Unpublished observations.

THE JOURNAL OF IMMUNOLOGY
Vol. 105, No. 3, September 1970

Printed in U.S.A.

THE EVOLUTION OF THE IMMUNE RESPONSE

VII. Antibody to Human "O" Cells and Properties of the Immunoglobulin in Lamprey[1]

BERNARD POLLARA, GARY W. LITMAN, JOANNE FINSTAD, JOHN HOWELL AND ROBERT A. GOOD

From the Pediatric Research Laboratories of the Variety Club Heart Hospital and the Departments of Microbiology and Biochemistry, University of Minnesota, Minneapolis, Minnesota 55455

Received for publication January 12, 1970

Lamprey produced agglutinins in high titer against Brucella organisms and the H antigens of human "O" cells. The antibody was shown to be labile at room temperature. The lamprey immunoglobulin was purified using Bio-Gel A 1.5 column and DE 52-cellulose column fractionation. Both purified immunoglobulin and antibody activity of serum were shown to have the electrophoretic mobility of an alpha globulin, a sedimentation velocity of 9S and a molecular weight of approximately 300,000. These characteristics indicate that the lamprey immunoglobulin is unique.

The sea lamprey, *Petromyzon marinus*, occupies a critical position in the phylogenetic development of immunity. Numerous investigations over a period of years have failed to demonstrate true adaptive immunity among the invertebrates (1, 2). Studies in these laboratories have failed to reveal immune responses to a variety of antigens in two species of hagfishes (3; J. Finstad, personal communication). However, recent findings by Thoenes and Hildemann suggest that hagfishes (*Eptatratus stoutii*) develop a feeble immune response after prolonged stimulation with keyhole limpet hemocyanin (4).

The sea lamprey was found to possess a system of lymphoid cells, a lymphoepithelial protothymus and lymphoid foci in spleen and protovertebral arch (5). Lamprey were able to respond with antibody production to few among many antigens tested, to develop delayed allergic responses to old tuberculin and to reject allografts of skin. These animals exhibited immunologic memory in both cell-mediated and humoral immunologic reactions (6). Our studies revealed that lampreys possess at least two proteins of gamma mobility which do not contain antibody but have iron-binding properties (7). Initial investigations suggested that the antibodies formed by lamprey against *Brucella abortus* had characteristics quite different from antibodies formed by the other primitive vertebrates including elasmobranchs (8–11), chondrosteans (12, 13), holosteans (14), dipnoid (15; G. W. Litman, personal communication), amphibia (16) and reptiles (17–19).

Marchalonis and Edelman (20) described primary immune responses in *Petromyzon marinus* to bacteriophage f2. They demonstrated that both high (14S) and low (6.6S) molecular weight (m.w.) immunoglobulin fractions contained this activity. Marchalonis and Edelman further maintained that the lamprey immunoglobulin molecules contain light and heavy chains similar to the immunoglobulins of higher vertebrates, but they recognized a uniqueness of the lamprey immunoglobulin since the chains seemed not to be covalently bonded. Boffa and Fine (21) reported that *Petromyzon marinus* possess low titers of agglutinins to the H surface antigen of human "O" cells and that immunization of lampreys results in an increase in titer of these agglutinins.

It is the purpose of this report to present immunologic studies on the response to human "O" cells and Brucella antigen in lamprey and to describe the purification and physiochemical characterization of the lamprey immunoglobulin.

[1] This work was aided by grants from The National Foundation-March of Dimes; the United States Public Health Service (AI-08372, AI-08677, AI-00292 and NB-02042); and the Minnesota Chapter, Arthritis Foundation.

MATERIALS AND METHODS

Animals. Both parasitizing and pre-spawning, senescent adult lamprey were obtained from the United States Bureau of Commercial Fisheries, Lamprey Research Station, Hammond Bay, Millersburg, Michigan. Animals were maintained in raceways and aquaria with free flowing fresh lake water. Parasitic lamprey were kept at temperatures between 15°C and 18°C. Parasitizing lamprey were fed by permitting feeding on teleost host fish. Senescent lamprey do not feed. Adult lamprey ranged in weight from 90 to 221 g.

Immune responses of parasitizing adult lamprey. Parasitizing adult lamprey were immunized by intramuscular injections of either 0.1 ml of packed type "O" human red blood cells or 1×10^{10} killed Brucella cells at monthly intervals for 3 months or at weekly intervals for 6 weeks. In all cases the lamprey were bled and killed 7 to 10 days following the last injection. Individual sera were stored at either −20°C or −70°C until used. Antibody titrations for human "O" cells and for Brucella were done by both the standard tube method and microtiter methods with the modification that in these studies titrations were incubated at 20°C or at 37°C.

Immune responses of senescent adult lamprey. Groups of pre-spawning, senescent adult lamprey were immunized with 0.1 ml packed human "O" red blood cells or with 1×10^{10} killed Brucella cells at monthly intervals for 2 months or at weekly intervals for 4, 6 or 9 weeks. Seven to 10 days after the last injection the animals were bled and killed. The individual sera were stored at −20°C until analyzed.

Hyperimmunization. In order to obtain sufficient quantities of "hyperimmune" serum, groups of 50 to 100 additional lamprey, either parasitizing or senescent, were immunized with 0.1 ml packed human "O" cells at weekly intervals for 6 or 9 weeks. The animals surviving the course of immunization were bled and killed 7 days following the last injection. All sera were individually titered. Only those sera with titers greater than 1:640 were used in the purification of lamprey immunoglobulin.

Natural antibody. Fifty normal lamprey sera were tested for naturally occurring antibodies against Brucella cells and human type "O" red blood cells. There was no demonstrable anti-Brucella activity in any of the sera and only 1 serum of the 50 showed slight agglutinating activity for human "O" cells in a titer of less than 1:20.

Characterization of the immunoglobulin. Preparative zonal electrophoresis was carried out using both starch and agar as support media (22). Analytic polyacrylamide gel electrophoresis was performed with a slight modification of the methods of Ornstein and Davis using 7.5%, pH 9.5, separating gels (23, 24). All runs were made at 4°C with a constant current of 5 mA/gel. The tracking dye employed was bromophenol blue, and the runs were allowed to proceed until the tracking dye reached a specific point at the anodal end of the separating gel thus insuring reproducibility of the runs and making R_f calculations possible.

Immunoelectrophoresis was carried out using a modification of the method of Scheidegger (25) with Noble agar, pH 8.6, in barbital buffer. Sera were chromatographed on Bio-Gel A 1.5 m (200 to 400 mesh) with an effective sieving range from 10,000 to 1,500,000 m.w. Columns with dimensions of 2 x 150 cm were equilibrated with 0.01 M phosphate, 0.15 M NaCl, pH 7.2 buffer containing 0.1% sodium azide. A pressure head of 75 cm was maintained throughout all runs.

Ion exchange chromatography on microgranular DE 52 (Whatman, H. Reeve Angel and Co., Clifton, N. J.) was used. In these preparations elution was stepwise using phosphate buffers in the range of 0.02 M to 0.2 M, pH 7.35, or by linear ionic strength gradient produced by a Varigrad gradient maker. Linearity of gradients was checked by conductivity measurements on individual fractions.

Andrews' column chromatography (26) was done on the above described Bio-Gel A 1.5-m columns. All molecular weight markers were tested for homogeneity by immunoelectrophoresis, polyacrylamide gel electrophoresis and analytical centrifugation in the Spinco model E ultracentrifuge. In all cases purity of the markers was confirmed by all three criteria. The colostral IgA which was used as a marker showed a tendency to aggregate as was seen on both the Andrews' column and ultracentrifugal analysis. The major portion of the IgA marker, however, was shown to be 11S. Under these conditions a plot of log molecular weight *vs* linear volume eluted obeyed linearity from 870,000 to 154,000. A slight deviation from linearity was seen when the plot was extended to include the 67,500 m.w. standard bovine serum albumin (BSA). This slight deviation would account for only a 10,000 m.w. increase in the range of concern of this report.

Sucrose density gradient ultracentrifugation was performed at 4°C using a SW 39 swinging bucket rotor in a Spinco model L-2 ultracentrifuge. Gradients were formed using a two chamber linear gradient apparatus equipped with a Technicon autoanalyser pump. Linearity of these gradients was confirmed by analysis in a prismatic refractometer.

RESULTS

Immune responses. Immune responses to *Brucella abortus* and human type "O" red blood cells are summarized in Table I. Lamprey respond with antibody production to both antigens with titers ranging from 1:20 to 1:10,240. Actively parasitizing lamprey seem to respond somewhat more vigorously to both antigens than do the senescent non-feeding lamprey. The highest geometric mean titer (GMT) of 1:2700 (range 1:640 to 1:10,240) was obtained in parasitic lamprey immunized with "O" cells, and the highest GMT with Brucella immunization was 1:370 (range 1:160 to 1:1280).

Several courses of immunization were used with both antigens. These data show that the most effective course of immunization was a weekly injection of human "O" cells for 4 or 6 weeks. Both parasitic and senescent lamprey given this course of immunization for 4 or 6 weeks had GMT of 1:1600 and 1:2700, respectively. Prolonged stimulation with "O" cells (for 9 weekly injections) did not seem to enhance the response.

Lamprey given Brucella cells with either course of immunization responded with lower titers than did those obtained after immunization to human "O" cells. Parasitic and senescent lamprey had anti-Brucella GMT of 1:370 (ranging from 1:160 to 1:1280) and 1:100 (ranging from 1:20 to 1:1280), respectively.

Comparing the methods of immunization for the two antigens, four to six weekly injections of "O" cells appear to evoke a maximum response while three monthly injections of Brucella cells give the maximum response observed in these studies. Again, responses of senescent animals to Brucella antigen were somewhat lower than those observed with actively parasitizing adults.

Both "O" cell agglutinin and Brucella agglutinin titers were determined at 37°C as well as at room temperature. With both antigens incubation at 37°C yielded significantly lower titers, often three or four tube differences in $\log_2$ dilutions. The titers reported in Table I were representative of those incubated at room temperature.

Specificity of the antibody. Specificity of the lamprey anti-"O" cell agglutinins was tested by studying absorption with "O" cells, Bombay cells (which lack H antigen), and by human A and B cells (S. Benson, personal communication). Further, soluble H antigen was used to block the response to "O" cells (M. Adinolfi, personal communication). In these studies absorption with "O" cells regularly reduced the titers to

TABLE I

Immune responses of parasitic and senescent adult lamprey given human "O" cells or killed Brucella cells

Stage of Life Cycle	No. Injected	No. Responding	Antigen	Type of Immunization	Time	GMT[a]	Reciprocal of Range
Parasitic	22	21	"O" cells	Monthly	3 mo	1:370	0–2,560[b]
Parasitic	5	5	Brucella	Monthly	3 mo	1:370	160–1,280
Parasitic	23	23	"O" cells	Weekly	6 wk	1:2700	640–10,240
Parasitic	7	7	Brucella	Weekly	6 wk	1:240	20–2,560
Senescent	35	30	"O" cells	Monthly	2 mo	1:26	0–640
Senescent	34	34	Brucella	Monthly	2 mo	1:120	20–640
Senescent	14	14	"O" cells	Weekly	4 wk	1:1600	320–5,120
Senescent	34	34	Brucella	Weekly	6 wk	1:100	20–1,280
Senescent	27	27	"O" cells	Weekly	9 wk	1:790	80–2,560

[a] GMT, geometric mean titer.
[b] Titer expressed as the reciprocal of the serum dilution.

insignificant levels, whereas absorption with Bombay, A or B cells did not significantly reduce the titers. Significant inhibition of agglutination was also obtained upon addition of soluble H substance prior to titration with "O" cells. These observations establish that the bulk of antibody formed against human "O" cells was directed against the H antigen.

Lability of the antibody. In the course of these studies it was noted that both Brucella antibody and antibody to the human "O" erythrocytes were labile. Storage at room temperature and particularly column manipulations at room temperature often resulted in decreases in titer. Similar losses in activity were also noted by Marchalonis and Edelman (20) in handling the f2 phage antibody.

Purification of lamprey immunoglobulin. Sera with anti-human "O" cell agglutinating activity were pooled and applied to 2 x 150 cm Bio-Gel A 1.5-m columns. Following an initial equilibration phase the column was eluted with phosphate-buffered saline, pH 7.3. After elution from the column the chromatographic fractions were checked for anti-human "O" cell agglutinating activity. The majority of the agglutinating activity following appropriate volume compensation was associated with the second peak immediately following the first major peak (Fig. 1). The first peak consisted of low density lipoprotein. The Bio-Gel fractions possessing the majority of the antibody activity were concentrated and applied to equilibrated columns of DE 52-cellulose. Fractions were eluted stepwise by ionic strength increases holding pH constant. A typical elution profile (Fig. 2) demonstrates that the majority of the agglutinating activity eluted between 0.04 M and 0.045 M phosphate, pH 7.35. Analysis of the fraction containing antibody activity revealed contamination by at least one major component. Recycling on DE 52 using an identical elution schedule (Fig. 3) yielded a product represented by one arc on immunoelectrophoresis (Fig. 4), one major band on polyacrylamide gel electrophoresis and a single symmetrical peak on analytical gel filtration on Bio-Gel A 1.5 m. The precise amount of antibody nitrogen present in our most homogeneous preparations has not been estimated. The problem is further complicated by the extreme instability and lability of the antibody preparations noted by both Marchalonis and Edelman and ourselves.

Sedimentation velocity and electrophoretic characteristics. The peak agglutinating activity of immune lamprey serum to Brucella cells was found to possess an $s_{20,w}$ value of approximately 9 as determined by zonal ultracentrifugation (Fig. 5)

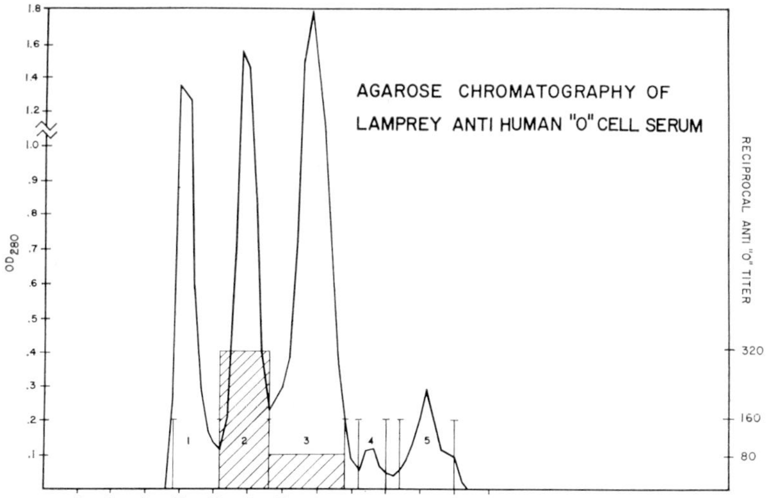

Figure 1. Chromatogram of whole immune lamprey serum from Bio-Gel A 1.5-m column demonstrating the elution characteristic of lamprey anti-human "O" cell antibody. The shaded area represents the antibody. Note that the majority of antibody is associated with the second peak eluted from the column. Small amounts of antibody were found in the third peak.

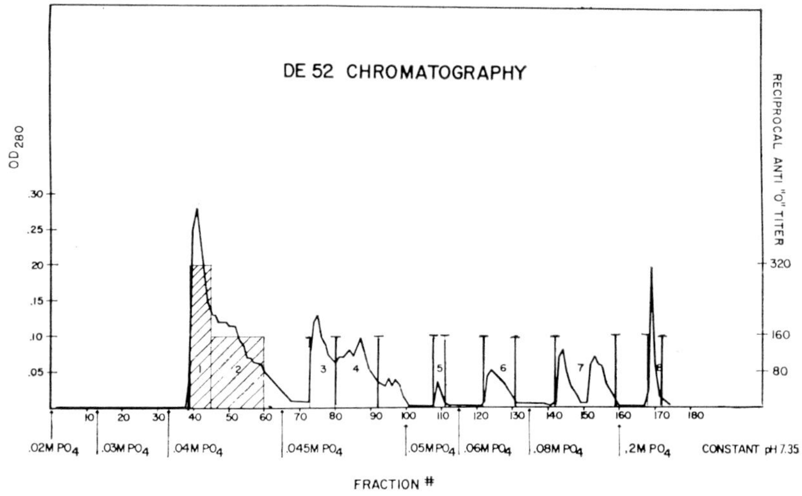

Figure 2. Further purification of lamprey immunoglobulin. Fraction II's obtained on Bio-Gel A 1.5 m were pooled and chromatographed on DE 52-cellulose. Note that the bulk of agglutinating activity eluted between 0.03 and 0.04 M phosphate pH 7.5.

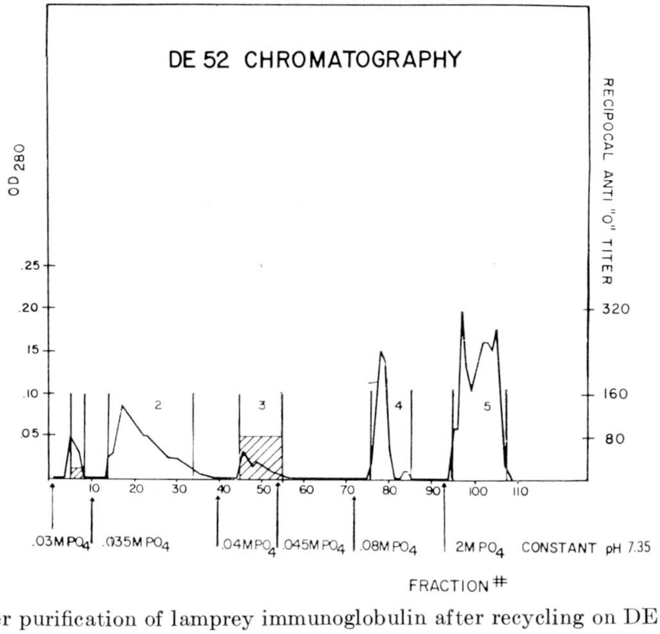

Figure 3. Further purification of lamprey immunoglobulin after recycling on DE 52. Upon recycling some antibody activity is found in a fraction eluted at 0.03 M phosphate; antibody activity is absent from a second fraction eluted at 0.035 M phosphate. Most of the antibody elutes between 0.04 and 0.045 M phosphate.

using the method of Fisher and Canning (27). Standard sucrose density gradient ultracentrifugation performed in 10% to 40% linear gradients showed the peak agglutinating activity to occur between the centrifugal boundary of ^{125}I-labeled human IgG (153,000 m.w.) and the centripetal boundary of ^{131}I-labeled paddlefish 19S immunoglobulin (870,000 m.w.).

Fractionation by starch and agar block electrophoresis at pH 8.6 in barbital buffer demonstrated agglutinating activity in a position immediately anodal to the point of application. This mobility agrees with that obtained by electrophoretic analysis of the purified lamprey immunoglobulin and is best described as having a beta 1 or alpha 2 mobility (Fig. 4). Acrylamide gel electrophoresis gave an R_f of 0.28. This value is coincident with the R_f calculated for the agglutinating activity for "O" cells in whole immune serum when gel slices were eluted and direct titers measured on the eluates.

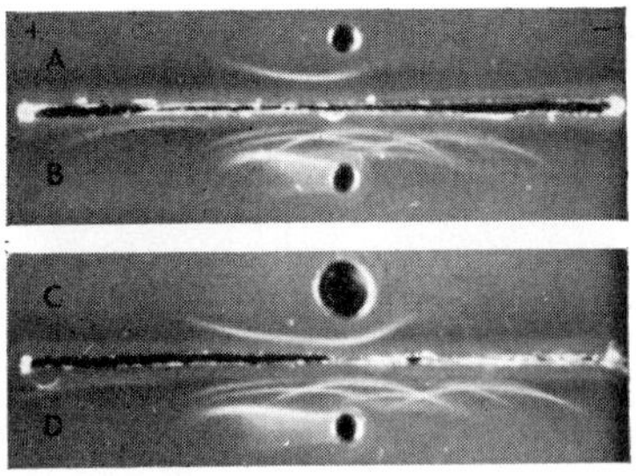

Figure 4. Immunoelectrophoretic analysis of the purified lamprey immunoglobulin. *A*, the single arc is the purified lamprey immunoglobulin after reaction with goat anti-whole lamprey serum. Note that the lamprey immunoglobulin migrates as a single arc in the alpha globulin region. *B*, the whole lamprey serum reacted against goat anti-whole lamprey serum. Cathode to right. *C*, the purified immunoglobulin has been applied in 5 × greater amount. Note: even with this concentration, the lamprey immunoglobulin appears as a single arc. *D*, for reference whole lamprey serum is reacted with the goat antiserum.

Molecular weight estimation. Bio-Gel A 1.5-m column chromatography of the purified immunoglobulin preparation and a series of molecular weight markers demonstrated the peak elution of purified lamprey immunoglobulin to be present between the descending boundary of the colostral IgA marker and the ascending boundary of human IgG marker (Fig. 6). When appropriate elution points were plotted as log molecular weight *vs* linear peak elution point volume, a straight line plot was obtained for the three immunoglobulin markers used, thus permitting extrapolation to a molecular weight of approximately 320,000 for the lamprey immunoglobulin (Fig. 7). Using this system similar molecular weights were determined for a radio-iodinated labeled eluate of the slice containing the peak agglutinating titer from polyacrylamide gel electrophoresis and the peak anti-human "O" cell agglutinating activity in whole immune lamprey serum.

Coincidence of anti-Brucella abortus and anti-human "O" cell activity. Of interest was the establishment of the physiochemical properties of two types of antibody to different antigens in the lamprey. Mixtures of anti-Brucella and anti-

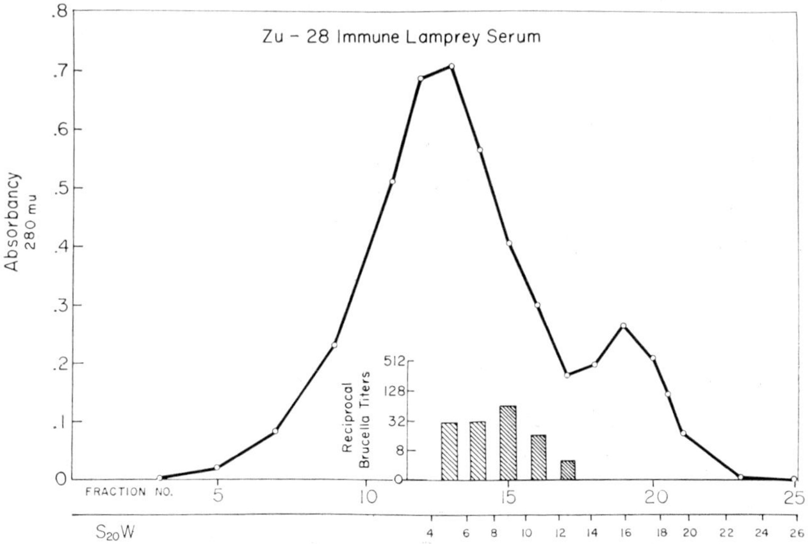

Figure 5. Sucrose density gradient separation of anti-Brucella lamprey serum using method of Fisher and Canning (27). Beckman B IV rotor. Sample volume 7 ml 10% to 20% sucrose, linear with rotor volume, phosphate buffer pH 7.5, μ = 0.2.

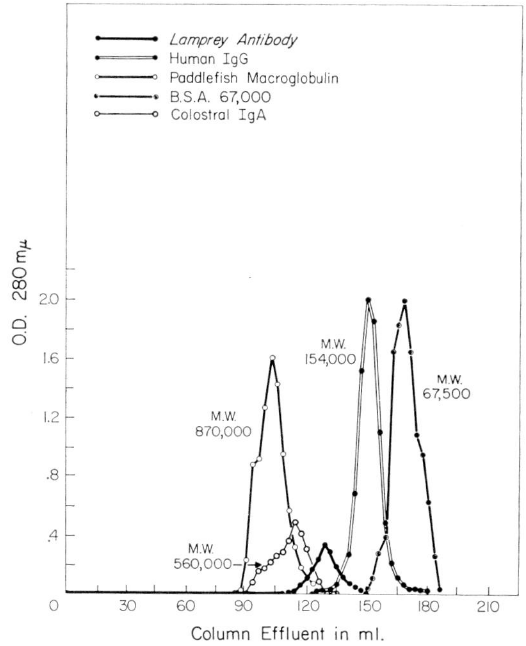

Figure 6. Analytical gel filtration of purified lamprey immunoglobulin compared with proteins of established molecular weight. The lamprey immunoglobulin eluted between the descending boundary of colostral IgA marker and the ascending boundary of the human IgG marker. These findings indicate that the molecular weight of lamprey immunoglobulin is unique.

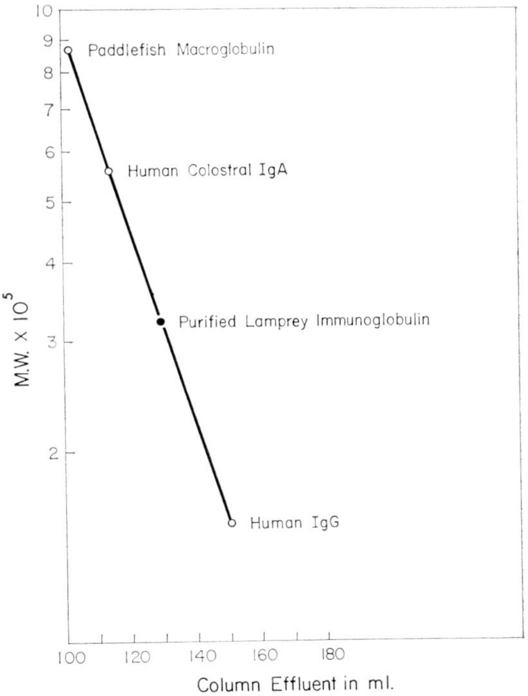

Figure 7. Andrews' plot of elution points of the three immunoglobulin markers illustrated in Figure 6. Molecular weight of lamprey immunoglobulin is approximately 300,000 by this method.

human "O" cell immune sera were applied to both Bio-Gel A 1.5-m and DEAE-cellulose columns and duplicate titers were run on each chromatographic fraction obtained. Agglutinating activity for both human "O" and Brucella cells was eluted at identical volumes thus establishing coincidence of the two antibodies within the resolution of the method employed.

DISCUSSION

These observations establish that antibody responses can be consistently obtained in the sea lamprey to both *Brucella abortus* antigen and type "O" human red blood cells. With repeated weekly immunizations high-titered serum to both antigens can be available for analysis. Comparative absorptions and agglutination inhibition studies established that the agglutinating antibody to human "O" cells is directed toward the H antigen. We thus confirm and extend observations of Boffa *et al.* (21), who originally found that lamprey serum contained an agglutinin for human "O" cells and that an immune reaction can be produced against this antigen in the lamprey.

At face value our studies of the physical and immunochemistry of the immunoglobulins of the lamprey seem to contradict certain findings of Marchalonis and Edelman (20) who, using neutralization of f2 phage, claimed that lamprey immunoglobulins, like immunoglobulins of sharks and other fishes, occur in both high and low m.w. forms and possess conventional light and heavy chain structure. Although our inability to obtain immune responses to several bacteriophages in the lamprey has precluded direct comparison of our findings with those reported by Marchalonis and Edelman, it seems clear to us that the immunoglobulin we are studying, and the only immunoglobulin we can demonstrate in the lamprey, has unique properties which contrast sharply with the immunoglobulin of mammals and of those heretofore described for various species of primitive vertebrates (8–19). The unusual molecular weight and electrophoretic mobility and, more importantly perhaps, the apparent lability dictate that this protein may have unusual structural features which require further analysis.

Acknowledgments. The authors wish to acknowledge the facilities and helpfulness of the members of the United States Bureau of Commercial Fisheries, Hammond Bay Lamprey Research Station and the Great Lakes Fisheries Research Board of Canada and the United States for collection and maintenance of experimental animals.

REFERENCES

1. Bang, F. B., Fed. Proc., *26:* 1664, 1967.
2. Good, R. A. and Papermaster, B. W., Advances Immun., *4:* 1, 1964.
3. Papermaster, B. W., Condie, T. M. and Good, R. A., Nature, *196:* 355, 1962.
4. Thoenes, G. H. and Hildemann, W. H. Symposium on Mechanisms of Antibody Formation, in Proceedings of Czechoslovak Academy of Sciences, Prague, 1969.
5. Finstad, J., Papermaster, B. W. and Good, R. A., Lab. Invest., *13:* 490, 1964.
6. Finstad, J. and Good, R. A., J. Exp. Med., *120:* 1151, 1964.
7. Webster, R. O. and Pollara, B., Comp. Biochem. Physiol., *30:* 509, 1969.
8. Marchalonis, J. J. and Edelman, G. M., J. Exp. Med., *122:* 601, 1965.
9. Clem, L. W. and Small, P. A., J. Exp. Med., *125:* 893, 1967.
10. Clem, L. W., DeBoutaud, F. and Sigel, M. M., J. Immun., *99:* 1226, 1967.
11. Suran, A. A., Tarail, M. H. and Papermaster, B. W., J. Immun., *99:* 679, 1967.
12. Fish, L. A., Pollara, B. and Good, R. A., in *Phylogeny of Immunity*, Edited by R. T. Smith, P. A. Miescher and R. A. Good, p. 99, University of Florida Press, Gainesville, Florida, 1966.
13. Pollara, B., Suran, A., Finstad, J. and Good, R. A., Proc. Nat. Acad. Sci., *59:* 1307, 1968.
14. Bradshaw, C. M., Clem, L. W. and Sigel, M. M., J. Immun., *103:* 496, 1969.
15. Marchalonis, J. J., Aust. J. Exp. Biol. Med. Sci., *47:* 405, 1969.
16. Marchalonis, J. J. and Edelman, G. M., J. Exp. Med., *124:* 901, 1966.
17. Grey, H. M., J. Immun., *91:* 819, 1963.
18. Lykakis, J. J., Immunology, *14:* 799, 1968.
19. Marchalonis, J. J., Ealey, E. H. M. and Diener, E., Aust. J. Exp. Biol. Med. Sci., *47:* 367, 1969.
20. Marchalonis, J. J. and Edelman, G. M., J. Exp. Med., *127:* 891, 1968.
21. Boffa, G. A., Fine, J. M., Drilhon, A. and Amouch, P., Nature, *214:* 701, 1967.
22. Kunkel, H. G. and Slater, R. J., Proc. Soc. Exp. Biol. Med. *80:* 42, 1952.
23. Ornstein, L., Ann. N. Y. Acad. Sci., *121:* 321, 1964.
24. Davis, B. J., Ann. N. Y. Acad. Sci., *121:* 404, 1964.
25. Scheidegger, J. J., Int. Arch. Allerg., *7:* 103, 1955.
26. Andrews, P., Biochem. J., *91:* 222, 1964.
27. Fisher, W. D. and Canning, R. E., Nat. Cancer Inst. Monogr., *21:* 403, 1966.

THE JOURNAL OF IMMUNOLOGY
Vol. 105, No. 3, September 1970
Printed in U.S.A.

AN *IN VITRO* CORRELATIVE ASSAY FOR THE IMMUNOSUPPRESSIVE ACTIVITY OF HORSE ANTI-RAT LYMPHOCYTE SERA: ESTIMATION OF LYMPHOCYTOPHILIC ANTIBODY ACTIVITY USING ^{51}Cr-LABELED THYMOCYTES

MICHAEL K. BACH, JOHN R. BRASHLER AND ROBERT J. PERPER

From the Department of Hypersensitivity Diseases Research, The Upjohn Company, Kalamazoo, Michigan

Received for publication January 5, 1970

An *in vitro* method for determining equine cytophilic antibody activity against rat lymphocytes is presented. Because of its reliance on a radioactive counting end point, the assay is rapid, sensitive and capable of handling large numbers of sera. There is a good correlation between the *in vitro* activity of these sera and their ability to prolong the survival of skin homografts in rats.

In the last few years the preparation of potent, heterologous antilymphocytic sera (ALS) for administration in model animal systems and for combatting allograft rejection in human transplant patients has received considerable attention. Interpretation of many of these studies has been difficult because no predictive assay was available to permit a meaningful regulation of the dose of immunosuppressive activity being administered to different animals, in different experiments, or when using different preparations of serum. It is now well known that lymphocytotoxicity or lymphoagglutinating activity does not correlate with the immunosuppressive potency of sera (1). Other features, notably those dealing with the mitogenic stimulation of lymphocytes *in vitro*, also have failed to yield correlations with immunosuppressive potency (2, 3). J. F. Bach *et al.* (4) have presented evidence for a correlation between the ability of ALS preparations to prolong the survival of skin allografts and their ability to inhibit the formation of "rosettes" between lymphocytes from unimmunized animals and sheep erythrocytes. While the assay is applicable to antisera against mouse and human lymphocytes, neither we nor the French group succeeded in using it with antisera against rat cells because of the very low incidence of natural rosette-forming cells in rat spleens.

We have recently presented preliminary evidence that there was a strong correlation between the ability of horse antirat lymphocyte sera (HARLS) to opsonize rat thymocytes and to prolong the survival of skin allografts in rats (5). The opsonizing activity of the sera had been estimated by counting the number of treated rat thymocytes adhering to a constant number of rat macrophages on a monolayer, a tedious and time-consuming process.

In the present communication, we present an improved method for the estimation of this cytophilic activity of ALS based on measurement of the radioactivity adhering to the macrophage monolayers after ^{51}Cr-labeled rat thymocytes pretreated with ALS are allowed to attach. In addition, several experiments dealing with the species specificity for the macrophages involved and the organ specificity for the lymphocytes are also presented.

MATERIALS AND METHODS

The preparation of antisera and their evaluation in prolonging the survival of L/Bn rat skin grafted to Lewis strain recipient rats have been described (6). Briefly, the prolongation of skin grafts was determined following a standard regimen of treatments with ALS consisting of administration (i.p.) of 1.5 ml/rat on days −1 and 0 (day of grafting), 1.0 ml to each on days +1 and +2 and 0.5 ml daily on days +3 through +8.

The preparation of rat peritoneal macrophage monolayers has been described (5). The monolayers used in this study were prepared on round, Red Label no. 2 coverslips, 12 mm in diameter (Arthur H. Thomas Co., Philadelphia, catalog no. 7022) which had been rinsed in water and alcohol before autoclaving. Unless otherwise indicated, the coverslips were seeded at a concentration of 1.5×10^6 leukocytes/50-mm Petri plate as determined by a cell count on a Coulter counter model A (threshold = 8, ACS = 5), placing 12 to 14 coverslips/plate. This resulted in a macrophage density of 100/mm² of surface area based on a direct count of the adhering cells after 48 hr of culture.

Preparation of ^{51}Cr-labeled lymphocytes. Lymphocytes were obtained from the thymus of 200-g male Sprague-Dawley rats unless otherwise indicated. Single cell suspensions of thymic and lymph node cells were prepared as described for thymocytes (7). Bone marrow was obtained from the long bones of the hind legs by perfusion with citrated saline with a syringe. Where indicated, purified lymphocytes were isolated from the cell suspensions by centrifugation over a solution of Hypaque-Ficoll (8).

The cells were concentrated by centrifugation at half maximal speed in an International Equipment Co. clinical centrifuge for 10 min and were suspended in twice their volume of medium RPMI 1634 (Grand Island Biological Co., Grand Island, N. Y.). One hundred microcuries of $Na_2{}^{51}CrO_4$ (specific activity 38 to 76 Ci/g) were added/ml of packed cells. The suspension was incubated at 37°C for 15 to 30 min, diluted with saline and washed 7 to 10 times with 10 volumes each of citrated saline/volume of packed cells to remove the soluble radioactivity. The specific activity of the washed cells, when determined on a Packard Tri-Carb model 314E liquid scintillation spectrometer in the presence of Diotol (9), was approximately 3 to 4 cpm/10^3 cells in a large number of experiments. The counting efficiency was 15%.

Incubation with HARLS and attachment to macrophages. The ^{51}Cr-labeled cells were resuspended at a concentration of 3×10^7/ml in medium RPMI 1634, and 1-ml amounts, containing serial twofold dilutions of the HARLS preparations to be assayed, were incubated at 37°C for 1 hr in duplicate. All HARLS were heated to 63°C for 10 min (5, 10) immediately before use and were not refrozen thereafter. At the end of the incubation, the tube contents were diluted to 5 ml with saline, the cells were sedimented by centrifugation at 300 × G for 10 min and the supernatant solution was removed. The cells could be washed in saline before final resuspension in medium RPMI 1634 without affecting the results. The resuspended cells, in a volume of 1 ml, were poured over a macrophage monolayer which had been rinsed in saline and placed in a disposable tray with 15-mm diameter cups (Linbro Chemical Co., Inc., New Haven, Conn., type FB 54). The cups were covered with Saran Wrap (Dow Chemical Co.) and the lymphocytes were allowed to attach for 1 hr at 37°C. The coverslips were rinsed by five or six immersions in two changes of saline and were placed into counting vials containing Diotol scintillator fluid.

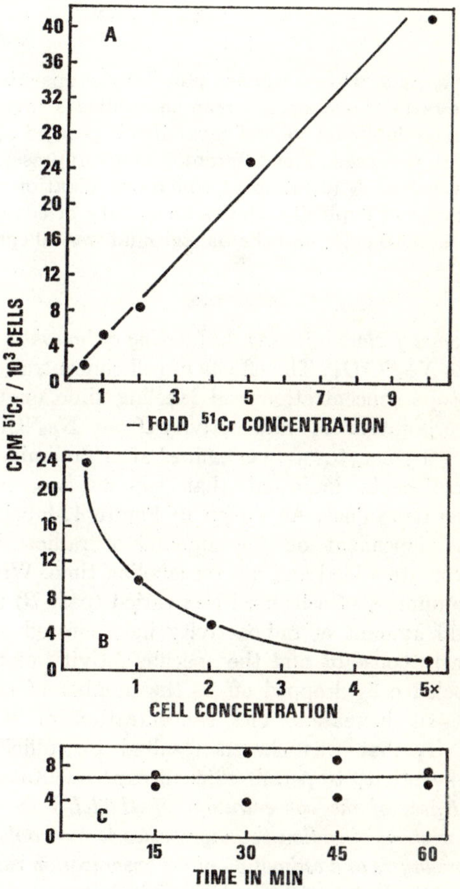

Figure 1A, effect of the $Na_2{}^{51}CrO_4$ concentration on the labeling of thymocytes. A suspension containing 3×10^8 cells/ml was incubated for 30 min at 37°C with various concentrations of $Na_2{}^{51}CrO_4$. The standard ("onefold") concentration was 100 μCi/ml. *B*, effect of cell concentration on labeling of thymocytes with $Na_2{}^{51}CrO_4$. Incubation was with 100 μCi/ml $Na_2{}^{51}CrO_4$ for 30 min. The 1 × cell concentration was 10^8 cells/ml. *C*, effect of incubation time on labeling of thymocytes with $Na_2{}^{51}CrO_4$. Incubation was with 100 μCi/ml $Na_2{}^{51}CrO_4$ at a cell concentration of 2×10^8 cells/ml.

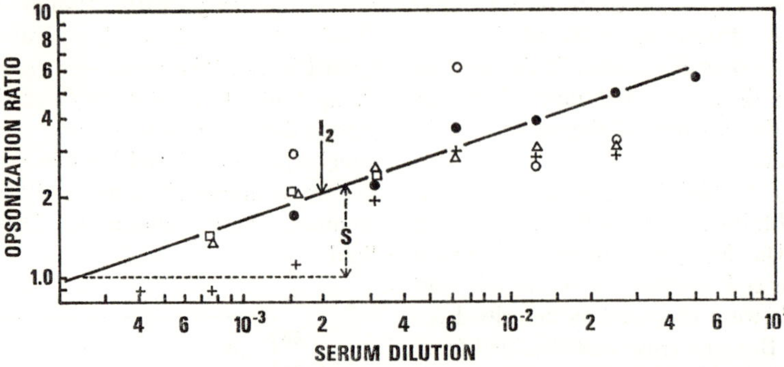

Figure 2. Dose-response plot for the opsonization of rat thymocytes by serial dilutions of HARLS. The ratio of average net cpm on duplicate coverslips exposed to treated thymocytes to the average net cpm on duplicate control coverslips is plotted as the opsonization ratio against the dilution of HARLS which was used. The different symbols represent results from experiments conducted on different days. The values I_2 (dilution at which opsonization ratio = 2.0) and S (slope of line as defined in text) are indicated. Typically, the radioactivity of cover slips exposed to untreated lymphocytes was approximately 200 cpm, and the background was 20 cpm.

RESULTS

Some factors affecting the labeling of lymphocytes with $Na_2{}^{51}CrO_4$. The effects of cell concentration, isotope concentration and labeling time on the incorporation of radioactivity from $Na_2{}^{51}CrO_4$ into thymocytes were examined after preliminary experiments indicated that labeling was not time dependent. As shown in Figure 1, labeling was dependent on the amount of radioactive chromate added and not on labeling time. When the number of cells used was varied (part *B*) the total amount of radioactivity incorporated was nearly constant and the specific activity of the labeled cells dropped off as the number of cells present increased. The concentration of $Na_2{}^{51}CrO_4$ that was chosen resulted in sufficient radioactivity to permit efficient experimentation.

Effect of the concentration of HARLS on the attachment of radioactive thymocytes to macrophage monolayers and estimation of the opsonization ratio. A typical plot of the relationship between dilutions of HARLS and opsonization ratio (OR) is shown in Figure 2. The results represent four independent experiments, each conducted on a different day. The OR is defined as the ratio of the average net cpm found on coverslips after attachment of HARLS-treated thymocytes to the average net cpm found on coverslips which were incubated with untreated thymocytes. All radioactive counts were corrected for background. The use of the OR permits comparisons from one experiment to the next despite variation in the specific activity of the labeled thymocytes. When different HARLS preparations were assayed, both the slope and the intercept of the dose-response plots varied. Thus, it seemed inappropriate to base estimates of the opsonizing activity of the preparations on either of these factors by itself. As already reported (5), the opsonization titer, OT, arbitrarily defined as the ratio of the slope (S) of the dose *vs* OR-response curve to its intercept (I_2), correlated with the *in vivo* immunosuppressive activity of the sera. I_2 is defined as the HARLS dilution at which the OR is 2.0. The slope, S, is defined as the change in the height of the plot along the OR axis for a 10-fold change in the HARLS concentration starting with the point at which the OR is 1.0 (i.e., log opsonization ratio = 0). This is equal to the ratio of the OR values for any 10-fold change in the ALS concentration (since antilog (log B- log A) = B/A). The reproducibility of the OT from one experiment to the next was ±1 dilution tube (standard deviation of ±78%).

Correlation between opsonization titer and the prolongation of skin allograft survival by HARLS. The OT's of 18 sera are plotted against their activity in prolonging skin allograft survival under standardized conditions in Figure 3. The linear correlation had a regression coefficient of 0.622, $p < 0.01$. When all the individual OR values for a given serum from various experiments were pooled to calculate a single OT, the correlation was 0.686. It should be clear that this log-log

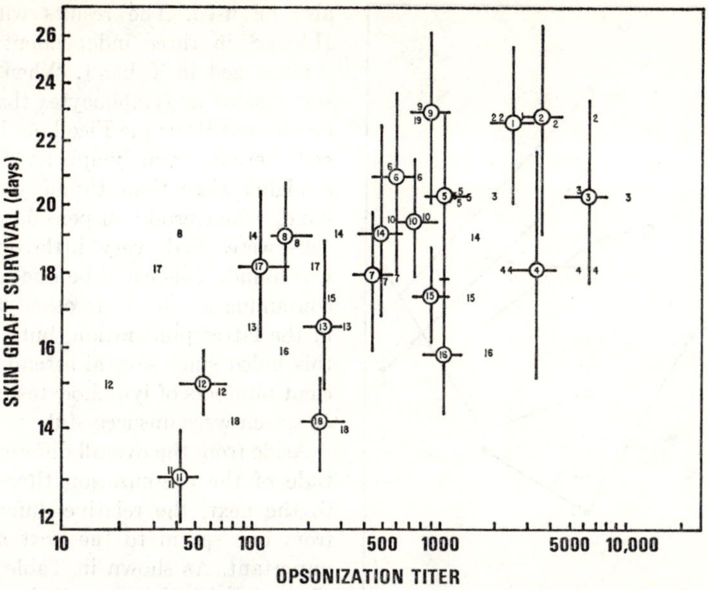

Figure 3. Correlation between the opsonization titers of 18 HARLS preparations and their activity in prolonging rat skin allograft survival. See *Materials and Methods* for details of skin graft evaluation, and Figure 2 for the derivation of the opsonization titer S/I_2. Survivals of control skin grafts were 13 to 14 days. Numbers represent results for individual determinations on each serum. Circles are titers obtained when all OR values for a given serum were pooled. Bars are 95% confidence limits.

correlation will break down at the left end of the plot since once the correlation line intersects the line where skin graft survival is equal to that of the controls, any further decrease in opsonizing potency of the sera will not be reflected in a decrease in the survival of skin grafts. Thus two sera having very low OT values were omitted from the calculation of the line of regression, since they clearly fell off the linear portion of the curve.

Variables affecting the reproducibility of the determination of the opsonization titer. In the previous report (5) we stated that, using the visual method of enumerating the ratio of the number of lymphocytes adhering per macrophage, the results were independent of the number of lymphocytes employed. When the same proportion of lymphocytes to macrophages (on the basis of the areas of the monolayers involved) was used in the radioactive assay, variable OT's were obtained even though the dose-response plots were linear. Furthermore, the OR values that were obtained in the radioactive assay never exceeded 10, whereas the visual assay often resulted in maximal values near 50. In the hope of finding conditions that would increase the maximum OR values in the radioactive method (thus increasing the slopes of the dose-response plots) and of improving the reproducibility of the assay, the effect of the concentration of macrophages on the monolayers and the effect of the concentration of the lymphocytes during attachment were examined. The radioactive method permitted this to be done over a much broader range than was feasible with visual counting. The results of two experiments are summarized in Figure 4. Large variations in the OT values were obtained with different numbers of thymocytes or macrophages. As the number of thymocytes used per determination was increased to 3×10^7 the values became more reproducible from experiment to experiment and from one macrophage concentration to another. Thus reproducibility depended more on the number of thymocytes that were used than on the number of macrophages on the monolayer or on the ratio of thymocytes to macrophages, and reproducibility was obtained only when 1 to 3×10^7 thymocytes were used for each determination. Although the use of lower macrophage concentrations might have increased the sensitivity of the assay, the variability introduced with the

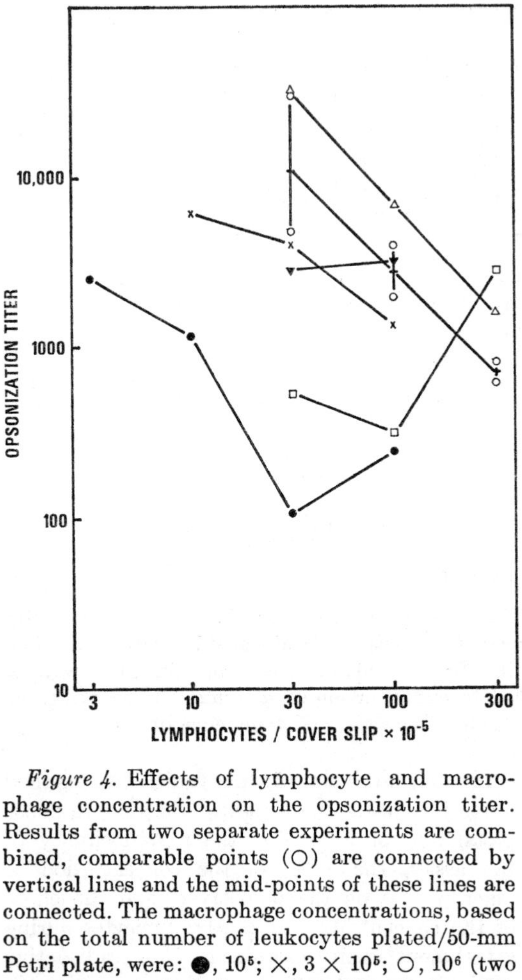

Figure 4. Effects of lymphocyte and macrophage concentration on the opsonization titer. Results from two separate experiments are combined, comparable points (○) are connected by vertical lines and the mid-points of these lines are connected. The macrophage concentrations, based on the total number of leukocytes plated/50-mm Petri plate, were: ●, 10^5; ×, 3×10^5; ○, 10^6 (two experiments included); △, 2×10^6; ▼, 3×10^6; □, 5×10^6.

changes in the abundance of macrophages in various preparations of peritoneal exudate cells dissuaded us from using these conditions. For routine assay, Petri plates were seeded with 1.5×10^6 macrophages and each coverslip was incubated with 3×10^7 thymocytes.

Effect of lymphocytes from different organs on the opsonization titer. Because of the ease with which large quantities of lymphocytes can be obtained in relatively pure form from the thymus, and because of the presumed desirability of inhibiting those immune responses which involve "thymus-derived" lymphocytes by treatment with ALS (11, 12), the standard assay was performed with crude cell suspensions from thymus. It was of interest, however, to determine whether lymphocytes from other lymphoid organs could also be used. The results with several active HARLS in three independent experiments are summarized in Table I. When either crude cell suspensions or lymphocytes that had been purified by the Hypaque-Ficoll method (8) were used, cells derived from lymph nodes frequently gave a higher titer than thymocytes. On the other hand, when crude suspensions of bone marrow cells were used, very little opsonizing activity was found. This could be due to the much larger contamination by cells other than lymphocytes in the latter preparation, but attempts to prove this failed since several attempts to purify sufficient numbers of lymphocytes from bone marrow or spleen were unsuccessful.

Aside from the overall differences in the magnitude of the opsonization titers from one tissue to the next, the relative differences in activity from one serum to the next are perhaps more important. As shown in Table I, if the activity of serum with thymus cells is taken as standard, the activities with the cells from other tissues were not in a constant relation to the activity with thymocytes. Experiments II and III contain an internal control as sera 4 and 5 were used in both: the ratio of activity of these sera (numbers in parentheses) remained the same during purification. Thus, it may be important to use thymus cells exclusively for the correlative assay and not to substitute other lymphoid cells (12).

Opsonization titers of HARLS using macrophages from other species. If the opsonizing activity of HARLS is due to a cytophilic antibody having specificity for rat lymphocytes, it is possible that similar activity can be demonstrated when macrophages from other species than the rat are employed. This is particularly important when the application of this assay to horse antihuman lymphocyte preparations (HAHLS) is considered since significant supplies of human macrophages are difficult to obtain. As shown in Figure 5, the correlation between the skin graft-prolonging activity of HARLS and the opsonization titers obtained using rabbit macrophages was as good as that when rat macrophages were used. A rank correlation between the factors, as well as a rank correlation between the opsonization titers using the two different macrophage preparations, was near perfect. On the other hand, no such correlations could be obtained using mouse peritoneal macrophages (Fig. 6). Similar results were obtained in two

TABLE I

Comparative opsonizing activity of various HARLS preparations when cells from different lymphoid organs were used

Experiment	Serum No.	Immunizing Antigen[a]	Skin Graft Survival[b]	Opsonization Titer[c]		
				Thymus	Lymph node[d]	Bone marrow[d]
			days			
I[e]	1	Spleen	22.9	830	1800 (2.1)	
	2	Spleen	19.6	770	830 (1.1)	
	3	Thymus	22.5	6200	1100 (0.18)	
II[e]	4	Thymus	22.7	2200	6200 (2.9)	450 (0.21)
	5	Thymus	21.0	1100	4300 (3.8)	630 (0.55)
	6	Thymus	18.7	2300	4000 (1.7)	230 (0.10)
	7	Spleen	19.1	1110		560 (0.50)
III[f]	4	Thymus	22.7	1300	4000 (3.0)	
	5	Thymus	21.0	1000	4000 (4.0)	
	8	Thymus	18.7	500	8300 (17)	
	9	Thymus	20.5	480	5900 (12)	

[a] Immunizing cells were lymphocytes from the tissue source indicated, which had been purified by the Hypaque-Ficoll method.

[b] Normal rejection time was 14.5 days.

[c] See text for derivation of opsonization titer.

[d] Values in parentheses are the ratio of opsonization titer with cells used to the titer when thymocytes were used.

[e] Crude cell suspensions were used for assay.

[f] Purified lymphocytes were used for assay.

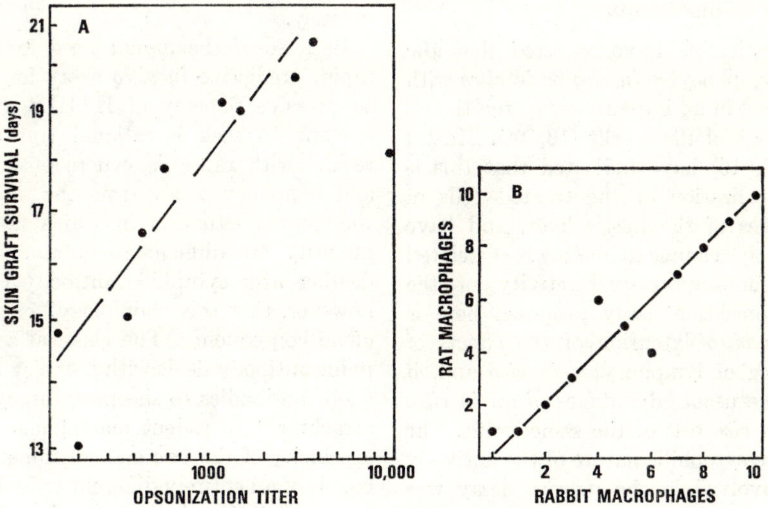

Figure 5. Correlation between opsonization titers using rat thymocyte and rabbit peritoneal macrophages and the skin graft-prolonging activity of various HARLS. Seventy-two-hour-old macrophage monolayers were prepared from peritoneal exudate cells from a single rabbit 6 days after i.p. stimulation with 0.5 g glycogen in 30 ml saline. *A*, plot of opsonization titer *vs* skin graft survival. *B*, rank correlation of opsonization titers using rat *vs* rabbit peritoneal macrophages.

separate experiments. When 24-hr monolayer cultures were used in place of 48- to 72-hr cultures, the results with the rabbit macrophages were not good. Perhaps this was due to the higher contamination of the rabbit macrophage monolayers by polymorphonuclear cells, which, while they might bind thymocytes, have no relation to the assay at hand. Thus, it may be possible

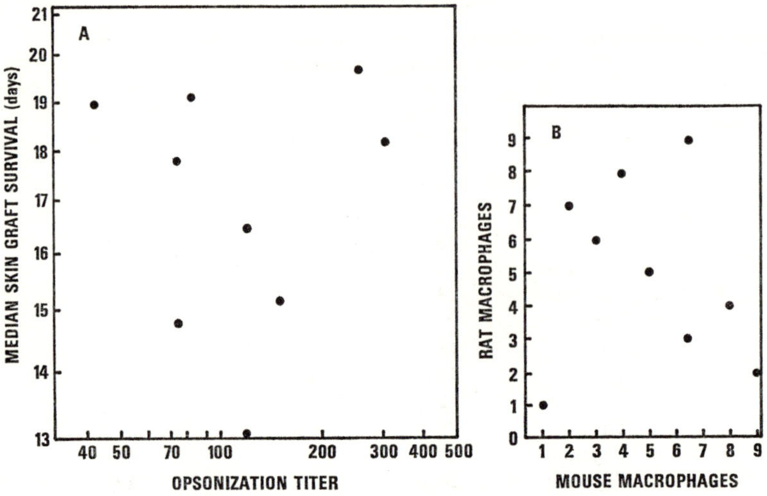

Figure 6. Correlation between opsonization titers using rat thymocytes and mouse peritoneal macrophages, and the skin graft-prolonging activity of various HARLS. Seventy-two-hour-old macrophage monolayers were prepared from peritoneal exudate cells from 10 mice 2 days after i.p. stimulation with 1 ml thioglycolate medium. *A*, plot of opsonization titer *vs* skin graft survival. *B*, rank correlation of opsonization titers using rat *vs* mouse macrophages.

to use macrophage cultures from another species for the assay of HARLS.

DISCUSSION

Several investigators have reported that the treatment of lymphocytes *in vivo* or *in vitro* with ALS has resulted in an impairment of the tissue-specific "homing" of these cells (13, 14). Martin and Miller (15, 16) have indicated that this is due to the localization of the treated cells in the macrophages of the host's liver, and have suggested that this change in homing is correlated with the immunosuppressive activity of the sera. The opsonization assay proposed here is possibly an *in vitro* extension of the effects of ALS on homing of lymphocytes *in vivo* and, if so, offers all the usual advantages of an *in vitro* test over an *in vivo* test of the same event. The evidence for the cytophilic nature of the antibody (antibodies) involved in the present assay was discussed in some detail in our previous report (5), as was the evidence that the assay was specific for cells from the species against which the sera had been prepared, for lymphocytes as contrasted to erythrocytes, and that it did not detect anti-IgG activity. Furthermore, differences between our assay and that proposed by Greaves *et al.* (17) were considered, and it was pointed out that the latter assay, because of its dependence on the complement system, was probably a very sensitive assay for the lymphocytotoxicity of the sera rather than their immunosuppressive potency.

Because of the urgent need for developing a rapid, predictive *in vitro* assay for the immunosuppressive potency of HAHLS, it seemed important to seek a rational translation of the results with rat cells, where both macrophages and lymphocytes are from the same species, to the human situation in which macrophages in quantity are difficult to obtain. The literature dealing with cytophilic antibody (18) disclosed, however, that this "homology" of cell types was of no consequence. The classical assay for cytophilic antibody deals with homologous or heterologous antibodies to sheep erythrocytes and their attachment to rodent macrophages. Clearly the specificity of the two ends of the antibody molecule is of an entirely different order of magnitude, the antigen-(erythrocyte or lymphocyte) combining site being highly specific and the cytophilic site having relatively broad specificity. In fact, the ability of a heterologous serum protein to bind to a cell to which the immunized animal has, presumably, never been exposed must be a function of the general properties of this class of molecules or of a cross-reactivity between the combining sites on the macrophages of the heterologous (horse in this case) host and those on the rat macrophages. Since clear differences in the specificity of the combining sites of macrophages of relatively closely related species have been demonstrated by prior studies such as those of Kossard and Nelson (19), there is no *a priori* reason to expect that the combining sites of human macrophages, rat macrophages, or those of any given other species will necessarily cross-react. On the other hand, there is good reason to believe that cross-reactivity will be demonstrable between some species. Our results (Figs. 5 and 6) indicate that there was good cross-reactivity between rat and rabbit macrophages and relatively poor cross-reactivity between rat and mouse macrophages even though taxonomically rats and mice are more closely related than are rats and rabbits. It must be kept in mind that other explanations for the observed discrepancy between results with rat and mouse macrophages exist. Thus, no attempt has been made to "characterize" the cells that adhere to the coverslips after 24 to 72 hr incubation. They are defined as macrophages on the basis of their ability to take up neutral red (20) and the fact that they have survived in culture for longer than polymorphonuclear cells are usually expected to survive (21). On the other hand, if it is recognized that there may be many cell types included in the classification of "macrophages" it seems very possible that cytophilic activity with a given antibody may be a property of only some of these cell types and that the abundance of these particular cells may differ enormously among species.

A number of factors may be involved in explaining the large variation in the opsonization titer with the number of lymphocytes and macrophages (Fig. 4). The attachment of the opsonized lymphocytes to the macrophages requires that the lymphocytes settle in close proximity to a macrophage on the monolayer. Naturally, the more lymphocytes that are used per determination (up to a certain point), the higher the chance that opsonized lymphocytes will attach in proportion to the fraction of the total lymphocyte population that is opsonized. Similarly, increasing the number of macrophages per coverslip should achieve the same end. On the other hand, if more lymphocytes are used during opsonization, more antibody will be required. This results in a marked reduction in the OT with increasing cell number even though the reproducibility of the assay seems to be improved. An unfortunate corollary of these results is the need for very large numbers of lymphocytes for executing these experiments. While this offers no problem when rat thymocytes are used, it precludes the use of peripheral lymphocytes from human donors even if the problems of tissue specificity (Table I) were surmountable.

In evaluating the data for possible correlation between OT and skin graft-prolonging activity, correlations in approximately the same range were obtained for linear, log-linear, or log-log correlation. In view of the relatively narrow standard deviation in the OT (one twofold dilution) and the much wider limits on the skin graft data it seems likely that much of the randomness in the results could be ascribed to the latter source.

The observation that different HARLS preparations had apparently different opsonizing activity towards cells from different lymphoid organs was to be expected. Several reports have suggested differences in the immunosuppressive activity of ALS preparations which were produced using lymphocytes from different organs (21–23). Studies in this laboratory have disclosed a difference in the temporal course of the antibody activity produced from the same horse depending on the nature of the antigens used and the method of immunization (24). Thus, even though some of the sera used in this study were from different bleedings of the same horse, it is not surprising that their relative activity against thymus and lymph node cells should differ. These findings offer hope that it may be possible to determine not only the desirable immunosuppressive activity of an ALS preparation (by using the intended target cells as the antigen to be opsonized) but also the degree of specificity, general immunosuppression, or toxicity of the serum by using other host cells for the assay.

Acknowledgment. We are indebted to Dr. John R. Schultz of our Biostatistical Department for the statistical evaluation of the results.

REFERENCES

1. James, K., Clin. Exp. Immun., *2:* 615, 1967.
2. Stevens, L. E., Keutel, H. and Reemtsma, K., Surg. Forum, *19:* 192, 1968.
3. Mosedale, B., Felstead, K. J. and Parke, J. A. C., Nature, *218:* 983, 1968.
4. Bach, J. F., Dormont, J., Dardenne, M. and Balner, H., Transplantation, *8:* 265, 1969.

5. Bach, M. K., Brashler, J. R. and Perper, R. J., Transplantation, *9:* 49, 1970.
6. Perper, R. J., Glenn, E. M., Yu, T. Z., Monovich, R. E. and Brunden, M. N., Proceedings of the International Symposium on Pharmacological Treatment in Organ and Tissue Transplantation, Milan, Italy (1969), In press.
7. Gray, G. D., Michelson, M. M. and Crim, J. A., Transplantation, *6:* 805, 1968.
8. Perper, R. J., Zee, T. W. and Mickelson, M. M., J. Lab. Clin. Med., *72:* 842, 1968.
9. Herberg, R. J., Anal. Chem., *32:* 42, 1960.
10. Kidd, J. G. and Friedwald, W. F., J. Exp. Med., *76:* 543, 1942.
11. Denman, A. M., Denman, E. J. and Holborow, E. J., Nature, *217:* 177, 1968.
12. Grabar, P., Antibiot. Chemother., *15:* 117, 1969.
13. Taub, R. N. and Lance, E. M., Immunology, *15:* 633, 1968.
14. Jooste, S., Lance, E. M., Levey, R. H., Medawar, P. B., Ruszkiewicz, M., Sharman, R. and Taub, R. N., Immunology, *15:* 697, 1968.
15. Martin, W. J. and Miller, J. F. A. P., Int. Arch. Allerg., *35:* 163, 1969.
16. Martin, W. J. and Miller, J. F. A. P., J. Exp. Med., *128:* 855, 1968.
17. Greaves, M. F., Tursi, A., Playfair, J. H. L., Torrigiani, G., Zamir, R. and Roitt, I. M., Lancet, *1:* 68, 1969.
18. Rabinovitch, M., Seminars Hemat., *5:* 134, 1968.
19. Kossard, S. and Nelson, D. S., Aust. J. Exp. Biol. Med. Sci., *46:* 51, 1968.
20. Gesner, B. M. and Howard, J. G., in *Handbook of Experimental Immunology*, Edited by D. M. Weir, p. 1019, F. A. Davis Co., Philadelphia, 1967.
21. Barth, R. F., Southworth, J. and Burger, G. M., J. Immun., *101:* 282, 1968.
22. Nagaya, H. and Sieker, H. O., Science, *150:* 1181, 1965.
23. Perper, R. J., Yu, T. Z. and Kooistia, J. B., Int. Arch. Allerg., *37:* 418, 1970.
24. Perper, R. J., Lyster, S. C., Monovich, R. E. and Bowersox, B. E., Transplantation, *9:* 447, 1970.

THE JOURNAL OF IMMUNOLOGY
Vol. 105, No. 3, September 1970
Printed in U.S.A.

STUDIES ON THE CYTOTOXIC IMMUNE REACTION

I. The Action of Antibodies on Normal and Regenerating Corneal Tissues[1]

W. MANSKI, G. EHRLICH AND F. M. POLACK

From the Departments of Microbiology and Ophthalmology, College of Physicians and Surgeons, Columbia University, New York, New York 10032

Received for publication December 11, 1969

Duck anti-rabbit cornea serum, which is cytotoxic to corneal epithelial or endothelial cells cultured *in vitro*, was found not to react with normal rabbit corneal tissue *in vivo*. No pathologic effects were observed after injecting such antiserum into the anterior chamber or intrastromally, or after repeated topical application to the corneal epithelium. Rabbit corneal tissues regenerating after injury were susceptible to damage by the anti-cornea serum. Corneal clouding developed after the antiserum was injected into the anterior chambers of eyes whose corneas had previously been injured by trauma or cold. In addition to pathologic changes in the endothelium, similar changes occurred in the epithelium after topical application of the antiserum. With the passage of time, the inflammatory response in the cornea gradually decreased in intensity, and the cornea became refractory to damage by antibody about 15 days after injury. The difference in the susceptibility to antibodies of regenerating as compared to normal tissue appears to be related to a difference in their cell membranes, which results in the accessibility of some antigens to cytotoxic antibodies during the active period of proliferation.

The cells of organized tissues are much more resistant to cytolysis by circulating antibody than are dispersed and suspended cells, such as erythrocytes, leucocytes or even platelets (1). Isoantibodies against grafted cells passively administered do not cause rejection of grafted organized tissue, but always cause rejection of transplants of the dispersed cells such as red or white blood cells (2). Even strong heteroimmune anti-tissue antisera do not usually produce diseases by a direct cytotoxic mechanism (3). The Masugi type of glomerulonephritis is exceptional, but does not primarily involve a cytolytic process (4, 5). The reason for the resistance of cells in organized tissue to the action of antibodies is not well understood.

A point of departure for our experiments was the observation that anti-tissue antibodies are strongly cytotoxic for cultured tissues (1, 6, 7). Since one of the basic differences between living tissues *in vivo* and *in vitro* lies in the respective rates of cell division, we produced an "activated state" in organized tissue *in vivo* by causing regeneration after various kinds of injuries. The cornea was selected for this study and the effects of anti-tissue antisera *in vivo* were investigated before and after injury to the cornea. The advantage of using the cornea for such an investigation is that the pathologic effects can be visually observed and graded.

[1] This work was supported by Research Grant EY 00198-12 from the National Institutes of Health.

MATERIALS AND METHODS

Animals. Three- to 4-month-old New Zealand albino rabbits weighing 2.7 to 3.2 kg were used. In a few instances the tests were performed on 3- to 4-week-old animals weighing 150 to 180 g.

Antigens. Whole corneas of mixed breed rabbits (Pel-Freez Biologicals, Inc., Rogers, Ark.) were homogenized and suspended in Hanks' balanced salt solution at a concentration of 100 mg wet tissue/ml. For some control experiments homogenates were made containing endothelial tissues from 10 corneas in 1 ml of Hanks' balanced salt solution to which 100 units penicillin and 100 μg streptomycin were added.

Antisera. Anti-rabbit cornea sera (DARCS) were produced in Muscovy ducks. A 1:1 mixture of antigen in complete Freund's adjuvant (*Mycobacterium butyricum*—Difco) was prepared. For each injection, 1 ml containing about 50 mg wet weight corneal tissue was injected into six separate points of the breast muscle. The first three immunizations were made weekly and the subsequent ones at monthly intervals. Immunization was continued for prolonged periods, in some instances up to 2 years. The normal duck sera used as controls and the immune sera were heat inactivated (56°C for 30 min).

Antibodies to the serum proteins in the corneal tissues were removed by absorbing the duck anti-rabbit cornea serum with 10 mg/ml of lyophilized pooled normal rabbit serum. Cellular antibodies were removed by absorption with about 0.3 ml of rabbit leucocytes from peritoneal exudate, using about 0.3 ml of pooled cells, packed by centrifugation, for each milliliter of duck anti-rabbit cornea serum. The procedure followed for collecting the inflammatory cells from peritoneal exudate was that described by Dixon, Weigle and Roberts (8). In both absorptions the mixtures were left for a week in the refrigerator, shaken each day and centrifuged. Before injection all the sera were filtered through a Pyrex sintered glass filter and tested for sterility.

The cytotoxic effect of the immune sera was tested on rabbit corneal epithelium or endothelium grown in tissue culture and graded + to +++. The methods used have been described in previous publications (6, 7). Sera obtained from the ducks before immunization were not cytotoxic.

The technique described by Strauss *et al.* (9) was used for fluorescein-labeling of duck anti-rabbit cornea and rabbit anti-duck γ globulin antisera. In the indirect fluorescent antibody method, excised corneal tissue slices were placed on glass slides and covered with one drop of conjugated rabbit anti-duck serum globulin and kept for 3 hr in a wet chamber. After washing with Hanks' balanced salt solution, the slides were examined under the fluorescence microscope.

Anesthesia. Before ocular injections or injury the rabbits were anesthetized by injecting Diabutal (30 mg/kg) into the marginal ear vein and the eyes were treated with one or two drops of proparacaine HCl (Squibb).

Tissue injury. a) Freezing: a cryogenic probe (2 mm diameter) filled with Dry Ice and absolute alcohol was applied to the central area of the cornea for 1 min. The epithelium and corneal endothelium regenerated completely within 4 to 5 days. For approximately 2 days after injury the cornea was cloudy due to edema but cleared as regeneration of the endothelium progressed. *b) Scraping:* a bent 30-gauge steel needle was used to penetrate the anterior chamber and an area of about 3 mm diameter of the endothelial layer was scraped off. Corneal edema of a mild degree appeared a few hours after scraping and subsided 1 or 2 days later. *c) Penetrating wounds:* a 3 mm-long stab wound with a razor blade was made in the central part of the cornea. No sutures were applied. Corneal cloudiness around the wound was present for 1 or 2 days. Thereafter the wound epithelialized.

Application of anti-cornea sera to corneal tissues in vivo. In one group of rabbits the endothelial layer was exposed to antibodies. One-tenth milliliter of antiserum was injected into the anterior chamber with a 27-gauge needle after previous extraction of an equal amount of aqueous humor. The injection was made at the upper limbus so that the animal's head could be fixed in a normal position to avoid leakage of the serum. Five-hundredths milliliter of immune serum was injected into the corneal stroma of rabbits of a second group. In a third group of rabbits, the immune serum was applied topically to the epithelial layer. One drop of anti-cornea serum was instilled over the cornea every 5 min for 1 hr and then every hour for 6 hr. In all cases the other eye was used as a control and was treated similarly with pooled normal duck serum. The eyes were examined with a slit lamp.

Histologic examination. Excised rabbit corneas were kept in a modified Carnoy's solution (35 ml absolute methyl alcohol and 10 ml glacial acetic acid) for 3 to 4 hr. After transfer to 50% alcohol for 5 to 10 min, the corneas were treated for 5 to 10 min with distilled water. The endothelial layer attached to Descemet's membrane with a thin layer of stroma was removed with an iris spatula and forceps under a dissecting microscope. The endothelial preparation was then placed on a gelatin-coated glass slide endothelial side up. After drying, the tissue was stained in Harris' hematoxylin (5 drops/ml) for 18 to 24 hr.

In some instances, paraffin sections were examined after hematoxylin staining.

RESULTS

In experiments on normal corneas *in vivo* 15 rabbits were given a single injection of 0.1 ml of a strongly cytotoxic anti-cornea serum

(+++DARCS) into the anterior chamber. Normal duck serum was injected in a similar manner into the other eye. No differences were observed between the control eyes and the eyes injected with anti-cornea serum. Both showed minimal conjunctival and iris congestion resulting from the anterior chamber tap. Forty-eight hours after injection both eyes were clear in all rabbits (see Fig. 1*a*) and they remained so for the rest of the experiment.

Fluorescein-labeled anti-cornea serum was injected similarly into four additional normal rabbits. Slit lamp examination revealed fluorescence in the anterior chamber for 16 hr and only traces at 24 hr. No fluorescence was observed in tissue sections at 48 hr. The indirect fluorescent antibody technique revealed a similar lack of antibody binding.

The same experiments were performed in three (3- to 4-week-old) animals with results essentially similar to those described above. The slight and transient symptoms found in the eyes treated with immune serum were similar to those found in the eyes treated with normal serum.

Another group of 12 rabbits received an intrastromal injection of 0.05 ml of +++DARCS in one eye and of normal duck serum in the other. These animals showed a transient stage of stromal haziness in both eyes which cleared after 48 hr. The injection was repeated in four rabbits on 4 consecutive days; their eyes were more inflamed than were those of rabbits that received only one injection, but the degree of inflammation was similar in the test and control eyes. The corneal structure as seen in histologic sections on the 4th day after a single injection was essentially normal. In one case after repeated injections the cornea was almost totally clear by the 4th day at which time a faint Wesseley ring developed; the ring disappeared 24 hr later.

Further control experiments were performed by applying antiserum topically to the normal epithelial layer of the corneas of five rabbits. As in the above experiments, no epithelial alterations developed. Both the direct and indirect fluorescence antibody techniques gave negative results.

In most of the experiments on regenerating tissues, corneal freezing or endothelial scraping was used as a method of injury. In both instances histologic studies showed that the endothelial layer was almost completely healed 4 days after the injury. The 4th day was selected as the most adequate early time to study cytotoxic reactions to anti-corneal sera. The anti-cornea sera were injected at the latest 21 days after injury. The majority of investigations were performed 7 days after injury (24 rabbits). The reactions obtained are shown in Figure 1. Figure 1*a* shows the lack of reactivity of normal cornea to anti-cornea serum injected into the anterior chamber. Figure 1*b* shows a cornea 7 days after freezing and 24 hr after the injection of normal duck serum. In both experiments only a mild transient reaction to puncture occurred, which had disappeared after 24 hr when the pictures were taken. Figures 1*c* and 1*d* show the reactions of rabbit corneas which were injured and then exposed to a strongly cytotoxic duck anti-rabbit cornea serum. As can be seen, a marked opacity developed which could be relatively localized, as in Figure 1*c*, or more diffuse, as exemplified in Figure 1*d*. This inflammatory reaction usually lasted 2 to 3 days. Similar strong cytotoxic reactions occurred in 10 animals tested 4 days after the endothelial injury. Further experiments were performed in groups of four rabbits at 10, 13, 15 and 21 days after injury. The resulting keratitis decreased with time elapsed between injury and exposure to anti-cornea antiserum. Fifteen days after injury a cytotoxic antiserum did not cause corneal turbidity and no pathologic changes were observed. A similar set of experiments performed in four rabbit eyes using weakly cytotoxic antisera produced milder pathologic alterations.

The histologic appearance of the corneal endothelium 7 days after freezing and 24 hr after exposure to normal and strongly cytotoxic duck anti-rabbit cornea serum is presented in Figure 2, where it may be seen (Fig. 2*a*) that 7 days after freezing the regenerating cornea exposed to normal duck serum showed no pathologic changes. In striking contrast, the cornea exposed to the cytotoxic antiserum showed destruction of large areas of endothelium (Fig. 2*b*), and under higher magnification leucocyte infiltration could be observed.

Polymorphonuclear cells, lymphocytes and macrophages that were present in the aqueous humor 1 day after corneal freezing could still be found 15 days after the injury. The injection, 4 to 7 days after freezing, of +++DARCS produced a significant augmentation of spindle-shaped cells, leucocytes and possibly modified endothelial cells (20 to 30/field) in this fluid.

Histologic sections of the cornea and of the limbal region were made from control and experimental animals and stained with hematoxylin.

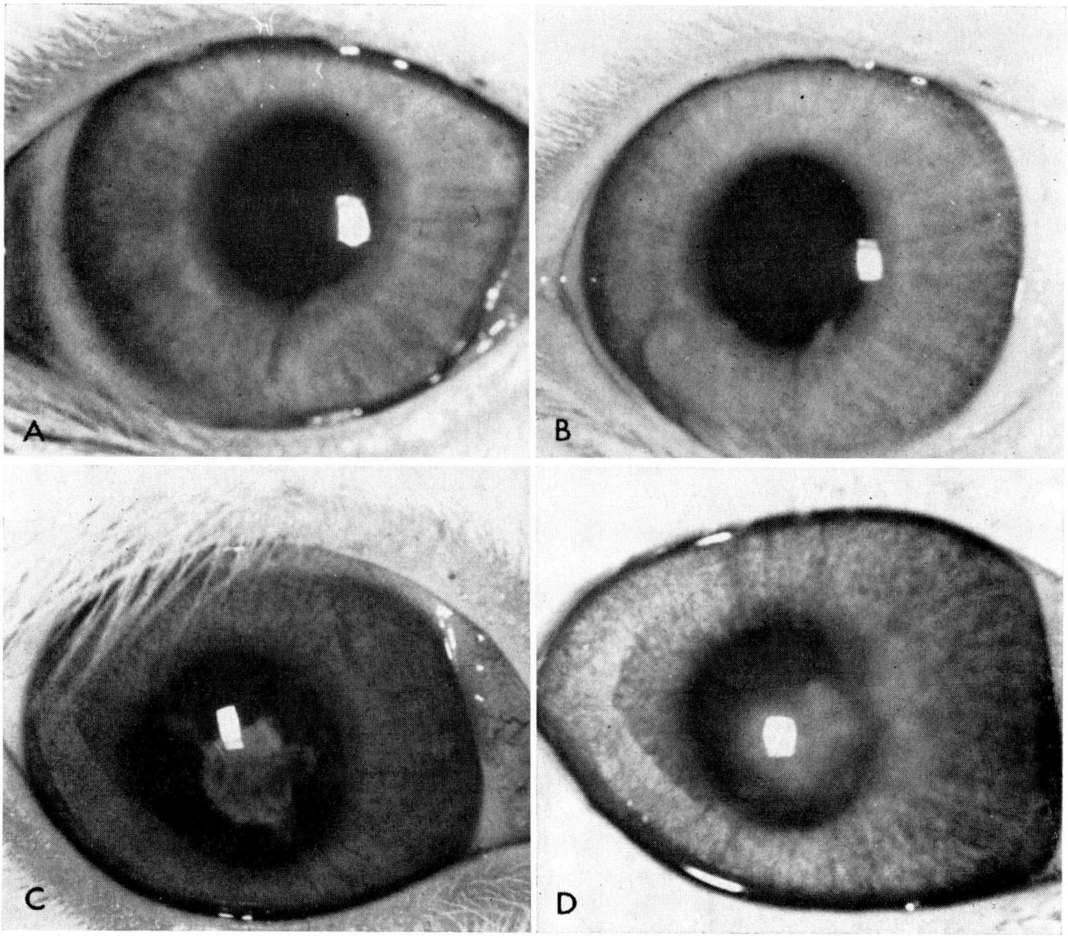

Figure 1. Corneal reactions *in vivo* 1 day after the injection into the anterior chamber of *a*, duck anti-rabbit cornea serum; *b*, normal duck serum 7 days after freezing the cornea; *c* and *d*, duck anti-rabbit cornea serum 7 days after freezing the cornea.

Sections of control eyes treated with normal duck serum (Fig. 3*a* and 3*c*) revealed no histologic alterations except occasional round cell infiltration at the limbus and ciliary body. Eyes treated with duck anti-rabbit cornea serum showed corneal edema (Fig. 3*b* and 3*d*), probably due to endothelial damage. Discrete round cell infiltration centrally and severe leucocytic infiltration at the limbus were observed. The cellular infiltrate consisted of polymorphonuclear leucocytes, lymphocytes and plasma cells, as can be seen more clearly under higher magnification in Figure 4. These changes are characteristic of a severe anterior uveitis.

The occurrence of inflammatory cells in the regenerating corneal endothelium as well as in the aqueous points to the possibility that the cytotoxic reactions might primarily involve leucocytes, because of antigens that they may share with corneal cells. In this case, the endothelial damage observed could be explained as a secondary reaction. To test such a possibility the anti-cornea serum was absorbed with centrifuged and washed rabbit peritoneal exudate cells. Such absorbed anti-cornea antiserum, when tested in six rabbits, showed little or no decrease in toxic effect on the corneal endothelium *in vivo*.

In addition, it is possible that during freezing some corneal endothelial antigens are freed, persist in the eye, and react with the anti-cornea serum in an Arthus-type reaction, thus, causing secondary damage to the regenerating corneal

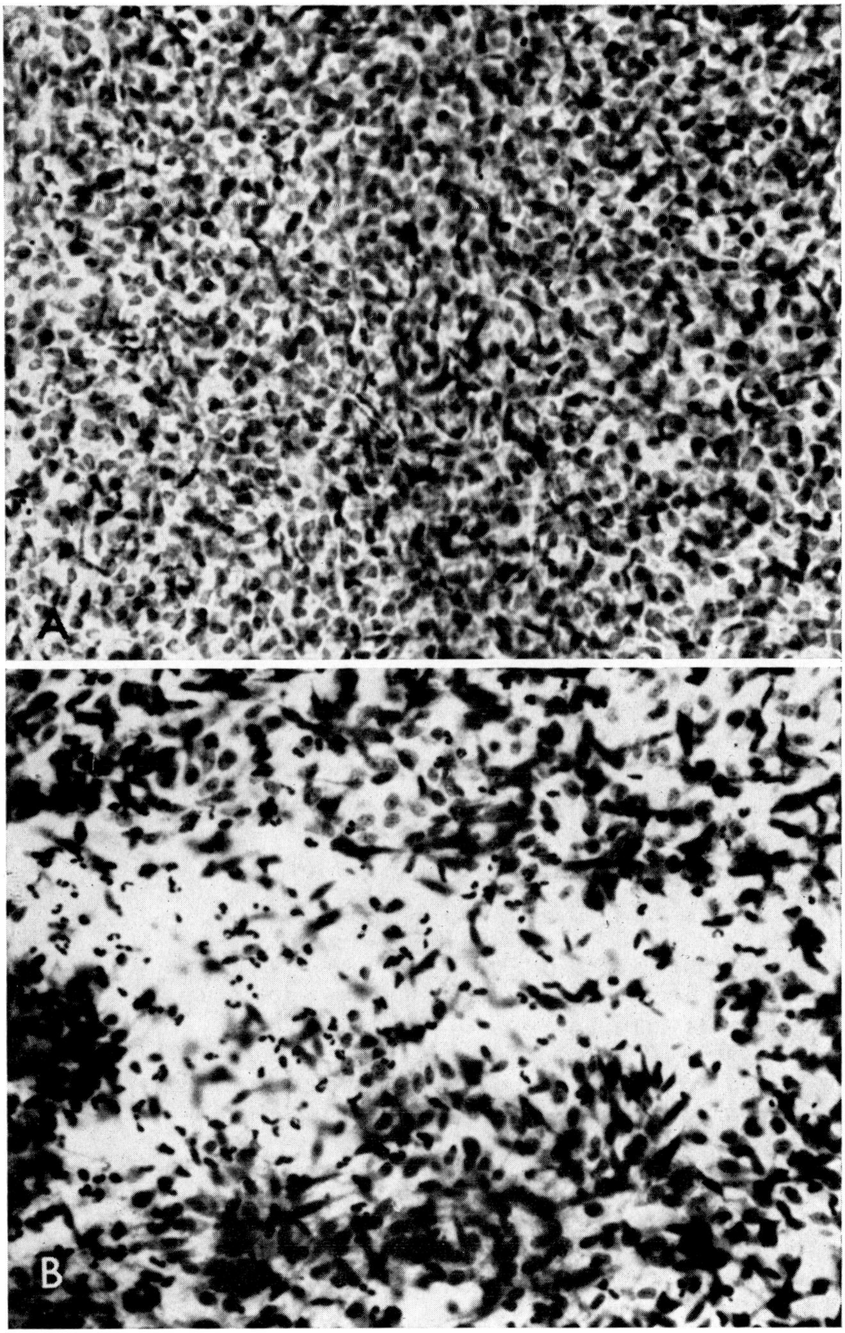

Figure 2. Rabbit corneal endothelium 7 days after freezing and 1 day after exposure to *a*, normal duck serum; *b*, +++cytotoxic duck anti-rabbit cornea serum (× 400).

endothelium. To rule out this possibility the following experiment was performed. Five-hundredths milliliter of an endothelial tissue homogenate in buffered saline containing streptomycin and penicillin was injected into the anterior chamber of one eye in each of four rabbits. Twenty-four hours after injection the eyes appeared normal. Seven days later the eyes were

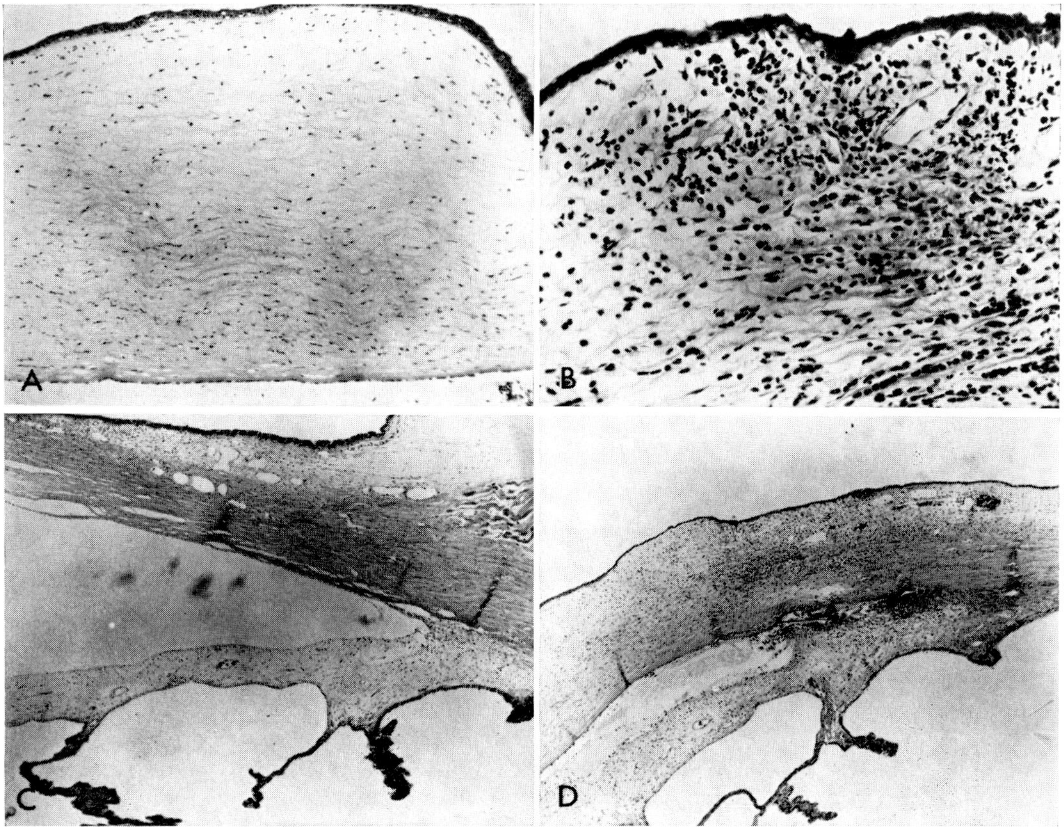

Figure 3. Histologic sections of the cornea (*a*, *b*—× 150) and limbus (*c*, *d*—× 100) 7 days after freezing and 1 day after injecting duck anti-rabbit cornea serum (*b*, *d*) and normal duck serum (*a*, *c*).

injected with 0.1 ml of anti-corneal serum. Except for a transient and mild traumatic reaction, the corneas were clear 24 hr after the injection and remained so during the next 7 days.

Regenerating corneal epithelium in 10 rabbits was exposed 7 days after freezing to duck anti-rabbit cornea serum and to normal duck serum. The antisera were repeatedly applied to the epithelial surface. Clinically, the keratitis induced by applying + + +DARCS to the multilayered epithelium was less pronounced than that caused in the monolayered endothelium, but again a clear difference from the control corneas exposed to normal duck serum could be observed. This is illustrated in Figure 5, which shows flat mounts of the regenerating corneal epithelium after exposure to normal and to immune serum. Destruction of epithelial cells and an influx of inflammatory cells (Fig. 5*b*) can be seen after exposure to + + +DARCS. The epithelium of the corresponding eyes, similarly regenerating but treated with normal duck serum, showed no lesions (Fig. 5*a*).

In 10 rabbits in which the process of corneal regeneration was induced by mechanical injury, a portion of the corneal surface about the same size as that produced by freezing was scraped without injury to Descemet's membrane. The results obtained 4 and 7 days after injury and 24 hr after challenge with normal and anti-cornea duck antiserum of weak and strong cytotoxicity were similar to those obtained when the injury was caused by freezing. Experiments in four rabbits in which normal and + + +DARCS sera were injected into the anterior chamber 7 days after a penetrating corneal wound (3 mm) likewise gave these results. Figures 6*a* and 6*b* show the difference between the reactions to normal and cytotoxic anti-cornea sera in such animals.

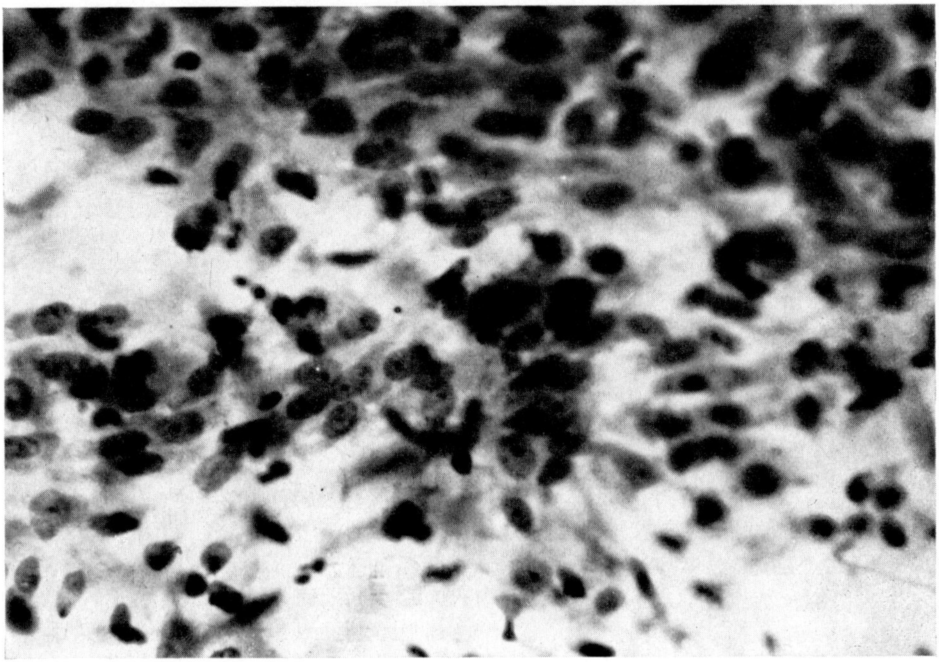

Figure 4. Inflammatory cells in the cytotoxic reaction of the regenerating rabbit cornea (× 800).

DISCUSSION

Destruction of the regenerating corneal endothelial or epithelial cells upon exposure to anti-cornea antibodies is the result of a cytotoxic immune reaction and appears not to be secondary to an Arthus-type reaction occurring around the corneal cells. This was proven in several control experiments. The continued reactivity of anti-cornea sera after absorption with serum proteins excludes a role of these antigens in the pathologic changes that were observed.

A possibility that anti-cornea sera react with endothelial cell antigens that are liberated by the primary injury and persist locally, thus producing an Arthus-type reaction, could be similarly excluded. When a suspension of homogenized corneal endothelium was injected into the anterior chamber, the eye showed no pathologic changes after exposure 7 days later to anti-cornea serum. The amount of endothelium used in such control experiments was approximately half that of a rabbit cornea, whereas mechanical or thermal injury involved less than 3% of the corneal endothelium.

Absorption of the duck anti-rabbit cornea serum with rabbit leucocytes did not significantly reduce its cytotoxicity. These experiments show that cross-reactions of anti-cornea sera with inflammatory cells cannot play an important part in evolution of the keratitis. This is supported, in addition, by the observation that inflammatory cells were still present in the regenerating cornea and in the aqueous humor 15 days after injury, when the cornea was again resistant to damage by specific antibodies.

The antigen or antigens that are involved in the cytotoxic response of the regenerating corneal tissue to anti-cornea antibodies must be present in the normal excised corneal tissue that was used for producing the cytotoxic antisera. The cytotoxic effects of anti-cornea sera on regenerating tissue and the absence of these effects on normal tissue *in vivo* appear therefore to be the consequence of the accessibility of certain antigens on cells of the regenerating tissue and lack of accessibility of the same antigens on cells of the normal cornea. This view is supported by the observation that neither direct nor indirect fluorescence antibody techniques demonstrated anti-corneal antibody binding by the normal cornea *in vivo*. Equally important, the area of regenerating cells after injury could be clearly seen on histologic examination as the one involved

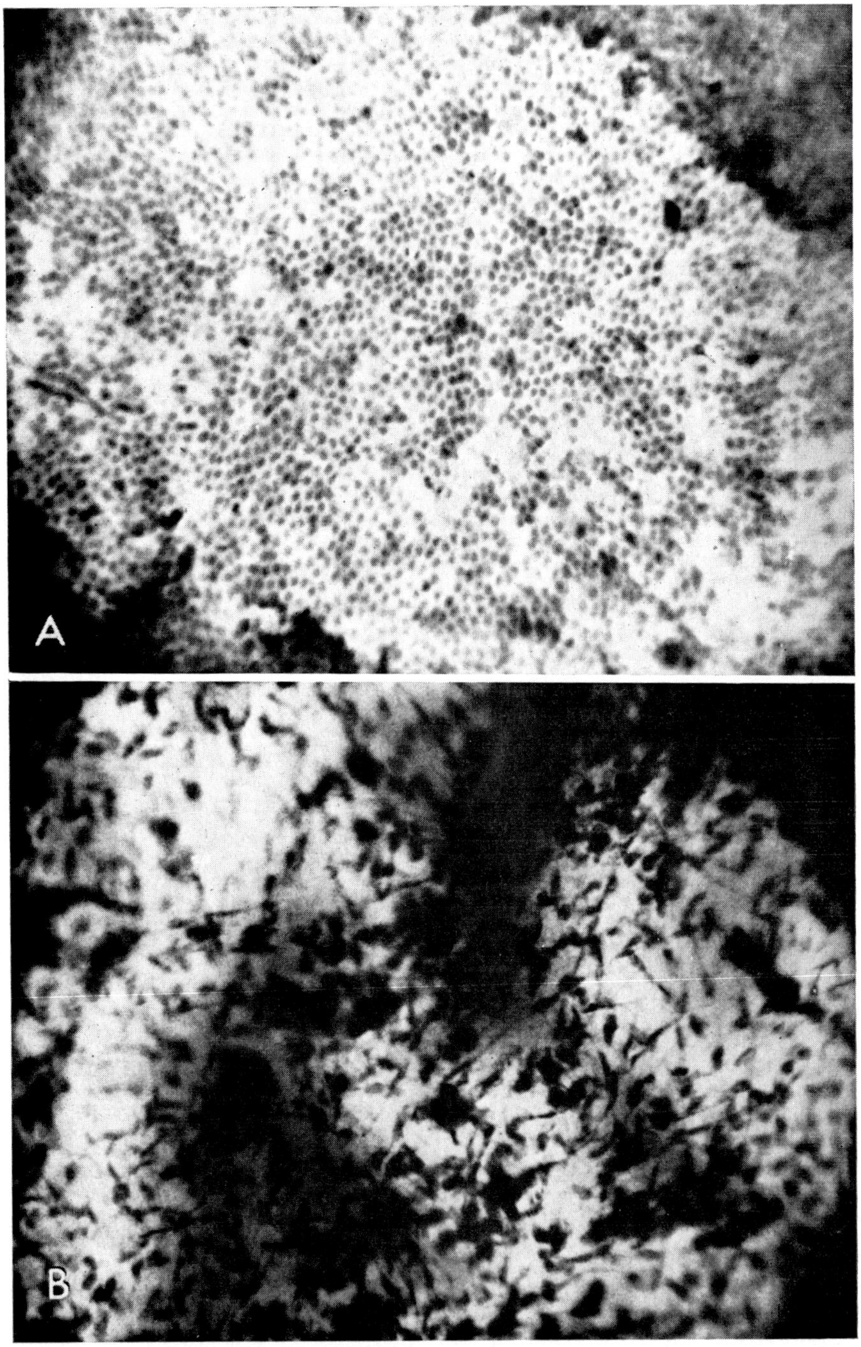

Figure 5. Rabbit corneal epithelium 7 days after freezing and 1 day after applying *a*, normal duck serum and *b*, +++duck anti-rabbit cornea serum (×200).

in the cytotoxic action of the anti-cornea antiserum.

In experiments (10) to be reported subsequently in detail, it was found that fluorescein-labeled anti-cornea sera exhaustively absorbed with the lyophilized soluble corneal fraction stain cell membranes and produce undiminished cytotoxic effects. Absorption with the saline-

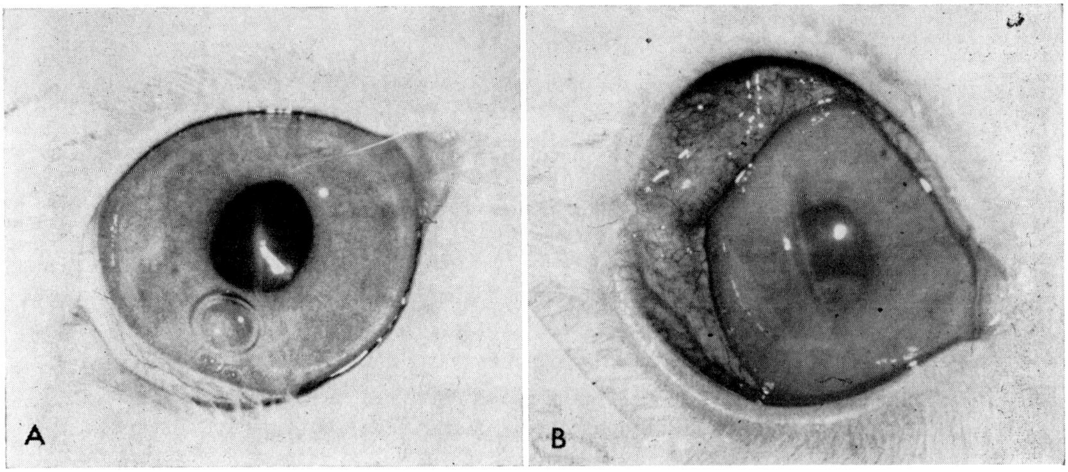

Figure 6. Corneal reactions *in vivo* 1 day after injection into the anterior chamber of *a*, normal duck serum and *b*, +++duck anti-rabbit cornea serum. The corneas of both eyes had been injured 7 days before the injection by inflicting a 3-mm penetrating wound.

extracted insoluble corneal cell residue removed the cytotoxic antibodies.

It appears that the accessibility of cell membrane antigens involved in the cytotoxic reaction *in vivo* may be related to the process of active proliferation. Such a process occurs in the corneal tissue *in vivo* by prior injury (11, 12) and exists in corneal tissue culture similarly sensitive to anti-cornea antibodies.

There must be a minimum number of cells in the "activated state" that are able to react with +++DARCS in order to produce clinical symptoms. Apparently, the number of such corneal cells in 3- to 4-week-old rabbits (13) is insufficient to induce an evident cytotoxic reaction.

The period of about 14 days after injury during which corneal tissue *in vivo* reacts with antibodies coincides with certain morphologic changes of the readapting endothelial, stromal and epithelial cells. A flatness of endothelial cells and a variation in cell size, which is generally larger than normal, can be observed only at this time (Fr. Vrabec, personal communication). Such morphologic differences between regenerating and normal corneal tissues are consistent with the view that a change in the cell membranes, which results in the accessibility of pre-existing tissue antigens to antibodies is the determining factor in the acquired sensitivity of organized tissues to anti-tissue antibodies.

The sensitivity of other regenerating tissues is now under investigation. This investigation is designed to ascertain the extent to which the experimental results herein described may have a general application to immunopathologic reactions.

REFERENCES

1. Bitensky, L., Brit. Med. Bull., *19:* 241, 1963.
2. Stetson, C. A., Advances Immun., *3:* 97, 1963.
3. Anderson, J. R., Brit. Med. Bull., *19:* 251, 1963.
4. Dixon, F. J. and Unanue, E. F., Advances Immun., *6:* 1, 1967.
5. Masugi, M., Beitr. Path. Anat., *91:* 82, 1933.
6. Ehrlich, G. and Halbert, S. P., J. Immun., *86:* 267, 1961.
7. Ehrlich, G., Halbert, S. P. and Manski, W., J. Immun., *89:* 391, 1962.
8. Dixon, F. J., Weigle, W. O. and Roberts, J. C., J. Immun., *78:* 56, 1957.
9. Strauss, A. L., Seegal, B. C., Hsu, K. C., Burkholder, P. M., Nastuk, W. L. and Osserman, K. S., Proc. Soc. Exp. Biol. Med., *105:* 184, 1960.
10. Manski, W., Ehrlich, G. and Polack, P., Fed. Proc., *27*(No. 2, Abst.)*:* 622, 1968.
11. Duke-Elder, S. and Leigh, A. G., *Diseases of the Outer Eye*, Vol. VIII, p. 604, C. V. Mosby Co., St. Louis, 1965.
12. Newell, F. W., Trans. Ophthal. Soc. U. K., *86:* 813, 1966.
13. von Sallmann, L., Caravaggio, L. L. and Grimes, P., Amer. J. Ophthal., *51:* 955, 1961.

THE JOURNAL OF IMMUNOLOGY
Vol. 105, No. 3, September 1970
Printed in U.S.A.

STUDIES ON THE CYTOTOXIC IMMUNE REACTION

II. The Action of Antibodies on Normal and Metabolically Inhibited Tissue Cultures[1]

W. MANSKI AND G. EHRLICH

From the Departments of Microbiology and Ophthalmology, College of Physicians and Surgeons, Columbia University, New York, New York 10032

Received for publication December 11, 1969

Rabbit corneal epithelium tissue culture kept at low temperature (6°C) or exposed to colchicine or puromycin (10 μg/ml) in the growth medium ceased to show cytotoxic effects in response to duck anti-rabbit corneal serum. The above loss of susceptibility to antibodies was found to be reversible. It was shown experimentally that the underlying mechanism involved primarily a loss of antibody binding by the inhibited tissue cultures.

In the preceding article (1) we reported that the normally resistant corneal epithelium and endothelium of rabbits become sensitive to cytotoxic antibodies after an "activated state" is induced in these tissues, for example, during cellular regeneration after previous injury. The experiments now to be described were designed to establish whether inhibition of the metabolic activity of a culture of corneal epithelium, which normally is sensitive to cytotoxic antibodies, causes inhibition of the cytotoxic effects of those antibodies. Additional experiments were performed to determine directly whether a decrease in the cytotoxic response of a metabolically-inhibited corneal epithelium culture to anti-cornea antibodies is related to a decrease in antibody binding or in susceptibility to bound antibodies.

MATERIALS AND METHODS

Immune sera. Duck anti-rabbit cornea sera were used. The immunization procedure was described in the preceding report (1).

Metabolic inhibitors. Colchicine (Pierce Chemical Co., Rockford, Ill.) and puromycin (Sigma Chemical Co., St. Louis, Mo.) were used.

Tissue cultures. The culture method used was a modification of one previously described (2, 3). Corneal epithelium from 10-day-old chinchilla rabbits of either sex was cut in 1- to 2-mm squares and explanted onto a thin layer of human cord serum on the bottom of 30-ml plastic tissue culture flasks (Falcon Plastics Co., Oxnard, Calif.). The feeding solution consisted of medium 199 with 10% newborn calf serum (Microbiological Associates, Inc., Bethesda, Md.). All cultures were incubated at 36.5°C. Each was washed and fed two or three times a week. When growth was at its peak (5 to 7 days), the cultures were washed with Hanks' balanced salt solution and, after its removal, were then exposed to 0.5 ml of undiluted antiserum. The cytotoxic effects of anti-cornea sera started with a rounding up of cells, and after 3 to 6 hr lead to a complete disorganization of the cell sheet. Control cultures were treated similarly except that normal duck serum was added. In no instance were cytotoxic effects observed.

RESULTS

Figure 1*a* shows a 6-day-old corneal epithelium culture kept for 2 days at 6°C. As can be seen, the cells exposed to low temperature did not change significantly from those not so exposed (Fig. 1*b*). After 7 days in the cold a rounding up of cells began, which after 14 days became more extensive.

A practically undiminished cytotoxic reaction resulted when corneal epithelium cultures grown for 5 to 8 days were kept for 2 days at 6°C before exposure to the anti-corneal antisera at 36.5°C. The culture seen in Figure 2*a* was kept for 48 hr at 6°C and was then exposed to antibodies at

[1] This work was supported by Research Grant EY 00198-12 from the National Institutes of Health.

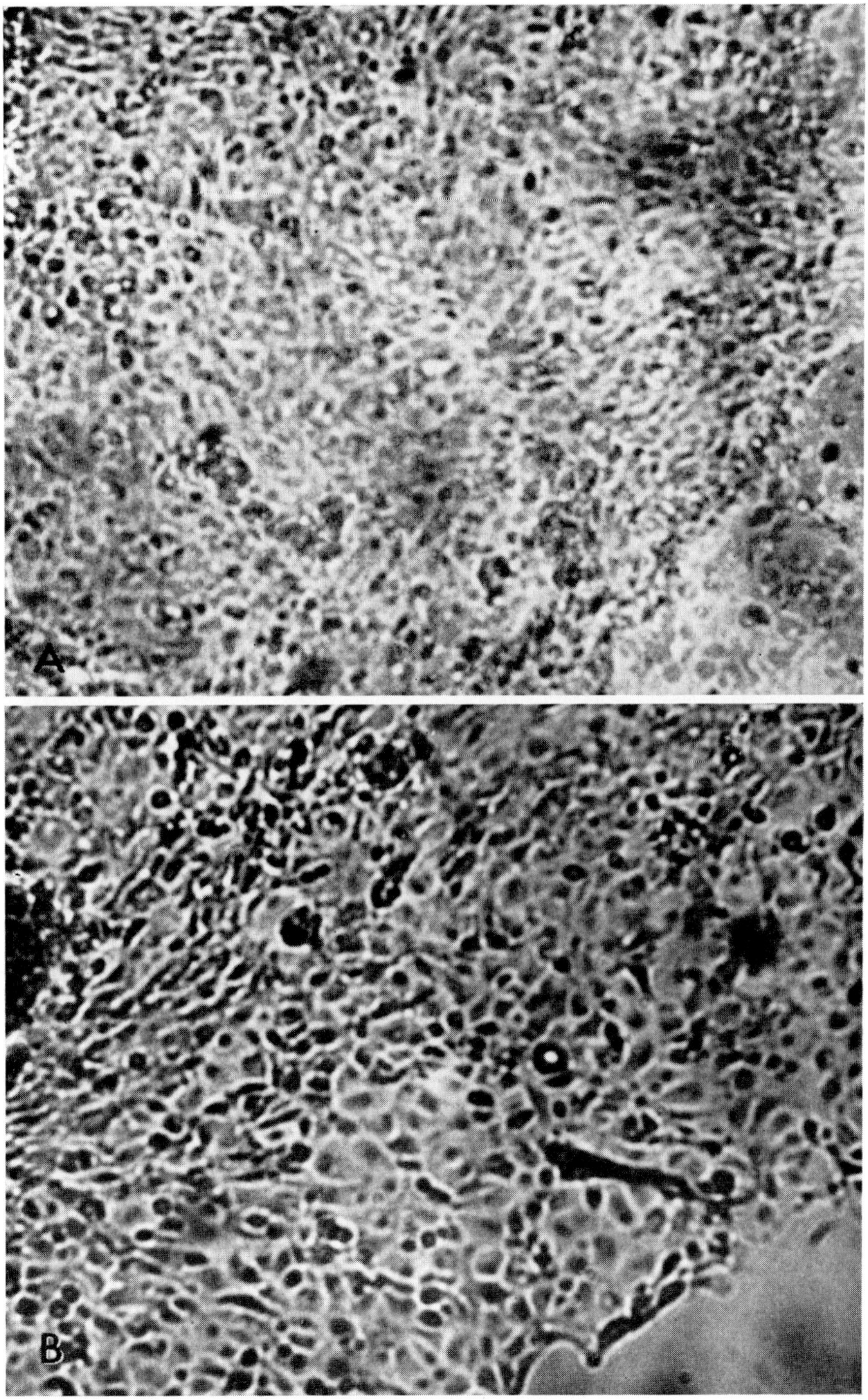

Figure 1. The response of rabbit corneal epithelium culture to cold. *a*, Culture after 2 days at 6°C; *b*, culture before exposure to cold. T-flask culture, phase contrast (×200).

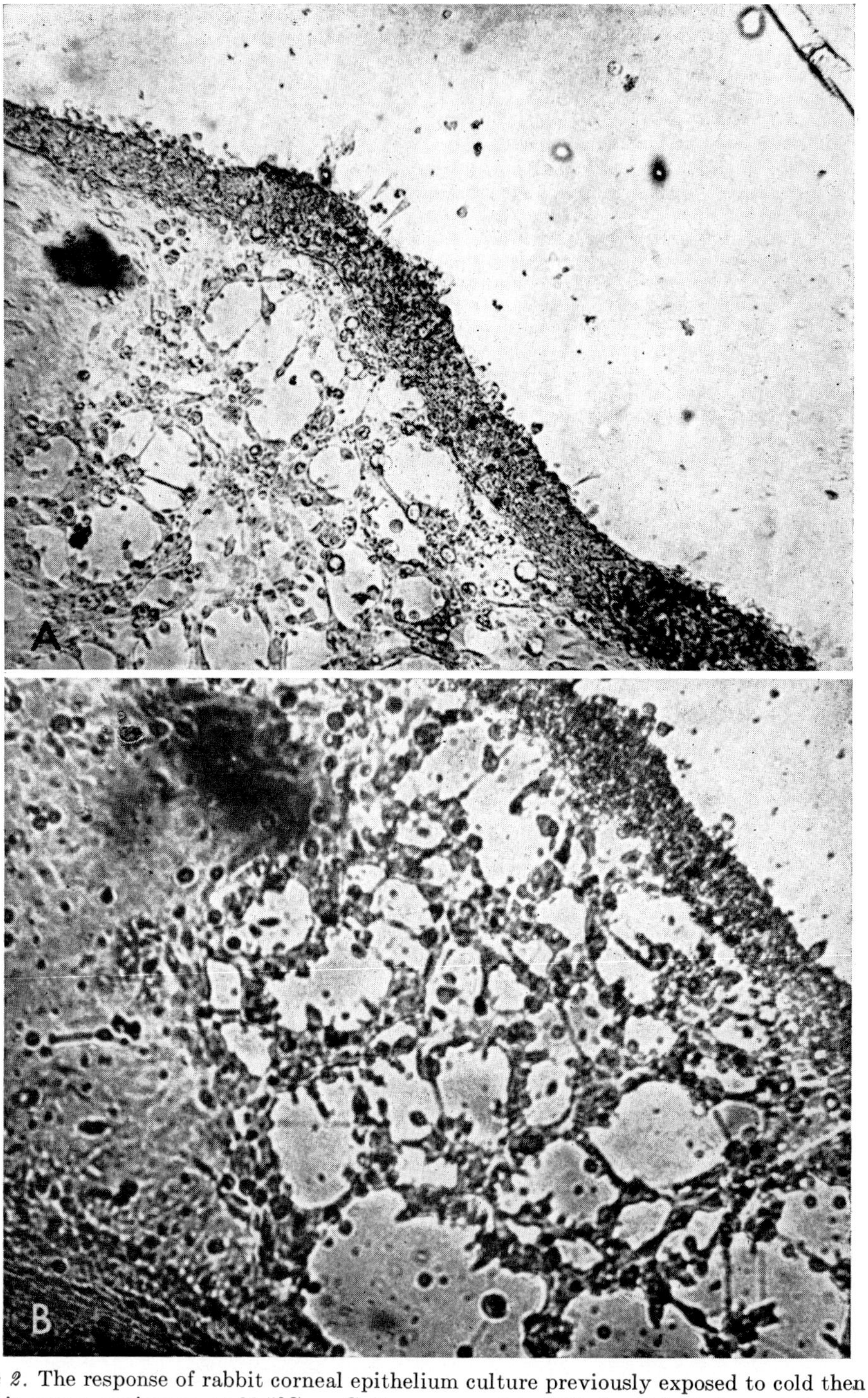

Figure 2. The response of rabbit corneal epithelium culture previously exposed to cold then to duck anti-rabbit cornea antiserum at 36.5°C. *a*, Culture exposed to 6°C, for 48 hr before adding antiserum; *b*, culture directly exposed to antiserum (control). T-flask culture, phase contrast (×100).

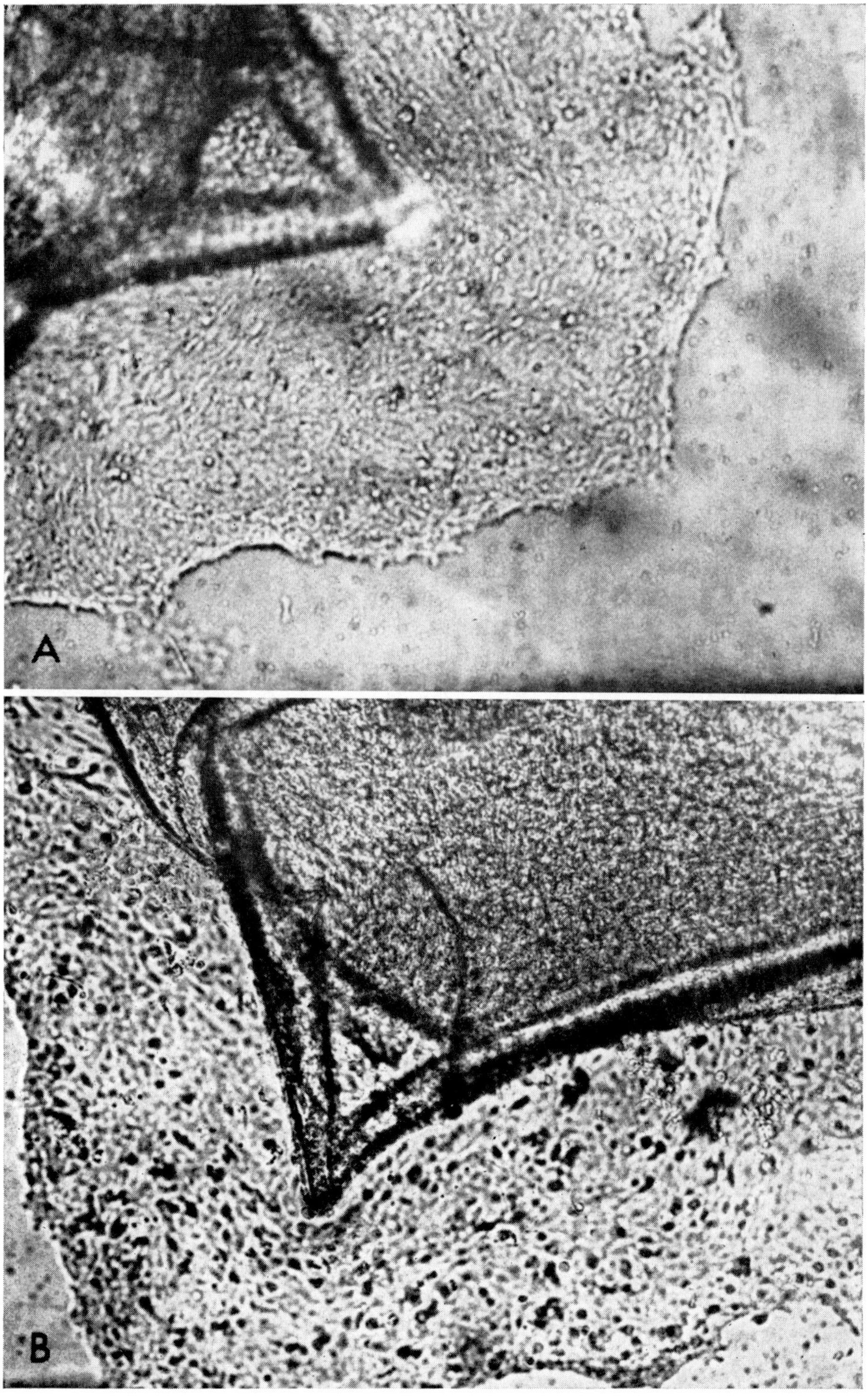

Figure 3. The response of rabbit corneal epithelium culture to duck anti-rabbit cornea antiserum at 6°C. *a*, Culture exposed to antiserum at 6°C for 18 hr; *b*, culture treated as in *a*, then washed and put in fresh growth medium at 36.5°C. T-flask culture, phase contrast (×100).

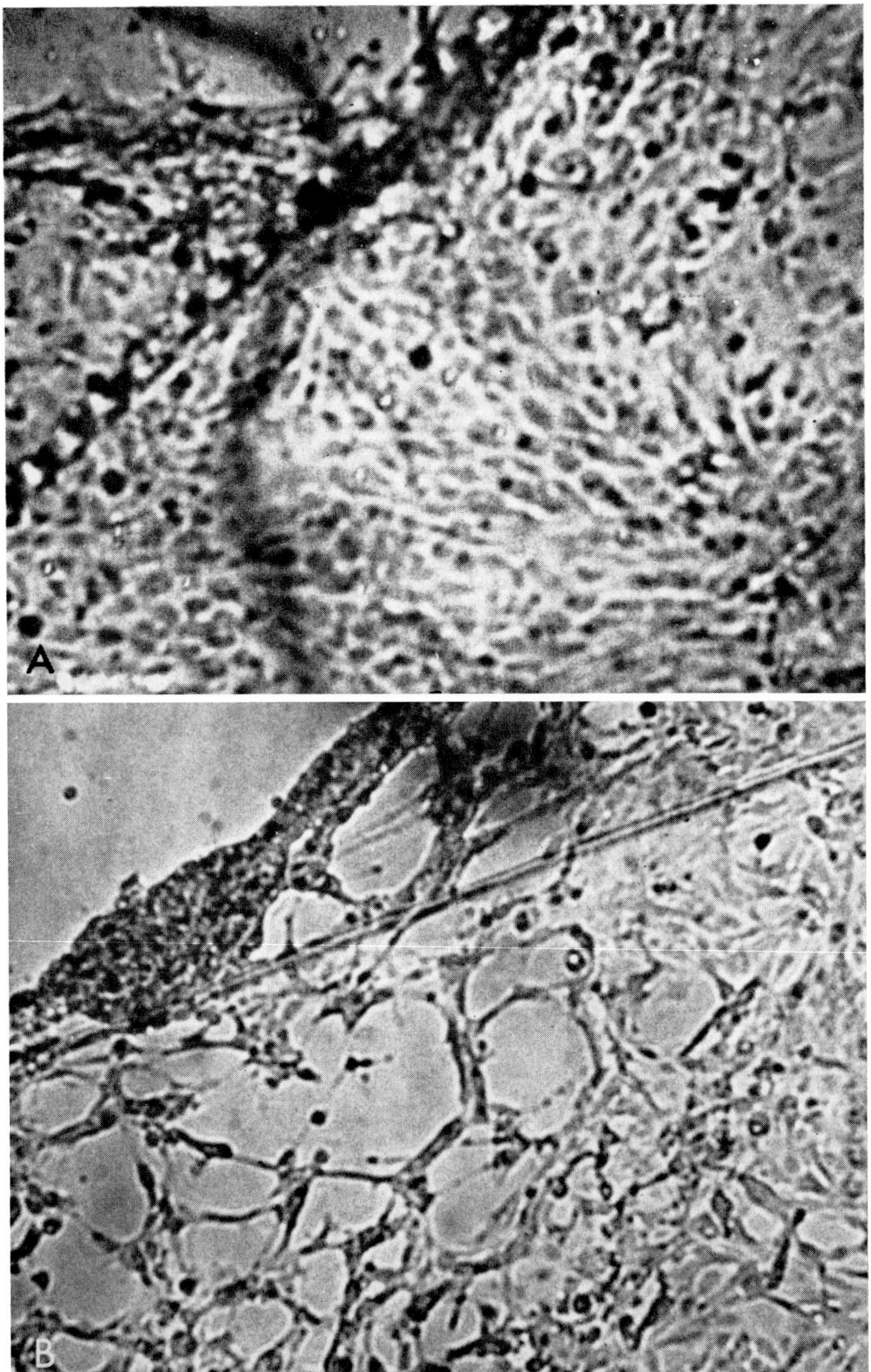

Figure 4. The binding of duck anti-rabbit cornea antibodies by a rabbit corneal epithelium culture at 36.5°C. *a*, Culture 90 min after adding antiserum; *b*, *culture a* washed and put in fresh growth medium at 36.5°C. T-flask culture, phase contrast (× 200).

36.5°C. The control culture in Figure 2*b* was not exposed to cold. The pictures were taken after 5 hr of contact between the tissue cultures and the antiserum at 36.5°C. The cytotoxic reaction was strong in both cultures, and there was only a faint indication that damage to the corneal epithelial cell sheet was somewhat greater in the tissue culture not exposed to cold.

In the above experiment the cooled cultures were brought to 36.5°C before addition of the antiserum. When a cold tissue culture and antiserum were kept together in the cold, no cytotoxic effects could be observed even after prolonged contact. The results of such an experiment can be seen in Figure 3*a*. In another experiment corneal epithelial cultures were first exposed to antiserum for 18 hr at 6°C, then after removal of the antiserum the cultures were thoroughly washed four times with cold balanced salt solution and finally warmed to 36.5°C in fresh growth medium. A tissue culture treated in such a way is seen in Figure 3*b*. Again no cytotoxic effects could be observed.

Cytotoxic antibody binding, however, could be demonstrated by similar experiments in tissue cultures kept at 36.5°C. This is seen in Figure 4. A corneal epithelium culture was exposed for 90 min to anti-cornea antibodies at 36.5°C. No evident change in the morphology could be observed at this time (*cf.* Fig. 4*a* with Fig. 1*a*). The antiserum was then removed and the tissue culture was washed four times with balanced salt solution and incubated further in a fresh medium. A strong cytotoxic reaction devel-

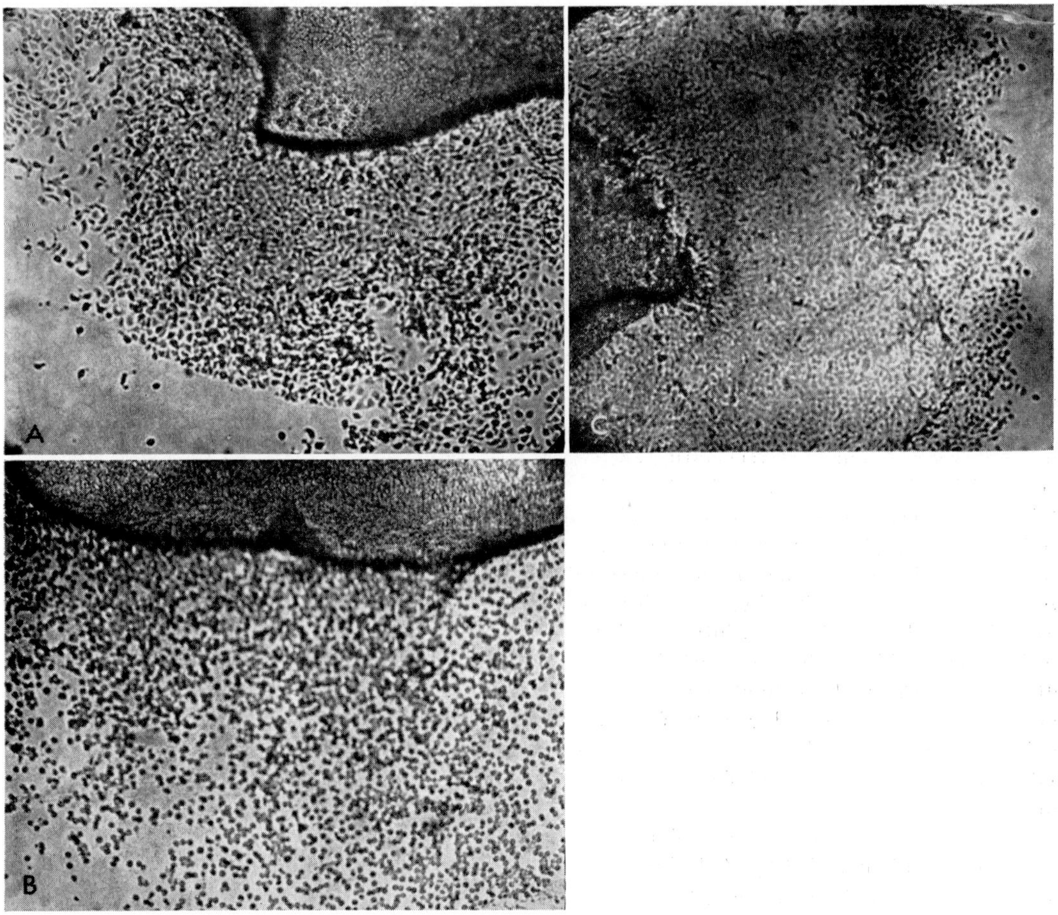

Figure 5. The effect of colchicine (10 μg/ml) on the response of a rabbit corneal epithelium culture to duck anti-rabbit cornea antiserum. *a*, Culture 5 hr after addition of colchicine; *b*, culture treated as in *a*, 5 hr after subsequent addition of antiserum; *c*, culture treated as in *b*, washed and put in fresh growth medium after 3 days. T-flask culture, phase contrast (× 100).

oped after an additional 3 to 4 hr in the growth medium alone (see Fig. 4*b*). The above experiments indicate that anti-tissue antibodies which are not bound by a tissue culture at 6°C are bound at 36.5°C, before morphologic changes in the tissue culture can be observed. Such a conclusion was confirmed in separate experiments testing the cytotoxic activity of the antisera removed from the above tissue cultures exposed at 6°C and 36.5°C. Only in the latter instance was a significant decrease in the cytotoxicity noted.

Additional experiments were done with chemical inhibitors such as puromycin (4, 5) and colchicine (6). Colchicine at 1 μg/ml decreased only slightly the susceptibility of the corneal tissue culture to anti-corneal antibodies. At 10 μg/ml the inhibitory effect of colchicine on the susceptibility of the corneal culture toward antibodies was much more pronounced. Figure 5*a* shows a 7-day-old corneal culture after 5 hr of exposure to 10 μg/ml of colchicine. At this concentration some rounding up of cells can be observed. A subsequent exposure of such colchicine-treated cultures to a strongly cytotoxic anti-cornea antiserum for 5 hr (Fig. 5*b*) produced an apparent increase of this effect. Changes of the same kind were found, however, in the control culture treated for the same length of time with normal serum. That the rounding up of cells was a result of the action of colchicine and not of antiserum was confirmed by an additional experiment in which it was shown that no binding of antibodies occurred in the tissue cultures exposed to colchicine. This can be seen in Figure 5*c*. A 7-day-old corneal epithelium culture was treated for 5 hr with 10 μg/ml colchicine and then exposed for the same length of time to anti-cornea antiserum (as in Fig. 5*b*). Finally, the culture was washed with balanced salt solution and fresh medium was added. Changes started to occur after 1 day. Figure 5*d* exhibits such a corneal epithelium culture after 3 days in fresh medium, and shows not only an absence of cytotoxic effect but restoration to a morphologically normal appearance.

Treatment of a corneal epithelium tissue culture for 3 to 5 hr with 10 μg/ml of puromycin similarly inhibited the reaction with duck anti-rabbit cornea antiserum. The tissue cultures at corresponding experimental stages were similar to the one obtained when colchicine was used as a metabolic inhibitor (see Fig. 5).

DISCUSSION

All the experiments indicate that metabolically inactive tissue cultures are insensitive to antibodies, in contrast to active ones. This raises the question whether metabolic activity in cultured cells primarily regulates the ability to bind antibodies, or to respond to bound antibodies.

The experiments presented in this report demonstrated that metabolically inhibited corneal tissue cultures did not bind anti-cornea antibodies. This was shown by transfer experiments in which the inhibited tissue cultures were exposed to antibodies and then washed and put in fresh growth medium. No cytotoxicity occurred. Active tissue cultures under otherwise identical conditions developed pronounced cytotoxic changes. The lack of antibody binding by tissue cultures that were metabolically inhibited, e.g., by cold, was found to be reversible immediately after removal of the cause of inhibition. It thus appears that the inability of the inhibited tissue culture to bind antibody does not reflect a loss of antigenic sites, but rather the inaccessibility of these sites to antibody when the tissue is in the inhibited state.

As shown in the previous report (1), the determining factor in the sensitivity to antibodies *in vivo* is related also to the accessibility of cell membrane antigens.

Normal corneal tissue *in vivo*, like metabolically inhibited tissue *in vitro*, is *insensitive* to antibodies, but activated corneal tissue in the intact animal is *sensitive* to antibodies, like corneal cells when cultivated *in vitro*.

In vitro as well as *in vivo* accessibility of the antigens involved in the cytotoxic reaction appears to be a response to the process of active proliferation.

REFERENCES

1. Manski, W., Ehrlich, G. and Polack, F. M., J. Immun., *105:* 755, 1970.
2. Ehrlich, G. and Halbert, S. P., J. Immun., *86:* 267, 1961.
3. Ehrlich, G., Halbert, S. P. and Manski, W., J. Immun., *89:* 391, 1962.
4. Nathans, D., Proc. Nat. Acad. Sci., *51:* 585, 1964.
5. Berenbaum, M. C., Brit. Med. Bull., *21:* 140, 1965.
6. Rihlman, B. A., *Action of Chemicals on Dividing Cells*, Prentice-Hall, Inc., Englewood Cliffs, N. J., 1966.

THE JOURNAL OF IMMUNOLOGY
Vol. 105, No. 3, September 1970

Printed in U.S.A.

THE INDUCTION OF BACTERIOPHAGE-NEUTRALIZING ANTIBODY BY MOUSE SPLEEN IMMUNOGENIC RNA

I. Preparation and Properties of Immunogenic RNA[1]

HERBERT B. HERSCOWITZ[2, 3] AND PETER STELOS

From the Department of Microbiology, Hahnemann Medical College, Philadelphia, Pennsylvania 19102

Received for publication June 16, 1969

RNA extracted from the spleens of Swiss Webster mice immunized with bacteriophage 81a, which infects *Streptococcus faecalis* var. *zymogenes*, induced the formation of specific phage-neutralizing antibody when added to nonimmune mouse spleen fragments in culture. Antibody formation could be elicited by the addition of immunogenic RNA derived from one inbred mouse strain to nonimmune spleen fragments from other inbred mouse strains. The activity of immunogenic RNA was inhibited by treatment with RNase, but not by DNase, trypsin, amylase or moderate amounts of pronase. The active RNA sedimented in the lightest fraction of a 5% to 20% linear sucrose gradient, and was estimated to have an average sedimentation coefficient of 8.2 S by analytical ultracentrifugation.

Many experiments have been described in which ribonucleic acid (RNA) fractions from an immune cell population (termed "immunogenic RNA") have been shown to transfer the capacity to produce specific antibody to a second, nonimmune cell population. Fishman and Adler (1) reported that RNA extracted from rat peritoneal exudate cells previously incubated *in vitro* with T2 phage induced the formation of anti-T2 phage neutralizing antibody in cultures of lymph node fragments derived from normal rats. The immune response was shown to be biphasic: an early rise, presumably of γM antibody, on day 4, and a second rise, presumably of γG antibody, on day 11 (2). Further studies using peritoneal exudate cells and lymph nodes from rabbits of distinct allotypes indicated that the γM antibody contained the allotypic specificity of the donor peritoneal exudate cells, whereas the γG antibody contained that of the recipient lymph node fragments (3). This finding suggests an informational role for RNA in the synthesis of γM antibody, and still another role for RNA, as yet undisclosed, in the synthesis of γG antibody.

Friedman (4) and Cohen and Parks (5) reported that RNA extracted from spleens of specifically immunized mice induced the formation of antibody when added to suspensions of nonimmune spleen cells. Cohen *et al.* (6) observed that the immunogenic activity of the spleen extract could be abolished by ribonuclease (RNase) treatment, but that it was unaffected by treatment with deoxyribonuclease (DNase), trypsin or amylase. The biologically active material sedimented in the 8 S to 12 S region as determined by sucrose density gradient centrifugation. These authors (6) also reported that the induction of antibody synthesis by spleen immunogenic RNA was strain-specific.

This paper describes the preparation and properties of an immunogenic RNA extracted from the spleens of mice immunized with a bacteriophage having for its host a Gram-positive bacterium. The following paper presents serologic and radiochemical evidence for the presence of antigenic material derived from the phage in immunogenic RNA.

[1] This work was supported by United States Public Health Service Grant AI-07137 and was presented in part at the 52nd Annual Meeting of the American Association of Immunologists in April, 1968, at Atlantic City, New Jersey.

[2] Recipient of United States Public Health Service Predoctoral Award 1-F1-GM-38, 593-01.

[3] Present address: Department of Microbiology, School of Medicine and Dentistry, Georgetown University, Washington, D. C.

MATERIALS AND METHODS

Immunization of animals. Female Swiss Webster mice (25 to 30 g) were injected intraperitoneally on alternate days for 3 weeks with 0.1-ml doses of 10^{10} plaque-forming units (PFU)/ml of a highly purified preparation of phage 81a infecting *Streptococcus faecalis* var. *zymogenes* (7). Blood samples were obtained by puncture of the venous plexus in the retro-orbital sinus. Three days after the final injection, the animals were killed, and their spleens removed and immediately frozen between blocks of solid CO_2.

RNA extraction. A modification (7) of the procedure of Homma and Graham (8) was used. A pool of 5 to 10 frozen spleens was thawed in 1 volume of 0.01 M sodium acetate buffer, pH 5, containing 0.2 M LiCl, 0.001 M $MgCl_2$, 0.5% sodium dodecyl sulfate, and 0.02% bentonite. It was homogenized by four to five strokes of a Teflon-coated pestle in a glass tissue-grinder that was mechanically driven at low speed. An equal volume of phenol containing 0.01% of 8-hydroxyquinoline and saturated with pH 5 acetate buffer was added to the homogenate. The mixture was shaken vigorously for 2 min, heated for 3 min at 60°C and cooled rapidly by immersion in an alcohol-solid CO_2 bath. The phases were separated by centrifugation for 10 min at 12,000 × G. The aqueous phase was removed, and the phenol phase was extracted by addition of one-half its volume of the pH 5 acetate buffer. The aqueous phases were pooled, and the pool was extracted twice more with one-half of its volume of hot phenol. It was then digested with 50 μg/ml of electrophoretically purified DNase (Worthington Biochemicals, Freehold, N. J.) for 30 min at 37°C. Two additional hot-phenol extractions were carried out to remove the DNase, and 2 volumes of cold 95% ethanol were added to 1 volume of the aqueous phase. After overnight storage at −20°C, the precipitated RNA was collected by centrifugation, washed three times with cold 66% ethanol, resuspended in 0.01 M sodium acetate buffer, pH 5, containing 0.2 M LiCl and 0.001 M $MgCl_2$, and dialyzed overnight at 4°C against 200 volumes of the same buffer. RNA concentration was determined spectrophotometrically, assuming an $A^{1\%}_{1\,cm}$, 260 nm of 333 (3). The RNA preparation showed an A_{260}/A_{280} ratio of 2.0. It contained 2 to 10 μg of protein/800 μg RNA, as measured by the method of Lowry *et al.* (9) using bovine serum albumin as standard, and 8 to 12 μg of DNA/800 μg RNA, as measured by the diphenylamine reaction (10) using salmon sperm DNA as a standard.

Culture of spleen fragments. Spleens were removed aseptically from 6 to 12 mice whose sera showed a background of less than 10% phage-neutralizing activity in the standard assay system. The spleens were cut into fragments measuring 1 to 3 mm^3 and six to eight of these were placed on the surface of an agar disc (7). The disc, 17 mm in diameter and 3 mm in height, was prepared with 0.7% Noble agar (Difco Laboratories, Detroit, Mich.) in medium 199 (Grand Island Biological Corp., Grand Island, N. Y.), and was inserted in the center of a 60- x 15-mm plastic Petri dish. Each dish contained 2 ml of medium 199 supplemented with 25% normal rabbit serum that was heat-inactivated (56°C, 30 min) and devoid of phage-neutralizing activity, 100 units/ml of penicillin G, 50 μg/ml of streptomycin, and 1 μg/ml of Fungizone. The pH of the medium was adjusted to 6.95. Immunogenic or normal RNA was added directly to the spleen fragments. Incubation of the cultures was carried out at 37°C in a moist atmosphere of 5% CO_2 in air; after 3 days 0.5 ml of fresh medium was added to the culture. Fluids from four to six replicate culture dishes were harvested after 5 days, centrifuged at low speed, and an equal volume of saturated ammonium sulfate (SAS) was added to the supernatants. The precipitates were washed twice with 50% SAS, resuspended in 1 ml of pH 8 borate-saline buffer, and dialyzed against this buffer. This step resulted in a four- to sixfold concentration of the tissue culture fluids.

Assay for phage-neutralizing antibody. The overlay-agar method was used (11). Samples containing 0.9 ml of concentrated culture fluid or serum were mixed with 0.1 ml of phage (2 × 10^9 PFU/ml). One-tenth milliliter of this mixture was added to 9.9 ml of a broth composed of 1% yeast extract, 1% Casamino acids, 0.2% K_2HPO_4, and 0.1% glucose (all from Difco, Detroit, Mich.). After mixing, 0.1-ml samples (in triplicate) were transferred to tubes containing the propagating bacteria in 0.7% agar that were maintained at 48°C. The ingredients were mixed and were poured over the surface of a 100- x 15-mm plastic Petri plate that contained 20 ml of solidified agar. This procedure was repeated after 45 min of incubation at 37°C of the samples (in triplicate) with the phage. Control samples consisted of 1) phage incubated with broth, 2) phage incubated with culture fluids form normal spleen fragments, and 3) phage incubated with culture fluids from normal spleen fragments treated with normal RNA extracts. After overnight incubation at 37°C, the plates were scored for plaques. In all of the controls, there was less than 10% variation in plaque counts of samples tested at 0 time and after 45 min of incubation.

Enzyme treatment. In some experiments portions of the RNA extract were treated with various enzymes after the third extraction with hot phenol. The enzymes were incubated with the immunogenic RNA for 30 to 60 min at 37°C and removed by two further phenol extractions. The RNA samples were then processed as above and tested for immunogenic activity.

Density gradient ultracentrifugation. Linear gradients containing 5% to 20% sucrose (RNase-free, Mann Biochemicals, New York) were formed in 5-ml centrifuge tubes using as diluent the pH 5 acetate buffer. Approximately 100 μg of RNA were layered over the gradient, and the tubes were centrifuged in a Spinco SW-39L rotor at 35,000 rpm for 4 hr at 0°C in a Spinco model L centrifuge. Five-drop fractions were collected from the bottom of the first tube and, after dilution, absorbency of the fractions at 260 nm was determined. The second tube was similarly fractionated, but the samples were not diluted. Fractions corresponding to those of the first tube that showed absorbency peaks were pooled, dialyzed, and tested for their immunogenic activity in cultures of normal spleen fragments.

RESULTS

Response of normal spleen fragments to immunogenic RNA. Figure 1 shows that normal spleen fragments stimulated with 100 μg of immunogenic RNA began to produce neutralizing antibody after the 1st day of incubation, reached a maximum on the 5th day, and then declined until the termination of the culture period on the 12th day. Repeated attempts to detect a second wave of antibody formation on or about the 11th day of culture, as reported by Fishman *et al.* (2), were unsuccessful.

The effect of increasing concentrations of immunogenic RNA on the production of neutralizing antibody is shown in Figure 2. In repeated experiments, exposure of spleen fragments to increasing amounts of RNA resulted in the formation of increasing amounts of neutralizing

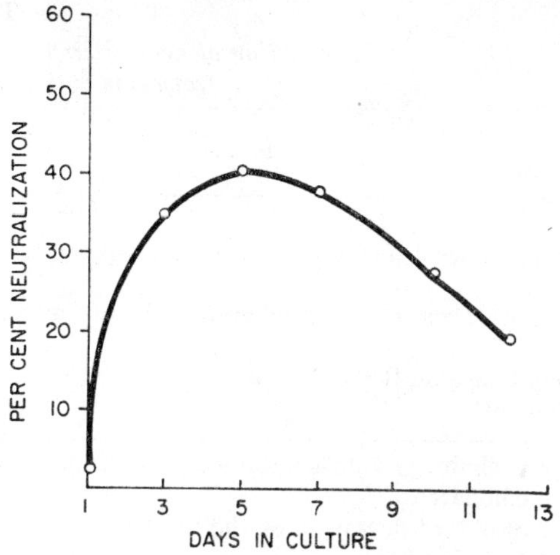

Figure 1. Production of neutralizing antibody by nonimmune spleen fragments after treatment with 100 μg of immunogenic RNA. Medium was changed completely and assayed for neutralizing antibody on days 1, 3, 5, 7, 10 and 12.

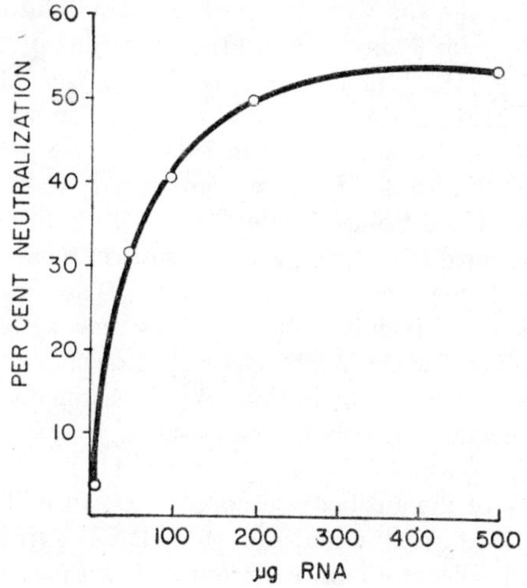

Figure 2. Neutralizing antibody of 5-day culture fluids induced by varying amounts of immunogenic RNA.

antibody. Beyond 200 μg of RNA, however, no appreciable increase in immunogenic activity was observed.

Lack of antibody formation in normal spleen fragments treated with phage. Attempts were made to induce antibody formation in nonimmune spleen fragments by incubating them directly with phage. In one experiment, spleen fragments

TABLE I

Induction of neutralizing antibody by direct stimulation of spleen fragments with phage or immunogenic RNA

Inducing Agent	No. of Plaques	Percentage Neutralization	p[a]
	mean ± *S.D.*[b]		
Streptococcal phage incubated with spleen fragments 1 hr	132.6 ± 3.9	1.3	NS[c]
Streptococcal phage incubated with spleen fragments 7 days	129.6 ± 3.9	3.8	NS
Immunogenic RNA, 140 μg	83.0 ± 6.7	38.2	<0.001
Control[d]	134.4 ± 5.8		

[a] Probability values obtained from Student's *t* test. Mean values of control and treated culture fluids are compared.

[b] Standard deviation of the mean.

[c] Not significant.

[d] Controls consisted of phage incubated in broth, in culture medium from nonimmune spleen fragment cultures, and in culture medium from normal spleen fragments incubated with RNA extracted from the spleens of nonimmune mice. Average value of the three is given.

were incubated with 4×10^{10} PFU of phage for 1 hr at 37°C. They were then washed to remove free phage and were cultured in the standardized system for 7 days. In another experiment, 4×10^{10} PFU of phage were added to the spleen fragments, and were allowed to remain in contact with the fragments for the 7-day culture period. The culture fluids were centrifuged at 40,000 rpm in the Spinco model L centrifuge for 2 hr to remove free phage, and the supernatants were tested for neutralizing activity. The results, which are given in Table I and are representative of several experiments, show that antibody synthesis could not be initiated by direct incubation of phage with spleen fragments.

Specificity of immunogenic RNA. The specificity of the antibody response is shown in Table II. The results indicate that RNA extracted from spleens of mice immunized with streptococcal phage was unable to induce significant levels of antibody directed against the T2 or T7 phages of *Escherichia coli*. It should be noted that sera from both spleen-RNA-donors and spleen-fragment-recipients usually had a high background level (15% to 20%) of neutralizing antibody against T2 and T7 coliphages.

TABLE II

Specificity of the antibody response induced by immunogenic RNA[a]

Test Antigen	No. of Plaques	Percentage Neutralization	p[b]
	mean ± *S.D.*[c]		
Streptococcal phage	80.3 ± 1.7	40.3	<0.001
Control	133.0 ± 3.7		
T2 coliphage	165.3 ± 11.6	6.8	NS[d]
Control	177.3 ± 6.6		
T7 coliphage	156.0 ± 4.0	6.4	NS
Control	166.6 ± 4.3		

[a] One hundred ninety-six micrograms of immunogenic RNA extracted from the spleens of mice immunized with the streptococcal phage. Culture fluids were taken after 7 days and tested for neutralizing antibody against the streptococcal phage and *E. coli* phages T2 and T7.

[b] Probability values obtained from Student's *t* test. Mean values of control (culture fluids from normal spleen fragments incubated in the absence of immunogenic RNA) and immune culture fluids are compared.

[c] Standard deviation of the mean.

[d] Not significant.

Immunogenicity of RNA in relation to strain specificity. RNA extracts were prepared from the spleens of A/He/J, BALB/c/J, B_6AF_1, and Swiss Webster mice previously immunized by the procedures already described. The immunogenicity of RNA from one mouse strain was tested in cultures of spleen fragments derived from all of the other strains of nonimmunized mice. The results, summarized in Table III, show that immune RNA from one mouse strain was capable of inducing neutralizing antibody in

TABLE III

Induction of neutralizing antibody by immunogenic RNA[a] derived from different mouse strains

Immune RNA Donor	Normal Spleen Fragment Recipient			
	A/He/J	BALB/c/J	B_6AF_1	Swiss Webster
	Percentage neutralization			
A/He/J	32	17[b]	26	25
BALB/c/J	23	27	39	9
B_6AF_1	18	39	33	49
Swiss Webster	6	54	45	48
Nonimmune Swiss Webster				
RNA control	13	9	0	1
Control[c]	13	13	0	11

[a] One hundred thirty-five micrograms of immunogenic RNA.

[b] All values above 17% neutralization are significant to the 1% confidence level.

[c] Control consisted of culture fluid from normal spleen fragments incubated in the absence of immunogenic RNA. Note the absence of significant levels of phage-neutralizing antibody in culture fluids of normal spleen fragments incubated with nonimmune RNA.

TABLE IV

Effect of enzymes on the induction of neutralizing antibody in cultures of normal spleen fragments by immunogenic RNA[a]

Enzyme	Enzyme: Substrate Weight Ratio	No. of Plaques	Percentage Neutralization	p[b]
		mean ± *S.D.*[c]		
RNase	1:100	111.6 ± 2.5	17.0	<0.01
	1:10	127.6 ± 2.6	4.9	NS[d]
	1:5	128.3 ± 3.3	4.5	NS
	1:1	132.3 ± 3.3	1.6	NS
DNase	1:10	83.0 ± 6.7	38.3	<0.001
Pronase	1:10	94.0 ± 5.1	30.6	0.001
	1:1	123.6 ± 3.7	8.0	NS
Trypsin	1:10	87.0 ± 4.6	35.3	<0.001
Amylase	20:1	83.3 ± 10.3	38.0	<0.001
None		84.6 ± 6.8	37.6	<0.001
Control[e]		134.4 ± 5.8		

[a] One hundred forty micrograms immunogenic RNA was treated with enzyme for 60 min at 37°C.

[b] Probability values obtained from Student's *t* test. Mean values of control and enzyme-treated are compared.

[c] Standard deviation of the mean.

[d] Not significant.

[e] Same as in Table I.

spleen fragments derived from most of the other strains. However, immune RNA from Swiss Webster mice was inactive in eliciting an antibody response in normal spleen fragments of A/He/J mice, and immune RNA from BALB/c/J mice was also inactive when added to normal spleen fragments of Swiss Webster mice.

Effect of enzymes on the immunogenicity of RNA. Several reports indicate that the immunogenic activity of RNA is eliminated by certain enzymes. The results given in Table IV show that digestion with DNase, trypsin and amylase had no effect on the ability of RNA to induce neutralizing antibody in cultures of normal spleen fragments. RNase, however, inhibited the reaction at all concentrations used. Pronase had virtually no effect on the response when added at a weight ratio of 1:10, whereas it reduced the response considerably at a weight ratio of 1:1.

Sedimentation properties of RNA. Fractionation of immunogenic RNA by sucrose density gradient centrifugation disclosed three peaks (Fig. 3), presumably having sedimentation coefficients of 30 S, 18 S and 6 to 12 S (12). Fractions from each of these peaks were tested for immunogenic activity. The data in Table V indicate that 20 μg of the 6 to 12 S peak was more immunogenic than 150 μg of the unfractionated material. The other two peaks showed very little immunogenicity. In the analytical ultracentrifuge, using ultraviolet optics, the 6 S to 12 S peak was found to have an average sedimentation coefficient of 8.2 Svedbergs.

DISCUSSION

To eliminate the contribution of endotoxin-like factors to the immunogenicity of RNA, a phage infecting a Gram-positive bacterium was chosen as antigen for these studies. Johnson *et al.* (13) found that the endotoxin derived from Gram-negative bacteria was capable of enhancing antibody formation to unrelated antigens. No such adjuvant effects have been attributed as yet to the cell constituents of Gram-positive bacteria. However, it was found that sera of nonimmunized mice had background levels of neutralizing antibody against the streptococcal phage ranging from 0 to 10%. This finding would indicate that the mice used in our studies harbored the host bacterium or its phage or both. The antigenic stimulus may also have been

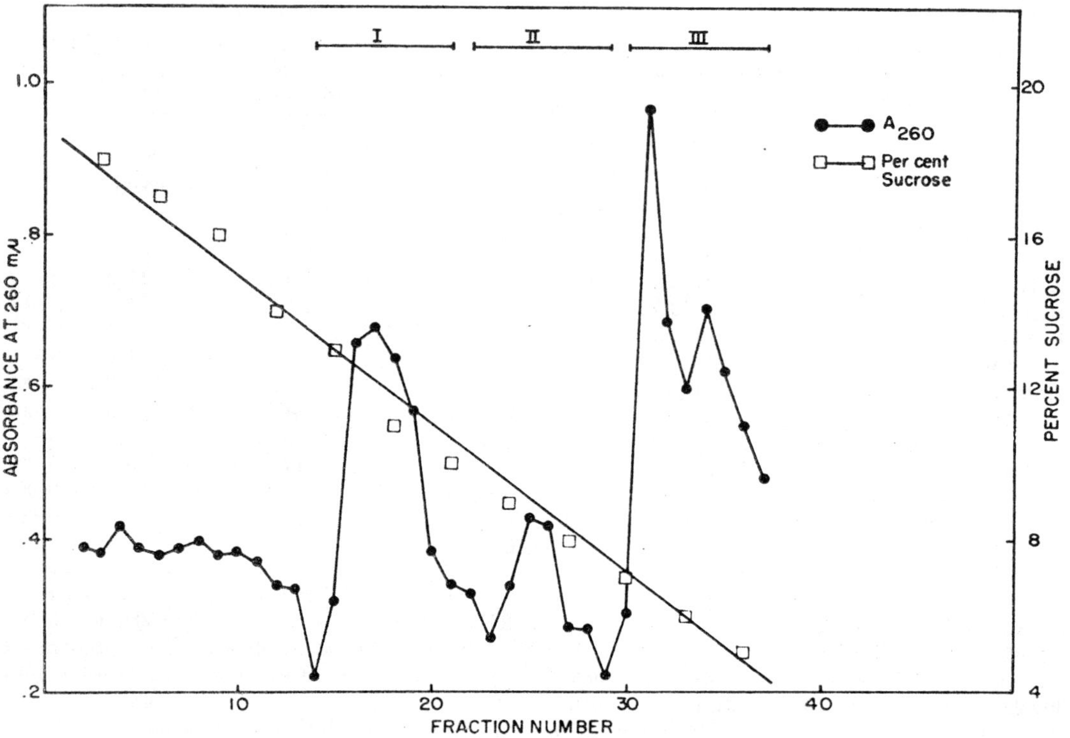

Figure 3. Fractionation of immunogenic RNA by sucrose density gradient centrifugation for 4 hr at 35,000 rpm in SW-39L rotor.

TABLE V

Immunogenic activity[a] of RNA fractionated by sucrose density gradient centrifugation

Fraction No.[b]	RNA Concentration	No. of Plaques	Percentage Neutralization	p[c]
	μg	Mean ± S.D.[d]		
1–13	20	89.3 ± 1.7	11.3	<0.05
14–21	17	90.3 ± 5.2	10.3	NS[e]
22–29	22	90.6 ± 4.2	10.0	NS
30–37	30	53.3 ± 4.0	47.0	<0.001
Unfractionated	150	62.3 ± 4.9	38.1	<0.01
Control[f]		100.6 ± 4.5		

[a] Immunogenic activity tested in cultures of normal spleen fragments.

[b] See Figure 3. Fraction 1 represents bottom of tube; fraction 37, top.

[c] Probability values obtained from Student's *t* test.

[d] Standard deviation of the mean.

[e] Not significant.

[f] Same as in Table I.

provided by unknown substances that were serologically related to the phage antigens. It would further indicate that the cultures of normal spleen fragments most probably contained some cells that had been "primed" prior to exposure of immunogenic RNA. Therefore, our results, as well as those of others based on similar experiments, suffer from the uncertainty originating from finding normal, immunologically competent cells that have never been stimulated by a given antigen or a substance containing cross-reacting antigenic determinants.

Evidence for the role of immunogenic RNA in the induction of the immune response came from experiments in which varying concentrations of phage, directly incubated with nonimmune spleen fragments, failed to induce an antibody response. It would thus appear that antigen must first be processed in some way before it can initiate antibody formation, as suggested by Fishman and Adler (14).

Unlike the results of Fishman *et al.* (2), we did not detect a second wave of antibody response in cultures of spleen fragments stimulated with immunogenic RNA. It should be noted, however, that their culture system as well as the source of immunogenic RNA differed markedly from the one described in this paper. Instead of rat lymph nodes, we used mouse spleens; and instead of RNA extracted from peritoneal exudate cells incubated *in vitro* with T2 phage, we used RNA extracted from the spleens of mice immunized *in vivo* with a streptococcal phage. A single peak of antibody formation following stimulation of nonimmune spleen cells with immunogenic RNA has also been observed by Bishop *et al.* (15).

The amount of neutralizing antibody induced in cultures of normal spleen fragments by immunogenic RNA was found to be dose-dependent, in the range of 5 to 200 μg of RNA in the standardized culture system. No further increase in the amount of neutralizing antibody was observed in cultures treated with larger amounts of RNA. A similar observation was reported by Cohen *et al.* (6), and suggests that either a saturation level had been reached by those spleen cells that were capable of taking up immunogenic RNA or that the spleen fragments contained only a limited number of potential antibody-producing cells.

Contrary to a previous report (6) that the conversion of nonimmune spleen cells to antibody-forming cells by RNA was strain-specific, our experiments would indicate that RNA from one strain of mice induces the formation of neutralizing antibody in normal spleen fragments derived from other mouse strains. This finding is not surprising in view of the report (16) that immunogenic RNA extracted from antigen-treated macrophages of mouse, rat, or rabbit could induce the formation of specific antibody when injected intraperitoneally into nonimmune mice. The lack of strain-specificity, and indeed of species-specificity, in the ability of immunogenic RNA to induce antibody formation in cultures of spleen fragments or animals not knowingly immunized would cast doubt on the ability of RNA alone to induce antibody formation.

In these experiments, inhibition of the induction of neutralizing antobody was observed after digestion of immunogenic RNA with RNase and high concentrations of pronase, but not with DNase, amylase and trypsin. The effect of RNase on immunogenic RNA has been reported by all workers using similar experimental systems, and it would indicate that the active material is intimately associated with an RNA fraction. The observation that the immunogenicity of RNA was inactivated only when it was treated with an equal weight of pronase agrees with a similar finding by Gottlieb *et al.* (17).

In early experiments, no attempt was made to remove the enzymes from immunogenic RNA before adding it directly to the spleen fragments in culture. Hence the enzymes could have acted on RNA, the spleen fragments, or the neutralizing antibody produced by the spleen fragments. If the enzymes were removed from the immunogenic RNA by further extraction with phenol, it was found that only RNase and pronase (at a weight ratio of enzyme to substrate of 1:1) abolished the immunogenicity of RNA (see Table IV). The inhibitory effect of high concentrations of pronase may well have resulted from its incomplete removal from immunogenic RNA. If pronase was present in the RNA extract, it could seep into the culture fluid and act directly on the neutralizing antibody that was produced by the spleen fragments. Pronase has been shown to abolish the neutralizing activity of antiserum to the streptococcal phage (18). This finding, however, does not rule out the possibility that the immunogenicity of RNA requires the presence of antigen, as postulated by others (19).

The immunogenic activity of the RNA extract was found to be associated with a fraction sedimenting in the 6 S to 12 S region, and agrees with the sedimentation value reported by others (1, 6, 14). Of interest is the greater immunogenicity on a weight basis of the 6 S to 12 S fraction as compared to the unfractionated RNA, and indicates that only a small part of the total RNA extract is immunogenically active. Ultracentrifugal analysis revealed that the active material had an average sedimentation coefficient of 8.2 S, which would correspond to a molecular weight of approximately 100,000 (6). An RNA of this size would be expected to function as a messenger RNA in the synthesis of a polypeptide of roughly 10,000 mol. wt., but it would not be of sufficient size to act in the synthesis of even the light chains (20,00 mol. wt.) of an immunoglobulin molecule.

Acknowledgments. The authors thank Dr. J. M. Hammel for supplying *Streptococcus faecalis* var. *zymogenes* and its bacteriophage 81a, and Miss M. Fitzgerald for her skillful technical assistance.

REFERENCES

1. Fishman, M. and Adler, F. L., J. Exp. Med., *117:* 595, 1963.
2. Fishman, M., van Rood, J. J. and Adler, F. L.,

Molecular and Cellular Basis of Antibody Formation, Edited by J. Šterzl, p. 491, Academic Press, New York, 1965.
3. Fishman, M., Adler, F. L. and Dray, S., J. Immun., *97:* 554, 1966.
4. Friedman, H., Science, *146:* 934, 1964.
5. Cohen, E. P. and Parks, J. J., Science, *144:* 1012, 1964.
6. Cohen, E. P., Newcomb, R. W. and Crosby, L. K., J. Immun., *95:* 583, 1965.
7. Herscowtiz, H. B., Thesis (Ph.D.), Hahnemann Medical College, Philadelphia, 1968.
8. Homma, M. and Graham, A. F., J. Cell Comp. Physiol., *62:* 179, 1963.
9. Lowry, O. H., Rosebrough, N. J., Farr, A. L. and Randall, R. J., J. Biol. Chem., *193:* 265, 1951.
10. Burton, K., Biochem. J., *62:* 315, 1965.
11. Adams, M. H., *Bacteriophages*, Interscience Publishers, New York, 1959.
12. Mach, B. and Vassalli, P., Proc. Nat. Acad. Sci., *54:* 975, 1965.
13. Johnson, A. G., Gaines, S. and Landy, M., J. Exp. Med., *103:* 225, 1956.
14. Fishman, M. and Adler, F. L., Cold Spring Harbor Symp. Quant. Biol., *32:* 343, 1967.
15. Bishop, D. C., Pisciotta, A. V. and Abramoff, P., J. Immun., *99:* 751, 1967.
16. Pinchuck, P., Fishman, M., Adler, F. L. and Maurer, P., Science, *160:* 194, 1968.
17. Gottlieb, A. A., Glišin, V. R. and Doty, P., Proc. Nat. Acad. Sci., *57:* 1849, 1967.
18. Herscowitz, H. B. and Stelos, P., Biochim. Biophys. Acta, *200:* 408, 1970.
19. Askonas, B. A. and Rhodes, J. M., Nature, *205:* 470, 1965.

THE JOURNAL OF IMMUNOLOGY
Copyright © 1970 by The Williams & Wilkins Co.

Vol. 105, No. 3, September 1970
Printed in U.S.A.

THE INDUCTION OF BACTERIOPHAGE-NEUTRALIZING ANTIBODY BY MOUSE SPLEEN IMMUNOGENIC RNA

II. Evidence for the Presence of Phage Antigen in Immunogenic RNA[1]

HERBERT B. HERSCOWITZ[2, 3] AND PETER STELOS

From the Department of Microbiology, Hahnemann Medical College, Philadelphia, Pennsylvania 19102

Received for publication June 16, 1969

Antigenic components derived from phage were detected in immunogenic RNA preparations extracted from immune mouse spleens. Injection of immunogenic RNA into previously immunized mice resulted in an anamnestic response, whereas challenge with non-immune RNA did not. Treatment of immunogenic RNA with mouse antiphage antibody reduced its ability to induce neutralizing antibody in cultures of normal spleen fragments. The extracted RNA was found to contain ^{14}C-labeled material derived from phage. These findings indicate the presence of antigen in RNA extracted from the spleens of immunized mice.

The *in vitro* production of antibody by normal lymphoid cells stimulated by RNA extracted from immunologically active cells ("immunogenic RNA") has been recently reviewed (1). Askonas and Rhodes (2) detected antigen in immunogenic RNA, and they postulated that antigen was essential for its immunogenicity. Friedman *et al.* (3) found that their immunogenic RNA contained antigenic fragments that reacted with specific antibody, as tested by the complement-fixation reaction. The presence of antigen in immunogenic RNA has also been reported by others (4–6). We report here further evidence for the role of antigen in the immunogenicity of RNA extracts.

MATERIALS AND METHODS

Animals and immunization. Adult female Swiss Webster mice (25 to 30 g) were used. The mice were immunized by intraperitoneal injections of 0.1-ml doses of 1 × 10^{10} plaque-forming units (PFU)/ml of bacteriophage 81a, which infects *Streptococcus faecalis* var. *zymogenes*, on alternate days for 3 weeks. When needed, blood was collected from the venous plexus of the retro-orbital sinus or by cardiac puncture.

Extraction of RNA. RNA was extracted from a pool of 5 to 10 spleens by a modification of the hot phenol method (7).

Phage neutralization assay. Neutralization tests were performed by adding 0.1 ml of a phage suspension containing 2 × 10^6 PFU/ml to 0.9 ml of the sample to be tested. Sera were assayed at dilutions of 1:10 and 1:50. All values expressed are for serum diluted 1:10 unless otherwise stated. At 0 time and after 45 min of incubation at 37°C, 0.1-ml portions of the mixture were withdrawn and assayed in triplicate by the agar overlay method (8). During this incubation period there was less than 10% variation in the control samples, indicating phage stability. The percentage of neutralization was calculated by comparing the ability of test samples to neutralize phage with that of controls, which consisted of the same amount of phage incubated in saline or in culture medium from spleen fragments of non-immune mice.

Preparation of ^{14}C-labeled bacteriophage. The host bacterial strain was grown overnight at 37°C in 3 ml of a chemically defined medium (9) containing 2.5 μCi of ^{14}C-*l*-leucine (180 mCi/mM, uniformly labeled, Tracerlab, Waltham, Mass.). The overnight culture was added to 200 ml of prewarmed defined medium containing 47.5 μCi of ^{14}C-*l*-leucine. After incubation at 37°C for 70

[1] This work was supported by United States Public Health Service Grant AI-07137.

[2] Recipient of United States Public Health Service Predoctoral Award 1-F1-GM-38, 593-01.

[3] Present address: Dept. of Microbiology, School of Medicine and Dentistry, Georgetown University, Washington, D. C.

min, 2.5 ml of a phage 81a stock containing 8 $\times 10^{11}$ PFU/ml was added and incubation continued until lysis occurred. The lysate was centrifuged at 12,000 $\times$ G for 20 min at 4°C to remove particulate matter. The supernatant fluid was dialyzed against several changes of 0.15 M NaCl at 4°C. The phage was concentrated by chromatography on DEAE-cellulose by a modification (10) of the procedure of Davison *et al.* (11), and further purified by banding in a cesium chloride density gradient (12). After dialysis against 0.15 M NaCl and sterilization by Millipore filtration, the phage was stored at −20°C until needed.

Radioactivity measurement. Radioactivity was determined in a liquid scintillation counter on samples to which BBS-3 solubilizer and Fluoralloy TLA scintillation fluid were added (Beckman Instruments Co., Palo Alto, Calif.).

RESULTS

Presence of phage antigen in immunogenic RNA. In order to detect phage antigen in the RNA extracted from the spleens of immune mice, a modification of the method of Friedman *et al.* (3) was used. The detection of phage antigen is based on the appearance of a secondary immune response upon injection of immunogenic RNA into mice previously immunized with phage 81a. A preimmune sample was obtained by pooling the sera from a group of 15 mice. Each mouse was given a primary intraperitoneal injection of 10^9 PFU of phage; 5 days later they were bled and their sera were pooled. Thirty days later the mice were bled again, and a serum pool was prepared. The animals were then divided into three groups. Mice in group 1 were each injected with 300 μg of immunogenic RNA. Group 2 mice were injected with an equivalent amount of RNA obtained from the spleens of nonimmune mice, and group 3 mice were injected with 10^9 PFU of phage 81a. All groups were bled 4 days after the secondary injection, and the pooled sera of each group was tested for neutralizing activity. As can be seen in Table I, the mice challenged with RNA extracted from the spleens of immune mice responded with the production of higher levels of neutralizing antibody than the mice challenged with RNA extracted from the spleens of nonimmune mice. The group challenged with phage 81a gave the greatest antibody response.

Reduction of RNA immunogenicity by absorption with mouse anti-phage serum. Further evidence for the presence of phage antigen in the immunogenic RNA extracts was indicated by absorption experiments with specific mouse anti-phage serum. The antiserum was obtained by pooling the sera from a group of 30 mice that had been hyperimmunized with phage as described above. An immunogenic RNA preparation, taken after the fourth phenol extraction, was divided into three fractions: to one was added 1 ml of pooled mouse anti-phage serum; to the second, 1 ml of pooled normal mouse serum; and to the third, 1 ml of saline. After a 30-min

TABLE I

Induction of a secondary antibody response in primed mice by immunogenic RNA

Group	No. of Mice	Source of Serum (Diluted 1:10)	No. of Plaques	Percentage Neutralization	p[a]
			mean ± *S.D.*[b]		
1–3	15	Preimmune	87.0 ± 6.3	6.5	NS[c]
1–3	15	Primary, after 5 days	77.3 ± 2.6	16.9	<0.01
1–3	15	Primary, after 30 days	62.0 ± 6.2	33.4	<0.01
1	5	Secondary, immunogenic RNA	39.6 ± 3.3	57.5	<0.001
2	5	Secondary, nonimmune RNA	64.2 ± 3.8	31.1	<0.01
3	5	Secondary, phage 81a	14.0 ± 2.4	84.9	<0.001
Control[d]		Normal	93.1 ± 4.5		

[a] Probability values obtained from Student's *t* test. Mean values of control and experimental are compared.

[b] Standard deviation of the mean.

[c] Not significant.

[d] Controls consisted of phage incubated in saline and in culture medium from nonimmune spleen fragment cultures. The average value of the two is given.

TABLE II

Effect of mouse anti-phage serum on the ability of immunogenic RNA to induce antibody formation in cultures of spleen fragments

Treatment of RNA	RNA Added	No. of Plaques	Percentage Neutralization	p[a]
	μg	*mean ± S.D.*[b]		
Mouse anti-phage serum	158	77.3 ± 3.9	16.9	<0.02
Normal mouse serum	154	61.0 ± 6.7	34.5	<0.01
Saline	136	53.0 ± 3.3	43.1	<0.01
Control[c]		93.1 ± 4.5		

[a] Probability values obtained from Student's *t* test. Mean values of control and treated are compared.
[b] Standard deviation of the mean.
[c] Controls consisted of phage incubated in saline and culture medium from nonimmune spleen fragment cultures. The average value of the two is given.

incubation period at 37°C with stirring, the fractions were centrifuged at low speed to remove a small amount of precipitate, and they were extracted twice more with phenol to remove serum proteins. The procedures previously described (7) were followed for the preparation and testing of the immunogenicity of the RNA extracts. Table II shows that treatment of immunogenic RNA with specific anti-phage serum reduced its ability to stimulate neutralizing antibody in nonimmune spleen fragments by 60% as compared to the neutralizing activity induced by the saline treated RNA. Similar treatment of immunogenic RNA with normal serum resulted in only a 20% reduction of neutralizing activity.

Presence of radioactivity in immunogenic RNA. In this experiment, 10 mice were each injected intraperitoneally on alternate days with six doses of 10^8 PFU of unlabeled phage followed by six doses of 1.5×10^8 PFU of ^{14}C-labeled phage (specific activity, 1.33×10^{-2} cpm/PFU). One day after the last injection, the mice were killed, their spleens were removed, and RNA was extracted from the combined spleens. Table III shows the distribution of radioactivity at various stages in the extraction, and indicates that most of the radioactivity was removed by the third stage. The radioactivity remained relatively constant from the fourth to the final stage. The finding of approximately equal amounts of radioactivity in the aqueous and phenol phases may be the result of a continuous degradation of highly polymerized RNA associated with ^{14}C-labeled protein fragments derived from the phage. Presumably such breakdown products would be soluble in either phase.

TABLE III

Determination of carry-over of ^{14}C-labeled antigen[a] in the immunogenic RNA[b]

Sample	Total cpm
Whole spleen homogenate (1.8 g wet weight)	8.0×10^4
1st and 2nd aqueous phases	3.0×10^4
1st and 2nd phenol phases	3.7×10^4
3rd aqueous phase	1.3×10^3
3rd phenol phase	1.6×10^3
4th aqueous phase	2.3×10^2
4th phenol phase	2.8×10^2
5th aqueous phase	2.3×10^2
5th phenol phase	2.5×10^2
6th aqueous phase	2.2×10^2
6th phenol phase	2.5×10^2
Precipitated RNA, before dialysis	2.5×10^2
Final RNA product, 450 μg/ml (3 ml)	2.5×10^2

[a] ^{14}C-labeled phage was injected intraperitoneally into 10 mice for 6 days following a 2-week immunization schedule with unlabeled phage.
[b] RNA was extracted from spleens and samples removed for radioassay at all stages during the extraction procedure.

DISCUSSION

The presence of phage antigen in immunogenic RNA was indicated by three types of experiments. In the first, the injection of RNA extracted from the spleens of immune mice into a group of mice previously immunized with the phage resulted in a statistically significant rise in neutralizing activity. No such increase in neutralizing activity was observed in similarly primed mice that were injected with RNA extracted from the spleens of normal mice. This finding supports the conclusion of Friedman *et al.* (3), who used a similar approach. In the second, absorption of the RNA extracted from the spleens of immune mice with specific mouse anti-phage serum resulted in a significant decrease in immunogenic activity as measured by the ability of RNA to induce the formation of neutralizing antibody in cultures of normal spleen fragments. The same conclusion was noted by Abramoff and Brien (6), who used RNA extracted from the spleens of chickens immunized with sheep red cells. The decrease in immunogenicity after absorption with normal mouse serum may have been caused by nonspecific precipitation of RNA by normal serum or by the background level of neutralizing antibody present in the normal serum used in this experiment, or by both. The third experiment indicated the presence of ^{14}C-labeled phage components in the RNA extracted from the spleens of mice immunized with this preparation. Although the amount of radioactivity incorporated into the phage was low, i.e., 1.33×10^{-2} cpm/PFU of phage, the amount found in the last aqueous extract was appreciable and accounted for approximately 0.3% of the radioactivity present in the homogenized pooled spleens.

Our results indicate that immunogenic RNA contains antigen or antigenic fragments. It would appear that a combination of RNA and antigen is responsible for the induction of antibody formation rather than RNA itself. It has been suggested that the RNA serves merely as a carrier of antigenic material (2). Until it can be shown that the RNA extracted from immunologically active cells is free of antigenic material, the role of RNA in the immune response would appear to be unknown.

Acknowledgment. We thank Miss M. Fitzgerald for her skillful technical assistance.

REFERENCES

1. Fishman, M., Ann. Rev. Microbiol., *23:* 199 1969.
2. Askonas, B. A. and Rhodes, J. M., Nature, *205:* 470, 1965.
3. Friedman, H. P., Stavitsky, A. B. and Solomon, J. M., Science, *149:* 1106, 1965.
4. Gottlieb, A. A., Glišin, V. R. and Doty, P., Proc. Nat. Acad. Sci., *57:* 1849, 1967.
5. Roelants, G. E. and Goodman, J. W., Biochemistry, *7:* 1432, 1968.
6. Abramoff, P. and Brien, N. B., J. Immun., *100:* 1210, 1968.
7. Herscowtiz, H. B. and Stelos, P., J. Immun., *105:* 771, 1970.
8. Adams, M. H., *Bacteriophages*, Interscience Publishers, New York, 1959.
9. Hammel, J. M., Thesis (M.S.), Pennsylvania State University, University Park, Pennsylvania, 1962.
10. Herscowtiz, H. B., Thesis (Ph.D.), Hahnemann Medical College, Philadelphia, 1968.
11. Davison, P. F., Freifelder, D., Hede, R. and Levinthal, C., Proc. Nat. Acad. Sci., *47:* 1123, 1961.
12. Thomas, C. A., Jr. and Abelson, J., in *Procedures in Nucleic Acid Research*, Edited by G. L. Cantoni and D. R. Davies, p. 556, Harper and Row, New York, 1966.

THE JOURNAL OF IMMUNOLOGY
Vol. 105, No. 3, September 1970

Printed in U.S.A.

Structural Studies of Immunoglobulin E. II. Amino Terminal Sequence of the Heavy Chain[1]

WILLIAM D. TERRY, MAKIO OGAWA AND SHAUL KOCHWA

From the National Institutes of Health, National Cancer Institute, Immunology Branch, Bethesda, Maryland 20014, Dartmouth Medical School, Department of Medicine, Hanover, New Hampshire 03755, and the Mount Sinai School of Medicine, Department of Medicine, New York, New York 10029

Determination of the primary structure of immunoglobulin proteins provides information that can be used to extend our knowledge of the structural relationship between different classes of immunoglobulins, as well as their genetic and evolutionary characteristics. Primary structural information will also be important ultimately in attaining an understanding of the antibody and non-antibody functional properties of these molecules.

Immunoglobulin E (IgE) is the most recently discovered of the human immunoglobulins and is the one, therefore, about which we have the least structural information. IgE antibodies bind antigens, and also have the capacity to sensitize receptors in human tissue for immediate hypersensitivity reactions (reviewed in 1). Structural studies of IgE will provide data for comparison with the amino acid sequences already determined for other classes of human immunoglobulins, and also may be useful in investigating the nature of the interaction between IgE molecules and cellular receptors. The large quantities of homogeneous protein required for such studies can now be isolated from a patient's serum that contains an IgE-myeloma protein (2). In this report, the sequence of the amino-terminal 21 amino acids of the heavy polypeptide chain (ε chain) of this myeloma protein is presented.

MATERIALS AND METHODS

Myeloma protein was isolated from the serum of Sha. by chromatography on DEAE-cellulose (Whatman DE-52) followed by gel filtration on Sephadex G-200 (Pharmacia). The isolated material was tested by immunoelectrophoresis and radial immunodiffusion and shown to contain IgE with λ light chains, contaminated with IgG (approximately 2%). Heavy chains were prepared by partially reducing the protein with 0.01 M dithioerythritol in 0.5 M Tris HCl buffer, pH 8.1, followed by alkylation with 0.04 M iodoacetamide. Polypeptide chains were separated by gel filtration through G-100 in 1 N acetic acid. The sequence of the amino-terminal 21 amino acids of the ε chain was determined with an automatic amino acid sequencer (Beckman Instruments, Inc., Fullerton, Calif., model 890A) using the methods and conditions described by Edman and Begg (3). The thiazolinone derivatives obtained from the sequencer were converted to phenylthiohydantoin-amino acids and identified and quantitated using the liquid-gas chromatographic methods of Pisano and Bronzert (4). DC-560 support was used in the coiled glass columns (4 ft x 0.2 mm) of a gas chromatograph (Varian Instruments, Inc.).

RESULTS AND DISCUSSION

The sequence of the amino-terminal 21 amino acids of the ε chain is compared with the sequences of three γ chains in Table I. It can be seen that the sequence of Sha. is highly homologous with that of Vin. (5), in that 17 of the 21 residues are identical. The sequences of Eu. (6) and He. (7) are also homologous with that of Sha., but are less similar to Sha. than is Vin. For example, Eu. and Sha. have identical residues at 11 positions, whereas He. and Sha. are identical at 9 positions.

Immunoglobulin heavy chains have been shown to consist of variable regions (approximately the amino-terminal 120 residues) and common regions (the remainder of the chain to the carboxy termi-

[1] This work was aided by Grants CA 04326, Dartmouth, AM 12912, and CA 04457 (Mount Sinai) from the United States Public Health Service, and by the Albert A. List, Frederick Machlin and Anna Ruth Lowenberg Research Funds (Mount Sinai).

TABLE I

Amino terminal sequence of ϵ chain (Sha.) compared with three γ chains[a]

Variable Subgroup	Protein	Class	1				5					10	
IV	Sha	ϵ	Glu	Val	Gln	Leu	*Met*	Glu	Ser	Gly	Gly	Gly	*Val*
	Vin	γ	Glu	Val	Gln	Leu	*Val*	Glu	Ser	Gly	Gly	Gly	*Leu*
II	He	γ	PCA	Val	Thr	Leu	Lys	Glu	Asn	Gly	Pro	Thr	Leu
I	Eu	γ	PCA	Val	Gln	Leu	Val	Gln	Ser	Gly	Ala	Glu	Val

Variable Subgroup	Protein	Class				15					20		22
IV	Sha	ϵ	*Val*	*Lys*	Pro	Gly	Gly	Ser	Leu	Arg	Leu	Ser	[ ]
	Vin	γ	*Ileu*	*Gln*	Pro	Gly	Gly	Ser	Leu	Arg	Leu	Ser	Cys
II	He	γ	Val	Lys	Pro	Thr	Glu	Thr	Leu	Thr	Leu	Thr	Cys
I	Eu	γ	Lys	Lys	Pro	Gly	Ser	Ser	Val	Lys	Val	Ser	Cys

[a] The bracket indicates failure to define a residue at position 22. This is expected if position 22 is a cysteine, since the cysteine would be linked to another cysteine by an intrachain disulfide bond, and would not be recovered following acid cleavage. Residues that are not identical in Sha. and Vin. are italicized. Sequence data are from the following references: Vin. (5); Eu. (6); He. (7).

nus) (6). The sequences of the variable regions have been divided into subgroups on the basis of sequence similarities. Eu. is a representative of subgroup I and He. represents subgroup II (7). The variable regions of Sha. and Vin. appear to belong to subgroup IV, which is characterized by a non-blocked amino terminus, glutamine at the third position and an invariant sequence of Glu-Ser-Gly-Gly from position 6 to 10 (8, 9). The ϵ chain sequence differs from that of seven other proteins of this variable region subgroup in that it has a methionine at position 5. In addition, methionine has not been seen at this position in any of 11 other immunoglobulin heavy chains that belong to other variable region subgroups. Further sequence studies will be required to determine whether additional unique residues are present in the ϵ chain. At the present time, only one other IgE-myeloma protein (N.D.) has been described (10). It will be interesting to compare the sequence of Sha. with that of N.D. and any additional E-myeloma proteins that are identified, to determine whether ϵ chain variable regions have characteristics that differentiate them from the other classes of immunoglobulins.

Portions of the Sha. sequence are identical to those found in other species. The sequence Glu-Ser-Gly in positions 6 to 8 (Table I) is also seen in some mouse myeloma heavy chains (L. Hood, D. McKean and M. Potter, unpublished), as well as in the predominant sequence of rabbit IgG heavy chains (11). As additional sequence data become available, it should be possible to define the evolutionary relationships of heavy chain variable regions.

It has been hypothesized that separate genes control synthesis of the variable and common regions of immunoglobulin heavy chains (7). If this hypothesis is correct, it would appear that there is a pool of variable region genes that can be integrated into heavy chain common region genes. The portion of the pool characterized by an unblocked amino terminal residue previously demonstrated in IgG, IgA, IgM and a γ heavy chain disease protein (5, 8, 9; A. Kaplan, L. Hood, H. Metzger and W. D. Terry, to be published) has now been shown also to be associated with IgE.

Acknowledgments. We wish to thank Mr. Robert Guyer and Mr. Matthew Miller for their excellent technical assistance.

REFERENCES

1. Ishizaka, K. and Ishizaka, T., J. Allerg., *42:* 330, 1968.
2. Ogawa, M., Kochwa, S., Smith, C., Ishizaka, K. and McIntyre, O. R., New England J. Med., *281:* 1217, 1969.

3. Edman, P. and Begg, G., Europ. J. Biochem., *1:* 80, 1967.
4. Pisano, J. J. and Bronzert, T. J., J. Biol. Chem., *244:* 5597, 1969.
5. Pink, J. R. L. and Milstein, C., FEBS Symposium on γGlobulins, Edited by F. Franek and D. Shugar, p. 177, Academic Press, Inc., 1969.
6. Edelman, G. M., Cunningham, B. A., Gall, W. E., Gottlieb, P. D., Rutishauser, U. and Waxdal, M. J., Proc. Nat. Acad. Sci., *63:* 78, 1969.
7. Cunningham, B. A., Pflumm, M. N., Rutishauser, U. and Edelman, G. M., Proc. Nat. Acad. Sci., *64:* 997, 1969.
8. Terry, W. D. and Ohms, J., Proc. Nat. Acad. Sci., In press.
9. Wang, A. C., Pink, J. R. L., Fudenberg, H. H. and Ohms, J., Proc. Nat. Acad. Sci., In press.
10. Johansson, S. G. O. and Bennich, H., Immunology, *13:* 381, 1967.
11. Wilkinson, J. M., Biochem. J., *112:* 173, 1969.

THE JOURNAL OF IMMUNOLOGY
Vol. 105, No. 3, September 1970

Printed in U.S.A.

Measurement of IgA Levels in Human Cord Serum by a New Radioimmunoassay[1]

W. FAULKNER AND L. BORELLA

From the Laboratories of Virology and Immunology, St. Jude Children's Research Hospital and The University of Tennessee Medical Units, Memphis, Tennessee 38101

Accurate determination of all classes of serum immunoglobulins during the perinatal period should provide not only basic information on the ontogenetic development of these proteins, but may also have diagnostic significance. For example, there is a relationship between high levels of cord sera IgM and congenital infections and between very low levels and adverse fetal outcome (1). With simple methods such as single radial diffusion, levels of IgG and IgM were readily determined in cord sera (2). In contrast, utilizing the same technique, measurable IgA was found in only 2 of 133 cord sera tested. More sensitive methods would have to be developed to determine whether this low incidence represents a true absence of IgA in cord sera or is due mainly to the relative insensitivity of the assay. This latter possibility is supported by the finding of Brascher and Hartley (3), who reported a 30% incidence of IgA in cord sera assayed by a more sensitive technique, electroimmunodiffusion.

In this report we describe a new radioimmunoassay for the determination of human IgA. It is based on the Single Antibody Millipore Filtration (SAMF) method reported by one of us (4) for measuring isotopically labeled albumin-antialbumin complexes. Concentrations of IgA as low as 100 ng were readily detectable with this assay, and by its use we have found measurable levels of IgA in all cord sera tested, thus demonstrating that the reported absence of IgA in cord sera was due mainly to the limited sensitivity of the methods previously utilized.

MATERIALS AND METHODS

Antigens and antisera. Purified human IgG, IgM and IgA globulins and sheep anti-IgG, IgM and IgA sera were obtained from Melpar, Inc., Falls Church, Va. The monospecificity of the antisera was determined by immunodiffusion. Precipitation lines developed only between each immunoglobulin and its specific antiserum, indicating the lack of cross-reacting antibodies against common light chains. For the immunoassay these reagents were diluted with 1% normal rabbit serum (NRS) in phosphate-buffered saline, pH 7.4 (PBS).

Labeling procedure. Purified human IgA (H IgA) was labeled with ^{125}I by the method of Webster *et al.* (5). After dialysis more than 95% of the radioactivity in this preparation was precipitable by 10% trichloroacetic acid.

Measurement of ^{125}I H IgA-anti-H IgA complexes. The procedure used was essentially the same as that described by Borella (4) for the determination of ^{125}I-labeled albumin-anti-albumin complexes. The principle and the fundamental steps of this immunoassay are shown in Figure 1. 1) A mixture of labeled antigen and antibody is filtered through a Millipore filter; 2) the free nonbound antigen passes through the filter, but the antigen-antibody complexes are retained; and 3) the radioactivity retained in the filter measures concentration of antibody-bound antigen in the reaction mixture. The instrument used for filtration has been described (4). To perform the assay, serial dilutions of anti-H IgA were added to constant amounts of ^{125}I H IgA; the mixtures were then incubated at 37°C from 1 to 48 hr and filtered through Millipore membranes. The filters were washed twice with 2 to 3 ml of PBS, placed in polyethylene tubes and counted in a Packard gamma counter.

Previously we reported that the conditions of this assay may vary for different antigen-antibody systems (4). Therefore, the following variables were investigated: 1) pore size of the filters, 2) the effect of protein concentration in nonspecific retention and 3) incubation time of the antigen-antibody mixture. It was found that for maximal retention of specific ^{125}I H IgA-anti-H IgA complexes with minimal nonspecific back-

[1] This work was supported by United States Public Health Service Clinical Center Grant CA-08480 and Training Grant CA-05176 from the National Cancer Institute and by ALSAC.

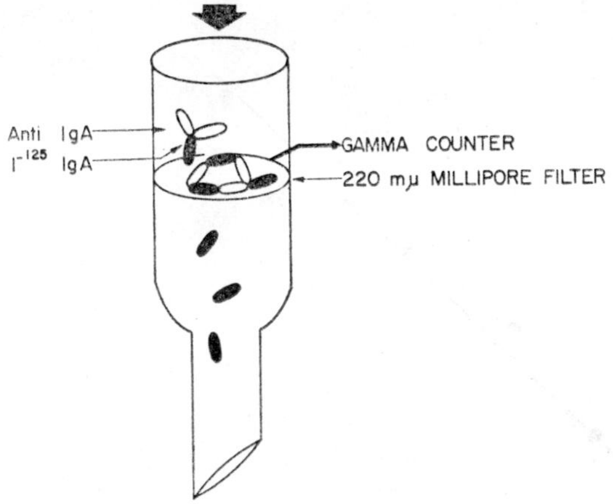

Figure 1. Schematic representation of the Single Antibody Millipore Filtration (SAMF) immunoassay.

ground, the following conditions were necessary: 1) filters with a uniform pore size of 220 mμ; 2) treatment of the filter with 10% NRS in PBS for a few minutes prior to filtration; and 3) 24-hr incubation of the antigen-antibody mixture before filtration. In all of the following assays these conditions were followed.

In the following step, the zone of equivalence (optimum binding of antibody with antigen) was determined as previously described (4). It was found that 1.0 ml of anti-H IgA diluted 1:3000 with 1% NRS in PBS specifically bound 0.2 μg of ^{125}I H IgA. Neither free ^{125}I H IgA nor anti-H IgA was detected in the filtered fluid. Therefore, this ratio of antigen and antibody was considered "equivalence" and was maintained throughout the following determinations. Specifically retained counts/min (SpRd cpm) were calculated by subtracting from the total cpm in the filter, the cpm retained in filters of mixtures where no antibody was added. All samples were run in duplicate.

Standard inhibitory curve. One-tenth-milliliter volume of increasing concentrations of either purified H IgA or human serum containing a known amount of IgA was added to tubes containing 1 ml of a 1:3000 dilution of anti-H IgA. Immediately thereafter 0.2 μg of ^{125}I H IgA in a volume of 1.0 ml was added to each tube, and the samples were gently mixed and incubated at 37°C for 24 hr before filtration. The percentage of inhibition was calculated by using the following equation:

$$\% \text{ Inhibition} = 100 \frac{\text{SpRd E} \times 100}{\text{SpRd}}$$

where "SpRd E" is the cpm retained in the filter of samples containing anti-IgA and ^{125}I IgA plus nonlabeled IgA; and "SpRd C" is cpm retained in the filters of mixtures containing only anti-IgA and ^{125}I IgA. A standard curve was derived from the values of percentage inhibition as a function of the nanograms of nonlabeled H IgA added to each sample.

Measurement of IgA in cord sera. Cord blood was collected from 60 consecutive newborns at the time of delivery. The serum was separated by centrifugation and stored at −20°C. For the immunoassay these sera were diluted 1:2.5, 1:5 and 1:10 with 1% NRS-PBS. One-tenth milliliter of each dilution was added to 1 ml of 1:3000 anti-H IgA. After gentle mixing, 0.2 μg ^{125}I H IgA in 1 ml of diluent was added to each tube. All dilutions were assayed in duplicate. Controls containing only ^{125}I H IgA and anti-H IgA and controls containing also known amounts of H IgA were included in each assay. Percentage inhibition below 20% or above 80% was not considered for evaluation and some sera were diluted further to fit the standard inhibition curve. The concentration of IgA in these sera was then determined by reading off the standard curve of concentration of IgA and multiplying this value by the dilution factor.

RESULTS

Specific retention of ^{125}I H IgA-anti-H IgA complexes on Millipore filters. We first tested whether the specific retention of ^{125}I H IgA was a function of the concentration of antibody added to a constant amount of ^{125}I H IgA. It was found that 90% to 100% of the ^{125}I-H IgA was retained on the filter when anti-H IgA was added in the antibody excess region. Below the equivalence zone throughout the antigen excess zone the amount of specifically retained ^{125}I H IgA decreased in a linear relationship to the decreasing concentration of antibody. The curve obtained was similar to that reported for ^{125}I bovine albumin-anti-albumin system (4). The specificity of this reaction was tested in several ways: 1) as previously described, no cross-reaction was detected by immunodiffusion between anti-H IgA and H IgM or H IgG; 2) the reaction was completely inhibited when 4 μg of nonlabeled H IgA were added to the anti-H IgA-^{125}I H IgA samples, but no inhibition occurred when 100 times higher concentrations of nonlabeled H IgG or H IgM were added; 3) retention of ^{125}I H IgA was less than 10% in samples containing only diluent and

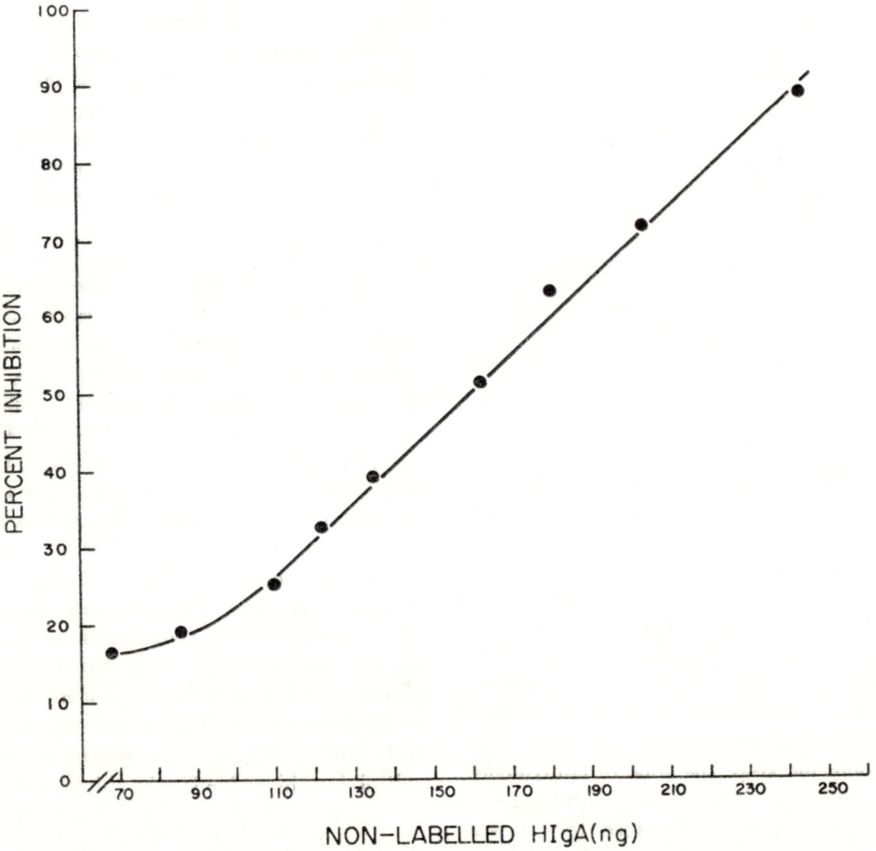

Figure 2. Standard curve obtained by adding increasing concentrations of non-labeled H IgA to constant amounts of ^{125}I H IgA-anti-H IgA. Each point is the mean of five determination.

in those incubated with high concentrations of anti-H IgG or H IgM antisera. These results demonstrate that the SAMF immunoassay measures ^{125}I H IgA specifically bound to anti-H IgA and that there is no cross-reaction with either IgM or IgG.

Standard inhibition curve. The correlation between concentrations of nonlabeled H IgA added to the H IgA antisera and the inhibition of specific retention of ^{125}I H IgA by the filter was investigated. Figure 2 shows that there was a linear relationship between inhibition and concentration of nonlabeled H IgA. The curve obtained was sigmoid, but a straight linear relationship was found between 20% and 80% inhibition. The reproducibility of the standard curve was tested in two ways. 1) We compared the inhibition curves obtained by adding either purified H IgA or normal human serum containing known quantities of IgA. 2) The inhibition assay was repeated on different days and the mean and standard deviation of each point in the curve were then calculated. It was found that the values were similar whether the inhibitor was purified H IgA or human serum IgA. The mean and standard deviation for 25%, 50% and 70% inhibition were 110 $\pm$ 17.8, 162 $\pm$ 8.6, 203 $\pm$ 8.2 ng of IgA, respectively.

Measurement of H IgA in cord sera. With the SAMF immunoassay, IgA was detected in all 60 consecutive cord sera tested. Two of these were from premature newborns; the remainder were from full-term infants with normal deliveries and no immediate complications. The lowest cord serum IgA concentration was 0.15 mg%. IgA was very high in two sera: 38 and 82.2 mg%. The first was from a premature; the second was from a full-term newborn. Excluding these two samples and a third from the other premature newborn, IgA concentration in the cord sera of full-term newborns ranged from 0.15 to 2.15 mg% with a mean value of 0.8 mg%. Five per cent of the sera

TABLE I

Correlation between IgA, IgM and IgG levels in cord sera

	Low IgA Group: Mean (Range)	High IgA Group: Mean (Range)	Difference between Groups[a]
IgA[b]	0.39 mg%	1.57 mg%	
	(0.15–0.57)	(1.02–2.15)	$p < 0.001$
IgM[c]	8.7 mg%	10.1 mg%	
	(5.6–16.8)	(7.2–19.0)	$p > 0.10$
IgG[c]	1040 mg%	1074 mg%	
	(840–1625)	(840–1200)	$p > 0.50$

[a] Calculated by Student's t test for small samples.

[b] Values determined by the SAMF radioimmunoassay.

[c] Values determined by single radial di ffusion

TABLE II

Comparison between IgA levels by the single radial diffusion method and the SAMF radioimmunoassay

	Serum No. 7[a]	Serum No. 48[a]	Purified IgA
	mg %	*mg %*	*mg %*
Single radial diffusion	35	78	200
SAMF radioimmunoassay	38	82	211

[a] Serum no. 7 from a premature and serum no. 48 from a full-term newborn had abnormally high IgA levels and were excluded from the analysis of IgA values for normal full-term infants.

had IgA values in the range of detection by the single radial immunodiffusion method (6), and in one-third the IgA concentration was within range of detection by electroimmunodiffusion (EID) (3, 6). These figures agree with those previously reported (2, 3, 7).

Correlation between IgA, IgM and IgG levels in cord sera. Several tests for the specificity of this assay were described above. However, we did not entirely exclude the possibility that variations in the concentrations of IgG or IgM could affect the immunoassay of IgA in cord sera. To test this, we measured by radial immunodiffusion the concentrations of IgM and IgG in two groups of cord sera, one with high, the other with low IgA levels. Then we determined whether the differences in the levels of IgA, IgG and IgM between these two groups were statistically significant. As shown in Table I, while the p value was <0.001 for IgA, it was >0.10 for IgM and >0.50 for IgG. These data indicate that the levels of IgA determined by the SAMF immunoassay were independent of the concentration of IgG or IgM in the cord sera tested.

Comparison between the single radial immunodiffusion method and the SAMF radioimmunoassay. When the cord sera were assayed by the single radial immunodiffusion method, only two had measurable IgA. These were the sera with abnormally high IgA values, previously excluded from the analysis of IgA levels in normal full-term newborns. We compared IgA levels in these two sera measured by the immunodiffusion method and the SAMF immunoassay (Table II). The values obtained with purified H IgA are also included. There was no difference in the results obtained with the two procedures. Thus, with concentrations of IgA above 2 mg%, the values obtained with both methods are comparable.

DISCUSSION

In this report we described a rapid, simple and sensitive method for measuring human IgA. With this immunoassay we were able to quantitate IgA in all cord sera tested, in contrast to the observations of other investigators. Using the single radial diffusion method, Buckley *et al.* (2) and McCracken *et al.* (7) found measurable IgA in 1.5% and 5.9%, respectively, of normal cord sera. On the other hand, Brasher and Hartley (3), using EID, detected IgA in 29.9% of newborn sera. Since the lower limits of detection were 2 mg% for the radial immunodiffusion method (6), from 0.5 to 0.8 mg% for EID (3, 6) and 0.1 mg% for the H IgA immunoassay, we conclude that this apparent discrepancy in results is due only to difference in methodology.

The main advantage of the SAMF radioimmunoassay is its sensitivity. Amounts of IgA as low as 0.1 μg could be measured. However, the specific activity of the ^{125}I H IgA used in this assay was not very high, and by increasing this specific activity a proportionally higher sensitivity may be achieved. Other advantages of the method are: 1) in contrast to other radioimmunoassays, the labeled antigen or antibody is not bound to insoluble materials (8) and the antigen is not precipitated by a double antibody complex (9), thus eliminating further steps and variables; 2) the procedure is performed in 24 hr; and 3) raw data could easily be incorporated into computerized programs.

A critical question in any assay for immunoglobulins is whether the antiserum is monospecific and thus only one class of immunoglobulin is being detected. This question becomes even more significant when the method is used to assay very low concentrations of IgA in sera containing higher levels of IgG and IgM. The following criteria were used to establish the specificity of this immunoassay. 1) By immunodiffusion, precipitation lines developed only between anti-IgA and IgA and not between anti-IgA and IgM or IgG. 2) While 100% of the total ^{125}I IgA was retained on the filter when anti-IgA was added to ^{125}I IgA, when anti-IgM or anti-IgG was added the retention of ^{125}I IgA was equal or lower than the nonspecific retention controls. 3) No inhibition occurred when purified H IgG or H IgM was added to the mixture of anti-H IgA-^{125}I H IgA in concentrations 100 times higher than that required for H IgA to produce 100% inhibition. 4) In the cord sera tested, there was no correlation between IgA concentrations as determined by the H IgA radioimmunoassay and levels of IgM or IgG as determined by radial immunodiffusion. 5) In two sera with concentrations of IgA in the range of sensitivity of radial immunodiffusion, there was agreement between the IgA values obtained by this method and by the SAMF radioimmunoassay. This was also true for purified H IgA.

These data are conclusive regarding the presence of IgA in all cord sera tested; however, no information was obtained about the maternal or fetal origin of IgA, or about the relationship between the levels of IgA in cord sera and concentrations of secretory IgA or gestational age. Future studies using this radioimmunoassay should provide answers to these questions and to whether subtle changes in IgA in newborns may be correlated with congenital infections and/or adverse fetal outcome. The SAMF IgA radioimmunoassay may also be adapted to measure antibodies in each of the immunoglobulin classes. In a report from this laboratory (10), G. Fitzgerald recently described a new technique using this immunoassay for quantitation of anti-influenza virus IgA antibodies in mouse lung washings. A similar method is now being developed to study kinetics of production of antibodies of each immunoglobulin class in humans.

Acknowledgments. The authors are grateful to Dr. Nancy Holland and the personnel of the Newborn Unit, St. Joseph Hospital, Memphis, Tennessee for supplying the cord sera used in this study.

SUMMARY

A new quantitative inhibition immunoassay for measurement of human IgA has been developed, based on the Single Antibody Millipore Filtration (SAMF) method of Borella. IgA labeled with ^{125}I was mixed with anti-human IgA serum, incubated for 24 hr at 37°C and filtered through a 220-mμ pore size Millipore filter. Labeled antigen-antibody complexes were retained by the filter while unbound ^{125}I IgA was filtered through. The concentration of IgA specifically bound to antibody was calculated by the radioactivity retained in the filter. Addition of nonlabeled IgA to the reaction mixture inhibited the binding of ^{125}I IgA by antibody. Between 20% and 80%, this inhibition was a linear function of the concentration of nonlabeled IgA. This immunoassay was used to measure the concentration of IgA in cord serum and all of 60 specimens had measurable levels of IgA. The mean value was 0.8 mg%, ranging from 0.15 mg% to 2.15 mg%. The SAMF immunoassay is rapid, reproducible and highly sensitive and should provide an ideal method for future studies on the ontogenetic development of IgA and its relationship to perinatal infections.

REFERENCES

1. Hardy, J. B., McCracken, G. H., Mellitis, E. D., Gilkeson, M. R. and Sever, J. L., J. Pediat., *75:* 1211, 1969.
2. Buckley, R. H., Younger, J. B. and Brumley, G. W., J. Pediat., *75:* 1143, 1969.
3. Brasher, G. W. and Hartley, T. F., J. Pediat., *74:* 784, 1969.
4. Borella, L., Anal. Biochem, *24:* 259, 1968.
5. Webster, R. G., J. Gen. Virol., *3:* 315, 1968.
6. Merrill, D., Hartley, T. F. and Claman, H. N., J. Lab. Clin. Med., *69:* 151, 1967.
7. McCracken, G. H., Handy, J. B., Chen, T. C., Hoffman, L. S., Gilkeson, M. R. and Sever, J. L., J. Pediat., *74:* 383, 1969.
8. Mann, D., Granger, H. and Fahey, J. L., J. Immun., *102:* 618, 1969.
9. Yalow, R. S. and Berson, S. A., J. Clin. Invest., *39:* 1157, 1960.
10. Fitzgerald, G. R., Bact. Proc., p. 186, 1970.

THE JOURNAL OF IMMUNOLOGY
Vol. 105, No. 3, September 1970
Printed in U.S.A.

Appendix and γM Antibody Formation. IV. Synergism of Appendix and Bone Marrow Cells in Early Antibody Response to Sheep Erythrocytes[1]

H. OZER[2] AND B. H. WAKSMAN

From the Department of Microbiology, Yale University, New Haven, Connecticut 06510

Earlier studies have shown that the γM antibody response in rabbits injected intravenously (i.v.) with low doses of heat-aggregated bovine γ globulin is abolished by lethal whole body irradiation but preserved in animals whose appendix and bone marrow are shielded (1). Antibody-forming cells, however, were not found in the appendix itself but in that part of the mesenteric lymph node draining the appendix and in the spleen (2). We show here that the early response of rabbits to sheep red blood cells (SRBC) also requires the presence of both appendix and bone marrow cells.

MATERIALS AND METHODS

New Zealand albino rabbits received 2×10^9 SRBC i.v., and their spleen cells were assayed 5 days later for direct plaque-forming cells (PFC) by a modification of the technique of Jerne *et al.* (3). Appendectomy, whole body irradiation (900 rads, central axis dose), and shielding of femoral bone marrow (after prior excision of both popliteal lymph nodes) were carried out by techniques already described (1, 2). Some animals were reinjected immediately after irradiation and 3 to 4 hr before immunization with 1 to 5×10^9 appendiceal cells i.v., while others received a similar number of allogeneic spleen cells. Control animals were reinjected with appendiceal cells disrupted by hypotonic lysis (in 20 ml distilled water) and two cycles of freeze-thawing; microscopic examination showed that no viable cells remained following this treatment.

RESULTS

The direct PFC response in the spleen, 5 days following SRBC injection, was almost completely abolished by the combination of appendectomy and lethal whole body irradiation. Shielding of the bone marrow or reinjection of living autologous appendiceal cells restored the response to a slight extent (Table I). The two in combination gave 5 to 10 times more PFC than either alone or than the sum of the two. This degree of restoration was slightly less, however, than that achieved by injecting a similar number of living spleen cells. The effect observed did not depend on an adjuvant effect of endotoxin present in the appendiceal cell preparation, since killed appendiceal cells failed to restore the PFC response. With the number of cells employed, the maximal response attained was less than the minimum seen in normal animals.

DISCUSSION

The data show that the early splenic antibody response to SRBC in the rabbit requires the presence of two cell types provided, respectively, by the bone marrow and the appendix. We thus confirm in a direct manner the results of extirpation experiments (4, 5), which suggest that the appendix, sacculus rotundus, and Peyer's patches in this species act as the source of a cell essential to γM antibody formation. Our finding also supports the hypothesis (2) that this cell is not immunocompetent in itself, but normally must migrate to peripheral lymphoid organs such as the spleen, where it can interact with antigen in cooperation with a marrow-derived cell. Since spleen cells respond in high degree to the SRBC stimulus, it is clear that antigen can act directly on progeny of the marrow and appendix (or similar organs) which have already entered the peripheral lymphocyte pool. However, in animals whose bone marrow and appendix are shielded during irradiation, antigen given directly into the appendiceal artery immunizes very effectively (1). This implies, in agreement with the present results, that cells of the appendix possess specific

[1] This work was supported by Grants AI-06112 and AI-06455 from the United States Public Health Service.

[2] Predoctoral Fellow, U.S.P.H.S. Medical Scientist Training Program GM 02044-01.

TABLE I
Cell cooperation in early antibody formation

Experimental Group[a]	No. of Rabbits	PFC/10^6 Spleen Cells Average (Range)		PFC × 10^3/Spleen Average (Range)	
Normal	5	201	(183–213)	174	(150–210)
Appendectomy + 900 rads					
(BM)	5	8.6	(7–19)	2.3	(1.8–2.5)
(App)	5	16	(9–28)	4.5	(0.4–10)
(BM + App)	5	91	(47–118)	33	(18–43)
(BM + App[b])	4	5.3	(3–7)	1.2	(0.7–1.7)
(Spleen)	4	132	(84–178)	90	(33–143)

[a] BM: Shielding of femoral marrow; App: 1 to 5 × 10^9 autologous appendiceal cells; Spleen: 1 to 5 × 10^9 allogeneic spleen cells.
[b] Hypotonic lysis and freeze-thawing.

reactivity for antigen before they leave to enter the peripheral pool.

We concluded in our previous study (2) that the failure of antibody-forming cells to appear in the appendix itself must depend on the absence of a required cooperating cell, such as that of the marrow, or more probably the absence of anatomic features which would favor interaction of antigen with the two cooperating cells. Since we show here that appendiceal cells alone give a minimal level of response to SRBC in irradiated recipients, the appendix apparently does not contain both types of cell or contains a markedly suboptimal proportion of marrow-derived cells. Our finding agrees in principle with the observation of Henry *et al.* (6) that anatomic relationships within the rabbit Peyer's patch do not favor the interaction of antigen with competent cells, but that this organ must normally serve as a source of reactive cells which migrate to other sites where they can be stimulated. These authors also conclude, however, that the cell populations of the Peyer's patch and of the spleen contain a similar number and proportion of cells reactive for SRBC. It is not improbable that the appendix and Peyer's patch are really different in this respect (see our discussion in 1, 2). Indeed Richter and his colleagues have shown that reactivity is restored in irradiated (1200 R) rabbits by cells of the sacculus rotundus, which resembles a large Peyer's patch, but not by appendiceal cells (7). Abdou and Richter (8) have provided indirect evidence that one of the cells of the sacculus rotundus is the direct precursor of the antibody-forming cells in such transfer experiments, but this finding does not permit a distinction between the two cell types involved.

These findings and those of other authors who have recently studied γM responses in the rabbit (1, 2, 4–8) provide an interesting contrast to the findings in rats and mice (see reviews in 9). In these species, the response to SRBC is in large part thymus-dependent and there is good evidence to show that thymus-derived and bone marrow-derived lymphocytes must cooperate, the antibody-forming cell originating directly from the marrow-derived partner. The function of the lymphoepithelial organs in the rabbit bowel is apparently not affected by thymectomy and irradiation (4, 5). There is, therefore, a strong presumption that in this species these organs may carry out part of the function usually ascribed to the thymus, namely, that related to γM responses.

REFERENCES

1. Hanaoka, M., Nomoto, K. and Waksman, B. H., J. Immunl., *104:* 616, 1970.
2. Hanaoka, M. and Waksman, B. H., Cell. Immun., Submitted.
3. Jerne, N. K., Nordin, A. A. and Henry C., in *Cell Bound Antibodies*, Edited by B. Amos and H. Koprowski, p. 109, Wistar Institute Press, 1963.
4. Konda, S. and Harris, T. N., J. Immun., *97:* 805, 1966.
5. Good, R. A., Cain, W. A., Perey, D. Y., Dent, P. B., Meuwissen, H. J., Rodey, G. E. and Cooper, M. D., In *Lymphatic Tissue and Germinal Centers in Immune Response*, Edited by L. Fiore-Donati and M. G. Hanna, Jr., p. 335, Plenum, New York, 1969.
6. Henry, C., Faulk, W. P., Kuhn, L., Yoffey, J. M. and Fudenberg, H. H., J. Exp. Med., *131:* 1200, 1970.
7. Richter, M., Rose, B. and Abdou, N. I., Int. Arch. Allerg., *38:* 269, 1970.
8. Abdou, N. I. and Richter, M., J. Immun., *104:* 1087, 1970.
9. *Antigen Sensitive Cells*, Edited by G. Möller, Vol. 1, Williams & Wilkins, Balto., 1969.

THE JOURNAL OF IMMUNOLOGY
Vol. 105, No. 3, September 1970

Relationship of Epstein-Barr Virus-Induced Membrane Antigens in Lymphoid Cells to Viral Envelop Antigens

PAUL GERBER AND GERALD GOLDSTEIN

From the Division of Biologics Standards, National Institutes of Health, Bethesda, Maryland, and the Department of Microbiology, University of Virginia, Charlottesville, Virginia

The etiologic relationship to Burkitt's lymphoma (BL) of a herpesvirus designated the Epstein-Barr virus (EBV) and the apparent role of a host immune defense in this disease have been the objects of intense investigation in recent years. The possible role of a host immune response in the clinical course of BL led Klein *et al.* (1) to initiate a search for tumor-specific surface antigens on BL cells. They employed the membrane immunofluorescence (MIF) method (2) to demonstrate the presence of surface antigens on biopsied and cultured BL cells. Their initial observations indicated that many BL patients, particularly those in long-term remission following chemotherapy, had membrane-reactive antibodies and it was suggested that these reactions were comparable to those observed with tumor-specific antigens in murine lymphomas (1). Subsequent reports by these investigators indicated that, although the MIF reaction depended on the presence of EBV in the reactive cells, the number of MIF-positive cells was about 10 times that of the EBV-positive cells (3). On the basis of serum absorption studies it was concluded that MIF and EBV antibodies were distinct (4). On the other hand, Dunkel and Zeigel (5) recently reported that the number of MIF-positive cells was comparable to the number of EBV-positive cells.

The present report describes preliminary results of our studies on the nature of MIF antigens on EBV-infected lymphoid cells. The following continuous lymphoid cell lines were grown in McCoy's medium with 20% fetal calf serum: a) Raji (6) and HRIK-P3J (7) cells derived from BL, the former free of detectable EBV, the latter containing from 5% to 50% of cells with intracellular immunofluorescent EBV antigen; and b) an EBV-transformed human lymphoid cell line designated the AV cells (8) containing up to 90% of infected cells. Twenty sera were tested from groups of five patients each with BL or infectious mononucleosis and from five normal human donors and chimpanzees. All sera were heated at 56°C for 30 min and were tested for complement-fixing antibodies to EBV with a partially purified viral antigen (9) using the microtiter technique. The MIF test was performed as follows: 1.5×10^6 viable cells were incubated with 0.05 ml serum diluted 1:10 in saline at 37°C for 30 min. Following three saline washes the cells were stained for 30 min at 37°C with fluorescein-isothiocyanate (FITC)-labeled goat anti-human IgG and washed again. For the direct MIF and blocking test (10) we used FITC-labeled globulin of sera from a normal human donor and from a BL patient (latter serum kindly furnished by Dr. Klein). When these stained cells were suspended in 50% glycerol-saline the surface staining ranged from dots and sectors to staining of the entire surface. Because of the spherical shape of the suspended cells only a portion of the cell membrane could be brought into focus. In order to facilitate the localization of MIF antigens we adopted a modification of Cerrotini's technique (11) in which the viable, stained cells were spread on a slide, air-dried, fixed in methanol for 5 min at room temperature and mounted in Elvanol. Such preparations showed distinctly stained membranes (Fig. 1).

The results obtained by this technique are summarized in Table I. The peripheral leukocytes of donor A failed to react with any of the sera. Seventy to eighty per cent of the EBV-transformed (AV) cells of this donor reacted with EBV-positive human and chimpanzee sera, but none reacted with EBV-negative sera. Similarly, the virus-free Raji cells were negative and the EBV-infected HRIK cells reacted only with EBV-positive sera. In an effort to clarify the relationship between MIF and EBV antibodies, a serum from a normal donor (B76) containing both antibodies was absorbed three consecutive times each with 40×10^6 viable Raji, HRIK or AV cells. The serum after such absorptions was then tested for MIF and EBV neutralizing activity.

The neutralization test was carried out by incubating equal volumes of serum and infectious EBV at 37°C for 1 hr. This mixture was inoculated into 1.5×10^6 NC 37 cells (a virus-free human lymphoid cell line obtained from Pfizer, New York, N. Y.). After 1 hr of incubation at 37°C the cells were resuspended in 3 ml of McCoy's medium with 20% fetal calf serum and were tested for intracellular, EBV-specific immunofluorescence after 6 to 7 days of incubation. The amount of virus used resulted in infection of about 15% of the cells in the virus control group. The neutralization endpoint was considered to be the highest serum dilution that caused a 90% or greater reduction in the number of EBV-positive cells. The results of these experiments are summarized in Table II. Absorption with Raji cells had no effect on either the MIF or neutralizing antibody titers. On the other hand, absorptions

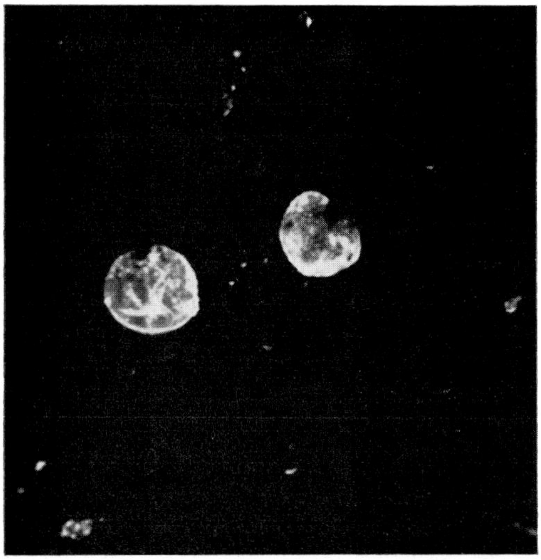

Figure 1. EBV-transformed lymphoid cells showing membrane immunofluorescence (× 400).

TABLE I

Results of indirect MIF tests

Test Cells	Saline Control	Human Sera		Chimpanzee Sera
		EBV⁻	EBV⁺	EBV⁺
Peripheral lymphocytes Donor A	0[a]	0	0	0
AV	0	0	40–80	30–70
Raji	0	0	0	0
HRIK	0	0	15–50	15–30

[a] Percentage positive.

TABLE II

Results of serum absorptions

Serum B76	MIF	Neutr.
Unabsorbed	160[a]	320[a]
Raji-absorbed	160	320
HRIK-absorbed	<10	<10
AV-absorbed	<10	<10

[a] Reciprocal of serum dilution endpoint.

with HRIK and AV cells removed both of these antibodies. These results suggest that antibodies directed against the EBV envelop and EBV-induced membrane antigens are closely related or identical. They were confirmed by the use of an anti-EBV rabbit serum which was prepared by multiple intravenous inoculations of semi-purified EBV consisting mainly of unenveloped particles. This hyperimmune serum, kindly furnished by Dr. B. Hampar, reacted in the immunoferritin test only with the capsid and not with the envelop of EBV (12). This capsid-specific antiserum failed to react in the indirect MIF test, did not block the direct MIF test and had no detectable EBV-neutralizing antibodies.

The results of these studies indicate that some of the surface antigens on EBV-transformed lymphoid cells and on cultured BL cells are closely related or identical. Antibodies reactive with these membrane antigens are specific for the EBV envelop, thus strongly suggesting that these membrane antigens share components with the viral envelop material.

SUMMARY

Immunofluorescent membrane antigens of Epstein-Barr virus-infected lymphoid cells from a normal donor and from a patient with Burkitt's lymphoma appear to be identical and to contain components of the viral envelop.

REFERENCES

1. Klein, G., Clifford, P., Klein E. and Stjernsward, J., Proc. Nat. Acad. Sci., *55:* 1628, 1966.
2. Möller, G., J. Exp. Med., *114:* 415, 1961.
3. Klein, G., Pearson, G., Nadkarni, J. S., Nadkarni, J. J., Klein, E., Henle, G., Henle, W. and Clifford, P., J. Exp. Med., *128:* 1011, 1968.
4. Pearson, G., Klein, G., Henle, G., Henle, W. and Clifford, P., J. Exp. Med., *129:* 707, 1969.

5. Dunkel, V. C. and Zeigel, R. F., J. Nat. Cancer Inst., *44:* 133, 1970.
6. Pulvertaft, R. J. V., Lancet *1:* 238, 1964.
7. Hinuma, Y., Konn, M., Yamaguchi, J., Wudarski, D. J., Blakeslee, J. R., Jr. and Grace, J. T., J. Virol., *1:* 1045, 1967.
8. Gerber, P., Whang-Peng, J. and Monroe, J. H., Proc. Nat. Acad. Sci., *63:* 740, 1969.
9. Gerber, P. and Birch, S. M., Proc. Nat. Acad. Sci., *58:* 478, 1967.
10. Goldstein, G., Klein, G., Pearson, G. and Clifford, P., Cancer Res., *29:* 749, 1969.
11. Cerottini, J. C. and Brunner, K. T., Immunology, *13:* 395, 1967.
12. Hampar, B., Gerber, P., Hsu, K. C., Martos, L. M., Walker, J. L., Siguenza, R. F. and Wells, G. A., J. Nat. Cancer Inst., In press.

THE JOURNAL OF IMMUNOLOGY
Vol. 105, No. 4, October 1970
Printed in U.S.A.

PASSIVE HEMAGGLUTINATION

II. Titration of Antibody against Determinants Unique for Aggregated Denatured Bovine Serum Albumin and Further Studies on Gelatin[1]

GERALD WOLBERG,[2] CHI TAN LIU AND FRANK L. ADLER

From the Department of Immunology, The Public Health Research Institute of the City of New York, Inc., New York, N. Y.

Received for publication June 5, 1970

Aggregates of mildly denatured bovine serum albumin (BSA) present antigenic determinants which are not found in native or denatured but unaggregated BSA. Antibody against these determinants appears early and often transiently in rabbits immunized with denatured or native BSA emulsified in Freund's incomplete adjuvant. Using agglutination of tanned red cells, coated by exposure to native or denatured BSA, to detect and measure antibody activity against BSA, it was shown that adding trace amounts of gelatin to the coating solution significantly reduces the sensitivity of the test. This effect is related to gelatin's highly efficient adsorption to tanned red cells. The degree of reduction in sensitivity varies with the antiserum tested.

Mild denaturation of bovine serum albumin (BSA) leads to the formation of two major products, one consisting of aggregates, the other of non-aggregated protein. Both were shown to sensitize tanned red cells to agglutination by antibody against BSA with vastly greater efficiency than native BSA (1). Data to be presented in this report show that in addition to, and apparently unrelated to, the modifications just described, mild denaturation causes the appearance of new antigenic determinants which are confined to the aggregated protein.

In the earlier paper we have also called attention to an inhibiting effect of gelatin upon the agglutination of BSA-coated tanned cells by specific antisera. The results of additional studies are now reported. They show that addition of minute amounts of gelatin to BSA greatly reduces the ability of the latter to effectively sensitize tanned red cells to agglutination by specific anti-BSA sera.

[1] This work was supported by Grant AI-06899 from the National Institute of Allergy and Infectious Diseases, National Institutes of Health.

[2] Supported by Postdoctoral Fellowship AI-30,261 from the National Institute of Allergy and Infectious Diseases, National Institutes of Health.

MATERIALS AND METHODS

The passive hemagglutination, gel filtration, and immunization procedures were described in a previous paper (1).

The quantitative precipitation tests employed standard procedures (2). The reaction was carried out in a total volume of 2.5 ml.

Electrophoretic fractionation of BSA was carried out in a block (9.5 x 18.5 x 0.8 cm) of 2% Noble agar by applying 150 volts for 18 hr at 4°C. The buffer used in the chambers and in preparing the agar was Veronal buffer, pH 8.6, μ = 0.05. The sample of BSA (20 mg in 1 ml) was mixed with 2.0 ml of 3% agar at 48°C and was applied to a slit in the block. For development by appropriate anti-BSA sera, longitudinal sections of the agar block containing the BSA fractions were embedded in 1% agar made in 0.85% NaCl.

Solutions of native BSA were prepared fresh daily. Denatured BSA was prepared by heating a 0.1% solution in 0.15 M phosphate buffer, pH 6.5, for 10 min at 70°C. Bacto gelatin was obtained from Difco Laboratories, Detroit, Mich. (control 491882).

RESULTS

Unique antigenic determinants in aggregated bovine serum albumin. Certain antisera from rabbits immunized with BSA contain not only antibodies reactive with native BSA but also antibodies specific for heated BSA. Quantitative precipitin data for one such serum, from a rabbit immunized with heated BSA, are shown in Figure 1. Heated BSA precipitated 165 μg Ab N/ml (OD_{280nm} of 0.330) while unheated BSA precipitated only 128 μg Ab N/ml (OD_{280nm} of 0.260). Tests for residual antibody activity in the supernatants showed that those from the equivalence and antigen excess zones of the reaction with heated BSA were free of demonstrable antibody. In contrast, antibody activity against heated BSA (on tanned cells) persisted far into antigen excess in the serum to which native BSA had been added. In fact (not shown in Fig. 1) even the addition of 50 times the equivalent dose of unheated BSA caused only a modest reduction (two tubes) in the agglutination titer of supernatants against tanned cells coated with heated BSA.

In further experiments it was found that the

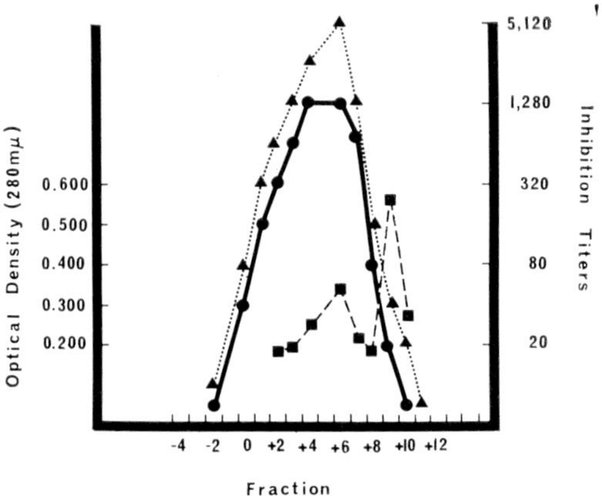

Figure 2. Inhibition of tanned cell agglutination by electrophoretically separated fractions of heated bovine serum albumin. ■, Protein concentration in eluates from agar block; ● and △ inhibition titers in the presence of antiserum 1:400 and 1:1000, respectively. Tanned cells coated with heated BSA were used. This serum (same as in Figure 1) had been absorbed before use with 10 times the equivalence dose of unheated BSA.

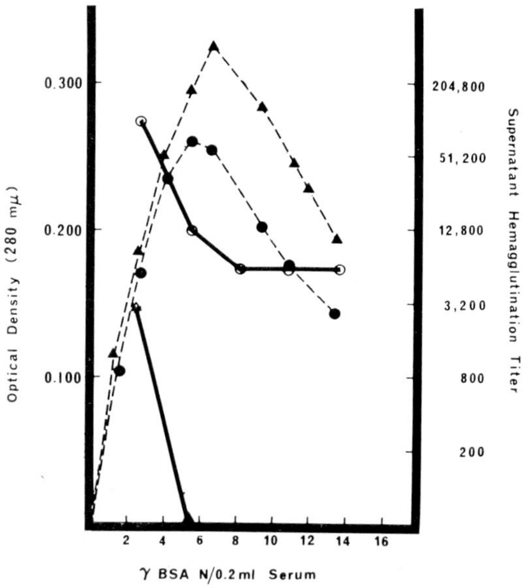

Figure 1. Quantitative precipitin and supernatant tests on an antiserum against heated bovine serum albumin. *Broken lines,* precipitin nitrogen determinations; *solid lines,* agglutination titers of supernatants against tanned cells optimally coated with heated BSA. ● ○ Unheated or ▲△ heated BSA in amounts indicated added to 0.2-ml amounts of serum. Serum was obtained 21 days after a first injection of 2 mg of heated BSA in incomplete Freund's adjuvant and 7 days after a booster injection of 2 mg of heated BSA in saline.

apparently unique antigenic determinants of heated BSA are confined to aggregates of the mildly denatured protein. When the serum employed in the precipitin tests just described was treated with 10 times the equivalent amount of unheated BSA and then was used in agglutination tests against tanned cells coated with heated BSA (Fig. 2), the reaction was readily inhibited by the slowly moving components of electrophoretically separated heated BSA and only poorly or not at all by that component which, though denatured (3), still moved with the mobility of native BSA. If the absorbed serum was used in a dilution of 1:400 the minimal inhibitory amounts of protein were the following (in micrograms of protein): unheated BSA >125; heated BSA 0.12; aggregated heated BSA (fractions +3 to +7, Fig. 2) 0.05 to 0.08; unaggregated heated BSA (fractions 9 and 10, Fig. 2) 7 to 9 μg. Thus there exists an approximately 100-fold difference in specific inhibition activities between denatured aggregated and non-aggregated BSA.

Heated BSA subjected to fractionation on a Sephadex G-200 column yielded confirmatory data. Once again the aggregated material recovered with the early eluates (peaks I and II of Figure 5*A* in (1)) had high specific inhibitory activity ranging from 0.02 to 0.09 μg whereas

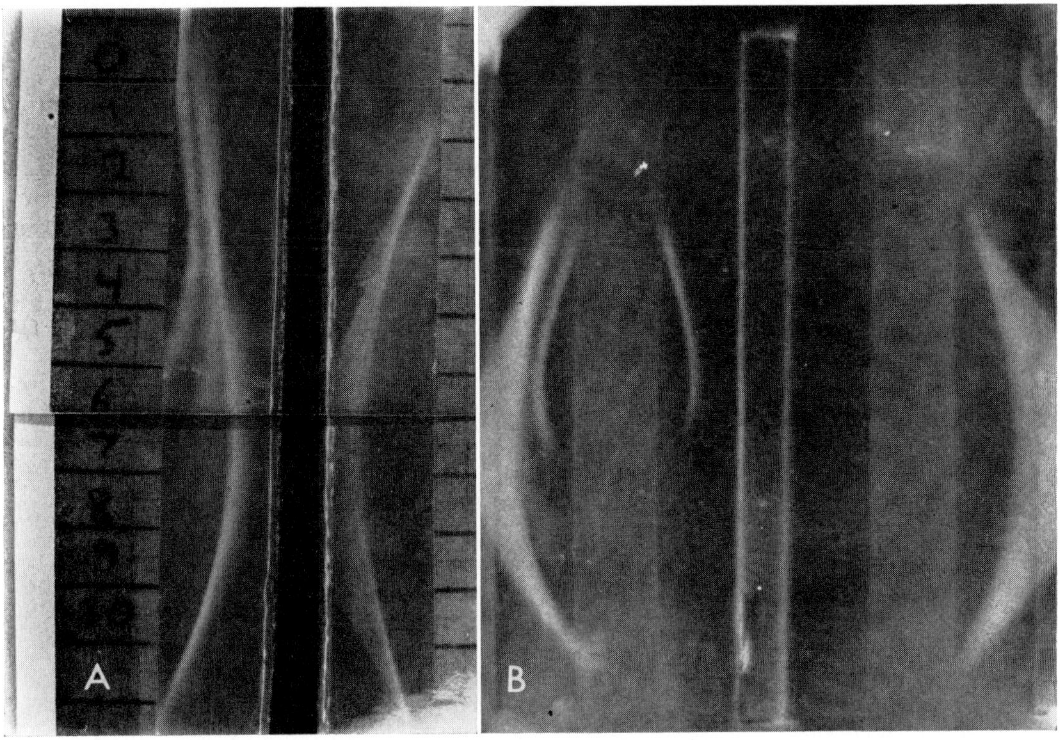

Figures 3A and 3B. Immunoelectrophoretic demonstration of antigenic differences between native BSA and the several fractions of heated BSA. Figure 3*A* shows the precipitin bands developed by an antiserum against heated BSA in electrophoretically separated native BSA (*right*) and in heated BSA (*left*). Figure 3*B* shows the development of precipitin bands in heated (*left*) and unheated (*right*) BSA by antiserum to heated BSA before (*lateral trenches on extreme left and right*) or after (*central trench*) absorption with excess unheated BSA.

the protein in the last peak had a specific activity of 4 to 8 μg.

Finally, it could be shown by immunoelectrophoresis that among the several precipitin bands developed between heated BSA and antiserum against heated BSA (Fig. 3*A*) there is one, in the region occupied by aggregates, which can be demonstrated by development with antiserum that has been exhaustively absorbed with unheated BSA (Fig. 3*B*).

It appears important to stress that antibody with the specificity just described appeared in the sera of all eight rabbits that were immunized with heated BSA and that it usually disappeared on continued immunization. It was not always formed in sufficient amounts to be demonstrable by precipitin procedures, but could readily be demonstrated by the tanned cell test. Finally, this antibody also appeared in the sera of some rabbits that were immunized with native BSA which, in freshly prepared solution, seemed to be completely devoid of the determinants under discussion. It is suggested that the emulsification of native BSA in Freund's adjuvant and possibly the *in vivo* "incubation" of the depot bring about sufficient denaturation and aggregation to account for this finding.

Inhibitory action of gelatin. We have reported previously that the substitution of gelatin for normal rabbit serum in the suspending medium for tanned cells coated with BSA led to reduced sensitivity toward agglutination by anti-BSA, and that the titer of "early" bleedings was more susceptible to this inhibition than that of "late" bleedings. We have also presented preliminary evidence that absorption of gelatin by the cells was responsible (1). Further studies, illustrated in Table I, have shown that under conditions of simultaneous exposure of tanned red cells to optimally sensitizing concentrations of BSA and different amounts of gelatin sensitization can be significantly reduced. Gelatin in amounts

TABLE I

The inhibitory effect of gelatin under conditions of simultaneous coating with BSA and gelatin

Gelatin	Native BSA (250 μg/ml)		Heated BSA[a] (4 μg/ml)	
	A[b]	B[b]	A[b]	B[b]
μg/ml				
500	2–3[c]	3		
250	3	3		
125	4	4–5		
62	3–4	6		
31	3–4	6–7	3	7
15	3–4	7	3	7
7	3–4	8	4	8
3.5	4–5	8	5	8
1.7	6	10	5–6	10
0.8	5–6	10	6	10
0.4	7	10	7–8	10
0.2	8	10	8	10
0.1	8	10–11	9	10
0.05	8	10–11	9	10
None	8	10–11	9	10

[a] A 0.1% solution of BSA in 0.15 M phosphate-buffered saline, pH 6.5, heated at 70°C for 10 min.

[b] A and B, sera from a BSA-immune rabbit obtained 3 and 21 weeks, respectively, after the initial immunizing injection.

[c] Titer: The last tube showing agglutination in a series of twofold dilutions starting with anti-BSA serum 1:100.

of 0.4 to 3.5 μg/ml effectively interfered with the sensitizing efficiency of 250 μg/ml of native BSA or that of 4 μg/ml of heated BSA. While the adverse effect of so little gelatin on the activity of 250 μg BSA is striking it has to be borne in mind that less than 2 μg of BSA is absorbed to the standard dose of tanned cells (1).

Gelatin, in contrast, appears to be adsorbed with a much greater efficiency, as shown by the data in Table II. It will be noted that a solution containing 500 μg of BSA and 1 μg gelatin/ml was freed of the inhibitory effect of gelatin by a single absorption with a standard dose of tanned cells. The eventual decrease in sensitizing activity after four or more successive absorptions has previously been described and discussed in terms of heterogeneity of the BSA with respect to coating efficiency. It would appear, therefore, that a substantial portion of the 1 μg gelatin/ml is adsorbed to the tanned cells and that the inhibition of agglutination should be viewed in terms of the presence of this amount

TABLE II

Sensitivity of successive batches of tanned cells exposed to BSA containing gelatin

Batch[a] TA cells	Titer	
	A[b]	B[b]
1	1600	12800
2	12800	51200
3	6400	51200
4	1600–3200	51200
5	1600–3200	51200
Control[c]	12800	51200

[a] Successive standard doses of tanned cells were incubated with a solution containing 500 μg BSA and 1 μg gelatin/ml.

[b] A and B, sera from a BSA-immune rabbit obtained 3 and 21 weeks, respectively, after the initial immunizing injection.

[c] Control: Cells incubated with a solution containing 500 μg BSA/ml.

of gelatin on cells that would absorb about 2 μg of BSA from a solution containing 250 μg unheated BSA/ml, or 0.2 μg of BSA from a solution containing 4 μg heated BSA/ml. Thus what appears to be interference by a trace of gelatin in the coating solution seems actually to be interference by an amount of gelatin on the cells that is similar to or greater than the amount of BSA that is adsorbed.

DISCUSSION

The appearance of new antigenic determinants in mildly denatured aggregated BSA and their absence in unaggregated denatured protein suggests that conformational changes related to aggregation are implicated in their emergence. Extensive studies on γ globulins (4, 5) have yielded much similar information. Studies on more drastically denatured BSA have either failed to reveal additions or deletions of antigenic determinants (6) or have shown a dominant specificity for the antigen used in immunization accompanied by some cross-reactivity with the native or denatured product (7). The complexity of the immunoelectrophoretic pattern among the aggregation products of mildly denatured BSA (Fig. 3) suggests that both loss and gain of antigenic determinants contribute to the heterogeneity of the products.

As has already been stated, antibodies with specificity for the new antigenic determinants appear early and tend to disappear on continued immunization. This observation reminds one of Habeeb's (8) finding that rabbits immunized with chemically modified BSA make antisera in which, with time, the antibody reactive with native BSA shows a significant relative increase over that specific for the derived products. It also parallels the observation of Hirose and Osler (5) on the transient production of antibody specific for "conformational determinants" in rabbits that were immunized with H polypeptide chains of human γ globulin. Whether this constitutes an instance of tolerance superseding immunity, or indicates some other regulatory factor in action cannot be answered at present.

That the injection of native BSA evokes antibody reactive with the new determinants of aggregates which cannot be removed by absorption of the antiserum with the immunizing antigen (native BSA) provides food for thought in connection with current speculations on the role of "antigen processing" *in vivo*. One can readily imagine situations in which an antigen A could give rise not only to anti-A but also to antibody against an unrelated antigen B (Fig. 3*B*) and that such antibody would escape detection by *in vitro* tests for lack of the proper test antigen. As already suggested, we think that denaturation and aggregation of the BSA during its emulsification in Freund's adjuvant is the most likely source of the immunogenic stimulus under discussion.

The data on the effect of gelatin are reported mainly to caution against indiscriminate use of this substance as a substitute for normal serum in performing tanned cell agglutination tests (2). Beyond this, they have significance in the light of observations by others (9) showing a "masking" of some adsorbed antigens as a result of the adsorption to the tanned cells of other, supposedly stronger antigens. Moreover, the very marked effect of 1 μg gelatin on the coating efficiency of 250 μg BSA suggests that trace contamination of the antigen used for coating, with gelatin or possibly with other antigenic or non-antigenic substances, might have profound effects on the sensitivity of the treated cells to agglutination by antibody specific for the coating antigen. Finally, to compound this difficulty, the results presented show that the adverse effect of a given gelatin preparation and dose is not uniform in that it is most pronounced when such cells are used in the titration of antibody obtained early in immunization. This most probably is but another manifestation of the requirement for higher antigen concentrations in the coating solution which appears to be characteristic of early antibodies of both IgM and IgG classes (1).

Acknowledgments. The authors wish to thank M. Stokes and M. Williams for technical assistance, and K. Kelly for secretarial assistance.

REFERENCES

1. Wolberg, G., Liu, C. T. and Adler, F. L., J. Immun., *103:* 879, 1969.
2. Kabat, E. A., *Kabat and Mayer's Experimental Immunochemistry*, 2nd Ed., Charles C Thomas, Springfield, Ill., 1961.
3. Štokrová, S. and Šponar, J., Coll. Czechoslov. Chem. Commun., *28:* 659, 1963.
4. James, K., Henney, C. S. and Stanworth, D. R., Nature, *202:* 563, 1964.
5. Hirose, S. and Osler, A. G., J. Immun., *98:* 618, 1967.
6. Draper, L. R. and Hirata, A. A., Immunology, *15:* 23, 1968.
7. Maurer, P. H., Sri Ram, J. and Ehrenpreis, S., Arch. Biochem., *67:* 196, 1957.
8. Habeeb, A. F. S. A., J. Immun., *101:* 505, 1968.
9. Linz, R. and Lecocq, E., Ann. Inst. Pasteur, *102:* 92, 1962.

THE JOURNAL OF IMMUNOLOGY
Vol. 105, No. 4, October 1970

Printed in U.S.A.

A PRE-ALBUMIN ACTIVATOR OF PREKALLIKREIN[1]

ALLEN P. KAPLAN[2] AND K. FRANK AUSTEN

From the Department of Medicine, Harvard Medical School at the Robert B. Brigham Hospital, Boston, Massachusetts 02120

Received for publication June 1, 1970

Chromatography of human serum on diethylaminoethyl cellulose reveals five peaks having bradykinin-generating activity. Kallikrein is found in peak 1, Hageman factor is found overlapping peaks 2 and 3, and a prekallikrein activator is found in peaks 2 through 5. Further purification of the prekallikrein activator by gel filtration, carboxymethyl cellulose chromatography, and elution from unstained sliced disc gels after electrophoresis gave purified material which appeared heterogeneous and had an estimated molecular weight of 30,000 to 40,000. Throughout each step of purification, the prekallikrein activator retained the ability to correct specifically the coagulation defect of Hageman factor deficiency. Prolonged dialysis of a partially purified preparation of active Hageman factor resulted in the development of pre-albumin bands in the position previously noted for the highly purified prekallikrein activator. The development of these bands and their associated clot-promoting and prekallikrein-activating abilities at low ionic strength and the prevention of these events at high ionic strength but under otherwise identical conditions are consistent with the direct derivation of the low molecular weight pre-albumin prekallikrein activator from active Hageman factor.

The biologically active nonapeptide, bradykinin, is a product of the action of the plasma enzyme, kallikrein, on its α2-globulin substrate, kininogen (1, 2). Bradykinin has been implicated in the regulation of the microcirculation of exocrine glands (3), and in the circulatory changes occurring after birth, such as constriction of umbilical vessels and the ductus arteriosus and vasodilatation of the pulmonary vasculature (4). Involvement of bradykinin as a mediator of the inflammatory process has been considered in a variety of pathologic states (5). A radioimmunoassay for the determination of circulating bradykinin (6) and a radial immunodiffusion assay for the measurement of plasma kininogen (7) have been developed in this laboratory. Further assessment of this system must include methods for determining the enzymes leading to the conversion of prekallikrein to kallikrein. This report describes a low molecular weight activator of prekallikrein and presents evidence to suggest that it is a derivative of Hageman factor.

[1] This investigation was supported by Grants AI-07722 and FR-05669 from the National Institutes of Health and a grant from The John A. Hartford Foundation, Inc.

[2] Special Fellow (Grant 5 FO3 AI42810) of the National Institute of Allergy and Infectious Diseases.

MATERIALS AND METHODS

Bradykinin triacetate (Sandoz Pharmaceuticals, Basle, Switzerland, or New England Nuclear Corp., Cambridge, Mass.) was used as the standard for native bradykinin. Antisera to γG, γA, γM, β lipoprotein, transferrin, albumin, and whole human serum were purchased from Behringwerke AG. Hexadimethrine (Polybrene) was a gift of Dr. Floyd McIntire, Abbott Laboratories (North Chicago, Ill.). Hageman factor deficient plasma was supplied by Dr. H. Nossel (New York, N. Y.), Dr. O. Ratnoff (Cleveland, Ohio), or Warner-Lambert Co. (Morris Plains, N. J.).

Collection of serum and plasma. Serum was prepared for the isolation of active enzymes by allowing 100 ml of blood to clot in 40-ml glass centrifuge tubes at room temperature. After 90 min, the tubes were rimmed, centrifuged at 900 $\times$ G for 20 min, and the serum was separated and dialyzed overnight at 4°C in 0.01 M PO_4 buffer, pH 7.8.

Plasma was prepared for the isolation of proenzymes. One hundred milliliters of blood were collected in 10-ml volumes in polypropylene tubes, each containing 9 mg of disodium ethylenediaminetetraacetic acid (EDTA) and 3.6 mg of hexadimethrine in 0.1 ml of 0.15 M saline. The tubes were immediately centrifuged at 900 × G for 20 min at 4°C. The plasma was separated using siliconized pipettes and was dialyzed for 6 hr at 4°C against three changes of 2 liters of 0.01 M PO_4 buffer, pH 7.8, containing 40 mg/liter hexadimethrine.

Diethylaminoethyl (DEAE)-cellulose chromatography. Thirty-five milliliters of dialyzed serum or plasma were applied to a 3.5- x 30-cm column of packed DEAE-cellulose equilibrated with 0.01 M PO_4 buffer, pH 7.8. The column was washed with 500 ml of the equilibrating buffer and eluted with a linear salt gradient of 2 liters of equilibrating buffer and 2 liters of 0.01 M PO_4 buffer, pH 7.8, containing 0.3 M NaCl. The column was run at 60 ml/hr and 12-ml fractions were collected. The eluate fractions were assayed for protein content (O.D. 280 nm), conductivity, and various intermediates of the kinin-forming sequence. Peaks having bradykinin-generating capacity were concentrated by ultrafiltration using a UM-10 membrane (Amicon Corp., Lexington, Mass.) to 5 to 10 ml and were then further concentrated by wall vacuum using Collodion bags No. 100 (Schleicher and Schuell, Inc., Keene, N. H.).

Sephadex G-100 filtration. A 5- x 80-cm column of Sephadex G-100 was equilibrated with 0.01 M PO_4 buffer, pH 7.8, 0.15 M NaCl. Samples of 2 to 4 ml were applied to the column and the pattern developed by upward flow at 30 ml/hr; 10-ml fractions were collected.

Carboxymethyl (CM)-cellulose chromatography. A 3.5- x 20-cm column of packed CM-cellulose was equilibrated with 0.01 M PO_4 buffer, pH 6.0. Twenty- to 30-ml samples, dialyzed in 0.01 M PO_4 buffer, pH 6.0, were applied to the column; the column was washed with 350 ml of equilibrating buffer; and a linear salt gradient using 1.5 liters of equilibrating buffer and 1.5 liters of 0.01 M PO_4 buffer, pH 6.0, containing 0.75 M NaCl was applied. The column was run at 60 ml/hr and 12-ml fractions were collected.

Disc gel electrophoresis. Analytic disc gel electrophoresis was performed at a running pH of 9.3 using the equipment and directions supplied by Buchler Instruments, Inc. Samples of 100 λ were routinely applied to the disc gels. After electrophoresis the protein bands were stained with Coomassie blue stain (8) and inspected visually.

In order to correlate the bands seen with their functional activity, a series of disc gels was run simultaneously. After staining one disc gel with Coomassie blue, this gel and the unstained gels were sliced into 1 mm sections using the gel column cutter described by Heideman (9). The unstained gel sections were crushed and the proteins were eluted from each section by suspension in 0.5 ml of 0.15 M NaCl. After standing at room temperature for 2 hr and at 4°C overnight, the polyacrylamide was sedimented by centrifugation and the supernatant separated.

Bradykinin assay. Bradykinin was routinely determined by bioassay utilizing the isolated guinea pig ileum (10) or by radioimmunoassay (6).

Kallikrein assay. Heat-inactivated plasma, prepared by heating fresh plasma at 61°C for 2 hr and dialyzing overnight against 0.15 M NaCl, was used as a substrate for kallikrein (11). A partially purified preparation of kininogen was prepared as described (7).

Kallikrein activity was determined by incubating 0.2 ml of enzyme source with 0.2 ml of heat-inactivated plasma or purified kininogen for 2 min at 37°C and then measuring the bradykinin generated by adding the mixture to the organ bath used for bioassay. Control tubes containing 0.2 ml of enzyme source or 0.2 ml of substrate were incubated and evaluated separately for bradykinin.

Prekallikrein assay. Two-tenths milliliter of prekallikrein source was incubated for 5 min at 37°C with 0.2 ml of material containing prekallikrein-activating components. Two-tenths milliliter of heat-inactivated plasma or purified kininogen was then added, the mixture incubated for 2 min at 37°C, and the bradykinin generated was measured. Control tubes containing 0.2 ml of prekallikrein source or 0.2 ml of prekallikrein-activating components were preincubated, incubated with substrate, and evaluated for bradykinin generated.

Assay of prekallikrein-activating components. Two-tenths milliliter of prekallikrein-activating components was incubated with either 0.2 ml of fresh plasma (12) or with 0.2 ml heat-inactivated plasma for 2 min at 37°C, and the bradykinin generated was measured. Materials capable of generating bradykinin from fresh plasma but not from heat-inactivated plasma lack kallikrein and presumably generate bradykinin by direct activation of prekallikrein or by formation of an activator of prekallikrein.

Hageman factor assay. The shortening of the partial thromboplastin time of Hageman factor deficient plasma was used as an assay for Hageman factor. Twenty-five thousandths milliliter of Hageman factor source was incubated for 1 min at 37°C with 0.025 ml of kaolin-"cephalin" reagent (13) and 0.025 ml of Hageman factor deficient plasma in siliconized glass tubes. Twenty-five thousandths milliliter of 0.05 M $CaCl_2$ was added and the clotting time determined at room temperature. The tubes were tilted each minute and the end point defined as the time interval required for the clot to adhere to the glass tube.

Utilization of the cephalin reagent with and without kaolin revealed whether or not the Hageman factor was already active.

RESULTS

Isolation and purification of a low molecular weight prekallikrein activator

DEAE-cellulose chromatography of serum and plasma. Five areas having bradykinin generating capacity were found when serum was chromatographed on DEAE-cellulose (Fig. 1) and the fractions assayed using fresh plasma. Peak 1 eluted with the starting buffer, released bradykinin from either fresh plasma, heat-inactivated plasma, or purified kininogen, and therefore contained kallikrein activity. Peaks 2 through 5 generated bradykinin from fresh plasma but not from heat-inactivated plasma or purified kininogen and thus contained prekallikrein activating components. Peaks 2 and 3 eluted immediately after application of the gradient, were poorly resolved, and varied in their relative magnitude. Peak 4 was not consistently observed and when present was always small. Peak 5 was invariably present, well resolved, and was found to increase in activity if dialysis of the serum was increased from 24 to 72 hr. A peak of clot-promoting activity demonstrable without kaolin was found overlapping peaks 2 and 3, and activity was detectable through peaks 4 and 5.

Plasma was chromatographed on DEAE-cellulose under the same conditions as for serum. A similar protein elution pattern was obtained

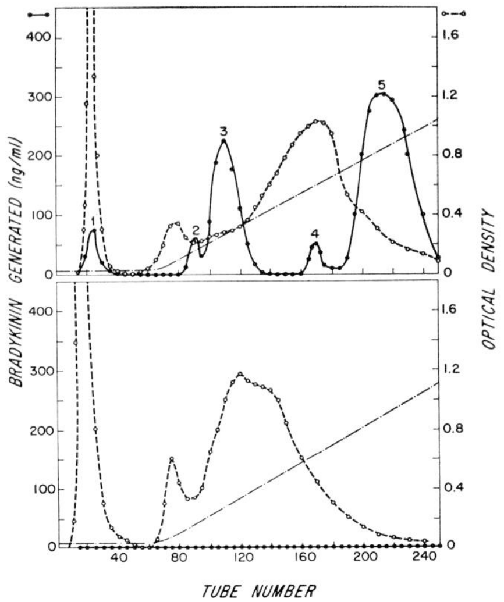

Figure 1. Bradykinin generated when human serum (*upper*) and human plasma (*lower*) are chromatographed on DEAE-cellulose. Conductivity was expressed as the corresponding molarity of NaCl. Peaks 2 and 3 eluted between 0.06 M and 0.10 M NaCl, peak 4 between 0.18 M and 0.20 M NaCl and peak 5 between 0.23 and 0.28 M NaCl.

but bradykinin-generating activity was absent when the fractions were assayed either with fresh plasma or heat-inactivated plasma. Incubation of the first protein peak from the chromatography of plasma with peaks 2, 3, 4, or 5 from serum yielded a mixture capable of generating bradykinin from heat-inactivated plasma or partially purified kininogen. The peaks from serum were known to contain prekallikrein-activating components because they released bradykinin from fresh plasma but not from heat-inactivated plasma which is deficient in prekallikrein. The action of peaks 2 through 5 from serum on the first protein peak of plasma reveals that the plasma peak contains prekallikrein and suggests that peaks 2 through 5 of serum are not necessarily different enzymes in the sequence. A peak of clot-promoting activity demonstrable only when kaolin was included in the incubation mixture was found in the same position as the clot-promoting activity seen in serum and was assumed to contain unactivated Hageman factor.

Peaks 3 or 5 from the DEAE-cellulose chromatography of serum were pooled, concentrated, dialyzed, and rechromatographed on DEAE-cellulose (Fig. 2). When peak 3 was rechromatographed, a peak of clot-promoting activity eluted in the same position as previously; however, the bradykinin-generating activity was now found in the position of peak 5. When peak 5 was rechromatographed, all of the applied activity was recovered in the same position.

Sephadex G-100 filtration. When peaks 3 or 5 from the DEAE-cellulose chromatography of serum were pooled, concentrated, and subjected to gel filtration, bradykinin-generating activity was found in two major peaks and a variable minor peak (Fig. 3). With peak 3, a peak of clot-promoting activity was found at 45% bed volume, with trailing into the areas containing bradykinin-generating activity. When the major peaks of bradykinin-generating activity from gel filtration of peak 3 or peak 5 were pooled, concentrated, and re-run on Sephadex G-100, they eluted in the same position.

Disc gel electrophoresis. The proteins detected by disc gel electrophoresis after subjecting serum to DEAE-cellulose chromatography and gel filtration are shown in Figure 4. When a disc gel of peak 3 material from DEAE-cellulose chromatography was sliced and each of the 32 slices eluted, clot-promoting activity was found throughout the last 10 slices at the cathodal end of the gel and bradykinin-generating activity was found associated with two prealbumin bands about 1 mm apart. When a concentrate of peak 5 from DEAE-cellulose chromatography was

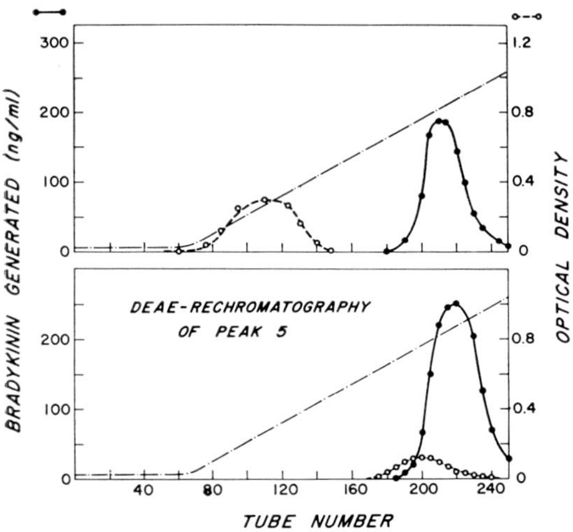

Figure 2. Rechromatography of peak 3 (*upper*) and peak 5 (*lower*) on DEAE-cellulose.

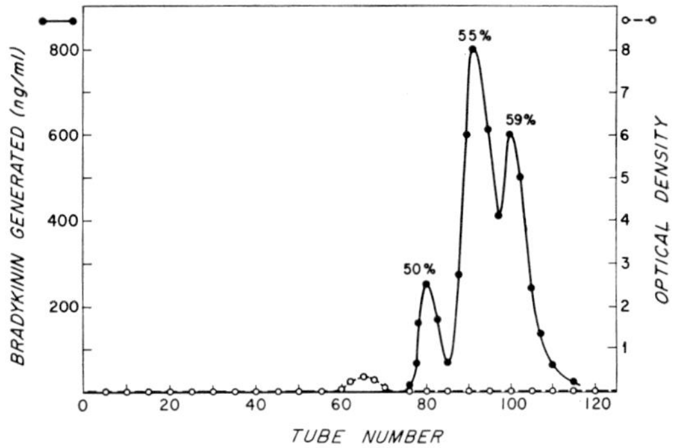

Figure 3. Gel filtration on Sephadex G-100 of peak 3 obtained from DEAE-cellulose chromatography of human serum. Above each peak having bradykinin-generating activity is the % bed volume at which it was found.

similarly electrophoresed, two corresponding prealbumin bands were seen which contained the bradykinin-generating activity. A concentrate of the two major peaks of bradykinin-generating activity obtained from Sephadex G-100 filtration of peak 3 or peak 5 again revealed bradykinin-generating activity associated with the prealbumin bands.

A concentrate of peak 3 or peak 5 from Sephadex G-100 was dialyzed against 0.01 M PO_4 buffer, pH 6.0, and chromatographed on CM-cellulose. In each case, all the bradykinin-generating activity was found in the effluent of starting buffer. The effluent was concentrated and disc gel electrophoresis performed. As shown in Figure 5, only albumin and two bands in the pre-albumin region were seen. When an unstained disc gel was sliced starting from the anodal end and assayed for bradykinin-generating activity using fresh plasma, only slices 7, 8 and 9 were positive (Fig. 6). Only the eluate from these slices shortened the partial thromboplastin time of Hageman factor deficient plasma. No shortening of the partial thromboplastin time of plasma thromboplastin antecedent (PTA), plasma thromboplastin component (PTC) or antihemophiliac globulin (AHG) deficient plasmas was observed.

Serial dilutions of a concentrate of the pre-albumin bands obtained from six disc gels of material purified by DEAE-cellulose chromatography, Sephadex G-100 filtration, and CM-cellulose chromatography were made in order to relate clot-promoting activity to bradykinin-generating activity (Fig. 7). At room tempera-

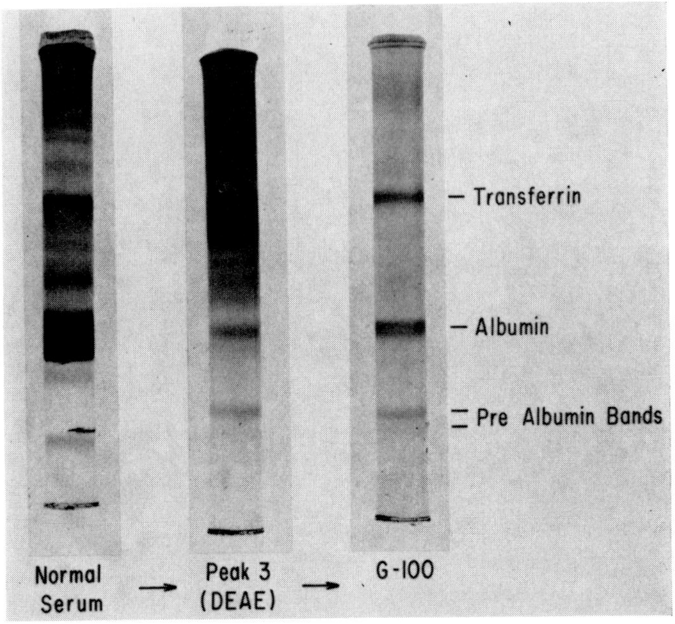

Figure 4. Disc gel electrophoresis of peak 3 obtained from DEAE-cellulose chromatography and of a pool of the two major peaks having bradykinin-generating activity after gel filtration.

ture the concentrated material gave a partial thromboplastin time of 3.5 min (control time: 30 min) and released 10 μg of bradykinin from fresh plasma. When the data are plotted on semi-log paper, a straight line relating clot promotion and bradykinin generation is obtained over a wide range.

Generation and function of a low molecular weight prekallikrein activator

Activation of prekallikrein. A concentrate of the pre-albumin disc gel eluate of material purified by DEAE-cellulose chromatography, Sephadex G-100 filtration, and CM-cellulose chromatography was incubated with prekallikrein isolated by DEAE-cellulose chromatography of plasma. Five minutes later, heat-inactivated plasma was introduced as a source of kininogen. This reaction mixture generated 4.0 μg of bradykinin, whereas no bradykinin was generated in the control mixtures lacking one of the three ingredients. Because of the associated clot-promoting activity, a portion of the disc gel eluate was incubated with hexadimethrine, 100 μg/ml, for 5 min at 37°C before being mixed with the prekallikrein and substrate sources. Hexadimethrine completely inhibited the clot-promoting activity of the disc gel eluate and, as shown in Table I, its bradykinin-generating capacity was reduced by 60%. Incubation of kallikrein with hexadimethrine had no effect upon its ability to generate bradykinin from heat-inactivated plasma.

Generation from Hageman factor. A preparation of unactivated Hageman factor obtained from DEAE-cellulose chromatography of human plasma was chromatographed on CM-cellulose. Hageman factor was eluted with 0.6 M NaCl and was apparently activated during chromatography in that kaolin was no longer necessary to demonstrate its clot-promoting ability. When a portion of the active Hageman factor preparation was dialyzed against 0.01 M phosphate buffer, pH 7.8, and allowed to stand for 1 week, its bradykinin-generating capacity increased sixfold whereas the starting material left in 0.6 M NaCl was unchanged. The Hageman factor preparation had no visible pre-albumin bands when disc gel electrophoresis was performed immediately after its elution and 1 week later (Fig. 8, disc 1), whereas the dialyzed preparation had generated three pre-albumin bands (Fig. 8, disc 2).

The bradykinin generated when comparable unstained discs of the dialyzed and non-dialyzed

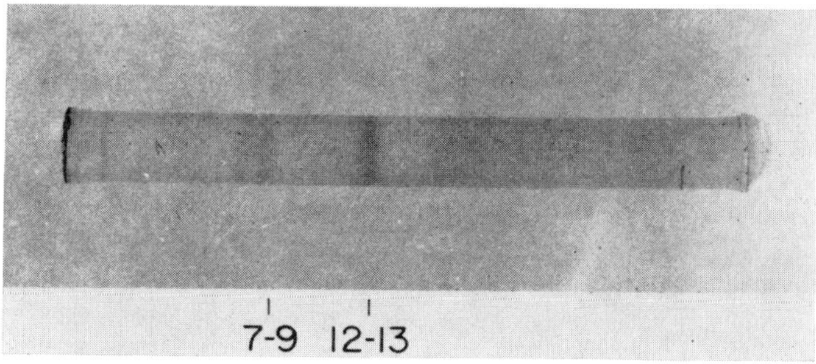

Figure 5. Disc gel electrophoresis of the peak having bradykinin-generating activity after chromatography on CM-cellulose. Beneath the gel is shown the slice numbers corresponding to the positions of the bands seen.

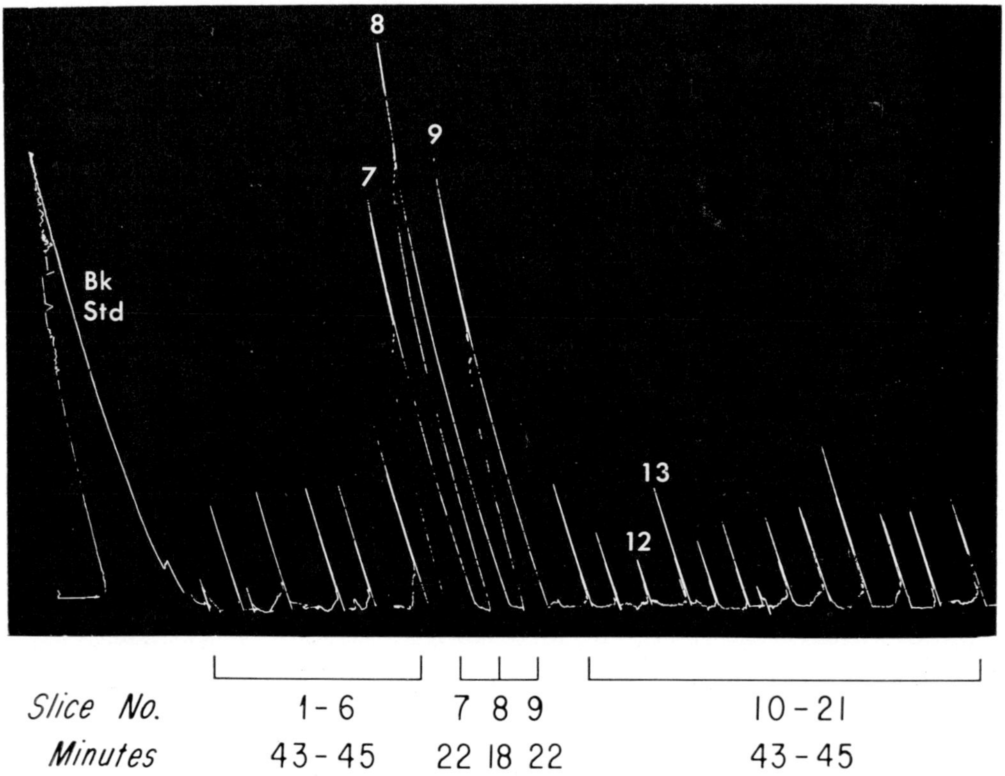

Figure 6. A chymograph recording of the contractions of the guinea pig ileum obtained when the disc gel slice eluates are assayed for bradykinin-generating ability. A 10 ng/ml bradykinin standard is shown on the left. Beneath is shown the partial thromboplastin times in minutes obtained with the disc gel slice eluates.

preparations were sectioned and each section assayed is shown in Table II. Disc gel 1 of the non-dialyzed material revealed clot-promoting and bradykinin-generating activities in slices 27 through 30 at the cathodal end. Disc gel 2 of the dialyzed preparation revealed bradykinin-generating activity in slices 27 through 30; however, 80% of the bradykinin-generating activity was found in slices 7 through 10 associated with the pre-albumin bands. Clot-promoting activity was found in slices 27 through 30; however, a small second area of clot-promoting activity was found extending from sections 7 through 10.

DISCUSSION

An activator of prekallikrein, having a molecular weight of 30,000 to 40,000 as estimated by gel filtration and found in the pre-albumin region after disc gel electrophoresis of a highly purified preparation, was generated when human blood was allowed to clot in glass. The previous observations of Webster (14) that DEAE-cellulose chromatography of human serum yields at least four peaks of activity (Fig. 1) capable of leading to the conversion of prekallikrein to kallikrein were confirmed. The demonstration that each peak directly activated partially purified prekallikrein suggested that each peak of activity did not represent a unique enzyme in the kinin-forming sequence. A further analysis of peak 3 and peak 5 revealed identical position of their bradykinin-generating activity upon gel filtration (Fig. 3) or disc gel electrophoresis (Fig. 4). It was inferred from these data that the complex elution profile of prekallikrein-activating ability reflected different molecular forms of the same protein in clotted blood. Rechromatography of peak 3 revealed a shift of bradykinin-generating activity (Fig. 2) to the region of peak 5 and was consistent with the finding that the activities of these two peaks were located in the same positions upon further purification.

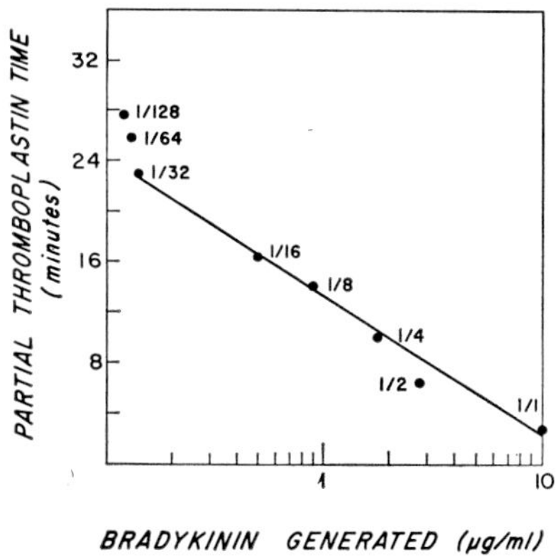

Figure 7. Clot-promoting activity *vs* bradykinin-generating activity of serial dilutions of the disc gel eluate.

In addition to the heterogeneity of the prekallikrein activator exemplified by the shift in activity from peak 3 to peak 5 upon rechromatography, there is a more constant heterogeneity revealed by the two major peaks of bradykinin-generating activity seen on gel filtration of either peak 3 or peak 5 and by the presence of two pre-albumin bands on disc gel electrophoresis of peak 3 or peak 5 before and after gel filtration. The yield of prekallikrein activator commencing

TABLE I

Activation of prekallikrein and inhibition by hexadimethrine[a]

A	+	B	+	C	Bradykinin Generated
					μg
Prekallikrein activator 0.025 ml	+ Saline 0.1 ml	Prekallikrein 0.01 ml		Heat-inactivated plasma 0.2 ml	4.0
Prekallikrein activator 0.025 ml	+ Hexadimethrine 0.1 ml	Prekallikrein 0.01 ml		Heat-inactivated plasma 0.2 ml	1.6
Prekallikrein activator 0.025 ml	+ Saline 0.1 ml	Saline 0.01 ml		Heat-inactivated plasma 0.2 ml	0.0
Prekallikrein activator 0.025 ml	+ Saline 0.1 ml	Prekallikrein 0.01 ml		Saline 0.2 ml	0.0
Saline 0.125 ml		Prekallikrein 0.01 ml		Heat-inactivated plasma 0.2 ml	0.0
Saline 0.025 ml	+ Hexadimethrine 0.1 ml	Kallikrein 0.01 ml		Heat-inactivated plasma 0.2 ml	8.5
Saline 0.125 ml		Kallikrein 0.01 ml		Heat-inactivated plasma 0.2 ml	8.5

[a] The mixtures in column A were incubated for 5 min at 37°C; B was then added, and after further incubation for 5 min at 37°C, C was introduced. After incubation for 2 min at 37°C, the bradykinin generated was measured.

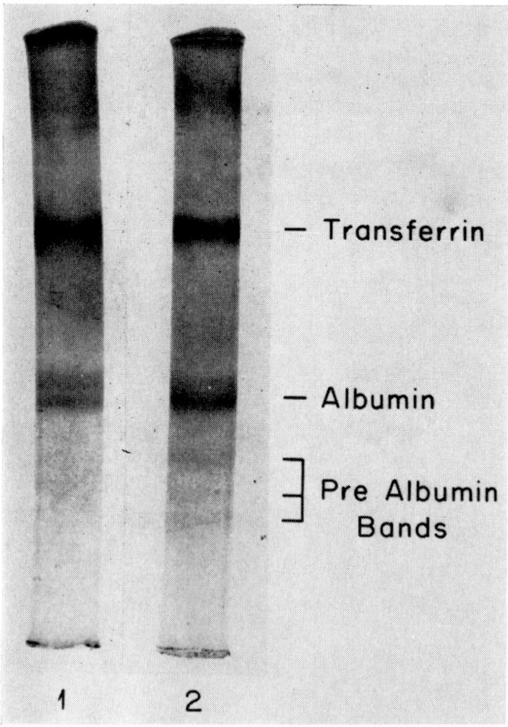

Figure 8. Disc gel electrophoresis of the Hageman factor preparation 1 week after its elution from CM-cellulose (disc 1) and after prolonged dialysis (disc 2).

with peak 5 from DEAE-cellulose chromatography of whole serum, and proceeding through gel filtration, CM-cellulose chromatography, and elution after electrophoresis in disc gels was 50 to 65%. This prekallikrein activator described previously in preliminary form (15) has also been noted by others. Poon and Movat (16) located such material on polyacrylamide electrophoresis as a pre-albumin, estimated its molecular weight to be 35,000, and concluded that it acts before kallikrein because it released bradykinin from fresh plasma but not from heated plasma. An apparently similar protein has been simultaneously described by Wuepper and Cochrane in the rabbit (17) and by Treloar and Movat in the guinea pig (18).

Human kallikrein does not adsorb to DEAE-cellulose, is present in the effluent with IgG in the starting buffer, and represents the major kininogenase present in human plasma (14, 19). Colman *et al.* (19), Eisen and Glenville (20) and Poon and Movat (16) have found one or more

TABLE II

Bradykinin generated from disc gel eluates[a]

Slice No.	Disc 1 Bradykinin		Disc 2 Bradykinin	
	A	B	A	B
	μg		μg	
1–6	0.0	0.0	0.0	0.0
7	0.0	0.0	0.5	2.0
8	0.0	0.0	1.5	5.0
9	0.0	0.0	1.5	5.0
10	0.0	0.0	2.0	6.0
11–26	0.0	0.0	0.0	0.0
27	0.7	2.0	0.7	1.0
28	0.7	2.0	0.7	1.0
29	0.4	1.5	0.3	0.6
30	0.4	1.5	0.2	0.5
31	0.0	0.0	0.0	0.0
32	0.0	0.0	0.0	0.0

[a] A refers to the bradykinin generated by the disc gel eluates incubated with fresh plasma. B refers to the bradykinin generated by the disc gel eluates incubated with prekallikrein and then with heat-inactivated plasma as described in *Materials and Methods*.

kininogenases which elute from DEAE-cellulose after application of a salt gradient. In the present study only a single peak of kallikrein activity was observed. Prekallikrein was also present in the effluent with IgG when plasma was subjected to DEAE-cellulose chromatography under the same conditions used for the preparation of kallikrein. McConnell and Mason have also prepared human prekallikrein from plasma utilizing heparin rather than hexadimethrine to inhibit the generation of bradykinin (21).

Two lines of evidence are consistent with the view that the prekallikrein activator is derived from Hageman factor. Peak 3 from DEAE-cellulose chromatography of human serum contained both active Hageman factor as assessed by shortening of the partial thromoboplastin time of Hageman factor-deficient plasma without the introduction of kaolin and prekallikrein activator as demonstrated by the direct conversion of prekallikrein to kallikrein. The shift of the prekallikrein activator from peak 3 to peak 5 after rechromatography of peak 3 on DEAE-cellulose was not accompanied by a parallel shift of the peak of clot-promoting activity. The bulk of clot-promoting activity remained in the same position representing active Hageman factor. However, definite Hageman factor activity was invariably associated with the prekallikrein activator following gel filtration, CM-cellulose chromatography, and elution of the pre-albumin bands from disc gel electrophoresis (Fig. 7). The bradykinin-generating ability of the prekallikrein activator was, in addition, inhibited by incubation with hexadimethrine, a Hageman factor inhibitor (Table I).

The concept that the prekallikrein activator is a derivative of Hageman factor was pursued by attempting to follow the biologic activities associated with the activation and subsequent elution of partially purified Hageman factor. Unactivated Hageman factor obtained by DEAE-cellulose chromatography of plasma was identified by its capacity to shorten the partial thromboplastin time of Hageman factor-deficient plasma in the presence of kaolin and was further purified by CM-cellulose chromatography. During the latter procedure the material became activated in that kaolin was no longer necessary for correction of Hageman factor deficiency. Analysis of this material by disc gel electrophoresis revealed that clot-promoting activity and bradykinin-generating activity were located at the cathodal region of the gel. Upon prolonged dialysis of active Hageman factor a sixfold increase in prekallikrein-activating ability was seen; concomitantly three bands appeared in the pre-albumin region associated with the capacity to correct Hageman factor-deficient plasma and to activate prekallikrein (Fig. 8). The lower two bands corresponded to the position of the highly purified prekallikrein activator (Fig. 5). The upper band may represent a derivative of higher molecular weight. The development of the pre-albumin bands with associated prekallikrein-activating ability and Hageman factor activity at low temperature under conditions of low ionic strength and the capacity of higher ionic strength to prevent the appearance of these events under otherwise identical conditions is consistent with the direct derivation of the prekallikrein activator from active Hageman factor. The alternative hypothesis that the prekallikrein activator is derived from the action of Hageman factor on a separate pro-enzyme is considered less likely.

Sequential activation of Hageman factor, PF/dil (permeability factor dilute), and kallikrein has been postulated to be the mechanism by which bradykinin is generated in human plasma. The literature presents much conflicting evidence concerning the existence of a precursor molecule (pro-PF/dil) distinct from Hageman factor which, when activated to PF/dil, will in turn convert prekallikrein to kallikrein (22–24). The activity termed PF/dil refers to the increased vascular permeability seen after the intradermal injection of guinea pigs with guinea pig plasma that had been diluted 100-fold with normal saline and allowed to stand in contact with glass for 1 hr. Human plasma was found to have an analogous permeability factor in the β globulin fraction (25). Kagen *et al.* (26, 27) in an attempt to isolate this factor, found two regions from a DEAE chromatogram which produced increased vascular permeability when injected into guinea pig skin; the first was a γ globulin which corresponded to the elution position of plasma kallikrein, and the second was a β globulin thought therefore to represent the activity seen upon dilution of plasma. The β globulin material, which could release bradykinin from fresh plasma but not from heat inactivated plasma (28), was thought to act before kallikrein in the sequence, possibly being the activator of prekallikrein, and was designated PF/dil. Margolis first demonstrated that Hageman factor is required for the formation of bradykinin in human plasma by glass (29, 30) and is required for the generation of PF/dil (31). Peak 3 seen in Figure 1 corresponds to the β globulin designated PF/dil as described by Kagen *et al.* and is the region in which Hageman factor is eluted (32). Nagasawa *et al.* (33) have reported that purified bovine Hageman factor can directly activate bovine prekallikrein; and Davies *et al.* (34) reported similar results using guinea pig Hageman factor and guinea pig prekallikrein. Hageman factor has, in addition, been shown to increase vascular permeability when injected into guinea pig skin (23). A possible explanation of these observations would appear to be that active Hageman factor is, in fact, PF/dil. However, upon activation of Hageman factor, a mixture is evolved which includes Hageman factor, the prekallikrein activator described here, and possibly intermediate sized fragments. The term PF/dil is best restricted to its original definition as a function developing upon dilution and should not be employed to designate any particular protein.

Acknowledgments. We are grateful to Dr. Anthony Britton of the Tufts-New England

Medical Center for determining the partial thromboplastin time on the pre-albumin prekallikrein activator using plasmas deficient in Hageman factor, PTA, PTC, and AHG. We are indebted to Miss Pamela Reducha for her proficient technical assistance.

REFERENCES

1. Pierce, J. V. and Webster, M. E., in *Hypotensive Peptides*, Edited by E. G. Erdos, N. Bach, F. Sicuteri and A. F. Wilde, p. 130, Springer-Verlag, New York, 1966.
2. Pierce, J. V., Fed. Proc., *27:* 52, 1968.
3. Lewis, G. P., in *Cystic Fibrosis*, Edited by R. Porter and M. O'Conner, p. 123, Little, Brown & Company, Boston, 1968.
4. Melmon, K. L., Cline, M. J., Hughes, T. and Nies, A. S., J. Clin. Invest., *47:* 1295, 1968.
5. Kellermeyer, E. W. and Graham, R. C., New England J. Med., *279:* 859, 1968.
6. Talamo, R. C., Haber, E. and Austen, K. F., J. Lab. Clin. Med., *74:* 816, 1969.
7. Spragg, J., Haber, E. and Austen, K. F., J. Immun., *104:* 1348, 1970.
8. Chrambach, A., Reisfeld, R. A., Wyckoff, M. and Zaccare, J., Analyt. Biochem., *20:* 150, 1967.
9. Heideman, M. L., Ann. N. Y. Acad. Sci., *121:* 501, 1964.
10. Rocha e Silva, M., Beraldo, W. T. and Rosenfeld, G., Amer. J. Physiol., *156:* 261, 1949.
11. Jonasson, O. and Becker, E. L., J. Exp. Med., *123:* 509, 1966.
12. Mason, B. and Miles, A. A., Nature, *196:* 587, 1962.
13. Kellermeyer, R. W. and Breckenridge, R. T., J. Lab. Clin. Med., *67:* 455, 1966.
14. Webster, M. E., Fed. Proc., *27:* 84, 1968.
15. Kaplan, A. P., Spragg, J., Gigli, I. and Austen, K. F., Fed. Proc., *29:* 491 (Abstract) 1970.
16. Poon, M. C. and Movat, H. Z., Fed. Proc., *29:* 689 (Abstract) 1970.
17. Wuepper, K. D. and Cochrane, C. G., Fed. Proc., *29:* 811 (Abstract) 1970.
18. Treloar, M. P. and Movat, H. Z., Fed. Proc., *29:* 576 (Abstract) 1970.
19. Colman, R. W., Mattler, L. and Sherry, S., J. Clin. Invest., *48:* 11, 1969.
20. Eisen, V. and Glenville, K. L. A., Brit. J. Exp. Path., *50:* 38, 1969.
21. McConnell, D. J. and Mason, B., Brit. J. Pharmacol., *38:* 490, 1970.
22. Webster, M. E. and Ratnoff, O. D., Nature, *192:* 180, 1961.
23. Ratnoff, O. D. and Miles, A. A., Brit. J. Exp. Path., *45:* 328, 1964.
24. Ratnoff, O. D., Prog. Hematol., *5:* 204, 1966.
25. Miles, A. A., Fed. Proc. (Suppl. 9) *20:* 141 (Abstract) 1961.
26. Kagen, L. J., Leddy, J. P. and Becker, E. L., Nature, *197:* 693, 1963.
27. Kagen, L. J., Leddy, J. P. and Becker, E. L., J. Clin. Invest., *42:* 1353, 1963.
28. Kagen, L. J., Brit. J. Exp. Path., *45:* 604, 1964.
29. Margolis, J., J. Physiol., *144:* 1, 1958.
30. Margolis, J., Nature, *181:* 635, 1958.
31. Margolis, J., Austral. J. Exp. Biol. Med. Sci., *37:* 239, 1959.
32. Shiffman, S., Rapaport, S. I., Ware, A. G. and Mehl, J. W., Proc. Soc. Exp. Biol. Med., *105:* 453, 1960.
33. Nagasawa, S., Takaheshi, H., Koida, M., Suzuki, T. and Schoenmaker, J. G., Biochem. Biophys. Res. Commun., *32:* 644, 1968.
34. Davies, C. E., Holman, G. and Lowe, S. S., Brit. J. Pharmacol. Chemother., *29:* 55, 1967.

THE JOURNAL OF IMMUNOLOGY
Vol. 105, No. 4, October 1970

Printed in U.S.A.

BIOLOGIC PROPERTIES OF A MOUSE IgG2a MYELOMA PROTEIN WITH ANTI-DINITROPHENYL ACTIVITY[1]

NOEL L. WARNER AND ZOLTAN OVARY[2]

From the Laboratory of Immunogenetics, The Walter and Eliza Hall Institute of Medical Research, Melbourne, Australia, and The Department of Pathology, New York University School of Medicine, New York, New York

Received for publication May 26, 1970

An NZB-derived IgG2a myeloma protein with anti-dinitrophenol (DNP) activity was assayed for its ability to elicit complement fixation (CF) and passive cutaneous anaphylaxis (PCA) in guinea pigs after it had been combined with DNP antigens. The myeloma protein agglutinates difluorodinitrobenzene-coupled red cells and this agglutination can be inhibited by monovalent DNP amino acids, albeit with approximately 1000-fold more inhibitor than that needed to inhibit agglutination by a mouse anti-DNP serum. Despite the ability to agglutinate DNP red cells, no passive hemolysis occurred. The myeloma protein gave reverse PCA reactions in guinea pig skin with as little as 0.12 μg and challenge by anti-mouse globulin. However, even with 40 μg per skin site, no PCA reactions could be elicited on challenge with DNP conjugates. It is concluded that the complete biologically active sites on IgG2a molecules for CF and PCA reactions are created by the energy of binding of the molecule to its antigen. The myeloma anti-DNP protein does not create these sites after antigen binding because of its extremely low affinity.

Antigenic studies of mouse myeloma proteins have shown that mouse immunoglobulins can be divided into at least five distinct classes: IgM, IgA, IgG1, IgG2a and IgG2b (1, 2). As with most mammalian species extensively studied, different biologic properties have been found to be associated with the various classes. Studies with fractionated antisera have shown that only IgG1 globulin will sensitize mouse skin *in vivo* (3–5) (passive cutaneous anaphylaxis, PCA), or mast cells *in vitro* (5), whereas only IgG2a globulin will sensitize guinea pig skin (5, 6). Complement fixation is given by IgM, IgG2a and IgG2b globulins (7). Although many of these studies have been performed with antibodies to the dinitrophenol (DNP) hapten no direct studies on the biologic properties of purified IgG2a anti-DNP antibodies have been made, as complete physical separation between IgG2a and IgG2b is at present not possible.

Several recent studies have demonstrated that some mouse and human myeloma proteins or Waldenström macroglobulins have anti-DNP antibody specificity (8–12, Warner, N.L., unpublished). However, in most cases where measurements of affinity of antibody activity to DNP have been made, low values of binding constants have been found. Despite this low binding activity, studies with monovalent haptens have confirmed that the reaction of the myeloma with the hapten is a specific antigen-antibody interaction.

In a recent series of studies on plasma cell tumors in NZB and (NZB × BALB/C) F_1 hybrid mice (Warner, N. L., to be published), an IgG2a myeloma protein was found which showed anti-DNP reactivity. Since IgG2a globulin antibodies will both fix complement and also give PCA and reverse PCA (RPCA) reactions in guinea pigs, we have tested this myeloma protein for these activities.

MATERIALS AND METHODS

Animals. Random bred Hartley strain guinea pigs were used as recipients for PCA tests.

[1] This is publication 1403 from The Walter and Eliza Hall Institute of Medical Research. This work was supported by National Institute of Health Grants AM-11234-03 and AI-03075-10, American Cancer Society Grant E-432 and by The Health Research Council, City of New York, Contract I-140.

[2] Health Research Council Career Scientist of the City of New York.

Antigens. Crystalline bovine serum albumin (BSA, Armour, lot 2266), five times crystallized hen's egg albumin (EA, Pentex, Inc., Ill., lot F-61) and bovine gamma globulin (BGG, Armour, lot X-30604) were dinitrophenylated as previously described (13). Various preparations were used and the numbers given in the text refer to the number of DNP groups/molecule of carrier protein, for example, DNP_9EA. Dinitrophenylated amino acids were obtained commercially (Mann Chemicals, New York, N. Y.) and were dissolved in slightly alkaline saline.

Antisera. A hyperimmune serum against DNP_{160} hemocyanin was prepared as previously described in A/J inbred mice (7). The serum was stored at −20°C until use. The titer of this serum expressed in hemagglutination units (the highest dilution which gave 50% agglutination of DNP-coated sheep erythrocytes) was 4000. A rabbit antiserum was also prepared against normal BALB/c mouse serum by repeated immunization with serum emulsified in complete Freund's adjuvant. The resulting serum had strong antibody activity against all classes of mouse immunoglobulins and was used for developing RPCA reactions. In preliminary studies it has been shown that 0.05 ml/mouse of this antiserum is sufficient to detect threshold amounts of IgG2a globulins by RPCA.

Mouse myeloma protein. Plasma cell tumor HPC-3 was induced in an inbred NZB mouse by three injections of mineral oil. The tumor was maintained in serial transplantation in (NZB × C57BL)F_1 mice and ascites fluid collected from mice carrying the tumor. This tumor actively secretes an IgG2a myeloma protein which was isolated from ascites fluid by starch gel electrophoresis in Veronal buffer, pH 8.2. Disc acrylamide electrophoresis and precipitation studies with iodinated (^{125}I) HPC-3 myeloma protein have confirmed that the preparation of HPC-3 is at least 95% purified myeloma IgG2a. The protein was lyophilized, stored and dissolved for use in phosphate-buffered saline at a concentration of 2.0 mg/ml. The extinction coefficient of this protein (1 mg/ml at 280 Å, 1 cm pathway) was 1.15.

Assays of antibody activity. $DNP_{37}BSA$ was coupled to thrice washed sheep erythrocytes and passive lysis tests were performed as previously described (14) with guinea pig serum as a source of complement. Briefly, 0.5 ml of antiserum or myeloma protein dilutions in Veronal buffer containing optimal amounts of Ca^{++} and Mg^{++}, 0.1 ml of 0.5% $DNP_{37}BSA$-coated sheep erythrocytes and 0.1 ml of guinea pig complement containing 12.5 H_{50} units/ml (a 1:15 dilution of our guinea pig complement stock) were mixed thoroughly. The tubes were then incubated at 37°C for 45 min; the last tube giving 50% lysis was taken as the endpoint.

For hemagglutination studies, DNP determinants were coupled to thrice washed sheep erythrocytes as described by Bullock and Kantor (15) using 1,3-difluoro-4,6-dinitrobenzene (Aldrich Chemical Co., Milwaukee, Wisc.) (DFDNB red cells). Hemagglutination assays were performed in microtiter trays with EDTA-glucose buffer (15). (The volume of each reactant was 0.05 ml.) For the inhibition tests, serial threefold dilutions of the various DNP inhibitors were made in buffer, DFDNB red cells (1%) were then added, followed by either the A/J anti-DNP serum diluted 1:1500 in buffer or HPC-3 myeloma protein, 2 mg/ml diluted 1:80 in buffer. (The volume of each reactant was 0.05 ml.) The trays were left for 6 hr and the 50% inhibition of agglutination determined (to within one-half of a tube dilution).

PCA tests in guinea pigs were made as previously described (16) with a sensitization period of 4 hr. Challenge was made with DNP-protein conjugates. RPCA tests with the HPC-3 protein were made as previously described (16), again with a 4-hr sensitization period using 2.0 ml of rabbit antiserum/guinea pig.

RESULTS

The anti-DNP activity of the HPC-3 myeloma protein has been compared to the anti-DNP hemocyanin serum in three different antibody assays, namely, passive lysis, PCA, and hemagglutination of DNP-coated cells. Since the first two assays depend not only on the anti-DNP site of the molecule but also on the Fc part of the molecule for biologic activity, we have first tested for anti-DNP activity in a hemagglutination system which does not involve biologic activity of immunoglobulins. The results in Table I show that the HPC-3 myeloma protein does agglutinate DFDNB red cells, albeit more weakly than the hyperimmune anti-DNP serum, the titer being 1:160 (0.0125 mg/ml) as compared to 1:4000 for the A/J anti-DNP serum. However, despite this ability to agglutinate DNP-coated cells, no lysis of DNP-coated cells could be detected with HPC-3 in passive lysis assays. Thus, in comparing the two assays, although only 2.5 times more A/J anti-DNP hemocyanin serum was required to give the lysis endpoint titer as compared to the agglutination endpoint, even 32 times more HPC-3 myeloma protein failed to give any detectable lysis.

In order to confirm that the agglutination of the DFDNB red cells is indeed an anti-hapten-specific reaction, inhibition studies with different DNP conjugates were performed. Serial dilutions of DNP conjugates were used with a fixed amount of anti-DNP antiserum or HPC-3 protein. In each case approximately twice the agglutinating dilution of antibody was used (1:80 HPC-3, and 1:1500 anti-DNP). The results in Table II show that monovalent DNP amino acids were capable of inhibiting the HPC-3-mediated agglutination of DFDNB red cells. However, approximately 500 to 1300 fold of the monovalent haptens were required to inhibit HPC-3 as compared to the anti-DNP serum, although, with the DNP protein conjugates, about the same amount of low DNP protein conjugates was needed to inhibit both myeloma and antibody and about 10 times less of the high DNP protein conjugates inhibited the myeloma protein than the antibody.

PCA reactions were induced with the A/J anti-DNP serum with challenge by either DNP_9EA or $DNP_{37}BSA$. An endpoint of approximately 1:1500 was observed with this serum. However, neither conjugate induced PCA reactions when even 40 μg of the HPC-3 protein was injected intradermally. In order to verify that the potential biologically active PCA site was indeed present on this myeloma protein, RPCA tests were performed. The results in Table III show that even 0.12 μg of the HPC-3 protein could be detected by RPCA tests.

Preliminary studies kindly carried out by Dr. T. Werblin (17) on the measurement of antibody affinity have given the following result for the HPC-3 myeloma protein: $K_0 = 7.94 \times 10^4$ and $-\Delta F° = 6.17$ kcal/mol at 4°C.

TABLE I

Hemagglutination and hemolysis of dinitrophenol-coated erythrocytes with anti-DNP antibody or myeloma protein

Source of Anti-DNP	Reciprocal of Anti-DNP Titer: Hemagglutination of DFDNB[a]-coated cells	Reciprocal of Anti-DNP Titer: Hemolysis of DNP_{37} BSA-tanned cells
A/J hyperimmune anti-DNP hemocyanin serum	4000	1600
HPC-3 myeloma protein 2 mg/ml	160	<5

[a] DFDNB, 1,3-difluoro-4,6-dinitrobenzene.

DISCUSSION

Studies with electrophoretically purified fractions of mouse antibodies (3–5) have shown that the IgG2 globulin isolated from sera of mice immunized to dinitrophenol antigens will agglu-

TABLE II

Inhibition of agglutination of dinitrophenylated erythrocytes

Inhibitor	Concentration of Inhibitor to Give 50% Inhibition of Hemagglutination		Relative Efficiency of Inhibitor with Antibody:Myeloma
	A/J anti-DNP hemocyanin serum[a] (1:1500)	HPC-3 myeloma[a] protein 0.025 mg/ml)	
N-DNP-*o*-di-L-tyrosine	2.5×10^{-8} M[b]	1.3×10^{-5} M[b]	520
ε-DNP-L-lysine	5.0×10^{-8} M	6.6×10^{-5} M	1300
N-DNP-β-alanine	10.0×10^{-8} M	12.5×10^{-5} M	1250
N-DNP-ΔL-ornithine	25.0×10^{-8} M	14.0×10^{-5} M	560
N,N-*bis*-DNP-L-lysine	10.0×10^{-8} M	1.0×10^{-5} M	100
$DNP_{3.4}EA$	10.0×10^{-8} M	32.0×10^{-8} M	3.2
$DNP_{3.7}BGG$	11.0×10^{-8} M	16.0×10^{-8} M	1.5
$DNP_{34}BSA$	30.0×10^{-8} M	4.0×10^{-8} M	0.13
$DNP_{28}BGG$	31.0×10^{-8} M	3.0×10^{-8} M	0.10

[a] Source of agglutinator of DFDNB-coated erythrocytes.

[b] Concentration of inhibitor required for 50% inhibition of agglutination, in molarity of dinitrophenol.

TABLE III

PCA and RPCA reactions with HPC-3 myeloma protein

Skin Site Injection[a]	Intravenous Challenge[b]	Skin Reaction[c]	Mean
		mm	
PCA			
A/J anti-DNP-hemocyanin serum			
0.2 μl	0.5 mg DNP_9EA	8, 14, 20, 20	15.5
0.10 μl	0.5 mg DNP_9EA	0, 6, 10, 10	6.5
0.05 μl	0.5 mg DNP_9EA	0, 0, 0, 10	2.5
0.15 μl	1.0 mg $DNP_{37}BSA$	10, 10, 10, 12	10.5
0.07 μl	1.0 mg $DNP_{37}BSA$	0, 8, 8, 10	5.5
HPC-3 myeloma protein			
40 μg	0.5 mg DNP_9EA	0, 0, 0, 0	0
20 μg	1.0 mg $DNP_{37}BSA$	0, 0, 0, 0	0
RPCA			
HPC-3 myeloma protein			
0.25 μg	2 ml RAMG[d]	0, 12, 13, 20	11.2
0.12 μg	2 ml RAMG	0, 6, 8, 15	7.2

[a] Intradermal injection in 0.1 ml.
[b] Challenge made 4 hr after intradermal skin injection.
[d] Individual reaction on 4 guinea pigs/sample.
[d] Polyvalent rabbit anti-BALB/c immunoglobulin.

tinate DFDNB-coupled red cells, will fix complement to give passive lysis of DNP-coated red cells, and by virtue of the IgG2a fraction (6), will fix to guinea pig skin to elicit PCA reactions on challenge with DNP-protein conjugates.

The results presented here show that a mouse myeloma protein of the immunoglobulin class IgG2a, despite having a specific anti-DNP reactivity capable of agglutinating DFDNB red cells, will not fix complement, and, in spite of sensitizing guinea pigs for RPCA, does not provoke PCA reactions with DNP-proteins. This therefore constitutes the first demonstration of failure of an antibody molecule to elicit its potential biologic properties despite specific antigen-antibody union.

In order to justify this statement, two essential points must be made; namely, that the myeloma protein does specifically combine with the DNP ligand, and that it does have the potential biologic properties of its immunoglobulin class.

Detection of DNP binding activity of this myeloma protein has been made using three methods. Studies to be published elsewhere (Warner, N. L., in preparation) have shown that HPC-3 will precipitate ^{125}I-labeled DNP-protein conjugates and that this precipitation can be inhibited by DNP-haptens. The results in Tables I and II show that the HPC-3 myeloma protein will agglutinate red cells coated with the DNP determinant and that this agglutination can also be inhibited by the monovalent DNP-haptens. Affinity measurements have also shown binding of the HPC-3 myeloma protein to DNP-haptens, albeit with a very low binding affinity.

That this myeloma protein is indeed an IgG2a globulin has been verified by specific inhibition of precipitation assays with highly specific rabbit anti-mouse IgG2a sera and with mouse allotype antisera specific for the $Ig\text{-}1^e$ allele (18).

The results in Table III, with the RPCA technique, demonstrate that sensitization of guinea pig skin occurs with as little as 0.12 μg/skin site, which is very similar to previous reports on RPCA with mouse IgG2a myeloma proteins (6). This demonstrates that the HPC-3 myeloma protein does indeed have a potential sensitization or "fixing" site.

Why then does the interaction of HPC-3 with a DNP antigen fail to elicit the PCA reaction or fix complement? One possible explanation lies in the concept that an alteration of the tertiary structure occurs on the gamma globulin molecule when the Fab portion reacts with its appropriate antigenic determinant. This alteration occurs only when the energy of interaction between the Fab portion and the antigenic determinant is sufficient.

It was shown that aggregation of the antibody molecule is necessary for complement fixation (19) and that the site of fixation of complement (C1 and, precisely, the C1q fragment) is on the Fc portion of the antibody molecule (20, 21). It is known that it is the aggregation of antibody molecule by the antigen which brings about the activation of the complement system. It is thought that C1q fixes to the Fc fragment, or that new sites for C1q develop on this portion when the antibody molecule is aggregated by its Fab portions.

It is also postulated that the interaction of the antibody-combining site with the antigenic determinant brings about modifications, which ultimately, through interaction with cell receptors on some cells, possibly mast cells, produce the liberation of vasoactive substances. These modifications (probably on the Fc portion) occur only when the energy of interaction between the antibody-combining site (in the Fab portion) and the antigenic determinant is sufficient. We are therefore suggesting that the energy of interaction between the myeloma anti-DNP site and DNP conjugates is insufficient to bring about this alteration in conformation.

These suggestions are supported by the following observations. a) The affinity measurements of myeloma anti-DNP binding usually show a weak binding constant (8, 9, 12) which may reflect that the myeloma antibody site is primarily specific for other antigens such as nucleic acid (22) or gamma globulin (11; Warner, N. L., unpublished). The binding constant for HPC-3 myeloma protein is very low ($-\Delta F^\circ = 6.2$ kcal/mol), much lower than was found with low affinity guinea pig antibodies (23). The data in Table II on the inhibition of agglutination with monovalent haptens already suggest the low values of the binding constant because about 1000 times more hapten was needed to inhibit HPC-3 than was necessary for an average mouse anti-DNP antibody. However, about the same amount was needed for low DNP-protein conjugates and about 10 times less is sufficient for the highly conjugated DNP-proteins (Table III). This observation is in accord with previous *in vivo* observations (24). b) Previous studies (24) on the effect of affinity on the elicitation of PCA reactions have indeed shown that much weaker reactions occur with low affinity antibodies than with high affinity antibodies. Low affinity antibodies do not produce PCA reactions when the bivalent hapten α-ε-*bis*-DNP-L-lysine is used as challenging antigen and low DNP-protein conjugates are much less effective than highly conjugated DNP-protein conjugates at inducing the PCA reaction.

The studies reported in this paper are also compatible with a recent report (25) on the ability of a mouse macroglobulin myeloma protein with anti-dextran activity to fix complement. In this series it was shown that MOPC 104 E protein reacts with a number of dextrans in a true antibody fashion. CF was studied by microcomplement fixation assays and it was found that the affinity of binding to various dextrans was proportional to the activity of the dextran in microcomplement fixation reactions. Thus, a certain minimal affinity of binding of the dextran to MOPC 104 E was necessary to permit CF to occur.

Further studies of this nature with human and mouse myeloma proteins of appropriate immunoglobulin classes would be of great value in eventually determining the approximate level of energy of binding required to create the completely active biologic site.

Acknowledgments. The excellent technical assistance of Diane Grail, Margaret Odgers and Mr. Gzaba de Szalay is most gratefully acknowledged.

REFERENCES

1. Fahey, J. L., Wunderlich, J. and Mishell, R., J. Exp. Med., *120:* 223, 1964.
2. Fahey, J. L., Wunderlich, J. and Mishell, R., J. Exp. Med., *120:* 243, 1964.
3. Nussenzweig, R. S., Merryman, C. and Benacerraf, B., J. Exp. Med., *120:* 315, 1964.
4. Fahey, J. L. and Barth, W. F., Nature, *206:* 730, 1965.
5. Ovary, Z., Vaz, N. M. and Warner, N. L., Immunology, In press.
6. Ovary, Z., Fahey, J. L. and Barth, W. F., J. Immun., *94:* 410, 1965.
7. Warner, N. L., Vaz, N. M. and Ovary, Z., Immunology, *14:* 725, 1968.
8. Eisen, H. N., Little, J. R., Osterland, C. K. and Simms, E. S., Cold Spring Harbor Symp. Quant. Biol., *32:* 75, 1967.
9. Eisen, H. N., Simms, E. S. and Potter, M., Biochemistry, *7:* 4126, 1968.
10. Schubert, D., Jobe, A. and Cohn, M., Nature, *220:* 882, 1968.

11. Hannestad, K., Clin. Exp. Immun., *4:* 555, 1969.
12. Ashman, R. F. and Metzgar, H., J. Biol. Chem., *224:* 3405, 1969.
13. Ovary, Z. and Benacerraf, B., Proc. Soc. Exp. Biol. Med., *114:* 72, 1963.
14. Bloch, K. J., Kourilsky, F. M., Ovary, Z. and Benacerraf, B., J. Exp. Med., *117:* 965, 1963.
15. Bullock, W. E. and Kantor, F. S., J. Immun., *94:* 317, 1965.
16. Ovary, Z., in *Immunological Methods*, Edited by J. F. Ackroyd, p. 259, Blackwell, Oxford, 1964.
17. Eisen, H. N., in *Methods in Medical Research*, Edited by H. N. Eisen, Vol. 10, p. 106, Year Book Medical Publishers, Inc., Chicago, 1964.
18. Herzenberg, L. A., Warner, N. L. and Herzenberg, L. A., J. Exp. Med., *121:* 415, 1965.
19. Osler, A. G. and Hill, B. M., J. Immun., *75:* 137, 1955.
20. Ovary, Z. and Taranta, A., Science, *140:* 193, 1963.
21. Müller-Eberhard, H. J. and Calcott, M. A., Immunochemistry, *3:* 500, 1966.
22. Schubert, D., Roman, A. and Cohn, M., Nature, *225:* 154, 1970.
23. Mancino, D., Paul, W. E., Benacerraf, B., Siskind, G. and Ovary, Z., J. Immun., *104:* 224, 1970.
24. Hurlimann, J. and Ovary, Z., J. Immun., *95:* 765, 1965.
25. Leon, M. A., Young, N. M. and McIntire, K. R., Biochemistry, *9:* 1023, 1970.

THE JOURNAL OF IMMUNOLOGY

Vol. 105, No. 4, October 1970
Printed in U.S.A.

AN IMMUNOLOGIC MARKER TECHNIQUE FOR THE CENDEHILL VACCINE STRAIN OF RUBELLA VIRUS

J. S. OXFORD AND C. W. POTTER

From the University of Sheffield, Virus Research Laboratory, Lodge Moor Hospital and the Department of Medical Microbiology, Sheffield University, Sheffield, England

Received for publication May 26, 1970

Rabbits were immunized with serial, intramuscular doses of low tissue culture passage "wild" and high passage "attenuated" strains of rubella virus. Rubella hemagglutination-inhibiting antibody was detected in animals immunized with two serial doses of 3 $\log_{10}$ TCD_{50}/ml of low passage strains. However, no antibody was detected in animals immunized with 3 $\log_{10}$ TCD_{50}/ml of the Cendehill vaccine strain of rubella virus. A reisolate virus from a person immunized with Cendehill rubella vaccine also had markedly reduced immunogenic properties in the rabbit. Experiments indicated that the Cendehill vaccine virus had a markedly decreased ability to infect rabbits by the intranasal route. The technique may be a useful marker test for this strain of rubella vaccine. The RA/27/3 and the HPV 77 rubella vaccine strains also had a reduced immunogenicity for rabbits but the results were too variable to be used as a marker test for these two strains.

The serial passage of rubella viruses in tissue cultures has resulted in the development of vaccine strains of virus with decreased virulence for man. The vaccine strains most extensively tested, HPV-77 (1), Cendehill (2) and RA/27/3 (3) produce a sub-clinical infection in the person immunized, while transmissibility to contacts is markedly reduced or absent. The possible teratogenic properties of these attenuated rubella virus strains have been incompletely documented to date (4, 5). Of particular importance, therefore, is the development of precise laboratory markers of the vaccine strains to monitor any spread in the community, and to ensure that any teratogenic effects occurring in vaccinees are not due to the intrusion of natural rubella infection. Several markers have been described for individual strains including increased interferon production (1), distinctive plaques (6) and increased cytopathic effects in infected tissue cultures (1). However, other workers have failed to confirm these findings (7–9).

Other studies have indicated a marked reduction in the ability of certain high passaged, attenuated strains of rubella virus to produce antibody after subcutaneous injection of rabbits (10) and a reduced ability to infect rabbits by the intranasal route (11). The present communication describes the application and limitations of this immunologic marker technique in the identification of four vaccines and four low passage "wild" strains of rubella virus.

MATERIALS AND METHODS

Tissue cultures. RK-13 cells were grown as monolayer cultures in "mixture 199" containing 5% inactivated calf serum. The cells were maintained in "mixture 199" containing 2% inactivated calf serum.

Viruses. The Shepherd/5 and Needham/4 strains of rubella virus were isolated in Sheffield from throat swabs of typical cases of rubella occurring in 1964 and have since received five and four passes in RK-13 cells respectively. The West Point/19 strain had received five passes in grivet monkey kidney (GMK) cells and 14 passes in RK-13 cells.

The Cendehill virus strains were supplied by Dr. C. Huygelen, Virus Laboratories R.I.T., Genval, Belgium, as low passage virulent and high passage attenuated viruses: three passes in GMK cells followed by 21 and 51 passes in primary rabbit kidney cells, respectively. These strains were passed a further three times in RK-13 cells in our laboratory. A reisolate of the Cendehill vaccine strain from the throat of a vaccinee, the Cendehill/Francis strain, was supplied by Dr. J. A. Dudgeon, the Hospital for

Sick Children, Great Ormond Street, London, W.C.1; it had been passed three times in RK-13 cells.

The RA/27/3 vaccine strain was supplied by Dr. S. Plotkin, Wistar Institute, Philadelphia. The strain had been passed 27 times in WI-38 cells. It was subsequently passed twice in human diploid cells and once in RK-13 cells.

The parent M33 virus and the HPV-77 vaccine strain derived from it were supplied by Dr. H. M. Meyer, Division of Biological Standards, National Institutes of Health, Bethesda, Md. The HPV-77 vaccine strain had been passed 77 times in GMK cells and 5 times in RK-13 cells. The parent M33 virus had received five passes in GMK cells and two passes in RK-13 cells. The HPV/duck embryo/Morley strain, supplied by Dr. J. A. Dudgeon, was a reisolate from a vaccinee immunized with the HPV-77/duck embryo tissue vaccine strain (12) and has subsequently been passed three times in RK-13 cells.

The Judith virus strain was supplied by Professor K. McCarthy, University of Liverpool, and has been passaged 54 times in RK-13 cells.

Viruses were titrated for infectivity using RK-13 cells. Cytopathic end-points were read at 12 days.

Immunization schedules. Young (12-week-old) New Zealand White rabbits weighing approximately 2 to 3 kg, were purchased from an accredited dealer. A separate room was used to house rabbits for each strain of rubella virus. All rabbits were tested for the presence of rubella HI antibody at a serum dilution of 1:4 before they were included in any experiment. No rubella HI antibody was detected initially in any of the 78 rabbits used in the experiments.

Unless otherwise stated, rabbits were immunized with 1.0-ml intramuscular doses of rubella virus diluted in maintenance medium to contain 3.0 $\log_{10}$ TCD_{50}/ml of infective virus on four occasions and at four weekly intervals. Blood samples were taken from the ear vein at 1- to 3-week intervals. In certain experiments rabbits were anesthetized with ether and inoculated intranasally with 1.0 ml of rubella virus (13).

Rubella hemagglutination-inhibition (HI) tests. Rubella virus hemagglutinin (HA) was prepared by ether-Tween treatment of the supernatant fluids removed from monolayer cultures of hamster fibroblast cells persistently infected with the HPV-77 vaccine strain of rubella virus (14). Sera were treated overnight at 4°C with a mixture of pigeon red blood cells and kaolin (15) and then heated at 56°C for 30 min. Eight HA units of rubella virus were used in the test, and pigeon cells (0.5%) were added immediately to the virus-serum mixtures. The buffer used for all dilutions in the test was 0.9% NaCl, 0.1% $CaCl_2$ (anhydrous), 0.1% $MgSO_4 \cdot 7H_2O$, 1% dextrose and 0.24% bovine serum albumin. The cells were allowed to settle at room temperature and hemagglutinin patterns were read after 1 hr. In some experiments sera were adsorbed with $MnCl_2$ (16).

RESULTS

Immunization of rabbits with low passage rubella strains. Groups of rabbits were immunized with intramuscular doses of two different low passage strains of rubella virus, Shepherd/5 and Needham/4. Each dose contained 3.0 $\log_{10}$ TCD_{50}/ml of virus, and was given at 0, 4, 8 and 16 weeks from the beginning of the experiments. Figure 1 shows the development of serum HI titers to rubella virus for individual animals over a period of 28 weeks. HI antibody to rubella virus was detected in the majority of animals by 8 weeks. In this experiment four serial injections of virus were required to produce antibody conversion in all rabbits although two of the six rabbits immunized with the Shepherd/5 strain of rubella produced HI antibody at 4 weeks after only one immunization. Considerable variation was apparent in the final HI antibody titers achieved in individual rabbits, and the range of HI antibody titers was 1:16 to 1:256.

Similar results were obtained with other strains of rubella virus with a low tissue culture passage history. Two out of four rabbits immunized with the West Point/19 rubella virus (Table I) strain produced HI antibody 5 weeks after the first immunizing dose, but two serial doses of virus were required to produce HI antibody in all four rabbits. Two rabbits immunized with a single dose of 3.0 $\log_{10}$ TCD_{50}/ml of M33 rubella virus produced HI titers of 1:48 after 4 weeks.

Immunization of rabbits with high passage rubella vaccine strains. Figure 2 shows the serum HI titers in individual rabbits immunized with four serial doses of 3.0 $\log_{10}$ TCD_{50}/ml of the Cendehill/57 rubella vaccine strain or a reisolate of this strain from a vaccinee (Cendehill/Francis). No rubella HI antibody was detected at a serum di-

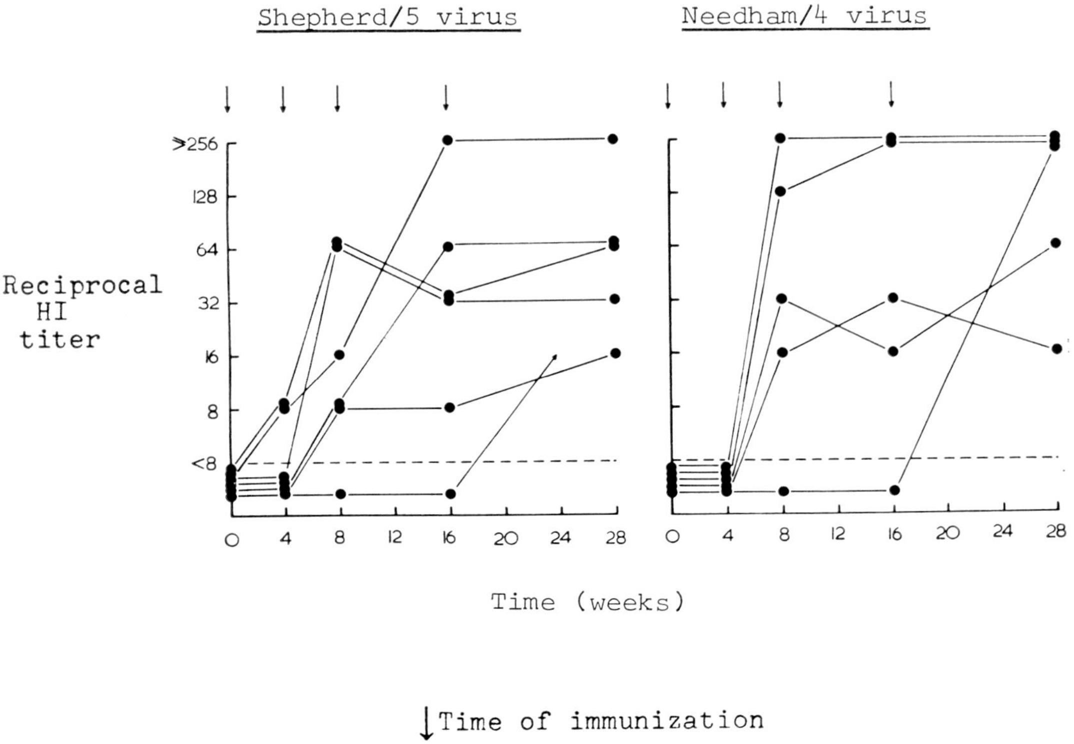

Figure 1. Serum HI antibody in rabbits immunized with low passage rubella strains

TABLE I

Production of HI antibody in rabbits immunized with different strains of rubella virus

Immunizing Virus	Virus Titer log_{10} TCD_{50}/ml and Route of Inoculation	No. of rabbits with HI Antibody (Time in Weeks)		
		5	7	10
West Point/19	3 log i.m.	2/4[a] (8, 32)[b]	2/4 (32, 32)	4/4 (32, 32, 128, 32)
HPV/Duck embryo/Morley	3 log i.m.	1/4 (4)	2/4 (4, 16)	3/4 (16, 16, 4)
RA/27/3	3 log i.m.	0/4	2/4 (4, 4)	2/4 (4, 4)
Judith/54	3 log i.m.	1/4 (4)	Not tested	4/4 (256, 16, 32, 4)
Cendehill/Francis	3 log i.v.	0/4	0/4	0/4
Cendehill/Francis	5 log i.m.	0/4	0/4	0/4
Cendehill/Francis	5 log i.v.	0/4	0/4	1/4 (4)

[a] $\frac{\text{No. of rabbits with HI antibody}}{\text{No. of rabbits inoculated}}$.

[b] Numbers in brackets are reciprocals of HI titers.

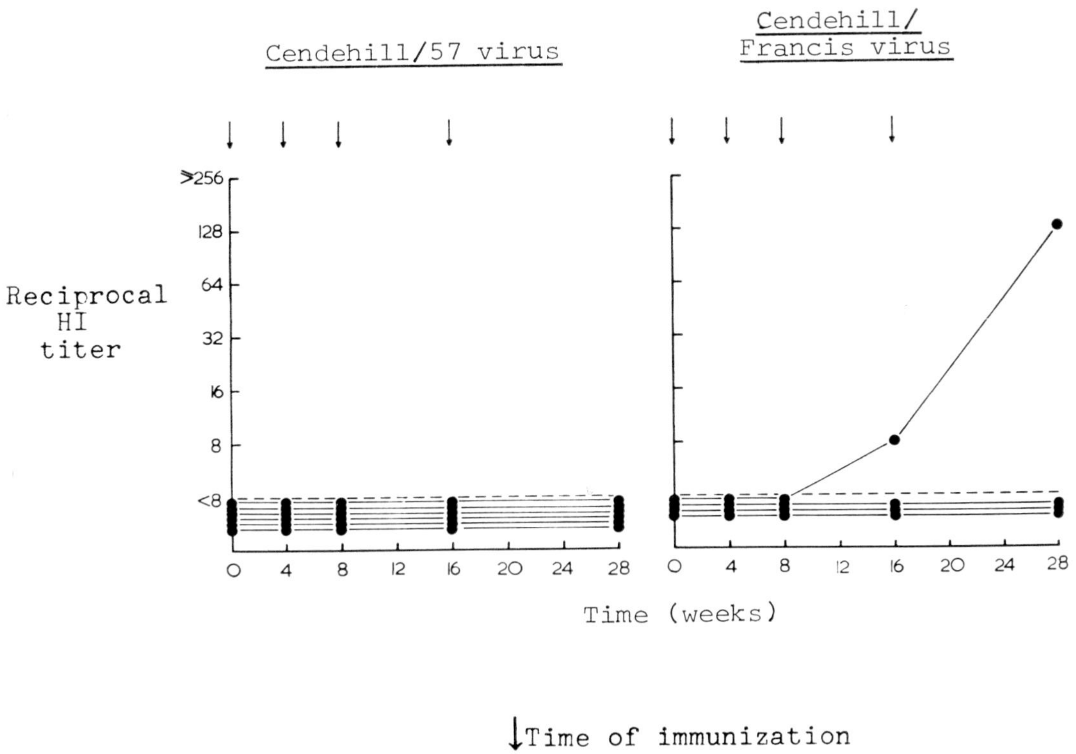

Figure 2. Serum HI titers in rabbits immunized with Cendehill rubella vaccine

lution of 1:4 in any of the animals immunized over a period of 28 weeks with Cendehill/57 virus. To test the possibility that the animals were incapable of responding to rubella virus antigens, a rabbit previously immunized with the Cendehill/57 strain was subsequently immunized at 28 and 32 weeks with two further 1.0-ml injections containing 4.0 $\log_{10}$ TCD_{50}/ml of low passage West Point/19 rubella virus. Four weeks after the first injection (32 weeks) the HI titer was 1:8 and this increased to 1:128 after the second injection. The remaining five rabbits in this group were immunized with a further two injections of Cendehill/57 virus but remained sero-negative until the experiment was terminated at 40 weeks.

Of particular importance is the characterization of strains reisolated from vaccinees in order to detect any reversion of marker properties. Rubella HI antibody was detected in one of a group of four rabbits after immunization with three serial intramuscular injections at 4-week intervals of the Cendehill/Francis reisolate strain (Fig. 2). The remaining three rabbits remained sero-negative until the experiment was terminated after 28 weeks. Two of the sero-negative rabbits were immunized with 4.0 $\log_{10}$ TCD_{50}/ml of low passage West Point/19 rubella virus at 28 weeks, and produced antibody titers of 1:64 and 1:128 after a further 3 weeks.

Rabbits were also immunized by different routes and with high and low infectivity titers of the Cendehill/Francis vaccine strain to determine whether these parameters were important variables in the marker test. Table I shows that one of four rabbits immunized intravenously with two doses of 5.0 $\log_{10}$ TCD_{50}/ml of the Cendehill/Francis strain produced rubella HI antibody. In contrast, no rubella HI antibody was detected in rabbits immunized intramuscularly with either 5.0 or 3.0 $\log_{10}$ TCD_{50}/ml of the same strain.

Table I also shows the serologic response of rabbits immunized with two other vaccine strains of rubella. Thus, rubella HI antibody was detected in a proportion of rabbits 7 weeks after a single immunizing dose of 3.0 $\log_{10}$ TCD_{50}/ml of either the HPV/duck embryo/Morley reisolate vaccine strain or the RA/27/3 vaccine strain. In addition, in a separate experiment rubella HI antibody (titers 1:128, 1:64 and 1:48) was detected in three rabbits immunized intramuscularly with two serial four weekly doses of 3.0 $\log_{10}$ TCD_{50}/ml of the HPV-77 vaccine strain.

Effect of intranasal inoculation of rabbits with rubella virus. Further experiments were carried out to determine whether the absence of rubella HI antibody in the majority of rabbits immunized with the Cendehill rubella vaccine strain or the Cendehill/Francis reisolate strain could be correlated with the inability of these strains to infect rabbits. Groups of rabbits were inoculated intranasally with the Cendehill/57 virus vaccine strain or with the low passage Shepherd/5 virus. Table II shows the serum HI antibody titers in the rabbits 4 weeks after inoculation. All animals inoculated with 2 to 4 $\log_{10}$ TCD_{50}/ml of the low passage strain, and a proportion of the rabbits inoculated intranasally with 1.0 $\log_{10}$ TCD_{50} of the low passage strain, produced HI antibody. In contrast, rabbits inoculated with 4.0 $\log_{10}$ TCD_{50} of the Cendehill/57 vaccine virus showed no evidence of infection. Thus, HI antibody was not detected at a serum dilution of 1:4 in any of these latter animals 8 weeks after inoculation.

The apparent absence of serum HI antibody to rubella virus in rabbits inoculated by the intramuscular or intranasal routes with the Cendehill vaccine virus strain could be attributed possibly to the use of rubella hemagglutinin from a single high passage stain of virus (HPV-77) in the HI test. Chessboard HI titrations were therefore performed using fresh, untreated HA prepared from the Shepherd/5, Cendehill/27, Cendehill/Francis, M33 and HPV/Duck embryo/Morley rubella strains. The sera used in the tests were from rabbits immunized with a single dose of 1.0 ml of these different strains of rubella. No significant antigenic difference was detected between the varying strains of rubella virus using this technique. In particular, HI antibody (titer 1:8) to the low passage Cendehill/27 strain of virus was detected in equivalent amounts in tests using HA produced by both the Cendehill/54 and HPV-77 vaccine strains of rubella virus. In addition, sera from rabbits immunized with four doses of Cendehill/57 rubella vaccine strain were adsorbed with $MnCl_2$ since it has been reported that kaolin treatment may remove specific HI antibody to viruses (16). However, no rubella HI antibody was detected in these sera.

TABLE II

Production of HI antibody in rabbits inoculated intranasally with rubella strains

Titer of Rubella Inoculated ($\log_{10}$ TCD_{50}/ml)	No. of Rabbits with HI Antibody 1 Month after Inoculation with: Cendehill 57 virus	Shepherd/5 virus	Reciprocal of HI Antibody Titers in Rabbits Inoculated with Shepherd/5 Rubella
4	0/3[a]	3/3	48, 48, 48
3	0/3	3/3	96, 48, 48
2	0/3	3/3	96, 128, 128
1	0/3	2/3	6, 12

[a] $\frac{\text{No. of rabbits with HI antibody}}{\text{No. of rabbits inoculated}}$.

DISCUSSION

An important criterion for the selection of markers of virus vaccine strains is reproducibility by different laboratories. Variable results of the application of certain proposed marker techniques for rubella vaccine viruses have been reported in the literature. Thus, although most studies have described the production of plaques in RK-13 cells by high passaged attenuated strains of rubella, others have also described plaque formation by "wild" low passage rubella strains (7, 8). The marker technique of increased interferon production by vaccine strains of rubella has also given variable results (9).

However, a property shared by both the attenuated HPV-77 and the Cendehill virus strains is that of altered pathogenicity for laboratory animals (1, 10). The markedly reduced ability of the Cendehill vaccine strain to produce serum HI antibody in serially immunized rabbits would seem a reproducible characteristic of this strain. However, since low levels of HI antibody were detected in a proportion of rabbits immunized intravenously with relatively large doses of the Cendehill vaccine virus, the experimental conditions must be controlled carefully. Some rabbits did not produce serum HI antibody after a single immunizing dose of 3.0 $\log_{10}$ TCD_{50} of wild strains of rubella, and it appears therefore that two serial intramuscular immunizations of 3.0 $\log_{10}$ TCD_{50} of virus are required to differentiate reliably between attenuated Cendehill virus and wild strains of rubella using this technique. The results of the present study suggest that the reduced capacity to produce antibody may be correlated with a decreased ability of the Cendehill strain to infect the rabbit.

An interesting feature of the Cendehill strain is that a reisolate from a vaccinee possessed the same marker characteristic of reduced immunogenicity for rabbits. It would seem particularly important to test further strains from rubella vaccinees to determine whether this marker is characteristic of all such reisolated Cendehill vaccine strains.

Parkman and Meyer (1) described the decreased pathogenicity of the HPV-77 rubella vaccine strain for monkeys. The present study indicated that this virus strain and a derivative, the HPV/duck embryo strain, also appeared to have a decreased immunogenicity for rabbits; however, the results were too variable for this to be used as a reliable marker of this strain. Of particular interest was the production of rubella HI antibody in all rabbits immunized with the Judith virus which has been passaged 54 times in continuous RK-13 cells. Further studies are required to determine whether the particular passage history of the Cendehill vaccine strain in primary rabbit cells has resulted in the selection of a virus strain with the characteristic property of decreased immunogenicity for rabbits.

No antigenic differences were detected between five different strains of rubella virus using the hemagglutination-inhibition test. For these studies the immune sera were from rabbits immunized with a single dose of virus to reduce the possibility of broadening antibody response after multiple doses of antigen. Similar results have been reported by Banatvala and Best (17). Minor serologic differences have been detected between different rubella virus strains using sensitive plaque reduction techniques, but these are unlikely to prove reliable markers of virulence (6, 11). Preliminary studies have indicated differences in the buoyant density of the hemagglutinin of different strains of rubella (18).

Acknowledgments. We thank Professor Sir Charles Stuart-Harris and Professor M. G. McEntegart for their encouragement and advice during the study. Miss Lynda Bebbington gave excellent technical assistance.

REFERENCES

1. Meyer, H. M., Parkman, P. D., Hobbins, T. E., Larson, E., Davis, W. J., Simsarian, J. P. and Hopps, H. E. Amer. J. Dis. Child., *118:* 155, 1969.
2. Prinzie, A., Huygelen, C., Gold, J., Farquhar, J. and McKee, J., Amer. J. Dis. Child., *118:* 172, 1969.
3. Plotkin, S. A., Farquhar, J. D., Katz, M. and Buser, F., Amer. J. Dis. Child., *118:* 178, 1969.
4. Vaheri, A., Vesikari, T., Okerblom, N., Seppala, M., Veronelli, J., Robbins, F. C. and Parkman, P. D., Amer. J. Dis. Child., *118:* 243, 1969.
5. Furukawa, T., Miyata, T., Kondo, K., Kuno, K., Isomura, S. and Takekoshi, T., Amer. J. Dis. Child., *118:* 262, 1969.
6. Fogel, A. and Plotkin, S. A., J. Virol., *3:* 157, 1969.
7. Morgan, J. R., *Symposia Series Immunobiological Standard,* Vol. II, Karger, Basle/New York, 1969.
8. Lawrence, G. D. and Gould, J., *Symposia Series Immunobiological Standard,* Vol. II, Karger, Basle/New York, 1969.
9. Vasington, P. J. and Douglas, A., *Symposia Series Immunobiological Standard,* Vol. II, Karger, Basel/New York, 1969.
10. Huygelen, C. and Peetermans, J., Arch. Ges. Virusforsch., *21:* 357, 1967.
11. Oxford, J. S., *Symposia Series Immunobiological Standard,* Vol. II, Karger, Basle/New York, 1969.
12. Buynak, E. B., Hilleman, M. R., Weibel, R. E. and Stokes, J., J.A.M.A., *204:* 195, 1968.
13. Oxford, J. S., J. Immun., *98:* 697, 1967.
14. Downie, J. C. and Oxford, J. S., J. Gen. Virol., *5:* 11, 1969.
15. Gitnick, G. L., Vincent, M. M., Auletta, A., Ley, A., Tzan, N. and Sever, J. L., Appl. Microbiol., *15:* 1244, 1967.
16. Mann, J. J., Rossen, R. D., Lehrich, J. R. and Kasee, J. A., J. Immun., *98:* 1136, 1967.
17. Banatvala, J. E. and Best, J. M., Lancet, *1:* 695, 1969.
18. Oxford, J. S. and Potter, C. W., J. Gen. Virol., *5:* 565, 1969.

THE JOURNAL OF IMMUNOLOGY

Vol. 105, No. 4, October 1970
Printed in U.S.A.

IMMUNOLOGIC DETECTION OF SINGLE-STRANDED DNA IN ADENO-ASSOCIATED SATELLITE VIRIONS[1]

E. V. BARNETT, K. TORIKAI AND H. D. MAYOR

From the Department of Medicine, University of California at Los Angeles, School of Medicine, and Department of Virology and Epidemiology, Baylor College of Medicine, Houston, Texas

Received for publication May 18, 1970

Double diffusion experiments with antibodies to single-stranded (s-s) DNA confirmed physicochemical data that adeno-associated satellite virions contain s-s DNA but the DNA extracted from such virions is double-stranded. Positive immunologic reactions of intact virions with sera from man and mouse with "autoimmune" disease and specifically immunized rabbits are consistent with the hypothetical role if viruses as immunogens or as the antigenic participants of immune-complex vasculitis.

Adeno-associated satellite viruses which replicate only in the presence of competent adeno virions have recently been classified as picodnaviruses (1) or parvoviruses (2). Similar small DNA viruses, some of which were originally thought to contain double-stranded (d-s) DNA (3) have now been shown to contain single-stranded (s-s) DNA (4). The DNA extracted from these virions is also s-s DNA (5). Like other parvoviruses, satellite viruses contain s-s DNA, but each virion appears to contain either a "plus" or a "minus" strand. Upon extraction, complementary plus and minus strands from individual particles can anneal to form double-stranded DNA molecules (6–8).

Immunodiffusion experiments with antibodies to s-s DNA obtained from immunized rabbits, humans with systemic lupus erythematosus (SLE) and New Zealand Black (NZB/b1) mice against satellite virions, s-s, and d-s DNA, and control antigens are reported here. Since the satellite virions were precipitated by antibody to s-s DNA, while the DNA isolated from these virions formed no prceipitates with antibodies to s-s DNA, the immunologic data support the physical evidence of s-s regions existing in the virions which are "renatured" to form d-s molecules on extraction (7, 8).

[1] Aided by Research Grants HE 05435 from the National Heart Institute, CA 04600 from the National Cancer Institute, National Institutes of Health, United States Public Health Service, and United States Public Health Service Research Grant AM 11170.

MATERIALS AND METHODS

Type 4 satellite virions purified by cesium chloride buoyant density ultracentrifugation (1.43 g/cm³) containing approximately 25 μg/ml of DNA were prepared (9). The 260/280 nm ratio of these purified preparations was 1.42. Control material of buoyant density 1.34 g/cm³ containing d-s adeno virions and light satellite virions (Torikai and Mayor, manuscript in preparation) with a total DNA content of 2 μg/ml were also prepared. A preparation of Kilham rat virus X-14 containing less than 0.2 μg of s-s DNA/ml and less than 0.6 μg of coat protein/ml, empty satellite particles (buoyant density 1.30 gm/cm³) containing no detectable nucleic acid by optical density profile but shown to contain 6 μg coat protein, reovirus type 3 containing 0.2 μg d-s RNA/ml and 3 μg coat protein/ml, rhinovirus type 14 containing 0.3 μg s-s RNA/ml plus 1.0 μg coat protein/ml, tissue culture fluid from green monkey kidney cell cultures containing 1% bovine serum albumin, d-s simian adenovirus, SV15 free from satellite and containing 0.3 μg d-s DNA/ml and 3.0 μg coat protein/ml were also prepared and used in the immunodiffusion experiments. S-s and native d-s calf thymus DNA (10) shown to be protein-free were used in concentrations of from 1 to 1000 μg/ml. Fetal calf serum as control antigen was also used in the immunodiffusion experiments. Isolated "renatured" DNA from satellite virus at concentrations of 1 and 10 μg/ml were also used in the immunodiffusion experiments.

Serum from rabbits immunized with s-s calf thymus DNA-rabbit serum albumin complexes (10), from patients with SLE, and from New Zealand Black mice served as the anti-s-s DNA sera in the immunodiffusion experiments. Antisera against density gradient-purified satellite virus were prepared in guinea pigs as reported previously (11, 12).

The immunodiffusion technique employed dilute agarose as previously described (10).

RESULTS

The intact virions formed precipitates with rabbit or human sera containing antibodies to s-s DNA (Table I, Fig. 1). The fraction from cesium chloride ultracentrifugation containing d-s adenovirus with a minor contaminant of s-s DNA satellite virions formed an equivocal line of precipitation at 72 hr only with the human antiserum. The X-14 concentrated Kilham rat virus (s-s DNA) formed a definite precipitate at 24 hr with the rabbit antibody, but not with serum from the SLE patient or the NZB mouse. Satellite and adenovirus capsids of buoyant density of 1.30 g/cm^3 (no detectable DNA) formed strong precipitin lines with all three sera within 24 hr (Fig. 2). This suggests that these capsids probably still contain a small polynucleotide component. No precipitates formed between the sera and reovirus type 3, rhinovirus, tissue culture fluid, fetal calf serum or the dialysate of satellite-free adenovirus SV15. DNA extracted from satellite virions (concentration 1 μg/ml or 10 μg/ml DNA but no detectable protein by the Lowry technique) formed no precipitins with the sera. When serum from rabbit 61-30, which had been immunized for over 2 years with s-s calf thymus DNA-rabbit serum albumin complexes, was diffused against satellite capsids, three precipitin lines formed, only one of which gave identity with s-s DNA (Fig. 3). At one side of the Ouchterlony plate shown in Figure 3 the

TABLE I

Precipitin tests with antigens and anti-DNA antibodies

Antigens	Antisera: Rabbit N 61-25-MRSA[a]	SLE-CAL[b]	NZB mouse 20A[c]
Type 4 satellite virions (1.43) (SS-DNA)	+	+	NT[d]
Adenovirus (1.34) (DS-DNA)	−	±	NT
K-14 Kilham rat virus (SS-DNA)	+	−	−
Satellite and adeno capsids (1.30)	+	+	+
Reovirus type 3 (DS-RNA)	−	−	−
Rhinovirus (SS-RNA)	−	−	−
Tissue culture fluid	−	−	−
Fetal calf serum	−	−	−
SV15 (0) (DS-DNA)	−	−	−
Satellite DNA 1 μg/ml	−	−	−
Satellite DNA 10 μg/ml	−	−	−

[a] Rabbit 61-25 immunized with s-s calf thymus DNA-methylated bovine serum albumin complexes. Serum forms precipitins with 1.5 to 1000 μg/ml s-s calf thymus DNA and with 100 to 1000 μg native calf thymus DNA.

[b] Serum from patient Cal with SLE forms precipitins with 15.0 to 1000 μg/ml s-s calf thymus but not with 1000 μg/ml native calf thymus DNA.

[c] Serum from 1-year-old NZB mouse 20A with anemia and nephritis forms precipitins with 10.0 to 1000 μg/ml s-s calf thymus DNA.

[d] Not tested.

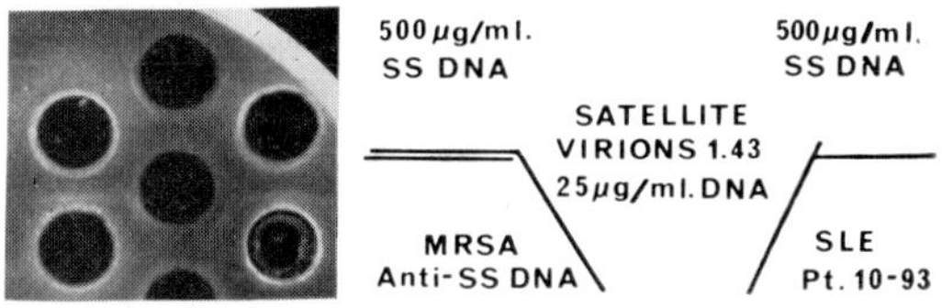

Figure 1. Double immunodiffusion of satellite virions against rabbit antibody to s-s DNA and against the serum from patient Pt. 10-93 with systemic lupus erythematosus. Both antisera form precipitin lines with the s-s DNA (calf thymus), 500 μg/ml.

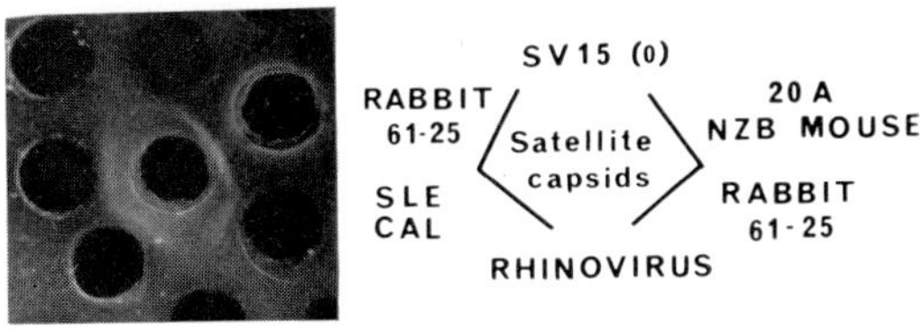

Figure 2. Double immunodiffusion of satellite capsids, simian virus 15 and rhinovirus preparations against antisera to s-s DNA from an immunized rabbit (61-25), patient CAL with systemic lupus erythematosus, and New Zealand black mouse 20A. All antisera form precipitin lines with satellite capsids but not with other viruses.

precipitin line formed between the SLE serum and satellite capsids seems identical to the midline of the three precipitin lines formed between serum 61-30 and satellite capsids. On the other side of the immunodiffusion plate, the precipitin line formed between satellite capsids and serum 61-30 is continuous with the precipitin line formed between SLE serum and satellite capsids. Supporting the evidence that all precipitin lines shown in Figures 1, 2 and 3 contained s-s DNA was the observation that when these immunodiffusion plates were stained with acridine orange and viewed in ultraviolet light they fluoresced yellow-green (13). However, prior incubation of the empty capsids (buoyant density 1.30 g cm³) with DNAse did not alter the precipitin bands formed by rabbit antisera. The detection of antigenic determinants of single-stranded DNA on adeno-associated satellite capsids is shown in Figure 4. Rabbit antibody (ASV-4) produced by immunization of rabbits with satellite virions gave a single dense line of precipitation when diffused against satellite capsids and formed no precipitin bands with single-strand calf thymus DNA. Furthermore, it was also shown by the quantitative complement fixation technique that the rabbit antibody induced by immunization with satellite virus did not fix complement in the presence of a variety of single-strand DNA concentrations. The precipitin band formed by the ASV-4 antiserum gave a line of complete identity with the precipitin lines formed between rabbit 61-31 and the satellite capsids. On the left-hand side of the Ouchterlony immunodiffusion plate the precipitin line formed between rabbit 61-31 serum and 500 μg/ml single-strand calf thymus DNA gives a line of partial identity

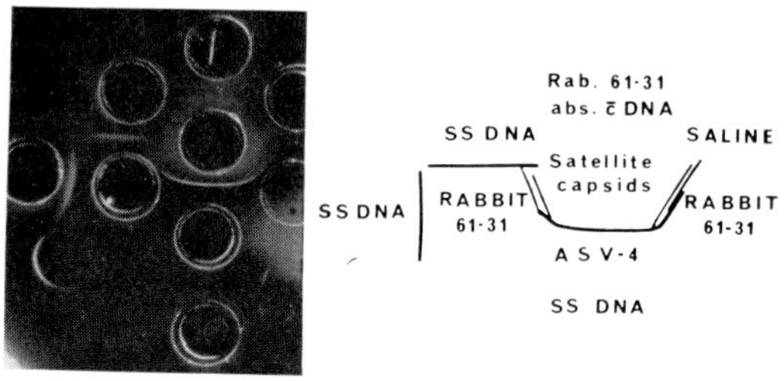

Figure 4. Double immunodiffusion of satellite capsids against anti-s-s DNA sera from rabbit 61-31 and rabbit antisera to adeno satellite V-4. The later anti-viral serum forms no precipitates with s-s DNA in the bottom well. The precipitin line formed between the antiviral serum (AS V-4) gives complete identity with one of the two precipitin lines formed between anti-s-s DNA rabbit 61-31 serum and complete or partial identity with a second line. The precipitin line formed between s-s DNA and anti-s-s DNA from rabbit 61-31 spurs over the two lines formed between satellite capsids and anti-s-s DNA. Anti-s-s DNA following absorption with s-s DNA (*top well*) forms no precipitin lines with s-s DNA or satellite capsids.

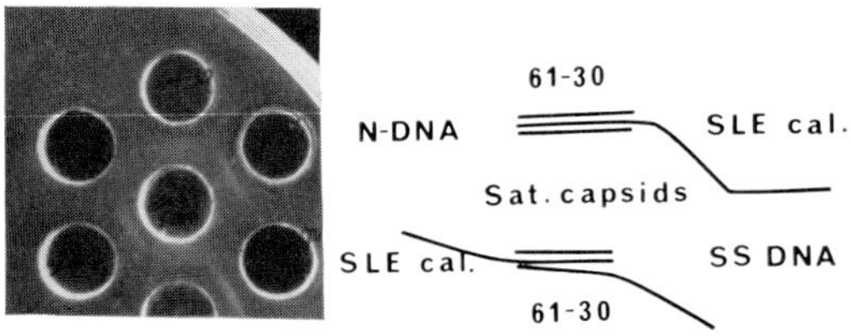

Figure 3. Double immunodiffusion of satellite capsids, N-DNA and s-s DNA against anti-s-s DNA sera from rabbit 61-30 and patient CAL with systemic lupus erythematosus. N-DNA (100 μg/ml) formed no precipitates with anti-s-s DNA sera. Three precipitin lines formed between satellite capsids and anti-s-s DNA from rabbit 61-30. One of these lines gave complete identity between the single precipitin line from between satellite capsids and anti-s-s DNA from the SLE patient. Another precipitin line of these three gave complete identity with the line formed between s-s DNA (calf thymus) and the rabbit (61-30) anti-s-s DNA.

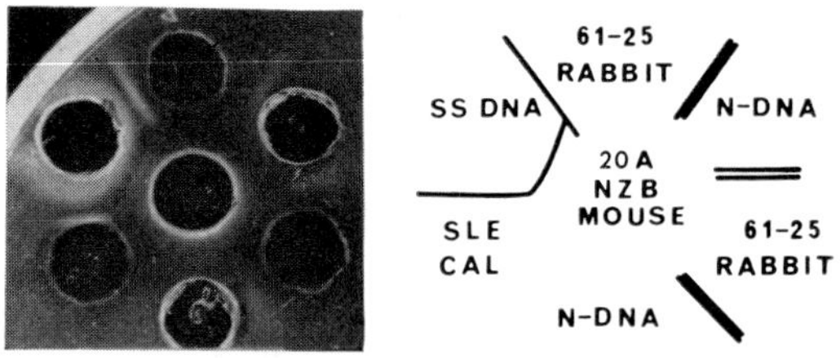

Figure 5. Double immunodiffusion of anti-s-s DNA sera from NZB mouse 20A, patient CAL with systemic lupus erythematosus, and rabbit 61-25 against calf thymus s-s DNA and N-DNA. The single precipitin line formed between s-s DNA and rabbit 61-25 anti-s-s DNA spurs over the one between s-s DNA and anti-s-s DNA from NZB mouse 20A. There is complete identity of line between s-s DNA and SLE CAL with the line between s-s DNA and the NZB mouse 20A-anti-sOs DNA serum. Two faint precipitin lines form between the N-DNA (1000 μg/ml) and rabbit 61-25 anti-s-s DNA.

with that formed between rabbit serum 61-31 and satellite capsids. This suggests that there are additional "s-s DNA determinants" on the calf thymus preparation that are not found on the satellite capsids.

In Figure 5 serum from rabbit 61-25 NZB mouse 20A and the SLE patient Cal gave a line of complete identity with s-s DNA for the latter two antisera and partial identity with the rabbit antibody. The same two precipitin lines formed between rabbit serum 61-25 and native calf thymus DNA concentration 1000 μg/ml at 48 hr can be attributed to presence in the N-DNA preparation of small amounts of s-s DNA antigenic determinants.

DISCUSSION

Serum from rabbits immunized with s-s calf thymus DNA-rabbit serum albumin complexes (MRSA pools) have been shown to react with s-s DNA and minimally or not at all with native calf thymus DNA by precipitin analysis (10), quantitative complement fixation, and radioimmuno assays (14). The precipitin lines formed between MRSA and s-s DNA give complete or partial identity with those formed between s-s DNA and serum from the SLE patient and the NZB mouse. Since one or more of these sera, each of which may have slightly different specificities for s-s DNA determinants, precipitated with satellite virions, we have confirmatory data that these virions with intact capsids contain s-s DNA. Precipitation of the material from Kilham's rat virus (containing s-s DNA) (4) by rabbit serum 61-25 is consistent with the DNA content of these virions and the specificity of the antibody. Absence of precipitation by the SLE serum and the mouse serum may be explained on the basis that the anti-s-s DNA antibodies in these sera are, a) in lower concentration, and b) of probably slightly different specificity. Precipitation of "empty" satellite capsids (buoyant density 1.30) by all three sera suggests that the capsids contain polynucleotides of sufficient size to form precipitates with antibodies directed primarily against s-s DNA (Fig. 2). Control antigens of d-s DNA and RNA virions, tissue culture fluid and fetal calf serum formed no precipitins. The dialysate of SV 15 containing d-s DNA, as anticipated, also formed no precipitates. The observation that DNA extracted from satellite virions formed no precipitates with the sera is consistent with the hypothesis that the extracted DNA undergoes some form of "renaturation." The "renatured" DNA thus has hidden its s-s DNA antigenic determinants.

Appropriate controls to exclude the possibility of reactions of complement components present in the sera with DNA were included by the demonstration that the heated sera shown to be complement free had identical precipitating activities. The possibility that there was aggregated IgG in the sera rather than antibodies to s-s DNA has been controlled in preceding experiments by demonstrating that heat aggregated rabbit human or mouse IgG did not give the reactions shown with the anti-s-s DNA antisera.

In recent years there have been a number of speculative reviews (15–17) dealing with the interrelationships of persistent viral infection and chronic diseases of man and animals characterized by immunoglobulin abnormalities (the so-called auto-immune diseases). Since "auto-antibodies" directed against s-s DNA are particularly prevalent in many of these disorders, the serologic cross-reaction of such antibodies with DNA of intact virions suggests the possibilty that the immunogens in such persistent infections are similar, and that the antigenic constituents of the circulating and deposited immune complexes may be similar agents. Furthermore, the documented heterogeneity of antibodies induced by nucleotide-containing antigens (18, 19), coupled with the data from this report, indicates the danger of interpreting serologic tests in clinical disorders of unknown etiology. The designation of "slow virus" diseases for disorders characterized by anti-viral antibodies should be as cautiously applied as the designation of "auto-immune" diseases for disorders characterized by auto-antibodies.

Acknowledgment. The technical services of Miss Margaret Alspaugh are greatfully acknowledged.

REFERENCES

1. Mayor, H. D. and Melnick, J. L., Nature *210:* 331, 1966.
2. Brailovsky, C., Ann. Inst. Pasteur, *110:* 43, 1966.
3. May, P., Niveleau, A., Berger, G. and Brailovsky, C., J. Mol. Biol., *27:* 603, 1967.
4. May, P. and May, E., J. Gen. Virol., *6:* 437, 1970.

5. McGeoch, D. J., Crawford, L. V. and Follett, E. H. C., J. Gen. Virol., *6:* 33, 1970.
6. Mayor, H. D., Jordan, L. E. and Ito, M., J. Virol., *4:* 191, 1969.
7. Mayor, H. D., Torikai, K., Melnick, J. L. and Mandel, M., Science, *100:* 140, 1969.
8. Rose, J. A., Burns, K. I., Hoggan, H. D. and Koczot, F. J., Proc. Nat. Acad. Sci., *64:* 863, 1969.
9. Mayor, H. D., Jamison, R. M., Jordan, L. E. and Melnick, J. L., J. Bact., *90:* 235, 1965.
10. Forsén, N. R., Alspaugh, M. and Barnett, E. V., Immunology, *19:* 669, 1970.
11. Ito, M., Melnick, J. L. and Mayor, H. D., J. Gen. Virol., *1:* 199, 1967.
12. Parks, W. P., Melnick, J. L., Rongey, R. and Mayor, H. D., J. Virol., *1:* 171, 1967.
13. Armstrong, J. A., Exp. Cell Res., *11:* 640, 1956.
14. Wold, R. T. and Farr, R. S., Fed. Proc., *28:* 696, 1969.
15. Hotchin, J., in *Current Topics in Microbiology and Immunology*, p. 33, Springer-Verlag, New York, 1967.
16. Isacson, T., Progr. Allerg., *10:* 256, 1967.
17. Asherson, G. L., Progr. Allerg., *12:* 192, 1968.
18. Lacour, F., Michelson, A. M. and Nahon, E., in *Nucleic Acids in Immunology*, p. 32, Springer-Verlag, New York, 1968.
19. Plescia, O. J., Imperato, S., Shimbor, C. and Braun, W., Fed. Proc., *27:* 683, 1968.

THE JOURNAL OF IMMUNOLOGY

Vol. 105, No. 4, October 1970
Printed in U.S.A.

PERSISTENT LYMPHOCYTIC CHORIOMENINGITIS VIRAL INFECTION

III. Virus-Anti-Viral Antibody Complexes and Associated Chronic Disease Following Transplacental Infection[1]

MICHAEL B. A. OLDSTONE[2] AND FRANK J. DIXON

From the Department of Experimental Pathology, Scripps Clinic and Research Foundation, La Jolla, California 92037

Received for publication May 13, 1970

Mice naturally infected transplacentally with lymphocytic choriomeningitis virus carry high titers of virus in their blood and tissues, make anti-viral antibody, and develop an associated chronic disease. The virus travels in the circulation in virus-IgG-complement(C) complexes. A study of the renal glomeruli of such transplacentally infected mice showed the presence of viral antigen, C3 and Ig at birth, and a progressive accumulation of virus-Ig complexes that led to death from glomerulonephritis in some mice by 2 weeks of age.

It has been known for over 30 years that lymphocytic choriomeningitis (LCM) virus can cause a life-long murine infection (1–5). Chronic LCM infection or the carrier state develops in mice either infected transplacentally (6) or inoculated with LCM virus shortly after birth (neonatal infection) (7–10). Previously it had been thought that persistently infected mice were not capable of making an anti-LCM viral immune response and were therefore immunologically tolerant (11–13). However, recent studies of neonatally infected LCM carriers indicate not only that these mice produce anti-LCM viral antibody, but that the interaction of anti-viral antibody with virus or virus-infected cells is responsible in part for the tissue injury associated with chronic LCM infection (10, 14).

This paper reports that transplacentally infected mice of several strains also carry persistently high titers of virus in their blood and tissues, make anti-viral antibody, and develop an associated chronic disease. Free anti-viral antibody could not be detected in the circulation presumably because of an excess of antigen or virus, but its presence could be inferred from immunologic precipitation of either IgG or C3 from the serum of these mice, which resulted in significant loss of serum viral infectivity. Study of the glomeruli of transplacentally infected mice showed deposits of viral antigen, C3 and IgG_2 at birth with accumulation of IgG_1 and IgA during the 1st week of life and IgM by the 3rd week. In contrast to neonatally infected mice, these mice had earlier and more severe disease which culminated in an earlier and higher mortality rate. Death from glomerulonephritis secondary to accumulation of virus-anti-viral antibody complexes occurred in some mice by 2 weeks of age.

MATERIALS AND METHODS

Mice. Breeders for SWR/J, C57BL/10 × DBA2 F_1 (hereafter called B10D2 old), and C3H inbred strains were obtained from Jackson Laboratories, Bar Harbor, Maine. Breeding was performed in our laboratory. Adult Swiss Webster (SW) mice, 10 to 15 g, were obtained from a local breeder. Random testing of mice indicated that they were free of LCM, polyoma and lactic dehydrogenase viral infections.

Parental virus carrier state. Newborn mice were inoculated with a 1000 × LD_{50} dose of virus prepared from infected isologous mouse brain within the first 15 hr of life. Details of virus passage, inoculation procedure and development of LCM carrier state have been reported (10,

[1] This is publication 413 from the Department of Experimental Pathology, Scripps Clinic and Research Foundation, La Jolla, California. This research was supported by United States Public Health Service Grants AI-09484 and AI-07007.

[2] Recipient of Career Development Award I KO4-A1 42580 AID from the United States Public Health Service.

15). Brother and sister virus carriers were mated to establish colonies of naturally infected LCM carrier mice.

Virus. Seed virus was mouse brain passage NIH strain CA1371 provided by Dr. Wallace Rowe, National Institute of Allergy and Infectious Diseases, Bethesda, Md. Methods of handling, diluting and titrating virus have been described (10, 15).

Ig and anti-LCM antibody in carrier mice. The sediment of washed kidney homogenate from carrier mice was suspended in 0.02 M glycine-HCl buffer, pH 3.2, 20 ml/g of kidney, and incubated at 37°C for 60 min with constant shaking in order to elute the deposited Ig. Technical details for detection of anti-LCM, antinuclear and anti-glomerular basement membrane antibodies have been reported (10).

Fluorescent antibody studies. Tissue blocks were snap-frozen in liquid nitrogen and sections 4 μ thick were cut, fixed and examined (16).

Procedures used for making antisera and their conjugation to fluorescein isothiocyanate (FITC) have been previously described (16). Rabbit anti-mouse IgG_1, anti-mouse IgG_2, anti-mouse IgA, and anti-mouse IgM were kindly supplied by Dr. Howard Grey. Rabbit anti-mouse IgM was absorbed with newborn mouse sera, anti-mouse IgG_1 was absorbed with mouse IgG_2, and anti-mouse IgG_2 was absorbed with IgG_1. Rabbit anti-mouse IgA was absorbed with purified mouse IgG_1, IgG_2 and IgM. After absorption all rabbit anti-mouse Ig sera were monospecific as judged by Ouchterlony and immunoelectrophoretic analysis.

Histology. Formalin-fixed paraffin sections of tissue were stained by hematoxylin and eosin and periodic acid-Schiff (PAS) methods.

Pathologic changes associated with LCM carrier state. LCM carrier and control mice of the strains under study were examined for clinical, immuno- and histopathologic changes from birth to 9 months of age. Clinical study consisted of daily observations, monthly weighings, and urinary protein determinations. Proteinuria was determined by the sulfosalicylic acid method (17) on 24-hr collections. Proteinuria over 5 mg/24 hr was considered abnormal.

RESULTS

Concentration of LCM infectious virus in tissues of 6-week-old LCM carrier mice. Tissues from four LCM carrier mice of SWR/J, B10D2 old and C3H strains showed wide interstrain variation in the concentration of infectious LCM virus (Table I). The SWR/J carriers had the highest concentration of infectious LCM virus, more than 2 logs greater than C3H carriers, which had the least.

Immunofluorescence study of carrier mice. Tissues (brain, liver, kidney, heart, skeletal muscle, lung, intestinal tract, lymph node, spleen and thymus) from five male and five female 6-week-old LCM carrier and control mice of SWR/J, B10D2 and C3H strains were studied for distribution of LCM antigen, host Ig and C3

TABLE I

Infectivity titers and immunofluorescent staining in 6-week-old mice after transplacental LCM infection

Strains	Blood	Brain		Liver		Kidney			
	Titer[a]	Titer	LCM Ag[b]	Titer	LCM Ag	Titer	LCM Ag	Ig[c]	C3[c]
SWR/J	4.8	5.4	+	5.6	+	6.1	+	++	++
B10D2 old	3.6	4.0	+	4.8	+	4.4	+	+	+
C3H	2.4	2.7	+	3.1	+	3.5	+	±	±

[a] Reciprocal of log dilution giving a 50% lethal endpoint per 0.03 ml of intracerebral inoculum. Number is the mean value of the LD_{50} endpoints obtained with organs from four individual mice. LD_{50} endpoints calculated by method of Reed and Muench (28).

[b] Degree of involvement as determined by direct immunofluorescence: 0, negative result; ±, less than 2% cells involved; +, 2% to 10% cells involved.

[c] Degree of glomerular involvement as determined by direct immunofluorescence: 0, no Ig deposit; ±, minimal Ig deposit, in general limited to the mesangial area; +, moderate Ig deposit in mesangial and peripheral capillary walls; ++, marked Ig deposits in mesangia and peripheral capillary walls. Neither Ig nor C3 was found deposited in any other tissues studied except in occasional areas of focal necrosis in the liver, heart and arteries.

(Table I) by the direct immunofluorescence technique. LCM antigen was found in the cell cytoplasm in all tissues studied, appearing as fine to coarse particles which fluoresced apple green after staining with fluorescein-labeled anti-LCM antibody. The greatest concentration of LCM antigen appeared in brain, liver and kidney. In contrast to widespread distribution of viral antigen there was accumulation of Ig and C3 only in the renal glomeruli and on occasion in focal areas of necrosis in liver, heart and arteries. Viral antigen, Ig and C3 were deposited in the glomeruli along basement membranes of capillaries and in the mesangia (Fig. 1). A difference among various strains of LCM carrier mice as to amount of glomerular-bound Ig was noted with most being present in SWR/J and least in C3H strain.

Nature of Ig deposited in the renal glomeruli. The Ig eluted from the glomeruli of SWR/J carrier mice when assayed in a microcomplement fixation test in the presence of added specific LCM antigen was shown to contain antibody to LCM virus (Table II). In addition, anti-LCM antibody made up about 60% of total eluted kidney Ig as indicated by absorption with LCM antigen. When 280 μg of eluted γ globulin were mixed with LCM-infected monkey kidney cells, approximately 160 μg of eluted γ globulin were absorbed as measured by the Mancini radial diffusion technique. No significant absorption occurred when γ globulin was absorbed with non-infected monkey kidney culture cells. Renal eluates from control SWR/J mice did not have detectable Ig. In these eluates, neither anti-nuclear antibody nor anti-glomerular basement membrane antibodies were detected at 280 μg Ig/ml concentration.

Time of appearance and class of glomerular bound Ig in SWR/J carrier mice. Kidneys from SWR/J fetuses and mice from birth to 3 months were studied for the presence of mouse Ig by the immunofluorescence technique. The results indicated that kidney-bound IgG, largely IgG_2, could be detected in over 50% of mice examined within the first 12 hr of life (Table III, Fig. 2). IgG_2 was found in the glomeruli of all mice examined after 3 days of age. IgG_1 was detectable in the glomeruli of some mice 3 to 14 days old and in all mice 21 days old. Its frequency diminished by 2 to 3 months. Heavy IgA deposits appeared by the 3rd day after birth (Fig. 3), diminished in intensity by the 3rd week and were uncommon by the 6th month. In contrast, the earliest IgM deposits formed at the end of the 1st week, increased by the 3rd week and were heaviest by 2 to 3 months.

Circulating virus-Ig complexes. The presence of LCM antigen, Ig and C3 along the glomerular capillary walls in irregular lumpy deposits suggested that these deposits represented trapped circulating virus-antibody complexes. Circulating virus-Ig complexes were present in the sera and plasma of transplacentally infected mice during the first several hours after birth and persisted throughout life (Table IV). The Ig in these complexes was largely of the IgG class. Immunologic precipitation of IgG from the sera of these mice resulted in a significant lowering of the infectivity of the sera, whereas no significant loss followed similar treatment with anti-mouse IgA or IgM (Table V). Mixtures of stock LCM virus and normal mouse IgG did not result in the formation of LCM-IgG complexes precipitable by anti-mouse Ig, indicating immunologic specificity of the complexes found in the sera of carrier mice.

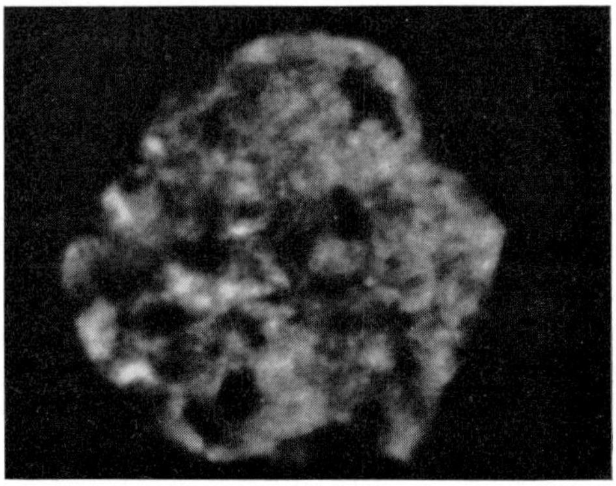

Figure 1. Renal glomerulus from a 6-week-old SWR/J mouse transplacentally infected with LCM virus. The preparation was stained with fluorescein-conjugated rabbit antiserum to mouse IgG. IgG is heavily deposited along peripheral walls of glomerular capillaries and in mesangial areas. Comparable results were obtained with fluorescein-conjugated rabbit antiserum to mouse C3. Following absorption of fluoresceinated antisera with mouse C3 and IgG, no staining occurred. Fluorescein-conjugated rabbit antisera to mouse albumin or rat fibrinogen did not stain the glomerulus.

TABLE II

Anti-LCM antibody eluted from kidneys of SWR/J mice after transplacental LCM infection[a]

	Dilution of Renal Eluate					
	1:5	1:10	1:50	1:100	1:200	1:400
	Hemolysis-OD readings 413 nm					
Kidney pool from carrier mice age:						
1 day	0.14	0.16	0.43	0.57	0.54	0.56
14 days	0.09	0.15	0.28	0.38	0.57	0.52
8 weeks	0.11	0.14	0.21	0.34	0.48	0.56
Kidney pool from uninfected mice age:						
1 day	0.54					
14 days	0.50					
8 weeks	0.52					
LCM Ag only	0.58					
C only	0.57					

[a] Microcomplement-fixation assay (29). One and two-tenths CH_{50} units were used in the assay. The antigen was specific LCM complement-fixing antigen. Any reading below 0.43 indicates 25% or more complement fixation and is considered significant.

Chronic disease associated with transplacental LCM infection. In SWR/J, B10D2 old and C3H strains a disease is associated with LCM carrier state after transplacental infection (Table VI). This disease is characterized clinically by increased proteinuria in SWR/J strain and increased mortality in SWR/J, B10D2 old and C3H mice. The increased severity of disease after transplacental infection as compared to neonatal infection was noted in all three strains. The transplacentally infected SWR/J mice had a 32% mortality by 3 months of age, 50% by 6 months, and 65% by 9 months compared to a 2% to 8% mortality by 3 to 9 months after neonatal infection. Similarly, C3H mice infected with LCM virus in the neonatal period rarely showed disease over a 2-year period but had a 21% mortality by 6 months and 42% by 9 months after transplacental infection.

Histopathologically, the cardinal manifestations of chronic disease after transplacental infection occurred in kidney, liver, heart, arteries and brain (Figs. 4, 5 and 6). In the kidney, the earliest manifestations of disease were glomerular endothelial and mesangial proliferation. Later, varying gradations of basement membrane thickening, intracapillary hyalinization and

TABLE III

Ig deposits in glomeruli of SWR/J mice after transplacental LCM infection[a]

Age	Serum Proteins Deposited in Renal Glomeruli							
	IgG	IgG_1	IgG_2	IgA	IgM	Alb	Fib	RabIgG
12 to 16 day embryo	0/5[b]							
First 12 hr after birth	18/33	1/8	8/8	0/8	0/8	0/8	0/8	0/8
3 days	4/4	2/4	4/4	4/4	0/4	0/4	0/4	0/4
7 days	6/6	2/6	6/6	6/6	1/6	0/6	0/6	0/6
10 days	2/2	2/2	2/2	2/2	1/2	0/2	0/2	0/2
14 days	6/6	2/6	6/6	6/6	2/6	0/6	0/6	0/6
21 days	5/5	5/5	5/5	5/5	3/5	1/5	1/5	0/5
2 to 3 months	10/10	5/10	10/10	6/10	10/10	2/10	2/10	0/10
Neonatally infected SWR/J carriers 2 to 3 months	10/10	5/10	10/10	4/10	7/10	0/10	0/10	0/10
Control SWR/J mice[c] 2 to 3 months	0/10	0/4	0/4	0/4	0/4	0/4	0/4	0/4

[a] Direct immunofluorescence technique was used for detection of mouse IgG, albumin (Alb), fibrinogen (Fib), and rabbit IgG (RabIgG). Indirect immunofluorescence assay was used to demonstrate mouse IgG_1, IgG_2, IgA and IgM. The kidney sections were stained with fluorescein-conjugated sheep anti-rabbit IgG after initial exposure to various absorbed monospecific rabbit anti-mouse immunoglobulin sera.

[b] Number of positive mice showing specific fluorescence/total number of mice assayed.

[c] Inoculated with 10^{-1} dilution of normal (non-infected) isologous brain at birth.

capillary occlusion developed. Renal disease was seen in several 7-day-old transplacentally infected mice and was severe in some 10- to 14-day-old SWR/J mice (Fig. 4). Renal disease was moderate to mild in B10D2 old and C3H mice. In the liver and heart scattered areas of parenchymal damage with mixed inflammatory infiltrates occurred in SWR/J by 4 weeks (Fig. 5) and B10D2 old by 6 months of age but were not observed in C3H mice. Location of the focal damage had no consistent relationship to either hepatic or cardiac architecture. In approximately 5% to 10% of SWR/J virus carrier mice of all ages an arteritis was detected (Fig. 6) which involved scattered vessels in heart, kidney, spleen and omentum. Histopathologically, its predominant features were mixed inflammatory infiltrates in and necrosis of the vessel wall. In addition, about 20% of SWR/J and 5% of B10D2 old mice by 6 months showed scattered perivascular round cell infiltration in the central nervous system. Associated with these inflammatory and necrotizing lesions, a lymphoid proliferation and mononuclear interstitial infiltration occurred predominantly in liver, kidney, lungs, and, to a lesser extent, spleen, pancreas, adrenals, omental fat, and heart tissues. No abnormalities were seen in the thymus or thymic-dependent areas of spleen and lymph node tissues.

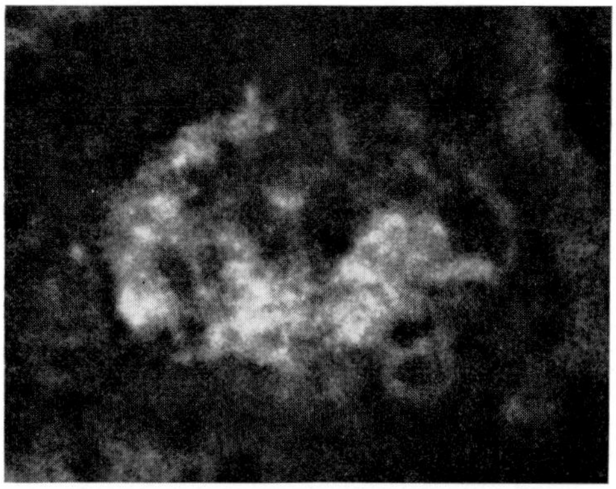

Figure 2. Renal glomerulus from an 8-hr-old SWR/J mouse transplacentally infected with LCM virus. The preparation was stained by indirect immunofluorescence technique using absorbed monospecific rabbit anti-mouse IgG_2 as the first layer followed by fluorescein-conjugated sheep anti-rabbit IgG. IgG_2 deposits are seen predominantly in the mesangial areas.

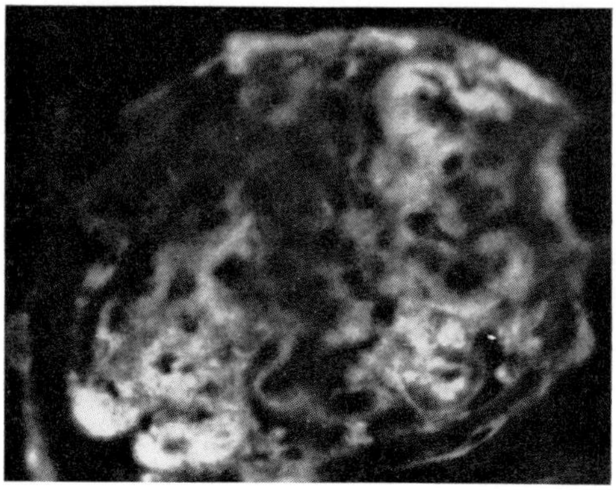

Figure 3. Renal glomerulus from a 3-day-old SWR/J mouse transplacentally infected with LCM virus. The preparation was stained by indirect immunofluorescence technique using absorbed monospecific rabbit anti-mouse IgA as the first layer followed by fluorescein-conjugated sheep anti-rabbit IgG. Heavy IgA deposits are seen along peripheral walls of glomerular capillaries and in the mesangial areas.

TABLE IV

Virus-Ig complexes in sera of SWR/J mice after transplacental LCM infection

Age of Infected Mice	Treatment of Infectious Sera	LD_{50}[a]
12 hr	Normal rabbit sera	2.0
	Anti-mouse IgG	0.4
	Anti-mouse albumin	1.7
7 days	Normal rabbit sera	3.6
	Anti-mouse IgG	0.5
	Anti-mouse albumin	4.0
2 months	Normal rabbit sera	4.4
	Anti-mouse IgG	0.8
	Anti-mouse albumin	4.1

[a] Reciprocal of log dilution giving a 50% lethal endpoint/0.03 ml intracerebral inoculum in 10 to 50 g SW mice. Six mice were used/log dilution.

DISCUSSION

Mice naturally infected transplacentally with LCM virus resemble neonatally infected mice in that they carry high titers of virus in blood and organs and make an anti-viral antibody response throughout life. However, their chronic disease associated with this anti-viral response is much more severe than that in neonatally infected mice. Although anti-viral antibody could

TABLE V

Virus-Ig complexes in sera of 2- to 3-month-old SWR/J mice after transplacental LCM infection

Treatment of Infectious Sera	Dilution of Treated Supernatants					LD_{50}
	2×10^{-1}	2×10^{-2}	2×10^{-3}	2×10^{-4}	2×10^{-5}	
Normal rabbit sera	6/6[a]	6/6	5/6	1/6	0/6	$2 \times 10^{-3.5}$
Anti-mouse IgG	1/6	0/6	0/6	0/6	0/6	$<2 \times 10^{-1}$
Anti-mouse IgA	5/5	6/6	2/6	1/6	0/6	$2 \times 10^{-2.9}$
Anti-mouse IgM	5/5	6/6	5/6	0/6	0/6	$2 \times 10^{-3.4}$
Anti-mouse C3	5/5	1/6	0/6	0/6	0/6	$2 \times 10^{-1.6}$
Anti-mouse albumin	6/6	6/6	6/6	0/6	0/6	$2 \times 10^{-3.5}$

[a] Number of specific deaths/total number of SW mice inoculated intracerebrally with treated supernatants.

TABLE VI

Mortality after transplacental LCM infection

Strain	Carrier State	Cumulative Mortality		
		3 Months	6 Months	9 Months
SWR/J	Control[a]	1/50[b]	1/50	2/50
	Neonatal[c]	1/50	2/50	4/50
	Transplacental[d]	28/86	45/86	56/86
B10D2 old	Control	0/50	0/50	2/50
	Neonatal	0/50	1/50	2/50
	Transplacental	4/34	4/19	—[e]
C3H	Control	0/50	1/50	1/50
	Neonatal	0/50	0/50	0/50
	Transplacental	4/47	8/38	12/18

[a] Mice inoculated with non-infected isologous brain at birth.

[b] Number of deaths/total number of mice.

[c] Mice inoculated i.c. with 1000 × LD_{50} dose of virus prepared from infected isologous mouse brain within first 15 hr of life.

[d] Mice naturally infected via transplacental route.

[e] Insufficient observations at this time.

not be detected in the circulation of transplacentally infected mice by conventional techniques, its presence could be inferred by the demonstration of circulating IgG-virus-C3 complexes. Circulating complexes could be detected on the day of birth and apparently persisted throughout life.

Study of the glomeruli of such mice showed a progressive accumulation of Ig, C3 and viral antigen in irregular deposits along the capillary walls and mesangia area with age. The Ig eluted from renal homogenates of these mice contained C-fixing antibody to LCM virus. Approximately 60% of the eluted Ig could be specifically absorbed by LCM-infected tissue culture cells but not by uninfected control cultures, indicating specific accumulation and concentration of anti-LCM antibody in the glomeruli.

The origin of Ig deposits found at birth in these mice is not clear. Under normal conditions little or no synthesis of Ig occurs in the developing fetus while transfer of Ig from the mother apparently takes place transplacentally and after birth through the neonatal intestine (18). Normally, in the newborn, IgM is not detected until 1 to 3 weeks and IgA until 4 to 6 weeks, whereas both IgG_1 and IgG_2 are present in low levels at birth and increase to adult levels by 2 weeks (19). However, the fetus may be capable of making antibodies when stimulated by appropriate antigens (20–22). The chronicity of LCM intrauterine infection suggests the possibility that an anti-viral immune response against the virus may be made by the fetus, and, if this is so, part of the IgG_2 deposits found at birth may be fetal in origin. The deposits of IgA which are detected on the 3rd day and diminish by the 3rd week parallel the time of expected absorption of antibodies from the gut in the nursing mouse (18, 23) and are probably maternal in origin, whereas the IgM deposits which appear later and increase as the mouse ages are most likely synthesized by the host.

Progressive accumulation of Ig-virus com-

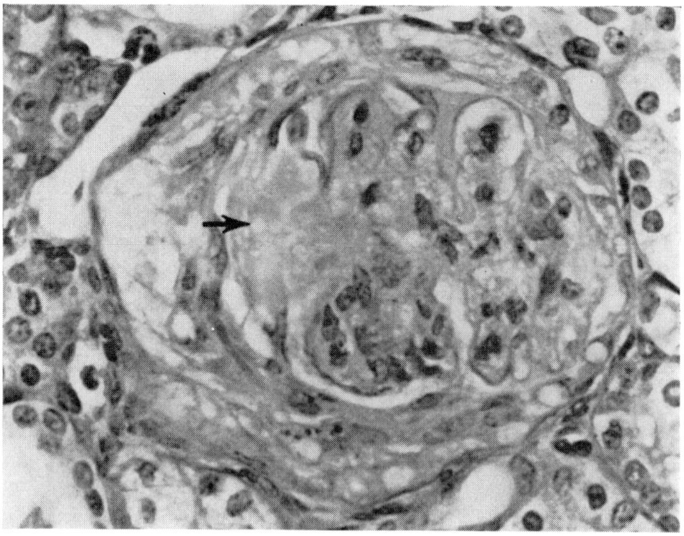

Figure 4. Light photomicrograph of a periodic acid-Schiff (PAS)-stained kidney section from a 14-day-old SWR/J transplacentally infected LCM carrier mouse. Extensive glomerular injury with proliferation of mesangial and epithelial cells and obliteration of Bowman's space are seen. *Arrow* indicates deposit of amorphous PAS positive material.

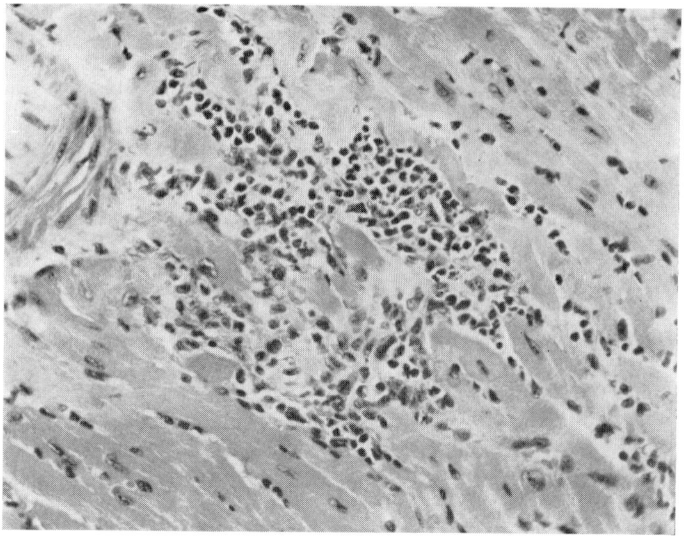

Figure 5. Light photomicrograph of a hematoxylin- and eosin-stained heart section from a 6-week-old SWR/J transplacentally infected LCM carrier mouse showing area of myocardial damage with infiltrating inflammatory cells.

plexes in the glomeruli is the principal cause of death in these mice. Hence, in this situation, a generalized infection with viremia appears to provide viral antigen which forms circulating complexes with antibody and C. There is no evidence to suggest that the virus itself has a primary injurious effect on the glomerulus so that this form of disease is not truly a "viral nephritis" but rather an immune complex nephritis similar to that developing in well recognized laboratory models in which soluble protein antigens, antibody and C combine to

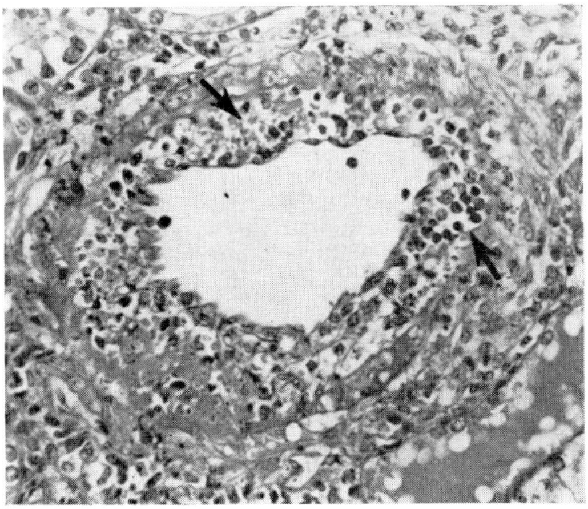

Figure 6. Light photomicrograph of a hematoxylin- and eosin-stained artery in a kidney section from a 14-day-old SWR/J transplacentally infected LCM carrier mouse. Necrosis and inflammation are seen throughout the wall of the vessel (*arrows*).

form circulating complexes that lodge in the kidney (24).

There are several possible explanations for the non-glomerular lesions. First, large amounts of circulating antigen-antibody complexes can cause focal hepatic (25) and myocardial necrosis and arteritis (26). In such situations the immune complexes may be seen lodged in the hepatic sinusoids or the medial wall of arteries. Whether the injury in these situations results from the deposits of the phlogogenic complexes is not known. Second, the transfer of anti-LCM antibody *in vivo* to LCM carrier mice causes acute necrotizing inflammation in regions of viral persistence followed by chronic mononuclear infiltrates (14). Similarly, addition of anti-LCM antibody and C to LCM-infected cells in culture has a prompt cytotoxic effect (27). Third, immune spleen or lymph node cells from isologous donors can injure LCM-infected cultures (27). Fourth, a cell-free soluble cytotoxin is released following incubation of immune lymphoid cells and virus. When this cytotoxin is added to infected or non-infected culture cells, cellular injury occurs (unpublished data). Any or all of these various immunologic mechanisms may be involved in the disease suffered by these chronically infected mice.

The early and severe nature of disease after transplacental infection is probably in part due to transfer of circulating maternal anti-LCM antibody or even virus-anti-viral antibody complexes. However, both the severity and time of onset of disease appeared strain-associated. As with neonatal infection, the SWR/J strain with the greatest amount of virus and antibody developed the earliest and severest disease, and the C3H strain with the least virus and antibody had the least disease. Preliminary experiments indicate that *in vitro* both C3H and SWR/J cell cultures are equally susceptible to initiation of LCM infection. However, the virus yield from SWR/J cultures is considerably greater than that from C3H cultures. The production of anti-viral inhibitors by either strain does not appear to account for this difference in viral replication (unpublished data).

Acknowledgments. The authors wish to thank Dr. Howard Grey both for advice and for providing several rabbit anti-mouse immunoglobulin sera, Antoinette Tishon for technical aid, and Phyllis Keim for preparing the manuscript.

REFERENCES

1. Traub, E., Science, *81:* 298, 1935.
2. Traub, E., J. Immun., *29:* 69, 1935.
3. Traub, E., J. Exp. Med., *64:* 183, 1936.
4. Traub, E., J. Exp. Med., *63:* 847, 1936.
5. Traub, E., J. Exp. Med., *68:* 229, 1938.
6. Traub, E., J. Exp. Med., *69:* 801, 1939.
7. Hotchin, J. and Cinits, M., Canad. J. Microbiol., *4:* 149, 1958.
8. Traub, E., Zbl. Bakt. (Orig.), *177:* 472, 1960.
9. Volkert, M. and Hannover, L., Acta Path. Microbiol. Scand., *60:* 577, 1964.
10. Oldstone, M. B. A. and Dixon, F. J., J. Exp. Med., *129:* 483, 1969.
11. Burnet, F. and Fenner, F., *The Production of Antibodies*, 2nd Ed., p. 104, Macmillan and Co., Ltd., Melbourne, 1949.
12. Hotchin, J., Cold Spring Harbor Symp. Quant. Biol., *27:* 479, 1962.
13. Volkert, M., *Perspectives in Virology*, Edited by V. M. Pollard, Vol. 4, p. 269, Harper and Row, New York, 1964.
14. Oldstone, M. B. A. and Dixon, F. J., J. Exp. Med., *131:* 1, 1970.
15. Oldstone, M. B. A. and Dixon, F. J., J. Immun., *100:* 355, 1968.
16. Oldstone, M. B. A. and Dixon, F. J., Amer. J. Path., *52:* 251, 1968.
17. Kingsbury, F., Clark, C., Williams, G. and Post, A., J. Lab. Clin. Med., *11:* 981, 1926.

18. Brambell, F. W. R., Lancet, *2:* 1087, 1966.
19. Fahey, J. L. and Barth, W., Proc. Soc. Exp. Biol. Med., *118:* 596, 1965.
20. Silverstein, A. M. Nature, *194:* 196, 1962.
21. Silverstein, A. M., Thorbecke, G., Kraner, K. and Lukes, R., J. Immun., *91:* 384, 1963.
22. Alford, C., Schaeffer, J., Blakenship, W., Straumfyord, J. and Cassady, G., New England J. Med., *277:* 438, 1967.
23. Morris, I. G., Proc. Roy. Soc. Ser. B., *148:* 84, 1957.
24. Dixon, F. J., Feldman, J. and Vazquez, J., J. Exp. Med., *113:* 899, 1961.
25. Fennell, R., Jr. and San Tamaria, A., Amer. J. Path., *41:* 521, 1962.
26. Cochrane, C. G. and Dixon, F. J., in *Textbook of Immunopathology*, Edited by P. Miescher and H. J. Müller-Eberhard, Vol. 1, p. 94, Grune and Stratton, New York, 1968.
27. Oldstone, M., Habel, K. and Dixon, F., Fed. Proc., *28:* 429, 1969.
28. Reed, L. and Muench, H., Amer. J. Hyg., *27:* 493, 1938.
29. Wasserman, E. and Levine, L., J. Immun., *87:* 290, 1961.

THE JOURNAL OF IMMUNOLOGY
Vol. 105, No. 4, October 1970
Printed in U.S.A.

IMMUNOPRECIPITATION ANALYSIS OF SOLUBLE COMPLEMENT-FIXING ANTIGENS OF DENGUE VIRUSES[1]

PHILIP K. RUSSELL, DUMRONG CHIEWSILP AND WALTER E. BRANDT

From the Department of Virus Diseases, Walter Reed Army Institute of Research, Washington, D. C. 20012

Received for publication May 13, 1970

Soluble complement-fixing antigens were obtained from brains of suckling mice infected with each of the four dengue serotypes. Brain suspensions were partially purified by clarification with protamine sulfate, precipitation of the antigen with ammonium sulfate, and gel filtration on Sephadex G-100. Antigenic relationships of the partially purified antigens were examined by complement-fixation and Ouchterlony type immunoprecipitation. Discrete precipitin lines were formed with soluble complement-fixing antigens and hyperimmune mouse ascitic fluid. An antigenic determinant common to all four dengue serotypes was demonstrated by both complement-fixation and immunoprecipitation. Cross-absorption experiments confirmed the presence of the group antigen. Spur formation indicated the presence of a unique type-specific antigen for each serotype. Immunoprecipitation patterns indicated that both group- and type-specific antigenic determinants were on the same molecule and that separate antibodies were formed to each determinant.

The basis of the observed antigenic interrelationships between dengue viruses is of considerable interest for taxonomic reasons and because of the suspected relationship of anamnestic antibody responses to the pathogenesis of the dengue shock syndrome (1, 2). The anamnestic responses observed after a second dengue infection are presumably due to antigen-sharing between dengue serotypes. Present knowledge of antigenic interrelationships within this group of arboviruses is based mainly on the results of three serologic methods: hemagglutination-inhibition (HI), complement-fixation (CF), and virus neutralization (N). Each of these tests measures the summation of the reactions of several viral antigens with their respective antibodies. The dengue viruses have been shown to have at least three structural polypeptides in the virion (3) and, in addition, at least three virus-specific nonstructural proteins are thought to be produced during replication of group B arboviruses (4, 5). Thus there is a probability that several independent antigen-antibody systems exist.

Serologic cross-reactions occur most extensively in the HI test, which forms the basis for the present classification of arboviruses (6). Dengue hemagglutinating antigens are physically heterogeneous; two physically distinct hemagglutinins have been recognized (7) and the number of antigenic groups involved is unknown. CF tests also demonstrate a high degree of cross-reactivity (8). The number of antigenic determinants and corresponding antibodies reacting in the CF tests using crude or acetone extracted antigens is also unknown, but at least three physically distinct particles with CF activity have been demonstrated (9).

Immunoprecipitation methods have demonstrated the presence of several antigenic components in crude antigens of group B arboviruses and such methods have been used for comparison and typing of dengue viruses (10, 11) and other group B arboviruses (12, 13). However, use of unpurified antigens and hyperimmune sera results in the formation of a variable number of precipitin lines which are difficult to interpret. The inability to accurately quantify any single antigenic determinant and corresponding antibody limits the value of immunoprecipitation with unpurified antigens.

[1] In conducting the research described in this report, we adhered to the "Guide for Laboratory Animal Facilities and Care," as promulgated by the Committee on Revision of the "Guide for Laboratory Animal Facilities and Care" of the Institute of Laboratory Animal Resources, National Academy of Sciences-National Research Council.

The finding and characterization of a soluble complement-fixation (SCF) antigen in dengue virus-infected tissues (9, 14) and subsequent development of methods for purification of SCF antigens of each serotype (15) allowed immunoprecipitin analysis to be carried out using a highly purified antigenic component. The biophysical characterization of these SCF antigens (16) provided a unique opportunity to correlate physical differences between SCF antigens of the four serotypes with antigenic differences. This report describes antigenic relationships among the SCF antigens of the four dengue viruses as determined by complement-fixation and double diffusion immunoprecipitation in agar.

MATERIALS AND METHODS

Viruses. Mouse adapted prototype strains of dengue-1 (Hawaii), dengue-2 (New Guinea "C"), dengue-3 (H-87) and dengue-4 (H-241) were obtained from Dr. William McD. Hammon. Before being received in our laboratory, these strains had undergone purification by terminal dilution in suckling mice.

Immune ascitic fluids. The antibody source for all serologic tests was hyperimmune ascitic fluids prepared in adult female mice by a modification of the method described by Brandt *et al.* (17). Adult female mice were inoculated subcutaneously (0.4 ml) and intramuscularly (0.1 ml) with 20% suspensions of infected suckling mouse brain on days 1 and 3. Freund's complete adjuvant (0.1 ml) was also injected intraperitoneally (i.p.) on day 3. A second series of injections of infected brain suspension (0.5 ml) was given i.p. on days 25 and 28 and Sarcoma-180 cells were also injected i.p. on day 28. Ascitic fluids were harvested on day 42, clarified by centrifugation, and stored at −20°C.

Purification of SCF antigens. The SCF antigens were prepared from each strain of dengue virus by methods previously described (15). Briefly, 1- to 2-day-old suckling mice were inoculated intracerebrally and virus-infected brains were harvested when the mice became moribund. A 20% suspension of infected suckling mouse brain was made in 0.02 M Tris-HCl, pH 8.2, and protamine sulfate was added to a final concentration of 2 mg/ml. The resulting precipitate was sedimented by centrifugation (9000 × G, 30 min) and discarded. Ammonium sulfate was then added to a final concentration of 60% saturation. The resulting antigen-containing precipitate was sedimented by centrifugation (9000 × G, 60 min) and redissolved in Tris-HCl buffer effecting a 10-fold concentration. The antigen was applied to a 5- x 80-cm column of Sephadex G-100 and eluted in phosphate-buffered saline. Fractions containing SCF antigen were concentrated by pressure filtration. A control antigen was made in a similar manner from uninfected mouse brains.

Crude CF antigens. Crude antigens were prepared by making a 20% suspension of infected suckling mouse brain in normal saline, allowing the suspension to remain at 4°C for 24 hr, and then clarifying by centrifugation at 9000 × G for 30 min.

Complement-fixation test. CF tests were carried out by a microtiter modification of methods described by Kent and Fife (18). In grid CF tests, antigens were diluted in tubes before they were added to the microtiter plates.

Immunodiffusion test. Ouchterlony plates were prepared in 8.5-cm diameter plastic Petri dishes using 1.0% agarose in 0.02 M Tris-buffered saline, pH 8.2. Agar was poured to a depth of 3 mm; 6-mm diameter wells were cut with 12-mm center to center distance. When filled, each well held approximately 0.1 ml of reagent. Before use in immunodiffusion tests, ascitic fluids were diluted to a uniform CF titer of 1:128, a 1:2 to 1:4 dilution in most instances. Antigens were similarly standardized to a CF titer of 1:256. For absorption experiments undiluted SCF antigens were mixed in equal proportions with undiluted ascitic fluid and held at 4°C for 18 hr. Precipitates were removed by centrifugation before using the adsorbed ascitic fluids in gel diffusion experiments.

RESULTS

The hyperimmune ascitic fluids had CF antibody titers of 1:512 to 1:1024 with homologous crude antigens. No reaction with control mouse brain antigens was observed. A significant reaction between each ascitic fluid and each heterologous crude antigen was observed (Fig. 1). The CF antibody titers of the same ascitic fluids were two- to fourfold lower when tested against homologous purified SCF antigens (Fig. 2) and an even greater difference in heterologous titers was noted. The dengue-4 ascitic fluid appeared specific when tested against SCF antigens, not

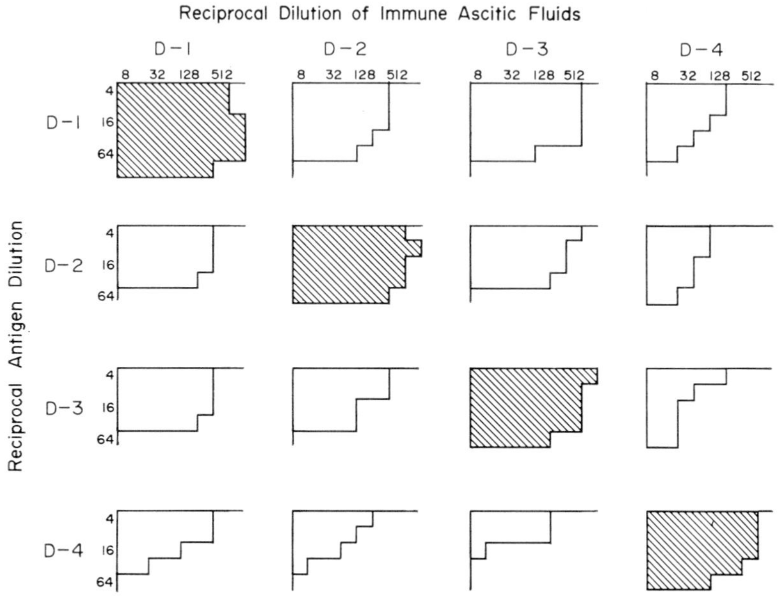

Figure 1. Complement-fixation tests using crude CF antigens and immune ascitic fluids. Homologous reactions are shaded.

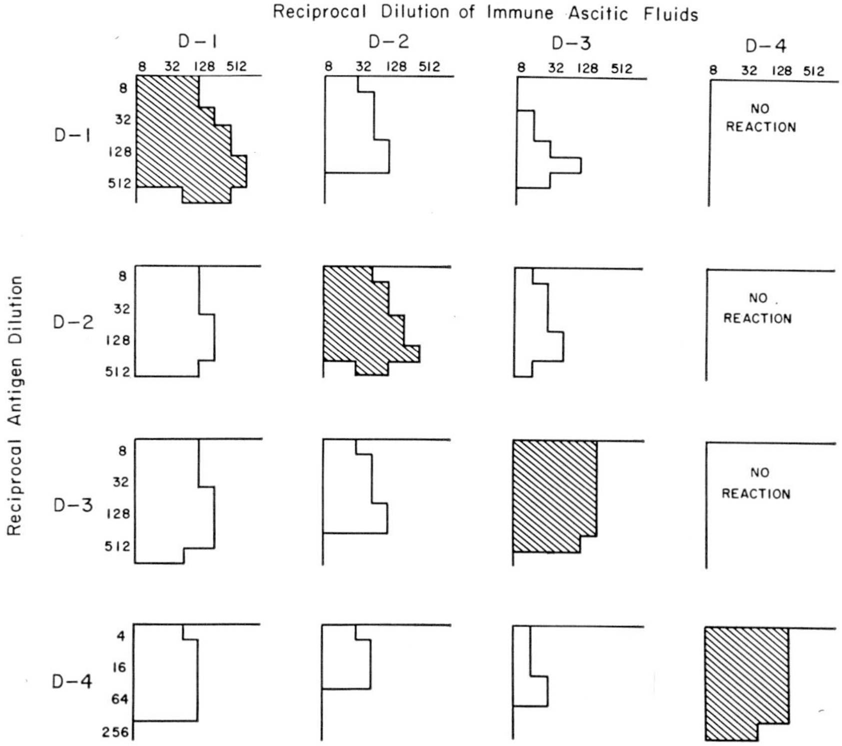

Figure 2. Complement-fixation tests using purified SCF antigens. Immune ascitic fluids are the same as in Figure 1. Homologous reactions are shaded.

reacting with heterologous SCF antigen preparations. Similarly, the dengue-3 ascitic fluid gave a much more specific pattern when tested against the purified antigens. Dengue-1 and dengue-2 ascitic fluids, however, exhibited a smaller difference in specificity between the crude antigens and the purified SCF antigens. The difference in the shape of the grids is striking. The SCF antigens usually produced a "post-zone" inhibition of complement-fixation in regions of relative antigen excess. With the crude saline antigens, however, inhibition due to antigen excess was noted only in the dengue-1 homologous reaction. In all other instances maximum antibody titers occurred with the highest concentration of crude antigen.

Immunodiffusion. The SCF antigens of prototype strains of dengue-1, 2, and 4 gave a single line when tested by the immunoprecipitin method with homologous and heterologous ascitic fluids. The SCF antigen preparations of dengue-3 produced a faint but unmistakable second line in addition to the major precipitin line of the SCF antigen.

The relationship observed between dengue-1 and dengue-2 SCF antigens by immunoprecipitation is depicted in Figures 3 to 6. When antigen was placed in the center well and antibody in the peripheral wells, the precipitin lines fused, forming a line of identity between both homologous and heterologous antibody sources (Figs. 3 and 4). However, when antibody was placed in the center well with antigen in the peripheral wells, a line of identity formed between adjacent homologous antigens, whereas, formation of a distinct spur was seen with heterologous antigens in adjacent wells, indicating partial identity (Figs. 5 and 6). When dengue-1 and dengue-2 ascitic fluids were tested against homologous and heterologous pairs of all the dengue SCF antigens, a spur of partial identity was seen with each pair (Figs. 7 and 8). This basic relationship was also true for dengue-3 and dengue-4. With dengue-3 or -4 antigen in the center well, homologous and heterologous antibody in adjacent outer wells

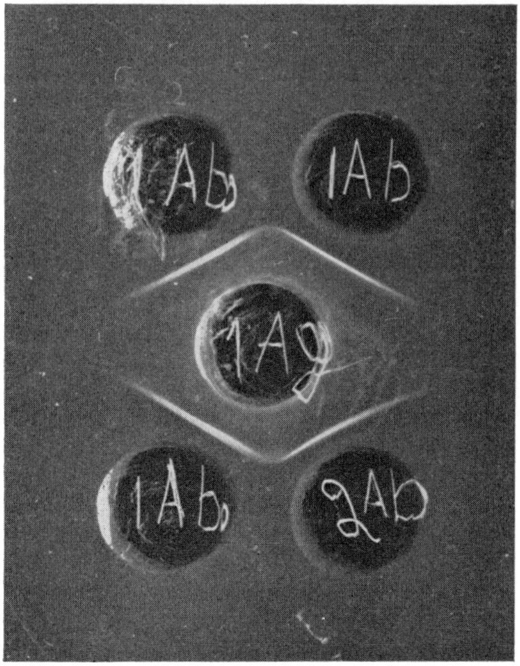

Figure 3. Relationship between dengue-1 SCF antigen (*center well*) and dengue-1 antibody (*upper wells*) and dengue-1 and dengue-2 antibody (*lower wells*). Note fusion of precipitin lines between homologous and heterologous antibody wells.

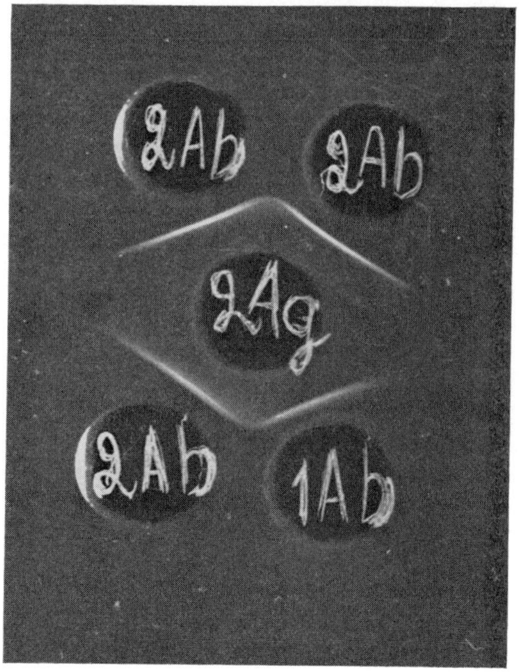

Figure 4. Relationship between dengue-2 SCF antigen (*center well*) and dengue-2 antibody (*upper wells*) and dengue-1 and dengue-2 antibody (*lower wells*). Note fusion of precipitin line between both homologous and heterologous antibody wells.

formed lines of identity. Conversely, dengue-3 antibody in the center well resulted in spur formation when heterologous antigens were placed in wells adjacent to the dengue-3 antigen. The dengue-4 ascitic fluid, however, formed a precipitin line only with homologous antigen.

The hypothesis that a common identical antigenic determinant is present on the SCF antigen of each serotype was tested by diffusing heterologous antigens in pairs against ascitic fluid of a third serotype. Lines of identity formed between pairs of heterologous antigens are shown in Figures 9 and 10.

Dengue-1, dengue-2 and dengue-3 ascitic fluids reacted with all three respective heterologous dengue serotypes but dengue-4 ascitic fluid apparently lacked antibody to the common antigenic determinant. Absorption of dengue-1 ascitic fluid with dengue-2 SCF antigen eliminated the immunoprecipitin reaction of the ascitic fluid with dengue-2, -3 and -4 antigens leaving only homologous antibody. Similarly, absorption of dengue-2 ascitic fluid with dengue-1 antigen removed antibody against dengue-1, -3 and -4 SCF antigens leaving antibody which reacted only with the homologous SCF antigen.

DISCUSSION

The ascitic fluids of mice hyperimmunized with antigen preparations known to be heterogeneous contain independent populations of antibodies to several different virus-specific antigenic determinants. Differences in degree of serologic cross-reactivity between serotypes as shown by different serologic methods which assay different antibody populations support this assumption. Cross-reactivity among the dengue serotypes in serologic tests may result from either the presence of one or more identical antigens possessed in common by each serotype, or from immunologic cross-reactions due to antibodies reacting with analogous antigenic determinants of similar but not identical structure, or a combination of both mechanisms. Lower CF antibody titers were ob-

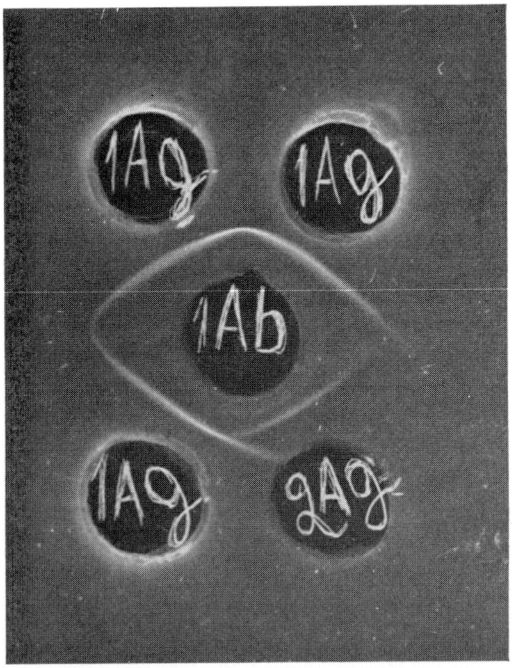

Figure 5. Relationship between dengue-1 antibody (*center well*) and dengue-1 SCF antigen (*upper wells*) and dengue-1 and dengue-2 SCF antigens (*lower wells*). Precipitin lines fuse between homologous antigen wells, whereas a spur is visible between heterologous antigen wells.

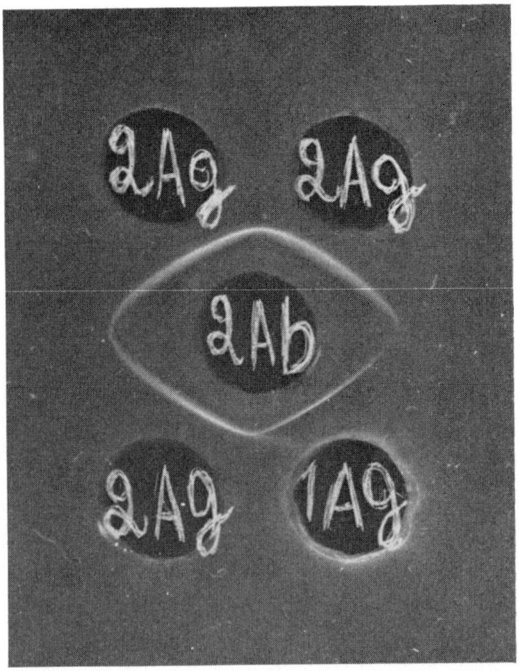

Figure 6. Relationship between dengue-2 antibody (*center well*) and dengue-2 SCF antigen (*upper wells*) and dengue-2 and dengue-1 SCF antigens (*lower wells*). Precipitin lines fuse between homologous antigen wells, whereas a spur is visible between heterologous antigen wells.

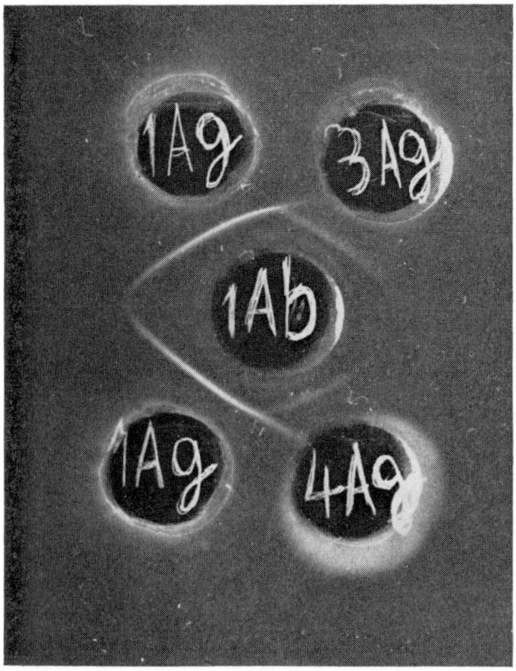

Figure 7. Relationship between dengue-1 antibody (*center well*) and dengue-1 and dengue-3 SCF antigens (*upper wells*) and dengue-1 and dengue-4 SCF antigen (*lower wells*). Spurs are visible between both pairs of antigens.

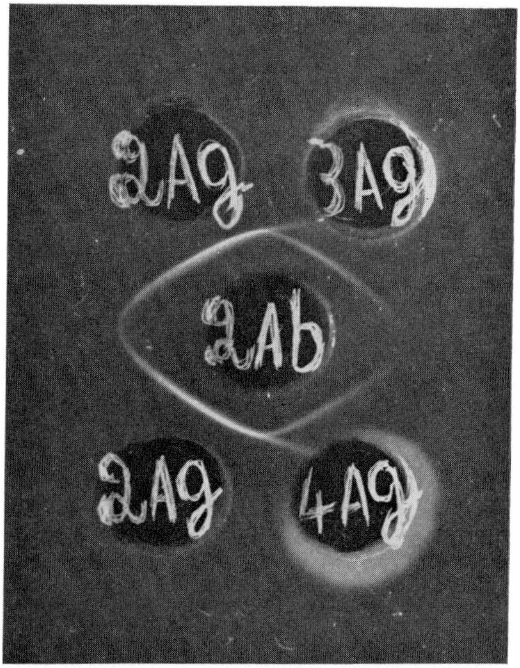

Figure 8. Relationship between dengue-2 antibody (*center well*) and dengue-2 and dengue-3 SCF antigens (*upper wells*) and dengue-2 and dengue-4 SCF antigens (*lower wells*). Spurs are visible between both pairs of antigens.

served when immune ascitic fluids were tested with SCF antigens than when crude saline antigens were used. This may be explained by the presence of an antigenic determinant (or determinants) in the crude saline antigen which is not present in the SCF preparations if the antibody directed against this component is in higher titer than antibodies directed against SCF antigen. In the case of dengue-4 ascitic fluid, heterologous reacting antibodies appeared to react only with antigens other than those present in SCF. Smith *et al.* demonstrated that, in addition to SCF, two hemagglutinins present in crude suspensions of dengue-2 infectious mouse brain or cell culture have CF reactivity (9). It appears that one or more of the CF-reactive antigenic determinants present on the hemagglutinins is not present in the SCF antigens. The SCF antigen has been shown to be a non-structural virus-specific antigen (Brandt, W. E., Cardiff, R. D. and Russell, P. K., unpublished data), thus it is not surprising that antibodies directed against SCF are separate from those directed against virion-associated antigens such as the hemagglutinins.

The antigenically active components in purified SCF antigen preparations have been shown to be proteins of a single molecular size (m.w. 39,000) when analyzed by gel filtration and electrophoresis on polyacrylamide gels (16). In some preparations of SCF antigen, another antigen was found as evidenced by the formation of a second immunoprecipitin line. This relative lack of purity of some of the SCF antigen preparations did not appear to affect the patterns of immunoprecipitation due to the major component and, hence, does not affect the interpretation of the results produced by SCF antigen *per se*.

The SCF antigen of each serotype, although of relatively small size, has both group and serotype-specific activity. SCF antigens of all four serotypes reacted with heterologous ascitic fluids when antigens were placed in the center wells. Fusion of the precipitin lines indicated the

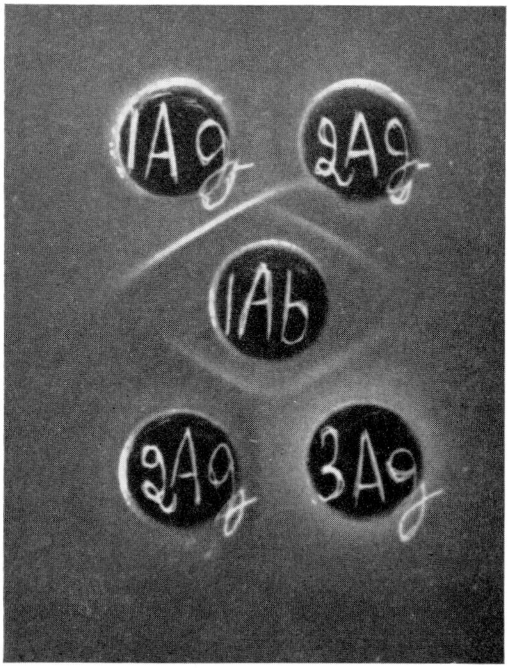

Figure 9. Relationship between dengue-1 antibody (*center well*) and dengue-1 and dengue-2 SCF antigens (*upper wells*) and dengue-2 and dengue-3 SCF antigens (*lower wells*). Fusion of precipitin lines without spur formation occurred between the two heterologous antigen wells.

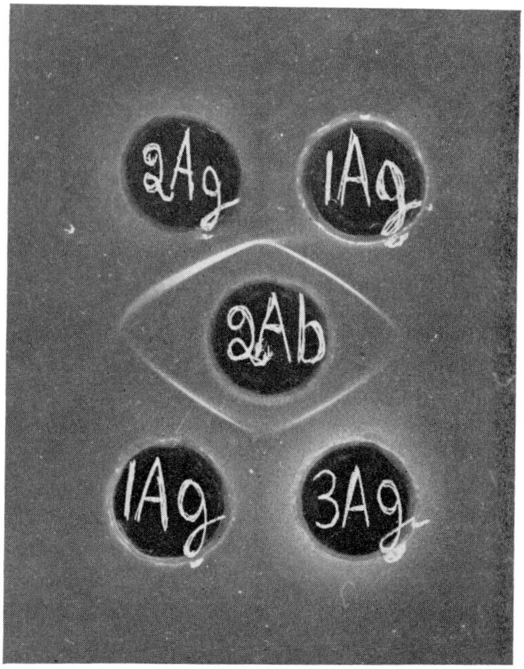

Figure 10. Relationship between dengue-2 antibody (*center well*) and dengue-2 and dengue-1 SCF antigens (*upper wells*) and dengue-1 and dengue-3 antigens (*lower wells*). Fusion of precipitin lines without spur formation occurred between the two heterologous antigen wells.

common identity of this group-specific antigenic determinant, as did formation of lines of identity with one ascitic fluid *vs* two heterologous antigens. The absorption experiments proved the presence of the common determinant.

Differentiation between SCF antigens of the four serotypes could only be demonstrated by spur formation when antibody was placed in the center well. This type of reaction, designated as a type IV reaction by Ouchterlony (19), occurs when two antigenic determinants are linked together on the same molecule and separate populations of antibodies are produced against each determinant. Thus, the interpretation most consistent with the results of our immunoprecipitin analysis is that the SCF antigen of each serotype has two determinant groups, one of which is identical to the corresponding site on SCF antigens of the other serotypes; in addition, each has a type-specific antigenic determinant which is unique for the serotype. Serologic cross-reactivity of dengue SCF antigens, therefore, appears to be due to antigen-sharing rather than to true immunologic cross-reactions.

The immunogenicity of the common antigenic determinant on the SCF molecule appeared quite variable between serotypes. Dengue-4 ascitic fluid had little or no antibody directed at the common antigenic determinant of SCF in spite of the demonstrated presence of the common antigenic site on the dengue-4 SCF antigen by both CF and precipitin tests. The intensity of precipitin lines produced by dengue-3 ascitic fluids with common antigens was low compared to dengue-1 and dengue-2 ascitic fluids. Biologic variation may be the most likely explanation since variation of this nature was noted between lots of dengue-2 ascitic fluids. Differences in immunogenicity due to structural differences or differences in relative amounts of SCF antigen in the immunizing antigens are also possibilities.

The demonstration of differences in electrophoretic mobilities between the SCF antigens of the four dengue serotypes (16) lead to the speculation that the structural differences which result in the electrical charge differences are related to the type-specific antigenic determinants.

The biologic role of SCF antigen and antibodies produced against it during infection remains to be evaluated. Since SCF antigen is a non-structural, virus-specific protein, antibodies against SCF do not affect the virion and presumably can play no role in defense against infection. The failure of antibody against dengue-2 SCF to neutralize dengue-2 virus supports this concept (Brandt, W. E., Cardiff, R. D. and Russell, P. K., unpublished data).

SCF antigen is produced in both infected cell cultures and infected suckling mice and has been shown to be present in the blood of infected mice (14). It may contribute to *in vivo* antigen-antibody reactions and, thus, be involved in the pathogenesis of disease. The anamnestic antibody response which occurs in second dengue infections has been incriminated in the pathogenesis of the dengue shock syndrome (2). Because of the group-specific antigenic site on the SCF antigen, an anamnestic immunologic response to this determinant would be expected to occur during a second dengue virus infection and, hence, the SCF antigen may play a role in pathogenesis of the dengue shock syndrome.

The demonstration of a group-specific determinant on the SCF molecule only partially explains the antigenic relationships between dengue viruses since serologic cross-reactions observed by tests dependent on virion-associated antigens, such as hemagglutination-inhibition, are unrelated to the SCF system. Similarly, the specificity of the neutralization test is unrelated to the type-specific antigenic determinant on the SCF antigen. Knowledge of the antigenic make-up of the SCF antigen emphasizes the requirement for similar data pertinent to the structural proteins of the virion.

REFERENCES

1. Halstead, S. B., Yamarat, C. and Russell, P. K., Jap. J. Med. Sci. Biol., *20:* 96, 1967.
2. Russell, P. K., Intavivat, A. and Kanchanapilant, S., J. Immun., *102:* 412, 1969.
3. Stollar, V., Virology, *39:* 426, 1969.
4. Westaway, E. G. and Reedman, B. M., J. Virol., *4:* 688, 1969.
5. Trent, D. W., Qureshi, A. A. and Swensen, C. C., Bact. Proc., p. 161, 1969.
6. Casals, J., Bull. W. H. O., *24:* 723, 1961.
7. Stollar, V., Stevens, T. M. and Schlesinger, R. W., Virology, *30:* 303, 1966.
8. Hammon, W. McD. and Sather, G. E., Milit. Med., *129:* 130, 1965.
9. Smith, T. J., Brandt, W. E., Swanson, J. L., McCown, J. M. and Buescher, E. L., J. Virol., *5:* 524, 1970.
10. Chan, Y. C., Nature, *206:* 116, 1965.
11. Ibrahim, A. N. and Hammon, W. McD., J. Immun., *100:* 86, 1968.
12. Hawkes, R. A. and Marshall, I. D., Amer. J. Epidem., *86:* 28, 1967.
13. Clarke, D. E., Bull. W. H. O., *31:* 45, 1964.
14. Russell, P. K., Brandt, W. E., Smith, T. J. and Buescher, E. L., Fed. Proc., *28:* 2, 1969.
15. Brandt, W. E., Smith, T. J., Buescher, E. L. and Russell, P. K., Bact. Proc., p. 186, 1969.
16. Cardiff, R. D., McCloud, T. G., Brandt, W. E. and Russell, P. K., Virology, *41:* 569, 1970.
17. Brandt, W. E., Buescher, E. L. and Hetrick, F. M., Amer. J. Trop. Med., *16:* 339, 1967.
18. Kent, J. F. and Fife, E. H., Jr., Amer. J. Trop. Med., *12:* 103, 1963.
19. Ouchterlony, O., in *Immunological Methods*, Edited by J. F. Ackroyd, F. A. Davis Co., Philadelphia, 1964.

THE JOURNAL OF IMMUNOLOGY
Vol. 105, No. 4, October 1970

STUDIES OF MALEYLATED CHAINS OF HUMAN IgM[1]

A. F. S. A. HABEEB, RALPH E. SCHROHENLOHER AND J. CLAUDE BENNETT[2]

From the Division of Clinical Immunology and Rheumatology, Department of Medicine and Departments of Microbiology and Biochemistry, University of Alabama in Birmingham, The Medical Center, Birmingham, Alabama 35233

Received for publication May 13, 1970

An approach to the isolation and physicochemical study of the chains of IgM is presented. The chains were separated after mild reduction in the absence of guanidine as the maleylated derivatives. The maleylated μ and κ chains were isolated in pure form with their intrachain disulfide bonds intact by gel filtration on Sephadex G-200 in Tris-glycine buffer, pH 8.9. Disulfide bond titration of these modified chains revealed 17 such bonds per 7S IgM subunit (5 interchain + 8 intrachain per 2 μ + 4 intrachain per 2 κ). These findings agreed well with the finding of 18 disulfides per subunit obtained on reduction of 19S IgM for 6 hr in 3M guanidine. The maleylated chains were soluble permitting the determination of the molecular weight from the sedimentation and diffusion coefficients in the absence of denaturing agent. The molecular weight determined from these values for the maleylated μ chain was 80,000 and that for the maleylated κ chain was 23,000. Based on the number of maleyl groups on the respective chains, the molecular weight of unmodified μ chain was 75,000 and that of unmodified κ chain was 22,000.

Studies of IgM have revealed that the molecule consists of five subunits of molecular weight 180,000 to 200,000 (1–3). Each subunit has been reported to consist of either two heavy chains and two light chains (1, 3) or of two heavy and three light chains (2). Mild reduction results in formation of 7S subunits in which the heavy and light chains are held together by non-covalent bonds. Dissociation of the heavy and light chains has been achieved by 1 M propionic acid. Such isolated heavy chains show a tendency to aggregate, which may be prevented by the presence of 6 M guanidine. Light chains isolated in this manner also have a tendency to form dimers (2).

The object of the present work was to isolate the heavy and light chains of IgM in the absence of denaturing agents as the maleylated derivatives. A note on this approach has already appeared (4). The introduction of maleyl groups resulted in electrostatic repulsions of sufficient magnitude to counteract hydrophobic and other non-covalent attractive forces, which hold the chains together. These maleylated chains were easily soluble in Tris-glycine buffer and suitable for physicochemical studies. Data obtained with the modified chains were compared with those reported in the literature.

MATERIALS AND METHODS

Materials. 5,5′-Dithiobis (nitrobenzoic acid)[3] reagent was obtained from Aldrich Chemical Co., Milwaukee, Wis.; trinitrobenzene sulfonic acid from Eastman Kodak Co., Rochester, N. Y.; maleic anhydride from Fisher Scientific Co., Westford, Mass.; Sephadex G-200 and blue dextran 2000 from Pharmacia Chemical Co., Piscataway, N. Y.; bovine serum albumin from Pentex, Inc., Kankakee, Ill.; human IgG and ovalbumin from Nutritional Biochemicals Corp., Cleveland, Ohio; and guanidine hydrochloride, ultra pure, from Mann Research Laboratories, New York, N. Y.

Isolation of IgM. Euglobulin was isolated from the plasma of a patient with Waldenström's

[1] This work was supported by grants from National Institutes of Health and the John A. Hartford Foundation, Inc., of New York.

[2] John and Mary R. Markle Scholar in Academic Medicine and Research. Career Development Awardee (K3 GM 25386).

[3] Abbreviations used are: IgM, immunoglobulin M; IgG, immunoglobulin G; DTNB, 5,5′-dithiobis (nitrobenzoic acid); IgMs, subunit if IgM; ML-, maleyl; SDS, sodium dodecyl sulfate.

macroglobulinemia by precipitation with a 15-fold excess of cold distilled water. The precipitate was resuspended in saline and the procedure was repeated twice. Ultracentrifugal analysis demonstrated that the resulting preparation contained only trace amounts of 7S materials in addition to the major macroglobulin component sedimentating at 19S and minor components sedimenting at 25S and 30S. The light chains of the IgM were type K.

Reduction of IgM and the maleylated chains in the absence and presence of guanidine. Disulfide reduction was performed with 0.05 M β-mercaptoethanol in 0.1 M sodium phosphate buffer, pH 7.0, containing 0.5 mg EDTA/ml essentially as described previously (5). The concentration of guanidine hydrochloride in the final reaction mixture varied from 0 to 5.1 M. The liberated sulfhydryl groups were determined by the DTNB reagent of Ellman (6) as described by Habeeb (7). The number of disulfide groups was calculated using a subunit molecular weight of 180,000, a μ chain molecular weight of 75,000, and κ chain molecular weight of 22,000.

Reduction and alkylation of IgM. A 2% solution of IgM in 0.1 M sodium phosphate buffer, pH 7.0, containing 0.5 mg EDTA/ml was reduced with 0.05 M β-mercaptoethanol at room temperature for 1 hr. Alkylation was carried out with a 1.6-fold molar excess of iodoacetamide, at pH 8.0 for 15 min. The completeness of reaction was tested with DTNB. After alkylation, the solution was dialyzed against water and freeze dried.

Reaction of reduced and alkylated IgM with maleic anhydride. Reduced and alkylated IgM solution (2%) in 0.1 M sodium phosphate buffer, pH 8.0, was reacted with maleic anhydride at room temperature for 30 min (8). A sufficient quantity of the anhydride was added as a stock solution (50 mg/ml) in dioxane to provide a threefold molar excess of reagent over the free amino groups. The pH of the reaction mixture was maintained at 8.0 by adding NaOH. After reaction, the protein (ML-IgMs) was dialyzed against water and freeze dried.

Determination of the extent of modification of amino groups. Free amino groups were determined by reaction with trinitrobenzene sulfonic acid (9, 10). A solution of unmodified IgM served as the standard and was considered to contain 100% free amino groups. Protein concentration was derived from absorbance at 280 nm, using an extinction coefficient, $E_{1cm}^{1\%}$ of 12.0 for IgM subunit (1).

Determination of the esterification of phenolic groups of tyrosine residues in ML-IgMs. The spectrophotometric method of Riordan and Vallee (11) which depends on the lability of the ester linkages to hydroxylamine was used. A solution of ML-IgMs in 0.05 M sodium borate buffer, pH 7.5, was treated with an equal volume of 0.2 M hydroxylamine hydrochloride previously adjusted to pH 7.5. Absorbance of treated and untreated ML-IgM was measured at 280 nm at intervals between 0 to 18 hr.

Determination of esterification of serine and threonine residues. In view of the recent observation that serine and threonine are esterified by acid anhydrides (12), the number of ester bonds formed with these amino acid residues was determined by reaction with hydroxylamine as described by Habeeb and Atassi (13). Glycine methyl ester HCl was used as a standard.

Fractionation of ML-IgMs on Sephadex G-200. Sephadex G-200 was allowed to swell in pH 8.9 Tris-glycine buffer (0.043 M Tris and 0.046 M glycine) for 1 week and then packed into a 3.5- x 100-cm column. Two hundred milligrams of ML-IgMs dissolved in 10 ml of buffer were applied to the column and eluted with the same Tris-glycine buffer. Fractions of 8 ml were collected and the absorbance was read at 280 nm. Protein peaks were pooled, dialyzed against water and freeze dried. Rechromatography in the same system was performed if necessary for further purification.

Disc electrophoresis. Electrophoresis was performed in 7.5% polyacrylamide gel using pH 8.9 Tris-glycine buffer (0.043 M Tris and 0.046 M glycine) as described previously (14) and also in pH 7.2 sodium phosphate-sodium dodecyl sulfate-urea buffer (15).

Amino acid analysis. Samples were hydrolyzed with constant boiling HCl in sealed tubes for 24 hr and subjected to amino acid analysis on the Beckman model 120 C automatic amino acid analyzer using 55-cm and 8-cm column separations for neutral and acidic, and basic amino acids respectively. Tryptophan was determined by reaction with *o*-nitrobenzene sulfenyl chloride in 99% formic acid for 3 hr (16).

Determination of sedimentation rates. Sedimentation analysis was carried out in a Spinco model E ultracentrifuge at a temperature of

20°C, using 12-mm single sector cells for the ML-IgMs and ML-μ chain preparations and a 12-mm cup type synthetic boundary cell for ML-κ chain preparations. Except where otherwise noted, samples were dissolved in the pH 8.9 Tris-glycine buffer. Measurements on patterns were made with a Nikon microcomparator. Concentrations of sedimenting materials were estimated from areas under boundaries, applying appropriate corrections for radial dilution. Sedimentation rates were calculated and corrected to standard condition ($s_{20,w}$) as described by Schachman (17, 18). The sedimentation rates of ML-μ chain and ML-κ chain at infinite dilution ($\mathring{s}_{20,w}$) were estimated by the linear extrapolation of the $s_{20,w}$ values determined at five different concentrations of the sample, using the method of least squares.

Determination of Stokes radius and diffusion coefficients. A 1.3- x 120-cm column was packed with Sephadex G-200 in the pH 8.9 Tris-glycine buffer. The column was calibrated with bovine serum albumin, human IgG, ovalbumin and blue dextran to obtain the value of the effective pore radius, as described previously (19). Data from Table III of Ackers (20) were used to calculate the Stokes radius of the ML-μ and ML-κ chains from their elution volume on the calibrated Sephadex column. The diffusion coefficient (D) was calculated from the Stokes radius (a) by the equation:

$$D = RT/6\pi\eta N a$$

where R is the gas constant (8.3×10^7 ergs degree^{-1} mol^{-1}); T is the absolute temperature; η is the viscosity of solvent; and N is Avogadro's number (6.02×10^{23}).

Diffusion studies on the ML-μ and ML-κ chains were also performed in a Spinco model E ultracentrifuge, using a double sector capillary type synthetic boundary cell and schlieren optics. The centrifuge was operated at 3617 rpm and the temperature was regulated at 20°C. Samples were analyzed in pH 8.9 Tris-glycine buffer. Pattern measurements were as described for the determination of sedimentation rates. Diffusion coefficients were calculated by the "maximum ordinate-area" method of Ehrenberg (21) and were corrected to standard conditions ($D_{20,w}$) as described by Schachman (17). The diffusion coefficient at infinite dilution ($\mathring{D}_{20,w}$) was estimated by linear extrapolation of the $D_{20,w}$ values obtained for two or four determinations at each of three different sample concentrations, using the method of least squares.

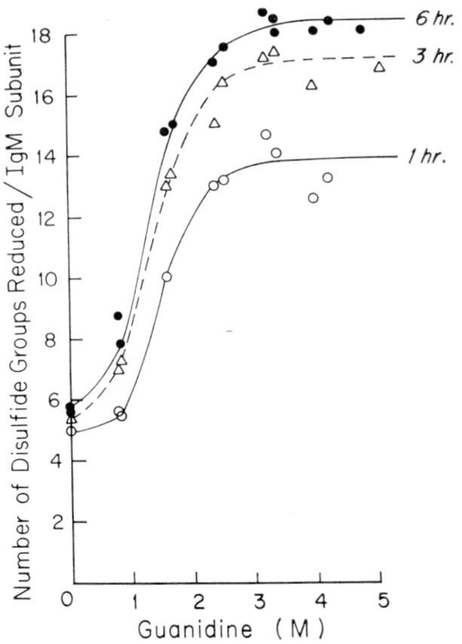

Figure 1. Number of disulfide bonds reduced in IgM in the absence and presence of guanidine at pH 7 with 0.05 M β-mercaptoethanol.

Calculation of molecular weights. Molecular weights were calculated from the $\mathring{s}_{20,w}$ values and $\mathring{D}_{20,w}$ values using the Svedberg equation (22). The partial specific volumes of μ and κ chains were assumed to be the same as that determined for the IgM subunit by Miller and Metzger (1). However, corrections were made to take into account the introducted maleyl groups in maleylated chains. This was calculated using the values published by Cohn and Edsall (23). The volume increase was 52.1 ml per maleyl group. Since a negatively charged maleyl group replaced a positively charged ammonium group, electrostriction due to charge was unchanged (23). The calculated partial specific volume of ML-μ chain (containing 50 maleyl groups) was 0.710 and that for ML-κ chain (containing 10 maleyl groups) was 0.717.

RESULTS

Reduction of IgM with β-mercaptoethanol. Figure 1 shows the number of disulfide bonds reduced per IgM subunit as a function of time and guanidine concentration. A maximum of approximately 5 bonds was reduced in the absence of guanidine which corresponded to interchain

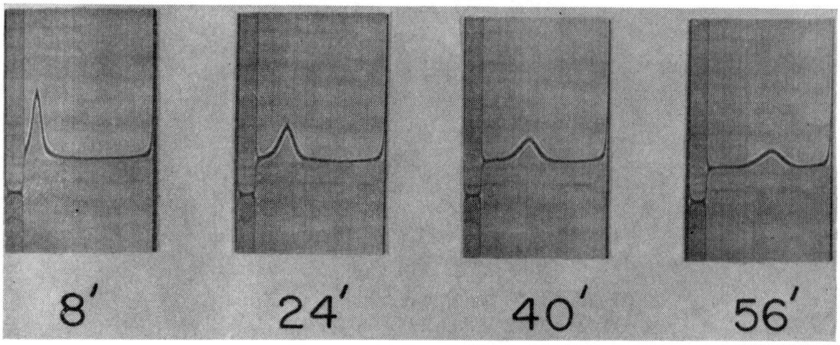

Figure 2. Ultracentrifugal patterns of reduced and alkylated unmodified IgM. Photographs were taken at the indicated times after acceleration to 59,780 rpm using a phase plate angle of 60°. Sedimentation in this and subsequent illustrations of ultracentrifugal patterns proceeds from left to right.

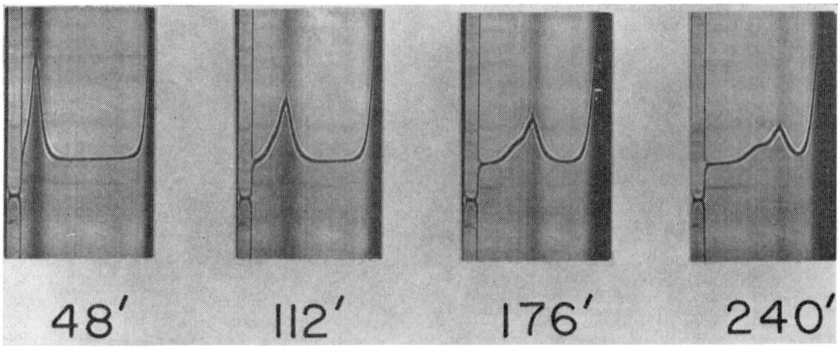

Figure 3. Ultracentrifugal patterns of reduced and alkylated ML-IgM. Photographs were taken at the indicated times after acceleration to 59,780 rpm using a phase plate angle of 60°.

and intersubunit disulfide bonds (as shown later by disc electrophoresis where light and heavy chains were formed). The progressive reduction of intrachain disulfide bonds took place on increasing both the guanidine concentration and time of reaction. A guanidine concentration of 3 to 3.5 M gave maximum reduction at any given time. A total of 18 disulfide bonds/IgM subunit were reduced with β-mercaptoethanol after 6 hr in guanidine. These corresponded to interchain, intersubunit and intrachain disulfide bonds.

Formation of IgM subunits. IgM was reduced in the absence of guanidine and alkylated as described. The preparation used in these studies had 4.4 disulfide bonds reduced/IgM subunit of 180,000. When subjected to ultracentrifugal analysis in the pH 8.9 Tris-glycine buffer, it showed a single boundary having an $s_{20,w}$ value of 6.6S at a protein concentration of 3.3 mg/ml (Fig. 2).

Reaction of IgM subunits with maleic anhydride. Reaction of reduced and alkylated IgM with maleic anhydride resulted in modification of 93% of the amino groups as determined by the trinitrobenzene sulfonic acid method. There was no observed esterification of the phenolic hydroxy group, but there was esterification of serine and threonine as determined by the hydroxylamine test. The maleylated subunit (ML-IgMs) showed two components upon ultracentrifugal analysis in the pH 8.9 Tris-glycine buffer (Fig. 3). When analyzed at a protein concentration of 7.3 mg/ml, the major component sedimented at 2.0S and the minor component sedimented at approximately 1.4S. It is evident that maleylation of IgM subunit produces two discrete molecular species which are detectable in the ultracentrifuge. These molecular populations represent the heavy and light chains (as shown by subsequent work described below).

Analysis of reduced and alkylated IgM by disc electrophoresis (Fig. 4) in sodium phosphate-SDS buffer indicated that heavy and light chains were produced by mild reduction (cleavage of

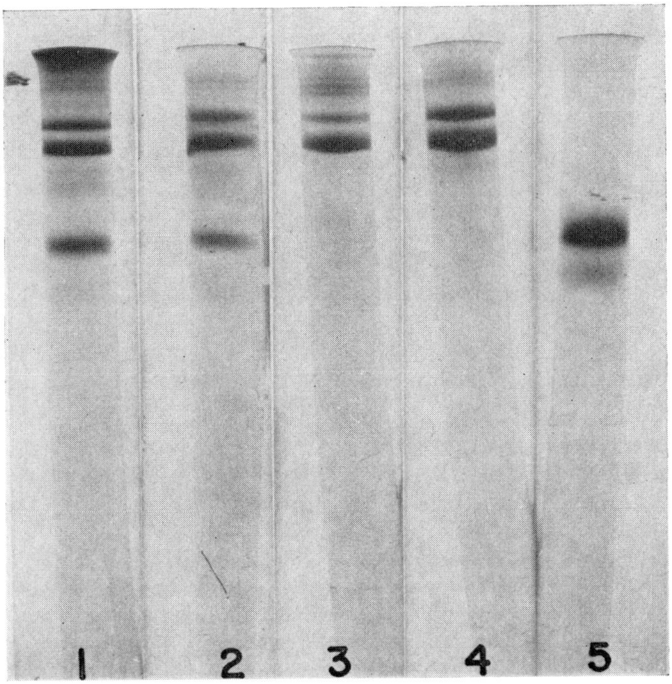

Figure 4. Disc electrophoresis in sodium phosphate-SDS buffer. *1*, IgMs; *2*, ML-IgMs; *3, 4 and 5*, pre-peak F1, F1 and F2, respectively, obtained by subjecting ML-IgMs to Sephadex chromatography (see Fig. 6).

about 5 disulfide bonds). The heavy chains appear as double bands in mildly reduced and alkylated IgM, but as only one band in extensively reduced and alkylated IgM (24). The ML-IgMs showed an electrophoretic pattern in this system similar to that of mildly reduced and alkylated IgM but with the absence of aggregates at the top of the gel.

When subjected to disc electrophoresis in the pH 8.9 Tris-glycine buffer (Fig. 5) reduced and alkylated IgM showed a single band near the top of the gel, but the maleylated derivative demonstrated dissociation into heavy and light chains. Replacement of the positively charged ammonium groups of lysine residues by negatively charged carboxyl groups introduced electrostatic repulsions of sufficient magnitude to counteract attractive non-covalent interactions that exist between the heavy and light chains.

Since the two components of maleylated reduced and alkylated IgM could be separated by both electrophoresis and ultracentrifugation in pH 8.9 Tris-glycine buffer, chromatography on Sephadex G-200 in pH 8.9 buffer was performed to fractionate the heavy and light chains.

Separation of heavy and light chains of ML-IgMs. Figure 6 shows the elution pattern of ML-IgMs from the Sephadex G-200 column with pH 8.9 Tris-glycine buffer. Two components of distinct molecular size were obtained corresponding to heavy and light chains (obtained as maleylated derivatives). Each protein peak was pooled, dialyzed and freeze dried. Disc electrophoresis in the pH 8.9 Tris-glycine system showed the progress of chain separation and homogeneity of each chain (Fig. 5). In some preparations a peak preceded the heavy chain on Sephadex chromatography. Disc electrophoresis in the sodium phosphate-SDS buffer indicated that the material was aggregated ML-μ chain (Fig. 4). It is evident from the results of the gel filtration and disc electrophoresis that the ML-μ and ML-κ chains were effectively separated from each other. They were, therefore, subjected to further chemical and physicochemical characterization.

Determination of intrachain disulfide bonds in ML-μ and ML-κ chains. In order to investigate whether the intrachain disulfide bonds were intact in the isolated maleylated chains, the

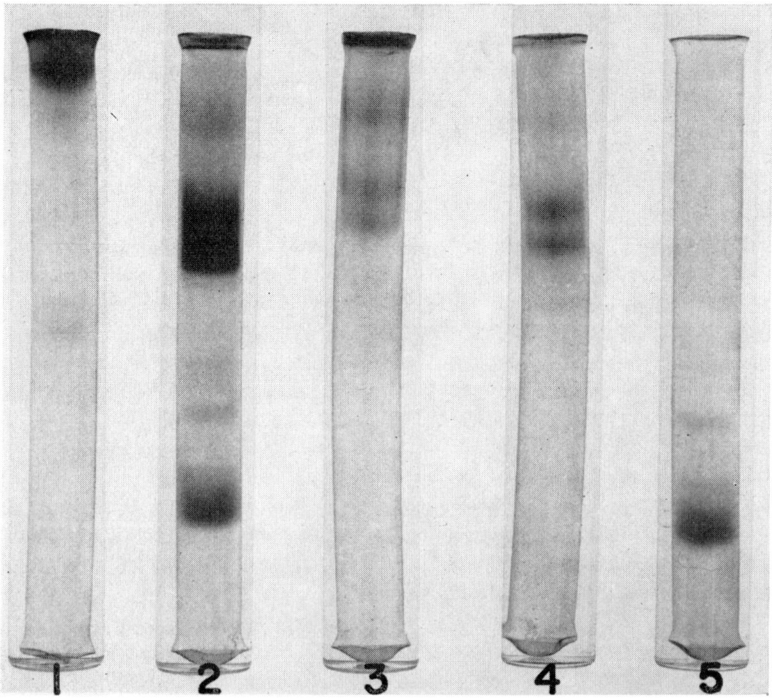

Figure 5. Disc electrophoresis in Tris-glycine buffer (symbols as in Fig. 4).

maleylated chains were reduced with β-mercaptoethanol in the absence and presence of guanidine. Figure 7 shows that 4 intrachain disulfide bonds were intact in the ML-μ chain and 1.6 in the ML-κ chain. All the intrachain disulfide bonds were reducible in 1 hr in the presence of 2 to 2.5 M guanidine. Increasing the time of reduction to 6 hr or increasing the concentration of guanidine to 5.1 M was without effect.

Amino acid analysis of ML-μ chain. Table I shows the number of amino acid residues/mol of heavy chain (molecular weight 75,000). The value of 7 half-cystine residues obtained by amino acid analysis compares favorably with 8 half-cystines determined by DTNB. Reaction with maleic anhydride, in addition to modifying 27 amino groups, resulted in esterification of 21 residues of serine, threonine, or both.

Sedimentation studies on ML-μ and ML-κ chains. The ML-μ and ML-κ chains each sedimented as a single boundary when analyzed in the pH 8.9 Tris-glycine buffer (Figs. 8 and 9). The relationship of sample concentration to the sedimentation rate is illustrated in Figure 10. The sedimentation rate at infinite dilution ($\mathring{s}_{20,w}$) was found to be 3.41S for ML-μ chains and 1.84S for ML-κ chains. A slight asymmetry of the boundaries was noted as sedimentation progressed. The effect of concentration on the sedimentation rate suggests that this was due to self-sharpening of the boundary (18). In contrast to the above results, aggregation was noted upon analysis of the ML-μ chain in the same buffer made 0.1 M with respect to sodium chloride.

Diffusion studies on ML-μ and ML-κ chains. The diffusion coefficients of both the ML-μ and ML-κ chains, as determined by the method of Ehrenberg (21), demonstrated positive concentration dependence, which appeared to be linear (Fig. 11). The diffusion coefficient at infinite dilution ($\mathring{D}_{20,w}$) of ML-μ chain was found to be 3.6×10^{-7} cm^2sec^{-1} and that for ML-κ chain was 6.9×10^{-7} cm^2sec^{-1}.

The Stokes radius of the ML-μ chain (obtained from the calibrated Sephadex column) was 6.6 nm and that of the ML-κ chain was 3.1 nm. Calculation of the diffusion coefficients gave values of 3.2×10^{-7} cm^2sec^{-1} and 6.8×10^{-7} cm^2sec^{-1} for the ML-μ chain and ML-κ chain, respectively.

Molecular weight of ML-μ and ML-κ chains. The molecular weight of the ML-μ chain, as

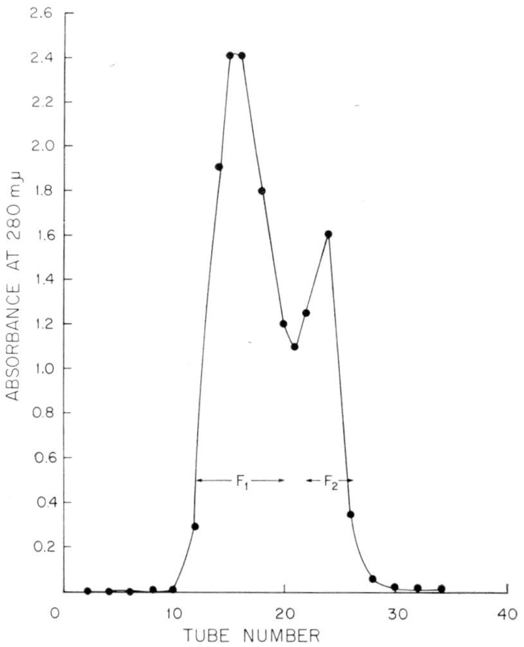

Figure 6. Elution pattern of ML-IgMs on Sephadex G-200 using pH 8.9 Tris-glycine buffer as eluant. F1 and F2 represent μ and κ chains, respectively, as shown from disc electrophoresis.

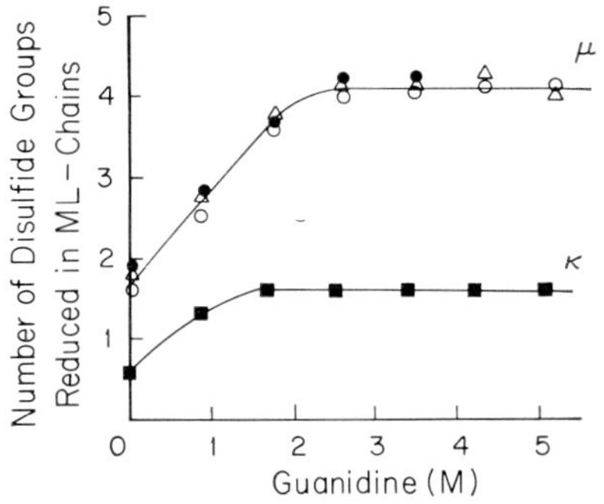

Figure 7. Susceptibility and number of disulfide bonds reduced in ML-μ and ML-κ chains in the absence and presence of guanidine. ML-μ chain—○, 1 hr; △, 3 hr; and ●, 6 hr; ML-κ chain—■, 1 hr.

calculated from the $D^{\circ}_{20,w}$ and sedimentation data, was 80,000 and that for ML-κ chain was 23,000. Since the ML-μ chain was found to contain approximately 50 maleyl groups, the molecular weight of the unmodified chain represented by the sample was 75,000. The presence of 10 maleyl groups/ML-κ chain indicated that the molecular weight of the unmodified κ chain was 22,000.

TABLE I

Amino acid analysis of the maleylated heavy chain of IgM[a]

	1	2	3	Mean	No. of Residues to Nearest Integer
Asp	51.5	51.5	51.0	51.3	51
Thr	60.0	60.5	59.0	60.0	60
Ser	69.0	70.5	69.0	69.5	70
Glu	65.0	67.0	65.0	65.7	66
Pro	39.0	43.5	38.0	40.2	40
Gly	43.0	43.0	42.7	42.9	43
Ala	41.0	41.0	41.0	41.0	41
Cys/$_2$	6.4	6.6	6.9	6.63	7
Val	51.0	53.5	51.5	52.0	52
Met	7.8	6.2	7.5	7.2	7
Ileu	18.5	19.0	18.3	18.6	19
Leu	48.0	49.0	49.0	48.7	49
Tyr	16.4	16.4	16.2	16.3	16
Phe	24.0	23.7	23.5	23.7	24
Glucosamine	8.7		8.1	8.4	8
Lys	29.0	31.2	27.4	29.3	29
His	10.0	11.6	9.3	10.3	10
Arg	29.0	30.0	28.6	29.2	29
Try	10.0				10
Cys/$_2$[b]	8.0	7.7	8.8	8.2	8
Ester groups[c]				21.0	21

[a] Number of amino acid residues/mol of heavy chain (molecular weight 75,000).

[b] Determined by DTNB as described in text after reduction with β-mercaptoethanol in 3 M guanidine HCl for 1 hr.

[c] Determined by hydroxylamine method.

DISCUSSION

Reduction of IgM under the mild conditions described in this report results in cleavage of about 5 interchain disulfide bonds/7S subunit. These subunits are made up of heavy and light chains held together by noncovalent bonds. Maleylation, which introduces electrostatic repulsions, resulted in complete dissociation of the μ and κ chains in pH 8.9 Tris-glycine buffer. Similar electrostatic repulsions introduced by succinylation have been found to result in complete dissociation of non-covalently linked subunits of proteins, e.g., hemerythrin, at neutral pH (25). After succinylation of partially reduced rabbit IgG, Lenard and Singer (26) were able to separate the heavy and light chains on Sephadex

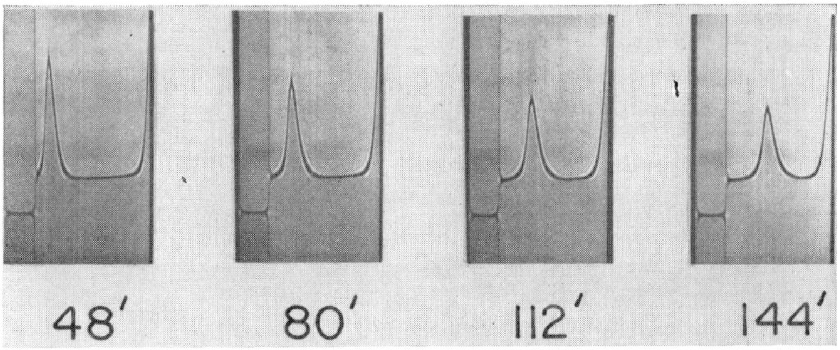

Figure 8. Ultracentrifugal patterns of ML-μ chain (7.3 mg/ml). Photographs were taken at the indicated times after acceleration to 59,780 rpm using a phase plate angle of 60°.

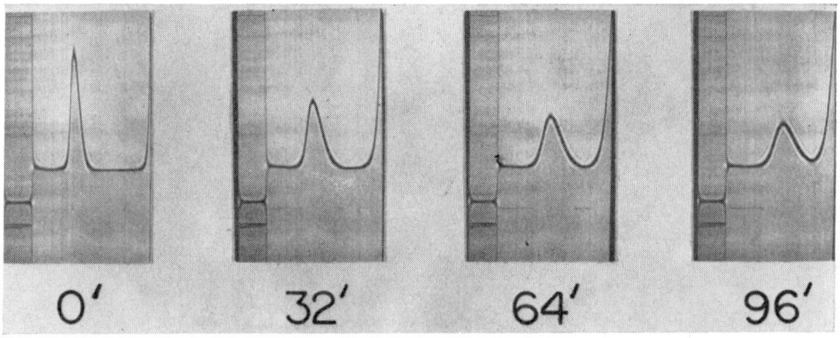

Figure 9. Ultracentrifugal patterns of ML-κ chain (7.1 mg/ml). Photographs were taken at the indicated times after acceleration of 59,780 rpm using a phase plate angle of 60°.

G-200 using 0.01 Tris buffer, pH 8.2. Recently, Bezkorovainy, *et al.* (27) separated human 7S and bovine colostral immunoglobulin into their heavy and light chains after succinylation of the reduced and alkylated immunoglobulins.

The maleylated μ and κ chains were isolated in pure form on a Sephadex G-200 column. Both chains had intact intrachain disulfide bonds. The μ chain was found to contain 4 intrachain disulfide bonds, which is in agreement with the data of Beale and Buttress (28), while the κ chain contained about 2. The total number of intrachain and interchain disulfide bonds/IgM subunit was 17 (5 interchain + 8 intrachain/2 μ + 4 intrachain/2 κ). This is in close agreement with the value of 18 disulfides/IgMs obtained when the whole molecule of IgM was reduced in the presence of 2.5 to 3 M guanidine for 6 hr. It is of note that the intrachain disulfide bond of both the maleylated μ and κ chains showed greater susceptibility to reduction than did those of whole 19S IgM (reduction was complete at 1 hr in 2.5 M guanidine).

The order in which reduction and maleylation

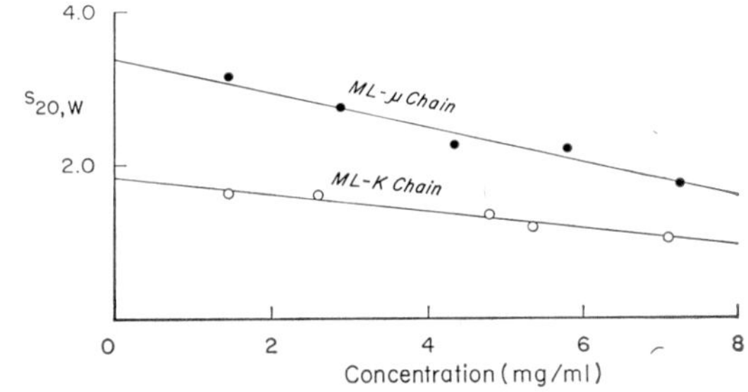

Figure 10. The dependence of the sedimentation coefficient of ML-μ and ML-κ chains on concentration.

is carried out is important to obtain chains with intact intrachain disulfide bonds. Reduction of native (19S) IgM permitted selective cleavage of interchain disulfide bonds, whereas reduction of maleylated IgM resulted in the additional cleavage of 3 or 4 intrachain disulfide bonds (Habeeb, unpublished data). These findings are in agreement with previous observations that succinylated bovine serum albumin and human γ globulin showed increased susceptibility of the

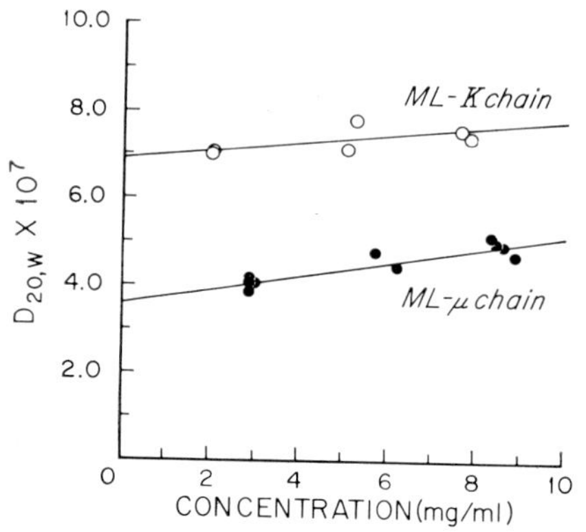

Figure 11. The dependence of the diffusion coefficient of ML-μ and ML-κ chains on concentration. $D_{20,w}$ is expressed in cm²/sec.

disulfide groups to reduction (5, 7, 26) presumably due to conformational changes.

The μ chain had a Stokes radius of 6.6 nm and the light chain 3.1 nm. These values are much higher than globular proteins of comparable molecular weights. Bovine serum albumin (m.w. 69,000) had a Stokes radius of 3.6 nm and trypsin (m.w. 23,800) had a Stokes radius of 1.94 nm. The increase in the Stokes radius found for the ML-μ and ML-κ chains is due to increased asymmetry as a result of maleylation and is in agreement with the previous findings of an increase in the Stokes radius of bovine serum albumin and human IgG on succinylation (5, 19). There was close agreement of the diffusion coefficients for ML-κ chains obtained from both the ultracentrifuge and Sephadex column studies. However, the diffusion coefficient of the ML-μ chain obtained by the Sephadex column study was slightly lower than that from the ultracentrifuge (3.2×10^{-7} cm² sec^{-1} compared to 3.57×10^{-7} cm² sec^{-1}). This deviation may be due to the great asymmetry and increased Stokes radius of the ML-μ chain and the fact that it is eluted close to the void volume of the column. Previous studies (5) on various succinylated bovine serum albumin derivatives showed a very close agreement of their diffusion coefficients determined by both the ultracentrifuge and Sephadex G-200 column.

Ultracentrifugal studies on immunoglobulin polypeptide chains usually require the presence of unfolding reagents, such as guanidine or urea, in order to prevent aggregation. However, aggregation of ML-immunoglobulin polypeptide chains, as demonstrated by the present study, can be prevented by low ionic strength and hence dilute buffer of the proper pH. Due to the high concentrations of guanidine or urea required when studying unmodified chains, corrections for the viscosity and density of the solvent are large. In contrast, such corrections are relatively small for the buffer used in the analysis of ML-immunoglobulin chains. Therefore, uncertainties arising out of such factors as the non-ideal nature of the experimental system and an inexact knowledge of the relative viscosity and density of the unfolding reagent under the conditions of the experiment are minimized.

Ultracentrifugal analysis of the maleylated protein derivatives as performed in the present study involved the sedimentation of highly charged molecules in a low ionic strength buffer. Such systems are subject to charge effect (29). As a result of this phenomenon, the observed sedimentation rate of a charged molecule at some finite concentration in a low ionic strength buffer is less than that which would be observed for the molecule at the same concentration in a buffer of high ionic strength. However, charge effects are inoperative at infinite dilution and sedimentation coefficients determined by extrapolation to zero concentration are considered to be free of charge effects (30). Kronman and Foster (30) observed that the error in determining the sedimentation coefficients of bovine serum albumin at infinite dilution in 0.02 M NaCl, pH 2, was at most 1%. Similarly, Habeeb (5) found that the $s^{\circ}_{20,w}$ for highly succinylated bovine serum albumin was free of charge effects.

The value of 75,000 for the molecular weight of the μ chain is slightly higher than the reported values of 70,000 for rabbit μ chain (3) and 66,000 for human μ chain (2). The reason for this apparent difference may be due to the use of aqueous buffer in this work as opposed to use of 5 M guanidine solution during ultracentrifugation by other workers. Confidence in the value of 75,000 and further support for the use of soluble derivatives of proteins for physicochemical studies stem from the close agreement of the value of molecular weight of κ chain (22,000) as determined in the present study with that found in the literature (2, 3). Previous studies on the μ chain from this macroglobulin by gel filtration on Sephadex G-200 in 5 M guanidine have also indicated a molecular weight of 75,000 (24).

Acknowledgments. The authors wish to acknowledge the capable technical assistance of Annette Jones, Freda Moore, Karin Acton and Wallis Harrison.

REFERENCES

1. Miller, F. and Metzger, H., J. Biol. Chem., *240:* 3325, 1965.
2. Suzuki, T. and Deutsch, H. F., J. Biol. Chem., *242:* 2725, 1967.
3. Lamm, M. E. and Small, P. A., Jr., Biochemistry, *5:* 267 1966.
4. Habeeb, A. F. S. A., Schrohenloher, R. E. and Bennett, J. C., Fed. Proc., *29:* 641, Abstract, 1970.
5. Habeeb, A. F. S. A., Arch. Biochem., *121:* 652, 1967.
6. Ellman, G. L., Arch. Biochem., *82:* 70, 1959.
7. Habeeb, A. F. S. A., Biochim. Biophys. Acta, *115:* 440, 1966.
8. Butler, P. J. G., Harris, J. I., Hartley, B. S. and Liberman, R., Biochem. J., *103:* 78P, 1967.
9. Habeeb, A. F. S. A., Anal. Biochem., *14:* 328, 1966.
10. Habeeb, A. F. S. A., Arch. Biochem., *119:* 264, 1967.
11. Riodan, J. F. and Vallee, B. L., Biochemistry, *3:* 1768, 1964.
12. Gounaris, A. D. and Perlmann, G. E., J. Biol. Chem., *242:* 2739, 1967.
13. Habeeb, A. F. S. A. and Atassi, M. Z., Immunochemistry, *6:* 555, 1969.
14. Habeeb, A. F. S. A., Arch. Biochem., *130:* 430, 1969.
15. Maizel, J. V., Jr., Science, *151:* 988, 1966.
16. Scoffone, E., Fontana, A. and Rocchi, R., Biochem. Biophys. Res. Commun., *25:* 170, 1966.
17. Schachman, H. K., *Methods in Enzymology*, Edited by S. P. Colowick and N. O. Kaplan, Vol. 4, p. 32, Academic Press, Inc., N. Y., 1957.
18. Schachman, H. K., *Ultracentrifugation in Biochemistry*, Academic Press, Inc., New York, 1959.
19. Habeeb, A. F. S. A., Biochim. Biophys. Acta, *121:* 21, 1966.
20. Ackers, G. K., Biochemistry, *3:* 723, 1964.
21. Ehrenberg, A., Acta Chem. Scand., *11:* 1257, 1957.
22. Svedberg, T. and Pederson, K. O., *The Ultracentrifuge*, Oxford University Press, London, 1940.
23. Cohn, E. J. and Edsall, J. T., *Proteins Amino Acids and Peptides*, p. 155, Rheinhold, New York, 1943.
24. Bennett, J. C., Arch. Biochem., *131:* 551, 1969.
25. Klotz, I. M. and Keresztes Nagy, S., Biochemistry, *2:* 448, 1963.
26. Lenard, J. and Singer, S. J., Nature, *210:* 536, 1966.
27. Bezkorovainy, A., Zschocke, R., and Grohlich, D., J. Immun., *104:* 648, 1970.
28. Beale, D. and Buttress, N., Biochim. Biophys. Acta, *181:* 250, 1969.
29. Pedersen, K. O., J. Phys. Chem., *62:* 1282, 1958.
30. Kronman, M. J. and Foster, J. F., Arch. Biochem., *72:* 205, 1957.

THE JOURNAL OF IMMUNOLOGY
Vol. 105, No. 4, October 1970

Printed in U.S.A.

IDENTIFICATION AND GENETIC CONTROL OF THE Mt-3 AND Mt-4 ALLOTYPES OF RABBIT SERUM α_2-MACROGLOBULIN[1, 2]

BERNARD H. BERNE,[3] SHELDON DRAY AND KATHERINE L. KNIGHT

From the Department of Microbiology, University of Illinois at the Medical Center, Chicago, Illinois

Received for publication May 12, 1970

Two rabbit serum α_2-macroglobulin (α_2M) allotypes, Mt-3 and Mt-4, which are distinct from the previously described Mtz1 and Mtz2 allelic allotypes of α_2M, were identified. The Mt-3 and Mt-4 allotypes are controlled by a pair of alleles at an autosomal locus that appears to be closely linked to the *Mtz* locus and not closely linked to the *Aa*, *Ab*, or *Af* immunoglobulin loci, or to the *Lpq* lipoprotein locus. Sera from *Mt-*^{3}*Mt-*^{4} heterozygous rabbits do not precipitate in agar gel double diffusion plates with either anti-Mt-3 or anti-Mt-4 antisera, but do inhibit the precipitation of each antiserum with serum from the corresponding homozygous rabbits. Serum from a heterozygous rabbit precipitates with a mixture of the two antisera, indicating that both Mt-3 and Mt-4 determinants are present on the same α_2M molecule and suggesting that Mt-3 and Mt-4 determinants are each present in a smaller number than that found on molecules from homozygous rabbits. Allelic exclusion does not occur at the molecular level in the *Mt-*^{3}*Mt-*^{4} heterozygous rabbit; in this respect, the Mt-3/Mt-4 system resembles the Mtz1/Mtz2 system, but is dissimilar from all other known serum allotype systems. Individual α_2M molecules possess allotypic specificities of both the Mtz1/Mtz2 and Mt-3/Mt-4 systems.

Genetic variants of serum proteins identified by differences in their antigenic properties with isoantisera are designated as allotypes. Allotypes of rabbit IgG[4] (1–3), IgM (4), and IgA (5) immunoglobulins, as well as of low-density lipoprotein (6), haptoglobin (7), α_1 aryl-esterase (8) and α_2-macroglobulin (α_2M), have been described. Allotypes have been used in elucidating the relationship of genetic control to the structure and cellular biosynthesis of these molecules (9–11).

The allotypes of α_2M previously described in reports from our laboratory (12, 13) were designated as Mtz1 and Mtz2. These were found to be controlled by a pair of allelic genes at an autosomal locus not closely linked to the heavy or light chain loci of immunoglobulins (12) or to the *Hph* haptoglobin (7), *Lpq* lipoprotein (14), or *Ess* esterase (8) loci. In *Mtz*^{1}*Mtz*^{1} or *Mtz*^{2}*Mtz*^{2} homozygous rabbits, nearly all α_2M molecules have the Mtz1 or the Mtz2 specificity, respectively. In an *Mtz*^{1}*Mtz*^{2} heterozygous rabbit, 60% to 80% of the α_2M molecules have both specificities, while the remaining molecules possess either Mtz1 or Mtz2. Hence, the allelic genes *Mtz*^{1} and *Mtz*^{2} contribute to the synthesis of the same molecule. Among the serum protein allotype systems investigated thus far, α_2M is the only one in which allelic exclusion does not occur at the molecular level. Because rabbit α_2M is a large glycoprotein molecule (m.w. approximately 850,000) and may have multiple polypeptide chains (15) and glycosidic residues, it seemed likely that additional allotypes might be found on this molecule, and that their discovery might further help to elucidate the structure and genetic control of the biosynthesis of this molecule.

This report describes the identification and

[1] Presented in part at the 54th Annual Meeting of the Federation of American Societies for Experimental Biology, Atlantic City, New Jersey, April 12–17, 1970.

[2] This investigation was supported in part by United States Public Health Service Grants AI 09241 and AI07043.

[3] In partial fulfillment of the requirements for the Doctor of Philosophy Degree in the Graduate College. Supported by a postdoctoral fellowship from the Schweppe Foundation.

[4] The nomenclature for the immunoglobulins is that suggested in Bulletin of the World Health Organization, *30:* 447, 1964.

genetic control of two additional allotypic specificities on the α_2M molecule. Studies on the genetic and immunochemical relationship of the new allotypic specificities to the previously described Mtz1 and Mtz2 allotypic specificities are presented.

MATERIALS AND METHODS

Rabbits. Rabbits descended from crosses of closed colonies of Flemish Giants and New Zealand Whites, originally obtained from the National Institutes of Health, were bred in our laboratories and used in these experiments. Sera, rabbits and pedigree data obtained from the Ax and AxBu colonies at The Jackson Laboratory, Bar Harbor, Maine, were kindly supplied by Dr. Richard R. Fox. Rabbits 656 and 807 were obtained from other colonies.

Analytical methods. Immunoelectrophoresis and allotyping were performed by double diffusion in agar gel plates, as previously described (2, 12). Sera which did not react to form precipitates with antisera were typed by inhibition of precipitation as described by Lichter (16). Analytical ultracentrifugation was performed in a Spinco model E ultracentrifuge using schlieren optics, as previously described (12).

Isolation of macroglobulin. The α_2M was prepared from serum by ultracentrifugation at 40,000 rpm followed by fractionation of the pellet together with the lowest 2 ml in the centrifuge tube on a Sephadex G-200 column, as previously described (12). The Sephadex gel filtration was performed in a saline borate buffer (0.16 M boric acid, 0.13 M NaCl, 0.035 M NaOH, pH 8.0). Further purification was accomplished by zone electrophoresis in a starch block using 0.05 M sodium barbital buffer (pH 8.6). After electrophoresis, α_2M was eluted from the starch with the saline borate buffer and again passed through a Sephadex G-200 column. Dilute fractions were concentrated by vacuum ultrafiltration.

Antisera. Rabbits were injected with the crude macroglobulin preparation isolated by ultracentrifugation and gel filtration. Rabbits were injected with macroglobulin emulsified in complete Freund's adjuvant as previously described (12). The goat (G-3) anti-rabbit macroglobulin antisera is the same as that described earlier. This antiserum had been absorbed with α_1M, resulting in a monospecific antiserum directed against α_1M. Rabbits selected to receive injections of αf_2M were typed for the Mtz1 and Mtz2 allotypes and injected with α_2M having the same Mtz specificities to ensure that any antibodies produced would not be directed against a known α_2M allotype (Mtz1 or Mtz2).

Purification of IgG immunoglobulin. Purified IgG immunoglobulin was successively precipitated with 18%, 14% and 12.5% sodium sulfate according to the procedure of Kekwick (17). Precipitates were dissolved in saline borate after each precipitation and reprecipitated with the next lower concentration of sodium sulfate. The final precipitate was dissolved in saline borate and further purified by gel filtration on a Sephadex G-200 column.

RESULTS

Identification of two new α_2-macroglobulin allotypes. By immunization of rabbits with macroglobulin preparations, using donors and recipients with the same Mtz allotypes, two antisera, anti-Mt-3 (Ax7) and anti-Mt-4 (El 75-3) were obtained which were specific for different serum allotypes of α_2M, designated as Mt-3 and Mt-4. A panel of 849 rabbit sera was typed by double diffusion in agar gel plates. Some sera precipitated only with anti-Mt-3, while other sera precipitated only with anti-Mt-4 (Fig. 1). The remaining sera did not precipitate with either of the two new antisera, but did inhibit the precipitation of anti-Mt-3 with allotype Mt-3 and anti-Mt-4 with allotype Mt-4, indicating that these sera had both the Mt-3 and Mt-4 allotypes (Fig. 1). The inhibition of precipitation was indicated by the shortening of the precipitin line proximal to the well containing serum with both Mt-3 and Mt-4 specificities (Fig. 1). Moreover, a serum (rabbit 656) which inhibited both antisera separately did precipitate with a mixture of anti-Mt-3 and Mt-4 (Figs. 2 and 3). In Figure 2, the isolated IgG antibody preparations were placed in adjacent wells; a precipitin band appeared in a position equidistant from each antibody well, indicating that both antibodies participated in the precipitation. When both antibodies were mixed in the same well, a precipitin reaction also occurred (Fig. 3). Thus, all sera tested possessed either the Mt-3, the Mt-4, or both allotypic specificities.

Immunoelectrophoresis of normal rabbit sera with anti-Mt-3 and anti-Mt-4 gave precipitin bands in the α_2 region. These bands were similar

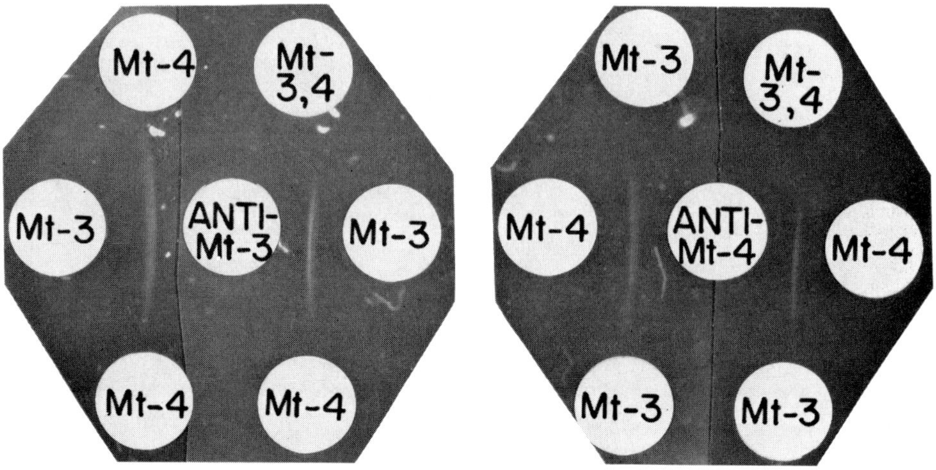

Figure 1. Double diffusion experiment in agar gel to demonstrate the method for typing rabbit sera by precipitation and inhibition of precipitation to determine allotypic specificities present. In both plates, antiserum is in the center well, serum from rabbit 656 is in the upper right well, and other sera are in the remaining peripheral wells. *Left*, reactions with anti-Mt-3; *right*, reactions with anti-Mt-4.

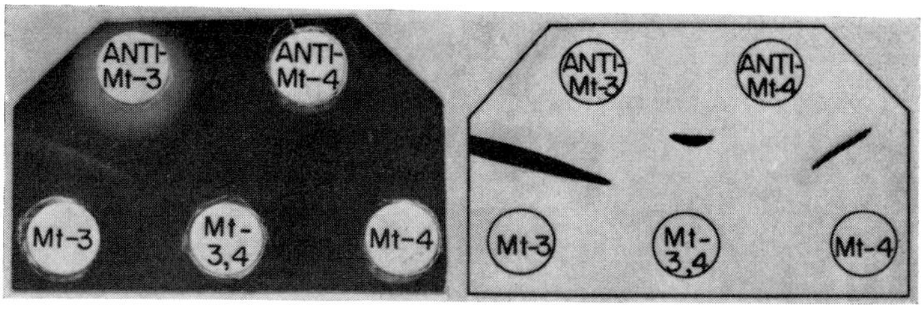

Figure 2. Double diffusion experiment in agar gel illustrating precipitation of sera (*bottom*) by IgG preparations of anti-Mt-3 and anti-Mt-4 antibodies (*top*). Serum from rabbit 656 is in the center well of the bottom row.

to those formed with anti-Mtz1, anti-Mtz2, and goat anti-rabbit α_2M (anti-α_2M) (Fig. 4).

Rabbit α_2M of allotype Mtz1Mt-3 was isolated by gel filtration and starch block electrophoresis. This purified preparation sedimented in the analytical ultracentrifuge almost entirely as a single symmetrical peak with a sedimentation coefficient of 16.3S, uncorrected for concentration; a small leading peak was also present (Fig. 5). This α_2M preparation gave a single similar precipitin band in the α_2 region on immunoelectrophoresis when reacted against goat anti-whole rabbit serum (anti-NRS), anti-α_2M, anti-Mtz1, or anti-Mt-3 (Fig. 6).

When serum with allotype Mt-4 was reacted in a double diffusion experiment with the IgG preparation of anti-Mt-4, a precipitin band formed which coalesced with the band formed with goat anti-rabbit α_2M (Fig. 7, *left*). Finally, when a purified α_2M preparation possessing Mtz1 and Mt-4 was reacted in a double diffusion experiment with the IgG preparations of anti-Mtz1 and anti-Mt-4, the precipitin bands which formed also coalesced (Fig. 7, *right*). Results similar to those shown in Figure 7 were also obtained with the Mt-3 allotypes. These data indicate that the Mt-3 and Mt-4 specificities, like the Mtz specificities, are found on α_2-macroglobulin molecules.

Genetic studies. Sera from all rabbits in our colony reacted with anti-Mt-3, whereas none reacted with anti-Mt-4. Sera from all rabbits in the Ax and AxBu colonies at The Jackson Laboratories reacted with one, the other, or both of these antisera. Seven of the nine possible combinations of phenotypes with respect to the

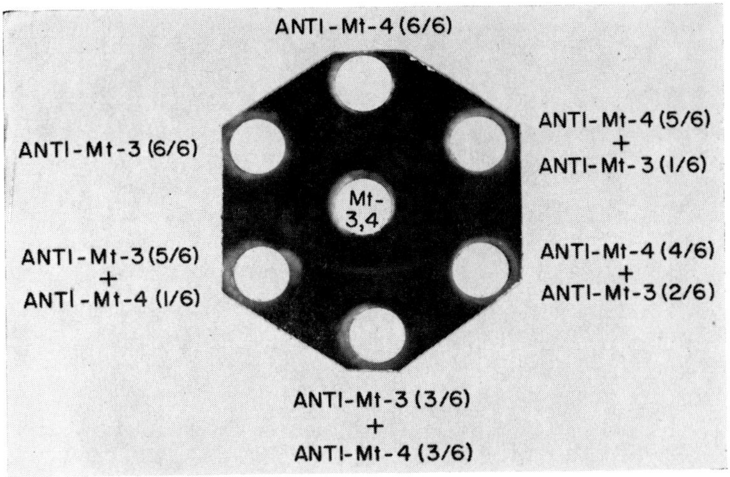

Figure 3. Double diffusion experiment in agar gel illustrating precipitation of serum from rabbit 656 (*center well*) by mixture of individual IgG preparations of anti-Mt-3 and anti-Mt-4 antibodies. The preparation of each antibody in the mixture is indicated in parentheses.

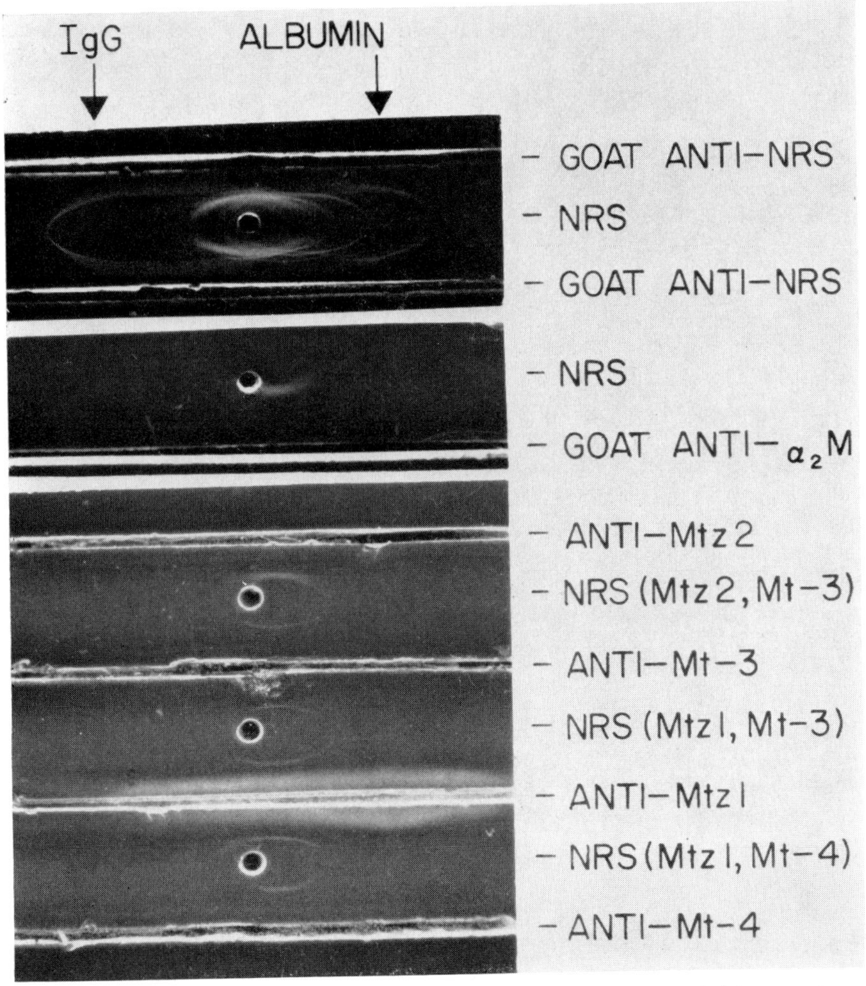

Figure 4. Immunoelectrophoresis in 1.5% Noble Agar showing the precipitin reaction of electrophoresed normal rabbit serum (NRS) with four different anti-allotype antisera, goat anti-rabbit α_2M antiserum (anti-α_2M), and goat anti-normal rabbit serum antiserum (anti-NRS). The anode is at the right.

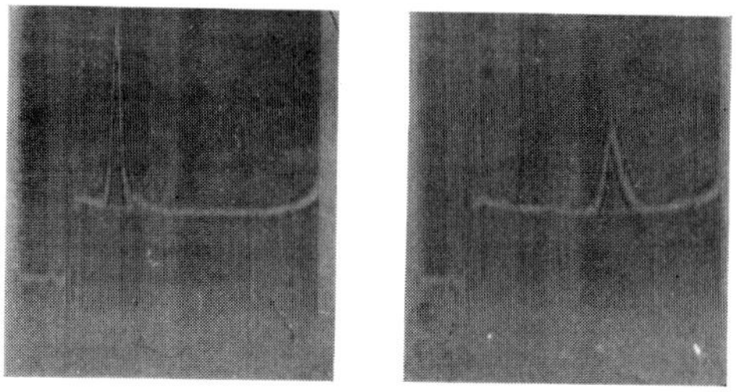

Figure 5. Ultracentrifuge pattern of purified α_2M in saline borate buffer, pH 8.0. The centrifuge was run at 52,000 rpm and 20°C. Photograph taken at 60° bar angle. Sedimentation is from left to right. *Left*, 17 min; *right*, 40 min after attaining speed.

four α_2M allotypes were found; the two combinations not found were Mtz2Mt-4 and Mtz2-Mt-3,4 (Table I).

In performing genetic studies with Mt-3 and Mt-4, it was postulated that homozygous rabbits were those whose sera precipitated with one of the two antisera, but which neither precipitated nor inhibited precipitation with the other antiserum. Rabbits whose sera showed inhibition of precipitation with both antisera were considered heterozygous. Those rabbits whose sera were precipitated by anti-Mt-3 were assigned the genotype $Mt\text{-}^3Mt\text{-}^3$, and those whose sera were precipitated by anti-Mt-4 were designated as

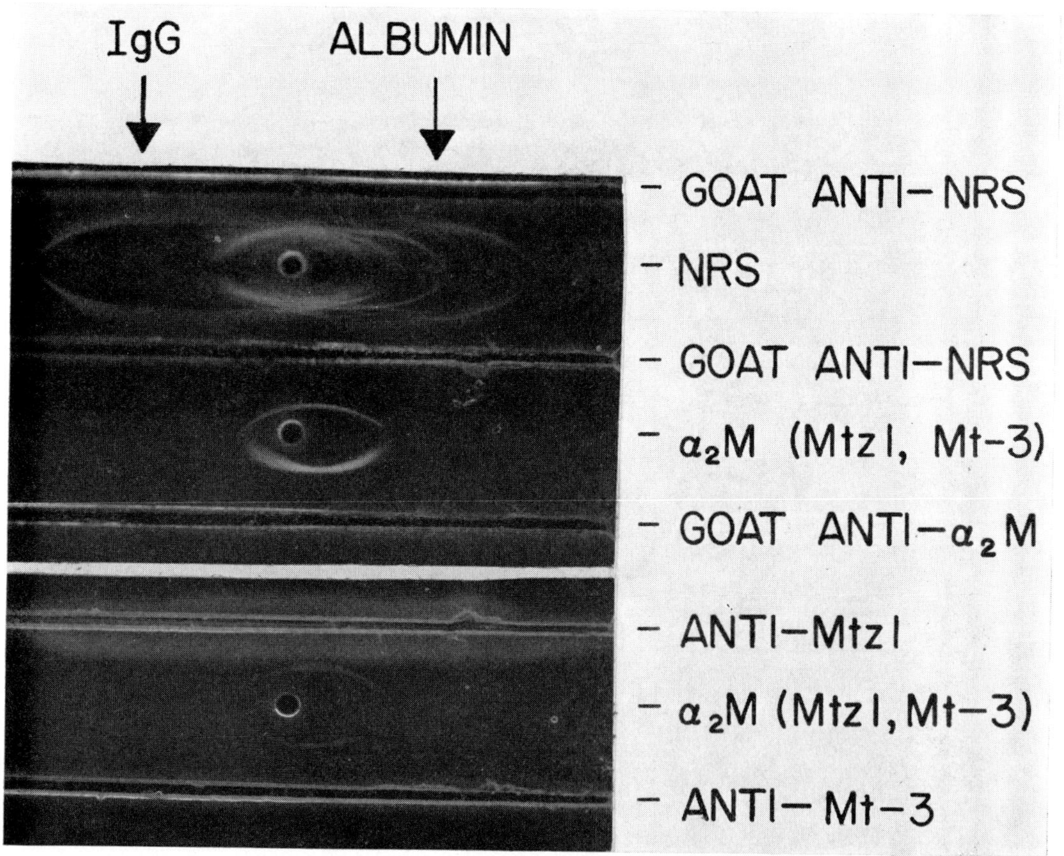

Figure 6. Immunoelectrophoresis in 1.5% Noble Agar showing the precipitin reaction of electrophoresed purified α_2M of allotype Mtz1 Mt-3 with goat anti-normal rabbit antiserum (anti-NRS), goat anti-rabbit α_2M antiserum (anti-α_2M), and anti-Mtz1 and anti-Mt-3 anti-allotype antisera. The reaction of anti-NRS with normal rabbit serum (NRS) is shown at the top for reference. The anode is at the right.

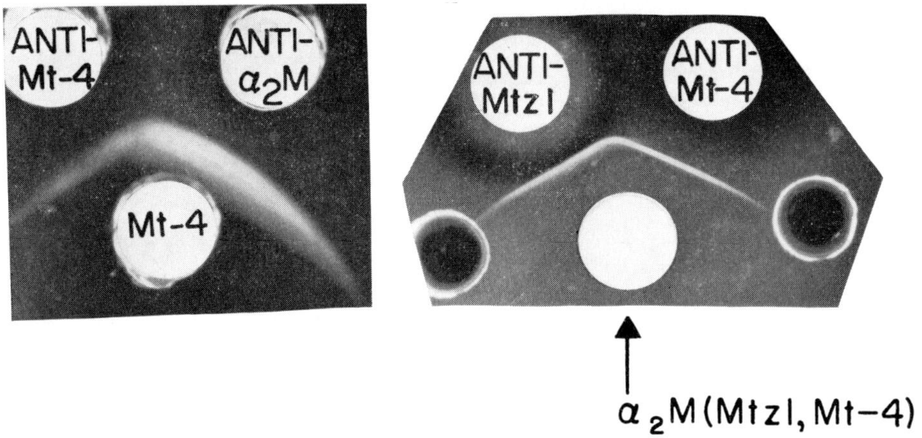

Figure 7. Double diffusion experiments in agar gel. *Left*, reactions of serum of allotype Mt-4 with goat anti-rabbit α_2M (anti-α_2M) and with an IgG preparation of anti-Mt-4 antibody; *right*, reactions of purified α_2M of allotype Mtz1Mt-4 with IgG preparations of anti-Mtz1 and anti-Mt-4 antibodies.

Mt-⁴Mt-⁴. Heterozygotes were designated as *Mt-³Mt-⁴*.

The number of phenotypes observed among 828 progeny of various matings are tabulated in Table II, together with the numbers expected if the two genes are alleles. The results are consistent with the hypothesis that the allotypes Mt-3 and Mt-4 are controlled by the allelic genes $Mt\text{-}^3$ and $Mt\text{-}^4$.

Since the Mtz^2 gene is presently absent from the Ax and AxBu colonies, and the $Mt\text{-}^4$ gene is absent from our colony, only a limited amount of data is available to test linkage hypotheses. The progeny of one pair, from differing origins, mated in our laboratory, is illustrated in Figure 8. All four progeny have genotypes identical to one or the other of their parents, consistent with close linkage of the $Mt\text{-}^3/Mt\text{-}^4$ and Mtz^1/Mtz^2 systems. The $Mtz^1Mt\text{-}^3/Mtz^2Mt\text{-}^3$ offspring of an $Mtz^1Mt\text{-}^3/Mtz^1Mt\text{-}^3 \times Mtz^1Mt\text{-}^4/Mtz^2Mt\text{-}^3$ mating was similarly consistent with close linkage. Three offspring were obtained from an $Mtz^1Mt\text{-}^3/Mtz^2Mt\text{-}^3 \times Mtz^1Mt\text{-}^4/Mtz^2Mt\text{-}^3$ mating, and their genotypes were also consistent with close linkage of the two systems. More progeny data are needed, however, before a definite conclusion can be drawn regarding linkage between the two allotypic systems of α_2M.

In a similar manner, the inheritance of the Aa (IgG heavy chain), Ab (IgG light chain), and Lpq (low-density lipoprotein) allotypes was determined in relation to the Mt-3/Mt-4 system.

TABLE I

Distribution of α_2M-phenotypes in selected rabbit populations

Phenotype	Ax and AxBu Colonies	University of Ill. Colony	Others[a]	Total
Mt-3 Mtz1	8	190	70	268
Mt-3 Mtz1,2	0	294	34	328
Mt-3 Mtz2	0	108	17	125
Mt-3,4 Mtz1	24	0	18	42
Mt-3,4 Mtz1,2	0	0	8	8
Mt-3,4 Mtz2	0	0	0	0
Mt-4 Mtz1	18	0	6	24
Mt-4 Mtz1,2	0	0	24	24
Mt-4 Mtz2	0	0	0	0
Total	50	592	177	819

[a] Includes other colonies and progeny of intercolony matings.

Results indicate that the $Mt\text{-}^3/Mt\text{-}^4$ locus is not closely linked to any of the loci determining these allotypes. Matings between $Mt\text{-}^3Mt\text{-}^4$ heterozygous does and $Mt\text{-}^3Mt\text{-}^3$ or $Mt\text{-}^4Mt\text{-}^4$ homozygous bucks produced 12 male progeny, 5 of which were heterozygotes, indicating that the $Mt\text{-}^3$ and $Mt\text{-}^4$ genes are not sex-linked.

DISCUSSION

Two allotypic specificities, designated Mt-3 and Mt-4, have been found on rabbit serum α_2-

TABLE II

Progeny test for segregation of the Mt-3 and Mt-4 allotypes at a single locus

Parental Phenotypes	Total Progeny		Phenotypes of Progeny		
			Mt-3	Mt-3,4	Mt-4
Mt-3 × Mt-3	762	O[a]	762	0	0
		E[b]	762	0	0
Mt-3 × Mt-4	13	O	0	13	0
		E	0	13	0
Mt-3 × Mt-3,4	18	O	9	9	0
		E	9	9	0
Mt-4 × Mt-3,4	23	O	0	12	11
		E	0	11.5	11.5
Mt-3,4 × Mt-3,4	12	O	4	5	3
		E	3	6	3

[a] O, observed.
[b] E, expected.

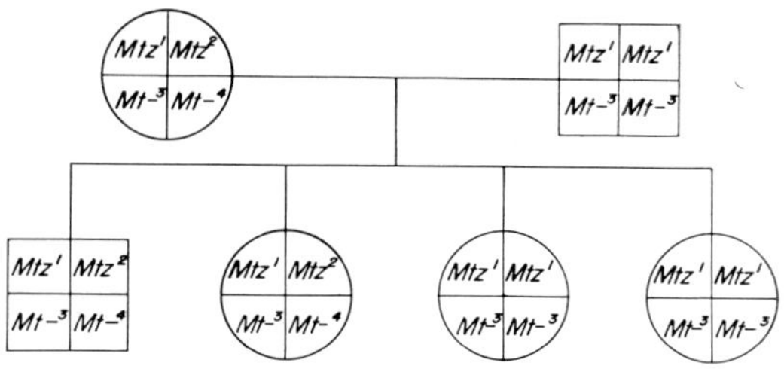

Figure 8. Pedigree of a rabbit family indicating that the Mtz1/Mtz2 and Mt-3/Mt-4 loci of α_2M may be closely linked.

macroglobulin molecules.[5] Antisera to these specificities were developed by immunization of rabbits with macroglobulin preparations from rabbits of the same α_2M allotype with respect to the previously described *Mtz* locus (12, 13). The distribution of phenotypes among 819 rabbits indicated that the Mt-3 and Mt-4 specificities were not identical to each other or to the Mtz1 or Mtz2 specificities. All rabbits tested possessed either Mt-3, Mt-4, or both allotypes. Data from 828 progeny of various matings indicate that the Mt-3 and Mt-4 allotypes are controlled by allelic autosomal genes, designated as $Mt\text{-}^3$ and $Mt\text{-}^4$, respectively. No evidence of a third allele at the $Mt\text{-}^3/Mt\text{-}^4$ locus was found. Progeny data of appropriate test crosses show that the $Mt\text{-}^3/Mt\text{-}^4$ locus is not linked to the *Aa* (immunoglobulin heavy chain), *Ab* (immunoglobulin light chain), *Af* (IgA) or *Lpq* (low-density lipoprotein) rabbit allotype loci.

[5] The general plan of notation used for rabbit immunoglobulin allotypes (18) is adapted for the α_2-macroglobulins. Since the allotypic specificities become known first, they are numbered in the sequence of discovery and listed with the prefix Mt, i.e., Mt-1, Mt-2, Mt-3, Mt-4. When progeny data are sufficient to establish a locus, a third letter is added; e.g., Mtz1 and Mtz2. A more complete designation for Mt-3 and Mt-4 must await further evidence as to whether these specificities are inherited by distinct loci or in phenogroup combinations with Mtz1 and Mtz2 at a single complex locus.

On immunoelectrophoresis, anti-Mt-3 and anti-Mt-4 antisera reacted against whole rabbit serum and purified rabbit α_2M of appropriate allotypes to give a similar band in the α_2 region to those obtained by reacting anti-Mtz allotype antisera and goat anti-rabbit α_2M antiserum against serum and α_2M. The specificity of the two antisera for α_2M was further established by the development of precipitin bands in agar gel double diffusion plates which coalesced with those obtained by the reaction of anti-Mtz allotype antisera and goat anti-rabbit α_2M antiserum against purified α_2M and whole rabbit serum.

Although the serum from $Mt\text{-}^3Mt\text{-}^3$ or $Mt\text{-}^4Mt\text{-}^4$ homozygous rabbits precipitated with the corresponding antiserum, the serum from $Mt\text{-}^3Mt\text{-}^4$ heterozygous rabbits did not precipitate with either anti-Mt-3 or anti-Mt-4. However, the serum from the heterozygotes did inhibit precipitin bands formed between the serum from each type of homozygous rabbit and the specific antiserum. The serum from the homozygote did not precipitate with the antiserum specific for the allelic allotype, nor did it inhibit the precipitin bands formed by reactions of that antiserum.

The presence of the Mt-3 and the Mt-4 specificities in the α_2M molecules of heterozygotes was confirmed by the fact that a mixture of the IgG antibody preparations of the two antisera did precipitate with serum from a heterozygous rabbit, while the individual antibody preparations did not. Additionally, this gave evidence that the two specificities are present on the same molecules in the serum of the heterozygotes. The α_2M molecules of a heterozygous rabbit probably possess an insufficient number of determinants of each specificity to form a lattice and to precipitate with a single antiserum, but, like monovalent haptens, they have the capability of inhibiting the precipitation of the antiserum with the α_2M molecules of a homozygote. In the heterozygous rabbit, however, the α_2M molecules apparently have a sufficient number of both the Mt-3 and Mt-4 determinants to form a precipitate when both antibodies are present together. Similar considerations also seem to be pertinent to the observation (previously unreported) that, in the Mtz1/Mtz2 system, sera from homozygous rabbits give denser precipitin bands in agar gel with specific antisera than do sera from heterozygous rabbits.

Macroglobulin from an $Mt^{-3}Mt^{-4}$ heterozygote (rabbit 807) had been used to immunize rabbit E175-3, which subsequently produced anti-Mt-4. Rabbit 807 serum did not precipitate with the anti-Mt-4 produced in response to the injection of rabbit 807 macroglobulin, but the serum did inhibit precipitation of the anti-Mt-4 with an $Mt^{-4}Mt^{-4}$ serum. The Mt-3/Mt-4 system thus illustrates the possibility of discovering allotypic specificities when the immunogen does not itself give a precipitate with the antiserum developed against it. A definite precipitate could be found with a single antiserum only by testing sera from animals other than the one providing the immunogen. The development of the anti-Mt-4 is analogous to the system described by Reichlin *et al.* (19), in which free monomeric kangaroo cytochrome *c* was injected into a rabbit. The resulting antiserum was shown to precipitate with polymeric kangaroo cytochrome *c* in agar gel, but not with the monomer. The monomer was able to inhibit precipitation of the polymer by the antiserum.

The linkage relationship of the Mt^{-3}/Mt^{-4} locus to the Mtz^1/Mtz^2 locus of α_2M is not yet clear. The genotypes of four progeny from an appropriate test cross were consistent with inheritance of Mtz1 and Mt-3 or of Mtz2 and Mt-4 in phenogroup combinations. The genotypes of four progeny from two other test crosses were consistent with inheritance of Mtz2 and Mt-3 or of Mtz1 and Mt-4 in phenogroup combinations. If the results of additional test crosses confirm these observations, this pattern of inheritance would resemble the complex loci of the *Lpq* lipoprotein (14) and *Af* IgA (20) allotypes.

Allelic exclusion apparently does not operate at the molecular level in the Mt-3/Mt-4 system, as both specificities are present on the α_2M molecules in the $Mt^{-3}Mt^{-4}$ heterozygous rabbits. Similarly, Mtz1 and Mtz2 specificities have also been found on the same α_2M molecules in Mtz^1-Mtz^2 heterozygotes (12). In this respect, the allotypic systems of α_2M are unique among the rabbit serum protein allotypes studied to date. Allelic exclusion in individual molecules has been reported as occurring at three immunoglobulin allotype loci, *Aa* (11, 21), *Ab* (11), and *Ac* (22) and at the *Lpq* low density lipoprotein (23) and the *Ess* α_1-aryl esterase (8) loci. At all of these loci, individual molecules in heterozygous rabbits each bear only one of the two specificities found in the serum. Allelic exclusion does not operate in the case of the *A* and *B* alleles of the *ABO* blood group system, in which both genes in a heterozygote contribute to the formation of a single complex mucopolysaccharide molecule (24).

Reactions of anti-Mtz and anti-Mt-3 or anti-Mt-4 antisera with sera of appropriate allotypes produce bands of partial or complete identity with each other in agar gel double diffusion plates. Therefore, at least some α_2M molecules carry both Mtz and Mt-3/Mt-4 specificities.

Allotypic specificities controlled by immunoglobulin loci, *Aa*, *Ab* (25), and *Ac* (26), have been identified with the heavy or light chains of the IgG molecule. The intramolecular location of the allotypic specificities of the α_2M molecule have not yet been investigated. Structural studies have indicated that the rabbit α_2M molecule has carbohydrate and may have more than one polypeptide chain (15); the allotypic specificities may reside in any of these constituents.

The α_2M molecule readily lends itself to studies on allotypes because of its large size (m.w. approximately 850,000) (15), which confers on it the possibility of possessing a greater number of allotypic specificities than are found on smaller molecules. Four α_2M allotypes have now been described in reports from this laboratory. All four specificities can be present on the same molecule; the two allelic pairs may determine antigenic sites located on different parts of the molecule.

REFERENCES

1. Oudin, J., J. Exp. Med., *112:* 107 and 125, 1960.
2. Dray, S., Young, G. O. and Gerald, L., J. Immun., *91:* 403, 1963.
3. Gilman-Sachs, A., Mage, R. G., Young, G. O., Alexander, C. and Dray, S., J. Immun., *103:* 1159, 1969.

4. Kelus, A. S. and Gell, P. G., Nature, *206:* 313, 1965.
5. Conway, T. P., Dray, S. and Lichter, E. A., J. Immun., *102:* 544, 1969.
6. Albers, J. J. and Dray, S., Biochem. Genet., *2:* 25, 1968.
7. Chiao, J. W. and Dray, S., Biochem. Genet., *3:* 1, 1969.
8. Albers, L. V., Dray, S. and Knight, K. L., Biochemistry, *8:* 4416, 1969.
9. Cebra, J., Colberg, J. and Dray, S., J. Exp. Med., *123:* 547, 1966.
10. Pernis, B., Chiappino, M. B., Kelus, A. S. and Gell, P., J. Exp. Med., *122:* 853, 1965.
11. Dray, S. and Nisonoff, A., Proc. Soc. Exp. Biol. Med., *113:* 20, 1963.
12. Knight, K. L. and Dray, S., Biochemistry, *7:* 1165, 1968.
13. Knight, K. L. and Dray, S., Biochemistry, *7:* 3830, 1968.
14. Albers, J. J. and Dray, S., J. Immun., *103:* 155, 1969.
15. Picard, J. J., Roels, H. A., Carbonara, A. O. and Heremans, J. F., in *Protides of the Biological Fluids, Proceedings of the 12th Colloquium, Bruges, 1964,* Edited by H. Peeters, p. 353, Elsevier, Amsterdam, 1965.
16. Lichter, E. A., J. Immun., *98:* 139, 1967.
17. Kekwick, R. A., Biochem. J., *34:* 1248, 1960.
18. Dray, S., Dubiski, S., Kelus, A., Lennox, E. S. and Oudin, J., Nature, *195:* 785, 1962.
19. Reichlin, M., Nisonoff, A. and Margoliash, E., J. Biol. Chem., *245:* 947, 1970.
20. Conway, T. P., Dray, S. and Lichter, E. A., J. Immun., *103:* 662, 1969.
21. Oudin, J., Biochem. Biophys. Res. Commun., *5:* 358, 1961.
22. Vice, J. L., Hunt, W. L. and Dray, S., J. Immun., *104:* 38, 1970.
23. Albers, J. J. and Dray, S., J. Immun., *103:* 163, 1969.
24. Watkins, W. M., Science, *152:* 172, 1966.
25. Feinstein, A., Gell, P. G. H. and Kelus, A. S., Nature, *200:* 653, 1963.
26. Mage, R., Young, G. O. and Reisfield, R. A., J. Immun., *101:* 617, 1968.

THE JOURNAL OF IMMUNOLOGY
Vol. 105, No. 4, October 1970

Printed in U.S.A.

THE EFFECT OF SELECTIVE MODIFICATION OF TRYPTOPHAN, LYSINE AND ARGININE RESIDUES OF BASIC BRAIN PROTEIN ON ENCEPHALITOGENIC ACTIVITY[1,2]

ROBERT H. SWANBORG

From the Department of Microbiology, Wayne State University, School of Medicine, Detroit, Michigan 48207

Received for publication May 12, 1970

Basic protein (BP), which caused experimental allergic encephalomyelitis in guinea pigs in a dose of 30 μg, was isolated from bovine brain. Studies were carried out to characterize the encephalitogenic determinant by means of selective and permanent modification of tryptophan, lysine and arginine residues of BP. When tryptophan residues of BP were altered by the addition of 0.045 μmol 2-hydroxy-5-nitrobenzyl bromide/mg BP, preparations exhibited a significant decrease in encephalitogenic activity. In contrast, acetylation of free amino groups of lysine with acetic anhydride, or modification of guanidinium groups of arginine with 2,3-butanedione, had no effect on the encephalitogenic activity of BP. These results suggest that tryptophan is an essential component of the encephalitogenic determinant, whereas lysine and arginine are probably not present in this site.

Specific chemical modification procedures have been employed by many investigators to study the contribution of individual amino acid side chains to the specificity of antigens (1–3) and to the biologic activity of enzymes (4) and antibodies (5–7). Previous findings from this laboratory (8) suggested that a similar approach might be useful to study the structure of the encephalitogenic determinant on the basic protein (BP) isolated from brain. It was reported that diazonium groups appeared to block this encephalitogenic site (8), although, since diazonium groups are known to couple to a variety of protein functional groups (9, 10), it was not possible from those studies to identify the amino acids which comprise this region of the molecule.

The present investigation describes the effect of more selective chemical modification of individual amino acids on the ability of BP to cause experimental allergic encephalomyelitis (EAE) in guinea pigs. The amino acids chosen for this study were tryptophan, which Eylar and Hashim (11, 12) have previously implicated as essential for encephalitogenic activity, and lysine and arginine, which were chosen because each is present in large amounts in BP (13, 14). Moreover, tryptophan, lysine and arginine are known to be reactive with diazonium compounds (9, 10). A preliminary report has been presented (15).

[1] This work was supported by Research Grant NS-06985 from the National Institute of Neurological Diseases and Stroke, United States Public Health Service, Bethesda, Maryland.

[2] Presented in part at the 1970 FASEB meeting (15), and at the Tenth International Congress for Microbiology, Mexico City, August 1970.

MATERIALS AND METHODS

Encephalitogenic protein. Basic protein (BP) was prepared from bovine brain (generously donated by National Packing Co., Detroit, Mich.) according to the method of Kies (16), as previously described (8). Briefly, BP was extracted from lyophilized, defatted brain with N/1 HCl at pH 2.0, then subsequently precipitated at half-saturation with ammonium sulfate, and the redissolved precipitate was dialyzed against pH 9.0 borate buffer (0.05 M) to precipitate additional contaminating proteins. The soluble dialysate was designated BP, and was lyophilized and stored at 4°C.

Modification of tryptophan. The method of Horton and Koshland (17) was employed. Fifty-milligram portions of lyophilized BP were dissolved in 5 ml of 8 M urea at pH 3. Then, 2 ml of 0.1 M 2-hydroxy-5-nitrobenzyl bromide (Eastman), which had been dissolved in methanol

(2), were added, and the reaction was allowed to proceed in the dark at 25°C for 1 hr. Uncombined reagent was then removed by passage through a column of Sephadex G-25, equilibrated with 8 M urea at pH 3. The modified BP (benzyl-BP) was eluted with the void volume and subsequently dialyzed against distilled water to remove the urea. The degree of coupling was determined spectrophotometrically at 410 nm, pH 11, employing a molar extinction coefficient of 18,000 M^{-1} cm^{-1} for the hydroxynitrobenzyl group (17). Control preparations consisted of BP dissolved in 8 M urea (pH 3), then dialyzed against distilled water (designated urea-control).

Modification of free amino groups. The free amino groups, primarily of lysine, were modified by acetylation, according to the method of Fraenkel-Conrat (18). BP was dissolved in distilled water, and adjusted to pH 8 with N/1 NaOH. Acetic anhydride was then added slowly, with stirring, at 4°C, for 1 hr, then dialyzed against distilled water. The acetylated BP was then exposed to pH 11 for 10 min to remove labile O-acetyl groups from tyrosine residues (18). The percentage of modification was determined by use of the ninhydrin test (19) which is specific for free amino groups.

Modification of arginine. The guanidinium group of arginine was modified with 2,3-butanedione, as described by Yankeelov *et al.* (20) and Grossberg and Pressman (7). Fifteen per cent 2,3-butanedione (Eastman Organic Chemicals, Rochester, N. Y.) in pH 8.2 borate buffer was adjusted to pH 8.8 with 5 N NaOH, and incubated at 25°C, in the dark, until the optical density of a 1:15 dilution, at 400 nm, exceeded 0.45. Then, one volume of this reagent was incubated with two volumes of BP dissolved in distilled water (1% concentration) at room temperature. The reaction was stopped at the appropriate time (1 to 24 hr) by adding N/1 HCl (7). The percentage of modification was determined spectrophotometrically, employing the Sakaguchi test, which is relatively specific for arginine (21).

Analytical methods. Zonal electrophoresis on cellulose acetate membranes was carried out as previously described (8). Protein concentration was determined by the biuret reaction (22) or by ultraviolet absorption at 280 nm, employing an extinction coefficient calculated by dry weight analysis according to previously reported procedure (23).

Immunization. Male Hartley strain guinea pigs, weighing 350 to 500 g, were given a single intradermal injection of BP, or modified BP, emulsified in Freund's complete adjuvant containing 8 mg/ml of *Mycobacterium butyricum.* The total volume injected was 0.1 to 0.2 ml. Animals were examined daily, and killed when definite symptoms of EAE were observed, or after 28 to 30 days.

Histology. At the time of death, the brains were fixed in formalin-saline. Paraffin sections were prepared, stained with hematoxylin and eosin, and examined microscopically for lesions of EAE. All sections were coded prior to staining and examined without knowledge of origin. Each slide was graded according to the following scheme: 0, no lesions; ±, small inflammatory lesions in a few fields; +, perivascular lesions in several fields; ++, extensive lesions in most fields (24).

RESULTS

When the bovine BP was subjected to cellulose acetate electrophoresis at pH 4.5, one component, which migrated toward the cathode, was seen. The ultraviolet extinction coefficient of BP at 280 nm was determined. It was calculated by dry weight analysis to be 6.0, using Beer's law. Encephalitogenic activity was determined by immunizing guinea pigs with a single intradermal injection of 30 μg BP in Freund's complete adjuvant. At least three of every four guinea pigs that received this dose of BP developed EAE within 21 days.

Several BP preparations were treated with 2-hydroxy-5-nitrobenzyl bromide in order to modify tryptophan residues. As illustrated in Table I, spectrophotometric determinations of the extent of coupling revealed that 0.045 μmol

TABLE I

Spectrophotometric determination of extent of modification of BP with 2-hydroxy-5-nitrobenzyl bromide, at pH 11, 410 nm, employing an extinction coefficient of 18,000 M^{-1} cm^{-1} [a]

Maximum 2-Hydroxy-5-Nitrobenzyl Bromide Coupled to BP	Reported Tryptophan Content of BP[b]
0.045 ± 0.001	0.050 μmol/mg BP
0.90 ± 0.02	1.0 mol/mol BP

[a] Horton and Koshland (17).
[b] Carnegie *et al.* (13).

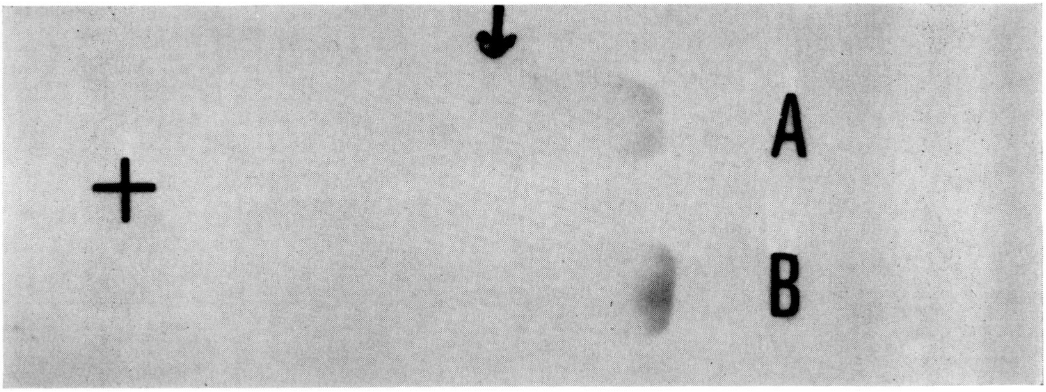

Figure 1. Cellulose acetate electrophoresis at pH 4.5 of: *A*, benzyl-BP at 0.3%; and *B*, unmodified BP at 0.6%. The arrow indicates the point of origin. The anode is to the left.

of reagent was bound/mg of BP. On a molar basis, this corresponds to 0.9 mol/mol BP, assuming the molecular weight of BP to be 20,000 (8, 16). These values were consistent for various benzyl-BP preparations modified as described, and agree reasonably well with the reported tryptophan content of BP (Table I) (13). It was not possible to increase the amount of reagent bound, even when the ratio of 2 hydroxy-5-nitrobenzyl bromide to BP was increased five-to-one, suggesting that maximum conjugation had probably been achieved.

When analyzed by cellulose acetate electrophoresis at pH 4.5, the benzyl-BP was similar to unmodified BP (Fig. 1). A single basic component with the same mobility as unmodified BP was observed.

Guinea pigs were immunized with benzyl-BP, emulsified in Freund's complete adjuvant. Control animals received BP which had been dissolved in 8 M urea (pH 3), then dialyzed against distilled water (urea-control). The results of three experiments are illustrated in Table II. One guinea pig of 28 that received benzyl-BP developed clinical and moderate histologic EAE 21 days after injection. Eight of the remaining animals injected with this material exhibited mild histologic EAE, 3 had moderate histologic disease, and 16 showed no lesions. In contrast, 8 of 13 guinea pigs that were immunized with the urea-control preparations developed clinical and severe histologic EAE in 10 to 16 days, and 2 additional animals exhibited mild histologic EAE. The unmodified BP preparation was also encephalitogenic in a dose of 36 μg. The results reported in Table II are representative of a series of experiments with benzyl-BP preparations. It appears from these findings that benzyl-BP is considerably less encephalitogenic than the urea-control material.

Other BP preparations were treated with acetic anhydride, which resulted in acetylation of free amino groups (18), primarily of lysine. The percentage of modification was calculated by the ninhydrin test (19). The degree of acetylation could be controlled by varying the amount of acetic anhydride added and the time of reaction. When acetylated BP was subjected to electrophoretic analysis, it was observed that mobility became progressively less basic with continued acetylation (Fig. 2). This would suggest that the positive charges on the free amino groups were neutralized by the acetylation procedure.

Table III illustrates the effect of acetylation on the encephalitogenic activity of BP. With the exception of a preparation in which 89% of the free amino groups had been modified, acetylated BP appears to be as encephalitogenic as unaltered BP. Subsequent attempts to prepare acetylated BP with 89% of the amino groups altered were unsuccessful.

2,3-Butanedione was employed to modify the guanidinium groups of arginine in BP preparations (7, 20). The percentage of unmodified arginine was determined by the Sakaguchi test (21). The extent of modification could be controlled to some degree by varying the time of reaction, although complete modification could not be achieved. These preparations also exhibited a somewhat less basic electrophoretic mobility than unaltered BP.

TABLE II

Encephalitogenic activity of benzyl-BP, containing 0.045 μmol reagent/mg BP, in guinea pigs

Antigen	Dose	Animals Tested	Experimental Allergic Encephalomyelitis				
			Clinical symptoms	Histologic[a]			
				0	±	+	++
	μg						
Benzyl-BP	100	6	0	4	1	1	0
	105	5	0	4	0	1	0
	110	8	1	4	3	1	0
	210	5	0	2	2	1	0
	220	4	0	2	2	0	0
Urea-control	87	4	2	1	1	0	2
	100	4	2	1	1	0	2
	110	5	4	1	0	0	4
Unmodified BP	36	4	3	1	0	1	2

[a] 0, No lesions; ±, small inflammatory lesions in a few fields; +, perivasular lesions in several fields; ++, extensive lesions in most fields (cf. ref. 24).

Analysis of 2,3-butanedione-treated BP by the ninhydrin method revealed that up to 30% of the free amino groups were also modified by this procedure, a finding which is in agreement with the studies of Grossberg and Pressman (7) for antibody molecules.

The effect of modification of arginine on encephalitogenic activity of BP is illustrated in Table IV. It can be seen that BP with 74% of the guanidinium groups modified—the maximum modification attainable—induces EAE in guinea pigs as readily as does unmodified BP.

DISCUSSION

Previous findings (8) strongly suggested that the encephalitogenic determinant includes amino acid side chains that are reactive with diazonium groups. It is known that diazonium compounds can interact covalently with a number of amino acids, including tyrosine, histidine, lysine, arginine and tryptophan (9, 10). Therefore, it was decided to attempt to characterize the encephalitogenic determinant by selective modification of these amino acids. The present investigation describes the effect of modification of tryptophan, lysine and arginine on the encephalitogenic activity of BP. Lamoureux *et al.* (25) have reported that iodination of the tyrosine and histidine residues of a basic encephalitogenic peptide derived from BP does not affect the ability of this peptide to elicit EAE, suggesting that tyrosine and histidine are not associated with this region of the molecule.

BP was modified with 2-hydroxy-5-nitrobenzyl bromide, a reagent that reacts predominantly with tryptophan, and to a lesser extent with cysteine (17). Since BP and related encephalitogenic proteins contain one tryptophan residue/molecule, but lack cysteine (11, 13, 14, 26), loss of encephalitogenic activity subsequent to treatment of the protein with 2-hydroxy-5-nitrobenzyl bromide would be directly attributable to modification of tryptophan (2, 5, 6, 17). This reagent reacts permanently and irreversibly with the indole group of tryptophan, forming an indolenine intermediate, with subsequent ring closure with suitable nearby nucleophilic groups (27). 2-Hydroxy-5-nitrobenzyl bromide has been employed to study the contribution of tryptophan to the biologic properties of antibodies (5, 6), and the antigenic determinants of sperm whale myoglobin (2).

Guinea pigs that were immunized with varying doses of benzyl-BP, even in excess of 200 μg, failed to develop clinical EAE, although some exhibited mild histologic disease. The occurrence of mild histologic EAE in some guinea pigs injected with benzyl-BP indicates that either additional minor encephalitogenic determinants exist, as Kibler *et al.* (14) have suggested, or alternatively, that a few unaltered BP molecules remain. In contrast, animals that received urea-control preparations developed clinical and severe histologic EAE, indicating that exposure of BP to 8 M urea does not induce conformational changes in the encephalitogenic determinant. The present investigation clearly shows that modification of tryptophan results in a significant decrease in the encephalitogenic activity of BP. One might conclude from this study that tryptophan is present in the encephalitogenic determinant. This would be in agreement with the findings of Eylar and Hashim (12), that cleavage of the C-tryptophyl bond of an encephalitogenic basic protein from bovine spinal cord results in loss of encephalitogenic activity. Al-

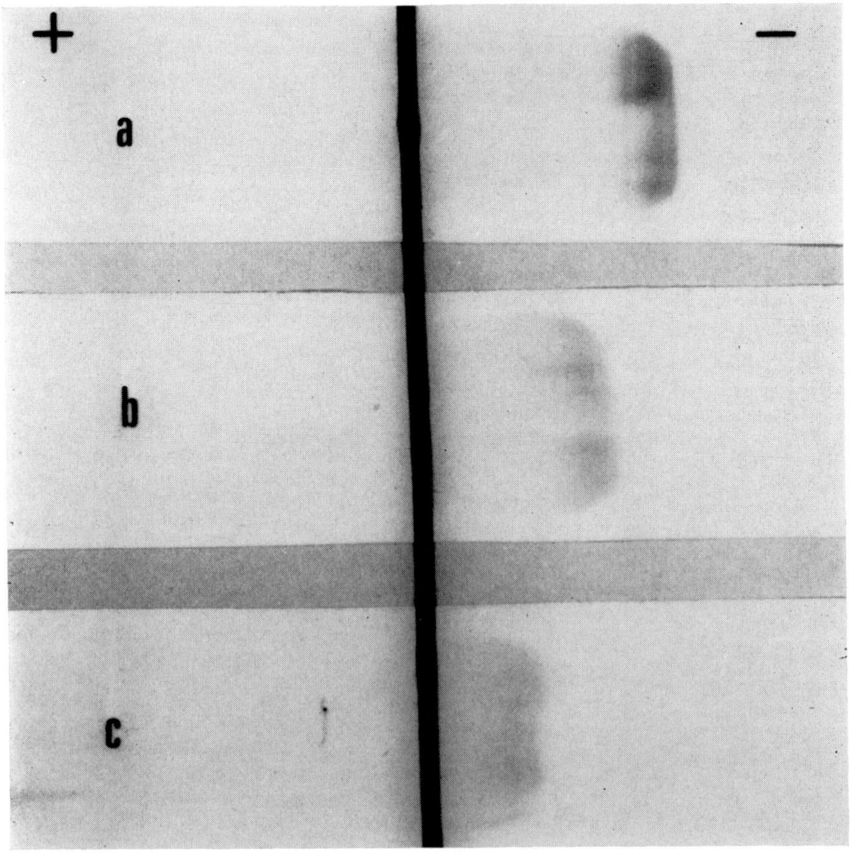

Figure 2. Cellulose acetate electrophoresis at pH 4.5 of: *a*, unmodified BP at 1%; *b*, acetylated BP, with 58% of the amino groups modified, at a concentration of 0.5%; and *c*, acetylated BP, with 89% of the amino groups modified, at a concentration of 0.4%. The vertical line represents the origin. The anode is to the left.

TABLE III

Encephalitogenic activity of acetylated BP in guinea pigs

Percentage of Amino Groups Modified	Dose	EAE
	μg	
43	63	3/4
58	40	3/4
89	36	0/4
0[a]	41	4/4
0	61	4/4
0	60	3/4

[a] Unmodified control BP, which was subjected to the same environmental changes as the modified preparations.

ternatively, it is possible that tryptophan contributes to the tertiary structure of the encephalitogenic determinant, but is not actually present in this site. Thus, loss of encephalitogenic activity might be due to conformational changes resulting indirectly from the modification of tryptophan. However, when considered in relation to previous work (11, 12), the present findings would seem to support the former hypothesis, i.e., that tryptophan is present in the encephalitogenic determinant.

When free amino groups of BP were acetylated with acetic anhydride, electrophoretic migration became progressively less basic with continued modification. On the other hand, the encephalitogenic activity of these preparations was similar

TABLE IV

Encephalitogenic activity of 2,3-butanedione-treated BP in guinea pigs

Percentage of Arginine Modified	Dose	EAE
	μg	
62	91	2/4
74	38	2/4
74	94	2/4
0[a]	38	2/4
0	94	3/4

[a] Unmodified control BP, which was subjected to the same environmental changes as the modified preparations.

to that of unmodified BP. The one exception was a preparation with 89% of the free amino groups modified. In view of unsuccessful attempts to prepare similarly acetylated BP, one might speculate that the inability of this particular preparation to cause EAE resulted from significant structural alterations brought about by the extensive modification. The use of acetic anhydride to permanently modify amino groups of enzymes (4) and antigens (1) is well established.

Grossberg and Pressman (7) have employed 2,3-butanedione to modify the active sites of antibodies directed against negatively charged haptens. They reported that approximately 71% of the arginyl residues could be modified, and that side reactions with amino groups resulted in the modification of approximately 25% of the lysyl residues. Our present findings with 2,3-butanedione-treated BP are in agreement with their studies (7). Up to 74% of the arginine in BP could be modified with this reagent. The ninhydrin test revealed that up to 30% of the free amino groups were also affected. Owing to the fact that acetylated BP retains encephalitogenic activity, this side-reaction of 2,3-butanedione with amino groups would not appear to interfere with the conclusions concerning the contribution of arginine to the encephalitogenic site. The observation that maximal modification of arginine in BP does not interfere with the ability of these preparations to elicit EAE would suggest that arginyl residues are not present in the encephalitogenic determinant.

Acknowledgments. The author wishes to thank Mrs. Susan R. Feldstein for her excellent technical assistance, and Drs. Frederick A. Zydeck and Richard R. Bennett, Division of Laboratory Animal Resources, Wayne State University, for the preparation of tissue sections.

REFERENCES

1. Sri Ram, J. and Maurer, P. H., Arch. Biochem. Biophys., *72:* 119, 1957.
2. Atassi, M. Z. and Caruso, D. R., Biochemistry, *7:* 699, 1968.
3. May, J. E. and Brown, R. K., Immunochemistry, *5:* 79, 1968.
4. Sri Ram, J., Terminiello, L., Bier, M. and Nord, F. F., Arch. Biochem. Biophys., *52:* 464, 1954.
5. Griffin, D., Tachibana, D. K., Nelson, B. and Rosenberg, L. T., Immunochemistry, *4:* 23, 1967.
6. Cohen, S. and Becker, E. L., J. Immun., *100:* 403, 1968.
7. Grossberg, A. L. and Pressman, D., Biochemistry, *7:* 272, 1968.
8. Swanborg, R. H., J. Immun., *102:* 381, 1969.
9. Howard, A. N. and Wild, F., Biochem. J., *65:* 651, 1957.
10. Tabachnick, M. and Sobotka, H., J. Biol. Chem., *235:* 1051, 1960.
11. Eylar, E. H. and Hashim, G. A., Proc. Nat. Acad. Sci., *61:* 644, 1968.
12. Eylar, E. H. and Hashim, G. A., Arch. Biochem. Biophys., *131:* 215, 1969.
13. Carnegie, P. R., Bencina, B. and Lamoureux, G., Biochem. J., *105:* 559, 1967.
14. Kibler, R. F., Shapira, R., McKneally, S., Jenkins, J., Selden, P. and Chou, F., Science, *164:* 557, 1969.
15. Swanborg, R. H., Fed. Proc., *29:* 373, 1970.
16. Kies, M. W., Ann. N. Y. Acad. Sci., *122:* 161, 1965.
17. Horton, H. R. and Koshland, D. E., Jr., J. Amer. Chem. Soc., *87:* 1126, 1965.
18. Fraenkel-Conrat, H., in *Methods in Enzymology*, Vol. 4, p. 251, Edited by S. P. Colowick and N. O. Kaplan, Academic Press, New York, 1957.
19. Rosen, H., Arch. Biochem. Biophys., *67:* 10, 1957.
20. Yankeelov, J. A., Jr., Mitchell, C. D. and Crawford, T. H., J. Amer. Chem. Soc., *90:* 1664, 1968.

21. Izumi, Y., Anal. Biochem., *10:* 218, 1965.
22. Gornall, A., Bardawill, C. and David, M., J. Biol. Chem., *177:* 751, 1949.
23. Shulman, S., Milgrom, F. and Swanborg, R. H., Immunology, *16:* 25, 1969.
24. Alvord, E. C., Jr. and Kies, M. W., J. Neuropath. Exp. Neurol., *18:* 447, 1959.
25. Lamoureux, G., Carnegie, P. R. and McPherson, T. A., Immunochemistry, *4:* 273, 1967.
26. Chao, L. P. and Einstein, E. R., J. Biol. Chem., *243:* 6050, 1968.
27. Loudon, G. M., Portsmouth, D., Lukton, A. and Koshland, D. E., Jr., J. Amer. Chem. Soc., *91:* 2792, 1969.

THE JOURNAL OF IMMUNOLOGY

Vol. 105, No. 4, October 1970
Printed in U.S.A.

STUDIES ON THE IMMUNE CAPABILITIES OF CHIROPTERA

I. Quantitative and Qualitative Nature of the Immune Responses in Bats to Bacteriophage φX174[1]

BETTY A. HATTEN, RAE ALLEN AND S. EDWARD SULKIN

From the Department of Microbiology, The University of Texas (Southwestern) Medical School, Dallas, Texas

Received for publication May 12, 1970

K values based on 90% neutralization of φX174 indicate that the response of bats held at 24°C and 37°C to immunization with multiple doses of 10^{10} plaque-forming units (PFU) was less and that production of ME-sensitive antibodies was more pronounced than in rabbits or guinea pigs. Neutralization of φX174 by early bat antibodies was especially dependent upon the presence of a heat-labile serum factor or factors. Once a response was elicited in bats (24°C), antibody production continued at a relatively high level for a long period of time. An anamnestic response was demonstrated at the latter time interval in which the quantity of predominantly ME-resistant antibodies, having minimal requirements for heat-labile factors, approached that induced earlier in guinea pigs. A rapid response with early conversion to ME-resistant antibodies was evoked in bats (24°C) after single doses of 10^{11} PFU of φX174 (without adjuvant) or 10^9 PFU of φX174 in complete adjuvant. Considerable dissociation of φX174 from bat antibodies occurred when less than 90% of the phage had been neutralized, but was not remarkable when inactivation was greater than 90%. The proportionate loss of anti-φX174 activity in relation to concentration of antibodies diminished upon dilution of bat plasma pools as the immune response progressed, suggesting that an increase in affinity of antibodies for φX174 had occurred, possibly in association with changes in the major type of antibody being produced. Potential effects of the nature and degree of antigenic stimulation upon immune responses in bats are discussed.

A preliminary study indicated that while the initial immune response of bats to multiple doses of an *E. coli* phage, φX174, was more rapid than in conventional laboratory animals, the magnitude and duration of their response appeared to be less (1). Bat antibodies were also more sensitive to mercaptoethanol and to dilution than rabbit and guinea pig antibodies. The immune response of bats to immunization with live Japanese B encephalitis virus was subsequently found to be quantitatively less, but qualitatively similar, to that produced in guinea pigs and at least two types of bat antibodies having characteristics of 19S and 7S immunoglobulins were demonstrated (2).

[1] This investigation was supported in part by National Science Foundation Grant GB-12611 (formerly GB-6612) and United States Public Health Service Research Grant AI-02316 from the National Institute of Allergy and Infectious Diseases.

This paper discusses continued studies on the quantitative and qualitative nature of the immune response in bats to φX174 and provides some information concerning the kinetics of phage inactivation by bat antibodies.

MATERIALS AND METHODS

Bats. Big brown bats (*Eptesicus f. fuscus*), kindly supplied by Professor James B. Cope, Earlham College, Richmond, Ind., were handled and maintained in the laboratory by methods previously described (3).

Bacteriophage. Preparation of purified φX174 was similar to that published earlier (1). Titers of purified and concentrated φX174 ranged between 10^{10} and 10^{11} plaque-forming units (PFU) /ml and when stored at −20°C showed no appreciable loss in titer over a 9- to 12-month period.

Preparation of antisera. All animals injected with multiple doses of phage initially received three weekly doses of 10^{10} PFU of ϕX174 subcutaneously followed by a single subcutaneous dose of 10^{10} PFU 8 weeks after the first inoculation. Plasma pools originally collected from six groups of bats held at 24°C and 37°C (bats 24°C and bats 37°C, respectively) each were combined into one large pool so that results indicated represent the average response of from 12 to 45 animals at every time interval examined. Results with rabbit and guinea pig antisera were obtained from pooled sera from 3 animals each. Globulin pools used for kinetic studies and to confirm inactivation rates where anti-ϕX174 activity was low were obtained by treatment of sera or plasma pools with saturated ammonium sulfate. The precipitated globulins were washed and reconstituted in buffered saline (pH 7.2) in a concentration so that neutralization in the range of 90% could be attained, when possible, after a short incubation period.

Bats receiving single immunizing doses of ϕX174 were inoculated subcutaneously with and without complete adjuvant. Mixtures consisting of equal volumes of phage and adjuvant were such that 0.1 ml of inoculum contained 10^9 PFU of ϕX174. Pools initially comprised of plasmas from eight bats were generally reduced to three or four animals at later time intervals due to the increased mortality rate among animals after several intra-cardiac bleedings.

Neutralization tests. Basic procedures followed in neutralization tests and for mercaptoethanol (ME) treatment of sera and plasma pools were identical to those described earlier (1, 4). Tests were generally carried out with 10^5 to 10^6 PFU of ϕX174 in the incubation tubes, but the concentration varied from 10^4 to 10^7 PFU depending on the conditions of the experiment. No differences in inactivation rates were revealed when representative sera were incubated with concentrations of ϕX174 in this range. K values calculated by the method of Adams (5) and indicated as log K in the figures are averages of several determinations made with neutralization in the range of 90%. Survival of ϕX174 after incubation with anti-globulin, recorded as the log of the surviving fraction, was also obtained from averages of several tests.

Dissociation tests. To determine if ϕX174 could be dissociated from antibody upon dilution, tests were carried out after phage had been incubated with anti-globulin pools for 30 min at 37°C and after continued incubation overnight at 4°C. Percentages of phage dissociating were calculated from differences in the amount of phage inactivated when mixtures of antigen and antibody were plated undiluted and after dilutions ranging up to 1:100 and 1:1000, respectively. Slopes of curves plotted from these results indicate that the percentages of phage dissociating within these ranges are proportional to the dilution of the mixture. Concentrations of anti-globulins used in the tests were selected so that the lowest dilution neutralized approximately 90% of the phage after 30 min incubation. The second dilution was generally a twofold dilution of the first which usually gave in the neighborhood of 80% neutralization in 30 min. Determinations carried out with similar dilutions of rabbit and guinea pig anti-globulins showed no appreciable dissociation of phage with either concentration of antibody or incubation times when antigen-antibody mixtures were diluted in a range up to 1:5000.

RESULTS

Immune response to multiple doses of ϕX174. K values based on 90% inactivation of ϕX174 by pooled guinea pig and rabbit antisera increased between the 3rd and 8th weeks and were comparable throughout the first 5 weeks, but by the 8th week anti-ϕX174 activity in the guinea pig serum pool was almost twice that of the rabbit pool (Figs. 1*a* and 1*b*). A sharp increase in anti-phage activity was detected in the guinea pig pool obtained 1 week after a booster dose of 10^{10} PFU of ϕX174 while only a slight increase was demonstrable in the pooled rabbit antisera collected at the same time. K values of 4-week and 9-week rabbit serum pools were reduced approximately 40% and 15%, respectively, by treatment with ME. Ten per cent of the anti-ϕX174 activity in the 9-week guinea pig pool was removed by ME treatment; none was removed from the 12-week pool. Anti-ϕX174 activity of 3-week and 12-week rabbit sera; and 3-, 4-, 5- and 8-week guinea pig sera was enhanced by ME treatment. Inactivation of the antisera and normal rabbit serum used in the dilution tubes resulted in a marked reduction in the K values of both rabbit and guinea pig pools. The propor-

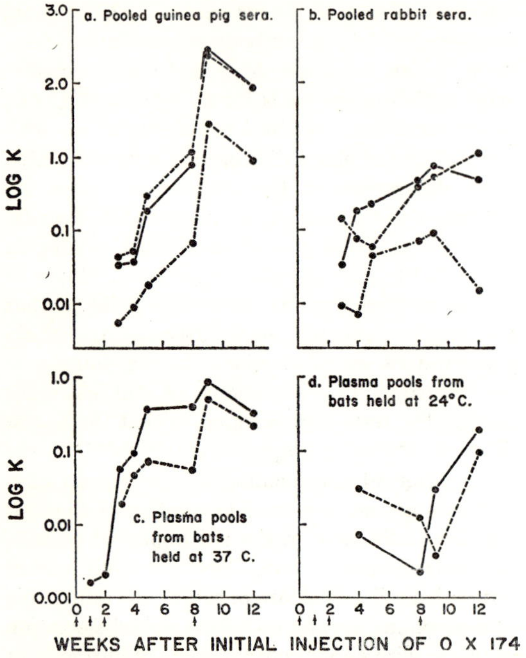

Figure 1. Immune response of guinea pigs (*a*), rabbits (*b*), bats 37°C (*c*) and bats 24°C (*d*) after multiple doses of ϕX174. Arrows indicate time intervals at which doses containing 10^{10} PFU were administered subcutaneously. *K* values, indicated as log K, are averages of results obtained with uninactivated, ●——●; ME-treated, uninactivated, ●-----●; and inactivated, ●·-·-·●, sera or plasma pools.

tionate loss in anti-ϕX174 activity observed with inactivated sera did not decrease during the 12-week period over which the anti-sera were collected.

Pooled plasmas from bats held at 37°C had increasing *K* values during the first 8 weeks with a two-fold increase 1 week after a booster dose of ϕX174 (Fig. 1*c*). *K* values of the bat (37°C) plasma pools were comparable to those obtained in rabbit antisera between 3 and 9 weeks, but were slightly lower in the 12-week pool. *K* values were decreased from 50% to 80% after ME treatment of 3-week to 9-week bat (37°C) plasma pools. Mercaptoethanol treatment of the 12-week pool resulted in a 30% reduction in *K* value. Plasma pools from bats held at 24°C showed little anti-ϕX174 activity during the first 5 weeks even when the globulins were precipitated and concentrated several times (Fig. 1*d*). Consequently, *K* values for

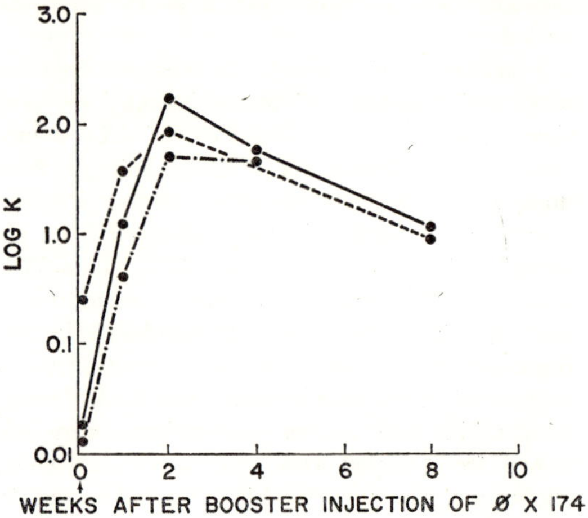

Figure 2. Immune response of bats (24°C) 3.5 years after multiple doses of ϕX174. Arrow indicates time interval at which a booster dose containing 10^{10} PFU was administered subcutaneously. *K* values, indicated as log K, are averages of results obtained with uninactivated, ●——●; ME-treated, uninactivated, ●-----●; and inactivated, ●·-·-·●, plasma pools.

plasma pools collected prior to the booster dose of phage could be determined only on those collected at 4 and 8 weeks. Approximately a 10-fold increase in *K* value occurred 1 week after a booster dose of ϕX174 given 8 weeks after initial injection of phage. Anti-ϕX174 activity was still increasing on the 12th week where it approached that of the comparable pool from bats held at 37°C. Anti-ϕX174 activity was enhanced in 4-week and 8-week bat (24°C) plasma pools treated with ME, but 9- and 12-week pools had greater loss of activity after treatment than the same plasma pools from bats held at 37°C. A previous study has shown that ME sensitive and resistant bat antibodies are characteristic of 19S and 7S immunoglobulins, respectively, when fractionated on DEAE-cellulose columns and by ultracentrifugation, and examined by immunoelectrophoresis (2). Removal of heat labile serum factors from the test system by inactivation of sera and bat plasma pools used in the experiments at 56°C for 30 min eliminated most of the anti-phage activity. Ninety per cent inactivation was never reached except with 8-, 9- and 12-week plasma pools from bats held at 37°C which had been allowed to incubate with ϕX174 for 2 hr at 37°C and then overnight at 4°C.

Duration of immunity to φX174 in bats held at 24°C. K values of a plasma pool from several bats (24°C) surviving 3.5 years after initial immunization with φX174 were high in comparison with those observed during the first 12 weeks after initial immunization (Fig. 2). A 10^{10} PFU dose of phage given to the survivors at this time brought about an immediate response with approximately a 70-fold increase in K value by the end of the 1st week. At the end of the 2nd week, the magnitude of the response approached that obtained earlier in guinea pigs after a booster dose of φX174. The greatest reduction in K value after ME treatment of plasma pools occurred 2 weeks after the booster dose of φX174, but most activity in all pools was ME resistant. While removal of heat labile factors decreased the rate of φX174 inactivation, K values could be determined for all inactivated pools and reduction in anti-φX174 activity was less than in guinea pig and rabbit antisera tested under similar conditions.

Immune response of bats to single doses of φX174. In order to determine whether bats were capable of responding to smaller doses of φX174, four groups of animals (24°C) were inoculated subcutaneously with 10^{11}, 10^{9}, 10^{7} PFU of φX174, and 10^{9} PFU of φX174 in complete adjuvant, respectively. While the response to 10^{7} PFU of φX174 was negligible and 90% inactivation was not reached until 20 weeks after inoculation of 10^{9} PFU of φX174, the responses to 10^{11} PFU of φX174 (without adjuvant) and 10^{9} PFU of φX174 in adjuvant were very good in comparison to that obtained in bats (24°C) after multiple doses of phage. K values could be determined for plasma pools from all time intervals tested in these two groups with the exception of pools collected 1 wk after immunization (Fig. 3). K values were comparable in the two groups although the maximum was reached more rapidly and declined earlier in plasma pools from animals receiving 10^{9} PFU of φX174 and adjuvant than in those receiving 10^{11} PFU of φX174. A more rapid conversion to ME-resistant antibodies was also detected in plasma pools from bats (24°C) injected with 10^{9} PFU of φX174 and adjuvant where virtually all anti-φX174 activity was ME resistant by the end of the 4th week. Almost no ME-resistant antibody was present in the 4-week plasma pool from bats receiving 10^{11} PFU of φX174, but most was ME resistant at 6 weeks

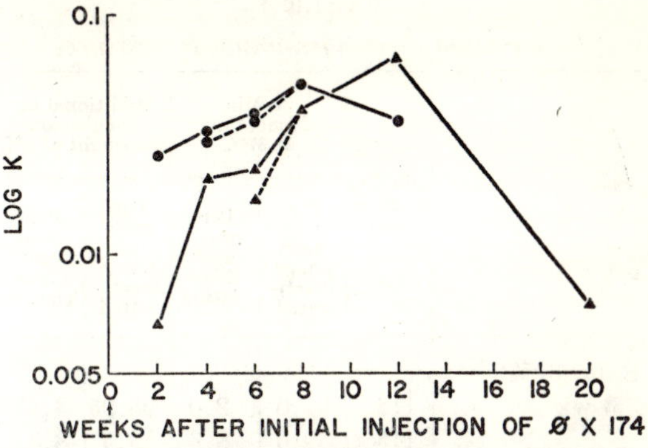

Figure 3. Immune response of bats (24°C) to single doses of φX174. Arrow at 0 time indicates time interval at which 10^{11} PFU, ▲; or 10^{9} PFU, ●, in complete adjuvant each were administered to a group of animals subcutaneously. K values, indicated as log K, are averages obtained with uninactivated, ——; and ME-treated, uninactivated, -----, plasma pools.

and all was resistant at 8 weeks. K values could not be determined in either group after ME treatment of plasma pools taken at earlier time intervals. Inactivation of sera and plasma pools used in the neutralization tests resulted in almost complete loss of anti-φX174 activity in all instances.

Kinetics of φX174 inactivation by bat antibodies. Preliminary experiments indicated that no significant dissociation occurred upon dilution of antigen-antibody mixtures containing φX174 and rabbit or guinea pig antibodies, but mixtures containing bat antibodies obtained after multiple injections of phage dissociated to varying degrees. Since it appeared that dissociation of φX174-bat antibody mixtures might be related to antibody concentration (1), dissociation tests were repeated using two dilutions of each bat globulin. The percentage of φX174 dissociating upon dilution of the mixtures was much less when 90% or more of the phage had been inactivated (Table I). Dilution of the antibodies approximately twofold decreased the percentage of phage inactivated after 30 min incubation and large proportions of φX174 could be dissociated by diluting the mixtures 1:100 at this time. Once 90% inactivation had been reached, the initial concentration of antibody had little effect upon the percentage of phage dissociating even when mixtures were diluted 1:1000.

After 90% or more of the phage had been in-

TABLE I

Dissociation of antigen-antibody mixtures

	Dilution of Antibody	30-Min Incubation at 37°C		Additional at Incubation Overnight at 4°C	
		Percentage[a] phage inactivated	Percentage[b] dissociation	Percentage phage inactivated	Percentage[c] dissociation
Bats (37°C)					
3 wk	1:2	91.0	2.0	96.95	3.45
	1:5	80.0	8.6	89.5	8.3
5 wk	1:40	91.0	1.03	98.9	1.35
	1:80	78.0	75.4	96.0	3.5
9 wk	1:80	96.0	4.0	98.5	2.2
	1:160	84.0	38.0	96.0	3.0
Bats (24°C)					
4 wk	1:5	89.05	7.5		
	1:10	66.0	90.0	97.7	5.3
12 wk	1.20	95.3	5.5	97.35	2.0
	1.40	78.2	62.0	89.5	4.7
3.5-yr	1:10	97.0	2.0	99.03	1.48
	1:50	50.0	34.0	98.27	0

[a] Percentage inactivation of phage in undiluted mixtures.

[b] Percentage dissociation of ϕX174 from mixtures when diluted 1:100 and allowed to stand at room temperature 15 min before plating.

[c] Percentage dissociation of ϕX174 from mixtures when diluted 1:1000 and allowed to stand at room temperature 15 min before plating.

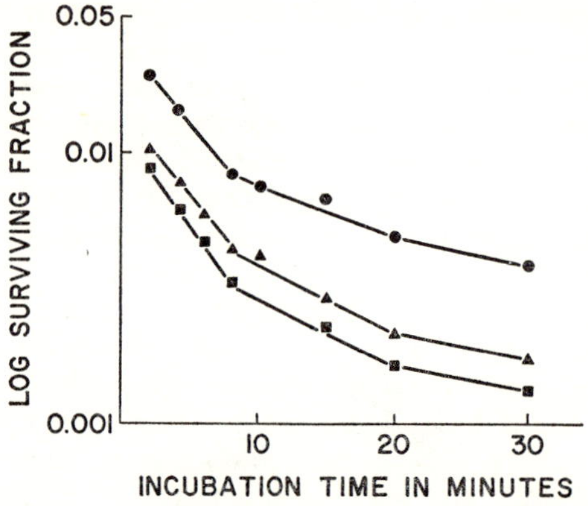

Figure 4. Inactivation curves obtained with 9-week bat (24°C, ●; and 37°C, ▲,) and guinea pig, ■, globulin pools showing similar secondary rates of ϕX174 neutralization.

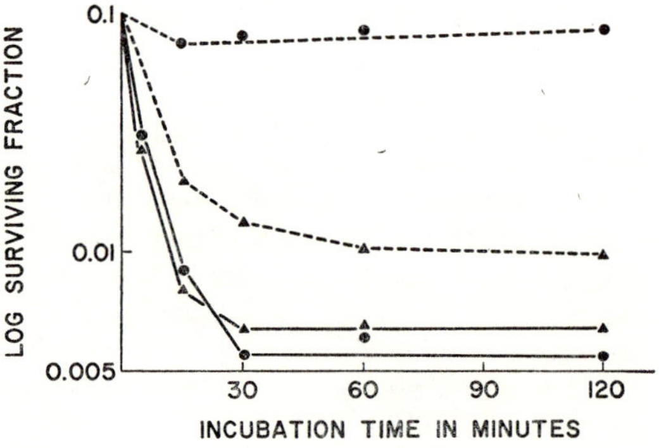

Figure 5. Inactivation of ϕX174 by 1:2, ——; and 1:5 -----, dilutions of bat (24°C) plasma pools collected 4 weeks, ●; and 6 weeks, ▲, after a single subcutaneous dose of 10^{11} PFU.

activated, inactivation rates were quite similar for all three animal species when inactivation curves of comparable globulin pools were compared. Inactivation curves with almost identical slopes shown in Figure 4 were obtained with 9-week bat (24 and 37°C) and guinea pig globulin pools from animals receiving multiple doses of ϕX174. Such results provide additional evidence that dissociation of ϕX174-bat antibody complexes is not excessive during latter stages of phage inactivation and suggests that bat antibodies are not unlike those of other animals in their secondary binding capacity.

Results indicating that loss of anti-ϕX174 activity upon dilution of bat plasma pools may be related to the developmental stage of the immune response and not entirely to decreased concentration of antibodies have been obtained. Figure 5 shows the rate of ϕX174 inactivation by plasma pools collected 4 weeks and 6 weeks after immunization of bats (24°C) with a single subcutaneous dose of 10^{11} PFU of ϕX174. When diluted 1:2, the plasma pools inactivated phage at about the same rate, but when tested in a 1:5 dilution, marked differences in the degree of phage inactivation occurring over a 2-hr incubation period were apparent. While a fivefold dilution of the 4-week plasma pool resulted in nearly complete loss of anti-ϕX174 activity, inactivation by a 1:5 dilution of the 6-week pool proceeded at about the rate anticipated from calculations based on results obtained when the pool was diluted 1:2. Treatment of the two pools with ME showed that a major portion of the anti-ϕX174 activity in the 6-week pool was ME resistant whereas most of that in the 4-week pool was

ME sensitive. These results suggest that bat antibodies produced during early phases of the immune response to ϕX174 have less affinity for specific antigen than those present later in the immune response and indicate that differences in affinity may be, at least partially, dependent upon the type of antibodies being produced.

DISCUSSION

This paper confirms and extends earlier results which led to the conclusion that the quantity and quality of antibodies produced in bats following immunization with ϕX174 was less than in guinea pigs and rabbits (1). Quantitatively the response of bats held at 37°C was similar to that obtained in rabbits, but declined more rapidly after a booster dose of phage. The response was characterized by production of considerable amounts of ME-sensitive antibody and induction of a true anamnestic response was not shown in bats held at 37°C. The response of animals kept at 24°C, on the other hand, was less and the production of ME-sensitive antibodies more pronounced than in those held at 37°C. Occasional enhancement of anti-ϕX174 activity after ME treatment of sera or plasma pools may indicate the presence of ME-sensitive "blocking" antibodies having a high affinity for ϕX174, but little neutralizing capabilities. Enhancement of antibody activity following ME treatment of antisera has been encountered by other workers (6).

Continued production of ME-sensitive antibodies as well as prolonged synthesis of antibodies has been related to persistence of antigen in several animals (7, 8). Presence of anti-ϕX174 antibodies, some of which were ME sensitive, long after immunization of bats (24°C) with multiple doses of ϕX174 suggests retention of phage by these animals. The immediate and dramatic response to a booster injection of ϕX174 3.5 years after initial immunization demonstrates that bats held at 24°C are capable of developing an adequate response to antigenic stimulation under certain conditions. Quantitative improvement in the immune response and early conversion to ME-resistant antibodies in bats receiving single doses of ϕX174 indicate that multiple doses of phage may have exceeded levels required for optimal antibody production.

Differences in the immune response of rabbits and guinea pigs can be accounted for on a dose per weight basis but on this basis alone does not justify differences between the response of guinea pigs and bats. That the much greater dose per weight ratio in bats compounded by lower metabolic rates of animals held at 24°C hampered efficient processing of antigen is feasible.

Induction of immune tolerance or exhaustion as a result of over-stimulation with antigens is well known (9–12). Suppression of anamnestic responses has also been attributed to titers of circulating antibodies above the level necessary for stimulation of new antibody synthesis (8, 13, 14). Presence of circulating antibodies could account for the poor secondary response observed in bats held at 37°C since animals held at 24°C, in which only small amounts of circulating antibody could be detected, had a relatively better response when given a booster dose of ϕX174 at the same time interval.

Neutralization of phage by early bat antibodies was especially dependent upon heat labile factors available in uninactivated sera, but antibodies present after a prolonged period of time had minimal requirements for these factors. Although no differences in heat labile serum factor requirements of early and late guinea pig and rabbit ϕX174 antibodies were detected, reports noting changes in complement requirements of neutralizing antibodies to both bacterial and animal viruses have been made (15, 16).

Dissociation of ϕX174 from bat antibodies was marked during early phases of inactivation but was not unusual during final stages. Slopes of inactivation curves indicate that secondary binding of ϕX174 by bat antibodies was similar to that obtained with guinea pig antibodies confirming that dissociation was not excessive during later stages of phage inactivation and substantiating earlier conclusions that equal numbers of bat and guinea pig antibodies are probably required to neutralize viral infectivity (2). While bat antibodies differ somewhat from rabbit and guinea pig antibodies produced under the same conditions, interaction between ϕX174 and antibody produced in bats is not unlike that described for several virus-antibody systems in which a primary, reversible phase of inactivation is followed by a secondary, irreversible phase (15). Affinity of bat antibodies for ϕX174 after a single dose of phage increased as the immune response progressed and seemed to be associated with the type of antibodies being produced. Increasing affinity of antibodies for specific antigen during development of an immune response is expected and differences in the affinity of early and late 19S and 7S antibodies have been shown (15, 17). The relative affinities of purified 19S and 7S bat antibodies for antigen have not been studied.

Results of studies on the immune response of bats to a variety of antigens tend to agree that their response is different from homeothermic animals, although perhaps no different than other hibernating mammals (18–21). The quantity and quality of antibodies synthesized by bats may be especially dependent upon the degree and nature of the antigenic stimulation since optimal conditions for maximum antibody production are more critical than in animals where metabolic processes are more stable. It has been proposed that more avid antibodies are bound by excess antigen *in vivo* and as a result are not detected by *in vitro* assays (8, 9). Bats are known to harbor infectious viruses for long periods of time (19, 22), and present indications are that phage may have persisted *in vivo* long after animals received multiple doses of ϕX174. Thus, apparent deficiencies in the immune response of bats, particularly with regard to the quantity and quality of circulating antibodies, are not conclusive evidence that a basic anomaly exists in the immune capabilities of this animal.

Acknowledgment. The authors thank Mary Louise Schulze for technical assistance, and LaRue Christian for care and maintenance of bats used in this study.

REFERENCES

1. Hatten, B. A., Allen, R. and Sulkin, S. E., J. Immun., *101:* 141, 1968.
2. Leonard, L. L., Allen, R. and Sulkin, S. E., J. Immun., *101:* 1168, 1968.
3. Sulkin, S. E., Allen, R. and Sims, R. A. Amer. J. Trop. Med., *12:* 800, 1963.
4. Uhr, J. W., Finkelstein, M. S. and Baumann, J. B., J. Exp. Med., *115:* 655, 1962.
5. Adams, M. H., *Bacteriophages*, p. 463, Interscience Publishers, Inc., New York, 1959.
6. Uhr, J. W. and Finkelstein, M. S., J. Exp. Med., *117:* 457, 1963.
7. Möller, G., J. Exp. Med., *127:* 291, 1968.
8. Good, R. A. and Möller, G., in *Immunological Tolerance: A Reassessment of Mechanisms of the Immune Response*, Proceedings of an International Congress, Brook Lodge, Augusta, Mich., Sept. 18–20, 1968, Edited by M. Landy and W. Braun, p. 215, Academic Press, New York, 1969.
9. Goidl, E. A., Paul, Wm. E., Siskind, G. W. and Benacerraf, B., J. Immun., *100:* 371, 1968.
10. Byers, V. and Sercarz, E. E., J. Exp. Med., *127:* 307, 1968.
11. Miller, J. F. A. P. and Nossal G. J. V., in, *Immunological Tolerance: A Reassessment of Mechanisms of the Immune Response*, Proceedings of an International Congress, Brook Lodge, Augusta, Mich., Sept. 18–20, 1968, Edited by M. Landy and W. Braun, p. 53, Academic Press, New York, 1969.
12. Dresser, D. W. and Mitchison, N. A., Advances Immun., *8:* 129, 1968.
13. Cerottini, J. C., McConahey, P. J. and Dixon, F. J., J. Immun., *103:* 268, 1969.
14. Uhr, J. W. and Möller, G., Advances Immun., *8:* 81, 1968.
15. Svehag, S. E., in *Progress in Medical Virology*, Edited by J. L. Melnick, Vol. 10, p. 1, S. Karger, New York, 1968.
16. Hampar, B., Notkins, A. L., Mage, M. and Keehn, M. A., J. Immun., *100:* 586, 1968.
17. Finkelstein, M. S. and Uhr, J. W., J. Immun., *97:* 565, 1966.
18. Fletcher, M. A., Sims, R., Allen, R. and Sulkin, S. E., Texas Rep. Biol. Med., *20:* 142, 1962.
19. Sulkin, S. E., Allen, R., Sims, R. and Singh, K. V., Amer. J. Trop. Med., *15:* 418, 1966.
20. McKenna, J. M., and Musacchia, X. J., Proc. Soc. Exp. Biol. Med., *129:* 720, 1968.
21. Jarslow, B. W., Proc. Nat. Acad. Sci., *61:* 69, 1968.
22. Sulkin, S. E., in *Progress in Medical Virology*, Edited by E. Berger and J. L. Melnick, Vol. 4, p. 158, S. Karger, New York, 1962.

THE JOURNAL OF IMMUNOLOGY
Vol. 105, No. 4, October 1970

Printed in U.S.A.

NATURAL AND ANTIBODY-INDUCED ADHERENCE OF GUINEA PIG PHAGOCYTIC CELLS TO AUTOLOGOUS AND HETEROLOGOUS THYMOCYTES[1]

ISRAEL SIEGEL

From the Robert A. Cooke Institute of Allergy, Department of Medicine, The Roosevelt Hospital, New York, New York

Received for publication May 8, 1970

Adherence of macrophages and thymocytes occurs in cell mixtures containing untreated guinea pig macrophages and autologous or homologous thymocytes. Morphologically the reaction resembles the adherence of guinea pig macrophages to heterologous lymphocytes which has been induced by moderate concentrations of antilymphocyte serum. There is relatively little natural adherence of guinea pig macrophages to rat, mouse, and rabbit thymocytes or to extra-thymic guinea pig lymphocytes. Adherence of autologous or homologous guinea pig macrophages and thymocytes occurs in the absence of serum but is augmented when guinea pig serum or gelatin is present. At high serum concentrations the adherence is often followed by phagocytosis of autologous thymocytes by the macrophages. When serum is incubated at 57°C for 30 min its ability to induce phagocytosis is abolished but its ability to enhance adherence is not. Dialysis of serum against salt solution does not affect its ability to enhance adherence or phagocytosis. Treatment of macrophages with trypsin completely abolishes the adherence of autologous macrophages and thymocytes. The degree of adherence of guinea pig neutrophils and eosinophils to autologous and homologous thymocytes exceeds their adherence to extra-thymic guinea pig lymphocytes or heterologous thymocytes but is less than the adherence of guinea pig macrophages. Comparative studies have indicated that the adherence of autologous macrophages and thymocytes does not occur through any of the known opsonic actions of circulating antibodies. It is postulated that adherence of autologous macrophages and thymocytes may participate in mechanisms which limit the number and circulation of thymocytes.

Conditions which lead to adherence of macrophages and lymphocytes have been generally associated with the presence or development of immune responses. Macrophages tend to adhere to and phagocytize cells in the presence of opsonic antibodies against the cells. Lymphocytes have also been shown to adhere to other cell types in the absence of detectable antibodies during certain delayed type immune responses *in vitro* (1). The action of opsonic antibodies which cause phagocytic cells to adhere to lymphocytes *in vitro* have been correlated with the immunosuppressive activity of antilymphocyte serum (ALS) (2). Cell transfer studies have identified the lymphocytes affected during immunosuppressive activity of ALS as thymocytes (3). Adherence of macrophages and lymphocytes likewise occurs through unknown mechanisms during the stimulation period when lymphocytes are transformed into blast cells. This has been postulated to aid in the transfer of stimulatory factors from macrophages to lymphocytes (4). During the initial stages of the present study, attempts were made to utilize macrophage-lymphocyte adherence as an index for the presence or absence of immune responses *in vitro*. It was found that there was little or no adherence of macrophages and lymphocytes when macrophages were mixed with heterologous (foreign) lymphocytes. There was, however, a significant macrophage-lymphocyte

[1] This work was supported by Grants AI-05861 and 5T1-AI-201 from the National Institute of Allergy and Infectious Diseases, United States Public Health Service.

adherence in mixtures containing normal guinea pig macrophages and autologous thymocytes (5, 6). This occurred in the absence of any known antibodies or immune stimuli. The adherence was highly specific, and resembled morphologically the adherence of guinea pig macrophages to heterologous lymphocytes which occurs in the presence of moderate concentrations of opsonins. This phenomenon will be described in greater detail and will be compared to the adherence of macrophages to lymphocytes which occurs through the action of antibodies against lymphocytes.

MATERIALS AND METHODS

Animals. The animals used in this study were 250 to 500 g Hartley guinea pigs, 2 to 3 kg New Zealand White rabbits, 30- to 40-g Swiss-Webster mice, and 75- to 200-g Sprague-Dawley rats. Random bred males and females were used.

Salt solutions. Unless otherwise specified, all cells and reagents were prepared in a phosphate-buffered modified Hanks' solution (7).

Cells. Peritoneal white cells were obtained by lavage of peritoneal cavities. The peritoneal white cell suspensions often contained varying numbers of red cells. Only white cell preparations in which the concentration of red cells did not exceed the concentration of white cells were used in this study. White cells obtained from the peritoneal cavity of untreated guinea pigs usually consisted of 70% to 90% relatively large mononuclear cells ($>12\ \mu$) and 10% to 30% eosinophils and relatively small mononuclear cells of the size ($<9\ \mu$) and morphology of small lymphocytes. Practically all of the relatively large peritoneal mononuclear cells were phagocytic (8) and were therefore classified as macrophages.

There were generally few or no neutrophils in peritoneal cell suspensions of untreated guinea pigs. Peritoneal white cells consisting predominantly of neutrophils were, however, obtained 4 to 8 hr after an initial lavage of the peritoneal cavity or intraperitoneal injection of 1 to 5 ml of salt solution.

Peripheral white cells were obtained from the buffy coat layer of heparinized guinea pig whole blood after the blood had been centrifuged for 10 min at 1200 rpm.

Guinea pig bone marrow cells were obtained from aspirations and washing of split tibias or fibulas.

Lymphocyte suspensions were obtained from the thymus or lymph nodes by crushing tissue fragments in a loose-fitting glass homogenizer. Most of the stroma and visible cell clumps which settled to the bottom of the tube by gravity were discarded during cell preparation. The final lymphocyte suspensions contained predominantly free cells. These consisted of 95% to 98% small lymphocytes and 2% to 5% larger cells. Spleen cells were obtained by similar methods and contained a heterogeneous cell population.

All cells were stored at 4°C and were used on the day of preparation. Cells were kept cold during preparation and handling by immersing the tubes in ice baths and by using refrigerated centrifuges at 4°C during cell washing.

Autologous adherence. The experimental procedures after cell preparation were conducted at room temperature and consisted of the following: a) lymphocytes obtained from the thymus or lymph nodes were mixed with peritoneal cells at a concentration of 6.25×10^6 lymphocytes and 1.25×10^6 macrophages/ml in a total volume of 0.3 to 0.5 ml; b) the lymphocyte-macrophage mixtures were sedimented immediately by centrifugation at 1700 to 2000 rpm for 15 to 30 sec; and c) the sediment was resuspended and examined under the phase microscope.

The degree of adherence of macrophages to lymphocytes was evaluated by the total number of lymphocytes which adhered to 100 to 150 randomly chosen macrophages. The average number of lymphocytes which adhered to one macrophage multiplied by 100 was called the adherence index (AI). Single lymphocytes or lymphocytes in aggregates were easily distinguishable under the phase microscope by their smaller size from other cell types. Eosinophils were distinguished from macrophages or other cell types by the presence of large refractile granules in the eosinophils. Different cell types were especially distinct under the phase microscope 15 to 30 min after the slides were prepared and the cell nuclei were clearly outlined. The correct identification of cell types was confirmed in air-dried or formaldehyde vapor-fixed smears stained with Wright's stain or by a general polychromatic stain (9). Gross differences between degrees of adherence were detected by the presence and absence or by the sizes of the macrophage-lymphocyte aggregates. These differences were useful in comparing mixtures which contained relatively dense aggregates in which cells could not easily be counted.

Cytophilic anti-rat lymphocyte serum. Guinea pigs weighing about 300 g were injected into both hind footpads with a total of 0.5 ml of complete Freund's adjuvant containing 5×10^8 rat thymocytes. This was followed 6 weeks later by an intramuscular injection of 9.5×10^7 rat thymocytes in 3.8 ml of salt solution. Serum was obtained from blood taken from these guinea pigs 6 days after the latter injection, and was tested for cytophilic anti-rat lymphocyte activity. The main criterion for cytophilic activity of serum was its ability to confer specific cytophilic activity upon previously inactive macrophages. The test consisted of the following procedures. About 5×10^6 macrophages from unimmunized guinea pigs were suspended in 0.2 ml of 50% serum from immunized guinea pigs which was to be tested for cytophilic activity. Control tubes contained an equal concentration of cells in 50% serum from unimmunized guinea pigs. The mixtures were incubated at 37°C for 30 min. The cells were washed three times after incubation and resuspended in salt solution. The macrophages were then mixed and sedimented with rat thymocytes and observed microscopically according to the same procedures and cell concentrations utilized for autologous adherence.

Antilymphocyte opsonin titer. Rat thymocytes at a concentration of 2.25×10^7/ml were incubated with twofold dilutions of anti-rat lymphocyte serum (ALS) at 37°C for 60 min. They were then washed three times and resuspended in their original concentrations in salt solution. The treated thymocytes were then mixed and sedimented with guinea pig macrophages under the same conditions used for detecting autologous adherence. The reciprocal of the highest dilution of ALS used to treat the thymocytes which caused over 50% of the macrophages to adhere to one or more thymocytes was considered as the opsonic titer of the serum.

Lysin. Rat thymocytes treated as above with ALS were incubated at 37°C for 60 min with a 1:30 dilution of fresh guinea pig serum (used as a source of complement). Lysis was detected by phase microscopic observations of the thymocytes. Lysed thymocytes were swollen and consisted mostly of large cytoplasmic vacuoles. The reciprocal of the highest dilution of ALS which caused over 50% of the thymocytes to lyse was considered as the lysin titer.

Agglutinins. This was the reciprocal of the highest dilution of serum which caused most of the thymocytes to form aggregates which were detectable when ALS-treated thymocytes were washed and then observed under the phase microscope.

Treatment with trypsin. Trypsin used was twice crystallized, salt free (Worthington Biochemical Corp., Freehold, N. J.). Macrophages at a concentration of 2.5×10^6/ml were incubated with twofold dilutions of trypsin at 37°C for 60 min. Control cells were incubated in salt solution only. Cells were washed twice and resuspended in salt solution, and then tested for adherence activity according to procedures described above for untreated macrophages.

Macrophage eluates. 1.5×10^7 macrophages with or without cytophilic activity were suspended in 0.5 ml salt solution and then heated at 55 to 60°C for 30 min. The cell suspension was then centrifuged, the sediment was discarded and the supernatant used as eluate.

RESULTS

Autologous adherence. Table I summarizes the degree of adherence of macrophages and lymphocytes in a variety of cell mixtures. The degree of adherence of macrophages to autologous or homologous thymocytes varied with cells obtained from different guinea pigs but was significantly larger than the degree of adherence of macrophages to heterologous thymocytes or autologous or homologous extra-thymic lymphocytes. The majority of the macrophages in autologous or homologous mixtures usually adhered to one or more thymocytes. The adhering thymocytes often formed rosettes around the surfaces of the macrophages (Fig. 1). This occurred either immediately after centrifugation of the cell mixtures or after 60 min in uncentrifuged tubes left at room temperature or incubated at 37°C. In contrast, most macrophages remained free in mixtures containing guinea pig macrophages and mesenteric lymph node lymphocytes or rat and mouse thymocytes (Fig. 2, Table I). Adherence occurred only occasionally and consisted in most cases of 1 to 2 thymocytes which adhered to a single macrophage. There was little or no adherence of lymphocytes to other cell types when lymphocyte preparations were not mixed with macrophage preparations. There was no obvious spontaneous aggregation of lymphocytes in unmixed suspensions observed up to 24 hr after preparation. Spontaneous aggregation of peritoneal white cells occasionally occurred. In practically all instances, however, the aggregates consisted of large peritoneal cells and contained few or no small lymphocytes.

The degree of adherence of guinea pig macrophages to heterologous lymphocytes obtained from the rabbit was similar to that obtained with lymphocytes from the rat and the mouse. The degree of adherence of guinea pig macrophages to autologous or homologous lymphocytes obtained

TABLE I

Adherence of guinea pig macrophages to lymphocytes

Lymphocytes		Adherence Index	
Source	No. of animals	Mean ± standard deviation	Range
Autologous thymus	37	145 ± 62	39–315
Autologous mesenteric lymph nodes	34	25 ± 18	6–83
Homologous thymus	12	194 ± 74	25–340
Rat thymus	10	13 ± 4	2–11
Mouse thymus	6	14 ± 5	6–20

from cervical and popliteal lymph nodes and the spleen was similar to that obtained with lymphocytes from the mesenteric lymph nodes. There was little or no adherence of guinea pig thymocytes to rat, mouse and rabbit peritoneal white cells, or to most cells present in guinea pig spleen and bone marrow cells.

Effects of serum. Adherence of autologous or homologous macrophages and thymocytes was augmented in the presence of autologous or homologous sera in the cell mixtures. Thus, in the presence of the sera the adherence index was increased (Table II) and a large proportion of macrophage-thymocyte aggregates contained more than one macrophage. The ability of serum to augment adherence was not affected by heating the serum at 57°C for 30 min or by dialysis of the serum against modified Hanks' salt solution. Augmentation of adherence was evident at a dilution of up to 1:250 of normal sera. There was relatively little augmentation of adherence by autologous or homologous serum in mixtures containing extra-thymic lymphocytes instead of thymocytes.

In the presence of 25% to 50% serum, but not in the presence of lower serum concentrations, thymocytes were frequently seen inside macrophages. This was evident at room temperature about 5 to 60 min after slides had been prepared according to the procedures described for ob-

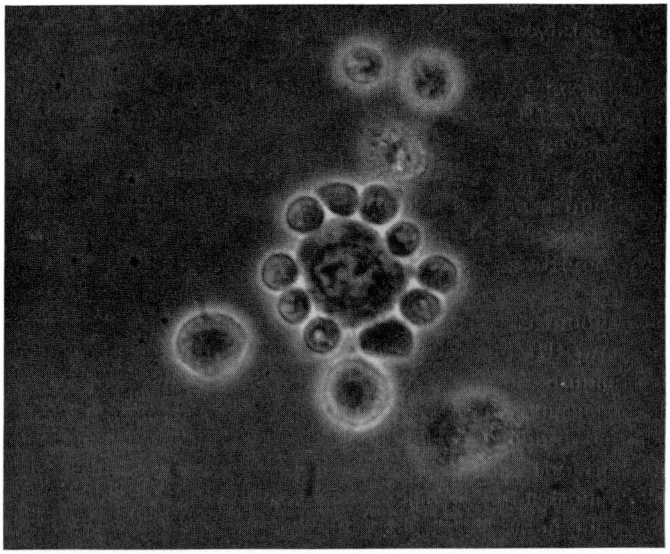

Figure 1. Untreated guinea pig macrophages and autologous thymocytes in salt solution

servation of adherence. In some cases the ingested thymocyte appeared to consist of a nucleus only surrounded by a relatively large refractive vacuole (Fig. 3). The ability of serum to cause phagocytosis under these conditions was not affected by dialyzing the serum against salt solution but was abolished by heating the serum at 57°C for 30 min. The adherence of macrophages to thymocytes was augmented not only by serum but also by 0.01% to 0.1% gelatine solution. Phagocytosis, however, was not induced by the gelatine solution.

Polymorphonuclear leukocytes. Peritoneal neutrophils and eosinophils adhered to autologous or homologous thymocytes to a larger extent than to heterologous thymocytes or autologous and homologous extra-thymic lymphocytes. The degree of adherence was, however, less than that of peritoneal macrophages obtained from the same guinea pig (Table II). This adherence was augmented by adding serum to the cell mixtures. Similar results were obtained with peripheral neutrophils.

Cytophilic thymocyte-macrophage adherence. Macrophages from unimmunized guinea pigs

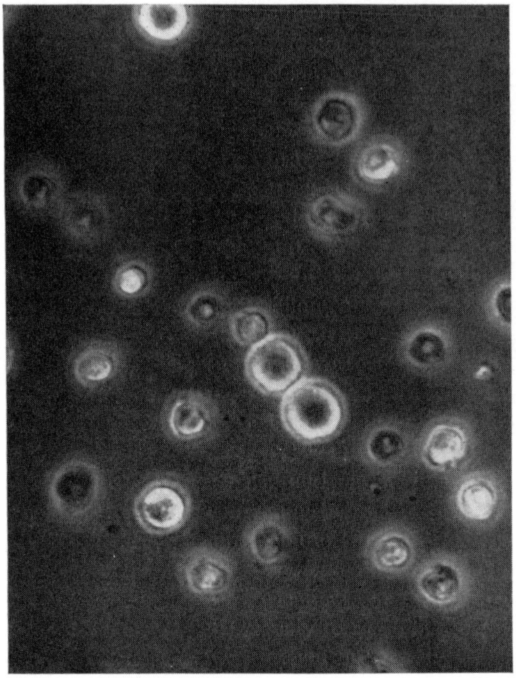

Figure 2. Untreated guinea pig macrophages and rat thymocytes in salt solution.

TABLE II

Adherence index in mixtures of guinea pig macrophages or neutrophils with autologous lymphocytes

	Without Serum		With Serum[a]	
	Thymocytes	Mesenteric lymph node lymphocytes	Thymocytes	Mesenteric lymph node lymphocytes
Macrophages	100	20	310	22
Neutrophils[b]	61	4	130	14

[a] Dilution of serum was 1:5.

[b] Peritoneal neutrophils and macrophages were obtained from the same guinea pig.

which were treated with cytophilic anti-rat lymphocyte serum adhered in the absence of serum to rat thymocytes and rat mesenteric lymph node lymphocytes, but not to rat red cells (Fig. 4). There was little or no adherence to mouse and rabbit lymphocytes. In contrast, macrophages exposed to sera of guinea pigs which were not immunized with rat thymocytes did not adhere to any of the rat cells.

Effect of trypsin. Autologous adherence was almost completely abolished by pretreatment of macrophages with 0.01% to 0.02% trypsin solution. Cytophilic adherence was likewise prevented by pretreatment of active macrophages with trypsin but required a minimal trypsin concentration of 0.125% to 0.25%. Exposure of trypsin-inactivated macrophages to guinea pig serum or heat eluates of active macrophages did not restore autologous adherence activity. In contrast, exposure of trypsinized macrophages to serum containing cytophilic activity or to heat eluates of macrophages which had cytophilic activity restored cytophilic activity to the macrophages. Similar effects of trypsin upon cytophilic activity and restoration of cytophilic adherence after trypsin digestion was reported by Weiser *et al.* (10).

Antibody-treated thymocytes. Guinea pig macrophages adhered to rat thymocytes in the absence of antiserum if thymocytes were pretreated with anti-rat lymphocyte serum. There was little or no adherence of guinea pig macrophages to untreated rat thymocytes or to rat thymocytes which have been treated with sera obtained from unimmunized guinea pigs. Table III illustrates the opsonic titers when untreated and trypsinized macrophages were utilized. In contrast to

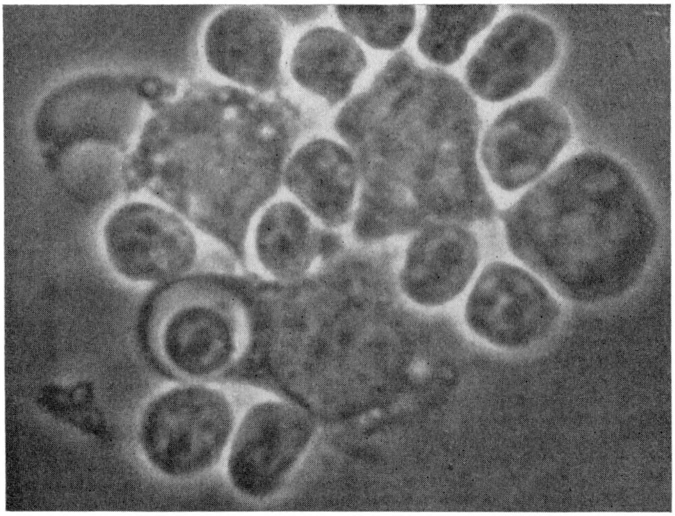

Figure 3. Guinea pig macrophages and autologous thymocytes in the presence of 1:3 dilution of autologous serum.

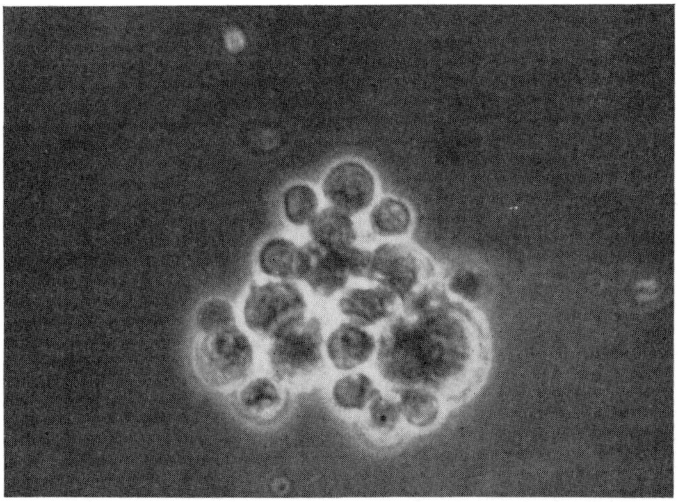

Figure 4. Guinea pig macrophages and rat thymocytes in salt solution. The macrophages had been previously treated with cytophilic anti-rat lymphocyte serum.

natural autologous adherence, treatment of macrophages with 0.1% trypsin solution did not affect their ability to adhere to antibody-pretreated thymocytes.

DISCUSSION

The main finding in this study is that adherence of phagocytic cells to autologous thymocytes occurs not only in the presence of antilymphocyte serum or during immune stimuli but also in mixtures in which antibodies against lymphocytes and immune stimuli by foreign antigens cannot be detected. The mechanism of this adherence is not known. One possibility is that guinea pig thymocytes possess nonspecific surface properties which make them more adherent to cells than thymocytes of other species or extra-thymic guinea pig lymphocytes. This is unlikely since there is little or no adherence of guinea pig thymocytes to heterologous macro-

TABLE III

Effect of treatment of macrophages with trypsin upon opsonic adherence of guinea pig macrophages and rat thymocytes

Liter	Untreated Macrophages	Trypsinized[a] Macrophages
Opsonin	8,000–16,000	8,000–16,000
Agglutinin	500–1,000	
Lysin	2,000–4,000	

[a] Macrophages were exposed to 0.1% trypsin at 37°C for 60 min.

phages and to a variety of guinea pig spleen and bone marrow cells. The results are more consistent with the notion that adherence of autologous macrophages and thymocytes is the result of the reciprocal action of highly specific factors. These factors are more specific than antilymphocyte antibody since they can distinguish not only between guinea pig cells and those of other species but also between thymic and extra-thymic lymphocytes.

Results obtained in this study indicate that adherence of autologous macrophages and thymocytes cannot be accounted for by any of the known circulatory antibody systems. It is not "immune adherence" since "immune adherence" requires the presence of both circulatory antibody and complement (11). Autologous macrophage-thymocyte adherence occurred in the absence of serum. Augmentation of adherence by serum also did not require complement, since this augmentation occurred in the presence of heat-inactivated serum. The synthesis of a significant quantity of extra-cellular materials by thymocytes or macrophages under the conditions used in this study is unlikely since the reaction occurred at room temperature immediately after cell washing.

Autologous macrophage-thymocyte adherence also cannot be explained by previous action of a natural autologous antibody upon guinea pig thymocytes. This is suggested by the differences in the behavior of normal and antibody-treated thymocytes. Antibody-treated rat thymocytes adhered to both heterologous and trypsin-treated macrophages while untreated guinea pig thymocytes adhered to neither.

The fact that pretreatment of macrophages with trypsin abolishes autologous adherence indicates that the phenomenon is associated with a protein or proteins present on the macrophage surface. This protein is probably not a cytophilic antibody. This is suggested by the fact that it is more susceptible to trypsin than cytophilic antibody and by the fact that autologous activity cannot be restored to trypsinized macrophages by treatments which restore cytophilic activity.

The functions of macrophage-thymocyte adherence are unknown and require further study. The adherence is likely to hinder the circulation and diminish the number of thymocytes. The latter possibility is supported by the observation that adherence may be associated with phagocytosis of and morphologic changes in the thymocytes. In addition autologous macrophage-thymocyte affinity may, under certain conditions, facilitate interactions between macrophages which have phagocytized antigen (12) and antigen sensitive-thymocytes or thymus-derived cells (13, 14).

Acknowledgment. I wish to thank Dr. William B. Sherman for his interest and encouragement during this work, and for helpful discussions.

REFERENCES

1. Rosenau, W. and Moon, H. D., J. Immun., *96:* 80, 1966.
2. Greaves, M. F., Tursi, A., Playfair, J. H. L., Torrigiani, G., Zamir, R. and Roitt, I. M., Lancet, *1:* 68, 1969.
3. Martin, W. J. and Miller, J. F. A. P., J. Exp. Med., *128:* 855, 1968.
4. McFarland, W. and Heilman, D. H., Nature, *205:* 887, 1965.
5. Siegel, I., Cell. Biol., *43:* 132a, 1969.
6. Siegel, I., J. Allerg. *46:* 190, 1970.
7. Martin, S. P. and Green, R., *Methods in Medical Research*, Edited by J. V. Warren, Vol. 7, p. 136, 1958.
8. Siegel, I. and Sherman, W. B., J. Allerg., *45:* 133, 1970.
9. Siegel, I., Stain Techn., *42:* 29, 1967.
10. Weiser, R. S., Heise, E., McIvor, K., Han, S. H. and Granger, G. A., *Cellular Recognition*, Edited by R. Smith and R. A. Good, p. 215, Appleton-Century-Crofts, New York, 1969.
11. Nelson, D. S., Advances Immun., *3:* 131, 1963.
12. Friedman, H. P., Stavitsky, A. B. and Salomon, J. M., Science, *149:* 1106, 1965.
13. Claman, H. N. and Chaperon, E. A., Transplant. Rev., *1:* 93, 1969.
14. Miller, J. F. A. P. and Mitchell, G. F., Transplant. Rev., *3:* 42, 1969.

THE JOURNAL OF IMMUNOLOGY
Vol. 105, No. 4, October 1970
Printed in U.S.A.

DEGRADATION OF IMMUNOGLOBULINS BY INTRACELLULAR PROTEASES IN THE RANGE OF NEUTRAL pH[1]

JOSEPH J. LoSPALLUTO, KURT FEHR[2] AND MORRIS ZIFF

From the Departments of Biochemistry and Internal Medicine (Rheumatic Diseases Unit), The University of Texas, Southwestern Medical School at Dallas, Texas

Received for publication May 3, 1970)

A proteolytic enzyme active in the range of neutral or slightly alkaline pH has been partially purified from a lysosome-containing granule fraction of human spleen. The molecular weight of the enzyme was estimated to be in the range of 15,000 to 30,000 by gel filtration, and it has a pH optimum of approximately 7.5 with bovine hemoglobin or human IgG as substrates. Its activity is stimulated by cysteine but is strikingly inhibited by diisopropylfluorophosphate. The enzyme is active against a variety of protein substrates including human IgM, IgG, IgA, albumin, and also bovine hemoglobin. The products of IgG and IgM digestion were studied most extensively. IgG was broken down into Fab and Fc fragments, which proved to be very similar in size and immunochemical properties to fragments produced by papain digestion. In addition, a slightly degraded product with a molecular weight in the range of 110,000 to 120,000 was observed, which was not distinguishable from intact IgG by immunodiffusion analysis. IgM was extensively degraded by the neutral protease, a large proportion being broken down to small, dialyzable fragments. Relatively small quantities of large fragments containing Fab and Fc(μ) determinants were found. Evidence was obtained that both Fab and Fc regions of the IgM molecule are degraded by this enzyme.

Proteolytic enzymes from human spleen, human synovium, and beef spleen lysosomes have been shown (1, 2) to digest immunoglobulin G at pH 3.5, giving rise to dialyzable products, partially degraded Fc and Fab fragments, Fab_2-like fragments, and a slightly degraded IgG with a molecular weight of approximately 135,000. The major enzyme involved under the conditions employed was cathepsin D. The pH activity profile of the lysosomal extracts also indicated proteolytic activity in the range of neutral pH with human IgG as substrate.

A number of reports indicate that proteases capable of digesting different protein substrates at neutral pH exist in various cells and tissue. Such neutral proteases have been found in human polymorphonuclear leucocytes (PMN) (3–6); PMN of cats, rats, and rabbits (7–9); rabbit monocytes (10); rat thyroid mast cells (11); human synovium (3, 12); rat brain (13); and also in blood serum (8). The substrates attacked by these enzymes included vascular basement membrane (5), elastin (6), collagen (4, 12), cartilage mucoprotein (3, 9), casein (7, 10), thyroglobulin (11) and hemoglobin (3, 8, 13). Whether the proteolytic activity at neutral pH is due to the same or different enzymes in various tissues is as yet unknown.

In this report, the effects on human IgG and IgM of a neutral protease from a lysosome-containing granular fraction from human spleen are described. The digestion products have been purified and characterized by various techniques including gel filtration, ultracentrifugation and Ouchterlony analysis. A fragment was isolated from digested IgG which showed a molecular weight of approximately 120,000 upon gel filtration and contained both Fab and Fc determinants. In addition, a mixture of digestion products containing Fab and Fc fragments was also found, which on immunodiffusion, gel filtration and ultracentrifugation were very

[1] This work was supported by Grant I-155 from the Robert A. Welch Foundation, and by Research Grant AM-09989 and Training Grant AM-05154 from the United States Public Health Service.

[2] Present address: Universitats Rheumaklinik, Gloriastrasse 25, 8006 Zurich, Switzerland.

similar to papain fragments. The amounts of small dialyzable products formed were considerably smaller than was previously observed at pH 3.5 with human spleen extracts (1).

IgM was also broken down by the neutral protease with the production of a large amount of dialyzable peptides. Evidence was obtained which indicated that the Fab as well as the Fc(μ) region of IgM was extensively degraded.

MATERIALS AND METHODS

Preparation of lysosomal proteases. Fresh human spleens obtained from individuals undergoing splenectomy because of abdominal trauma were used to prepare lysosomes. The method of preparation was the same as described previously (1) with the following changes. After removing the nuclear fraction (nuclei, intact cells, heavy cell debris) by centrifugation at 800 × G for 10 min, the supernatant was centrifuged at 35,000 × G for 20 min. At this speed, a greater yield of the granular fraction was obtained. This contained the bulk of cathepsin D and β-glucuronidase activity. The granular fraction was washed once with Tris-NaCl buffer, pH 8.5 (0.05 M Tris, 0.2 M NaCl, 0.25% sodium azide). It was then resuspended in the same buffer and the enzymes were liberated by freezing and thawing five times.

Enzyme assays. Proteolytic activity was assayed using as substrate either a 2% solution of purified human IgG (in some experiments human fraction II[3] was used) or denatured bovine hemoglobin (14) in 0.15 M NaCl and measuring the TCA-soluble polypeptides at 280 nm as described earlier (1). In several instances, the method of Lowry *et al.* (15) was also employed. For preparative studies, IgG purified from commercial human fraction II or from serum (Ripley)[4] containing anti-D antibody was used.

IgG was purified by applying fraction II to a column of DEAE-cellulose and eluting with 0.01 M phosphate at pH 7.5. Digestion of human serum albumin (HSA) (Pentex, Inc., Kankakee, Ill.) was measured according to the method of Lapresle and Webb (16) using a 10% solution of HSA as substrate. Digestion of IgG with papain and pepsin was carried out according to Porter (17) and Nisonoff *et al.* (18), respectively.

[3] Fraction II from pooled human plasma (American Red Cross) obtained from E. R. Squibb and Sons, New York, N. Y.

[4] Kindly supplied by Dr. Marion Waller.

Most assays for neutral protease activity were carried out with either 2% human IgG or 10% bovine hemoglobin as substrate in 0.05 M Tris buffer, pH 7.5, 0.2 M NaCl, in the presence of 0.02% sodium azide. In studies of inhibition or stimulation, cysteine was added to a final concentration of 0.01 M and iodoacetamide and diisopropylfluorophosphate (DFP) to final concentrations of 1×10^{-2} M and 1×10^{-3} M, respectively. β-Glucuronidase was assayed by the method of Gianetto and DeDuve (19).

In order to isolate and study degradation products, 100 mg of IgG were digested with partially purified enzyme at 37°C in Tris buffer, pH 7.5, in the presence of 0.01 M cysteine and 0.02% sodium azide for 24 to 48 hr. The IgM protein studied in these experiments was obtained from the serum of a patient (B.B.) with rheumatoid arthritis. IgM was purified by gel filtration through a 2.5- x 90-cm Sephadex G-200 column at pH 4.0 (0.1 M acetate buffer containing 0.1 M glycine and 0.02% sodium azide). The IgM component, which emerged at the void volume, was further purified by gel filtration through a 2.5- x 90-cm column of Bio-Gel A 5 M to remove large aggregates. The product contained 90% to 95% of a 19S component on ultracentrifugation and was essentially free of other immunoglobulins. IgM was digested for 44 hr under the same conditions as those employed for IgG.

Chromatographic procedures. Various enzyme preparations were chromatographed at 4°C on columns of Bio-Gel A 1.5 M (Bio-Rad Laboratories, Richmond, Calif.) with Tris-NaCl buffer at pH 8.5. The separated components were concentrated by pressure ultrafiltration through UM-10 Diaflo membranes (Amicon Corp., Cambridge, Mass.) before assaying for proteolytic activity. Protein content was determined by the biuret colorimetric assay (20).

Digests of IgG were chromatographed through columns of agarose A 1.5 M, Sephadex G-200 and G-100 (Pharmacia, Uppsala, Sweden) using Tris-NaCl buffer of pH 8.5 or pH 7.5. Molecular size estimates from gel filtration experiments (21, 22) were carried out using ovalbumin (Pentex, Inc., Kankakee, Ill.), HSA human IgG, IgM and myoglobin as markers. To calculate the protein concentration in IgG and IgM digests from 280 nm absorbance measurements, the extinction coefficients of 13.0 and 11.0, respecively, were employed for 1% solutions of the immunoglobulins in saline.

Ultracentrifugation. Ultracentrifugation was carried out in a model E analytical ultracentrifuge in a 30-mm cell at 47,760 rpm.

Electrophoresis. Electrophoresis in polyacrylamide gel was carried out with Canalco equipment (model G, Canalco Industrial Corp., Bethesda, Md.). Samples usually containing 100 or 200 μg of proteins in 0.1 ml were mixed with 0.1 ml of 10% sucrose, applied to the top of the spacer gel, and run without the use of a sample gel.

Immunologic procedures. To characterize chromatographic fractions, Ouchterlony double diffusion in agar was carried out using goat antisera directed against human IgG, its Fab and Fc fragments, and human IgM, IgA, and whole serum (Hyland Laboratories, Los Angeles, Calif.).

RESULTS

Intracellular distribution of neutral protease activity. The results of assays of subcellular fractions for proteases active at pH 7.5 are shown in Table I. Although the supernatant fraction contained a significant proportion of the total activity, it is evident that the bulk of the enzymatic activity was in the granule fraction (lysosomes and mitochondria). Assays of the same fractions for the lysosomal enzymes, β-glucuronidase and acid protease (mainly cathepsin D), showed similar distribution of all three activities in subcellular fractions. The neutral protease activity, like that of β-glucuronidase and the acid protease, appears to be associated mainly with lysosomes.

Fractionation of the granule extract. Since in previous experiments (1) it was observed that the total proteolytic activity of lysosome extracts against IgG in the range of neutral pH was considerably less than that at pH 3.5, attempts were made to determine whether the activity in the two pH ranges was due to the same or different enzymes. Lysosome extracts were therefore fractionated on columns of Bio-Gel A 1.5 M with Tris-NaCl buffer, pH 8.5. The results of fractionation of the granule extract from one human spleen (Fig. 1) show seven or eight different components. The fractions corresponding to each of the major components were pooled, concentrated to a volume equal to that of the original extract, and assayed for proteolytic

TABLE I

Distribution of neutral protease in subcellular fractions

Subcellular Fraction	Percentage Total Enzymatic Activity		
	Protease[a] (pH 7.5)	Protease[a] (pH 3.5)	β-Glucuronidase[b]
Nuclear	19.1	19.9	16.3
Lysosomes + mitochondria	35.6	43.2	24.9
Supernatant	9.2	34.4	27.6

[a] Protease activities measured with denatured hemoglobin as substrate.

[b] Measured with phenolphthalein glucuronide as substrate.

activity at pH 3.5 and pH 7.5 with human IgG (plasma fraction II) as substrate. In a parallel control experiment, enzyme and IgG were incubated separately, mixed after the 2-hr incubation period and then precipitated with TCA. The bars in the diagram indicate proteolytic activity at pH 3.5 and pH 7.5. Acid protease activity is clearly confined to peak 4, whereas neutral protease activity appears chiefly in peaks 5 and 6.

The active fractions were combined and further purified by a second gel filtration. The activity of this protease was studied untreated and after treatment with cysteine, iodoacetamide and DFP. For these experiments, assays were performed by mixing 10 mg of substrate and 0.17 mg of enzyme, either untreated or treated with the compounds mentioned above, in a total volume of 1.0 ml. Control tubes were prepared containing 0.17 mg/ml of enzyme alone, 20 mg/ml of substrate alone and, in addition, either enzyme or substrate with each of the compounds listed. All tubes were incubated for 2 hr at 37°C and pH 7.5, and assayed tubes were then precipitated by adding 1.0 ml of 10% TCA. In the case of the controls, 0.5 ml of the separately incubated substrate-containing solutions (20 mg/ml) was mixed with 1.0 ml of the incubated enzyme solution (0.17 mg/ml) and immediately precipitated by adding 0.5 ml of 20% TCA. Enzyme activity was expressed as the difference in absorbance at 280 nm between assay and control TCA supernatant solutions. The results obtained were similar when the method of Lowry *et al.* (15) was employed on TCA supernatant solutions.

The neutral protease activity was enhanced by

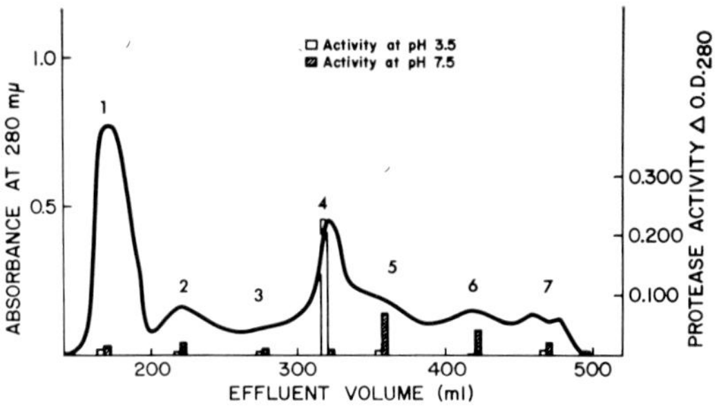

Figure 1. Gel filtration of lysosome extract on a Bio-Gel A 1.5 M column (2.5 x 80 cm). Eight and three-tenths milliliters of extract (from 60 g of human spleen) were applied. Proteins were eluted with 0.05 M Tris buffer, pH 8.5, containing 0.2 M NaCl, 0.02% NaN_3 and 0.001 M ethylenediaminetetraacetic acid sodium salt (EDTA). For assay of protease activity, fractions were pooled and concentrated to 8 ml. Protease activity is expressed as the difference in absorbance at 280 nm between control and experimental TCA supernatants after incubation for 1 hr at 37°C.

TABLE II

Properties of neutral protease

Treatment of Enzyme	Substrate: Human IgG — Enzyme activity ΔO.D. 280 nm	Human IgG — Relative activity[a]	Bovine hemoglobin — Enzyme activity ΔO.D. 280 nm	Bovine hemoglobin — Relative activity[a]
None	0.121	1.00	0.557	1.00
Iodoacetamide 1×10^{-2} M	0.126	1.04	0.618	1.11
DFP 1×10^{-3} M	0.000	0.00	0.094	0.17
Cysteine 5×10^{-3} M	0.279	2.31	0.725	1.30
Cysteine 5×10^{-3} M Iodoacetamide 1×10^{-2} M	0.179	1.48	0.536	0.96
Cysteine 5×10^{-3} M DFP 1×10^{-3} M	0.045	0.37	0.157	0.28

[a] Ratio of activity to that of untreated enzyme.

cysteine, strikingly inhibited by DFP, and inhibited by iodoacetamide only after stimulation by cysteine (Table II). The greater enhancement with IgG as substrate as compared

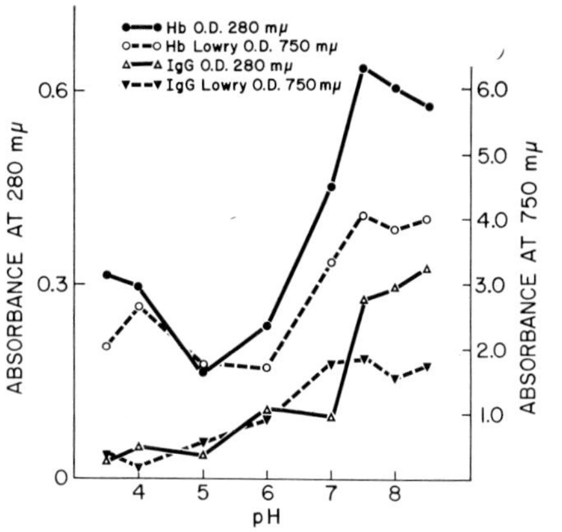

Figure 2. pH profile of neutral protease activity with two different substrates. Estimations by absorbance at 280 nm with IgG as substrate, △——△; with hemoglobin as substrate, ●——●; and, by the Lowry method, with IgG as substrate, ▼-----▼; and with hemoglobin as substrate, ○-----○. Lowry values are calculated as absorbance at 750 nm per milliliter of TCA supernatant.

with hemoglobin suggests that reducing disulfide bonds of the IgG substrate exposes sites more readily accessible to attack by the enzyme.

pH profile of the neutral protease. The variation with pH of the activity of partially purified neutral protease using hemoglobin and IgG as substrates is shown in Figure 2. Measurements were made on the TCA supernatant using both the method of Lowry *et al.* and absorbance at 280 nm. Significantly increased activity was observed over a relatively narrow range of pH, i.e., 7.0 to 8.0, with an optimun at pH 7.5, when both hemoglobin and IgG were used as substrates.

Degradation of human IgG by partially purified neutral protease. In preliminary experiments, it was observed that treating IgG with lysosomal extracts in the absence of cysteine digested relatively little IgG. However, when the proteases of peaks 5 and 6 (Fig. 1) were incubated with IgG at pH 7.5 in the presence of cysteine, considerable digestion was observed. Gel filtration of the digests on agarose A 1.5 M (Fig. 3) showed three major peaks containing 42%, 33%, and 25% of the applied protein, respectively. Approximately 75% of the IgG was significantly altered in this experiment. The proteins of peak A emerged at an elution volume indicating the presence of both intact IgG and slightly digested fragments.

The proteins of peak A were further fractionated by recycling twice through Bio-Gel A 1.5 M and once through a Sephadex G-100 column. A major component (A_p) isolated by these gel filtration procedures emerged in a position indicating a molecular weight of 110,000 to 120,000 (Table III). On ultracentrifugal analysis, its sedimentation velocity was 5.8S compared with 6.7S measured for intact IgG under the same conditions (Table III). On electrophoresis through polyacrylamide gel (Fig. 4), moreover, it moved slightly ahead of intact IgG. Although these observations show a distinct difference in size from intact IgG, immunodiffusion experiments indicated complete identity with intact IgG (Fig. 5, *a* and *b*). This component could not be distinguished from a fragment (A_{bov}) isolated earlier in this laboratory (1) from bovine spleen protease digests of IgG at low pH and which, upon ultracentrifugation and gel filtration, had a molecular size slightly smaller than intact IgG. The A_{bov} component was also not distinguishable from intact IgG on immunodiffusion. On ultracentrifugation under the same conditions, however, the A_{bov} was somewhat heavier than the neutral protease product, A_p, having a sedimentation coefficient of 6.2S. Moreover, in experiments in which such fragments obtained from anti-D antibodies were used to coat type O, Rh-positive human erythrocytes, the two products were shown to have different antigenic specificity (2). In addition, since they retained the ability to react with and sensitize D cells, it was concluded that the antigen-binding site of these fragments had not been destroyed by enzymatic digestion at either acid or neutral pH.

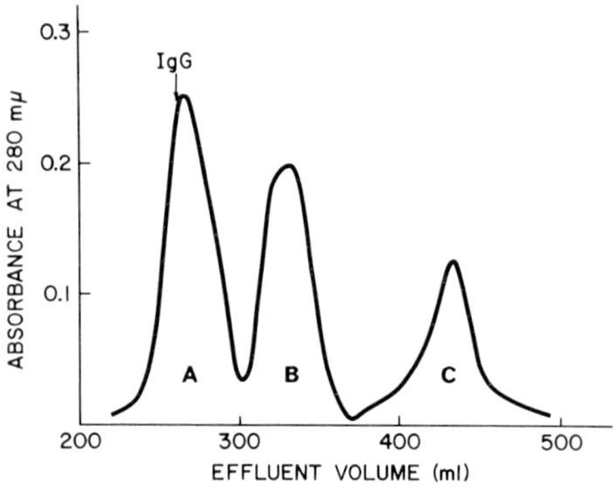

Figure 3. Fractionation of a neutral protease digest of human IgG on Bio-Gel A 1.5 M. One hundred milligrams of IgG were incubated 38 hr at pH 7.9 with 6.3 mg of enzyme protein in the presence of 0.01 M cysteine. Elution was with Tris-NaCl buffer, pH 8.5.

The components of peak B showed considerably greater electrophoretic mobility than component A_p, while peak C, which consisted mostly of dialyzable peptides, showed no detectable bands (Fig. 4). Ouchterlony analysis of peak B was consistent with the presence of Fab and Fc fragments in this fraction (Fig. 6*a*). On comparison with Fab and Fc fragments produced

TABLE III

Properties of IgG digestion products

Sample	Percentage of Total Protein	Molecular Weight (Gel Filtration)	Ultracentrifugal Analysis: Concentration	Ultracentrifugal Analysis: Sedimentation coefficient	Ouchterlony Analysis
			mg/ml		
IgG[a]		150,000	2.4	6.7S	
Ap[b]	28	110,000–120,000	2.4	5.8S	Same as IgG with anti-Fab and anti-Fc
B[c]	33	50,000	2.0	3.9S	Fab + Fc (same as papain digest)
C	25	<10,000			
Papain digest of IgG[a]		50,000	2.0	3.8S	Fab + Fc

[a] IgG was purified by DEAE-cellulose chromatography of Ripley serum. Fractions Ap and B were obtained from digests of the same IgG.

[b] Fraction A (Fig. 2) was purified by recycling twice through Bio-Gel A 1.5 M and once through Sephadex G-100.

[c] Fraction B (Fig. 2).

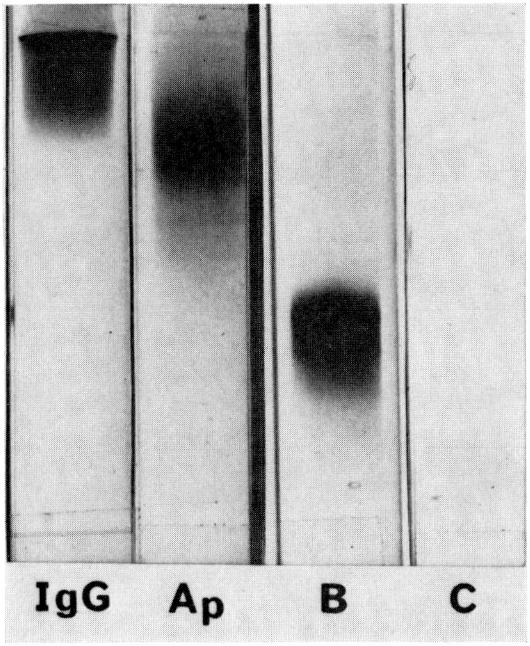

Figure 4. Polyacrylamide gel electrophoresis of IgG and various neutral protease digestion products. A_p (peak A, Fig. 3) further purified by gel filtration twice through Sephadex G-200 (2.5- x 85-cm columns); B (peak B, Fig. 3) further purified by gel filtration through 1.5- x 80-cm column of Sephadex G-100; C (peak C, Fig. 3) is mostly dialyzable material.

by papain, complete identity was found (Fig. 6*a*). The Fc components of both papain-digested IgG and peak B were identical with the Fc portion of intact IgG; however, the Fab moieties of each were antigenically deficient when compared with the Fab segment of intact IgG (Fig. 6, *b* and *c*).

On gel filtration through Sephadex G-100, peak B was eluted with the same volume as the mixture of Fab and Fc produced by papain digestion. The elution volume of products by both papain and neutral protease digests was consistent with molecular weights of approximately 50,000. The heterogeneity of peak B was also suggested by its electrophoretic pattern in polyacrylamide gel (Fig. 4). On ultracentrifugation in 0.15 M NaCl at a concentration of 2 mg/ml of protein, peak B had a sedimentation velocity of 3.9S while the papain fragments had a sedimentation velocity of 3.8S. When peak B was used to sensitize type O, Rh-positive erythrocytes, the cells were agglutinated by goat anti-Fab serum. Thus, the antigen-binding site in Fab fragments appeared to be unaltered by digestion at neutral pH. Using the hemagglutination test to detect newly exposed or previously hidden antigenic sites, it was shown that all human sera tested contained agglutinators directed to cells coated with fragments produced at both neutral

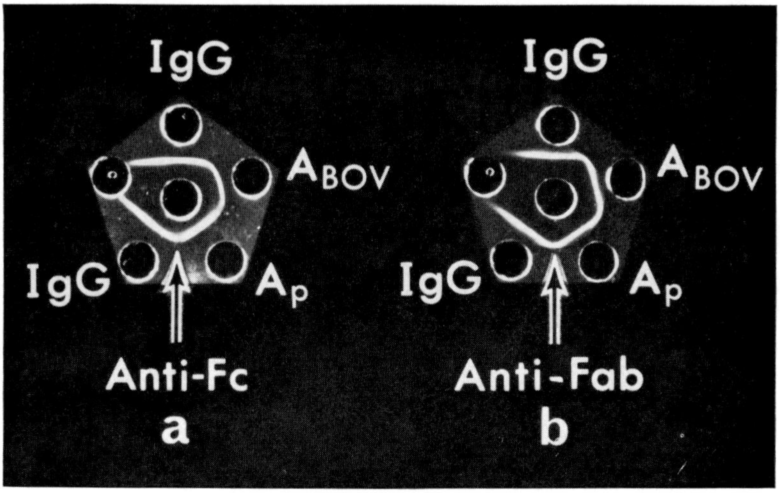

Figure 5. Ouchterlony analysis of purified component A (Fig. 3). *a*, Center well, goat anti-Fc; A_{bov} is a fragment of IgG of approximately 135,000 molecular weight obtained from digests with bovine spleen lysosomal extract at pH 3.5. A_p = component A purified by gel filtration on Sephadex G-200. It shows no difference from IgG or component A_{bov}. *b*, Center well, anti-Fab; again, A_p shows no difference from IgG.

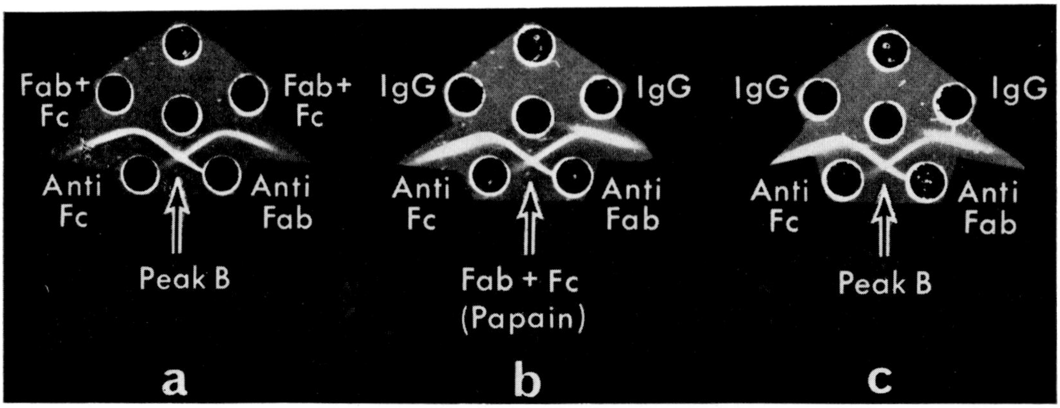

Figure 6. Ouchterlony analysis of peak B (Fig. 3). *a*, Peak B, in center well. Both Fc and Fab components are present in this fraction and are identical with lines obtained with a papain digest of IgG containing a mixture of Fab and Fc. *b*, A mixture of Fab and Fc produced by papain digestion was placed in the center well. The papain digest, Fab + Fc, shows reaction of identity with IgG when tested with anti-Fc but of partial identity with IgG when tested with anti-Fab. *c*, Peak B, in center well, shows reaction of identity with IgG when tested with anti-Fc, but of partial identity with IgG when tested with anti-Fab. Shows also the great similarity between peak B and a papain digest.

and acid pH (2). However, in experiments in which such fragments were used to sensitize type O, Rh-positive cells, their exposed antigenic sites appeared not to be identical to the sites exposed by papain digestion, since Fab fragments from papain digests could not inhibit serum agglutinators for these antigenic sites (2).

Peak C consisted chiefly of dialyzable, non-TCA precipitable fragments of substrate. The extensively degraded fragments of IgG present in peak C could have arisen from either or both Fab and Fc regions of the molecule. No definite conclusions could be drawn, however, from the data obtained.

Degradation of human IgM by neutral proteases. In order to study the effect of neutral proteases on human IgM, IgM with rheumatoid factor activity was prepared by gel filtration of serum from a patient with rheumatoid arthritis through Sephadex G-200 at pH 4.0, followed by filtration through Bio-Gel A 5 M. Fifty milligrams of this preparation were then digested with 3 mg of partially purified enzyme (pool 6, Fig. 1) for 44 hr at 37°C and pH 8.0 in the presence of 0.01 M cysteine. The digestion mixture was then applied to a column of Bio-Gel A 1.5 M. The elution pattern (Fig. 7) showed at least seven components. The first contained a small amount of protein which, on the basis of its gel filtration properties and its failure to penetrate the separating polyacrylamide gel on electrophoresis, behaved like undigested IgM or its polymers. Polyacrylamide electrophoresis of components 2 to 4 (Fig. 7) showed considerable heterogeneity in the digestion products. The small amount of protein of component 5 migrated in the same region as component 4 and most likely represents the trailing edge of peak 4. The components labeled 6 and 7 in the diagram were both dialyzable. They were presumably washed out of the gels on staining since both gave no protein bands on polyacrylamide. The inset photograph number 6 illustrates the result obtained with both 6 and 7.

On Ouchterlony analysis (Fig. 8), it can be seen that peaks 1, 2 and 3 contain both Fc (μ) and Fab determinants. On the basis of these observations, and on the basis of its gel filtration characteristics and sedimentation coefficient (Table IV), peak 2 appears to contain subunits of IgM (IgMs) which can be produced by reduction in the absence of enzyme. Peaks 3, 4 and 5 consist of various fragments of IgM. Peak 3 proteins were slightly more than 100,000 in molecular weight, peak 4 approximately 48,000, and peak 5 approximately 20,000. The presence of Fab determinants and little or no Fc(μ) determinants in fragments such as peak 4 indicates that the Fc(μ) region of the molecule is extensively degraded by the neutral protease. The small

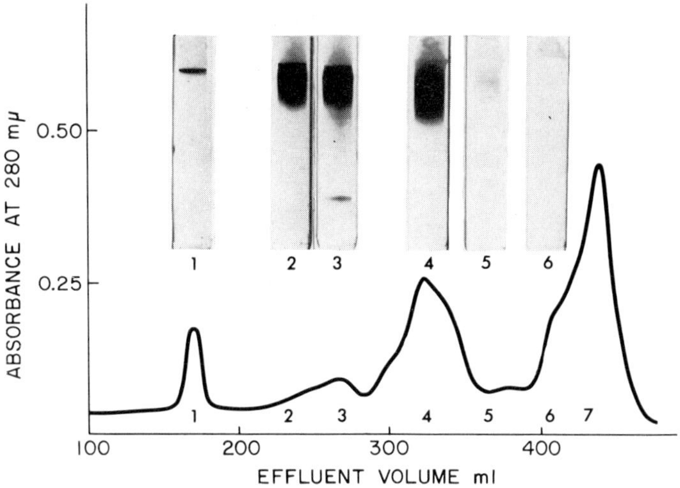

Figure 7. Fractionation of a neutral protease digest of human IgM on Bio-Gel A 1.5 M. One hundred and six milligrams of IgM with rheumatoid factor activity were incubated in Tris-NaCl buffer, pH 7.5, at 37°C for 44 hr in the presence of 0.01 M cysteine, 0.02% sodium azide, and 5.7 mg of partially purified neutral protease. Elution was with the Tris-NaCl buffer, pH 8.5. Polyacrylamide gel electrophoresis of peaks 1 to 6 is shown. Peak 1 protein did not penetrate the separating gel and peaks 5 and 6 showed no discrete bands. The pattern obtained with peak 7 (not shown here) also showed no discrete bands.

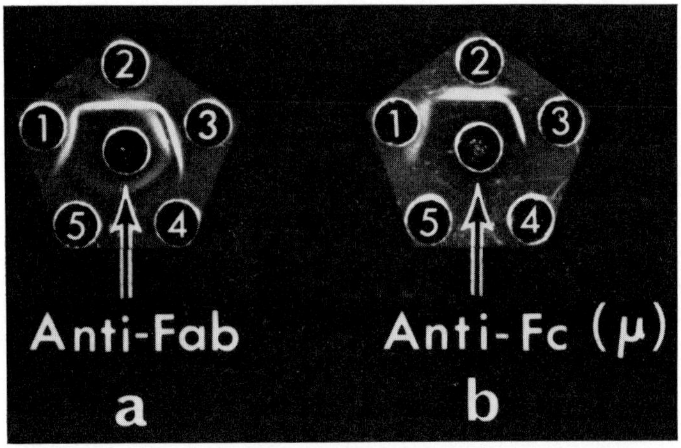

Figure 8. Ouchterlony analysis of neutral protease digestion products of IgM. *a*, Center well, anti-Fab. Peaks 1 to 5 contain Fab determinants. No reaction of peaks 6 or 7 with anti-Fab was observed. Peak 1 contains undigested IgM. *b*, Center well, anti-Fc (μ). Fc component was present in peaks 1 to 3. Little or no Fc (μ) antigen was found in peaks 4 and 5. No reaction was observed with peaks 6 and 7.

amount of fragment in peak 5 appeared to consist mainly of Fab determinants with only traces of Fc(μ) antigens remaining (Fig. 8). Their molecular weight of something less than 20,000 estimated from gel filtration indicates that the F(ab) region of the IgM must also have undergone degradation. Peaks 6 and 7 consisted chiefly of digestion products of IgM too small to precipitate with TCA.

Digestion of other proteins by neutral protease. In addition to bovine hemoglobin, human IgG and IgM, an IgA myeloma protein and HSA were also digested to determine the extent of their breakdown to TCA soluble products by neutral proteases. At pH 7.5, all were hydrolyzed to some degree, i.e. 0.9% of the HSA, 1.1% of the IgA, 2.2% of the IgG, 5.3% of the hemoglobin and 5.8% of the IgM were reduced to TCA soluble

TABLE IV

Digestion of IgM (B.B.)

Fraction	Percentage of Total[a] Protein Recovered	Molecular Weight by Gel Filtration	Ultracentrifugal Analysis		Ouchterlony Analysis
			Concentration	Sedimentation coefficient	
			mg/ml		
1	8.4	900,000	1.0	19.0S	Same as IgM
2	7.4	180,000	1.6	7.6S	Same as IgM
3	5.3	~120,000	2.3	5.4S	Fc (μ) Fab
4	32.4	48,000	2.0	3.8S	Fc (μ) Fab
5	3.0	16,000	1.4	1.6S	Small amounts of Fab, Fc (μ)
6	9.6	<10,000	1.4	<1S	NR[b]
7	33.9	<5,000	1.2	1S	NR[b]

[a] Recovery 87% of total protein applied.
[b] NR, no reaction with anti-Fab or anti-Fc (μ).

fragments in a 2-hr period. Further studies are required, however, to establish the nature of the digestion products, particularly of the IgA and of other IgM proteins.

DISCUSSION

Intracellular proteolytic enzymes active in the range of neutral pH are associated with the lysosome-containing granular fraction of human spleen. Since the main protease activity of this tissue appears to be due to cathepsin D (1), the question arises as to whether activity in the range of neutral pH can be ascribed to residual activity of cathepsin D. The evidence is that separate enzymes are involved since the cathepsin D activity emerges (Fig. 1) from Bio-Gel columns in a separate fraction from the neutral proteases, and cysteine enhances the neutral protease activity while it has no effect on cathepsin D activity (21). Moreover, the pH profile of the neutral protease after partial purification by gel filtration (Fig. 2) shows considerably greater activity in the range of neutral pH with two substrates than at pH 3.5 or pH 4.0, the optimal region for cathepsin D. We have concluded, therefore, that a neutral protease with a molecular weight in the range of 15,000 to 30,000 by gel filtration is present in lysosomes from human spleen homogenates. This enzyme is capable of digesting a variety of substrates including denatured hemoglobin, IgG and IgM, and to a much lesser extent IgA and HSA. The total neutral protease activity present in lysosome extracts appears to be less than that of the acid proteases when measured with the same substrates. Although both the acid and neutral protease activities appear to be associated with the lysosome fraction, they may or may not be associated with the same subpopulation of lysosomes as cathepsin D (23).

It is difficult, at present, to relate the neutral protease described here to others reported in the literature. Proteolytic enzymes such as trypsin and chymotrypsin are not activated by thiol compounds, although like it they are inhibited by DFP. Plasmin can degrade human IgG in a fashion similar to that described here (24, 25), but is not affected by cysteine. The spleen protease described here is similar to the leucocyte protease active against vascular basement membrane at neutral pH (5) in that both are inhibited by DFP and not by iodoacetamide. From this and a number of other reports involving neutral proteases (3, 4, 6, 9, 11, 12), similarities with the present enzyme are observed. For the present, however, no definite conclusions can be drawn on the relation of the enzyme reported here to those previously described.

As for other known lysosomal proteases, cathepsin A was not enhanced by cysteine when assayed with a synthetic substrate and has a pH optimum of 5.7 (26). Cathepsins B and C are enhanced by cysteine but, in contrast to the present enzyme, are completely inhibited by iodoacetamide (27–30). In addition the molecular weight of 210,000 found for bovine cathepsin C (29), an enzyme with very low proteinase activity, is much greater than the value of 15,000 to 30,000 estimated for the present enzyme. Cathepsins D and E, described by LaPresle and Webb (31), have clearly different pH profiles. Thus, it seems clear that none of the known cathepsins are responsible for the activity observed.

In several reports (32–34), a thiol-dependent protease has been observed in tissues of active Arthus lesion sites. This enzyme, which is probably released from neutrophils and macrophages in the Arthus lesions, has been partially purified but has not been characterized sufficiently to compare with the human spleen enzymes studied here.

The results of digestion of human IgG indicate that the bulk of the products, Fab and Fc fragments, are similar to those found in papain digests (17). However, a product such as the 5.8S component (Table III), which represents a mildly degraded fragment of IgG, has not been described in papain digests. Whether this component is generated by the same protease which brings about the more extensive splitting observed or is produced by another enzyme in the partially purified preparation is not clear. The Fab and Fc fragments produced in these experiments, while indistinguishable from papain fragments by immunodiffusion and physicochemical tests, were clearly distinguishable by serologic tests. In these tests, the agglutination by serum agglutinators of human type O, Rh-positive erythrocytes coated with enzymatically produced fragments (from a sample of IgG containing anti-Rh activity) was not inhibited by fragments prepared by papain digestion (2). These results indicate that the neutral protease attacks IgG at a site different from papain. Although the digestion products have not been compared serologically with those obtained here, it is possible that the type of digestion observed in the present studies is similar to that obtained with other enzymes such as ficin and bromelin (35) since these enzymes, like papain, gave rise to mixtures of Fab and Fc fragments with a sedimentation coefficient of 3.5S.

Human IgM was also degraded by neutral protease from spleen, but analysis of the digestion mixture was somewhat more complicated than with IgG. The identification of the major products of digestion indicate considerable alteration of the IgM. Component 5 (Table IV), for example, had a molecular weight of less than 20,000, and on Ouchterlony analysis contained Fab but little or no Fc (μ) antigenic determinants. The last two components to be eluted (numbers 6 and 7) contained small, non-TCA precipitable digestion products of the substrate. On the other hand, peak 2 emerged from the column in a position indicating that it consists most likely of monomers (IgM)'s of the 19S IgM. Ouchterlony analysis showed that peak 2 was identical in its reactions with anti-Fab and anti-Fc (μ) with IgM's produced by reduction of the 19S IgM in the absence of enzyme. In addition, its sedimentation coefficient of 7.6S was similar to that of IgM's prepared by reduction of 19S IgM.

Further analysis of the elution pattern of the IgM digest shown in Figure 7 indicates that, of the total IgM incubated with enzyme, approximately 80% had been degraded to fragments smaller than the IgM monomer (IgM)'s. The protein in peak 3 contained both Fab and Fc (μ) antigenic determinants, whereas those of peak 4 contained only F(ab) determinants. The lower molecular fragments in peaks 5, 6 and 7 (Fig. 7, Table IV) gave little or no reaction with anti-Fab and anti-Fc (μ). The quantity of protein degraded to these small fragments, correcting for the enzyme added, indicated that both the Fab and the Fc(μ) had been broken down to the point where they no longer were precipitated by TCA.

Intracellular proteases probably play an important role in cellular metabolism, particularly in the processes of phagocytosis and digestion. Of the various intracellular proteolytic enzymes which have been studied, most, if not all, are associated with the lysosomal granules. Although a spectrum of different types of activity is present, no specific biologic function has been ascribed to any one enzyme other than that of involvement in the general process of catabolism. However, this group of enzymes, particularly those found in macrophages, may well play an important role in the immune response to protein antigens. A body of evidence indicates that antigens are "processed" in macrophages (36–39). However, studies of the fate of antigens in macrophages have indicated that both soluble (40, 41) and particulate (42, 43) antigens are degraded to the point where their immunogenicity would be expected to be lost. Yet, if processing of protein antigens in macrophages involves intracellular proteases, these proteases must permit the survival of fragments of sufficient size to retain immunogenicity. Because it appears to degrade immunoglobulins to fragments ranging in size from small dialyzable pieces to fragments only slightly smaller than the starting material even after prolonged digestion, the neutral protease described here may, by its action on these as well as other protein antigens, either intracellularly or extracellularly (if released by the cells), play a key role in the immune response. Acid proteases, on the other hand, because they are active in a limited low pH range, may well be concerned chiefly with catabolism of proteins within phagosomes.

The fact that antibody proteins, particularly IgG, have antigen-binding sites on their Fab regions which are relatively resistant to the intracellular neutral proteases suggests a possible explanation for the known inhibition of antibody formation by specific antibody, particularly of the IgG variety (44–46). Even small amounts of antibody, by combining with antigen, might, by virtue of their protease-resistant Fab region, protect parts of the antigen molecules from degradation by neutral protease and hence prevent the "antigen processing" necessary to induce antibody formation. On the other hand, IgM proteins, such as the one studied here, appear to be more readily degraded by the neutral protease, both in their Fab and Fc regions. Antibodies of this type therefore would inhibit the immune response to their specific antigens less effectively. In fact, IgM antibodies to Salmonella antigens have been shown to be poor inhibitors of the immune response (46). It may be, however, that individual human IgM antibodies will differ in their sensitivity toward neutral proteases, and the same may also prove to be true for IgA antibodies. The one sample of IgA studied, which was obtained from the serum of a patient with multiple myeloma, appeared to be relatively resistant to digestion at neutral pH.

Acknowledgments. We are grateful for the competent technical assistance of Joanna Allen and Barbara Smith.

REFERENCES

1. Fehr, K., LoSpalluto, J. and Ziff, M., Fed. Proc., *28:* 496, 1969.
2. Fehr, K., LoSpalluto, J. and Ziff, M., Arthritis Rheum., *11:* 822, 1968.
3. Ziff, M., Gribetz, H. J. and LoSpalluto, J., J. Clin. Invest., *39:* 405, 1960.
4. Lazarus, G. S., Brown, R. S., Daniels, J. R. and Fullmer, H. M., Science, *159:* 1483, 1967.
5. Janoff, A. and Zeligs, D., Science, *161:* 702, 1968.
6. Janoff, A. and Scherrer, J., J. Exp. Med., *28:* 1137, 1968.
7. Grob, D., J. Gen. Physiol., *29:* 219, 1946.
8. Grob, D., J. Gen. Physiol., *33:* 103, 1949.
9. Weissmann, G. and Spilberg, I., Arthritis Rheum., *11:* 162, 1968.
10. Hayashi, H., Tokuda, A. and Udaha, K., J. Exp. Med., *112:* 237, 1960.
11. Pastan, I. and Almquist, S., Endocrinology, *78:* 350, 1966.
12. Evanson, J. M., Jeffrey, J. J. and Krane, St. M., Science, *158:* 499, 1967.
13. Marks, N. and Lajtha, A., Biochem. J., *97:* 740, 1965.
14. Anson, M. C., J. Gen. Physiol., *22:* 79, 1939.
15. Lowry, O. H., Rosebrough, N. J., Farr, A. L. and Randall, R. J., J. Biol. Chem., *193:* 265, 1951.
16. Lapresle, C. and Webb, T., Biochem. J., *76:* 538, 1960.
17. Porter, R. R., Biochem. J., *73:* 119, 1959.
18. Nisonoff, A., Wissler, F. C., Lipman, L. N. and Woernly, D. L., Arch. Biochem. Biophys., *89:* 230, 1960.
19. Gianetto, R. and deDuve, C., Biochem. J., *59:* 433, 1955.
20. Gornall, A. G., Bardawill, C. J. and David, M. M., J. Biol. Chem., *177:* 751, 1949.
21. Andrews, P., Biochem. J., *91:* 222, 1964.
22. Andrews, P., Biochem. J., *96:* 595, 1965.
23. Bowers, W. E. and deDuve, C., J. Cell Biol., *32:* 339, 1967.
24. Segouris, J. T., Vox Sang., *13:* 71, 1967.
25. Merler, E., Rosen, F. S., Salmon, S., Grain, Y. D. and Janeway, C. A., Vox Sang., *13:* 102, 1967.
26. Lichtenstein, N. and Fruton, J. S., Proc. Nat. Acad. Sci., *46:* 787, 1960.
27. Greenbaum, L. M. and Fruton, J. S., J. Biol. Chem., *226:* 173, 1957.
28. Tallan, H. H., Jones, M. E. and Fruton, J. S., J. Biol. Chem., *194:* 793, 1952.
29. Metrione, R. M., Neves, A. G. and Fruton, J. S., Biochemistry, *5:* 1597, 1966.
30. Planta, R. J. and Gruber, M., Biochim. Biophys. Acta, *89:* 403, 1964.
31. LaPresle, C. and Webb, T., Biochem. J., *84:*
32. Hayashi, H., Udaka, K., Koono, K. and Yoshimura, M., Brit. J. Exp. Path., *43:* 575, 1962.
33. Hayashi, H., Miyoshi, H., Nitta, R. and Udaka, K., Brit. J. Exp. Path., *43:* 564, 1962.
34. Koono, M., Muto, M. and Hayashi, H., Tohoku J. Exp. Med., *94:* 231, 1968.
35. Waller, M., Curray, N. and Mallory, J., Immunochemistry, *5:* 577, 1968.
36. Franzl, R. E., Nature, *195:* 457, 1962.
37. Fishman, M. and Adler, F. L., in *Immunopathology, IIIrd International Symposium*, Edited by P. Grabar and P. Miescher, Benno Schwabe, Basel, 1963.
38. Fishman, M. and Adler, F. L., J. Exp. Med., *117:* 595, 1963.
39. Fishman, M., Hammerstrom, R. A. and Bond, V. P., Nature, *198:* 549, 1965.
40. Ehrenreich, B. A. and Cohn, Z. A., J. Cell Biol., *38:* 244, 1968.

41. Ehrenreich, B. A. and Cohn, Z. A., J. Exp. Med., *129:* 227, 1968.
42. Perkins, E. H. and Makinodan, T., J. Immun., *94:* 765, 1965.
43. Perkins, E. H., Nettesheim, P. and Morita, T., J. Reticuloendothel. Soc., *3:* 71, 1966.
44. Uhr, J. W. and Baumann, J. B., J. Exp. Med., *113:* 395, 1961.
45. Sahiar, K. and Schwartz, R. S., Science, *145:* 395, 1964.
46. Fink, C. W. and LoSpalluto, J. J., Immunology, *12:* 259, 1967.

THE JOURNAL OF IMMUNOLOGY
Vol. 105, No. 4, October 1970

Printed in U.S.A.

CELLULAR AND ANTIBODY REACTIONS TO STREPTOCOCCAL M PROTEIN TYPES 1, 3, 6 AND 12[1]

LAUREN M. PACHMAN[2] AND EUGENE N. FOX[2]

From the Variety Club Research Center of La Rabida-University of Chicago Institute and the Department of Pediatrics, University of Chicago, Chicago, Illinois

Received for publication May 3, 1970

Immunization with purified M protein, a component of the group A streptococcal cell wall, induces the formation of circulating antibody and delayed cutaneous hypersensitivity (DCH). The specificity of these responses was evaluated in guinea pigs and man, using types 1, 3, 6 and 12 M protein. In a study of 10 human adults, delayed hypersensitivity and circulating antibody to more than one M protein was usually present. In several individauls, *in vitro* cellular reactivity to several M proteins was found in the absence of detectable DCH and antibody. Female Hartley guinea pigs sensitized with specific M proteins were reactive to homologous and, to a lesser extent, heterologous serotypes when DCH or spleen cell reactivity was determined. High titer homologous antisera reacted with heterologous M proteins measured by passive hemagglutination; only opsonic antibody was type-specific. Cellular responses to M proteins, assayed by spleen cell reactivity and inhibition of peritoneal exudate cell migration 6 months after sensitization when antibody was no longer detectable, were as great as when titers were high. Unimmunized controls, or those given Freund's adjuvant without M protein manifested negative skin tests, did not produce circulating antibody or respond with significant cellular proliferation when challenged with M proteins.

Infection with group A beta hemolytic Streptococcus usually confers on the host type-specific protection which may be life long. One component of the streptococcal cell wall is M protein, and after exposure to the bacteria or the isolated M protein, a subject usually develops delayed hypersensitivity and circulating antibodies to M protein (1, 2). Type-specific opsonic antibody (anti-M) is protective, and can be detected *in vitro* by the indirect bactericidal test of Lancefield (3, 4). However, this antibody does not always persist, making difficult the identification of not only a previously infected host, but also the particular type of Streptococcus involved (5). The precise relationship of delayed hypersensitivity to systemic protection has not yet been established, but the delayed response is induced after immunization of guinea pigs (6) and man (7) with vaccines containing M protein. Inasmuch as opsonic antibody is type-specific, it was of interest to determine if other immunologic assays would discriminate between individual types of M protein as well. These studies were designed to evaluate the specificity of the host response to M protein types 1, 3, 6 and 12 as measured by delayed cutaneous hypersensitivity (DCH), lymphocyte stimulation, inhibition of macrophage migration and antibody titers.

MATERIALS AND METHODS

Test subjects. Ten healthy adults, five male and five female, were used for human studies. Female Hartley guinea pigs from a closed colony, weighing 350 to 450 g, were used for animal experiments.

Antigens. Group A beta hemolytic streptococcal M proteins, types 1, 3, 6 and 12, were prepared as previously described (8). Intermediate strength tuberculin purified protein derivative (PPD, Parke, Davis and Co., Detroit, Mich.) was used for human skin testing, and lyophilized PPD (a gift from Dr. Fischer of

[1] This investigation was supported by United States Public Health Service Grant AI 04342.

[2] La Rabida Children's Hospital and Research Center, East 65th Street at Lake Michigan, Chicago, Illinois 60649.

Parke, Davis and Co.) was made up to the appropriate concentration for cell stimulation studies and animal skin testing. Bovine serum albumin (BSA, fraction V, Armour Pharmaceutical Company, Chicago, Ill.) served as a protein control, and phytohemagglutinin (PHA, Wellcome Research Laboratories, Beckenham, England) was added to some cell cultures as a mitogenic stimulus.

Skin tests. DCH was assessed in man by intradermal injection of intermediate strength PPD or 1.0 μg of M protein in 0.1 ml saline. The extent of the erythema and induration was measured at 24 and 48 hr. Guinea pigs were tested for DCH by intradermal injection of 30 μg of antigen in 0.1 ml, and the sites were measured 18 hr later.

Immunization. Groups of guinea pigs were tested for DCH 1 week after footpad injection of 0.2 ml of complete Freund's adjuvant emulsified with an equal volume of saline or with 40 μg of M protein in saline. Other groups of animals were given two additional subcutaneous injections of adjuvant either with saline or with 20 μg of M protein in saline at 2-week intervals (see text). Two weeks after the final injection, blood was drawn for passive hemagglutination tests and opsonic antibody assay, and spleens were obtained for cell culture. Other variations in route of injection and suspending adjuvant are indicated in the text.

Serologic tests. Anti-M antibody was assayed by hemagglutination of tanned group O human erythrocytes sensitized with M protein (8). The indirect bactericidal test of Lancefield (9) was used with slight modification (8) and was considered positive for opsonic antibody if four bacterial dilutions exhibited at least a 0.5 log diminution when compared with the preimmunization serum. Guinea pig sera were obtained by the method of Hirsch *et al.* (10) to eliminate nonspecific opsonins.

Cellular reactivity. Human lymphocytes were isolated from heparinized (10 μ/ml) peripheral blood by passage through absorbent cotton columns as previously outlined (11). The cells were suspended in Eagle's minimal essential medium, spinner modification (MEM, Grand Island Biological Co., Grand Island, N. Y.) containing per milliliter: 20% fetal calf serum (FCS, Grand Island Biological, heated at 56°C), 50 units of penicillin, 50 μg streptomycin, and 2 mM L-glutamine. Each 1 ml of culture contained 2×10^6 cells, 20 μg of antigen or PHA in 16- x 100-mm disposable glass tubes (Bellco, Vineland, N. J.) and was maintained at 37°C in 5% CO_2 and air. Duplicate cultures and controls were made for the PHA response, terminated at day 3, and antigen stimulation studies, terminated at day 5. Guinea pig spleen cells were obtained by mincing the tissue, pressing it through a 60-mesh stainless steel wire screen and washing the cells three times in Hanks' solution at 37°C. The cells were suspended in MEM to contain per milliliter: 7×10^6 cells; 10% FCS; 4 mM L-glutamine; 50 units of penicillin; 50 μg of streptomycin; and 50 μg of antigen.

Determination of DNA synthesis: One microcurie of ^{3}H-methylthymidine, specific activity 1.9 Ci/mmol (Schwarz BioResearch, Orangeburg, N. J.) was added to each culture. After 4 hr, the cultures were centrifuged at 150 × G for 10 min at 4°C. The supernatant liquid was removed and the cells were frozen and thawed once. The DNA was extracted twice with cold 5% trichloroacetic acid (TCA) and twice with cold absolute methanol. Each precipitate was dissolved in 0.3 ml of solubilizer (NCS, Nuclear Chicago, Chicago, Ill.) and 10 ml of scintillator, Liquifluor, (New England Nuclear Corp., Boston, Mass.) containing 6 g 2,5-diphenyloxazol and 0.075 g *p*-bis-(5-phenyloxazolyl) benzene/liter of toluene. The radioactivity was measured in a Packard Tri-Carb liquid scintillation counter (model 3320, Packard Instruments, Downers Grove, Ill.) and expressed as the counts/min (cpm)/culture ± the standard error of the mean (S.E.).

Macrophage migration. Guinea pigs were injected intraperitoneally (i.p.) with 15 ml of mineral oil (Marcol 52, Humble Oil and Refining Co., Downers Grove, Ill.) and the injection tract was sealed wth Aeroplast (Parke, Davis and Co., Detroit, Mich.). Four days later the peritoneal exudate cells were harvested and washed three times in Hanks' solution containing heparin (10 units/ml). Migration chambers were prepared with a slight modification of the method of David *et al.* (12), using flame-sealed micro-sampling pipettes (50 μl, Corning, Chicago, Ill.). At least two chambers containing two tubes each were used for every assay, and the area of migration of the exudate cells was measured at 24 and 48 hr. The area of migration was measured with a net micrometer placed in an 8 × ocular in an inverted microscope with a 2.5 × objective. The

TABLE I

Human reactions to various serotypes of M protein

Subject[a]	Assay	Antigen				
		PBS	12 M	3 M	1 M	PPD
1. R.N., 25, F	Skin test[b]	0	2.5[c]	2.8	1.0	
	HA		1:100	1:400	1:200	
	Mean cpm[d] (DNA synthesis)	154	7,857	2,414	1,073	
2. D.C., 25, M	Skin test	0	1.8	1.0	1.2	0
	HA		1:400	1:400	1:400	
	Mean cpm (DNA synthesis)	36	767	469	106	149
3. R.Mc., 25, M	Skin test	0	1.2	1.7	0.4	3.0
	HA		1:100	1:100	1:400	
	Mean cpm (DNA synthesis)	52	3,089	65	645	3,169
4. M.A., 21, M	Skin test	0	0	0	0	1.2
	HA		1:200	1:200	0	
	Mean cpm (DNA synthesis)	10	70	542	39	74
5. L.R., 30, F	Skin test	0	3.5	2.5	1.2	2.0
	HA		1:100	1:400	1:100	
	Mean cpm (DNA synthesis)	52	8,735	11,592	3,152	2,595
6. B.D., 30, F	Skin test	0	1.5	1.5	0.2	0
	HA		1:400	1:800	1:100	
	Mean cpm (DNA synthesis)	759	5,859	5,295	2,576	461
7. C.M., 23, M	Skin test	0	1.2	1.7	0.7	1.5
	HA		1:1600	1:800	1:400	
	Mean cpm (DNA synthesis)	87	2,152	1,294	216	695
8. V.F., 26, F	Skin test	0	0	0	0	0
	HA		0	1:400	0	
	Mean cpm (DNA synthesis)	81	940	1,849	1,321	327
9. G.A., 26, M	Skin test	0	1.4	2.0	0.5	1.3
	HA		1:400	1:200	1:400	
	Mean cpm (DNA synthesis)	290	2,173	2,496	2,362	2,618
10. L.W., 35, F	Skin test	0	2.2	3.0	0	1.8
	HA		1:800	1:400	1:200	
	Mean cpm (DNA synthesis)	89	803	293	2,212	653

[a] Initials, age and sex of subject.
[b] Intradermal skin test antigen in 0.1 ml: intermediate strength PPD, 1 μg of M protein, or saline.
[c] Diameter of skin of reaction at 24 hr (in centimeters).
[d] Mean of triplicate cultures; uptake of ^{3}H-thymidine by peripheral blood lymphocytes in culture with and without antigen.

vertical diameter of the area of migration was multiplied by the horizontal diameter and the results are given as the ratio of the area of migration in those chambers to which antigen had been added over the area of migration of the controls. Results obtained in this manner did not differ significantly from those obtained by tracing the projected area of migration in the conventional manner (12).

Histologic examination. Biopsies of guinea pig skin were taken from sites of DCH 18 hr after testing. Sections were fixed and stained with hematoxylin and eosin and examined by light microscopy.

RESULTS

Human response to M proteins. Reactivities to streptococcal M proteins types 1, 3 and 12 were evaluated in man using: a) the delayed cutaneous response, b) measurements of circulating antibody, and c) *in vitro* lymphocyte stimulation. The results of observations obtained from 10 adults are presented in Table I. Negative cutaneous response to M proteins did not correlate with either circulating antibody titers or lymphocyte stimulation. In general, if a subject exhibited DCH to one M protein, some degree of reactivity was observed toward the other M proteins, making determinations of the specificity of the response difficult. Animal studies were initiated in order to clarify these findings.

DCH to M proteins in guinea pigs. Hartley guinea pigs were selected after initial trials with other varieties of albino guinea pigs showed positive skin tests to M proteins in the unimmunized animals, or inconsistent skin test reactions in the immunized ones. Uninjected Hartley guinea pigs were consistently negative to M protein when sera or skin test responses were studied throughout their lives. Sensitization with 40 μg of M protein in complete Freund's adjuvant conferred DCH on almost all the recipients when they were challenged with 30 μg of M protein 7 days after sensitization. At this time no circulating antibody could be detected by the passive hemagglutination test. The results obtained when groups of animals were sensitized and challenged with different M proteins are tabulated in Table II. Injection with complete Freund's adjuvant and saline produced sensitization to PPD alone. Animals immunized with M protein reacted to the homologous antigen, but the incidence of positive DCH reactions elicited by heterologous

TABLE II

Delayed cutaneous hypersensitivity to streptococcal M proteins in guinea pigs[a]

Sensitizing Antigen	Skin Test Antigen					
	PPD	12 M	3 M	1 M	6 M	Saline
Complete Freund's adjuvant	*16/16*	0/16	0/16	0/16	0/4	0/16
Complete Freund's adjuvant + 12 M	16/16	*16/16*	4/16	5/16	2/4	0/16
Complete Freund's adjuvant + 3 M	20/20	14/20	*19/20*	11/20	4/4	0/20
Complete Freund's adjuvant + 1 M	20/20	7/20	7/20	*20/20*	3/4	0/20
Complete Freund's adjuvant + 6 M	4/4	4/4	2/4	4/4	*4/4*	0/4

[a] Guinea pigs were sensitized with complete Freund's adjuvant mixed with saline or with 40 μg of M protein in saline and skin tested 7 days later with 30 μg of antigen in 0.1 ml. The results are expressed as the number of animals with greater than 0.5 cm diameter of erythema and induration 18 hr after skin test, divided by the total number tested. Homologous systems are italicized.

M proteins was variable. The degree of cross-reactivity was not reciprocal; many animals sensitized with 3 M were highly reactive to 12 M and 1 M, but the converse was not true. Histologic examination of the skin test site at 18 hr revealed edema and an intense round cell infiltration characteristic of the delayed cutaneous reaction in the guinea pig.

Circulating antibodies. The specificity of the passive hemagglutination test was next investigated by obtaining sera from guinea pigs before and at various times throughout the immunization period. When high antibody titers to the homologous antigen appeared, the specificity of the antibody reactivity was tested with M proteins of other serotypes. The results are shown in Table III as the mean hemagglutination titers in the homologous and heterologous systems. The range of values was extensive, but titers were usually highest when tested against the homologous antigen. Equal doses of M protein were not equally immunogenic; protein obtained

TABLE III

Cross-reactions of immune guinea pig sera[a]

Sensitizing Antigen	Mean Hemagglutination Titer (Antigen on Tanned RBC)			
	12 M	3 M	1 M	6 M
Complete Freund's adjuvant	0 [13][b]	0 [13]	0 [13]	0 [13]
Complete Freund's adjuvant + 12 M	*9,169* (25,600–800)[c] [13]	3,307 (12,800–200) [13]	30,666 (102,400–6,400) [9]	285 (800–0) [7]
Complete Freund's adjuvant + 3 M	2,988 (12,800–0) [9]	*11,155* (51,200–400) [9]	2,560 (6,400–0) [5]	<100 [4]
Complete Freund's adjuvant + 1 M	175 (400–100) [4]	900 (1,600–400) [4]	*32,000* (51,200–25,600) [4]	
Complete Freund's adjuvant + 6 M	0 [4]	100 [4]	125 (400–0) [4]	*2,600* (6,400–800) [4]

[a] Guinea pigs were sensitized with complete Freund's adjuvant containing saline or 40 μg of M protein in saline given in divided doses in the footpads, followed by two subcutaneous injections of adjuvant alone or containing 20 μg of M protein, administered at 2-week intervals. Sera were collected 2 weeks after the final injection and assayed for antibody by passive hemagglutination. Homologous systems are italicized.

[b] Number of animals [ ].

[c] Range of hemagglutination titers, as reciprocal ( ).

from type 6 did not elicit a high homologous titer and little cross-reactivity was observed. In addition, no opsonic antibody to type 6 could be detected by the indirect bactericidal test. However, specific opsonic antibodies were found in the sera of guinea pigs immunized with types 1, 3 and 12 M protein, if the sera were harvested in the cold (Table IV). Preimmunization sera from all the animals (data not presented in the table) did not show opsonic activity.

Spleen cell stimulation by M protein. The specificity of the *in vitro* cellular response to antigenic challenge with M proteins was investigated. Groups of guinea pigs were immunized by several routes with M proteins either in solutions, precipitated with aluminum hydroxide (APM), or in complete Freund's adjuvant. The serologic and cellular responses were then evaluated. From the results presented in Table V it is seen that complete Freund's adjuvant given in the footpad was the most efficient procedure for stimulating cell sensitization and antibody production.

The response of spleen cells from animals immunized with different M proteins was evaluated using heterologous and homologous M proteins, PPD, and BSA as *in vitro* stimulants. Immunization with any single M protein resulted in sensitization of spleen cells so that *in vitro* challenges with homologous as well as heterologous M types were stimulatory (Table VI). However, control animals immunized with Freund's adjuvant alone responded only to PPD.

Persistence of cellular reactivity. Guinea pigs were immunized in the footpads with a single dose of 40 μg of 12 M protein in complete Freund's adjuvant or with adjuvant mixed with saline. Animals in group A were killed 3 months after sensitization and the *in vitro* response of their spleen cells to antigenic stimulation was determined. The remaining animals in group B were maintained for 6 months until circulating antibodies were no longer detectable by hemagglutination. The animals were then killed and their spleen cell reactivity was determined. Table VII shows that spleen cells responded

TABLE IV

Bactericidal specificity of "plasma sera" from guinea pigs immunized with three types of M Protein[a]

Sensitizing Antigen	Animal No.	Bactericidal Activity[b] for Dilutions of Bacteria: 1:4	1:16	1:64	1:256
		Type 3			
Freund's adjuvant	1	−	−	−	−
	2	−	−	−	−
	3	−	−	−	−
3 M	4	+	+	+	+
	5	−	−	+	+
	6	+	+	+	+
12 M	7	−	−	−	−
	8	−	−	−	−
	9	−	−	−	−
1 M	10	−	−	−	−
	11	−	−	−	−
	12	−	−	−	−
		Type 12			
Freund's adjuvant	1	−	−	−	−
	2	−	−	−	−
	3	−	−	−	−
3 M	7	−	−	+	+
	8	−	−	−	−
	9	−	−	−	−
12 M	4	+	+	+	+
	5	−	−	+	+
	6	−	+	+	+
1 M	10	−	−	−	−
	11	−	−	−	−
	12	−	−	−	−
		Type 1			
Freund's adjuvant	1	−	−	−	−
	2	−	−	−	−
	3	−	−	−	−
12 M	4	−	−	−	−
	5	−	−	−	−
	6	−	−	−	−
3 M	7	−	−	−	−
	8	−	−	−	−
	9	−	−	−	−
1 M	10	+	+	+	+
	11	+	+	+	
	12	−	+	+	+

[a] Guinea pigs were sensitized with complete Freund's adjuvant, with or without 40 μg of M protein, given in divided doses in the footpads, followed by two subcutaneous injections of adjuvant containing saline or 20 μg of M protein administered at 2-week intervals. The sera were collected in the cold, 2 weeks after the final injection, and the specific opsonic activity was determined using homologous and heterologous streptococci.

[b] +, Indicates bactericidal activity (see *Materials and Methods*).

equally to antigenic challenge, whether or not the donor possessed circulating antibody.

Another *in vitro* assay of cellular reactivity employed inhibition by type 12 M protein of the migration of peritoneal exudate cells taken from sensitized guinea pigs. The results in Figure 1 indicate that cells taken from immunized animals were susceptible to inhibition by antigen, independent of the level of circulating antibody.

DISCUSSION

Studies by Lancefield (5) have shown that type-specific opsonic antibodies can be detected in man for as long as 12 years after infection with a known streptococcal serotype. No correlation exists between the severity of the initial infection and the persistence of type-specific opsonic antibody. The identification of a population susceptible to a particular type of streptococcal infection must therefore rest on other evidence. This is of practical consideration in the selection of subjects at risk who might be eligible to receive M protein vaccines (7).

Cellular reactivity to crude M protein was first documented by Lawrence (2, 13) in man when he transferred leukocytes from skin test-positive individuals to skin test-negative hosts, and induced conversion of the delayed response. However, the type-specificity of the reaction was not investigated. In the present study of 10 adults, delayed hypersensitivity to one M protein was usually accompanied by positive reactions to other serotypes. In addition, *in vitro* lymphocyte stimulation was obtained in the absence of demonstrable DCH and circulating antibody. Crude M protein and other streptoccal products have been reported to stimulate hyman lymphocytes *in vitro*, but type-specificity and correlation with other assays of immunity were not investigated (14–18).

Animal experiments were designed to clarify the type-specificity of reactions to M protein. Circulating antibody was measured by passive hemagglutination and opsonization. Cellular reactivity to antigen was assessed *in vivo* by skin testing and *in vitro* by lymphocyte stimulation and inhibition of sensitized guinea pig macro-

TABLE V

A comparison of routes of administration and adjuvants for antibody production and DNA synthesis by sensitized guinea pig spleen cells

Sensitizing Antigen and Route[a]	Mean 12 M HA Titer	^{3}H-Thymidine Uptake by Spleen Cells (Ratio Mean CPM ± S.E.)	
		12 M/C	PPD/C
None, (6)[b]	0	1.220 ± 0.187	0.940 ± 0.237
I. Soluble 12 M intramuscular (4)	1:100	1.370 ± 0.345	1.673 ± 0.375
II. APM-12 intraperitoneal (4)	1:200	1.208 ± 0.365	1.123 ± 0.428
III. APM-12 footpad (5)	1:400	1.758 ± 0.307	0.962 ± 0.124
IV. APM-12 intramuscular (8)	1:400	2.264 ± 0.350	1.598 ± 0.393
V. Complete Freund's adjuvant + 12 M footpad (7)	1:8000	10.06 ± 2.97	20.30 ± 6.05

[a] Guinea pigs sensitized and immunized by a variety of routes were bled and spleens removed 2 weeks after the final injection. Spleen cells were assayed for stimulation of DNA synthesis after *in vitro* exposure to 12 M protein or PPD. The results are expressed as the mean CPM of the antigen stimulated cells divided by the control cultures ± standard error. The schedule of sensitization for each group of animals was as follows. I: 40 μg of 12 M protein given intramuscularly, followed by 20 μg at 2-week intervals; II: 40 μg 12 M in 3 mg $Al(OH)_3$ given intraperitoneally (i.p.) at 2-week intervals; III: the same schedule and adjuvant as (II) except given in the footpad; IV: the same schedule and adjuvant as (II) except given intramuscularly; V: 40 μg of 12 M protein suspended in complete Freund's adjuvant, followed by two subcutaneous injections of 20 μg 12 M protein in Freund's adjuvant, given at intervals of 2 weeks.

[b] Number of animals in each experiment.

TABLE VI

Cross-reaction of streptococcal M proteins demonstrated by stimulation of DNA synthesis in sensitized guinea pig spleen cells[a]

Sensitizing Antigen	Ratio of cpm in Cultures Containing Antigen Divided by cpm Controls					
	PPD	12 M	3 M	1 M	6 M	BSA
Complete Freund's adjuvant (7)[b]	*21.98* ± 8.14	1.38 ± 0.46	0.79 ± 0.076	0.89 ± 0.11		1.33 ± 0.29
Complete Freund's adjuvant + 12 M (7)	20.30 ± 6.05	*10.06* ± 2.97	2.27 ± 0.58	7.67 ± 3.04		0.95 ± 0.15
Complete Freund's adjuvant + 3 M (4)	14.59 ± 2.17	14.36 ± 7.89	*4.85* ± 1.30	6.18 ± 2.74		1.09 ± 0.37
Complete Freund's adjuvant + 1 M (4)	26.05 ± 11.03	6.81 ± 2.42	3.76 ± 1.15	*7.06* ± 1.34		1.02 ± 0.15
Complete Freund's adjuvant + 6 M (4)	15.56 ± 9.02	6.18 ± 3.60	10.78 ± 6.05	13.65 ± 6.37	*16.15* ± 6.97	1.74 ± 0.29

[a] Guinea pigs were sensitized with complete Freund's adjuvant containing saline or 40 μg M protein, given in divided doses in the footpads, followed by two subcutaneous injections of adjuvant, with or without 20 μg of 12 M protein given at 2-week intervals. The results are expressed as the mean counts per minute (cpm) of triplicate cultures, each containing 50 μg of antigen, divided by the mean cpm of the control cultures ± the standard error. The results of the homologous systems are italicized.

[b] The number of animals in each experiment.

TABLE VII

A comparison of DNA synthesis in spleen cells from guinea pigs with and without circulating antibodies[a]

Animal No.	Sensitizing Antigen	Postimmunization 12 M HA Titer		Postimmunization Spleen Cultures—Mean cpm in Response to: Saline	Postimmunization Spleen Cultures—Mean cpm in Response to: 12 M
Group A		3 months	6 months	3 months	
1	Complete Freund's adjuvant	0		373	562
2	Complete Freund's adjuvant	0		290	382
3	Complete Freund's adjuvant + 12 M	1:3200		560	3018
4	Complete Freund's adjuvant + 12 M	1:800		339	2970
5	Complete Freund's adjuvant + 12 M	1:3200		695	1705
Group B		3 months	6 months	6 months	
6	Complete Freund's adjuvant	0	0	205	308
7	Complete Freund's adjuvant	0	0	535	467
8	Complete Freund's adjuvant + 12 M	1:3200	0	206	1411
9	Complete Freund's adjuvant + 12 M	1:1600	0	502	3656
10	Complete Freund's adjuvant + 12 M	1:3200	0	651	3186

[a] Two groups of guinea pigs were immunized with a single injection of Freund's adjuvant containing saline or 12 M protein. Group A was killed 3 months later and hemagglutination titers and spleen reactivity were assayed. Group B was evaluated 6 months after sensitization.

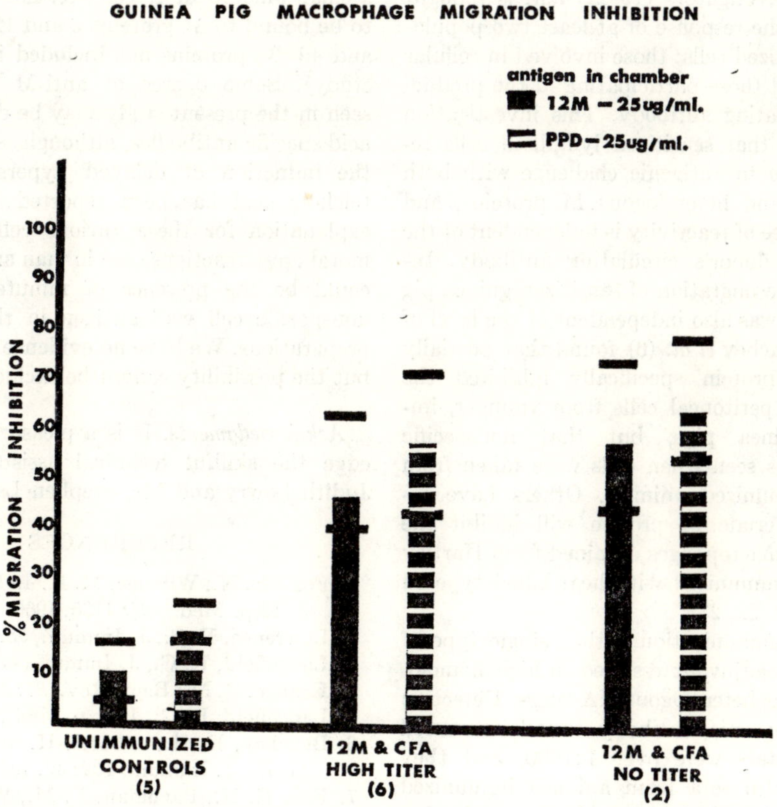

Figure 1. Peritoneal exudate was obtained from three groups of guinea pigs: 1) unimmunized; 2) immunized with 12 M and complete Freund's adjuvant 3 months before harvest, high titer circulating antibody present in donors; and 3) immunized with 12 M and complete Freund's adjuvant 6 months before harvest, circulating antibody no longer at detectable levels. Migration of the peritoneal exudate cells was measured in the absence of antigen, and when either 12 M or PPD were added to the chambers.

phage migration. Hartley guinea pigs were selected for immunization with individual M proteins after screening confirmed that unimmunized animals weighing from 300 to 900 g did not spontaneously develop DCH to M proteins. These findings were at variance with those of Beachey *et al.* (6), who found that older, normal random-bred guinea pigs developed DCH to partially purified M proteins. Our data, obtained from animals weighing from 300 to 400 g, indicated that immunization with Freund's adjuvant alone did not produce responsiveness to M protein, despite induction of reactivity to PPD. Immunization with specific M proteins resulted in DCH to homologous types and, to some degree, reaction to heterologous ones.

The specificity of *in vitro* cellular reactivity to M proteins was investigated after the optimum route and adjuvant for immunization had been established. *In vitro* antigenic stimulation of guinea pig lymphocytes has been evaluated by a number of investigators (19–21) and is thought to represent the response of at least two populations of sensitized cells: those involved in cellular reactivity and those participating in the production of circulating antibody. This investigation demonstrates that sensitized lymphoid cells respond *in vitro* to antigenic challenge with both homologous and heterologous M proteins, and that the degree of reactivity is independent of the level of the donor's circulating antibody. Inhibition of the migration of sensitized guinea pig exudate cells was also independent of the level of antibody. Beachey *et al.* (6) found that partially purified M protein specifically inhibited the migration of peritoneal cells from younger, immunized guinea pigs, but that nonspecific inhibition was seen when cells were taken from older, unimmunized animals. Others have reported that crude M protein will inhibit the spreading of macrophages obtained from Hartley guinea pigs immunized with heat-killed type 24 streptococcus (22, 23).

Repeated immunization with a single type of M protein in adjuvant resulted in high homologous as well as heterologous HA titers. Detection of specific opsonic antibody usually occurred when HA titers were over 1:1600, and they were present in sera from animals immunized with types 1, 3 and 12 M protein. Immunization with type 6 M protein resulted in low homologous titers, lower heterologous ones and no opsonic antibody. Throughout the experiment, pre- and post-immunization sera to be tested for opsonic antibodies were collected in the cold to prevent the release of nonspecific opsonins (10). Although cellular response to antigen, manifested either by DCH or *in vitro* stimulation, reflected previous contact with M proteins in the guinea pig or immunized humans (7), it is apparent from the experiments presented here that opsonic antibody is the most reliable type-specific assay of exposure to group A streptococcal M protein.

The observed cross-reactions using M proteins in humoral and cellular assays of sensitization may be due to several factors. Shared antigenic determinants between serotypes 3 and 12 M protein were demonstrated by Wittner and Fox (24). These determinants, revealed by immunodiffusion spurs, absorption and quantitative precipitation experiments, showed a significant antigenic similarity. In addition, it has been recently demonstrated in this laboratory (25) that a small amount of glycerol-teichoic acid appears to be bound to M proteins 6 and 12 (as well as 2 and 49, M proteins not included in the present study). Some degree of anti-M cross-reaction seen in the present study may be due to teichoic acid specific antibodies, although no evidence for the induction of delayed hypersensitivity by teichoic acid has been reported (26). A third explanation for these various cellular and humoral cross-reactions seen in man and guinea pigs could be the presence of minute amounts of nonspecific cell wall antigen in the M protein preparations. We have no evidence for the latter, but the possibility cannot be excluded.

Acknowledgments. It is a pleasure to acknowledge the skillful technical assistance of Mrs. Judith Lowry and Mr. Stephen Lau.

REFERENCES

1. Fox, E. N., Wittner, M. K. and Dorfman, A., J. Exp. Med., *124:* 1135, 1966.
2. Lawrence, H. S., J. Immun., *68:* 159, 1952.
3. Lancefield, R. C., J. Immun., *89:* 307, 1962.
4. Krause, R. M., Bact. Rev., *27:* 369, 1963.
5. Lancefield, R. C., J. Exp. Med., *110:* 271, 1959.
6. Beachey, E. H., Alberti, H. and Stollerman, G. H., J. Immun., *102:* 42, 1969.
7. Fox, E. N., Pachman, L. M., Wittner, M. K. and Dorfman, A., J. Infect. Dis., *120:* 598, 1969.
8. Fox, E. N., J. Immun., *93:* 826, 1964.
9. Lancefield, R. C., J. Exp. Med., *106:* 525, 1957.

10. Hirsch, J. G., J. Exp. Med., *112:* 15, 1960.
11. Pachman, L. M., Blood, *30:* 601, 1967.
12. David, J. R., Al-Askari, A., Lawrence, H. S. and Thomas, L., J. Immun., *93:* 264, 1964.
13. Lawrence, H. S., Proc. Soc. Exp. Biol. Med., *110:* 271, 1959.
14. Francis, T. C. and Oppenheim, J. J., Fed. Proc., *28:* 553, 1969.
15. Passaleva, A., Romagnani, S., Ricci, N., Leri, A. and Salvadori, R., Folia Allerg., *14:* 621, 1967.
16. Ky, N. T. and Halpern, B., Rév. Franc. Allerg., *7:* 203, 1967.
17. Lyampert, I. M., Smirnova, M. N. and Semina, N. A., J. Hyg. Epidem., *11:* 160, 1967.
18. Lau, H. S. and Scherago, M., J. Bact., *94:* 1722, 1967.
19. Oppenheim, J. J., Wolstencroft, R. A. and Gell, P. G. H., Immunology, *12:* 89, 1967.
20. Knight, S., Ling, N. R., Snell, S. and Oxnard, O. E., Immunology, *9:* 565, 1965.
21. Mills, J. A., J. Immun., *97:* 239, 1966.
22. Dekaris, D., Fauve, R. M. and Raynaud, M., J. Immun., *103:* 1, 1969.
23. Dekaris, D., Faure, R. M., Alouf, J. E. and Raynard, M., Ann. Inst. Pasteur, *116:* 602, 1969.
24. Fox, E. N. and Wittner, M. K., J. Immun., *100:* 39, 1968.
25. Wittner, M. K. and Fox, E. N., Fed. Proc., *29:* 637, Abstract, 1970.
26. McCarty, M. and Morse, S. I., Advances Immun., *4:* 249, 1964.

THE JOURNAL OF IMMUNOLOGY
Vol. 105, No. 2, October 1970
Printed in U.S.A.

GENETIC CONTROL OF THE IMMUNE RESPONSE IN MICE

II. A Two-Way Selection Experiment for Specific Immunologic Competence[1]

DAVID L. GASSER[2, 3]

From the Mammalian Genetics Center, Department of Zoology, The University of Michigan, Ann Arbor, Michigan 48104

Received for publication April 29, 1970

The production of agglutinating antibodies to the Ea-1a erythrocytic alloantigen in *Mus musculus* has previously been shown to be controlled by a single Mendelian recessive factor when strain YBR was crossed with BALB or CBA. It has now been determined that when YBR is crossed with C57BL/10, responsiveness is dominant and a strong nongenetic effect occurs. When positive assortative matings were made between YBR-B10 F2 segregants, a significant response to selection occurred, and estimates of the heritability of the response could be obtained. After one additional generation of selection the high responder line included 81% responders while the low responder line included no responders.

In a previous report (1) the ability of the inbred mouse strains YBR, CBA and BALB to produce agglutinating antibodies to the Ea-1a antigen, which is present on the red cells of some wild mice, was shown to be under genetic control. When the responding strain YBR was crossed with either of the nonresponding strains, CBA or BALB, the responder trait behaved as if determined by a simple Mendelian recessive factor which was linked to the agouti locus in linkage group V.

In this report a second genetically determined response to the same antigen is described. The responding strain YBR was crossed with the nonresponding strain C57BL/10, and the responder trait behaved as a dominant character. Segregation data suggest that more than one genetic factor may be involved, and linkage tests indicate that this system is distinct from the *Ir-2* system previously reported.

MATERIALS AND METHODS

Animals. The YBR/a (YBR) strain is a subline started in 1962 from YBR/HeWiHa mice obtained in 1959 from Dr. T. S. Hauschka of the Rosewell Park Memorial Institute. The C57BL/10ScSn (B10) strain was obtained in 1968 from The Jackson Laboratory, Bar Harbor, Maine. The mice which supplied the red cells for immunization were derived from wild mice trapped in the Ann Arbor area in 1961 and 1962 by Dr. M. L. Petras.

Immunization procedure. The donor animals of type *Ea-1*[a] were bled from the retroorbital plexus and the blood was suspended in 4% sodium citrate. After washing three times in saline, the cells from the various donors were pooled and suspended in five volumes of Freund's complete adjuvant (Difco Laboratories, Detroit, Mich.).

Recipients which were about 8 weeks old at the time of primary immunization received 0.2 ml of this suspension injected s.c. over the scapular region. Beginning 3 weeks later, the mice received 10 i.p. boosters at 4- to 5-day intervals, each consisting of 0.2 ml of a suspension of donor red cells in physiologic saline (1:10).

Assay. The assay for hemagglutinating antibodies was the same as previously described (1).

[1] Parts of this study were taken from a thesis submitted to The Horace H. Rackham School of Graduate Studies in partial fulfillment of the requirements of the degree of Doctor of Philosophy.

[2] This study was supported in part by a National Institutes of Health predoctoral genetics training grant, NIH-5-T01-GM-00071-12; in part by a National Institutes of Health postdoctoral fellowship, 1-F02-GM-33,294-01; and by NSF GB-7241.

[3] Present address: Immunobiology Research Unit, Department of Medical Genetics, University of Pennsylvania, School of Medicine, Philadelphia, Pennsylvania 19104.

Seminal vesicle protein (Svp) typing. The electrophoretic typing procedure for *Svp* of Platz and Wolfe (2) was used. Seminal vesicles were dissected from the mice, the fluid was suspended in saline, and the suspension was centrifuged. One drop of supernatant was mixed with 50 drops of sample gel, and Davis's method of acrylamide gel electrophoresis was followed (3).

RESULTS

Evidence for segregation. Animals of the parental strains YBR and B10 and the F_1, F_2, and backcross generations were immunized and tested for their ability to produce hemagglutinating antibodies. The results are shown in Table I. The value of the heterogeneity X^2 is highly significant ($X^2 = 73.56$, d.f. $= 6$, $p < 0.005$). Since all environmental conditions were kept as constant as possible (animal care conditions, age at immunization, method of immunization, etc.), the most likely explanation for this heterogeneity would seem to be that genetic segregation is occurring in crosses (d) through (g). This conclusion is supported by the data of Table III and Figure 1, which are discussed below.

Influence of nongenetic variation. The fact that not all of the YBR mice, the B10 mice, and the YBR-BI0 F_1 hybrids have the same responder phenotype could be due to either genetic or nongenetic variation. This question was examined by making assortative matings by responder phenotype and immunizing the progeny. This has been done using F_1 hybrids as parents, with the results as shown in Table II. These data show that there was no significant difference in the proportion of responders in the progeny of responder parents as compared with the progeny of nonresponder parents ($X^2 = 0.009$, $p > 0.90$). Since all F_1 hybrids between two isogenic strains are expected to have the same genetic endowment, we are led to conclude that the variation within the F_1 generation and presumably that in the parental strains as well resulted from nongenetic factors. This type of inheritance has generally been referred to as threshold inheritance (4, 5), or to use another terminology, we may say that penetrance is incomplete. This implies that within the constraints imposed by genetic factors, whether an animal can respond is randomly determined.

TABLE I

Segregation data for parental, F1, F2, and backcross generations in YBR and B10 mice

Animals	Responders	Nonresponders
(a) YBR	27	4
(b) B10	4	17
(c) YBR-B10 F_1	18	9
(d) (YBR-B10)F_1 × YBR	25	1
(e) (YBR-B10)F_1 × B10	16	49
(f) YBR-B10 F_2	27	50
(g) (YBR-B10 F_1 × B10) × B10	3	14

Heterogeneity $X^2 = 73.56$, d.f. $= 6$, $p < 0.005$

TABLE II

Positive assortative matings of F1 parents: phenotypes of the progeny

Mating	Responders	Nonresponders	Responders
			%
(a) F_1 responder × F_1 responder	14	24	37
(b) F_1 nonresponder × F_1 nonresponder	13	26	33

Contingency $X^2 = 0.009$, $p > 0.90$

TABLE III

Artificial selection for responsiveness and nonresponsiveness

	Responders	Nonresponders	Responders	h^2
			%	
(a) YBR-B10 F2[a]	27	50	35	
(b) F_2 responder × F_2 responder	21	12	64	0.45
(c) F_2 nonresponder × F_2 nonresponder	5	32	14	0.60

[a] Line (a) represents the sum of lines (a) and (b) in Table II.

Estimate of heritability. If genetic segregation is occurring, the variation in the F_2 should result not only from nongenetic factors, but from genetic factors as well. When positive assortative matings were made using F_2 mice as parents, the results shown in Table III were obtained. The offspring of these two types of matings differed significantly in the proportion of responders ($X^2 = 4.80$, d.f. $= 1$, $p < 0.05$). In fact, the F_2 nonresponder parents produced offspring among which the frequency of responders did not differ significantly from that of the B10 parental strain ($X^2 = 0.03$, $0.75 < p < 0.90$).

These matings permit an estimate to be made of the relative contributions of genetic and nongenetic factors. Falconer's method (5) of determining the *realized heritability* has been applied with the results as shown in the last column of Table III. The fact that the second h^2 is greater than the first can be attributed primarily to the recessivity of nonresponsiveness. Although these estimates of heritability cannot be regarded as being very precise, they demonstrate that a measurable component (about 45% to 60%) of the variation can be attributed to genetic factors.

Selection for responsiveness and nonresponsiveness was continued for one additional generation, in which the F_3 responder parents produced 81% (13/16) responders among their F_4 progeny, while the nonresponder parents produced no responders (0/6). The results of this two-way selection experiment are summarized in Figure 1. The fact that a progressive differentiation could be made between the two lines until the high responder line included 81% responders and the low responder line included no responders provides convincing evidence that this trait is largely under genetic control. The proportion of responders in the F_4 generation of the "high line" did not differ significantly from that in the YBR parental strain, and the proportion of responders in the "low line" did not differ significantly from that in the B10 parental strain. The small number of generations required to achieve this result suggests that this responder trait is determined by relatively few genes.

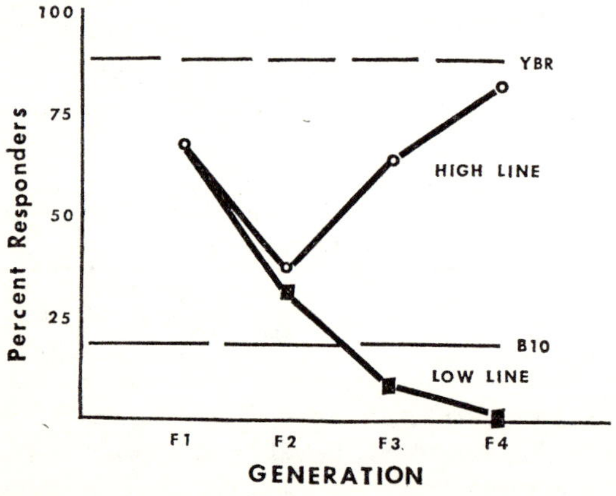

Figure 1. Summary of two-way selection for response to the Ea-1a antigen.

Test for linkage with Svp. When YBR was crossed with CBA or BALB, responsiveness to *Ea-1* antigens was determined by a single locus designated *Ir-2*, which was linked to the agouti locus (1). Since YBR and B10 are both nonagouti strains, linkage to agouti cannot be tested directly. These strains do segregate for a biochemical marker, *Svp*, which is closely linked to agouti (3), so linkage of the responder trait to the chromosomal region containing agouti can be tested. The data of Table IV do not suggest any association between these traits. This suggests that the genetic basis of the response described in this report is distinct from the *Ir-2* system but the participation of the *Ir-2* region in a multigenic system is not ruled out.

DISCUSSION

In these experiments there was no evidence that the titer of the response was genetically determined, but rather that the all-or-none phenomenon of the ability to produce antibody seemed to be under genetic control. Since the phenotype is not a graded character, most of the standard methods used for estimating the number of loci in quantitative genetics cannot be

TABLE IV

Test for linkage between seminal vesicle protein Svp and the responder trait in YBR × B10 crosses

Generation	Svp^a		Svp^a/Svp^b		Svp^b		X^2	P
	Responders	Nonresponders	Responders	Nonresponders	Responders	Nonresponders		
(a) YBR-B10 F_2	4	6	7	10	3	2	0.83	0.50–0.75
(b) (YBR-B10)F_1 × B10			3	11	4	9	0.02	0.90

applied. Although a single-locus mode of inheritance (subject to nongenetic influences) has not been ruled out, the complexity of the system may well indicate that multiple genetic factors are involved.

An hypothesis recently discussed by Jerne (6) predicts that histocompatibility antigens would determine the antigenic diversity to which an animal could respond. At least three cases are now known in which the *H-2* region appears to influence specific immunologic competence (7, 8, 9). In a previous report (1) another gene affecting response to *Ea-1* antigens was found to be linked to agouti, and therefore to *H-3* and *H-6*, and could in fact be identical to one of these two loci.

Jerne's hypothesis is consistent with the idea that nongenetic variation could occur in these systems since antibody diversity is generated in a random process, but that genetic constraints will be placed on the system by histocompatibility loci. On the basis of Jerne's hypothesis, one might expect multigenically determined immune responses to occur since there are many histocompatibility loci, and the response to a given antigen need not always be associated with only one of these loci. Experiments are in progress to determine whether the genetic system described in this report might be associated with histocompatibility loci.

Acknowledgments. It is a pleasure to acknowledge the help and advice of Professors M. Foster, D. C. Shreffler, G. W. Nace, and A. G. Johnson.

REFERENCES

1. Gasser, D. L., J. Immun., *103:* 66, 1969.
2. Platz, R. D. and Wolfe, H. G., J. Hered., *60:* 187, 1969.
3. Davis, B. D., Ann. N. Y. Acad. Sci., *121:* 404, 1964.
4. Wright, S., Genetics, *19:* 506, 1934.
5. Falconer, D. S., *Introduction to Quantitative Genetics*, Ronald Press Co., New York, 1960.
6. Jerne, N. K., in *Immunological Surveillance*, Edited by R. T. Smith and M. Landy, Academic Press, New York, In press.
7. McDevitt, H. O. and Tyan, M. L., J. Exp. Med., *128:* 1, 1968.
8. Rathbun, W. E. and Hildemann, W. H., Genetics, *61:* s49, 1969.
9. Vaz, N. M. and Levine, B. B., Fed. Proc., *29:* 825, Abstract, 1970.

THE JOURNAL OF IMMUNOLOGY
Vol. 105, No. 4, October 1970

Printed in U.S.A.

IMMUNOLOGIC RESPONSES OF PACIFIC HAGFISH

III. Serum Antibodies to Cellular Antigens[1]

D. SCOTT LINTHICUM[2] AND W. H. HILDEMANN

From the Department of Medical Microbiology and Immunology, University of California, Los Angeles, California 90024

Received for publication April 29, 1970

Hagfish serum contains naturally-occurring agglutinins which react to different degrees with heterogenetic, but non-Forssman antigens on the erythrocytes of various vertebrates. These antibodies of generally low activity were found to reside in the macroglobulin (IgM) fraction, but became undetectable after heating serum at 56°C for 30 min. Specific production of antibodies against sheep erythrocytes was regularly inducible, given suitable tactics of immunization. Hagfish which received weight-adjusted dosages every 14 days over a 70-day period at 18°C showed 2^3- to 2^5-fold rises in specific hemagglutination titers. Induced antibodies were heat stable and displayed a high degree of specificity for sheep cell antigens. Chromatographic and immunoelectrophoretic analyses showed the naturally-occurring and induced antibody activity to be limited to a major macroglobulin fraction similar to but distinguishable from the IgM of higher vertebrates. Hagfish, despite their "most primitive vertebrate" status, are capable of vigorous production of antibodies to at least certain cellular and soluble antigens. The extent of their immunogenetic library and immunologic memory invites further investigation.

Hagfish are Agnathan cyclostomes with numerous primitive traits and they may well represent an important stage in the early evolution of vertebrates. Evaluation of their immunologic potentialities should help to elucidate the evolution of immune responsiveness in higher vertebrates. Because earlier investigations (1, 2) had failed to detect any specific induced immunity in Pacific hagfish, this species erroneously became a negative hero in the "phylogeny of immunity."

Actually, the capacity to recognize and reject skin allografts was found to be well developed in hagfish (abbr. hags). Chronic allograft rejection characteristic of weaker histocompatibility barriers was the rule, but accelerated second-set reactions revealed the induction of specific immunity as well as persistent immunologic memory (3). Moreover, hagfish also produce serum antibodies to both soluble and cellular antigens. Macroglobulin antibodies of the IgM-type were evoked in high titers following parenteral immunization with soluble keyhole limpet hemocyanin (KLH) as shown by both passive hemagglutination and gel diffusion-precipitation methods (4). Although chromatographic fractionation of antisera and purification of components showed the KLH antibodies to belong to the IgM class, the immunologic memory suggested by rising titers of specific antibody was not reflected in any major change in the quality of antibodies detected.

The present study is concerned with serum antibody responses to cellular antigens, especially those induced by sheep erythrocytes and detectable by hemagglutination. The molecular class of immunoglobulins involved and the specificity of both naturally-occurring and induced agglutinins were also investigated.

MATERIALS AND METHODS

Hagfish. Adult hagfish (*Eptatretus stoutii*) ranging in length from 20 to 35 cm were used in these studies. These animals were collected in deep (38 to 40 fathoms), cool (10° to 13°C) water

[1] This work was supported by National Institutes of Health Grant AI-07970.

[2] Supported by an National Science Foundation summer scholarship grant from the Committee for Advanced Science Training (CAST), 700 State Drive, Los Angeles, California 90037, and by the Los Angeles Chapter of the American Cancer Society.

near Point Dume off the coast of Southern California. They were acclimatized to large aquariums with circulating sea water and were held at 18.5° ± 0.5°C throughout the experiments. Satisfactory though probably not optimal conditions for keeping hags healthy in captivity have been reported (3, 4). They were fed mainly on fish or beef liver. After repeated bleedings and injections, the hags tended to stop normal feeding and were then force-fed at 2-week intervals with homogenized beef liver by oral insertion of a plastic catheter into the gut.

Anesthesia and bleeding. Tricaine methanesulfonate (Ayerst Laboratories Inc., New York, N. Y.) was most satisfactory; animals placed in this anesthetic at a concentration of 70 mg/liter of sea water became quiescent in about 30 min at 18°C. Additional cooling of the hags by exposure to sea-ice prolonged the anesthesia. Hagfish were bled from the tail sinus using a syringe with 25-gauge needle. Blood was pooled in the tail sinus by gentle pushing along the body wall with the forefinger and thumb. This tail sinus is described by Jensen (5) as an "open space" into which the arterial blood is discharged by the caudal heart. Serum was collected following centrifugation of the blood which was allowed to clot for at least several hours in the cold. Completion of clotting may take 24 hr, but is accelerated by agitation of the blood sample.

Detection of serum antibodies. Hemagglutination tests were performed in 10- x 75-mm test tubes containing 0.2 ml serum or antiserum dilutions plus 0.2 ml of a 2% suspension (v/v) of washed erythrocytes. A 1.2% saline control tube was used for each batch of red cells, although the saline concentration is not critical for the success or sensitivity of the test. Specific agglutination was most sensitively determined in all instances by clumping of the cell "button" as revealed by tapping the tubes gently, following just sufficient centrifugation to sediment the cells. Similar titers of hemagglutinating antibodies were also detectable with smaller volumes by sedimentation of test erythrocytes in microtiter plates (Cooke Engineering Company, Alexandria, Va.) without centrifugation. To delineate the specificity of naturally-occurring agglutinins in hagfish sera, a variety of vertebrate erythrocytes were tested. Injections of sheep erythrocytes for immunization were given subcutaneously, which is equivalent in hagfish to an intravascular route.

Immunoelectrophoretic and serum fractionation procedures. The immunoelectrophoretic microtechnique (6) utilized barbital buffer, pH 8.6, for the electrode vessel and agar gel. A 1% agarose (Mann Research Laboratories, New York, N. Y.) and buffer mixture was poured on 26- x 76-mm slides to give a 2 mm gel thickness. Anti-hagfish-globulin serum was produced in adult rabbits. Six-tenths milliliter of a mixture of hagfish serum and complete Freund adjuvant (2:1) was injected intradermally into the footpads. Booster injections (0.1 to 0.15 ml) were given after 2 weeks and antiserum was harvested after 10 days or later. Precipitation bands were scored after incubation of the test slides for at least 48 hr at 4°C. These slides were subsequently dried and stained with Amido black 10 B for preservation and photography.

Isolation of serologically active immunoglobulin was first attempted by a method involving sodium sulfate precipitation (7), but reactive preparations were not obtained. Both quick-batch chromatography, using the rapid method of Stanworth (8), and column chromatography methods yielded active immunoglobulin fractions. Sephadex G-200 gel filtration was done on a Sephadex K-25/100 column (Pharmacia, Uppsala, Sweden) having upward flow adapters. The gel was equilibrated with 0.2 M NaCl, 0.1 M Tris-HCl buffer containing trace metals (0.1% solution of 1.0 M $MgCl_2$ and 0.15 M $CaCl_2$) at pH 8.0 and at 5°C. Hag serum samples were dialyzed for several hours against this buffer before being placed on the column. Using a pressure head of 14 cm with a flow rate of about 10 ml/hr, 5-ml fractions were collected at 5°C. Protein concentrations were monitored by UV absorbancy at 280 nm, and fractions were concentrated by negative pressure dialysis prior to testing for hemagglutinating activity.

Ion exchange chromatography with DEAE-cellulose was performed at 5°C on a 1.5- x 45-cm column. Whole serum or fractions from G-200 chromatography were dialyzed against 0.015 M Tris-HCl at pH 8.0, which served as the starting buffer. Elution was accomplished by an increasing NaCl gradient from 0.1 M to 0.4 M NaCl in 0.015 M Tris-HCl, pH 8.0, passed through the column. Immunoglobulin fractions were again concentrated by negative pressure dialysis.

RESULTS

Naturally-occurring antibodies. Fresh normal hag serum regularly contains saline agglutinins for sheep red cells at a 1:4 or 1:8 titer. This reactivity remains intact for up to 14 days storage at 4°C or after freezing for several days at −20°C or −195°C. However, these agglutinins are heat-labile, since hag sera heated at 56°C for 30 min lost all antibody activity, whereas induced antibodies retained their activity. Agglutination tests at 4°C showed weaker reactions, whereas room temperature (~20°C) yielded the highest titers.

Tests of normal hag serum against red cells of representative vertebrates are summarized in Table I. These results ranged from essentially no reactivity for hagfish, shark and chicken cells to titers as high as 1:32 for iguana and mouse cells. Mice of quite different strains and humans of different blood groups behaved similarly, so no alloantigens in these species were responsible for the observed reactions. Hagfish apparently lack normal alloantibodies as evidenced by no significant agglutination of red cells from other hags. Presumably one or more heterogenetic cellular antigens in the various species tested is reactive with the normal hag agglutinins. The Forssman "antigen" in the broader sense is not involved, since chickens, mice and men all have this specificity in common (9). Given the scavenger role of hags, which live at the bottom of coastal bays, the finding of naturally-occurring agglutinins is hardly surprising. Indeed, hagfish also possess agglutinins for antigens of sea urchin (*Strongylocentrotus purpuratus*) sperm.

TABLE I

Reactions of normal hagfish serum with erythrocytes of representative vertebrates

[a] Two per cent suspensions of erythrocytes were made in isotonic saline. Final readings were made after 3 hr at 22°C. The entries show the number of hagfish sera with the indicated titer.

Erythrocyte Species	No. of Hagfish Sera Tested	Reciprocal of Agglutination Titer				
		<4	4	8	16	32
Hagfish (*E. stoutii*)	10	10				
Shark (*C. venturiosm*)	6	6				
Bass (*P. clataratus*)	6	0	0	4	2	
Iguana (*C. pectinata*)	6	0	0	0	1	5
Bullfrog (*R. catesbeiana*)	6	4	2			
Chicken	6	6				
Mouse (C3H)	6	0	0	0	4	2
Mouse (A/J)	2	0	0	0	1	1
Rat (Fischer)	6	0	0	4	2	
Sheep	10	0	4	6		
Human (AB)	6	4	0	1	1	
Human (O)	6	1	2	3		

Induced antibodies. Several schedules of immunization with sheep red cells were tried in attempts to induce elevated antibody titers. Two groups of three adult hags kept at 18°C each received a total of eight injections of 2.5×10^7 or 5.0×10^7 cells, respectively, at 7-day intervals. Repeated bleedings at 14-day intervals indicated slight increases followed by actual decreases in antibody levels; no significant changes in titer or degree of agglutination were found. Since these animals all died within 2 months after the experiments were begun, we suspected that cumulative antigen overdosages or the stress of frequent trauma may have impaired their immune responsiveness.

Two additional groups of three hagfish each were immunized with body weight-adjusted dosages of sheep cells at 14- rather than 7-day intervals. Smaller hags weighing about 50 g received 2.5×10^7 cells/injection, and larger hags weighing about 150 g received 10^8 cells/injection. These results are summarized in Figure 1. All the hags that survived the course of injections at both cell dosages showed a substantial rise in titer of 3 to 5 doubling dilutions. Two fish reached a peak titer of 1:128 after 70 days. Other variations in the tactics of immunization were tried with other hagfish. However, hemagglutination titers of up to 1:1024 have been obtained more recently, within a 3-month period after initial stimulation.

These induced antibodies were specific for sheep cell antigens since increased reactivity toward burro erythrocytes was not elicited. Burro red cells, non-cross-reactive with sheep cells, were, however, agglutinated by the wide spectrum "natural" antibodies. Human and mouse erythrocytes also reacted similarly to burro cells. In addition to showing induced specificity, the hag antibodies evoked by sheep cells were also heat stable after 30 min at 56°C. The antibodies produced after specific immuniza-

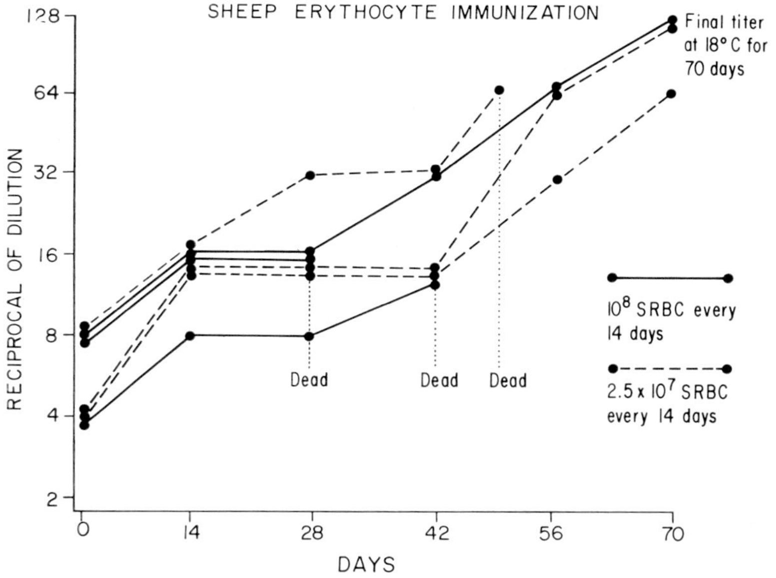

Figure 1. Hemagglutinin titers induced in hagfish which received weight-adjusted dosages of sheep red cells injected every 14 days over a period of 70 days. Hagfish were bled 14 days after each injection.

tion remained active for up to 60 days when stored at 4°C.

Hagfish are slow to replenish blood cells lost by excessive bleeding. Thus, frequent bleeding appears to be counterproductive and probably accounts for lower antibody levels as well as premature death of the experimental animals. Several attempts to induce neutralizing antibodies to T2 coliphage in hagfish have surprisingly yielded negative results, although non-immune clearance of phage from the circulation is readily achieved over a wide dosage range. More refined experiments with this potentially sensitive model system are underway. Conceivably hagfish may fail to respond or may respond poorly to certain immunogens which are quite potent in higher vertebrates.

Immunoglobulin identification. The immunoelectrophoretic and chromatographic components of hagfish serum were described in a previous paper (4). Upon fractionation on Sephadex G-200 columns, most hagfish serum protein is located in the first (IgM) peak. The second peak appears as a distinctive shoulder off the first, while a third peak represents low molecular weight protein always present in much lower concentration. Naturally-occurring hemagglutinins against sheep cells in hagfish serum have consistently been found in the first G-200 peak. Induced antibodies, at titers as high as 1:1024 in some recent experiments, were also concentrated in the high molecular weight protein excluded by G-200. This localization of antibody activity was also confirmed by ion exchange chromatography of whole serum and of G-200 fractions on DEAE-cellulose. Immunoelectrophoresis revealed IgM-like mobility in the G-200 fractions with agglutinating activity.

The immunoelectrophoretic separation of hagfish serum proteins following sodium sulfate precipitation, quick-batch DEAE, or G-200 chromatography is shown in Figure 2, with purified mouse IgM for comparison. The antibody-containing globulin is just on the positive side of the well following DEAE separation (*2*) which corresponds to the active G-200 fraction (*3*) in the same position. This hag immunoglobulin is clearly distinguishable from mouse IgM on an immunoelectrophoretic basis, and as noted below, on the basis of sedimentation coefficient also. Whether prolonged immunization may lead eventually to production of lower molecular weight antibodies remains to be tested critically.

Ultracentrifugal analysis of normal hagfish serum and plasma under various conditions consistently revealed four major protein peaks, all with rather stable sedimentation coefficients.

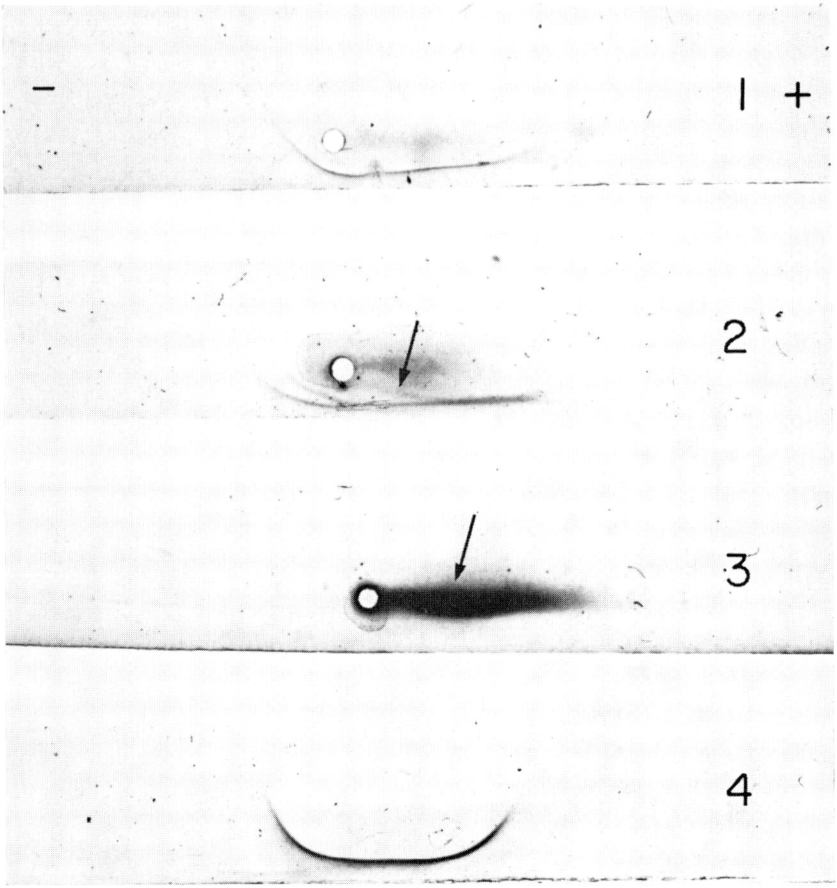

Figure 2. Immunoelectrophoretic distribution of hagfish serum protein fractions following sodium sulfate precipitation (*1*), quick-batch DEAE chromatography (*2*) and Sephadex G-200 chromatography (*3*). The active immunoglobulin fractions are indicated by arrows. Similar but distinctive mouse IgM is illustrated for comparison (*4*). The diffuse band in (*3*) is often seen after hag IgM is obtained by G-200 fractionation and then reconcentrated; it probably results from aggregation of the IgM.

$s_{20,w}$ values for the macroglobulin peak containing the naturally-occurring antibody activity ranged from 22.2 to 24.8 with an average of 23.8 in a series of 20 runs. These closely similar values held despite considerable variation in diluents and protein concentration. The higher value of 28S found earlier (4) with a purified IgM fraction probably reflects some abnormal aggregation. This additional study will be presented in detail elsewhere after more data are available on induced antibodies in high concentration.

DISCUSSION

Hagfish have rarely survived for more than 3 months, even in constantly renewed ocean water, under the conditions of repeated immunization and bleeding described. Beyond the obvious stress of handling, repetitive blood loss in these animals definitely appears to be debilitating. To achieve optimal antibody production, better conditions of maintenance should be sought. This consideration is surely pertinent to all specialized marine animals subjected to experimental stress over an extended period of time.

The apparent absence of low molecular weight antibodies (6S to 11S) in hagfish in our studies is not convincing. Whereas 19S antibodies to *Salmonella* antigens in nurse sharks are already detectable at 30 days after initial immunization, 7S antibodies were isolated only after nearly a year of immunization at about 25°C (10). That hagfish, like various invertebrates and mammals, give a prompt bactericidal "antibody" response to certain Gram-negative bacteria (11) is also of interest. These heat-labile bactericidins are not typical immunoglobulins, but they do behave like macroglobulins on passage through a Sephadex G-200 column. Hagfish antibodies against sheep erythrocytes or KLH appear to be restricted to the IgM-type based on their chromatographic, immunoelectrophoretic and ultracentrifugal characteristics. In various molecular properties, including carbohydrate content, hagfish immunoglobulins resemble those described for lampreys (12) and for elasmobranch fishes (13).

Only tentative comparisons of immunologic competence at different phylogenetic levels are now possible. Perhaps hagfish and other primitive fishes are incapable of reaching the mammalian norm or standard by one or more of the following criteria: a) genetic library or repertoire of responsiveness to broad *vs* narrow spectrum of potential antigens, b) development and duration of immunologic memory, c) limitations in spectrum of cellular or humoral responses, d) molecular classes and quality of antibodies inducible (14). Each of these points invites further study. Possible limitations may exist, for example, in immunogenetic repertoire or immunologic memory among the classes of fishes. However, conspicuous differences in association constants and low efficiency of detection of 7S antibodies in fishes can be misleading. Clem and co-workers (15) recently found rates and levels of 2,4-dinitrophenyl (DNP) antibody production in sharks and groupers similar to those of mammals. Thus, the notion that lower vertebrates characteristically show more sluggish responses than mammals to equivalent doses of antigen is quite doubtful.

Teleost fish (16) and even elasmobranchs (13, 15) exhibit at least two antibody populations with distinct molecular properties which suggest transitional stages in the evolution of immunoglobulins. Based on distinctive properties of the heavy polypeptide chains, the Australian lungfish is the least advanced vertebrate now known to possess more than one major class of immunoglobulins (17). Immunoglobulins similar to the IgG class of mammals are surely present in anuran amphibians (18) and may have first appeared at the phylogenetic level of teleost fishes. Whether the molecular equivalents of mammalian IgA, IgD, or IgE antibodies also occur in ectothermic vertebrates remains to be studied conclusively.

Although hagfish may lack a discrete thymus and well developed peripheral lymphoid tissues, preliminary results show specific immunofluorescence of hag blood lymphocytes from animals actively making antibodies to sheep erythrocytes. Diverse lymphocytes, granulocytes, and macrophages are found in hag blood and coelomic fluid (4), consistent with the direct evidence of general immunocompetence in this primitive Agnathan. The apparent absence of plasma cells and germinal centers in certain primitive fishes (19) may have little fundamental significance in view of the mammalian-like spectrum of cell types clearly shown to produce antibodies to sheep erythrocytes in teleost fish (20).

Hagfish and certain invertebrates have been found to be highly resistant to irradiation and nitrogen mustard by comparison to mammals and other vertebrates (21). This difference was correlated with the supposed absence of "a lymphoid system capable of immunologic adaptation" in hags. Since we now know this immunologic distinction to be invalid, the resistance to radiation and alkylating agents cited may be attributable to a combination of low environmental temperature (15°C) and short-term experiments with a maximum observation period of 54 days. Differential lymphocyte sensitivity (22) and physiologic recovery from radiation damage as a function of low water temperature (23) are well known in ectothermic vertebrates.

Acknowledgment. The authors are much indebted to Mrs. Lynda Frautnick and Mrs. Mary Morgan for technical assistance.

REFERENCES

1. Good, R. A. and Papermaster, B. W., in *Advances in Immunology*, Edited by F. J. Dixon, Jr. and J. H. Humphrey, vol. 4, p. 1, Academic Press, New York, 1964.
2. Papermaster, B. W., Condie, R. M., Finstad, J. and Good, R. A., J. Exp. Med., *119:* 105, 1964.
3. Hildemann, W. H. and Thoenes, G. H., Transplantation, *7:* 506, 1969.
4. Thoenes, G. H. and Hildemann, W. H., in *Developmental Aspects of Antibody Formation and Structure*, Czechoslavakian Academy of Science, Prague, In press.

5. Jensen, D., Sci. Amer., *214:* 82, 1966.
6. Hirschfeld, J., in *Handbook of Immunodiffusion and Immunoelectrophoresis*, Edited by O. Oucherlony, p. 139, Ann Arbor Science Publishers, Ann Arbor, 1968.
7. Thurston, J. R., Rheins, M. S. and Buehler, E. V., J. Lab. Clin. Med., *49:* 647, 1957.
8. Stanworth, D. R., Nature, *188:* 156, 1960.
9. Boyd, W. C., *Fundamentals of Immunology*, 4th Ed., p. 196, Interscience Publishers, New York, 1966.
10. Fidler, J., Clem, L. W. and Small, P. A., Comp. Biochem. Physiol., *31:* 365, 1969.
11. Acton, R. T., Weinheimer, P. F., Hildemann, W. H. and Evans, E. E., J. Bact., *99:* 626, 1969.
12. Marchalonis, J. J. and Edelman, G. M., J. Exp. Med., *127:* 891, 1968.
13. Clem, L. W. and Leslie, G. A., in *Phylogeny of Immunoglobulin Structure and Function*, Edited by M. Adinolfi, Spastics Society International Medical Publications, London, In press.
14. Hildemann, W. H., Transplant. Proc., *2:* 253, 1970.
15. Clem, L. W., Transplant. Proc., *2:* 260, 1970.
16. Trump, G. N. and Hildemann, W. H., Immunology, In press.
17. Marchalonis, J. J., Aust. J. Exp. Biol. Med. Sci., *47:* 405, 1969.
18. Marchalonis, J. J., Transplant. Proc., In press.
19. Pollara, B., Finstad, J. and Good, R. A., in *Advances in Experimental Medicine and Biology*, Edited by L. Fiore-Donati and M. G. Hanna, Jr., Vol. 5, p. 1, Plenum Press, New York, 1969.
20. Chiller, J. M. Hodgins, H. O. Chambers, V. C. and Weiser, R. S., J. Immun., *102:* 1193, 1969.
21. Finstad, J., Fänge, R. and Good, R. A. in *Advances in Experimental Medicine and Biology*, Edited by L. Fiore-Donati and M. G. Hanna, Jr., Vol. 5, p. 21, Plenum Press, New York, 1969.
22. Stearner, S. P., J. Exp. Zool., *115:* 251, 1950.
23. Owen, R. D. and Hildemann, W. H., Radiation Res., *12(4):* 119, 1960.

The Journal of Immunology
Vol. 105, No. 4, October 1970

Printed in U.S.A.

A CYTOLYTIC SYSTEM FOR THE *IN VITRO* DETECTION OF CELL-MEDIATED IMMUNITY TO SOLUBLE ANTIGEN

CHRISTOPHER S. HENNEY

From the World Health Organization Immunology Research and Training Centre, 21 rue du Bugnon, Lausanne, Switzerland

Received for publication April 23, 1970

An *in vitro* cytotoxic test is described for the demonstration of cell-mediated immunity to soluble antigen. This system has been used to study the development of a cytotoxic splenic lymphocyte population in the guinea pig after immunization with dinitrophenylated human IgG (DNP-HGG). As "target" cells, ^{51}Cr-labeled mouse mastocytoma cells were used, and were coupled to DNP-HGG with 1-ethyl-3-(3-dimethylaminopropyl) carbodiimide HCl. "Target" cell destruction was assessed by comparing the rates of ^{51}Cr release from these cells in the presence of splenic lymphocytes from specifically sensitized animals with that released in the presence of the same number of lymphocytes from unimmunized animals. The mastocytoma cells were found to be preferable to erythrocytes as carriers of antigen, in that they were more sensitive to membrane permeability changes. Splenic lymphocytes from guinea pigs immunized with DNP-HGG caused specific lysis of DNP-HGG-coated mastocytoma cells. Cells coated with DNP-BSA and HGG were lysed to a lesser extent, while cells coated with antigens immunochemically unrelated to the antigen used for sensitization were not lysed to any greater extent than that observed with lymphocytes from unimmunized animals. Several factors distinguished cytolysis by "sensitized" lymphocytes from that mediated by serum antibody in the presence of complement. Cytolysis by lymphocytes was not inhibited by anti-guinea pig immunoglobulin antisera. The total cytolytic activity of splenic lymphocytes did not parallel measured serum antibody. The specificity of cytolysis by splenic lymphocytes from animals immunized with DNP-HGG was markedly carrier-dependent.

It is becoming increasingly evident that cell-mediated immunity plays an important role in a variety of defense mechanisms and disease processes. This awareness has given rise to much interest in the mechanisms by which cell-mediated immunity is effected, and has consequently led to the development of several *in vitro* correlates of different aspects of cell-mediated immunity (1–3).

Perhaps the most widely used of these *in vitro* models are the various macrophage-inhibition techniques (1, 4). These are based on the finding that contact between antigen and lymphocytes from a specifically sensitized animal leads to the release of soluble mediators which are capable of inhibiting the migration of normal macrophages and other leucocytes. These techniques are reproducible and provide a sensitive index of cell-mediated immunity against bacteria, proteins, and even haptens (5). The tests are, however, by their very nature, only an indirect measurement of the presence of "sensitized"[1] lymphocytes.

The demonstration that lymphoid cells from immunized donors are cytotoxic for cells carrying antigens to which the cell donor is sensitized has led to the development of another series of *in vitro* tests for cell-mediated immunity (6). These systems, which measure directly the lytic activity of "sensitized" lymphocytes, can be readily adapted to a quantitative approach by incorporating ^{51}Cr (as sodium chromate) into the antigen-carrying (or "target") cell, and following the kinetics of target cell destruction by measuring ^{51}Cr release from these cells. This

[1] The term "sensitized" lymphocytes is used here to describe populations of cells from specifically immunized animals; "normal" lymphocytes refers to the same population from unimmunized animals.

approach has been used most effectively by Brunner *et al.* (3, 7) to study allograft immunity in mice. Such cytolytic techniques have obvious advantages in their directness, their specificity, and their adaptability to quantitation. They are generally applicable, however, only to systems involving cell surface antigens and as such have found particular use in the study of histocompatability in these systems. Attempts have been made to broaden the applicability of these systems by passively coupling soluble antigens to carrier cells, notably the coupling of purified protein derivative (PPD) to chicken erythrocytes using tannic acid (8, 9); but the amount of lysis of these "target" cells by lymphocytes from tuberculin-sensitive animals was low, and the system therefore was rather insensitive.

The present paper describes a cytotoxic technique for demonstrating "sensitized" lymphocytes after immunization with a soluble antigen, dinitrophenylated human IgG (DNP-HGG). The technique has been used successfully to follow the development of a cytotoxic lymphocyte population in guinea pig spleen after administration of this antigen. A preliminary account of this work has been given (10).

MATERIALS AND METHODS

Antigens

Human IgG. This was prepared from normal serum by diethylaminoethyl (DEAE)-cellulose chromatography. The fraction eluted with 0.005 M phosphate buffer, pH 8.0, was concentrated by ultrafiltration. The preparation was shown to be homogeneous by gel diffusion precipitin analysis and by immunoelectrophoresis, with sheep and rabbit antisera against whole human serum.

Dinitrophenylated human IgG (DNP-HGG). The above IgG preparation was dinitrophenylated by the method of Eisen *et al.* (11). To a solution containing 100 mg of protein in 5 ml of phosphate-buffered saline was added a 100-fold molar excess of 2,4-dinitrobenzene sulfonic acid dissolved in 1 ml of 1 M Na_2CO_3. The pH of the reaction mixture was adjusted to 10.4 by adding more 1 M Na_2CO_3. The mixture was then rotated gently for 24 hr at room temperature. The number of DNP groups/molecule protein, calculated on the basis that the molar extinction coefficient of DNP-lysine at 360 nm is 17,400, was found to be between 10 and 12.

Dinitrophenylated bovine serum albumin (DNP-BSA). A sample of BSA (Behringwerke A. G., Marburg-Lahn, Germany) was dinitrophenylated in the same manner as that described for IgG. The preparation was found to contain 11 DNP groups/molecule BSA.

All antigens were passed through Millipore filters (0.21 μ pore diameter) immediately before use.

Cells

Erythrocytes. Chicken and sheep erythrocytes were obtained from venous blood and stored in Alsever's solution.

Mastocytoma cells. Mouse mastocytoma cells (P815 of the DBA/2 strain) were those originally described by Dunn and Potter (12) and were harvested from cultures in modified Eagle's medium supplemented with 10% inactivated calf serum. Cell cultures were kindly provided by Dr. K. T. Brunner (ISREC Lausanne).

Lymphocytes. Guinea pig splenic lymphocytes were prepared essentially by the method described by Brunner *et al.* (3). Spleens from both immunized and non-immunized animals were removed aseptically, and homogenized by hand in glass grinders containing modified Eagle's medium with fourfold excess amounts of amino acids and vitamins. The cell suspension was centrifuged at 1500 rpm for 5 min and the sediment was resuspended and allowed to stand for 1 hr at 4°C. The cells remaining in the supernatant were washed twice and resuspended in Eagle's medium containing 10% inactivated calf serum. The number of viable lymphocytes was determined by the trypan blue exclusion test. The cell suspension was adjusted to a known concentration.

Radio-labeling of cells with ^{51}Cr. Erythrocytes and mastocytoma cells were labeled with ^{51}Cr in the same way. Cells were washed twice in sterile Tris-buffered saline and 2.0 ml of the cell suspension, at a concentration of 2×10^6 cells/ml, were incubated with 0.2 ml sodium ^{51}Cr (specific activity, 100 μCi/μg Cr) for 30 min at 37°C. The cell suspension was then centrifuged at 1500 rpm for 5 min and washed three times with sterile Tris-buffered saline.

Preparation of "target" cells

Erythrocytes. Sheep and chicken erythrocytes were washed three times with Tris-buffered saline, pH 7.2, and labeled with ^{51}Cr as described above.

One million ^{51}Cr-tagged cells in 0.5 ml of Tris-buffered saline were incubated with 3 ml of a solution of DNP-HGG containing 2.5 mg protein/ml, and with quantities of 1-ethyl-3-(3-dimethylaminopropyl) carbodiimide HCl (ECDI) ranging in concentration from 0.2 to 20 mg in 0.5 ml of phosphate-buffered saline. After standing at room temperature for 1 hr the cell suspension was centrifuged at 1500 rpm for 5 min and washed twice with Eagle's medium containing 10% inactivated calf serum.

Mastocytoma cells. One million ^{51}Cr-labeled mastocytoma cells were suspended in 0.5 ml Tris-buffered saline, pH 7.2, and 3 ml of a 2.5 mg/ml solution of DNP-HGG (or the same concentration of other antigens) were added. One minute later, 0.5 ml of a 500-μg/ml solution of ECDI was added. After inversion, the cells were incubated at room temperature for 1 hr and then washed three times in Eagle's medium containing 10% inactivated calf serum. Concentrations of ECDI greater than 1.5 mg/ml proved toxic for the cells while concentrations below 200 μg/ml yielded cells which were not agglutinated by antisera directed against the antigens used for coupling.

The mouse mastocytoma cells were also coupled to DNP-HGG with tannic acid. Five million ^{51}Cr-labeled mastocytoma cells were incubated with 7.5 mg of DNP-HGG in 3 ml of Tris-buffered saline, and quantities of tannic acid ranging from 1 to 100 mg were added. After incubation at room temperature for 1 hr, the cells were washed twice in Eagle's medium containing 10% inactivated calf serum.

Bisdiazotized benzidine (BDB) was also used as an agent for coupling antigen to ^{51}Cr-labeled mastocytoma cells. Benzidine·HCl was diazotized as described by Gordon *et al.* (13). Five-tenths milliliter of dilutions of this BDB preparation ranging from 1:20 to 1:500 in Tris-buffered saline was added to 5×10^6 ^{51}Cr-labeled mastocytoma cells, and 1 min later 3 ml of DNP-HGG (2.5 mg/ml) were added. The solution was mixed and then incubated at room temperature for 15 min and the cells were then sedimented and washed three times with Eagle's medium containing 10% inactivated calf serum.

Assay of "target" cell destruction. Lymphocytes and "target" cells were mixed either in 5-ml sterile plastic tubes (Falcon Plastics, Inc., Culver City, Calif.), or in Leighton tubes, so the final reaction volume of 0.4 ml usually contained 10^7 lymphocytes and 10^5 "target" cells. The tubes were saturated with a CO_2-air mixture, stoppered, and then incubated at 37°C either in an upright position, or in the case of the Leighton tubes, on a rocking platform which cycled every 15 sec from the horizontal to a final angle of tilt of 7°. At various times after incubation up to 9 hr, 1 ml of Tris-buffered saline was added to representative tubes. Each assay was performed on duplicate tubes. These tubes were centrifuged at 1500 rpm for 5 min and 1 ml of supernatant fluid was withdrawn and assayed for ^{51}Cr. The value obtained was corrected for the volume of fluid which was left with the cell sediments. This was also counted for ^{51}Cr, and the amount of ^{51}Cr in the supernatant was expressed as a percentage of the total ^{51}Cr which was originally cell associated. The percentage of cell-associated ^{51}Cr liberated after lysis with distilled water was between 75% and 80%.

Antigen-binding capacity of serum. The capacity of serum to bind DNP-HGG was determined in serum samples taken at various times after immunization with this protein, as previously described (14), using ^{131}I-labeled DNP-HGG and a rabbit antiserum reacting with both guinea pig $\gamma 1$ and $\gamma 2$ immunoglobulins.

RESULTS

Adult guinea pigs of the Hartley strain weighing approximately 400 g were immunized in the rear footpads with 50 μg DNP-HGG in complete Freund's adjuvant. The animals were exsanguinated 14 days later, and splenic lymphocyte preparations were obtained. These cells were tested for their cytotoxicity towards sheep and chicken erythrocytes coupled with DNP-HGG using ECDI and towards similarly coupled mouse mastocytoma cells. Splenic lymphocyte preparations from unimmunized animals were used as controls. Fifty million lymphocytes were incubated in sterile plastic tubes at 37°C with 10^5 "target" cells in a reaction volume of 0.4 ml. The amount of "target" cell destruction was assessed after 3, 6 and 9 hr of incubation, by measuring ^{51}Cr release. The results are shown in Table I. DNP-HGG-coupled erythrocytes were not lysed by the lymphocyte preparations, although such erythrocytes were readily lysed in the presence of complement and guinea pig antisera against DNP-HGG, indicating that the protein was effectively coupled to the erythrocyte

TABLE I

Cytolysis of DNP-HGG coated cells by lymphocytes

Time of Incubation 37°C	% ^{51}Cr Release[a] from:											
	DNP-HGG chicken red cells[b]				DNP-HGG sheep red cells				DNP-HGG mastocytoma cells			
	"Sensitized"[c] lymphocytes		"Normal"[d] lymphocytes		"Sensitized" lymphocytes		"Normal" lymphocytes		"Sensitized" lymphocytes		"Normal" lymphocytes	
	Mean	Range	Mean	Range	Mean	Range	Mean	Range	Mean	Range	Mean	Range
hr												
3	7.6	7–8	7.5	7–9	8.2	8	8.8	8–10	18.0	16–21	10.5	8–12
6	10.3	9–12	9.8	9–13	10.6	9–11	10.2	10–11	26.2	24–29	12.0	11–14
9	12.2	11–14	12.0	11–13	11.8	10–13	11.0	10–13	33.1	29–35	14.8	12–16

[a] Values shown are, in general, means of four assays; duplicates were performed on two separate occasions. Ranges are rounded off to the nearest integer.

[b] In all cases 5×10^7 lymphocytes were used and 10^5 "target" cells.

[c] Splenic lymphocytes obtained from guinea pigs 14 days after immunization with 50 μg DNP-HGG.

[d] Splenic lymphocytes obtained from unimmunized animals.

surface. The mouse mastocytoma cells, on the other hand, were, under identical conditions, readily lysed in the presence of lymphocytes from specifically immunized animals, and to a much greater extent than with lymphocytes from unimmunized animals. These findings confirm previous reports (10, 15) that such mastocytoma cells are more susceptible to alterations in membrane permeability and to specific lysis than are erythrocytes. The mastocytoma cells thus seemed to provide a sensitive index of the presence of specifically sensitized lymphocytes to passively coupled antigen.

A number of agents (ECDI, tannic acid, BDB) were used to covalently link antigen to the erythrocyte and mastocytoma cell surfaces. In the case of erythrocytes, although hemagglutination studies showed that antigen coupling readily occurred in each case, there was never a significant lysis of these cells by lymphocyte preparations. With mastocytoma cells, ECDI proved the most suitable coupling agent. Empirical studies showed for a variety of antigens (DNP-HGG; DNP-BSA; HGG-BSA) that 0.5 ml of ^{51}Cr-labeled mastocytes (10^6 cells) plus 3 ml of 2.5 mg/ml antigen and 0.5 ml of 500 μg/ml ECDI gave the optimal conditions for antigen coupling and subsequent specific lysis by lymphocytes. At ECDI concentrations above 2000 μg/ml much spontaneous lysis of mastocytoma cells was noted, and at concentrations below 250 μg/ml antigen coupling was inefficient.

BDB coupled antigen efficiently to the mastocytoma cells (as evidenced by agglutination studies) but lysis could not be achieved either with antibody and complement or with lymphocytes from specifically sensitized animals. Tannic acid-treated mouse mastocytoma cells were invariably spontaneously lysed by the concentrations necessary for antigen coupling.

The effect of lymphocyte concentration on "target" cell lysis was tested by mixing between 10^6 and 3×10^7 lymphocytes from specifically sensitized animals (8 days after immunization with 50 μg DNP-HGG in complete Freund's adjuvant in the rear footpads) with between 10^4 and 10^5 "target" cells (DNP-HGG-coated mouse mastocytoma cells) in a 0.4-ml reaction volume. This gave a lymphocyte to "target" cell ratios of between 100:1 and 3000:1. The same number of lymphocytes from unsensitized animals was used as a control. The results are shown in Table II. The rate of ^{51}Cr release was unaffected by the presence of lymphocytes from unimmunized animals. There was a direct correlation, however, between the rate of "target" cell destruction and the number of lymphocytes present from DNP-HGG-immunized animals. The values of lymphocyte to "target" cell ratios required for extensive lysis in this system are much higher than those observed in systems involving transplantation antigens (3, 7); a phenomenon which almost certainly reflects the lower number of "sensitized" lymphocytes which resulted from the administration of soluble antigen as compared with

TABLE II

Effect of lymphocyte concentration on cytolysis

Ratio Lymphocytes:Target Cells[a]	% ^{51}Cr Release 9 Hr 37°C			
	"Sensitized" lymphocytes[b]		"Normal" lymphocytes[c]	
	Mean[d]	Range	Mean	Range
100:1	15.3	14–16	12.3	11–15
200:1	22.1	18–25	11.6	10–13
500:1	29.4	28–30	13.2	11–15
1000:1	31.8	30–34	12.8	11–14
3000:1	33.7	31–35	11.4	10–15

[a] DNP-HGG-coupled mouse mastocytoma cells.

[b] Splenic lymphocyte preparation obtained 8 days after immunization with 50 μg DNP-HGG in complete Freund's adjuvant via the rear footpads.

[c] Splenic lymphocyte preparation from unimmunized guinea pigs.

[d] Values are means of four estimations; duplicate tubes were tested on two separate occasions. Ranges are rounded off to the nearest integer.

TABLE III

Specificity of cytolysis by splenic lymphocytes 8 days after immunization with DNP-HGG

Antigen Coupled to "Target" Cell	% ^{51}Cr Released from 10^5 "Target" Cells in 9 Hr at 37°C by:			
	"Normal" lymphocytes[a]		"Sensitized" lymphocytes[a]	
	Mean[b]	Range	Mean[b]	Range
DNP-HGG	16	14–17	30	28–31
DNP-BSA	17	15–18	22	21–22
HGG	15	14–16	18	15–20
BSA	15	14–16	14	14
None	14	14–17	14	14–15

[a] In each case 5×10^7 lymphocytes were used.

[b] Means of four estimations; duplicate estimations were done on two separate occasions. Ranges are rounded off to the nearest integer.

the number obtained after exposure to cellular antigens in histocompatability systems.

The specificity of the cytolysis obtained with "sensitized" lymphocytes was assessed by measuring the cytolytic capacity of splenic lymphocyte preparations obtained 8 days after immunization with 50 μg DNP-HGG in complete Freund's adjuvant, for uncoated mastocytoma cells, and for the same cells coupled with DNP-HGG, DNP-BSA, HGG and BSA. As previously, 5×10^7 lymphocytes were mixed with 10^5 "target" cells and the rate of "target" cell destruction was assessed by estimating the amount of ^{51}Cr release after 3, 6 and 9 hr of incubation at 37°C. The collective release over the 9-hr period is shown in Table III. DNP-HGG-coated mastocytes were lysed most effectively by "sensitized" lymphocytes; DNP-BSA and HGG-coated cells were lysed slightly more effectively by these lymphocytes than by the cell preparations from unimmunized animals. On the other hand, BSA-coated mastocytoma cells and the uncoated cells were lysed to the same extent by lymphocytes from both normal and DNP-HGG-immunized animals. Thus, the requirement on the "target" cell surface of antigens which are immunochemically related to the antigen used for sensitization would argue strongly in favor of specific cytolysis.

As antigen-coated mastocytoma cells are readily lysed by antibody in the presence of complement (authors' unpublished observations), it was necessary to demonstrate that the cytolysis observed in the presence of "sensitized" lymphocytes was not a function of humoral antibody possibly associated with the lymphocyte preparations. A comparative study was thus made of the lysis of "target" cells by "sensitized" lymphocytes and by antibody in the presence of complement. One hundred thousand DNP-HGG-coupled mouse mastocytoma cells were mixed either with 5×10^7 lymphocytes from specifically sensitized animals (8 days after 50 μg of DNP-HGG in complete Freund's adjuvant) or with 0.1 ml of a 1:4 dilution of a guinea pig antiserum against DNP-HGG (15 μg antibody) and 0.1 ml of a 1:2 dilution of fresh rabbit serum. (When fresh guinea pig serum was used as a source of complement only weak lysis was observed.) The kinetics of "target" cell destruction were assessed in each case (Fig. 1). Lysis by antibody and complement was extremely rapid, lysis being complete within 1 hr. Lysis by sensitized lymphocytes, on the other hand, proceeded slowly and was not complete even after 9 hr of incubation.

The effect of the addition to these systems of several rabbit antisera specific for guinea pig immunoglobulins provided further evidence for distinguishing lysis mediated by lymphocytes from that mediated by serum antibody (Table IV). To the test systems employed above were added dilutions of rabbit antisera corresponding to approximately 20 μg antibody. "Target" cell destruction was assessed as previously. None of

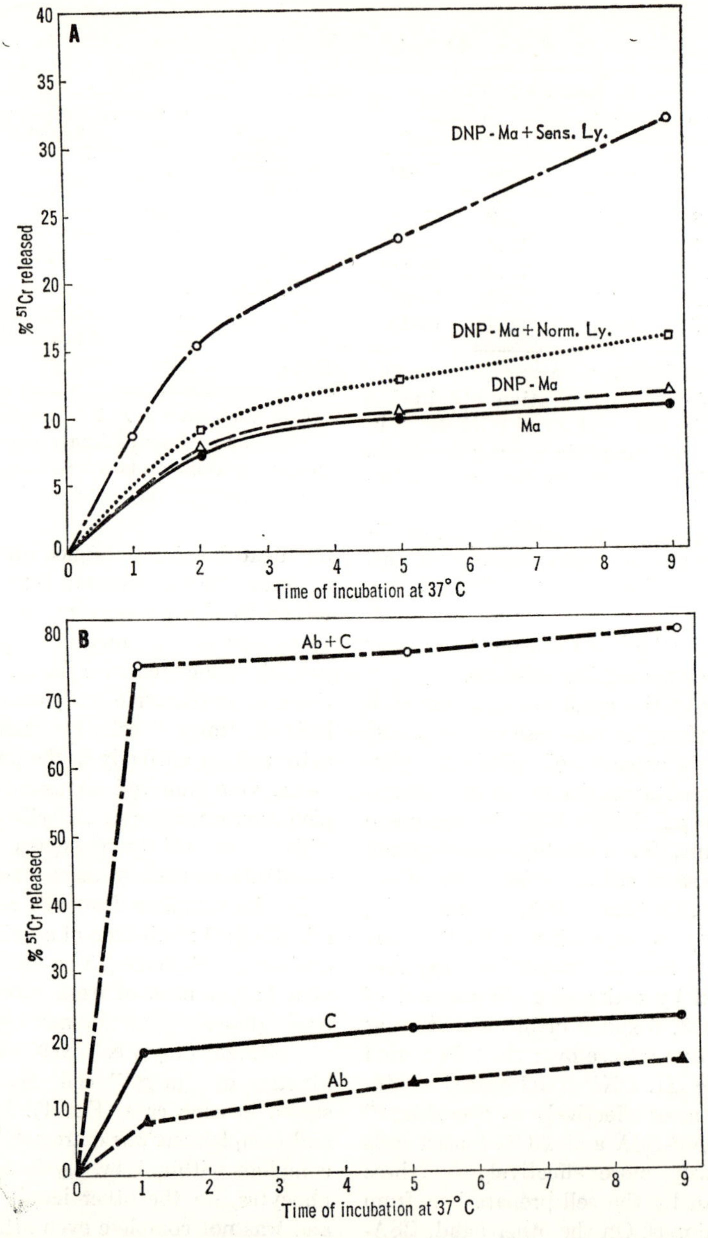

Figure 1. Percentage of ^{51}Cr released from 10^5 DNP-HGG-coated mouse mastocytoma cells by (*upper*) 5×10^7 lymphocytes from both unimmunized and specifically sensitized animals and (*lower*) by antibody in the presence of complement. *Upper:* Ma, cultured mastocytoma cells before antigen coupling; DNP-Ma, the same cells after coupling with DNP-HGG; DNP-Ma + Norm Ly, coupled cells in the presence of lymphocytes from unimmunized animals; DNP-Ma + Sens Ly, coupled cells in the presence of lymphocytes from specifically immunized animals. *Lower:* Ab, guinea pig anti-DNP-HGG antibody (~15 μg); C, fresh rabbit serum; Ab + C, a mixture of antibody and complement.

the antisera affected cytolysis by "sensitized" lymphocytes, but all had a marked effect on antibody-mediated lysis—an antiserum reacting with both the Fab and Fc fragments of guinea pig γ1 and γ2 immunoglobulins effectively annulled antibody-mediated lysis, without any demonstrable effect on lysis by "sensitized" lymphocytes. These findings support the concept that

TABLE IV

Effect of anti-immunoglobulin antisera on specific cytolysis induced by antibody and by "sensitized" lymphocytes

Antiserum[a]	% Inhibition of ^{51}Cr Release[b] over 6 Hrs Incubation at 37°C:	
	Antibody[c] + C[d] (mean[e])	'Sensitized'[f] lymphocytes (mean)
Anti-γ1 (Fc specific)	30	<1.0
Anti-γ2 (Fc specific)	49	<1.0
Anti-γ1 + γ2 (Fab and Fc)	85	2.2

[a] Rabbit antisera corresponding to approximately 20 μg antibody were added in each case.

[b] From 10^5 DNP-HGG coupled mouse mastocytoma cells.

[c] Guinea pig antiserum against DNP-HGG. Approximately 15 μg of antibody were used.

[d] Fresh rabbit serum, used as a source of complement.

[e] Mean values of an experiment performed in duplicate.

[f] Splenic lymphocytes obtained 8 days after immunization with 50 μg of DNP-HGG in complete Freund's adjuvant.

the lysis of antigen-coupled mastocytoma cells by sensitized lymphocytes is an index of cell-mediated immunity in these animals rather than of a humoral immune response.

In an attempt to increase the sensitivity of the lysis of "target" cells by lymphocytes from immune animals, the lymphocyte-"target" cell suspensions were gently rocked in order to increase the likelihood of contact between "sensitized" lymphocytes and "target" cells. Suspensions composed of 10^5 DNP-HGG-coated mouse mastocytoma cells and 10^7 lymphocytes (from either unimmunized animals or from animals 14 days after sensitization with DNP-HGG) were mixed in a 0.4-ml reaction volume in Leighton tubes, and placed at 37°C on a rocking platform. The rate of "target" cell destruction under these conditions was compared with that of identical tubes stored vertically. The results are given in Table V. As can be seen, although nonspecific lysis was increased somewhat upon agitation in the manner described, there was an increase in the specific rate of ^{51}Cr release, as well as an overall increase in specific lysis under these conditions.

This rocking system was employed in tests to follow the development of cytotoxic activity in spleen cells obtained from guinea pigs after administration of DNP-HGG. Adult Hartley strain guinea pigs were immunized with 50 μg of DNP-HGG in complete Freund's adjuvant via the rear footpads. Pooled splenic lymphocyte preparations were made from three animals on days 4, 7, 14, 21 and 28 after antigen administration. Ten million lymphocytes were added to 10^5 DNP-HGG-coated mouse mastocytoma cells in

TABLE V

The effect of agitation on "target" cell lysis

Time of Incubation 37°C	% ^{51}Cr Release[a] from 10^5 "Target" Cells[b]			
	No agitation		With agitation[c]	
	"Normal"[d] lymphocytes	"Sensitized"[e] lymphocytes	"Normal"[d] lymphocytes	"Sensitized"[e] lymphocytes
hr				
3	10.2	15.0	13.6	31.1
6	11.8	17.5	18.4	39.8
9	14.5	21.0	22.9	52.4

[a] Values are means of experiments performed in duplicate.

[b] DNP-HGG-coupled mouse mastocytoma cells.

[c] On a rocking platform cycling every 15 sec from the horizontal to a final angle of tilt of 7°.

[d] 10^7 splenic lymphocytes from unimmunized guinea pigs.

[e] 10^7 splenic lymphocytes obtained 14 days after immunization with 50 μg of DNP-HGG in complete Freund's adjuvant.

TABLE VI

Development of splenic lymphocyte population cytotoxic for DNP-HGG-coated mastocytoma cells at differing times after immunization with DNP-HGG

Time After Immunization[a]	% ^{51}Cr Specifically Released[b] from 10^5 DNP-HGG-Coated Mastocytoma Cells by 10^7 Splenic Lymphocytes (Incubation Time)	
	3 Hr	9 Hr
days		
4	0	1.8
7	3.1	13.6
14	5.8	20.4
21	8.3	19.4
28	10.6	18.7

[a] With 50 μg DNP-HGG in complete Freund's adjuvant.

[b] % ^{51}Cr released in presence of 10^7 lymphocytes from immunized animals minus that obtained in the presence of the same number of cells from unimmunized controls. Values are means of experiments performed in duplicate.

Leighton tubes. The tubes were agitated in the manner described above and the rate of ^{51}Cr release was estimated after incubation for 3 and 9 hr. Lymphocytes from unimmunized animals were used as controls on each occasion. The amount of specific lysis (the percentage of ^{51}Cr release induced by sensitized lymphocytes minus that obtained with normal lymphocytes) was calculated (Table VI). Specific cytolysis was observed from day 7 after immunization, and the extent of "target" cell destruction over the first 3 hr of incubation increased throughout the 28 days studied (Table VI). The overall amount of "target" cell destruction (9-hr values), however, reached a peak by day 14 and thereafter no increase in the total percentage of cells lysed was observed.

DISCUSSION

Evaluation of the significance of the cell-mediated immune response depends upon the development of specific and quantitative test systems. By analogy with studies on humoral immunity there is a need for a variety of test systems for this evaluation, as the classical systems for measurement of cell-mediated immunity, viz, delayed hypersensitivity skin testing, macrophage migration inhibition and cytolytic tests, undoubtedly measure different parameters of the response. Cytolytic tests have, in their directness and their adaptation to quantitative approaches, many advantages over the skin tests and macrophage inhibition techniques and have been used to great effect in the study of allograft immunity (3, 7, 16).

Previous attempts to increase the applicability of these tests by passively coupling antigen to erythrocytes have resulted in "target" cells which are only slowly lysed by "sensitized" lymphocytes and which require incubation times up to 48 hr, at which time the nonspecific release of ^{51}Cr from "target" cells is rather high (9). In this study advantage has been taken of the properties of the mouse mastocytoma cell as a suitable carrier for antigen. These cells, although relatively resistant to lysis under normal culture conditions, can readily be specifically lysed both by antibody and by sensitized lymphocytes. Coupling of soluble antigen to the mastocytoma cell surface using ECDI does not apparently in itself alter the permeability of the cell to internally labeled ^{51}Cr, but such cells are readily lysed in the presence of lymphocytes from animals immunized with DNP-HGG. Under the same conditions, coupled erythrocytes were not lysed.

Using a rocking platform device, up to 55% of the total ^{51}Cr associated with the cells is released into the supernatant within 9 hr at 37°C in the presence of "sensitized" lymphocytes. Such lysis is not affected by the presence of anti-immunoglobulin antisera, a finding which clearly differentiates this mode of lysis from that obtained by serum antibody.

The specificity of lymphocyte-mediated cytolysis is shown by the finding that "target" cells coated with the antigen used for immunization were lysed the most effectively, cross-reacting antigens to a lesser extent, while those cells coated with unrelated antigen were not specifically lysed.

The kinetics of "target" cell destruction by splenic lymphocytes were found to vary with time after immunization. Over the 28-day period the amount of "target" cell destruction over a 3-hr incubation period increased progressively, although the total specific lysis observed over a 9-hr incubation period reached a maximum 14 days after sensitization and then remained constant. The reason for this is unknown. It might imply that there is a maximal number of "target" cells present that are susceptible to lysis and, as this value would appear to be less than the amount of ^{51}Cr released from these cells by antibody and complement (55% *vs* approximately 80%), one might infer that there is a particular antigenic distribution requirement on the "target" cell surface either for recognition by the "sensitized" lymphocyte or for cytolysis. If this is the case, one could interpret the increased rate of lysis over the first 3-hr incubation period as being reflective of the number of "sensitized" lymphocytes present in the reaction medium. When this number of cells exceeds a certain number (attained by day 14) the amount of ^{51}Cr released after a 9-hr incubation would thus represent the total ^{51}Cr specifically releasable from this "target" cell population by "sensitized" lymphocytes.

The usefulness of cytotoxic tests has already been demonstrated in histocompatability studies, and their specificity for cell-mediated immunity established (3, 7, 16). The modifications described here, which allow the study of cell-mediated responses to soluble antigens, widely increase their scope.

Since different species may be used to provide "target" cells and "sensitized" lymphocytes, and since a wide variety of antigens may be covalently linked to the "target" cells (besides those antigens described in this study PPD has also been successfully used), it seems likely that such systems may prove to have general applicability in the study of cell-mediated immunity.

Acknowledgments. I am grateful to Dr. D. S. Rowe for his encouragement and aid throughout this study; to Dr. K. T. Brunner for introducing me to many of the techniques employed and for providing the mastocytoma cells, and to Miss Katharina Hug for her excellent technical assistance.

REFERENCES

1. George, M. and Vaughan, J. H., Proc. Soc. Exp. Biol. Med., *111:* 514, 1962.
2. Oppenheim, J. J., Fed. Proc., *27:* 21, 1968.
3. Brunner, K. T., Mauel, J., Cerottini, J. C. and Chapuis, B., Immunology, *14:* 181, 1967.
4. David, J. R., J. Exp. Med., *122:* 1125, 1965.
5. David, J. R., Lawrence, H. S. and Thomas, L., J. Immun., *93:* 279, 1964.
6. Perlmann, P. and Holm, G., Advances Immun., *11:* 117, 1969.
7. Brunner, K. T., Mauel, J., Rudolf, H. and Chapuis, B., Immunology, *18:* 499, 1970.
8. Perlmann, P. and Holm, G., in *Mechanisms of Inflammation Induced by Immune Reactions*, Edited by P. Miescher and P. Grabar, p. 325, Schwabe & Co., Basel, 1968.
9. Perlmann, P., Perlmann, H., Wasserman, J. and Packalén, T., Int. Arch. Allerg., *38:* 204, 1970.
10. Henney, C. S., Nature, 226: 1167, 1970.
11. Eisen, H. N., Carsten, M. E. and Belman, S., J. Immun., *73:* 296, 1954.
12. Dunn, T. B. and Potter, M., J. Nat. Cancer Inst., *18:* 587, 1957.
13. Gordon, J., Rose, B. and Sehon, A. H., J. Exp Med., *108:* 37, 1958.
14. Henney, C. S. and Ishizaka, K., J. Immun., *101:* 896, 1968.
15. Chapuis, B., Int. Arch. Allerg., In press.
16. Rosenau, W., Fed. Proc., *27:* 34, 1968.

THE JOURNAL OF IMMUNOLOGY
Vol. 105, No. 4, October 1970
Printed in U.S.A.

HIDDEN RHEUMATOID FACTORS REACTING WITH "Non a" AND OTHER ANTIGENS OF NATIVE AUTOLOGOUS IgG[1]

PER IVAR GAARDER[2] AND JACOB B. NATVIG

From the Institute of Immunology and Rheumatology, Rikshospitalet University Hospital, Oslo, Norway

Received for publication April 17, 1970

Several rheumatoid factor activities were revealed in 14 rheumatoid sera after the separation of IgM rheumatoid factors from inhibiting autologous IgG by gel filtration. These included a "new" specificity, anti-"non a." Anti-Ga, found in 14 sera, anti-Gm(a), found in 10, and anti-"non a," found in 6, were the most frequently detected rheumatoid factor specificities, while anti-Gm(g) was found in one serum. The anti-"non a" and anti-Ga rheumatoid factors reacted with antigens present in native autologous IgG. The original anti-Gm(p) and anti-Gm(e) rheumatoid sera contained anti-"non a" together with anti-Ga, and the respective original anti-Rh antibodies carried both the "non a" and Ga antigens. Gm(p) and Gm(e) appeared to be identical in part with "non a" and in part with Ga, and thus were not regular Gm types. The antigen for rheumatoid anti-"non a" was found to be located on the pFc′ fragment of IgG. In contrast, the antigen for anti-Ga was present on Fc, but not on the pFc′ fragment. Thus two distinct molecular regions of Fc were involved in the rheumatoid factor reactions.

Rheumatoid factors are antibodies against IgG. They react with IgG from a number of species, including man. Certain rheumatoid factors with anti-Gm specificities seem to show an isospecific reaction (1–6). However, increasing attention has been focused on the reactivity of rheumatoid factors with autologous IgG (2–14). Of particular significance is the finding in rheumatoid sera of complexes with a high sedimentation coefficient of 22S and above, which consist of IgM rheumatoid factor bound to IgG (15). IgG rheumatoid factors and autologous IgG form intermediate complexes with sedimentation coefficients between 7S and 19S (16, 17). Reactivity of rheumatoid factors with autologous IgG has also been shown in hemagglutination systems (5, 8, 11–13). Such reactivities may often be hidden in rheumatoid sera because of an excess of inhibiting autologous IgG (12, 14, 18). A frequently occurring rheumatoid factor, anti-Ga, with a clear specificity for an antigen, Ga, common to the IgG1, IgG2 and IgG4 subclass proteins, was reported by Allen and Kunkel (12).

[1] This study was supported by a grant from Anders Jahre's Foundation for the Advancement of Science.

[2] Fellow of the Norwegian Research Council for Science and the Humanities.

One of the antigens involved in rheumatoid factor reactions is the genetic antigen Gm(a) (19) on IgG1 molecules (20, 21). The antigen antithetically related to Gm(a) within the IgG1 subclass, is "non a," which has recently been delineated by employing properly absorbed heteroantisera against isolated "non a" positive myeloma proteins (22). Since this antigen is also present in all IgG2 and IgG3 proteins and thus in all normal human sera, a possible rheumatoid factor with anti-"non a" specificity is likely to be hidden due to complexing with "non a" positive autologous IgG. It was recently suggested (22) that the rheumatoid factor systems used for the detection of Gm(p) (23) and Gm(e) (24) at least partly measured "non a." Gm(p) seemed to have a similar molecular localization to that of "non a" (25), and the original anti-Gm(p) and anti-Gm(e) rheumatoid sera showed pronounced prozone phenomena (23, 26) suggesting specific inhibitors in the antiserum (27).

In the present study, rheumatoid factors with specificity for the "non a" antigen were demonstrated. This was achieved by separating IgM rheumatoid factors from the potentially inhibiting autologous IgG in strongly positive rheumatoid sera, and neutralizing interfering rheumatoid factors that might be related to IgG antigens other than "non a." The previously described anti-Gm(p) and anti-Gm(e) sera were also shown to contain anti-"non a" activity.

MATERIALS AND METHODS

Rheumatoid sera. Fourteen sera from randomly selected patients with strongly seropositive rheumatoid arthritis were obtained from Oslo Sanitetsforenings Rheumatism Hospital. The titers in the anti-Rh Ripley test varied from 1024 to 8192. Serum Ga was kindly provided by Dr. H. G. Kunkel, serum P.C.E. 64 (the original anti-Gm(e)) by Dr. C. Ropartz, and serum Po (the original anti-Gm(p)) by Dr. M. Waller. All sera were stored in the frozen state at −20°C until they were used.

Heterologous antisera. The heterologous anti-"non a" antisera were obtained from cynomologous monkeys and baboons, immunized with "non a" positive myeloma proteins. The antisera were absorbed with "non a" negative myeloma proteins and pepsin-digested pooled human IgG (22). Anti-IgM and anti-IgG were produced in rabbits by immunization with isolated monoclonal macroglobulins and pooled human IgG respectively, and absorbed and tested for specificity as previously described (28, 29).

Anti-Rh antisera. Incomplete anti-Rh antisera with Gm(a), (b), (f) and (g) specificities respectively were used, as previously described (28). The Gm(a) anti-Rh also carried Gm(x), but no attempts were made to distinguish between anti-Gm(a) and anti-Gm(x) in this study. Anti-Rh Ripley and the original Gm(p) anti-Rh Moore were kindly provided by Dr. M. Waller, and the original Gm(e) anti-Rh 61 by Dr. C. Ropartz. For red cell coating, washed human OR_1R_2 erythrocytes were incubated with anti-Rh antibodies for 1.5 hr at 37°C, then washed four times, and used as a 1% suspension in the hemagglutination tests.

Myeloma proteins and macroglobulins. Myeloma proteins (IgG and IgA) from sera of patients with multiple myeloma and macroglobulins (IgM) from patients with Waldenström's macroglobulinemia were isolated by starch block electrophoresis (30). Some of the myeloma sera were kindly provided by Dr. H. G. Kunkel.

Preparation of fragments of pooled human IgG. Pooled human IgG was obtained from AB Kabi, Stockholm, Sweden. Heavy and light chains were obtained by reduction and alkylation of IgG, and subsequent isolation at low pH by G-100 Sephadex gel filtration (28). $F(ab')_2$ fragments were obtained by pepsin digestion (29), Fab and Fc fragments by papain digestion and isolation through starch block electrophoresis (28, 31), pFc′ fragments by mild pepsin digestion and isolation through G-150 Sephadex chromatography, and Fc′ by subsequent papain digestion of pFc′ as previously described (32).

Gel filtration. Serum samples of 4 ml were fractionated on a Sephadex G-200 column, 3.2 cm x 90 cm, employing a 0.1 M acetate buffer pH 4.0 and upward flow of 20 ml/hr at room temperature. Prior to application, sera were dialyzed against the eluant buffer and filtered through a Millipore filter, pore diameter 1.2 μ. Serum Ek was also fractionated on Sephadex G-200 in phosphate-buffered saline, (PBS), pH 7.4, in a similar way. Optical density of the effluent was measured continuously at 280 nm by a LKB Uvicord Absorptiometer. Fractions of 6.7 ml were collected by a mechanical fraction collector. With each serum, three major peaks were eluted. The fractions corresponding to each of the peaks were pooled, omitting the last fractions of the first peak and the first fractions of the second peak (Fig. 1). The fractions were concentrated by dialysis against a solution of polyethyleneglycol, m.w. >17,000, subsequently dialyzed against PBS in the cold, and stored at −20°C until they were used. This procedure gave in the initial peak, eluted corresponding to void volume, IgM rheumatoid factors separated from the potentially inhibiting IgG, which was eluted in the second peak. In each case the concentrated initial peak was shown by double diffusion in agarose to contain IgM and no, or only a trace of, IgG. IgM

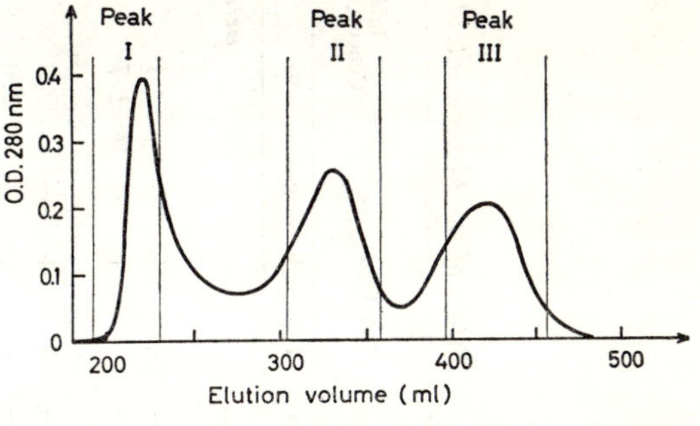

Figure 1. Gel filtration of serum Ek on Sephadex G-200 at pH 4.0. The fractions of the three peaks were pooled as indicated by the vertical lines.

TABLE I

Titers of the 14 rheumatoid sera (Se) and their IgM fractions (IgM) against red cells coated with various anti-Rh antibodies

Serum	Gm Type				IgM Concentration		Titers against Red Cells Coated with[a]								Rheumatoid Factor Specificities Detected			
							Gm(a) anti-Rh 3091		Gm(f) anti-Rh 3066		Gm(b) anti-Rh 3109		Gm(g) anti-Rh 4752		Anti-Ga	Anti-Gm(a)	Anti-"non a"	Anti-Gm(g)
	a	f	b	g	Se	IgM	Se	IgM	Se	IgM	Se	IgM	Se	IgM				
					mg/ml													
Group I																		
Ek	−	+	+	−	2.1	1.2	128p[b]	256	<1	128	<1	32	<1	16	+	+	+	−
Fo	−	+	+	−	1.7	0.65	256p	256	<1	128	<1	64	<1	32	+	+	+	−
Group II																		
He	−	+	+	−	2.3	1.0	256	128	<1	32	<1	<1	<1	<1	+	+	+	−
Ro	−	+	+	−	6.0	1.15	512p	128	<1	16	<1	<1	<1	<1	+	+	+	−
Pe	−	+	+	−	0.96	0.70	<1	256	<1	64	<1	<1	<1	<1	+	−	−	−
Ow	−	+	+	−	1.6	0.63	512p	256	<1	16	<1	<1	<1	<1	+	+	+	−
Lö	+	−	−	+	1.6	1.3	128p	256	<1	16	<1	<1	<1	<1	+	+	−	−
Ha	+	−	−	+	1.25	0.70	<1	64	<1	16	<1	<1	<1	<1	+	+	+	−
Sk	+	−	−	+	1.55	0.26	<1	32	<1	4	<1	<1	<1	<1	+	+	−	−
Ad	+	+	+	+	1.7	0.84	64p	32	<1	16	<1	<1	<1	<1	+	+	−	−
La	+	+	+	+	1.15	0.86	<1	128	<1	32	<1	<1	<1	<1	+	−	−	−
Mo	+	+	+	+	1.5	0.65	<1	64	<1	16	<1	<1	<1	<1	+	−	−	−
Fr	+	+	+	+	1.7	1.25	64p	64	<1	32	<1	<1	<1	<1	+	−	−	−
Group III																		
Th	−	+	+	−	2.4	0.80	1024p	256	<1	128	<1	<1	256	64	+	+	−	+

[a] Controls: Unsensitized cells and serum or IgM fraction: no agglutination. Sensitized cells and saline: no agglutination. Rabbit anti-human γ globulin and sensitized cells: titers 8000 to 16,000.

[b] p, Denotes prozone.

concentrations of each serum and initial peak, determined by the radial diffusion technique (33), are shown in Table I. The material of this peak will subsequently be called the IgM fraction. In each serum, strong rheumatoid factor activity was detected in the IgM fractions. No rheumatoid factor activity was detected in the second and third peaks, which contained mostly IgG and albumin, respectively.

Hemagglutination procedures. All hemagglutination tests were performed in tubes. Each tube contained one drop of serum or IgM fraction, one drop of inhibiting material or PBS, one drop of neutralizing material or PBS, and one drop of a 1% suspension of anti-Rh-coated red cells. The tubes were left for 15 min at room temperature before the cell suspension was added. They were left for another 15 min, spun down, and the degree of agglutination was recorded after resuspension. Whenever possible, master dilutions were made. In inhibition experiments, an amount of agglutinator giving a 2 to 3+ reaction, corresponding to approximately four agglutinating units, was commonly used.

Gm typing. Because all the sera contained rheumatoid factor activity, Gm typing was performed on the IgG material of the second peak from gel filtrations (28).

RESULTS

Agglutination experiments to detect hidden rheumatoid factor activities. The 14 rheumatoid sera and their IgM fractions obtained by gel filtration at pH 4.0 were tested for agglutination of red cells coated with Gm(a), Gm(f), Gm(b) and Gm(g) anti-Rh antibodies respectively (Table I). To detect prozone phenomena, the sera were always tested undiluted and in fourfold dilutions up to at least 1:64. Nine of the sera and all the 14 IgM fractions agglutinated the Gm(a)-coated red cells. In contrast, none of the sera agglutinated the Gm(f)-coated cells, whereas all the IgM fractions showed such activity. In two IgM fractions new activities, not present in whole serum, were detected with Gm(b)- and Gm(g)-coated cells. In one case, reaction with Gm(g)-coated cells was obtained both with whole serum and the IgM fraction. In Table I the sera are divided into three groups according to their reaction patterns. IgM fractions Ek and Fo of group I reacted with Gm(a)-, Gm(f)-, Gm(b)- and Gm(g)-coated cells. In group II, comprising the majority of the sera, reaction of the IgM fractions was seen only with Gm(a) and Gm(f)-coated cells. IgM fraction Th of group III also reacted with Gm(a)- and Gm(f)-coated cells, but in addition both whole serum and IgM fraction strongly agglutinated Gm(g)-coated cells. Similar results were obtained with several other anti-Rh sera of the Gm(a), (f), (b) and (g) specificities.

The IgM fraction from separation of serum Ek on Sephadex G-200 at pH 7.4 gave essentially the same reaction pattern as whole serum. This clearly indicated that new activities were revealed by gel filtration at pH 4.0. No agglutinating activity was found in the second or third peaks from gel filtration.

Although cells sensitized with Gm(a) anti-Rh reacted with most whole sera, several sera showed distinct prozones, irrespective of their Gm type. In contrast, the IgM fractions gave good reactions without significant prozones. By coating the red cells less heavily, the sera gave either weaker reactions with more pronounced prozones, or no reactions. By adding a large excess of anti-Rh serum for red cell coating, some activity was also seen in sera, together with pronounced prozones, even with Gm(f)-, Gm(b)- and Gm(g)-coated cells. However, these reactions were weaker than those obtained when using Gm(a) anti-Rh. With heavy sensitization, most of the IgM fractions of group II (Table I) reacted weakly with Gm(b)- and Gm(g)-coated cells. This might be due partly to the slight inhomogeneity of the anti-Rh antibodies used.

Inhibition studies. The IgM fraction Ek from group I (Table I) was chosen for further studies, since the serum itself agglutinated only the Gm(a)-coated cells, whereas the IgM fraction from separation at low pH reacted with all four test systems.

First the reaction of IgM fraction Ek with the Gm(b)-coated cells was investigated. The IgG3 Gm(b) molecules contain the "non a" antigen, but not the Ga antigen. Thus anti-Ga antibodies would not be detected in this test system. Clear inhibition was obtained with Gm(f+a−) IgG1 proteins and all IgG2 and IgG3 proteins irrespective of their Gm types (Table II). No inhibition was obtained with either IgG4, Gm(a) IgG1 proteins, including the Chinese Gm(fa) myeloma protein Ch, or with IgA or IgM proteins. The same inhibition pattern was seen with several other myeloma proteins of each of the

TABLE II

Inhibition of the reaction of IgM fraction Ek with Gm(b)[a]-coated red cells by various myeloma proteins

Class and Genetic Type of Myeloma Protein	Concentration of Inhibitor in mg/ml[b]						No Inhibitor
	1.0	0.5	0.25	0.12	0.06	0.03	
IgG1 Gm(za) Ke	2	2	2	2	2	2	2
Gm(f) Gr	0	0	0	0	2	2	
Gm(fa) Ch[c]	2	2	2	2	2	2	
IgG2 Gm(n) Ne	0	0	0	0	1	2	
Gm(−) Ts	0	0	0	0	0	2	
IgG3 Gm(b) Pr	0	0	0	0	±	2	
Gm(g) Vi	0	0	0	±	2	2	
IgG4 Gm(−) Ge	2	2	2	2	2	2	

[a] Anti-Rh 3109.
[b] Controls: Inhibitor and coated cells: no agglutination. Further controls as in Table I.
[c] A Chinese myeloma protein.

IgG subclasses and genetic types, and was similar to that previously described for the "non a" antigen employing heteroantisera.

Red cells coated with Gm(f) anti-Rh, which contain both the Ga and "non a" antigens, were also used to detect hidden anti-"non a." In the first test inhibition was seen only with those myeloma proteins containing both the "non a" and Ga antigens, i.e., Gm(f) IgG1 and IgG2 proteins (Table III, first column). However, when the anti-Ga activity of the IgM fraction Ek was neutralized with Gm(a) myeloma proteins, which are "non a" negative but Ga positive, a clear "non a" inhibition pattern was obtained (Table III, second column). When the anti-"non a" was neutralized with Ga negative, "non a" positive IgG3 proteins, inhibition was obtained with all IgG1, IgG2, and IgG4 proteins, but not with IgG3 (Table III, third column). This inhibition pattern corresponded to the distribution of the Ga antigen. The IgM fraction Ek thus contained both anti-Ga and anti-"non a." The anti-Ga specificity could also be demonstrated directly by utilizing Gm(a)-coated cells, which do not carry "non a," and by employing the original Ga anti-Rh. In the latter system the anti-"non a" had to be neutralized by an IgG3 myeloma protein.

Both the anti-"non a" and anti-Ga were shown to be inhibited by high concentrations of negative myeloma proteins (5 to 10 mg/ml), and by such proteins after heat aggregation, in concentrations above 1 to 2 mg/ml. This might be caused in part by slight contamination of the myeloma protein preparations with normal γ globulin.

A rheumatoid anti-"non a" activity was also demonstrated in IgM fraction Fo. By neutralizing the co-existent anti-Ga activity with a Gm(a) IgG1 myeloma protein as previously described, a weak anti-"non a" activity could also be demonstrated in IgM fractions He, Ro, Ow, and Ha. Anti-"non a" was thus present in 6 of the 14 rheumatoid sera tested. By further hemagglutination inhibition studies, evidence for anti-Ga was found in all 14, for anti-Gm(a) in 10, and for anti-Gm(g) in 1 of the sera (Table I). Anti-Gm(b) was not detected. Both the anti-Ga and the anti-"non a" activities were readily inhibited by the autologous IgG of the second gel filtration peak.

Specificity of the rheumatoid factors in the original anti-Gm(p) serum Po and the original anti-Gm(e) serum P.C.E. 64. Since previous studies had raised the question of possible anti-"non a" activity in the anti-Gm(p) and anti-Gm(e) sera, their IgM fractions were further studied. The IgM fractions of both sera contained anti-Ga activity detectable in hemagglutination inhibition studies using Gm(a)-coated cells. However, in reaction with the Gm(f)-coated cells after neutralizing the anti-Ga specificity, a "non a" inhibition pattern appeared, clearly showing that sera Po and P.C.E. 64 contained the anti-"non a" specificity similar to that of heterologous origin and of IgM fraction

TABLE III

Inhibition of agglutinating activities in IgM fractions Ek, Po and P.C.E. 64 and of heterospecific anti-"non a" by IgG, IgA and IgM proteins

Class and Genetic Type of Inhibitor[b]	IgM Fraction Ek with Gm(f) anti-Rh[a]	IgM Fraction Ek with Gm(f) anti-Rh[a] Neutr.[c]	IgM Fraction Ek with Gm(f) anti-Rh[a] Neutr.[d]	IgM Fraction Ek with Gm(a) Anti-Rh	IgM Fraction Ek with Gm(b) Anti-Rh	IgM Po(Anti-Gm(p)) with Gm(f) Anti-Rh (Neutr.)[c]	IgM P.C.E. 64 (Anti-Gm (e)) with Gm(f) Anti-Rh (Neutr.)[c]	Hetero-anti-"non a" Gm(f) Anti-Rh
IgG1 Gm(za) Ke,Br	>1.0[e]	>1.0	0.12	0.12	>1.0	>1.0	>1.0	>1.0
Gm(f) Cu,Gr,67,So	0.06	0.06–0.12	0.12	0.06	0.12	0.03–0.12	0.06	0.008–0.015
Gm(fa) Ch[f]	>1.0	>1.0	0.12	0.12	>1.0	>1.0	>1.0	>1.0
IgG2 Gm(n) Ne,TP,46,Su,68	0.12	0.06	0.12	0.12	0.12	0.12	0.12	0.008
Gm(−) Ts,Thi,Nm,Sm,Wi	0.06	0.12	0.12	0.12	0.06	0.06	0.06	0.015
IgG3 Gm(b) Pr,Bru,Jo,Le	>1.0	0.06	>1.0	>1.0	0.06	0.12	0.25	0.015
Gm(g) Vi,Lau,Col	>1.0	0.06	>1.0	>1.0	0.12	0.12	0.12	0.008
IgG4 Gm(−) Ge,07,58,81	>1.0	>1.0	0.12–0.25	0.12	>1.0	>1.0	>1.0	>1.0
IgA Ta,Cou	>1.0	>1.0	>1.0	>1.0	>1.0	>1.0	>1.0	>1.0
IgM 3067,37,79,08	>1.0	>1.0	>1.0	>1.0	>1.0	>1.0	>1.0	>1.0

[a] The same anti-Rh sera as in Table I were used for red cell coating.

[b] Because of scarcity of material not all inhibitors were titrated to their endpoints.

[c] Neutralization of anti-Ga by IgG1 Gm(a) proteins. Without neutralization no inhibition was obtained with IgG3 proteins, as shown for IgM fraction Ek in this table.

[d] Neutralization of anti-"non a" by IgG3 proteins.

[e] Lowest concentration in mg/ml giving inhibition.

[f] A Chinese myeloma protein.

Ek (Table III). In addition, a "non a" inhibition pattern was obtained with a test system employing the IgM fractions Po and Ek and red cells coated with the original Gm(p) anti-Rh Moore, but since the anti-Rh Moore is specific for Gm(f) and thus contains the Ga antigen, appropriate neutralization of anti-Ga was necessary. The original Gm(e) anti-Rh 61 was also shown to react with rheumatoid anti-"non a" of IgM fractions Ek and Po, but because the material was scarce this test was not performed with the IgM fraction of the anti-Gm(e) serum P.C.E. 64. Anti-Rh 61 also contained the Ga antigen.

Molecular specificity of anti-"non a" and anti-Ga rheumatoid factors. The inhibition of rheumatoid anti-"non a" (Ek, Po, P.C.E. 64) by pooled human IgG and its fragments and chains was also tested. Inhibition was obtained consistently with whole IgG, heavy chains, Fc and pFc′ fragments. Inhibition of anti-Ga in IgM fractions Ek and Ga was also tested, utilizing red cells coated with Gm(a) anti-Rh and the original Ga anti-Rh. The anti-Ga activity was inhibited by IgG, heavy chains and Fc fragments, but in contrast to the "non a" system no inhibition was obtained with pFc′ fragments. Neither anti-"non a" nor anti-Ga was inhibited by light chains, $F(ab')_2$, Fab or Fc′ fragments, although appropriate antigenic activity was demonstrated in these materials. Rheumatoid and heterospecific anti-"non a" showed the same molecular specificities in all these tests.

Detection of rheumatoid anti-Ga in whole serum. Nine of the 14 rheumatoid sera gave a strong reaction with Gm(a)-coated cells, although prozones were commonly observed, even in Gm(a−) sera. This indicated that the reactions might be due to other activities than anti-Gm(a). The reaction of Gm(a)-coated cells and whole serum Ek was inhibited by all IgG1, IgG2 and IgG4 myeloma proteins, but not by IgG3, thus showing specificity for the Ga antigen. A similar inhibition pattern suggestive of anti-Ga was also seen when using cells coated with anti-Rh Ripley and a few other diagnostic anti-Rh antibodies in reaction with serum Ek and some other rheumatoid sera. In serum Ek, the pattern became clear only after neutralizing the strong anti-"non a" activity. However, it was not possible to obtain an equally clear "non a" inhibition pattern in whole serum Ek by neutralizing the anti-Ga activity.

Other rheumatoid factor specificities. In reaction with Gm(g)-coated cells serum Th showed an anti-Gm(g) specificity. However, the reaction of the IgM fraction with the Gm(g)-coated cells was inhibited not only by IgG3 Gm(g) myeloma proteins, but also by IgG1 and IgG2 proteins. No inhibition was obtained by IgG4 or several IgG3 Gm(b) myeloma proteins. The same inhibition pattern was also demonstrated with Gm(f)-coated cells and IgM fraction Th. With Gm(g)-coated cells the Gm(g) IgG3 myeloma proteins exerted a stronger inhibitory effect than the IgG1 and IgG2 proteins, but with Gm(f)-coated cells no such difference could be seen. In three additional IgM fractions other specificities were also seen, which were not investigated further in the present study.

DISCUSSION

Rheumatoid factor activities were revealed in all the 14 rheumatoid sera tested after separation of the IgM rheumatoid factors from the potentially inhibiting IgG by gel filtration at pH 4.0. In hemagglutination inhibition tests these activities were completely inhibited by the patients' own IgG. These findings are in accordance with those of Allen and Kunkel (12), and support previous observations that rheumatoid factors show a distinct autospecificity (4, 7–18). Some findings indicate that rheumatoid factors would react easily with denatured IgG (34). However, the GM(a), Gm(x), Gm(b), Gm(g), and Ga antigens are all present in intact native IgG molecules. This is also the case with the antigen for rheumatoid anti-"non a" defined in the present study. The anti-Ga specificity is probably one of the main specificities of rheumatoid factors (12). The major specificity obtained in ultracentrifugal studies (9), and a "general" rheumatoid factor activity detected by hemagglutination (21), appeared to be very similar, or identical, to the anti-Ga specificity. Also in the present study, anti-Ga was the major specificity, found in all the 14 rheumatoid sera tested, while anti-Gm(a) was present in only 10, anti-"non a" in 6 sera, and anti-Gm(g) in 1 serum. The Ga, "non a," and Gm(a) antigens, together with the Gm(x), Gm(b), and Gm(g) antigens, may together cover the majority of rheumatoid factor activities in most sera.

Ten of the 14 sera reacted with the Gm(a)-coated cells. This may be due partly to the fact that all patients were selected on the basis of strong seropositivity, and that this test system detected both of the two major rheumatoid factor specificities, anti-Ga and anti-Gm(a). By increasing the degree of red cell coating with the Gm(f), Gm(b), and Gm(g) anti-Rh sera, some of the rheumatoid whole sera reacted weakly with marked prozone phenomena. But with the same degree of sensitization, Gm(a) anti-Rh appeared to be more efficient than Gm-(f), Gm(b), and Gm(g) anti-Rh in detecting rheumatoid factor specificities directed against autologous IgG. With all test systems the degree to which rheumatoid factor activities were hidden in whole sera appeared to be dependent on the strength of the test system used. With low sensitization the isospecificity of rheumatoid factors was usually detected, whereas with strong sensitization autospecific rheumatoid factors were also revealed, fitting well with the observations of Aho *et al.*, (5). Rheumatoid anti-Ga could be demonstrated directly in several whole sera, utilizing red cells coated with anti-Rh Ripley, Gm(a) anti-Rh 3091, and certain other Ga positive anti-Rh antibodies of high serum titers.

Beside the anti-Ga specificity, it is mainly the anti-Gm(a), anti-Gm(x), anti-Gm(b), and anti-Gm(g) which have shown rheumatoid factors to be specifically directed against well defined antigens on the IgG molecules (26). In addition, a rheumatoid anti-"non a" was demonstrated in 6 of the 14 rheumatoid sera tested. Previously the "non a" antigen has been detected by hetero-antisera. The rheumatoid anti-"non a" in six sera showed the same inhibition pattern with IgG subclass proteins as heterospecific anti-"non a." This strongly indicated that the same antigen is involved in these reactions. However, the sensitivity of the rheumatoid anti-"non a" was similar to that of other rheumatoid factors (4), with end points of hemagglutination inhibition reactions at higher concentrations of inhibitor than when heteroantisera were employed. Moreover, the reactions were inhibited by "non a" negative IgG myeloma proteins in high concentrations or in the heat-aggregated form. Five of the six sera containing anti-"non a" were themselves Gm(a−). Thus all proteins of the major subclass IgG1 in these five sera were "non a" positive.

The genetic antigen Gm(p) has previously been found to be present on Fc fragments of IgG1 Gm(f+a−) myeloma proteins (25), but not on a Gm(f+a+) Chinese myeloma protein (G. Kronvall, personal communication). The antisera Po and P.C.E. 64 used for the detection of Gm(p) (23) and Gm(e) (24) respectively both showed marked prozone phenomena, indicating the presence of inhibitors (26, 27). Our study demonstrated the presence in these two sera of anti-"non a" and anti-Ga. These were also shown to be the specificities involved in the original Gm(p) system with anti-Rh Moore. The original Gm(e) anti-Rh 61 also contained the "non a" and Ga antigens. These findings indicate that Gm(p) and probably also Gm(e) are identical in part with "non a" and in part with Ga, and thus are not regular Gm types. In studies with Gm(e) (35), quantitative rather than qualitative differences among human sera were observed, similar to those with "non a" (22). The presence also of anti-Ga in the original anti-Gm(p) and anti-Gm(e) sera explains why inhibition has previously been obtained only with IgG1 and IgG2 proteins (36), containing both the "non a" and Ga antigens, and not with IgG3 proteins, which are Ga negative. Lack of inhibition with IgG3 was also seen in the present study when anti-Ga was not neutralized (Table III).

The molecular localization of the antigens for rheumatoid anti-"non a" and anti-Ga clearly indicates that different areas of the IgG molecules are involved in rheumatoid factor reactions. The Ga antigenic site is located in the Fc region of heavy chains (12), but the present investiga-

TABLE IV

Antigens of various IgG subclass proteins involved in rheumatoid factor reactions

Subclass	Gm Type	Fc Fragment of IgG: N-terminal part	Fc Fragment of IgG: pFc′ fragment
IgG1	zax	Ga	a and x
	f	Ga	"non a"
IgG2	n+	Ga	"non a"
	n−	Ga	"non a"
IgG3	g	g	"non a"
	b	b[1]	"non a"
IgG4[a]	—	Ga	?

[a] An anti-gG4 rheumatoid factor specificity has recently been demonstrated (39; J. B. Natvig, unpublished).

tion showed that it is not present on the pFc′ or Fc′ fragments. This indicated that its localization is probably further toward the N-terminal part of the Fc fragment, or that the integrity of this part of Fc is needed for antigenic activity. On the other hand, rheumatoid anti-"non a," as previously shown also for heterospecific anti-"non a" (32), was inhibited by pFc′ fragments, which also contain the antigens for rheumatoid anti-Gm(a) and anti-Gm(x) (21).

The rheumatoid factor specificities studied here cover antigens in all subclasses and genetic variants of IgG, (Table IV). Moreover, several IgG subclass proteins contained the antigen for two rheumatoid factor specificities. For example, IgG1 proteins contained the Ga and Gm(a) or "non a" antigens, IgG2 Ga and "non a," and IgG3 "non a" and Gm(g) or Gm(b^1). Previously, no rheumatoid anti-Gm(f) had been found (37, 38), while rheumatoid anti-Gm(a) is frequent. However, the rheumatoid anti-"non a" reported here is directed against an antigen, called "non a," located on the pFc′ part of the Fc fragment of those Gm(f) molecules lacking the Gm(a) antigen. Thus this antigen for rheumatoid anti-"non a" could not be distinguished from the "non a" antigen previously described (22, 32).

One serum contained anti-Gm(g) and another specificity (possibly anti-"non-b") related to Gm(g) IgG3 proteins and also to other IgG molecules. Further investigations on the latter rheumatoid factor specificity are needed.

The reactivity of rheumatoid factors with these distinct IgG antigens, Gm(a), Gm(x), Gm(b), Gm(g), Ga, and "non a," gives additional evidence that rheumatoid factors are a population of specific antibody molecules directed against well-defined antigenic determinants on the IgG molecule. The rheumatoid factor activity, as seen in whole serum, probably constitutes the sum of several such narrow specificities.

REFERENCES

1. Grubb, R., Immunopathology, First International Symposium, p. 359, Schwabe, Basel/Stuttgart, 1959.
2. Harboe, M., Acta Path. Microbiol. Scand., *50:* 89, 1960.
3. Fudenberg, H. H. and Kunkel, H. G., J. Exp. Med., *114:* 257, 1961.
4. Tan, E. M. and Kunkel, H. G., Advances Immun., *4:* 351, 1964.
5. Aho, K., Harboe, M. and Leikola, J., Immunology, *7:* 403, 1964.
6. Fudenberg, H. H. and Franklin, E. C., Ann. N. Y. Acad. Sci., *124:* 884, 1965.
7. Singer, J. M. and Plotz, C. M., Arthritis Rheum., *1:* 142, 1958.
8. Aho, K., Harboe, M. and Sievers, K., Vox Sang., *10:* 225, 1965.
9. Schur, P. H. and Kunkel, H. G., Arthritis Rheum., *8:* 468, 1965.
10. Normansell, D. E. and Stanworth, D. R., Immunology, *10:* 527, 1966.
11. Tönder, O., Natvig, J. B. and Milgrom, F., Arthritis Rheum., *9:* 703, 1966.
12. Allen, J. C. and Kunkel, H. G., Arthritis Rheum., *9:* 758, 1966.
13. Bandilla, K. K. and McDuffie, F. C., Arthritis Rheum., *12:* 74, 1969.
14. Bluestone, R., Goldberg, L. S. and Cracchiolo, A., III, Lancet, *2:* 878, 1969.
15. Franklin, E. C., Holman, H. R., Müller-Eberhard, H. J. and Kunkel, H. G., J. Exp. Med., *105:* 425, 1957.
16. Kunkel, H. G., Müller-Eberhard, H. J., Fudenberg, H. H. and Tomasi, T. B., J. Clin. Invest., *40:* 117, 1961.
17. Chodirker, W. B. and Tomasi, T. B., Jr., J. Clin. Invest., *42:* 876, 1963.
18. Hannestad, K., Clin. Exp. Immun., *3:* 671, 1968.
19. Grubb, R. and Laurell, A.-B., Acta Path. Microbiol. Scand., *39:* 390, 1956.
20. Kunkel, H. G., Allen, J. C. and Grey, H. M., Cold Spring Harbor Symp. Quant. Biol., *29:* 443, 1964.
21. Natvig, J. B. and Turner, M. W., Nature, *225:* 855, 1970.
22. Natvig, J. B., Kunkel, H. G. and Joslin, F. G., J. Immun., *102:* 611, 1969.
23. Waller, M., Hughes, R. D., Townsend, J. I., Franklin, E. C. and Fudenberg, H. H., Science, *142:* 1321, 1963.
24. Ropartz, C., Rivat, L. and Rousseau, P.-Y., Proceedings of the Ninth Congress of the International Society of Blood Transfusion, p. 455, Karger, Basel/New York, 1964.
25. Kronvall, G., Vox Sang., *10:* 303, 1965.
26. Natvig, J. B. and Kunkel, H. G., Series Hematol., *I, 1:* 66, 1968.
27. Oreskes, I. and Plotz, C. M., J. Immun., *94:* 567, 1965.
28. Natvig, J. B., Kunkel, H. G., Yount, W. J. and Nielsen, J. C., J. Exp. Med., *128:* 763, 1968.
29. Natvig, J. B., Immunology, *19:* 125, 1970.
30. Kunkel, H. G., Meth. Biochem. Anal., *1:* 141, 1954.
31. Porter, R. R., Biochem. J., *73:* 119, 1959.

32. Turner, M. W., Mårtensson, L., Natvig, J. B. and Bennich, H., Nature, *221:* 1166, 1969.
33. Mancini, G., Carbonara, A. O. and Heremans, J. F., Immunochemistry, *2:* 235, 1965.
34. Edelman, G. M., Kunkel, H. G. and Franklin, E. C., J. Exp. Med., *108:* 105, 1958.
35. Steinberg, A. G., Muir, W. A. and McIntire, S. A., Amer. J. Hum. Genet., *20:* 258, 1968.
36. Rivat, L., Ropartz, C., Burtin, P. and Cruchaud, A., Nature, *225:* 1136, 1970.
37. Grubb, R., Kronvall, G. and Mårtensson, L., Ann. N. Y. Acad. Sci., *124:* 865, 1965.
38. Natvig, J. B., Acta Path. Microbiol. Scand., *66:* 188, 1966.
39. van Loghem, E. and de Lange, G., Vox Sang., *18:* 81, 1970.

THE JOURNAL OF IMMUNOLOGY
Vol. 105, No. 4, October 1970

THE KINETICS OF *IN VIVO* TOLERANCE INTRODUCTION IN MICE[1]

SAROJ DAS AND SIDNEY LESKOWITZ

From the Department of Pathology, Tufts Medical School, Boston, Massachusetts 02111

Received for publication April 14, 1970

C57BL/6 mice were rendered immunologically tolerant by an intraperitoneal injection of 200 μg of bovine γ globulin (BGG). An intraperitoneal injection of 1 mg of polyornithine (poly-O) given from 24 hr before to 5 hr after the injection of BGG produced immunity rather than tolerance. After 8 hr the induction of tolerance by BGG was no longer reversible by the poly-O. In a further test of the induction period of tolerance, washed spleen cells were transferred to x-irradiated recipients which were then immunized. If spleen cells were removed from donor mice as little as 4 hr after they had been injected with 2 mg of BGG, significant loss of ability to produce immunity in recipients was seen.

Much is known about the practical aspects of the induction of tolerance to protein antigens in adult animals. At the same time considerable uncertainty exists about the mechanism by which such tolerance is induced. To evolve a comprehensive view of tolerance more information is required on the time course or kinetics of its induction following exposure to antigen. In view of reports in the literature placing the period required for induction of tolerance anywhere from several hours (1, 2) to several days (3, 4) it was felt useful to re-explore the phenomenon. Using bovine γ globulin (BGG) as antigen in C57BL/6 strain mice our findings are consistent with reports that the induction of tolerance *in vivo* is rapid and requires a period of hours rather than days.

MATERIALS AND METHODS

Animals. Male inbred C57BL/6 mice, 8 to 10 weeks old when obtained from Jackson Laboratories, Bar Harbor, Maine, were used throughout.

Bovine γ globulin (BGG) was purchased from Pentex, Inc., Kankee, Ill.

Poly-L-ornithine-HBr (poly-O) (m.w. 130,000 lot T-1218) was purchased from Mann Research Laboratories, New York, N. Y.

Induction of tolerance. A saline solution of BGG (25 mg/ml) was centrifuged at 30,000 rpm for 30 min in a Spinco model L centrifuge with a No. 50 rotor. Protein determination on the supernatant before and after centrifugation revealed that less than 4% of the protein was sufficiently aggregated to appear in the pellet. The supernatant was collected and suitable dilutions of BGG were made in 1% normal mouse serum to stabilize the protein. Induction of tolerance was attempted with the appropriate dose of antigen injected intraperitoneally into groups of mice in a volume of 0.2 ml.

Challenge. One week after the injection of the tolerance-inducing dose of BGG, the mice were immunized with 100 μg of BGG incorporated into complete Freund's adjuvant (8.5 parts mineral oil, 1.5 parts Arlacel-A, 5 mg/ml killed mycobacteria). A total volume of 0.1 ml was given in the two hind feet. To test the efficacy of the immunization, a normal group of mice was immunized with the antigen in adjuvant for each experiment.

Determination of immune status. One week after immunization all mice were given a tracer dose of about 4 μg BGG labeled with ^{131}I. Whole body counts on each mouse were done daily by placing the anesthetized mouse in a plastic vial into a Baird-Atomic well type 810C crystal coupled to a model 530 spectrophotometer. All animals were given 0.1% KI in drinking water 48 hr prior to injection of the tracer dose and for as long as counting studies continued.

Iodination. The BGG used was labeled with ^{131}I by a modification of the method described by McConahey and Dixon (5) using chloramine-T. Usually 250 μg of BGG were conjugated with 25 to 30 μCi of carrier-free ^{131}I using 100 μg chloramine-T and a reaction time of 10 min. The reaction was stopped with 100 μg of sodium metabi-

[1] This work was supported by Grant AI 01289 from the United States Public Health Service.

sulfite and unconjugated ^{131}I was removed by passage through a Bio-Gel P-2 column using 0.05 M phosphate buffer, pH 7.0, for elution. The dose of antigen usually given was about 4 to 5 μg of BGG containing about 0.3 μCi of ^{131}I.

Treatment with poly-L-ornithine. A saline solution of poly-O-was adjusted to pH 7 before use. Preliminary studies indicated that doses above 10 mg/mouse were quite toxic. A dose of 1 mg given intraperitoneally in a volume of 0.2 ml was used in this study.

Analysis of data. Total body counts for all animals in the study were performed immediately after injection of the tracer dose and then daily for as long as required. Total body counts per minute were corrected each day for radioactive decay, and plotted against time on semilogarithmic paper. All experiments were performed on groups of five or more mice and the results for each group were averaged every day after applying the correction factor for decay. When experiments were not done all at once, control groups were run each time and all results were averaged.

Passive transfer of spleen cells. Donor mice were rendered tolerant by intravenous injection of 2 mg of BGG. At 24-hr and 5-day intervals the animals were killed, their spleens removed and cell suspensions prepared by gently pressing the spleens through stainless steel mesh screens and rinsing with Eagle's minimum essential medium (MEM). The cells were gently centrifuged and washed twice with MEM before use. One spleen equivalent was injected intravenously into each recipient in a volume of 0.5 ml. Recipients were given 800 R x-irradiation (1.95 mm Cu half value layer, 51 R/min) several hours prior to use. They were then injected i.p. with 25 units of heparin a few minutes before receiving the cells. One week after cell transfers all mice were immunized with 100 μg BGG in complete Freund's adjuvant (CFA). Nonimmune controls were given adjuvant alone. Seven days later the immune status of all animals was tested by injecting them with about 5 μg of ^{131}I-labeled BGG and doing daily whole body counting.

In a subsequent experiment spleens were removed 4 and 24 hr after the tolerance-inducing injection of BGG. These were teased, washed, and given to x-irradiated recipients as above. Two days later all animals were immunized with 100 μg BGG in CFA and their immune status was tested 10 days later by challenge with 5 μg of ^{131}I-labeled BGG.

RESULTS

To determine an effective dose for induction of tolerance, groups of mice were injected i.p. with 20 μg, 200 μg and 2 mg of BGG and then immunized with 100 μg of BGG in adjuvant. In Figure 1 are seen the results following the administration of the challenge dose of ^{131}I-labeled BGG. Immune mice cleared over 90% of the label in 24 hr and by 48 hr had whole body counts only slightly above background levels. All groups of treated mice were tolerant and showed a clearance rate indistinguishable from normal nonimmunized controls. In all experiments it was found that normal or tolerant mice exhibited a biphasic clearance of ^{131}I-labeled BGG with approximately 40% to 50% being excreted in the first 24 hr. The residual material then disappeared at a slower rate. In a separate experiment 2 μg of BGG were found to be ineffective in producing unresponsiveness.

Since 20 μg were found to be the minimum effective dose producing a uniform tolerance, 10 times that dose was used in subsequent experiments. The effect of a polycationic stimulator of the reticuloendothelial system on the induction of tolerance was studied by injecting 1 mg of poly-O intraperitoneally at various intervals before, during, and after the injection of the tolerance-inducing dose of BGG. Mice were then immunized and challenged with ^{131}I-labeled BGG as before. In this experiment no animals treated

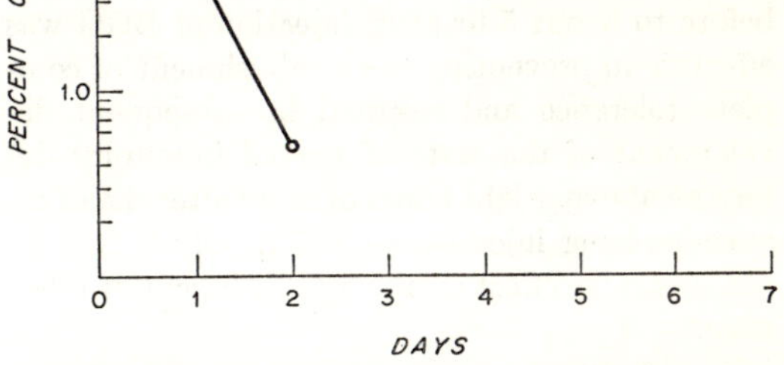

Figure 1. Elimination of ^{131}I-labeled BGG in control, immune, and BGG-treated mice. ×——×, Freund adjuvant (FA) alone (av. 8); ○——○, 100 μg BGG in FA (av. 6); △-----△, 0.02, 0.2 or 2 mg of BGG first, then 100 μg BGG in FA (av. 20).

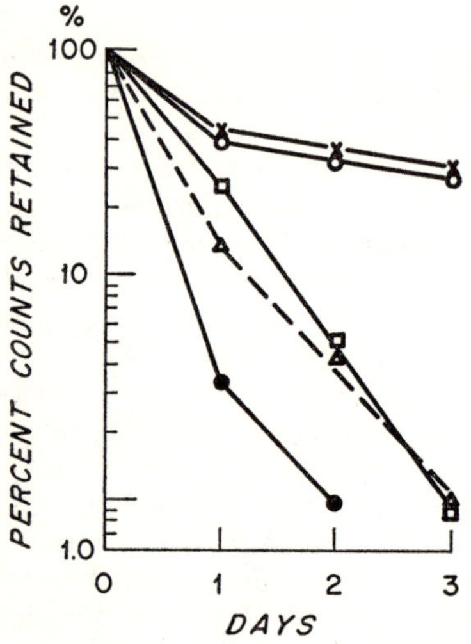

Figure 2. The effect of polyornithine (1 mg) on the induction of tolerance by 200 μg BGG in mice. ×——×, BGG alone (av. 9); △-----△, 1 mg poly-O 24 hr before BGG (av. 8); ○——○, 1 mg poly-O 24 hr after BGG (av. 6); ●——●, no BGG (av. 5); □——□, 1 mg poly-O with BGG (av. 9).

with poly-O and the tolerizing dose of BGG ever achieved a degree of immune elimination comparable to the immunized control animals. A typical result seen in Figure 2 shows that the type of immune response achieved by animals treated with poly-O either 24 hr or just before injection of 200 μg of BGG was distinctly different from tolerant animals but fell somewhat short of the rapidity of clearance in fully immune animals. This degree of partial immunity was similar for all treatment groups in which any effect was noticed.

In Table I are seen the results when poly-O was administered at various times around the injection of the tolerance-inducing dose of 200 μg of BGG. Treatment with poly-O from 48 hr before to about 5 hr after injection of BGG was effective in preventing the establishment of complete tolerance and resulted in subsequent development of the state of partial immunity described above. Eight hours or more after the tolerance-inducing injection of BGG, poly-O had no demonstrable effect on the establishment of tolerance.

To determine whether poly-O was effective in converting a tolerance-inducing injection of BGG into an immunizing event, mice treated with poly-O and BGG were tested 1 week later with a tracer dose of ^{131}I-labeled BGG for the existence

TABLE I

Effect of polyornithine (Poly-O) on induction of tolerance by 200 μg BGG in mice

Treatment	Time of Injection of Poly-O Relative to BCG	Number	Immune Status
	hr		
1 mg poly-O	−48	5	All immune
1 mg poly-O	−24	3	All immune
1 mg poly-O	−5	7	All immune
1 mg poly-O	0	7	All immune
1 mg poly-O	+5	4	All immune
1 mg poly-O	+8	5	1 immune, 4 tolerant
1 mg poly-O	+16	5	All tolerant
1 mg poly-O	+24	3	All tolerant
Nothing		10	All tolerant

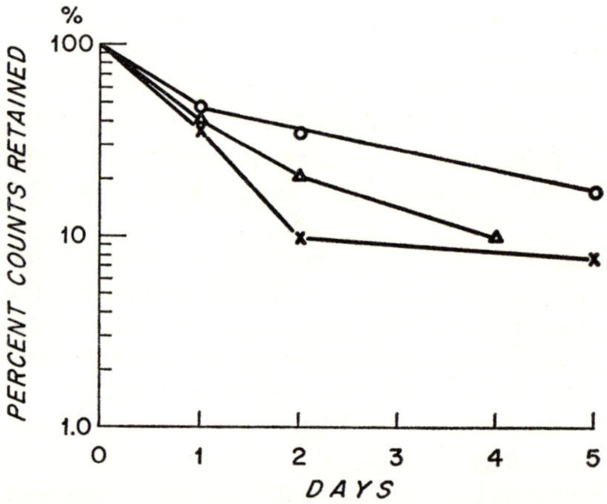

Figure 3. The effect of polyornithine on the conversion of a tolerance-inducing injection of BGG to an immunizing one. ○——○, 200 μg BGG alone (av. 7); ×——×, 1 mg poly-O 24 hr before BGG (av. 6); □——□, 1 mg poly-O 5 hr after BGG (av. 5).

of an immune state. As seen in Figure 3, a slight but consistent indication of a more rapid clearance of the test dose of ^{131}I-labeled BGG was obtained in mice treated with poly-O 24 hr before or 5 hr after the tolerance-inducing dose of BGG. The accelerated clearance of tracer BGG, most apparent at 48 hr, suggested the presence of a small immune response as a result of injection of BGG and poly-O 1 week previously.

To determine whether poly-O had a direct effect on the metabolism and clearance of the BGG, groups of mice were treated at intervals before and after injection of a tracer dose of ^{131}I-labeled BGG. When 1 mg of poly-O was given 24 hr before or 5 hr after a dose of ^{131}I-labeled BGG, small but consistent increases in the rate of clearance were noted such that by 48 hr treated animals had excreted about 10% more of the ^{131}I label than controls.

The results obtained *in vivo,* which suggested that induction of tolerance could not be reversed with poly-O after about 8 hr, were re-examined by a passive transfer system used by Golub and Weigle (4), in an attempt to confirm the observed brevity of induction time. This test was chosen to attempt to overcome the difficulties in assessing the kinetics of tolerance induction in the *in vivo* system when competing events produced by antigen in an immunizing and a tolerance-inducing form are simultaneously present (4). To establish an appropriate dose of antigen for induction of tolerance and a suitable time after transfer of cells for testing immune status, it was first necessary to determine how long the tolerance produced at various dose levels persisted. Groups of mice were given either 2 mg or 0.2 mg of BGG and allowed to rest 2, 4 or 8 weeks before immunization with 100 μg BGG in CFA. One week later they were tested for an immune response in the usual way.

The results shown in Figure 4 indicate that a dose of 2 mg BGG produced a complete unresponsiveness for up to 4 weeks prior to immunization (open circles). After 8 weeks mice exhibited a partial immunity which indicated an escape from tolerance (open squares). The 0.2-mg dose of BGG was similarly effective up to 4 weeks (open triangles), but the degree of tolerance produced did not seem to be as profound as that achieved with 2 mg BGG. A slightly accelerated immune clearance was observed at 2 and 4 weeks with the lower dose as compared with the higher dose of BGG. After 8 weeks a higher degree of responsiveness was seen indicative of an escape from tolerance. These results suggested that a 2-mg dose of BGG be used to produce tolerance in animals prior to transferring their spleen cells to irradiated recipients.

Since the half-life of BGG was sufficiently long (6) to allow significant amounts to be circulating at the times when the spleen cells were to be removed and transferred, it was necessary to check the possible carry-over of free antigen by the cells being transferred. A group of mice was given 2 mg of ^{131}I-labeled BGG and killed 24 hr and 5 days after injection to study the localization of the antigen. Approximately 0.2% of the total residual body count was found in the spleen, the bulk being in the blood. Washed spleen cell suspensions prepared for passive transfer were found to contain only trace amounts of radioactivity indicating a possible carry-over of less than 0.4 μg antigen for one spleen equivalent of cells.

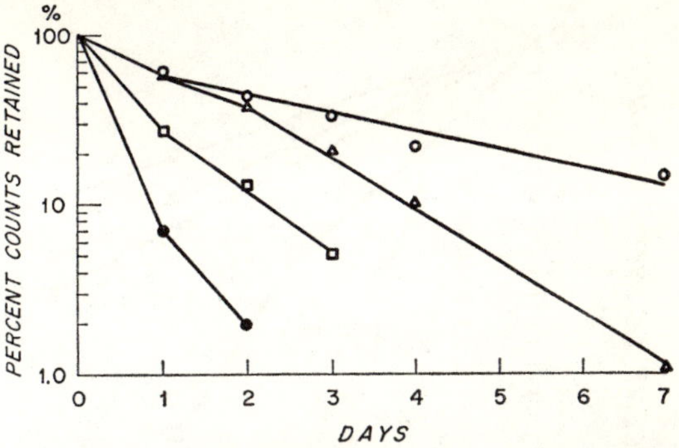

Figure 4. The persistence of tolerance induced in mice by 2.0 or 0.2 mg of BGG. ○——○, Control, 2 mg BGG at 2 and 4 weeks (av. 6); □——□, 0.2 mg BGG at 2 and 4 weeks (av. 6); □——□, 2 mg and 0.2 mg BGG at 8 weeks (av. 6); ●——●, immune (av. 14).

In the first experiment spleen cells from mice rendered tolerant by 2 mg of BGG given 1 and 5 days before the spleens were removed were transferred to x-irradiated recipients in the proportion of one spleen equivalent per recipient. All mice were immunized 1 week after cell transfers and tested a week later for immune responsiveness. In addition two groups of irradiated mice receiving normal spleen cells were used; one was immunized with BGG in CFA in the usual way and one received only CFA without antigen. The degree of immunity achieved by irradiated mice given normal spleen cells and immunized in the usual way (open squares) was somewhat less than that seen previously for normal immune animals (Fig. 5). The two groups of x-rayed mice receiving cells taken from animals treated with BGG 1 (crosses) or 5 days (open triangles) previously showed a high degree of unresponsiveness indicating that the transferred cells were largely tolerant to BGG.

To increase the degree of immunity achieved by the control group irradiated mice were immunized 2 days after transfer of spleen cells, but were not tested until 10 days later. Thus, while this pro-

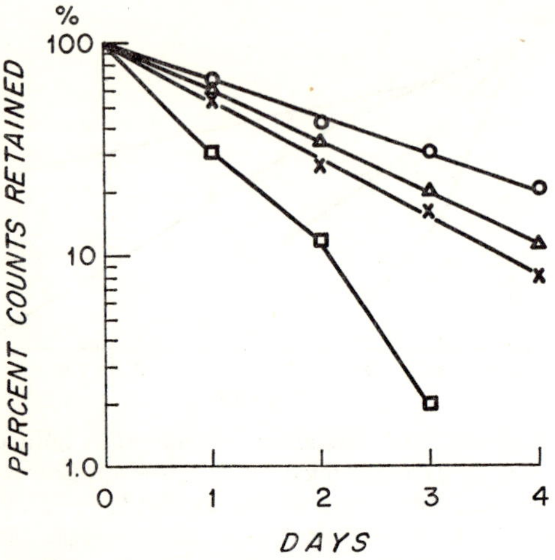

Figure 5. The immune response 7 days after immunization with 100 μg BGG in CFA in x-irradiated mice receiving spleen cell transfers. ○——○, Normal spleen cells, nonimmunized (av. 4); □——□, normal spleen cells, immunized (av. 5); △——△, spleen cells 5 days after BGG (av. 7); ×——×, spleen cells 24 hr after BGG (av. 6).

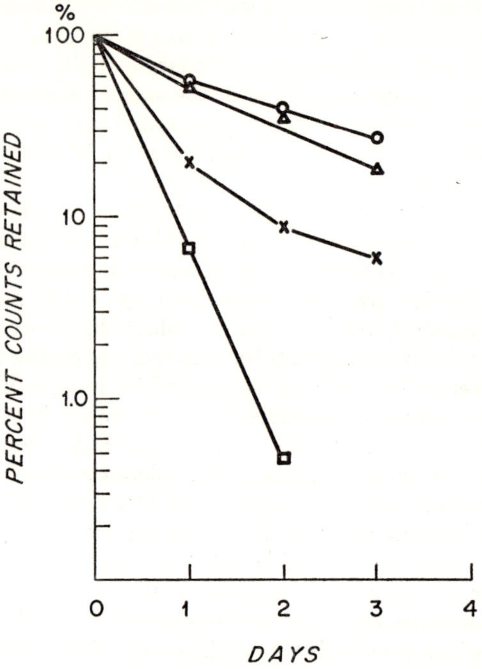

Figure 6. The immune response 10 days after immunization with 100 μg BGG in CFA in x-irradiated mice receiving spleen cell transfers. ○——○, Normal spleen cells, nonimmunized (av. 6); □——□, normal spleen cells, immunized (av. 8); △——△, spleen cells 24 hr after BGG (av. 6); ×——×, spleen cells 4 hr after BGG (av. 9).

vided a longer interval for immunization, the total time which elapsed after injection of the cells did not exceed that of the first experiment nor did it impinge on the limits of tolerance persistence. Control animals receiving normal spleen cells after irradiation developed a good immune response as judged by their rate of clearance of the tracer dose of BGG (Fig. 6). By contrast animals receiving spleen cells from donors treated with 2 mg of BGG 24 hr previously had an antigen clearance rate not significantly different from unimmunized controls, indicating a high degree of tolerance in the transferred cells. Mice receiving spleen cells from donors treated with BGG only 4 hr previously also showed a significantly altered rate of clearance, indicating that a high degree of tolerance existed in the transferred cells.

DISCUSSION

The operational event in the development of tolerance has been variously considered to be: a) a direct interaction between antigen and a receptor on the immunocompetent cell (cf. 7), b) a maturation process during which the cell develops to a sensitive stage in which it reacts to antigen by becoming suppressed or eliminated (3), c) an end stage development of all immunocompetent cells leading to exhaustion by "terminal differentiation" of responding cells (8), and d) an interaction of immunocompetent cells with antigen after it has been processed by some other type of cell (9, 10).

One possible way of distinguishing among the various possibilities would be to determine the time required for the development of tolerance. Those theories encompassing direct interaction of antigen and cells (with or without "processing") might be thought to be rapid reactions whose rate-limiting step would be the diffusion or dissemination of antigen. The other theories requiring some maturational event or cell differentiation would presumably require more time.

As a possible approach to the solution of this problem, some investigators have utilized *in vitro* systems involving direct exposure of cells to antigen and have estimated that several hours are required to produce tolerance with lipopolysaccharide and flagella antigens (1, 2). Other attempts to produce tolerance *in vitro* with protein antigens have been unsuccessful (9, 11). Another approach has been to interrupt the induction of tolerance *in vivo* by eliminating the antigen with a degrading enzyme (3) or by adding an adjuvant capable of converting a tolerance-inducing dose of antigen to one that immunizes (12, 13). These methods have in general suggested that several days are required, which is consistent with the notion of a maturational event.

As an additional contribution it was thought desirable to investigate the action of a nonspecific stimulator of the reticuloendothelial system, polyornithine, on the kinetics of induction of tolerance. When poly-O was administered 24 hr before or 5 hr after a nonimmunizing injection of BGG, slight but definite degrees of immunity were observed (Fig. 3). When it was injected between 48 hr before to about 8 hr after a tolerance-inducing dose of BGG it successfully inhibited the induction of tolerance and led to significant immune clearance rates after immunization. Administering it after 8 hr no longer reversed the course of tolerance induction. These results suggested a much shorter induction period of tolerance than similar experiments utilizing endotoxin (13) in which it was observed that administration as much as 2 days after a tolerance-inducing dose of human γ globulin (HGG) would still suffice to reverse the course of tolerance induction.

Golub and Weigle (4) found that 0.5 mg of HGG required 5 days to produce tolerance in C57BL/6 mice. Cells removed from such donors before 5 days conferred complete responsiveness on irradiated recipients, while cells removed after 5 days were unresponsive.

Using a similar experimental protocol Mitchison (11) found that 2 hr of *in vivo* exposure to 50 mg of bovine serum albumin (BSA) or human serum albumin (HSA) conferred appreciable unresponsiveness on transferred blood leukocytes, but spleen cells required slightly longer exposures of up to 24 hr. Our results are more compatible with these findings in that the experiments with poly-O and passive transfer of spleen cells both suggested an induction period only hours long before the establishment of irreversible tolerance.

Differences in antigen, mode of immunization and method of assay of immune response make it difficult to reconcile these results with Golub and Weigle's estimate of a 5-day latent period (4) or Dresser's even longer estimate (6). The present studies and those of Golub and Weigle (4) while comparable in technical details differ somewhat in result. Both utilized a protocol of immunization and testing that might be less than optimal and measure only the response to major determinants. The all or none nature of the conversion at 4 days from an immune to a tolerant state in their studies (4) could be explicable on the basis of an assay which classifies an animal in only one of two ways, immune or tolerant.

A number of other circumstances could account for the differences observed in the induction period. The combination of a potentially less immunogenic molecule (BGG *vs* HGG) for the mouse and a more toleragenic route of injection (intravenous *vs* intraperitoneal) might have produced an apparently more rapid induction of tolerance in the experiments described in this paper.

In any event, the ability to produce a more rapid induction of tolerance *in vivo* by altering such factors as the antigen and its rate of dissemination together with the evidence concerning its induction *in vitro* (1, 2, 9) would appear to rule out the necessity for a maturational process in the induction of tolerance.

REFERENCES

1. Britton, S., J. Exp. Med., *129:* 469, 1969.
2. Diener, E. and Armstrong, W. D., J. Exp. Med., *129:* 591, 1969.
3. Brooke, M. S., Nature, *204:* 1319, 1964.
4. Golub, E. S. and Weigle, W. O., J. Immun., *99:* 624, 1967.
5. McConahey, P. J. and Dixon, F. J., Int. Arch. Allerg., *29:* 185, 1966.
6. Dresser, D. W., Int. Arch. Allerg., *35:* 259, 1969.
7. Leskowitz, S., Ann. Rev. Microbiol., *21:* 157, 1967.
8. Sterzl, J., Nature, *209:* 416, 1966.
9. Scott, D. W. and Waksman, B. H., J. Immun., *102:* 347, 1969.
10. Collotti, C. and Leskowitz, S., J. Exp. Med., *131:* 571, 1970.
11. Mitchison, N. A., Immunology, *15:* 531, 1968.
12. Brooke, M. S., Nature, *206:* 635, 1965.
13. Golub, E. S. and Weigle, W. O., J. Immun., *98:* 1241, 1967.

THE JOURNAL OF IMMUNOLOGY

Vol. 105, No. 4, October 1970
Printed in U.S.A.

PROTEIN A FROM *STAPHYLOCOCCUS AUREUS*

X. Complement-Fixing Activity of Complexes between Protein A and Myeloma IgG or Papain Fragments of IgG[1]

G. STÅLENHEIM AND J. SJÖQUIST

From the Wallenberg Laboratory, Department of Biochemistry, Faculty of Pharmacy, University of Uppsala, Uppsala, Sweden

Received for publication April 13, 1970

Myeloma IgG proteins become equally anticomplementary when aggregated with protein A from *Staphylococcus aureus* and thus contain equally efficient C-fixing sites. Furthermore, Fc fragments aggregated with protein A inactivate complement. Sheep erythrocytes stabilized with glutaric dialdehyde and coated with protein A were agglutinated by normal human IgG, by myeloma IgG, by fragment Fc from IgG, but not by fragment Fab. Thus protein A is a sensitizing substance for aldehyde-treated cells.

If normal IgG is heated it denatures and becomes complement-fixing (C-fixing (1)) (2). It has been reported that myeloma proteins from different patients differ considerably in this property, some preparations lacking C-fixing ability completely (3–6). The ability to fix C does not seem to be correlated to Gm characters, InV types or the electrophoretic mobility of the IgG (4, 6). Most investigators believe the differences to be due to the various tendencies of different myeloma proteins to aggregate. Alternatively it has been suggested that the differences could be due to structural variations in the region of IgG where the "C-fixing site" is located (4). Among the four subgroups of human IgG, 1, 2 and 3 have been found to fix C (7).

There is no doubt that at least most of the C-fixing property of IgG resides in the Fc fragment (8–10), probably in the N-terminal part of the fragment (10, 11). Probably more than one site in the immunoglobulin is involved, and some of the C-fixing activity seems to be located to the $F(ab')_2$ fragment (12, 13).

Protein A from *S. aureus* is likewise known to react with the Fc part of the IgG molecule (14). Non-immune human IgG as well as IgG from most animal species reacts in this manner. It has recently been shown that protein A reacts with the IgG subgroups 1, 2 and 4 but not with 3 (15). Except for the anomalous combining site on the IgG and the reactivity with nonimmune IgG, the reaction has the characteristics of a normal antigen-antibody reaction (16).

The work described here shows that myeloma protein in complex with protein A inactivates complement and that this property is not correlated to the ability of heat-aggregated myeloma proteins to fix complement. It has been furthermore shown that protein A-Fc complexes fix complement.

MATERIALS AND METHODS

Preparation of protein A. Protein A was prepared by digestion of *S. aureus* with lysozyme as previously described. It was further purified by chromatography on DEAE-Sephadex and Sephadex G-150 (17, 18).

Preparation of human IgG. Normal human IgG was prepared as previously described (16). Myeloma IgG was prepared from sera of patients with myelomatosis (19).

Preparation of papain-digested fragments from myeloma protein. Papain digestion of two human myeloma IgG-1 was performed according to a technique modified from that of Porter (20). The protein was dissolved in 0.1 M phosphate buffer, pH 7.1, containing 2 mM EDTA·2Na and 0.01 M cysteine-hydrochloride. One part mercuripapain (Worthington Biochemical Corp;

[1] This work was supported by grants from the Medical Faculty, University of Uppsala, from Konung Gustaf V:s 80-årsfond, the Swedish Medical Research Council and the Swedish Cancer Society.

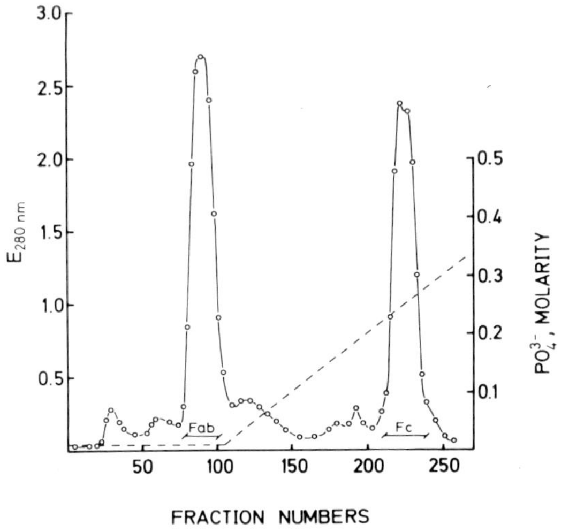

Figure 1. Chromatography on DEAE-Sephadex of papain-digested myeloma IgG (AL). *Unbroken line,* optical density of the eluate at 280 nm; *dashed line,* molarity of phosphate in the eluant. Pooled fractions indicated. For details see *Materials and Methods.*

Freehold, N. J.) was added to 100 parts of protein. Digestion was allowed to proceed for 30 min at 37°C. It was stopped by adding iodoacetamide in fivefold molar excess over cysteine, adjusting the pH to 8.0 and incubating at 20°C for 30 min. The digest was then dialyzed against 0.01 M phosphate buffer, pH 8.0, containing 2 mM EDTA·2Na. The papain fragments were separated on a DEAE-Sephadex column (Pharmacia Fine Chemicals, Uppsala) equilibrated with 0.01 M phosphate buffer, pH 8.0. The Fab fragment was eluted with this buffer and then a linear gradient was applied going from 0.01 to 0.35 M phosphate (Fig. 1). The Fc peak appeared at a phosphate concentration of about 0.25 M. The pooled Fab and Fc fractions were separately dialyzed against distilled water and lyophilized.

Heating of normal and myeloma IgG. In order to aggregate IgG, a 2% (w/v) solution of the protein in Veronal-buffered saline (VBS) was heated at 63°C for 20 min and then rapidly cooled to room temperature.

Protein determination. Protein concentration was determined by reading the absorbancy at 280 nm (21).

Precipitation in gel. 1% agar (Special Agar Noble Difco) in 0.05 M Tris-HCl, pH 7.2, was used in the gel precipitation test. The microgel diffusion method was used with 10 μl reactant in each well.

Complement (C) fixation. C determination and fixation were performed as previously described (16).

Protein A determination was performed with the hemagglutination technique previously described (16).

Fixation of protein A to aldehyde-treated erythrocytes. Red blood cells were coated with protein A by a method modified from that of Ling (22). Sheep blood was collected from individual sheep using sodium citrate as anticoagulant. The erythrocytes were spun down and washed three times in saline. A 50% cell suspension in saline was made up. A 25% solution of glutaric dialdehyde (GA) was neutralized with 10% sodium carbonate. One and a half volumes of neutralized GA, 5 volumes of saline and 1 volume of 0.015 M phosphate buffer, pH 8.0, were mixed and 1 volume of the 50% cell suspension was added. The suspension was left at 4°C under continuous gentle stirring for 24 hr. The cells were collected by centrifugation and washed four times with saline. A 10% cell suspension in saline containing 0.1% sodium azide was prepared.

One volume of the 10% suspension was washed three times in 0.015 M phosphate buffer, pH 6.0, and suspended in 0.5 volume of this buffer containing 250 μg protein A/ml. The suspension was heated to 50°C under continuous stirring for 1 hr. The cells were collected by centrifugation, washed three times in saline and suspended in 0.1 volume of saline containing 0.2% (w/v) bovine serum albumin (BSA) and 0.1% (w/v) sodium azide. The cells were stored at 4°C. The suspension was diluted 20-fold for use. The sample to be tested was serially diluted in a microhemagglutination plate. To 50 μl of each dilution was added 50 μl of cell suspension. The pattern was read after 2 hr.

RESULTS

Heat-treated IgG. Samples of heat-treated myeloma or normal IgG were added to approximately 50 CH_{50} units of C. After incubation at 4°C for 19 hr, the remaining C was determined and the amount of IgG fixing 25 CH_{50} units was calculated. This figure was more than 200 μg for three of the five myeloma IgG proteins tested (AL, GL and TJ). About 40 μg of one myeloma protein (EG) and about 90 μg of another (SE)

TABLE I

Reaction between protein A and normal IgG, myeloma IgG and papain fragments as measured by precipitation and hemagglutination. Complement fixation of normal IgG, myeloma IgG and papain fragments after treatment with protein A and with heat[a]

	Lowest Concentration Precipitating with 0.05% Protein A in Gel	Precipitation with Protein A in Tube	Lowest Concentration Agglutinating Protein A-Coated GA Cells	Protein Fixing 25 CH_{50} after Protein A Treatment	Protein Fixing 25 CH_{50} after Heat Treatment
	μg/ml		*μg/ml*	*μg*	*μg*
AL-γ	600–1200	–	4–8	13	>200[b]
Se-γ	150–300	–	4–8	13	86
EG-γ	2500–5000	–	4–8	13	39
GL-γ	300–600	+	4–8	21	≫200[c]
TJ-γ	150–300	+	1–2	24	>200[b]
Normal γ	150–300	+	1–2	30	50
Fc[AL]	NP[d]	–	8–16	12	NT[d]
Fc[Se]	NP	–	8–16	17	NT
Fab[AL]	NP	–	>100[e]	NT	NT
Fab[Se]	NP	–	>100	NT	NT

[a] For experimental conditions see *Materials and Methods.*

[b] Amount of protein tested (200 μg) showed almost no C fixation.

[c] Amount of protein tested (200 μg) showed no C fixation.

[d] NP, no precipitate; NT, not tested.

[e] Amount tested (100 μg/ml) showed no agglutination.

were needed to fix 25 CH_{50}. Fifty micrograms of normal human IgG (heat-aggregated) fixed 25 CH_{50}.

Protein A and IgG. Two of the myeloma IgG proteins (GL and TJ) and normal human IgG precipitated with protein A in tubes. The five myeloma proteins and normal IgG all formed precipitates with protein A in the gel diffusion test. When dilutions of the IgG preparations were tested for the ability to agglutinate protein A-coated GA cells, all displayed such activity, the concentration needed to effect agglutination ranging from 1 to 8 μg/ml. The point of equivalence between protein A and an immunoglobulin was determined in the following way. To a dilution series of the immunoglobulin a constant amount of protein A was added. The mixtures were incubated at 37°C for 90 min and at 4°C overnight. The protein A remaining in solution was estimated by hemagglutination. With the highest concentrations of immunoglobulin no protein A was detected, with decreasing concentrations more and more protein A was left free in solution. The highest dilution of immunoglobulin at which no free protein A was found indicated the point of equivalence.

Protein A and normal or myeloma IgG were mixed in proportions corresponding to the equivalence point, incubated at 37°C for 90 min and at 4°C overnight. The product was tested for free protein A, using the hemagglutination technique. Samples of appropriate dilutions were added to about 50 CH_{50} units of C. Remaining C was determined after 19 hr at 4°C and the C-fixing capacity of the IgG treated with protein A was calculated (Table I). All immunoglobulins tested were found to have excellent C-fixing properties under these conditions. Three of the myeloma proteins (AL, Se and EG) were needed in amounts less than half that of normal IgG to fix 25 CH_{50}. Two of the proteins (GL and TJ) had to be added in about the same amount as normal IgG. All IgG proteins had higher C-fixing capacities when aggregated by protein A than when aggregated by heat. All protein A was eliminated in all cases as determined by hemagglutination. Even the myeloma proteins found to be "poor C-fixers" after heat aggregation fixed C well when protein A was used as the aggregating agent.

In order to better define the C-fixing component in the IgG-protein A mixture, the incubation mixture of one myeloma protein (AL) and protein A was treated with ammonium sulfate to half saturation (16). Precipitate and supernatant were separated by centrifugation and the precipitate washed twice with two-thirds saturated ammonium sulfate. The supernatant and the dissolved precipitate were dialyzed against VBS and tested for C-fixing activity. The supernatant had no such capacity, whereas the precipitate fixed C as did the mixture before precipitation. No free protein A was found in the supernatant or in the dissolved precipitate.

Papain fragmentation. Two myeloma IgG-1 proteins (AL and Se) were digested by papain and the fragments purified on a DEAE-Sephadex column (Fig. 1). The fragments were set up in gel diffusion tests with goat antiserum against human IgG (Fig. 2*a*) and rabbit antiserum against fragment Fc (Fig. 2*b*). In Figure 2*a* it can be seen that there are single distinct precipitation lines between the antiserum well on one hand and the Fc- and Fab-fragment wells on the other. There are "reactions of nonidentity" between the Fab- and Fc arcs. Figure 2*b* shows that there is no Fc-determinant in the Fab-fractions from the two myeloma proteins.

Papain fragments and protein A. The papain fragments from the myeloma proteins (AL and Se) were separately mixed with protein A. Fragment Fc and protein A were mixed in amounts corresponding to the equivalence point. Since fragment Fab does not react with protein A, it was used in the same amount as Fc. After incubating the mixtures at 37°C for 90 min and at 4°C overnight, assays for free protein A were performed. Fragment Fab did not react with protein A, whereas fragment Fc from both myeloma proteins bound all protein A added. The Fab-protein A mixture was not assayed for C-fixing capacity since free protein A could react with and render the immunoglobulin of the guinea pig serum C fixing (16). Fc plus protein A was found, however, to fix complement. Samples containing 12 μg (AL) and 17 μg (Se) of Fc fragment, respectively, fixed 25 CH_{50} units. After precipitating the soluble complex between protein A and the Fc fragment of one of the myelomas (AL) with ammonium sulfate it was found that all the C-fixing activity resided in the washed precipitate. Dilutions of Fc fragment from either of the two myeloma proteins agglutinated protein A-coated GA cells. None of the Fab preparations was found to have such activity (Table I).

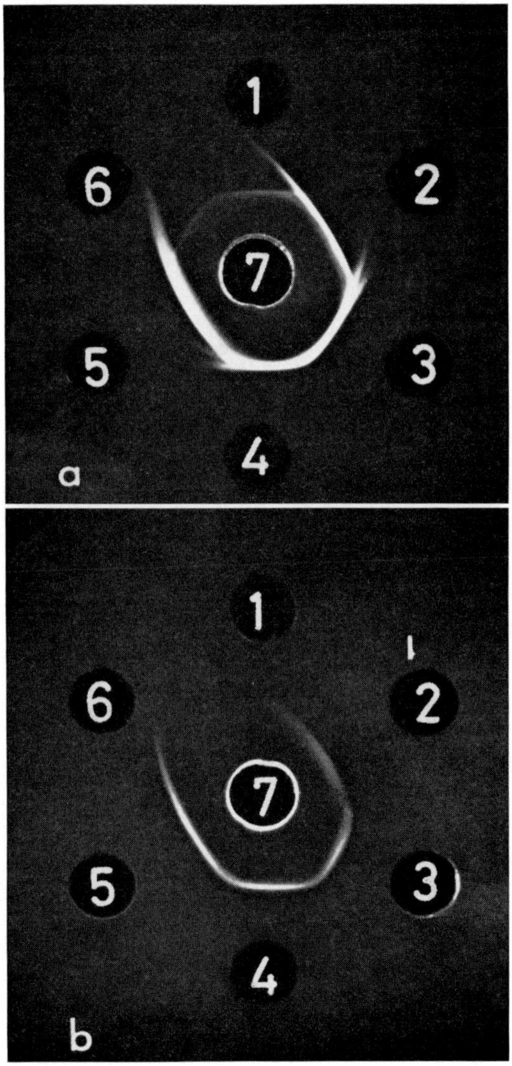

Figure 2. Gel diffusion pattern with *a*) goat antiserum against human IgG and *b*) rabbit antiserum against fragment Fc from human IgG. *1*, Fragment Fab from myeloma IgG Se; *2*, fragment Fc from myeloma IgG Se; *3*, myeloma IgG Se; *4*, myeloma IgG AL; *5*, fragment Fc from myeloma IgG AL; *6*, fragment Fab from myeloma IgG AL; *7*, antiserum. Ten microliters of a 1 mg/ml solution of each protein was applied.

DISCUSSION

It has been found that protein A can be attached to the surface of altered erythrocytes (23, 24). Live and Ranu (23) found that aldehyde-treated, tanned, and protein A-coated cells were agglutinated by normal human sera and by rabbit antisera to *S. aureus* type Cowan I. Normal rabbit sera and myeloma proteins did not react in their experiments. We have found, however, that normal human IgG and myeloma IgG as well as Fc fragments from myeloma IgG agglutinate glutaric dialdehyde-treated, protein A-coated red cells. Live and Ranu washed the cells in normal rabbit serum, which under certain conditions could produce "spontaneous agglutination." This may be an essential difference between our techniques.

Two myeloma proteins of the IgG-1 type were digested by papain and the fractions were subsequently purified on DEAE-Sephadex. The products were homogeneous as tested by agar gel diffusion and showed no cross-reactivity when tested with specific antisera. The preparations of Fab fragments completely lacked the capacity to agglutinate protein A-coated GA cells. Fc preparations, however, agglutinated these cells. In contrast to other results (23–25) our experiments clearly show that protein A is attached to aldehyde-treated cells. In this form the protein reacts both with intact myeloma IgG and with the Fc prepared from it.

We confirmed previous findings that some myeloma IgG proteins fix complement after heat denaturation whereas others do not (3–6). However, after reaction with protein A, different myeloma IgG proteins had almost identical complement-fixing properties. There was no correlation between the complement fixing properties of an IgG after heat treatment and after reaction with protein A. Differences in precipitability of IgG's by protein A were not accompanied by differences in C-fixing activity. The results indicate that the different myeloma IgG proteins used in these experiments are functionally related with respect to complement-fixing properties. As expected, the reaction product of protein A and the Fc fragment fixed complement.

Acknowledgments. The skillful technical assistance of Mrs. L. Möller and the secretarial work of Mrs. M. Gustafson are gratefully acknowledged.

REFERENCES

1. Nomenclature Committee, Bull. W.H.O., *39:* 935, 1968.
2. Ishizaka, T. and Ishizaka, K., Proc. Soc. Exp. Biol. Med., *101:* 845, 1959.
3. Frommhagen, L. H. and Fudenberg, H., J. Immun., *89:* 336, 1962.
4. Laurell, A-B. and Nilsson, U., Acta Path. Microbiol. Scand., *59:* 79, 1963.
5. Cooper, R. G., J. Lab. Clin. Med., *63:* 404, 1964.
6. Morse, J. H., J. Immun., *95:* 722, 1965.
7. Ishizaka, T., Ishizaka, K., Salmon, S. and Fudenberg, H., Fed. Proc., *25:* 489, 1966.
8. Müller-Eberhard, H. J., Adv. Immun., *8:* 1, 1968.
9. Ishizaka, K., Ishizaka, T. and Sugahara, T., J. Immun., *88:* 690, 1962.
10. Utsumi, S., Biochem. J., *112:* 343, 1969.
11. Turner, M. W., Stanworth, D. R., Normansell, D. E. and Bennich, H. H., Biochim. Biophys. Acta., *188:* 265, 1969.
12. Schur, P. H. and Becker, E. L., J. Exp. Med., *118:* 891, 1963.
13. Cerottini, J.-C. and Fitch, F., Int. Arch. Allerg., *34:* 188, 1968.
14. Forsgren, A. and Sjöquist, J., J. Immun., *97:* 822, 1966.
15. Kronvall, G. and Williams, R. C., Jr., J. Immun., *103:* 828, 1969.
16. Sjöquist, J. and Stålenheim, G., J. Immun., *103:* 467, 1969.
17. Forsgren, A. and Sjöquist, J., Acta Path. Microbiol. Scand., *75:* 466, 1969.
18. Forsgren, A., Acta Path. Microbiol. Scand., *75:* 481, 1969.
19. Sjöquist, J., Nature, *210:* 1182, 1966.
20. Porter, R. R., Biochem. J., *73:* 119, 1959.
21. Crumpton, M. J. and Wilkinson, J. M., Biochem. J., *88:* 228, 1963.
22. Ling, N. R., Brit. J. Haemat., *7:* 299, 1961.
23. Live, I. and Ranu, R. S., J. Bact., *96:* 14, 1968.
24. Löfkvist, T., Int. Arch. Allerg., *29:* 240, 1966.
25. Grov, A., Acta Path. Microbiol. Scand., *76:* 629, 1969.

THE JOURNAL OF IMMUNOLOGY
Vol. 105, No. 4, October 1970

Printed in U.S.A.

CHARACTERIZATION OF A MONOCLONAL CANINE MACROGLOBULIN

J. DONALD CAPRA AND ARTHUR I. HURVITZ

From The Rockefeller University, New York City, and The Department of Microbiology, Mount Sinai School of Medicine of The City University of New York, 10 East 102nd Street, New York, New York 10029

Received for publication April 4, 1970

A monoclonal γM immunoglobulin was isolated from the serum of a dog with a disease that resembled Waldenström's macroglobulinemia clinically and pathologically. The protein was characterized by physical, chemical and immunologic analysis. The molecular weight was 880,000, the $s^0_{20,w}$ was 17.6, and it contained 6.80% carbohydrate. The amino acid content was similar to that of rabbit γM and quite different from human γM, but the amino acid content of the canine light chains was very similar to the composition of human λ chains. Antisera prepared against human γM proteins reacted in gel diffusion studies with the canine immunoglobulin and some antisera prepared against the canine γM reacted with certain human γM preparations.

Studies with human myeloma proteins and Waldenström's macroglobulins have contributed greatly to our understanding of normal immunoglobulins and antibodies (1, 2). The examination of similar homogeneous proteins from species other than man should be productive in elucidating immunoglobulin structure in these species as well as exploring phylogenic aspects of immunoglobulins. The finding of a dog with macroglobulinemia afforded the opportunity to isolate and study a canine macroglobulin. A preliminary report of these findings has been presented elsewhere (3).

MATERIALS AND METHODS

Animal. A 10-year-old male mixed breed dog with retinopathy, anemia, hematuria, and elevated serum viscosity had a total serum protein of 11.8 g% with an abnormal β spike accounting for 7.0 g%. Neither abnormal urinary proteins nor osteolytic lesions were detected. Plasmapheresis resulted in a clinical remission. This case is similar to Waldenström's macroglobulinemia as described in man. Further clinical details as well as necropsy studies will be reported elsewhere (4).

Immunologic techniques. The γM was isolated from Le dog serum by zone electrophoresis on polyvinyl copolymer (Pevikon). Further purification was accomplished by gel filtration on Sephadex G-200 (Pharmacia, Uppsala) 270-325 mesh. γG and γM were resolved by upward flow on a 2.5-cm by 100-cm column. Microimmunoelectrophoresis was carried out as described by Scheidegger. Antisera to the Le dog γM and to the heavy and light chains were prepared in rabbits by giving multiple subcutaneous injections of 2 mg over a 2- to 3-month period. The anti-γM antisera were rendered individually specific by absorption with pooled normal dog serum. The various anti-human γM and anti-human μ chain sera were similarly prepared and had been used in this laboratory for several months prior to this study.

Ultracentrifugation. All studies were performed on a Spinco model E analytical ultracentrifuge equipped with schlieren optics. Twelve-millimeter double sector cells were run at 20°C and 56,640 rpm. Plate measurements were made according to procedures described by Trautman (5). A partial specific volume of 0.72 was assumed in correcting the sedimentation coefficients to $s^0_{20,w}$. Studies were performed on whole sera diluted 1:1 with phosphate-buffered saline, pH 7.2 (PBS). The isolated γM protein was studied in PBS as well as pH 4.0 acetate buffer, 0.1 M. Studies on γMs were performed after dialyzing the γM into pH 8.2 Tris buffer, 0.5 M, made 0.2 M in β-mercaptoethanol. Sedimentation constants at infinite dilution were derived from plots of $s_{20,w}$ *vs* concentration.

Molecular weights were determined by the method of Kegeles and Sia (6) using the field relaxation procedure. Fluorochemical Fc 43 (Beck-

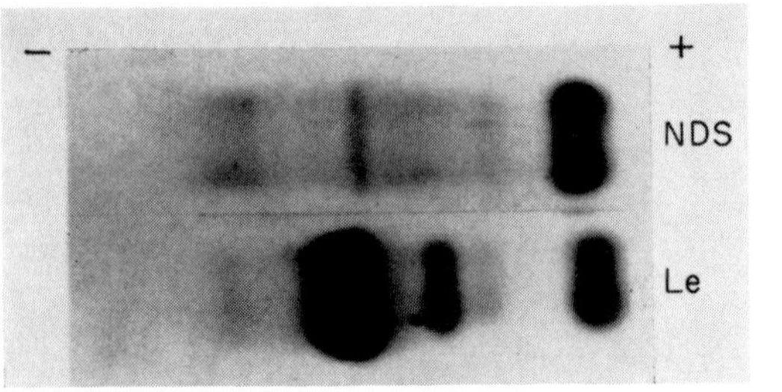

Figure 1. Cellulose acetate electrophoresis of Le dog serum with normal dog serum for comparison.

man/Spinco Division, Palo Alto, Calif.) was used in a capillary synthetic boundary cell. Molecular weights were determined in pH 7.2 PBS as well as 0.1 M acetate buffer, pH 4.0. The method of calculation has been described (7).

Viscosity studies. All solutions introduced into the viscometers were repeatedly filtered through a Millipore filter pad. The density of the solutions was measured with a 5-ml capillary vent pyknometer. Procedures for determining the relative viscosity as well as the intrinsic viscosity have been described (7).

Chemical studies. Amino acid analyses were performed according to the method of Spackman, Stein and Moore (8) using a Spinco model 121 amino acid analyzer on samples of protein hydrolyzed in 6 N HCl at 110°C for 20 hr in evacuated, sealed Pyrex tubes. Completely reduced and alkylated samples as well as performic acid-oxidized samples were run in duplicate. N-terminal amino acids were determined by the dansyl technique (9). Sialic acid was determined by the method of Aminoff (10), neutral sugars by the gas-liquid chromatographic method of Lehnhardt and Winzler (11), and hexosamines by amino acid analyzer.

RESULTS

Immunologic studies. Figure 1 depicts the cellulose acetate electrophoresis of Le dog serum with normal dog serum shown for comparison. A very large band in the β region and a faster less prominent α-2 band is seen. Albumin and γ globulin appear diminished. The β peak was isolated by zone electrophoresis and purified by gel filtration and it corresponded to the large β peak on cellulose acetate electrophoresis.

Immunoelectrophoresis of Le dog serum is shown in Figure 2. The antisera used were made against human immunoglobulins and were rendered class specific by appropriate absorption. The only precipitin line noted is against the anti-human γM and corresponds to the β peak on cellulose acetate electrophoresis. Under identical conditions normal dog serum gives precipitin arcs on immunoelectrophoresis against anti-human γG but not against the anti-human γM used here, indicating that in Le serum there is less γG than in normal dog serum. Immunoelectrophoresis with antiserum made against Le light chains, as well as against a canine Bence Jones protein (to be reported separately), identified the α-2 band on cellulose acetate electrophoresis as serum Bence Jones protein. Free light chains were not detected in the urine.

The shared antigenicity of the Le canine γM and human γM was studied with several antisera made against human γM proteins. Figure 3 shows that human γM spurs over Le dog γM using anti-human γM antisera. This was seen with all of nine antisera made against human macroglobulins. The converse experiment with anti-pooled dog γM antisera showed Le γM spurring over human γM.

Figure 4 shows the patterns of reactivity of

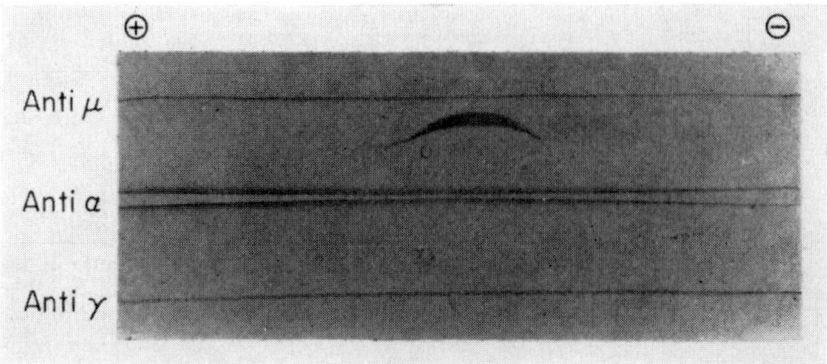

Figure 2. Immunoelectrophoresis of Le dog serum. Antisera were made against whole human immunoglobulins and were absorbed to render them class specific.

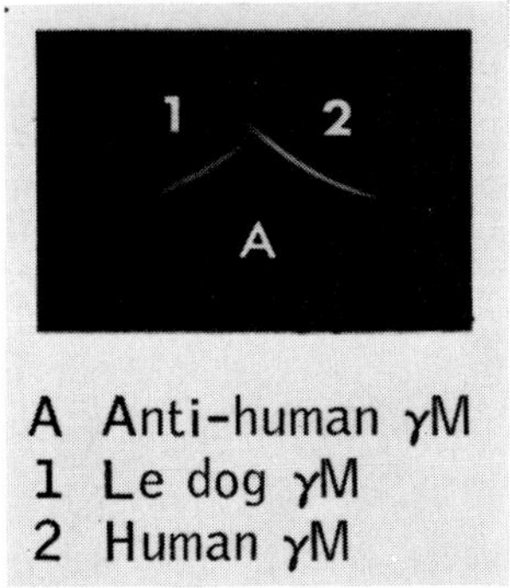

Figure 3. Gel diffusion study showing the relationship between Le γM (*1*) and human γM (*2*) with anti-human γM (*A*).

Le γMs with various anti-human γM antisera. Five antisera showed the pattern in Figure 4*A* with Le γMs not precipitating with anti-human γM antisera, but inhibiting the precipitation of Le γM as well as human γMs. Two antisera showed the pattern in Figure 4*B* with Le γMs not precipitating with anti-human antisera, inhibiting Le γM precipitation, but not appreciably inhibiting precipitation with human γMs. Two anti-human γM antisera did precipitate Le γMs, although human γMs spurs over Le γMs as shown in Figure 4*C*. Three antisera prepared against human μ chains did not react in agar gel precipitation tests with either Le γM or Le γMs.

Three antisera prepared against Le dog γM when absorbed with pooled normal dog serum still reacted with Le γM but not with γM prepared from pooled dog serum, thereby indicating individual antigenic specificity. Two of these antisera reacted in gel diffusion experiments with all of nine human γM λ proteins and all of five γM κ proteins.

Physical studies. Analytical ultracentrifugation of whole serum diluted with an equal volume of phosphate-buffered saline is shown in Figure 5. A homogeneous peak is seen in the 19S region as well as a small peak at 28S. The isolated and purified Le γM was studied at concentrations from 1.7 mg/ml to 20 mg/ml and an S *vs* C plot was constructed. The $s^0_{20,w}$ was 17.6. γMs was prepared by dialyzing Le γM at 20 mg/ml into 0.5 M Tris, pH 8.2, made 0.2 M in β-mercaptoethanol. By subsequent dilution with this same buffer γMs was analyzed at several concentrations and the $s^0_{20,w}$ was found to be 6.7.

The molecular weight of the Le γM protein was determined by two methods. By the Svedberg equation from the above data a molecular weight of 862,000 was obtained. By the field relaxation procedure of Kegeles and Sia (6) a value of 877,000 was found. By sodium dodecyl sulfate acrylamide gel electrophoresis the Le μ chain had a molecular weight of 65,000 and the Le light chain had a molecular weight of 24,200.

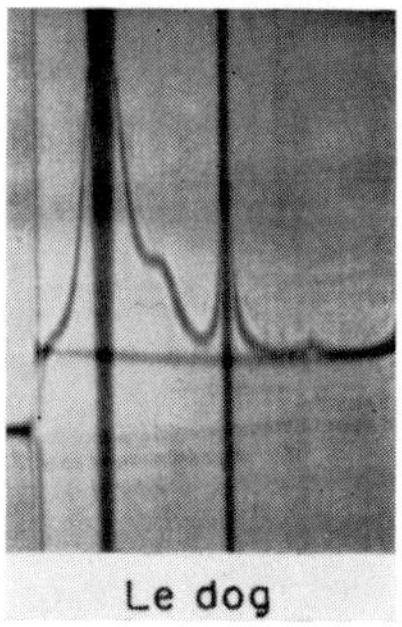

Figure 5. Analytical ultracentrifugation of Le dog serum diluted 1:1 with phosphate-buffered saline. Sedimentation is left to right. Photograph taken 24 min after reaching two-thirds maximum speed of 56,640 rpm.

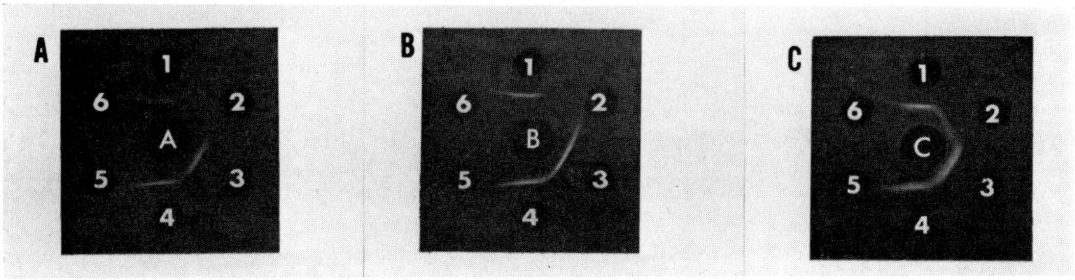

Figure 4. Gel diffusion study showing the relationship between Le γM (*well 1*), Le γMs (*well 2*), human γMs (*well 3*), human γM (*well 4*), and saline (*wells 5 and 6*). *A*, anti-human γM R-15; *B*, anti-human γM R-120; *C*, anti-human γM R-14.

TABLE I

Amino acid content of various γM globulins

	Human[a] γM	Rabbit[b] γM	Le Dog γM
Lysine	360	261	344
Histidine	124	114	148
Arginine	308	207	197
Aspartic acid	610	503	525
Threonine	678	660	558
Serine	912	737	763
Glutamic acid	752	611	680
Proline	468	437	484
Glycine	476	520	476
Alanine	363	429	402
Half cystine	136	105	98
Valine	592	579	541
Methionine	67	83	82
Isoleucine	222	221	238
Leucine	523	471	476
Tyrosine	245	210	238
Phenylalanine	280	245	238
Tryptophan	158		141
Total	7274	6393	6661

[a] Average of three human γM globulins, from Suzuki and Deutsch (24).

[b] Pooled rabbit γM, from Dalen, Seijen and Gruber (28).

In the analytical ultracentrifuge there was no significant reduction in the molecular weight of the whole γM when it was determined in pH 4.0 acetate buffer, nor did 6 M urea significantly alter the S value.

The relative viscosity of the initial serum was 7.7 at 20°C. The isolated purified Le γM was studied at several concentrations and the intrinsic viscosity was determined by extrapolation to 0.155 dl g^{-1}.

Chemical analysis. The amino acid analysis of Le γM is shown in Table I. The data from the literature of human and rabbit γM have been converted to residues/mol in order to make them comparable, and they are depicted on a bar histogram in Figure 6. Figure 6, *A* and *B*, demonstrates the marked differences between rabbit, canine and human γM, and Figure 6*C* shows that excepting lysine and histidine, canine and rabbit γM are rather similar in amino acid composition.

The amino acid analysis of the isolated Le μ chains and light chains is shown in Table II. As can be seen, the human model of 10 heavy and 10 light chains appears to best fit the Le dog γM data as there is good correlation between the content of each residue in the light and heavy chains multiplied by 10 and the analysis of the total protein. Table III shows a comparison of the Le μ chains and the average of three human μ chains as well as Le light chains and the average of four human λ chains. Lambda chains were chosen because canine light chains are blocked at the N terminus and they are thus presumed to be more closely related to the human λ chain. The comparison is shown graphically in Figure 6, *D* and *E*. The similarity of Le light chains and human λ chains stands in contrast to the marked differences apparent between the Le μ chains and human μ chains. Virtually all the differences between human and Le γM (see Fig. 6*B*) are explained by differences in their respective heavy chains.

N-terminal amino acids on both Le heavy and light chains were undetectable. Thus, presumably, they are pyrrolidone carboxylic acid as in most human μ and λ chains. Carbohydrate analysis was performed on the whole molecule as well as the separate chains. None was detected on the light chains but the whole molecule contained 6.80% carbohydrate with 0.92% sialic acid, 2.10% N-acetylglucosamine, 0.16% fucose, 2.31% mannose and 1.31% galactose. The total nitrogen content was 14.4%.

DISCUSSION

Immunoglobulins with molecular weights of 1 million were described in 1937 by Heidelberger and Pedersen (12) and their relationship to the 7S γ globulins has been clarified in recent years. Studies on human myeloma proteins and 19S Waldenström macroglobulins have greatly expanded our knowledge of normal γ globulins. To date, except for man, only the mouse has been known to spontaneously develop monoclonal γM proteins (13, 14), and while virtually every vertebrate species studied has γM immunoglobulins, structural studies in most species have been hampered by the lack of homogeneous proteins. While myeloma is not a rare disease among dogs, only a few canine homogeneous immunoglobulins have been studied. The one well studied example is a polymeric γA myeloma first described by Medway *et al.* (15) and later studied by Rockey and Schwartzman (16). This protein apparently existed wholly as a dimer with a S

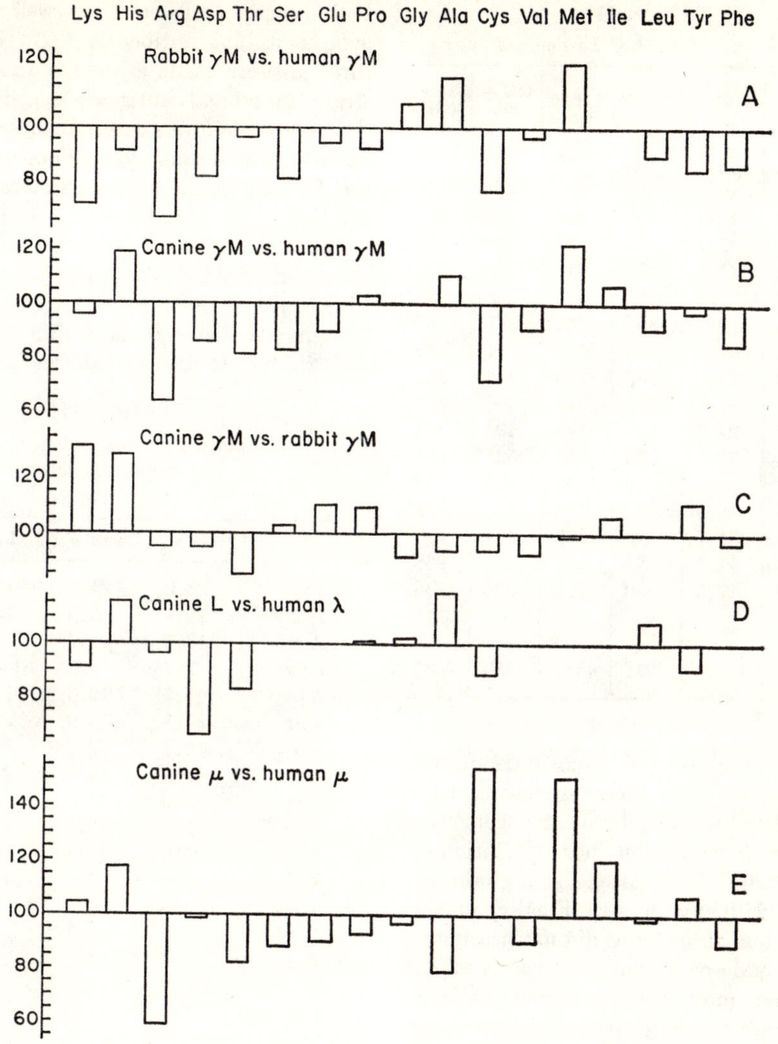

Figure 6. Bar histogram comparing the amino acid content of various γM, light and μ chains

rate of 9.8, which became 6.8 on reduction. Recently Vaerman and Heremans (17) have shown that all normal canine serum γA exists as a dimer which is converted to the monomer by reduction. Several studies suggest that canine light chains closely resemble human λ chains. The N-terminal amino acid is blocked and is presumed to be pyrrolidone carboxylic acid.

Patterson, Roberts and Pruzansky (18) and Johnson, Vaughan and Swisher (19) have elucidated from four to six classes of canine immunoglobulins and the latter group has identified antibodies in all classes. Canine γM is presumed to be a 19S immunoglobulin, but it has been thought to be antigenically less related to human γM than canine γA is to human γA. In double diffusion studies Vaerman and Heremans (20) found that only 4 of 30 antisera prepared against human γM would precipitate with canine γM while 13 of 17 antisera prepared against human γA reacted with canine γA. However, all of the antisera to human γM employed in our study showed varying degrees of cross-reactivity with the canine macroglobulin. The pattern of reactivity of the canine γMs (Fig. 4) with anti-human γM suggests that the major shared determinants are involved in the arrangement of the subunits and are therefore conformational.

TABLE II

Amino acid content of Le dog γM

	L	H	L × 10	H × 10	10H + 10L	Total Protein
Lys	10.0	25.0	100	250	350	344
His	3.7	10.6	37	106	143	148
Arg	5.0	13.5	50	135	185	197
Cys	3.3	7.7	33	77	110	98
Asp	12.2	41.7	122	417	539	525
Thr	20.5	37.1	205	371	576	558
Ser	30.6	46.2	306	462	768	763
Glu	21.8	44.3	218	443	661	680
Pro	15.9	29.0	159	290	449	484
Gly	18.1	31.5	181	315	496	476
Ala	16.3	24.0	163	240	403	402
Val	16.8	35.3	168	353	521	541
Met	0	6.5	0	65	65	82
Ile	5.5	18.8	55	188	243	238
Leu	14.7	34.7	147	347	494	476
Tyr	8.4	14.7	84	147	231	238
Phe	5.0	17.5	50	175	225	238
Try						141
	207.8	438.1	2078	4381	6459	6661

However, the reactivity of some antisera with the γMs suggests that there are some determinants unrelated to the subunit arrangement as well. Neither precipitation nor inhibition of precipitation with the isolated Le μ chain was demonstrated with any antisera. Finally, antisera made against human μ chains did not precipitate with Le γM, γMs or μ chains. It was therefore concluded that most of the shared antigenic determinants are related to polymeric specificity.

In humans with multiple myeloma or macroglobulinemia it is not difficult to show that the protein product that appears in the serum is homogeneous. These proteins are of a single class and light chain type and a single light chain subgroup. They contain certain genetic markers to the exclusion of others. However, the proof of monocolonality in the dog is less definitive for as yet no subclasses of canine γM have been described, nor are there any genetic markers in the dog. Also, the λ class of light chains is predominant in the dog (21). Therefore to prove that this protein is monoclonal one has to show a single amino acid residue at each position (these studies are in progress). However, individual antigenic specificity has been demonstrated for all myeloma and macroglobulins of both human and mouse as well as for homogeneous rabbit antibodies (22). The fact that three antisera made against the Le γM demonstrate individual antigenic specificity suggests that the protein has determinants which are not shared in the normal dog pool of γ globulins and the Le γM is therefore considered monoclonal pending sequence analysis.

Physical studies on canine γM and human γM are summarized in Table IV. By several criteria canine γM appears to be slightly smaller than human γM although it is difficult to compare data from different laboratories in this instance.

TABLE III

Amino acid composition of canine and human heavy and light chains

	Le μ	Human μ(1)	Le L	Human λ(2)
Lys	25.0	24.0	10.0	11.0
His	10.6	9.0	3.7	3.2
Arg	13.5	22.7	5.0	5.2
Cys	7.7	5.0	3.3	5.0
Asp	41.7	42.0	12.2	14.7
Thr	37.1	45.0	20.5	20.5
Ser	46.2	52.0	30.6	30.5
Glu	44.3	49.0	21.8	21.5
Pro	29.0	31.0	15.9	15.5
Gly	31.5	32.3	18.1	15.2
Ala	24.0	30.3	16.3	18.2
Val	35.3	39.3	16.8	16.9
Met	6.5	4.3	0	0
Ile	18.8	15.7	5.5	5.5
Leu	34.7	35.3	14.7	13.7
Tyr	14.7	13.7	8.4	9.2
Phe	17.5	19.3	5.0	5.0
Try				3.5
	438.1	469.8	207.8	214.1

TABLE IV

Physical properties of canine and human γM

	Molecular Weight	$S^0_{20,w} \times 10^{13}$	(η) dl/g
Le canine γM	882,000[a] 877,000[b]	17.6	0.155
Le canine γMs	175,000[a]	6.7	0.071
Human γM[c]	890,000[a]	17.9	0.162
Human γMs[c]	185,000[a]	7.07	0.080

[a] Svedberg equation.
[b] Field relaxation.
[c] Miller and Metzger (23).

Our average molecular weight (879,000) is 2% below the value of Miller and Metzger (23). This lower molecular weight is reflected in the lower $s^0_{20,w}$ (17.6 *vs* 17.9) for the γM and the lower $s^0_{20,w}$ for the γMs (6.7 *vs* 7.07). Finally, the amino acid analysis reveals a protein smaller by 8% than the average of three human γM proteins of Suzuki and Deutsch (24). The similar intrinsic viscosity values further suggest similar tertiary conformation.

Studies on the amino acid content of Le dog γM and its heavy and light chains reveal that the content of the light chain is remarkably similar to the human λ chain. This similarity between the amino acid content of canine λ chains and human λ chains is not wholly unexpected as the mouse κ chain sequence is quite homologous to the human κ chain. In fact, the mouse κ chain sequence is more homologous to the human κ chain sequence than the human κ chain is to the human λ chain (21). Thus, the variable regions of human κ and λ chains have about a 50% sequence difference with three to five gaps and the constant regions a 60% sequence difference with two to four gaps. On the other hand, mouse κ and human κ variable regions differ by only 36% to 42% and their respective constant regions by only 41% without any gaps (25). Thus, the more stable evolutionary pattern of the canine and human λ chain is consistent with previous data. Sequence studies are under way at present to document more fully these presumed homologies.

The major amino acid content differences between human and canine γM seem to be related to their respective heavy chains. The canine μ chains have over 50% more cystine and methionine and 20% more histidine and isoleucine, but 40% less arginine and 20% less threonine and alanine than its human counterpart. Our comparative data are not wholly internally consistent because the amino acid content of the γM proteins reported by Suzuki and Deutsch (24) is not corrected for light chain type (not specified), while the human λ chain comparative data were generated from four human λ chains that have been sequenced (26). However, even with these reservations, the comparisons point out the relative similarities of the light chains *vs* the relative dissimilarities of the heavy chains.

Our data are most consistent with a model of γM with 10 heavy chains and 10 light chains. The recently suggested model of human γM consisting of 10 heavy and 15 light chains (24) would not be consistent with these data.

The N-terminal amino acids were unavailable for dansylation and even 50 mg of purified heavy and light chains did not reveal significant amounts of N-terminal amino acid, indicating that as in the human the N terminus of both chains may be blocked, presumably by cyclized glutamic acid.

Carbohydrate analysis revealed somewhat less carbohydrate than has generally been reported for human macroglobulins. However, the report of Davie and Osterland (27) divided the human γM proteins into two groups on the basis of their carbohydrate content. Their group I contained an average of 10.69 ± 1.49% carbohydrate and their group II 7.71 ± 0.65%. Le canine γM would therefore more closely resemble their group II proteins.

The delineation of a monoclonal macroglobulin in the dog as well as our recent finding of several more dogs with myeloma present an opportunity to do further structural studies on these proteins. Questions such as the variability of λ chains in another species, studies on the constant regions as an independent elucidation of κ/λ evolutionary divergence as well as the study of an additional species for species-specific residues should prove of interest and such sequence studies are now in progress.

Acknowledgments. It is a pleasure to acknowledge the excellent technical assistance of Vicki Ecker and Bonnie Gerber. One of us (J.D.C.) would like to thank Dr. Henry Kunkel in whose laboratory most of this work was done. Dr. John Gregory assisted in the carbohydrate analysis and we are grateful for his help.

REFERENCES

1. Grey, H. M. and Kunkel, H. G., J. Exp. Med., *120:* 253, 1964.
2. Cohen, S. and Milstein, C., Advances Immun., *7:* 1, 1967.
3. Hurvitz, A. I., and Capra, J. D., Fed. Proc., *29:* 357, 1970.
4. Hurvitz, A. I., Haskins, D. and Fischer, C., J. Amer. Vet. Med. Assoc., In press.
5. Trautman, R., J. Phys. Chem., *60:* 1211, 1956.
6. Kegeles, G. and Sia, C. L., Biochemistry, *2:* 906, 1963.

7. Capra, J. D. and Kunkel, H. G., J. Clin. Invest., In press.
8. Spackman, D. H., Stein, W. H. and Moore, S., Anal. Chem., *30:* 1190, 1958.
9. Doolittle, R. F., Biochem. J., *9:* 742, 1965.
10. Aminoff, D. F., Biochem. J., *81:* 384, 1961.
11. Lehnhardt, W. F. and Winzler, R. J., J. Chromatogr., *34:* 471, 1968.
12. Heidelberger, M. and Pedersen, X. O., J. Exp. Med., *65:* 393, 1937.
13. Clausen, J., Rask-Nielsen, R., Christensen, H. E., Lontie, R. and Heremans, J., Proc. Soc. Exp. Biol. Med., *103:* 802, 1960.
14. McIntire, K. R., Asofsky, R. M., Potter, M. and Kuff, E. L., Science, *150:* 361, 1965.
15. Medway, W., Weber, W. T., O'Brien, J. A. and Krawitz, L. J., J. Amer. Vet. Med. Ass., *150:* 386, 1967.
16. Rockey, J. H. and Schwartzman, R. M., J. Immun., *98:* 1143, 1967.
17. Vaerman, J. and Heremans, J. F., Immunochemistry, *6:* 779, 1969.
18. Patterson, R., Roberts, M. and Pruzansky, J. J., J. Immun., *101:* 687, 1968.
19. Johnson, J. S., Vaughan, J. H. and Swisher, S. N., J. Immun., *98:* 935, 1967.
20. Vaerman, J. and Heremans, J. F., Immunochemistry, *5:* 425, 1968.
21. Hood, L., Gray, W. R., Sanders, B. G. and Dreyer, W. J., Cold Spring Harbor Symp. Quant. Biol., *32:* 133, 1967.
22. Braun, D. G. and Krause, R. M., J. Exp. Med., *128:* 969, 1968.
23. Miller, F. and Metzger, H., J. Biol. Chem., *240:* 3325, 1965.
24. Suzuki, J. and Deutsch, H. F., J. Biol. Chem., *242:* 2725, 1967.
25. Hood, L., Grant, J. A. and Sox, H. C., in Developmental Aspects of Antibody Formation and Structure, Prague, June 28, 1969, In press.
26. Edelman, G. M. and Gall, W. E., Ann. Rev. Biochem., *38:* 415, 1969.
27. Davie, J. M. and Osterland, C. K., J. Exp. Med., *128:* 699, 1968.
28. Dalen, A. V., Seijen, G. H. and Gruber, M., Biochim. Biophys. Acta, *147:* 421, 1967.

THE JOURNAL OF IMMUNOLOGY
Vol. 105, No. 4, October 1970

Printed in U.S.A.

ANTIBODY PRODUCTION BY HOST CELLS IN X-IRRADIATED RECIPIENTS OF ALLOGENEIC SPLEEN CELLS[1]

U. STORB AND R. S. WEISER

From the Departments of Microbiology and Biological Structure, School of Medicine, University of Washington, Seattle, Washington 98105

Received for publication April 1, 1970

Experiments were performed to test the hypothesis that two different cells, a radiosensitive antigen reactive cell and a radioresistant precursor of the antibody producing cell collaborate in antibody synthesis. Twenty-four hours following 500 R x-irradiation, experimental recipient group C mice were injected with normal allogeneic spleen cells and sheep red blood cells (SRBC). Control recipients of group A were irradiated similarly and injected with SRBC alone while control recipients of group B were irradiated similarly and injected simultaneously with SRBC and allogeneic spleen cells from heavily irradiated (1000 R) mice. Five to 10 days after antigen injection, the numbers of plaque-forming cells (PFC) of donor and host origin were determined in the spleens of the three groups. The contribution of donor and host PFC was distinguished by the use of anti-histocompatibility sera. On day 5, the spleens of mice in group C contained 26 times as many PFC as did the spleens of mice in group A. Of these, 80% were donor cells and 20% were of host type. Thus more than five times as many host PFC developed in group C than in group A. At least some of the stimulatory effect on host PFC was independent of the normal donor spleen cells because the spleens of control group B contained twice as many PFC as did those of control group A. On days 6 and 7, the PFC in group C decreased, while those in control group A increased, possibly due to alloimmune reactions between donor graft and recipient. The injection of antidonor H-2 serum into group C on day 3 suppressed the development of PFC of both donor and recipient type. Evidently survival of donor cells beyond day 3 was necessary for the enhanced recipient PFC response. It is concluded that existing data establish the importance of cell interactions in the immune response but do not prove the existence of an antigen-sensitive cell capable of transmitting antigen-specific information to the precursor of the antibody-producing cell.

It has been shown that the antibody response involves two phases: a radiosensitive induction phase and a radioresistant production phase (1). One reason for this dichotomy may be the participation of two different cell types in the antibody response (2, 3) with different functions and radiosensitivities. Support for a cellular separation of the functions of antigen recognition and antibody synthesis has been published recently (4). According to this two-cell hypothesis antigen-reactive cells (ARC) and antibody-forming cell precursors (AFCP) are different and must interact to stimulate antibody synthesis.

[1] This work was supported by Graduate Research Training Grant CA 05040 from the National Cancer Institute, National Institutes of Health, United States Public Health Service.

The present experiments were designed to test the hypothesis that radiosensitive ARC trigger radioresistant AFCP to form antibody. The immune response to sheep red blood cells (SRBC) in sublethally x-irradiated mice (500 R) infused with nonimmune allogeneic spleen cells was studied; irradiated control mice received SRBC alone. The donor and host cells were distinguished by the use of antisera specific for histocompatibility antigens. It was expected, if the two-cell hypothesis of antibody formation is correct and if ARC are more radiosensitive than AFCP, that surviving AFCP in the irradiated host would be stimulated by the ARC in the transfused spleen cells and lead to a response in which the number of plaque-forming cells (PFC) of host type would exceed PFC in control animals.

MATERIALS AND METHODS

Unless otherwise specified the following materials and methods were used.

Animals. Three- to 6-month-old male and female mice of the C57BL/Ks strain served as recipients and spleens were obtained from inbred A/Jax donor mice.

Experimental design. Mice of the C57BL/Ks strain were irradiated with 500 R x-ray. Twenty-four hours after irradiation animals in the experimental group were given an intravenous (i.v.) dose of 4×10^7 A/Jax spleen cells from mice of the same sex together with an i.v. injection of 0.1 ml of a 30% suspension of thrice-washed SRBC in physiologic saline containing M/100 Sorensen's phosphate buffer, pH 7.2 (PBS). Two groups of irradiated control mice were injected with SRBC and Hanks' balanced salt solution (HBSS) or with SRBC and 4×10^7 spleen cells from A/Jax mice given 1000 R 4 hr before spleen removal. The spleen cells from the two sources at the time they were injected were equally viable. The mice were bled and killed 5 to 10 days after injecting SRBC, i.e., 6 to 11 days after irradiation, and their spleens were removed aseptically. The following procedures were carried out: 1) the mice were weighed after x-irradiation and immediately before death, 2) the spleen weights and/or the total number of spleen cells were determined, 3) PFC were measured using a modification of the direct Jerne plaque test, 4) the spleens were assayed for total numbers of direct PFC of donor and recipient types by treating the cells with appropriate alloimmune sera (see below) and guinea pig complement, and 5) serum hemagglutinins were determined.

Irradiation of mice. Mice received whole body irradiation with a General Electric Maxitron x-ray machine under the following conditions: 200 Kv, 30 ma; 60 R/min dose rate at 70 cm distance with 0.25 mm Cu plus 1.0 mm Al filters. The animals were kept in a circular Plexiglas container during irradiation.

Preparation of donor spleen cells. Single cell suspensions (6) were prepared aseptically from the spleens of several A/Jax mice, and, after washing twice in HBSS, were suspended in HBSS to yield 10^8 cells per milliliter.

Preparation of cytotoxic alloimmune sera and ascites. Alloimmune sera were obtained as follows. Mice of the A/Jax strain were injected i.p. once a week with a suspension of twice-washed C57BL/Ks cells equivalent to one-quarter of a spleen, one-quarter of the thymus gland and one-half of a lymph node. Ten days after the 10th injection, the mice were bled; sera from a pool of these mice, when tested with C57BL/Ks erythrocytes, gave hemagglutinin titers averaging 1:500.

Anti-A/Jax alloantibodies were obtained in the ascites of C57BL/Ks mice, as described by Munoz (7). Mice of the C57BL/Ks strain were injected at weekly intervals for 4 weeks with 0.1 to 0.2 ml of fresh sarcoma I ascites, removed from an A/Jax mouse 6 days after i.p. inoculation with tumor, and thereafter at weekly intervals with 0.1 ml of a 1:1 emulsion of 12 times freeze-thawed sarcoma I ascites and Freund's complete adjuvant. Ascites first appeared at about 6 weeks. After 8 weeks ascitic fluid was withdrawn every 8 to 10 days; the mice were rechallenged each time with frozen-thawed tumor cells immediately after withdrawing the fluid. Fibrin was spooled from the clotted fluid with a capillary pipette; the fluid from individual samples was cleared by centrifugation and tested for hemagglutinins with A/Jax erythrocytes. Ascitic fluids with titers ranging from 1:256 to 1:4000 were obtained, and those with titers of 1:1000 and higher were pooled.

Alloimmune serum or ascitic fluid pools were heat inactivated (30 min at 56°C), absorbed with SRBC and stored at −70°C in small samples.

Determination of the cytotoxicity and specificity of alloimmune sera and ascitic fluid. The toxicity of the alloimmune sera (or ascitic fluid) for A/Jax and for C57BL/Ks spleen cells was tested in the presence of guinea pig complement.

Equal volumes of diluted alloimmune serum plus fresh guinea pig serum diluted 1:4 and a suspension of spleen cells containing 2 to 5×10^6 cells/ml were mixed and kept at 37°C for 1 hr. The percentages of damaged cells were then determined using the dye exclusion test with 0.1% trypan blue. The cytotoxicity of each serum was specific for normal spleen cells (Table I) and was concentration-dependent (not shown). Table I (columns (6) and (7) also shows that the percentage of cells of each strain in a mixture of A/Jax and C57BL/Ks spleen cells can be determined with reasonable accuracy. Similar results were obtained using immune spleen cells or peritoneal exudate cells from mice of the two strains.

TABLE I

Specificity of alloimmune sera for A/Jax and C57BL/Ks spleen cells

Cells	% of Nonviable Cells after Treatment with				Validity of Method for Determining Cell Origin: % A/Jax cells	
	Anti-A/Jax serum + C	Anti-C57BL/Ks serum + C	Anti-A/Jax serum + anti-C57BL/Ks serum + C	C control	Known	Calculated[a]
(a) A/Jax	100	1	ND[b]	9	100	100
(b) C57BL/Ks	5	96	ND	8	0	0
(c) A/Jax + C57BL/Ks	14	77	ND	7	19	9
(d) A/Jax + C57BL/Ks	41	52	95	3	41	44
(e) A/Jax + C57BL/Ks	53	27	ND	6	68	69

[a] $$\text{\% A/Jax cells} = \frac{(\text{\% nonviable cells with anti-A/Jax serum} + \text{C}) - (\text{\% nonviable cells with C})}{[(\text{\% nonviable cells with anti-A/Jax serum} + \text{C}) - (\text{\% nonviable cells with C})] + [(\text{\% nonviable cells with anti-C57BL/Ks serum} + \text{C}) - (\text{\% nonviable cells with C})]}$$

Example (e): $$\text{\% A/Jax cells} = \frac{53 - 6}{(53 - 6) + (27 - 6)} = 69.$$

[b] ND, not done.

TABLE II

The reliability of treatment with allo-antisera for identifying the histocompatibility types of PFC

Spleen Cell Suspension Containing PFC	PFC[a] after Treatment of Cell Suspension with:						
	Nothing	Anti-A/Jax serum 1:32	Anti-A/Jax serum 1:64	Anti C57BL/Ks serum 1:10	Anti C57BL/Ks serum 1:20	Normal Serum 1:10	Normal Serum 1:20
A/Jax	46	4	3	27	27	22	30
C57BL/Ks	187	93	69	1	2	59	68
A/Jax + C57BL/Ks	110	51	40	15	12	66	44
	(117)[b]	(49)	(36)	(14)	(15)	(41)	(49)

[a] Two plates contained either 2×10^5 A/Jax or C57BL/Ks cells or a mixture of 1×10^5 A/Jax and 1×10^5 C57BL/Ks spleen cells obtained 5 days after i.p. injection of 0.2 ml 30% SRBC.

[b] The numbers in parentheses designate the numbers of PFC expected in the respective mixtures of A/Jax and C57BL/Ks spleen cells.

Use of specific alloimmune sera or ascitic fluid for identifying donor and recipient antibody-producing cells. A modification of the method of Harris *et al.* (8) was used to identify donor and recipient antibody-producing cells in the Jerne test. A suspension of spleen cells in HBSS containing 2×10^6 cells/ml was mixed with an equal volume of fresh guinea pig serum diluted 1:4 in PBS and an equal volume of alloimmune serum or ascitic fluid diluted in HBSS. Control mixtures consisted of complement-containing cell suspensions mixed with an equal volume of a mixture of diluted normal A/Jax and C57BL/Ks serum. The mixtures were incubated at 37°C and carefully shaken every 10 min. After 1 hr the cells were centrifuged at $200 \times$ G for 5 min and resuspended in 0.2 ml of HBSS. To each tube was added 1.8 ml of a warm (45°C) mixture consisting of one part Difco Noble agar (1.4% in HBSS), one part of medium 199 containing 1 mg DEAE dextran/ml, and one-tenth part 10% (v/v) SRBC in PBS. The mixture was poured rapidly into 100- x 15-mm plastic Petri plates (Falcon Plastics, Inc., Oxnard, Calif.) containing a solidified bottom layer of 1.4% agar in HBSS. The plates were incubated at 37°C for 90 min, flooded with 2 ml of guinea pig serum diluted 1:8, and reincubated for another hour. Plaques were counted under a dissecting microscope.

Table II shows the number of plaques obtained after treatment with various sera. The antisera specifically suppressed plaque formation by PFC of the respective phenotypes. In a mixture of immune A/Jax and C57BL/Ks cells treated with either of the two alloimmune sera approximately the expected number of cells was inhibited.

Incubation with normal serum or with non-specific alloimmune serum always depressed the number of PFC substantially as compared with untreated samples. However, the nonspecific effects of the two alloimmune sera were similar (Table II). Therefore, in order to estimate the absolute number of PFC of donor origin and of host origin in a chimera, the percentage of PFC of each type (as determined with the two respective alloimmune sera) was simply related to the total number of PFC developing without any treatment. For example, the number of donor cells in a C57BL/Ks recipient of A/Jax cells was determined as follows:

No. A/Jax PFC/spleen

$$= \frac{(\text{No. PFC after anti-C57BL/Ks serum}) \times (\text{PFC/spleen (untreated)})}{(\text{No. of PFC after anti-C57BL/Ks serum}) + (\text{No. of PFC after anti-A/Jax serum})}.$$

Thus, the number of A/Jax PFC in the mixture of 10^5 C57BL/Ks and 10^5 A/Jax spleen cells in Table II = $(15 \times 110)/(15 + 51) = 25$. This number is reasonably close to the known input of 23 A/Jax PFC.

Since the action of the antisera was concentration-dependent (unpublished data), the following conditions were used throughout the experiments. The anti-A/Jax, anti-C57BL/Ks, and normal sera were diluted 1:32, 1:10 and 1:15, respectively. A control preparation of cells treated with both anti-A/Jax serum 1:32 and anti-C57BL/Ks serum 1:10 was included and usually yielded no PFC.

The data were analyzed statistically using the Student *t* test (9).

RESULTS

Various responses are compared in table III for three groups of C57BL/Ks mice. Mice of experimental group C were injected intravenously with SRBC and normal allogeneic spleen cells from A/Jax mice 24 hr after they had been irradiated with 500 R. Mice of control group A were similarly irradiated and injected with SRBC alone. Mice of control group B were similarly irradiated and injected with SRBC; in addition they received allogeneic spleen cells harvested from A/Jax mice 4 hr after x-irradiation with 1000 R. The results are shown in Table III. In control group A on day 5, the PFC/spleen averaged 25 while the total number of spleen cells averaged 10.2×10^6. In contrast, in experimental group C on day 5, the PFC of recipient origin averaged 136 while the total number of spleen cells averaged 23×10^6. Thus, experimental group C showed a statistically significant stimulatory effect on day 5 in that there were about 5.5 times more recipient PFC and about 2.3 times more total spleen cells than in control group A. In addition, in experimental group C on day 5, there were 506 PFC of host origin; these PFC and PFC noted on days 6 and 7 were not included in obtaining the values for p as compared to controls that had no donor response.

On succeeding days, however, the PFC/spleen and the body weight index decreased in group C, whereas they increased in group A. This decrease in the anti-SRBC response of experimental group C may have been due to the onset of a graft-*vs*-host and/or a host-*vs*-graft reaction. This idea is supported by the decrease in body weights of mice of experimental group C (Table III), whereas the weights of control mice remained essentially unchanged. The behavior of serum hemagglutinins in the experimental group also supports the concept that the anti-SRBC response is inhibited by an allogeneic reaction in group C. Thus, serum hemagglutinins showed a mean peak of 57 on day 6 and then declined while titers in control group A were markedly lower and reached a delayed peak on day 8.

The finding that at 5 days experimental group C mice produced more PFC of recipient origin than did control group A mice required elaboration. The following two alternative possibilities were considered: 1) that donor cells undergoing an anti-SRBC response provided surviving lymphoid cells of the irradiated recipient with specific information; and 2) that donor cells provided nonspecific factors such as nucleotides, which served to stimulate recipient cells to form antibody.

To test the second possibility, we used spleen cells from A/Jax mice given 1000 R 4 hr before spleen removal as a source of nonspecific factors. As shown in Table III, control group B yielded more than twice as many total spleen cells and PFC/spleen as did control group A. Moreover the PFC were all of recipient type, and the total

TABLE III

Five responses of x-irradiated C57BL/Ks group C mice injected with SRBC and donor A/Jax spleen cells as compared to irradiated control groups A and B[a]

Group[b]	Day after Injection of SRBC: 5	6	7	8	10
1. PFC/spleen					
A	25 (20)	141 (2)	172 (9)		
B	53 (15)$^{+}$				
C:exp[c]	136 (19)$^{A++B+}$	107 (2)	19 (2)		
2. Spleen weight in mg					
A		28 (4)	40.6 (22)	52 (6)	92 (2)
B	67 (8)		73 (22)$^{++}$	74 (8)	
C:exp	67 (8)	132 (4)$^{A++}$	117 (2)$^{A++B+}$	142 (6)$^{A++B++}$	119 (2)
3. Mean body weight index, i.e., % of original weight					
A and B[d]		97.7 ± 4.3 (20)	106 ± 7.8 (14)	102 ± 2.9 (13)	102.5 ± 3.5 (2)
C:exp		96.0 ± 7.1 (14)	95 ± 8.3 (14)$^{AB+}$	92 ± 14.2 (5)	88.5 ± 2.1 (2)$^{AB+}$
4. Total cells/spleen (× 10⁶)					
A	10.2 (30)	13.0 (10)	17 (9)		
B	20.8 (15)$^{++}$				
C:exp	23.0 (19)$^{A++}$	29.3 (10)$^{A++}$	25 (9)$^{A+}$		
5. Serum agglutinin titer					
A		0 (8)	1.8 (18)	5.5 (6)	0 (2)
B			2.7 (14)	0 (8)	
C:exp		57 (14)	29 (6)	26 (6)	8 (2)

[a] Control irradiated groups A and B received no spleen cells and irradiated A/Jax spleen cells, whereas experimental group C received unirradiated A/Jax spleen cells. The numbers in parentheses designate the number of mice in the respective groups, and blank spaces indicate no data.

[b] p Values are designated by A for group C:exp *vs* group A:control and by B for group C:exp *vs* group B:control and by $^{++}$ if <0.001 and by $^{+}$ if 0.025 to 0.001. Group B *vs* group A is simply indicated by $^{++}$ or $^{+}$.

[c] The increments of PFC from donors in experimental group C on days 5, 6 and 7 were 506, 18 and 112, respectively, but these were not used to obtain p values. Numbers given represent the mean host PFC.

[d] The two sets of controls were pooled because their weight indices were similar.

cell population in the spleens was largely of recipient origin (Table IV). The number of PFC/10^6 host cells (2.5 to 3.1×10^6 cells on day 5) was similar in control groups A and B. In contrast, recipients of group C had averages of 12.9 or 29×10^6 cells on day 5. Thus despite the low numbers of total host spleen cells (Table IV), recipients of group C produced significantly more host PFC/spleen than did recipients of group B (Table III).

The stimulating effect of normal donor cells on recipient cells was shown when the recipients of group C were treated with anti-donor alloimmune serum 3 days after receiving the donor cells (Table V). In controls injected with normal C57BL/Ks serum, the number of PFC of both donor and host type was depressed to some degree even though the total number of spleen cells was increased slightly as compared with mice not receiving serum. Anti-donor alloimmune serum

TABLE IV

Donor and host cells in the spleens of irradiated C57BL/Ks mice injected with normal (group C) or x-irradiated (group B) A/Jax spleen cells[a]

Exp. No. (No. of Recipient Mice)	Cells Injected	Per-centage of Host Cells	Mean No. Donor Cells/Spleen $\times 10^{-6}$	Mean No. Host Cells/Spleen $\times 10^{-6}$	Host PFC/10^6 Host Cells
XIV (5)	Normal	7%	36.4	2.7	29
(7)	Irradiated[b]	95%	1.0	18.5	2.6
XV (7)	Normal	31%	10.5	4.8	12.9
(8)	Irradiated[b]	85%	3.3	18.5	3.1

[a] Six days after 500 R, 5 days after injection of A/Jax spleen cells and SRBC.

[b] Spleen cells obtained from A/Jax mice 4 hr post x-irradiation with 1000 R.

depressed donor PFC to 9.5% and host PFC to 43% of the values shown by controls injected with normal serum. This indicates that the survival of donor cells beyond the 3rd day was necessary for their enhancing effect on host cells.

DISCUSSION

The present experiments have shown that depressed antibody synthesis of host cells imposed by sublethal x-irradiation can be partially restored by injecting normal allogeneic spleen cells. Partial rather than complete restoration may have occurred because of histocompatibility differences between graft and host. Two findings in mice of group C, which suggest that a graft-*vs*-host reaction occurred, were lack of weight gain and a marked decrease in the number of PFC of host type/spleen after day 5 as compared to mice of control group A (Table III).

The partial restoration of the x-irradiated host's antibody response by normal spleen cells in group C may have been due to either nonspecific or specific factors supplied by donor cells. The possibility that the restoration of host cells observed was due to nonspecific rather than specific factors supplied by donor cells is suggested by the observation that heavily irradiated donor cells in group B, which failed to produce anti-SRBC antibody, stimulated antibody production by host cells, albeit less effectively than did non-irradiated donor cells in group C. Other studies have shown that various compounds such as cell breakdown products or oligoribonucleotides can partially restore immune responses impaired by x-irradiation (for a review see Braun and Firshein (10)). Irradiated thymus cells have also been noted to cause stimulation of host cells (11). Since the greater recovery accomplished with non-irradiated donor cells cannot be ascribed with certainty to either nonspecific or specific effects, our experiments do not establish the existence of a radiosensitive antigen reactive cell (ARC) and a radioresistant precursor of the antibody-producing cell (AFCP).

The importance of cell interactions in the immune response was first stressed by Claman *et al.* (12), who showed a synergism of bone

TABLE V

Effects of injecting x-irradiated C57BL/Ks recipients of allogeneic spleen cells (group C) with anti-donor alloserum[a]

Cells Injected	Serum Injected	Mean No. Cells/Spleen	PFC/Spleen		
			Total	D[b]	H[b]
Normal A/Jax Spleen	None	20.6 (3)[c]	1250	790	460
Normal A/Jax Spleen	Normal[d]	26.5 (8)	560	410	150
Normal A/Jax Spleen	Anti-H Alloserum[e]	15.0 (8)	103	39 (9.5%)[f]	64 (43%)[f]
None	None	11.4 (9)	7	0	7

[a] All mice were injected with SRBC 24 hr post irradiation and tested 5 days later.

[b] D = PFC of donor type. H = PFC of host type.

[c] In parentheses, number of mice pooled.

[d] Five-tenths milliliter of normal C57BL/Ks serum injected i.p. 3 days after spleen cell and SRBC injection.

[e] Five-tenths milliliter of C57BL/Ks anti-A/Jax alloserum injected i.p. 3 days after spleen cell and SRBC injection.

[f] The values in parentheses represent percentages of PFC counts in mice given normal serum.

marrow and thymus cells in restoring the immunocompetence of irradiated mice. Experiments by Mitchell and Miller (13) established that in this situation the bone marrow cells and not the thymus cells produce antibody. They postulated (4) that the thymus cells serve as antigen-reactive cells (ARC) and stimulate bone marrow cells (AFCP) to develop into antibody-producing cells. This hypothesis has since been tested in various systems (14–21).

The crucial questions regarding the nature of the cell interactions involved in antibody production and the cell type(s) that possess the genetic information for the antibody specificity have not been answered. Equivocal results were offered by the adoptive transfer of cells from tolerant animals. Playfair (19) found that bone marrow cells from tolerant animals and not thymus cells lacked immunocompetence, whereas Miller (20) made the opposite observation.

Mitchell and Miller (21) concluded from the following experiment that thymocytes must react with antigen before they can interact with bone marrow cells to promote an antibody response. Thymus cells mixed with SRBC were "incubated" in a heavily irradiated "intermediate host." Spleen cells from these intermediate hosts were able to restore the immunocompetence of irradiated second hosts injected with bone marrow much better than spleen cells from intermediate hosts immunized with unrelated antigens. However, in this system it was not possible to determine whether the antibody-producing cells in the secondary host were of bone marrow origin. Thus, it is possible that the PFC were derived from cells of the first host which had survived irradiation and had transformed into antigen-specific memory cells with the nonspecific support of the thymus cells.

In summary, the experimental data currently available establish the importance of cellular interactions in the antibody response. However, the question of whether the genetic information determining antibody specificity is transcribed in the antibody-producing cell or received by it from an ARC is unresolved. The effect of thymus cells in adoptive transfer experiments may be of a nonimmunologic nature, similar to the nonspecific effects observed in our experiments with irradiated allogeneic cells; or the stimulation may be similar to the enhancement of bone marrow colony growth *in vitro* by cell crowding (22). Probably it will be necessary to use more defined systems, such as *in vitro* culture (16, 23, 24), to eliminate uncontrolled interactions between cell systems *in vivo*.

REFERENCES

1. Dixon, F. J., Talmage, D. W. and Maurer, P. H., J. Immun., *68:* 693, 1952.
2. Storb, U. and Weiser, R. S., J. Reticuloendothel. Soc., *5:* 81, 1968.
3. Storb, U., Bauer, W., Storb, R., Fliedner, T. M. and Weiser, R. S., J. Immun., *102:* 1474, 1969.
4. Miller, J. F. A. P. and Mitchell, G. F., J. Exp. Med., *128:* 801, 1968.
5. Jerne, N. K. and Nordin, A. A., Science, *140:* 405, 1963.
6. Howard, J. G., Brit. J. Exp. Path., *42:* 72, 1961.
7. Munoz, J., Proc. Soc. Exp. Biol. Med., *95:* 757, 1957.
8. Harris, S., Harris, T. N. and Ogburn, C. A., J. Immun., *99:* 447, 1967.
9. Hill, A. B., Principles of Medical Statistics, 7th Ed., Oxford University Press, New York, 1961.
10. Braun, W. and Firshein, W., Bact. Rev., *31:* 83, 1967.
11. Claman, H. N., Chaperon, E. A. and Selner, J. C., Proc. Soc. Exp. Biol. Med., *128:* 462, 1969.
12. Claman, H. N., Chaperon, E. A. and Triplett, R. F., Proc. Soc. Exp. Biol. Med., *122:* 1167, 1966.
13. Mitchell, G. F. and Miller, J. F. A. P., J. Exp. Med., *128:* 821, 1968.
14. Richter, M. and Abdou, N. I., J. Exp. Med., *129:* 1261, 1969.
15. Mosier, D. E., J. Exp. Med., *129:* 351, 1969.
16. Mosier, D. E. and Coppleson, L. W., Proc. Nat. Acad. Sci., *61:* 542, 1968.
17. Abdou, N. I. and Richter, M., J. Exp. Med., *129:* 757, 1969.
18. Nossal, G. J. V., Cunningham, A., Mitchell, G. F. and Miller, J. F. A. P., J. Exp. Med., *128:* 839, 1968.
19. Playfair, J. H. L., Nature, *222:* 882, 1969.
20. Miller, J. F. A. P., Rev. Franc. Étud. Clin. Biol., *14:* 614, 1969.
21. Mitchell, G. F. and Miller, J. F. A. P., Proc. Nat. Acad. Sci., *59:* 296, 1968.
22. Metcalf, D., J. Cell Physiol., *72:* 9, 1968.
23. Mishell, R. I., Dutton, R. W. and Raidt, D. J., in *Hemic Cells in Vitro*, Edited by P. Farnes, p. 83, The Williams and Wilkins Co., Baltimore, 1969.
24. Haskill, J. S., Byrt, P. and Marbrook, J., J. Exp. Med., *131:* 57, 1970.

THE JOURNAL OF IMMUNOLOGY
Vol. 105, No. 4, October 1970

Printed in U.S.A.

THE EFFECT OF AGING ON HUMAN SERUM IMMUNOGLOBULIN CONCENTRATIONS[1]

C. E. BUCKLEY, III AND F. C. DORSEY

From the Allergy and Clinical Immunology Division, Department of Medicine and the Biostatistics Division, Department of Community Health Sciences, and the Center for the Study of Aging, Duke University Medical Center, Durham, North Carolina

Received for publication March 30, 1970

Single radial diffusion was used to measure the concentration of IgG, IgA and IgM in sera of 811 healthy individuals aged from birth to 92 years. Evaluation of age, race and sex differences was accomplished by multivariate analysis on $\log_e$ transformed data using age as a linear covariate for each race-sex group within the 0 to 13, 14 to 27, 28 to 54 and 55 to 92 year age spans. Age contrasts between all groups were highly significant ($p < 0.0001$), while race and sex contrasts within all groups revealed only a significant difference in IgG related to race ($p < 0.0133$). Maximum serum immunoglobulin concentrations were reached in the third decade. Highly significant changes related to aging occur in older individuals as well as early in life. Average IgM concentrations decreased significantly by the sixth decade ($p < 0.0005$). Average IgG decreased significantly from the third through the sixth decade ($p < 0.0027$). Changes in serum IgA after maturity were small and not significant. These observations document the occurrence of a relative hypoglobulinemia in healthy older individuals.

The relationship between changes in serum immunoglobulin concentrations and immunologic diseases in adults is often obscure. Current difficulties in identifying alterations relevant to disease may result from several factors: the degree of departure from normal confidence intervals is usually small in comparison to dysimmunoglobulinemias occurring early in life; other sources of biologic variation, such as race (1) and sex (2, 3) tend to obscure disease-related changes. Aging is another source of biologic variation only indirectly related to disease. Significant age-related changes occur prior to adult life (4). Relatively little is known of the immunoglobulin content of the serum of humans late in life, a period associated with an increased frequency of disease. As a consequence observations of serum immunoglobulin concentrations in older patients are difficult to interpret. A systematic study of serum immunoglobulin concentrations throughout the life-span of man is a necessary requisite for the identification of disease-related changes.

[1] This work was supported by grants from the United States Public Health Service (AI-07499, 5-K3-AI-14797, HD-00668) and the American Medical Association (AMA-ERF).

The concentrations of IgG, IgA and IgM were measured in the serum of 811 apparently healthy humans ranging in age from birth to 92 years. This work represents a part of continuing studies of the immunologic aspects of aging in man. Biometric analysis of these data suggests that valid contrasts of serum immunoglobulin concentrations between healthy and diseased adults are not possible without adequate control of biologic variation related to age.

MATERIALS AND METHODS

Subjects. Sera were obtained from apparently healthy individuals who were free of complaints related to acute or chronic disease and exhibited no obvious abnormalities. The subjects included professional and paramedical hospital personnel, healthy family members and friends of patients who provided blood donations, and older individuals who are members of longitudinal study populations under periodic survey by the Duke University Center for the Study of Aging.

Preparation of antigens and antisera. Blood

was collected by phlebotomy and serum separated within 1 hr. Sera were frozen at −20°C until analyzed and retained at 4°C during the period of analysis.

Purified human immunoglobulins were used as antigens and primary reference standards. Each immunoglobulin was prepared from serum by a combination of gel filtration and ion exchange chromatography. Human IgG was prepared from Cohn fraction II[2] human γ globulins and from sera of patients with heterogenous hyperglobulinemia and myeloma. Human IgA was prepared from the sera of patients with IgA multiple myeloma and from one patient with increased heterogenous IgA. Human IgM was prepared from the sera of two patients with monoclonal macroglobulinemia, a patient with cryomacroglobulin (5) and a patient with heterogenous macroglobulinemia (6).

Gel exclusion chromatography with G-200 Sephadex or P-300 Bio-Gel was performed on a 15-cm x 150-cm column as an initial enrichment step. Immunoglobulins in eluate peaks were initially identified by microimmunoelectrophoresis (7) with a polyvalent antiserum to human serum proteins. More recently single radial diffusion (8) against monospecific antisera has also been used in order to identify eluate fractions enriched with the desired human immunoglobulin. Chromatography was repeated on the same column after concentration of the desired eluate fraction by lyophilization.[3] Solutions of each partially purified human immunoglobulin were chromatographed on a 5- x 100-cm DEAE Sephadex A-5 column. The resin bed and protein solution were equilibrated with a 0.01 M ionic strength, pH 8, Tris-propionate buffer, and elution was carried out with a continuous gradient developed by pH 7, 0.05 M ionic strength Tris-propionate buffer adjusted to a final ionic strength of 0.45 M with sodium chloride. Eluate fractions were monitored by measurement of the optical density, evaluated immunochemically and concentrated by lyophilization. Purified antigens were further characterized by analytical ultracentrifugation[4] and further immunochemical analysis. Preparations having immunochemical or physicochemical evidence of impurities were rechromatographed under the same conditions, or alternately were chromatographed on CM-Sephadex A-50 after equilibration with a pH 5.0, 0.01 M ionic strength acetate buffer. Elution was accomplished with a continuous gradient developed by a pH 6, 0.5 M ionic strength acetate buffer.

The apparently immunochemically pure globulins obtained were adjusted to a pH of 5.5 and dialyzed into 0.01 M sodium chloride. Each solution of IgG and IgA was adjusted to a concentration range between 1% and 4% and each IgM solution to between 0.3% and 0.5%. Each preparation was sterilized by ultrafiltration prior to measurement of concentration by drying duplicate amounts to minimal weight at 107° ± 0.2°C in a forced draft oven. All samples contained more than 20 mg protein and were weighed on an analytical balance having a precision of ±0.0002 g. Weights obtained were corrected for the salt content of the initial solution and the concentration of each primary reference standard solution expressed in milligrams/milliliter of solution. The concentrations of some primary reference standard solutions were also evaluated in the analytical ultracentrifuge using Rayleigh interference optics (η = 0.000465 for 2.5 mg/ml, λ = 546 nm). Estimates of concentration by these two methods agreed within ±2%.

All antisera were prepared in goats. The quantity of primary reference standard used as antigen solution for each injection varied between 0.3 and 1.0 mg in a volume of 1 ml. Each antigen was homogenized with an equal volume of mixed complete Freund's adjuvant and injected intramuscularly in divided doses into each goat at weekly intervals for a period of 6 to 8 weeks. Booster doses of antigen prepared as an alum toxoid (9) were used twice monthly thereafter. Approximately 200-ml bleedings were obtained every 2 weeks after the development of precipitating antibodies, usually after the 4th week of immunization.

Each harvest of antiserum was evaluated for antibody to other human serum proteins by microimmunoelectrophoresis. Apparently monospecific antisera were evaluated against a panel of 12 or more κ and λ purified human L chains (Bence Jones proteins). Antibody activity to L chains or to other human serum proteins was

[2] Pentex, Inc., Kankakee, Ill.

[3] Centrifugal Freeze Dryer, Model 30P1/662, Edwards High Vacuum Ltd., Manor Royal, Crawley, Sussex, England.

[4] Model E Analytical Ultracentrifuge, Beckman Instruments, Palo Alto, Calif.

removed by absorption with an appropriate antigen containing serum or partially purified antigen. After absorption each pool of goat antiserum was precipitated three times with ammonium sulfate (24 g/100 ml of serum or solution), dialyzed into physiologic saline, sterilized by ultrafiltration, and portions were sealed in 10-ml vials closed with a rubber bung and aluminum seal. Each antiserum globulin preparation was again evaluated for potency and specificity, dated and labeled, and retained at −70°C until used. These goat antibody globulin preparations contained 90% or better 7S protein by ultracentrifugation and antibody activity was two- to fourfold greater than in neat serum.

Quantitation of immunoglobulin concentrations. The quantity of IgG, IgA and IgM in serum was measured by a modification of the single radial diffusion method (8, 10). Equal volumes (6 to 10 μl) of serum or antigen-standard were measured with a 50-μl[5] syringe or micropipette[6] into 3.6-mm wells cut in agar containing optimally diluted monospecific antisera to each human immunoglobulin. Each diffusion plate was allowed to incubate in a moist chamber at room temperature. Diffusion was allowed to progress 4 hr for IgG and IgA and 12 hr for IgM. At the end of the diffusion the precipitate rings were photographed with the aid of an indirect light source. The photographed diameter of diffusion was measured with needle point calipers and a microcomparator. Initially, concentrations of each unknown immunoglobulin were estimated by interpolation of the diameter observed on a semilog graph of values obtained with a previously quantitated and diluted secondary reference standard (SRS) run on the same plate. More recently interpolated concentrations were calculated by a least squares regression of the $\log_e$ of the unknown SRS standards against observed diameters on a programmed calculating machine.[7] These calculated regressions allow computation of known values and an estimate of minimal error. Replicate dilutions of the SRS, placed geometrically about each plate in such a way as to maximize error due to loading of wells and leveling the plate, were used to calculate the percentage standard error of the regression. Replicate determinations on each unknown serum on different days were done until the average estimates of concentration obtained agreed within the experimental limits of the method. The coefficient of variation of regression obtained by this technique currently averages 5.12% for IgG, 5.75% for IgA and 10.0% for IgM.

Analysis and presentation of data. Graphic plots of the cumulative frequency of serum concentrations observed in healthy individuals are curvilinear. The same frequency distribution plotted against logarithmically transformed serum concentrations is linear. Therefore, statistical evaluations of the serum immunoglobulin concentrations observed in healthy individuals were accomplished by multivariate analysis (11) on the $\log_e$ of the value observed. Data were categorized as to the race, sex and age of each individual. Age was initially treated as a variate. In the analysis presented in this report, age is treated as a linear covariate within each of the four age spans of human life in which similar age-related trends occur.

RESULTS

The ranges of serum concentrations of IgG, IgA and IgM observed throughout the life of man are presented in Figure 1. This figure shows the confidence interval derived from the antilog of the two standard deviation interval about the means of sequential groups of healthy people from birth into the 10th decade of life. The magnitude of the variation observed differed considerably throughout life. However, the largest variance for equal sized groups was less than fourfold greater than the smallest variance observed. IgG reaches maximum variation and concentration between the second and fourth decades of life. IgA concentration approximates the range of adult values by puberty, but continues to increase slowly through the third decade and shows increasing variation throughout life. IgM increases until the beginning of the second decade when it reaches maximum concentration and it reaches maximum variance by the fifth decade of life. Average IgG and IgM concentrations decrease toward neonate values beyond the fifth decade of life.

On the basis of the age-related trends pictured in Figure 1, data were divided into four age

[5] Hamilton Company, Inc., P.O. Box 307, Whittier, Calif.

[6] Eppendorf Pipet, Brinkman Instruments, Inc., Cantioque Road, Westbury, N. Y. 11590.

[7] Wang Laboratories, Inc., Tewksbury, Mass. 01876.

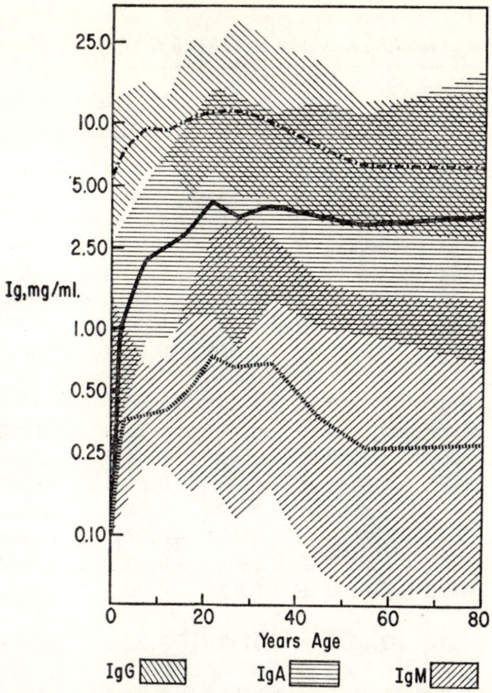

Figure 1. This graph presents the means and confidence intervals of serum immunoglobulin concentrations observed throughout the life of apparently healthy man. Note the logarithmic scale. The cross-hatched areas represent the measured confidence intervals for each immunoglobulin. The mean IgG (-·-·-), mean IgA (——), and mean IgM (-----) show the relative magnitude of age-related trends and the basis for selection of age spans used for statistical analysis of these data.

spans: 0 to 13 years, 14 to 27 years, 28 to 54 years, and 55 to 92 years. Multivariate analysis of the $\log_e$ of each value with the age of each apparently healthy individual as a different covariate for each age-race-sex group was accomplished in order to make use of age spans in which the transformed serum concentrations might approximate a linear function of age. The results of this analysis are presented in Table I as the age-adjusted mean and the standard error of the mean, and the slope and standard error of the slope within each of the 16 age-race-sex groups. All values presented in Table I are expressed as the $\log_e$ of units of W.H.O. reference standard 67/95. Mean values and slopes not statistically different from zero are identified. A graphic summary of these mean immunoglobulin concentrations and significant slopes is shown in Figure 2, which also presents an estimate of the variation between each race and sex in relation to the magnitude of change observed with aging. Age-race-sex groups having significant age-related changes within each age span are presented as a line. Group means without statistically significant within group age effects are presented as single points at the mean age for the group. The general variation observed in group means and the time in life when race and sex differences are maximum are represented by the stippled areas in Figure 2.

Generally, the magnitude of variation between different race and sex groups parallels the overall variation presented in Figure 1. Sex differences in whites were less than in blacks. Higher serum immunoglobulin concentrations were observed in blacks. Females have slightly higher serum IgM concentrations than males, but black females do not maintain this apparent difference into older age. The largest source of variation observed was related to age. In addition to the well documented increases in serum immunoglobulin during the first two decades of life, large age-related changes occur after maturity. IgM concentrations in older individuals decrease to values near those early in life. IgG decreases from the third through the sixth decade of life. Changes in IgG with age in blacks are less precipitous than in whites. Age-related changes of IgA in adults were small in comparison to changes in IgG and IgM.

Statistical comparisons of differences in serum immunoglobulin concentrations between age groups were made. These results are presented in Table II, which lists probabilities that the differences observed could occur by chance alone. The probability that the mean difference or slope difference observed is not different from zero is presented for the adjusted mean and slope of each immunoglobulin for every possible contrast in the four selected age spans of life. Significant differences were found throughout life in all age spans for all immunoglobulins with but two exceptions: IgM in the interval from 0 to 27 years and IgA within the 28- to 92-year interval. Simultaneous contrasts between all age groups were highly significant for all immunoglobulins ($p < 0.0001$) with respect to both mean and slope differences. A similar simultaneous contrast of race and sex differences within all age groups (Table III) suggests that only race differences

TABLE I

Serum immunoglobulin concentrations of apparently healthy humans from birth to old age

Group	No.	Mean Age ± S. D		IgG[a]	IgA[a]	IgM[a]
White males	47	6.2 ± 4.9	(1)[b]	4.1864 ± 0.0942	1.8567 ± 0.1936	3.9072 ± 0.1785
			(2)[c]	0.0557 ± 0.0118	0.2294 ± 0.0244	0.0384 ± 0.0225[d]
	55	20.0 ± 4.2	(1)	4.7487 ± 0.2619	4.1811 ± 0.5388	4.1447 ± 0.4963
			(2)	0.0060 ± 0.0049	0.0155 ± 0.0263[d]	0.0343 ± 0.0242[d]
	93	42.8 ± 3.3	(1)	5.5882 ± 0.2162	4.5415 ± 0.4445	6.1269 ± 0.4098
			(2)	−0.0253 ± 0.0049	0.0012 ± 0.0101[d]	−0.0390 ± 0.0093
	121	66.3 ± 8.8	(1)	3.8885 ± 0.2743	3.7506 ± 0.5638	4.4917 ± 0.5198
			(2)	0.0073 ± 0.0040[d]	0.0132 ± 0.0084[d]	−0.0053 ± 0.0077[d]
White females	43	4.6 ± 4.8	(1)	4.5342 ± 0.0084	0.7988 ± 0.1742	3.5007 ± 0.1606
			(2)	0.0192 ± 0.0127[d]	0.3365 ± 0.0261	0.1138 ± 0.0240
	63	19.7 ± 3.4	(1)	4.6726 ± 0.2925	3.5289 ± 0.6011	4.4382 ± 0.5543
			(2)	0.0096 ± 0.0145[d]	0.0464 ± 0.0299[d]	0.0293 ± 0.0275[d]
	66	43.3 ± 8.9	(1)	5.2746 ± 0.2438	4.4964 ± 0.5010	6.4197 ± 0.4620
			(2)	−0.0170 ± 0.0055	−0.0038 ± 0.0113[d]	−0.0388 ± 0.0104
	104	67.6 ± 9.3	(1)	3.2749 ± 0.2853	3.2344 ± 0.5864	3.3081 ± 0.5407
			(2)	0.0155 ± 0.0041	0.0150 ± 0.0085[d]	0.0113 ± 0.0079[d]
Black males	41	3.9 ± 4.3	(1)	4.1356 ± 0.0843	2.5512 ± 0.1733	3.9586 ± 0.1598
			(2)	0.0867 ± 0.0146	0.1866 ± 0.0300	0.0582 ± 0.0276
	19	20.7 ± 2.9	(1)	3.5219 ± 0.6586	1.1855 ± 1.3535[d]	2.9042 ± 1.2480[d]
			(2)	0.0874 ± 0.0313	0.1632 ± 0.0644	0.0891 ± 0.0594[d]
	29	40.6 ± 7.4	(1)	5.7566 ± 0.4174	4.3165 ± 0.8579	5.3767 ± 0.7910
			(2)	−0.0120 ± 0.0101[d]	0.0189 ± 0.0207[d]	−0.0100 ± 0.0191
	14	73.7 ± 10.5	(1)	6.8263 ± 0.7760	6.5533 ± 1.5948	5.6989 ± 1.4704
			(2)	−0.0254 ± 0.0104	−0.0224 ± 0.0214[d]	−0.0191 ± 0.0197[d]
Black females	32	3.7 ± 3.7	(1)	4.4689 ± 0.1009	1.7188 ± 0.2074	3.8320 ± 0.1912
			(2)	0.0623 ± 0.0191	0.3022 ± 0.0393	0.0816 ± 0.0362
	24	20.0 ± 4.8	(1)	5.2200 ± 0.3502	4.7301 ± 0.7198	3.7407 ± 0.6637
			(2)	−0.0047 ± 0.0170[d]	0.0017 ± 0.0349[d]	0.0702 ± 0.0322
	42	43.7 ± 7.2	(1)	4.7722 ± 0.3785	4.9701 ± 0.7779	5.3798 ± 0.7172
			(2)	−0.0011 ± 0.0085[d]	−0.0136 ± 0.0175[d]	−0.0447 ± 0.0161
	18	66.4 ± 9.9	(1)	3.7432 ± 0.6508	4.2112 ± 1.3376	1.7964 ± 1.2333[d]
			(2)	0.0130 ± 0.0096[d]	0.0042 ± 0.0199[d]	0.0317 ± 0.0183[d]

[a] All values expressed as $\log_e$ of units of W.H.O. reference standard 67/95.
[b] (1), age adjusted mean ± standard error of the mean.
[c] (2), slope ± standard error of the slope.
[d] Statistically not different from zero, $p < 0.05$.

in IgG are significant ($p < 0.0133$). These comparisons indicate that changes in serum immunoglobulin concentration occur throughout life, and that age-related differences are much more important than those related to race and sex.

Even though race and sex differences throughout life are minor in comparison to age-related trends, it was of interest to evaluate in which age range these differences are important. Table III presents the results of race, sex and first order interaction contrasts within each of the four age ranges studied. In the 0- to 13-year range mean IgG differences related to sex ($p < 0.0004$), and mean IgA differences related to race ($p < 0.0001$) and sex ($p < 0.0001$) could be detected. The covariate relationship of age on serum IgG was different in each race ($p < 0.0124$) and sex ($p < 0.0383$) and the age effect on serum IgA was different in each sex ($p < 0.0004$). In the next age span, 14 to 27 years,

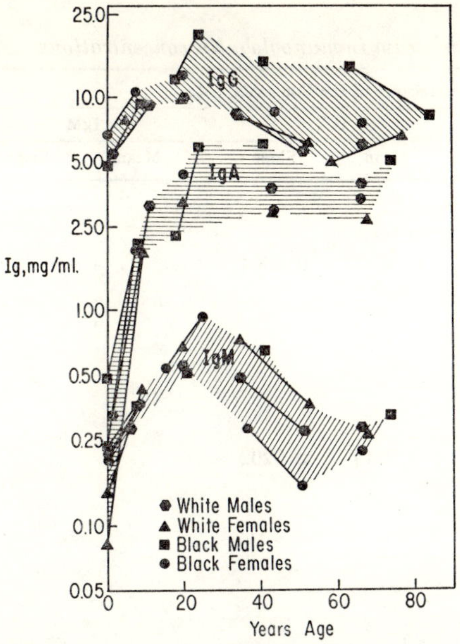

Figure 2. The means of each race and sex group within each age span for each immunoglobulin are shown as a function of age. Lines between two points within an age span represent statistically significant covariant effects within the particular age span; other group means in which the covariant effect of age was not significant are shown as a single point. Note the relative magnitude of age related variation in contrast to average differences related to race and sex.

significant differences were restricted to the covariate effect of age on IgG in each sex ($p < 0.0277$) and mean and slope sex-race interaction effects for IgG and IgA. A difference in mean IgG related to sex was marginally significant in the 28- to 54-year age span ($p < 0.0437$). Late in life, in the 55- to 92-year age range, mean differences in IgG for race ($p < 0.0022$) and sex ($p < 0.0011$) and differences in the covariate effect of age on IgG with respect to race ($p < 0.0210$) and sex ($p < 0.0029$) were detected. Similar mean and slope differences related to sex exist for IgM ($p < 0.0132$, 0.0195). First order interaction effects were also significant for IgG.

DISCUSSION

Well documented changes in serum immunoglobulin concentrations occur during human development (4). It has generally been assumed that changes beyond early adult life are small and of trivial consequence in comparison to those observed during the developmental years. Major emphasis in studies of healthy adults has been placed on differences related to race (1) and sex (2, 3). Prior studies of the serum of older individuals have led to various conclusions. Studies of serum globulin concentrations by electrophoresis suggest that γ migrating globulins increase with age (12–14). Other investigators have concluded on the basis of studies of a small number of subjects that IgG and IgM increase in older individuals (14). Thus, the present data obtained by a quantitative immunochemical technique in a very large population of older healthy humans do not confirm earlier studies.

The information presented in this report identifies age-related changes as the major source of biologic variation in serum immunoglobulin concentrations. Although changes related to race and sex can be identified, these are small and can only be reliably identified early in life or in older age. It was of interest that blacks

TABLE II

Significant age-related changes in human serum immunoglobulin concentrations

Age Range of Grouped Contrasts	Significance of the Contrasts, p<					
	IgG		IgA		IgM	
	Mean	Slope	Mean	Slope	Mean	Slope
years						
0–13 *vs* 14–27		0.0122	0.0001	0.0001		
0–13 *vs* 28–54	0.0001	0.0001	0.0001	0.0001	0.0001	0.0001
0–13 *vs* 55–92		0.0001	0.0001	0.0001		0.0001
14–27 *vs* 28–54	0.0029	0.0007	0.0301	0.0116	0.0001	0.0001
14–27 *vs* 55–92		0.0001	0.0001	0.0001		0.0001
28–54 *vs* 55–92	0.0043	0.0027			0.0008	0.0005
All age groups	0.0001	0.0001	0.0001	0.0001	0.0001	0.0001

TABLE III

Significant race, sex and race-sex differences in human serum immunoglobulin concentrations

Age Range	Contrast	Significance of the Contrasts, p<					
		IgG		IgA		IgM	
		Mean	Slope	Mean	Slope	Mean	Slope
years							
0–13	Race		0.0124	0.0001			
	Sex	0.0004	0.0383	0.0001	0.0004		
	Race-sex interaction						
14–27	Race						
	Sex		0.0277				
	Race-sex interaction	0.0334	0.0177	0.0149	0.0202		
28–54	Race						
	Sex	0.0437					
	Race-sex interaction						
55–92	Race	0.0022	0.0210				
	Sex	0.0011	0.0029			0.0132	0.0195
	Race-sex interaction	0.0220	0.0466				
0–92	Race		0.0133				
	Sex						
	Race-sex interaction						

maintained relatively high serum IgG concentrations to a later point in adult life than whites. It is uncertain whether this difference is of genetic or environmental origin. However, a similar prolongation of increased IgM serum concentrations could not be demonstrated in blacks, suggesting that if this difference is of environmental origin, a similar ecologic effect does not involve IgM.

One of the most striking changes observed in these studies is the marked increase in variability of serum immunoglobulin concentrations with age. Only a small portion of this trend could be related to the expression of differences associated with race and sex later in life (Fig. 2). Similar biologic variability as a function of aging has been identified in studies of other attributes of growth and development. For example, Tyler and Norris have observed a similar augmentation in variance in the weight of beagle dogs as a function of age (15). This augmented variation tends to diminish the certainty with which other biologic effects can be identified and diminishes the usefulness of measurements in adults as a discriminator of health and disease.

Despite these reservations the fall in serum immunoglobulin concentrations with advancing age suggests an age-related abiotrophy of selected cells responsible for producing immunoglobulin molecules. The maintenance of concentrations of IgA suggests that this immunoglobulin may be of relatively greater importance with advancing age.

Comparable changes in immunity related to aging have been demonstrated in mice by Makinodan and Peterson, who measured the primary antibody-forming potential of fixed numbers of spleen cells from donors of varying age (16). These investigators found no age-related differences in the time of doubling of the antibody response of spleen cells passively transferred to irradiated and challenged recipients.

Instead, a decrease in the number of responsive cells occurred with age. A similar decrease in the population of immunologically responsive cells could account for the age-related abiotrophy identified by these studies of human serum immunoglobulin concentrations. The relevance of this phenomena to senescence and degenerative changes associated with aging and with diseases common in older humans remains to be explored. While the observed age-related changes in serum immunoglobulin concentration do not provide direct evidence of altered immunologic function in older individuals, they do provide the basis for the expectation of decreased complement fixing, precipitating and perhaps agglutinating antibody activity in older individuals. Antibody activity decreases with age (14). The extent to which this apparent decrement is made up by antibody activity within the IgA and other immunoglobulin classes having different modes of optimal serologic expression is important in diagnostic serologic studies in older individuals. The concentrations of immunoglobulin within each class may be important determinants of changes in humoral hypersensitivity reactions characteristic of disease states and their varied manifestations depending upon the age of the afflicted individual. Thus, the identification of age-related changes in immunoglobulin concentration throughout life provides additional evidence of the importance of resolution of disease-related changes in antibody activity in terms of the actual immunoglobulin classes involved.

The method of statistical analysis used to evaluate these data was adequate for the task, but is not necessarily optimal. The use of long age spans weakens the applications that can be made from the data in Table I. We have made preliminary studies and categorized large patient populations and healthy controls into each of 27 possible categories evolved from the three possible alterations (high, normal, low) of three immunoglobulins. Each contrast was made with respect to the appropriate confidence interval for the individuals' age, race and sex. The computed confidence intervals at the extremes of the age spans used in this report are very wide. When these wide confidence intervals are used to categorize individuals near the extremes of the selected age spans, the estimate of normal fails to sharply discriminate individuals who differ greatly from mean age for the selected age interval. Circumvention of this difficulty with smaller age spans and the identification of the frequency and kind of immunoglobulin alterations found in healthy individuals will be the subject of a separate report.

The magnitude and importance of the age effect are the major objects of this report. In preliminary analyses when age was evaluated as a variate, highly significant differences related to the race and sex of the individual could be readily identified. These differences were similar to those reported previously (2, 3). Age differences of contrasted groups did not differ significantly. When the same data are analyzed with age as a covariate, many of these differences related to race and sex disappear leaving only those reported in Table III. This observation suggests that some of the previously reported alterations related to race and sex are primarily a consequence of race-sex differences in the effect of aging. A second possible source of difference may be related to differences in the age distribution of the healthy subjects. The evidence presented in this report indicates the importance of either controlling age effects as a covariate, or alternately using age-matched controls (17) in the evaluation of serum immunoglobulin alterations in disease states. Interpretations based on data in which age effects are not controlled are at risk.

REFERENCES

1. Rowe, D. S., McGregor, I. A., Smith, S. J., Hall, P. and Williams, K., Clin. Exp. Immun., *3:* 63, 1968.
2. Butterworth, M., McClellan, B. and Allansmith, M., Nature, *214:* 1224, 1967.
3. Stoop, J. W., Zegens, B. J. M., Sander, P. C. and Ballieux, R. E., Clin. Exp. Immun., *4:* 101, 1969.
4. Buckley, R. H., Dees, S. C. and O'Fallon, W. M., Pediatrics, *41:* 600, 1968.
5. Turkington, R. W. and Buckley, C. E., III, Amer. J. Med., *40:* 156, 1966.
6. Whitehouse, A. C., Buckley, C. E., III and McCarter, J., Amer. J. Med., *43:* 609, 1967.
7. Scheidegger, J. J., Int. Arch. Allerg., *7:* 103, 1955.
8. Mancini, G., Carbonara, C. O. and Heremans, J. F., Immunochemistry, *2:* 235, 1965.
9. Kabat, E. A., in *Kabat and Mayer's Experimental Immunochemistry*, 2nd Ed., p. 133, Charles C Thomas, Springfield, Ill., 1961.
10. Fahey, J. L. and McKelvey, E. M., J. Immun., *94:* 84, 1965.
11. Starmer, C. F. and Grizzle, J. E., *A Computer*

for Analysis of Data by General Linear Models, Institute of Statistics Mimeo Series No. 560, University of North Carolina, Chapel Hill, N. C., 1968.
12. Karel, J. L., J. Amer. Geriat. Soc., *4:* 667, 1956.
13. Das, B. C., Canad. J. Biochem. Physiol., *39:* 569, 1961.
14. Haferkamp, O., Schlettwein-Gsell, D., Schwick, H. G. and Storiko, K., Gerontologia, *12:* 30, 1966.
15. Tyler, S. A. and Norris, W. P., Growth, *32:* 235, 1968.
16. Makinodan, T. and Peterson, W. J., J. Immun., *93:* 886, 1964.
17. Buckley, C. E., III and Dorsey, F. C., Ann. Int. Med., *72:* 37, 1970.

THE JOURNAL OF IMMUNOLOGY
Vol. 105, No. 4, October 1970

DEGRADATION OF IMMUNOGLOBULIN G BY LYSOSOMAL ACID PROTEASES[1]

KURT FEHR,[2] JOSEPH LoSPALLUTO[3] AND MORRIS ZIFF[4]

From the Department of Internal Medicine (Rheumatic Diseases Unit) and the Department of Biochemistry, University of Texas Southwestern Medical School at Dallas

Received for publication March 2, 1970

Enzyme preparations from bovine spleen, human spleen, and lysosomal fractions of human synovial membrane tissue have been shown to degrade human IgG at pH 3.5. The major proteolytic activity is due to cathepsin D. The products of digestion have been shown to consist of fragments of IgG ranging from a slightly altered IgG with a molecular weight of approximately 135,000 to extensively degraded Fc and partially degraded Fab fragments.

Intracellular proteases or cathepsins have been demonstrated in a wide variety of human tissues and in specific types of cells including fibroblasts (1), mast cells (2), polymorphonuclear leucocytes (3–5) and macrophages (6, 7). The localization of these enzymes in lysosomes has been well documented, notably by deDuve and co-workers (8, 9). The widespread distribution of tissue proteases suggests that these enzymes are directed at multiple physiologic substrates; and the degradation of numerous proteins by lysosomal proteases from different tissues of a variety of experimental animals and man has received considerable attention (2, 3–5, 10–14).

In recent years, it has been shown that neutrophils and macrophages phagocytize immune complexes under varying conditions in animals (15–19) and in man (20, 21). The phagocytized complexes are thereby exposed to the lysosomal enzymes and digested (22). In addition, studies in experimental animals have shown that protease activity is released into the circulation in significant amounts (23) and, as a result, complexes may be exposed to the proteolytic activity of the lysosomal enzymes both intracellularly and extracellularly.

To assay protease activity, hemoglobin has been used as substrate in many instances (24, 25) and synthetic peptide substrates specific for cathepsins A, B, or C have been used in others (26). Albumin is also readily digested and has been used as a substrate for rabbit, bovine and human cathepsins (27–29). In this report, the effect of lysosomal enzymes from bovine and human spleen and human synovial tissue on human immunoglobulin G (IgG) is described. Fragmentation has been observed not only at low pH, but also, to a lesser extent, at neutral pH. Two types of large fragments have been purified from the digests and characterized. In addition, other, less clearly defined breakdown products have been observed.

MATERIALS AND METHODS

Preparation of lysosomal proteases. Fresh beef spleen or human spleen was placed in ice cold 0.25 M sucrose, freed of connective tissue, minced with scissors, and suspended in 1:10 (w/v) cold 0.25 M sucrose. All subsequent manipulations were made in the cold. The tissue was then homogenized in a Potter-Elvehjem homogenizer with a Teflon pestle (Tri-R, Jamaica, N. Y.) at 2000 to 3000 rpm. Microscopic examination of the homogenate showed disruption of most of the cells. The procedure followed from this point onward was essentially that of Weissman and Thomas (30). After centrifugation at 800 ×

[1] Supported by Grant I155, Robert A. Welch Foundation; Grant AI-05479, National Institute of Arthritis and Metabolic Diseases; and Project Grant AM-09989 from the United States Public Health Service.

[2] Present address: Universitäts rheumaklinik, Gloriastrasse 25, 8006 Zurich, Switzerland.

[3] All correspondence should be addressed to Dr. LoSpalluto, Dept. of Biochemistry.

[4] Recipient, Research Career Award, National Institutes of Arthritis and Metabolic Diseases, National Institutes of Health.

G for 10 min at 2°C, the sediment, termed the nuclear fraction, was resuspended in 1:5 (w/v) 0.25 M sucrose. This fraction contained unbroken cells, nuclei, and cellular debris. It was saved for assay of proteolytic activity. The supernatant was centrifuged for 20 min at 15,000 × G, which sedimented the main portion of the lysosomes and included the light mitochondria. The sediment, termed the granular fraction, was washed once with 1:10 (w/v) 0.25 M sucrose and then resuspended in 1:5 (w/v) 0.25 M sucrose. In some experiments 0.15 M NaCl was used to wash and resuspend the granular fraction. After sedimentation at 15,000 × G, the supernatant and the washes were assayed for proteolytic activity. All four fractions were then alternately frozen and thawed five times, centrifuged at 15,000 × G for 20 min and the solutions stored at −20°C.

The human spleens extracted were obtained from 15- to 35-year-old individuals who had undergone splenectomy following abdominal trauma. The synovial membrane extract was prepared from the inflamed synovial tissue resected at synovectomy from the knee joint of a patient with psoriatic arthritis. Lysosomal proteases were prepared from synovial membrane in the same manner as described above.

Digestion procedures and assay of enzyme activity. Prior to use, the enzyme preparations were dialyzed against 0.15 M saline in the cold before they were used. Digestions were carried out in 0.15 M saline or in suitable buffers with 0.02% sodium azide added as a preservative. The pH of the mixtures was adjusted to 3.5 with 0.2 M HCl immediately before incubation. Proteolytic activity was assayed by a procedure similar to that of Lapresle and Webb (28, 31) using a 1% solution of human IgG or bovine hemoglobin as substrate in 0.15 M NaCl containing 0.02% sodium azide. Cysteine was added in a final concentration of 0.002 M. Undigested or slightly digested protein was precipitated by adding an equal volume of 10% TCA. After centrifugation, the non-precipitable protein was estimated by ultraviolet absorption at 280 nm. The protein concentration of the enzyme preparation was determined by the biuret method' (32) using human serum albumin as a standard. To calculate the protein concentration from 280-nm absorbance, an extinction coefficient of 13.0 for a 1% solution of human IgG in saline was employed. Controls were run in parallel with experimental samples by incubating the substrate and enzyme separately at the same pH and mixing the two immediately before adding TCA. In experiments designed to study the effects of cysteine, iodoacetamide or diisopropyl fluorophosphate (DFP) on the acid protease, enzyme prepared from a human spleen lysosome fraction and partially purified by gel filtration through Bio-Gel A 1.5 M was employed. Tubes containing enzyme alone or enzyme plus the compounds listed above were incubated for 1 hr at 37°C, pH 7.5. Portions were then removed for assay. The assays were performed by mixing 10 mg of substrate (human IgG or bovine hemoglobin) and 0.15 mg of enzyme untreated or pretreated as described above. The total volume of each tube was 1.0 ml. Control tubes containing enzyme alone (0.15 mg/ml), substrate alone, 20 mg/ml, and each of these with the various compounds listed above were prepared. After incubation for 2 hr at 37°C, pH 3.5, assay solutions were precipitted by adding 1.0 ml of 10% TCA. For controls, 0.5 ml of the substrate (20 mg/ml) was mixed with the 1.0 ml of enzyme solution (0.15 mg/ml) and immediately precipitated by adding 0.5 ml 20% TCA. Enyzme activity was then determined by measuring absorbance of supernatant solutions at 280 nm.

Purification of human IgG. Commercial human fraction II was purified by chromatography on a column of DEAE-cellulose equilibrated with 0.01 M phosphate buffer at pH 7.5. The first two-thirds of the first protein peak eluted was pooled, dialyzed against 0.15 M NaCl, and concentrated by ultrafiltration to 20 mg/ml. The preparation showed the presence of only IgG by agar double diffusion and immunoelectrophoretic analysis. It showed only one component when tested with horse anti-human serum and gave no reaction with antisera to IgM and IgA.

Chromatographic procedures. In order to study the nature of the digestion products of human IgG by the lysosomal proteases, the various digestion mixtures were chromatographed through Sephadex G-200 or G-100 columns (Pharmacia, Uppsala, Sweden), using for elution acetate-glycine buffer, pH 3.9, (0.1 M acetate, 0.1 M glycine containing 0.02% sodium azide) or Tris-NaCl buffer, pH 7.5, (0.05 M Tris, 0.2 M NaCl containing 0.02% sodium azide). For molecular size estimates from these gel filtration experiments, ovalbumin (Pentex, Inc., Kankakee,

Ill.), human serum albumin (Armour Pharmaceutical Company, Kankakee, Ill.), human IgG, fibrinogen, and myoglobin were employed as markers. The semi-logarithmic plot of molecular weights of the markers against elution volume of the respective protein peaks gave straight lines (33) for each of the columns which were used for estimating the molecular weights of the digestion products.

Protein fractions were concentrated by pressure ultrafiltration through UM-10 Diaflo membranes (Amicon Corp., Cambridge, Mass.).

Immunologic procedures. To characterize chromatographic fractions, double diffusion in agar was carried out using goat antisera to human IgG and its Fab and Fc fragments, human IgM, human IgA and whole human serum (Hyland Laboratories, Los Angeles, Calif.).

RESULTS

Digestion of IgG by lysosomal proteases. The effect of pH on the digestion of human IgG is shown in Figure 1. Both bovine and human spleen preparations showed major proteolytic activity between pH 3.0 and pH 4.0 after 30 min of incubation. Both preparations also showed a second smaller peak of activity at a pH between 7.0 and 8.0. This activity was detected with the human lysosomal fraction only after longer incubation times. The relation between amount of digestion and concentration of enzyme was linear over at least a fivefold range of enzyme concentration.

An attempt was made to separate and purify the acid proteases. The bovine and human spleen

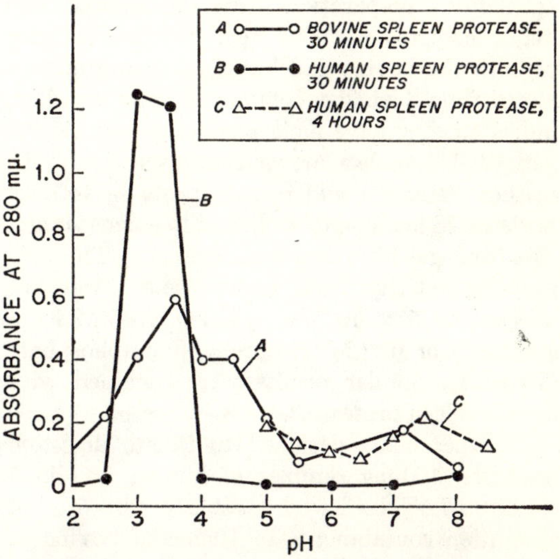

Figure 1. pH activity profile of bovine and human spleen proteases. Ten milligrams of human IgG plus 0.95 mg of beef spleen enzyme or 1.7 mg of human spleen enzyme. The pH was adjusted after initial mixing and readjusted during incubation. Total volume 1.0 ml.

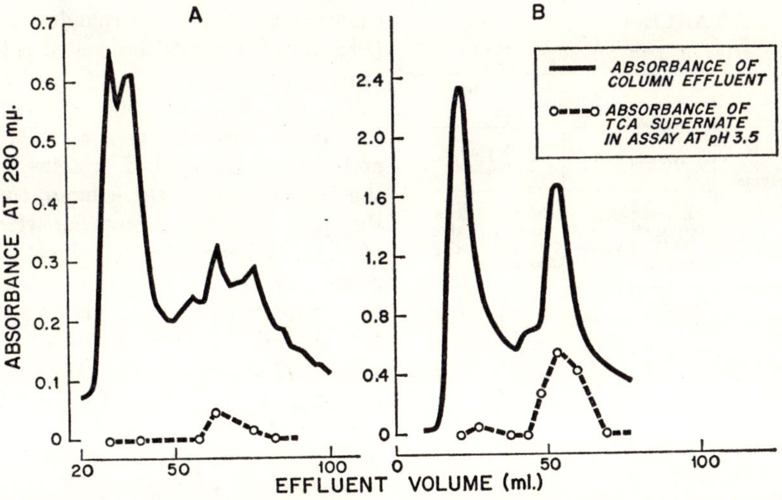

Figure 2. Fractionation of (*A*) 45 mg of bovine spleen and (*B*) 47 mg of human spleen enzymes on Sephadex G-100 columns (1.2 × 80 cm) at 4°C. Eluting buffer 0.05 M Tris-0.2 M NaCl, pH 7.5; fraction volume 2 ml. For determination of protease activity, the samples were dialyzed against 0.15 M NaCl and assayed at pH 3.5 with HSA as substrate.

enzyme preparations were concentrated by ultrafiltration at 4°C and applied to Sephadex G-100 in Tris-NaCl buffer, pH 7.5. Chromatography was carried out at 2°C. Fractions of the eluates were dialyzed in the cold against saline and assayed for protease activity with human IgG. Both preparations (Fig. 2) showed two major components. The acid protease activity of both the bovine and human preparation was eluted from Sephadex columns in volumes which indicated they have molecular weights of 56,000 and 49,000 molecular weight respectively. In neither instance could neutral protease activity be detected in amounts sufficient to estimate their size from gel filtration measurements. The acid protease activity from human spleen was not affected by 5 × 10^{-3} M cysteine, 10^{-2} M iodoacetamide or 10^{-3} M diisopropyl fluorophosphate (Table I). Similar results were obtained with bovine spleen protease.

In experiments designed to isolate digestion products, 100-mg samples of human IgG in 5 ml of 0.15 M NaCl were incubated with 5 ml of a solution containing 8 to 10 mg of bovine or human spleen enzyme in 0.15 M NaCl for 18 hr or longer at 37°C in the presence of 0.02% sodium azide. The pH of the reaction mixture was adjusted to 3.5 immediately after mixing and checked at various time intervals. The small decrease in pH which sometimes occurred was

TABLE I

Properties of acid protease

Treatment of Enzyme	Substrate			
	Human IgG		Bovine hemoglobin	
	Enzyme activity[a] (O.D. 280 nm)	Relative activity[b]	Enzyme activity (O.D. 280 nm)	Relative activity
None	0.120	1.00	0.487	1.00
Cysteine 5 × 10^{-3} M	0.117	0.98	0.445	0.91
Cysteine 5 × 10^{-3} M Iodoacetamide 1 × 10^{-2} M	0.135	1.12	0.485	1.00
Cysteine 5 × 10^{-3} M DFP 1 × 10^{-2} M	0.123	1.03	0.466	0.96

[a] Enzyme activity is expressed as the difference in absorbance at 280 nm between assay and control tubes of TCA supernatant solutions.

[b] Ratio of activity to that of untreated enzyme.

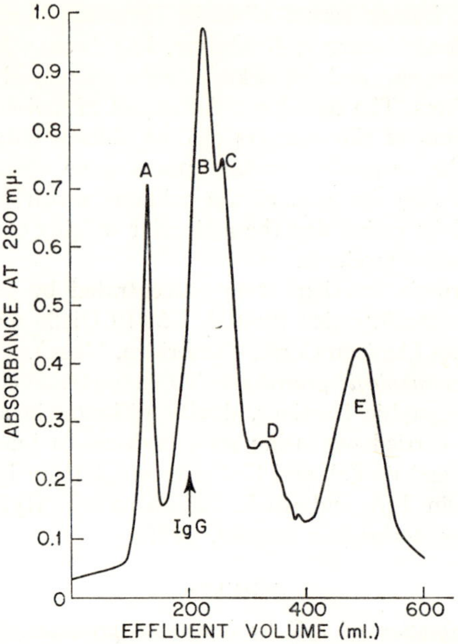

Figure 3. Fractionation of a digest of human IgG by beef spleen protease. One hundred milligrams of IgG digested with 9.5 mg of beef spleen proteases at pH 3.5 for 30 hr at 37°C. Gel filtration through Sephadex G-200 (2.5 × 90 cm) in 0.05 M Tris, 0.2 M NaCl pH 7.5 containing 0.02% NaN_3. Five-milliliter fractions collected.

corrected by adding 1 N NaOH. Gel filtration of the products of digestion with bovine spleen enzyme at pH 3.5 on Sephadex G-200 resulted (Fig. 3) in five peaks, designated A through E, in order of their elution.

The proteins of the first component A, which in various experiments comprised between 10 and 30% of the applied proteins, emerged with the void volume of the column, thus indicating that they consisted, at least in part, of aggregates of IgG. When untreated IgG substrate was passed through the same Sephadex G-200 column in acetate-glycine buffer, pH 3.9, about 20% of the applied IgG was recovered as aggregate. When IgG at the same concentration was allowed to stand at 37°C and pH 3.5 for 24 hr in the absence of enzyme, almost 75% of the applied protein emerged as an aggregate.

The second component, B, comprised 47 to 69% of the applied protein. In a number of experiments, this component consistently emerged from the column slightly later than intact IgG and consisted of fragments of approxi-

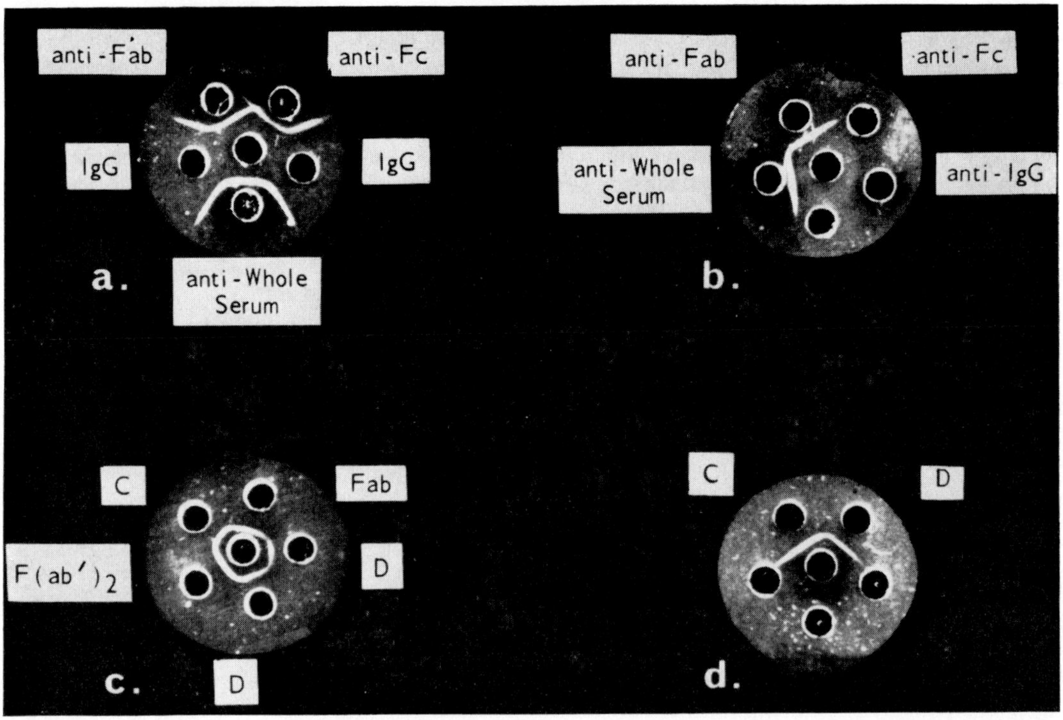

Figure 4. Ouchterlony analysis of components obtained upon digestion of human IgG at pH 3.5 using beef spleen protease. *a*, Component B (see Figure 5) in center well, showing identity with IgG when tested with anti-Fab, anti-Fc, and anti-whole human serum; *b*, component C in center well. The precipitation lines with anti-Fab and anti-whole serum show complete identity. No precipitation lines are seen with anti-Fc and anti-IgG absorbed with Fab (papain); *c*, The relation between component C, $F(ab')_2$ (pepsin), Fab (papain), and component D. Center well contains anti-Fab. Complete identity between C, D, and Fab is seen; component D, however, has an antigen deficiency with respect to $F(ab')_2$; *d*, Ouchterlony analysis of component D (Fig. 6). The precipitation line with anti-Fab (*center well*) shows antigenic deficiency when compared with fraction C ($F(ab)_2$). Only faint lines were seen with anti-Fc. No data on D with anti-Fc is shown.

mately 135,000 molecular weight. Fraction C consisted of fragments in the range of 100,000 molecular weight.

Resolution of fractions B and C was achieved by recycling through Sephadex G-200 three times. Ouchterlony analysis of B with goat anti-Fab and anti-Fc showed lines indicating the presence of both Fab and Fc antigens. Analysis with anti-whole human serum showed complete identity between component B and intact purified IgG (Fig. 4*a*).

To determine whether the difference in chromatographic behavior between this component and intact IgG reflected a real difference in size, both the fragment as well as intact IgG were analyzed in the ultracentrifuge at three different concentrations. The extrapolated $s_{20,w}$ values of component B and IgG were found to be 6.3 and 7.0, respectively. In addition, hidden antigens were observed in component B which were not detectable in intact IgG (34).

Ouchterlony analysis of purified fraction C (Fig. 4*b*) showed that this component contained no antigenic determinants reacting with anti-Fc and anti-IgG absorbed with Fab, but gave strong reactions with anti-Fab and anti-whole human serum. These findings, in conjunction with the measurement of a molecular weight for fraction C of 100,000 by gel filtration, and an $s_{20,w}$ of 5, indicate a molecule of the Fab_2 type. Comparison of this fraction (Fig. 4*c*) with those obtained from pepsin and papain digested IgG by Ouchterlony agar diffusion against anti-Fab showed reactions of complete identity. In addition, ultracentrifugation of the lysosomal protease derived Fab_2 and pepsin derived Fab'_2 at a concentration of 5 mg/ml showed in each case a sedimentation coefficient of 5.0S.

Component D comprised 7 to 13% of the applied protein. It had a molecular size in the range of 40,000 to 50,000 by gel filtration measurement and reacted with anti-Fab (Fig. 4*c*) as well as with anti-Fc. In attempts to purify this component further by rechromatography on Sephadex-G 100 at pH 7.5, it became evident that further degradation into smaller fragments occurred on standing. In several experiments it was possible to separate fragments with molecular weights of 11,000 to 19,000 from fragments in the range of 40,000 to 47,000. The fragments in the 40,000 to 47,000 range reacted with anti-Fab and showed antigenic deficiency when compared with pepsin Fab'_2 (Fig. 4*c*) and component C (Fab_2) isolated from the same digest (Fig. 4*d*). The smaller fragments reacted with anti-Fc. The presence of fragments smaller than 50,000 molecular weight, with Fab determinants which were antigenically deficient when compared with Fab_2 from the same digest, shows that these fragments are further degraded by lysosomal proteases. The further digestion of the proteins of fraction D was undoubtedly due to acid protease activity which was present in this region of the chromatogram.

The Fc part of the molecule appears to be much more susceptible to attack by lysosomal protease than the Fab fragments, as is the case with other proteolytic enzymes. In no instance was it possible to recover Fc fragments of a size comparable to those obtained from a papain digest of IgG (35). Moreover, the reactions of fragments with Fc determinants and anti-Fc were considerably weaker than would be expected from the amounts of Fab_2 and Fab fragments found.

Component E, comprising about 18% of the applied IgG, emerged in a volume indicating a molecular weight of less than 12,000. These fragments were not precipitated by TCA. No further characterization of the polypeptides of this peak was attempted.

Degradation of human IgG by human spleen proteases at pH 3.5. Both at acid pH and in the range of pH 7 to 8, human IgG was attacked by extracts of human spleen lysosomes. The proteolytic activity of these extracts at pH 3.5 was considerably greater than at pH 7.5 and, for this reason, only acid protease digests were further studied at this time. The proteolytic activity at neutral pH will be described in a future report.

In order to characterize the products of digestion, 100-mg samples of IgG were incubated at 37°C with lysosome extracts containing 8 mg of protein for 8 hr at pH 3.5. The pH of the incubation mixture was measured from time to time and little change was observed over the time course employed. The reaction mixture was then applied directly to a column of Sephadex G-200 and gel filtration was carried out with 0.1 M Tris buffer at pH 7.5. The chromatographic pattern obtained (Fig. 5) shows a number of differences from that obtained with bovine protease digests. It is immediately evident that little or no aggregated IgG remained in the digest, since very little protein emerged in the region labeled A, i.e., before an undigested IgG marker would appear. The ascending limb of the first main component, labeled B, consisted in part of undigested IgG. Little or no protein behaving like the "135,000" component (Fig. 3, Table II) was

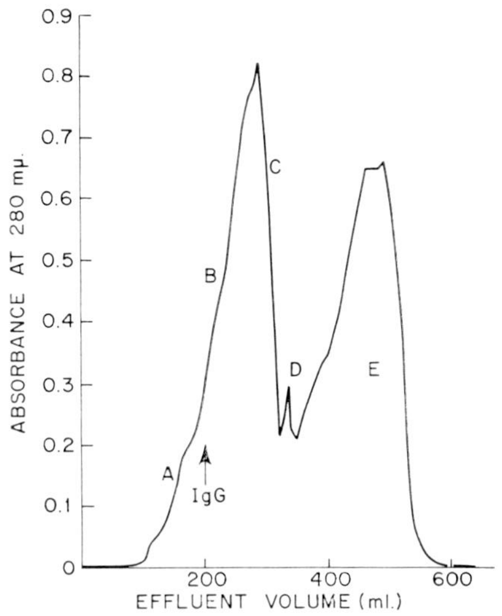

Figure 5. Fractionation on Sephadex G 200 (2.5 × 90 cm) of a human spleen protease digest of human IgG using 100 mg IgG and 8.4 mg of protease at pH 3.5 for 8 hr at 37°C. Total volume 7.5 ml. Proteins eluted with Tris-NaCl, pH 7.5; 2.5 ml fractions collected. Relatively large non-TCA precipitable peak (E) is seen. Little aggregated IgG (A), little IgG, and little of peak B remain. A large amount of digestion product (E) is non-TCA precipitable.

TABLE II

Properties of digestion products of IgG

Source of Enzymes	Chromatographic Product	Properties: Molecular size	Properties: Sedimentation coefficient	Antigenic Analysis
Bovine spleen lysosomes (Fig. 5)	B	~135,000	6.3S	Same as IgG
	C	100,000	5.0S	Fab_2
	D	<50,000		Fab, F′ab, F′c
	E	<12,000		
Human spleen lysosomes (Fig. 7)	B			IgG
	C	100,000	5.1S	Fab_2
	D	15–50,000		Fab, F′ab, F′c
	E	<12,000		
Human synovium lysosomes (Fig. 8)	B	150,000–175,000		IgG
	C	100,000	5.0S	Fab_2
	D	15–50,000		Fab, F′ab, F′c
	E	<12,000		

detectable in this region. The bulk of the protein of the first chromatographic peak, labeled C, was purified by recycling through Sephadex G-200. The final product emerged from the column in a volume which indicated its molecular weight was approximately 100,000. In addition, this component gave a single peak with a sedimentation coefficient of 5*S* on ultracentrifugation, the same as that found in the bovine protease digest (Table II). On Ouchterlony analysis component C was indistinguishable from component C obtained in the bovine protease digests in that it gave precipitation lines with anti-Fab but not with anti-Fc.

After purification by recycling through Sephadex G-100 columns, component D was found to contain a mixture of fragments ranging in size from 15,000 to 50,000 and which reacted with anti-Fab and gave faint reactions with anti Fc. A similar mixture of products was observed in bovine protease digests (component D, Fig. 3).

Component E consisted of non-TCA precipitable material. It was evident from the size of this peak that the extent of digestion to small peptides was considerably greater than that obtained with the bovine protease preparation.

Effect of synovial membrane lysosomal proteases on human IgG at pH 3.5. Lysosymes were prepared from 2 g of inflamed synovial tissue. The lysosomal extract obtained contained 1 mg of protein/ml. The specific enzymatic activity, when assayed by the TCA precipitation method using human IgG as substrate, was approximately two-thirds of that of the beef spleen preparation. Digestion was carried out at pH 3.5 in 0.15 M NaCl and the mixture subsequently fractionated by gel filtration through Sephadex G-200 using acetate-glycine buffer at pH 3.9. Figure 6 shows a pattern similar to that obtained with the beef spleen digests prepared at acid pH except for differences in the amounts of the various products.

Analytical ultracentrifugation of fraction B under the same conditions as those employed for the corresponding fragments from the beef spleen protease digests indicated that it consisted mainly of intact IgG. On immunodiffusion, component C reacted with anti-Fab and not with anti-Fc. This fraction had an $s_{20,w}$ of 5.0, a value identical to that obtained for the component C of bovine spleen and human spleen digests. Fraction D contained a distinct Fab component and exhibited weak reactivity with the anti-Fc serum (Table II).

DISCUSSION

Extracts of both human and bovine spleen lysosome digest human immunoglobulin G in the range of pH 3.0 to 4.0. The enzyme active in this pH region was not affected significantly by preincubation at neutral or acid pH with cysteine, iodoacetamide, or DFP. These observations suggest that cathepsins B and C are not responsible for the activity observed since these enzymes

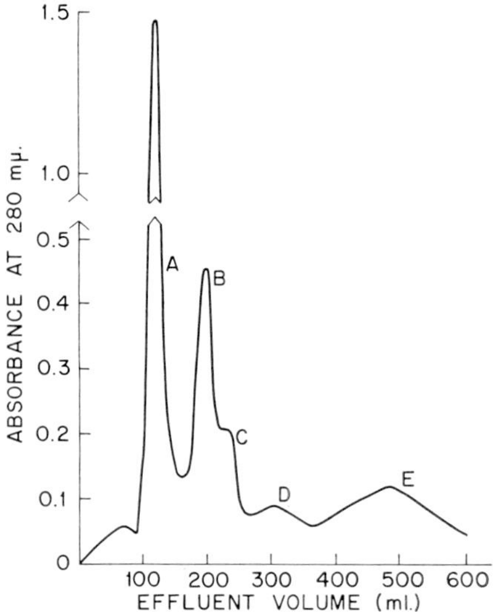

Figure 6. Fractionation of a human synovial membrane protease digest of human IgG. Forty-four milligrams of human IgG digested with 2.2 mg of protease; incubation at pH 3.5 for 24 hr at 37°C. Eluted with 0.1 M acetate-0.1 M glycine buffer, pH 3.9, containing 0.02% NaN_3; 2.5 ml fractions collected. Small non-TCA precipitable peak E is seen. A large amount of aggregated IgG, peak A, and IgG, peak B, remain.

are stimulated by cysteine and completely blocked by iodoacetamide (13, 26, 36). Cathepsins A and E, which require no sulfhydryl activation and are not inhibited by iodoacetamide have pH optima of 5.7 and 2.5 respectively (31, 37). At these pH values, lysosomal protease activity toward human IgG was minimal.

It has been shown by *Press et al.* (38) that only a small part of the total beef or rabbit spleen proteolytic activity can be attributed to cathepsins A and E, and that cathepsin D accounts for approximately two-thirds of the total proteolytic activity of beef spleen homogenates. Moreover, the pH activity curves of the crude homogenate and purified cathepsin D from rabbit spleen are almost identical (28). Both crude and purified preparations also cause a similar type of albumin fragmentation (27, 28), suggesting that cathepsin D accounts for the bulk of the proteolytic activity in rabbit spleen. In agreement with present observations utilizing IgG as substrate, this enzyme has a pH optimum in the range of 3.2 to 4.0 when assayed with albumin (28, 29) or hemoglobin (38, 39), requires no sulfhydryl compounds, and is not blocked by alkylating agents. Furthermore, the pH activity curves of bovine and human spleen proteases using human IgG as substrate in the present experiments were similar to those described for bovine, rabbit, and human cathepsin D with HSA and hemoglobin as substrate (28, 29, 38, 39).

The molecular weight range of cathepsin D from beef spleen and rabbit liver has been estimated to be 50,000 to 58,000 (38, 39), while preparations from rat brain, hog thyroid, and bovine dental pulp fibroblasts showed molecular weights ranging from 35,000 (1) to 60,000 (40). In this report, estimated values of 56,000 for beef spleen and 49,000 for human spleen protease support the conclusion that the chief proteolytic activity at low pH with human IgG as substrate is due to cathepsin D.

In bovine protease digests of human IgG carried out at a pH of 3.5 to 4.0, two major fragments were found, with molecular sizes in the range of 135,000 and 100,000 and with sedimentation coefficients of 6.3S and 5.0S, respectively (Table II). The larger fragment differed from intact IgG on gel filtration and ultracentrifugation, but not in its antigenic characteristics, as determined by immunodiffusion tests. Ouchterlony analysis, in fact, demonstrated complete identity with IgG. Precipitin lines were also developed with anti-Fab and anti-Fc.

A fragment of human IgG similar to the 135,000 molecular weight fragment has also been demonstrated following treatment of IgG with plasmin (41). This product, with $s_{20,w}$ of 6.5, retains antibody activity, but appears to lack antigenic sites on the L chain. It also does not fix complement in its aggregated state suggesting that part of the H chains has also been digested.

The 100,000 molecular weight fragment here described closely resembles Fab'_2 produced by pepsin digestion (42). This is indicated by its behavior on ultracentrifugation, gel filtration, and immunochemical analysis. With respect to the latter, reaction was observed only with anti-Fab serum.

Fc and Fab antigenic determinants were observed in the peak D region of the Sephadex G-200 chromatograms, a region where proteins with molecular weights of approximately 50,000 emerged. On immunodiffusion this mixture gave reactions of identity with Fab fragments isolated from papain digests and also reacted with anti-Fc. On repeated gel filtration through Sephadex G-100, proteins reactive with anti-Fc could be recovered in fractions containing protein fragments smaller than 19,000 molecular weight. Since the amounts recovered were much smaller than would be expected from the quantities of IgG employed and of other major fragments found, it seems likely that the proteases emerging from the columns in the same volume as the Fc fraction had further degraded it into smaller components.

By means of repeated Sephadex G-100 gel filtration of the Fab-containing fraction, peak D protein with the characteristics of Fab and with a molecular weight in the range of 40,000 to 47,000 was obtained. On immunodiffusion analysis, this protein was antigenically deficient when compared with the Fab_2 isolated from the same digest in the form of component C.

Extracts of human spleen lysosomes with high acid protease activity gave more extensive degradation of IgG than those from bovine spleen lysosomes. The major product was a 100,000 molecular weight fragment reacting with anti-Fab but not with anti-Fc, and identical with Fab'_2. Fragments with the characteristics of partially degraded Fab and Fc were also found. Little intact IgG or fragments such as the 135,000 molecular weight component B were found in these digests. Digestion of IgG by proteases obtained from tissue of an inflamed human synovial membrane resulted in less overall breakdown than that obtained with beef spleen proteases but similar types of fragments were found.

The results obtained suggest that the main acid protease of bovine spleen, human spleen, and human synovial membrane, which appears to be cathepsin D, attacks IgG in the same region of the heavy chains as pepsin. The exact point of attack, however, appears to be different from that of pepsin, since agglutinators of the type described by Osterland *et al.* (43) in human sera which react with the Fab_2 fragment from lysosomal protease digests are not inhibited by Fab'_2 fragments produced by pepsin digestion (34).

A possible sequence of reactions leading to the type of degradation of IgG described is shown schematically in Figure 7. Early steps in this sequence would involve degradation of the Fc region of IgG and production of fragments of various sizes such as components D and E (Figs. 3, 5 and 6). The 135,000 molecular weight moiety observed on digestion with bovine spleen protease (Fig. 3) is most likely one of the early reaction products. In time, more extensive digestion of the Fc region takes place giving rise to an Fab_2 fragment similar in size to that produced by pepsin digestion. Further degradation of this fragment then occurs, leading to Fab fragments and their degradation products (F'ab). In time, even the relatively resistant Fab region of IgG would be expected to be completely digested. A similar sequence probably also occurs in pepsin digests although the most familiar products are those obtained after 18 hr at pH 4.5.

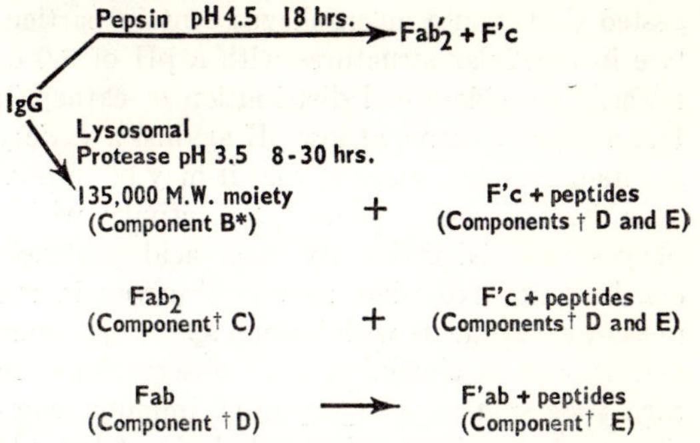

Figure 7. Hypothetical reaction sequence in the degradation of IgG by lysosomal proteases at pH 3.5.

Fab-like fragments of IgG, with sedimentation coefficients in the range of 3S to 5S, have been observed by Lawrence and Williams in sera from normal individuals and from patients with a variety of diseases (44). These authors have also shown that such circulating fragments of IgG interact with intact serum IgG and that the complexes formed are dissociated in isotonic salt solution both at neutral pH and at pH 4.0. Circulating fragments of the type described by Lawrence and Williams appear to have characteristics similar to those of the fragments found in lysosomal protease digests and may well be formed *in vivo* by the action of these enzymes Complexes of the type described may also be formed (44) when Fab or Fab_2 fragments are infused into animals. Rapid elimination of such complexes may explain the relatively short half life of Fab or Fab_2 fragments (41, 45–48).

Fragmentation of IgG such as described here may be effected not only by lysosomal enzymes but also by non-lysosomal and presumably extracellular enzymes. With regard to intracellular digestion, Roux in 1925 (49) first suggested that mouse macrophages contain particulate intracellular structures with a pH of 3.0 or lower. The widespread distribution of cathepsin D, an enzyme active at low pH against a variety of intact proteins, suggests that it may be responsible for the major proteolytic activity within phagosomes. Digestion by such acid proteases can be quite extensive, as was observed in the present experiments with human spleen lysosome extracts particularly. These observations in turn suggest that phagocytosed immune complexes can be digested intracellularly at low pH to produce IgG fragments, some of which may be released only after extensive digestion to small peptides or amino acids (50).

During the preparation of this manuscript a report on the degradation of rabbit IgG by a granular fraction from rat and rabbit spleen appeared (51). No purification or characterization of the enzymatic activity was attempted, nor was the extent of digestion of the rabbit IgG as great as that observed in the studies reported here, particularly when enzyme preparation from human spleen was used.

Acknowledgment. We are grateful to Joanna Allen and Barbara Smith for their competent technical assistance.

REFERENCES

1. Schwabe, C. and Kalnitsky, G., Biochemistry, *5:* 158, 1966.
2. Pastan, I. and Almquist, S., Endocrinology, *78:* 350, 1966.
3. Ziff, M., Gribetz, H. J. and LoSpalluto, J., J. Clin. Invest., *39:* 405, 1960.
4. Janoff, A. and Zeligs, D., Science, *161:* 702, 1968.
5. Weissmann, G. and Spilberg, I., Arthritis Rheum., *11:* 162, 1968.
6. Cohn, Z. A. and Wiener, E., J. Exp. Med., *118:* 991, 1963.
7. Hayashi, H., Tokuda, A. and Udaka, K., J. Exp. Med., *112:* 237, 1960.
8. DeDuve, C., Pressman, B. C., Gianetto, R., Wattiaux, R. and Applemans, F., Biochem. J., *59:* 604, 1955.
9. Bowers, W. E. and DeDuve, C., J. Cell Biol., *32:* 349, 1967.
10. Fell, H. B. and Dingle, J. T., Biochem. J., *87:* 403, 1963.
11. Weston, P. D., Barrett, A. J. and Dingle, J. T., Nature, *222:* 285, 1969.
12. Woessner, J. F., Biochem. J., *97:* 855, 1965.
13. Metrione, R. M., Neves, A. G. and Fruton, J. S., Biochemistry, *5:* 1597, 1966.
14. Cochrane, C. G. and Aikin, B. S., J. Exp. Med., *124:* 733, 1966.
15. Cochrane, C. G., J. Exp. Med., *118:* 489, 1963.
16. Kniker, W. T. and Cochrane, C. G., J. Exp. Med., *122:* 83, 1965.
17. Cochrane, G., Unanue, E. R. and Dixon, F. J., J. Exp. Med., *122:* 99, 1965.
18. Ward, P. A. and Cochrane, C. G., J. Exp. Med., *121:* 215, 1965.
19. Baum, J., Stastny, P. and Ziff, M., J. Immun., *93:* 985, 1964.
20. Hollander, J. L., McCarty, D. J., Astorga, G. and Castro-Murillo, E., Ann. Int. Med., *62:* 271, 1965.
21. Astorga, G. and Bollet, A. J., Arthritis Rheum., *8:* 511, 1965.
22. Wasi, S., Mu-kay, R. K., Macmorine, D. R. L. and Movat, H. Z., Brit. J. Exp. Path., *47:* 411, 1966.
23. Wasi, S., Uriuhara, T., Taichman, N. S., Murray, R. K. and Mowat, H. Z., Experientia, *22:* 196, 1966.
24. Anson, M. L., J. Gen. Physiol., *23:* 695, 1940.
25. Appelmans, F., Wattiaux, R. and DeDuve, C., Biochem. J., *59:* 438, 1955.
26. Tallan, H. H., Jones, M. E. and Fruton, J. S., J. Biol. Chem., *194:* 793, 1952.
27. Lapresle, C., Kaminiski, M. and Tanner, C. E., J. Immun. *82:* 94, 1959.
28. Lapresle, C. and Webb, T., Biochem. J., *76:* 538, 1960.
29. McMaster, P. B. and Webb, T., Ann. Inst. Pasteur, *104:* 90, 1963.
30. Weissman, G. and Thomas, L., J. Exp. Med., *116:* 433, 1962.
31. Lapresle, C. and Webb, T., Biochem. J., *84:* 455, 1962.
32. Gornall, A. G., Bardawill, C. J. and David, M. M., J. Biol. Chem., *177:* 751, 1949.
33. Andrews, P., Biochem. J., *96:* 595, 1965.
34. Fehr, K., LoSpalluto, J. and Ziff, M., Fed. Proc., *28:* 496, 1969.
35. Porter, R. R., Biochem. J., *73:* 119, 1959.
36. Greenbaum, L. M. and Fruton, J. S., J. Biol. Chem., *226:* 173, 1957.
37. Lichtenstein, N. and Fruton, J. S., Proc. Nat. Acad. Sci., *46:* 787, 1960.
38. Press, E. M., Porter, R. R. and Cebra, G., Biochem. J., *74:* 501, 1960.
39. Barrett, A. J., Biochem. J., *104:* 601, 1967.
40. Marks, N. and Lajtha, A., Biochem. J., *97:* 74, 1965.
41. Janeway, C. A., Merler, E., Rosen, F. S.,

Salmon, S. and Grain, J. D., New England J. Med. *278:* 919, 1968.

42. Nisonoff, A., Wissler, F. C., Lipman, L. N. and Woernly, D. L., Arch. Biochem., *89:* 230, 1960.
43. Osterland, C. K., Harboe, M. and Kunkel, H. G., Vox Sang., *8:* 133, 1963.
44. Lawrence, T. G. and Williams, R. C., J. Exp. Med., *125:* 233, 1967.
45. Wochner, R. D., Strober, W. and Waldmann, T. A., J. Exp. Med., *126:* 207, 1967.
46. Spiegelberg, H. L. and Weigle, W. O., J. Exp. Med., *121:* 323, 1965.
47. Fahey, J. L. and Robinson, A. G., J. Exp. Med., *118:* 845, 1963.
48. Spiegelberg, H. L. and Weigle, W. O., J. Exp. Med., *123:* 999, 1966.
49. Roux, P., J. Exp. Med., *41:* 399, 1925.
50. Cohn, Z. A. and Wiener, E., J. Exp. Med., *118:* 1009, 1963.

1. Motas, C. and Ghetie V., Immunochemistry, *6:* 547, 1969.

THE JOURNAL OF IMMUNOLOGY

Vol. 105, No. 4, October 1970
Printed in U.S.A.

CELLULAR RECOGNITION BY MOUSE LYMPHOCYTES *IN VITRO*

II. Specific Stimulation by Histocompatibility Antigens in Mixed Cell Culture[1, 2]

W. H. ADLER, T. TAKIGUCHI, B. MARSH AND R. T. SMITH

From the Tumor Biology Unit, Department of Pathology, University of Florida College of Medicine, Gainesville, Florida 32601

Received for publication February 27, 1970

The *in vitro* stimulation of mouse spleen cells by foreign histocompatibility antigens is described. Spleen cells from mice less than 3 weeks of age could not be stimulated in mixed lymphocyte cultures. They were also deficient in their ability to stimulate adult allogeneic cells in mixed lymphocyte cultures. The ability of the cells to be stimulated by histocompatibility antigens was correlated in time with their ability to stimulate allogeneic cells. Stimulation of mouse spleen cells was accomplished by allogeneic spleen cells with differences at the H-2 locus or at the H-3, H-13 loci, and with soluble H-2 antigen. F_1 hybrid spleen cells were stimulated by parental strain spleen cells or by parental strain red blood cell stroma. Immunization with allogeneic spleen cells was found to transiently affect the degree of stimulation obtained in mixed lymphocyte cultures of spleen cells from the immunized mice mixed with mitomycin-treated cells of the strain used for immunization. The cells from immunized animals also showed an increased degree of stimulation when reacted in MLC with allogeneic cells sharing some of the H-2 antigens of the strain used for the immunization. Immunization did not affect the degree of stimulation obtained in MLC of cells from strains with weak histocompatibility differences. The possible explanations of *in vitro* lymphocyte stimulation by histocompatibility antigens of allogeneic or semi-allogeneic cells are discussed.

In mixed lymphocyte cultures (MLC), the reactivity of a lymphoid cell population toward target cells of differing phenotype is assayed and this reaction shows many characteristics which have been interpreted as a primary immune reaction to cell surface antigens *in vitro*. This method has proven to be a valuable tool for investigating cellular recognition, and the histocompatibility antigens of man (1, 2), rat (3, 4) and mouse (5, 6) have been studied in this way. The full potentialities of the laboratory mouse for examining genetic aspects of cellular recognition have not as yet been exploited, however, for lack of a simple and reliable culture system which supports the appropriate mixed cell reactions. The first paper in this series (7) reported cultural conditions in which lymphoid cells survived for prolonged periods and mitogen-stimulated DNA synthesis and its metabolic and morphologic antecedents occurred. Phytohemagglutinin (PHA)- and specific antigen-stimulated cell transformation and DNA synthesis were characterized under a variety of conditions.

This paper described experiments showing that the same culture system supports mixed cell reactions involving primary stimulation by both major and minor histocompatibility antigens. The data further establish that prior immunization results in enhanced *in vitro* reactivity over that of a primary response, and that augmented reactivity is related to the specific antigenic determinants exposed to the immunized strain. Evidence is presented that F_1 hybrid cells are stimulated by cells from either parental strain.

[1] This work was supported in part by research grants from the National Institutes of Health (HD-00384), the American Cancer Society (ACS-T-463), an American Cancer Society Institutional Grant (IN-62-G), and a National Institute of General Medical Sciences Training Grant (GM-01996).

[2] Work done as National Institute of Allergy and Infectious Diseases trainee (5 TI AI-0128).

MATERIALS AND METHODS

Cell culture technique. The cell culture technique employed here has been described in detail in the preceding paper of this series (7). Briefly, the medium consisted of RPMI-1640 obtained from Grand Island Biological Company, Grand Island, New York, to which was added 100 units of penicillin and 100 μg of streptomycin/ml, together with 5% fresh, heated (56°C for 30 min) human serum obtained from a single donor for each experiment. Fifteen $\times$ 10^6 reacting cells were distributed to each tube containing 3 ml of this medium. Unless indicated otherwise, an equal number of target cells was added to the tube prior to incubation. The tubes were incubated at 37°C in 80% humidity and 5% CO_2 in air for 72 hr. Tritiated thymidine (Schwarz/Mann, Orangeburg, N. Y.; specific activity 1.9 Ci/mmol) was added during the final 24 hr of incubation. ^{3}H-thymidine incorporation was assayed as described previously. Average values are shown for experiments in which duplicate tubes were examined; mean values and ranges are given for experiments involving three to five replicate tubes; and the mean values and the standard error (S.E.) of the mean are given for those in which there were six or more tubes. The range of values for replicate tubes rarely exceeded plus or minus 10% for the mixed cell culture method employed here. In all experiments involving mixed cell cultures, the controls included tubes containing reacting cells plus syngeneic mitomycin treated target cells.

Preparation of target cells. Mitomycin-C (Nutritional Biochemicals Corp., Cleveland, Ohio) was used in a modification of the method of Bach and Voynow (8) to prevent tritiated thymidine incorporation by target cells in the reaction. Target cells were incubated 30 min at 37°C in 0.5 ml of Eagle's minimum essential medium (MEM), containing 50 μg mitomycin-C, or other indicated amounts, and then washed by gentle centrifugation with the addition of 5 ml of fresh medium twice before the addition of the reacting cell suspension and 3 ml of medium.

Radiation of target cells was delivered by a General Electric Maxitron at 250 kv, 15 mA, through 0.5 mm copper and 1.0 mm aluminum, at a rate of 600 R/min to a total value of 6000 R.

Mice. Mice employed for all of these studies were production stock derived from inbred lines maintained in these laboratories or purchased from the Jackson Laboratories, Bar Harbor, Maine. The congenic resistant sublines of C57BL/10 came from the production or research stock of the Jackson Laboratories, as did the F_1 hybrids and appropriate parental strains.

Cell preparations for experiments involving animals of varying ages were derived from litters born in this laboratory.

Mice were immunized by a single i.p. injection of 50 $\times$ 10^6 allogeneic spleen cells contained in 0.1 ml of MEM; the spleen cells were harvested from these recipients at varying intervals thereafter, and used as reacting cells in mixed cell culture with the appropriate blocked allogeneic and syngeneic target cells.

Soluble H-2 antigen employed for experiments described here was kindly supplied as a lyophilized powder by D. A. L. Davies (Searle Research Laboratories, High Wycombe Bucks, England). This preparation was redissolved and sterilized by passage through a Millipore filter and then added in the indicated amounts to the appropriate reacting cells. This preparation had been made from spleen cells of the B10-M strain mice by a procedure described elsewhere by Davies (9).

Erythrocyte stroma were prepared by hypotonic lysis of thrice-washed A/J erythrocytes, followed by repeated washing and centrifugation in saline to remove soluble protein and hemoglobin. The red cell stroma were then lyophilized for subsequent use in the experiments as described.

PHA-P was obtained from Difco, Inc.; 10 μl were added to the appropriate culture as described in the text.

RESULTS

Two methods have been employed in other lymphocyte culture systems for the purpose of discriminating between the contribution of each cell population in mixed lymphocyte reactions; irradiation of the target cells at a dose level which prevents cell division, or treatment of target cells with compounds having the property of inhibiting DNA synthesis such as mitomycin-C (10, 11). Both methods were employed here in examination of the one-way reaction. The amount of mitomycin-C required in this system for optimal effects was determined by assaying the reactivity of mouse spleen cells to PHA after incubation with varying concentrations of mitomycin-C, then comparing ^{3}H-thymi-

TABLE I

Effect of treatment with various amounts of mitomycin-C upon PHA stimulation of ³H-thymidine incorporation by A/J spleen cells[a]

Amount of Mitomycin-C	³H-Thymidine Incorporation (CPM/Tube; Mean and Range)	
	Control	PHA
μg		
0	9,357 (9,149–9,703)	140,675 (137,890–143,089)
25	234 (226–241)	2,952 (2,509–3,376)
50	53 (49–56)	490 (461–529)
75	50 (48–54)	188 (167–199)
100	53 (48–60)	154 (130–191)
200	47 (46–49)	184 (142–218)

[a] In this experiment, the effect of varying concentrations of mitomycin-C upon PHA stimulation of 15×10^6 spleen cells/tube was determined. The cells were incubated 30 min at 37°C with the indicated amount of mitomycin-C in 0.5 ml of culture medium, then washed twice by centrifugation with 5 ml of fresh medium before incubation with or without PHA for 48 hr. ³H-thymidine was added for the final 24 hr. The data shown are mean values and the range of three to five paired determinations.

dine incorporation of these cells with that of unstimulated cells. Table I shows an experiment in which A/J spleen cells required 50 μg of mitomycin-C/15×10^6 cells for complete inhibition of incorporation in control cells, and for nearly complete inhibition of PHA-stimulated ³H-thymidine incorporation. Inasmuch as PHA represents the most potent stimulus available, it was concluded that treatment with 50 μg was adequate to insure minimal participation by the target cell population in a one-way reaction. This level appeared not to provide an excess which could elute into the medium and interfere with ³H-thymidine incorporation by the unblocked population, providing the ratio between reacting and target cells was appropriately low. When very large numbers of mitomycin-treated cells were added to 15×10^6 reacting cells (see below), incorporation of ³H-thymidine was slightly less than that stimulated by comparable numbers of irradiated target cells. This suggests that in very high target cell concentrations, and despite washings, mitomycin-C may be released into the medium and exert an inhibitory effect upon DNA synthesis of the untreated cell populations. Other evidence substantiating this point has been reported recently (11).

Six thousand roentgens were established as an adequate level of irradiation to stop essentially all DNA synthesis in normal mouse spleen cell populations, both in mixed allogeneic cell cultures where both cell types were irradiated, and in PHA-treated cells.

Time course of allogeneic stimulation in the one-way mixed cell culture. After preliminary studies established a satisfactory ratio between target and reacting cells and appropriate methods of blocking target cell reactivity, the time course of the one-way mixed cell reaction was examined further. ³H-thymidine was added 24 hr before the culture was terminated, and the degree of stimulation was assayed at various intervals for 5 days. The results with all the strains investigated are exemplified by the response of C57BL/6 reacting to A/J target cells shown in Figure 1. Optimal reactivity in terms of ratio of incorporation, i.e., ³H-thymidine incorporation stimulated by allogeneic target cells, divided by that of the syngeneic combination, occurred when the culture was terminated at 72 hr. High levels of incorporation on day 1 are characteristic of spleen cell populations *in vitro* under these conditions, regardless of the stimulus employed (7).

Dose response relationships in mixed cell reactions. Early experiments with mixed cell cultures suggested that the optimal ratio between numbers of target and reacting cells was not identical for each strain combination. An example of the dose response relationship for three combinations is shown in Figure 2. In this experiment, C57BL/6 spleen cells were mixed with varying numbers of mitomycin-treated CBA, A, or A × C57BL/6 F_1 hybrid cells, and ³H-thymidine incorporation stimulated in this mixture was compared with that stimulated by syngeneic cells. Optimal stimulation was obtained at target cell/reacting cell ratios between 0.5 and 1.0. In its reactions to A strain, C57BL/6 showed opti-

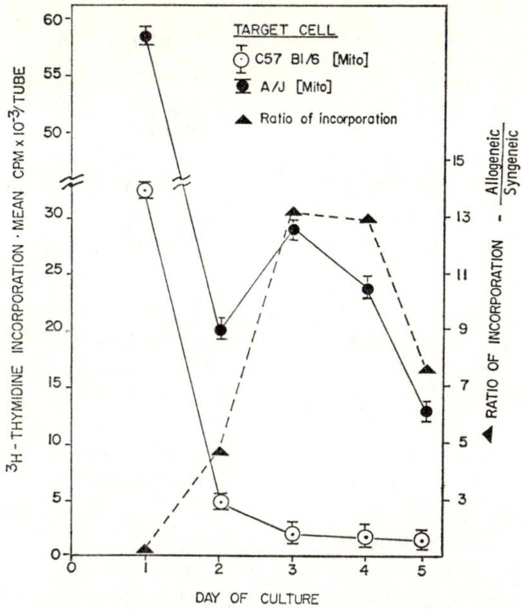

Figure 1. Time course of ^{3}H-thymidine incorporation into C57BL/6 spleen cells in mixed cell culture with mitomycin-treated A/J target cells. In this experiment, replicate tubes containing 15 × 10^6 C57BL/6 cells were mixed with 10 × 10^6 A/J spleen cells and ^{3}H-thymidine was added at 0, 24, 48, 72 or 96 hr. The cultures were terminated 24 hr later. The data shown represent the mean and range of the values obtained.

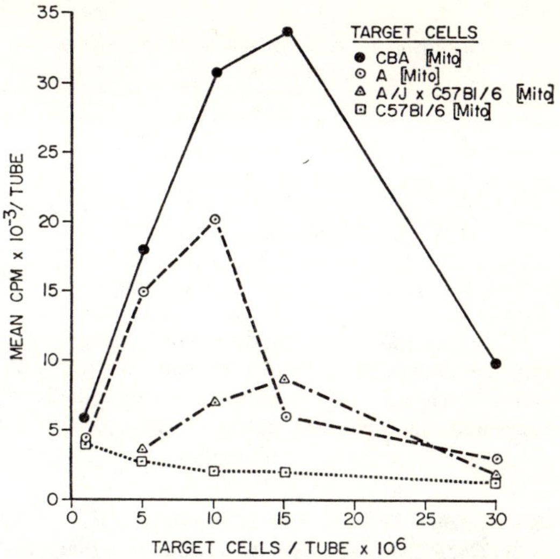

Figure 2. Dose-response relationship between ^{3}H-thymidine incorporation by C57BL/6 spleen cells stimulated in culture by various numbers of A/J, CBA, C57BL/6 and F_1 hybrid cells. Varying numbers of mitomycin-treated A/J, CBA, C57BL/6 or (A/J × C57BL/6) F_1 target cells were added to tubes containing 15 × 10^6 C57BL/6 spleen cells in culture medium containing serum of a single donor; ^{3}H-thymidine was added at 48 hr and the cultures were terminated at 72 hr. Each point represents the mean value for three to five replicate tubes.

mal stimulation when 10 × 10^6 target cells were added. At 15 × 10^6 cells, there was considerably less stimulation. In strongly reacting combinations such as C57BL/6 reacting with CBA, this ratio was less critical. It was especially necessary to test varying ratios of reacting to target cells in order to detect maximum stimulation in weakly reacting combinations.

Highly reproducible stimulation in mixed cell culture required that the serum from a single donor be used for medium on successive days. Table II illustrates results of four successive tests in which A spleen cells were reacted in mixed cell culture with mitomycin-treated C57BL/6 target cells. This high order of reproducibility permitted studies of changing reactivity of cells over varying periods of time and in animals of differing ages.

Effect of age of reacting and target cell donor upon allogeneic stimulation in mixed cell culture. Newborn mice are known to give far less vigorous *in vivo* primary responses to histocompatibility antigens than their mature counterparts (12). Immunologic tolerance, in fact, is induced in many strain combinations when allogeneic cells are introduced in large quantity during the early days of life (13). Despite this, immunologic competence of newborn lymphoid cells has been apparently demonstrated by their capacity to react to foreign histocompatibility antigens (14), and to restore immunologic competence when given to an irradiated syngeneic recipient (15). Results reported in the previous paper of this series (7) indicated a deficiency of spleen cells taken from newborn mice, in their susceptibility to PHA stimulation *in vitro*. It was of interest, therefore, to examine the *in vitro* reactivity of newborn spleen cells to foreign histocompatibility antigens.

Mixed cell cultures in which the reacting cells were derived from animals of differing age were compared in cultures in which the target cells were taken from mature donors. The results of such experiments are indicated in Table III.

TABLE II

Stimulation of A/J spleen cells by mitomycin-treated C57BL/6 target cells in mixed cell culture: Reproducibility of results using medium from a single serum donor[a]

Day	^{3}H-Thymidine Incorporation (Mean CPM/Tube and Range)		Ratio of Incorporation: Allogeneic/Syngeneic
	A/J [mito]	C57BL/6 [mito]	
0	4,610 (4,480–4,840)	16,514 (16,166–17,137)	3.6
2	4,680 (4,550–4,873)	16,936 (16,069–17,710)	3.8
4	4,704 (4,428–5,034)	16,955 (15,123–18,409)	3.6
8	4,540 (4,400–4,660)	16,248 (14,560–17,500)	3.6

[a] In this experiment, medium containing fresh serum from a single donor was employed on successive days as shown. 15 × 10[6] A/J spleen cells/tube were reacted with an equal number of A/J [mito] target cells; ^{3}H-thymidine was added at 48 hr and the experiment was terminated at 72 hr. The values shown represent the mean and range of three to five replicate tubes.

TABLE III

Relationship between age of reacting spleen cells from C57BL/6 mice and stimulation by mitomycin-treated mature A/J cells in mixed cell culture[a]

Age of Donors of C57BL/6 Reacting Cells	^{3}H-Thymidine Incorporation Stimulated by Syngeneic and Allogeneic Mitomycin-Treated Target Cells (Mean CPM/Tube)		Ratio of Incorporation: Allogeneic/Syngeneic
	C57BL/6 (syngeneic)	A/J (allogeneic)	
days			
7	1,514	1,851	1.2
10	1,661	1,659	1.0
14	1,249	1,644	1.4
21	1,284	2,260	1.8
28	1,482	3,101	2.1
35	1,723	4,469	2.6
56	1,664	6,669	4.1

[a] Spleen cells for this experiment were harvested from groups of a single pool of C57BL/6 litters at the indicated ages; 15 × 10[6] cells/tube were incubated 72 hr with 15 × 10[6] mitomycin-treated A/J cells from 4-month-old donors. ^{3}H-thymidine was added for the last 24 hr of culture. A single serum donor was used for the medium throughout the experiment. The values represent the means of duplicate tubes.

In the experiments shown, C57BL/6 cells from donors of varying ages were reacted with syngeneic C57BL/6, or allogeneic A/J, mitomycin-treated target cells. The results demonstrate the absence of allogeneic stimulation before 10 days of age; thereafter, the capacity to respond increased, but did not reach mature levels until 6 to 8 weeks of age.

Several explanations for this lack of response in early life seem plausible. The relative proportion of lymphocytes and other cell types in the reacting cell population changes rapidly during this period (16). Macrophages in particular appear deficient in newborn animals since their immune responses are significantly enhanced by transfer of these cells from the mature syngeneic host (17). Biochemical and enzymatic mechanisms in the first days of life also differ in major ways from those of the mature individual. These conditions could create cultural or metabolic requirements not satisfied by a culture medium in which mature cells are stimulated. A relative deficiency of newborn lymphoid cells might also exist in the number of receptor sites which bind the human anti-mouse lymphocyte globulin. It is conceivable that such a deficit might fail to provide a necessary threshold level of stimulation for any of the *in vitro* mouse cell reactions; however, developing spleen cell populations do become responsive to PHA significantly sooner than they respond to allogeneic cells.

Cellular recognition in mixed cell culture appears to involve contact between antigenically disparate surfaces (18, 19). Therefore, it would be important for both the reacting cell and the target cell in this system to have sufficient antigenic representation to provide for recognition triggered stimulation. A deficiency in histocompatibility determinents on the spleen cell membrane of newborn animals might be responsible for recognition failure. Using serologic techniques Möller and others (20, 21) have established that this appears to be the case.

In an attempt to examine this question further, mixed cell cultures were prepared between reacting cells derived from mature donors and target cells derived from animals of ages varying

TABLE IV

Effect of age of donor on capacity of C57BL/6 target cells to stimulate mature A/J reacting cells in mixed cell culture[a]

Age of Donor of Mitomycin-Treated Target Cells	^{3}H-Thymidine Incorporation by Mature A/J Spleen Cells (Mean CPM/Culture and Range Value)	Ratio of Incorporation: Allogeneic/Syngeneic
Mature A/J	1,881 (1,862–1,929)	
3-day C57BL/6	3,032 (3,003–3,062)	1.6
7-day C57BL/6	4,553 (4,220–4,729)	2.4
90-day C57BL/6	11,671 (10,479–12,748)	6.2

[a] In this experiment spleen cells were taken from groups of donors of the indicated age, treated with mitomycin-C, washed three times, then 15 × 10[6]/tube were cultured 72 hr with 15 × 10[6] A/J spleen cells from a mature donor. ^{3}H-thymidine was added for the final 24 hr of culture. Incorporation values represent mean and range values of three to six replicate tubes.

[b] Ratio of incorporation represents incorporation stimulated by allogeneic cells of differing age divided by that stimulated by mature syngeneic cells.

from newborn to 90 days of age. The results of such experiments are shown in Table IV. Target cells derived from immature donors were found deficient in capacity to stimulate mature allogeneic reacting cells. The capacity to stimulate reached mature levels before 90 days as shown here, and by 6 weeks in other experiments.

These data, taken with those of Möller (20) strongly suggest that one major source of the age deficiency demonstrated in the mixed cell reaction involving newborn cell populations is the relative lack of H-2 representation on the surface of the immature lymphoid target cells used to stimulate the reaction. This has been discussed more fully elsewhere (7).

Comparison of primary cellular recognition determined by various major and minor histocompatibility loci. A variety of combinations of spleen cells from various mouse strains, differing at the H-2 locus, were employed in mixed cell culture, using mature donors, the same serum donors for medium, and an identical culture assay system. A single 1:1 ratio of reacting to target cell was used for this experiment although it was shown (Fig. 2) that this ratio is not optimal for every combination. The results, given in the upper section of Table V, show the ^{3}H-thymidine incorporation by A/J, C57BL/6, CBA, BALB/c and DBA/2 reacting in one-way mixed cell culture with mitomycin-blocked target cells derived from mouse strains of differing and identical H-2 alleles.

Each of the combinations in which histoincompatibility is demonstrable by tissue grafting gave significant ^{3}H-thymidine incorporation in the allogeneic over the syngeneic combination in culture. Total incorporation values varied widely among the strain combinations. When expressed as ratio of incorporation, however, a relatively narrow range of stimulation in excess of syngeneic incorporation was shown, between 2.4 and 6.5. The single exception was the reaction between C57BL/6 and CBA [mito] which gave 13-fold stimulation, and a high total incorporation value. The reciprocal culture result—CBA and B57BL/6 [mito]—fell within the ratio range of the others, but had nearly identical total incorporation.

On the assumption that H-2 incompatibility was solely responsible for the mixed cell culture reactions observed, attempts were made to relate the known antigenic determinant mosaics involved in each combination to a total incorporation or ratio of incorporation.[3] For example, only one antigenic determinant, H-2[5], is shared in the combination C57BL/6-CBA; the other 16 determinants differ. C57BL/6 could conceivably recognize and react to six different antigens on CBA, and CBA to eight on C57BL/6. This does, indeed, give a strong reaction in both directions, and exceptionally high incorporation ratio when C57BL/6 reacted to CBA [mito].

However, in the case of C57BL/6 reacting to A/J where eight different antigens are present, and six are shared, lower levels of incorporation and a low ratio were found; in this case, the optimal number of mitomycin-treated A/J cells was 10 × 10[6] (Fig. 2). As a result of this type of analysis, it could be concluded that the degree of incorporation in a given mixed cell culture tested at a 1:1 cell ratio could not be accounted for simply in terms of the numbers of individual H-2 antigenic differences or similarities involved.

All of the strains involved presumably differ also at multiple minor histocompatibility loci; it

[3] These correlations were based upon the data on individual H-2 antigenic distribution set forth in reference (22) and modified in minor aspects based upon personal communications with Jackson Laboratories.

TABLE V

Comparison of stimulation of ³H-thymidine uptake by spleen cells from various mouse strains in mixed cell culture with mitomycin-C blocked allogeneic target cells[a]

Reacting Cell and Pertinent Histocompatibility Data	Mitomycin-Treated Target Cell and Pertinent Histocompatibility Data	³H-Thymidine Uptake by Reacting Cells: Mean CPM/tube ± S.E.	Ratio of incorporation: allogeneic/syngeneic
A/J [H-2ᵃ]	A/J	3,766 ± 123	
	BALB/c [H-2ᵈ]	13,194 ± 359	3.6
	C57BL/6 [H-2ᵇ]	17,358 ± 630	4.7
	CBA [H-2ᵏ]	24,251 ± 162	6.5
	(A/J × C57BL/6) F_1 [H-2ᵃ/H-2ᵇ]	7,725 ± 459	2.4
C57BL/6 [H-2ᵇ]	C57BL/6	2,651 ± 154	
	BALB/c [H-2ᵈ]	6,407 ± 210	2.4
	CBA [H-2ᵏ]	35,550 ± 1,273	13.4
	A/J [H-2ᵃ]	6,380 ± 330	2.4
	(CBA × C57BL/6) F_1 [H-2ᵏ/H-2ᵇ]	13,126 ± 57	5.0
	(A/J × C57BL/6) F_1 [H-2ᵃ/H-2ᵇ]	7,860 ± 155	2.9
CBA [H-2ᵏ]	CBA	9,466 ± 406	
	C57BL/6 [H-2ᵇ]	34,311 ± 819	3.6
	A/J [H-2ᵃ]	34,711 ± 1,035	3.7
	(CBA × C57BL/6) F_1 [H-2ᵏ/H-2ᵇ]	17,186 ± 392	1.8
BALB/c [H-1ᵇ, H-2ᵈ]	BALB/c	1,680 ± 85	
	C57BL/6 [H-2ᵇ]	8,510 ± 457	5.1
	A/J [H-2ᵃ]	6,964 ± 38	4.2
	DBA [H-1ᵃ H-2ᵈ]	4,304 ± 308	2.4
DBA-2 [H-1ᵃ, H-2ᵈ]	DBA	2,768 ± 131	
	BALB/c [H-1ᵇ, H-2ᵈ]	6,834 ± 301	3.9

[a] In this series of experiments, 15×10^6 reacting cells/3-ml tube were tested with the 15×10^6 mitomycin-treated target cells; ³H-thymidine was added at 48 hr and the test was terminated at 72 hr. Each reacting cell was tested against the series of target cells in medium containing serum from the same donor, but the various reacting lines were tested in different sera; thus, the incorporation data are not necessarily comparable between strains. In each experiment, 5 to 10 replicate tubes were included in the mean value and calculated standard error. All of the differences shown are significant at a p value of 0.01 or less.

seemed probable therefore that these latter differences also contributed to the recognition process and the eventual degree of stimulation observed. The results of testing the combination of DBA/2 and BALB/c, which share all antigens of the H-2ᵈ allele but differ at at least two other known loci, gave significant reactions in both directions. The incorporation achieved, in fact, was about one-half that stimulated by these strains reacting to the strong H-2 differences.

When parental strains were combined in mixed cell culture with various F_1 hybrids as the target cell, the levels of incorporation were approximately one-half of that attained when the allogeneic parental strain was the target cell. The exception to this finding was C57BL/6 reacting to A × C57BL/6 F_1 hybrid cells. In this case the dose response relationship (Fig. 2) indicated that the optimal ratio of cells was different for the two combinations. Compared at optimal stimulation, the A × C57BL/6 F_1 hybird gave nearly one-half the value of the allogeneic combination as that found in the other cases. These data are consonant with the known codominance of H-2 in its antigenic representation on the cell surface of F_1 hybrids (20). Such cells have approximately one-half the antigenic representation of the parental strain as revealed by the absorption technique.

Allogeneic stimulation by a soluble purified histocompatibility antigen preparation. Purified membrane antigen derived from B10-M mouse spleen

TABLE VI

Stimulation of ³H-thymidine incorporation into allogeneic spleen cells by a purified soluble H-2ᶠ antigen[a]

Reacting Cell Source	³H-Thymidine Incorporation in Cultures with Varying Amounts of Soluble H-2^f[b] Extract—mean CPM/Tube; (Range); [Ratio of Incorporation]				
	0	10 μg	50 μg	100 μg	1,000 μg
C57BL/6 [H-2^b]	5,544 (5,108–5,904)	6,957 (6,528–7,196) [1.26]	10,030 9,268–10,678) [1.86]	9,397 (8,902–10,168) [1.69]	1,265 (1,243–1,287) [0.23]
A/J [H-2^a]	12,255 (12,016–12,715)	22,461 (21,824–23,461) [1.84]	27,192 (26,326–28,390) [2.22]	23,112 (22,862–23,297) [1.88]	
A/J × C57BL/6 F_1 [H-2^a × H-2^b]	8,038 (7,905–8,211)	12,483 (12,607–12,702) [1.56]	11,548 (11,344–11,935) [1.43]	9,253 (9,108–9,368) [1.14]	
B10-M [H-2^f]	14,301 (13,054–15,971)	10,009 (9,398–11,774) [0.72]	12,477 (11,092–12,489) [0.87]	12,029 (11,092–12,489) [0.84]	

[a] In this experiment, 15 × 10⁶ spleen cells/tube from syngeneic or allogeneic donors were incubated 72 hr with the indicated amounts of soluble H-2ᶠ extract. The results shown represent the mean values and range of three to five replicate tubes. The values for ratio of incorporation shown in brackets, represent the mean incorporation value for tubes to which varying amounts of antigen was added. Serum from a single donor was used for the experiment.

[b] H-2ᶠ antigen derived from spleen cells of B10-M strain mice was provided by Dr. D. A. L. Davies, Searle Research Laboratories, England.

has been prepared by enzyme solubilization and shown to have antigenic properties closely related to those of the intact cell (9). These properties include specific reactivity in a blocking reaction in which known anti-H-2 antisera are absorbed with the purified antigen and cytotoxicity of the antisera is thereby blocked. In addition, this soluble preparation can immunize allogeneic recipients as indicated by a second set graft rejection. These membrane preparations can be further fractionated into a number of moieties having the individual isoantigenic determinants known to constitute this H-2 allele. Since it has been demonstrated here that *in vitro* stimulation of spleen cell cultures by mitomycin-treated allogeneic cells is, for the most part, related to H-2 locus histocompatibility differences, the effect of a purified membrane preparation containing H-2 antigenic activity was tested for its capacity to stimulate allogeneic cells. A soluble H-2 antigen from B10-M mice (H-2ᶠ) was provided by Davies. Varying amounts of H-2 extract were added to spleen cell cultures from allogeneic and syngeneic mice and ³H-thymidine incorporation was compared. The results are given in Table VI. The H-2ᶠ antigen stimulated an increase in total ³H-thymidine uptake and ratio of incorporation by C57BL/6, A/J and C57BL/6 × A/J F_1 spleen cell cultures over that of cultures to which no antigen was added. The antigenic preparation did not stimulate syngeneic B10-M cells.

A dose response effect was observed, in which peak stimulation varied between 10 and 50 μg/tube among the three reacting cell lines, and inhibition occurred at higher doses. This is similar to the dose response effect observed in primary mixed cell reactions, and in experiments in which SRBC stroma or the soluble antigen, PPD, was added to appropriate immune cell populations.

Although it is probable that the H-2ᶠ purified membrane preparation contains antigens determined by other than the H-2 locus, these data add to others establishing that this locus alone is responsible for a major share of the stimulation between H-2 incompatible cells in this culture system.

One-way mixed cell cultures between C57BL/10

TABLE VII

Stimulation of ³H-thymidine incorporation in spleen cells from congenic resistant strains of mice by cells differing at the H-2 or H-3, H-13 loci[a]

Reacting Cell and Pertinent Histocompatibility Data	Mitomycin-Treated Target Cell and Pertinent Histocompatibility Data	Tritiated Thymidine Incorporation by Reacting Cells: Mean CPM ± S.E.	Tritiated Thymidine Incorporation by Reacting Cells: Ratio of incorporation: allogeneic/syngeneic
Experiment 1-250, C57BL/10 [$H\text{-}2^b$, $H\text{-}3^a$, $H\text{-}13^a$]	C57BL/10	311 ± 25	
	B10-D2 [$H\text{-}2^d$, $H\text{-}3^a$, $H\text{-}13^a$]	2,315 ± 55	7.4
	B10-LP [$H\text{-}2^b$, $H\text{-}3^b$, $H\text{-}13^b$]	482 ± 23	1.6
B10-LP [$H\text{-}2^b$, $H\text{-}3^b$, $H\text{-}13^b$]	B10-LP	594 ± 20	
	C57BL/10 [$H\text{-}2^b$, $H\text{-}3^a$, $H\text{-}13^a$]	894 ± 5	1.5
	B10-D2 [$H\text{-}2^d$, $H\text{-}3^a$, $H\text{-}13^a$]	4,264 ± 58	7.2
B10-D2 [$H\text{-}2^d$, $H\text{-}3^a$, $H\text{-}13^a$]	B10-D2	679 ± 13	
	C57BL/10 [$H\text{-}2^b$, $H\text{-}3^a$, $H\text{-}13^a$]	4,660 ± 16	6.9
	B10-LP [$H\text{-}2^b$, $H\text{-}3^b$, $H\text{-}13^b$]	4,164 ± 46	6.1
Experiment 2-78 B10-LP [$H\text{-}2^b$, $H\text{-}3^b$, $H\text{-}13^b$]	B10-LP	6,551 ± 29	
	C57BL/10 [$H\text{-}2^b$, $H\text{-}3^a$, $H\text{-}13^a$]	10,757 ± 432	1.6
C57BL/10 [$H\text{-}2^b$, $H\text{-}3^a$, $H\text{-}13^a$]	C57BL/10	4,423 ± 109	
	B10-LP ($H\text{-}2^b$, $H\text{-}3^b$, $H\text{-}13^b$]	20,115 ± 985	4.5
Experiment 2-83 B10-LP [$H\text{-}2^b$, $H\text{-}3^b$, $H\text{-}13^b$]	B10-LP	2,696 (2,055–3,150)	
	C57BL/10 [$H\text{-}2^b$, $H\text{-}3^a$, $H\text{-}13^a$]	3,558 (3,414–3,780)	1.3
Experiment 2-139 B10-LP [$H\text{-}2^b$, $H\text{-}3^b$, $H\text{-}13^b$]	B10-LP	2,556 (2,288–2,705)	
	C57BL/10 [$H\text{-}2^b$, $H\text{-}3^a$, $H\text{-}13^a$]	3,268 (3,100–3,486)	1.3

[a] Four experiments in which 15×10^6 reacting spleen cells were mixed with 15×10^6 mitomycin-treated target spleen cells of the indicated origin, and incubated for a total of 72 hr. ³H-thymidine was added during the final 24 hr of culture. Different serum donors were used for the medium in each experiment. Experiments 1-250 and 2-78 consisted of 10 or more replicate tubes in each category; the data are given as mean values ± S.E. Experiments 2-83 and 2-89 consisted of three to five replicate tubes; the mean and range values are shown. The differences shown for incorporation values between syngeneic and allogeneic combinations are significant at a p value of 0.1 or less.

and the congenic resistant inbred sublines, B10-LP and B10-D2. The multiple histocompatibility loci by which the available inbred strains of mice differ make it essentially impossible to attribute the results of mixed cell cultures to a single set of antigens of a histocompatibility allele. However, the ready availability of a few congenic resistant (CR) sublines of C57BL/10 offered the opportunity for examining cellular recognition of isolated single H-2 alleles and the combined effect of two minor histocompatibility loci, H-3 and H-13. The results are exemplified by four such experiments, conducted identically, but at different times, with different lots of the mice, and in media derived from different serum donors (Table VII). When the mixed cell reactions involved spleen cells derived from CR lines differing at H-2, a high degree of reactivity was found. The total levels and ratios of incorporation were strikingly similar in the reactions of B10-D2 [$H\text{-}2^d$] and mitomycin treated C57BL/10 [$H\text{-}2^b$] or B10-LP [$H\text{-}2^b$], as well as in the reciprocal culture in which $H\text{-}2^b$ reacted to $H\text{-}2^d$. These results confirm that antigens determined by the H-2 locus alone can stimulate a high degree of ³H-thymidine incorporation. Moreover, the data show that in terms of ratios of incorporation, the reactions are approximately equivalent in the reciprocal culture. This suggests that the net stimulatory effect of the same antigens represented is approximately equal in the two lines.

These experiments also demonstrate consistent and significant stimulation in mixed cell culture by antigens determined by minor histocompatibility loci. This stimulation occurred regardless of which participant was treated with mitomycin. Although statistically significant and reproducible, the degree of stimulation observed was usually less than that seen in reactions involving H-2 differences. The graft rejection time for these combinations, according to Berrian and McKhann (23), is 24 days when C57BL/10 is the donor. In some experiments, B10-LP target cells were more stimulatory to C57BL/10 than the reciprocal combination (e.g., experiment 2-78), but this was not consistently observed. The relationships between graft rejection times among other CR lines, and the degree of *in vitro* reactivity in mixed cell cultures involving these lines, are being further investigated.

Allogeneic stimulation of F_1 hybrid spleen cells by parental strain alloantigens. The observations of Snell (24) and others (25, 26) have shown that F_1 hybrid or semi-syngeneic mice provide a less favorable environment for the growth of parental strain tumors than does the syngeneic host. Depending upon the model, this is termed syngeneic preference, hybrid resistance, hybrid hyper-reactivity, or allogeneic inhibition. The *in vitro* equivalent of the phenomenon in mice, also termed allogeneic inhibition, has been studied in detail by Hellström (26), Möller (27) and others (28). Their systems involve reactions between lymphoid cells and target cell populations under a variety of conditions with endpoints determined by inhibition of cell growth or cytotoxicity. Each of the techniques requires, however, the presence of PHA, or heterologous anti-lymphocyte globulin in order to detect specific allogeneic cytotoxicity or colony inhibition. Huemer *et al.* (6) have reported a PHA-free system containing 20% horse serum, in which F_1 hybrid cells derived from parental strains congenic except at the H-2 locus are significantly stimulated to incorporate ^{3}H-thymidine in mixed culture by mitomycin-treated parental strain cells. Wilson (4), on the other hand, interpreted his data as showing no clear-cut *in vitro* inhibition or stimulation of F_1 rat lymphoid cells by the parental strain. Harrison *et al.* (29) also failed to demonstrate, using chromosomal markers, what they considered to be significant increase in F_1 mitoses when F_1 hybrid mouse spleen cells were mixed with parental strain in diffusion chambers and implanted *in vivo*.

One of the early observations using the mouse cell culture system reported here was that F_1 hybrid spleen cells were consistently stimulated in mixed cell cultures by parental strain cells. This type of experiment has been repeated many times with differing strain combinations and conditions, always revealing significant stimulation of F_1 hybrid spleen cells by mitomycin-blocked parental strain cells. Table VIII gives data exemplifying these results. For example, A/J × C57BL/6 F_1 cells were reacted with both parental strains (experiments 1-156, 1-160 and 1-171) on three successive occasions in medium having serum from different donors, with significant ratio of incorporation values over the syngeneic combination between 1.5 and 2.1 for the A/J parent target cells, and 2.5 and 2.8 for the C57BL/6 parent. Similar findings (experiments 1-242 and 1-280) were obtained with CBA × C57 BL/6 F_1 hybrids. Irradiated target cells (experiment 2-28) also stimulated the C57BL/6 × A F_1 hybrid strain.

In view of the universal failure of F_1 hosts to reject allografts from either parental strain, explanations of this phenomenon other than primary immune recognition, as suggested by Huemer (6), or recognition of some novel type, as postulated by Möller and Möller (30), were considered. It seemed possible, for example, that stimulation of the F_1 hybrid by the parental strain cell might be the nonspecific result of the elaboration of a mitogenic factor or factors by blocked target cells, as described by Kasakura and Lowenstein (31) and observed in this laboratory (unpublished). This explanation cannot be excluded, but as discussed elsewhere (to be published) is probably invalid. Experiments were performed attempting to exclude all participation by the parent strain target cell in the reaction. To do this, advantage was taken of the representation of H-2^a antigens on the membrane of A/J mouse erythrocytes. Stromal preparations from such cells contain H-2^a but presumably cannot participate in any active metabolic process or release mitogens. Varying amounts of A/J RBC stroma were added to cultures of A/J × C57BL/6 F_1 hybrid spleen cells and the effects were com-

TABLE VIII

Stimulation of ^{3}H-thymidine incorporation in F_1 hybrid spleen cells by target cells and erythrocyte stroma of parental origin[a]

Expt. No.	Reacting Cell	Target Cell	Incorporation of ^{3}H-Thymidine (Mean CPM/Tube and Range)[b]	Ratio of Incorporation: Allogeneic/Syngeneic
1-156	(A/J × C57BL/6) F_1	(A × C57BL/6) F_1 [mito]	923 (903–957)	
	(A/J × C57BL/6) F_1	A/J [mito]	1,386 (1,254–1,486)	1.5
	(A/J × C57BL/6) F_1	C57BL/6 [mito]	2,497 (2,254–2,673)	2.7
1-160	(A/J × C57BL/6) F_1	(A × C57BL/6) F_1 [mito]	3,512 (3,380–3,727)	
	(A/J × C57BL/6) F_1	A/J [mito]	7,007 (6,870–7,216)	2.0
	(A/J × C57BL/6) F_1	C57BL/6 [mito]	9,675 (9,263–9,954)	2.8
1-171	(A/J × C57BL/6) F_1	(A/J × C57BL/6) F_1 [mito]	3,024 (2,727–3,430)	
	(A/J × C57BL/6) F_1	A/J [mito]	6,199 (5,654–6,816)	2.1
	(A/J × C57BL/6) F_1	C57BL/6 [mito]	7,418 (6,792–7,954)	2.5
2-28	(A/J × C57BL/6) F_1	(A/J × C57BL/6) F_1 [x-ray]	3,226 (3,114–3,422)	
	(A/J × C57BL/6) F_1	A/J [x-ray]	4,272 (4,231–4,368)	1.3
	(A/J × C57BL/6) F_1	C57BL/6 [x-ray]	4,489 (4,424–4,563)	1.4
2-48	(A/J × C57BL/6) F_1		11,610 (11,125–12,026)	
	(A/J × C57BL/6) F_1	A/J RBC stroma[c]	20,353 (19,907–21,130)	1.9
	A/J		10,800 (10,642–10,833)	
	A/J	A/J RBC stroma	10,298 (10,132–10,502)	
	C57BL/6		10,682 (10,327–11,304)	
	C57BL/6	A/J RBC stroma	15,915 (15,153–16,462)	1.5
1-242	(CBA × C57BL/6) F_1	(CBA × C57BL/6) F_1 [mito]	5,914 (5,841–6,039)	
	(CBA × C57BL/6) F_1	CBA [mito]	10,780 (10,499–11,001)	1.8
	(CBA × C57BL/6) F_1	C57BL/6 [mito]	13,459 (12,911–14,004)	2.3
1-280	(CBA × C57BL/6) F_1	(CBA × C57BL/6) F_1 [mito]	4,492 (3,992–4,841)	
	(CBA × C57BL/6) F_1	CBA [mito]	10,820 (10,499–11,101)	2.4
	(CBA × C57BL/6) F_1	C57BL/6 [mito]	11,798 (10,911–12,450)	2.6

[a] To 15 × 10^6 reacting spleen cells/tube, containing 3 ml of medium, were added 15 × 10^6 target cells which had been either treated with mitomycin-C [mito], or irradiated with 6000 R [x-ray]. The cultures were incubated a total of 72 hr, and ^{3}H-thymidine was added for the last 24 hr. Different serum donors were used for the medium in the various experiments.

[b] Mean and range values of triplicate or quadruplicate determinations.

[c] Five-tenths milligram of A/J erythrocyte stroma was added to the indicated tubes before incubation.

pared with those of such preparations on either parental strain. Experiment 2-48 exemplifies the results of such tests, indicating that stroma stimulate significant ^{3}H-thymidine incorporation in the semi-syngeneic F_1 hybrid as well as the allogeneic parent strain.

This reaction seems to be most appropriately termed allogeneic stimulation. It appears to be no different in character from other primary recognition demonstrated between cells having H-2 and minor histocompatibility differences. Nor is it necessarily "non-immune," since the consequences of recognition demonstrated in allogeneic systems would not be possible in the F_1 hybrid in which there is *de facto* tolerance of parental strain histocompatibility antigens. The question, therefore, is whether any of these primary recognition responses are immune in

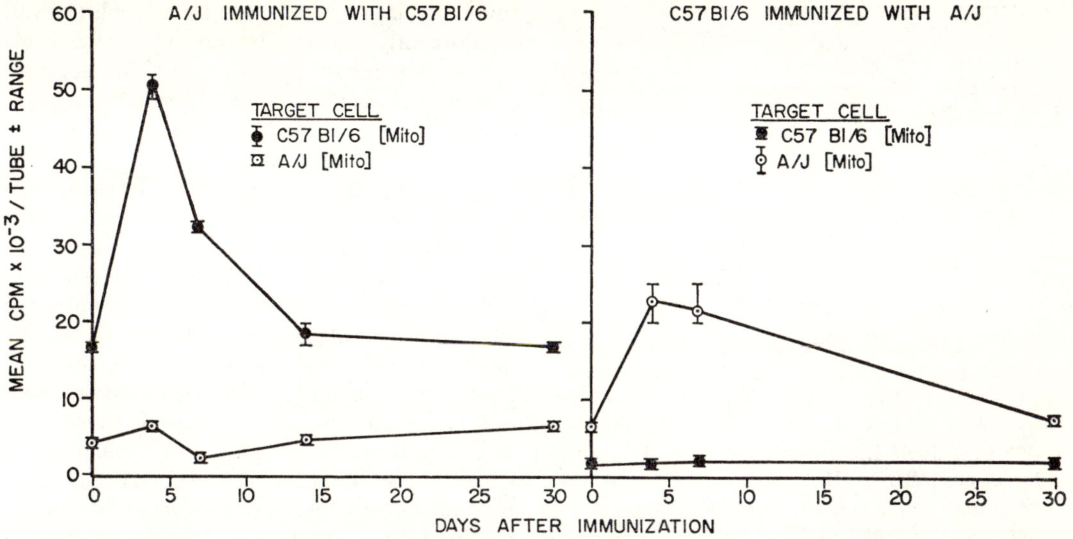

Figure 3. Specific stimulation of ^{3}H-thymidine incorporation by A/J and C57BL/6 spleen cells at intervals after immunization of the donor with allogeneic cells. Time course of response of groups of C57BL/6 and A/J mice to immunization with a single i.p. injection of 50×10^{6} spleen cells from the other strain. The data represent incorporation of ^{3}H-thymidine into 15×10^{6} cells of the reacting population taken from immunized donors at the indicated intervals, stimulated by 15×10^{6} mitomycin blocked syngeneic or allogeneic spleen cells. Each point represents the average value of three tubes and the range.

character, i.e., whether they lead to the generation of memory in the form of augmented cellular or antibody-mediated recognition and its consequences. Experiments to examine this question will be described next.

Effects of immunization on ^{3}H-thymidine incorporation stimulated by allogeneic spleen cells in mixed cell culture. Previous studies of rat mixed lymphoid cell cultures (32) have indicated that prior immunization of the donors of the reacting cells with an appropriate alloantigen did not increase ^{3}H-thymidine incorporation stimulated by specific allogeneic cells. In contrast, mouse cells in the sealed diffusion chamber culture systems (29) showed an increase in the number of mitoses in the cells of one member of a mixed cell reaction when the donor had been previously immunized with spleen cells of the other strain.

Since the mixed cell reaction *in vitro* appeared to reveal primary recognition of histocompatibility differences, paralleling first set graft rejection, it was of interest to determine whether this reaction was enhanced by immunization. The donors of reacting cells in mixed cell culture were immunized by a single injection of allogeneic spleen cells. Donor cells were taken at intervals after immunization and cultured with mitomycin-treated allogeneic cells of the same strain used for immunization. The results of typical experiments employing reciprocal strain combinations are shown in Figure 3. Marked increase in incorporation over that of cells from unimmunized donors was characteristic of cell populations taken 4 to 6 days after immunization.

In both of these strain combinations, and in others studied, this increase in reactivity was transient and returned to pre-immunization levels 2 to 4 weeks after immunization. No increase in the specifically antigen sensitive cell population appeared to accrue from the primary recognition process, i.e., no detectable cell-mediated memory resulted.

When attempts were made to immunize congenic resistant mice with allogeneic cells representing H-3, H-13 locus differences, i.e., B10-LP immunized with C57BL/10 (Fig. 4), overall incorporation in mixed cell culture of both syngeneic and allogeneic combinations increased over the 30-day interval examined. The ratio of incorporation increased slightly at 7 to 14 days, but the significance of this difference is doubtful. On the 4th day after immunization, incorporation

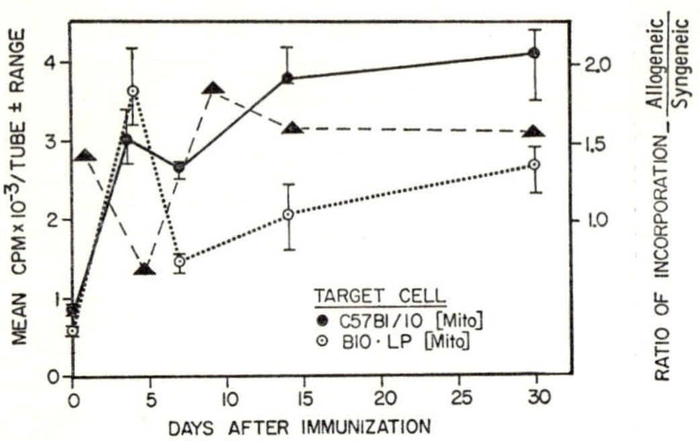

Figure 4. Specific stimulation of ^{3}H-thymidine by B10-LP spleen cells at intervals after immunization with C57BL/10 cells. Time course of the response of groups of B10-LP mice (H-2^{b}, H-3^{b} H-13^{b} to a single i.p. injection of 50×10^{6} spleen cells from C57BL/10 (H-2^{b}, H-3^{a}, H-13^{a}). The data shown represent mean values for three to five tubes and the range of ^{3}H-thymidine incorporation into 15×10^{6} B10-LP spleen cells taken from immunized donors and cultured 72 hr with 15×10^{6} syngeneic or allogeneic mitomycin treated target cells. ^{3}H-thymidine was added at 48 hr.

in mixed cell cultures of C57BL/10 immune B10-LP spleen cells, and C57BL/10 target cells and of syngeneic B10-LP target cells was nearly equal; in fact, the syngeneic mixture usually exceeded the allogeneic one.

This phenomenon is probably explained by the persistence of living C57BL/10 cells in the spleens of the injected B10-LP on the 4th day after immunization. This chimeric cell population should be equally capable of being stimulated by B10-LP or by C57BL/10 target cells. Additional evidence has been obtained recently (unpublished) that an early, short-lived chimeric state exists in the spleen even when living immunocompetent H-2 incompatible cells are injected into an allogeneic host.

It is concluded from these experiments that in the putatively immunized B10-LP, persistent C57BL/10 cells in the spleen preclude demonstration of any additive stimulus which might have resulted from additional exposure *in vitro* to C57BL/10 antigen. Further attempts to examine immunization with non-H-2 antigens will probably require immunogenic stimuli which are either non-replicating or do not create a chimeric state.

Effect of immunization on stimulation by allogeneic cells which partially share H-2 antigen determinants of the immunizing strain. It has been demonstrated above that incorporation of ^{3}H-thymidine into mixed allogeneic cell cultures can be transiently increased by immunizing the reacting cell donor with H-2 incompatible allogeneic cells of the target strain. This effect of immunization presumably reflects an increase in the numbers of cells among the spleen cell population which are sensitive to each of the differing specific H-2 isoantigens. The H-2 locus determines multiple individual antigens (H-2 isoantigens) which can be identified serologically in intact cells (33) and in purified cell membranes (9). Isoantigenic antisera are usually raised in strains selected for minimum numbers of isoantigenic differences and for relative immunogenicity, then absorbed with cells carrying appropriate antigens. It seems quite probable, therefore, that *in vitro* stimulation in mixed cell culture also reflects the sum of reactions of sub-populations of cells which respond to the individual isoantigenic determinants. Some preliminary tests of this hypothesis have been made by immunizing mice with allogeneic cells and determining whether the resultant immune cell populations are stimulated by other strains which share some, but not all, of the isoantigenic determinants.

C57BL/6 and A/J mice were immunized with prleen cells from A/J or C57BL/6. The *in vitro* seactivity of the C57BL/6 or A/J strain cells from the immunized donor was then tested in mixed cell culture with mitomycin-treated A/J, BALB/c CBA or B10-M spleen cells. The incorporation levels attained were compared with those of cells from unimmunized A/J or C57BL/6 (Table IX). In this type of experiment, immunized C57BL/6 mice should respond to the H-2^{a} isoantigens present on the A/J cells used for immunization, but also to the same isoantigens present on BALB/c (H-2^{d}) and CBA (H-2^{k}). The control, A/J spleen cells after immunization with C57BL/6 spleen cells, should be stimulated by C57BL/6 isoantigens (H-2^{b}), but not by B10-M (H-2^{f}) spleen cells with which it shares no isoantigens.

The results show, as described in the previous section, that immunization with allogeneic cells augments the responsiveness of spleen cell populations from the immunized animals in mixed cell cultures. The increased reactivity is not limited to stimulation by the strain with which they were immunized. The reactivity extended to those strains which share isoantigens with the immunizing strain. This shared augmentation is not simply

TABLE IX

Stimulation of ³H-thymidine incorporation into spleen cells from immune and non-immune mice in mixed cell culture with allogeneic cells sharing H-2 antigenic determinants[a]

Reacting Cell	³H-Thymidine Incorporation (Mean CPM/Tube and Range)				
	C57BL/6	A/J	BALB/c	CBA	B10-M
A/J	12,700 (12,450–12,950)	3,028 (2,874–3,181)			9,698 (8,797–10,667)
A/J immunized with C57BL/6 spleen cells[b]	24,453 (24,450–24,456)	3,148 (3,023–3,192)			10,548 (8,918–12,718)
C57BL/6	1,396 (1,106–1,609)	9,846 (9,153–10,980)	11,071 (10,174–11,771)	27,049 (25,960–28,897)	
C57BL/6 immunized with A/J spleen cells[b]	1,529 (1,457–1,609)	25,071 (22,664–29,892)	16,382 (12,182–18,631)	72,345 (70,107–74,587)	

[a] The antigenic determinants constituting the alleles of these strains, according to Snell (22) are as follows: A/J [H-2ᵃ]—1, 3, 4, 5, 6, 8, 10, 11, 13, 14, 25, 27, 28, 29; C57BL/6 [H-2ᵇ]—2, 5, 6, 14, 22, 27, 28, 29, 33; BALB/c [H-2ᵈ]—3, 4, 6, 8, 10, 13, 14, 27, 28, 29, 31; B10-M [H-2ᶠ]—1, 7, 8, 9, 27; CBA [H-2ᵏ]—1, 3, 5, 8, 11, 25, 32. Therefore, A/J injected with C57BL/6 spleen cells could be immunized by H-2 isoantigenic determinants 2, 22 and 33; B10-M contains none of these H-2 antigenic determinants. C57BL/6 injected with A/J spleen cells could be immunized by the H-2 antigens 1, 3, 4, 8, 10, 11, 13 and 25; of these antigens, CBA shares 1, 3, 8, 11 and 25 and BALB/c shares 3, 4, 8, 10 and 13.

[b] In these experiments A/J or C57BL/6 mice were immunized by a single intraperitoneal injection of the allogeneic spleen cells (50×10^6). Spleen cells were taken from the immunized mice 5 days after injection and examined in mixed cell cultures with mitomycin-treated A/J, C57BL/6, BALB/c, B10-M or CBA spleen cells. The cultures were terminated at 72 hr. The values shown represent means of four or five replicate tubes.

a nonspecific increase in the number of potentially reactive cells in the immunized spleen cell population. A/J cells after immunization with C57BL/6 are not stimulated by mitomycin-treated B10-M spleen cells to a greater extent then are cells from non-immune A/J mice. B10-M does not share any H-2 antigenic determinants with C57BL/6 that are not also shared with A/J.

These data, therefore, provide evidence that specific isoantigenic components of H-2 are recognized individually as foreign in the mixed cell reaction. This implies that sub-populations of the antigen-sensitive cells from immunized animals recognize individual antigenic determinants and that overall incorporation must, therefore, reflect the summation of reactivities of sub-populations to the individual determinants. Studies with multiple combinations of congenic resistant lines differing at H-2 alone will be required for further substantiation of this concept.

DISCUSSION

This series of experiments has demonstrated that the culture system previously shown to be satisfactory for supporting *in vitro* antigen-stimulated proliferative responses of mouse lymphoreticular cells (7) also permits the detection of primary and immune stimulation in one-way mixed lymphocyte cultures and with cell derived antigens. These reactions are similar to those previously described in that there is a requirement for an anti-mouse lymphocyte globulin, an age determined susceptibility to stimulation, and comparable dose-response relationships.

Interpretation of *in vitro* mixed cell interactions is subject to several assumptions. It is assumed, for example, that incorporation of tritiated thymidine assayed during the final 24 hr of a 3-day culture is proportional to the number of cells that are stimulated to synthesize DNA by interaction with a specific antigen. It has been shown that the degree of blast transformation in this *in vitro* system (7) actually parallels DNA synthesis. The studies of Wilson on rat lymphocytes (4) and of Marshall *et al.* (34) on human lymphocytes showed that tritiated thymidine incorporation reflects proliferation of a sub-population of antigen-sensitive cells. Their data also indicated that recruitment of non-antigen sensitive cells probably does not represent a significant contribution to the reaction. Thus, it is reasonable to assume that tritiated thymidine incorporation in the mouse MLC is a measure of the degree of stimulation of antigen-sensitive cells in the spleen cell population.

Interpretation of these data is also based upon the assumption that the reaction is essentially uni-directional—that the target cell block, whether by x-irradiation or mitomycin treatment, effectively limits the DNA synthesis detected by tritiated thymidine incorporation to the untreated cell population. Evidence that this is the case includes the findings that both mitomycin-C and x-irradiation almost completely abolished incorporation by spleen cells stimulated with PHA, a relatively powerful stimulus. In addition, reactive cells were readily stimulated by purified H-2 alloantigenic cellular membrane preparations. These observations support the assumption that significant residual bi-directionality is not required for reactivity of the unblocked cell population. Huemer's findings are also consistent with this conclusion (6). The data do not exclude the possibility that under certain circumstances bi-directionality might account for fractional stimulation in otherwise weakly reacting combinations. It has been found recently, for example (35), that nonspecific as well as specific mitogenic factors are produced even by heavily irradiated cells, when these target cells are placed in contact with reactive cell populations having differing alloantigens. It is conceivable that in the mouse MLC, blocked target cells could release a nonspecific mitogenic factor upon recognition of alloantigens on the reacting cell population. This would give a false indication of recognition and seriously affect interpretation of resultant thymidine incorporation. Especially would this be true in the case of F_1 hybrids reacting to parental cells. This problem was resolved both in the case of combinations involving H-2 antigenic differences and in F_1 hybrid reacting to parent, through the use of purified H-2 antigen or erythrocyte stroma as the stimulant. Purified membrane antigens representing exclusively minor histocompatibility locus differences have not been available. With this exception the reactions can be considered to be effectively uni-directional as regards the assumption that the DNA synthesis assayed represents recognition exclusively by the reacting cell population.

A third assumption upon which MLC interpretation depends, particularly in attempts to correlate the level of incorporation with *in vivo* histoincompatibility, is that antigen-reactive cells are represented equally in the spleens of the strains compared. Although precise data on interstrain variation in this context are not available, the variable course of immunologic maturation as concerns recognition of histoincompatibility throughout the life span is known (36). This factor is exemplified in the rigorous age dependence of recognition in MLC reported here, and suggests caution in relating MLC results to graft rejection times. In general, H-2 differences gave vigorous proliferative responses *in vitro*, while weaker, non-H-2 differences associated with long allograft rejection times gave lesser degrees of stimulation. Exceptions were significant, however, for in the case of BALB/c reacting to DBA/2, incorporation was quite high, nearly equaling some H-2 combinations as also shown by Festenstein (37, 38) although graft rejections times in this combination are prolonged (39).

Within the limits of validity of these assumptions, consideration can be given to the nature of the recognition phenomenon as revealed in MLC. The most straightforward formulation would be that the reactive member of the pair in cell-cell interaction is simply stimulated by membrane antigen through direct contact with the target cell surface or by antigen released by the target cell into the medium. The antigen would be considered to react with pre-existing sterically specific receptors on the reacting cell surface. This model has the virtue of being a direct conceptual extension of other cell recognition phenomena in which antigen and antigen-reactive cells interact, and is most consistent with the primary response to purified membrane antigens and the isoantigenic determinant specificity of immune cell populations. It is also consistent with the findings that F_1 hybrid cells stimulate about one-half of the level of incorporation in parental strain cells as the allogeneic combination.

Another model of cell-cell interaction which

might be considered is that the degree of incorporation is not related strictly to antigenic recognition by the responding cell population, but to the sum of reciprocal antigenic differences in the combination. No correlation was found, however, between the sum of such differences on serologic grounds and the level of incorporation achieved in MLC between non-congenic lines. Recent studies employing such lines led Huemer to conclude that the degree of incorporation is not correlated with the sum of differences of isoantigens (6). If individual isoantigens varied considerably in capacity to stimulate in MLC, however, this would invalidate all comparisons based upon the assumption of equal strength.

A third possible model is related to one suggested by Möller and Lundgren (40) that recognition of non-identity is the basis of primary stimulation by alloantigens; i.e., that any cell surface or cell antigen which fails the test of identity is nonspecifically interpreted as foreign and the stereotyped consequences of recognition are thereby triggered. This model would require that all alloantigens of a given class give roughly equivalent responses whether triggered by a single or multiple isoantigenic determinant. Above a threshhold level stimulus, no relation would be found between degree of difference revealed by serologic tests and level of incorporation. Variation in levels of incorporation between strains could be attributed to differences in the pool size of the sub-population of alloantigen sensitive cells in the spleen. Data on primary recognition of alloantigens reported here and elsewhere (4, 6) appear quite consistent with this model. However, the specific isoantigenic recognition characteristics of immune populations cannot be reconciled with it, unless it is assumed that primary and immune recognition in this system involve different cell systems. This possibility is considered below.

Of central interest is the frequent assertion that the MLC represents the equivalent of a primary immune response by an antigen-sensitive cell population relieved by virtue of *in vitro* conditions of the feed-back control systems and space limitations of the intact organism. Some insight into this question and a basis for speculation on the nature of immunologic memory is gained by evaluating in MLC the results of immunization with alloantigens. Immunization with allogeneic spleen cells increased the *in vitro* reactivity of spleen cell populations in MLC. This increment was transient, disappearing about 4 weeks after immunization. The time course was very similar to that observed with sheep erythrocyte immunization, examined previously (7), in which increased *in vitro* reactivity was maximal 4 days after cell injection and fell off rapidly after that. The spleen cells from BCG immunized animals showed peak reactivity to PPD at 4 weeks after immunization and had fallen to nearly non-immune levels 12 weeks following injection (7). In each circumstance, therefore, the number of antigen reactive cells, as reflected by thymidine incorporation, rose to a peak value after contact with antigen and fell to background levels after a relatively short interval.

Interpreted literally, these data suggest that no residual increase in antigen-reactive cells follows an antigenic experience, as detected in this system. This interpretation has two potential flaws. The memory cell population of the spleen accruing after an antigenic experience may not exert a full effect during the 3-day culture period employed. For example, memory cell recognition could be expressed in proliferative responses which have different kinetics than with primary recognition and require 3 to 5 days for expression. A second possibility in interpretation is that the sensitivity of the assay system may be insufficient to detect small incremental increases in the numbers of antigen reactive cells in the spleen cell population after an antigenic experience. If these major questions can be resolved, the body of evidence presented here could be interpreted to indicate that in the MLC system employed, immunologic memory after a given antigenic experience may not be reflected in an increase in the population of antigen-reactive cells which can respond subsequently to the antigen. If this is correct, then it is necessary to postulate that there is a second population of antigen-sensitive cells associated perhaps with immunospecific antibody formation, and that it is the accrual of this population which represents memory. Further examination of these speculative issues is intrinsically within the capability of the *in vitro* technique reported here.

Acknowledgment. We wish to thank Mrs. Penny Marquette for her help in the preparation of this manuscript.

REFERENCES

1. Bain, B., Vas, M. R. and Lowenstein, L., Blood, *23:* 108, 1964.

2. Bach, F. and Hirshhorn, K., Science, *143:* 813, 1964.
3. Silvers, W. K., Wilson, D. B. and Palm, J., Science, *155:* 703, 1967.
4. Wilson, D. B., J. Exp. Med., *126:* 625, 1967.
5. Dutton, R. W., J. Exp. Med., *122:* 759, 1965.
6. Huemer, R. P., Keller, L. S. and Lee, K. D., Transplantation, *6:* 706, 1968.
7. Adler, W. H., Takiguchi, T., Marsh, B. and Smith, R. T., J. Exp. Med., *131:* 1049, 1970.
8. Bach, F. W. and Voynow, N. K., Science, *153:* 545, 1966.
9. Davies, D. A. L., Transplantation, *5:* 31, 1967.
10. Djordjevic, B. and Kim, J. H., J. Cell Biol., *38:* 477, 1968.
11. Elves, M. W., Nature, *223:* 90, 1969.
12. Medawar, P. B. and Woodruff, M. F. A., Immunology, *1:* 27, 1958.
13. Billingham, R. E., Brent, L. and Medawar, P. B., Nature, *172:* 603, 1953.
14. Howard, J. G. and Michie, D., Transplant. Bull., *29:* 1, 1962.
15. Urso, I. S., Congdon, C. C. and Owen, R. D., Proc. Soc. Exp. Biol. Med., *100:* 395, 1959.
16. Metcalf, D., *The Thymus in Immunobiology*, Hoeber Medical Division, Harper & Row, New York, 1964.
17. Argyris, B. F., J. Exp. Med., *128:* 459, 1968.
18. Amos, D. B. and Bach, F. H., J. Exp. Med. *128:* 623, 1968.
19. Smith, R. T. and Good, R. A., (Editors), *Cellular Recognition*, Appleton-Century-Crofts, New York, 1969.
20. Möller, G., J. Immun., *90:* 271, 1963.
21. Schlessinger, M., J. Immun., *94:* 350, 1965.
22. Snell, G. D. and Stimpfling, J. H., *Biology of the Laboratory Mouse*, p. 473, Blakiston Division, McGraw-Hill, New York, 1966.
23. Berrian, J. H. and McKhann, C. F., J. Nat. Cancer Inst., *25:* 111, 1969.
24. Snell, G. D. and Stevens, L. C., Immunology, *4:* 366, 1961.
25. Huemer, R. P., Cancer Res., *29:* 610, 1969.
26. Hellström, K. E., Nature, *199:* 614, 1963.
27. Möller, E., Science, *147:* 873, 1965.
28. Malchow, H., Zeiss, I. M., Szenberg, W. A. and Fischer, H., Int. Arch. Allerg., *35:* 495, 1969.
29. Harrison, G. A., Owen, J. J. T. and Ritter, M. A., Nature, *219:* 302, 1968.
30. Möller, G. and Möller, E., Nature, *208:* 260, 1965.
31. Kasakura, S. and Lowenstein, L., Nature, *219:* 652, 1968.
32. Wilson, D. B., Silvers, W. K. and Norell, P. C., J. Exp. Med., *126:* 655, 1967.
33. Hämmerling, V., Aoki, T., de Harven, E., Boyse, E. and Old, L., J. Exp. Med., *128:* 1461, 1968.
34. Marshall, W. B., Valentine, F. T. and Lawrence, H. S., J. Exp. Med., *130:* 327, 1969.
35. Hardy, D. L., Ling, N. R. and Knight, S. C., Nature, *223:* 511, 1969.
36. Teague, P. O., Yunis, E. J., Rodey, G., Fish, A., Stutman, O. and Good, R. A., Lab. Invest., *22:* 121, 1970.
37. Festenstein, H., Ann. New York Acad. Sci., *129:* 567, 1966.
38. Festenstein, H., Exerpta Medica International Congress Series, *131:* 214, 1966.
39. Prehn, R. T. and Main, J. M., J. Nat. Cancer Inst., *15:* 191, 1954.
40. Möller, G. and Lundgren, G., in *Cellular Recognition*, edited by R. T. Smith and R. A. Good, p. 177, Appleton-Century-Crofts, New York, 1969.

THE JOURNAL OF IMMUNOLOGY
Copyright © 1970 by The Williams & Wilkins Co.

Vol. 105, No. 4, October 1970
Printed in U.S.A.

IMMUNOLOGIC TOLERANCE TO *ESCHERICHIA COLI* SOMATIC ANTIGEN ASSESSED BY BACTERIOLYTIC AND HEMOLYTIC PLAQUE ASSAYS[1, 2]

JERRY L. ALLEN[3] AND HERMAN FRIEDMAN

From the Departments of Microbiology, Albert Einstein Medical Center and Temple University Medical School, Philadelphia, Penna.

Received for publication February 26, 1970

Immunologic tolerance to the somatic antigen of *E. coli* 0127:B8 was induced in neonatal mice by multiple injections with a lipopolysaccharide (LPS) antigen during the first weeks of life. The immune response of neonatally treated animals, as well as that of non-treated control mice, was assessed by two different kinds of immunoplaque assays: 1) direct bacteriolysis of viable *E. coli* in agar gel, and 2) hemolysis of sheep erythrocytes coated with specific antigen. Mice treated with differing amounts of LPS, and a variety of injection schedules, developed a marked tolerance as assessed by the indirect hemolytic plaque assay, as well as by serum hemolysin and hemagglutination tests. In contrast, significant numbers of plaque-forming cells were detected in spleens of neonatally treated mice when the direct bacteriolytic assay was used. Similarly, there were higher bacterial agglutinin titers in the sera of these animals. Larger numbers of antibody-forming cells were detected by the hemolytic assay in the spleens of control mice after challenge immunization than in neonatally treated animals. Significant numbers of bacteriolytic plaque-forming cells were present in the spleens of "tolerant" animals, in contrast to the marked suppression of hemolytic cells. These findings suggest that tolerance to bacterial antigens as complex as the somatic extracts of *E. coli* results in tolerance to "major" antigenic determinants and a concomitant immunity to some but not all of the "minor" antigens which fail to coat onto carrier erythrocytes.

Specific immunologic tolerance has been induced in many animal species with a large variety of antigens, including tissue allografts, serum proteins, haptens, foreign erythrocytes, and bacterial products (1–4). Most studies of tolerance have been concerned mainly with serum antibody responses or allograft immunity. However, in recent years it has become feasible to directly enumerate antibody-producing cells in lymphoid tissues of tolerant as well as normal animals directly, using localized immunoplaque assays (5–9). In the case of tolerance to sheep erythrocytes, specific hemolysin-forming cells are absent or greatly reduced in lymphoid tissues of mice treated as neonates with multiple injections of red blood cells. Induction of complete or prolonged tolerance to red blood cells is generally difficult to achieve in adult animals without simultaneous use of immunosuppressive drugs (10).

Recent models developed with bacterial systems have shown that tolerance can be induced with lipopolysaccharide (LPS) somatic antigens derived from *Shigella paradysenteriae* or *Escherichia coli*, as well as with flagellar antigens of Salmonella (7, 8, 11–14). In most instances, markedly reduced numbers of antibody-forming cells to these antigens occur in lymphoid tissues of the tolerant animals. Such studies, as well as earlier investigations with erythrocytes (15, 16), have suggested that, at the cellular level, tolerance may reflect "terminal exhaustion" of antibody-forming cells or their precursors. Supporting this hypothesis is the observation that specific antibody formation may occur during tolerance "induction." However, another alternative remains to be explored — that many or perhaps

[1] Supported in part by research grants from the National Science Foundation (GB 6251).

[2] Presented, in part, at the 68th Annual Meeting, American Society for Microbiology, Detroit, Michigan, May 1968.

[3] Post-doctoral fellow, National Institutes of Allergy and Infectious Diseases (No. 1-F2-A1-38012-01).

even most of these antibody-forming cells have specificity toward "minor" rather than "major" antigenic portions of the complex mosaic of proteins and polysaccharides present in the antigenic extracts used for tolerance induction (17).

In the present study two separate kinds of immunoplaque assays were used to assess the specificity of tolerance of mice to *E. coli* somatic antigen (18–20). One assay was the indirect hemolytic plaque procedure using erythrocytes specifically, sensitized with LPS derived from *E. coli*; the other method was the direct bacteriolytic plaque assay using viable *E. coli* as the indicator target cell. It was anticipated that these experiments would reveal whether a significant immune response was involved in tolerance induction and whether such a response was specific for either major or minor antigenic components of the antigen.

METHODS AND MATERIALS

Animals. NIH Albino A mice were used for this study, as described elsewhere (17, 19, 20). Pregnant females were kept in individual cages until litter delivery and the newborns were left with their mothers until weaned at 3 to 4 weeks of age (17).

Antigen. The lipopolysaccharide somatic antigen (LPS), extracted by the phenol method from *Escherichia coli* 0127:B8 (Difco Laboratories, Detroit, Mich.) was used as described previously (19, 20).

Antigen injection for immunization and induction and tolerance. The LPS was suspended in sufficient saline to prepare the appropriate concentrations for injection into newborn or adult mice. For purposes of immunization, a solution containing 100 μg LPS was injected into 6- to 8-week old test animals. For tolerance induction, newborn mice were injected i.p. with different concentrations of LPS. Most groups were injected two to three times per week. Littermates were injected with saline only.

Determination of immune response. At weekly intervals, six animals from each experimental and control group were bled individually from the retro-orbital plexus to obtain serum specimens for antibody determination (17, 19, 20). The mice were then killed and their spleens removed to determine the number of antibody plaque-forming cells (PFC) to *E. coli* and sheep red blood cells (RBC) (19, 20). Other mice from each group were challenged with LPS at 6 to 8 weeks of age (usually 2 weeks after the last injection) and sacrificed 5 days later to determine their cellular and humoral antibody responses. The number of bacterial (B-PFC) or hemolytic (H-PFC) PFC per spleen and per million spleen cells was determined for each animal and the averages were calculated for each group (17–20).

RESULTS

Immunization of adult mice with graded doses of *E. coli* LPS resulted in a rapid appearance of specific antibody-forming cells. There was a peak of 50,000 or more PFC per spleen 5 days after immunization of control mice (Fig. 1). Both the bacteriolytic and indirect hemolytic procedures showed a rapid rise in PFC, from a level of several hundred before immunization to a level of several thousand or more on the 2nd and 3rd day after immunization. The number of PFC decreased to a level of approximately 10 to 20 thousand on days 7 to 10 and less than 5000 on days 14 to 21.

The number of PFC was determined by both

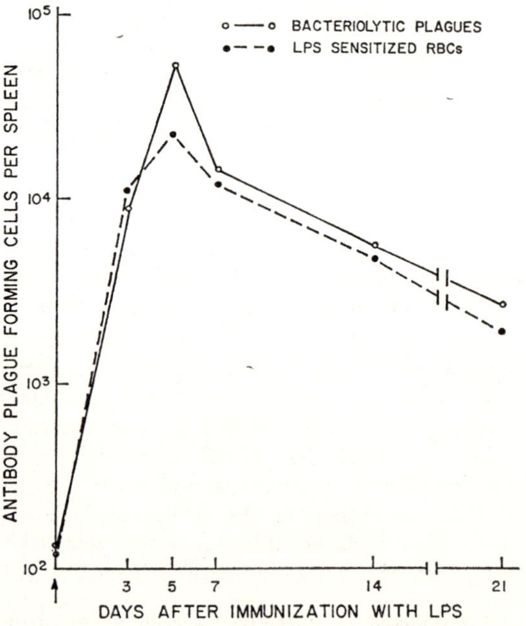

Figure 1. The cytokinetics of antibody-forming cells to *E. coli*, as assessed by the passive hemolytic and direct bacteriolytic plaque method. Young adult mice were given a single injection of 50 μg LPS (*arrow*). Each point represents the average splenic response of 5 to 6 mice on the day indicated.

TABLE I

Development of cellular and humoral antibody in neonatal mice injected with 20 μg E. coli LPS

Age When Tested[a]	Antibody Plaque Response (per Spleen)			Serum Antibody Titer (Means)	
	Bacteriolysis (viable *E. coli*)	Passive hemolysis (LPS-RBC)[b]	Hemolysis (control RBC)	Bacterial agglutination	Passive hemagglutination
days					
7	5	5	5	1:2	<1:2
14	18	25	5	1:2	<1:2
21	4212	41	287	1:128	<1:2
28	1980	200	150	1:128	<1:2
35	1755	1130	920	1:64	<1:2

[a] Five to six mice tested (entire spleen) at age indicated; each mouse injected twice weekly with LPS during time period indicated.

[b] Not corrected for number of PFC to unsensitized RBC (third column).

TABLE II

Appearance of antibody-forming cells to E. coli in spleens of mice given LPS during first 6 weeks of life

LPS Dose[a]	Mouse Group	Plaque-Forming Cells per Spleen[b]		
		Bacteriolytic	Passive hemolytic[c]	Hemolytic (control RBC)
μg				
10	Neonatally treated[d]	7,480	2,380	2,772
	Normal controls	94,250	45,220	2,000
1.0	Neonatally treated[d]	26,100	7,200	5,400
	Normal controls	30,000	97,440	2,040
0.1	Neonatally treated[d]	11,950	7,650	1,800
	Normal controls	13,000	14,800	1,800

[a] Concentration of antigen used for challenge immunization at 8 weeks of life.

[b] Antibody plaque response in spleens of 5 to 8 mice per group 5 days after i.p. challenge with the indicated concentrations of antigen.

[c] Not corrected for number of PFC to unsensitized RBC (third column).

[d] Mice injected i.p. from birth to 6 weeks of life two to three times weekly with the indicated dose of *E. coli* LPS.

assays in spleens of neonatally injected mice during the first weeks of life. Mice injected with 20 μg LPS twice weekly from the day of birth had different numbers of PFC when tested by either assay during the first 5 weeks of age (Table I). Very few, if any PFC had developed during the first 2 weeks of life, regardless of which assay procedure was used. There were approximately 4000 B-PFC per spleen in 3-week-old treated animals, and about one half that number at 4 and 5 weeks of life. In contrast, few if any H-PFC were detected in spleens of neonatally treated mice during the first 3 to 4 weeks of life. By the 5th week there were approximately 1100 H-PFC in the spleens of this group of mice. However, there were over 900 PFC per spleen to untreated S-RBC, indicating that only about 200 of the PFC were specific for the LPS.

Analysis of serum antibody titers also suggested that the unresponsiveness was directed mainly toward the LPS and not to other antigens which might be present on the intact bacterial cells (Table I). For example, there was no titer greater than 1:2 in the serum of mice injected with LPS during the first 5 weeks of life, as assessed by the indirect hemagglutination or hemolytic method. However, direct bacterial agglutination tests with the same sera indicated titers of 1:64 to 1:128 by the 3rd to 5th week of life.

Injections of lower doses of LPS during the first weeks of life also resulted in the appearance of lower or insignificant numbers of H-PFC, and lower hemolysin titers to LPS, as compared to larger numbers of B-PFC and higher bacterial agglutinin titers. Furthermore, challenge immunization of such neonatally treated mice revealed a marked suppression in their subsequent responsiveness to LPS (Table II). Mice injected several times weekly with either 10, 1.0 or 0.1 μg LPS during the first 6 weeks of life had markedly depressed cellular and humoral responses when challenged with LPS at 8 weeks of age, as compared to control mice injected only once with a similar immunizing dose of LPS (Table II). For example, mice treated neonatally with 10 μg LPS had approximately 2380 H-PFC after challenge with 10 μg LPS at 8 weeks of life, as compared to the 45,000 H-PFC per spleen in control mice challenged at the same age. Furthermore, the number of cells forming antibody to untreated sheep RBC exceeded the number against LPS-coated erythrocytes, suggesting a complete absence of antibody-forming cells to LPS in the spleens of these animals. The number of B-PFC in the spleens of these mice, as assessed by the bacteriologic assay with viable *E. coli*, was also suppressed as compared to the response of control mice. However, the suppression was not as marked as that observed with the indirect hemolytic assay.

There was a lower degree of suppression in mice injected neonatally with the 1.0- and 0.1-μg doses of LPS. Such mice had relatively more PFC than those treated with the higher dose of LPS during the first weeks of life. However, the number of H-PFC was reduced significantly as compared to the controls, especially when the increased number of PFC to red blood cells was subtracted from the number of LPS-specific PFC.

Control experiments with *E. coli* LPS and similar extracts from other bacterial species indicated the specificity of the antibody plaque response in spleens of normal and neonatally treated mice. The PFC to the *E. coli* antigen could be inhibited by incorporation of homologous *E. coli* LPS into the test agar, whereas heterologous LPS preparations were without effect.

DISCUSSION

These results indicate that immunologic responsiveness of mice to the somatic antigen of *E. coli* can be readily suppressed by multiple injections of LPS during the first weeks of life. No suppression occurred after a single injection on the day of birth (unpublished observations). However, mice inoculated twice weekly with 20 μg LPS, or with daily injections of lower doses of antigen, developed specific tolerance, as assessed by subsequent challenge immunization with this antigen. Both serum antibody and the development of PFC were suppressed. The greatest degree of suppression was evident when the antibody response was determined by passive hemolytic techniques using LPS-sensitized erythrocytes, rather than by direct bacteriolysis or agglutination with intact *E. coli*.

These divergent findings suggest that the bacterial assay detected antibody formation to "minor" antigens in the LPS preparation which were present in or on intact microorganisms but which did not "coat" onto the indicator erythrocytes used as a carrier for the LPS in the hemolytic tests. It is also plausible that only the major antigenic component(s) of the LPS preparation could sensitize the red blood cells. Thus, use of such sensitized RBCs as the indicator would permit only detection of antibody formation to the major antigen.

The presence of small amounts of minor or contaminating antigens in the LPS preparation would be expected eventually to stimulate antibody formation after repeated injections into young mice. The absence of these antigens on the sensitized RBC would result in failure to detect the reciprocal PFC, even if the appropriate immunocompetent cells were present in the spleen cell population. On the other hand, the bacteriolytic plaque procedure, using viable *E. coli*, should provide detection of antibody-forming cells to both the major and minor antigens. Such plaques would be indistinguishable from each other. Thus, detection of bacteriolytic PFC in the spleens of test mice during induction of immunologic tolerance, as well as after challenge immunization, could reflect the heterogeneity of both the antigen used for injection and the population of corresponding antibody-forming cells.

The results of this study are relevant to other reports concerning tolerance to microbial antigens. In previous studies it was observed that mice injected with *Shigella* antigen at birth develop a relatively prolonged tolerance characterized by depressed serum antibody and immunoplaque responses (21–22). Sheep RBC coated with *Shigella* extract were used for those assays (22). No information was available concerning the response of tolerant mice to antigens which had not coated onto the red blood cells, since direct bacteriolysis of *Shigella* has not thus far been achieved. In studies somewhat similar to these, Britton (13, 14) reported that tolerance is induced in mice injected either as neonates or adults with *E. coli* lipopolysaccharide. Challenge immunization consisted of inoculation with bacterial vaccine. However, the immune response of both control and tolerant mice was assessed by an indirect hemolytic plaque assay using red cells coated with the *E. coli* extract, rather than by utilizing intact and viable bacteria. A "cyclic" appearance of antibody-forming cells to the *E. coli* was observed in control animals, and a depressed response in the tolerant mice. However, the assay used excluded the possibility of obtaining data on the nature and specificity of the immune response to the challenge vaccine, since the antibody-forming cells to those bacterial determinants other than the ones coating onto the indicator red cells would not be detected.

REFERENCES

1. Hasek, M., Lengerova, A. and Hraba, T., Advances Immun., *1:* 1, 1961.

2. Smith, R. J., Advances Immun., *1:* 67, 1961.
3. Dresser, D. W. and Mitchison, N. A., Advances Immun., *8:* 129, 1968.
4. Hraba, T., Monographs in Allergy, Vol. *3*, S. Karger Co., Basel, 1968.
5. Rowley, D. A. and Fitch, F. W., J. Exp. Med., *121:* 683, 1965.
6. Friedman, H., Nature, *205:* 508, 1965.
7. Friedman, H., J. Bact., *92:* 820, 1966.
8. Friedman, H., J. Bact., *96:* 1124, 1968.
9. Hraba, T. and Merchant, B., J. Immun., *102:* 229, 1969.
10. Aisenberg, A. C., J. Exp. Med., *125:* 833, 1967.
11. Diener, E. and Armstrong, W. D., Lancet, *2:* 1281, 1967.
12. Armstrong, W. D., Diener, E. and Shellam, G. R., J. Exp. Med., *129:* 393, 1969.
13. Britton, S., Immunology, *16:* 513, 1969.
14. Britton, S., Immunology., *16:* 527, 1969.
15. Sterzl, J., Nature, *209:* 416, 1966.
16. Sterzl, J., Cold Spring Harbor Symp. Quant. Biol., *32:* 493, 1967.
17. Friedman, H., in *Immunologic Tolerance*, Edited by M. Landy and W. Braun, p. 31, Academic Press, New York, 1969.
18. Schwartz, S. A. and Braun, Science, *149:* 200, 1965.
19. Friedman, H., Allen, J. and Landy, M., J. Immun. *103:* 204, 1969.
20. Friedman, H., Allen, J. and Rosenzweig, J., Proc. Soc. Exp. Biol. Med., *131:* 353, 1969.
21. Friedman, H., J. Immun., *96:* 289, 1966.
22. Friedman, H., J. Bact., *92:* 820, 1966.

THE JOURNAL OF IMMUNOLOGY
Vol. 105, No. 4, October 1970

Printed in U.S.A.

BIOLOGIC ACTIVITIES OF PEROMYSCUS $7S\gamma_1$ AND $7S\gamma_2$ GLOBULINS

J. COE, L. PEEL AND R. F. SMITH

From the United States Department of Health, Education, and Welfare, Public Health Service, National Institutes of Health, National Institute of Allergy and Infectious Diseases, Rocky Mountain Laboratory, Hamilton, Montana 59840

Received for publication February 20, 1970

Peromyscus $7S\gamma_1$- and $7S\gamma_2$-globulins which contained antibody to hen egg albumin (HEA) were isolated, quantitated, and tested for their ability to mediate passive cutaneous anaphylaxis (PCA) and to fix complement. Peromyscus antibody of the $7S\gamma_2$ class induced a PCA reaction in guinea pigs with as little as 4.9 ABC units of antibody/milliliter. With 40 times as much $7S\gamma_1$ antibody, however, no PCA reaction was produced in guinea pigs. In contrast, only Peromyscus $7S\gamma_1$ anti-HEA induced the PCA reaction in Peromyscus. Complement fixation and hemolysis of HEA-conjugated erythrocytes were found only with antibodies of the $7S\gamma_2$ class.

The functional significance of the various classes and subclasses of immunoglobulins (Ig) has become more apparent as their unique biologic capacities have been studied. In the guinea pig and mouse (*Mus musculus*), the major serum Ig, the 7S γ globulins, consist of two separate classes, $7S\gamma_1$ and $7S\gamma_2$, which differ in their capacity to fix complement and to induce the passive cutaneous anaphylaxis (PCA) reaction (reviewed in reference 1). $7S\gamma_1$- and $7S\gamma_2$-globulins have also been defined in the deer mouse (*Peromyscus maniculatus artemisiae*) (2). In this report we compare the ability of these two 7S Ig classes to fix complement and to produce a PCA reaction in the guinea pig and Peromyscus. The biologic activities of the $7S\gamma_1$- and $7S\gamma_2$-globulins of Peromyscus appear to be similar to those of the mouse and guinea pig.

MATERIALS AND METHODS

Animals. Peromyscus maniculatus artemisiae were trapped locally and reared in the laboratory. Hartley guinea pigs weighing 250 to 300 g were obtained from a local source.

Antigen. Hen egg albumin (HEA), recrystallized five times, was obtained from K & K Laboratories, Plainview, N. Y. and labeled (2) with ^{131}I (Nuclear Science and Engineering, Pittsburgh, Pa.).

Antibody production. Peromyscus mice were inoculated in the footpads or intraperitoneally (i.p.) with 0.25 ml of a complete Freund's emulsion containing 50 μg HEA and 0.5 mg of killed *Mycobacterium tuberculosis*. Twenty-one days later the animals were inoculated i.p. with 0.25 ml of an incomplete Freund's emulsion containing 100 μg of HEA, and similar inocula were then given at 3-week intervals. Some Peromyscus developed ascites and 13 to 20 ml of peritoneal fluid could be obtained from individual mice. Individual ascitic fluids and pooled sera were tested for anti-HEA content by gel diffusion and radioimmunoelectrophoresis (2). All sera were obtained at least 8 weeks after primary inoculation.

Immunoglobulin fractionation. Peromyscus $7S\gamma_2$ Ig was isolated from immune serum by DEAE-cellulose chromatography, as previously described (2). $7S\gamma_2$ and $7S\gamma_1$ Ig were obtained by Pevikon block preparative electrophoresis (2) of $7S\gamma_1$-γ_2 anti-HEA preparations. These were obtained by absorption of immune serum or ascitic fluid with an HEA immunoabsorbent prepared by conjugating HEA with a *p*-aminophenacetyl ether of cellulose (3). The immune serum or ascitic fluid was mixed with the HEA immunoabsorbent and after 12 hr at 4°C, the mixture was washed with phosphate-buffered saline (pH 7.2) and the antibody eluted with 0.03 M glycine-HCl buffer, pH 3.0. Pevikon fractions containing only $7S\gamma_1$- or $7S\gamma_2$-globulins were pooled and concentrated by negative pressure dialysis. The purity of these preparations was verified by gel diffusion analysis with specific antisera to the $7S\gamma_1$-, $7S\gamma_2$- and γM-globulins and also antiserum to whole Peromyscus serum. The protein concentration was determined by measuring the optical density (O.D.) at 280 nm with an extinction coefficient of $E_{280}^{1\%} = 14.2$ (2). Both 7Sγ_1 and 7Sγ_2 anti-HEA preparations produced precipitin reactions with HEA in gel diffusion analysis.

Antibody quantitation. The amount of HEA antibody in the 7Sγ_1 and 7Sγ_2 preparations was determined by Farr's antigen-binding technique (4). Briefly, fivefold dilutions of the anti-HEA serum were made in 1:10 normal hamster serum: borate buffer solution after an initial 1:10 dilution of the test serum in borate buffer (pH 8.3). HEA-^{131}I (0.5 μg protein in 0.5 ml of 1% normal hamster serum:borate buffer) was added to duplicate 0.5 ml portions of the test dilution and, with the appropriate controls, left at 4°C overnight. One milliliter of filtered saturated ammonium sulfate was added, mixed immediately and centrifuged after 30 min incubation at 4°C. The precipitates were washed once with 3 ml of 50% saturated ammonium sulfate and counted in a well-type scintillation counter with a NaI crystal. The dilution of antiserum which would have combined with 33% of the added antigen was determined by interpolation and the ABC-33 values for 0.5 μg HEA protein were calculated. One ABC unit is the amount of antibody which combines with one μg HEA protein and the ABC value is the number of ABC units in 1 ml of undiluted serum. One practical reason for using this procedure is that the antibody activity can be quantitated with very small amounts of serum. An estimate of the amount of antibody can be derived from the ABC-33 value as follows. The ABC-33 value is the amount (in micrograms) of antigen protein bound by 1 ml of serum with a fixed excess of free antigen. For antibody of high affinity the antigen binding may approach saturation at the level of antigen excess employed. The mol ratio of antibody to antigen would then be close to 1:2 and the weight ratio of 7S anti-HEA to HEA $= \frac{1}{2} \times (165{,}000/45{,}000) = 1.83$. Then the minimum amount of antibody protein (micrograms/milliliter) in the sample would be 1.83 × ABC value. Antibody to HEA commonly has an antibody-antigen weight ratio at equivalence of about 9:1 (5, and unpublished data). Therefore, the approximate amount (μg) of HEA protein at equivalence would be $\frac{1}{9} \times 1.83 \times$ ABC value or 0.2 × ABC value for a high avidity antiserum. This value would represent the optimum amount of HEA protein to demonstrate complement fixation (see Discussion).

PCA test. One-tenth milliliter of test antiserum was injected intracutaneously into the shaved area of guinea pigs and after a 2½- to 3-hr interval, 1.0 mg of HEA in 1 ml of 0.5% Evans blue dye solution was injected intravenously. For control purposes, guinea pigs were also injected sequentially with the Evans blue dye and HEA solution. Each preparation was tested in two to four guinea pigs. A positive control skin test with a standard guinea pig anti-HEA serum was included to validate the PCA reactivity of each guinea pig. Diameters of the blue skin reactions were measured and the results recorded. Tests for PCA reactions in Peromyscus were performed similarly except that 0.025 ml of antiserum was injected intracutaneously and 2 to 3 hr later 0.25 ml of 1% Evans blue dye and 0.25 ml of HEA (10 mg/ml) were sequentially injected intravenously. Bluing of skin test sites was not detected when Evans blue dye was given alone.

Complement fixation (CF) procedure. A pool of fresh normal guinea pig sera was divided into small portions which were quick frozen at −70°C and stored at −20°C. Complement titer (CH_{50} units/ml) was determined according to Kabat (6). This guinea pig serum retained full hemolytic activity during these studies. For each day's experiment, a new vial was thawed and diluted with Veronal buffer-0.1% bovine serum albumin (VB-BSA) solution as required for the CF procedure.

Rabbit anti-sheep-erythrocyte serum was purchased from Baltimore Biological Laboratory, Baltimore, Md. A stock solution, 1:50 dilution of this serum in phosphate-buffered saline, was stored at 4°C and further diluted 1:25 before adding it to the erythrocytes.

The sheep-erythrocyte suspension was prepared by (6) diluting the red cells in VB-BSA so that the clear lysate obtained by mixing 1 ml of this suspension with 14 ml of 0.1% K_2CO_3 gave an optical density reading (O.D.) of 0.700 on a Beckman DU spectrophotometer at 541 nm. The sensitized erythrocytes (EA) were prepared by using a ratio of 1:1:8 of sheep-erythrocyte suspension, hemolytic antibody, and VB-BSA respectively and contained 1×10^8 EA/ml.

The micro-CF technique of Wasserman and Levine (7) was used with some modifications. Five-tenths milliliter of an appropriate dilution of anti-HEA globulin (containing 0.06 to 0.09 ABC-33 units of antibody), 0.5 ml of different concentrations of HEA and 0.5 ml of complement were incubated at 4°C for 18 hr. After addition of 0.2 ml EA to each experimental and control tube, the mixtures were incubated at 37°C for 1 hr and then cooled in an ice bath. The tubes were centrifuged at 1500 rpm for 10 min and the O.D. of the supernatant fluids was analyzed at 413 nm. All tests were performed in duplicate with volumetric or lambda pipettes.

Hemagglutination and hemolysis of HEA-conjugated erythrocytes. Washed sheep erythrocytes were coupled to HEA by bis-diazotized benzidine (8) and hemagglutinin titers of $7S\gamma_1$ and $7S\gamma_2$ anti-HEA preparations were determined by twofold dilutions. Hemolysis of the HEA-conjugated erythrocytes (9) was performed as follows: Twofold dilutions of the anti-HEA fractions were made in 1% BSA-Veronal buffer and guinea pig complement (10) was added. After addition of HEA-conjugated erythrocytes, the tubes were incubated for 1 hr at 37°C, and then centrifuged (1500 rpm for 10 min) and the O.D. of the supernatant was read at 413 nm. Appropriate controls for specificity of hemolysis and for the O.D. of individual components were included. The relative lysis in individual dilutions was determined by comparing the O.D. of the supernatants with that obtained after 100% lysis of a sensitized cell standard.

RESULTS

Four $7S\gamma_2$ anti-HEA and five $7S\gamma_1$ anti-HEA preparations were tested for PCA reactions in guinea pigs (Table I). Positive reactions were obtained with the $7S\gamma_2$ preparations and could be elicited with 4.9 to 11.5 ABC units of antibody/ml. The $7S\gamma_1$ anti-HEA preparations never elicited a PCA reaction in guinea pigs, even with antibody concentrations up to 224.5 ABC units/ml. However, when PCA was tested in Peromys-

TABLE I

Passive cutaneous anaphylaxis (PCA) in guinea pigs and Peromyscus with Peromyscus $7S\gamma_1$ and $7S\gamma_2$ antibody to hen egg albumin

Prep.	Class of Antibody	ABC Units/ml	PCA Reactions in Guinea Pigs at Given Dilutions of Anti-HEA							Approximate Guinea Pig PCA Endpoint (ABC Units)	Peromyscus PCA Reactions with Undiluted Anti-HEA
			Undil.	1:4	1:8	1:10	1:50	1:100	1:250		
1	$7S\gamma_2$	429.0				17 × 17[a]	12 × 15	9 × 9		8.6	0,0[b]
						15 × 15	14 × 14	0			
						14 × 17	12 × 12	0			
						12 × 17		0			
2	$7S\gamma_2$	39.6		10 × 10	10 × 10	0				4.9	0,0
				12 × 12	10 × 10	0					
				11 × 11							
3	$7S\gamma_2$	1155.0				17 × 17		13 × 13	0	11.5	0,0
						18 × 18		12 × 12	0		
								12 × 13	0		
								12 × 12	0		
4	$7S\gamma_2$	44.6		14 × 15	5 × 5	0				5.6	0,0
				10 × 10	10 × 10	0					
				13 × 13							
				5 × 5							
5	$7S\gamma_1$	79.2	0,0,0							>79.2	7 × 11, 6 × 6
6	$7S\gamma_1$	35.6	0,0							>35.6	6 × 11, 9 × 8
7	$7S\gamma_1$	14.5	0,0							>14.5	6 × 10, 6 × 8
8	$7S\gamma_1$	47.8	0,0							>47.8	10 × 10, 10 × 10
9	$7S\gamma_1$	224.5	0,0							>224.5	14 × 14, 6 × 7

[a] Diameters (mm) of bluing in PCA reaction (individual skin tests).

[b] Some of the Peromyscus $7S\gamma_2$ anti-HEA produced reactions of diffuse bluing less than 5 mm in diameter; 0 = no PCA reaction (individual skin tests).

TABLE II

Complement fixation by Peromyscus 7Sγ_1 and 7Sγ_2 antibody to hen egg albumin

Prep.	Class of 7S Antibody	ABC Units/ml	ABC Units Used	Average O.D. of Standard[a]	Complement Fixation with Given Amount of HEA (µg/0.5 ml) 0.100	0.050	0.025	0.0125	0.006	0.003
1	γ_2	429	0.0605	0.680				0.370[b] (46%)	0.445 (35%)	0.545 (20%)
2	γ_2	39.6	0.0635	0.590				0.390 (34%)	0.500 (12%)	0.550 (7%)
3	γ_2	1155	0.0695	0.605				0.075 (88%)	0.225 (63%)	0.445 (26%)
4	γ_2	44.6	0.0800	0.615				0.165 (73%)	0.260 (58%)	0.495 (21%)
5	γ_1	79.2	0.0792	0.550				0.600 (0%)	0.540 (2%)	0.600 (0%)
6	γ_1	35.6	0.0890	0.800	0.810 (0%)	0.800 (0%)	0.790 (1%)	0.800 (0%)	0.800 (0%)	0.765 (4%)
7	γ_1	14.5	0.0905	0.755	0.720 (4.5%)	0.715 (5%)	0.700 (7%)	0.780 (0%)	0.755 (0%)	0.740 (2%)
8	γ_1	47.8	0.0905	0.790	0.790 (0%)	0.785 (<1%)	0.800 (0%)	0.795 (0%)	0.800 (0%)	0.790 (0%)
9	γ_1	224.5	0.0900	0.810	0.790 (2%)	0.795 (2%)	0.800 (1%)	0.780 (3%)	0.780 (3%)	0.805 (<1%)
10	γ_1	39.9	0.0887	0.795	0.790 (<1%)	0.790 (<1%)	0.795 (0%)	0.780 2%)	0.790 (<1%)	0.790 (<1%)

[a] 100% lysis of EA.

[b] Upper figure, optical density of lysed sensitized erythrocytes (EA) due to unfixed complement lower figure (in parentheses), % of complement fixed.

cus skin, discrete bluing reactions were detected with Peromyscus 7Sγ_1 antibody only and not with 7Sγ_2 antibody (Table I).

These same 7Sγ_1 and 7Sγ_2 preparations, plus an additional 7Sγ_1 preparation (no. 10), were tested for their ability to fix complement (Table II). HEA antibodies of the 7Sγ_2 globulin class consistently fixed complement in the presence of HEA. The six 7Sγ_1 preparations were tested in a wide range of antibody-antigen ratios without detectable CF.

A 7Sγ_2 anti-HEA and two 7Sγ_1 anti-HEA preparations (nos. 4, 8 and 10—Table II) were tested for hemagglutination and hemolysin titer (Fig. 1). These three preparations had similar ABC values and also similar hemagglutination titers. However, hemolysis of the HEA-conjugated erythrocytes was detected only with the 7Sγ_2 anti-HEA.

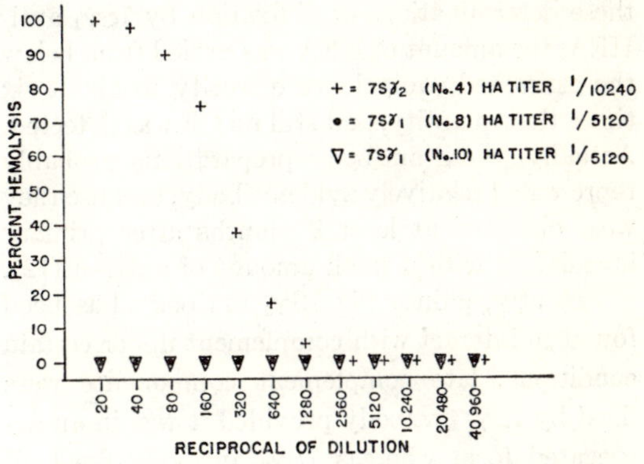

Figure 1. Hemolysis of HEA-conjugated sheep erythrocytes by peromyscus 7Sγ_2 and 7Sγ_1 anti-HEA. The 7Sγ_2 and 7Sγ_1 preparations contained similar amounts of antibody (ABC 33 = 39.9 to 47.8) and had similar hemagglutinin titers (1:5120 and 1:10,240); however, hemolysis was detected only with 7Sγ_2 anti-HEA.

DISCUSSION

This paper presents evidence for a qualitative difference in biologic activity of the 7Sγ_1- and 7Sγ_2-globulins of Peromyscus. Small amounts of Peromyscus 7Sγ_2 antibody produced positive PCA reactions in guinea pigs while much larger amounts of 7Sγ_1 antibody did not. However, the PCA response was reversed if the test were made on the homologous species. Also, comparable amounts of the two globulins had similar hemagglutination titers but hemolysis of the HEA-conjugated erythrocytes was produced only by $7S\gamma_2$ antibody. In addition, with the same amount of $7S\gamma_1$ antibody as the quantity of $7S\gamma_2$ which was sufficient to fix most of the complement in the CF test, no fixation was detectable.

It is well known (11) that the plot of complement fixation *vs* antigen concentration is very similar to the precipitin curve for many antigen-antibody systems, with the ratio of antibody to antigen at equivalence about the same in both cases. When one compares the complement-fixing abilities of two antibody preparations, not only should the quantities of antibody be the same but also similar equivalence ratios of antigen should be used. Since there was not enough serum to do a precipitin curve, or even a complete CF curve on every sample, an estimate of the amount of antibody (1.83 × ABC value) and the antigen equivalence point (0.2 × ABC value) was made from the ABC value. However, if the affinity between antibody and antigen is not great, the antibody concentration (micrograms/milliliter) will be more than 1.83 × ABC value and the equivalence amount of HEA (μg) will probably be greater than 0.2 × ABC value. Therefore, in these determinations of C fixation by $7S\gamma_1$ anti-HEA, the amount of HEA was varied from below the estimated equivalence quantity to about six times that quantity, and still no CF was detected. Actually, these antibody preparations probably represented relatively avid antibody, because they were obtained at least 2 months after primary inoculation with a small amount of antigen (12).

Recently, guinea pig $7S\gamma_1$ antibody has been found to interact with complement under certain conditions; late complement components were fixed by $7S\gamma_1$ antibody provided it was in an aggregated form whereas $7S\gamma_2$ antibody fixed all complement components when either preformed complexes or antigen and antibody were incubated with complement (13). Under similar conditions, fixation of complement components might also be detected with Peromyscus $7S\gamma_1$-globulin. In addition, it is apparent that even within a given Ig class not all the antibody molecules are capable of fixing complement. For instance, antibodies in the IgM class which did not fix complement have been reported in the rabbit (14), mouse (15) and guinea pig (16) and the ability of rabbit IgM antibody to fix complement was related to the charge of the IgM molecule (14). A similar heterogeneity of CF antibodies within the $7S\gamma_1$ and $7S\gamma_2$ classes may also exist. In the present study only the more cathodally migrating $7S\gamma_2$ globulins and anodally migrating $7S\gamma_1$ globulins could be isolated and examined.

The F_c pieces of the Peromyscus $7S\gamma_1$ and $7S\gamma_2$ globulins do not share any detectable antigenic determinants (2). Presumably, structural differences in the F_c portion of the molecule are responsible for the distinctive biologic activities of these two 7S globulins. The similarities between the known biologic activity of the $7S\gamma_1$ $7S\gamma_2$ globulin classes in the guinea pig, mouse and Peromyscus suggest that the functional role of these 7S globulins had developed in an ancestor common to these three rodents.

REFERENCES

1. Bloch, K. J., Progr. Allerg., *10:* 84, 1967.
2. Coe, J. E., J. Immun., *103:* 639, 1969.
3. Chou, C. T., Cinader, B. and Dubiski, S., Int. Arch. Allerg., *32:* 583, 1967.
4. Farr, R. S., J. Infect. Dis., *103:* 239, 1958.
5. Heidelberger, M. and Kendall, F. E., J. Exp. Med., *62:* 697, 1935.
6. Kabat, E. A., *Kabat and Mayer's Experimental Immunochemistry*, 2nd Ed., p. 149, Charles C Thomas, Springfield, Ill., 1961.
7. Wasserman, E. and Levine, L., J. Immun., *87:* 290, 1961.
8. Stavitsky, A. B. and Arquilla, E. R., J. Immun., *74:* 306, 1955.
9. Arquilla, E. R. and Stavitsky, A. B., J. Clin. Invest., *35:* 458, 1956.
10. Arquilla, E. R. and Finn, J., J. Exp. Med., *122:* 770, 1965.
11. Kabat, E. A., *Kabat and Mayer's Experimental Immunochemistry*, 2nd Ed., p. 216, Charles C Thomas, Springfield, Ill., 1961.
12. Eisen, H. N. and Siskind, G. W., Biochemistry, *3:* 996, 1964.
13. Sandberg, A. L., Osler, A. G., Shin, H. S. and Oliveira, B., J. Immun., *104:* 329, 1970.
14. Hoyer, L. W., Borsos, T., Rapp, H. J. and Vannier, W. E., J. Exp. Med., *127:* 589, 1968.
15. Plotz, P. H., Colten, H. and Talal, N., J. Immun., *100:* 752, 1968.
16. Linscott, W. D. and Hansen, S. S., J. Immun., *103:* 423, 1969.

THE JOURNAL OF IMMUNOLOGY
Vol. 105, No. 4, October 1970

Printed in U.S.A.

ANTIGENICITY OF POLYPEPTIDES (POLY α AMINO ACIDS): IMMUNOGENICITY OF A HOMOPOLYMER DERIVATIVE[1]

PAUL H. MAURER

From the Department of Biochemistry, Jefferson Medical College, Thomas Jefferson University, Philadelphia, Pennsylvania 19107

Received for publication February 14, 1970

The γ-2-N ethyl morpholinyl derivative of the homopolymer polyglutamic acid (PAMEG) was immunogenic in rabbits but not in mice or humans. The specificity of the PAMEG-anti PAMEG reaction has been shown. The immunogenic behavior of PAMEG is analogous to polymers of D amino acids.

Homopolymers of amino acids *per se* generally are non-immunogenic (1, 2). The one exception noted so far has been the response of guinea pigs against polyproline (3, 4). One of the first proposed synthetic plasma expanders of amino acids to be tested for immunogenicity was polyglutamic acid (5). However, because of its high net negative charge, it had adverse effects on several blood components. Subsequent developments therefore led to synthesis of a more neutral charged analogue of polyglutamic acid (PGA). This polymer poly γ-2-N-ethyl-morpholinyl ethyl glutamic acid (PAMEG) has been studied for immunogenicity in several species. The unexpected finding that this polymer is immunogenic in rabbits but not in humans is the basis of this report.

The polymer PAMEG was supplied by Drs. E. R. Blout and E. Simons of Harvard Medical School. As prepared (6) it had a molecular weight of about 70,000.

The initial screening for immunogenicity in rabbits employed injections in the footpads with either 10 μg, 100 μg or 1 mg of polymer in complete adjuvant. Bleedings were taken weekly for 2 months. The animals were then reinjected subcutaneously with the same amount of polymer and exsanguinated 2 weeks later. In another experiment eight rabbits were immunized with 100 μg of polymer and bled weekly for 6 weeks. They then received another injection of the polymer and were bled periodically for 8 months.

The procedure for immunization of humans was similar to that employed previously with other polymers (7). Volunteers were bled, skin tested with PAMEG (0.1 ml of 1 mg/ml) and then given two intramuscular injections of the polymer in solution 3 days apart. Three groups of individuals received the total dose of PAMEG as indicated: eight volunteers, 1 mg; seven volunteers, 10 mg; seven volunteers, 80 mg. Ten days and 3 weeks after the last injection, the bleedings and skin testing were repeated. For initial testing of rabbit sera the PCA (passive cutaneous anaphylaxis) reaction in guinea pigs was performed (8). Challenging injections consisted of 1 ml of a solution of 500 μg polymer and 0.5 % Evans blue dye. The micro precipitin reaction was employed for determining the amounts of antibody N/ml of serum (9). With rabbit sera 0.2 to 2.0 ml of serum was used. With human sera, because of the low levels of antibody generally produced, 3.0 ml of serum were employed. The range of PAMEG added was 0.6 to 2.5 μg N.

The results obtained in rabbits indicated that 10 μg and 100 μg were immunogenic but that 1 mg was not (Table I). Reimmunization of 8 rabbits with 100 μg PAMEG produced 100% positive reactors. All the sera that elicited positive PCA reactions also gave precipitin reactions (7 to 50 μg antibody N/ml of serum).

In addition to the biologic test (PCA) for antibody the precipitates formed with PAMEG and rabbit serum were soluble in excess PAMEG (1 mg/ml). Tanned red blood cells "coated" with PAMEG were agglutinated specifically by

[1] This work was supported by Contract DADA17-67-C-7021 from the Department of the Army, Office of the Surgeon General and United States Public Health Service Grants AI-07825 and TIAI-00334 from the National Institute of Allergy and Infectious Diseases. Paper 35 in a series of Antigenicity of Polypeptides (Poly α Amino Acids).

TABLE I

Immune response of rabbits against PAMEG

Dose Injected	Response[a]	Antibody Precipitated per ml Serum[b]
		μg N
10 μg (I)[c]	2/3	12–60
100 μg (I)	2/3	10–90
100 μg (II)	8/8	15–60
1 mg	0/3	

[a] Number of positive sera/number of sera tested; all sera that were positive by PCA reaction also gave precipitin reactions.

[b] Range of antibody N precipitated.

[c] Number in parentheses refers to experiment number.

rabbit antisera and were inhibited by the presence of excess PAMEG. However, the precipitates that formed with all the human sera, 6 to 18 μg N/ml (1 pre- and 2 post-immunization bleedings) did not dissolve in "excess PAMEG" even when incubated for 1 week at room temperature.

In some ways PAMEG can be considered to behave as a D amino acid polymer, especially as it is poorly degraded by known enzymes, i.e., pepsin, trypsin and chymotrypsin (E. R. Blout and E. Simons, personal communication). The definite rabbit response obtained with 100 μg, but not with 1 mg, is also reminiscent of the dose requirements for immunogenicity *vs* tolerogenicity observed with D amino acid polymers (10–12).

It appears that PAMEG has a slight positive charge on the N atom of its morpholino ring and this might have contributed to its immunogenic potential. Perhaps the PAMEG interacts "*in vivo*" with some negatively charged carrier protein which then becomes the true immunogen. The data presented with the human sera indicate that such a nonspecific interaction is indeed possible.

This postulated mechanism of "*in vivo*" complexing with proteins might also be important in explaining the immunogenicity of polymers of αD amino acids. In our previous studies, αD amino acid polymers were shown to be significantly more immunogenic in rabbits and guinea pigs when complexed with immunogenic carriers such as methylated or phosphorylated bovine serum albumin (13). In addition to the non-immunogenicity of PAMEG in man reported here, no responses have been obtained in mice and guinea pigs. The rabbit has been the only species to show a response.

Acknowledgment. The author wishes to thank Miss Maria Filinska for technical assistance and the contributions of Drs. M. Egan and C. Merryman to some aspects of this study.

REFERENCES

1. Maurer, P. H., Progr. Allerg., *8:* 1, 1964.
2. Sela, M., Advances Immun., *5:* 29, 1966.
3. Jasin, H. E. and Glynn, L. E., Immunology, *8:* 95, 260, 1965.
4. Brown, P. C. and Glynn, L. E., Immunology, *15:* 589, 1968.
5. Maurer, P. H., Proc. Soc. Exp. Biol. Med., *96:* 394, 1957.
6. Kulkarni, R. K. and Blout, E. R., J. Amer. Chem. Soc., *84:* 3971, 1962.
7. Maurer, P. H., Gerulat, B. F. and Pinchuck, P., J. Exp. Med., *116:* 521, 1962.
8. Ovary, Z., Progr. Allerg., *5:* 459, 1958.
9. Maurer, P. H., Gerulat, B. F. and Pinchuck, P., J. Biol. Chem., *239:* 922, 1964.
10. Janeway, C. A., Jr. and Sela, M., Immunology, *13:* 29, 1967.
11. Stupp, Y. and Sela, M., Biochim. Biophys. Acta, *140:* 349, 1967.
12. Gill, T. J., Papermaster, D. S. and Mowbray, J. F., J. Immun., *95:* 794, 1965.
13. Maurer, P. H. and Pinchuck, P., in *Nucleic Acids in Immunology*, Edited by O. J. Plescia and W. Braun, p. 301, Springer-Verlag, New York, 1968.

THE JOURNAL OF IMMUNOLOGY
Vol. 105, No. 4, October 1970

Printed in U.S.A.

COMPLEMENT FIXATION: THE EFFECTS OF IgG AND IgM ANTIBODY CONCENTRATION ON C1-BINDING AFFINITY[1]

WILLIAM D. LINSCOTT

From the Department of Microbiology, University of California, San Francisco Medical Center, San Francisco, California 94122

Received for publication February 6, 1970

When red cells were reacted with increasing amounts of IgG antibody, the number of sites capable of binding C1 increased in a non-linear manner with constantly decreasing rate. At low antibody multiplicities, all of these sites bound C1 with approximately the same affinity, as shown by nearly complete C1 transfer at an ionic strength (μ) close to 0.06. As the amount of antibody increased, a heterogeneity in C1-binding affinities appeared, such that increasing amounts of C1 failed to transfei at μ = 0.059 but did transfer at μ = 0.140. It is suggested that this heterogeneity in C1 binding to IgG may reflect different C1-binding affinities of antibody doublets, triplets, etc. When red cells were reacted with increasing amounts of IgM antibody, the number of C1-binding sites increased linearly. The slope of the plotted curves of these data was close to 1. These sites bound C1 with a range of affinities that was constant, providing all sites were saturated with C1, over a wide range of IgM concentrations. If the antibody:C1 ratio exceeded approximately 1.5:1, a selection in favor of more firmly bound C1 appeared, so that the proportion of cell-bound C1 which transferred at any ionic strength below 0.14 became inversely proportional to the antibody concentration. It is suggested that this heterogeneity in C1 binding to IgM may reflect differences in the number of antibody combining sites which are occupied by antigen.

Recent preliminary results from this laboratory indicated that the first component of guinea pig complement (C1)[2] is bound to IgG immune complexes with an affinity which is proportional to the antibody concentration (1). This suggested that IgG antibody doublets, triplets, etc. might each have a characteristic C1-binding affinity. The present paper reports further investigations on this problem, and presents evidence that IgM antibodies also display a heterogeneity of C1-binding affinities, possibly related to the number of antibody combining sites which are occupied by antigen.[3]

METHODS AND MATERIALS

The methods and materials have been reported previously (2). In brief, 15-week IgG and IgM antibody fractions from a rabbit immunized with boiled sheep E stroma were used at different concentrations to sensitize sheep E. These sensitized cells, along with unsensitized controls, were then washed and reacted with suitable amounts of functionally pure guinea pig C1, under optimal conditions for each antibody class (2, 3). After further washing, these cell preparations were lysed with distilled water to facilitate later separation from the intact EAC4 used for the assay, and then reconstituted to isotonicity with concentrated buffer. Aliquots were then mixed

[1] This work was supported in part by United States Public Health Service Grant AI 06464 and American Cancer Society Grant E-529.

[2] Abbreviations used in this paper include Ab (antibody), E (erythrocytes), C1 (first component of complement), C2 (second component of complement), C4 (fourth component of complement), EA (sheep erythrocytes sensitized with antibody), SA (antibody-sensitized antigenic site on an erythrocyte, capable of fixing C1), and EAC1, EAC4, SAC1, etc., where the above definitions also apply.

[3] C1-binding affinity is used here to refer to the relative strength of the bond between IgG or IgM antibody molecules and associated C1, as measured by the ionic strength which must be attained before the C1 will dissociate into the fluid phase.

with receptor EAC4 and incubated under a variety of conditions of temperature and ionic strength, to allow C1 to transfer from the donor cells to the EAC4. The lysed donor stroma were then removed along with the supernatant fluid after centrifugation, and the numbers of SAC14 generated during transfer were measured by saturating the cells with C2, followed by EDTA-complement to provide an excess of the remaining components needed for lysis. After correction for nonspecific C1 binding by unsensitized red cells (2, 4), the average number of molecules of C1 per original donor cell was calculated from the relative concentrations of donor and receptor cells, using the negative natural log of (1 minus the per cent lysis) (2, 4).

RESULTS

To determine the effect of IgG concentration on the amount of C1 transfer and the optimal ionic strength (μ) for transfer, E were sensitized with eight different concentrations of IgG antibody, in twofold dilutions from 1:20 to 1:2560. After washing, all cell preparations were treated at 0°C with sufficient C1 to provide about 90 molecules/cell. The cells were then washed in the cold at $\mu = 0.037$, lysed with water, reconstituted to isotonicity, and portions were assayed by the C1 transfer technique at 30°C. The results are shown in Figure 1. In the upper half the data are presented as the actual average number of molecules of C1 transferred from each cell, at five different ionic strengths. It is readily apparent that IgG dilutions from 1:80 to 1:320 produced cells capable of binding and releasing near maximal amounts of C1. Higher dilutions provided insufficient antibody to bind more than a part of the C1 offered, as shown by a reduced amount of transfer. More importantly, the larger amounts of antibody present in the 1:20 and 1:40 dilutions also resulted in a restricted total amount of C1 transferred at the highest μ, although the same amount of C1 should have been taken up by these cells as by those treated with antibody 1:80, 1:160 or 1:320 (C1 was limiting at all antibody dilutions from 1:20 to 1:320). It can also be seen that there was a marked increase in the ionic strength required for a given amount of C1 transfer, roughly proportional to the increase in antibody concentration. It would appear from the curves that an ionic strength considerably

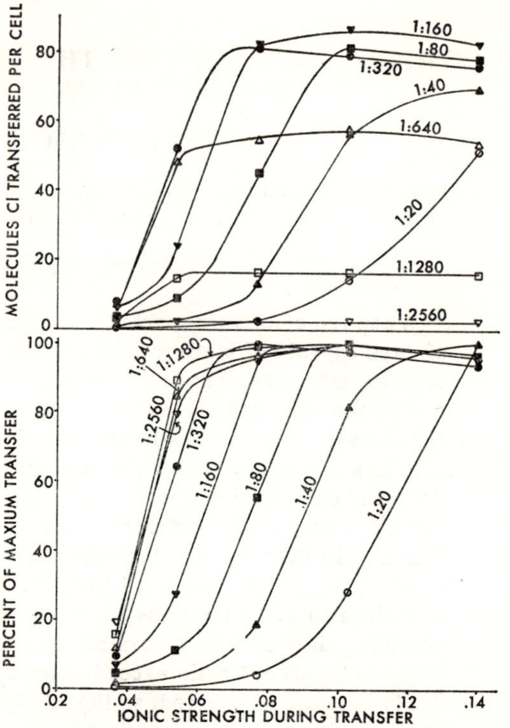

Figure 1. Effect of IgG antibody concentration on the ionic strength required for maximum C1 transfer.

above 0.15 would be required for maximal transfer with the highest antibody concentration.

It is, of course, possible that reduced C1 transfer with high antibody concentrations might have resulted from secondary effects of agglutination. Microscopic examination of all cell preparations after reaction with C1 showed a moderate amount of agglutination with antibody diluted 1:20 (some clumps, but most containing fewer than 10 red cells), while with antibody diluted 1:40 there was almost no agglutination (3 to 4 cells/clump, at the most). At higher dilutions no agglutination was seen.

In the lower half of Figure 1, where each point is plotted as the percentage of maximum C1 transfer obtained for that particular antibody dilution, the pronounced and regular increase in the ionic strength required for a given degree of transfer with each increment in antibody is more easily seen. This effect first appeared at the 1:640 dilution, far below the agglutination level, and continued up to the highest amount of antibody used. Other studies showed that a 1:640 dilution of this IgG preparation contains enough antibody to generate approximately 150 C1-fixing sites/cell, and theoretical considerations discussed elsewhere predict that with this amount of antibody virtually all the molecules should be present as singlets or doublets at the cell surface, with perhaps 1 to 2 triplets/cell at the most (1, 5). Thus, essentially all of the C1 fixed to cells sensitized with this amount of antibody or less should be bound to IgG doublets (since singlets do not fix C1), and an estimate of the ionic strength required for complete transfer of C1 from these cells should indicate what ionic strength is required to dissociate C1 from such doublets. Inspection of the curves in the lower half of Figure 1 indicates that C1 transfer from cells prepared with antibody dilutions of 1:640 or higher is more than 90% complete at about μ = 0.06, while from cells treated with large amounts of antibody there is almost no transfer at a similar ionic strength.

The effect of antibody concentration is even more clearly shown in Figure 2, where these same data are plotted as number of molecules of C1 transferred per cell at each ionic strength, over the range of antibody concentrations employed. A sharp decrease in transfer at higher antibody concentrations is apparent at each ionic strength tested, as is a plateau of maximum transfer occurring at a dilution of about 1:320, beyond which antibody is in excess relative to C1. The estimates of numbers of IgG doublets, triplets, etc., expected at each antibody dilution were derived from computer data based on "occupancy problem" theory, assuming 600,000 Forssman sites/cell and given that approximately 150 doublets/cell are generated with this IgG preparation diluted 1:640, in moderate C1 excess. Of course, with the limited amount of C1 offered in this experiment (about 90 molecules/cell), it would not be expected that each site capable of fixing C1 would be able to do so, but if there is a differential C1-binding affinity, dependent upon how many closely associated molecules of IgG cooperate in the binding of a single molecule of C1 (1), then the more antibody used to sensitize the cell, the greater the proportion of a limited amount of C1 that should be bound strongly and released for transfer only at high ionic strength. The data obtained in this experiment are in accord with such a concept.

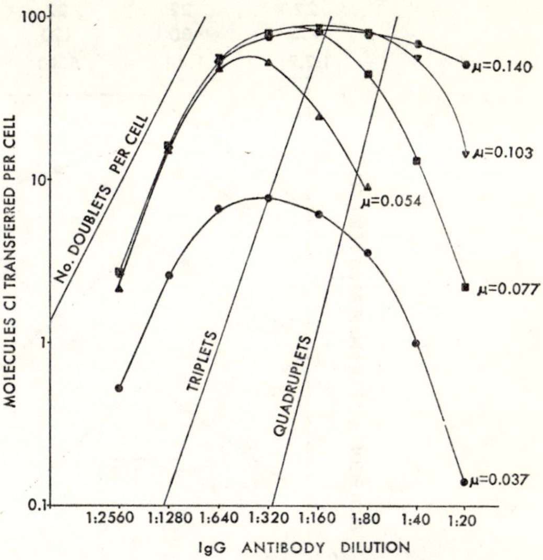

Figure 2. Inhibition of C1 transfer at high IgG antibody concentrations, and homogeneity of C1-binding affinities at low antibody concentrations.

Since preliminary work had indicated that a somewhat similar effect could be obtained with IgM antibodies as well, an experiment much like the above was designed using antibodies of this class. The main difference was that each IgM concentration was tested against two different amounts of C1, supplying about 22 and 350 molecules of C1/cell respectively. Also, all the IgM-sensitized and control cells were washed with EDTA buffer to remove any possible rabbit C1 (from the antibody preparation) before reaction with guinea pig C1 for 15 min at 30°C (μ = 0.065). After repeated washing at room temperature (μ = 0.037), the cell preparations were lysed with water, reconstituted to isotonicity, and appropriate dilutions were then reacted with EAC4 at four different ionic strengths, for 1 hr at 0°C. The amounts of C1 transferred under these conditions are shown in Figure 3. First of all, note the distinct separations between curves at different ionic strengths, to the left of the inflection points. This is in sharp contrast to the almost superimposed nature of similar portions of the IgG curves shown in Figure 2 (except at μ = 0.037, where transfer is very strongly inhibited). (A similar contrast between IgM and IgG is also apparent in Figures 7 and 8.) This suggests that when amounts of IgG antibody

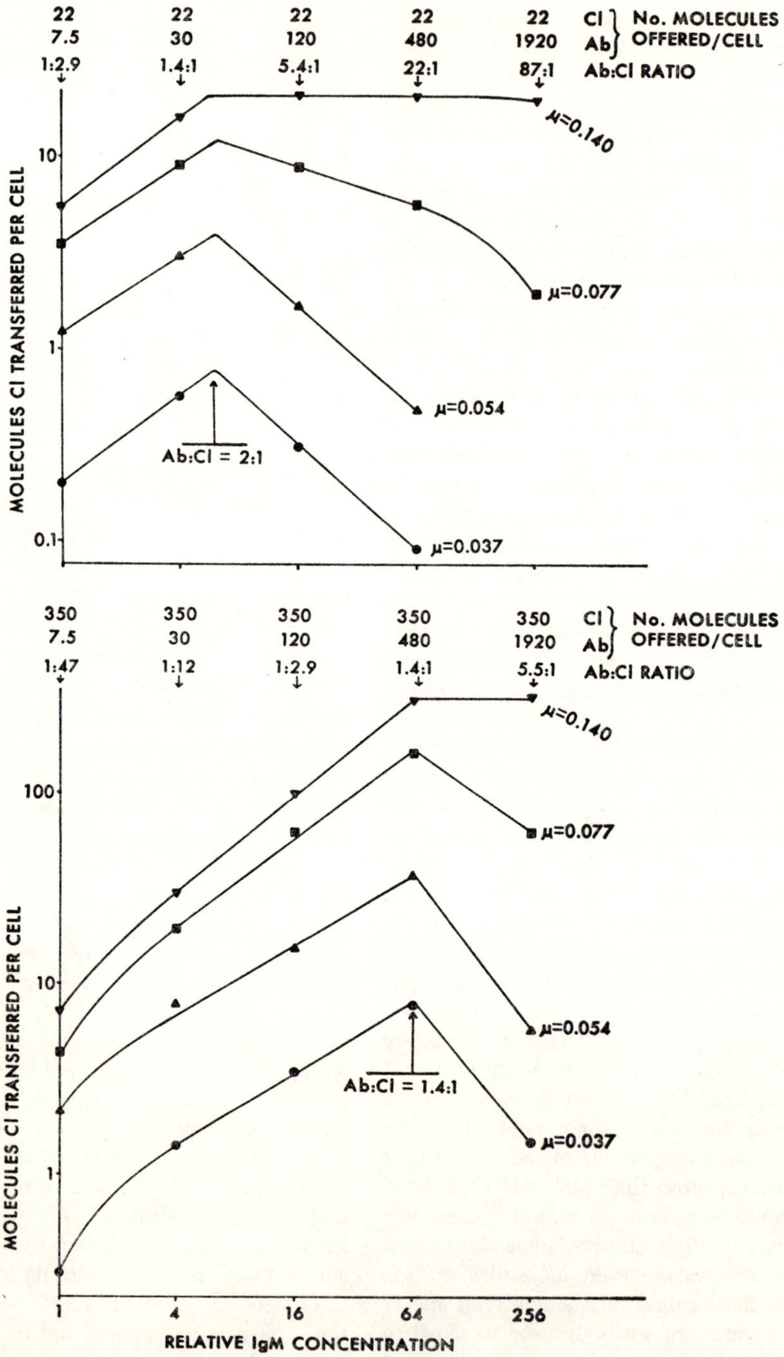

Figure 3. The effect of IgM antibody:C1 ratio on the affinity of C1 binding, and selection for high affinity binding at high IgM concentrations.

sufficient to generate doublets, but insufficient for triplet formation, are used then all C1-fixing sites bind C1 at about the same affinity, as shown by the similar amounts of transfer obtained at all ionic strengths between about 0.054 and 0.14 in Figure 2 (also see upper half of Figure 1 and reference 1). On the other hand, IgM antibodies at any concentration appear to offer a range of

C1-binding affinities, which are progressively overcome with each increment in ionic strength during transfer. The plateau seen at $\mu = 0.14$, and the 90 to 99% efficiency of the transfer reaction (3, 6), indicate that even the highest IgM binding affinity for C1 is overcome at $\mu = 0.14$. This appears not to be true for IgG (upper half of Figure 1).

The other important aspect of Figure 3 relates to the antibody:C1 ratio. As is apparent from the shift in the inflection points of the transfer curves with change in C1 concentration, the important factor governing what proportion of C1 will be bound to IgM at each affinity is not the antibody concentration *per se*, but the antibody:C1 ratio. If C1 is present in relative excess, as it is to the left of the inflection points, then all or nearly all of the antibody molecules will have fixed C1, and the entire spectrum of binding affinities will be represented upon transfer. But when more antibody is present than C1, there should be a selection in favor of the highest-affinity sites so that, at ionic strengths below 0.14, the amount of C1 transfer is inversely proportional to antibody concentration. This is in agreement with the data shown in Figure 3. The antibody:C1 ratio at which selection starts to occur seems quite sharply defined with IgM, being about 2:1 for the lower C1 concentration and 1.4:1 for the higher. The difference may represent a somewhat reduced efficiency of C1 fixation at the lower C1 concentration.

There seemed to be a possibility that spontaneous aggregation of the IgM preparation during storage might have created antibody dimers or trimers which could produce foci capable of high-affinity C1 binding at the red cell surface. Such an effect was sought by centrifuging the IgM preparation at high speed in a sucrose gradient and testing equivalent amounts of antibody from the monomer and dimer regions of the gradient. They gave essentially identical results, ruling out this mechanism as a possible explanation for the above observations.

It was felt that if C1 binding to IgG doublets and triplets did occur at discrete affinities, it might be possible to demonstrate this directly in the form of a step-wise increase in transfer with increasing ionic strength. Accordingly, red cells were sensitized with as high a concentration of IgG as could be used without marked agglutination, in order to produce a large number of antibody triplets as well as doublets. These cells and

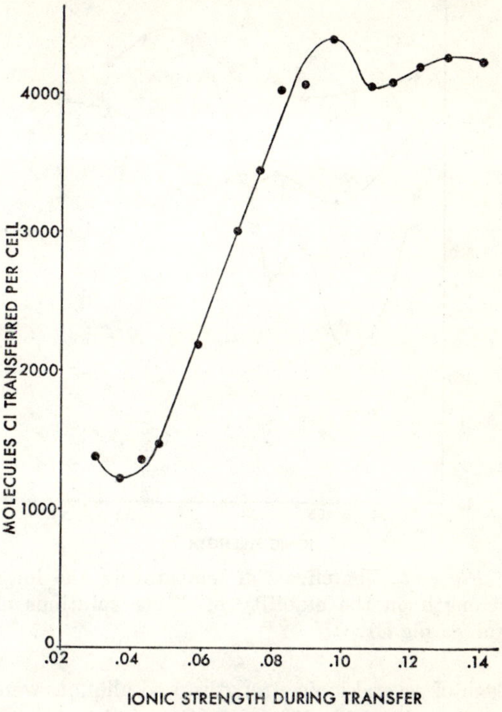

Figure 4. The effect of ionic strength on C1 transfer from heavily IgG-sensitized cells.

unsensitized controls were then treated with approximately a 10-fold excess of C1, washed, lysed and tested for transfer over a closely-spaced series of different ionic strengths. The results are shown in Figure 4, and have been confirmed on several occasions. There appears to have been some transfer even at low ionic strengths, but this might possibly have resulted from C1 release during lysis of the cells with water. It did not occur when smaller amounts of antibody and C1 were used in other experiments. As can be seen, there was an abrupt increase in transfer above $\mu = 0.05$ and an apparent double peak of maximum transfer with a trough between, but no clear indication of a step-wise increase. It might be argued that the "double peak" depends upon a single point (although duplicate tubes agreed quite closely), but several similar protocols have yielded similar results.

In an effort to understand the complexity of the upper portion of this curve, it was decided to reexamine the stability of guinea pig C1 under conditions approximating those found during transfer. A very dilute solution of C1 (about 5×10^8 effective molecules/ml) was prepared at

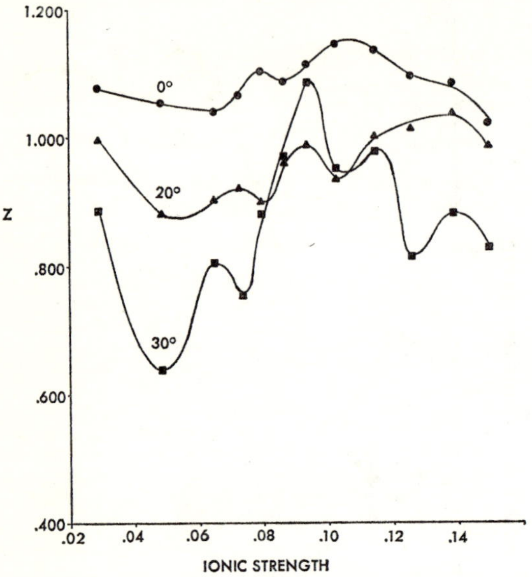

Figure 5. The effects of temperature and ionic strength on the stability of dilute solutions of guinea pig C1.

each of several ionic strengths, and aliquots were incubated at 0°, 20° or 30°C for 30 min. All samples were then brought to 0°C, and restored to μ = 0.094 by adding two volumes of cold buffer at appropriate ionic strengths. Aliquots of 0.5 ml were then incubated with an equal volume of EAC4 (1.5 × 10^8/ml, μ = 0.037) for 10 min at 30°C, before addition of excess C2 and EDTA-complement. The effects of temperature and ionic strength upon these dilute C1 solutions are shown in Figure 5. Although the finer details of these curves were not always reproducible, certain aspects were quite constant: a) less inactivation at 0°C than at 20°C or 30°C, regardless of μ; b) less inactivation at 30°C than at 20°C at certain intermediate μ; c) very strong inactivation at 30°C, μ = 0.04 to 0.07; and d) multiphasic curves at 20 to 30°C and intermediate μ, usually with a trough at 30°C at about the same μ as shown in the upper part of the curve in Figure 4.

It thus appeared likely that C1 transfer from IgG antibody at 30°C was complicated by the effects of ionic strength not only on the dissociation of C1 from SAC1 and its fixation to SAC4, but also on the stability of fluid-phase C1 itself. Since C1 stability was in general better at temperatures below 30°C, an attempt was made to duplicate the experiment shown in Figure 4, but

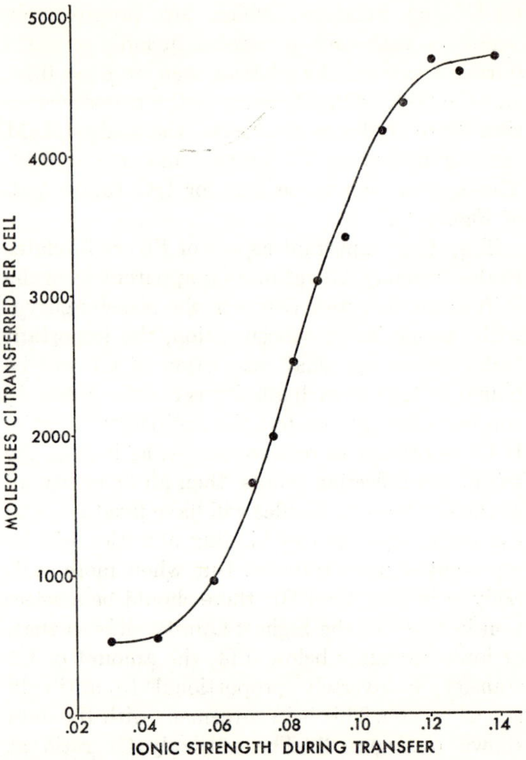

Figure 6. The effect of ionic strength on C1 transfer from heavily IgM-sensitized cells.

using 15°C and 20°C instead of 30°C. Transfer was markedly slower, however, and incomplete.

A similar experiment was then carried out using IgM antibodies instead of IgG. Since C1 dissociates more completely from IgM at 0°C than at higher temperatures, transfer is best carried out at 0°C (3, 7), where C1 inactivation effects should be minimal. As can be seen from Figure 6, a much smoother curve was obtained, but how much of this was due to greater C1 stability at 0°C, and how much to the lack of a doublet-triplet transition step is unclear. It can be seen that a sharp increase in transfer occurred at about μ = 0.05, as with IgG, but the curve rose somewhat less steeply, reaching a maximum at μ = 0.12 to 0.14. (The difference in transfer between μ = 0.122 and μ = 0.13 represents the difference between 79.9% lysis and 79.2%.)

It could be estimated from Figure 1 that C1 should transfer from IgG doublets at about μ = 0.06, and possibly from triplets at about μ = 0.10 to 0.14. It could also be predicted on a statistical

TABLE I

Attempt to measure numbers of cell-bound IgG doublets and triplets by C1 transfer at 2 different ionic strengths

Relative IgG Ab Conc.	Relative C1 Conc.	Final μ at Transfer	Molecules C1 Transferred/Cell	Corrected Molecules C1 Transferred/Cell	Doublets + Triplets	Doublets	Triplets
None	1	0.059	1.3				
		0.140	2.0				
None	4	0.059	7.0				
		0.140	11				
None	16	0.059	79				
		0.140	96				
None	64	0.059	676				
		0.140	788				
1	1	0.059	33.0	32	33	32	1
		0.140	35.1	33			
2	4	0.059	218	211	222	211	11
		0.140	233	222			
4	16	0.059	734	655	756	655	101
		0.140	852	756			
8	64	0.059	2220	1544	2476	1544	932
		0.140	3264	2476			

basis how many doublets would have to be generated/cell before triplets would start to appear (approximately 150), and the rate at which doublets and triplets would accumulate as more antibody was added (as the square and the cube respectively, of the increase in antibody concentration). An attempt was made to compare these predictions with experimental observation. Previous experiments had suggested that it was difficult to attain C1 "excess" in attempting to saturate IgG-sensitized red cells with C1 (3), so it was elected to supply C1 at a fixed ratio to IgG antibody, in an amount based on the predicted increase in number of C1-fixing (doublet) sites as the amount of antibody was successively doubled. (It was later determined that from 14 to 23 molecules of C1 had actually been offered/site capable of binding and transferring C1.) Table I shows the experimental setup. Twofold increments in the amounts of IgG antibody and fourfold increments in the amounts of C1 were added to a standard number of red cells, with a washing at 37°C, $\mu = 0.15$ interposed before the addition of C1, to remove non-avidly bound antibody (2). Unsensitized control cells were also treated with each C1 concentration employed. After thoroughly washing at 0°C, $\mu = 0.037$ to remove uncombined C1, the cells were lysed in cold water, restored to isotonicity at $\mu = 0.037$, and diluted in cold buffer, $\mu = 0.037$. Then 100-μl portions were mixed with 1-ml portions of EAC4 (7.5×10^7/ml) at $\mu = 0.061$ (for transfer from doublets) or $\mu = 0.15$ (for transfer from doublets plus triplets). After incubation for 40 min at 30°C, the contents of each tube were diluted with 8 ml of $\mu = 0.037$ buffer and centrifuged, and the lysed EAC1 stroma were removed with the supernatant fluid. The EAC4 were then reacted with C2 and EDTA-complement in the usual manner, to determine the amount of C1 which had transferred. The results are shown in Table I and Figure 7. The corrected number of molecules of C1 transferring/cell at $\mu = 0.059$ (final μ of mixture), which could represent transfer from IgG doublets, was subtracted from the number transferring at $\mu = 0.14$, which could represent doublets plus triplets, to give a possible estimate of the number of triplets/cell. Interestingly enough, when plotted logarithmically these points gave a straight line with a slope of 3.3 (expected = 3.0), but in absolute numbers they exceeded by fivefold or more the number of triplets predicted on a statistical basis. As has usually been found in this laboratory, the total number of C1-fixing sites increased with an initial slope considerably steeper than 2.0, which then decreased at higher antibody concentrations. The corrections for C1 bound to unsensitized cells are

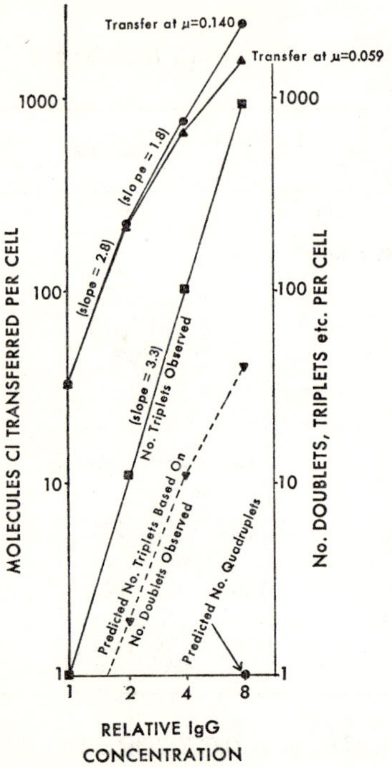

Figure 7. Attempt to measure numbers of cell-bound IgG doublets and triplets by C1 transfer at two different ionic strengths.

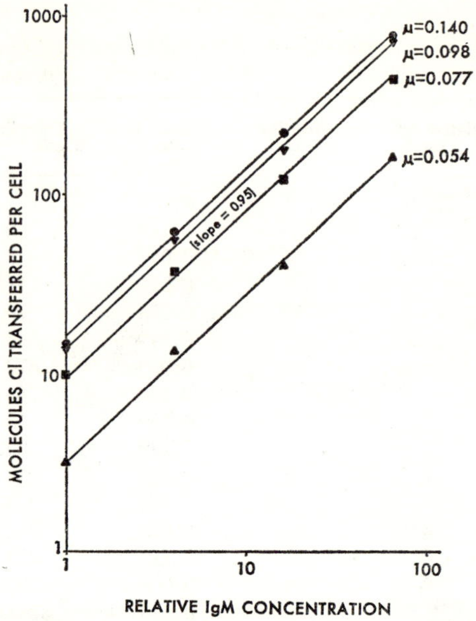

Figure 8. Constant range of C1-binding affinities over wide range of IgM antibody concentrations (C1 in excess).

uncomfortably high at high C1 concentrations, but no way has been found to reduce this appreciably without causing marked losses from the sensitized cell population. Note that, as also shown in Figures 1 and 2, there was essentially no heterogeneity of C1 binding at the lowest antibody concentration (transfer at $\mu = 0.059$ and $\mu = 0.14$ almost the same).

A similar experiment was done with IgM, using doubling dilutions of IgM antibody and doubling dilutions of C1 (offering approximately seven molecules of C1/molecule of antibody), and carrying out the transfer reaction at four different ionic strengths instead of two. The results, in Figure 8, stand in sharp contrast to those with IgG, and confirm those presented earlier in Figure 3. The lines connecting amounts of C1 transferred at different antibody concentrations but the same ionic strength do not converge at lower antibody concentrations, but instead are parallel over the whole range studied, indicating that the same proportion of cell-bound C1 transferred at each increment in ionic strength, regardless of the absolute antibody concentration (all points being in relative C1 excess). Thus, the heterogeneity of C1 binding by IgM appears to extend uniformly over a wide range of antibody concentrations, whereas C1 binding by IgG appears to be homogeneous at low antibody concentrations and to become progressively stronger as the amount of antibody is increased, even though the ratio of antibody to C1 is relatively constant (increasing discrepancy between transfer at $\mu = 0.059$ and $\mu = 0.14$ in Figure 7).

DISCUSSION

The events taking place during C1 transfer are probably quite complex. C1 must first dissociate from the sites to which it was bound, a process which is proportional to the ionic strength (3, 4). This dissociation is also directly proportional to the temperature for IgG antibody, and inversely proportional for IgM (3, 7). The dissociated C1, in order to be detected in the transfer assay, must then bind to a site possessing both antibody and C4 (SAC4), a reaction for which the optimal ionic strength is about $\mu = 0.04$ for IgG and $\mu = 0.065$ for IgM, and the optimal temperatures 0° and 30°C respectively (3, 8, 9). The fact that sites containing C4 in addition to antibody bind C1 more firmly than sites containing antibody alone (3), undoubtedly contributes to the completeness of transfer and the great efficiency which can be attained. This efficiency, which may be as high as 90% to 99% (3, 6), appears to fall off sharply with IgG when the antibody concentration exceeds a certain level (upper part of Figure 1). This effect may also account for the gradually decreasing slope of the IgG dose-response curve usually seen in this laboratory (Fig. 7), as more and more C1 reacts with sites which fail to release it at $\mu = 0.15$, the highest ionic strength at which transfer to EAC4 can be carried out. This problem has not been encountered with IgM.

An additional complexity affecting C1 transfer is the ionic strength-dependent inactivation of fluid-phase C1. This inactivation, which is partially reversible but only at much higher C1 concentrations than those existing during transfer, increases with time, temperature and ionic strength, and with decreasing C1 concentration (10). The C1 concentrations present during transfer, and those used in the inactivation experiment shown in Figure 5, are at least 50-fold lower than those used in the cited studies (10). C1 inactivation might account for the reduced C1 recovery from IgG at $\mu = 0.140$ as compared with $\mu = 0.077$ or 0.103, shown in Figures 1 and 2. Such an effect should be much less with IgM, since transfer from this antibody class is most rapid at 0°C, where C1 is most stable.

The attempt to detect a step-wise increase in C1 transfer from IgG, corresponding to a doublet-triplet transition (Fig. 4), was unsuccessful. In addition to complications introduced by C1 inactivation, averaging effects may have been produced by the conflict between the ionic strength requirement for optimal reaction of free C1 with SAC4, and the higher ionic strength necessary for dissociation of C1 from some IgG complexes. Additionally, the transition in C1 release from doublets to triplets with increasing ionic strength may not have been sufficiently abrupt to produce the anticipated result. Nevertheless, the release of essentially all the bound C1 at an ionic strength of approximately $\mu = 0.06$, when cells were sensitized with amounts of IgG insufficient to generate appreciable numbers of antibody triplets (Fig. 1 and reference 1), argues both for a homogeneity of C1-binding affinities at low IgG concentration and for C1 release from IgG doublets at about $\mu = 0.06$.

The C1 binding heterogeneity which was observed at higher concentrations of IgG was reflected in the steady increase in ionic strength needed for equivalent C1 transfer with increasing antibody concentration (Fig. 1), and in the increasing discrepancy between transfer at $\mu = 0.059$ and at $\mu = 0.140$ when antibody and C1 were both increased to maintain relative C1 excess (Fig. 7). This binding heterogeneity might reflect a variability in the configuration of the antigenic determinants at the cell surface, but its absence at low antibody concentration and rapid increase with increasing antibody concentration would seem to argue against this explanation. On the other hand, if it were due to spontaneous aggregation of the IgG solution during storage, with consequent deposition of preformed "dimer" and "trimer" complexes at the cell surface, it would be expected that the relative proportions of these complexes, and therefore the C1-binding heterogeneity, would remain constant at different IgG concentrations. Such, however, was not the case. Secondary effects of agglutination on C1 binding were ruled out by microscopic examination of cell preparations. If the heterogeneity were a reflection of whether one or both of the antibody combining sites were occupied by antigen, then it should have been constant at all antibody concentrations short of near-saturation, but was not. The simplest explanation which seems consistent with the data is that IgG triplets bind C1 more avidly than do IgG doublets, and that higher aggregates bind C1 even more firmly. This variability only occurs, however, if the cells have reacted with sufficient antibody to generate appreciable numbers of higher-affinity binding sites. In the case of very high antibody concentrations recovery of cell-bound C1 appears to be incomplete, presumably because some is bound so firmly it is not released even at $\mu = 0.140$.

Human C1q is capable of binding unaggregated human IgG weakly in free solution, as detected in the analytical ultracentrifuge (11). This has been interpreted as a weak expression of the much stronger binding which occurs when the antibody is distorted by complexing with antigen. The valence of C1q for IgG is approximately six (each molecule of C1q can bind up to six molecules of unaggregated IgG), and in IgG excess most of the complexes formed have a sedimentation velocity indicating that three or more molecules of IgG are bound/molecule of C1q (11, and Müller-Eberhard, H. J., personal communication). This suggests that the stability of these complexes increases with the number of molecules of IgG bound, and *if* these data can be extrapolated to the guinea pig C1 transfer system, they would lead to the prediction that C1 should be bound more tightly by IgG triplets than by doublets, and more tightly still by higher aggregates. The spatial coordinates involved in the generation of a "doublet" or "triplet" are as yet unknown.

There remains to be explained the fact that, in the experiment designed to detect IgG triplets (Fig. 7), the number detected exceeded by several-fold the number expected, although the rate of increase was quite close to that predicted (slope = 3.3 instead of 3.0). It might be that the theory on which the prediction was based was inappropriate; the assumption of transfer from doublets at about $\mu = 0.06$ or higher and from triplets at $\mu = 0.14$ might be in error; or the association of IgG molecules into doublets and triplets at the cell surface might not be a random process. In the absence of data about the spatial arrangement of Forssman determinants and antibody doublets, triplets, etc. at the cell surface, the "occupancy problem" theory employed seemed most appropriate for the task at hand (5), and the reasons for choosing the ionic strengths indicated have already been discussed. As to the randomness of doublet and triplet formation, there are some findings which may bear on this question. It has been my own experience that C1-fixing sites do *not* increase uniformly as the square of the IgG concentration (12), but rather that, in the range of from one to a few sites per cell the increase is much faster than this, and not constant but continuously decreasing so that at intermediate antibody concentrations the slope may indeed appear to be about 2. At higher antibody concentrations it decreases even further. This variability is clearly shown in Figure 7, and its possible significance has already been discussed. I have also been unable to attain "C1 excess" when attempting to saturate IgG-sensitized cells with C1; each increment of C1, even in the range of 50 to 100 times the number of C1-binding sites available, produces a further increase in the amount of C1 fixed by a given amount of IgG antibody (3), whereas such a problem has never been encountered with IgM. It seems possible that C1, because of its multivalent nature (11, 13, 14), and its greater stability when complexed with higher aggregates of IgG, might be able to bring about the re-positioning of IgG molecules at the cell surface, thus inducing the appearance of more doublets and triplets than expected on a statistical basis. In order for this to occur, the affinity between C1 and IgG complexes at 0°C, $\mu = 0.037$ to 0.065, would have to exceed that of the antibody combining site for the antigen. That this effect could be sufficiently large to account for the discrepancies observed in Figure 7 seems unlikely. It has been shown, however, that with very low-avidity IgM antibodies C1 *can* increase the avidity of the bond between antibody and antigen, leading to an increase in the number of molecules of antibody which bind to the antigen (15).

With regard to the C1-binding heterogeneity observed with IgM antibodies, my interpretation is quite different from that with IgG. Of the ways in which binding heterogeneity might be generated, agglutination effects were clearly ruled out by microscopic examination after reaction with C1 and during washing. Possible spontaneous aggregation of the IgM preparation during storage was not a factor, because equivalent amounts of "monomer" and "dimer" obtained after ultracentrifugation in a sucrose gradient gave essentially identical results. The possibility of IgM doublet and triplet formation at the cell surface would be quite remote at the antibody concentrations employed, and in addition such a mechanism should not give uniform heterogeneity over a wide range of antibody concentrations, as was observed. A more likely possibility is that C1-binding affinity with IgM may vary as a function of the number of antibody combining sites which are actually occupied by antigen. In any reaction mixture, regardless of antibody concentration (as long as saturation of the antigen by antibody was not approached), there should be similar proportions of IgM molecules in all permissible binding configurations with cell surface antigens. If these different configurations represent a range of potential C1-binding affinities, then whether or not selection occurs for the highest-affinity sites would depend solely on whether there were more or fewer molecules of C1 than needed to occupy all available sites. If more, then all antibody sites would bind C1 and the proportion of C1 molecules transferring at a given ionic strength would be constant regardless of the antibody concentration (portions of curves to the left of the inflection points in Figure 3, and Figure 8). If less, then C1 would tend to occupy the highest-affinity sites first, and the proportion of bound C1 transferring at any ionic strength below $\mu = 0.14$ would diminish with increasing antibody concentration (portions of curves to the right of the inflection points in Figure 3). The experimental data fit this prediction quite well, and argue against antigenic diversity as the cause for C1-binding heterogeneity. The fact that selection seems to have begun at antibody:C1 ratios slightly greater than 1:1 may reflect an inefficiency of C1 capture when antibody is not in relative excess, and in fact the lower C1 concentration did require a higher antibody:C1 ratio than the higher C1 concentration (2:1 *vs* 1.4:1), as might have been expected.

If C1-binding affinity to IgM is proportional to the number of antibody combining sites which are occupied, then it would be expected that this binding affinity would be less if the number of antigenic determinants on the red cell surface were reduced. In recent experiments anti-hapten IgM was reacted with hapten-coupled red cells, followed by C1 fixation and transfer, and the C1 binding heterogeneity in this system was much lower than that observed with the anti-Forssman system. In addition, *all* C1 transferred at an ionic strength of about 0.10, and the affinity of C1 binding was proportional to the amount of hapten coupled to the red cell (unpublished data).

The IgM molecule in many ways resembles an IgG pentamer: it has 10 H and 10 L chains, 5 Fc-like fragments and 10 combining sites (16). Thus, it might not be unrealistic to expect that it would have 5 potential sites which could bind C1. If this is the case, then steric hindrance is probably responsible for the fact that each cell-fixed IgM molecule is capable of binding only a single molecule of C1 (4, 8, 12). However, as more of the 10 antibody combining sites are actually occupied by antigen, it seems possible that progressive distortion of the molecule might bring into play more sites capable of reacting with C1, thus binding the single C1 molecule into place with increasing affinity.

REFERENCES

1. Linscott, W. D., J. Immun., *102:* 1322, 1969.
2. Linscott, W. D., J. Immun., *102:* 986, 1969.
3. Linscott, W. D., J. Immun., *102:* 993, 1969.
4. Borsos, T. and Rapp, H. J., J. Immun., *95:* 559, 1965.
5. Feller, W., *An Introduction to Probability Theory and its Applications*, 2nd Ed., John Wiley & Sons, New York, 1957.
6. Colten, H. R., Borsos, T. and Rapp, H. J., Science, *158:* 1, 1967.
7. Colten, H. R., Borsos, T. and Rapp, H. J., *Protides of the Biological Fluids*, Vol. 15, p. 471, Elsevier, Amsterdam, 1967.
8. Borsos, T. and Rapp, H. J., J. Immun., *91:* 851, 1963.
9. Tamura, N. and Nelson, R. A., Jr., J. Immun., *101:* 1333, 1968.
10. Colten, H. R., Borsos, T. and Rapp, H. J., J. Immun., *100:* 799, 1968.
11. Müller-Eberhard, H. J., Ann. Rev. Biochem., *38:* 389, 1969.
12. Borsos, T. and Rapp, H. J., Science, *150:* 505, 1965.
13. Müller-Eberhard, H. J. and Kunkel, H. G., Proc. Soc. Exp. Biol. Med., *106:* 291, 1961.
14. Ewald, R. W. and Schubart, A. F., J. Immun., *97:* 100, 1966.
15. Rosse, W. F., Borsos, T. and Rapp, H. J., J. Immun., *100:* 259, 1968.
16. Franklin, E. C. and Frangione, B., Ann. Rev. Med., *20:* 155, 1969.

THE JOURNAL OF IMMUNOLOGY
Vol. 105, No. 4, October 1970
Printed in U.S.A.

STUDIES ON THE MECHANISM OF HEAT AGGREGATION OF HUMAN γG[1]

WIPRECHT AUGENER AND HOWARD M. GREY[2]

From the Department of Experimental Pathology, Scripps Clinic and Research Foundation La Jolla, California 92037

Received for publication January 6, 1970

The intact proteins and Fab and Fc fragments of normal γG and myeloma proteins of the four γG subclasses were studied for their susceptibility to heat aggregation. It was found that in the case of normal γG and myeloma proteins of the two major subclasses, γG1 and γG2, aggregation of the intact protein correlated with aggregation of the Fab fragment, whereas the Fc fragments of these proteins did not aggregate appreciably. In the case of the two minor subclasses, γG3 and γG4, the Fc fragment was also a contributing factor in the formation of heat aggregates. Aggregation could be partially reversed (54% to 73%) by treatment with 8 M urea, indicating that both disulfide bonds and non-covalent interactions were responsible for the formation of the aggregates. It was also found that heat aggregation of γG1 protein leads to a conformational change in the Fab which renders it extremely susceptible to proteolysis. The significance of these findings with respect to the mechanism by which aggregation results in the enhanced biologic activity of the Fc fragment is discussed.

Heating of γ globulin has been used extensively over the past 10 years as a means of aggregating γ globulin in such a manner that it simulates the biologic reactivity of antigen-antibody complexes. Little is known however, of the physical and chemical effects of heat aggregation on the γ globulin molecule. The fact that only a portion of normal γG can be heat aggregated indicates a structural heterogeneity associated with this property (1). This structural heterogeneity is further demonstrated by the fact that only certain γG myeloma proteins are susceptible to heat aggregation (2). The purpose of our investigation was to determine the subunit structure within γG responsible for heat aggregation, and to investigate some of the structural changes that occur in the γG molecule upon heating.

[1] This is publication 391 from the Department of Experimental Pathology, Scripps Clinic and Research Foundation, La Jolla, California. This investigation was supported by United States Public Health Service Grant A1-07007, Atomic Energy Commission Contract AT(04-3)-410, American Heart Association Grant 67-795 and United States Public Health Service Training Grant 5T1 GM 683.

[2] Established Investigator of the American Heart Association. Present address: National Jewish Hospital and Research Center, Denver, Colorado 80206. All requests for reprints should be addressed to Dr. Grey.

MATERIALS AND METHODS

Immunoglobulin isolation. Normal γ globulin (HGG) was purified from a preparation of Cohn fraction II of normal human serum by DEAE chromatography using a sodium phosphate buffer of 0.01 M, pH 7.6. Myeloma proteins were isolated by zone electrophoresis (3) of sera obtained from patients with multiple myeloma. Light chain type and γG heavy chain subclasses were determined by the use of specific antisera. Gm typing was performed by hemagglutination inhibition methods (4) using the tube technique with anti-Rh/Gm (a+)-coated human type O red cells and anti-Gm (a+) reagents (Behringwerke AG).

Papain digestion. Enzymatic fragments were obtained by papain digestion of HGG and myeloma proteins and isolated by zone electrophoresis as previously described (5) except for the following modification. For γG3 the digestion time was shortened to 30 min, and for γG2 the digestion was prolonged to 60 min in the presence of 0.1 M mercaptoethanol instead of 0.01 M cysteine.

Immunodiffusion. The purity of the isolated

proteins was verified by immunoelectrophoresis using rabbit anti-whole human serum for the intact γG globulins and a rabbit anti-human γG for the Fab and Fc fragments (6). Quantitation of Fab and Fc fragments was done by radial immunodiffusion using rabbit antiserum which was made specific for the Fab and Fc fragments by suitable absorption (7).

Carbohydrate moiety. Determination of hexosamine, L-fucose, hexose, and sialic acid was performed as previously described (8).

Heat aggregation. Proteins were aggregated by heating them for 30 min at 63°C in barbital-buffered saline, pH 7.8. During this procedure, the concentration was 7 to 10 mg/ml of intact HGG and myeloma protein, 5 to 7 mg/ml of the Fab fragment and 3 to 7 mg/ml of Fc fragment. The concentration of the fragments was chosen so that the molar concentration of fragments was similar to that of the intact protein. Aggregation was evaluated by examining the sedimentation pattern in a Spinco model E ultracentrifuge at 56,1000 rpm. The concentration of unaggregated protein was determined by measuring the area of the different ultracentrifuge peaks according to the method of Trautmann (9).

Sulfhydryl blocking. Proteins were treated with a 2000-fold molar excess of iodoacetamide to protein in 0.5 M Tris buffer, pH 8.2, while heating. Treatment with parachloromercuribenzoate (PCMB) was done with a 50-fold molar excess of PCMB to protein in 0.02 M Tris-buffered saline, pH 8.6, while heating (10). Reduction and alkylation were carried out for 1 hr at room temperature with 0.2 M mercaptoethanol in 0.5 M Tris buffer, pH 8.2, followed by alkylation in the cold for 1 hr with a 50% molar excess of recrystallized iodoacetamide and dialysis against phosphate-buffered saline (PBS).

RESULTS

Aggregation of γG1 myeloma proteins and fragments. To determine the subunit of γG responsible for heat aggregation, several γG1 myeloma proteins were initially chosen for study. These proteins were typed for light chain type and Gm (a+, a−) allotype. Hexose, hexosamine, fucose and sialic acid determinations were also done on these proteins. After heating for 30 min at 63°C the extent of aggregation varied from one protein to the next. The data contained in Table I confirmed the results of Morse (2) in that heat aggregation did not correlate with light chain type or Gm allotype, but additionally showed that aggregation did not correlate with the amount and distribution of carbohydrate on the protein, since the carbohydrate moiety present on the Fc portion of all tested proteins did not differ significantly from one another in hexose, hexosamine, sialic acid or fucose content.

TABLE I

Aggregation of γG1 myeloma proteins upon heating for 30 min at 63°C

Myeloma Protein	Gm Allotype	L-chain Type	Carbohydrate		Analytic Ultracentrifuge
			Distribution	Amount	% Aggregation
Fis	a−	κ	Fc	3%	32
Ing	a−	κ	Fc	3%	>90
Mor	a−	λ	Fc	3%	44
Mur	a+	κ	Fc	3%	38
Pap	a−	κ	Fc	3%	<5
Pea	a−	λ	Fc	3%	—[a]
Qua	a−	λ	Fc	3%	>90
Way	a+	λ	Fc	3%	>90
Wil	a−	κ	Fab + Fc	6%	>90
Van	a+	κ	Fc	3%	—[a]

[a] Cryoglobulins which did not visibly aggregate upon heating but could not be tested in the ultracentrifuge because of their cryoglobulin nature.

The finding that myeloma proteins with probably identical constant regions differed in their susceptibility to heat aggregation (e.g., proteins Pap and Ing) suggested that the variable region of the molecule might be the important structure in determining aggregation. Therefore, Fab and Fc fragments were isolated and tested. Figure 1 shows the ultracentrifuge pattern of the intact protein, and Fab and Fc fragments of an aggregating (Qua) and non-aggregating (Pap) protein. Neither the intact protein nor the papain fragments of protein Pap aggregated appreciably, whereas the intact protein and Fab fragment of protein Qua were heat aggregated to greater than 90% as evidenced by the almost absent monomer γG and Fab peaks. In contrast, the heated Fc fragment of Qua did not aggregate at all. Table II summarizes the results obtained with eight γG1 proteins and their fragments. None of the Fc fragments aggregated appreciably, whereas aggregation of the Fab fragments correlated well with that of the intact γG1 protein.

Aggregation of γG2, γG3 and γG4 myeloma

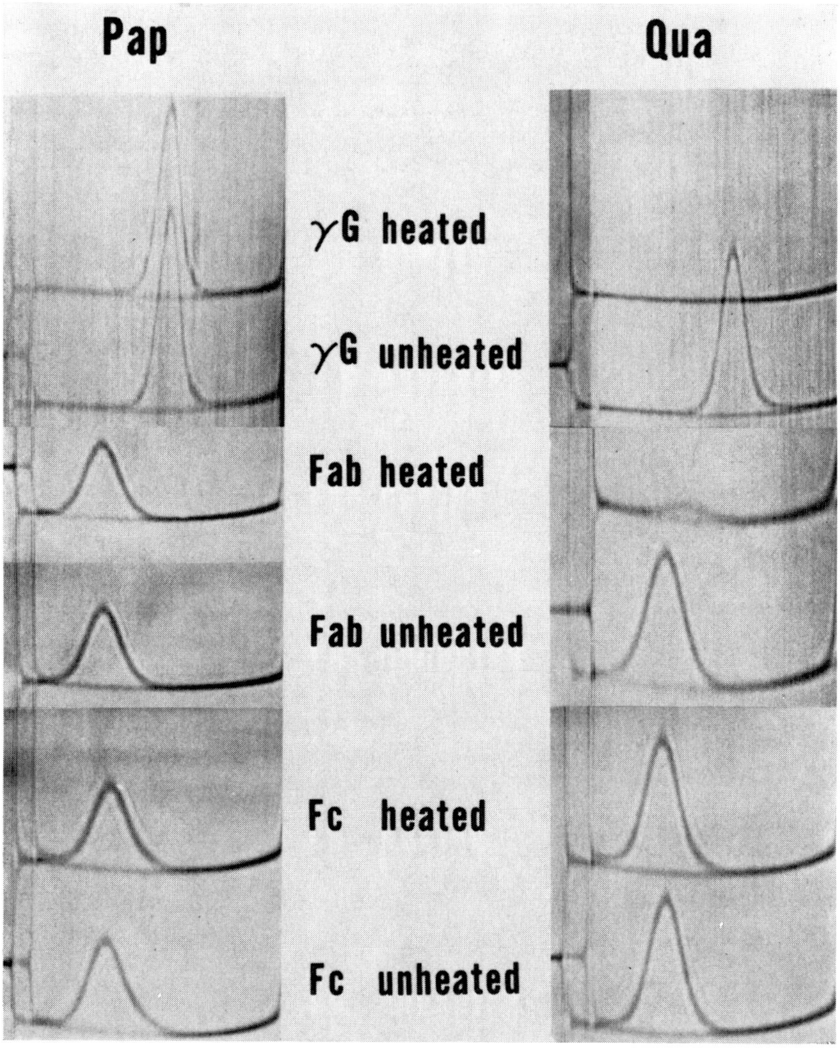

Figure 1. Ultracentrifuge pattern of an aggregating (Qua) and a non-aggregating (Pap) γG1 myeloma protein and their Fab and Fc fragments after 64 min at 56,100 rpm. The protein concentrations of heated and unheated samples were the same. Aggregation of Qua intact protein and Fab are indicated by the almost complete loss of the monomer γG and Fab peaks in the heated samples.

proteins and their fragments. To determine whether the data obtained with γG1 proteins accurately represented the situation as it exists for all γG immunoglobulins, the heat aggregability of the other γG subclasses was also studied. As shown in Table III, it was found that in contrast to the findings with γG1, the Fc fragments of γG3 and γG4 proteins were quite heat susceptible and that the Fc fragment of γG2 proteins were slightly more susceptible to aggregation than the Fc fragment of γG1 proteins.

Aggregation of normal γG and fragments. To determine if the findings with myeloma proteins were significant with respect to the aggregation of normal γG, heat aggregation experiments were performed on the Fab, Fc, and intact protein of normal HGG. The results shown in Table III demonstrate that upon heating for 30 min at 63°C, 30% of the HGG aggregated, 28% of the Fab fragment aggregated, and 7% of the Fc fragment aggregated. This preponderance of Fab aggregation is in accordance with the data ob-

TABLE II

Aggregation of γG1 myeloma proteins and their Fab and Fc fragments

Myeloma Protein	% Aggregation		
	Intact protein	Fab fragment	Fc fragment
Ing	>90	>90	<5
Mor	44	40	9
Mur	38	41	<5
Pap	<5	<5	<5
Pea	—[a]	26	8
Qua	>90	>90	<5
Van	—[a]	25	9
Way	>90	>90	12

[a] Cryoglobulins which did not visibly aggregate upon heating.

TABLE III

Aggregation of intact protein and papain fragments from normal γG and myeloma proteins of different subclasses

Myeloma Protein	Subclass	% Aggregation		
		Intact protein	Fab fragment	Fc fragment
Dah	2	32	53	26
Taf	2	60	80	32
Fel	3	>90	>90	>90
Jon	3	>90	42	55
Kup	3	—[a]	<5	64
Man	3	—[a]	17	90
Heb	4	18	<5	46
Ger	4	28	7	71
Normal γG	—	30[b]	28[b]	7[b]

[a] Cryoglobulins which visibly did not aggregate upon heating.

[b] Mean of three determinations.

TABLE IV

Effect of sulfhydryl-blocking reagents and urea on heat aggregation

Treatment		% Aggregation		
Before heating[a]	After heating	Normal γG	γG1 (Qua)[b]	γG3 (Jon)[c]
—[d]	—	30	67	73
Iodoacetamide	—	51	>95	>95
PCMB	—	47		
Partial reduction and alkylation	—	58		
Iodoacetamide	Urea	<5	<5	11
—	Urea	8	31	24

[a] A 2000-fold molar excess of iodoacetamide over protein or a 50-fold molar excess of PCMB was added prior to heating and was present during the heating as well. Partial reduction and alkylation was performed before heating and the reagents were dialyzed off before heating.

[b] Heat aggregated for 10 min at 63°C.

[c] Heat aggregated for 20 min at 63°C.

[d] No treatment.

tained with myeloma proteins since it would be expected that results with normal γG would be similar to the data obtained with γG1 and γG2 proteins as these two subclasses make up about 90% of normal γG.

An attempt was made to characterize the type of interaction responsible for the aggregation of γG proteins. Specifically we wanted to evaluate the possibility that intermolecular disulfide bond formation was involved (Table IV). To evaluate the role of disulfide bonds in the aggregation process two approaches were used: 1) the effect of inhibition of disulfide interchange on the heat aggregability of proteins was evaluated by adding PCMB or iodoacetamide to the reaction mixture before heating or partially reducing and alkylating proteins before heating; 2) the ability of reagents such as urea to dissociate the aggregates was evaluated. In the course of performing the experiments with urea it became obvious that urea itself was capable of causing aggregation by means of disulfide interchange reactions. To eliminate this complication, when aggregated proteins were to be treated with urea, this was done in the presence of iodoacetamide. These experiments were done on normal γG, an aggregating γG1 and γG3 myeloma protein. The treatment with the SH-blocking reagents did not prevent or decrease the tendency of these preparations to aggregate. Rather, all three preparations showed an increase in aggregation after this treatment. The reason for this increase is unknown at the present time. When the preparations were subsequently treated with urea, 90% or more of the aggregates dissociated, thereby confirming that heat aggregation performed under these conditions was almost entirely due to non-covalent interactions. The effect

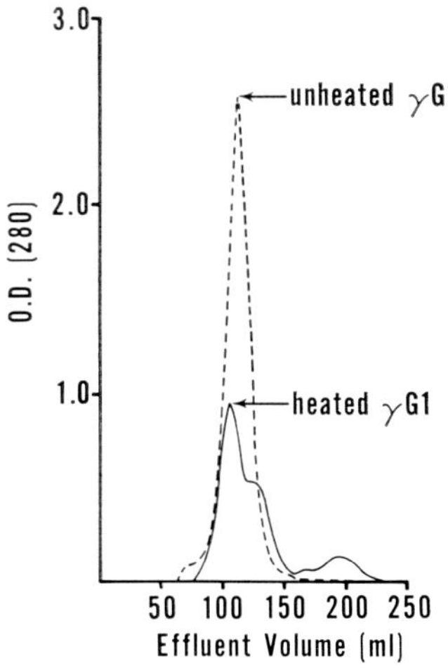

Figure 2. Sephadex G-100 filtration of papain digests from heated and unheated γG1 myeloma protein (Qua). The unheated sample gave a single symmetrical peak which contained Fab and Fc fragments. The heated digest gave a peak corresponding to the unheated digest which contained Fc and a prominent shoulder which contained partially degraded Fab. A second broad peak contained non-dialyzable peptides.

of urea on the heat-aggregated proteins whose SH groups were not blocked was less complete. Urea treatment dissociated 54% to 73% of the aggregates.

It would appear from these results that heat aggregation can occur in the almost complete absence of disulfide bonded aggregates, but that under the conditions usually used for heat aggregation (i.e., in the absence of SH-blocking reagents) one quarter to one half of the aggregates are disulfide linked.

Effect of heat aggregation on susceptibility to proteolysis. In order to obtain some information regarding the conformational changes that take place in γG upon heat aggregation, the relative susceptibility of a heated γG1 protein (Qua) to proteolysis by papain was compared with an unheated sample of the same protein. Heated and unheated proteins were digested for 1 hr with 1% papain. It was noted that the grossly turbid heat-aggregated solution became almost clear after papain treatment, only 4% of the total protein being present in insoluble form. The digested proteins were dialyzed against PBS and were then placed on a Sephadex G-100 column equilibrated in PBS. Protein determinations done after the dialysis step indicated that 30% of the heat-aggregated, papain-digested protein was lost as dialyzable peptides, whereas no loss occurred upon dialysis of the unheated, papain-digested protein. Figure 2 illustrates the gel filtration pattern produced by the papain digests of the heated and unheated proteins. Whereas the unheated digest produced a single symmetrical peak which contained both Fab and Fc fragments, the heated digest gave a peak corresponding in position to the peak of the unheated digest and a prominent shoulder on the descending limb as well as a broad peak of non-dialyzable peptides. Immunodiffusion analysis demonstrated that the major peak consisted predominantly of Fc fragment with little if any Fab fragment. The shoulder present on the descending limb contained Fab fragments which, when examined by immunodiffusion and ultracentrifugation, were antigenically deficient to the Fab fragment of the unheated digest and were considerably smaller as judged by the elution volume and a sedimentation coefficient of 1.8S compared to 3.6S for the Fab of the unheated digest. Radial diffusion analysis indicated that the heated digest contained 81% of the Fc fragment present in the unheated digest, whereas it contained less than 20% of intact Fab. Exact quantitation of the intact Fab was made difficult due to the presence of the antigenically deficient Fab which had a higher diffusion coefficient than the intact Fab. These data indicate that heating resulted in a conformational change in the Fab so that it became extremely susceptible to proteolysis by papain, whereas the Fc fragment showed little increase in susceptibility to proteolysis.

DISCUSSION

The salient findings of the present study were: 1) In normal γG and in γG1 and γG2 myeloma proteins the major structure responsible for heat aggregation is located in the Fab fragment while both Fab and Fc fragments can contribute to the heat aggregation of proteins in the γG3 and γG4 subclasses. 2) Experiments with sulfhydryl-blocking reagents and urea indicate that both non-covalent interactions and intermolecular disulfide bonds contribute to the formation of the aggregates. 3) In proteins in which the Fab fragment aggregates (γG1, γG2), the structural changes that take place are such that the Fab fragment is rendered unusually susceptible to extensive proteolysis by papain. The structure within γG responsible for aggregation has not been previously investigated; however, perhaps because of the relation between the Fc and the biologic properties exhibited by aggregated γG, it had been postulated (10) that the Fc fragment was responsible for the phenomenon of aggregation. However, the finding by Morse that aggregation did not correlate with L chain type, γG subclass or Gm allotypes suggested that proteins with probably identical constant regions and, therefore, identical Fc pieces, differed in their susceptibility to heat aggregation (2). In light of current information on the sequence of heavy and light chains of γG, these data strongly suggested that the constant portion of the molecule was not of primary importance in the heat aggregability of a γG protein. In the present study, when γG1 myeloma proteins were heated the data of Morse were confirmed, and it was also found that the carbohydrate composition of myeloma protein did not correlate with the susceptibility of the protein to heat aggregation. When isolated Fab and Fc fragments of normal γG and of myeloma proteins of the different γG subclasses were heated it was found that the Fc fragments of normal γG and γG1 myeloma proteins did not aggregate to a significant degree and that of γG2 aggregated only slightly, whereas the extent of aggregation of the Fab fragment correlated well with that of the intact proteins. These data demonstrated that the Fab portion of the molecule is the structure primarily involved in aggregation of normal γG globulin. This correlation between the data obtained with normal γG and with γG1 and γG2 proteins is to be expected since these two subclasses make up about 90% of normal γG. The data obtained with γG3 and γG4 proteins indicated that the Fc fragment is involved in the heat aggregation of these proteins. The two γG4 proteins studied showed very little heat aggregation of their Fab fragments. Also, none of the four cryoglobulins included in the study visibly aggregated. Whether decreased susceptibility to heat is a property of all γG4 proteins and all γG cryoglobulins must await further studies on more of these relatively rare proteins.

The aggregation process was a result of intermolecular non-covalent interactions as well as intermolecular disulfide bonds. In the three preparations studied between one-half and three-quarters of the aggregates were composed solely of non-covalently linked molecules as evidenced by their dissociation in 8 M urea. That intermolecular disulfide bond formation is not essential to the aggregation process was strongly suggested by the experiments shown in Table IV. Partial reduction and alkylation or heating in the presence of sulfhydryl-blocking reagents did not decrease (and actually increased) the tendency for γG to aggregate, whereas these procedures were almost completely effective in blocking intermolecular disulfide interchange from occurring. Why the alkylated preparations aggregated to a greater extent than the untreated proteins is unknown. Alkylation of cysteine and/or other residues may alter the protein sufficiently to change its thermal lability. This possibility is supported by studies on myoglobin in which the effect of alkylation of histidine residues on the heat denaturation of this protein was studied. It was found that the alkylated protein underwent the changes in optical rotatory dispersion typical of denaturation at slightly lower temperatures than the unaltered protein (11).

When heat aggregates of γG1 were treated with papain under the same conditions used for the digestion of monomeric molecules, it was found that only the Fc fragment was obtained in good yield, whereas the Fab fragment was to a great extent digested into either non-antigenic or antigenically deficient, low molecular weight material. This experiment indicated that upon heating there was a conformational change in the structure of the Fab which rendered the Fab abnormally susceptible to proteolysis. This instability of the heated Fab is of particular interest since it would appear to be in direct contrast to the conformational change that the Fab undergoes upon binding of hapten where it has been shown that the tertiary structure becomes more stable than the native Fab and less susceptible to both proteolysis (12) and the denaturing effects of guanidine HCl (13).

Both heat-aggregated γG and antibody γG aggregated by specific antigen demonstrate similar biologic activities involving the Fc fragment that are difficult to demonstrate with unaggregated γG (14–17). This has led to speculation as to the mechanism by which aggregation causes an enhanced activity of the Fc fragment. On the one hand, it has been postulated that aggregation of γG globulin results in a critical conformational change in the molecule which reveals or alters the Fc binding site so that it can react more efficiently (18). On the other hand, the increased efficiency of binding may merely reflect the greater proximity and increased number of binding sites per macromolecule which results from aggregation of γG (19). Since heat aggregation and antigen-antibody aggregation lead to extremely different conformational changes in the Fab portion, it would appear unlikely that both processes would secondarily lead to the same conformational change within the Fc portion of the molecule. For this reason we favor the postulate that an increase in number and proximity of binding sites is the main factor involved in the greatly enhanced expression of biologic activity which occurs upon aggregation of γG.

REFERENCES

1. Christian, C. L., J. Exp. Med., *108:* 139, 1958.
2. Morse, J. H., J. Immun., *95:* 722, 1965.
3. Kunkel, H. G., Meth. Biochem. Anal., *1:* 141, 1954.
4. Natvig, J. B. and Kunkel, H. G., Series Hematol., *1:* 66, 1968.
5. Grey, H. M. and Kunkel, H. G., Biochemistry, *6:* 2326, 1967.
6. Scheidegger, J. J., Int. Arch. Allerg., *7:* 103, 1955.
7. Mancini, G., Vaerman, J.-P., Carbonara, A. O. and Heremans, J. F., in *Protides of the Biological Fluids*, Proceedings of the 11th Colloqium, Bruges, 1963, p. 370, Elsevier, Amsterdam, 1964.
8. Abel, C. A., Spiegelberg, H. L. and Grey, H. M., Biochemistry, *7:* 1271, 1968.
9. Trautmann, R. J., J. Phys. Chem., *60:* 1211, 1956.
10. Henney, C. S. and Stanworth, D. R., Immunology, *9:* 139, 1965.
11. Clark, J. F. and Gurd, F. R. N., J. Biol. Chem., *242:* 3257, 1967.
12. Grossberg, A. L., Markus, G. and Pressman, D., Proc. Nat. Acad. Sci., *54:* 942, 1965.
13. Cathou, R. E. and Haber, E., Biochemistry, *6:* 513, 1967.
14. Laurell, A. B. and Nilson, U., Acta Path. Microbiol., *59:* 79, 1963.
15. Cooper, R., J. Lab. Clin. Med., *63:* 404, 1964.
16. Edelman, G. M., Kunkel, H. G. and Franklin, E. C., J. Exp. Med., *108:* 105, 1958.
17. Christian, C. L., J. Immun., *84:* 112, 1960.
18. Glynn, L. E., Holborow, E. J. and Johnson, G. D., Proc. Roy. Soc. Med., *50:* 469, 1957.
19. Edelman, G. M., Kunkel, H. G. and Franklin, E. C., J. Exp. Med., *108:* 105, 1958.

THE JOURNAL OF IMMUNOLOGY
Vol. 105, No. 4, October 1970

COMMUNICATIONS

Streptococcal M Protein Vaccines, Rheumatic Fever and Human Histocompatibility Antigens[1]

EUGENE N. FOX AND RAYMOND D. A. PETERSON

From the Variety Club Research Center and the Sprague Regional Tissue Typing Center of La Rabida Children's Hospital and Research Institute, University of Chicago, Chicago, Illinois 60649

Hirata and Terasaki (1) recently reported that allogeneic antisera against human lymphocytes were specifically inhibited by group A streptococcal M protein, type 1. They suggested from this observation that shared antigenic determinants between M proteins (particularly type 1) and human histocompatibility antigens could lead to autoimmune phenomena resulting in the post-streptococcal sequelae of rheumatic fever or acute glomerulonephritis. However, militating against this hypothesis were their observations that M proteins of serotypes 3, 4, 5, 6, 12 and 14 were inactive in absorbing allogeneic antibodies. Hyperimmune sera from rabbits immunized with any of the above M proteins, including type 1, were not cytotoxic for human lymphocytes. Furthermore, more than 2 mg of type 1 M protein/ml of allogeneic antiserum was required for absorption in order to detect a diminution in the cytotoxic activity.

Our work on the development of a streptococcal vaccine for human use, employing alum-precipitated M proteins (APM) to induce primary type-specific immunity (2), obviously impinges on the observations of Hirata and Terasaki. During the past several years we have explored the possibility that M proteins might share antigenic determinants with human tissue antigens. Our studies have shown that type 12 M protein would not absorb the autoantibodies to human heart that often appear in the sera of children with rheumatic fever (3). We have not, however, published our studies regarding M protein and human transplantation antigens, but in view of the report by Hirata and Terasaki it seems appropriate to do so now.

We have made two approaches to the question of whether M protein shares antigenic determinants with human histocompatibility antigens. The first was to ascertain whether high-titer rabbit antisera to a spectrum of M proteins would be cytotoxic to human lymphocytes. Antisera to M types 1, 2, 12 and 49 were tested against human lymphocytes possessing HL-A antigens 1, 2, 4, 5, 7, 8, 9, 11 plus 4a and 4b. Cytotoxicity was assayed in a conventional microcytotoxicity system (4). None of the rabbit anti-M sera were cytotoxic. Appropriate positive controls ruled out anticomplementarity of the rabbit sera. The second approach was to look for cytotoxic antibodies in the sera of 97 children with rheumatic fever and 58 children immunized with type 12 vaccine. We used a panel of lymphocytes for eight persons. These cells possessed antigenic specificities designated HL-A 1, 2, 3, 5, 7, 8, 11, plus 4a and 4b. Obviously many other antigens were also represented but the aforementioned were clearly identified.

Table I summarizes the results of the cytotoxic assay for HL-A antibodies in the sera of 97 acute and convalescent rheumatic fever (RF) patients. These patients' sera were obtained between 1 and 6 weeks after admission to the La Rabida Children's Hospital. All patients were in the acute phase of their disease at the time of admission; the extent of cardiac involvement ranged from no demonstrable damage to massive pancarditis. Many of these sera exhibited antiheart antibodies as detected by indirect immunofluorescence with frozen sections of human and mouse myocardium (3). Approximately one-third of the RF sera contained bactericidal (opsonic) antibodies specific for type 1 streptococcus when assayed by Lancefield's method (5). However, none of these type 1 sera, nor any RF sera regardless of the anti-M specificity, exhibited cytotoxicity for human lymphocytes in the presence of complement. It should be noted that type 1 streptococcus is rarely associated with acute glomerulonephritis but is one

[1] This work was supported in part by a contract (PH-43-68-83) of the Vaccine Development Branch, National Institutes of Allergy and Infectious Diseases, National Institute of Health.

TABLE I
Analysis of 97 rheumatic fever sera

Bactericidal Assay	Cytotoxic Assay[a]
Streptococcus type 1 No. assayed: 64 No. positive: 29	
	No. assayed: 64 No. positive: 0
Streptococcus type 12[b] No. assayed: 37 No. positive: 19	
33 sera not assayed for bactericidal activity	No. assayed: 33 No. positive: 0

[a] Each serum assayed with lymphocytes from eight donors.

[b] These sera were from the same lot of 64 assayed for anti-1 activity. Approximately 10 were bactericidal for both serotypes.

of the more common types responsible for RF. Type 12 has been notorious for many years as a nephritogenic and rheumatogenic streptococcus (6). Sera from 58 infants who received three subcutaneous injections of APM-12 vaccine (2) were not cytotoxic for the lymphocytes of our panel.

Acknowledgment. We greatly appreciate the skilled technical assistance of Mrs. Peggy Dunbar and Mr. Frank Seepersad.

SUMMARY

Within the limits of our techniques, we could not demonstrate any serologic cross-reactions between streptococcal M proteins and human histocompatibility antigens, nor could we detect antibodies to human transplantation antigens in persons during the acute or convalescent phases of rheumatic fever, or subsequent to the administration of streptococcal M protein vaccine.

REFERENCES

1. Hirata, A. A. and Terasaki, P. I., Science, *168:* 1095, 1970.
2. Fox, E. N., Pachman, L. M., Wittner, M. K. and Dorfman, A., J. Infect, Dis., *120:* 598, 1969.
3. Fox, E. N. and Grossman, B. J., J. Immun., *102:* 970, 1969.
4. Amos, D. B., Bashir, H., Boyle, W., MacQueen, M. and Tiilikainen, A., Transplantation, *7:* 220, 1969.
5. Lancefield, R.C., J. Exp. Med., *106:* 525, 1957.
6. Stollerman, G. H., J. Infect. Dis., *120:* 258, 1969

THE JOURNAL OF IMMUNOLOGY
Vol. 105, No. 4, October 1970

Printed in U.S.A.

Subgroup-Specific Antigenic Marker on Immunoglobulin λ Chains: Identification of Three Subtypes of the Variable Region[1]

FRANK W. TISCHENDORF, MARGRIT M. TISCHENDORF AND ELLIOTT F. OSSERMAN[2]

From the Department of Medicine, Tübingen University, Germany, and the Department of Pathology, Columbia University College of Physicians and Surgeons, New York, N. Y.

Three distinct classes of human κ light polypeptide chains have been detected immunochemically (1). The three antigenic types correspond to the three basic variable sequences designated as κ_{I}, κ_{II} and κ_{III} (2). In previous reports (3, 4) we described two specificity region subgroups of human λ chains tentatively called (St^+) and (St^-), differing in antigenic determinants localized on the variable (V) or NH_2-terminal region of the λ molecule.

In the course of studies on the delineation of the (St^-) subgroup with various antisera, several rabbit antisera were encountered which showed differences among (St^-) type Bence Jones proteins and λ chains of myeloma proteins in immunodiffusion analysis. Similar differences were found for the (St^-) type proteins of normal serum. The antigens involved correlate with certain structures of the V region of the λ polypeptide chain.

Myeloma proteins and Bence Jones proteins were isolated and typed with respect to subgroup (4). The antisera used for distinguishing different St antigens were prepared by immunizing rabbits with λ Bence Jones protein St. Twelve rabbit antisera were made against six randomly chosen Bence Jones proteins of the (St^-) type. Antiserum produced against two Bence Jones proteins, proteins 111 (5) and Ku (4), contained antibodies with the specificity described below. All immunizations were carried out with complete Freund's adjuvant.

Light chains were prepared essentially in the usual fashion (6) from pooled and individual normal γG-globulin and myeloma proteins of subclasses γG_1, γG_2 and γG_3. After reduction and alkylation, light and heavy chains were separated by gel filtration with 0.1 M formic acid as the dissociating agent. The sequence of the NH_2-terminal four amino acids was determined by subjecting native λ chains to sequential amino-terminal (Edman) degradation (7). The phenylthiohydantoin (PTH) derivatives were identified by thin-layer silica gel chromatography.

Antiserum to Bence Jones protein 111 proved to be the strongest. It reacted specifically with 17 of 80 myeloma λ chains and Bence Jones proteins and intact γG-globulin in immunodiffusion analysis. Absorption with a pool of

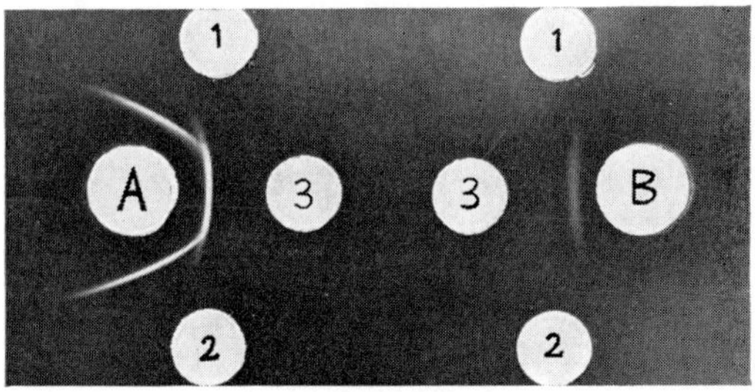

Figure 1. The reaction of three λ chains of different subgroups with the unabsorbed (*A*) and the (111^+) specific antiserum (*B*). Protein Sg of subgroup III (*well 3*) gives spur over the adjacent precipitin line of proteins HBJ 7 of subgroup I (*well 1*) and S1 of subgroup II (*well 2*) with the antiserum in the central well *A*. The antiserum in the central well *B* was completely absorbed with normal serum and Bence Jones protein Br (subgroup I).

The nomenclature used is that recommended for human γ G-globulins by Kunkel, H. G., Fahey, J. L., Franklin, E. C., Osserman; E. F. and Terry, W. D., Bull. W.H.O., *35:* 953, 1966.

Abbreviations for amino acid residues: Lys, lysine; Arg, arginine; Asp, aspartic acid; Ser, serine; Glu, glutamic acid; Ala, alamine; Val, valine; Leu, leucine; Tyr, tyrosine; PCA, pyrrolidone carboxylic acid. The first amino acid of protein 111 is designated Tyr-2, and so forth. A deletion at the first position is indicated by [].

[1] Presented in part at the 54th annual meeting of the American Society of Biological Chemists, Atlantic City, New Jersey, April, 1970.

[2] American Cancer Society Research Professor of Pathology (Immunology and Oncology).

deficient proteins having C-terminal regions identical to that of the immunizing protein, as judged by sequence and fingerprint studies, and normal serum left antibodies only to the V region of the same 17 proteins (Fig. 1). These were termed (111^+) and the negative proteins were designated (111^-). The distinctive antigenic sites were also detected on light chain preparations of pooled and individual normal γG-globulin in an inhibition system using an intrabasin absorption technique. In this technique the peripheral wells of an Ouchterlony rosette were first filled with the materials to be tested (3 mg protein in 0.5 ml buffer solution) and subsequently with the antiserum. Normal light chains inhibited the precipitation of (111^+) λ chains (center well) by the (111^+) specific antiserum.

Edman degradation of (111^+) light chains gave the results presented in Table I. According to the data the presence of tyrosine in position 2 and a deletion in position 1 is a characteristic of (111^+) polypeptide chains. In two proteins a serine-tyrosine-interchange was found at position 2. In contrast to the data obtained for (111^+) light chains, 10 proteins of the (St^+) and 22 proteins of the $St^-/111^-$ type had blocked N-termini indicating the presence of NH_2-terminal pyrrolidone carboxylic acid. Antigenic typing of protein Sh (8) which has the NH_2-terminal residue Ser-2 gave ambiguous results in the Ouchterlony double diffusion test. Its (111^+) character was finally established by precipitin-inhibition analyses.

TABLE I

N-terminal sequences of (111^+) λ chains and the 190 lys/arg polymorphism of the C region[a]

Specimen	Position				
	1	2	3	4	190
111	[ ]	Tyr	Glu	Leu	Arg
Be	[ ]	Tyr	Val	Leu	Arg
Bt	[ ]	Tyr	Glu	Leu	Arg
Fr	[ ]	Tyr	Glu	Leu	Arg
Ke	[ ]	Tyr	Val	Leu	Arg
Kern (15)	[ ]	Tyr	Ala	Leu	Arg
Pf	[ ]	Ser	Glu	Leu	Arg
Sh (8)	[ ]	Ser	Glu	Leu	Arg
Yo	Ser	Tyr	Glu	Leu	Arg
119	[ ]	Tyr	Glu	Leu	Arg
X (14)	[ ]	Tyr	Asp	Leu	Arg
Ku	[ ]	Tyr	Val	Leu	Lys
Sg	[ ]	Tyr	Val	Leu	Lys

[a] See references 16 to 19.

TABLE II

Prototype amino acid residues of completely sequenced Bence Jones proteins representative for the three antigenic subgroups[a]

Sub-group	Antigenic Type	Specimen	Prototype Amino Acid Residues (New Numbering System)																		
			1	2	13	17	21	25	28a	28b	28c	38	41	46	50	52	68	69	88	95	96	109
I	$St^+/111^-$	Ha (8)	PCA		Thr	Arg						Leu		Leu		Lys	Thr	Ser	Ala		Ala	
II	$St^-/111^-$	Bo (8)	PCA					Thr	Val	Gly		His			Val				Ser			
III	$St^-/111^+$	X (14)	[ ]	Tyr		Thr	Thr	Asp	[ ]	[ ]	[ ]	Arg	Gln	Val					Gln			
		Kern (15)	[ ]	Tyr		Thr	Thr	Asp	[ ]	[ ]	[ ]	Arg	Gln	Val					Gln			
		Sh (8)	[ ]	**Ser**		Thr	Thr	Asp	[ ]	[ ]	[ ]	**Lys**	Gln	Val					**Asn**			

[a] The subgroups are defined by correlated amino acid differences and by amino acid gaps. Bold-face type indicates individually specific differences.

The studies clearly indicate that three specificity-region subgroups of human λ immunoglobulin chains can be distinguished antigenically. Of 80 λ chains tested for the (St^+) and (111^+) specific determinants, 24% were (St^+) (group I), 21% were (111^+) (group III) and 55% contained neither of these two determinants (group II). The distinctive determinants are "hidden" antigenic sites, i.e., they are inaccessible in the intact γ globulin but present on free light chains. Data on a small number of λ Bence Jones proteins suggest three to four fundamental sequences (9–12).

When sequences are known, the (St^+) type proteins can be distinguished from those of the (St^-) type by characteristic amino acid residues at positions 13, 17, 38, 46, 52, 68, 69, 88 and 96. (St^+) type chains follow the prototype sequence of the Ha protein (8, 13).

The present studies provide evidence that (111^+) type proteins follow the sequence of protein X (14). Like the overwhelming majority of the (111^+) λ polypeptide chains tested, Bence Jones protein X and another completely sequenced specimen, protein Kern (15), begin with the NH_2-terminal residue Tyr-2 and are (111^+) as determined in our laboratory. In contrast to these results the completely sequenced protein Bo (8) was (St^-) and (111^-), probably representing the antigenic subgroup II. (111^+) light chains show subgroup specific amino acid residues at positions 1, 2, 17, 21, 25, 28, 38, 41, 46 and 88 (Table II).

With the delineation of the (111^+) marker a second specificity region antigen has become available in the λ class of γ globulin. Since light chains are involved in combining activity of antibody such specificity region antigens may prove to be important in an understanding of the antibody problem. Preliminary studies on light chain preparations of γG-globulin of 12 normal individuals appear to exclude the allelic nature of subgroup I and III.

The results indicate that at least three germ line genes encode the specificity or V region of λ chains. Since the (111^+) genetic locus already controls 21% of λ polypeptide chains, which represent the fairly homogeneous group III, it appears that not more than a small number of genes encode the V region.

Acknowledgment. We wish to acknowledge the help given us by Dr. B. Wittmann-Liebold in learning the Edman degradation method. We thank Mrs. Dagmar Pfarr for technical assistance, and Dr. W. Pruzanski and Dr. D. Bergsagel for the kind supply of Bence Jones proteins. This work was supported in part by a grant from the Deutsche Forschungsgemeinschaft.

REFERENCES

1. Solomon, A., J. Exp. Med., *130:* 1295, 1969.
2. Milstein, C., Nature, *216:* 330, 1967.
3. Tischendorf, F. W., Proceedings of the XIIth Congress of the International Society of Hematologists, New York, 1968.
4. Tischendorf, F. W. and Osserman, E. F., J. Immun., *102:* 172, 1969.
5. Van Eyk, H. G. and Monfoort, C. H., Biochim. Biophys. Acta, *86:* 410, 1964.
6. Fleischman, J. B., Pain, R. H. and Porter, R. R., Arch. Biochem. Biophys., *Suppl. 1:* 174, 1962.
7. Erikson, S. and Sjöquist, J., Biochim. Biophys. Acta, *45:* 290, 1960.
8. Putnam, F. W., Shinoda, T., Titani, K. and Wikler, M., Science, *157:* 1050, 1967.
9. Cohn, M., 8n *Nucleic Acids in Immunology* Edited by O. J. Plescia and W. Braun, p. 671, Springer-Verlag, Berlin, 1968.
10. Hood, L. and Ein, D., Nature, *220:* 764, 1968.
11. Langer, B., Steinmetz-Kayne, M. and Hilschmann, N., Hoppe Seyler Z. Physiol. Chem., *349:* 945, 1968.
12. Tischendorf, F. W., in *Structure, Genetics and Formation of Antibodies*, *49:* 100, Behringwerk-Mitteilungen, 1969.
13. Tischendorf, F. W. and Tischendorf, M. M., Europ. J. Biochem., *13:* 398, 1970.
14. Milstein, C., Clegg, J. B. and Jarvis, J. M., Biochem. J., *110:* 631, 1968.
15. Ponstingl, H., Hess, M., and Hilschmann, N., Hoppe Seyler Z. Physiol. Chem., *349:* 867, 1968.
16. Appella, E. and Ein, D., Proc. Nat. Acad. Sci., *57:* 1449, 1967.
17. Tischendorf, F. W. and Osserman, E. F., Z. Naturforsch., *22b:* 1337, 1967.
18. Milstein, C., Biochem. J., *104:* 280, 1967.
19. Quattrocchi, R., Cioli, D. and Baglioni, C., Nature, *216:* 56, 1967.

THE JOURNAL OF IMMUNOLOGY
Vol. 105, No. 4, October 1970
Printed in U.S.A.

Serologic Evidence That Infectious Canine Hepatitis Virus Commonly Infects Humans and Is Related to Human Adenovirus Type 8

KENDALL O. SMITH, WARREN D. GEHLE AND WILLIAM T. KNIKER

From the Departments of Microbiology and Pediatrics, The University of Texas Medical School at San Antonio, 7703 Floyd Curl Drive, San Antonio, Texas 78229

We have been interested in the possibility that viruses commonly occurring in household pets and other domestic animals infect man. Human infection with infectious canine hepatitis virus (ICHV) has been suspected in the past, but evidence for this has been meager. Studies on the relationship of ICHV to human disease have been largely limited to veterinary workers (1) or to determining whether ICHV causes human hepatitis (2). ICHV, a canine adenovirus, was of particular interest to us in regard to human infection because Sarma *et al.* showed it to be oncogenic for hamsters (3). We reported recently that ICHV can infect human cells *in vitro* and initiate the synthesis of small amounts of new virus, and that infected human cells produce tumor-specific antigens (4). We also found that ICHV can frequently be isolated from the kidneys of dogs (5). This is not surprising because most dogs periodically receive doses of live attenuated ICHV vaccine for the prevention of infectious hepatitis and probably harbor virus for extended periods of time.

This study was undertaken to determine by immunologic methods whether ICHV infects man. ICHV shares a common complement-fixation (CF) antigen with human adenoviruses, making the CF test useless for distinguishing between canine and human adenovirus antibody (6). Carmichael and Barnes (7), however, showed that ICHV and human adenovirus type 4 did not cross-react in neutralization tests. Therefore, we employed this technique to determine whether humans have antibody to ICHV and whether ICHV will cross-react with other known human adenoviruses in the neutralization test. The following report presents evidence that ICHV-specific antibody is present in a high proportion of the healthy human population and that there is a one-way cross-reaction between ICHV and human adenovirus type 8 (Ad-8) neutralizing antibody. Cross-neutralization between ICHV and other human adenoviruses was not found.

MATERIALS AND METHODS

We used ICHV, strain Utrecht, originally obtained from the American Type Culture Collection and passaged about 10 times in Madin dog kidney (MDCK) cells. Ad-8 was from the Research Reference Reagents Branch, National Institute of Allergy and Infectious Diseases (NIAID), National Institutes of Health (NIH), and was passaged once in KB cells or human amnion (HA) cells before use.

Reference adenovirus antisera were obtained from the Research Reference Reagents Branch, NIAID, NIH and from the National Communicable Disease Center (NCDC) except for one ICHV antiserum which we prepared in guinea pigs at the Division of Biologics Standards (DBS), NIH. Reference human antisera were used at dilutions sufficient to give 4 to 250 neutralizing doses of antibody against the homologous virus.

For cultivation of ICHV we used MDCK cells originally obtained from Microbiological Associates, Inc. Human amnion (strain FL) and KB cells from Microbiological Associates, Inc. were used for cultivation of Ad-8. Basal Eagle's medium plus 10% fetal calf serum, glutamine and neomycin (20 μg/ml final concentration) was used for cell cultivation. Five or ten per cent serum-containing medium was used to maintain cells for up to 48 hr after inoculation. Larger quantities of cells were produced in plastic flasks. Cells planted in Petri dishes for virus assays were incubated in a 5% CO_2 atmosphere.

Antibody was titrated as we described before (5). Equal volumes of serially diluted serum or globulin were mixed with ICHV suspensions containing $10^{4.0}$ infectious units/0.2 ml or with suspensions containing $10^{1.5}$ infectious units of Ad-8/0.2 ml. The mixtures were incubated for 1 hr at 26°C, then inoculated on cells in Petri plates (Falcon Plastics, Inc., Los Angeles, Calif.) as indicated below. Sera and globulin preparations were routinely heat-inactivated at 56°C for 20 min before use. Positive neutralization in this report is defined as suppression of more than 80% infectivity (fivefold decrease).

Virus titrations were done as described previously (4, 5, 8). Briefly, cell cultures in plastic Petri plates were aspirated free of growth medium, inoculated with 0.2-ml volumes of appropriately diluted virus and the virus was allowed to adsorb for 1 hr (plates were agitated frequently). After maintenance medium was added, each dish was incubated for 40 to 48 hr at 37°C, washed, then fixed and stained by the indirect immunofluorescence method to reveal virus-infected cells. For this purpose we used hyperimmune serum prepared in guinea pigs against highly purified ICHV (described in Table II as anti-ICHV-DBS), and fluorescein conjugated anti-guinea pig globulin (Colorado Serum Co.). Because ICHV and Ad-8 share group antigens, fluorescence labeling with anti-ICHV sera worked equally well for either virus. Infected cell foci were quantitated as described in previous reports (4, 5, 8).

Human adult sera were from normal individuals undergoing routine serologic tests and pregnant women receiving pre-natal care in Bexar County, Texas (ages ranged from 15 to 66). Children's sera, obtained through the courtesy of Dr. Fernando A. Guerra, came from individuals hospitalized in the Pediatric wards of the Bexar County Teaching Hospital. Their ages ranged from 6 months to 12 years; none had immunologic disorders, liver disease or significant infections.

Globulin was precipitated from sera by mixing equal volumes of chilled serum and saturated aqueous ammonium sulfate. The precipitates were sedimented by centrifugation, dissolved in phosphate-buffered saline and dialyzed against changes of phosphate-buffered saline before use.

RESULTS

Neutralization of ICHV by adult human sera; evidence that ICHV-neutralizing activity is due to an immune globulin. Initial screening of several adult human sera at dilutions of 1:2 and 1:6 for ICHV-neutralizing antibody yielded several sera which neutralized the virus. Two of the positive sera were selected for globulin precipitation in order to determine whether the neutralizing substance was in the globulin fraction, which would be consistent with its being antibody. The results obtained with one of these sera are shown in Table I. It is seen that the neutralizing activity was quantitatively recovered in the globulin fraction, which suggests that the neutralizing substance is antibody. Similar results were obtained with the other serum. Further testing of adult human sera showed that a high percentage contained neutralizing activity at dilutions of 1:2 or greater and, on titration, the neutralizing titers ranged as high as 1:162. Commercially available human γ globulin (Lederle Laboratories, 16.5%) was titrated and found to have a titer of 1:36.

TABLE I
Infectious canine hepatitis virus (ICHV) neutralization by whole human serum and its globulin fraction

Specimen	Neutralization of ICHV[a]				
	1:6	1:8	1:54	1:162	1:486
Whole serum	+	+	+	−	−
Globulin	+	+	+	−	−

[a] Dilutions neutralizing >80% ICHV = +.

Serologic relationship between ICHV and human Ad-8. Although Carmichael and Barnes (7) found that ICHV and human adenovirus type 4 did not cross-react in neutralization tests, we wanted to exclude the possibility that ICHV cross-reacts with other known human adenovirus types. Each of the available reference anti-human adenovirus sera was tested for neutralizing activity against ICHV (antisera used included those prepared against adenoviruses 1 to 31). None of these sera neutralized ICHV except the two prepared against human Ad-8. Anti-Ad-8 (NIH) was produced in rabbits for the NIH and anti-Ad-8 (NCDC) was produced for the National Communicable Disease Center in horses. It is significant that these two anti-Ad-8 sera were prepared in different places, at different times and with different passages of prototype Ad-8.

The extent of the cross-reactions between ICHV and human Ad-8 was further studied by quantitative reciprocal neutralization tests, the results of which are shown in Table II. It can be seen that anti-Ad-8 neutralized ICHV and Ad-8 at about the same antibody titers, but that anti-ICHV did not neutralize Ad-8, even at extremely high antibody concentrations (1:10

TABLE II

Relationships between infectious canine hepatitis virus (ICHV) and human adenovirus type 8 neutralizing antibody

Virus	1/Neutralization Titer			
	Anti-ICHV (NIH)	Anti-Ad-8 (NIH)	Anti-ICHV (DBS)	Anti-Ad-8 (CDC)
ICHV	1,620	20	43,740	20
Ad-8	<10	20	<10	60

dilutions of specific anti-ICHV sera (NIH and DBS) failed to neutralize Ad-8, although 1:1620 and 1:43,740 dilutions of these sera, respectively, neutralized ICHV). It can be concluded from these experiments that infections with Ad-8 would probably give rise to antibody which would neutralize ICHV, but that *infection with ICHV would probably not elicit neutralizing antibody to Ad-8*. It became apparent, therefore, that ICHV-positive human sera should be tested for antibody to human Ad-8.

Testing of ICHV antibody positive sera for antibody to Ad-8. The likelihood that a high percentage of adults would have detectable neutralizing antibody to Ad-8 seemed remote, in view of the literature indicating that Ad-8 neutralizing antibody occurs only rarely in the general population and is usually associated with individuals with acute kerato-conjunctivitis (9). Nevertheless, we selected 10 human sera which were strongly positive in neutralizing ICHV (having titers of 1:18 to 1:162) and reacted these with Ad-8 at dilutions of 1:2 and 1:6. No neutralizing antibody to Ad-8 was detected in any of the 10 sera. We conclude, on the basis of these results, that these 10 sera contained ICHV-specific antibody, but no specific Ad-8 antibody.

Later, each of the 53 ICHV-positive sera found during this study was screened at a 1:2 dilution for neutralizing antibody to Ad-8, with negative results in all except five cases. These five sera, which were doubly positive for ICHV and Ad-8, were excluded from subsequent study in order to avoid confusion by the one-way cross-reaction between these two viruses (these are not described further in this paper). On the basis of these experiments we can conclude that our assumptions above were correct, i.e., that human infection with ICHV does not elicit neutralizing antibody to Ad-8.

TABLE III

Incidence of infectious canine hepatitis virus (ICHV) antibody in sera from humans of different ages

Age Group	ICHV Positive[a] Sera/Total Sera Tested	Percentage of Sera ICHV Positive
yr		
0.5–5	2/9	22
6–12	1/7	14
13–19	15/20	75
20–26	11/13	85
27–33	7/10	70
34–40	7/9	78
41 and over	10/12	83

[a] Neutralized >80% ICHV at a serum dilution of 1:2 or greater.

Relationship between age and incidence for ICHV antibody. Table III presents a summary of the findings in various age groups. It is clear that the incidence of ICHV-neutralizing activity is low in childhood. By teen age (13 to 19 years), half of the tested individuals had developed ICHV antibody. It is noteworthy that about 80% of adults have ICHV antibody and that the highest titers of antibody were found in this group.

DISCUSSION

Adenovirus type 8 seems to be unique among human adenoviruses in its relationship to ICHV. The cross-reaction was in only one direction, i.e., antibody to Ad-8 neutralized ICHV, but anti-ICHV did not neutralize Ad-8. This might suggest the possibility that ICHV and Ad-8 have a common origin or that one is an adapted strain of the other in a new host. The fact that ICHV grows to very high titers in homologous species (canine) cells (over $10^{9.0}$ infectious units/ml), whereas Ad-8 grows poorly in human cells ($10^{3.0}$ infectious units/ml maximum) might suggest that Ad-8 is a human-adapted ICHV strain. However, preliminary experiments indicate that Ad-8 does not grow well on primary passage in canine cells, which suggests that this may not be true. Further studies are underway to determine whether repeated passage of ICHV or Ad-8 in human or canine cells, respectively, results in adaptation of either virus so as to more closely resemble the other.

The failure of ICHV antibody to neutralize

Ad-8 made it easy to recognize this specific antibody in human sera. Since Ad-8 antibody neutralizes ICHV, the occasional Ad-8 positive serum was simply deleted from consideration in this study. It is clear that about 80% of adults have ICHV antibody, and the majority of children develop antibody by their mid-teens. The mean ICHV antibody titer we observed in individuals from Texas was 1:18, which is consistent with the titer observed in pooled human γ globulin (1:36).

The high incidence of ICHV antibody in humans may reflect periodic contact with dogs over a period of years. Many veterinarians give attenuated, live ICHV vaccine to dogs at yearly intervals, and the vaccine virus is almost certainly shed into the human environment. Often dogs live in intimate contact with their owners, providing opportunity for continuous exposure to a virus which is notably resistant to inactivation (10).

Our *in vitro* experiments with ICHV in human cells (4) showed that the virus did not replicate well or spread from cell-to-cell. However, we found that substantial quantities of viral antigens, including tumor-specific antigens, are produced by ICHV-infected human cells *in vitro*. The observed high incidence of ICHV-neutralizing antibody in humans and the frequent occurrence of substantial antibody titers suggest that most humans are periodically stimulated by ICHV antigen, either by repeated re-infection by dogs or by protracted release of viral antigens from a few long-lived, abortively infected cells. Neutralizing antibody appears during childhood and is found in nearly all people by middle age.

The fact that ICHV is oncogenic for hamsters (3) makes widespread natural human infection with this virus worthy of attention. However, a recent study revealed no evidence of antibody to ICHV tumor antigen in human cancer patients' sera (11).

ADDENDUM

We have prepared antibody to Ad-8 by repeatedly injecting the footpads of guinea pigs with density gradient-purified virus and Freund's complete adjuvant. This antibody neutralized Ad-8 at a dilution of 1:1400 but did not neutralize ICHV at the lowest antibody dilution tested (1:20). Since 70 doses of Ad-8 neutralizing antibody failed to neutralize ICHV, it appears that a serologic relationship between Ad-8 and ICHV cannot be demonstrated with neutralizing antibody prepared against purified virus in guinea pigs.

REFERENCES

1. Govaerts, A., Arch. Ges. Virusforsch., *10:* 395, 1960.
2. Bech, V., Proc. Soc. Exp. Biol. Med., *100:* 135, 1959.
3. Sarma, P. S., Vass, W., Huebner, R. J., Igel, H., Lane, W. T. and Turner, H. C., Nature, *215:* 293, 1967.
4. Gehle, W. D. and Smith, K. O., Proc. Soc. Exp. Biol. Med., *131:* 87, 1969.
5. Smith, K. O., Dunlap, R. C., Thiel, J. F., Newman, J. T. and Palmer, A. E., Proc, Soc. Exp. Biol. Med., *133:* 560, 1970.
6. Kapsenberg, J. A., Proc. Soc. Exp. Biol. Med., *101:* 611, 1959.
7. Carmichael, L. E. and Barnes, F. D., Proc. Soc. Exp. Biol. Med., *107:* 214, 1961.
8. Thiel, J. F. and Smith, K. O., Proc. Soc. Exp. Biol. Med., *125:* 892, 1967.
9. Jawetz, E., Thygeson, P., Hanna, L., Nicholas, A. and Kimura, S., Proc. Soc. Exp. Biol. Med., *92:* 91, 1956.
10. Fastier, L. B., Vet. Res., *70:* 623, 1958.
11. Gilden, R. V., Kern, J., Lee, Y. K., Rapp, F., Melnick, J. L., Riggs, J. L., Lennette, E. H., Zbar, B., Rapp, H. J., Turner, H. C. and Huebner, R. J., Amer. J. Epidem., *91:* 500, 1970.

THE JOURNAL OF IMMUNOLOGY
Copyright © 1970 by The Williams & Wilkins Co.

Vol. 105, No. 4, October 1970
Printed in U.S.A.

Herpes-Like Virus (EB Virus) in Continuous Lymphoblastoid Cell Lines from Patients with Viral Hepatitis

DAVID P. STEVENS,[1] LEWELLYS F. BARKER,[2] HOPE E. HOPPS AND HARRY M. MEYER, JR.

From the Laboratory of Viral Immunology, Division of Biologics Standards, National Institutes of Health, Bethesda, Maryland 20014

In 1968, 21 continuous lymphoblastoid tissue culture cell lines were established in this laboratory from the peripheral blood of individuals with diagnosed acute infectious hepatitis (IH) (1). Concurrent attempts to establish similar cultures from normal subjects yielded a significantly lower number of continuous lines. These lines have been maintained in rapidly dividing suspension culture for 9 to 12 months.

Similar cell lines have been derived from individuals with lymphoma, leukemia (2, 3) infectious mononucleosis (4), serum hepatitis (5) and other infectious diseases (6) as well as from presumably normal "healthy" donors (7, 8). Most have been shown to contain the Epstein-Barr virus (EBV), a herpes-like virus.

The present report summarizes studies employing immunofluorescence (IF) and electron-microscopic techniques to determine whether EBV or any other viral agents were present in our cell lines which could be associated either with IH or with the lymphoproliferative phenomenon observed *in vitro* by leukocytes from patients with IH.

MATERIALS AND METHODS

Cells for the experiments described in this report were cultivated in 250-ml plastic tissue culture flasks (Falcon Plastics Co., Los Angeles, Calif.) The flasks were tightly closed and incubated at 35°C on a rocking platform (Bellco Glass Co., Vineland, N. J.) which rocked at 2 oscillations/min. Culture growth medium, consisting of Roswell Park Memorial Institute medium 1640 (7) supplemented with 20% fetal bovine serum and glutamine, was changed every 3 to 4 days. The predominant cell types in these suspension cultures were immature and atypical lymphoblasts with occasional mature small lymphocytes (1). The viable cell count, determined by trypan blue exclusion, doubled every 24 hr under optimal culture conditions.

Cells for IF studies were air dried at 35°C on ethanol-cleaned slides and fixed in acetone at room temperature for 7 min. Fixed preparations were stored at −70°C until stained. For the detection of EBV antigen, cells from 3 lines derived from normal donors and 13 lines from individuals with IH were overlayed for 30 min at room temperature with a 1:10 dilution of a known positive human antiserum (8). This antiserum was obtained from a patient who was 2 months convalescent from infectious mononucleosis; the anti-EBV titer of the serum was 1:80 in our indirect IF test. After rinsing with phosphate-buffered saline, the cells were overlayed with a 1:5 dilution of fluorescein-conjugated caprine anti-human γ globulin (Baltimore Biological Laboratory, Cockeysville, Md.) for 30 min at room temperature. Slides were read under ultraviolet illumination. Appropriate serum and cell controls were employed in all tests. Anti-EBV antibodies were determined with twofold dilutions of plasma specimens from each cell line donor by the same indirect IF method. Here a positive Burkitt tumor cell line, EB_3, was employed as the indicator cell.

Thin section preparations were prepared as described by Moore *et al.* (9). Briefly, cells were pelleted by low-speed centrifugation, fixed in 2% glyceraldehyde followed by 1% osmium tetroxide at 4°C for 1 hr and embedded in a mixture containing equal parts of propylene oxide and Epon. Sections (0.5 μ to 0.15 μ in thickness) were examined using a JEM electron microscope. No fewer than 1200 to 1500 individual cells were screened from each cell line.

RESULTS AND DISCUSSION

Typical EBV fluorescence was observed in 5 of 13 IH cell lines but not in the three lines

[1] Present address: Department of Medicine, University Hospitals, Cleveland, Ohio 44106.

[2] Requests for reprints should be sent to Dr. Lewellys F. Barker, Division of Biologics Standards, National Institutes of Health, Bethesda, Maryland 20014.

from normal donors. In most instances, cells containing EBV antigen were rare, usually less less than 0.2% of cells. Granular cytoplasmic fluorescence, probably resulting from staining of γ globulin present in the cells, was observed in almost all lines overlayed with normal saline followed by the anti-human globulin-fluorescein dye conjugate. Plasma specimens from all IH leukocyte donors from whom cell lines were established and from all the normal leukocyte donors regardless of whether a line was established or not were found to contain anti-EBV antibodies at the screening dilution of 1:10 at the time the blood was obtained for attempted establishment of cell lines.

Examination with the electron microscope of thin section preparations from a total of 14 IH cell lines revealed EBV in 5 lines. One line derived from a normal donor carried EBV (Table I). No other virus-like particles were observed. Utilizing a variety of techniques, including immunofluorescence, challenge with cytopathic viruses, hemadsorption, interferon assay and inoculation onto monolayer cultures of human primary, diploid and continuous cell lines, no other viruses were demonstrated in these cell lines.

It seems unlikely that the presence of EBV in these lines indicates that it plays an etiologic role in classical infectious hepatitis because a) significant rises in anti-EBV titer have not been found in viral hepatitis (10), and b) EBV is larger and more labile than the purported properties of the agent of viral hepatitis (11).

TABLE I

Cell lines positive for Epstein-Barr virus (EBV) as demonstrated by immunofluorescence (IF) and electron microscopy (EM)

Cell Line No.	EBV Demonstrated by	
	IF	EM
BS-HLH-12[a]	+	+
BS-HLH-14	−	+
BS-HLH-16	+	+
BS-HLH-17	+	−
BS-HLH-18	+	+
BS-HLH-21	−	+
BS-HLH-24	+	−
BS-HLN-3	−	+

[a] Designations BS-HLH and BS-HLN are for lymphoblastoid cell lines derived from patients with hepatitis and from a normal donor, respectively (1).

It is also unlikely that the finding of EBV in lines derived from patients with IH indicates a *unique* role of the virus in lymphoproliferation in IH. Rather, it seems probable that prior infection with the virus—perhaps with a resulting latent infection—is a necessary preceding event for the establishment of cultures from any donor, regardless of his state of health at the time of blood donation. All individuals from whom lymphoblastoid lines were established in this laboratory—both normal and with IH—possessed antibodies to EBV at the time blood was drawn for establishing cultures, indicating prior active infection by the virus at some undetermined time. This is not surprising since antibodies to EBV are widespread in the general population (12). EBV has been found in continuous lymphoblastoid cell cultures derived from peripheral blood of individuals with numerous diseases, including infectious mononucleosis (13), serum hepatitis (14), and leukemia (3), as well as from normal donors (7, 8). To our knowledge, no permanent lymphoblastoid cultures have ever been established from individuals who did not possess antibodies to EBV except upon addition of that virus to the leukocytes *in vitro* (15).

Failure to find EBV in more than eight lines may be attributed to the length of time the cells had been in culture (over 4 months) before they were examined for the virus. It has been suggested that cultivation techniques which are optimal for cell growth may lead to loss of the virus from the cells (13). Most of the lines were found to contain EBV in a very small percentage of cells tested (often less than 0.5%).

The reason for the increased lymphoproliferation observed in patients with IH compared to that of normal donors remains a matter for speculation. It may be due to an agent that is undetectable by present techniques. An alternative hypothesis is that it represents an *in vitro* manifestation of increased immunologic activity of leukocytes which have been antigenically stimulated *in vivo*, perhaps by a hepatitis virus. Increased tritiated thymidine uptake by lymphocytes *in vitro* has been demonstrated in several disease states in which increased immunologic activity due to a variety of antigens probably was present (16).

In summary, we suggest the following hypothesis, based on currently available data, for the finding of increased lymphoblastoid proliferation in peripheral leukocytes from patients with infectious hepatitis. Prior infection of the donor by EBV with a resulting chronic or latent infection of peripheral leukocytes (probably lymphocytes) is necessary for the establishment of continuous suspension cultures *in vitro*, regardless of the state of health of the donor at the time leukocytes are obtained for culture. Given this background of EBV infection, the cells of donors who recently have been exposed to antigenic stimulation—presumably viral in the case of IH—possess increased potential for proliferation into permanent culture *in vitro*.

Acknowledgments. Excellent technical assistance was provided with immunofluorescent staining by Mrs. Eva Brown, and with tissue cultures by Mrs. Barbara C. Meyer, Mr. Daniel Jackson and Mr. Audry J. Shawver. Electron microscopy was performed by Mr. D. Stewart, Melpar, Inc., Falls Church, Virginia, under Contract NIH-69-2013.

REFERENCES

1. Stevens, D. P., Barker, L. F., Fike, R., Hopps, H. E. and Meyer, H. M., Jr., Proc. Soc. Exp. Biol. Med., *132:* 1042, 1969.
2. Iwabata, S. and Grace, J. T., N. Y. J. Med., *64:* 2279, 1964.
3. Moore, G. E., Grace, J. T., Citron, P., Gerner, R. and Burns, A., N. Y. J. Med., *66:* 2757, 1966.
4. Pope, J. H., Nature, *216:* 810, 1967.
5. Glade, P. R., Hirshaut, Y., Douglas, S. D. and Hirschhorn, K., Lancet, *2:* 1273, 1968.
6. Glade, P. R., Paltrowitz, I. M. and Hirschhorn, K., Bull. N. Y. Acad. Med., *45:* 647, 1969.
7. Moore, G. E., Gerner, R. E. and Franklin, H. A., J. A. M. A., *199:* 519, 1967.
8. Gerber, P. and Monroe, J. H., J. Nat. Cancer Inst., *40:* 855, 1968.
9. Moore, G. E, Kitamura, H. and Toshima, S., Cancer, *22:* 245, 1968.
10. Henle, G., Henle, W. and Diehl, V., Proc. Nat. Acad. Sci., *59:* 94, 1968.
11. Hillis, W. D., Johns Hopkins Med. J., *120:* 176, 1967.
12. Gerber, P. and Birch, S. M., Proc. Nat. Acad. Sci., *58:* 478, 1967.
13. Diehl, V., Henle, G., Henle, W. and Kohn, G., J. Virol., *2:* 663, 1968.
14. Douglas, S. D., Glade, P. R., Fudenberg, H. H. and Hirschhorn, K., J. Virol., *3:* 520, 1969.
15. Gerber, P., Whang-Peng, J. and Monroe, J. H., Proc. Nat. Acad. Sci., *63:* 740, 1969.
16. Wood, T. A. and Frenkel, E. P., Amer. J. Med., *42:* 92, 1967.

THE JOURNAL OF IMMUNOLOGY
Vol. 105, No. 4, October 1970
Printed in U.S.A.

Enhancement by Reducing Agents of the Transformation of Human and Rabbit Peripheral Lymphocytes[1]

MICHAEL W. FANGER,[2] DAVID A. HART, J. VIVIAN WELLS[3] AND ALFRED NISONOFF

From the Department of Biological Chemistry, University of Illinois at the Medical Center, Chicago, Illinois 60612

Lymphocytes may be stimulated to undergo transformation into blast cells by a variety of nonspecific chemical agents, or by antiglobulin or antilymphocyte antisera. Antigens act as mitogenic agents on lymphocytes from sensitized animals (1–3).

We have now observed that the action of various mitogens on human and rabbit peripheral lymphocytes is markedly enhanced in the presence of the reducing agents, L-cysteine, glutathione, or sulfite.

Rabbit peripheral lymphocytes were isolated, purified on a cotton-wool column and cultured as described previously (4). Human leukocytes were obtained from the blood of normal individuals by allowing the cells to settle in 10% Plasmagel (Laboratoire Roger Bellon, Neuilly, France). The leukocyte-rich layer was removed and the cells were washed several times with 20% decomplemented fetal calf serum in Eagle's minimal essential medium (MEM). Leukocytes were cultured (4) at a concentration of 10^6 cells/ml. Rabbit lymphocytes were cultured for 48 hr and human leukocytes for 108 hr; 24 hr before harvest, 5 μCi of ^{3}H-thymidine (6.7 Ci/mM) was added to the rabbit lymphocyte

TABLE I

Enhancement of PHA-stimulated transformation of human peripheral leukocytes by L-cysteine[a]

Donor	Reagent Added	Concentration of Cysteine (M)[b]			
		No cysteine added	1×10^{-3}	5×10^{-3}	1×10^{-2}
		counts/min incorporated[c]			
JH	None	1370 ± 390	1090 ± 130	1220 ± 120	1230 ± 120
	PHA (20 μg)	67,140 ± 13,000	129,000 ± 14,000	130,000 ± 9,000	228,000 ± 18,000
	PHA (50 μg)	97,800 ± 10,000	171,000 ± 8,000	245,000 ± 30,000	245,000 ± 27,000
	NRS[d] (50 μl)	1320 ± 150	470 ± 190	570 ± 150	500 ± 90
	Anti-IgG[e] (50 μl)	1500 ± 250	950 ± 150	1780 ± 70	1670 ± 220
JVW	None	360 ± 50	190 ± 20	160 ± 10	150 ± 10
	PHA (40 μg)	17,500 ± 750	45,000 ± 11,000	52,900 ± 5000	89,600 ± 100
RWR	None	90 ± 10	90 ± 10	130 ± 30	100 ± 10
	PHA (40 μg)	14,500 ± 500	42,900 ± 10,000	48,000 ± 2000	29,800 ± 4500

[a] Experiments conducted with cells from donor JH used 5 μCi of ^{3}H-thymidine 24 hr before harvest; experiments with cells from JVW and RWR used 2 μCi. Cysteine was added to the cell culture before the other reagent.

[b] Final molar concentrations.

[c] Counts/min of ^{3}H-thymidine incorporated into 1.33×10^6 cells ± average deviation of duplicate cultures.

[d] Normal rabbit serum.

[e] Rabbit anti-human IgG antiserum.

[1] This work was supported by grants from the National Science Foundation (GB-5424) and the National Institutes of Health.

[2] Postdoctoral Fellow of the National Institutes of Health.

[3] Supported by University of California Training Grant HE-05677 (USPHS) and the Royal Australasian College of Physicians.

TABLE II

Enhancement by L-cysteine of the transformation of rabbit lymphocytes caused by PHA or antiglobulin reagents[a]

Donor	Reagent Added	Concentration of Cysteine (M)[b]: No cysteine added	1×10^{-3}	5×10^{-3}	1×10^{-2}
		counts/min incorporated[c]			
Rabbit					
R1	None	340 ± 10	480 ± 50	330 ± 30	90 ± 10
	PHA (50 μg)	7190 ± 130	11,300 ± 800	16,000 ± 1900	6800 ± 50
	Anti-Fc (1.0 mg)	2710 ± 110	4700 ± 600	3600 ± 150	1000 ± 50
	Anti-Fab (0.5 mg)	1950 ± 150	4200 ± 500	3600 ± 250	1200 ± 130
	Anti-Fab (1.0 mg)	2580 ± 80	4000 ± 250	3400 ± 100	1000 ± 50
	Anti-Fab Fab′ (0.5 mg)	260 ± 10	310 ± 10	200 ± 10	50 ± 10
	Anti-Fab Fab′ (1.0 mg)	160 ± 30	230 ± 20	130 ± 20	50 ± 10
	Anti-b5 (20 μl)	1730 ± 230	6100 ± 500	3300 ± 100	1300 ± 100
R2	None	90 ± 10	90 ± 10	120 ± 10	20 ± 10
	PHA (25 μg)	1860 ± 290	1100 ± 170	7000 ± 100	960 ± 100
R4	None	840 ± 60	660 ± 30	390 ± 10	100 ± 10
	PHA (50 μg)	9600 ± 150	26,000 ± 3000	31,000 ± 3500	26,860 ± 140
	Anti-Fc (1.0 mg)	2430 ± 300	4000 ± 200	3100 ± 600	3700 ± 300

[a] Abbreviations used: anti-Fc, the IgG fraction of goat anti-rabbit fragment Fc; anti-Fab, the IgG fraction of goat anti-rabbit Fab; anti-Fab Fab′, the Fab′ fragment of anti-Fab; anti-b5, rabbit antiserum directed to the b5 determinants of rabbit IgG.

[b] See Table I.

[c] Counts/min of ^{3}H-thymidine incorporated into 6.7×10^5 cells ± average deviation of duplicate cultures.

[d] The allotype of rabbit R1 was a1,b5.

cultures and either 5 μCi or 2 μCi of ^{3}H-thymidine to the human leukocyte cultures. Radioactivity incorporated into DNA was determined as described previously (4).

The preparation of IgG fractions of goat anti-rabbit fragment Fc and antirabbit fragment Fab has been described (4). Antiserum to allotype b5 of rabbit immunoglobulin was generously provided by Dr. S. Dray. A rabbit antiserum of high titer was prepared against human IgG purified by precipitation with Na_2SO_4 and chromatography on diethylaminoethyl cellulose (5, 6). Phytohemagglutinin P (PHA) was obtained from Difco Laboratories, Detroit, Mich.; reduced glutathione from the Sigma Chemical Co., St. Louis, Mo.; and L-cysteine from Mann Research Laboratories, New York, N. Y.

Enhancement of transformation of human peripheral leukocytes by PHA in the presence of L-cysteine is shown in Table I. L-Cysteine alone had no stimulatory effect in the presence or absence of normal rabbit serum. When PHA was present, L-cysteine at optimal concentration increased thymidine incorporation by a factor of 2.5 to 5. No stimulation by rabbit anti-human IgG was observed either in the presence or absence of cysteine. The failure of rabbit antihuman IgG to stimulate blast transformation appreciably is in accord with results of Holt *et al.* (7) although other investigators have observed transformation (8).

The data in Tables II and III indicate that L-cysteine, reduced glutathione or sulfite had no stimulatory effect on cultured rabbit lymphocytes. However, each compound markedly enhanced the mitogenic activity of antiglobulin reagents (IgG fractions of goat anti-rabbit Fab or anti-rabbit Fc antisera) or that of PHA. The only exception was observed with the lymphocytes of rabbit R3; no significant enhancement of the mitogenic activity of PHA was caused by glutathione. In other experiments

TABLE III

Enhancement by reducing agents of the transformation of rabbit lymphocytes stimulated by PHA or antiglobulin reagents[a]

Donor	Mitogenic Agent	Reducing Agent	Concentration of Reducing Agent (M)[b]				
			0	10^{-4}	5×10^{-4}	10^{-3}	5×10^{-3}
			counts/min incorporated[c]				
Rabbit							
R4	None	Sulfite	840 ± 60	1000 ± 200	1020 ± 20	960 ± 10	
	PHA[d]	Sulfite	9600 ± 150	17,700 ± 800	20,700 ± 2600	13,600 ± 800	
	Anti-Fc[d]	Sulfite	2430 ± 300	4010 ± 10	4100 ± 350	2400 ± 100	
	None	Glutathione[e]	840 ± 60	800 ± 200		1000 ± 20	1000 ± 300
	PHA	Glutathione	9600 ± 150	9600 ± 200		20,200 ± 1600	34,600 ± 300
	Anti-Fc	Glutathione	2430 ± 300	2900 ± 200		4400 ± 300	8300 ± 300
R3	None	Glutathione	160 ± 10	180 ± 10		200 ± 20	
	PHA	Glutathione	1410 ± 20	2580 ± 120		4610 ± 20	
	Anti-Fc	Glutathione	2840 ± 160	2050 ± 450		3240 ± 50	

[a, b, c] See Table II.

[d] Fifty micrograms of PHA or 1.0 mg anti-Fc were used in these experiments.

[e] Reduced form.

thymidine incorporation caused by antiglobulin reagents or PHA was increased by a factor of 1.6 to 3.8 in the presence of an optimal concentration of reducing agent. In the most extensive studies, carried out with lymphocytes of rabbit R1 (Table II), enhancement by L-cysteine was observed on stimulation with PHA, with IgG fractions of goat anti-rabbit Fc or anti-rabbit Fab antisera, and with rabbit anti-b5 antiserum. The Fab′ fragment of goat anti-rabbit Fab was not mitogenic, as previously noted (4), and this result was not affected by the presence of reducing agent.

The results show consistent enhancement by reducing agents (L-cysteine, glutathione or sulfite) of the blast transformation of human or rabbit lymphocytes. The transforming reagents tested were PHA, IgG fractions of goat anti-rabbit Fab and anti-rabbit Fc, and anti-rabbit allotype b5 antiserum. Reducing agents alone consistently failed to cause stimulation; nor did they induce transformation when mixed with nonmitogenic reagents (rabbit anti-human IgG or univalent goat anti-rabbit Fab antibodies).

The mechanism of enhancement cannot be deduced from the present data. The reducing agents may act as metabolites, through their effect on the redox potential of the system, or by activation of SH-requiring enzymes. An obvious possibility is that reducing agents cleave disulfide bonds on the membrane and thus render the cells more sensitive to mitogenic agents. Elucidation of the mode of action of these reagents may provide information relevant to an understanding of the mechanism of blast transformation of lymphocytes.

REFERENCES

1. Ling, N. R., *Lymphocyte Stimulation*, John Wiley & Sons, Inc., New York, 1968.
2. Sell, S. and Asofsky, R., Progr. Allerg., *12:* 86, 1968.
3. Naspitz, C. K. and Richter, M., Progr. Allerg., *12:* 1, 1968.
4. Fanger, M. W., Hart, D. A., Wells, J. V. and Nisonoff, A., J. Immun., In press.
5. Kekwick, R. A., Biochem. J., *34:* 1248, 1940.
6. Levy, H. B. and Sober, H. A., Proc. Soc. Exp. Biol. Med., *103:* 250, 1960.
7. Holt, L. J., Ling, M. R. and Stanworth, D. S., Immunochemistry, *3:* 359, 1966.
8. King, R. A., Messner, R. P. and Williams, R. C., Jr., Arthritis Rheum. *12:* 597, 1969.

THE JOURNAL OF IMMUNOLOGY
Vol. 105, No. 4, October 1970
Printed in U.S.A.

A Method for Typing Rabbit Sera for the A14 and A15 Allotypes with Cross-Linked Antisera

S. LANDUCCI TOSI AND R. G. MAGE

From the Osservatorio di Genetica Animale, Via Pastrengo 28, Torino, Italy, and the Laboratory of Immunology, National Institute of Allergy and Infectious Diseases, National Institutes of Health, Bethesda, Maryland 20014

The allotypes A14 and A15 are allelic specificities on immunoglobulin-G (IgG) of rabbits (1, 2). They are located on the Fc portion of IgG and are genetically linked to specificities associated with the *a* locus which are localized on the Fd portion. Their assignment to a separate locus (*e* locus) awaits a definite solution of one of the crucial questions of immunogenetics, that is, whether the heavy polypeptide chain of a given immunoglobulin is the product of one or two genes. The A14 and A15 allotypes provide very useful markers. For example, by quantitating the distribution of a1, a2, A14 and A15 among IgG molecules from heterozygous rabbits of known pedigree, we are able to evaluate whether genetic information from maternal and paternal chromosomes contributes to individual IgG molecules (3). In contrast to the *a* locus markers, the A14 and A15 markers are exclusively localized on IgG. Therefore, a useful criterion for the purity of an immunoglobulin of another class is the absence of A14 or A15 specificity (Landucci Tosi, S., Mage, R. G. and Lawton, A. R., in preparation). In addition, in conjunction with the Ms markers (4), which are present only on IgM, they could be used to test for linkage between genes for μ and γ chains of the rabbit.

Rabbit sera have been typed for A14 and A15 by a hemagglutination-inhibition test (1) because no anti-A14 or anti-A15 antisera have been found so far which possess precipitating activity. We have shown that anti-A14 and anti-A15 antisera, when rendered insoluble by cross-linking, maintain their specific binding properties (3). We now report a typing procedure which tests for A14 and/or A15 by inhibition of the specific binding of ^{125}I-labeled IgG to cross-linked antisera.

The same rabbit sera and anti-A14 and anti-A15 antisera described in a previous paper (3) were used. IgG was prepared from animals of known genotype by sodium sulfate precipitation and DEAE chromatography as previously described (3). Purity was checked by disc electrophoresis on polyacrylamide gels (5), omitting urea. Iodination was performed by the method of Greenwood *et al.* (6). Specific activities ranged from 3 to 5 $\times$ 10^5 cpm/μg. Free ^{125}I was less than 2% in the final preparation. Antisera were cross-linked by the method of Avrameas and Ternynck (7) as previously described (3). They were resuspended in saline containing 0.014 M sodium phosphate (PBS), pH 7.9, to two to five times the original antiserum volume.

Assay conditions

Binding curves. A fixed amount (50 μl) of labeled IgG, diluted in PBS containing 5% bovine serum albumin (BSA Armour Cohn fraction V powder) to provide 5000 to 10,000 cpm was distributed in small conical plastic tubes. Increasing amounts of the cross-linked antisera were added, with care being taken to keep the suspension homogeneous. Volumes were equalized to 100 μl with PBS. Incubation on a revolving wheel prevented sedimentation of the insoluble antiserum. After 24 hr at room temperature, the tubes were centrifuged for 30 min at 1500 $\times$ G and 50 μl of supernatant were transferred to a second tube (top tube). Both tubes (top and bottom) were counted in a well-type crystal scintillation counter. The percentage of labeled antigen that was bound to the insoluble antibody was calculated as follows:

$$\frac{(\text{cpm - bottom}) - (\text{cpm top})}{\text{total cpm}} \times 100.$$

In Figure 1*a* and 1*b* the binding curves of A14 and A15 IgG to the corresponding antisera are shown. Only antisera that bound more than 70% of the labeled antigen were used for the inhibition assay.

Inhibition assay. To 30 μl of labeled IgG

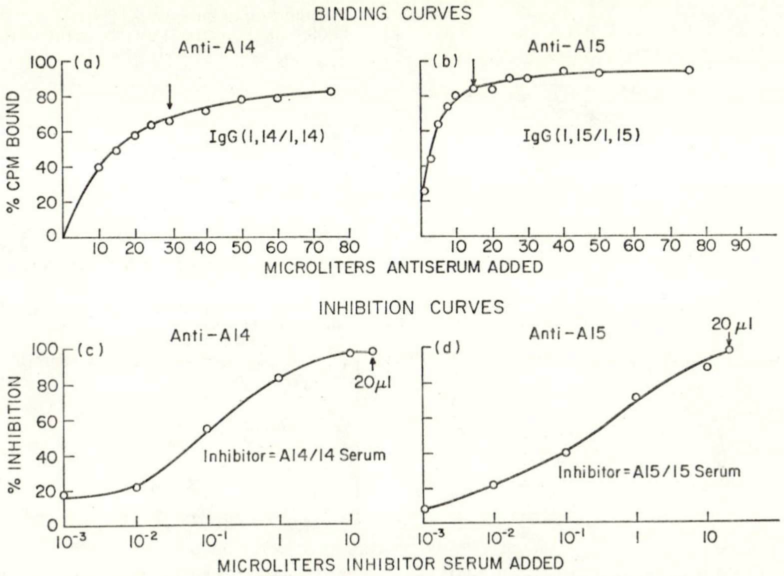

Figure 1. Binding curves (*a*) and (*b*). Increasing volumes of cross-linked antisera were added to a fixed amount of ^{125}I-labeled IgG (about 7000 cpm). Non-specific binding of 1,15/1,15 IgG by anti-A14 antiserum and of 1,14/1,14 IgG by anti-A15 antiserum was less than 5%. Arrows indicate antiserum volume selected for the performance of inhibition curves. Inhibition curves (*c*) and (*d*). Inhibition of binding of ^{125}I-IgG by unlabeled antigen. Increasing volumes of normal rabbit sera (inhibitor) were added to a fixed amount of ^{125}I-IgG. After mixing, the selected antiserum volume (30 μl for anti-A14, 15 μl for anti-A15) was added. Arrows indicate volume of inhibitor serum chosen for the performance of routine typing.

(5000 to 10,000 cpm), 20 μl of the sera under test were added. This volume was ordinarily enough to give almost complete inhibition as shown in Figure 1*c* and 1*d*. After careful mixing, the amount of cross-linked antiserum known to give 80% of maximum binding (marked by arrows in Figure 1*a* and 1*b*) was added. The following controls were included in the assay: 1) measurement of binding without added inhibitor; 2) measurement of non-specific binding to an unrelated antiserum or in the absence of added antiserum; and 3) test with a known negative and a known positive serum. For the inhibition assay, the incubation time was reduced to 3 hr, with a loss of binding of 9.5% compared to a 24-hr incubation. Inhibition was expressed in the following manner:

$$\text{Percentage of inhibition} = 100 - \frac{\%\ \text{binding with inhibitor}}{\%\ \text{binding without inhibitor}} \times 100$$

Theoretically, a serum positive for the allotype under test should give 100% inhibition and a negative serum 0%. Actually, due in part to technical variability and in part to the broad range of IgG concentration in normal rabbit sera, negative sera gave up to 20% inhibition and positive sera gave down to 65%. However the distinction between the negative and positive classes of sera was always clear cut and unequivocal. A comparison of the present test with the hemagglutination-inhibition assay was done with 27 sera (four homozygous for A14, five for A15, and eighteen A14–15 heterozygotes) and no discrepancies were found. In conclusion, the present method offers some practical advantages because a) being an all-or-none assay, it does not require performance of serial dilutions and is thus technically simpler, and b) the results are obtained in a short time, are unequivocal and are fully reproducible.

The same system can be applied without major modification to tests of antisera for their anti-A14 and anti-A15 activity. Addition to the system of an untreated antiserum would be expected to cause competition for the available antigen, and since no precipitation occurs there should be inhibition of binding. Figure 2 shows that this is indeed the case. Three different cross-linked anti-A14 antisera were completely

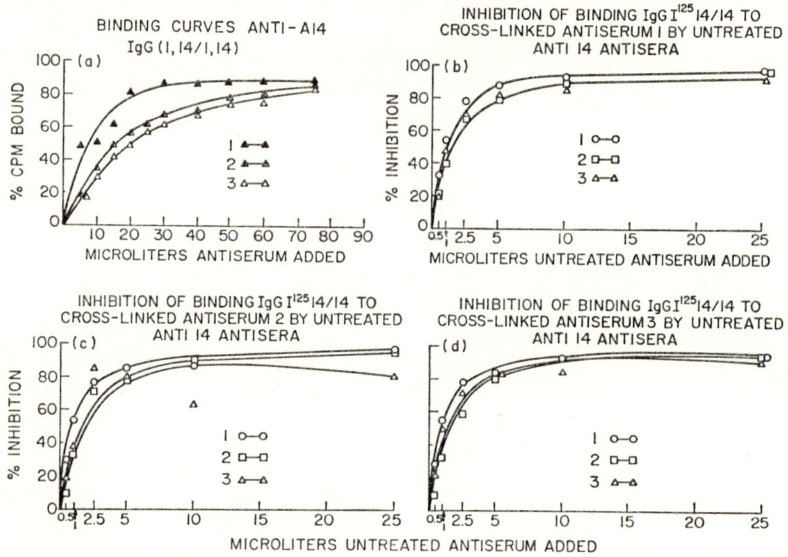

Figure 2. (*a*) Binding curves obtained with three different anti-A14 antisera. Increasing volumes of cross-linked antisera were added to a fixed amount of ^{125}I-labeled IgG (about 7000 cpm). (*b*, *c* and *d*) Inhibition of binding of cross-linked antisera by non-cross-linked antisera. Increasing volumes of untreated antisera were added to a fixed amount (20 μl for 1; 40 μl for 2 and 50 μl for 3) of cross-linked antisera. After mixing, ^{125}I-labeled 1,14/1,14 IgG was added.

inhibited by each non-cross-linked anti-A14 antiserum. Thus with one cross-linked specific antiserum available, the presence of the same antibody specificity in other sera can be evaluated without going through the cross-linking procedure each time. A quantitative inhibition curve also provides an estimate of the relative strength of the antisera.

REFERENCES

1. Dubiski, S., J. Immun., *103:* 120, 1969.
2. Dubiski, S., in *Protides of the Biological Fluids* XVII, Edited by H. Peeters, Pergamon Press, Los Angeles, in press.
3. Landucci Tosi, S., Mage, R. G. and Dubiski, S., J. Immun., *104:* 641, 1970.
4. Kelus, A. S. and Gell, P. G. H., Nature, *206:* 313, 1965.
5. Reisfeld, R. A. and Small, P. A., Science, *152:* 1253, 1966.
6. Greenwood, F. C., Hunter, W. M. and Glover, J. S., Biochem. J., *89:* 114, 1963.
7. Avrameas, S. and Ternynck, T., J. Biol. Chem., *242:* 1651, 1967.

THE JOURNAL OF IMMUNOLOGY
Vol. 105, No. 4, October 1970
Printed in U.S.A.

Predominant Contribution of IgA Antibody-Forming Cells to an Immune Response Detected in Extraintestinal Lymphoid Tissues of Germ-free Mice Exposed to Antigen by the Oral Route[1]

H. BAZIN, G. LEVI AND G. DORIA

From the CNEN-Euratom Immunogenetics Group, Laboratory of Animal Radiobiology, C.S.N., Casaccia (Rome), Italy, and the Department of Experimental Medicine, Cliniques Universitaires St. Pierre, Louvain, Belgium

The immune response in germ-free mice given ferritin by oral route was claimed by Crabbé *et al.* (1) to be almost exclusively localized in the intestinal mucosa and to belong to antibody-forming cells of the IgA class. The contribution of extraintestinal tissues to this reponse was limited to very few immunocytes, only four of which, localized in the mesenteric lymph node, could be identified for their Ig class and found to belong to IgA.

Walters and Jackson (2), Wortis *et al.* (3) and Sell *et al.* (4) were able to show by the Jerne technique (5) the appearance of relevant numbers of hemolytic plaque-forming cells (PFC) of the IgA class, as well as of the other classes (IgM, IgG_1, IgG_{2a}, IgG_{2b}), in the spleen of conventional mice immunized by proper doses of sheep red blood cells (RBC) given by the parenteral route.

In the present work the immune response of germ-free mice immunized by the oral route was investigated in extraintestinal lymphoid tissues. Using sheep RBC as antigen and the direct and indirect (6, 7) Jerne technique, it has been possible to screen large populations of cells and to identify the Ig classes of antibodies produced at the cellular level.

MATERIALS AND METHODS

Animals. Germ-free male and female N.M.R.I. mice, 3 to 5 months old, were kept in Trexler-type isolators.

Immunization. The mice were immunized orally by allowing them to drink a 5% suspension of washed sheep RBC in a sterile conservative medium (Sclavo, Siena, Italy) diluted 1:1 with sterile water. Control mice were given sterile drinking water. In one experiment to study the primary response, mice were exposed to antigen continuously for variable periods of time up to 25 days. In another experiment to study the secondary response, mice were given antigen during 15 days, sterile water for a subsequent 10 days, and then antigen again for variable periods of time up to 77 days. A third group of mice was immunized parenterally by the intraperitoneal injection of 1 ml of 1% sheep RBC (2×10^8 cells).

Detection of PFC. Separate cell suspensions were prepared from spleen and lymph nodes of normal or immunized mice by teasing apart each tissue in Eagle's medium. Portions of each cell suspension were plated with sheep RBC, according to the Jerne technique (5). Indirect plaques of a given Ig class were developed and estimated from counts on four Petri dishes in which the direct plaques had already been developed, marked, and counted. Two dishes were overlaid with anti-Ig class monospecific antiserum properly diluted, the other two dishes with phosphate-buffered saline as controls. After overnight incubation at 4°C and washing, guinea pig complement was added to the four dishes for 1 hr at 37°C. The net number of plaques resulting from antibodies of the specific Ig class was calculated from the difference between counts on antiserum and control dishes.

Antisera. Antisera specific for each mouse Ig class were prepared in rabbits and tested as previously described (8).

RESULTS AND DISCUSSION

Table I shows the primary and secondary response to sheep RBC in the spleen of orally immunized germ-free mice. Both primary and secondary responses were characterized by the appearance of a remarkable number of PFC secreting antibodies of the IgA class. In the primary response these antibody-forming cells were detected 14 days after the beginning of

[1] This work was supported by CNEN-Euratom Association Contract. Publication No. 630 of the Euratom Biology Division.

immunization and their number increased thereafter. In the secondary response IgA-PFC could not be found after 6 days of antigenic restimulation. This shows that if the antigen administration is interrupted for 10 days, the number of IgA-PFC drops to 0 as in the spleen of unstimulated controls. The numbers of IgA-PFC were higher in the secondary than in the primary response, although the profiles of both responses were roughly the same. It can be seen that the values of IgA-PFC in the secondary response apparently decline after day 25 despite the continuous exposure to antigen.

As to the PFC belonging to the other Ig classes, a slight primary response could be detected on day 25. Upon antigenic restimulation, while the IgM-PFC response was not clearly detected, the IgG-PFC response was low but consistent, especially in the case of IgG_1-PFC. PFC in the spleen of unimmunized controls were found to belong to the IgM class only, and their number

TABLE I

PFC per spleen in germ-free mice orally immunized with sheep RBC

Immune Response	Primary				Secondary				
Days of oral immunization	0	6	14	25	6	11	25	33	77
No. of mice	7	2	6	6	2	2	3	4	4
Classes of PFC									
IgM	83	80	94	524	145	72	264	83	105
IgA	0	0	254	2967	0	310	7200	5500	3500
IgG_1	0	0	0	167	0	50	230	157	235
IgG_{2a}	0	0	0	46	0	0	230	110	10
IgG_{2b}	0	0	0	40	0	0	10	10	10

was comparable to that reported by Nordin (9) for germ-free mice.

The immune response in lymph nodes was evaluated by the number of PFC/10^6 nucleated cells owing to the difficulty of recovering all cells from each node. PFC were detected in the mesenteric lymph node, but not in peripheral lymph nodes (axillary, brachial and inguinal). IgM-PFC were found to contribute only to the primary response, in which they reached a maximum value of 33 PFC/10^6 cells on day 14 and subsequently declined to the control level (7.8 PFC/10^6 cells) on day 25. As to the IgG-PFC, 7 PFC/10^6 cells were detected on day 25 only in the IgG_1 class. The majority of PFC belonged to the IgA class. In Table II, IgA-PFC/10^6 nucleated lymph node cells and IgA-PFC/10^6 nucleated spleen cells are compared. The onset of the immune response by IgA-PFC seems predominant in the mesenteric lymph nodes for both primary and secondary responses. This observation supports the hypothesis that the IgA immune response to sheep RBC given by oral route might spread from intestinal to extraintestinal tissues through the lymphatic vessels. It has, indeed, been proposed (1) that an immune response initiated in the intestinal mucosa may predominantly be effected by IgA-antibody-forming cells owing to the local great abundance of these cells, which then can migrate elsewhere. It has also been postulated that antigen may be processed somehow in the gut and become more suitable for inducing the appearance of IgA-antibody-forming cells in extraintestinal tissues.

IgA-PFC could be detected in extraintestinal lymphoid tissues after oral or parenteral immunization. The origin of IgA-PFC in these tissues is not known. So far as the parenteral route is concerned, several findings (2–4, 10)

TABLE II

PFC of the IgA class per 10^6 nucleated cells in the spleen and mesenteric lymph node of germ-free mice orally immunized with sheep RBC

Immune response	Primary				Secondary		
Days of oral immunization	0	6	14	25	6	11	25
No. of mice	7	2	6	6	2	2	3
Spleen	0.00	0.00	1.48	17.27	0.00	1.10	21.00
Mesenteric lymph node	0.00	ND[a]	53.00	15.09	0.33	2.70	15.60

[a] Not done.

indicate that higher doses of antigen are required for the appearance of PFC of the IgA class than for PFC of the other classes in the spleen of conventional mice immunized with sheep RBC. Under our experimental conditions, the spleens of germ-free mice immunized by the parenteral injection of 2×10^8 sheep RBC showed very few IgA-PFC in comparison to the number of PFC of the other Ig classes, as found by Sell *et al.* (4). Upon parenteral immunization the requirement of a high antigen dose for the appearance of IgA-antibody forming cells in the spleen is compatible with the existence of a small number of PFC precursors in this tissue. However, it is also possible that when antigen is given in high doses it may reach a large population of cells in the lamina propria of the gut through the blood stream and trigger a local response of the IgA class (11). Such a response may later involve extraintestinal lymphoid tissues by the mechanisms previously considered (1). Migration and homing of lymphatic cells are well known to occur and may account, more specifically, for a flow of IgA immunocytes moving from the lamina propria of the gut to the mesenteric lymph nodes and the spleen, and back to the lamina propria (12–14).

SUMMARY

Germ-free mice exposed to sheep RBC by the oral route displayed an immune response in extraintestinal lymphoid tissues. Such a response in the spleen and mesenteric lymph nodes was characterized by a high percentage of PFC of the IgA class, and is at variance with that found after parenteral immunization.

REFERENCES

1. Crabbé, P. A., Nash, D. R., Bazin, H., Eyssen, H., Eyssen, H. and Heremans, J. F., J. Exp. Med., *130:* 723, 1969.
2. Walters, C. S. and Jackson, A. L., J. Immun., *101:* 541, 1968.
3. Wortis, H. H., Dresser, D. W. and Anderson, H. R., Immunology, *17:* 93, 1969.
4. Sell, S., Park, A. B. and Nordin, A. A., J. Immun., *104:* 483, 1970.
5. Jerne, N. K. and Nordin, A. A., Science, *140:* 405, 1963.
6. Dresser, D. W. and Wortis, H. H., Nature, *208:* 959, 1965.
7. Sterzl, J. and Riha, I., Nature, *208:* 858, 1965.
8. Bazin, H. and Malet, F., Immunology, *17:* 345, 1969.
9. Nordin, A. A., Proc. Soc. Exp. Biol. Med., *129:* 57, 1968.
10. Plotz, P. H., Talal, N. and Asofsky, R., J. Immun., *100:* 744, 1968.
11. Bazin, H., Path. Biol., In press.
12. Gowans, J. L. and Knight, E. J., Proc. Roy. Soc. Ser. B., *159:* 257, 1964.
13. Griscelli, C., Vassalli, P. and McCluskey, R. T., J. Exp. Med., *130:* 1427, 1969.
14. Hall, J. G. and Smith, M. E., Nature, *226:* 262, 1970.

THE JOURNAL OF IMMUNOLOGY
Copyright © 1970 by The Williams & Wilkins Co.

Vol. 105, No. 4, October 1970
Printed in U.S.A.

Experience with a Mixed Lymphocyte-Tumor Reaction as a Method of Detecting Antigenic Differences between Normal and Neoplastic Cells

STEVEN P. KANNER, MICHAEL R. MARDINEY, JR.[1] AND RICHARD J. MANGI

From the Section of Immunology and Cell Biology, National Cancer Institute, Baltimore Cancer Research Center, 3100 Wyman Park Drive, Baltimore, Maryland 21211

The need to detect both antigenic differences between host and autochthonous tumor and host reactivity to tumor has assumed increasing importance in modern cancer immunology. The development or evaluation of tumor specific antibodies and the colony inhibition technique (1) have been the main methods employed. Recently, both the leukocyte migration-inhibition test (2) and the mixed lymphocyte reaction (MLR) (3) have also been used to evaluate host reactivity to tumor (or in the latter case, antigenic differences between normal and neoplastic cells). Andersen, Bendixen and Shiodt (2) demonstrated that an extract of autologous mammary carcinoma could specifically inhibit migration of host leukocytes *in vitro* and Fridman and Kourilsky (3), using the MLR, demonstrated stimulation of lymphocytes by autologous leukemic cells. Fridman and Kourilsky could not determine whether the responses observed were those of lymphocytes presensitized to tumor antigen or were first recognition responses characteristic of the MLR.

In order to detect antigenic differences between host and syngeneic tumor, we have evaluated some of the factors of a mixed lymphocyte-tumor reaction (MLTR), using the murine mixed lymphocyte reaction as established in this laboratory (4). Two tumor systems have been studied: the P388 lymphoma (5) syngeneic to the DBA/2 mouse, and the B16 melanoma (6) syngeneic to the C57BL/6 mouse. The experiments which follow describe the reactivity of syngeneic nonimmune lymphocytes obtained from animals with no prior exposure to syngeneic tumor cells.

P388 lymphoma cells were obtained in ascitic form from 8- to 12-week-old male DBA/12 mice. The B16 melanoma, a subcutaneous tumor, was obtained from 8- to 12-week-old male C57BL/6 mice. Splenic lymphocytes were obtained from normal adult mice as previously described (4). Suspensions of melanoma cells were made in a similar manner. All cultures were performed in RPMI medium 1630 containing 20% mule serum. Reactant lymphocytes were cultured alone at a concentration of 2.5×10^6 cells/ml and in the MLTR at a concentration of 1.25×10^6 cells/ml. Tumor cells (irradiated and unirradiated) were cultured at various concentrations alone and in mixed cultures. Studies of the reaction of DBA/2 lymphocytes and P388 lymphoma cells were both of the one-way and two-way type. Only one-way lymphocyte reactivity (lymphocytes *vs* irradiated tumor cells) was studied in the lymphocyte-B16 melanoma system. Reactivity was determined by thymidine incorporation measured over 4-hr periods by the addition of 2 μCi of ^{3}H thymidine (sp. act. 1.9 Ci/mmol) as previously described (4, 7). The methods of culture, cellular irradiation, evaluation of thymidine incorporation, autoradiograph production, morphologic study and statistical evaluation were similar to those previously described (4, 7).

Various concentrations of gamma-irradiated (15,000 R) lymphoma cells were cultured alone. One-half milliliter of each of these concentrations was placed in one-way cultures with 0.5 ml of DBA/2 lymphocytes (2.5×10^6/ml). ^{3}H thymidine incorporation was measured on days 5 and 6. Greater stimulation was observed on day 5 and these data are plotted in Figure 1. Maximal stimulation was initiated by 6.28×10^4 lymphoma cells. In repeated experiments, the number of gamma-irradiated lymphoma cells necessary for stimulation ranged between 2.5×10^4 and 2.5×10^5. No stimulation was observed when equal quantities of lymphocytes and gamma-irradiated tumor were incubated together.

Daily plots, over a 9-day period, of thymidine incorporation of simultaneous one-way and two-way reactions between P388 lymphoma cells and DBA/2 lymphocytes are presented in Figures 2 to 4. The curve profiles of the two-way reaction experiment (Fig. 2) and the P388 one-way reac-

[1] Requests for reprints should be sent to Dr. Michael R. Mardiney, Jr., Head, Section of Immunology and Cell Biology, Baltimore Cancer Research Center, 3100 Wyman Park Drive, Baltimore, Maryland 21211.

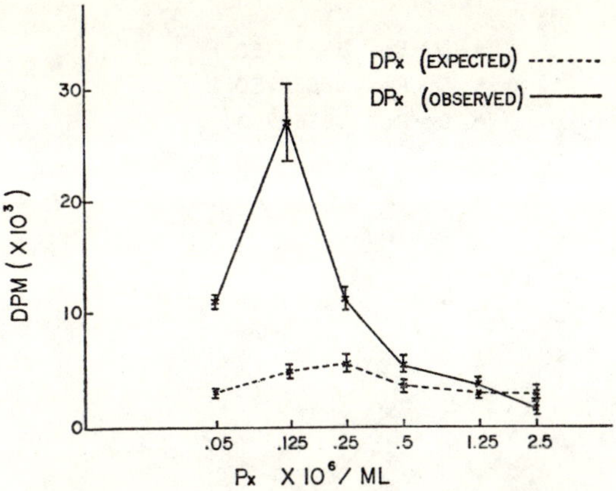

Figure 1. One-way MLTR of 1.25×10^6 DBA/2 (D) lymphocytes and varied concentrations of gamma-irradiated P388 lymphoma cells (P_x). The numbers on the abscissa represent the concentrations of P_x used in unmixed cultures. One-half of these concentrations was used in mixed cultures (DP_x observed). DP_x (expected) $-\frac{1}{2}$ D cultured alone + $\frac{1}{2}$ P_x cultured alone.

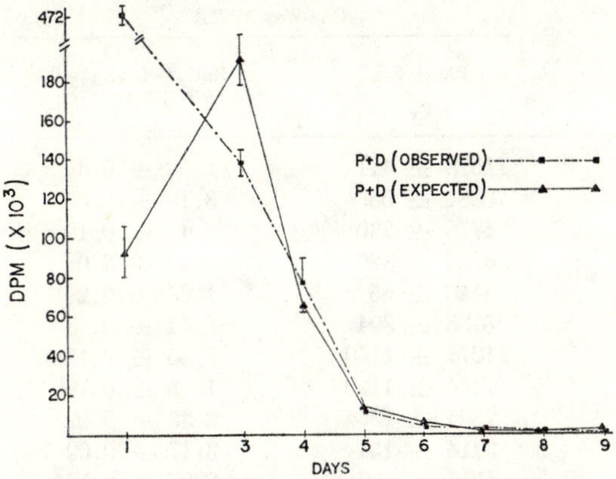

Figure 2. Two-way MLTR. P = P388 cells; D = DBA/2 lymphocytes. Concentration of controls: D = 2.5×10^6; P = 0.5×10^6. One-half milliliter of each control was used in mixed culture.

tion experiment (Fig. 3) (lymphoma reactant) were essentially the same. Enhanced activity was observed only on day 1. These curves contrast to the one-way experiment (lymphocyte reactant) depicted in Figure 4. Enhanced activity occurred from days 4 through 7 with peak activity on day 5. In 10 one-way lymphocyte-irradiated tumor experiments, peak stimulation occurred on day 6 in 7 and day 5 in 3 (Table I).

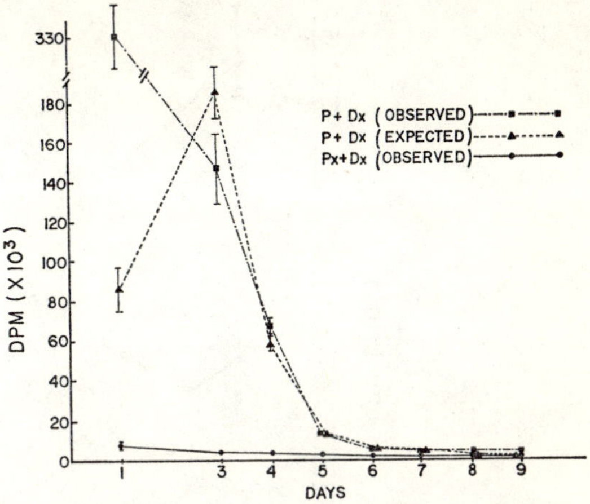

Figure 3. One-way MLTR (tumor reactant). P = P388 cells; D = DBA/2 lymphocytes; P_x = 15,000 R: D_x = 450 R. Control and experimental cell concentrations as in Figure 2. Expected results determined as in Figure 1.

Two experiments were performed in which C57BL/6 lymphocytes were incubated with varied concentrations of gamma-irradiated (15,000 R) melanoma cells and thymidine incorporation was measured on days 4, 5 and 6. The results of these experiments were identical. In general, lymphocytes were stimulated in increasing fashion as the concentration of melanoma cells and days of incubation increased. Table II lists the results of one of these experiments.

DISCUSSION

The mixed lymphocyte reaction is considered an *in vitro* recognition phenomenon analogous to the recognition which occurs *in vivo* during the evolution of first-set graft rejection. The murine mixed lymphocyte reaction has been previously shown to develop peak reactivity on day 5 or 6 with occasional peaks on day 7 (4). No reactivity has been demonstrated when lymphocytes were incubated with syngeneic irradiated lymphocytes (R. J. Mangi and M. R. Mandiney, Jr., to be published). The sensitivity of the two-way reaction is greater than that of the one-way reaction although the latter is sensitive enough to detect histocompatibility differences of both H2 and at individual minor loci (to be published). The results of the experiments described here suggest that a one-way mixed lymphocyte-tumor reaction can be used to detect antigenic differences between host and syngeneic tumor.

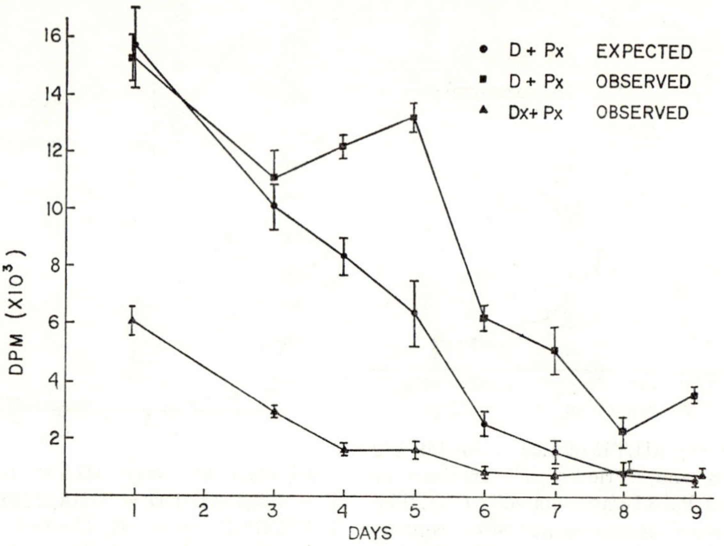

Figure 4. One-way MLTR (lymphocyte reacant). Concentrations and symbols as in Figures 2 and 3.

TABLE I

One-way MLTR between DBA/2 lymphocytes and P388 cells

Experiment[b]	Control: DPM ± S.E. Cells Alone		One-Way MLTR	
	D[c]	P_x[d]	DPM ± S.E. DP_x	Ratio[a] of increased activity ± S.D.
1	10880 ± 15	188 ± 34[e]	11528 ± 411	2.08 ± 0.35
1	10880 ± 15	2248 ± 330[f]	20384 ± 65	3.10 ± .05
2	2214 ± 509	1781 ± 50[e]	4778 ± 230	2.4 ± 0.19
3	4946 ± 10	1333 ± 305[f]	6760 ± 329	2.15 ± 0.08
4	5322 ± 1125	104 ± 5[e]	4440 ± 55	1.63 ± 0.29
5	4818 ± 614	275 ± 24[f]	6138 ± 394	2.41 ± 0.18
6	6179 ± 604	3033 ± 472[e]	11271 ± 1150	2.45 ± 0.15
7	8130 ± 608	3712 ± 182[f]	7154 ± 1100	1.23 ± 0.19
8	6418 ± 1166	322 ± 82[e]	7884 ± 1554	2.33 ± 0.09
9	1955 ± 110	132 ± 25[f]	3414 ± 154	3.17 ± 0.09
10	3245 ± 946	167 ± 21[e]	4015 ± 630	2.35 ± 0.17

[a] Ratio of increased activity $= \frac{2 \times \text{cell mix}}{\text{Sum of cells cultured alone}}$.

[b] Experiments 2, 3 and 7 peaked on day 5; the remainder peaked on day 6.

[c] D, DBA/2 lymphocytes (2.5×10^6/ml).

[d] P_x, gamma-irradiated P388 cells.

[e] 1×10^5 cells/ml.

[f] 5×10^5 cells/ml.

Peak reactivity in the one-way MLTR (lymphocyte reactant) occurred on days 5 and 6 and is analogous in occurrence to the normal one-way mixed lymphocyte reaction. This system differed from the normal reaction in that the number of tumor cells necessary to initiate stimulation was not necessarily equal to the total number of cells in the reacting lymphocyte population. We observed two extremes in our experiments. Although equivalent concentrations of irradiated lymphoma cells did not stimulate normal lymphocytes, smaller concentrations were

TABLE II

Ratio of increased activity (± S.D.) in one-way MLTR of C57BL/6 lymphocytes-B16 melanoma[a]

Stimulating Cell Concentration (× 10^6)	Days		
	4	5	6
M_x[b] 0.05	2.06 ± .002	2.04 ± 0.09	3.76 ± 0.08
M_x 0.1	2.95 ± 0.02	2.76 ± 0.15	5.24 ± 0.12
M_x 0.25	3.85 ± 0.04	4.35 ± 0.03	6.72 ± 0.44
M_x 0.5	3.54 ± 0.003	6.39 ± 0.05	11.30 ± 0.14
M_x 1.0	5.30 ± 0.02	9.11 ± 0.18	6.27 ± 0.02
M_x 2.5	5.39 ± 0.04	5.68 ± 0.18	7.06 ± 0.14

[a] Ratio of increased activity $= \frac{2 \times \text{cell mix}}{\text{Sum of cells cultured alone}}$.

[b] M_x, gamma-irradiated melanoma cells; 0.5 ml of each of the concentrations listed were used as stimulants in the MLTR.

effective stimulants. In contrast, C57BL/6 lymphocytes responded to concentrations of B16 melanoma cells similar to the concentration of stimulating lymphocytes in a standard one-way reaction.

We have observed that cell concentration is important in detecting the standard mouse mixed lymphocyte reaction (4). It does not appear that differences in size between the tumor cells and the normal spleen lymphocytes cause the results observed since both populations of tumor cells occupy approximately the same volume (approximately three times that of normal splenic lymphocytes). Whether toxic or inhibitory factors are secreted by the P388 tumor cell population is not known. Further experimentation should elucidate this phenomenon. It is important to emphasize this observation since reactivity in other systems may be missed if only one stimulating concentration of tumor is used. Further, in order to obtain peak reactivity in our system, it was also essential to assay cultures during periods of possible optimal stimulation.

Continued use of the MLTR will hopefully confirm its effectiveness in detecting antigenic differences between normal and neoplastic cells. It may also be expected that this test may allow for a practicable and sensitive assay of host reactivity to tumor.

SUMMARY

A one-way mixed lymphocyte-tumor reaction having kinetics of DNA synthesis similar to those of the standard mixed lymphocyte reaction is described. This reaction may prove to be effective in detecting both antigenic differences between normal and neoplastic cells and host reactivity to tumor.

REFERENCES

1. Hellstrom, I. and Hellstrom, K. E., Int. J. Cancer, *4:* 587, 1969.
2. Andersen, V., Bendixen, G. and Shiodt, T., Acta Med. Scand., *186:* 101, 1969.
3. Fridman, W. H. and Kourilsky, F. M., Nature, *224:* 277, 1969.
4. Mangi, R. J. and Mardiney, M. R., Jr., J. Immun., *105:* 90, 1970.
5. Evans, V. J., La Rouk, J. F., Yosiga, T. H. and Potter, M., Exp. Cell Res., *32:* 212, 1963.
6. *Handbook on Genetically Standardized Jax Mice*, Edited by E. L. Green, p. 57, Bar Harbor Times Publishing Co., Bar Harbor, Maine, 1968.
7. Bredt, A. B. and Mardiney, M. R., Jr., Transplantation, *8:* 763, 1969.

THE JOURNAL OF IMMUNOLOGY
Vol. 105, No. 5, November 1970

BIOCHEMICAL DEMONSTRATION OF THE ACTIVATABLE ESTERASE OF THE RABBIT NEUTROPHIL INVOLVED IN THE CHEMOTACTIC RESPONSE[1]

PETER A. WARD AND ELMER L. BECKER[2]

From the Immunobiology Branch, Armed Forces Institute of Pathology, Washington, D. C. 20305, and Walter Reed Army Institute of Research, Washington, D. C. 20012.

Received for publication June 29, 1970

Direct biochemical evidence is provided that the rabbit blood neutrophil contains a precursor esterase involved in the cell response to the chemotactic stimulus $C\overline{567}$, and that contact of the cell with chemotactic factor leads to activation of the proesterase. Rabbit blood leukocytes contain esterase 1, that is, an enzyme capable of hydrolyzing acetyl-DL-phenylalanine β-naphthyl ester. This activity can be ascribed largely, if not entirely, to the presence of neutrophils. Comparing blood leukocytes with peritoneal (exudate) neutrophils, the former cells contain greater esterase activity as well as greater chemotactic responsiveness. Treatment of blood leukocytes, but not peritoneal neutrophils, with chemotactic factor results in the acquisition of esterase activity ("esterase activation") and chemotactic deactivation (loss of chemotactic responsiveness). By using highly purified complement and preparative (density gradient) ultracentrifugation, and employing agents that dissociate the macromolecular chemotactic factor, the phenomena of chemotactic activity, esterase-activating capacity and deactivating potential have been shown to be interrelated and clearly ascribable to $C\overline{567}$. The esterase that appears in the blood leukocyte as a result of interaction with $C\overline{567}$ can be identified as esterase 1, on the basis of exquisite sensitivity to inhibitory effects of phosphonate compounds at very low concentrations (10^{-8} M). These data provide direct biochemical support for the original hypothesis that the chemotactic response of the neutrophil to the complement chemotactic factor $C\overline{567}$ involves an interaction which results in the conversion of the cell-bound proesterase to an active esterase. The biochemical role of this esterase in the kinetic behavior of the granulocyte is not known. This information may have special relevance to at least four other phenomena in which activation of a protesterase to an active esterase as the cause of an "allergic response" has been postulated on the basis of indirect evidence.

Several series of *p*-nitrophenyl ethyl phosphonates inhibit the chemotactic response of the rabbit peritoneal neutrophil to the complement-derived chemotactic factor, $C\overline{567}$. (1) The importance of the *p*-nitrophenyl ethyl phosphonates in this connection is that they are irreversible inhibitors of a class of enzymes, the so-called "serine esterases." The phosphonates have the following general structure:

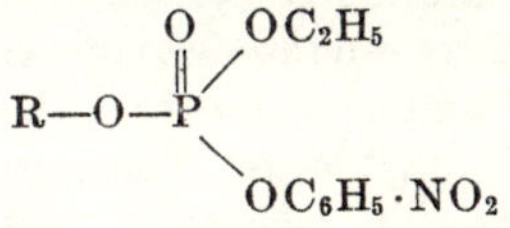

The inhibitory activity of the phosphonates varies with changes in the structure of the R group to give the so-called "inhibition profiles." The different serine esterases can be differentiated from one another by means of the different inhibition profiles that they give with the various series of phosphonates (2).

To explain the nature of the inhibition of

[1] Supported by Grant AI-07291-AIA from the National Institutes of Health, Bethesda, Maryland 20014, under the auspices of Universites Associated for Research and Education in Pathology, Inc.

[2] Present address: Department of Pathology, University of Connecticut, School of Medicine, Farmington, Connecticut.

phosphonate esters, we hypothesized that the chemotaxis of rabbit neutrophils induced by $C\overline{567}$ involves the activation of a leukocyte esterase, termed the "activatable esterase." It was further supposed that the activatable esterase exists in an enzymatically inert form on the cell and is thus insusceptible to inhibition by the phosphonates. On contact of the leukocyte with $C\overline{567}$, the serine esterase becomes activated and susceptible to phosphonate inhibition (1, 3).

Subsequent work aimed at substantiating this hypothesis showed that incubation of rabbit polymorphonuclear leukocytes (hereafter called leukocytes) with $C\overline{567}$ induced a progressive decrease in the chemotactic responsiveness of the leukocyte; the cells were "deactivated" (3). Deactivation was prevented if the phosphonate ester was present during incubation of leukocytes with the chemotactic factor. The profiles of inhibition of deactivation (protection against deactivation) were the same as the inhibition profiles of chemotactic responsiveness to $C\overline{567}$ determined in previous studies, implying that the same activatable esterase was involved in both chemotaxis and deactivation. Aromatic amino acid derivatives also protected against deactivation and this protection was specific; non-aromatic amino acid derivatives did not protect (3). In addition, the aromatic amino acid derivatives directly and specifically inhibited chemotaxis. In view of these results the original hypothesis was expanded: "The activatable esterase of the rabbit polymorphonuclear leukocyte is a serine esterase with a special affinity for aromatic amino acid derivatives, that is, the activatable esterase is an aromatic amino acid esterase" (4).

In the immediately preceding paper (4) we showed that the rabbit peritoneal leukocyte has not one but three esterases capable of hydrolyzing the aromatic amino acid ester, acetyl-DL-phenylalanine β-naphthyl ester. These esterases were termed esterase 1, esterase 2 and esterase 3. Esterase 1 is inhibited by phosphonates in concentrations between 10^{-8} to 10^{-9} M; under the same circumstances, 10^{-4} M to 10^{-6} M is required to inhibit esterase 2, and esterase 3 is not inhibited at all. The inhibition profiles of esterase 1 differ profoundly from those of esterase 2 but are essentially the same as the activatable esterase, as determined both by inhibition of chemotaxis and protection against deactivation (3). It was tentatively concluded that esterase 1 is the activated form of the activated esterase.

Using rabbit peritoneal polymorphonuclear leukocytes it proved impossible to show the presence of an inert precursor form of esterase 1. To explain this failure, we considered the possibility that a very large proportion of the precursor form of the activatable esterase might have become activated in the migration of the leukocyte to the peritoneal cavity in response to glycogen. Based upon this reasoning we have turned in this work to the rabbit blood polymorphonuclear leukocyte as a source of acetyl-DL-phenylalanine β-naphthyl esterase activity with the hope that more of the activatable esterase might be in the precursor form.

This paper will present the evidence that rabbit blood leukocytes possess acetyl-DL-phenylalanine β-napthyl esterase activity in an inert form. This can be activated by treatment of the leukocyte with the chemotactic factor $C\overline{567}$. When activated, the esterase has the properties associated with esterase 1. In the precursor form it is insusceptible to inhibition by phosphonate esters.

MATERIALS AND METHODS

Buffer. Unless otherwise stated, the buffer (TGS) used throughout consisted of 0.15 M NaCl, 0.005 M tris (hydroxymethyl) aminomethane, pH 7.3 (Fisher Scientific Company, Silver Spring, Md.) and 0.1% gelatin (Difco Laboratories, Detroit, Mich.).

Leukocytes. These experiments were confined to studies with rabbit leukocytes. Neutrophilic granulocytes (neutrophils) in essentially pure (98% or better) suspension were obtained from the rabbit peritoneal cavity 5 hr after the injection of 0.1% glycogen in saline (5). Blood leukocytes were obtained by the method of Boyüm (6) using the following modification: 30 ml of 50% sodium diatrizoate (Hypaque, Winthrop Laboratories, New York, N. Y.) were added to 11.5 ml distilled water. One volume of diluted Hypaque was added to 4 volumes of 6% dextran (m.w. 240,000, Pharmachem Corporation, Bethlehem, Pa.) in water. Rabbit blood collected in ethylenediaminetetraacetic acid (EDTA), pH 7.3, using 1 volume EDTA/49 volumes blood, was overlaid on the diluted Hypaque. After settling for 1.5 hr at 25° C, the leukocyte-rich supernatant was removed and the cells were obtained by centrifugation at 500 × G for 10 min. In all experiments except those listed in Table I this procedure for obtaining leukocytes was followed.

A second procedure, suggested by Dr. Peter Henson (La Jolla, California), for obtaining blood leukocytes was also employed. Blood to which EDTA (see above) was added as anticoagulant was centrifuged at 3000 × G for 20 min at 5° C. The resulting buffy coat was aspirated; it was rich in mononuclear cells. The sedimented red cells contained most of the neutrophils. This mixture of red cells and neutrophils was added to an equal volume of 2.5% gelatin in saline. After 30 min at 25° C, the bulk of the red cells had settled out. The neutrophil-rich supernatant was centrifuged at 500 × G for 5 min to obtain the leukocytes. The cell preparations were then washed and resuspended in TGS. By selecting one of these three preparations it was possible to have a suspension rich in red cells, mononuclear cells or neutrophils.

Considerable problems in obtaining adequate numbers of neutrophils (1.5 to 2.5 × 10^8) were encountered with rabbit blood, largely due to the low ratio of neutrophils to other leukocytes. In some experiments it was possible to raise the proportion of blood neutrophils from the usual 25% to >60% by mating the rabbit for a brief period (5 min) before cardiac puncture. This in no way appeared to affect the enzyme (esterase) status or the functional (chemotactic) capacity of the blood neutrophils. We are indebted to Dr. Henson for suggesting this technique.

Chemotactic assay. The micropore filter technique was used, employing the *in vitro* chambers previously described (5). Micropore filters of 0.65 μ pore size were employed. These permit movement of neutrophils, but not of mononuclear cells. After the chambers were incubated for an appropriate period the filters were removed from the chambers, stained and mounted on glass slides. Five fields at high power were randomly selected and the total number of cells which migrated below the uppermost monolayer were counted. This number was the measure of the chemotactic activity of the neutrophils. Unless otherwise indicated, the chemotactic factor employed for measuring the degree of deactivation was a culture filtrate (diluted to 10% in medium 199) obtained by incubation of an untyped strain of *Escherichia coli* in medium 199 for 24 hr at 37° C (7). This permitted the use of a standardized chemotactic agent in each experiment.

Chemotactic factors. All experiments unless otherwise noted used partially purified rabbit $\overline{C567}$. Procedures previously described in detail (5) were employed for the production and partial purification of $\overline{C567}$. Briefly, the euglobulin fraction of rabbit serum was obtained by isoelectric precipitation, followed by ion exchange chromatography. The resulting C567 was activated by incubation with sensitized red cell stromata containing the first four reacting components of rabbit complement. A portion of the C567 preparation was set aside before activation and served as a control for subsequent experiments. Another series of chemotactic preparations consisted of supernatants from intermediate complexes made from highly purified components of human complement; there were kindly supplied by Drs. Hans J. Müller-Eberhard and Otto Götze (Scripps Clinic and Research Foundation, La Jolla, Calif.). The complexes were made using sensitized sheep red cells to which were added highly purified human C1, C4, oxidized C2, and C3. Various additional highly purified components were then added, the mixture was incubated at 37° C for 30 min (neutral pH) and the supernatant was then obtained by centrifugation.

Acetyl-DL-phenylalanine β-naphthyl ester. This substrate was obtained from Mann Research Laboratories of New York. For use, 8 mg were dissolved in 3 ml of N,N-dimethyl formamide and 6 ml of acetone (both solvents were reagent grade from Fisher Scientific Company, Silver Spring, Md.). Immediately before the cells were to be assayed one volume of the substrate solution was added to nine volumes of TGS.

Coupling reagent. 11.5 mg of fast scarlet salt, GGN (General Dyestuff Company, Chicago, Ill.) were freshly dissolved in 7.5 ml of distilled water just before use.

Esterase assay. The esterase assay was fundamentally the same as described previously, in that the β naphthol set free by the action of the esterase (APNe-ase) on the substrate, acetyl-DL-phenylalanine β-naphthyl ester, was measured by the intensity of the orange-yellow color it forms when conjugated to the fast scarlet diazonium salt (4). The assay used previously was insufficiently sensitive, mainly due to the red cells and leukocytes competing with the substrate for the diazonium salt. This difficulty was overcome by precipitating the cells and protein with acetone (thus stopping the enzyme reaction) before adding the coupling reagent.

In the present procedure, 0.5 ml of cells containing 1×10^7 polymorphonuclear leukocytes was added to 2.0 ml of substrate. The suspension of cells and substrate were incubated at 37° C with shaking. Samples of 0.5 ml were removed at 0, 15, 30 and 45 min, or at other indicated intervals, and added to 1 ml of acetone. The precipitated cells and protein were centrifuged and the supernatant was added to 0.15 ml of the coupling reagent. After standing 20 min the resulting color was read at 485 nm in a model 300 Gilford spectrophotometer. Any turbidity which developed was removed by recentrifugation. Appropriate blanks were treated in the same way.

This assay was used for all experiments in which the chemotactic factor was employed to activate the cell esterase. Under these circumstances the 45-min reading (period of incubation of substrate with cells) was employed. For experiments comparing the esterase activity of blood and peritoneal leukocytes, the previously described assay procedure was employed using 5- or 10-min periods of incubation of cells with substrate. In this latter assay the presence of red cells tends to depress apparent activity. This makes even more significant the finding of greater esterase activity in the blood leukocytes.

Pre-incubation of cells with phosphonates. In all experiments except those in which the activity of blood and peritoneal leukocytes were compared, the leukocytes were pretreated with phosphonate in order to inactivate esterase 1 and 2 and reduce the background level of esterase activity. The cells in TGS in a volume not exceeding 10 ml in TGS were incubated for 15 min at room temperature with 5×10^{-5} M *p*-nitrophenyl ethyl 5-chloropentylphosphonate. At the end of this time 200 ml of TGS were added, the cells were centrifuged, and the tubes were thoroughly drained. The cells were then further washed in 200 ml TGS and then brought to 2.0×10^7/ml polymorphonuclear leukocytes in TGS. Large volumes were used to wash the cells in order to be certain that any residual phosphonate was below that required to inhibit esterase 1, that is, below 10^{-8} to 10^{-9} M.

Deactivation. The extent of deactivation (see above and (3)) is determined by the following calculation: the ratio of the chemotactic counts of cells treated with chemotactic factor to the counts of cells not treated with chemotactic factor, times 100, subtracted from 100, is the percentage deactivation.

Inhibitors. CBZ-glutamyl-L-tyrosine (Mann Research Laboratories, New York, N. Y.) and fumaropimaric acid (see reference 8 for source) were added to the appropriate $C\overline{567}$ preparation to give a final concentration of 0.005 M. It has been shown that these agents cause dissociation of the $C\overline{567}$ complex whether or not the complex is chemotactically active (8, 9). The mixture was then added to the leukocyte suspension, incubated for 30 min at 25° C and TGS added. The cells were centrifuged, resuspended in TGS and then assayed for chemotactic responsiveness as well as esterase activity.

Ultracentrifugal separation. When high speed centrifugation in a sucrose density gradient was carried out, samples of 0.2 ml were overlaid on a sucrose gradient, from 7.5% to 35% sucrose in phosphate buffer, pH 7.3, ionic strength 0.05. Using a B60 International Equipment Company (Needham, Mass.) ultracentrifuge, sedimentation proceeded at 5° C for 15 hr at 55,000 rpm in a swinging bucket rotor (SB405). Samples were collected by perforation of the bottom of the appropriate tube.

RESULTS

Correlation of enzyme activity with neutrophil content of blood leukocyte preparation. Previous experiments using cells in peritoneal exudates indicated that APNe-ase activity was a function of the number of neutrophils present. It nevertheless became necessary to determine if in the leukocyte preparations from peripheral blood the esterase activity could be due to cells other than the neutrophil. Cells were fractionated by centrifugation followed by red cell sedimentation in the presence of gelatin, as described above. The results of two experiments are summarized in Table I. In preparation A there was unusually good separation of granulocytes from mononuclear cells (including lymphocytes and monocytes). The contribution of esterase activity by the mononuclear cells was trivial, and red cells had no demonstrable activity. In the B preparations less effective separation of the leukocytes was achieved. The esterase activity in the 2B

TABLE I

Association of APNe-ase activity with neutrophils present in blood leukocyte preparations

Preparation	Number of Cells Present			Esterase Activity[b]
	Leukocytes ($\times 10^{-6}$)			
	Neutrophils	Mononuclears[a]	Red cells ($\times 10^{-7}$)	
1A	10	3.2	8.5	0.765
1B	2.2	10	40	0.030
1C	0	0	40	0.000
2A	4.0	6.0	1.6	0.560
2B	2.5	9.5	2.5	0.225
2C	<0.1	<0.1	1.7	0.075

[a] Includes both monocytes and lymphocytes.
[b] Increase in the optical density readings at 485 nm after 10 min incubation at 37° C.

preparation was probably due to the presence of 2.5×10^6 neutrophils, although whether the mononuclear cells added any activity could not be directly ascertained. The findings from these and other experiments indicate that the APNe-ase activity in preparations of blood leukocytes can be accounted for either completely or in very large part by the neutrophils.

Esterase activity and chemotactic responsiveness in blood and peritoneal leukocytes from the same rabbit. In 20 different rabbits both blood leukocytes and peritoneal neutrophils were compared for esterase activity. In 15 animals comparisons were made both of the total esterase activity (against acetyl-DL-phenylalanine β-naphthyl ester) and of the chemotactic responsiveness of the blood leukocytes and the peritoneal neutrophils obtained from the same animal (Table II). The blood leukocyte had more activity than the peritoneal neutrophil and this difference was statistically highly significant, amounting to 40% to 50% in four instances. In only three cases did peritoneal neutrophils contain more enzyme activity, and this difference failed to exceed 25%. The possibility exists that in the blood leukocyte preparations the additional amount of esterase activity could be due to the presence of mononuclear cells. However, in at least three different preparations the numbers of non-neutrophil leukocytes were sufficiently small (<10% of the neutrophils) as to render this possibility unlikely.

The blood leukocytes were chemotactically more active on the average. The differences in chemotactic responsiveness were less evident than the differences in esterase activity, but nevertheless they were statistically highly significant. Although these experiments were made difficult by the occasional presence of large numbers of red cells in the blood leukocyte preparations, they nevertheless indicate that the blood neutrophil has a greater content of APNe-ase activity as well as a greater capacity for chemotactic responsiveness than does the peritoneal neutrophil. The latter cell, it should be stressed, is an exudate cell.

TABLE II

Differences in esterase activity and chemotactic responsiveness of blood and peritoneal leukocytes from same rabbit

Animal No.	Total Esterase Activity in Leukocytes[a]			Chemotactic Responsiveness[b]		
	Blood	Peritoneal	Difference[c]	Blood	Peritoneal	Difference[d]
9	0.525	0.180	0.345	350	250	100
10	0.255	0.230	0.025	270	220	50
11	0.635	0.325	0.310	220	220	0
1	0.380	0.215	0.165	120	75	45
2	0.935	0.710	0.225	45	110	−65
3	0.510	0.430	0.080	220	140	80
14	0.760	0.465	0.295			
15	0.610	0.460	0.150			
16	0.615	0.520	0.095	125	180	−55
17	0.405	0.230	0.175	125	150	−25
37	0.490	0.400	0.090	250	100	150
38	0.480	0.360	0.120	230	120	110
40				170	180	−10
41	0.340	0.225	0.115	120	130	−10
42	0.790	0.930	−0.140	250	150	100
43	0.550	0.560	−0.010	90	140	−50
44	0.390	0.275	0.115	125	210	−85
45	0.600	0.390	0.125	180	240	−60
6	0.505	0.720	0.115			
16	0.510	0.390	0.120			
17	0.305	0.390	−0.090			
46				200	95	105
47				170	160	10
48				130	120	10
51				170	100	70

[a] Hydrolysis of acetyl-DL-phenylalanine β-naphthyl ester after 5 min incubation with 1×10^6 neutrophils at 37°C.
[b] Chemotactic response to bacterial factor (see text).
[c] Mean difference ± standard error = 0.121 ± 0.028, $p < 0.01$.
[d] Mean difference ± standard error = 43 ± 13.

TABLE III

Comparison of activities of esterases 1, 2 and 3 in blood and peritoneal leukocytes from the same rabbit

Experiment No.	Blood Cell Esterases[a]			Peritoneal Cell Esterases		
	1	2	3	1	2	3
41	0.480	0.020	0.095	0.460	0.090	0.040
42	0.250	0.030	0.060	0.115	0.040	0.060
43	0.840	0.040	0.060	0.700	0.000	0.090
6	0.465	0.030	0.010	0.350	0.040	0.000
16	0.455	0.025	0.030	0.655	0.065	0.000
17	0.235	0.070	0.000	0.355	0.035	0.000
43	0.500	0.020	0.030	0.500	0.060	0.000
44	0.350	0.035	0.005	0.245	0.010	0.020
45	0.550	0.035	0.015	0.420	0.045	0.010
37	0.430	0.050	0.010	0.370	0.030	0.000
38	0.660	0.100	0.030	0.620	0.060	0.010

[a] Different esterase activities are defined according to reference 4. Preparations have been adjusted to contain 1×10^7 neutrophils.

Comparison of three esterases in blood and peritoneal leukocytes. By pretreating leukocytes with 5-chloropentyl phosphonate at concentrations of 4×10^{-5} or 1×10^{-7} M it is possible to discern the contributions of three different esterases capable of hydrolyzing acetyl-DL-phenylalanine β-naphthyl ester (4). In Table III the results are given, comparing once again blood leukocytes with peritoneal neutrophils obtained from the same rabbit. With both blood and peritoneal leukocytes the preponderant activity was found to be due to esterase 1, with usually less than 20% of the total activity being attributable to esterases 2 and 3. In general, the content of esterase 1 was higher in blood leukocytes compared to peritoneal leukocytes. This expands the findings presented in Table II, where the contributions of the individual esterases were not defined. Although blood leukocytes compared to peritoneal leukocytes generally had more activity in terms of esterases 2 and 3, the only firm conclusion to be drawn from these experiments is that most of the esterase activity in blood and peritoneal leukocytes is due to esterase 1.

The increase of esterase activity induced by contact of blood leukocytes with partially purified chemotactic factor. Blood leukocytes (0.5 ml containing usually 1×10^7 neutrophils)[3] were treated with 0.3 ml of various preparations consisting of a C567-rich fraction (not chemotactically active) or a $\overline{C567}$-rich fraction (chemotactically activated with EAC1-4 stromata in TGS buffer). After incubation for 15 min at 25°C, the cells were diluted with 4 ml of TGS, centrifuged at 500 × G for 5 min, then resuspended either in TGS for the esterase assay or in medium 199 (with 10% homologous serum) for the chemotaxis assays. A compilation of the results from 12 experiments (Table IV) makes it clear that incubation of blood leukocytes with $\overline{C567}$ leads to a statistically significant increase in esterase activity in the treated cells, concomitant with a reduction in the chemotacic responsiveness of the same batch of cells. The increased enzyme activity, while rarely exceeding a 20% increment in cell esterase activity, was nevertheless definite and reproducible. Incubation of leukocytes with C567 had little, if any, effect on either esterase or chemotactic activity. Not listed here is the finding that esterase activity in the C567 and $\overline{C567}$ preparations was negligible (equivalent to the blank control). This indicates that the increased esterase activity in the leukocytes was not due to addition (for instance, by absorption) to the rabbit leukocyte of an enzyme present in the $\overline{C567}$ preparation.

Demonstration that the acquired esterase is due to cell interaction with $\overline{C567}$. Since the $\overline{C567}$ was only partially purified, it became necessary to determine if the newly acquired esterase activity of the blood leukocyte was, in fact, attributable

[3] In this and all succeeding experiments, leukocytes were pretreated with 5×10^{-5} M 5-chloropentyl phosphonate as described in *Materials and Methods* in order to reduce pre-existing esterase activity.

TABLE IV

Induction by chemotactic factor of increased esterase activity with concomitant loss of chemotactic responsiveness of blood leukocytes

	Esterase Activity		Chemotactic Activity	
	No. of experiments	O.D. at 485 nm	No. of experiments	Cells in 5 fields
Difference in values of leukocytes treated with $\overline{C567}$ and those treated with C567	12[a]	+0.037 ± 0.012[b] (p > 0.01, <0.02)	11	−82 ± 12 (p < 0.01)
Differences in values of leukocytes treated with C567 and those treated with buffer	8	−0.008 ± 0.012	7	−17 ± 18

[a] In some experiments there were insufficient leukocytes for buffer control. In one experiment, the chemotactic responsiveness of the cells was not determined.

[b] All similar values represent mean difference ± standard error. The values in the lower half of the chart are not statistically significantly different.

to an effect of $\overline{C567}$ on the leukocyte. In order to determine this, two different experiments were carried out. In the first, supernatants with chemotactic activity were obtained after incubating sensitized sheep erythrocytes with supernatants containing all of the first seven components of human complement to which varying amounts of C5 had been added. Preparations from these highly purified components are described in the section on *Materials and Methods*. The assays done on each of the five complement preparations to which 1×10^7 blood neutrophils and different amounts of C5 were added included assessment of chemotactic activity (in 100 μl), ability of the preparations to cause leukocyte deactivation (loss of chemotactic responsiveness after incubation of leukocytes with preparations), and leukocytic esterase-activating capacity of the complement-derived material. The latter two procedures were done essentially as described in experiments where the partially purified $\overline{C567}$ was employed (see prior section) and the assays were performed on the same batch of cells. After incubation of blood leukocytes with complement containing supernatants the cells were washed with and resuspended (following centrifugation) in TGS. One portion (2×10^6 neutrophils) was removed for assay of chemotactic responsiveness to the bacterial factor, while the other (containing 2×10^7 neutrophils) was retained for the esterase assay. Figure 1 shows very clearly that when 1 μg C5 was used (the optimal concentration) there was a definite increase of esterase activity (ΔOD. = 0.060) following contact of

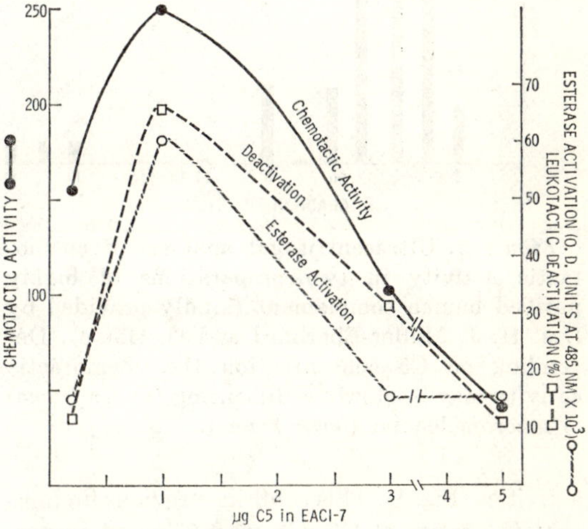

Figure 1. Comparison of three activities (chemotaxis, deactivation and esterase activation in the neutrophil) in purified human complement preparations as a function of the amount of C5.

leukocytes with the chemotactic factor made with highly purified components. In addition Figure 1 also demonstrates that there exists within a given preparation a very good correlation between chemotactic activity and the ability of the sample to deactivate (chemotactically) the leukocyte and to activate (cause the cell to acquire) the esterase that hydrolyzes acetyl-DL-phenylalanine β-napthyl ester. For reasons that are not evident, the amount of C5 used in the C1-7 preparations significantly influenced the three activities just mentioned. Excessive quantities of C5 result in a sharp drop-off in all three

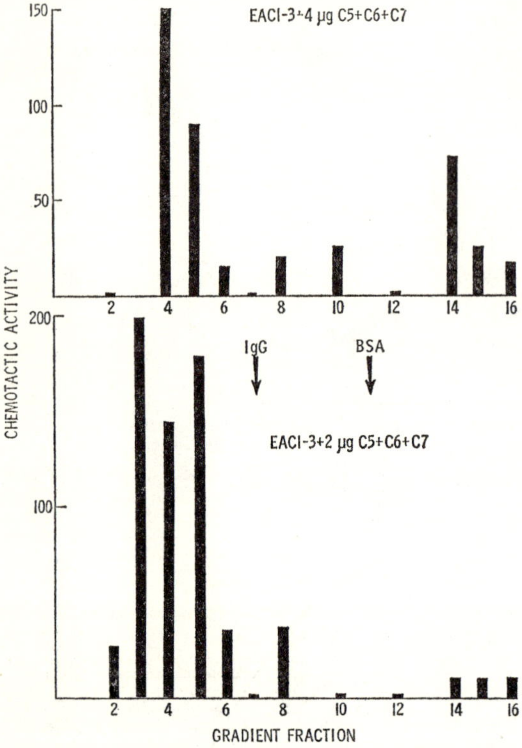

Figure 2. Ultracentrifugal analysis of chemotactic activity in two preparations of highly purified human complement (kindly provided by Drs. H. J. Müller-Eberhard and O. Götze). Depending on C5 concentration the chemotactic activity may be slowly sedimenting (*upper frame*) or macromolecular (*lower frame*).

activities (Fig. 1). This confirms previous findings that the ratios of C5, C6, and C7 used in preparing the activated trimolecular complex influenced the amount of chemotactic activity (5, 9). The controls for this experiment consisted of leukocytes treated with TGS, or treated with a preparation C1-7 in which C5 was lacking. This complement preparation was devoid of chemotactic activity. The leukocytes treated with these preparations showed no deactivation and no esterase activation.

Either the chemotactic factor C5a or C$\overline{567}$ could have been responsible for the results pictured in Figure 1. In order to distinguish which chemotactic factor was responsible, the supernatants from the interactions of C1-7 were analyzed by density gradient ultracentrifugation (Fig. 2). When a lower amount of C5 was used (2 μg), the chemotactic activity was entirely of the rapidly sedimenting variety, that is, macromolecular (Fig. 2, lower frame), whereas preparations made from a higher amount of C5 (4 μg) had biphasic chemotactic activities (Fig. 2, upper frame). These results indicate that with 2 μg C5, the only detectable chemotactic activity produced was of high molecular weight, that is, C$\overline{567}$. By increasing the amount of C5 to 4 μg there was some indication of the appearance of a chemotactic factor of low molecular weight, presumably C5a. These results are similar to previous findings (10). As shown in Figure 2, maximum esterase activation and chemotactic activity were produced when 1 μg C5 was used in the mixture. This, taken with the results of the ultracentrifugal studies, indicates that the esterase activation pictured in Figure 1 is a function of C$\overline{567}$. To what extent C5a can also activate the proesterase of the leukocyte is presently not known.

Because only limited numbers of preparations derived from highly purified complement components could be obtained, another experiment was devised to determine indirectly whether the phenomenon of esterase activation could be attributed to an effect of C$\overline{567}$ (Table V). C$\overline{567}$ as well as C$\overline{567}$-rich preparations to which CBZ-glutamyl-L-tyrosine or fumaroprimaric acid had been added were used. Each agent has been demonstrated to cause dissociation of the trimolecular complex, and thus disappearance of its biologic (chemotactic) activity (8, 9). Each compound precluded the ability of C$\overline{567}$ to cause esterase activation in the blood leukocytes, although controls showed the anticipated increment in esterase activity of nearly 10% (Table V). Unfortunately, the amount of deactivation of leukocytes induced by the C$\overline{567}$-rich preparation was sufficiently low as to prevent a correlation with the esterase activation. These data provide indirect confirmation of the direct demonstration (Figs. 1 and 2), using highly purified complement components, that C$\overline{567}$ is the agent responsible for esterase activation.

Characteristics of the esterase activity induced by contact of leukocytes with chemotactic factor. From the results of the previous experiments it is clear that contact of blood leukocytes with C$\overline{567}$ causes an increase of esterase activity. However, there are three esterases in the polymorphonuclear leukocyte capable of hydrolyzing acetyl-DL-phenylalanine β-naphthyl ester (4), and thus it

TABLE V

Effects of agents that dissociate $\overline{\text{C567}}$ on esterase activation and chemotactic deactivation of blood leukocytes

Tube No.	C567[a]	Inhibitor	Esterase Activity		Chemotactic Responsiveness	Deacti-vation
		0.005 M	*O.D. at 485 nm*	*Δ O.D.*	*cells/5 fields*	*%*
1	Activated	CBZ-glutamyl tyrosine	0.315	−0.010	190	5
2	Non-activated	CBZ-glutamyl tyrosine	0.325		220	
3	Activated	Fumaropimaric acid	0.315	0.000	250	0
4	Non-activated	Fumaropimaric acid	0.315		240	
5	Activated	None	0.345	0.030	150	25
6	Non-activated	None	0.315		200	

[a] See *Materials and Methods* for description of activated and non-activated C567.

TABLE VI

Ability of phosphonates to inhibit in blood leukocytes esterase activity induced by contact with chemotactic factor

Experi-ment	Tube No.	C567	Phosphonate[a]	Esterase Activity		Chemotactic Response	Deactivation
			M	*O.D. at 415 nm*	*Δ O.D.*	*cells in 5 fields*	*%*
A	1	Activated	None	0.555	0.055	50	62
	2	Non-activated	None	0.500		130	
	3	Activated	1×10^{-7}	0.500	0	80	48
	4	Non-activated	1×10^{-7}	0.500		150	
	5	Activated	1×10^{-8}	0.535	0.015	50	67
	6	Non-activated	1×10^{-8}	0.520		150	
B	1	Activated	None	0.325	0.030	70	44
	2	Non-activated	None	0.295		125	
	3	Activated	1×10^{-8}	0.305	0.005	60	66
	4	Non-activated	1×10^{-8}	0.300		110	
	5	None	None	0.285		150	

[a] 5-Chloropentyl phosphonate.

became necessary to identify the esterase activity induced by the chemotactic factor. In doing so, advantage was taken of the very widely differing susceptibilities of the three esterases to inhibition by the phosphonate esters (see reference 4 and above).

In these experiments 2×10^7 cells previously treated with 5×10^{-5} M *p*-nitrophenyl ethyl 5-chloropentylphosphonate (see *Materials and Methods*) were incubated with partially purified chemotactic factor ($\overline{\text{C567}}$) or with a chemotactically inactive factor (C567) for 10 min. Then the *p*-nitrophenyl ethyl 5-chloropentylphosphonate at the appropriate concentration was added and incubation continued for another 10 min. The total volume was 0.5 ml. At the end of this time 2×10^6 cells were removed for chemotaxis. All cells were washed in TGS. To the remaining cell batch, substrate was added and the esterase activity was determined. Control cells not incubated with inhibitor were otherwise treated in the same way.

The results of two experiments are seen in Table VI. Cells treated with $\overline{\text{C567}}$ (Exp. A and B) showed a 10% increase in esterase activity and correspondingly a loss of chemotactic responsiveness (deactivation) compared to cells treated with C567. Incubation with 1×10^{-8} M *p*-nitrophenyl ethyl 5-chloropentylphosphonate for 10 min was sufficient to abolish completely or almost completely this increased activity. Four other experiments not shown here gave essentially the same results. The only known esterase capable of being inhibited by such low concentrations of phosphonate after only 10 min incubation is esterase 1.

DISCUSSION

The experiments reported in Tables II, III and IV imply that the blood neutrophil can be differentiated from the peritoneal neutrophil both by its greater chemotactic responsiveness and its increased esterase content. Although the differences between the cells from the two sources are not major, they are nevertheless consistent and reproducible. There is a possibility that the increased esterase activity of the blood leukocyte might be due to contamination with other cells. This can largely be discounted. The old assay procedure (4) was used in these experiments. This meant that the presence of red cells (and there were 5×10^7 to 2×10^8 red cells/1×10^7 neutrophils in these preparations) would tend to decrease rather than enhance esterase activity by tying up the coupling reagent. The data in Table I indicate that the overwhelming bulk, if not all, of esterase 1 activity in blood leukocytes can be ascribed to the neutrophils. Similarly, in unpublished experiments using the glass bead procedure no activity was found in preparations low in neutrophils but relatively enriched in lymphocytes. Thus, the results indicate that the blood neutrophil is a more active cell than the peritoneal neutrophil, the peritoneal leukocyte apparently having at least partially exhausted its enzyme content by responding to the stimulus (glycogen) that caused it to accumulate in the peritoneal cavity. This is in accord with our original idea that the peritoneal neutrophil has too little esterase to allow it to be detected directly. Presumably, however, there is enough to allow it to give a detectable chemotactic response to the chemotactic factor. In other words, the chemotactic assay is, not unexpectedly, a more sensitive indicator for the presence of the proesterase than the direct biochemical assay.

The amount of esterase activity which can be demonstrably activated by contact of the blood leukocyte with chemotactic factor is small, being at most no more than 10% to 20% of the preexisting esterase activity. The technical conditions under which such small activity can be reproducibly evoked are critical and must be rigidly observed. The assay procedure must be of sufficient sensitivity, and this is why the modification of the esterase assay described in *Materials and Methods* is so important. A sufficient number of blood leukocytes must be employed, at least 1×10^7 polymorphonuclear leukocytes being required. The background esterase must be decreased to the greatest extent possible by pre-treatment of leukocytes with phosphonates, otherwise any increment would be well within experimental error. Lastly, but not of least importance, the chemotactic factor must be of sufficient potency that the contact of chemotactic factor with leukocytes leads to at least 50% deactivation or, preferably, more.

The ability of the $C\overline{567}$ arising from highly purified human complement component to activate esterase shows not only that the activation is due to the chemotactic factor but also that it is not a function restricted to rabbit $C\overline{567}$. This is what is expected from the capacity of human as well as rabbit $C\overline{567}$ to deactivate rabbit leukocytes. Whether the other chemotactic factors, C3a and C5a, can also activate esterase is not known at present. This is presently under study.

The fact that the esterase activity arising after contact of the rabbit leukocyte with chemotactic factor is irreversibly inhibited by 10^{-7} to 10^{-8} M phosphonate after only 10 min incubation at room temperature (Table VI) clearly identifies the acquired activity as esterase 1.

The results depicted in Table VI have one further important implication. The cells were pretreated with 5×10^{-5} M phosphonate for 15 min before contact with the chemotactic factor. Yet, after contact with chemotactic factor, esterase 1 activity appeared and was inhibited by concentrations of phosphonate 500 to 5000 times less than this, which must mean that the acquired esterase 1 activity before contact with the chemotactic factor existed in a form that was insusceptible to phosphonate inhibition.

In the preceding paper (4) we showed that the inhibition profiles of an aromatic amino esterase, esterase 1, obtained with the several homologous series of phosphonate esters are the same as those found for the activatable esterase in both chemotactic factor dependent inhibition (3) of chemotaxis and protection against deactivation. In this paper we have demonstrated that the same aromatic amino acid esterase exists in a precursor form which is insusceptible to the inhibitory effects of phosphonates until it is activated. We have also shown that the precursor form of this aromatic amino acid esterase is capable of being activated by interaction of the cell with the macromolecular chemotactic factor, $\overline{C567}$. Thus, all five of the conditions previously set forth (4) as being necessary to be fulfilled in order to prove our hypothesis that the activatable esterase is an aromatic amino acid esterase have been fulfilled; the ring of evidence is complete.

Although we have a synthetic substrate for the aromatic amino acid esterase we still do not know its nature, its natural substrate, or where the precursor form is situated on the cell. This all remains for further investigation. We suspect it is a proteolytic enzyme but at present this is only a working hypothesis. The way is now open, however, for the isolation in pure state of the activated form of the proesterase as the first step in the study of the nature of the activatable esterase and its relation to the chemotactic process.

Previous work has led to the conclusion that the activation of an activatable esterase is responsible for the release of histamine from sensitized guinea pig lung (11) and from rat peritoneal cells sensitized with homocytotropic antibody (12) upon addition of antigen, from rat peritoneal cells to which rabbit and anti-rat γ globulin is added (13) and erythrophagocytosis by rabbit neutrophils (14). In each case, the only evidence for such a conclusion has derived from the employment of phosphonate esters. The present work presents a direct biochemical approach that we hope can be employed in these other systems.

REFERENCES

1. Ward, P. A. and Becker, E. L., J. Exp. Med., *125:* 1001, 1967.
2. Becker, E. L. and Ward, P. A., J. Exp. Med., *125:* 1021, 1967.
3. Ward, P. A. and Becker, E. L., J. Exp. Med., *127:* 693, 1968.
4. Becker, E. L. and Ward, P. A., J. Exp. Med., *129:* 569, 1969.
5. Ward, P. A., Cochrane, C. G. and Müller-Eberhard, H. J., J. Exp. Med., *122:*322, 1965.
6. Böyum, A., Scand. J. Clin. Lab. Invest., *21* (Suppl. 97)*:* 9, 1968.
7. Ward, P. A., Lepow, I. H. and Newman, L. J., Amer. J. Path., *52:* 725, 1968.
8. Ward, P. A., Cochrane, C. G. and Müller-Eberhard, H. J., Immunology, *11:* 141, 1966.
9. Glovsky, M. M., Ward, P. A., Becker, E. L. and Halbrook, N. J., J. Immun., *102:* 1, 1969.
10. Ward, P. A., in *Cellular and Humoral Mechanisms in Anaphylaxis and Allergy*, Edited by H. Z. Movat, p. 279, S. Karger, Basel, 1969.
11. Becker, E. L. and Austen, K. F., J. Exp. Med., *120:* 491, 1964.
12. Becker, E. L. and Austen, K. F., J. Exp. Med., *124:* 379, 1966.
13. Austen, K. F. and Becker, E. L., J. Exp. Med., *124:* 397, 1966.
14. Pearlman, D. S., Ward, P. A. and Becker, E. L., J. Exp. Med., *130:* 745, 1969.

The Journal of Immunology
Vol. 105, No. 5, November 1970
Printed in U.S.A.

RELEASE OF VIRUS INHIBITOR FROM TUBERCULIN-SENSITIZED PERITONEAL CELLS STIMULATED BY ANTIGEN[1]

LEONARD M. MILSTONE[2] AND BYRON H. WAKSMAN

From the Department of Microbiology, Yale University, New Haven, Connecticut 06510

Received for publication June 22, 1970

Tuberculin-sensitized mouse peritoneal cells exposed to purified protein derivative release an interferon-like virus inhibition within 24 hr. Release appears to require the interaction of specifically sensitized lymphocytes and sensitized or unsensitized macrophages.

Cell-mediated hypersensitivity appears to be important in lesion production and normal recovery from many viral diseases (1, 2). To date, no satisfactory mechanism has been proposed to explain the role that this type of reaction plays in the normal recovery process. Glasgow's report that Chikungunya virus can elicit increased interferon production from specifically sensitized cells (3) suggests a mechanism by which some form of cellular immunity might influence the recovery process. This laboratory and others (4), however, have failed to duplicate his results so that his model is not amenable to further study at present. We undertook the present study to determine whether a virus inhibitor is produced under conditions which conform to a well-studied *in vitro* model of cell-mediated hypersensitivity, the *in vitro* tuberculin reaction.

MATERIALS AND METHODS

Animals. Six-week-old BALB/c mice were obtained from Jackson Laboratories, Bar Harbor, Maine.

Sensitization. Heat-killed *Mycobacterium tuberculosis* hominis (Tbc), obtained through the kindness of I. S. Danielson, Lederle Laboratories, Pearl River, N. Y., ground to a fine powder and suspended in Bayol F (BF) (Humble Oil and Refining Co.), was injected into three footpads so that each mouse received 100 μg Tbc in a volume of 0.1 ml (5). Control mice received 0.1 ml BF distributed to three footpads. Footpad testing (see *Results*) and *in vitro* studies were performed 10 days after sensitization.

Virus. Vesicular stomatitis virus (VSV), Indiana strain, obtained from the World Health Organization Arbovirus Reference Laboratory of the Yale Arbovirus Research Init, was passaged once in suckling mice and stored as a lyophilized suspension of 10% brain in phosphate-buffered saline (PBS) containing 0.75% bovine albumin.

Culture media. Peritoneal cells were harvested in a medium consisting of Roswell Park Memorial Institute medium 1640 (Microbiological Associates, Bethesda, Md.), 20% heat-inactivated fetal calf serum (Grand Island Biological Co., Grand Island, N. Y.), sodium heparin (Organon, West Orange, N. Y.), 10 units/ml, potassium penicillin (Squibb & Sons, New York, N. Y.), 100 units/ml, and streptomycin sulfate (Eli Lilly & Co., Indianapolis, Ind.), 100 μg/ml. Peritoneal cells were maintained in the same medium except that it contained no heparin. Purified protein derivative (PPD) (Parke, Davis & Co., Detroit, Mich.), 25 μg/ml, was included in the medium in half the cultures. L cells were grown in a medium consisting of MEM-E (Grand Island Biological Co.), 10% calf serum (Flow Laboratories, Rockville, Md.), and antibiotics as above. The agar overlay consisted of medium 199-E plaque (Grand Island Biological Co.), 2% calf serum, 1% Ionagar no. 2 (Oxoid), and antibiotics. The second agar overlay contained, in addition, neutral red (Allied Chemical, New York, N. Y.), 67 μg/ml. All dilutions were made with a medium consisting of medium 199-E, 2% calf serum and antibiotics.

[1] This study was supported by United States Public Health Service Grants AI-06112 and AI-06455 and was taken from a thesis submitted to the Medical School of Yale University in partial fulfillment of the requirements for the degree of Doctor of Medicine.

[2] Present address: Department of Medicine, University of Oregon School of Medicine, Portland, Oregon 97201.

Culture of mouse peritoneal cells (6). Mice were rapidly killed with ether, and the abdominal skin was washed with 70% ethanol and reflected. Cold medium, 1.5 ml/mouse, was introduced into the previously unstimulated peritoneal cavities and then withdrawn. Pooled cell suspensions from 40 to 50 mice were centrifuged at 300 × G for 5 min at 4°C. The supernatant was aspirated, and the cells were resuspended in maintenance medium and distributed to 75-ml (25-mm^2) plastic screw-top flasks (Falcon Plastics, Inc., Oxnard, Calif.) so that each flask contained 5 × 10^6 cells in a final volume of 4.0 ml. Flasks were gassed with 5% CO_2:95% air, tightly capped, and incubated at 37°C.

Cell separation (7). Peritoneal exudate was prepared as above, and 10^7 cells/flask were incubated 1 hr at 37°C. Non-adherent cells were removed, placed in new flasks, and incubated an additional hr. Cells remaining non-adherent after this second incubation were designated "lymphocytes." Adherent cells from the first incubation were rinsed gently twice and thereafter considered to be "macrophages."

Plaque inhibition assay (8). Monolayers of L cells (clone 929), obtained through the courtesy of Dr. Hilton B. Levy, National Institutes of Health, Bethesda, Md., were prepared in 6-cm multiwell plastic plates (Linbro Chemical Co., New Haven, Conn.) by incubating 1.5 × 10^6 cells for 2 days at 37°C in a humidified 5% CO_2 atmosphere. Fluids to be tested for viral interference were centrifuged 20 min at 12,350 × G, diluted, applied in 2.0-ml volumes to the cell sheets, and allowed to incubate there for 24 hr at 37°C. After removal of the fluids and washing of the cell sheets with PBS, 30 to 100 plaque-forming units of VSV were applied to the cells. At 1 and 40 hr after applying the virus, the cell sheets were overlaid with agar. Plaques were counted at 44 to 48 hr.

RESULTS

Footpad reactions. The efficacy of the sensitization procedure was demonstrated by comparing the responses to PPD and to diluent alone injected into a hind footpad of tuberculin-sensitized and control mice (Fig. 1). Routine hematoxylin and eosin-stained sections showed intense mononuclear cell infiltration with edema and necrosis on both dorsal and ventral aspects of feet from sensitized mice injected with PPD, while the feet of all other animals showed only mild polymorphonuclear cell infiltrates at the site of injection.

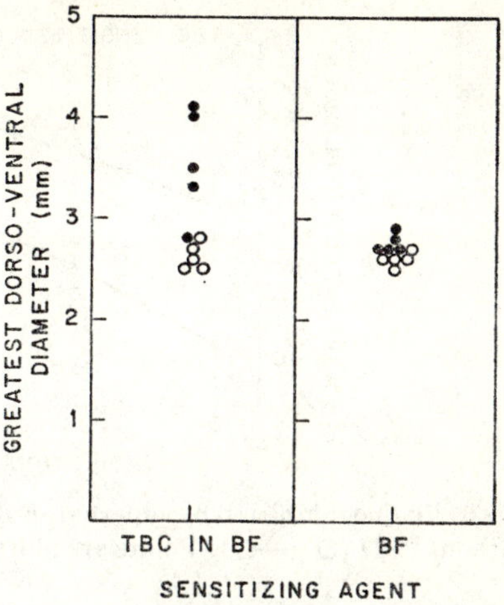

Figure 1. Footpad measurements 24 hr after challenge and 11 days after sensitization. Mice were challenged with PPD, 25 μg in 0.05 ml diluent (●) or 0.05 ml diluent (○).

Production of virus inhibitor by crude cell preparation. Peritoneal cells were obtained from untested littermates of the mice used for footpad testing. These cells were incubated with or without PPD for 24 hr at 37°C, and the resulting supernatants were assayed for their ability to inhibit VSV plaque formation. Supernatants from sensitized cells incubated with PPD produced more plaque inhibition than did supernatants from the same pool of cells incubated without PPD (Fig. 2). No significant difference in inhibition was observed between supernatants of cells from control mice incubated with and without PPD.

Production of virus inhibitor by combinations of lymphocytes and macrophages. Purified lymphocytes and macrophages were prepared from sensitized and control mice. Incubation with carbon particles (Pelikan C$^{11/1431}$) for 1 hr showed that 63% of the crude cell preparation, 97% of the macrophages and 7% of the lymphocytes ingested carbon. Combinations of sensitized and normal cells of each type were incubated 24 hr with or without PPD, and their supernatants were assayed for VSV plaque inhibitor. Only cultures containing sensitized lymphocytes produced significantly more of the inhibitor in the presence of PPD than in its absence (Table I). Before calcu-

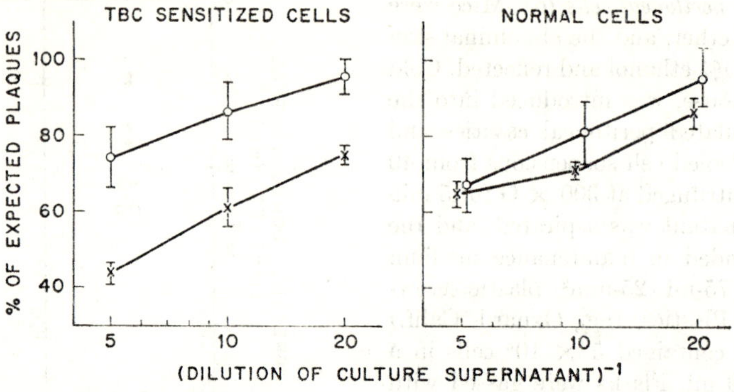

Figure 2. Plaque inhibition by supernatants from crude peritoneal cells incubated with PPD (X——X) and without PPD (O——O). Points are plotted ± one standard error of the mean.

TABLE I

Plaque inhibition by supernatants from combinations of sensitized and normal lymphocytes and macrophages

In Vivo Sensitization[a]		*In Vitro* Challenge	Dilution of Culture Supernatant					
			1:5		1:10		1:20	
Lymphocytes	Macrophages		No. of plaques[b]	p[c]	No. of plaques	p	No. of plaques	p
Tbc	Tbc	PPD	14 ± 2.9	<0.3	14 ± 1.1	<0.03	17 ± 1.7	<0.01
Tbc	Tbc	Diluent	18 ± 2.4		19 ± 1.9		28 ± 2.4	
Tbc	BF	PPD	10 ± 3.5	<0.001	22 ± 5.6	<0.3	12 ± 2.0	<0.01
Tbc	BF	Diluent	18 ± 1.3		21 ± 2.2		23 ± 1.8	
BF	Tbc	PPD	17 ± 1.4	<0.2	17 ± 2.4	<0.8	18 ± 2.0	<0.3
BF	Tbc	Diluent	13 ± 2.1		21 ± 2.7		21 ± 1.1	
BF	BF	PPD	12 ± 1.8	<0.5	12 ± 1.1	<0.2	20 ± 2.7	<0.1
BF	BF	Diluent	15 ± 2.8		16 ± 2.6		13 ± 1.7	

[a] Tbc, tuberculin sensitization; BF, injection of Bayol F.

[b] Average from nine plates for each dilution: triplicate determinations of three identical samples ± one standard error of the mean. Without added peritoneal cell supernatant, VSV produced 35 and 27 plaques, respectively, on L cells pretreated with PPD in diluent and with diluent alone.

[c] From Student's t test.

lating t values, the raw data were adjusted by a factor compensating for the increase in VSV plaques produced by PPD alone.

DISCUSSION

In vitro models of cell-mediated hypersensitivity have led to the identification of several lymphocyte products—a migration inhibition factor (9), a cytotoxic factor (10), a chemotactic factor (11), and a blastogenic factor (12)—which are detected in maximal concentration in the culture medium within 24 hr of adding antigen to sensitized cells and which induce characteristic changes in suitable target cells. When macrophages are the target, they become more active in terms of size and stickiness (13–15) and an increased ability to suppress intracellular replication of bacteria (16) or viruses (17). The problem raised by the present study, as well as by Glasgow's work, is whether the virus inhibitor released by sensitized peritoneal cells exposed to specific antigen is a lymphocyte product or a product of activated macrophages.

Lymphocytes produce interferon-like virus inhibitors under a variety of experimental conditions which are unrelated to the immunologic status of the donor (18, 19). Green *et al.* (20) reported increased interferon production by specifically sensitized lymphocytes cultured with antigen, occurring only when the cells were undergoing blast transformation at 4 days. In our study the virus inhibitor was produced in less than 24 hr, and thus the time course resembles that of the early release phenomena described in cell-mediated immune responses. A single experiment done in this laboratory appeared to confirm the finding of Green *et al.* that sensitized lymphocytes alone exposed to antigen did not produce increased inhibitor within 24 hr.

The results presented in this paper show that a mixture of sensitized lymphocytes and sensitized or normal macrophages produced a virus inhibitor when stimulated by antigen. Both cell types seem to be necessary for the observed result, but the nature of their interaction needs to be further explored.

Macrophages obtained from peritoneal cavities stimulated with glycogen or glass beads "spontaneously" produce far more interferon than macrophages from unstimulated peritoneal cavities (21). Since activated macrophages obtained from inflammatory exudates (6) bear many similarities to macrophages activated immunologically (15), it is tempting to speculate that the biochemical expression of this activity is similar in both cases. Interferon production by stimulated macrophages would, of course, be quite distinct from the immunologic mechanism described by Green and his colleagues.

Acknowledgment. The authors are deeply grateful to Dr. Robert E. Shope for his patient instruction in virologic techniques and for the encouragement he so generously imparts.

REFERENCES

1. Flick, J. A. and Pincus, W. B., J. Exp. Med., *117:* 663, 1963.
2. Seligman, M., Fudenberg, H. H. and Good, R. A., Amer. J. Med., *45:* 817, 1968.
3. Glasgow, L. A., J. Bact., *91:* 2185, 1966.
4. Subrahmanyan, T. P. and Mims, C. A., J. Reticuloendothel. Soc., *7:* 32, 1970.
5. Kantor, F. S., Fed. Proc., *29:* 701, 1970.
6. Cohn, Z. A. and Benson, B., J. Exp. Med., *121:* 153, 1965.
7. Bloom, B. R. and Bennett, B., Science, *153:* 80, 1966.
8. Wagner, R. R., Levy, A. H., Snyder, R. M., Ratcliff, G. A., Jr. and Hyatt, D. F., J. Immun., *91:* 112, 1963.
9. David, J. R., Proc. Nat. Acad. Sci., *56:* 72, 1966.
10. Ruddle, N. H. and Waksman, B. H., J. Exp. Med., *128:* 1267, 1967.
11. Ward, P. A., Remold, H. G. and David, J. R., Science, *163:* 1079, 1969.
12. Wolstencroft, R. A. and Dumonde, D. C., Immunology, *18:* 599, 1970.
13. Waksman, B. H. and Matoltsy, M., J. Immun., *81:* 220, 1958.
14. Bennett, B. and Bloom, B., Proc. Nat. Acad. Sci., *59:* 756, 1968.
15. Mooney, J. J. and Waksman, B. H., J. Immun., In press.
16. Mackaness, G. B., in *Infectious Agents and Host Reactions*, Edited by J. Mudd, pp. 61–75, W. B. Saunders Co., Philadelphia, 1970.
17. Benedict, A. A. and McFarland, C., Nature, *181:* 1742, 1958.
18. Gresser, I., Proc. Soc. Exp. Biol. Med., *108:* 799, 1961.
19. Friedman, R. M. and Cooper, H. L., Proc. Soc. Exp. Biol. Med., *125:* 901, 1967.
20. Green, J. A., Cooperband, S. R. and Kibrick, S., Science, *164:* 1415, 1969.
21. Smith, T. J. and Wagner, R., J. Exp. Med., *125:* 559, 1967.

THE JOURNAL OF IMMUNOLOGY
Vol. 105, No.5, November 1970

Printed in U.S.A.

ABROGATION OF IMMUNOLOGIC UNRESPONSIVENESS BY WHOLE MOLECULES AND FRAGMENTS OF CROSS-REACTING IMMUNOGLOBULINS[1, 2]

R. W. SCALES[3] AND J. M. CRUSE

From the Department of Biology, Immunology Research Unit, University of Mississippi, The Graduate School, University, Mississippi 38677

Received for publication June 16, 1970

A state of immunologic tolerance to a given antigen can be terminated by the injection of a cross-reacting antigen provided that the degree of cross-reactivity is within certain limits. The present investigation was designed to test the ability of human γG or its fragments to terminate tolerance to bovine γG or its fragments and *vice versa*. γG of both species was isolated by DEAE-cellulose chromatography and digested by mercuripapain. C57BL mice were injected with 1.0 mg of tolerogen and 20 days later were immunized with 0.2 mg of the cross-reacting antigen in Freund's incomplete adjuvant. Seven days after the last immunizing injection, ^{125}I-tolerogen was injected intraperitoneally and the course of elimination followed by whole body counting. Sera were assayed for antibodies to the tolerogen by gel diffusion, immunoelectrophoresis and passive hemagglutination. Results of this investigation demonstrated that tolerance to bovine γG in mice may be terminated by injection of human γG or its fragments. Likewise, tolerance to human γG in mice may be terminated by injection of bovine γG or its fragments.

A state of immunologic tolerance to serum proteins can be induced in numerous animal species (1–3). This tolerance is specific in that the response to challenge with an antigenically unrelated substance is not impaired. Immunologic tolerance to a given antigen can be terminated by immunization with a cross-reacting antigen provided that the degree of cross-reactivity is within certain limits (4–6). It has been demonstrated that tolerance to bovine serum albumin (BSA) in rabbits can be terminated following immunization with human serum albumin (15% cross-reactivity with anti-BSA). Sheep serum albumin (76% cross-reactivity with anti-BSA) was unable to do so.

Other systems include termination of tolerance to: bovine gamma globulin (BGG) by immunization with human gamma globulin (HGG) (7); serum proteins by immunization with the proteins substituted with diazonium derivatives of various acids (5, 8).

The present investigation was designed to demonstrate the effect of human γG (HγG) on tolerance in mice to bovine γG (BγG) and *vice versa*. To gain new information concerning the specificity of immunologic tolerance, experiments were designed to test the effect of enzymatically produced fragments of both γG species on tolerance to the intact molecule of both γG species.

MATERIALS AND METHODS

Mice. Adult male C57BL/6J mice (The Jackson Laboratory, Bar Harbor, Maine), 4 to 5 months of age, were used in all studies. Mice were never less than 8 weeks old when given the first injection of protein.

Antigens. Commercial lyophilized preparations of human HGG (lot 32) and BGG (lot 29) were obtained from Pentex, Inc., Kankakee, Ill. Both proteins were routinely purified on a glass chromatographic column, 2.5- x 35-cm, of diethyl-

[1] Part of the material contained in this paper was presented at the 54th Annual Meeting of the Federation of American Societies for Experimental Biology in Atlantic City, N.J., 1970.

[2] This work was supported in part by grants from the Brown-Hazen Fund of Research Corporation, New York, N.Y. and from the State of Mississippi, provided through Legislative House Bill HR1133.

[3] Present address: Department of Microbiology, University of Florida College of Medicine, Gainesville, Florida.

aminoethyl cellulose (DEAE-cellulose), equilibrated with 0.01 M phosphate buffer, pH 8.0. After chromatographic separation, the eluates containing γG were concentrated using a Diaflo ultrafiltration unit (Amicon Corp., Lexington, Mass.) or by dialysis against a high molecular weight substance, e.g., Ficoll (Pharmacia, Uppsala, Sweden) or polyvinylpyrrolidone (PVP). The protein solutions were stored at 4°C as concentrated solutions.

Antisera. Antisera used to test the purity of all antigen preparations, including immunoglobulin fragments (see below), were obtained from the following sources: rabbit anti-BGG, batch 649B, and rabbit anti-human γG, batch 1506 M, Behringwerke AG (Marburg, Lahn); goat anti-human Fab, lot 8259E003A1, and goat anti-human Fc, lot 8258E005A1, Hyland Laboratories, Los Angeles, Calif.

Analytical ultracentrifugation. Ultracentrifugation of papain-digested γG was performed in a Spinco model E ultracentrifuge. After reaching a speed of 56,100 rpm, photographic plates were obtained at 8-min intervals.

Enzymatic hydrolysis of γG. Digestion of HγG and BγG was performed according to the method of Porter (9). One hundred milligrams of γG were incubated with 1 mg of twice crystallized papain (Mann Research Laboratories, New York, N. Y.) in 0.15 M phosphate-buffered saline solution, pH 7.0, containing 0.01 M cysteine and 0.002 M ethylenediaminetetraacetate (EDTA). The concentration of γG in each digest was 30 mg/ml of phosphate-buffered saline solution. Digestion was allowed to proceed for 4 hr at 37°C (10). The digests were then dialyzed against 0.01 M phosphate buffer, pH 7.6.

Removal of undigested γG. The digests were placed on a 2.5- x 85-cm Sephadex column (Pharmacia, Uppsala, Sweden) filled with Sephadex G-100 and equilibrated with 0.01 M phosphate buffer, pH 7.6. The flow rate was adjusted to 10 ml/hr using a Mariotte flask maintained at a hydrostatic pressure of 15 cm. Two-milliliter fractions were collected, and the protein distribution was monitored at 280 nm using a Uviscan III (Buchler Instruments, Inc., Fort Lee, N. J.). Figure 1 shows the ultracentrifugal pattern of a papain digest of HγG, free of undigested material. The sedimentation coefficient was 3.61S.

Isolation of papain digestion fragments. Human Fab and Fc fragments were isolated by the method of Franklin (11). Papain digests were applied to a column of carboxymethylcellulose (CM-cellulose), equilibrated with 0.01 M phosphate buffer, pH 7.6. A gradient of NaCl up to 0.4 M was established after collection of the protein that came off with the initial buffer front. The two peaks thus obtained were chromatographed separately on DEAE-cellulose, equilibrated with 0.01 M phosphate buffer, pH 8.0, and a gradient up to 0.3 M NaCl was established. Fab fragments were eluted with the starting buffer and Fc fragments were eluted shortly after the gradient was started. All fractions were dialyzed against 0.15 M phosphate-buffered saline solution, concentrated, and stored at 4°C.

Bovine papain digests were separated into electrophoretically slow and fast fragments by starch block electrophoresis as described by Chase and Williams (12). Papain digests, free of undigested BγG, were equilibrated to the electrophoretic buffer (barbital buffer, pH 8.6, μ = 0.05) by dialysis. Electrophoresis was performed at 4°C for 18 hr employing a voltage of 5 V/cm. The block was then cut into 1-cm segments and each segment was eluted with 0.15 M NaCl. Protein determination was performed by the Folin-Ciocalteu method as described by Kabat (13).

Induction of tolerance. All tolerogen preparations were centrifuged at 30,000 × G for 1 hr to remove any aggregated material that might have an adjuvant effect (2). The standard concentration for the intact molecule preparation was 10 mg/ml. Fc fragments were injected at a concentration of 20 mg/ml. Adult mice were inoculated intraperitoneally with 0.1 ml of a soluble preparation of tolerogen in 0.15 M NaCl. Controls received 0.1 ml of 0.15 M NaCl.

Immunization. Twenty days after tolerogen injection mice were inoculated subcutaneously with 0.1 mg of the immunogen incorporated into 0.1 ml of Freund's incomplete adjuvant. One injection was administered weekly for a total of 3 weeks.

Iodination. Except for minor modifications, the method of McConahey and Dixon (14) was used for labeling protein. For the reaction buffer 0.1 M phosphate, pH 7.0, was used in place of 0.05 M phosphate buffer, pH 7.0. ^{125}Iodine in carrier-free form (New England Nuclear Corp., Boston, Mass.) was added to the protein solution at a concentration such that the degree of iodination was slightly less than one atom of ^{125}I per mole-

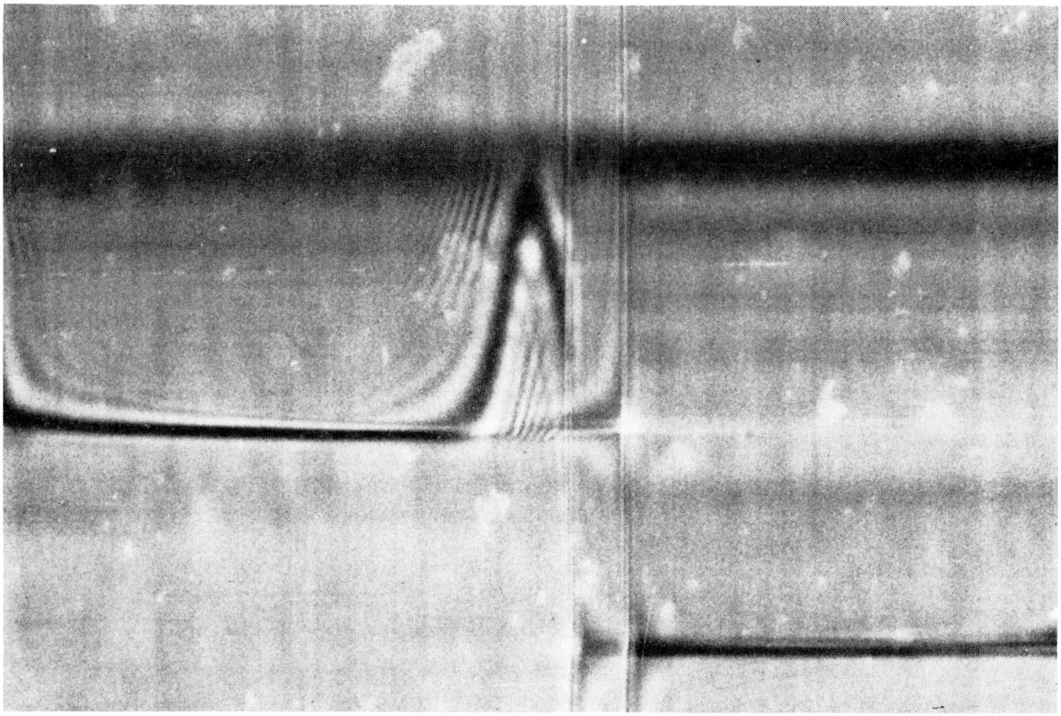

Figure 1. Photograph of schlieren pattern taken in a Spinco model E ultracentrifuge after 40 min at 56,100 rpm. Sample of papain-digested HγG, free of undigested material, in 0.15 M NaCl, adjusted to pH 7.0 with NaOH.

cule of protein. Chloramine T was added to the protein-iodide mixture at a concentration of 10 μg/mg of protein. Ten minutes after addition of chloramine T, an equal amount of sodium metabisulfite, dissolved in distilled water, was added to stop the reaction. Non-protein-bound iodide was removed by dialysis against several changes of cold 0.15 M phosphate-buffered solution, pH 7.0. Dialysis was continued until the dialysate registered background.

Antigen elimination. To prevent thyroid uptake of ^{125}I, potassium iodide, at a concentration of 0.1%, was added to the drinking water 1 week before the mice received the labeled protein. Seven days post immunogen injection, experimental and control mice were inoculated intraperitoneally with 20 μg of labeled tolerogen. The course of elimination was followed by whole body counts using a Packard Tri-Carb liquid scintillation spectrophotometer equipped with an Armac tandem (Packard Instrument Co., Downer's Grove, Ill.). All counts were corrected for background and radioisotope decay.

Analysis of antisera. In addition to the antigen elimination assay, individual sera were analyzed by passive hemagglutination (PHA) tests, immunoelectrophoresis and gel diffusion.

RESULTS

Dose requirements for induction of tolerance. In the majority of previous tolerance studies involving gamma globulin as the antigen, the whole gamma globulin fraction was used. Commercial preparations of Cohn fraction II gamma globulin (e.g., HGG and BGG) contained all of the major classes of immunoglobulin (γG, γM, and γA) in addition to a beta globulin component inherent in these preparations. Some components were tolerogenic while others were immunogenic. Therefore, experiments were performed to determine whether the dose threshold established for HGG and BGG (whole gamma globulin fraction) was the same for HγG and BγG.

Various quantities of HγG and BγG were injected intraperitoneally into adult mice. Twenty days later these mice were challenged with HγG

TABLE I

The effect of HγG on the response to immunization with HγG in Freund's incomplete adjuvant

Dose	Degree of Tolerance[a]		
	+	±	−
mg			
10	5/5[b]		
5	5/5		
1	5/5		
0.5	5/5		
0.1	5/5		
0.05		3/5 (1.48)[c]	2/5 (2.20)
0			5/5 (2.50)

[a] +, Tolerant; ±, partially tolerant; −, immune.

[b] Number of mice tolerant or immune of total injected.

[c] Average hemagglutination titer expressed as the reciprocal of the $\log_{10}$.

and BγG incorporated into Freund's incomplete adjuvant. Seven days after challenge individual sera were analyzed by PHA tests; mice were recorded as tolerant, partially tolerant, or immune.

As shown in Table I, all mice receiving quantities of HγG greater than 0.1 mg became tolerant. Injection of 0.05 mg of HγG resulted in a shift to partial tolerance. Two of five mice were non-tolerant and had an average hemagglutinin titer ($\log_{10}$ reciprocal) of 2.20. Three mice, although producing antisera of low titer, were less responsive than non-tolerant, immunized controls.

A similar experiment, using BγG as the antigen, yielded essentially the same results. However, the shift to partial tolerance occurred at a dose of 0.01 mg rather than 0.05 mg, indicating that the threshold concentration for induction of tolerance was lower for BγG than HγG. These data demonstrated that the dose requirements for the induction of tolerance to HγG and BγG did not differ significantly from the dose required for tolerance to HGG and BGG.

Effects of cross-reacting γG on tolerance to γG. As a basis for determining whether tolerance involving cross-reacting antigens was terminated, elimination patterns of various controls were obtained. As shown in Figure 2, the manner in which mice eliminated antigen depended on their immune status and the labeled antigen injected. Those mice immunized with HγG incorporated into Freund's incomplete adjuvant and injected with ^{125}I-HγG (a homologous system) eliminated the labeled antigen rapidly. The group of mice that received only ^{125}I-HγG showed an exponential rate of elimination, characteristic of the *in vivo* half-life of HγG. When mice received HγG in Freund's incomplete adjuvant and later were injected with ^{125}I-BγG (a cross-reacting system), the rate of elimination was faster than the normal catabolic rate but slower than the rate observed in the homologous system. This was due to the 15% cross-reactivity between HγG and anti-BγG. Since this pattern represented the type of elimination that would be observed in tolerant mice immunized with a cross-reacting antigen and then injected with labeled tolerogen, tolerance was considered terminated in mice showing this pattern.

In addition, the hemagglutination of red blood cells coated with the tolerogen confirmed that tolerance was terminated.

Immunization of BγG-tolerant mice with HγG terminated the tolerant state to BγG as shown in Table II. Seven of 10 mice eliminated ^{125}I-BγG in a manner characteristic of partial tolerance (conversely, hyporesponsiveness). The average hemagglutinin titer ($\log_{10}$ reciprocal) was 1.77. All 10 mice produced precipitating antibody to the immunogen (HγG), but no precipitating antibody to the tolerogen (BγG) was detected.

Controls tolerant to BγG and immunized with BγG did not show an immune elimination of a subsequent injection of labeled BγG nor did these controls produce significant titers of hemagglutinating antibodies. A second group of controls, non-tolerant mice immunized with BγG, demonstrated an elimination of HγG characteristic of partially tolerant mice. The elimination of BγG in these same mice followed an immune elimination pattern.

The converse of the above experiment, i.e., termination of tolerance to HγG and BγG, yielded similar results. However, HγG was relatively more efficient than BγG in terminating tolerance to its cross-reacting counterpart.

Effects of human Fab and Fc on tolerance to BγG. Five of eight mice tolerant to BγG and immunized with human Fab showed a partial immune elimination of a subsequent injection of labeled BγG (Fig. 3). The elimination pattern was similar to that observed in termination of tolerance by intact HγG. Hemagglutination of red blood cells coated with bovine slow or fast fragments indicated that the antibody response

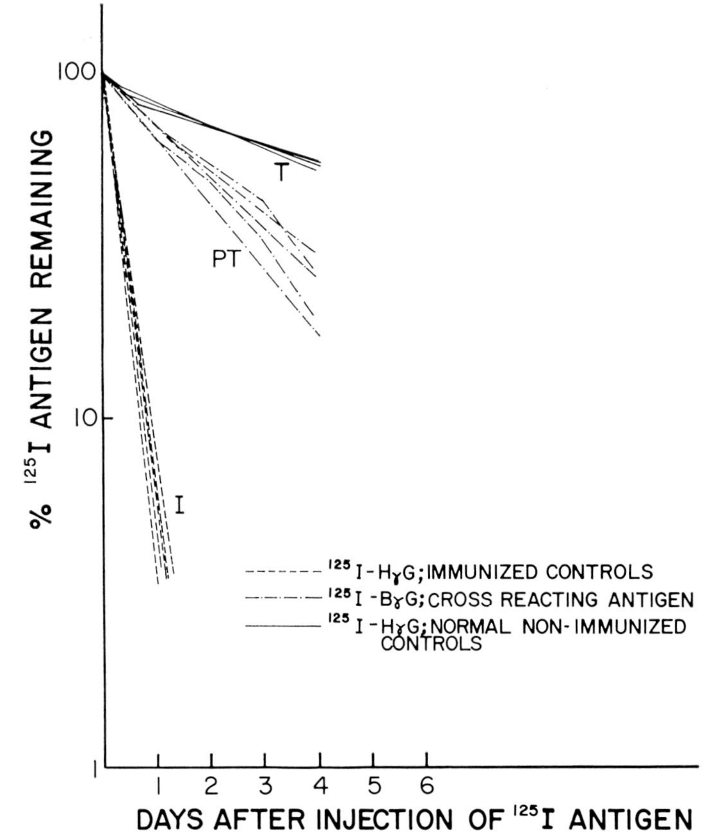

Figure 2. The elimination of ^{125}I-HγG and ^{125}I-BγG from mice immunized with HγG. *T*, tolerant; *PT*, partially tolerant; *I*, immune.

was directed against the antigenic determinants located on the bovine slow fragment but not on the bovine fast fragment. Bovine slow and fast fragments appear to be analogous to human Fab and Fc, respectively, on the basis of *in vivo* half-life, electrophoretic mobility, and in showing reactions of partial identity in gel diffusion media with the parent, intact molecule.

When BγG-tolerant mice were immunized with human Fc (Table III), the rate of elimination of labeled BγG and the number of mice showing an immune elimination were diminished. The antibody response of these mice, although of low titer, was directed against bovine fast fragment. Control mice, tolerant to BγG but not immunized with human Fab or Fc, showed an elimination pattern typical of tolerant mice.

Effects of bovine fragments on tolerance to HγG. The apparent lower efficiency with which BγG terminated tolerance to HγG also extended to the papain-produced slow and fast fragments of BγG.

TABLE II

The effect of HγG on mice tolerant to BγG

Tolerogen	Immunogen	Immune Elimination of Tolerogen	Average HA Titer	Gel Precipitins
		positive/total	*log₁₀ reciprocal*	*positive/total*
BγG	HγG	7/10	1.77	0/10
BγG	BγG	0/10	0.48	0/10
BγG		0/10		0/10

Bovine fast fragment (analogous to human Fc) demonstrated relatively little ability to terminate tolerance to HγG (Fig. 4). Only 3 of 10 mice tolerant to HγG and immunized with bovine fast fragment eliminated HγG at a rate consistent with that observed in partially tolerant mice.

In contrast, HγG-tolerant mice that were immunized with bovine slow fragment (analogous to human Fab) were rendered non-tolerant to HγG as evidenced by an immune elimination of

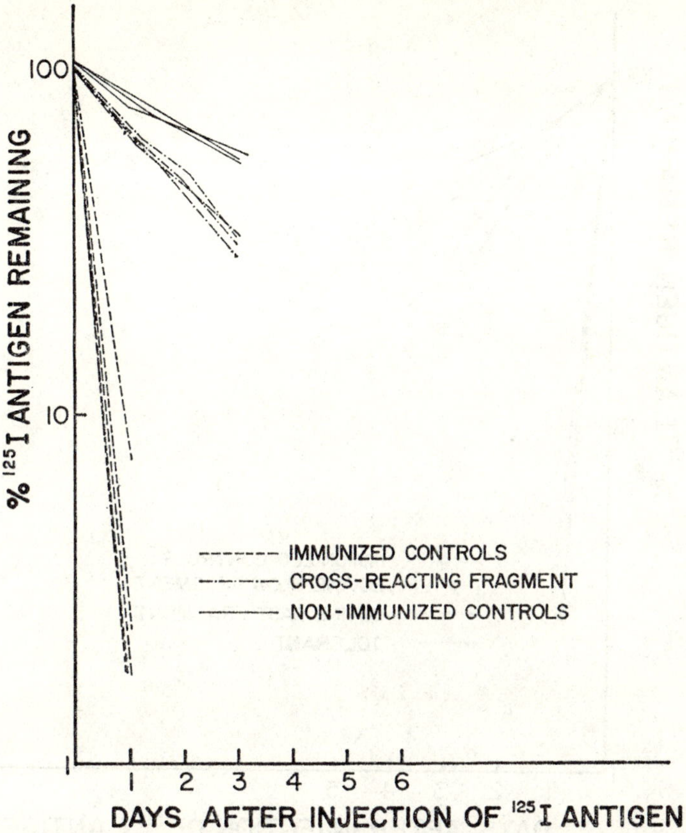

Figure 3. The elimination of ^{125}I-BγG from mice tolerant to BγG and immunized with human Fab.

labeled HγG. The sera of these mice were analyzed by passive hemagglutination of red blood cells coated with human Fab or Fc. Cells coated with human Fab but not with human Fc were agglutinated to a titer of 1.75 ($\log_{10}$ reciprocal), indicating that the immune elimination of HγG was due to antibodies directed against the Fab portion of the molecule.

Effects of bovine fragments on tolerance to human Fc. Table IV shows the effects of bovine slow and fast fragments on tolerance to human Fc. When 10 mice tolerant to human Fc were immunized with bovine slow fragment, tolerance did not terminate as judged by the failure of all mice to eliminate a subsequent injection of labeled Fc fragment. Agglutinating antibodies were not detected in any of the sera.

A second group of mice tolerant to human Fc was immunized with bovine fast fragment. Three of 10 mice eliminated a subsequent injection of human Fc and contained agglutinating antibodies to human Fc in their sera.

TABLE III

The Effect of human Fab and Fc on tolerance to BγG

Tolerogen	Immunogen	Immune Elimination of Tolerogen	Average HA Titer
		positive/total	*$\log_{10}$ reciprocal*
BγG	Human Fab	5/8	1.41
BγG	Human Fc	4/10	0.48
BγG		0/10	

Human Fc-tolerant mice that were immunized with human Fc failed to show an immune elimination of the same antigen, indicating that tolerance in this group of mice was still in effect. All non-tolerant mice that received an inoculation of human Fc in Freund's incomplete adjuvant showed a rapid immune elimination of human Fe and produced anti-Fc sera of relatively high titer.

DISCUSSION

Dose requirements for induction of tolerance. Results of the first section of this investigation dem-

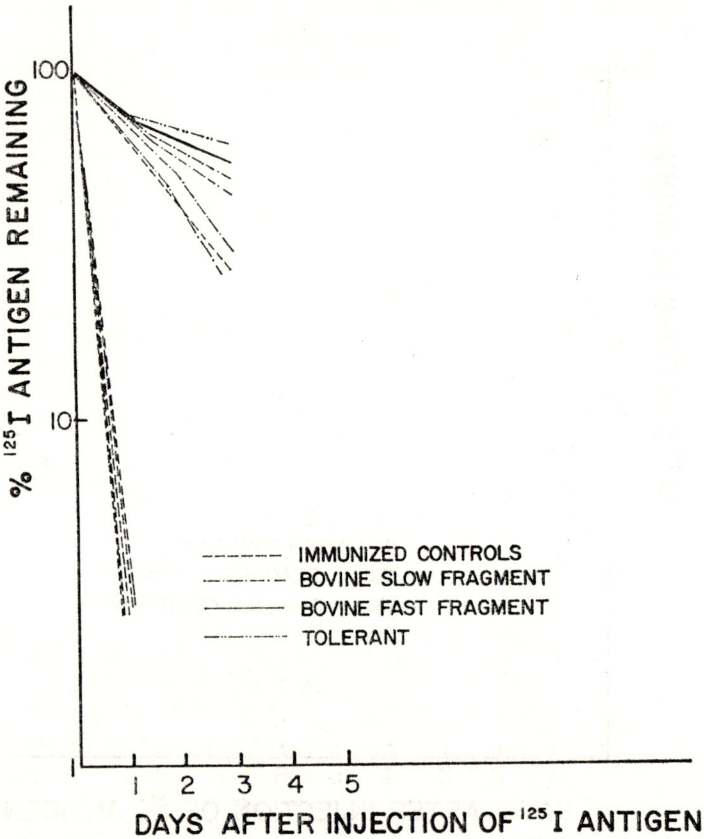

Figure 4. The elimination of ^{125}I-HγG from mice tolerant to HγG and immunized with bovine slow and fast fragments.

onstrated that a state of immunologic tolerance to HγG, BγG, and papain-produced fragments was induced in adult C57BL/6J mice. This unresponsiveness was not abrogated even when the tolerogen was administered in an immunogenic form, i.e., in Freund's incomplete adjuvant.

Mice that received as little as 0.05 mg of soluble antigen showed a degree of partial tolerance. Quantities of antigen greater than 0.05 mg rendered all mice completely tolerant. The use of relatively purified, deaggregated antigens prevented the sporadic immune responses observed in investigations by others (2).

Mice were rendered tolerant to γG by quantities of antigen on the order of 40 mg of protein/kg body weight (80 mg/kg body weight in the case of human Fc). These parameters placed the present investigation in the category of high zone tolerance. The induction of low zone tolerance was not investigated in these experiments. However, based on the data of Dresser (2), who used BGG as the tolerogen and CBA mice as experimental animals, low zone tolerance is probably applicable in the present system.

Tolerance induced with 1.0 mg of soluble protein antigen lasted at least 6 weeks. This is in agreement with findings of other investigators (15) in which unresponsiveness in newborn mice

TABLE IV

The effect of bovine slow and fast fragments on mice tolerant to human Fc

Tolerogen	Immunogen	Immune Elimination of Tolerogen	Average HA Titer
		positive/total	*log₁₀ reciprocal*
Human Fc	Bovine_{slow}	0/10	
Human Fc	Bovine_{fast}	3/10	0.47
Human Fc	Human Fc	0/8	
	Human Fc	8/8	2.60

rendered tolerant to BGG lasted for as long as 6 weeks. Thus, it was established that the immune elimination observed in tolerance-terminated animals was not due to spontaneous recovery from tolerance. In support of this concept is the observation that none of the tolerant animals immunized with tolerogen 6 weeks after tolerance induction produced antibodies to the tolerogen.

Larger quantities of human Fc fragments were used for tolerance induction because of the somewhat shorter *in vivo* half-life of approximately 3 days in mice (16). The induction of tolerance to human Fab and bovine slow fragments was not investigated. Fab fragments have a half-life of 0.5 day. Thus, it would have required relatively large amounts of antigen for the threshold dose to persist throughout the 3- to 5-day induction period.

The minimum tolerogenic dose of HγG and BγG was found to be 0.05 mg, which is compatible with the data reported by Dietrich and Weigle (17). The effectiveness of this low dose, especially for induction in adults, was due to the route of administration and the fact that soluble proteins were poor antigens in mice. In administering antigen intraperitoneally, the slow exposure of antigen to antibody-producing cells, as in subcutaneous or intradermal injection, was avoided. In addition, the use of relatively pure proteins, free of aggregates and other immunogenic components (e.g., γA), rendered the tolerogen preparations even less immunogenic.

Effects of cross-reacting γG on tolerance to γG. This section of the study was performed to ascertain whether the parameters established by other investigators using the BGG-HGG cross-immunization system of tolerance termination in rabbits were applicable to the BγG-HγG combination in mice. In doing so, this system served as a baseline for studies on the effect of antigen fragments on tolerance to the intact, parent antigen molecule.

The data presented in these experiments demonstrated that tolerance to BγG was terminated by immunization with the cross-reacting antigen, HγG. The 15% cross-reactivity between HγG and anti-BγG made the HγG-BγG. combination an ideal system for testing tolerance termination. Weigle (7) reported that human serum albumin (HSA), which cross-reacted to the extent of 15% with anti-BSA, terminated tolerance to BSA in rabbits. HGG, which also cross-reacted to 15% with anti-BGG, terminated tolerance to BGG in rabbits.

It appears that in order for a cross-reacting antigen to terminate tolerance, it must be different enough to be recognized as foreign and to stimulate immunocompetent cells, and yet similar enough to cross-react within certain limits. Antigens that are closely similar to the tolerogen would not be recognized as foreign by immunocompetent cells. It should be expected that a species of γG globulin closely related to HγG, e.g., other primate γG globulin, might not terminate tolerance because of its overall antigenic similarity to HγG.

Certainly, the phylogenetic relationship of an antigen to a given host determines to a large extent the tolerogenicity of that antigen. Provided that there is no inherent predisposition to nonreactivity, the more distantly related an antigen is to a given host, the more determinants there should be for the immune mechanism to recognize as foreign. With an increase in the number of antigenic determinants, greater numbers of immunocompetent cells must be inhibited or eliminated for tolerance to be induced. However, with closely related antigens fewer cells would be affected, and thus tolerance would be more easily broken.

This could possibly account for the relatively greater efficiency of HγG in terminating tolerance to BγG compared with termination of HγG tolerance by BγG. Within the parameters used in the present system, BγG might be more tolerogenic than HγG. Thus, termination of tolerance might be more easily accomplished.

Several mechanisms could account for termination of tolerance by cross-reacting antigens. The lymphocyte was found to be the target cell affected in tolerance. Therefore, it appeared that the lymphocyte and/or its precursors and progeny were the cells affected by cross-reacting antigens.

A cross-reacting antigen in tolerant animals may be recognized as foreign on the basis of its overall antigenic dissimilarity to the tolerogen. Consequently, it would be allowed to confront the immune recognition apparatus of host cells. Weigle (4) suggested that once the antigen passed this initial recognition barrier, antibody synthesis occurred resulting in the production of antibodies that reacted with determinants specific for the cross-reacting antigen as well as tolerated determinants.

According to this theory tolerance affected only the initial recognition step and not the antibody-producing step. The question then arises whether the antibody is directed specifically against previously tolerated, individual determinants or whether the antibody represents an "overlap" due to the intimate association of tolerated and non-tolerated determinants. The "antibody overlap" alternative received experimental support from Spiegelberg and Weigle (18) who observed that intact HγG did not terminate tolerance to human Fc fragments in rabbits. The results of the present investigation provided additional support for this concept.

Siegel (19) postulates that cross-reacting antigens stimulate those cells that might not have been inhibited or eliminated during the induction of tolerance. The ability of cross-reacting γG to terminate tolerance to γG would support this theory and that proposed by Weigle.

Dissection of the tolerance-terminating ability of cross-reacting γG. Mice tolerant to BγG and immunized with human Fab fragments became non-tolerant as evidenced by immune elimination of BγG. Thus, it appeared that the cross-reactivity between BγG and HγG was located, in part, on the Fab portion of HγG. Likewise, mice tolerant to BγG and immunized with human Fc were rendered non-tolerant. However, the results indicated that the termination of tolerance to BγG by human Fc fragments as compared with human Fab fragments was relatively less efficient. Not only was the elimination of BγG less marked but the hemagglutinin titers were relatively low.

Assuming that a defined degree of cross-reactivity is required for termination of tolerance, these data suggest that the cross-reacting determinants of HγG and BγG are located in the Fab region of HγG and the corresponding region of BγG. This concept is supported by the evidence that species-specific antigenic determinants of various γG globulin species are located mainly on the Fc portions of the molecules (20). The Fc portions of various γG homologues, therefore, might not cross-react sufficiently because of a lack of shared determinants.

It is suggested that this cross-reactivity is due, in part, to determinants on the light chains. Each Fab fragment is composed of one light chain (kappa or lambda type) and the Fd portion of one heavy chain. The interspecies homology of kappa chains is greater than the intraspecies homology of kappa and lambda chains (21).

When mice tolerant to HγG were immunized with bovine slow or fast fragments, a tolerance-terminating ability similar to that of human Fab and Fc was observed. Bovine fast fragments (analogous to human Fc) did not appear to have a pronounced effect on the tolerant state. Bovine slow fragments (analogous to human Fab), however, stimulated the production of antibodies capable of eliminating HγG and agglutinating red blood cells coated with HγG.

The most distinct effect of γG fragments in terminating tolerance was observed in mice tolerant to human Fc and immunized with bovine slow or fast fragments. Ten mice tolerant to human Fc and immunized with bovine slow fragments failed to show an immune elimination of a subsequent injection of labeled human Fc. Three of 10 mice tolerant to human Fc and immunized with bovine fast fragments showed an immune elimination of human Fc and agglutinated red cells coated with human Fc. The rate of elimination was relatively slow, approaching the rate of elimination of tolerant mice. The hemagglutinin titers of these mice were relatively low also.

These results are consistent with the findings mentioned above. Although Fc homologues contained species-specific determinants, it might be expected that the Fc fragments of various species also would show weak homologies.

REFERENCES

1. Dixon, F. J. and Maurer, P. H., J. Exp. Med., *101:* 245, 1955.
2. Dresser, D. W., Immunology, *5:* 378, 1962.
3. Biro, E. C. and Garcia, G., Immunology, *8:* 411, 1965.
4. Weigle, W. O., J. Exp. Med., *114:* 111, 1961.
5. Weigle, W. O., J. Exp. Med., *116:* 913, 1962.
6. Weigle, W. O., J. Immun., *94:* 177, 1965.
7. Weigle, W. O., Immunology, *7:* 239, 1964.
8. Dietrich, F. M., Nature, *213:* 496, 1967.
9. Porter, R. R., Biochem. J., *73:* 119, 1959.
10. Gergely, J., Stanworth, O. R., Jefferis, R., Normansell, D. E., Henney, C. S. and Pardoe, G. I., Immunochemistry, *4:* 101, 1966.
11. Franklin, E. C., J. Clin. Invest., *39:* 1933, 1960.
12. Chase, M. W. and Williams, C. A. (Editors), *Methods in Immunology and Immunochemistry*, Vol. II, p. 63, Academic Press, New York, 1968.

13. Kabat, E. A., in *Kabat and Mayer's Experimental Immunochemistry*, 2nd Ed., p. 556, Charles C Thomas, Springfield, Ill., 1961.
14. McConahey, P. J. and Dixon, F. J., Int. Arch. Allerg., *29:* 185, 1966.
15. Thorbecke, G. T., Siskind, G. W. and Goldberger, N., J. Immun., *87:* 147, 1961.
16. Spiegelberg, H. L. and Weigle, W. O., J. Exp. Med., *121:* 323, 1965.
17. Dietrick, F. M. and Weigle, W. O., J. Immun., *92:* 167, 1964.
18. Spiegelberg, H. L. and Weigle, W. O., J. Immun., *98:* 1020, 1967.
19. Siegel, I., J. Theor. Biol., *24:* 171, 1969.
20. Weir, D. M. (Editor), *Handbook of Experimental Immunology*, F. A. Davis Co., Philadelphia, 1967.
21. Putnam, F. W., Science, *163:* 633, 1969.

The Journal of Immunology
Vol. 105, No. 5, November 1970
Printed in U.S.A.

IMMUNOCHEMICAL AND BIOLOGIC PROPERTIES OF RAT IgE

I. Immunochemical Identification of Rat IgE[1]

DANIEL J. STECHSCHULTE,[2] ROBERT P. ORANGE[3] AND K. FRANK AUSTEN

From the Department of Medicine, Harvard Medical School at the Robert B. Brigham Hospital, Boston, Massachusetts 02120

Received for publication June 16, 1970

An electrophoretically fast, antigenically unique rat immunoglobulin with hapten specificity has been identified and termed IgE. Monospecific antiserum for rat IgE removed from rat antiserum the biologic activities attributed to rat homocytotropic antibody. Thus, the immunoglobulin class of rat homocytotropic antibody is IgE.

Antigenically distinct rat immunoglobulins demonstrated initially by immunoelectrophoresis (1–3) and subsequently by radioimmunoelectrophoresis include IgGa, IgGb, IgM, γ1 and IgA (4–7). An additional immunoglobulin, termed mast cell-sensitizing (8), anaphylactic (9), or homocytotropic antibody (10), has been defined on the basis of unique functional characteristics. These include the capacity to persist at a skin site in the rat for weeks as assessed by mediation of passive cutaneous anaphylaxis (PCA) (8, 9) and the ability to prepare mast cells passively *in vitro* for antigen-induced release of histamine and serotonin (8, 10, 11).

The known physicochemical properties of the rat homocytotropic antibody are a fast electrophoretic mobility, a molecular size of approximately 8S, and a susceptibility to inactivation by heat or 2-mercaptoethanol (9, 12–14). The elution characteristics of rat homocytotropic antibodies with ion-exchange chromatography are identical to those of γ1 (13–16). However, absorption of rat antiserum with specific anti-rat γ1 (11) had no effect on the titer of homocytotropic antibody as assessed by the capacity either to mediate PCA or to prepare mast cells for the antigen-induced release of histamine. Thus, the available data on the functional, physicochemical and antigenic characteristics of rat homocytotropic antibody suggest that it is not a member of one of the known classes of rat immunoglobulin.

The present studies describe the preparation of an antiserum to rat homocytotropic antibody which fails to recognize rat IgGa, IgGb, IgA, IgM or γ1 but does precipitate an electrophoretically fast rat immunoglobulin with antigen binding capacity. Further, this antiserum used as an immunoabsorbent, removes the biologic activity attributed to rat homocytotropic antibody. The unique immunoglobulin class of rat homocytotropic antibody is designated IgE.

MATERIALS AND METHODS

Bovine serum albumin (BSA, Pentex Inc.) and keyhole limpet hemocyanin (KLH, Mann Research Laboratories, Inc.) were purchased from the suppliers. Dinitrophenyl bovine serum albumin (DNP-BSA) and dinitrophenyl keyhole limpet hemocyanin (DNP-KLH) were prepared according to the method of Eisen *et al.* (17) and contained 20 and 1.83×10^3 haptenic groups/mol of protein, respectively.

Antisera containing hapten-specific homocytotropic antibody were prepared by injecting Sprague-Dawley rats weighing 250 to 350 g (Gofmoor Farms) intramuscularly with 1 mg of an aqueous solution of DNP-KHL and simultaneously injecting intraperitoneally 1.0 ml of heat-killed *Bordetella pertussis* vaccine (2×10^{10} organisms/ml) obtained from Dr. E. S. Barclay (Merck Sharp and Dohme). These antisera were obtained 10 to 12 days after immunization and individual sera were tested for the capacity to mediate PCA after a 48-hr latent period as described (9). Approximately one-half of the DNP-

[1] This work was supported by Grants AI-07722 and FR-05669 from the National Institutes of Health, and a grant from the John A. Hartford Foundation, Inc.

[2] Postdoctoral Fellow of the National Arthritis Foundation.

[3] Postdoctoral Research Fellow of the Helen Hay Whitney Foundation.

KLH antisera were positive for PCA at a dilution of 1:50; two-thirds of these were positive at dilutions of greater than 1:100. Sera with comparable PCA titers were pooled and stored at −70°C.

The antisera were fractionated by ion-exchange chromatography using diethylaminoethyl (DE-52) cellulose microgranules (Reeve Angel, Clifton, N. J.) and Sephadex G-200 gel filtration (5, 7). The identification of rat immunoglobulins in chromatographic fractions was achieved by Ouchterlony analysis in 1% agar using monospecific antisera to rat IgGa, IgGb, IgA, IgM and γ1 (7). Immuno- and radioimmunoelectrophoretic techniques performed as previously described (5) were utilized to detect the ability of precipitated immunoglobulins to bind radiolabeled antigen. The rabbit anti-rat Fab antiserum was that described (7).

RESULTS

Preparation of specific antiserum to rat homocytotropic antibody

Homocytotropic antibody rich immunogen. The globulins in pooled homocytotropic antisera were precipitated in a solution of 50% $(NH_4)_2SO_4$. The precipitate was washed with a 33% solution of $(NH_4)_2SO_4$, resuspended and equilibrated in a volume of 0.01 M, pH 7.5 phosphate buffer equal to one-third the starting serum volume. Eighty milliliters of this material were applied to a 4.5- x 100-cm column of DE-52 cellulose equilibrated with 0.01 M, pH 7.5 phosphate buffer. The proteins were eluted by the step-wise addition of phosphate buffers as shown in Figure 1. Homocytotropic antibody in the unconcentrated eluate as detected by PCA was eluted with the 0.05 M, pH 5.5 phosphate buffer. This fraction was concentrated by ultrafiltration (Amicon Corporation, Lexington, Mass.) to 8 ml, dialyzed against phosphate buffered saline (PBS), pH 7.2, and applied to a 4.5- x 100-cm column of Sephadex G-200 equilibrated with PBS. The distribution of the homocytotropic antibody in the resulting chromatogram is shown in Figure 2. The fractions containing homocytotropic antibody were pooled and concentrated to a volume of 8 ml. The protein concentration of this material was estimated by absorption spectrophotometry at 280 nm; the O.D./μg N/ml was assumed to be 0.01.

Immunization. Homocytotropic antibody-rich immunogen was emulsified with an equal volume of complete Freund's adjuvant (Difco). One milliliter of this emulsion containing 114 μg of protein was injected into the footpads of guinea pigs immediately after the intravenous injection of 5 mg of rat IgG in 1 ml of 0.15 M NaCl. The IgG was isolated from hyperimmune rat antiserum as described (5) and was administered to suppress the antibody response to this immunoglobulin (18). Three weeks later the guinea pigs were boosted intradermally with the same quantity of immunogen in 0.15 M NaCl and their sera were harvested after 10 days. The guinea pig globulins were concentrated to one-third the starting volume by precipitation in 50% $(NH_4)_2$-SO_4, resuspension in and extensive dialysis against 0.15 M NaCl.

Absorption. Some of these concentrated guinea pig globulins were absorbed sequentially with rat

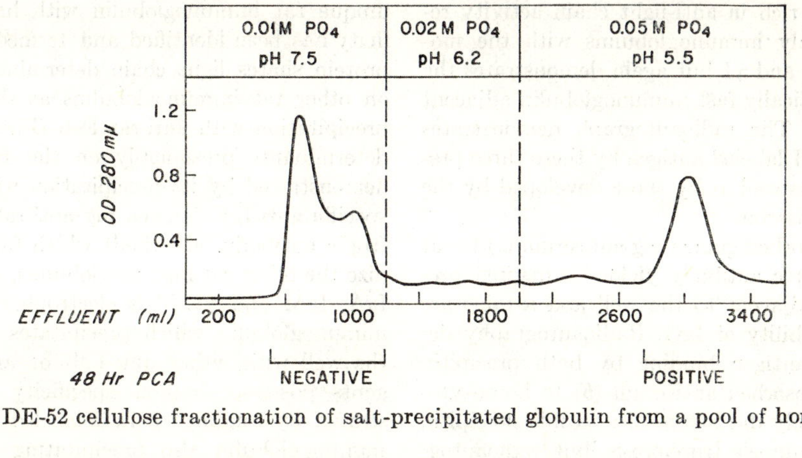

Figure 1. DE-52 cellulose fractionation of salt-precipitated globulin from a pool of homocytotropic antisera.

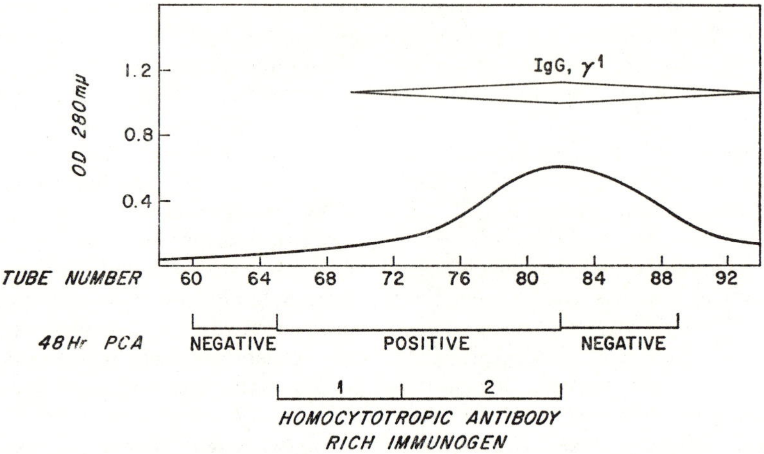

Figure 2. Sephadex G-200 gel filtration of the concentrated PCA-positive fraction obtained on DE-52 cellulose chromatography (Fig. 1). The fractions were collected in 10.5-ml volumes per tube at a flow rate of 15 ml/hr. In later immuno- and radioimmunoelectrophoretic studies the PCA positive fractions were divided and labeled as indicated.

IgG and newborn rat serum cross-linked with glutaraldehyde (19). These absorbed antisera did not react with IgG, IgA, IgM or γ1 immunoglobulins in either Ouchterlony or immunoelectrophoretic analyses.

Immunochemical recognition of rat homocytotropic antibody

The rat homocytotropic antibody-rich immunogen was divided into two portions (1 and 2) as shown in Figure 2 and analyzed by immuno- and radioimmunoelectrophoresis (Fig. 3). Rabbit anti-rat Fab antiserum (*a*) demonstrates both an immunoglobulin with γG mobility and a faster immunoglobulin adjacent to the well. Analysis with unabsorbed rabbit anti-rat IgG antiserum (*d*) which is rich in anti-light chain activity reveals not only immunoglobulins with the mobility of IgG and γ1 but again demonstrates the electrophoretically fast immunoglobulin adjacent to the well. The radioautograph demonstrates binding of ^{125}I-labeled antigen by these three precipitin arcs as well as by those developed by the anti-Fab antiserum.

The unabsorbed guinea pig antiserum (*c*) to rat homocytotropic antibody yielded a distinct precipitin arc adjacent to the well and a faint arc with the mobility of IgG. Radioautography demonstrates antigen binding by both precipitin lines. The absorbed antiserum (*b*) to homocytotropic antibody did not form a visible precipitin arc on immunoelectrophoresis but radioautography demonstrated antigen binding in an electrophoretically fast band adjacent to the well.

The absorbed antiserum to rat homocytotropic antibody which recognized only an electrophoretically fast immunoglobulin was examined for its ability to remove homocytotropic antibody from rat antiserum. As shown in Table I, the PCA titer of rat antiserum capable of yielding a lesion 10 mm in diameter decreased from 1:80 to 1:10 after absorption. Absorption with a comparable amount of either normal guinea pig serum or guinea pig anti-rat IgGa had no effect on the PCA titer.

DISCUSSION

An electrophoretically fast, antigenically unique rat immunoglobulin with hapten specificity has been identified and termed IgE. This protein shares light chain determinants present on other rat immunoglobulins as shown by its precipitation with anti-rat Fab (Fig. 3). Unique determinants presumably on the H chain are demonstrated by its precipitation with a monospecific anti-IgE (guinea pig anti-rat homocytotropic antibody, absorbed) which fails to recognize the other rat immunoglobulins, IgGa, IgGb, IgA, IgM and γ1. This electrophoretically fast immunoglobulin which precipitates adjacent to the well with either anti-Fab or anti-IgE reagents possesses hapten specificity as demonstrated by binding of radiolabeled antigen. An immunoglobulin also precipitating adjacent to

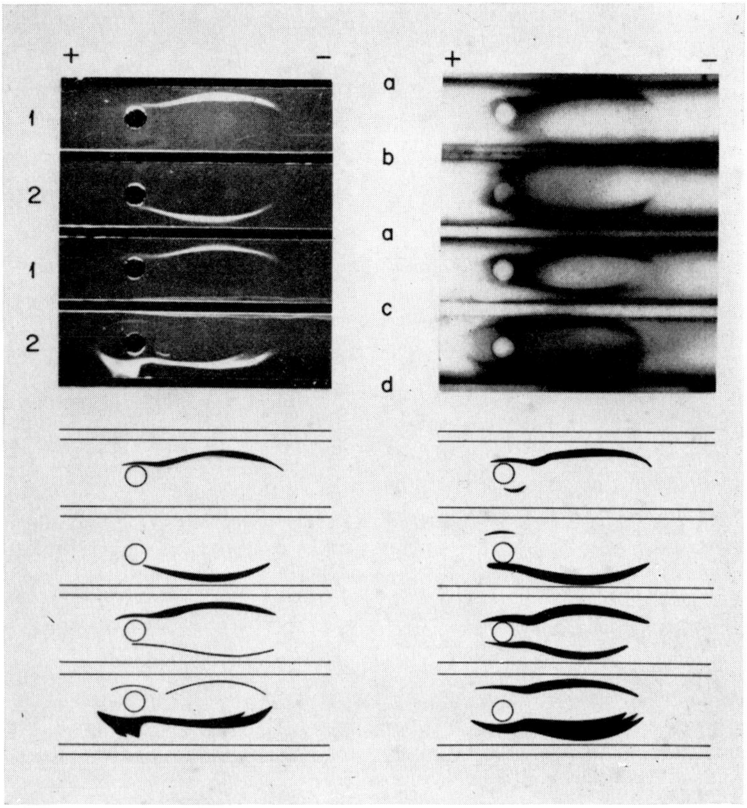

Figure 3. Immuno- and radioimmunoelectrophoretic analyses of homocytotropic antibody-rich immunogen divided as shown in Figure 2.

TABLE I

Removal of the PCA activity of rat antiserum[a]

Dilutions of Homocytotropic Antiserum	Absorbent					
	Normal guinea pig serum		Anti-rat homocytotropic antibody (absorbed)		Anti-rat IgGa	
	mm		*mm*		*mm*	
1:10	13	3+[b]	11	2+	14	3+
1:20	13	3	9	1	13	3
1:40	11	2	5	1	10	2
1:80	10	2	0	0	10	2

[a] Samples of rat DNP-KLH antiserum were incubated with an equal volume of each absorbent with constant stirring at 37°C for 1 hr and then at 4°C for 1 hr. The samples were centrifuged at 30,000 × G for 30 min and the supernatants then tested for 48 hr PCA activity.

[b] PCA reactions in rat skin were recorded by diameter (millimeters) and intensity of blueing (1+ to 3+) and the results expressed as the mean obtained from three rats.

the well and binding radiolabeled antigen has recently been recognized in the serum of rats infected with the nematode, *Nippostrongylus brasiliensis* (20).

In order to isolate rat IgE-rich material for use as an immunogen its presence throughout the fractionation procedures was monitored by its ability to mediate PCA after a 48-hr latent period. The trace nature of this immunoglobulin required that a 240-ml pool of rat antisera with a PCA titer of greater than 1:50 be processed by salt precipitation, ion-exchange chromatography (Fig. 1) and gel filtration (Fig. 2) to yield approximately 4 mg of IgE rich material. Since this material was known to contain electrophoretically fast IgG, the animals were pretreated with electrophoretically slow IgG to suppress the antibody response to this immunoglobulin class. Nonetheless, the antiserum obtained weakly recognized this immunoglobulin class as well as $\gamma 1$. To remove these reactivities, the antiserum was absorbed sequentially with glutaraldehyde cross-linked IgG and newborn rat serum resulting in a monospecific reagent for rat IgE.

Monospecific antiserum for rat IgE (Fig. 3) was capable of removing from rat antiserum the biologic activity attributable to homocytotropic antibody (Table I). The specificity of this absorption was demonstrated by the failure of antisera to rat IgGa or normal guinea pig serum to effect a reduction in biologic activity. It should also be noted that the activities removed by specific absorption include both the capacity to prepare rats for PCA (Table I) and mediation of the antigen-induced intraperitoneal release of histamine and slow-reacting substance of anaphylaxis (SRS-A) (21). Further, rat tissues sensitized with homocytotropic antibody as demonstrated by antigen challenge also manifest a cutaneous change in vascular permeability or the intraperitoneal release of histamine and SRS-A when challenged with anti-rat IgE. Thus, the unique immunoglobulin class of homocytotropic antibody is IgE.

Acknowledgments. The authors gratefully acl knowledge the untiring and proficient technica-assistance of Mrs. C. R. Wesley and Mrs. F. S. Frasier.

REFERENCES

1. Arnason, B. G., De Vaux St-Cyr, C. and Relyveld, E. H., Int. Arch. Allerg., *25:* 206, 1964.
2. Nussenzweig, V. and Binaghi, R. A., Int. Arch. Allerg., *27:* 355, 1965.
3. Binaghi, R. A. and Sarandon de Merlo, E., Int. Arch. Allerg., *30:* 589, 1966.
4. Banovitz, J. and Ishizaka, K., Proc. Soc. Exp. Biol. Med., *125:* 78, 1967.
5. Bloch, K. J., Morse, H. C. and Austen, K. F., J. Immun., *101:* 650, 1968.
6. Bistany, T. S., Tomasi, Jr., T. B. and Butler, V. P., Fed. Proc., *28:* 820 (abstract), 1969.
7. Stechschulte, D. J. and Austen, K. F., J. Immun., *104:* 1052, 1970.
8. Mota, I., Ann. N.Y. Acad. Sci., *103:* 264, 1963.
9. Binaghi, R. A. and Benacerraf, B., J. Immun., *92:* 920, 1964.
10. Becker, E. L. and Austen, K. F., J. Exp. Med., *124:* 379, 1966.
11. Austen, K. F. Bloch, K. J., Baker, A. R. and Arnason, B. G., Proc. Soc. Exp. Biol. Med., *120:* 542, 1965.
12. Binaghi, R. A., Benacerraf, B., Bloch, K. J. and Kourilsky, F. M., J. Immun., *92:* 927, 1964.
13. Jones, V. E. and Ogilvie, B. M., Immunology, *12:* 583, 1967.
14. Bloch, K. J. and Wilson, R. J. M., Immunology, *100:* 629, 1968.
15. Stechschulte, D. J., Austen, K. F. and Bloch, K. J., J. Exp. Med., *125:* 127, 1967.
16. Jones, V. E., Immunology, *16:* 589, 1969.
17. Eisen, H. N., Belman, S. and Carsten, M. E., J. Amer. Chem. Soc., *75:* 4583, 1953.
18. Henney, C. S. and Ishizaka, K., J. Immun., *103:* 56, 1969.
19. Avrameas, S. and Ternynck, T., Immunochemistry, *6:* 53, 1969.
20. Frick, O. L. and Pickart, L., J. Allerg., *45:* 123 (abstract) 1970.
21. Orange, R. P., Stechschulte, D. J. and Austen, K. F., J. Immun., *105:* 1087, 1970.

THE JOURNAL OF IMMUNOLOGY
Vol. 105, No. 5, November 1970

Printed in U.S.A.

IMMUNOCHEMICAL AND BIOLOGIC PROPERTIES OF RAT IgE

II. Capacity to Mediate the Immunologic Release of Histamine and Slow-Reacting Substance of Anaphylaxis (SRS-A)[1]

ROBERT P. ORANGE,[2] DANIEL J. STECHSCHULTE[3] AND K. FRANK AUSTEN

From the Department of Medicine, Harvard Medical School at the Robert B. Brigham Hospital, Boston, Massachusetts 02120

Received for publication June 16, 1970

Rat IgE identified by its physicochemical and antigenic characteristics was shown to mediate the immunologic release of both histamine and slow-reacting substance of anaphylaxis (SRS-A) in the rat. The antibodies in homocytotropic antiserum which mediated histamine and SRS-A release after a 2-hr latent period were shown to be heat-labile, to elute on DE-52 cellulose chromatography and Sephadex G-200 gel filtration in the fractions known to contain rat IgE, and to sediment as an approximately 8S immunoglobulin on sucrose density gradient ultracentrifugation. Absorption with mono-specific guinea pig anti-IgE strikingly reduced the capacity of homocytotropic antiserum to mediate passive cutaneous anaphylaxis or the intraperitoneal release of histamine and SRS-A, thereby establishing that these biologic activities of homocytotropic antiserum are attributable to an antigenically unique rat immunoglobulin. The release of histamine and SRS-A mediated by rat IgE is dependent on the participation of the mast cell but does not require the circulating polymorphonuclear (PMN) leukocyte or an intact complement system, thus differing from the PMN leukocyte- and complement-dependent pathway to SRS-A release mediated by the IgGa antibodies of hyperimmune serum.

Rat homocytotropic antibody represents a unique class of immunoglobulin in the rat capable of sensitizing homologous mast cells *in vivo* (1–3) and *in vitro* (4, 5) for the antigen-induced release of histamine and serotonin. These antibodies appear in low titer, and only transiently, in the primary response of rats immunized with protein antigens or hapten-protein conjugates (1, 2), while rats repeatedly infected with the nematode, *Nippostrongylus brasiliensis* (6, 7), exhibit higher and more persistent antibody titers. The reaction of passive cutaneous anaphylaxis (PCA) mediated by homocytotropic antibody has an optimal latent period for sensitization of 48 to 72 hr (1, 7) and is completely suppressed by pretreatment of rats with a combination of histamine and serotonin antagonists (8). Homocytotropic antibody also prepares rats for the intraperitoneal (i.p.) release of histamine following the same sensitization period used for PCA (9). Preliminary studies (9) have indicated that whole rat antiserum containing high titers of hapten-specific homocytotropic antibody mediates the i.p. release of not only histamine but also slow-reacting substance of anaphylaxis (SRS-A), providing a 2-hr latent period is employed.

Rat homocytotropic antibody is known to be a trace immunoglobulin of fast electrophoretic mobility, has a molecular size greater than the 7S IgG globulins, and is susceptible to inactivation by heat or 2-mercaptoethanol (2, 6, 7, 10). As demonstrated in the preceding paper (11), the biologic and chemical properties ascribed to rat homocytotropic antibody are characteristic of an antigenically unique rat immunoglobulin termed IgE. The present paper establishes that rat IgE antibody is involved in the release of both histamine and SRS-A, that the mast cell is an es-

[1] This work was supported by Grants AI-07722 and FR-05669 from the National Institutes of Health.

[2] Postdoctoral Research Fellow of the Helen Hay Whitney Foundation.

[3] Postdoctoral Fellow of the National Arthritis Foundation.

sential cellular prerequisite for the release of both mediators, that serum complement is not necessary for this reaction, and that the release of both mediators is inhibited by disodium cromoglycate. This reaction sequence is clearly differentiated from the IgGa-mediated, polymorphonuclear (PMN) leukocyte- and complement-dependent release of SRS-A in this species.

MATERIALS AND METHODS

Bovine γ globulin (BGG) and bovine serum albumin (BSA) were obtained from Pentex, Inc., and keyhole limpet hemocyanin (KLH) from Mann Research Laboratories. Dinitrophenyl conjugates of BGG (DNP-BGG), BSA (DNP-BSA) and KLH (DNP-KLH) were prepared according to the method of Eisen *et al.* (12).

Materials employed to deplete rats of various cellular and humoral agents

Pharmacologic agents. Diethylcarbamazine citrate (Hetrazan, Lederle Laboratories), disodium cromoglycate (Intal, Fison's Pharmaceuticals) and cytosine arabinoside (Cytarabine, The Upjohn Co.) were gifts of the manufacturers.

Rabbit antisera against various cellular elements. Rabbit antisera directed against rat peritoneal mast cells (Ra anti-RMC), rat polymorphonuclear leukocytes (Ra anti-RPMN), and rat thymic lymphocytes (Ra anti-RTL) were prepared as described in references 13, 3 and 14, respectively. Rabbit anti-rat platelet antisera (Ra anti-RPL) were prepared as follows: Blood from the carotid artery of 20 rats was collected in polypropylene tubes, immediately mixed with 0.2 M ethylenediaminetetraacetic acid (EDTA, Fisher Scientific Co.), and centrifuged at 4°C at 220 × G for 20 min. The platelet-rich plasma was aspirated using siliconized Pasteur pipettes and the platelets were sedimented by centrifugation at 1500 × G for 20 min at 4°C. The platelets were resuspended in Tyrode's solution without Ca^{++} or Mg^{++} containing 0.005 M EDTA, and were washed three times. The final suspension was standardized to 4×10^9 platelets/ml. The platelet suspension (0.5 ml) was emulsified in an equal volume of complete Freund's adjuvant (Difco Laboratories) and the emulsion was injected into the four footpads of albino rabbits. Three to 4 weeks later, the rabbits were exsanguinated and the sera stored at −70°C.

Preparation of cobra venom factor. Cobra venom factor (CoVF) was prepared from the lyophilized venom of the cobra *Naja naja* (Calbiochem) by DEAE-cellulose chromatography as described by Ballow and Cochrane (15). Three units of CoVF as defined in reference 15 were injected intravenously (i.v.) into Sprague-Dawley rats 18 hr before an experiment. Whole serum complement determinations (CH_{50}) were carried out according to the method of Mayer (16).

Antibody preparations employed to mediate the release of histamine and SRS-A

Hyperimmune rat antisera were obtained by injecting into the footpads of male Sprague-Dawley rats (Gofmoor Farms) 4.0 mg of DNP-BGG in 0.5 ml of 0.15 M saline emulsified in 0.5 ml of complete Freund's adjuvant. The rats were exsanguinated 21 to 28 days later, and the antisera stored at −70°C. These hyperimmune antisera contained IgGa, IgGb and γ1 hapten-specific antibodies as determined by radioimmunoelectrophoresis (17); they did not mediate a 48-hr PCA reaction in the rat (18). The monospecific rabbit and guinea pig antisera against rat immunoglobulins were the reagents described by Stechschulte and Austen (19).

Rat antiserum containing homocytotropic antibody was obtained by injecting rats intramuscularly (i.m.) in both thighs with 1.0 mg of DNP-KLH or DNP-BGG and simultaneously injecting the rats i.p. with 1.0 ml of a heat-killed *Bordetella pertussis* vaccine (2×10^{10} organisms/ml) obtained from Dr. E. S. Barclay (Merck, Sharp and Dohme). The rats were exsanguinated 10 to 12 days later and the sera stored at −70°C. These homocytotropic antisera contained IgE hapten-specific antibody (11) and are capable of preparing rats for 48-hr PCA reactions at dilutions of 1:50 or greater. Small quantities of specific IgGa, IgGb, and γ1 were also present.

Sephadex G-200 gel filtration (19) and chromatography (17) using DE-52 cellulose microgranules (Reeve Angel, Clifton, N. J.) were performed as described. Sucrose density gradient ultracentrifugation was carried out according to the method of Martin and Ames (20) using a Beckman model L2-65B ultracentrifuge equipped with an SW-50 rotor.

Preparation of rats for the antigen-induced release of histamine and SRS-A

Male Sprague-Dawley rats weighing 250 to 350 g and of similar size in each experiment were prepared for the immunologic release of histamine and SRS-A by the i.p. injection of whole antiserum or its fractions diluted in 1.0 ml of 0.15 M NaCl. After a 2-hr latent period, except when otherwise cited in the text, the animals were challenged by the i.p. injection of 2.0 mg of DNP-BSA in 5.0 ml of Tyrode's solution containing heparin, 50 μg/ml. Five minutes later, the animals were stunned and exsanguinated; the peritoneal fluid was harvested, centrifuged, and the supernatant collected as described (3). Pharmacologic inhibitors were diluted in 1.0 ml of 0.15 M saline and injected i.p. 30 sec before challenge with specific antigen. Histamine and SRS-A were bioassayed on the atropinized guinea pig ileum as described (3). One unit of SRS-A refers to the concentration required to produce a contraction of the guinea pig ileum equal in amplitude to that produced by 5 ng histamine base/ml in that assay. The results of each experiment are expressed as the mean value for the three or four rats in each group.

RESULTS

Male Sprague-Dawley rats were injected i.p. with rat antiserum containing hapten-specific homocytotropic antibody and after various time intervals, the animals were challenged by the i.p. injection of specific antigen (Fig. 1). The maximal release of histamine was observed using latent periods ranging from 2 to 48 hr. In contrast, the release of SRS-A was maximal at 2 hr and declined to barely detectable levels by 12 to 24 hr. The capacity of the antiserum to prepare rats for the release of both mediators was lost on heating at 56°C for 4 hr.

A comparison was made of the ability of hyperimmune antiserum and homocytotropic antiserum to mediate the i.p. release of histamine and SRS-A before and after heating at 56°C for 4 hr (Table I). The capacity of hyperimmune antiserum to mediate the release of SRS-A is not altered by heating, whereas there is a marked reduction in histamine and SRS-A release when homocytotropic antiserum is heated at 56°C for 4 hr.

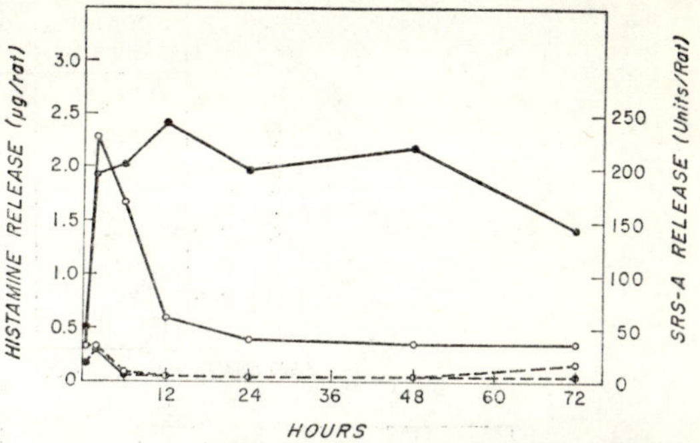

Figure 1. The effect of varying the latent period between the i.p. injection of 0.25 ml of homocytotropic anti-DNP-KLH antiserum (PCA titer at 48 hr = 50) on the subsequent antigen-induced release of histamine (●——●) and SRS-A (○——○). The effect of heating the homocytotropic antiserum at 56°C for 4 hr is also indicated (-----).

TABLE I

Histamine and SRS-A release in rats prepared with hyperimmune or homocytotropic antiserum[a]

Antibody Preparation	56°C for 4 hr	Histamine Release	SRS-A Release
		μg/rat	*units/rat*
Hyperimmune	−	1.0	142
Hyperimmune	+	0.4	177
Homocytotropic	−	6.7	600
Homocytotropic	+	1.7	174

[a] Rats were prepared by injecting i.p. 0.5 ml of hyperimmune anti-DNP-BGG antiserum (1.3 mg of hapten-specific antibody protein/ml) or 0.25 ml of homocytotropic anti-DNP-KLH antiserum (PCA titer at 48 hr = 200).

The capacity of an IgE-containing fraction from homocytotropic antiserum to mediate the antigen-induced release of histamine and SRS-A. Figure 2 describes a typical elution pattern obtained when 10 ml of homocytotropic antiserum were separated by step-wise elution from DE-52 cellulose columns (17). As determined by immuno- and radioimmunoelectrophoretic analyses, fraction 1 contained IgGa, fraction 2 contained IgGa and IgGb, and fraction 4 contained electrophoretically "fast" IgGa and γ1. Fractions 3, 5 and 6 contained small amounts of IgGa and γ1. Only fraction 7 contained rat IgM. The capacity to prepare rats for a 48-hr PCA reaction and the i.p. release of histamine and SRS-A resided predominantly in fraction 4.

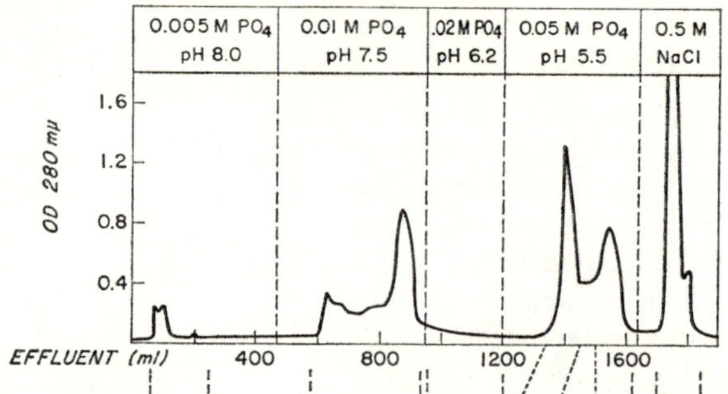

FRACTIONS	1	2	3	4	5	6	7	Starting Pool
48 Hr PCA TITER	0	0	0	50	5	0	0	50
HISTAMINE RELEASE (μg/rat)	0.16	0.16	0.52	7.74	0.73	0.37	0.08	6.70
SRS-A RELEASE (units/rat)	29	29	46	696	112	12	14	541

Figure 2. Fractionation of rat homocytotropic anti-DNP-KLH antiserum on a DE-52 cellulose column by the step-wise addition of phosphate buffers. The effluent fractions were pooled as noted above, concentrated to the original volume by ultrafiltration, dialyzed against 0.15 M saline, evaluated for PCA activity at 48 hr, and tested for the ability of 0.25 ml to prepare the rat peritoneal cavity for antigen-induced histamine and SRS-A release after a 2-hr latent period.

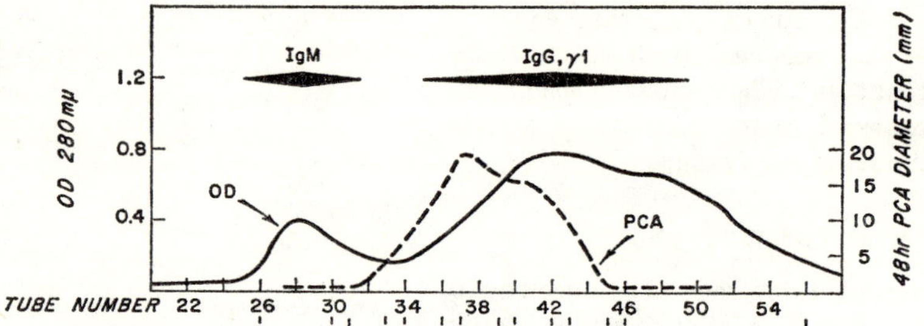

HISTAMINE RELEASE (μg/Rat)	0.19	0.15	2.6	9.2	6.9	3.4	0.3
SRS-A RELEASE (Units/Rat)	<10	15	21	121	86	60	5

Figure 3. Fractionation of fraction 4 (see Fig. 2) by Sephadex G-200 gel filtration. Rat IgM was added to the applied sample and the chromatogram developed with phosphate-buffered saline, pH 7.2. The effluent sample in each tube was evaluated for its immunoglobulin content by Ouchterlony analysis. The effluent fractions were pooled as noted above, concentrated to the original volume by ultrafiltration, tested for PCA activity at 48 hr and for the ability of 1.0 ml to prepare the rat peritoneal cavity for antigen-induced histamine and SRS-A release after a 2-hr latent period.

Fraction 4 was separated by Sephadex G-200 gel filtration (Fig. 3). The capacity to mediate the 48-hr PCA reaction and the i.p. release of histamine and SRS-A were maximal in the eluate pools recovered from the ascending limb of the 7S peak. These activities did not correlate with the peak concentrations of IgG or γ1 but rather with the distribution of hapten-specific IgE antibody (11). Further evidence of a difference in molecular size between IgE and 7S IgGa antibodies was obtained by sucrose density gradient ultracentrifugation (Fig. 4). The peak activity derived from fraction 4 sedimented more rapidly than the main protein peak and in relation to the albumin marker was compatible with an immunoglobulin of about 8S molecular size. In comparable experiments with hyperimmune antiserum to DNP-BGG, the IgGa (fraction 1) was associated with the protein peak and a sedimentation rate of about 7S. The biologic activity of IgGa after fractionation by either Sephadex G-200 gel filtration or sucrose density gradient ultracentrifugation was stable when the preparation was heated at 56°C for 4 hr.

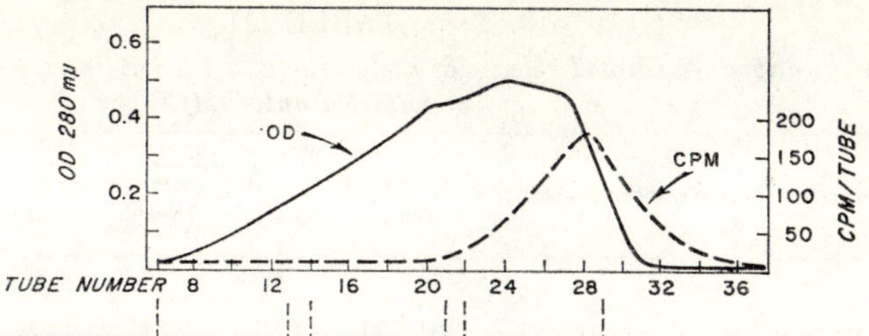

HISTAMINE RELEASE (µg/Rat)	Unheated	0.59	1.51	0.25
	56°C - 4hr	0.08	0.25	0.16
SRS-A RELEASE (Units/Rat)	Unheated	60	158	64
	56°C - 4hr	31	27	30

Figure 4. Sucrose density gradient ultracentrifugation of fraction 4 (see Fig. 2). A trace amount of ^{125}I-labeled rabbit serum albumin was added to the sample as a marker (-----). A gradient was developed using 10% and 30% sucrose. Fractions were pooled as depicted, diluted to starting serum volume and divided into two portions, one of which was heated at 56°C for 4 hr. The capacity of 1.0 ml of the fractions to mediate histamine and SRS-A release was then determined.

Removal of the biologic activity of homocytotropic antiserum by absorption with specific anti-IgE. As shown previously (11), absorption of homocytotropic antiserum with mono-specific guinea pig anti-rat IgE markedly reduced the 48-hr PCA titer. The capacity of homocytotropic antiserum absorbed with this mono-specific guinea pig anti-rat IgE to mediate the release of histamine and SRS-A in the peritoneal cavity was reduced by 74% and 64% respectively (Table II). The effects of absorption with normal guinea pig serum were inconsistent.

Cellular prerequisites for the antigen-induced release of histamine and SRS-A mediated by homocytotropic antibody. In an attempt to determine the cellular prerequisites for the homocytotropic antibody-mediated release of histamine and SRS-A, rats were pretreated with various pharmacologic and biologic agents in order to deplete the animals of certain cell types. As shown previously (3), rats pretreated with distilled water demonstrate a marked reduction in the number of free peritoneal mast cells as assessed by measurement of the residual cellular histamine concentrations as well as a reduction in tissue histamine (21). Rats pretreated with distilled water and prepared with homocytotropic antiserum or a fraction 4 derived therefrom by DE-52 chromatography demonstrated a significant suppression of both histamine and SRS-A release upon subsequent challenge with specific antigen (Table III). Depletion of the peritoneal mast cell population with Ra anti-

TABLE II

Removal of the biologic activity of homocytotropic antiserum by absorption with specific anti-IgE antiserum[a]

Homocytotropic Antiserum	Peritoneal Fluid		
	Histamine residual	Histamine release	SRS-A release
	µg/rat	*µg/rat*	*units/rat*
Unabsorbed	42	7.6	379
Absorbed with anti-rat IgE	30	2.1	154
Absorbed with normal guinea pig serum	36	10.0	284

[a] Samples of rat DNP-KLH antiserum were incubated with one-half volume of each absorbent with constant stirring at 37°C for 1 hr and then at 4°C for 1 hr. The samples were centrifuged at 30,000 × G for 30 min and the supernatant antiserum was removed. Rats were prepared by injecting i.p. 0.3 ml of antiserum.

RMC also prevented the antigen-induced release of histamine and SRS-A mediated by homocytotropic antiserum or fraction 4 (Table III).

Pretreatment of rats with cytosine arabinoside (22) resulted in an 80% reduction in the absolute neutrophil count but had no effect on the peritoneal mast cell population. In confirmation of earlier experiments (3), a marked neutropenia resulted in suppression of SRS-A release in rats prepared with hyperimmune antiserum (Table

TABLE III

Homocytotropic antibody-mediated release of histamine and SRS-A in rats pretreated with distilled water[a] or with Ra anti-RMC[b]

Antibody Preparation	Pretreatment Procedure	Peripheral Blood				Peritoneal Fluid		
		WBC	Poly	Lymph	Mono	Histamine residual	Histamine release	SRS-A release
						μg/rat	*μg/rat*	*units/rat*
Homocytotropic antiserum	—	10,800	21	74	5	27.0	3.7	286
	Distilled water	9,700	16	77	7	0.06	0.5	144
Fraction 4	—	13,500	19	75	6	17.3	6.4	503
	Distilled water	15,650	29	66	5	0.03	0.7	60
Homocytotropic antiserum	—	11,350	18	67	15	26.3	3.00	132
	Ra anti-RMC	17,300	26	64	10	0.05	0.01	24
Fraction 4	—	10,100	28	68	4	24.0	4.70	300
	Ra anti-RMC	11,300	25	69	6	0.01	0.05	19

[a] Rats were prepared by injecting i.p. 0.25 ml of homocytotropic anti-DNP-KLH antiserum (PCA titer at 48 hr = 50) or 0.2 ml of fraction 4 of homocytotropic anti-DNP-KLH antiserum. Distilled water (20 ml) was administered i.p. 4 days before the experiments.

[b] Rats were prepared by injecting i.p. 0.3 ml of homocytotropic anti-DNP-BGG antiserum (PCA titer at 48 hr = 20) or 0.25 ml of fraction 4 of homocytotropic anti-DNP-KLH antiserum. Ra anti-RMC (2.5 ml) was injected i.p. 16 hr before experiment.

TABLE IV

Hyperimmune and homocytotropic antibody-mediated release of histamine and SRS-A in rats pretreated with cytosine arabinoside[a]

Antibody Preparation	Pretreatment Procedure	Peripheral Blood				Peritoneal Fluid		
		WBC	Poly	Lymph	Mono	Histamine residual	Histamine release	SRS-A release
						μg/rat	*μg/rat*	*units/rat*
Hyperimmune	—	6830	38	60	2	7.5	0.4	289
Hyperimmune	Cytosine arabinoside	2990	12	83	5	15.0	0.4	90
Homocytotropic	—	8700	38	59	3	24.0	8.7	270
Homocytotropic	Cytosine arabinoside	3300	17	81	2	14.0	11.6	271
Fraction 4	—	8580	47	51	2	21.0	10.1	188
Fraction 4	Cytosine arabinoside	3020	22	78	0	15.0	7.3	189

[a] Rats were prepared by injecting i.p. 0.5 ml of hyperimmune anti-DNP-BGG antiserum (2.7 mg of hapten-specific antibody/ml) or 0.5 ml of homocytotropic anti-DNP-KLH antiserum (PCA titer at 48 hr = 100) or 0.5 ml of fraction 4 of the homocytotropic antiserum. Cytosine arabinoside, 150 mg/kg, was injected subcutaneously daily for 7 days before the experiments.

IV). In contrast, rats prepared with homocytotropic antiserum or fraction 4 demonstrated no suppression of the antigen-induced release of histamine or SRS-A.

The specificity of the cellular requirement for the homocytotropic antibody-mediated release of histamine and SRS-A was further studied in rats pretreated with Ra anti-RTL to effect a marked lymphopenia or with Ra anti-RPL to induce a thrombocytopenia (Table V). The

TABLE V

Homocytotropic antibody-mediated release of histamine and SRS-A in rats pretreated with Ra anti-RTL and Ra anti-RPL[a]

Antibody Preparation	Pretreatment Procedure	Peripheral Blood					Peritoneal Fluid		
		WBC	Poly	Lymph	Mono	PL	Histamine residual	Histamine release	SRS-A release
							μg/rat	*μg/rat*	*units/rat*
Homocytotropic antiserum	—	9,700	22	70	8	269,000	25.0	6.72	155
	Ra-anti-RTL	4,075	64	29	7	218,000	28.5	5.62	145
	Ra anti-RPL	9,525	42	54	4	17,500	36.0	8.20	206
Fraction 4	—	8,200	36	61	3	144,000	20.0	7.00	625
	Ra anti-RTL	2,780	62	32	6	224,000	22.5	6.30	760
	Ra anti-RPL	8,620	41	55	5	10,000	15.0	5.40	531

[a] Rats were prepared by injecting i.p. 0.25 ml of homocytotropic anti-DNP-KLH antiserum (PCA titer at 48 hr = 200) or 0.25 ml of fraction 4 of homocytotropic anti-DNP-KLH antiserum. Ra anti-RTL (0.3 ml) or Ra anti-RPL (1.0 ml) was injected i.v. 4 hr before antigen challenge.

greater than 80% reduction in the absolute number of circulating lymphocytes after pretreatment with Ra anti-RTL was not associated with significant suppression of the immunologic release of histamine and SRS-A mediated by homocytotropic antiserum or fraction 4. Pretreatment of rats with Ra anti-RPL effected a greater than 90% reduction in circulating platelets without suppressing the homocytotropic antibody-mediated release of histamine and SRS-A.

Pharmacologic inhibition of the homocytotropic antibody-mediated release of histamine and SRS-A. Previous experiments (8), indicating that disodium cromoglycate inhibits the homocytotropic antibody-mediated release of histamine, were extended to demonstrate inhibition of SRS-A release as well. Table VI demonstrates that the inhibition of the antigen-induced release of histamine and SRS-A mediated by fraction 4 of homocytotropic antiserum using various doses of disodium cromoglycate occurred in dose-response fashion. Diethylcarbamazine also inhibited SRS-A release in a dose-response fashion without affecting the release of histamine.

The administration of CoVF reduces the CH_{50} of the serum and markedly suppresses the immunologic release of SRS-A mediated by hyperimmune antiserum (3). This observation was confirmed in the experiment described in Table VII. In contrast, such pretreatment did not suppress the release of histamine and SRS-A mediated by a fraction 4 of homocytotropic antiserum.

TABLE VI

Effects of disodium cromoglycate and diethylcarbamazine on the homocytotropic antibody-mediated release of histamine and SRS-A[a]

Disodium Cromoglycate	Histamine Release	SRS-A Release
mg/kg	*μg/rat*	*units/rat*
0	2.9	176
0.0001	3.4	207
0.001	2.6	121
0.01	0.9	69
1.00	0.3	23
Diethylcarbamazine		
mg/kg		
0.0	12.9	154
1.0	12.7	126
5.0	15.0	81
10.0	12.5	75
20.0	12.3	49

[a] Rats were prepared by injecting i.p. 0.25 ml of fraction 4 of homocytotropic anti-DNP-KLH antiserum (PCA titer of fraction 4 at 48 hr = 100).

DISCUSSION

Rat IgE identified by both its physicochemical and antigenic characteristics was shown to mediate the immunologic release of both hista-

TABLE VII

Hyperimmune and homocytotropic antibody-mediated release of histamine and SRS-A in rats pretreated with CoVF[a]

Antibody Preparation	Pretreatment Procedure	CH_{50}	Peritoneal Fluid		
			Histamine residual	Histamine release	SRS-A release
			μg/rat	*μg/rat*	*units/rat*
Hyperimmune		102	18.0	0.67	462
Hyperimmune	CoVF	0.5	15.0	0.29	75
Fraction 4		122	18.0	9.7	157
Fraction 4	CoVF	0.5	12.0	7.3	230

[a] Rats were prepared by injecting i.p. 0.5 ml of hyperimmune anti-DNP-BGG antiserum (1.8 mg of hapten specific antibody/ml) or 0.5 ml of fraction 4 of homocytotropic anti-DNP-KLH antiserum. Three units of CoVF were injected i.v. in 1.0 ml of 0.15 M saline 18 hr before the experiment.

mine and SRS-A. The antibodies in homocytotropic antiserum which mediated histamine and SRS-A release were demonstrated to be heat-labile (Table I), to elute on DE-52 cellulose chromatography and on Sephadex G-200 gel filtration in the fractions known to contain IgE (Figs. 2 and 3) (11) and on sucrose density gradient ultracentrifugation had a molecular size of approximately 8S (Fig. 4). Absorption with monospecific guinea pig anti-rat IgE reduced strikingly the capacity of homocytotropic antiserum to mediate the reaction of PCA (11) or the i.p. release of histamine and SRS-A (Table II) thereby establishing that these biologic activities of homocytotropic antiserum are the function of rat IgE.

Earlier studies (18) with rat homocytotropic antiserum and a 48-hr latent period, optimal for the PCA reaction, had demonstrated the capacity of this antiserum to mediate the release of histamine without SRS-A. Using a 4-hr latent period (8), homocytotropic antisera with low 48-hr PCA titers used in dilutions of 1:20 to 1:50 also did not mediate the release of significant concentrations of SRS-A. The subsequent observation (23) that human IgE antibody mediated the *in vitro* antigen-induced release of histamine and SRS-A from monkey lung tissue after a 2-hr sensitization period prompted reexamination of the biologic activity of the rat homocytotropic antibody. Preliminary experiments (9) revealed that antibody of higher titer used in the same or lesser dilutions than previously described (8) mediated SRS-A and histamine release if the latent period was shortened to 2 hr. The optimal latent period for the immunologic release of SRS-A mediated by homocytotropic antiserum appeared to be 2 hr, and at 12 hr release was barely detectable; whereas, the capacity to mediate the release of histamine persisted for 48 to 72 hr (Fig. 1). This persistence is consistent with the fixation of the antibody to the target cell, while the limited duration of the ability to release SRS-A suggests the action of an immune complex.

Previous studies have demonstrated that in rats prepared with heterologous (24) and homologous (3, 25) hyperimmune antisera the subsequent antigen-induced release of SRS-A requires the presence of the PMN leukocyte but not the peritoneal mast cell or circulating lymphocyte. Whereas the PMN leukocyte was again established as a cellular prerequisite for the antigen-induced release of SRS-A mediated by hyperimmune antiserum (Table IV), depletion of this cell type had no effect on the release of SRS-A or histamine mediated by homocytotropic antiserum or a partially purified antibody fraction derived therefrom. In contra-distinction, depletion of the peritoneal mast cells by pretreatment of rats with distilled water or Ra anti-RMC (Table III) markedly suppressed the antigen-induced release of SRS-A and histamine mediated by homocytotropic antiserum or fraction 4. The induction of a marked lymphopenia using Ra anti-RTL or a profound thrombocytopenia using Ra anti-RPL was not associated with significant suppression of the biologic activity of homocytotropic antibody (Table V). Thus, only the mast cell was shown to be a cellular prerequisite for the immunologic release of histamine and SRS-A mediated by hapten-specific IgE antibody.

Studies (8, 18) demonstrating that disodium

cromoglycate inhibited the homocytotropic antibody-mediated release of histamine have been confirmed and extended to show that SRS-A release is also suppressed (Table VI). This agent suppressed the release of both mediators in a dose-response fashion with doses of 0.01 mg/kg (1.7 μM concentration i.p.) resulting in about 50% inhibition. Diethylcarbamazine suppressed the release of SRS-A mediated by homocytotropic antibody but was without effect on the concomitant release of histamine (Table VI). This agent also inhibited the IgGa-mediated release of SRS-A (3, 8). These observations suggest that diethylcarbamazine may act at some common point in the immunologic pathways initiated by the interaction of antigen with IgGa or IgE antibodies which leads to the formation and release of SRS-A independent of the cellular prerequisites.

The heat stable 7S IgGa antibodies present in hyperimmune serum (17) which mediate the antigen-induced release of SRS-A require the presence of the PMN leukocyte and serum complement (Tables IV and VII). This pathway may involve the formation of an immune complex, activation of the complement system with elaboration of chemotactic principles (26, 27) and phagocytosis of the complex (28). In contrast, the pathway initiated by the heat-labile IgE antibody and antigen has the mast cell as a cellular prerequisite and exhibits no requirement for the PMN leukocyte (Table IV) or the complement system (Table VII).

Acknowledgments. The authors gratefully acknowledge the untiring and proficient technical assistance of Mrs. C. R. Wesley and Mrs. F. S. Frasier. We are grateful to Mrs. P. Daub for her assistance with the platelet determinations.

REFERENCES

1. Mota, I., Immunology, *7:* 681, 1964.
2. Binaghi, R. A. and Benacerraf, B., Immunology, *92:* 920, 1964.
3. Orange, R. P., Valentine, M. D. and Austen, K. F., J. Exp. Med., *127:* 767, 1968.
4. Mota, I., Ann. N. Y. Acad. Sci., *103:* 264, 1963.
5. Becker, E. L. and Austen, K. F., J. Exp. Med., *124:* 379, 1966.
6. Jones, V. E. and Ogilvie, B. M., Immunology, *12:* 583, 1967.
7. Bloch, K. J. and Wilson, R. J. M., J. Immun., *100:* 629, 1968.
8. Orange, R. P. and Austen, K. F., Proc. Soc. Exp. Biol. Med., *129:* 836, 1968.
9. Orange, R. P., Stechschulte, D. J. and Austen, K. F., Fed. Proc., *28:* 1710, 1969.
10. Binaghi, R. A., Benacerraf, B., Bloch, K. J. and Kourilsky, F. M., Immunology, *92:* 927, 1964.
11. Stechschulte, D. J., Orange, R. P. and Austen, K. F., J. Immun., *105:* 1082, 1970.
12. Eisen, H. N., Belman, S. and Carsten, M. E., J. Amer. Chem. Soc., *75:* 4583, 1953.
13. Valentine, M. D., Bloch, K. J. and Austen, K. F., J. Immun., *99:* 98, 1967.
14. Guttman, R. D., Carpenter, C. B., Lindquist, M. D. and Merrill, J. P., J. Exp. Med., *126:* 1099, 1967.
15. Ballow, M. and Cochrane, C. G., J. Immun., *103:* 944, 1969.
16. Mayer, M. M., in *Kabat and Mayer's Experimental Immunochemistry*, 2nd Ed., p. 133, Charles C Thomas, Springfield, Ill., 1961.
17. Bloch, K. J., Morse, H. C. and Austen, K. F., J. Immun., *101:* 650, 1968.
18. Morse, H. C., Bloch, K. J. and Austen, K. F., J. Immun., *102:* 327, 1969.
19. Stechschulte, D. J. and Austen, K. F., J. Immun., *104:* 1052, 1970.
20. Martin, R. G. and Ames, B. N., J. Biol. Chem., *236:* 1372, 1961.
21. Fawcett, D. W., Anat. Rec., *121:* 29, 1955.
22. Glenn, E. M., Bowman, B. J. and Koslowske, T. C., Biochem. Pharmacol., Supp.: 27, 1968.
23. Ishizaka, T., Ishizaka, K., Orange, R. P. and Austen, K. F., J. Immun., *104:* 335, 1970.
24. Orange, R. P., Valentine, M. D. and Austen, K. F., Science, *157:* 318, 1967.
25. Orange, R. P. and Austen, K. F., in *Cellular and Humoral Mechanisms in Anaphylaxis and Allergy*, Edited by H. Z. Movat, p. 196, S. Karger, Basel, 1969.
26. Ward, P. A., Cochrane, C. G. and Müller-Eberhard, H. J., Immunology, *11:*141,1966.
27. Ward, P. A. and Newman, L. J., J. Immun., *102:* 99, 1969.
28. Gigli, I. and Nelson, R. A., Exp. Cell Res., *51:* 45, 1968.

THE JOURNAL OF IMMUNOLOGY
Vol. 105, No. 5, November 1970
Printed in U.S.A.

IMMUNOCHEMICAL AND BIOLOGIC PROPERTIES OF RAT IgE

III. Modulation of the IgE-Mediated Release of Slow-Reacting Substance of Anaphylaxis by Agents Influencing the Level of Cyclic 3′,5′-Adenosine Monophosphate[1]

WILLIAM J. KOOPMAN[2], ROBERT P. ORANGE[3] AND K. FRANK AUSTEN

From the Department of Medicine, Harvard Medical School at the Robert B. Brigham Hospital, Boston, Massachusetts 02120

Received for publication June 16, 1970

The antigen-induced release of slow-reacting substance of anaphylaxis (SRS-A) in rats prepared with IgE antibody is markedly influenced by agents which act to increase or decrease the levels of cellular cyclic 3′,5′-adenosine monophosphate (cyclic-AMP). Three lines of evidence indicate that the intracellular accumulation of cyclic-AMP suppresses SRS-A release: β-adrenergic stimulation with isoproterenol or epinephrine is inhibitory; methylxanthine derivatives inhibit in a dose-response fashion; and synergism is observed when isoproterenol and aminophylline are used together. Conversely, depletion of cellular cyclic-AMP through direct α-adrenergic stimulation with norepinephrine enhances IgE-mediated SRS-A release. Agents known to be specific α- or β-adrenergic antagonists were employed to establish the specificity of the effects observed with the catecholamines. The β-adrenergic blocking agent, propranolol, prevents the inhibition observed with isoproterenol but has no effect on that observed with aminophylline. The α-adrenergic blocking agent phenoxybenzamine prevents the enhancement of SRS-A release achieved with norepinephrine and enhances the inhibition produced with epinephrine. The implication that the intracellular accumulation of cyclic-AMP inhibits the IgE-mediated release of SRS-A is further supported by the observation that exogenous administration of dibutyryl cyclic-AMP inhibits SRS-A release in a dose-response fashion.

Previous studies in this laboratory (1, 2) have demonstrated that rat IgE antibodies are capable of preparing rats for the intraperitoneal (i.p.) release of both histamine and slow-reacting substance of anaphylaxis (SRS-A) after a 2-hr latent period. These mediators are also released when monkey (3) or human lung (4–6) slices are sensitized with human IgE and challenged with specific antigen. The release of histamine mediated by human IgE from lung tissue (6) or peripheral leukocytes (7, 8) is inhibited by agents capable of increasing intracellular levels of cyclic 3′,5′-adenosine monophosphate (cyclic-AMP). Preliminary studies with monkey lung fragments (9) have revealed that agents leading to an accumulation of cyclic-AMP inhibit the capacity of human IgE to mediate the antigen-induced release of SRS-A as well as histamine. The present studies describe the modulating effect of cyclic-AMP *in vivo* on the IgE-mediated release of SRS-A in the rat; pharmacologic agents which are known to increase endogenous cyclic-AMP levels are inhibitory, whereas agents which decrease cyclic-AMP levels enhance the IgE-mediated release of SRS-A.

[1] This work was supported by Grants AI-07722 and FR-05669 from the National Institutes of Health, and a grant from the John A. Hartford Foundation, Inc.

[2] Predoctoral Fellow, Harvard Medical School.

[3] Postdoctoral Research Fellow of the Helen Hay Whitney Foundation.

MATERIALS AND METHODS

Materials. Dinitrophenyl bovine serum albumin (DNP-BSA) and dinitrophenyl keyhole limpet hemocyanin (DNP-KLH) were prepared as described in a preceding paper (1).

Rat antiserum rich in IgE antibody was obtained from rats immunized with DNP-KLH and a heat-killed *Bordetella pertussis* vaccine as previously described (1). All antisera utilized in this study were capable of preparing rats for 48-hr passive cutaneous anaphylaxis (PCA) reactions (10) at dilutions of at least 1:50.

Isoproterenol hydrochloride (Isuprel, Winthrop Laboratories), norepinephrine bitartrate (Levophed, Winthrop Laboratories), epinephrine hydrochloride (Adrenalin, Parke, Davis and Company), aminophylline (Searle and Company), phenoxybenzamine hydrochloride (Dibenzyline, Smith, Kline and French Laboratories), propranolol hydrochloride (Inderal, Ayerst Laboratories), and dibutyryl adenosine 3′,5′-cyclic monophosphate (Calbiochem) were purchased. Diethylcarbamazine citrate (Hetrazan, Lederle Laboratories) and disodium cromoglycate (Intal, Fison's Pharmaceuticals) were the agents utilized in the preceding paper (2).

The antihistamine, mepyramine maleate (Neo-Antergan), was obtained from Merck, Sharp and Dohme and histamine diphosphate was supplied by Mann Research Laboratories. A partially purified preparation of SRS-A was obtained by ethanol extraction (11).

Methods. Male Sprague-Dawley rats (Gofmoor Farms) of comparable weight in each experiment were prepared for the i.p. release of SRS-A by the i.p. injection of homologous antiserum containing IgE antibody diluted 1:2 to 1:5 in 1.0 ml of 0.15 M saline. After a 2-hr latent period, the animals were challenged with DNP-BSA, the peritoneal fluid was harvested and centrifuged, and the supernatant was collected and bioassayed as described previously (2). One unit of SRS-A is defined arbitrarily in reference 2. The results of each experiment were expressed as the mean SRS-A release for the three or four rats in each group. Because of variability within each group, mean inhibition of less than 25% was not considered significant. Pharmacologic agents tested for their ability to modulate the antigen-induced release of SRS-A were diluted in 1.0 ml of 0.15 M saline and injected i.p. 30 sec before challenge of the rats with specific antigen which was diluted in 5.0 ml Tyrode's solution containing heparin. The concentration of each agent used is expressed in the text on a molar basis assuming that the final i.p. concentration of each agent was diluted in 6.0 ml. Each agent was tested in at least three separate experiments.

Agents appearing to modulate the IgE antibody-mediated release of SRS-A were tested for their effect on the bioassay by two methods. An SRS-A standard was assayed in the presence of various concentrations of each active agent and the concentration of each agent producing end-organ inhibition was determined. In addition, a concentration of each agent which produced 100% inhibition of the *in vivo* immunologic release of SRS-A was injected i.p. into unsensitized rats, and the peritoneal fluid harvested 5 min later was tested for its ability to interefere with the bioassay of an SRS-A standard. No agent used in this study was administered to rats in a concentration which would interfere with the bioassay of SRS-A.

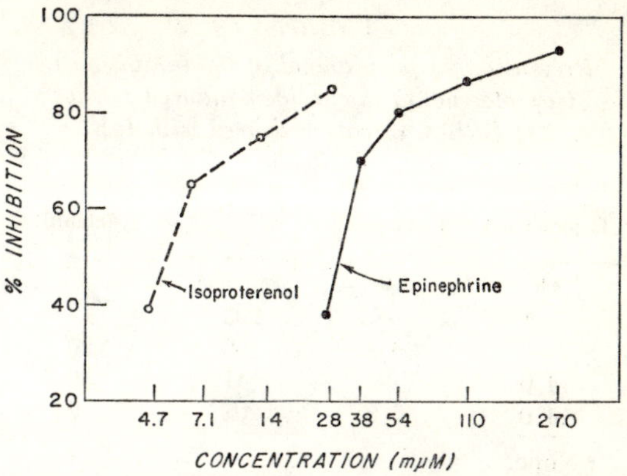

Figure 1. Comparison of the ability of isoproterenol and epinephrine to inhibit the antigen-induced release of SRS-A in rats prepared with IgE antibody.

RESULTS

Modulation by sympathomimetic amines of the IgE antibody-mediated release of SRS-A

Inhibition of the immunologic release of SRS-A by β-adrenergic agents. Initial experiments were conducted to determine the effects of various doses of the predominantly β-adrenergic agent (12) isoproterenol on the IgE antibody-mediated release of SRS-A. Sprague-Dawley rats prepared by the i.p. injection of IgE antibody were injected i.p. with various concentrations of isoproterenol 30 sec before challenge with specific antigen. As depicted in Figure 1, isoproterenol inhibited the antigen-induced release of SRS-A in a dose-response fashion; i.p. concentrations of about 5 nM resulted in 50% inhibition.

TABLE I

Prevention by propranolol of the inhibition by isoproterenol of the antigen-induced release of SRS-A in rats prepared with IgE antibody

Isoproterenol	Propranolol	Mean SRS-A Release	% Inhibition
nM	*nM*	*units/rat*	
—[a]	—	203	—
—	36.3	160	20
14.0	—	41	80
14.0	36.3	208	0

[a] None.

TABLE II

Enhancement by norepinephrine of the antigen-induced release of SRS-A mediated by IgE antibody

Norepinephrine	Phenoxybenzamine	Mean SRS-A Release	% Increase
nM	*nM*	*units/rat*	
—[a]	—	325	—
58.4	—	467	44
—	0.67	378	16
58.4	0.67	363	12

[a] None.

Epinephrine, a sympathomimetic agent possessing both α- and β-adrenergic activity (12), also inhibited the release of SRS-A in a dose-response fashion. The i.p. concentration yielding 50% inhibition was seven times greater on a molar basis than that required with isoproterenol. Alpha-adrenergic blockade with phenoxybenzamine enhanced the inhibitory activity of epinephrine. Pre-treatment of rats with concentrations of epinephrine (27 nM) and phenoxybenzamine (0.66 nM) which alone did not suppress SRS-A release resulted in 50% inhibition when employed together.

The inhibition observed using isoproterenol was reversed by the β-adrenergic blocking agent, propranolol. As shown in Table I, a non-inhibitory dose of propranolol completely prevented the 80% inhibition achieved with a 14 nM concentration of isoproterenol.

Enhancement of the immunologic release of SRS-A by α-adrenergic agents. Preliminary experiments with the predominantly α-adrenergic agent (12) norepinephrine revealed that the dose range 5.8 to 58.4 nM consistently enhanced the IgE-mediated release of SRS-A. As shown in Table II, the enhancing activity of norepinephrine was prevented by the simultaneous administration of the α-adrenergic blocking agent, phenoxybenzamine.

Inhibition by a methylxanthine derivative of the IgE antibody-mediated release of SRS-A

Aminophylline, a methylxanthine derivative, inhibited the IgE-mediated release of SRS-A in a dose-response fashion; 50% inhibition was observed using an i.p. concentration of 3.7 μM (Fig. 2). The inhibitory activity of aminophylline was not prevented by the simultaneous administration of propranolol (Table III); in contrast, propranolol completely prevented the inhibition observed with isoproterenol in the same experiment.

Experiments were next conducted to determine the effect of the simultaneous administration of isoproterenol and aminophylline on the IgE-mediated release of SRS-A (Table IV). Isoproterenol in a concentration of 4.7 nM resulted in 33% inhibition of SRS-A release whereas the same dose administered simultaneously with a non-inhibitory concentration of aminophylline (1.0 μM) produced 68% inhibition. The same non-inhibitory dose of aminophylline increased the inhibition observed with 14.1 nM isoproterenol. The combination of the non-inhibitory dose of aminophylline and the lower dose of isoproterenol yielded more inhibition than a threefold increase in the concentration of isoproterenol administered alone.

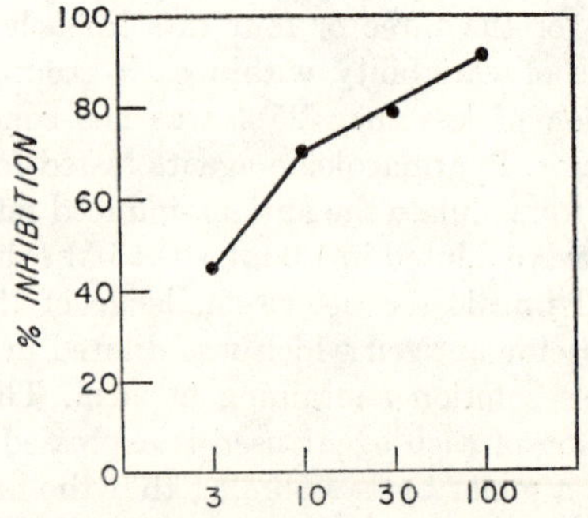

Figure 2. Inhibition by aminophylline of the antigen-induced release of SRS-A in rats prepared with IgE antibody.

TABLE III

Effect of propranolol on the inhibition by isoproterenol and aminophylline of the antigen-induced release of SRS-A in rats prepared with IgE antibody

Isoproterenol	Aminophylline	Propranolol	Mean SRS-A Release	% Inhibition
nM	*μM*	*nM*	*units/rat*	
—[a]	—	—	161	—
—	—	27.0	129	20
—	5.0	—	97	40
—	5.0	27.0	110	32
6.1	—	—	42	74
6.1	—	27.0	171	0

[a] None.

TABLE IV

Synergistic effect of aminophylline and isoproterenol in inhibiting the antigen-induced release of SRS-A in rats prepared with IgE antibody

Isoproterenol	Aminophylline	Mean SRS-A Release	% Inhibition
nM	*μM*	*units/rat*	
—[a]	—	273	—
—	1.0	316	0
4.7	—	182	33
4.7	1.0	88	68
14.1	—	131	52
14.1	1.0	33	88

[a] None.

Inhibition by dibutyryl cyclic-AMP of the IgE antibody-mediated release of SRS-A

The synergistic effect of isoproterenol and aminophylline is consistent with inhibition of SRS-A release by accumulation of endogenous cyclic-AMP (13). The exogenous administration of dibutyryl cyclic-AMP inhibited the subsequent immunologic release of SRS-A in a dose-response fashion (Fig. 3); an i.p. concentration of 0.43 mM dibutyryl cyclic-AMP resulted in 50% inhibition.

The effect of agents which influence the cyclic-AMP system on the inhibitory activity of diethylcarbamazine and disodium cromoglycate

Diethylcarbamazine. Previous studies have demonstrated that the antifilarial agent diethylcarbamazine prevents the IgE-mediated release of SRS-A in the rat (2) and in monkey lung slices (9) while simultaneously permitting the tissues to become desensitized. Attention was now directed toward determining whether its site of action was similar to that of isoproterenol or aminophylline. A non-inhibitory concentration of aminophylline (1.0 μM) failed to increase the activity of an inhibitory concentration of diethylcarbamazine (Table V). This lack of synergism suggested that diethylcarbamazine was not acting in a manner identical to isoproterenol. The failure of propranolol (Table V) to prevent the inhibitory effect of diethylcarbamazine corroborates this view.

When diethylcarbamazine was examined in combination with the catecholamines, it demon-

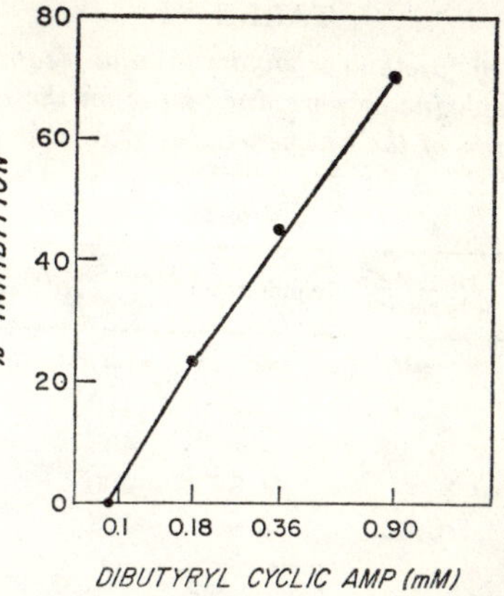

Figure 3. Inhibition by dibutyryl cyclic-AMP of the antigen-induced release of SRS-A in rats prepared with IgE antibody.

TABLE V

Effects of aminophylline or propranolol on the inhibition by diethylcarbamazine of the antigen-induced release of SRS-A in rats prepared with IgE antibody

Diethylcarbamazine	Aminophylline	Mean SRS-A Release	% Inhibition
mM	*μM*	*units/rat*	
—[a]	—	535	—
2.5	—	246	54
—	1.0	507	5
2.5	1.0	309	42
	Propranolol		
	nM		
—	—	522	—
—	18.2	799	—
4.5	—	145	72
4.5	18.2	109	79

[a] None.

TABLE VI

Effects of diethylcarbamazine and isoproterenol, epinephrine or norepinephrine on the inhibition of the antigen-induced release of SRS-A in rats prepared with IgE antibody

Expt.	Diethylcarbamazine	Isoproterenol	Mean SRS-A Release	% Inhibition
	mM	*nM*	*units/rat*	
A	—[a]	—	410	—
	0.42	—	438	7
	—	3.8	400	3
	0.42	3.8	178	57
		Epinephrine		
		nM		
B	—	—	362	—
	0.42	—	335	7
	—	16.0	314	13
	0.42	16.0	72	80
		Norepinephrine		
		nM		
C				
	—	—	410	—
	0.42	—	438	+7
	—	58.4	799	+94
	0.42	58.4	332	−19

[a] None.

TABLE VII

Effects of isoproterenol and aminophylline on the inhibition by disodium cromoglycate of the antigen-induced release of SRS-A in rats prepared with IgE antibody

Expt.	Disodium Cromoglycate	Aminophylline	Mean SRS-A Release	% Inhibition
	μM	*μM*	*units/rat*	
A	—[a]	—	488	—
	1.0	—	267	45
	—	1.0	501	0
	1.0	1.0	388	22
		Isoproterenol		
		nM		
B	—	—	441	—
	3.0	—	175	60
	—	3.8	253	43
	3.0	3.8	198	55

[a] None.

strated a remarkable capacity to influence their action. Non-inhibitory doses of diethylcarbamazine combined with non-inhibitory doses of isoproterenol or epinephrine yielded 57 and 80% inhibition, respectively (Table VI, Expts. A and B). The same non-inhibitory dose of diethylcarbamazine completely prevented the 94% increase in SRS-A release achieved with norepinephrine (Table VI, Expt. C).

Disodium cromoglycate. Disodium cromoglycate represents another previously investigated agent which inhibits the IgE-mediated release of SRS-A (2). A non-inhibitory dose of aminophylline did not increase the effect of an inhibitory dose of disodium cromoglycate (Table VII, Expt. A). Furthermore, the combination of inhibitory doses of disodium cromoglycate and isoproterenol provided essentially the same inhibition as that observed with either agent used alone (Table VII, Expt. B).

DISCUSSION

Adenyl cyclase is a membrane-bound enzyme (14, 15) present in all mammalian cells examined to date except non-nucleated erythrocytes (13). The interaction of β-adrenergic agents with postulated β-receptors in tissues results in the activation of adenyl cyclase (16) and the formation of cyclic-AMP from adenosine triphosphate. A phosphodiesterase in cytoplasm catabolizes cyclic-3′,5′-AMP to 5′-AMP; methylxanthine derivatives appear to be competitive inhibitors of the phosphodiesterase enzyme (13). The intracellular accumulation of cyclic-AMP due to increased synthesis, decreased catabolism, or both, may result in activation of an enzyme (17, 18) or, as in the case of the glycogen synthetase system (19), inactivation of an enzyme. This study presents evidence that agents which act to increase or decrease cellular cyclic-AMP levels modulate the antigen-induced, IgE-mediated release of SRS-A.

Three lines of evidence indicate that the intracellular accumulation of cyclic-AMP results in inhibition of the IgE-mediated release of SRS-A. The predominantly β-adrenergic agents isoproterenol and epinephrine inhibited SRS-A release in a dose-response fashion (Fig. 1); the relative potency of these agents was consistent with their β-adrenergic activity (13). The methylxanthine derivative aminophylline (Fig. 2) also inhibited the IgE-mediated release of SRS-A in a dose-response manner. Finally, synergism was observed between isoproterenol and aminophylline in inhibiting the antigen-induced release of SRS-A (Table IV). Sutherland *et al.* (13) have established the synergistic action of methylxanthine derivatives and β-adrenergic agents as an important criterion for the implication of the cyclic-AMP system in a reaction sequence.

Evidence indicating that decreased cellular levels of cyclic-AMP enhance the release of SRS-A is both direct and indirect. Predominantly α-adrenergic stimulation with norepinephrine is known to be capable of decreasing cellular levels of cyclic-AMP in some tissues (16) and in the present experiments enhanced the release of SRS-A (Tables II and VI, Expt. C). Beta-adrenergic blockade using propranolol, which presumably limited the response to endogenous catecholamines to α-adrenergic stimulation, also enhanced the release of SRS-A in some experiments (Table V) but was not as consistent (Table III) as direct α-stimulation.

The specificity of the effects observed with the catecholamines was established by preventing their action by agents known to be specific α- or β-adrenergic antagonists. The β-adrenergic blocking agent propranolol prevented the inhibition achieved with isoproterenol (Tables I and III) but had no effect on that observed with aminophylline. The α-adrenergic antagonist phenoxybenzamine not only reversed the enhancement of SRS-A release observed with the α-adrenergic agent norepinephrine (Table II) but also enhanced the inhibition with the mixed α-β-adrenergic agent epinephrine. The administration of norepinephrine to sensitized rats in the absence of antigen challenge did not result in the release of SRS-A, suggesting that the cyclic-AMP system modulates the release of SRS-A by acting at some point subsequent to antigen-antibody interaction.

The implication that the intracellular accumulation of cyclic-AMP results in inhibition of the IgE-mediated release of SRS-A was supported by the observation (Fig. 3) that exogenous administration of dibutyryl cyclic-AMP also inhibited the antigen-induced release of SRS-A in a dose response fashion. This alkylated cyclic nucleotide is believed to enter cells more readily and be more slowly catabolized than cyclic-AMP itself (20).

Previous studies have demonstrated that diethylcarbamazine effectively inhibits the release of SRS-A mediated by IgE antibodies (2). The present study demonstrated that diethylcarbamazine is unlike isoproterenol in that there was no synergism with aminophylline and no reversal of inhibition by propranolol (Table V). The capacity of diethylcarbamazine to potentiate the action of epinephrine and to prevent the enhancing effect of norepinephrine (Table VI) was similar to the action of the α-adrenergic antagonist phenoxybenzamine (Table II). However, phenoxybenzamine has not been found to inhibit in a dose-response fashion when used alone and in preliminary experiments did not potentiate the inhibitory activity of the predominantly β-adrenergic agent isoproterenol. Indeed, the marked potentiation of the action of isoproterenol as well as epinephrine by diethylcarbamazine (Table VI) is reminiscent of the synergism observed between β-adrenergic agents and aminophylline. The similarity of the action of diethylcarbamazine to aminophylline is further supported by the preliminary finding that both agents prevent the norepinephrine-induced enhancement of SRS-A release.

In contrast to diethylcarbamazine, disodium cromoglycate, which also inhibits the IgE-mediated release of SRS-A (2), did not potentiate the inhibitory activity of isoproterenol or aminophylline (Table VII). These findings suggest that disodium cromoglycate inhibits the antigen-induced release of SRS-A by an action independent of the cyclic-AMP system.

Acknowledgments. The authors gratefully acknowledge the excellent technical assistance of Mrs. C. R. Wesley and Mrs. F. S. Frasier.

REFERENCES

1. Stechschulte, D. J., Orange, R. P. and Austen, K. F., J. Immun., *105:* 1082, 1970.
2. Orange, R. P., Stechschulte, D. J. and Austen, K. F., J. Immun., *105:* 1087, 1970.
3. Ishizaka, T., Ishizaka, K., Orange, R. P. and Austen, K. F., J. Immun., *104:* 335, 1970.
4. Parish, W. E., Nature, *215:* 738, 1967.
5. Sheard, P., Killingback, P. G. and Blair, A. M. J. N., Nature, *216:* 283, 1967.
6. Assem, E. S. K. and Schild, H. O., Nature, *224:* 1028, 1969.
7. Lichtenstein, L. M. and Margolis, S., Science, *161:* 902, 1968.
8. Lichtenstein, L. M., in *Cellular and Humoral Mechanisms in Anaphylaxis and Allergy*, Edited by H. Z. Movat, p. 176, S. Karger, Basel, 1969.

9. Ishizaka, T., Ishizaka, K., Orange, R. P. and Austen, K. F., Fed. Proc., *29:* 575 (Abstract), 1970.
10. Mota, I., Immunology, *7:* 681, 1964.
11. Orange, R. P., Stechschulte, D. J. and Austen, K. F., Fed. Proc., *28:* 1710, 1969.
12. Ahlquist, R. P., Amer. J. Physiol., *153:* 586, 1948.
13. Sutherland, E. W., Robison, A. G. and Butcher, R. W., Circulation, *38:* 279, 1968.
14. Devoren, P. R. and Sutherland, E. W., J. Biol. Chem., *238:* 3016, 1963.
15. Sutherland, E. W., Rall, T. W. and Mennon, T., J. Biol. Chem., *237:* 1220, 1962.
16. Robison, G. A., Butcher, R. W. and Sutherland, E. W., Ann. N.Y. Acad. Sci., *139:* 703, 1967.
17. DeLonge, R. J., Kemp, R. G., Riley, W. D., Cooper, R. A. and Krebs, E. G., J. Biol. Chem., *243:* 2200, 1968.
18. Rizack, M. A., J. Biol. Chem., *239:* 392, 1964.
19. DeWulf, H. and Hers, H. G., Europ. J. Biochem., *6:* 558, 1968.
20. Pasternak, T., Sutherland, E. W. and Henion, W. F., Biochim. Biophys. Acta, *65:* 558, 1962.

THE JOURNAL OF IMMUNOLOGY
Vol. 105, No. 5, November 1970

FURTHER STUDIES ON GUINEA PIG SKIN SENSITIZING ACTIVITIES OF HUMAN MYELOMA PROTEINS[1]

ZOLTAN OVARY,[2] HENRY G. KUNKEL AND FENNEKE G. JOSLIN

From the Department of Pathology, New York University School of Medicine, New York City 10016 and The Rockefeller University, New York City 10021

Received for publication June 12, 1970

Guinea pigs may be sensitized for reverse passive cutaneous anaphylaxis (RPCA) by the following human γG subclasses: γG1, γG3 and γG4. Native or reduced and alkylated γG2 and γE are unable to do so. Sensitization is independent of the light chain type and also of Gm determinants. Incomplete molecules from heavy chain diseases of subclasses γG1, γG3 or γG4, but not of subclass γG2, may sensitize guinea pig skin. RPCA reactions may be obtained with anti-light chain antibodies with γG1, γG3 or γG4.

It has been shown that reverse passive cutaneous anaphylaxis (RPCA) can be produced in guinea pigs with γG antibodies of several species (1–4). In addition, it is known that RPCA can be produced by some, but not all, myeloma proteins (5). Human and mouse γA and γM, and human γD and γE, are ineffective as are some of the subclasses of mouse and human myelomas (6–9). Sensitization of guinea pig skin for RPCA depends upon some as yet unidentified structure on the Fc portion of the molecule. Fc fragments obtained from rabbit or human antibodies or from γG pools were as effective as the intact γG molecules, whereas the Fab or $F(ab')_2$ fragments were ineffective (10, 11).

In the present paper human γG myeloma proteins of various subclasses with various Gm specificities and with either kappa or lambda chains were investigated for their ability to sensitize the guinea pig for RPCA reactions. Sensitization by incomplete γG molecules obtained from patients with "heavy chain disease," by Fc fragments of different subclasses of human γG myeloma proteins, and by one γE myeloma protein, was also investigated. Finally, it was shown that RPCA reactions can be produced with antibodies specific for kappa or lambda L chain determinants.

[1] This work was supported by National Institutes of Health Grant AI-03075-10 and by the Health Research Council, City of New York, under Contract I-140.

[2] Health Research Council Career Scientist of the City of New York.

MATERIALS AND METHODS

Antigens. Because of previous problems with myeloma proteins containing small amounts of normal γ globulin contaminants, the proteins used in the present study were selected from a much larger group on the basis of relative freedom of such contaminants. Separate typing studies with sensitive genetic typing systems as well as heavy and light chain subgroup typing by hemagglutination inhibition had furnished an accurate assessment of purity (12, 13). The proteins were isolated in most instances by a combination of zone electrophoresis and gel filtration as described previously (14).

The heavy chain disease proteins were obtained from multiple sources. Protein Cr was kindly furnished by Dr. Edward Franklin, protein Gi by Dr. Donald Feinstein and protein Ha by Dr. Kurt Bloch. These were isolated primarily by zone electrophoresis.

Papain splitting of myeloma proteins was carried out as described previously (13). Proteins of the γG2 class were reduced and alkylated first.

Antibodies. All antibodies were tested undiluted in double diffusion in agar (Ouchterlony) using pattern D Hyland plates (Hyland Laboratories, Los Angeles, Calif.).

1. Guinea pig anti-human γ-globulin (Gp anti-HuγG). A pool of sera from 20 guinea pigs hyperimmunized with human Cohn fraction II in Freund's complete adjuvant was used. It contained 6 mg of antibody protein/ml. In scanning experiments it was seen that 0.04 ml of this serum gave strong RPCA reactions with

threshold amounts (2 μg/ml) of the immunizing antigen and with several γG1 specimens. From this pool, 0.05 ml was used per guinea pig for challenge. This antibody gave one strong line in double diffusion in agar against all antigens except against Ha (γG4 heavy chain disease) and for this reason this antibody was not used in RPCA reactions when the Ha heavy chain disease protein was investigated.

2. Rabbit anti-kappa antibody (Rab-anti-k). Rabbits were hyperimmunized with kappa Bence Jones proteins in Freund's complete adjuvant (Difco Labs., Detroit, Mich.) and the sera absorbed with lambda Bence Jones and γG1 lambda proteins. This antibody gave one strong line in double diffusion in agar against kappa myeloma proteins of subclasses γG1, γG3 and γG4 with kappa chains, but did not react with γG1, γG3 or γG4 with lambda chains.

3. Rabbit anti-lambda antibody (Rab-anti-l). Rabbits were hyperimmunized with a γG1 lambda myeloma protein in Freund's complete adjuvant (Difco Labs). The sera were absorbed with a γG1 kappa myeloma protein. This serum gave one strong line in double diffusion in agar against γG1, γG2, γG3 or γG4 lambda myeloma proteins and against γE myeloma protein, but no line was obtained with any of the myeloma proteins with kappa chains.

4. Monkey anti-γG4 antibody (M anti-γG4). A monkey was hyperimmunized with a γG4 kappa myeloma protein in Freund's complete adjuvant. This serum, in double diffusion in agar, gave one strong line against myeloma proteins with κ chains and with Ha heavy chain disease protein, but gave no lines against γG1 lambda myeloma proteins.

From the two rabbit and the monkey antisera 0.2 ml was used per guinea pig.

RPCA. RPCA was performed as previously described (2, 3). Briefly, 0.1 ml of the antigens diluted in 0.15 M NaCl was injected intradermally on the backs of newly shaved guinea pigs. Not more than 12 injections were made per guinea pig. Five animals were used in each experiment. Three concentrations of each antigen were used (20, 10 and 5 μg of protein/ml); when the strongest concentration did not give RPCA reactions the experiment was repeated with 50 μg of protein/ml of this antigen. The period between sensitization and challenge was 5 hr. Challenge was made by intravenous injection of the antibody in 1 ml of 0.5% Evans blue dye in 0.15 M NaCl. The rabbit sera and the monkey serum were absorbed before use with fresh guinea pig serum (0.1 ml of fresh guinea pig serum was mixed with 1 ml of antiserum, then the mixture was centrifuged at 15,000 rpm for 30 min). This treatment was necessary to render the sera nontoxic for guinea pigs. In fact, before absorption with guinea pig serum, these sera frequently produced generalized blueing of the guinea pigs. Thirty to 45 min after challenge the animals were killed, the skin reflected, and the diameter of the reactions measured on both sides of the skin.

Animals. Hartley strain albino guinea pigs of either sex weighing 300 ± 50 g were used for RPCA reactions.

RESULTS

In every subgroup there were proteins with either kappa or lambda chains (Table I). There was no difference in skin-sensitizing activity if the H chains were linked to kappa or lambda type L chains. The three subgroups (γG1, γG3 or γG4) which are capable of sensitizing guinea pig skin for RPCA reactions did so equally well with kappa or lambda L chains. On the other hand, the γG2 subgroup which is unable to sensitize the guinea pig skin (7) did not sensitize when this protein had kappa or lambda chains. The γG2 protein was reduced and alkylated to investigate whether this treatment would reveal some hidden structure which might have skin-sensitizing ability; however, no such property appeared.

Strong RPCA reactions could be produced with anti-L chain antibodies. Antibodies with anti-kappa specificities produced good RPCA reactions with myeloma proteins with kappa L chains but did not provoke any reaction with myeloma proteins with lambda L chains and *vice versa*, i.e., antibodies with anti-lambda specificities provoked RPCA reactions only with myeloma proteins with lambda L chains.

The structure necessary for sensitization of guinea pig skin is not dependent upon the genetically determined different Gm specificities: γG1 with az, axz or f specificities were equally effective, as were the γG3 with either b or g specificities. Proteins of the γG4 class were all effective

TABLE I

RPCA reactions in guinea pigs sensitized with different human gamma G subclasses

Antigen	H Chain Class	Gm Type	L Chain Class	Amounts Injected Intradermally in μg Protein/ml				Antiserum for Challenge
				50	20	10	5	
Ch	γG1	af	k	nd[a]	17[b]	16	12	Gp anti-HuγG
Ja		az	k	nd	16	12	11	Gp anti-HuγG
Dr		az	k	nd	16	15	12	Gp anti-HuγG
Ti		az	k	nd	18	16	13	Gp anti-HuγG
Kl		az	k	nd	20	18	16	Gp anti-HuγG
Kl		az	k	nd	16	12	10	Rab-anti-k
Do		f	k	nd	16	13	11	Gp anti-HuγG
Ne		f	k	nd	17	13	10	Gp anti-HuγG
Ne		f	k	0	0	0	0	Rab-anti-l
Ni		az	l	nd	18	15	15	Gp anti-HuγG
De		axz	l	nd	18	16	12	Gp anti-HuγG
Li		f	l	nd	16	14	12	Gp anti-HuγG
Tr		f	l	nd	20	16	15	Gp anti-HuγG
Tr		f	l	nd	20	16	15	Rab-anti-l
Tr		f	l	0	0	0	0	Rab-anti-k
Ne	γG2	n+	l	0	0	0	0	Gp anti-HuγG
Th		n−	k	0	0	0	0	Gp anti-HuγG
Da		n+	k	0	0	0	0	Gp anti-HuγG
Da reduced and alkylated		n+	k	0	0	0	0	Gp anti-HuγG
Do	γG3	b+	k	nd	16	12	9	Gp anti-HuγG
Li		b+	l	nd	15	15	10	Gp anti-HuγG
Vi		g	l	nd	16	14	12	Gp anti-HuγG
Ge	γG4	4a	k	nd	17	12	8	Gp anti-HuγG
He		4b	k	nd	15	12	10	Gp anti-HuγG
He		4b	k	nd	18	14	12	M anti-γG4
1154		4a	k	nd	14	9	tr[c]	Gp anti-HuγG
Ro		4a	k	nd	18	10	tr	Gp anti-HuγG
La		4a	k	nd	18	16	12	Gp anti-HuγG
Ma		4a	k	nd	17	13	9	Gp anti-HuγG
St		4a	l	nd	16	12	10	Gp anti-HuγG
St		4a	l	nd	13	10	6	M anti-γG4
St		4a	l	nd	0	0	0	Rab-anti-k
Heavy Chain Disease								
Cr	γG1	Non a		nd	20	16	12	Gp anit-HuγG
Gi	γG2	n		0	0	0	0	Gp anti-HuγG
Zu	γG3	b		nd	20	16	15	Gp anti-HuγG
Ha	γG4	4a		nd	18	15	6	M anti-γ4
Ne Fc	γG1			nd	20	16	12	Gp anti-HuγG
Ti Fc	γG1			nd	18	15	13	Gp anti-HuγG
Le Fc	γG3			nd	20	13	13	Gp anti-HuγG
Ge Fc	γG4			nd	17	14	10	Gp anti-HuγG
Ge Fc	γG4			0	0	0	0	Rab-anti-k
Sh	γE			0	0	0	0	Rab-anti-l

[a] Not done.

[b] Mean diameter in millimeters of the reactions obtained in five guinea pigs.

[c] Trace.

regardless of their 4a or 4b typing (15). The γG2 proteins with the n+ or n− specificities were ineffective.

The Fc fragments behaved exactly as the intact proteins from which they were split off, similar to what was observed with rabbit Fc fragment (10, 11). When antibody directed against the Fc fragment was used for challenge, as in the case of M anti-γG4, good RPCA reactions could be obtained.

Proteins from heavy chain diseases were also investigated γG1, γG3 and γG4 heavy chain disease proteins are capable of sensitizing guinea pig skin for RPCA reactions, whereas γG2 heavy chain disease protein is not.

The γE myeloma protein (Sh) which has lambda light chains did not give RPCA reactions with Rab-anti-l serum. The control γG1 with lambda light chain (Tr) gave good RPCA reactions in the same guinea pig. This γE protein gave one strong line with the challenging rabbit antiserum in double diffusion in agar.

DISCUSSION

It has been shown that human γG antibodies and γG myeloma proteins are capable of sensitizing the guinea pig skin for PCA and RPCA reactions (3, 5), and that the human γG2 subgroup is ineffective (7).

In previous studies it has been shown that the L chain type linked to the H chain has no influence on the sensitizing ability of the γG myeloma proteins and also that the Fc fragment of the γG2 myeloma protein is unable to sensitize the guinea pig skin (7). In these studies it has also been shown that the Fc fragments of the γG1 and γG3 subgroups of human myeloma proteins are capable of sensitizing the guinea pig skin for RPCA. It has been shown that anti-kappa (7) or anti-lambda (8) chain antibodies are able to elicit RPCA reactions in the guinea pig. However, a systematic study of the sensitizing ability of Fc fragments derived from all types of human myeloma proteins capable of sensitizing the guinea pig skin or all types of heavy chain disease proteins has never been made, nor have the effects on skin sensitization of the genetically determined variations such as the Gm specificities of the H chains been previously studied. The present studies confirm and extend these previous observations and show that three of the subgroups: γG1, γG3 or γG4 from heavy chain disease proteins are able to sensitize the guinea pig skin, whereas the fourth: γG2 heavy chain disease protein is unable to do so. Moreover, it was confirmed that both anti-kappa or anti-lambda antibodies are effective in challenging the respective antigens.

The importance of the Fc fragment in sensitization was also shown by experiments where Fc-hapten conjugates were used (16). Good RPCA reactions could be obtained with anti-hapten antibody against Fc-hapten conjugates provided the number of the haptenic group was kept under a critical level. Presumably crowding the Fc fragment with too many haptenic groups created conditions such as steric hindrance or others which prevented sensitization.

The genetically determined Gm specificities do not influence sensitization of the guinea pig skin for any of the γG subgroups. This is somewhat surprising in view of the multiple differences that are known to be present in the Fc portions; in the case of Gm(g) *vs* Gm(b) for the γG3 subgroup at least five separate antigens are involved (17).

It appears probable that the genetic variants have less influence in the tertiary or quaternary configuration of the γG molecule than subgroup variations. The recent findings on great variations in disulfide bridges of the different subgroups support this interpretation (18).

Ishizaka *et al.* (9) showed that γE is unable to sensitize guinea pigs for RPCA reactions. This fact was confirmed, however, using anti-light chain serum instead of specific anti-γE. With this modification it is possible to obtain controls on the same animal with γG1 myeloma protein of the same L chain type as the γE under investigation.

REFERENCES

1. Bier, O. G. and Siqueira, M., Int. Arch. Allerg. *6:* 391, 1955.
2. Ovary, Z., Immunology, *3:* 19, 1960.
3. Ovary, Z., in *Immunological Methods, C.I.O.M.S. Symposium*, Edited by J. F. Ackroyd, Blackwell Scientific Publications, p. 259, Oxford, 1964.
4. Humphrey, J. H. and Mota, I., Immunology, *2:* 19, 1959.
5. Franklin, E. C. and Ovary, Z., Immunology, *6:* 434, 1963.
6. Ovary, Z., Barth, W. F. and Fahey, J. L., J. Immun., *94:* 410, 1965.
7. Terry, W. D., J. Immun., *95:* 1041, 1966.
8. Ovary, Z., J. Immun., *102:* 790, 1969.

9. Ishizaka, T., Ishizaka, K., Bennich, H. and Johansson, S. G. O., J. Immun., *104:* 854, 1970.
10. Ovary, Z. and Karush, F., J. Immun., *86:* 146, 1961.
11. Ovary, Z., Fed. Proc., *24:* 94, 1965.
12. Natvig, J. B. and Kunkel, H. G., Series Haematologica, *1:* 66, 1968.
13. Kunkel, H. G., Natvig, J. B. and Joslin, F. G., Proc. Nat. Acad. Sci. *62:* 144, 1969.
14. Litwin, S. D. and Kunkel, H. G., J. Exp. Med., *125:* 847, 1967.
15. Kunkel, H. G., Joslin, F. G., Penn, G. M. and Natvig, J. B., J. Exp. Med., In press.
16. Hurlimann, J. and Ovary, Z., J. Immun., *95:* 765, 1965.
17. Natvig, J. B., Kunkel, H. G., Yount, W. J. and Nielsen, J. C., J. Exp. Med., *128:* 763, 1969.
18. Frangione, B., Milstein, C. and Pink, J. R. L., Nature, *221:* 154. 1969.

THE JOURNAL OF IMMUNOLOGY
Copyright © 1970 by The Williams & Wilkins Co.

Vol. 105, No. 5, November 1970
Printed in U.S.A.

APPARENT FALSE-POSITIVE REACTIONS IN A SEROLOGIC TEST FOR SYPHILIS AND PRESENCE OF ANTINUCLEAR FACTOR IN HYBRIDS OF NZB AND A/J MICE[1]

LESLIE C. NORINS, LESLIE C. LOGAN AND MARJORIE A. LANTZ

From the Venereal Disease Research Laboratory, Venereal Disease Branch, State and Community Services Division, National Communicable Disease Center, Health Services and Mental Health Administration, Public Health Service, United States Department of Health, Education, and Welfare, Atlanta, Georgia 30333

Received for publication June 12, 1970

NZB mice and their hybrids develop many features resembling human autoimmune disease. Apparent false-positive reactions in a routine cardiolipin-antigen serologic test for syphilis (rapid plasma reagin (18-mm circle) card test) were found in 32.3% of male and 2.0% of female (A/J × NZB)F_1 mice, and also in a small percentage of NZB mice and F_2 hybrids. Antinuclear factor was also found in the serum of a significant percentage of the animals. The (A/J × NZB)F_1 hybrids may be useful as models for the study of the false-positive serologic tests for syphilis which occur in autoimmune disease.

It is recognized that false-positive (sometimes called "biologic false-positive") reactions in routine cardiolipin-antigen serologic tests for syphilis may herald or accompany diseases classified as autoimmune, such as lupus erythematosus (LE) and Hashimoto's thyroiditis (1), but the cause of the false-positive phenomenon in autoimmune disease remains conjectural. An animal model might be useful in its elucidation.

Mice of the NZB strain, and hybrids of that strain with others, spontaneously develop many features which resemble human autoimmune disease; e.g., NZB mice develop Coombs-positive hemolytic anemia (2) and antinuclear factor (ANF) (3), and (NZB × NZW)F_1 mice develop LE cells and glomerulonephritis (4). It was of interest to determine if NZB mice or their hybrids develop false-positive reactions in serologic tests for syphilis.

In the present study, sera from NZB mice, A/J mice, and hybrids of the two strains were tested. The A/J mice were selected to breed with NZB mice since A/J mice have been reported to have a high incidence of ANF (5). We report here the finding of a significant incidence of apparent false-positive serologic tests for syphilis, and the presence of ANF, in (A/J × NZB)F_1 mice.

MATERIALS AND METHODS

Mice. Several breeder pairs of NZB mice were obtained through the generosity of Drs. N. Warner, H. Holman, L. Herzenberg, K. Lange, and E. Hook. Additional NZB mice were bred from these by brother-sister matings. A/J mice were purchased from Jackson Laboratory (Bar Harbor, Maine). Because NZB females are notoriously poor mothers, F_1 hybrids of NZB and A/J mice were always derived by mating an NZB male with an A/J female. Mice were fed *ad libitum* on water and commercial antibiotic-free mouse food pellets. Throughout this study, all mice were kept in cages on a single rack of shelves in an animal room which was maintained at about 20°C.

Sera. When mice were 12 to 16 months of age they were anesthetized with ether and exsanguinated by cardiac puncture. Serum was separated from the clotted blood and stored at −20°C until tested.

Serologic tests for syphilis. To minimize chances of destroying any labile reactivities, the sera were manipulated as little as possible before testing. Because it can be performed on unheated serum, the "rapid plasma reagin" (RPR) (18-mm circle) card test (6) was the routine

[1] Trade names are used for identification only and do not represent an endorsement by the Public Health Service or the United States Department of Health, Education, and Welfare.

cardiolipin-antigen serologic test for syphilis performed on each fresh serum sample. This RPR card test incorporates finely powdered charcoal in the cardiolipin antigen suspension, which makes it possible to view agglutination macroscopically. Field evaluations on human sera have shown the procedure to have an overall sensitivity and specificity comparable to the more widely performed VDRL slide test (6), for which sera must be heated before they are tested. The remaining portion of each serum sample was stored at −20°C until the fluorescent treponemal antibody-absorption (FTA-ABS) test could be performed. This procedure, which is very sensitive and specific for treponemal infection in humans, was carried out on mouse serum by using the technique for testing human serum (6), except that a fluorescein-conjugated rabbit antiserum to mouse globulin (Microbiological Associates, Bethesda, Md.) was used to demonstrate mouse antibodies attached to the *Treponema pallidum* antigen.

Immunofluorescent test for ANF. This indirect fluorescent antibody procedure, in which nuclei of human peripheral leucocytes serve as antigen, was carried out and the fluorescence scored as previously described for mouse serum (3).

RESULTS

The results summarized in Table I show that 32.3% of male and 2% of female (A/J × NZB) F_1 mice reacted in a routine serologic test for syphilis, the RPR (18-mm circle) card test. In the small number of F_2 hybrids available for testing, the reactivity occurred in males. NZB mice showed 2% to 4% reactivity, and no reactivity was found in A/J mice (though only four male A/J mice were available for testing). All sera reactive in the card test were tested in the FTA-ABS procedure, and were nonreactive.

All 16 sera reactive in the card test were also tested for the presence of ANF. Seven of the 11 male (A/J × NZB)F_1 reactors had an ANF intensity of 2+ or greater, as did the one female reactor. Six of the seven male reactors and the female reactor showed the homogeneous staining of nuclei previously described for NZB and other mice (3). The other male reactor showed a bright "ring" pattern of peripheral staining of the nucleus. The "brown fur" F_2 reactor was also ANF-positive, but the F_2 "white fur" reactor was ANF-negative. No "black fur" F_2 mice were tested. The two NZB reactors were ANF-negative.

TABLE I

Reactivity of NZB, A/J and A/J × NZB mice in a serologic test for syphilis

Mice (Age 12–16 Mos)	RPR (18-mm Circle) Card Test		
	No. tested	No. reactive	% reactive
NZB			
Male	39	1	2.5
Female	27	1	3.7
A/J			
Male	4	0	0.0
Female	20	0	0.0
(A/J × NZB)F_1			
Male	34	11	32.3
Female	48	1	2.0
(A/J × NZB)F_2			
White fur			
Male	12	1	8.3
Female	6	0	0.0
Brown fur			
Male	7	1	14.2
Female	9	0	0.0
Black fur	None		

Eighteen sera from (A/J × NZB) F_1 females nonreactive in the card test were also tested for ANF. Fourteen (77.7%) were reactive. Five of these ANF reactors showed homogeneous staining of nuclei, but the other nine showed the bright "ring" pattern of peripheral staining of the nuclei, or the nucleoli, or both.

DISCUSSION

Although many autoantibodies and other features resembling human autoimmune disease have been described in NZB mice and their hybrids (reviewed in (4) and (7)), to our knowledge this is the first report of reactive serologic tests for syphilis in such mice. The probability is strong that the reactions we found in the non-treponemal test are false positive, for no treponemal infection is known to be endemic to mice, and the animals had never been inoculated with pathogenic treponemes. Also, the finding of a reactive cardiolipin-antigen test with a non-reactive FTA-ABS test is comparable to the serologic results seen with human sera which give reactions considered to be false positive. However, we offer the caution that the FTA-ABS procedure we used has not been appraised in mice experimentally inoculated with *T. pallidum*, so its sensitivity for a *T. pallidum* infection is not known.

The observation of ANF in the mouse sera which gave apparent false-positive tests for syphilis is consistent with the fact that ANF and false-positive syphilis reactions can occur together in human sera; both in patients with lupus erythematosus and other autoallergic diseases, and even in apparently healthy persons (1). The presence of reactivity in the serologic test for syphilis was not correlated with the presence of ANF, since ANF was found both in card test-reactive and card test-nonreactive sera.

A striking difference of our findings from the human situation is that most of the apparent false-positive reactions we observed were in male mice. False-positive reactions in cardiolipin-antigen tests are known to occur in male humans, but in reported series of human cases females outnumber males by two or three to one (1). Our results with inbred mice and their hybrids also suggest that genetic factors may contribute to the causation of false-positive tests for syphilis, a possibility which fits with the familial aggregation of false-positive results noted in some human cases (1). The finding that false-positive reactions occurred more frequently in the F_1 mice than in either of the parent strains resembles the pattern of certain other autoimmune phenomena noted in NZB hybrids; e.g., lupus erythematosus cells are more frequent in (NZB $\times$ NZW) F_1 mice than in either the NZB or NZW parent strains (4).

Although the various serologic tests for syphilis which use cardiolipin antigens are, as a group, roughly comparable in their overall rate of false-positive reactivity, it is important to point out that the different tests may not agree with each other on every individual specimen or, indeed, on certain categories of specimens. For example, the VDRL slide test often gives false-positive reactions with sera from leprosy patients whereas the RPR (18-mm circle) card test rarely does so. Thus, it is possible that other flocculation or complement-fixation tests using cardiolipin antigens may detect percentages of reactivity lesser or greater than those reported here.

Acknowledgments. We thank Mr. E. A. Tolliver for care of the mice, Dr. A. Scotti for help in reviewing the data, and Mrs. Virginia Falcone for counsel on serologic aspects of the study.

REFERENCES

1. Harvey, M. A. and Shulman, L. E., *Lupus Erythematosus*, Edited by E. L. Dubois, p. 104, McGraw Hill, Inc., New York, 1966.
2. Holmes, M. C. and Burnet, F. M., Ann. Int. Med., *59:* 265, 1963.
3. Norins, L. C. and Holmes, M. C., J. Immun., *93:* 897, 1964.
4. Braverman, I. M., J. Invest. Derm., *50:* 483, 1968.
5. Friou, G. J. and Teague, P. O., Science, *143:* 1333, 1964.
6. United States Department of Health, Education and Welfare, Manual of Tests for Syphilis, 1969 Revision, United States Public Health Service Publication No. 411, U. S. Government Printing Office, Washington, D. C., 1969.
7. Holmes, M. C., *Proceedings 11th Congress International Society Blood Transfusions*, Sydney, 1966; Bibl. Haemat., No. 29, Part 2, p. 454, Karger, Basel/New York, 1968.

THE JOURNAL OF IMMUNOLOGY
Vol. 105, No. 5, November 1970
Printed in U.S.A.

ROLE OF LYMPHOID CELLS IN PASSIVE TRANSFER WITH PLASMA OF DELAYED HYPERSENSITIVITY IN GUINEA PIGS[1]

J. M. DUPUY[2] AND R. A. GOOD[3]

From the Pediatric Research Laboratories of the Variety Club Heart Hospital, University of Minnesota, Minneapolis, Minnesota 55455

Received for publication June 11, 1970

Specific skin reactions to purified protein derivatives could frequently be transferred with plasma or serum from heavily irradiated sensitized guinea pigs. Splenic lymphocytes from a non-sensitized animal that had been incubated for 90 minutes with plasma capable of transferring sensitivity became able to effect such a transfer. Latex particles, red blood cells, or thymocytes could not effect the transfer nor could spleen cells treated *in vitro* with large amounts of mitomycin C. It is concluded that only certain lymphoid cells may have receptors at their surfaces for attachment of the factor that is responsible for transferring sensitivity, and that the viability and the ability of these cells to replicate are essential for the passive transfer of delayed hypersensitivity.

In previous papers we have reported studies of the transfer of sensitivity to purified protein derivative (PPD) (1) and to DNP-BSA (bovine serum albumin) in guinea pigs (2) and to skin graft rejection in mice (3) using plasma from immunized, x-irradiated donors. These experiments were based on the work of Clark *et al.* (4–6), who showed that rejection of renal allografts could be attributed to non-cellular factors in blood following irradiation. Antibodies of β and γ mobility do not participate in this form of transfer of cell-mediated immunity (2, 7). Instead, the biologically active material was found to migrate rapidly, and was located in albumin or prealbumin fractions on agar electrophoresis. It was also found that normal spleen cells incubated with plasma from immunized, x-irradiated donors could pick up the factor and then participate in the transfer of sensitivity to normal recipients (1).

On the basis of these observations we have postulated that a factor(s) responsible for cell-mediated immunity is released from the sensitized lymphoid cells into the plasma after x-irradiation, and that it is this factor, possibly the immunoprotein of the thymus-dependent system, which we are studying. Alternatively, our data might be compatible with the view that we are working with a form of transfer factor (8) capable of specifically mobilizing and recruiting host cells to specific cell-mediated responses. The studies reported herein were carried out to examine further the nature of the factor and to better define the characteristics of the cell involved in interaction with the factor and transfer of immunity.

MATERIALS AND METHODS

Animals and immunizations. Outbred Hartley strain female guinea pigs weighing 300 to 500 g (Oak Crest Rabbitry, Loretto, Minn.) were immunized with two injections of 0.2 ml of bacillus Calmette-Guérin (BCG) vaccine (Eli Lilly Co., Indianapolis, Ind.) given 2 weeks apart in the posterior footpads. Two weeks after the second immunization, animals were given 1000 R of x-radiation (tissue dose). Three days later they were bled and the plasma from groups of 20

[1] This work was aided by grants from the American Thoracic Society, The National Foundation-March of Dimes, U. S. Public Health Service (NB-02042, AI-08677), American Cancer Society, and American Heart Association.

[2] J. M. D. was supported by fellowships from the Commissariat Général du Plan d'Equipement et de la Productivité (France), the University of Minnesota, and the Eli Lilly Company. Present address: Unité de recherches d'hépatologie infantile—Laboratoire d'immunologie, Bicêtre, France.

[3] American Legion Memorial Research Professor, Regents' Professor of Pediatrics and Microbiology, University of Minnesota.

donors was pooled and kept at −70°C. Each plasma pool was individually tested for its ability to transfer sensitivity to PPD after i.p. injection into normal guinea pigs as described previously (1). Only positive groups of pooled plasma were used for further experiments.

In vitro incubation

In some experiments, prior to incubation with spleen cells, plasma from immunized x-irradiated donors was treated with either RNase, DNase, or trypsin.

RNase. Five times crystallized bovine RNase (Mann Research Laboratories, New York, N. Y.) concentration of 1 mg/ml; incubation at 37°C for 30 min.

DNase. Once crystallized bovine DNase (Mann Research Laboratories) concentration of 1 mg/ml; incubation at 37°C for 1 hr.

Trypsin. Twice crystallized (Nutritional Biochemicals Corporation, Cleveland, Ohio). Plasma was incubated with trypsin in concentrations of 5 mg/ml for 1 hr at 37°C at pH 8. Each day 1 ml of treated plasma was used for incubation.

Materials used for incubation with plasma

Latex particles. Polystyrene latex—10% solids (Dow Chemical Company, Midland, Mich.). One-tenth milliliter of latex particles was incubated with 1 ml of plasma at 37°C, pH 8.2, with continuous agitation for 30 min. Particles were then sedimented at 10,000 rpm for 10 min and resuspended in 5 ml of Eagle's minimal essential medium (MEM) (Grand Island Biological Company, Grand Island, N.Y.). One milliliter of the final suspension was injected i.p. daily into each recipient for 5 successive days.

Guinea pig erythrocytes. Packed erythrocytes were used after having been washed three times in saline. Each day 1 ml of packed erythrocytes was incubated at 37°C for 90 min with plasma from immunized, x-irradiated donors, then washed three times with MEM and resuspended in 5 ml of MEM. One milliliter of the final suspension was injected i.p. into each recipient. The same procedure was carried out on each of 5 successive days.

Cell suspensions. Thymuses, peripheral lymph nodes, and spleens were removed, minced in MEM, then gently passed through a wire mesh screen. Before incubation, a white cell count was performed and viability was determined by trypan-blue exclusion. One milliliter of each suspension was incubated with 1 ml of plasma at 37°C for 90 min with constant shaking, washed three times in MEM, and the cells were then resuspended in 5 ml of the same medium. Before i.p. injection of 1 ml/recipient, white cell count and viability were determined for the final suspensions. The same procedure was performed on 5 successive days. As controls, similar cell suspensions were incubated with plasma from immunized non-irradiated, or irradiated non-immunized donors.

Mitomycin-treated cells. Spleen cells were treated with mitomycin C (Sigma Chemical Company, St. Louis, Mo.). Dilutions of 200 μg and 20 μg/10^8 cells/ml were used. Cells were incubated with mitomycin C at 37°C for 20 min in the dark, washed in 30 volumes of MEM, and then used for incubation with plasma as described above.

Experimental designs

Transfer of delayed hypersensitivity (DH) with plasma or serum. In these experiments a total of 8 to 10 ml of plasma from BCG-immunized, x-irradiated guinea pigs was injected i.p. into normal recipients on three successive days. Either fresh plasma or plasma treated at 56°C for 30 min was used.

Transfer of DH with different materials incubated in vitro with plasma. A total of approximately 3 to 3.5 × 10^8 viable, nucleated spleen cells or thymocytes with 1 ml of packed erythrocytes was injected i.p. after incubation and washing into each recipient on 5 successive days.

In both experimental designs, the recipients were skin tested with 10 μg of PPD 6 days after the last i.p. injection. PPD in 0.1 ml of diluent was injected intradermally (i.d.) into the skin of the backs of the test animal after shaving. The injection site was inspected at 2, 4, 18, or 24 hr after skin tests. A positive reaction, 18 or 24 hr after i.d. injection, consisted of erythema greater than 5 mm in diameter plus induration ($^+$ weak; $^{++}$ moderate; $^{+++}$ strong). In some instances, biopsy samples were taken at 24 hr, prepared in the usual way and stained with hematoxylin and eosin.

RESULTS

Two hours following i.d. injection of 10 μg of PPD, none of the recipient guinea pigs in any of the experiments showed positive reactions. Positive reactions characterized by erythema with induration appeared 4 to 6 hr after PPD injection, reached a peak between 11 and 18 hr and began to subside by 24 hr. Histologic examination of the biopsy from positive skin reactions showed mononuclear cell infiltration.

Transfer of sensitivity with plasma or serum. As shown in Table I, heated plasma or serum and fresh plasma were able passively to transfer PPD sensitivity to normal recipients.

TABLE I

Passive transfer of sensitivity to PPD in guinea pigs with fresh or heated plasma and serum from BCG-immunized, X-irradiated donors

Recipient Injections of[a]	PPD[b] Sensitivity in Normal Recipients after Transfer	Intensity of Reaction Range of	
		Erythema diameter	Induration[c]
		mm	
Fresh plasma	2/3	7–9	+
Heated plasma (56°C for 30 min)	2/3	7–10	+; ++
Serum	4/5	7–10	+; ++

[a] All recipients were given, on three successive days, a total of 8 to 10 ml of plasma or serum from BCG-immunized, x-irradiated donors.

[b] Test dose 10 μg in all experiments, 6 days after the last injection.

[c] Induration was noted as: 0, absent; +, weak; ++, moderate.

Transfer of DH with passively-sensitized materials. These studies were carried out to test the ability of different materials to pick up the factor responsible for the passive transfer of DH after *in vitro* incubation with plasma from sensitized irradiated donors. In experiments shown in Table II, erythrocytes, latex particles and thymocytes incubated in such a plasma and injected into recipients uniformly failed to transfer sensitivity to PPD. On the contrary, transfer of sensitivity to PPD was achieved by injecting normal guinea pig spleen cells or lymph node cells incubated with plasma for 90 min. Transfer of sensitivity did not occur when spleen cell suspensions were incubated *in vitro* for 10 mins only. In control groups, sensitivity to PPD was not transferred in recipients injected with spleen cells incubated with plasma from donors previously immunized but not irradiated, or from non-immunized and irradiated donors.

As shown in Table III, sensitivity to PPD was transferred to normal recipients with spleen cells incubated with plasma which had been treated, prior to incubation, with RNase, DNase or trypsin. Concentrations of 20 μg of mitomycin C/ml did not prevent transfer of sensitivity when mitomycin C-treated spleen cells were injected into normal recipients after incubation with plasma. However, higher concentrations of

TABLE II

Studies on transfer of sensitivity to PPD with different materials incubated with guinea pig plasma

State of Plasma Donors		*In Vitro* Incubation			PPD[b] Sensitivity in Normal Recipients
Immunized	X-irradiated	Treatment of plasma	Material used for incubation with plasma[a]	Incubation time at 37°C	
				min	
+	+	None	Erythrocytes	90	0/5
+	+	None	Latex particles	90	0/5
+	+	None	Thymocytes	90	0/5
+	+	None	Spleen cells	10	0/5
+	+	None	Spleen cells	90	3/5
+	+	Heated[c]	Spleen cells	90	3/5
+	+	None	Lymph node cells	90	4/4
+	−	None	Spleen cells	90	0/5
−	+	None	Spleen cells	90	0/5

[a] A total of 3 to 3.5 × 10^8 spleen cells, thymocytes or lymph node cells, 1 ml of packed erythrocytes and 0.10 ml of latex particles was injected i.p., after incubation and washing, in each guinea pig recipient during 5 successive days.

[b] Test dose 10 μg injected i.d. 6 days after the last injection.

[c] Plasma was heated at 56°C for 30 min.

TABLE III

Passive transfer of PPD sensitivity with guinea pig spleen cells incubated with plasma

Treatment prior to Incubation		PPD[c] Sensitivity in Normal Recipients after Cell Transfer	Intensity of Reaction Range of	
Plasma[a]	Spleen cells[b]		Erythema diameter	Induration
			mm	
RNase (1 mg/ml)	None	4/5	6–9	+; ++
DNase (1 mg/ml)	None	3/5	6–8	+
Trypsin (5 mg/ml)	None	3/5	7–10	+
None	Mitomycin C (200 μg/ml)	0/5		
None	Mitomycin C (20 μg/ml)	2/3	6–8	+
None	None	7/10	6–10	+; ++

[a] Each day 1 ml of plasma from immunized, x-irradiated donors was incubated for 90 min at 37°C with guinea pig spleen cell suspension.

[b] A total of 3 to 3.5 × 10^8 spleen cells were incubated, washed, then injected i.p. into each recipient during 5 successive days.

[c] Test dose 10 μg injected i.d. 6 days after the last injection.

mitomycin C (200 μg/ml) did prevent transfer of sensitivity (Table III).

DISCUSSION

The experiments described here were done to test further the passive transfer of cell-mediated immunity with cell-free plasma. Serum, as well as fresh or heated plasma from BCG-immunized lethally x-irradiated donors, passively transferred sensitivity to PPD in more than 50% of the recipients. Normal non-immunized guinea pig spleen cells incubated with the plasma capable of this transfer appeared to pick up the factor from the plasma and transfer sensitivity to recipients after i.p. injection.

In previous experiments the factor was shown to have been depleted from the plasma when the same plasma was used for a second incubation with new spleen cells (3). When the period of incubation of plasma with spleen cells was shortened from 90 to 10 min, none of the five guinea pigs injected with the incubated spleen cells had a positive reaction after PPD injection. This would indicate that absorption of the factor by the cells is an active phenomenon. When materials such as latex particles, guinea pig erythrocytes or thymocytes were used for incubation, passive transfer of sensitivity to PPD did not occur. These observations would seem to indicate that the material responsible for transfer has a high cytophilic activity, but that this requires specific sites, which are present only on certain cells. It seems from these and prior investigations that the cells involved are lymphocytes, and perhaps thymus-dependent lymphocytes. In earlier work, for example, we were unable to passively transfer skin allograft rejection when mice thymectomized as newborns were injected with plasma from lethally irradiated donors that rejected the specific allograft (J. M. Dupuy, O. Stutman and R. A. Good, unpublished). One explanation might be the lack, in thymectomized animals, of a cell population specific for binding or processing the factor.

Four of five animals were found to be positive when spleen cells were injected after incubation with RNase-treated plasma. Positive transfer was also obtained after DNase and trypsin treatment of the plasma. These experiments must be interpreted with caution since only one enzyme dose was tested.

Bloom *et al.* (9) showed that sensitized guinea pig cells treated with 100 μg/ml of mitomycin C would not transfer delayed hypersensitivity whereas leucocytes treated with a lower dose of mitomycin C would do so. In our experiment, passive transfer of sensitivity occurred when spleen cells were treated with 20 μg of mitomycin/ml prior to incubation with plasma. Higher concentrations of mitomycin C (200 μg), however, prevented the transfer. In the latter experiment, cell viability ranged from 65% to 80% before i.p. injection. The inability of the cells to transfer sensitivity after treatment with a large dose of mitomycin C could result from failure of the cells to pick up the factor from the plasma or to transfer it to the host cells. An alternative explanation is that despite apparently good viability, the cells treated with mitomycin C *in vitro* had been damaged. Nonetheless, such a relationship would also favor the active participation of cells in the transfer process and development of the sensitivity.

Acknowledgment. The technical assistance of Mr. J. H. Wicks is gratefully acknowledged.

REFERENCES

1. Dupuy, J. M., Perey, D. Y. E. and Good, R. A., Lancet, *1:* 551, 1969.
2. Dupuy, J. M. and Good, R. A., J. Immun., In press.
3. Dupuy, J. M., Perey, D. Y. E. and Good, R. A., J. Immun., *104:* 1523, 1970.
4. Clark, D. S., Foker, J. E., Gewurz, H., Good, R. A. and Varco, R. L., Surgery, *62:* 770, 1967.
5. Clark, D. S., Good, R. A. and Varco, R. L., Lancet, *1:* 8, 1968.
6. Foker, J. E., Clark, D. S., Pickering, R. J., Good, R. A. and Varco, R. L., Surgery, *66:* 42, 1969.
7. Dupuy, J. M., Kalpaktosoglou, P. and Good, R. A., J. Immun., *104:* 1384, 1970.
8. Lawrence, H. S., Advances Immun., *11:* 195, 1969.
9. Bloom, B. R., Hamilton, L. D. and Chase, M. W., Nature, *201:* 689, 1964.

THE JOURNAL OF IMMUNOLOGY
Vol. 105, No. 5, November 1970
Printed in U.S.A.

PROTEIN A REACTIVITY WITH MOUSE IMMUNOGLOBULINS

Structural Relationship between Some Mouse and Human Immunoglobulins[1]

GÖRAN KRONVALL, HOWARD M. GREY[2] AND RALPH C. WILLIAMS, JR.

From the Department of Medicine, Bernalillo County Medical Center, School of Medicine, University of New Mexico, Albuquerque, New Mexico 87106 and the Department of Experimental Pathology, Scripps Clinic and Research Foundation, La Jolla, California

Received for publication June 8, 1970

Reactivity with staphyloccal protein A in normal mouse serum was localized to the electrophoretic γ region. After absorption of normal mouse serum with a protein A-containing *Staphylococcus aureus* strain, Cowan I, the γ globulin line could not be detected by immunoelectrophoresis. Similar absorption of a mixture of Fab and Fc fragments from mouse γG localized the activity in the Fc piece. To define this protein A reactivity further, M-components isolated from various mouse plasma cell tumor lines were studied. All six γ2a, γ2b and γ3 mouse myeloma globulins tested reacted with protein A, whereas four M-components of the γ1, γA and γM mouse immunoglobulin classes did not react. One human IgD and one IgE myeloma globulin were also tested. Neither reacted with protein A. Protein A reactivity thus seems to be a characteristic of mouse γ2a, γ2b, γ3 globulins as well as human IgG-1, -2 and -4 globulins.

Protein A reactivity of γ globulin mediated by Fc was originally described for human IgG (1). Other reports have confirmed this finding (2–5). Studies on rabbit γG (6) as well as guinea pig γ1 and γ2 globulins (7, 8) have shown a similar reactivity with protein A for the Fc region. Since the Fc part of immunoglobulins is inherited in a simple Mendelian way (9), we felt that we could obtain further information on protein A-reactive structures by using isolated myeloma globulin. In a study of human myeloma globulins, IgG-1, -2 and -4, molecules were found to react with protein A, whereas IgG-3 molecules were nonreactive (3). In addition, 20 IgA and 20 IgM human M components have been reported as negative (10). No other human serum proteins combined with protein A (10). Phylogenetic studies have indicated that mice also seem to contain protein A-combining γ globulins with a reacting Fc structure similar to that in humans (10). In the current study we found evidence for such a specific combination. Myeloma globulins from the mouse were also available to us and this permitted a correlation to immunoglobulin types: γ2a, γ2b and γ3 globulin molecules showed protein A reactivity. In addition, we attempted to study the possible biologic significance of soluble complexes formed between mouse γ globulins and protein A.

[1] This investigation was supported in part by United States Health Service Grant AI-07007, Atomic Energy Commission Contract AT (04-3)-410, and American Heart Association Grant 67-795 and in part by Grants AM 13690-01 and AMAI 13824-01 from the United States Public Health Service. It is Publication 383 from the Department of Experimental Pathology, Scripps Clinic and Research Foundation, La Jolla, Calif.

[2] Established Investigator of the American Heart Association.

MATERIALS AND METHODS

Protein A. Staphylococcal protein A was partially purified according to Jensen (11) as described previously (3).

Human myeloma globulins. Protein A-precipitating IgG myeloma globulins used in the test for protein A reactivity were isolated by zone electrophoresis (12). Purity of the myeloma globulins was checked by immunoelectrophoresis. An IgD myeloma globulin was kindly provided by Dr. H. Spiegelberg, La Jolla, California. The IgE myeloma globulin studied was a gift from Dr. Kimishige Ishizaka, Denver, Colorado.

Mouse γ globulin. Normal pooled mouse serum

was from Swiss Webster mice (Simonsen Laboratories, Inc., Gilroy, Calif.). Inbred strains of mice (Table I) were from Dr. Edmond Yunis, Minneapolis, Minnesota. Fractions from normal mouse serum were isolated by zone electrophoresis on starch block (12). The protein content was measured by the modified Folin method (13). Pooled fractions were concentrated to 3 mg/ml and analyzed by immunoelectrophoresis. The γ globulin peak from zone electrophoresis of normal mouse serum showed strong anti-protein A reactivity, and was further subjected to papain digestion using an enzyme to substrate ratio of 1:100 w/w in 0.01 M phosphate buffer, pH 7.3, containing 0.15 M NaCl, 0.01 M cysteine and 0.002 M EDTA. The mixture was incubated at 37°C for 1 hr. Digestion was stopped by dialysis. The fragments were separated from undigested γ globulin by gel filtration on Sephadex G-100 equilibrated with phosphate-buffered saline (PBS, 0.15 M NaCl, 0.01 M phosphate, pH 7.3) at 4°C. These fragments were identified by their mobility in immunoelectrophoresis using a commercial anti-mouse γ globulin antiserum (Microbiological Associates Inc., Bethesda, Md.). Protein A-reactive fragments were defined by absorption with a strain of *Staphylococcus aureus*, Cowan I, containing protein A, followed by immunoelectrophoresis.

Mouse myeloma globulins. Mouse myeloma globulins from various lines of plasma cell tumors were isolated from mouse serum by zone electrophoresis on starch block (12) and when necessary also by Sephadex G-200 gel filtration (14). MOPC 21 (γ1) PC5 (γ2a), MOPC 141 (γ2b) and MOPC 104 (γM) mouse tumors were from Dr. Michael Potter, Bethesda, Maryland, and J 606 (γ3) and S 121 (γA) mouse tumors were from Dr. Melvin Cohn, La Jolla, California. Isolated myeloma globulins from mice with plasma cell tumors RPC 23 (γ1), MOPC 173 (γ2a), MOPC 213 (γ2a) and MOPC 195 (γ2b) were kindly provided by Dr. Michael Potter, Bethesda, Maryland.

Protein A reactivity. Tests for protein A reactivity of serum fractions, γ globulins, and myeloma globulins were performed using the inhibition technique of Seligmann (15) as described previously (3). Precipitation and inhibition in this test system by human (3, 15) and animal (10) γ globulins indicate the presence of similar protein A-reacting structures.

Absorption with staphylococci. Absorption of protein A-reacting serum components with staphylococci was performed according to Lind and Mansa (16) with modifications. An equal volume of normal human or mouse serum was added to the pellet of washed fresh bacteria. The mixture was incubated at 20°C for 10 min, the bacteria were spun down at 10,000 G for 10 min, and the supernatants absorbed a second time. The second supernatant was subsequently tested by immunoelectrophoresis.

Immunoelectrophoretic localization of protein A reactivity. Serum and other test samples were subjected to routine electrophoresis in agar gel (0.05 M Veronal buffer, pH 8.6). Two troughs were cut on both sides of the single well. In the trough closer to the well 20 μl of a preparation of partially purified protein A was added. The other trough contained 20 μl of a rabbit antiserum raised against formalinized staphylococci of strain Cowan I which has large amounts of protein A. Protein A formed a precipitation line with the anti-staphylococcal antiserum. The presence of protein A-reacting molecules in the test sample caused a deflection or inhibition of the precipitation line between the troughs. The position of this reactivity was compared with an immunoelectrophoretic analysis of the test sample run simultaneously.

RESULTS

Protein A reactivity of mouse sera. Pooled serum from normal mice has previously been shown to

TABLE I

Protein A reactivity of sera from inbred strains of mice[a]

Strain		Strain	
A/Bi	I	C57BL/6	I
A/Jax	I	C58	I
AKR/J	I	DBA/2 fB	I
BALB/c	I	D8	I
CBA	I	I	I
C3H	I	NZB	I
C3HfB	I	NZW	I
C57BL/Ks	I	SJL/J	I
C57BL/1 Bi	I	T6	I
C57BL/4	I		

[a] All sera tested showed inhibition (I) of the precipitation between a human myeloma globulin and staphylococcal protein A.

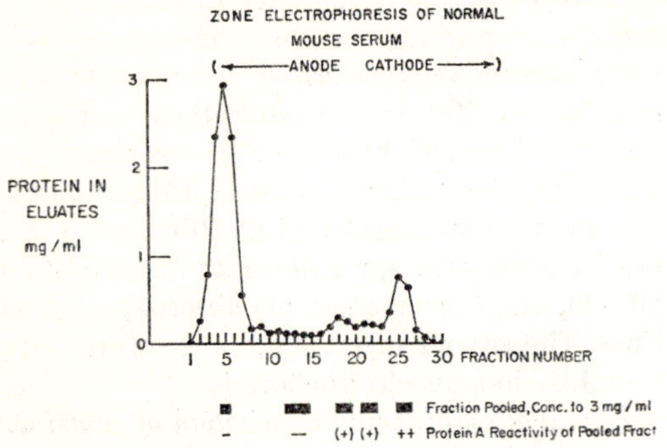

Figure 1. Protein A reactivity in mouse serum. Fractions from zone electrophoresis of normal mouse serum were pooled as indicated and tested for protein A reactivity after they were concentrated to 3 mg/ml of protein. The γ globulin fraction contained the bulk of the reactivity. Some activity was also present in the β-γ_1 region. Albumin and α globulins did not react with protein A.

possess anti-protein A activity (10). Sera from 19 inbred strains of mice were analyzed; all of them showed inhibition of the precipitation between a human IgG myeloma globulin and protein A (Table I).

Localization of protein A reactivity in mouse serum. Pooled serum from Swiss Webster mice was separated by zone electrophoresis. Pools from representative portions of the separated fractions were concentrated and analyzed by immunoelectrophoresis (Fig. 1). Fraction 5 contained albumin and fractions 25 to 26, γ globulin. When analyzed for protein A reactivity, the γ globulin pool (fractions 25 to 26) showed marked inhibition. Pools containing fractions 21 to 22 and 18 to 19 showed β globulins on immunoelectrophoresis in addition to some γ globulin, and were only slightly inhibitory in tests for protein A reactivity. Pools containing α globulins and albumin were completely negative.

Two additional approaches were utilized to determine which serum components from mice reacted with protein A. Absorption of reactive serum components to a protein A-containing *Staphylococcus aureus*, Cowan I, strain was performed first. When normal mouse serum was absorbed with this strain the γ globulin line disappeared completely in immunoelectrophoresis (Fig. 2*A*). The second method utilized immunologic inhibition. After electrophoretic separation of serum in agar gel, protein A and a rabbit antistaphylococcal antiserum were allowed to diffuse from two troughs on either side. Protein A combining molecules in the serum sample interfered with the precipitation line and caused arcing or inhibition. The position of this arc corresponded to γ globulin. It was evident from these three approaches that the protein A reactivity in normal mouse serum was a characteristic of γ globulins only.

Protein A reactivity of mouse γ globulin fragments. Papain digests of mouse γ globulin containing Fab and Fc fragments were analyzed before and after absorption with *S. aureus*, Cowan I. Such absorption resulted in loss of the fast (Fc) fragment with no apparent effect on the slow (Fab) fragment in immunoelectrophoresis (Fig. 3). Clearcut affinity of protein A for mouse Fc fragment of γ globulin was therefore evident.

Protein A reactivity of mouse myeloma globulins. Since the protein A reactivity of mouse γG was localized to the Fc fragment, it seemed clear that this activity must be correlated to heavy chain types analogous to previous findings in the human (3). Mouse myeloma globulins of various types were therefore tested for protein A reactivity (Table II). Two isolated γ1 and one γA, as well as one γM, myeloma globulins were nonreactive. On the other hand, all three γ2a and two γ2b, as well as the newly discovered representative of the γ3 immunoglobulin class (17), were positive. The γ3 myeloma globulin showed precipitation whereas all five γ2a and γ2b myeloma globulins were inhibitory. Among the 10 mouse myeloma globulins tested, the correlation to heavy chain type was thus clearly distinct.

Protein A reactivity of normal human serum. For comparative purposes experiments similar to those documented above for mouse serum were performed using normal human serum and the Cowan I strain of *S. aureus*. Absorption of human serum with the protein A-containing staphylococcal strain, Cowan I, almost complately removed the IgG precipitation line (Fig. 2*B*) analogous to the results obtained for mouse serum. Furthermore, when electrophoretically separated human serum was allowed to interact in a protein A precipitating system in agar as described above, the activity was localized to γ globulins. One human IgD and one IgE myeloma globulin were also tested for protein A reactivity. Both were non-reactive, indicating absence of protein A-combining structures on these human myeloma globulins.

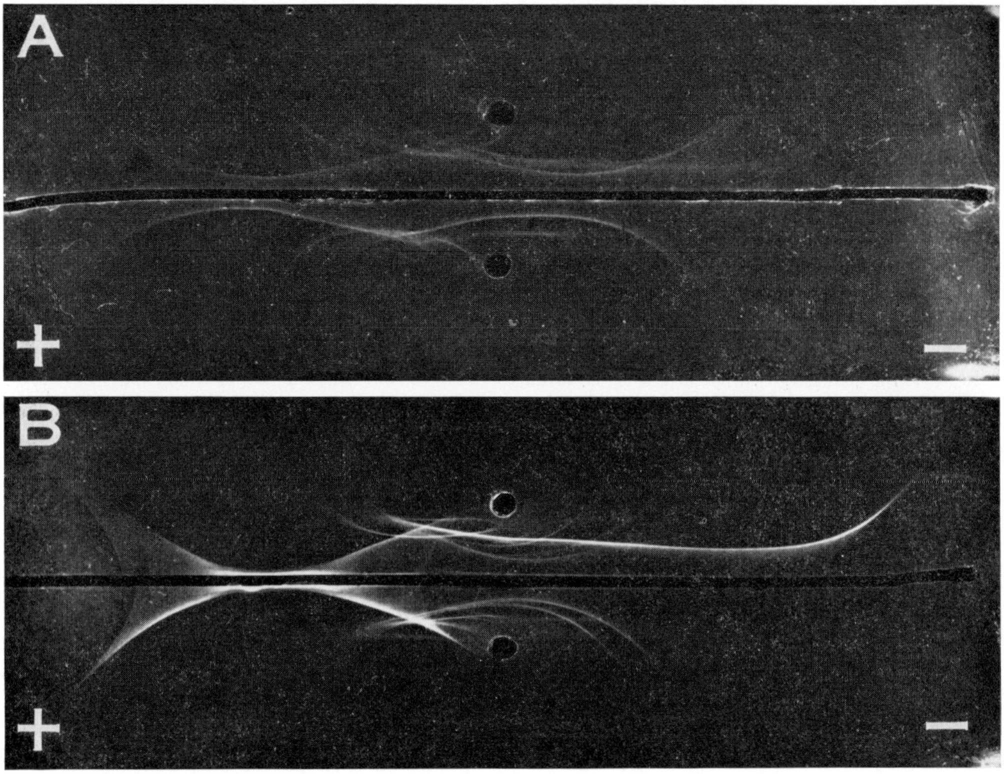

Figure 2. A, immunoelectrophoresis of normal mouse serum (*upper well*) and the same serum after absorption with *S. aureus*, strain Cowan I (*lower well*). The trough was filled with rabbit anti-mouse antiserum. Mouse serum absorbed with the protein A-containing Cowan I strain lacks the γ globulin line which normally extends into the most cathodal region. *B*, immunoelectrophoresis of normal human serum (*upper well*) and the same serum after absorption with *S. aureus*, Cowan I strain (*lower well*). The trough contained rabbit anti-human antiserum. The γG globulin line is almost completely gone after absorption with the protein A-containing Cowan I strain.

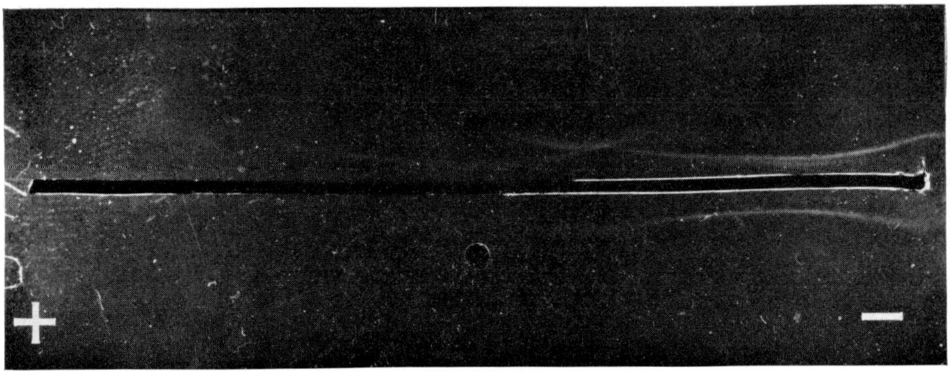

Figure 3. Immunoelectrophoresis of papain fragments (*upper well*) obtained from mouse γ globulin as well as the same preparation after absorption with *S. aureus*, Cowan I (*lower well*). After absorption with this protein A-containing strain the fast Fc fragment is absent.

TABLE II

Protein A reactivity of mouse myeloma globulins

γ1	γ2a	γ2b	γ3	γA	γM
MOPC 21-N[a]	MOPC 173-I[b]	MOPC 141-I	J 606-P[c]	S 121-N	MOPC 104-N
RPC 23-N	MOPC 213-I	MOPC 195-I			
	PC 5-I				

[a] N = No interaction.
[b] I = Inhibition.
[c] P = Precipitation.

Effect of intravenous injection of protein A in mice. Since mouse γ2-globulin molecules showed inhibition in the protein A-test system, it seemed possible that soluble complexes prepared between protein A and mouse γ globulin might be capable of inducing vasculitis or nephritis. Accordingly, from 10 to 500 μg of protein A were injected into the tail veins of eight normal Swiss Webster mice. No immediate untoward reactions were noticed. The eight animals, as well as untreated controls, were killed 2 days after injection. The kidneys were removed, pieces were fixed or frozen and then sectioned for ordinary light microscopy. Some sections were stained with fluorescein isothiocyanate (FITC)-conjugated γ globulin from rabbit anti-mouse γG antiserum (Microbiological Associates Inc., Bethesda, Md). No lesions were seen using either technique. Four mice were also injected five times intravenously with 10-μg doses of protein A every other day for 8 days and then killed. The kidneys of these mice appeared normal and did not show lesions by conventional hematoxylin and eosin staining or by immunofluorescent staining using anti-γG conjugates. Thus, no pathologic relationship was noted between the inhibition reaction (presumably soluble complexes) of mouse γG and protein A and the development of renal lesions.

DISCUSSION

Protein A from *S. aureus* combines with the Fc part of human IgG-1, -2 and -4 molecules (3). This reaction was originally described as "nonspecific" and "pseudoimmune" (1) to distinguish it from ordinary antibody activity localized in the variable portions of the Fab fragment. The reaction between protein A and immunoglobulin G is, however, a rather specific one. The distinct subgroup pattern as well as the reactivity of immunoglobulin subfragments indicates that very specific structures of some immunoglobulin heavy chains are involved (3, 4). For example, in this regard it differs completely from the phytohemagglutinins or lectins which react with carbohydrate structures on many serum proteins (18–20).

In a previous study, we utilized the specific reaction between protein A and immunoglobulins to study the phylogenetic evolution of the human γ heavy chain (10). We found protein A-reactive structures present in 61 out of 62 mammalian sera tested, which suggested the presence of a common γ chain precursor. Kinetic studies on the interaction between human γ globulin and protein A on the bacterial cell wall gave values for the equilibrium constant of approximately 4×10^7 liters/mol (21). This value exceeds that of hapten-antibody reactions and thus emphasized the high specificity of the reaction.

A number of antibody-mediated reactions have been shown to be induced by staphylococcal protein A through its reactivity with the Fc part of human γ globulin. In γ globulin excess both guinea pig (22) and human complement (23) are consumed. An Arthus-like reaction is produced in rabbits passively sensitized with human γ globulin (24). Both an immediate and a delayed type of reaction can be induced upon intracutaneous injection of protein A in humans (25). It therefore seems clear that any evaluation of the inflammatory response in states of staphylococcal disease must take into account this specific reaction with γ globulin. Since considerable experimental work on staphylococcal infections has been done in mice, a precise knowledge of which immunoglobulin types are capable of combining with protein A is essential in such studies.

Previous work has indicated that serum from normal mice contains protein A-combining components (10). Moreover, the phylogenetic pattern suggests that γ globulins are responsible for this activity. In this study we have confirmed the inhibitory reactivity of pooled normal mouse serum in the test system used. Sera from 19 inbred strains of mice were also inhibitory (Table I). The protein A reactivity of normal mouse serum was found by three different techniques to be present on γ globulins only (Fig. 1 and 2). The reacting serum component was specifically localized to the Fc piece (Fig. 3). The reaction between staphylococcal protein A and γ globulin, which shows such a high degree of specificity in the human, thus presents a strikingly similar pattern in the mouse.

The availability of myeloma globulins from the mouse permitted a closer definition of protein A-reactive immunoglobulins in this species. We found a strict correlation of protein A reactivity to immunoglobulin classes; γ2a, γ2b and γ3 globulins being positive whereas γ1, γA and M were nonreactive. A summary of our present knowledge of protein A reactivity of human and mouse immunoglobulins is shown in Table III. Since reaction with protein A seems to indicate the presence of specific structures inherited in the Fc part of some human and mouse heavy chains, these common structures should eventually be correlated by analyzing amino acid sequences. The fingerprint technique has already revealed identity between some peptides from mouse γ2a and γ2b myeloma globulins (26).

TABLE III

Protein A reactivity of human and mouse immunoglobulins

Human	Mouse
IgG 1 +[a]	—[b]
2 +	
3 —	γ2a +
4 +	γ2b +
IgA —	
	γ3 +
IgM —	
	γA —
IgD —	
	γM —
IgE —	

[a] + represents that protein A reactivity was present.

[b] — indicates that protein A reactivity was absent.

The Fc portion of γG immunoglobulins carries various biologically active structures. These activities are inherited in the different H-chain subtypes in different patterns (Table IV). In the human, complement fixation is mediated by IgG-1 and IgG-3 molecules and to a lesser extent by IgG-2 molecules (27, 28). The cytophilic and opsonic sites reside in IgG-1 and IgG-3 molecules (29, 30). Guinea pig skin reactivity is mediated by IgG-1, -3 and -4 globulins (31). *In vivo* catabolism of the different human IgG subclasses appears to be similar for all except IgG-3 which shows a more rapid turnover (32, 33). In the mouse, complement activation is mediated by γ2a and γ2b antibodies (18, 34, 35) whereas the reactivity of guinea pig skin is a quality of γ2a molecules only (18, 34, 36). The catabolic rate differs between the immunoglobulin classes with 17%, 13% and 25% catabolism per day for γ1, γ2a and γ2b globulins respectively (37). Taking the available data on the biologic activities of human and mouse immunoglobulins, it is clear that there is no correlation between protein A reactivity and any other biologic characteristics of γG (Table IV). Protein A reactivity is therefore an expression of a very distinct γ globulin structure.

TABLE IV

Comparative summary of biologic activities of human and mouse immunoglobulins

Activity	Human				Mouse			
	IgG-1	IgG-2	IgG-3	IgG-4	γ1	γ2a	γ2b	γ3
Protein A reactivity (3)	+[a]	+	—[b]	+	—	+	+	+
Complement fixation (18, 27, 28, 34, 35)	+	(+)	+	—	—	+	+	—
Guinea pig skin reactivity (18, 31, 34, 36)	+	—	+	+	—	+	—	—
In vivo catabolism (32, 33, 37)	S[c]	S	R[c]	S	S	S	R	S

[a] + indicates activity was positive.

[b] — indicates activity was negative.

[c] S denotes slow and R denotes rapid catabolism of immunoglobulins in that species.

It is of interest that when the patterns of biologic reactivities of human and mouse γG are compared, only human IgG-1 and mouse γ2a are similar. All other subclasses show different combinations of biologic activities. These data would argue against a direct phylogenetic relationship between human and mouse subclasses and would be more compatible with the concept that the subclasses arose independently after the evolutionary divergence of mouse and man. Recent amino acid sequence data of the Fc fragments are in keeping with this hypothesis (38).

Protein A reactivity in the guinea pig is a characteristic of both γ1 and γ2 antibodies (8). Intravenous injection of protein A in the guinea pig causes an anaphylactic reaction (39). This was felt to be due to the reaction between protein A and γ1 molecules. Since mouse γ1 molecules seem to lack protein A reactivity, an anaphylactic reaction from injected protein A would not be expected in this animal. Such a lack of reactivity has been shown not only for mice but also for rabbits and rats (39). We have confirmed this observation in mice, since no adverse effects were noted even after intravenous injection of as much as 0.5 mg of protein A. Since the principal mode of reaction of mouse γ globulin and protein A is by formation of soluble complexes, the *in vivo* reaction with protein A might also give rise to immune complex disease. However, our experiments showed no such effect as judged by the normal macro- and microscopic appearance of the kidneys in injected animals. No deposits of mouse γG were seen. Thus, we did not observe immune complex disease resulting from *in vivo* complex formation between protein A and mouse γ globulin.

The mouse has been extensively used as an experimental animal in staphylococcal research (40, 41). Although protein A reacts with the "wrong" part of human γ globulin molecules, it is still capable of giving rise to several types of immunologic phenomena (22–25, 42). Protein A can also act as an agglutinogen (43). The role of protein A in staphylococcal disease is still unclear. Future experimental approaches to the immunology of staphylococcal infections using various animal models must, however, take the reaction between protein A and γ globulin into account. The results obtained in the current study showing protein A reactivity in γ2a, γ2b and γ3 molecules could help to clarify some serologic phenomena and pathophysiologic mechanisms in staphylococcal infections. The unexpected finding of agglutinating was well as fluorescent antibodies against staphylococci in germ-free mice (44) might be explained on this basis.

Acknowledgment. We acknowledge the fine technical assistance of Miss Almera Seber and the secretarial expertise of Miss Shirley Cordova. We are indebted to Dr. William Doughty for evaluating mouse kidney specimens by light microscopy.

REFERENCES

1. Forsgren, A. and Sjöquist, J., J. Immun., *97:* 822, 1966.
2. Kronvall, G., Acta Path. Microbiol. Scand., *69:* 619, 1967.
3. Kronvall, G. and Williams, R. C., Jr., J. Immun., *103:* 828, 1969.
4. Kronvall, G. and Frommel, D., Immunochemistry, *1:* 124, 1970.
5. Nickerson, D. S., White, J. G., Kronvall, G., Williams, R. C., Jr. and Quie, P. G., J. Exp. Med., *131:* 1039, 1970.
6. Forsgren, A. and Sjöquist, J., J. Immun., *99:* 19, 1967.
7. Forsgren, A., J. Immun., *100:* 921, 1968.
8. Forsgren, A., J. Immun., *100:* 927, 1968.
9. Natvig, J. B., Kunkel, H. G., Yount, W. J. and Nielson, J. C., J. Exp. Med., *128:* 763, 1968.
10. Kronvall, G., Seal, U. S., Finstad, J. and Williams, R. C. J., J. Immun., *104:* 140, 1970.
11. Jensen, K., Thesis, Ejnar Munksgaard, Copenhagen, 1959.
12. Kunkel, H. G.: In *Methods of Biochemical Analysis*, p. 41, Interscience Publishers, Inc., New York, 1954.
13. Lowry, O. H., Rosebrough, N. J., Farr, L. A. and Randall, R. J., J. Biol. Chem., *193:* 265, 1951.
14. Killander, J., Acta Soc. Med. Upsal., *68:* 230, 1963.
15. Seligmann, M., Meshaka, G., Hurez, D. and Hihaesco, C., *VIth International Symposium on Immunopathology*, p. 229, Grune & Stratton, Inc., New York, 1965.
16. Lind, I. and Mansa, B., Acta Path. Microbiol. Scand., *73:* 637, 1968.
17. Grey, H. M., Hirst, J. W. and Cohn, M., Fed. Proc., *29:* 704, Abs., 1970.
18. Goldstein, I. J. and So, Lucy L., Arch Biochem. Biophys., *111:* 407, 1965.

19. Leon, M. A., Science, *158:* 1325, 1967.
20. Morse, Jane H., Immunology, *14:* 713, 1968.
21. Kronvall, G., Quie, P. G. and Williams, R. C., Jr., J. Immun., *104:* 273, 1970.
22. Sjöquist, J. and Stålenheim, G., J. Immun., *103:* 467, 1969.
23. Kronvall, G. and Gewurz, H., Clin. Exp. Immun., *7:* 213, 1970.
24. Gustafson, G. T., Sjöquist, J. and Stålenheim, G., J. Immun., *98:* 1178, 1967.
25. Martin, R. R., Crowder, J. G. and White, A., J. Immun., *99:* 269, 1967.
26. Potter, M., Lieberman, R. and Dray, S., J. Mol. Biol., *16:* 337, 1966.
27. Ishizaka, T., Ishizaka, K., Salmon, S. and Fudenberg, H. H., J. Immun., *99:* 82, 1967.
28. Kohler, P. F. and Müller-Eberhard, H. J., Science, *163:* 474, 1969.
29. Huber, H. and Fudenberg, H. H., Int. Arch. Allerg., *34:* 18, 1968.
30. Messner, R. P. and Jelinek, J., Submitted for publication.
31. Terry, W. D., J. Immun., *95:* 1041, 1965.
32. Spiegelberg, H. L., Fishkin, B. G. and Grey, H. M., J. Clin. Invest., *47:* 2323, 1968.
33. Morell, A., Terry, W. D. and Waldmann, T. A., J. Clin. Invest., *49:* 673, 1970.
34. Nussenzweig, R. S., Merryman, C. and Benacerraf, B., J. Exp. Med., *120:* 315, 1964.
35. Müller-Eberhard, H. J. and Grey, H. M., Personal communication to: Warner, N., Vaz, N. M. and Ovary, Z., Immunology, *14:* 725, 1968.
36. Ovary, Z., Barth, W. F. and Fahey, J. L., J. Immun., *94:* 410, 1965.
37. Fahey, J. L. and Sell, S., J. Exp. Med., *122:* 41, 1965.
38. Pink, J. R. L., Buttery, S. H., deVries, G. M. and Milstein, C., Biochem. J., *117:* 33, 1970.
39. Gustafson, T. T., Stålenheim, G., Forsgren, A. and Sjöquist, J., J. Immun., *100:* 530, 1968.
40. Ekstedt, R., Ann. N. Y. Acad. Sci., *128:* 301, 1965.
41. Mudd, S., In *Infectious Agents and Host Reactions*, Edited by S. Mudd, p. 197, W. B. Saunders Co., Philadelphia, 1970.
42. Dossett, J., Kronvall, G., Williams, R. C., Jr. and Quie, P. G., J. Immun., *103:* 1405, 1969.
43. Kronvall, G.: Acta Path. Microbiol. Scand., *B78:* 127, 1970.
44. Cohen, J. O., Newton, W. L., Cherry, W. B. and Updyke, E. L., J. Immun., *90:* 358, 1963.

THE JOURNAL OF IMMUNOLOGY
Vol. 105, No. 5, November 1970

CROSS-REACTIONS AMONG GROUP A STREPTOCOCCI

III. The M and R Antigens of Type 43 and Serologically Related Streptococci

GROVE G. WILEY AND PAULINE N. BRUNO

From the Alfred I. du Pont Institute, Wilmington, Delaware 19899

Received for publication June 5, 1970

Antigens in type 43 streptococci were studied, which were responsible for confusing cross-reactions among numerous strains isolated during recent years from patients with streptococcal illness, notably pyodermas, sometimes complicated by acute glomerulonephritis. Bactericidal activity, which was either reciprocal or in one direction only, accompanied precipitin cross-reactions between type 43 and the other cross-protective types 33, 41, 52, 53, 56, Ross, C506 and G_1. The experiments reported here showed that the cross-protective antibodies could be separated from the type-specific M antibodies by absorption with a strain which shared cross-protection, leaving only type-specific M antibodies. Absorption with one of these strains removed precipitin antibodies for the rest of the cross-reacting strains as well. This indicates that these reactions depend on the same antigenic determinants, and as far as tested, the cross-protective antibodies were removed also. The precipitin reactions between type 43 and strains P24037A and AD996 depended upon one of two non-protective R antigens, R_1, which these strains shared with the type 43 representative strain, C126/21. The second R antigen, R_2, has not been found in types other than 43 or independent of R_1. In other work, a non-protective antigen was also found on M^+ and M^- variants of strain C107/24, the type 33 representative strain. This antigen accounted for positive precipitin tests with M^- variants and anti-M sera. It has not been found in cocci of other types.

Studies of cross-reactions among group A streptococci revealed numerous cross-precipitin reactions between type 43 cocci and other types. Bactericidal activity accompanied some of these precipitin reactions but not others. For example, antisera of eight heterologous types inhibited multiplication of type 43 cocci to some extent and type 43 antisera were inhibitory in the reciprocal reactions for at least five of these (1, 2 and unpublished observation). Other strains, which cross-reacted in precipitin tests with type 43 and multiplied well in blood, indicating the presence of an M antigen, did not participate in either one-way or reciprocal protection with type 43 cocci, so that obviously antigens other than M were functioning in the precipitin tests.

The present work shows that some type 43 strains have, in addition to the M antigen, with its type-specific and cross-protective antigenic determinants, two heretofore unrecognized, non-protective antigens which occur in acid extracts of type 43, along with the M antigen. One of these is found in extracts of two other previously undescribed types as well. They probably represent R antigens of the kind described by Lancefield (3). One of them has been responsible for confusing strains of heterologous type with those belonging to type 43.

It was important to investigate the antigens involved in these cross-reactions in order to find ways, if possible, of avoiding them. Also, a more detailed knowledge of the antigenic structure of type 43 cocci seemed particularly important because of their close serologic relationship to numerous heterologous strains. In recent years, these have accounted for much streptococcal disease, especially pyodermas. Acute glomerulonephritis sometimes follows these infections.

MATERIALS AND METHODS

Streptococcal strains. The methods of handling and preserving cultures in this laboratory have been described in an earlier report (1). Certain strains tested in these experiments carried previously unrecognized M antigens. When two or more such strains shared an identical M antigen, as demonstrated in bactericidal and agar gel diffusion tests, they were referred to, for convenience, as a type, designated by a strain number or name.

Strain C126/21, the type 43 representative strain, and DS2519 shared identical M antigens, but not R antigens. DS2618, which lacked an M antigen, was considered to be a non-virulent, type 43 M^- variant because of its R antigenic composition. These strains were supplied by the National Communicable Disease Center, Atlanta, Georgia. With the exception of C506, the following strains with heterologous M antigens were serologically related to C126/21 through one of the R antigens. AD996 and C632/Rb6 (type AD996) and P24037A, which was representative of the satellite strains described by Chapman *et al.* (4), shared an identical R antigen with C126/21. C506 (type C506) is included as an example of a strain which shared protective antigenic determinants with type 43 strains as well as with other types which participate in cross-protection with type 43. These strains (listed in Table IV) have been described previously (1, 2). C632/Rb6 and C506 were obtained from Dr. Rebecca C. Lancefield, P24037A from Dr. Lewis Wannamaker, and AD996 from the collection of strains in this laboratory.

In slide agglutination tests, strains C126/21, DS2618 and DS2519 reacted with type 3, NCDC agglutinating antiserum; P24037A with types 3 and 5; C506 with type 28; AD996 with type 12; and C632/Rb6/20 with types 3, 13, B3264.

Capillary precipitin tests and streptococcal extracts. Precipitin tests were performed by the method of Swift *et al.* (5) with absorbed antisera and M extracts prepared by alcohol precipitation of crude extracts according to the method of Lancefield (6). Concentrated M extracts for the agar gel tests were prepared by taking up the final alcohol precipitate of M extracts in 0.1 the usual volume of saline. These are referred to in the text and figures as 10x M extracts.

Antisera. The preparation of vaccines and streptococcal antiserum are described in a previous publication (1).

Double diffusion tests. These tests have been described in another publication from this laboratory (7) and were carried out with optimal dilution of 10x M extracts and absorbed antisera.

Indirect bactericidal or protection tests. Positive results in bactericidal tests, like those of tests of mouse protection, depend upon factors which promote phagocytosis of cocci with subsequent suppression of their multiplication, and, like tests of mouse protection, they are generally believed to indicate immunity or protection from infection. They are, therefore, often referred to as protection tests and the inhibition of multiplication which they measure is called protection.

The test, as it is performed here, has been described in detail (8). Briefly it consists of rotating for 3 hr at 37°C mixtures of dilutions of streptococci. These had been grown in filtered beef heart infusion broth containing 20% of the donor's serum and resuspended in silicone-stoppered, 7- x 10-mm glass test tubes containing the filtered broth without serum (0.1 ml), with normal rabbit serum or with antiserum (0.05 ml), and heparinized normal human blood (0.25 ml). One-tenth milliliter of this mixture was then plated in sheep blood agar. After incubating overnight, the amount of growth was reported as L, PL or TM, depending upon whether the sheep blood was laked, partially laked (confluent hemolysis) or there were too many colonies to count, respectively. When possible, the colonies were counted and their number recorded. The total number of chains present after rotation can be calculated by multiplying the figure in the tables by four.

RESULTS

The three double diffusion tests in Figure 1 demonstrate the antigens present in various strains of type 43 cocci. The extract of C126/21, the type representative strain, in the lower left well in each test, reacted with the homologous antiserum in the upper well to form three bands, a broad one next to the serum well and two fine, discrete lines nearer the antigen well. In the first test a variant of C126/21, obtained by picking colonies from tryptose infusion blood agar with hyaluronidase, formed two lines which joined the broad and the fine center band of the parent culture. Eight of twelve colonies yielded cultures which reacted to form three bands and four produced two like the variant shown in the figure. Strain DS2519 in the center test formed only the broad band, and was thought to lack an R antigen until antisera against these cocci became available. Tests with such sera showed that DS2519 cocci have an R antigen serologically distinct from the others encountered in these experiments. In the third test with DS2618 only two fine lines are present, the broad band being absent.

The work to be presented demonstrates that the broad band was formed by the M anti-M reaction and that the antigens responsible for the two fine lines were not associated with protection. They were designated R antigens, R_1 being the center line and R_2 the one next to the antigen well. The M and R antigenic composition of the strains is summarized in Table I along with the corresponding capillary precipitin tests. AD996 and P24037A are included in these data as examples of heterologous strains which shared the R_1 antigen of type 43.

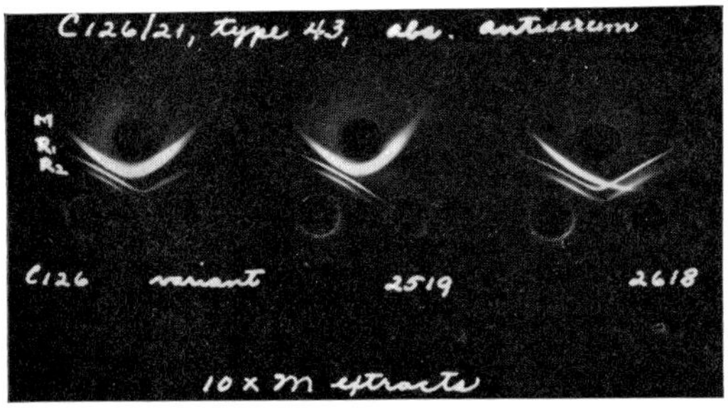

Figure 1. The agar gel tests illustrate the M and R antigens of four type 43 cultures. The type representative strain, C126/21, shows three bands. The M reaction is next to the serum well, R_2 next to the extract well, and R_1 between. In these tests the C126 variant lacked R_2; DS2519, R_1 and R_2; and DS2618, the M reaction.

A total of eight type 43 cultures of independent origin were examined in agar gel tests. Two carried all three of the antigens, four M and R_1, one M only, and one R_1 and R_2, M being absent. It is presumed that this M^- culture, DS2618, which failed to multiply in blood, and was therefore M deficient, was a degraded type 43 culture, although the only evidence in favor of this interpretation was the presence of the R_2 antigen, which has not yet been found in strains of heterologous type.

The M antigen of type 43 cocci. There is good reason to believe that the C126/21 M anti-M reaction formed the broad band in the agar gel tests. For example, DS2519 cocci, which lacked both type 43 R antigens and whose extracts gave a reaction of identity with this band, absorbed the antibodies responsible for the reaction from C126/21 antiserum (Fig. 2, upper test) and the bactericidal activity of the serum as well (Table II).

Strain DS2618, which had the two type 43 R antigens but lacked the broad band (Fig. 1), failed to multiply in blood and was therefore considered to be M antigen deficient, a conclusion justified by the failure of these cocci to absorb bactericidal antibodies from C126/21 antiserum (Table II).

Also, heterologous types which participated

TABLE I

M and R antigens of type 43 and related strains

M Extracts	Type 43 Antigens Agar Gel and Bactericidal Tests	Capillary Precipitin Tests Antisera		
		C126/21 absorbed		DS2519 absorbed
		Type 1[a] M R_1 R_2	AD996[a] M R_2	type 1 M
C126/21	M R_1 R_2	++++	++++	++++
C126/21 variant	M R_1	++++	++++	++++
DS2519	M	++++	++++	++++
DS2618	R_1 R_2	+++	±[b]	−
AD996	R_1	+++[b]	−	−
P24037A	R_1	+++	−	−

[a] C126/21 antiserum absorbed with type 1 cells demonstrated M and both R antigens, DS2519 serum M only, since these cocci lacked the type 43 R antigens. Heterologous AD996 cocci shared R_1 with C126/21 and therefore removed R_1 but not M antibodies. See Figures 1 and 3.

[b] R_1 interfered with the type identification of heterologous strains such as AD996 and P24037A. R_2 was rarely demonstrable in standard extracts, and required more concentrated extracts for its detection.

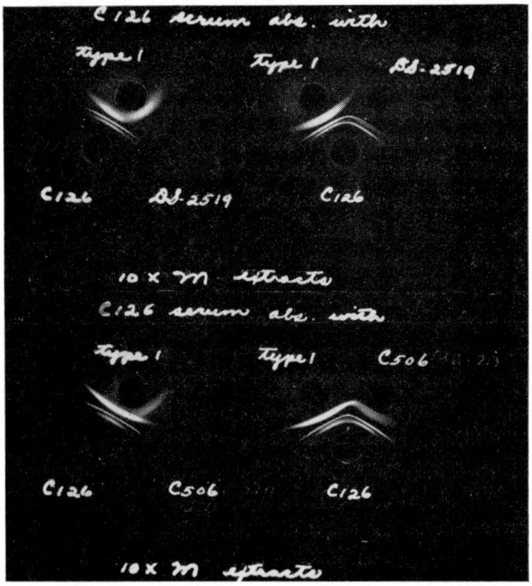

Figure 2. The upper two tests show identity between the M reactions of DS2519 and C126/21. Absorption of C126/21 antiserum with the type 43 R-deficient DS2519 cocci removed M but not R antibodies from the serum. The bactericidal test in Table II confirms this interpretation. In the lower two tests, strain C506 which shared cross-protection with C126/21, reacted with partial interference with the M band of C126/21. Absorption of the type 43 serum with C506 cocci diminished but did not abolish the M reaction. These results correspond with those of the bactericidal tests (Table III).

in cross-protection with C126/21 cocci gave the previously described reaction of partial interference with the broad band (1). An example is shown in the first test in the lower part of Figure 2 with an extract of strain C506. The cross-protective relationship of this strain to C126/21 is examined in the next section. Thus, both the type-specific and cross-protective reactions involved the broad band next to the serum well.

The type-specific and cross-protective antigenic determinants of C126/21 cocci. The bactericidal tests in Table III with C126/21 antiserum and cocci and a cross-reacting strain, C506, which has an M antigen of its own, are examples of the separation of cross-protective from type-specific antibodies. The test on the left side of the table with C126/21 serum, which was bactericidal for both C126/21 and C506 cocci, shows that absorption of the homologous antiserum with C506 cocci diminished the homologous bactericidal effect of the serum somewhat but did not eliminate it. This, then, represents the type 43 M anti-M reaction from which the cross-protective C506 antibodies were removed as shown in the test on the right side of the table with C506 cocci. The intensity of the broad type 43 M band in agar gel was diminished somewhat but not abolished by absorption with the cross-reactive strain (second test, lower part of Fig. 2).

The ever-present question in this work has been whether these numerous cross-protective reactions among the different types (1, 2) depend upon the same or several different antigenic determinants. Evidence is accumulating to indicate that many of these reactions, at least, depend upon the same determinants, although the possibility of some exceptions has not been eliminated. Examples are given in Table IV. When type 43 antiserum was absorbed with either of two cross-protective strains, C506 or G_1, precipitin antibodies for both strains were removed as well as those for the rest of the strains listed in the table, and as far as tested cross-protective bactericidal antibodies have been removed as well. The results indicate a serologic similarity among all of the cross-protective antigenic determinants.

The R antigens of type 43 cocci. Lancefield designated certain non-protective, streptococcal antigens, whose biologic significance is unknown, by the letter R. These antigens are extracted from the cocci by heat and acid and therefore appear in acid extracts of streptococci. They may be confused with M antigens and lead to errors in the type identification by the precipitin method, since some at least are not type-specific. For example, type 28 R antigen also occurs in some strains of types 2 and 48 and even in certain groups other than A, such as B, C and G (9, 10). The R antigens vary in their susceptibility to digestion by proteolytic enzymes. The type 28 R antigen is susceptible to digestion by pepsin but resists trypsin (9). Both enzymes digest the 3 R antigen of strain D58. A further characteristic of these antigens is their presence on M^- as well as M^+ variants.

The antigens responsible for the two fine lines in agar gel tests with extracts of C126/21 (Fig. 1) apparently belong in the category of R antigens, because they provided no protection

TABLE II

M antibodies confer protection; R antibodies do not

Antisera	Summary of Type 43 Antibodies[a]			Bactericidal Tests[b] C126/21 Cocci, Type 43		
				Inoculum		
				7500	750	75
				Results		
Normal rabbit serum				L	L	PL
C126/21 absorbed with type 1	M	R_1	R_2	2	0	0
C126/21 absorbed with DS2519[c]		R_1	R_2	L	L	PL
DS2519 unabsorbed	M			5	0	0
Type 28[d] unabsorbed				L	L	PL
				Inoculum		
				10500	1050	105
				Results		
Normal rabbit serum				L	L	PL
C126/21 unabsorbed	M	R_1	R_2	0	0	0
C126/21 absorbed with DS2618	M			5	0	0
Type 13 unabsorbed				L	L	PL

[a] Summary is based on results of agar gel and bactericidal tests.

[b] L, PL and TM indicate that the blood agar plates were laked, partially laked or that there were too many colonies to count, respectively. Figures represent the number of colonies present in the plates.

[c] DS2519 cocci have type 43 M but lack type 43 R antigens. DS2618 cocci have R_1 and R_2 but no M antigen.

[d] Type 28 R antigen is serologically distinct from the type 43 R antigens.

TABLE III

Type-specific and cross-protective reactions of C126/21

Antisera	Precipitin Tests M Extracts		Bactericidal Tests					
	C126/21	C506	C126/21 Cocci, Type 43			C506 Cocci, Type C506		
			Inocula					
			4300	430	43	2570	257	25
			Results					
Normal rabbit serum			L	L	PL	L	L	PL
C126/21 unabsorbed			0	0	0	17	0	0
C126/21 absorbed with type 1[a]	++++	++	0	0	0	149	17	2
C126/21 absorbed with C506[a]	++++	–	5	1	0	L	L	PL
Type 6 unabsorbed			L	L	PL	L	L	PL

[a] Only C506 cocci shared cross-protection with C126/21. Type 1 did not.

for the cocci against the bactericidal properties of normal human blood, were susceptible to digestion by both trypsin and pepsin, occurred on both M^+ and M^- variants of type 43 cocci and one, R_1, was not type-specific. They were serologically independent of type 28 and 3 R antigens, however, since antisera against these antigens failed to react with the type 43 R antigens.

Their non-protective nature was illustrated by the failure of the M^- strain, DS2618, with both R_1 and R_2, to multiply in blood. These cocci also failed to absorb bactericidal antibodies from C126 antisera (Table II). R_1 was not type-specific, being shared by strains with independent M antigens. Two such strains, AD996 and C632/Rb6/20, had identical, previously undescribed M antigens and both carried the R_1 antigen. An example is shown in Figure 3, left test, where the center line of the C126/21 reaction (R_1) connects in a reaction of identity with the AD996 line. Absorption of C126/21 antiserum with this strain removed R_1 antibodies as shown in the other agar gel test in Figure 3,

TABLE IV

Evidence that cross-protective reactions depend on the same antigenic determinant

Capillary Precipitin Tests				
M extract	Type	C126/21, type 43 antiserum absorbed with cells of		
		Type 1	G_1	C506
C107/24	33	++	−	−
C101/21	41	++	−	−
C126/21	43	++++	+++	+++
A871/14	52	++	−	−
Ross	Ross	+++	−	−
C506	C506	++	−	−
G_1	G_1	++	−	−

With the exception of C126/21 none of these strains have a type 43 R_1 or R_2 antigen. The precipitin reactions here are distinct from the R reactions, depending upon *cross-protective antigenic determinants*, and as far as tested the cross-reacting bactericidal antibodies for all of the strains were absorbed by any one of the strains along with the precipitin antibodies.

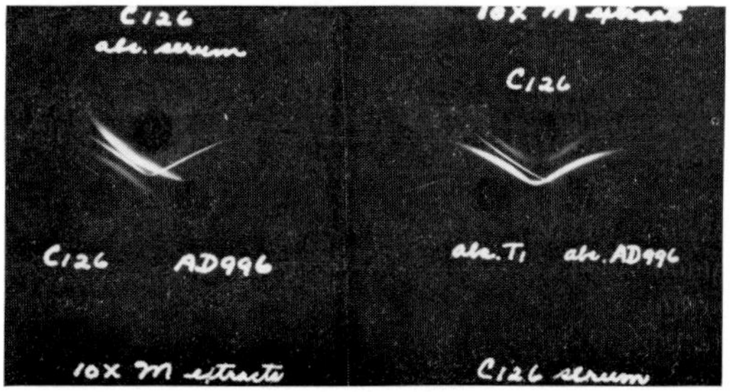

Figure 3. Heterologous AD996 cocci have an antigen identical with the R_1 antigen of C126/21 cocci. Absorption of type 43 antiserum with AD996 cocci removed R_1 but not M and R_2 antibodies.

but failed to remove bactericidal antibodies (Table V). The serologically distinct M antigens of AD996 and C126/21 were demonstrated by completely negative reciprocal bactericidal tests. The connection between a heterologous strain from Dr. Wannamaker's laboratory, P24037A, one of the satellite strains (4), and C126/21 also depended upon the R_1 antigen.

The R_2 antigen of C126/21 has not been found in types other than 43 nor has it been encountered independently of R_1. The possibility that the two R bands were formed by the splitting of a single band during diffusion of

TABLE V

Demonstration that absorption of R_1 antibodies did not affect the bactericidal reactions

Antisera	Bactericidal Test C126 Cocci, Type 43			
	Inoculum			
	4700	470	47	4
	Results			
Normal rabbit serum	L	L	PL	TM
C126/21 absorbed with type 1	11	0	0	0
C126/21 absorbed with AD996	1	0	0	0
Type 6 unabsorbed	L	L	PL	48

C126/21 and AD996 with serologically distinct M antigens share the type 43 R_1 antigen. See Figure 3 and Table 1.

antigen and antibody in agar was considered and rejected because absorption of C126/21 antisera with AD996 cocci removed the R_1 but not the R_2 reaction, and R_1 variants lacking R_2 were frequently encountered.

Capillary precipitin tests with a limited number of groups other than A (B, C, F and G) have failed to reveal either of the R antigens.

DISCUSSION

The possible role of cross-protective reactions in streptococcal immunity has been considered in earlier papers (1, 2) in which it was suggested that cross-protection among types, as measured in bactericidal tests, might be a factor in acquired immunity if a corresponding situation occurs *in vivo*. Thus, infection with one of the cross-protective strains might, in addition to type-specific immunity, confer some protection against other types which share cross-protective antigenic determinants. This possibility has not yet been investigated.

From a more practical point of view, it is important to understand the fundamental nature of these cross-reactions so that they can be eliminated and with them the confusion in the identification of streptococcal types. To a considerable extent this has been accomplished with type 43. For example, experiments reported here and elsewhere have shown that in addition to the type-specific protective determinants of the M antigen, type 43 cocci also carry cross-protective antigenic determinants, demonstrable in bactericidal tests with normal human blood and hyperimmune rabbit antiserum, which are shared by at least eight other group A streptococcal types. These are types 33, 41, 52, Ross and G_1 (1, 2) and 53, 56 and C506 (unpublished observations). Other confusing cross-reactions depended upon one of two non-protective antigens which have been identified as R antigens, R_1 and R_2, analogous to that described by Lancefield for certain type 3 cocci, although the type 43 antigens were serologically independent of this antigen. The R_1 antigen accounted for the serologic connection in precipitin tests between type 43 and two additional, serologically distinct types designated AD996 and P24037A.

Fortunately, it was less difficult to eliminate a formidable list of cross-reactions from sera intended for identification of type 43 cocci than a first glance suggested. Evidence of the kind presented in Table IV showed that the cross-protective precipitin reactions depended upon the same antigenic determinants. Thus, absorption of C126/21 antiserum with one of the cross-protective strains, such as G_1, which was especially useful for this purpose, removed precipitin reactions for the rest of the strains as well, leaving type-specific M antibodies. In this way, it was possible to eliminate the cross-protective reactions without absorption with numerous other related types.

After such absorption, R antibodies remained so that the sera cross-reacted with strains sharing the R_1 antigen, such as AD996 and P24037A (Table I). Absorption with DS2618 cocci having both R_1 and R_2 antigens but no type 43 M antigen removed antibodies for both of the R antigens without diminishing the type 43 M antibodies. Thus, absorbing type 43 sera with one of the cross-protective strains and with DS2618 cocci yielded a strongly bactericidal serum free of major cross-reactions. In practice, when sera cross-reacted feebly with strains other than those described above, such cocci were also included in the absorption.

Apparently, non-protective antigens like the type 43 R antigens occur more frequently than has been suspected and account for many confusing results in capillary precipitin tests. The D58 and type 28 R antigens of Lancefield have been referred to previously. Another example, encountered in this laboratory, explained the apparent paradox of a type 33 variant of C107/24, which failed to multiply in blood and was therefore presumably M^-, reacting strongly in precipitin tests with highly bactericidal, anti-M serum. Agar gel diffusion tests revealed the absence of the M antigen on the cocci and the presence of what proved in subsequent absorption and bactericidal experiments to be a non-protective antigen. This accounted for the positive precipitin reaction with anti-M serum. The same findings and interpretation were made independently in another laboratory (W. K. Harell, personal communication). It has not yet been determined whether this antigen occurs in other types. At any rate, it would be prudent to eliminate its antibodies from antisera by absorption with the M^- variant.

Acknowledgments. The authors wish to thank Dr. Rebecca C. Lancefield for her valuable advice during this work and acknowledge the able technical assistance of Mrs. Carobelle Hanssmann, Mrs. Annie P. van der Lek and Mrs. Priscilla Moses.

REFERENCES

1. Wiley, G. G. and Bruno, P. N., J. Exp. Med., *128:* 959, 1968.
2. Wiley, G. G. and Bruno, P. N., J. Immun., *103:* 1969.
3. Lancefield, R. C., J. Exp. Med., *108:* 329, 1958.
4. Chapman, S. S., Johnson, D. R. and Dudding, B. A., American Society for Microbiology, Bact. Proc., p. 72, 1969.
5. Swift, H. F., Wilson, A. T., and Lancefield, R. C., J. Exp. Med., *78:* 127, 1943.
6. Lancefield, R. C., J. Exp. Med., *47:* 91, 1928.
7. Wilson, A. T. and Wiley, G. G., J. Exp. Med., *118:* 527, 1963.
8. Wiley, G. G. and Wilson, A. T., J. Exp. Med., *113:* 451, 1961.
9. Lancefield, R. C. and Perlmann, G. E., J. Exp. Med., *96:* 83, 1952.
10. Lancefield, R. C., J. Exp. Med., *106:* 525, 1957.

THE JOURNAL OF IMMUNOLOGY
Vol. 105, No. 5, November 1970

ANTIGENIC PROPERTIES OF CHEMICALLY MODIFIED COLLAGEN

R. TIMPL, I. WOLFF, W. MEIGEL, B. PONTZ, C. STEFFEN AND K. KÜHN

From the Max-Planck-Institut für Eiweiss- und Lederforschung, München, Germany, and the Institute of Immunology, University of Vienna, Austria

Received for publication June 5, 1970

Acid-soluble calf collagen was modified by succinylation, methylation or deamination. These modified collagens showed no loss of serologic activity when investigated with antibodies detecting three distinct groups of antigenic determinants on unmodified collagen. A single antiserum exhibiting a very rare specificity did not, however, react with methylated collagen. Treatment of collagen with strong alkali which results in a complete deamidation and probably also in a removal of terminal peptide sequences caused the destruction of the protease-labile antigenic determinants but had no effect on the other. In rabbit antisera to methylated or succinylated collagen mainly antibodies specific for the modified collagen were detectable. These antibodies are adapted to haptenic structures since they could be effectively inhibited by γ-methyl glutamic acid and succinylated ϵ-amino caproic acid, respectively. In antisera to deamidated collagen, antibodies of this kind could not be demonstrated.

Recent studies demonstrated several distinct antigenic determinants on soluble calf collagen, one of which can be removed from the native molecule by the action of various proteases and is probably localized in a non-helical terminal region of the molecule (1–3). Cross-reaction studies revealed a high degree of species specificity (4). A second class of species-specific determinants is stable against proteolytic attack (2) and was recently assigned to sequences of the middle region of the molecule (3). The same stability was found for a third group of antigenic determinants, which could be demonstrated on all collagens independent of the species origin (4).

The rod-like collagen molecule is a triple helix composed of three polypeptide chains that are held together by non-covalent bonds. Mild denaturation disrupts this structure and the resulting single chains are in a random coil configuration (5). All studies except one (1) have demonstrated that denatured collagen retains full serologic activity. Most investigators, therefore, now agree (6–8) that the antigenic determinants of collagen so far characterized are not dependent on the conformation of the molecule. The ability of small collagen peptides to inhibit anti-collagen antibodies (7, 9, 10) supports this view. These results provide a basis for investigating the structure of the different antigenic determinants by fragmentation methods (3). In a second approach to elucidate the antigenic structure synthetic peptides corresponding to typical collagen sequences were employed and pronounced cross-reactions with antibodies to collagen have been reported (10, 11). Antigens with chemically modified amino acid side chains have not yet been used as a third possible way to get information about the structure of antigenic determinants of collagen. In the present study the effect of a chemical modification on the serologic activity of collagen was therefore investigated. Additionally, antisera were prepared against modified collagens and the specificity of the antibodies was characterized as directed mainly to the sites of modification.

MATERIALS AND METHODS

Isolation and chemical modification of acid-soluble collagen. Soluble collagen was isolated from calf skin by extraction with citrate buffer, pH 3.7, and was purified by two precipitations (3). This collagen was modified by either methylation, succinylation, deamination or deamidation as already described (12–14). The groups affected by these treatments and the extent of the modifications obtained are summarized in Table I.

For the serologic studies the different collagens were denatured by dissolving in 2 M KSCN or by treating in acidic solution at 50°C (2). Suc-

TABLE I

Chemical characterization of modified calf collagen obtained by different methods

Treatment (Reference)	Groups Affected and Extent of Modification	Calculated from:
Methylation at 25°C (13)	Free carboxyl groups, 100%	Titration, methoxyl analysis
Succinylation (13)	ε-amino groups, >95%	Titration
Deamination by nitric acid (14)	ε-amino groups, >98%	Amino acid analysis
Deamidation at pH 14 (12)	Amide groups, 100%	Nesslerization after hydrolysis with 2 M HCl
	Intramolecular cross-links, 95%	Ultracentrifugation

cinylated collagen which is insoluble under acidic conditions was converted into a random coil configuration by a similar heating process at neutral pH. Deaminated collagen is completely insoluble in common protein solvents and detergents and was therefore used only in absorption studies.

Preparation of haptens. Gamma-methyl glutamic acid and β-methyl aspartic acid were obtained according to an established procedure (15). The hydrochloride salts of these esters were recrystallized from ethanol:ether (3:1, v/v) and had uncorrected melting points of 154° to 156°C and 184° to 186°C, respectively. The quantitative elemental analysis was in good agreement with the calculated values.

Succinylated ε-amino caproic acid. An equimolar mixture of succinic anhydride and ε-amino caproic acid was heated for 15 min at about 60°C. The product obtained was recrystallized from ethanol and had an uncorrected melting point of 78° to 81°C. A quantitative analysis was in accordance with the values for the cyclic imide:

Calculated:	C 56.33%	H 7.09%	N 6.57%
Found:	C 56.60%	H 7.23%	N 6.38%

The imide was converted to the open amide by addition of two equivalents of dilute NaOH (pH maintained at 11). The solution was neutralized with HCl and used directly in the inhibition studies.

Antisera. Rabbits were injected with 1 to 2 mg of native or denatured acid-soluble calf collagen incorporated into complete Freund's adjuvant. After 14 days a booster injection of 5 mg of antigen without adjuvant was given intraperitoneally. Animals which showed an insufficient response were treated for a second time in the same way.

The antisera were collected 5 days after the last injection, checked for their specificity using the passive hemagglutination-inhibition method and classified according to the following scheme (2). *P-specificity:* antibodies directed to protease-labile, species-specific determinants; *S-specificity:* antibodies directed to protease-stable, species-specific determinants; and *A-specificity:* antibodies directed to general collagen determinants.

The S-specific antibodies were further subdivided by means of a positive or negative cross-reaction with rat collagen into the subgroups S1 and S2, respectively (4). In this study two types of antibody solutions were used: antisera exhibiting *per se* a restricted specificity for a distinct group of antigenic determinants or antibodies separated from single sera according to their specificity by an immunoadsorbent technique (16). Both gave identical results.

As for collagen, antisera were prepared against methylated collagen, succinylated collagen and deamidated collagen. Two rabbits (155 and 156) received methylated collagen together with $Al(OH)_3$ according to a schedule previously applied for hydroxylamine-treated collagen (17).

Immunoadsorbent studies. Denatured calf collagen was coupled to carboxymethyl cellulose by the aid of a water-soluble carbodiimide (18). The resulting immunoadsorbents contained 12% to 20% conjugated collagen as revealed by hydroxyproline analyses. A column was prepared from 10 to 20 g material in phosphate-buffered saline, pH 7.2, and was used for the absorption of 20 ml of antiserum against modified collagen. After each passage the column was regenerated by elution with collagen peptides (16) but no attempt was made to isolate and characterize the eluted antibodies.

Serologic technique. The passive hemagglutination method was applied throughout (2). For this purpose tanned human red cells were coated with 0.001% collagen denatured by 2 M KSCN. Under these conditions methylated collagen caused some unspecific clumping of the tanned red cells and was therefore employed without impaired sensitizing efficacy at concentrations as low as 0.0002% to 0.0005%. For the inhibition tests the collagens were denatured by a heating procedure.

Titrations were performed on a glass plate. In inhibition tests an equal amount of inhibitor (antigen or hapten) was added to twofold progressive dilutions of the antiserum. The activity is expressed as the decrease of the original titer of the serum.

Deaminated collagen could be used only in absorption experiments which were carried out as described earlier (19). Controls included absorptions with insoluble collagen and with quartz; the latter one has been used for grinding both insoluble collagen preparations.

RESULTS

Studies with antibodies to unmodified collagen. Acid-soluble collagens, modified either by methylation, succinylation or deamidation, were compared in hemagglutination-inhibition tests with unmodified collagen for their ability to inhibit antibodies specific for different antigenic determinants on collagen (Fig. 1). The A-specific antibodies which are directed to the general collagen determinants could be inhibited by all of the modified collagens. The activity was slightly less than that for unmodified collagen but could be considerably increased by a 10-fold increase in the inhibitor concentration. Similar results were found for antibodies possessing the specificity S1. On the contrary, P-specific antibodies which detect protease-labile determinants could be inhibited only by methylated and succinylated collagen.

In these experiments a single antiserum having the specificity S2 was also studied but the results have not been included in Figure 1. This specificity differs from S1 inasmuch as the corresponding antigenic determinant was not detectable on rat collagen (4). Only succinylated and deamidated collagen were able to inhibit the S2-specific antibodies. Methylated collagen proved to be completely inactive.

Absorption experiments revealed an unimpaired serologic activity for deaminated collagen when compared with insoluble collagen. Typical examples for each type of specificity are given in Table II.

Specificity of antisera against modified collagen. The rabbit antisera to the different modified collagens were titrated in passive hemagglutination against red cells coated with collagen or with the respective modified collagen. The titers of the sera were reexamined after a passage through a collagen immunoadsorbent (Table III). Additionally, the serologic activity of modified and unmodified collagen was compared in inhibition tests for which representative examples are given in Table IV.

Most of the antisera to succinylated or methylated collagen reacted mainly with the corresponding antigen and exhibited no or only a

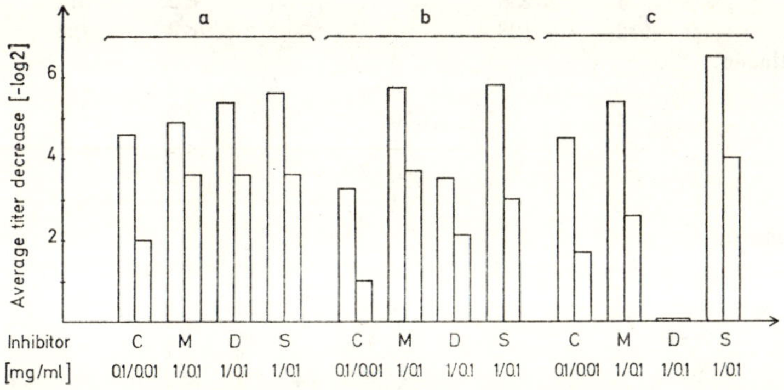

Figure 1. Hemagglutination-inhibition of anti-collagen antibodies by unmodified collagen (C), methylated collagen (M), deamidated collagen (D) and succinylated collagen (S). Red cells were coated with unmodified collagen. *a*, A-specific antibodies (average of 7 sera); *b*, S1-specific antibodies (average of 3 sera); *c*, P-specific antibodies (average of 11 sera).

very low activity for unmodified collagen. This result was found with the agglutination technique as well as in the agglutination inhibition studies. A minor antibody fraction was occasionally found which reacted with unmodified collagen. It could be completely removed on the immunoadsorbent without concomitant reduction in the titer for modified collagen. Therefore, it seems very likely that the main antibody fraction in these sera is specifically adapted to structural pecularities of the modified collagen. This has been proved by inhibition studies with haptens which presumably correspond to those groups introduced into the collagen molecule by the chemical methods. The antibodies to methylated collagen could be significantly inhibited by γ-methyl glutamic acid but not at all by β-methyl aspartic acid and by both parent amino acids (Table V). Likewise, the antibodies to succinylated collagen are completely inhibited by succinylated ϵ-amino caproic acid whereas succinate was devoid of activity (Table VI). An exchange of the active haptens between both systems did not result in any reduction in titer.

TABLE II

Effect on anti-collagen sera of absorption with insoluble collagen or deaminated collagen

Serum No.; Type of Specificity	Reciprocal Titer after Absorption with[a]		
	Quartz[b]	Insoluble collagen	Deaminated collagen
219; A	256	NT[c]	<8
230; A	128	<8	<8
163; S1	128	<8	<8
95; S2	512	8±	32±
119; P	1024	<8	<8
235; P	512	<8	<8

[a] Titrated with collagen-coated red cells.
[b] Same titer as prior to absorption.
[c] NT, not tested.

TABLE III

Titer of antisera to various modified collagens before and after absorption on a collagen immunoadsorbent

Antiserum against:	Reciprocal Titer with[a]							
	Original antiserum				Absorbed antiserum			
	C	M	S	D	C	M	S	D
Methylated collagen, no.								
151	4	16			<2	32		
152	<4	64			<2	64		
153	1024	128			2	64		
155	4	1024				NT[b]		
156	4	1024				NT		
182	4	128			4	256		
184	4	256			<2	512		
185	512	128			<2	128		
Succinylated collagen, no.								
174	4		256		<2		256	
175	<2		64		<2		64	
176	<2		256		<2		256	
177	<2		64			NT		
Deamidated collagen, no.								
240	4			64	<2			<2
241	<2			8	<2			<2
242	<2			16	<2			<2
243	8			64	<2			<2

[a] Red cells coated with collagen (C), methylated collagen (M), succinylated collagen (S) or deamidated collagen (D).
[b] NT, not tested.

TABLE IV

Inhibition of antisera to modified collagen by the corresponding antigen and unmodified collagen

Inhibitor (mg/ml)	Reciprocal Titer for Antiserum against[a]		
	Methylated collagen no. 182	Succinylated collagen, no. 175	Deamidated collagen no. 240
0.15 M NaCl	128	64	64
Methylated collagen (0.1)	<2		
Succinylated collagen (0.1)		<2	
Deamidated collagen (0.1)			<2
Collagen (1.0)	128	64	4

[a] In each case the corresponding antigen was used for coating the red cells.

TABLE V

Inhibition by haptens of antibodies to methylated collagen

Inhibitor (mg/ml)	Reciprocal Titer for Red Cells Coated with Methylated Collagen for Antiserum No.[a]						
	151	152	155	156	182	184	185
0.15 M NaCl	32	64	1024	1024	128	512	128
γ-Methyl glutamic acid (10)	4	8	128	128	<4	64	8
β-Methyl aspartic acid (10)	16	64	512	512	64	512	128
Glutamic acid (10)	32	64	1024	1024	128	512	128
Aspartic acid (10)	32	64	1024	1024	128	512	128

[a] Antisera which showed a reaction with collagen were used after absorption on a collagen immunoadsorbent.

Furthermore, these haptens could not inhibit antibodies to unmodified collagen.

The antisera to deamidated collagen correspond to the antisera against the other modified collagens above insofar as they preferentially agglutinate red cells coated with the modified collagen. The results of the absorption and inhibition studies (Tables III and IV) provide, however, no evidence for the presence of antibodies specifically directed to groups generated by the deamidation of collagen.

DISCUSSION

The different antigenic determinants of unmodified collagen as investigated by the aid of antibodies with restricted specificity do not depend on an intact conformational structure (6). The results obtained with the chemically modified collagens can, therefore, be interpreted in terms of a participation of discrete amino acid side chains in the combining sites of this antigen. It seems highly probable that the ε-amino groups of lysine are not involved since succinylation as well as deamination do not influence the serologic activity of collagen. This is also true for the free carboxyl groups of glutamic and aspartic acid with the exception of the very rarely recognized determinant, S2. Succinylated and methylated collagen are soluble in neutral solvents, even at very low ionic strength. As a side result of the present findings one can assume that both are suitable for certain serologic studies for which native acid-soluble collagen cannot be easily applied.

The protease-labile antigenic determinants of calf collagen have recently been located in nonhelical terminal regions of the molecule (3). Degradation of the amide groups makes collagen unreactive for antibodies directed to such determinants. A simultaneous destruction of intramolecular cross-links (12) under the alkaline conditions employed in the deamidation reaction raises the question as to which change the loss of serologic activity can be related. Since it is probable that the cross-links are destroyed by a removal of terminal sequences in which they are located, a simultaneous removal of these antigenic determinants may have been the inevitable consequence.

TABLE VI

Inhibition by haptens of antibodies to succinylated collagen

Inhibitor (mg/ml	Reciprocal Titer with Red Cells Coated with Succinylated Collagen for Antiserum No.[a]			
	174	175	176	177
0.15 M NaCl	256	128	32	256
Succinylated ε-amino caproic acid (1) (0.1)	<2 2	<2 16	<2 <2	<2 64
Succinate (10)	256	64	16	128
ε-Amino caproic acid (10)	256	128	32	256

[a] Antisera which showed a reaction with collagen were used after absorption on a collagen immunoadsorbent.

As was found for collagen in this report, Habeeb (20) obtained no evidence for the participation of the ϵ-amino groups in the antigenic determinants of bovine serum albumin. The same was claimed for the carboxyl groups of this antigen (21). On the other hand, succinylation of serum β-lipoprotein (22) or deamination of ovalbumin (23) caused a considerable loss of the serologic activity. Since in these particular cases both forms of treatment cause marked alterations in conformation, there still remains doubt as to which of these changes was responsible for destroying the antigenic structure.

Although methylated and succinylated collagen possess virtually all of the original antigenic determinants, in rabbits they primarily elicit antibodies which must be considered as strictly specific for the chemically modified groups, i.e., as antibodies directed to haptens. From the relatively low inhibiting capacity of γ-methyl glutamic acid, it may be concluded that some adjacent amino acids play an additional role in this determinant. However, the esterified amino acid should be considered as the immunodominant group like succinylated lysine in the other system. The depression of the antibody titer to collagen in these sera may reflect a phenomenon of antigenic competition between different determinants on the same carrier molecule, similarily as reported for proteins carrying two different haptens (24, 25). Closer to our findings is the observation that serum albumin, modified by succinylation followed by nitroguanidination, still reacts with 71% of the antibodies directed to the unmodified antigen but causes a strongly depressed synthesis of anti-albumin antibodies (20). In collagen such an effect seems to be very easily induceable since antisera to hydroxylamine-treated collagen also contain mainly antibodies specific for aspartic acid hydroxamate (26).

A heavily succinylated albumin also elicits antibodies that recognize the succinyl group. Yet, the larger antibody fraction in these sera is directed to areas on the molecule which are newly created by conformational changes (20). Although such antibodies have not been detected so far in the antisera to succinylated collagen, there is no certainty that they are absent.

In a recent report Slobin (27) postulated that the recognition of a haptenic determinant depends on the extent of conformational changes provoked by the introduction of this foreign structure. Physicochemical studies gave no evidence that methylation or succinylation of collagen is accompanied by a gross alteration of the triple helix structure although small changes in some regions of the molecule may exist (13). Since both modified collagens give rise to antibodies to very small haptens these models may be useful to study such general questions as the role of foreignness or conformational alterations for the induction of hapten-specific antibodies.

REFERENCES

1. Davison, P. F., Levine, L., Drake, M. P., Rubin, A. L. and Bump, S., J. Exp. Med., *126:* 331, 1967.
2. Steffen, C., Timpl, R. and Wolff, I., Immunology, *15:* 135, 1968.
3. Pontz, B., Meigel, W., Rauterberg, J. and Kühn, K., Europ. J. Biochem., In press.
4. Timpl, R., Wolff, I., Wick, G., Furthmayr, H. and Steffen, C., J. Immun., *101:* 725, 1968.
5. Engel, J., Arch. Biochem., *97:* 150, 1962.
6. Steffen, C., Timpl, R. and Wolff, I., Z. Immunitaetsforsch., *134:* 91, 1967.
7. Kirrane, J. A. and Robertson, W. van B., Immunology, *14:* 139, 1968.
8. Michaeli, D., Kamenecka, H., Benjamini, E., Kettman, J. R., Leung, D. Y. K. and Miner, R. C., Immunochemistry, *5:* 433, 1968.
9. Steffen, C. and Timpl, R., Z. Immunitaetsforsch., *129:* 469, 1965.
10. Kettman, J. R., Benjamini, E., Michaeli, D. and Leung, D. Y. K., Biochem. Biophys. Res. Commun., *29:* 623, 1967.
11. Borek, F., Kurtz, J. and Sela, M., Biochim. Biophys. Acta, *188:* 314, 1969.
12. Kühn, K., Zimmer, E., Waykole, P. and Fietzek, P., Z. Physiol. Chem., *333:* 209, 1963.
13. Rauterberg, J. and Kühn, K., Z. Physiol. Chem., *349:* 611, 1968.
14. Kühn, K., Grassmann, W. and Hofmann, U., Z. Naturforsch., *13b:* 154, 1958.
15. Coleman, D., J. Chem. Soc., p. 2294, 1951.
16. Timpl, R., Wolff, I., Furthmayr, H. and Steffen, C., Immunology, *15:* 145, 1968.
17. Steffen, C., Timpl, R. and Wolff, I., Z. Immunitaetsforsch., *124:* 476, 1962.
18. Weliky, N., Weetall, H. H., Gilden, R. V. and Campbell, D. H., Immunochemistry, *1:* 219, 1964.
19. Steffen, C., Timpl, R. and Wolff, I., J. Immun., *93:* 656, 1964.
20. Habeeb, A. F. S. A., J. Immun., *99:* 1264, 1967.

21. Sri Ram, J. and Maurer, P. H., Arch. Biochem., *83:* 223, 1959.
22. Gotto, A. M., Levy, R. J., Rosenthal, A. S. and Fredrickson, D. S., Nature, *219:* 1157, 1968.
23. Maurer, P. H. and Heidelberger, M., J. Amer. Chem. Soc., *73:* 2076, 1951.
24. Amkraut, A. A., Garvey, J. S., and Campbell, D. H., J. Exp. Med., *124:* 293, 1966.
25. Brody, N. J., Walker, J. G. and Siskind, G. W., J. Exp. Med., *126:* 81, 1967.
26. Steffen, C., Timpl, R. and Wolff, I., Nature, *213:* 497, 1967.
27. Slobin, L. I., Nature, *225:* 698, 1970.

THE JOURNAL OF IMMUNOLOGY
Vol. 105, No. 5, November 1970

Printed in U.S.A.

ACTIVATION OF NORMAL RABBIT MACROPHAGE MONOLAYERS BY SUPERNATANTS OF ANTIGEN-STIMULATED LYMPHOCYTES[1]

JOHN J. MOONEY[2] AND BYRON H. WAKSMAN

From the Departments of Pathology and Microbiology, Yale University School of Medicine, New Haven, Connecticut 06510

Received for publication June 3, 1970

Tuberculin- or HSA-sensitized rabbit lymph node cells, harvested at 10 to 14 days, and normal rabbit lymph node cells were incubated for 24 hr alone or in the presence of specific or heterologous antigen. The supernatants prepared from these lymph node cell cultures were added to duplicate or triplicate monolayer cultures of peritoneal macrophages from normal rabbits, each macrophage being exposed to soluble products released *in vitro* by 10 lymph node cells. After 24 and 48 hr of continuous exposure to the undiluted supernatants, 150 to 300 cells in each flask were scored for adherence and ameboid activity. Macrophages exposed to supernatants from mixtures of sensitized cells with specific antigen had two to five times greater numbers of ameboid cells at 24 and 48 hr than did monolayers of the same macrophages exposed to control supernatants, and twice as many cells remained adherent at 48 hr. Thus, factors released by sensitized lymphocytes cause activation of normal macrophages. It is suggested that a similar mechanism may be responsible for cell-mediated immunity in systems involving microbial antigens.

The present study was derived from two quite different lines of investigation. Recent studies of cell-mediated immunity show that "sensitized" lymphocytes stimulated by antigen release mediators which may activate or kill various target cells (1). Secondly, the macrophages of animals with such infections as tuberculosis manifest "cellular immunity," an apparently nonspecific ability to suppress intracellular replication of various microorganisms (2, 3). Mackaness and his colleagues have demonstrated a striking parallel of the latter property with activation of macrophages, as shown by their ability to spread on glass or plastic surfaces, but have inferred from passive transfer experiments that it depends on specific delayed sensitivity mediated by sensitized lymphocytes (4). Our object was to determine whether such sensitized lymphocytes, when they react with specific antigen, release substances capable of stimulating normal macrophages to an activated state.

[1] This work was supported by United States Public Health Service Research Grants AI-06112 and AI-06455, and Training Grant AI-00291, and was reported in preliminary form at the American Society for Experimental Pathology, Atlantic City, New Jersey, April 13, 1970.

[2] Postdoctoral Trainee, United States Public Health Service Grant HTS-5153.

MATERIALS AND METHODS

Immunization. Four-kilogram New Zealand albino rabbits (males and virgin females) were obtained from local suppliers, separately housed, and fed a diet of Purina rabbit chow and water *ad libitum.* After pentobarbital anesthesia, one shaved toepad on each of the four limbs was injected with either 0.1 ml of complete Freund's adjuvant containing 0.3 mg of heat-killed tubercle bacilli or 0.1 ml of complete Freund's adjuvant emulsion containing 1 mg of human serum albumin (HSA) (Hyland Co., Los Angeles, Calif., lot 0490E090A1).

Harvesting of lymph node cells. For each experiment, either tuberculin- or HSA-sensitized lymph node cells (SLNC) from the draining axillary and popliteal lymph nodes of two rabbits, 10 to 14 days after immunization, were pooled and normal lymph node cells (NLNC) were obtained from the mesenteric nodes of two unsensitized rabbits and similarly pooled. In each case, the cells were teased out into medium 199/Earle's base (199/E supplied by the Yale Laboratory of Epidemiology and Public Health) containing 100 units of penicillin and 100 μg of streptomycin/ml. The resulting suspensions were passed through sterile gauze, washed once in 199/E by centrifugation at 250 × G for 10 min, resuspended in fresh medium, and counted in hemocytometer chambers.

Lymph node cell cultures. Portions of the two LNC pools were suspended at a concentration of 10^7 cells/ml in 199/E containing either 5% or 20% (v/v) heat-inactivated, pooled normal rabbit serum, and antibiotics. After gassing with a 5% CO_2-95% air mixture, these were incubated for 24 hr at 37°C in the presence of specific or heterologous antigen (Ag), 10 to 20 μg PPD (Parke-Davis & Co., Detroit, Mich.), 100 μg HSA (Hyland, lot 0490E090A1), or 100 μg ovalbumin (Worthington Biochemicals, Freehold, N. J.)/ml, usually in a total volume of 50 ml in 250-ml Falcon plastic flasks. Supernatants were prepared by centrifugation at 400 × G for 10 min from the following incubation mixtures: SLNC + Ag, SLNC + heterologous Ag, SLNC only, NLNC + Ag, NLNC + heterologous Ag, NLNC only, medium + Ag, medium + heterologous Ag, medium only. In other experiments, supernatants were prepared from these incubation mixtures: SLNC + Ag, SLNC only, and SLNC only to which Ag was added at the end of the incubation period. All supernatants were stored at −20°C, and used within 7 days of preparation.

Macrophage monolayer cultures. In most experiments, a given set of supernatants was added to macrophage monolayers obtained from each of two unsensitized donors. Peritoneal exudates were induced by using a 350- to 400- ml infusion of glycogen (Pfanstiehl Laboratories, Inc., Waukegan, Ill.) at a concentration of 1 mg glycogen/ml saline. The exudates were harvested 36 to 48 hr later by injecting 150 ml of phosphate-buffered saline (PBS) containing heparin (Organon, Inc., West Orange, N. J.) 10 units/ml, and collecting the cell suspension by gravity. The usual yield was 1.5 × 10^8 leukocytes/rabbit, 85% to 90% being mononuclear cells. Donor rabbits were used only once. Each cell suspension was centrifuged at 250 × G for 7 min, and resuspended in 199/E containing antibiotics and 20% heat-inactivated serum from the same batch used to prepare the LNC culture supernatants of the same experiment. The cells were counted by hemocytometer chamber, gently resuspended, and portions of each suspension added to 30-ml Falcon plastic flasks. These were then gassed and incubated without shaking for 30 min at 37°C. The time elapsing between collection of the cells and their deposition in medium and serum was minimized by processing each of the two mononuclear exudates of an experiment separately. After the 30-min incubation, nonadherent cells were removed by agitation and a single wash with 199/E. Each previously prepared LNC supernatant was then added to duplicate or triplicate culture flasks containing the macrophage monolayers, the flask contents gassed, and the flasks incubated at 37°C in an atmosphere of 5% CO_2-95% air for 48 hr. Each cultured macrophage was continuously exposed to soluble products released by approximately 10 LNC.

Evaluation of cellular activity. Twenty-four hours after adding the LNC supernatants to the macrophage monolayers, the living, adherent cells were individually examined by light microscopy at six equally spaced points approximately 1 cm from the edge of the flask surface on which the monolayer was growing. Each adherent cell in a 450 × field, measuring 0.053 mm^2 as defined by a Howard eyepiece micrometer disc (A. H. Thomas, Inc., Philadelphia, Pa.) was classified as either rounded or ameboid by the following criteria: a) rounded cells had no visible pseudopods or ruffled limiting membranes, and the periphery of the centrally-located nucleus very nearly extended to the plasma membrane of the cell. b) ameboid cells had pseudopods, ruffled membranes, and an eccentrically-placed nucleus. Most of the rounded and ameboid cells had a small number of tiny, refractile, round bodies in their cytoplasm suggestive of lipid droplets. At 48 hr the nonadherent cells and medium were removed from each flask, and the adherent cells were fixed by exposing them to 1.25% glutaraldehyde in PBS for 10 min at 4°C. They were then gently washed with PBS, overlayed with another volume of PBS, and stored at 4°C. The fixed, adherent cells were counted and scored for ameboid activity in the same manner as at 24 hr. The number of nonadherent cells in the supernatant medium was determined by hemocytometer counts.

Computation of results. The mean numbers of adherent cells/field at 24 and 48 hr and the standard error of these means (SEM) were determined for each flask. The numerical value of the SEM was usually 5% to 7% of the mean.

The number of adherent cells/flask was determined by multiplying the mean number of cells/field (0.053 mm²) times 4.7 × 10⁴, since the flask surface is 25 cm² in area. The total number of ameboid cells/flask was determined in a similar manner. The number of cells actually counted in a single flask at either 24 or 48 hr ranged between 150 and 300.

RESULTS

Culture supernatants prepared by incubating LNC from tuberculin-sensitized donors with

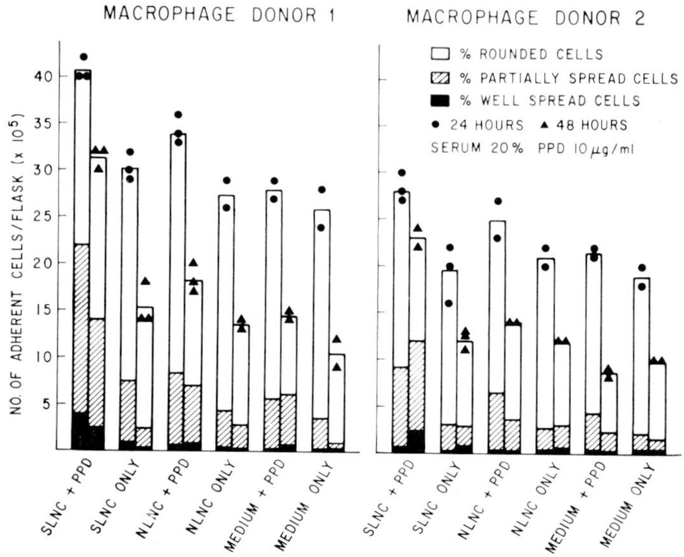

Figure 1. Adherence and ameboid activities of macrophage monolayers from two different donors exposed to the same batch of supernatants. Each bar represents the mean number of adherent cells of 2 to 3 flasks.

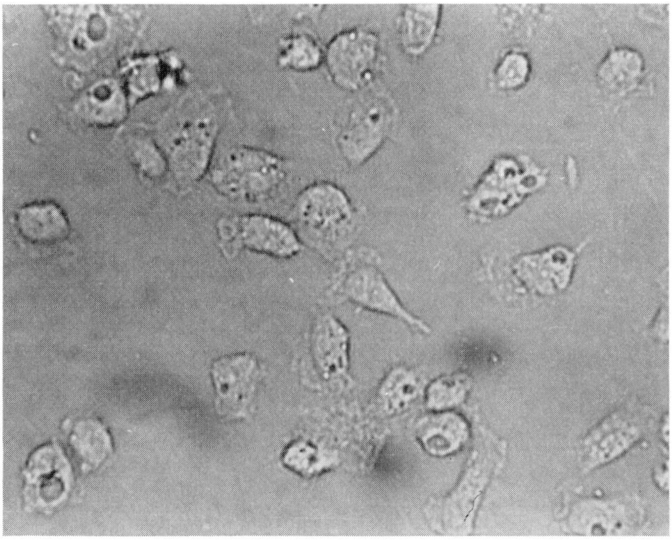

Figure 2. Unstained macrophage monolayers fixed with 1.25% glutaraldehyde in phosphate-buffered saline for 10 min at 4°C × 450, after 48 hr of continuous exposure to tuberculin-sensitized lymph node cells + PPD (10 μg/ml) supernatant.

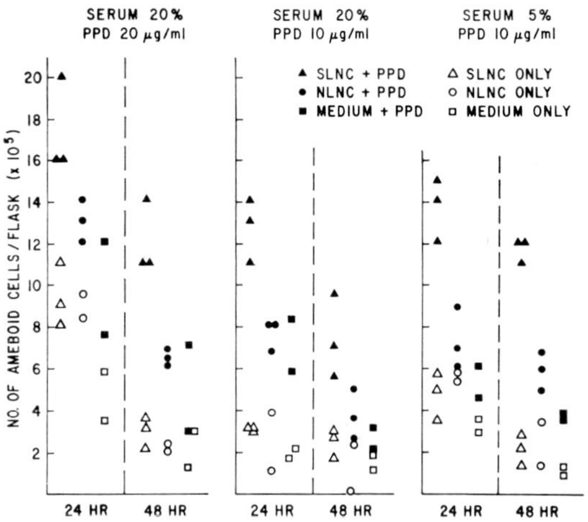

Figure 3. Scatterplots of ameboid cells/flask for three experiments in which different batches of supernatants containing different amounts of heat-inactivated serum or antigen were applied to macrophage monolayers from three different donors.

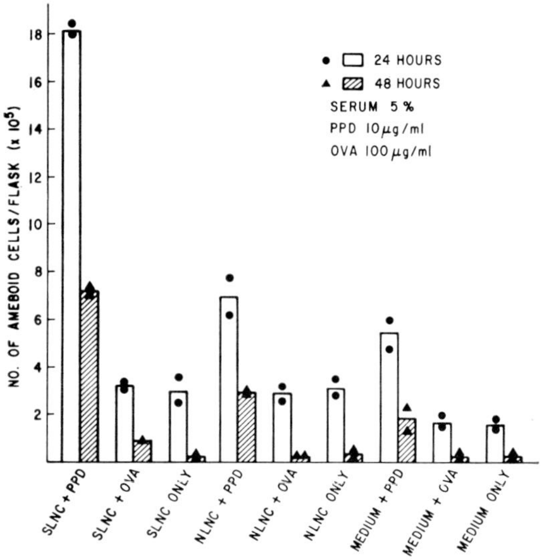

Figure 4. Specificity of macrophage activation in an experiment with tuberculin-sensitized lymph node cells. Ovalbumin (OVA) serves as the heterologous antigen. Each bar represents the mean of duplicate cultures.

PPD produced apparent stimulation of macrophages by several criteria, as illustrated by the data of a single experiment (Fig. 1). More macrophages remained at 48 hr in flasks to which this supernatant had been added than in any to which the various control supernatants were added. Also a larger proportion (and absolute number) of surviving cells remained adherent to the plastic surface of the flasks at 24 and 48 hr, and of these, many more were partially or completely spread and obviously ameboid (Fig. 2). Control cultures differed little from each other except that there was some stimulatory effect of PPD alone on macrophage activity.

The effect of the SLNC + PPD supernatant was reproducible when two different concentrations of PPD were employed (10 μg or 20 μg/ml) to stimulate the LNC and the macrophages were cultured in either 5% or 20% serum (Fig. 3). Macrophage monolayers obtained from different normal rabbits differed somewhat in their quantitative responses to the same batch of LNC supernatants, although their pattern of responses to the same batch of LNC supernatants was qualitatively the same (Fig. 1). The SLNC + PPD effect was immunologically specific; SLNC exposed to the unrelated antigen ovalbumin did not produce an active supernatant (Fig. 4). Addition of PPD to a "SLNC only" supernatant immediately before it was placed on monolayers did not result in stimulation of the macrophages (Fig. 5).

Supernatants prepared from HSA-immunized SLNC + HSA also produced stimulation of ameboid activity in macrophage monolayers from unsensitized rabbits, whereas HSA alone had no stimulatory effect (Figs. 6 and 7*A*). Monolayers exposed to a culture supernatant prepared by incubating these sensitized LNC with both HSA and PPD also showed enhanced ameboid activity during the 48-hr period of observation. Among cells exposed to SLNC + HSA substantial numbers of multinucleated giant cells (8 to 15 nuclei/cell) appeared at 48 hr, but such cells were not observed in monolayers exposed to either the SLNC + HSA + PPD or tuberculin-sensitized LNC + PPD supernatants. Ameboid cells of cultures stimulated by supernatants containing PPD rarely had more than 2 to 3 nuclei per cell. Addition of HSA to a HSA-sensitized "SLNC only" supernatant immediately before it was placed on monolayers did not result in stimulation of the macrophages (Fig. 7*B*).

Table I summarizes experiments in which counts of both adherent and nonadherent cells were obtained after 48 hr of culture. The stimulatory effect described above is consistently observed with the active supernatants prepared by

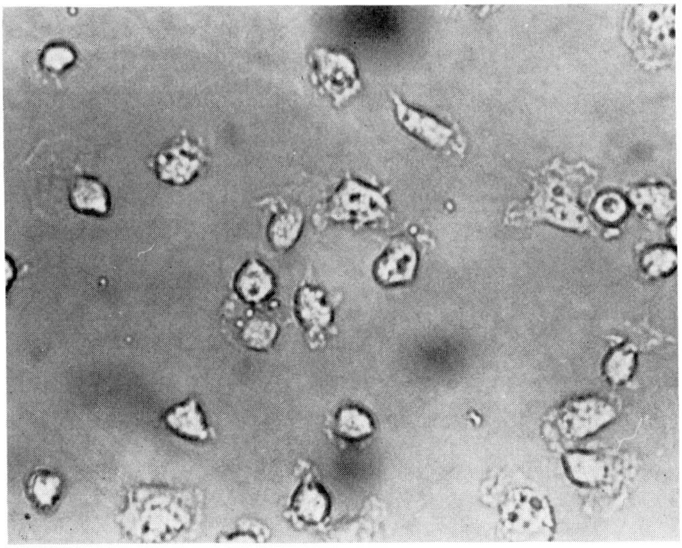

Figure 5. As in Figure 2 but after 48 hr of continuous exposure to "tuberculin-sensitized lymph node cells only" supernatant to which PPD (10 μg/ml) was added shortly before the addition of the supernatant to the culture flask.

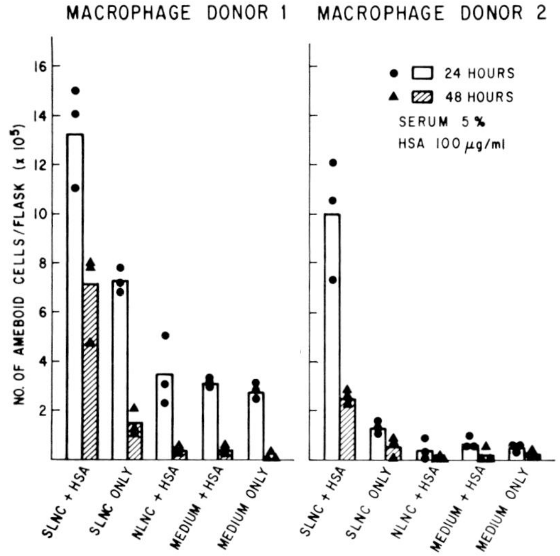

Figure 6. Stimulation of ameboid activity in monolayers exposed to supernatants from HSA-sensitized lymph node cells reacting with specific antigen. Each bar represents the mean number of ameboid cells observed in duplicate or triplicate cultures.

incubating sensitized lymph node cells with the appropriate antigen. At 48 hr, the media prepared by incubating SLNC without Ag or with heterologous Ag contained (with one exception) twice as many detached cells as those supernatants prepared by incubating the same pools of SLNC with the specific sensitizing antigen.

DISCUSSION

The present findings represent an extension of our earlier observation that macrophages in peritoneal exudates of tuberculin-sensitive guinea pigs, when exposed to tuberculoprotein under favorable conditions *in vitro*, showed marked, apparently specific cell activation. Small basophilic monocytes were transformed within 24 hr into large macrophages filled with phagocytic vacuoles and showed greatly improved survival over controls (5). The findings presented here demonstrate that a similar effect is induced in normal rabbit macrophages by exposure to mediator(s) released from sensitized rabbit lymph node cells interacting with specific antigen. This activation may be accompanied by an increase in lysosomes and their content of hydrolases, such as acid phosphatase (6–8). Fauve and Dekaris (9) in experiments lasting 30 min have observed an early inhibition of spreading.

Recently, much attention has been given to a number of effects of substances released by activated lymphocytes on various target cells *in vitro* (1, 10). These include: inhibition of macrophage migration, chemotactic effects on macro-

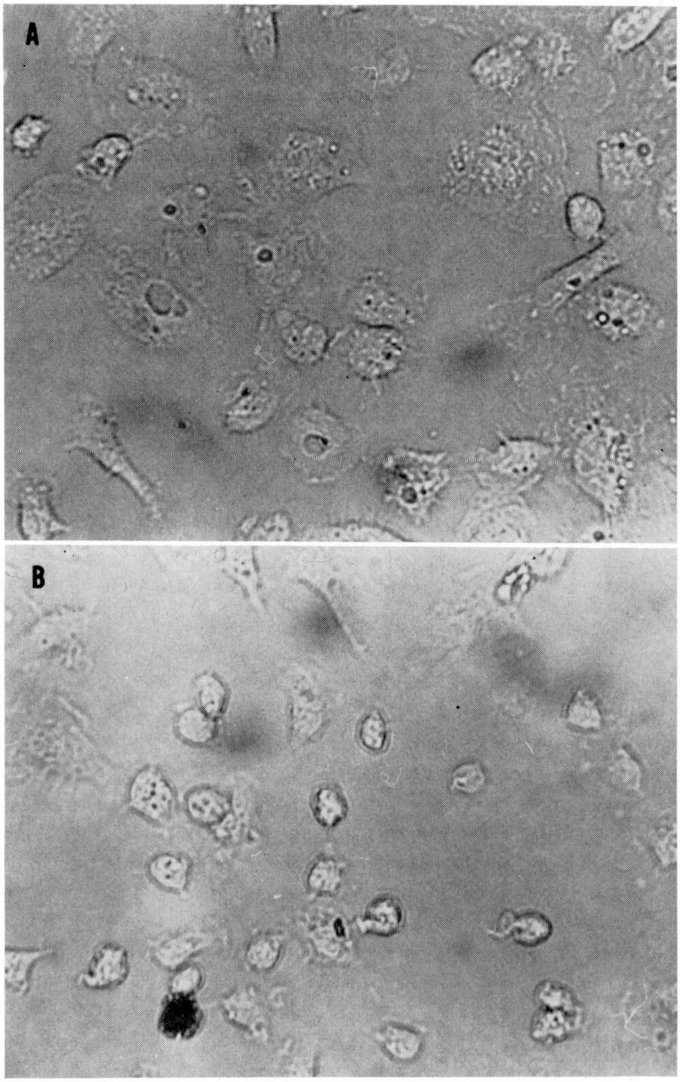

Figure 7. Unstained macrophage monolayers fixed with 1.25% glutaraldehyde in phosphate-buffered saline for 10 min at 4°C × 450. *A*, after 48 hr of continuous exposure to HSA-sensitized lymph node cells + HSA (100 μg/ml) supernatant; *B*, after 48 hr of continuous exposure to "HSA-sensitized lymph node cells only" supernatant to which HSA (100 μg/ml) was added shortly before the addition of the supernatant to the culture flask.

phages, the killing of fibroblasts and other target cells, and mitogenesis and blastogenesis in lymphocytes. The present work adds other phenomena to this list: the stimulation of macrophage spreading and motility. Several of these phenomena may depend on similar mechanisms. Activation, if sufficiently intense, may lead to cell death, as suggested by Granger (11). However, in the experiments of David (12) and Bloom and Bennett (13), the macrophages were not killed, and the observed inhibition of their migration may well have depended on the stickiness shown here, which is characteristic of activated macrophages such as those from BCG-infected animals (3). The chemotactic effect must also represent increased activity at the level of the surface membrane. Fibroblast cultures which are destroyed by these substances also show an early increase in intracellular acid phosphatase, suggesting an early phase of activation before

TABLE I

Supernatant activity and cell counts at 48 hr[a]

Exudate Cells Originally Added	Test Antigen	Adherent Cells		Ameboid Cells		Nonadherent Cells	
		SLNC + Ag	SLNC only	SLNC + Ag	SLNC only	SLNC + Ag	SLNC only
200	PPD	34	23	11	4	7	15
100	PPD	31	15	15	3	11	20
80	PPD	23	12	12	4	16	17
80	PPD	19	9	10	1	14	23
80	PPD	28	12	12	2	6	10
80	PPD	22	7[b]	8	1[b]	11	24[b]
70	PPD	32	17	12	3	13	26
50	PPD	17	15	6	2	3	10
80	HSA	13	13	7	1	4	13
80	HSA	12	9	2.5	0.5	12	21
80	HSA + PPD	21	13	10	1	5	13
80	HSA + PPD	17	9	5	0.5	8	21

[a] Mean number of cells/flask ($\times 10^5$) in duplicate or triplicate sets of flasks.
[b] SLNC + OVA.

death (14). The identity of the mediator in our cultures of rabbit cells is as yet unknown. It is a plausible hypothesis that it may be either migration inhibitory factor or chemotactic factor. Its possible relationship to factors in "conditioned medium" in which L-cells or other cells have been grown, which can stimulate peritoneal macrophages to divide actively, remains to be determined (15).

These findings are relevant to events in the intact organism, since it has been established that the macrophages in such peritoneal exudates as we used here are derived from the bone-marrow (16, 17) and are thus comparable to the marrow-derived hematogenous monocytes which form the predominant infiltrating cells in delayed reactions (18). As noted earlier, cell-mediated immunity against microbial pathogens is closely paralleled by an activated state of peritoneal and other macrophages. These cells are able to suppress intracellular replication both of the specific organism to which the animal is immune and of other unrelated organisms. Specific immunity may be transferred to normal animals by transfer of lymphocytes; if antigen is given to the recipient, a state of nonspecific immunity develops (4). Our experiment provides the *in vitro* counterpart of this observation. On the other hand, by transferring macrophages from the immunized animal, one may convey nonspecific immunity limited to the cells actually transferred (19). Mackaness' formulation is thus borne out by our tissue culture study. Histologic and histochemical observation on tuberculous lesions also show that the appearance of tuberculin sensitivity and the accompanying activation of macrophages, with an increase of lysosomal enzymes, are followed by a rapid decrease in intracellular organisms (8). Thus, activated macrophages, a *sine qua non* of cell-mediated immunity, must be produced after release of these soluble mediators in the intact animal.

Acknowledgments. We gratefully acknowledge the assistance of Dr. Zanvil A. Cohn, Rockefeller University, and Dr. Elisha Atkins, Yale University, both of whom generously donated the facilities of their laboratories to one of us (J.M.) at various stages in the pursuit of these experiments. Dr. Michael Kashgarian of Yale University assisted us with the photography.

REFERENCES

1. *Mediators of Cellular Immunity*, Edited by H. S. Lawrence and M. Landy, Academic Press, New York, 1969.
2. Mackaness, G. B., J. Exp. Med., *120:* 105, 1964.
3. Blanden, R. V., Lefford, M. J. and Mackaness, G. B., J. Exp. Med., *129:* 1079, 1969.
4. Mackaness, G. B., J. Exp. Med., *129:* 973, 1969.
5. Waksman, B. H. and Matoltsy, M., J. Immun., *81:* 220, 1958.
6. Adams, D. O., Biesecker, J. L. and Koss, L. G., Fed. Proc., *29:* 359 (Abstract), 1970.

7. Cohn, Z. A. and Benson, B., J. Exp. Med., *121:* 835, 1965.
8. Dannenberg, A. M., Jr., Meyer, O. T., Esterly, J. R. and Kambare, T., J. Immun., *100:* 931, 1968.
9. Fauve, R. M. and Dekaris, D., Science, *160:* 795, 1968.
10. Ward, P. A., Remold, H. G. and David, J. R., Science, *163:* 1079, 1969.
11. Granger, G. A., in *Mediators of Cellular Immunity*, Edited by H. S. Lawrence and M. Landy, p. 324, Academic Press, New York, 1969.
12. David, J. R., Fed. Proc. *27:* 6, 1968.
13. Bloom, B. R. and Bennett, B. Fed. Proc., *27:* 18, 1968.
14. Ruddle, N. H. and Waksman, B. H., J. Exp. Med., *128:* 1267, 1968.
15. Virolainen, M. and Defendi, V., in *The Wistar Institute Symposium Monograph #7*, p. 67, Edited by V. Defendi and M. Stoker, The Wistar Institute Press, Philadelphia, 1967.
16. Volkman, A. and Gowans, J. L., Brit. J. Exp. Path., *46:* 62, 1965.
17. van Furth, R. and Cohn, Z. A., J. Exp. Med., *128:* 415, 1968.
18. Lubaroff, D. M. and Waksman, B. H., J. Exp. Med., *128:* 1437, 1968.
19. Miki, K. and Mackaness, G. B., J. Exp. Med., *120:* 93, 1964.

THE JOURNAL OF IMMUNOLOGY
Vol. 105, No. 5, November 1970
Printed in U.S.A.

HYDROCORTISONE RESISTANCE OF GRAFT *VS* HOST ACTIVITY IN MOUSE THYMUS, SPLEEN AND BONE MARROW[1]

J. JOHN COHEN,[2] MICHAEL FISCHBACH[3] AND HENRY N. CLAMAN

From the Division of Clinical Immunology, Department of Medicine, University of Colorado Medical School, Denver, Colorado 80220

Received for publication June 2, 1970

The effects of corticosteroids on the graft *vs* host activity of thymus, spleen and bone marrow were studied. Adult BALB/c mice were given 2.5 mg of hydrocortisone intraperitoneally 2 days before killing. The number of nucleated cells in their spleens was 21% of control values; in bone marrow, 79%; and in thymus, only 6%. When equal numbers of thymus cells from hydrocortisone-treated and control animals were administered to neonatal CAF_1 recipients, the hydrocortisone-thymus was by far the more active at initiating the graft *vs* host (GvH) reaction, as measured by splenomegaly. Similarly, when equal numbers of spleen or bone marrow cells from hydrocortisone-treated or normal mice were transferred to normal adult CAF_1 recipients, the hydrocortisone-spleen and hydrocortisone-bone marrow were significantly more active at initiating GvH. It is suggested that a population of cells which is not involved in GvH is preferentially destroyed by hydrocortisone in each of these organs. The corticosteroid-resistant thymus cells, which have previously been shown to exist in the medulla, thus have characteristics of peripheral lymphoid cells.

Knowledge of the cells involved in the graft *vs* host (GvH) reaction, and of their origins, is of great importance both theoretically and clinically. Although GvH activity of organs such as the spleen is thymus-dependent (1, 2) the thymus itself contains few cells capable of initiating the reaction (3). Blomgren and Andersson (4) have found that these few cells are located in the thymus medulla. They destroyed the thymus cortex by injecting intact A/Sn donors with 2.5 mg of cortisone acetate; the medulla, which is cortisone-resistant (5, 6), was, cell for cell, about 10 times as active as was the whole gland at inducing splenomegaly in F_1 recipients. In this test system, the GvH activity of donor spleen differed from that of thymus in that spleen GvH activity was not enhanced after cortisone treatment. This suggested that the GvH capacity of the spleen is not restricted to a cortisone-resistant population, as is that of the thymus. Because the mouse spleen appears to be a composite of thymus-derived and marrow-derived cells (with regard to hemolysin formation) (7), we found it surprising that the spleen did not contain a corticosteroid-resistant population of cells with high GvH activity. Therefore, we have investigated the response to corticosteroids of the GvH initiator cells in the thymus, spleen and bone marrow. Unlike Blomgren and Andersson, we found that the GvH activity of all three tissues is corticosteroid-resistant.

[1] This work was supported by the Medical Research Council of Canada and United States Public Health Service Grants AI-00013 and AM-10145.

[2] Fellow of the Medical Research Council of Canada.

[3] Summer trainee, United States Public Health Service.

MATERIALS AND METHODS

Mice. Male A/J mice, 8- to 12-weeks old, were obtained from Jackson Laboratories, Bar Harbor, Maine. Female BALB/c mice 8 to 10 weeks old were obtained from the breeding colony of the American Medical Center, Denver. Four-day-old (BALB/c × A/J) F_1 (CAF_1) mice from our own colony were used as recipients of thymus cells; 8- to 10-week-old male CAF_1 mice used in other experiments were from Jackson Laboratories.

Cell suspensions. Thymus or spleen cell suspensions were prepared by pressing those organs through a 60-mesh screen into cold Eagle's spinner-type minimal essential medium (MEM). Bone marrow was flushed from the cavities of femurs with a syringe and needle containing cold MEM. The cells were passed through 20- and 26-gauge needles to disrupt clumps. All suspensions were centrifuged at 400 × G for 5 min, the supernatant fluids discarded, and cells resuspended with MEM so that the desired number of cells for transfer was contained in 0.1 ml for 4-day-old recipients, and 0.5 ml for adults.

Corticosteroid treatment. Preparations used were cortisone acetate suspension (Intra) and hydrocortisone acetate suspension (Cortril, Pfizer Laboratories, New York). Each was administered intraperitoneally (i.p.), 2.5 mg/mouse, 2 days before the donors were killed, unless otherwise noted. Dilutions, when necessary, were made with sterile saline. Control animals received a similar volume of sterile saline.

Graft vs host assay. Because so few cells are recovered from thymuses of hydrocortisone-treated donors (see Results), and because normal thymus has such weak GvH activity, it was necessary to use 4-day-old recipients for thymus assays. These animals were given 6 × 10^6 thymus cells i.p. from normal or hydrocortisone-treated parental (BALB/c) or F_1 donors on day 0, and killed on day 8.

For assay of bone marrow and spleen GvH activity, adult CAF_1 recipients were given the appropriate inoculum intravenously on day 0, and killed on day 8. The relative spleen weight (RSW) (the spleen weight (mg) divided by the body weight (g)) was computed. Spleen index is the ratio of the mean RSW of the animals receiving test cells to the mean RSW of the animals receiving F_1 cells.

RESULTS

Dose of hydrocortisone vs organ cellularity. To determine optimal dosage of hydrocortisone acetate, groups of six adult A/J mice were given various doses of the drug i.p. on day −2. On day 0, they were killed and nucleated cells in the thymus, spleen and femurs were counted in a hemocytometer. Yields of thymus and bone marrow cells/organ were so low that they were each pooled; the total cell yield was divided by the number of organs used. The curves show (Fig. 1) that each organ has a population of cells which is easily destroyed by hydrocortisone, and a population of cells resistant to hydrocortisone.

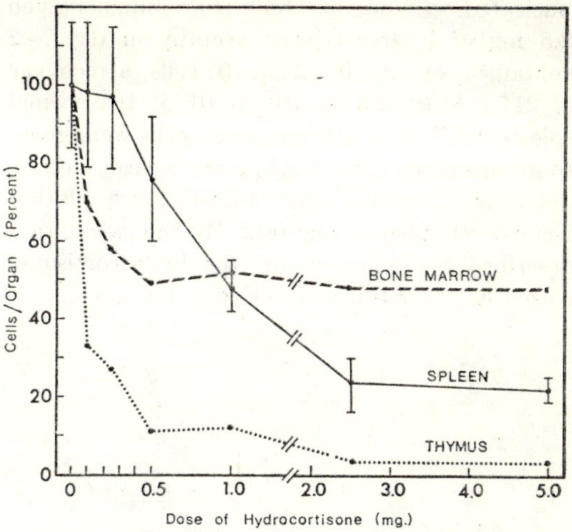

Figure 1. Fraction of nucleated cells remaining in thymus, spleen and bone marrow of A/J mice after treatment with various doses of hydrocortisone acetate 2 days before killing. Means and 95% confidence limits are given for spleen.

The resistant population comprises about 50% of the marrow, 20% of the spleen and only 3% of the thymus. Viability of the nucleated cells obtained was in every case 90% or greater by the trypan blue method. Because the effects of hydrocortisone were nearly maximal at a dose of 2.5 mg/mouse, this dose was used in subsequent studies.

Enhancement of thymus GvH with hydrocortisone. BALB/c donors were given 2.5 mg of hydrocortisone acetate i.p. on day −2, and their thymuses were removed at day 0 (hydrocortisone-thymus). Recovery of nucleated cells was 2.6 × 10^6/thymus, or 6% of control yields (45 × 10^6). Three litters of 4-day-old CAF_1 recipients were used. One-third of each litter received 6 × 10^6 normal BALB/c thymus cells, another third received 6 × 10^6 hydrocortisone-thymus cells, and the remaining third received 6 × 10^6 normal CAF_1 thymus cells. A mean spleen index of 2.77 (2.56 to 2.99, 95% confidence limits) was obtained with the nine animals receiving hydrocortisone-thymuses compared to 1.28 (1.21 to 1.35, 95% confidence limits) for the eight recipients of normal thymuses. Thus, the GvH activity of this organ is resistant to hydrocortisone.

Enhancement of spleen GvH with hydrocortisone. Normal BALB/c spleens contained 105 × 10^6

nucleated cells/organ. Those from animals given 2.5 mg of hydrocortisone acetate on day −2 contained, on day 0, 22 × 10^6 cells, a recovery of 21%. From 2.5 × 10^6 to 10 × 10^6 normal spleen and hydrocortisone-spleen cells were given to groups of six adult CAF_1 mice. Spleen indices, determined 8 days after transfer, are plotted against cell dose in Figure 2. By the calculation described by Simonsen (8) the hydrocortisone-spleen was four times as active as normal spleen.

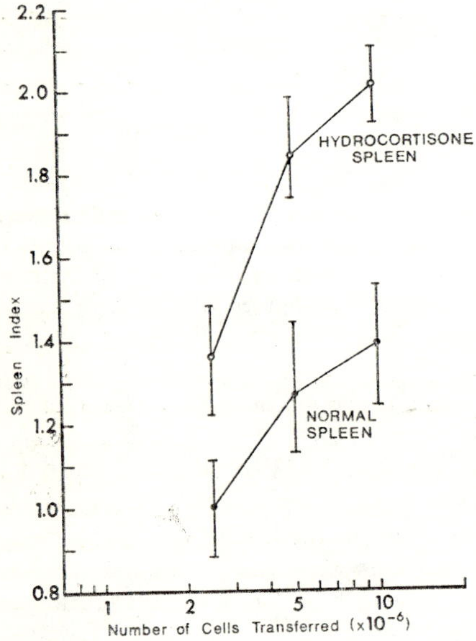

Figure 2. Graft *vs* host reactivity of various doses of spleen cells from normal and hydrocortisone acetate-treated BALB/c mice injected into adult CAF_1 recipients. The spleen index shown is the ratio of relative spleen weights of the experimental group to those of a control group receiving normal CAF_1 spleen cells. Means and 95% confidence limits are given. Each group contained six mice.

Enhancement of bone marrow GvH with hydrocortisone. Normal BALB/c mice yielded, on the average, 8.1 × 10^6 cells/femur; normal A/J mice, 12.8 × 10^6; and normal CAF_1, 11.0 × 10^6. Mice of each strain were given 2.5 mg of hydrocortisone acetate on day −2. On day 0, the BALB/c mice had 6.4 × 10^6 cells/femur (79% of normal); the A/J had 6.5 × 10^6 cells/femur (51%); and the CAF_1 10.2 × 10^6 cells/femur (93%). Thirty million nucleated cells of each type were injected into groups of adult CAF_1 mice. Spleen weights determined 8 days later (Table I) show no splenomegaly induced by normal or hydrocortisone-treated CAF_1 (i.e., syngeneic) cells (groups A and B). This dose of normal BALB/c cells was also inactive (group C), while hydrocortisone-BALB/c cells produced significant splenomegaly (group D). Normal A/J cells had slight GvH activity (group E), and GvH was significantly enhanced if the cells were from hydrocortisone-treated donors (group F).

Comparison of steroid preparations. Similar groups of BALB/c mice were given 2.5 mg i.p. of either hydrocortisone acetate or cortisone acetate. Two days later, spleen and thymus were removed and the nucleated cells counted. Suspensions of spleen cells were made, and 5 × 10^6 cells were transferred to groups of six adult CAF_1 mice. The effects of hydrocortisone and cortisone acetate at this dosage were virtually indistinguishable (Table II).

DISCUSSION

These experiments show that the thymus, spleen and bone marrow of mice have different proportions of corticosteroid-sensitive cells. Each organ has GvH potential and this immunologic reactivity is concentrated in each case, in the *corticosteroid-resistant cells.* Since the GvH re-

TABLE I

Graft vs host reactivity of 30 × 10^6 bone marrow cells from normal and hydrocortisone-treated BALB/c A/J and CAF_1 donors transferred to adult CAF_1 recipients

Group	Cells Transferred	No. of Recipients	Recipient Spleen Index
A	Normal CAF_1	14	1.00 (0.88–1.12)[a]
B	Hydrocortisone-CAF_1	7	0.93 (0.82–1.04)
C	Normal BALB/c	16	0.93 (0.82–1.04)
D	Hydrocortisone-BALB/c	18	1.28 (1.07–1.46)
E	Normal A/J	12	1.15 (1.04–1.26)
F	Hydrocortisone-A/J	6	1.47 (1.29–1.65)

[a] Mean and 95% confidence limits.

TABLE II

Effects of hydrocortisone acetate and cortisone acetate treatment of BALB/c donors on the cellularity of thymus and spleen, and on the graft vs host reactivity of spleen

Pretreatment of Spleen Donors	Mean Cells/Thymus	Mean Cells/Spleen	Recipient Spleen Index[a]
None	77×10^6	93×10^6	1.35 (1.23–1.46)[b]
Hydrocortisone acetate	3.3×10^6	24×10^6	1.86 (1.72–1.99)
Cortisone acetate	4.1×10^6	30×10^6	1.80 (1.63–1.98)

[a] Six adult CAF_1 mice each received 5×10^6 spleen cells i.v. and were killed 8 days later.

[b] Means and 95% confidence limits.

action is thymus-dependent, it is most instructive to examine the thymus first.

It is something of a paradox that functions which are known to be absent in thymus-deprived animals are often poorly restored by thymus cell suspensions (9). Thymus grafts, on the other hand, are more effective in restoring immunocompetence to thymectomized animals (10). A possible explanation is that cells arise in the thymus in a state of functional immaturity and can become immunologically active only in an intact thymus. Dynamic studies (11) have shown that some thymus lymphocytes originate in the cortex, move into the medulla and leave the gland by the circulation. Weber demonstrated (12) that pig thymus medullary cells will stimulate with phytohemagglutinin (a widely accepted index of immunocompetence), but cells from the thymic cortex will not. We have here confirmed the finding of Blomgren and Andersson (4), that corticosteroid-resistant thymic cells (probably identical with thymic medullary cells (6)) contain virtually all of that gland's GvH initiator potential. A similar conclusion was reached in 1964 by Warner (13) using chicken thymus. This finding may help in understanding the development of thymus-dependent cells. Thus, it may be that in the thymic cortex, cells are corticosteroid-sensitive and immunoincompetent, but those that have reached the medulla are corticosteroid-resistant cells which can initiate the GvH reaction. This transformation may be the result of cell maturation which might be mediated by a humoral factor. It would be of interest to know if thymus factors can confer corticosteroid-resistance on otherwise susceptible cells.

It is also possible that thymus medulla has GvH potential because it contains active cells of extrathymic origin—perhaps from the bone marrow. The bone marrow appears functionally analogous to the bursa of the fowl, and bursa-derived cells have been detected in the chicken thymus medulla (14). If the GvH potential of the thymus medulla is due to these immigrant cells, the thymus itself must have an active role in the development of their potential. This conclusion follows from the fact that the peripheral lymphoid tissues are seriously deprived of GvH activity if the thymus is removed (1). This thymic effect may be humoral or may involve the recently observed phenomenon of cell cooperation in the initiation of the GvH reaction (15). Perhaps a bone marrow-derived cell reaches the thymic medulla through the circulation and there interacts with a mature thymus-derived cell; the combination might then be the corticosteroid-resistant GvH initiator which Blomgren and Andersson described.

The thymic medulla, therefore, contains corticosteroid-resistant, phytohemagglutinin-responsive, GvH-producing cells, which may leave the thymus as long-lived cells and enter the circulating pool of lymphocytes. The thymic medulla, in this view, is a peripheral rather than a central type of lymphoid organ.

We were able to detect GvH activity in normal A/J bone marrow, and in both A/J and BALB/c marrow after corticosteroid treatment. The splenomegaly assay for bone marrow GvH, using normal F_1 recipients, has proved difficult in the hands of several workers (4, 16, 17). We have found that reproducible results are obtained provided suitable strains are used, sufficient cells are transferred, and the intravenous route is employed. Thus, a thymus-dependent activity in the bone marrow (GvH) is resistant to corticosteroids. This was recently shown to be true for stimulation by phytohemagglutinin, another thymus-dependent bone marrow function (17).

In the spleen, about 80% of the cells can be destroyed by corticosteroid treatment without affecting the GvH initlator potentiai of the organ as a whole. In other words, the corticosteroid spleen is (cell for cell) more efficient as an initiator of GvH. This finding is different from that of Blomgren and Andersson (4). The difference between corticosteroid preparations in their study and ours does not seem to explain the discrepancy (cf. Table II). It is possible that they used a dose of steroid which, in their animals, affected the thymus but not the spleen. In our system, a dose of hydrocortisone was found that had a profound effect on thymus cellularity, but little on the spleen (approximately 0.25 mg). It is possible that, in the strain used by Blomgren and Andersson (A/Sn), 2.5 mg of cortisone had a similar differential effect.

The mechanism through which corticosteroids appear to enhance the GvH activity of thymus, spleen and bone marrow is probably the destruction of immunologically irrelevant cells. The remaining populations are therefore, cell for cell, more potent in GvH.

The cells destroyed by corticosteroids are not immunologically inert in other systems, however, since corticosteroids greatly reduce the capacity of spleens to transfer hemolysin production to irradiated recipients (18). We are using corticosteroids to investigate the relationship of the cells involved in the GvH reaction and humoral antibody production.

Acknowledgments. The authors acknowledge with pleasure the expert technical assistance of Miss Martha Post and the secretarial work of Miss Lenore Shapiro.

REFERENCES

1. Miller, J. F. A. P. and Mitchell, G. F., Nature, *214:* 994, 1967.
2. Dalmasso, A. P., Martinez, C. and Good, R. A., Proc. Soc. Exp. Biol. Med., *110:* 205, 1962.
3. Billingham, R. E. and Silvers, W. K., J. Exp. Zool., *146:* 113, 1961.
4. Blomgren, H. and Andersson, B., Exp. Cell Res., *57:* 185, 1969.
5. Dougherty, T. F., Berliner, M. L., Schneebeli, G. L. and Berliner, D. L., Ann. N.Y. Acad. Sci., *113:* 825, 1964.
6. Ishidate, M. and Metcalf, D., Aust. J. Exp. Biol., *41:* 637, 1963.
7. Claman, H. N. and Chaperon, E. A., Transplant. Rev., *1:* 92, 1969.
8. Simonsen, M., Progr. Allerg., *6:* 349, 1962.
9. Yunis, E. J., Hilgard, H., Sjodin, K., Martinez, C. and Good, R. A., Nature, *201:* 784, 1964.
10. Miller, J. F. A. P. and Osoba, D., Physiol. Rev., *47:* 437, 1967.
11. Borum, K., Scand. J. Haemat., *5:* 339, 1968.
12. Weber, W. T., J. Cell Physiol., *68:* 117, 1968.
13. Warner, N. L., Aust. J. Exp. Biol. Med. Sci., *42:* 401, 1964.
14. Droge, W. and Strominger, J. L., Fed. Proc., *29:* 698, 1970.
15. Cantor, H. and Asofsky, R., J. Exp. Med., *131:* 235, 1970.
16. Owens, A. H., Jr. and Santos, G. W., J. Exp. Med., *128:* 277, 1968.
17. Dicke, K. A., Tridente, G. and van Bekkum, D. W., Transplantation, *8:* 422, 1969.
18. Levine, M. A. and Claman, H. N., Science, *167:* 1515, 1970.

THE JOURNAL OF IMMUNOLOGY
Vol. 105, No. 5, November 1970
Printed in U.S.A.

A METHOD FOR PREPARING SPECIFIC FLUORESCEIN-CONJUGATED ANTIBODY REAGENTS USING BENTONITE IMMUNOADSORBENTS[1]

MARGARET A. REISBERG,[2] ROGER D. ROSSEN AND WILLIAM T. BUTLER

From the Departments of Microbiology and Medicine, Baylor College of Medicine, and the Laboratories of Immunology Research, the Veterans Administration and the Methodist Hospitals, Houston, Texas 77031

Received for publication June 1, 1970

A simple, rapid, and reproducible method is described for the preparation of fluorescein-conjugated specific antibody reagents. Bentonite clay was used to adsorb and insolubilize antigen. Release of antigen from bentonite particles was prevented by treating the adsorbed antigen with a water-soluble carbodiimide reagent. The resulting immunoadsorbent could be used both to isolate homologous antibody and to remove cross-reacting antibodies from heterologous antisera. These immunoadsorbents were reusable, well-adapted to batch techniques, and stable on storage at −70° to 4°C for periods in excess of 1 year. Prior isolation of antibody globulin is not required before fluorescein conjugation when antibody is to be isolated subsequently by immunoadsorbents. The quantity of fluorescein isothiocyanate (FITC) used for conjugation of the antiserum was rigorously controlled by adding 1-μl portions of dissolved FITC, so that subsequent fractionation to remove excessively labeled globulin is not required. With these methods highly specific antibody reagents can be prepared in a single working day when homologous antigen is already available. More than 95% of the protein in such conjugates has antibody activity as measured by the ability to bind to homologous antigen. When used to locate antigen in tissue, the antibody reagents exhibit virtually no background fluorescence.

Conventional fluorescein-labeled antibody conjugates may contain antibodies which have undesirable specificities. For this reason it is preferable to purify the antibody conjugates by adsorption to insolubilized antigen from which the specific antibody can subsequently be eluted free of undesired labeled antibodies. Although a variety of immunoadsorbents is available for this purpose, the preparation of most of them is a complex and costly procedure, and may be applied to only a limited variety of antigens (1). In this study, we used bentonite-bound homologous antigen to provide a simple and rapid means for isolating and purifying fluorescein-conjugated antibodies highly specific for immunoglobulin heavy chain antigens.

[1] This work was supported in part by The Veterans Administration Hospital, Houston, Texas, and by Grant HE-05435 from the National Heart Institute and Grant RR-00350 from the General Clinical Research Center Branch, National Institutes of Health, Bethesda, Maryland.

[2] Reprint requests should be addressed to William T. Butler, M.D., Immunology Research Laboratory, The Veterans Administration Hospital, Houston, Texas 77031.

MATERIALS AND METHODS

Antigens. Human IgG was prepared from normal human serum by electroconvection (E. C. Apparatus Co., Philadelphia, Pa., model EC135) (2) or DEAE-cellulose ion exchange batch chromatography (3). Its purity was confirmed by immunoelectrophoresis at concentrations up to 20 mg/ml.

Human IgA was prepared from the serum of a patient with myeloma by a combination of sodium sulfate precipitation (20%, w/v), gel filtration on Sephadex G-200, and starch block zone electrophoresis. Remaining contaminants were removed by adsorption with an immunoadsorbent coated with sheep antiserum to the whole serum of an IgA-deficient individual (see preparation of immunoadsorbents.) The IgA was shown to be immunoelectrophoretically pure at a protein concentration of 14 mg/ml.

Human IgM was prepared from the serum of

a patient with macroglobulinemia by a combination of sodium sulfate precipitation (30%, w/v) gel filtration through Sephadex G-200, and starch block zone electrophoresis. At a concentration of 3 mg/ml it was shown to be free of contaminating serum proteins by immunoelectrophoresis.

Equine IgG was isolated from normal equine serum by electroconvection or DEAE-cellulose ion exchange chromatography (2, 3). The protein preparation contained IgG_a, IgG_b, and IgG_c, but lacked IgG_T (4) when tested by immunoelectrophoresis at concentrations up to 40 mg/ml.

Bence Jones proteins were used as sources of κ and λ light polypeptide chains. These proteins were bound to bentonite and used to remove antibody specific for light chains from the antibody reagents that were to be made specific for heavy chain antigens.

Antisera. Antisera were obtained from sheep hyperimmunized with the purified human IgA, IgM, IgG, and equine IgG using Freund's complete adjuvant (Difco Laboratories, Detroit, Mich.). The antisera to human IgM and equine IgG were specific for the immunizing antigen as demonstrated by immunoelectrophoresis. The contaminating antibodies present in other antisera were eliminated along with other nonspecific protein during the initial specific antibody isolation (see below).

Preparation of specific immunoadsorbents. Proteins were trace-labeled with radioactive iodine (^{125}I or ^{131}I) by either of two methods (5, 6). Each protein antigen was bound to the particles of a stock bentonite suspension with a carbodiimide reagent (CDI) as described previously (7). The stock bentonite suspension (1.8 mg bentonite/ml contained particles which sedimented at centrifugal forces between 40 and 400 $\times$ G; those particles requiring greater or lesser forces to sediment were discarded. To obtain maximum antigen binding with the antigens used in this study, 1.5 mg protein was added/mg bentonite. Unbound protein was removed by washing with a solution of 0.15 M NaCl, buffered at pH 7.4 with 0.01 M sodium phosphate (PBS). The washed immunoadsorbent was then counted for radioactivity and the adsorbent-bound protein concentration was adjusted to 1 mg/ml.

Adsorbents that were reused were washed with PBS, eluted with 0.05 M phthalate-HCl buffer, pH 2.4, and promptly neutralized by resuspension in PBS.

Preparation of fluorescein-conjugated antiserum. Either whole antiserum or the globulin fraction obtained after precipitation with 20% (w/v) sodium sulfate was conjugated with fluorescein isothiocyanate (FITC; Sylvana Chemical Co., Milburn, N. J.) at 0 to 2°C by the following technique: The protein was diluted to 10 mg/ml with 0.15 M NaCl which was buffered at pH 9.5 by adding 10% (v/v) 0.5 M carbonate-bicarbonate buffer. To 25 mg of FITC in a 5-ml glass beaker was added 0.05 ml of acetone, followed by 1.0 ml of 0.5 M carbonate-bicarbonate buffer, pH 9.5; the solution was mixed for approximately 1 min. An amount of this solution equivalent to 6 μg of FITC per milligram of protein to be conjugated was immediately added to the prechilled protein solution; the FITC was added in increments of 1 μl/sec using a 50-μl syringe fitted with a repeating dispenser (no. 705 50-μl syringe, PB 600 repeating dispenser, Hamilton Co., Whittier, Calif.) while the reaction mixture was stirred continuously.

This mixture was incubated for 5 min at 4°C and dialyzed against PBS to remove unreacted FITC. The excess FITC could also be removed by column chromatography or gel filtration, in which case the mixture was incubated 30 to 60 min to allow completion of the conjugation reaction. If specific antibody was to be isolated immediately after conjugation, the reaction mixture was incubated for 30 to 60 min and then neutralized; the unreacted FITC was not removed since it was eliminated during the isolation procedure.

Preparation of monospecific antibody reagents. The procedure for the preparation of specific antibody to the γ-chain of human IgG antigen is described in Figure 1. Ten milliliters of FITC-labeled sheep globulin containing 100 mg protein were exposed to 20 mg of adsorbent-bound IgG for 2 hr at 24°C with intermittent agitation. After centrifugation (1500 $\times$ G, 20 min, 4°C) the IgG immunoadsorbent-antibody complex was washed four times with 20 ml of PBS; antibody was eluted by the addition of 6.0 ml of 0.05 M phthalate-HCl buffer, pH 2.8, at 4°C with intermittent agitation for 30 min. We have noted, however, that with some antigen-antibody complexes, pH as low as 2.4 is required to elute the antibody. The bentonite-bound IgG was removed by sedimentation (1500 $\times$ G, 20 min, 4°C); the supernatant containing the isolated antibody was dialyzed against PBS at pH 7.4. An equal volume of normal sheep serum was added to the purified antibody to minimize the loss of specific antibody that will otherwise occur by adsorption to glassware and to nonspecific sites on the immunoadsorbents used subsequently for additional purification. Antibodies to other than γ-chain were removed by sequential adsorptions with an excess amount of IgM, IgA and κ and λ light chain immunoadsorbents (2 hr at 24°C with intermittent agitation).

Antibody specific for μ-chain was isolated with an IgM-bentonite adsorbent and then adsorbed with λ, κ, IgG or Cohn fraction II and IgA adsorbents under the conditions outlined above.

In the preparation of antibody specific for the α-chain, the IgA adsorbent was used to isolate antibody that was then adsorbed with κ, λ, IgG or Cohn fraction II and IgM adsorbents.

The antibody specific for equine IgG was prepared by adsorption and elution of antibody from an equine IgG adsorbent. Antibodies cross-reacting with human IgG were removed by adsorption with human IgG or Cohn fraction II immunoadsorbents.

Specific antibody reagents were stored at −70°C in 0.4-ml quantities in Beckman microfuge polyethylene centrifuge tubes. The solutions were thawed immediately before use, mixed by inversion, and centrifuged (7000 × G, 15 min at 4°C) to remove any suspended material.

Determination of staining characteristics of FITC-conjugated specific antibody reagents. Frozen tissue sections were cut at 4 to 6 μ, fixed in 95% ethanol, rehydrated with saline buffered at pH 7.4, and stained with FITC-labeled specific antibody reagents as described previously (8). Tissue sections of human lymphoid tissue from agammaglobulinemic and immunologically normal individuals and sections from normal human hearts and rejected human cardiac allografts (9) were examined with a Leitz Ortholux microscope

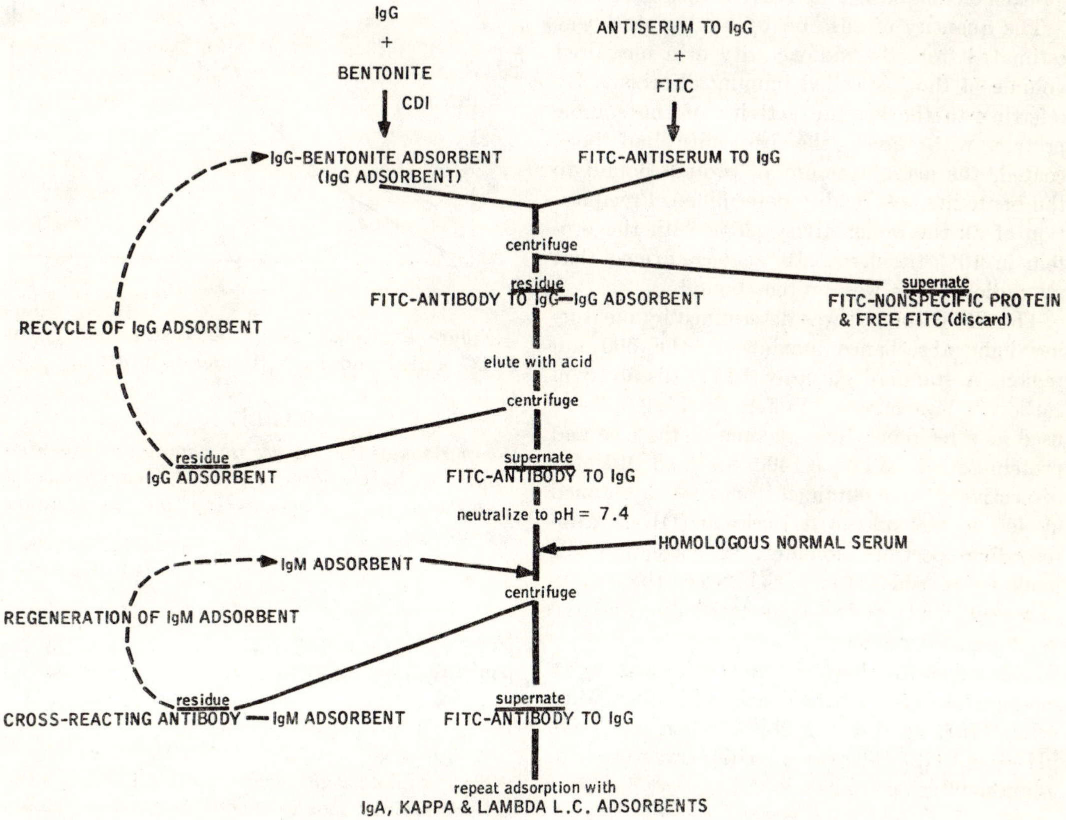

Figure 1. Preparation of fluorescein-conjugated antibody specific for human γ-chain antigens. (FITC = fluorescein isothiocyanate; CDI = carbodiimide reagent; L.C. = light chain.)

fitted with Corning 7-60 and 7-57 excitation filters and Kodak K 430, K 460, and K 510 barrier filters. The intensity of fluorescent staining was graded 1 to 4+ on coded slides by the same observer each day who had no knowledge of the slide numbering system or the origin of the tissue sections.

Other Methods. Protein concentration was estimated by the Lowry modification of the Folin technique (10), the biuret method (11), or from its optical absorbance at 280 nm. The latter method could not be used for solutions containing FITC or phthalate buffer because the absorbance of the FITC dye or phthalate ions at this wavelength introduces a significant error. The presence of FITC or phthalate ions did not interfere with either the Lowry or biuret protein determination. The presence of carbodiimide interfered with the Lowry technique, but not with either of the other two methods. Serial dilutions of human IgG and of a normal serum protein mixture were prepared for each technique and used as reference standards.

The quantity of adsorbent-bound protein was estimated from the radioactivity of a measured volume of the suspended immunoadsorbent. By referring to the specific activity of the soluble protein with which the bentonite had been coated, the actual amount of protein bound to the bentonite was readily determined. Precipitation of all the radioactivity along with the protein in 10% trichloroacetic acid confirmed that all radioactivity was protein bound.

The FITC content was determined by measuring light absorbance maxima in the 500 nm region. A standard curve of FITC dissolved in carbonate-bicarbonate buffer, pH 9.5, was used as a reference. The maxima of the free and protein-bound FITC at 490 nm and 497 nm, respectively, were obtained from spectra scanned at 400 to 600 nm on a Beckman DK-1 ratio-recording spectrophotometer. No correction was made for possible differences between the extinction coefficients of the conjugated dye and the unconjugated standard.

Immunoelectrophoresis was performed by a modification of the Scheidegger microtechnique, using 0.75% agarose in barbital buffer, $\mu = 0.05$, pH = 8.2 (12). The same medium was used for immunodiffusion studies.

RESULTS

Relationship between quantity of FITC added and FITC bound to protein. Varying quantities of FITC were coupled to equal portions of the globulin fractions of different immune sera. The same FITC solution was used for all mixtures; reaction time, volume and temperature were held constant. The results are seen in Figure 2. A molar ratio of FITC to protein (F:P) of about 1.6 could be obtained by adding 2.5 mols FITC/mol protein (assumed molecular weights of 389

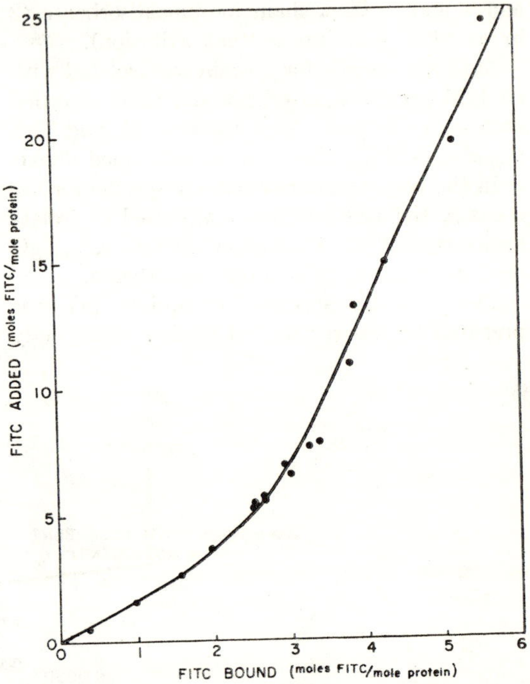

Figure 2. Relationship between quantity of FITC added and FITC bound to protein.

TABLE I

Comparison of the changes in molar F:P ratio seen in: (A) lightly labeled and (B) heavily labeled antibody[a] conjugates during the purification procedure

	Molar F:P Ratio	
	A	*B*
FITC in reaction mixture	2.5	13.0
FITC-conjugated globulin	1.6	4.5
Purified antibody after isolation	1.0	3.5
Purified antibody after adsorption with		
Kappa immunoadsorbent	1.0	2.0
Lambda immunoadsorbent	1.0	1.9
IgM immunoadsorbent	1.0	0.7
IgA immunoadsorbent	1.0	0.7

[a] Antibody to human γ-chain antigen.

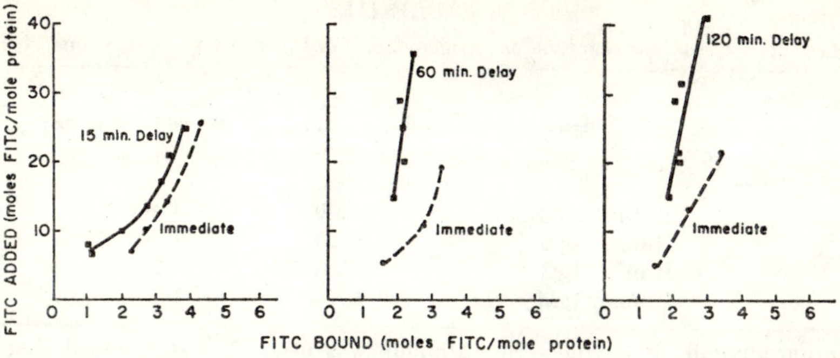

Figure 3. Effect of delaying the addition of dissolved FITC on the quantity of FITC bound to protein.

and 160,000, respectively, in this experiment). It was found, however, that when specific antibody was isolated from FITC-conjugated globulin solutions, the molar F:P ratio would decrease by about 20% to 40%, but then would remain constant during the subsequent adsorptions with heterologous immunoadsorbents (Table I*A*). However, when the protein was more heavily conjugated, the molar F:P ratio decreased successively with each adsorption (Table I*B*). This was possibly due to loss of more heavily conjugated antibody molecules by nonspecific adsorption to the heterologous immunoglobulin adsorbents. When McDevitt *et al.* (13) precipitated specific antibody from a conjugated globulin solution, they also observed a decrease in F:P ratio similar to that noted here. Presumably, more heavily conjugated molecules fail to precipitate, so that the average F:P ratio of the specific precipitate is lower.

Stability of FITC in solution. It was found that once FITC was dissolved, it had to be added immediately to the chilled protein solution ready for conjugation. A delay at this stage decreased the degree of conjugation, apparently due to the inactivation of FITC (Fig. 3). The maximum FITC inactivation occurred during the 1st hour after dissolution; no additional effect was observed during the 2nd hour.

Capacity of the bentonite for various antigens (Table II). The capacity of the particles in 100 ml of stock bentonite suspension (180 mg bentonite) for binding protein ranged from 98 mg for equine IgG down to 25 mg for whole human serum. It was possible to increase the capacity of the bentonite for proteins which bind less readily to bentonite, both by repeated adsorptions and by increasing the adsorption period.

TABLE II

Capacity of bentonite for protein

Protein	Protein Bound[a]	% of Added Protein Bound
	mg	
Human IgG	60–90	50–75
Human IgA	36–40	30–33
Human IgM	50	42
Human serum albumin	50	42
Bence Jones protein (Kappa)	40	33
Bence Jones protein (Lambda)	30	25
Whole human serum deficient in IgA	25–35	21–29
Equine IgG	75–98	62–82

[a] To the particles from 100-ml stock bentonite suspension (120 to 180 mg bentonite) were added 120 mg of radioactive labeled protein, followed by 120 mg carbodiimide. Adsorption was for 1 hr at 24°C. The amount of protein bound was determined by a measure of the radioactivity of the protein bound to the bentonite particles, after removing unbound protein by washing with PBS.

Capacity of the immunoadsorbent for homologous antibody (Table III). Capacity was determined by adding various known quantities of precipitating antibody to measured amounts of adsorbent antigen (Fig. 4). This technique was developed with a human serum albumin (HSA) rabbit anti-HSA system. It can be seen that the maximum capacity of 1.4 mg antibody/mg adsorbent-bound HSA was more readily determined at the lower concentrations of antigen. Using this same method the maximum capacity of a human IgG adsorbent for specific antibody was 0.9 mg/mg adsorbent IgG. However, this was achieved in gross antibody excess where subsequent recovery of total added antibody was

TABLE III

Comparison of capacity of various carriers for antigen and of antigen-bound immunoadsorbents for antibody

Carrier	Antigen	Capacity		
		Mg antigen per mg carrier	Mg antibody per mg antigen bound to carrier	Mg antibody per mg immunoadsorbent
Bentonite	Serum[a] albumin	0.40	0.4–1.7	0.08–0.36
Bentonite	Human IgA	0.25	0.1–0.35	0.02–0.08
Bentonite	Human IgG	0.45–0.75	0.2–0.9	0.09–0.68
Bentonite	Human IgM	0.25	0.3–0.6	0.075–0.15

[a] Human serum albumin or bovine serum albumin was used. It was assumed that both types of albumin reacted similarly for purposes of comparison.

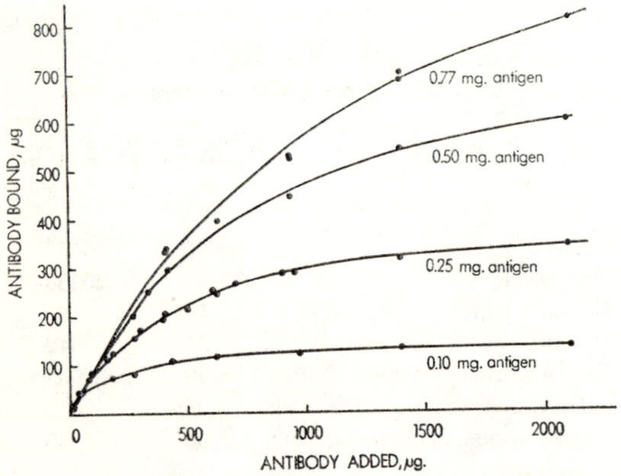

Figure 4. Determination of maximum capacity of bentonite immunoadsorbent. Adsorbent antigen was human serum albumin (HSA). Anti-HSA was produced in rabbits. Bound antibody (*ordinate*) represents the quantity of protein which could be eluted from each of four quantities of adsorbent antigen after these had been equilibrated with various known quantities of antibody.

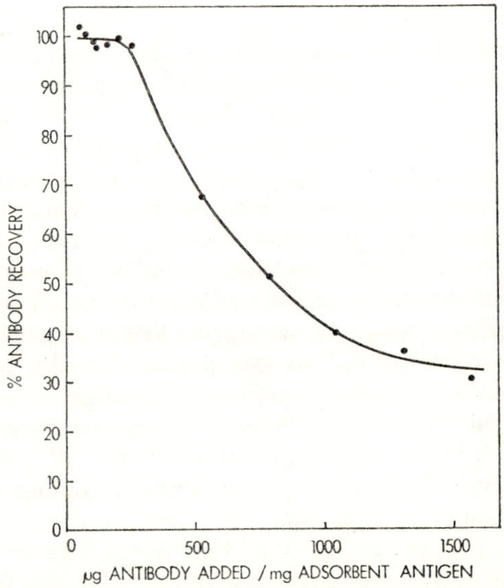

Figure 5. Illustrates the percentage of the sheep anti-human IgG added which may be subsequently recovered by acid elution from an homologous IgG adsorbent equilibrated with various known quantities of anti-IgG.

low as can be seen in Figure 5. For the most economical and efficient preparation of the FITC-specific antibody reagents, the ratio of added antibody to adsorbent antigen was selected so that approximately 50% of the antibody in the conjugate would be isolated. With the human IgA immunoadsorbent it was possible to isolate up to 0.25 mg antibody per milligram adsorbent antigen; the capacity of the IgM adsorbent was approximately 0.56 mg/mg antigen. However, a systematic study of the capacities of the IgM and IgA immunoadsorbents was not carried out.

Reuse of immunoadsorbents. Antigen immunoadsorbents could be reused for additional antibody isolations. In fact the efficiency of the adsorbent for antibody isolation increased approximately 10% after the initial isolation. However, approximately 3% of the bentonite particles containing adsorbent antigen were lost during each antibody isolation, due primarily to adsorption onto glassware and a failure to completely sediment during centrifugation. Thus, adsorbent antigen eventually becomes depleted.

Stability of immunoadsorbent. The stability of the adsorbent was such that after 9 months, only 1% of the antigen bound to bentonite had been released. (This loosely bound antigen can be removed by washing with PBS before use.) Specific antibody was isolated with adsorbents that had been stored for a year at 4°C. The protein-bentonite bond was not affected by three freeze and thaw cycles at either −20°C or −70°C, as indicated by the loss of only 0.3% of the antigen from the adsorbent.

The use of homologous, unconjugated, non-antibody protein to prevent specific antibody losses during adsorption with heterologous immunoglobulin adsorbents. We found that adding homologous, non-antibody, unconjugated protein to solutions of specific antibody minimized loss of specific antibody on glassware and nonspecific sites of the immunoadsorbents. The effect of non-antibody protein on subsequent antibody recovery can be seen in Table IV. Sheep antibody specific for human IgG, isolated with a human IgG immunoadsorbent, and adsorbed with equine IgG bound to a bentonite adsorbent, was labeled with ^{131}I. A portion of the purified antibody was mixed with PBS and another portion with normal sheep serum; samples of both portions were adsorbed either with a series of other human immunoglobulin adsorbents to remove antibodies not specific for the γ-chain or repeatedly with freshly prepared equine IgG adsorbent which had not previously been used to isolate antibody. Repeated adsorption with an equine IgG adsorbent measured only nonspecific antibody loss since cross-reacting antibody had been removed by a prior adsorption. The data in Table IV suggest that the addition of normal sheep serum reduced the loss of purified antibody during subsequent adsorptions and that a significant portion of this specific antibody may be lost solely because proteins tend to adhere nonspecifically to bentonite particles and glassware. Some of this loss might be prevented by combining all the heterologous immunoadsorbents used to adsorb a given antibody, subjecting the isolated antibody thereby to a single, rather than multiple adsorptions.

Immunochemical qualities of the FITC-conjugated specific antibody

Immunochemical test of specificity. Antibody isolated by adsorption to a homologous antigen immunoadsorbent was eluted, labeled with ^{125}I and reexposed to an unlabeled homologous antigen immunoadsorbent. When antibody specific for γ-chain was tested under these conditions, 95.1% (0.3% average deviation based on quadruplicate analyses) of the antibody reagent was readsorbed to the human IgG immunoadsorbent and therefore considered "active" antibody.

Protein purity. Contamination of the antibody reagent with adsorbent antigen was less than 0.1%. This was determined by measuring the radioactivity of the antibody reagent when the adsorbent antigen had been labeled with ^{125}I. Actually, more antigen was released from the bentonite during elution, but 98% of the contaminating antigen was removed by centrifugation when it precipitated as an immune complex during neutralization (7).

Previous experiments have shown that approximately 0.02% of the nonspecific protein in the initial reaction mixture was contained in the isolated antibody solution (7). Actually, about 1% of the nonspecific protein was adsorbed to the immunoadsorbent, but most remained bound during the acid elution so that significant contamination of the specific antibody reagent did not occur.

The FITC-labeled specific antibody concentration ranged from 0.070 to 0.38 mg/ml in the antibody reagents used in this study.

Fluorescent staining characteristics of FITC-conjugated specific antibody reagents

Specificity was determined by the following tests. 1) The removal of specific antibody from the FITC-conjugated antibody reagents by adsorption to homologous antigen immunoadsorbents eliminated all the fluorescent staining normally observed in tissue sections of a heart known to contain bound immunoglobulin. 2) The use of unconjugated homologous antibody preparations for specific inhibition (blocking) by Coons' technique (14) eliminated staining that was normally observed (Table V). Unconjugated heterologous antibody did not diminish the fluorescent staining of tissues (Table V).

Effect of unconjugated nonspecific protein. When unconjugated nonspecific protein was added to the antibody, specific fluorescent reactions, observed on the sarcolemma and muscle, were enhanced (Table VI*A*). Thus the antibody could be used at higher dilutions, thereby conserving the reagent. Moreover, nonspecific staining was absent at higher dilutions.

Effect of molar F:P ratio. Using an antibody reagent with a molar F:P ratio above 1.0 increases nonspecific staining, without increasing the specific fluorescence (Table VI*B*). However, an antibody preparation with a low molar F:P ratio, 0.31, while free of nonspecific staining

TABLE IV

Effect of added non-antibody protein on loss of specific antibody during adsorption with other immunoadsorbents

Immunoadsorbent Used for Adsorption[a]	Loss of Specific Antibody (Anti-human IgG)													
	In PBS diluent							In sheep serum						
	Protein present before adsorption	Loss on immuno-adsorbent[b]	Loss on glassware	Total loss on this adsorption[c]		Total accumulated loss		Protein present before adsorption	Loss on immuno-adsorbent	Loss on glassware	Total loss on this adsorption		Total accumulated loss	
	μg	μg	μg	μg	(%)	μg	(% of original)	μg	μg	μg	μg	(%)	μg	(% of original)
I. Loss on cross-reacting antigen adsorbents:														
Human IgM	277	43	21	64	(23)	64	(23)	277	15	0	15	(5.4)	15	(5.4)
Human IgA	213	33	6	39	(18)	103	(37)	262	31	7	38	(15)	53	(19)
Human kappa	174	28	22	50	(29)	153	(55)	224	28	16	44	(20)	87	(31)
Human lambda	124	14	22	36	(29)	189	(68)	180	18	24	42	(23)	129	(47)
II. Loss on non-cross-reacting antigen adsorbents:[d]														
Equine IgG	142	17	18	35	(25)	35	(25)	142	7	1	8	(5.6)	8	(5.6)
Equine IgG	107	16	0	16	(15)	51	(36)	134	6	0	6	(4.5)	14	(10)
Equine IgG	91	17	8	25	(27)	76	(54)	128	5	13	18	(14)	32	(22)
Equine IgG	66	23	19	42	(64)	118	(83)	110	10	3	13	(12)	45	(32)

[a] The adsorption was for 2 hr at 24°C.

[b] The antibody loss on the adsorbent was measured by the ^{131}I counts remaining on the immunoadsorbent after centrifugation.

[c] Total antibody loss was evaluated by the difference between antibody added and antibody recovered. The antibody recovery after the adsorption was measured by the ^{131}I radioactivity in a sample of the supernatant from each successive adsorption. The amount of antibody in this sample, corrected to the total volume, was a measure of total antibody recovery.

[d] Antibodies reacting with equine IgG were removed before the adsorptions described in part II.

TABLE V

Determination of specificities of FITC-conjugated specific antibody reagents by blocking with an unconjugated antibody preparation[a]

Unconjugated Antibody Preparation Used for Blocking (Type)	Fluorescent Staining after Reaction with FITC-Conjugated Specific Antibody Reagents		
	Anti-human γ	Anti-human α	Anti-human μ
Anti-human γ-chain[b]	1+	4+	4+
Anti-human γ-chain[c]	0	4+	4+
Anti-human α-chain[c]	4+	0	4+
Anti-human μ-chain[c]	4+	4+	0

[a] Frozen sections of human heart known to contain bound immunoglobulin (9) were treated first with an unconjugated specific antibody preparation for 30 min, washed in PBS, and then treated with FITC-labeled specific antibody and again washed with PBS.

[b] Purified antibody prepared and made specific with immunoadsorbents.

[c] Commercial preparation: Hyland Laboratories, Los Angeles, Calif.

reactions, exhibited greatly reduced specific fluorescence.

DISCUSSION

Binding protein to bentonite clay by means of a carbodiimide reagent appears to be one of the most simple, rapid and inexpensive methods to prepare insoluble antigen in terms of both reagents and equipment. Because of their high ratio of surface area to volume the bentonite immunoadsorbents are peculiarly adapted to batch methods. Since only centrifugation then is required to recover the bentonite-bound antigen, no specialized equipment such as columns or fraction collectors are required. Bentonite clay also is not subject to solubilization by bacterial enzymes, as are the cellulose derivatives, or to denaturation, as would occur with protein carriers. Thus, bentonite clay stock suspensions do not require refrigerated storage before antigen binding. Moreover, the bentonite is non-antigenic, so there are no extraneous antigenic determinants to cross-react with the specific immune system under study. The versatility of the technique is illustrated by its applicability to a variety of antigens. The capacity of the bentonite carrier for antigen and of the antigen adsorbent for antibody compares favorably with that observed with other immunoadsorbent systems (15–20).

The stability of the immunoadsorbent is limited only by the stability of the bound protein. Because of the wide temperature range over which the protein-bentonite bond is stable (4°C to −70°C), a storage temperature can be selected that will be optimum for the protein bound to the bentonite.

Furthermore, bentonite immunoadsorbents can be reused, and indeed are more efficient for antibody isolation after the initial use (Table IV). The protein used for the first adsorption apparently saturates the nonspecific binding sites so that during subsequent adsorptions, specific antibody is not bound to such nonspecific sites. Antibody bound to nonspecific sites cannot be recovered since it is not quantitatively eluted with an acid buffer (7). Antibody recovery on even the initial isolation can be increased by prior adsorption of the immunoadsorbent with normal serum proteins so that less antibody is lost on nonspecific sites.

To fully utilize the bentonite immunoadsorbent system to purify antibody, it is necessary that non-antibody protein be added to the isolated antibody after its initial elution from the immunoadsorbent. Otherwise, substantial quantities of specific antibody protein will be lost if it is necessary to adsorb the purified antibody with other antigen immunoadsorbents. Nonspecific protein in excess saturates the nonspecific sites irreversibly with nonspecific protein, thereby allowing the specific antibody to reversibly attach to the specific antigen-binding sites from which recovery is high. In addition, when these adsorbents are used specifically to purify fluorescein-labeled antibodies, the presence of unconjugated, non-antibody protein enhances the specific fluorescence (Table VI*A*) so that the antibody reagent can be used at higher dilutions and thereby conserved.

Even with immunoadsorbent-prepared antibody conjugates that are highly specific, we have found that to avoid nonspecific staining reactions on tissue sections, the molar fluorescein to protein ratio must not greatly exceed unity or nonspecific staining will occur. Only 6 mg FITC/g protein were found to be optimal, approximately ⅛ of the quantity generally advocated (50 mg FITC/g protein). Goldstein *et al.* (21) previously observed that conjugates made with 6 to 8 mg FITC/g protein exhibited less nonspecific staining than those more highly conjugated. If a low input of

TABLE VI

Improvement of the tissue-staining characteristics of highly specific fluorescein-conjugated anti-γ-chain antibody by addition of unlabeled, non-antibody protein and by control of the molar F:P ratio

A. Effect of the addition of non-antibody protein

Tissue	Diluent	Dilution	Fluorescent Staining: Specific		Nonspecific	
			Sarcolemma	Muscle	Connective tissue	Interstitial spaces
Positive heart[a]	PBS	1:2	4+	4+	1+	1+
Positive heart	NSS[b]	1:2	4+	3+	1+	1+
Positive heart	PBS	1:6	1+	1+	0	0
Positive heart	NSS	1:6	3+	2+	0	0
Positive heart	PBS	1:12	±	±	0	0
Positive heart	NSS	1:12	2+	2+	0	0

B. Effect of molar F:P ratio[c]

Tissue	Molar F:P Ratio	Sarcolemma	Muscle	Connective tissue	Interstitial spaces
Positive heart	1.71	3+	4+	1+	0
Negative heart[d]	1.71	0	1+	1+	0
Positive heart	1.21	3+	3+	0	0
Negative heart	1.21	±	0	±	1+
Positive heart	0.90	2+	2+	0	0
Negative heart	0.90	0	0	0	0
Positive heart	0.58	3+	2+	0	0
Negative heart	0.58	0	0	0	0
Positive heart	0.31	1+	±	0	0
Negative heart	0.31	0	0	0	0

[a] Human heart tissue known to contain bound immunoglobulins (9).

[b] Normal sheep serum.

[c] All antibody solutions adjusted to same protein and specific antibody concentration before testing on tissue.

[d] Heart tissue control negative for bound IgG.

FITC is used, ion-exchange chromatography or similar operations to obtain antibody molecules with a designated degree of conjugation is not required.

Since it is not necessary to use purified globulin solutions for FITC conjugation if an immunoadsorbent is ultimately to be used to isolate the conjugated antibody, one may start with whole antiserum and prepare a FITC-conjugated specific antibody reagent in only one working day when purified homologous antigen is available. This time includes that required to prepare the bentonite carrier, bind antigen to the bentonite, conjugate the antiserum, isolate the antibody and adsorb with heterologous immunoadsorbents.

Acknowledgments. The authors are grateful to Michael Johnson and Ruth Rickaway for expert technical assistance.

REFERENCES

1. Silman, I. H. and Katchalski, E., Ann. Rev. Biochem., *35:* 873, 1966.
2. Bier, M., *Electrophoresis*, Academic Press, Inc., New York, 1959.
3. Strauss, A. J., Kemp, P. G., Jr., Vannier, W. E. and Goodman, H. C., J. Immun., *93:* 24, 1964.
4. Rockey, J. H., Klinman, N. R. and Karush, F., J. Exp. Med., *120:* 589, 1964.
5. McFarlane, A. S., Nature, *182:* 53, 1958.
6. Hunter, W. M. and Greenwood, F. C., Nature, *194:* 495, 1962.
7. Carpenter, R. R. and Reisberg, M. A., J. Immun., *100:* 873, 1968.
8. Rossen, R. D., Morgan, C., Hsu, K. C., Butler, W. T. and Rose, H. M., J. Immun., *100:* 706, 1968.
9. Rossen, R. D., Butler, W. T., Reisberg, M. A., Brooks, D. K., Leachman, R. D., Milam,

J. D., Mittal, K. K., Montgomery, J. R., Nora, J. J. and Rochelle, D. G., J. Immun., To be published.
10. Lowry, O. H., Rosebrough, N. J., Farr, A. L. and Randall, R. J., J. Biol. Chem., *193:* 265, 1951.
11. Kabat, E. A., *Kabat and Mayer's Experimental Immunochemistry*, 2nd Ed., p. 559, Charles C Thomas, Springfield, Illinois, 1961.
12. Campbell, D. H., Garvey, J. S., Cremer, N. E. and Sussdorf, D. H., *Methods in Immunology*, W. A. Benjamin, Inc., New York, 1963.
13. McDevitt, H. O., Peters, J. H., Pollard, L. W., Harter, J. G. and Coons, A. H., J. Immun., *90:* 634, 1963.
14. Coons, A. H., Creech, H. J., Jones, R. N. and Berliner, E., J. Immun., *45:* 159, 1942.
15. Gurvich, A. E., Kuzovleva, O. B. and Tumanova, A. E., Biokhimiia, *26:* 803, 1961.
16. Behrens, M. M., Inman, J. K. and Vannier, W. E., Arch. Biochem., *119:* 411, 1967.
17. Robbins, J. B., Haimovich, J. and Sela, M., Immunochemistry, *4:* 11, 1967.
18. Onoue, K., Yagi, Y. and Pressman, D., Immunochemistry, *2:* 181, 1965.
19. Avrameas, S. and Ternynck, T., J. Biol. Chem., *242:* 1651, 1967.
20. Takahashi, M., Yagi, Y. and Pressman, D., J. Immun., *100:* 1169, 1968.
21. Goldstein, G., Slizys, I. S. and Chase, M. W., J. Exp. Med., *114:* 89, 1961.

THE JOURNAL OF IMMUNOLOGY
Copyright © 1970 by The Williams & Wilkins Co.

Vol. 105, No. 5, November 1970
Printed in U.S.A.

HETEROGENEITY OF BLASTOGENIC FACTORS PRODUCED *IN VITRO* BY ANTIGENICALLY STIMULATED AND UNSTIMULATED LEUKOCYTES[1]

SHINPEI KASAKURA[2]

From the Division of Hematology, Royal Victoria Hospital, Montreal 112, Canada

Received for publication June 1, 1970

Blastogenic factor derived from antigenically stimulated or unstimulated leukocyte cultures was studied. Cell-free medium (CFM) from unmixed leukocyte cultures was frequently stimulatory for both autologous and allogeneic cells. However, the blastogenic factor usually stimulated allogeneic cells much more than autologous cells. The blastogenic factor which is stimulatory only for allogeneic cells may be a soluble form of histocompatibility antigen. The CFM preparations that were the most stimulatory toward allogeneic cells were not necessarily the most active toward autologous cells. The two types of stimulatory activity showed no correlation. It seems probable that CFM from unmixed cultures of leukocytes contains at least two components: a) a specific blastogenic factor (histocompatibility antigen), and b) a nonspecific stimulatory factor (probably identical to the "potentiating factor" described by Janis and Bach). Blastogenic factor was produced *in vitro* by tuberculin-sensitive leukocytes in response to PPD-stimulation. The production of this factor was antigenically-specific, but once produced, it was as active for autologous cells as for allogeneic cells. This factor is not histocompatibility antigen. The continuous presence of antigen was not required for activity. This factor may be different from the "lymphocyte-activating factor" described by Valentine and Lawrence. When the medium was changed every 2 days, the blastogenic factor was produced repeatedly until the culture died. The present findings indicate that the blastogenic factor produced by PPD-stimulation differs from that which is produced in unmixed cultures and which is stimulatory only for allogeneic cells. However, it is not known whether there are differences between the blastogenic factor arising from PPD-stimulation and the factor which is produced in unmixed cultures and which stimulates autologous cells.

A number of substances have been found to stimulate the transformation of peripheral blood lymphocytes to blast cells *in vitro*. Among these are antigens such as tuberculin-purified protein derivative (PPD), which stimulates the lymphocytes of previously sensitized donors (1, 2), and allogeneic leukocytes bearing foreign histocompatibility antigens (mixed leukocyte reaction) (3, 4). A form of stimulation related to the mixed leukocyte reaction is the induction of transformation by "blastogenic factor," a material that is released into the surrounding medium in leukocyte cultures (5–7). Tuberculin-sensitive human lymphocytes cultured with tuberculin elaborate "mitogenic factor" which stimulates blastogenesis of allogeneic and autologous lymphocytes (8–10), and "lymphocyte-activating material" which causes non-sensitive lymphocytes to respond to tuberculin *in vitro* by transformation and proliferation (11). It has also been reported (12) that cell-free medium from antigenically stimulated or unstimulated leukocyte cultures sometimes contains a non-specific factor which potentiates antigen-induced lymphocyte transformation.

In the present study, blastogenic materials derived from the medium of antigenically stimulated or unstimulated leukocyte cultures were investigated. The specific aim of these studies was to clarify the relation between the various stimulatory factors reported in the literature.

[1] This work was supported by Medical Research Council of Canada Grant MA-3886.

[2] Scholar of the Medical Research Council of Canada.

MATERIALS AND METHODS

Leukocyte suspensions. The subjects were normal volunteers. Venous blood was drawn into a heparinized syringe (preservative-free heparin, 20 units/ml) and allowed to sediment at 37°C for 1 hr. The blood was then centrifuged at 25 × G for 5 min, and the supernatant plasma, containing leukocytes, platelets, and a few erythrocytes, was drawn off.

Culture methods. The leukocytes were suspended in medium 199 (Microbiological Associates, Bethesda, Md.) containing 20% fresh autologous plasma and penicillin (100 units/ml). In every instance the leukocyte count was approximately 1500 cells/mm³. For each culture, 4 ml of cell suspension was placed in a 17- x 100-mm disposable plastic culture tube (Falcon Plastics Co., Los Angeles, Calif.) and kept at 37°C.

Blastogenic factor from unmixed leukocyte cultures. Cell-free culture medium (CFM) was prepared from cultures of leukocytes from single donors as described previously (5). The culture medium was collected from unmixed cultures after 5 days' incubation, and centrifuged at 1500 × G for 15 min to remove cells. Blastogenic activity of the cell-free medium (CFM) was assessed as described previously (5), by adding the preparation (2 ml/culture tube) to cultures of fresh autologous or allogeneic leukocytes, incubating for 7 days, and measuring cellular uptake of ³H-thymidine.

Blastogenic factor produced in vitro by leukocytes in response to tuberculin-stimulation. Leukocyte suspensions (usually tuberculin-sensitive cells) were divided into two parts: one part was used as the test culture and PPD (Parke, Davis & Co., Detroit, Mich.) was added in a dose of 1.25 μg/ml; the other served as a control and no PPD was added. Both cultures were incubated at 37°C for 30 min, and then the cells were sedimented, washed twice in medium 199, and finally resuspended in fresh medium 199 with 20% plasma. After incubation for 5 days, the culture medium was collected from the test and control cultures, and centrifuged at 1500 × G for 15 min to remove cells. There were then two cell-free culture media: a) cell-free medium from PPD-stimulated leukocyte cultures (test cell-free medium); b) cell-free medium from cultures of identical cells not exposed to PPD (control cell-free medium). Both the test cell-free medium and the control cell-free medium were added separately to fresh cultures of autologous or allogeneic leukocytes. ³H-thymidine was measured after incubation for 7 days at 37°C.

Assessment of blastogenic activity. Each culture was prepared in triplicate and incubated at 37°C for 7 days. At the end of the incubation period, ³H-thymidine (New England Nuclear Corp., Boston, specific activity 2.5 Ci/mmol) was added to the culture tubes to give a concentration of 1 μCi/ml. After 2 hr at 37°C, the cells were washed three times with cold physiologic saline. Five-tenths milliliter of hydroxide of Hyamine (Packard Instrument Co., Inc., Downer's Grove, Ill.) was added to each tube to digest the cells. The tubes were kept in the dark at room temperature for 2 days, and then their contents were transferred to glass counting vials with two washings of absolute ethyl alcohol, 0.3 ml each. The vials were heated for 1.5 hr at 75°C. Fifteen milliliters of 0.3% PPO (2,5-diphenyloxazole) and 0.01% POPOP (1,4-bis-2-(5-phenyloxazolyl)-benzene) in toluene was added, and the vials were counted in a Tri-Carb Liquid Scintillation Spectrophotometer (Packard Instruments). Quenching was determined by using an automatic external standard and counting efficiency was nearly identical for the samples within each experiment. The results were expressed as counts/minute/culture. In some experiments DNA was extracted by the Schmidt-Tannhauser technique (13), except that the concentration of potassium hydroxide was decreased to 0.5 N. The radioactive content of the DNA fraction was estimated in a liquid scintillation counter, with an automatic external standard. The concentration of the DNA present in each preparation was determined by measuring the optical density at 260 nm in a spectrophotometer. The results were expressed as counts/minute (cpm) per 10 μg of DNA.

Smears were made from one of the culture tubes in some experiments, and stained with Jenner-Giemsa. The radioactive count was found to correlate with the number of lymphoblastoid cells in the smears.

RESULTS

Fifty-seven experiments were performed in which CFM from cultures of leukocytes from single subjects was added to fresh autologous or allogeneic leukocytes. In these experiments, the degree of stimulation was expressed as ³H-thymidine uptake (cpm) by the cells grown in the stimulating cell-free medium minus the counts/minute of identical cells grown without adding CFM. Figure 1 shows the comparative response of autologous and allogeneic leukocytes

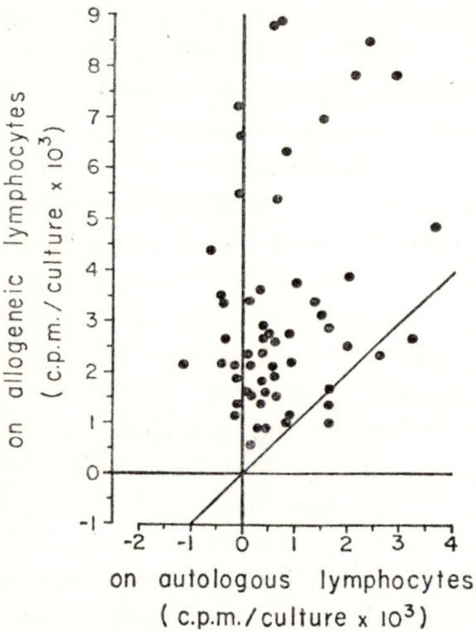

Figure 1. Comparative response of autologous and allogeneic leukocytes to the cell-free medium (CFM) from 5-day unmixed leukocyte cultures. The degree of stimulation of the blastogenic factor was expressed as counts/minute obtained in the experimental cultures minus the counts/minute in the cultures of corresponding cells without added CFM stimulant. Each point above the diagonal solid line represents the positive difference in counts/minute of allogeneic over autologous cellular cultures stimulated by a given "CFM."

to a given "CFM." Fifty-three of 57 CFM preparations stimulated allogeneic leukocytes more than autologous leukocytes. While CFM was stimulatory for all cultures of allogeneic leukocytes, it inhibited uptake of thymidine by 13 cultures of autologous cells below the value obtained for control cultures. The CFM preparations that were the most stimulatory toward allogeneic cells were not necessarily the most active toward autologous cells. The two types of stimulatory activity in the CFM preparations showed no correlation ($r = 0.26$; $p > 0.05$).

Table I shows the effect of leukocyte washing on *in vitro* production of blastogenic factor. Leukocyte suspensions were divided into two parts: one part was washed twice in medium 199 and then cultured; the other was cultured without washing. The stimulatory activity of the CFM from each of these 5-day cultures was tested on fresh autologous or allogeneic cells. In many experiments, CFM from cultures of washed cells was much more stimulatory for both autologous and allogeneic leukocytes than

TABLE I

The effect of washing on the production of a blastogenic factor in cell-free medium (CFM) by leukocytes cultivated in vitro

Expt. No.	^{3}H-Thymidine Uptake (cpm/10 µg DNA)[a]			
	Allogenic leukocytes with CFM from cultures of		Autologous leukocytes with CFM from cultures of	
	Unwashed cells	Washed[b] cells	Unwashed cells	Washed cells
1	1,749[c]	1,299	−256	−323
2	1,211	2,345	430	−241
3	3,143	6,143	1,097	2,422
4	3,583	5,428	226	4,712
5	1,786	6,407	1,380	2,247
6	6,071	12,912	537	6,785
7	1,054	3,228	−799	−152

[a] The stimulatory activity of CFM was expressed as counts/minute obtained in the cultures of leukocytes with CFM after subtraction of the counts/minute in the control cultures of corresponding cells without CFM.

[b] Leukocytes were washed twice in medium 199 and then cultured for 5 days before preparation of CFM.

[c] Mean values for triplicate cultures.

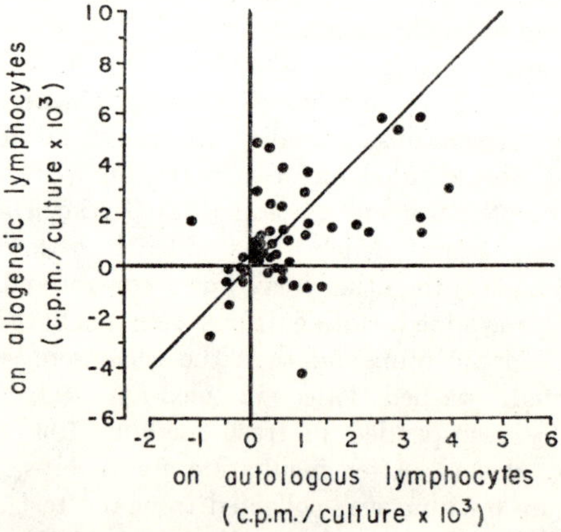

Figure 2. Comparative response of autologous and allogeneic cells to the blastogenic factor produced by the PPD-stimulation of leukocytes. Activity was expressed as counts/minute obtained in the experimental cultures minus the counts/minute in control cultures with the supernatants from corresponding cells not exposed to PPD. The diagonal line represents the border between negative and positive differences in counts/minute of allogeneic over autologous cellular cultures stimulated by a given "PPD-induced CFM."

TABLE II

The effect of CFM source on lymphocyte stimulation: PPD-positive vs negative donors

Donors of Responding Cells	^{3}H-Thymidine Uptake (cpm/10 μg DNA)[a] from CFM Source:			
	B (268)[b]	R (−40)	D (10,779)	H (4,595)
	cpm/10 μg DNA			
B (−)[c]	−7[d]	N.D.[e]	909	588
R (−)	N.D.	−355	882	739
D (+)	188	N.D.	2,150	1,136
H (+)	N.D.	−1,153	3,984	1,428

[a] The stimulatory activity of CFM from PPD-stimulated leukocyte cultures was expressed as counts/minute obtained in the experimental cultures after subtracting the counts/minute obtained with control (CFM from cultures not exposed to PPD).

[b] Figures in parentheses indicate ^{3}H-thymidine uptake in the original cultures of PPD-stimulated cells from which CFM was obtained.

[c] Tuberculin skin test: (+) = positive after a skin test with the first strength of PPD; (−) = negative after a skin test with the second strength of PPD.

[d] Mean value for triplicate cultures.

[e] Not tested.

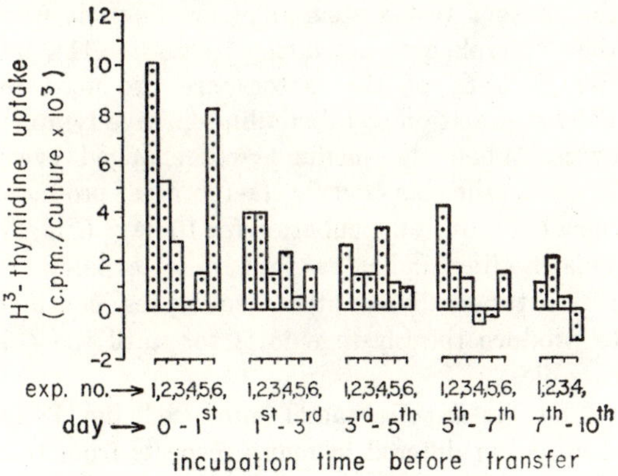

Figure 3. Production of blastogenic factor in cultures of PPD-stimulated leukocytes during different time intervals. CFM was prepared from the test (PPD-stimulated) and control (not exposed to PPD) cultures which had been incubated during different time intervals. Blastogenic activity of the test and control CFM was assessed by adding these preparations separately to cultures of fresh autologous cells, incubating for 7 days, and measuring cellular uptake of ^{3}H-thymidine. The activity of PPD-stimulated blastogenic factor (CFM) was expressed as described in Figure 2.

was the CFM from cultures of unwashed cells.

To determine whether the blastogenic factor which accumulates in cultures of lymphocytes stimulated by PPD is as active for autologous cells as for allogeneic cells, cells were exposed to PPD for 30 min, washed twice, and then incubated in fresh medium *without* added antigen ("test" cultures). Parallel "control" cultures were treated identically except that PPD was not added. The CFM from these 5-day "test" and "control" cultures was added to cultures of fresh autologous and allogeneic cells, and the stimulation measured after incubation for 7 days. The results are illustrated in Figure 2, and are expressed as ^{3}H-thymidine counts/minute from cultures containing "test" medium, minus counts from cultures with "control" medium. This was done to isolate the effects of PPD-stimulated blastogenic factor from those of the "autologous" and "allogeneic" factors described above. It is apparent (Fig. 2) that this PPD-stimulated blastogenic factor was as active for autologous cells as for allogeneic cells ($r = 0.46$; $p = 0.001$).

Table II shows that the production of this blastogenic factor was antigenically specific. Supernatants from cultures of PPD-stimulated leukocytes from tuberculin-negative subjects lacked blastogenic activity or were even inhibitory. The effect of the blastogenic factor, however, appeared nonspecific since this factor was stimulatory for cells from both tuberculin-positive and negative subjects.

Figure 3 shows production of the blastogenic factor over successive time intervals. The maximal amount of the blastogenic factor was produced during the first 24 hr in most experiments. When the medium was changed every 2 days, this factor was produced repeatedly but in successively lesser amounts. In two experiments (nos. 4 and 5), new production of the blastogenic factor discontinued completely after 5 days.

DISCUSSION

In earlier studies we suggested that the blastogenic factor in the medium of leukocyte cultures might be a histocompatibility antigen (5, 7). However, this conclusion would certainly conflict with a recent report stating that CFM from unmixed leukocyte cultures, on the average, stimulates autologous and allogeneic cells to the same extent (12). The present study showed that the CFM from unmixed leukocyte cultures was frequently stimulatory for both autologous and allogeneic cells. This finding suggests that the CFM contains the "nonspecific potentiating factor" described by Janis and Bach (12). However, this CFM stimulated allogeneic leukocytes much more than did autologous cells (Fig. 1). The present study also showed that while the blastogenic factor was always stimulatory for allogeneic cells, it was inhibitory for autologous cells in 13 of 57 experiments. It has been reported that blastogenic factor from unmixed leukocyte cultures from one monozygotic twin sister showed no stimulation with cells from the other twin sister, but definitely stimulated cells from unrelated donors (14). Also, CFM from mixed leukocyte cultures from the monozygotic twin sisters produced no blastogenesis when added to cells from one of the original donors (14). Therefore, at least some component of the blastogenic factor is antigenically-specific and might be a soluble form of histocompatibility antigen. Viza *et al.* (15) have shown that purified HL-A antigens cause blastogenesis when added to cultures of allogeneic lymphocytes from single donors. Mannick *et al.* (16) have observed that CFM recovered from cultures of dog spleen can induce homograft sensitivity.

In the present study the CFM preparations that were the most stimulatory toward allogeneic cells were not necessarily the most active toward autologous cells. The two types of stimulatory activity in these cell-free culture media showed no correlation (Fig. 1). This finding suggests that separate molecules may be responsible for each activity. It seems pertinent that CFM from unmixed cultures of leukocytes contains at least two components: a) a specific blastogenic factor (probably histocompatibility antigen), and b) a nonspecific stimulatory factor (probably the "potentiating factor" described by Janis and Bach (12)).

Blastogenic factor production is accelerated in mixed cultures as compared with cultures from single donors (5), showing that some extra process takes place in the mixtures. This process can occur in the absence of HL-A antigenic differences between a pair of donors and obvious blast-cell transformation (14). In the present study, washing of leukocytes accelerated subsequent production of blastogenic factor by these cells (Table I). It is therefore conceivable that non-immunologic membrane phenomena may accelerate the production of blastogenic factor.

It has been reported by others that blastogenic factor is produced by tuberculin-sensitive lymphocytes in response to PPD-stimulation (8–10). It is, however, not known from these reports whether the presence of antigen is required for activity of this blastogenic factor since in these experiments the active supernatants contained antigen. It would be important to clarify this point in order to distinguish this factor from the "lymphocyte-activating factor" described by Valentine and Lawrence (11). The latter factor requires antigen to get a blastogenic effect (11). In the present experiments we also found the production of blastogenic factor by tuberculin-sensitive leukocytes in response to PPD-stimulation. However, in the present study the amount of residual antigen in the supernatant was diminished greatly by exposing the sensitive cells to PPD for only 30 min, washing them twice, and then allowing them to continue in culture for a further 5 days without added antigen. While there always remained a trace of antigen, it seems most unlikely that this trace was involved in the activity. Therefore, the blastogenic factor recognized by the present test system may be different from the "lymphocyte-activating factor" (11), although both of the factors are produced by PPD-stimulation of tuberculin-sensitive lymphocytes. When the medium was changed every 2 days, the blastogenic factor was produced repeatedly during incubation for 10 days (Fig. 3). This finding indicates that once exposed to PPD, tuberculin-sensitive leukocytes continue to produce the blastogenic factor until the culture dies.

The blastogenic factor produced by PPD-stimulation differed in many respects from that which was produced in unmixed leukocyte cultures and which was stimulatory only for allogeneic cells. These differences were as follows: *a) The specificity of production.* The blastogenic factor from PPD-stimulated cultures was produced *in vitro* only by tuberculin-sensitive lymphocytes when triggered by tuberculin antigen (Table II, and reference 8). The factor from unmixed leukocyte cultures was produced in all the unmixed leukocyte cultures (Fig. 1). *b) The specificity of effect.* Once produced, blastogenic factor from PPD-stimulated cultures was as active for autologous cells as for allogeneic cells

(Fig. 2). It has already been shown that the stimulatory effect of the "allogeneic" blastogenic factor from unmixed cultures is antigenically specific (Fig. 1, and reference 14). Therefore, the blastogenic factor produced by PPD-stimulation of tuberculin-sensitive cells probably is different from the "allogeneic" blastogenic factor.

It is not known from the present study whether there are differences between the blastogenic factor produced by PPD-stimulation and that produced in unmixed cultures and which stimulates autologous cells.

Acknowledgments. The author wishes to thank Dr. B. A. Cooper and Dr. B. Bain for helpful discussion of the manuscript, and Mrs. S. Lazar and Miss R. Harrington for skilled technical assistance.

REFERENCES

1. Pearmain, G., Lycette, R. R. and Fitzgerald, P. H., Lancet, *1:* 637, 1963.
2. Schrek, R., Amer. Rev. Resp. Dis., *87:* 734, 1963.
3. Bain, B., Vas, M. and Lowenstein, L., Blood, *23:* 108, 1964.
4. Bach, F. and Hirschhorn, K., Science, *143:* 813, 1964.
5. Kasakura, S. and Lowenstein, L., Nature, *208:* 794, 1965.
6. Gordon, J. and MacLean, L. D., Nature, *208:* 795, 1965.
7. Kasakura, S. and Lowenstein, L., Transplantation, *5:* 459, 1967.
8. Maini, R. N., Bryceson, A. D. M., Wolstencroft, R. A. and Dumonde, D. C., Nature, *224:* 43, 1969.
9. Spitler, L. E. and Lawrence, H. S., J. Immun., *103:* 1072, 1969.
10. Spitler, L. E. and Fudenberg, H. H., J. Immun., *104:* 544, 1970.
11. Valentine, F. T. and Lawrence, H. S., Science, *165:* 1014, 1969.
12. Janis, M. and Bach, F. H., Nature, *225:* 238, 1970.
13. Schmidt, G. and Tannhauser, S. J., J. Biol. Chem., *161:* 83, 1945.
14. Kasakura, S., Nature, In press.
15. Viza, D. C., Degani, O., Dausset, J. and Davies, D. A. L., Nature, *219:* 704, 1968.
16. Mannick, J. A., Graxiani, J. T. and Egdahl, R. H., Transplantation, *2:* 321, 1964.

THE JOURNAL OF IMMUNOLOGY
Copyright © 1970 by The Williams & Wilkins Co.

Vol. 105, No. 5, November 1970
Printed in U.S.A.

PHYSICAL SEPARATION OF HEMOPOIETIC STEM CELLS FROM CELLS CAUSING GRAFT-*VS*-HOST DISEASE

I. Sedimentation Properties of Cells Causing Graft-*vs*-Host Disease[1]

R. A. PHILLIPS AND R. G. MILLER

From the Department of Medical Biophysics, University of Toronto and The Ontario Cancer Institute, Toronto, Ontario, Canada

Received for publication May 28, 1970

The goal in these experiments was to obtain a physical separation of the cells causing graft-vs-host disease (GVHD) from hemopoietic stem cells. Because these two types of cells were thought to differ in size, a cell separation method, velocity sedimentation, that separates cells primarily on the basis of cell volume was used. To test the effectiveness of this separation procedure, spleen and bone marrow from donor mice were fractionated and GVHD activity in the various fractions was assayed by injecting the cells into appropriate recipients. These experiments showed that for both tissues GVHD is caused by a homogeneous population of small cells having a sedimentation velocity at 4°C and unit gravity of 3 mm/hr. Because hemopoietic stem cells are known to sediment at 4.0 mm/hr under these conditions, it was concluded that hemopoietic stem cells in the mouse can be physically separated by velocity sedimentation from the cells that cause GVHD.

Immunologically competent cells in allografts of bone marrow can react against the transplantation antigens of the recipient causing an often fatal graft-*vs*-host disease (GVHD). The observation that the cells causing GVHD are different from the hemopoietic stem cells required for animal survival (1) suggests an obvious method for preventing this disease: selective removal of the cells that cause GVHD. The numerous attempts at selective removal fall into three categories:

1. Incubation of bone marrow cells under empirically defined conditions such that the cells causing GVHD are selectively destroyed or inhibited (2). The major disadvantage of these methods is that they are seldom applicable to species other than the one for which they were developed (3).

2. Treatment of donors and recipients with large doses of immunosuppressive drugs. Although this method has been used successfully in animals (4, 5), it is not an attractive method for man; pretreatment involves excessive risk to the donor, and early treatment of the recipient may inhibit function of the graft because of sensitivity of the stem cells to many of the immunosuppressive agents used (6).

3. Physical separation of hemopoietic stem cells from cells involved in GVHD. Dicke *et al.* showed that hemopoietic stem cells are less dense than cells that cause GVHD and that separation can be achieved by flotation of cells in gradients of bovine serum albumin (1).

Physical separation might be expected to be the best method. However, there are several disadvantages in the use of density gradients to separate stem cells from the cells that cause GVHD. Even after careful standardization of their method for preparing density gradients, Shortman and Szenberg found significant animal-to-animal variation in the density of cells causing GVHD in chickens (7). Worton *et al.* were unable to obtain precise reproducibility in the density distributions of hemopoietic stem cells in the mouse (8). Dicke *et al.* found that conditions which gave the desired separation of GVHD cells with mouse bone marrow did not work well for primate bone marrow (9). We, therefore, sought to find a more reproducible physical method for separating hemopoietic stem cells from cells that cause GVHD.

[1] This work was supported by the Donner Canadian Foundation, the National Cancer Institute of Canada, and the Medical Research Council (Grant MA-3766).

Previous data indicated that velocity sedimentation might separate the two types of cells. Worton *et al.* showed that murine hemopoietic stem cells detected by colony formation in the spleens of irradiated recipients have a modal sedimentation velocity of 4 mm/hr (8). Under the same conditions, we have observed that the immediate progenitors of antibody-producing cells in bone marrow, which might be closely related to the cells that initiate GVHD, have a sedimentation velocity of 3 mm/hr (10). The results of this paper demonstrate that the cells responsible for GVHD cosediment with the immediate progenitors of antibody-producing cells and can be physically separated from hemopoietic stem cells.

MATERIALS AND METHODS

Mice. C3H/HeJ mice were purchased from Jackson Laboratories (Bar Harbor, Maine). F_1 hybrids between C3H/HeOci and C57BL/6JOci (hereafter referred to as $C3B6F_1$) were bred in the animal facilities at the Ontario Cancer Institute. Animals were 8- to 10-weeks old at the start of an experiment. In some experiments genetically anemic mice of genotype W/W^v were used (11, 12); co-isogenic, normal littermates served as controls and recipients. These mutant mice were obtained from the mouse colony at the Ontario Cancer Institute or purchased from the Jackson Laboratory. All mice were kept two to a cage and allowed free access to food and water.

Irradiation. All recipient mice were irradiated with a ^{137}Cs irradiator (13) at a dose rate of 102 rads/min for a total dose of 950 rads.

Cell suspensions. Bone marrow cell suspensions were obtained by aspirating phosphate-buffered saline (PBS) through the marrow cavities of femurs of donor mice. This yielded single cell suspensions with only a few cell clumps. Suspensions of spleen or lymph node cells were prepared by cutting the organ into small pieces with scissors and aspirating the pieces in and out of a disposable plastic syringe. If the suspension was to be used for a cell separation experiment, it was washed once by centrifugation for 10 min at $700 \times G$ in a refrigerated centrifuge and the pellet of cells resuspended in PBS. Filtration through a capillary array filter (Mosaic Fabrications, Sturbridge, Mass.) with a pore size of 37 μ removed most small cell clumps and fibrous debris which might still be present.

Assay for spleen cells that cause GVHD. Transplantation of parental spleen cells into irradiated F_1 recipients causes an acute form of GVHD ending in death of the recipients 2 to 3 weeks after transplantation. The degree of mortality has been used as a measure of the GVHD activity in the suspension of spleen cells (14). Although the mortality in this situation is commonly ascribed to GVHD, the irradiated recipients could die either from GVHD or from a failure of the transplanted stem cells to protect the recipients from radiation-induced anemia. To use mortality as a measure of cells causing GVHD, it was necessary to ensure that the irradiated animals did not die from a lack of stem cells. Therefore, irradiated $C3B6F_1$ recipients were injected with 5×10^5 syngeneic bone marrow cells, a number sufficient to protect the irradiated recipients from the lethal effects of the radiation but not large enough to interfere with the induction of GVHD caused by injecting parental spleen cells. A test of this assay is shown in Table I. Eighty per cent of the recipients that received only bone marrow cells survived for 100 days (group 1). However, when such recipients were also given 2×10^6 parental spleen cells, there was 100% mortality (group 3). The only effect of the added

TABLE I

Assay for GVHD activity in spleen

Group	Cells Transplanted	Genotype of Recipient	Time to 50% Mortality	% Survival at 100 days[a]
			days	
1	5×10^5 $C3B6F_1$ bone marrow	$C3B6F_1$	>100	80 (9/11)
2	2×10^6 C3H spleen	$C3B6F_1$	13	0 (0/10)
3	2×10^6 C3H spleen + 5×10^5 $C3B6F_1$ bone marrow	$C3B6F_1$	22	0 (0/12)

[a] The numbers in parentheses give the numbers of survivors over the number of animals initially injected.

syngeneic bone marrow on the GVHD appears to have been to slightly delay the onset of mortality (compare groups 2 and 3). These data indicate that irradiated F_1 mice protected with small numbers of syngeneic bone marrow cells are suitable recipients for measuring GVHD activity in suspensions of parental spleen cells.

Cell separation. The method has been described previously (15). In brief, the cell suspension is allowed to sediment under gravity through a gradient of fetal calf serum or bovine serum albumin (BSA) in PBS. The density of the gradient is chosen to be always significantly less than the density of the cells. Under these conditions, we have shown that the rate of fall of each cell is nearly proportional to the square of its radius and depends little on other parameters, such as cell or gradient density. To achieve a separation, 80 ml of a cell suspension at a concentration of 6×10^6 cells/ml in 0.3% BSA in PBS was placed in the bottom of a cylindrical chamber with a conical shaped bottom. The cells were lifted to the top of the cylinder by introducing a non-linear 0.5% to 2% BSA gradient underneath the cell band through an orifice at the apex of the conical bottom. The chamber used had a diameter of 24 cm resulting in a cell band at the top of the gradient which was 1.7 mm wide. The cells were allowed to sediment through the BSA gradient for approximately 3.5 hr at 4°C. At the end of this time, 60-ml fractions were collected through the bottom of the chamber and the concentration of cells in each fraction measured with an electronic cell counter.

As an example, the detailed procedure for determining the sedimentation distribution of the spleen cells that cause GVHD was as follows. A suspension of C3H spleen cells was fractionated as just described. The cells in each fraction were spun down ($700 \times G$ for 10 min at 4°C), and the pellet of cells was resuspended in 5.5 ml of PBS containing 1×10^6 C3B6F_1 bone marrow cells/ml; 0.5 ml of this mixture was injected into each of 10 irradiated C3B6F_1 recipients. Thus, the recipients in each group received $\frac{1}{11}$th of the cells in that fraction, plus 5×10^5 C3B6F_1 bone marrow cells. The purpose of the C3B6F_1 bone marrow was to protect all the recipients from radiation-induced anemia, as described in the previous section.

It is important to note that cell separation techniques can be used in two ways: 1) to obtain a pure population of cells with a particular function or 2) to determine some physical property, such as sedimentation velocity of a class of cells. In the first case, the results should be expressed as activity per cell or as enrichment over control. In the second use, however, only the activity per fraction is important. In the experiments described here we wanted to know the sedimentation profile of cells causing GVHD and therefore we measured activity per fraction. The sedimentation was done such that most (more than 99.9%) of the spleen cells were distributed over 20 equal-sized fractions. A constant proportion of each fraction was tested for GVHD activity by injection into 10 irradiated recipients, making a total of 200 mice for each gradient. The total number of spleen cells processed, 4.8×10^8, was more than enough to cause a fatal GVHD in 200 mice. Even if the cells causing GVHD had been spread uniformly throughout the gradient they would have been detected in the assay.

RESULTS

Transplantation of allogeneic spleen cells. The initial experiments were done using the model system of van Bekkum (14) for studying GVHD in mice: transplantation of parental spleen cells into F_1 recipients. In mice, the GVHD produced by spleen cells is much more severe than that produced by bone marrow and should be easier to investigate. The sedimentation profile of the cells causing GVHD in a suspension of C3H spleen cells was determined as described (Fig. 1). The upper panel shows the distribution of nucleated cells (solid line) and erythrocytes (dashed line). The data have been plotted in terms of sedimentation velocity rather than fraction number since past experience has shown that the sedimentation velocity of a particular cell type is a reproducible parameter (16). The nucleated cell distribution is identical to those we have presented previously (15, 16); peaks of nucleated cells at 2 and 3 mm/hr are the dominant features. Recent data (16) indicate that most of the cells in the peak at 2 mm/hr cannot take up the vital dye, fluorescein diacetate (17), and are thus probably non-viable.

The lower panel in Figure 1 shows the survival of mice 80 days after they were given cells from the corresponding regions of the upper panel. Deaths occurred primarily in those mice

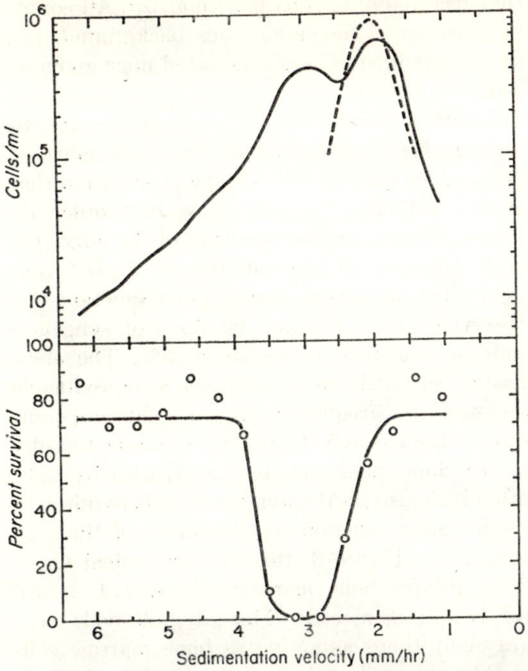

Figure 1. Sedimentation distribution of spleen cells responsible for GVHD. Spleen cells from C3H mice were separated as described, and individual fractions were tested for GVHD activity by injection into 10 irradiated C3B6F$_1$ recipients given 5×10^5 syngeneic bone marrow cells. The upper panel shows the distribution of nucleated cells (*solid line*) and erythrocytes (*dashed line*). Eighty days after transplantation the survivors in each group were tabulated. The percent survival of mice given cells from each fraction is given in the lower panel. The direction of sedimentation is from right to left. The position of the initial layer of cells is at a sedimentation velocity of 0 mm/hr.

that received cells with a sedimentation velocity between 2.5 and 3.5 mm/hr. These data indicate that GVHD is caused by a single, homogeneous population of small cells, probably small lymphocytes (18).

Assay for bone marrow cells that cause GVHD. Irradiated C3B6 F$_1$ mice given C3H bone marrow cells survive almost as well as mice given syngeneic bone marrow so that mortality cannot be used as an assay for GVHD. Therefore, it was necessary to devise a more sensitive assay for the cells in bone marrow that cause GVHD. The assay used was based on experiments reported by Willard and Smith (19). These authors measured the ability of syngeneic grafts of lymphoid cells

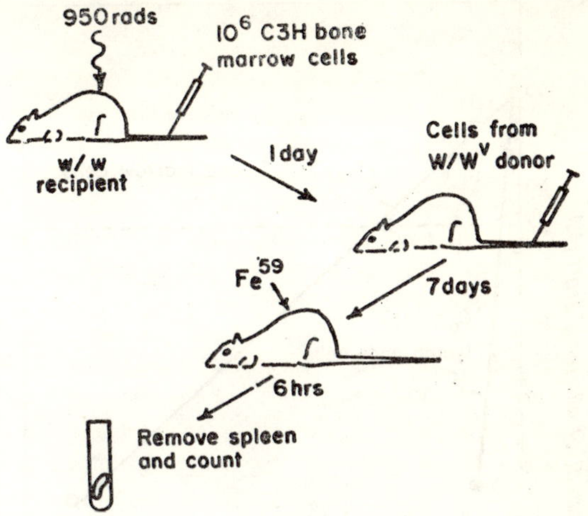

Figure 2. Assay for immunocompetent cells in tissues from W/W^v donors. See text for details of the experimental design.

to suppress the function of bone marrow allografts growing in irradiated recipients and found that the degree of graft suppression was dependent on the number of lymphoid cells injected. Thus, inhibition of the function of the allograft could be used as a quantitative measure of the capacity of the syngeneic lymphoid cells to react against the foreign histocompatibility antigens of the allograft. The lymphoid cells detected in this assay are probably the same ones that cause GVHD.

The principal attraction of this technique is its simplicity. Function of the allograft can be determined by measuring the incorporation of radioactive iron into the spleens of the recipients. However, to adapt this assay for measuring GVHD activity in samples of bone marrow, it is essential that syngeneic bone marrow not contribute to the incorporation of ^{59}Fe. This requirement can be met using mice of genotype W/W^v. These mice have a genetic defect that prevents hemopoietic stem cells from functioning normally (11) to the extent that there is no detectable erythropoiesis in irradiated recipients given only cells from W/W^v donors. Although the hemopoietic system in these mice is defective, their immune system is normal (20) and can react against allogeneic cells (12).

The experimental design using W/W^v mice is shown in Figure 2. Irradiated recipients, coisogenic with W/W^v mice, were given 10^6 bone marrow cells from an allogeneic donor, in this

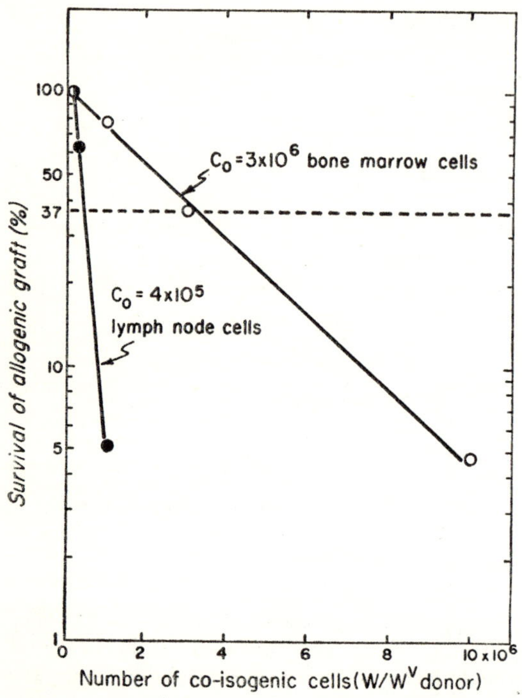

Figure 3. Allograft survival in recipients given different numbers of isologous cells from W/W^v donors. Irradiated (950 rads) recipients, co-isogenic with W/W^v, were given 1×10^6 bone marrow cells from C3H donors. One day later, these recipients received lymph node cells (*closed circle*) or bone marrow cells (*open circles*) from W/W^v donors. Seven days later, function of the allograft was determined by measuring uptake of ^{59}Fe. Relative graft survival was calculated by taking as 100% survival the counts/minute in the recipients that received only C3H bone marrow cells. The slope of each curve is expressed as the number of cells required to reduce survival to 37% (1/e).

case, C3H/HeJ. Twenty-four hours after the bone marrow graft, the recipients were given different numbers of cells from W/W^v donors. If the suspension of cells from W/W^v donors contains cells capable of causing GVHD, they should react against the C3H allograft. Allograft function was assessed 7 days after injection of the W/W^v cells by measuring ^{59}Fe incorporation in the spleens of the recipients. For this purpose 0.2 μCi of ^{59}Fe was injected intraperitoneally into the mice; 6 hr later their spleens were removed and the whole spleen counted in a well-type scintillation counter. Graft function was expressed as a ratio of the counts in the experimental group divided by the counts in the controls that received only C3H bone marrow. All counts were corrected for endogenous background, i.e., the counts in spleens of irradiated mice given no cells.

Figure 3 shows the results of an experiment testing this assay, not only for bone marrow, but also for lymph node. On the expectation that graft inactivation would follow first order kinetics, we plotted the logarithm of the surviving graft function *vs* the number of W/W^v cells injected. Exponential loss of graft function was observed with increasing numbers of syngeneic cells for survival values above 5%. The slope of the survival curve provides a reproducible measure of frequency of immunocompetent cells in the tissue being tested. A simple measure of the slope, analogous to the D_0 used by radiation biologists, is the number of cells required to reduce graft function to 37% (1/e) of the control. From Figure 3, this number, called C_0, is 3×10^6 for bone marrow cells and 4×10^5 for lymph node cells. Thus, lymph node cells are eight times as active as bone marrow cells in this assay. The relatively low activity in bone marrow may be the reason why GVHD is mild in irradiated mice given allogeneic bone marrow cells.

Transplantation of allogeneic bone marrow cells. A bone marrow suspension from W/W^v donors was separated by velocity sedimentation. A constant proportion ($\frac{1}{11}$th) of each fraction was transplanted into co-isogenic, irradiated recipients that had received a graft of C3H bone marrow cells 24 hr earlier. Function of the C3H allograft was measured by iron incorporation 7 days after injection of the fractions from the gradient as explained in the preceding section. The results are shown in Figure 4. The upper panel again shows the distribution of nucleated cells and erythrocytes. The major difference between this curve and the one in Figure 1 is the presence in bone marrow of a large number of cells with sedimentation velocities between 3.5 and 4.5 mm/hr. Cells in this region of the gradient were examined microscopically and the majority were granulocytes. The lower panel shows relative allograft function in groups of recipients given cells from corresponding fractions of the gradient. Suppression of the C3H allograft occurred only in recipients given bone marrow cells sedimenting at 3 mm/hr. The shape of the distribution, once again, indicates that the cells capable of reacting against foreign tissues are a

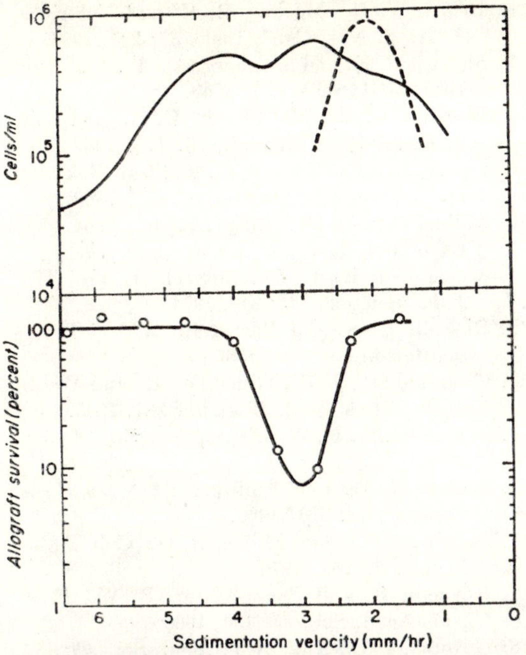

Figure 4. Sedimentation distribution of bone marrow cells causing GVHD. Bone marrow from W/W^v donors was separated and tested for its ability to inhibit an allograft of C3H bone marrow cells growing in irradiated recipients, co-isogenic with W/W^v. The upper panel shows the distribution of nucleated cells (*solid line*) and erythrocytes (*dashed line*). The lower panel shows the relative survival of a C3H allograft in recipients given cells from the various fractions.

homogeneous population of small, slowly sedimenting cells.

DISCUSSION

The most important conclusion to be derived from these data is that hemopoietic stem cells can be separated from cells involved in GVHD by velocity sedimentation. Figure 5 shows the probable sedimentation distributions of these two cells for mouse tissue. The sedimentation distribution of CFU is taken from the data of Worton *et al.* (8). The curve for GVHD was derived from the data in Figure 4. Although there is some overlap in the two distributions, fractions from the bottom of the gradient should contain stem cells and few, if any, cells capable of causing GVHD. For the mouse, we predict that transplantation of stem cells with sedimentation velocities greater than 4.5 mm/hr will protect irradiated recipients without the occurrence of

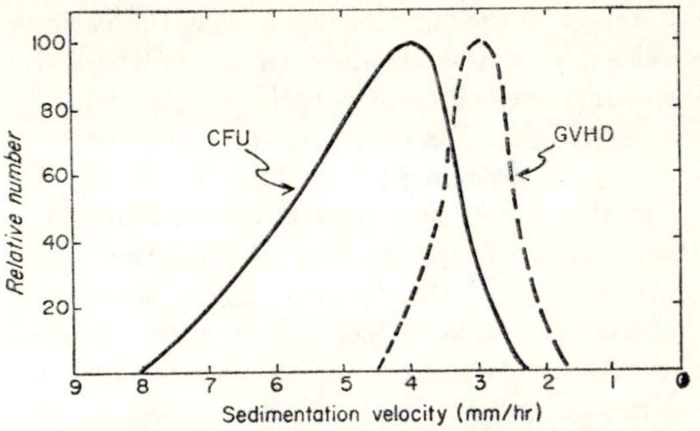

Figure 5. Proposed sedimentation distribution of hemopoietic stem cells and cells causing GVHD. The distribution of stem cells is taken from the CFU distribution described by Worton *et al.* (8). The distribution of bone marrow cells causing GVHD is taken from the data in Figure 4.

GVHD. Preliminary experiments with spleen and bone marrow confirm this prediction, but further experiments are necessary to determine the extent to which these fractions can repopulate the hemopoietic and immune systems of both syngeneic and allogeneic recipients.

The feasibility of using cell separation in the transplantation of human bone marrow has recently been demonstrated by de Konig *et al.* (21). These investigators used flotation in density gradients to achieve a partial separation of hemopoietic stem cells from cells causing GVHD. The fraction enriched in stem cells was then injected into a child with lymphopenic immunologic deficiency. Although there were symptoms of a mild GVHD 2 to 3 weeks after transplantation, the patient recovered and was eventually shown to have both his hemopoietic and immune systems repopulated by donor cells. If the separation procedure could be improved, transplantation could be considered in patients where GVHD is more severe than in patients with immunologic deficiency diseases.

The principal advantage of velocity sedimentation over density separation is that the former appears to be readily adaptable to species other than the mouse. As mentioned above, the density conditions that give suitable separation of mouse cells do not work for cells from primates (9). However, sedimentation profiles are reproducible from one species to another. Sedimentation profiles of bone marrow obtained either from humans (22) or from rats (23) are essentially identical to those obtained from mice. The only differences in the distributions among the various species are in the absolute values of the sedimentation velocities for each of the various classes of cells. For example, the sedimentation velocity for human granulocytes is 6.0 mm/hr while that for mouse cells is only 4.5 mm/hr. However, most importantly, the relative positions of each of the various classes of cells is unchanged from one species to another. Preliminary work has been done on determining the sedimentation profiles of immunocompetent cells and hemopoietic stem cells in human marrow. It appears that the various cell populations are located in the same relative positions as in the mouse (22).

Acknowledgments. These experiments were carried out with the excellent technical assistance of Mr. R. Kuba, Mrs. J. Madrus, and Miss H. Mooney.

REFERENCES

1. Dicke, K. A., van Hooft, J. I. M. and van Bekkum, D. W., Transplantation, *6:* 571, 1968.
2. Uphoff, P. E., Nature, *222:* 1089, 1969.
3. van Putten, L. M., Balner, H., Muller-Berat, C. N., de Vries, M. J. and van Bekkum, D. W., Bibl. Haemat., *29:* 574, 1968.
4. Floersheim, G. L. and Ruszbiewicz, M., Nature, *222:* 854, 1969.
5. Thomas, E. D., Kasakura, S., Cavino, J. A., Swisher, S. N. and Ferrebee, J. W., Ann. N. Y. Acad. Sci., *120:* 362, 1964.
6. Bruce, W. R., Meeker, B. E. and Valeriote, F. A., J. Nat. Canc. Inst., *37:* 233, 1966.
7. Shortman, K. and Szenberg, A., Aust. J. Exp. Biol. Med. Sci. *47:* 1, 1969.
8. Worton, R. G., McCulloch, E. A. and Till, J. E., J. Cell. Physiol., *74:* 171, 1969.
9. Dicke, K. A., Tridente, G. and van Bekkum, D. W., Transplantation, *8:* 422, 1969.
10. Miller, R. G. and Phillips, R. A., Proc. Soc. Exp. Biol. Med., In press.
11. McCulloch, E. A., Siminovitch, L. and Till, J. E., Science, *144:* 844, 1964.
12. Russell, E. S. and Bernstein, S. E., Transplantation, *5:* 142, 1967.
13. Cunningham, J. R., Bruce, W. R. and Webb, H. P., Phys. Med. Biol., *10:* 381, 1965.
14. van Bekkum, D. W., Transplantation, *2:* 393, 1964.
15. Miller, R. G. and Phillips, R. A., J. Cell. Physiol., *73:* 191, 1969.
16. Phillips, R. A. and Miller, R. G., Cell Tissue Kinet., *3:* 263, 1970.
17. Rotman, B. and Papermaster, B. W., Proc. Nat. Acad. Sci., *55:* 134, 1966.
18. Gowans, J. L., Ann. N.Y. Acad. Sci., *99:* 432, 1962.
19. Willard, H. G. and Smith, L. H., Transplantation, *4:* 56, 1966.
20. Mekori, T. and Phillips, R. A., Proc. Soc. Exp. Biol. Med., *132:* 115, 1969.
21. de Konig, J., Dooren, L. J., van Bekkum, D. W., van Rood, J. J., Dicke, K. A. and Radl, J., Lancet, *1:* 1223, 1969.
22. Amato, D., Iscove, N. N., Cowan, D. H. and McCulloch, E. A., Exp. Haemat., *20:* 8, 1970.
23. McCool, D., Miller, R. J., Painter, R. H. and Bruce, W. R., Exp. Cell Res., In press.

THE JOURNAL OF IMMUNOLOGY
Copyright © 1970 by The Williams & Wilkins Co.

Vol. 105, No. 5, November 1970
Printed in U.S.A.

PRODUCTION OF CONGENITAL MALFORMATIONS USING TISSUE ANTISERA

VIII. Effectiveness of Reduced, Alkylated and Digested Anti-Kidney Antibodies[1]

J. ROBERT BRAGONIER,[2] MICHAEL M. FRANK AND ROBERT L. BRENT

From the Laboratory of Clinical Investigation, National Institute of Allergy and Infectious Diseases and the National Institute of Child Health and Human Development, Bethesda, Maryland 20014; and the Department of Pediatrics and Radiology, Stein Research Center, The Jefferson Medical College, Philadelphia, Pennsylvania 19107

Received for publication May 27, 1970

Studies have been performed in a model teratologic system in which congenital malformations are produced in offspring by injecting sheep anti-rat kidney antiserum into pregnant rats on day 8 of gestation. To determine whether the antiserum produces its effects simply by combining with antigen, or whether direct participation of nonspecific mediators of immunologic damage is required, the antibody molecule was structurally altered by two methods: (1) a globulin fraction of the antiserum was reduced and alkylated to dissociate IgM antibody and destroy the complement-fixing ability of IgG antibody, and (2) a globulin fraction was digested with pepsin to destroy the Fc fragment of IgG. Both modified fractions retained the capacity to produce congenital malformations. This result suggests that complement and other nonspecific mediators are not involved in the immunologic damage which results in malformations in this system. The finding lends support to the proposition that this teratogenic antiserum acts by interfering sterically with normal yolk sac function during a critical period of fetal development.

In 1961 it was first reported that injection of antirat kidney antiserum into pregnant rats causes congenital malformations in their offspring (1). Many of the variables in this teratologic model have since been systematically examined (2–7). For example, the time of administration and dosage of antiserum have been shown to be critical; a dose of antiserum which malforms 86% and kills 19% of fetuses when administered on day 8 of gestation causes malformation in only 25% and 14% of fetuses when given on gestational days 7 and 10, respectively. Increasing that dose three times on day 8 of gestation increases the mortality rate from 19% to 97%.

Three possible mechanisms of teratogenesis have been proposed (4): 1) direct effect of the antiserum upon the developing embryo, 2) direct effect on placental trophoblast or extraembryonic membranes, and 3) indirect effect on the embryo resulting from biochemical or physiologic alterations in the maternal organism. Considering the first alternative, studies using fluorescent antibody techniques have failed to support a direct effect on the embryo; no gross *in vivo* localization of labeled antibody was observed in the young embryo. (The possibility of direct effect could not be excluded, however. A small number of cytotoxic antibody molecules could cause cell death without being visible by fluorescence microscopy). It has also been impossible to rule out the third alternative. Localization of labeled antiserum has been observed in the basement membrane of maternal kidney glomeruli, adrenal, liver and spleen (5), and maternal rats exhibited marked proteinuria and weight loss following injection (1). However, the second possibility has seemed the most likely, for several reasons. First, anti-rat placenta antiserum produces malformations indistinguishable from those produced by anti-rat kidney antiserum (3), despite the fact that no localization of fluorescent-labeled antibody could be observed on the trophoblast or

[1] This work was supported in part by Grant HD 630 from the National Institutes of Health, United States Public Health Service, Department of Health, Education and Welfare.

[2] Present address: Department of Obstetrics and Gynecology, University of California, Los Angeles, Harbor General Hospital, 1000 West Carson Street, Torrance, California 90509.

amnion. Second, specific deposition of labeled antibody does occur on the basement membrane of the developing yolk sac (5). Third, antibody raised in rabbits to yolk sac basement membrane has proven to be highly teratogenic (7). Finally, trypan blue, a teratogenic chemical dye (8, 9), also localizes in the yolk sac membrane and is felt to act by interfering with yolk sac function (4, 10).

If it could be demonstrated that the anti-kidney antibody acts directly by combining with antigen, rather than indirectly through the participation of nonspecific mediators of immunologic damage, the case for its acting via steric interference with normal yolk sac function would be strengthened. The present study attempted to make that distinction by determining the teratogenic effectiveness of antiserum after its secondary biologic effects were destroyed by structural alteration of the antibody molecules.

MATERIALS AND METHODS

The sheep anti-rat kidney antiserum utilized in these studies was obtained from a large pool which has been extensively characterized in previous studies (4–7). Its LD_{50} term for 8-day-old rat embryos was 175 mg/kg. The teratogenic threshold was 100 mg/kg; at a dose of 75 mg/kg the antiserum produced no malformations, mortality, or growth retardation.

For reduction and alkylation, the lyophilized antiserum was reconstituted in distilled water (70 mg/ml) and centrifuged at 45,600 × G for 30 min to precipitate agglomerates. To the supernatant was added an equal volume of 5.4 molal ammonium sulfate; after 15 min of incubation and centrifugation in the cold, the globulin precipitate thus formed was taken up in a small volume of distilled water and dialyzed overnight against 0.15 M saline at 4°C. The dialyzed fraction was then diluted to twice the original antiserum volume with 0.15 M saline and made 0.1 M with respect to Tris buffer (pH 7.4). Dithioerythritol was dissolved to a concentration of 0.02 M and the solution incubated for 1 hr at 37°C. The reaction mixture was chilled at 0°C for 15 min and a 10% molar excess of iodoacetamide added. After incubation for 1 hr at 0°C, the mixture was dialyzed at 4°C overnight against 0.15 M saline and cleared by centrifugation at 45,600 × G for 30 min. Protein nitrogen was determined by the Kjeldahl method which allowed similar doses of treated and non-treated globulin fraction to be prepared for injection, despite different methods of treatment.

For alteration of the antiserum by digestion with pepsin, two volumes of 27% sodium sulfate solution were added to one volume of reconstituted antiserum. After a 3 hr incubation at room temperature, the globulin precipitate was centrifuged at 30,000 × G for 10 min at room temperature and redissolved in one-half volume of 0.1 M sodium phosphate buffer (pH 8.0). The globulin fraction was twice reprecipitated in one-half volume of 27% sodium sulfate and the final precipitate redissolved in sodium phosphate buffer. It was dialyzed overnight at 4°C against 0.15 M saline and then against 0.2 M sodium acetate buffer (pH 4.1).

Protein concentration of the dialyzed fraction was estimated from its optical density at 280 nm after hydrolysis with sodium hydroxide. Twenty micrograms of pepsin dissolved in sodium acetate buffer was then added per milligram of protein and the solution incubated overnight at 37°C. The digested fraction and a control sample incubated at pH 4.1 without pepsin were carefully adjusted to pH 7.7 to pH 7.8 with sodium hydroxide and cleared by centrifugation at 45,600 × G for 20 min. Both samples were compared by ultracentrifugal analysis to confirm adequacy of digestion.

Complement fixation blocks were prepared on Microtiter plates (Cooke Engineering Company, Alexandria, Virginia). Homogenized, lyophilized rat kidney was reconstituted in distilled water (70 mg/ml) and used as a stock antigen solution. Details of the microtechnique have previously been reported (11). Microprecipitin tests were performed according to the method of Preer (12).

To determine the teratogenic effect of treated and control fractions, pregnant rats were obtained by mating rats at 5 p.m. and examining the females for vaginal sperm the following morning, which time was considered to be the beginning of the first day of pregnancy. After 8 days of pregnancy, the maternal rats were lightly anesthetized, and a small abdominal incision was made in order to observe the number and condition of sites where embryos had implanted (implantation sites, Tables I and II). The incision was closed and the animal injected with a particular dose and preparation of antiserum. Small volumes were

Figure 1. Results of microprecipitin test. *Left to right*, pepsin-digested globulin fraction, control immune globulin fraction, pepsin-digested fraction without antigen, antigen without antibody. Precipitin bands with the pepsin-digested fraction, although decreased in number and slightly different in configuration, are clearly present. Additional controls, including control immune globulin fraction without antigen and normal serum with antigen, also demonstrated no precipitation.

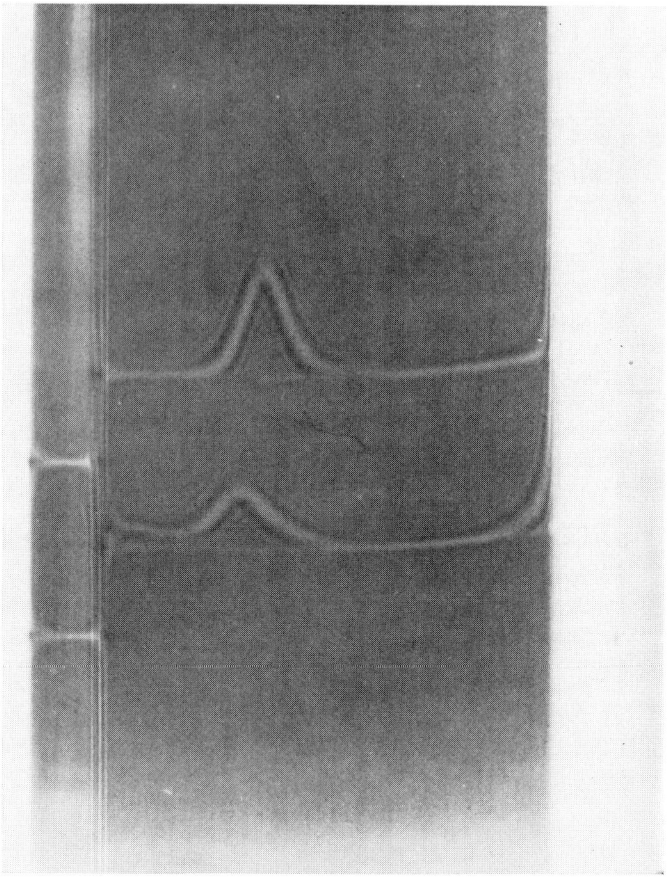

Figure 2. Ultracentrifugal comparison of control immune globulin fraction (*above*) and pepsin digested globulin fraction (*below*). The rate of sedimentation of the pepsin-digested fraction can be seen to be slower than that of the undigested material.

TABLE I

Effects of injection of reduced and alkylated sheep anti-rat kidney globulin into 8-day pregnant rats

No. of Pregnant Rats	Preparation of Sheep Anti-Rat Kidney Antiserum	Dose (in mg/kg of Pregnant Rat)	Route of Administration	Total No. of Implantation Sites (Pre-injection) in Treated Group	Per Cent Resorptions at Term (Mortality)	Average Term Weight of Fetuses	Per Cent Malformations Observed at Term
						g	
3	Reduced and alkylated globulin fraction	100	i. v.	19	5.2	4.643	5.5
4		200	i. p.	42	14.2	4.595	27.5
12		350	i. p.	137	33.3	4.278	73.9
6	Control globulin fraction	100	i. v.	67	21	4.179	96.2
10		200	i. p.	102	27.4	3.895	89.1
10		350	i. p.	122	75.4	3.424	53.3

TABLE II

Effects of injection of pepsin-digested sheep anti-rat kidney globulin into 8-day pregnant rats

No. of Pregnant Rats	Preparation of Sheep Anti-Rat Kidney Antiserum	Dose (in mg/kg of Pregnant Rat)	Route of Administration	Total No. of Implantation Sites (Pre-injection) in Treated Group)	Per Cent Resorptions at Term (Mortality)	Average Term Weight of Fetuses	Per Cent Malformations Observed at Term
						g	
3	Pepsin-digested globulin fraction	100	i. v.	43	7.5	3.963	5.0
5		175	i. p.	47	37	4.008	85.7
6	Control globulin fraction	100	i. v.	72	13.8	3.942	74.1
3		175	i. p.	33	100		

given intravenously. Dilute preparations which necessitated administering more than 2 ml were given intraperitoneally. The animals were allowed to proceed to term, and after 21 days, the rats were sacrificed and the fetuses delivered by cesarean section. The number of resorptions was recorded. The fetuses and placentae were weighed and placed in Bouin's fixative. After several days the fetuses were dissected and the incidence of congenital malformations was determined.

RESULTS

Microtiter two-dimensional block titration with reduced and alkylated and pepsin-digested fractions showed no complement fixation starting at dilutions of 1:10. Control globulin fractions fixed complement at dilutions of 1:320 and 1:160 respectively, demonstrating that at least 97% and 94% of complement-fixing activity was abolished by these methods of treatment.

Molecules altered by both methods maintained their ability to precipitate with homogenized rat kidney antigen (Fig. 1). Precipitin bands formed were clearly present, although decreased in number and, following reduction and alkylation, in intensity.

The rate of sedimentation of the pepsin-digested globulin fraction of serum was slower than that of the undigested material (Fig. 2). Lack of symmetry of the slow peak suggests slight contamination with undigested globulins, but in an amount insufficient to account for the results of animal injection.

Results of the biologic experiments are summarized in Tables I and II. The reduced and alkylated nephrotoxic globulin is a potent teratogen and causes definite growth retardation when administered at higher dosage levels. In a previously reported study, 97 embryos from uninjected animals of this strain, operated upon on day 8 of gestation, had 8.2% mortality, 1.7% malformations, and weighed 4.80 ± 0.31 g (± one standard deviation) (2). Only borderline effectiveness is noted at the 100 mg/kg dose.

Even with unmodified teratogenic antiserum, however, there is a sharp cutoff or threshold for teratogenicity when administered at this stage of gestation; although the LD_{50} term dose of the antiserum is 175 mg/kg and malformations and growth retardation are seen at a dose of 100 mg/kg, no effect is seen after a dose of 75 mg/kg. It appears that the globulin fraction has suffered some loss of potency during reduction and alkylation, but biologic variability within the test system precludes statistical verification of this loss. For example, using unmodified whole antiserum, the LD_{50} term dose may cause from 100% resorption to 15% to 20% resorption with 30% malformations in different litters within the same strain.

With the pepsin-digested fraction, distinct growth retardation was noted at a dose of 100 mg/kg, although the malformation and mortality rates were at a borderline level. At a higher dosage, this treated fraction also proved to be a potent teratogen with accompanying significant embryonic mortality.

DISCUSSION

It has previously been reported that complement-fixing activity of antibody requires the presence of intact disulfide bridges. Extensive reduction and alkylation of disulfide bonds destroys complement fixation while leaving antigen binding sites intact (13, 14). Our findings with sheep anti-rat kidney antibody are in agreement with that premise. Treatment with dithioerythritol and iodoacetamide caused a loss of complement-fixing ability of the globulin fraction without destroying its ability to precipitate with rat kidney antigen or produce the same spectrum of congenital malformations. This fact implies that complement fixation is not involved in the process of immune teratogenesis.

Studies of pepsin-digested antiserum lead to similar conclusions. Pepsin treatment of an antibody molecule is known to destroy the integrity of the F_c fragment, and with it, the capacity to produce many of its biologic effects. In this experiment, loss of complement-fixing activity with preservation of antigen-binding function and teratogenic capacity of the antiserum was again verfiied. The teratogenic effect of the antibody is thus independent of any biologic functions mediated nonspecifically through presence of an intact F_c fragment.

That modified antisera are not teratogenic at the lower doses administered is consistent with the previously observed threshold for malformations in this test system. As mentioned, a 25% reduction in dose at the threshold level completely abolishes the biologic effect of the antiserum. The 100 mg/kg dose of both preparations thus appears to be below the threshold, suggesting a loss of potency during structural modification which is supported by the data at higher doses. This loss in potency is not of the same order of magnitude as the loss in complement-fixing activity which the altered fractions manifest, however.

The anti-rat kidney antibody thus appears able to produce malformations simply by combining with its antigen. Because of the broad range of organ systems which may be malformed by the antibody, it seems unlikely that these malformations result from destruction of specific embryonic cells important to subsequent normal development. The critical period in embryogenesis seems to be of sufficiently short duration to make highly unlikely the possibility that the maternal immune system causes the observed malformations through its response to heterologous cell-bound globulin. That malformations might occur secondary to derangement of maternal organ systems other than the immune system remains a possibility. Nonetheless, these observations best support the hypothesis that teratogenic anti-kidney antibody is directed against yolk sac basement membrane and produces malformations by interfering sterically with normal yolk sac function during a critical period of fetal development.

Acknowledgment. The authors would like to thank Dr. J. S. Johnson for performing the ultracentrifugal analyses.

REFERENCES

1. Brent, R. L., Averich, E. and Drapiewski, V. A., Proc. Soc. Exp. Biol. Med., *106:* 523, 1961.
2. Brent, R. L., Amer. J. Anat., *115:* 525, 1964.
3. Brent, R. L., Proc. Soc. Exp. Biol. Med., *125:* 1024, 1967.
4. Brent, R. L., Amer. J. Anat., *119:* 555, 1966.
5. Slotnick, V. and Brent, R. L., J. Immun., *96:* 606, 1966.
6. Brent, R. L., Fed. Proc., *27:* 622, 1968.
7. Brent, R. L. and Johnson, A., Fed. Proc., *26:* 701, 1967.

8. Fox, M. H., Goss, C. M. and Bordeaux, L. F., Anat. Rec., *130:* 302, 1958.
9. Beck, F., Spencer, B. and Baxter, J. S., Nature, *187:* 605, 1960.
10. Wilson, J. G., Shepard, T. H. and Gennar, J. F., Anat. Rec., *145:* 300, 1963.
11. Fauci, A. S., Frank, M. M. and Johnson, J. S., J. Immun., *105:* 215, 1970.
12. Preer, J. R., Jr., J. Immun., *77:* 52, 1956.
13. Wiedermann, G., Miescher, P. A. and Franklin, E. C., Proc. Soc. Exp. Biol. Med., *113:* 609, 1963.
14. Wiedermann, G., Ovary, Z. and Miescher, P. A., Proc. Soc. Exp. Biol. Med., *116:* 448, 1964.

THE JOURNAL OF IMMUNOLOGY
Vol. 105, No. 5, November 1970
Printed in U.S.A.

CHARACTERIZATION OF SURFACE ANTIGEN ON CELLS INFECTED BY FIBROMA VIRUS[1]

WAYNE A. F. TOMPKINS, NORMAN A. CROUCH, S. S. TEVETHIA[2] AND WILLIAM E. RAWLS[3]

From the Department of Virology and Epidemiology, Baylor College of Medicine, Houston, Texas

Received for publication May 25, 1970

Cells infected with fibroma virus developed a surface antigen which could be detected by immunofluorescence. Sera from rabbits with regressed fibroma-induced tumors reacted with the surface of viable fibroma-infected cells, but not with cells infected with vaccinia virus or herpesvirus. Serum prepared against vaccinia virus, herpesvirus, SV40 virus and rabbit papilloma virus failed to react with fibroma-infected cells. The surface antigen appeared to be a late antigen and was dependent upon viral DNA synthesis. The antibody reaction was not to intact virions attached to the cell surface. The antigen persisted in association with the cell membrane long after infectious virus had decreased to low levels. A temporal relationship existed between the surface antigen measured by the fluorescent antibody technique and the antigen measured by the macrophage migration-inhibition test. Antibody reactive against the surface antigen developed in rabbits with growing fibromas and the antibody titer increased as the tumors regressed. The possible role of cell-mediated and humoral immune responses against this membrane-associated antigen in tumor regression is discussed.

Cells transformed by oncogenic DNA or RNA viruses develop specific antigens at the cell surface (1, 2). These antigens mediate the development of immunity in the host against the transplantation of cells transformed by the homologous viruses (3, 4). In the case of the DNA tumor virus system, the tumor cells are free of infectious virus or viral antigens and the tumor-specific transplantation antigens (TSTA) at the cell surface are virus-specific but are not a part of the virion. However, in the RNA tumor virus system, both TSTA and viral antigens are expressed at the cell surface (2). The viral antigens may therefore play some role in the rejection of the tumors induced by RNA viruses.

Fibroma virus induces the formation of benign tumors in adult rabbits, which generally contain infectious virus. However, these tumors regress completely in a short period of time and cellular immunity may play a role in the tumor regression (5, 6). Cellular immune reactions are directed towards the antigen[4] present at the surface of cells altered by the virus infection. This conclusion has been reached using the macrophage migration-inhibition test. Peritoneal exudate cells from rabbits showing tumor regression are inhibited from migrating from the glass capillaries in the presence of cells infected with the fibroma virus (7).

The present study was undertaken to investigate the nature of the specific antigen present at the surface of fibroma-infected rabbit kidney cells by means of the immunofluorescence test using sera from animals immune to fibroma virus. The immune response of rabbits to the

[1] This investigation was supported by Grants CA 04600 from the National Cancer Institute, HE 05435 from the National Heart Institute and Training Grant 2-T1-AI-74 from the National Institute of Allergy and Infectious Diseases, National Institutes of Health.

[2] Recipient of Research Career Development Award 1-K3-CA-38,614 from the National Cancer Institute, National Institutes of Health.

[3] Recipient of Research Career Development Award 5-K3-AI-25,943 from the National Institute of Allergy and Infectious Diseases, National Institutes of Health.

[4] The term antigen is used throughout this paper in the full realization that multiple antigens may be present.

specific surface antigen has been correlated with the appearance and regression of fibroma tumors.

MATERIALS AND METHODS

Cells. LLC-RK_1 cells, a continuous line of rabbit kidney cells, were kindly supplied by Dr. James C. Chan, Department of Medicine, Indiana University, Indianapolis, Ind. These cells were at the 240th passage. A cloned line of New Zealand White rabbit kidney cells (DRK_3) was obtained from Dr. Harry C. Hinze, Department of Medical Microbiology, University of Wisconsin Medical School, Madison, Wis. Primary rabbit kidney cells were prepared from 3-week-old New Zealand White rabbits by previously described methods (8). Continuous cell lines were grown in medium 199, supplemented with 10% fetal bovine serum (FBS), 100 μg streptomycin/ml, 100 units of penicillin/ml, and the pH was adjusted to 7.2 with a 7.5% solution of $NaHCO_3$. This medium was used in all experiments involving continuous rabbit kidney cell lines. Primary rabbit kidney cells were grown in Eagle's medium supplemented with 10% FBS, glutamine, antibiotics, and $NaHCO_3$.

Viruses and virus assay. The Patuxent strain of Shope fibroma virus (9) was prepared in primary rabbit kidney cells grown in 16-oz bottles by inoculating the cultures with approximately 1×10^7 pock-forming units (PFU) of virus and harvesting after 48 hr of incubation at 37°C. The infected cells were frozen and thawed three times, sonicated for 1 min at 10 kc to release cell-bound virus and centrifuged for 10 min at 1000 rpm. The WR strain of vaccinia virus and the KOS strain of type 1 herpesvirus were prepared in the same manner. Fibroma virus was assayed by pock formation on DRK_3 monolayers as described previously (9). Vaccinia virus and herpesvirus were assayed in primary rabbit kidney cells by the plaque method (10).

Inhibitors. Cytosine arabinoside (20 μg/ml) and hydroxyurea (5×10^{-3} M) were used as DNA inhibitors and cycloheximide (10 μg/ml) was used as an inhibitor of protein synthesis. The compounds were solubilized at the desired concentration in the cell culture medium.

Virus infection of cultures for immunofluorescence studies. Confluent monolayers of rabbit kidney cells in 60- x 15-mm plastic Petri dishes (Falcon Plastics, Oxnard, Calif.) were inoculated with 0.2 ml of fibroma virus at a multiplicity of 2 to 3 PFU/cell. After 2 hr adsorption at room temperature, the monolayers were washed once with 5 ml of Tris-buffered saline (TBS), pH 7.4, refed with 5 ml of medium 199 with 10% FBS, and incubated at 37°C in an atmosphere of 5% CO_2 in air. Cultures were harvested for immunofluorescence studies at various intervals after infection. Cultures inoculated with vaccinia or herpesvirus were treated in the same manner.

Immunofluorescence test. The indirect immunofluorescence test employing viable cells for the demonstration of surface antigens was performed as described by Tevethia *et al.* (11). Briefly, the cells growing in tissue culture were dispersed with 0.25% trypsin and 0.2% Versene, resuspended in Eagle's medium with 10% FBS and centrifuged at 1000 rpm for 5 min. The cell pellets were resuspended in TBS, counted, and portions containing 1×10^6 cells were dispensed in 13- x 100-mm plastic test tubes (Falcon Plastics) and washed twice more with TBS. After the final wash, the cell pellet was resuspended in 0.1 ml of test serum and mixed by gentle pipetting. After incubating at 37°C for 45 min, the cells were washed three times with 1 ml of TBS and reacted with 0.1 ml of baboon anti-rabbit γ globulin conjugated with fluorescein isothiocyanate. After incubation for 30 min at 37°C, the cells were washed three times with TBS, drained, suspended in a few drops of buffered glycerol (pH 7.0), and examined under a Zeiss fluorescence microscope. Cells showing a bright fluorescence ring around the surface were considered positive. Controls in each test included normal rabbit serum and non-infected cells. Also, a direct immunofluorescence test was carried out using rabbit anti-fibroma γ globulin conjugated with fluorescein isothiocyanate.

Preparation of immune sera. Young adult male New Zealand White rabbits were inoculated intradermally (i.d.) with 1×10^6 PFU of fibroma virus into each of four sites on the shaved backs. Tumors grew for 10 to 12 days and had completely regressed by 3 weeks as described previously (7). The rabbits were inoculated with a second dose of virus on the 4th week after the first injection. These animals demonstrated no tumor development but showed a strong delayed hypersensitivity reaction to the virus. The animals were bled by cardiac puncture 10 to 14 days after the second injection of virus.

Rabbit serum immune to the WR strain of

vaccinia virus was prepared in the same way by two schedules of i.d. inoculation of vaccinia virus. Antiserum to the KOS strain of herpesvirus was prepared by one intraperitoneal (i.p.) inoculation of 7×10^7 PFU of virus followed 3 weeks later by the i.p. injection of 1×10^8 PFU of virus. The rabbits were bled 10 days after the second inoculation. All sera were heat inactivated at 56°C for 1 hr and stored at −20°C. Immune sera to SV40 and Shope papilloma virus were generously supplied by Dr. Janet Butel.

Macrophage migration-inhibition test. Fibroma tumors were induced on the backs of young adult rabbits as described. One week after the tumors had completely regressed, peritoneal exudates were induced by injecting 40 ml of sterile paraffin oil. The exudate cells were harvested 72 hr later and processed for testing in the macrophage migration inhibition test as previously described (7). The antigens to be tested in the migration inhibition test were prepared from rabbit kidney cells in Petri dishes inoculated with 2 to 3 PFU of fibroma virus/cell. At the time of harvest the cells were collected as described for the fluorescent antibody test. Cells from four plates were resuspended in 2 ml of TBS, subjected to three cycles of freeze-thawing and sonicated for 1 min at 10 kc. The infected cell homogenates were diluted 1:40 in Eagle's medium containing 10% FBS plus 5% normal rabbit serum and incorporated into migration chambers containing immune or nonimmune peritoneal exudate cells packed in capillary tubes. The area of migration of the macrophages from the capillary tubes was measured after 24 hr of incubation at 37°C as previously described (7).

Electron microscopy. Cultures of RK_1 cells grown in 16-oz bottles were infected with 1×10^7 PFU of fibroma virus and incubated at 37°C. The cells were removed from the glass surface by the same methods used for preparing cells for the immunofluorescence test. The cells were pelleted and processed for thin section electron microscopy as described by Rhim *et al.* (12).

RESULTS

Demonstration of surface antigen of rabbit kidney cells infected with fibroma virus by immunofluorescence. RK_1, DRK_3, and primary rabbit kidney cells infected with fibroma virus were tested after incubation for 48 hr at 37°C using four different sera collected from rabbits hyperimmune to fibroma virus. All four sera reacted positively in the immunofluorescence test. The reaction reveals a fluorescent ring around the cell (Fig. 1). Approximately 80% to 100% of the cells showed this membrane fluorescence. Normal rabbit sera did not show this reaction with the fibroma-infected cells (Table I). Subsequent experiments were performed using RK_1 cells and serum number 4 (Table I).

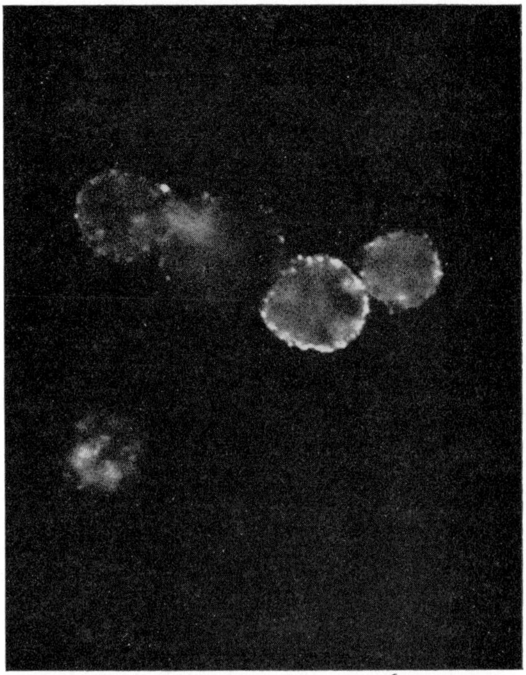

Figure 1. Surface immunofluorescence reaction of RK_1 cells infected with fibroma virus.

Specificity of the surface immunofluorescence reaction. The specificity of the reaction was examined by reacting fibroma-infected RK_1 cells with sera containing antibodies to several other DNA viruses (Table II). Antisera containing antibodies to the SV40, vaccinia or herpesvirus antigens did not react with fibroma virus-infected cells, nor did a serum containing antibodies to Shope papilloma virus. Similarly, fibroma-immune serum did not react with cells infected with vaccinia virus, herpesvirus or SV40, although the homotypic sera reacted strongly with vaccinia- or herpes-infected cells. It is noteworthy that cells infected with vaccinia virus or herpesvirus for 24 hr or greater showed weak fluorescence with heterotypic sera or normal sera. This fluorescence was markedly less than that observed with the homotypic sera and was not present at 18 hr after infection.

The reaction at the surface of the fibroma-infected cells was mediated by immunoglobulins, since partially purified γ globulin reacted specifically with fibroma-infected cells in the indirect immunofluorescence test. Also, rabbit anti-fibroma γ globulins conjugated with fluorescein isothiocyanide reacted specifically with the fibroma virus-infected cells in the direct immunofluorescence test.

TABLE I

Detection of cell surface antigen by immunofluorescence in cells infected with fibroma virus

Rabbit No.	Sera from Rabbits Infected with	Cell Types Infected with Fibroma Virus[a]		
		RK_1[b]	DRK_3[b]	PRK[b]
1	Fibroma	3+[c]	4+	2+
2	Fibroma	4+	4+	2+
3	Fibroma	4+	4+	2+
4	Fibroma	4+	4+	3+
5	No virus	0	0	0
6	No virus	0	0	0

[a] Cells were tested 48 hr after inoculation with 2 to 3 PFU of fibroma virus per cell.

[b] Uninfected cells did not react in the immunofluorescence test. RK_1 and DRK_3 are established lines of rabbit kidney cells. PRK, primary rabbit kidney cells.

[c] Results recorded as estimated intensity of the observed fluorescence: 4+, maximum fluorescence observed; 0, no fluorescence.

The effects of inactivation of fibroma virus and metabolic inhibitors on the appearance of the surface antigen. The requirement for the live virus to induce the synthesis of surface antigen was examined by inoculating RK_1 cells with fibroma virus suspension inactivated by heating at 56°C for 60 min. The inactivated virus failed to induce the synthesis of specific surface antigens.

The effect of DNA inhibitors and protein inhibitors on the synthesis of specific surface antigens was studied by inoculating RK_1 cells with 2 to 3 PFU of fibroma virus per cell. Some cultures received medium containing 20 μg/ml of cytosine arabinoside. Others received medium containing 5×10^{-3} M hydroxyurea, or 10 μg/ml of cycloheximide. Control cultures received medium without inhibitors. After 24 hr incubation at 37°C, the cells were harvested and tested for surface antigen. The surface antigen could not be detected in cultures in which protein synthesis was inhibited with cycloheximide (Table III). In the presence of the DNA inhibitors, cytosine arabinoside and hydroxyurea, there was marked reduction in the intensity of the fluorescence observed. Similar results were obtained when the

TABLE II

Specificity of surface antigen detected by the immunofluorescence test

Virus Used to Prepare Antiserum	Serum Dilution	Fluorescence Reaction: Virus Used to Infect Cells[a]				
		Fibroma	Vaccinia	Herpesvirus	SV40	No virus
Fibroma	Undiluted	3+[b]	0	0	0	0
	1:2	3+	0	0	0	0
	1:4	3+	NT[c]	NT	NT	0
	1:8	2+	NT	NT	NT	0
Vaccinia	Undiluted	0	4+	0	0	0
	1:4	0	4+	0	0	0
Herpesvirus	Undiluted	0	0	4+	NT	0
	1:4	0	0	4+	NT	0
SV40	Undiluted	0	NT	NT	NT	0
Shope papilloma	Undiluted	0	NT	NT	NT	0
None	Undiluted	0	0	0	0	0
	1:4	0	0	0	0	0

[a] RK_1 cells were used 24 hr after infection with fibroma and SV40 virus and 18 hr after infection with vaccinia and herpesvirus.

[b] See Table I.

[c] NT, not tested.

TABLE III

Effect of metabolic inhibitors on the appearance of surface antigen of fibroma-infected cells

Infected Cells Treated with	Fluorescence Reaction with[a]	
	Immune serum	Normal serum
None	3+	0
Cytosine arabinoside[b] (20 μg/ml)	1+	0
Hydroxyurea[b] (5×10^{-3} M)	1+	0
Cycloheximide[b] (10 μg/ml)	0	0

[a] Test performed 24 hr after infection of RK_1 cells with 2 to 3 PFU of fibroma virus per cell.

[b] Inhibitors added to virus inoculum and to the culture medium.

experiments were repeated using DRK_3 and primary rabbit kidney cells.

Temporal relationship of appearance of the surface antigen and of the antigen inhibiting migration of macrophages. Previous studies have demonstrated that peritoneal exudate cells from rabbits immune to fibroma virus failed to migrate over monolayers of cells infected with fibroma virus. This implied that the peritoneal exudate cells were reacting to fibroma-induced antigen at the cell surface (7). The temporal relationship between the appearance of surface antigen detected by immunofluorescence and the antigen-mediated inhibition of migration of peritoneal macrophages was examined by testing cells at intervals after infection with fibroma virus by the two assay procedures. The results shown in Table IV indicate that surface antigen detected by the immunofluorescence test became detectable as early as 6 hr after adsorption and persisted for 120 hr (the longest period tested). The reaction at 6 hr was weak but complete rings were evident. The intensity of the reaction increased up to 24 hr and remained essentially unchanged thereafter.

Significant inhibition of the migration of macrophages was first seen with antigens prepared from cells infected 12 hr earlier with fibroma virus. The degree of inhibition increased with antigens harvested after the infected cells had been incubated for 24 hr and 48 hr. These data confirm our previously published data which showed strong inhibition of migration of macrophages by cells infected 24 to 120 hr before testing (7).

The effect of cytosine arabinoside on the appearance of the antigens which inhibited macrophage migration was also examined. Antigens prepared from cells infected with fibroma virus and incubated for 48 hr in the presence of 20 μg/ml of cytosine arabinoside failed to inhibit the migration of macrophages obtained from sensitized rabbits.

Examination of fibroma-infected cells by electron microscopy. The antigens detected by the immunofluorescence reaction and by the inhibition of macrophage migration could represent virus particles aggregated at the cell membrane. The possibility was explored by examining infected cells in the electron microscope.

An examination of 50 infected cells between 2 and 5 days after infection revealed that no virus particles were associated with the cytoplasmic membranes. Large quantities of cytoplasmic virus were seen in over 80% of the cells examined At 2 days after infection, cytoplasmic inclusions containing mature virus were evident, and by 5 days after infection, many inclusions lacked mature virus and appeared empty. No budding of virus at the cell membrane or virus particles attached to the cell membrane was observed (Fig. 2).

TABLE IV

Time of appearance of immunofluorescence-reacting surface antigen in fibroma virus-infected cells and of the antigen as measured by the inhibition of migration of macrophages from immune animals

Hr Post-Infection[a]	Immunofluorescence Reaction with		% Inhibition of Migration[b]	
	Immune serum	Normal serum	Immune peritoneal exudate cells	Normal peritoneal exudate cells
0	0[c]	0	8	4
2	0	0	1	3
4	0	0	11	9
6	1+	0	10	8
12	2+	0	29	17
24	3+	0	51	11
48	3+	0	64	14
72	4+	0	NT[d]	NT
120	4+	0	NT	NT

[a] RK_1 cell cultures inoculated with 2 to 3 PFU of fibroma virus per cell and harvested at various intervals.

[b] Per cent inhibition =

$$\left[1 - \frac{\text{area of migration with antigen}}{\text{area of migration without antigen}}\right] \times 100.$$

[c] See Table I.

[d] NT, not tested.

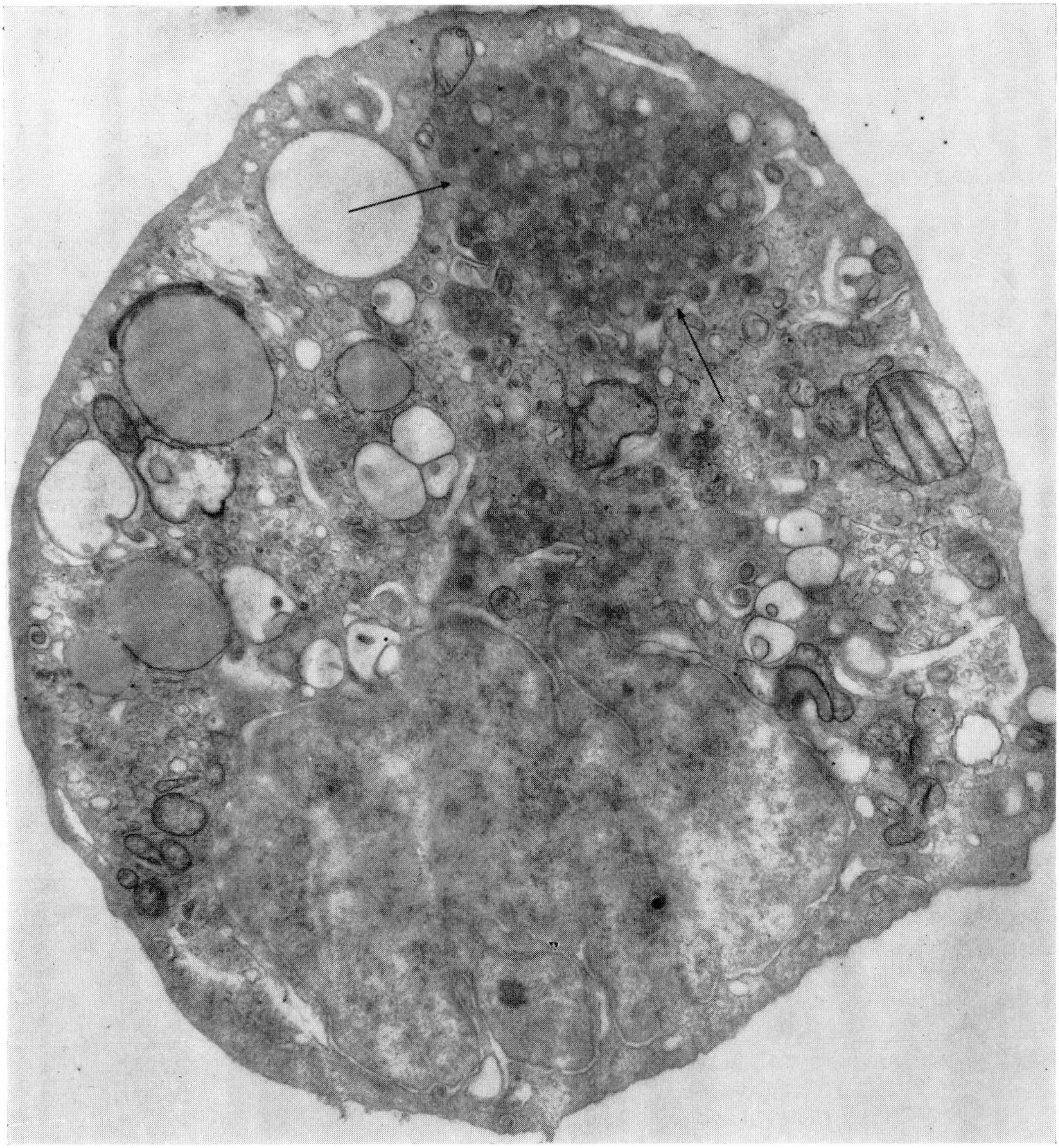

Figure 2. Electron micrograph of RK_1 cell infected with fibroma virus and incubated 4 days at 37°C. Fibroma virus particles are readily observed in cytoplasmic inclusion (*arrows*) but no virus particles are seen at the cell membrane.

The production of antibodies to the surface antigen of fibroma-infected cells in rabbits infected with fibroma virus. Rabbits injected i.d. with fibroma-infected cells develop tumors at the site of inoculation. The tumors grow to maximum size in 10 to 12 days after infection, and then completely regress by 20 to 22 days (7). The relationship between the development of antibodies to the surface antigens of fibroma-infected cells and tumor regression was examined. Adult male rabbits were inoculated at four i.d. sites with 4×10^6 PFU of fibroma virus each and bled at intervals over a period of 4 to 28 days after inoculation. The sera were examined by the

TABLE V

The appearance of antibodies to fibroma-specific surface antigen in rabbits inoculated intradermally with fibroma virus

Time of Serum[a] Collection	Surface Fluorescence on RK_1 Cells Infected with Fibroma Virus[b] for Serum Dilution		
	Undiluted	1:2	1:4
days			
5	0[c]	0	0
6	1+	0	0
7	1+	0	0
8	2+	0	0
9	2+	0	0
10	2+	0	0
14	3+	1+	0
17	3+	1+	1+
19	4+	1+	1+
25	4+	2+	1+
27	4+	4+	2+
28	4+	4+	2+

[a] Rabbits inoculated intradermally with 1×10^6 PFU of fibroma virus at each of four sites.

[b] RK_1 cells tested 24 hr after infection with 2 to 3 PFU of fibroma virus per cell.

[c] See Table I.

indirect immunofluorescence test using RK_1 cells infected with fibroma virus 24 hr before testing.

The results presented in Table V show that low levels of antibody reacting with surface antigen appeared between days 6 and 7 after inoculation. At this time, only 10% to 30% of the cells showed complete rings and the intensity of the reaction was weak. Between days 7 and 14 the number of positive cells increased to 80% to 90%; however, the intensity of the reaction remained weak and the sera did not react at 1:2 dilutions. Between days 14 and 28, when the tumors were regressing, the sera showed an increasing titer of surface-reacting antibody as measured by the intensity of fluorescence and the higher dilutions (1:4) at which the sera were reactive.

DISCUSSION

Infection of cell monolayers with fibroma virus results in the production of virus progeny in the cell cytoplasm. RNA synthesis is first noted 6 hr after infection at which time there is also a marked increase in viral DNA synthesis in the cytoplasm. This DNA synthesis is maximal at 8 hr after infection and has ceased by 14 hr after infection (13). Most of the newly synthesized virus remains cell-associated; maximal amounts of infectious virus were observed at 2 days after infection, and the titer of infectious virus decreases rapidly thereafter (7, 14). The infected cells do not display cytolysis but instead undergo characteristic alterations of cell morphology and show evidence of a loss of contact inhibition. These alterations are readily observed at 48 to 72 hr after infection of the monolayers, and they persist for many days.

The present study demonstrates the appearance of an antigen on the surface of fibroma-infected primary cells or continuous cell lines of rabbit kidney which reacted with fibroma hyperimmune serum in the immunofluorescence test. The antigen appeared to be specific for fibroma virus since sera containing antibodies to vaccinia virus, herpesvirus, SV40 virus or rabbit papilloma virus failed to react with the infected cells. In addition, cultures inoculated with vaccinia virus, herpesvirus or SV40 virus failed to react in the immune fluorescence test with fibroma hyperimmune serum, although the surfaces of the respective cells reacted against homotypic sera.

An absolute requirement for protein synthesis for induction of the antigen in fibroma cells was demonstrated. Treatment of infected cell cultures with inhibitors of viral DNA synthesis (cytosine arabinoside and hydroxyurea) reduced the surface immunofluorescence to barely detectable levels. Studies of the kinetics of appearance of the surface antigen showed that strong surface immunofluorescence appeared only after the infected cells had been incubated for 12 or more hr. The surface antigen persisted for at least 5 days (the longest period tested). The appearance of the antigen after viral DNA synthesis had occurred and the inhibition of the appearance of the antigen by DNA inhibitors indicate that the surface antigen is a late antigen which is dependent upon viral DNA replication for its expression.

Electron microscopic observations showed the virus particles to be localized within the cytoplasm of the infected cell, and no virus particles were found associated with the cell membrane. Even 4 and 5 days after infection, when a strong immunofluorescence reaction of surface antigen was observed and few intact virus particles were found in the cytoplasmic inclusions, there were still no virus particles associated with the cell surface. These observations suggest that the surface antigen induced by fibroma virus is separate from the intact virion and persists at the surface of the cell even after the inclusions have been emptied of most of the infectious virus. Whether the antigen represents nonstructural antigen or viral antigen which is not incorporated into the intact virion remains to be determined.

The data confirm and extend the work of Miyamoto and Kato (15), who detected specific antibody to the antigen of fibroma-infected cells employing the immune hemadsorption test and the immunofluorescence test. The data are different from that reported by Ueda *et al.* (16), who examined cells infected with vaccinia virus for surface antigens using direct immunofluorescence. These authors found an earlier appearance of the antigen and no reduction in the surface immunofluorescence reaction in the presence of cytosine arabinoside. The authors suggested that the vaccinia-induced surface antigen was an early antigen which was not dependent upon viral DNA synthesis.

Rabbits inoculated intradermally with fibroma virus develop palpable tumors at the site of inoculation. The tumors reach maximal size by 10 to 12 days, after which time they undergo regression, and complete resolution of the lesions is accomplished by 3 weeks after infection. Evidence for a cellular immune response to the virus infection becomes apparent by day 5 or 6 after infection when a positive cutaneous delayed hypersensitivity reaction develops and when the migration of peritoneal exudate cells from infected rabbits is inhibited by fibroma virus antigens (7).

The present study indicates that antibody to the surface antigen of fibroma-infected cells appears on the day 7 after infection and remains at a low titer until the tumors begin to regress. As tumor regression proceeded between days 10 and 25 after infection, a parallel increase in the titer of antibody reacting to the surface antigen was observed. The low level of antibody to the surface antigen during the period of tumor growth and early stages of regression suggests that the antibody might adsorb to the infected cells, thus being removed from the circulation; with tumor regression, more antibody would be available in the circulation and this could explain the increased levels of antibody. Evidence for such a phenomenon in a number of neoplasias has been described (3, 11). However, it seems more likely that the increase in titer of the antibody reacting to the surface antigen reflects a shift from the production of IgM globulin to IgG globulin.

Our previous studies have demonstrated a cell-mediated immune response against intact monolayers of cells infected with fibroma virus using the macrophage migration inhibition test (7). The appearance of the antigen which inhibits the migration of macrophages from immune rabbits parallels that of the antigen which reacts in the surface immunofluorescence test, and both antigens persist on the infected cells for at least 5 days. This suggests that the antigen measured by one of the two techniques is the same.

It is our hypothesis that the surface antigen as demonstrated by *in vitro* techniques on cells infected in culture is produced at the surface of fibroma-induced tumor cells *in vivo*. This antigen could function as a transplantation antigen and elicit both a humoral antibody and a cellular immune response. Although it has been possible to demonstrate both a cellular immune response and an antibody immune response to the surface antigens of cells infected with fibroma virus, the significance of either response in the process of tumor regression has not been established. Both immune responses are present early after tumor induction, and both are reactive during the period of tumor growth and regression.

Acknowledgments. The authors wish to express their gratitude to Mrs. Doris Petronella for excellent assistance and to Mrs. Liane Jordan for the electron microscopy.

REFERENCES

1. Klein, G., Ann. Rev. Microbiol., *20:* 223, 1966.
2. Pasternak, G., Advances Cancer Res., *12:* 2, 1969.
3. Hellström, K. E. and Hellström, I., Advances Cancer Res., *12:* 117, 1969.
4. Law, L. W., Cancer Res., *29:* 1, 1969.
5. Allison, A. C. and Friedman, R. M., J. Nat. Cancer Inst., *36:* 859, 1966.
6. Allison, A. C., J. Nat. Cancer Inst., *36:* 869, 1966.
7. Tompkins, W. A. F., Adams, C. and Rawls, W. E., J. Immun., *104:* 502, 1970.
8. Melnick, J. L. and Wenner, H. A., in *Diagnostic Procedures for Viral and Rickettsial Diseases*, 4th Ed., pp. 529–602, American Public Health Association, New York, 1969.

9. Tompkins, W. A. F., Walker, D. L. and Hinze, H. C., J. Virol., *4:* 603, 1969.
10. Rawls, W. E., Tompkins, W. A. F. and Melnick, J. L., Amer. J. Epidem., *89:* 547, 1969.
11. Tevethia, S. S., Couvillion, L. A. and Rapp, F., J. Immun., *100:* 358, 1968.
12. Rhim, J. S., Jordan, L. E. and Mayor, H. D., Virology, *17:* 342, 1962.
13. Ewton, D. and Hodes, M. E., Virology, *33:* 77, 1967.
14. Hinze, H. C. and Walker, D. L., J. Bact., *88:* 1185, 1964.
15. Miyamoto, H. and Kato, S., Biken J., *11:* 343, 1968.
16. Ueda, Y., Ito, M. and Tagaya, I., Virology, *38:* 180, 1969.

THE JOURNAL OF IMMUNOLOGY
Vol. 105, No. 5, November 1970
Printed in U.S.A.

ANTIBODY RESPONSES TO TWO SYNTHETIC POLYPEPTIDES: THE ROLE OF THE THYMIC EPITHELIAL RETICULUM[1]

MARVIN L. TYAN AND HUGH O. McDEVITT

From the Life Sciences Division, Stanford Research Institute, Menlo Park, California 94025 and Stanford School of Medicine, Palo Alto, California 94305

Received for publication May 18, 1970

Thymectomized, lethally irradiated mice that normally respond well to the synthetic polypeptide (T,G)-A--L but poorly to (H,G)-A--L were protected with liver cells and a thymus graft from fetal mice of a strain that responds to these antigens in the opposite manner. All chimeras failed to respond to (T,G)-A--L, but 24 of 27 responded well to (H,G)-A--L. Moreover, when thymectomized mice that respond well to (H,G)-A--L but poorly to (T,G)-A--L were lethally irradiated, protected with syngeneic fetal liver cells, and grafted with thymus from newborn mice of a strain that normally responds well to both antigens, the resultant chimeras responded to (H,G)-A--L only. These data indicate that the control of the antibody response to these two antigens is expressed through a cell type(s) present in the liver during embryonic life. While it is apparent that the presence of the thymus was essential for a detectable response to these synthetic polypeptides, the phenotypic expression of the response was independent of the genotype of the thymic epithelial reticulum.

When adult, thymectomized mice are exposed to a lethal dose of x-radiation and are protected with hemopoietic and lymphoid stem cells from bone marrow or fetal liver, they subsequently have a marked impairment of their ability to reject foreign skin grafts and to produce antibody to some, but not all, antigens (1–4). It has been shown, however, that lymphoid precursors obtained from the livers of mouse embryos as early as the 9th to 12th day of gestation (i.e., prior to the appearance of the thymic rudiment) give rise to cells that are able to produce γG_{2a} and γG_1 immunoglobulins in thymectomized, irradiated hosts as well as they do in nonoperated controls (5, 6). Further, the progeny of these transferred lymphoid stem cells are capable of a detectable, though impaired, 7S antibody response to sheep erythrocytes in the absence of the thymus (7). Thus it would appear not only that immunoglobulin production *per se* is largely thymus-independent, but that lymphoid stem cells have the innate ability to respond to at least certain of the antigens present on sheep erythrocytes.

The above observations suggested that the thymus-stem cell interaction in these, and perhaps in other experimental models (8, 9), was primarily quantitative in nature. That is, the thymus increased the number of effector cells committed to a response, but did not appear to confer specificity or qualitative change upon that response. Preliminary studies on the genetically controlled response to the synthetic polypeptide (T,G)-A--L in radiation chimeras (10) suggested that although the thymus was essential for a detectable response to this antigen, the ability to respond well was dependent upon the genotype of the donor stem cells rather than upon the genome of the reticuloepithelial thymus. The following studies were performed in an effort to more clearly delineate the interaction between the thymus and the precursors of the effector cells in the regulation of this genetically controlled immune response.

MATERIALS AND METHODS

Antigens. The antibody responses of various strains of inbred mice to a series of multichain synthetic polypeptide antigens are quantitative traits under a dominant-determinant-specific type

[1] From the Naval Radiological Defense Laboratory, San Francisco, California (disestablished in November 1969). This work was supported in part by Office of Naval Research, Contract N00014-70-C-0068 and by National Institutes of Health Grant AI-07757.

of genetic control (11, 12). That is, a given strain of mouse may respond poorly, if at all, to one of the antigens while a second strain will respond quite well. These antigens are composed of a polylysine backbone with side chains of poly-DL-alanine and, in the case of the two antigens used in these experiments, terminating in short random sequences of either tyrosine and glutamic acid, (T,G)-A--L, or histidine and glutamic acid, (H,G)-A--L. It has been shown recently that the genetic mechanism controlling these antibody responses is closely linked to the major histocompatibility locus (H-2) of the mouse (13, 14). It was found that all strains of the same H-2 type (except $H\text{-}2^d$) exhibit a similar pattern of immune response to these antigens regardless of the remainder of the strain's genetic background. Of the more frequently used mouse strains, $H\text{-}2^b$ and most $H\text{-}2^d$ mice respond well to (T,G)-A--L and poorly to (H,G)-A--L; the reverse is true for $H\text{-}2^a$ and $H\text{-}2^k$ strains. Although the differences were clearly quantitative, high responder mice will on occasion be termed responders, and low responder mice will be termed nonresponders.

Mice. The hosts were thymectomized, 12- to 16-week-old, male C3H/J or (C57BL/6 × DBA/2)F_1, B6D2F_1, and (C3H × C57BL/6)F_1 mice. The mice were thymectomized 1 to 4 weeks before use, and complete absence of the thymus was confirmed grossly and microscopically when the experiments were terminated.

Donors. Fetal liver cells were obtained from 16- to 20-day-old C3H/J or CBA/J embryos. The livers were dissected free of maternal blood or tissue contamination, minced and suspended in medium 199 (Difco Laboratories, Detroit, Mich.) and injected i.p. into the hosts shortly after irradiation. Each recipient was given approximately 50×10^6 viable nucleated cells.

Thymuses were obtained from CBA/J, C57BL/6J or (C3H × C57BL/6)F_1 mice within 12 hr of their birth. One or two lobes were implanted under the capsule of the left kidney of the thymectomized host within 2 hr after irradiation. When the experiments were terminated, the presence or absence of the graft was determined grossly and microscopically.

Of the mouse strains used, B6D2F_1 respond well to (T,G)-A--L and poorly to (H,G)-A--L; the reverse is true for C3H and CBA mice. (C3H × C57BL/6)F_1 mice respond well to both antigens.

Irradiation. The C3H mice received 840 rads and the B6D2F_1 and (C3H × C57BL/6)F_1 mice 870 rads whole-body x-radiation (250 kvp, 15 ma; half value layer, 1.5 mm Cu).

Immunizations. Sixty days after irradiation the mice were given a primary stimulus with 10 μg of (T,G)-A--L in complete Freund's adjuvant, administered subcutaneously in the inguinal area. Twenty-one days later they received 10 μg of antigen in saline intraperitoneally; 10 days after this they were bled from the retro-orbital plexus and the serum was stored at −20°C until use. Immunization with (T,G)-A--L was repeated 100 days after irradiation, and 10 days after blood was drawn they were immunized in an identical manner with (H,G)-A--L. Previous work has shown that responder-to-responder radiation chimeras are able to produce significant amounts of antibody to these antigens by 45 days after irradiation (6, 10).

Antibody assay. The antibody response was measured by an antigen-binding capacity assay using iodinated (^{125}I) antigens (11–13). The sera were assayed individually at a dilution of 1:250. Previous work has shown that (1) 0 to 5% antigen is bound at all dilutions of normal mouse serum; (2) the antibody produced by nonirradiated, nonresponder mice to either (T,G)-A--L or (H,G)-A--L is 0 to 27% antigen-bound; and (3) 0 to 5% antigen is bound by the sera of nonresponder-to-nonresponder radiation chimeras immunized twice with either antigen. On this basis, a chimera was not considered to have responded to a given antigen unless its serum, at a dilution of 1:250, bound more than 30% of the antigen. The results are reported as the number of mice responding to a given antigen per total number of mice immunized and as the mean percentage of antigen bound.

RESULTS AND DISCUSSION

Thymectomized, lethally irradiated mice that normally respond well to (T,G)-A--L (B6D2F_1) were given liver cells and a thymus graft from nonresponder fetuses (CBA) and immunized with (T,G)-A--L 60 and 100 days after irradiation (Table I). All chimeras failed to respond to (T,G)-A--L (mean antigen bound < 5%), but 24 of 27 responded well to (H,G)-A--L (mean antigen bound 53%). Similarly, when thymectomized C3H mice that respond well to (H,G)-A--L but poorly to (T,G)-A--L were protected with

TABLE I

Response to (T,G)-A-L and (H,G)-A-L by thymectomized, lethally irradiated B6D2F₁ mice given CBA fetal liver cells and thymus graft[a]

Thymus Implant Intact	No. Responding to (T,G)-A--L		Mean % ppt.[b]	No. Responding to (H,G)-A--L	Mean % ppt.[b]
	1°	2°			
Yes	0/44	0/41	<5	24/27	53
No	0/8	0/8	<5	0/8	<5

[a] B6D2F₁ mice respond well to (T,G)-A--L and poorly to (H,G)-A--L; the reverse is true with CBA mice. The mice were immunized with (T,G)-A--L 60 days (1°) and 100 days (2°) after irradiation.

[b] Percentage of antigen precipitated by sera diluted 1:250.

TABLE II

Response to (T,G)-A--L and (H,G)-A--L by thymectomized, lethally irradiated C3H mice given C3H fetal liver cells and a (C3H × C57BL/6)F₁ thymus graft[a]

Thymus Implant Intact	No. Responding to (T,G)-A--L		Mean % ppt.[b]	No. Responding to (H,G)-A--L	Mean % ppt.[b]
	1°	2°			
Yes	0/14	0/14	<5	13/14	47
No	0/2	0/2	<5	0/2	<5

[a] C3H mice respond well to (H,G)-A--L and poorly to (T,G)-A--L. (C3H × C57BL/6)F₁ mice respond well to both antigens. The mice were immunized as in Table I.

[b] Percentage of antigen precipitated by sera diluted 1:250.

TABLE III

Response to (T,G)-A--L and (H,G)-A--L by thymectomized, lethally irradiated (C3H × C57BL/6)F₁ mice given C3H fetal liver cells and a C57BL/6 thymus graft[a]

Thymus Implant Intact	No. Responding to (T,G)-A--L		Mean % ppt.[b]	No. Responding to (H,G)-A--L	Mean % ppt.[b]
	1°	2°			
Yes	0/4	0/4	<5	4/4	36
No	0/1	0/1	<5	0/1	<5

[a] C3H mice respond well to (H,G)-A--L and poorly to (T,G)-A--L; the reverse is true with regard to C57BL/6 mice. (C3H × C57BL/6)F₁ mice respond well to both antigens. The mice were immunized as in Table I. The surviving chimeras were moderately runted.

[b] Percentage of antigen precipitated by sera diluted 1:250.

syngeneic fetal liver cells and grafted with thymus from a strain that responds well to both antigens, (C3H × C57BL/6)F₁, or when a thymectomized host that can respond to both antigens was given liver cells from a strain that responds poorly to (T,G)-A--L and a thymus graft from a strain that responds well, the resultant chimeras failed to respond to (T,G)-A--L but responded well to (H,G)-A--L (Tables II and III). In the experiments presented in Table III, the chimeras were moderately runted, perhaps as a result of a graft-*vs*-host response on the part of the thymic lymphocytes (C57BL/6 *vs* (C3H × C57BL/6)F₁; parental-F₁). No response was elicited in any of the above chimeras when the thymus graft was absent.

In these experiments the genetic control of the immune response appeared to be expressed through a cell type(s) present in the fetal liver and was independent of the genotype of either the host or the thymus donor. These findings are in accord with previous work (6) showing that lymphoid stem cells obtained from responder embryos are capable of responding well to (T,G)-A--L after "maturation" under the influence of the thymus of a nonresponder strain. Although it is apparent from these and other experiments (6, 7, 10) that the reticuloepithelial thymus promotes antibody production in response to most antigens, its role with regard to these two synthetic polypeptides and to sheep erythrocytes seems to be nonspecific. That is, lymphoid precursors have the innate ability to produce γG_{2a} antibody to sheep blood cells; while the thymus increases the number of effector cells committed to this response, it does not appear to be directly involved in antigen recognition or processing (7). It has been demonstrated in these experiments that the phenotype of the antibody response to (T,G)-A--L and (H,G)-A--L is dependent upon the genotype of the stem cell rather than on that of the thymic epithelial reticulum.

Given the present findings, it seems reasonable to conclude that bone marrow (or fetal liver cells) is the source of the precursors of antibody-forming cells, and is also the ultimate source of thymus-passaged, antigen-reactive cells capable of interacting with (T,G)-A--L or (H,G)-A--L. However, these studies do not bear on the question of whether the genetic control of the ability to respond to these antigens is expressed in a bone marrow-derived, antibody-producing cell, a thymus-passaged, antigen-reactive cell, or in a third cell type.

REFERENCES

1. Miller, J. F. A. P., Nature, *195:* 1318, 1962.
2. Miller, J. F. A. P., Doak, S. M. A. and Cross, A. M., Proc. Soc. Exp. Biol. Med., *112:* 785, 1963.
3. Cross, A. M., Leuchars, E. and Miller, J. F. A. P., J. Exp. Med., *119:* 835, 1964.
4. Tyan, M. L., Cole, L. J. and Herzenberg, L. A., Proc. Soc. Exp. Biol. Med., *124:* 1161, 1967.
5. Tyan, M. L. and Herzenberg, L. A. Proc. Soc. Exp. Biol. Med., *129:* 952, 1968.
6. Tyan, M. L., Cole, L. J. and Herzenberg, L. A., in *Advances in Transplantation*, Proceedings of the First International Congress of the Transplantation Society, Edited by J. Dausset, J. Hamburger, and G. Mathe, p. 87, Munksgaard, Copenhagen, 1968.
7. Tyan, M. L., Herzenberg, L. A. and Gibbs, P. R., J. Immun., *103:* 1283, 1969.
8. Miller, J. F. A. P. and Mitchell, G. F., J. Exp. Med., *128:* 801, 1968.
9. Mitchell, G. F. and Miller, J. F. A. P., J. Exp. Med., *128:* 821, 1968.
10. Tyan, M. L., McDevitt, H. O. and Herzenberg, L. A., Transplant. Proc., *1:* 548, 1969.
11. McDevitt, H. O. and Sela, M., J. Exp. Med., *122:* 517, 1965.
12. McDevitt, H. O. and Sela, M., J. Exp. Med., *126:* 969, 1967.
13. McDevitt, H. O. and Tyan, M. L., J. Exp. Med., *128:* 1, 1968.
14. McDevitt, H. O., and Chinitz, A., Science, *163:* 1207, 1969.
15. Claman, H. N., Chaperon, E. A. and Triplett, R. F., J. Exp. Med., *122:* 1167, 1966.

THE JOURNAL OF IMMUNOLOGY
Vol. 105, No. 5, November 1970

Printed in U.S.A.

A TYPE-SPECIFIC IMMUNODIFFUSION TECHNIQUE FOR THE CALIFORNIA ENCEPHALITIS VIRUS GROUP[1]

F. M. WELLINGS,[2] G. E. SATHER AND W. McD. HAMMON

From the Department of Epidemiology and Microbiology, Graduate School of Public Health, University of Pittsburgh, Pittsburgh, Pennsylvania

Received for publication May 18, 1970

The development and evaluation of a California encephalitis virus (CEV) type-specific immunodiffusion (ID) technique is described. Agreement between this typing method and the more conventional complement-fixation test ranged from 96.2% to 100%. To date, type-specific rabbit antisera used in the system have been prepared against Keystone, trivittatus, BFS 283, snowshoe hare, LaCrosse and Jamestown Canyon antigens. A type-specific reaction was obtained with rabbit anti-San Angelo serum following absorption with BFS 283 antigens. However similar absorption of rabbit anti-Tahyna, anti-Lumbo and anti-Jerry Slough sera failed to produce a type-specific response. By screening isolates initially in the ID test using a CEV grouping serum, reacting isolates can quickly be identified by the type-specific antisera in the ID test. The technique is relatively inexpensive and can be performed readily by a technically competent technician in a modicum of time.

Twenty-five years ago the first California encephalitis virus (CEV) isolations were made from mosquitoes in Kern County, California, by Hammon and Reeves (1). Since that time, the originals and subsequent worldwide isolates have been compared by complement fixation (CF), neutralization (N), and to a limited degree, by hemagglutination-inhibition (HI) tests. In all tests, extensive cross-reactivity has been noted, although the CF and N tests have distinguished the homologous systems on the basis of higher titers as shown recently by Sather and Hammon (2).

Murphy and Coleman (3) initiated the use of the double diffusion in agar gel technique to differentiate members of the CEV group. Their identification relied on the nature of the homologous system response, characterized by the formation of unique precipitin arcs and depicted by "individual or multiple dense arcs." These were referred to as major precipitin reactions as opposed to minor reactions in which faint precipitin lines were noted. However, it was pointed out, and has been subsequently observed by us, that the number of lines and relative density of individual arcs varied considerably with the antigens and antisera used. The individual antigen-antibody reactions were frequently difficult to interpret. Therefore, investigations were carried out to develop a system in which only the homologous reactants would precipitate. This report describes the development and evaluation of a CEV type-specific immunodiffusion (ID) technique.

[1] These studies were supported in part by Public Health Service Research Grant AI-02686 from the National Institute of Allergy and Infectious Diseases, and in part under the sponsorship of the Commission on Viral Infections, Armed Forces Epidemiological Board, they were supported by the U. S. Army Medical Research and Development Command, Department of the Army, under Contract DA-49-193-MD-2042. In conducting the research described in this report, the investigators adhered to the "Guide for Laboratory Animal Facilities and Care," as promulgated by the Committee on the Guide for Laboratory Animal Resources, National Academy of Sciences-National Research Council.

[2] In part from a thesis submitted to the Graduate School of Public Health, University of Pittsburgh, as partial requirement for the Doctor of Science in Hygiene degree while the recipient of a fellowship under a Training Grant in Epidemiology from the National Institute of General Medical Sciences, National Institute of Health, United States Public Health Service 5 TO1 GM 00010, supplemented by General Research Support Grant FR 054 51 from the National Institutes of Health.
Present address: Epidemiology Research Center, 4001 Tampa Bay Boulevard, Tampa, Florida 33614.

MATERIALS AND METHODS

Viruses used. The 11 prototypes and additional 2 strains of the CEV group used in this study were: a) California encephalitis (BFS 283) passage 4 (P4) and P19 TDP III[3] (4); b) Trivittatus P18 (5) and B63-373B P6 (6); c) Keystone (TA-26) P4 (7) and Waycross P2 (8); d) Snowshoe hare P15 (9); e) LaCrosse 177 P5 (10); f) Melao (TRVL 9375) P? (11); g) Tahyna (strain "92") P20 (12); h) Lumbo P5 (13); i) San Angelo (20-230) P17 (14); j) Jamestown Canyon (61 V-2235) P3 (15); k) Jerry Slough (BFS-4470) P5 (16).

One other arbovirus included in this study for comparative purposes was Guaroa P12 (17).

All of the aforementioned viruses were available in this department in the form of seed viruses (20% infected suckling mouse brain homogenates in 50% inactivated normal rabbit serum-infusion broth, centrifuged at 1000 × G for 20 min, the supernatant ampouled in 0.7- to 0.9-ml amounts, sealed, and stored at about −65°C).

In addition to the prototype viruses, virus isolates made at the Florida State Board of Health, Encephalitis Research Center were available as mosquito, tissue, and/or early passage mouse brain suspensions.

Infected brains. Each of the seed viruses was passaged intracerebrally (i.c.) in pathogen-free 2- to 4-day-old white Swiss suckling mice (Charles River Breeding Laboratories) to provide infected brains for the preparation of antigens and vaccines. When a majority of the animals exhibited signs of encephalitis, they were killed. Brains were harvested aseptically and stored at approximately −70°C in a Revco deep freezer until needed.

Antigens. Antigens used in this study were of three types: *a) Fifty per cent suckling mouse brain (SMB) antigen.* Infected suckling mouse brains (ISMB) were homogenized with a pestle in a chilled mortar in the presence of sterile alundum, diluted to a 50% homogenate with cold Tris-buffered saline at pH 8.0 and clarified by centrifugation at 27,000 × G for 20 min. The supernatant was distributed in 1-ml amounts in Wasserman tubes and stored at about −20°C. Normal mouse brains (NMB) were similarly prepared. *b) Twenty per cent antigen.* Original isolates from mosquitoes from Florida were passaged IC in SMB and those mice developing signs of encephalitis were killed. From two to five brains were harvested and homogenized in 2 ml of a 50% normal inactivated rabbit serum-infusion broth diluent, giving approximately a 20% suspension. These were prepared and supplied by Dr. Lewis and co-workers at the Encephalitis Research Center, Tampa, Florida. *c) Sucrose acetone (SA)-extracted antigen.* The preparation was made according to the method of Clarke and Casals for hemagglutinating antigens (18), omitting the final lyophilization procedure.

Antisera. Antisera were prepared in albino rabbits weighing approximately 5 to 6 lb and purchased from Hazleton Laboratory, Inc., Falls Church, Va. The rabbits were inoculated with a live virus vaccine prepared as a 20% ISMB homogenate in phosphate-buffered saline, pH 7.4, and clarified by centrifugation at 13,200 × G for 30 min. The primary immunization given each rabbit was 4 ml of vaccine, inoculated intramuscularly (i.m.) in 2-ml amounts into each hindquarter. No adjuvants were used. Booster inoculations when given consisted of an i.m. injection of 2 ml of the vaccine at 2-week intervals following the primary immunization. The anesthetized animals were bled under pentobarbital anesthesia before each inoculation and at 2-week intervals following a single immunization. Animals were exsanguinated by cardiac puncture at 4, 6 or 8 weeks after the primary immunization. Sera were frozen at −20°C in 2-ml amounts.

Mouse ascitic fluid. This was prepared in adult white Swiss mice by intraperitoneal administration of ISMB vaccines in combination with adjuvants in a prolonged series. Animals were tapped at various intervals and the fluids were pooled. The fluid was found to be very broadly reactive by CF and neutralization tests within the CEV group.

Immunodiffusion technique. Two methods of double diffusion in two dimensions were used, both employing the micro-modification of Mansi (19) and Ouchterlony (20). Various agar-buffer systems and a variety of well sizes were tested. The following is the standard methodology adopted. Three milliliters of a 1% agarose-Tris[4]-buffered saline (0.05 M Tris; 0.15 M NaCl) Merthiolate (0.01%) molten preparation at pH

[3] Terminal dilution passage 3.

[4] Trizma base: Reagent Grade, Sigma Chemical Co., St. Louis, Mo.

8.0 was pipetted onto each 1- x 3-in precleaned microscope slide. The coated slides were kept at room temperature until the agar had gelled, then placed in a humidified chamber and either used immediately or stored at 4°C until used. A 3-mm central well, surrounded by six peripheral wells of the same size, at a 3-mm distance from the periphery of the central well to the edge of each satellite well, was cut in the agar on the day of the test. The slide was then placed on a moistened filter paper in a Petri dish. Absorption of the antisera with NMB to remove antibodies formed against non-viral antigens was accomplished by a modification (21) of the method of Dray and Young (22) in which the absorbing antigen was placed in the serum well, allowed to diffuse for 2 hr at room temperature and the residual then removed. The well was refilled with the test serum and antigens were placed in the surrounding wells. The prepared slides were stored at room temperature in a humidified atmosphere until read.

The second method utilized plastic Petri dishes. Twelve milliliters of the molten agarose-Tris-buffered saline at pH 8.0 was pipetted into each Petri dish. When the agar had gelled, the lids were replaced and the dishes were stored at room temperature or at 4°C in a plastic bag containing moistened paper towels. Once sealed, these bags preserved the plates for an indefinite period. The day of the test, as many as eight patterns/plate were cut in the agar.

Reading and recording of results. A viewing box was constructed according to the specifications obtained from Dr. Philip Coleman, National Communicable Disease Center, Atlanta, Georgia. This provided an indirect light source which served for direct reading and for photography. A 4× magnifying hand lens facilitated direct reading. Reaction patterns were recorded at intervals from 18 to 96 hr although the reactions were usually complete by 24 hr. Photographs were taken with a 35-mm reflex camera using a high resolution panchromatic film (Kodak, High Contrast Copy, M135–36).

RESULTS

Initially, rabbit antisera were prepared against Keystone, trivittatus, and BFS 283 antigens. Two weeks following the primary immunization the rabbits were bled and the sera tested by ID. Figure 1*A* is a schematic representation of results obtained when NMB-absorbed rabbit anti-BFS 283 serum was tested against NMB and 11 CEV antigens. A reaction occurred only with the homologous system. However, when NMB-absorbed serum from this same rabbit drawn 2 weeks after a second injection was tested, the antibody spectrum had broadened extensively. Figure 1*B* is a schematic representation of these results. Precipitin lines were formed with all the CEV antigens in the test. However, no reactions occurred with the NMB or Guaroa antigens.

Figure 2 presents further evidence for the specificity of this test. Rabbit anti-Keystone serum, drawn 2 weeks following primary immunization, was tested against NMB and five CEV antigens. In pattern 1, the serum was absorbed with NMB for 2 hr. Reactions were noted only with the two Keystone strains, Keystone and Waycross. In pattern 2, absorption with Keystone antigen was carried out and the precipitin reactions were precluded showing that both reacting antigens were the same, and that reactions in pattern 1 were type-specific.

A trial of this ID typing technique was carried out using 48 unknown viruses, including isolates from Florida and other sections of the country. Four antisera were employed: Keystone, trivittatus, and BFS 283 type-specific rabbit antisera (single injection early bleeding) and a group-specific mouse ascitic fluid (repeated injections with adjuvant) prepared against BFS 283. Preparations of 20% ISMB or sucrose acetone antigens were numbered and only after the ID identifications were made was the code broken and results compared with those obtained by the more conventional CF method. Table I shows the results. There was complete agreement between the two typing systems insofar as the ID typing could be carried out with the reagents on hand. Twenty-four were Keystone, 16 were trivittatus, and none was BFS 283. Four typed as members of the CEV group (no reaction with any of the three type-specific antisera but positive with the group-specific) and four were not CEV isolates (no reactions). These latter were shown to be members of the Bunyamwera group by the CF test.

Through the cooperation of the Encephalitis Research Center (ERC), Tampa, mosquito and mammalian isolates from 1966 and 1967 were made available for ID typing. All the CEV and a number of the non-CEV isolates were run in a

A. *S*, rabbit anti-BFS 283 serum drawn 2 weeks after primary immunization

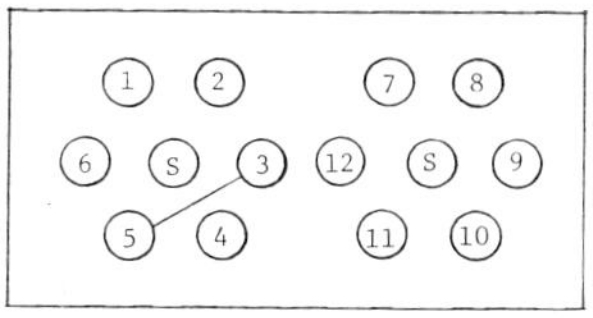

1, NMB; *2*, Keystone; *3*, Waycross; *4*, BFS 283; *5*, San Angelo; *6*, LaCrosse; *7*, Snowshoe hare; *8*, Jamestown Canyon; *9*, Malao; *10*, Trivittatus; *11*, Tahyna; *12*, Lumbo

B. *S*, rabbit anti-BFS 283 serum drawn 2 weeks after booster given 2 weeks after primary immunization

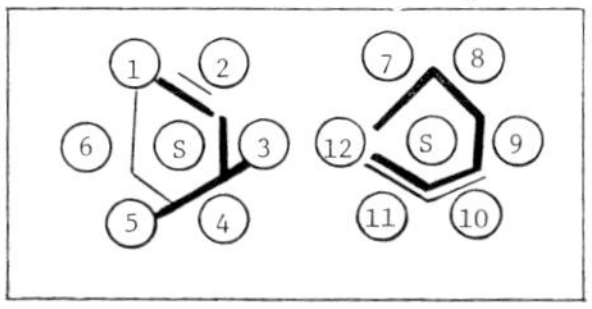

1, NMB; *2*, Keystone; *3*, Trivittatus; *4*, BFS 283; *5*, Jamestown Canyon; *6*, LaCrosse; *7*, Malao; *8*, Tahyna; *9*, Lumbo; *10*, Snowshoe hare; *11*, San Angelo; *12*, Guaroa

Figure 1. Immunodiffusion patterns with various antigens of normal mouse brain-absorbed rabbit anti-BFS 283 serum drawn 2 weeks after initial immunization and 2 weeks following booster inoculation.

Pattern 1 Pattern 2

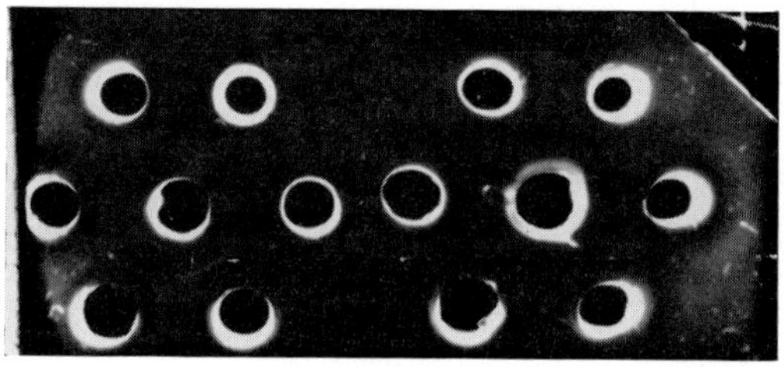

Antigens

1, NMB
2, Keystone
3, Trivittatus
4, Waycross
5, BFS 283
6, Snowshoe hare

Pattern 1 Pattern 2

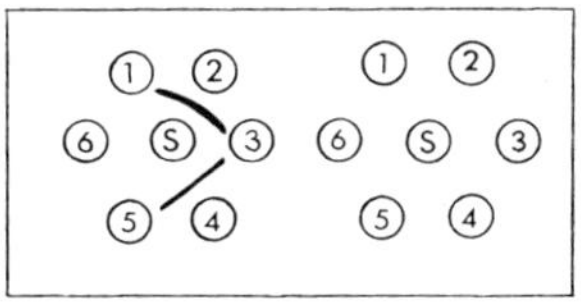

Schematic representation of photograph above
Wells numbered 1–6 in both patterns beginning at 11 o'clock and proceeding clockwise. Antigens the same in both patterns. Serum in central wells absorbed with: NMB in Pattern 1; Keystone antigen in Pattern 2.

Figure 2. Rabbit anti-Keystone serum drawn 2 weeks after primary immunization reacted against various California encephalitis virus antigens.

blind test against Keystone, trivittatus, and LaCrosse type-specific and BFS 283 group-specific rabbit antisera in dilutions of 1:1, 1:2 and 1:4. In 1966, using the CF test, the ERC had identified their isolates by group only, but in 1967, isolates were typed by CF as well. Table II shows the source of identification of the 1966 isolates as determined by both tests. There was an overall agreement of 98.8% (83/84). One antigen, L66-5506.03 P3, had been identified by the CF test as a member of the CEV group. However, it failed to react in the ID test with any of the antisera at any dilution.

In separate tests and of particular interest were 2 of 14 original mosquito suspensions (2 ml of 25% normal rabbit serum-saline/50 mosquitoes) tested which reacted directly as antigens in the ID test. Both of these suspensions of *Aedes atlanticus-tormentor* mosquitoes yielded Keystone isolates and were collected at Big Bend during the weeks of July 13 and July 20. Apparently the number of infected mosquitoes in these pools

TABLE I

Results of typing California encephalitis virus isolates by immunodiffusion and complement fixation tests

Test Systems	Identity and No. of Isolates				
	Keystone	Trivittatus	CEV[a] group	Not CEV group	Total tested
Complement fixation	24	16	4	4	48
Immunodiffusion	24	16	4	4	48

[a] California encephalitis virus.

was exceptionally high. Virus present in the remaining 12 mosquito suspensions could be detected and identified only after suckling mouse passage.

Results of the original CF and later ID identifications of the 1967 isolates are shown in Table III. The overall agreement between the two tests was 96.2% (75/78). Three isolates had been originally identified as Keystone using the CF test but they failed to react in the ID tests. Fifty-three per cent of the ISMB isolates tested were first passage SMB material. All non-reactants were among this group. However, it was determined that for these non-reactive antigens, only two or three mice had been harvested when sick. Death of the other litter mates did not ensue until 2 to 5 days later. In addition, each group of two or three brains had been homogenized and suspended in 2 ml of diluent and then further diluted 1:10 for inoculation into additional litters for the preparation of CF antigens. The unused portion of the 10^{-1}

TABLE II

Identification of 1966 virus isolates by immunodiffusion and complement fixation tests

Source	Immunodiffusion Test			Complement Fixation Test[a]	
	Keystone	Trivittatus	Not CEV[b]	CEV	Not CEV
Aedes					
atlanticus	61	2	0	63	0
infirmatus	4	1	1	6	0
taeniorhynchus	1	1	1	2	1
Anopheles					
crucians	0	0	2	0	2
Culex					
salinarius	0	0	1	0	1
Rabbit	6	0	0	6	0
Cotton rat	2	0	1	2	1
Total	74	4	6	79	5

[a] Encephalitis Research Center Laboratory identification.
[b] California encephalitis virus group.

TABLE III

Identification of 1967 virus isolates by immunodiffusion and complement fixation tests

Source	Immunodiffusion Test			Complement Fixation Test[a]		
	Keystone	Trivittatus	Not CEV[b]	Keystone	Trivittatus	Not CEV
Aedes						
atlanticus	49	0	4	50	0	3
infirmatus	11	4	3	12	4	2
Anopheles						
crucians	0	0	2	0	0	2
Cotton rat	0	0	1	0	0	1
Sentinel rabbit	1	0	1	2	0	0
House mouse	0	0	1	0	0	1
Rat fetus	0	0	1	0	0	1
Total	61	4	13	64	4	10

[a] Encephalitis Research Center Laboratory identification.
[b] California encephalitis virus group.

dilution was ampouled, shell frozen and stored at −70°C until used in the ID test. Thus they represented a brain WT/VO dilution of $>10^{-2}$ and the titers of suspensions were undoubtedly very low.

To date, type-specific rabbit antisera have been prepared against the following CEV antigenic types: Keystone, trivittatus, BFS 283, snowshoe hare, LaCrosse and Jamestown Canyon. Rabbit antisera drawn at 2 weeks following initial immunization against San Angelo, Tahyna, Lumbo, and Jerry Slough failed to react in the ID system. A second injection evoked a broad group-specific response. However, a type-specific reaction did occur with the San Angelo undiluted hyperimmune serum following absorption with BFS 283 antigen. Conversely, such absorption of the remaining three undiluted hyperimmune sera failed to produce a type-specific response.

DISCUSSION

The classical serologic methods of arbovirologists are very time consuming, expensive, and specificity is frequently relatively poor. These disadvantages are compounded in the CEV group because of the poor hemagglutinins produced by many of these agents. Therefore, the more complicated and expensive CF and N tests have been used almost routinely to differentiate CEV isolates.

Murphy and Coleman (3) introduced the double diffusion in agar gel technique as a less time consuming and less costly method for CEV identification. They succeeded in identifying eight antigenic subgroups on the basis of "unique homologous arcs." In our hands, rabbit antisera prepared in the absence of adjuvant but with multiple immunizations failed to show this discrimination in some instances and it was difficult or impossible to decide which of the many complicated patterns did in fact appear to be unique. If this test were to receive general acceptance in a laboratory in which technicians less skilled in the sophisticated interpretation of immunodiffusion reaction patterns were to perform the test, a more discriminating or specific technique would be needed. Therefore, the type-specific antisera discussed herein were prepared. Why three of the nine prototypes failed to elicit an early type-specific immune response in rabbits is not understood. It is recognized that this may be simply the expression of the rabbits' immunologic incompetency. However, the probability of selecting two such animals for each of three virus prototypes and two immunologically competent ones for all others is relatively insignificant. It would appear to be more probable that the difference is virus-related, i.e., perhaps different strains and/or passage levels may have elicited the early type specific response. The large immunizing inocula may also have interfered with the formation of the precipitating antibody which we believe to be closely related to, if not identical with, the CF antibody. Kolman *et al.* (23) have demonstrated considerably lower titers of CF antibody in rabbits following a threefold immunizing dose of Tahyna virus as compared with a small immunizing dose (>1:128 *vs* 1:32). Whether this phenomenon is the result of virus interference and/or interferon production was not stated.

Certain of the early type specific antisera were treated with 2-mercaptoethanol (2-ME) for immunoelectrophoretic studies (to be published). No loss of precipitating antibodies was noted. It has been shown by other workers (24, 25) that CF antibody is not associated with the 2-ME sensitive IgM fraction. Therefore, if CF and precipitating antibodies are analogous, as we believe they are, no loss in the latter following 2-ME treatment would have been expected.

Much additional work needs to be done to explain the antigenic variations in the CEV group. However, since type-specific antisera can be produced against six of the most frequently isolated viruses of the CEV group and the seventh can be produced by absorption of a hyperimmune serum and a type-specific reaction obtained, there is little doubt that differentiation of the majority of the CEV isolates can be a relatively simple procedure using the technique described herein. Screening of isolates should be carried out with broadly reacting hyperimmune mouse ascitic fluids or rabbit hyperimmune antisera prepared against BFS 283. Those reacting can then be identified by testing against the type-specific antisera.

Many advantages of the ID system over the conventional techniques are apparent, particularly if large numbers of isolations are being made. Six isolates can be tested against eight sera in a single Petri dish which in most instances would be sufficient for identification, provided the test sera were selected with perspicacity. All materials needed for the test are relatively inexpensive and can be kept readily available. In addition, a technically competent technician can perform these tests in a modicum of time.

In conclusion, the ID technique, using type-specific rabbit immune sera, appears to offer advantages over the conventional CF technique for the routine identification and typing of members of the CEV group. The usefulness and reliability of the technique have been demonstrated under diagnostic laboratory conditions.

REFERENCES

1. Hammon, W. McD. and Reeves, W. C., Calif. Med., *77:* 303, 1952.
2. Sather, G. E. and Hammon, W. McD., Amer. J. Trop. Med., *16:* 548, 1967.
3. Murphy, F. A. and Coleman, P. H., J. Immun., *99:* 276, 1967.
4. Hammon, W. McD., Reeves, W. C. and Sather, G. E., J. Immun., *69:* 493, 1952.
5. Eklund, C. M., No. 96 in Taylor, R. M., *Catalogue of Arthropod-borne Viruses of the World*, United States Public Health Service Publication No. 1760, 1967.
6. Lewis, A. L., Hammon, W. McD., Sather, G. E., Taylor, D. J. and Bond, J. O., Amer. J. Trop. Med., *14:* 451, 1965.
7. Bond, J. O., Hammon, W. McD., Lewis, A. L., Sather, G. E. and Taylor, D, J., Pub. Health Rep., *81:* 607, 1966.
8. Chamberlain, R. W., Sudia, W. D., Coleman, P. H., Johnston, J. G., Jr. and Work, T. H., Amer. J. Epidem., *89:* 82, 1969.
9. Burgdorfer, W., Newhouse, V. F. and Thomas, L. A., Amer. J. Hyg., *73:* 344, 1961.
10. Thompson, W. H., Kalfayan, B. and Anslow, R., Amer. J. Epidem., *81:* 245, 1965.
11. Spence, L., Anderson, C. R., Aitkens, T. H. G. and Downs, W. G., Amer. J. Trop. Med., *11:* 687, 1962.
12. Bardos, V. and Danielova, V., J. Hyg. Epidem. (Praha), *3:* 264, 1959.
13. Kokernot, R. H., McIntosh, B. M., Worth, C. B., DeMorais, T. and Weinbren, M. P., Amer. J. Trop. Med., *11:* 678, 1962.
14. Grimes, J. E., Garza, E. H. and Irons, J. V., Eleventh Annual Meeting of the American Society of Tropical Medicine and Hygiene, Atlanta, Georgia, Oct. 31–Nov. 3, 1962.
15. LaMotte, J. C., Jr., No. 177 in Taylor, R. M., *Catalogue of Arthropod-borne Viruses of the World*, United States Public Health Service Publication No. 1760, 1967.
16. Reeves, W. C., No. 176 in Taylor, R. M., *Catalogue of Arthropod-borne Viruses of the World*, United States Public Health Service Publication No. 1760, 1967.
17. Groot, H., Oya, A., Bernal, C. and Barretto-Reyes, P., Amer. J. Trop. Med., *8:* 604, 1959.
18. Clarke, D. H. and Casals, J., Amer. J. Trop. Med., *7:* 561, 1958.
19. Mansi, W., J. Comp. Path. Therap., *67:* 297, 1957.
20. Ouchterlony, O., Progr. Allerg., *5:* 1, 1958.
21. Ibrahim, A. N., Proc. Soc. Exp. Biol. Med., *130:* 784, 1969.
22. Dray, S. and Young, G. O., Science, *129:* 1023, 1959.
23. Kolman, J. M., Mal Kora, D., Marhoul, Z., in Symposium on Arboviruses of the California Complex and the Bunyamwera group, Bratislavia, Oct. 18–21, 1966.
24. Bellanti, J. A., Russ, S. B., Holmes, G. E. and Buescher, E. L., J. Immun., *94:* 1, 1965.
25. Best, J. M., Banatvala, V. E. and Watson, D., Lancet, *1:* 65, 1969.

THE JOURNAL OF IMMUNOLOGY
Vol. 105, No. 5, November 1970

Printed in U.S.A.

THE PREVENTION OF AUTOIMMUNITY TO THE THYROID AND ALLERGIC THYROIDITIS BY ANTIGENIC COMPETITION

PHILIP R. B. McMASTER AND MICHAEL KYRIAKOS

From the Laboratory of Microbial Immunity, National Institute of Allergy and Infectious Diseases, National Institutes of Health, Bethesda, Maryland, and the Department of Surgical Pathology, Barnes Hospital, Washington University School of Medicine, Saint Louis, Missouri

Received for publication May 18, 1970

When bovine gamma globulin (BGG) is mixed with thyroid extract in Freund's complete adjuvant, the BGG competes with the thyroid extract and inhibits the development of allergic thyroiditis as well as the production of antibody and delayed sensitivity to thyroid extract. The amount of BGG required to inhibit the production of thyroiditis, anti-thyroid antibody and delayed sensitivity to thyroid extract depends in part upon the amount of thyroid antigen used to immunize and in part upon the location of the two antigens.

In a series of elegant experiments, Adler (1) and his associates proved that an injection of bovine gamma globulin (BGG) could inhibit the immune response to a simultaneous or subsequent injection of ferritin. This phenomenon, termed antigenic competition, has been studied with other sets of antigens including hemocyanin *vs* rabbit globulin (2), red cell antigen *vs* mouse histocompatibility antigen (3) and selected brain antigens *vs* encephalitogenic antigen (4). The results of these experiments indicate that the ability of one antigen to inhibit the immune response to another may be a general property with many antigen pairs. Accordingly, it seemed likely that antigenic competition could alter the development of autoimmunity to the thyroid and the consequent production of allergic thyroiditis. The present study was undertaken to examine this possibility and to clarify some of the conditions that promote that competition.

MATERIALS AND METHODS

Animals. The Rabbit and Rodent Section of the National Institutes of Health supplied the guinea pigs used in these studies.

Antigens. Thyroid glands of Hartley strain and NIH strain guinea pigs were used to prepare thyroid extract for immunization, and the glands of strain 13 guinea pigs were used to make thyroid extract to measure delayed skin reactivity and antibody titers. To prepare the extract, the thyroid glands were ground with four times their weight of physiologic saline and the product was centrifuged to yield a clear supernatant, as described previously (5). This stock thyroid extract was stored at −20°C. For use it was thawed and, if necessary, diluted with saline or mixed with a saline solution of one of the following three antigens: BGG, bovine serum albumin (BSA), or *Limulus hemocyanin*, at the concentrations described below.

Immunization. For immunization 3 volumes of each antigen preparation were emulsified with 1 volume of complete adjuvant composed of Bayol F and Arlacel A (80:20) containing killed *Mycobacterium tuberculosis* strain $H_{37}Rv$ at a concentration of 4 mg/ml. Groups of five strain 13 guinea pigs were then injected intradermally (i.d.) with small portions of the emulsion in multiple sites in the hind feet, hind legs, and posterior flank until each animal had received a total of 1 ml.

Skin tests. The animals were skin tested by injecting intradermally in the flank 0.1 ml of a saline solution of the desired antigen, i.e., the stock thyroid extract, BGG (1 mg N/ml), BSA, (1 mg N/ml) or hemocyanin (4 mg N/ml). The reactions were measured at 24 hr to determine the average diameter, in millimeters, of the induration and erythema. Using these measurements the reaction was graded on a 1 to 4 plus scale as described elsewhere (6).

Antibody titers. After the skin tests had been read, the animals were anesthetized with Nembutal and bled by cardiac puncture to obtain serum for antibody tests. The agglutination tests were performed on serial twofold dilutions of the antiserum using bentonite particles coated with the appropriate antigen as the indicator (5). The reciprocal of the highest dilution which gave specific agglutination of the particles was recorded as the titer.

Histologic preparation and examination of thyroid glands. Unless otherwise stated, the animals were skin tested, bled and thyroidectomized 6.5 weeks after immunization: a time when the degree of thyroiditis was expected to be maximal (5). Once the thyroid glands were removed, they were fixed in 10% formalin and embedded in paraffin. Fourteen serial sections were cut at 6 μ and stained with hematoxylin and eosin. The presence of a significant mononuclear leukocytic infiltrate was considered to establish the presence of allergic thyroiditis. The histologic severity of the disease was graded on a 1 to 4 plus scale as previously described (5).

RESULTS

Effect of immunization with thyroid extract and with thyroid extract plus BGG. Three groups of five strain 13 guinea pigs were immunized with 0.4 mg of thyroid extract N in complete Freund's adjuvant. For comparison, six other groups, each composed of five strain 13 guinea pigs, were immunizaed with an emulsion that contained the same amount of thyroid antigen plus 1 mg BGG N. Four and one-half, 7 and 11 weeks later selected groups were examined. At each of these intervals, one of the groups that had been immunized with thyroid extract alone and one immunized with thyroid extract and BGG were skin tested with thyroid extract. In addition one other group that had been immunized with thyroid extract and BGG was skin tested with BGG. Twenty-four hours after the start of the skin tests, the animals were bled and thyroidectomized, to obtain sera and tissue for analysis. Table I illustrates the results of these studies. Animals immunized with an emulsion of Freund's adjuvant and thyroid extract developed significant thyroiditis, moderate to high levels of anti-thyroid antibody and strong delayed reactions to thyroid. However, the addition of 1 mg of BGG N to the immunizing emulsion prevented the development of thyroiditis. This amount of BGG also inhibited the production of detectable levels of anti-thyroid antibody and of delayed sensitivity to the thyroid. Although the BGG inhibited the immune response to the thyroid, it did stimulate the production of a high level of antibody and dealyed sensitivity to itself.

Quantity of BGG required to inhibit thyroditis produced in response to 0.8 mg thyroid extract N (Table II). A high dose of BGG (1.0 mg N) completely prevented the development of thyroiditis in animals injected with a high dose of thyroid extract (0.8 mg N). In competition with this amount of thyroid extract, a lower dose of BGG (0.1 mg N) prevented the development of the disease in some animals and partly inhibited its production in others. When competing with

TABLE I

Comparative effects of immunization with thyroid extract and with thyroid extract mixed with BGG at various time intervals

Immunized with	Skin Tested with	Weeks after Immunization	Average Degree of Thyroiditis	Average Degree of Delayed Sensitivity to		Reciprocal of Average Antibody Titer to	
				Thyroid	BGG	Thyroid	BGG
Thyroid[a]	Thyroid	4.5	1.7	3	—[b]	22	0
		7	2.2	4	—	16	0
		11	1.6	3	—	8	0
Thyroid[c] and BGG	Thyroid	4.5	0	0	—	0	1000
		7	0	0	—	0	1000
		11	0	0	—	0	2600
Thyroid[c] and BGG	BGG	4.5	0	—	2	0	1000
		7	0	—	3	0	1000
		11	0	—	3	0	4000

[a] Animals immunized with 0.4 mg thyroid extract N.

[b] —, Not skin tested.

[c] Animals immunized with 0.4 mg thyroid extract N and 1 mg BGG N.

TABLE II

Effect of immunization with 0.8 mg thyroid extract N mixed with selected amounts of BGG

BGG N	Average Degree[a] of Thyroiditis	Average Degree of Delayed Sensitivity to[a]		Reciprocal of Average[a] Antibody Titer to	
		Thyroid	BGG	Thyroid	BGG
mg					
0.0	2.0	3.0	—[b]	26	0
1.0	0.0	1.0	3.0	1.5	1,000
0.1	0.8	1.4	3.8	13	4.0
0.01	1.8	3.0	4.0	24	1
0.001	2.0	3.2	0.0	18	0

[a] Animals examined 6.5 weeks after immunization.

[b] —, Not skin tested.

TABLE III

Effect of immunization with 0.08 mg thyroid extract N mixed with selected amounts of BGG

BGG N	Average Degree[a] of Thyroiditis	Average Degree of Delayed Sensitivity to[a]		Reciprocal of Average Antibody Titer to[a]	
		Thyroid	BGG	Thyroid	BGG
mg					
0.0	1.1	3.0	—[b]	7.4	—
1.0	0.0	0.0	—	0.0	820
0.1	0.0	0.6	3	0.8	64
0.01	0.1	2.6	4	0.2	28
0.001	1.2	2.8	3	4.0	4.6
0.0001	1.1	2.6	0	4.8	0

[a] Animals examined 6.5 weeks after immunization.

[b] —, Not tested.

this high dose of thyroid extract, an even lower amount of BGG (0.01 mg N) did not appear to inhibit the development of the disease at all, for animals immunized with such a mixture had as much disease (grade 2+) as those given 0.8 mg of thyroid extract N alone.

Quantity of BGG required to inhibit thyroiditis produced in response to a low dose of thyroid extract (0.08 mg N) (Table III). Guinea pigs inoculated with 0.08 mg of thyroid extract N ordinarily developed grade 1+ thyroiditis. However, when doses of BGG as low as 0.01 mg of N were mixed with this amount of thyroid extract, the development of thyroiditis was inhibited in nearly all the animals.

Effect of BGG on antibody and delayed hypersensitivity to the thyroid (Table II). Adding BGG to the immunizing emulsion altered the production of antibody and delayed hypersensitivity to the thyroid. Animals that were injected with the high dose of thyroid extract (0.8 mg N) developed high titers of antibody and intense levels of delayed sensitivity to the thyroid antigen. When 1.0 mg of BGG N was added to the high dose of thyroid extract for immunization, the animals produced only low anti-thyroid antibody titers and low levels of delayed hypersensitivity to the thyroid. When a reduced dose of BGG (0.1 mg N) was employed with the same high dose of thyroid for immunization, the animals developed significantly higher titers of serum anti-thyroid antibody and somewhat higher levels of delayed sensitivity to the thyroid. However, if the amount of BGG was still further reduced (0.01 mg N), the production of anti-thyroid antibody and delayed sensitivity to the thyroid were hardly inhibited at all (Table II).

The inhibitory effect of small amounts of BGG in the immunizing emulsion upon the anti-thyroid immune response was more pronounced in animals given the low dose of thyroid extract (0.08 mg N) (Table III). In these animals, the development of antibody to the thyroid was greatly inhibited by the three higher concentrations of BGG (1.0, 0.1 and 0.01 mg of BGG N). In addition, delayed hypersensitivity to thyroid was also severely inhibited by the two higher concentrations of BGG (1.0 and 0.1 mg of BGG, N). However, significant delayed reactions to the thyroid extract (26 mm in diameter) developed in the animals immunized with an emulsion containing the lower dose of BGG (0.01 mg of BGG N).

Antigenic competition with other antigens. The competitive effects of two other antigens, BSA and *Limulus hemocyanin*, were also studied. When mixed with 0.8 mg of thyroid extract N, 1.4 mg of BSA N moderately reduced the degree of thyroiditis, anti-thyroid antibody titer, and delayed sensitivity to the thyroid. Moreover, 3 mg of *Limulus hemocyanin* N totally prevented the production of the disease as well as detectable antibody and delayed hypersensitivity (Table IV).

Effect of inoculating the competing and inciting antigen separately. The influence of the position of the competing antigen (BGG) and the inciting antigen (thyroid) was studied. When the animals were immunized with thyroid emulsified in com-

TABLE IV

Effect of immunization with thyroid extract and with thyroid extract mixed with either BSA or hemocyanin

Immunized with	Average Degree of Thyroiditis[a]	Reciprocal of Average Anti-thyroid Antibody Titer[a]	Average Degree of Delayed Sensitivity to Thyroid[a]
Thyroid[b]	2.2	12	4.0
Thyroid and BSA[c]	1.3	1.6	1.6
Thyroid and hemocyanin[d]	0.1	0	0.2

[a] Animals examined 6.5 weeks after immunization.

[b] Eight-tenths milligram of thyroid extract N.

[c] One and four-tenths milligrams of BSA N used/animal.

[d] Three milligrams of *Limulus hemocyanin* N.

plete adjuvant in one hindquarter and the competing antigen (BGG) in the other, they developed as much thyroiditis, anti-thyroid antibody and delayed sensitivity to the thyroid as the controls given just thyroid extract.

DISCUSSION

Although the etiology of autoimmunity to the thyroid in man remains obscure, it seems possible that an infectious agent might disrupt a portion of the gland, thereby releasing autoantigen in such a form that it could immunize and cause disease. If, however, antigenic competition might modify the development of autoimmunity, then that competition might be a determining factor in the development of allergic thyroiditis.

Such a concept is predicated on the assumption that antigens can compete with thyroid antigens and alter the frequency and intensity of autoimmunity. The experiments reported herein indicate that that assumption is valid.

It was shown that all the antigens studied—BGG, BSA or hemocyanin—may inhibit the development of experimental allergic thyroiditis when incorporated in the immunizing emulsion along with the thyroid extract. Indications are that the nature of the antigen required to inhibit the development of autoimmunity does not appear to be highly restricted, because BGG, BSA, and hemocyanin all competed effectively despite having great differences fro : the thyroglobulin molecule in charge, size, and antigen structure.

Certain conditions that promote antigenic competition were also clarified by the experiments. The BGG competed effectively only when it was inoculated in the same region as the thyroid antigen. In addition, the amount of BGG required to inhibit the production of thyroiditis did not depend solely upon the animal or the nature of the adjuvant but varied with the amount of thyroid extract against which it had to compete.

Similarly, the amount of BGG required to inhibit the formation of anti-thyroid antibody and delayed sensitivity to the thyroid varied directly with the amount of thyroid extract used. When high doses of thyroid extract were used to immunize, only high doses of BGG gave a pronounced inhibition of these factors. However, when a lower dose of thyroid extract was used, even a low dose of BGG was sufficient to inhibit antibody and delayed sensitivity to the thyroid. In general, antigenic competition reduced the anti-thyroid antibody titer and delayed sensitivity to the thyroid to roughly the same extent. However, one salient exception to this generality is of interest, for it may help clarify some aspects of the pathogenesis of the disease. One group of animals (those given 0.08 mg of thyroid extract N and 0.01 mg of BGG N, Table III) made very little anti-thyroid antibody, yet they had a significant level of delayed sensitivity to the thyroid. Nevertheless, four out of five of them did not have any detectable thyroiditis. It is not yet known whether all forms of delayed sensitivity are the same or whether there may be different types, as there are classes of antibody. Moreover, it is not known whether delayed sensitivity to one determinant group on a molecule, such as thyroglobulin, must necessarily produce the same tissue reaction as delayed sensitivity to another determinant on the same molecule. Nevertheless, despite these problems, the results of these experiments add to the evidence that delayed skin sensitivity to thyroid extract by itself does not necessarily produce thyroiditis. Whether it can, however, influence the degree of thyroiditis by acting in concert with other agents remains to be studied.

The number and variety of cells stimulated by

thyroid antigen and by the competing antigens remains undetermined. However, the fact that many antigens can compete with thyroglobulin would indicate that the production of anti-thyroid antibody and delayed hypersensitivity in this experimental system involves, at some point, the participation of cells that react to many antigens rather than just a few or only one (7, 8). Similarly, the precise site and biochemical path in the cell at which the antigens compete also remain to be determined. It may be that the antigens compete in or on a cell type involved with the early part of the immune response, and interfere with antigenic recognition or with the processing of antigens. Alternatively the competing antigen may act at a later point and interfere with the production or use of specific messenger RNA (9).

REFERENCES

1. Adler, F. L., Progr. Allerg., *8:* 41, 1964.
2. Adler, F. L., J. Immun., *78:* 201, 1957.
3. Eidinger, D., Khan, A. S. and Millar, K. G., J. Exp. Med., *128:* 1183, 1968.
4. Einstein, E. R., Csejtey, J., Davis, W. J. and Rauch, H. C., Immunochemistry, *5:* 567, 1968.
5. McMaster, P. R. B., Lerner, E. M., II and Exum, E. D., J. Exp. Med., *113:* 611, 1961.
6. McMaster, P. R. B., Lerner, E. M., II, Kyriakos, M. and Mueller, P. S., J. Immun., *99:* 201, 1967.
7. Amkraut, A. A., Garvey, J. S. and Campbell, D. H., J. Exp. Med., *124:* 293, 1966.
8. Schechter, I., J. Exp. Med., *127:* 237, 1968.
9. Fishman, M. and Adler, F. L., in *Proceedings of the 3rd International Symposium on Immunopathology*, Edited by P. Grabar and P. A. Miescher, p. 79, B. Schwabe, Basel, 1963.

THE JOURNAL OF IMMUNOLOGY
Vol. 105, No. 5, November 1970
Printed in U.S.A.

CONVERSION OF SOLUBLE IMMUNE COMPLEXES INTO COMPLEMENT-FIXING AGGREGATES BY IgM-RHEUMATOID FACTOR[1]

JOSEPH T. TESAR[2] AND FRANK R. SCHMID

From the Section of Arthritis-Connective Tissue Diseases, Department of Medicine, Northwestern University-McGaw Medical Center, Chicago, Illinois 60611

Received for publication May 18, 1970

Complement fixation was studied after aggregation of soluble immune complexes by IgM-rheumatoid factors (RF). Such aggregates fixed larger amounts of complement than did soluble complexes alone. The extent of this reaction was dependent upon the antigen-antibody ratio in the complex. Complement-fixing ability of those complexes formed near equivalence could be further enhanced by IgM-RF, while those formed in greater antigenic excess with little or no ability to fix complement could be aggregated and converted into complement-fixing units by IgM-RF. The composition of complexes that most readily reacted with RF to form aggregates contained two or more molecules of IgG antibody. Within the aggregate, the major share of complement fixation was mediated by the RF component rather than the IgG antibody. These observations are consistent with the view that RF blocks the binding site on IgG for complement and substitutes its own instead. Under the conditions employed, this substitution resulted in a net increase in complement fixation.

Rheumatoid factor (RF) exists as an IgM antibody[3] with major specificity directed toward antigenic determinants on the IgG molecule that are revealed by aggregation (2, 3). In this reaction, RF fixes complement (4–6). Conditions responsible for such fixation remain largely unexplored and, in fact, earlier reports indicated absence or inhibition of complement activation by RF (7–10). The present study investigates some of the features of complement fixation in this double antibody system in which IgM-RF binds to IgG antibody present in immune complexes of varying antigen-antibody ratios. Complement fixation was shown to be enhanced for those IgG complexes formed near equivalence that already possessed this ability. Smaller complexes formed in greater antigen excess that lacked this ability could be aggregated by RF into complement-fixing units. The RF component in the aggregate of RF and immune complex was found to be responsible for the major share of the observed complement fixation.

[1] This work was supported by Grants AM 11513 and AM 5069 from the United States Public Health Service, and by the Illinois Chapter, Arthritis Foundation.

[2] Recipient of Laidlaw Fellowship in Rheumatic Diseases.

[3] While RF of the IgG and IgA classes have also been described (1), the data in this report will be limited to RF of the IgM class.

MATERIALS AND METHODS

Rheumatoid factor. Human sera with strong agglutinating titers were inactivated at 56°C for 30 min and absorbed with washed sheep red cells to remove Forssman antibodies. Such serum (5 to 15 ml) was incubated for 16 hr at 4°C with about 450 mg of human IgG (Cohn fraction II) made insoluble by cross-linkage with bis-diazotized benzidine (11). The mixture was sedimented by low speed centrifugation and the sediment resuspended and washed three times with 0.15 M NaCl. RF was eluted in small volumes (5 to 10 ml) of 0.3 M acetate buffer (pH 4.0) and bovine gelatin (5 mg/ml) was added. The IgM fraction was obtained by ultracentrifugation of the acid eluate on a discontinuous density gradient of 10% to 40% sucrose in acetate buffer pH 4.0. This fraction was dialyzed overnight in the cold against 0.1 M glycine, 0.05 M saline buffer, pH 7.0. Portions of purified RF were stored at −20°C until used. On immunoelectrophoresis, IgM was the only protein present but in some preparations trace amounts of IgG were noted. An occasional preparation was found to be anticomplementary and was discarded. Agglutinating titers were determined by a microtiter modification of the sheep cell agglutination procedure using cells coated with one-quarter the amount of rabbit amboceptor needed for agglutination. The reciprocal of the titer present in 1 ml of a given preparation was considered as the number of agglutinating units of the preparation. IgM protein content of some preparations was quantitated by measuring their optical densities at 280 nm, based upon an extinction coefficient ($E_{1cm}^{1\%}$) obtained in our laboratory of 12.6.

Bovine serum albumin (BSA). Crystalline BSA (Pentex, Inc., Kankakee, Ill.) was used for immunization of rabbits as well as for preparation of immune complexes. Labeling with ^{131}I was performed according to the method of McConahey and Dixon (12).

Anti-bovine serum albumin (anti-BSA). Anti-BSA antibodies were raised in four rabbits by injections of BSA in Freund's adjuvant over a period of 12 months. No precipitating activity against human serum albumin or against the non-albumin fractions of rabbit serum was found by immunodiffusion and immunoelectrophoresis in agar. The sera were pooled and their antibody content was determined in a quantitative precipitation test. One milliliter of anti-BSA serum contained 10.4 mg of antibody protein. This antibody after elution from a BSA immunoadsorbent made by the method of Avrameas and Ternynck (13) was found to be almost exclusively IgG globulin by immunoelectrophoresis against antisera both to whole rabbit serum and to rabbit immunoglobulin G.

Reduction and alkylation of anti-BSA antiserum (ME-anti-BSA). Anti-BSA antiserum, diluted 10-fold in phosphate saline buffer, pH 7.0, was treated for 3 hr at 37°C with 2-mercaptoethanol at a final concentration of 0.1 M according to the method of Wiedermann *et al.* (14). The serum was dialyzed against 0.02 M iodoacetamide in phosphate saline buffer, pH 7.2, for 4 hr at room temperature and overnight against the buffer alone at 4°C. Precipitated protein was removed by centrifugation for 30 min in a Beckman preparative ultracentrifuge at 35,000 rpm in a SW-39 rotor. The antibody content was again determined by the quantitative precipitation technique. Only slight loss of antibody activity was noted. Antibody levels of such treated sera were adjusted to equal the level of untreated antibody.

Human complement preparations. Sera of healthy young individuals free of RF activity were absorbed three times for 10 min at 0°C with washed, cooled sheep red cells to remove anti-Forssman antibodies. The absorbed serum was centrifuged at 7,500 × G for 15 min at 4°C to remove red cell remnants. Portions of serum were kept frozen at −65°C until used. Complement titer was determined by the method of Mayer (15) with the following modifications. Volumes of all reagents were scaled down to 40%, that is, the final volume in the reaction mixture was 3.0 ml and contained 2×10^8 sheep erythrocytes. Values obtained in these reduced volumes were corrected to those of a 100% volume system in the final calculation. Sensitized sheep red cells were coated with optimal amounts of rabbit IgM hemolytic antibody that had been separated from whole serum by G-200 Sephadex gel filtration. The IgM antibody was shown to be free of IgG by immunodiffusion against anti-rabbit IgG antiserum and, when coated on sheep red cells, did not react with RF in an agglutination test.

Complement fixation. The ability of immune complexes and RF to fix complement was determined in the conventional two-phase system (16). In the first phase, a quantity of human serum containing from 2.0 to 6.0 CH_{50} units of complement was added to mixtures of BSA antigen, IgG anti-BSA antibody, and IgM-RF in a final volume of 2.6 ml. The amount of IgG antibody in a given experiment was held constant and the amount of BSA antigen was varied to provide immune complexes with the same IgG content but differing antigen-antibody ratios. All reagents were kept at 4°C and were added within a span of 5 to 10 min in the following order: antigen, antibody, RF and complement. The text mixture was then incubated for the time periods and temperatures indicated. Immediately afterwards, in the second phase, the amount of complement remaining after fixation was determined using sheep erythrocytes coated with optimal amounts of IgM rabbit hemolysin. The use of IgM hemolysin precluded the binding of RF to sensitized erythrocytes, a condition that would have influenced the complement determination (Schmid, F. R., Roitt, I. M. and Rocha, M. J., unpublished observations). These assays for residual complement were made at 37°C for 60 min upon portions of the phase-one mixture suitably diluted for measurement of hemolysis. Volumes of all reagents were reduced to 40% of the standard volume, as noted earlier, but all calculations were expressed in terms of the 100% system. Appropriate correction for nonspecific decay of complement during incubation was made from reaction mixtures lacking BSA antigen.

The slope (1/n) of the Van Krogh equation used to calculate the amount of complement fixed in these experiments was found to be 0.35 rather than the usual value of 0.2. Such a change in slope, reflecting a change in the kinetics of complement fixation, most likely was due to consumption of certain complement components whose initial concentration was marginal in the small amounts of complement that were employed (17, 18).

Ultracentrifugal studies. BSA, labeled with ^{131}I, anti-BSA antiserum, and IgM-RF were mixed in a volume of 1.0 ml phosphate-buffered saline, pH 7.2. After incubation at 37°C for 90 min, the sample was layered on top of a 4.5 ml continuous sucrose gradient (10% to 50%) and centrifuged in a Spinco model L ultracentrifuge at 40,000 rpm (96,592 × G) for 16 hr in a SW-50 rotor. Fractions were collected by gravity through a pin hole made in the bottom of the tube and radioactive counts determined in a well-type scintillation counter.

RESULTS

Precipitation of BSA-anti-BSA immune complexes by RF. To tubes containing 1 ml of rabbit anti-BSA antiserum (1050 μg antibody protein) increasing amounts of BSA were added (Fig. 1*A*). A second row of tubes, set up in parallel, received, in addition, 100 agglutinating units of an RF preparation. After incubation at 37°C for 90 min to equal the time used in complement fixation experiments reported below, each precipitate was separated and washed three times by centrifugation at 7500 × G for 30 min. The precipitin curve showed maximal precipitation of complexes at equivalence (100 μg BSA protein) and solubilization of complexes in antigen excess. Addition of RF increased the total amount of protein precipitated over the entire range of the curve with the greatest differential effect noted between two and five times equivalence.

Precipitation of BSA-ME-anti-BSA immune complexes by RF. Experiments carried out with anti-BSA antiserum which had been treated with 2-mercaptoethanol (ME) yielded results similar to those obtained with untreated antiserum (Fig. 1*B*). The precipitin curve formed with ME-anti-

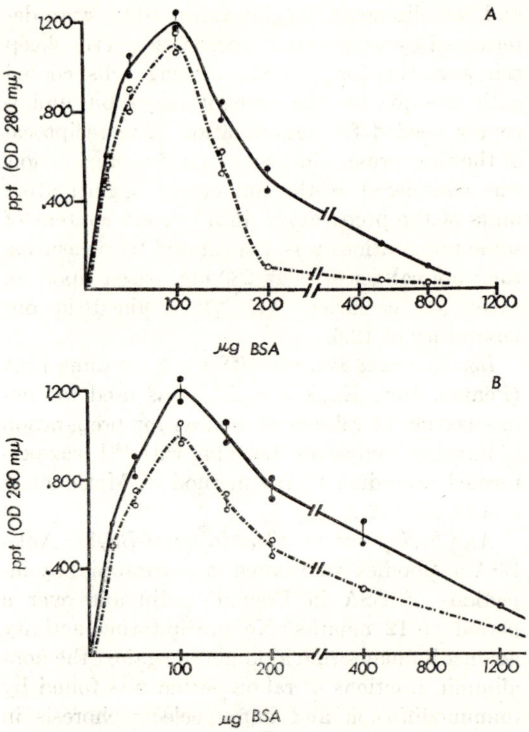

Figure 1. Quantitative precipitin curves formed by immune complexes and rheumatoid factor (RF). Lines drawn through the means of two experiments. Order of addition of reagents: bovine serum albumin (BSA), rabbit IgG anti-BSA antiserum, and RF. Incubation at 37°C for 90 min. Protein content of each precipitate after dissolution in 0.1 M NaOH determined by spectroscopy at 280 nm. *A*, complexes formed by increasing amounts BSA with a constant amount anti-BSA (1050 μg antibody protein) shown by interrupted line. Similar complexes to which a constant amount RF (100 agglutinating units) had been added shown by solid line. *B*, complexes formed by increasing amounts BSA with a constant amount anti-BSA, treated with mercaptoethanol (1050 μg antibody protein) shown by interrupted line. Similar complexes to which a constant amount RF (100 agglutinating units) had been added shown by solid line.

BSA, however, showed larger amounts of precipitation on the descending limb than that formed with untreated complexes. This effect and our observation in other experiments that the combination of ME-anti-BSA antiserum and RF in the absence of BSA produced slight degrees of complement fixation suggested that reduction and

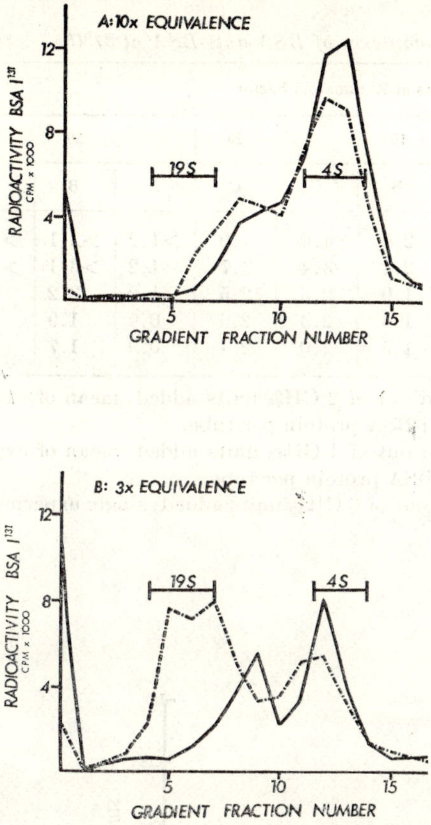

Figure 2. Aggregation of soluble immune complexes formed at antigen-antibody ratios of 3 and 10 times equivalence by IgM-rheumatoid factor. Equal amounts of anti-BSA protein (13 μg) in each set of complexes as well as equal numbers of radioactive counts of ^{131}I attached to the BSA component. Ultracentrifugal separation of these complexes according to their mass on a continuous sucrose density gradient (10 to 50%). The 4S region of the gradient determined by the free BSA peak; the 19S region by an IgM-RF marker in another gradient lacking immune complexes. *A*, complexes formed at 10 times equivalence (-----) compared to a parallel set of complexes to which 200 agglutinating units of RF had been added (——). *B*, complexes formed at three times equivalence (-----) compared to a parallel set of complexes to which 200 agglutinating units of RF had been added (——).

alkylation had caused the formation of small amounts of IgG aggregates in the antiserum.

Aggregation of soluble immune complexes by RF. The size of immune complex to which RF most readily binds was defined by ultracentrifugal studies. Immune complexes prepared at antigen-antibody ratios of 10 (Fig. 2*A*) and 3 times (Fig. 2*B*) equivalence contained the same amount of anti-BSA protein (13 μg) as well as the same number of radioactive counts of ^{131}I attached to the BSA component. Separation of these complexes according to their mass was accomplished on a continuous sucrose density gradient (10% to 50%). The majority of the complexes at both 10 and 3 times equivalence were distributed in the 19S or lighter regions of the gradient. When compared to a parallel system of complexes to which 200 agglutinating units of RF had been added, it can be seen that some soluble complexes had been aggregated into larger masses. At 10 times equivalence, RF caused a slight increase in the quantity of aggregated material that sedimented to the bottom of the gradient. The bulk of small-size complexes was unaffected. At three times equivalence, however, a substantial increase in the amount of aggregates occurred, most of which was derived from the combination of RF with BSA-anti-BSA complexes of the size that had segregated in the 19S region of the gradient.

Complement fixation by immune complexes and RF at 37°C. The ability of immune complexes and RF to fix complement was tested under conditions of time and temperature of incubation similar to those used in the precipitin reaction. From 2 to 6 CH_{50} units of complement were added in rapid succession to tubes that had received BSA, anti-BSA, and various amounts of RF. These were incubated for 90 min at 37°C and residual complement was determined by adding red cells sensitized with IgM hemolysin (Table I). Smaller amounts of complement were useful in detecting minimal amounts of fixation as well as any anti-complementariness in the reagents while larger amounts permitted assay over the full range of fixation. BSA-anti-BSA complexes alone fixed considerable complement at equivalence and lesser amounts in antigen excess. Addition of increasing amounts of RF in each instance increased the amount of complement fixed.

That a direct relationship existed between the degree to which RF aggregated and precipitated immune complexes and its ability to influence complement fixation may be readily seen in Figure 3. Fifty agglutinating units of RF were tested in this comparison but the relative amount of RF in the precipitin reaction was only one-tenth that used in complement fixation since larger amounts

TABLE I

Complement fixation by rheumatoid factor and complexes of BSA-anti-BSA at 37°C

Equivalence of Complex	Agglutinating Units of Rheumatoid Factor											
	0			5		10			20	50		
	A[a]	B[b]	C[c]	A	B	A	B	C	C	A	B	C
1 ×	1.1	2.1	3.8	1.1	2.5	1.2	2.6	4.0	4.0	>1.2	>3.1	>4.2
2 ×	0.2	1.6	3.0	0.7	1.9	1.1	2.4	3.4	3.7	1.2	>3.1	>4.2
5 ×	0.1	1.4	2.0	0.3	1.5	0.5	1.9	2.3	2.5	1.2	2.2	3.5
10 ×	0	1.4	1.6	0.2	1.5	0.3	1.6	2.3	2.6	0.9	1.9	3.1
20 ×	0	<1.4	1.3	0.1	<1.4	0.2	1.5	2.0	2.4	0.9	1.7	3.1

[a] A, number of CH_{50} units of human complement fixed out of 2 CH_{50} units added; mean of experiments using three different RF preparations; 10.4 μg anti-BSA protein per tube.

[b] B, number of CH_{50} units of human complement fixed out of 4 CH_{50} units added; mean of experiments using two different RF preparations; 10.4 μg anti-BSA protein per tube.

[c] C, number of CH_{50} units of human complement fixed out of 6 CH_{50} units added; single experiment; 20 μg anti-BSA protein per tube.

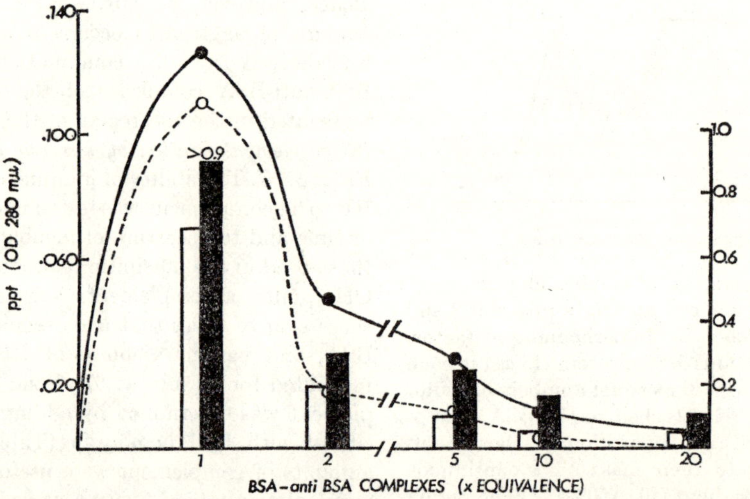

Figure 3. Relationship between amount of precipitate formed and complement fixed by immune complexes and IgM-rheumatoid factor. Precipitin curves formed by BSA-anti-BSA complexes (-----) and by BSA-anti-BSA complexes and RF (——), using 100 μg anti-BSA antibody protein and 50 RF agglutinating units. Complement fixation was assayed for BSA-anti-BSA complexes (▯) and for BSA-anti-BSA complexes and RF (▮) using 10 μg anti-BSA antibody protein, 50 RF agglutinating units and 2.0 CH_{50} units of complement per assay.

of immune complexes were necessary for accurate quantitation of the amount of precipitate formed. Nevertheless, increases in amounts of complexes precipitated by RF were associated with proportionally increased levels of complement fixation.

Complement fixation by RF after interaction with non-complement-fixing immune complexes. Treatment of anti-BSA antiserum with 2-mercaptoethanol (ME) markedly reduced its capacity to fix complement while leaving intact both its ability to react with BSA and its antigenic determinants for RF (Fig. 1*B* and Table II). Little or no complement was fixed by complexes formed with ME-anti-BSA at all equivalences in the presence of 2.0 to 6.0 CH_{50} units of complement. Addition of increasing amounts of RF increased the amounts of complement fixed with each type

TABLE II

Complement fixation by rheumatoid factor and complexes of mercaptoethanol-treated BSA-anti-BSA at 37°C

Equivalence of Complex	Agglutinating Units of Rheumatoid Factor											
	0			5		10			20	50		
	A[a]	B[b]	C[c]	A	B	A	B	C	C	A	B	C
1 ×	0	1.2	1.4	1	1.8	>1.2	2.5	2.5	3.1	>1.2	>2.8	4.0
2 ×	0	<1.2	0.9	0.8	1.3	>1.2	2.4	2.4	3.0	>1.2	>2.8	3.9
5 ×	0	<1.2	0.5	0.6	1.2	0.9	1.7	1.9	2.5	>1.2	2.8	3.8
10 ×	0	<1.2	0.5	0.6	1.2	0.7	1.6	1.8	2.3	1.2	2.6	3.5
20 ×	0	<1.2	0.3	0.5	1.2	0.6	1.3	1.9	2.3	1.1	2.4	3.5

[a] A, number of CH_{50} units of human complement fixed out of 2 CH_{50} units added; 10 μg ME-anti-BSA protein per tube.

[b] B, number of CH_{50} units of human complement fixed out of 4 CH_{50} units added; 10 μg ME-anti-BSA protein per tube.

[c] C, number of CH_{50} units of human complement fixed out of 6 CH_{50} units added; 20 μg ME-anti-BSA protein per tube.

TABLE III

Complement fixation by rheumatoid factor and complexes of BSA-anti-BSA and BSA-mercaptoethanol-treated anti-BSA at 4°C

Equivalence of Complexes	Agglutinating Units of Rheumatoid Factor							
	0		10		20		50	
	A[a]	B[b]	A	B	A	B	A	B
1 ×	4.4	0	4.7	0	4.7	0	>4.7	0
2 ×	2.8	0	4.4	0	4.6	0	>4.7	0
5 ×	1.5	0	2.1	0	3.7	0	4.3	0
10 ×	0.5	0	1.2	0	2.8	0	4.3	0
20 ×	0	0	0.4	0	2.3	0	2.6	0

[a] A, number of CH_{50} units of human complement fixed out of 6 CH_{50} units added; 20 μg anti-BSA antibody protein per tube.

[b] B, number of CH_{50} units of human complement fixed out of 6 CH_{50} units added; 20 μg ME-anti-BSA antibody protein per tube.

TABLE IV

Effect of anti-rabbit globulin antiserum, treated by mercaptoethanol, on complement fixation by immune complexes at 37°C

Equivalence of Complex	BSA-Anti-BSA		BSA-Anti-BSA, ME-Treated	
	Complex alone	Anti-IgG-ME added[a]	Complex alone	Anti-IgG-ME added[a]
1 ×	1.1[b]	0.4	0.2	0
2 ×	0.9	0	0	0
10 ×	0.1	0.1	0	0

[a] Mercaptoethanol-treated goat anti-rabbit globulin antiserum (0.1 ml).

[b] Number of CH_{50} units of human complement fixed out of 2.0 CH_{50} units added; 10 μg anti-BSA protein (predominantly rabbit IgG), either untreated or treated with mercaptoethanol (ME), added to each tube.

of ME-complex to approximately the same levels noted previously for the untreated complexes. These results suggested that the RF component in the aggregate was mainly responsible for the fixation of complement.

Complement fixation by RF and complexes in the cold. Since complement fixation by IgM antibodies has been shown to be inhibited in the cold (19), the ability of IgM-RF to fix complement at 4°C was explored (Table III). When 6.0 CH_{50} units of complement were added, BSA-anti-BSA complexes alone consumed considerable complement. The addition of RF resulted in a further increase of complement fixation comparable to that noted at 37°C. ME-treated immune complexes alone fixed no complement in the cold and in contrast to the results with untreated complexes no increase in complement fixation was found after additions of large amounts of RF.

Effect of IgG antiglobulin serum treated with ME on complement fixation by BSA-anti-BSA complexes. To further dissect the respective contributions of IgM-RF and of IgG antibody in mediating complement fixation, attempts were

TABLE V

Effect of mercaptoethanol-treated anti-human IgM antiserum on complement fixation by IgM-rheumatoid factor and ME-treated BSA-anti-BSA complexes

Equivalence of Complexes	BSA-Anti-BSA Complex			ME-treated BSA-anti-BSA Complex		
	Complex alone	RF added[a]	RF and anti-IgM ME added[b]	Complex alone	RF added[a]	RF and anti-IgM ME added[b]
1 ×	0.8[c]	1.1	0.8	0	1.0	0.1
2 ×	0.6	1.0	0.6	0	1.0	0.1
10 ×	0	0.9	0	0	0.7	0

[a] Rheumatoid factor, 40 aggutinating units.

[b] Rheumatoid factor, 40 agglutinating units and goat anti-human IgM antiserum, treated with mercaptoethanol.

[c] Number of CH_{50} units of human complement fixed out of 2.0 CH_{50} units added; 10 μg anti-BSA protein, either untreated or treated with mercaptoethanol, added per tube.

made to aggregate immune complexes with an RF that had been rendered inactive as a complement-fixing antibody. These attempts using urea treatment (20), however, were unsuccessful because such treatment also markedly reduced the ability of RF to combine with IgG. Therefore, an alternative approach was used in which an IgG antiglobulin which had been treated with ME was substituted for the IgM-RF, the assumption being that if RF restored complement fixation to ME-treated antibody by physical aggregation of the immune complexes, antiglobulins of another immunoglobulin class might also do so. Goat anti-rabbit globulin of the IgG class treated by ME did not by itself fix appreciable amounts of complement. Neither did it restore complement fixation to ME-treated BSA-anti-BSA complexes (Table IV). Rather, it further reduced the complement fixation of untreated BSA-anti-BSA complexes.

Effect of anti-human IgM antiserum, treated by ME, on complement fixation by RF and immune complexes. If complement was fixed mainly by RF in the aggregate, the addition of a ME-treated IgG antiserum against human IgM might be expected to neutralize this function of RF. As before, BSA-anti-BSA complexes fixed complement and the addition of RF increased this amount (Table V). Addition of ME-treated anti-IgM caused a decrease in complement fixation, which was even more striking when the underlying anti-BSA antibody had also been treated by mercaptoethanol.

DISCUSSION

Complement fixation noted in these experiments was increased after aggregation of soluble immune complexes by IgM-rheumatoid factor. The types and amounts of immune complexes that could be aggregated were closely correlated with their ability to generate complement fixation. Of the various molecular ratios of antigen and antibody studied, complexes containing two or more IgG molecules reacted most readily with IgM-RF. Those formed in great antigen excess (10 times equivalence), in which the predominant complex consisted of two antigen molecules and one antibody molecule (21), could be only minimally aggregated by RF. In addition, in other experiments not recorded, centrifugation of mixtures of complexes and RF to remove precipitates also depleted their ability to fix complement. The specific quality resident in larger complexes that enabled them to be bound more effectively by RF was not determined. It is not clear from our studies whether two or more IgG molecules bound in a complex are necessary to provide the properly spaced, multiple attachment sites for strong binding by polyvalent IgM-RF or whether conformational changes develop within the IgG molecule when incorporated into larger size complexes that reveal new antigenic determinants for RF binding.

Once bound, RF confers additional complement fixation upon the aggregate. Data have been presented to support the view that IgM-RF itself, rather than the IgG antibody, offers the major combining site for this fixation. Particularly convincing in this respect are the experiments performed at 37°C in which ME-treated BSA-anti-BSA complexes were reacted with RF. About the same quantity of complement was fixed as that fixed by RF and complexes formed with untreated antibody. Since the ME-treated complexes by themselves consume only small amounts of complement, the greater part of complement fixation must have resulted from the activity of RF. That it probably did not result from the restoration of activity to the ME-treated IgG component by its physical aggregation with RF was shown by failure of a non-complement-fixing antiglobulin to reconstitute complement fixation. Furthermore, IgM-RF lost its ability to fix complement with ME-treated complexes in the cold, a finding consistent with the inactivity of other IgM antibodies at this temperature (19). Finally, this effect of RF also was inhibited by the addition of an antibody to human IgM which had been treated with mercaptoethanol to destroy its own complement-fixing ability. The simplest explanation of these data would postulate that RF blocks the complement-fixing site on IgG through steric interference since both antigenic determinants for RF (22) and the site for complement fixation (23) are located on the Fc portion of IgG. IgM-RF bound to IgG then becomes the major site for complement attachment.

A smaller degree of complement fixation by the aggregate, however, appeared to be mediated in some cases by IgG antibody as well. This can be inferred from persistence of fixation in the RF-complex aggregate containing untreated IgG antibody after the IgM-RF reaction had been blocked with non-complement-fixing antibody to IgM (Table V). IgG reactivity would also account for the complement fixation noted in the cold for RF-complex aggregates containing untreated IgG antibody since complement fixation by such IgG antibody is less influenced at this temperature than is IgM antibody (19). These data indicate that not all sites on IgG for complement attachment are blocked by RF; that, indeed, some remain available for direct interaction with complement.

Although able to enhance complement fixation, IgM-RF in these aggregates is relatively less efficient on a weight basis than is the IgG antibody in the complex alone. Estimates of the correlation between agglutinating titers and protein concentrations of several of our purified IgM-RF indicate a range of 1 to 2 μg RF protein per agglutinating unit. Since RFs eluted from an IgG immunoadsorbent such as ours have been shown to contain little non-antiglobulin protein contamination (1), it can be assumed that most of this protein is active antibody. Utilizing previous data, we estimate that 3 to 5 times as much IgM-RF protein (Table II, 50 RF, column C) was required to fix about 3 out of 6 CH_{50} units of complement as did 20 μg IgG antibody (Table I, 0 RF, column C). On a molar basis, the concentration of IgM-RF approaches that of IgG. Nevertheless, its effectiveness compared to IgG is still far less than that found for IgM antibody attached to antigen on a red cell membrane (24). In this respect, IgM-RF behaves as does an IgM antibody directed against blood group substance A (25). Such antibody also was less efficient for complement fixation when bound to antigen in a soluble complex than when bound to antigen on a red cell membrane. Thus, while RF converts weak or inert complement-fixing complexes into aggregates with greater complement fixation, its ability to do so is modest in comparison to conventional cell-bound IgM antibody.

The sum total of the evidence presented in previous reports (4–6) and in the present study justifies the conclusion that RF is capable of complement fixation *in vitro*. Furthermore, it is likely that a similar mechanism for complement fixation occurs *in vivo*. Injection of small doses of autologous aggregated globulin into the joints of seropositive patients with quiescent rheumatoid arthritis elicits an acute inflammatory response. The same quantity of such material injected into the joints of normal persons is without effect (26). The presence of conversion products of the third component of complement in synovial fluid correlates well with RF in the serum (27). RF has been found in a close spatial relationship to deposits of IgG and components of the complement system in the inflamed synovium of patients with rheumatoid arthritis (28, 29). RF can promote phagocytosis of soluble aggregates of gamma G globulin (30, 31). Vaughan and coworkers have shown an association between lowered levels of complement in the synovial fluid and inclusion bodies containing IgM (possibly RF) in polymorphonuclear phagocytes of the joint fluids (32). Recently, Hurd *et al.* (33) were able to induce the formation of such inclusions in leucocytes of the joint fluid of patients without RF after exogenous RF has been added. McCormick *et al.* (34) showed that RF-containing human sera would potentiate the severity of the first stage of nephrotoxic serum nephritis in rats. This stage is mediated by the action of complement with heterologous antibody bound to the renal basement membrane. Our study documents the conditions under which mixtures of soluble immune complexes with little or no ability to fix complement can be converted to complement-fixing agents by RF. Viewed in this light, RF assumes a modest role in complement-mediated reactions and provides a mechanism for a more active or persistent inflammatory response.

Acknowledgments. The authors are grateful to Miss Maria J. Rocha for expert technical help, to Mrs. Sharon Kunitz for assistance in preparation of the manuscript, and to the American Red Cross for supplies of human gamma globulin, Cohn fraction II.

REFERENCES

1. Torrigiani, G. and Roitt, I. M., Ann. Rheum. Dis., *26:* 334, 1967.
2. Christian, C. L., J. Exp. Med., *108:* 139, 1958.
3. Edelman, G. M., Kunkel, H. G. and Franklin, E. C., J. Exp. Med., *108:* 105, 1958.
4. Zvaifler, N. J. and Schur, P., Arthritis Rheum., *11:* 523, 1968.
5. Davis, J. S., IV, Arthritis Rheum., *11:* 475, 1968.
6. Schmid, F. R. and Rocha, M. J., J. Lab. Clin. Med., *72:* 1014, 1968.
7. Bernhard, G. C., Cheng, W. and Talmage, D. W., J. Immun., *88:* 750, 1962.
8. Heimer, R., Levin, F. M., Primack, A., Corcos, J. M. and Nosenzo, C., J. Immun., *89:* 382, 1962.
9. Heimer, R., Levin, F. M. and Kahn, M. F., J. Immun., *91:* 866, 1963.
10. Davis, J. S., IV and Bollet, A. J., J. Immun., *92:* 139, 1964.
11. Butler, V. P., Jr. and Vaughan, J. H., Immunology, *8:* 144, 1965.
12. McConahey, P. J. and Dixon, F. J., Int. Arch. Allerg., *29:* 185, 1966.
13. Avrameas, S. and Ternynck, T., Immunochemistry, *6:* 54, 1969.
14. Wiedermann, G., Miescher, P. A. and Franklin, E. C., Proc. Soc. Exp. Biol. Med., *113:* 609, 1963.
15. Mayer, M. M., in *Kabat and Mayer's Experimental Immunochemistry*, 2nd Ed., p. 149, Charles C Thomas, Springfield, Ill., 1961.
16. Mayer, M. M., in *Kabat and Mayer's Experimental Immunochemistry*, 2nd Ed., p. 214, Charles C Thomas, Springfield, Ill., 1961.
17. Osler, A. G. and Hill, M. B., J. Immun., *75:* 137, 1955.
18. Levine, L., Mayer, M. M. and Rapp, H. J., J. Immun., *73:* 435, 1954.
19. Cunniff, R. V. and Stollar, B. D., J. Immun., *100:* 7, 1968.
20. Cunniff, R. V. H., Cole, H. H. and Stollar, B. D., J. Immun., *101:* 695, 1968.
21. Singer, S. J. and Campbell, D. H., J. Amer. Chem. Soc., *74:* 1794, 1952.
22. Kunkel, H. G. and Tan, E. M., in *Advances in Immunology*, edited by F. J. Dixon and H. G. Kunkel, Vol. 4, p. 363, Academic Press, New York, 1964.
23. Müller-Eberhard, H. J., Nilsson, U. R., Dalmasso, A. P., Polley, M. J. and Calcott, M. A., Arch. Path., *82:* 205, 1966.
24. Borsos, T. and Rapp. H. J., Science, *150:* 505, 1965.
25. Ishizaka, T., Tada, T. and Ishizaka, K., J. Immun., *100:* 1145, 1968.
26. Restifo, R. A., Lassier, H. J., Rawson, A. J., Rockey, J. H. and Hollander, J. L., Ann. Intern. Med., *62:* 285, 1965.
27. Zvaifler, N. J., J. Clin. Invest., *48:* 1532, 1969.
28. Fish, A. J., Michael, H. F., Gewurz, H. and Good, R. A., Arthritis Rheum., *7:* 267, 1966.
29. Rodman, W. S., Williams, R. C., Jr., Bilka, P. J. and Müller-Eberhard, H. J., J. Lab. Clin. Med., *69:* 141, 1967.
30. Parker, R. and Schmid, F. R., J. Immun., *88:* 519, 1962.
31. Astorga, G. and Bollet, A. J., Arthritis Rheum., *7:* 288, 1964.
32. Vaughan, J. H., Barnett, E. V., Sobel, M. V. and Jacox, R., Arthritis Rheum., *11:* 125, 1968.
33. Hurd, R. E., LoSpalluto, J. and Ziff, M., Arthritis Rheum., *12:* 304, 1969.
34. McCormick, J. N., Day, J., Morris, C. I. and Hill, A. G. W., Clin. Exp. Immun., *4:* 17, 1969.

THE JOURNAL OF IMMUNOLOGY
Vol. 105, No. 5, November 1970

Printed in U.S.A.

STRUCTURAL AND ANTIGENIC RELATIONSHIPS BETWEEN AVIAN IMMUNOGLOBULINS

III. Antigenic Relationships of the Immunoglobulins of the Chicken, Pheasant and Japanese Quail[1]

GERRIE A. LESLIE[2] AND ALBERT A. BENEDICT

From the Department of Microbiology, University of Hawaii, Honolulu, Hawaii 96822

Received for publication May 1, 1970

Ring-necked pheasants, Japanese quail and chickens have 7S immunoglobulins that are antigenically related to each other. It was demonstrated that the cross-reactions were due to similar antigenic determinants on the H and L chains and Fab and Fc fragments. The L chains of the chicken and pheasant were antigenically identical whereas the quail L chains reacted only weakly with the other two. It was concluded that the antigenic structure of QG was much more different from either CG or PG than CG or PG were from each other. The H chains of each of the IgM's shared antigenic determinants.

Our previous studies have shown that the predominant serum immunoglobulin of the chicken, pheasant and Japanese quail has a sedimentation coefficient of about 7S (1) and a molecular weight of ca. 170,000 daltons (2). In addition, these three immunoglobulins share several other properties such as dissociation after reduction in alkaline buffers (1), formation of Fab and Fc fragments following papain digestion (3) and aggregation in "high-salt"-containing buffers (4). The reduction characteristics, high molecular weight and aggregation phenomenon differentiate these immunoglobulins from the typical IgG of man. Considerably fewer data are available on the IgM of chickens, pheasants, and Japanese quail than on their 7S immunoglobulins. However, reduction of chicken (5, 6) and quail IgM (1) results in ~6.5S and ~5.7S subunits whereas pheasant IgM (1) yields only ~6.1S subunits. As with chicken IgM (5), reduction of pheasant IgM caused the release of some light chains (1) at neutral pH.

The similar physicochemical properties of chicken, pheasant, and quail 7S immunoglobulins prompted an examination of the antigenic relationships among these immunoglobulins. The purpose of the present study was to determine whether the cross-reacting antigenic determinants of these avian IgG immunoglobulins were located in both their heavy and light polypeptide chains, and in both Fab and Fc fragments. The long range goal of this study is to identify chemically those antigenic determinants (amino acid sequence) that have been conserved between closely related avian species.

MATERIALS AND METHODS

Preparation of immunoglobulins, polypeptide chains and enzymatically produced fragments. The 7S and ~17S immunoglobulins were the same as those described previously (1). The heavy (H) and light (L) polypeptide chains were prepared by reduction with mercaptoethanol (ME), alkylation with iodoacetamide and gel filtered on Sephadex G-200 columns equilibrated with 1 M propionic acid (1). The preparation and isolation of papain and pepsin fragments of chicken, pheasant and quail 7S immunoglobulins have been described (3). In this report the 7S immunoglobulins of the chicken, pheasant and Japanese quail will be designated as CG, PG and QG respectively.

Antisera. Rabbits were immunized by a series of footpad and intramuscular injections with: 1)

[1] This investigation was supported in part by United States Public Health Service Research Grant AI05660-05 and Training Grant AI00243-05 from the National Institute of Allergy and Infectious Diseases.

[2] Present address: Department of Microbiology, University of Florida, College of Medicine, Gainesville.

chicken, pheasant or quail serum, 2) the respective immunoglobulin and in some cases, isolated polypeptide chains or enzymatically produced fragments. A pheasant anti-chicken 7S serum was prepared by inoculating a pheasant with chicken 7S immunoglobulin in complete Freund's adjuvant (Difco Laboratories, Detroit, Mich.). Several abbreviations will be used for the antisera that have been employed, namely, a-QG1, a-PG1, a-CG1, which represent rabbit antisera to Q-globulins, P-globulins, and C-globulins. Bracketed letters behind the antiserum designation indicates that the antiserum has been absorbed with the material indicated in the bracket.

Immunodiffusion. The methods used for immunodiffusion were described previously (1).

RESULTS

Studies of intact 7S immunoglobulins. Antisera obtained from rabbits immunized with chicken (a-CG1), pheasant (a-PG1) or quail (a-QG1) globulins contained antibodies capable of precipitating the homologous 7S immunoglobulin as well as the two heterologous 7S immunoglobulins (Fig. 1, *A*, *B* and *C*). The intensities of the various spurs seen in these figures suggested that the chicken and pheasant 7S immunoglobulins (CG and PG) were antigenically more closely related to one another than was quail 7S immunoglobulin (QG) to either of the other two.

Antigenic studies of H and L chains from 7S immunoglobulins. Heavy chains (H) isolated from propionic acid columns are only sparingly soluble in the commonly employed buffer systems. For this reason the H chains, and in some cases the L chains, were dissolved in 0.5 M propionic acid.

The anti-chicken 7S H chain antiserum reacted with C, P and Q heavy chains (Fig. 1*D*). The precipitin bands of P and Q heavy chains showed reactions of partial identity with the C heavy chains. However, even after staining, it was not possible to assess the reaction between P and Q heavy chains (i.e., partial identity or identity). It is possible that the presence of propionic acid in the area of the precipitates interfered with precipitate formation or in some way changed the antigenic properties of the H chains. The distance between the antigen and antibody wells in these experiments was quite large (ca. 1 cm) and thus the concentration of protein in the environment of the precipitate should have been very low. In order to clarify this relationship, the three intact 7S immunoglobulins were studied using the same antiserum (Fig. 1*E*). Both PG and QG showed a reaction of partial identity with CG. The very short spur between CG and PG and the longer spur between CG and QG indicated a closer antigenic relationship between the former pair than between the latter. A small spur between PG and QG indicated that the pheasant H chain shares more determinants with the chicken H chain than does the quail H chain. CG and PG gave reactions of partial identity with isolated quail H chains (Fig. 1*F*) when analyzed with a a-QG1 antiserum. There was no indication that chicken or pheasant L chains were being detected with the a-QG1 antiserum.

As an initial approach to the study of L chain relationships, CG, PG and QG were tested against a rabbit anti-chicken L chain serum. The CG and PG gave a reaction of identity whereas QG gave only a very weak diffuse band (not shown). The a-CG1 and a-PG1 antisera when reacted with the isolated L chains likewise showed that P and C light chains were antigenically identical whereas only a trace of precipitation was seen in the area of Q light chains (Fig. 2*A* and *B*). It should be pointed out that the a-PG1 forms double precipitin bands with the isolated C and P light chains (Fig. 2*B*). Whether this represents two antigenic types of L chains (K and λ?) or monomer-polymer relationships has not been determined. The a-QG1 antisera reacted very poorly with C and P light chains. In fact, Figure 2*C* shows that quail L chains give a band of apparent non-identity with CG and PG, but the L chain precipitin line is very weak and short once it crosses the CG and PG precipitin lines, indicating some antigenic relatedness. Similar observations were made when chicken L chains and QG were tested with a-CG1 antisera (Fig. 2*D*).

Absorption studies. In an attempt to substantiate the previous findings on the relationships of the intact 7S immunoglobulins and their constituent polypeptide chains, various absorption experiments were carried out.

The a-CG1 (PG) antiserum gave a reaction of identity between CG and chicken H chains, thus showing that the anti-L chain antibodies had been removed. This antiserum did not react with PG, QG or chicken L chains. The fact that QG was not detected suggested that the antigenic

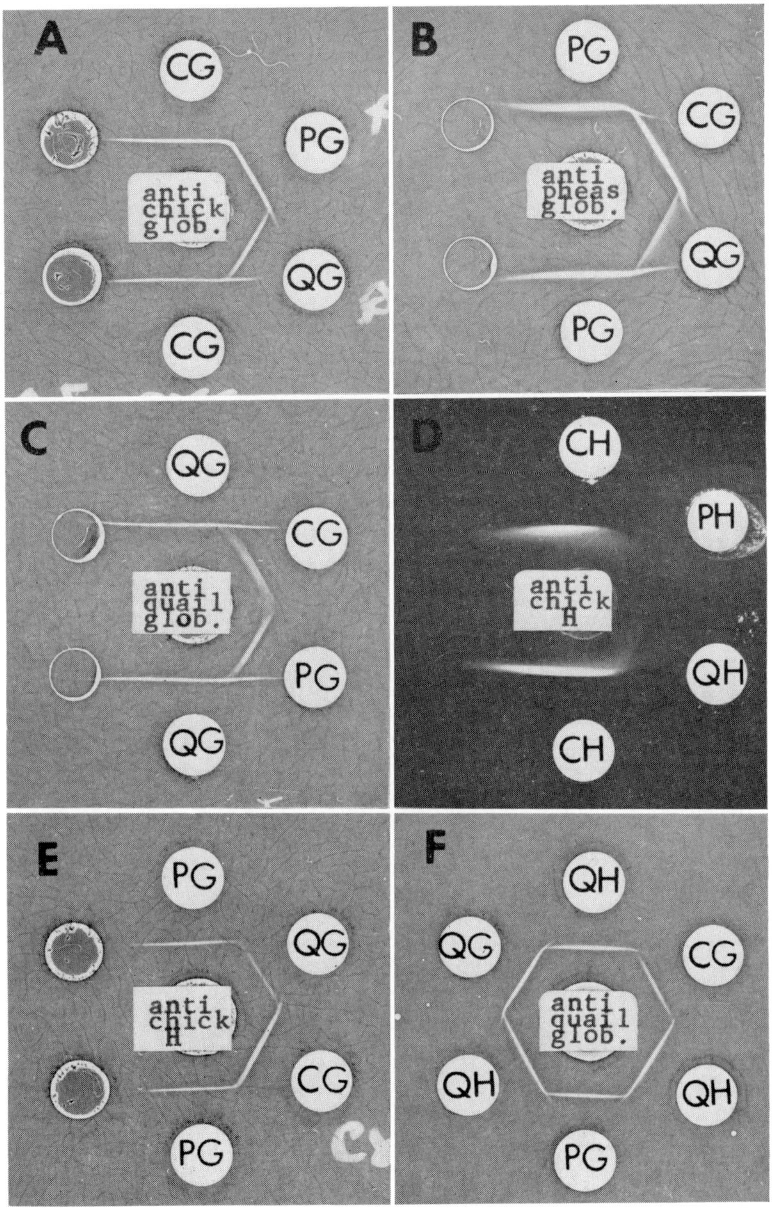

Figure 1. Double diffusion of chicken (C), pheasant (P) and quail (Q) 7S immunoglobulins and their H chains (CH, PH, QH) with rabbit antisera made against CG, PG, QG and chicken H chains.

determinants present on QG (or most of the determinants) which were detected with a-CG1 also were present on PG, so that absorption removed all or most of the antibodies reacting with both PG and QG. A similar pattern developed when a-PG1 antiserum was absorbed with CG and reacted with the three immunoglobulins and the homologous polypeptide chains. A line of identity formed between PG and pheasant H chains, whereas no reaction occurred with CG, QG or pheasant L chains. This observation again demonstrated that determinants of QG that react with a-PG1 are in common with some of the determinants present on CG.

In contrast to the results obtained using absorbed a-PG1 and a-CG1 antisera, the a-QG1

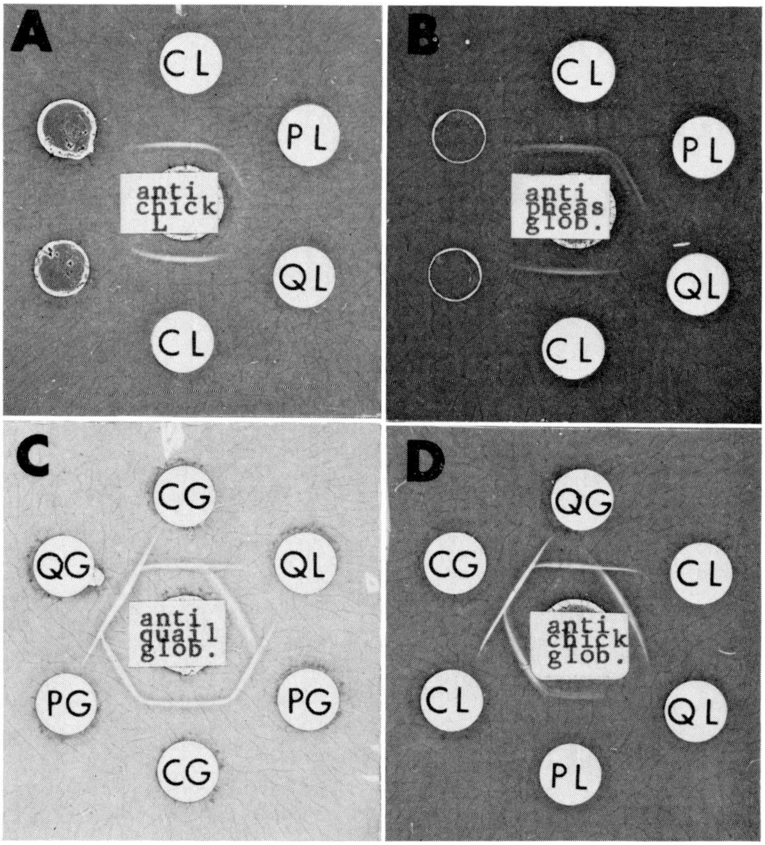

Figure 2. Double diffusion of chicken, pheasant and quail 7S immunoglobulins (CG, PG, QG) and their L chains (CL, PL, QL). All antisera were prepared in rabbits.

(CG) reacted with the homologous H and L chains as well as with PG. A reaction of partial identity occurred between PG and QG, as well as between QG and quail H chains. Quail H chains gave a reaction of non-identity with quail L chains. Rabbit a-QG1 (PG), showed a pattern identical to that seen with a-QG1 (CG) except that PG was not precipitated whereas CG was precipitated. The results obtained using absorbed a-QG1 were confirmed using a different antiserum and different antigen preparations.

It is well recognized that in order to prepare highly specific antisera for the detection of minor antigenic variations in proteins one should immunize an animal of a closely-related species or even a member of the same species but of a different genetic constitution. To test the antigenic relationship between pheasant and chicken H and L chains, a pheasant anti-chicken 7S immunoglobulin (anti-CG) antiserum was used. A line of identity formed between CG and chicken H chains and no reaction was observed with chicken L chains. Thus the pheasant appears to recognize only antigenic determinants that are associated with chicken H chains.

Antigenic analysis of Fab fragments. When reacted with rabbit anti-chicken Fab antiserum, CG and PG showed a reaction of partial identity and QG was not detected (Fig. 3*A*). However, the PG precipitin line gave evidence of interruption in the area of QG diffusion, suggesting a blocking activity by soluble complexes. The same antiserum gave a reaction of partial identity between chicken and pheasant Fab fragments but in contrast to Figure 3*A*, a very faint precipitin band formed with quail Fab (Fig. 3*B*). This band gave a reaction of partial identity with both pheasant Fab and quail Fab. The a-CG1 antiserum gave a line of identity between chicken Fab and pheasant Fab and a line of

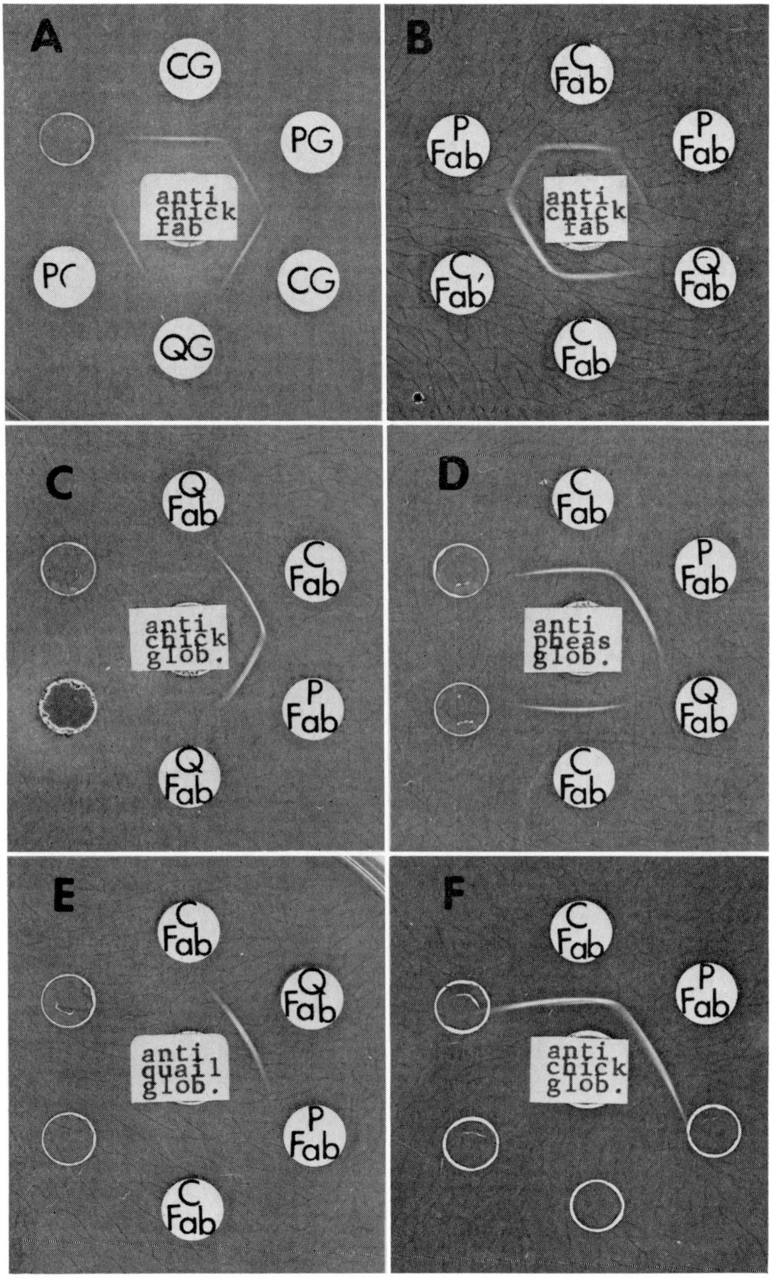

Figure 3. Antigenic relationships between chicken (C), pheasant (P) and quail (Q) Fab fragments. Double diffusion analysis of chicken, pheasant and quail 7S immunoglobulins (CG, PG, QG); chicken, pheasant and quail Fab fragments (C-Fab, P-Fab, Q-Fab). Rabbit antisera made against CG, PG and QG and chicken Fab fragments were added to the center wells.

partial identity between quail Fab and the other two fragments (Fig. 3*C*). A similar reaction of identity between chicken Fab and pheasant Fab was given with a-PG1 (Fig. 3*D*), and a-QG1 antiserum (Fig. 3*E*). The a-PG1 gave a line of partial identity between quail Fab and the Fab of the other two birds (Fig. 3*D*) and the a-QG1 gave a reaction of partial identity between quail

Fab and the Fab fragments of chickens and pheasants (Fig. 3*E*).

The importance of employing several different antisera, when studying antigenically related material, is demonstrated in Figures 3*C* and 3*F*. Chicken and pheasant Fab fragments were antigenically identical when analyzed with a-CG1 antisera (Fig. 3*C*), whereas a different a-CG1 antiserum showed a very short spur indicating partial identity (Fig. 3*F*).

Antigenic analysis of Fc. Using a specific rabbit anti-chicken Fc antiserum, PG showed a partial identity to CG and QG showed a partial identity with CG and PG. As noted previously, the reaction of QG with the heterologous antiserum was very weak (not shown). The partial identity of chicken and pheasant Fc fragments was confirmed with the isolated Fc fragments (Fig. 4*A*). A pheasant anti-CG antiserum detected CG and chicken Fc but not chicken Fab or QG. The quail Fc fragment has not been highly purified. However, by immunoelectrophoresis chicken and pheasant Fc are detected with a-QG1 antisera. A reaction of partial identity was observed between chicken Fc and QG when a-QG1 (Fig. 4*B*) and a-PG1 antisera were employed.

The antigenic relationship of chicken, pheasant and quail IgM. Figure 4*C* shows that chicken, pheasant and quail IgM share some common antigenic determinants. These determinants must be located on the H chains since the antiserum was prepared by absorption with the homologous 7S immunoglobulin. Similar observations were made with anti-pheasant and anti-quail IgM with the exception that the heterologous IgM molecules showed a partial identity with the homologous one.

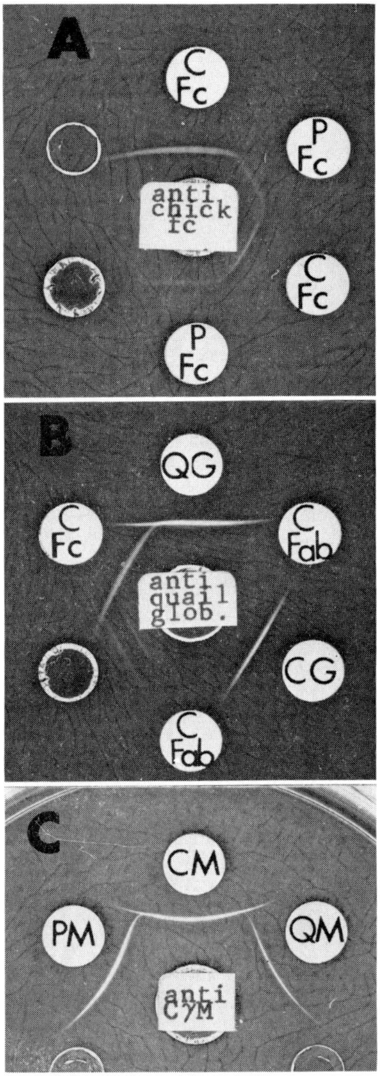

Figure 4. Double diffusion of chicken, pheasant and quail 7S immunoglobulins (CG, PG, QG), their papain fragments (Fab and Fc) and IgM (PM, CM, QM).

DISCUSSION

The similarity in several of the physicochemical and immunochemical properties of chicken, pheasant and Japanese quail 7S immunoglobulins (1–4), as well as the close taxonomic relationship of these birds suggested that the immunoglobulins may also share antigenic determinants.

The ideal method for comparing these molecules would obviously be one that provides the complete amino acid sequence. Generally, however, such methods are slow, and require large amounts of fairly homogeneous protein. Gel diffusion, while being less informative than amino acid sequences, gives data depending to a great extent on primary structure.

The results of these studies demonstrated that each species' 7S immunoglobulin is related to the others by means of some common antigenic determinants on the H chains, L chains, Fab fragments, and Fc fragments. By using several different antisera it was possible to show that, with one possible exception, the observed reactions were reactions of partial identity. The one

TABLE I

A summary of the antigenic relationships between avian immunoglobulins

Test Antigens	Rabbit Antisera to	Reaction by Double Diffusion	
		Identity	Partial identity
~7S immunoglobulins	Chicken (a-CG1) globulins		P and Q[a]
			C and Q
	Pheasant (a-PG1) globulins		C and P
			C and Q
			P and Q
	Quail (a-QG1) globulins	P and C	
			C and Q
			P and Q
Heavy chains	Chicken heavy chains		C and Q
			C and P
			P and Q
Light chains	Chicken light chains	C and P	
			C and Q
			Q and P
Fab	Chicken Fab fragment		C and P
			C and Q
			P and Q
	Pheasant globulins	C and P	P and Q
			Q and C
Fc	Chicken Fc fragment		C and P
			C and Q
IgM	Chicken IgM		C and P
			C and Q
	Pheasant IgM		C and P
			Q and P
	Quail IgM		Q and C
			Q and P

[a] C, chicken; P, pheasant; Q, quail.

exception was the reaction between chicken and pheasant L chains. Several different antisera showed them to be antigenically identical. One thing became very clear as these experiments were being carried out: the antigenic structure of QG was much more different from either CG or PG than CG or PG were from each other. A summary of the antigenic relationships is given in Table I. The techniques employed in these experiments did not allow measurement of the degree of cross-reaction; other techniques could be used to affix numerical values to the degree of relatedness.

On the basis of N-terminal and C-terminal amino acid analysis, most chicken L chains have been assigned to the K subclass although some of the λ type have been suggested (6). In this regard, two precipitin bands were sometimes seen with isolated chicken and pheasant L chains.

Antisera directed towards either C-IgM or Q-IgM detected all three macroglobulins. The shared determinants must have been located on the H chains since each antiserum was prepared by absorption of rabbit anti-whole globulin antisera with the homologous 7S immunoglobulin. In this regard, it has been reported that human IgM cross-reacts with chicken IgM whereas human IgG does not cross-react with chicken 7S immunoglobulin (Methta and Tomasi, personal communication to G.A.L.).

The classification of non-mammalian immunoglobulins has become somewhat of an enigma. Many of the properties used to classify human immunoglobulins are based on characteristics of the H chains, although characteristics such as whole molecule molecular weight and carbohydrate are also important. Recent studies have shown that chicken (2, 7–9), pheasant and quail 7S immunoglobulins (2) have a molecular weight of 170,000 to 180,000 daltons, which is 20,000 to 30,000 daltons greater than that of human IgG. Furthermore, the L chains of chicken 7S are the same size as those of human IgG whereas the H chains are about 17,000 daltons heavier as determined by extensive reduction and gel filtration (9) or ~10,000 daltons heavier as determined by ultracentrifugation (R. T. Hersh, R. T. Kubo, G. Dressman and A. A. Benedict, to be published). Since the H chains of these three birds are antigenically related and many of the other physicochemical properties are similar, it is felt that they belong to the same immunoglobulin class.

Since this study was completed an interim designation for the 7S immunoglobulins of lower vertebrates has been suggested by Leslie and Clem. They state that immunoglobulins that are ~7S, electrophoretically slow and do not closely align themselves with any of the described human immunoglobulins should be called IgY (9, 10). It should be emphasized that this is not necessarily a permanent designation since eventually amino acid sequences may indeed show that the IgY in question has a human counterpart.

REFERENCES

1. Leslie, G. A. and Benedict, A. A., J. Immun. *103:* 1356, 1969.
2. Hersh, R. T., Kubo, R. T., Leslie, G. A. and Benedict, A. A., Immunochemistry, *6:* 762, 1969.
3. Leslie, G. A. and Benedict, A. A., J. Immun., *104:* 810, 1970.
4. Kubo, R. T. and Benedict, A. A., J. Immun., *103:* 1022, 1969.
5. Benedict, A. A., Seventh International Congress on Biochemistry, Abstracts, p. 979, Tokyo, 1967.
6. Hood, L., Gray, W. R., Sanders, B. G. and Dreyer, W. J., Cold Spring Harbor Symp. Quant. Biol., *32:* 133, 1967.
7. Gallagher, J. S. and Voss, E. W., Immunochemistry, *6:* 199, 1969.
8. Orlans, E., Rose, M. E. and Marrack, J. R., Immunology, *4:* 262, 1961.
9. Leslie, G. A. and Clem, L. W., J. Exp. Med., *130:* 1337, 1969.
10. Clem, L. W. and Leslie, G. A., in *Immunology and Development*, p. 62, Spastics International Medical Publications, London, 1969.

THE JOURNAL OF IMMUNOLOGY
Vol. 105, No. 5, November 1970

IMMUNOLOGIC PROPERTIES OF THE MAIN ENCEPHALITOGENIC PEPTIDE FROM THE BASIC PROTEIN OF HUMAN MYELIN[1,2,3]

VANDA A. LENNON,[4] ANN V. WILKS[5] AND PATRICK R. CARNEGIE[6]

From the Clinical Research Unit, Walter and Eliza Hall Institute of Medical Research, and The School of Biochemistry, University of Melbourne, Parkville, 3052, Australia

Received for publication May 1, 1970

The encephalitogenic basic protein from human brain was digested with pepsin and encephalitogenic peptides were isolated. Two overlapping peptides containing 15 and 22 amino acids had similar encephalitogenicity as the parent protein. Both peptides induced delayed hypersensitivity to the protein but no detectable circulating antibody in guinea pigs. There was a striking correlation between the occurrence of experimental autoimmune encephalomyelitis and low yields of peritoneal exudate cells. The main encephalitogenic determinant resides within the sequence Ser-Arg-Phe-Ser-Trp-Gly-Ala-Glu-Gly-Gln-. We postulate that the integrity of this region of the basic protein of myelin is vital to the normal functioning of the central nervous system. These small peptides should be of value in investigating the role of delayed hypersensitivity in autoimmune disease.

Our knowledge of the nature of the antigen in the central nervous system (CNS) which induces experimental autoimmune encephalomyelitis (EAE) has increased considerably since 1965. The antigen was claimed by Kies (1) to be a basic protein of myelin, and by Lumsden *et al.* (2, 3) to be a peptide. The controversy was resolved by the discovery (4, 5) that peptide encephalitogens were produced by the action of an acid proteinase during the isolation of the basic protein from acetone powders of CNS tissue. This led to attempts to isolate and characterize encephalitogenic fragments of the basic protein (5, 6). Eylar and Hashim (7) found that digestion of the bovine protein with pepsin yielded a potent encephalitogenic peptide which contained tryptophan.

We herein describe the isolation, amino acid sequence and immunologic properties of peptides which contain the main encephalitogenic determinant of the basic protein of human myelin.

MATERIALS AND METHODS

Isolation of basic protein. The encephalitogenic basic protein was isolated (1) from human brains obtained 12 hr after death. It was purified by ion-exchange on carboxymethyl Sephadex followed by gel filtration in 0.1 N HCl on Sephadex G-75 (5). The content of tryptophan was determined with 2-hydroxy-5-nitrobenzyl bromide (8).

Isolation of peptides. The basic protein (250 mg) was digested for 3 hr at 38°C with 4 mg of pepsin (Worthington Biochemical Corp., Freehold, N. J.) in 11 ml of 5% formic acid. The digest was fractionated on a 135- x 5.2-cm column of Sephadex G-50 with 1% acetic acid as solvent. Peptides containing tryptophan were found with the Ehrlich reagent in two zones eluted with a volume approximately 2.42 and 2.66 times the exclusion volume of the column. These zones were concentrated on a rotary evaporator at 30°C and fractionated by preparative electrophoresis on Whatman 3MM paper in pH 6.5 pyridine-acetate buffer (9) for 1 hr with 3000 volts. Edge strips were used to locate the zones which stained for tryptophan; these zones were fractionated by

[1] Presented in part at the Annual Meeting of the Australian Society of Immunologists, December 1969.

[2] This work was supported by grants from the Australian Research Grants Committee, National Health and Medical Research Council of Australia and the National Multiple Sclerosis Society, New York (Grant 591-A-4).

[3] Publication 1419 from The Walter and Eliza Hall Institute of Medical Research.

[4] Clinical Research Unit, The Walter and Eliza Hall Institute of Medical Research, Royal Melbourne Hospital, Victoria, 3050, Australia.

[5] Russell Grimwade School of Biochemistry, University of Melbourne, Victoria, 3052, Australia.

preparative paper chromatography by stitching them on to 3MM paper and developing with *n*-butanol-pyridine-acetic acid-water (15:10:3:12; by volume). The zones containing tryptophan were again located and further purified by preparative paper electrophoresis with pyridine acetate buffer, pH 3.5. Three homogeneous peptides called P1, P2 and P3 (Fig. 1) which contained tryptophan were eluted with 0.01 N NH_3 and characterized. The procedure for determining the amino acid sequence was similar to that used to characterize the tryptic peptide which contained tryptophan (9); full details will be published elsewhere.

Induction of EAE. Outbred adult guinea pigs of both sexes were injected into the two hind footpads with basic protein or peptides in Freund's complete adjuvant (FCA) (10). The guinea pigs were killed by bleeding from the heart under chloroform anesthesia at various times up to 33 days or when severe clinical EAE occurred. Sera were stored at −20°C. Brains and spinal cords were removed immediately and processed for histologic examination (10).

Antibody assay. The antigen-binding capacity of all sera was measured by radioimmunoassay using gel filtration (11–13). The human basic protein was labeled with ^{125}I and separated from free inorganic iodide on a column of Sephadex G-75 with 0.1 N HCl as solvent. The iodinated antigen was selected from the center of the peak of labeled protein, and was stored in 0.1 N HCl for not more than 3 weeks at 4°C. The specific activity was approximately 9 μCi/μg.

Fivefold dilutions of each serum were prepared using normal rabbit serum as diluent. The samples of sera (0.1 ml) were held for 24 hr at 4°C with 0.9 ml of Tris acetate buffer, pH 7.4, and 10 μl of ^{125}I-basic protein (0.04 μg) in a siliconized Technicon sample cup. An antigen-binding curve was constructed for each serum and the dilution of serum at which 40% of the antigen was bound was used as the reference point for estimating the antigen-binding capacity of 1 ml of undiluted serum (11). This point was always on the linear aspect of the curve and non-immune sera invariably bound less than 15% of the ^{125}I-basic protein.

Iodination of tryptophan peptide. Peptide P2, which contained tyrosine, was iodinated by the lactoperoxidase method (14) and separated from free inorganic iodide by paper electrophoresis at pH 6.5. ^{125}I-P2 was used in the radioimmunoassay procedure described above.

Competitive inhibition assay. A rabbit was hyperimmunized with basic protein in FCA to obtain a standard immune serum. The ability of the test antigens, in 10 μl of 0.05 N acetic acid, to inhibit competitively the binding of 40 ng of ^{125}I-basic protein added to 10 μl of this serum was assayed (11).

Skin tests for delayed hypersensitivity. Guinea pigs were tested once, from 11 to 16 days after immunization, using both basic protein (15 μg) and mycobacterial antigen (PPD, 1 μg) in 0.1 ml of normal saline. Test sites were read as positive if there was erythema and induration at 24 and 48 hr. Equivocal test sites were excised and examined histologically.

In vitro delayed hypersensitivity. The technique for testing the inhibition of macrophage migration from capillary tubes (15, 16) was used with slight modification, namely that peritoneal exudates were induced by the injection of 20 ml of sterile paraffin oil and after 4 days the peritoneal cells were harvested in 80 ml of Eisen's balanced salt solution with 10 units of preservative-free heparin/ml. Cells were washed three times in a graduated centrifuge tube and their packed volume was measured. They were made up to a 6% (by volume) suspension in Eagle's minimum essential medium (MEM) supplemented with 15% fetal calf serum (Commonwealth Serum Laboratories, Melbourne), penicillin G 100 units/ml and streptomycin 100 μg/ml, and transferred to capillary tubes.

The test antigens, basic protein (5 nmol/ml) peptide P2 (1.5 nmol/ml) and PPD (15 μg/ml), were prepared in MEM and added to Mackaness-type culture chambers in which the capillaries were mounted in pairs on a glass cover slip. At least two chambers were prepared for each antigen tested. After 24 hr at 37°C the area occupied by the migrating cells was measured. The mean of the four or more areas of migration in the presence of test antigen was compared with the mean of four areas of migration of the cells from the same animal cultured in the absence of antigen. The difference between the mean of the two areas, representing the degree of inhibition by antigen, was calculated. Differences were tested by Student's *t* test and inhibition was considered significant with p values <0.01.

RESULTS

Isolation of tryptophan peptides. The encephalitogenic basic protein from human brain was shown to contain 1 mol of tryptophan/mol, assuming a molecular weight of 19,000. However because there were several bonds close to tryptophan which were susceptible to digestion by pepsin, several peptides containing tryptophan were present in the peptide map of the digest. The three major peptides, P1, P2, and P3 (Fig. 1), were easily isolated by a combination of gel filtration, paper electrophoresis and chromatography. Because of their hydrophobic nature they were retarded by adsorption on the dextran gel. The yield of each peptide was approximately 0.05 μmol/μmol of protein taken for digestion; this low yield is consistent with there being multiple sites for digestion and with the losses known to be associated with paper electrophoresis and chromatography.

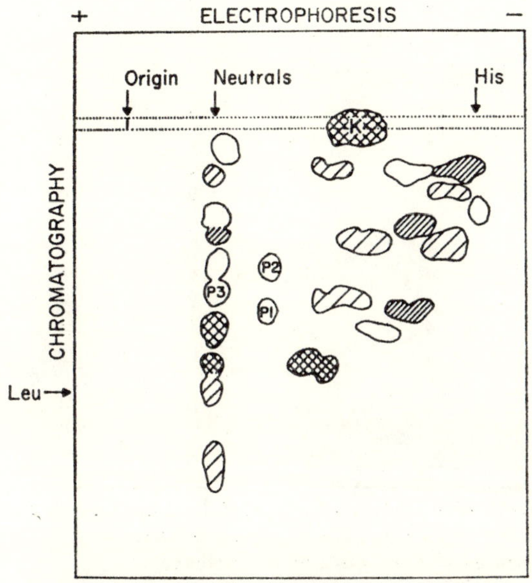

Figure 1. Peptide map of peptic digest of encephalitogenic basic protein from human myelin. Electrophoresis was at pH 6.5 in pyridine acetate buffer for 1 hr with 3000 volts; *n*-butanol-pyridine-acetic acid-water (15:10:3:12, by volume) was the solvent for chromatography. The position of amino acid markers is shown. Hatching indicates the relative intensity of the spots stained with ninhydrin. The tryptophan peptides are labeled P1, P2 and P3.

Amino acid sequence of the peptides. Figure 2 gives the amino acid sequence around the sole tryptophan in the basic protein. Peptide P1, P2 and P3 contained 15, 22 and 19 amino acids respectively.

Encephalitogenicity of peptic peptides. A total of 57 guinea pigs was injected with the peptic peptides P1 and P2; 35 animals had clinical EAE and 44 had histologic lesions in the CNS. The mean day of onset of EAE in animals injected with the peptic peptides was 15 (range 11 to 21 days).

In Table I the encephalitogenic activity of the tryptophan peptides is compared with that of the human basic protein. Peptides P1 and P2 on a molar basis had an activity comparable with that of the basic protein; however, as the peptides are approximately one-tenth the molecular weight of the parent basic protein, they are more potent on a weight basis. Their encephalitogenicity was similar to that of the analogous peptides from the bovine protein (7). Both peptides induced clinical disease and histologic lesions in the CNS. However, peptide P3, which lacks the N-terminal

Pepsin Pepsin
↓ ↓
NH_2–Ser–Arg–Phe–Ser–Trp–Gly–Ala–Glu–Gly–Gln–Arg–Pro–Gly–
1 2 3 4 5 6 7 8 9 10 11 12 13

Pepsin Pepsin
↓ ↓
Phe–Gly–Tyr–Gly–Gly–Arg–Ala–Ser–Asp–Tyr–Lys COOH
14 15 16 17 18 19 20 21 22 23 24

Peptide P1 consists of the amino acids 1 to 15 inclusive
Peptide P2 consists of the amino acids 1 to 22 inclusive
Peptide P3 consists of the amino acids 4 to 22 inclusive
Region underlined must be intact for induction of clinical EAE.

Figure 2. Amino acid sequence of the main encephalitogenic determinant isolated from a peptic digest of the human basic protein.

TABLE I

Encephalitogenic activity of peptides from a peptic digest of the basic protein of human myelin

Immunogen (in FCA)	Dose	No. of Guinea Pigs[a]	Clinical EAE[b]		Histologic EAE[c]
			Mild	Severe	
	pmol				
Human basic protein (1 pmol = 19 ng)	5000	4	0	4	4
	2500	4	0	4	4
	500	4	0	4	4
	50	4	0	4	4
	5	4	1	0	1
Peptide P1 (15 amino acids)	1800	11	1	8	11
	180	4	2	2	4
	18	4	0	0	2
	1.8	4	0	0	4
Peptide P2 (22 amino acids)	1600	3	0	3	3
	950	4	0	4	4
	400	4	0	2	4
	30	4	2	1	4
	3	4	3	0	2
Peptide P3 (19 amino acids)	2160	4	0	0	4
FCA		23	0	0	0

[a] Guinea pigs were immunized in both hind footpads with a total volume of 0.1 ml containing the immunogen in 50 µl of saline and an equal volume of Freund's complete adjuvant (FCA).

[b] Mild = loss of righting reflex and incontinence; severe = paralysis and incontinence.

[c] Perivascular infiltration of mononuclear cells in the CNS.

$\underset{1}{\text{Ser}}$-$\underset{2}{\text{Arg}}$-$\underset{3}{\text{Phe}}$ residues, induced only histologic lesions and not clinical disease.

Antigenicity of peptic peptides. Guinea pigs with EAE induced by the human basic protein usually had circulating antibody to the basic protein: sera from 17 guinea pigs were tested 14 or more days after injection and 15 contained antibody; the mean antigen-binding capacity was 4.27 µg of ^{125}I-basic protein/ml of serum (range 0.2 to 16 µg/ml).

Sera from 45 guinea pigs injected with different doses (see Tables I and IV) of peptides P1 and P2 were tested between 14 and 33 days. Although 28 of the 45 had clinical EAE, none had detectable antibody to ^{125}I-basic protein. Sera from three guinea pigs with EAE induced with peptide P2 were tested for ability to bind ^{125}I-P2 in the radioimmunoassay; no binding was detected. Moreover there was no binding of ^{125}I-P2 by either a guinea pig or rabbit antiserum with antigen-binding capacities for ^{125}I-basic protein of 2.24 µg/ml and 139 µg/ml respectively.

Peptides P1, P2 and P3 were compared with the basic protein for their ability to inhibit competitively the binding of the ^{125}I-basic protein by hyperimmune rabbit serum. Whereas 0.025 nmol of basic protein gave 50% inhibition of binding of ^{125}I-basic protein, 25 nmol of each of the peptides gave no inhibition.

Skin tests. All sites injected with basic protein and PPD appeared normal at 4 hr. None of the control sites injected with saline showed erythema or induration at 24 or 48 hr and none of the animals injected with only FCA gave a reaction to basic protein.

Maximum erythema, in most cases accompanied by induration, was seen at 24 hr in four of the five animals immunized with peptide P1 and tested with basic protein (Table II). The diameter of erythema in two of the five animals was less than the arbitrary criterion of 8 mm (17), but both sites showed perivascular accumulation of mononuclear cells in the dermis when examined histologically at 48 hr.

TABLE II

Occurrence of delayed hypersensitivity to encephalitogenic basic protein assessed by skin testing in individual guinea pigs with EAE 11 to 16 days after immunization

Immunogen	Dose	Test Antigen		
		PPD	Basic protein	EAE (Severe)
	pmol			
P1 (in FCA)	1800	ND[a]	+[b]	+
	1800	−[c]	+	+
	1800	−	+	+
	500	+	+	+
	500	+	−	−
FCA	−	+	−	−
	−	+	−	−
	−	ND	−	−

[a] ND, not done.

[b] +, Eight millimeters or more of erythema with or without induration at 24 hr; or 4 to 8 mm of erythema with histologic lymphocytic infiltration of the dermis at 48 hr.

[c] −, No skin reaction.

TABLE III

Occurrence of low yield of peritoneal exudate cells in guinea pigs injected with encephalitogenic basic protein and peptic peptides

Occurrence of EAE	No. of Guinea Pigs Yielding a Packed Volume of Peritoneal Cells[a]	
	<0.05 ml	>0.05 ml
Clinical signs	13	1
Histologic signs only	1	4
None	0	16
Total	14	21

[a] A volume of 0.05 ml of packed cells contains $26 \pm 1 \times 10^6$ peritoneal exudate cells. This was the minimum volume for statistically valid cell migration inhibition procedures.

Studies with peritoneal exudate cells. A problem was encountered in obtaining sufficient peritoneal exudate cells from some of the guinea pigs which were immunized with encephalitogens and FCA. When guinea pigs had clinical EAE insufficient cells were recovered from the peritoneal washings to permit statistically significant numbers to be tested by the *in vitro* method for delayed hypersensitivity (Table III).

The occurrence of inhibition of macrophage migration in those guinea pigs from which a good yield of peritoneal cells was obtained is shown in Table IV. With cells from control animals, there was no inhibition of migration with all concentrations of brain antigens. Hughes and Newman (18) found that the greatest incidence of inhibition of macrophage migration in guinea pigs immunized and tested with basic protein occurred between 11 and 28 days, but in our studies with animals injected with peptides as test antigen, there was no inhibition before 12 days. Hence we have cited only the results in guinea pigs tested on day 12 or later.

In seven of eight animals immunized with basic protein, there was significant inhibition of migration of their peritoneal cells by basic protein, and in three there was inhibition by peptide P2. Of

TABLE IV

Occurrence of delayed hypersensitivity to encephalitogenic basic protein and peptic peptides in individual guinea pigs assessed by macrophage migration inhibition test

Immunogen	Dose	Test Antigen		
		PPD	Basic protein	Peptide P2[a]
	pmol			
Basic protein	50	ND[b]	+[c]	+
	50	+	+	−[d]
	50	ND	ND	+
	50	+	+	ND
	50	+	+	ND
	500	ND	−	ND
	500	+	+	ND
	500	+	+	ND
	1250	ND	+	ND
	1250	ND	ND	+
Peptide P1 (15 amino acids)	500	+	+	ND
	500	ND	−	ND
	500	ND	+	ND
	500	−	−	ND
Peptide P2 (22 amino acids)	50	ND	+	−
	50	+	+	+
	50	ND	ND	+
	360	ND	+	ND

[a] The small amount of peptide available limited the number of these tests.

[b] ND, not done.

[c] +, Significant inhibition of migration ($p < 0.01$).

[d] −, No significant inhibition.

the animals immunized with peptides P1 and P2, the migration of cells from five of the seven tested with basic protein was significantly inhibited and the migration of cells from two of three tested with peptide P2 was significantly inhibited.

DISCUSSION

The encephalitogenic basic protein comprises approximately 30% of the total protein of myelin of the CNS (19) and is composed of 170 amino acids. From a peptic digest we isolated two peptides, P1 and P2, which contained 15 and 22 amino acids. These were, in a molar comparison with the whole protein, as effective as the protein in inducing EAE in guinea pigs. This finding is not surprising because the basic protein exists as an unfolded non-helical molecule (20), and therefore we would expect the main encephalitogenic area to be contained in a short linear sequence of amino acids. The two overlapping peptides P1 and P2 contained the sole tryptophan of the basic protein and shared the first 15 amino acids (Fig. 2). In the bovine basic protein the corresponding region around the tryptophan residue differed only in the addition of a glycine residue, and the analogous peptide retained full encephalitogenicity (7). As the corresponding bovine and human peptides have different C-terminal sequences, the encephalitogenic determinant must reside within the first 10 residues of the peptides. Disruption of this sequence (Fig. 2, underlined) by chymotrypsin and N-bromosuccinimide (7), trypsin (10) and pepsin (P3, Table I and (7)) abolished the ability to induce clinical EAE.

Although peptide P3, which lacks the N-terminal $\underset{1}{\text{Ser}}$-$\underset{2}{\text{Arg}}$-$\underset{3}{\text{Phe}}$ residues, did not induce clinical EAE, lymphocytic infiltration characteristic of EAE was observed in the brain and spinal cord. This lack of correlation between clinical and histologic signs of disease has been emphasized in recent studies with different strains of guinea pigs (21) and in suppression experiments (22).

Although the area around tryptophan appears to be the main encephalitogenic determinant, it is not the sole region of the basic protein which can induce EAE. A second encephalitogenic polypeptide of 45 amino acids, with a high proportion of arginine and lysine, was isolated by Kibler (23) from the bovine protein. We isolated the analogous region from a peptic digest of the human protein (peptide K, Fig. 1); however, in studies in our laboratory (Carnegie, P. R., unpublished data) 500-fold greater quantities of this peptide were required to induce an incidence of clinical EAE similar to that induced by peptide P2. This second encephalitogenic determinant in no way overlaps with that containing tryptophan. A third determinant of 21 amino acids can be isolated from the N-terminal region of the human protein but in comparison with P2 on a molar basis, 1000 times as much was necessary to produce the same incidence of clinical EAE (10).

Peptide P1 and P2 induced delayed hypersensitivity detectable *in vivo* and *in vitro* but no detectable circulating antibody to the parent protein. This is consistent with previous studies with encephalitogenic protein in which the occurrence of EAE correlated well with that of delayed hypersensitivity (17, 18) but poorly with that of humoral antibody (24, 25; Lennon and McPherson, unpublished data). Our smallest encephalitogenic peptide contained only 15 amino acids but it may well be possible to remove several amino acids from the C-terminal end and still retain activity, because Schlossman *et al.* (26) showed that a modified hepta-peptide (α-N-dinitrophenyl-hepta-lysine) could induce delayed hypersensitivity.

We found a striking correlation between the occurrence of EAE and low yields of peritoneal exudate cells (Table III). This could be due to the massive release *in vivo* of migration inhibitory factor (27) by sensitized lymphocytes after their contact with specific antigen in the CNS. Similarly Nelson and Boyden (28) found in guinea pigs that disappearance of macrophages from peritoneal exudates after injection of specific antigen was characteristic of delayed hypersensitivity. Moreover Yoshida *et al.* (29) found in rats and guinea pigs that there was an abrupt drop in numbers of circulating blood monocytes after intravenous injection of specific antigens to which they exhibited delayed hypersensitivity.

Peptides P1 and P2, in contrast to the basic protein, failed to induce any detectable humoral antibody when administered with the same dose, route and mode of presentation; the sensitivity of the assay system was such that antibody in a hyperimmune rabbit serum could be detected up to a dilution of 1:10,000. It is conceivable that antibody to the encephalitogenic determinant, if it were produced, is absorbed from the serum *in vivo* by the target organ, as occurs in experimental allergic thyroiditis (30) and experimental and human glomerulonephritis (31, 32).

Why is the region around the tryptophan residue of the basic protein of human myelin such an effective autoantigen? Is it because it is more efficiently processed than the other determinants in the afferent limb of the immune response? This area in contrast to the protein as a whole is hydrophobic rather than highly basic. Burnet (33) suggested that in delayed hypersensitivity the effective antigen may be transported on the lipoprotein membrane of a carrier cell and thus rendered highly sensitizing to the lymphoid system. The amino acid composition of this determinant would suggest a ready ability to react with such a lipoprotein surface.

However, an ability of these peptides simply to act as potent inducers of delayed hypersensitivity is not sufficient to explain their action in inducing EAE. To explain why sensitization to this small determinant causes paralysis, we postulate that in certain regions of the brain, for example, at the junction of the neurone and oligodendroglial cell, the area around tryptophan in the basic protein in its native state is not "buried" among the other proteins and lipids of myelin but is "exposed." Thus this "tryptophan area" might be readily accessible to attack by sensitized lymphocytes; moreover if it forms a vital part of the structure of myelin, damage caused by an immune reaction could widely disrupt the functional integrity of the central nervous system.

Acknowledgments. The authors thank Miss D. Hutchieson for technical assistance, and Mr. A. Bargebos and Drs. G. S. M. Robson and D. H. Hicks for histologic assistance. We also thank Dr. I. R. Mackay for reviewing the manuscript.

Note added in proof: Eylar *et al.* (34) have revised their original sequence for the bovine encephalitogenic determinant (7). The corrected sequence shows that the human and bovine determinants are identical except for an Arg to Lys substitution at position 11 (Fig. 2). Dr. Eylar supplied us with a synthetic peptide of only 11 amino acids, which comprised residues 1 to 11, inclusive. This peptide induced the same clinical and immunologic responses as did P1, and produced severe EAE and delayed hypersensitivity in guinea pigs at doses of 5 nmols (all of three animals) and 0.5 nmols (three of four animals).

REFERENCES

1. Kies, M. W., Thompson, E. B. and Alvord, E. C., Ann. N. Y. Acad. Sci., *122:* 148, 1965.
2. Lumsden, C. E., Robertson, D. M. and Blight, R., J. Neurochem., *13:* 127, 1966.
3. Carnegie, P. R. and Lumsden, C. E., Immunology, *12:* 133, 1967.
4. Nakao, A., Davis, W. J. and Einstein, E. R., Biochim. Biophys. Acta, *130:* 163, 1966.
5. Carnegie, P. R., Bencina, B. and Lamoureux, G., Biochem. J., *105:* 559, 1967.
6. Chao, L-P. and Einstein, E. R., J. Biol. Chem., *243:* 6050, 1968.
7. Eylar, E. H. and Hashim, G. A., Proc. Nat. Acad. Sci., *61:* 644, 1968.
8. Eylar, E. H. and Hashim, G. A., Arch. Biochem. Biophys., *131:* 215, 1969.
9. Carnegie, P. R., Nature, *223:* 958, 1969.
10. Carnegie, P. R., McPherson, T. A. and Robson, G. S. M., Immunology, in press.
11. McPherson, T. A. and Carnegie, P. R., J. Lab. Clin. Med., *72:* 824, 1968.
12. McPherson, T. A. and Carnegie, P. R., Anal. Biochem., *30:* 307, 1969.
13. McPherson, T. A., Ph.D. thesis, University of Melbourne, Victoria, Australia, 1968.
14. Marchalonis, J. J., Biochem. J., *113:* 299, 1969.
15. George, M. and Vaughan, J. H., Proc. Soc. Exp. Biol. Med., *111:* 514, 1962.
16. David, J. R., Al-Askari, S., Lawrence, H. S. and Thomas, L., J. Immun., *93:* 264, 1964.
17. Shaw, C.-M., Alvord, E. C., Kaku, J. and Kies, M. W., Ann. N. Y. Acad. Sci., *122:* 318, 1965.
17. Hughes, D. and Newman, S. E., Int. Arch. Allerg., *34:* 237, 1968.
19. Eng, L. F., Chao, F. C., Gerstl, B., Pratt, D. and Tavaststjerna, M. G., Biochemistry, *7:* 4455, 1968.
20. Palmer, F. B. and Dawson, R. M. C., Biochem. J., *111:* 629, 1969.
21. Stone, S. H., Lerner, E. M. and Goode, J. H., Proc. Soc. Exp. Biol. Med., *132:* 341, 1969.
22. Leibowitz, S., Lessof, M. H. and Kennedy, L. A., Clin. Exp. Immun., *3:* 753, 1968.
23. Kibler, R. F., Shapira, R., McKneally, S., Jenkins, J., Selden, P. and Chou, F., Science, *164:* 577, 1969.
24. Lamoureux, G., Carnegie, P. R., McPherson, T. A. and Johnston, D., Clin. Exp. Immun., *2:* 601, 1967.
25. Alvord, E. C., in *The Central Nervous System,* Edited by O. T. Bailey and D. E. Smith, p. 52, The Williams and Wilkins Co., Baltimore, 1968.
26. Schlossman, S. F., Yaron, A., Ben-Efraim, S. and Sober, H. A., Biochemistry, *4:* 1638, 1965.

27. Bloom, B. R. and Bennett, B., Science, *153:* 80, 1966.
28. Nelson, D. S. and Boyden, S. V., Immunology, *6:* 264, 1963.
29. Yoshida, T., Benacerraf, B., McCluskey, R. T. and Vassalli, P., J. Immun., *102:* 804, 1969.
30. Nakamura, R. M. and Weigle, W. O., J. Exp. Med., *130:* 263, 1969.
31. Lerner, R. A. and Dixon, F. J., J. Exp. Med., *124:* 431, 1966.
32. Lerner, R. A., Glassock, R. J. and Dixon, F. J., J. Exp. Med., *126:* 989, 1967.
33. Burnet, F. M., Nature, *218:* 426, 1968.
34. Eylar, E. H., Caccam, J., Jackson, J. J., Westall, F. C. and Robinson, A. B., Science, *168:* 1220, 1970.

THE JOURNAL OF IMMUNOLOGY
Vol. 105, No. 5, November 1970

THE TERMINATION OF IMMUNOLOGIC UNRESPONSIVENESS TO BSA IN RABBITS

II. Response to a Subsequent Injection of BSA[1]

DAVID C. BENJAMIN[2] AND WILLIAM O. WEIGLE[3]

From the Department of Experimental Pathology, Scripps Clinic and Research Foundation, La Jolla, California

Received for publication April 4, 1970

Rabbits made unresponsive to BSA at birth were given two courses of immunization with various cross-reacting albumins and a subsequent injection of BSA. The same fraction of unresponsive rabbits as control rabbits responded to this subsequent injection by producing antibody reactive with BSA. Normal control rabbits were found to produce higher levels of antibody than did the previously unresponsive rabbits. Assays for both antibody-producing cells in the spleens and serum antibody of the previously unresponsive rabbits showed that 1) the subsequent injection of BSA failed to recruit precursor cells specific for BSA, 2) those cells primed by the injections of the terminating antigens were exhausted by multiple injections of BSA, and 3) unresponsiveness appeared to be terminated to all determinants shared between BSA and the terminating antigen. Following immunization of either normal or BSA unresponsive rabbits with cross-reacting albumins, a subsequent injection of BSA resulted in the production of antibody specific for the cross-reacting albumin which could not be absorbed with BSA. The response in normal rabbits to the determinants on the BSA unrelated to the determinants on the cross-reacting antigen was secondary in nature.

It has previously been shown that following the termination of immunologic unresponsiveness to BSA in rabbits by immunization with cross-reacting albumins, the rabbits will respond to a subsequent injection of BSA (1–3). However, the ability to respond to BSA is lost with time and the rabbits eventually return to the unresponsive state. This phenomenon not only has a direct bearing on the nature of immunologic unresponsiveness, but has some interesting implications regarding the mechanisms involved in autoimmunity and the perpetuation of autoimmune diseases. The present report is concerned with a further investigation of the response to injections of BSA in rabbits whose unresponsive state to BSA was terminated by the injection of certain heterologous albumins. Experiments were designed to investigate both the specificity of the response to BSA and the number of antigenic determinants involved in the termination of the unresponsive state.

[1] Publication 397 from the Department of Experimental Pathology, Scripps Clinic and Research Foundation, supported by United States Public Health Service Grant AI-07007 and Atomic Energy Commission Contract AT (04-3)-410.

[2] This work was performed during the tenure of a United States Public Health Service Predoctoral Fellowship (5-F01-GM-29, 481-04) from the National Institute of General Medical Sciences. Data taken, in part, from a dissertation submitted to the Department of Biology, University of California, San Diego, in partial fulfillment of requirements for the degree of Doctor of Philosophy. Present address: Department of Biology, The Johns Hopkins University, Baltimore, Maryland 21218.

[3] Recipient of United States Public Health Service Research Career Award 5-K6-GM-6936.

MATERIALS AND METHODS

Animals. All rabbits used in these studies were of the New Zealand White strain.

Antigens. Commercial preparations of serum albumins were obtained from the following sources: bovine (BSA), Armour Pharmaceutical Co., Lot D71209; human (HSA), supplied through the courtesy of the American Red Cross and prepared by the Squibb Pharmaceutical Co., Lot 591R. Serum albumins from sheep (SSA), pig (PSA), horse (ESA), guinea pig (GPSA), and chicken (CSA) were prepared from whole serum by the method of Schwert (4). Rabbit γG-globulin (RγG) was prepared by diethylaminoethyl (DEAE) cellulose chromatography. Albumins were trace labeled with $^{131}I(I^*)$ according to the method of McConahey and Dixon (5), and samples were counted in a gamma scintillation counter with a sodium iodide crystal.

Protein nitrogen. Protein nitrogen determinations were carried out by a modification of the micro-Kjeldahl technique (6) using a Technicon AutoAnalyzer (Technicon Corporation, Tarrytown, N. Y.).

Induction of immunologic unresponsiveness to BSA. The unresponsive state to BSA was induced by injecting 100 mg during the first 24 hr of life followed by 400 mg in two equal doses before the 5th day of life. This procedure has proved sufficient to make *all* the rabbits thus treated unresponsive for as long as 6 months (3).

Termination of unresponsiveness to BSA. The unresponsive state to BSA was terminated by giving two courses of PSA, HSA, ESA, or GPSA spaced 2 weeks apart. Each course consisted of four daily injections of 20 mg subcutaneously followed by 30 mg/kg body weight intravenously on day 5. Seven days after the last injection all the rabbits were bled and the sera were tested for antibody against several albumins (7). Subsequent injections of BSA were given either 4 or 8 weeks after the last injection of heterologous albumin.

Antibody determinations. Precipitating antibody was measured by the quantitative method of Talmage and Maurer (8) using I* antigen and the results are reported as μg antibody N/1.0 ml of serum. Tests for binding antibody were performed by the ammonium sulfate technique of Farr (9) employing 1.0 μg I* antigen N and increasing dilutions of antisera, and the results are reported as micrograms of I* antigen N bound to the globulin present in 1.0 ml of serum.

Dissociation rates. The avidity of antibody for BSA was determined as described in the previous paper (10).

Amplifying antibody. Amplifying antibody (anti-RγG) was prepared by intramuscular injections of squirrel monkeys with Freund's adjuvant containing 0.5 to 2.5 mg RγG and 0.3 mg mycobacteria. Three weeks later each monkey received 1.5 mg of heat-aggregated, alum-precipitated RγG intramuscularly in the thigh. The monkeys were bled 4 weeks after the last injection and those sera showing a strong precipitin band with RγG in agar were pooled.

Complement. Pooled sera from male Hartley strain guinea pigs weighing approximately 500 g were absorbed at 0°C for 30 min with rabbit erythrocytes. This serum was stored at −70°C and used at a 1:2.5 dilution in balanced salt solution (BSS) (11) and contained amplifying antibody at a final dilution of 1:50.

Hemolytic plaque assay. The method described here is based on the monolayer plaque assay technique reported by Petersen and Ingraham (12) but modified for use with protein antigens covalently coupled to the surface of rabbit red blood cells by use of a soluble carbodiimide (1-ethyl-3-(3-dimethylaminopropyl)-carbodiimide, The Ott Chemical Co., Muskegon, Mich.). Albumin was conjugated to rabbit erythrocytes as described by Daniels and Weigle (11), except that a 10-fold higher concentration of red cells was used (A. Cunningham, personal communication). Just before use the cells were washed with BSS and diluted 1:2.5 in BSS. Rabbit spleen cells were prepared as previously described (11) and serial dilutions (1:10) were made in BSS. For plaquing, 0.05 ml of the red cell suspension was pipetted into disposable test tubes in an ice bath, guinea pig complement (0.05 ml) was added followed by 0.1 ml of the appropriate spleen cell suspension. The contents of the tube were mixed and 0.01 ml was transferred to an Ingraham plaque assay slide (Bellco Glass Co., Vineland, N. J.). The cell mixture was spread over the assay area by means of a glass coverslip which was lowered into position with coverglass forceps. Molten petrolatum was used to seal the edges and the slides were incubated in a moist chamber at 37°C for 2 to 3 hr. Rabbit red blood cells without conjugated antigen were used as controls for background activity. After this period, the slides were removed and the plaques enumerated by observation under the 7× lens of a Spencer stereoscope (American Optical Co., Buffalo, N. Y.). The number of plaques was corrected for background and is reported as plaque-forming cells/million spleen cells plated.

Inhibition of plaque formation with soluble antigens. The amount of antigen conjugated to the red cells was estimated (11) and a 1000-fold molar excess of either soluble BSA or soluble terminating antigen was added to the complement source used in the plaque assay above. The soluble antigen was then in 1000-fold excess over that on the red cells and any spleen cells producing antibody that would react with this soluble antigen would not produce a plaque. Soluble egg albumin (a noncross-reacting antigen) was used as a specificity control.

RESULTS

Binding antibody. Both BSA-unresponsive and normal rabbits were given 20 mg I*-BSA intravenously 1 month after the last injection of heterologous albumin. These animals were exsanguinated 4 days after the level of protein bound I* decreased to 0.2% of that initially injected (as determined by precipitation with an equal volume of 20% TCA). Here some differences between unresponsive and normal animals were apparent. Following injection of BSA, the levels of binding antibody produced in the unresponsive animals were less than in the normal animals (Table I), not only to the terminating antigens and tolerated antigen, but to the other albumins as well. This was true regardless of which albumin had been used to terminate the unresponsive state. Of the 22 unresponsive rabbits thus treated, 20 had terminated unresponsiveness, since antibody reacting with BSA was produced. All the normal rabbits responded to BSA by producing anti-BSA.

The injection of BSA appeared to stimulate the production of antibody nonreactive with BSA, since the titers to the terminating antigen in both the unresponsive animals and normal rabbits were higher than the titers to BSA. This difference did not seem to be due to the residual antibody from the terminating injections, since 32 of 35 normal and 20 of 22 unresponsive rabbits had an excess of antibody over the sum of this residual antibody and the anti-BSA following BSA injection (if the half-life of the antibody was taken into account). This suggests that BSA is nonspecifically inducing the formation of antibodies reactive with the terminating antigen or more likely that some sites on BSA are immunogenic but not antigenic. The response to BSA appeared to be a secondary response since the titer to BSA following BSA injection was greater than the titer to BSA following the terminating injections (7) and the antigen clearance patterns were more characteristic of a secondary response than of a primary response.

Precipitating antibody and dissociation rates. After a subsequent injection of BSA, significant differences were seen between unresponsive and normal rabbits in the amount of antibody precipitating with the previously tolerated antigen, the terminating antigen, and some of the other albumins tested. In all cases the amount of precipitating antibody to any given albumin was greater in the normal than in the unresponsive animals (Table II), and in all cases the fraction of the total antibody produced in response to this BSA injection was greater than antibody from sera obtained 7 days after injection of the heterologous serum albumin (7). As seen with the antigen-binding capacities, the titer to the terminating antigen was higher than the titer to the injected antigen BSA.

Dissociation rate studies showed that the avidity of sera from normal animals was higher than that from previously unresponsive rabbits and was usually more avid than previously reported (7) for antibody in sera obtained after the heterologous albumin injections (Table III).

Specificity of the antibody produced following termination and a subsequent injection of BSA. Results reported elsewhere (7) suggest that the unresponsive rabbits possess the same cellular potential to produce antibody as does the normal rabbit since, regardless of which albumin was used to terminate the unresponsive state, there were no differences in the amount of antibody produced by normal and unresponsive rabbits. Following a subsequent injection of BSA, however, there were significant differences in the quantity of antibody produced which reacted with BSA. Experiments were carried out to determine if this quantitative difference between normal and previously unresponsive rabbits was a result of a difference in the specificity of the response to the BSA. Serum specimens from BSA-unresponsive rabbits and from normal rabbits (following termination and a subsequent injection of BSA) were absorbed at equivalence with either BSA or with the terminating antigen. After removal of the precipitate, these absorbed sera were then assayed for binding antibody in the presence of a 100-fold excess of the absorbing antigen as inhibitor. Absorption

TABLE I

Mean antigen-binding capacities[a] of sera from normal and BSA-unresponsive rabbits after two courses of various soluble albumins and a subsequent injection of BSA[b]

Terminating Antigen	Status	Albumin Tested										
		BSA		PSA		ESA[c]	HSA		GPSA		SSA[c]
		Pre[d]	Post	Pre	Post	Post	Pre	Post	Pre	Post	Post
PSA	Unresp.[e]	0.7 ± 0.4[f]	19.5 ± 3.5	23.3 ± 5.6	55.1 ± 10.2	4.7 ± 1.7		3.4 ± 1.0		7.8 ± 3.1	8.1 ± 2.1
	Normal	1.4 ± 0.4	52.5 ± 11.7	35.7 ± 7.6	114.1 ± 20.2	16.1 ± 3.8		13.2 ± 3.3		25.5 ± 10.0	29.1 ± 9.6
	P		0.01 < P < 0.02		0.01 < P < 0.02	0.01 < P < 0.02		0.01		0.1	0.02 < P < 0.05
HSA	Unresp.	0	27.1 ± 15.8		11.5 ± 6.2	7.8 ± 4.2	23.5 ± 2.9	50.1 ± 21.5		23.2 ± 14.1	9.9 ± 5.1
	Normal	1.6 ± 0.7	88.4 ± 16.7		47.7 ± 9.9	17.8 ± 2.8	29.4 ± 4.7	114.9 ± 17.7		54.4 ± 12.3	69.0 ± 17.9
	P		0.01 < P < 0.02		P < 0.01	0.05 < P < 0.1		0.02 < P < 0.05		0.1 < P < 0.2	P < 0.01
GPSA	Unresp.	0	30.7 ± 11.2		40.9 ± 18.7	16.1 ± 5.4		20.1 ± 7.8	25.4 ± 4.8	67.3 ± 22.1	33.2 ± 14.8
	Normal	1.1 ± 0.5	59.2 ± 13.8		75.3 ± 19.1	23.0 ± 2.7		44.8 ± 8.3	47.6 ± 8.8	136.3 ± 26.0	54.6 ± 15.4
	P		0.1 < P < 0.2		0.2 < P < 0.3	0.3 < P < 0.4		0.02 < P < 0.05		0.05 < P < 0.1	0.3 < P < 0.4

[a] Micrograms of antigen N bound by the globulin (precipitated with 50% saturated $(NH_4)_2SO_4$ present in 1.0 ml of serum).
[b] Twenty micrograms of I*-BSA given i.v. 4 weeks after the last injection of heterologous albumin.
[c] Pre-bleedings taken immediately before the I* injections were not analyzed.
[d] Pre-bleeding taken immediately before I*-BSA injection to determine residual antibody from the injections of heterologous albumins.
[e] Unresp., unresponsive.
[f] Standard error of the mean.

TABLE II

Mean precipitating antibody[a] from normal and BSA-unresponsive rabbits after two courses of various soluble albumins and a subsequent injection of BSA[b]

Terminating Antigen	Status	Antigen Tested					
		BSA	PSA	HSA	ESA	GPSA	SSA
PSA	Unresp.[c]	12.6 ± 3.2[d]	24.8 ± 8.3	0.9 ± 0.7	0.1 ± 0.2	0.7 ± 0.5	4.1 ± 1.4
	Normal	64.2 ± 20.0	92.5 ± 24.4	1.1 ± 0.4	2.2 ± 0.8	6.4 ± 4.4	40.7 ± 18.0
	P	0.02	0.01 < P < 0.02	0.8	0.01 < P < 0.02	0.2 < P < 0.3	0.05 < P < 0.1
HSA	Unresp.	22.1 ± 11.4	6.0 ± 3.8	35.1 ± 17.7	1.5 ± 1.0	1.2 ± 0.8	9.9 ± 6.0
	Normal	161.2 ± 46.1	32.8 ± 9.9	132.1 ± 28.2	9.9 ± 3.2	21.1 ± 10.7	137.8 ± 49.5
	P	0.01	0.02 < P < 0.05	0.01	0.02 < P < 0.05	0.05 < P < 0.1	0.02
GPSA	Unresp.	12.6 ± 4.0	5.2 ± 2.4	1.7 ± 1.1	0.9 ± 0.9	49.1 ± 18.2	6.0 ± 2.4
	Normal	80.4 ± 13.1	26.5 ± 14.0	4.3 ± 1.5	2.9 ± 0.9	128.1 ± 22.4	48.6 ± 10.6
	P	P < 0.01	0.1 < P < 0.2	0.1 < P < 0.2	0.1 < P < 0.2	0.01 < P < 0.02	P < 0.01

[a] Micrograms of antibody N/milliliter of serum.
[b] Twenty micrograms of I*-BSA given i.v. 4 weeks after the last injection of heterologous albumin.
[c] Unresp., unresponsive.
[d] Standard error of the mean.

of sera from unresponsive animals with BSA removed all the antibody reactive with BSA but left some residual antibody reactive not only with the terminating antigen, but also with some of the other albumins (Table IV). Absorption of sera from unresponsive rabbits with the terminating antigen removed all the antibody. Thus in the unresponsive rabbit no specific anti-BSA was formed even following a response to BSA. Absorption of sera from normal rabbits with BSA removed all antibody reactive with BSA, but as with the unresponsive rabbits left some antibody reactive with the terminating antigen and with several other albumins. In contrast to the unresponsive animal, absorption of the normal sera with the terminating antigen left some antibody reactive with BSA and removed all the antibody reactive with the terminating antigen. The normal rabbit, therefore, produced some specific anti-BSA in response to the BSA booster injection. The amount of specific anti-BSA found in normal rabbits injected with HSA was greater than that produced in normal rabbits given only a single injection of BSA and may be due to the presence of antibody left over from the terminating injections which complexes with the BSA and increases its immunogenicity.

TABLE III

Mean dissociation rates of antibody from normal and BSA-unresponsive rabbits after two courses of various soluble albumins and a subsequent injection of BSA

Terminating Antigen	Status	No. of Animals	Dissociation Rate[a]
PSA	Unresp.[b]	7	19.7 ± 3.0
	Normal	11	31.1 ± 3.0
	P		0.01 < P < 0.02
HSA	Unresp.	10	24.8 ± 9.3
	Normal	14	93.2 ± 18.2
	P		0.01

[a] Time in minutes for 50% of the initially bound I*-BSA to dissociate from antibody and be replaced by unlabeled BSA.

[b] Unresp., unresponsive.

The effect of passive anti-BSA on the primary response to BSA in normal rabbits. Normal rabbits, 12 weeks of age, were given varying amounts of passive anti-BSA intravenously ranging from 0 to 30 mg antibody N. Two days later these animals were given 25 mg I* BSA protein intravenously and the immune elimination of this labeled antigen was followed. Four days after immune elimination the rabbits were bled and the precipitating antibody to BSA was determined. It can be seen that the amount of anti-BSA produced (Table V) increased with increasing amounts of passive antibody and the onset of immune elimination was shortened (Fig. 1). Beyond a certain level, however, the passive antibody loses its effect (Table V, 30 mg passive antibody N), presumably because the complexes

TABLE IV

Specificity of antibody from normal and BSA-unresponsive rabbits following two courses of various soluble albumins and a subsequent injection of BSA

Terminating Antigen	Absorbing Antigen	Status	Antigen-Binding Capacity[a]					
			BSA	PSA	HSA	ESA	GPSA	SSA
PSA	BSA	Unresp.[b]	0	39.0	0.3	3.3	0.3	1.4
		Normal	0	105.0	0.2	3.1	11.6	6.9
PSA	PSA	Unresp.	0	0	0	0	0	0
		Normal	2.4	0	0	0	0	1.0
HSA	BSA	Unresp.	0	0	19.5	5.4	0.6	0
		Normal	0	3.3	67.4	4.0	10.2	4.6
HSA	PSA	Unresp.	0	0	0	0	0	0
		Normal	22.3	4.0	0	0.3	1.8	25.2

[a] Micrograms of antigen N bound by the globulin (precipitated with 50% saturated $(NH_4)_2SO_4$) present in 1.0 ml of serum.

[b] Unresp., unresponsive.

TABLE V

Effect of passive antibody on the primary response to BSA in rabbits

Antibody[a]	No. of Animals	Anti-BSA N
mg		*mg*
0	7	1.61
1.0	4	1.87
3.0	6	4.81
8.0	12	5.19
16.0	6	6.14
30.0	6	1.48

[a] Milligrams of anti-BSA N injected i.v. 2 days before 25 mg I*-BSA.

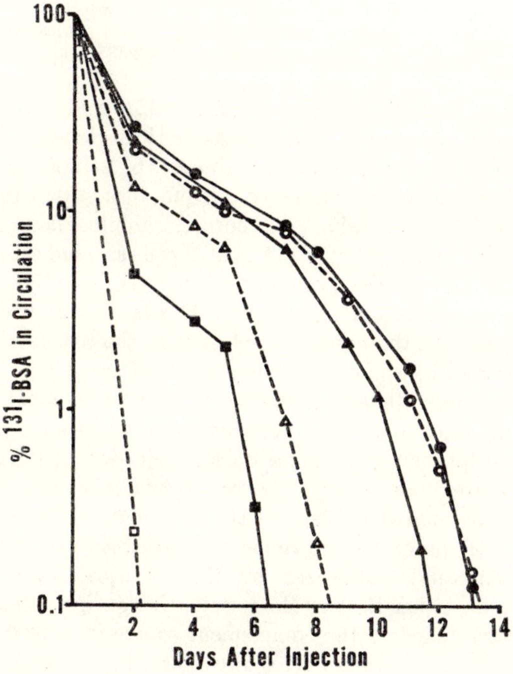

Figure 1. Serum elimination patterns of ^{131}I-BSA in rabbits after injecting different amounts of passive anti-BSA N. ●, no anti-BSA; ○, 1.0 mg anti-BSA; ▲, 3.0 mg anti-BSA; △, 8.0 mg anti-BSA; ■, 16.0 mg anti-BSA; □, 30.0 mg anti-BSA.

formed with the I* BSA were large enough to be rapidly removed by the reticuloendothelial system.

Determinants on BSA to which tolerance was terminated. In order to determine whether unresponsiveness was terminated to either a few or many of the determinants which BSA shares

TABLE VI

Antibody-combining activity following sequential absorption[a] of sera from normal and BSA-unresponsive rabbits after two courses of pig serum albumin and a subsequent injection of BSA

Animal No.	Pre-titer[b]	Absorption No.			
		I	II	III	IV
		Unresponsive			
1	30.7	24.4[c]	10.2	5.6	2.9
2	26.4	23.8	7.5	5.7	2.6
3	13.5	5.5	4.4	1.6	0.2
4	18.5	6.6	5.2	3.2	2.2
5	13.5	8.4	7.3	5.0	1.7
6	5.7	4.0	3.5	2.6	1.5
7	28.4	22.1	9.7	6.4	2.8
		Normal			
8	24.8	23.1	18.8	9.2	5.0
9	31.4	23.1	10.8	8.4	1.8
10	26.1	20.1	9.8	8.1	2.8
11	115.5	86.5	63.4	40.3	8.3
12	67.3	31.7	26.7	13.7	6.0
13	75.9	39.6	28.4	23.4	14.9
14	117.5	77.0	46.9	32.9	14.7
15	35.6	20.8	18.2	8.7	4.3
16	50.1	30.0	25.7	21.1	8.6

[a] Sera sequentially absorbed with four cross-reacting albumins in order of their increasing reactivity with the sera.

[b] BSA antigen-binding capacity before absorption.

[c] BSA antigen-binding capacity.

with the terminating antigen, sera from normal and unresponsive rabbits following injections of PSA and a subsequent injection of BSA were absorbed sequentially with various albumins and the sera were assayed after each absorption for its antigen-binding capacity to BSA. These assays were carried out in the presence of a 100-fold excess of each of the antigens with which it had been absorbed. For example, sera from rabbit 1 (Table VI) was absorbed first with HSA and assayed against BSA in a 100-fold excess of HSA; this absorbed serum was then absorbed with ESA and assayed against BSA in a 100-fold excess of both HSA and ESA; absorptions were then carried out with GPSA and SSA in that order. In this way the first absorption would remove antibody to determinants that BSA shares with HSA; the second with ESA; the third with GPSA, and the fourth with SSA. The order of

TABLE VII

Mean plaque-forming response to a booster injection of BSA or CSA following termination of unresponsiveness by human or equine serum albumin

Status	No. of Animals	Booster Antigen	Terminating Antigen	PFC/10^6 Spleen Cells Plated					
				R-BSA[a] / —	R-TA[b] / —	R-BSA / I-BSA[c]	R-TA / I-BSA	R-BSA / I-TA	R-TA / I-TA
Unresp.[d]	12	BSA	ESA	2181	4280	0	2220	0	0
Normal	5	BSA	ESA	1312	3993	0	2463	154	0
Unresp.	7	None	ESA	0	3	0	1	1	1
Normal	9	None	ESA	0	2	0	2	0	0
Unresp.	12	BSA	HSA	765	2366	0	1633	0	0
Normal	6	BSA	HSA	947	2017	1	1495	466	6
Unresp.	7	CSA	HSA	2	27	0	0	0	0

[a] Antigen on red cell (R) against which spleen cells were assayed.
[b] TA, terminating antigen.
[c] Soluble antigen added as inhibitor (I).
[d] Unresp., unresponsive.

absorption varied for each serum and the antigen with the lowest antigen-binding capacity was the first used. The results of these absorptions are given in Table VI. In every serum (both unresponsive and normal) the titer to BSA decreased with each absorption and after the last absorption there was still some antibody reactive with BSA. In the normal animals this residual antibody was greater than the amount of specific anti-BSA produced (i.e., could not be absorbed out with the terminating antigen) and probably represents some antibody that is produced to determinants shared by BSA and PSA but not the other albumins.

It therefore seems that unresponsiveness was terminated to at least five determinants that BSA shares with PSA, e.g., in rabbit 1 (Table VI), determinants shared by BSA, PSA and HSA; determinants shared by BSA, ESA and PSA; determinants shared by BSA, PSA and GPSA; determinants shared by BSA, PSA and SSA; and determinants shared by BSA and PSA. This represents only a minimal number, since some determinants may be shared by several albumins and absorption with other albumins would only tend to increase this number.

Plaque-forming response to an injection of BSA in rabbits following immunization with heterologous albumins. Twelve-week-old unresponsive rabbits and normal rabbits (of equivalent age and weight) were given two 1-week courses of immunization with HSA or ESA. Two months later these animals were given 20 mg BSA intravenously. Their spleens were removed 4 days later and assayed for plaque-forming cells against BSA-coated red cells and against either ESA- or HSA-coated red cells in the presence or absence of soluble albumins as inhibitors of plaque formation. In both unresponsive and normal rabbits plaques were found to both BSA-coated cells and red cells coated with the terminating antigens (Table VII). The number of plaques to BSA-coated cells was less than the number of plaques to the terminating antigen in every animal tested. These plaque-forming cells were not left over from the terminating injections since those normal or unresponsive rabbits not receiving a booster injection of BSA showed few (if any) plaque-forming cells against either antigen (Table VII).

In order to determine the specificity of the antibody synthesized by these plaque-forming cells, either BSA or the terminating antigen used was added to the complement source in a 1000-fold molar excess over that estimated to be on the surface of the red cells. Soluble egg albumin, in the same molar excess, had no effect on plaque formation. Soluble BSA inhibited the formation of all plaques to BSA by spleen cells from both unresponsive and normal animals (Table VII). However, when BSA was added to the terminating antigen assay system, some plaques were found to terminating antigen-coated cells. The number of plaques to the terminating antigen in the presence of BSA inhibitor was approximately equal to the difference in plaques between BSA and terminating antigen-coated cells in the absence of inhibitor. These results parallel the serologic results where absorption of both un-

TABLE VIII

Kinetics of the plaque-forming response to a BSA booster injection following termination of unresponsiveness by equine serum albumin

Days after Booster	Status	PFC/10⁶ Spleen Cells					
		R-BSA[a] / —	R-ESA / —	R-BSA / I-BSA[b]	R-ESA / I-BSA	R-BSA / I-ESA	R-ESA / I-ESA
4	Unresp.[c]	2181	4280	0	2220	0	0
4	Normal	1312	3992	0	2463	154	0
7	Unresp.	314	482	0	166	0	0
7	Normal	407	678	0	303	131	1
10	Unresp.	20	59	1	43	0	0
10	Normal	32	43	0	15	1	0

[a] Antigen on red cell (R) against which spleen cells were assayed.
[b] Soluble antigen added as inhibitor (I).
[c] Unresp., unresponsive.

responsive and normal sera with BSA left some antibody reacting with the terminating antigen while removing all that would react with BSA. The addition of soluble terminating antigen as inhibitor showed quite different results. In the unresponsive animal the terminating antigen inhibited all plaque formation to both BSA and terminating antigen-coated cells. However, in the normal animal some residual plaques to BSA-coated cells were found (Table VII). Again, these results parallel those serologic results presented above where absorption of sera from unresponsive animals with the terminating antigen removed all antibody whereas absorption of normal sera left some antibody that reacted with BSA.

In order to determine whether the excess antibody reacting with the terminating antigen but not with the tolerated antigen was due to specific stimulation by BSA or to a nonspecific (trephocytic) induction, rabbits whose unresponsive states were terminated with HSA were given a booster injection of CSA (instead of BSA) which does not detectably cross-react with either BSA or HSA. These rabbits were killed 4 days after the CSA injection and their spleens assayed for antibody-forming cells to BSA- or HSA-coated red cells. The response to BSA was specific since the injection of this noncross-reacting CSA did not cause significant increase in the number of plaque-forming cells (Table VII).

Kinetics of the response to a BSA booster injection following termination of unresponsiveness to BSA. Normal and unresponsive rabbits were immunized with ESA and given a booster injection of BSA 2 months later. Their spleens were removed at 4, 7, or 10 days after this injection and assayed for plaque-forming cells against BSA- or ESA-coated red cells in the presence and absence of soluble albumin inhibitors. The results are given in Table VIII. The plaque-forming ability of these spleen cells decreased after 4 days and returned to essentially zero by day 10, as shown for a normal response to BSA (13). At each time the number of plaque-forming cells to the terminating antigen ESA exceeded those against the injected antigen BSA. Addition of BSA inhibited all BSA plaque formation in both unresponsive and normal animals, but left some plaque-forming cells to ESA. Addition of ESA inhibitor removed plaques to ESA in all animals but left some residual plaques to BSA-coated cells in the normal rabbit. These specific BSA plaques reached a peak somewhere between 4 and 7 days after the BSA booster and returned to zero by day 10.

Plaque-forming response to a second injection of BSA in rabbits following termination of unresponsiveness to BSA. Normal and unresponsive rabbits were immunized with two courses of soluble ESA as above. One month after the last injection these animals received 20 mg BSA intravenously. A second injection of BSA was given 2 months after the first and their spleens were removed and assayed for plaque-forming cells 4 days later. The number of plaque-forming cells in the unresponsive rabbits decreased following the second injection of BSA (Table IX) when the spleen cells were assayed against BSA- or ESA-coated red cells in the presence or ab-

TABLE IX

Plaque-forming response to a second injection of BSA in normal and unresponsive rabbits following termination of unresponsiveness with equine serum albumin

Status	No. of BSA Injections	PFC/10⁶ Spleen Cells					
		R-BSA[a] / —	R-ESA / —	R-BSA / I-BSA[b]	R-ESA / I-BSA	R-BSA / I-ESA	R-ESA / I-ESA
Unresp.[c]	1	2181	4280	0	2220	0	0
	2	580	1215	1	525	5	1
Normal	1	1312	3992	0	2463	154	0
	2	2796	4167	0	1413	640	2

[a] Antigen on red cell (R) against which spleen cells were assayed.
[b] Soluble antigen added as inhibitor (I).
[c] Unresp., unresponsive.

sence of soluble inhibitors. The unresponsive animal still did not produce a specific response to BSA. In normal rabbits the response to this second injection showed quite a different pattern. In the absence of any inhibitor the number of cells producing anti-BSA increased, while the number producing plaques to ESA-coated cells remained the same. Again, all the BSA plaques were inhibited with soluble BSA. However, the number of cells not inhibited by BSA decreased (from 2463 to 1413). The number of plaque-forming cells to BSA-coated cells (in the presence of ESA as inhibitor) increased from 154 to 640 as would be expected of a normal secondary response to specific BSA determinants.

DISCUSSION

It is suggested by the above data that BSA cannot stimulate differentiation and proliferation of precursor cells in either "virgin" unresponsive or unresponsive rabbits previously immunized with a cross-reacting albumin, whereas the albumin used to terminate the unresponsive state can do so. Rabbits whose unresponsive states to BSA were terminated following injections of various cross-reacting antigens made an immune response to a subsequent injection of BSA. However, none of the antibody produced was specific for BSA, in that it all was removed by absorption with the albumin used to terminate the unresponsive state. These serologic findings are supported by the cellular events occurring in the spleens of the rabbits. Following a subsequent injection of BSA all of the rabbits had plaque-forming cells (PFC) in their spleens to both red cells coated with BSA and red cells coated with the terminating antigen. Studies on inhibition of plaque formation by soluble albumins showed that the spleens of the normal rabbits, but not the unresponsive rabbits, contained cells making antibody specific for BSA. It appears that following injection of BSA into BSA-unresponsive rabbits, memory cells are not recruited from precursor cells, but once the memory cells are recruited by cross-reacting antigens BSA can then cause the conversion to antibody-producing cells, which results in antibody only to determinants shared with the cross-reacting antigens. The larger amount of antibody made by the normal rabbits probably is the result of the stimulation of new precursor cells specific for BSA. Such stimulation or recruitment would not occur in the previously unresponsive rabbit despite immunization with a cross-reacting albumin.

Although following the termination of the unresponsive state the rabbits respond for a limited period of time to subsequent injections of BSA, the responsive state is limited and the rabbits tend to return to the unresponsive state. The spleens of unresponsive rabbits immunized by a cross-reacting albumin and given two subsequent injections of BSA contained considerably fewer antibody-producing cells to BSA after the second injection of BSA than after the first. In contrast, normal rabbits immunized with a cross-reacting albumin and given two subsequent injections of BSA contained considerably more cells producing antibody to BSA after the second injection. These findings are in agreement with previous observations showing that following termination of the unresponsive state to BSA with either chemically altered BSA (14) or heterologous albumins (1), multiple injections of BSA resulted in an eventual decrease in antibody synthesis and a return to the unresponsive state. Byers and Sercarz (15) have shown that the specific immunologic memory can be exhausted by a single large dose of antigen 3 to 6 months after a primary dose of the same antigen. Furthermore, sequential booster injections of aqueous preparations of S III polysaccharide into rabbits previously immunized with S III pneumococci led to a progressive decrease in the antibody response (16). These latter observations and the present results could best be explained by a failure of the antigen to recruit new precursor cells and by an exhaustion of memory cells.

It does not appear that the relative location of the related determinants on BSA and the heterologous albumins is involved in the termination of the unresponsive state. It was previously suggested that the location of some of these determinants on BSA was such that neither immunity nor unresponsiveness could be induced to them following injection, whereas their locations on the cross-reacting albumin were more advantageous in that they could elicit an antibody response (17). However, this possibility seems unlikely, since it appears that unresponsiveness is terminated to all determinants of the tolerated antigen that are shared or related to those on the terminating antigen. Sera from both unresponsive and normal rabbits immunized first with PSA and then given an injection of BSA showed the same qualitative reaction with BSA after each sequential absorption with four cross-reacting albumins. In these assays designed to determine the presence of five determinants to which unresponsiveness had been terminated, all five were found to be involved. This number is minimal, since the albumins used share some determinants and absorption with any one, in all probability, would remove antibody reactive not only with itself and BSA but also with some of the other albumins. Absorption of hyperimmune anti-BSA serum with any given mammalian albumin very seldom removed all antibody reactive with all other albumins (18). Furthermore, mixtures of albumins were more effective than single albumins in termination of the unresponsive state to BSA (3). It is possible that the entire spectrum of determinants on BSA may be found in a mixture of a large number of albumins and that the injection of this mixture would result in termination of unresponsiveness to all the determinants on BSA.

If the site of unresponsiveness to BSA in the rabbit was at the thymus-derived cell and the bone marrow-derived cell (or its counterpart in the rabbit[4]) was unaffected, containing a normal complement of precursor cells with receptor sites, all of the events observed with the termination of immunologic unresponsiveness could be readily explained. As suggested previously, a defect at only the thymus-derived cell would permit the presence of a normal complement of precursor cells in rabbits rendered unresponsive to BSA. Since thymus-derived cells containing receptors for cross-reacting albumins would be present in rabbits unresponsive to BSA, interaction could take place between thymus-derived cells (via determinants specific to the terminating albumin) and the bone marrow-derived cells (via determinants related to BSA) resulting in a normal response to BSA-related determinants. A defect at the thymus-derived cell also would explain 1) the ability of BSA to stimulate an immune response after termination of the unresponsive state, 2) the failure of subsequent injections of BSA to result in antibody specific for BSA, and 3) the return to the unresponsive state following termination. Following the termination of unresponsiveness, subsequent injections of the previously tolerated BSA would be expected to result in an immune response if memory cells could be stimulated directly without a synergistic interaction with thymus-derived cells. Production of antibody specific for determinants on BSA would not be expected, since BSA would still be unable to recruit precursor cells. Exhaustive differentiation of memory cells to antibody-producing cells, in the absence of further recruitment, would result in a return to the unresponsive state. It may be suggested further that the inhibition of the termination of unresponsiveness by simultaneous injections of the tolerated BSA and the terminating albumin results from a direct competition between the free BSA and the related

[4] Recent data by Richter, M. and Abdou, N. I. (J. Exp. Med., *129:* 1261, 1969) suggest that bone marrow cells are not precursor cells, but may be similar to the antigen-reactive cell of the mouse thymus. In this communication the thymus-derived cell is referred to as antigen-reactive, non-precursor cells, while the bone marrow cell is referred to as antigen-reactive, precursor cells.

determinants on the thymus cell-bound terminating albumin for receptors on the bone marrow-derived precursors.

The possible events involved in the termination of immunologic unresponsiveness to BSA may have some implications to some autoimmune diseases if, as has been suggested (3), the mechanisms between these two phenomena (in some cases) may be the same. In any event, the cellular events postulated in the termination of immunologic unresponsiveness could also be postulated for at least certain autoimmune phenomena.

The failure of rabbits to respond to specific BSA determinants following the termination of the unresponsive state has considerable bearing on other explanations of events involved in the termination of unresponsiveness. Paul *et al.* (19) suggested that once termination occurs a subsequent injection of previously tolerated antigen would result in an antibody response to determinants on BSA not shared with the terminating antigen. Bretscher and Cohn (20) proposed that once unresponsiveness was terminated, the cross-reacting antibody formed might act as a carrier and that a subsequent injection of BSA could result in a response to BSA specific determinants. Since a specific response to BSA does not occur following termination of unresponsiveness, neither of these viewpoints is tenable. The proposal of Bretscher and Cohn would be more compatible with the present data if the carrier antibody was in the form of a receptor on a cell different than the one destined to produce antibody, a possibility that they considered (20).

Normal rabbits injected first with a cross-reacting albumin and later with BSA produced an enhanced primary response to the determinants on BSA unrelated to those present on the first albumin injected. Not only was the cellular response to the unrelated determinants of a greater magnitude but it also occurred earlier than in rabbits injected with only BSA. A secondary response to determinants on BSA related to the first albumin occurred in both normal and previously unresponsive rabbits. The enhanced immune response in normal rabbits to unrelated determinants on BSA may have been the result of small amounts of residual antibody present in the circulation. It has been shown in the present studies that the presence of circulating antibody results in an enhanced response to a primary injection of excess BSA. Similar observations with other soluble proteins have been made by others (21, 22).

The injection of BSA into either normal or unresponsive rabbits previously immunized with a cross-reacting albumin results in the production of antibody specific for the cross-reacting antigen. Absorption studies showed that the antibody stimulated by BSA could be absorbed by the cross-reacting albumin injected previously, but not by BSA. Similar observations have been reported by Dixon and Maurer (23). In addition, it was shown that the injection of BSA following a previous injection of a related albumin resulted in the appearance in the spleen of a large number of cells producing antibody to the related albumin that could not be inhibited with BSA. This does not appear to be a nonspecific stimulation of antibody, since the injection of an albumin unrelated to the first albumin was ineffective. It appears that some determinants on BSA are capable of reacting with cell receptors stimulating the production of antibody that cannot effectively react with these same determinants. The host animal may be a more sensitive detector of an effective interaction between cell receptor and antigen than the test tube assay for the products resulting from the interaction.

REFERENCES

1. Weigle, W. O., J. Immun., *92:* 791, 1964.
2. Linscott, W. D. and Weigle, W. O., J. Immun., *95:* 596, 1965.
3. Weigle, W. O., *Natural and Acquired Immunologic Unresponsiveness*, World Publishing Company, Cleveland, Ohio, 1967.
4. Schwert, G. W., J. Amer. Chem. Soc., *79:* 139, 1957.
5. McConahey, P. J. and Dixon, F. J., Int. Arch. Allerg., *29:* 185, 1966.
6. Ferrari, A., Ann. New York Acad. Sci., *87:* 792, 1960.
7. Benjamin, D. C. and Weigle, W. O., J. Exp. Med., *132:* 66, 1970.
8. Talmage, D. W. and Maurer, P. H., J. Infect. Dis., *92:* 288, 1953.
9. Farr, R. S., J. Infect. Dis., *103:* 239, 1958.
10. Grey, H. M., J. Immun., *91:* 90, 1963.
11. Daniels, J. C. and Weigle, W. O., J. Immun., *101:* 1223, 1968.
12. Petersen, B. and Ingraham, J., Immunochem., *6:* 379, 1969.
13. Daniels, J. C. and Weigle, W. O., J. Immun., *101:* 1230, 1968.
14. Weigle, W. O., J. Exp. Med., *116:* 913, 1962.
15. Byers, V. S. and Sercarz, E. E., J. Exp. Med., *127:* 307, 1968.

16. Paul, W. E., Benacerraf, B., Siskind, G. W., Goidl, A. and Reisfeld, R. A., J. Exp. Med., *130:* 77, 1969.
17. Weigle, W. O., J. Exp. Med., *114:* 111, 1961.
18. Weigle, W. O., J. Immun., *87:* 599, 1961.
19. Paul, W. E., Siskind, G. W. and Benacerraf, B., Immunology, *13:* 147, 1967.
20. Bretscher, P. A. and Cohn, M., Nature, *220:* 444, 1968.
21. Terres, G. and Wolins, W., J. Immun., *86:* 361, 1961.
22. Weigle, W. O., J. Immun., *92:* 113, 1964.
23. Dixon, F. J. and Maurer, P. H., J. Immun., *74:* 418, 1955.

THE JOURNAL OF IMMUNOLOGY
Vol. 105, No. 5, November 1970

IN VITRO INDUCTION OF SULFANILIC ACID-SPECIFIC ANTIBODIES BY RNA EXTRACTED FROM RAT SPLEEN[1]

D. S. JURAS[2] AND P. ABRAMOFF

From the Department of Biology, Marquette University, Milwaukee, Wisconsin

Received for publication April 2, 1970

Rats were immunized with bovine serum albumin (BSA) or sulfanilic acid conjugated to BSA (sa-BSA) and RNA was extracted from spleens that were synthesizing antibody. The extracted RNA was used to induce sulfanilic acid-specific plaque forming cells (PFC) in a population of non-immune isologous cells *in vitro*. The induction was specific, since a significant number of PFC appeared in the presence of RNA from sa-BSA but not from either BSA-immunized or non-immunized rats. Sucrose gradient analysis of extracted RNA showed most of the immunogenic activity to be associated with light RNA (4 to 12S). The immunogenic activity of RNA was inhibited by RNase, partially inhibited by pronase, and not affected by DNase. Agglutination inhibition used to detect antigen associated with immunogenic RNA gave negative results. Analysis of RNA extracted from spleens of rats immunized with radioactive sulfanilic acid conjugated to BSA showed that radioactivity was not preferentially associated with immunogenic RNA.

Two major classes of cells have been shown to be involved in the immune response: macrophages with the capacity to degrade antigens (1) and lymphoid cells with the capacity to form antibodies (2). Studies on peritoneal cells demonstrate that macrophages form an RNA-antigen complex which induces production of specific antibodies in non-immune lymphoid cells (3–8). Biochemical analysis of the complex indicates that its immunogenicity is due to an antigen attached to immunologically nonspecific RNA (7–12). This RNA-antigen moiety is associated with heavy RNA (28S) (11). In addition, an antigen-free, immunogenic light RNA (5 to 7S or 8 to 10S) has also been isolated (13, 14). However, since the peritoneal cell population consists of approximately 90% macrophages and 10% lymphocytes, the cellular origin of these RNA's is uncertain.

These two classes of cells can be separated by a glass-adherence technique, and RNA isolated from the adherent (mostly macrophage) and non-adherent (mostly lymphocyte) cells. Studies of the immunogenicity of RNA extracted from such separated cells indicate that both RNA complexed with antigen and antigen-free RNA originate within the macrophage (14). On the other hand, studies of the molecular specificity of antigen-induced RNA indicate that a unique species of RNA is formed by lymphocytes (15, 16). Because different assay techniques were used in these two studies, it is not possible to definitely establish that the antigen-free RNA isolated from adherent cells is identical with the unique RNA isolated from non-adherent cells; but there is a reasonable likelihood that this is the case.

That an antigen stimulates the formation of new molecular species of RNA within lymphoid cells is implied by several experiments. For example, it has been shown that the amount of RNA per cell increases in the spleen after antigen injection (17), and that this is correlated with the formation of a new species of RNA (18, 19). Furthermore, RNA isolated during this biochemically active period is immunogenic *in vivo* and *in vitro* (20–25). Analysis of the immunogenic RNA indicates that it is light (21), and that it appears to be free of serologically detectable antigen (25). However, its immunogenic activity can be suppressed by antiserum specific for the antigen used to immunize RNA donors (24, 25). These results imply the presence of antigenic components with RNA. Thus, further studies are needed to determine whether an antigen must

[1] This work was supported by a Training Grant in Developmental Biology, 5T1-HD27, from the National Institutes of Health.

[2] Present address: Department of Biological Sciences, De Paul University, Chicago, Illinois.

be associated with lymphoid cell RNA for antibody production to occur.

The present study shows that spleen cells of rats immunized with sulfanilic acid conjugated to bovine serum albumin form RNA which induces sulfanilic acid-specific antibodies in nonimmune isologous cells *in vitro*. Furthermore, tracer studies of the sulfanilic acid indicate that the immunogenicity of lymphoid cell RNA is not due to an antigenic moiety associated with it.

MATERIALS AND METHODS

Animals. Charles River male albino rats[3] weighing 180 to 280 g were used for these studies.

Antigens. Bovine serum albumin (BSA) and sulfanilic acid conjugated to BSA (sa-BSA) were used. The sulfanilic acid was conjugated to BSA fraction V using the method of Campbell *et al.* (26). After conjugation, the sa-BSA was precipitated (1:1 v/v saturated $(NH_4)_2SO_4$). The resulting precipitate was resuspended (0.15 M NaCl-0.05 M Tris buffer, pH 7.4) and dialyzed (at 4°C, 48 hr, four changes of above buffer containing 0.01% Merthiolate). The amount of sa-BSA recovered was determined by Nessler's protein nitrogen test (26).

Immunization. Rats were injected with a total of 5 mg of either BSA or sa-BSA antigen as follows: 0.2 ml (1 mg) intravenously; and 0.2 ml (1 mg) (emulsified in Freund's complete adjuvant, 1:1 v/v) intraperitoneally, subcutaneously, intramuscularly, and into the hind footpads. At various times after antigen injection, rats were anesthetized and bled by cardiac puncture. Their spleens were then removed and immediately placed in chilled Eagle's minimal essential medium (MEM) until used for plaque studies. Serum was separated from clotted blood by centrifugation and stored at −20°C until needed.

Assay for humoral and cellular antibodies. Sheep red blood cells (SRBC) were washed and resuspended in twice their volume of 0.15 M NaCl (containing 1% dextrose and adjusted to pH 7 with 0.1 M disodium phosphate). For the conjugation of sulfanilic acid to SRBC, the procedure of Ingraham (27) was used. The nonconjugated and conjugated SRBC were standardized colorimetrically.

Starting with a 1:2 dilution of serum, 0.4 ml of serial dilutions was incubated with 0.1 ml of 1% SRBC or sa-SRBC for 2.5 hr at 25°C. After centrifugation, the agglutination titer of the serum was recorded.

Spleen cells of rats immunized either with BSA or sa-BSA were tested for plaque-forming cells (PFC) using the following modification of the procedure described by Merchant and Hraba (28). Spleens were minced in Eagle's MEM and the resulting cell suspension was diluted to 5×10^7 viable nucleated cells/ml as determined by the trypan blue dye exclusion technique. One-tenth milliliter of red blood cells (O.D. 540 = 1) and 0.2 ml of spleen cell suspension were mixed with 2 ml of the agar (Difco Noble) and poured into Petri plates. The latter were incubated at 37°C for 1 hr, then guinea pig complement (diluted 1:5) was added and incubation was continued for another 2 hr.

Extraction of RNA. On day 8 after antigen injection, RNA was extracted at 1° to 4°C from homogenized spleen tissue (1:10 v/v tissue in 0.14 M NaCl-0.05 M potassium acetate buffer, pH 6, containing 0.001 M EDTA and 5% BRIJ58 detergent, using a Potter-Elvehjem ground glass tissue grinder) to which washed bentonite was added (final concentration 2 mg/ml) immediately after homogenization.

Successive phenol extractions were made (first, 1:1 v/v homogenate in distilled, H_2O-saturated phenol, stirred 15 min; next centrifuged 10 min at 12,000 × G in a Sorvall RC-2B centrifuge, interphase and phenol layers re-extracted twice with buffer 2:1 v/v; then, all aqueous extracts pooled, re-extracted with phenol 2:1 v/v, and centrifuged at 17,000 × G for 10 min). The RNA in the final aqueous layer was precipitated overnight with 2 volumes of 95% ethanol at −20°C. The precipitate was washed three times with 70% ethanol in 0.15 M NaCl-0.05 M potassium acetate and resuspended in 0.15 M NaCl-0.05 M Tris buffer, pH 7.4.

The amount of RNA extracted was determined using both the orcinol test (29) and absorbance at 260 nm. The DNA was determined by the diphenylamine test (30), and protein by the method of Lowry *et al.* (31). The following standards were used for the above determinations: yeast RNA, thymus DNA, and BSA fraction V. The results indicated that 0.062 ± 0.028 mg of DNA and 0.198 ± 0.04 mg of protein were present/mg of extracted RNA.

[3] The Charles River Breeding Laboratory, Inc., North Wilmington, Massachusetts.

Fractionation of RNA. For the fractionation of RNA, linear sucrose gradients (5% to 20%) were prepared in 0.01 M Tris buffer pH 7.2, supplemented with 0.004 M $MgCl_2$, 0.025 M KCl. One milliliter containing 1 to 1.5 mg of RNA was layered over the 30-ml gradient and the tubes were centrifuged for 14 hr at 24,000 rpm in a Spinco SW 25.1 swinging bucket rotor. One-milliliter fractions were collected manually by puncturing the bottom of the tube. The amount of RNA per fraction was determined by reading O.D. units at 260 nm.

Assay for the inductive activity of RNA. All procedures were conducted under aseptic conditions. The spleens were minced in Eagle's MEM supplemented with 10% fetal calf serum. The isolated cells were centrifuged at 4°C for 10 min at 2000 × G and the pellet was resuspended in Eagle's MEM.

Various amounts of RNA were added to non-immune cells (2 × 10^7 viable cells/ml final concentration) in culture tubes (15 x 125 mm) and the suspension was incubated at 37°C for 12 hr on a roller drum. The pH of the medium was periodically adjusted to 7.4 by bubbling 5% CO_2 into the tubes. After incubation, the tubes were rapidly cooled in an ice bath and centrifuged for 10 min. The pellets were resuspended in Eagle's MEM (5 × 10^7 cells/ml) and the cell suspensions were kept at 4°C until plated to determine the number of PFC.

When enzymes were used, 0.1 ml containing 10 μg RNase,[4] DNase,[5] or pronase[6] was added to 0.1 ml of RNA. After incubation of the sample for 30 min at 37°C, 1 ml containing 2 × 10^7 cells was added and the sample reincubated for 12 hr.

Enzyme assays. The RNA (50 to 100 μg) was incubated at 37°C either with RNase, DNase or pronase (10 μg/ml). A perchloric acid test was used to assay enzyme activities (32). The results showed that after 30 min of incubation, 70.8%, 0.7% and 23.0% (w/v) of RNA was degraded by RNase, DNase, and pronase, respectively. Longer incubation of RNA with RNase did not result in an increase of perchloric acid-soluble components, while incubation with DNase or pronase showed a gradual increase of such components.

Determination of antigen associated with RNA

Agglutination-inhibition test. Various dilutions of antisera (0.2 ml rat anti-SRBC or anti-sa-SRBC) of known titer were incubated with RNA (10 to 20 μg in 0.2 ml). After 30 min at 37°C, 0.1 ml of 1% SRBC or sa-SRBC was added, and the tubes were reincubated for 2 hr at room temperature, centrifuged, and examined for agglutination.

Detection of radioactive antigen associated with RNA. ^{35}S-sulfanilic acid[7] (spec. act., 30 mCi/mmol, 3 mCi contained in 1 ml) was coupled to BSA (100 mg in 5 ml saline) using the same procedure as for non-radioactive BSA. The total recovery of ^{35}S-sa-BSA was 60% (spec. act., 20.6 μg/mg BSA).

Rats weighing 210 ± 10 g were injected with 35.5 μg of ^{35}S-sa-BSA. Freund's adjuvant and the same injection routes were used as for non-radioactive sa-BSA injections. The animals were killed at 5 hr and 3, 7 and 8 days after injection, and RNA was extracted from the spleens. A modification of the method of Mans and Novelli (33) was used to determine radioactive labeling of RNA extracted from rats injected with ^{35}S-sa-BSA. One volume of RNA (10 to 100 μg) was precipitated with one volume of 10% trichloracetic acid (TCA) containing 0.1 mg yeast RNA/ml TCA. After 2 to 3 hr at 4°C, the precipitate was collected on a Whatman No. 3 MM filter paper disk using negative pressure (Millipore). The disks were washed twice with 5% TCA containing carrier sulfanilic acid and RNA, and once with ethanol-ether (1:1). The filters were dried and placed in counting vials to which was added 5 ml of scintillation fluid (0.4% 2,5-diphenyloxazole, 0.01% 1,4-bis-2(5-phenyloxazole) benzene in toluene), and the samples were then counted in a Packard liquid scintillation spectrometer.

RESULTS

Induction of antibodies to sulfanilic acid. Agglutination titers and number of PFC were determined on four to six rats killed 1 to 20 days after immunization with sa-BSA, BSA in Freund's adjuvant, or adjuvant alone. For each spleen, two to three plates containing sa-SRBC or SRBC

[4] Bovine pancreas RNase (protease free) type 1-A, 5× crystallized, Sigma Chemical Company, St. Louis, Missouri.

[5] Bovine pancreas DNase, 1× crystallized, Sigma Chemical Company, St. Louis, Missouri.

[6] Pronase, B grade, Calbiochem, Los Angeles, California.

[7] Nuclear Chicago Corporation, Des Plaines, Illinois.

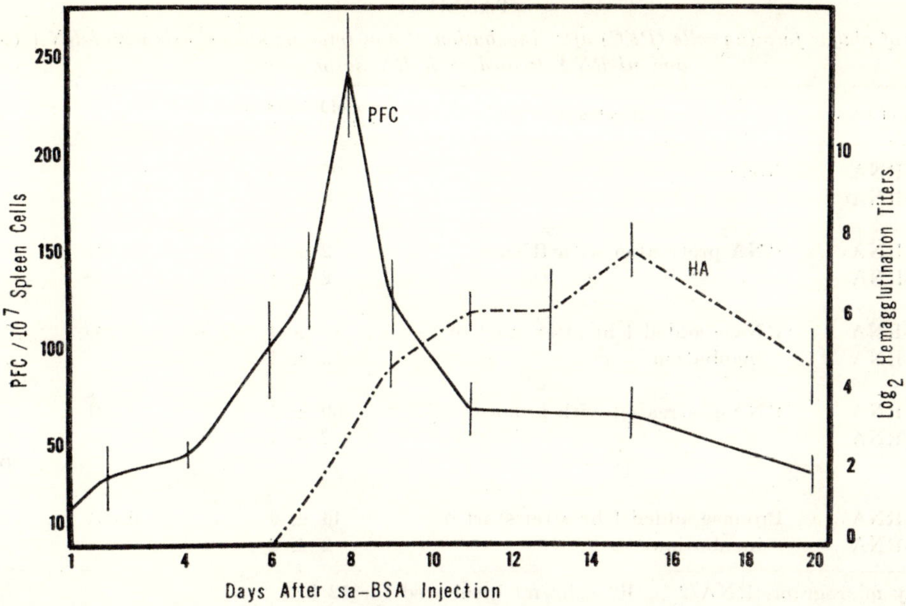

Figure 1. **Primary response in rats immunized with sa-BSA in Freund's adjuvant; plaque-forming cells (PFC) in spleens and hemagglutination titers (HA) of sera. Means ± S.E. are represented by vertical bars on a graph.**

were used. The number of PFC in spleens of non-immunized rats was 7 to 20 $\pm$ 3/10^7 spleen cells; the numbers of PFC in spleens of rats immunized with BSA or adjuvant alone were also found to lie in this range. However, the animals immunized with sa-BSA produced significant numbers of PFC in the plates containing sa-SRBC. As shown in Figure 1, the peak PFC number was reached on day 8, and this was followed by an increase of humoral antibody which agglutinated only sa-SRBC but not SRBC.

Induction of antibody activity by RNA from spleens of rats immunized with sa-BSA. Three rats were immunized with sa-BSA in Freund's adjuvant and three rats were injected with adjuvant alone. On day 8 after antigen injection both groups of rats were killed and spleen RNA was extracted. (We designate spleen cell RNA from rats immunized with sa-BSA as: i-RNA(sa-BSA); that from rats injected with adjuvant alone as: ni-RNA.) Non-immune spleen cells (2×10^7 cells/ml) were incubated with 25 to 200 μg of the extracted RNA. Then the cells were plated with SRBC or sa-SRBC. The cell cultures exposed to either i-RNA(sa-BSA) or ni-RNA produced virtually the same number of PFC to SRBC (10 $\pm$ 2) as those to which no RNA,

TABLE I

Number of plaque-forming cells (PFC) after incubation of non-immune spleen cells with i-RNA (sa-BSA) or ni-RNA

Amount of RNA Added[a]	No. of PFC/10^7 Non-Immune Spleen Cells Plated with sa-SRBC[b]	
	i-RNA (sa-BSA)	ni-RNA
μg		
25	34 ± 1	0
50	53 ± 2	6 ± 1
100	95 ± 3	8 ± 1
150	81 ± 3	5 ± 1
200	78 ± 2	12 ± 2

[a] Micrograms of RNA/2×10^7 cells/ml incubated for 12 hr.

[b] Backgrounds (plaques on plates containing SRBC alone) were subtracted in all cases. Means ± S.E. were based on three experiments with two plates/sample (N = 6).

or RNA extracted from BSA-injected animals, was added. The final results are shown in Table I. These data indicate specificity of response in that the number of PFC in the cultures exposed to i-RNA(sa-BSA) was about 10 times higher than after exposure to ni-RNA. The data also show

TABLE II

Number of plaque-forming cells (PFC) after incubation of non-immune spleen cells with i-RNA (sa-BSA) and ni-RNA treated with RNase or pronase

Type of RNA[a]	Treatment	No. of PFC/10^7 Non-Immune Spleen Cells[b]	P_1[c]	P_2[d]
i-RNA	None	97 ± 8		
ni-RNA		4 ± 3		
i-RNA	RNA pretreated with RNase	2 ± 1	0.001	
ni-RNA		2 ± 1		
i-RNA	RNase added 1 hr after start of incubation	89 ± 4	0.100	
ni-RNA		2 ± 1		
i-RNA	RNA pretreated with pronase	60 ± 1	0.001	
ni-RNA		2 ± 1		
				0.200
i-RNA	Pronase added 1 hr after start of incubation	46 ± 9	0.001	
ni-RNA		2 ± 2		

[a] Fifty micrograms RNA/2 × 10^7 cells/ml incubated for 12 hr.

[b] Background (plaques on plates containing SRBC) PFC were subtracted from all samples. Means ± S.E. were based on two experiments, three plates/sample (N = 6).

[c] Probability of difference between PFC numbers being at least as great as observed due to random sampling: case for untreated *vs* enzyme-treated i-RNA.

[d] As for [c]: case for pronase-pretreated *vs* pronase-post-treated i-RNA.

that the amount of i-RNA(sa-BSA) required for maximum PFC number was about 100 μg/2 × 10^7 cells.

That i-RNA(sa-BSA) conferred antibody activity on non-immune cells was indicated by the fact that after pre-treatment with RNase, this RNA lost most of its inductive activity (Table II). However, when RNase was added after incubating non-immune cells with i-RNA(sa-BSA) for 1 hr there was no significant reduction in plaque numbers.

On the other hand, pronase added either before or after incubation of cells with i-RNA(sa-BSA) prevented formation of PFC to a significant extent. Since pronase is a proteolytic enzyme, it might be thought to inhibit formation of plaques by degrading antibody protein. This possibility was tested by incubating spleen cells isolated from SRBC immunized rats with pronase and assaying the cells for plaque formation. Since the numbers of plaques of enzyme-treated and untreated samples were about the same (Table III), the likelihood that pronase degraded antibody protein originating in i-RNA(sa-BSA) incubated cells appears to be slight.

Effects of fractionated i-RNA on non-immune cells. As a reference for determining molecular species present in rat spleen RNA isolated on sucrose gradients, ^{35}S-sa-BSA(3.9S) was used. Three identical sucrose gradients were prepared: to the first was added 1 mg ni-RNA/ml; to the second, 0.05 mg ^{35}S-sa-BSA (5.4 × 10^5 cpm)/ml; and to the third, 1 mg ni-RNA mixed with 0.05 mg ^{35}S-sa-BSA/ml. All gradients were centrifuged simultaneously and 1-ml fractions were collected. The distribution patterns of RNA, ^{35}S-sa-BSA, and the mixture of the two conformed with each other for all three gradients (Fig. 2). Since ^{35}S-sa-BSA gave a single peak coinciding with RNA fraction III, an approximate assignment of S values for RNA could be made (18): fraction I was estimated to contain 26 to 34S; fraction II, 12 to 26S; and fraction III, 4 to 12S.

Studies of plaque formation by non-immune cells after incubation with unfractionated and fractionated i-RNA(sa-BSA) showed that most of the inductive activity was concentrated in fraction III (Table IV). The plaque-forming efficiency of fractionated i-RNA (PFC/50 μg fractionated i-RNA/PFC/50 μg non-fractionated i-RNA) was 3.2 in fraction III, 1.6 in fraction II, and 1.1 in fraction I. The RNase treatment of

TABLE III

Effect of pronase on plaque formation by spleen cells from rats immunized with SRBC

Experimental Conditions		PFC/10^7 Spleen Cells[a] Incubated for a Total of	
Mode of enzyme used	Enzyme solution	3 hr	7 hr
30 min in buffer at 37°C prior to start of all incubation	Buffer + pronase	203 ± 9	171 ± 12
	Buffer	159 ± 12	187 ± 16
Added to culture at 1 hr after start of all incubation	Buffer + pronase	170 ± 15	143 ± 2
	Buffer	162 ± 8	137 ± 20

[a] The number of plaque-forming cells (PFC) before incubation was 143 ± 16. Means ± S.E. were based on five plates/cell culture (N = 5). The differences between pronase and control (buffer) samples were found to be statistically insignificant.

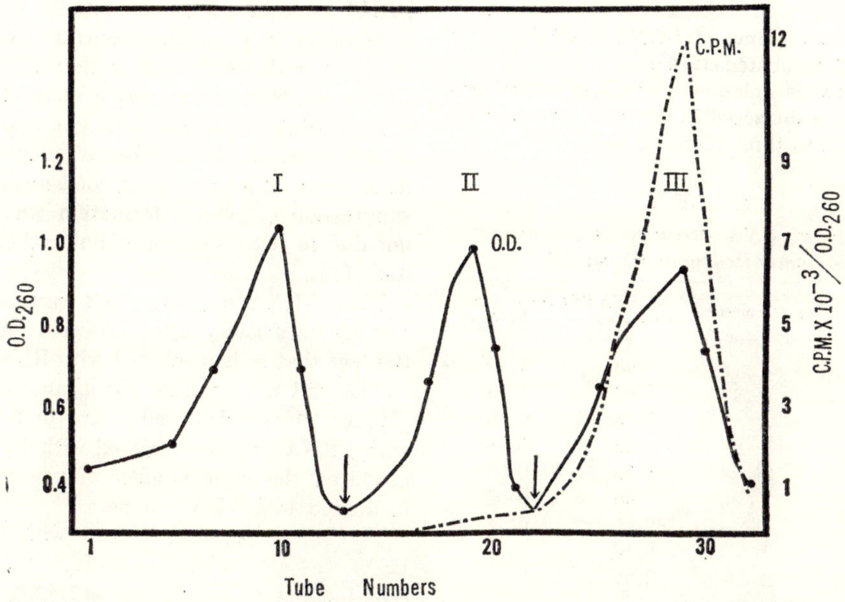

Figure 2. Sucrose gradient sedimentation patterns of ni-RNA and ^{35}S-sa-BSA. A mixture of rat spleen RNA and ^{35}S-sa-BSA was separated on a linear (5% to 20%) sucrose gradient. The optical density units (O.D.) of ni-RNA and counts/min (cpm) of ^{35}S-sa-BSA/sample tube are reported. For the studies of induction of antibody activity by RNA fractions I, II and III, the samples within each fraction were pooled. The arrows point to the tubes where fractions were separated for pooling.

i-RNA(sa-BSA) inhibited the activity in all fractions; DNase did not have any significant effects on any fraction. Pronase, as in previous studies, seemed to reduce plaque formation.

When plaque formation produced by ni-RNA was studied as above, no net increase in plaque numbers was observed.

Agglutination-inhibition test. Neither fractionated nor unfractionated i-RNA samples showed agglutination-inhibition of SRBC or sa-SRBC in the presence of their specific antisera.

Detection of ^{35}S-sa-BSA associated with i-RNA. The results of several attempts to detect an association of ^{35}S-sa-BSA with spleen RNA are presented in Table V. After injection of ^{35}S-sa-BSA, the radioactivity associated with 5-hr RNA was approximately 10 times larger than that associated with 3 to 8 day RNA. The latter is virtually the same as that of the *in vitro* control.

If the above radioactivity data are recalculated on the basis of percentage of injected antigen, they are in agreement with the findings of

TABLE IV

Number of plaque-forming cells (PFC) after incubation of non-immune spleen cells with i-RNA (sa-BSA) fractionated on sucrose gradient

i-RNA (sa-BSA) Fractions[a]	No. of PFC/10^7 Non-Immune Spleen Cells[b]			
	No enzyme added	RNase added	DNase added	Pronase added
Unfractionated i-RNA (sa-BSA)	33	7	41	25
Fraction I	35	8	38	29
Fraction II	52	10	47	40
Fraction III	106	15	99	80

[a] Forty micrograms of i-RNA (sa-BSA)/2 × 10^7 cells/ml incubated 12 hr.

[b] Backgrounds (plaques on plates containing SRBC) were subtracted in all cases. Means were based on two to three plates/sample.

TABLE V

Radioactivity of RNA extracted from spleens of rats immunized with ^{35}S-sa-BSA

Time after Injection[a]	No. of Spleens	Mg RNA Extracted	NanoCi/mg RNA
5 hr	2	4.45	1.20
	2	2.94	1.58
	3	5.48	0.90
	3	3.63	0.89
3 days	2	5.39	0.05
7 days	2	7.45	0.05
7 days	3	12.97	0.16
8 days	2	6.16	0.06
Control[b]	2	3.21	0.17

[a] 35.5 μCi injected into each rat.

[b] 71 μCi added to the homogenate of two spleens immediately before RNA extraction.

Garvey *et al.* (34, 35) for ^{35}S-sa-BSA retention and association with RNA in rabbit liver.

Since the specific activity (nanoCi/mg RNA) of RNA 3 to 8 days after injection was too low for further analysis of labeled RNA, only that at 5 hr was used for fractionation on sucrose gradients. Two sucrose gradients containing i-RNA were employed for each batch of extracted i-RNA. The radioactivity was found to be distributed uniformly through the entire gradient. At no time was any evidence obtained for a differential increase of radioactivity in any one particular fraction of i-RNA.

DISCUSSION

This investigation provided reasonably clear evidence for two basic facts concerning cellular immune responses: first, that hapten-induced lymphoid cell i-RNA stimulates antibody production in non-immune lymphoid cells, and second, that the antigen present at this time is not immunogenic. The data obtained here and by other investigators supporting these conclusions may be summarized as follows. When i-RNA(sa-BSA) was incubated with a constant number of non-immune cells, the number of PFC obtained was directly dependent on i-RNA concentration up to 100 μg/ml. In fact, the increase in PFC with i-RNA concentration was initially linear. This dependence is in distinct contrast to that produced by ni-RNA. It is true that an increase in i-RNA(sa-BSA) concentration above 100 μg/ml did not result in a corresponding increase of PFC. However, since the number of viable cells remained the same at all RNA concentrations used, suppression of plaque formation was probably not due to toxic substances but rather to RNA itself (36).

That i-RNA(sa-BSA) itself carries the immunogenic activity into the cell is implied by the fact that cells incubated with RNase-treated i-RNA did not produce significant numbers of plaques. Also, when cells were first incubated with i-RNA and then treated with RNase, they produced the same number of plaques as cells incubated with i-RNA alone.

The role of protein present with i-RNA(sa-BSA) was also investigated. It was found that cells incubated with i-RNA(sa-BSA) pre-treated with pronase produced the same number of plaques as cells first incubated with i-RNA and then with pronase. The number of PFC in both experimental groups was reduced to approximately 55% of that in the control group (cells incubated with i-RNA). Because pronase contains RNase-like activity, interpretation of these results regarding the role of protein in evoking antibody activity is difficult. Nevertheless, one must argue that if protein alone is immunogenic, pre-treatment of RNA with pronase should abolish formation of plaques (7). As seen above, only partial reduction in PFC occurred. Moreover, addition of pronase to the cells pre-incubated with i-RNA also reduced the number of PFC. The results might also be due to pronase effects on antibody protein or cell permeability, but it seems unlikely that any significant number of antibody molecules were degraded by pronase because cells from immunized rats, when incubated with pronase *in vitro*, continued to form the same number of plaques as did controls. Thus, it is plausible to assume that pronase, by virtue of its proteolytic activity, may alter cell permeability and enter the cell, where it degrades i-RNA.

That immunogenic activity was carried by i-RNA(sa-BSA) was also supported by the findings that most of the activity was associated with light RNA(4–12S). Thus, i-RNA(sa-BSA) appeared to be concentrated in that size range which corresponds to the i-RNA isolated from mouse spleens immunized with SRBC (8 to 12S) (21) and to i-RNA from peritoneal cells stimulated by bacteriophage (8–10S) (13). Furthermore, it appeared to be in the range of RNA sizes having the highest template activity (6 to 12S) (18, 19) and a base composition different from the RNA of non-immunized animals (8 to 12S and 18S) (15). The size correlation suggests, but does not prove, that i-RNA investigated in the present study has properties similar to the above RNA's, namely, lymphoid cell origin, template activity, and a unique base composition.

None of several different techniques used to detect antigen associated with lymphoid cell i-RNA gave positive results (21–23). Similarly, in the present study, antigen could not be detected by agglutination-inhibition using either unfractionated i-RNA(sa-BSA) or the fractionated i-RNA contained in any single sucrose gradient collection tube. Seeking a more sensitive assay technique to detect antigen, an attempt was made to correlate the immunogenic activity of i-RNA-(sa-BSA) with radioactive antigen retained with i-RNA. Since i-RNA(sa-BSA) induced sulfanilic acid-specific PFC, the presence of radioactivity with i-RNA would be presumptive evidence for a sulfanilic acid antigen (37).

As seen in Table V, although radioactivity was associated with i-RNA at early (5 hr) post-injection times, at all later times there is no significant (relative to control) attachment of radioactivity to i-RNA. These facts imply that antigen was not selectively attached to i-RNA when the immune response was at its maximum.

When combined density gradient and tracer techniques were used to determine whether there there was a preferential association of ^{35}S-labeled antigen with any particular i-RNA fraction, the results were negative. That is, for 5-hr i-RNA, the distribution of ^{35}S over the density gradient fractions was completely uniform. By implication, 8-day i-RNA similarly had no antigen preferentially attached to any one particular fraction. This inference is indirectly supported by several studies showing that radioactive antigen peaks at those densities where immunogenic macrophage RNA is concentrated (5, 7–12). Since the 8-day i-RNA was probably derived from lymphoid cells, the absence of a peak was not unexpected.

In conclusion, the inductive (4 to 12S) fraction of i-RNA(sa-BSA) in rat spleen lymphoid cells at the time of peak immune response evoked sulfanilic acid-specific antibody in non-immune cells. Any antigen component that might have been associated with this i-RNA(sa-BSA) appeared to be non-immunogenic.

Acknowledgments. The authors are grateful to Dr. B. Merchant, National Institutes of Health, who provided sa-BSA for the preliminary studies and gave valuable advice on some techniques. Also, thanks are due to Dr. A. V. Pisciotto for his advice and to Mrs. N. Brien for her capable technical assistance.

REFERENCES

1. Cohn, Z. A., Adv. Immun., *9:* 163, 1968.
2. Dutton, R. W., Adv. Immun., *6:* 253, 1967.
3. Fishman, M., J. Exp. Med., *117:* 837, 1961.
4. Fishman, M. and Adler, F. L., J. Exp. Med., *117:* 595, 1964.
5. Askonas, A. and Rhodes, J. M., Nature, *205:* 470, 1965.
6. Friedman, H. P., Stavitsky, A. B. and Solomon, J. M., Science, *149:* 1106, 1965.
7. Gottlieb, A. A., Glisin, V. R. and Doty, P., Proc. Nat. Acad. Sci., *57:* 1849, 1967.
8. Gottlieb, A. A., Science, *165:* 592, 1969.
9. Gottlieb, A. A., J. Reticuloendothel. Soc., *5:* 270, 1968.
10. Gottlieb, A. A., Biochemistry, *8:* 2111, 1969.
11. Gottlieb, A. A. and Strauss, D. S., J. Biol. Chem., *244:* 3324, 1969.
12. Roelants, G. E. and Goodman, J. W., Biochemistry, *7:* 1432, 1968.
13. Fishman, M. and Adler, F. L., Cold Spring Harbor Symp. Quant. Biol., *32:* 343, 1967.
14. Fishman, M. and Adler, F. L., in *Nucleic Acids in Immunology*, Edited by, Plescia, D. J. and Braun, W., p. 439, Springer-Verlag, New York, 1968.
15. Cohen, E. P., Proc. Nat. Acad. Sci., *57:* 673, 1967.

16. Cohen, E. P. and Raska, K., Jr., in *Nucleic Acids in Immunology*, Edited by Plescia, D. J. and Braun, W., p. 573, Springer-Verlag, New York, 1968.
17. Juhasz, A. and Rose, B., Canad. J. Biochem., *41:* 2983, 1963.
18. Mach, B. and Vassali, P., Proc. Nat. Acad. Sci., *54:* 975, 1965.
19. Mach, B. and Vassali, P., Science, *150:* 622, 1965.
20. Cohen, E. P. and Parks, J. J., Science, *144:* 1012, 1964.
21. Cohen, E. P., Newcomb, R. W. and Crosby, L. K., J. Immun., *95:* 583, 1965.
22. Friedman, H., Science, *146:* 934, 1964.
23. Friedman, H., Biochem. Biophys. Res. Commun., *17:* 272, 1964.
24. Abramoff, P. and Brien, N., J. Immun., *100:* 1210, 1968.
25. Friedman, H., in *Nucleic Acids in Immunology*, Edited by Plescia, D. J. and Braun, W., Jr., p. 505, Springer-Verlag, New York, 1968.
26. Campbell, D. H., Garvey, J. S., Cremer, N. E. and Sussdorf, D. H., in *Methods in Immunology*, W. A. Benjamin Inc., New York, 1963.
27. Ingraham, S. J., J. Infect. Dis., *91:* 268, 1952.
28. Fraenkel-Conrat, H., Singer, B. and Tsugita, A., Virology, *14:* 54, 1961.
29. Mejbaum, W., Hoppe-Seyler Z. Physiol. Chem., *258:* 117, 1939.
30. Dische, Z., in *The Nucleic Acids*, Vol. 1, Academic Press, New York, 1955.
31. Lowry, O. H., Rosebrough, N. J., Farr, A. L. and Randall, R. J., J. Biol. Chem., *193:* 265, 1951.
32. Josefssom, L. and Lagerstedt, S., in *Methods of Biochemical Analysis*, Edited by D. Glick, Vol. 9, p. 64, Interscience Publishers, 1962.
33. Mans, R. J. and Novelli, G. D., Arch. Biochem. Biophys., *94:* 48, 1961.
34. Garvey, J. S. and Campbell, D. H., J. Exp. Med., *105:* 361, 1957.
35. Garvey, J. S., Campbell, D. H. and Mannick, L. D., J. Exp. Med., *125:* 111, 1967.
36. Morini, J. C., Londner, M. V., Font, M. T. and Rabasa, S. L., Experientia, *25:* 640, 1969.
37. Ingraham, J. S., J. Infect. Dis., *89:* 109, 1951.

THE JOURNAL OF IMMUNOLOGY
Vol. 105, No. 5, November 1970

STUDIES ON EQUINE IMMUNOGLOBULINS

II. Antigenic Interrelationships among Horse IgG, IgG(T) and Antipneumococcal γ_1-Component[1]

CHARLES M. HELMS[2] AND PETER Z. ALLEN

From the Department of Microbiology, University of Rochester School of Medicine and Dentistry, Rochester, New York 14620

Received for publication March 30, 1970

A comparative antigenic analysis of horse IgG, IgG(T) and γ1-component was carried out by immunodiffusion. In addition to sharing antigenic determinants in common with the L chain and Fab fragment of IgG, IgG(T) and γ1-component each share a similar set of antigenic determinants in common with the Fc fragment of horse IgG. γ1-Component can be further shown, however, to share an additional set of antigenic determinants in common with the Fc fragment of IgG-globulin which is absent from IgG(T). Based on the immunologic data, schematic models for the antigenic structures of horse IgG, IgG(T) and γ1-component are proposed.

Eight antigenically distinct immunoglobulins have been recognized and described by Rockey (1) and Rockey *et al.* (2) among isolated horse anti-*p*-azophenyl-β-D-lactoside antibodies: γGa, γGb, γGc, γA[3], 10Sγ1, γM, and two immunoglobulins of γ1-mobility which remain to be further studied and classified. An antibody of γ1-mobility, which is heterogeneous in its sedimentation behavior and forms salt dissociable aggregates, has also been isolated from hyperimmune horse antibacterial sera (3–5). Originally termed "atypical macroglobulin" (3, 4), this horse immunoglobulin has also been referred to as "AI" or "aggregating immunoglobulin" (5), γ1-component (6) and IgB (7). γ1-Component[4] has been shown to be antigenically distinct from horse IgG, IgG(T) and IgM globulins (5). While γ1-component appears to be physicochemically distinct from other horse antibodies and may represent a ninth antigenic type of horse immunoglobulin, its relationship to anti-lactoside antibodies of γ1-mobility isolated by Rockey (1) is not yet established.

Of the horse immunoglobulins so far isolated, the antigenic structure of the IgG-globulins has been most extensively studied. Unique H chain specific antigenic determinants of γGa, γGb, and γGc anti-Lac. antibodies have been localized on the Fc region of the heavy chain (1, 8). Similar to data obtained with the immunoglobulins of other animal species (9), antigenic determinants shared with other horse immunoglobulin classes have been found to occur on the L chains and Fab fragment of IgG (1, 8, 10, 11). Antigenic determinants common to the Fc region of IgG and IgG(T) have also been reported (1, 11, 12). Relatively little is known about the antigenic structure of γ1-component and its relationship to other horse immunoglobulin classes.

In an earlier study (13), five antigenic specifi-

[1] This investigation was supported by United States Public Health Service Research Grant AI-06534 from the National Institute of Allergy and Infectious Diseases. Support, in part, was also obtained from General Research Grant FR 05403, National Institutes of Health.

[2] Predoctoral Fellow, supported by United States Public Health Service Training Grant TI AM-1004-05, Clinical Investigator Training Program, Department of Medicine, University of Rochester School of Medicine and Dentistry.

[3] The following synonyms have also been applied to this horse immunoglobulin: 7S β_{2A}, T-component, IgA(T), IgT, IgG(T) and γT. In the present study the designation IgG(T) will be used to refer to this immunoglobulin.

[4] The noncommital designation "γ1-component" is retained throughout this study, since it is at present not yet established whether this antibody constitutes a separate immunoglobulin class or is a subclass of IgG.

cities (Fc_1, Fc_2, Fab_{sp}, L and L_{sp}) associated with the horse IgG molecule and its fragments were recognized by immunodiffusion analysis of papain digestion products, heavy and light chains of normal serum IgG-globulins, employing rabbit anti-IgG reagents. In the present study, antigenic interrelationships among IgG, γ1-component and IgG(T) were examined by immunodiffusion analysis employing reagents directed against antigenic specificities associated with various parts of the horse IgG molecule. Based on the immunologic data obtained, schematic models of the antigenic structures of horse IgG, γ1-component and IgG(T) are proposed to illustrate antigenic relationships among these three immunoglobulins and to show the location of common and unique antigenic determinants.

MATERIALS AND METHODS

IgG-globulin. Horse IgG-globulin was isolated from pooled normal horse serum and commercial fractions of horse γ globulin (fraction II, Pentex, Corp., Kankakee, Ill.) by DEAE-cellulose column chromatography as described in earlier studies (13–15). Isolated IgG was rechromatographed and represents protein comprising the ascending limb of the peak eluted from DEAE-cellulose by 0.01 M phosphate, pH 8.0, starting buffer.

Papain digestion fragments and polypeptide chains of horse IgG-globulin. F'c, Fc and Fab fragments and heavy and light chains of horse IgG-globulin were prepared according to procedures described by Porter (16) and Fleischman *et al.* (17). The isolation and purification of these antigens have already been described in detail (15).

IgG(T)-globulin. IgG(T)-enriched fractions were isolated from a commercial globulin fraction of equine antitoxin (Eli Lilly and Co., Indianapolis, Ind.) using a modification of the method described by Weir and Porter (11). Antitoxin (40,000 units) were equilibrated with 0.01 M phosphate pH 8.0 starting buffer and then applied to a 4- x 42-cm column of DEAE-cellulose. IgG was eluted from the column by starting buffer, as well as by 0.02 M phosphate buffer, pH 8.0. IgG(T)-containing fractions were then eluted by 0.05 M phosphate buffer, pH 6.3. A fraction rich in IgG(T) antitoxin, but containing a readily detectable IgG contaminant, was obtained by pooling the peak tubes eluted by 0.05 M phosphate buffer, pH 6.3.

As shown in Figure 1, when diffused against specific anti-IgG reagent, the IgG(T) antitoxin preparation (well 2) gave a band showing complete fusion with the band formed by purified horse IgG (well 1), thereby demonstrating the presence of an IgG contaminant. When diffused against a specific anti-IgG(T) reagent (Fig. 1*B*), IgG(T), well 2, gave a single band of precipitation.

Antipneumococcal γ1-component. Antipneumococcal γ1-component was isolated from 5- to 10-ml portions of hyperimmune type II antipneumococcal horse serum H513 Bl.55 (3/14/39) by salt or hapten dissociation. Thoroughly washed immunoprecipitate, formed by adding an equivalent amount of type II pneumococcal capsular polysaccharide (SII) to antiserum made 0.01 M in disodium ethylenediaminetetraacetic acid, was suspended in 2 ml of 15% NaCl and incubated at 37°C for 1 hr with frequent agitation. Precipitate remaining insoluble after this time was spun down and extracted twice more with strong salt. Supernatant fluids from the three extractions were combined, dialyzed overnight against 0.15 M saline, and concentrated by negative pressure dialysis. A small amount of precipitate formed during dialysis and concentration which was removed by centrifugation and discarded.

Hapten dissociation of γ1-component from (SII-H513 anti-SII) immunoprecipitates, using 15% sodium glucuronate (18–21), was carried out following a procedure identical to that described for salt extraction.

Solutions of antipneumococcal γ1-component were also readily prepared from horse antiserum by hapten solubilization of immunoprecipitates formed with Oxycel, a cross-reacting antigen. Washed immunoprecipitate formed by adding an equivalent amount of oxidized cellulose (Oxycel, 12% COOH, Eastman Chemical Products, Kingsport, Tenn.) to serum H513 could be almost entirely solubilized in a few drops of 5% sodium glucuronate (18).

When examined by immunoelectrophoresis with rabbit anti-normal horse serum, all preparations of antipneumococcal γ1-component isolated from serum H513 gave an arc of precipitation confined to the γ1 region. In immunodiffusion analysis, isolated γ1-component failed to show any reactivity with reagents specific for IgG and IgG(T) (Fig. 1), as well as IgM.

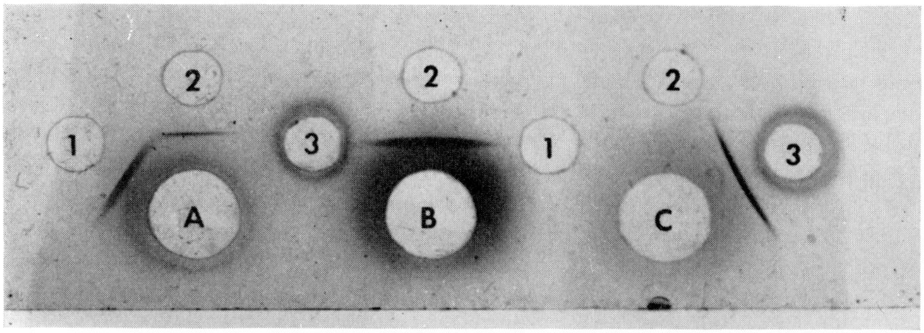

Figure 1. Immunodiffusion analysis of horse immunoglobulin preparations. Center wells contain: *A*, anti-IgG (reagent RH3-3C absorbed with γ1-component); *B*, anti-IgG(T) (reagent R7-1C absorbed with IgG); *C*, anti-γ1-component (RH17-3C absorbed with IgG). Peripheral wells contain: *1*, horse IgG; *2*, IgG(T) antitoxin preparation containing an IgG contaminant; *3*, γ1-component (H 513 anti-S II-Oxycel precipitate dissolved in 5% sodium glucuronate).

The sedimentation velocity of isolated γ1-component from serum H513 showed a marked heterogeneity dependent upon protein concentration and ionic strength as described for "atypical macroglobulin" (3, 4) and "aggregating immunoglobulin" (5) of hyperimmune horse antibacterial sera. Hapten-dissociated γ1-component isolated from serum H513, at 4.5 mg/ml in 0.15 M NaCl, showed two rapidly sedimenting components: a major 11.1 $s_{20,w}$ component and a minor 26.9 $s_{20,w}$ component. The minor 26.9 S component may represent highly aggregated γ1-component or soluble antigen-antibody complex. At approximately one-half the original protein concentration (2.3 mg/ml in 0.15 M NaCl) the same preparation sedimented as a major 8.9 $s_{20,w}$ peak with some heavier material present as a low plateau on the leading edge. At one-fourth the original concentration (1.2 mg/ml in 0.15 M NaCl) a major 8.3 $s_{20,w}$ peak was observed. The ionic strength of solvent employed also affected the sedimentation velocity. Salt-dissociated antibody at 4 mg/ml in 0.15 M NaCl sedimented as a major 8.0 $s_{20,w}$ peak, while the same preparation in 1.0 M NaCl sedimented with a 6.7 $s_{20,w}$ peak.

Through an exchange of reagents with Dr. G. Sandor of the Institut Pasteur, it was established by immunodiffusion that the γ1-component isolated from H513 antipneumococcal horse serum is immunologically indistinguishable from the "atypical macroglobulin" described earlier by Sandor (3, 4).

Pepsin digestion of horse γ1-component. Purified γ1-component (5.6 mg), isolated from antiserum H513, was treated with pepsin for 18 hr at 37°C in 2.5 ml 0.2 M acetate buffer, pH 4.5, at an enzyme to substrate ratio of 2:100 (w/w). As a control, γ1-component at the same concentration was subjected to identical treatment, except that pepsin was omitted. Digestion was stopped by adjusting the pH to 7.5 with 0.4 M Tris base and the digest centrifuged to remove traces of insoluble material. During digestion, white floccules of precipitate formed which readily dissolved when the pH was finally adjusted. No precipitates formed in controls.

Horse antipneumococcal sera. Hyperimmune sera H513 Bl.55 (3/14/39), H485 Bl.53 (3/14/39) were obtained from the New York State Department of Health through the kindness of Jesse L. Hendry. These sera were obtained from horses after repeated intravenous inoculations with type II and type VIII pneumococcal vaccine, respectively. Sera were absorbed with pneumococcal C polysaccharide and stored at 4°C in the presence of phenol (0.25%) and Merthiolate (0.0001%).

Pneumococcal polysaccharide. Type II pneumococcal capsular polysaccharide (SII) was prepared by the method of Heidelberger *et al.* (22). Type VIII (S VIII) pneumococcal capsular polysaccharide was isolated essentially as described for type III polysaccharide (22) and purified by copper precipitation (23).

Rabbit antisera. Anti-normal horse serum (anti-NES, RH1-5C) was prepared by immunizing rabbits with pooled normal horse serum according to a regimen previously described (13). Anti-IgG reagents (R2-2C and RH3-3C) were obtained by immunization with purified horse IgG emulsified in complete Freund's adjuvant. Reagents (RH3-3C abs. and R2-2C abs.) specific for the Fc region of horse IgG were prepared by absorbing anti-IgG sera with purified Fab fragment. Such sera designated as anti-$IgG_{Fc_{1,2}}$ reagents react with both F′c and Fc fragments. Anti-IgG_{Fc_2} reagent (R2-2C abs.) prepared by absorbing anti-$IgG_{Fc_{1,2}}$ serum with F′c fragment is reactive only with Fc fragment (13).

A reagent (R7-1C abs.) specific for IgG(T) was prepared by absorbing with IgG globulins, serum from rabbits immunized with isolated IgG(T) tetanus antitoxin provided by Prof. R. R. Porter (11).

Rabbit antisera to horse IgM-globulins and horse γ1-component were prepared employing a technique used by Treffers and Heidelberger (24) in early studies on antigenic relationships among horse antibodies. Washed antigen-antibody complexes, precipitated from horse antipneumococcal sera, were emulsified with complete Freund's adjuvant so as to provide about 1 mg protein/ml emulsion. Rabbits were given several courses of immunization with antigen, each course separated from the next by a minimum of 4 weeks. Each course of immunization lasted 3 weeks and consisted of weekly 0.2- to 0.4-ml subcutaneous injections of antigen in either the footpads or back. Three weeks after the final injection, rabbits were bled from the marginal ear vein. Antisera RH17-3C and R1(8-8)-1C were obtained from rabbits immunized with specific precipitates formed from horse anti-SII serum H513 and horse anti-VIII serum H485, respectively. By absorption of RH17-3C serum with IgG-globulins, a reagent specific for γ1-component was obtained. A reagent specific for horse IgM was prepared by absorbing antiserum R1(8-8) with horse γ1-component, IgG and IgG(T) globulins.

Immunoelectrophoresis and immunodiffusion. Immunoelectrophoresis and immunodiffusion in two dimensions were carried out as previously described (13–15).

RESULTS

Antigenic relationship between horse γ1-component and IgG. An antigenic similarity between horse γ1-component and horse IgG is evident from the reaction of partial identity shown by these antigens in immunodiffusion analysis. When diffused against anti-IgG (Fig. 2*A*), IgG (well 1) gave a band of precipitation which fuses with, but spurs over, the band given by γ1-component (well 2). Partial fusion demonstrates the occurrence of antibodies with a specificity directed against determinants common to both γ1-component and IgG, while spurring of IgG over γ1-component shows the presence of anti-IgG antibodies specific for determinants present only on IgG.

Antigenic determinants shared by both γ1-component and IgG are located only in part on the L chain of IgG. As shown in figure 2*A*, when diffused against anti-IgG, γ1 component (well 2) and IgG (well 1) each gave a band of precipitation which spurred over that given by L chain (well 4). Spurring of γ1-component over purified L chain indicated that anti-IgG antibodies reactive with determinants other than those on isolated L chain were precipitated by γ1-component. Thus, antigenic determinants shared by isolated L chain and γ1-component alone could not account for all the cross-reactivity shown by γ1-component.

Antigenic determinants shared by both γ1-component and IgG are also localized on the Fab fragment of IgG. As shown in figure 2*A*, γ1-component (well 2) gave a band which fused with and spurred over the band given by isolated Fab fragment of IgG (well 3). This same pattern of reactivity persists even after the removal of L chain reactivity from anti-IgG by absorption with purified L chain (Fig. 2*B*). Thus, in addition to sharing L chain determinants with IgG and its Fab fragment, γ1-component also possesses antigenic configurations unique to the Fab fragment not detected on isolated L chain. Such determinants have been previously identified and termed Fab_{sp} (13). The spurring of γ1-component over Fab fragment (Fig. 2*A* and 2*B*) suggests that anti-IgG antibodies specific for determinants on the Fc portion of the IgG molecule are also precipitable by γ1-component. That γ1-component shares determinants in common with the Fc fragment of IgG is evident from immunodiffusion findings shown in figure 2*C*. γ1-Component (well 2 gives a band of precipitation with anti-$IgG_{Fc_{1,2}}$. This reagent shows no reactivity with Fab fragment (well 3) or L chain (well 4), but does give a band of precipitation with intact horse IgG (well 1) and its Fc fragment (well 5). That some, but not all, Fc determinants of IgG are shared with γ1-component is evident from the spurring of IgG and its Fc fragment over γ1-component.

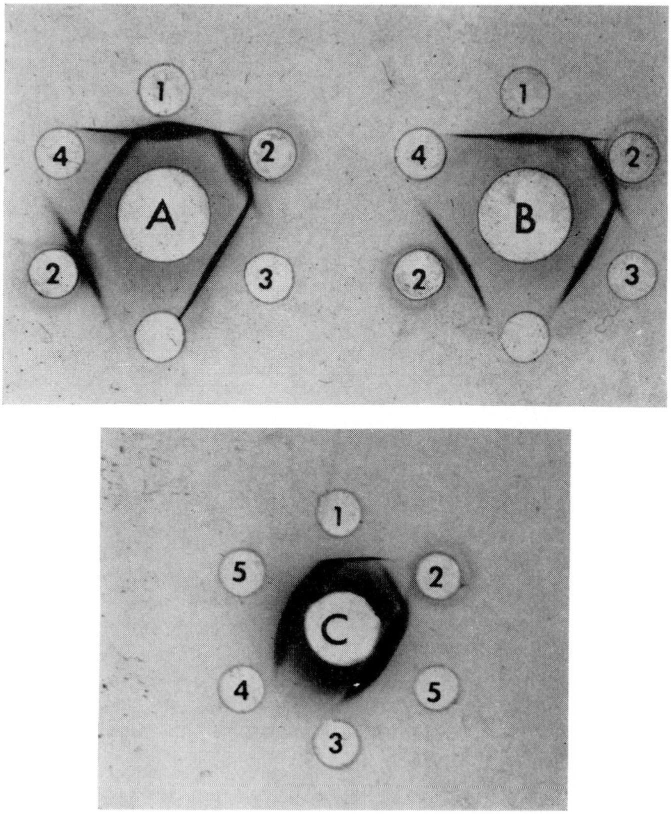

Figure 2. Antigenic comparison of horse γ1-component with horse IgG, its L chain, Fab and Fc fragments by immunodiffusion analysis. Center wells contain: *A*, anti-IgG (RH 3-3C); *B*, anti-IGg absorbed with L chain (RH 3-3C L abs.); *C*, anti-IgG$_{Fc1,2}$ (anti-IgG serum RH 3-3C absorbed with Fab fragment). Peripheral wells contain: *1*, horse IgG; *2*, γ1-component; *3*, Fab fragment; *4*, L chain; *5*, Fc fragment.

Effect of pepsin digestion on the antigenic structure of γ1-component. The effect on immunologic reactivity of treating purified γ1-component with pepsin is shown in Figure 3. Pepsin-treated antipneumococcal γ1-component (well 2) failed to react with a reagent specific for γ1 component (well A) or a reagent specific for the Fc fragment of IgG (well B); untreated γ1-component (well 1), however, retains its reactivity with both these reagents. Pepsin digests contained only a single component of slow γ2 mobility found to be immunologically indistinguishable from Fab fragment of IgG (Fig. 3*C*, well 3) when diffused against anti-IgG.

Antigenic relationships between γ1-component and IgG(T). Absorption studies were carried out to establish the relationship of antigenic determinants shared by γ1-component and IgG, to determinants shared by IgG(T) and IgG (1, 11). Portions of anti-IgG were absorbed with IgG(T) or γ1-component and the absorbed sera were then tested for reactivity with IgG, its Fc and Fab fragments, L chain as well as IgG(T) and γ1-component. Results obtained from immunodiffusion analyses are summarized in Table I. Data obtained with anti-IgG absorbed with L chain or Fab are also included for comparison.

In order to demonstrate that all the antibody present in anti-IgG serum RH3-3C was specific for and precipitable by horse IgG, a portion of serum was absorbed with IgG. As shown in Table I, after absorption with horse IgG, antiserum RH3-3C failed to give bands in immunodiffusion with γ1-component, IgG(T), IgG, Fc and Fab fragment as well as L chain. Absorption of anti-IgG with either IgG(T) or γ1-component com-

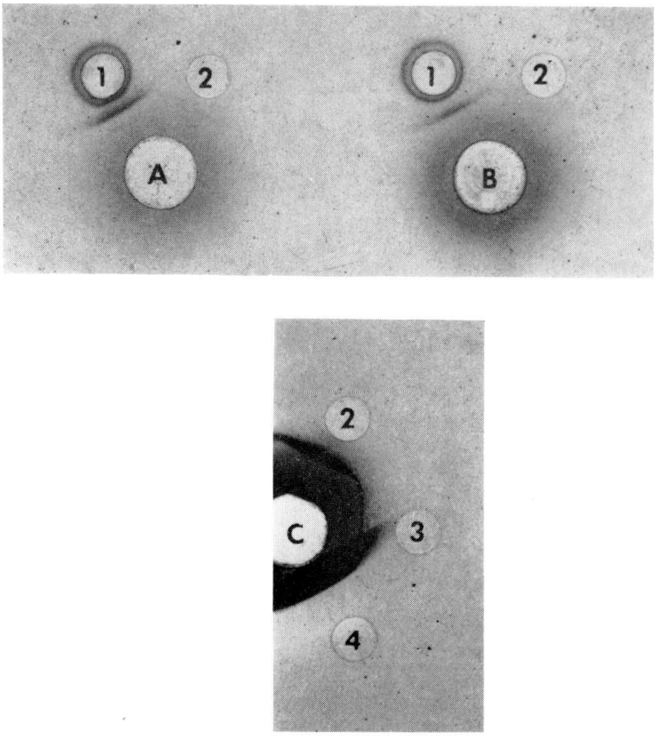

Figure 3. Effect of pepsin digestion on the immunologic reactivity of γ1-component. Central wells contain: *A*, anti-γ1-component (RH 17-3C abs.); *B*, anti-$IgG_{Fc1,2}$ (anti-IgG RH 3-3C absorbed with Fab); *C*, anti-IgG (RH 3-3C). Peripheral wells contain: *1*, γ1-component exposed to 0.2 M acetate buffer, pH 4.5, at 37°C for 18 hr; *2*, γ1-component treated with pepsin; *3*, Fab fragment of horse IgG, produced with papain; *4*, IgG.

TABLE I

Immunodiffusion behavior of anti-horse IgG before and after absorption with various antigens

Antiserum	Antigen Used for Absorption	Reactivity in Immunodiffusion with					
					Fragment or subunit of IgG		
		IgG	IgG(T)	γ1-comp.	Fc	Fab	L chain
Anti-IgG (serum RH3-3C)	None	+	+	+	+	+	+
	IgG	−	−	−	−	−	−
	γ1-component	+	−	−	+	−	−
	IgG(T)	+	−	+	+	−	−
	L chain of IgG	+	+	+	+	+	−
	Fab fragment	+	+	+	+	−	−

pletely eliminated reactivity with Fab and isolated L chain. Thus, both IgG(T) and γ1-component possess most if not all the L chain (1) and Fab-specific (Fab_{sp}) determinants associated with Fab fragment of IgG(13). The behavior of these absorbed sera with Fab fragment and L chain was the same as that of anti-IgG absorbed with Fab fragment, but differs, however, from that of anti-IgG absorbed with L chain. Anti-IgG absorbed with L chain fails to react with isolated L chain, but shows reactivity with Fab fragment. This reactivity persists due to the presence of Fab_{sp} specific antibodies not precipitable by isolated light chain (13).

Anti-IgG absorbed with Fab fragment retains reactivity not only with IgG and its Fc fragment, but with IgG(T) and γ1-component as well, thus confirming that IgG(T) and γ1-component share antigenic determinants in common with Fc fragment of IgG. As summarized in Table I, absorption of anti-IgG with IgG(T) removed reactivity with IgG(T), leaving behind antibodies capable of precipitating not only with IgG and its Fc fragment but also with γ1-component. This finding shows that IgG(T) lacks some determinants present on γ1-component which are shared with Fc fragment of IgG. Anti-IgG absorbed with γ1-component, on the other hand, while continuing to show reactivity with IgG and its Fc fragment, ails to react with IgG(T) as well as γ1-component. These immunodiffusion findings suggest the existence of two groups of antigenic determinants: one group shared by the Fc fragment of IgG with IgG(T) and γ1-component while the other group is shared only by the Fc fragments of IgG and γ1-component.

Immunodiffusion with anti-Fc reagents. The behavior of IgG, IgG(T) and γ1-component with anti-IgG_{Fc2} reagent (R2-2C abs.), and anti-$IgG_{Fc1,2}$ in immunodiffusion is shown in Figures 1, 2 and 4*A*. A preparation of IgG(T) antitoxin, known to contain about 10% IgG (wells 3 and 6), gave two bands of precipitation. The band formed closer to the antigen well is identified as the IgG contaminant by its complete fusion with the band given by purified horse IgG in adjacent well 2. The

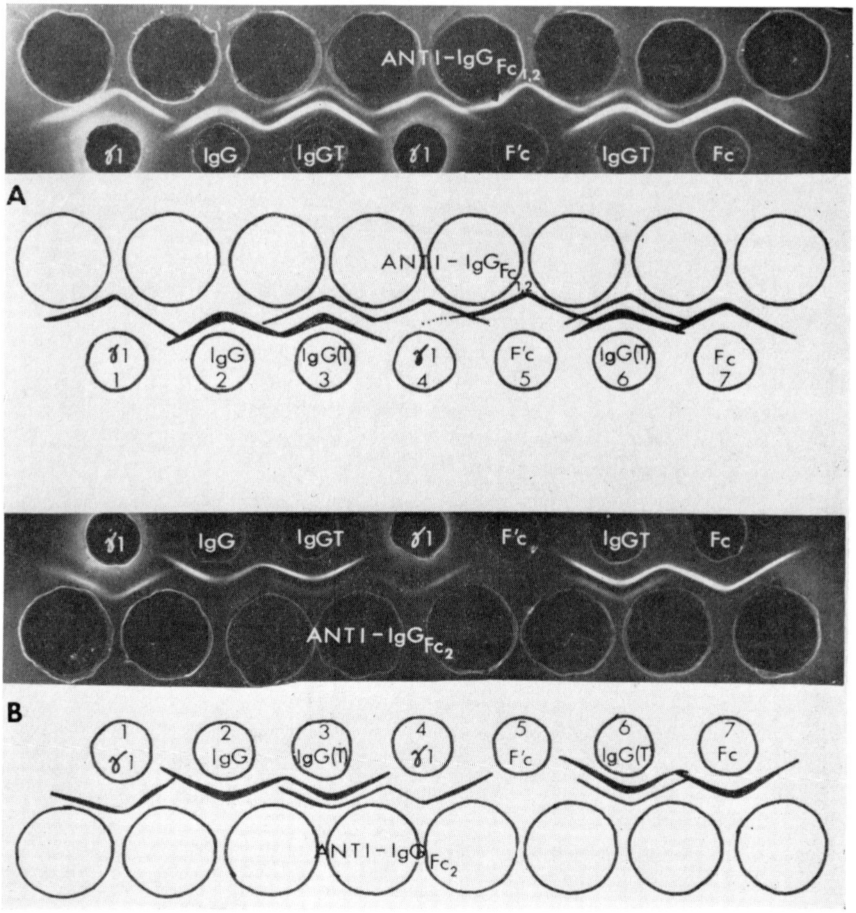

Figure 4. Immunodiffusion behavior of horse IgG, its Fc and F′c fragments, γ1-component, and IgG(T) with anti-Fc reagents. Wells labeled anti-$IgG_{Fc1,2}$ contain anti-IgG serum R2-2C absorbed with Fab fragment. Wells labeled anti-IgG_{Fc2} contain anti-IgG serum R2-2C absorbed with Fab and F′c fragments.

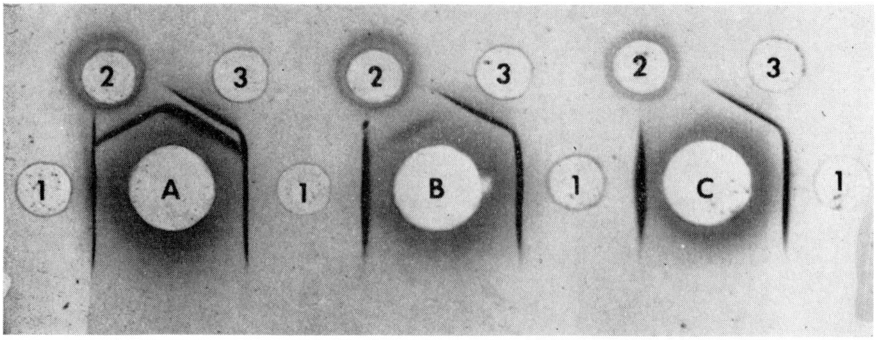

Figure 5. Immunodiffusion behavior of horse IgG, antipneumococcal γ1-component and IgG(T) with anti-horse immunoglobulin reagents. Center wells contain: *A*, anti-IgG$_{Fc1,2}$ (R2-2C absorbed with Fab); *B*, anti-IgG$_{Fc1,2}$ absorbed with IgG(T); *C*, anti-IgG$_{Fc1,2}$ absorbed with γ1-component. Peripheral wells contain: *1*, IgG; *2*, γ1-component; *3*, IgG(T) antitoxin containing about 10% IgG.

single band given by IgG (well 2) shows partial fusion and spurs over the band given by γ1-component (well 1) and IgG(T) (well 3), demonstrating both IgG(T) and γ1-component to be antigenically related to Fc fragment of IgG. The band of precipitation given by γ1-component (well 4) and IgG(T) (well 3) shows complete fusion indicating the presence of anti-Fc antibodies cross-reactive with determinants also present on IgG(T) and γ1-component.

F′c fragment (Fig. 4*A*, well 5) gave a single band of precipitation with anti-IgG$_{Fc1,2}$ which intersects the band formed by the IgG(T) component in well 6 and γ1-component (well 4). These immunodiffusion findings show that some of the determinants shared by Fc fragment of IgG, IgG(T), and γ1-component are absent or not detectable on F′c fragment. Absorption of anti-IgG$_{Fc1,2}$ with F′c fragment fails to eliminate reactivity with IgG(T) (wells 3 and 6) or γ1-component (wells 1 and 4, Fig. 4*B*). These data show that determinants shared by IgG(T), γ1-component and the Fc fragment of IgG are not confined to the isolated F′c fragment of IgG (i.e., are not uniquely Fc$_1$ determinants).

Immunodiffusion data obtained with a specific anti-IgG$_{Fc1,2}$ reagent (Fig. 5*A*) gave a single band of precipitation with IgG (well 1) and γ1-component (well 2), while two bands of precipitation were obtained with the IgG(T) equine antitoxin mixture (well 3). The IgG contaminant of the mixture is identifiable as the band closest to well 3 by its complete fusion with purified equine IgG in well 1. The more rapidly diffusing IgG(T) constituent gives a band which forms closer to the central well A. Although not clearly evident in Figure 5*A*, γ1-component (well 2), shows a faint spur over the IgG(T) band. That IgG(T) lacks antigenic determinant groupings cross-reactive with anti-IgG$_{Fc1,2}$ which are present on γ1-component is evident from Figure 5*B*. As seen in Figure 5*B*, following absorption of anti-IgG$_{Fc1,2}$ with IgG(T), reactivity with IgG(T) is removed leaving behind reactivity with γ1-component (well 2) and IgG (well 1). Absorption of anti-IgG$_{Fc1,2}$ with γ1-component (Fig. 5*C*) results in the complete loss of reactivity with IgG(T) as well as γ1-component.

DISCUSSION

Like the immunoglobulins of other species, horse immunoglobulins possess both common and unique antigenic determinants. Elucidation of antigenic interrelationships among horse immunoglobulins, as well as antigenic relationships to immunoglobulins of other species, not only provides independent, immunologic evidence for structural homologies, but also provides additional, useful criteria for classification as already demonstrated with human (25) and canine (26) immunoglobulins.

Eight antigenically distinct horse anti-hapten antibodies have been described by Rockey (1) which possess unique antigenic determinants localized on the H chain portion of the molecule. The failure of anti-L chain reagents to distinguish among heavy chain types has established that these immunoglobulins share common light chain determinants (1, 8).

Antigenic and structural relationships between horse IgG and IgG(T) have been examined by several workers (1, 2, 8, 11, 12, 27–29) and extensive reciprocal cross-reaction as well as considerable structural homology was reported for both immunoglobulins. Cross-reactions were shown to be mediated only in part by common light chain determinants (1, 11). In addition to class-specific or unique determinants, common antigenic determinants were also found localized on the pepsin-susceptible Fc portion of the heavy chain of both horse IgG and IgG(T) (1, 11).

While the γ1-component of horse antibacterial sera (3, 4) has been shown to be antigenically distinct from IgM, IgG and IgG(T) (5), an antigenic analysis of determinants shared by γ1-component in common with IgG and IgG(T) has not been previously carried out. As demonstrated by immunodiffusion data (Fig. 2) and absorption studies summarized in Table I, horse antipneumococcal γ1-component shows extensive cross-reactivity with anti-IgG sera. This cross-reaction is mediated by antigenic determinants localized in various regions of the γ1-component molecule. Antigenic determinants shared by both γ1-component and IgG are localized not only on L chain and Fab fragment (Fig. 2, *A* and *B*), but also occur on Fc fragment of IgG. The finding that anti-IgG reagents rendered specific for Fc by absorption with Fab fragment retain their cross-reactivity with γ1-component (Figs. 2*C* and 4) demonstrates the occurrence of similar antigenic determinants on γ1-component and the Fc portion of IgG globulin.

Evidence that cross-reactive determinants are localized on the Fc portion of the γ1-component molecule is provided by immunodiffusion data obtained with pepsin-digested γ1-component. As shown in Figure 3, treatment of purified antipneumococcal γ1-component with pepsin results in a loss of unique γ1-component determinants and the production of an antigen immunologically indistinguishable from the Fab fragment of IgG, as well as a loss of cross-reactivity with reagents specific for Fc fragment of IgG. Similarly, peptic digestion of horse IgG(T) results in the production of a 5S $F(ab')_2$-like component (1, 11, 28, 29) and a loss of cross-reactivity with reagents specific for IgG heavy chains (1).

Absorption and immunodiffusion analysis (Table I and Figs, 4 and 5) provide data showing that the cross-reaction of horse γ1-component with anti-IgG is mediated at least in part by the same antigenic determinants shown by others (1, 11) to be shared by the Fc portion of the heavy chains of horse IgG and IgG(T) globulins. This is established by the findings that: 1) horse anti-IgG sera absorbed with Fab fragment fail to provide specific anti-Fc reagents and retain cross-reactivity with both γ1-component and IgG(T); 2) anti-IgG absorbed with γ1-component no longer cross-reacts with IgG(T), while absorption of anti-IgG with IgG(T) does not eliminate cross-reactivity with γ1-component.

Immunologic findings obtained in the present study are readily explained by the existence of two sets of common antigenic determinants localized in Fc portion of the heavy chains of horse IgG, IgG(T), and γ1-component. While one set of common determinants occurs on each of the three immunoglobulins, another set of antigenic determinants shared by IgG and γ1-component is absent from IgG(T).

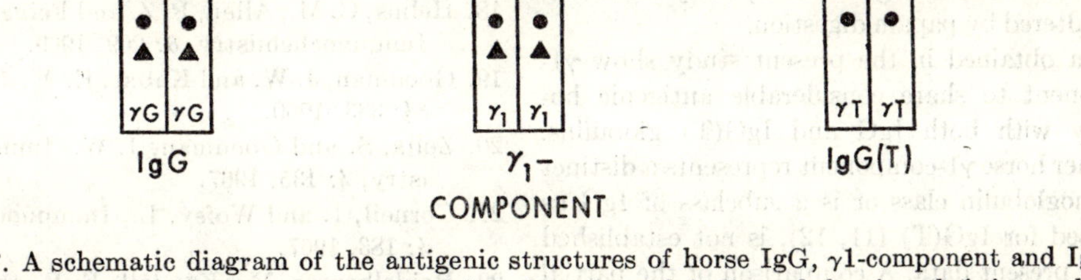

Figure 6. A schematic diagram of the antigenic structures of horse IgG, γ1-component and IgG(T) illustrating antigenic specificities associated with each immunoglobulin and showing their interrelationships. The symbols γG, γ1 and γT, shown in Fc region, represent unique antigenic determinants. Solid triangles, solid circles, and the symbols L and Fab_{sp} represent common or shared determinants.

A schematic diagram of the antigenic structures of horse IgG, γ1-component and IgG(T), summarizing immunologic relationships among these immunoglobulins is illustrated in Figure 6. Common antigenic groupings shared by each horse immunoglobulin include L chain determinants localized entirely on the light chain (1, 13), as well as determinants associated with Fab fragments termed Fab_{sp} which may require the association of both H and L chains for expression (13). Each immunoglobulin possesses unique antigenic determinants (represented by symbols γG, γ1, γT in Figure 6) associated with the Fc portion of the molecule. This pepsin-susceptible portion of the heavy chain also carries, however, common antigenic determinants, some (Fig. 6, solid circle) shared by each of the three immunoglobulins, others (represented by solid triangles) common only to IgG and γ1-component.

Common antigenic determinants shared by the Fc portion of γ1-component, IgG and IgG(T) are not demonstrable by immunodiffusion on the isolated F′c fragment of horse IgG. Horse F′c fragment was shown in a previous study (13) to exhibit in immunodiffusion only some of the antigenic determinants (Fc_1) occurring on the Fc fragment; others (Fc_2) were demonstrable only with intact Fc fragment. As shown in figure 4*B*, anti-IgG_{Fc_2} reagent (anti-$IgG_{Fc_{1,2}}$ absorbed with F′c) continues to react with both IgG(T) and γ1-component. Thus, at least some of the determinants common to the Fc regions of IgG, IgG(T) and γ1-component are associated with the Fc_2 domain.

The failure to detect common Fc determinants on the F′c fragment cannot, however, be interpreted as proof that such determinants are missing from or localized outside the F′c fragment. As discussed by Irimajiri *et al.* (30) for the immunologic properties of human F′c fragment, secondary, tertiary or quaternary structural features required for immunologic activity may have become altered by papain digestion.

Data obtained in the present study show γ1-component to share considerable antigenic homology with both IgG and IgG(T) globulins. Whether horse γ1-component represents a distinct immunoglobulin class or is a subclass of IgG as proposed for IgG(T) (11, 12), is not established by the present data. A comparison of the partial amino acid sequences of the Fc regions of IgG, IgG(T) and γ1-component would provide data useful in elucidating the structural basis of antigenic homology and assist in the classification of horse γ1-component.

Acknowledgment. The authors wish to express their appreciation to Dr. George Sandor and Mlle. F. Audibert of the Institut Pasteur for the gift of horse antibacterial fraction and for examination of the specificity of anti-horse immunoglobulin reagents.

REFERENCES

1. Rockey, J. H., J. Exp. Med., *125:* 249, 1967.
2. Rockey, J. H., Klinman, N. R. and Karush, F., J. Exp. Med., *120:* 589, 1964.
3. Sandor, G., Korach, S. and Mattern, P., Nature, *204:* 794, 1964.
4. Sandor, G. and Korach, S., Ann. Inst. Pasteur, *111:* 7, 1966.
5. Zolla, S. and Goodman, J. W., J. Immun., *100:* 880, 1968.
6. Helms, C. M. and Allen, P. Z., Fed. Proc., *27:* 684, 1968.
7. Sandor, G. and Audibert, F., Comp. Rend. Acad. Sci., *270:* 1538, 1970.
8. Klinman, N. R., Rockey, J. H., Frauenberger, G. and Karush, F., J. Immun., *98:* 587, 1966.
9. Cohen, S. and Porter, R. R., Advances Immun., 4: 287, 1964.
10. Hill, W. C. and Cebra, J. J., Biochemistry, *4:* 2575, 1965.
11. Weir, R. C. and Porter, R. R., Biochemistry, *100:* 63, 1966.
12. Weir, R. C., Porter, R. R. and Givol, D., Nature, *212:* 205, 1966.
13. Helms, C. M. and Allen, P. Z., Immunochemistry, *7:* 401, 1970.
14. Johnston, S. L. and Allen, P. Z., J. Immun., *100:* 955, 1968.
15. Allen, P. Z., Berger, B. M. and Helms, C. M., J. Immun., *101:* 1023, 1968.
16. Porter, R. R., Biochem. J., *73:* 119, 1959.
17. Fleischman, J. R., Pain, R. H. and Porter, R. R., Arch. Biochem. Biophys., Supplement, *1:* 174, 1962.
18. Helms, C. M., Allen, P. Z. and Feingold D. S., Immunochemistry, *6:* 269, 1969.
19. Goodman, J. W. and Kabat, E. A., J. Immun., *84:* 333, 1960.
20. Zolla, S. and Goodman, J. W., Immunochemistry, *4:* 135, 1967.
21. Corneil, I. and Wofsy, L., Immunochemistry, *4:* 183, 1967.
22. Heidelberger, M., Kendall, F. E. and Scherp, H. W., J. Exp. Med., *64:* 559, 1936.
23. Jones, J. K. N. and Perry, M. B., J. Amer. Chem. Soc., *79:* 2787, 1957.

24. Treffers, H. P. and Heidelberger, M., J. Exp. Med., *73:* 125, 293, 1941.
25. World Health Organization Bulletin, *30:* 447, 1965, reprinted in Immunochemistry, *1:* 145, 1964.
26. Vaerman, J. P. and Heremans, J. F., Immunochemistry, *5:* 425, 1968.
27. Schwick, G. and Schultze, H. E., *Protides of the Biological Fluids*, Edited by H. Peters, p. 162, Elsevier Publishing Company, Amsterdam, 1960.
28. Schultze, H. E., Haupt, H., Heide, K., Heimberger, N. and Schwick, H. G., Immunochemistry, *2:* 273, 1965.
29. Cohen, J. J., Myers, J., Rose, B. and Goodfriend, L., Canad. J. Biochem., *42:* 1787, 1964.
30. Irimajiri, S., Franklin, E. C. and Fragione, B., Immunochemistry, *5:* 383, 1968.

THE JOURNAL OF IMMUNOLOGY
Vol. 105, No. 5, November 1970

Printed in U.S.A

HYPERSENSITIVITY TO ASCARIS ANTIGENS

V. Production of Homocytotropic Antibodies in the Rabbit[1]

GILL STREJAN AND DAN H. CAMPBELL

From the Department of Bacteriology and Immunology, University of Western Ontario, London, Canada and the Division of Chemistry and Chemical Engineering, California Institute of Technology, Pasadena, California

Received for publication March 30, 1970

Rabbits immunized with soluble, crude *Ascaris* extracts, or with extracts adsorbed on $Al(OH)_3$ produced homocytotropic (Hc) antibodies after both primary and secondary antigenic stimulations. The antigen emulsified in complete Freund's adjuvant proved ineffective. While reduction and alkylation inactivated most of the antibody preparations, heating of the antisera at 56°C indicated that both heat resistant and heat sensitive Hc antibodies are being produced and may coexist in the same serum.

The ability of rabbits to produce several types of homologous anaphylactic (homocytotropic) antibodies was reported recently and the accumulated evidence suggested that the type produced depended on the nature of the antigen and on the route and immunization schedule (1–5). Rabbits immunized with dinitrophenyl-bovine γ globulin (DNP-BGG) conjugates emulsified in complete Freund's adjuvant produced a type of homocytotropic (Hc) antibody which appeared early (6 to 9 days) after a primary antigenic stimulation, disappeared after relatively short periods of time (21 to 30 days), but failed to reappear after secondary stimulation (1, 3). In electrophoresis the antibody migrated as a fast γ globulin (γ 1) and was inactivated by heat (2 hr at 56°C) and by 0.1 M 2-mercaptoethanol (with alkylation). Rabbits immunized with tetanus toxoid adsorbed on aluminium phosphate produced an early homocytotropic antibody which could be detected in the circulation for as long as 133 days. An anamnestic response was also elicited (4). The antibody was resistant to heat and to sulfhydryl reagents (without alkylation). The skin-sensitizing activity was recovered from the fast γ region in electrophoresis and was eluted from a diethylaminoethyl cellulose column with a 0.05 M phosphate buffer. The antibody belonged to a class of immunoglobulin other than IgG, IgM or IgA.

Recently a third type of skin-sensitizing antibody was produced in rabbits by footpad administration of relatively large amounts of bovine serum albumin emulsified in Freund's incomplete adjuvant (5). The antibody was described as a heat-stable IgG which could be isolated in both fast and slow γ globulin regions from block-electrophoresis; the homologous PCA reaction was complement dependent.

Rabbits infected with *Schistosoma mansoni* cercariae developed sera with high Hc titers after 7 to 12 weeks. An abrupt return of Hc antibodies was observed in 50% of the animals subjected to a second infection 36 weeks after the initial exposure (6).

In previous studies it was found that extracts derived from *Ascaris suum* adult worms were very powerful inducers of Hc antibodies in rats (7), Rhesus monkeys (8) and in man (9). The present study is concerned with the production of Hc antibodies in rabbits immunized with *Ascaris* crude extracts. The results will show that the extracts may induce the production of at least two distinct types of Hc antibodies which were detected in both primary and anamnestic sera.

MATERIALS AND METHODS

Antigens. Crude *Ascaris* extract was prepared from homogenized *Ascaris suum* specimens, as described previously (10).

Animals. White, male rabbits, of the New

[1] This investigation was supported by MRC of Canada Grant MA-3072 and by Public Health Service Research Grant AI-1339, from the National Institute of Allergy and Infectious Diseases (Contribution 4024 from the Gates and Crellin Laboratories of Chemistry and Church Laboratory of Chemistry and Biology, California Institute of Technology).

TABLE I

Method of Immunization	Group No.	No. of Rabbits	Injected at Days[a]
3 mg soluble *Ascaris* extract, subcutaneously	1[b]	2	0, 14, 21, 30 and 60
3 mg soluble *Ascaris* extract, first injection intravenously, the others subcutaneously	2[b]	2	0, 14, 21, 30 and 60
3 mg *Ascaris* extract emulsified in complete Freund's adjuvant, intramuscularly	3[b]	2	0, 14, 21, 30 and 60
	4	2	0 and 45
3 mg *Ascaris* extract adsorbed on $Al(OH)_3$, intramuscularly.	5[b]	2	0, 14, 21, 30 and 60
	6	4	0, 14 and 21
	7	2	0 and 45

[a] Days on which antigen was administered.

[b] One rabbit from these groups received an additional intramuscular injection of 3 mg *Ascaris* of extract in $Al(OH)_3$ on day 120.

Zealand strain, weighing between 2000 and 2500 g were used throughout the experiments.

Immunization procedure. Rabbits were divided into several groups and were injected with crude *Ascaris* extract as shown in Table I. The rabbits were bled at various intervals over a period of 130 days after the initial antigenic stimulation and their sera were stored at −20°C until tested. Hyperimmune, precipitating rabbit anti-*Ascaris* sera were prepared as previously described (8).

Passive cutaneous anaphylaxis (PCA). White male rabbits were injected intradermally, on a shaved area of the back, with 0.1-ml volumes of rabbit serum, or with serum dilutions made in borate-buffered saline, pH 8.4. As many as 30 skin sites per rabbit could be injected; each sample was tested on two, sometimes on four, rabbits. The challenge was given 72 hr later and consisted of an intravenous injection of 3 mg of crude *Ascaris* extract in a total volume of 2 ml, containing 1% Evans blue solution. The reactions were recorded, in millimeters of diameter, 45 min after the challenge.

Reduction and alkylation. PCA-positive rabbit sera were reduced and alkylated as follows; 0.1-ml volumes of 0.1 M 2-mercaptoethanol solution were added to 0.9 ml of serum and the mixtures were incubated for 60 min at room temperature. Alkylation was carried out by incubating the reduced samples for 60 min at room temperature with 10% excess iodoacetamide solution in borate-buffered saline, pH 8.4 (0.11 M final concentration). For control, a few unreduced serum samples were treated only with iodoacetamide (0.11 M final concentration). All the serum samples were dialyzed overnight at 4°C against borate-buffered saline, pH 8.4, and were then tested by PCA reactions in rabbits.

TABLE II

Production of homocytotropic antibodies: primary response[a]

Method of Immunization[b]	Group No.	No. PCA Positive/ No. Injected
Soluble extract, subcutaneously	1	2/2
Soluble extract, intravenously	2	0/2
Antigen emulsified in complete Freund's adjuvant	3, 4	1/4
Antigen adsorbed on $Al(OH)_3$	5, 6, 7	5/8

[a] Homologous PCA reactions performed with preimmunization sera were all negative.

[b] One rabbit from these groups received an additional intramuscular injection of 3 mg of *Ascaris* extract in $Al(OH)_3$ on day 120.

Heat inactivation. One-milliliter volumes of PCA-positive sera were incubated for 2, 4 or 6 hr in a water bath at 56°C. At the end of the incubation period the heated sera as well as the unheated controls were tested by PCA reactions in rabbits.

Immunoelectrophoresis was carried out on microscope slides (11) using 1% Noble agar in Na Barbital-HCl buffer, pH, 8.2 = 0.025. After development of the precipitin arcs, the slides were washed, dried and stained with Ponceau S.

RESULTS

Production of homocytotropic antibodies after primary antigenic stimulation. Of 16 rabbits immunized with the crude *Ascaris* extract, eight produced detectable amounts of Hc antibodies after a single antigenic stimulation (Table II). Of those, one rabbit showed an abortive response, with circulating Hc antibodies detectable only at days 6 and 7; the rest had circulating Hc antibodies 14 days after the primary stimulation. The most effective means of eliciting this response occurred when the soluble antigen was administered subcutaneously and the antigen was adsorbed on $Al(OH)_3$.

TABLE III

Production of homocytotropic antibodies following secondary injections

Method of Immunization[a]	Group No.	No. PCA Positive/No. Immunized
Soluble extract, subcutaneously	1, 2	4/4
Antigen emulsified in complete Freund's adjuvant	3, 4	0/4
Antigen adsorbed on $Al(OH)_3$	5, 6, 7	8/8

[a] One rabbit from these groups received an additional intramuscular injection of 3 mg of *Ascaris* extract in $Al(OH)_3$ on day 120.

Anamnestic response. All rabbits were given a number of booster injections (see Table I), were bled at various intervals and their sera were tested for the presence of Hc antibodies by homologous PCA. The results are summarized in Table III. With the exception of the group receiving the antigen in complete Freund's adjuvant, all the rabbits had circulating Hc antibodies in their sera. The individual responses of rabbits after both primary and secondary injections are shown in Table IV. The PCA titers ranged from 1:1 to 1:90 and varied considerably from rabbit to rabbit and in individual animals from one bleeding to another. The evolution of the Hc antibody titers in rabbits 934 and 941 is represented graphically in Figure 1. In both animals, each booster injection triggered an abrupt return, or a sharp increase of Hc antibodies in the serum. On the other hand, the titers

TABLE IV

Homologous PCA reactions with rabbit sera following primary and secondary responses

Rabbit No.	Group No.[a]	Days after Primary Stimulation									
		14[b]	21[b]	30[b]	60[b]	70	90	120[b]	123	127	130
		Reaction[c]/reciprocal of titer[d]									
934	1	7/1	10/1	25/10	5/1	20/30	20/10	0	14/3	20/10	17/3
935	1	10/1		20/10	25/10	25					
936	2	0	5/1	20/5	10/1	22	5				
937	2	0	0	20/5	14	25	17	0	<5	20	15
938	3	15/10	5/1	0	0	0	0				
939	3	0	0	0	0	<5	0	0	0	0	0
940	5	20/5	20/1	20/5	20	10	0				
941	5	22/10	25/20	25	22/30	22/90	18/30	0	12/10	20/30	20/10
949	6	14/5	10/1	20/5							
950	6	0	15/1	22/5							
951	6	5/1	0	5/1							
952	6	0	15/1	22/5							

Rabbit No.	Group No.[a]	4	5	6	7	8	10	12	20	45[b]	48	50	52	56
967	4	0	0	0	0	0	0	0	0	0	0	0	0	0
968	4	0	0	0	0	0	0	0	0	0	0	0	0	0
969	7	0	0	10/1	10/1	0	0	0	0	0	5	10	12	10
970	7	0	0	0	0	0	0	0	0	0	8	12	12	10

[a] For immunization procedures see Table I.

[b] Days at which booster injections were given (after bleeding).

[c] The intensity of PCA reactions was recorded in millimeters diameter, 45 min after the intravenous challenge.

[d] Reciprocal of the highest serum dilution giving a positive PCA reaction of at least 5 mm diameter.

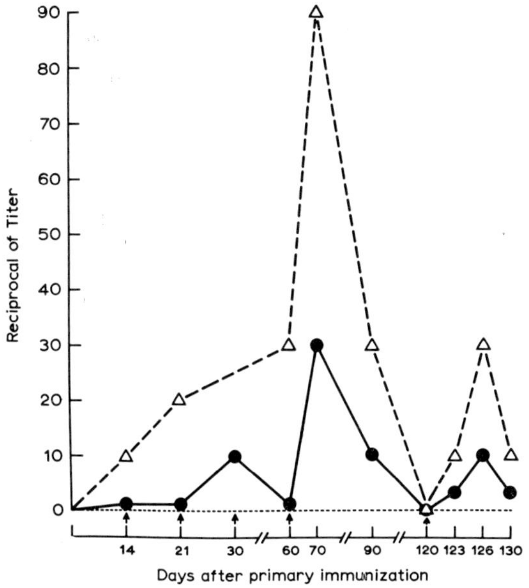

Figure 1. Evolution of homocytotropic antibody titers in two rabbits immunized with crude *Ascaris* extract; ●——●, rabbit 934; △-----△, rabbit 941. Arrows indicate secondary antigenic stimulations.

declined relatively fast after reaching their peaks. The sharp differences between the two animals may be attributed to the different immunization procedures employed: soluble extract was administered subcutaneously for rabbit 934, and extract adsorbed on $Al(OH)_3$, was injected intramuscularly for rabbit 941.

From a total of 16 rabbits immunized with *Ascaris* extracts, only 3 failed to produce detectable levels of Hc antibodies. All 3 belonged to the group immunized with the antigen in complete Freund's adjuvant. A fourth rabbit in this group (No. 938) showed a good but short-lived primary response; then, despite four additional injections, the Hc antibodies failed to reappear. Similar findings were obtained with anti-*Ascaris* hyperimmune sera, after prolonged immunizations with the antigen emulsified in complete Freund's adjuvant. Of five hyperimmune rabbit anti-*Ascaris* sera tested none had detectable levels of Hc antibodies.

To find whether a correlation existed between the level of Hc and precipitating antibodies in the serum, PCA-positive and negative anti-*Ascaris* sera were tested by immunoelectrophoresis against *Ascaris* crude extracts. A few

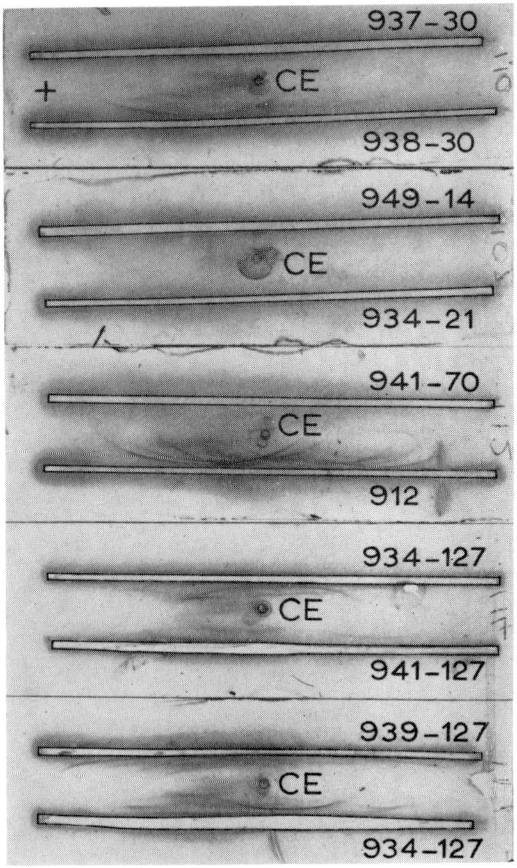

Figure 2. Agar immunoelectrophoretic analysis; CE, *Ascaris* crude extract; 912, rabbit anti-*Ascaris* hyperimmune serum; 937-30, serum of rabbit 937 obtained at day 30, a.s.o. (stained with Ponceau S).

patterns are presented in Figure 2. No direct correlation could be found between the number and intensity of the precipitin arcs on one hand and the intensity of the PCA reactions on the other. However, negative correlations were recorded in several instances. Sera of rabbits 912, 938 (day 30) and 939 (day 127) that were negative in homologous PCA reactions gave more precipitin arcs against the crude *Ascaris* extract than did sera with high titers of Hc antibody (rabbits 949, day 14; 941, day 70; and 941, day 127). It is interesting to note that sera 912, 938 and 939 were obtained from rabbits immunized with *Ascaris* extract emulsified in complete Freund's adjuvant.

Sensitivity to sulfhydryl reagents. A number of

TABLE V

Sensitivity of rabbit Hc antibodies to reduction and alkylation

Rabbit	Day[a]	PCA Reactions	
		Treated[b]	Control[c]
		mm	
938	14	0	11
949	14	0	20
949	30	0	15
935	30	0	8
940	30	0	11
941	30	0	16
941	70	7	15
941	130	11	15
952	30	0	10
934	70	5	18
934	130	0	14
937	130	<5	18

[a] Day of bleeding, after primary injection.

[b] Serum samples were reduced with 0.1 M 2-mercaptoethanol and alkylated with 0.11 M iodoacetamide.

[c] Serum samples were treated with 0.11 M iodoacetamide.

PCA-positive sera were reduced with 0.1 M 2-mercaptoethanol and alkylated with iodoacetamide as described. Both reduced and control samples were compared in PCA tests on the same rabbits (Table V). Most of the sera were completely inactivated by reduction and alkylation; however, a few sera with relatively high titers of Hc antibodies partially retained their skin-sensitizing properties.

Heat treatment. A number of PCA-positive rabbit anti-*Ascaris* sera were heated for 2, 4 or 6 hr at 56°C and were then compared by homologous PCA reactions with the untreated controls. The PCA-positive sera tested may be divided into two groups (Table VI). One group contains antibodies completely inactivated after heating for 2 hr at 56°C (serum 938-14, 934-21, 934-30 and 935-30). The second group of sera contains apparently a mixed population of heat sensitive and heat resistant Hc antibodies, as seen in sera 949-14 and 941-90 in which a considerable decrease in PCA activity was recorded after the first 2 hr of heating but sufficient residual PCA activity was still present at the end of 4 or 6 hr. Sera 934-70 and 941-70 showed practically no decrease in PCA activity even after 6 hr of incubation at 56°C, however, when these sera were

TABLE VI

Sensitivity of Hc antibodies to heat

Rabbit No.	Day[a]	Group No.	PCA Reactions			
			Control[b]	Heated at 56°C		
				2 hr	4 hr	6 hr
			mm			
938	14	4	11	0	ND[c]	ND
949	14	6	20	13	12	0
934	21	1	5	<5	0	0
934	30	1	11	0	0	0
934	70	1	25	20	21	25
935	30	1	20	0	0	0
940	30	5	11	<5	0	0
941	21	5	20	20	10	ND
941	70	5	22	18	18	18
941	90	5	18	5	5	5
941	130	5	25	22	25	24

[a] Day of bleeding, after primary injection.

[b] Unheated serum samples.

[c] Not determined.

diluted 5- or 10-fold before heating, a sharp decrease (but not complete inactivation) of PCA activity was recorded after 6 hr of incubation at 56°C. These results suggest that rabbits immunized with crude *Ascaris* extracts produce at least two different populations of Hc antibodies that can be distinguished on the basis of their different heat stabilities.

DISCUSSION

Earlier studies have indicated that rabbits are capable of producing at least two different kinds of homocytotropic antibodies, depending on the nature of the antigen as well as on the schedule and route of immunization. In the present study rabbits were immunized by various procedures with a highly complex antigenic mixture, represented by the crude *Ascaris* extract, and the production of Hc antibodies was followed after primary and anamnestic stimulations. The results have indicated that from a total of 16 rabbits, 8 produced detectable levels of Hc antibodies after a single injection and 12 after a number of secondary stimulations. Of the methods of immunization employed, the antigen emulsified in complete Freund's adjuvant was the least effective since the production of Hc antibodies was elicited in only one of four rabbits immunized. It is interesting to note that even in that rabbit (No. 938) the Hc antibodies were no longer detectable 30 days after the primary stimulation and could not be recalled despite the administration of four additional injections. Moreover, five rabbit hyperimmune sera obtained after prolonged immunization with *Ascaris* extracts in complete Freund's adjuvant had no circulating Hc antibodies. This observation seems to confirm the previously reported failure to elicit an anamnestic response in rabbits, after footpad administration of dinitrophenyl-bovine γ globulin (DNP-BGG) conjugates, emulsified in complete Freund's adjuvant (1, 3, 12). On the other hand, the report that a high percentage (65%) of rabbits produced "reaginic" antibodies after a primary stimulation with DNP-bovine serum albumin conjugates in complete Freund's adjuvant, and that 50% of these animals showed an anamnestic response (13), could not be corroborated. Immunization procedures employing complete Freund's adjuvant represent the method of choice for the production of high levels of precipitating antibodies in the rabbit. It is possible that large amounts of precipitating antibodies as elicited by antigens in complete Freund's adjuvant would inhibit the production of Hc antibodies. The immunoelectrophoretic patterns obtained (Fig. 2) suggest a negative correlation between the level of precipitating and Hc antibodies. It must be pointed out, however, that this evidence is equivocal since no accurate quantitative data could be obtained from a complex precipitating system such as the crude *Ascaris* extract and its antibodies. The antigen adsorbed on $Al(OH)_3$ proved the most effective in eliciting the production of relatively high levels of anti-*Ascaris* Hc antibodies. Five of eight rabbits responded after a primary stimulation; all eight rabbits responded after a secondary injection. The anamnestic responses were characterized by a sharp increase or an abrupt return of circulating Hc antibodies, within 72 hr after restimulation. Anamnestic Hc antibody responses were reported previously when the antigens were given in $Al(OH)_3$ (4, 14) and a preferential Hc antibody production was observed recently when rabbits were injected with small doses of alum-precipitated DNP-BGG conjugates (15). It must be mentioned however that the *Ascaris* extract injected subcutaneously without adjuvant was also effective in eliciting Hc antibodies (rabbits 934 and 935).

Although Hc antibodies are characterized as 2-mercaptoethanol-sensitive and heat-sensitive immunoglobulins, Lindqvist (4) has recently reported the presence of a highly heat-resistant (32 hr at 56°C) rabbit Hc antibody. In the present experiments, reduction and alkylation completely inactivated the skin-sensitizing property of the anti-*Ascaris* antibodies, with the exception of serum 941, day 70 and day 130, and serum 934, day 70. It is interesting to note that these sera had the highest Hc antibody titers and therefore the relative stability to reduction might be explained on quantitative grounds. On the other hand, the heat inactivation experiments suggested that qualitatively different Hc antibody populations were produced; one which was destroyed after 2 hr of incubation at 56°C, the other was resistant even after 6 hr at 56°C. The two types could coexist in the same serum as shown in sera 949-14 and 941-90 in which, despite a sharp drop in PCA activity recorded after 2 hr of incubation, a certain degree of skin-sensitizing activity was present after 4 or 6 hr of heating. Although sera with high titers of Hc were in general more heat resistant than the low-titered ones (serum 941-70 *vs* serum 941-90) the heat stability was not due to quantitative differences. This is illustrated by the fact that serum 949-14 with a titer of 1:10 was more heat resistant than serum 935-30 or 934-30, also with a titer of 1:10 (see Table VI). Recently, a heat stable antibody which is complement dependent and homologous skin-sensitizing was produced after immunizing rabbits with large doses of bovine serum albumin in incomplete Freund's adjuvant (5). This antibody was described as a 7S IgG and was recovered in both fast and slow electrophoretic fractions of γ globulins. On the basis of physicochemical and immunochemical properties, this antibody was different from the heat stable Hc antibody described by Lindqvist (4). Studies on the anti-*Ascaris* Hc antibodies (16) have shown that both heat-resistant and heat-sensitive types were recovered from diethylaminoethyl cellulose columns in the same fraction and that neither type belonged to the IgG class. The present evidence indicates that rabbits produce both heat-resistant and heat-sensitive skin-sensitizing antibodies. The two types described in the present report might belong to different immunoglobulin classes. On the other hand they could represent different segments of an antibody population displaying a wide spectrum of idiotypic specificities, hence a certain degree of structural microheterogeneity, within the same immunoglobulin class.

Acknowledgments. The authors wish to thank Dr. R. G. E. Murray for his interest and Mrs. Pamela Cowley for her excellent technical assistance in the present investigation.

REFERENCES

1. Zvaifler, N. J. and Becker, E. L., J. Exp. Med., *123:* 935, 1966.
2. Onoue, K., Yagi, Y. and Pressman, D., J. Exp. Med., *123:* 173, 1966.
3. Zvaifler, N. J. and Barbaro, J., Int. Arch. Allerg., *31:* 465, 1967.
4. Lindqvist, K. J., Immunochemistry, *5:* 525, 1968.
5. Henson, P. and Cochrane, C., J. Exp. Med., *129:* 158, 1969.
6. Zvaifler, N. J., Sadun, E. H., Becker, E. L. and Schoenbechler, M. J., Exp. Parasit., *20:* 278, 1967.
7. Strejan, G. and Campbell, D. H., J. Immun., *101:* 628, 1968.
8. Malley, A., Amkraut, A., Strejan, G. and Campbell, D. H., J. Immun., *101:* 292, 1968.
9. Kailin, E. W., Rossbach, E. A. and Walzer, M., J. Allerg., *21:* 225, 1950.
10. Strejan, G. and Campbell, D. H., J. Immun., *98:* 893, 1967.
11. Scheidegger, J. J., Int. Arch. Allerg., *7:* 103, 1955.
12. Zvaifler, N. J. and Robinson, J., J. Immun., *102:* 947, 1969.
13. Strannegard, Ö. and Yurchision, A., Immunology, *16:* 387, 1969.
14. Richerson, H. B., Cheng, H. and Seebohm, P., J. Immun. *101:* 1291, 1968.
15. Revoltella, R. and Ovary, Z., Int. Arch. Allerg., *36:* 282, 1969.
16. Strejan, G. and Campbell, D. H., Fed. Proc. *29:* 639 (abstract), 1970.

THE JOURNAL OF IMMUNOLOGY
Vol. 105, No. 5, November 1970

PROCARBAZINE AS AN IMMUNOSUPPRESSANT IN ANIMALS

P. BRIAN STEWART AND ROSALIND BELL

From the Department of Pharmacology, Pharma-Research Canada, Ltd., 250 Hymus Boulevard, Pointe Claire, Montreal 730, P.Q., Canada

Received for publication March 25, 1970

Procarbazine, a methylhydrazine derivative, has been shown to be a potent immunosuppressant in mice, rats and rabbits. Procarbazine was much more effective if given continuously, starting 21 days before exposure to antigen or grafting and for 7 days after (procarbazine day −21 regimen) than if given 2 days before and continued for 13 days after (procarbazine day −2 regimen). Its action was best demonstrated in mice. Procarbazine prolonged the survival of skin grafts in strains incompatible and compatible at the H_2 locus. It was also capable of prolonging second set skin grafts in the H_2 compatible model, and is the only chemical immunosuppressant that can do this. It also suppressed completely circulating hemagglutinins to SRBC. In rabbits, the procarbazine day −21 regimen produced a prolongation of skin allograft survival and significantly depressed the level of humoral antibodies to bovine serum albumin, but less effectively than in the mouse. This could be due to the fact that rabbits could tolerate only one-twentieth of the procarbazine dosage on a weight basis, as the mouse.

Effective suppression of the immune response by chemicals has been a long sought after goal. Progress in this field has been recently reviewed by Gabrielson and Good (1). Of all the diverse chemical groups discussed, they selected the methylhydrazines as the group to watch as a result of the work by Floersheim (2–4). Stewart and Cohen (5) confirmed the profound effect that procarbazine, one of the methylhydrazine group, had in prolonging the survival of skin allografts in mice, and showed also that it was highly effective in suppressing humoral antibody to sheep erythrocytes, and in suppressing the number of plaque-forming cells (PFC) from the spleen. It was also shown (6) that procarbazine was effective as an immunosuppressant in the rat and rabbit, and in these studies procarbazine compared favorably with antilymphocyte serum (ALS).

The present study was undertaken to ascertain more fully the immunosuppressant properties of procarbazine. No special attempt was made to induce tolerance. By use of maximally tolerated daily doses in several species, the effect on both cell-mediated immunity and humoral antibody production was noted.

MATERIALS AND METHODS

Mice. The inbred strains of mice were obtained from the Jackson Laboratories, Bar Harbor, Maine.

Rats. Sprague-Dawley rats were obtained from the Canadian Breeding Laboratories, Montreal.

Rabbits. Random-bred white and black New Zealand (NZ) male rabbits were obtained from local dealers.

Skin grafting. The technique used in mice was described by Bliss (7). The recipients were always the same sex as the donors. In the first set skin grafts, the dressings were removed on day 8, and in the second set grafts they were removed on day 5. The grafts were inspected daily and were considered rejected when more than half the area of the graft was scabbed over.

Full thickness pinch ear grafts measuring approximately 2 cm x 1 cm were taken from black NZ male rabbits and placed in the dorsum of the ear of white NZ male recipients. They were secured in place by sutures. The dressings were removed on day 5 and the grafts inspected daily. They were considered rejected when they had lost their elasticity and had become hard.

Immunization. Day 0 was the day of immunization and grafting, and events occurring before this time are a negative, and thereafter a positive, figure.

The mice were immunized with 0.1 ml and the rats with 0.2 ml of a thrice-washed 30% suspension of sheep red blood cells (SRBC) given intraperitoneally. The rabbits were immunized intravenously with 100 mg of bovine serum albumin (BSA) (Armour Laboratories, Chicago, Ill.) dissolved in 5 ml of saline. The rats were immunized with 1.0 mg of BSA in 0.2 ml of incomplete Freund's adjuvant, given into the footpads of the hind paws.

Procarbazine dosage. Procarbazine (N-isopropyl-α-(2-methylhydrazino))-p-toluamide was kindly supplied by Hoffmann-La Roche (Nutley, N. J.) as the hydrochloride. Procarbazine was given in either of two dosage schemes. In the first, it was given daily from day −21 to day 0 in the maximum tolerated dose; at day 0 the dosage was reduced by a half, and treatment was stopped on day 7. This treatment is referred to in the text as the procarbazine day −21 regimen. In the second scheme, the same daily dose was given from day −2 to day 13 (or until day 3 in the plaque-forming cell test), and this is referred to as the procarbazine day −2 regimen. The maximum daily dose that could be tolerated in the procarbazine day −21 regimen was determined. In mice this was 150 mg/kg by intraperitoneal injection (i.p.). A few mice were given 300 mg/kg i.p., but this had to be lowered after a few days. In rats, the maximum tolerated daily dose was 35 mg/kg subcutaneously (s.c.), and in rabbits the dose was 7.5 mg/kg s.c.

Measurement of humoral antibody. The direct hemagglutination titers to SRBC and the indirect hemagglutination titers to BSA were determined using a microtiter technique (8). The BSA was coupled to the sheep erythrocytes using the bisdiazotized benzidine method (9). The antisera in the indirect hemagglutination test were absorbed against sheep erythrocytes before use. Serial twofold dilutions were made with the appropriate normal serum diluted 1:100 in phosphate-buffered saline (pH 7.4), using plastic trays with multiple wells. An equal volume of a 3% suspension of SRBC, or SRBC with BSA coupled to them was added to each dilution and allowed to stand overnight. Agglutination was obvious, and the results were expressed as the negative logarithm to the base 2 of the highest dilution showing agglutination. All antisera were run in duplicate with the appropriate controls. No naturally occurring antibodies to SRBC or BSA were discovered in unimmunized animals or unimmunized controls bled at the same time as the treated ones in these experiments.

Antigen-binding capacity (ABC) test. The amount of humoral antibody to BSA in rats was measured using the test of Farr (10) but using normal rat serum as the diluent. The ABC_{33} results were expressed as the γ^{131}I-BSA N bound/ml of undiluted serum when 0.2 γ^{131}I-BSA N was the amount of antigen added.

Plaque-forming cell test. The PFC test was done on day 4 as described by Jerne *et al.* (11). The results were expressed as the percentage suppression in the total number of PFC/spleen in the treated group compared to the immunized controls, after adjustment for the background plaques in the unimmunized controls.

RESULTS

Effect on the survival of first set skin grafts in mice. Two models of differing histocompatibility strengths were used to test the effectiveness of the procarbazine. In the first, the strains used were incompatible at the H_2 locus. The donors were C57BL/10ScSnJ and were $H_2{}^b$ at the H_2 allele, while the recipients, AKR/J were $H_2{}^k$. This was the model with the stronger histocompartibility differences, but the procarbazine day −21 regimen produced a prolongation to an average of 20.8 days compared to 10.3 days in the controls (Table I). In the second, weaker histocompatibility model the strains were both $H_2{}^k$, the donors being the C3H/HeJ inbred strain and the recipients again were the AKR/J strain. However, there were multiple differences at other non-H_2 histocompatibility loci, so that it added up to quite a strong histocompatibility difference, although weaker than the H_2 incompatible model.

The procarbazine day −21 regimen produced a striking prolongation of skin allograft survival to 51.3 days on the average, compared to 12.4 days for the controls. The procarbazine day −2 regimen produced a prolongation to an average of 30.5 days, which although a significant prolongation over the controls, was much less effective than the day −21 regimen (Table I).

Effect on the survival of second set skin grafts in mice. The H_2 compatible model was used and the first set skin grafts were rejected in the expected time. Second set skin grafts were done 5 weeks

TABLE I

Prolongation of first set skin allografts in mice in the H_2 incompatible and H_2 compatible models by procarbazine

Strain: Donor	Strain: Recipient	Treatment	No.	Mean Allograft Survival	95% Confidence Limits
				days	
C57BL/10 ScSnJ	AKR/J	None	36	10.3	9.9–10.7
(H-2[b])	(H-2[k])	Procarbazine, day −21	15	20.8	13.5–28.1
C3H/HeJ	AKR/J	None	40	12.4	12.0–12.8
(H-2[k])	(H-2[k])	Procarbazine, day −21	18	51.3	47.0–55.6
		Procarbazine, day −2	28	30.5	27.1–33.9

TABLE II

Prolongation of second set skin allografts in mice in the H_2 compatible model by procarbazine

Strain: Donor	Strain: Recipient	Treatment	No.	Mean Allograft Survival	95% Confidence Limits
				days	
C3H/HeJ	AKR/J	None	21	7.0	6.8–7.2
(H-2[k])	(H-2[k])	Procarbazine, day −21	12	32.0	28.2–35.8

after the first. Procarbazine was started 21 days before and stopped 7 days after doing the second graft from the same donor strain. This treatment produced a prolongation of skin allograft survival to a mean of 32 days, compared to the accelerated rejection of 7.0 days in the controls (Table II). This was a highly significant finding and meant that the procarbazine day −21 regimen was able to erase immunologic memory as ALS is claimed to do (12, 13).

Effect of procarbazine on humoral antibody production in mice. The day −21 regimen was effective in completely suppressing circulating hemagglutinins to SRBC in all mice when tested on day 13 (Table III). This was even more impressive as treatment had to be stopped for 5 out of the 8 on day 1, but the other three were continued on treatment until day 7. In contrast, the procarbazine day −2 regimen hardly affected the level of circulating hemagglutinins. This demonstrated the need to give procarbazine well in advance of antigen.

Suppression of PFC in mice by procarbazine. In contrast to the inability of procarbazine day −2 to suppress the level of circulating hemagglutinins, this same dosage scheme produced a 99.8% suppression of the PFC in the spleen when tested on day 4 (Table IV). In a few mice given the

TABLE III

Suppression of humoral antibody to SRBC in mice

Treatment	−Log 2 Hemagglutination Titer[a] at Day 13: 0	4	5	6	7	8	9	10
None		1[b]	3	2	1	4	4	3
Procarbazine, day −21	8[c]							
Procarbazine, day −2		2	1	4	1	1		

[a] SRBC 0.1 ml of 30% suspension.

[b] Numbers represent the number of animals with the given titer.

[c] Five of the eight had to stop treatment on day 1.

procarbazine day −21 regimen, the number of PFC were reduced below the number found in the unimmunized controls.

This finding must mean that the cells producing circulating hemagglutinins to SRBC are much less sensitive to the action of procarbazine than those producing the same antibody in the spleen. This is not peculiar to procarbazine as ALS, which produces almost as much suppression of the PFC in the spleen, is also not as effective in sup-

TABLE IV

Suppression of PFC in AKR mice by procarbazine

Immunization	Treatment	No.	Total PFC/Spleen	Suppression
			range	%
None	None	7	143 (43–376)	
SRBC	None	10	30,885 (13,800–58,032)	
SRBC	Procarbazine, day −2	10	187 (90–658)	99.8

TABLE V

Suppression of the humoral antibody response in rats to BSA and SRBC by procarbazine

Treatment	Humoral Antibody Response of Rats at Day 14	
	BSA: ABC_{33} ± SEM[a]	SRBC: Mean −Log 2 hemagglutination titer ± SEM
None	0.32 ± 0.07 (12/12)[b]	5.3 ± 0.8 (12/12)
Procarbazine, day −2	0 (0/14)	3.3 ± 0.8 (9/15)
Procarbazine, day −21		1.0 ± 0.3 (5/10)

[a] ABC_{33} expressed as γ^{131}I-BSA N bound/ml of undiluted serum when 0.2 γ^{131}I-BSA N was the amount of antigen added.

[b] Numbers in parentheses represent the ratio of animals in the group making antibody.

pressing circulating hemagglutinins to SRBC in mice (5, 6).

Effect of procarbazine on humoral antibody production in rats. The effect of procarbazine in suppressing humoral antibody production in rats was tested using two antigens, BSA and SRBC. Against the weaker antigen, BSA, the procarbazine day −2 regimen was able to completely suppress the production of humoral antibody in all 14 rats when tested at day 14, using the Farr test (Table V). This same dosage scheme was much less effective against SRBC and 9 out of the 15 rats produced appreciable amounts of circulating hemagglutinins. The procarbazine day −21 regimen, on the other hand, was much more effective, as 5 out of the 10 rats produced none at all and the remaining 5 had a very significant reduction with a mean $-\log_2$ titer for the whole group of 1.0 compared to 5.3 for the untreated controls (Table V). It was interesting that, unlike in the mouse, the procarbazine day −21 regimen was unable to suppress circulating hemagglutinins to SRBC completely. Thus, while procarbazine was a powerful immunosuppressant of circulating antibody in the rat, it was not as effective as in the mouse. Its effect on skin grafts in the rat was not tested.

Effect of procarbazine in rabbits. The procarbazine day −21 regimen prolonged the survival of skin allografts from black NZ donors to 11.1 ± 0.7 SEM days on the average in the 14 treated white NZ recipients, compared to an average of 7.6 ± 0.7 SEM days in the controls (Fig. 1). These same

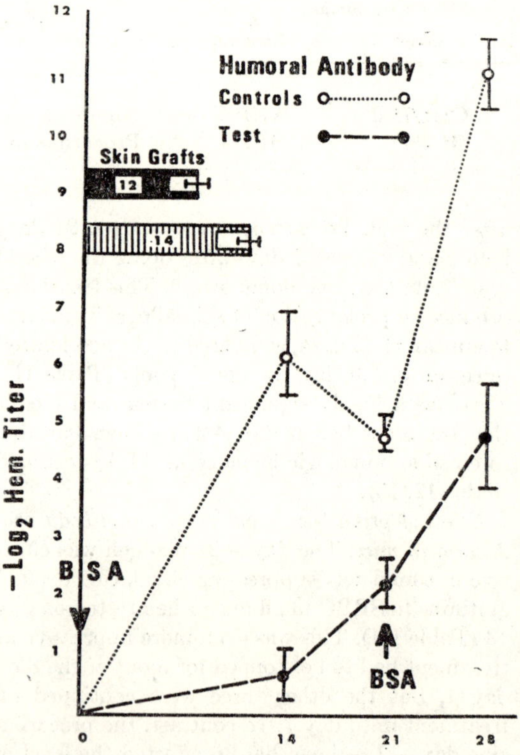

Figure 1. Prolongation of skin graft survivals by procarbazine treatment, and marked suppression in the same rabbits of the primary and secondary antibody response to BSA. Mean skin graft survival in days for controls is given in the hatched area, and for procarbazine-treated animals in the lined area. Numbers in bars represent the animals in each group. Standard error of the mean is shown for each point. One hundred micrograms of BSA were given at the arrows, on days 0 and 21.

rabbits were immunized intravenously on day 0, the day of grafting, with 100 mg of BSA. All controls made a normal primary response with a mean $-\log_2$ titer of 6.2 ± 0.7 SEM on day 14, and 4.8 ± 0.3 SEM on day 21. The procarbazine-treated rabbits had a marked suppression of humoral antibody production. Two out of the 5 tested on day 14 made no antibody, but by day 21, 12 out of the 13 tested had detectable antibody although the mean $-\log_2$ titer of 2.2 ± 0.4 SEM was substantially below that of the controls (Fig. 1). Both groups of rabbits were given another dose of 100 mg BSA i.v. on day 21, and the anti-BSA titer was determined on day 28. The procarbazine-treated rabbits had an increase in the anti-BSA titers, the mean $-\log_2$ in these rabbits being 4.8 ± 0.9 SEM and 3 out of the 13 tested made no detectable antibody. This was significantly below the level in the control group of 11.2 ± 0.6 SEM where all 13 made antibody.

Thus, procarbazine had a significant effect in suppressing cell-mediated immunity, as judged by the prolongation of the survival of skin grafts, and also a profound effect in depressing the level of humoral antibody to BSA.

A striking finding in this experiment was the narrow dosage range with procarbazine. Preliminary experiments showed that 10 mg/kg s.c. killed all animals within 3 to 4 weeks. A dose of 5 mg/kg s.c. was almost without effect, but was also nontoxic. The dosage used in this experiment produced 4 deaths out of 18 rabbits in the original group. Two rabbits died on day 1, the day after grafting, after 22 days on continuous treatment; another on day 8, 1 day after treatment was stopped; and the last on day 12, 5 days after cessation of therapy. The 14 survivors showed no ill effects apart from some weight loss, and they recovered and were healthy throughout the rest of the experiment.

A final experiment was done to see if procarbazine could erase the secondary response to BSA after a normal primary response had been allowed to become established. A control group of seven rabbits and a test group of six rabbits were immunized on day 0 with 100 mg of BSA i.v. At day 21, the rabbits were bled and the anti-BSA titers measured. All rabbits in both groups made a normal primary response; the control group had a mean $-\log_2$ titer of 5.0 ± 0.4 SEM and the test group a mean $-\log_2$ titer of 4.3 ± 0.5 SEM (Fig. 2). The test group was then started on procarbazine, 7.5 mg/kg s.c. daily, and this was continued until day 26, when it was reduced to 5.0 mg/kg s.c. daily until day 48. Both groups were bled at day 40 and again at day 49. At day 40, the test group had a mean $-\log_2$ titers of 1.8 ± 0.6 SEM compared to 2.7 ± 0.2 SEM for the controls. After a second immunization of 100 mg BSA i.v. on day 42, both groups had a substantial increase in the amount of humoral antibody. The test group increased to a mean $-\log_2$ titer of 6.3 ± 1.8 SEM and the control group to 9.7 ± 1.1 SEM, and all rabbits in both test and control groups made detectable antibody. It is extremely debatable whether procarbazine had any effect at all on the established primary response. Even after 19 days of continuous treatment, there was still a significant amount of BSA antibody when tested at day 40, and the reduction in the amount of antibody in the test group compared to the

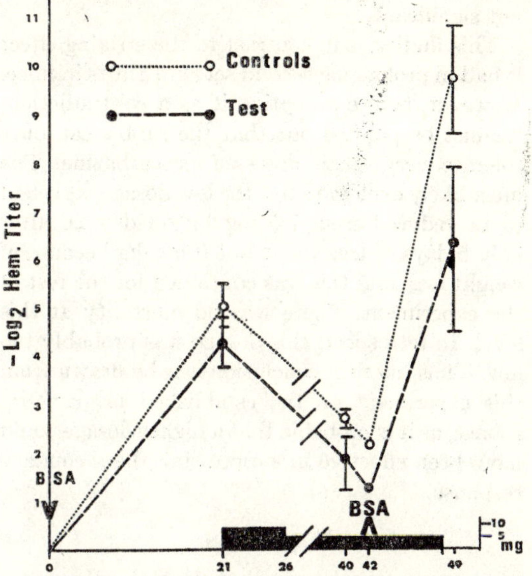

Figure 2. Effect of procarbazine treatment on the established primary response to BSA. Procarbazine treatment was begun on day 21 after a normal primary response to BSA had been established, and was continued until day 48. A second challenge of BSA on day 42 resulted in near normal secondary response of the procarbazine treated rabbits. All rabbits made antibody to BSA and none were tolerant. Dosage of procarbazine in mg/kg s.c. is shown by the hatched area. Standard error of the mean is shown for each point.

controls in the secondary response was probably not significant.

This finding is in contrast to the striking effect it had in prolonging second set skin grafts in mice. However, before accepting it as a contradiction, it must be pointed out that the rabbit can only tolerate very small doses of procarbazine. The most likely explanation is the low dosage, as it had to be reduced from 7.5 mg/kg on day 26 after only 5 days of treatment to 5.0 mg/kg because of weight loss, and this was continued for the rest of the experiment. There was no mortality at this level. In retrospect, this dosage was probably too low. Thus, no firm conclusion can be drawn from this experiment on the established primary response, as it is probable that a higher dosage could have been effective in suppressing the secondary response.

DISCUSSION

These results showed that procarbazine was a potent immunosuppressant. Its action was best demonstrated in the mouse, and it is the only chemical immunosuppressant in our experience that will prolong the survival of skin allografts in this species. Its potency was further underlined, in that it was able to prolong the survival of second set skin grafts, a feat accomplished so far only by ALS (12, 13). Procarbazine suppressed completely circulating antibodies to SRBC, and produced complete suppression of PFC in the spleen.

Procarbazine was also effective in other species, but to a lesser degree. In the rat, it suppressed completely the production of antibody to BSA and substantially reduced the amount of antibody to SRBC. In rabbits, procarbazine prolonged the survival of skin allografts and markedly reduced the amount of humoral antibody to BSA. Although procarbazine produced significant immunosuppression in the rabbit, it was much less than in the mouse. This was almost certainly due to the fact that the rabbit could only tolerate about one-twentieth of the mouse dose, on a weight basis. These small doses, compared to the mouse, especially in the established primary response experiment, probably limited its immunosuppressant action in rabbits. Why it is so toxic in rabbits compared to mice is unexplained.

The mode of action of procarbazine as an immunosuppressant is not fully understood. The most likely explanation is that it works by depleting lymphocytes. Floersheim (3) found a 70% reduction in mice in circulating lymphocytes after 28 days of treatment, and Possanza and Stewart (14) noted an 80% reduction after procarbazine treatment in rats. Procarbazine also produced a depletion of lymphoid tissue as judged by the size of the spleen in mice. In our PFC experiments, procarbazine-treated mice invariably had spleens half the weight of the immunized controls.

A possible explanation for this effect on lymphocytes was put forward by Weitzel *et al.* (15), who showed that procarbazine and two of its metabolites inhibited the transport of nucleosides into lymphocytes. If this explanation is correct, it could mean that the action of procarbazine would be more on developing than on mature lymphocytes. It must be noted, however, that these cells were from mice with lymphatic leukemia, and the results may not hold for normal cells.

Another interesting finding was the necessity for the long treatment with procarbazine before exposure to antigen. Floersheim (2) noted that skin grafts survived longer in mice if procarbazine was given 1 or 2 weeks before grafting. Our results showed that the procarbazine day −21 regimen was clearly much more immunosuppressant than the day −2 one, but no intermediate points were tried. However, this work, taken in conjunction with Floersheim's, indicates that procarbazine requires 1 to 3 weeks of treatment before grafting or immunization for its best immunosuppressant action.

A disturbing feature which has been recently noted by Penn *et al.* (16) is the induction of tumors by immunosuppressants. This danger may apply also to procarbazine. Kelly *et al.* (17) reported that procarbazine and some of its metabolites induced pulmonary tumors and leukemia in certain strains of mice. Grunberg and Prince (18) confirmed the induction of pulmonary tumors in mice by procarbazine, but not the leukemia. They also noted that hamsters were resistant to tumor induction with procarbazine. Our experience with several hundred AKR mice of a known high leukemic strain treated with procarbazine has been negative. Although our work was not designed to detect the onset of cancer, any animal that was sick or dying during the course of the experiment had a postmortem, and random postmortems were also performed on the survivors, but did not reveal any neoplastic disease. However, it does raise the whole question of the carcinogenicity of immunosuppressants. There may be a correlation, as commented by Medawar (19), between the potency of the immunosuppressant and its ability to produce neoplasms. The only common feature between ALS, azathioprine and procarbazine, all known to induce tumors, is their immunosuppressive properties. It should also be remembered in this context that proven carcinogens such as benz-a-anthracenes and methylcholanthrenes have the ability to produce long lasting suppression of the immune response (20–22). This interference with the immune response may have some part to play, as yet undetermined, in their capability to induce tumors.

Acknowledgments. We thank Miss. H. Baier and Mr. Mike Holeczek for their excellent technical help, and also Mrs. Esther Davies for preparation of the figures.

REFERENCES

1. Gabrielson, A. E. and Good, R. A., Advances Immun., *7:* 92, 1967.
2. Floersheim, G. L., Nature, *211:* 638, 1966.
3. Floersheim, G. L., Science, *156:* 951, 1967.
4. Floersheim, G. L., Transplantation, *8:* 392, 1969.
5. Stewart, P. B. and Cohen, V., Science, *164:* 1082, 1969.
6. Stewart, P. B. and Bell, R., Laval Med. (In press), 1970.
7. Bliss, J. Q., Transplantation, *3:* 730, 1965.
8. Sever, J. L., J. Immun., *88:* 320, 1962.
9. Pressman, D., Campbell, D. H. and Pauling, L., J. Immun., *44:* 101, 1942.
10. Farr, R. S., J. Infect. Dis., *103:* 239, 1958.
11. Jerne, N. K., Nordin, A. A. and Henry, C., in *Cell Bound Antibodies*, Edited by B. Amos and H. Koprowski, p. 109, Wistar Institute Press, Philadelphia, 1963.
12. Monaco, A. P., Wood, M. L., Gray, J. G. and Russell, P. S., J. Immun., *96:* 229, 1966.
13. Levey, R. H. and Medawar, P. B., Ann. N. Y. Acad. Sci., *129:* 164, 1966.
14. Possanza, G. J. and Stewart, P. B., Clin. Exp. Immun., *6:* 291, 1970.
15. Weitzel, G., Schneider, F., Kumner, D. and Ochs, H. Z., Krebsforsch. Krebsbekaempf., *70:* 354, 1968.
16. Penn, I., Hammond, W., Brettschneider, L. and Starzl, T. E., Transplant. Proc., *1:* 106, 1969.
17. Kelly, M. G., O'Gara, R. W., Yancey, S. T., Gadekar, K., Botkin, C. and Olivierio, V. T., J. Nat. Canc. Inst., *42:* 337, 1969.
18. Grunberg, E. and Prince, H. N., Chemotherapy, *14:* 65, 1969.
19. Medawar, P. B., Proc. Roy. Soc. Ser. B., *174:* 155, 1969.
20. Malmgren, R. A., Bennison, B. E. and McKinley, T. W., Jr., Proc. Soc. Exp. Biol. Med., *79:* 484, 1952.
21. Stjernsward, J., Antibiot. Chemother. (Basel), *15:* 213, 1969.
22. Ball, J. K., Sinclair, N. R. and McCarter, J. A., Science, *152:* 650, 1966.

THE JOURNAL OF IMMUNOLOGY
Vol. 105, No. 5, November 1970
Printed in U.S.A.

THE EVOLUTION OF THE IMMUNE RESPONSE

VIII. Structural Studies of the Lamprey Immunoglobulin[1]

G. W. LITMAN, D. FROMMEL, J. FINSTAD, J. HOWELL, B. W. POLLARA AND R. A. GOOD

From the Pediatric Research Laboratories of the Variety Club Heart Hospital and the Department of Microbiology, University of Minnesota, Minneapolis, Minnesota 55455

Received for publication February 12, 1970

Highly purified preparations of radiolabeled lamprey immunoglobulin have been employed to study the structure of the immunoglobulin of this primitive vertebrate. The identity of the labeled material with that of the native immunoglobulin has been established. The lamprey immunoglobulin appears to be unique among vertebrate immunoglobulins since it has a unique molecular weight, electrophoretic mobility, and sedimentation velocity. It is also extremely labile and dissociates in solvents in a complex manner. The observations presented show that this molecule lacks counterparts of heavy and light chains and does not possess interchain disulfide linkages between its major subunits. A structural model based on its dissociation behavior is presented and the implications of such a structure in terms of molecular function and phylogenetic development are discussed.

The sea lamprey has been studied in phylogenetic perspective as a modern representative of one of the most primitive deviations in the evolutionary development of adaptive immunity. Antibody production in the lamprey has been demonstrated to few among many antigens (1, 2) with responses to human "O" cells and *Brucella* antigens being highly reproducible (3).

In previous studies, we have presented evidence that the lamprey immunoglobulin does not appear to be related to other immunoglobulins, according to several physicochemical parameters (3). This immunoglobulin, when compared to other vertebrate immunoglobulins, was shown to have an unusual molecular weight, sedimentation properties and electrophoretic mobility. Marchalonis and Edelman (2) studied the immunoglobulin of sea lamprey immunized with f_2 phage. They observed that the lamprey immunoglobulin had both high and low molecular weight forms, multiple chain structure, and heavy chains similar to the μ type. They recognized, however, uniqueness of this molecular form. They reported that the antibody studied was extremely labile and that interchain disulfide bonds were absent. The purpose of this communication is to describe studies with the purified radiolabeled immunoglobulin of the sea lamprey. Our studies emphasize the uniqueness of the immunoglobulin in terms of its lability, solution dissociation behavior, and lack of true counterparts of vertebrate heavy and light chains. On the basis of these data, we propose a model for this immunoglobulin which suggests that the lamprey immunoglobulin reflects a crucial stage in the phylogenetic development of immunity.

MATERIALS AND METHODS

Animals. Lampreys were obtained and immunized as previosuly described (1, 3). Sera were obtained from animals which had been immunized by six or nine weekly injections of human "O" cells as previously reported (3).

Purification of the immunoglobulin. Purification of the lamprey immunoglobulin was carried out by column chromatography as described (3). However, a modification was introduced by using a linear type of gradient elution, instead of stepwise increases in ionic strength. For a 1.5- x 30-cm column of cellulose DE 52 (Whatman, H. Reeve Angel and Co., Clifton, N. J.), an

[1] Aided by grants from The National Foundation, March of Dimes; the United States Public Health Service (AI-08372, AI-00292, NB-02042, and HE-05222); and the Minnesota Chapter, Arthritis Foundation.

ionic strength gradient employing 200 ml of 0.05 M Tris-HCl, pH 8.0, and 200 ml of 0.25 M Tris-HCl, pH 8.0, was used. Antibody activity was determined as previously described (3).

Immunoelectrophoresis and polyacrylamide gel electrophoresis. Immunoelectrophoresis and polyacrylamide gel electrophoresis were performed as described (3). Polyacrylamide gels (4.8 cm) were sliced into 24 sections of 2 mm each in a gel slicer. For elution from the gel the slices were incubated in 1 ml of 0.02 M Tris-HCl, 0.15 M NaCl, pH 8.0, for 24 hr with frequent agitation.

Sources and characterizations of carrier proteins. Carrier proteins used in thse studies included human IgG (Mann Research, Inc., New York, N. Y.), judged pure by immunoelectrophoresis when tested against a horse antiserum to whole human serum. The IgM used was purified from a plasmaphoresis sample of a patient with Waldenström's macroglobulinemia. Purification was accomplished by initial euglobulin precipitation followed by gel filtration on Bio-Gel A 1.5 m, 200 to 400 mesh (Bio-Rad Laboratories, Richmond, Calif.). The final preparation was judged pure by immunoelectrophoretic analysis. A human IgG preparation, enriched in dimer forms, was obtained by passage of Cohn Fr. II (E. R. Squibb & Sons, New York, N. Y.) over a DEAE-Sephadex A-50 column, equilibrated with 0.015 M Na-phosphate, pH 6.6 buffer. Analytical gel filtration on Bio-Gel A 1.5 m showed approximately 20% of this preparation to be composed of dimer.

Radioiodination of purified immunoglobulin. Radioiodination of lamprey immunoglobulin was carried out using the chloramine T oxidation as described by McConahey and Dixon (4). All labeling procedures were carried out at 0°C and iodination was adjusted to give approximately 0.5 mol of iodine/mol of protein with an $E_{1\,cm\,280nm}^{1\%} = 14$ assumed and a molecular weight of 320,000. Free iodine was removed by extensive dialysis at 4°C with multiple changes of 0.02M Tris-HCl, 0.15 M NaCl, pH 8.0 for 48 hr. More than 95% of the radioactivity was precipitable after addition of TCA. All radioactive measurements were made on a dual channel scintillation counter (Nuclear Chicago, model 4223).

Reduction and alkylation in neutral aqueous buffers. Reduction and alkylation in neutral buffers were carried out on samples dialyzed extensively against 0.15 M Tris-HCl, 0.15 M NaCl, pH 8.0, at 4°C. Reductions were made at calculated molar ratios with fresh lots of Dithiothreitol (DTT) (Calbiochem, Los Angeles, Calif.) for 40 min at room temperature. Alkylations were performed at twofold ratios over reductant, using recrystallized iodoacetamide (K & K Laboratories, Plainview, N. Y.) for 20 min at 0°C. The samples were dialyzed against either phosphate-buffered saline or against 1 N propionic acid, at a 100-fold excess over sample volume, for 6 to 8 hr before application to a Sephadex G-200 column, 2.5 x 100 cm, in 1 N propionic acid.

Reduction and alkylation in 6 M guanidine-HCl. Reduction and alkylation in 6 M guanidine-HCl were achieved by dialyzing samples against 6 M guanidine-HCl (Eastman, Rochester, N. Y.) adjusted to pH 8.0 with Tris. Reductive procedures were performed for 40 to 60 min at 23°C. Alkylation was carried out with recrystallized iodoacetamide at 23°C for 2 hr in a twofold molar excess over DTT. The samples were dialyzed against 6 M guanidine-HCl, pH 5.0, before application to either Sephadex G-200 or G-150 columns equilibrated in the same solvent.

Radioautography. The dipping technique described by Messier and Leblond (5) was used with minor modification. Periods of development varied from 1 to 8 weeks depending on the relative activity of the ^{125}I-labeled immunoglobulin preparations.

Estimation of molecular weight. Molecular weights were determined by column chromatography on Bio-Gel A 1.5 m, 200 to 400 mesh, Sephadex G-200 and G-150, and by using the relationship $\sqrt{K_D}$ *vs* $\sqrt{\text{m.w.}}$ as proposed by Andrews (6). The columns used in this study were calibrated with selected markers so as to give molecular weight estimates of all proteins eluting in the validity range of the Andrews' plot. The molecular weights of the markers employed were: human IgG, 150,000; mercaptalbumin, 138,000; human μ chains, 70,000; human γ chains, 50,000; ovalbumin, 45,000; human light chains, 22,500; and sperm whale myoglobin, 17,800 (7). Linearity was realized for all proteins on Bio-Gel A 1.5 m, 200 to 400 mesh, and Sephadex G-200 and G-150 columns. To estimate the molecular weights in various chromatographic solvents, 0.01 M Na-phosphate-0.15 M NaCl, pH 7.2, 1 N propionic acid, and 6 M guanidine-HCl, pH 5.0, were used.

RESULTS

Dissociation of lamprey immunoglobulin during storage. Dilute solutions of lamprey immunoglobulin dissociated when stored for periods as short as 3 days (Fig. 1). For example, apparent in the immunoelectrophoretic analysis is the presence of two components having a different electrophoretic mobility than that of the native protein. When analyzed by gel filtration, stored preparations appeared to contain up to several components: aggregated material and subunits with an approximate molecular weight of 150,000 and 75,000 respectively. These values were estimated by gel filtration on Bio-Gel A 1.5 m. Double diffusion analysis of the latter two subunits, however, revealed complete identity indicating a common structural origin. Antibody activity to human blood group "O" cells was not observed with the isolated subunits whereas the preparation before gel filtration contained agglutinating activity for human type "O" cells. It must be noted that the agglutination patterns of stored, partially degraded preparations did not resemble those of whole immune sera, with anti-"O" cell agglutinating activity.

Identity of radiolabeled sea lamprey immunoglobulin with immunoglobulin of whole serum. Lamprey immunoglobulin, prepared by a combination of gel filtration on Bio-Gel A 1.5 m and ion exchange chromatography on cellulose DE 52, was shown on immunoelectrophoresis to consist of a single line of slow α mobility. On polyacrylamide gel electrophoresis, the immunoglobulin behaved as a broad band, usually accompanied by two rather faint bands, one cathodal and one anodal to the main band (Fig. 2). After radioactive labeling of immunoglobulin preparations, the iodinated products were subjected to various analyses to assure complete coincidence of chromatographic (molecular sieve) and electrophoretic behavior of the iodinated lamprey immunoglobulin with the immunoglobulin as it exists in both whole serum and in purified preparations. Iodinated immunoglobulin was chromatographed with whole immune serum on Bio-Gel A 1.5 m and complete coincidence of the labeled product with whole serum agglutinating activity was confirmed. When the iodinated product was chromatographed with purified immunoglobulin on the same agarose column, identical elution patterns were observed. When iodinated immunoglobulin was added to whole immune lamprey serum and subjected to polyacrylamide

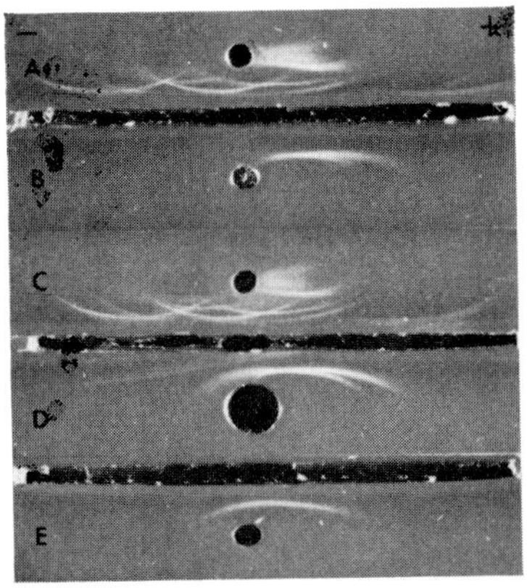

Figure 1. Dissociation behavior of purified lamprey immunoglobulin after storage. *A*, whole lamprey serum; *B*, purified lamprey immunoglobulin stored at 4°C for 1 week; *C*, whole lamprey serum; *D*, purified lamprey immunoglobulin stored for 1 week at 4°C, 5× application; *E*, nondissociated purified lamprey immunoglobulin. Developed with goat anti-whole lamprey serum. Anode is on the right.

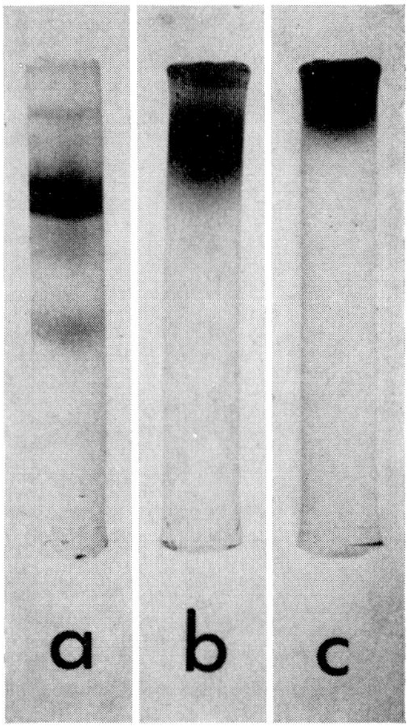

Figure 2. Comparative polyacrylamide gel electrophoresis of immunoglobulins from higher vertebrates and lamprey immunoglobulin. *A*, lamprey immunoglobulin; *B*, *Amia calva* 7S immunoglobulin; *C*, human IgG. Note the different Rf of the lamprey immunoglobulin.

gel electrophoresis, identical Rf values of 0.28 were obtained for agglutinating activity from whole serum, purified lamprey immunoglobulin, and purified and labeled immunoglobulin. Radioimmunoelectrophoresis of labeled immunoglobulin performed with whole immune lamprey serum and normal lamprey serum as carrier, when developed with goat anti-lamprey serum, revealed a single arc with a pattern corresponding to the purified immunoglobulin (Fig. 3).

To further confirm the identity of the radiolabeled immunoglobulin with immunoglobulin in native state, an antiserum to the radiolabeled immunoglobulin was produced. Immunization of rabbits with the radiolabeled immunoglobulin preparations, emulsified in complete Freund's adjuvant, yielded antrasie which revealed a

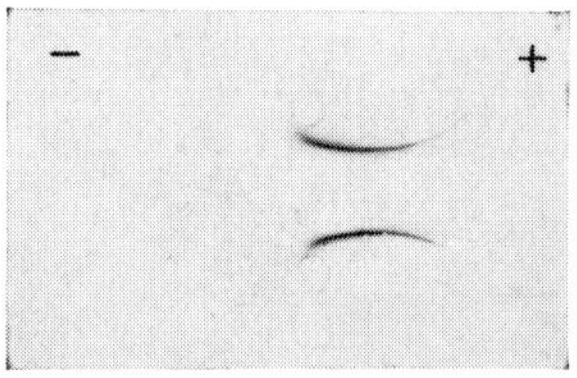

Figure 3. Radioimmunoelectrophoresis of ^{125}I-labeled lamprey immunoglobulin. ^{125}I lamprey immunoglobulin added to whole immune lamprey serum (*upper*) and whole normal lamprey serum (*lower*). Immunoelectrophoretic patterns are developed with goat anti-lamprey serum. Anode is on the right.

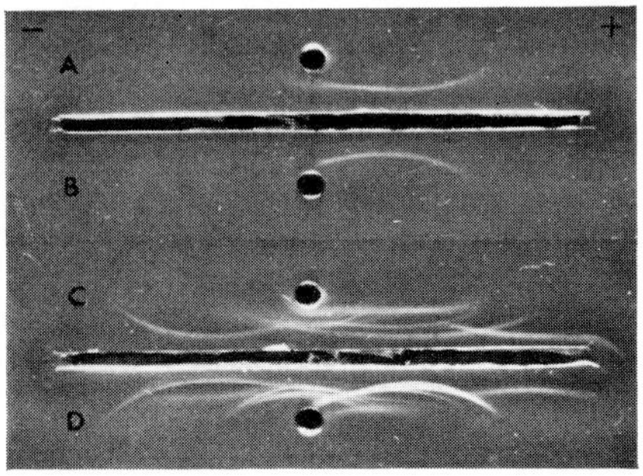

Figure 4. Antigenic analysis of ^{125}I-labeled lamprey immunoglobulin. *A*, whole normal lamprey serum; *B*, whole immune lamprey serum. Antisera is rabbit anti-^{125}I lamprey immunoglobulin. *C*, whole normal lamprey serum; *D*, whole immune lamprey serum. Antisera is goat anti-lamprey whole serum. Anode is on the right. Note that the antisera reveal only a single arc of α mobility.

single precipitin arc when tested against both normal and immune lamprey serum (Fig. 4). When these antisera were incubated with whole lamprey serum containing antibody to human "O" cells, the antibody titer of the lamprey serum was significantly reduced. Since structural studies required maintenance of the native molecular weight, chromatography of labeled lamprey immunoglobulin with carrier human IgG, enriched in dimers, on Bio-Gel provided a reliable check of the persistence of a size identical to that of native lamprey immunoglobulin. Both possess a molecular weight of approximately 300,000.

Reduction of lamprey immunoglobulin in carrier human IgM. As previously described (8), dissociation of human IgM to 7S subunits can be readily effected by reduction with DTT at 50-fold molar excess over protein and subsequent alkylation with iodoacetamide. A mixture of human IgM and lamprey immunoglobulin, when subjected to such treatment, resulted in a conversion of the carrier IgM to 7S subunits; however, the elution profile of the lamprey immunoglobulin remained unchanged (Fig. 5).

Dissociation behavior in propionic acid. Weak organic acids have been extensively employed in studies of chain dissociation of immunoglobulins from higher vertebrates. The role of such weak acids in the dissociation of lamprey immunoglobulin was investigated using human IgG and human IgM as protein carriers. Chromatography of non-reduced and non-alkylated lamprey immunoglobulin using IgG as carrier showed a complex dissociation behavior characterized by three discernible, reproducible peaks with a portion of the labeled material eluting in the void volume of the Sephadex G-200 column (Fig. 6*A*). Reduction at 100-fold molar excess of DTT over protein and subsequent alkylation showed the labeled material to behave as a single peak eluting in the same position as did the last peak of non-reduced, non-alkylated immunoglobulin. A molecular weight of approximately 90,000 was assigned to this peak (Fig. 6*B*). Alkylated lamprey immunoglobulin (without prior reduction), chromatographed together with conventionally reduced and alkylated human IgG, gave an elution pattern similar to that obtained for reduced and alkylated lamprey immunoglobulin (Fig. 6*C*).

Behavior after complete reduction and alkylation in 6 M guanidine-HCl. Lamprey immunoglobulin

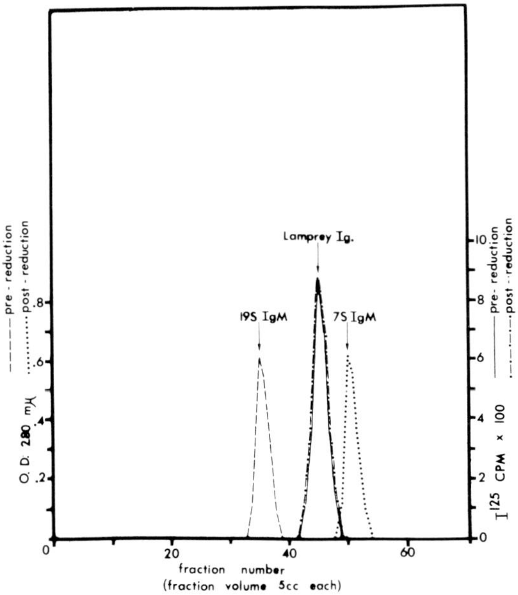

Figure 5. Behavior of ^{125}I-labeled lamprey immunoglobulin in carrier human IgM during reduction with DTT at a 50-fold molar ratio over protein. Human IgM pre-reduction (-----); post-reduction (····). Lamprey immunoglobulin pre-reduction (——); post-reduction (·-·-·). Note that the lamprey immunoglobulin shows no reduction in size after treatment with DTT. By contrast human IgM undergoes reduction to 7S subunits. Chromatography on Bio-Gel A 1.5 m.

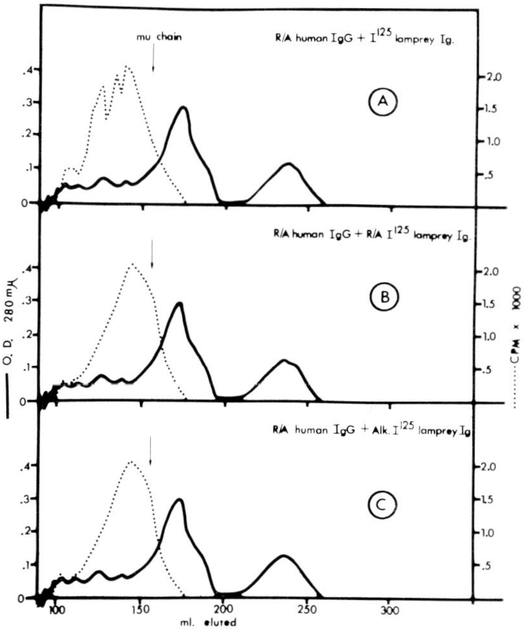

Figure 6. Comparative chromatographic behavior on Sephadex G-200 in 1 N propionic acid of ^{125}I-labeled lamprey immunoglobulin in carrier human IgG under various conditions of reduction and alkylation. *A*, ^{125}I-labeled lamprey immunoglobulin added after reduction and alkylation of human IgG; *B*, ^{125}I-labeled lamprey immunoglobulin reduced and alkylated with human IgG. *C*, ^{125}I-labeled lamprey immunoglobulin alkylated and added to reduced and alkylated human IgG. (↓) denotes elution position of μ chains.

was also subjected to reduction at 250-fold molar excess of DTT over protein in 6 M guanidine-HCl in an effort to separate subunits comparable to heavy and light chains of higher vertebrate immunoglobulins. When radiolabeled immunoglobulin was added to human IgG (previously reduced and alkylated in 6 M guanidine-HCl, pH 8.2) and subsequently chromatographed on Sephadex G-150 in 6 M guanidine-HCl, the radioactivity distributed as a single symmetrical peak, eluting along the ascending limb of the human γ chain peak (Fig. 7*A*). A molecular weight of approximately 140,000 was assigned to the fraction containing the radiolabeled lamprey immunoglobulin. Alkylation alone or reduction and alkylation of the lamprey immunoglobulin did not modify the elution pattern of the major peak of the radiolabeled immunoglobulin on Sephadex G-150 in 6 M guanidine-HCl (Fig. 7*B* and 7*C*). However, a small peak, eluting between the human light chain and the ascending boundary of the dialyzable peptides was observed in the reduced and alkylated preparation. To obtain this small fragment by reduction in 6 M guanidine-HCl, a molar ratio (DTT/protein) of 100 was found to be effective.

DISCUSSION

The sea lamprey is reported to be among the most primitive vertebrates capable of producing circulating antibody to various antigenic challenges. The antigens studied to which the lamprey has responded thus far are all particulate and include *Brucella abortus*, f_2 phage and human blood group "O" cells. Specificity of the antibody has been confirmed in all cases and with human blood group "O" cells the antibody seems to be directed only to the H surface antigen.

Deviations from the well established lines of

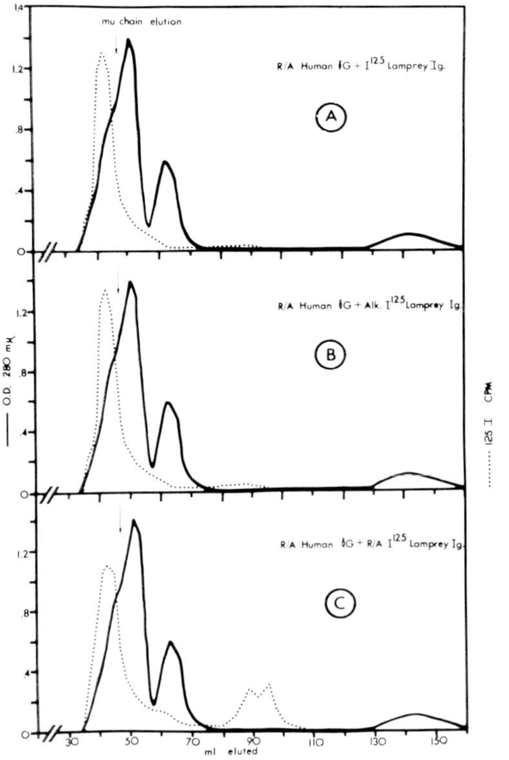

Figure 7. Comparative chromatographic behavior on Sephadex G-150 in 6 M guanidine-HCl of lamprey immunoglobulin in carrier human IgG. *A*, ^{125}I-labeled lamprey immunoglobulin added after reduction and alkylation of human IgG; *B*, ^{125}I-labeled lamprey immunoglobulin alkylated and added to reduced and alkylated human IgG; *C*, ^{125}I-labeled lamprey immunoglobulin reduced and alkylated with human IgG. (↓) denotes the elution position of isolated μ chains. No evidence for either light or heavy chains of the μ or γ types of higher vertebrates was found by this method of analysis.

immunoglobulin evolution were apparent in the sea lamprey from a standpoint of gross physical properties alone (2, 3). Studies of representative immunoglobulins of elasmobranchs, chondrosteans, teleosts, and holosteans have established a general pattern of immunoglobulins which seem to belong to two classes designated 19S and 7S from evaluation of sedimentation velocity measurements (9–13). The heavy chains of both classes seem to be of the μ type and resemble those of mammalian IgM. Beginning at the level of the dipnoid fishes, evidence exists for two antibody populations with distinct heavy chains (14).

Marchalonis and Edelman, using sucrose density ultracentrifugation of whole immune lamprey serum, demonstrated that the antibodies to f_2 phage resided in both 6.6S and 14S fractions (2). Further, they described immune response conversion from high to low molecular weight, similar to the 19S to 7S shift of higher vertebrates. The antibodies, unlike those described for any vertebrate to date, resided in a serum fraction which migrated anodaly on zone electrophoresis of whole immune serum. Attempts at assigning a molecular weight utilizing high speed equilibrium ultracentrifugation proved to be difficult and suggested that dissociation was occurring. The authors clearly recognized as being unique to this species the general instability of immune serum to f_2 and the propensity of purified immunoglobulin to break down (2).

Our previous studies showed that long-term immunization with human "O" cells resulted in the production of antibodies which were associated with a 9S fraction as determined by sucrose density ultracentrifugation and preparative zonal ultracentrifugation (3). A change in antibody size was not found. Also notable is the lack of a serum fraction possessing a sedimentation velocity comparable to mammalian macroglobulins when whole serum is analyzed by ultracentrifugation (15). Among all vertebrates, the absence of heavy molecular weight protein seems to be unique to Ostracoderm-derived species (9, 10, 11, 15). The molecular weight of 320,000 we obtained for the purified immunoglobulin was extrapolated from column chromatography determinations. Attempts at assigning molecular weights of the purified immunoglobulin by analytical ultracentrifugation failed when aggregation and dissociation occurred in the course of the runs.

We observed the serum antibody activity to reside in an anodal migrating fraction. The combination in acrylamide gel electrophoresis of molecular sieve and separation based on charge permitted the establishment of an Rf value for the purified immunoglobulin and the whole serum antibody activity which further differentiated the lamprey immune protein from that of any other purified immunoglobulin thus far described. We, too, encountered extreme lability of the molecule and demonstrated in this report dissociation products by immunoelectrophoretic analysis.

From studies of the dissociation behavior of the protein in 1 N propionic acid, with and without prior reduction and alkylation Marchalonis and Edelman concluded that the lamprey immunoglobulin, under both sets of conditions, eluted in a manner similar to that of heavy and light chains. Their profile did not, however, resemble classic heavy and light chain elution patterns. No attempts at more complete dissociation in 8 M urea or 6 M guanidine-HCl were made (2). Molecular weight estimates of the isolated chains were difficult to interpret, but it appeared as if the molecules consisted of two types of chains, bound together by non-covalent linkages. Vertical starch gel electrophoresis indicated that the heavy chains possessed migration properties roughly comparable to μ chain structure (2).

Our studies of the dissociation of lamprey immunoglobulin in various solvents confirmed that non-covalent interactions were involved in maintaining the structural integrity of lamprey immunoglobulin. We did not, however, find counterparts of heavy and light chains comparable to those found in other vertebrate immunoglobulins. On the basis of our findings, we propose a four chain model which is based primarily on a native molecule of 320,000 m.w. and on the spontaneous dissociation of such a molecule to subunits of approximately 150,000 and 75,000 m.w. (Fig. 8). These subunits are antigenically identical. The basic subunit yielded in 1 N propionic acid, after alkylation alone or reduction and alkylation, possesses a molecular weight of approximately 90,000. Since alkylation alone generated the basic subunit, it was assumed that the polydispersity observed with native lamprey immunoglobulin, when chromatographed in 1 N propionic acid, was due to disulfide interchange. Reduction and alkylation in 6 M guanidine-HCl did not yield a true counterpart of either μ, γ or light chains. Only a fragment with a size considerably smaller than light chains was obtained by this procedure.

The molecular weight of the major subunit obtained in 6 M guanidine-HCl was in the order of 140,000. The differences existing in molecular weight estimations of the lamprey immunoglobulin in various solvents might be explained by the observations that, unlike other vertebrate immunoglobulins and their subunits, lamprey immunoglobulin had an exceedingly high content of α helix, as estimated by circular dichroic analysis (16). The elevated helicity would be lost in the interaction with guanidine-HCl, a hydrogen bond donor capable of maintaining proteins in the disulfide-limited random coil configuration. Since it was necessary to determine molecular weight of the native antibody molecule in neutral buffers, other types of vertebrate immunoglob-

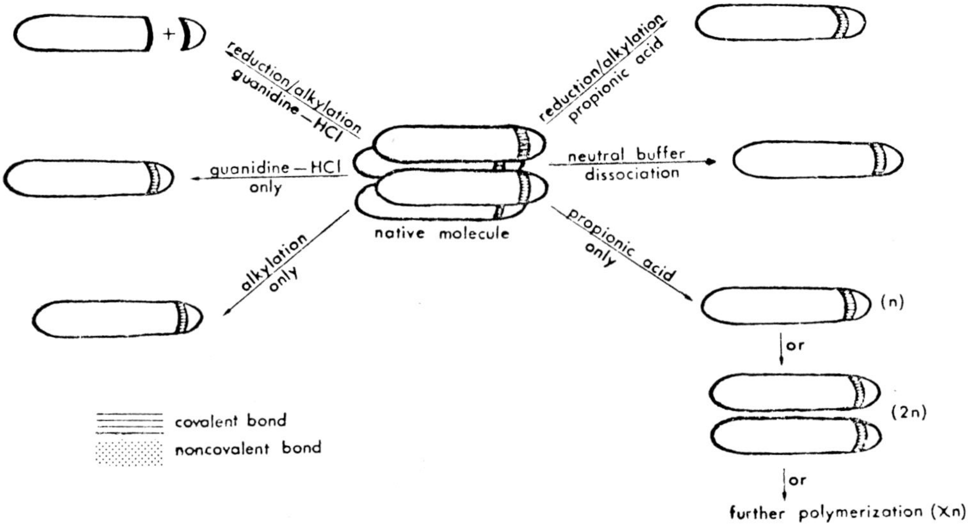

Figure 8. Proposed structural model based on the dissociation behavior in various solvents and under different conditions of reduction and alkylation.

ulins were used as markers (3). The possible unfolding in guanidine-HCl with a concomitant increase in Stokes' radius would give an increase in the apparent molecular weight of the dissociated subunits and would, therefore, provide an explanation for the apparently conflicting results n the estimates of molecular weights.

Assignment of the lamprey immunoglobulin into a scheme of vertebrate immunoglobulin evolution requires caution. The subunit structure and molecular weights indicate a unique position for the lamprey immunoglobulin which may be far removed from the general directions of vertebrate immunoglobulin evolution. Its ready dissociation into subunits and loss of activity during purification differ markedly from the more stable structures of higher vertebrate immunoglobulins. We feel that in its solution characteristics the lamprey immunoglobulin may resemble the behavior of invertebrate agglutinators (17, 18) and thus provide a link between adaptive immunity and more primitive forms of specific reactions. Particularly critical will be comparative studies of the lamprey immunoglobulin with the hagfish immunoglobulin recently described by Thoenes and Hildemann (19).

REFERENCES

1. Finstad, J. and Good, R. A., J. Exp. Med., *120:* 1151, 1964.
2. Marchalonis, J. J. and Edelman, G. M., J. Exp. Med., *127:* 891, 1968.
3. Pollara, B., Litman, G., Finstad, J., Howell, J. and Good, R. A., J. Immun., *105:* 738, 1970.
4. McConahey, P. J. and Dixon, F. J., Int. Arch. Allerg., *29:* 185, 1966.
5. Messier, B. and Leblond, C. P., Proc. Soc. Exp. Biol. Med., *96:* 7, 1957.
6. Andrews, P., Biochem. J., *91:* 222, 1964.
7. Edelman, G. M. and Gall, W. E., Ann. Rev. Biochem., *38:* 415, 1969.
8. Miller, F. and Metzger, H., J. Biol. Chem., *240:* 3325, 1965.
9. Marchalonis, J. and Edelman, G. M., J. Exp. Med., *122:* 601, 1965.
10. Clem, L. W. and Small, P. A., J. Exp. Med., *125:* 893, 1967.
11. Clem, L. W., De Boutaud, F. and Sigel, M. M., J. Immun., *99:* 1226, 1967.
12. Suran, A. A., Tarail, M. H. and Papermaster, B. W., J. Immun., *99:* 679, 1967.
13. Pollara, B., Suran, A. A., Finstad, J. and Good, R. A., Proc. Nat. Acad. Sci., *59:* 1307, 1968.
14. Marchalonis, J. J., Aust. J. Exp. Biol. Med. Sci., *47:* 405, 1969.
15. Roberts, R. C. and Seal, U. S., Comp. Biochem. Physiol., *16:* 327, 1965.
16. Litman, G. W., Rosenberg, A. and Good, R. A., Fed. Proc., *29:* 774, 1970.
17. Marchalonis, J. J. and Edelman, G. M., J. Molec. Biol., *32:* 453, 1968.
18. Acton, R. T., Bennet, J. C., Evans, E. E. and Schrohenloher, R. E., J. Biol. Chem., *244:* 4128, 1969.
19. Thoenes, G. H. and Hildemann, W. H., *Immunological Responses of Pacific Hagfish. II. Serum Antibody Production to Soluble Antigen*, Czechoslovak Academy of Science Symposium, Prague, June 1969.

THE JOURNAL OF IMMUNOLOGY
Vol. 105, No. 5, November 1970

COMMUNICATIONS

Heterogeneity of Carbohydrate Content of Human IgA Myeloma Proteins

AN-CHUAN WANG AND H. HUGH FUDENBERG

From the Department of Microbiology and the Department of Medicine, University of California, San Francisco, California 94122

Immunoglobulins are highly heterogeneous (1) in many respects. For example, structural analysis of the protein portion of myeloma proteins indicated that almost all the heavy and light chains thus far studied differed in amino acid sequences (2) with only a few exceptions (3; I. M. Cesari, M. G. Weigert and M. Cohn, to be published). Heterogeneity also exists in the carbohydrate content of isolated IgG protein. Studies on the carbohydrate moiety of immunoglobulins have demonstrated that the carbohydrate is covalently bonded to the protein portion (4–6) at multiple attachment sites on the heavy and in some cases also on the light chains (7, 8). Extensive analysis of the carbohydrate portion of IgG class myeloma proteins indicated that the hexose content of each IgG myeloma protein differs and does not correlate with the antigenic subclass of heavy or light chains (9). In the present study, human IgA class myeloma proteins were analyzed in order to determine whether the heterogeneity of carbohydrate content is limited to the IgG class only or is also present in other classes of immunoglobulins.

MATERIALS AND METHODS

Human IgA proteins were isolated from sera of myeloma patients as described previously (10).

Hexose determination. A modified anthrone reaction (11) was used. Each immunoglobulin sample (containing 0.01 mg to 0.2 mg of hexoses) was dissolved in 1 ml of cold H_2O, to which 5 ml of ice bath-cooled anthrone reagent (1.4 g anthrone, 500 ml concentrated H_2SO_4 and 200 ml H_2O) was added. The mixture was shaken and heated in a 100°C water bath for 10 min. The optical density was read at 620 nm in a Zeiss spectrophotometer. An equimolar mixture of galactose and dextrose was used as the standard.

Hexosamine determinations. Immunoglobulin samples were hydrolyzed under nitrogen in sealed tubes at 100°C for 14 hr. They were vacuum dried and put on small columns of Dowex 50-X8 (H^+) in H_2O. All neutral and acidic amino acids pass through when eluted with H_2O. Afterward, hexosamines and basic amino acids were eluted from the columns with 0.5 N HCl. The later eluates were subsequently analyzed in a Spinco automatic amino acid analyzer model 120C. Glucosamine and galactosamine came off the long column as distinct peaks after the phenylalanine peak.

Sialic acid determination. The thiobarbituric acid method (12) was used. Sialic acid residues were cleaved from proteins by hydrolysis with 0.2 ml of 0.1 N H_2SO_4 for 1 hr at 80°C. One-tenth milliliter of periodate solution (0.2 M metasodium periodate in 9 M H_3PO_4) was added to each sample. The mixture was shaken and allowed to stand at room temperature for 20 min. One milliliter of arsenite solution (10% sodium arsenite in a solution of 0.5 M sodium sulfate and 0.1 N H_2SO_4) was added and the mixture was shaken until a yellow-brown color disappeared. Three milliliters of thiobarbituric acid solution (0.6% in 0.5 M sodium sulfate) was added, and the mixture was shaken, heated in a boiling water bath for 15 min, and cooled in an ice water bath for 5 min. The solution was subsequently extracted with 4.3 ml of cyclohexanone. The optical density of the organic phase was determined at 549 nm in a Zeiss spectrophotometer. The amount of sialic acid was calculated by the following equation:

$$\mu\text{mols of sialic acid} = 0.075 \times \text{O.D.}_{549}$$

Fucose determination. The primary cysteine-sulfuric acid procedure (13) was used. Immunoglobulin samples were dissolved in 1 ml of cold H_2O, to which 4.5 ml of ice bath-cooled 86% H_2SO_4 was added. After 1 min the mixture was shaken in an ice water bath, then transferred to a tap water bath for 2 min, and finally placed in a boiling water bath for 10 min. After being cooled in a tap water bath, 0.1 ml of a 3% solution of cysteine hydrochloride was added. The optical density was measured in a Zeiss spectrophotometer, $O.D._{396}$ minus $O.D._{427}$ being taken as the measurement of fucose. One-hundredth milligram to 0.05 mg of L-fucose was used as standard.

RESULTS AND DISCUSSION

The results of carbohydrate analysis of IgA proteins isolated from the sera of myeloma patients are summarized in Table I. Among seven IgA proteins examined, the content of hexoses ranged from 2.5% to above 15%, of hexosamines from 0.7% to 3.6%, of sialic acid from 0.4% to 2.0%, and of fucose from 0.18% to 0.76%. In general, more than fourfold differences were found between the highest and the lowest values of all four kinds of carbohydrate tested. These results clearly indicate that, like IgG immunoglobulins (10), IgA immunoglobulins are also heterogeneous in their carbohydrate content.

No correlation was found between the carbohydrate content and the light chain type of a given IgA (Table I). This is what would be expected from work reported previously (14, 15), that most of the carbohydrate moiety of immunoglobulins is attached to the carboxy-terminal half of heavy chains, and that most of the light chains do not contain any carbohydrate.

TABLE I

Carbohydrate analysis of human IgA myeloma proteins

Proteins		Heavy Chain Subclass	Am(1)[a] Marker	Type of Light Chain	Hexoses	Hexosamines		Sialic Acid	Fucose
						Glucosamine	Galactosamine		
For	P[b]	?[c]	−	λ	11.6	3.5	None	1.1	0.54
	M[b]	?[c]	−	λ	12.0	3.4	None	1.2	0.67
Bro	P	α1	−	λ	2.7	1.8	0.97	1.7	0.18
	M	α1	−	λ	2.5	2.0	0.70	1.6	0.20
Pod	P	α1	−	κ	13.8	0.5	0.22	1.1	0.76
	M	α1	−	κ	17.0	0.7	0.26	1.2	0.68
Blo		α1	−	λ	3.3	1.7	0.71	2.0	0.19
Zap		α2	+	λ	3.8	3.6	None	0.4	0.32
Low		α2	+	κ	5.4	3.0	None	2.0	0.23
Her	P	α2	+	λ	5.9	3.2	None	0.8	0.38
	M	α2	+	λ	5.0	2.9	None	0.8	0.53

[a] Am(1) typing was done by a passive hemagglutination method (16).

[b] P, polymer; M, monomer.

[c] See text for explanation.

Four of the IgA's studied were found to exist in both monomeric and polymeric forms. These two forms of each IgA were separated by gel filtration on Sephadex G-200 columns (0.02 M Tris, 0.15 M NaCl, pH 8.0), and were subjected to carbohydrate analysis independently. The results showed that the polymer and the monomer of each IgA had similar amounts of carbohydrate, suggesting that the carbohydrate portion probably is not directly contributing to the polymerization of IgA molecules.

Examination of the antigenic subclass and the Am(1) genetic marker (16) of heavy chain of a given IgA and its carbohydrate content also failed to show clear-cut correlations; but it is interesting that galactosamine was found in all three IgA proteins belonging to the IgA_1 subclass, and was not present in any of the three IgA's belonging to the IgA_2 subclass (Table I). This is in agreement with Abel and Grey's observation (17), that one galactosamine-containing peptide was found in IgA_1 but not in IgA_2 heavy chains; however, since their data have been published only in abstract form, it is not known how many proteins they studied. We hesitate to conclude that all IgA_1 heavy chains lack galactosamine, because ambiguous results were obtained with protein For, which was classified as IgA_1 by Feinstein and Franklin (18) and as IgA_2 by Vaerman and Heremans (19) using subclass-specific antisera. The absence of light chain dimer on urea starch gel electrophoresis (20) again suggests that For probably belongs to the IgA_1 subclass since the vast majority of the IgA_1's have their light chains covalently bonded to heavy chains by disulfide bridges (21). Perhaps more than two subclasses of IgA exist, and antisera used in different laboratories do not detect identical antigenic determinants on the IgA molecule. A search for additional IgA subclasses in humans is currently in progress in our laboratory.

Acknowledgment. The authors thank Dr. J. J. Ludowieg for technical advise, Mr. A. Epstein for technical assistance, and Dr. J. R. L. Pink for comments and criticisms. This work was supported by the Jane Coffin Childs Memorial Fund, American Cancer Society Grant T-386, and a grant from the United States Public Health Service, AI-09813-01. Dr. Wang is a fellow of the National Foundation for Genetics and Neuromuscular Diseases.

SUMMARY

Carbohydrate determinations were performed on seven human IgA myeloma proteins, four of them in both monomeric and polymeric form. The results showed that IgA molecules are heterogeneous in carbohydrate content, that the carbohydrate portion probably does not contribute directly to the polymerization of IgA molecules, and that the IgA_2 subclass does not appear to possess galactosamine.

REFERENCES

1. Edelman, G. M. and Gall, W. E., Ann. Rev. Biochem., *38:* 415, 1969.
2. Milstein, C. and Pink, J. R. L., Progr. Biophys. Mol. Biol., *21:* 209, 1970.
3. Wang, A. C., Wang, I. Y. F., McCormick, J. and Fudenberg, H. H., Immunochemistry, *6:* 451, 1969.
4. Smith, E. L., Greene, R. D. and Bartner, E., J. Biol. Chem., *164:* 359, 1946.
5. Nolan, C. and Smith, E. L., J. Biol. Chem., *237:* 446, 1962.
6. Clamp, J. R. and Putnam, F. W., J. Biol. Chem., *239:* 3233, 1964.
7. Edmundson, A. B., Sheber, F. A., Ely, K. R., Simonds, N. B., Hutson, N. K. and Rossiter, J. L., Arch. Biochem. Biophys., *127:* 725, 1968.
8. Melchers, F., Biochemistry, *8:* 938, 1969.
9. Abel, C. A., Spiegelberg, H. L. and Grey, H. M., Biochemistry, *7:* 1271, 1968.
10. Wang, A. C., Goodman, J. W. and Fudenberg, H. H., J. Immun., *103:* 1149, 1969.
11. Scott, T. A., Jr. and Melvin, E. H., Anal. Chem., *25:* 1656, 1953.
12. Warren, L., J. Biol. Chem., *234:* 1971, 1959.
13. Dische, Z., Meth. Biochem. Anal., *2:* 313, 1955.
14. Fleischman, J. B., Pain, R. H. and Porter, R. R., Arch. Biochem. Biophys., Supplement 1, page 174, 1962.
15. Edelman, G. M. and Gally, J. A., Proc. Nat. Acad. Sci., *51:* 846, 1964.
16. Vyas, G. N. and Fudenberg, H. H., Proc. Nat. Acad. Sci., *64:* 1211, 1969.
17. Abel, C. A. and Grey, H. M., Fed. Proc., *28:* 495, 1969.
18. Feinstein, D. and Franklin, E. C., Nature, *212:* 1496, 1966.
19. Vaerman, J. P. and Heremans, J. F., Science, *153:* 647, 1966.
20. Grey, H. M., Abel, C. A., Yount, W. J. and Kunkel, H. G., J. Exp. Med., *128:* 1223, 1968.
21. Jerry, L. M., Kunkel, H. G., Grey, H. M. and Osserman, E. F., Fed. Proc., *29:* 257, 1970.

THE JOURNAL OF IMMUNOLOGY
Copyright © 1970 by The Williams & Wilkins Co.

Vol. 105, No. 5, November 1970
Printed in U.S.A.

Inhibition of Guinea Pig Complement by Aromatic Amidine and Guanidine Compounds[1]

DAVID H. BING

From the Department of Microbiology and Public Health, Michigan State University, East Lansing, Michigan 48823

The enzymatically active form of the first component of guinea pig complement, $C\bar{1}$,[2] has been postulated to have an anionic binding site (1). The evidence for such a site is based on the ability of guinea pig $C\bar{1}$ to hydrolyze N-tosyl arginine methyl ester (2). Examination of the competitive enzyme kinetics of $C1\bar{s}$, the esterase enzyme which is part of the macromolecular complex constituting human $C\bar{1}$, has provided direct evidence for an anionic binding site (3). This report describes the inhibition of the early acting components of guinea pig complement by aromatic amidine and guanidine compounds in the hemolysis of sheep erythrocytes sensitized with anti-Forssman antibody (EA). The data are consistent with inhibition at the level of $C\bar{1}$, and further substantiate the evidence for an anionic binding site on guinea pig $C\bar{1}$.

The compounds employed in this study were α phenylguanidine, *p*-aminobenzamidine, benzamidine and trimethylphenylammonium. Benzamidine and trimethylphenylammonium were obtained as HCl salts from K & K Fine Chemicals Laboratories (Jamaica, N. Y.) and recrystallized from hot ethanol twice before use. Alpha phenylguanidine and *p*-aminobenzamidine were synthesized according to published procedures (3). Each was recrystallized to constant melting point from ethanol. The *p*-aminobenzamidine had a melting point of 289 to 290°C (literature melting point = 290 to 291°C). Infrared spectrometry (KBr pellet) indicated γ_{max} (cm^{-1}) 1675 ($C = N^+$, amidine). Phenylguanidine had a melting point of 283 to 284°C. Infrared spectrometry (KBr pellet) indicated V_{max} (cm^{-1}) 1675 (C = NH, imine) and 1520 (C = NH, imine).

Sheep blood was collected into Alsever's solution and aged 2 weeks before use. Antiserum prepared against boiled stromata (4) was used to prepare EA. Retired breeders were obtained from the guinea pig colony at the Michigan State Public Health Laboratories, Lansing, Michigan, and exsanguinated by cardiac puncture. The blood was allowed to clot overnight at 4°C, the clot and cells were removed by centrifugation, and the serum was stored at −60°C. Isotonic triethanolamine-buffered saline (TBS) containing 0.1% gelatin (Difco), 0.00015 M $CaCl_2$ and 0.005 M $MgCl_2$ was used for all experiments (5). EA and functionally pure C2 were prepared according to procedures described by Nelson *et al.* (6). Functionally pure $C\bar{1}$ was prepared using the method of Borsos and Rapp (7). The method of Tamura and Nelson was used to prepare EAC4 cells (8). C2 was assayed using the procedure described by Mayer (4); $C\bar{1}$ was assayed at an ionic strength of 0.15 employing 100 effective molecules of C2 per cell added and 0.5-ml portions of EAC4 (5×10^8 cells/ml). The concentrations of $MgCl_2$ and $CaCl_2$, reaction times and temperatures of incubation were identical to those described by Nelson *et al.* (6). C EDTA was prepared by diluting fresh guinea pig serum 1:100 in TBS containing 0.04 M EDTA.

Inhibitors were made to a final concentration of 2×10^{-3} M in TBS containing 0.1% gelatin, 0.00015 M $CaCl_2$ and 0.005 M $MgCl_2$. Each was mixed individually with an equal volume of $C\bar{1}$ (4.85×10^7 effective molecules/ml) or C2 (7.5×10^9 effective molecules/ml), or EAC4 (2×10^8 cells/ml) or C EDTA (diluted 1:50 in TBS containing 0.08 M EDTA). Each mixture was incubated at 0°C for 30 min and then at 30°C for 30

[1] This work was supported by a grant from the National Institutes of Health 1-R01-AM 1369-01 ALY. Article Number 5143 from the Michigan State Agricultural Experiment Station.

[2] The terminology for the complement system is that suggested in the Bulletin of the World Health Organization, *39:* 935, 1968.

min before assaying for inhibitory activity at the appropriate point in the reaction consisting of:

$$\mathrm{EAC4} \xrightarrow[\substack{20\ \mathrm{min} \\ 30^\circ\mathrm{C}}]{C\bar{1}} \mathrm{EAC1,4} \xrightarrow[\substack{20\ \mathrm{min} \\ 30^\circ\mathrm{C}}]{\mathrm{C2}} \mathrm{EAC1,4,2} \xrightarrow[\substack{60\ \mathrm{min} \\ 37^\circ\mathrm{C}}]{\mathrm{C\ EDTA}} \mathrm{lysis.}$$

The amounts of each reactant were 0.4 ml of EAC4 (1×10^8 cells/ml), 0.2 ml of $C\bar{1}$ (2.42×10^7 effective molecules/ml), 0.2 ml of C2 (3.25×10^9 effective molecules/ml) and 1.5 ml of C EDTA. At the end of the incubation period at 37°C, 3.5 ml of cold 0.15 M NaCl was added, the tubes were centrifuged and lysis was measured by determining spectrophotometrically at 410 nm the hemoglobin that was released. The final concentration of every inhibitor in the reaction mixture was 8.7×10^{-5} M except when the inhibitor was mixed with C EDTA. In this case it was 6.5×10^{-4} M. The percentage of inhibition was determined by comparison with a control treated identically but containing no inhibitors. This control gave 70% lysis when compared to the same amount of cells lysed with 1.9 ml of whole serum diluted 1:100 in TBS with 0.005 M $MgCl_2$ and 0.00015 M $CaCl_2$. Other controls included a $C\bar{1}$ control (no $C\bar{1}$ added), a C2 control (no C2 added) and a C EDTA control (no C EDTA added). The results are shown in Table I.

These results indicate that cationic amidine and guanidine aromatic compounds can inhibit the early acting components of complement. The composite results suggest that the primary site of action is on $C\bar{1}$; with the exception of *p*-aminobenzamidine, none of the compounds were inhibitory except when present during the reaction of $C\bar{1}$ with EAC4. As C4 is apparently the natural substrate of $C\bar{1}$, the data are consistent with the inhibitors competing with C4 for a site on $C\bar{1}$. Presumably this site has an anionic character. The results with *p*-aminobenzamidine suggest

TABLE I

Percentage inhibition of hemolysis by aromatic cationic inhibitors[a]

Inhibitor	Inhibitor Added to			
	EAC4	$C\bar{1}$	C2	C EDTA
Alpha phenylguanidine: 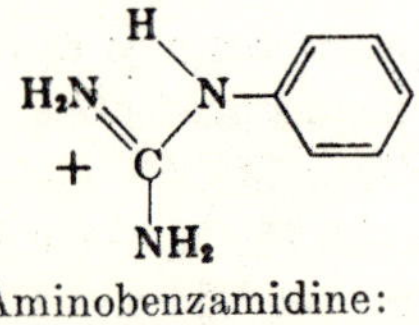	17.7[a]	60.2	3.2	0.0
p-Aminobenzamidine: 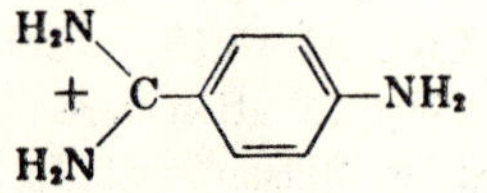	25.6	40	29.2	0.0
Benzamidine: 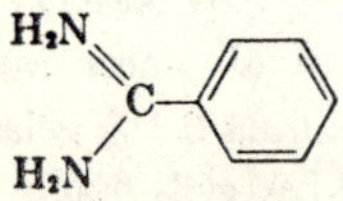	20	23.9	6.9	0.0
Trimethylphenylammonium: 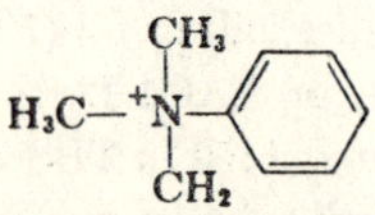	12.9	33.6	7.1	2.5

[a] Each value is the average of triplicate determinations.

that this compound inhibits both C$\overline{1}$ and perhaps the C $\overline{4,2}$ enzyme (the C3 convertase) (9). Trimethylphenylammonium, which does not inhibit human C1$\bar{s}$, apparently inhibits guinea pig C$\overline{1}$. This difference in activity may represent a difference in structure of the guinea pig C$\overline{1}$ enzyme. Further studies on the interaction of purified components in the absence of EA will be necessary to clarify all of these points.

REFERENCES

1. Becker, E. L., in *Ciba Foundation Symposium: Complement*, Edited by G. E. W. Wolstenholme and J. Knight, p. 64, Little, Brown & Co., Boston, 1965.
2. Becker, E. L., J. Immun., *77:* 462, 1956.
3. Bing, D. H., Biochemistry, *8:* 4503, 1969.
4. Mayer, M. M., in *Kabat and Mayer's Experimental Immunochemistry*, 2nd Ed., p. 133, Charles C Thomas, Springfield, Ill., 1961.
5. Haines, A. L. and Lepow, I. H., J. Immun., *92:* 456, 1964.
6. Nelson, R. A., Jr., Jensen, J., Gigli, I. and Tamura, N., Immunochemistry, *3:* 111, 1966.
7. Borsos, T. and Rapp, H. J., J. Immun., *91:* 851, 1963.
8. Tamura, N. and Nelson, R. A., J. Immun., *99:* 582, 1967.
9. Müller-Eberhard, H. J., Advances Immun., *8:* 2, 1968.

THE JOURNAL OF IMMUNOLOGY
Copyright © 1970 by The Williams & Wilkins Co.

Vol. 105, No. 5, November 1970
Printed in U.S.A.

Use of Immunoadsorption Techniques in the Preparation of Chemical Agammaglobulinemia[1]

D. FROMMEL, J. M. DUPUY, G. W. LITMAN AND R. A. GOOD

From the Departments of Pediatrics, Microbiology and Pathology, University of Minnesota, Minneapolis, Minnesota 55455

Currently the use of affinity chromatography has been directed toward selective purification of proteins (1). Specific antibodies have been obtained in high yield using columns of Sepharose coupled either to haptens or to protein antigens (2). It is the purpose of this communication to report the application of these newly developed immunoadsorbents to selective removal of immunoglobulins from serum by passage on a Sepharose anti-light chain antibody column.

Preparation of the immunoadsorbent. Antiserum to guinea pig light chain was prepared by immunizing a goat with an IgG light chain pool, emulsified in complete Freund's adjuvant (3). In double diffusion analysis this antiserum reacted strongly with the κ type light chains whereas the precipitin reaction against the λ type of light chains though present was significantly weaker.

Five and six-tenths grams of CNBr (37.5 mg/ml of Sepharose), dissolved in water, were added with stirring at room temperature to 150 ml of packed Sepharose 4 B (Pharmacia Chemicals, Piscataway, N. J.), contained in 300 ml of 0.05 M sodium bicarbonate buffer, pH 9.0. The pH of the suspension was immediately raised to 11.2 with 2.5 N NaOH. Addition of NaOH was continued until the pH remained stable. The suspension was then washed with 12 liters of cold bicarbonate buffer. One and five-tenths grams of goat IgG, obtained from the anti-light chain serum and dissolved in 75 ml of bicarbonate buffer, pH 8.4, were added to the activated, washed Sepharose. The coupling reaction was allowed to proceed for 16 hr at 2°C, with slow stirring. Unbound goat IgG was removed by washing the Sepharose in a 2.4- x 45-cm column with phosphate-buffered saline, pH 6.8, until the O.D. of the effluent at 280 nm was less than 0.005.

Source of immune guinea pig sera. Sera from guinea pigs immunized with DNP_{25}-BGG[2] (4) and from guinea pigs immunized with BCG and x-irradiated before bleeding (5) were employed.

Immunoadsorption. Five-milliliter amounts of immune guinea pig serum were applied to the Sepharose column. The initial elution phase was performed at room temperature at a rate of 10 ml/hr. After a void volume of 100 ml, proteins were eluted in a broad peak over approximately 80 ml. Proteins eluted below $O.D._{280nm} = 0.05$ were not used for pooling and concentrating the recovered proteins to initial volume. In one experiment, 5 mg of ^{125}I-radiolabeled IgG_2 (6) were added to the serum. The proteins bound to the immunoadsorbent were recovered at 2°C with either 0.1% acetic acid or 0.2 M glycine-HCl, pH 2.3.

RESULTS

Six $\times$ 10^{-2} μM of goat IgG/ml of Sepharose or 92% of the goat IgG were coupled by the described procedure. On immunoelectrophoresis, the eluate, readjusted to initial concentration, was devoid of IgG_2, IgG_1 and IgM (Fig. 1); in double diffusion analysis, no precipitin reaction could be visualized with the treated serum using monospecific antiserum to guinea pig IgG_1 and IgG_2. In seven experiments an average of 18.5% of the total serum proteins was retained on the immunoadsorbent columns, an amount which corresponded to the immunoglobulin concentration of immune guinea pig serum (7). In two of seven experiments, the adsorption was incomplete. Recycling of the eluate on a small column (1 $\times$ 15 cm) resulted in complete adsorption of the immunoglobulins. When radiolabeled IgG_2

[1] This work was aided by grants of the Graduate School, University of Minnesota, American Heart Association, American Thoracic Society, National Foundation-March of Dimes and United States Public Health Service (AI-00292, AI-00798 and AI-08677).

[2] Abbreviations used: DNP-BGG: 2,4-dinitrophenyl bovine γ globulin (the subscript refers to the average number of DNP groups/molecule of conjugated protein); BCG, Bacille Calmette-Guérin; PPD, purified protein derivative.

was chromatographed, only 2% of the radioactivity was found in the major protein eluate. However, 29% of the radioactivity was recovered with neutral aqueous buffer at a Ve/Vo = 5.5 to 8.5 and represents immunoglobulins with λ type light chains which were less firmly bound to the immunoadsorbent.

As shown in Table I, the treated anti-BGG-DNP serum no longer exhibited antibody activities as shown in passive hemagglutination (8, 9), precipitin reactions and passive cutaneous anaphylaxis using sensitization periods of 4 and 18 hr (10).

The ability to transfer delayed hypersensitivity to PPD with plasma (11) was not abolished by the immunoadsorption procedures. This finding supports prior conclusions that this form of transfer of cellular immunity is not due to conventional immunoglobulins. Further, this observation suggests that the components involved in transfer of delayed hypersensitivity have no common antigenic relationship to light chain determinants.

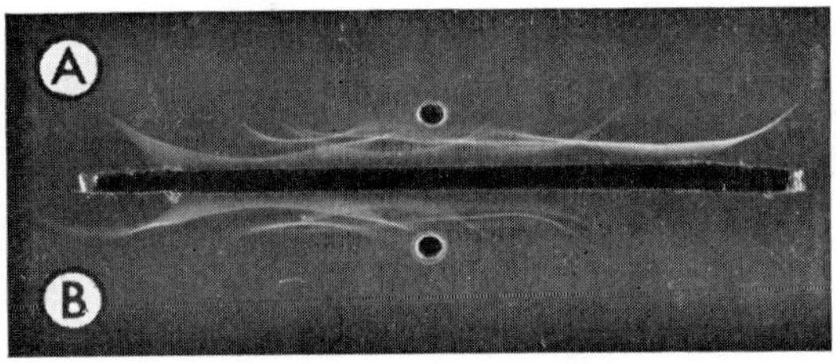

Figure 1. Immunoelectrophoretic pattern of native immune guinea pig serum (*A*) and immune guinea pig serum after adsorption (*B*), as revealed by a goat anti-guinea pig (normal) serum.

TABLE I

Biologic activity of immune guinea pig serum anti-BGG-DNP before and after immunoadsorption

	Native Immune Serum	Immune Serum after Immunoadsorption
Passive hemagglutination		
Anti-DNP_{25}-BGG	1:10,240	<1:10
Anti-DNP_{43}-BSA	1:20,480	<1:10
Precipitin titer		
vs DNP_{25}-BGG	1:16	Neg
vs DNP_{43}-BSA	1:32	Neg
PCA		
With 2 mg of DNP_{43}-BSA as antigen	1:2500	<1:10

Recovery of the Sepharose immunoglobulins bound to the column was unsatisfactory when using 0.1% acetic acid; with the glycine-HCl buffer, 80% to 85% of the guinea pig immunoglobulins could be eluted, but most of the IgM fraction had been denatured.

Selective and complete removal of a protein class from serum can be achieved easily and reproducibly by use of antibody coupled to agarose derivatives. The efficiency of such procedures can be increased following the suggestions of Cuatrecasas (12).

Serum rendered totally agammaglobulinemic will be useful as a source of homologous serum in cell culture work. Serum selectively deprived of one immunoglobulin class, through the use of monospecific anti-heavy chain reagents, will be helpful in analyzing complex immune reactions.

Acknowledgments. We are grateful to Drs. Michael E. Lamm and V. Nussenzweig, New York University School of Medicine, for evaluation of our antiserum and our treated guinea pig sera. The able technical assistance of Miss Vân Nguyen was appreciated.

REFERENCES

1. Cuatrecasas, P., Wilchek, M. and Anfinsen, C. B., Proc. Nat. Acad. Sci., *61:* 636, 1968.
2. Wofsy, L. and Burr, B., J. Immun., *103:* 380, 1969.
3. Nussenzweig, V., Franklin, E. C. and Benacerraf, B., J. Immun., *93:* 1015, 1964.
4. Benacerraf, B., Ovary, Z., Bloch, K. J. and Franklin, E. C., J. Exp. Med., *117:* 937, 1963.
5. Dupuy, J. M., Kalpaktsoglou, P. and Good, R. A., J. Immun., *104:* 1384, 1970.
6. McConahey, P. J. and Dixon, F. J., Int. Arch. Allerg., *29:* 185, 1966.
7. Binaghi, R., J. Immun., *97:* 159, 1966.
8. Gold, E. R. and Fudenberg, H. H., J. Immun., *99:* 859, 1967.
9. Stavitsky, A. B., J. Immun., *72:* 360, 1954.
10. Ovary, Z., in *Immunological Methods*, edited by J. F. Ackroyd, p. 259, F. A. Davis Company, Philadelphia, 1964.
11. Dupuy, J. M., Perey, D. Y. E. and Good, R. A., Lancet, *1:* 551, 1969.
12. Cuatrecasas, P., J. Biol. Chem., *245:* 3059, 1970.

THE JOURNAL OF IMMUNOLOGY
Vol. 105, No. 5, November 1970

Pepsin Digestion of Mouse Antibody[1]

FRANCIS B. CASEY[2] AND SEI TOKUDA[3]

From the Department of Microbiology, The University of New Mexico, School of Medicine, Albuquerque, New Mexico 87106

In 1960 Nisonoff *et al.* described a method of producing $F(ab')_2$ fragments from human and rabbit IgG antibodies (1). The immunoglobulins are mixed with pepsin (3% by weight) in 0.1 M acetate buffer, pH 4.5. The mixture is stirred for 18 hr at 37°C. The enzymatic action is terminated by raising the pH to 7.0 and by precipitating the globulins in 18% (w/v) sodium sulfate. This precipitate contains a relatively homogeneous preparation of 5S $F(ab')_2$ antibody fragments. Recently, Sinclair (2) reported that when this procedure is followed for mouse γ globulins, the pepsin-digested material is grossly contaminated with intact 7S antibodies. In order to obtain the 5S material it was necessary to subject

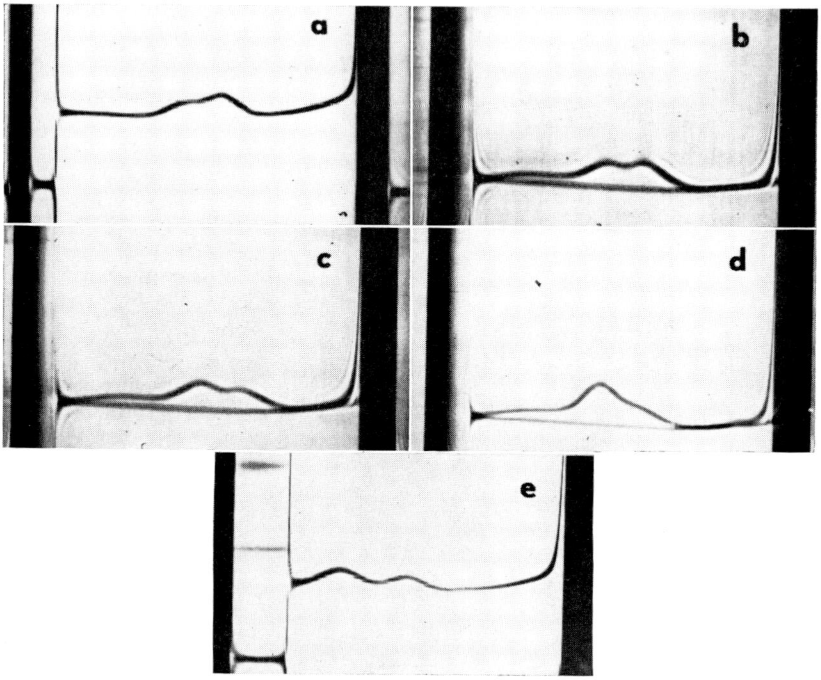

Figure 1. Schlieren patterns of pepsin-treated mouse γ globulin after varying periods of enzyme digestion. Direction of sedimentation is from left to right. *a*, 18 hr, fast peak = 6.8S, slow peak = 5.0S; *b*, 24 hr, fast peak = 6.7S, slow peak = 5.0S; *c*, 30 hr, fast peak = 6.7S, slow peak = 4.9S; *d*, 44 hr, fast shoulder = 6.7S, peak = 4.9S; *e*, 56 hr, fast peak = 5.1S, slow peak = 2.2S. Slow shoulders on *b*, *c* and *d* represent the pepsin which was not removed from the enzyme-γ globulin mixture.

[1] This investigation was supported in part by United States Public Health Service Research Grant CA 10129 from the National Cancer Institute.

[2] Recipient of United States Public Health Service Predoctoral Fellowship No. F01 GM 34484 from the National Institute of General Medical Sciences. Present Address: Experimental Pathology Laboratory, USARIEM, Natick, Massachusetts 01760.

[3] Recipient of United States Public Health Service Research Career Development Award No. K4 GM 14893 from the National Institute of General Medical Sciences.

the pepsin digest to sucrose density gradient ultracentrifugation for 40 hr at 40,000 rpm, at 4°C. We have also encountered difficulties in preparing mouse $F(ab')_2$ according to the method described by Nisonoff *et al.* The purpose of this communication is to characterize the time relationship in the pepsin digestion of mouse γ globulin in order to determine a procedure that may be used to obtain mouse $F(ab')_2$ in high yield and relatively free of contaminating 7S antibody.

Mouse γ globulin was prepared from whole mouse serum by three successive precipitations in one-third saturated ammonium sulfate. The γ globulin was dialyzed overnight against 0.1 M acetate buffer, pH 4.5, prior to incubation with 3% pepsin at 37°C for varying periods of time. Portions of the pepsin and γ globulin mixture were obtained after 18, 24, 30, 44 and 56 hr of incubation. The pH of the mixture was adjusted to 7.0 to stop the enzyme reaction. The entire reaction mixture was then dialyzed against saline. Preparations digested for 18 and 56 hr, used in a previous study (3), were used for comparison. These 18- and 56-hr samples differed from the other samples in that the globulins had been precipitated by sodium sulfate before analytical centrifugation. The protein concentration of each sample was adjusted to approximately 4.5 mg/ml. Each sample was then subjected to analytical ultracentrifugation at 56,100 rpm at 20°C, using a type D rotor and the standard double sector cell. The phase plate analyzer angle was set at 60°. Examination of the schlieren patterns obtained (Fig. 1) revealed that after 18 hr of incubation the digestion was only 45% complete. Degradation of the 7S antibody into its 5S fragments took place between 44 and 56 hr of incubation. Since the 56-hr sample from an earlier experiment had been separated from pepsin by sodium sulfate precipitation, the substantial 2.2S peak represents a further degradation product of pepsin digestion.

These findings suggest that in order to obtain sufficient quantities of mouse 5S antibody according to the methods described by Nisonoff *et al.* it is necessary to extend the incubation time from 18 hr to at least 44 to 50 hr. If it can be determined by analytical ultracentrifugation or change in biologic activity, such as loss of hemolysin titer, that all the 7S antibody has been digested, then the necessity of sucrose gradient ultracentrifugation can be eliminated. However, even though passage through a gradient is required, the extended digestion period will increase the yield of 5S $F(ab')_2$ fragments.

REFERENCES

1. Nisonoff, A., Wissler, F. C., Lipman, L. N. and Woernley, D. L., Arch. Biochem. Biophys., *89:* 230, 1960.
2. Sinclair, N. R. S., Nature, *220:* 1048, 1968.
3. Casey, F. B. and Tokuda, S., J. Immun., *104:* 1569, 1970.

THE JOURNAL OF IMMUNOLOGY
Vol. 105, No. 5, November 1970
Printed in U.S.A.

Homologous Serum Passive Cutaneous Anaphylaxis in Guinea Pigs Mediated by Two γ1 or γ1-Type Heat-Stable Globulins and a Non-γ1 Heat-Labile Reagin

W. E. PARISH

From the Lister Institute of Preventive Medicine, Elstree, Hertsfordshire, England

Immunoglobulins with properties like those of human IgE (reaginic antibodies) occur in several laboratory animals, particularly the rat after antigenic injection (1, 2) or helminth infestation (3), the mouse after antigenic injection (4, 5) or helminth infestation (6), and the rabbit after antigenic injection (7, 8) and helminth infestation (9). Apart from a heat-labile antibody reported in guinea pigs infected with *Trichinella spiralis* (10), which conferred passive cutaneous anaphylactic (PCA) sensitivity on homologous skin for 21 days, reagin-like antibodies have not hitherto been described in guinea pigs, despite this animal's extreme susceptibility to anaphylaxis.

Benacerraf and Ovary and their associates (11, 12) described two 7S immunoglobulins in guinea pigs, a γ1 which sensitized homologous tissues anaphylactically, and a γ2 which did not. The investigations described below now reveal at least three antibodies in guinea pig sera capable of sensitizing homologous tissues anaphylactically. The first is the γ1 globulin (12) that is heat-stable at 60°C, confers good PCA activity after a latent period of 4 hr, and persists in skin for 3 to 4 days. The second, a previously undescribed antibody, is closely associated with the γ1 globulin and shares some of its antigenic determinants, is heat-stable, gives little or no PCA sensitivity after a latent period of 4 hr, but strong sensitivity after 16 hr which persists for 7 and occasionally for 9 days. The third anaphylactic sensitizing antibody resembles reaginic antibodies in other species; it is heat-labile at 56°C after 1 hr and induces a sensitivity that persists for 28 days.

Antisera were judged to contain 4-day persisting antibody when they conferred good PCA activity at 4 hr, which was weak or absent on the 4th day, and to contain 7-day persisting antibody when at 4 hr there was no PCA activity or less than that at 16 hr, but the activity remained strong at 4 days and persisted weakly to the 7th day. Thus sera containing both antibodies gave strong PCA responses at 4 hr and 4 days and weak ones at 7 days (anti-β-lactoglobulin in Table I). Reagin-like antibody is easily differentiated by its heat-lability and persistence in skin for 21 days. Hereafter, the PCA antibody persisting for about 4 days is referred to as 4-day antibody; that persisting 7 days as the 7-day antibody.

Fifty Hartley strain guinea pigs were sensitized to picryl chloride by injecting 50 μg in 0.3 ml of complete Freund's adjuvant divided between each hind footpad. On the 15th and 17th days, 3% picryl chloride in absolute alcohol was applied to a 4-mm area of shaved skin. In all cases it elicited typical delayed-type reactions. On the 45th day, 0.1 ml of a solution containing 5 μg of picryl chloride combined with guinea pig serum albumin was injected into a hind footpad, and the injection was repeated in alternate feet each week for 18 weeks. Another 50 guinea pigs were sensitized to β-lactoglobulin with 50 μg in aluminum hydroxide gel, half into each hind footpad; after 14 days 5 μg β-lactoglobulin in aluminum hydroxide was injected weekly for 12 weeks into the pad or dorsum of a foot, all four feet being injected in rotation. Blood samples were taken from the ear or by cardiac puncture once a week; at intervals some animals from each group were bled out. Individual sera, or pools from 10 animals, unheated or heated at 56°C for 1 hr were tested in 0.1-ml volumes by PCA in guinea pigs, which were challenged with picryl chloride-egg albumin or β-lactoglobulin at 4 hr, and 7 and 21 days after sensitization. In further tests, recipients were challenged daily.

The PCA titers at various intervals after sensitization (Table I) illustrate the difference in persistence of anaphylactic sensitivity conferred by the antisera. Samples taken 19 and 30 days after sensitization to picryl chloride were inactive. At 58 days, 13 days after the injections of picryl chloride-guinea pig albumin had started, all the animals had a heat-stable antibody that conferred little or no cutaneous anaphylactic sensitivity at 4 hr but did so at 16 hr, the sensitivity persisting for 7 to 9 days. The antibody was formed by all

TABLE I

Homologous PCA titers of anti-picryl chloride and anti-β-lactoglobulin sera

Days after Primary Sensitization	Antigen	No. of Sera	Mean Titers[a] and Character of PCA Antibody				No. of Sera with Reagin
			Heat stable "4-hr"	Heat stable "4-day"	Heat stable "7-day"	Heat labile "21-day"	
19	pic chl	50	0	0	0	0	0
	β-lact	50	16	2	0	0	0
30	pic chl	45	0	0	0	0	0
	β-lact	45	128	4	0	0	0
58	pic chl	40	16	128	4	4	1
	β-lact	40	512	128[b]	2	0	0
77	pic chl	30	32	256	4	4	4
	β-lact	30	1024	128[b]	4	2	9

[a] Sum of titers divided by number of sera with activity, to nearest doubling dilution.

[b] Too diffuse to measure accurately.

the animals and the titers increased with further injections.

On the 77th day another antibody was found in four of the remaining 30 animals. This antibody was heat-labile and sensitized skin for 21 to 28 days, when the reaction was about 10 mm in diameter on the subcutaneous surface 30 min after intravenous challenge. The titers were 1:2, 1:4, 1:4 and 1:8.

The results with animals sensitized to β-lactoglobulin (Table I) were different. Antibody conferring PCA activity at 4 hr was present on the 19th day, and its titer increased as sensitization proceeded. It had a weak affinity for skin, for although reactions following challenge at 4 hr were discrete, they were less so at 16 hr, and animals sensitized with high-titer sera and challenged at 16 hr, and 1 or 2 days, either died of anaphylaxis or had a diffuse subcutaneous exudation of the blue indicator dye, sometimes leaving pale areas at the sites of sensitization. This latter event prevented the detection of 7-day antibody or reagin in the same sera until the dye had diffused away on the 4th or 5th day.

Beta-lactoglobulin with aluminum hydroxide was better than picrylchloride at evoking the reagin-like antibody, which was formed by 9 of 30 guinea pigs, though in low titers (1:2 or 1:4).

Beta-lactoglobulin in Freund's adjuvant behaved differently from that in aluminum hydroxide as it induced formation of the γ1 4-day antibody but no 7-day antibody or reagin. Similarly bovine serum albumin (BSA), bovine γ globulin (BGG) and dinitrophenylated (DNP) egg albumin (13) in solution or in Freund's complete adjuvant evoked 4-day antibody but no 7-day or reaginic antibody. However, DNP-egg albumin in aluminum hydroxide induced formation of 7-day antibody detected in recipients challenged with DNP-BSA, much like that of animals sensitized to picryl chloride, although some sera contained both 4-day and 7-day antibodies. No reaginic anti-DNP antibody was found to any of these antigens other than picryl chloride and β-lactoglobulin. It is evident from these tests that the adjuvant as well as the antigen influences the type of antibody formed.

The persistence of PCA sensitivity for 7 days was not due to the presence of greater amounts of antibody than in sera with 4-day sensitivity. To the contrary, the titer of some 4-day anti-BSA and anti-BGG sera at 16 hr was about four times greater than that of the 7-day anti-picryl chloride sera. The persistence of 7-day sensitivity was an expression of a qualitative change in antibody activity. This was demonstrated by sensitizing guinea pigs on one flank with anti-BSA or anti-BGG sera, and on the other flank with anti-picryl chloride serum, all at the same PCA titer at 16 hr, and challenging daily with both antigens. At 2 to 3 days there was diffuse subcutaneous exudation of dye on the anti-bovine sites and little response at 4 to 5 days, whereas the anti-picryl chloride sites gave discrete reactions up to the 7th or 8th day, although diminishing in size and intensity. It thus appears that loss of PCA sensitivity to the bovine antigens is partly due to elution of the antibody from the site of injection, whereas that lost to picryl chloride is due to decay of antibody remaining at the site.

An attempt was made to separate the three different antibody activities in a pool of anti-β-lactoglobulin sera on DEAE cellulose, by stepwise elution with a phosphate buffer. Both the 4- and 7-day activity was eluted with the γ1 globulin-rich fractions, and although some fractions contained 4-day activity only, all fractions containing 7-day activity contained also 4-day activity. Reagin-like antibody was never recovered from the column, probably because of its low concentration.

Similar partial separation was also obtained by electrophoresis of the anti-β-lactoglobulin serum in agar gels, cutting out strips and testing the globulins eluted from them for PCA activity (12). Four-day PCA activity was found throughout the region of the $\gamma 1$ arc, but the 7-day activity, together with 4-day activity, was found in the fast region of the arc near the well of origin.

Treatment of whole anti-β-lactoglobulin serum with rabbit anti-$\gamma 1$-globulin eliminated nearly all the heat-stable PCA activity; the residual activity could not be identified. The anti-$\gamma 1$ globulin did not affect the reagin-like antibody.

Thus in guinea pig serum, three antibodies may mediate PCA in the homologous species, although two of them are distinguishable only by their biologic activity. The first antibody is the $\gamma 1$ globulin first recognized by Benacerraf and Ovary (11, 12). It is heat-stable at 56°C for 1 to 2 hr. PCA sensitivity occurs after a latent period of 4 hr and persists for about 4 days, although it tends to diffuse from the injected sites after 16 hr, so that high-titer antisera sensitize the recipient to generalized anaphylaxis or to a diffuse skin reaction. This antibody follows sensitization with most antigens tested, with or without adjuvant.

The second antibody shares antigenic determinants with the $\gamma 1$ globulin and may be a variety of it. It is also heat-stable. The latent period for PCA sensitization is about 16 hr; there is little or no sensitization after 4 hr, which distinguishes it from the previous antibody. The PCA titer is highest on the 3rd or 4th day when the 4-day $\gamma 1$ antibody activity disappears, and it persists in low titer to the 7th or 8th day. The reactions in the skin after challenge are always discrete. This antibody is induced by certain antigens only, whose effectiveness is influenced by the nature of the adjuvant. With the correct choice of antigen and adjuvant and after prolonged sensitization, all the animals formed the antibody.

The third antibody is not a $\gamma 1$ globulin and resembles the reagin-like antibody found by Catty (10) in guinea pigs infected with trichinella. It is heat-labile at 56°C for 1 hr, it confers PCA sensitivity for up to 28 days and the lesions remain discrete, although small. Only two antigens induced formation of the antibody, which was found in very low titers in a few animals.

Anaphylaxis, to which guinea pigs are extremely susceptible, appears to be mediated mainly by heat-stable immunoglobulins. However, reagin-like antibodies can be induced in a small proportion of animals after parenteral sensitization. The situation may be analogous to that of atopy in man; for although IgE globulins are present in nearly all human sera, they are more abundant in persons susceptible to atopic (anaphylactic) disorders (14, 15) who form about 16% of the population (16). Similarly, inbred strains of mice vary in their ability to form reagin (5), and in this species aluminum hydroxide is an effective adjuvant, as it has proved to be in the guinea pig. Reagin in guinea pigs appeared after prolonged sensitization, whereas in rats (1, 2), mice (4, 5) and rabbits (7) it appears early.

REFERENCES

1. Mota, I., Immunology, *7:* 681, 1964.
2. Binaghi, R. A., Benacerraf, B., Bloch, K. J. and Kourilsky, F. M., J. Immun., *92:* 927, 1964.
3. Ogilvie, B. M., Immunology, *12:* 113, 1967.
4. Mota, I., Immunology, *12:* 343, 1967.
5. Revoltella, R. and Ovary, Z., Immunology, *17:* 45, 1969.
6. Mota, I., Sadun, E. H., Bradshaw, R. M. and Grove, R. W., Immunology, *16:* 71, 1969.
7. Zvaifler, N. J. and Becker, E. L., J. Exp. Med., *123:* 935, 1966.
8. Strannegard, O. and Yurchison, A., Immunology, *16:* 387, 1969.
9. Hogarth-Scott, R. S., Int. Arch. Allerg., *32:* 201, 1967.
10. Catty, D. *Immunology of Nematode Infections. Trichinosis in Guinea Pigs as a Model*, S. Karger, Basel, 1969.
11. Benacerraf, B., Ovary, Z., Bloch, K. J. and Franklin, E. C., J. Exp. Med., *117:* 937, 1963.
12. Ovary, Z., Benacerraf, B. and Bloch, K. J., J. Exp. Med., *117:* 951, 1963.
13. Ovary, Z. and Benacerraf, B., Proc. Soc. Exp. Biol. Med., *114:* 72, 1963.
14. Johansson, S. G. O., Lancet, *2:* 951, 1967.
15. Heiner, D. C. and Rose, B., J. Allerg., *45:* 30, 1970.
16. Van Arsdel, P. P. and Motulsky, A. G., Acta Genet. Statist. Med., *9:* 101, 1949.

THE JOURNAL OF IMMUNOLOGY
Vol. 105, No. 5, November 1970

Ultrastructural Analysis of Hemolysin-Forming Cell Clusters

I. Preliminary Observations[1]

GEORGE C. SAUNDERS AND WILLIAM S. HAMMOND

From the Department of Pathology, University of Colorado Medical Center, Denver, Colorado 80220, and the Denver Veterans Administration Hospital, Denver, Colorado 80220

Following *in vitro* stimulation of mouse spleen cells with sheep red blood cell antigens (SRBC) many of the resulting hemolysin-forming cells have been found to be associated with cell clusters (1, 2). We have initiated a series of studies designed to investigate the interrelationships of the various cell types found within these clusters. We report here preliminary morphologic observations of hemolysin-forming cell clusters.

Dissociated mouse spleen cells were cultured in the presence of SRBC using Saunders' (3) modification of Marbrook's (4) technique. After 48 hr of incubation, the spleen cells were carefully recovered and transferred into 15-ml centrifuge tubes which were then placed in an icebucket. Cell clusters were allowed to settle out in the cold for 10 min. The supernatant containing the remainder of the cells and medium was discarded. The recovered cell clusters were analyzed for hemolytic activity by the method of Jerne and Nordin (5). Cell clusters clearly showing hemolytic activity were isolated and prepared for electron microscopy in a manner similar to that of Harris, Hummeler and Harris (6). The entire agar plate was fixed for 10 min by flooding it with cold 2.5% glutaraldehyde in 0.1 M cacodylate buffer, pH 7.4. Hemolytic plaques with their central clusters were cut out, fixed further in a 2:1 mixture of 1% OsO_4 and 2.5% glutaraldehyde in cacodylate buffer, postfixed in uranyl acetate, and embedded in Vestopal or Araldite-Epon. Sections were examined with either a Siemens 100 or a Philips EM-300 electron microscope.

We have examined hemolysin-forming clusters containing from as few as 6 to as many as 250 viable cells. Large amounts of debris from autolyzed cells have been observed within all clusters examined. Autolyzed erythroid, lymphoid and phagocytic cells have been identified in the clusters. No degenerating (nor intact) polymorphonuclear leucocytes have been observed, probably because these short-lived cells are beyond recognition at the time the cultures are harvested. Viable cells that persist in the clusters are plasma cells in various stages of differentiation, small and medium sized lymphocytes, blast cells and macrophages.

In most of the clusters examined, we have observed a similar cell arrangement (Fig. 1). Macrophages (in some clusters more than one macrophage is present) are surrounded by plasma cells, small and medium sized lymphocytes and undifferentiated blast cells. These units generally contain 6 to 10 cells seen in a single plane of section. The small clusters usually contain one of these macrophage units while large clusters contain several. Frequently morphologically similar cells occur in pairs. While there is much interdigitation of the microvillar projections of adjacent cells (Figs. 2 and 3) we have not found any evidence of cytoplasmic bridges between cells.

We are currently examining cell clusters in cultures obtained at shorter and longer periods of incubation after antigenic stimulation to establish intracellular changes as well as changes in cell associations that may occur during the course of the response.

Acknowledgments. We greatly appreciate and acknowledge both the interpretative help of Dr. A. E. Vatter and the excellent technical assistance of Mrs. M. Alders and Mr. D. Swartzendruber.

[1] This investigation was supported by United States Public Health Service Grant AI-08269 and Denver Veterans Administration Institutional Grant 1570.

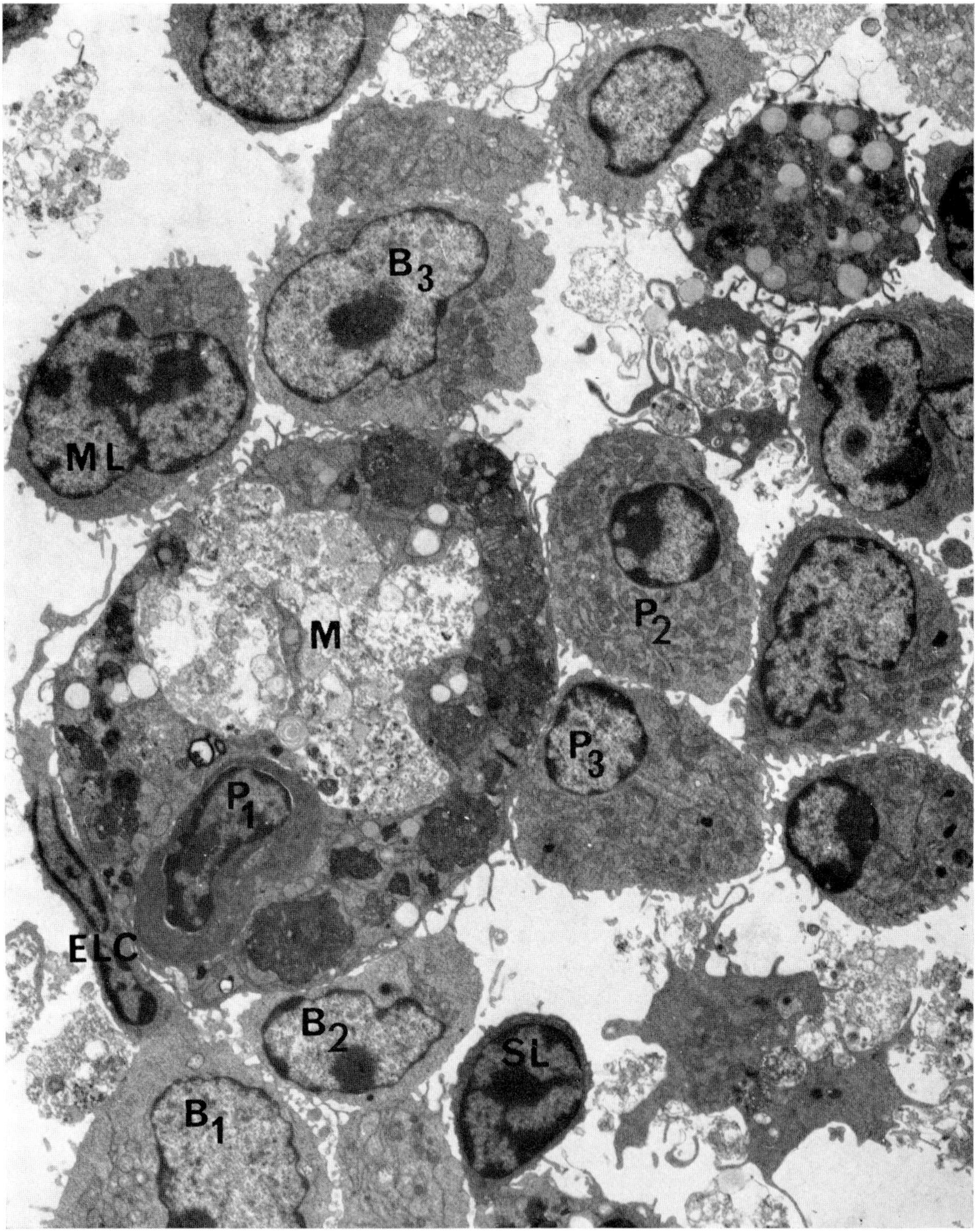

Figure 1. Portion of a large hemolysin-forming cell cluster illustrating the cell types seen in the basic unit. *M*, macrophage (with entrapped plasma cell, P_1); $P_{1,2,3}$, blast cells; *ELC*, elongated lymphoid cell; *ML*, medium lymphocyte; $P_{2,3}$, plasma cells. Observe the pairing of B_1 and B_2, and P_2 and P_3. Such pairing of morphologically similar cells is quite common. *SL*, small lymphocyte (× 3500).

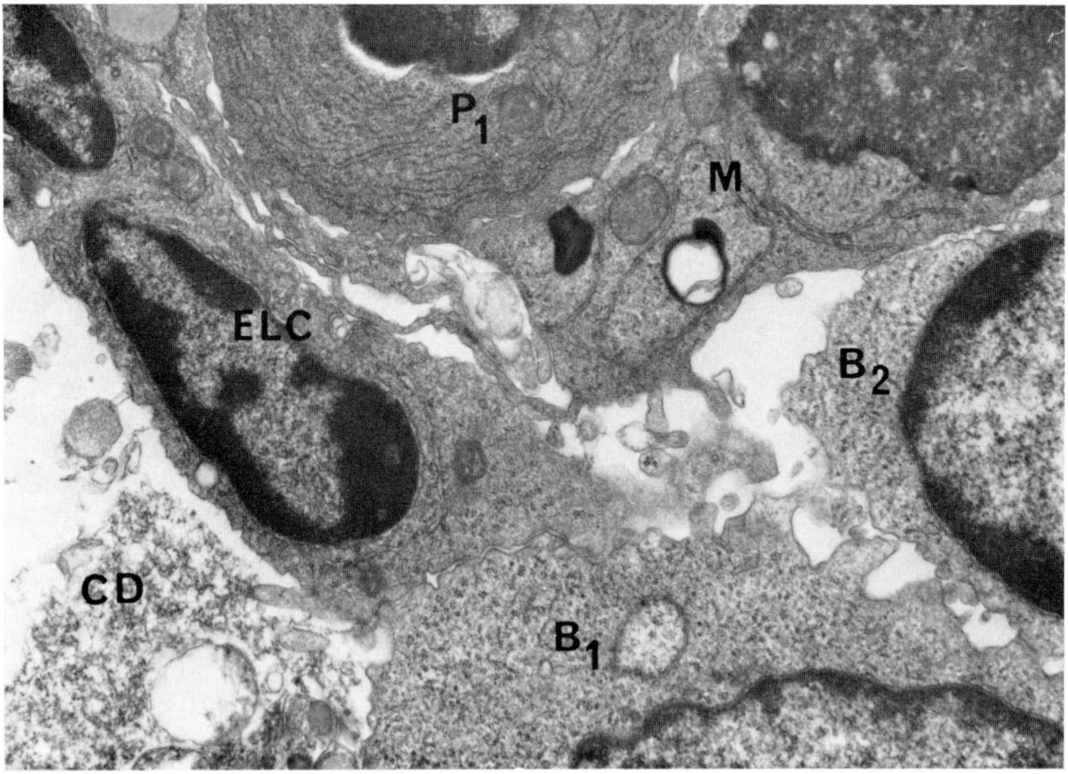

Figure 2. Higher power micrograph of a portion of the basic unit illustrated in Figure 1. *M*, macrophage; P_1, entrapped plasma cell; $B_{1,2}$, blast cells; *ELC*, elongated lymphoid cell; *CD*, cell debris. Note these points of interest: 1) Large number of spiral polysomes in $B_{1,2}$; 2) the complex membrane relationships of all cells pictured; 3) the absence of cytoplasmic cross-bridging between cells. The association of the ELC with M depicted here has been seen quite frequently (× 23,600).

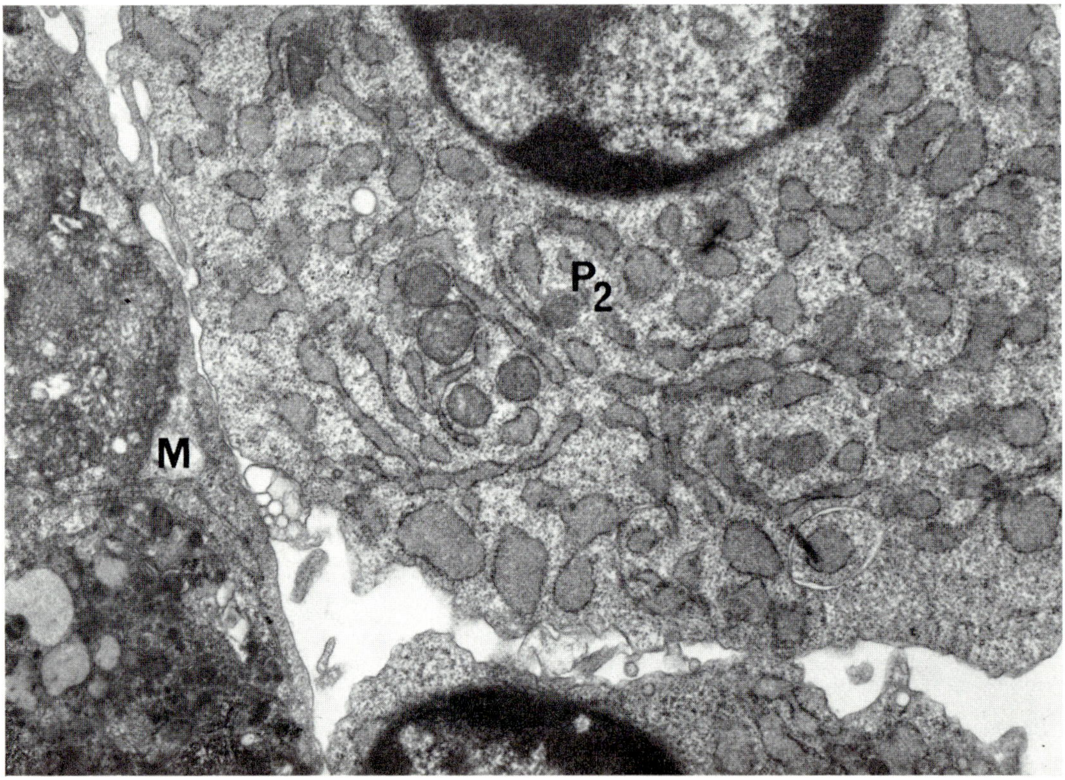

Figure 3. Higher power micrograph of another portion of the basic unit illustrated in Figure 1. This figure illustrates the association of plasma cell P_2 with the macrophage (*M*). Again note the absence of cytoplasmic cross-bridging between cells (× 35,900).

REFERENCES

1. Mosier, D. E., J. Exp. Med., *129:* 351, 1969.
2. Pierce, C. W. and Benacerraf, B., Science, *161:* 1002, 1969.
3. Saunders, G. C., J. Exp. Med., *130:* 543, 1969.
4. Marbrook, J., Clin. Exp. Immun., *3:* 367, 1968.
5. Jerne, N. K. and Nordin, A. A., Science, *140:* 405, 1963.
6. Harris, T. N., Hummeler, K. and Harris, J., J. Exp. Med., *123:* 161, 1966.

THE JOURNAL OF IMMUNOLOGY
Copyright © 1970 by The Williams & Wilkins Co.

Vol. 105, No. 5, November 1970
Printed in U.S.A.

Lymphocytes and Yellow Fever
I. Transient Virus Refractory State following Vaccination of Man with the 17-D Strain

E. FREDERICK WHEELOCK, STEPHEN T. TOY AND RUNE L. STJERNHOLM

From the Department of Preventive Medicine, Case Western Reserve University, Cleveland, Ohio 44106

The often observed presence of lymphocytes at sites of virus replication *in vivo* suggests that these cells are actively involved in the host defense against viral infections. In order to define more clearly the antiviral role of lymphocytes, a model viral infection in man was needed for study. For this purpose the infection produced by the 17-D vaccine strain of yellow fever virus was selected for study since it produces an asymptomatic infection in man associated with transient low titers of virus and interferon in the blood, followed by the development of long-lasting immunity (1).

Previous *in vitro* studies with each human leukocyte type have revealed that 17-D virus induces interferon production in monocytes and lymphocytes and replicates to high titers in monocytes and in phytohemagglutinin-stimulated lymphocytes (2). Also, experiments with monkeys have indicated that 17-D virus replicates in the lymph nodes draining the site of inoculation (3).

We report here the observation that peripheral lymphocytes stimulated with phytohemagglutinin support 17-D virus replication *in vitro*, but lose their capacity to do so when removed from circulation between the 7th and 11th days following yellow fever virus vaccination.

The 17-D vaccine strain of yellow fever virus (4) was obtained from the National Drug Company (Philadelphia, Pa.) as a standard vaccine preparation. The virus seed was prepared by replication in the C-13 clone of baby hamster kidney cells and stored in 2-ml amounts at −70°C. The 17-D virus seed contained 2×10^8 50% tissue culture infective doses ($TCID_{50}$)/ml, when titered in C-13 monolayers.

Samples from infected lymphocyte cultures were assayed for virus by the tube dilution method in monolayers of C-13 cells grown in 16- x 125-mm glass culture tubes. Titrations employed eight tubes/10-fold dilution and the 50% endpoint was calculated by the method of Reed and Muench (5). Differences in titer of more than 0.5 $\log_{10}$ (3.2-fold) were considered to be significant.

Six non-immune young adult male volunteers who had never received yellow fever vaccine, had never been in yellow fever endemic area, and had no history of encephalitis were selected for the initial study. No yellow fever virus-specific neutralizing antibody was detected in their sera. None of the volunteers had evidence of a viral infection for the week prior to 17-D virus vaccination.

Immediately before and on selected days following vaccination, 60 ml of peripheral venous blood was withdrawn from each of the subjects. Lymphocytes were separated from other leukocyte types by passage of leukocyte-rich plasma through a column of siliconized glass beads as described previously (6). The lymphocytes were washed twice by centrifugation and suspended in Eagle's minimum essential medium supplemented with 4% tryptose phosphate broth, 10% unheated fetal calf serum, 1.75 g/liter sodium bicarbonate, 1% glutamine, penicillin and streptomycin. The cell concentration was adjusted to 2×10^6 cells/ml and each culture tube received 4 ml of the cell suspension. Cells prepared by this technique usually consisted of 98% to 100% lymphocytes.

From each sample of blood two cultures were prepared and inoculated with 17-D virus at a virus-to-cell multiplicity of 10. Following 2 hr incubation at 37°C, the lymphocytes were washed twice with phosphate-buffered saline by centrifugation and the cells resuspended in the original volume of growth medium. PHA (PHA-P, Difco) at a concentration of 25 μg/ml was added to one of each set of two cultures, and the cultures were then incubated at 37°C in the presence of 5% CO_2 in air. On selected days thereafter, 2 ml were removed from all the cultures without disturbing the lymphocytes which had settled to the bottom of each culture tube. The samples were rapidly frozen and

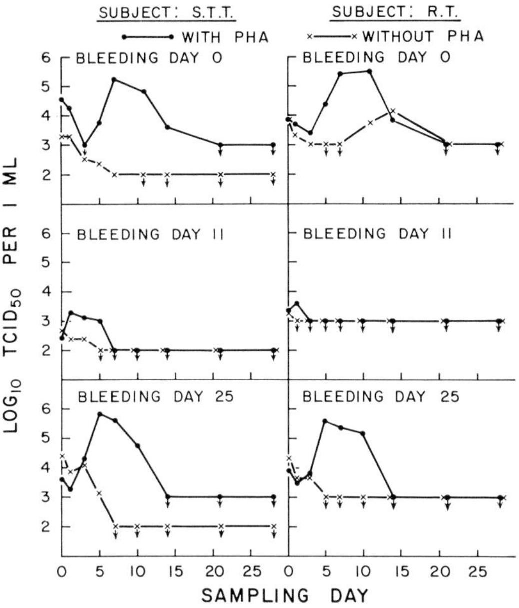

Figure 1. Replication of 17-D yellow fever virus in human lymphocytes removed from donors on selected days after vaccination.

stored at −70°C until assayed for virus. Two milliliters of fresh medium were added back to each culture and the cells were gently swirled to mix the medium. Thus, at all times the initial volume of medium was present over the cells.

Figure 1 illustrates the 17-D virus growth curves in cultures of human lymphocytes from two donors on various days after vaccination. The PHA-stimulated, pre-vaccination cultures (day 0) supported the replication of 17-D virus; no significant replication occurred in the unstimulated cultures. Occasionally, slight virus replication occurred in unstimulated lymphocytes. This replication was probably due to virus production in a few spontaneously transformed lymphocytes (2). PHA-stimulated lymphocytes removed 1, 3, and 5 days after vaccination also supported 17-D virus replication. However, lymphocytes withdrawn on days 7, 9, and 11 after vaccination (see Figure 1 for day 11 growth curve) failed to support virus replication when treated with PHA. Lymphocytes from one of the additional volunteers did not lose their ability to synthesize 17-D virus. Of possible relevance to the absence of a virus refractory period in this donor was his participation in a routine tuberculin testing program on the day of 17-D vaccination.

By day 25 following vaccination, PHA-treated lymphocytes from five of the six donors were once again able to support 17-D virus replication. PHA-treated lymphocytes removed from the donor with the extended refractory period were still incapable of supporting virus replication on the 76th day following vaccination. However, lymphocytes removed from this donor 248 days post-vaccination had regained this capacity.

The development of a transient anti-17-D virus state in lymphocytes during the post 17-D vaccination period may be due to one or more of the following four mechanisms:

1. "Virus refractory" lymphocytes may develop resistance to the biochemical stimulatory effects of the PHA needed by these cells for 17-D virus replication (2). A number of RNA and DNA containing viruses have been reported to infect lymphocytes and render them resistant to stimulation by PHA (7, 8).

2. 17-D virus refractory lymphocytes may produce greater than normal quantities of interferon or be more sensitive to the action of interferon, thereby preventing virus replication *in vitro*.

3. Virus refractory lymphocytes may develop a transient immunologic response to the virus in the form of either a) released or cell-bound, virus-specific antibody or b) sensitization to and cytotoxic activity against 17-D virus-producing cells (9, 10).

4. 17-D virus-refractory lymphocytes may undergo a biochemical alteration which blocks replication of 17-D virus.

Hotta (11) has reported the development of a delayed hypersensitivity cutaneous reaction during the early stages of dengue virus infections of man. The transient post-vaccination anti-17-D virus state of peripheral human lymphocytes may reflect their participation in a cell-mediated immune response to the viral infection and indicate that these cells are actively involved in the recovery process.

SUMMARY

Human lymphocytes can support the replication of 17-D yellow fever virus when stimulated *in vitro* with phytohemagglutinin. Between 7 and 11 days following vaccination with 17-D virus, peripheral lymphocytes lose their ability to support virus replication but regain this capacity by the 25th day post-vaccination.

Acknowledgments. We thank Juanita Ruffier and Carolyn Jimmerson for their technical assistance. This work was conducted under the auspices of the Commission on Viral Diseases of the Armed Forces Epidemiological Board and was supported in part by Contract DADA17-68-C-8047 of the United States Army Medical Research and Development Command, and in part by United States Public Health Service Grant 5K03-CA31815.

REFERENCES

1. Wheelock, E. F. and Sibley, W. A., New England J. Med., *272:* 194, 1965.
2. Wheelock, E. F. and Edelman, R., J. Immun., *103:* 429, 1969.
3. Theiler, M., in *Yellow Fever*, Edited by G. K. Strode, Chapter 2, McGraw-Hill, New York, 1951.
4. Theiler, M. and Smith, H. H., J. Exp. Med., *65:* 787, 1937.
5. Reed, L. J. and Muench, H. A., Amer. J. Hyg., *27:* 493, 1938.
6. Edelman, R. and Wheelock, E. F., J. Virol., *2:* 440, 1968.
7. Montgomery, J. R., South, M. A., Rawls, W. E., Melnick, J. L., Olsen, G. B., Dent, P. B. and Good, R. A., Science, *157:* 1068, 1967.
8. Willems, F. Th. C., Melnick, J. L. and Rawls, W. E., Proc. Soc. Exp. Biol. Med., *130:* 652, 1969.
9. Ruddle, N. H. and Waksman, B. H., Science, *157:* 1060, 1967.
10. Toy, S. T. and Wheelock, E. F., Bact. Proc., p. 166, 1970.
11. Hotta, S., J. Infect. Dis., *90:* 10, 1952.

THE JOURNAL OF IMMUNOLOGY
Vol. 105, No. 5, November 1970
Printed in U.S.A.

Plasma Kinin System: Proenzyme Components[1]

KIRK D. WUEPPER,[2] ERNEST S. TUCKER, III[3] AND CHARLES G. COCHRANE

From the Department of Experimental Pathology, Scripps Clinic and Research Foundation, La Jolla, California 92037

Cell-free blood plasma contains a discrete system of protein components which, upon activation, leads to generation of kinins (1, 2). These polypeptide fragments of the parent substrate kininogen have profound effects on small blood vessels and smooth muscle and evoke the sensation of pain. Minutes following injection into the skin, kinins mimic many signs of inflammation.

One or more of the components necessary for kinin generation in plasma is exquisitely labile and readily activates under usual conditions of enzyme purification (3, 4). In great part for this reason, identification of the various components and determinants of the exact sequence of activation in the kinin-forming system has not been possible (5, 6). Indeed, abundant confusion exists regarding the numbers of different components acting in the sequence, and the numbers of components at any one stage. Much of this stems from a lack of purification and quantitation, and from the fact that partially or fully activated components have been employed that are subject to alteration in impure mixtures. We report herein the isolation and purification of three major proteins in precursor form and describe their sequence of activation. These studies were reported in part previously (7–10).

In eleven separate experiments, 275 to 600 ml of rabbit plasma were treated with hexadimethrine bromide[4] (HBr) (11), fractionated with ammonium sulfate, and applied to columns of diethylaminoethyl (DEAE) cellulose as described in Figure 1. Portions of all fractions eluted from DEAE with a sodium chloride gradient were analyzed for kinin-releasing enzymes and for the substrate kininogens (see legend to Figure 1 for methods). No active kininogenase could be demonstrated in chromatographed fractions of HBr-protected plasma.

As trypsin is known to activate a kinin-releasing enzyme (13, 14) and to release kinin from kininogen (15), 0.2 ml of fractions obtained from DEAE chromatography was treated with 4 μg of trypsin for 20 min at 37°C, pH 7.3. Trypsin was then neutralized with an excess of trypsin inhibitor from lima beans (50 μg). Such treatment generated kininogenase and esterolytic activity for benzoyl-L-arginine ethyl ester (BAEe) in proteins eluting from a single region of the column (Fig. 1, region I).

In order to identify kininogen in fractions from DEAE columns, 25 to 40 mU of kininogenase in 0.2 ml, pH 7.6, or trypsin, 4 μg, was added to 0.2 ml from the fractions of the column in the presence of 8-hydroxyquinoline and incubated 60 min at 37°C. Assay for kinin under either circumstance revealed the presence of kininogen in a single common region (Fig. 1, region II). The kinin released from substrate by kininogenase or trypsin was rapidly inactivated by chymotrypsin 10 μg/ml or carboxypeptidase B, 10 μg/ml. Further isolation of kininogen by gel filtration, cation exchange chromatography and disc-gel electrophoresis revealed a single molecular species, as will be reported separately.

In order to find whether the trypsin-activated esterase was an intermediate in the activation sequence capable of activating another arginine esterase or possessing auto-catalytic activity, a known amount of the enzyme was added to fractions eluted from DEAE cellulose as above. After incubation at 37°C for 1 hr, the synthetic substrate BAEe was added and further incubated. No additional arginine esterase was generated nor was evidence for autoactivation obtained.

[1] This is Publication 398 from the Department of Experimental Pathology, Scripps Clinic and Research Foundation, La Jolla, California. The work was supported by United States Public Health Service Grant AI-07007, National Multiple Sclerosis Society Grant 459 and a Grant-in-Aid of the American Heart Association (supported in part by the Long Beach Heart Association).

[2] Special Research Fellow of the United States Public Health Service (AM 40086-01).

[3] Special Fellowship of the United States Public Health Service (AM 36626-02).

[4] Generously provided by E. A. Pritchett, Abbott Laboratories, North Chicago, Illinois.

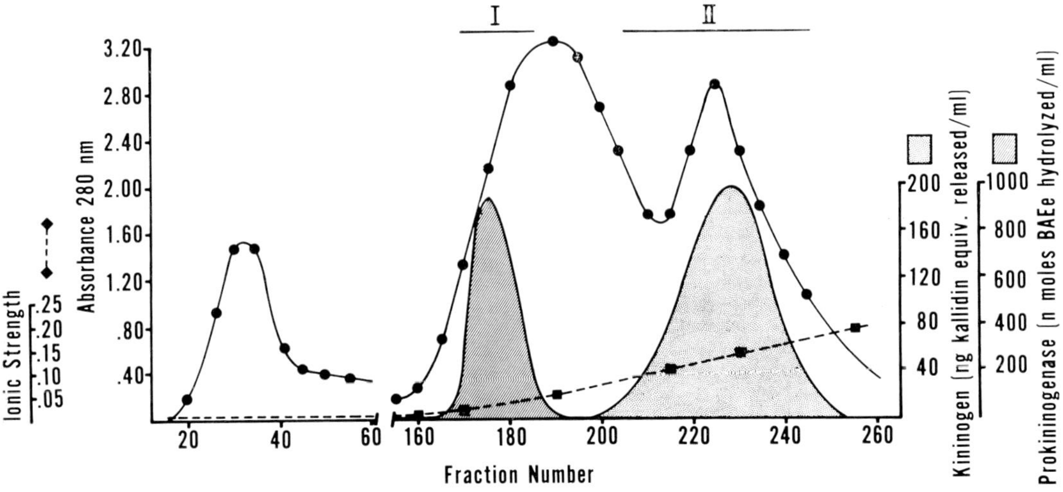

Figure 1. Chromatography of rabbit plasma proteins on DEAE cellulose. Arterial blood was collected in citrate dextrose, pH 6.8. Siliconized needles and glassware or plastic were used throughout. Cells were removed by centrifugation and hexadimethrine bromide (HBr) 50 μg/ml was added to the plasma. Proteins were salted out at 0°C with neutral ammonium sulfate containing HBr and neutral ethylenediamine tetraacetate (EDTA) 0.001 M. The fraction soluble at 33% but insoluble at 50% saturation was obtained and dialyzed against the initial buffer solution (SB) consisting of phosphate buffer, 0.0075 M, pH 8, HBr and EDTA; the final ionic strength was 0.01. The sample was applied to a column of diethylaminoethyl (DEAE) cellulose 0.74 mEq/g equilibrated with SB. After proteins excluded from the column eluted in SB, a gradient of 0.5 M sodium chloride in SB was started. While the use of DEAE cellulose is reported here, we have subsequently found DEAE Sephadex A-50 to be more satisfactory. Kininogenase was assayed by its ability to release a kinin from its substrate, kininogen, isolated from rabbit plasma. The kinin was measured routinely by bioassay. In addition, the ability of this enzyme to hydrolyze the synthetic amino acid substrate, benzoyl-L-arginine ethyl ester (BAEe) was determined by differential spectrophotometry (12). The increased absorbance at 253 nm due to hydrolysis of BAEe was compared with known quantities of benzoyl-L-arginine. The amount of enzyme giving hydrolysis of 1 μmol/min was taken as one unit (U). Kininogen was determined by treating fractions with trypsin or kininogenase in the presence of neutralized 8-hydroxyquinoline. Kinins were assayed on the estrus rat uterus in Tyrode's solution. The amplitude of contractions was recorded on a moving chart (Phipps & Bird, Richmond, Va.), and was compared to those given by known quantiies of kallidin (Sandoz, Basel, Switzerland). Samples were expressed in equivalents of kallidin required to produce the same response.

Finally, no kininogenase inhibitor was identified during this procedure in the chromatographed globulin preparations.

The prokininogenase we have identified has been purified further by rechromatography on DEAE cellulose, gel filtration, sucrose gradient ultracentrifugation and disc gel electrophoresis in acrylamide. The final product is over 1200-fold purified with respect to starting plasma and behaves in all separatory procedures as a single homogeneous molecular entity (7).

Kininogenase in 0.1 ml volume was injected into the skin of rabbits which had received an earlier intravenous injection of Evans blue dye 25 mg/kg. Increased vascular permeability was perceptible at 5 min and the reaction was fully developed 15 min following injection. The minimum dose giving increased permeability (2 x 2 mm) was 5 mU; permeability increased in a log-dose relationship to a maximal response (8 x 7 mm) with 70 mU. The reaction was unaffected by the intracutaneous injection of the antihistamine chlorpheniramine maleate, 10 μg in 0.1 ml, 15 min before the kinin-releasing enzyme.

To study the activation of prokininogenase, contact factors of the clotting system were adsorbed to silica dioxide particles (as diatomaceous earth, DE), by exposing fresh plasma in citrate-dextrose and 0.01 M EDTA to DE

TABLE I

Physical characteristics of components of the rabbit plasma kinin system

	Prokininogenase Activator (PKA)	Prokininogenase	Kininogenase	Kininogen
Gel filtration[a]				
Diffusion coefficient	8.2	4.5	4.6	4.8
Sucrose gradient ultracentrifugation[b]				
S-coefficient	2.6	4.5	4.0	3.8
Molecular weight[c]	32,000	99,900	86,300	79,000
Isoelectric fractionation[d]				
pI	4.6	5.9	5.4	5.2
Polyacrylamide gel electrophoresis[e]				
Mobility	Pre-albumin	gamma	beta	alpha

[a] Gel filtration was performed on columns of Sephadex G-150 or G-200 (Pharmacia, Uppsala, Sweden). Columns were calibrated with marker substances, IgG globulin, bovine albumin and cytochrome C, whose diffusion coefficients were known. Eluting buffer was saline buffered with phosphate, pH 7.3, with a flow rate of 10 to 12 ml/hr.

[b] Sedimentation coefficients were ascertained by ultracentrifugation at 45,000 rpm for 15 hr in linear gradients of 5% to 25% sucrose dissolved in PBS. ^{131}I-IgG and ^{125}I-BSA were added to samples as reference markers.

[c] Calculated from sedimentation and diffusion coefficients.

[d] Isoelectric fractionation was carried out in 110-ml columns with polyampholytes (Ampholine; LKB Instruments, Stockholm, Bromma). Appropriate ranges of 2 pH units were purchased from the manufacturer and distributed in a 0 to 45% sucrose gradient. The sample was introduced at the midpoint of the gradient and run at 600 volts, 0°C for 24 to 48 hr. Fractions were collected, the pH determined and samples brought to pH 7.5 for assay.

[e] Disc electrophoresis was done in 6% to 9% acrylamide gels in Tris-glycine, pH 8.3, buffer with bromphenol blue as tracking dye (17).

(10 mg/ml) 60 min, 25°C, pH 6.8, followed by washing the particles exhaustively in buffered saline containing EDTA 0.001 M. Suspensions of DE with adsorbed plasma factors (2 mg) were incubated 1 hr with eluted fractions of the anion exchange column and the generation of kininogenase and esterase activity was assayed. Fractions from region I only were again found to contain the activable precursor of kininogenase.

To ascertain whether clot-promoting substances were directly responsible for prokininogenase activation, eluates were prepared from the DE adsorbate of plasma by treating with 2 M sodium chloride at pH 7. After removal of the DE by centrifugation and dialysis to remove salt, the eluate was found to promote clotting in human factor XII or factor XI (but not factor IX)-deficient plasma[5] (16) and to convert prokininogenase to the active enzyme. The two activities were readily separated in acrylamide gel electrophoresis at pH 8.3: the prokininogenase activator migrated rapidly to the anode, whereas the clot-promoting factors were identified at the top of the gel. These two substances are clearly differentiated by function and by strikingly different physical characteristics (Table I).

The prokininogenase activator (PKA) was isolated and characterized by gel filtration, isoelectric fractionation, sucrose gradient ultracentrifugation and electrophoresis in alkaline acrylamide gels. Its physicochemical features along with the changes in the physical characteristics of its substrate, prokininogenase, after activation by PKA are shown in Table I. Of note, the activation of prokininogenase is attended by a distinct decrease in sedimentation rate and change in overall charge of the molecule.

PKA did not accelerate clotting in human plasma deficient in clotting factors XII, XI or IX. The substance did not cause lysis of fibrin

[5] Human plasmas deficient in clotting factors XII, XI or IX were kindly supplied by Dr. S. I. Rappoport, Los Angeles, California.

plates after incubation at 37°C for 24 hr (18), nor did it hydrolyze the synthetic substrate BAEe or release a kinin from kininogen. The only natural substrate we have identified for this substance is the prokininogenase.

In order to find the precursor of PKA, rabbit plasma was salted out with ammonium sulfate and subjected to the same separatory procedures described in footnotes to Table I and Figure 1. In preliminary studies, it has been shown that a precursor of PKA can be identified by addition of DE, ellagic acid, or trypsin. This precursor behaves in anion exchange chromatography and isoelectric focusing as a β globulin, and sediments at 4.6S.

Kininogenase and PKA have not only different physical properties and substrate specificities but are inhibited quite differently by trypsin inhibitors. At final inhibitor concentrations of 10^{-4} M or less, kininogenase (50 mU) is inhibited by diisopropyl fluorophosphate (DFP), Trasylol, and soy bean trypsin inhibitor. PKA is inhibited by DFP, phenyl methyl sulfonyl fluoride, and lima bean trypsin inhibitor. Neither enzyme is sensitive to egg white trypsin inhibitor or heparin.

DISCUSSION

The results of these investigations gave valuable information concerning the components of the plasma kinin-forming system. When plasma was fractionated in the presence of an inhibitor of the contact phase of blood coagulation, stable proenzyme components and kininogen could be isolated and characterized by methods which tend to prevent protein denaturation and aggregation. In this fashion we found in rabbit plasma and, similarly, in human plasma, a single kininogen. Spragg, Haber and Austen have also reported a single kininogen in human plasma (19). Furthermore, a single kinin-releasing enzyme (kininogenase, kallikrein) was isolated as a precursor, prokininogenase. The availability of this highly purified proenzyme provided a substrate to permit the identification and isolation of a new enzyme we have termed prokininogenase activator (PKA) from rabbit and human plasma. Going one step further, PKA has been shown to derive from a precursor itself. When the physicochemical characteristics of the precursor and active forms of PKA and kininogenase are compared, distinct changes were found in mass and charge, suggesting in each case that activation occurs by limited hydrolysis of the precursor.

These findings are somewhat at variance with other proposals regarding the activation of prokininogenase (prekallikrein) in various species. Nagasawa and associates showed direct activation of a preparation of bovine prekallikrein by treatment with bovine clotting factor XII (20). By contrast, Margolis suggested clotting factor XI may participate in kallikrein activation along with factor XII (21). Kinin generation by exposure to glass surfaces has been reported as normal, however, in human plasma deficient in XI (22, 23). Others have suggested that a permeability factor (PF/dil) generated for a brief period of time by simple dilution of fresh serum acts as an intermediary between clotting factor XII and a kinin-releasing enzyme (24, 25). The present studies demonstrate the presence of a low molecular weight activator of prokininogenase which differs from PF/dil in many physical and chemical parameters. It resembles activators recently reported that release kinin from fresh but not heated plasma (26). The relationship of PKA and its precursor to factor XII is under current investigation.

SUMMARY

Precursor enzyme components and kininogen of the plasma kinin-forming system were isolated from rabbit plasma treated with hexadimethrine bromide. Employing highly purified components, only a single kininogen and a single kininogenase were identified. The precursor of kininogenase, prokininogenase, was selectively activated by a unique low molecular weight acidic enzyme termed prokininogenase activator (PKA). PKA activated prokininogenase by limited proteolysis causing a change in mass and charge. PKA itself was generated from a larger more basic precursor upon contact with negatively charged surfaces of mild trypsinization.

REFERENCES

1. Kraut, H., Frey, E. K. and Werle, E., Z. Physiol. Chem., *222:* 73, 1933.
2. Webster, M. E., Fed. Proc., *27:* 84, 1968.
3. Eisen, V., J. Physiol., *166:* 496, 1963.
4. Armstrong, D., Mills, G. L. and Stewart, J. W., in *International Symposium on Vasoactive Polypeptides: Bradykinin and Related Kinins*, Edited by M. Rocha e Silva and

H. A. Rothschild, p. 167, Proc. III Int'l. Cong. Farmacol., Sao Paulo, 1967.

5. Mason, B. and Miles, A. A., Nature, *196:* 587, 1962.
6. Webster, M. E., in *Cellular and Humoral Mechanisms of Anaphylaxis and Allergy*, Edited by H. Z. Movat, p. 207, S. Karger, Basel, 1969.
7. Wuepper, K. D., Tucker, E. S., III and Cochrane, C. G., Fed. Proc., *28:* 363, 1969.
8. Tucker, E. S., III and Wuepper, K. D., Fed. Proc., *28:* 363, 1969.
9. Wuepper, K. D. and Cochrane, C. G., Fed. Proc., *29:* 811, 1970.
10. Lawrence, T. G., Cochrane, C. G. and Tucker E. S., III, Fed. Proc., *29:* 576, 1970.
11. Eisen, V., Brit. J. Pharmacol., *22:* 87, 1964.
12. Schwert, G. W. and Takenaka, Y., Biochim. Biophys. Acta, *16:* 570, 1955.
13. Werle, E., Forell, M. M. and Maier, L., Arch. Exp. Path. Pharmakol., *225:* 369, 1955.
14. Webster, M. E. and Ratnoff, O. D., Nature, *192:* 180, 1961.
15. Rocha e Silva, M., Beraldo, W. T. and Rosenfield, G., Amer. J. Physiol., *156:* 261, 1949.
16. Nossel, H. L., in *The Contact Phase of Blood Coagulation*, F. A. Davis, Philadelphia, 1964.
17. Davis, B. J., Ann. N. Y. Acad. Sci., *121:* 404, 1964.
18. Lieberman, J., Lab. Invest., *19:* 466, 1968.
19. Spragg, J., Haber, E. and Austen, K. F., Fed. Proc., *28:* 363, 1969.
20. Nagasawa, S., Takahashi, H., Koida, M., Suzuki, T. and Schoenmakers, J. G. G., Biochem. Biophys. Res. Commun., *32:* 644, 1968.
21. Margolis, J., *in Hypotensive Peptides*, Edited by E. G. Erdös, N. Back and F. Sicuteri, p. 198, Springer-Verlag, New York, 1966.
22. Ratnoff, O. D. and Miles, A. A., Brit. J. Exp. Path., *45:* 328, 1964.
23. Margolis, J., J. Physiol., *144:* 1, 1958.
24. Kagan, L. J., Leddy, J. P. and Becker, E. L., J. Clin. Invest., *42:* 1353, 1963.
25. Becker, E. L., Wilhelm, D. L. and Miles, A. A., Nature, *183:* 1264, 1959.
26. Kaplan, A. P., Spragg, J., Gigli, I. and Austen, K. F., Fed. Proc., *29:* 491, 1970.

THE JOURNAL OF IMMUNOLOGY
Vol. 105, No. 6, December 1970

TRANSFER OF THE DELAYED HYPERSENSITIVITY SKIN REACTION IN THE GUINEA PIG USING RNA-TREATED LYMPHOID CELLS[1]

R. E. JUREZIZ,[2] D. E. THOR AND S. DRAY

From the Department of Microbiology, University of Illinois at the Medical Center, Chicago, Illinois, and the Division or Biologics Standards, National Institutes of Health, Bethesda, Maryland

Received for publication August 13, 1970

Ribonucleic acid extracts from the lymph nodes of guinea pigs sensitive to purified protein derivative, brain antigen, α,DNP-oligolysine and ϵ,DNP-oligolysine were shown to confer on syngeneic nonsensitive guinea pig lymphoid cells the ability to transfer for each antigen the delayed hypersensitivity skin reaction to nonsensitive guinea pigs. Successful transfers were obtained using intraperitoneal injections of approximately 10^9 nonsensitive lymphoid cells previously incubated for 15 to 30 min at 37°C with 120 to 300 μg/ml of RNA.

Reports from this laboratory (1, 2) have described the ability of RNA extracts from lymph nodes of skin test positive individuals to transfer tuberculin and histoplasmin sensitivity to nonsensitive human lymph node cell suspensions using a modification of George and Vaughn's (3) cell-migration-inhibition assay as a correlate to delayed hypersensitivity. Subsequently, it was shown that RNA extracts obtained from the lymph nodes of guinea pigs sensitive to purified protein derivative (PPD) or coccidioidin were capable of transferring sensitivity to nonsensitive guinea pig peritoneal exudate cells using the cell-migration-inhibition assay (4). This latter work was recently extended by Thor and Schlossman (5) using inbred guinea pigs and better defined antigens, i.e., α,DNP-oligolysine and ϵ,DNP-oligolysine.

These previous transfer experiments with RNA extracts have all utilized *in vitro* cell-migration-inhibition as the assay for delayed hypersensitivity. We now report an extension of these studies using the classical *in vivo* delayed skin tests as the assay of delayed hypersensitivity. The ability of nonsensitive lymphoid cells to transfer delayed hypersensitivity after incubation with RNA extracts obtained from sensitive cells was demonstrated using four antigens: tuberculin, an extracted brain antigen, α,DNP-oligolysine and ϵ,DNP-oligolysine.

MATERIALS AND METHODS

Antigens for sensitization of guinea pigs. Two milligrams of *bacillus Calmette-Guérin* (BCG, Research Foundation and University of Illinois, Chicago, Ill.) were used to sensitize random bred guinea pigs. Male strain 2 guinea pigs were injected with α,DNP-$\overline{\text{Lys}_{8.4}}$ (150 μg)[3] or ϵ,DNP-$\overline{\text{Lys}_{14}}$ (150 μg)[3] incorporated into 1 ml of complete Freund's adjuvant (Baltimore Biological Laboratory, Cockeysville, Md.). Strain 13 inbred guinea pigs were injected with an oil emulsion containing either 2.5 mg *Mycobacterium tuberculosis* H37Rv[3] or 2.5 mg of *M. tuberculosis* H37Rv[3] plus 50 mg of lyophilized spinal cord from random bred guinea pigs. The antigens were given in multiple sites in the footpads and nuchal area.

Antigens for skin testing of guinea pigs. Five micrograms of purified protein derivative (PPD, Difco Laboratories, Detroit, Mich.) were used to skin test all random bred guinea pigs. The strain 2 inbred guinea pigs were skin tested with 10 μg of α,DNP-$\overline{\text{Lys}_{8.4}}$ and 10 μg of ϵ,DNP-$\overline{\text{Lys}_{14}}$. The strain 13 animals were skin tested with 10 μg of PPD[3] and with 15 μg of brain antigen.

The brain antigen was prepared from randomly bred albino guinea pigs. The brains were removed

[1] This investigation was supported by United States Public Health Service Research Grant AI-08576-01, from the National Institute of Allergy and Infectious Diseases.

[2] Supported by a fellowship from the Life Insurance Medical Research Fund.

[3] The authors wish to thank Dr. Stuart F. Schlossman for providing the DNP-oligolysine preparations and Dr. Sotiros D. Chaparas for providing the *M. tuberculosis* and PPD.

and immediately frozen in a Dry Ice-acetone bath and stored at −70°C. Frozen brains from 40 animals (32 g) were quickly homogenized in distilled water with a Waring Blendor, refrozen, lyophilized and stored as a lyophilized powder at 4°C. This lyophilized brain powder was extracted with chloroform-methanol according to the procedure of Kies (6). The defatted residue was then extracted in HCl essentially by the method of Nakao *et al.* (7). The dried residue was suspended in 10 volumes (w/v) of 0.05 M HCl and the pH was adjusted to 1.8. This mixture was stirred for 20 to 24 hr at 4°C and then centrifuged at 10,000 rpm for 20 min. The residue was re-extracted with 5 volumes (w/v) 0.05 M HCl for 20 to 24 hr. The two supernatant fluids were neutralized with NH_4OH and saturated with $(NH_4)_2SO_4$, resulting in a precipitate which was exhaustively dialyzed against distilled water and lyophilized. All dialysis tubing was boiled for approximately 2 hr in 1% acetic acid to reduce the pore size. The lyophilized product was dissolved in 0.05 M NaOAc, pH 4.6, and applied to a Whatman CM-32 cellulose column equilibrated in the same buffer. The NaCl concentration of the eluting buffer was increased stepwise and a fraction between 0.3 M NaCl and 0.6 M NaCl was collected, dialyzed against distilled water and lyophilized. This material was dissolved in 0.85% NaCl (150 μg/ml) for skin testing.

Isolation of RNA. Lymph nodes were excised and frozen in crushed Dry Ice and stored at −70°C until needed. The RNA extracts of lymph nodes were obtained by hot phenol extraction as previously described in detail (4). Particular care was taken to use 10 to 12 ml of the aqueous phenol extraction buffer and an equal amount of 88% phenol for each gram of tissue used. This precaution has made it unnecessary to do more than three phenol extractions in order to obtain an $O.D._{260}/O.D._{280} \geq 2$, thus minimizing possible adverse effects of the phenol on the RNA.

Collection and preparation of lymph node and spleen cell suspensions. Guinea pigs injected with complete Freund's adjuvant, incomplete adjuvant, *M. tuberculosis* H37Rv or animals which had never been previously injected were used as cell donors. The animals were first anesthetized and exsanguinated by cardiac puncture. Then the lymph nodes and spleens were removed asceptically and kept in iced Hanks' balanced salt solution containing 5 units/ml heparin. The lymph nodes and spleens were carefully trimmed of fat and separately minced using scissors and forceps and were sieved through a stainless steel screen (40 mesh) to separate the large remaining pieces of tissue. These pieces of tissue were then resuspended in fresh Hanks' balanced salt in a Petri dish, teased again, gently compressed with a disposable syringe plunger to express as many cells as possible and sieved. Although this method yields somewhat fewer cells, the cell viability was generally higher than that obtained when the tissue fragments were forced through the stainless steel screen with a syringe plunger. This procedure was repeated four to six times with the non-sieved tissue. The cells were collected in siliconized 40-ml conical glass tubes, centrifuged at 1000 rpm for 10 min and pooled. The cells were suspended in Eagle's basal media and washed at least four times before being transferred to 12-ml disposable plastic tubes.

Incubation of cells RNA extracts and injection into guinea pigs. The RNA extracts were dissolved in a minimum of Hanks' balanced salt solution and the concentration was determined spectrophotometrically assuming 1 mg of RNA/ml yields an $O.D._{260}$ of 20. The cells were suspended in isotonic Roswell Park Memorial Institute media 1640 (Media Services, National Institutes of Health) containing 75 mM N-Tris (hydroxymethyl) methyl-2-amino-ethanesulfonic acid to which was added 67 μg of *l*-epinephrine (Eastman Organic Chemicals, Rochester, N. Y.) and approximately 2.5 mg of RNA in a total volume of 10 ml. After 15 to 30 min incubation at 37°C, the cells were centrifuged at 1000 rpm for 10 min, resuspended in 10 ml of Eagle's basal media and injected intraperitoneally into guinea pigs of the same sex and strain as the donor cells. Recipient guinea pigs were never skin tested before receiving RNA-treated cells.

Skin testing. Sites for skin testing on the dorsal surface were prepared by first shaving in the direction of hair growth and removing the short remaining stubble by very carefully shaving against the direction of hair growth. Sites showing a reddened area of irritation after the latter procedure were not used for skin testing. Depilatories were at no time used in preparing skin test sites. Random bred albino guinea pigs were injected intradermally with 0.1 ml of a mixture of 1 μg of PPD and 1×10^7 nonsensitive peritoneal exudate cells which had been previously incubated with approximately 500 μg of RNA from a PPD sensitive donor. Strain 13 animals were skin

TABLE I

Skin reactions observed in random bred guinea pigs 24 hr after intradermal injections of PPD (1 μg) mixed with nonsensitive guinea pig peritoneal exudate cells (NS-PEC, 1 × 10⁷) with or without incubation in RNA (226 to 289 μg/ml) from the lymph nodes of PPD sensitive guinea pigs

Recipient Guinea Pig	Donor Guinea Pig	RNA Pool	24-Hr Skin Reactions		
			PPD + NS-PEC	NS-PEC incubated with RNA from PPD sensitive guinea pigs	PPD + NS-PEC incubated with RNA from PPD sensitive guinea pigs
			mm	*mm*	*mm*
RB-1	RB-21	A	4 x 5		7 x 9
RB-2	RB-21	A	3 x 3		8 x 8
RB-3	RB-22	A	4 x 4		7 x 9
RB-4	RB-22	A	3 x 3		7 x 7
RB-5	RB-23	B	2 x 2		6 x 6
RB-6	RB-23	B	2 x 3		8 x 7
RB-7	RB-24	C	5 x 4		12 x 11
RB-8	RB-24	C	3 x 4		9 x 8
RB-9	RB-25	D	2 x 3		10 x 8
RB-10	RB-25	D	3 x 3		9 x 7
RB-11	RB-26	E	3 x 3		8 x 8
RB-12	RB-26	E	2 x 1		9 x 7
RB-13	RB-27	F		4 x 3	11 x 12
RB-14	RB-27	F		4 x 4	9 x 10
RB-15	RB-28	G		3 x 4	11 x 9
RB-16	RB-28	G		5 x 5	12 x 11
RB-17	RB-29	H		3 x 2	10 x 10
RB-18	RB-29	H		4 x 4	14 x 12
RB-19	RB-30	I		3 x 4	8 x 7
RB-20	RB-30	I		3 x 3	10 x 9

tested with both 15 μg of the purified brain antigen and 10 μg of PPD. Strain 2 animals were skin tested with both 10 μg of α,DNP-oligolysine and with 10 μg of ε,DNP-oligolysine. All animals were observed at 4 to 6 hr and at 20 to 24 hr for both erythema and induration; however, all values reported represent the diameters of induration even though the larger reactions observed gave diameters of erythema exceeding the diameters of induration by as much as 4 mm.

RESULTS

Preliminary experiments with random bred guinea pigs. Before a sufficient number of inbred guinea pigs was available, attempts were made to demonstrate the ability of RNA extracts obtained from sensitized guinea pigs to confer skin reactivity on random bred albino guinea pigs. For this purpose, RNA extracts were used which had previously been shown by the cell-migration-inhibition assay to be active in conferring PPD sensitivity on nonsensitive peritoneal exudate cells (PEC) (4). Nonsensitive PEC obtained as described previously (4) were incubated with the RNA extracts, centrifuged and re-suspended in TC-199 medium containing 10 μg/ml of PPD. Random bred albino guinea pigs were injected intradermally with a 0.1-ml suspension containing 1 × 10⁷ viable treated cells; at 24 hr, induration ranging from 6 mm to 14 mm in diameter was observed at the injection sites (recipients RB-1 to RB-20, Table I). These skin reactions were greater than those observed in the same animals (RB-1 to RB-12) which were injected with untreated PEC plus PPD (1 to 5 mm) and also greater than those observed in the same animals (RB-13 to RB-20) which received RNA-treated PEC but without PPD (2 to 5 mm).

Assay of RNA extract activity by cell-migration inhibition. One large pool of an RNA extract was prepared from the lymph nodes of numerous strain 13 guinea pigs which had been sensitized with 2.5 mg *M. tuberculosis* H37Rv and had skin tests of 15 to 21 mm induration 11 to 12 days after the sensitizing injection. Four RNA pools were obtained from the lymph nodes of strain

TABLE II

Mean migration indices obtained when nonsensitive strain 13 guinea pig peritoneal exudate cells were incubated with pools of RNA obtained from strain 13 animals sensitized with either M. tuberculosis or spinal cord plus M. tuberculosis

RNA Pool	Sensitizing Antigens	Mean Migration Indices	
		Brain antigen	PPD
J	*M. tuberculosis*	110 ± 3	31 ± 2
K	Spinal cord + *M. tuberculosis*	37 ± 2	33 ± 2
L	Spinal cord + *M. tuberculosis*	22 ± 2	26 ± 2
M	Spinal cord + *M. tuberculosis*	70 ± 8	80 ± 6
N	Spinal cord + *M. tuberculosis*	33 ± 3	32 ± 3

13 guinea pigs which had been injected with 50 mg of spinal cord and 2.5 mg of *M. tuberculosis* H37Rv; for each of these pools, five to eight animals were injected and the lymph nodes from four to six of these animals were excised 7 days after injection. The lymph nodes were not excised from one or two remaining guinea pigs which went on to develop paralysis by day 14. Nonsensitive PEC were incubated with each of the five RNA pools, centrifuged, resuspended in TC-199 medium and assayed by inhibition of cell migration in the presence of 10 μg/ml PPD or a 5% extract of strain 13 guinea pig brain as described by Hughes and Field (8). The mean migration indices (4) obtained indicated that pools J, K, L and N were clearly active, whereas pool M had borderline activity (Table II). Only pools J, K, L and N were used in the following experiments.

Syngeneic transfer of the skin test to PPD by nonsensitive cells treated with RNA from PPD sensitive donors. Strain 13 guinea pigs which had not been previously skin tested were skin tested with PPD and brain antigen between 58 and 64 hr after receiving an intraperitoneal injection of nonsensitive lymph node cells (LNC) or spleen cells (SpC) previously incubated with *l*-epinephrine and the RNA extract (pool J) derived from the LNC of PPD sensitive strain 13 guinea pigs (Table III, animals I13-1 to I13-7). For the skin sites injected with PPD, the induration observed at 20 to 24 hr varied from 7 to 14 mm and all skin test sites showed marked erythema as well. Skin test sites injected with brain antigen, a non-cross-reacting antigen, gave reactions varying from 0 to 3 mm with negligible erythema. A common pool of cells was used for recipient animals I13-4 and I13-5 and also for animals I13-6 and I13-7. Other strain 13 guinea pigs from this colony which had not been previously injected were skin tested with PPD and no reaction larger than 3 mm of induration and negligible erythema was observed.

Syngeneic transfer of the skin test to brain antigen by nonsensitive cells treated with RNA from a sensitized donor. Strain 13 guinea pigs were skin tested with PPD and brain antigen between 58 and 64 hr after receiving an intraperitoneal injection of nonsensitive LNC or SpC previously incubated with *l*-epinephrine and RNA (pools K, L or N) derived from the lymph nodes of strain 13 guinea pigs injected with spinal cord and *M. tuberculosis* 7 days previously (Table III, animals I13-8 to I13-15). The skin test sites injected with brain antigen varied from 6 to 11 mm of induration with considerable erythema. The skin test sites of animals I13-8 and I13-9 injected with PPD were 3 to 5 mm and are considered negative. On the other hand, animals I13-10 and I13-11 showed positive skin tests of 10 x 8 mm and 6 x 7 mm with PPD. The positive reactions on the PPD skin test sites of the remaining animals can not be considered to be due to the effects of the RNA on the cells because the cells used for incubation with the RNA extracts came from donors injected with complete Freund's adjuvant. This procedure was used in an effort to obtain a larger number of cells with which to attempt to create the disease, experimental allergic encephalomyelitis; however, none of the animals showing positive skin tests to the brain antigen developed clinical symptoms of the disease. The skin test with brain antigen in animal I13-10 showed an area of 8 x 8 mm nonerythematous induration with an apparently hemorrhagic 2- x 2-mm central area at 4 hr, and animal I13-11 showed a skin reaction with brain antigen of 17 x 18 mm of nonerythematous in-

TABLE III

Skin reactions observed in strain 13 guinea pigs when tested 56 to 64 hr after intraperitoneal injection of nonsensitive spleen cells (SpC) or lymph node cells (LNC) incubated for 15 to 30 min at 37°C with l-epinephrine (6.7 μg/ml) and RNA extracts from the lymph nodes of animals sensitized to either M. tuberculosis or spinal cord plus M. tuberculosis

Recipient Guinea Pig	Cells Transferred				RNA Extracts		24-Hr Skin Reactions	
	Pretreatment of donor guinea pig	Source	Viability	No. viable cells transferred	Guinea pigs sensitive to PPD (pool J)	Guinea pigs sensitive to brain protein (pools K, L, N)	PPD (10 μg)	Brain antigen (15 μg)
			%		μg RNA/ml	μg RNA/ml	mm	mm
I13-1	None	SpC	87	2.19×10^9	160		8 x 8	1 x 1
I13-2	Incomplete adjuvant	LNC	92	1.09×10^9	160		7 x 8	0 x 0
I13-3	Incomplete adjuvant	LNC	88	9.33×10^8	248		10 x 9	2 x 3
I13-4	None	SpC	86	1.10×10^9	234		8 x 9	1 x 1
I13-5	None	SpC	86	1.10×10^9	234		9 x 8	1 x 2
I13-6	None	SpC	85	1.12×10^9	248		14 x 12	3 x 3
I13-7	None	SpC	85	1.12×10^9	248		13 x 12	2 x 1
I13-8	Incomplete adjuvant	LNC	84	8.74×10^8		120	4 x 5	8 x 8
I13-9	None	SpC	91	2.59×10^9		120	3 x 3	7 x 8
I13-10	None	SpC	89	1.27×10^9		297	10 x 8	9 x 8
I13-11	None	SpC	86	2.30×10^9		226	6 x 7	11 x 10
I13-12	Complete adjuvant	LNC	91	3.95×10^9		270	9 x 10	8 x 8
I13-13	Complete adjuvant	LNC	91	3.95×10^9		270	10 x 11	7 x 8
I13-14	Complete adjuvant	SpC	91	3.84×10^9		314	11 x 11	6 x 7
I13-15	Complete adjuvant	SpC	91	3.84×10^9		314	9 x 9	6 x 7

duration with an apparently hemorrhagic central zone of 8 x 8 mm at 4 hr. No other recipient animals showed such reactions with either brain antigen or with PPD. A common pool of cells was used for recipient animals I13-12 and I13-13 and also for animals I13-14 and I13-15.

Syngeneic transfer of the skin test to α,DNP-oligolysine by nonsensitive cells treated with RNA from a sensitized donor. A previous report has demonstrated that RNA extracts from the lymph nodes of α,DNP-oligolysine and ε,DNP-oligolysine are capable of transferring sensitivity in the cell-migration-inhibition assay (5). Such studies were not repeated on these RNA pools because of the limited availability of these two antigens. Guinea pigs were skin tested with α,DNP-oligolysine and ε,DNP-oligolysine between 58 and 64 hr after receiving an intraperitoneal injection of nonsensitive LNC or SpC previously incubated with l-epinephrine and RNA derived from the lymph nodes of strain 2 guinea pigs injected with α,DNP-oligolysine in complete Freund's adjuvant 14 days previously (Table IV, animals I2-1 to I2-7). For the skin test sites injected with α,DNP-oligolysine, the induration observed at 20 to 24 hr varied from 6 to 15 mm and the skin test sites showed marked erythema. Skin test sites injected with ε,DNP-oligolysine gave reactions varying from 0 to 2 mm of induration with negligible erythema. A common pool of cells was used for recipient animals I2-1 and I2-2 and for animals I2-3 to I2-7.

Syngeneic transfer of the skin test to ε,DNP-oligolysine by nonsensitive cells treated with RNA from a sensitized donor. Strain 2 guinea pigs were skin tested with α,DNP-oligolysine and ε,DNP-

TABLE IV

Skin reactions observed in strain 2 guinea pigs when tested 56 to 64 hr after intraperitoneal injection of syngeneic nonsensitive spleen cells (SpC) or lymph node cells (LNC) incubated for 15 to 30 min at 37°C with l-epinephrine (6.7 μg/ml) and RNA extracts from the lymph nodes of animals sensitized to α,DNP-oligolysine or ε,DNP-oligolysine

Recipient Guinea Pig	Cells Transferred				RNA Extracts		Skin Reactions	
	Pretreatment of donor guinea pig	Source	Viability	No. viable cells transferred	From guinea pigs sensitive to α, DNP-oligolysine	From guinea pigs sensitive to ε, DNP-oligolysine	α,DNP-oligolysine (10 μg)	ε,DNP-oligolysine (10 μg)
			%		μg RNA/ml	μg RNA/ml	mm	mm
I2-1	Complete adjuvant	LNC	70	1.15×10^9	250		7 x 8	2 x 2
I2-2	Complete adjuvant	LNC	70	1.15×10^9	250		8 x 6	0 x 0
I2-3	None	SpC	88	1.36×10^9	297		10 x 11	2 x 2
I2-4	None	SpC	88	1.36×10^9	297		11 x 11	1 x 2
I2-5	None	SpC	88	1.36×10^9	297		12 x 11	1 x 1
I2-6	None	SpC	88	1.36×10^9	297		15 x 15	1 x 2
I2-7	None	SpC	88	1.36×10^9	297		11 x 12	2 x 2
I2-8	Complete adjuvant	LNC	70	1.15×10^9		228	1 x 2	9 x 10
I2-9	Complete adjuvant	LNC	70	1.15×10^9		228	0 x 0	8 x 9
I2-10	None	SpC	88	1.36×10^9		249	1 x 1	12 x 12
I2-11	None	SpC	88	1.36×10^9		249	2 x 3	12 x 12
I2-12	None	SpC	88	1.36×10^9		249	2 x 3	17 x 17
I2-13	None	SpC	88	1.36×10^9		249	2 x 2	11 x 12
I2-14	None	SpC	88	1.36×10^9		249	1 x 2	10 x 9

oligolysine between 58 and 64 hr after receiving an intraperitoneal injection of nonsensitive LNC or SpC previously incubated with *l*-epinephrine and RNA derived from the lymph nodes of strain 2 guinea pigs injected with ε,DNP-oligolysine in complete Freund's adjuvant 14 days previously (Table IV, animals I2-8 to I2-14). For skin test sites injected with ε,DNP-oligolysine, the induration observed at 20 to 24 hr varied from 8 to 17 mm and all skin test sites showed marked erythema. Skin test sites injected with α,DNP-oligolysine gave reactions varying from 0 to 3 mm induration with negligible erythema. A common pool of cells was used for recipient animals I2-8 and I2-9 and for animals I2-10 to I2-14.

Effects of l-epinephrine on adoptive transfers. Strain 13 guinea pigs were skin tested with PPD and brain antigen between 58 and 64 hr after receiving an intraperitoneal injection of PPD sensitive LNC or SpC which were previously incubated either with or without *l*-epinephrine (Table V). Animals I13-16 and I13-17 received equal portions of a common pool of LNC with the cells for animal I13-16 being incubated with *l*-epinephrine and the cells for animal I13-17 being incubated without *l*-epinephrine. The PPD skin tests observed at 20 to 24 hr were not significantly different: 10 x 10 mm induration *vs* 9 x 9 mm induration. Animals I13-18 and I13-19 received equal amounts of a common pool of SpC and were treated in the same manner as the previous two recipients. The PPD skin tests in these two animals were not significantly different: 8 x 9 mm induration with *l*-epinephrine and 9 x 9 mm induration without *l*-epinephrine. Animals I13-20, I13-21 and I13-22 were skin tested 58 to 64 hr after receiving an intraperitoneal injection of LNC from animals injected with 2.5 mg *M. tuberculosis* 14 days previously. The PPD skin test site presented an indurated reaction of 13 to 18 mm at 20 to 24 hr. In all these experiments, the brain antigen elicited at most a 2 x 2 mm indurated reaction.

Attempts to actively sensitize guinea pigs with

TABLE V

Skin reactions to PPD observed in strain 13 guinea pigs when tested 56 to 64 hr after syngeneic transfer of PPD sensitive cells given intraperitoneally with or without prior incubation in l-epinephrine

Recipient Guinea Pig	PPD Sensitive Cells Transferred				24-Hr Skin Reaction	
	Source[a]	Viability	No. viable cells	Incubated with *l*-epinephrine[b]	PPD (10 μg)	Brain antigen (15 μg)
		%			*mm*	*mm*
I13-16	Lymph node	88	1.58×10^9	Yes	10 x 10	2 x 2
I13-17	Lymph node	88	1.58×10^9	No	9 x 9	2 x 2
I13-18	Spleen	91	1.53×10^9	Yes	8 x 9	0 x 0
I13-19	Spleen	91	1.53×10^9	No	9 x 9	1 x 1
I13-20	Lymph node	89	9.98×10^8	No	15 x 15	2 x 2
I13-21	Lymph node	86	1.42×10^9	No	18 x 16	2 x 2
I13-22	Lymph node	90	1.12×10^9	No	15 x 13	1 x 2

[a] In recipients I13-16 to I13-19, the guinea pigs serving as cell donors were injected with complete Freund's adjuvant containing 500 μg *M. tuberculosis* 14 days before use. In recipients I13-20 to I13-22 the cell donors were injected with Freund's adjuvant containing 2.5 mg *M. tuberculosis* 14 days before use.

[b] Six and seven-tenths micrograms per milliliter *l*-epinephrine for 15 to 30 min.

RNA extracts. Three strain 2 guinea pigs were each given an intraperitoneal injection of RNA extract (2.11 mg) obtained from guinea pigs sensitized with α,DNP-oligolysine. This amount of RNA was equivalent to the total amount of RNA used in the incubations with nonsensitive cells and was obtained from a pool which was shown to actively convert nonsensitive cells so that they would transfer the skin reactions. After 14 days, each of the animals were skin tested with both α,DNP-oligolysine and ε,DNP-oligolysine and negative reactions were observed, 2 mm of induration with negligible erythema being the largest. Two strain 2 animals each received an intraperitoneal injection of an RNA extract (2.49 mg) from guinea pigs sensitized with ε,DNP-oligolysine. Fourteen days later these animals were skin tested with both α,DNP-oligolysine and ε,DNP-oligolysine and negative reactions were again observed with a 2-mm reaction being the largest.

Attempted syngeneic transfer of the skin test to ε,DNP-oligolysine by nonsensitive cells treated with epinephrine and ε,DNP-oligolysine. In five separate experiments 1.54×10^9 to 2.20×10^9 viable spleen cells from strain 2 guinea pigs were incubated with 6.7 μg/ml of epinephrine and 25 μg of ε,DNP-oligolysine in a total volume of 10 ml and incubated at 37°C for 15 to 30 min. Cells were centrifuged, the supernatant fluid was discarded and the cells were resuspended in fresh tissue culture media. These cells were then injected intraperitoneally into nonsensitive strain 2 recipients. After receiving these treated cells, skin testing was done 3, 17 and 31 days later with both α,DNP-oligolysine and ε,DNP-oligolysine. Skin tests varied from 1 to 3 mm of induration with negligible erythema with both antigens and at the three times tested.

DISCUSSION

The results presented in this report demonstrate that RNA extracts isolated from the lymph nodes of guinea pigs sensitive to PPD, brain antigen, α,DNP-oligolysine and ε,DNP-oligolysine are capable of transferring the classical *in vivo* delayed skin test. These transfers were accomplished by intraperitoneally injecting into nonsensitive guinea pigs a 10 ml suspension of 8.7×10^8 to 4.0×10^9 nonsensitive lymphoid cells which had been previously incubated for 15 to 30 min with 120 to 314 μg/ml of RNA. In these transfers, the delayed skin reactions ranged in diameter of induration as follows: with PPD, 8 to 14 mm; with brain antigen, 6 to 11 mm; with α,DNP-oligolysine, 6 to 15 mm; and with ε, DNP-oligolysine, 8 to 17 mm. The specificity of the transferred reaction was indicated by the correlation of the skin test with the sensitivity of the donor of the RNA extract: e.g., when RNA from a PPD sensitive animal was used, the skin test was negative (0 to 3 mm) with brain antigen; when RNA from an α,DNP-oligolysine sensitive animal was used, the skin test was negative (0 to 2 mm) for ϵ,DNP-oligolysine and vice versa.

The RNA extracts used to transfer sensitivity to brain antigen were obtained from animals receiving 2.5 mg *M. tuberculosis* as well as homogenized spinal cord in oil adjuvant. Furthermore, since Stone (9) has reported that strain 13 guinea pig cells obtained five to seven days after sensitization were optimum for adoptive transfer of allergic encephalomyelitis, we chose to extract the RNA from lymph nodes taken seven days after sensitization with spinal cord rather than waiting 14 days after sensitization as was done in the experiments using the other antigens. Although all of the recipient animals gave positive skin tests to brain antigen none of the animals had developed symptoms of allergic encephalomyelitis 1 month after receiving the RNA-treated cells. Two of the animals gave negative (2 x 3 mm) or borderline (4 x 5 mm) skin reactions to PPD. The explanation for this result is not clear but it might have occurred because of the lower amount of RNA used, e.g., with two other guinea pigs in which approximately twice the amount of RNA was used, the skin reactions were positive, 6 x 7 mm and 8 x 10 mm. Another possible explanation is that the RNA was obtained after 7 days compared with 14 days for the seven guinea pigs that received RNA from animals sensitized with *M. tuberculosis* alone.

In the initial experiments using random bred guinea pigs only the sites receiving both PPD and cells treated with RNA extracts from the lymph nodes of PPD sensitive animals developed reactions considered positive, 6 to 14 mm of induration. However, in contrast to the negative controls observed in the inbred guinea pigs, these control reactions developed clear cut erythema as well as induration (1 to 5 mm) although in no experiment did the size of the reactions at the control sites exceed those observed at the sites receiving PPD- and RNA-treated cells. For this reason, it was felt that conclusive results were not obtainable with this procedure and the results obtained are considered only suggestive of successful transfers.

The use of epinephrine in the incubation of lymphoid cells with RNA extracts seemed to be necessary since all of our attempts to transfer sensitivity without epinephrine did not succeed. The actual mechanism of epinephrine action in carrying out these successful transfers is unknown but it is thought to involve facilitation of RNA uptake by the lymphoid cells. Previous successful *in vitro* transfers of cellular immunity using RNA extracts without epinephrine have been reported using 72-hr human lymph node cell suspensions (2), using guinea pig peritoneal exudate cells (4) and using 72-hr guinea pig lymph node suspensions (5). It may be significant that these three successful reports which have not required epinephrine for successful transfers have all utilized populations of cells which are known to be phagocytic. Furthermore, the lack of successful transfers using lymph node cells or spleen cells which have not been incubated with epinephrine or cultured 72 hr stands in contrast to the successful transfers of anti-sheep red blood cell antibody formation using RNA extracts in rabbits. Whether this difference observed between the transfer with RNA extracts of antibody formation and the transfer of cellular immunity represents a basic difference in mechanism or can simply be explained on the basis of differing technical procedures is at present unresolved. Two other possible effects of epinephrine were explored: epinephrine might act to amplify or otherwise alter a minimal response or it might act to increase the reactivity of the cells towards small amounts of antigen. The results presented show that incubation with epinephrine does not alter the magnitude of skin reactions in adoptive transfers; neither does epinephrine alter the threshold for active sensitization.

Attempts to transfer delayed skin reactions were unsuccessful in five separate guinea pigs receiving intraperitoneal injections of spleen cells incubated with ϵ,DNP-oligolysine as well as epinephrine indicating that the presence of antigen alone in our RNA extracts is not sufficient to explain the results observed. Furthermore, five other guinea pigs received intraperitoneal injections of 2 to 2.5 mg of RNA from α,DNP-oligolysine and ϵ,DNP-oligolysine sensitive animals and no positive skin tests were observed 14 days later. Although these experiments might suggest that these RNA extracts contained no immunogenic RNA-antigen complexes, the possibility remains that the RNA may have been degraded by ribonuclease *in vivo* thus destroying the immunogenicity of the complex. RNA-antigen complexes which have been shown to be capable of conferring on nonsensitive cells the ability to produce specific antibody are inactivated by ribonuclease (10); however, no such complexes have been demonstrated as yet in our RNA extracts active in cellular immune reactions. The experiments of Adler *et al.* (11) and Bell and Dray (12) suggest that the intact RNA required for activity in such extracts may have an informational role. In their experiments, RNA extracts converted lymphoid cells to produce IgM antibody with the light chain genetic markers of the RNA donor. Perhaps, in our delayed hypersensitivity system, the RNA may also act by directing the synthesis of an effector molecule such as migration inhibitory factor.

The history of attempts to transfer delayed hypersensitivity reactions using subcellular extracts is clouded by numerous failures from the time Chase (13) first reported on adoptive transfer of tuberculin sensitivity. Bloom and Chase (14) have reviewed and analyzed this problem and its difficulties in detail and reference should be made to their review for further information. In contrast to the difficulties encountered using crude cell lysates, several workers have successfully demonstrated the transfer of sensitivity of cellular immune responses *in vitro* using RNA extracts (15, 16, 17). Furthermore, Mannick and Egdahl (18) have demonstrated that RNA extracts were able to transfer homograft immunity *in vivo* as evidenced by a second set rejection phenomenon. Sabbidini and Sehon (19) have presented similar *in vivo* results using mice. More recently, Alexander *et al.* (20) have described an RNA extract capable of conferring partial protection in a rat tumor system. Our results are consistent with these reports for other cellular immune systems and extend a previous report (4) of *in vitro* transfer of cellular immune reactions with RNA extracts to include demonstration of the transfer with RNA extracts of delayed skin reactions in the guinea pig, a species which previously has been the subject of numerous unsuccessful attempts to transfer delayed skin reactions with subcellular extracts.

REFERENCES

1. Thor, D. E. and Dray, S., J. Immun., *101:* 51, 1968.
2. Thor, D. E. and Dray, S., J. Immun., *101:* 469, 1968.
3. George, M. and Vaughn, J. H., Fed. Proc., *8:* 514, 1962.
4. Jureziz, R. E., Thor, D. E. and Dray, S., J. Immun., *101:* 823, 1968.
5. Thor, D. E. and Schlossman, S., Fed. Proc., *28:* 629, 1969.
6. Kies, M. W., Ann. N. Y. Acad. Sci., *122:* 161, 1965.
7. Nakao, A., Davis, W. J. and Einstein, E. R., Biochim. Biophys. Acta, *130:* 163, 1966.
8. Hughes, D. and Field, E. J., Int. Arch. Allerg., *33:* 45, 1968.
9. Stone, S. H., Science, *134:* 619, 1961.
10. Gottlieb, A. A., Science, *165:* 592, 1969.
11. Adler, F. L., Fishman, M. and Dray, S., J. Immun., *97:* 554, 1966.
12. Bell, C. and Dray, S., J. Immun., *103:* 1196, 1969.
13. Chase, M. W., Proc. Soc. Exp. Biol. Med., *59:* 134, 1945.
14. Bloom, B. R. and Chase, M. W., Progr. Allerg., *10:* 151, 1967.
15. Fong, J., Chin, D. and Elberg, S. S., J. Exp. Med., *118:* 371, 1963.
16. Wilson, D. B. and Wecker, E. E., J. Immun., *97:* 512, 1966.
17. Gerughty, R. M., Rosenau, W. and Moon, H. D., J. Immun., *97:* 700, 1966.
18. Mannick, J. A. and Egdahl, R. H., J. Clin. Invest., *43:* 2166, 1964.
19. Sabbadini, E. and Sehon, A. H., Int. Arch. Allerg., *32:* 55, 1967.
20. Alexander, P., Delorme, E. J., Hamilton, L. D. G. and Hall, J. G., Nature, *213:* 569, 1967.

THE JOURNAL OF IMMUNOLOGY
Vol. 105, No. 6, December 1970

SPECIFIC INHIBITION OF AN ANTI-HAPTEN IMMUNE RESPONSE BY CHEMICAL MODIFICATION OF CELLS[1]

DAVID NAOR,[2] ROBERT I. MISHELL AND LEON WOFSY

From the Department of Bacteriology and Immunology, University of California, Berkeley, California 94720

Received for publication August 10, 1970

Reaction of mouse spleen cells with 2,4,6-trinitrophenyl sulfonate (TNPS) resulted in suppression of an *in vitro* anti-TNP antibody response without diminishing the response to carrier sheep red blood cells (SRBC). The anti-TNP response of unreacted spleen cells could also be inhibited specifically by addition of small fractions of TNPS-reacted cells, indicating that the specific inhibition is not primarily due to direct chemical modification by TNPS of anti-TNP cellular receptor sites. These results illustrate some of the considerations involved in applying affinity labeling to the problem of antigen receptors on lymphocytes. They also suggest a general procedure for suppressing a particular antibody response with appropriately modified homologous cells.

Recent studies have begun to explore the reaction of possible affinity labeling reagents with immunocompetent cells (1, 2). This approach arises logically from recognition of the presence of immunoglobulin receptor sites on lymphocytes (3), as well as from the successful utilization of affinity labeling for the specific chemical modification of antibody- and enzyme-combining sites (4) and cell-membrane bound receptor protein (5).

In the experiments of Plotz (1), the reaction of 4-hydroxy-3-iodo-5-nitrophenylacetic acid azide from mice primed against NIP-chicken γ globulin (NIP-CGG) resulted in the specific inhibition of the anti-NIP response in adaptively transferred mice, while the response to CGG remained almost unchanged. Segal *et al.* (2) obtained very similar results in a tissue culture system when they reacted α-N-bromoacetyl-ϵ-N-(2,4 dinitrophenyl)-lysine (BADL) or N-bromoacetyl-N′-(2,4 dinitrophenyl)-ethylenediamine (BADE) with spleen explants from mice primed against DNP-protein conjugates. Both groups concluded that the selective inhibition observed was the consequence of affinity labeling of specific antibody receptor sites.

We have conducted a series of experiments aimed at examining some complexities involved in the attempt to apply affinity labeling to the study of specific antibody receptor sites on immunocompetent cells. We have reacted cells with 2,4,6-trinitrophenyl sulfonate (TNPS) and subsequently observed drastic depression of the anti-TNP antibody response to *in vitro* stimulation with TNP-modified sheep red blood cells (TNP-SRBC), while the anti-SRBC response was undiminished. This specific inhibition of an anti-hapten immune response can be shown, however, *not* to be due in significant measure to affinity labeling reactions at anti-TNP receptor sites. For, when TNP-modified spleen cells are mixed with unmodified spleen cells in ratios ranging from 1:9 to 1:2, the anti-TNP response of the *unreacted* cell population is also specifically and sharply curtailed. This indirect, but specific, inhibition of antibody response by mixing reacted and unreacted cells—an effect observed earlier by Plotz in his anti-NIP studies[3]—raises significant questions about what criteria should be developed in determing whether cellular

[1] This study was supported by the United States Public Health Service, National Institutes of Health, Grant AI-06610.

[2] International Postdoctoral Fellow, United States Public Health Service Fellowship 5-FO5-TW-1509-02. Permanent address: The Hebrew University, Hadassah Medical School, Jerusalem.

[3] Private communication from P. Plotz. This observation is referred to in a paper presented by P. Plotz at the Third Sirgrid Juselius Foundation Symposium, Helsinki, Finland, June 22–25, 1970; to be published.

TABLE I

Specific inhibition of anti-TNP response by reaction of cells with TNPS, 1×10^{-3} M[a]

Expt. No.	Reacted Cells, Fraction	Unreacted Cells, Fraction	Anti-SRBC Response		Anti-TNP Response[b]		
			PPM	% of activity	PPM	% of activity	% of activity expected[c]
1	0	1.0	2018	100	287	100	
	1.0	0	2252	112	82	29	
	0.5	0.5	1730	86	57	20	65
2	0	1.0	570	100	141	100	
	1.0	0	692	121	32	23	
	0.5	0.5	818	143	26	18	62
	0.25	0.75	536	94	45	32	83
	0.1	0.9	600	105	44	31	93
3[d]	0	1.0	622 ± 96	100	386 ± 46	100	
	1.0	0	892 ± 125	143	140 ± 12	36	
	0.25	0.75	578 ± 63	93	156 ± 14	40	84
	0.1	0.9	458 ± 23	74	233 ± 14	60	96

[a] The cells were preincubated with TNPS, 1×10^{-3} M, washed three times and reincubated with 0.1% TNP-SRBC.

[b] Anti-TNP activity was assayed in experiments 1 and 2 with TNP-BRC; in experiment 3, the assay was performed with TNP-HRC.

[c] This value is calculated on the basis of the prediction that given numbers of reacted and unreacted cells will contribute the same number of ppm when mixed as they would in separate populations. See "expected activity" in Results.

[d] The experiment was done in triplicate. The results show the average and the standard errors.

receptors have been modified selectively by an affinity labeling reagent.

MATERIALS AND METHODS

All of the following procedures and techniques were done aseptically. Three-month-old $B_6D_2F_1$ X mice (The Jackson Laboratory, Bar Harbor, Maine) were primed 3 days before the experiment with 0.2 ml of 0.5% SRBC, but not preimmunized against TNP conjugates.[4] The mice were killed by cervical dislocation. The spleens were removed and teased in balanced salt solution (BSS) (6). The rough particles of the cell suspension were removed by gravitation, and the cells were washed once and resuspended in BSS at a concentration of 4×10^7 cells/ml. From 3 to 6 ml of this suspension were transferred to Petri dishes (60 × 15 mm) and TNPS (Nutritional Biochemicals, Cleveland, Ohio) was added at a final concentration ranging from 10^{-6} M to 10^{-2} M. After 2.5 hr of incubation on a shaker at 4°, the cells were washed three times with 10 ml BSS and resuspended at a final concentration of 15×10^6 cells/ml in Eagle's minimal essential medium supplemented as previously described (6). One milliliter aliquots of chemically modified cell suspensions (reacted cells), non-modified cell suspensions (unreacted cells), or mixtures of both were cultured as described by Mishell and Dutton (6) and stimulated with 0.1% TNP-SRBC according to the procedure of Kettman and Dutton (7). Four days later the cells were harvested and assayed for plaque-forming cells (PFC) by a modified Jerne technique (6). Horse red blood cells or burro red blood cells coupled with TNP (TNP-HRC and TNP-BRC, respectively) were utilized in assaying for anti-TNP PFC (7). There is negligible cross-reaction between these red cells and SRBC.

[4] Private communication from J. Kettman and R. Dutton, who have found that priming against ed cell carriers results in an enhanced anti-TNP response to subsequent *in vitro* immunization with TNP-red cells.

RESULTS

Table I shows the results of three experiments in which cells were modified with 1×10^{-3} M

TABLE II

Specific inhibition of anti-TNP response by reaction of cells with TNPS, 3 × 10⁻³ M[a]

Reacted Cells, Fraction	Unreacted Cells, Fraction	Anti-SRBC Response		Anti-TNP Response		
		PPM	% of activity	PPM	% of activity	% of activity expected[b]
0	1.0	2400	100	739	100	
1.0	0	3800	158	140	19	
0.25	0.75	3830	159	238	32	80

[a] The cells were preincubated with TNPS, 3×10^{-3} M, washed three times and reincubated with 0.1% TNP-SRBC; the assay for anti-TNP PFC was performed with TNP-HRC.

[b] This value is calculated on the basis of the prediction that given numbers of reacted and unreacted cells will contribute the same number of ppm when mixed as they would in separate populations. See "expected activity" in Results.

TNPS. The anti-TNP response of the reacted cells was about 25% that of the control unreacted cells. The anti-SRBC response of the reacted cells was the same as or even slightly higher than that of unreacted cells. Moreover, small fractions of reacted cells specifically inhibited the anti-TNP response of unreacted cells when they were mixed together in the *in vitro* cultures. "Expected activity" levels indicated for the cell-mixing experiments (Table I) were calculated on a proportionate basis from the number of anti-TNP PFC (ppm) found in the separate populations of reacted and unreacted cells. For example, in experiment 1, Table I, when a 50/50 mixture of reacted and unreacted cells was examined, the "expected" level represented the sum of 41 ppm (half of 82 ppm) and 143 ppm (half of 287 ppm), or 184 ppm (65% of the 287 ppm unreacted cell control value); the level of anti-TNP PFC found was 57 ppm (20% of 287 ppm). Cell mixtures in which the unreacted cell fraction was only 0.25 or 0.10 also showed marked reduction of the "expected" anti-TNP response, whereas the anti-SRBC response in the mixed cell populations was not significantly diminished. Experiment 3, Table I, was done in triplicate and the p values were calculated; both the reacted and mixed cell populations differed from unreacted cells in the anti-TNP response, $p < 0.01$.

Results of another experiment, in which the TPNS reagent concentration was raised to 3×10^{-3} *M*, are summarized in Table II. The reacted cells showed 19% of the anti-TNP response of the unreacted cells; mixed cell populations with 25% reacted cells showed 32% of the control anti-TNP activity, whereas the activity "expected" was 80%. The reacted and mixed cell populations showed slight *increases* in the anti-SRBC response.

When cells were reacted at TNPS concentrations of 10^{-2} M, both the anti-TNP and the anti-SRBC responses were eradicated. Preincubation of cells with 10^{-4} M TNPS (Table III) specifically reduced the anti-TNP response to 25 to 40% of unreacted control values, but in two of three experiments, activity levels in mixed cell populations were found to be the same as "expected" values. Pre-incubation of cells at 10^{-5} and 10^{-6} M concentrations of TNPS resulted in some reduction of the anti-TNP response, 55 to 70% of control values for unreacetd cells, but mixed cell populations showed no

TABLE III

Specific inhibition of anti-TNP response by reaction of cells with TNPS, 1 × 10⁻⁴ M[a]

Expt. No.	Reacted Cells, Fraction	Unreacted Cells, Fraction	Anti-SRBC Response		Anti-TNP Response		
			PPM	% of activity	PPM	% of activity	% of activity expected[b]
1	0	1.0	1650	100	381	100	
	1.0	0	1840	112	155	41	
	0.50	0.50	1528	93	178	47	70
2	0	1.0	6168	100	660	100	
	1.0	0	5540	90	234	35	
	0.50	0.50	6590	107	492	74	68
3	0	1.0	2362	100	402	100	
	1.0	0	3099	131	101	25	
	0.5	0.5	2642	112	241	60	62

[a] The cells were preincubated with TNPS, 1×10^{-4} M, washed three times and reincubated with 0.1% TNP-SRBC; the assay for anti-TNP PFC was performed with TNP-HRC.

[b] This value is calculated on the basis of the prediction that given numbers of reacted and unreacted cells will contribute the same number of ppm when mixed as they would in separate populations. See "expected activity" in Results.

inhibition of unreacted by reacted cells. With all concentrations of TNPS in the range of 1×10^{-6} M to 3×10^{-3} M, no inhibition of the anti-SRBC response was effected.

DISCUSSION

This study on the chemical modification of mouse spleen cells with TNPS has: 1) revealed some of the problems in applying the method of affinity labeling to specific receptors on antibody precursor cells, and 2) demonstrated an adaptable procedure for selective inhibition of a particular antibody response.

Cell suspensions pre-incubated with 10^{-3} M TNPS showed a striking decrease in anti-TNP response, while their anti-SRBC response remained intact or was slightly increased (Tables I and II), thus simulating the effect that might be anticipated from affinity labeling of anti-TNP cellular receptors. However, *in vitro* cultures composed of only 10 to 25% reacted cells, and the rest unreacted cells, showed a similar degree of suppression of the level of the anti-TNP response and no change, or a slight increase, in the anti-SRBC response (Tables I and II).

From these results we conclude that the inhibition of the anti-TNP response by reaction with TNPS has been *specific*, but essentially *indirect*, i.e., not primarily the result of affinity labeling of cellular anti-TNP receptors. The extensive nonspecific modification of cell surface proteins with TNPS apparently converts many cells into specific inhibitors whose TNP groups can block anti-TNP receptor sites on the same or other cells.

The fact that the TNP-white cells inhibit the *in vitro* anti-TNP response, whereas TNP-SRBC stimulate it, may reflect that the former are modified, but *homologous*, mouse cells and cannot provide sufficient carrier determinants for significant antibody response. At the same time, compared to the use of free hapten as a reversible inhibitor of anti-hapten receptors, homologous cells with multiple hapten sites should be superior receptor-blocking reagents. Because haptens conjugated to homologous cells may thus serve as efficient inhibitors of a specific anti-hapten antibody response, such selective immune suppression by chemical modification of immunocompetent cells cannot be accepted as proof that the specific antibody receptor sites have been labeled covalently and, therefore, inactivated.

In these studies, when cells were reacted with concentrations of TNPS of 10^{-4} M (Table III) or below, some specific depression of the anti-TNP response resulted, but an inhibitory effect of reacted on unreacted cells could not be demonstrated unequivocally. This observation might be attributed to some chemical modification of specific anti-TNP receptors, but even the absence of the inhibitory cell mixing effect is not an adequate criterion for such direct labeling. It is possible that the modification of cell surface proteins in the vicinity of specific receptors allows neighboring interactions that may block receptor sites strongly, but non-covalently. Thus, even at levels of modification insufficient to convert reacted cells into effective inhibitors of unreacted cells, the inactivation of the reacted cells themselves may be more or less indirect. This especially might be the case where the reagent used is ineffective for affinity labeling of a particular antibody-combining site: e.g., if the antibody (receptor) site lacks residues reactive with a given reagent. TNPS, which reacts primarily with lysine amino or free sulfhydryl groups on proteins (8), is probably a poor affinity labeling reagent for anti-TNP antibodies, since most antibody-combining sites evidently lack these functional groups (9).

Since the mechanism of affinity labeling involves covalent bond formation after the ligand-reagent is non-covalently complexed at the active site (4), the best evidence for such labeling of specific cellular receptors is the ability of a reversibly binding inhibitor to protect against inactivation by the reagent (5). Plotz has reported data suggesting limited protection in some experiments in the anti-NIP system (1), so that part of the observed decrease in anti-hapten response was probably due to direct receptor modification.

When possible objectives of affinity-labeling studies with lymphoid cells are considered, major difficulties are readily apparent. Since cells with antigen reactive receptors of any given specificity occur at a frequency as low as 10^{-5} to 10^{-6} in a normal population of lymphocytes (10), a very highly enhanced affinity-labeling reaction (4) may be obscured by nonspecific reactions which are summed over the total number of cells present. Even an individual affinity-labeled cell, reacted specifically at thousands of replicate receptor sites (11), might be difficult to distinguish from a chemically modified lymphocyte with unrelated receptor specificity, since specific receptor must comprise only a tiny percentage of the cell membrane protein exposed to the labeling reagent. In any case, the cumulative level of nonspecific modifications in the system almost certainly would nullify specific approaches to isolating the few affinity-labeled cells.

Affinity labeling can be a useful approach to the problem of isolation and characterization of cellular receptor sites in systems where the number of cells bearing the specific receptor is sufficiently high to permit separation of affinity-labeled protein from other proteins in cell membrane fractions. Such a favorable situation obviously is not found in normal lymphocyte populations. Because of these considerations, it seems more reasonable to isolate antigen reactive cells without chemical modification, exploiting their affinity for specific cellular immunoadsorbents (12, 13).

While chemical modification of immunocompetent cells with putative affinity-labeling reagents can produce complicating influences on the function of cells in the immune response, the cell-mixing experiments reported here suggest an important direction for further studies. Where, either for theoretical or potential clinical purposes, it is desired to suppress a particular immune response without effecting other immunocompetent cells, the introduction of appropriately modified homologous cells into an otherwise intact (unmodified) cell population may prove to be a valuable tool.

The extent to which this approach may be adapted to a variety of systems remains to be examined. The present study is necessarily limited in that we are comparing, *in vitro*, a primary anti-hapten response with a primed anti-carrier response. While our chemical modification procedures distinguish between the anti-TNP and anti-SRBC responses on a specific basis, there may also be some factors of a more general (nonspecific) nature that influence variably the stability of immunocompetent cells which differ in type or in stage of differentiation. It may also be the case that homologous cells of different types may not all be readily transformed by chemical modification into specific inhibitors of an immune response. For example, in preliminary experiments, TNP-conjugated mouse thymocytes and irradiated spleen cells seem to be less effective as inhibitors than similarly modified populations of red cells or non-irradiated spleen cells. These problems should be clarified by further investigation and as progress is made in developing additional *in vitro* anti-hapten responses.

REFERENCES

1. Plotz, P. H., Nature, *223:* 1373, 1969.
2. Segal, S., Globerson, A., Feldman, M., Haimovich, J. and Givol, D., Nature, *223:* 1374, 1969.
3. Sulitzeanu, D., Bact. Rev., *32:* 404, 1968.
4. Singer, S. J., Advances Protein Chem., *22:* 1, 1967.
5. Changeux, J. P., Podleski, T. R. and Wofsy, L., Proc. Nat. Acad. Sci., *58:* 2063, 1967.
6. Mishell, R. I. and Dutton, R. W., J. Exp. Med., *126:* 423, 1967.
7. Kettman, J. and Dutton, R. W., J. Immun., *104:* 1558, 1970.
8. Okuyama, T. and Satake, K., J. Biochem. (Tokyo), *47:* 454, 1960.
9. Wofsy, L. and Singer, S. J., Biochemistry, *1:* 1031, 1962.
10. Jerne, N. K., Cold Spring Harbor Symp. Quant. Biol., *32:* 591, 1967.
11. Byrt, P. and Ada, G. L., Immunology, *17:* 503, 1969.
12. Wigzell, H. and Anderson, B., J. Exp. Med., *129:* 23, 1969.
13. Truffa-Bachi, P. and Wofsy, L., Proc. Nat. Acad. Sci., *66:* 655, 1970.

THE JOURNAL OF IMMUNOLOGY
Vol. 105, No. 6, December 1970

CANINE SECRETORY IMMUNOGLOBULINS: IDENTIFICATION OF SECRETORY COMPONENT[1]

JOHN RICKS,[2] MARY ROBERTS AND ROY PATTERSON

From the Departments of Microbiology and Medicine, Northwestern University-McGraw Medical Center, Chicago, Illinois

Received for publication August 7, 1970

Immunoglobulin A was demonstrated in canine tracheal secretions, saliva, tears, nasal secretions and colostrum. Another molecular species, presumably canine secretory component, was demonstrated in colostrum, tracheal secretions and tears. The IgA in colostrum was purified by a combination of Sephadex G-200 and DEAE-cellulose chromatography, and an antiserum which reacts with IgA and secretory component was prepared against this purified IgA. Immunoglobulins G, A and M were measured semiquantitatively in colostrum and milk and compared to serum values. Immunoglobulin A has the highest colostrum to serum ratio, IgG has the next highest and IgM is usually found in higher concentration in serum than in colostrum. The actual concentrations of IgG, IgA and IgM in the colostrum, however, varied widely among the six dogs studied.

Johnson and Vaughan described six immunoglobulin classes in the dog (1). One of these immunoglobulins, Int.S γ_1, has a sedimentation coefficient greater than that of IgG but less than that of IgM and has a high colostrum to serum concentration ratio. Antigenic determinants unique to colostral IgA were reported briefly in the initial publication (1) but these findings could not be duplicated with other antisera (2, 3). Vaerman, Heremans and van Kerckhoven (4, 5) identified Johnson and Vaughan's Int.S γ_1 as canine IgA on the basis of its reaction with antisera prepared against human IgA. IgA has been found in canine colostrum, milk, bronchial secretions, saliva, tears, hepatic bile and intestinal fluid (1, 2, 6, 7).

The present report describes the purification of canine colostral IgA and the preparation of antisera which recognize antigenic determinants present in colostral IgA but absent in serum IgA. Canine secretory component was separated from colostral IgA. IgA was found in several canine secretions and secretory component was found in some of these secretions. Colostrum to serum ratios were determined for IgG, IgA and IgM.

[1] This work was supported by the Life Insurance Medical Research Fund and the Ernest S. Bazley Asthma Research Fund.

[2] Submitted in partial fulfillment of requirements for the degree of Doctor of Philosophy in Microbiology.

MATERIALS AND METHODS

Preparation of clarified colostrum. Colostrum was collected from adult outbred female dogs during and up to 6 hr after parturition by manual expression from the mammary glands. The fat was separated by centrifugation at 15,000 × G for 20 min at 4°C; this was repeated, if necessary, to provide complete separation.

Purification of IgA from colostrum. Preparations of clarified colostrum were fractionated on Sephadex G-200 columns using a buffer of 0.15 M NaCl and 0.1 M Tris-HCl, pH 8.2. Peak I fractions from the Sephadex G-200 columns which contained IgA were pooled and concentrated by pervaporation and applied to a diethylaminoethyl (DEAE)-cellulose column which had been equilibrated with 0.005 M phosphate buffer, pH 8.0. Elutions from the DEAE-cellulose column were made with 0.005 M, 0.020 M, 0.040 M, 0.10 M and 0.30 M phosphate buffers, all of pH 8.0. The fractions were collected and tested by gel diffusion and immunoelectrophoresis against rabbit anti-normal dog serum (anti-NDS) and sheep anti-human IgA.

Anti-immunoglobulin sera. Anti-human IgA produced in sheep (Melpar, batch SHA01) was found to cross-react with canine IgA. Goat anti-human IgM (Hyland, lot 8211H 004A1) cross-reacted with canine IgM. The preparation of rabbit anti-dog IgG and anti-NDS has been previously described (8).

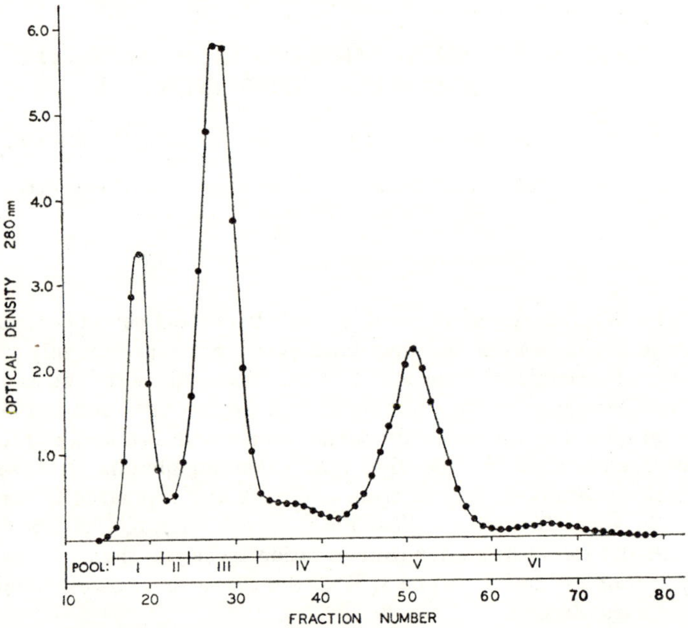

Figure 1. Clarified colostrum from dog 6 separated on a 2.5- x 35-cm Sephadex G-200 column and pooled as shown by horizontal lines.

Antisera specific for dog colostral IgA were raised in two rabbits by the injection of 1 mg of purified colostral IgA in complete Freund's adjuvant containing 5 mg/ml heat-killed *Mycobacterium tuberculosis.* The rabbits were injected at the end of 2 weeks and again 3 months later with 0.5 mg IgA in incomplete Freund's adjuvant. They were bled periodically and exsanguinated 5 months after the initial injection. The antisera were absorbed with IgG fractions prepared as previously described (8).

Gel diffusion and immunoelectrophoresis. Gel diffusion and immunoelectrophoresis were performed in 0.85% agar gel. Electrophoresis was carried out in barbital buffer, 0.05 μ, pH 8.2, at a constant voltage of 150 V.

Quantitation of immunoglobulins in colostrum. Immunoglobulins in colostrum were quantitated by the radial immunodiffusion technique of Mancini, Carbonara and Heremans (9). Hyland Immuno-plates for measuring human IgM were used to measure dog IgM concentrations. Canine IgG and IgA concentrations were determined using 0.85% agar plates made with an appropriate concentration of anti-dog IgG or anti-dog IgA. The calibration of these plates is described in the *Results.*

Collection of other secretions. Dog tracheal secretions were collected by aspiration from surgically prepared tracheal pouches as described by Wardell, Chakrin and Payne (10). Dog tears, saliva and nasal secretions were collected from dogs anesthetized with sodium pentobarbital and injected intravenously with 15 mg of pilocarpine hydrochloride (6% Isoptocarpine, Alcon Laboratories, Inc., Fort Worth, Texas).

RESULTS

Purification of canine colostral IgA. The results of Sephadex G-200 chromatography of clarified colostrum are shown in Figure 1. The fractions were pooled as indicated; pool I corresponded to the void volume of the column. IgA was found in pool I by gel diffusion against anti-human IgA. Pool I was chromatographed on a DEAE-cellulose column and the results of this separation are shown in Figure 2. The peak which eluted with 0.10 M phosphate buffer contained only IgA by analysis using gel diffusion against anti-human IgA, anti-human IgM and anti-dog IgG. The peak eluted with 0.30 M phosphate buffer contained IgA and IgM. Analysis of the 0.10 M peak by immunoelectrophoresis developed with anti-NDS showed only one band, consistent with IgA by its β_2 migration.

Preparation and specificity of anti-canine IgA.

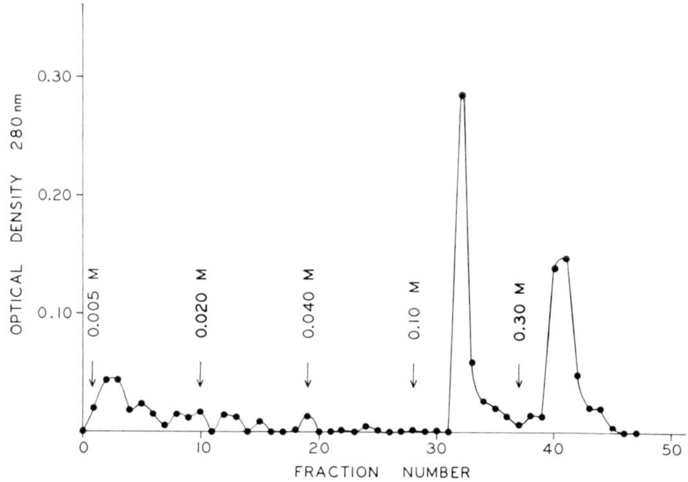

Figure 2. Separation of material from Sephadex G-200 peak I (Fig. 1) on a 1- x 5-cm DEAE-cellulose column. Eluting buffers were pH 8.0 phosphate of 0.005 M, 0.020 M, 0.040 M, 0.10 M and 0.30 M.

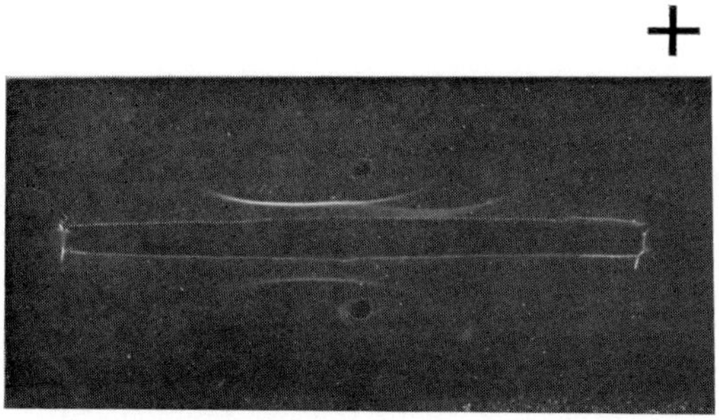

Figure 3. Immunoelectrophoresis of colostrum (*upper well*) and normal dog serum (*lower well*) developed with anti-IgA serum absorbed with canine IgG (anti-IgA_{abs}).

The Sephadex peak I fraction of colostrum which eluted from DEAE-cellulose with 0.10 M phosphate buffer was used to immunize rabbits. When these antisera were tested in immunoelectrophoresis against normal dog serum, only bands corresponding to IgG and IgA were found. Antibodies reacting with IgG were removed by absorption of the antisera with a sample of dog $IgG_{2a,b}$ prepared from normal canine sera by DEAE-cellulose chromatography.

The results of electrophoresis of clarified colostrum and normal dog serum developed with this absorbed anti-IgA are shown in Figure 3. A single line, IgA, developed against electrophoresed normal dog serum. Two bands occurred, however, against clarified colostrum. As seen in Figure 3, these two bands showed a reaction of partial identity, the band corresponding electrophoretically to serum IgA having the extra antigenic determinants. This antiserum, therefore, reacted with one protein in normal dog serum and two proteins in normal dog colostrum. When this antiserum was absorbed with whole normal dog serum and then used to develop electrophoresed normal dog serum and dog colostrum, the antiserum only reacted with material in the colostrum (Fig. 4). As seen in Figure 4 the absorbed antiserum once again reacted with IgA and the second band in colostrum, but this time the reaction was one of identity, indicating that the antiserum recognized no antigenic differences between the two materials. Thus the antigenic determinants on the molecules making up the extra band are

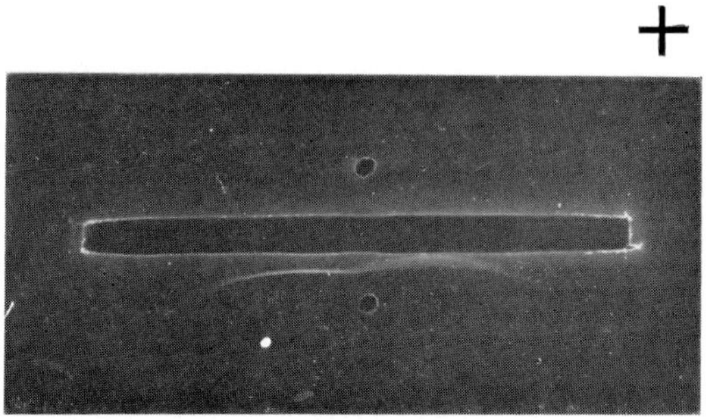

Figure 4. Immunoelectrophoresis of normal dog serum (*upper well*) and colostrum (*lower well*) developed with anti-IgA serum which had been absorbed with normal dog serum.

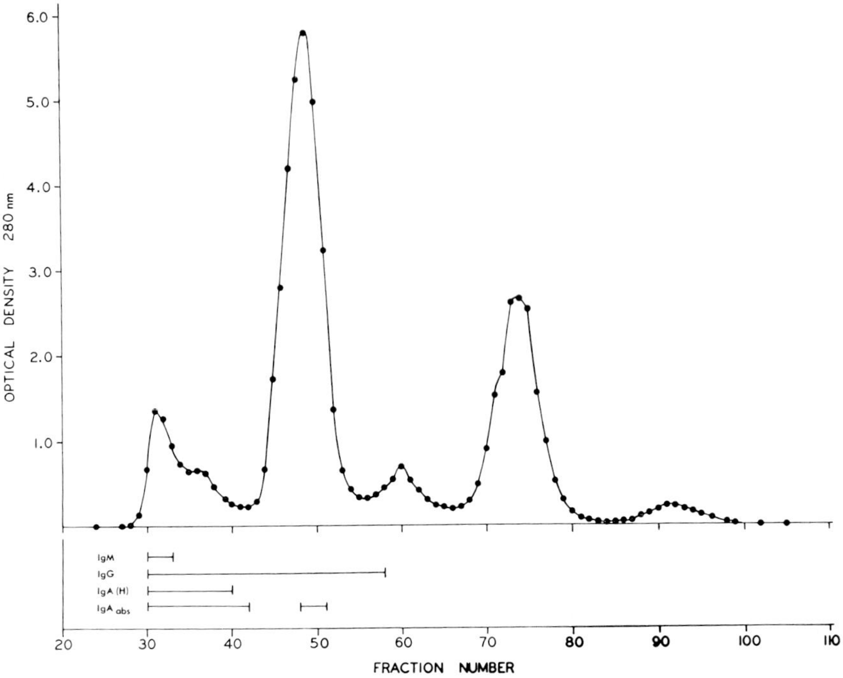

Figure 5. Clarified colostrum from dog 6 separated on a 2.5- x 120-cm Sephadex G-200 column. Immunoglobulins were localized as shown by gel diffusion against anti-human IgM, anti-dog IgG, anti-human IgA (H) which reacted only with the α chains, and anti-dog IgA_{abs} which reacted with determinants on the α chains as well as with determinants on the secretory component.

also present on at least some of the IgA molecules in canine colostrum, but are not present in dog serum.

Localization of immunoglobulins in colostrum by Sephadex G-200 fractionation. Immunoglobulins M, G and A were all found in colostrum by gel diffusion. The localization of these three immunoglobulins in Sephadex G-200 fractions of clarified colostrum is shown in Figure 5. IgM was localized to the main part of peak I. A small amount of IgG was also present in peak I, but the precipitin lines did not show strongly until tube 40. The IgG extended completely through peak II and into peak III. Two anti-IgA sera were used to localize IgA in the fractions. The first (anti-IgA(H)) was a commercial preparation which was specific for the α chains of human immunoglobulin A. The second (anti-IgA_{abs}) was the antiserum prepared as discussed in the previous section and absorbed with canine IgG to remove anti-L chain antibodies. The anti-IgA(H) antiserum showed IgA localized in peak I and the shoulder on the trailing edge of peak I. The anti-IgA_{abs} antiserum, on the other hand, showed two locations with activity. The first corresponded with the anti-IgA (H) findings (tubes 30 to 42, Fig. 5), whereas the second region of precipitation with the anti-IgA_{abs} antiserum occurred under peak II (tubes 48 to 51). These two areas of reactivity were separated by five tubes of material which did not precipitate with the anti-IgA_{abs} antiserum.

Other clarified colostrum fractions from this dog were pooled as shown in Figure 1. The pools were concentrated and dialyzed against 0.15 M NaCl. These samples were electrophoresed and developed with the anti-IgA_{abs} antiserum. The results are shown in Figure 6. The IgA is located only in pools I and II, whereas the other protein is located only in pools III and IV. No reaction occurred with the material in pools V and VI. The protein in pools III and IV migrates identically to the anodally migrating protein in Figure 3 which showed a reaction of partial identity with IgA from colostrum.

Determination of the relative concentrations of immunoglobulins in canine colostrum. Estimations of the concentration of immunoglobulins G, A

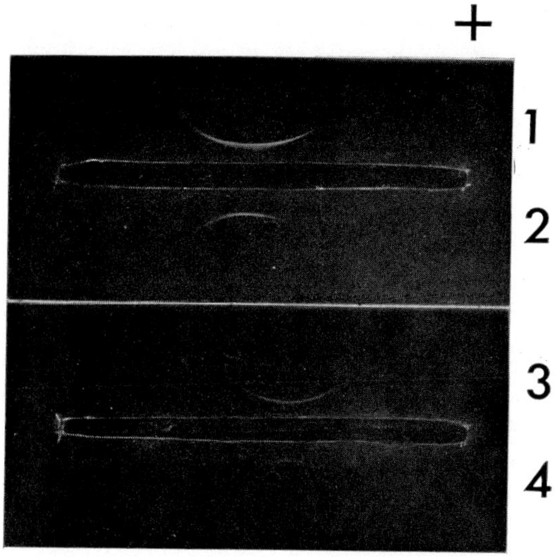

Figure 6. Immunoelectrophoresis of pools I (*1*), II, (*2*), III (*3*) and IV (*4*) from the Sephadex G-200 fractionation of clarified colostrum shown in Figure 1. The troughs contain anti-IgA_{abs}.

and M in colostrum and milk were made by the radial immunodiffusion method of Mancini, Carbonara and Heremans (9). To calibrate the plates, a standard pool of normal dog serum and 1:2, 1:5, 1:10 and 1:20 dilutions of this serum were made. Preliminary studies showed that a 1:10 dilution of colostrum would fall close to the 5% to 100% values of immunoglobulin concentration in normal dog serum; therefore, 1:10 dilutions of clarified colostrum were used in plates calibrated with dilutions of normal dog serum. In this way the immunoglobulin concentrations in colostrum can be expressed as the percentage of the standard normal serum concentrations.

The standard curves for IgA, IgG and IgM are shown in Figure 7. The log concentration *vs* diameter of precipitin ring relationship is very close to linear. The diameter of the ring produced by colostrum samples is used to determine the immunoglobulin level relative to the standard serum level. The results of such determinations on six different samples of colostrum and two samples of milk are shown in Table I. Immunoglobulins G and A are found consistently in higher concentrations in colostrum than in serum. Immunoglobulin M is found in lower concentration in colostrum than in serum. Relative to the serum concentration, IgA is by far the major immunoglobulin in colostrum. In canine milk collected 47 and 49 days after parturition, IgA is the only immunoglobulin measured which is in higher concentration in the milk than in serum.

Immunoglobulin A in other secretions. Unconcentrated dog tracheal secretions, tears, saliva and nasal secretions were examined for content of IgA. All of these secretions showed IgA arcs on immunoelectrophoresis developed with anti-canine IgA antiserum. The extra arc which gives a reaction of partial identity with IgA, shown in colostrum in Figures 3, 4 and 6, was found in unconcentrated tears and tracheal secretions, but not in unconcentrated saliva or nasal secretions.

DISCUSSION

The method used in this study to purify colostral IgA is a relatively simple technique which yields small amounts of purified IgA.

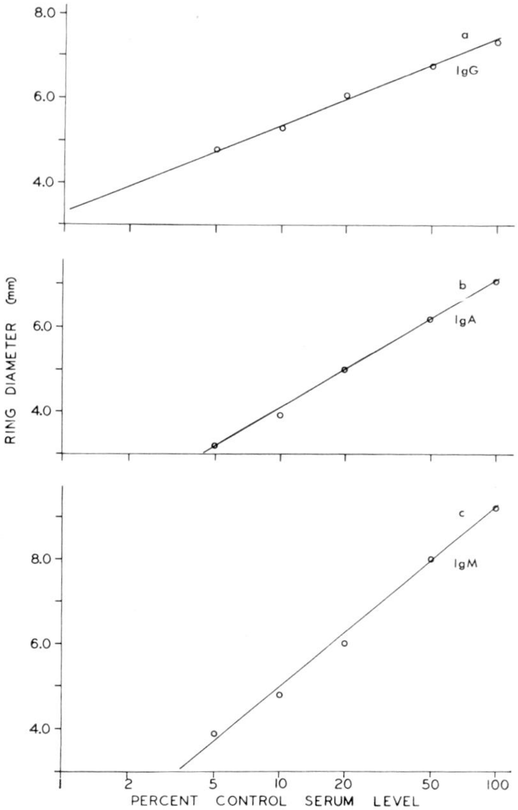

Figure 7. Calibration curves using whole serum pool (100%), 1:2 (50%), 1:5 (20%), 1:10 (10%) and 1:20 (5%) dilutions of the serum pool. *a*, Curve for IgG; *b*, curve for IgA; *c*, curve for IgM.

TABLE I

Immunoglobulin concentrations in canine colostrum and milk relative to pooled normal serum levels

Sample	Per Cent of Standard Serum Values		
	IgG	IgA	IgM
Dog 1 colostrum	350	1350	52
Dog 2 colostrum	200	1350	50
Dog 3 colostrum	440	1100	85
Dog 4 colostrum	550	5000	76
Dog 5 colostrum	130	1350	40
Dog 6 colostrum	160	3300	42
Dog 3 milk (day 47)	4	400	11
Dog 3 milk (day 49)	3	860	9

IgA prepared in this way showed no impurities when it was electrophoresed and developed with antisera against NDS, colostrum or saliva. Furthermore, when this preparation was used to hyperimmunize two rabbits, neither of the rabbits made detectable antibody to any component of colostrum except to IgA and to a constituent of colostrum which gave a reaction of partial identity with colostral IgA on immunoelectrophoresis and gel diffusion. This assumes that the absorption with IgG removed only anti-light chain antibodies. That this is the case is likely since the IgG preparation used to absorb the anti-IgA antiserum contained only $IgG_{2a,b}$ and the immunoglobulins which would be expected to contaminate the IgA preparations would be IgG_1 and IgM.

Anti-dog IgA antiserum has been prepared by Johnson and Vaughan (1), Vaerman and Heremans (4) and Reynolds and Johnson (2). The original anti-IgA made by Johnson and Vaughan was able to detect antigenic differences between salivary IgA (Int.S γ_1) and serum IgA (1) but serum from this rabbit later lost its ability to distinguish between serum and salivary IgA (2). The anti-IgA antiserum described in the present report consistently distinguishes two components of colostrum, tracheal secretions and tears. These two components show reactions of immunologic partial identity, the extra antigenic sites being on the IgA molecule. When the anti-IgA antiserum is absorbed with whole dog serum, the antibodies specific to the IgA molecule as well as to light chains are removed. The antiserum no longer reacts with the serum IgA, but now gives a reaction of identity with colostral IgA and the "extra" component in colostrum. This "extra" component in colostrum is probably analogous to the secretory component which has been described in other species (11). Free canine secretory component was localized to peaks II and III of a Sephadex G-200 fractionation of colostrum. The finding of free secretory component in canine colostrum is consistent with observations in the human. Free human secretory piece has been found in peaks II and III of Sephadex G-200 fractionations of human colostrum (12, 13).

Vaerman and Heremans (7) reported colostrum:serum and milk:serum ratios for IgM, IgG_{2c}, $IgG_{2a,b}$, IgG_1, IgA, transferrin and albumin during the first 31 days after parturition in one dog. In general, the values reported here agree with those obtained by Vaerman and Heremans. However, the degree of variability of measurements from the six dogs studied here indicates that samples of colostrum from different dogs may differ greatly in the concentration of immunoglobulins. The values given in Table I are relative to a standard dog serum with respect to IgG, IgA and IgM. If these are expressed as colostral Ig:serum Ig in the same dog, the values range from 1.2 to 5.7 for IgG, 7.3 to 39 for IgA and 0.75 to 1.0 for IgM for day 0 colostrum. Vaerman and Hereman's dog gave colostrum: serum ratios of 1.3 for IgG_{2c}, 1.8 for $IgG_{2a,b}$, 1.1 for IgG_1, 0.45 for IgM and 14 for IgA. The main feature to be noted in all 7 dogs is, of course, the marked concentration of IgA in colostrum compared to serum levels. IgG is also consistently present in colostrum in higher concentrations than in serum, but IgM is always present in the same or lower concentration in colostrum compared to serum. After the first few days, however, the composition of milk is quite different from that of colostrum. The concentrations of IgG and IgM drop to negligible amounts and the concentration of IgA drops markedly, although it is still four to eight times the IgA concentration of serum. Vaerman and Heremans obtained a value of six times the serum concentration in milk obtained at 20 days. In view of the report by Gillette and Filkins (14) that the maximum absorption of antibody in the puppy occurs from 8 to 15 hr after birth, this initially high immunoglobulin concentration of colostrum seems to be the most economical way to give the pups maternal immunoglobulins early in life.

The present detection of IgA in saliva, tears,

nasal secretions and tracheal secretions extends the number of external secretions of the dog which have been studied for IgA content. Vaerman and Heremans (7) detected IgA in saliva, tears, bile, milk and intestinal secretions. Reynolds and Johnson described IgA in canine colostrum (2) and intestinal secretions (6), and Johnson and Vaughan described IgA in canine saliva, bronchial secretions and colostrum (1).

REFERENCES

1. Johnson, J. S. and Vaughan, J. H., J. Immun., *98:* 923, 1967.
2. Reynolds, H. Y. and Johnson, J. S., J. Immun., *104:* 1000, 1970.
3. Reynolds, H. Y. and Johnson, J. S., Fed. Proc., *29:* 641, 1970.
4. Vaerman, J. P. and Heremans, J. F., Immunochemistry, *5:* 425, 1968.
5. Vaerman, J. P., Heremans, J. F. and van Kerkhoven, G., J. Immun., *103:* 1421, 1969.
6. Reynolds, H. Y. and Johnson, J. S., J. Immun., *104:* 888, 1970.
7. Vaerman, J. P. and Heremans, J. F., Immunochemistry, *6:* 779, 1969.
8. Patterson, R., Roberts, M. and Pruzansky, J. J., J. Immun., *101:* 687, 1968.
9. Mancini, G., Carbonara, A. O. and Heremans, J. F., Immunochemistry, *2:* 235, 1965.
10. Wardell, J. R., Jr., Chakrin, L. W. and Payne, B. J., Amer. Rev. Resp. Dis., In press.
11. Tomasi, T. B., Jr., Tan, E. M., Soloman, A. and Prendergast, R. A., J. Exp. Med., *121:* 101, 1965.
12. Van Munster, P. J. J., Stodinga, G. B. A. and Poels-Zanders, S., Immunology, *17:* 165, 1969.
13. Mestecky, J., Kraus, F. W. and Voight, S. A., Immunology, *18:* 237, 1970.
14. Gillette, D. D. and Filkins, M., Amer. J Physiol., *210:* 419, 1966.

THE JOURNAL OF IMMUNOLOGY

Vol. 105, No. 6, December 1970
Printed in U.S.A.

INTERSPECIES "TRANSFER" OF DELAYED HYPERSENSITIVITY *IN VITRO* WITH RNA EXTRACTS[1]

RONALD E. PAQUE[2] AND SHELDON DRAY

From the Department of Microbiology, University of Illinois at the Medical Center, Chicago, Illnioïs 60680

Received for publication August 5, 1970

When nonsensitive guinea pig peritoneal exudate cells (PEC) were incubated *in vitro* with RNA extracts from rhesus monkeys with delayed sensitivity to purified protein derivative (PPD) alone, or PPD and coccidioidin, the PEC were inhibited in their migration from capillary tubes in the presence of specific antigen. These data suggest that interspecies conversion of "nonsensitive" guinea pig PEC to "sensitive" cells was accomplished with monkey RNA extracts.

The mechanism whereby isolated "immune" ribonucleic acid (RNA) extracts are able to convert "nonsensitive" immunocompetent cell populations in both humoral antibody and delayed hypersensitivity systems is under active investigation (1–5). Transplantation and tumor immunity have been used as *in vivo* assays of cellular immunity to demonstrate specific conversion by RNA of nonsensitized lymphoid cells to an immunologically reactive state (6, 7). In these experiments, the RNA and the recipient cells were derived from animals of the same species. For example, Mannick and Egdahl (6) demonstrated that rabbit RNA extracts were able to elicit a second set graft rejection in outbred rabbits. On the other hand, in some experiments, the RNA and recipient cells were derived from animals of different species (8, 9).

Thus far in our laboratory, experiments involving transfer of immunologic reactivity with RNA extracts have been done *in vitro*, and with donor RNA and recipient cells being taken from animals of the same species. Thus, extracts of RNA prepared from humans strongly skin test positive to PPD, coccidioidin, or histoplasmin have been shown to transfer specific immunologic reactivity to "nonsensitive" human lymph node cells cultured 72 hr *in vitro* as assayed by the cell migration-inhibition method (10). Similar results were observed with PPD and coccidiodin antigens when analogous experiments were done *in vitro* with peritoneal exudate cells of "nonsensitive" guinea pigs (11). Other *in vitro* assays have also been used when reporting intraspecies transfer of cellular immunity with RNA extracts (12–15). We now report that RNA extracts from the lymph nodes and spleen of rhesus monkeys skin test positive to PPD or coccidioidin can cross the species barrier and transfer PPD or coccioidin sensitivity *in vitro* to peritoneal exudate cells of "nonsensitive" guinea pigs, as assayed by the cell migration-inhibition correlate of delayed hypersensitivity.

[1] This investigation was supported by United States Public Health Service Research Grant AI-08576-01, from the National Institute of Allergy and Infectious Diseases.

[2] United States Public Health Service Postdoctoral Fellowship AM-40739-01.

MATERIALS AND METHODS

Experimental animals and sensitization. Rhesus monkeys, *Macacca mulatta*, sensitized to PPD alone, or PPD and coccidioidin were used as RNA donors. Two monkeys had been naturally infected with *Mycobacterium tuberculosis* and exhibited strongly positive skin tests 48 hr after intrapalpebral injection with 5 μg of PPD. Two monkeys were injected with coccidioidin incorporated into complete Freund's adjuvant (2 ml of a 1:100 stock dilution of coccidioidin, Cutter Laboratories, Berkeley, California, was incorporated in 2.0 ml of Freund's complete adjuvant containing 500 μg/ml of *Mycobacterium butyricum*, Difco Laboratories, Detroit, Michigan); 0.25 to 0.5 ml of the mixture was injected in each footpad and subcutaneously on the back of the neck. Three weeks later, strongly positive skin tests were obtained by intrapalpebral injection of 0.1 ml of a 1:100 stock solution of coccidioidin.

Random bred, albino Rockefeller guinea pigs

were used as the source of peritoneal exudate cells. The guinea pigs were sensitized by injection of each footpad with 0.25 ml of a mixture containing 2 mg of heat-killed *M. tuberculosis* H37 Ra (Difco Laboratories, Detroit, Mich.) dissolved in 1 ml of saline and emulsified in 1 ml of Freund's complete adjuvant containing 500 μg/ml of *M. butyricum*.

Preparation of RNA extracts. Separate pools of RNA were extracted from the lymph nodes and spleens of sensitized rhesus monkeys. The RNA extraction was carried out by a modification of the procedure described by Scherrer and Darnell (16). Lymph nodes and spleens were excised and immediately frozen on Dry Ice. Using a Virtis homogenizer, the tissues were homogenized for 10 to 15 min at 4°C in distilled phenol containing 0.1% 9-hydroxyquinoline saturated with 0.01 M NaOAc, 0.5% sodium dodecyl sulfate, and 4 μg/ml of polyvinyl sulfate. An equal volume of NaOAc containing 0.5 mg/ml of bentonite was added to the tissue homogenate. The mixture was heated to 55 to 60°C with stirring, rapidly cooled to 4°C in an ice water bath and centrifuged at 40,000 × G at 4°C for 10 min. The aqueous phase containing the RNA was removed with a Pasteur pipet and an equal amount of buffer-saturated phenol was added. The extraction was repeated three times or until the $OD_{260}:OD_{280}$ ratio ≧ 2. After the last extraction, the aqueous phase was precipitated with 95% ethanol and stored at −20°C until needed. The RNA was dissolved in 1 ml of 0.3 M NaOAc buffer and reprecipitated at least three times with 95% ethanol before use with guinea pig cells.

Collection of guinea pig peritoneal exudate cells (PEC). After the abdominal area was shaved, guinea pigs were injected intraperitoneally with 30 ml of light mineral oil. Three days later the animals were sacrificed by cervical dislocation, a small patch of skin was cut away, and a sterile trocar was inserted into the peritoneal cavity. The peritoneal cavity was washed at least three times by draining 150 to 200 ml of cold Hanks' balanced salt solution (HBSS) containing 6 units of heparin/ml from a separatory funnel connected by rubber tubing to the trocar. The rubber tubing was disconnected from the separatory funnel and the fluid from the peritoneal cavity was drained into 50-ml, siliconized, sterile glass centrifuge tubes. To obtain the PEC, the fluid was centrifuged at 140 × G for 10 to 15 min at 25°C. The PEC were then washed two to four times in cold HBSS and pooled.

Incubation of guinea pig peritoneal exudate cells with monkey RNA. Before incubating monkey RNA with "nonsensitive" guinea pig peritoneal exudate cells (NS-GP-PEC), the RNA extracts were centrifuged at 40,000 × G for 10 min at 4°C. The ethanol used to store the RNA was drawn off with a Pasteur pipet connected by rubber tubing to a suction flask. The RNA was carefully dissolved in 0.3 to 1.0 ml of HBSS without heparin. With each incubation, the $OD_{260}:OD_{280}$ ratio of the RNA was determined in a Gilford model 240 spectrophotometer and found to be ≧ 2.

Guinea pig peritoneal exudate cells (10^7 to 10^9 PEC in 0.2 to 0.5 ml of HBSS) were incubated for 20 min at 37°C in 5% CO_2 with 500 to 1600 μg of rhesus monkey RNA (Rh-RNA) and gently shaken. The PEC that were used as controls without Rh-RNA were incubated in 0.3 to 0.5 ml of HBSS only. After incubation, the RNA treated and untreated PEC were centrifuged at 140 × G for 5 min, the supernatant fluid was discarded, and the PEC were resuspended in tissue culture medium 199 containing 0.2% glutamine, 10% guinea pig serum, and 5% fetal calf serum (Grand Island Biological Co., Grand Island, N. Y.). These cells were used immediately in the capillary tube-cell migration assay.

Capillary tube-cell migration assay. The capillary tube-cell migration assay was essentially the same as that described by Jureziz, Thor and Dray (11). In these experiments, the Sykes-Moore tissue culture chambers were filled with tissue culture medium 199 (TCM-199) containing 0.2% glutamine, 10% guinea pig serum, 5% fetal calf serum, 50 μg/ml of streptomycin, and 50 units/ml of penicillin. Media to be used in appropriate chambers contained the following antigens: PPD (10 μg/ml, Parke Davis and Co., Detroit, Mich.), histoplasmin (30 μg/ml), and coccidioidin (1:100,000 final concentration of a stock 1:100 dilution, Cutter Laboratories, Berkeley, Calif.). The chambers were incubated 36 to 48 hr at 37°C. After incubation, the areas of cell migration were determined by planimetry with a Nikon 6 C comparator profile projector, and migration indices were calculated by the method of George and Vaughn (17).

TABLE I

Migration indices of guinea pig peritoneal exudate cells (PEC) in the presence of PPD after incubation of "nonsensitive" guinea pig PEC with monkey spleen RNA (SpC-RNA) or monkey lymph node RNA (LNC-RNA) from rhesus monkeys skin test sensitive to PPD

Reference		Controls				RNA-Converted PEC + Specific Antigen	
Exp. No.	PEC	PEC + PPD	PEC + SpC-RNA	PEC + LNC-RNA	PEC + SpC-RNA + Hist.	PEC + SpC-RNA + PPD	PEC + LNC-RNA + PPD
1	1.00	0.93	ND[a]	1.02	ND	ND	0.42
2	1.00	0.81	1.01	0.91	0.99	0.32	0.31
3	1.00	1.09	ND	1.08	ND	ND	0.14
4	1.00	0.87	0.99	1.05	ND	0.38	0.56
5	1.00	0.96	1.04[b]		0.89	0.57[b]	

[a] ND, not done.

[b] Pooled RNA from LNC and SpC.

RESULTS

Conversion of "nonsensitive" guinea pig peritoneal exudate cells with RNA extracted from lymph nodes and spleen of rhesus monkeys skin test "sensitive" to PPD. "Nonsensitive" guinea pig peritoneal exudate cells (NS-GP-PEC) were incubated with RNA extracts from lymph nodes and spleens of rhesus monkeys which were skin test positive to PPD. The RNA-converted NS-GP-PEC were inhibited in their migration from capillary tubes in the presence of PPD; the migration indices (MI) ranged from 0.14 to 0.57 in the experiments shown in Table I. When PPD was not present, the RNA-converted GP-PEC were not inhibited in their migration; the MI ranged from 0.91 to 1.05. The presence of a nonspecific antigen, histoplasmin, also failed to inhibit the migration; the MI were 0.89 and 0.99. As expected, the untreated PEC were not inhibited in the presence of PPD; the MI were 0.81 to 1.09 (Table I).

The RNA extracts of lymph nodes and spleen of PPD-sensitive rhesus monkeys could possibly have quantities of PPD antigen, or RNA-antigen complexes (18–20). The RNA extracts were assessed for obvious contamination with PPD by testing the ability of the RNA extracts to inhibit the migration of PPD-sensitive GP-PEC (Table II). Whereas the sensitized PEC were inhibited in their migration by 10 μg/ml of PPD (MI = 0.28 to 0.35), these same PEC were not inhibited by a nonspecific antigen (MI = 0.99 and 1.14), by the RNA extracts (MI = 0.96 to 1.10), or by RNA extracts plus a nonspecific antigen (MI = 1.01 and 1.21) (Table II).

Conversion of "nonsensitive" guinea pig peritoneal exudate cells with RNA extracted from lymph nodes of rhesus monkeys skin test "sensitive" to coccidioidin and PPD. To further evaluate the specificity of the RNA conversion, monkeys sensitive to coccidioidin as well as to PPD were used. The NS-GP-PEC were incubated with the RNA extracted from the lymph nodes of these monkeys (Rh-LNC-RNA). As shown in Figure 1, for one experiment with one pool of NS-GP-PEC, these RNA-treated cells were inhibited in their migration from capillary tubes in the presence of coccidioidin (MI = 0.31) or PPD (MI = 0.52), but not by histoplasmin (MI = 1.24) or in the absence of antigen (MI = 1.21). The untreated NS-GP-PEC were not inhibited by any of the antigens (histoplasmin MI = 1.10, coccidioidin MI = 1.01, and PPD MI = 0.94).

Similar results were observed in two other experiments. Inhibition of migration was seen when coccidioidin was added to NS-GP-PEC + Rh-LNC-RNA (the coccidioidin MI = 0.39 and 0.23). When PPD was present, inhibition was seen in one of these experiments (MI = 0.37), but was inconclusive in the other experiment (MI = 0.70). No inhibition was observed in controls without antigen (MI = 1.09 and 0.75) or in untreated NS-GP-PEC in the presence of antigen (PPD MI = 0.91 and 0.88, coccidioidin MI = 0.88 and 0.73.

TABLE II

Migration indices of PPD "sensitive" guinea pig peritoneal exudate cells (PEC) incubated with monkey lymph node RNA extracted from rhesus monkeys which are skin test positive to PPD

Exp. No.	Sensitized PEC Alone	Sensitized PEC + PPD[a]	Sensitized PEC + Hist.	Sensitized PEC + LNC-RNA	Sensitized PEC + Rh-SP-RNA + Hist.
1	1.00	0.28	0.99	0.96	1.21
2	1.00	0.34		1.10	
3	1.00	0.35	1.14	1.09	1.01

[a] Skin tests of guinea pigs used in experiment 1 were 10 mm by 11 mm; experiment 2, 12 mm by 14 mm; and experiment 3, 8 mm by 10 mm.

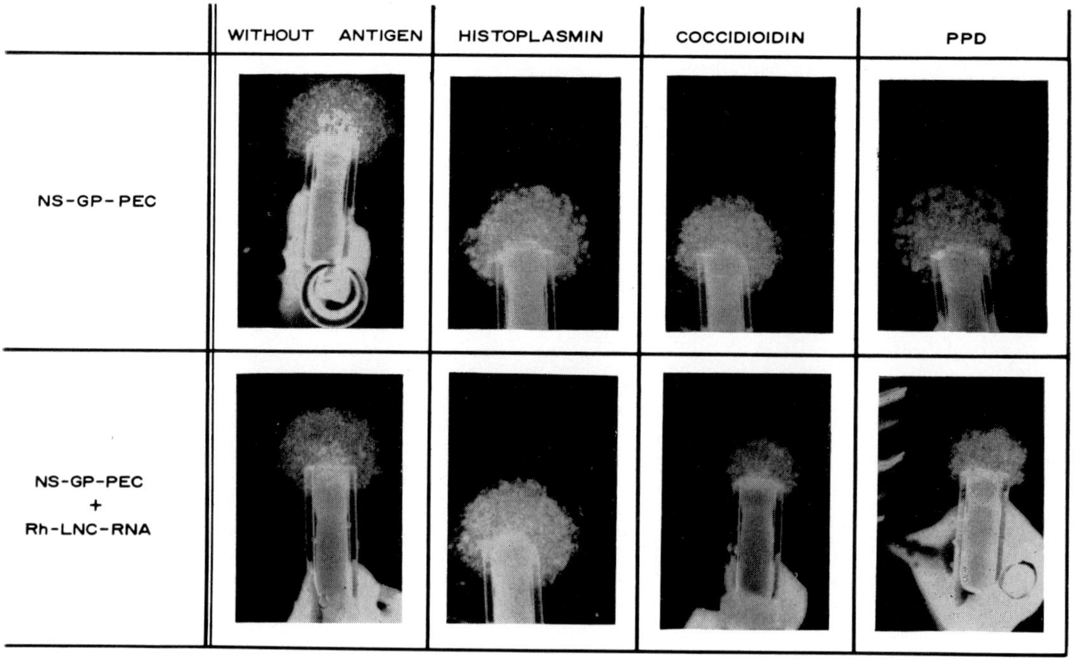

Figure 1. Capillary tube migration: *Top row,* NS-GP-PEC incubated in the presence of histoplasmin (MI = 1.10), coccidioidin (MI = 1.01) and PPD (MI = 0.94). *Second row,* NS-GP-PEC incubated with rhesus monkey lymph node RNA (Rh-LNC-RNA) alone (MI = 1.21), in the presence of histoplasmin (MI = 1.24), coccidioidin (MI = 0.31) and PPD (MI = 0.52).

DISCUSSION

Our results indicate that RNA extracted from lymphoid cells of rhesus monkeys (Rh-RNA) sensitized to PPD or coccidioidin are able to convert PEC of guinea pigs to an immunologically reactive state as indicated by their migration inhibition in the presence of the specific antigen. In the absence of specific antigen, or the presence of a nonspecific antigen, the Rh-RNA-converted GP-PEC were not inhibited in their migration.

One explanation for the activity of these RNA extracts is that RNA-antigen complexes are present which act as potent immunogens, and thus, are able to sensitize lymphoid cells *in vitro.* The "super antigen" concept is supported by the data of several investigators who have reported the presence of antigen, or antigen fragments in RNA extracted from immunized animals (18–20). In our experiments the Rh-RNA was not analyzed for the presence of antigen; however, incubation of 500 to 1500 μg of "PPD-sensitive" Rh-RNA with PPD-sensitive GP-PEC failed to inhibit their migration. Thor and Dray (10) also reported that PPD-sensitive human lymph node cells cultured 72 hr *in vitro* were not inhibited in the presence of "PPD-sensitive" human RNA. Although the amount of antigen in the RNA extracts was insufficient to be detected by cell migration inhibition, the possibility that sufficient antigen was present for sensitization *in vitro* cannot be excluded. In addition, these RNA extracts were susceptible to RNAse which indicated that intact RNA was necessary for conversion (10).

The requirement for intact RNA suggests that the RNA itself has an informational role and utilizes the biosynthetic machinery of the "nonsensitive" cell to direct the synthesis of a factor, e.g., possibly migration inhibition factor (21–23) which accounts for the inhibition of migration of GP-PEC. Moreover, recent work in the rabbit by Adler, Fishman and Dray (1) and Bell and Dray (2) in an antibody system suggests that RNA may indeed have an informational role. In rabbits, IgM antibody (1, 2) as well as IgG antibody (24) produced by recipient spleen cells possess the allotypic specificity of the RNA donor.

Thus, although it is easier to accept the idea that one species of lymphoid cells could be actively sensitized by an RNA-antigen complex from another species, these RNA extracts may also have an information role in our delayed hypersensitivity experiments (11). McCarthy (25) reports that mammalian ribosomal RNA's from widely different species are easily hybridized and are quite similar in their base composition, although our RNA extracts probably contain much more than ribosomal RNA. Clarification of the mechanism for the activity of the RNA extracts might evolve with the isolation and characterization of specific RNA responsible for conversion, or possibly when the effector molecules (21–23) in delayed hypersensitivity are isolated and genetic markers for them are found.

Species barriers apparently do not exist in a number of systems where delayed hypersensitivity is assessed. Baram and Condoulis (26) report that monkey "transfer factor," which may or may not include an RNA moiety, is able to sensitize human lymphocytes *in vitro*. Ramming and Pilch (9) have reported that tumor isografts in mice are inhibited *in vivo* by injection of syngeneic mouse spleen cells incubated *in vitro* with RNA extracted from guinea pigs immunized with mouse tumor. Alexander *et al.* (8) also reported partial tumor regression in rats receiving footpad injections of RNA extracts from sheep immunized with rat sarcoma.

Our results are consistent with previous observations whereby RNA from one species apparently can confer immunologic reactivity on immunocompetent lymphoid cells of another species. That primate RNA is effective in converting lymphoid cells of another species may present important consequences in present day methods of immunization, immunotherapy of tumors, transplantation and immunosuppression in man.

Acknowledgments. The authors wish to extend grateful thanks to Suzanne Starn for excellent technical assistance, and to Dr. Leon Le Beau for taking the photographs.

REFERENCES

1. Adler, F. L., Fishman, M. and Dray, S., J. Immun., *97:* 554, 1966.
2. Bell, C. and Dray, S., J. Immun., *103:* 1196, 1969.
3. Fishman, M., J. Exp. Med., *114:* 837, 1967.
4. Mitsuhashi, S., and Sato, K., J. Bact., *84:* 592, 1962.
5. Spiers, R. S., Science, *140:* 71, 1963.
6. Mannick, J. A. and Egdahl, R. N., Ann. Surg. *156:* 356, 1962.
7. Sabbadini, E. and Sehon, A. H., Int. Arch. Allerg., *32:* 55, 1967.
8. Alexander, P., Delorme, E. J., Hamilton, L. O. G. and Hall, J. G., Nature, *213:* 569, 1967.
9. Ramming, K. P. and Pilch, Y. H., Science, *168:* 492, 1970.
10. Thor, D. E. and Dray, S., J. Immun., *101:* 459, 1968.
11. Jureziz, R. E., Thor, D. E. and Dray, S., J. Immun., *101:* 823, 1968.
12. Lolekha, S., Dray, S. and Gotoff, S. P., J. Reticuloendothel. Soc., *7:* 649, 1970.
13. Wilson, D. B. and Wecker, E. E., J. Immun., *97:* 512, 1966.
14. Gerughty, R. M., Rosenau, W. and Moon, H. D., J. Immun., *97:* 700, 1966.
15. Thor, D. E. and Schlossman, S., Fed. Proc., *28:* 629, 1969.
16. Scherrer, K. and Darnell, J. E., Biochem. Biophys. Res. Comm., *7:* 486, 1962.
17. George, M. and Vaughan, J. H., Proc. Soc. Exp. Biol. Med., *111:* 514, 1962.
18. Gottlieb, A. A., J. Reticuloendothel. Soc., *5:* 270, 1968.
19. Campbell, D. H. and Garvey, J. S., Immunology, *3:* 261, 1963.
20. Friedman, H. P., Stavitsky, A. B. and Solomon, J. M., Science, *149:* 1106, 1965.
21. Bennet, B. and Bloom, B. R., Transplantation, *5:* 996, 1967.
22. Ruddle, N. H. and Waksman, B. H., Science, *157:* 1060, 1967.
23. Granger, G. A. and Kolb, W. P., J. Immun., *101:* 111, 1968.
24. Bell, C. and Dray, S., J. Immun., *105:* 541, 1970.
25. McCarthy, B. J., *Progress in Nucleic Acid Acid Research and Molecular Biology*, Vol. 4, pp. 144–145, Academic Press, New York, 1966.
26. Baram, P. and Condoulis, W., J. Immun., *104:* 769, 1970.

THE JOURNAL OF IMMUNOLOGY
Vol. 105, No. 6, December 1970

THYMUS DEPENDENCY OF THE IMMUNE RESPONSE TO HEMOCYANIN: AN EVALUATION OF THE ROLE OF MACROPHAGES IN THYMECTOMIZED MICE[1]

EMIL R. UNANUE[2]

From the Department of Experimental Pathology, Scripps Clinic and Research Foundation, La Jolla, California

Received for publication August 3, 1970

The role of the thymus in the immune response to keyhole limpet hemocyanin (KLH) was studied in the mouse. Adult mice were thymectomized, lethally irradiated and reconstituted with bone marrow cells. The immune response to KLH was greatly impaired by thymectomy. Only some thymectomized mice could respond to large doses of KLH but in low amounts. The thymectomized mice did not respond to KLH bound to live macrophages nor to KLH administered simultaneously with an adjuvant like beryllium. Macrophages from both thymectomized and control mice handled KLH similarly.

That the thymus may influence the induction of an immune response to allogeneic grafts and to some foreign red cells, proteins, bacteria and viruses is a well established fact (1–4). This influence is best shown in murine species by studying either neonatally thymectomized mice (1) or adult thymectomized mice that are lethally irradiated (and protected by transplantation of syngeneic cells from the bone marrow) (5). The role of the thymus is believed to be enacted by lymphocytes that migrate into lymphoid organs and form part of the recirculating pool of cells (6, 7). Thymus cells apparently proliferate upon interaction with antigen (9, 10), do not synthesize antibodies (8), but help, in some undetermined way, the immunocompetent cells derived from the bone marrow for the formation of antibody (8; reviewed in 11, 12). Whether the thymus influences the immune response to all antigens and, if so, the extent of thymus dependency among different immunogens, is not known. To obtain answers to these important considerations we may have to evaluate the influence of the thymus in the immune response to antigens that vary in form, physicochemical composition, immunogenic strength, etc.

In the present paper, the role of the thymus in the immunologic response of the mouse to the hemocyanin from *Megathura crenulata* (keyhole limpet hemocyanin, KLH) is reported. We thought that perhaps the response to KLH, a relatively strong immunogen, might not depend greatly upon thymic function. However, KLH proved to be a markedly "thymus-dependent" antigen. Thymectomized mice responded poorly to KLH unless they were reconstituted with thymus cells. Immunization with KLH, whether administered in large doses, combined with an adjuvant like beryllium or bound to live macrophages, did not heighten significantly the poor immune response of the thymectomized mice.

Additionally, the capacity of macrophages from normal and thymectomized mice to handle and carry KLH to immunocompetent cells of normal mice has been evaluated in this study. Since macrophages appear to be one of the targets of cell-mediated immunities that are highly influenced by the thymus, perhaps a defect in the handling of KLH by macrophages of thymectomized mice would be observed. However, the capacity of macrophages from thymectomized mice to take up KLH and to interact with immunocompetent cells was not impaired.

[1] This is publication 427 from the Department of Experimental Pathology, Scripps Clinic and Research Foundation, La Jolla, California 92037. This work was supported by United States Public Health Service Grant AI 07007 and a Tuberculosis and Respiratory Disease Association of California Grant-in-Aid.

[2] Dr. Unanue is a Senior Fellow of the American Cancer Society (California Division).

MATERIALS AND METHODS

Mice. A/St, CBA/St and (CBA × A)F1 from Strong Research Laboratories, San Diego, Calif., of either sex were used in the different experiments.

Antigen. The antigen was the hemocyanin from *Megathura crenulata* (keyhole limpets, KLH), in its associated form of about 7.5 × 10^6 molecular weight (13).

Antibody determinations. An antigen-binding capacity test (Farr) using a coprecipitation method with rabbit anti-mouse Ig sera was used. The rabbit anti-mouse Ig sera precipitated all known classes of mouse Ig. The details of this assay have been published previously (13). Radioiodinated (^{125}I) KLH was used as the antigen. Iodination was made by a chloramine T procedure (14) to a specificity of about 1 μCi/μg. The dilution of antisera that binds 33% of the KLH (0.4 μg KLH N per reaction test) was taken as the end point (ABC-33). Titers are expressed as μg of KLH N bound per milliliter of undiluted serum. The percentage of KLH bound at a 1:2 dilution of serum is reported whenever the degree of binding of KLH to serum is too low to calculate an ABC-33 value.

Protocol for studying the immune response to KLH in thymectomized and sham thymectomized mice. Mice of 8 to 12 weeks of age were thymectomized and after 2 weeks were given 850 R of whole body x-irradiation followed immediately by an intraperitoneal (i.p.) injection of syngeneic bone marrow cells (usually 5 to 10 × 10^6). Four weeks later the mice were immunized with KLH i.p. (from 1 μg to 3 mg in different experiments); 2 to 4 weeks later mice were bled and a secondary challenge usually of 50 μg of KLH i.p. was then administered. Mice were bled again 7 and 14 days later and then sacrificed and autopsied. Remnants of thymus were investigated by gross and histologic analysis. About 5% of the mice had thymus remnants. The data on these mice have been omitted from the study. Control studies were performed on mice treated in the same way except that at surgery the thymus was not removed (sham thymectomy). Mortality varied from 25 to 50%. The surviving mice were healthy and gained as much weight as normal mice.

The primary response of mice to KLH is usually poor, but upon a second challenge a brisk anamnestic response is easily attained. Usually there is a 2-fold increase in the secondary ABC-33 titer for every 10-fold increase in antigen when priming with 1 to about 500 μg of KLH (and boosting always with 50 μg). There is little increase in the antibody titer (primary or secondary) when priming with more than 500 μg.

Cells. Bone marrow cells were obtained from tibia and femur of 6- to 8-week-old mice. Thymus or spleen cells were harvested by gentle teasing under sterile conditions. Macrophages were obtained from the peritoneal cavity of mice three days after an i.p. injection of 1.5 ml of 10% proteose-peptone (Difco Laboratories, Detroit, Mich.) (15). The peritoneal exudates contained 10^7 cells, three-fourths of which were typical macrophages.

Experiments with macrophages. Thymectomized and sham thymectomized mice were immunized with KLH bound to live macrophages from normal syngeneic mice. The exact details of the live macrophage transfer system have been given previously (13, 15). In essence, the macrophages were obtained from the peritoneal cavity of normal mice and exposed to associated ^{125}I KLH *in vitro*. A suspension of 30 × 10^6 macrophages was incubated with 1 mg of ^{125}I-KLH, for 1 hr, in 6 ml of Eagle's minimum essential medium (Grand Island Biological Co., Berkeley, Calif., catalogue 109G). After several washes the content of ^{125}I-KLH in the live cells was determined in a gamma ray spectrometer. The cells were injected, i.p., into mice which were boosted 3 weeks later with 50 μg of KLH i.p. and then bled for determination of the secondary antibody response.

In other experiments the handling and immunogenicity of KLH by macrophages from thymectomized and sham thymectomized mice was evaluated. The peritoneal macrophages were obtained from mice 2 weeks after lethal irradiation and bone marrow reconstitution. The macrophages were exposed to KLH for 1 hr, as described above, washed and transferred into normal mice which were then studied immunologically.

Adjuvants. The effect of an adjuvant like beryllium sulphate (Be salt) (16) on the response of the thymectomized mice to KLH was evaluated. One hundred micrograms of Be salt (0.5 ml in 0.9% NaCl) was given i.p. with 10 μg of KLH. Four weeks later a secondary challenge

TABLE I

The immune response of thymectomized and sham thymectomized A/St mice to KLH[a]

KLH	No. of BMC[b]	Secondary Antibody Response			
		Thymectomized		Sham thymectomized	
		Responder/total	Antibody titer (geometric mean) μg KLH N/ml	Responder/total	Antibody titer (geometric mean) μg KLH N/ml
200 μg 4 weeks apart	10^7	4/8	3.9 (1.2–23.0)[c]	9/9	239 (22–614)
1 μg followed 4 weeks later with 50 μg	5×10^6	2/7	(<1 and 6.0)	6/6	4.5 (1.0–17.0)
1 μg followed 4 weeks later with 50 μg	50×10^6	0/4		11/11	20.8 (4.0–76)
1 μg together with 100 μg Be salt followed 4 weeks later with 50 μg	5×10^6	1/9	(5.8)	ND[d]	ND

[a] Thymectomized and sham thymectomized mice were given 850 R of whole body x-irradiation followed by bone marrow cells. Four weeks later the mice were immunized as described. The titers represent a secondary response.

[b] BMC, bone marrow cells.

[c] Figures in parentheses show the range of values.

[d] ND, not done.

with 50 μg i.p. was administered, and the mice were subsequently tested for their secondary antibody response. One hundred micrograms of Be salt, which is the optimal dose, enhances the response to KLH about 10- to 20-fold in normal mice. (J. R. Schmidtke and E. R. Unanue, unpublished results.)

RESULTS AND DISCUSSION

Mice that were sham thymectomized, irradiated with a lethal dose of x-rays and reconstituted with 5 to 10 $\times$ 10^6 bone marrow cells were capable of responding immunologically to KLH given 4 to 8 weeks following irradiation. Two weeks after irradiation the response was about one-half of that present at 4 weeks. The immune response of these irradiated and reconstituted mice was as strong as that of normal untreated mice. In contrast, thymectomized mice treated in the same way, i.e., irradiated and transplanted with bone marrow, responded very poorly. The number of thymectomized mice that responded immunologically varied among several experiments from 0 to approximately 50%; however, the titer of the responding mice (except in few occasional mice) was at the most about one-fifth that of the sham thymectomized mice. Representative experiments are shown in Table I and Figure 1. In the experiment shown in Figure 1 the initial immunizing dose of KLH was varied from 3 μg to 3 mg. (In the case of the immune response to sheep red cells, the difference in response between thymectomized and normal mice was reduced as the dose of antigen was increased (4, 17).) The dose of KLH had some effect, albeit small, on the response of thymectomized mice. Note that in one experiment of Table I the number of bone marrow cells injected after irradiation was increased to 50 $\times$ 10^6 without any appreciable effect on the capacity of thymectomized mice to respond to KLH. The number of bone marrow cells, however, did make a difference in the extent of the response of the sham thymectomized mice.

Macrophage bound KLH. KLH was administered to thymectomized and sham thymectomized mice in live macrophages. The macrophages were obtained from the peritoneal cavity of normal A/St mice previously injected i.p. with peptone and exposed *in vitro* to KLH. Both groups, thymectomized and sham thymectomized, received 6 $\times$ 10^6 macrophages containing 3 μg of

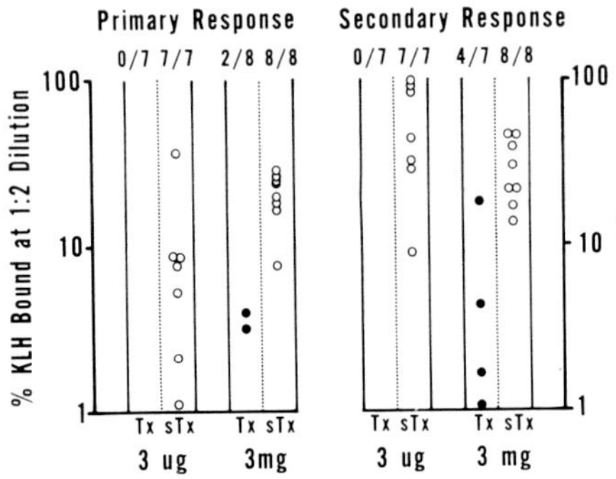

Figure 1. (CBA × A)F1 thymectomized (Tx) and sham thymectomized (sTx) mice were immunized with 3 μg or 3 mg of KLH; 3 weeks later all mice were challenged with 50 μg i.p. Primary antibody studies were made 21 days after immunization. Each symbol represents the antibody titer of individual mice. The number of mice making antibody over the total mice in a group is represented at the top of each column. Primary antibody titers are given as the percentage of KLH bound at 1:2 dilution of sera; secondary antibody titers are given as ABC-33 values.

KLH followed 3 weeks later by a secondary challenge of 50 μg of free KLH. In this transfer system some of the injected macrophages migrate into the spleen and can initiate an immune response, apparently, by presenting non-pinocytosed antigen to the immunocompetent cells (13).

The immune defect of the thymectomized mice was not corrected by presenting the KLH in macrophages. All five sham thymectomized mice made an immune response to KLH bound in live macrophages with a mean secondary antibody titer of 3.9, while none of the seven thymectomized mice made a detectable antibody response.

The handling of KLH by macrophages from both sham thymectomized and thymectomized mice was evaluated. Macrophages from thymectomized mice could take up KLH as effectively as normal macrophages (1.0% *vs* 1.3% of the KLH after 1 hr of *in vitro* culture). A/St mice received 2 μg of KLH in 6 × 10^6 macrophages from either normal or thymectomized mice and were boosted 3 weeks later with 50 μg of free KLH i.p. The nine normal mice that received KLH in live macrophages from normal donors responded with a mean secondary titer of 5.4. The seven mice that received the same amount of KLH, but in macrophages obtained from thymectomized mice, responded with a titer of 4.9 which was not statistically different from the above group. Hence, we did not find abnormalities in the handling of an antigen like KLH by macrophages which would satisfactorily explain the hyporesponsiveness of thymectomized mice.

Adjuvants. Neonatally thymectomized mice can be made to respond to some antigens if these are administered with immunologic adjuvants (18). In one experiment, the thymectomized mice were given Be salt, a potent adjuvant that may carry some of its effect by stimulating macrophages (16). Thymectomized mice, however, immunized with KLH and Be salt were as unresponsive as those immunized only with KLH (Table I).

Reconstitution with thymus cells. Injection of thymocytes reconstituted the immune response of the thymectomized mice. Reconstitution was shown most clearly when thymocytes were injected together with the KLH 4 weeks after lethal irradiation and bone marrow transplant (Table II).

Amounts of KLH in the spleen of thymectomized mice. About 100 μg of ^{125}I-KLH were administered i.p. into each of 3 normal and 3 thymectomized A/St mice; the mice were sacrificed the next day, at which time blood radioactivity was negligible, and the amount of radioactivity in the spleen was determined. Both normal and thymectomized mice had comparable amounts of radioactivity in the spleen (0.05 to 0.1%).

TABLE II

Reconstitution of thymectomized A/St mice with thymocytes[a]

Treatment	Thymocytes	Secondary Antibody Response: Responder/total	Secondary Antibody Response: Antibody titer geometric mean (range) (μg KLH N bound/ml of serum)
Thymectomy	No	1/5	1.6
Thymectomy	10^8	5/5	181 (129–273)
Sham thymectomy		12/12	101 (92–430)

[a] Thymectomized and sham thymectomized mice received 850 R of whole body x-irradiation followed by 10^7 bone marrow cells. All mice received 50 μg of KLH i.p. twice, 1 month apart, starting 4 weeks after irradiation. The titers of antibody represent the secondary response. One group of thymectomized mice received 10^8 thymus cells, i.p., together with the first injection of KLH.

In essence, the induction of an immune response by the mouse to a large protein antigen like KLH is markedly dependent upon the presence of a thymus. Thymocytes could restore completely the immunocompetence of thymectomized mice. Two points should be analyzed briefly. First, results suggest that the deficiency of the thymectomized mice was not associated with a defective system for trapping antigen. Clearly the spleens from both normal and thymectomized mice took up comparable amounts of KLH and, furthermore, large doses of KLH (which might have overridden a deficient antigen trapping system) had a relatively small effect on the immune response of the thymectomized mice. Hence, the function of thymocytes may be other than effective transportation of antigen to bone marrow-derived lymphocytes in the antibody-forming organs. Second, in thymectomized mice there was no indication of a functional impairment of macrophages when handling KLH. Furthermore, thymectomized mice failed to respond to KLH either bound to live macrophages or administered together with a potent stimulator of the reticuloendothelial system (beryllium). One must conclude that the interaction of KLH bound to live macrophages with bone marrow-derived lymphocytes would not be sufficient to initiate an immune response unless thymus-derived lymphocytes were also present. Perhaps one role of macrophages in the inductive process of immunity may be to favor the meeting of thymus and bone marrow-derived lymphocytes with antigen. The chances of interaction of two classes of lymphocytes, which presumably are genetically selected and few in number, with the few molecules of antigen that escape catabolism must be quite small. The macrophages favor the cell-antigen interactions since 1) many are situated in the areas of traffic of cells in the lymphoid tissues and 2) they can concentrate and hold a few molecules of antigen on their plasma membrane for relatively long periods of time (13).

Acknowledgments. We thank Dr. Sun Lee for performing most of the thymectomies and for teaching us the technique, and Miss Roberta Coss and Miss Rosemarie Peña for excellent technical assistance.

REFERENCES

1. Miller, J. F. A. P., Proc. Roy. Soc. Ser. B., *156:* 415, 1962.
2. Papermaster, B. W., Dalmasso, A. P., Martinez, C. and Good, R. A., Proc. Soc. Exp. Biol. Med., *111:* 41, 1962.
3. Martinez, C., Dalmasso, A. P. and Good R. A., Nature, *194:* 1289, 1962.
4. Taylor, R. B., Nature, *199:* 873, 1963.
5. Leuchars, E., Cross, A. M. and Dukor, P., Transplantation, *3:* 28, 1965.
6. Miller, J. F. A. P. and Osoba, D., Physiol. Rev., *47:* 437, 1967.
7. Weissman, I. L., J. Exp. Med., *126:* 291, 1967.
8. Mitchell, G. F. and Miller, J. F. A. P., J. Exp. Med., *128:* 821, 1968.
9. Davies, A. J. S., Leuchars, E., Wallis, V. and Koller, P. C., Transplantation, *4:* 438, 1966.
10. Davies, A. J. S., Leuchars, E., Wallis, V., Merchant, R. and Elliot, E. V., Transplantation, *5:* 222, 1967.
11. Miller, J. F. A. P. and Mitchell, G. F., Transplantation Rev., *1:* 3, 1969.
12. Claman, A. N. and Chaperon, E. A., Transplantation Rev., *1:* 92, 1969.
13. Unanue, E. R. and Cerottini, J.-C., J. Exp. Med., *131:* 711, 1970.
14. McConahey, P. J. and Dixon, F. J., Int. Arch. Allerg., *29:* 189, 1966.
15. Unanue, E. R. and Askonas, B. A., Immunology, *15:* 287, 1968.
16. Unanue, E. R., Askonas, B. A. and Allison, A. C., J. Immun., *103:* 71, 1969.
17. Sinclair, N. R. St. C. and Elliot, E. V., Immunology, *15:* 325, 1968.
18. Cone, R. E. and Johnson, A. G., Bact. Proc., p. 91, 1970.

THE JOURNAL OF IMMUNOLOGY
Vol. 105, No. 6, December 1970
Printed in U.S.A.

BIOLOGICAL AND CHEMICAL PROPERTIES OF NATURAL ANTIBODIES IN THE NURSE SHARK[1]

STUART RUDIKOFF, EDWARD W. VOSS[2] AND M. MICHAEL SIGEL

From the Department of Microbiology, University of Miami School of Medicine, Miami, Florida, the University of Illinois, Urbana, Illinois and the Lerner Marine Laboratory, Bimini, Bahamas

Received for publication July 29, 1970

Immunoglobulin was purified from serum of the nurse shark by gel filtration and ion exchange chromatography. The purified immunoglobulin was used in a mixed agglutination assay by sensitizing chicken or pigeon erythrocytes and reacting the sensitized cells with unsensitized erythrocytes from other species. Strong positive reactions were obtained with erythrocytes from several species.

Further studies revealed the presence of a natural antibody to DNP. The antibody activity was associated primarily with 19S immunoglobulin and was characterized by low affinity. Although it did not bind to a DNP immunoadsorbent, it could be adsorbed following precipitation with DNP-BSA (bovine serum albumin). Enzymatic digestion yielded 5S subunits which showed the same DNP-binding activity as the intact molecule. Antibody purified by precipitation with DNP-BSA was found to agglutinate red blood cells and bind guanosine monophosphate.

Normal nurse shark serum has been previously reported to react with a wide variety of antigens including viruses, bacteria, erythrocytes from many species and DNP-conjugated proteins (1, 2). This wide range of reactivity raises the question as to whether the activity is due to the presence of a large number of antibody molecules with different specificities or a smaller number of molecules capable of reacting with several antigens. This report is concerned with a characterization of this activity and the molecules involved in this system.

MATERIALS AND METHODS

Sera. Normal nurse shark sera was obtained as previously described by Clem *et al.* (3).

Fractionation of normal immunoglobulin. Fractionation and chromatography buffers consisted of 0.005 M phosphate buffer, pH 7.4, containing sodium chloride at various ionic strengths. Ascending Sephadex G-200 gel filtration was performed on a 10-cm x 100-cm column at 4°C. Chromatography buffer was used at an ionic strength of 0.21. The flow rate was maintained at 140 to 150 ml/hr and 20-ml fractions were collected.

DEAE-cellulose chromatography was performed at room temperature on 2.5-cm x 40-cm columns. Protein was eluted with an increasing salt gradient prepared in a Buchler Varigrad. Starting buffer was used at an ionic strength of 0.04 with limit buffer at an ionic strength of 0.5.

Serologic assays. Activity to sheep erythrocytes was determined by a microtiter hemagglutination assay. One volume of sample was diluted in one volume of 0.02 M EDTA-saline. An additional two volumes of diluent were added followed by one volume of sheep E (1×10^8) in gelatin-Veronal buffer containing Ca^{++} and Mg^{++} (4). Plates were shaken for 10 min at 30°C and then allowed to settle at room temperature.

Mixed agglutination assays were employed to study the range of erythrocyte activity. Chicken or pigeon erythrocytes were sensitized with purified immunoglobulin by incubation at 30°C for 60 min and overnight in the cold. The sensitized erythrocytes were then washed three times in cold buffer and resuspended to approximately 1×10^8 cells/ml. The sensitized cells

[1] This investigation was supported by United States Public Health Service Research Grants AI-05758 and AI-08288 from the National Institute of Allergy and Infectious Diseases. Part of the equipment used was purchased with funds provided by the American Cancer Society, Florida Division, Inc.

[2] Present address: Department of Microbiology, University of Illinois, Urbana, Illinois.

were mixed with unsensitized erythrocytes from a variety of species and incubated at 30°C for 30 min and then 0°C for 30 min. Samples were removed and observed microscopically for mixed agglutination.

Preparation of antigens. DNP- and TNP-conjugated proteins were prepared as described by Eisen (5). Acetylated bovine serum albumin (BSA) was prepared by reacting BSA, pH 9.0, with acetic anhydride in approximately 100 molar excess of the number of substitutable lysine residues.

Forssman antigen was kindly supplied by Dr. R. A. Fugmann. The antigen was prepared from a methanol extract of horse kidney.

Purification of natural antibody to DNP. Ten milliliters of heat-inactivated (56°C, 30 min) normal serum were mixed with 10 ml DNP-BSA (4 mg/ml) and incubated for 60 min at 37°C and overnight in the cold. The precipitate was removed and washed three times in cold, 0.05 M phosphate buffer, pH 8.0. The antibody was eluted from the precipitate with 0.1 M DNP hapten and the elution mixture applied to a DEAE-Dowex chromatography column. The bottom layer (2 cm x 5 cm) consisted of Dowex 1-X8 (J. T. Baker Chemical Co.) and the top layer (2 cm x 10 cm) DEAE-cellulose. Columns were equilibrated in 0.1 M phosphate buffer, pH 8.0.

Purification of normal rabbit immunoglobulin. Normal rabbit sera was precipitated three times with 25% sodium sulfate at final concentrations of 18, 14 and 12.5%. Precipitates were dissolved in saline borate buffer, pH 8.0, and then dialyzed against 0.175 M phosphate buffer, pH 6.9. The material was then applied to a DEAE-cellulose column equilibrated in the dialysis buffer.

Preparation of immunoadsorbent. DNP immunoadsorbent was prepared as described by Robbins *et al.* (6) and modified according to the method of Gallagher and Voss (7).

Ultracentrifugation. Analytical ultracentrifugation was performed as previously described (8). Samples were dissolved in 0.05 M phosphate buffer, pH 8.0. Rotor speed was 44,700 rpm.

Polyacrylamide gel electrophoresis. Polyacrylamide gel electrophoresis was performed according to the method of Ornstein (9) and Davis (10).

Equilibrium dialysis. Equilibrium dialysis was performed as described by Voss *et al.* (8).

Preparation of rabbit antisera. Antisera to whole shark serum and shark immunoglobulin were prepared as previously described (4). Initial antiserum to nurse shark immunoglobulin was kindly supplied by Dr. L. W. Clem. Subsequent antisera were raised by giving rabbits two injections of purified immunoglobulin incorporated in Freund's adjuvant or were purchased from Kallestad Laboratories, Inc., Minneapolis, Minn.

Immunoelectrophoresis. Immunoelectrophoresis was performed as described by Jensen (4). Slides were coated with 1% agarose in barbital buffer, pH 8.6, and runs were made for 45 to 60 min.

Ouchterlony analysis. Double diffusion in agar was performed in 1% Noble agar in phosphate-buffered saline, pH 7.4.

EXPERIMENTAL RESULTS

Purification of immunoglobulin. Normal nurse shark serum was fractionated by Sephadex G-200 gel filtration. The elution profile contained three protein peaks as has been reported previously by Clem *et al.* (3). Fractions from the first peak containing the highest HA activity for sheep erythrocytes were pooled, concentrated and applied to DEAE-cellulose columns equilibrated in 0.005 M phosphate buffer, ionic strength 0.04, pH 7.4. The protein was eluted with an increasing salt gradient and the major protein peak containing the HA activity was found to elute between 0.08 M and 0.12 M NaCl.

Immunoelectrophoresis of the concentrated DEAE protein peak containing HA activity using a rabbit anti-whole nurse shark serum reagent revealed a single protein component which was identified as IgM in agar diffusion with a specific antisera. This preparation will be referred to as purified immunoglobuiin fraction.

Mixed agglutination assays. The purified immunoglobulin fraction was found to agglutinate a variety of erythrocytes. In order to determine whether the diverse hemagglutinating activity was associated with separate molecules or was resident in single molecules, a mixed erythrocyte agglutination assay was employed. Chicken or pigeon erythrocytes were sensitized with purified immunoglobulin and then thoroughly washed to remove unbound protein. The sensitized cells were reacted with unsensitized erythrocytes from a variety of species and observed microscopically for mixed agglutination. Figure 1 depicts mixed agglutination observed with sheep and manatee erythrocytes as indicator cells. Similar results were obtained with human O erythrocytes, but

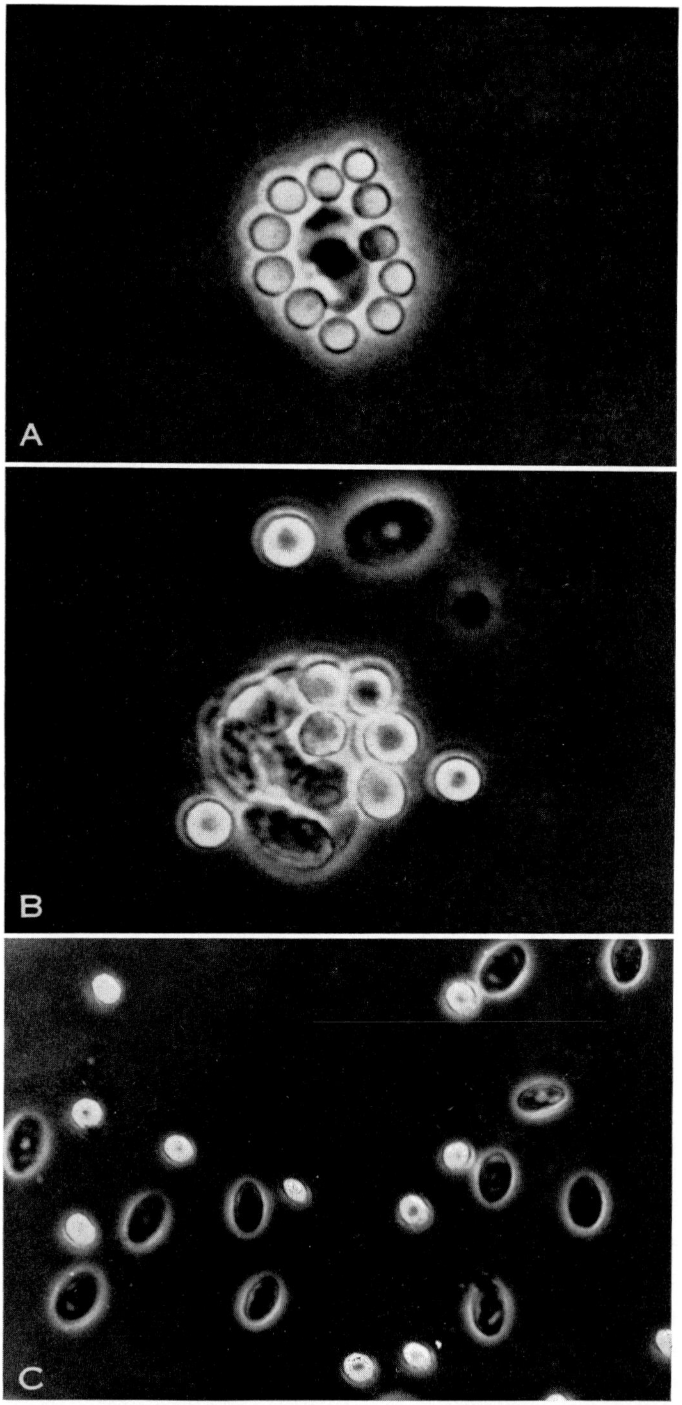

Figure. 1. A (*upper*), mixed agglutination of chicken and sheep erythrocytes; B (*center*), mixed agglutination of chicken and manatee erythrocytes; C (*lower*), control of unsensitized chicken and manatee erythrocytes.

only a very weak reaction was observed with rabbit erythrocytes as indicator cells. The positive mixed agglutination reaction could have resulted from aggregation of antibody molecules. This possibility was considered unlikely because ultracentrifuge studies (see below) have failed to demonstrate molecules with sedimentation coefficients greater than 19S. Other alternative explanations are the presence of multiple reactive sites on the same antibody molecule or the recognition by the shark natural antibody of antigens shared by the various cells. One such antigen may be the classical Forssman substance and the difference observed with Forssman positive and Forssman negative cells may be relevant to this point. A further possibility would be the assembly of $F(ab)_2$ subunits with different specificities into 19S molecules. This seems unlikely in that essentially all of the $F(ab)_2$ subunits prepared by pepsin digestion of natural antibody to DNP (see below) demonstrated DNP-binding activity.

Absorption of immunoglobulin with Forssman antigen. In order to assess the role of Forssman antigen in the wide range of reactivity, experiments were conducted employing Forssman antigen extracted from horse kidney. Purified immunoglobulin was incubated with the antigen for 60 min at 37°C and then overnight in the cold. The antibody-antigen complexes were removed by centrifugation and the supernatant was titrated along with a sample of the starting material. Results of an absorption experiment are presented in Table I. As can be readily seen, the titers to sheep, pigeon, and human O and A erythrocytes were drastically reduced by the Forssman absorption. Rabbit erythrocytes which are known to be Forssman negative were titrated as a control and no decrease in titer was found after absorption.

Precipitation of normal serum with DNP and TNP conjugated proteins. Further studies with normal sera revealed that a precipitate was formed upon the addition of DNA-BSA. BSA alone caused no precipitation, but TNP-BSA produced a similar reaction as with DNP-BSA. As shown in Table II, fluorescein-conjugated BSA or naphthalene coupled to BGG gave negative results. That the precipitation reaction was not due to the blocking of lysine residues was shown by the lack of precipitation with acetylated BSA.

TABLE I
Absorption of IgM with Forssman antigen

	Hemagglutination Titer			
	ShE	Pigeon E	Hu O	Hu A
Starting material	±640	5120	±2560	±640
Absorbed material	±20	±80	±40	±40

TABLE II
Precipitation of normal serum with various antigens[a]

Antigen	Precipitation
BSA	–
Acetylated BSA	–
BGG	–
$Fluorescein_{10}$-BSA	–
$Naphthalene_{19}$-BGG	–
2,4-DNP_{34}-BSA	+++
2,4,6-TNP_{38}-BSA	+++

[a] Reaction mixture contains 1 ml of serum and 1 ml of antigen (4 mg/ml).

The precipitation of DNP-BSA could be inhibited by DNP-lysine haptens.

Previous studies have shown that shark antibodies elicited by immunization with DNP-hemocyanin could be purified by means of adsorption to a DNP-immunoadsorbent (8). Repeated attempts were made to purify the anti-DNP activity from normal serum by this procedure. Serum was incubated with the adsorbent for 60 min at 37°C and then several hours in the cold. The adsorbent was then removed by centrifugation and the supernatant was tested along with unadsorbed serum. One-milliliter aliquots of serum were reacted with 1 ml of increasing antigen concentrations for 60 min at 37° and overnight in the cold. The precipitates were removed by centrifugation, washed twice in cold 0.05 M PO_4 buffer, pH 8.0, and dissolved in 0.1 M NaOH. Absorbance was determined at 280 and 360 mμ. Figure 2 shows that the immunoadsorbent did not remove the natural antibody from the serum. Thus, the natural antibody differed from induced antibody by its failure to bind to an immunoadsorbent.

As can be seen in the quantitative precipitin

curves, no true zone of antigen excess is seen, even at antigen concentrations as high as 10 mg/ml. Analysis of the precipitates for antigen recovery (Fig. 3) revealed that at the point of maximum precipitation of antibody (4 mg/ml) only about 10% of the antigen was found in the precipitate. When the supernatant from the precipitation reaction was reacted with rabbit antisera to nurse shark immunoglobulin, an additional 30 to 35% of the antigen was precipitated. These results suggest that a significant amount of the natural antibody to DNP is bound in soluble complexes and does not precipitate.

Purification of proteins with anti-DNP activity. Since the natural antibody to DNP was shown not to bind to an immunoadsorbent, purification was accomplished from immune precipitates. An equal volume of serum and DNP-BSA (4 mg/ml) were mixed and incubated for 60 min at 37°C and overnight in the cold. The precipitate formed was removed by centrifugation and washed

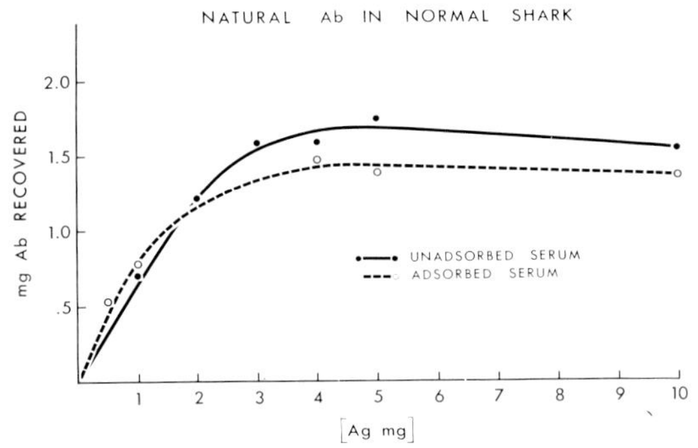

Figure 2. Quantitative precipitin curve of normal shark serum precipitated with DNP-BSA.

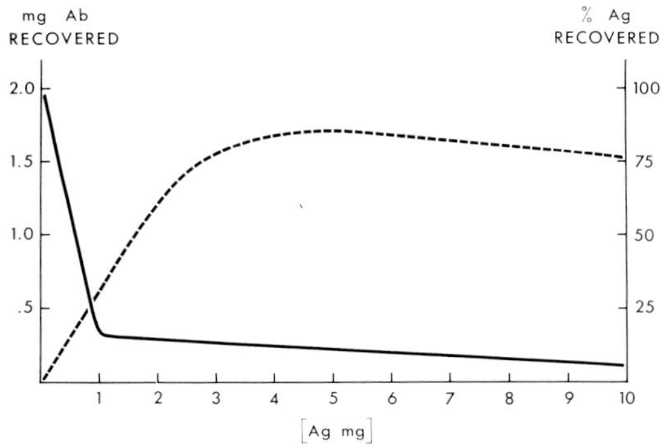

Figure 3. Antigen recovery in the quantitative precipitin test. -----, Antibody recovery; ——, antigen recovery.

three times in cold buffer. The antibody was eluted from the precipitate with 0.1 M DNP hapten and the elution mixture placed on a double layered DEAE-Dowex column for removal of antigen and hapten. Interestingly, after purification from immune precipitates the natural antibody was found to then bind (i.e., adsorb) to the DNP immunoadsorbent.

Characterization of proteins with anti-DNP activity. Analytical ultracentrifugation of the purified anti-DNP antibody as seen in Figure 4 revealed two protein peaks. A large homogeneous peak with a corrected sedimentation coefficient of 19S was found along with a small 7S peak. Polyacrylamide gel electrophoresis (Fig. 5) revealed the 7S molecule to migrate similarly to the rabbit 7S immunoglobulin controls. Due to the small amount of 7S protein it could not be determined whether or not this molecule was an immunoglobulin. Immunoelectrophoresis of the purified preparation (Fig. 6) revealed a single line of precipitation with typical IgM mobility. However, the 7S protein, if it were not IgM, may not have been present in high enough concentration to produce a precipitin line. Double diffusion in agar of the purified protein using a rabbit anti-nurse shark immunoglobulin reagent resulted in the formation of a strong precipitin line. These results confirmed the previous assumption that the purified protein was in fact nurse shark natural antibody.

A valence could not be determined for the antibody by equilibrium dialysis apparently due to low affinity. The association constant was estimated to be less than 10^4 liters/mol. Protein concentrations as high as 3.5 mg/ml were used but saturation of the sites could not be achieved.

Subunit structure and activity of natural antibody to DNP. In order to determine subunit structure and activity the natural antibody was labeled with ^{125}I by the ICl method using $Na^{125}I$. Iodination was designed for four groups per 7S subunit. The reaction is approximately 50% efficient so that about two groups are found per subunit.

The labeled IgM was mixed with purified normal rabbit IgG to a final concentration of 6.0 mg/ml (rabbit IgG) and dialyzed against 0.1 M acetate buffer, pH 4.5, for 24 hr. Pepsin (Worthington Biochem. Corp., Freehold, N. J.) dissolved in the dialysis buffer was added to the antibody mixture to equal a 1:100 (enzyme:antibody) weight ratio. The proteolytic reaction was allowed

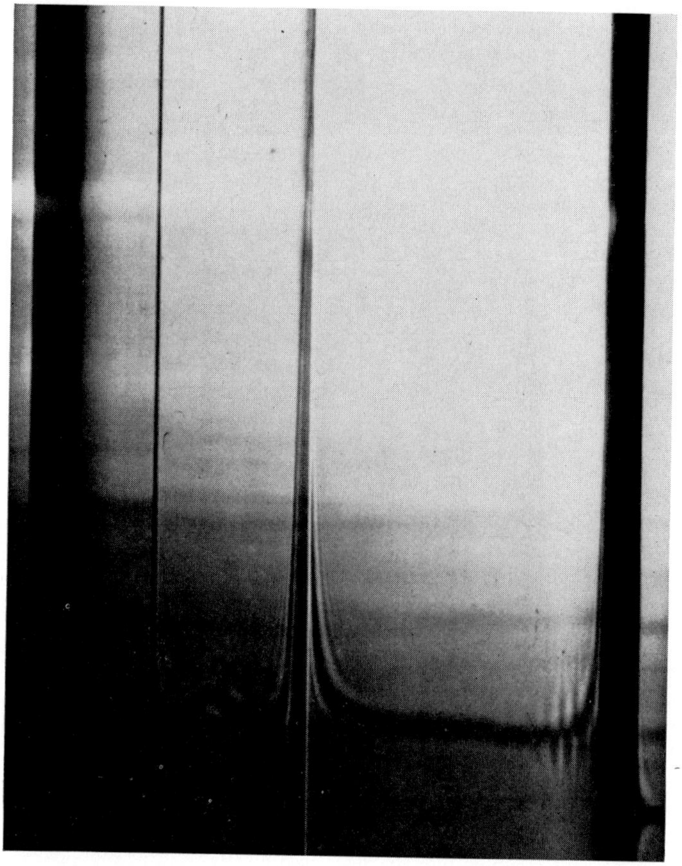

Figure 4. Ultracentrifuge profile of purified anti-DNP antibody (A_{278} 9.4)

to proceed for 20 hr at 37°. The digested protein was then precipitated in 50% ammonium sulfate and removed by centrifugation. The precipitate was dissolved in 0.05 M phosphate buffer, pH 8.0, and dialyzed against the same buffer.

At this point two samples were removed for determination of subunit size and activity (see below). A sample was applied to a calibrated Sephadex G-200 column (2 cm x 80 cm) equilibrated in 0.05 M phosphate buffer, pH 8.0. Elution of the protein with the equilibration buffer revealed a single peak of radioactivity with a sedimentation coefficient of 5S. This subunit is assumed to be the $F(ab)_2$ formed upon degradation of the Fc region by the enzyme.

The remainder of the protein digest was subjected to reduction with mercaptoethanol and alkylation with iodoacetamide. The protein was dialyzed against 0.1 M Tris, pH 8.0, and mercaptoethanol was added to a final concentration of 0.01 M. Reduction was carried out for 1 hr and then iodoacetamide was added to a final concentration of 0.02 M for 1 hr. The reduced and alkylated material was dialyzed against 0.05 M phosphate buffer, pH 8.0, and subunit size was determined as described above.

The major peak of activity eluted in the area corresponding to a sedimentation coefficient of 3.5S. This subunit is assumed to be the F(ab) moiety resulting from the splitting of $F(ab)_2$ by mercaptoethanol.

Activity of the labeled 19S antibody was determined by the ability to bind to a DNP immunoadsorbent. Activity of the iodinated 19S molecule was found to range from 86 to 98%. The $F(ab)_2$ pepsin product exhibited virtually the same activity as the intact 19S molecule indicating that the DNP-binding activity is localized in the F(ab) regions.

Multiple reactivity of the natural anti-DNP antibody. The antibody purified by DNP precipitation was tested for specificity. It was found to agglutinate sheep and pigeon erythrocytes and it bound guanosine monophosphate in equilibrium dialysis. Attempts were made to inhibit the sheep cell agglutination with DNP and DNP-lysine haptens at concentrations ranging from 100 μg to 5 mg/ml. No inhibition was observed at any of the concentrations tested.

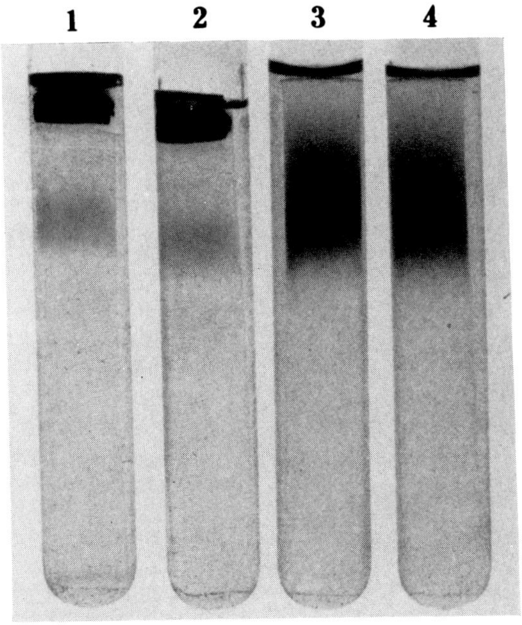

Figure 5. Polyacrylamide gel electrophoresis in 6 M urea of purified shark anti-DNP antibody (*tubes 1* and *2*) and normal rabbit immunoglobulin (*tubes 3* and *4*).

DISCUSSION

From the results of the mixed agglutination assays it is apparent that the shark possesses a natural antibody capable of reacting with erythrocytes from a variety of species. This activity could result either from the recognition of a common antigen or the presence of a multispecific antibody.

The demonstration of a large drop in titer to sheep, pigeon, and human O and A erythrocytes following absorption with Forssman antigen suggests that the red cell activity may be due to recognition of Forssman or Forssman-"like" antigens. The observation that significant titers to the various erythrocytes tested remain after Forssman absorption and the lack of reduction in titer to Forssman negative rabbit cells indicates the presence of at least one other class of antibody besides the one involved in the mixed agglutination. This contention is further supported by the extremely weak mixed agglutination of sensitized pigeon erythrocytes with rabbit indicator cells. This second class of antibody is then presumably directed against antigens specific to the various erythrocytes.

Normal shark serum precipitates DNP-conjugated proteins. This activity, like the hemagglutination activity, is associated with IgM immunoglobulin and has been found in all of 12 sera tested. All sera tested were also capable of agglutinating DNP-coated erythrocytes and usually in very high titers. Both the precipitation and passive hemagglutination reactions can be inhibited by DNP-lysine. The precipitation re-

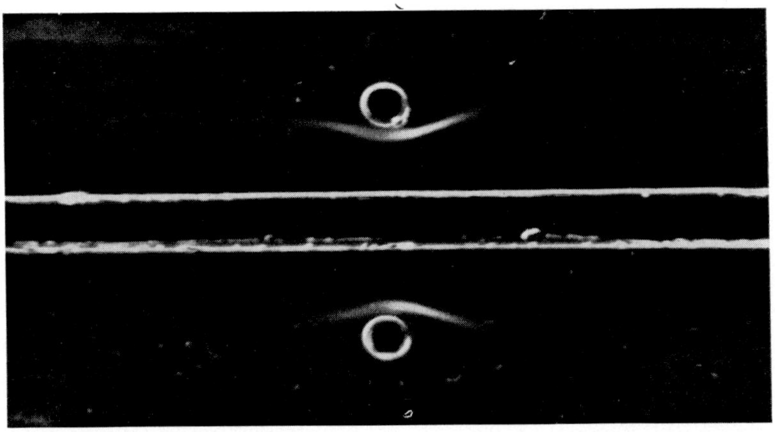

Figure 6. Immunoelectrophoresis of two purified shark anti-DNP antibody preparations developed with rabbit anti-nurse shark whole serum.

action was characterized as to some specificity in that TNP could be substituted for DNP but there was no precipitation of fluorescein and naphthalene conjugates or the protein carriers alone, i.e., BSA, BGG. The validity of reactions with DNP has recently been questioned as an immunologic phenomenon because of their high frequency. In this connection we would like to site our unpublished observations that purified shark anti-BGG antibody did not agglutinate DNP-coated cells indicating that specific antibody of the shark does not react with this hapten. The precipitation with DNP provided the means for purification of antibody. As was mentioned above the natural antibody was not readily removed from whole serum by immunoadsorption. It is interesting that following precipitation the antibody could be successfully adsorbed by the immunoadsorbent. At this time we cannot explain this phenomenon.

Our data show that not only were the serologic activities associated with immunoglobulin but that the binding of DNP occurred in the $F(ab)_2$ fragments. In this respect the reactive molecules behaved as typical antibodies.

Why should shark serum react with DNP and with such a diverse array of antigens which are not known to be present in their environment? One possibility is that the shark's immune mechanism is degenerate but this is not very likely in view of the high degree of immunologic specificity observed in induced antibodies. It is of course possible that these reactions result from the recognition of an antigenic determinant shared by a large variety of antigens—a determinant which may escape recognition by the normal immune mechanisms of more highly evolved species. The original discovery by Eisen *et al.* (11) of reactivity with DNP in human myeloma proteins has sparked wide surveys for this reactivity. In addition to mouse myelomas (12, 13), substantial anti-DNP precipitating reactions have been noted in normal sera of gars and bowfins (14). Using a phage neutralization technique Haimovich *et al.* (15) demonstrated significant anti-DNP activity in the sera of normal rabbits and Leslie and Clem (16) found low levels of activity in the normal sera of bufos, chickens and certain fishes. It is of special interest that activity with this hapten has also been observed in a large segment of normal human sera (17) and in rheumatoid factor (18).

Multiple reactivity has been previously reported for several proteins. Smith and Potter (19) found that antibody from carp immunized with DNP-BSA also reacted with DNA and various DNA derivatives and analogs. Schubert *et al.* (12, 13) have reported a number of mouse myelomas with activity against various combinations of purine 5-acetyl uracil adenosine monophosphate, DNP and TNP. Hannestad (18) has recently reported an IgM rheumatoid factor which precipitates aggregated IgG and also reacts with DNP- and TNP-conjugated proteins.

The multiple reactivity described for carp antibody, myeloma protein and rheumatoid factor was found to be inhibited by either of two antigens each of which was bound by the protein, suggesting that the same active site is involved in the binding of both antigens. In the shark, however, the ability of natural anti-DNP antibody to agglutinate sheep erythrocytes is not inhibited by DNP haptens. This observation suggests two possible explanations: 1) the binding of DNP and sheep erythrocytes may take place at different sites on the molecule, and 2) the active site may be large enough to accomodate the DNP hapten and still react with a sheep cell antigen. Winkelhake and Voss (20) have recently reported that rabbit antibodies induced with TNP-guanosine appear to have separate "sites" or "cavities" for the binding of TNP and the guanosine carrier within a single combining site. Thus the shark combining site may similarly have separate areas capable of binding different antigens.

REFERENCES

1. Rudikoff, S., Sigel, M. M. and Voss, E. W., Fed. Proc., *29:* 771, 1970.
2. Sigel, M. M., Voss, E. W., Rudikoff, S., Lichter, W. and Jensen, J. A., Miami Winter Symposium, 1, In press.
3. Clem, L. W., De Boutaud, F. and Sigel, M. M., J. Immun., *99:* 1226, 1967.
4. Jensen, J. A., J. Exp. Med., *130:* 217, 1969.
5. Eisen, H. N., Meth. Med. Res., *10:* 94, 1964.
6. Robbins, J. B., Haimovich, J. and Sela, M., Immunochemistry, *4:* 11, 1967.
7. Gallagher, J. S. and Voss, E. W., Immunochemistry, *6:* 199, 1969.
8. Voss, E. W., Russell, W. J. and Sigel, M. M., Biochemistry, *8:* 4866, 1969.
9. Ornstein, L., Ann. N. Y. Acad. Sci., *121:* 321, 1964.

10. Davis, B. J. Ann. N. Y. Acad. Sci., *121:* 404, 1964.
11. Eisen, H. N., Little, J. R., Osterland, C. K. and Sims, E. S., Cold Spring Harbor Sympos. Quant. Biol., *32:* 75, 1967.
12. Schubert, D., Jobe, A. and Cohn, M., Nature, *220:* 882 1968.
13. Schubert, D., Roman, A. and Cohn, M., Nature, *225:* 154, 1970.
14. Bradshaw, C. M., Personal communication.
15. Haimovich, J., Tarrab, R., Sulica, A. and Sela, M., J. Immun., *104:* 1033, 1970.
16. Leslie, G. A. and Clem, L. W., J. Immun., *103:* 613, 1969.
17. Brandriss, M. W., Nature, *221:* 960, 1969.
18. Hannestad, K., Clin. Exp. Immun., *4:* 555, 1969.
19. Smith, M. A. and Potter, M., Fed. Proc., *28:* 819, 1969.
20. Winkelhake, J. L. and Voss, E. W., Biochemistry, *9:* 1845, 1970.

THE JOURNAL OF IMMUNOLOGY
Vol. 105, No. 6, December 1970
Printed in U.S.A.

IMMUNOCHEMICAL STUDIES ON THE INTERACTION BETWEEN STAPHYLOCOCCAL PROTEIN A AND γG GLOBULIN[1]

GÖRAN KRONVALL, RONALD P. MESSNER AND RALPH C. WILLIAMS, JR.

From the Department of Medicine, University of New Mexico, Bernalillo County Medical Center, Albuquerque, New Mexico 87106

Received for publication July 29, 1970

Reactivity with staphylococcal protein A is a characteristic of IgG-1, -2 and -4 molecules. Human myeloma globulins of these types either precipitate with protein A or are capable of inhibiting such precipitation. In the present study chemical modifications of human myeloma globulins showed distinct effects on the reactivity with protein A. Carbamylation changed a precipitin reaction to one of inhibition. Acetylation rendered myeloma globulins completely non-reactive with protein A. Quantitative precipitin curves for the reaction between normal human γG or various myeloma globulins and staphylococcal protein A revealed marked quantitative differences with varying amounts of soluble complexes formed. Analytical ultracentrifugation of γG preparations with and without protein A revealed similar differences. No intermediate sized complexes were detected. Our results confirm a previous hypothesis that precipitation in this system is a secondary reaction after the primary combination between protein A and the Fc site on human γG globulin. Ultracentrifugational data also indicated that protein A may be univalent, structurally or functionally, in its reaction with γG.

Protein A from *Staphylococcus aureus* combines with the Fc part of human γG-1, -2, and -4 molecules (1–4). Myeloma globulins combining with protein A either give rise to precipitation or inhibit such precipitation in the test system (2). These two different types of reactivity do not correlate with heavy or light chain groups (2). It was hypothesized that both reactions detect the same protein A combining structures on γG. This assumption was strengthened by phylogenetic studies (5). Furthermore, the equilibrium constants for the reaction between cell wall-associated protein A and either precipitating or inhibiting myeloma globulins were found to be approximately the same (6). Since precipitation between protein A and human γG globulin therefore seemed to involve mechanisms other than the primary combination between γG and protein A, further experiments were undertaken to define the structures involved.

[1] This investigation was supported by Grants ROI AM-13690-01, AMAI-13824-01 and AMAI-13789-01 from the United States Public Health Service.

MATERIALS AND METHODS

Protein A reactivity. Protein A was partially purified as described previously (2) from *S. aureus*, strain Cowan I, according to Jensen (7). Tests for determination of protein A reactivity were performed in agar gel using the method of Seligmann *et al.* (8) as described previously (2).

Myeloma sera and globulins. Sera with high concentrations of myeloma globulins were used in some experiments for determination of electrophoretic mobilities or for double diffusion in agar gel. Myeloma globulins were also isolated by zone electrophoresis on starch block (9). H chain subgroup determinations were kindly performed by Dr. William Yount, Rockefeller University, New York. Light chains were typed with monospecific absorbed rabbit antisera (10). Gm types were determined as described previously (11, 12). Several isolated myeloma globulins, tested for heat aggregability (13), were kindly provided by Dr. Howard M. Grey, Scripps Institute, La Jolla, California.

Chemical modification of myeloma globulins. Acetylation of isolated human myeloma globulins and normal human pooled γG (Cohn fraction II) was accomplished with acetic anhydride according to the method of Ljaljevic, Ljaljevic and Parker (14) using saturated sodium acetate as buffer. Treatment with potassium cyanate (carbamylation) was performed by the method of Chen, Grossberg and Pressman (15) as modified by Ljaljevic *et al.* (14). The amidination procedure was adopted from Wofsy and Singer (16). Ethylacetimidate and dimethylproprionimidate were prepared by the method of McElvain and Nelson (17). After each modification, control and treated samples were dialyzed for 24 hr against two changes of phosphate-buffered saline (PBS, 0.15 M NaCl, 0.01 M phosphate, pH 7.4) and adjusted to equal protein concentration. The degree of substitution attained with each treatment was monitored by the ninhydrin technique for determination of free amino groups (18).

Quantitative precipitin curves. To 0.1 ml of γ globulin preparations containing 1 mg/ml, increasing amounts of protein A were added. The total volume was brought to 0.5 ml with PBS. Mixtures were incubated at 37°C for 1 hr and then for 3 days at 4°C. Precipitates were spun down and washed twice with cold PBS. After drying the precipitates at room temperature, 50 μl of 0.1 N NaOH were added and the amount of protein determined according to Folin with modifications (19). For studying the development of precipitates by time, protein A was added to γ globulin preparations at equivalence. Mixtures were incubated at 4°C and the amount of precipitate determined after 1, 2, 3 and 6 days of incubation.

Serum electrophoresis. The relative electrophoretic mobilities of myeloma globulins were determined from electrophoretic separations on cellulose acetate using the Microzone Electrophoresis System (Beckman Instruments, Inc. Spinco Division, Palo Alto, Calif.).

Analytical ultracentrifugation. Samples of various immunoglobulins, with and without protein A, were studied in a Beckman Analytical Ultracentrifuge, model E. Protein A or an equal volume of PBS, as a control, was added immediately before the run. All preparations were dissolved in PBS. Pictures were taken with 8-min intervals after the rotor had reached its final speed of 59,780 rpm.

RESULTS

Effect of chemical modification of myeloma globulins on protein A reactivity. Samples of normal pooled γG globulin as well as two protein A precipitating (*HO, HE*) and one inhibiting (*HU*) myeloma globulin were separately acetylated, carbamylated and amidinated and subsequently tested for protein A reactivity (Table I). Acetylation of all preparations rendered them completely non-reactive with protein A. Amidination did not drastically alter reactivity with protein A. Of three precipitating γ globulin preparations tested, two were unchanged and in one a slight decrease in the amount of precipitate was noted. Carbamylation of normal γG and myeloma globulins *HO* and *HE*, however, changed the type of reactivity from one of precipitation to inhibition. During treatment of γ globulins with acetic anhydride, free amino-, sulfhydryl and phenolic and aliphatic hydroxyl groups are substituted with acyl groups with a resultant increase in negative charge. Amidination substitutes amidine groups on free amino groups and causes no change of charge. Carbamylation results in substitution of carbamyl groups in sulfhydryl and amino groups and increases the net negative charge. Changes in charge or tertiary structure of the γ globulin resulting from acetylation and carbamylation made it difficult to attribute the changes in reactivity noted to substitution of specific chemical groups. However, the apparent separation of precipitation from

TABLE I

Summary of results of protein A reactivity obtained with chemically modified human γ globulin preparations

Control	Acetylation		Carbamylation		Amidination	
	% substitution[a]	Reactivity	% substitution[a]	Reactivity	% substitution[a]	Reactivity
Normal γG (P[b])	65	—[c]	88	I[b]	65	P
HO[d] (P)	70	—	48	I	80	P
HE[b] (P)	75	—	32	I	85	P
HU[b] (I)	65	—	90	I	95	I

[a] Calculated on the basis of ninhydrin reaction.
[b] P, precipitation; I, inhibition.
[c] —, Absence of reactivity.
[d] Purified myeloma globulins.

primary reactivity with protein A after carbamylation suggested that different structures were involved in these two processes.

Relation between ability to precipitate protein A and heat aggregability of myeloma globulins. One explanation for the two types of protein A reactivity (precipitation and inhibition) might lie in a correlation with another characteristic of individual myeloma globulins: nonspecific heat aggregability of γG molecules (13, 20). Nine myeloma globulins previously tested for heat aggregability at 63°C for 30 min were therefore analyzed for type of protein A reactivity (Table II). There was no correlation between precipitation of protein A and the ability to aggregate when treated with heat. These two phenomena, therefore, seem to be expressions of different structural characteristics of immunoglobulin molecules.

Spurring phenomena between myeloma globulins in tests detecting protein A reactivity. It was noted that a few myeloma globulins formed a spur with other myeloma globulins used in test systems detecting protein A reactivity. Among 20 protein A-precipitating myeloma sera tested in the present study, two (*MP* and *MA*) formed a spur with the myeloma serum or globulins used in the test system (Fig. 1). One of these two, *MP* had been extensively characterized in a previous study (21). This myeloma globulin is known to have anti-streptolysin O (ASO) activity in the Fab fragments. Anti-protein A activity was found only in H chain preparations. Since this isolated myeloma globulin showed Fc-mediated protein A reactivity, the spurring phenomenon could not be attributed to any additional reactivity with staphylococcal antigens.

TABLE II

Lack of correlation between heat aggregability of human γG myeloma globulins and their mode of reaction with protein A[a]

Myeloma Globulin	Heat Aggregability	Protein A Reactivity
Pap	0	Precipitation
Qua	4	Precipitation
Mur	0	Inhibition
Fis	0	Inhibition
Sla	1–2	Precipitation
Gre	0	Precipitation
Wil	4	Inhibition
Ing	4	Inhibition
Way	4	Precipitation

[a] Heat aggregability is indicated by figures, from 0 (no aggregation) to 4 (maximal aggregation).

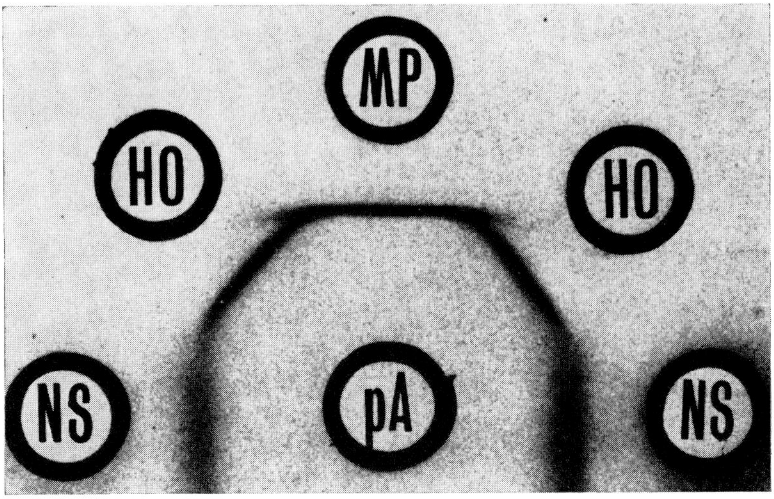

Figure 1. Spur formation between myeloma globulins *MP* and *HO*. The precipitin line between staphylococcal protein A (*center well*) and *MP* (*upper well, marked MP*) extends beyond the partial fusion with the lines obtained between protein A and *HO* (*wells marked HO*). For comparison, the diffuse precipitation between normal human serum (*side wells, marked NS*) and protein A is also included and seen to fuse diffusely with the *HO*-protein A lines.

Effect of salt concentration and pH variation on protein A reactivity. Since changes in the medium can influence immune precipitation in gel (22–24) we performed immunodiffusion tests with protein A-reacting systems at low and high salt concentrations, in buffers of various pH, as well as in the presence of Dextran 500. The spurring phenomenon by myeloma globulin *MP* with myeloma globulin *HO* and the inhibition of the precipitin reaction between protein A and myeloma globulin *HO* by other myeloma globulins, as well as the behavior of three precipitating and nine other inhibiting myeloma globulins, were studied. The media used included 0.10, 0.15, 0.50 and 1.0 M NaCl in 0.05 M Veronal buffer, pH 8.6; 0.15 M Tris-HCl buffers, pH 9.6 and 7.2; 0.15 M NaCl in 0.01 M phosphate, pH 6.0 and also 40 mg Dextran 500/ml of agar. No differences in the types of reactivity were noted among the tests in the various media. Thus, the type of protein A reactivity—whether spurring, precipitation, or inhibition—was not changed by a simple alteration of the surrounding medium.

Relation between electrophoretic mobility and protein A reactivity. The difference between precipitating and non-precipitating antibodies has been attributed to differences in molecular charge (25). This might be correlated to the ability to precipitate with protein A. The electrophoretic mobility of 15 protein A-precipitating and 17 inhibiting myeloma globulins was therefore determined from cellulose acetate electrophoresis of the sera. Precipitation or inhibition in tests for protein A reactivity was determined for the isolated components. The means and variances for the electrophoretic mobilities of the two groups were calculated and analyzed by the *t* test for differences between means. There was no significant difference between the electrophoretic mobilities of the protein A precipitating myeloma globulins as compared to those of the inhibiting.

Differences among γ globulin preparations in quantitative precipitation of protein A. Since the different behavior in immunodiffusion of myeloma globulins with the same primary reactivity for protein A seemed to depend upon secondary characteristics of the immunoglobulin molecules themselves, techniques of quantitative precipitation were employed to define these differences. Equal amounts of myeloma globulin *MP* (spurring) and *HO* (precipitating), as well as pooled normal γG (Cohn fraction II, further purified on DEAE-cellulose), were added to increasing amounts of protein A. The amount of precipitate formed differed markedly (Fig. 2). One hundred per cent of the myeloma globulin molecules *MP* and *HO* should theoretically combine with protein A and similarly 92% of normal γ globulin. However, *HO* gave 2.4 times more and *MP* 3.1 times more protein precipitate at equivalence than did normal human γG globulin (Fig. 2*A*). Increasing the time of incubation of the precipitin reaction up to 6 days did not affect the relative amounts of precipitate formed by the three preparations (Fig. 2*B*). We have previously found that a precipitating myeloma globulin showed the same affinity for cell wall-associated protein A as a myeloma globulin which gave inhibition (6). The differences in amount of precipitate formed during quantitative precipitation seemed, therefore, possibly due to the presence of soluble complexes. Myeloma globulin *MP* was obviously more capable of precipitating out protein A than myeloma globulin *HO*. The spurring of *MP* with *HO* might therefore have been due to precipitation of soluble *HO*-protein A complexes by *MP*.

Analytical ultracentrifugation. Ultracentrifugational analysis of protein A-γG mixtures was performed in an effort to further define soluble complexes formed as indicated by the precipitin curves. When myeloma globulin *HO* was mixed with protein A at a ratio of 5:1 w/w to a final γG concentration of 4.3 mg/ml, heavy precipitation occurred immediately. This precipitation was spun down to the bottom of the cell when the rotor reached 10,000 rpm. No intermediate peaks were observed during the run. The original peak had the same uncorrected S value of 6.2 as the markedly reduced peak in the test cell. Normal human *F II* was tested similarly at a ratio to protein A of 5:1 with a final γG concentration of 4.5 mg/ml. When mixed with protein A, a slowly occurring precipitation was noted. This precipitate had reached the bottom of the cell at 10,000 rpm. Like the experiment with myeloma globulin *HO*, a reduction of the γG peak was noted without a change of uncorrected S value (6.15S). The reduction of the peak was not as marked, though, as for *HO*. The inhibiting myeloma globulin *HU* was also analyzed with and without protein A in the ultracentrifuge. No reduction of the peak was seen at the final

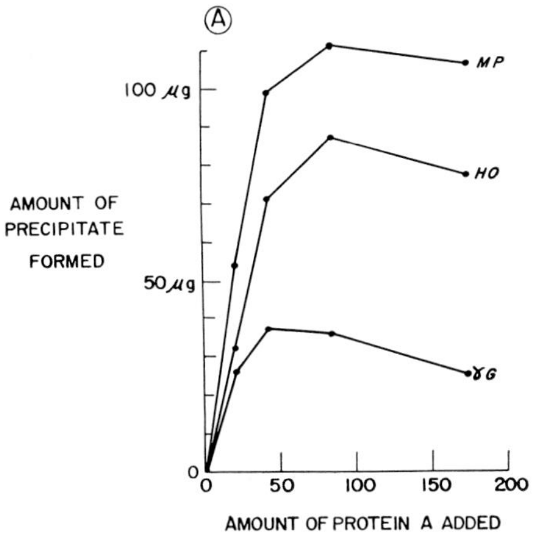

Figure 2. Quantitative precipitation of a partially purified protein A preparation by pooled normal human γG globulin (*curves marked γG*), myeloma globulin *HO* (*curves marked HO*) and *MP* (*curves marked MP*). Figure 1*A* shows quantitative precipitin curves obtained with the same amount (100 μg) of the various γ globulin preparations. *HO* yields 2.4 times and *MP* 3.1 times more precipitate at equivalence when compared to normal γG. Figure 1*B* shows that these differences are not merely due to differences in the rate of precipitation.

γG concentration of 7.8 mg/ml. Protein A was added at a ratio of 1:5 w/w to *HU*. The sedimentation constant, however, showed a significant change from 6.18 for the control to 5.74 for the sample with protein A. No complexes with higher sedimentation rates than that of γG were noted in this case either. Similar ultracentrifugational studies with the inhibiting myeloma globulin AL at varying ratios of pA added (10:1, 5:1, 2.5:1, w/w) showed the same result. The combination of protein A with inhibiting myeloma globulins in excess thus does not give rise to multiple complexes of γG. Protein A therefore seems to be univalent in its reaction with the specific receptor on the Fc part of γG.

DISCUSSION

The two types of protein A reactivity found for human myeloma globulins, precipitation or inhibition, appear to detect similar protein A combining structures (2). This theory is supported by their presence in myeloma globulins with identical Fc structures as judged from H chain type and Gm group (2, 26) and also by the fact that the equilibrium constant for the reaction of one representative of each of the two types of reactivities with cell wall-associated protein A was essentially the same (6). Since the protein A molecules were fixed to the cells in this latter system, any further secondary reactivity therefore was prevented. In the current experiments reported above using chemically modified γ globulins, it became clear that precipitation with protein A depends on molecular configurations different from primary protein A reacting structures. This was evident from the results obtained after carbamylation which showed that the ability to precipitate with protein A could be lost without loss of reactivity. We can therefore postulate a two-step reaction for the precipitation of protein A by human γ globulin:

$$\mathrm{PA} + \gamma\mathrm{G} \underset{}{\overset{K^1}{\rightleftharpoons}} \underset{\text{Soluble complexes}}{\mathrm{pA}\gamma\mathrm{G}} \overset{K^2}{\rightleftharpoons} \underset{\text{Precipitate}}{[\mathrm{pA}\gamma\mathrm{G}]}$$

Since there are no exact data yet available on optimal molar ratios in the reactions, no figures are included in the postulated reaction scheme. The first equilibrium constant, K^1, is already known to be approximately 4 to 4.5 × 10^7 liters/mol (6). The second constant, K^2, is dependent on still unknown γ globulin factors with an apparent wide variation for different myeloma globulins. Precipitin curves (Fig. 2) show a difference in the amount of precipitate formed with myeloma globulin *HO* and *MP*. *HO* represents the majority of precipitating myeloma globulins regarding its reactivity with protein A and gives only about 80% of the most of precipitate formed with the spurring myeloma globulin *MP*. A smaller value of K^2 for the reaction between protein A and *HO* as compared to the reaction with *MP* might explain the spurring phenomenon.

The precipitation phenomenon has for over three decades generally been held to be due to lattice formation via the specific γG receptors for antigen on multivalent antigenic structures (27). Other data, however, have pointed to additional γ globulin factors to be involved (22, 25). Other authors studying rabbit γG antibodies have shown that carbamylation, while not changing the initial reaction with antigen, markedly slows down the secondary reaction leading to precipitation (28). Results obtained during this study using chemically modified myeloma globulins as well as normal human γ globulin indicated the necessity for assuming a two-step reaction in the precipitation with protein A. This system therefore provides new evidence for precipitation as a secondary reaction and also, with the availability of reacting myeloma globulins, offers an experimental model for the precipitation phenomenon.

Although precipitation seems to depend on certain structures on γG altered by carbamylation, no direct correlation to known structural features has been found. The change in charge and tertiary structure on carbamylation does not allow a direct interpretation that amino- or sulfhydryl groups are involved in precipitation. It appears, however, that the variation in carbohydrate of individual γ globulin molecules (29–31) may not be a determining factor for precipitation. The inability of Fc fragments to precipitate supports this view (1, 3). Other inherent characteristics of myeloma globulins, heat aggregability (13, 20), electrophoretic motility, and charge, did not correlate with the ability to precipitate with protein A. Two recently recognized characteristics of immunoglobulins are the subgroups of the variable portions of the light and heavy chains (22, 32, 33). It is possible that precipitation of protein A might correlate to some of these subgroups or certain combinations thereof.

The results from ultracentrifugational experiments with *HU* and *Fr II* with and without protein A are in line with the quantitative precipitin curves showing differences in the amount of aggregates formed. The results with *HU* seem very intriguing. The change in S value would indicate that protein A combined with γG, giving a less dense molecular configuration. There is a conspicuous absence of soluble aggregates of sizes that would have resulted from bivalent or multivalent protein A molecules. This may explain the lack of renal lesions when protein A was injected intravenously into mice (34). The absence of multiple complexes of γG also means that the protein A molecules are either structurally or functionally univalent with regard to the reactivity with the Fc-combining site on γG.

Acknowledgments. The fine technical assistance of Miss Almera Seber and the secretarial expertise of Miss Shirley Cordova are gratefully acknowledged.

REFERENCES

1. Forsgren, A. and Sjöquist, J., J. Immun., *97:* 822, 1966.
2. Kronvall, G. and Williams, R. C., Jr., J. Immun., *103:* 828, 1969.
3. Kronvall, G. and Frommel, D., Immunochemistry, *7:* 124, 1970.
4. Nickerson, D. S., White, J. G., Kronvall, G., Williams, R. C., Jr. and Quie, P. G., J. Exp. Med., *131:* 1039, 1970.
5. Kronvall, G., Seal, U. S., Finstad, J. and Williams, R. C., Jr., J. Immun., *104:* 140, 1970.
6. Kronvall, G., Quie, P. G. and Williams, R. C., Jr., J. Immun., *104:* 273, 1970.
7. Jensen, K., Thesis, Ejnar Munksgaard, Copenhagen, 1959.
8. Seligmann, M., Meshaka, G., Hurez, D. and Mihaesco, C., in *Immunopathology, IVth International Symposium*, Edited by P. Grabar and P. A. Miescher, p. 229, Grune & Stratton, New York, 1965.
9. Kunkel, H. G., in *Methods of Biochemical Analysis*, p. 141, Interscience Publishers, Inc., New York, 1954.
10. Levi, D. F., Williams, R. C., Jr. and Lindström, F. C., Amer. J. Med., *44:* 922, 1968.
11. Mårtensson, L., J. Exp. Med., *120:* 1169, 1964.
12. Litwin, S. D. and Kunkel, H. G., J. Exp. Med., *125:* 847, 1967.
13. Augener, W. and Grey, H. M., Fed. Proc., *29:* 303 (abstract), 1970.
14. Ljaljevic, M., Ljaljevic, J. and Parker, C. W., J. Immun., *100:* 1041, 1968.
15. Chen, C. C., Grossberg, A. L. and Pressman, D., Biochemistry, *1:* 1025, 1962.

16. Wofsy, L. and Singer, S. J., Biochemistry, *2:* 104, 1963.
17. McElvain, S. M. and Nelson, W., J. Amer. Chem. Soc., *64:* 1825, 1942.
18. Yemm, E. W. and Cocking, E. C., Analyst, *80:* 209, 1955.
19. Lowry, O. H., Rosebrough, N. J., Farr, A. L. and Randall, R. J., J. Biol. Chem., *193:* 265, 1951.
20. Morse, J. H., J. Immun., *95:* 722, 1965.
21. Kronvall, G., Acta Path. Microbiol. Scand., *69:* 619, 1967.
22. Kleczkowski, A., Immunology, *8:* 170, 1965.
23. Kubo, R. T. and Benedict, A. A., J. Immun., *103:* 1022, 1969.
24. Hellsing, K., Biochemistry J., *114:* 151, 1969.
25. Carter, B. G. and Harris, T. N., Immunology, *12:* 75, 1967.
26. Natvig, J. B., Kunkel, H. G., Yount, W. J. and Nielsen, J. C., J. Exp. Med., *128:* 763, 1968.
27. Marrack, J. R., Medical Research Council, Special Report Series, No. 194, 1934.
28. Feinman, L., Cohen, S. and Becker, E. L., J. Immun., *103:* 395, 1969.
29. Hillman, A., Hillman, G. and Hohss, F., Z. Naturforsch., *8b:* 28, 1953.
30. Laurell, C. B., Laurell, H. and Waldenström, J., Amer. J. Med., *22:* 14, 1957.
31. Thorpe, N. O. and Deutsch, H. F., Immunochemistry, *3:* 317, 1966.
32. Cunningham, B. A., Pflumm, M. N., Rutishauser, U. and Edelman, G. M., Proc. Nat. Acad. Sci., *64:* 997, 1969.
33. Hood, L. and Talmage, D. W., Science, *168:* 325, 1970.
34. Kronvall, G., Grey, H. M. and Williams, R. C., Jr., J. Immun., In press.

THE JOURNAL OF IMMUNOLOGY
Vol. 105, No. 6, December 1970
Printed in U.S.A.

ELECTRON MICROSCOPIC STUDY OF INHIBITION OF MACROPHAGE MIGRATION IN DELAYED HYPERSENSITIVITY[1]

A. COLLIER SMYTH AND LEON WEISS[2]

From the Department of Anatomy, The Johns Hopkins University School of Medicine, Baltimore, Maryland 21205

Received for publication July 27, 1970

The migration of peritoneal cells from guinea pigs with delayed hypersensitivity to bacillus Calmette-Guérin was studied by light and electron microscopy. To permit satisfactory morphologic study and monitoring of cell migration, cells were concentrated in clots whose open interstices were accessible to medium. This clot technique, compared to the commonly used capillary tube, provided: 1) better viability and more uniform morphology, 2) better sampling for electron microscopy, 3) more uniform exposure to antigen, and 4) the opportunity to use fewer cells. Suspension cultures of spleen cells were also examined. Among peritoneal exudate cells from sensitized animals, purified protein derivative (PPD) induced clumping of macrophages, an increase in the number of their microvilli, and some cell death. Many of the clumped cells bore numerous microvilli which intertwined with those of contiguous cells. No intracellular differences between sensitized and control macrophages or lymphocytes, exposed or not exposed to antigen, were discernible. Sensitized cells exposed to PPD in suspension cultures were disc-shaped and clumped. Control cells were flattened on the flask floor, angulated and usually separated. We believe that both the rounded form of the macrophages and their clumping may contribute to the lack of migration.

The *in vitro* migration of peritoneal macrophages harvested from animals displaying delayed hypersensitivity is inhibited in the presence of the sensitizing antigen (1). Inhibition requires the presence of a small number of sensitized lymphocytes (2) (sensitized cells are those harvested from an animal displaying delayed hypersensitivity to the antigen in question) which, stimulated by the sensitizing antigen, release a protein of about 70,000 molecular weight (3). This protein, designated migration inhibitory factor (MIF), inhibits migration of macrophages derived from sensitized or from normal animals (3). This phenomenon of macrophage migration-inhibition has been termed an *in vitro* correlate of delayed hypersensitivity because it is demonstrated only by a cell population containing lymphocytes from delayed hypersensitive animals, has the same specificity as delayed hypersensitivity and is not dependent upon humoral antibody (4). There have been several studies of the structure of cells involved in this *in vitro* phenomenon. Rich and Lewis (5), who first reported this phenomenon, described cell death resulting from exposure of sensitized cells to very high concentrations of antigen. By examination of living preparations using low power phase microscopy, Fauve and Dekaris (6) described a decreased capacity of sensitized macrophages to spread on a glass surface after exposure to antigen. Bartfeld and Kelly (7) demonstrated, under the light microscope, the presence of groups of lymphocytes and macrophages in a culture of peritoneal exudate cells containing the sensitizing antigen.

We present the results of a light and electron microscopic study of macrophages and lymphocytes in a system displaying inhibition of macrophage migration using peritoneal cells from guinea pigs with delayed hypersensitivity to bacillus Calmette-Guérin (BCG). To permit satisfactory morphologic study we concentrated peritoneal cells not in capillary tubes, as is com-

[1] This study was supported by United States Public Health Service Grant 5R01 AM11381 10 HEM.

[2] Research Career Development Awardee, United States Public Health Service.

monly done, but in clots whose interstices are accessible to the medium. We also examined monolayer macrophage cultures made from spleen cells. We observed that sensitized macrophages, lymphocytes, and also granulocytes aggregate in the presence of purified protein derivative (PPD). This aggregation, due in part to interlacing microvilli, correlates with the inhibition of macrophage migration and is a more sensitive and more constant index of sensitivity than the inhibition of migration.

MATERIALS AND METHODS

Animals. Fifteen Duncan Hartley randomly bred albino male guinea pigs weighing 500 to 700 g were used.

Sensitization. Animals were sensitized by eight simultaneous intradermal injections, each of 0.1 ml of a suspension of live BCG (obtained from Dr. Arthur Dannenberg, Johns Hopkins University, School of Hygiene). Sensitivity was tested by paravertebral intradermal injection of 0.1 ml containing 10 μg PPD (PPD for this experiment was provided by Dr. Fisher, Parke-Davis, Detroit, Mich.) in the shaved skin. Animals were judged to be sensitive if induration and erythema exceeded 15 mm in 24 hr. Within 2 weeks of confirming a guinea pig as sensitive it was used as a source of cells.

Harvest of peritoneal cells. Eight sensitized animals and seven control animals were studied. Guinea pigs were killed by ether inhalation alone or together with exsanguination by cardiac puncture. The ventral abdominal wall was shaved, washed with soap, and treated successively with betadine, ether and alcohol. Sterile conditions were maintained throughout the experiment. The peritoneal cavity was opened and 100 ml of Hanks' balanced salt solution (BSS) (Microbiological Associates, Bethesda, Md.) was poured in and swashed about. The animal was then quickly turned over a funnel (15 cm diameter) inserted into a 250-ml Erlenmeyer flask so that the BSS, carrying free peritoneal cells (70% monocytes and macrophages, 20% lymphocytes, 10% eosinophils), drained from the peritoneal cavity into the funnel and flask. Then the spleen was removed and placed in a plastic Petri dish (see below). Animals stimulated to increase macrophage exudation with Bayol F or other irritant were not used in this study. Such stimulation induces large vacuoles in macrophages which interfere with morphologic study. Enough macrophages were obtained without such peritoneal irritation.

Macrophage migration system. The capillary tube commonly used to assess macrophage migration was not suitable for an ultrastructural study because the cells within the tube would often show vacuolization, loss of organelles and even cellular lysis; these are changes consistent with insufficient diffusion of nutrients and wastes within the capillary tube. Accordingly a clot was devised which held the cells together yet permitted a sufficiently free exchange of medium to maintain cellular viability and morphology. Moreover it allowed monitoring of migration from its edges. This free exchange also provided uniform exposure to antigen. The clot required fewer cells than the capillary tube technique and was easier to handle for electron microscopic fixation and embedding. Interestingly, in their report of this migration-inhibition phenomenon, Rich and Lewis used a clot to hold the cells (5).

The peritoneal cell suspension from the Erlenmeyer flask was spun in six test tubes at 289 × G for 4 min, resuspended in Eagle's medium, consolidated to one test tube, and recentrifuged. The supernatant was pipetted off completely and the concentrated cell mass thoroughly dispersed in 2 drops of fresh guinea pig plasma to which 1 drop of thrombin (Parke-Davis) was added. This cellular clot was sliced into approximately 16 pieces, each about 2 mm in diameter. Each piece was affixed to a non-cellular clot layered over the base of a 3-cm tissue culture Petri dish (Falcon Division, Becton, Dickinson and Co., Rutherford, N. J.), four cellular pieces/Petri dish. Three milliliters of medium were then added. In experimental cultures the medium contained 30 or 3 μg PPD/ml, 20% guinea pig serum (all serum used was prepared from control guinea pigs and heat inactivated) and Eagle's minimum essential medium (Microbiological Associates, Bethesda, Md.). In control dishes the medium consisted only of Eagle's medium with 20% guinea pig serum. The preparations were incubated at 37.5°C in a desiccator with 5% CO_2 and water-saturated atmosphere for 24 hr.

The plasma for the above clots was obtained by guinea pig heart puncture using 3.8% sodium citrate as the anticoagulant (1 ml/20 to 30 ml blood). The clot layered over the bottom of the Petri dish was made with plasma diluted 3:1

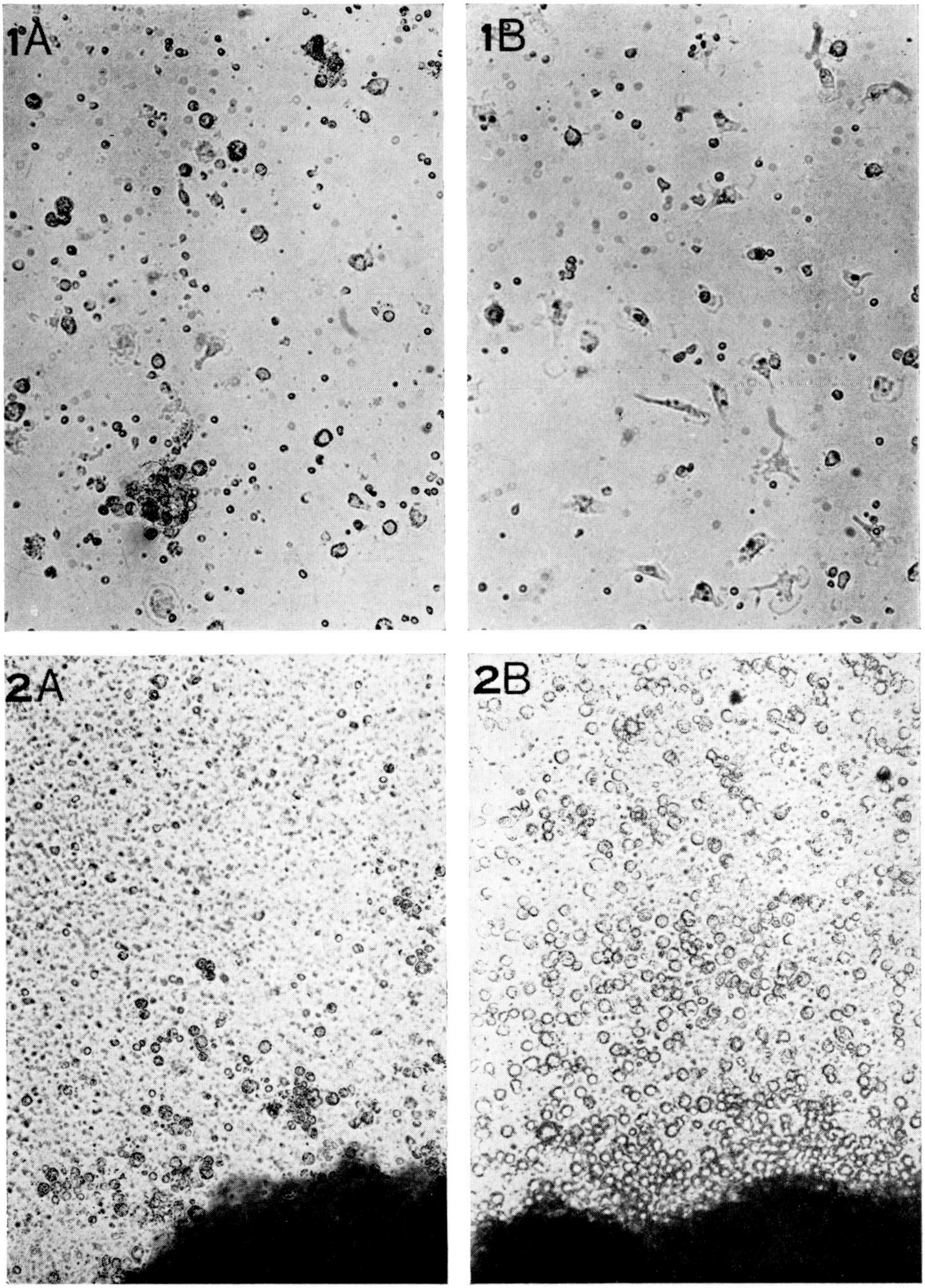

Figure 1. Cultures of sensitized spleen cells after 24 hr incubation and a change of culture medium (× 150). *A*, cultured with 30 μg PPD/ml (note large clumps of cells and rounded shapes); *B*, cultured without antigen (note flattened angulated cells).

Figure 2. Migration of macrophages from clot after 24 hr incubation and glutaraldehyde fixation (× 175). *A*, sensitized cells exposed to 30 μg PPD/ml (note clumping and small area of migration); *B*, control cells exposed to 30 μg PPD/ml, showing only part of the halo of migrated cells. Granular background in both *A* and *B* is the non-cellular clot layered over the base of the Petri dish.

with Hanks' BSS and thrombin. The clot containing the cells was made with full strength plasma and thrombin.

Light microscopy. The spleen cell cultures and macrophage migration from clots were observed and photographed using phase objectives on a Unitron inverted microscope. The cell migration was measured in a double blind fashion with a micrometer and changing the depth of focus from cell to micrometer level. The recorded migration was an average of 10 readings from a given Petri dish containing four clots. The spleen cell cultures were observed in a similar double blind fashion and the degree of aggregation rated. Toluidine blue-stained araldite-embedded sections of the cell-containing clots were observed by bright field microscopy.

Electron microscopy. All the clots involved in the migration experiments were studied under the electron microscope. After decanting the culture media, the cells in the clots were fixed *in situ* with 2.5% glutaraldehyde in 1.067 M cacodylate buffer with 1% sucrose, for 4 to 8 hr. Migration was measured during fixation because some cloudiness in the medium and some free floating cells interfered with visibility in the living cultures. After rinsing several times with cacodylate buffer the cells were post-fixed in 1% OsO_4 for 45 min at 0°C and then rinsed in buffer, also at 0°C. The cell-containing clots were then gently removed from the Petri dish, sliced to appropriately sized pieces, dehydrated in several changes of 70%, 95%, and pure ethanol, cleared in three changes of propylene oxide and embedded in Durcupan ACM Araldite (Roboz Surgical Co., Washington, D. C.) using regular BEEM capsules. After 36 hr of polymerization at 55°C the blocks were thin-sectioned on a Porter-Blum MT-II microtome. Gray sections were picked up on bare grids and stained for 2 min with uranyl acetate at 55°C and 2 min with lead citrate at room temperature. Sections were studied in a Siemens Elmiskop I. Microvillous cell projections were counted from electron micrographs of randomly selected areas. The cell perimeter was measured with a map measure (Keuffel and Esser). The number of microvilli were then expressed per micron of cell perimeter.

RESULTS

The migration and morphology in each of the following six situations was studied after 24 hr incubation: control guinea pig cells exposed to high, low, or no dose of PPD; sensitized guinea pig cells exposed similarly. Spleen cells from sensitized guinea pigs were cultured for 24 hr, some with high dose PPD, others with no PPD.

Splenic cultures. Here the formation of clusters and spherical masses of cells exposed to PPD was vivid. As the masses built up only a small portion of their surface could be attached. As a result they were relatively easily loosened from the floor of the flask by light to moderate agitation of the flask. The clumping was best displayed after the floating cells were removed and the medium replenished (Fig. 1*A*). The control cultures had only 10% to 20% of the clumps and these were perhaps one quarter the size of those in the cultures containing PPD (Fig. 1*B*). In addition, the cells in the experimental cultures were rounded (Fig. 1*A*). Those in controls, on the other hand, were flattened on the floor of the flask, angulated, and displayed an undulating membrane (Fig. 1*B*).

Macrophage migration. With sensitized donors and cells in 30 μg PPD/ml the inhibition of macrophage migration was observed consistently in eight experiments. The halo of cells surrounding the clots measured less than 0.3 mm from the clot edge while control situations demonstrated more than 1 mm of migration (Table I). In those halos where inhibition was manifest, the cells were seen to clump in small groups (Fig. 2*A*). In the larger halos of control cells exposed to PPD and of all cells not exposed to PPD, smaller and many fewer clumps were present (Fig. 2*B*). At concentrations of 3 μg PPD/ml the migration inhibition of sensitive macrophages was less consistent and less marked (Table I). Nonetheless, the clumping of sensitive cells, largely mac-

TABLE I

Cellular migration from clot edge

Exp. No.	Sensitized Guinea Pig: No antigen	Sensitized Guinea Pig: 3 μg PPD/ml	Sensitized Guinea Pig: 30 μg PPD/ml	Control Guinea Pig: No antigen	Control Guinea Pig: 3 μg PPD/ml	Control Guinea Pig: 30 μg PPD/ml
		mm			*mm*	
1	1.7	1.3	0.2	1.6	1.4	1.1
2	1.2	1.3	0.1	1.5	1.5	1.3
3	1.4	0.7	0.2	1.9	1.6	0.9
4	1.5	0.8	0.1	1.2	1.3	1.5
5	1.1	0.9	0.2	1.3	1.1	0.9
6	1.8	1.1	0.2	1.6	1.3	1.1
7	1.9	1.3	0.2	1.6	1.4	1.5
8	1.5	1.0	0.2			

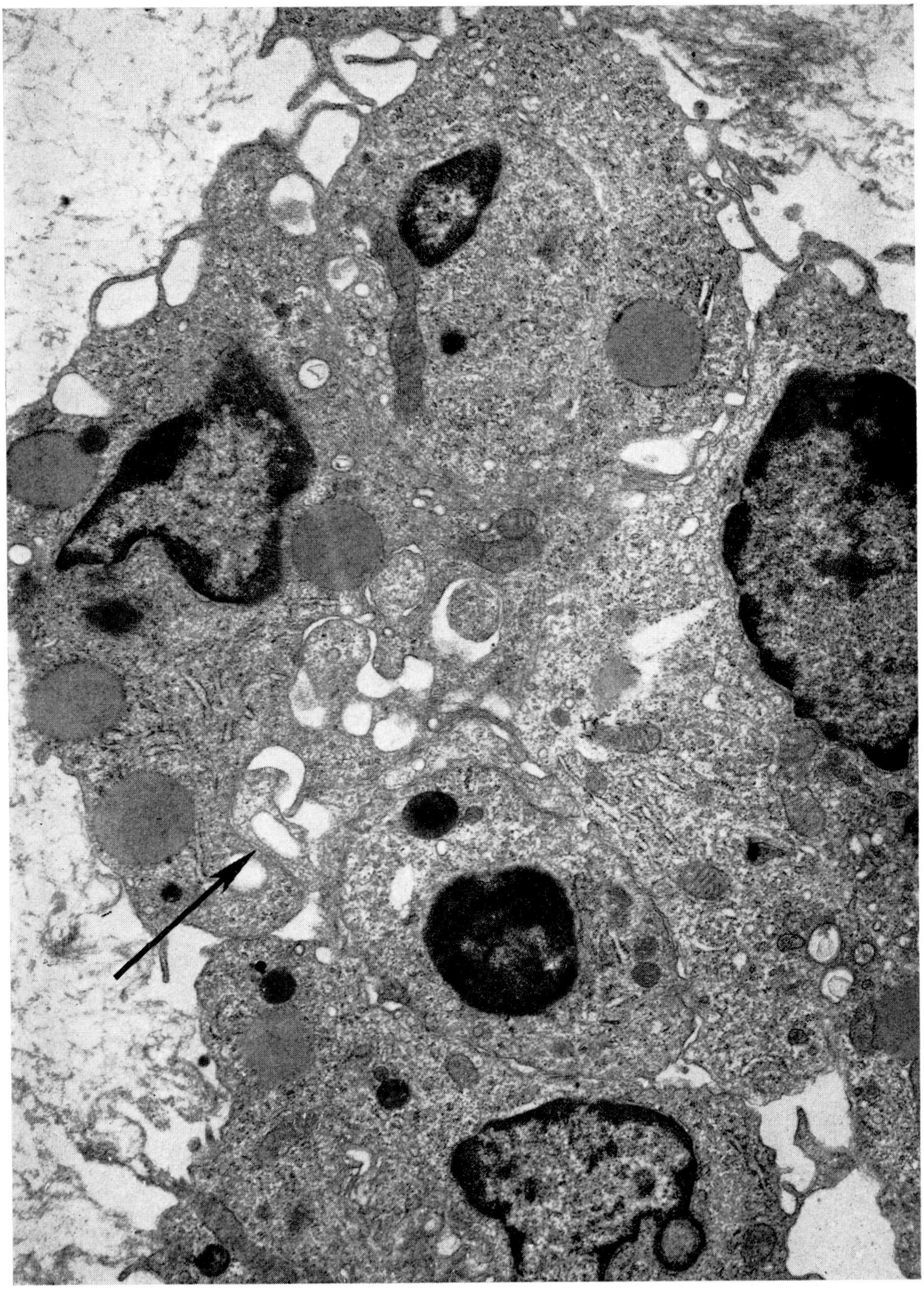

Figure 3. Sensitized macrophages in clot after 24 hr incubation with 3 μg PPD/ml. Note aggregation and interdigitation of microvilli (*arrow*) ($\times$ 12,000).

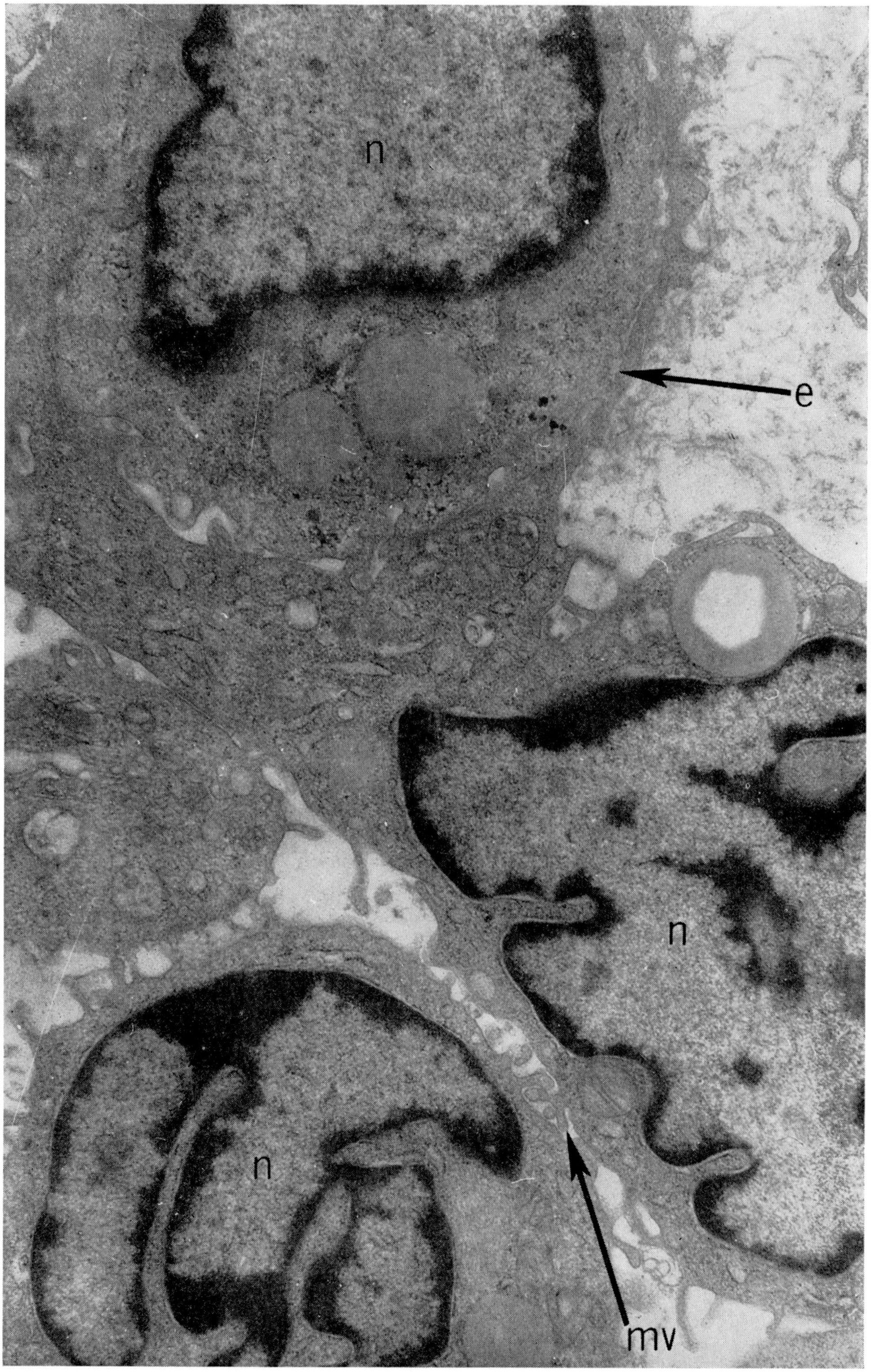

Figure 4. Sensitized macrophages in clot after 24 hr incubation with 30 μg PPD/ml. Note complex nuclei (*n*), interdigitation of microvilli (*mv*), and partial engulfment or indentation of one macrophage by another (*e*) ($\times$ 8,500).

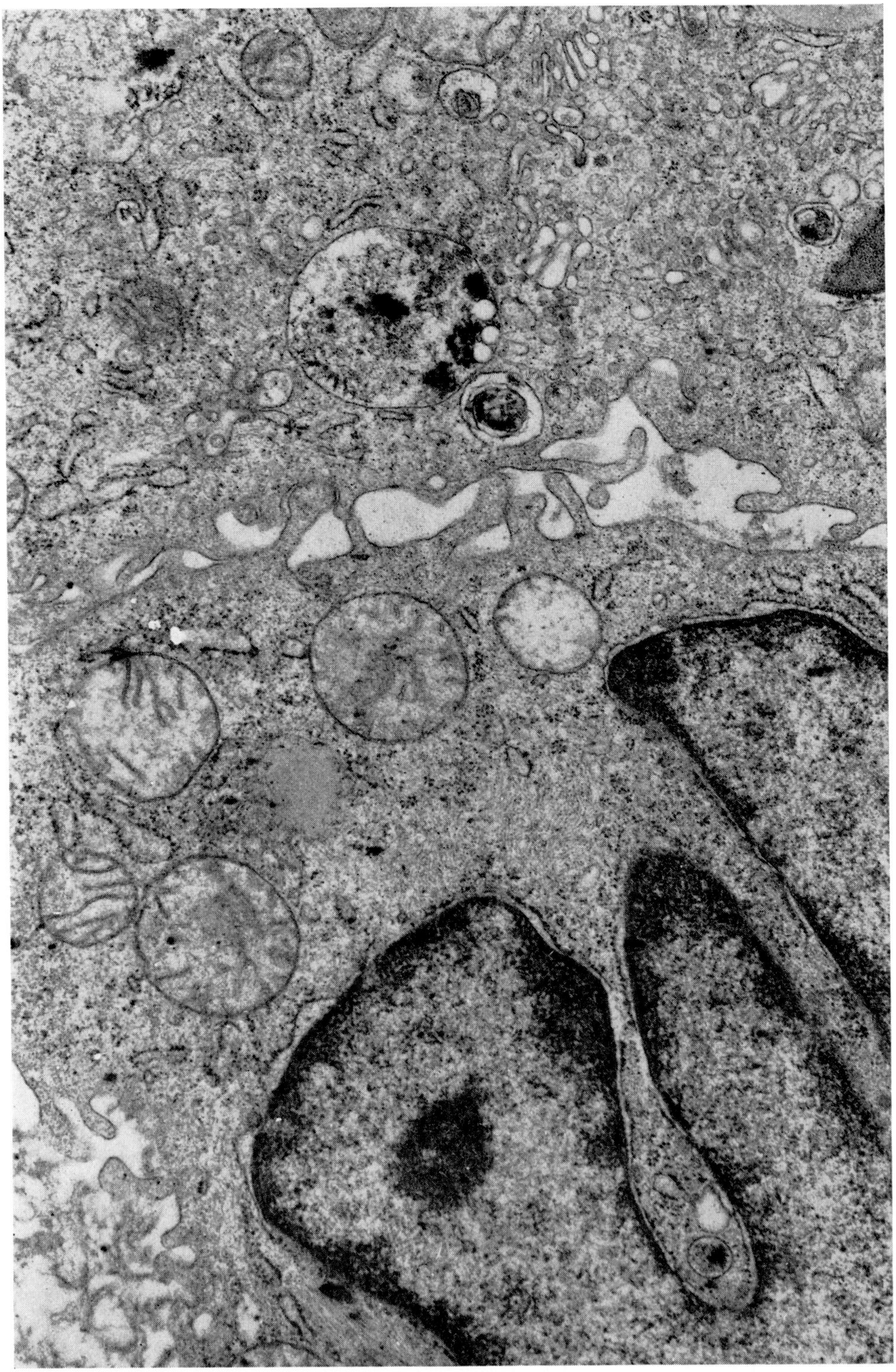

Figure 5. Sensitized macrophages in clot after 24 hr incubation with 30 μg PPD/ml. Note complex nucleus and interdigitation of microvilli ($\times$ 37,000).

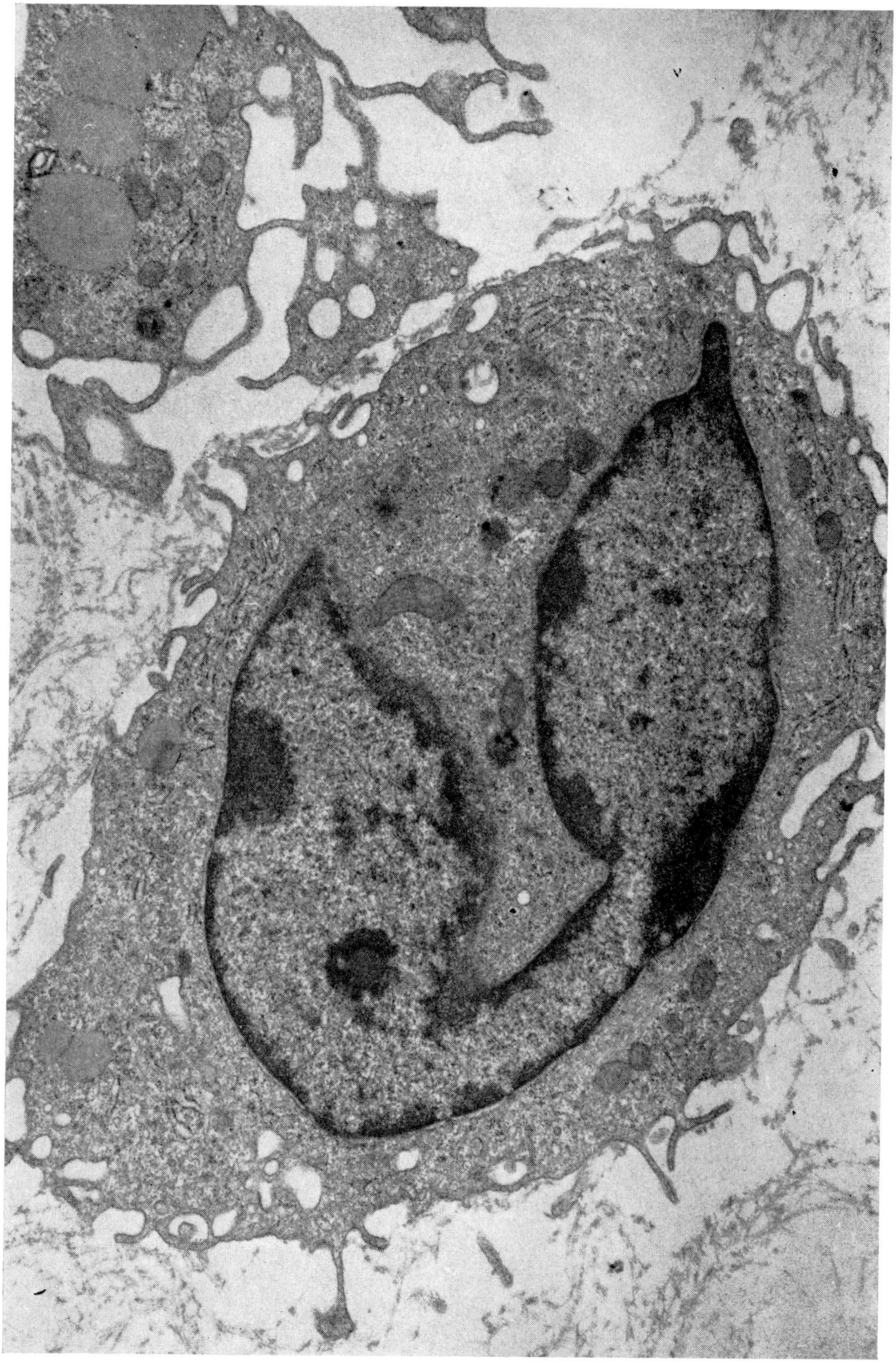

Figure 6. Sensitized macrophage in clot after 24 hr incubation with 3 μg PPD/ml. Note numerous microvilli (× 14,000).

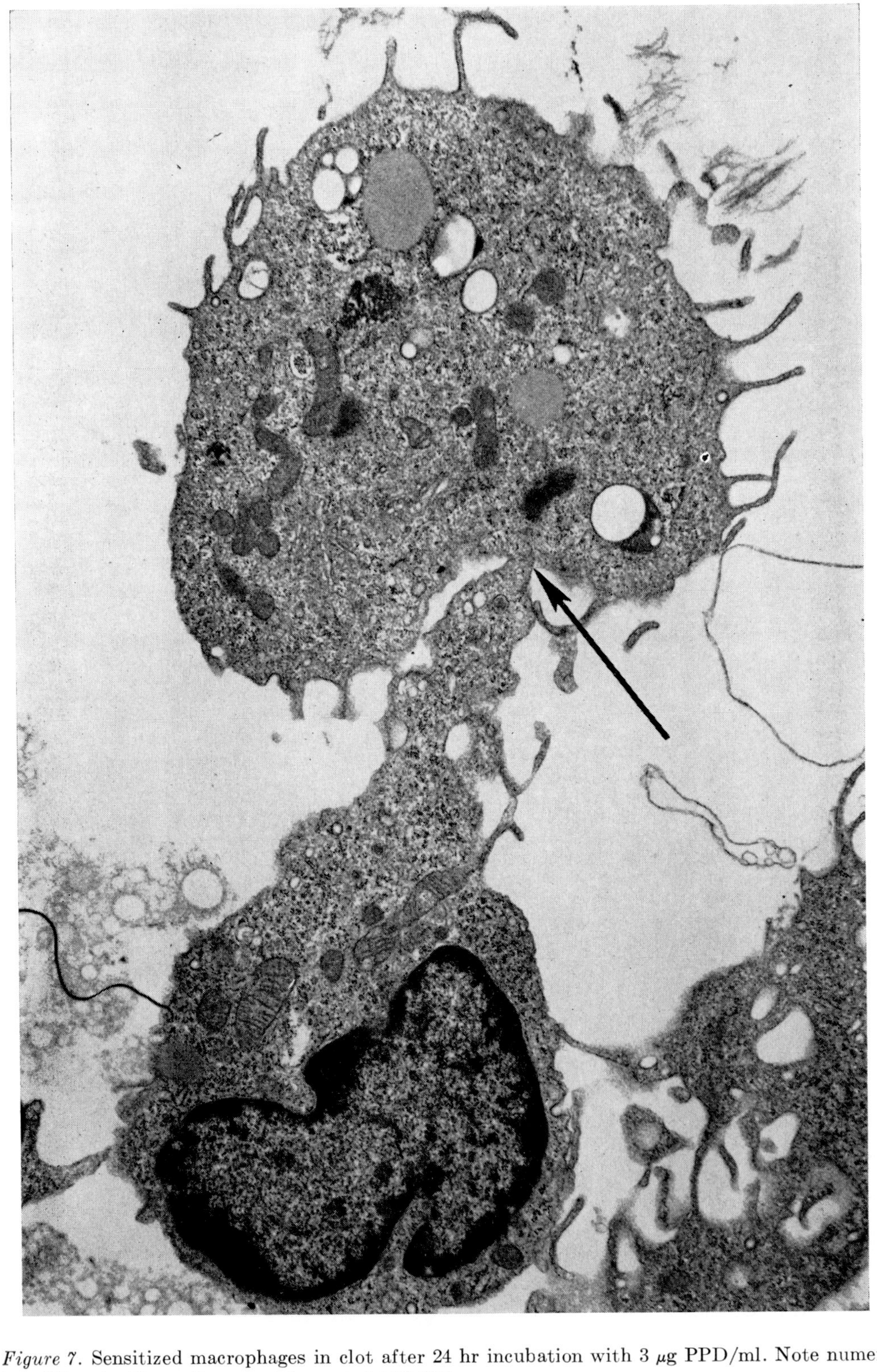

Figure 7. Sensitized macrophages in clot after 24 hr incubation with 3 μg PPD/ml. Note numerous microvilli and cell to cell contact (*arrow*) (× 12,000).

rophages, within the clots was definite at both high and low concentrations of PPD, but more marked at the former (Fig. 3). This was apparent in both light microscopic examination of clot sections and in electron microscopic observations. In most instances the clumping occurred without evident giant cell formation. Here the cells, which were almost exclusively macrophages, showed

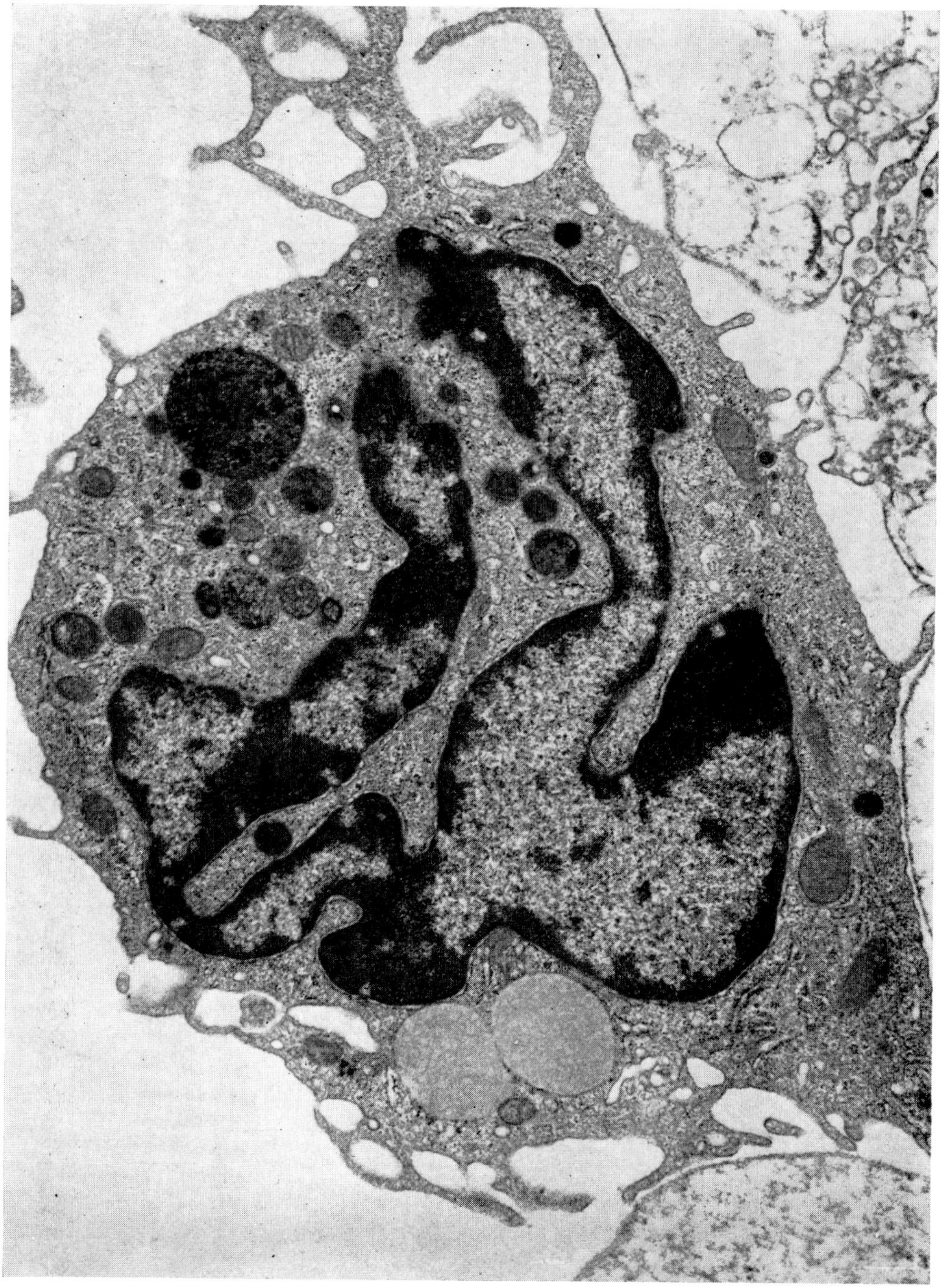

Figure 8. Sensitized macrophage in clot after 24 hr incubation without antigen. Note abundance of microvilli can occur in control situation (× 13,000).

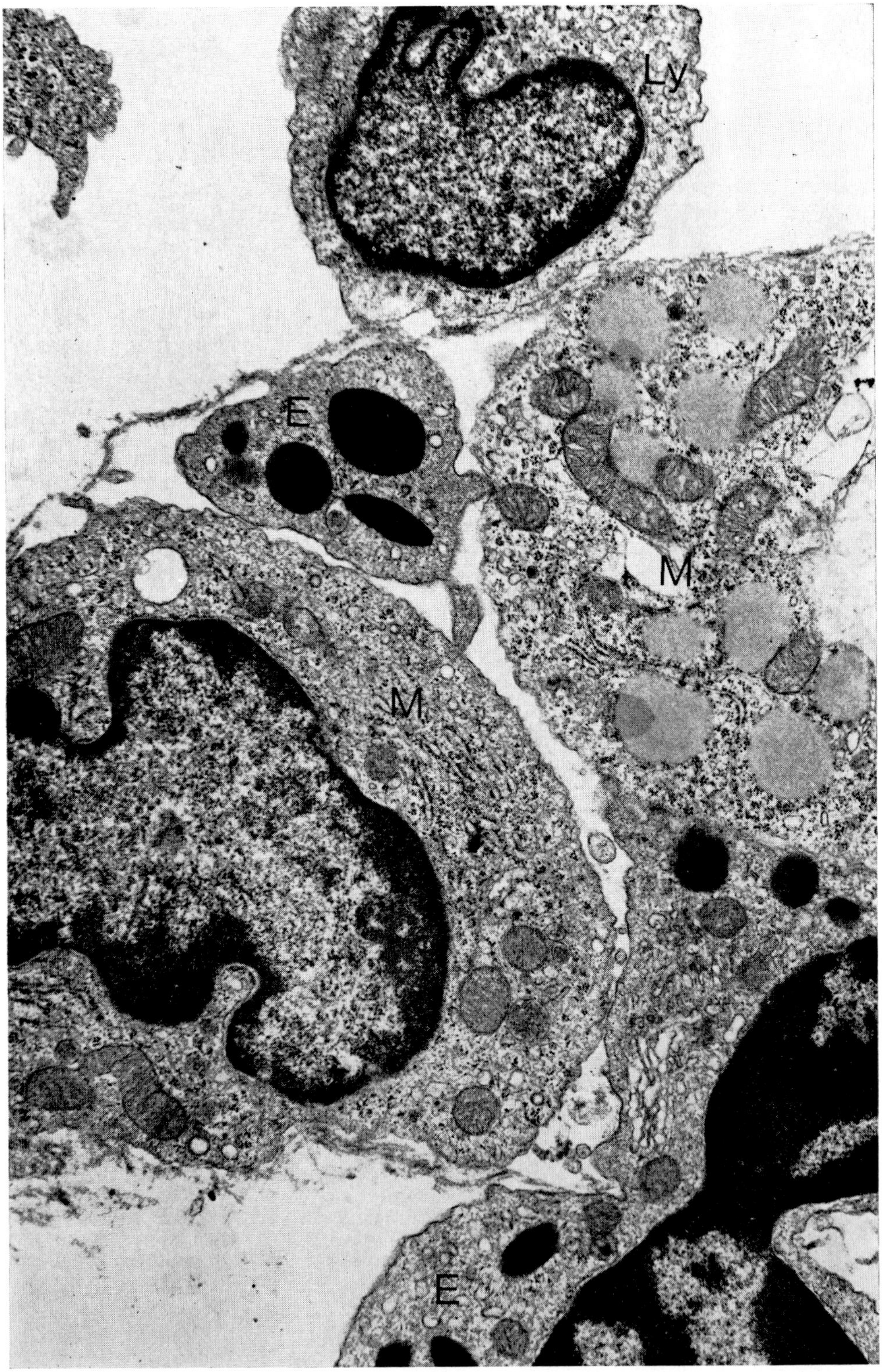

Figure 9. Sensitized macrophage(s) (*M*), eosinophil(s) (*E*), and lymphocyte (*Ly*) in clot after 24 hr incubation without PPD. Note relative lack of microvilli (× 14,000).

slender angulated short microvilli by means of which contiguous cells appeared to become entangled with one another (Figs. 3 to 5). The presence of these cytoplasmic processes was characteristic of experimental cultures (Figs. 3 to 7). They were observed in controls as well (Fig. 8), but a relative scarcity was the rule (Fig. 9), even in clumps.

Close analysis of electron micrographs of 104 randomly selected macrophages, all from sensitized guinea pigs, but half exposed to 3 μg PPD/ml and half not exposed to antigen, revealed a marked difference in the prevalence of microvilli between the two populations (Fig. 10). The mean number of these microvilli/micron of cell perimeter (microvilli/μ) was 0.545 microvilli/μ in macrophages exposed to low dose PPD (variance = 0.099) and 0.295 microvilli/μ in macrophages not exposed to antigen (variance = 0.060). The probability of our data representing a chance observation, assuming the mean values of these two populations is identical, is less than 1 in 10^5. Comparative examination of the extreme values of microvilli/micron helps clarify the difference. Twenty-nine per cent of sensitized macrophages exposed to PPD had 0.7 or greater microvilli/μ while only 8% of those not exposed to PPD had similar values. At the opposite extreme 25% of those not exposed to PPD had 0 to 0.1 microvilli/μ while only 4% of those exposed to antigen had so few processes (Fig. 10).

Giant cells involving three or more macrophages were occasionally observed in experimental cultures with high PPD concentrations. Some macrophages had marked cytoplasmic vacuolization and a degenerated pleomorphic labyrinthine nucleus consistent with cell death (Fig. 11). These cells were difficult to find in control cultures (1% in a count of 100 macrophages in the electron microscope), more prevalent in sensitized cells exposed to low PPD (5% of 100 macrophages counted), and common in high PPD exposure of sensitized cells (15% of 100 macrophages counted). No differences in the incidence of vacuolated macrophages were noted between sensitized cells not exposed to PPD and control cells exposed to high PPD concentration. No intra-cellular differences, other than the toxic changes mentioned, were noted on comparing sensitized and control macrophages exposed to PPD. Macrophages often contained small fat droplets.

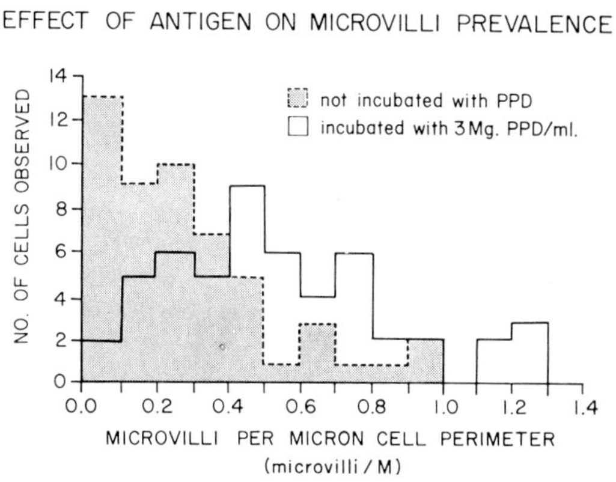

Figure 10. The prevalence of microvilli in 104 sensitized macrophages exposed to low dose or no antigen for 24 hr. The mean number of microvilli/μ after antigen exposure was 0.545 microvilli/μ (variance = 0.999) and 0.295 microvilli/μ (variance = 0.060) without antigen.

Granulocytes, especially eosinophils, were present. In all cultures these were often partially degranulated. They displayed slender cytoplasmic processes and a tendency to entanglement, but to a lesser degree than macrophages.

Lymphocytes were frequently encountered, sometimes within aggregates. These were often large (11 to 20 μ in diameter) and possessed polyribosomes and segments of rough endoplasmic reticulum. These, as macrophages, would often contain fat droplets. No significant structural difference was observed between lymphocytes from sensitized and control guinea pigs exposed to identical concentrations of PPD.

DISCUSSION

In peritoneal exudate cells derived from animals sensitized to BCG, PPD induced increased clumping of macrophages and possibly accelerated giant cell formation. Many of the clumped cells bore numerous microvilli which intertwined with those of contiguous cells. Sensitized cells exposed to PPD were disc-shaped in culture. Control cells, in contrast, were flattened on the floor of the flask and angulated, a conformation associated with motility. We believe that both the clumping of cells and the rounded form of the macrophages contributed to the lack of migration of sensitized cells exposed to antigen. These phenomena occurred to a lesser degree in the presence of concentrations of PPD too low to consistently inhibit migration. We cannot be

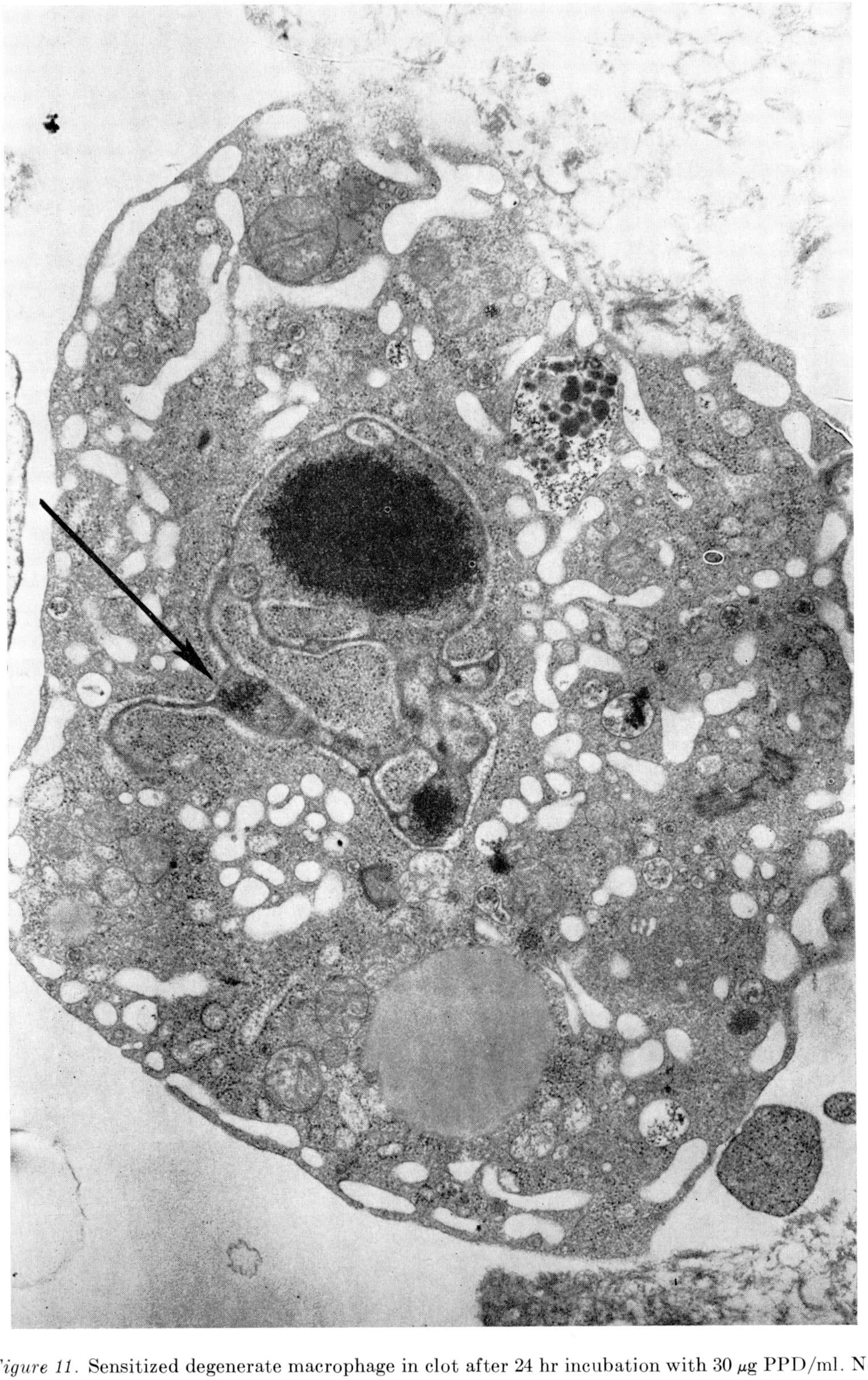

Figure 11. Sensitized degenerate macrophage in clot after 24 hr incubation with 30 μg PPD/ml. Note marked cytoplasmic vacuolization and degenerate pleomorphic nucleus (*arrow*) (× 18,000).

certain that these differences are due to migration inhibitory factor (MIF), macrophage aggregation factor (MAF) (8), or any other characteristic thought to be limited to delayed hypersensitivity rather than immediate hypersensitivity. Antibody is certainly produced to PPD in this *in vitro* system. The presence of clumping and rounded cells in systems where the preponderant response is immediate hypersensitivity has not been investigated.

The transformation of mononuclear cells into macrophages and epithelioid cells occurs readily in tissue culture. This transformation does not depend upon delayed hypersensitivity. It is promoted by low oxygen tension, low pH, and crowding. But even in avian cells where this transformation occurs readily, several days are usually required to bring it to consummation (9). The inhibition of migration as occurs in cells in capillary tubes and in clots in delayed hypersensitivity occurs within 24 hr, presumably before crowding, and its sequelae play significant roles. As observed in our macrophage cultures derived from spleen, moreover, the clumping of sensitized macrophages in the presence of sensitizing antigen was evident within 30 min of setting up the culture before pH shift, significant cell division or crowding.

Nelson (10) has studied peritoneal macrophages *in situ* after the intraperitoneal injection of PPD in tuberculin-sensitive guinea pigs. He noted that clumps of macrophages, in which contiguous cells showed intertwined microvilli, adhered to the peritoneal lining, and displayed incipient giant cell formation. Clearly our results in tissue culture confirm Nelson's *in vivo* observations. Nelson has suggested that increased macrophage adherence, both to other macrophages and to other structures, i.e., the clot in our experiment, may explain apparent decreased motility.

Granger (11) has demonstrated the production of a soluble nonspecific cell toxin, lymphotoxin (LT), by stimulated lymphocytes. The morphologic indications of LT effect on target cells observed under the light microscope are cytoplasmic vacuolization, the rounding up of the cells, and finally cell rupture. We too noted cell vacuolization and rounding up in our material. Their prevalence in our experience was proportional to the concentration of antigen to which the sensitized lymphocytes were exposed. Sundesmo, working with Granger (11), has studied mouse L cells exposed to human LT, using electron microscopy. He has observed plasma membrane blebbing and extension of many cytoplasmic processes by the target cells. Again we have noted similar changes in our guinea pig macrophages incubated with antigenically stimulated lymphocytes. Finally, Granger has found that partially purified preparations of human LT can inhibit the migration of guinea pig peritoneal macrophages from capillary tubes. The similarities between Granger's and our findings indicate that lymphotoxin may be actively involved in our system and may account for many of the changes described.

We have as yet no insight into any lymphocytic changes associated with the elaboration of migration inhibitory factor, a process which presumably occurs in our cultures. Lymphocytes are not uncommon. A number contain polyribosomes and some rough endoplasmic reticulum and a well developed Golgi apparatus; these are organelles signifying protein synthesis and secretion. Perhaps lymphocytes producing MIF are among these cells.

The implications of cell clumping induced by a specific protein extend beyond the field of immunology. Specific cell aggregation is a significant factor in major embryologic pathways of differentiation, for example. The possibility that different polypeptides have the potential to induce aggregation of specific cell types, such as macrophages in delayed hypersensitivity, requires investigation.

Acknowledgment. The authors express their sincere appreciation to Mrs. Prudence H. Smyth for her excellent technical assistance.

REFERENCES

1. George, M. and Vaughan, J. H., Proc. Soc. Exp. Biol. Med., *111:* 514, 1962.
2. David, J. R., Lawrence, H. J. and Thomas, L., J. Immun., *93:* 274, 1964.
3. Bloom, B. R. and Bennett, B., Fed. Proc., *27:* 13, 1968.
4. David, J. R., Fed. Proc., *27:* 6, 1968.
5. Rich, A. R. and Lewis, M. R., Bull. Johns Hopkins Hosp., *50:* 115, 1932.

6. Fauve, R. M. and Dekaris, D., Science, *160:* 795, 1968.
7. Bartfeld, H. and Kelly, R., J. Immun., *100:* 1000, 1968.
8. Somsak, L., Dray, S. and Gotoff, S. P., J. Immun., *104:* 296, 1970.
9. Weiss, L. and Facett, D. W., J. Histochem. Cytochem., *1:* 47, 1953.
10. Nelson, D. J., *Macrophages and Immunity,* p. 152, J. Wiley and Sons, Inc., New York, 1969.
11. Granger, G. A., in *Perspectives in Immunology, Mediators of Cellular Immunity,* Edited by H. J. Lawrence and M. Landy, p. 324, Academic Press, New York, 1969.

THE JOURNAL OF IMMUNOLOGY
Vol. 105, No. 6, December 1970

Printed in U.S.A.

PRIMARY REJECTION OF HOMOLOGOUS INTRAPERITONEAL FIBROBLASTS: AN ELECTRON MICROSCOPIC STUDY[1, 2]

LEON WEISS[3] AND PRUDENCE SMYTH

From the Department of Anatomy, The Johns Hopkins University, School of Medicine, Baltimore, Maryland

Received for publication July 27, 1970

This is an electron microscopic study of the rejection of a simple graft. 2×10^6 L cells (a tissue culture culture strain of fibroblasts derived from C_3H mice) are injected intraperitoneally into BALB/cJ mice. Following the injection intraperitoneal nodules 2 to 4 mm in diameter appear by day 2 and remain until days 5 to 7. The surface of the nodules is covered by histiocytes and L cells. These cells bear surface projections and are strikingly similar to mesothelium. Each nodule displays a central zone, and inner and outer shells. The outer shell is dominated by L cells; a few macrophages, plasma cells, lymphocytes and granulocytes are present. The inner shell contains many L cells, many macrophages, and lymphocytes, and relatively few plasma cells and mast cells. Host cells and L cells are in close touch, their contiguity increased by interdigitation of filiform cytoplasmic processes. Cytoplasmic continuity is seldom observed. Emperipolesis is occasionally noted. Especially toward the inner part of this shell both L cells and host cells are vacuolated and show other signs of damage. In certain nodules the L cell surface shows virus-like particles on stalk-like processes. The central zone is necrotic, often caseous. At the junction of the central zone and inner shell fluid necrotic material lies between vital cells and is taken into lysosomes of macrophages and, to a lesser extent, of other cell types. Some collagen is present throughout the nodule. Rarely are the nodules vascularized. During the rejection of the nodules, Peyer's patches, abdominal lymph nodes, and the spleen are enlarged by L cells. Changes similar to those present in the nodules are observed in these lymphatic structures.

Rejection of solid tissue homografts is a complex process associated with vascular changes, infiltration by diverse cellular types, large scale degeneration, and necrosis. Rosenau and Moon (1–4) and other workers (5–10) developed simplified systems wherein sensitized immunologically competent cells and cells isogenous with the sensitizing graft cells are isolated and then permitted to interact in tissue culture; thereby are isolated the essential cellular reactants in the terminal phases of a graft rejection. And indeed, the target graft cells are destroyed in a manner very much as grafts are rejected, *viz.*, cell-to-cell contact is required, the system does not require extrinsic complement, and humoral antibody does not appear relevant. Yet this useful simplified system is both limited and complex. The appearance in this reaction of significant numbers of plasma cells containing an immunoglobulin has been observed (11, 12). The reaction may parallel the essence of solid tissue graft rejection or it may depend upon humoral antibody and be related to the phenomenon of the "white graft."

The very simplification of the reaction and its advantages eliminate essential preliminary steps. Should it consititute a paradigm of homograft rejection, it does so only for the terminal phases. The production of humoral antibody in certain models depends upon the sequential action of at least two immunologically competent cells (13–15). These include antigen sensitive cells released from the thymus which, after reacting

[1] This work was presented at the American Association of Anatomists Meeting in Chicago, 1970. Anat. Rec., *166:* 48, 1970.

[2] This study was supported by Grant 5 R01 AM11381-10 from the United States Public Health Service.

[3] Research Career Development Awardee, United States Public Health Service.

with antigen, interact with cells derived from bone marrow, which actually elaborate antibody. This sequence may be preceded by the action of macrophages on the antigen (16, 17).

Such sequences, should they exist in delayed hypersensitivity, and they appear to (18), would be absent in this tissue culture system. Certainly the initial contact between homologous cell and host and the reactions in lymph node and spleen are not on view.

In their induction of sensitized spleen cells Rosenau and Moon (1) injected L cells as an intraperitoneal graft. These cells formed nodules which could be vascularized, were infiltrated with lymphoid cells and were rejected. These nodules, along with free L cells in the peritoneum, draining lymph nodes and spleen, appear to constitute a complete and simple type of *in vivo* system. It is more complete and more complex than the tissue culture systems and less complex than solid organ transplants.

Accordingly we have undertaken an electron and light microscopic study of the primary rejection of grafts of homologuos fibroblasts ("L" cells) injected as concentrated suspensions into the peritoneum of BALB/cJ mice. In fact, this material has been gathered from animals undergoing the very sensitization required for the tissue culture studies already reported. Our objectives are to study the interactions of homologous and host cells, to note changes in lymph nodes and spleen, and to relate these findings both to those from tissue culture systems and from grafts of solid tissues.

MATERIALS AND METHODS

Animals. Six- to 8-week-old female albino mice of the BALB/cJ strain were obtained from the Jackson Memorial Laboratories, Bar Harbor, Maine.

Media. L-929 fibroblast suspensions were used.[4] The cells were washed and resuspended in Hanks' balanced salt solution (BSS).[4]

Procedure. Fourteen mice were injected intraperitoneally, one time, with a suspension of 2 $\times$ 10^6 viable L cells in 0.25 ml Hanks' BSS. Two mice per day, beginning day 1 after injection, were sacrificed by cervical dislocation and their peritoneal cavities were opened. Clumps or nodules of cells, approximately 2 mm in diameter, floated freely in the fluid of the peritoneal cavity or adhered to the mesentery. These nodules were removed with ease by pipette and placed whole into fixative (Karnovsky's formaldehyde-glutaraldehyde) for 4 to 6 hr, then rinsed in cacodylate buffer (0.067 M, pH 7.4) with 1% sucrose. The nodules were post-fixed in 2% OsO_4 for 90 min, dehydrated in alcohols, cleared in propylene oxide, and embedded in Araldite (Durcupan ACM).[5]

Nodules were sectioned on a Porter-Blum MTII Ultra-Microtome. Sections for light microscopy, 1 to 3 μ in thickness, were stained with toluidine blue.

Approximately 150 nodules were studied.

OBSERVATIONS

Pattern of response

Peritoneal nodules were observed from 2 to 5 days after injections of L cells into non-sensitized animals. Seldom were nodules present before 2 days and rarely were they evident after 7 days. They were most numerous 4 to 5 days after injection, when as many as 10 to 15 nodules could be recovered per animal. By 6 days only 3 to 4 were found.

In animals sensitized by two or more monthly injections the nodules followed a less predictable pattern: fewer appeared, and when they did they remained a shorter time, typically 24 to 72 hr.

Gross observations

The nodules were largest on days 4 to 5 at which time they were 2 to 4 mm in diameter. They were translucent to opaque cream-colored bodies. Often they were mulberry-shaped, suggesting multicentric origin or fusion.

Blood vessels were not observed penetrating these nodules. Almost always the nodules were free in the peritoneal cavity dispersed through the peritoneum, somewhat concentrated in the gutters of the posterior wall, in folds of mesentery and upon the viscera. The nodules could easily be removed with a medicine dropper. There was slightly more clear fluid in the peritoneal cavity than normal but no other suggestion of inflam-

[4] Supplied by Baltimore Biological Laboratories, Baltimore, Md.

[5] Obtained frum Roboz Surgical Instrument Co., Inc., Washington, D. C.

mation. No increased vascularization was observed. The animals were not different in appearance or manner from normal. Peyer's patches and mesenteric and retroperitoneal lymph nodes were enlarged 2 to 3 times normal volume, and were tense and translucent. The spleen was not grossly changed.

Light microscopic observations

Nodules. In most of the nodules three zones were discernible by low power light microscopy: *viz.*, a central zone and inner and outer circumferential bands (Fig. 1). The central zone was necrotic. Nuclei, dense angulated cells, disrupted cells, cell debris, and a dense, irregular ground were present. The zone resembled caseous necrosis. The inner circumferential band contained host and graft cells in close contact and with evidence of damage (Figs. 2 and 3). It contained deeply basophilic pleomorphic lymphoid cells and macrophages in large numbers and many L cells. Lymphocytes and plasma cells in this zone were vacuolated, sharply angulated, degenerated, and otherwise altered. The outer circumferential band consisted of L cells, many of which were proliferating, and lymphoid cells, macrophages and granulocytes, whose structure and shape suggested movement. Here L cells and host cells seldom showed evidence of damage. The very outermost layer of cells showed a scalloped contour and occasionally displayed filiform processes.

Nodes. For 2 to 3 days after injection of L cells the lymph nodes of the posterior abdominal wall and Peyer's patches were crowded with L cells to a degree that it was difficult to separate cortex from medulla. Large zones of the node appeared to consist of sheets of L cells. In several days this was succeeded by marked macrophage activity. Single L cells and L cells in small clusters were closely surrounded by lymphocytes or plasma cells or macrophages. Post-capillary lymph nodes were moderately crowded with intra-endothelial lymphocytes. By 9 to 11 days, the node could appear normal.

Spleen. The spleen contained many L cells in white pulp and marginal zone soon after inoculation. Within 3 to 4 days the L cells were absent and there was little change from normal, the difference being more marked phagocytosis.

Electron microscopy of nodules

Outer circumferential band. This was made up of an outermost or surface layer and a subsurface shell or band.

The outermost layer, providing the peritoneal surface, bore filiform processes. The cell types making up this layer were for the most part histocytes or macrophages. Many L cells were present and some lymphocytes and granulocytes as well. Little phagocytosis was evident (Figs. 4 and 5). Beneath the surface layer, L cells in large numbers and occasional lymphocytes, plasma cells, mast cells and polymorphonuclear granulocytes were present (Figs. 6 and 7). A fair number of L cells and a few lymphoid cells were in division. The cells in this layer showed no evidence of damage or major structural modification. These cells often bore filiform processes and formed a loose feltwork of interdigitating processes. These processes could often be capped by concentric densities which appeared to be virus bodies (Fig. 6).

Intermediate band. Here structural modifications were present (Figs. 8 to 10). A few mast cells were usually present. Occasionally polymorphonuclear leukocytes were seen. Macrophages, lymphocytes, plasma cells and L cells were present in large numbers. Lymphocytes predominated over plasma cells by a ratio of approximately 2:1. Many of the plasma cells and lymphocytes were sharply angulated and vacuolated. Contiguity, but no cytoplasmic continuity, was observed between L cells and lymphocytes, plasma cells and macrophages. Many cells were severely degenerated and dead. A dense material, perhaps representing a fluid material derived from dead cells, lay between these cells forming slender strands varying in contour, thickness, density and consistency (Figs. 9 to 11). This material was taken up into lysosomes as secondary material in the formation of definitive lysosomes (Fig. 9). The inner layers of the intermediate band contained a large proportion of degenerated and dead cells (Figs. 10 and 11).

Central region or core. Here the cells were dead (Figs. 10 and 11). It was possible to recognize residues of different cell types—but in most instances the cells were so changed as to be unrecognizable.

DISCUSSION

The L cells in our experiments were injected into the peritoneal cavity as a cellular suspension. Undoubtedly, small clusters of cells likely formed nodules intraperitoneally. It is likely that the nodules were produced both by adhesion of L cells and by their proliferation. Within minutes, moreover, single or small groups of L cells were likely carried to lymph nodes and spleen. Within a few hours the peritoneal clusters of L cells were likely complexed with host cells.

Differences exist between this dispersed cell graft and a graft of solid tissue. A solid tissue graft may release cells which are taken up by the draining lymph nodes and spleen. A sufficient number of such cells may reach lymphatic tissue to induce sensitivity in the draining node or the spleen. As well, circulating cells of the host enter and interact with the solid graft and then leave it for local and remote lymph nodes and the spleen. There they may proliferate or induce changes or reactions in other cells. As a next step, sensitized cells and many non-sensitized cells lie at the base of the graft or re-enter it, after which the graft is rejected (19). The dispersed cellular graft behaves somewhat differently, primarily in that large numbers of graft cells quickly enter the draining lymphatic tissue. Further, the small size of the graft, i.e., single cells or small nodules of cells, makes it far more vulnerable to immune attack. Humoral antibody, considered inoperative or a minor factor in the rejection of solid tissue grafts, may play a significant factor in the rejection of cell suspensions. The dispersed cells may well be compared, in distribution and perhaps in the kind of reaction they elicit, to such invasive organisms as tubercle bacilli. Small nodules of grafted cells, moreover, need not depend upon vascularization to facilitate interaction with the host. We emphasize, however, that where cells injected as a dispersion coalesce and divide to form nodules of some size, they display the features of solid tissue grafts and, as we have shown, appear to have similar interactions with lymphoid cells. It is likely, however, that the cells of these moderate-sized nodules, because of the reactions elicited by their more dispersed cohorts, have antibody play upon them in rather high concentration.

The zonation of the nodule was consistent and striking. The absence of reaction as evident by cell damage in the outer band might have been due to a combination of just-entered host cells and proliferating graft cells. By the time there was morphologic evidence of interaction of host immunologically competent cells and graft cells, the interacting cells had been covered by a layer of proliferating and accreting L cells. The evidence of interaction was found largely in the intermediate layer. When the damaging interaction was complete, the result was a central zone of necrotic cells. The absence of evident reaction in the superficial cells suggests the absence or minor role of any circulating humoral antibody, although the nodular zonation may be interpreted differently. The central necrotic zone may have been due to an insufficient blood supply. The intermediate zone of damaged reactive cells may have represented nothing more than incipient degenerative changes en route to anoxic necrosis. The outer layer, just thick enough to be nourished by peritoneal fluid, would remain in good condition; however, the disappearance of these nodules, their morphology, the absence of necrosis in avascular masses of similar size and porosity, and the evidence from

---

Figure 1. A nodule of L cells undergoing rejection. Three zones may be recognized. In the center is a spherule of necrotic cells. It is surrounded by an inner circumferential band or shell, whose width is the distance between arrow tips. The tissue here is dark and partially vacuolated. Damaged cells are conspicuous. The outer shell, a light one, consists of L cells, many of them dividing, and host cells. Neither graft nor host cells appear damaged in this shell. Both host cells and L cells, presumably freshly arrived, form the surface of the nodule. Toluidine blue stain, Araldite embedded (× 75).

Figure 2. The outer band of a nodule. At the peritoneal surface several vacuolated cells (*arrows, m*) are likely macrophages. Near the right margin of the plate is a granulocyte (*arrow, g*). Within the nodule are several basophilic cells, likely plasma cells (*arrows, pc*). Note the mix of host cells and the large L cells (*arrows, L*). Toluidine blue stain, Araldite embedded (× 500).

Figure 3. The junction between the necrotic and reactive zones. Most of the cells at the bottom of the figure are dead. Although some cellular structures, such as granules and nuclei, may be recognized, much of this zone is amorphic debris. At the top of the field, L cells and some host cells, perhaps plasma cells or lymphocytes (*arrows*), can be recognized. Toluidine blue stain, Araldite embedded (× 500).

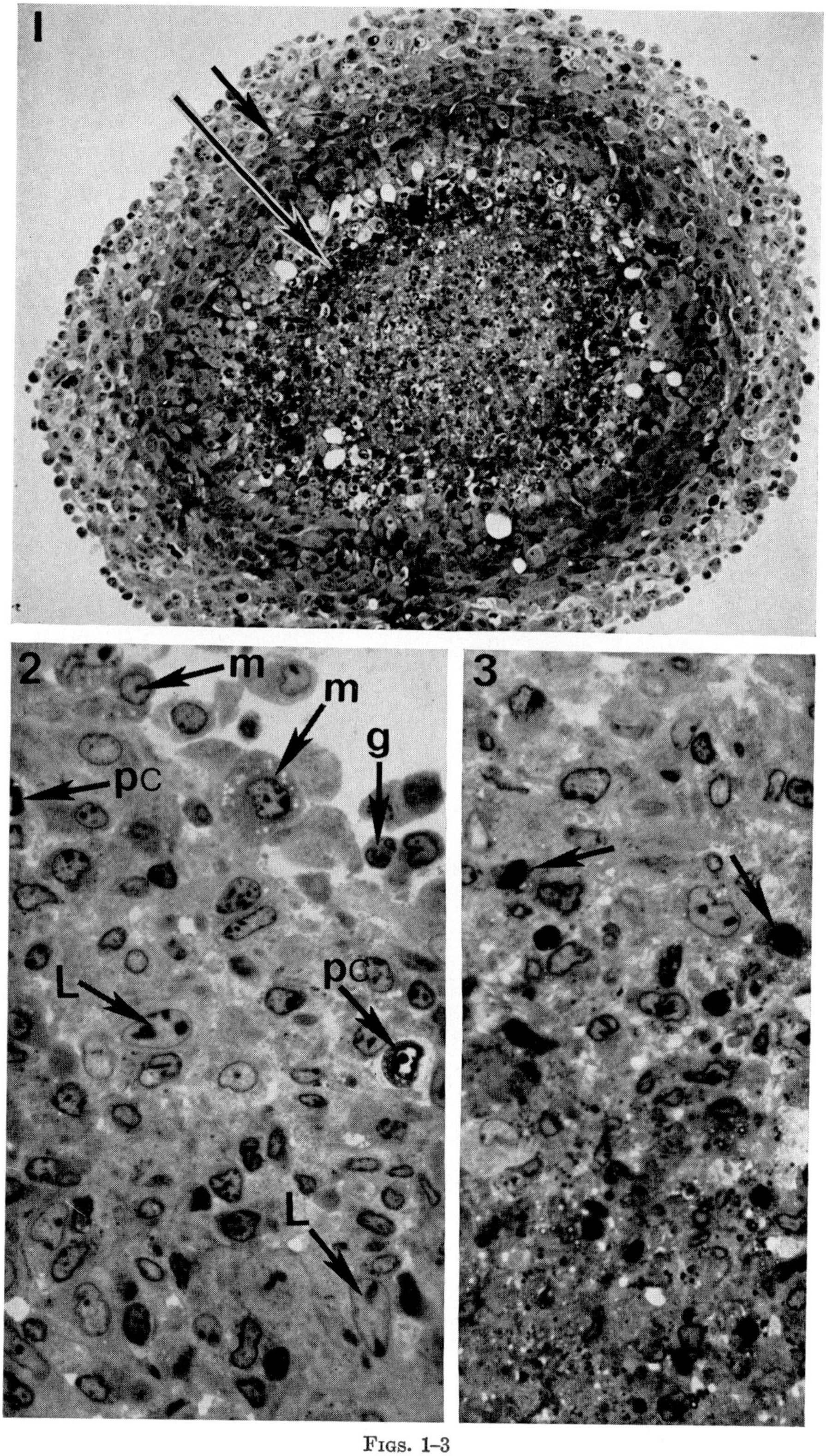

FIGS. 1–3

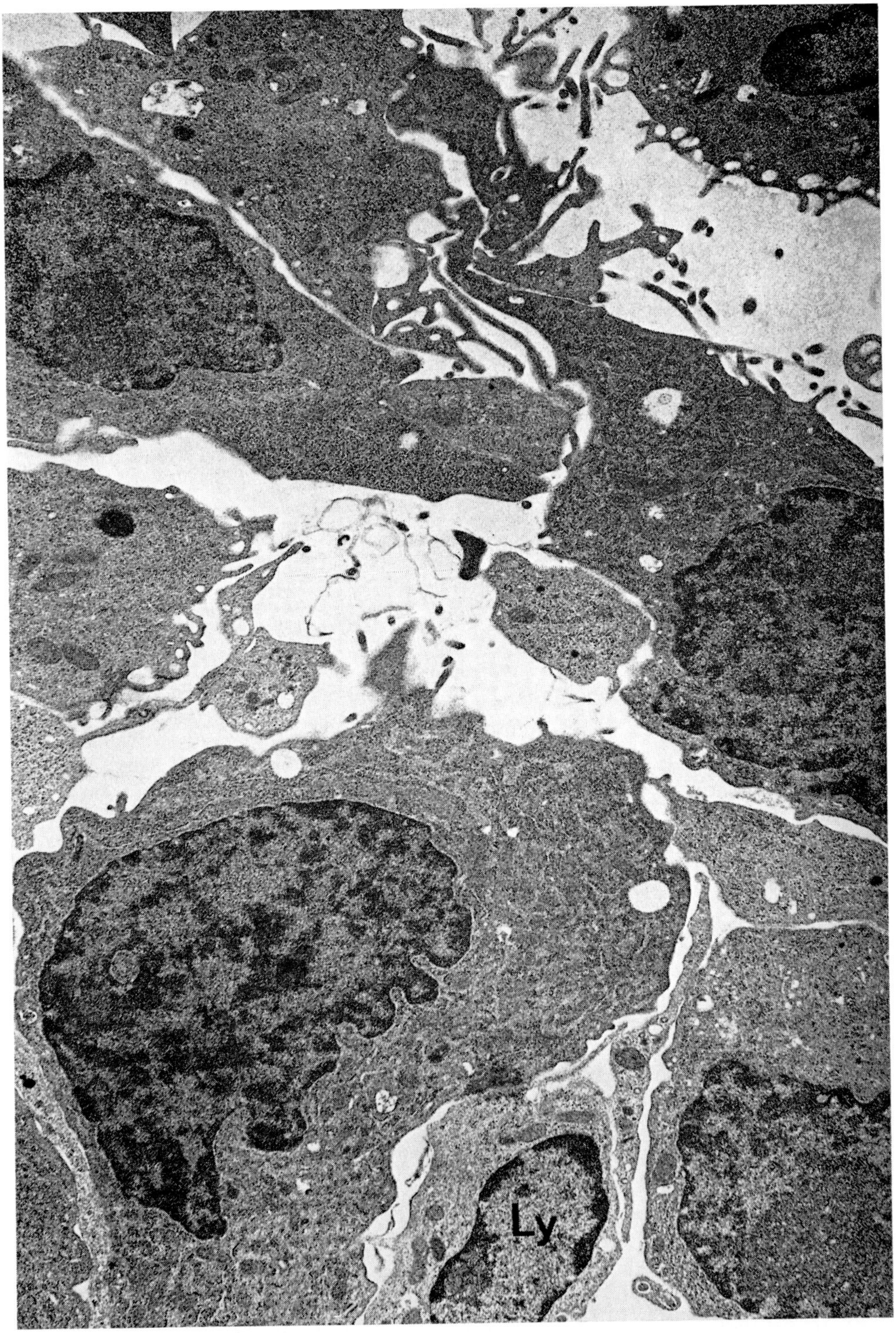

Figure 4. The peritoneal surface of a nodule. Here, as is common, the cells at the surface are separated by clear intercellular fluid. Long microvilli in large numbers are evident. A cell in the right upper corner appears loosely adherent to the nodule. The surface of the nodule, rich in microvilli, is made in large part of L cells. The L cells show dilated sacs of rough ER, perhaps containing material precursor to collagen. The villi of some of the microvilli of the L cells are tipped with a dense material which appears to be virus (see Fig. 6). At the bottom of the field a lymphocyte (*Ly*) is contiguous to an L cell. See Figures 5 to 8 (× 12,000).

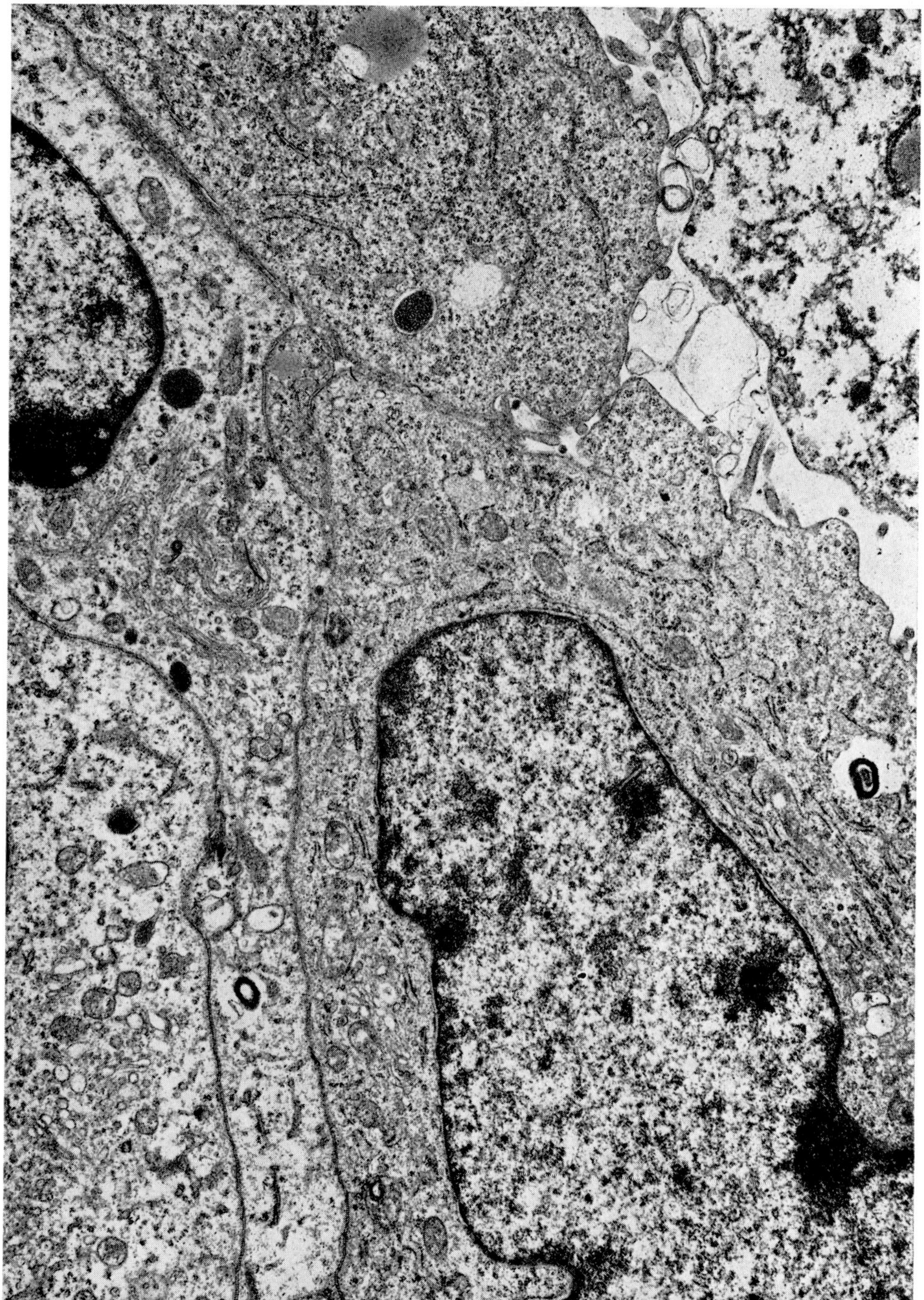

Figure 5. The peritoneal surface of a nodule. Most of the cells are macrophages. They lie close together and display short microvilli. A dead cell, apparently adherent to the surface, is in the right upper corner. Compare the dense lysosomes with Figures 9 to 11 and the surface with Figure 4 (× 18,000).

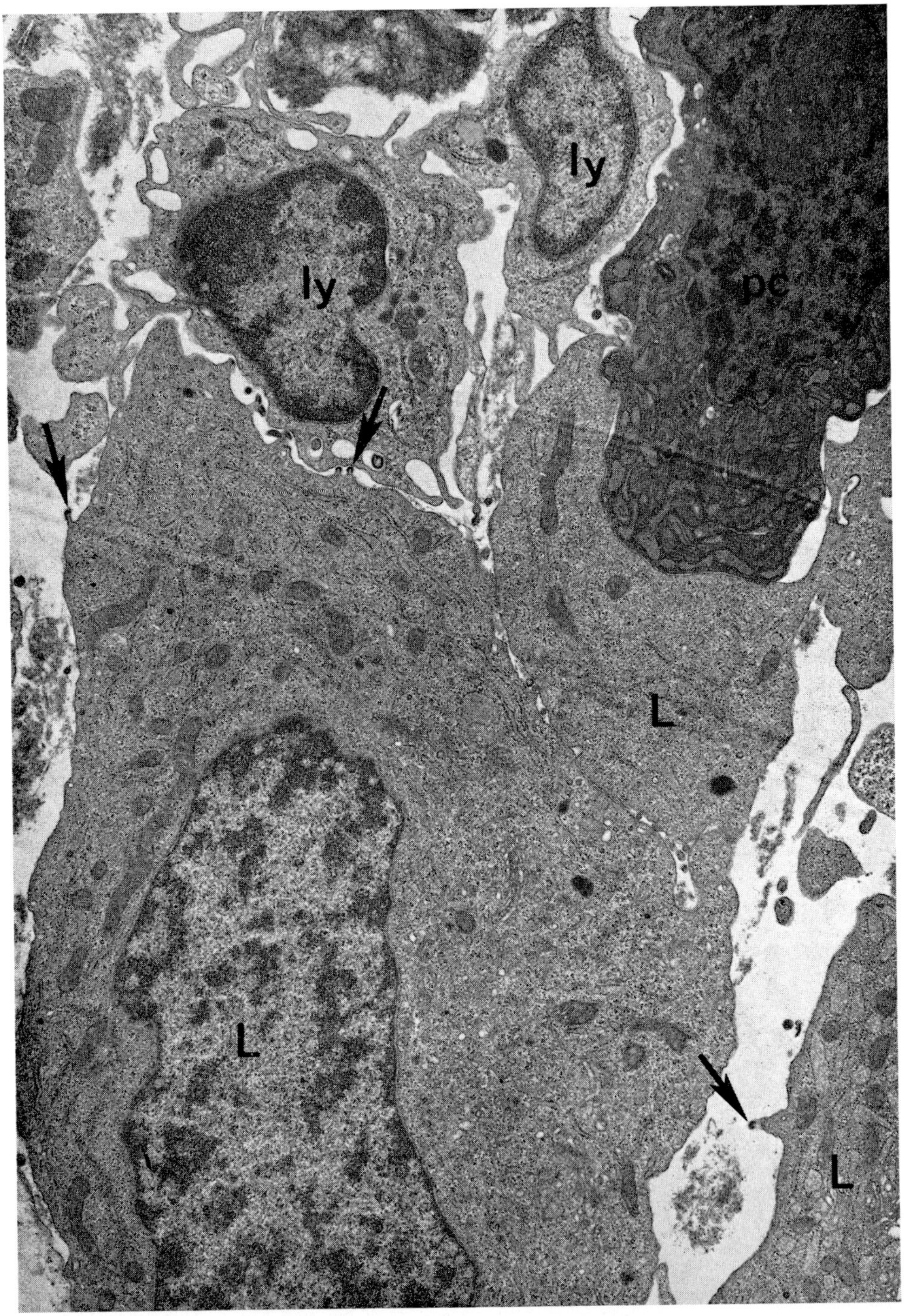

Figure 6. This field is taken from the outer band, several cell layers below the surface. The cells are loosely packed. L cells (*L*) occupy the lower two-thirds of the field. Note the contiguity of L cells with a plasma cell on the right (*pc*) and with the microvilli of two lymphocytes (*ly*). The microvilli of the L cells are tipped with virus-like structures (*arrows*) (× 10,500).

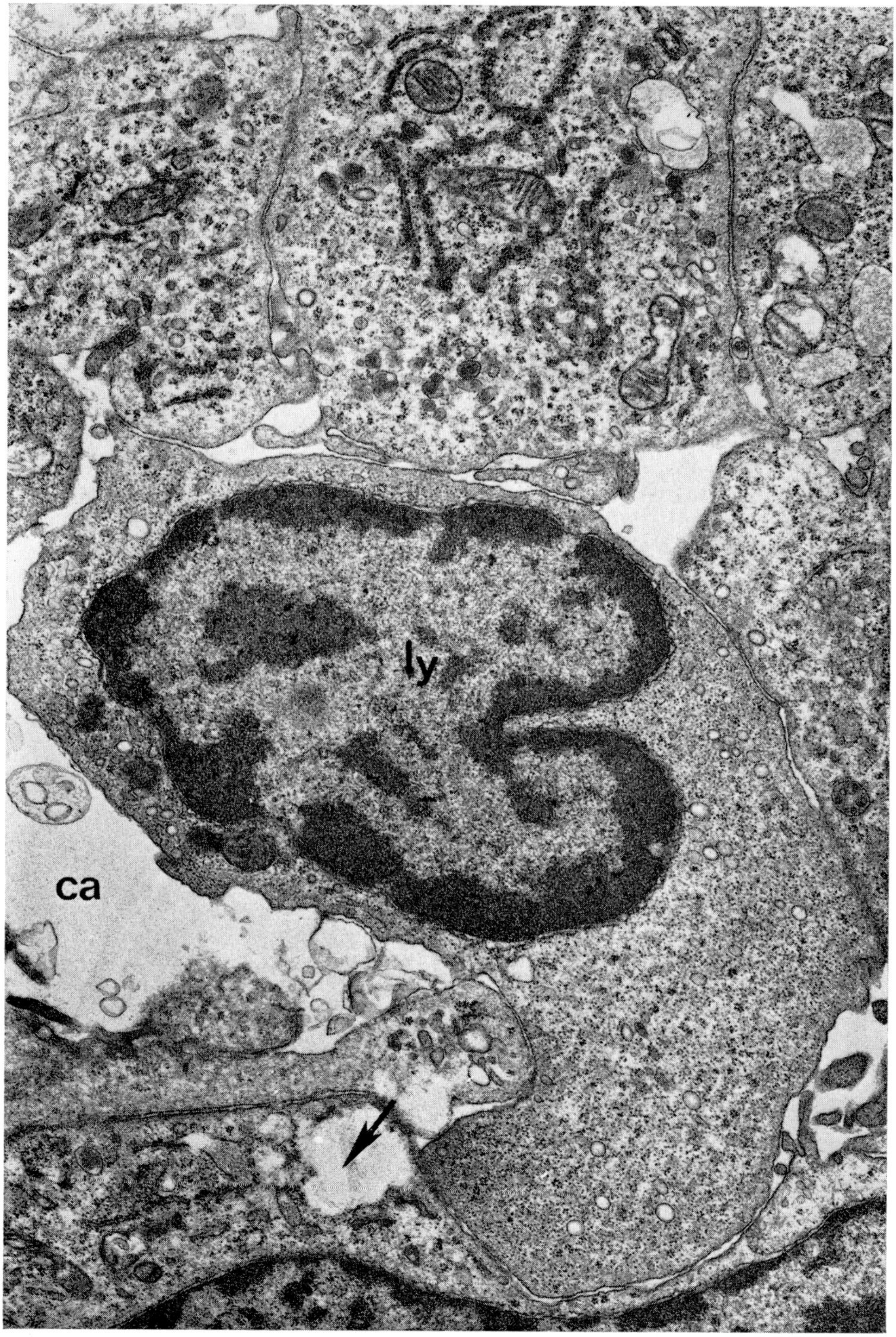

Figure 7. This field is at the junction of inner and outer bands. A lymphocyte (*ly*) with polyribosomes occupies the center of the field and extends a broad uropodal process to an L cell at the lower margin. The L cell shows evidence of damage (*arrow*). The top of the field is occupied by macrophage cytoplasm. The clear area on the left margin (*ca*) is not completely extracellular. Much of it is comprised of lucent cytoplasmic processes or fragments (× 18,000).

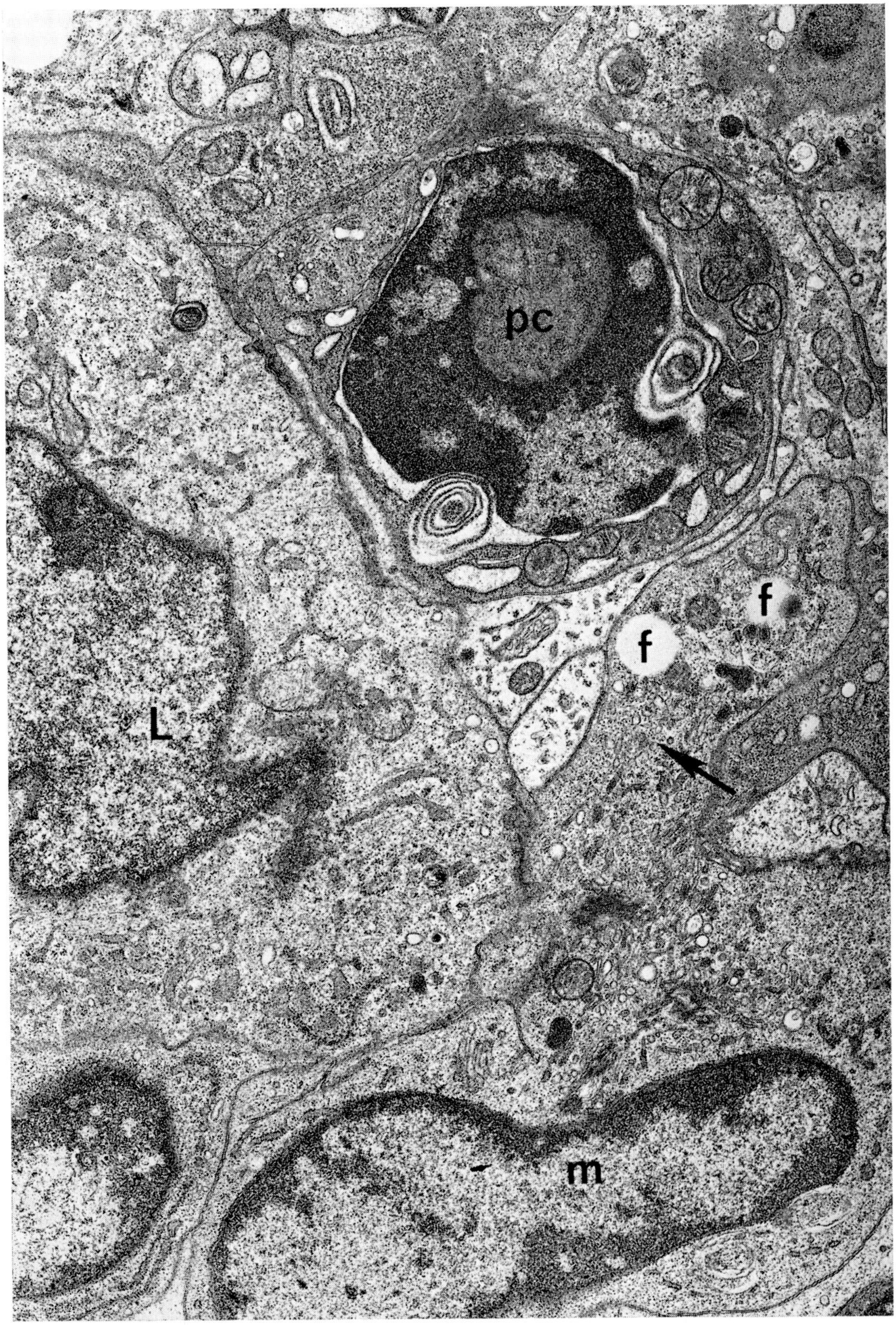

Figure 8. Here, deep in the outer band, a plasma cell (*pc*) whose angulated nucleus and cytoplasmic whorls suggest degeneration, is close against an L cell (*L*). A macrophage (*m*) is at the bottom of the field, with a broad cytoplasmic tongue (*arrow*) extending up to the plasma cell. The clear spaces in this tongue (*f*) likely represent dissolved fat. To the left of the macrophage is a lymphoid cell containing some rough endoplasmic reticulum (× 18,000).

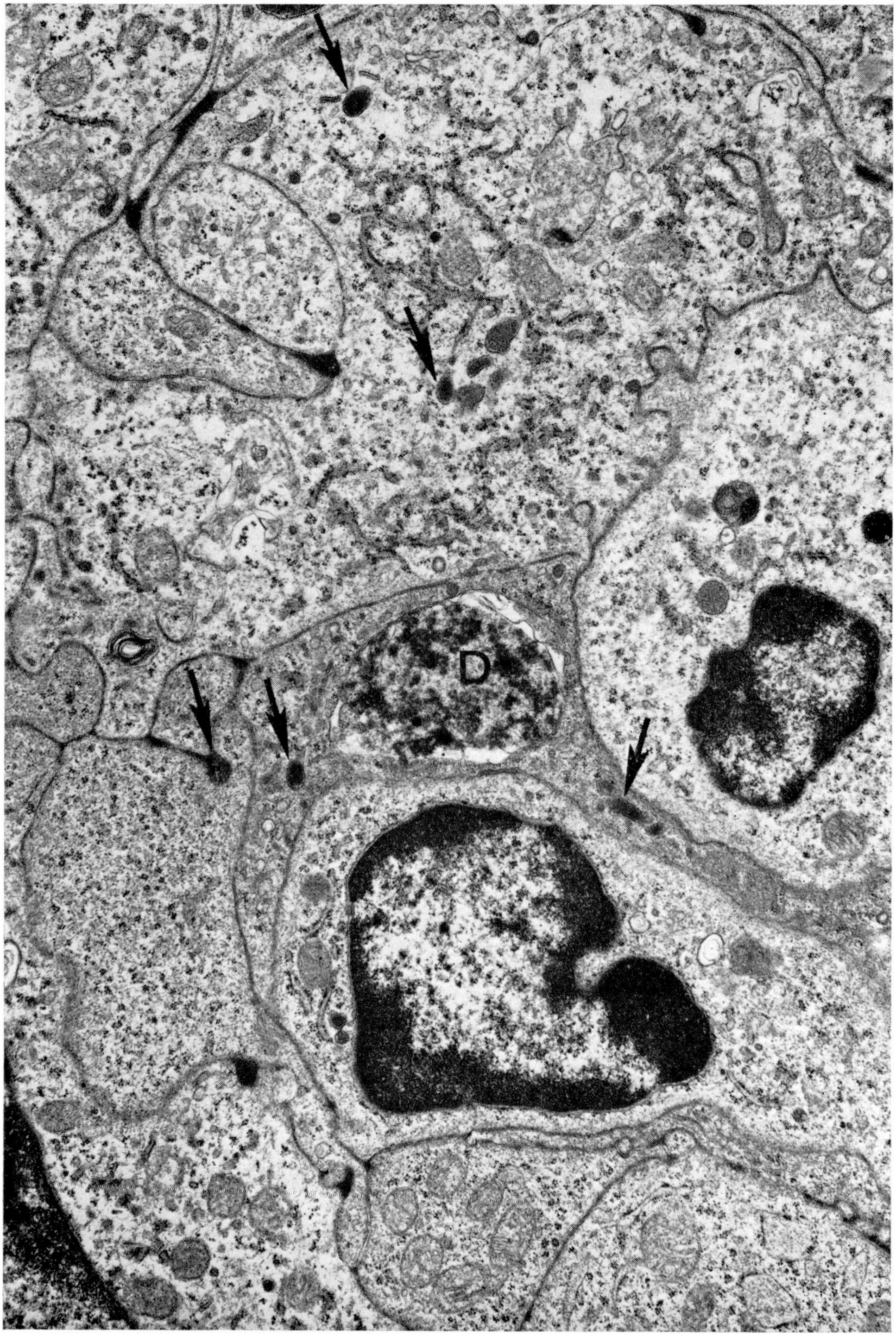

Figure 9. This field is in the deep inner band at its junction with the necrotic core. L cells, lymphoid cells and macrophages are closely packed. The dense extracellular material represents a fluid material derived from dead cells (see Figs. 10 and 11). There are several configurations which likely indicate the incorporation of this cell-derived extracellular material into lysosomes (*arrows*). Note the intracellular dead cell (*D*) membrane-bounded in a macrophage (× 17,000).

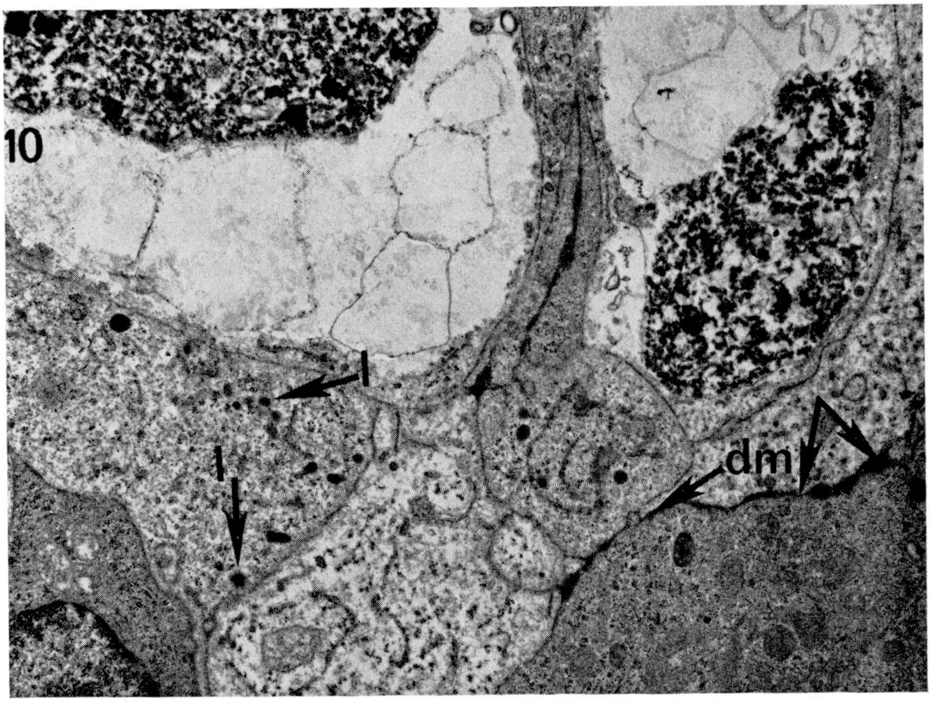

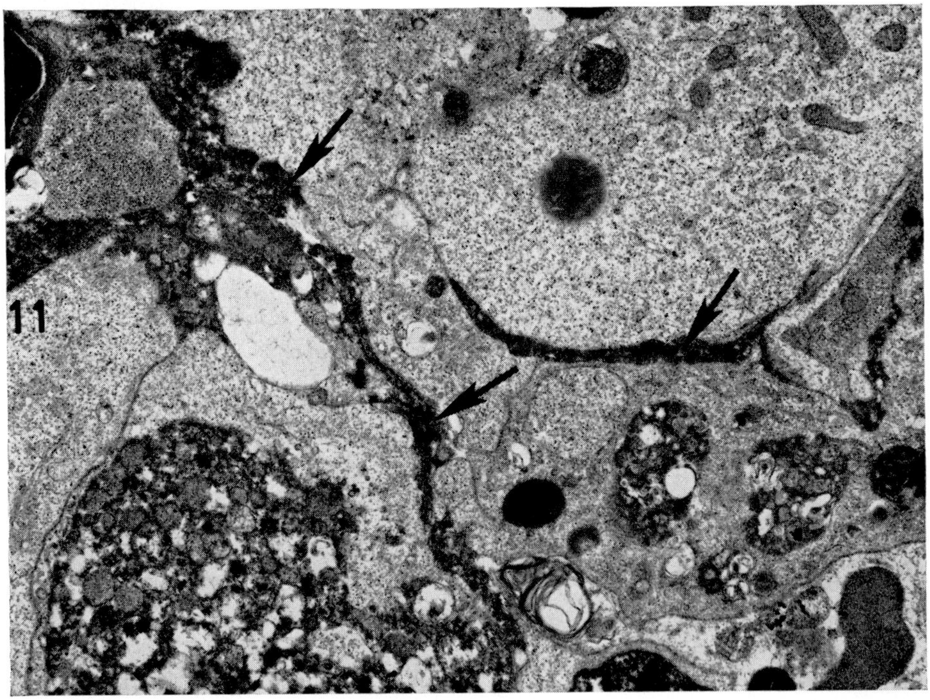

Figure 10. This field, as that in Figure 9, is at the border of the inner band and the necrotic zone. The cells at the lower edge belong to the inner band and appear vital. Note the dense material lying in slender bands between the cells (*arrows, dm*). A large number of lysosomes, appearing to contain this dense material, are present (*arrows, l*). Two dead cells are at the top. Their cytoplasm is markedly vacuolated and lucent, the nuclei dense and coarsely granular (× 16,500).

Figure 11. This field, slightly more superficial than Figure 10, is also at the junction of the necrotic zone and the inner band. Most of the cells here appear vital—a large number of phagocytic vacuoles are present. Here the necrotic cellular character of the extracellular bands of material (*arrows*) is evident. Presumably this material, further digested and altered, becomes the dense, more uniform material represented in Figures 9 and 10, which is incorporated into lysosomes (× 18,000).

tissue culture and that accumulated by Rosenau and Moon and others in this system (1–10) point to an immunologic basis or component for these cellular changes.

The elongation and microvilli of the surface cells created an appearance similar to that of the mesothelial cells lining the surface of the peritoneal cavity and to that of the fibroblasts forming the surface of synovial membrane. L cells were in the surface layer of the nodules studied here and might be plentiful there, but the dominant surface cells appeared to be histiocytes or macrophages. The microvilli were similar to those shown by lymphocytes in other immunologic or related reactions (20–22).

Within the nodule, the formation of definitive lysosomes in macrophages was marked, particularly in the deep intermediate zone contiguous to the necrotic center. A dense granular material, the residue of dead cells which occasionally contained cellular structures, lay as an evidently liquid material between the vital cells of the deep intermediate zone. Many examples of this material and its incorporation into lysosomes and cytoplasmic vacuoles were present. If cellular materials modify the immunologic role of macrophages, perhaps through their influence on the enzyme content, this large scale incorporation of graft protoplasm into host macrophages is significant.

A close relationship between vital host cells and graft cells was evident in the nodule. Lymphocytes and plasma cells lay close upon L cells, but close relationships between all cell types—lymphocytes, plasma cells, macrophages, granulocytes and L cells—occur. These cells may be pressed closely together. More distinctively, they are loosely interwined by a large number of long slender cytoplasmic processes. Such processes are common in lymphoid cells, less developed in granulocytes and L cells. While cell contact was intimate, no tight junctions or cytoplasmic union was observed except for occasional binucleated cells or multinucleated cells. Not uncommonly, cytoplasmic processes were capped by dense thickenings which appear to be viral in form.[6] These structures are a frequent, if inconstant, finding in electron micrographs of L cells, and their role in the process of rejection is not yet possible to assign. Viral material may be epiphenomenal to the process of graft rejection or be antigenic and contribute to the host response.

Significant differences mark these nodules from the interactions of L cells and lymphoid cells in tissue culture, where the lymphoid cells are taken from sensitized hosts. Although plasma cells were a constant and significant cell type in the nodules, the large-scale increase in plasma cells noted in the tissue culture system using spleen cells from animals sensitized by three injections of L cells was not observed here. A control for the tissue culture system, *viz.*, the addition of non-sensitized spleen cells to L cells in culture (12) bears closer comparison with the nodules studied here. A slow, small, but definite increase in a number of globulin-producing cells among the lymphoid cells attached to the L cells occurs in tissue culture. As in the nodules, the death of L cells occurs in such cultures. The mechanism of that death, in culture or in peritoneum, whether by high affinity antibody (22), antibody of a conventional sort, or nonspecific toxic factors, remains unknown.

[6] We are indebted to Dr. Junius Clark, who has collaborated in phases of this work (12), for identifying these structures as resembling paramyxovirus, myxovirus or murine leukemia virus.

REFERENCES

1. Rosenau, W. and Moon, H. D., J. Nat. Cancer Inst., *27:* 471, 1961.
2. Rosenau, W., in *Cell-Bound Antibodies*, Edited by B. Amos and H. Koprowski, p. 75, Wistar Institute Press, Philadelphia, 1963.
3. Rosenau, W. and Moon, H. D., J. Immun., *89:* 422, 1962.
4. Rosenau, W. and Moon, H. D., J. Immun., *96:* 80, 1966.
5. Govaerts, A., J. Immun., *85:* 515, 1960.
6. Koprowski, H. and Ferandes, M. V., J. Exp. Med., *116:* 467, 1962.
7. Wilson, D. B., J. Cell Comp. Physiol., *62:* 273, 1963.
8. Vainio, T., Koskimies, O., Perlmann, P., Perlmann, H. and Klein, G., Nature, *204:* 453, 1964.
9. Taylor, H. E. and Culling, C. F. A., Lab. Invest., *14:* 178, 1965.
10. Moller, E., J. Exp. Med., *122:* 11, 1965.
11. Weiss, L. J. Immun., *101:* 1346, 1968.
12. Clark, J. M. and Weiss, L., J. Immun., *103:* 1006, 1969.
13. Miller, J. F. A. and Mitchell, G. F., J. Exp. Med., *128:* 801, 1968.

14. Mitchell, G. F. and Miller, J. F. A., J. Exp. Med., *128:* 821, 1968.
15. Claman, H. N. and Chaperon, E. A., Transplant. Rev., *1:* 92, 1969.
16. Fishman, M. and Adler, F. L., J. Exp. Med., *117:* 595, 1963.
17. Humphry, R., and White, R., *Immunology for Students of Medicine*, F. A. Davis Co., Philadelphia, 1970.
18. Siskind, G. W. and Benacerraf, B., Advances Immun., *10:* 1, 1969.
19. Billingham, R. E. and Silvers, W. K., *The Immunobiology of Transplantation*, Prentice Hall Inc., Englewood Cliffs, N. Y.
20. Smyth, C. and Weiss, L., In press.
21. McFarland, W. and Schechter, G. P., Blood, *35:* 683, 1970.
22. Granger, *Perspectives in Immunology: Mediators of Cellular Immunity*, ed. H. S. Lawrence and M. Landy, p. 324, Academic Press, New York, 1969.

THE JOURNAL OF IMMUNOLOGY
Vol. 105, No. 6, December 1970
Printed in U.S.A.

AN *IN VITRO* MODEL OF THE ANAMNESTIC RESPONSE OF RABBIT LYMPH NODE CELL SUSPENSIONS TO KEYHOLE LIMPET HEMOCYANIN[1, 2]

HERBERT B. HERSCOWITZ[3, 4] AND ABRAM B. STAVITSKY

From the Department of Microbiology, School of Medicine, Case Western Reserve University, Cleveland, Ohio 44106

Received for publication July 27, 1970

Suspensions of popliteal lymph node cells from rabbits primed with keyhole limpet hemocyanin (KLH) were stimulated *in vitro* with KLH to give an anamnestic response. Newly synthesized IgG antibody as determined by the incorporation of radioactive leucine was first detected in the culture medium on days 2 and 3, reached a peak on days 5 to 7 and declined thereafter. The antigen-stimulated cells also synthesized increased amounts of non-antibody proteins, including α, β and γ globulins, which accounted for over 90% of the incorporated radioactivity. Both antibody and protein syntheses were antigen dose-dependent and required contact of primed cells with KLH for several hours. The synthesis of DNA and RNA increased in antigen-stimulated cells and preceded the appearance of radioactive antibody.

Considerable information about the events and mechanisms of the antibody response has been gained by the use of *in vitro* systems in which antigen is incubated with lymphoid cells or organ fragments (1–5). However, it has been difficult to study some aspects of the antibody response with these *in vitro primary* systems because of the small number of cells which are engaged and the small amounts of antibody and nucleic acids which are synthesized; therefore, increasing use is being made of the *in vitro anamnestic* systems (6, 7) which do not possess these limitations.

The present study had as its objective the development of a model of the *in vitro* anamnestic response which would lend itself to the exploration of the many cellular, subcellular and molecular aspects of the antibody response. Keyhole limpet hemocyanin was employed as antigen because it induces the synthesis of high concentrations of antibody, evokes a high level of immunologic memory and involves large numbers of cells in the synthesis of antibody (8; J. P. Gusdon and A. B. Stavitsky, unpublished observations). Antigen was added to isolated lymph node cells rather than to organ fragments in order to improve the quantitation and reproducibility of the *in vitro* antibody response. A very sensitive and specific assay for newly synthesized antibody, including antibody of low affinity (9)—the coprecipitation assay (10)—was employed to assure that *de novo* synthesis rather than release of preformed antibody (11) occurred. The data which are presented indicate that the objective of the study has been realized.

MATERIALS AND METHODS

Animals. Female, random bred, albino rabbits weighing 6 to 7 lb were purchased from a local dealer. The animals were housed individually, and were fed Purina chow and given water *ad libitum.*

Antigens. Five time crystallized egg albumin (EA) and bovine gamma globulin, fraction II were obtained from Pentex, Inc., Kankakee, Ill. Keyhole limpet hemocyanin (KLH) was obtained

[1] This study was supported by United States Public Health Service Grant 5RO1 AI-01865 and was presented in part at the 54th Annual Meeting of the American Association of Immunologists in April 1970 at Atlantic City, New Jersey.

[2] Please address requests for reprints to Dr. Stavitsky, Department of Microbiology, School of Medicine, Case Western Reserve University, Cleveland, Ohio 44106.

[3] Recipient of United States Public Health Service Postdoctoral Award 1F2 AI-38593.

[4] Present address: Department of Microbiology, School of Medicine, Georgetown University, Washington, D.C. 20007.

as an ammonium sulfate precipitate from the Pacific Bio-Marine Supply Co., Venice, Calif. Its purification and properties will be presented elsewhere (H. B. Herscowitz, W. W. Harold and A. B. Stavitsky, manuscript in preparation). Briefly, after dialysis and low speed centrifugation, the KLH was fractionated on DEAE-cellulose columns as described by Askonas and Rhodes (12). The first eluted peak was concentrated, dialyzed and fractionated by gel filtration on Bio-Gel A5M (Bio-Rad Laboratories, Richmond, Calif.). The first peak was again concentrated, dialyzed against 0.15 M phosphate-buffered saline, pH 7.2, and sterilized by filtration through a Millipore filter pad. The protein concentration, as determined by absorbance at 280 nm, was adjusted to 2 mg/ml, assuming an $E^{1\%}_{1\,cm} = 18.0$. The purified KLH showed one major component by double diffusion in agar, immunoelectrophoresis, disc electrophoresis and analytical ultracentrifugation.

Antisera. Rabbits were injected weekly with 2 mg of alum-precipitated (13) egg albumin into the hind footpads and with 2 mg of soluble EA intravenously for 4 weeks. Hyperimmune anti-KLH sera were produced by repeated injections of 2 mg alum-precipitated KLH into the hind footpads and intravenously for several months. For the preparation of serum, blood was collected by cardiac puncture 7 days after the last injection of antigen. All sera were heated at 56°C for 30 min and stored at −20°C until used.

Production of primed lymph node cells. Rabbits were primed by the injection of 1 mg of alum-precipitated KLH into each hind footpad. One to 9 months later they were bled, sacrificed and their popliteal lymph nodes were removed.

Preparation of cell cultures. The popliteal lymph nodes were removed aseptically, trimmed of fat, weighed and teased apart with stainless steel wire screens. The resulting cell suspensions were filtered through gauze and washed three times in Hanks' balanced salts solution (14) by alternate suspension and centrifugation of the cells for 10 min at 1000 rpm in an International PR-2 refrigerated centrifuge. The cells were counted in a hemocytometer and adjusted to a concentration of 2×10^7 nucleated cells/ml. Cell viability was determined by the trypan blue dye exclusion method (15). Cells were then suspended in 1 ml of a complete medium which included minimal essential medium, Eagle's, spinner modification, minus leucine (Grand Island Biological Co., Grand Island, New York), 10% normal rabbit serum (Grand Island Biological Co.), 2 mM glutamine (Grand Island Biological Co.), minimal essential medium nonessential amino acids (Grand Island Biological Co.), 100 units/ml of penicillin and 50 μg/ml of streptomycin. ^{14}C-*l*-leucine (210 to 250 mCi/mM, New England Nuclear, Boston, Mass.) at 0.5 μCi/ml of medium was the precursor for antibody synthesis. Soluble KLH was added to a portion of the cell suspension, while saline was added to another portion which served as control. The cells were then rotated on a drum (1 revolution/6 min) at 37°C. Each cell suspension was centrifuged and then washed three times in 3 ml of balanced salts solution to remove antigen and then resuspended in 1 ml of complete medium. The culture medium was changed completely every 2 days and media from at least five tubes were pooled. After centrifugation at 10,000 × G for 10 min, the culture fluids were dialyzed against several liters of saline and stored at −20°C until assayed.

For the assay of DNA and RNA synthesis, 0.25 μCi of ^{14}C-2-thymidine (New England Nuclear Corp.; specific activity >50 mCi/mM) and 0.25 μCi of ^{14}C-2-uridine (New England Nuclear Corp.; specific activity >50 mCi/mM) were employed, respectively. The cells were pulsed for 5 to 24 hr after which time a 1000-fold excess of unlabeled, chilled uridine or thymidine was added to dilute the labeled intracellular pools and to terminate further incorporation. The cells were sedimented and washed three times in balanced salts solution, the supernatants were discarded and the cell pellet was frozen and stored at −20°C until assays were done.

Assays of synthesis of macromolecules. The incorporation of ^{14}C-leucine into protein was assayed by adding 200 μg of bovine gamma globulin to 0.1 ml of culture fluid, bringing the volume to 1 ml with 0.15 M phosphate-buffered saline, pH 7.2, and then adding 1 ml of cold 10% trichloracetic acid (TCA). After 1 hr at 4°C the precipitate was collected on a Millipore filter pad (type RAWP) which was washed three times with 5% TCA and then glued (Elmer's Glue-All, Borden Chemical Co., New York, N. Y.) to an aluminum planchet for counting in a low background Nuclear Chicago gas flow counter.

The coprecipitation method (10, 16) was employed for the assay of newly synthesized antibody. Labeled protein(s) (nonspecific radioactivity) other than anti-KLH antibody was removed from the culture medium by coprecipitation with EA-rabbit anti-EA serum at equivalence. The precipitates were removed by centrifugation, resuspended in saline, collected on Millipore filter pads and counted as previously described. Usually 10 to 15 nonspecific coprecipitations were required to reduce the background to 50 cpm or fewer. Two specific coprecipitations—employing unlabeled KLH and hyperimmune rabbit anti-KLH serum—at equivalence were performed to assay labeled anti-KLH antibody. The sum of the counts per minute in the two specific coprecipitations was corrected by subtraction of the counts per minute in the final nonspecific coprecipitation. The values expressed are counts per minute in antibody/2×10^7 nucleated cells. A *stimulation index* was computed as the ratio of counts per minute in antibody from fluids of antigen-stimulated cultures to counts per minute in antibody from fluids of non-antigen-stimulated cultures.

Incorporation of ^{14}C-leucine into protein and antibody was inhibited by the addition of various amounts of unlabeled leucine to antigen-stimulated cell cultures which normally were induced to synthesize protein and antibody.

In a few experiments the culture fluids from primed cells which had been stimulated with antigen *in vitro* were assayed both by the coprecitation technique and by a modified Farr technique (17) employing ^{125}I-KLH and precipitation of the antigen-antibody complex with goat anti-IgG serum. The coprecipitation technique revealed the presence of labeled antibody to KLH and the antigen-binding technique the presence of IgG antibody to KLH.

DNA and RNA synthesis were assayed by the method of Kahan (18). Cultures were prepared in triplicate and assayed separately; an average value is presented as cpm/2×10^7 nucleated cells. Replicate determinations on a single sample varied by 10% or less.

Antibody titration. At the time of sacrifice, the rabbits were bled and serum was prepared. Levels of anti-KLH serum antibody were titrated by passive hemagglutination (19).

Characterization of antibody. Two and one-half milliliters of culture fluid were layered on a 1.5- x 90-cm column of G-200 Sephadex (Pharmacia Fine Chemicals, Inc., Piscatwawy, N. J.). Elution was effected with 0.15 M phosphate-buffered saline, pH 7.2.

Six-tenth milliliter of culture fluid was layered on 4.5 ml of a 10 to 40% sucrose (w/v) gradient in 0.15 M phosphate-buffered saline, pH 7.2. The gradients were placed in an SW-39L rotor and centrifuged for 18 hr at 35,000 rpm at 0°C. Fractions were collected by puncture of the bottom of the tube, and 24 fractions of approximately 0.20 ml each were obtained and assayed for protein by optical density at 280 nm, radioactive protein by TCA precipitability and anti-KLH antibody by coprecipitation.

Radioimmunoelectrophoresis. Culture fluids were concentrated 10-fold by treatment with Ficoll (Pharmacia Fine Chemicals, Inc.) and were subjected to immunoelectrophoresis on microscope slides (20). The precipitin bands were developed by the addition of goat anti-rabbit whole serum (diluted 1:3 in 0.15 M NaCl) or soluble KLH (0.65 mg/ml) to the center trough. After exhaustive washing with 0.15 M NaCl, the slides were dried and stained with 1% buffalo black (Allied Chemical Co., Morristown, N. J.) in glacial acetic acid:methanol:water (10:45:45 v/v). After destaining with the above solution, the slides were dried and fixed to a sheet of Lucite (8 x 10 in) with Double-Stick Scotch tape. Radioautographs were prepared by direct contact of the slides with Kodak medical x-ray film, type NS-54T (Eastman Kodak, Rochester, New York) for 6 to 8 weeks. The autographs were developed in Diafine developer (Baumann Photo-Chemical Corp., Chicago, Ill.).

RESULTS

Requirements for induction of the in vitro anamnestic response. Table I presents typical results of experiments which indicated that popliteal lymph node cells from non-immunized rabbits were not induced to synthesize antibody upon addition of KLH. This table also indicates that exposure of KLH-primed cells to 50 or 200 μg of a heterologous antigen (bovine gamma globulin) did not induce these cells to synthesize anti-KLH antibody, whereas exposure to 200 μg of KLH did.

It should be noted that lymph node cells from rabbits which were not previously exposed to KLH and from KLH-primed animals synthesized low levels of antibody to KLH. Com-

TABLE I

Requirements for the induction of the in vitro anamnestic response

Previous Exposure to KLH	Antigen for *In Vitro* Stimulation[a]	Counts per Minute in Antibody[b]	Stimulation Index[c]
None	Saline	75	
	10 μg KLH	70	0.93
	200 μg KLH	90	1.20
1 mg KLH 4 months previously	Saline	71	
	200 μg KLH	760	10.7
	50 μg BGG	69	0.97
	200 μg BGG	77	1.08

[a] Popliteal lymph node cell suspensions were incubated with antigen for 24 hr.

[b] Culture fluids were obtained at the peak of the response, on day 7, and were assayed by coprecipitation for ^{14}C-labeled antibody.

[c] Stimulation index = Counts per minute in antibody in fluids from KLH-stimulated cells/Counts per minute in antibody in fluids from saline control cells.

ment upon these data will be made in the *Discussion.*

Lymph node cells which were removed from rabbits as early as 1 month and as late as 9 months after priming were stimulated to synthesize antibody *in vitro*. Although this parameter was not investigated in detail, it appeared that the capacity to manifest an anamnestic response waned with increase in time between *in vivo* priming and *in vitro* antigenic stimulation.

Synthetic and cellular events

Time course of syntheses. Figure 1 shows that the addition of 200 μg of KLH to popliteal lymph node cells which had been primed 3 months previously induced the onset of antibody synthesis by day 3, a rise to a maximum on day 5 and a decline thereafter. On day 5—the peak of response—these cells incorporated 30,000 cpm into TCA-insoluble material, presumably protein, and only 320 cpm into specific antibody. The rise in total protein synthesis was closely paralleled by the rise in specific antibody synthesis.

Repeated attempts to prolong the period of protein and/or antibody synthesis beyond the 7th day were rarely successful, perhaps because of the rapid drop in viability of the cell suspension (see next section).

Cell viability. Table II indicates that there was a rapid drop in cell number and viability in both control and antigen-stimulated cultures after the 1st day in culture. However, the antigen-stimulated cultures appeared to retain viability for a longer time than the control cultures.

Effect of time of exposure to antigen. Antigenically primed lymph node cells were exposed to 200 μg of KLH for varying periods of time. Figure 2 shows that labeled antibody clearly in excess of that in control cultures was detected in the medium on day 3 of culture of cells exposed to antigen for 24 hr. Incubation of the cells with antigen for 15 min or 1 hr was insufficient to induce any discernible response. Exposure of the cells for 3 hr caused a minimal but definite response and contact for 5 hr induced still a greater and more prolonged response. Because exposure for 24 hr evoked a maximal response this period was routinely employed.

Effect of antigen concentration. The effect of

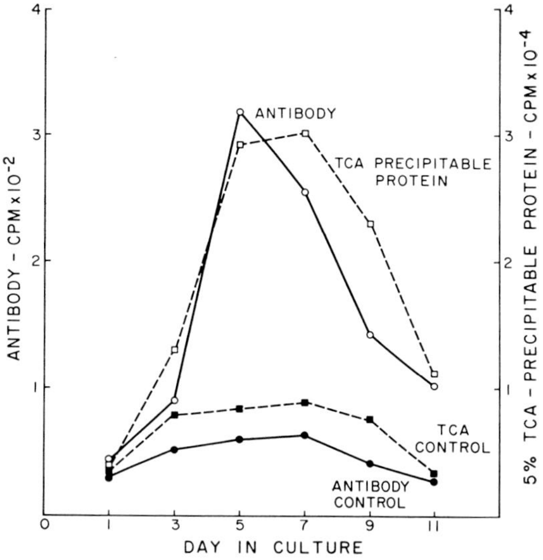

Figure 1. Time course of synthesis of extracellular protein and specific antibody by 2 × 10^7 KLH-stimulated lymph node cells. Each point is the arithmetic mean of triplicate samples. Cells were stimulated with 200 μg of KLH for 24 hr. Control cells were stimulated with an equal volume of Hanks' balanced salts solution. Culture fluids were completely changed on the days indicated and fresh medium including ^{14}C-leucine added.

antigen concentration on the synthesis of TCA-precipitable radioactivity, nonspecifically coprecipitable radioactivity and specific antibody was next determined. Figure 3 indicates that exposure of primed cells to 10 μg of KLH for 24 hr stimulated all of these syntheses, but not as much as did exposure to 100 μg. Exposure to 200 μg of antigen stimulated antibody synthesis even more, did not further stimulate the synthesis of TCA-precipitable radioactivity and was less stimulatory to the synthesis of nonspecific radioactivity than 100 μg of KLH. Addition of concentrations of KLH above 200 μg were less stimulatory than the addition of 100 or 200 μg; indeed stimulation approached that evoked by 10 or 50 μg of antigen. Of the total number of counts per minute incorporated into TCA-precipitable protein at the peak of the response (10,050 cpm), about 23% was incorporated into nonspecific radioactivity and 2% into antibody (920 cpm). The effects of increased concentration of antigen on the synthesis of antibody and of TCA-precipitable protein and nonspecific radioactivity were similar.

TABLE II

Viability of KLH-stimulated and control lymph node cell suspensions

Day of Culture	Antigen	Total Cell Count[a]	Viable Cell Count[b]	Percentage Viability
0	None	2.08×10^7	2.0×10^7	96
	KLH (200 μg)	2.04×10^7	2.0×10^7	96
1	None	1.28×10^7	9.9×10^6	77
	KLH (200 μg)	1.49×10^7	1.3×10^7	90
3	None	7.1×10^6	2.3×10^6	32
	KLH (200 μg)	6.7×10^6	2.9×10^6	40
5	None	4.8×10^6	8.0×10^5	16
	KLH (200 μg)	5.1×10^6	1.4×10^6	27
7	None	2.8×10^6	2.0×10^5	7
	KLH (200 μg)	2.9×10^6	4.0×10^5	14

[a] One-tenth milliliter of cell suspension was removed for total cell count.

[b] Viability was determined on a 0.1-ml sample by the trypan blue dye exclusion technique. Samples were incubated with trypan blue for 5 to 10 min before counting.

Sequence of RNA, DNA and antibody synthesis. In another series of experiments primed lymph node cells were exposed to 100 μg of KLH and were pulse-labeled with labeled thymidine or uridine or leucine to determine the time course of RNA, DNA and antibody syntheses. As shown in Figure 4, antigenic stimulation resulted in the synthesis of RNA beginning on day 2 with a rapid ascent to peak on day 5 and the synthesis of DNA beginning at about the same time and

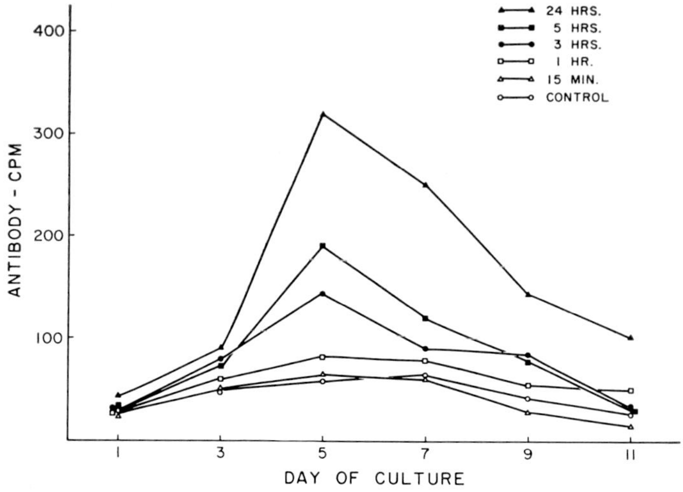

Figure 2. The effect of time of exposure to antigen on the induction of the *in vitro* anamnestic antibody response. Cells were exposed to 200 μg of KLH for the indicated times. Excess antigen was removed by washing with balanced salts solution and centrifugation. Culture fluids including radioactive leucine were changed completely on the indicated days. Each point is the arithmetic mean of duplicate samples and represents the counts per minute incorporated by 2×10^7 cells.

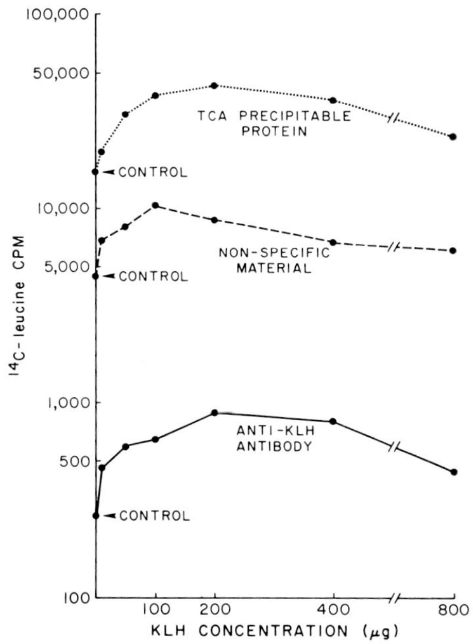

Figure 3. The effect of antigen concentration on the synthesis of TCA-precipitable protein, nonspecifically coprecipitable protein and specific antibody. Culture fluids were assayed at the peak of the response on day 6. Nonspecific material represents counts per minute coprecipitated by the heterologous EA-anti-EA system.

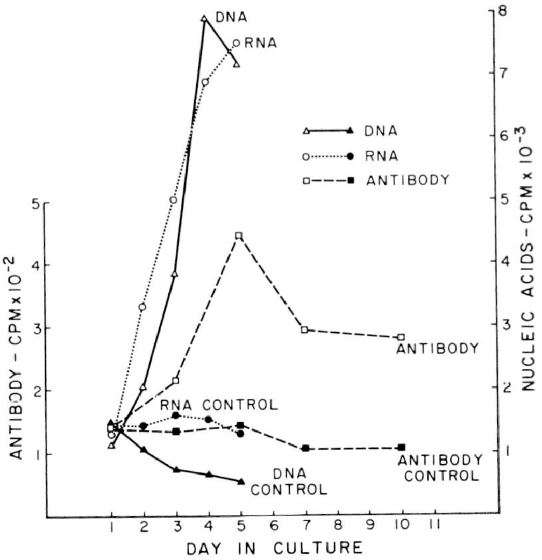

Figure 4. Time course of DNA, RNA and antibody synthesis following KLH stimulation of primed lymph node cells. Cells were exposed to 100 μg of KLH for 24 hr. Cultures were terminated on the indicated days for assay of DNA and RNA synthesis. Each point represents the arithmetic mean of quadruplicate determinations. Control cells were incubated in balanced salts solution.

ascending to a peak on day 4. Labeled antibody appeared in the culture medium by day 3, rose to its peak on day 5 and declined thereafter. Although not shown in the figure, the synthesis of RNA and DNA decreased after day 5.

Characterization of products of induction

Gel filtration. Culture fluids from cells exposed to 200 μg of KLH for 24 hr and then cultured for an additional 6 days were applied to a column of G-200 Sephadex. As shown in Figure 5, the fluid was resolved into three protein peaks on the basis of optical density. The first peak eluted from the column contained 19S material and most of the newly synthesized TCA-precipitable protein. The second peak included 7S material and a moderate amount of the labeled TCA-precipitable protein. The third peak corresponded to albumin (5S) and included lower concentrations of radioactive TCA-precipitable material. The fractions from each of these peaks were pooled and samples of the pools were then assayed for labeled anti-KLH antibody by the coprecipitation technique. It was found that the 7S peak contained most of the specific antibody radioactivity (213 cpm). Culture fluids from control cells did not contain any TCA-precipitable radioactivity in the 7S region or labeled antibody in the 19S or 7S peaks.

Sucrose density gradient centrifugation. Figure 6 presents the results of the sucrose density gradient fractionation and subsequent analysis of culture fluids removed on day 7 from cells exposed to 100 μg of KLH. Two protein peaks were obtained, a major peak (B), corresponding to material in the 5 to 7S region, and a minor peak (A), corresponding to the 19S region. Analysis of each fraction revealed that most of the TCA-precipitable radioactivity was in peak B, which is in contradistinction to the results obtained with gel filtration. However, analysis of the fractions for labeled antibody by coprecipitation confirmed the findings by gel filtration that most of the radioactivity was in the 5 to 7S region. Culture fluids from unstimulated cells showed similar optical density and TCA-precipitable protein profiles; however, virtually no incorporation of ^{14}C-leucine into antibody occurred.

Percentage of antibody which is IgG globulin. The analyses of the culture fluids by gel filtration and sucrose density gradient ultracentrifugation followed by coprecipitation with KLH-anti-KLH serum strongly suggested that most of the newly synthesized antibody was IgG. However, more rigorous evidence was desirable. Replicate samples of culture fluids from cells which had been

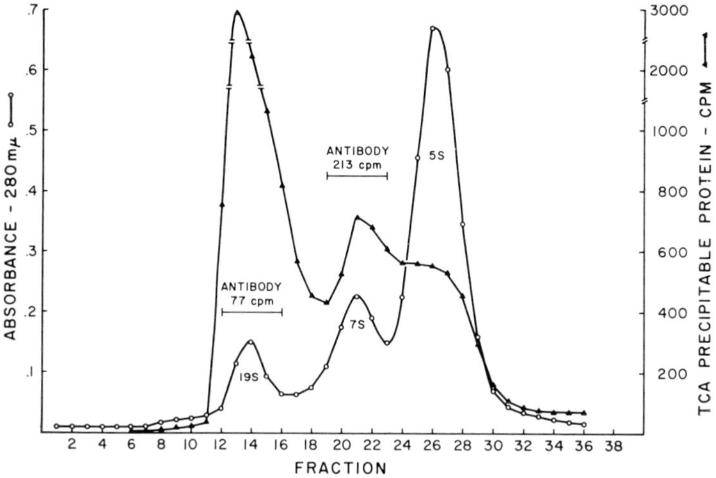

Figure 5. Gel filtration on G-200 Sephadex of fluids from cultures of lymph node cells stimulated with 200 μg of KLH for 24 hr. Culture fluids removed at the peak of the response (day 7) were assayed. The "19S peak" pool was prepared from fractions 12 to 16 and the "7S peak" pool from fractions 19 to 23.

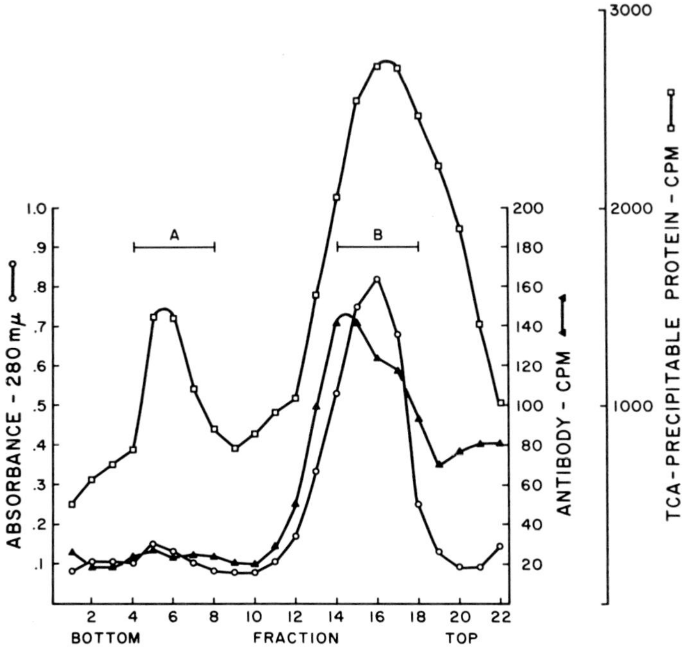

Figure 6. Sucrose density gradient ultracentrifugation of fluids from lymph node cells stimulated with 100 μg of KLH for 24 hr. One-half milliliter of culture fluid (day 6) was layered on a 4.5-ml gradient of 10 to 40% sucrose and centrifuged for 18 hr at 35,000 rpm. After collection of fractions from triplicate samples all analyses were performed without dialysis as it had previously been observed that sucrose did not interfere. The line designated A brackets the 19S region, whereas the line designated B brackets the 5 to 7S region.

stimulated with 200 μg of KLH were first treated with EA-*sheep* anti-EA serum in order to remove nonspecific radioactivity and not add *rabbit* IgG immunoglobulin. These samples were then assayed for labeled antibody by coprecipitation with KLH-anti-KLH or for labeled IgG protein by coprecipitation with rabbit IgG globulin and a specific goat antiserum to rabbit IgG. The data summarized in Table III indicate that 87.5 to 96.8% of the counts per minute associated with anti-KLH antibody could be accounted for as IgG globulin and thus support the conclusion that virtually all of the newly synthesized antibody is IgG.

TABLE III

Percentage of anti-KLH antibody which is IgG globulin

Day of Culture	CPM[a]		Percentage IgG
	Anti-KLH antibody	IgG immunoglobulin[b]	
1	131	117	89.3
3	163	150	92.0
5	221	214	96.8
7	146	136	93.1
9	112	98	87.5

[a] On basis of 2×10^7 cells.

[b] Labeled IgG immunoglobulin was determined by coprecipitation with goat anti-rabbit IgG and rabbit IgG at equivalence. The rabbit IgG was prepared by DEAE-cellulose chromatography and showed a single component by immunoelectrophoresis and double diffusion in agar when tested with goat anti-rabbit whole serum.

Radioimmunoelectrophoresis. Radioimmunoelectrophoresis was utilized to gain independent evidence about the nature of the proteins synthesized following *in vitro* stimulation with KLH. Culture fluids from control cells and cells stimulated with KLH were concentrated and then electrophoresed in agar. As illustrated in Figure 7, after development of precipitin lines with goat anti-whole rabbit serum and staining, the normal electrophoretic pattern of rabbit serum was observed. These lines are for the most part due to the presence of normal rabbit serum in the culture medium. Exposure of the slide to x-ray film revealed the presence of labeled α, β and γ globulins in the culture fluids from KLH-stimulated cells and labeled α, β and γ globulins of lesser density in the fluids from the control cells. The lower portion of Figure 7 presents an immuno-

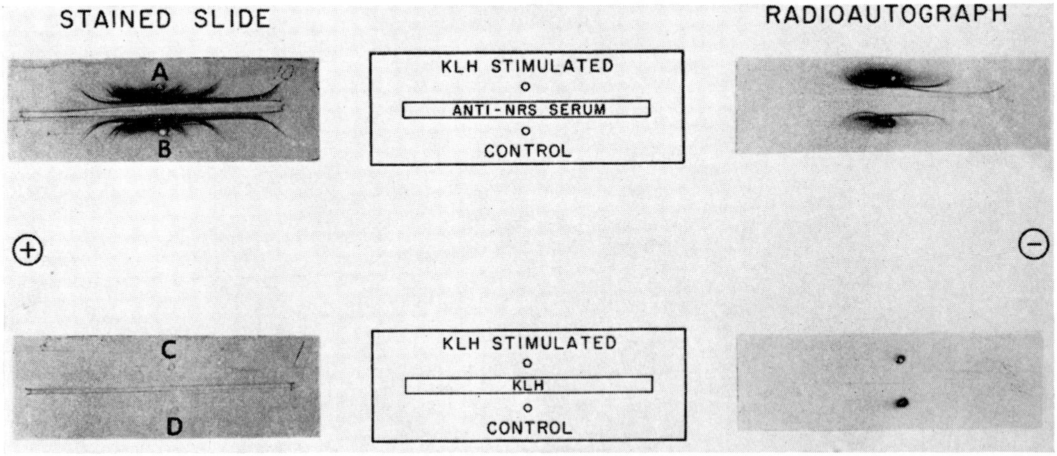

Figure 7. Radioimmunoelectrophoretic analysis of culture fluids from cells exposed to KLH. Cells were exposed to 200 μg of KLH for 24 hr and cultured for an additional 6 days. Culture fluids were concentrated 10-fold by treatment with Ficoll. *Well A* contained culture fluid from cells stimulated with KLH; *B*, culture fluid from control cells; *C*, culture fluid from KLH-stimulated cells plus unlabeled hyperimmune anti-KLH serum; *D*, culture fluid from control cells plus unlabeled hyperimmune anti-KLH serum. The trough between the *wells A and B* contained goat anti-rabbit serum diluted 1:3 with 0.15 M NaCl; the trough between *wells C and D* contained soluble KLH (0.65 mg/ml). The x-ray film was exposed for 6 weeks. The arc in the lower autoradiograph was retouched by the artist to make it more readily visible in the photograph.

electrophoretic pattern of concentrated culture fluids to which enough unlabeled rabbit anti-KLH serum was added so that visible precipitin bands could be detected in the agar when KLH was added to the trough. The stained slides show the presence of a single component with γ mobility in the region where IgG is normally found when culture fluid from stimulated cells was used. This component was absent in culture fluids from control cells. The corresponding radioautograph shows a short, but distinct, arc resulting from the reaction of KLH with a radioactive IgG protein. Control culture fluids did not give rise to a radioactive γ globulin arc. The lower intensity of staining and radiolabel in the lower slide further indicate that only a small percentage of the newly synthesized protein has specific antibody activity.

DISCUSSION

The objective of this study was to develop an *in vitro* model of the anamnestic response to KLH. The availability of numerous data on the native response to this antigen (8, 10, 21–24) made it feasible to compare many features with the *in vitro* system. Antigenic stimulation of primed cells in both systems induces the synthesis of IgG antibody as well as small amounts of IgM antibody (24). The predominant IgG anamnestic antibody response is in contrast with the primary response to KLH which includes the synthesis of both classes of antibody (21). Both *in vitro* and *in vivo* antibody synthesis begins on days 2 to 3 after antigenic stimulation and attains a peak on days 4 to 5 (8). The extent of antibody synthesis in cpm/2 $\times$ 10^7 cells is also comparable (8; H. B. Herscowitz and A. B. Stavitsky, unpublished observations). In both systems the initial synthesis of RNA and DNA is followed by the synthesis of antibody and of non-antibody proteins (A. B. Stavitsky, unpublished observations). Stimulation of RNA synthesis has been noted (25) and cellular proliferation is a prominent feature of the response to secondary stimulation *in vivo* (26, 27). Experiments to be reported elsewhere (H. B. Herscowitz and A. B. Stavitsky, manuscript in preparation) indicate that cellular synthesis of both RNA and DNA is required for induction of the *in vitro* anamnestic response to KLH.

The antigen-stimulated cell suspension contained a higher percentage of viable cells than did the control cells. This observation is consistent with the view that some of the cells responded to antigenic stimulation by undergoing differentiation and/or mitosis which rendered them more stable *in vitro* than the unstimulated cells.

It has been observed that immunized animals synthesize increased amounts of proteins which apparently do not have antibody activity (28, 29). The current experiments indicated that most of the newly synthesized protein did not have antibody activity and that it included α, β and γ globulins. In a recent study (7) it was also inferred that only a relatively small percentage of the newly synthesized protein in the culture medium was antibody. In the experiments done to date there has been close correlation between the induction of antibody synthesis and the induction of the synthesis of proteins which do not have antibody activity. However, it is not known whether a single cell or cell type synthesizes both antibody and non-antibody proteins; manipulation of various parameters of the system may bring about dissociation of the induction of synthesis of antibody and non-antibody proteins. Thus far only non-antibody proteins which are found in the culture medium and thus are either secreted or released upon autolysis of cells have been observed. Since these proteins are also produced upon *in vivo* stimulation of rabbits with KLH (J. D. Folds, T. L. Roszman and A. B. Stavitsky, manuscript in preparation) they are characteristic of the anamnestic response. The possibility that one or more of these non-antibody proteins plays a regulatory role in the antibody response (30) is attractive.

About 25% of the counts per minute which are incorporated into protein is associated with material which is coprecipitated by the EA-anti-EA system—indeed by almost any precipitating antigen-antibody system (31). The nature of this material is not known, but its binding to aggregated antigen-antibody systems suggests that it may include one or more of the components of complement (31).

Antibody to particulate and soluble antigens has been observed in the serum of animals which have not been immunized with these antigens (32). It has not been established whether these so-called "natural" antibodies were actively synthesized and, if so, what were the organ and cellular sites of their synthesis. The *in vitro* experiments (Table I) indicate that popliteal lymph node cells from unimmunized rabbits synthesize protein which is specifically coprecipitated with unlabeled KLH-anti-KLH serum. These molecules belong to both the IgM and IgG globulin classes (22) and their antibody activity has also been shown by the passive hemagglutination (19) and Farr (17) procedures. It is assumed that the antibody to KLH which is synthesized by lymph node cells of unimmunized rabbits was induced by exposure to cross-reacting antigen(s).

A lesser stimulation of protein and antibody synthesis occurred when amounts of KLH in excess of 200 μg were added to primed lymph node cells. It is unclear at this time whether this lesser stimulation is analogous to the induction of partial immunologic tolerance. Complete inhibition of induction by addition of excess antigen was not observed in the *in vitro* system. It may be relevant that it has been difficult to induce complete tolerance to KLH *in vivo* (33), perhaps because of its great immunogenicity. In a study in which the anamnestic response to bovine albumin was elicited by injection into mice of primed cells plus this antigen, exposure of the cells to excess antigen not only did not stimulate antibody synthesis but failed to promote DNA synthesis (34). These observations coupled with the lesser stimulation of total protein synthesis in the present study suggest that the induction of immunologic unresponsiveness is accompanied by a general inability of the involved cells to synthesize macromolecules.

A comparison of the results obtained with the *in vitro* model of the response to KLH and with other systems which employed different antigens, different assays and organ as well as cell cultures reveals some similarities and apparent differences. Predominantly IgG antibody was synthesized (7, 35), although some IgM antibody also was produced. In one study (36) the peak of the anamnestic antibody response to bovine albumin or diphtheria toxoid occurred on the 9th day rather than on the 5th to 7th day as in the KLH system. However, lymph node fragments were utilized in that study and experiments in this laboratory revealed that much more antibody is synthesized per unit number of cells when cell rather than fragment cultures are utilized (D. H. Plotkin and A. B. Stavitsky, unpublished observations). Others (37) observed that an *in vitro* secondary response could be induced by exposure of lymph node fragments from primed rabbits to bovine albumin for 15 sec to 2 min, whereas in our system exposure to KLH for 15 min did not evoke an antibody response. These rabbits were primed by footpad injections of antigen in Freund's adjuvant, followed by a similar injection into the footpads and intravenously 10 days later and removal of the nodes 1 month later. Thus these rabbits may have possessed cells of much higher affinity for antigen than our rabbits which were primed by a single injection of alum-precipitated KLH into each hind footpad and removal of the nodes 1 to 9 months later. Alternatively, some antigens may be more reactive with cellular receptors than others.

The induction of tolerance to bovine albumin by addition of large amounts of this antigen to primed lymph node fragments was also reported. However, the hemagglutination assay for antibody was employed and it is known (A. B. Stavitsky, unpublished observations) that the coprecipitation assay is manyfold more sensitive than the hemagglutination technique; it is, therefore, conceivable that antibody synthesis would have been detected even in the presence of an overdose of antigen, if a more sensitive assay had been used.

In its present state of development the *in vitro* model has some limitations. Cell viability falls off rapidly in the system which precludes study of the phase of decline of the response as has been done *in vivo* (8). Moreover, stimulation of antibody synthesis seems to require much more antigen than does the native system. Thus 2×10^7 cells had to be exposed to 100 μg of KLH for maximal induction, which corresponds to the injection of 1000 μg of KLH into a lymph node which contains 2×10^8 cells; however, an anamnestic response can be induced by the injection of 10 to 100 μg (A. B. Stavitsky, unpublished observations). The lower efficiency of utilization of antigen for induction *in vitro* may be caused by inefficient processing of antigen because of a paucity of macrophages in the isolated cell suspension, failure to rock the system, or impaired function of cells which were damaged during the isolation procedure.

Despite these obvious drawbacks the *in vitro* model already is suitable for the study of many features of the anamnestic antibody response. Subsequent papers will present the results of experiments with this model (H. B. Herscowitz, W. W. Harold and A. B. Stavitsky, manuscript in preparation; H. B. Herscowitz and A. B. Stavitsky, manuscript in preparation).

Acknowledgment. The authors are grateful to Mr. Weldon W. Harold for his expert technical assistance.

REFERENCES

1. Tao, T. W. and Auerbach, R., J. Exp. Med., *124:* 1001, 1966.
2. Adler, F. L., Fishman, M. and Dray, S., J. Immun., *97:* 554, 1966.
3. Mosier, D. E., Science, *158:* 1575, 1967.
4. Robinson, W. A., Marbrook, J. and Diener, E., J. Exp. Med., *126:* 347, 19C7.
5. Mishell, R. I. and Dutton, R. W., J. Exp. Med., *126:* 423, 1967.
6. Michaelides, M. C. and Coons, A. H., J. Exp. Med., *117:* 1035, 1963.
7. Godfrey, H. P., Yashphe, D. J. and Coons, A. H., J. Immun., *102:* 317, 1969.
8. Schoenberg, M. D., Moore, R. D., Stavitsky, A. B. and Gusdon, J. P., J. Cell. Physiol., *71:* 133, 1968.
9. Steiner, L. A. and Eisen, H. N., J. Exp. Med., *127:* 1143, 1967.
10. Stavitsky, A. B. and Gusdon, J. P., Bact. Rev., *30:* 418, 1966.
11. Michael, J. G., J. Exp. Med., *124:* 205, 1966.
12. Askonas, B. A. and Rhodes, J. M., Nature, *205:* 407, 1965.
13. Kabat, E. A., *Experimental Immunochemistry*, 2nd ed., Charles C Thomas, Springfield, Ill., 1961.
14. Hanks, J. H. and Wallace, R. E., Proc. Soc. Exp. Biol. Med., *71:* 196, 1949.
15. Phillips, H. J. and Terryberry, J. E., Exp. Cell. Res., *13:* 341, 1957.
16. Gusdon, J. P., Stavitsky, A. B. and Armentrout, S. A., Proc. Nat. Acad. Sci., *58:* 1189, 1967.
17. Farr, R. S., J. Infect. Dis., *103:* 239, 1958.
18. Kahan, F. M., Anal. Biochem., *2:* 107, 1960.
19. Stavitsky, A. B., J. Immun., *72:* 360, 1954.
20. Scheidegger, J. J., Int. Arch. Allerg., *7:* 103, 1955.
21. Roszman, T. L. and Stavitsky, A. B., Fed. Proc., *29:* 572, 1969.
22. Stavitsky, A. B., in *Nucleic Acids in Immunology*, Edited by O. J. Plescia and W. Braun, p. 447, Springer-Verlag, Inc., New York, 1968.
23. Bauer, D. C. and Stavitsky, A. B., Proc. Nat. Acad. Sci., *47:* 1667, 1961.
24. Bauer, D. C., Mathies, M. J. and Stavitsky, A. B., J. Exp. Med., *117:* 889, 1963.
25. Mach, B. and Vassalli, P., Proc. Nat. Acad. Sci., *54:* 975, 1965.
26. Dutton, R. W. and Eady, J. D., Immunology, *7:* 40, 1964.
27. Urso, P. and Makinodan, T., J. Immun., *90:* 897, 1963.
28. Dixon, F. J., Maurer, P. H., Weigle, W. O. and Deichmiller, M. P., J. Exp. Med., *103:* 425, 1956.
29. Humphrey, J. H., in *La Tolerance Acquise et La Tolerance Naturelle a L'Egard de Substances Antigeniques Definies*, p. 401, Centre National de la Recherche Scientifique, Paris, 1963.
30. Ambrose, C. T., J. Exp. Med., *130:* 1003, 1969.
31. Keston, A. S. and Katchen, B., J. Immun., *76:* 253, 1956.
32. Boyden, S., Advances Immun., *5:* 1, 1966.
33. Weigle, W. O., J. Immun., *96:* 319, 1966.
34. Mäkelä, O. and Mitchison, N. A., Immunology, *8:* 549, 1965.
35. Bullock, W. W. and Rittenberg, M. B., Immunochemistry, *7:* 310, 1970.
36. Yashphe, D. J. and Coons, A. H., J. Immun., *102:* 306, 1969.
37. Richter, M. and Singhal, S. K., Int. Arch. Allerg., *37:* 225, 1970.

THE JOURNAL OF IMMUNOLOGY
Vol. 105, No. 6, December 1970
Printed in U.S.A.

STUDIES ON RABBIT LYMPHOCYTES *IN VITRO*

XIII. The Induction of Blast Transformation with the F (ab′)² and Fab Fragments of Anti-Lymphocytic, Anti-IgG and Anti-Allotypic Globulins[1]

STEWART SELL,[2, 3] RUTH A. MASCARI AND STEPHANIE J. HUGHES[3]

From the Department of Pathology, University of Pittsburgh School of Medicine, Pittsburgh, Pennsylvania

Received for publication July 20, 1970

The effect of the divalent and univalent fragments of the immune globulins of burro anti-rabbit lymphocyte serum (BALS), sheep anti-rabbit IgG (SAG) and rabbit anti-rabbit allotypic IgG (RAG) on rabbit lymphocytes *in vitro* was tested. The divalent (F(ab′)²) fragments of each immune globulin stimulated lymphocytes to transform. The univalent fragments (Fab) of SAG and RAG were also stimulatory, but the univalent fragment of BALS was not stimulatory. A different type of reaction site distribution or stimulatory mechanism for BALS in contrast to SAG and RAG is suggested.

Both the divalent (F(ab′)²) and univalent fragment (Fab) of sheep immune globulin to rabbit IgG have been found to stimulate the induction of lymphocyte transformation *in vitro* (1). In contrast, only the divalent fragment of anti-human lymphocyte globulins and rabbit anti-mouse lymphocyte globulins were found to be stimulatory by other workers (2, 3), the univalent fragments being inactive. In addition, Greaves *et al.* (4) were able to block immunologic reactions to antigen of sensitized human lymphocytes by the univalent (Fab) fragment of anti-L chain, but did not find that such antisera induced transformation of human lymphocytes. Because of this apparent discrepancy, the univalent and divalent fragments of immune globulins to rabbit lymphocytes, rabbit-IgG and rabbit immunoglobulin allotype b4 were tested for lymphocyte transforming capacity *in vitro*.

[1] This work was supported by Grants AI-07125-05 from the National Institute of Allergy and Infectious Diseases, National Institutes of Health, and GB-8361 from the National Science Foundation.

[2] S.S. is the recipient of Research Career Development Award 1-K3-AI-23,308 from the National Institutes of Health.

[3] Present address: Department of Pathology, University of California at San Diego, La Jolla, California 92037.

MATERIALS AND METHODS

Lymphocyte cultures. Lymphocyte suspensions were obtained from the blood of rabbits of known allotype by gelatin sedimentation and cultured *in vitro* as described previously (5). After 44 hr *in vitro* 1 μCi^{3}H thymidine (^{3}Hdt) was added to each culture. At 48 hr each culture suspension was processed for determination of ^{3}HdT uptake and for microscopic evaluation (6).

Preparation of antisera-anti-lymphocytic serum. A burro anti-rabbit lymphocyte serum (BALS, kindly supplied by Dr. Joanne Southworth, Duke University) was prepared by multiple intramuscular injections of washed rabbit spleen cell suspensions.

The whole BALS had a hemagglutin titer of 1:2056 which could be absorbed by rabbit erythrocytes. The leukoagglutinin ti er of 1:512, the leukocytotoxicity titer of 1/64 and the ability of the whole BALS to stimulate transformation of rabbit lymphocytes were not significantly affected by erythrocyte absorption. The lymphocyte agglutination, cytotoxic and stimulating activity were eluted from a diethylaminoethyl cellulose (DEAE) column largely by 0.05 M NaCl in 0.005 M phosphate buffer at pH 8.0 while the majority of the hemagglutinating activity was found in fractions eluted at higher salt concentrations. The hemagglutinating activity was eluted in the breakthrough volume

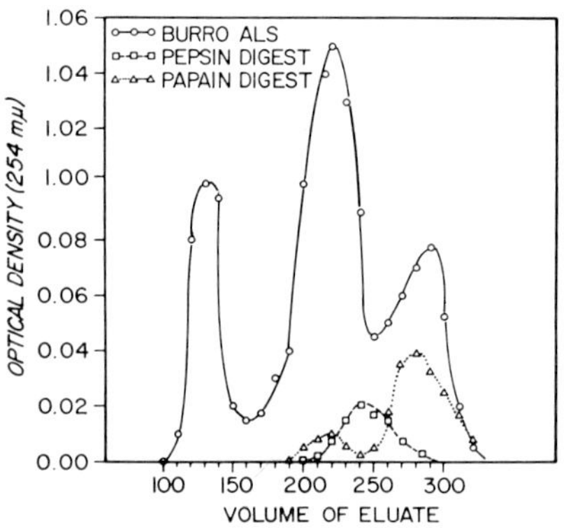

Figure 1. Fractionation of burro-anti-lymphocyte serum (BALS) and the pepsin and papain digest of the immune globulin of BALS on Sephadex G-200. The major peak of the pepsin digest is eluted at a volume between the 7S and 4S serum proteins. The papain digest is eluted as a major peak at a similar void volume as serum albumin. These void volumes are consistent with the known molecular weights of the F(ab′)² and Fab fragments of IgG.

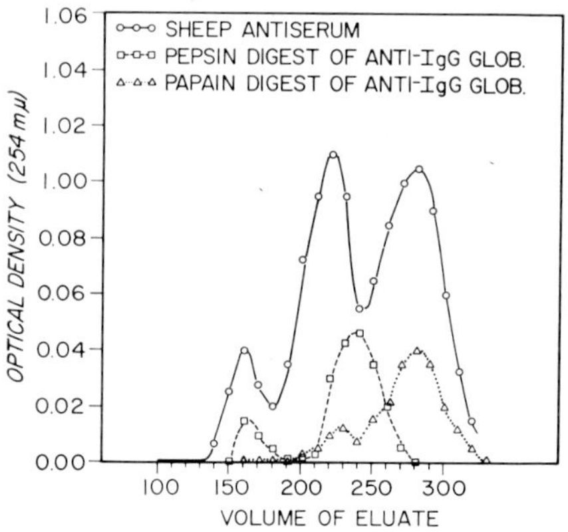

Figure 2. Fraction of sheep-anti-rabbit IgG (SAG) and the pepsin and papain digest of the immune globulins of SAG on Sephadex G-200. The pepsin and papain digests are eluted at a void volume consistent with the known molecular weights of the F(ab′)² and Fab fragments of the IgG, respectively.

of a Sephadex G-200 column while the anti-lymphocytic activities appeared later in the 7S protein peak (7).

Sheep anti-rabbit IgG (SAG) was prepared as described previously by immunizing sheep with DEAE prepared rabbit IgG. This antiserum did not react with IgA or IgM (8).

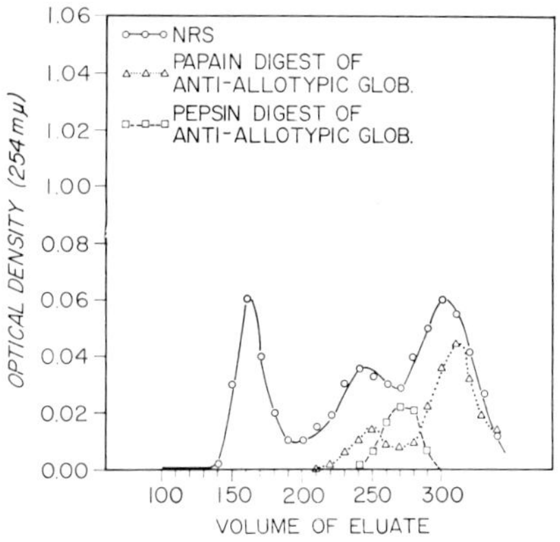

Figure 3. Fractionation of normal rabbit serum (NRS) and the pepsin and papain digests of rabbit-anti-allotype b4 immune globulins (RAG) on Sephadex G-200. The pepsin and papain digests are eluted at a void volume consistent with the known molecular weights of the F(ab′)² and Fab fragments of IgG.

TABLE I

Effect of ALG fragments on agglutination of rabbit lymphocytes

Preparation	Log_2 Agglutination Titers
IgG	7
F(ab′)²	8
Fab	3[a] (1/2 ALS)
	6[a] (1/10 ALS)

[a] The Fab preparation inhibited the agglutination of a 1:2 dilution of whole ALS at a 1:8 dilution and a 1:10 dilution of ALS at a 1:64 dilution. The Fab dilutions were incubated with the rabbit lymphocytes prior to the addition of the ALS.

Rabbit anti-rabbit immunoglobulin b4 (RAG) was prepared as described previously by immunizing a non-b4 rabbit with antigen-antibody complexes containing b4 antibody (9).

Immune globulin fragments. The IgG of each antiserum used was obtained by DEAE chromatography. The eluting buffers were as follows: BALS, 0.05 N NaCl in 0.005 M phosphate, pH 8.0; SAG, 0.01 M phosphate, pH 8.0; RAG, 0.0175 M phosphate pH 6.8. These conditions have been found to yield immunochemically pure IgG (1, 7, 9).

Pepsin and papain digestions of each of these immune globulin preparations were carried out according to standard conditions as described

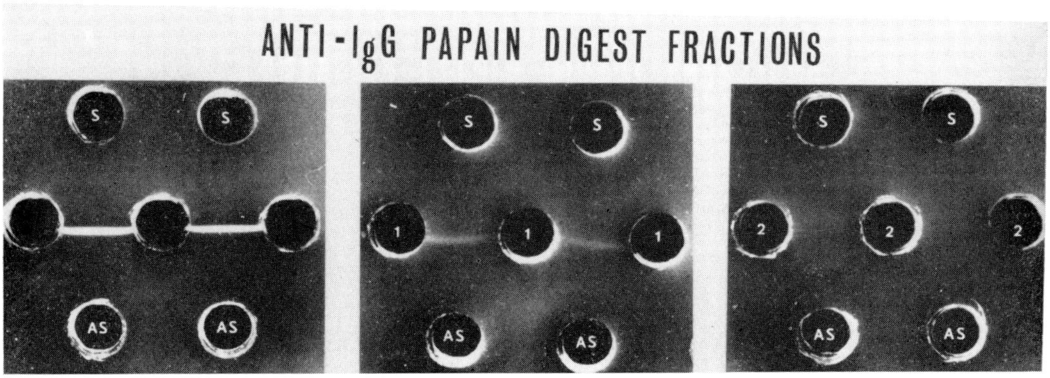

Figure 4. The reaction of the first and second elution peaks of the papain digest of SAG with rabbit IgG. The upper wells were filled with whole rabbit serum (*S*). The lower wells were filled with SAG (*As*). The three middle wells of the left plate were kept empty. The first S-G 200 peak concentrate was placed in the three center wells of the middle figure (*1*). The second S-G 200 peak concentrate was placed in the three outer wells of the right hand figure (*2*). The second peak concentrate (Fab fragment) inhibited the precipitin being produced by SAG reacting with serum. The first peak concentrate (*1*) inhibited the reaction only slightly, and did show a faint reaction with the whole serum (not reproducible in figure).

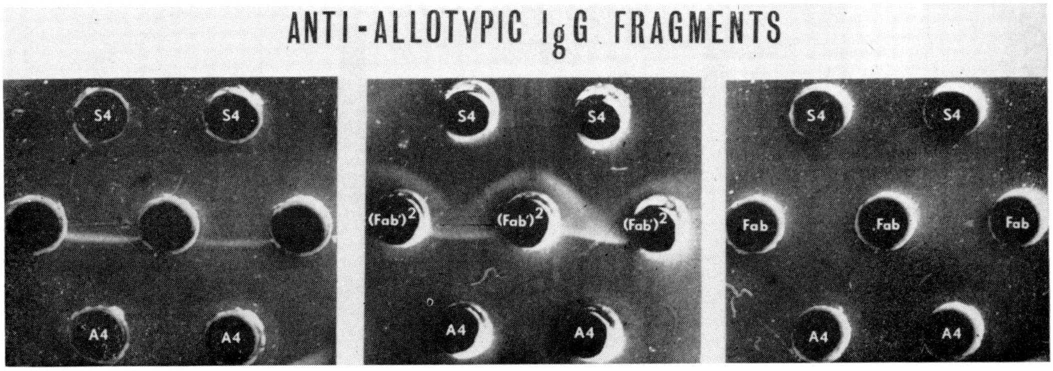

Figure 5. The reactions of the $F(ab')^2$ and Fab fragments of rabbit anti-b4 immune globulin (RAG) with whole b4 rabbit serum. The upper wells were filled with normal b4 rabbit serum (*S4*); the lower wells were filled with RAG (*A4*). The three wells of the left handed plate were kept empty. The three wells of the center plate were filled with the $F(ab')^2$ fragment of RAG, while the three wells of the right hand plate were filled with the Fab fragment of RAG. The $F(ab')^2$ fragment produced precipitin lines with b4 serum. The Fab fragment did not form precipitin lines with S4 but inhibited the reaction of RAG (*A4*) with b4 serum (*S4*).

previously (1). Following each digestion, the digestion mixtures were passed through a Sephadex G-200 column using 0.2 M Tris-buffered saline at pH 8.0. The elution patterns obtained are illustrated in Figures 1 to 3 and compared to those of whole serum. The eluates comprising each peak were concentrated by evaporation dialysis and tested for *in vitro* activity. The pepsin fragment of BALS-immune globulin agglutinated lymphocytes while the papain fragment inhibited agglutination (Table I). The SAG and RAG immune globulin fragments were tested for precipitating activity or precipitation inhibition activity by double-diffusion in agar as described previously (1). The pepsin fragments precipitated with the homologous antigen; the papain fragments inhibited the precipitation of the whole antiserum with antigen (Figs. 4 and 5).

TABLE II

Effect of burro ALG fragments on rabbit lymphocytes in vitro

	Mg[a]	Experiment 1		Experiment 2	
		Percentage blasts	Counts/10 min	Percentage blasts	Counts/10 min
Control		<1	606	<1	368
Pepsin	5.8	Toxic	537		
$F(ab')^2$	2.9	2+	1640	2+	3907
	1.2	2+	2532	2+	1506
Papain	3.2	<1	619		
Fab	1.6	<1	444	<1	677
	0.6	<1	376	<1	602
IgG	4.2			3+	1374
	0.5[b]	4+	4712		

[a] 0.3 ml NRS added to each culture.
[b] First peak of Sephadex G-200 fraction of papain digest.

RESULTS

The effect of the addition of each immune globulin fragment preparation and its undigested IgG fraction upon rabbit lymphocytes *in vitro* is given in Tables II–IV. The whole IgG and $F(ab')^2$ fragments of BALS, SAG and RAG were each reactive in inducing blast transformation of rabbit lymphocytes *in vitro*. In contrast the univalent (Fab) fragment of BALS was not stimulatory while the univalent fragments of SAG and RAG were stimulatory.

DISCUSSION

The present data show that the univalent fragments of anti-IgG and anti-allotypic immune globulins stimulate rabbit lymphocyte transformation, but the univalent fragment of anti-lymphocytic globulin is not stimulatory. In general, while univalent fragments can be shown to bind to antigens, such reactions do not necessarily activate the biologic processes that the reaction of the divalent antibody fragment with antigen does (10, 11). On the other hand, univalent fragments have been reported to be active in blocking of *in vitro* immunologic reactions mediated by sensitized cells (4), in suppression of antibody formation (12), in tumor enhancement (13, 14) and in modulation of TL antigens (15). Both univalent and divalent fragments are not active in reactions requiring the fixation of complement, or when given *in vivo*, most likely because of the rapid catabolism of these fragments *in vivo* (16, 17).

The site and mechanism of action of lympho-

TABLE III

Effect of sheep anti-IgG fragments on rabbit lymphocytes in vitro

	Mg[a]	Experiment 1		Experiment 2	
		Percentage blasts	Counts/10 min	Percentage blasts	Counts/10 min
Control		1	764	1	368
Papain	3.0	Toxic			
Fab	1.5	24	2698	22	1927
	0.6	12	2125	7	1650
	0.3	14	2103	8	1791
IgG	1.0	37	3046		
	0.3	51	2964	44	2825

[a] 0.3 ml calf serum added to each culture.

TABLE IV

Effect of anti-allotypic IgG fragments on rabbit lymphocytes in vitro

	Mg[a]	Experiment 1		Experiment 2	
		Percentage blasts	Counts/10 min	Percentage blasts	Counts/10 min
Control		2	375	1	307
Pepsin	1.0	33	2764	29	2018
$F(ab')^2$	0.3	23	1667	34	1998
Papain	2.3	12	1477	9	847
Fab	0.5	10	641	13	1333
	0.2	3	323	1	326
Anti-4	4.5[b]	12	1585	11	1478
	2.0	5	1459	5	1297
	1.0	6	981		

[a] 0.5 ml non-Ab4 normal rabbit serum added to each culture.
[b] Estimated.

cyte stimulating agents remains obscure. The dose response of lymphocyte cultures to various stimulating agents suggests a multiple hit stimulus for the induction of transformation. For both anti-immunoglobulin and anti-lymphocyte induced transformation a large excess of antibody molecules per lymphocyte is required. Yet, both phenomena are characterized by a dose response that gives inhibition at extreme excess (1, 3, 8, 18, 19). Although this inhibition may due to C dependent toxicity in some cases (20), in others C does not need be present for inhibition to occur (1, 3, 8). Perhaps lymphocytes require distortion of surface structures to be stimulated. A distortion of the lymphocyte membrane might be accomplished by an unequal distribution of determinants leading to a concentration of reactant agents at a given area. If more reactant molecules are added, then more molecules would be available to react more evenly over the surface of the responding cell and distortion prevented.

The difference in the lymphocyte transformation activity of the univalent fragments of ALG compared to those of anti-IgG or anti-allotypic antibodies may be due to a difference in the distribution of surface antigenic determinants on lymphocytes. The antigenic determinants with which the univalent fragments of anti-IgG and anti-allotypic antibodies react may be closer together permitting reacting univalent fragments to be located close to one another. Immunoglobulins may be concentrated at one pole of the reactive cell (21) while the lymphocyte determinants that react with xenogeneic ALG may be more uniformly distributed (22, 23). If either a given mass of reacting agents or a close association of univalent fragments is needed to "trigger" lymphocyte transformation then a localization of immunoglobulin determinants on a given area on the cell surface might be responsible for the stimulatory activity of the univalent fragments of anti-immunoglobulins. If the cellular determinants which react with anti-lymphocytic antibodies are more separated, close approximation of the univalent fragments of ALG would not occur.

The augmentation of anti-allotypically induced lymphocyte transformation by a second anti-allotypic serum that does not react with the lymphocytes directly but reacts with the first anti-allotypic serum *also* suggests that some mass effect of the association or close approximation of antibodies may be necessary for the induction of transformation (24). For example, if a2a2b6b6 lymphocytes are first treated with an anti-a2 serum raised in an a1a1b6b6 rabbit, a certain transformation response will occur. If an anti-a1 serum raised in an a3a3b6b6 rabbit is also added a significant increase in the transformation response occurs (piggy-back augmentation).

The failure of Greaves *et al.* (4) to find transforming activity in the Fab fragments of a rabbit anti-human L chain may be due to the more difficult demonstration of lymphocyte transformation of human lymphocytes by anti-immunoglobulins (25–27), to a peculiar property of their particular Fab preparation, to a different localization of distribution of immunoglobulin on human lymphocytes, or to other, as yet unknown, differences between human and rabbit lymphocytes.

ALG and anti-immunoglobulin sera used in the present experiments were obtained from different species, and differences in the lymphocyte transforming capacity might be due to different properties of the immune globulins isolated from different species. However, the Fab fragments of a potent sheep anti-rabbit lymphocyte globulin were also tested in our laboratory and found to be ineffective in inducing lymphocyte transformation.

REFERENCES

1. Sell, S., J. Immun., *98:* 786, 1967.
2. Woodruff, M. F. A., Reid, B. and James, K., Nature, *215:* 591, 1967.
3. Reithmuller, G., Reithmuller, D., Stein, H. and Housen, P., J. Immun., *100:* 969, 1968.
4. Greaves, M. F., Torrigiani, G. and Roitt, I. M., Nature, *222:* 885, 1969.
5. Sell, S., Lowe, J. A. and Gell, P. G. H., J. Immun., *104:* 103, 1970.
6. Sell, S. and Gell, P. G. H., Immunology, *16:* 285, 1969.
7. Storey, J., Hughes, S. J. and Sell, S., Fed. Proc., *28:* 294, 1969.
8. Sell, S., J. Exp. Med., *125:* 289, 1967.
9. Sell, S. and Gell, P. G. H., J. Exp. Med., *122:* 423, 1965.
10. Fahey, J. L., Adv. Immun., *2:* 41, 1962.
11. Cohen, S. and Milstein, C., Adv. Immun., *7:* 1, 1967.
12. Tao, T. and Uhr, J. W., Nature, *212:* 208, 1966.
13. Chard, T., French, M. E. and Batchelor, J. R., Transplant., *5:* 1266, 1967.

14. Chard, T., Immunology, *14:* 583, 1968.
15. Lamm, M. E., Boyse, E. A., Old, L. J., Lisowska-Berstein, B. and Stockert, E., J. Immun., *101:* 99, 1968.
16. Spiegelberg, H. L. and Weigle, W. O., J. Exp. Med., *121:* 323, 1965.
17. Spiegelberg, H. L. and Weigle, W. O., J. Immun., *95:* 1034, 1965.
18. Grasbeck, R., Nordman, C. T. and de la Chapelle, A., Acta Med. Scand., *412* (Suppl.): 39, 1964.
19. Sell, S., J. Exp. Med., *125:* 393, 1967.
20. Holt, L. J., Ling, N. R. and Stanworth, D. S., Immunochemistry, *3:* 359, 1966.
21. Raff, M. C., Sternberg, M. and Taylor, R. B., Nature, *225:* 553, 1970.
22. Cerottini, J. C. and Brunner, K. T., Immunology, *13:* 395, 1967.
23. Aoki, T., Hammerling, V., de Harven, E., Boyse, E. A. and Old, L. J., J. Exp. Med., *130:* 979, 1969.
24. Sell, S., Lowe, J. A. and Gell, P. G. H., J. Immun., *104:* 114, 1970.
25. Oppenheim, J. J., Rogentine, G. N. and Terry, W. D., Immunology, *16:* 123, 1969.
26. Greaves, M. F., Roitt, I. M., Zamir, R. and Carnaghan, R. B. A., Lancet, *2:* 1317, 1967.
27. King, R. A., Messner, R. P. and Williams, R. C., Arth. Rheum., *12:* 597, 1969.

The Journal of Immunology
Copyright © 1970 by The Williams & Wilkins Co.

Vol. 105, No. 6, December 1970
Printed in U.S.A.

IMMUNOSUPPRESSION BY LEUKEMIA VIRUSES

IV. Effect of Friend Leukemia Virus on Antibody-Precursors as Assessed by Cell Transfer Studies[1]

WALTER S. CEGLOWSKI AND HERMAN FRIEDMAN

From the Departments of Microbiology, Temple University School of Medicine and Albert Einstein Medical Center, Philadelphia, Pennsylvania

Received for publication July 20, 1970

Spleens of mice infected with Friend leukemia virus (FLV) were assayed for antibody-precursor cells by an indirect cell transfer method. Drug-treated syngeneic mice were used as immunologically inert recipients. Varying numbers of spleen cells from either normal control or FLV-infected animals were injected intravenously into the recipient mice, followed immediately by challenge immunization with sheep erythrocytes. At various times thereafter spleens of the recipients were tested for the number of individual antibody-forming cells, as well as for hemolytic antibody foci, regarded as clusters of progeny antibody-forming cells. There was a significant diminution in the number of both plaque-forming cells (PFC) and foci in recipients of spleen cells from donor mice infected with FLV. The greatest suppression occurred when donors were infected 7 to 14 days before sacrifice. There was a slight to moderate suppression when the donor spleen cells were obtained from animals infected shortly before sacrifice.

The calculated number of antibody-precursor cells present in the donor spleen cell suspension from infected mice was less depressed than would be expected from the suppression observed in the number of PFC appearing directly in the spleens of infected and directly immunized mice. Although the pool of spleen cells capable of responding to antigen and developing into PFC was depleted in spleens of infected animals, it appeared that there was also a secondary effect by virus on the proliferative capacity of such precursor cells and their progeny. The nature and significance of immune suppression at the cellular level are discussed in relation to the mechanism of virus-induced leukemogenesis.

Infection of susceptible adult mice with a leukemia-inducing virus such as Friend leukemia virus (FLV) results in a marked immunosuppression (1–6). There is a rapid diminution in the number of individual antibody-forming cells in the spleens of infected animals after challenge immunization with an antigen such as sheep erythrocytes or *Escherichia coli* (3–7). The greatest suppression results when virus infection occurs before immunization. Furthermore, the degree of suppression is directly related to the dose of virus for infection.

[1] This study was supported in part by research grants from the American Cancer Society, Inc. (T-382D), the Damon Runyon Memorial Fund for Cancer Research, Inc. (DRG-1037) and the National Science Foundation (GB-7719).

Although both cellular and humoral antibody formation is affected by leukemia-inducing viruses, the mechanism whereby immunologic suppression occurs has not been elucidated (6–9). A number of studies, including those involving the transfer of spleen cells from normal immunized mice to leukemia virus-infected recipients, suggest that these viruses do not directly affect lymphoid cells already committed to antibody formation (9, 10). On the other hand, preliminary studies using adoptive cell transfer procedures have indicated that the precursors of antibody-forming cells may be affected (10–11). Nevertheless, it is still not known whether immunosuppression occurs at the level of precursor cells, antigen "sensitive" cells, or cells which "process" antigen, such as macrophages.

In an effort to delineate the mechanism of immunosuppression induced by leukemogenic viruses in experimental mice, studies were performed in which spleen cells from FLV-infected mice were adoptively transferred at various times after infection to normal recipient mice treated with immunosuppressive drugs. Sheep erythrocytes were then injected into the recipients to stimulate antibody plaque-forming cells, as well as antibody "foci" regarded as "clones" of immune cells derived from the transferred cell population (11–16). Serum titers of the recipient mice were also determined. Although the number of individual antibody-forming cells appearing in the spleens of recipient mice injected with spleen cells from infected donors was markedly suppressed, there was no clear-cut relationship between such depression and diminished numbers of specific antibody foci.

METHODS AND MATERIALS

Animals. Inbred female BALB/c mice, obtained from Flow Research Animals, Inc., Dublin, Va., were used as described previously (5).

Tumor virus and infection. FLV was passaged in BALB/c mice and used as described previously (5). For purposes of infection, groups of 10 to 25 donor mice were infected by intraperitoneal (i.p.) inoculation of a 10^1 dilution of a clarified stock spleen homogenate (5). Splenomegaly was used as an indicator of infection. In addition, selected mice were autopsied and histologic examination made of the spleen and other organs.

Antigens and immunization. Sheep red blood cells (RBC), obtained commercially in Alsever's solution, were used as described previously (5). For immunization, mice were injected i.p. with 0.5 ml of a standardized 10% sheep RBC suspension.

Preparation of donor cell suspensions. Either control or infected donor mice, usually in groups of five or more, were sacrificed and their spleens were excised. Single cell suspensions were prepared by "teasing" with needles and forceps in 5 ml of cold sterile Hanks' solution. The cell suspensions were washed three times by serial centrifugation in the cold and resuspended in Hanks' balanced salt solution. The cell concentration was adjusted to contain 1×10^8 nucleated cells per milliliter. The number of viable leukocytes was determined by performing cell counts with a hemocytometer, using trypan blue stain. One-tenth-milliliter volumes of such cell suspensions, or appropriate dilutions, were transferred by the intravenous (i.v.) route to groups of recipient animals treated 24 hr previously with cyclophosphamide at a dose of 300 mg/kg and busulfan at a dose of 25 mg/kg of body weight. Such treated animals were incapable of responding to sheep erythrocytes by forming antibody plaques for a period of at least 10 days. All experiments were repeated four to six times.

Localized hemolytic plaque assay. The localized hemolytic plaque assay in agar gel was used to determine the number of antibody plaque-forming cells (PFC) in spleens of donor and recipient mice, as described previously (3–5). Only plaques detected after a single incubation with complement were enumerated. These were considered to be due to cells releasing high-efficiency 19S IgM hemolysins. For purposes of calculation the average number of plaques appearing on four separate plates was used to determine the number of PFC per recipient spleen.

Detection of antibody foci in recipient spleens. The hemolytic antibody focus method was performed with frozen spleen sections as described previously. In brief, recipient mice were killed, their spleens obtained, and one-half of each organ was rapidly frozen with Freon gas at $-60°C$. Thin sections (6 μ thick) were cut with a cryostat. Sequential sections were placed on the surface of previously prepared agar plates containing sheep erythrocytes. Following incubation for 1 hr at 37°C, the plates were treated with complement and incubated for 30 min, exactly as for the single cell plaque technique. Discrete zones of hemolysis coinciding with individual lymphoid follicles were enumerated and considered to be clusters on hemolysin-forming cells.

Experimental design. Groups of BALB/c mice, either uninfected controls or those injected with FLV at various times, such as 0, 3, 7 or 14 days before sacrifice, were used as donors (Fig. 1). Spleen cell suspensions were prepared from these animals and transferred i.v. to groups of drug-treated recipient mice. The recipients were injected i.p. immediately after cell transfer with sheep erythrocytes. At varying intervals thereafter, generally 3, 6, 9 and 12 days, at least five recipients from each group were sacrificed, their

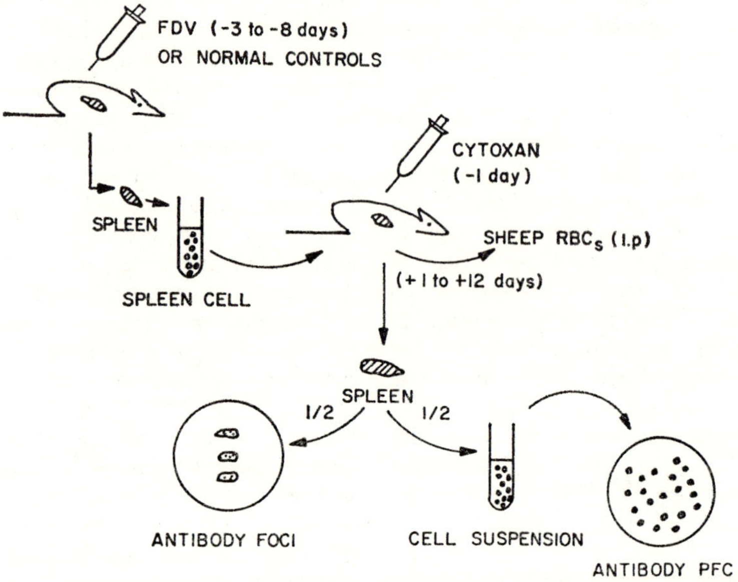

Figure 1. Schematic representation of experimental design to determine proliferative capacity of antibody-precursor cells to sheep erythrocytes in spleens of normal and FLV-infected donor mice.

spleens excised and the number of PFC determined (Fig. 1). One-half of each spleen from representative mice was rapidly frozen and sagittal sections were cut for the assay of the number of hemolytic foci (11, 17). After incubation of the sections on plates with sheep red blood cells (RBC), and treatment with complement, zones of hemolysis coinciding with individual lymphoid follicles could be readily observed on most plates and enumerated (Fig. 1). In general, drug-treated animals never responded with more than one or two foci when injected with RBC alone, without donor spleen cells. The foci occurring with spleen sections from recipient mice receiving either normal or FLV-infected donor cells were considered to be caused by the proliferation of individual antibody-precursor cells (11–16). The average number of foci was determined for at least three to five sections from a single spleen and the average number for five or more recipient mouse spleens per group was calculated. The total number of foci in recipient spleens was correlated with the number of individual PFC determined either from the other half of the same spleen or with the average number calculated for spleen cell pools. In most experiments, serum hemagglutinin titers of recipient mice were also determined.

In other experiments, groups of donor mice were infected with various dilutions of FLV 9 days before sacrifice. Spleen cell suspensions were prepared and inoculated i.v. into drug-treated recipients which were subsequently immunized with sheep RBC. Nine days after transfer, the recipients were killed and the number of PFC per spleen was determined.

RESULTS

Antibody PFC in recipient spleens. The number of PFC observed in the spleens of recipient mice after cell transfer and immunization is presented in Table I. Transfer of cells from normal mice, followed by immunization with RBC, resulted in the appearance of very few PFC in the spleens of recipient animals 3 days later. A significant increase occurred on the 6th day, with the largest number (approximately 5000) occurring 9 days after cell transfer. The number of PFC then declined to a level of approximately 1000 per spleen on day 13. Hemagglutinin (HA) titers in the range of 1:16 to 1:32 occurred at this time.

Drug-treated mice given spleen cells from donor animals infected the day of cell transfer showed similar kinetics of PFC appearance (Table I). However, the peak number was generally 50% lower than that appearing in the control recipients. The HA titers were only

TABLE I

Appearance of PFC to sheep RBC in spleens of recipient mice given spleen cells from normal or FLV-infected donor mice

Donor Group[a]	No. of Antibody PFC in Recipient Spleens on Day[b]				Recipient Serum Antibody (Mean)
	+3	+6	+9	+13	
Normal control	4.0×10^0	2.0×10^3	4.7×10^3	1.3×10^3	1:16
FLV-infected same day	4.0×10^0	1.6×10^3	2.1×10^3	1.9×10^3	1:8
FLV-infected + 3 days	7.4×10^0	1.2×10^2	7.8×10^2	1.8×10^2	1:2
FLV-infected + 7 days	4.0×10^0	1.2×10^2	2.8×10^2	1.4×10^1	<1:2
FLV-infected + 14 days	4.0×10^0	9.7×10^1	1.0×10^2	7.0×10^1	<1:2

[a] Groups of normal or FLV-infected donors used as source of pooled spleen cells.

[b] Drug-treated recipient mice injected i.v. with 20×10^6 spleen cells from indicated donors and immunized with sheep RBC; five animals tested per group on day indicated.

TABLE II

Calculated number of PFC expected on peak day (+9) in recipient spleens if entire donor spleen cell suspension were transferred

Donor Mouse Group[a]	Calculated No. of PFC in Recipient Spleens		Peak No. of Splenic PFC in Mice Infected with FLV before Immunization	
	No.	Percentage of control	No.	Percentage of control
Control	4.7×10^4	100	5.8×10^4	100
FLV-infected same day	2.1×10^4	40	3.4×10^4	58
FLV-infected + 3 days	1.0×10^4	21	8.8×10^3	15
FLV-infected + 7 days	9.4×10^3	20	1.6×10^3	3
FLV-infected + 14 days	7.2×10^3	15	2.3×10^2	0.3

[a] Infected mice injected i.p. with FLV on indicated day before sacrifice and cell transfer.

moderately lower than those occurring in control animals. Spleen cells derived from animals infected 3 days before cell transfer were less capable of proliferating and/or differentiating into antibody plaque formation (Table I). HA titers in the sera of these mice were rarely greater than 1:2.

Spleen cells obtained from mice infected 1 week or longer before sacrifice and transfer were markedly less competent to respond to RBC in recipient animals. Transfer of cells from mice infected 7 days earlier resulted in fewer than 300 PFC in the spleens of the drug-treated animals on the expected peak day after cell transfer (Table I). Serum HA titers were negligible. There was an even greater suppression in the number of PFC in recipient mice when the donors were infected 14 days before cell transfer.

Since the magnitude of the PFC suppression in recipient mice was directly related to the time interval between infection and cell transfer, it seemed possible that there was a "dilution" effect on the number of antibody-forming cells by non-functional leukemia cells. However, the calculations presented in Table II make it unlikely that cell dilution could account completely for the observed depression of PFC formation. The calculated number of PFC which, theoretically, would result if an entire donor spleen had been transferred to an individual recipient is presented for each group. It seems apparent that even if one compensates for the difference in spleen cell number between infected and control donor animals, there is a consistent decrease in the number of cells capable of responding to antigen and forming PFC as a function of time between infection and cell transfer. For comparative purposes, the number of PFC observed on the 4th day following direct immunization of control and FLV-infected mice is presented (Table II).

It should be noted that the calculated number and experimentally observed number of PFC in spleens of non-infected control mice were similar.

Mice infected the same day as cell transfer appeared to have a slightly greater suppression in the number of PFC when determined by cell transfer assay as compared to the number of PFC which appeared after direct immunization. On the other hand, mice infected 3 to 14 days before immunization or sacrifice had a greater suppression in the number of direct PFC, i.e., more antibody-forming cells appeared in recipient spleens following cell transfer than would have been expected on the basis of direct assay for PFC in similar donor spleens (Table II).

Appearance of antibody foci in recipient spleens. Previous studies have shown that drug-treated mice were suitable recipients for antibody-forming cells and their precursors transferred from normal donor mice (11, 18, 19). Furthermore, pilot experiments showed that spleen cells from donor mice infected with FLV had fewer antibody-precursor cells, as revealed by assay for antibody foci in spleens of drug-treated recipients (10). However, there was no information concerning the cytokinetics of foci formation in mice given spleen cells from normal or FLV-infected donors. In the present study, groups of drug-treated mice were injected with graded numbers of spleen cells from normal or infected mice, plus sheep erythrocytes, and then assayed for splenic foci 1, 3, 6 and 12 days later. As evident in Figure 2, there was a rapid appearance of antibody foci in spleens of mice given cells from a normal donor. The largest peak number of foci, generally 20 to 30 per recipient spleen, appeared after transfer of approximately 10 to 30 million or more nucleated spleen cells from control animals (Figs. 2 and 3). The peak number occurred on the 9th day after transfer and immunization, regardless of the number of cells transferred (Fig. 2). The earliest rise in foci number occurred on day 3; many more appeared on day 6. There were generally many fewer foci on day 12 unless larger numbers of cells were transferred. The absolute number of foci per recipient spleen was generally consistent for a given group of mice.

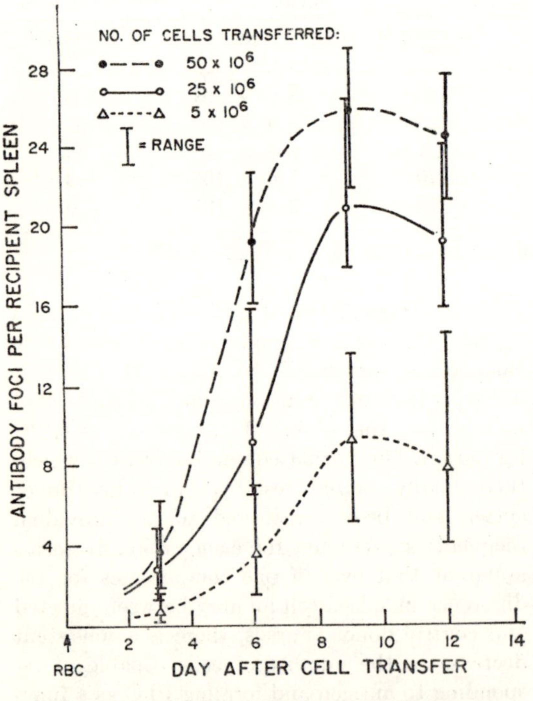

Figure 2. Cytokinetics of appearance of antibody foci to sheep erythrocytes in spleens of drug-treated recipient mice injected i.v. with varying numbers of spleen cells from normal donor mice, followed immediately by i.p. challenge with 4×10^8 RBC. Each point represents the average number of foci in sequential sections of spleens of four to eight recipient mice on day indicated after cell transfer.

Consistently fewer foci appeared in spleens of recipient mice given spleen cells from donor animals infected with FLV (Table III and Fig. 3). The lowest number occurred when the time interval between infection and cell transfer was the longest. For example, when FLV infection occurred 7 days before cell transfer there was a four- to sixfold decrease in the number of foci per recipient spleen, as compared to the number induced by approximately the same quantity of normal donor cells. There was a smaller difference when spleen cells were derived from donors infected 3 days before sacrifice; there was little difference when donors were infected on the day of sacrifice.

In the quantitative studies it was found that approximately 5 to 10 times as many spleen cells were required from 8-day infected donor animals to give the same number of foci as spleen cells from normal donors (Fig. 3). Spleen cells from 3-day infected animals were also less competent than "normal" cells (Fig. 3). The increase in spleen size and cellularity between days 3 to 14 after infection did not appear to account entirely for these differences. Since each focus of antibody activity is generally considered to be due to

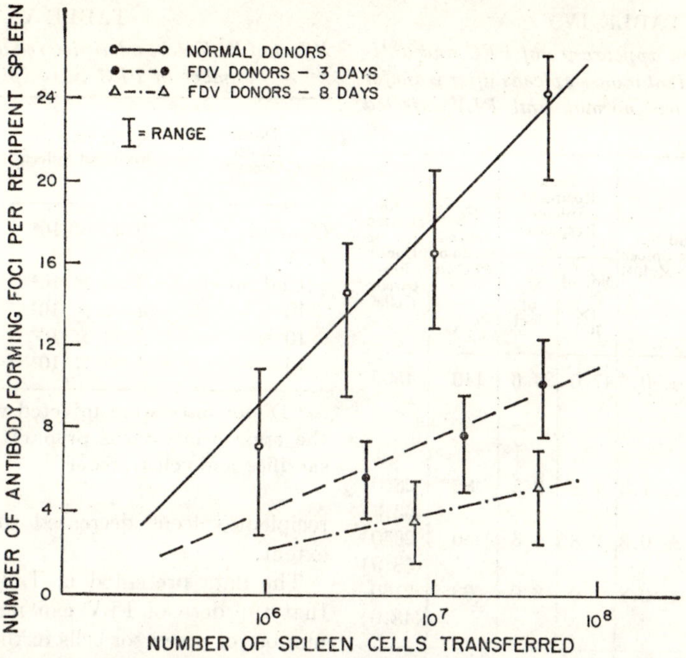

Figure 3. Relation between the number of nucleated spleen cells transferred and the average number of hemolytic antibody foci appearing in the spleens of drug-treated recipient mice 9 days after i.v. transfer of spleen cells from normal or FLV-infected donor mice. All recipients were challenged i.p. with 4×10^8 sheep RBC immediately after cell transfer. Each point represents the average number of hemolytic foci in spleens of 5 to 10 mice injected with the indicated number of spleen cells.

TABLE III

Appearance of antibody foci to sheep RBC in spleens of recipient mice at various times after transfer of spleen cells from either normal or FLV-infected donor mice

Donor Mouse Group[a]	Number of Foci per Recipient Spleen on Day[b]				
	+1	+3	+6	+9	+12
Normal control	1.1 ± 0.9	2.5 ± 1.3	11.5 ± 3.6	24.6 ± 5.3	16.5 ± 5.8
FLV-infected same day	—	1.8 ± 1.5	6.4 ± 2.1	15.3 ± 4.6	12.8 ± 4.9
FLV-infected + 3 days	1.3 ± 0.5	1.6 ± 2.5	3.8 ± 2.0	9.5 ± 2.6	8.2 ± 1.2
FLV-infected + 7 days	—	<1	2.8 ± 0.6	5.3 ± 1.9	4.5 ± 1.2
FLV-infected + 14 days	—	<1	1.3 ± 1.2	3.0 ± 1.2	—

[a] Groups of mice either untreated or infected with FLV on day indicated before sacrifice.

[b] Drug-treated recipient mice given approximately 20×10^6 spleen cells from indicated donor group and 3 to 5 animals tested for splenic foci on day indicated after cell transfer and challenge immunization with sheep RBC.

proliferation of an individual antibody-precursor cell (12–14), it is apparent from Table IV that the number of such cells was significantly depressed in spleens of infected animals, without regard to spleen size or cell number. However, the calculated number of precursor cells in FLV-infected donor spleens was not as low as would be expected from the number of foci in a recipient spleen. For example, there was a three- to fourfold increase in the number of nucleated spleen cells in mice infected 7 to 14 days before to sacrifice (Table IV). Transfer of spleen cells from these mice to drug-treated recipients resulted in fewer PFC and foci as compared to transfer to spleen cells from normal donors. The observed ratio of PFC to foci in a recipient decreased from a

TABLE IV

Relationship between appearance of PFC and antibody foci in recipient mouse spleens after transfer of splenocytes from normal and FLV-infected donor mice

Donor Mouse Group[a]	Total No. Donor Spleen Cells ($\times 10^8$)	Peak Recipient Splenic Response[b]		Observed Ratio of PFC to Foci	Calculated No. of Donor Precursor Cells[c]
		No. of PFC ($\times 10^2$)	No. of foci		
Normal	1.8 ± 0.6	47.0	24.6	140	4500
FLV-infected:					
3 days	2.9 ± 1.2	7.8	9.5	82	2850 (63.3)
7 days	5.1 ± 0.3	2.8	5.3	50	2650 (58.9)
14 days	7.2 ± 0.8	1.0	3.0	33	2160 (48.0)

[a] Infected mice injected with 10^{-1} dilution dose of FLV on indicated day relative to cell transfer; 20×10^6 viable nucleated cells pooled from at least five donor mice and injected i.v. into groups of drug-treated recipients.

[b] Recipient mice challenged immediately after cell transfer with sheep RBC; assayed 9 days later for PFC and foci.

[c] Calculated from the average number of foci per recipient group; adjusted for percentage of donor cells transferred times factor of 20; ( ) = percentage of control.

level of 140:1 with cells from normal donors to a low of 50:1 and 33:1 in recipients of spleen cells from 7- to 14-day infected donors, respectively (Table IV). The number of transferred cells from infected mice represented a smaller proportion of the donor cell population than did the control cells. Thus the total number of precursor cells in the donor cell population was multiplied by the dilution factor (11). In addition, since only about 5% of transferred cells have been shown to lodge or remain in the recipient spleen, the total number of precursor cells calculated for each donor spleen was multiplied by a factor of 20 (12–14). Based on these calculations it is evident from Table IV that the number of precursor cells in spleens of infected mice decreased to a low of only 45% of control values, even though the number of foci and PFC in

TABLE V

Effect of FLV dose administered to donor mice on the number of PFC in recipient spleens

Donor Mouse Group[a]	No. of PFC per Recipient Spleen	Calculated No. of PFC in Donor Spleen if Entire Spleen Cell Suspension Were Transferred
Control	2.30×10^3	1.15×10^4
FLV Dose		
Undiluted	4.30×10^0	4.09×10^2
10^{-1}	1.02×10^2	2.55×10^3
10^{-2}	2.13×10^2	2.66×10^3
10^{-3}	1.96×10^3	9.80×10^3

[a] Donor mice were injected with 0.5 ml i.p. of the appropriate virus preparation 9 days before sacrifice and cell transfer.

recipient spleens decreased to a much greater extent.

The data presented in Table V demonstrate that the dose of FLV can markedly affect the number of precursor cells in the spleens of donor mice. There appears to be a direct relationship between the dose of the virus and the reduction in the number of precursor cells. The greater the dose of virus, the greater the reduction in the number of precursor cells. This agrees with our earlier studies on the effect of FLV dose on the primary immune response (5) and secondary (4) immune response to sheep RBC.

DISCUSSION

The mechanism of immunosuppression induced by tumorigenic viruses is unknown. Many complex events obviously occur at the cellular and molecular levels after infection of a susceptible animal with a leukemia virus such as FLV. It is also obvious that complex cellular and molecular events occur during immunogenesis. Nevertheless, a direct effect of a leukemia virus on antibody-forming cells or their precursors is still only speculative. In this regard, it has been proposed that leukemia viruses may supress immunity by interfering with specific cellular components of the immune system, such as mature immunocompetent cells, antigen sensitive cells, or as yet uncharacterized precursor stem cells (1–3, 6, 8, 11, 20–22). It is also possible that immunosuppression is caused by interference with antigen "handling" or processing cells (1, 6).

Various studies supporting each of the above possibilities have been reported in recent years.

It should be noted, however, that the reports implicating committed antibody-producing cells have been based on studies performed only late in the course of the disease (6, 21, 22, 24, 25). On the other hand, studies demonstrating that immunologic suppression occurs early in the disease process support the concept that induction of immunity, and not its maintenance or continuation, appears to be the most sensitive step of immunogenesis affected by leukemia viruses (3–10).

Recent studies have indicated that typical virus-like particles may be present in many lymphoid cells presumably containing or secreting specific antibody (24, 25). A study by Siegel, Neher and Morton failed to demonstrate similar leukemia viruses in hemolysin secreting plaque-forming cells from mice infected with a leukemia virus before immunization (26). On the other hand, an ultrastructural study in this laboratory showed that many antibody plaque-forming cells from mice infected with FLV contained typical virus particles, suggesting that virus infection and antibody formation may not be mutually exclusive processes at the single cell level (27). The significance of these findings in relation to the mechanism of immunosuppression is not yet celar.

The results of the present study extend earlier observations concerning the nature of the cells involved in immunosuppression induced by FLV. Appearance of individual PFC to sheep erythrocytes or *E. coli* somatic antigen is markedly reduced in the spleens and lymph nodes of mice infected with FLV before immunization (2–5, 7, 8, 10, 11). In contrast, there is generally little or no immunosuppression when virus infection occurs *after* immunization. Similarly, cell transfer studies showed that FLV infection had little effect on individual antibody-forming cells adoptively transferred from normal immunized donor mice into infected recipients (9). The corollary experiments performed in this study, i.e., transfer of spleen cells from FLV-infected animals into non-infected recipients, demonstrated a markedly depressed antibody response as assessed on both the cellular and humoral levels. For these experiments drug-treated mice were used as immunologically inert recipients. The localized hemolysis in agar gel method was used to enumerate individual PFC and antibody foci in recipient spleens.

It is generally recognized that a discrete antibody focus in a recipient spleen represents the site of proliferation of individual antibody-precursor cells and their progeny present in the donor spleen cell population (11–16). Transfer of splenocytes from a normal donor into a drug-treated recipient, followed immediately by challenge immunization with sheep erythrocytes, resulted in the appearance of a maximum number of antibody foci 9 days later. These foci are considered to represent the progeny of only a portion of the transferred cell suspension, since a maximum of about 5% of the donor cells appear to lodge in a recipient spleen (11–16). Thus, the number of antibody-precursor cells in a donor spleen cell suspension is usually calculated by using a factor of 20 to take into account the relatively low number of cells which localize in a recipient spleen. Similar studies from a number of laboratories have resulted in relatively similar estimates of approximately 5000 antibody-precursor cells to sheep erythrocytes in the spleen of a typical adult mouse (12–16).

Each antibody focus in a recipient mouse spleen is considered to contain at least 100 individual PFC. For example, in the present study it was found by assay of equal halves of an individual recipient spleen that there was a ratio of about 140:1 for PFC to foci. Such results suggest that a single antibody focus may be derived from an individual precursor cell which undergoes a relatively large number of divisions following stimulation with antigen. If this assumption is correct, it would follow that the 5000 or so precursor cells present in the spleen of an immunized mouse should have the capacity of proliferating into approximately 500,000 detectable PFC at the peak of the response. However, there are rarely more than 50,000 PFC to sheep erythrocytes in the spleen of an actively immunized mouse, regardless of strain or antigen dose used. It thus seems apparent that only a relatively small number of potential precursor cells in a spleen are stimulated by antigen and develop into PFC. Proliferation of each of 500 precursor cells into 100 progeny PFC following a single injection of antigen would be sufficient to account for 50,000 PFC. Similarly if 10% of the antibody-precursors in the spleen of an FLV-infected mouse were also stimulated by antigen, and if each would result in at least 100 progeny PFC, there should be a peak of at least 20,000 PFC in the spleens of infected mice. This num-

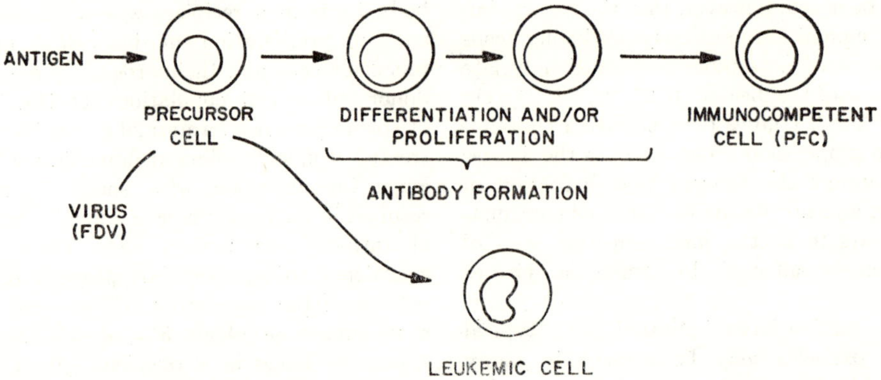

Figure 4. Postulated mechanism of action of FLV infection on immunologic responsiveness of mice. Virus may "compete" with antigen for limited number of antibody-precursor cells, diverting such cells from immunogenesis into leukemogenesis.

ber is based on the finding that the maximum suppression of precursor cells in spleens of infected mice, as assessed by the foci assay, is approximately 50%. In actuality, however, often fewer than 2000 PFC appear in the spleens of mice infected with FLV 3 to 7 days earlier (2–5). Thus, if each competent precursor cell in an FLV-infected mouse spleen could proliferate into at least 100 progeny PFC, as occurs in a normal spleen, it would seem that fewer than 10% are recruited after antigen stimulation. It is also possible that the precursor cells in an infected spleen have a much lower capacity for proliferation, as compared to those in a normal animal. This can be due to continued infection of precursor cells *and* their progeny during the course of infection, rather than infection of precursor cells by virus only at the time of antigen stimulation (Fig. 4).

The discrepancy between the degree of depression of the calculated number of antibody-precursor cells and the actual number of individual PFC in the spleens of FLV-infected animals suggests that immunosuppression associated with leukemogenesis is not due exclusively to inactivation of antibody-precursor cells. If this were the case, a 95% depression in the number of PFC in an infected animal should be a reflection of a similar depression in the calculated number of precursor cells. In addition, since immunosuppression is somewhat less marked early in the disease, such as on days 1 and 3, there should also be less suppression at this time in the number of calculated precursor cells. In this regard, a difference in the ratio of PFC to foci was evident in spleens of mice as a function of time. It seems unlikely, however, that the greater suppression in the number of PFC, as compared to foci, later in the disease was due to merely "dilution" with neoplastic cells. Nevertheless, the increase in spleen cell number had to be considered in the transfer experiments since there were approximately 4 to 6 times as many cells in spleens of 7- or 14-day infected mice, as compared with normal controls. Appropriate calculations indicated a 50% decrease in the number of precursor cells present in an entire donor spleen from mice infected with FDV, as compared to controls.

These results indicate a quantitative deficiency in the number of cells capable of proliferating into antibody-producing cells in spleens of leukemic mice, as compared with control animals, and also revealed that there is a moderate dilution of such cells by other cell types which may be insensitive to sheep erythrocytes, possibly because of previous commitment to other functions after infection with the virus.

Acknowledgments. The capable technical assistance of Mrs. Leoney Mills, Mrs. Vivian Simmons and Mrs. Dawn Burnside is acknowledged.

REFERENCES

1. Odaka, T., Ishii, H., Yamaura, K. and Yamamoto, T., Jap. J. Exp. Med., *36:* 277, 1966.
2. Salaman, M. H. and Wedderburn, N., Immunology, *10:* 445, 1966.
3. Ceglowski, W. S. and Friedman, H., Proc. Soc. Exp. Biol. Med., *126:* 662, 1967.

4. Ceglowski, W. S. and Friedman, H., J. Nat. Cancer Inst., *40:* 983, 1968.
5. Ceglowski, W. S. and Friedman, H., J. Immun., *101:* 594, 1968.
6. Salaman, M. H., Antibiot. Chemother., *15:* 393, 1969.
7. Hirano, S., Ceglowski, W. S., Allen, J. L. and Friedman, H., J. Nat. Cancer Inst., *43:* 1337, 1969.
8. Wedderburn, N. and Salaman, M. H., Immunology, *15:* 439, 1968.
9. Ceglowski, W. S. and Friedman, H., J. Immun., *103:* 460, 1969.
10. Ceglowski, W. S. and Friedman, H., Bact. Proc., p. 90, 1969.
11. Friedman, H. and Ceglowski, W. S., Nature, *218:* 1232, 1968.
12. Kennedy, J. C., Simminovitch, L., Till, J. E. and McCulloch, E. A., Proc. Soc. Exp. Biol. Med., *120:* 868, 1965.
13. Kennedy, J. C., Till, J. E., Simminovitch, L. and McCulloch, E. A., J. Immun., *96:* 973, 1966.
14. Playfair, J. H. L., Papermaster, B. W. and Cole, L. E., Science, *149:* 998, 1965.
15. Claman, H. N., Chaperon, E. A. and Triplett, R. F., Proc. Soc. Exp. Biol. Med., *122:* 1167, 1966.
16. Claman, H. N., Chaperon, E. A. and Triplett, R. F., J. Immun., *97:* 828, 1967.
17. Young, I. and Friedman, H., in *Germinal Centers in Immune Responses*, p. 102, Springer-Verlag, New York, 1967.
18. Santos, G., J. Immun., *97:* 587, 1967.
19. Neale, N., Mills, L. and Friedman, H., Bact. Proc., p. 90, 1967.
20. Cremer, N. O., Taylor, D. O. and Hagens, S. J., J. Immun., *96:* 495, 1966.
21. Siegel, B. V. and Morton, J. I., Immunology, *10:* 559, 1966.
22. Siegel, B. V. and Morton, J. I., Proc. Soc. Exp. Biol. Med., *123:* 467, 1966.
23. Bendinelli, M., Immunology, *14:* 837, 1968.
24. Cremer, N. E., Taylor, D. O. N. and Lennette, E. H., J. Nat. Cancer Inst., *42:* 695, 1969.
25. Oshiro, L. S., Cremer, N. E., Taylor, D. O. N. and Lennette, E. H., J. Nat. Cancer Inst., *43:* 1109, 1969.
26. Siegel, B. V., Neher, G. H. and Morton, J. I., Lab. Invest., *20:* 347, 1969.
27. Koo, G. C., Friedman, H. and Ceglowski, W. S., Bact. Proc., p. 82, 1970.

THE JOURNAL OF IMMUNOLOGY
Copyright © 1970 by The Williams & Wilkins Co.

Vol. 105, No. 6, December 1970
Printed in U.S.A.

HUMAN IMMUNOLOGIC RESPONSE TO SOLUBLE ANTIGENS

I. Hypersensitivity Induced by a Hapten-Altered Native Protein[1, 2]

MICHAEL W. BRANDRISS AND WARD E. BULLOCK, JR.[3]

From the Division of Immunology and Infectious Disease, Department of Medicine, Rochester General Hospital and the University of Rochester School of Medicine and Dentistry, Rochester, New York 14621

Received for publication July 16, 1970

Volunteers were injected intradermally and subcutaneously with soluble dinitrophenyl-human serum albumin (DNP-HSA) conjugates. Some responded with increasing titers of mercaptoethanol-sensitive agglutinating antibody to DNP-coupled red cells and some developed immediate type wheal and flare skin reactivity. Serum from one of these subjects was capable of passive transfer of DNP-specific wheal and flare reactions.

Thirty-eight of the 55 subjects developed delayed type skin reactions to DNP-HSA. These tended to be maximal in intensity at 24 hr after testing and declined or disappeared by 48 hr in contrast to classic delayed type reactions such as those to tuberculin which are usually prominent at 48 hr. There were also differences in both gross and histologic appearance between DNP-HSA and tuberculin reactions. The response of peripheral leukocytes to antigen *in vitro* measured by increased DNA synthesis was considerably less to DNP-HSA than it was to tuberculin in individuals who displayed skin reactivity to both. Passive transfer of delayed reactivity to DNP-HSA with dialysates of peripheral leukocytes from sensitive individuals could not be accomplished.

In contrast to the characteristic persistence of delayed sensitivity to tuberculin or other microbial antigens, delayed hypersensitivity to DNP-HSA developed early in the course of sensitization and then declined markedly in intensity or disappeared entirely with time and repeated testing. We suggest that this is a general characteristic of the human immune response to the administration of soluble antigens. This may be a distinct form of immunologic response that can be separated from both the serum antibody response and the classic delayed hypersensitivity that is induced by microbial infections or by administration of antigens in complete Freund's adjuvant.

In man, delayed skin reactivity to tuberculin and coccidioidin can be transferred from a hypersensitive donor to a previously nonreactive recipient with a dialyzable fraction of donor peripheral leukocytes (1). Major advantages in the further characterization of "transfer factor" would be offered by a system involving low molecular weight artificial chemicals with well-defined antigenic determinants, or other antigens absent in nature, to which a minimal degree of underlying sensitivity would not be expected. In a previous experiment a high degree of contact sensitivity to dinitrochlorobenzene was produced in normal volunteers but this was not transferable with leukocyte dialysate (2). Immunization to soluble dinitrophenyl-human serum albumin (DNP-HSA) conjugates was then undertaken in an attempt to produce transferable intradermal type hypersensitivity. The present report describes the delayed and immediate type re-

[1] This work was presented in part at the annual meeting of the American Association of Immunologists, Atlantic City, New Jersey, April 1968.

[2] This study was supported by United States Public Health Service Grants AI 07352 and AI 07964 from the National Institute of Allergy and Infectious Diseases.

[3] Present address, Division of Infectious Disease, Department of Medicine, University of Kentucky School of Medicine, Lexington, Kentucky 40506.

sponses, antibody formation and the *in vitro* reactivity of peripheral leukocytes that occurred in humans in response to immunization with DNP-HSA conjugates. The delayed sensitivity that developed differed from classical delayed type hypersensitivity in several respects. It resembled that first described in humans by Jones and Mote (3, 4) and may represent a distinct form of immunologic response.

MATERIALS AND METHODS

Volunteers. Volunteers were adult male inmates of the Attica State Prison, Attica, N. Y. The donors for transfer experiments had normal liver function tests and no history of hepatitis, jaundice, blood transfusion or drug addiction.

Antigens. Human serum albumin (HSA) was prepared from pooled plasma (E. R. Squibb & Sons, N. Y.). On immunoelectrophoresis against burro (provided by Dr. Lawrence Chessin) and rabbit (Behring Diagnostics Inc., Woodbury, N.Y.) anti-whole human sera only albumin was detected in this preparation. Dinitrophenyl-human serum albumin (DNP-HSA) was prepared by reacting 1-fluoro-2,4-dinitrobenzene (Matheson Coleman and Bell, Cincinnati, Ohio) with HSA in a molar ratio of 100:1 in aqueous solution at room temperature and alkaline pH. The degree of substitution was controlled by varying the pH from 9.0 to 10.5 by addition of 0.1 N NaOH, and the time of incubation from 60 to 90 min. The reaction was stopped at the desired time by addition of a molar excess of glycylglycine (Mann Research Laboratories Inc., N. Y.) as described by Carter *et al.* (5) for the preparation of picryl proteins. DNP-glycylglycine was removed by dialysis and the DNP-HSA was concentrated by ultrafiltration, dialyzed against pyrogen-free normal saline (Baxter Laboratories, Morton Grove, Ill.) and passed through 0.45-μ pore size Millipore filters (Millipore Corporation, Bedford, Mass.). Before use, all preparations were checked for sterility by incubation in thioglycolate broth at 37°C for 5 days. The molar ratio of DNP groups to protein was determined by ultraviolet absorption at 360 nm (6). Keyhole limpet hemocyanin (KLH) was obtained as an ammonium sulfate precipitate (Pacific Bio-Marine Supply Co., Venice, Calif.). It was dialyzed against 0.15 M phosphate-buffered NaCl, pH 7.0, until the KLH was in solution free of ammonium sulfate. It was then purified according to the method of Weigle (7), and dinitrophenylated in the same manner as was HSA. The molar concentration of DNP groups was determined by 360-nm absorption, but the molar ratio of DNP groups to protein could not be precisely determined because of apparent breakdown of the KLH molecule during conjugation. Dinitrophenyl-cellulose (DNP-AEC) was prepared by direct conjugation of 2,4-dinitrobenzenesulfonic acid (Eastman Organic Chemicals, Rochester, N. Y.) to aminoethyl cellulose (Bio-Rad Laboratories, Richmond, Calif.) as described by Cheng and Talmage (8).

Antibody assay. Agglutination of DNP-coupled group O human red cells as described by Bullock and Kantor (9) was used with some modifications. One-tenth milliliter of a 1% suspension of DNP-coupled cells was added to 0.1 ml of serial twofold dilutions of sera in tubes. Although it was practical to read settling patterns with anti-DNP test sera from hyperimmunized rabbits, this procedure was less reliable with the lower titered human sera. Instead of reading patterns, therefore, the cells were allowed to settle for 30 min and were then centrifuged at 1000 rpm for 2 min. The supernatant serum was removed, 0.1 ml of diluent was added and agglutination was read after gently tapping the tubes. Passive cutaneous anaphylaxis was performed in guinea pigs according to the method of Ovary (10). Beginning at a 1:10 dilution, serial twofold dilutions of serum in 0.1 ml volume were injected intradermally, 4 to 6 hr before intravenous injection of DNP-HSA, in amounts up to 20 mg. Standard Ouchterlony gel diffusion technique was used to screen for precipitating antibody (11).

In vitro response. DNA synthesis by peripheral leukocytes was assayed by incorporration of ^{3}H-thymidine as described by Moorehead and McFarland (12) with slight modification. Leukocytes were separated from heparinized blood and were placed in 13- x 100-mm screw cap glass culture tubes in tissue culture medium 199 (Microbiological Associates, Bethesda, Md.) containing 20% autologous plasma. One-tenth to 0.15 ml of DNP-HSA was added to triplicate sets of 3-ml cultures containing approximately 6×10^6 cells. Cultures were harvested on day 5, 75 min after addition of 1.5 μCi ^{3}H-thymidine (6 μCi/mmol) (Schwartz Bioresearch Inc., Orangeburg, N. Y.). Radioactivity of the washed, trichloroacetic acid-precipitated DNP containing protein was measured in a Mark I Nuclear-Chicago scintillation counter. The counting efficiency of individual samples was determined by the channels ratio method (13) using external standardization from a barium source. Results were expressed in counts per minute (cpm) per culture. In each experiment, one triplicate set of cultures was kept as a control without the addition of antigen. The antigen preparations contained either 26 or 43 groups of DNP per molecule of HSA. There was no significant difference *in vitro* in either toxic or stimulatory effects between the two conjugates and the results are combined in the text and figures. Concentration of DNP-HSA is expressed as milligrams of HSA protein. Other stimulants added to cultures were tuberculin; purified protein derivative (PPD) (kindly supplied by Parke Davis & Co., Ann Arbor, Mich.), 5.0 μg per culture; streptolysin-O (Schwartz Bioresearch Inc., Orangeburg, N. Y.), 0.1 ml (0.8 hemolytic doses per culture); and phytohemagglutinin M (Difco Laboratories, Detroit, Mich.), 0.1 ml per culture.

Immunization and skin testing. An initial dose of 1 mg DNP-HSA in 0.05 ml solution was given intradermally and observed for 20 min for any evidence of immediate type wheal and flare reactivity and for any systemic reactivity. The remaining 9 mg in approximately 0.45 ml were then given intradermally and subcutaneously in an adjacent site on the same forearm. Subsequent doses were injected in a similar fashion except for the more sensitive subjects in whom no more than 2 mg were used as a test dose.

Preparation of leukocyte dialysate and attempts at transfer of sensitivity. The methods adopted from Lawrence *et al.* (1) and previously described in detail (2) were followed. Leukocytes were separated from 500 ml of donor blood, lysed by freezing and thawing, treated with DNAse and dialyzed against approximately 100 volumes of distilled water. The dialysate was lyophilized, redissolved in 2 to 3 ml of sterile, pyrogen-free water and injected into normal individuals.

RESULTS

Because, in the absence of adjuvants, one might expect small rather than large amounts of antigen to be effective in producing delayed type sensitivity, a wide range of immunizing doses was explored. Initially, three groups of four subjects each received weekly or bi-weekly intradermal injections of either 2 μg, 10 μg or 100 μg of DNP-HSA. Of these individuals injected with 100 μg or less, none developed definite hypersensitivity. Subsequently one of three subjects injected with 1 mg became sensitive, and as a result of this experience, 10-mg initial immunizing doses were employed thereafter. No untoward systemic reactions to injection of DNP-HSA occurred at any time.

Following the initial dose, repeated injections of 2 to 10 mg of DNP-HSA were given to 55 individuals. This large number was necessary because of the variability of the response and the observation that, in almost all of the subjects who were followed for more than a few weeks, the degree of sensitivity declined or disappeared entirely with repeated testing. The subjects received conjugates containing either 22 to 26 groups of DNP/molecule of HSA or of 45 to 50 groups of DNP/molecule of HSA (Table I). Injections were given on day 0, usually on day 3 or 4, on 7 or 8 and weekly or bi-weekly thereafter. One group of eight subjects received an initial immunizing dose and then was not tested again until day 17. Later in these studies, as the course of declining skin reactivity became apparent, test doses were omitted after the first several weeks for periods of up to 5 months in some subjects.

TABLE I

Response of 55 humans to repeated intradermal and subcutaneous injections of soluble dinitrophenyl-human serum albumin (DNP-HSA) conjugates

	22 to 26 Groups DNP per Molecule HSA	45 to 50 Groups DNP per Molecule HSA	Total
Delayed type, skin reactivity	15/22[a] (66%)	23/33 (70%)	38/55 (69%)
Immediate wheal and flare reaction	1/16 (6%)	10/26 (38%)	11/42[b] (26%)
Rise in serum agglutinating activity to DNP-coupled red cells	6/20 (30%)	24/32 (75%)	30/52[b] (58%)

[a] Numerator = number of subjects who developed type of reactivity indicated; denominator = number of subjects injected.

[b] Wheal and flare reactivity and rise in agglutinating antibody developed later than did delayed type reactivity (see *Results*). Some of the 55 subjects were not followed long enough to evaluate these two types of response adequately.

Table I summarizes three types of immune responses that were seen. These were a delayed type of skin reactivity, immediate wheal and flare reactions and a rise in agglutinating activity of serum to DNP-coupled red cells. A fourth type of response, increased incorporation of ^{3}H-thymidine into DNA by peripheral leukocytes in response to antigen, was also observed. No statistically significant correlation could be made in this group of subjects between the appearance of any one type of reactivity and any other.

1. Delayed hypersensitivity to DNP-HSA

Thirty-eight of the 55 subjects developed delayed type reactivity. The moderately substituted conjugates (22 to 26 groups/molecule) and the heavily substituted ones were equally effective in their capacity to induce delayed hypersensitivity (Table I). The reactions were warm, erythematous, edematous and often pruritic. Although grossly comparable in intensity, they were more diffuse than typical tuberculin reactions with poorly defined borders of induration and they varied in size from those that were 10 mm in diameter to reactions covering most of the forearm. Reactions were maximal 24 hr after testing and were usually inapparent by 48 hr.

If reactivity appeared at all it did so by day 8 in all subjects who were tested at that time and by day 17 in those who were not tested at day 8. The maximal degree of skin reactivity was evident by day 8 to 17 and for the next 2 to 3 weeks. After 4 to 5 weeks, there was usually a decline in intensity of the reactions and in almost all subjects this was definite by 7 to 8 weeks. The decline could not be correlated with the appearance of hemagglutinating antibody or wheal and flare reactivity. In many, delayed type reactions disappeared entirely with repeated testing beyond 7 to 8 weeks. Figure 1 illustrates the appearance of a moderate reaction and the typical decline with time.

In an attempt to determine if the decrease in reactivity was caused by frequent skin testing, injections were discontinued at 3 to 7 weeks in a group of nine subjects. These subjects were retested 3 to 5 months later and again at 9 to 10 months. In eight of the nine, reactivity at the

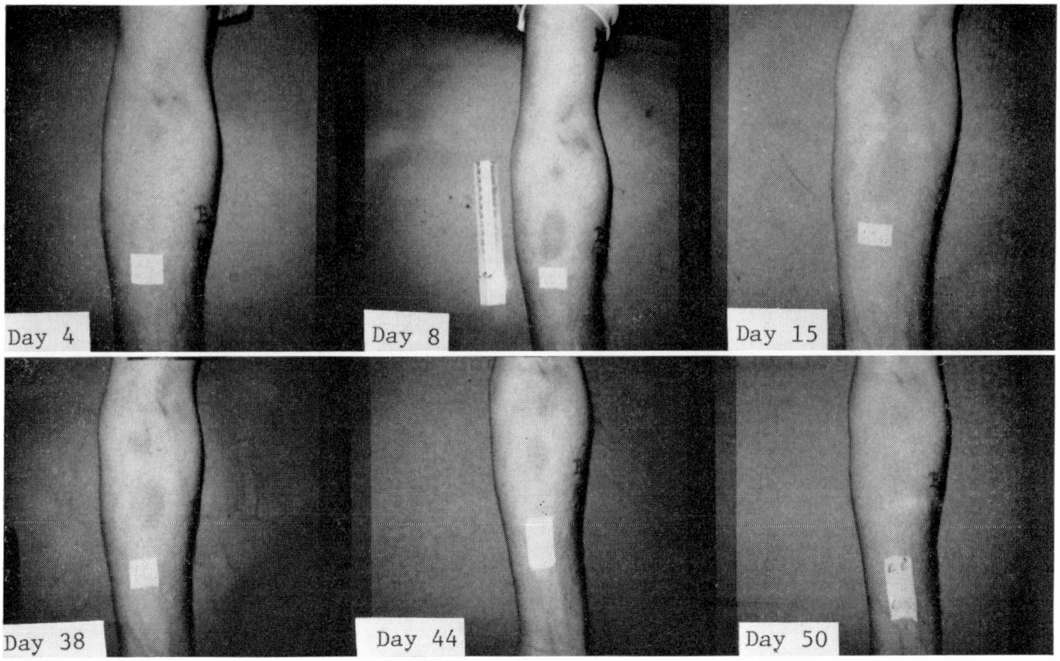

Figure 1. Reactions at 24 hr to intradermal injections of DNP-HSA. *Day* refers to number of days after first injection DNP-HSA. Two injections, a small preliminary test dose, and, 30 min later, the remainder of the test dose, were given on each occasion. Reactivity was most intense on days 8 and 15, had definitely declined by day 44 and was absent by day 50.

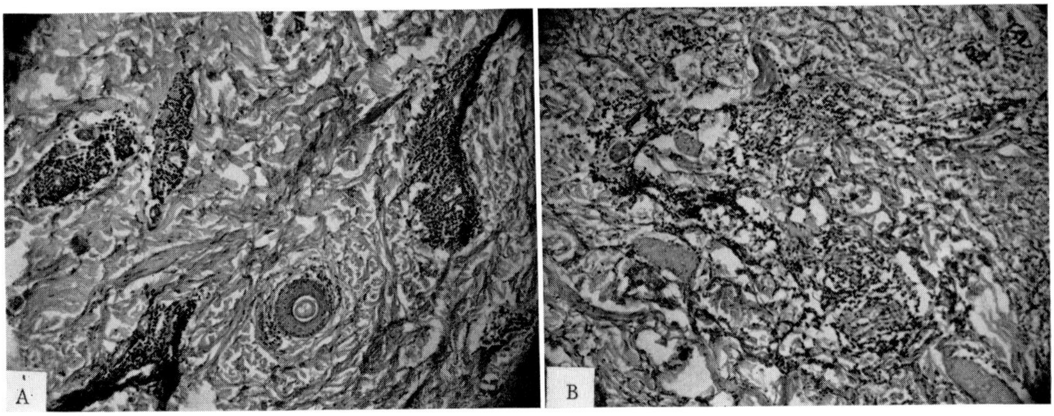

Figure 2. Biopsies of 24-hr reactions to DNP-HSA (*A*) and PPD (*B*). The inflammatory reaction to DNP-HSA is entirely perivascular. This was typical of the DNP-HSA reactions. The PPD reaction shows a more diffuse inflammatory infiltrate in the dermis.

time of these late test doses had further declined or had disappeared. In one subject reactivity increased between 4 weeks and 3 months but had declined further at 5 months.

Histologic studies. Five punch biopsies of DNP-HSA delayed type reactions and three of tuberculin reactions were compared. The histologic appearance was similar, both showing a perivascular infiltrate that was composed predominantly of small lymphocytes and larger mononuclear cells. A few small collections of neutrophils that were seen in the tuberculin reactions were not seen in the DNP-HSA reactions. The cellular infiltrate in both was predominantly perivascular, although more strikingly so in the DNP-HSA reactions. In the tuberculin reactions there was a greater tendency to an accompanying diffuse infiltrate of cells throughout the dermis (Fig. 2).

Specificity. Ten subjects who were immunized with DNP-HSA were tested on opposite arms with DNP-HSA and DNP-KLH conjugates (Table II). The dose of DNP-KLH injected contained approximately one-half the number of DNP groups and three times the amount of protein by weight as the simultaneously injected DNP-HSA. Conjugates corresponding more closely to DNP-HSA were difficult or impossible to prepare because of the high molecular weight of the native KLH molecule and its apparent breakdown during conjugation. Four of these 10 individuals (nos. 1 to 4, Table II) demonstrated moderate reactions to DNP-KLH in the order of one-sixth to one-half the diameter of induration of the DNP-HSA reactions. One (no. 5) had similar reactions to the two conjugates. One (no. 6) developed no induration to DNP-KLH, although a 22- x 20-mm area of erythema appeared. The other four (nos. 7 to 10) had no discernible reac-

TABLE II

Specificity of delayed type skin reactions to dinitrophenyl-human serum albumin (DNP-HSA) and dinitrophenyl-keyhole limpet hemocyanin (DNP-KLH) in humans

Sensitizing Antigen	Subject Number	Test Antigen	
		DNP-HSA	DNP-KLH
DNP-HSA	1	45 x 30[a] ++[b]	15 x 15 +
	2	120 x 80 +	15 x 13 +
	3	45 x 35 ++	10 x 9 +
	4	15 x 14 +	10 x 8 +
	5	15 x 15 ±	15 x 15 +
	6	13 x 13 +	0[c]
	7	35 x 30 +	<4
	8	10 x 10 ±	0
	9	20 x 15 +	<4
	10	10 x 10 ±	0
DNP-KLH	1	0	45 x 35 ++
	2	0	40 x 35 ++
	3	0	30 x 38 ++

[a] Millimeters of induration. Accompanying area of erythema was similar size or larger.

[b] ±, Barely palpable induration; +, mild induration; ++, moderate induration.

[c] A 22- x 20-mm area of erythema was present although there was no palpable induration.

tivity to DNP-KLH. Three individuals who were sensitized to DNP-KLH had no reactions to simultaneously administered DNP-HSA (Table II). In this circumstance, doses of DNP-HSA given contained twice the weight of protein and 12 times the number of DNP groups as the DNP-KLH injected. The reactivity, then, seemed to have carrier protein specificity although some cross-reactivity did occur.

Attempts to transfer delayed sensitivity. Four of the most sensitive subjects who reacted well to 2 mg or less of DNP-HSA were selected as donors. One donor per recipient was used. A local site was prepared by injection of 0.1 ml of dialysate (see *Materials and Methods*) intradermally in one forearm. The remainder of the dialysate was injected subcutaneously in the upper arm. Twenty-four hours later the local site was challenged by injection of 2 mg DNP-HSA intradermally. At the same time, 10 mg DNP-HSA was injected intradermally and subcutaneously in the opposite forearm to test for systemic transfer of reactivity. DNP-HSA skin tests at both locally prepared and remote sites were negative in all four recipients.

In vitro studies. Varying amounts of DNP-HSA, from 10 μg to 10 mg, were added to peripheral leukocyte cultures from sensitive individuals who were selected on the basis of positive 24-hr skin tests. The effect of antigen dose on DNA synthesis by peripheral leukocytes from sensitive subjects is illustrated in Figure 3. DNP-HSA was not toxic to leukocyte cultures as determined by trypan blue dye exclusion studies and by normal ^{3}H-thymidine uptake in response to PPD, streptolysin-O and phytohemagglutinin M in the presence of DNP-HSA. When a total of 0.4 mg DNP-HSA or less was added, little or no stimulation of DNA synthesis occurred. Addition of 3.3 mg caused maximal stimulation among the doses tested, whereas addition of 10 mg yielded no increase or a slight decrease in cpm compared to 3.3 mg (Fig. 3). Thereafter, the 3.3-mg dose was used in all control and sensitive cultures.

Figure 4 illustrates the effect of addition of DNP-HSA to peripheral leukocyte cultures of normal controls compared to sensitized subjects. A significant increase in DNA synthesis occurred when DNP-HSA was added to 14 triplicate cell cultures from 12 nonsensitized control individuals. The ratio of counts with antigen to those without ranged from 1.0 to 12.2, exceeded 3.0 in only 4 of the 14 and averaged 3.3. In 10 triplicate

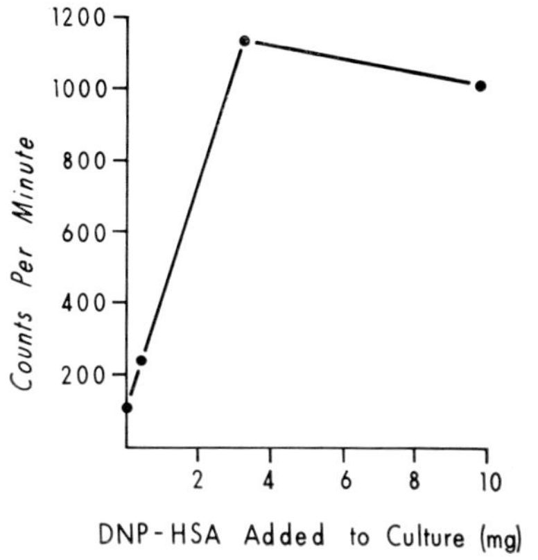

Figure 3. Effect of antigen dose on uptake of ^{3}H-thymidine by peripheral leukocytes. Each point represents the mean value of four individuals.

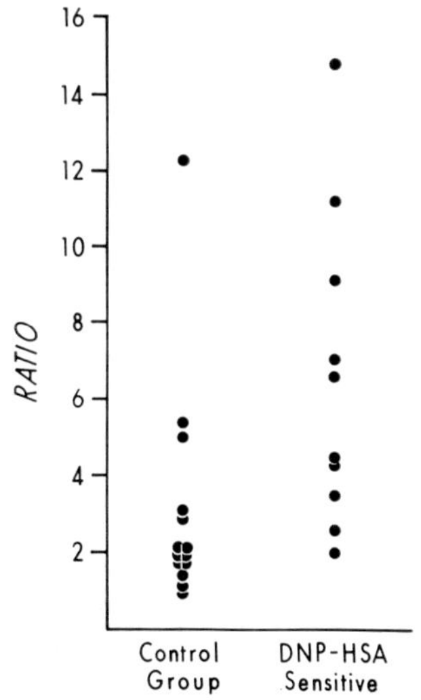

Figure 4. ^{3}H-thymidine incorporation into DNA by peripheral leukocytes in response to DNP-HSA. Points represent ratio of counts per minute (cpm) with antigen added to culture to cpm without antigen. Control group consists of 14 determinations in 12 normal, nonsensitized subjects; sensitive group consists of 10 subjects sensitized to DNP-HSA. The difference between the two groups is significant at 1% level by the two-sample rank test.

cultures from sensitized subjects, the ratio of cpm with antigen to those without ranged from 2.0 to 14.8, exceded 3.0 in 8 of the 10 and averaged 6.4. The difference between the control and sensitized

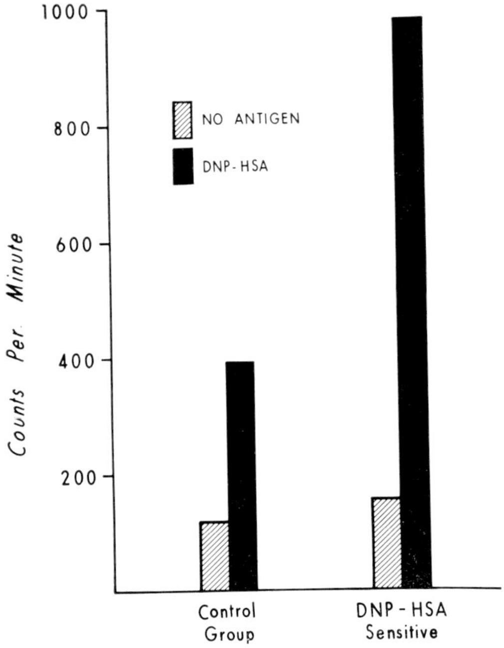

Figure 5. ^{3}H-thymidine incorporation into DNA by peripheral leukocytes in response to DNP-HSA: mean values for 14 determinations in 12 nonsensitized control and 10 sensitized subjects.

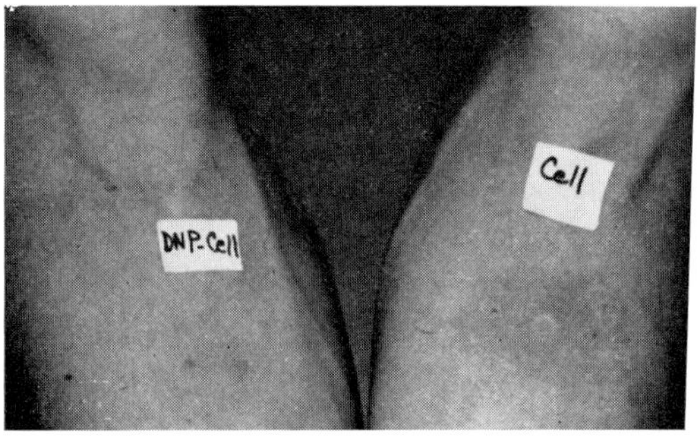

Figure 6. Wheal and flare reactions to DNP-HSA 20 min after challenge of skin sites that were passively sensitized 48 hr earlier with serum from a hypersensitive donor. The right arm (labeled DNP-cell) was injected with a 0.1 ml aliquot of serum that had been adsorbed with DNP-amino-ethyl cellulose (DNP-AEC), the left arm (labeled cell) with another 0.1 ml aliquot that was adsorbed with unaltered AEC. Challenge was with 1 mg DNP-HSA in 0.05 ml of solution. There was no reaction at the DNP-AEC-adsorbed site. A 13-mm wheal with a 45-mm surrounding area of erythema appeared at the AEC-adsorbed site.

individuals considered as ratio of cpm with antigen to cpm without antigen was significant at the 1% level by the two-sample rank test (14). Figure 5 compares the mean response of the control and DNP-HSA sensitized groups. In the control group, the mean cpm in cultures without added antigen was 119 and with antigen was 390. In the sensitive group, the mean cpm without antigen was 153 and with antigen was 979.

Simultaneously with these studies, aliquots of cells from the same individuals were put in culture with PPD in order to compare the magnitude of the response to DNP-HSA to that of a standard antigen. Seven of the DNP-HSA-sensitive subjects reacted with 15 mm or more of induration to intermediate strength PPD. In these subjects, the ratio of cpm with PPD to cpm without varied from 9 to 60 with a mean of 28, more than four times the mean response to DNP-HSA.

2. Immediate type reactions

Immediate type reactions developed in 11 of 42 subjects who were followed long enough for evaluation (Table I). The frequency of sensitization was greater with the highly substituted conjugates ($^{10}/_{26}$) than with the moderately substituted ones ($^{1}/_{10}$), although the difference is not quite significant statistically ($p > 0.05$, < 0.1). To evaluate wheal and flare reactions in actively sensitized subjects, DNP-HSA was injected in approximate volumes of 0.005 to 0.02 ml. Injection of 200 μg DNP-HSA produced wheals of more than 30 mm with pseudopods in some individuals and in the most sensitive subjects, wheal and flare reactions could be elicited by injections of as little as 20 μg, a dose considerably less than that required to elicit delayed reactions. Wheal and flare reactivity almost always appeared later in the course of sensitization than did the delayed reactions, usually requiring 2 weeks to 2 months and sometimes longer to become definite. There was often an increase in the intensity of these reactions in the first several months. In contrast to delayed reactivity, wheal and flare reactions persisted as long as the subjects were followed, in some cases for more than 2 years. Serum from one of the most sensitive individuals was capable of passive transfer of wheal and flare reactions to normal subjects. In one experiment, 0.1 ml of pre-immune donor serum was injected intradermally in the forearm of a normal recipient and 0.1 ml of hyperimmune serum from the same donor was injected in the other forearm. Forty-eight hours later these sites were challenged by injection of 1 mg DNP-HSA in a volume of 0.05 ml. There was no reaction at 20 min at the pre-immune serum site. At the hyperimmune site, an edematous 13-mm wheal with a 40-mm surrounding area of erythema developed. In a second experiment, hyperimmune serum from the same donor was used in another normal recipient. Before injection, one aliquot of serum was adsorbed with DNP-AEC while another aliquot was adsorbed with unaltered AEC. The recipient was then tested in the same manner. There was no reaction at the site of DNP-AEC-adsorbed serum, whereas a 13-mm wheal with a 45-mm area of surrounding erythema appeared at the unaltered AEC-adsorbed site (Fig. 6). Reagenic activity, then, was removed by adsorption of serum with the DNP group attached to an unrelated, insoluble carrier.

3. Serum antibody

Early in this study, it was noted that about 80% of normal pre-immune sera exhibited some agglutinating activity for DNP-coupled red cells. Titers were usually 1:8 or less, although they were as high as 1:64 in 5 of 56 sera tested. The agglutinating activity was abolished by treatment with 0.2 M mercaptoethanol for 2 hr, was present in the γ globulin containing fractions of serum and was specifically inhibited by DNP ligands as previously reported (15). A consistent increase of two tubes or more over pre-immunization titers followed the injection of DNP-HSA conjugates in more than half of the subjects (Table I). The frequency of antibody response was significantly greater ($p < 0.01$) with injection of highly substituted conjugates ($^{24}/_{32}$) than with moderately substituted ones ($^{6}/_{20}$). The response, although definite in these individuals, was never dramatic in magnitude, the highest post-immunization titer recorded being 1:512. The post-immunization agglutinating activity was also sensitive to treatment with 2-mercaptoethanol. The rise in titer of agglutinating antibody usually occurred by day 7 to 14, had some tendency to rise slightly higher in the next 2 or 3 weeks and then to plateau with time and repeated testing. No booster effect of later DNP-HSA injections was seen. Neither precipitating nor PCA-reacting antibody was ever detected.

DISCUSSION

The delayed hypersensitivity induced in man by injection of soluble DNP-HSA conjugates differed in several respects from classic tuberculin type sensitivity or the delayed reactivity induced in animals by similar conjugates incorporated in complete Freund's adjuvant. Skin tests were maximal in intensity at 24 hr, faded partially or entirely by 48 hr and, although grossly comparable in intensity to tuberculin reactions, tended to be more diffuse with poorly circumscribed borders of induration. Histologically the appearance was similar to that of tuberculin reactions, although the distribution of the cellular infiltrates was more strikingly perivascular.

In contrast to the characteristic persistence of reactivity, once established, to tuberculin or to other bacterial, viral or fungal antigens, reactivity to DNP-HSA appeared early in the course of sensitization and then declined rapidly in intensity or disappeared entirely with time and repeated testing. In this respect the reactions are similar to those previously described in humans to soluble foreign proteins by Jones and Mote (3, 4) and by Simon and Rackeman (16), and also to those induced in guinea pigs by several investigators (17–20). In an extension of the present study to the use of a foreign protein, a similar pattern of response in man to injection of soluble keyhole limpet hemocyanin was observed (21). That the same transient type of delayed reactivity that was produced with DNP-HSA has been produced in man by several investigators using different antigens and dosage schedules (4, 16, 21) suggests that this type of reactivity is a general characteristic of the human immune response to soluble foreign protein or hapten-altered native protein.

Whether this "Jones-Mote" reactivity and classical tuberculin sensitivity represent basically different types of delayed immunologic responses is not clear (22, 23). Because variations in macroscopic or microscopic appearance of skin tests are not necessarily reliable differential criteria but may be simply a function of the physical and chemical characteristics of the particular antigens involved (24), other criteria are required. One that might be applied is that of specificity. Immunization of animals with hapten-conjugated protein results in a hapten-specific serum antibody response, whereas elicitation of delayed skin reactivity requires the homologous carrier protein (25, 26). In the present experiments, although cross-reactivity did exist, some carrier specificity could also be demonstrated by using both DNP-HSA and DNP-KLH conjugates. In this respect, then, these Jones-Mote reactions do resemble classical delayed type reactions to hapten-protein conjugates. Similar carrier specificity for delayed reactions has been reported in humans immunized with picryl-protein conjugates (27).

It would be desirable to apply cellular criteria to the question of possible heterogeneity of delayed type responses. Of the various criteria available, the release of substances such as migration inhibitory factor secondary to leukocyte-antigen interaction seems to be most clearly related to classic delayed type hypersensitivity. Two studies employing this system in guinea pigs, one with picryl-proteins (28) and another with polysaccharides (20), have demonstrated the development of a transient state of macrophage migration inhibition after immunization with antigen in soluble form or in incomplete adjuvant. This may well represent a cellular counterpart to the course of Jones-Mote skin reactivity that follows sensitization with soluble antigens.

In a recent study, Richerson *et al.* (29) using azobenzenearsonate conjugates in guinea pigs showed that immunogenic requirements for the production of Jones-Mote sensitivity more closely resembled those for antibody production than for delayed sensitivity. Carrier requirements for elicitation of skin reactions, however, were different from those that are antibody mediated. The authors suggested that the Jones-Mote reaction is a distinct form of immunologic response distinguishable from both delayed hypersensitivity and classic antibody-mediated reactions. Employing special histologic preparations, they also described a basophilic infiltrate that was distinctive for the Jones-Mote skin reaction (29).

Taken together, these results suggest that in experimental animals Jones-Mote and tuberculin sensitivity are fundamentally different types of immune response. This distinction may apply to man as well.

Although a practical technique for the study of macrophage migration inhibition in man was not available to us at the time of this study, some attempts to compare the two types of reactivity on the cellular level were made. In contrast to the relative ease with which tuberculin sensitivity can be transferred (1), four attempts at local and systemic transfer of delayed reactivity to DNP-HSA were unsuccessful. Skin sensitivity to tuberculin and other bacterial or fungal products is accompanied by a specific response to antigen of peripheral leukocytes in cell culture which can be demonstrated by increased DNA synthesis. This system was utilized in a second attempt to compare tuberculin and Jones-Mote reactivity on a cellular level. Although we could demonstrate a response to DNP-HSA conjugates in sensitized humans, it was not as consistent and in magnitude was less than one-fourth the response to PPD in individuals sensitive to both, although the most highly reactive individuals to DNP-HSA were selected. While the results of these two experiments may indicate differences between the Jones-Mote and classic delayed types of sensitivity, it is possible that they reflect no more than quantitative factors, inasmuch as the amounts of DNP-HSA required to elicit both *in vivo* and *in vitro* responses are far larger than those of PPD.

The transient nature of the Jones-Mote reactions is not as easily explained on a simple quantitative basis. In previous studies in humans, foreign protein antigens were used and the early phase of delayed sensitivity that developed was usually succeeded by the appearance of wheal and flare reactivity (4, 16). Interference with the expression of delayed sensitivity by immediate type reactions might be thought to occur in those cases. The present experiment differs in that wheal and flare reactions developed in only a minority of the subjects and delayed reactivity disappeared whether or not immediate reactions or a serum antibody response occurred.

The characteristic persistence of wheal and flare reactivity and the ability to produce agglutinating antibody to DNP-HSA are in contrast to the evanescence of the delayed hypersensitivity observed. It is apparent, then that these antibody-mediated reactions, as well as persistent tuberculin type sensitivity, have different requirements for antigen than does the transient delayed type skin response observed in these experiments. It seems improbable that simple quantitative differences in the amounts of antigen presented or retained or in the magnitude of antigenic stimulus are responsible. Amounts of DNP-HSA that were sufficient to induce delayed type reactions grossly and histologically comparable in intensity to tuberculin reactions were ineffective in maintaining this state of sensitivity despite repeated and frequent administration. This could not be attributed to excessive antigen administration because smaller immunizing doses failed to induce a state of sensitivity and omission of test doses for prolonged periods did not avert its disappearance; nor could it be ascribed to an inhibitory effect of detectable circulating or cell-fixed antibody.

The results of the present study obviously do not provide a definitive answer to the question of heterogeneity of delayed type responses in man. However, in conjunction with previous studies and those in experimental animals, they emphasize the possibility that in man the delayed sensitivity induced to soluble antigens and that resulting from natural infection typified by tuberculin sensitivity are fundamentally different types of immune response. This is an important consideration in the selection of antigens suitable for evaluation of immune competence in man, particularly if the ability to develop classic delayed hypersensitivity is taken to reflect the capacity to express cellular immune responses in general. An alternative to intradermal sensitization with soluble antigens is the application of dinitrochlorobenzene, dinitrofluorobenzene or picryl chloride which regularly results in contact sensitivity in normal individuals (3, 27, 30). Whether this represents a basically identical phenomenon is not entirely clear either, but it is a classic form of delayed reactivity which may correspond better to tuberculin type reactivity.

For evaluation of the primary antibody response DNP-HSA cannot be recommended because of the feeble and inconsistent response in normals. Kantor and Bullock (27) described a more consistent response in man using picryl-HSA conjugates but the antibody formed was almost entirely mercaptoethanol-sensitive. The injection of KLH regularly results in antibody production in normals as originally reported by Swanson and Schwartz (31). Both mercaptoethanol-sensitive and -resistant antibodies were formed (31) and with Sephadex G-200 gel filtration it can be confirmed that both IgG and IgM antibodies are present. (M. W. Brandriss, unpublished observations.) Therefore, this is probably the most effective antigen available at present to detect major deficiencies in the human primary antibody response.

The wheal and flare reactivity to DNP-HSA that developed in about 20% of the subjects may be useful in further investigating human reagenic antibody to a well-defined determinant. That at least one serum was capable of passive transfer of DNP-specific reactivity further expands this possibility.

Acknowledgments. The authors wish to express their appreciation to the inmates of the Attica State Prison who participated in this study and to the Warden and the administration for their help and cooperation.

REFERENCES

1. Lawrence, H. S., Al-Askari, S., David, J., Franklin, E. C. and Zweiman, B., Trans. Assoc. Amer. Physicians, *76:* 84, 1963.
2. Brandriss, M. W., J. Clin. Invest., *47:* 2152, 1968.
3. Jones, T. D. and Mote, J. R., New England J. Med., *210:* 120, 1934.
4. Mote, J. R. and Jones, T. D., J. Immun., *30:* 149, 1936.
5. Carter, T. H., Macris, N. T. and Chase, M. W., Fed. Proc., *25:* 611, 1966.
6. Little, J. R. and Eisen, H. N., in *Methods in Immunology and Immunochemistry*, Edited by C. A. Williams and M. W. Chase, p. 131, Academic Press, Inc., New York and London, 1967.
7. Weigle, W. O., Immunochemistry, *1:* 295, 1964.
8. Cheng, W. C. and Talmage, D. W., J. Immun., *97:* 778, 1966.
9. Bullock, W. E. and Kantor, F. S., J. Immun., *94:* 317, 1965.
10. Ovary, Z., Progr. Allerg., *5:* 460, 1958.
11. Ochterlony, O., Progr. Allerg., *5:* 1, 1958.
12. Moorehead, J. F. and McFarland, W., Nature, *211:* 1157, 1966.
13. Bush, E. T., Anal. Chem., *35:* 1024, 1963.
14. Goldstein, A., *Biostatistics, an Introductory Text*, The MacMillan Company, New York, 1964.
15. Brandriss, M. W., Nature, *221:* 960, 1969.
16. Simon, F. A. and Rackemann, F. M., J. Allerg., *5:* 439, 1934.
17. Dienes, L., Arch. Path., *21:* 357, 1936.
18. Salvin, S. B., J. Exp. Med., *107:* 109, 1958.
19. Raffel, S. and Newell, J. M., J. Exp. Med., *108:* 823, 1958.
20. Gerety, R. J., Ferraresi, R. W. and Raffel, S., J. Exp. Med., *131:* 189, 1970.
21. Brandriss, M. W. and Chessin, L. N., Fed. Proc., *28:* 569, 1969.
22. Uhr, J. W., Physiol. Rev., *46:* 359, 1966.
23. Turk, J. L., in *Delayed Hypersensitivity*, Edited by J. L. Turk, pp. 21–30, John Wiley & Sons, Inc., New York, 1967.
24. Gell, P. G. H. and Benacerraf, B., Advances Immun., *1:* 319, 1961.
25. Benacerraf, B. and Gell, P. G. H., Immunology, *2:* 53, 1959.

26. Salvin, S. B. and Smith, R. F., J. Exp. Med., *111:* 465, 1965.
27. Kantor, F. S. and Bullock, W. E., J. Allerg., *43:* 349, 1969.
28. Carpenter, R. R. and Brandriss, M. W., J. Exp. Med., *120:* 1231, 1964.
29. Richerson, H. B., Dvorak, H. F. and Leskowitz, S., J. Immun., *103:* 1431, 1969.
30. Good, R. A., Varco, R. L., Aust, J. B. and Zak, S. J., Ann. N. Y. Acad. Sci., *64:* 882, 1957.
31. Swanson, M. A. and Schwartz, R. S., New England J. Med., *277:* 163, 1967.

THE JOURNAL OF IMMUNOLOGY
Copyright © 1970 by The Williams & Wilkins Co.

Vol. 104, No. 6, December 1970
Printed in U.S.A.

LYMPHOCYTOTOXIC ANTIBODY RESPONSE TO CARDIAC ALLOTRANSPLANTATION IN MAN[1]

I. Correlation with Post-Transplantation Clinical Course

KAMAL K. MITTAL, ROGER D. ROSSEN, WILLIAM T. BUTLER,[2] ARMEAD H. JOHNSON, ROBERT D. LEACHMAN, JAMES J. NORA, DONALD G. ROCHELLE AND DAVID K. BROOKS

From the Departments of Microbiology, Medicine and Pediatrics, Baylor College of Medicine and the Laboratories of Immunology Research, The Methodist and Veterans Administration Hospitals, Houston, Texas

Received for publication July 13, 1970

Lymphocytotoxic antibodies were found in sera collected prior to transplantation from 3 (14%) of 22 cardiac allograft recipients. Of sera collected after transplantation, multiple samples from 15 of 28 patients (54%) contained lymphocytotoxins. These antibodies were found especially frequently in sera from patients who died of infection or who succumbed after repeated episodes of threatened allograft rejection. The findings of the present study suggest that development of lymphocytotoxic antibodies in cardiac allograft recipients is an ominous sign which, within 1 month after transplantation, may identify individuals who will experience an unfavorable clinical course.

Although cell-mediated immune mechanisms have generally been credited with the primary role in allograft rejection (1), a growing body of evidence indicates that humoral antibodies may also participate in those events which lead to graft failure (2–9). Graft failure associated with deposition of humoral antibodies occurs particularly frequently when the recipient already has established immunity to antigens present in the allograft (6–9). It is therefore possible that humoral immune mechanisms, possibly reflecting a high incidence of pre-existing sensitization, may play a significant role in cardiac allograft rejection. The present work was undertaken to evaluate the incidence of lymphocytotoxic antibodies in sera from cardiac allograft recipients before and at intervals after transplantation and to determine whether development of these antibodies in an individual was associated with a poor prognosis.

[1] This work was supported in part by Grants HE-05435 and RR-00350 from the National Institutes of Health and The Veterans Administration Hospital, Houston, Texas.

[2] Address reprint requests to William T. Butler, M.D., Director, Immunology Research Laboratory, Veterans Administration Hospital, Houston, Texas 77031.

MATERIALS AND METHODS

Twenty-four pre-transplant sera from 22 recipients and 312 post-transplant sera from 28 cardiac allograft recipients were evaluated for the presence of lymphocytotoxic antibodies using the microcytotoxicity test and lymphocytes from 40 or more random normal donors (10, 11). Sera were tested undiluted and frequently also in two-fold serial dilutions (up to 1:32) made in McCoy's 5a medium (11). Sera were judged to be cytotoxic if they reacted with lymphocytes from 9% or more of normal donors tested (11). Although in some studies of renal transplant recipients (7) a higher level of reactivity (cytotoxic activity against ≥20% of random donor lymphocytes rather than ≥9% as in the present study) has been used to identify sera which contain antibody, such criteria applied to the present data would exclude 4 of the 5 positive pre-transplantation sera (2 of the 3 patients with positive sera) but only 8 of the 132 positive post-transplantation sera from 4 out of the 15 patients recognized as forming cytotoxic antibodies.

The clinical courses of 16 of the 28 recipients were examined in detail. Cases which were not studied in detail included 5 from whom multiple serum samples were not obtained and 7 who died within the first 8 days after cardiac transplantation. The 16 patients who satisfied these criteria were grouped into 3 classes: A) those who died from overwhelming infection (4 patients); B) those who died of rejection after a "poor" clinical course characterized by multiple episodes of threatened allograft rejection requiring intensive immunosuppressive therapy (7 patients who, in general, exhibited decreased exercise tolerance and remained in the hospital during most of the post-transplant period); C) those who are still alive and functioning normally (2 patients) or who died of rejection after a period of excellent cardiac function during which they enjoyed normal exercise tolerance (3 patients).

Immunofluorescence studies were carried out as previously described (12). Tissue from cardiac allografts was collected at autopsy and stored at −70°C until studied. Sections were treated with fluorescein-conjugated antibodies specific for the heavy chains of human IgG, IgA and IgM and evaluated for immunoglobulin found within the sarcolemma, muscle fibrils and vasculature. Appropriate controls to evaluate the specificity of the conjugated antibodies were included in these studies (12).

TABLE I

Incidence of lymphocytotoxic antibodies in sera of cardiac allograft recipients before and after transplantation

	No. Positive/No. Tested	
	Patients	Sera
Pre-transplantation	3/22 (14%)	5/24 (21%)
Post-transplantation (patients surviving > 1 month)	13/19 (68%)	127/285 (45%)
Post-transplantation (patients surviving ≤1 month)	2/9 (22%)	5/27 (19%)
Post-transplantation (all patients)	15/28 (54%)	132/312 (42%)

RESULTS

Prior to transplantation, sera from the cardiac allograft recipients showed a relatively low frequency of lymphocytotoxic antibodies. Sera from only 3 individuals contained such antibodies. One month or more after transplantation approximately half of the sera from over half of the patients tested exhibited lymphocytotoxic activity (Table I). Although no allograft recipient developed cytotoxic antibodies prior to the sixth day, the frequency with which these antibodies were detected increased rapidly during the first 2 months following transplantation. Such antibodies were detected most frequently in sera from individuals who later succumbed to infection and in a somewhat lower incidence in sera from patients who experienced recurrent problems with threatened allograft rejection (Table II, Fig. 1).

Sera from individuals who enjoyed a relatively comfortable post-transplantation course had the lowest frequency of cytotoxic antibody (group C, Tables II and III). These patients also lived longer after transplantation. Of the 5 individuals in group C, 4 returned full time to work or to school. Two of them (nos. 2 and 6) developed symptoms consistent with diminished cardiac output after 20 and 25 weeks of normal activity and died subsequently of irreversible rejection. A third member of this group (no. 4) died in his sleep at 266 days without premonitory symptoms. The other 2 remain well and active over 24 months after transplantation. Among these 5 patients, only sera from no. 4 consistently exhibited lymphocytotoxic activity, while antibodies were not detected in sera from the other 4. In contrast, sera from most of the patients who experienced a "poor" clinical course or who died from infection showed antibody activity in the majority of the sera tested.

There was no correlation between the frequency with which lymphocytotoxic antibodies were found in the sera of these patients and the frequency with which immunoglobulin was identified in sections from the transplants which were examined by immunofluorescence after death (Table II, rank correlation test, $p > 0.10$). However, patients who died of infection had significantly less immunoglobulin deposited within the transplanted hearts than individuals who died from rejection after a "poor" clinical course (Table IV), even though the patients who succumbed to infection had had the highest incidence of circulating cytotoxins antemortem.

DISCUSSION

Lymphocytotoxic antibodies develop relatively frequently in heart transplant recipients, particu-

TABLE II

Incidence of circulating lymphocytotoxic antibodies during the first 5 months post-transplantation: comparison with deposition of immunoglobulin within the cardiac allograft at necropsy

Patient No.	Serologic Studies: No. Lymphocytotoxic Sera/No. Sera Tested (at Months Post-Transplantation)					Immunofluorescent Studies of Heart at Necropsy: Frequency of Bound Immunoglobulin (Sections Positive/Sections Tested)		
	1	2	3	4	5	Sarcolemma-bound IgG	Total Ig[a] bound	IgM bound
				A. Dead of infection				
3	1/3	4/5	1/2			ND	ND	ND
7	0/4	5/5				3/3	11/22	3/7
27	5/5	3/3				1/4	8/33	3/11
43	10/12	10/10	1/1		1/1	ND	ND	ND
Total	16/24	22/23	2/3		1/1	4/7	19/55	6/18
				B. Dead of rejection after "poor" clinical course				
1	0/2	0/3	1/4	0/2	0/4	1/2	8/15	2/5
5	0/2	0/4	0/4	1/3	0/1	1/3	16/27	5/9
15	3/3	2/2	2/2	3/3	5/5	ND	ND	ND
19	0/3	0/2	2/3	2/2		3/3	13/23	3/8
32	4/6					3/3	16/16	5/6
37	5/5	1/1				3/3	14/25	4/8
41	3/23	20/21	0/5	1/5		ND	ND	ND
Total	15/44	23/33	5/18	7/15	5/10	11/14	67/106	19/36
				C. Alive, or dead of rejection after "good" clinical course				
2	0/1	0/3	0/2	1/1	0/3	0/8	11/85	2/29
4	2/4	4/5	2/2	1/1	1/1	ND	ND	ND
6	0/3	0/1	0/3	0/4	0/2	ND	ND	ND
10	0/16	0/8					Alive	
28	1/7	0/3	0/1	0/3			Alive	
Total	3/31	4/20	2/8	2/9	1/6	0/8	11/85	2/29

[a] Total Ig bound, sum of sections showing immunoglobulin of all major classes bound in sarcolemma, muscle fibers or vessels.

larly in those who experienced an unfavorable clinical course. Thus the results of the present study are in accord with what has been seen previously with human renal allografts (7, 9). The striking difference in incidence of these antibodies in sera from patients who had a relatively favorable outcome as compared with results with sera from those who did not do well was apparent within the first month after transplantation. This observation suggests that assay for these antibodies may be useful in predicting the long-term prospects of cardiac allograft recipients.

The high incidence of cytotoxins in post-transplantation sera from cardiac allograft recipients may reflect that cardiac disease sufficiently severe to require transplantation does not result in diminished immunologic reactivity as does uremia (13). Coming to transplantation without significant pre-transplant immunosuppression the cardiac recipient is challenged with foreign histocompatibility antigens both in the allograft and in the leukocytes present in the blood used to support his circulation during open heart surgery. The diversity of the antigenic specificities of the antibodies found in the sera of the cardiac allograft recipients indicates that these patients have been stimulated by a wide variety of histocompatibility antigens (14). In addition, the higher frequency of cytotoxic antibodies among sera from cardiac as compared to renal allograft recipients might suggest that cardiac allografts have a relatively limited capacity to absorb the antibodies produced (7). However, immunofluorescent studies have shown that there is extensive deposition of all major classes of immunoglobulin within human cardiac allografts regardless of the cause of death (12). On the other hand, the circulating lymphocytotoxins in these patients have been shown to be almost exclusively 19S (14) the only major species of immunoglobulin which distributes relatively poorly extravascularly (15). Thus, it is possible that 7S lymphocytotoxins are formed, but are readily absorbed by the graft leaving insufficient quantities in the serum to be detected by the microcytotoxicity test. The deposition of immunoglobulin is so extensive and begins so soon after transplantation in many cases that it seems likely that a relatively more vigorous immune response rather than decreased absorption of antibody within the graft explains why the incidence of cytotoxins is more frequent among sera from the cardiac allograft recipients (12).

The frequency with which cytotoxic antibodies are found in the serum bears no necessary relationship to the frequency with which deposits of immunoglobulin may be detected within the allograft (Table II). Thus, individuals who succumbed to infection had a significantly higher incidence of serum lymphocytotoxins than did those who died of rejection after an unfavorable clinical course. But patients who died of infection had considerably less immunoglobulin bound within the allograft at the time of death (Table IV). This may reflect that the individuals who died of rejection on the average survived longer and therefore had more time for deposits of immunoglobulin to accumulate, or that the humoral response in patients who died of rejection led to the formation of more avid antibodies. Alternatively, it is conceivable that the majority of the lymphocytotoxins in the infected patients' sera were not directed at unique alloantigens present in the graft but were specific for antigens in leukocytes introduced as a result of blood transfu-

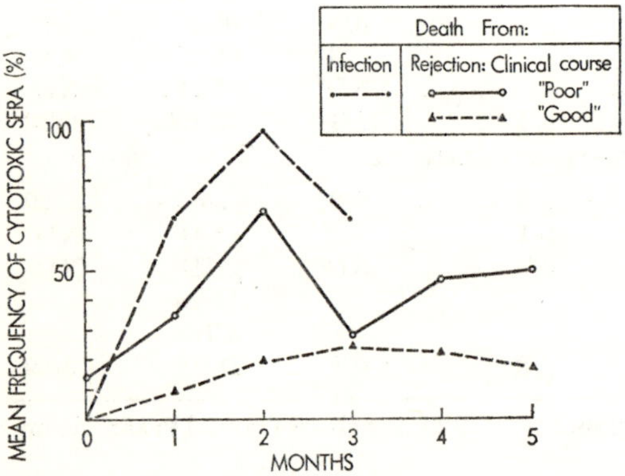

Figure 1. Average incidence of lymphocytotoxic antibodies in sera collected serially from 16 human cardiac allograft recipients following transplantation (see Table II for further details). The 14% incidence in pre-transplant sera from the group who had a "poor" clinical course and died of rejection is due to the presence of antibodies in the sera from only one of these seven patients (no. 15).

TABLE III

Incidence of cytotoxic antibody in relation to clinical course

	Clinical Course		
	Died of infection	Experienced a "poor" clinical course[a]	Experienced a "good" clinical course[a]
Positive sera	41	73	15
Negative sera	10	73	72
Average survival	78 days	156 days	>379 days[b]

$\chi^2 = 13.09$, $p < 0.001$
d.f. = 1 (comparing data in first 2 columns)
$\chi^2 = 89.2$, $p < 0.001$
d.f. = 2 (comparing data in all 3 columns)

[a] Totals include 39 sera in addition to those shown in Table II from patients who survived beyond the 5th month.

[b] Includes 2 patients who are still alive at >730 days.

TABLE IV

Incidence of bound immunoglobulin in allografts of patients at necropsy

	Succumbed to Infection	Succumbed to Rejection after "Poor" Clinical Course	Significance
No. sections with bound Ig[a] (all classes)	19	67	$\chi^2 = 10.8$, $p < 0.001$ d.f. = 1
No. sections without bound Ig	36	39	
No. sections with bound IgM	6	19	$\chi^2 = 2.9$, $0.05 < p < 0.10$ d.f. = 1
No. sections without bound IgM	12	17	

[a] Ig, immunoglobulin.

sion or for cross-reacting antigens present in the microorganisms responsible for the infection (16).

No definite role for these antibodies in the rejection of cardiac allografts can be assigned at present. Of the three patients who had pre-existing antibody, one experienced irreversible cardiac arrest immediately after surgery, but the histology of the lesions seen in the allograft was not consistent with hyperacute rejection (6). The other 2 individuals survived 177 and 498 days respectively. The longest survivor was the only one whose pre-transplant sera when tested retrospectively showed a low positive correlation (r = 0.32) with reactions of sera known to be specific for one of the antigens for which he was mismatched. This patient, however, suffered recurrent episodes of threatened allograft rejection and was bedridden continuously after transplantation. The patient who survived 177 days experienced little difficulty with rejection but succumbed to peritonitis secondary to rupture of a colonic diverticulum. Thus among these cardiac allograft recipients there are no individuals whose course exactly parallels that seen in renal allograft recipients who possess circulating antibodies to donor antigens prior to transplantation, and, as a result, experience hyperacute rejection of the new kidney (6–9). On the other hand, cytotoxins were found much more frequently in those patients who experienced recurrent problems with threatened allograft rejection (Tables II and III). Moreover, in these cardiac allograft recipients, deposition of immunoglobulin within the intima and media of the large and medium sized arteries has been directly associated with the evolution of intimal fibroplasia (12), a proliferative lesion of the structures lining the artery which is known to result in the obliteration of the lumen of arteries in both renal and cardiac allografts (17, 18). Thus the development of lymphocytotoxic antibodies in the sera of a cardiac allograft recipient is an ominous prognostic sign. Clinically it matters little whether these antibodies are a primary factor in the rejection process or whether their presence in a given individual simply indicates that the total immunologic response to the allograft is unusually vigorous.

Acknowledgments. The authors gratefully acknowledge the cooperation and aid of Doctors M. E. DeBakey, E. B. Diethrich, G. Noon, D. A. Cooley, R. D. Bloodwell, G. L. Hallman, D. J. Fernbach and J. D. Milam.

We also wish to acknowledge the outstanding technical assistance of Carrol Cagel, Sandy Farrow, Lucetta Guillory, Lucy Kormeier, Margaret A. Reisberg, Ruth Rickaway, Harold Summerlin and Julie Wareing.

REFERENCES

1. Russell, P. S. and Winn, H. J., N. England J. Med., *282:* 786, 848, 896, 1970.
2. Terasaki, P. I., Akiyama, T., McClelland, J. D. and Cannon, J. A., Ann. N. Y. Acad. Sci., *99:* 645, 1962.
3. Najarian, J. S. and Perper, R. J., Surgery, *62:* 213, 1967.
4. Dubernard, J. M., Carpenter, C. B., Busch, G. J., Diethelm, A. G. and Murray, J. E., Surgery, *64:* 752, 1968.
5. Hampers, C. L., Kolker, P. and Hager, E. B., J. Immun., *99:* 514, 1967.
6. Kissmeyer-Nielsen, F., Olsen, S., Petersen, V. P. and Fjeldborg, O., Lancet, *2:* 662, 1966.
7. Morris, P. J., Williams, G. M., Hume, D. M., Mickey, M. R. and Terasaki, P. I., Transplantation, *6:* 392, 1968.
8. Patel, P. and Terasaki, P. I., N. England J. Med., *280:* 735, 1969.
9. Jeannet, M., Pinn, V. W., Flax, M. H., Winn, H. J. and Russell, P. S., N. England J. Med., *282:* 111, 1970.
10. Mittal, K. K., Mickey, M. R., Singal, D. P. and Terasaki, P. I., Transplantation, *6:* 913, 1968.
11. Mittal, K. K., Rossen, R. D. and Butler, W. T., *Histocompatibility Testing 1970*, Munksgaard, Copenhagen, 1970.
12. Rossen, R. D., Butler, W. T., Reisberg, M. A., Brooks, D. K., Leachman, R. D., Milam, J. D., Mittal, K. K., Montgomery, J. R., Nora, J. J. and Rochelle, D. G., J. Immun., Submitted for publication.
13. Butler, W. T., Rossen, R. D., Hersh, E. M., Beall, A. C., Jr., Morgen, R. O., Diethrich, E. B. and DeBakey, M. E., Laval Med., *41:* 156, 1970.
14. Johnson, A. H., Butler, W. T., Rossen, R. D. and Mittal, K. K., J. Immun., *105:* 1432, 1970.
15. Barth, W. F., Wochner, R. D., Waldmann, T. A. and Fahey, J. L., J. Clin. Invest., *43:* 1036, 1964.
16. Hirata, A. A. and Terasaki, P. I., Science, *168:* 1095, 1970.
17. Porter, K. A., Owen, K., Mowbray, J. F., Thomson, W. B., Kenyon, J. R. and Peart, W. S., Brit. Med. J., *2:* 639, 1963.
18. Milam, J. D., Shipkey, F. H., Lind, C. J., Jr., Nora, J. J., Leachman, R. D., Rochelle. D. G., Bloodwell, R. D., Hallman, G. L. and Cooley, D. A., Circulation, *41:* 519, 1970,

THE JOURNAL OF IMMUNOLOGY
Vol. 105, No. 6, December 1970

LYMPHOCYTOTOXIC ANTIBODY RESPONSE TO CARDIAC ALLOTRANSPLANTATION IN MAN[1]

II. Characterization of Antigenic Specificities and Immunoglobulin Class

ARMEAD H. JOHNSON, WILLIAM T. BUTLER,[2] ROGER D. ROSSEN AND KAMAL K. MITTAL

From the Departments of Microbiology and Medicine, Baylor College of Medicine, The Methodist and Veterans Administration Hospitals, Houston, Texas

Received for publication July 13, 1970

Sera of 4 of 7 patients who developed a strong lymphocytotoxic response after cardiac transplantation showed a possible association with known histocompatibility groups. In 3 of these 4 patients the antibodies appeared to have specificity for antigens known to be present in donor but not in recipient lymphocytes. Thirty sera from the 7 cardiac allograft recipients were fractionated by sucrose density gradient ultracentrifugation. In each sample lymphocytotoxic activity was detected exclusively in the 19S region. In contrast, 3 sera from 2 renal transplant patients showed detectable lymphocytotoxic activity only in the 7S region. Among possible explanations for these results are that 7S antibodies were preferentially absorbed by the cardiac allografts or that these sera contain substances which block the action of 7S lymphocytotoxins.

Humoral antibodies against donor tissue antigens form following allotransplantation of skin (1, 2), kidney (3, 4) and heart (5, 6) in man. The high incidence of lymphocytotoxins in sera from heart allograft recipients who die relatively early after an unfavorable clinical course suggests that these antibodies may participate to an important degree in cardiac allograft rejection (6). Moreover, abundant immunoglobulin of all major classes has been found in allografts of patients who develop cardiac rejection (7).

To evaluate further the humoral lymphocytotoxic antibody response to human cardiac allografts, the antigenic specificities and the sedimentation characteristics of these antibodies were studied to determine whether the antibodies were directed against histocompatibility antigens known to be present in the cells of the donor and whether their physical characteristics corresponded to those of the immunoglobulins bound to the cardiac allografts at the time of death (7).

[1] This study was supported in part by Research Grants HE-05435 and RR-00350 and Training Grant AI-00325 from the National Institutes of Health and by The Veterans Administration Hospital, Houston, Texas.

[2] Address reprint requests to William T. Butler, M.D., Director, Immunology Research Laboratory, Veterans Administration Hospital, Houston, Texas 77031.

MATERIALS AND METHODS

Selection of sera

Sera were collected from 28 cardiac and 2 renal allograft recipients at approximately bi-weekly intervals and were kept at either −70°C or at 4°C after adding 0.1% sodium Merthiolate. Presence of lymphocytotoxic antibodies was determined by the microcytotoxic technique (8, 9). Sera found to be lymphocytotoxic were further tested in serial dilutions up to 1:32 against lymphocytes from an additional 40 normal donors and the antigenic specificities of these sera were analyzed by comparison with the reactions of known anti-HL-A sera tested simultaneously. The known antisera defined the following groups: HL-A1, HL-A2, HL-A3, HL-A9, HL-A5, HL-A7, HL-A8, HL-A12, VR4a and VR4b. The earliest and the latest post-transplantation samples which were cytotoxic for cells from ≥9% of random normal donors were selected for fractionation (6). In patients who survived for several months, additional samples which contained cytotoxic activity were also studied.

Sucrose density gradient ultracentrifugation

Exactly 0.2 ml of undiluted, whole serum was layered onto a 4.8-ml, 10% to 40% linear sucrose gradient in 0.15 M NaCl, buffered with 0.01 M Na phosphate, pH 7.4 (PBS), and centrifuged at 60,000 rpm (358,207 × G) for 12 hr at 5° to 7°C (10). Thirty-four to 37 fractions were collected by puncturing the tubes from below and were kept at −70°C until assayed. The concentrations of IgM, IgG and IgA in the fractions were measured by single radial diffusion[3] in agar (11) and the mid-point of the concentration distribution for IgM and IgG were used respectively as internal position markers for the sedimentation of 19S and 7S proteins. Normal lymphocytes remained alive in 5% sucrose, 20% sucrose and 40% sucrose under the conditions of the microcytotoxicity test. In addition, serum samples previously shown to contain cytotoxic activity associated with either IgM or IgG by Sephadex G-200 column chromatography were tested in serial dilutions up to 1:32 in McCoy's 5a medium and in 5%, 20% and 40% sucrose in PBS. Lymphocytotoxic titers in sucrose were never more than one tube lower than were those in McCoy's medium alone, and no significant difference was noted between titers in various concentrations of sucrose. In all, 30 sera from 7 cardiac and 3 sera from 2 renal allograft recipients were fractionated by this technique.

Gel filtration on Sephadex G-200

Sera were fractionated using upward flow elution on a 2.5 x 90 cm column of Sephadex G-200.[4] The flow rate was maintained at approximately 8 ml/hr with a peristaltic pump, and elution was carried out using 0.15 M NaCl buffered with 0.01 M Na phosphate, pH 7.4. Three-milliliter fractions were collected and were individually concentrated approximately 5-fold by placing the fluid within cellulose dialysis casings and spreading dry Sephadex G-200 on the outside of the bags. Concentrated fractions were kept at −70°C until assayed.

[3] The following goat anti-human immunoglobulin sera were used: Lots 8257E004A1 and 8257H001A1 (γ chain), Lots 8211H003A1 and 8211E004A1 (μ chain), Lots 8212D003A1 and 8212H005A1 (α chain), Hyland Laboratories, 4501 Colorado Blvd., Los Angeles, Calif.

[4] Pharmacia Inc., Uppsala, Sweden.

RESULTS

Antigenic specificity of lymphocytotoxic sera

Sera from 15 of the 28 cardiac allograft recipients contained cytotoxic reactivity (6). Sufficient sera were available from 7 of these 15 patients for further analysis and fractionation. The HL-A specificities of the sera from the 7 patients are presented in Table I. The reactions of sera from patient 32 correlated with those of sera known to be specific for HL-A8 and HL-A9, antigenic groups present in the donor's but not in the patient's own cells, but not with reactions of sera specific for the HL-A3 and HL-A5 groups for which the recipient was also mismatched. The patient also formed antibodies with HL-A7 and HL-A1 specificities although he was not mismatched for these groups. Another patient, no. 19, mismatched only for HL-A9, formed lymphocytotoxic antibodies which showed a suggestive association with HL-A9. Reactions of 6 of 7 lymphocytotoxic sera from patient no. 15 correlated with those of sera specific for HL-A9, an antigen present in lymphocytes from his donor. Antibodies with HL-A3 or HL-A7 specificities were also found in 2 sera from patient 15 although he was not mismatched for these groups. Patient 27 formed antibodies with HL-A9 and HL-A7 specificities; however, he was known to have been mismatched only for HL-A3 and VR4b. Reactions of lymphocytotoxic antibodies which developed in 3 patients (nos. 37, 41 and 43) did not correlate with those of any of the known anti-HL-A sera.

Characterization of lymphocytotoxic antibodies in organ allograft recipients

A. Fractionation by sucrose density gradient ultracentrifugation. Figure 1 shows the results obtained by fractionating a serum obtained from one of the cardiac patients by sucrose density gradient ultracentrifugation. These results are representative of those which occurred with all sera from the cardiac recipients. Lymphocytotoxic activity was found exclusively in the 19S region of the gradient and the titer of the activity appeared to parallel the IgM concentration of the fractions. In contrast, all 3 sera from the 2 renal recipients showed lymphocytotoxic activity exclusively in the 7S region of the gradient (Table II and Fig. 2).

Figure 3 shows a comparison of the sedimenta-

TABLE I

Lymphocytotoxic activity of post-transplantation sera from cardiac recipients

Patient Code No.	Days of survival	Cause of Death	Serum Sample Tested	Lymphocytotoxic Activity of Sera		Correlation with HL-A Groups[a]
			days post-transplantation	*titer*	*% positive*[b]	*group (r value)*
32	13	Rejection	11	1:16	30	HL-A7(0.46) *HL-A9*(0.73)[a]
			13	>1:32	52	HL-A1(0.36) *HL-A8*(0.36)[a] *HL-A9*(0.68)[a]
37	37	Rejection	30	1:8	13	None
			32	1:16	78	None
			36	1:16	36	None
27	47	Infection	13	1:2	14	None
			20	1:4	25	HL-A7(0.58)[c] HL-A9(0.50)[c]
			25	1:4	17	HL-A7(0.42)[c] HL-A9(0.57)[c]
			33	1:4	20	HL-A9(0.41)[c]
			39	1:4	100	None
			47	1:2	98	None
41	99	Rejection	26	1:16	52	None
			39	1:32	37	None
			48	1:8	25	None
			79	1:8	10	None
			92	Undil.	11	None
19	126	Rejection	28	Not done	7	*HL-A9*(0.34)[a]
			90	1:2	100	None
			104	1:2	100	None
43	143	Infection	24	1:2	15	None
			31	1:4	24	None
			38	1:8	42	None
			92	1:8	60	None
			141	1:4	20	None
15	409	Rejection	13	1:8	21	HL-A7(0.37) *HL-A9*(0.57)[a]
			123	1:8	90	None
			152	1:8	27	*HL-A9*(0.36)[a]
			252	1:16	73	*HL-A9*(0.41)[a]
			257	1:16	51	HL-A3(0.36) *HL-A9*(0.34)[a]
			312	1:2	15	*HL-A9*(0.43)[a]
			409	1:2	44	*HL-A9*(0.36)[a]

[a] Groups for which the patient was mismatched are italicized. The HL-A groups present on lymphocytes of donors and recipients were established by histocompatibility testing done retrospectively in all cases by Dr. Paul Terasaki and in 3 cases prospectively in our laboratory.

[b] % Positive, number of positive reactions/total number cells tested × 100.

[c] Donor lymphocytes in this case were tested and lacked HL-A7 and HL-A9.

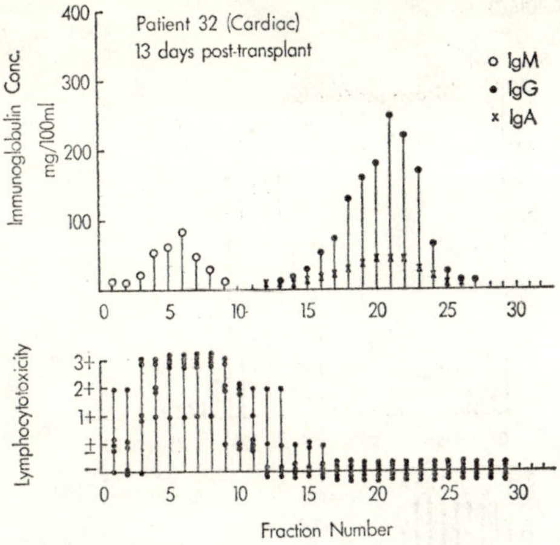

Figure 1. Serum from cardiac patient 32 fractionated by sucrose density gradient ultracentrifugation. The concentrations of IgM, IgG and IgA in each fraction are shown in the top half of the graph. Lymphocytotoxic activity in sequential fractions is shown in the lower half. Lymphocytotoxic activity is measured by the increase in percentage of lymphocytes that are killed in the fraction. (Negative, 0 to 4%; ±, 5 to 9%; 1+, 10 to 19%; 2+, 20 to 79%; and 3+, 80 to 100% dead cells.) Lymphocytotoxicity is represented with a dot. The reactions with lymphocytes from 5 different individuals are shown for each fraction.

tion behavior of the lymphocytotoxic activity in 2 sera from the same cardiac recipient 152 and 252 days respectively following transplantation; the fractions from both sera were tested against lymphocytes from the same panel of donors. The strength of the 19S lymphocytotoxic activity appeared to increase between days 152 and 252. Note also that the mean peak IgG concentration of the later serum sample is nearly double that of the earlier specimen; yet despite this increase, no 7S lymphocytotoxic antibodies were detected. Based on analysis of the immunoglobulin concentrations in the density gradients, mean peak values for total serum IgG concentration do not vary appreciably among the cardiac and the renal recipients. However, the mean peak IgM concentration in the density gradients from the cardiac recipients was 5-fold greater than in the renal recipients (Table II).

B. Gel filtration on Sephadex G-200. Seven sera from 2 renal transplant patients showed lymphocytotoxic activity in fractions containing IgG but no detectable IgM. Four sera from one cardiac recipient showed lymphocytotoxic activity in fractions containing IgM in the absence of detectable IgG. Some of the fractions from each peak also contained IgA, but since IgA does not fix complement (12), the cytotoxic activity was not attributed to this immunoglobulin.

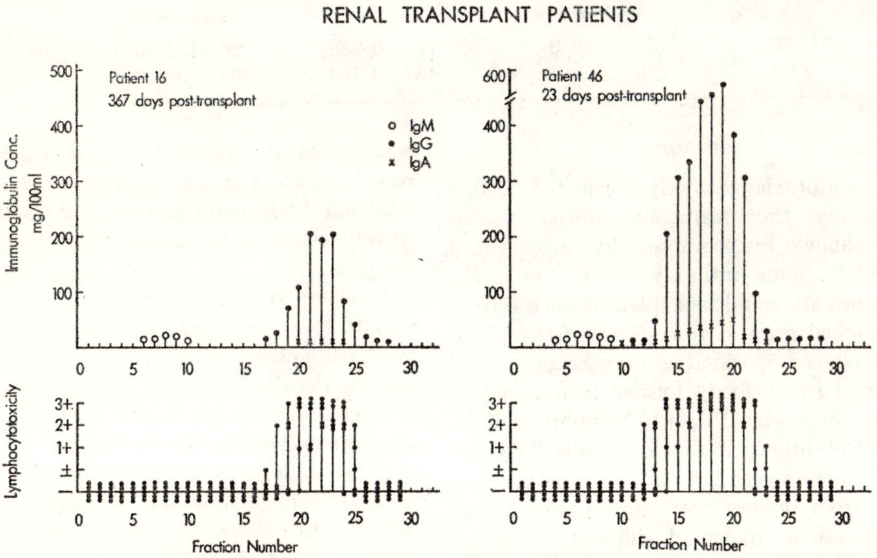

Figure 2. Sucrose density gradient ultracentrifugation of serum from renal patients 16 and 46 showing the immunoglobulin concentrations and the lymphocytotoxic activity in sequential fractions (see Figure 1 for explanation).

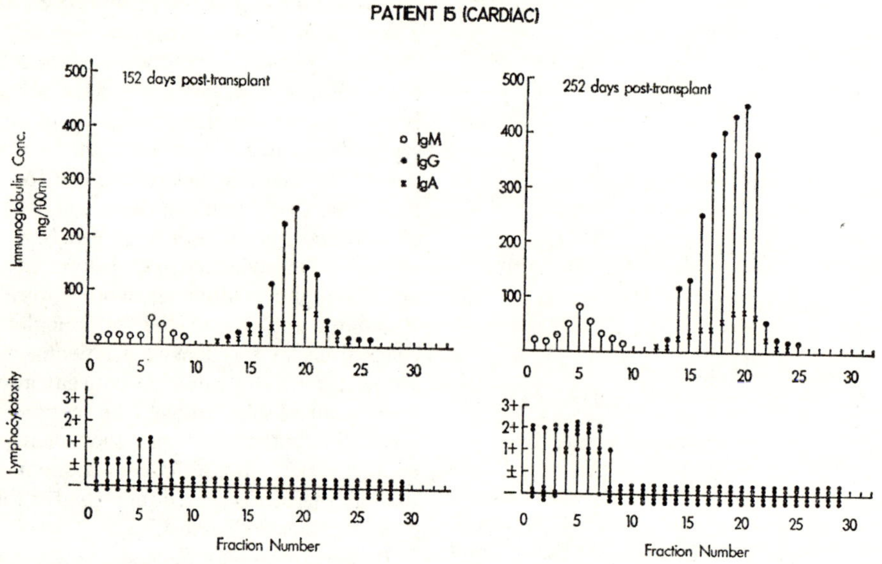

Figure 3. Comparison of the lymphocytotoxic activity of 2 sera from cardiac patient 15, fractionated by sucrose density gradient ultracentrifugation. Note the increase in the lymphocytotoxic activity in the 19S region (see Figure 1 for explanation).

TABLE II

Sucrose density gradient ultracentrifugation studies of 33 post-transplantation sera

Patients Studied	No. of Sera Fractionated	Location of Lymphocytotoxicity in Sucrose Density Gradient		Peak Immunoglobulin Conc. (mg./100 ml)		
		19 S region	7 S region	IgM	IgG	IgA
		no. of sera			*mean (range)*	
7 cardiac	30	30	0	77 (30–280)	296 (130–500)	96 (36–175)
2 renal	3	0	3	16 (13–18)	293 (80–600)	20 (7–44)

DISCUSSION

Lymphocytotoxic antibody formed following human cardiac transplantation showed association with known histocompatibility groups in 4 of 7 patients. Some antibody specificities in the sera, but not all, could be explained on the basis of mismatched groups from donor to recipient. The unexplained specificities may be accounted for either a) by antibody formed in response to transfused leukocytes (13), or b) by failure to identify all of the antigens in the donor cells. The high percentage of damaged lymphocytes among those obtained from donors with severe intracranial injury sometimes makes it difficult to obtain reliable typing results (unpublished personal experience). The lack of correlation of the reactions of cytotoxic sera from 3 cardiac recipients (nos. 37, 41 and 43) with those of known HL-A reactive sera raises the possibility that these patients responded to antigens which cannot be identified with our known antisera or that their sera are weakly reactive for a large number of HL-A antigens.

Antibody responses usually show class heterogeneity (14); therefore, the detection of lymphocytotoxic activity only in the 19S region of the sucrose density gradients in sera from cardiac recipients was an unexpected finding. Activity was detected exclusively in the 19S region in sera obtained as long as 13 months after transplantation, by which time the antibodies formed in response to most antigenic stimuli are predominately of the IgG class. In contrast, lymphocytotoxic activity in post-transplant sera from the 2 renal recipients was detected only in the 7S region of the gradients and was seen as early as 2 weeks post-transplantation. Stocker *et al.* (15), however, have reported finding IgG associated lymphocytotoxic activity in sera from only 1 patient whereas IgM associated activity was found in sera from 3 of 4 patients who developed renal allograft rejection.

The mean peak IgM concentration in the fractions from the sucrose density gradients of sera from cardiac allograft recipients was 5 times that of the mean peak IgM concentration of sera from renal recipients, suggesting that serum IgM levels increased after transplantation in the cardiac patients. Moreover, the IgG concentration of the fractions did not fall, suggesting that failure to detect 7S lymphocytotoxic antibody was not due to a generalized inhibition of IgG synthesis.

Sera from 5 patients whose rejected cardiac allografts were studied by immunofluorescence were included in the present study. Deposits of IgG were seen in tissue sections from these hearts more commonly than IgA or IgM except in arteries where IgG and IgM deposits were seen with equal frequency and IgA only rarely (7). Since the majority of the cardiac allograft recipients possessed anti-heart antibodies prior to transplantation (7), the immunoglobulin bound in the heart may represent in part a perpetuation of an auto-allergic response to cardiac tissue antigens. Nevertheless, the failure to detect other than 19S lymphocytotoxins in sera from these patients could be explained by one or more of the following:

1. Low levels of 7S lymphocytotoxic antibody are present but below the threshold of sensitivity of the microcytotoxicity test. Nothing in our data can exclude this possibility.

2. 7S lymphocytotoxic antibodies are present but their expression is inhibited by "blocking" antibodies. Since the assay system used is complement dependent, it is possible that a population of non-complement-fixing 7S antibodies, possibly of the IgA class or a subclass of IgG, is present in sufficient quantity to effectively block the attachment of the IgG antibodies to the antigen binding sites on the lymphocytes. This possibility is currently being examined in detail.

3. 7S lymphocytotoxic antibody is sufficiently avid to be preferentially adsorbed by the allograft. This hypothesis is particularly attractive in view of the immunofluorescence findings (7).

4. There is a preferential decrease in synthesis of 7S lymphocytotoxic immunoglobulin due to the high doses of immunosuppressive drugs which the cardiac patients received. In general, the cardiac recipients received considerably higher doses of corticosteroids than did the renal recipients, although both groups received comparable doses of azathioprine and anti-lymphocytic globulin. Moreover, the cardiac recipients received large doses of corticosteroids beginning at the time of transplantation, whereas, in the renal patients at this center, corticosteroids are usually not administered until signs of acute rejection appear. It has been reported that patients immunosuppressed with azathioprine (16) and prednisolone (17) exhibit a predominately IgM response to keyhole limpet hemocyanin and to bacterial flagellin, although small amounts of IgG antibody may also be produced to these antigens.

5. 7S lymphocytotoxic antibodies are not formed in response to cardiac transplantation. Although this conclusion seems unlikely in view of the immunofluorescence data, it is possible that the IgG and IgA molecules bound in the cardiac tissue were not cytotoxic. Williams *et al.* (5) were unable to detect lymphocytotoxic antibodies in the circulation of 3 cardiac allograft recipients who underwent acute rejection, although in all 3 cases antibodies could be eluted from the rejected hearts which were demonstrable by immune adherence to kidney cells and in 1 of 2 cases serum antibodies prior to allografting could be detected by immune adherence to donor kidney cells.

Acknowledgments. We thank the following persons for their excellent technical assistance: Carrol Cagel, Sandra Farrow, Lucetta Guillory, Lucy Kormeier and Julie Wareing.

REFERENCES

1. Walford, R. L., Martin, D. C., Troup, G. M. and Goodwin, W. E., *Histocompatibility Testing 1965*, Copenhagen, Munksgaard, 1966.
2. Colombani, J., Colombani, M. and Dausset, J., Ann. N. Y. Acad. Sci., *120:* 307, 1964.
3. Williams, G. M., Lee, H. M., Weymouth, R. F., Harlan, W. R., Holden, K. R., Stanley, C. M., Millington, G. A. and Hume, D. M., Surgery, *62:* 204, 1967.
4. Morris, P. J., Williams, G. M., Hume, D. M., Mickey, M. R. and Terasaki, P. I., Transplantation, *6:* 392, 1968.
5. Williams, G. M., DePlanque, B., Graham,

W. H. and Lower, R. R., New England J. Med., *281:* 1145, 1969.

6. Mittal, K. K., Rossen, R. D., Butler, W. T., Johnson, A. H., Leachman, R. D., Nora, J. J., Rochelle, D. G. and Brooks, D. K., J. Immun., *105:* 1427, 1970.
7. Rossen, R. D., Butler, W. T., Reisberg, M. A., Brooks, D. K., Leachman, R. D., Milam, J. D., Mittal, K. K., Montgomery, J. R., Nora, J. J. and Rochelle, D. G., J. Immun., Submitted for publication.
8. Mittal, K. K., Mickey, M. R., Singal, D. P. and Terasaki, P. I., Transplantation, *6:* 913, 1968.
9. Mittal, K. K., Rossen, R. D. and Butler, W. T., *Histocompatibility Testing 1970*, Munksgaard, Copenhagen, 1970.
10. Martin, R. G. and Ames, B. N., J. Biol. Chem., *236:* 1372, 1961.
11. Fahey, J. L. and McKelvey, E. M., J. Immun., *94:* 84, 1965.
12. Ishizaka, T., Ishizaka, K., Borsos, T. and Rapp, H., J. Immun., *97:* 716, 1966.
13. Hammond, D., Mattiuz, P. and Curtoni, E. S., *Histocompatibility Testing 1967*, Copenhagen, Munksgaard, 1967.
14. Pike, R. M., Bact. Rev., *31:* 157, 1967.
15. Stocker, J. W., McKenzie, I. F. C. and Morris, P. J., Nature, *222:* 483, 1969.
16. Swanson, M. A. and Schwartz, R. S., New England J. Med., *277:* 163, 1967.
17. Rowley, M. J., Mackay, I. R. and McKenzie, I. F. C., Lancet, *2:* 708, 1969.

THE JOURNAL OF IMMUNOLOGY
Vol. 105, No. 6, December 1970

IMMUNE HEMOLYSIS AND THE FUNCTIONAL PROPERTIES OF THE SECOND (C2) AND FOURTH (C4) COMPONENTS OF COMPLEMENT

I. Functional Differences among C4 Sites on Cell Surfaces[1, 2]

TIBOR BORSOS,[3] HERBERT J. RAPP AND HARVEY R. COLTEN

From the Biology Branch, Immunochemistry Section and The Molecular Separations Unit, National Cancer Institute, National Institutes of Health, Bethesda, Maryland 20014

Received for publication July 2, 1970

Evidence is presented that EAC4 (one of the intermediate products of immune hemolysis: E, sheep erythrocytes; A, hemolytic antibody; C4, the fourth component of complement) carry at least five types of SAC4 (S, a single site of initiation of C fixation) on their surface. Four of these SAC4 can be distinguished from one another by their activity with C1 (the activated first component of complement), C2 (the second component of complement) and the late acting components. The four types are: SAC4 hemolytically competent with guinea pig and with rat C-EDTA serum diluted with Na-ethylenediaminetetraacetate); SAC4 competent with rat C-EDTA only; SAC4 capable of utilizing C2 but not leading to a lytic site; and SAC4 capable of leading to lysis only in the presence of IgM hemolysin. The fifth type of site can be detected by the uptake of radiolabeled C4 and is probably not hemolytically active.

The fourth component of complement (C4) is one of the natural substrates of the activated first component of complement ($C\bar{1}$) (1). As a consequence of the interaction of cell bound $C\bar{1}$ with C4, some of the C4 molecules bind to the cell, while the rest remain in the fluid phase in an altered form that is incapable of further interaction with $C\bar{1}$ (2). It is known that some C4 molecules bind to the cell surface and some to the IgG hemolysin (3, 4). It has been claimed that some bound C4 are hemolytically inactive (5), i.e., are incompetent. The lack of competence of some of the bound C4, among other possibilities, may be due to their inability to interact with C2, or to the inability of the SAC$\bar{1}4\bar{2}$ to interact with one or more of the late acting components usually supplied in the form of guinea pig (GP) C-EDTA (guinea pig serum diluted 1:50 in 0.01 M Na-ethylenediaminetetraacetate, pH 7.6).

We have presented evidence for the existence of at least two types of SAC4 (6) both of which can react with C2 but only one of which is convertible to S* by gp C-EDTA. Miyakawa, *et al.* (7) have shown that rat C-EDTA is about 10 to 20 times more efficient than gp C-EDTA in the titration of guinea pig C4. This latter finding suggests the existence of two types of SAC$\bar{1}4\bar{2}$: one competent with rat and with gp C-EDTA, and the other with rat C-EDTA only.

In this report and in the accompanying papers we present evidence that indicates that there are at least five different kinds of SAC4 on EAC4.

MATERIALS AND METHODS

Source and preparation of sheep erythrocytes, guinea pig complement (gp C), partially purified gp C2 and isotonic Veronal-buffered saline (VBS) have been described (8). Isotonic Veronal-buffered saline-sucrose (VBS-sucrose, $\mu = 0.065$) was prepared as described in reference (9). EAC4 were prepared as described in (6). Briefly, EA were converted to EAC$\bar{1}$ by the addition of $C\bar{1}$; the EAC$\bar{1}$ were then mixed with C-EDTA. The

[1] A preliminary version of this paper was presented at the Complement Workshop, Harvard Medical School, Boston, Mass., June 3–5, 1968 (J. Immun., *101:* 811, 1968).

[2] The terms and abbreviations used in this paper conform to the recommendations outlined in "Nomenclature of Complement," Bull. W.H.O., *39:* 935, 1968.

[3] Please send reprint requests to Dr. T. Borsos, National Institutes of Health, Building 37, Room 2C-28, Bethesda, Md. 20014.

resulting cells have no other measurable C components but C4 on their surface. "Mock EAC4" were prepared exactly as EAC4 except no $C\bar{1}$ was added to the EA; such cells have no measurable C components on their surface. Ethylenediaminetetraacetate (EDTA)-buffer and C-EDTA were prepared as given in reference (10). Partially purified guinea pig and human $C\bar{1}$ were prepared by zonal ultracentrifugation (11) and titrated as described in reference (12). Titrations of C2 and determinations of t_{max} were performed as described in (13) with the exception that the interaction of cells with C2 occurred in VBS-sucrose (μ = 0.065). Titrations of C4 were carried out according to a modification of the method of Hoffmann as described in (14). The number of molecules of $C\bar{1}$ taken up by EAC4 was determined by the $C\bar{1}$ fixation and transfer test (15). The method of Sitomer *et al.* (16) was used to determine the relative number of C4 on EAC4 from the number of effective molecules of C2 adsorbed to EAC4.

IgG and IgM hemolysins were separated from rabbit antiserum to boiled stromata of sheep red blood cells by DEAE-cellulose and Sephadex chromatography as follows: IgG—10 ml of serum were mixed with 90 ml of distilled water and the solution was passed through a DEAE column (at pH 7.4, in 0.015 M NaCl). After the diluted serum passed through the column, the column was rinsed with 100 ml of 0.015 M NaCl, and the eluate and rinse fluids were pooled and concentrated to 10 ml with a UM-10 membrane in an Amicon Diaflo cell, (Amicon Corp., Cambridge, Mass.). Immunoelectrophoretic analysis showed that this concentrate contained IgG but no other detectable protein.

IgM–the column of DEAE was rinsed further with 500 ml of 0.015 M NaCl, and was then eluted with 0.25 M NaCl. The effluent (100 ml) was then concentrated to 5 ml with a UM-10 membrane in a Diaflo cell. The concentrate was placed on a Sephadex G-200 column (60 x 4.5 cm) and was eluted with 0.15 M NaCl. The first protein peak was pooled and concentrated on a Diaflo cell to about 10 ml. Immunoelectrophoretic analysis showed that this concentrate contained IgM, a small amount of α globulin and no other detectable protein. Cells sensitized with IgM and IgG antibody are designated EIgM and EIgG.

Guinea pig serum containing proteins internally labeled with ^{14}C amino acids was obtained by injecting 500-g female Hartley guinea pigs with yeast protein hydrolysate (Schwarz BioResearch, Inc., Orangeburg, N. Y., 1500 μCi/mg). Each guinea pig was injected both intravenously and intraperitoneally (i.v. and i.p.) and each received a total of 350 μCi. To determine the time for optimal labeling of molecules that behave like C4, guinea pigs were bled daily for 4 days after the injection of the ^{14}C-labeled amino acids. Serum was separated immediately from each blood sample and frozen at $-40°C$. On the 5th day EAC4 were prepared from each of the radioactive samples and from a serum sample that was obtained just before the injection of the ^{14}C-labeled amino acids. "Mock EAC4" were also prepared from each of the serum samples. ^{14}C activity in EAC4 preparations was determined as follows: 5.0 ml of each of the washed EAC4 and each of the washed "mock EAC4" (each containing 1.5×10^8 E/ml) were placed in separate Corex test tubes and centrifuged in a Servall RC-2 centrifuge for 5 min at $13,300 \times G$. The packed cells were lysed in 10 ml of water and the stromas were collected by centrifugation in the Servall centrifuge for 30 min at $34,800 \times G$. The stromas were resuspended in 0.6 ml of NCS reagent (Nuclear Chicago Corp., Des Plaines, Ill.) and were quantitatively transferred to counting vials in a final volume of NCS reagent of 1 ml. To each vial 10 ml of scintillation fluid (solution of 5 g of 2,5-diphenyloxazole and 0.1 g of 1,4-bis [2-(5-phenoxazolyl)] benzene in 1 liter of toluene) were added and each sample was counted for 10 min in a Packard Tri-Carb liquid scintillation spectrometer.

The data in Figure 1 show that of the four samples of serum the 24-hr sample generated EAC4 with the highest cpm. It can also be seen that radioactive molecules that behave like C4 disappear from serum in a first order fashion with a half life of about 47 hr. The data in the figure have been corrected for counts found in "mock EAC4"; they varied between 0 and 4 cpm.

Antiserum to gp C4 was prepared by injecting rabbits i.v. once a week for 3 weeks, each time with 5×10^9 EAC4 made at 30°C. The rabbits were bled 1 week after the last injection. The serum was heated to 56°C for 0.5 hr and was absorbed with EA. The absorbed serum does not agglutinate EA, and has no effect on the

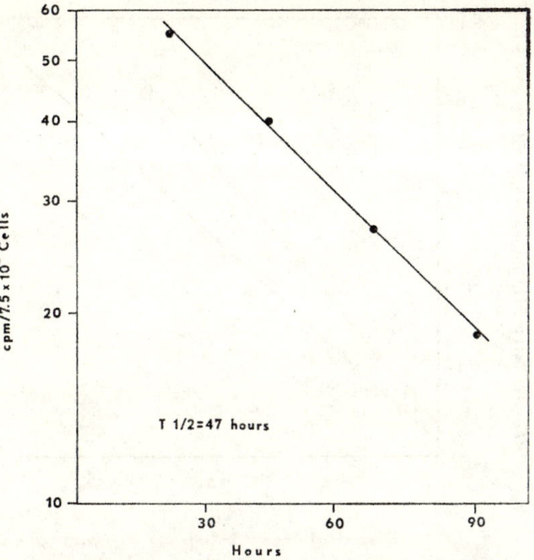

Figure 1. The amount of ^{14}C label in C4 molecules as a function of time after pulse labeling at 0 time with ^{14}C-labeled amino acids. The amount of radioactive C4 was determined at each time interval by the amount of uptake of ^{14}C by EAC$\bar{1}$ from guinea pig serum in the presence of EDTA.

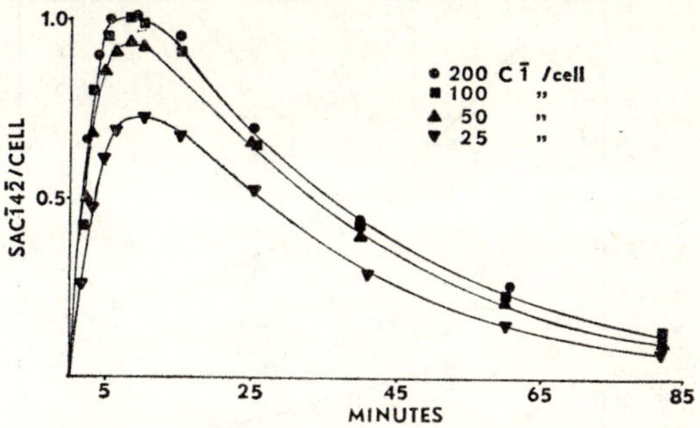

Figure 2. Determination of t_{max} as a function of C$\bar{1}$ concentration. Temperature, 30°C; ionic strength, 0.065; cell concentration, 1.5 × 10^8 EAC4/ml.

hemolytic activity of gp C1, gp C2 and gp C-EDTA.

TABLE I

Uptake of radiolabeled C4

	Counts Per Min/3 × 10^9 E
EAC4 0°C	21
Mock EAC4 0°C	9
EAC4 30°C	100
Mock EAC4 30°C	17

RESULTS

t_{max} *Determinations with EAC4 made at 0° and 30°C.* In the first experiment we determined the optimal amount of C$\bar{1}$ required to generate EAC$\bar{1}$4 from EAC4. The data in Figure 2 show the results of t_{max} experiments with EAC$\bar{1}$4 in which batches of EAC$\bar{1}$4 were generated from EAC4 with 200, 100, 50 and 25 effective C$\bar{1}$ molecules/cell. It is seen that 100 C$\bar{1}$ molecules/cell were sufficient to supply C$\bar{1}$ in excess, i.e., t_{max} and the efficiency of conversion of EAC$\bar{1}$4 to EAC$\bar{1}$4$\bar{2}$ were independent of C$\bar{1}$ concentration. Although this figure does not show it, we found that the same amount of C$\bar{1}$/cell was needed for the conversion of EAC4 made at 0°C and at 30°C. The data in Table I show the amount of C$\bar{1}$ taken up by the EAC4 as a function of the amount offered to the EAC4. It is seen that of 25, 50 and 100 molecules of C$\bar{1}$ offered to the cell, about 75% were recoverable from the cells. However, of the 200 C$\bar{1}$ offered to cells, only about 55% were accounted for on the cells. These results suggest that EAC4 prepared under these experimental conditions have not more than 100 C$\bar{1}$ and, therefore, not more than 100 SAC$\bar{1}$4 on their surface. These results were expected since the EAC4 were prepared with a dilution of antiserum that supplied about 200 C$\bar{1}$-fixing IgM molecules/cell.

In the next experiment we determined the t_{max} with EAC4 made at 0°C and 30°C. Both cells were converted to EAC$\bar{1}$4 with 200 C$\bar{1}$/cell. The t_{max} was determined for both cells with the same amount of C2 and with guinea pig C-EDTA as the converting agent. Two points emerge from the data presented in Figure 3. First, in confirmation of our earlier results (6), EAC4 prepared at 0°C are about twice as efficient in utilizing C2 in a hemolytically active form of SAC$\bar{1}$4$\bar{2}$ than EAC4 made at 30°C. Second, EAC4 made at 0°C have a t_{max} of about 3.8 to 4.0 min while those made at 30°C have a t_{max} of about 1.5 to 2.0 min. With the aid of the equation that relates t_{max} to the concentration of SAC$\bar{1}$4 (13) we calculated that EAC4 made at 30°C contain about 2.7 times more SAC$\bar{1}$4 capable of utilizing C2 than EAC4 made at 0°C. It is evident, however, that the 2.7-fold increase in the number of SAC$\bar{1}$4 was accompanied by a 50% decrease

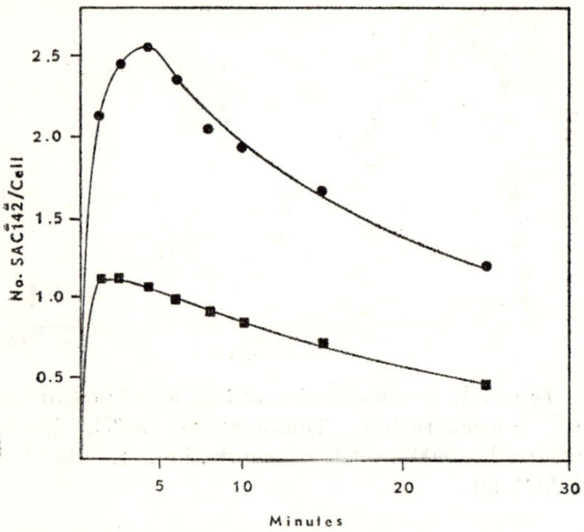

Figure 3. Determination of t_{max} with EAC4 made at 0°C (●) and at 30°C (■). Cells were converted to EAC$\bar{1}$4 with 200 C$\bar{1}$ molecules/cell. Temperature, 30°C; ionic strength, 0.065; cell concentration, 1.5 × 10^8 EAC4/ml. The t_{max} determinations were done with the same amount of C2.

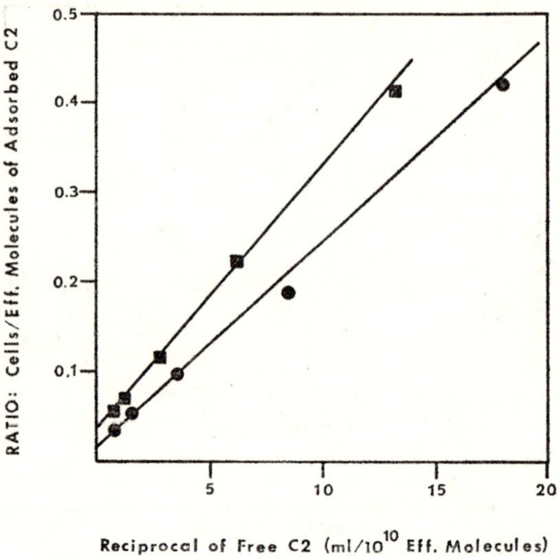

Figure 4. Adsorption of C2 to EAC4 made at 0°C (■) and 30°C (●). Conditions as described in reference 16.

in the number of hemolytically competent SAC$\bar{1}$4.

2. Adsorbtion of C2 to EAC4. In this experiment we investigated the removal of C2 from the fluid phase by EAC4 made at 0°C and at 30°C. The data in Figure 4 show that the two adsorption curves are different and that they intercept the y axis at different points. From the y intercept we have calculated that EAC4 made at 30°C contain at least twice the number of sites capable of adsorbing C2 than EAC4 made at 0°C.

3. Inhibition of SAC4 by antiserum to C4. This experiment was designed to quantitate the inhibition by anti-C4 antiserum of the hemolytic activity of cell bound C4. Portions of EAC4 (made at 30°C and at 0°C) were incubated with equal volumes of different dilutions of anti-C4 antiserum. The number of non-inhibited SAC4 was then determined and plotted as a function of decreasing antiserum concentration. The data in Figure 5 show that 2.5 times more antiserum was required to inhibit to the same extent EAC4 made at 30°C than at 0°C. This number was calculated by finding a multiplication factor which was required to make the two curves superimposable. We concluded from this calculation that EAC4 made at 30°C contained about 2.5 times more C4 than EAC4 made at 0°C.

4. Uptake of ^{14}C-labeled C4. We also studied the generation of EAC4 at 30°C and at 0°C with guinea pig serum that contained protein labeled internally with ^{14}C amino acids. As controls "mock EAC4" were prepared with the radiolabeled guinea pig serum. The data in Table II summarize the results obtained with these cell preparations. We found that EAC4 made at 30°C contained about 7 times more cpm, about 3 times more SAC$\bar{1}$4 as determined by t_{max} measurements, and about 2.8 times more bound C4 as determined with the anti-C4 antiserum inhibition test, than EAC4 made at 0°C. These data may indicate that nonfunctional C4 may also be taken up by the cells; however, we cannot exclude the possibility that serum proteins other than C4 were taken up as well. This latter possibility is unlikely because little or no radiolabeled protein was taken up by "mock EAC4."

The experiments cited so far showed that there are at least two types of SAC4 on EAC4: one type whose interaction with C2 results in the formation of a hemolytically competent site and the other type whose interaction with C2 results in a hemolytically incompetent site. They also showed that the ratio of these two types of SAC4 changes depends on the physical conditions

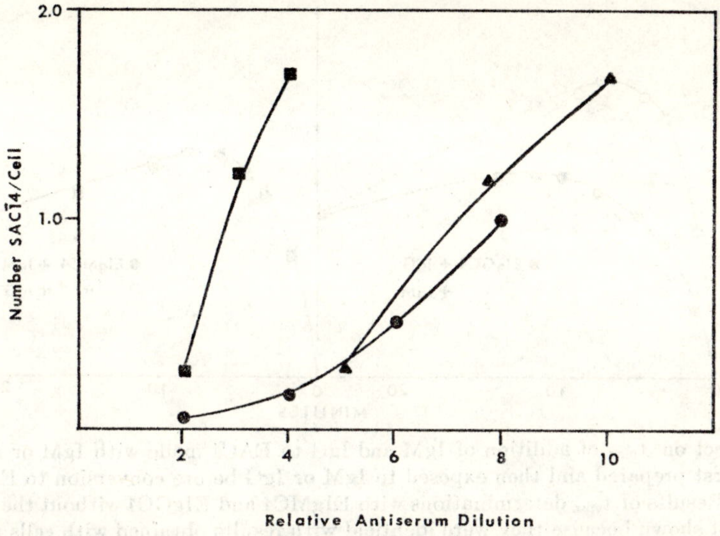

Figure 5. Inhibition of EAC4 activity by anti-C4 antiserum. ●, EAC4 made at 0°C; ■, EAC4 made at 30°C. By multiplying each point on the curve obtained with EAC4 made at 30°C by a factor of 2.5 the curve with the triangles was obtained.

TABLE II

Uptake of C$\bar{1}$ by EAC4 as a function of C$\bar{1}$ concentration

	Number of Effective C$\bar{1}$ Molecules/EAC4			
C$\bar{1}$ input/EAC4	200	100	50	25
C$\bar{1}$ found/EAC4	112	77	39	18

during the preparation of EAC4. The next experiment will show that in addition to these kinds of sites there are at least two more kinds of SAC4 that can be found on EAC4.

5. t_{max} Determinations with EAC4 made with IgG and IgM hemolysins. Two batches of EAC4 were made at 0°C: one with EIgM and one with EIgG. Each cell preparation was divided into three portions. One portion of each was converted directly to EAC$\bar{1}$4, the second of each was exposed to the same amount of IgM that was used in the preparation of EIgMC4, and the third portion of each was exposed to the same amount of IgG that was used in the preparation of EIgGC4. The four cell preparations that were exposed to the immunoglobulins the second time were then washed and converted to EAC$\bar{1}$4. t_{max} determinations were then done and the results are presented in Figure 6. It is seen that the addition of IgG hemolysin to EIgMC4 or to EIgGC4 had no effect on t_{max} of these cells; furthermore, the addition of IgM to EIgMC4 had no effect on the t_{max} of the cells. In contrast, the addition of IgM to EIgGC4 yielded cells with a shorter t_{max} and with an increased ability to utilize hemolytic C2. As calculated from the t_{max} equation, the observed shift in t_{max} from 12 to 6 min represents about a threefold increase in the concentration of SAC$\bar{1}$4.

6. Interaction of SAC4 with guinea pig and with rat C-EDTA. In all of the foregoing experiments, interaction of SAC$\bar{1}$4 with C2 was studied with cells that had more than five competent C4 molecules/cell, i.e., the addition of excess C1, excess C2 and excess gp C-EDTA resulted in the lysis of all of the cells. The next experiment was performed with EAC4 that had limited amounts of C4/cell, i.e., the ultimate extent of lysis (less than 100%) was a function only of C4 and independent of the other guinea pig reagents. The experiment was performed as follows. One volume of EAC$\bar{1}$ (1.5×10^8 E/ml, 200 C$\bar{1}$/E) was mixed at 0°C with the same volume of C4. The mixture was incubated for 20 min and washed once with VBS-sucrose. Portions of the cells then were mixed with different concentrations of gp C2, incubated for 25 min at 30°C and mixed with gp C-EDTA (1:50) or with rat C-EDTA (1:3). The degree of lysis was then determined in each

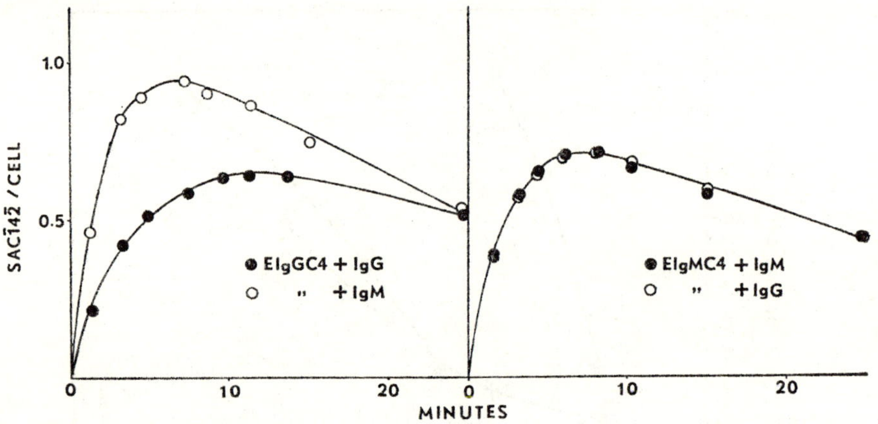

Figure 6. Effect on t_{max} of addition of IgM and IgG to EAC4 made with IgM or IgG. EIgMC4 and EIgGC4 were first prepared and then exposed to IgM or IgG before conversion to EAC$\bar{1}$4 with 200 C$\bar{1}$ molecules/cell. Results of t_{max} determinations with EIgMC4 and EIgGC4 without the addition of either antibody are not shown because they were identical with results obtained with cells after the addition of immunoglobulin of the class used to make the EAC4.

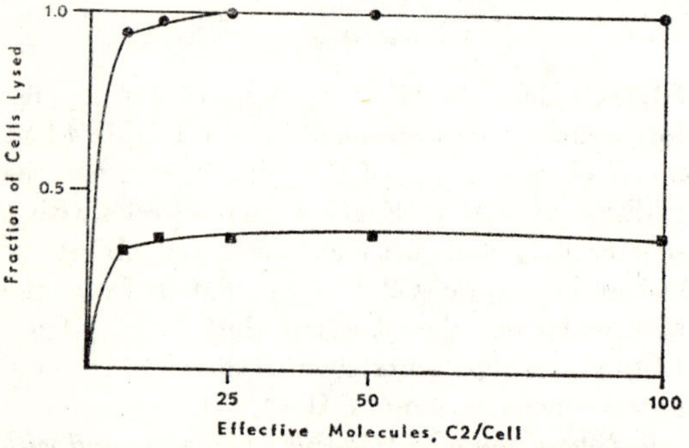

Figure 7. Lysis of EAC$\bar{1}$4 as a function of guinea pig C2 concentration. The cells were made with 200 C$\bar{1}$ molecules/cell and with about 0.5 effective molecules of C4 as determined with guinea pig reagents. Converting agents: guinea pig C-EDTA 1:50 (■); rat C-EDTA 1:3 (●).

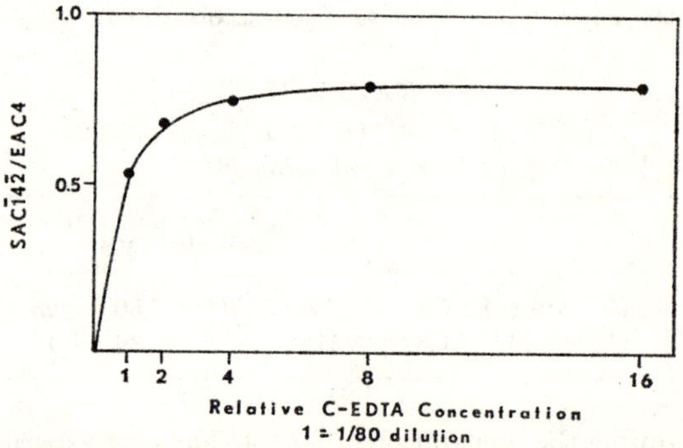

Figure 8. Lysis of EAC$\bar{1}4\bar{2}$ as a function of guinea pig C-EDTA concentration. The cells were prepared with 200 effective molecules of C$\bar{1}$, 1 effective molecule of C4 and 100 effective molecules of C2, all with respect to guinea pig C-EDTA as the converting agent.

mixture after 60 min incubation at 37°C. The data in Figure 7 show that while the fraction of cells lysed was 0.40 with gp C-EDTA over a wide range of C2 concentration, under the same conditions all of the cells were lysed by rat C-EDTA.

The data in Figure 8 show that the fraction of cells lysed was the same over a wide range of gp C-EDTA concentration. The cells for this experiment were exposed to about 100 effective C2 molecules/cell.

DISCUSSION

It may be concluded from the results presented in this report that the number of sheep erythrocytes (E) that can be lysed by hemolytic antibody (A) and complement (C) depends among other things, on the conditions under which C4 (the fourth component of complement) interacts with SAC$\bar{1}$ (a site on the surface of EAC$\bar{1}$ consisting of antigen, specific antibody and the activated form of the first component of complement).

This conclusion is based on the following observations. First, we found that depending on the temperature at which interaction between SAC$\bar{1}$ and C4 occurs, the uptake of C4 molecules by a given number of SAC$\bar{1}$ is variable. For example, about two to three times more C4 was demonstrated by t_{max} measurement, measurement of the amount of anti-C4 antibody required to inhibit C4 activation, and by adsorption of C2 on cells prepared at 30°C than on those prepared at 0°C. By measuring the uptake of ^{14}C-labeled C4 we found seven times more C4 on EAC4 made at 30°C than on those made at 0°C. Nevertheless, as detected with gp C-EDTA, there are more hemolytically competent SAC$\bar{1}$4 on EAC$\bar{1}$4 made at 0°C than on those made at 30°C. Second, IgG on EA generates some SAC4 that cannot utilize C2 until IgM is added to the cells. Third, EAC$\bar{1}4\bar{2}$ made with guinea pig reagents have SAC$\bar{1}4\bar{2}$ on their surface that are not hemolytically competent with gp C-EDTA but are detectable with rat C-EDTA.

It follows from these observations that if the ratio of incompetent to competent C4 is large, then the amount of C wasted will also be large; thus, the susceptibility of a given cell to lysis by antibody and C may depend on how and where these components are fixed to the cell.

The experiments also raise the question of the relation between the number of SAC$\bar{1}$ and the number of C4 (competent and incompetent) fixed by each SAC$\bar{1}$. From the t_{max} experiments with different numbers of C$\bar{1}$/cell, it was seen that for each EAC4 made at 0°C about 50 to 100 C$\bar{1}$ molecules/cell were sufficient to convert every SAC4 to SAC$\bar{1}$4 (competent and incompetent). When EAC4 were made at 30°C, 2.5 to 3.0 times more C4 molecules/cell were taken up than at 0°C; nevertheless, the same amount of C$\bar{1}$ (50 to 100 molecules/cell) was necessary for cells made at 30°C as for cells made at 0°C to supply excess C$\bar{1}$ for the t_{max} determination. These cells, therefore, have not more than 100 SAC$\bar{1}$4/cell. Since a 2.5-fold increase in the number of SAC$\bar{1}$4 interacting with C2 was accompanied by a loss of 50% of competent SAC$\bar{1}$4 we could estimate the number of SAC$\bar{1}$4 on the two types of cells in the following manner: if the cells made at 0°C had 40 SAC4, then for cells made at 30°C, $40 \times 2.5 = 100$ SAC4/cell (the limit set by the number of C$\bar{1}$/cell). Of these 100 SAC4, however, only 20 were competent because only half as many competent SAC$\bar{1}$4 were found on EAC4 made at 30°C than on those made at 0°C.

The experiments so far discussed the competence of SAC$\bar{1}4\bar{2}$ with gp C-EDTA as converting agent.

When the effect of converting agent on the competence of SAC$\bar{1}4\bar{2}$ was investigated, we observed that cells that have about 0.5 competent SAC$\bar{1}$4 with gp C-EDTA had at least 10 times that number when rat C-EDTA was used as the converting agent.

One of the interpretations of the above observation is that the number of SAC$\bar{1}$4/EAC$\bar{1}$4 exceeds the upper limit set by the number of C$\bar{1}$ on the cell. This interpretation requires that under conditions where C4 is not limiting with respect to gp C-EDTA, rat C-EDTA still detects sites that are not detectable with gp C-EDTA. The observation of Miyakawa *et al.* (10, confirmed by Mayer and by us) that both C4 and C2 titers are increased 10- to 20-fold when rat C-EDTA was used instead of gp C-EDTA supports the above conclusion. We also considered the possibility that the inability of gp C-EDTA to convert all SAC$\bar{1}4\bar{2}$ to S* is due to an inhibitor in gp C-EDTA. This is unlikely for two reasons. First, the extent of lysis of EAC$\bar{1}4\bar{2}$ is independent of gp C-EDTA concentration at high levels of C-EDTA, and second, it has been shown that gp C-EDTA is capable of detecting all SAC$\bar{1}4\bar{2}$ (as in the titration of C$\bar{1}$) when C$\bar{1}$ is the limiting reagent (17). Furthermore, rat and gp C-EDTA are equally effective in the titration of C$\bar{1}$ (18); likewise, EAC4 made at 0°C and at 30°C are equally competent for C$\bar{1}$ titrations (6). Thus, a decrease in the competence of the EAC4 with respect to C2 and the late acting components of guinea pig complement does not affect the competence of the EAC4 with respect to C$\bar{1}$.

The discrepancy between the estimate of the number of hemolytically active C$\bar{1}4\bar{2}$ sites and the estimate of the number of C$\bar{4}\bar{2}$ complexes led us to a more detailed investigation of the interaction of C1, C4 and C2 at a hemolytically active site on the cell surface. The results of these studies are presented in the next paper in this series (19).

Acknowledgments. The authors wish to thank Mrs. Jo Anne LeFever and Mrs. Gwendolyn Smith Brown for their competent technical assistance.

REFERENCES

1. Müller-Eberhard, H. J. and Lepow, I. H., J. Exp. Med., *121:* 819, 1965.
2. Mardiney, M. R., Jr., Müller-Eberhard, H. J. and Feldman, J. D., Amer. J. Path., *53:* 253, 1968.
3. Harboe, M., Brit. J. Haemat., *10:* 339, 1964.

4. Willoughby, W. F. and Mayer, M. M., Science, *150:* 907, 1965.
5. Cooper, N. R. and Müller-Eberhard, H. J., Immunochemistry, *5:* 155, 1968.
6. Borsos, T. and Rapp, H. J., J. Immun., *99:* 263, 1967.
7. Miyakawa, Y., Sekine, T., Shimada, K. and Nishioka, K., J. Immun., *103:* 374, 1969.
8. Mayer, M. M., in *Kabat and Mayer's, Experimental Immunochemistry*, 2nd Ed., p. 133, Charles C Thomas, Springfield, Ill., 1961.
9. Rapp, H. J. and Borsos, T., J. Immun., *91:* 826, 1963.
10. Rapp, H. J. and Borsos, T., J. Immun., *96:* 913, 1966.
11. Colten, H. R., Bond, H. E., Borsos, T. and Rapp, H. J., J. Immun., *103:* 862, 1969.
12. Borsos, T. and Rapp, H. J., J. Immun., *91:* 851, 1963.
13. Borsos, T., Rapp, H. J. and Mayer, M. M., J. Immun., *87:* 310, 1961.
14. Borsos, T. and Rapp, H. J., J. Immun., *94:* 510, 1965.
15. Borsos, T. and Rapp, H. J., J. Immun., *95:* 559, 1965.
16. Sitomer, G., Stroud, R. M. and Mayer, M. M., Immunochemistry, *3:* 57, 1966.
17. Colten, H. R., Borsos, T. and Rapp, H. J., Science, *158:* 1590, 1967.
18. Opferkuch, W., Rapp, H. J., Colten, H. R. and Borsos, T., Immunochemistry, Submitted for publication.
19. Opferkuch, W., Rapp, H. J., Colten, H. R. and Borsos, T., J. Immun., Submitted for publication.

The Journal of Immunology
Vol. 105, No. 6, December 1970

Printed in U.S.A.

INHIBITION OF LEUKOCYTE MIGRATION: AN EVALUATION OF THIS *IN VITRO* ASSAY OF DELAYED HYPERSENSITIVITY IN MAN TO A SOLUBLE ANTIGEN[1]

STEVEN A. ROSENBERG and JOHN R. DAVID

From the Department of Surgery, Peter Bent Brigham Hospital, and the Department of Medicine Robert Breck Brigham Hospital, Harvard Medical School, Boston, Massachusetts

Received for publication July 2, 1970

An *in vitro* assay of delayed hypersensitivity in man, modified from the method of Søborg and Bendixen, was evaluated. This assay is based on the inhibition of migration of human peripheral leukocytes in the presence of specific soluble antigen. Twelve of 13 individuals who were skin test positive to tuberculin showed inhibition of leukocyte migration when incubated with 100 μg/ml of soluble purified protein derivative. Only 1 of 12 skin test negative individuals showed a similar inhibition of leukocyte migration. Analysis of the migrating populations showed that the migration of mononuclear cells and not of neutrophils was inhibited.

The lack of a simple and rapid *in vitro* test for delayed hypersensitivity in man has been a limiting factor in studying the role of delayed hypersensitivity in a variety of human diseases. In 1967, Søborg and Bendixen (1, 2) described an *in vitro* test based on the inhibition of the migration of human peripheral leukocytes that correlated with the presence of delayed hypersensitivity *in vivo* to brucella antigens. Since that time they have used this test to study a wide variety of antigens (3–6). Several groups, however, have reported their inability to successfully use this technique to demonstrate delayed hypersensitivity to soluble tuberculoprotein antigens *in vitro* (7, 8). The suspicion that soluble antigens could not be used in this human assay has limited its potential application.

After considerable effort and minor modification of the technique, we have successfully used this test as a correlate of human delayed hypersensitivity to soluble tuberculin antigens. The study of other soluble antigens should likewise be feasible.

[1] This work was supported in part by a Research Training Grant from the National Institutes of Health and grants from the United States Army and the Atomic Energy Commission, and by AI-07685, Cancer Contract Grant NIH 69-2061, and AM-5577-09 from the N. I. H.

MATERIALS AND METHODS

Materials. Medium 199, horse serum and Hanks' balanced salt solution (HBSS) were obtained from Microbiological Associates, Inc., Bethesda, Md. Heparin sodium, 1000 U.S.P. units/ml with benzyl alcohol preservative, was obtained from Organon, Inc., West Orange, N. J. Fifty-milliliter plastic syringes were obtained from Becton, Dickenson and Co., Rutherford, N. J., and 16- x 125-mm plastic tissue culture tubes from Falcon Plastics, Oxnard, Calif. Mackaness-type chambers were manufactured to order by Berton Plastics, South Hackensack, N. J. Coverslips (No. 1½ 22 mm in diameter), Dow Corning silicone stopcock grease and paraffin wax were obtained from Fisher Scientific Co., Boston, Mass., and melting point capillary tubes (1.4 mm inner diameter, 100 mm length) from A. H. Thomas, Co., Philadelphia, Pa. Lyophilized tuberculin purified protein derivative (PPD) free of preservative was obtained from the National Institute of Allergy and Infectious Diseases, Bethesda, Md. Intermediate (0.0001 mg/0.1 ml) and second strength (0.005 mg/0.1 ml) PPD skin test antigens were obtained from Parke, Davis and Co., Detroit, Mich.

Preparation of glassware. Capillary tubes and coverslips were siliconized by immersion in Dricote (Fisher Scientific Co.). They were heated to 170°C in an oven for 2.5 hr. Capillary tubes were cleaned by flowing copious amounts of warm and distilled water through them. No detergent was used. Coverslips were cleaned with 7 × detergent (Linbro Chemical Co., New Haven, Conn.). They were then extensively rinsed with warm followed by distilled water. Coverslips were individually dried, first with gauze and then with lens tissue to remove all lint. They were then sterilized with dry heat. All other glassware was sterilized in an autoclave.

Skin tests. Blood was drawn from individuals before giving them an intradermal injection of 0.1 ml intermediate strength PPD. The skin site was examined for the presence of erythema and induration after 48 hr. Second strength PPD was injected if the results of the first test were ambiguous. An area of induration greater than 10 mm in diameter was considered to represent a positive test. All skin test negative individuals in this series had areas of induration less that 3 mm in diameter.

Leukocyte migration assay. Fifty milliliters of blood were drawn into a plastic syringe containing 1 to 2 ml of heparin. The blood was distributed into four 15-ml plastic tissue culture test tubes and allowed to settle for 1 hr at 37°C. After settling of the red blood cells, all but the bottom 0.5 cm of plasma was aspirated and transferred to another plastic test tube. The cell suspension was centrifuged at 250 × G for 5 min. All centrifugations were done at 20°C. The plasma was aspirated and discarded and the cell pellet was resuspended in warmed HBSS by repeated pipetting. The use of a vibrating mixer was avoided because this causes cell damage. The suspension was centrifuged at 250 × G for 5 min and washed twice more with HBSS. The final cell pellet was suspended in medium 199 containing 10% horse serum and adjusted to a cell concentration of about 70 million cells/ml.

This cell suspension was aspirated into a 10-cm long capillary tube leaving about one-third of the tube empty. This empty end of the capillary was closed by heating in a fine gas flame. The capillary was then placed horizontally in a Petri dish to cool. After cooling, the capillaries were centrifuged at 2000 × G for 10 min at 20°C. About 10 capillaries could be prepared from a 50-ml blood sample.

The migration was carried out in specially constructed Mackaness-type chambers. A coverslip was attached to the chamber using melted wax and the chamber was filled with standard medium (medium 199 containing 10% horse serum) with and without added antigen. Solutions containing antigen were filtered through a Millipore filter, 0.45 μ pore size.

The capillaries were cut 1 mm below the cell-liquid interface, immediately placed in the chamber and anchored firmly with a small drop of silicone grease. A second coverslip was added and sealed in place with melted wax. One capillary was placed in each chamber.

The chambers were incubated perfectly flat for 24 hr at 37°C. The migratory area was then projected and traced onto paper. The area of migration was measured with a planimeter. The migration in the presence and absence of antigen was compared using the following formula:

$$\text{Migration ratio (MR)} = \frac{\text{Area of migration in presence of antigen}}{\text{Area of migration in absence of antigen}}$$

Design of double blind test. To test the correlation of inhibition of leukocyte migration with *in vivo* delayed hypersensitivity, a double blind test was performed on 25 individuals. For each individual half of the capillaries were incubated in the presence of 100 μg PPD/ml and the other half with no antigen present. All tests were conducted at least in duplicate and many in quadruplicate.

Tuberculin was injected after drawing the blood sample. Since the assay was completed in 24 hr, the results of the skin test were not known at the time of evaluating the *in vitro* test. For the majority of patients the migration areas were also traced and measured without a knowledge of which chambers contained antigen and which did not.

RESULTS

Initial studies on 62 patients using a variety of modifications of this technique were unsuccessful. Several aspects of the technique were altered before deriving the method as described above. The results obtained in the study of 25 consecutive individuals are presented in Figure 1. Twelve of 13 skin test positive individuals had a migration ratio of 0.85 or less whereas only 1 of 12 skin test negative individuals had a migration ratio this low. An example of the inhibition of migration in the presence of antigen is shown in Figure

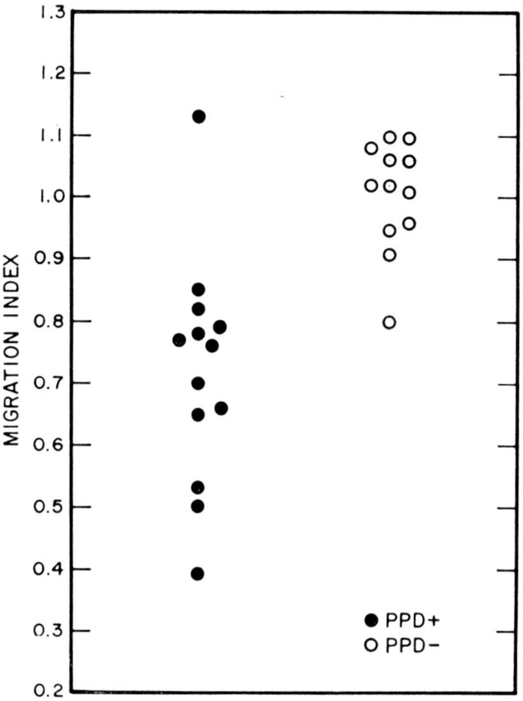

Figure 1. Results of the leukocyte migration assay on 25 consecutive individuals. The migration index is the ratio of the migration area in the presence of antigen to that in the absence of antigen.

2. The average value of the migration ratio for skin test negative individuals was 1.01 ± 0.09 (standard deviation) and that for skin test positive individuals was 0.72 ± 0.18. These two populations are significantly different with a Student's *t* test probability of less than 0.001.

Differential counts were performed on the original blood and final leukocyte suspension of many of the patients that were tested. The final leukocyte suspension was slightly enhanced in mononuclear type cells compared with the original blood. Most final suspensions contained about 40% mononuclear cells. Greater than 95% of the leukocytes were viable as tested by their ability to exclude trypan blue both before packing into the capillary tube and after 24 hr of migration. The appearance of inhibited leukocyte migration cultures was usually that of a dense inner area surrounded by a much lighter "halo." It was noted that only this dense inner area could be inhibited by specific antigen in sensitized individuals. In many cases the "halo" of surrounding cells did not show inhibition of migration.

To determine the relative cell concentrations of the inner and outer migration areas the coverslip was carefully removed from several chambers and a 25-gauge needle was used to take cell samples from the inner core of migration and from the halo. Differential counts were performed on Wright-stained preparations of these cells. The results are shown in Table I. The cell composition of the inner migrating area is similar to that added to the capillary tube. The outer halo, however, is composed almost entirely of neutrophils, suggesting that only the mononuclear cells are inhibited from migrating. In four preliminary experiments lymphocytes isolated from peripheral blood by the method of Rocklin *et al.* (9) were incubated with low levels of specific antigen (50 units/ml streptokinase-streptodornase) for 24 to 72 hr. This concentration of antigen was not high enough to inhibit leukocyte migration directly. The cell-free supernatants from these cultures inhibited the migration of leukocytes obtained from other individuals compared with supernatants from lymphocytes incubated in the absence of antigen to which antigen was later added.

Experiments were performed which demonstrated that incubation of cells from a PPD negative skin test individual in plasma or serum from a skin test positive individual did not cause inhibition of migration of these negative cells in the presence of specific antigen. Thus, this specific reactivity to antigen was not transferred to cells from plasma or serum.

DISCUSSION

The use of macrophage migration-inhibition as an *in vitro* correlate of delayed hypersensitivity in experimental animals (10–12) suggested that this principle might be useful in developing an assay for use in humans. Thor *et al.* (13) and Rocklin *et al.* (9) demonstrated that mediators produced by the incubation of sensitized human peripheral lymphocytes with specific antigen could be used to inhibit the migration of guinea pig macrophages. This test is a useful *in vitro* correlate of delayed hypersensitivity in humans, though the performance of each test requires up to 7 days.

In 1967, Søborg and Bendixen demonstrated that the migration of human peripheral leuko-

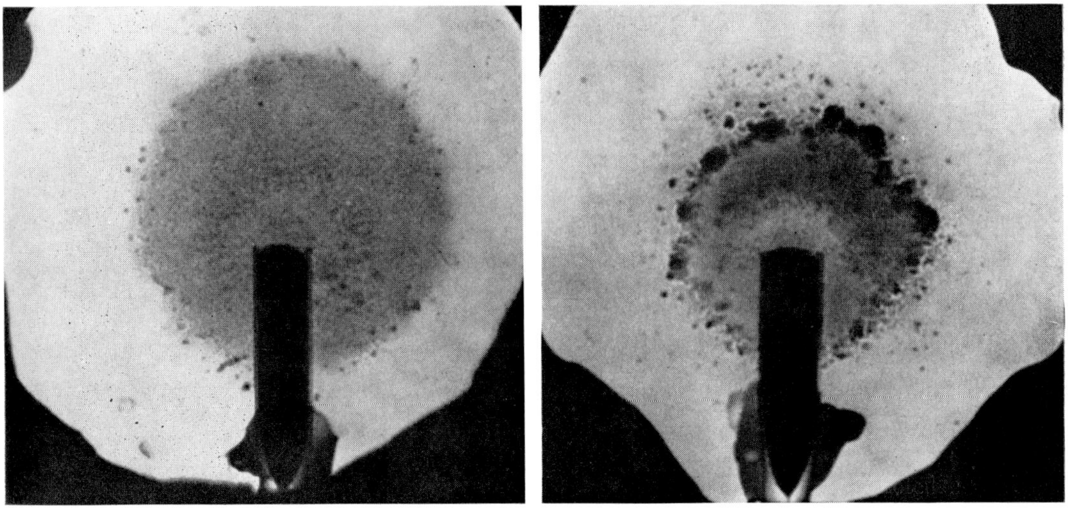

Figure 2. Appearance of normal leukocyte migration (*left*) and inhibited migration in the presence of PPD (*right*) of leukocytes from a PPD skin test positive individual.

TABLE I

Cell composition in migration field[a]

Position in Migration Field	Neutrophils		Mononuclear Cells	
	(1)	(2)	(1)	(2)
	%		%	
Center	57	58	43	42
Periphery ("Halo")	88	92	12	8

[a] Two experiments are shown.

cytes was inhibited in the presence of specific antigen and suggested that this direct and rapid test could be used as a specific *in vitro* test of human delayed hypersensitivity (1, 2). They demonstrated that migration-inhibition *in vitro* using (killed) brucella organisms as antigens showed excellent correlation with results of skin tests to brucella. They also used this technique in a variety of studies of delayed hypersensitivity using particulate antigens (3–6).

A number of investigators, however, have had difficulty using this technique successfully (7, 8; J. R. David and S. Lawrence, and O. Meyers and J. R. David, unpublished). The inability of several groups to demonstrate leukocyte migration inhibition using tuberculoprotein (PPD) antigens has led to a suspicion that the technique was not applicable to the study of soluble antigens.

The potential value of this simple and rapid test led us to investigate intensively its usefulness as an *in vitro* correlate of delayed hypersensitivity in man using soluble antigens. Our initial attempts to repeat and modify the methods of Søborg and Bendixen were uniformly unsuccessful. We studied 62 individuals and were unable to correlate the *in vitro* test with the skin test. Using the methods described by Kaltreider *et al.* (7) and by Lockshin (8) we corroborated their observations that the method as they described it does not work successfully. Many modifications of the procedure were made before obtaining the correlations shown in Figure 1.

Technical comments on the method. The following technical points are thought to be especially important for successful application of the test, though it cannot be said with assurance that any one of them is absolutely essential.

1. Heparin preserved with benzyl alcohol, not phenol, should be used.

2. The use of 0.6% dextran to aid red blood cell settling seems to interfere with migration-inhibition.

3. Collection of leukocyte-rich plasma should not include the bottom 0.5 to 1.0 cm of plasma, thus resulting in a mononuclear cell-enriched leukocyte population.

4. Capillary tubes and coverslips should be siliconized. Migration of leukocytes on unsiliconized glass is different from that on siliconized glass.

5. Leukocyte migration begins within minutes after preparation of the chambers. The capillary tip empties of cells but gradually refills during the next 24 hr. Failure to refill the capillary tip usually signifies decreased cell viability and may interfere with the results.

6. A high concentration of antigen should be used. In general, an antigen concentration just below a dose that causes nonspecific toxicity should be used.

7. Only the dense inner area of migration should be measured. This can often be more easily distinguished from the lighter surrounding halo by using a partially indirect light source.

8. All migrations should be run at least in duplicate, preferably in triplicate. Migration areas should be evaluated without a knowledge of the presence or absence of antigen in the chamber. Reproducible results depend on the meticulous application of the above technique.

Correlation with in vivo delayed hypersensitivity The results of the *in vitro* test showed excellent correlation with the presence or absence of a positive skin test, though there was no correlation between the degree of migration inhibition and the size of the positive skin test.

One false positive and one false negative result occurred in the 25 people studied. Of particular interest is the one skin test positive individual who did not show inhibition of leukocyte migration in the presence of soluble PPD. This person, in fact, had the highest migration ratio of any person tested, and her cells actually showed enhanced migration in the presence of antigen. She was a 47-year-old woman who shortly after *in vitro* testing was suspected of having active tuberculosis and had the largest skin test reaction to intermediate strength PPD of any patient in the series. Her *in vitro* test was performed before therapy was instituted. None of the other patients in this series was suspected of having tuberculosis. Specific enhancement of migration in the presence of antigen has also been noted in animal experiments and remains unexplained (14). The finding that plasma factors could not transmit reactivity to a negative person's cells argues against the role of cytophilic antibodies in this assay system.

Inhibition of macrophage migration in guinea pigs has been extensively studied and shown to correlate only with delayed hypersensitivity and not with humoral types of immune response (15, 16). In the guinea pig system inhibition of a relatively pure macrophage population is seen. The finding reported in this paper that the mononuclear cells of human peripheral blood and not the neutrophils are inhibited lends credence to comparisons with the better characterized guinea pig test system.

Soluble materials resulting from the contact of sensitized lymphocytes with specific antigen can be used to inhibit guinea pig macrophage migration. Thor *et al.* (13) and Rocklin *et al.* (9) have demonstrated that such soluble substances from human lymphocytes can also be used to inhibit the migration of guinea pig macrophages. It is thus of interest that in preliminary experiments we have noted that supernatants resulting from the incubation of purified human lymphocytes from one person with specific antigen can also cause the inhibition of migration of leukocytes from a second person. The intermediate role of soluble mediators in this leukocyte migration-inhibition assay thus seems likely.

This assay based on the inhibition of leukocyte migration is a rapid assay of delayed hypersensitivity in man. It can be used to study particulate and soluble antigens and should be useful in the study of a variety of human diseases.

Acknowledgment. We would like to acknowledge the excellent technical assistance of Miss J. Durant.

REFERENCES

1. Søborg, M., Acta Med. Scand., *182:* 167, 1967.
2. Søborg, M. and Bendixen, G., Acta Med. Scand., *181:* 247, 1967.
3. Bendixen, G., Scand. J. Gastroent., *2:* 214, 1967.
4. Søborg, M. and Halberg, P., Acta Med. Scand., *183:* 101, 1968.
5. Nerup, J., Andersen, V. and Bendixen, G. Clin. Exp. Immun., *4:* 355, 1969.
6. Clausen, J. E. and Søborg, M., Acta Med. Scand., *186:* 227, 1969.
7. Kaltreider, H. B., Soghor, D., Taylor, J. B. and Decker, J. L., J. Immun., *103:* 179, 1969.
8. Lockshin, M. D., Proc. Soc. Exp. Biol. Med., *132:* 928, 1969.
9. Rocklin, R. E., Meyers, O. L. and David, J. R., J. Immun., *104:* 95, 1970.
10. George, M. and Vaughan, J. H., Proc. Soc. Exp. Biol. Med., *111:* 514, 1962.

11. Bloom, B. R. and Bennett, B., Science, *153:* 80, 1966.
12. David, J. R., Proc. Nat. Acad. Sci., *56:* 72, 1966.
13. Thor, D., Jureziz, R. E., Veach, S. R., Miller, E. and Dray, S., Nature, *219:* 755, 1968.
14. Svejcar, J. and Johanovsky, J., Z. Immunitaetsforsch., *131:* 301, 1966.
15. David, J. R., Al-Askari, S., Lawrence, H. S. and Thomas, L., J. Immun., *93:* 264, 1964.
16. David, J. R., Lawrence, H. S. and Thomas, L., J. Immun., *93:* 279, 1964.

THE JOURNAL OF IMMUNOLOGY

Vol. 105, No. 6, December 1970
Printed in U.S.A.

THE MITOGENIC EFFECTS OF ENDOTOXIN AND STAPHYLOCOCCAL ENTEROTOXIN B ON MOUSE SPLEEN CELLS AND HUMAN PERIPHERAL LYMPHOCYTES[1, 2]

DUANE L. PEAVY,[3] WILLIAM H. ADLER AND RICHARD T. SMITH

From the Tumor Biology Unit, Department of Pathology, University of Florida College of Medicine, Gainesville, Florida 32601

Received for publication June 29, 1970

The effects of Salmonella endotoxin and staphylococcal enterotoxin B (SEB) were examined *in vitro* on mouse and human lymphocyte populations from unsensitized subjects. These substances were found to be extremely stimulatory to mouse spleen cells as measured by ^{3}H-thymidine incorporation. In regards to size, general morphologic features, and staining properties, the cell cultures appear identical to cultures stimulated by phytohemagglutinin (PHA). However, endotoxin failed to stimulate human peripheral lymphocytes while PHA and SEB produced a response over a wide dosage range. Attempts to detect stimulation of human lymphoid cells by endotoxin using various mammalian sera as augmentors were unsuccessful.

The administration of bacterial endotoxins produces various pathologic, physiologic and immunologic effects, including leucocytosis (1), fever (2), shock (3), the Shwartzman reaction (4), inhibition of antibody formation (5), changes in blood coagulation (6), release of endogenous pyrogens (7), and death.

Stetson (8, 9) first proposed that the major effects of endotoxin might be explained as an interaction of endotoxin with antibody, or as an expression of naturally occurring hypersensitivity to the lipopolysaccharide. Stetson's reasoning was based in part upon the observation that local and systemic administration of tuberculin produced endotoxin-like biologic effects in tuberculin-sensitized animals. Tuberculin shock has been reexamined recently with comparable findings. Involvement of hypersensitivity-like mechanisms has been further implicated by the work of Landy *et al.* (10), who described decreased sensitivity to the effects of endotoxin in germ-free animals. In addition, Heilman and Bast (11) found that endotoxin inhibited macrophage migration from mouse spleen explants, and Wiener *et al.* (12) reported endotoxin to be cytotoxic for mouse peritoneal leucocytes.

Recent studies have shown that lymphoreticular cells respond to a variety of stimuli *in vitro* including phytohemagglutinin (PHA), PPD in sensitive cells, staphylococcal filtrates, and streptolysin S, by the production of a group of biologically active molecules (13). Those reported include a macrophage-inhibiting factor, mitogenic factors, transfer factor, interferon, an inhibitor of DNA synthesis, and a cytotoxic agent termed lymphotoxin. A reasonable extension of Stetson's hypothesis, therefore, would be that the various stimulators react with populations of responsive lymphoreticular cells *in vivo*, and initiate stereotyped transformation responses comparable to those seen *in vitro*. The release of the potent effector molecules would, in turn, mediate the observed physiologic responses. Some evidence for this possibility is found in the morphologic changes in the mouse spleen after PHA injection (14). The findings to be reported here indicate that transformation of mouse cells does occur in response to endotoxin and staphylococcal enterotoxin B (SEB), and are thus consistent with Stetson's hypothesis.

[1] This work was supported in part by research grants from the National Institutes of Health (HD-00384), the American Cancer Society (ACS-T-463), an American Cancer Society Institutional Grant (IN-62-G), and a National Institute of General Medical Science Training Grant (GM-01996).

[2] Presented in part at the annual meeting of the Federation of American Societies for Experimental Biology, Atlantic City, New Jersey, April, 1970.

[3] Work done as National Institute of Allergy and Infectious Diseases trainee, grant TI-AI-0128.

MATERIALS AND METHODS

Animals. Mice used for this study were either taken from inbred stocks maintained in this laboratory or purchased directly from R. B. Jackson laboratories, Bar Harbor, Maine.

Lymphocyte culture. The tissue culture conditions employed were those described by Adler *et al.* (15). This technique allows long-term viability, transformation, and cell division of mouse lymphoid cells in response to general mitogens and immunologically specific antigens. Briefly, the tissue culture medium consisted of Roswell Park Memorial Institute (RPMI) medium 1640 (Grand Island Biological Co., Grand Island, N. Y.) supplemented with 5% fresh, heat-inactivated human serum with 100 units of penicillin and 100 μg of streptomycin/ml. Suspensions of spleen cells were prepared by mincing the tissue with scissors and pushing the fragments through a 60-mesh steel screen. The fragments were then drawn through a 25-gauge needle to produce a suspension of single cells. Cells were washed once with RPMI 1640, counted, centrifuged gently, and the pellet resuspended in complete medium. Suspensions prepared in this manner consisted usually of 95% mononuclear cells. The material to be tested was added in indicated amounts to tubes before incubation. All cultures were grown in 12-ml screw-capped, disposable plastic tubes (No. 2037, Falcon Plastics Co., Los Angeles, Calif.), containing 3 ml of culture medium and 15 × 10^6 mononuclear cells/tube. The culture tubes were incubated at 37°C, loosely capped in an air atmosphere of 80% humidity and 5% CO_2, inclined at an angle of 5 degrees.

Human peripheral blood lymphocytes were prepared as follows. Heparinized whole blood was diluted with 6% dextran in normal saline (McGraw Laboratories, Glendale, Calif.) to a final concentration of 2% dextran, and placed upright in a 37°C incubator for 2 hr. The supernatant was removed with a pipet and the cells were collected by gentle centrifugation. The cell pellet was then resuspended in RPMI 1640 and a total and differential count performed. The cells were again collected by centrifugation and finally suspended in tissue culture medium consisting of RPMI 1640 and 20% fetal calf serum, and an antibiotic mixture at the same concentrations as before. Each culture consisted of 5 × 10^6 mononuclear cells in 4 ml culture media, and was incubated under identical conditions as those previously described for the mouse spleen cells.

Lymphocyte cultures were treated with one of the following test substances: (1) Phytohemagglutinin P (PHA-P, Difco); (2) *Salmonella typhimurium* type 7 endotoxin (LPS), obtained from Dr. Joseph Shands, Department of Microbiology, University of Florida, and prepared according to the method of Westphal *et al.* (16); and (3) staphylococcal enterotoxin B (SEB), obtained from Dr. Sigurd Normann, Department of Pathology, University of Florida, and prepared by the method of Schantz *et al.* (17).

Method for assaying cell stimulation

Blast transformation. The occurrence of blast transformation was determined by light microscopy of May-Grünwald-Giemsa stained cell populations (18) using the morphologic criteria described by Marshall and Roberts (19). The results are expressed as percentage of cells in the total population of mononuclear cells scored as lymphoblasts.

^{3}H-thymidine incorporation assay. DNA synthesis was measured by the incorporation of ^{3}H-thymidine into acid insoluble material as previously described (15). One microcurie of tritiated thymidine (Schwarz Bioresearch, specific activity 1.9 Ci/mmol; 1 μCi/2 μl) was added to all tubes for the final 24 hr of the culture period. At termination, the cultures were centrifuged and the cell pellet was washed twice with cold saline and twice with 5% trichloroacetic acid at 4°C. The resultant precipitates were then washed once with methanol, air dried, and solubilized in Nuclear Chicago Solubilizer (Nuclear Chicago Corp., Des Plaines, Ill.) (NCS - 0.25 ml/culture). Fifteen milliliters of scintillation fluid (PPO 5 g/L, POPOP 100 mg/L in toluene) were added to the solubilized precipitates and the solution was transferred to screw-top vials. The vials were counted in a Beckman model CPM-100 liquid scintillation counter. This technique gave replicate values consistently within 5% to 10%. The data obtained are presented either as mean values of three to five replicate tubes, or as a ratio of incorporation obtained by dividing the mean counts/minute of antigen-stimulated cultures by the mean counts/minute of control cultures.

RESULTS

When Salmonella endotoxin (LPS) and staphylococcal enterotoxin B (SEB) were added to cultures of mouse spleen cells, the constellation of effects observed was identical to those when PHA was used for stimulation as previously reported (15). The dose response relationship for both SEB and LPS are shown in Figure 1. It will be seen that the general relation was similar for each stimulant, as measured by ^{3}H-thymidine incorporation. Incorporation increased with increasing concentrations of mitogen and beyond peak levels additional mitogen gave progressive inhibition of incorporation. Maximal stimulation of this number of cells under these conditions was found when 10 μg SEB, 100 μg LPS or 5 μl PHA/tube were added. These amounts were used in all subsequent experiments to obtain peak stimulation.

The time course of stimulation by these three substances, in terms of ^{3}H-thymidine incorporation, is given in Figure 2, and in terms of blast transformation in Figure 3. Blast transformation was stimulated by PHA, LPS, or SEB in 50% to 60% of the cell population by

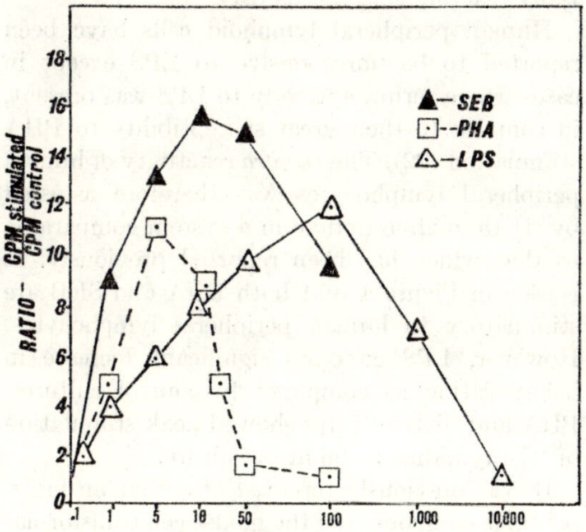

Figure 1. Dose response relationship of A/J spleen cells reacting to PHA, SEB or LPS. 15 × 10^{6} cells/tube in 3 ml culture medium were incubated with the indicated substance for 72 hr. ^{3}H-thymidine incorporation was measured during the last 24 hr of culture. Mean values and ratio of incorporation were calculated from triplicate simulated and control cultures.

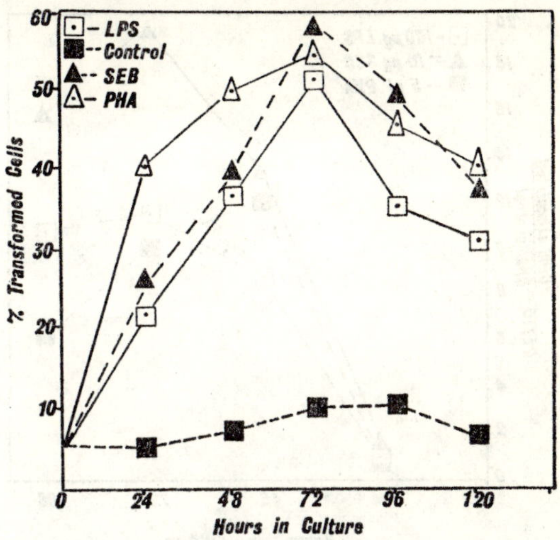

Figure 2. Time course of blast transformation of A/J spleen cells responding to PHA, LPS or SEB. The occurrence of blast transformation was determined by staining cell preparations on the indicated day. Results are expressed as percentage of the cell population scored as lymphoblasts and the averages represent triplicate cultures.

the end of the 3rd day of culture. This proportion decreased slightly thereafter. Unstimulated control cultures showed spontaneous transformation ranging between 5% and 9% lymphoblasts at the end of the same period. The large mononuclear cells had a blast-like appearance with a large nucleus and a small rim of basophilic cytoplasm. The cytoplasm appeared granular, highly vacuolated and often had small rounded pseudopodia protruding from the periphery. Nucleoli were present in some cells although they were not preponderant. Thus, according to the morphologic and histochemical criteria of Marshall and Roberts (19) these blast-like forms were indistinguishable from cells stimulated by PHA.

The time course of blast transformation paralleled precisely that of incorporation of a 24-hr pulse of ^{3}H-thymidine. Maximum incorporation in PHA-stimulated cultures was found between 24 and 48 hr, occurring some 12 to 24 hr before peak incorporation in cultures stimulated by LPS or SEB. The magnitude of ^{3}H-thymidine incorporation in response to LPS and SEB stimulation, however, was equal to or greater than the response to PHA stimulation.

Inasmuch as marked strain differences in responsiveness to the lethal effects of endotoxin

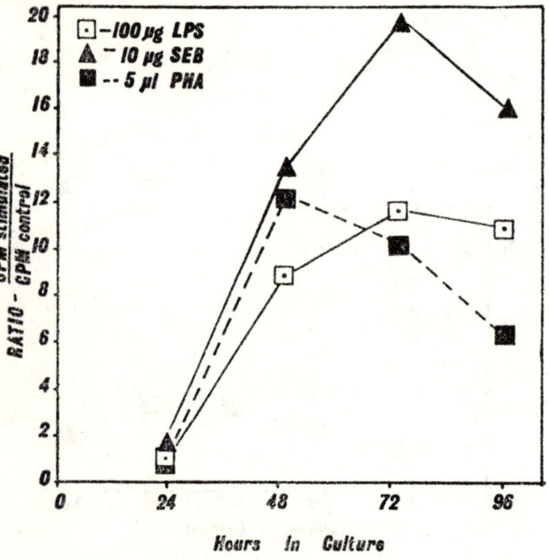

Figure 3. Time course of ³H-thymidine incorporation by A/J spleen cells responding to SEB, PHA, or LPS. 15 × 10⁶ cells/tube in 3 ml medium were incubated for indicated times with and without test antigens. DNA synthesis was measured by ³H-thymidine incorporation over the last 24 hr of each period. Mean values and ratio of incorporation were calculated for triplicate stimulated and control cultures.

are reported (20), it was of interest to determine whether such differences in *in vitro* responsiveness occurred. Accordingly, the effects of LPS and SEB at concentrations extending over a 100-fold range were determined in a variety of different mouse strains. Optimal stimulation, both in terms of total thymidine incorporation and discrimination as expressed by the ratio of incorporation was obtained at the dose of 100 μg LPS and 10 μg SEB/culture for each strain studied. Similar studies involving PHA stimulation, reported earlier (15), showed great strain variability in responsiveness as indicated by total incorporation and the ratio of incorporation under identical conditions. Table I shows the results of the effects of PHA, SEB, and LPS with different inbred strains, using concentrations which gave maximum stimulation. It is interesting that DBA-2, which was minimally stimulated by PHA, was stimulated strongly by both SEB and LPS. On the other hand, BALB/c was most responsive to SEB and PHA and possessed only average sensitivity to LPS. These differences in responsiveness to PHA, SEB and LPS among the various strains are unexplained; they may reflect

TABLE I

Effects of PHA, LPS and SEB on mouse spleen cells taken from various strains[a]

Source of Spleen Cells	³H-Thymidine Incorporation in Cultures of 15 × 10⁶ Cells from Each Spleen			
	Control	PHA	LPS	SEB
	mean cpm/tube			
A/J	8,256	122,590	126,378	184,236
BALB/c	11,011	199,709	98,520	353,506
C57BL/6	9,550	139,786	122,763	234,850
DBA-2	25,645	102,103	331,253	385,239
B1OM	9,855	107,345	122,611	191,677

[a] In these experiments, four to six replicate tubes, each containing 15 × 10⁶ cells from various inbred strains, were cultured for 72 hr with or without mitogen treatment. ³H-thymidine incorporation was assayed during the last 24 hr of culture and the results were expressed as mean counts/minute/tube. PHA-stimulated cultures were terminated at 48 hr, while SEB and LPS were terminated at 72 hr.

genetic difference in membranes or environmental experience, but the simplest explanation would be dissimilarity in the subpopulations of potentially reacting spleen cells (21).

Human peripheral lymphoid cells have been reported to be unresponsive to LPS except in cases where serum antibody to LPS was present, in contrast to their great susceptibility to PHA stimulation (22). The *in vitro* reactivity of human peripheral lymphocytes was therefore assessed by ³H-thymidine uptake in a system comparable to that which has been reported previously. It is seen in Figure 4 that both PHA and SEB are stimulatory to human peripheral lymphocytes. However, LPS gave no significant increase in incorporation as compared to control cultures. PHA and SEB cultures showed peak stimulation of ³H-thymidine at 96 hr of culture.

It was previously reported (15) that an indispensable component of the mouse cell transformation system *in vitro* was an anti-mouse lymphocyte globulin, which occurs normally in human serum and in that of certain other species (23). The culture conditions employed here for human cells contained fetal calf serum, and therefore no component analogous to the anti-lymphocyte globulin. Attempts were made to provide this by using a similar, naturally occurring anti-human lymphocyte globulin of rabbit serum

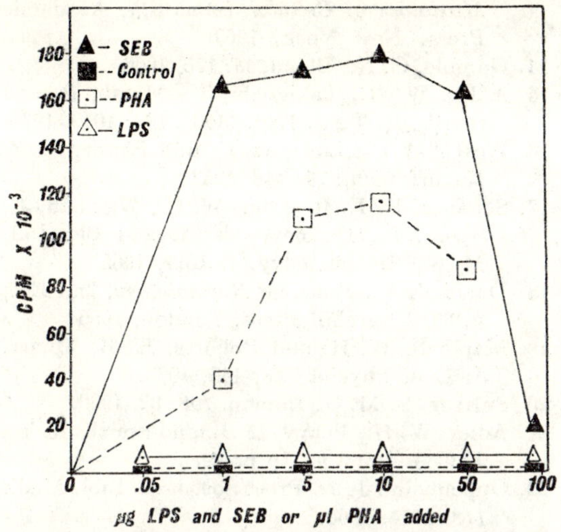

Figure 4. Dose response relationship of human peripheral lymphocytes reacting to PHA, LPS or SEB. 5 × 10^6 human peripheral lymphocytes/tube in 4 ml of culture medium were incubated with and without test antigen for 4 days. ^{3}H-thymidine incorporation was again measured during the last 24 hr of incubation. Mean values and ratio of incorporation were calculated from triplicate stimulated and control tubes.

TABLE II

Comparison of various supplemented media in their capacity to stimulate human peripheral lymphocytes[a]

Type of Media Employed	^{3}H-Thymidine Incorporation (mean cpm/tube)		
	Control	LPS	Ratio of incorporation: LPS/control
	mean cpm/tube		
10% autologous serum	462	635	1.37
20% fetal calf serum	1,119	932	0.83
1% normal rabbit serum	859	1,308	1.52
5% normal rabbit serum	1,650	1,157	0.70
10% normal rabbit serum	2,559	881	0.34

[a] In this experiment various mammalian sera were used to supplement the culture media in order to detect stimulation of human peripheral lymphocytes by *Salmonella typhimurium* endotoxin. 5 × 10^6 cells in 4 ml/tube were incubated with or without endotoxin for 96 hr, ^{3}H-thymidine was added, and the experiment was terminated at 120 hr. The values given represent means of three replicate tubes.

(24) for supporting the *in vitro* response to LPS. As will be seen from Table II, this serum, over a range of concentrations, failed to permit stimulation of human lymphocytes by LPS. Although this species difference remains to be solved, it may represent the differences in populations of reacting cells which are present in mouse spleens, but which are not found in human peripheral blood.

DISCUSSION

These studies show that transformation and thymidine incorporation occur in mouse lymphoid cells in response to Salmonella endotoxin (LPS) and staphylococcal enterotoxin B (SEB). In their morphologic features, and the intensity of ^{3}H-thymidine incorporation, these responses are entirely identical to those in cell cultures stimulated by PHA (15). Additional evidence that these responses are similar was established by a comparable dose-response relationship and by the observation that a peak response affected 50% to 60% of cultured cells. Although variation exists with different endotoxin preparations (unpublished), the magnitude of the responses induced by LPS and SEB was equal to, or greater than that stimulated by PHA. However, time studies indicated that peak thymidine incorporation lagged 24 hr behind that of PHA-activated cultures.

Whether these phenomena result from the immunologic or pharmacologic properties of the two classes of macromolecules is not presently known. Responses to LPS and SEB could represent alterations of lymphocyte membrane permeability (25) and be construed as nonspecific effects like PHA or denote specific recognition and induction of cell-mediated responses comparable to those of tuberculin on sensitized cells.

Finally, the physiologic significance of the biologically potent effector molecules characteristically elaborated during proliferation of spleen cells has yet to be assessed. It is quite conceivable that molecules which have the properties of activating macrophages, attracting polymorphonuclear leucocytes, inhibiting DNA synthesis and attacking cell membranes *in vitro* could play a significant role in the pharmacologic action of such toxins *in vivo*. If this proves to be the case, it can be anticipated that additional complexities such as host-derived inhibitors will be encountered. It can be expected that at some point these molecules affect the blood coagulation complex, and perhaps the terminal complement components.

REFERENCES

1. Bryant, R. E., Des Prez, R. M. and Rogers, D. E., Yale J. Biol. Med., *40:* 192, 1967.
2. Atkins, E. A., Phys. Rev., *40:* 580, 1960.
3. Thomas, L., Zweifach, B. W. and Benacerraf, B., Trans. Assoc. Amer. Phys., *70:* 54, 1957.
4. Shwartzman, G., J. Exp. Med., *48:* 247, 1928.
5. Whany, H. Y. and Neter, E. J., Immunology, *98:* 948, 1967.
6. Des Prez, R. M., J. Exp. Med., *120:* 305, 1964.
7. Atkins, E. A. and Snell, E. S., *The Inflammatory Process*, p. 495, Academic Press, New York, 1965.
8. Stetson, C. A., J. Exp. Med., *94:* 347, 1951.
9. Stetson, C. A., J. Exp. Med., *93:* 489, 1951.
10. Landy, M., Whitley, J. L., Michael, J. G., Woods, M. W. and Newton, M. L., Proc. Soc. Exp. Biol. Med., *109:* 352, 1962.
11. Heilman, D. H. and Bast, R. C., J. Bact., *93:* 15, 1967.
12. Wiener, E., Beck, A. and Shilo, M., Lab. Invest., *14:* 475, 1965.
13. Lawrence, H. S. and Landy, M., editors, *Mediators of Cellular Immunity*, Academic Press, New York, 1969.
14. Gamble, C. N., Blood, *28:* 175, 1966.
15. Adler, W. H., Takiguchi, T., Marsh, B. and Smith, R. T., J. Exp. Med., *131:* 1049, 1970.
16. Westphal, O., Lüderitz, O. and Bister, F., Z. Naturforsch., *76:* 148, 1952.
17. Schantz, E. J., Roessler, W. G., Wagman, J., Spero, L., Dunnery, D. A. and Bergdoll, M. S., Biochemistry, *4:* 1011, 1965.
18. Dacie, J. V., *Practical Haematology*, 2nd Ed., p. 39, Churchill Press, London, 1956.
19. Marshall, W. H. and Roberts, K. B., Quart. J. Exp. Physiol., *48:* 146, 1963.
20. Sultzer, B. M., J. Immun. *103:* 32, 1969.
21. Adler, W. H., Peavy, D. L. and Smith, R. T., J. Cell. Immun., In press.
22. Oppenheim, J. J., Proc. Soc. Exp. Biol. Med., *118:* 1014, 1965.
23. Landy, M., Michael, J. G., Tranpani, R. J., Achinstein, B., Woods, M. W. and Shear, M. J., Cancer Res. *20:* 1279, 1960.
24. Herberman, R., Transplantation, *8:* 813, 1969.
25. Braun, W., Yajima, Y. and Nakano, M., in *La Structure et les Effets Biologiques des Produits Bactériens Provenant des Germes Gram-Negatifs, Colloque International, Paris, 1967*, p. 229 Centre National de la Recherche Scientifique, Paris, 1969.

THE JOURNAL OF IMMUNOLOGY
Vol. 105, No. 6, December 1970

MECHANISMS OF PASSIVE SENSITIZATION

I. Presence of IgE and IgG Molecules on Human Leukocytes[1]

KIMISHIGE ISHIZAKA,[2] HISAO TOMIOKA[2] AND TERUKO ISHIZAKA[2]

From the Children's Asthma Research Institute and Hospital, Denver, Colorado 80204

Received for publication June 26, 1970

Immunoglobulins E and G were detected on human leukocytes by autoradiography. Evidence was obtained that specifically purified anti-human γE antibody combined with basophilic leukocytes from both normal and atopic individuals, and that anti-γG antibody bound with neutrophils and monocytes. Upon passive sensitization, E myeloma protein bound with basophils and normal γG bound with neutrophils and monocytes. The results show that basophils have receptor sites for γE, and that both neutrophils and monocytes have receptor sites for γG. Binding of the Fc fragments, but not the F(ab′)$_2$ fragments, of E myeloma protein with basophils indicated that γE combines with basophils through the Fc portion of the molecules. The binding of γE with basophils appears to be a process of passive sensitization for both antigen-induced and antibody-induced histamine release from leukocytes.

Sensitization for reaginic hypersensitivity reactions involves binding of reaginic antibodies with tissue constituents. Levy and Osler (1) succeeded in passively sensitizing normal human leukocytes with atopic patients' sera for antigen-induced histamine release. Evidence has been accumulated that the immunoglobulin responsible for the antigen-induced histamine release is γE. The antibody specific for γE, but not the antibodies specific for the other immunoglobulin classes, released histamine from the leukocytes of atopic patients (2) and passive sensitization of normal leukocytes with a γE-rich serum or E myeloma protein increased the sensitivity of the leukocytes to anti-γE (2, 3). These findings indicate that γE is present on/in the leukocytes and that reaction of cell-bound γE with either allergen or anti-γE is responsible for the histamine release.

The present experiments were undertaken to identify the sensitized cells. In view of our previous observation that γE-containing cells were not detectable in human leukocytes by fluorescent antibody techniques (4), autoradiography was applied to increase the sensitivity. The leukocytes from both atopic patients and normal individuals were treated with radioactively labeled anti-γE or anti-γG and smears of the cells were examined by autoradiography. Attempts were also made to sensitize the leukocytes with radioactive E myeloma protein or normal γG. The results show that γE is present on/in basophilic leukocytes whereas γG is present on neutrophils and monocytes.

MATERIALS AND METHODS

Immunoglobulins. E myeloma protein was isolated from the serum of myeloma patient PS by diethylaminoethyl (DEAE)-cellulose column chromatography and gel filtration (5). The Fc and F(ab′)$_2$ fragments of the protein were obtained by digestion with either papain or pepsin as described in a previous article (3). Normal γG was purified from human serum by DEAE-cellulose column chromatography. Protein eluted from the column with 0.005 M phosphate buffer, pH 8.0, was concentrated.

Antibodies specific for γG and γE. Monospecific antiserum to γE was obtained by immunizing

[1] This work was supported by Research Grant AI-04985 from the United States Public Health Service. A part of the data was presented before the 26th Annual Meeting of the American Academy of Allergy in New Orleans, Louisiana, on February 16, 1970.

[2] Present address: Department of Medicine, The Johns Hopkins University, School of Medicine at The Good Samaritan Hospital, Baltimore, Md. 21212. Reprint requests should be sent to K. I. at the above address.

rabbits with the Fc fragments of E myeloma protein and then absorbing with the Fab fragments of the protein (3). The antiserum against γG was obtained by immunizing rabbits with normal γG. The antiserum was rendered specific for the immunoglobulin by absorption with the Fab fragments of the protein.

The anti-γE and anti-γG antibodies were specifically purified using immunosorbents which were prepared by aggregating the respective immunoglobulin with glutaraldehyde (6). To a 2% solution (5 ml) of each immunoglobulin in acetate buffer, pH 4.9, 300 mg of cellulose powder (Cellex N-1) and 10 mg of glutaraldehyde (Eastman Organic Chemicals, Rochester, N. Y.) were added, and the mixtures were stirred for 2 hr at room temperature. Insoluble aggregates were washed thoroughly with cold distilled water and with 0.1 M glycine buffer, pH 2.5, and resuspended in saline. The suspension was adjusted to pH 8 and insoluble precipitates were washed several times with borate-buffered saline.

Approximately 15 ml of anti-γE or anti-γG serum were added to the γE- or γG-immunosorbent. After stirring overnight at 3°C, the precipitates were washed four times with borate-buffered saline and then extracted three times with 5 ml of 0.1 M glycine buffer, pH 3.0. The supernatant was adjusted to pH 7.0, dialyzed against borate-buffered saline and concentrated. The concentration of class-specific antibodies in the final preparations was measured by the quantitative precipitin reaction using the Fc fragments of E myeloma protein or normal γG. The precipitating antibodies in the anti-γE and anti-γG preparations were 68% and 72% of total protein, respectively.

Radio-labeling technique. E myeloma protein, its fragments, γG and the antibodies specific for each immunoglobulin class were labeled with ^{125}I or ^{131}I by the method of McConahey and Dixon (7) using chloramine T. Two to 3 mCi of ^{125}I (Cambridge Corp., Cambridge, Mass.) or ^{131}I (Abbott Laboratories, North Chicago, Ill.) were used to label 1 mg of protein in 1 ml of 0.05 M phosphate buffer, pH 7.0.

Measurement of γE in serum. Quantitative measurement of γE concentration in human sera was carried out by the inhibition of the ^{125}I Fc-anti-γE reaction by the samples. The tests were set up in duplicate. An appropriate dilution of serum samples and twofold dilutions

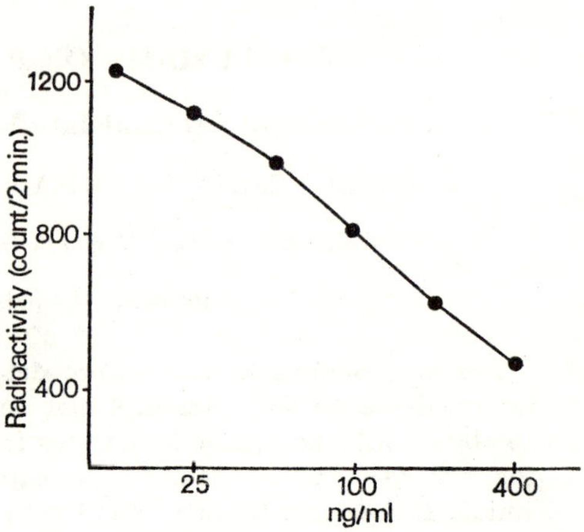

Figure 1. A dose-response curve illustrating the inhibition of the binding of ^{125}I-Fc fragments to anti-γE by standard serum.

of standard serum[3] containing 12.5 ng/ml to 400 ng/ml of γE were made in 0.1% human serum albumin (HSA) (Nutritional Biochemical Corp., Cleveland, Ohio). Two-tenths milliliter of each of the dilutions was mixed with 0.1 ml of anti-γE diluted in 600 μg/ml of normal rabbit γG. The amount of anti-γE added to each tube was 50 ng. Two controls, i.e., a mixture of 0.2 ml of 1 mg/ml HSA with anti-γE, and standard serum plus normal rabbit γ globulin, were set up. The tubes were kept for 1 hr at room temperature, and 20 ng (0.1 ml) of ^{125}I-labeled Fc fragment of E myeloma protein in 0.1% HSA were added to each tube. After another 1 hr, a goat antiserum specific for rabbit γG (Antibody, Inc., Davis, Calif.) was added and the tubes were kept overnight at 3°C. The amount of the anti-rabbit γG added to precipitate the rabbit immunoglobulin was about twice the equivalence amount. The precipitates were washed four times with cold borate-buffered saline and radioactivity of the precipitate was measured with an automatic gamma counter (Nuclear Chicago Corp., Chicago, Ill.). In order to estimate γE concentration in each serum, radioactivity of each precipitate was interpolated to a standard curve obtained with serial dilutions of reference serum (Fig. 1).

[3] The reference standard serum was kindly supplied by Dr. David Rowe, World Health Organization. The serum contained 10,000 units of IgE per milliliter which corresponded to 10 μg/ml measured by the method of Johansson *et al.* (8).

Isolation of leukocytes and histamine release. Leukocytes were isolated from the blood of two atopic patients and four normal individuals by the method of Lichtenstein and Osler (9). The cells were washed twice with Tris buffer, pH 7.6, containing 0.025 M Tris, 0.12 M NaCl, 0.005 M KCl and 0.3 g of HSA per liter (Tris-A buffer). Histamine release experiments by anti-γE were carried out by the same procedure as that described in a previous article (2). The medium for the experiment was Tris-A buffer containing 6×10^{-4} M $CaCl_2$ and 10^{-3} M $MgCl_2$ (Tris-ACM buffer). Unless specified, the reaction medium contained 1% fresh rabbit serum to enhance histamine release. After incubation for 40 min at 37°C with appropriate concentrations of anti-γE, the cells were centrifuged and histamine in the supernatant fluids was measured by a spectrophotofluorometric technique (9).

The experiments on antigen-induced histamine release were carried out by the method of Lichtenstein and Osler (9) using purified antigen E from ragweed pollen extract, (fraction IVc prepared according to King *et al.* (10) for the Committee on Standardization of Allergen).

Passive sensitization of leukocytes. The procedure described by Levy and Osler (1) was followed. Serum from patient AR containing 16 μg/ml of γE (2), normal γG, E myeloma protein, Fc or $F(ab')_2$ fragments of the myeloma protein were diluted in Tris-A buffer, pH 7.4, containing 4×10^{-3} M ethylenediaminetetraacetate (EDTA) and 10 μg/ml of heparin. The concentration of respective protein in the final dilution was 3 μg/ml. Leukocytes were suspended in one of the solutions and the suspension containing 10^7 leukocytes/ml was incubated at 37°C for 2 hr for passive sensitization.

Autoradiography. The isolated leukocytes were incubated at 0°C for 30 min with ^{125}I-labeled anti-γE or anti-γG in Tris-A buffer containing 0.01 M EDTA. In some experiments, the cells were passively sensitized with ^{125}I- or ^{131}I-labeled immunoglobulin by the method described above. The cells treated with either anti-immunoglobulin or purified immunoglobulin were washed five times at 4°C with Tris-A buffer containing 0.01 M EDTA. Smears of the leukocytes were stained with 0.25% toluidine blue in absolute ethanol for 5 min, and then stained with 0.05% toluidine blue in phosphate buffer, pH 8.4, for a few seconds. Some smears were stained with May-Grünwald Giemsa solution. In order to prevent photochemical fogging, the slides were coated with 0.5% celloidin (K and K Laboratories, Plainview, N. Y.) dissolved in a mixture of 50% ethanol and 50% ether, and quickly dried. The slides were then covered with Nuclear Track Emulsion NTB 2 (Eastman Kodak, Rochester, N. Y.). After 2 to 3 weeks, one smear of each specimen was developed every week. In some experiments, smears of leukocytes were fixed with absolute ethanol for 5 min and coated with Nuclear Track Emulsion before staining. These slides were stained with either toluidine blue or May-Grünwald Giemsa solution after development.

RESULTS

As preliminary experiments, serum γE levels and the sensitivity of leukocytes to anti-γE were examined. It was found that leukocytes from two atopic patients, having high γE levels, released more than 50% of the histamine upon exposure to anti-γE. Among the four normal individuals, having either normal or low serum γE levels, leukocytes from only one person (LC) released more than 50% of the histamine. Maximal histamine release from leukocytes of the other two individuals by the optimal concentration of anti-γE was 46% and 39%, respectively. The leukocytes of another person (MH) did not release a significant amount of histamine upon incubation with 0.005 to 1.0 μg N/ml of anti-γE (Table I).

Leukocytes from the four normal individuals were incubated in a 1:5 dilution of serum AR containing anti-ragweed γE antibody and the sensitized cells were exposed to antigen E. Passive sensitization for antigen-induced histamine release was successful only in one case (CL) (Table I). Fifty per cent of the total histamine was released from sensitized cells with 0.02 μg/ml of antigen E, but the same cells before sensitization did not release a significant amount of histamine with 0.01 to 0.1 μg/ml of the antigen.

Similarly, leukocytes from three normal individuals were sensitized with 3 μg/ml of E myeloma protein and both sensitized and unsensitized cells were challenged with anti-γE. As reported in a previous article (3), sensitivity of the leukocytes from LC to anti-γE increased upon passive sensitization. The sensitivity of

TABLE I

Serum γE level and sensitivity of leukocytes to anti-γE

Subject	Serum γE	Anti-γE (μg N/ml) Required for 50% Histamine Release	Passive Sensitization with	
			Reaginic ab[a]	γE[b]
	μg/ml			
Atopic				
AR	11.0	0.00005	ND[c]	ND
EL	0.56	0.0004	ND	ND
Non-atopic				
LC	0.16	0.005	+	+
HT	0.12	(0.02)[d]	−	ND
KI	0.048	(0.02)[d]	−	−
MH	0.048	(>1.0)[d]	−	−

[a] Passive sensitization was carried out with serum AR. Both sensitized and unsensitized cells were incubated with antigen E for histamine release.

[b] Cells were sensitized in 3 μg/ml of E myeloma protein and challenged with anti-γE.

[c] ND, not done. Leukocytes from both patients released histamine by antigen E.

[d] The concentration of anti-γE in parentheses represents that required for giving maximal histamine release. In HT and KI maximal histamine released by anti-γE was 46% and 39%, respectively. Leukocytes from MH did not release a significant amount of histamine in the range of 0.005 to 1.0 μg N/ml of anti-γE.

cells from the other two individuals (KI, MH) did not change after passive sensitization.

Binding of anti-γE and anti-γG with leukocytes. Leukocytes were isolated from the blood of both atopic and normal individuals and resuspended in Tris-A buffer containing 0.01 M EDTA. One-half of the suspension was incubated for 30 min at 0°C with ^{125}I-labeled anti-γE and the rest was incubated with ^{125}I-labeled anti-γG. The concentration of the antibodies in the final suspension was 0.1 μg antibody nitrogen/ml. Smears of the cells were stained with toluidine blue, coated with celloidin and then coated with Nuclear Track Emulsion. Autoradiographs of the leukocytes treated with anti-γE showed that only 1 to 2% of nucleated cells gave a significant number of grains over the cells, and these cells were identified as basophilic leukocytes (Fig. 2, *a* and *b*). Almost all cells containing metachromatic granules were labeled, whereas the number of grains over the other cells, i.e., neutrophils, eosinophils, small lymphocytes and monocytes was not significant. In order to confirm this finding, the number of grains over each basophilic leukocyte and those over the other cells were counted. For each slide, 100 cells of each type were examined and the distribution of different leukocytes giving a certain number of grains was plotted. A representative result is shown in Figure 3*a*. In the autoradiograph, less than 10 grains per cell was not significant as compared with background. It is clear that 96% of the basophilic leukocytes gave a significant number of grains, whereas over 99% of the neutrophils, eosinophils, small lymphocytes and monocytes did not. A significant number of grains was found over some large or medium sized lymphocytes in the smear. The number of grains over the lymphocytes was usually less than that over the basophils and about 1% of the medium and large lymphocytes were labeled with anti-γE. The experiments on leukocytes from two atopic patients and four normal individuals gave comparable results. In all the cases, anti-γE labeled basophilic leukocytes preferentially. However, an average number of grains per basophilic leukocyte was different from one case to another. When leukocytes from atopic patient AR and the cells from the normal individual, KI, were treated under the same condition, the average number of grains per basophilic leukocyte was 60 to 70 for AR as compared with 20 to 30 for KI.

When leukocytes were treated with ^{125}I-labeled anti-γG, approximately one-half of the cells were labeled and most of such cells were identified as neutrophilic leukocytes and monocytes (Fig. 2, *c* and *d*). Basophilic leukocytes, showing metachromatic staining with toluidine blue, did not give a significant number of grains. Distribution of each cell type giving a different number of grains is shown in Figure 3*b*. It is clear that more than 95% of the neutrophils were labeled, whereas essentially none of the basophils, eosinophils or small lymphocytes were labeled. Approximately 65% of the monocytes showed a significant number of grains on autoradiographs. In addition, 1 to 5% of the medium and large lymphocytes were labeled with anti-γG. These results were confirmed with leukocytes from four normal and two atopic individuals.

Leukocytes from these subjects were treated with ^{125}I-labeled normal rabbit γG; however, no leukocytes showed a significant number of grains on autoradiographs.

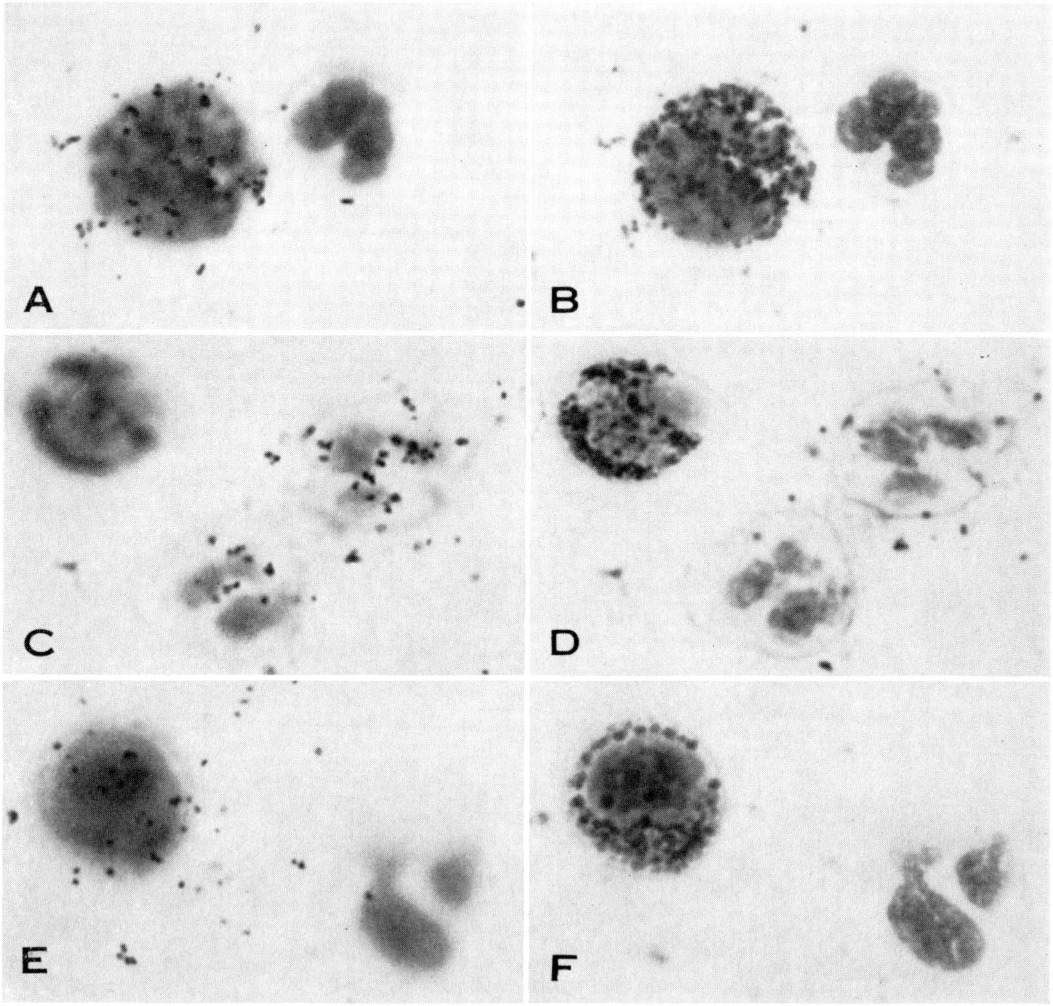

Figure 2. Autoradiography of leukocytes treated with ^{125}I-anti-γE (*A*, *B*). ^{125}I-anti-γG (*C*, *D*) and ^{131}I-E myeloma protein (*E*, *F*). Microscope was focused to grains in (*A*, *C*, *E*). The same cells are focused in (*B*, *D*, *F*). Magnification, × 1000; toluidine blue staining. Four weeks exposure for *A* and *C*, 8 weeks exposure for *E*. The results show that anti-γE bound with basophils but not with neutrophils (*A*, *B*); anti-γG bound with neutrophils but not with basophils (*C*, *D*); E myeloma protein bound with basophils but not with neutrophils (*E*, *F*).

Combination of γE and γG on leukocytes upon passive sensitization. Specific binding of anti-γE with basophils and of anti-γG with neutrophils and monocytes suggested the possibility that γE and γG have an affinity for different leukocytes. To test this, leukocytes isolated from a normal individual (LC), whose cells were passively sensitized with γE reaginic antibody for antigen-induced histamine release, were sensitized with 3 μg/ml of either ^{131}I- or ^{125}I-labeled E myeloma protein. When smears of these cells were stained with toluidine blue, coated with celloidin and then with Nuclear Track Emulsion, none of those cells treated with ^{125}I-labeled E myeloma protein gave a significant number of grains in autoradiographs. However, basophilic leukocytes treated with ^{131}I-labeled E myeloma protein showed grains after exposure for 2 months (Fig. 2, *e* and *f*). The number of grains over each cell was counted for 100 each of the different leukocytes. As shown in Figure 3*c* approximately 60% of basophil leukocytes gave significantly

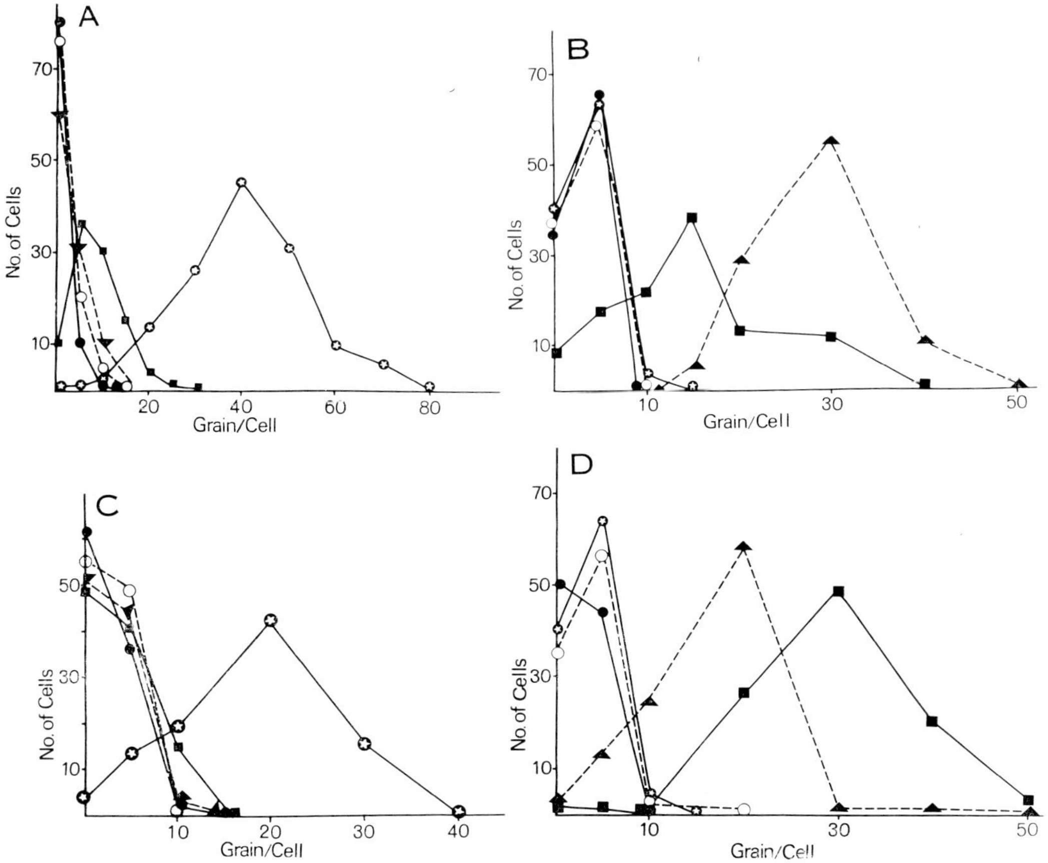

Figure 3. Distribution of leukocytes giving different numbers of grains on autoradiographs. Distribution of basophils, ⊛——⊛; neutrophils, ▲-----▲; eosinophils, ○-----○; monocytes, ■——■; and small lymphocytes, ●——●. Leukocytes treated with ^{125}I-anti-γE (*A*), ^{125}I-anti-γG (*B*), those passively sensitized with ^{131}I-E myeloma protein (*C*) or ^{131}I-γG (*D*).

more grains than the other leukocytes. The results indicate that E myeloma protein has an affinity for basophils.

The possibility remained that only one-half of the basophilic leukocytes could be passively sensitized. In order to increase the sensitivity of autoradiography, unstained smears of the γE-treated cells were coated directly with Nuclear Track Emulsion. Autoradiographs were developed after 4 to 5 weeks' exposure and the cells were stained with toluidine blue through the emulsion. It was found that staining characteristics of basophilic granules were lost by exposure of the slides to developer and fixer. Nevertheless, most of the labeled cells had s-shaped nuclei and their shape and staining characteristics were different from those of neutrophils, eosinophils or lymphocytes. In order to identify these cells, they were compared with the cells labeled with ^{125}I-anti-γE in a previous experiment. Smears of leukocytes treated with ^{125}I-anti-γE were covered with Nuclear Track Emulsion, developed after 2 to 3 weeks' exposure and then stained with toluidine blue. Staining characteristics of the cells labeled with anti-γE were the same as those labeled with ^{125}I-γE. Since 99% of the cells combining anti-γE were identified as basophils in a previous experiment, it appears that most of the cells combining with γE are probably basophilic leukocytes. Furthermore, the percentage of cells labeled with γE of the total leukocytes was comparable to the percentage of basophilic leukocytes in the original leukocyte suspension (Table II). It appears that almost all basophilic leukocytes combined with γE.

TABLE II

Comparisons between the percentage of basophilic leukocytes and the percentage of leukocytes labeled with ^{125}I-γE

Subject	Basophilic Leukocytes	Labeled Cells
	(% of total)	(% of total)
LC	2.1	2.1
KI	1.2	1.1
HT	1.0	1.4

The leukocytes isolated from the same individuals were sensitized with 3 μg/ml of ^{125}I-labeled normal γG by the same procedure. Smears were stained with either toluidine blue or May-Grünwald Giemsa solution and autoradiographs were made. A significant number of grains was first observed over monocytes and then neutrophils. Eosinophils, basophils and lymphocytes were not labeled with γG. The distribution of leukocytes with different numbers of grains is shown in Figure 3*d*.

In a previous article (3) we showed that the Fc fragments of E myeloma protein passively sensitize human leukocytes for reversed type histamine release. Thus, the Fc fragments and $F(ab')_2$ fragments of the myeloma protein were labeled with ^{131}I or ^{125}I, and leukocytes from normal individuals were sensitized with each of the fragments. Autoradiographs of the cells treated with ^{131}I-Fc showed that 20% of the basophils were labeled. Direct coating of unstained smears of ^{125}I-Fc-treated cells with Nuclear Track Emulsion showed that more than half of the basophils in the original leukocyte suspension were radiolabeled, and staining characteristics of the labeled cells were the same as those labeled with anti-γE or E myeloma protein. When the same leukocyte suspensions were treated with the $F(ab')_2$ fragments, which had a specific radioactivity slightly higher than that of ^{125}I-Fc, only a few monocytes but no basophils had only slightly more grains than background after a long exposure. The results indicate that γE combines with basophilic leukocytes through the Fc portion of the molecule.

DISCUSSION

The present data clearly show that anti-γE preferentially binds with basophilic leukocytes, and indicate the presence of γE on the cells. Affinity of γE for basophils was confirmed by passive sensitization experiments. After the leukocytes were incubated with E myeloma protein, the immunoglobulin was detected on basophils but not on the other leukocytes. Neither human γG nor rabbit γG bound with basophils. These findings indicate that basophils have receptor sites for γE. The experiments also show that the Fc fragments but not the $F(ab')_2$ fragments of E myeloma protein bind with basophils. The results are in accord with previous findings that Fc fragments sensitize human leukocytes for reversed type (anti-γE-induced) histamine release (3) and that the Fc fragments, but not the $F(ab')_2$ fragments, block passive sensitization of human skin with reaginic antibodies (3). They also strongly suggest that binding of γE with basophils is a process of passive sensitization of leukocytes.

The present experiments demonstrate that anti-γG bind with both neutrophils and monocytes and that normal γG binds with these cells upon passive sensitization. Evidence of γG binding with monocytes was shown by LoBuglio *et al.* (11) as well as Huber *et al.* (12, 13) through the demonstration that red cells coated with γG antibody bound with monocytes. The lack of rosette formation of red cell-γG antibody complexes around neutrophils in their experiments appears to be contradictory to our findings that neutrophils bind more anti-γG than monocytes. When the leukocytes were treated with ^{131}I-γG, however, the number of grains over monocytes was significantly more than that over neutrophils (cf. Fig. 3, *b* and *d*). It appears that neutrophils bind γG more firmly than monocytes, and that replacement of γG on neutrophils by external γG may be less than that which occurs on monocytes upon passive sensitization. In any event, it is apparent that both monocytes and neutrophils have receptor sites for γG.

In addition to the granulocytes, a small proportion of lymphocytes was labeled with both anti-γE and anti-γG. The number of cells combining with the antibodies was less than 0.05% of the total lymphocytes and was restricted to medium and large lymphocytes. In our previous study (4) in which γE-forming cells were demonstrated by a fluorescent antibody technique, 1 out of 2000 peripheral lymphocytes in the blood of patient AR was stained by anti-γE. Since autoradiography employed in the present experiments is more sensitive than the fluorescent antibody technique, by which γE on basophils was not detectable, the lymphocytes combining anti-immunoglobulin may be the cells forming the immunoglobulin. Sell (14, 15) has reported that antibodies against major immunoglobulin classes induced blast transformation of rabbit lymphocytes and more recent work in our laboratory showed that both anti-γE and anti-γG induced transformation of human lymphocytes obtained from both normal and atopic individuals (unpublished data).

Preferential binding of anti-γE with basophils strongly suggests that the combination of the antibody with basophil-bound γE results in the release of histamine from the cells. Graham *et al.* (16) reported that about 50% of the total histamine in human blood is associated with basophils. More recently, Pruzansky and Patterson (17) reported that basophils contain at least 85% of the total histamine in blood. Since an optimal concentration of allergen or anti-γE releases practically all the histamine in leukocytes in some cases, histamine in basophils should have been released by the reagent.

The presence of γE on basophils seems to be essential for sensitization. Lichtenstein *et al.* (18) have shown a rough correlation between serum γE level in atopic patients and maximal histamine release from their leukocytes by anti-γE. More recently, Levy *et al.* (19) reported that leukocytes from a normal individual who lacked γE in her serum did not release histamine upon exposure to anti-γE and that only 3 ng/ml of E myeloma protein successfully sensitized her leukocytes for anti-γE induced histamine release. However, the presence of γE on basophils is not sufficient for the anti-γE-induced histamine release. It was shown in the present experiment that leukocytes from a normal individual (MH), who had 48 ng/ml of γE in her serum, did not release a significant amount of histamine upon exposure to anti-γE. Her basophils actually contained γE as demonstrated by the specific binding of anti-γE with the cells.

A discrepancy between the presence of γE on basophils and sensitization for histamine release was observed in passive sensitization experiments as well. Levy and Osler (1) reported that leukocytes from only one out of five normal individuals accepted passive sensitization for antigen-induced histamine release. The present experiments confirmed and extended their findings. Among the four normal individuals studied, the leukocytes from only one person (CL) were sensitized for both antigen-induced and antibody-induced histamine release. When the leukocytes were incubated with ^{131}I-labeled E myeloma protein for passive sensitization, binding of the protein with basophils was demonstrated in all of the four cases. The results for passive sensitization indicate that basophils from blood of both "acceptor" and "nonacceptor" subjects bind γE. It is apparent that the allergen-γE antibody reaction (or anti-γE-γE reaction) on basophils from some of the nonacceptors (i.e., MH) did not lead to the release of histamine. The possibility still remains that the quantity of γE or γE antibody bound with cells upon passive sensitization is different depending on the source of cells, and basophils from nonacceptors fail to combine a sufficient amount of γE. On the other hand, evidence has been accumulated that the release of histamine is controlled by biochemical factors involved in the enzymatic sequences following the antigen-antibody reaction. Lichtenstein *et al.* (18, 20) reported that catecholamines such as isoproterenol and epinephrine, as well as theophylline, inhibited both antigen-induced and antibody-induced histamine release without preventing antigen-antibody reactions. Both the quantitation of cell-bound γE and further analysis of biochemical processes will be required to elucidate the mechanisms of histamine release.

REFERENCES

1. Levy, D. A. and Osler, A. G., J. Immun., *99:* 1062, 1967.
2. Ishizaka, T., Ishizaka, K., Johansson, S. G. O. and Bennich, H., J. Immun., *102:* 884, 1969.
3. Ishizaka, K., Ishizaka, T. and Lee, E. H., Immunochemistry, In press.
4. Tada, T. and Ishizaka, K., J. Immun., *104:* 377, 1970.
5. Ishizaka, T., Ishizaka, K., Orange, R. P. and Austen, K. F., J. Immun., *104:* 335, 1970.
6. Avrameas, S. and Ternynck, T., Immunochemistry, *6:* 53, 1969.
7. McConahy, P. J. and Dixon, F. J., Int. Arch. Allerg., *99:* 185, 1966.
8. Johansson, S. G. O., Bennich, H. and Wide, L., Immunology, *14:* 265, 1968.
9. Lichtenstein, L. M. and Osler, A. G., J. Exp. Med., *120:* 507, 1964.
10. King, T. P., Norman, P. S. and Cornell, J. T., Biochemistry, *3:* 458, 1964.

11. LoBuglio, A. F., Cotran, R. S. and Jandl, J. H., Science, *158:* 1582, 1967.
12. Huber, H. and Fudenberg, H., Int. Arch. Allerg., *34:* 18, 1968.
13. Huber, H., Polley, M. J., Linscott, W. D., Fudenberg, H. and Müller-Eberhard, H. J., Science, *162:* 1281, 1968.
14. Sell, S., J. Exp. Med., *125:* 289, 1967.
15. Sell, S., J. Exp. Med., *125:* 393, 1967.
16. Graham, H. T., Lowry, O. H., Wheelwright, F., Lenz, A. M. and Parish, H. H., Blood, *10:* 467, 1955.
17. Pruzansky, J. J. and Patterson, R., Int. Arch. Allerg., *37:* 98, 1970.
18. Lichtenstein, L. M., Levy, D. A. and Ishizaka, K., Immunology, In press.
19. Levy, D. A., Chen, J. L. and Ishizaka, K., Fed. Proc., *29:* 575 (Abstract), 1970.
20. Lichtenstein, L. M. and Margolis, S., Science, *161:* 902, 1968.

THE JOURNAL OF IMMUNOLOGY
Vol. 105, No. 6, December 1970

MECHANISMS OF ENDOTOXIN TOLERANCE

VII. The Role of the Liver[1]

SHELDON E. GREISMAN[2] AND CELESTE L. WOODWARD

From the Departments of Medicine and Physiology, University of Maryland School of Medicine, Baltimore, Maryland

Received for publication June 25, 1970

Immunologic mechanisms contribute to the development of pyrogenic tolerance to bacterial endotoxins. The present studies test the concept that the hepatic Kupffer cell is the "target" tissue protected by these immune mechanisms.

The pyrogenic response of healthy acclimatized New Zealand rabbits to a purified *Escherichia coli* endotoxin administered by ear vein was characterized by a classic biphasic febrile response, an initial early phase (60- to 90-min peak) and a later second phase (180-min peak). Tolerance induced by repetitive daily ear vein administration of the endotoxin resulted in ablation of the second febrile phase, but only minimal reductions of the early phase. These responses were then contrasted with those induced when the *E. coli* endotoxin was presented directly to the hepatic Kupffer cell by perfusion through chronically implanted hepatic portal venous cannulae.

Direct hepatic perfusion with endotoxin resulted in diminution or ablation of the early phase of fever in both non-tolerant and tolerant animals. This effect was seen in 3 of 12 non-tolerant and all of 21 tolerant animals. Reticuloendothelial blockade with thorotrast consistently restored the early fever phase following portal vein administration of the endotoxin in the tolerant animals. In contrast to the early febrile response, direct hepatic perfusion with endotoxin enhanced the second febrile phase in the non-tolerant animals; the second febrile phase, however, remained markedly inhibited in 17 of the 21 tolerant animals tested.

Analysis of these findings indicates: 1) extra-hepatic mechanisms dominate the first phase of the biphasic febrile response to bacterial endotoxin in the rabbit, 2) hepatic mechanisms dominate the second phase of the biphasic febrile response to endotoxin, 3) the liver of the tolerant rabbit clears directly perfused endotoxin more efficiently than the liver of the non-tolerant animal and 4) despite the more efficient uptake of directly perfused endotoxin by the liver of the tolerant rabbit, the second phase of fever usually remains markedly inhibited.

The findings fully support the concept that tolerance to the pyrogenic activity of bacterial endotoxin is based upon increased uptake of the toxin by hepatic Kupffer cells which have become refractory to further release of endogenous pyrogen.

It has long been recognized that intravenous administration of bacterial endotoxins into laboratory animals or man results in increasing resistance to its pyrogenic and toxic activities. The evolution of such resistance to the fever-producing activity of endotoxin has been recently shown to involve two temporally distinct phases. The early phase, occurring within hours, appears to be mediated by development of specific refractoriness at the cellular level; the subsequent mechanisms involve the elaboration of transferable protective humoral factors, including anti-"O" antibodies (1–4). The present studies are concerned with defining the "target" cells responsible for pyrogenic tolerance, i.e., the cell population that is initially rendered specifically refractory to endotoxin and then subsequently

[1] This work was supported by United States Public Health Service Research Grant AI-07052 and by the Frank C. Bressler Research Fund.

[2] Recipient of Research Career Award 2-K3-HE-15,237 from the National Institutes of Health.

protected by the elaboration of the humoral factors.

Considerable experimental evidence indicates that fever induced by bacterial endotoxin is mediated by release of intermediate tissue pyrogens which act upon the thermoregulatory centers of the hypothalamus (5–7). For a number of years, the granulocyte was considered the exclusive source of intermediate tissue pyrogen (endogenous pyrogen) released by endotoxin (5, 8). Subsequently, however, isolated peritoneal and lung macrophages of rabbits and blood monocytes of man also were found capable of elaborating an endogenous pyrogen when stimulated *in vitro* with endotoxin (9–11). In 1964, Fukuda and Murata (12, 13), utilizing extracts of liver obtained from dogs after intravenous typhoid vaccine administration, concluded that endotoxin fever was mediated by release of an hepatic pyrogen, and that endotoxin tolerance was associated with failure of such release. These findings, however, were hardly convincing since no precautions were taken to exclude participation of contaminating blood leucocytes in the hepatic preparations. In 1968, Dinarello, Bodel, and Atkins (14) demonstrated that isolated suspensions of rabbit hepatic Kupffer cells released significant quantities of endogenous pyrogen when incubated *in vitro* with bacterial endotoxin, and that such release was markedly diminished if the Kupffer cells were incubated with serum from tolerant donors or obtained from endotoxin tolerant animals. These investigators postulated that the Kupffer cell may play a key role in the pathogenesis of endotoxin fever, and that increased uptake of endotoxin by such cells that have become refractory to the endotoxin may account for pyrogenic tolerance. The present studies were designed to assess critically the role of the Kupffer cell as the "target" tissue in endotoxin tolerance by examining the pyrogenic response of acclimatized rabbits to bacterial endotoxin perfused directly through the liver via chronically implanted hepatic portal venous catheters.

MATERIALS AND METHODS

Syringes, needles and glassware were either of the sterile, pyrogen-free disposable type (Becton, Dickinson, and Co., Rutherford, N. J.) or were heated overnight in a dry air oven at 200°C to eliminate extraneous pyrogens.

Hepatic portal vein cannulation. Healthy New Zealand albino rabbits weighing approximately 2 kg and obtained from a uniform source were anesthetized with sterile, pyrogen-free pentobarbital (Diabutal, Diamond Laboratories, Inc., Des Moines, Iowa). The shaven abdominal wall was prepared with 2% tincture iodine and 70% alcohol and covered with sterile drapes, and the colon was exposed through an abdominal incision utilizing aseptic technique and instruments previously heated overnight in a dry air oven at 200°C. A fine polyethylene catheter (PE 10, Clay Adams Inc., N. Y.), previously rinsed repeatedly both internally and externally with alcohol and then with pyrogen-free sterile saline, was inserted into a small mesenteric vein and threaded proximally until the tip of the cannula lay adjacent to the liver. Intravascular catheter positioning was checked by repeated aspiration and flushing of blood samples, and the cannula was then tied in place at its insertion into the mesenteric vein. The free end of the cannula was brought out of the abdomen by threading it through an 18-gauge sterile needle inserted into the lateral abdominal wall. The cannula was filled with sterile, pyrogen-free saline and sealed, the wound was closed with sterile silk sutures and the cannula and wound were covered with a plastic dressing. Sutures were removed after 7 days; the plastic dressing was replaced to protect the cannula. After 4 weeks of convalescence, the protective plastic dressing was removed and the animals were acclimatized for pyrogen studies.

Pyrogen assay. Animals were loosely restrained by chain collars in Fiberglas stalls and acclimatized for 18 to 24 hr in an air-conditioned room at 70°F. Thermistor probes were inserted 6 in. into the rectum and connected to a recording telethermometer (Yellow Springs Instrument Co., Yellow Springs, Ohio). Temperatures were monitored 1 to 2 hr before each study; animals exhibiting initial temperatures greater than 104°F or varying more than 0.3°F in any 30-min control period were excluded. Mean fever curves were constructed by averaging the temperature increments at each 30-min period after endotoxin injection. The bacterial endotoxin employed was a Boivin type preparation of *Escherichia coli* endotoxin, 0127B8 (Difco Laboratories, Detroit, Mich.) suspended in pyrogen-free, sterile saline. The endotoxin, contained in 2 ml/kg volumes, was warmed to 39°C and infused over a 2-min

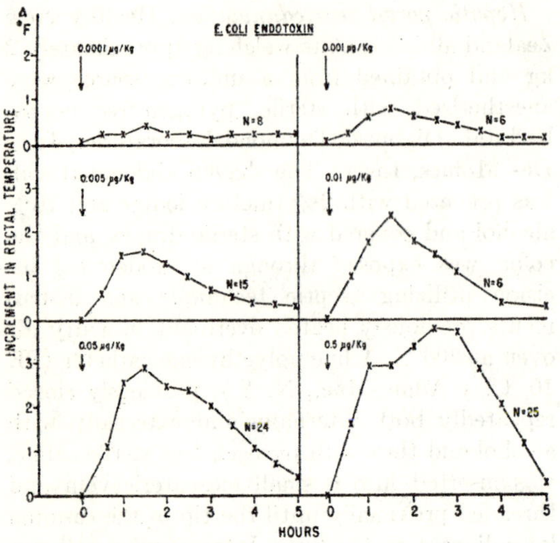

Figure 1. Relationship of mean febrile response to dosage of *E. coli* endotoxin administered by *ear vein* to healthy acclimatized groups of non-tolerant New Zealand rabbits.

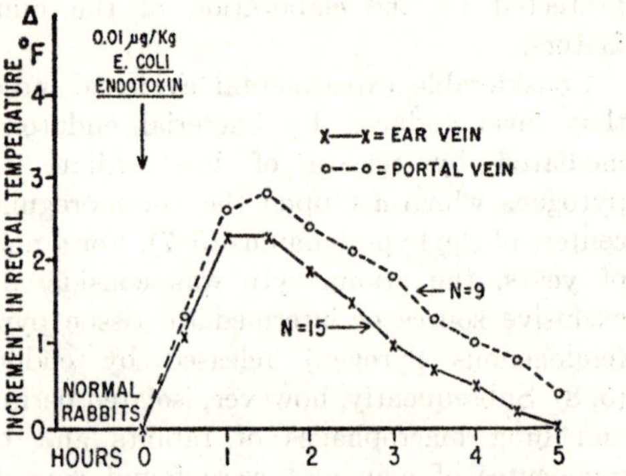

Figure 2. Comparative mean febrile responses to 0.01 µg/kg *E. coli* endotoxin administered via ear vein and via chronically implanted hepatic portal venous cannulae in healthy non-tolerant rabbits.

period. Residual endotoxin in the portal vein cannula was flushed into the animal with pyrogen-free sterile saline. In preliminary studies, endotoxin dose-response relationships, with respect to ear vein administration, were carefully defined (Fig. 1).

Upon completion of each series of studies, proper portal venous catheter placement was checked by infusion of 10 ml of 1% trypan blue. Animals exhibiting leakage of dye into the peritoneal cavity or mesentery were excluded. Characteristically, in those animals accepted for inclusion in the study, intense bluing of the liver occurred upon infusion of trypan blue through the portal venous cannula, with minimal bluing of extra-hepatic organs. The striking contrast to the intense blue staining of all tissues, liver and extra-hepatic, following ear vein administration of trypan blue provided a vivid illustration of the phagocytic efficiency of the liver when directly presented with the colloidal dye.

RESULTS

Portal vein infusion of endotoxin into non-tolerant animals. To analyze the influence of direct perfusion of the normal liver with bacterial endotoxin on the febrile response, it is necessary to avoid overwhelming the clearance capabilities of this organ. Otherwise, uncleared endotoxin will enter the general circulation and induce effects upon extra-hepatic sites that could mask the hepatic effects of the toxin. Therefore, the smallest test dose of *E. coli* endotoxin (0.01 µg/kg) capable of evoking both an early (60- to 90-min) and an unequivocal late febrile response (1°F at 180 min) was employed for the non-tolerant animal studies (see Fig. 1). Figure 2 illustrates that infusion of this test dose of endotoxin via the portal venous cannula evoked a febrile response in 9 of 12 animals tested which retained the same general contour as that seen in 15 control animals given the endotoxin by ear vein; the magnitude of the febrile response, however, in terms of fever area was 33% greater after portal vein infusion. From dose-response data, Figure 1, it is apparent that the animals responded to the endotoxin perfused directly through the liver as would be expected had they received fivefold greater quantities (i.e., 0.05 µg/kg) of the endotoxin by ear vein. It is also apparent that this increment in febrile response was expressed primarily in the later (post 60 min) portion of the fever curve. Three of the 12 non-tolerant animals tested by injection of the endotoxin via portal vein cannulae exhibited no febrile response for the initial 60 to 90 min (Fig. 3); a febrile response then ensued resembling, after the 2nd hr, the augmented late reaction seen in the previous 9 non-tolerant animals given the endotoxin by portal vein infusion. The absence of the initial 60-min febrile response after the portal vein infusion of endotoxin was not based upon a nonspecific refractory state, because re-injection of the endotoxin via ear vein

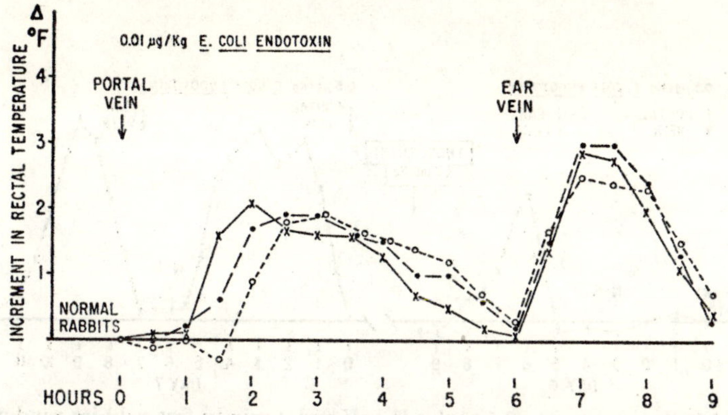

Figure 3. **Febrile responses to 0.01 μg/kg *E. coli* endotoxin administered via chronically implanted portal venous cannulae, and then via ear vein in three additional healthy non-tolerant rabbits.**

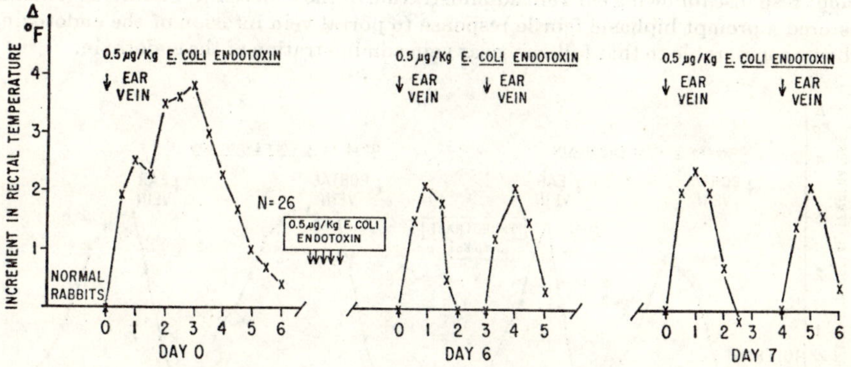

Figure 4. Initial biphasic and subsequent tolerant monophasic febrile response patterns following daily ear vein injections of 0.5 μg/kg *E. coli* endotoxin in healthy control rabbits.

evoked a brisk febrile response within 60 min, Figure 3.

The above findings demonstrate that when compared to ear vein administration, direct hepatic perfusion of endotoxin into non-tolerant animals can a) inhibit the early or initial 60-min febrile phase and b) augment the later phase of the febrile response to this toxin. Since the inhibition of the early febrile phase after portal vein infusion of endotoxin could be reversed by re-administering the toxin by ear vein, such inhibition must be based upon sequestration of the endotoxin by the liver. The corollary of this conclusion is that the augmentation of the later febrile response is also related to hepatic sequestration of the endotoxin. These basic premises are fully supported by the subsequent studies performed in tolerant animals.

Portal vein infusion of endotoxin into tolerant animals. To analyze the influence of direct perfusion of the tolerant animal liver with bacterial endotoxin, it was necessary to first establish the pattern of the tolerant febrile response to the endotoxin administered by ear vein, Figure 4. Employing 0.5 μg/kg *E. coli* endotoxin, a classic biphasic febrile response was initially elicited after ear vein administration which fell within the sensitive portion of the dose-response range (see Fig. 1). On days 6 and 7 following daily ear vein administration of the endotoxin, only the early fever phase was evident, reduced slightly in magnitude compared to the initial early response. Re-administration of the endotoxin by ear vein after the monophasic fever had subsided re-evoked a comparable monophasic response.

A second group of 21 animals was now rendered tolerant as in the above studies by daily ear vein administration of 0.5 μg/kg *E. coli* endotoxin. However, testing in this group was performed on day 6 by administration of the endotoxin by

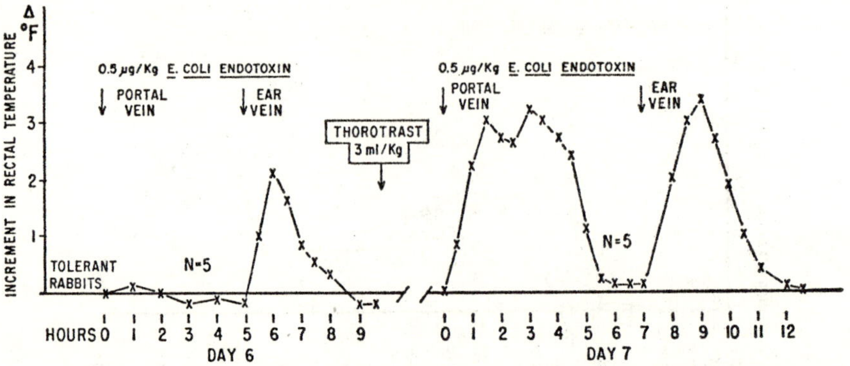

Figure 5. Mean febrile response to 0.5 μg/kg *E. coli* endotoxin in five rabbits rendered tolerant by six prior daily ear vein injections of toxin. The endotoxin on day 6 was administered via chronically implanted portal vein cannulae. Note complete absence of a febrile response, in contrast to the characteristic prompt response following ear vein administration of the endotoxin. Thorotrast administered via ear vein restored a prompt biphasic febrile response to portal vein infusion of the endotoxin, the early phase now being comparable to that following ear vein administration of the endotoxin.

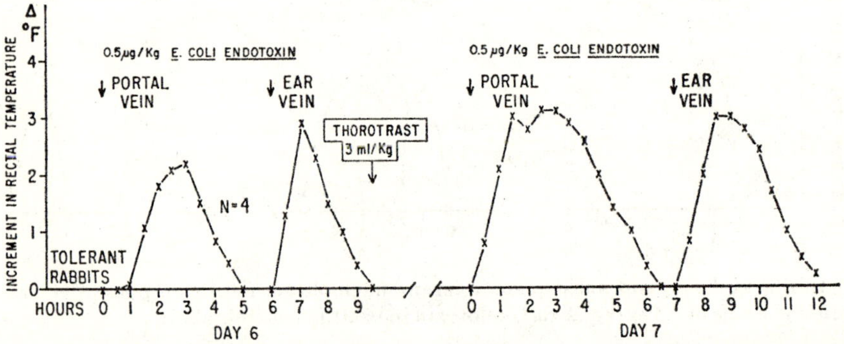

Figure 6. Mean febrile response to 0.5 μg/kg *E. coli* endotoxin in four rabbits rendered tolerant as in Figure 5. The endotoxin on day 6 was administered via chronically implanted portal vein cannulae. Note the absence of the early febrile response, but development of an unequivocal delayed febrile response. In contrast, note the prompt response to ear vein administration of the endotoxin. The effect of Thorotrast is similar to that described in Figure 5.

portal vein cannulae. Three general types of febrile responses were seen. 1) Five animals exhibited no febrile response, Figure 5. In contrast, re-administration of the endotoxin by ear vein evoked a brisk monophasic fever. Thorotrast (3 ml/kg) was then injected by ear vein, and the following day the endotoxin was re-perfused via the portal vein cannula. A prompt biphasic febrile response ensued, the early febrile phase now being comparable to that produced by ear vein administration of the toxin. 2) Four tolerant rabbits given the endotoxin by portal vein cannula exhibited no febrile response during the initial 60 min. A substantial response then ensued, peaking at 3 hr, Figure 6. In contrast, re-administration of the endotoxin by ear vein evoked a prompt febrile response which attained its peak at 60 min. Thorotrast was then given by ear vein; the following day, portal vein administration of the endotoxin evoked the same febrile response pattern seen in group 1 animals. 3) In 12 tolerant animals, portal vein infusion of the endotoxin evoked prompt monophasic fevers; the responses, however, were consistently lower in amplitude than those produced after ear vein administration of the endotoxin, Figure 7. Portal vein administration of the endotoxin after Thorotrast had been given by ear vein resulted in the same febrile response pattern observed in the previous groups.

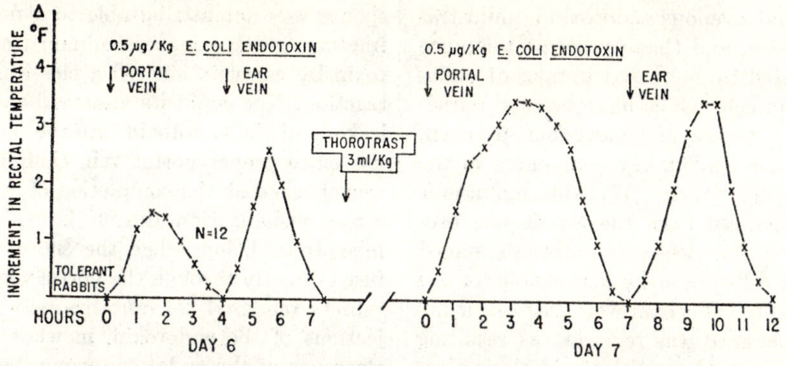

Figure 7. Mean febrile response to 0.5 µg/kg *E. coli* endotoxin in 12 rabbits rendered tolerant as in Figure 5. The endotoxin on day 6 was administered via chronically implanted portal vein cannulae. Note the prompt monophasic fever which, however, was consistently lower in amplitude than that evoked after ear vein administration of the toxin. The effect of Thorotrast is similar to that described in Figure 5.

It is apparent from the above data that the febrile responses of tolerant rabbits to direct hepatic perfusion of endotoxin are consistently and appreciably modified from those seen after ear vein administration of the toxin. It is also apparent that Thorotrast markedly alters the febrile response pattern following portal vein administration of the endotoxin. The significance of these findings will now be considered.

DISCUSSION

The acquisition of pyrogenic tolerance to bacterial endotoxin in the rabbit involves two temporally distinct mechanisms. Tolerance that appears within hours is directly related to endotoxin dosage, is not associated with increments in anti-"O" antibody titers and exhibits no inter-endotoxin specificity (3). Such tolerance, however, is not simply a generalized refractory state. When small doses (under 1 µg) of endotoxin are employed, this early tolerance is specific, i.e., full responsiveness persists to heterologous pyrogens such as influenza virus, old tuberculin, and staphylococcal enterotoxin B (2, 3). Since plasma at this time transfers no detectable tolerance, and since large amounts of fresh whole blood fail to restore responsiveness, it was concluded that this rapidly acquired phase of tolerance is mediated by a specific cellular refractory state, and that the refractory target cell is not the granulocyte (2). Whether the refractory state represents an immunologic desensitization to a common toxophore antigen or simply a pharmacologic depletion of susceptible target cells (2, 3) remains to be determined. The second or late phase of pyrogenic tolerance develops several days after endotoxin injection. When a single intravenous immunizing injection is employed, this late phase of tolerance is in large part specific for the particular immunizing endotoxin preparation and is dependent upon its "O" antigenicity (3). Thus two distinct mechanisms, cellular "desensitization" and anti-"O" antibody, appear to contribute to acquired resistance to bacterial endotoxins (2–4). In addition, a third mechanism is involved. In immunosuppressed (6-mercaptopurine treated or splenectomized) rabbits, transferable humoral tolerance factors appear after several days of daily intravenous endotoxin injections despite the absence of detectable increments in anti-"O" antibodies (15, 16). The nature of such humoral factors will be the subject of a later report. The present studies are concerned with the target cells responsible for pyrogenic tolerance, i.e., the cell population that is initially rendered specifically refractory to endotoxin and subsequently protected by anti-"O" antibody and the accompanying other humoral factors.

It is presently well established that fever following intravenous administration of bacterial endotoxin in several animal species is mediated by an endogenous pyrogen released from host tissues (5). This material enters the circulation and appears to evoke fever by acting upon the thermoregulatory centers of the hypothalamus (6, 7). On the basis of a series of remarkable *in vitro* studies, Dinarello, Bodel, and Atkins (14) recently suggested that the hepatic Kupffer cell may comprise a major source of endogenous pyrogen after intravenous endotoxin administration in the rabbit, and that pyrogenic tolerance may be mediated by increased uptake of endotoxin by Kupffer cells which have become refractory to further release of endogenous pyrogen. Since the Kupffer cell is a key component of the reticuloendothelial system (17), this hypothesis differs fundamentally from the classic one proposed by Beeson. The Beeson hypothesis assumed that the target cells primarily responsible for the febrile response to endotoxin were extra-reticuloendothelial; tolerance was regarded as resulting simply from enhanced uptake of circulating endotoxin by the reticuloendothelial system, thus diverting the toxin from the primary target sites (18).

To evaluate the importance of the Kupffer cell in the pyrogenic response to endotoxin, the toxin was presented directly to these reticuloendothelial cells by perfusion through chronically implanted hepatic portal venous cannulae. Selection of the proper endotoxin test dose and interpretation of the results were guided by the following basic principles derived from numerous control studies employing the *ear vein* route of toxin administration. a) Small quantities of purified endotoxin consistently evoke a rapidly appearing, monophasic fever, peaking at 1 to 1.5 hr; b) larger doses of endotoxin evoke a second fever peak, yielding the classical biphasic febrile response; this second or late febrile phase interrupts the waning early response at 1.5 to 2 hr and attains its peak at approximately 3 hr; c) repetitive daily injections of endotoxin rapidly evoke tolerance, characterized by ablation of the second febrile peak with only minor reductions in the first peak, i.e., tolerance to purified toxin is expressed primarily by inhibition of the second or late phase of the febrile response.

When the smallest dose of *E. coli* endotoxin capable, upon injection by ear vein, of eliciting both an early and an unequivocal late temperature elevation was perfused directly through chronically implanted portal vein cannulae of 12 healthy non-tolerant acclimatized rabbits, a latent period of 1 hr elapsed before any temperature elevation ensued in 3 of the animals. Such ablation of the early phase of the febrile response was never observed during previous studies in hundreds of normal acclimatized rabbits given comparable doses of the same endotoxin preparation by ear vein. The absence of the early febrile response was not attributable to a nonspecific refractory state, since re-administration of the toxin by ear vein elicited a classical brisk early reaction. Nor could its absence be attributed to leakage of the endotoxin into the peritoneal cavity, since proper portal vein cannula placement was checked at the completion of the studies by direct visualization during infusion of trypan blue. In addition, when the endotoxin was perfused directly through the portal vein of 21 other rabbits rendered tolerant by daily ear vein injections of the endotoxin, in whom the hepatic clearance of the endotoxin would be expected to be more efficient than in the non-tolerant group (19), the initial 60-min febrile response was reduced or entirely prevented in all animals. When these tolerant animals were then given the endotoxin by ear vein, the classical initial brisk 60-min febrile response was restored. Since direct hepatic perfusion of endotoxin was capable of inhibiting the initial 60-min febrile response in both normal and tolerant animals, it is concluded that the early febrile phase of the biphasic fever that characterizes the response to endotoxin administration by ear vein is based primarily upon an effect of the toxin on extra-hepatic mechanisms. Critical additional support for this conclusion was obtained by blocking (with thorotrast) hepatic uptake of the endotoxin perfused through the portal vein catheter; the blunted or absent early febrile phase was thereby consistently restored, and was now comparable to the response elicited by ear vein infusion of the toxin.

The extra-hepatic mechanisms responsible for the prompt febrile response after ear vein administration of endotoxin are not known. Endogenous pyrogen release from granulocytic and monocytic cells appears most likely (5, 9–11), but the contribution of a direct action of the endotoxin on the thermoregulatory portions of the central nervous system remains a distinct possibility (20).

In contrast to the initial 60-min febrile response, the later or second phase of the febrile response was not inhibited when the endotoxin was perfused directly through the portal venous cannulae. Indeed, in the non-tolerant rabbits, the second febrile phase was actually greater following portal vein perfusion of endotoxin than in control animals given the same dose of toxin by ear vein. From dose-response data, the hepatic-perfused animals responded with respect to the late phase of fever as would be expected had they been given approximately five times the dose of endotoxin by ear vein. Moreover, those non-tolerant animals that exhibited no febrile response during the initial 60 min after direct hepatic perfusion of endotoxin also exhibited enhanced later febrile responses. These findings are especially important for two reasons. First, as discussed above, the absence of the initial fever phase after portal vein infusion denotes enhanced sequestration of the directly perfused endotoxin by the liver, and thus more definitively implicates this organ as the mediator of the augmented late febrile reaction. Second, a biphasic febrile response can be elicited by large amounts of endogenous pyrogen, i.e., endogenous pyrogen *per se* can induce not only a prompt fever, but also a late febrile response, apparently by mobilizing a second wave of endogenous pyrogen (5, 21–23). The absence of a prompt febrile response therefore indicates that the augmented late febrile response can be related directly to the hepatic sequestration of toxin, and not to a second wave of endogenous pyrogen mobilized in response to an initial wave from extra-hepatic sources. The above considerations point to two distinct mechanisms for the biphasic febrile response induced by bacterial endotoxins in the rabbit, one rapidly acting and extra-hepatic, the other slower in onset and hepatic in origin. The subsequent considerations illustrate how this hypothesis supports the concept of the "target" role of the Kupffer cell in endotoxin tolerance.

As already indicated, tolerance after repetitive single daily ear vein injections of purified bacterial endotoxin is characterized by reduction in the second phase of fever with only minimal reductions in the early phase. Rabbits with chronically implanted portal vein cannulae, rendered tolerant to endotoxin such that only the early monophasic fevers were evoked by ear vein injections, responded to the same dose of endotoxin administered via portal venous cannulae in one of three ways: 1) no febrile response; 2) a small prompt monophasic fever; or 3) a slowly evolving fever, beginning after a latent period of 60 min and peaking near 3 hr. In group 1 animals, the absence of any initial 60-min febrile response indicates that the endotoxin failed to reach the systemic circulation in physiologically active amounts, because subsequent re-administration of the endotoxin by ear vein consistently elicited a brisk febrile response within 60 min. Such findings not only clearly demonstrate the ability of hepatic cells to inhibit the early febrile response to endotoxin, but also illustrate the high endotoxin extraction efficiency of the liver of these tolerant animals. The absence of any later fever denotes that the hepatic cells which sequestered the directly perfused endotoxin, in contrast to the non-tolerant animals, were refractory and released no detectable endogenous pyrogen. In group 2 animals, exhibiting a small prompt monophasic febrile response, the ability of the liver to clear the endotoxin during its first hepatic passage was apparently not sufficiently enhanced to prevent some toxin from reaching the systemic circulation and evoking a detectable early response; diversion of the endotoxin through collateral channels may have contributed to this result. Nevertheless, in contrast to the majority of non-tolerant animals, this initial 60-min febrile response was always less than that elicited when the endotoxin was injected via ear vein, indicating at least some enhancement of hepatic sequestration of the toxin. The minimal fever at 3 hr, as in group 1 animals, again demonstrates that despite the enhanced uptake of endotoxin, tolerant hepatic cells are refractory and release minimal endogenous pyrogen. In the group 3 animals, the absence of fever during the initial 60 min further demonstrates the high efficiency of the tolerant liver in sequestering the portal vein infused endotoxin, because subsequent ear vein perfusion of the toxin evoked the classical brisk 60-min febrile response. However, from the later pyrogenic response, peaking at 3 hr, it can be inferred that the sequestered endotoxin remained capable of initiating the release of some hepatic pyrogen. An alternative possibility, that the sequestered endotoxin was released from the liver after the initial hour and then acted upon extra-hepatic tissues, is unlikely from kinetic studies of radioactively labeled endotoxin distribution in tolerant rabbits (19). Another alternative, that the late febrile response was mediated by mobilization of a second wave of endogenous pyrogen in response to an initial wave generated from extra-hepatic tissues, is excluded by the absence of any initial febrile response (5, 21–23). Presumably, therefore, the hepatic cells in the group 3 animals were not as completely refractory to endotoxin as were those in the previous groups of tolerant animals, and such observations provide important additional support for the participation of the liver in the pathogenesis of the second phase of the biphasic febrile response to bacterial endotoxin.

Thorotrast administration consistently led to re-appearance (or enhancement) of the second phase of the biphasic febrile response in all groups of tolerant animals given the endotoxin by portal vein cannulae. The mechanisms underlying such resurgence of the second febrile phase are not defined. The phenomenon might be related to abrogation of hepatic Kupffer cell refractoriness by Thorotrast, or alternatively, to "blockade" of the Kupffer cell with consequent diversion of the endotoxin to those extra-hepatic tissues that remain responsive to endotoxin despite tolerance induction as demonstrated by Dinarello, Bodel and Atkins (14). Presently available evidence (1, 14, 24) supports this latter interpretation, and studies to confirm this mechanism of Thorotrast action are currently in progress.

The present findings, considered together with earlier observations that the liver clears the major portion of circulating endotoxin, even after ear vein administration (19), provide the basis for four fundamental principles: 1) extra-hepatic mechanisms dominate the first phase of the biphasic febrile response to endotoxin; 2) hepatic mechanims dominate the second phase of the biphasic febrile response to endotoxin; 3) the liver of the tolerant rabbit clears directly perfused endotoxin more efficiently than the liver of the non-tolerant animal; and 4) despite the more efficient uptake of directly perfused endotoxin by the liver of the tolerant rabbit, the second phase of fever usually remains markedly inhibited. These *in vivo* findings fully support the concept of Dinarello, Bodel and Atkins (14) that tolerance to the pyrogenic activity of bacterial endotoxin is based upon increased uptake of the toxin by hepatic Kupffer cells which have become refractory to further release of endogenous pyrogen.

REFERENCES

1. Greisman, S. E. and Woodward, W. E., J. Exp. Med., *121:* 911, 1965.
2. Greisman, S. E., Young, E. J. and Woodward, W. E., J. Exp. Med., *124:* 983, 1966.
3. Greisman, S. E., Young, E. J. and Carozza, F. A., Jr., J. Immun., *103:* 1223, 1969.
4. Greisman, S. E. and Young, E. J., J. Immun., *103:* 1237, 1969.
5. Atkins, E., Physiol. Rev., *40:* 580, 1960.
6. Jackson, D. L., J. Neurophysiol., *30:* 586, 1967.
7. Cooper, K. E., Cranston, W. I. and Honour, A. J., J. Physiol., *191:* 325, 1967.
8. Herion, J. C., Walker, R. I. and Palmer, J. G., J. Exp. Med., *113:* 1115, 1961.
9. Atkins, E., Bodel, P. and Francis, L., J. Exp. Med., *126:* 357, 1967.
10. Hahn, H. H., Char, D. C., Postel, W. B. and Wood, W. B., Jr., J. Exp. Med., *126:* 385, 1967.
11. Bodel, P. T. and Atkins, E., New England J. Med., *276:* 1002, 1967.
12. Fukuda, T. and Murata, K., Nature, *204:* 690, 1964.
13. Fukuda, T. and Murata, K., Jap. J. Physiol., *15:* 169, 1965.
14. Dinarello, C. A., Bodel, P. T. and Atkins, E., Trans. Assoc. Amer. Physicians, *81:* 334, 1968.
15. Wolff, S. M., Mulholland, J. H., Ward, S. B., Rubenstein, M. and Mott, P. D., J. Clin. Invest., *44:* 1402, 1965.
16. Carozza, F. A., Jr., Young, E. J., Workman, J. B. and Greisman, S. E., J. Reticuloendothel. Soc., *5:* 574, 1968.
17. Benacerraf, B., Biozzi, G., Halpern, B. N. and Stiffel, C., in *Physiopathology of the Reticuloendothelial System*, Edited by B. N. Halpern, p. 52, Blackwell Scientific Publications, Oxford, 1957.
18. Beeson, P. B., J. Exp. Med., *86:* 39, 1947.
19. Carey, F. J., Braude, A. I. and Zalesky, M., J. Clin. Invest., *37:* 441, 1958.
20. Bennett, I. L., Jr., Petersdorf, R. G. and Keene, W. R., Trans. Assoc. Amer. Physicians, *70:* 64, 1957.
21. Atkins, E. and Huang, W. C., J. Exp. Med., *107:* 415, 1958.
22. Moses, J. M. and Atkins, E., J. Exp. Med., *114:* 939, 1961.
23. Bornstein, D. L., Bredenberg, C. and Wood, W. B., Jr., J. Exp. Med., *117:* 349, 1963.
24. Greisman, S. E., Carozza, F. A., Jr. and Hills, J. D., J. Exp. Med., *117:* 663, 1963.

THE JOURNAL OF IMMUNOLOGY
Vol. 105, No. 6, December 1970
Printed in U.S.A.

SPECIFICITY OF RESPIRATORY SECRETION ANTIBODY AGAINST INFLUENZA VIRUS[1]

R. H. WALDMAN, F. M. WIGLEY AND P. A. SMALL, JR.

From the Departments of Medicine and Microbiology, University of Florida College of Medicine, Gainesville, Florida 32601

Received for publication June 25, 1970

Serum, sputum and nasal secretion neutralizing antibody rises were measured against A_2/Taiwan/64, A_2/Hong Kong/68 and A/PR8 influenza viruses and parainfluenza type 1 virus in volunteers who had been immunized with A_2/Taiwan/64 virus. There was approximately an eightfold rise in sputum, nasal wash and serum antibody to the homologous virus, and no rise to parainfluenza type 1 virus. There was no serum antibody rise to A/PR8 or A_2/Hong Kong viruses, but in sputum and nasal washing there was approximately a three- to fourfold rise. Absorption studies with homologous and heterologous virus indicate that the heterologous response is due mainly to cross-reacting antibody. This could mean that secretory IgA is less specific than serum IgG. If these findings are substantiated for other viruses, it is possible that protection against a broad range of viruses may be inducible with fewer vaccines than would be expected on the basis of serologic studies.

It has been shown that respiratory secretion antibody is important in mediating protection against several viruses that infect the respiratory tract (1, 2). Respiratory secretion antibody to influenza virus has been effectively stimulated by aerosol immunization (3, 4) and this method has been shown to lead to protection during an influenza epidemic (5, 6). Antigenic changes in the influenza viruses frequently occur; however, these changes have always been based on tests made with serum antibody. Since the antibody that protects against influenza virus infection may be that located in respiratory secretions, this study was undertaken to compare the degree of specificity of respiratory secretion antibody and serum antibody.

MATERIALS AND METHODS

Volunteers. Male prisoner volunteers aged 20 to 40 years were from the Florida State Prison at Raiford. They were healthy in every way except that they all smoked and could produce, with varying amounts of difficulty, some early morning sputum.

Vaccine. Vaccine was commercially available formalin-inactivated bivalent influenza vaccine[2] in general use in 1967–1968. The vaccine contained 300 chick-cell agglutination (CCA) units of A_2 (Asian) strains (150 CCA units each of A_2/Japan/170/62 and A_2/Taiwan/1/64 influenza virus) and 300 CCA units of a B strain/0.5 ml.

Specimens. Nasal washings were obtained as previously described (7). In brief, 10 ml of phosphate-buffered saline, pH 7.4, was instilled into the posterior nose and forcefully expelled. The fluid contained various amounts of mucus. The supernatant fluid was homogenized, centrifuged, and then used for antibody and immunoglobulin determinations.

Early morning expectorations of sputum were collected in sterile cups during spontaneous coughing and then frozen at −20°C. A few drops of 0.1% sodium azide were added to inhibit bacterial growth. The sputum was dialyzed for 24 to 48 hr with distilled water and homogenized in tissue grinders (8). Enough phosphate-buffered saline, pH 7.4, was added during homogenization to obtain a homogenate of sufficiently low viscosity so that centrifugation at 2000 rpm for 30 min separated the homogenate into two phases. The amount of saline added resulted in a 50 to 100% dilution of the specimen. The supernatant fluid was used for antibody and immunoglobulin determinations. All specimens of nasal washings and sputum were heated for 30 min at 56°C

[1] This work was supported by Army Grant DADA17-69-C-9179, NIH Grant 5TIAI0128-10 and The Irwin Strasburger Foundation.

[2] Zonimmune was kindly provided by Eli Lilly and Co., Indianapolis.

before antibody determinations to reduce the possibility of bacterial contamination.

Immunization procedure. Twenty-five hundredths milliliter of vaccine was sprayed into the posterior oropharynx during rapid, deep inspiration. This was followed by a spray of 0.125 ml into each nostril with a DeVilbiss No. 286 atomizer which emits particles averaging 40 μ in diameter.[3]

Absorption of antibody with virus. Five-tenths-milliliter samples of pooled nasal secretions or sputum specimens, concentrated by positive pressure dialysis, were mixed with an equal volume of concentrated monovalent A_2 vaccine, concentrated monovalent Hong Kong vaccine, or saline. The vaccines were concentrated by centrifugation at 40,000 rpm in a Beckman model L2-65B ultracentrifuge for 10 min and resuspension in $\frac{1}{10}$ of the original volume. The mixtures were incubated for 30 min at 37°C, overnight at 4°C, and then centrifuged as above. The sediment was discarded and the supernatant was analyzed for virus neutralizing activity.

Immunoglobulin determinations. The quantity of immunoglobulin was measured by the single radial diffusion precipitin method in agar (9). Specific antisera to serum IgA (WHO M-21-E) IgG (M-19-B), and IgM (M-24-B) were used at a final concentration of 1:50 in the agar, giving a sensitivity of 0.01 mg/ml. The WHO standard serum (67/97) was used.

Removal of IgA and IgG by precipitation with specific antisera. Specific antisera (described immediately above) were added in small increments to samples until no further precipitate could be detected (10).

Hemadsorption-inhibition-neutralizing activity. Specimens were tested against 32 to 320 $TCID_{50}$ of A_2/Taiwan/1/64 (A_2), A_2/Hong Kong/8/68 (HK), and A/PR8 (A_0) influenza viruses, and parainfluenza type 1 virus (Para), by the neutralization test previously described (11).

RESULTS

Antibody titers. The virus neutralizing antibody titers against the homologous and heterologous virus strains are shown in Tables I and II and summarized in Figure 1. There was a significant (fourfold or greater) rise in serum antibody titer against A_2 in 16 of the 17 volunteers, in 1 of 17 against HK, but in none of the same sera against A_0 or Para. There was a mean rise in serum titer of 8-fold against A_2, 1.1-fold against HK, 1.0-fold against A_0, and 1.0-fold against Para.

In sputum there was a significant rise in titer against A_2 in all of the 17 volunteers; against HK there was a significant sputum antibody rise in 10 of 17, against A_0 in 8 of 17, and against Para in 0 of 17. The mean titer rises were 8.5-fold for A_2, 3.0-fold for HK, 2.5-fold for A_0, and 1.0-fold for Para.

In nasal washings there was a significant neutralizing antibody titer rise against A_2 in 15 of the 17 volunteers. Against the heterologous strains there were significant rises in 8/17, 6/17, and 0/17 against the HK, A_0, and Para, respectively. The mean titer rises were 11.3-fold, 3.7-fold, 2.3-fold and 1.0-fold for A_2, HK, A_0, and Para, respectively.

The antibody rises were significantly greater ($p < 0.005$ by Student's t test) against the homologous strain compared with any of the heterologous strains, for serum, sputum or nasal washing. Comparing the antibody rises against the heterologous influenza strains with that of Para there was no significant difference in the serum rise against the three strains ($p > 0.1$); however, there was a significant difference in the sputum and nasal wash antibody rise against HK or A_0 compared with the rise against Para ($p < 0.005$). Comparison of the serum, sputum or nasal wash rises against HK and A_0 revealed no statistical difference ($p > 0.1$). When the serum rise against the homologous strain was compared with the sputum rise or the nasal washing rise against the homologous strain there was no significant difference ($p > 0.1$). However when the serum rise against either HK or A_0 was compared with the sputum or nasal washing rise, it was found that the serum rise is significantly less than the sputum or nasal washing rises ($p < 0.0005$).

The data on the immunoglobulin class of the homologous and heterologous antibody are shown in Table III. Absorption of the IgA from the pooled sputum or nasal wash specimens led to a marked reduction in the neutralizing antibody titer to both the homologous and heterologous strain tested. On the other hand, removal of the IgG led to no reduction in the antibody titers.

The data on the absorption of the antibody

[3] The atomizer was kindly provided by the DeVilbiss Company, Somerset, Penn., and the data by Dr. E. G. Lierke, of DeVilbiss Co.

TABLE I

Antibody response and immunoglobulin A concentration in 17 volunteers immunized by aerosol with bivalent influenza vaccine

Vol. No.	Specimens	Influenza Neutralizing Antibody Titers						Parainfluenza Neutralizing Antibody Titers (Para)		Immunoglobulin A Concentration	
		A_2/Taiwan/1/64 (A_2)		A_2/Hong Kong/8/68 (HK)		A/PR8 (A_0)					
		Pre	Post	Pre	Post	Pre	Post	Pre	Post	Pre	Post
1	Serum	1:32	1:256	<1:4	<1:4	1:8	1:8	<1:4	<1:4	N.D.[a]	N.D.
	Sputum	<1:1	1:2	<1:1	1:1	<1:1	1:2	1:1	1:1	0.32[b]	0.36
	Nasal	1:1	1:2	<1:1	1:1	<1:1	1:2	1:1	1:1	0.14	0.18
2	Serum	1:128	1:512	<1:4	<1:4	1:32	1:32	<1:4	<1:4	N.D.	N.D.
	Sputum	<1:1	1:2	<1:1	1:2	1:1	1:4	<1:1	<1:1	0.61	0.54
	Nasal	1:2	1:16	<1:1	<1:1	<1:1	1:1	<1:1	<1:1	0.25	0.32
3	Serum	1:32	1:128	1:4	1:4	1:8	1:8	<1:4	<1:4	N.D.	N.D.
	Sputum	<1:1	1:8	<1:1	1:4	<1:1	1:2	<1:1	<1:1	0.27	0.20
	Nasal	1:1	1:16	<1:1	1:8	<1:1	1:2	<1:1	<1:1	0.25	0.25
4	Serum	1:16	1:64	<1:4	<1:4	1:16	1:16	1:32	1:16	N.D.	N.D.
	Sputum	<1:1	1:8	<1:1	1:2	<1:1	<1:1	1:2	1:4	0.32	0.25
	Nasal	<1:1	1:8	<1:1	1:2	1:1	1:2	1:1	1:1	N.D.	N.D.
5	Serum	1:64	1:1024	1:8	1:8	1:16	1:16	<1:4	<1:4	N.D.	N.D.
	Sputum	<1:1	1:4	<1:1	1:1	<1:1	1:2	1:1	<1:1	0.25	0.30
	Nasal	<1:1	1:8	<1:1	<1:1	1:1	1:2	1:1	1:1	0.12	0.14
6	Serum	1:64	1:1024	1:4	1:16	1:32	1:32	1:32	1:32	N.D.	N.D.
	Sputum	1:2	1:32	<1:1	<1:1	1:1	1:2	1:1	<1:1	0.81	0.69
	Nasal	1:1	1:8	<1:1	1:4	<1:1	1:1	1:2	1:4	N.D.	N.D.
7	Serum	1:16	1:128	<1:4	<1:4	1:8	1:8	<1:4	<1:4	N.D.	N.D.
	Sputum	1:1	1:4	<1:1	1:2	<1:1	<1:1	<1:1	1:1	0.27	0.35
	Nasal	<1:1	1:8	<1:1	1:1	<1:1	1:1	1:1	1:1	0.15	0.19
8	Serum	1:12	1:1024	<1:4	1:4	1:8	1:8	1:32	1:32	N.D.	N.D.
	Sputum	<1:1	1:16	<1:1	1:2	<1:1	1:2	<1:1	<1:1	N.D.	N.D.
	Nasal	1:1	1:8	<1:1	1:1	<1:1	1:2	<1:1	<1:1	N.D.	N.D.
9	Serum	1:32	1:512	1:4	1:4	1:16	1:16	<1:4	1:4	N.D.	N.D.
	Sputum	<1:1	1:4	<1:1	<1:1	<1:1	1:1	1:1	<1:1	0.65	0.48
	Nasal	<1:1	1:8	<1:1	1:1	<1:1	1:1	<1:1	<1:1	N.D.	N.D.
10	Serum	1:256	1:256	<1:4	<1:4	1:64	1:128	1:4	1:4	N.D.	N.D.
	Sputum	1:1	1:16	<1:1	<1:1	<1:1	1:1	<1:1	<1:1	0.55	0.69
	Nasal	<1:1	1:1	<1:1	1:8	1:2	1:8	<1:1	1:1	0.09	0.09
11	Serum	1:32	1:1024	1:4	1:4	1:16	1:16	<1:4	<1:4	N.D.	N.D.
	Sputum	1:1	1:16	<1:1	1:1	<1:1	1:1	<1:1	1:1	0.75	0.55
	Nasal	<1:1	1:16	<1:1	1:2	1:1	1:1	<1:1	<1:1	N.D.	N.D.
12	Serum	1:64	1:512	1:8	1:8	1:16	1:16	<1:4	<1:4	N.D.	N.D.
	Sputum	1:1	1:4	<1:1	1:4	<1:1	1:1	<1:1	<1:1	N.D.	N.D.
	Nasal	<1:1	1:8	<1:1	1:8	<1:1	1:1	1:1	<1:1	0.18	0.18

TABLE I—*Continued*

Vol. No.	Specimens	Influenza Neutralizing Antibody Titers						Parainfluenza Neutralizing Antibody Titers (Para)		Immunoglobulin A Concentration	
		A_2/Taiwan/1/64 (A_2)		A_2/Hong Kong/8/68 (HK)		A/PR8 (A_0)					
		Pre	Post	Pre	Post	Pre	Post	Pre	Post	Pre	Post
13	Serum	1:32	1:256	1:8	1:8	1:32	1:32	<1:4	<1:4	N.D.	N.D.
	Sputum	<1:1	1:2	<1:1	1:2	<1:1	1:2	<1:1	<1:1	0.18	0.20
	Nasal	<1:1	1:32	<1:1	1:1	<1:1	1:2	<1:1	<1:1	N.D.	N.D.
14	Serum	1:8	1:128	1:4	1:8	1:8	1:8	1:32	1:16	N.D.	N.D.
	Sputum	<1.1	1:2	<1:1	1:1	<1:1	1:4	<1:1	<1:1	0.25	0.30
	Nasal	1:1	1:8	<1:1	1:1	<1:1	<1:1	1:1	1:1	0.20	0.25
15	Serum	1:32	1:256	1:4	1:4	1:16	1:8	<1:4	<1:4	N.D.	N.D.
	Sputum	<1:1	1:4	<1:1	1:2	<1:1	<1:1	<1:1	<1:1	N.D.	N.D.
	Nasal	<1:1	1:16	<1:1	1:2	<1:1	1:1	1:1	1:1	0.18	0.21
16	Serum	1:128	1:1024	<1:4	<1:4	1:32	1:32	1:16	1:16	N.D.	N.D.
	Sputum	1:2	1:8	<1:1	1:4	<1:1	1:1	<1:1	<1:1	0.42	0.51
	Nasal	1:1	1:2	<1:1	1:8	1:1	1:1	1:1	1:1	0.20	0.18
17	Serum	1:32	1:256	<1:4	<1:4	1:8	1:8	<1:4	1:4	N.D.	N.D.
	Sputum	<1:1	1:16	<1:1	1:2	<1:1	1:2	<1:1	<1:1	0.55	0.42
	Nasal	1:1	1:8	<1:1	<1:1	<1:1	1:1	<1:1	<1:1	0.20	0.25

[a] N.D., not done.

[b] Milligrams/milliliter.

activity with homologous and heterologous virus is shown in Table IV. When the specimens were absorbed with the classical A_2 virus, there was a reduction in the virus neutralizing activity of 75% to 87.5% against A_2, 50% to 75% against HK, and 50% to 75% against A_0. When the specimens were absorbed with HK, the titer drop was 50% to 75% against A_2, while it was 75% against HK, and 50% to 75% against A_0. Antibody titers in nasal washings and sputum are generally low (explicable by the fact that the total immunoglobulin content of recovered respiratory secretions is on the order of 1 mg/ml, while that of serum is about 15 mg/ml) making absorption studies impossible except in specimens with exceptionally high titers. In addition, serial absorptions lower the titers by dilution and make differences small. This coupled with the relatively large amount of material needed for absorption studies and subsequent antibody determinations at low titers (requiring 2 ml of specimen), limited the number of specimens which were suitable for absorption studies to two, and only one of these could be serially absorbed.

Immunoglubulin concentrations. The immunoglobulin concentrations are shown for all the specimens in Table I. In no instance do the pre- and postimmunization specimens from one individual vary more than 30%.

DISCUSSION

The present study indicates a difference in the extent of cross-reactivity or specificity between serum IgG and secretory IgA anti-influenza antibodies. This is suggested by the finding that, following aerosol immunization with the classical A_2 influenza vaccine, nasal secretion and sputum antibody titers rose significantly against heterologous virus strains, i.e., HK and A_0, while serum antibody titers did not. This can be explained by either or both of the following two mechanisms. Either the secretory system when stimulated by influenza antigens produces a wider range of antibody species, or the individual antibody molecules produced are less specific. In the former case, absorption of the antibody with one antigen should not remove the antibody to the others. In the latter case it should. The data strongly favor

TABLE II

Mean antibody titer rise in 17 volunteers immunized by aerosol with bivalent influenza vaccine

	A_2[a]	HK[b]	A_0[c]	Para[d]
Serum	3.0[e] ±1.1	0.2 ±0.6	0.0 ±0.4	0.0 ±0.5
Sputum	3.1 ±1.1	1.6 ±1.0	1.3 ±0.9	−0.1 ±0.6
Nasal	3.5 ±1.4	1.9 ±1.4	1.2 ±0.7	0.0 ±0.4

[a] Antibody titers measured against A_2/Taiwan/1/64 influenza virus.

[b] Antibody titers measured against A_2/Hong Kong/8/68 influenza virus.

[c] Antibody titers measured against A/PR8 influenza virus.

[d] Antibody titers measured against parainfluenza type 1 virus.

[e] Log_2 geometric mean neutralizing antibody titer rise (± standard error of the mean).

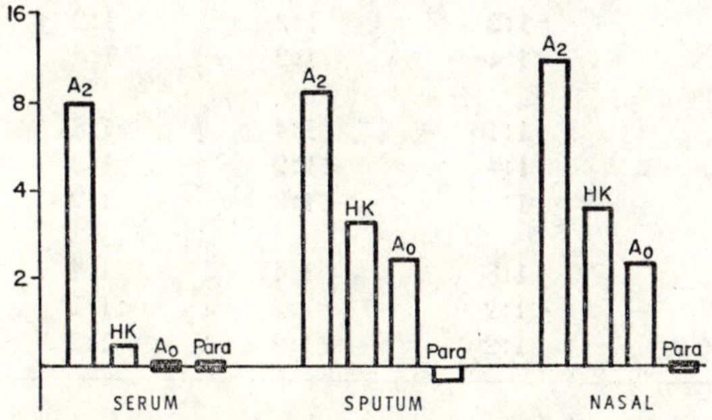

Figure 1. Reciprocals are shown of geometric mean fold-increases in neutralizing antibody titers against A_2/Taiwan/1/64 (A_2), A_2/Hong Kong/8/68 (HK), and A/PR8 (A_0) influenza viruses, and parainfluenza type 1 virus (Para), measured on serum, sputum and nasal washing samples from 17 volunteers immunized by aerosol against A_2/Taiwan/1/64 virus.

the latter possibility. The data show, however, that in most instances, the antibody titer is lowered more against the absorbing virus than against the other virus strains, indicating that some of the heterologous response may be due to stimulation of antibody that reacts only with the heterologous virus strains and not with the homologous strain.

Two experiments support the contention that the heterologous activity is antibody, and not simply nonspecific virus neutralization. These are: (A) the experiment which shows that both the homologous and heterologous activity are removed by absorption of the specimens with anti-IgA antiserum; and (B) the finding that the neutralizing activity is not completely nonspecific, i.e., Para was not neutralized by the respiratory secretions. It is still conceivable that IgA acts as a nonspecific virus inhibitor, but it is difficult to explain why there should be a rise in nonspecific inhibitors after immunization.

The respiratory secretion IgA levels show little variation (30%) between pre- and postimmunization specimens in each individual, which is in agreement with the findings of Rossen, *et al.* (12). This finding would rule out the possibility that the secretory antibody titer changes were simply a concentration phenomenon.

The results of this study are of possible significance in two respects. First, they may indicate that secretory IgA antibody is less specific than serum IgG antibody. However, because influenza virus is made up of many antigens, studies in animals using haptens would be helpful to further elucidate this point. There are other studies which would support the finding that IgA antibody may be less specific. Alford *et al.* (13) noted after infection with A_2/Bethesda/10/63 influenza virus, a slight rise in nasal wash neutralizing antibody titer against A/PR8 influenza virus (mean twofold rise in eight volunteers), but no rise in titer against A_1/FM1 or B/Lee influenza viruses, or parainfluenza type 1, and no serum antibody rises against these heterotypic viruses. Heterologous resistance lasting at least 5 weeks after an initial infection, using rhinovirus of different serotype, has been described (14). Interferon as an important explanation of this phenomenon has been ruled out (15). There are several studies which may indicate that intestinal antibody reacts more broadly to bacterial antigens than does serum antibody (16, 17). In rabbits and humans, after infection or immunization with *Salmonella* or *Shigellae*, coliform agglutinins appeared in feces (coproagglutinins) and serum, but the latter was more transient and the titers were lower (17). The rise and fall of the cross-reacting coproagglutinins roughly paralleled that against the infecting or immunizing agent.

Secondly, the practical application of these results may be significant. There is mounting evidence that respiratory secretion antibody is important in protection against respiratory viral

TABLE III

Immunoglobulin absorptions

Specimen	Absorbed with	Immunoglobulin Concentration			Antibody Titer	
		IgA	IgG	IgM	A_2	HK
Sputum	Saline	0.52[a]	0.16	<0.05	1:16[b]	1:8
	Anti-γA	0.07	0.14	<0.05	1:2	<1:2
	Anti-γG	0.41	<0.05	<0.05	1:16	1:8
Nasal washing	Saline	0.35	0.09	<0.05	1:32	1:8
	Anti-γA	<0.05	0.11	<0.05	1:2	1:2
	Anti-γG	0.41	<0.05	<0.05	1:16	1:8

[a] Milligrams/milliliter.
[b] Neutralizing antibody titer.

TABLE IV

Absorption with influenza virus

Specimen	Absorbed with	Neutralizing Antibody Titers		
		A_2/Taiwan/64	A_2/Hong Kong/68	A/PR8
Sputum	Saline	1:16	1:8	1:8
	A_2/Taiwan/64	1:2	1:2	1:2
	A_2/Hong Kong/68	1:4	1:2	1:4
Nasal washing	Saline	1:16	1:4	1:8
	A_2/Taiwan/64	1:4	<1:2	1:2
	A_2/Hong Kong/68	1:8	<1:2	1:2
Nasal washing	Saline × 2	1:8	1:4	1:4
	A_2/Taiwan/64 × 2	<1:2	1:2	<1:2
	A_2/Hong Kong/68 × 2	1:2	<1:2	1:2

infections (1, 2, 5). If aerosol immunization with A_2 leads to production of some neutralizing antibody to HK, then possibly protection against the Hong Kong variant might result from the use of the classical A_2 vaccine by aerosol. This has been tested in a recent field trial, and the results were consistent with the conclusion that there was protection against HK mediated by respiratory secretion antibody stimulated by A_2 (6). If there is cross-protection, then this would be important early in an epidemic caused by a new strain of A-influenza virus, as occurred in late 1968. In the present study, the volunteers were immunized before the emergence of the A_2/Hong Kong influenza epidemic. All volunteers were aged 20 to 40 years, so none had been exposed to that virus previously.

As noted above, volunteers recovering from a rhinovirus infection with one strain are resistant to challenge with another serologically distinct, serologically non-cross-reacting strain, despite the absence of serum antibody to the second strain (14). It is conceivable that these strains could be "secretologically" related and that the resistance noted was due to cross-reacting respiratory secretion antibody stimulated by the first infection. This is a readily testable hypothesis, and if borne out, it could make vaccine development against the multitudes of respiratory viruses much more feasible.

REFERENCES

1. Cate, T. R., Rossen, R. D., Douglas, R. G., Jr., Butler, W. R. and Couch, R. B., Amer. J. Epidem. *84:* 352, 1966.
2. Smith, C. B., Purcell, R. H., Bellanti, J. A. and Chanock, R. M., New England J. Med., *275:* 1145, 1966.
3. Waldman, R. H., Kasel, J. A., Fulk, R. V., Mann, J. J., Togo, Y., Hornick, R. B.,

Heiner, G. T. and Dawkins, A. T., Nature, *218:* 594, 1968.
4. Fulk, R. V., Fedson, D. S., Huber, M. A., Fitzpatrick, J. R., Howar, B. F., and Kasel, J. A., J. Immun., *102:* 1102, 1969.
5. Waldman, R. H., Mann, J. J. and Small, P. A., Jr., J. A. M. A., *207:* 520, 1969.
6. Waldman, R. H., Bond, J. O., Levitt, L. P., Hartwig, E. C., Prather, E. C., Baratta, R. L., Neill, J. S., and Small, P. A., Jr., W. H. O. Bull., *41:* 543, 1969.
7. Rossen, R. D., Butler, W. T., Cate, T. R., Szwed, C. F. and Couch, R. B., Proc. Soc. Exp. Biol. Med., *119:* 1169, 1965.
8. Masson, P. L., Heremans, J. F. and Prignot, J., Biochim. Biophys. Acta, *111:* 446, 1965.
9. Mancini, G., Carbonara, A. O. and Heremans, J. F., Immunochemistry, *2:* 235, 1965.
10. Fireman, P., Vannier, W. E. and Goodman, H. C., J. Exp. Med. *117:* 603, 1963.
11. Chanock, R. M., Parrott, R. H., Cook, K., Andrews, B. E., Bell, J. A., Reicheldefer, T., Kapikian, A. Z., Mastrota, F. M. and Huebner, R. J., New England J. Med., *258:* 297, 1958.
12. Rossen, R. D., Schade, A. L., Butler, W. T. and Kasel, J. A., J. Clin. Invest., *45:* 768, 1966.
13. Alford, R. H., Rossen, R. D., Butler, W. T. and Kasel, J. A., J. Immun., *98:* 724, 1967.
14. Fleet, W. F., Couch, R. B., Cate, T. R. and Knight, V., Amer. J. Epidem., *82:* 185, 1965.
15. Cate, T. R., Douglas, R. G., Jr. and Couch, R. B., Proc. Soc. Exp. Biol. Med., *131:* 631, 1969.
16. Raettig, H. Round Table Conference on Vaccines from Salmonella, Shigella, *V. cholerae*. Berne, October 1969.
17. Barksdale, W. L. and Ghoda, A., J. Infect. Dis., *89:* 53, 1951.

THE JOURNAL OF IMMUNOLOGY
Vol. 105, No. 6, December 1970
Printed in U.S.A.

REQUIREMENT FOR CROSS-LINKAGE IN THE STIMULATION OF TRANSFORMATION OF RABBIT PERIPHERAL LYMPHOCYTES BY ANTIGLOBULIN REAGENTS[1]

MICHAEL W. FANGER,[2] DAVID A. HART, J. VIVIAN WELLS[3] AND ALFRED NISONOFF

From the Department of Biochemistry, University of Illinois at the Medical Center, Chicago, Illinois 60612

Received for publication June 24, 1970

Fab′ fragments of goat anti-rabbit fragment Fab and anti-rabbit fragment Fc were ineffective in the stimulation of transformation of rabbit peripheral lymphocytes. $F(ab')_2$ fragments had stimulatory activity comparable to that of the intact IgG antibody. Combination of Fab′ fragments of both goat anti-rabbit Fc and anti-rabbit Fab with the lymphocytes was demonstrated by their capacity to inhibit specifically transformation by the corresponding, intact antibody; in addition, transformation was observed when rabbit lymphocytes, pretreated with univalent fragments of goat anti-rabbit Fc, were subsequently allowed to react with bivalent antibody directed to the univalent fragments. These results indicate that the triggering of transformation by antiglobulin reagents is accomplished through cross-linkage of membrane constituents. Such a mechanism may be relevant to the stimulation of sensitive lymphocytes by antigen and thus may aid in providing a basis for understanding the mechanism of induction and paralysis in the immune response.

Bivalent antibody directed to lymphocytes, to immunoglobulins or to other antigenic structures on the surface of lymphocytes can initiate cellular division as observed morphologically or by the uptake of isotopically-labeled DNA precursors (1–6). The capacity of monovalent fragments of antibody to cause such *in vitro* transformation is at present unclear. Sell has reported that Fab fragments of sheep antibody directed to rabbit IgG stimulate rabbit lymphocytes to transform into blast cells and to synthesize DNA, although Fab fragments from burro antibodies directed to rabbit lymphocytes were non-stimulatory (4, 5).

The data of Woodruff *et al.* (6) suggest that univalent fragments do not cause transformation of human lymphocytes. In their experiments, Fab′ fragments obtained from horse antibodies directed to human thymocytes did not cause the incorporation of labeled uridine into the nucleic acid of human peripheral lymphocytes. The bivalent $F(ab')_2$ fragments of these antibodies were, however, as active as untreated antibody in stimulating the uptake of isotope.

The resolution of this problem should be of particular importance, since it relates to the mechanism of transformation by antibody, and also because of a possible close similarity between this phenomenon and that of transformation of sensitized lymphocytes by antigen. The stimulation of division of lymphocytes *in vivo* as seen, for example, in the secondary immune response may well have the same basic triggering mechanism as the transformation *in vitro* by antibody directed to antigens on lymphocytes.

In the present investigation, carried out with goat antibodies directed to rabbit Fab or Fc fragments, we have consistently been unable to obtain a significant degree of transformation of rabbit lymphocytes with Fab′ fragments of the goat antibodies, although $F(ab')_2$ fragments were comparable in activity to intact goat antibody. In most instances Fab′ fragments specifically inhibited transformation by the antibody from

[1]This work was supported by grants from the National Science Foundation (GB-5424) and the National Institutes of Health (AI-06281).

[2]Postdoctoral Fellow of the National Institutes of Health.

[3]Supported by University of California Training Grant HE-05677 (United States Public Health Service) and the Royal Australasian College of Physicians.

which they were derived. Moreover, it was possible to initiate transformation by adding Fab′ fragments specific for rabbit immunoglobulin followed by bivalent antibody directed to the Fab′. The results suggest that, in the systems investigated, cross-linkage is essential for transformation.

MATERIALS AND METHODS

Preparation of antibodies and antibody derivatives. IgG fractions were prepared from goat or rabbit antisera by precipitation with Na_2SO_4 at final concentrations of 18% and 14% (7) followed by chromatography on DEAE-cellulose in 0.0175 M phosphate buffer, pH 6.9 (8). $F(ab')_2$ fragments were prepared by digestion of 100 to 300 mg of IgG with 2% pepsin at 37°C in 0.1 M acetate buffer, pH 4.1 (9); the period of digestion was 4 hr for goat IgG and 8 hr for rabbit IgG. Mixtures were then neutralized to pH 7 with 0.1 M NaOH and applied to a 600-cm³ column of Sephadex G-150. The protein comprising the major symmetrical peak was pooled, concentrated by vacuum dialysis and refiltered on the same column. The second filtration gave a single peak which, on ultracentrifugal analysis in each case had an $s_{20,w}$ value of 4.4 to 4.6 at a concentration of 6 to 8 mg/ml and no discernible contamination.

Fab′ fragments were prepared by reducing the $F(ab')_2$ fragment with 0.007 M dithiothreitol at 37°C for 2 hr, pH 7.0. Iodoacetic acid, neutralized to pH 7, was added to a final concentration of 0.015 M. After 2 hr at 37°C, the reduced and alkylated protein was applied to a 400-cm³ column of Sephadex G-100. Fragment Fab′ was eluted with 0.15 M NaCl, concentrated by vacuum dialysis and refiltered on the same column. In each case the major component eluted had a sedimentation coefficient, $s_{20,w}$, of 3.1 to 3.3 at a concentration of 7 mg/ml; no other components were detectable.

Rabbit fragments Fab and Fc were prepared by digesting rabbit IgG with 1% by weight of papain (10) at 37°C for 4 to 5 hr. Fragment Fc crystallized upon dialysis of the digest against cold neutral buffer and was recrystallized by dissolving in water at 52°C and refrigerating. Fragment Fab was purified by passing the digest, after removal of crystals, through a column of carboxymethycellulose equilibrated with 0.02 M sodium acetate, adjusted to pH 6. Fragment Fc was dissolved in 0.1 M acetate buffer, pH 5, for inoculations.

Goats were inoculated subcutaneously with 1.5 to 2 mg of rabbit fragment Fab or Fc, incorporated in complete Freund's adjuvant. This was repeated at 2-week intervals until a strongly precipitating antiserum was obtained. Antisera to fragment Fc also contained small amounts of antibody directed to fragment Fab. Such sera were absorbed by adding rabbit fragment $F(ab')_2$ at equivalence. After removal of the precipitate an additional 50 to 100 μg of $F(ab')_2$ per ml of antiserum was added. Sera from bleedings taken on three different occasions were used for preparing the antibodies against both Fab and Fc fragments. The goat anti-rabbit Fab was prepared from bleedings taken 6 weeks (anti-Fab-1), 20 weeks (anti-Fab-2), and 52 weeks (anti-Fab-3) after the initial injection. The sera were used individually. Goat anti-rabbit Fc was prepared from bleedings of two goats obtained 11 weeks (anti-Fc-1), 16 weeks (anti-Fc-2), and 24 weeks (anti-Fc-3) after the initial injection; sera of the two goats taken at the same time were pooled. In addition, bleedings of both goats producing anti-Fc were taken 43 weeks after the initial injection and used without pooling.

Rabbit anti-goat $F(ab')_2$ antiserum was prepared by injecting subcutaneously at 3-week intervals 3- to 5-mg quantities of goat $F(ab')_2$ in complete Freund's adjuvant. Bleedings were taken weekly, starting immediately before the third injection.

Lymphocyte cultures. Lymphocytes were isolated under sterile conditions. Normal rabbits were bled from an ear vein into a heparinized container. After diluting the red cells with a half-volume of 3% Knox gelatin, they were allowed to settle for 45 min at 37°C in an inverted syringe. The upper, white cell layer was removed and centrifuged at 300 × G for 20 min. The cell pellet was suspended in 24 ml of Eagle's minimum essential medium (MEM) and 6 ml of fetal calf serum that had been incubated at 56°C for 30 min to inactivate complement. The cell suspension was passed through a cotton wool column (3 g cotton wool washed with 4 liters H_2O) equilibrated with 20% fetal calf serum in MEM. After elution with 70 ml of 20% fetal calf serum in MEM, the cells were centrifuged at 300 × G for 20 min. The pellet, comprising more than 95% small lymphocytes, was resuspended in

MEM and cells were counted with a Neubauer hemacytometer. Cultures were set up in 17- x 100-mm plastic tubes, each containing 10^6 cells, 0.4 ml decomplemented fetal calf serum, 800 units of penicillin, 800 μg of streptomycin, 1.4 mg glutamine, and MEM to a final volume of 2 ml.

The cells were incubated at 37°C in 5% CO_2-95% air in a Hotpack incubator. Periodically, viability was tested by measuring uptake of trypan blue by the cultured cells; viability exceeded 70% in all cases. After 24 hr, 5 μCi of ^{3}H-methyl-thymidine (New England Nuclear Corp., Boston, Mass.; 6.7 Ci/mM) in 50 μl MEM was added to each tube. Twenty-four hr later each sample was centrifuged at 1000 × G for 12 min and the supernatant discarded. The cells were lysed by freezing and thawing seven times in 1 ml of a hypotonic solution containing 0.0008 M KH_2PO_4 and 0.002 M $MgCl_2$ at pH 6.7; 2.5 ml of 10% trichloroacetic acid was then added to each tube at 0°C. The tubes were centrifuged at 1000 × G for 12 min at 0°C and the supernatants were decanted. The pellet was washed three times with 2 ml of 5% trichloroacetic acid, once with 2 ml 80% ethanol, and once with 2 ml acetone. After drying, samples were solubilized in 0.15 ml 90% formic acid. One hundred-microliter portions were added to 15 ml of a toluene-methanol (3:1) solution containing 4 g of 2,5-diphenyloxazole and 200 mg of 1,4-bis-(2,4-methyl-5 phenyloxazolyl)-benzene/liter. Counting was performed in a Packard Tri-Carb liquid scintillation counter.

Other materials and methods. Phytohemagglutinin (PHA) was obtained from Difco Laboratories as "Bacto-phytohemagglutinin P" and used as a 1 mg/ml solution in MEM. L-Glutamine, penicillin, streptomycin and fetal calf serum were obtained from the Grand Island Biological Company.

Sedimentation velocity analyses of F(ab')$_2$ and Fab' fragments in phosphate-buffered saline, pH 7.0, were performed in double-sector cells in a Spinco model E analytical ultracentrifuge at 20°C and 59,780 rpm; the solvent was placed in the second compartment. Sedimentation coefficients were corrected to water as solvent at 20°C.

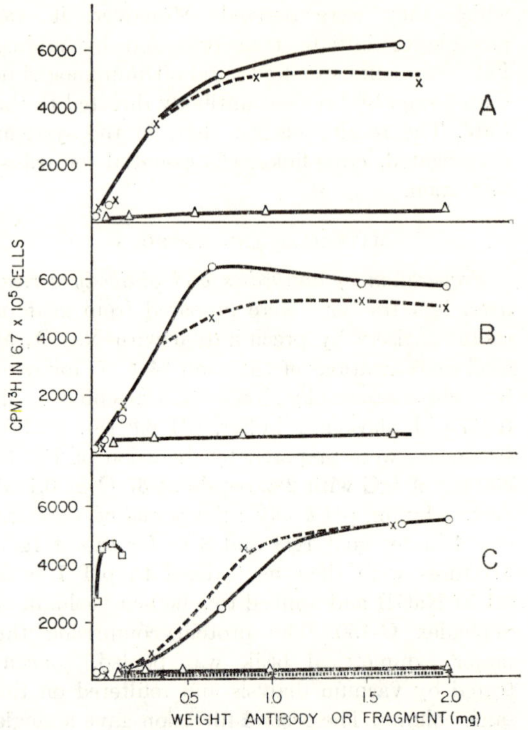

Figure 1. Stimulation of incorporation of ^{3}H-thymidine into rabbit peripheral lymphocytes by three preparations of goat anti-rabbit fragment Fc described in the text. *A*, anti-Fc-1; *B*, anti-Fc-2 *C*, anti-Fc-3. ○, IgG fraction of the goat antiserum; ×, F(ab')$_2$ fragments of the IgG; △, Fab' fragments; □, phytohemagglutinin; ▮▮▮, nonspecific goat IgG.

RESULTS

Transformation by antiglobulin reagents. Figures 1*A*, 1*B* and 1*C* show the effects of goat anti-rabbit Fc and of fragments of that antibody on thymidine uptake by rabbit peripheral lymphocytes. The curves were obtained with anti-Fc-1 (earlier bleeding), anti-Fc-2 (intermediate bleeding) and anti-Fc-3 (late bleeding), respectively.

In each set of experiments Fab' fragments of the goat antibody caused little if any stimulation. The untreated antibody and F(ab')$_2$ fragments were comparable in their transforming activities, causing a maximal uptake of thymidine 20 to 25 times as great as that of the unstimulated control, in which the average radioactivity incorporated was 230 cpm/10^6 cells.

Figure 1*C* also shows the transforming capacity of phytohemagglutinin, which gave maximal stimulation comparable to that of anti-Fc, but at a considerably lower concentration. Nonspecific goat IgG did not stimulate thymidine uptake.

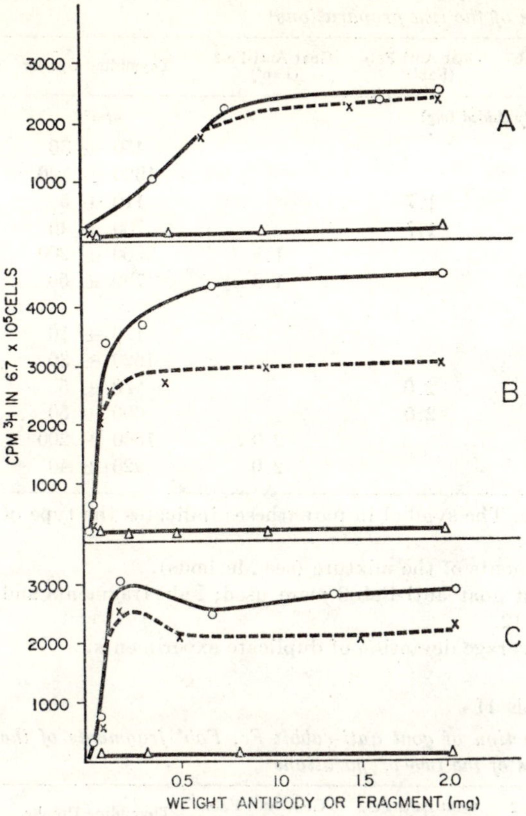

Figure 2. Stimulation of incorporation of ^{3}H-thymidine into rabbit peripheral lymphocytes by three preparations of goat anti-rabbit Fab fragments described in the text. *A*, anti-Fab-1; *B*, anti-Fab-2; *C*, anti-Fab-3. ○, IgG fraction of the goat antiserum; ×, F(ab′)$_2$ fragments of the IgG; △, Fab′ fragments.

Figures 2*A*, 2*B*, and 2*C* show the results of similar experiments in which goat anti-rabbit Fab, rather than anti-Fc, was used for stimulation. Again F(ab′)$_2$ fragments possessed a large fraction of the stimulatory activity of the intact goat IgG. Fab′ fragments had no activity. The amount of thymidine uptake was about one-half to two-thirds as great as that observed with anti-Fc.

Inhibition of transformation by Fab′ fragments. Table I shows the degree of transformation by an IgG fraction of goat anti-rabbit Fab, by Fab′ fragments of goat anti-rabbit Fab, and by mixtures of the intact goat IgG and its Fab′ fragments. Less than optimal amounts of the anti-Fab antibodies were employed in order to permit the use of a large molar excess of Fab′ fragments over intact antibody in the mixtures. The presence of Fab′ fragments of goat anti-rabbit Fab resulted in a significant decrease in the amount of thymidine uptake caused by the intact goat anti-rabbit Fab (Expts. 2 and 4 and Expts. 8 and 10). That this inhibition was specific was shown by the inability of the Fab′ fragments of anti-Fc-2 to affect the transformation by intact goat anti-rabbit Fab antibody (Expts. 2 and 5 and Expts. 8 and 11, Table I).

Table II presents similar experiments utilizing goat anti-rabbit Fc rather than anti-Fab. In two series of experiments, with lymphocytes from rabbits F-70 and F-64, univalent goat antibodies significantly inhibited transformation by the intact goat IgG. In the third series, the goat Fab′ fragments showed slight stimulatory activity and failed to cause inhibition. Inhibition of stimulation by univalent goat antibodies directed to rabbit fragment Fc was also observed in other experiments using different lymphocyte preparations and goat anti-Fc-1. Again, inhibition of transformation was specific; univalent fragments of goat anti-rabbit Fab did not affect transformation by anti-Fc (Expts. 2 and 5, and Expts. 8 and 11, Table II).

Effect of cross-linkage on transformation. In view of the finding that Fab′ fragments of antiglobulin reagents did not stimulate transformation, it was of interest to ascertain the effect of a reagent capable of cross-linking the Fab′ fragments after their attachment to cells. The reagent used for cross-linking was the F(ab′)$_2$ fragment of rabbit antibody directed to goat Fab′. (The goat antibody was specific for rabbit fragment Fc; this precluded the use of a rabbit IgG fraction as the cross-linking antibody, since it could react as an antigen with the goat antibody used.)

The experiments in Table III were carried out with Fab′ fragments of the goat anti-Fc-2 preparation and peripheral lymphocytes from four different nonimmunized rabbits. In two of the four sets of experiments thymidine uptake was stimulated slightly by the Fab′ fragments. In all cases (Expts. 3, 7, 13 and 20) cross-linkage by rabbit F(ab′)$_2$ fragments of antibody directed to the goat Fab′ fragments caused considerable enhancement of thymidine uptake; the rabbit F(ab′)$_2$ fragments alone had no significant effect. Also, antigen-antibody complexes formed by the mixture of nonspecific goat Fab′ fragments with F(ab′)$_2$ fragments of rabbit anti-goat Fab′ did

TABLE I

Transformation of rabbit lymphocytes by an IgG fraction of goat anti-rabbit Fab, Fab′ fragments of the goat antibody, and mixtures of the two preparations[a]

Lymphocyte Donor (Rabbit)	Expt.	Nonspecific Goat (IgG)	Goat Anti-Fab (IgG)[b, c]	Goat Anti-Fab (Fab′)[c]	Goat Anti-Fc-2 (Fab′)	Thymidine Uptake
		Quantity Added (mg)				*cpm*[d]
F-66	1	0.5				450 ± 30
	2		0.16			1620 ± 190
	3			1.7		110 ± 5
	4		0.16	1.7		700 ± 40
	5		0.16		1.8	2000 ± 200
	6				1.8	790 ± 50
F-70	7	0.5				170 ± 10
	8		0.2			1620 ± 30
	9			2.0		70 ± 5
	10		0.2	2.0		600 ± 50
	11		0.2		2.0	1660 ± 200
	12				2.0	220 ± 40

[a] These preparations are described under methods. The symbol in parentheses indicates the type of fragment utilized.

[b] Added 1 hr after the addition of all other components of the mixture (see Methods).

[c] In experiments 1 to 6 Fab′ fragments and IgG of goat anti-Fab-3 were used; Fab′ fragments and IgG of goat anti-Fab-2 were used in experiments 7–12.

[d] Counts/minute of tritium in 6.7×10^5 cells ± average deviation of duplicate experiments.

TABLE II

Transformation of rabbit lymphocytes by an IgG fraction of goat anti-rabbit Fc, Fab′ fragments of the goat antibody, and mixtures of the two preparations[a]

Lymphocyte Donor (Rabbit)	Expt.	Non-Specific Goat (Fab′)	Goat Anti-Fc-2 (IgG)[b]	Goat Anti-Fc-2 (Fab′)	Goat Anti-Fab (Fab′)[c]	Thymidine Uptake
		Quantity Added (mg)				*cpm*[d]
F-70	1	0.5				170 ± 10
	2		0.35			1700 ± 180
	3			2.0		220 ± 40
	4		0.35	2.0		950 ± 10
	5		0.35		2.0	1600 ± 50
	6				2.0	70 ± 5
F-64	7	0.5				450 ± 50
	8		0.3			1610 ± 200
	9			1.6		590 ± 50
	10		0.3	1.6		1020 ± 30
	11		0.3		1.8	1670 ± 30
	12				1.8	570 ± 30
F-66	13	0.5				450 ± 30
	14		0.35			1000 ± 90
	15			1.8		750 ± 50
	16		0.35	1.8		1740 ± 50
	17		0.35		2.0	980 ± 30
	18				2.0	110 ± 10

[a, b] See Table I.

[c] In experiments 5 and 6 the Fab′ fragments of anti-Fab-2 were utilized; nonspecific goat Fab′ was used in experiments 11 and 12, and Fab′ fragments of goat anti-Fab-3 in experiments 17 and 18.

[d] See Table I.

TABLE III

Enhancement of lymphocyte transformation by antibody directed to goat Fab′ fragments specific for rabbit immunoglobulin[a]

Lymphocyte Donor (Rabbit)	Expt.	Nonspecific Goat (Fab′)	Goat Anti-Fc-2 (Fab′)	Rabbit Anti-Goat Fab′ (F(ab′)$_2$)	Rabbit Anti-Goat Fab′ (Fab′)[b]	Thymidine Uptake
		Quantity Added (mg)				*cpm*[c]
F-38	1					230 ± 30
	2		1.1			650 ± 25
	3		1.1	1.3		1750 ± 60
	4			1.3		260 ± 20
F-58	5					180 ± 20
	6		0.8			820 ± 10
	7		0.8	1.0		2790 ± 60
	8			1.0		290 ± 10
	9[d]		0.8		1.0	600
	10[d]				1.0	260
F-66	11					550 ± 20
	12		0.9			820 ± 60
	13		0.9	1.2		1740 ± 60
	14			1.2		620 ± 10
	15	0.9				710 ± 50
	16	0.9		1.2		910 ± 10
F-70	17					170 ± 15
	18		0.8			210 ± 10
	19			1.0		210 ± 10
	20		0.8	1.0		650 ± 20
	21	0.8				260 ± 10
	22	0.8		1.0		190 ± 10

[a, b, c] See footnotes *a*, *b*, and *d*, Table I. This table shows the effect on lymphocyte transformation of a reagent (F(ab′)$_2$ fragments of rabbit anti-goat Fab′) capable of cross-linking lymphocyte-bound molecules (Fab′ fragments of goat anti-rabbit Fc). In the cross-linking experiments Fab′ fragments of goat anti-rabbit Fc were incubated with lymphocytes for 1 hr, and F(ab′)$_2$ fragments of rabbit anti-goat Fab′ were then added.

[d] Single analysis. The lack of activity of rabbit Fab′ fragments in this system was confirmed in other experiments (see text).

not cause stimulation (Expts. 16 and 22). Finally, monovalent rabbit Fab′ fragments directed to goat Fab′, which would not be expected to form cross-links, were nonstimulatory when added to cells preincubated with the Fab′ fragments of goat anti-rabbit Fc (Expt. 9). Similar results were obtained by using lymphocytes from four other rabbits. In all cases, the bivalent, F(ab′)$_2$ fragment of rabbit anti-goat Fab′ stimulated thymidine uptake (two- to fourfold) when added to lymphocytes pretreated with the Fab′ fragments of goat anti-rabbit Fc. Univalent, Fab′ fragments of rabbit anti-goat Fab′, under the same conditions, were nonstimulatory.

Additional experiments were carried out to determine whether a mixture of Fab′ fragments of goat antibodies directed to rabbit fragments Fc and Fab, respectively, might stimulate thymidine uptake. The results were negative (Table IV). In other experiments it was shown that the presence of rabbit IgG completely blocked transformation of rabbit lymphocytes by goat anti-rabbit Fab or by goat anti-rabbit Fc (Table V).

Studies, not tabulated, were also conducted with the Fab′ fragments of the two goat anti-rabbit Fc antibodies obtained from bleedings taken 43 weeks after the initial injection. Again, Fab′ fragments of goat anti-rabbit Fc antibody

TABLE IV

Effect on lymphocyte transformation of mixtures of Fab′ fragments of goat anti-rabbit Fc and of anti-rabbit Fab[a]

Expt.	Goat Anti-Fab-2 (IgG)	Goat Anti-Fc-2 (IgG)	Goat Anti-Fc-2 (Fab′)	Goat Anti-Fab-2 (Fab′)	Nonspecific Goat (Fab)	Thymidine Uptake
	Quantity Added (mg)					*cpm*[b]
1						165 ± 15
2			0.25	0.25		60 ± 5
3			0.5	0.5		45 ± 5
4			1.0	1.0		40 ± 5
5			2.0	2.0		60 ± 5
6					0.8	260 ± 10
7		0.35				1700 ± 180
8		2.0				1900 ± 60
9	0.2					1620 ± 30
10	2.0					2630 ± 25

[a] See Table I.
[b] See footnote *d*, Table I.

TABLE V

Effect of rabbit IgG on the transformation of rabbit lymphocytes by goat anti-rabbit Fab and goat anti-rabbit Fc[a]

Expt	Nonspecific Rabbit IgG	Goat Anti-Fab-2[b] (IgG)	Goat Anti-Fc-2[b] (IgG)	Thymidine Uptake
	Quantity Added (mg)			*cpm*[c]
1	0.5			140 ± 10
2		0.5		2000 ± 100
3	0.5	0.5		160 ± 40
4			0.5	2900 ± 100
5	0.5		0.5	210 ± 10

[a,b,c] See footnotes *a*, *b* and *d*, Table I.

were non-stimulatory, but transformation (three- to fourfold increases in thymidine incorporation) could be obtained by first incubating the cells with the goat Fab′ directed to rabbit Fc and then adding a cross-linking reagent ($F(ab')_2$ fragment of rabbit anti-goat Fab′).

DISCUSSION

Univalent Fab′ fragments of goat IgG specific for Fab or Fc fragments of rabbit IgG were generally ineffective in causing transformation of rabbit peripheral lymphocytes, as measured by incorporation of ^{3}H-thymidine. In most experiments the goat Fab′ frgaments specifically inhibited the transforming activity of the corresponding intact goat antibody. Bivalent $F(ab')_2$ fragments of goat antibody were approximately as active as the untreated antibody.

The ineffectiveness of goat Fab′ fragments directed to rabbit Fab in causing lymphocyte transformation was shown with antibodies isolated from a goat after periods of immunization of 6, 20 and 52 weeks. Antibodies from different bleedings were tested because combining affinity usually increases during prolonged immunization. The Fab′ fragments of antibody directed to rabbit fragment Fc were prepared from the pooled antisera of two goats, also taken at various time intervals. Negative results were obtained in all but a few experiments, in which slight stimulation by univalent fragments directed to rabbit fragment Fc was observed.

That the Fab′ fragments used combined with lymphocytes was shown by the transformation which resulted upon subsequent addition of $F(ab')_2$ fragments of a rabbit antibody directed to goat Fab′ fragments. Since $F(ab')_2$ fragments are bivalent they are capable of forming cross-links, either on the surface of one cell or between cells. There was no stimulatory effect when the lymphocytes were preincubated with non-specific goat Fab′ fragments. Also, rabbit Fab′ fragments directed to goat Fab′, in contrast to rabbit $F(ab')_2$ of the same specificity, did not cause stimulation of the pretreated lymphocytes. These findings and the effectiveness, in general, of bivalent antibodies directed to antigens present on lymphocyte surfaces, suggest that cross-linking is essential for lymphocyte transformation mediated by antibodies.

In four of five sets of experiments (Tables I

and II) Fab′ fragments of goat antibody directed to rabbit Fab or rabbit Fc significantly inhibited transformation by untreated goat antibody directed to the corresponding antigen. This blocking effect provides further evidence both for the attachment of the Fab′ fragments to lymphocytes and the necessity of cross-linkage for transformation.

The stimulatory effect of goat anti-rabbit Fab or goat anti-rabbit Fc was eliminated when rabbit IgG was added to the reaction mixture (Table V). Evidently the IgG reacted with the goat antibody and prevented its interaction with lymphocytes. In addition to providing evidence for the specificity of the goat antibodies, this experiment also shows that antigen-antibody complexes did not cause stimulation. The failure of immune complexes to stimulate transformation was also noted in Experiments 16 and 22, Table III, in which nonspecific goat Fab′ fragments and rabbit anti-goat Fab′ were present in the same mixture. Gell (11) has reported that complexes of IgG of allotype b^4 with anti-b4 antibody failed to cause transformation of rabbit lymphocytes. These results are in apparent contrast to those obtained with human leukocytes which are stimulated to transform by various immune complexes in the presence (12) or absence (13) of complement.

The finding that univalent fragments do not stimulate rabbit lymphocytes is consistent with the data of Woodruff *et al.* (6), who measured incorporation of uridine into RNA of human peripheral lymphocytes after addition of horse immunoglobulin directed to human thymocytes. Our data, however, apparently contrast with those of Sell (4, 5) who consistently observed transformation of rabbit lymphocytes by univalent fragments of sheep anti-rabbit IgG, although univalent fragments of burro anti-rabbit lymphocyte antibody were not stimulatory. These results were interpreted (5) as suggesting a different type of recognition site or stimulatory mechanism for anti-IgG and anti-lymphocyte antibodies.

The difference between our results and those of Sell may possibly be attributable to the fact that we utilized goat rather than sheep antibodies. Also, Sell used Fab fragments from antibodies directed to rabbit IgG whereas we studied Fab′ fragments of antibodies directed to rabbit fragments Fab and Fc. It seems improbable, however, that the difference in results could be due merely to a difference in receptors since a mixture of Fab′ fragments of anti-Fc and anti-Fab antibodies, which should correspond quite closely to univalent anti-IgG in its properties, did not induce transformation of lymphocytes (Table IV). It also seems doubtful that this difference in results could reflect a lack of saturation of the lymphocyte receptor sites in our experiments since the concentrations of the Fab′ fragments used (2×10^{-5} M) were sufficient to inhibit stimulation by untreated goat anti-rabbit Fc or goat anti-rabbit Fab (Tables I and II) and, moreover, were considerably above those concentrations of antibody or $F(ab')_2$ fragments (6×10^{-7} M to 3×10^{-6} M) which were maximally stimulatory.

A recent observation by Sell *et al.* (14) on the augmentation of transformation by anti-allotypic antibodies, upon addition of a second antiserum directed to allotypic determinants of the first, seems relevant to our findings. They suggested that the increased stimulation reflects a requirement for the close approximation of two antibody molecules reacting with a given lymphocyte. It seems consistent with our data to interpret this augmentation as the result of enhanced cross-linkage on the cell membrane in a manner analogous to that observed when rabbit lymphocytes were treated with univalent goat anti-rabbit Fc, followed by bivalent antibody directed to goat Fab′ (Table III). It is possible that stimulation of transformation requires a minimal number of cross-links on the cell membrane; this could account for the enhancement by a second cross-linking agent. It is also conceivable that the rate and number of cell divisions are influenced by the degree of cross-linkage.

The relation of the stimulation of specific immunocompetent cells by antigen to the transformation of nonimmune lymphocytes by antiglobulin reagents has not been defined. One can, however, imagine that the reactions involved in these phenomena have a common basis. If cross-linkage were important to antigenic stimulation of sensitive cells, it might be expected that; a) polyvalent, but not monovalent antigens, would be stimulatory and b) monovalent antigen could inhibit specifically transformation by polyvalent antigen. Such a finding has been reported by Francis and Paul (15), who observed that the hapten, ε-2,4-dinitrophenyl-L-lysine, inhibited transformation of sensitized guinea pig lymphocytes by a dinitrophenyl-protein conjugate. This result seems analogous to those reported in Tables I and II on the inhibition of transformation by univalent antibody fragments.

It is of interest to consider our data in the context of an hypothesis of Bretscher and Cohn (16, 17) for the induction of antibody formation. They propose that antibody production is induced as a consequence of the "stretching" of receptors (antibodies) on an antigen-sensitive cell, resulting from their interconnection by a polyvalent antigen. Our results would be interpreted in a similar manner on the assumption that receptors on a peripheral lymphocyte (in this case, antigen) undergo some modification in properties upon cross-linkage by a bivalent antibody. The mechanisms could not, however, be identical since the model of Bretscher and Cohn assumes that the Fab regions of a bivalent antibody, acting as receptor, are caused to undergo separation after binding of antigen. Such a mechanism would not apply when the receptor is an antigen, although cross-linkage is common to the two mechanisms. It seems conceivable, and consistent with the data, that the linking of receptors may in some manner alter the configuration of the cell membrane, and that this acts as a triggering mechanism leading to differentiation. Furthermore, blocking of transformation by monovalent fragments of antibody may be relevant to the mechanism proposed by Bretscher and Cohn (16) for the induction of tolerance by monomeric antigens.

REFERENCES

1. Gräsbeck, R., Norman, C. T. and DeLa Chapelle, A., Acta Med. Scand. (Suppl.), *412:* 39, 1964.
2. Holt, L. J., Ling, N. R. and Stanworth, D. R., Immunochemistry, *3:* 359, 1966.
3. Sell, S., J. Exp. Med., *125:* 393, 1967.
4. Sell, S., J. Immun., *98:* 786, 1967.
5. Sell, S., Fed, Proc., *29:* 301, 1970.
6. Woodruff, M. F. A., Reid, B. and James K., Nature, *215:* 591, 1967.
7. Kekwick, R. A., Biochem. J., *34:* 1248, 1940.
8. Levy, H. B., and Sober, H. A., Proc. Soc. Exp. Biol. Med., *103:* 250, 1960.
9. Nisonoff, A., Wissler, F. C., Lipman, L. N. and Woernley, D. L., Arch. Biochem., *89:* 230, 1960.
10. Porter, R. R., Biochem. J., *73:* 119, 1959.
11. Gell, P. G. H., *Mediators of Cellular Immunity*, Edited by H. Sherwood Lawrence and M. Landy, p. 13, Academic Press, New York, 1969.
12. Bloch-Shtacher, N., Hirschhorn, K. and Uhr, J. W., Clin. Exp. Immun., *3:* 889, 1968.
13. Möller, G., Clin. Exp. Immun., *4:* 65, 1969.
14. Sell, S., Lowe, J. A., and Gell, P. G. H., J. Immun., *104:* 114, 1970.
15. Francis, T. C. and Paul, W. E., Nature, *226:* 173, 1970.
16. Bretscher, P. A. and Cohn, M., Nature, *220:* 444, 1968.
17. Cohn, M., *Immunological Tolerance*, Edited by M. Landy and W. Braun, p. 281, Academic Press, New York, 1969.

THE JOURNAL OF IMMUNOLOGY
Copyright © 1970 by The Williams & Wilkins Co.

Vol. 105, No. 6, December 1970
Printed in U.S.A.

PROPERTIES OF SOLUBLE IMMUNE COMPLEXES[1]

ROBERT W. LIGHTFOOT, JR.,[2] RONALD E. DRUSIN AND CHARLES L. CHRISTIAN[2]

From the Department of Medicine, Columbia University College of Physicians and Surgeons, and the Edward Daniels Faulkner Arthritis Clinic of the Presbyterian Hospital, New York, New York

Received for publication June 22, 1970

Immune complexes have been prepared using oligovalent hapten-protein conjugates as antigens. Antigens with a valence of less than four exhibited restricted reactivity with antibody in the complement-fixation and precipitin reactions, and formed predominantly soluble immune complexes. The complexes thus formed were characterized with respect to density and antibody: antigen (Ab:Ag) composition. Complexes with a density greater than that of 19S proteins, with an Ab:Ag ratio of 5:2 or more, were found to fix complement more efficiently and to have a relatively short intravascular half-life. Complexes less dense than 19S proteins fixed complement poorly and had a prolonged intravascular existence. In situations where antigenic valence restricted precipitate formation, precipitation could be enhanced by human or rabbit complement, and this appeared to be predominantly an effect of C1q.

Numerous studies in recent years have elucidated the pathogenic events leading to the development of nephritis in animals with chronic serum sickness (1, 2). Previous work has indicated that animals destined to develop immune complex nephritis during prolonged intravenous immunization with a fixed daily dose of heterologous albumin synthesize predominantly non-precipitating antibodies that form soluble complexes with the corresponding antigens (3). Although the basis for this type of immune response is not known with certainty, current data support the thesis that failure of antigen to precipitate with antibody in these situations results from a limited recognition of the multiple antigenic determinants on complex antigens (3). With such a concept, heterologous serum albumins would function, with non-precipitating antisera, as oligovalent antigens.

In the present studies, a haptene system was used for the preparation of oligovalent haptene-protein conjugates and the subsequent formation, with anti-haptene antibody, of soluble immune aggregates of different complexities. The molecular character of complexes was estimated, and studies of their biologic properties were performed.

[1] This work was supported in part by grants from the United States Public Health Service, The John A. Hartford Foundation, Inc., and the Health Research Council of the City of New York.

[2] Present address: Hospital for Special Surgery, 535 East 70th Street, New York, N. Y. 10021.

MATERIALS AND METHODS

Antisera. Dinitrophenyl (DNP) groups were heavily conjugated to human γ globulin (HGG), bovine serum albumin (BSA), or keyhole limpet hemocyanin (KLH) using the technique of Benacerraf and Levine (4). These antigens (0.1 to 1.0 mg/ml) were mixed with an equal volume of complete Freund's adjuvant and used as immunogens. Random bred albino rabbits received four weekly injections of 0.4 ml of DNP-BSA or DNP-KLH plus adjuvant into the toe pads. A goat was immunized with six weekly intramuscular injections of DNP-HGG-adjuvant mixture. Sera were obtained 1 week after the last injection and stored at −20°C. Several rabbits were immunized a second time with a single intramuscular injection of DNP-HGG in adjuvant. Sera containing anti-HGG were absorbed with heat-aggregated HGG before the globulin was isolated and behaved in all respects like the other sera. Unless otherwise specified, all sera and globulin preparations were heated at 56°C for 30 min before use.

Precipitating and non-precipitating antisera against human serum albumin (HSA) were available from rabbits injected (i.v.) daily with soluble antigen for several weeks or more (3).

Immunoglobulins were obtained by ammonium

sulfate fractionation and subsequent isolation of the second peak on a Sephadex G-200 column (5). For some experiments, purified anti-DNP antibody was prepared according to the method of Farah *et al.* (6).

Antigens. HGG (Cohn fraction II) was obtained from the American Red Cross and serum albumins and KLH from Pentex, Inc., Kankakee, Ill., and Pacific Marine Laboratory, Venice, Calif., respectively.

Radioiodination with ^{125}I and ^{131}I was accomplished with the iodine monochloride method of McFarlane (7).

DNP was conjugated to ^{125}I-labeled rabbit serum albumin (RSA) using 2,4-dinitrochlorbenzene (DNCB) (4). The conjugates were dialyzed extensively against phosphate-buffered saline (PBS), pH 7.4, and aggregates removed by chromatography on Sephadex G-100. Haptene: protein ratios were estimated by adjusting these preparations to equivalent protein concentrations and comparing the optical density at 360 nm to that of conjugates prepared with ^{14}C-DNCB. The degree of conjugation of the latter was determined by liquid scintillation counting.

Immonologic techniques. Sucrose density gradient centrifugation was performed as described previously (3) in a gradient of 15 to 45% sucrose in PBS spun in a Spinco SW-56 rotor for 16 hr at 40,000 rpm. Standard techniques were used for precipitin (8), microcomplement fixation (9), and passive cutaneous anaphylaxis (PCA) analyses (10).

Rheumatoid factor was precipitated from rheumatoid serum by adding heat-aggregated HGG. The resultant precipitate was washed with PBS, dissolved in glycine-HCl buffer (pH 3.2) and the IgM component isolated by zone centrifugation in an acid gradient. Serum lacking the 11S component of complement (C1q) was prepared by adding heat-aggregated HGG to serum in the presence of sodium EDTA (0.01 M) and separating the supernatant after incubation at 0°C for several hours.

Intravascular clearance of antigen was evaluated by injecting 0.1- to 0.2-ml volumes into the tail veins of random-bred white mice and aspirating 50-μl samples of blood from the retro-orbital venous plexus at intervals thereafter. In certain instances mice were passively immunized 30 min before the clearance determination by injecting antiserum i.v. Samples obtained during clearance were pipetted into 2 ml of saline, and 2 ml of 20% trichloroacetic acid (TCA) were added. TCA-precipitable radioactivity in a given sample was expressed as a percentage of that present in the sample obtained at 2 min.

RESULTS

The reactivity of DNP-RSA conjugates with anti-DNP antisera in precipitin and C fixation reactions is illustrated in Figures 1 and 2. Conjugates with haptene:protein ratios of less than four were weakly or nonreactive. At approximate equivalence in the precipitin reaction, 80% of $DNP_{6.8}RSA$ was precipitated. As the ratio of haptene to protein decreased below this level, there was decreasing precipitation and proportional increase in the amounts of soluble complex formed as determined by gradient centrifugation. Conjugates with ratios in the range of 2 to 3 formed almost exclusively soluble complexes.

Figure 3 illustrates the influence of accessory serum factors on the precipitin reactions of $DNP_{6.2}RSA$ with anti-DNP globulin. With normal rabbit serum (NRS) as diluent, there was enhanced precipitation of antigen at equivalence and in antigen excess. This property—absent in heated NRS or serum depleted of C1q—was most marked in antigen excess. The effect of human rheumatoid factor on the precipitin reaction of

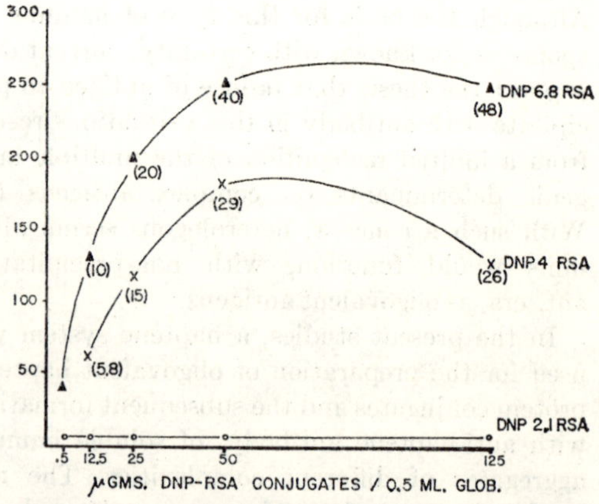

Figure 1. **Precipitin reactions of DNP-RSA (^{125}I) conjugates added to 0.5 ml rabbit anti-DNP globulin. The figures in parentheses indicate μg of ^{125}I-RSA in immune precipitates. In antibody excess, the molecular ratios of immune reactants (antibody-antigen) in precipitates were 4.3 and 5.7 for DNP_4RSA and $DNP_{6.8}RSA$, respectively.**

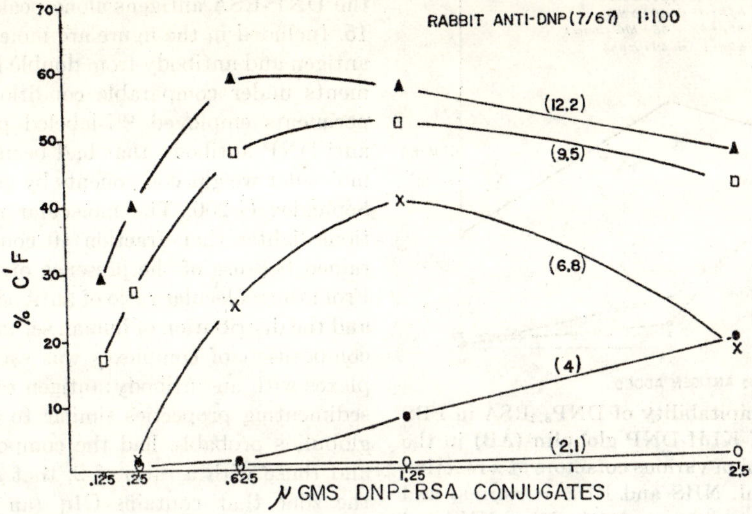

Figure 2. **Micro C fixation reactions of DNP-RSA conjugates with rabbit anti-DNP antiserum. The figures in parentheses indicate haptene:protein ratios of conjugates.**

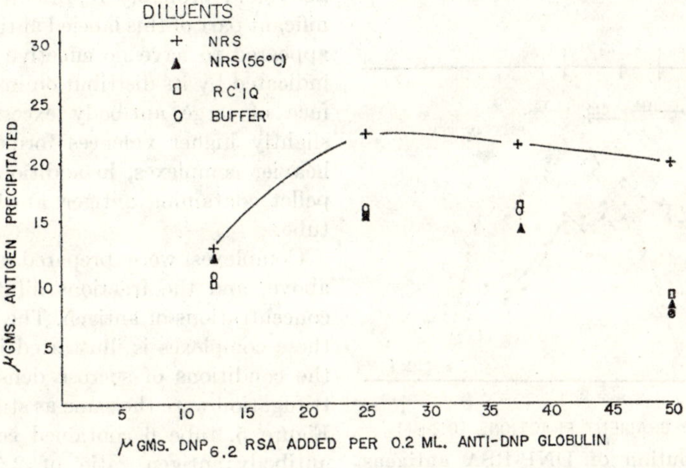

Figure 3. **Effect of accessory serum (rabbit) factors on the precipitation of $DNP_{6.2}RSA$ with rabbit anti-DNP globulin. The total reaction volume of 0.9 ml contained 0.5 ml of the serum reagents.**

$DNP_{8.2}RSA$ is illustrated in Figure 4. In other studies, this property of anti-γ globulin factors, in the zone of antigen excess, could be demonstrated with purified rheumatoid factor. Although normal human serum had negligible effect on precipitation of the relatively multivalent antigen $DNP_{8.2}RSA$, its effect using antigens of lower valence (e.g., $DNP_{4.1}RSA$) was more striking than that of NRS, shown in Figure 3.

The molecular character of immune complexes formed with low valence DNP conjugates was determined by zonal centrifugation. Figure 5 illustrates such a study using two DNP-RSA conjugates with haptene:protein ratios of 1.2 and 1.9, respectively. The complexes were formed in an excess of antibody by adding 50 μg of antigen to 0.5 ml anti-DNP sera, followed by incubation at 37°C for 1 hr and 4°C for 16 hr. Prior to density gradient analysis, any precipitate formed was removed by centrifugation at 2500 rpm for 1 hr at 4°C. In the case of antigens $DNP_{1.2}RSA$ and $DNP_{1.9}RSA$ no precipitate

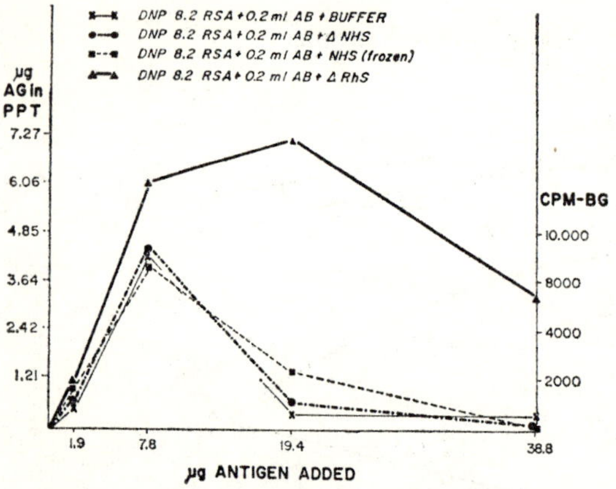

Figure 4. Precipitability of $DNP_{8.2}RSA$ in PBS with 0.2 ml anti-KLH-DNP globulin (AB) in the presence of 0.1 ml of various cofactors at a reaction volume of 0.5 ml. NHS and RHS = normal and rheumatoid human sera, respectively. △ NHS and △ RHS = sera heated to 56°C for 30 min.

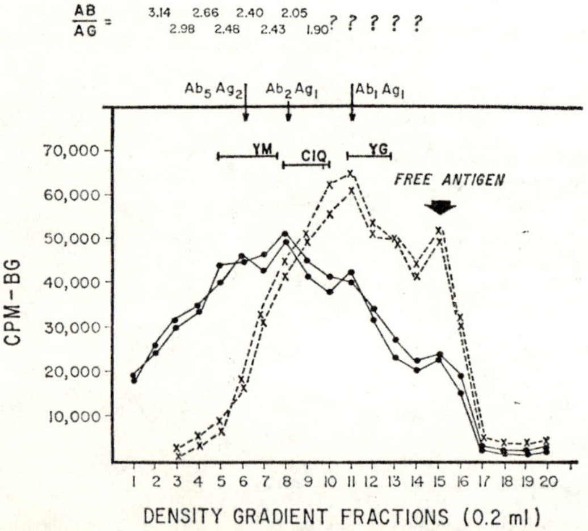

Figure 5. Distribution of DNP-RSA antigens in sucrose gradients; 50 μg of $DNP_{1.9}RSA$ (●——●) or 55 μg $DNP_{1.2}RSA$ (X——X) were reacted with 0.5 ml rabbit anti-DNP sera at 37°C for 60 min and 4°C for 24 hr. Data shown are from simultaneous duplicate runs, with top of gradient to *right*. Numbers at *top* of graph indicate molar ratios of antibody to antigen in various fractions based on double label experiments. *Arrows* signify probable composition of complexes in various fractions. Positions of IgM (γM), IgG (γG) and C1q (C1Q) markers are shown.

formation occurred (see Fig. 1). The distribution of human serum markers is indicated: IgM concentrations were maximal in fractions 5 to 8, Clq in 8 to 10, IgG in 11 to 13, while albumin and the DNP-RSA antigens alone peaked in fraction 15. Included in the figure are molecular ratios of antigen and antibody from double labeled experiments under comparable conditions. These experiments employed ^{131}I-labeled purified rabbit anti-DNP antibody that had been freed of high molecular weight components by gel filtration on Sephadex G-200. The molecular ratios in fractions lighter than fraction 10 could not be obtained because of the presence of free antibody. From the molecular ratio of antibody and antigen and the distribution of human serum proteins, the composition of complexes was estimated. Complexes with an antibody:antigen ratio of 2.5 and sedimenting properties similar to serum macroglobulins probably had the composition Ab_5Ag_2 and those with a ratio of 2, that sediment near the zone that contains C1q (an 11S marker), the composition Ab_2Ag_1. The bulk of complex which formed with $DNP_{1.2}RSA$ (in fraction 11) had a density only slightly greater than free antibody and probably represented Ab_1Ag_1. A significant part of this labeled antigen ($DNP_{1.2}RSA$) appeared to have no effective DNP valence, as indicated by its distribution in fraction 15 in the face of large antibody excess. Antigens with slightly higher valences formed predominantly heavier complexes, in addition to a substantial pellet containing antigen at the bottom of the tube.

Complexes were prepared on a gradient as above, and the fractions diluted to equivalent concentrations of antigen. The clearance rates of these complexes is illustrated in Figure 6. Since the conditions of sucrose density gradient centrifugation were the same as studies illustrated in Figure 5, tube 6 contained complexes with an antibody:antigen ratio of 2.5 and a density equivalent to IgM. These complexes were rapidly cleared from circulation, the 50% clearance level being obtained in approximately 20 min. Complexes in tubes 10 and 12, corresponding in density to C1q, were cleared more slowly. Above a certain minimum dose clearance rate is inversely related to number of particles injected. Therefore these data could be interpreted as showing no more than that a given amount of antigen in the lower gradient zones was contained in a smaller number of particles than at the top of the gradient. The finding of identical clearance data over a fourfold range of injected dose of antigen suggested that the observed differences were not dose-dependent.

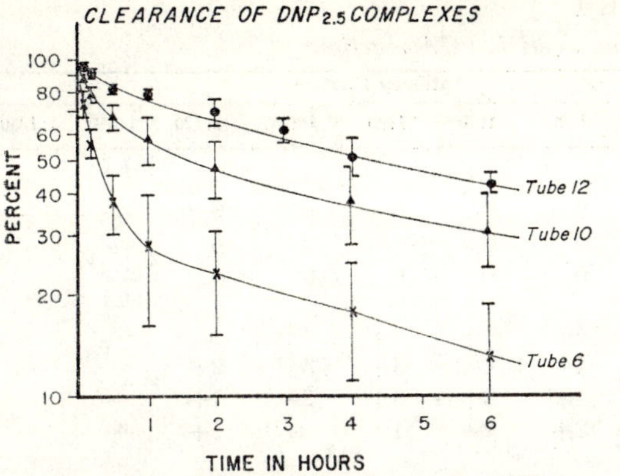

Figure 6. Clearance rates of $DNP_{2.5}RSA$ injected in the form of complexes (containing 30 to 40 μg Ag) obtained from various fractions of a gradient like that in Figure 5. Points represent average values plus or minus one standard deviation for the eight mice in each group and were not significantly different over a fourfold range of antigen concentration.

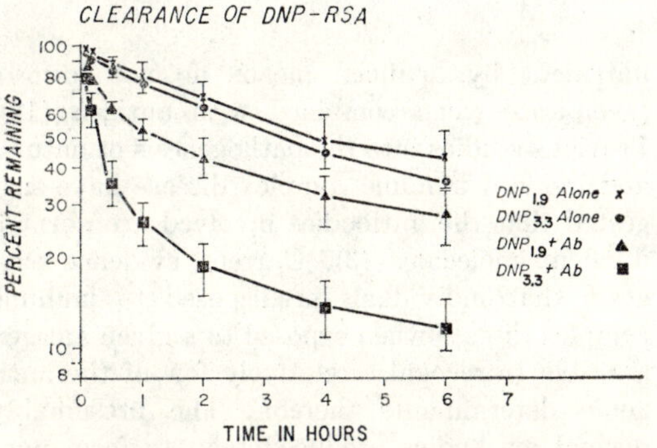

Figure 7. Clearance rates of 6 μg of $DNP_{1.9}RSA$ or $DNP_{3.3}RSA$ in mice pre-injected with 0.2 ml PBS (×, ●) or 0.2 ml rabbit anti-DNP (▲, ■). Points represent mean ± 1 S.D. for four mice in each group.

Figure 7 illustrates the fate of two DNP-RSA conjugates in mice passively immunized with an amount of rabbit anti-DNP antibody twice that required for maximal clearance rates. The rapid clearance of complex formed with $DNP_{3.3}RSA$, comparable to that of 6 in Figure 6, is evident while the clearance rate of $DNP_{1.9}RSA$ after about 1 hr is not significantly more rapid than antigen alone. In spite of this, zone centrifugation of mouse serum obtained at 6 hr showed that more than 50% of the labeled antigen remained complexed to antibody.

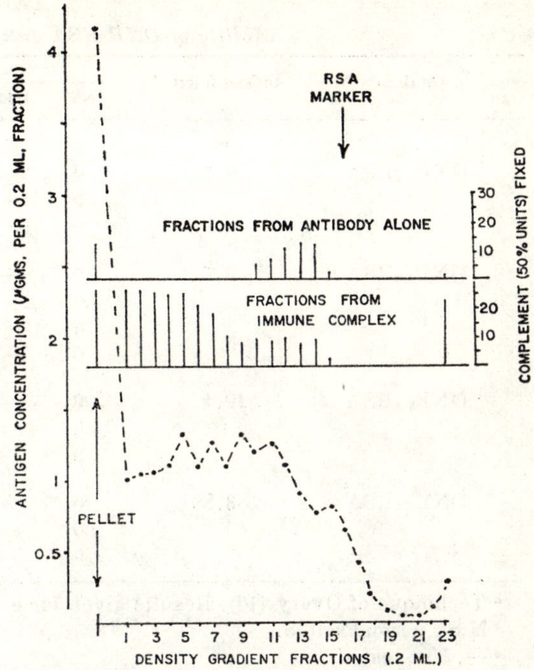

Figure 8. Sucrose gradient distribution of complexes formed with DNP_4RSA (^{125}I-labeled). The fractions (0.2 ml) obtained from sedimentation of 0.5 ml of anti-DNP globulin alone or of 0.5 ml of anti-DNP globulin to which 35 μg of DNP_4RSA had been added were analyzed for anti-complementary activity by incubating each fraction with 0.5 ml of 1:10 diluted guinea pig serum. (●-----● = antigen concentration.)

Corroborative data were obtained in the HSA-rabbit anti-HSA system. Rabbit sera forming heavy (19S) complexes with HSA *in vitro* (3) effected significantly more rapid clearance of ^{131}I-HSA than antisera forming lighter soluble complexes.

Figure 8 summarizes an analysis for anti-complementary (AC) activity of zonal centrifugation fractions from immune complex formed with $DNP_{4.1}RSA$. Comparable fractions from zonal centrifugation of the complex or the antibody globulin alone were incubated with 30 CH_{50} units of guinea pig C and the residual activity was determined after incubation at 37°C for 1 hr and overnight at 0°C. Some AC activity was present in fractions 10 to 15 and in the pellet of the antibody preparation. Fractions 1 to 7 of the complexes formed with $DNP_{4.1}RSA$ demonstrated marked AC effect while fractions 7 to 12, which contained equivalent concentrations of antigen

TABLE I

Ability of DNP-RSA antigens to elicit PCA reaction[a]

Antigen	Antigen Injected	Antibody Dilution								
		NS[b]	1:10	1:20	1:40	1:80	1:160	1:320	1:640	1:1280
	μg									
$DNP_{1.6}RSA$	9.7	0	2+	2+	0	0	0	0	—[c]	—
		0	1+	0	0	0	0	0	—	—
		0	0	0	0	0	0	0	—	—
$DNP_{8.2}RSA$	9.7	0	4+	4+	4+	3+	1+	tr	—	—
		0	4+	4+	4+	3+	3+	2+	—	—
		0	3+	4+	3+	3+	2+	1+	—	—
		0	2+	2+	2+	1+	tr	1+	—	—
$DNP_{1.6}RSA$	19.4	0	—	—	3+	3+	2+	1+	1+	0
		0	—	—	3+	2+	1+	1+	0	0
		0	—	—	1+	tr	tr	0	0	0
$DNP_{8.2}RSA$	3.88	0	—	—	4+	4+	4+	2+	1+	0
		0	—	—	4+	4+	3+	2+	2+	tr
		0	—	—	2+	3+	2+	1+	1+	0

[a] Technique of Ovary (10). Results given for each guinea pig tested.

[b] N.S., normal saline.

[c] —, Not tested.

in complex form, did not possess significantly more AC activity than fractions from the globulin alone. Buffer control tubes, containing no anti-complementary substances, contained 30 CH_{50} units. When the conditions for the study of AC activity were less sensitive than those illustrated in Figure 8, only fractions 1 to 7 and the pellet had activity, and AC activity/μg of antigen in complex was greatest for the pellet fraction.

Table I summarizes PCA analysis of two DNP-RSA conjugates. Equivalent amounts of $DNP_{1.6}$-RSA and $DNP_{8.1}RSA$, the latter of which was reactive in precipitin and CF systems, were tested in guinea pigs sensitized with rabbit anti-DNP-KLH globulin. The more heavily conjugated antigen was much more effective in eliciting PCA, but when the amount of $DNP_{1.6}$-RSA was increased fivefold so as to equalize the dose of the haptene moiety, the difference was less marked.

DISCUSSION

According to current concepts of precipitate formation (11), any limitation on the valence of either antigen or antibody should restrict the insolubility of the resultant immune complexes by interfering with lattice formation. It is well established that antibody molecules rendered univalent by artificial means do not form a precipitate when combined with antigen (12). Previous studies into the pathogenesis of natural and induced immune complex disease have suggested that the antibodies involved are normal, divalent molecules (3). Current evidence suggests that individuals predisposed to immune complex disease when exposed to a given antigen are able to recognize relatively few of the antigenic determinants thereon. The presumably normal antibodies produced tend to form non-precipitating complexes with the "oligovalent" antigen, because of the restrictions imposed on lattice formation by the limited antigenic valence.

The production of disease by such complexes requires two further assumptions: that these complexes are cleared from the intravascular space in a way different from that of the classical opsonized particle, with greater distribution to areas outside the reticuloendothelial system (e.g., kidney), and that, once cleared, they initiate the inflammatory process by activation of the complement, kinin or related systems. Therefore, it would seem relevant for both theoretical and practical reasons to examine the properties of immune complexes formed using antigens whose valences can be varied in a controlled way.

Previous studies on the properties of immune complexes have utilized immune precipitates solubilized in excess antigen (13–15). The composition of such complexes is dependent on the degree of antigen excess. In the system reported here, the Ag:Ab ratio of a complex is limited by the valence of the antigen molecule, as long as an excess of antibody is present.

Early work by Pauling *et al.* (16) demonstrated the anticipated effect of antigenic valence on the precipitation of haptenic groups coupled to relatively small organic carrier molecules. In some instances, variations from the expected were attributed to steric effects of rigidity of the carrier molecule. Using the benzyl penicilloyl haptenic group, Levine and Redmond also noted similar hindrance effects when small carrier molecules with high haptene:carrier ratios were employed (17). With the use of larger carriers, effective immunologic valence approached the chemical valence (haptene:carrier ratio). In the present study, the relatively large and complex carrier molecule, rabbit serum albumin, should have largely eliminated these steric factors. The effect on precipitation of increasing the valence of the DNP-RSA antigens is consistent with the lattice theory. In situations of borderline precipitability the presence of complement caused a substantial increase in precipitation of antigen, and this appeared to be due primarily to the action of C1q. Prior work by Paul and Benacerraf has indicated that in agar diffusion C1 may cause precipitation of otherwise insoluble immune complexes (18). This phenomenon has been used to detect soluble immune complexes in biologic fluids (19). Maurer and Talmage have previously demonstrated the ability of complement to increase antigen, antibody and total protein precipitated, emphasizing that, when low titered antisera were used, complement nitrogen became a significant fraction of total precipitate nitrogen. This effect was most pronounced in the region of antigen excess as in the present study, and was shown to be highly dependent on the species from which both complement and the immune complexes were obtained (20). In the present study results have been expressed in terms of augmentation in micrograms of antigen precipitated to avoid the question of whether the increases in total precipitate nitrogen were due solely to coprecipitation of complement nitrogen with already insoluble complexes.

The diminished fixation of complement in the region of antigen excess in the classical complement fixation curve implies an effect of size of immune complex on complement-fixing ability, as suggested by Heidelberger and Mayer (11). The data presented here indicate a direct correlation between antigenic valence, precipitability and ability to fix complement. The density gradient data provided further evidence that size is an important correlate of complement-fixing ability.

The results of the PCA reaction are consistent with the report of Ishizaka and Ishizaka (21) indicating a requirement for some aggregation of antibody for the elicitation of cutaneous allergy. Recent work by Mancino *et al.* (22) has suggested that monovalent DNP conjugates can elicit PCA if injected in the proper dose. It is not known whether antigen aggregation undetectable by usual physicochemical means was responsible for these findings. The ability of $DNP_{1.6}RSA$ at higher concentrations to elicit PCA in the present study may have been due in part to such an effect, as well as to the presence of trace amounts of more heavily conjugated DNP-RSA molecules insufficient to elicit PCA at the lower dose.

The data presented here suggest an apparent paradox, in that antigens and complexes with the requisite ability to produce injury or inflammation (CF, PCA) are also rapidly eliminated from the bloodstream and should, therefore, be unlikely participants in syndromes presumably caused by chronically circulating soluble immune complexes. Several possible situations could provide a resolution of this paradox. The levels of circulating complexes in disease states may be so great that clearance by the reticuloendothelial system is retarded, allowing time for deposition elsewhere. Such an explanation presumes a continual influx of soluble antigen into the vascular compartment, analogous to prolonged daily intravenous immunization in experimental serum sickness. It is also possible that small complexes with a long intravascular half-life may aggregate subsequent to their deposition in tissue and thus develop the biologic properties necessary for inducing disease. That immune deposits in the renal glomerulus are in a state of flux was suggested by the work of Valdes *et al.* (23) on induced serum sickness in which daily injections to maintain "antigen excess" apparently resulted in gradual removal of these deposits. Finally, although the present report emphasizes the hypothetical role of soluble complexes, formed from nonprecipitating antibodies, in the pathogenesis of immune complex disease, it must be stated that complexes formed from precipitating reactants, even with rapid clearance from circulation, may mediate immunologic injury in chronic serum sickness.

Several studies have suggested a role for complement in hastening the clearance of opsonized particles (24). If the more rapid clearance of larger complexes (mol. wt. 10^6 or greater) is dependent on interaction with complement, depletion of complement by a sustained immunologic process might prolong their intravascular existence. If subsequently deposited in proximity to the circulation, they might then be able to compete for complement components, provoking inflammation while contributing to prolonged hypocomplementemia.

The implications of the data provided by this study suggest that multiple factors are important in defining the *in vitro* and intravascular behavior of a given immune complex. Other factors as well may be operative at the tissue level. Continued efforts to elucidate these mechanisms would seem to be in order.

Acknowledgment. The capable technical assistance of Miss Diva Negrao is greatly appreciated.

REFERENCES

1. Dixon, F. J., Feldman, J. D. and Vazquez, J. J., J. Exp. Med., *113:* 899, 1961.
2. Cochrane, C. G. and Hawkins, D., J. Exp. Med., *127:* 137, 1968.
3. Pincus, T., Haberkern, R. and Christian, C. L., J. Exp. Med., *127:* 819, 1968.
4. Benacerraf, B. and Levine, B. B., J. Exp. Med., *115:* 1023, 1962.
5. Kabat, E. A., in *Kabat and Mayer's Experimental Immunochemistry*, 2nd Ed. p. 762, Charles C Thomas, Springfield, Ill., 1967.
6. Farah, F. S., Kern, M. and Eisen, H. N., J. Exp. Med., *112:* 1195, 1960.
7. McFarlane, A. S., in *Mammalian Protein Metabolism*, Edited by H. N. Munro, and J. B. Allison, Vol. 1, p. 331, Academic Press, Inc., New York, 1964.
8. Kabat, E. A., in *Kabat and Mayer's Experimental Immunochemistry*, 2nd Ed., p. 72, Charles C Thomas, Springfield, Ill., 1967.
9. Wasserman, E. and Levine, L., J. Immun., *87:* 290, 1961.
10. Ovary, Z., in *Immunological Methods*, Edited by J. F. Ackroyd, p. 259. F. A. Davis Co., Philadelphia, 1964.
11. Heidelberger, M. and Mayer, M. M. Advances Enzym., *8:* 71, 1948.
12. Porter, R. R., Biochem. J., *73:* 119, 1959.
13. Weigle, W. O. and Maurer, P. H., J. Immun., *79:* 211, 1957.
14. Edelman, G. M., Kunkel, H. G. and Franklin, E. C., J. Exp. Med., *108:* 105, 1958.
15. Morton, J. I. and Deutsch, H. F., Arch. Biochem., *64:* 26, 1956.
16. Pauling, L., Pressman, D., Campbell, D. H., Ikeda, C. and Ikawa, M., J. Amer. Chem. Soc., *64:* 2994, 1942.
17. Levine, B. B. and Redmond, A. P., J. Clin. Invest., *47:* 556, 1968.
18. Paul, W. E. and Benacerraf, B., J. Immun., *95:* 1067, 1965.
19. Agnello, V., Winchester, R. J. and Kunkel, H. G., Arthritis Rheum., *12:* 654, 1969.
20. Maurer, P. H. and Talmage, D. W., J. Immun., *70:* 435, 1953.
21. Ishizaka, K. and Ishizaka, T., J. Immun., *101:* 68, 1968.
22. Mancino, D., Tigelaar, R. E., and Ovary, Z., J. Immun., *103:* 750, 1969.
23. Valdes, A. J., Senterfit, L. B., Pollack, A. D. and Germuth, F. G., Jr., Johns Hopkins Med. J., *124:* 9, 1969.
24. Spiegelberg, H. L., Miescher, P. A. and Benacerraf, B., J. Immun., *90:* 751, 1963.

THE JOURNAL OF IMMUNOLOGY
Vol. 105, No. 6, December 1970
Printed in U.S.A.

ROSETTE FORMATION IN RELATION TO ACTIVE SYNTHESIS OF ANTIBODY[1]

NEOMI MOAV[2] AND T. N. HARRIS

From The Children's Hospital of Philadelphia and the Department of Pediatrics, University of Pennsylvania, School of Medicine, Philadelphia, Pennsylvania

Received for publication June 22, 1970

Studies were done on the requirement for an active synthetic process for the production of rosettes by mouse spleen cells, and on the relation of rosette-forming cells (RFC) to plaque-forming cells (PFC). Evidence for an active process was obtained by injection of mice with actinomycin D on the day of antigen injection. This prevented the appearance of both RFC and PFC. In other approaches, the inhibiting agents were applied *in vitro* to suspensions of cells producing rosettes. Rosette formation was inhibited on incubation at 37°C, in contrast with 4°C, by inhibitors of protein synthesis, cycloheximide and puromycin, and by anti-metabolites, iodoacetate and arsanilic acid.

The most direct evidence that rosettes and plaques can be produced by the same cells was obtained by differential density centrifugation. Following bovine plasma albumin density gradient centrifugation of original spleen cell suspensions, both rosettes and plaques were found to be produced by cells of the same, relatively low, density. When such suspensions were first incubated for rosette formation, however, the RFC, now in rosettes, were found in a fraction of higher density, intermediate between that of white blood cells and red blood cells. The number of plaques produced by this higher density fraction was found to be markedly increased over the analogous fraction from original spleen cell suspensions, in which rosettes had not been formed.

The nature of the receptors on the cell surface involved in rosette formation was examined in several ways. It was shown that rosette formation could be inhibited by exposure of the cells to an excess of antigen or to anti-IgG serum or its Fab fragments. The rosettes were partially sensitive to complement, indicating that IgM molecules as well as IgG molecules can be involved in rosette formation.

Two methods have been used extensively for investigating *in vitro* production of antibodies against sheep red blood cells (SRBC) by isolated cells: the hemolytic plaque technique described by Jerne *et al.* (1) and by Ingraham and Bussard (2), and the rosette test described by Zaalberg (3) and by Nota *et al.* (4). Since rosette formation requires only the presence of antibody on the surface of the rosette-forming cell (RFC), in contrast to the secretion and diffusion of antibody required for antibody plaque formation, the question has arisen whether plaque formation and rosette formation are two manifestations of the same phenomenon, with different thresholds of detection, or whether they represent different populations of cells which have different levels of activity in antibody synthesis and secretion. This question has been studied by several authors, with conflicting conclusions (5–8).

In an approach to this problem we have compared the kinetics of appearance of plaque-forming cells (PFC) and rosette-forming cells (RFC) in the spleen following immunization, the effect of the immunizing dose of antigen on their appearance and the effects of various antimetabolites and protein inhibitors on rosette formation. Some properties of the cell receptors involved in the formation of rosettes have been studied, and,

[1] This investigation was supported by United States Public Health Service Research Grant HE04598 from the National Heart and Lung Institute and Grant T-526B of the American Cancer Society.

[2] Present address: Department of Microbiology, Tel Aviv University, Tel Aviv, Israel.

finally, the distribution profiles of PFC and RFC have been compared in fractions obtained from centrifugation, in bovine plasma albumin density gradients, of original spleen cell suspensions and of rosette preparations made with such suspensions.

MATERIALS AND METHODS

Materials and chemicals. Bovine plasma albumin (BPA) (fraction V) was obtained from the Armour Co., Chicago, Illinois.

Goat anti-mouse IgG and fetal calf serum were obtained from Microbiological Associates, Bethesda, Md. All fetal calf sera were assayed for toxic effect on mouse cells by incubating mouse RBC with the serum for 1 hr at 37°C. Serum that lysed the RBC was not used.

Sheep blood, from Baltimore Biological Laboratory, Baltimore, Md., was kept in Alsever's solution.

Shigella paradysenteriae Z11 were grown in brain heart infusion medium (Difco Laboratories, Detroit, Mich.), centrifuged and washed several times with phosphate-buffered saline (PBS) and killed by exposure to ethyl alcohol at 70%. A sterile 10% stock suspension of Shigella in PBS was used for immunization.

Shigella O antigen was extracted by pyridine from *Shigella paradysenteriae* according to Goebel *et al.* (9).

Puromycin dihydrochloride was obtained from Nutritional Biochemical Co., Cleveland, Ohio; cycloheximide (Actidione) from The Upjohn Co., Kalamazoo, Mich.; and agarose from L'Industrie Biologique Francaise, S. A. Gennevilliers (Seine), France.

Immunization. C57BL/6 male mice, from The Jackson Laboratory, Bar Harbor, Maine, were injected intraperitoneally with 0.2 ml of washed 50% SRBC for both primary and secondary immunization. For immunization with *Shigella paradysenteriae*, 0.2 ml of 1:100 dilution of a 10% stock suspension was similarly injected.

Preparation of mouse spleen cells. Mice were killed by cervical dislocation. The spleens were excised and teased on a stainless steel no. 80 mesh screen. The cells were washed through the screen with Eagle's medium supplemented with 10% fetal calf serum to disperse most of the large aggregates, and then centrifuged at 1500 rpm for 10 min at 4°C.

Hemolytic plaque assay. The direct hemolytic plaque assay was performed as described by Jerne *et al.* (1).

The indirect (facilitated) plaque test, for the detection of cells presumably releasing 7S antibodies, was carried out according to the method described by Sterzl and Riha (10) and Dresser and Wortis (11).

Rosette test. Cells obtained from mouse spleens immunized with SRBC were washed once with Eagle's medium. Eagle's minimal essential medium, 100 ml, was supplemented with 200 mM glutamine, 1.0 ml; 50 × minimal essential amino acids, 2.0 ml; 100 × nonessential amino acids, 1.0 ml; 100 × vitamins, 1.0 ml; 100 mM sodium pyruvate 1.0 ml (all obtained from Flow Laboratories, Rockville, Md.); and 10% fetal calf serum (Microbiological Associates). The pH was adjusted to pH 7.2 with sodium bicarbonate, 7.5%. The rosette test was performed in a final volume of 1.0 ml of Eagle's medium containing 20 to 30 million cells of spleen or lymph node, and 2% SRBC. The cell suspensions were incubated for 1 to 2 hr at 37°C without shaking and the rosettes were then counted in a hemacytometer.

Anti-Shigella rosettes. The rosette test was modified to assay for cells producing antibodies against Shigella. A 30% suspension of SRBC was incubated on a roller for 30 min at 37°C with an equal volume of pyridine extracted Shigella O antigen at a final concentration of 0.25 mg/ml. The antigen-coated SRBC were washed three times with PBS and mixed with cells obtained from Shigella-immunized animals for rosette formation, as in the usual rosette test.

Preparation of BPA. Bovine plasma albumin was deionized by the procedure of Leif and Vinograd (12). The density of BPA obtained by this procedure was approximately 1.106 g/cm^3 and the pH was adjusted to 7.2 with Na_2CO_3. Solutions of lower density were prepared by diluting the original solution with balanced salt solution 1:1 (v/v). (The composition of the salt solution in g/liter is: 7.61 NaCl, 0.389 KCl, 1.52 $MgCl_2 \cdot 6H_2O$.) The density of the diluted solution was approximately 1.060 g/cm^3. Densities of BPA solutions were determined from their refractive indices, measured with a Bausch and Lomb refractometer at room temperature. The density of the BPA solution was calculated from the refractive index as reported earlier (12).

Fractionation of cells by density gradient centrifu-

gation. Cell suspensions obtained from mouse spleens or rabbit lymph nodes were mixed into 2.5 ml of the BPA with density of 1.106 g/cm³. A linear gradient was prepared by mixing this BPA-cell mixture with 2.5 ml of BPA of density 1.060 g/cm³. The tube was centrifuged for 30 min at 5000 rpm at 4°C, in an SW25 rotor.

RESULTS

A. Kinetics of the appearance of rosette-forming cells and plaque-forming cells following immunization with sheep red blood cells

The kinetics of appearance of rosette-forming cells (RFC) and plaque-forming cells (PFC) by mouse spleen cells were compared following primary and secondary injection of sheep red blood cells (SRBC). Adult C57BL/6 mice were injected with 0.2 ml of a 50% suspension of SRBC. At daily intervals after the injection, three mice were sacrificed and a pooled spleen cell suspension was prepared for determination of the number of RFC, direct PFC (19S) and plaques facilitated by anti IgG (7S). It was found (Fig. 1*a*) that RFC appeared on the 3rd day and increased to a peak level on the 5th and 6th days. Direct hemolytic PFC (19S) appeared on the 4th day; the number rose to a peak on the 5th day, and then declined rapidly. Indirect plaques (facilitated by anti-mouse IgG) appeared on the 7th day, with an increase to the 9th day which was accompanied by an increase in number of RFC. The mice were given a second injection of SRBC, in the same amount, 1 month after the primary dose, and similar observations were made. In this case (Fig. 1*b*) the number of rosettes and plaques (facilitated, in the secondary response) was higher than that seen in the primary response. In both the primary and secondary response, then, the appearance of RFC, and the increase and decrease in their number, paralleled the changes in numbers of PFC.

Similar experiments were carried out with SRBC injected at various doses—0.2 ml of SRBC in suspensions of 2%, 10%, 25%, 50% and 75%. Groups of mice were injected one or two times with the respective doses of SRBC, and on the 5th day after the primary or secondary injection the mice were sacrificed and their spleens were assayed for RFC and total PFC. It was found that for a first injection, 0.2 ml of 25% SRBC was the optimal dose for both plaque and rosette

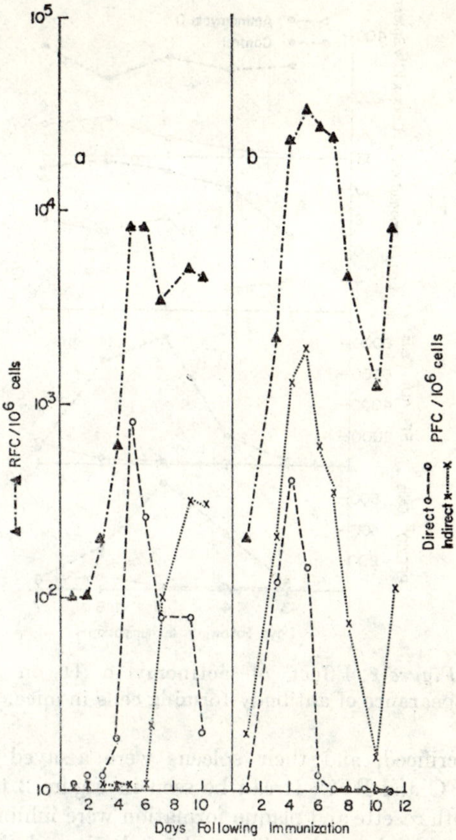

Figure 1. The appearance of rosette-forming cells and plaque-forming cells in mouse spleen following primary (*a*) and secondary (*b*) injection of SRBC.

formation. For secondary immunization, injection of 0.2 ml of 50% SRBC gave the highest number of both rosettes and total plaques. The hemagglutinin titers did not show significant differences among the various doses.

B. Rosette formation in relation to synthesis of antibody

1. Effect of actinomycin D on the immune response. Since actinomycin D inhibits transcription of RNA *in vivo* or *in vitro* (13), the effect of actinomycin D on the formation of rosettes and plaques was examined. Groups of primed mice were injected with 8 μg of actinomycin D 5 hr before they were immunized with 0.2 ml of 50% SRBC, whereas control primed mice were injected only with SRBC. At various intervals after the injection of actinomycin mice were

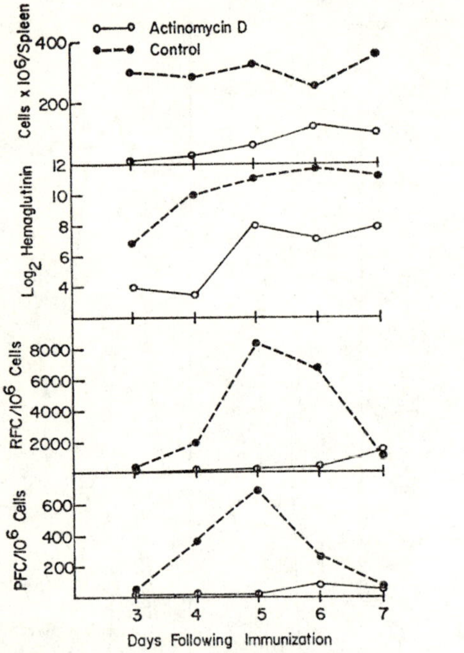

Figure 2. Effect of actinomycin D on the appearance of antibody-forming cells in mice.

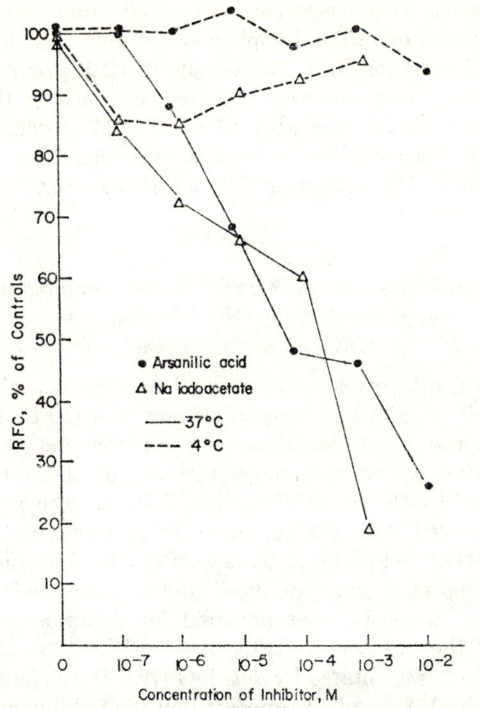

Figure 3. Effect of arsanilic acid and Na iodoacetate on rosette formation.

sacrificed, and their spleens were assayed for PFC and RFC. It can be seen in Figure 2 that both rosette and plaque formation were inhibited completely on days 3, 4 and 5 following administration of the inhibitor. A partial recovery can be seen on days 6 and 7. The actinomycin also caused a marked reduction in the number of cells per spleen and a decrease in serum hemagglutinin titers, which were lower by $\log_2$ 4–6 than those of the control mice. These results indicate that RFC behave in a similar way to PFC in terms of sensitivity to actinomycin D, and that RNA is required for the formation of rosettes.

2. Effect of antimetabolites on rosette formation. The effect of two antimetabolites on the formation of rosettes was examined. These were sodium iodoacetate and arsanilic acid, both known to inhibit enzymes required for the normal metabolism of cells (14). Spleen cells obtained from mice 5 days after a secondary immunization with SRBC were incubated for 2 hr at 37°C with SRBC and arsanilic acid or iodoacetate at several concentrations, and rosette preparations were made. The number of rosettes in each preparation is shown as a percentage of the control, incubated without the inhibitor. In Figure 3 it can be seen that both of these inhibitors had a pronounced effect on rosette formation, when incubated with the cells at 37°C. However, when the cells were incubated with the same concentrations of arsanilic acid or iodoacetate for 2 hr at 4°C no reduction in the number of rosettes was observed.

The results indicate that rosette formation is an active process which requires normal metabolism of cells, when carried out at 37°C. The rosettes formed at 4°C are presumably due to pre-existing antibody at the cell surface and therefore are insensitive to the inhibitor.

3. Effect of inhibitors of protein synthesis on rosette formation. Treatment of antibody-forming cells from spleens of SRBC injected mice with inhibitors of protein synthesis, puromycin or cycloheximide, has been found to cause a reduction in antibody formation (15–16). These observations were applied to rosette formation by incubating spleen cells obtained from mice 5 days after a secondary injection of SRBC with puromycin or cycloheximide at various concentrations before producing rosettes at 37°C and at 4°C. It can be seen (Fig. 4) that both agents caused a marked decrease in the number of

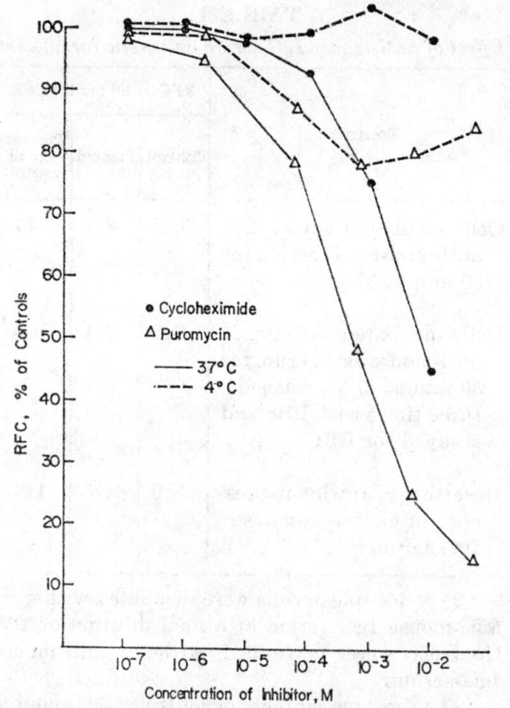

Figure 4. Effect of cycloheximide and puromycin on rosette formation.

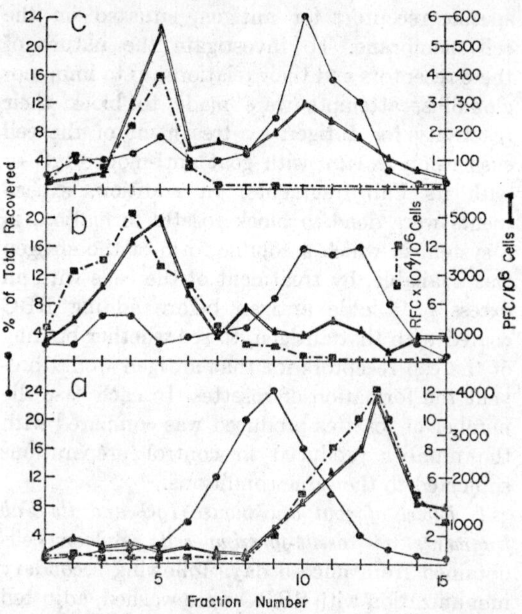

Figure 5. Distribution of plaque-forming cells and rosette-forming cells on bovine plasma albumin density gradients. Spleen cells obtained from mice 5 days after secondary immunization with SRBC. Original cell suspension (*a*) or rosette preparations (*b* and *c*) were centrifuged on BPA density gradients for 30 min at 5000 rpm.

rosettes formed in the 37°C incubation. On the other hand, in the 4°C incubations no such progressive decrease in rosettes was observed. In separate experiments it was shown that incubation of suspensions of preformed rosettes with various concentrations of puromycin or cycloheximide did not reduce the number of rosettes in comparison to control preparations. Thus, the inhibitors affected only the active process of antibody synthesis required for the formation of rosettes.

4. Nutritional requirements for rosette formation. In order to maintain antibody synthesis *in vitro* it is essential to supply the nutritional requirements of the cells, which are basically the precursors for synthesis of nucleic acids and proteins, and a source of energy. The nutritional requirements for rosette-forming cells were studied in spleen cells obtained from mice 5 days following secondary immunization with SRBC. The cells were suspended in Hanks' salt solution and incubated for 2 hr at 37°C to exhaust the pools of precursors in the cells. The cells were then washed once with Hanks' solution to remove excess antibody or other cell products which might have been released into the medium during the incubation period. The cells were then resuspended in Eagle's solution (Hanks' base) supplemented with either a mixture of amino acids, 10% fetal calf serum, or both. SRBC were added and the cells were incubated for 2 hr at 37°C for rosette formation.

The number of rosettes formed by cells suspended in Eagle's medium with 10% FCS was used as a control. In the Hanks' salt solution alone only 33% of the rosettes were formed. Supplementing this solution with a mixture of amino acids increased the number of rosettes to 88%, supplementing with fetal calf serum, to 92%, and adding both, 98%. Neither of the supplements had any effect on the number of rosettes formed when the cells were incubated at 4°C.

C. The nature of the receptors on rosette-forming cells

The reaction of spleen cells with antigen involved in rosette formation appears to involve specific receptors for antigen, situated on the cell membrane. To investigate the nature of these receptors and their relationship to immunoglobulins, attempts were made to block their reactivity for antigen by treatment of the cell suspension *in vitro* with goat anti-mouse IgG or with its Fab fragments. In addition, experiments were done to block rosette formation, in a system in which a soluble form of the antigen was available, by treatment of the cells with an excess of soluble antigen before adding RBC coated with that antigen, to see whether binding of the cell receptors for that antigen would prevent the formation of rosettes. In each case the number of rosettes produced was compared with the number produced in control preparations subjected to the same conditions.

1. Effect of goat anti-mouse IgG and its Fab fragments on rosette-forming cells. Spleen cells obtained from mice 5 days following secondary immunization with SRBC were washed, adjusted to a concentration of 20 to 30 $\times$ 10^6 cells in 0.5 ml of Eagle's medium, and incubated for 30 min at 37°C with an equal volume of goat anti-mouse IgG serum which had been heated to 56°C for 30 min and absorbed with SRBC. SRBC were added directly, and the cell suspension was incubated for 1 hr at 37°C. The results, in the upper row of Table I, show that pretreatment of the spleen cells *in vitro* with goat anti-mouse IgG serum caused an inhibition of rosette formation to less than half of the control level. In other portions of the cell suspension, the excess anti-mouse IgG serum was washed away after the first 30 min of incubation and the rosette preparation was then made. The rosette counts of the controls were considerably lower, reflecting the effect of the additional washing and resuspension of the cells following exposure to the goat antiserum, as seen in the second row of Table I, but the rosette count of the treated cell suspension showed considerably less reduction, to 80% of the control level. Finally, when the goat anti-mouse IgG serum was not used in a pretreatment of the spleen cells but, rather, was added at the beginning of the incubation of spleen cells and SRBC for rosette formation, there was an increase in the number of the rosettes formed to approximately 150% of the control level. (The higher control level here, relative to the top row of the table, reflects the shorter total incubation at 37°C.)

TABLE I

Effect of anti-mouse IgG serum on rosette formation[a]

Treatment	RFC $\times$ 10^3 per 10^6 Cells		
	Control	Treated	Percentage of control[b]
Cells incubated with goat anti-mouse IgG serum for 30 min at 37°C	20.2	8.7	43
Cells incubated with goat anti-mouse IgG serum for 30 min at 37°C, washed three times with PBS and assayed for RFC	8.8	7.1	80
Rosette preparation in presence of goat anti-mouse IgG serum	28.0	41.5	148

[a] 25 $\times$ 10^6 spleen cells were incubated with goat anti-mouse IgG serum at a final dilution of 1:2. Controls were performed without anti-mouse IgG-serum.

[b] The three percentages of control rosette counts are mean values from 20 experiments.

This increase in the number of rosettes formed might be due to an orientation of rosette-producing antibodies at the surface of the RFC by anti-IgG, which could increase the efficiency of the antibody in binding the RBC. To test this possibility, the rosette test was performed in the presence of univalent Fab fragments prepared from anti-mouse IgG serum. Fab fragments were prepared by digestion of the antibody molecules with 0.25 mg/ml papain for 2 hr at 37°C as described by Ogburn *et al.* (17). Rosette tests were done in the presence of various dilutions of the preparation of anti-mouse IgG Fab fragments. A pronounced reduction in the number of RFC was observed (Table II). These results show that rosette formation was progressively inhibited with increasing concentration of the Fab fragments of anti-mouse immunoglobulin. This would be consistent with the presence of immunoglobulin receptors on the cell surface.

2. Inhibition of anti-Shigella rosettes with soluble Shigella antigen. Spleen cells obtained from mice 5 days following secondary immunization with Shigella were suspended at a concen-

TABLE II

Effect of anti-mouse IgG Fab fragments on rosette formation

Final Dilution of Fab Fraction	RFC × 10[3] per 10[6] Cells	Percentage of Control
	50.0	100
1:128	42.0	85
1:64	35.0	70
1:32	26.0	52
1:16	17.5	35
1:8	12.5	25
1:4	8.5	17

tration of 25×10^6/ml in Eagle's medium containing 0.5 mg/ml of soluble Shigella antigen. Following incubation for 30 min at 37°C in roller tubes, a portion of the cell suspension was removed and the rosette test was performed with Shigella-antigen-coated SRBC. The remaining cells were washed four times with PBS to remove excess antigen. Following each wash a sample of cells was removed and assayed for rosette formation.

It can be seen in Table III that preincubation of the cells with the antigen inhibited formation of rosettes. After extensive washing of the cells there was a slight recovery to 36% of the number of rosettes in the control preparation. This might in part be due to some dissociation of antigen from the antibody on the cell surface.

3. Effect of 2-mercaptoethanol (2-ME) on rosette formation. In order to determine the type of antibody, 19S or 7S, causing rosette formation at various intervals after primary immunization, cells obtained on days 3 and 10 were examined for production of rosettes upon treatment with 2-ME. Spleen cells were incubated for 2 hr at 37°C with SRBC in presence of 2-ME at concentrations from 0.01 M to 0.1 M. The number of rosettes formed under these conditions was compared to the control, incubated without 2-ME. It was found that the sensitivity of rosettes to 2-ME treatment was greater at day 3 than at day 10. At 0.1 M 2-ME, only 8% of the rosettes at day 3 were resistant to 2-ME, in comparison with 35% resistant rosettes formed by spleen cells at day 10.

The effect of 2-ME was also tested on preformed rosettes, produced by spleen cells obtained at days 5 and 12. After rosette formation,

TABLE III

Inhibition of anti-Shigella rosettes with soluble Shigella antigen

Conditions for Rosette Formation	Percentage of Control
Incubation with soluble Shigella antigen	7.7
Wash	
1	12.2
2	16.0
3	36.5
4	36.4
Incubation without the antigen (control)	100

2-ME was added at a final concentration of 0.1 M, and the rosettes were counted after further incubation for 2 hr at 37°C. Of rosettes produced with 12-day cells, 75% to 100% were resistant to 2-ME, in comparison with 25% to 50% in the case of 5-day cells.

To test for direct cytotoxicity of the 2-ME on the spleen cells, these were incubated for 2 hr at 37°C with 0.1 M 2-ME before doing trypan blue dye exclusion tests. No toxic effect on the spleen cells was shown by 2-ME at the concentration used, although higher concentrations of 2-ME caused some increase in trypan blue-stained cells, as well as some lysis of SRBC.

On the basis of the difference in sensitivity to 2-ME it can be concluded that rosettes can be formed by both 19S and 7S antibody. On the early days following immunization the rosettes were formed largely by 19S antibody, and later, by the 7S antibody.

D. Correlation between plaque-forming cells and rosette-forming cells on bovine plasma albumin density gradients

Spleen cells obtained from mice 5 days following secondary immunization were layered on BPA density gradients and centrifuged for 30 min at 5000 rpm in an SW25 rotor. Fractions were collected, and the cells were washed once with PBS to remove the BPA. Each fraction was divided into three portions, for determination of cell number, and plaque and rosette formation. Figure 5*a* shows that the peak of the PFC and RFC were in the same fraction, indicating that the plaques and the rosettes were formed by cells of the same range of density.

Previous experiments had shown that rosettes can be concentrated within the total cell population, by using BPA density gradients (18). After centrifugation in such gradients the rosettes are found near the bottom of the BPA gradient. If RFC and PFC are two different cell populations, then, following rosette formation, the appearance of the PFC at the top of the gradient (Fig. 5*a*) should not be affected by the fact that the RFC, now included in rosettes with the higher density RBC, are near the bottom. However, if the plaques and the rosettes are formed by the same cell population, then the shift of the RFC from the top of the gradient to the bottom should result in a similar shift in the peak of the PFC.

Rosettes were prepared from spleen cells obtained from mice 5 days following secondary immunization with SRBC. The preparations were layered on BPA density gradients and centrifuged for 30 min at 5000 rpm in the SW25 rotor. Fractions were collected, washed once with PBS and assayed for the number of nucleated cells, rosettes and PFC. As can be seen from Figure 5*b* all the rosettes appeared close to the bottom of the gradient, and the peak of the PFC corresponded to the peak of the rosettes. These results suggest that the rosettes and the plaques are formed by the same cell population.

In some of the experiments two peaks of PFC were observed, one at the top of the gradient and another corresponding to the peak of the RFC at the bottom of the gradient (Fig. 5*c*). The fact that not all the PFC were found at the bottom of the gradient in these experiments can be explained by the fact that the cells were incubated with the SRBC for only 1 hr at 37°C to form rosettes, and not all of the RFC formed rosettes in 1 hr. The antibody-producing cells which had not formed rosettes within the period of incubation would appear, as PFC, at the top of the gradient. Another possible explanation is that some of the rosettes produced by the RFC might have dissociated, so that some of these cells would appear, as PFC, at the top of the gradient.

DISCUSSION

Rosette production in relation to an active process of synthesis of antibody. The requirement for *de novo* biosynthesis of nucleic acid and protein for the formation of rosettes was demonstrated by the effects of inhibitors such as actinomycin D, puromycin and cycloheximide. Actinomycin D, when injected into the animal 5 hr before immunization, was found to suppress rosette formation completely in cells obtained 4 and 5 days after immunization, with partial recovery on days 6 and 7. Because it has been shown (19) that actinomycin D blocks transcription of RNA, it can be concluded that synthesis of RNA is required for the formation of rosettes as well as for plaque formation. These results are in agreement with experiments of others in which it was shown that plaque formation and other indications of the immune response can be inhibited with actinomycin D (1, 13, 20, 21).

In terms of the *in vitro* incubation for the production of rosettes, the question of whether the antibody by which rosettes are formed is being actively synthesized by the RFC or simply released from an intracellular pool in the cells arises in part because rosette formation requires only a small amount of antibody, relative to the amount required for plaque production. The approach taken to this question was to apply relevant reagents such as inhibitors of protein synthesis or antimetabolites to rosette-forming cells at 37°C and at 4°C, because the difference in production of rosettes at the two temperatures would reflect a contribution due to synthesis of antibody during the incubation for rosette formation. Both the inhibitors of protein synthesis examined, puromycin and cycloheximide, caused a progressive decrease in the number of rosettes produced at 37°C, with increasing concentration of the inhibitor, but not a similar effect at 4°C. Two antimetabolites, arsanilic acid and sodium iodoacetate, also caused decreased rosette formation at 37°C, again with no similar effect on the cells at 4°C. The possibility that the inhibitors act by damaging the cells rather than by inhibiting a metabolic pathway was ruled out by the demonstration that the inhibitors had no detectable cytotoxic effects on the cells at concentrations which inhibited rosette formation. Since antimetabolites have been shown to decrease the number of plaques produced by antibody-forming cells (21–25), these data again show a similarity of an active process of antibody formation in rosette production and plaque production.

The nutritional requirements for rosette formation also support the conclusion that an active synthetic process is involved in the formation of rosettes.

The receptor sites on RFC. The reaction of antibody-producing cells of lymph node and spleen with antigen, as expressed by rosette formation, suggests that the newly synthesized antibody molecules, still attached to the cell surface, can act as specific receptors for the antigen. It has been shown that these "cell receptors" can be blocked with the immunizing antigen, with anti-mouse IgG serum, or with its Fab fragments, which is consistent with this view. The possibility that the inhibitory effect of the anti-mouse IgG serum on the formation of the rosettes is due to steric inhibition cannot be excluded; however, the fact that anti-IgG Fab fragments also inhibited rosette formation suggests that the inhibition is more likely due to binding rather than steric inhibition.

The data on the susceptibility of the rosette-forming cells to 2-ME indicate that both 7S and 19S antibodies can form rosettes. Incubation of rosette-forming cells with 0.1 M of 2-ME, the same concentration used for reducing 19S antibody activity in the serum (26), caused reduction in the number of rosettes formed. The susceptibility of the rosettes to 2-ME was greater on days 3 to 5 following immunization than on days 10 to 12, indicating that the rosettes which formed early after immunization are due primarily to 19S antibody and those produced later after immunization are mainly due to 7S antibody.

In another system, Biozzi *et al.* (27) used specific anti-γ_1 and anti-γ_2 serum to inhibit rosette formation by guinea pig lymph node cells. McConnell *et al.* (28) inhibited rosette formation by mouse lymph node cells with anti-μ and anti-γ heavy chain sera. It can therefore be concluded that several classes of antibody molecules attached to the cell surface can form rosettes. Inhibition of rosette formation by anti-immunoglobulin serum does not imply that the surface antibodies are in a unique form specific for RFC because plaques, which are formed by release of antibody molecules, can also be inhibited with anti-immunoglobulin sera (10, 29).

The relation between RFC and PFC. It has been shown that in a suspension of cells from stimulated lymph organs the number of cells forming rosettes is consistently higher that the number of cells which produce plaques. The question has arisen whether the rosettes and the plaques are being produced by the same cell population or by two distinct cell populations.

From the kinetics experiments it can be seen that the time of appearance and the relative frequency on successive days after immunization were quite similar for RFC and for PFC, direct (19S) and indirect (7S), in the primary and secondary responses, respectively. Similar results have been reported by Biozzi *et al.* (30, 31). Also, the effect of antigen dose on the immune response was similar for plaque and rosette formation, suggesting that both the RFC and PFC were stimulated to a similar degree by the same dose of antigen injected.

It seems reasonable that a larger quantity of antibody is required to cause a visible zone of hemolysis by diffusion into the gel medium than to agglutinate SRBC at the surface of the antibody-producing cell. Cunningham and Szenberg (32) and Golub *et al.* (33) recently showed that the method of hemolytic plaque formation in gel as originally described is not sensitive enough to reveal cells that are producing relatively small amounts of hemolytic antibody. They described a more sensitive method of plaque formation in thin layers that can detect about three times more antibody-producing cells than the classical Jerne's technique. Similarly, Nossal *et al.* (34) have recently described a considerably more sensitive adaptation of the gel technique originally described by Ingraham and Bussard (2).

In our approach to the question of whether the difference between the number of rosettes and plaques reflects a difference in sensitivity of the two detection methods rather than a difference in the nature of the antibody or the cell types, we used the concentration of cells by density gradient centrifugation. The advantage of this method over methods of isolating single cells, which have been used in other studies on this question, is that it allows the testing of a large number of cells for their ability to form rosettes, plaques, or both under various experimental conditions. When the original cell suspensions were fractionated on BPA density gradients and each fraction was assayed for PFC and RFC simultaneously, both curves followed the same density profile. However, the possibility remained that it was not the same cells which caused plaque and rosette formation, but merely cells in the same range of density.

An approach directed more particularly at the RFC was to allow rosette formation to proceed, to then centrifuge the suspension on a BPA density gradient and to assay each fraction for PFC. The RFC, now included in units of higher density, the rosettes, appeared near the bottom of the gradient, and a new peak of plaque production was also found in these fractions. If the PFC were formed by a cell population other than that of the RFC, they should have remained at the top of the gradient at the same range of density as in the original cell suspension, and not be affected by the fact that the rosettes were at the bottom of the gradient. The shift, however, in the peak of the plaques following the fractionation of the rosette preparation indicates that the same cells can produce rosettes and plaques. In some of the experiments there was a small peak of PFC which was not shifted toward the high density region following fractionation of the rosette suspension. This might be due to the fact that the incubation for rosette formation was for only 1 hr, so that not all of the potential RFC actually formed rosettes. Some of the potential RFC could have appeared at the low-density region of the gradient and have given rise to plaques. Another possibility is that some of the rosettes were dissociated during the fractionation procedure and the cells then appeared at the lower density region, with other antibody-forming cells.

The conclusion of these experiments is, then, that the same cells can produce rosettes and plaques. These results are in agreement with the results of two recent studies. Zaalberg *et al.* (7) allowed spleen cells to produce rosettes, then added complement and anti-IgG in agar-free medium for further incubation. At the end of the incubation period he showed that 90% of the rosettes were lysed by complement, either directly or after the addition of anti-IgG. Cunningham *et al.* (8) used agar-free medium to form plaques first, then removed the PFC from the media, washed them from the complement and added fresh SRBC. He found that all of the PFC were able to form rosettes under these conditions, but only some of the RFC produced plaques when complement and anti-IgG were added. On the other hand, Shearer and Cudkowicz (5) reported that RFC did not produce plaques when embedded in agar with complement and anti-IgG. The reason for the conflicting results might be the use of agar *vs* agar-free medium for lysing the rosettes. It is possible that the amount of complement that reached the agglutinates of SRBC around the lymphoid cells was not enough to lyse the SRBC or that it was not enough to cause a visible zone of hemolysis when embedded in agar.

REFERENCES

1. Jerne, N. K., Nordin, A. and Henry, C., in *Cell Bound Antibodies*, Edited by B. Amos and H. Koprowski, p. 109, The Wistar Institute Press, Philadelphia, 1963.
2. Ingraham, J. and Bussard, A., J. Exp. Med., *119:* 667, 1964.
3. Zaalberg, O. B., Nature, *202:* 1231, 1964.
4. Nota, N. R., Liacopoulos-Briot, M., Stiffel, C. and Biozzi, G., C. R. Acad. Sci. (D) (Paris), *259:* 1277, 1964.
5. Shearer, G. M. and Cudkowicz, G., J. Immun., *101:* 1264, 1968.
6. Zaalberg, O. B., Van der Neul, V. A. and Van Twisk, J. M., Nature, *210:* 544, 1966.
7. Zaalberg, O. B., Van der Neul, V. A. and Van Twisk, J. M., J. Immun., *100:* 451, 1968.
8. Cunningham, A. J., Smith, J. B. and Mercer, E. H., J. Exp. Med., *124:* 701, 1966.
9. Goebel, W. F., Binkley, F. and Perlman, E., J. Exp. Med., *81:* 315, 1945.
10. Sterzl, J. and Riha, I., Nature, *208:* 858, 1965.
11. Dresser, D. W. and Wortis, H. H., Nature, *208:* 859, 1965.
12. Leif, R. C. and Vinograd, V., Proc. Nat. Acad. Sci., *51:* 520, 1964.
13. Lazda, V. and Starr, J. L., J. Immun., *95:* 254, 1965.
14. Hochster, R. M. and Quastel, J. H., *Metabolic Inhibitors*, Academic Press, New York, 1963.
15. Ambrose, C. T., Bact. Rev., *30:* 403, 1966.
16. Rose, N. R., Haber, J. H. and Calabresi, P., Proc. Soc. Exp. Biol. Med., *128:* 1121, 1968.
17. Ogburn, C. A., Harris, T. N. and Harris, S., J. Immun., *99:* 713, 1967.
18. Moav, N. and Harris, T. N., Proc. Soc. Exp. Biol. Med., *128:* 407, 1968.
19. Kahn, E., Kahn, F. M. and Hurowitz, J., J. Biol. Chem., *238:* 2391, 1963.
20. Uhr, J. W., Science, *142:* 1476, 1963.
21. Strander, H., Immunology, *10:* 45, 1966.
22. Storb, U., Chiller, J. M. and Weiser, R. S., Proc. Soc. Exp. Biol. Med. *131:* 835, 1969.
23. Mazzur, S. R., Ellsworth, B. and Paucker, K., J. Immun., *98:* 638, 1967.
24. Fitch, F. W., Roseman, J. M., Rowley, D. A.

and Berenbaum, M. C., Nature, *218:* 972, 1968.
25. Roseman, J. M., Leserman, L. D., Fitch, F. W. and Rowley, D. A., J. Immun., *102:* 1002, 1969.
26. Deutsch, H. F. and Morton, J. I., Science, *125:* 600, 1957.
27. Biozzi, G., Binaghi, R. A., Stiffel, C. and Mouton, D., Immunology, *16:* 349, 1969.
28. McConnell, I., Munro, A., Gurner, B. W. and Coombs, R. R. A., Int. Arch. Allerg., *35:* 209, 1969.
29. Estwick, N., Merchant, B. and Sturdivant, B., Fed. Proc., *28:* 3093, 1969.
30. Biozzi, G., Stiffel, C. and Mouton, D., *Immunity, Cancer, and Chemotherapy*, Edited by E. Mihich, Academic Press, Inc., New York, 1967.
31. Biozzi, G., Stiffel, C., Mouton, D., Bouthillier, Y. and Decreusefonol, C., Immunology, *14:* 7, 1968.
32. Cunningham, A. J. and Szenberg, A., Immunology, *14:* 599, 1968.
33. Golub, E. S., Mishell, R. I., Weigle, W. O. and Dutton, R. W., J. Immun., *100:* 133, 1968.
34. Nossal, G. J. V., Bussard, A. E., Lewis, H. and Mazie, J. C., J. Exp. Med., *131:* 894, 1970.

THE JOURNAL OF IMMUNOLOGY
Vol. 105, No. 6, December 1970
Printed in U.S.A.

BIOLOGIC ACTIVITIES OF LYMPH NODE CELLS FRACTIONATED ON BOVINE PLASMA ALBUMIN[1]

NEOMI MOAV[2] AND T. N. HARRIS

From The Children's Hospital of Philadelphia and the Department of Pediatrics, University of Pennsylvania, School of Medicine, Philadelphia, Pennsylvania

Received for publication June 22, 1970

For the study of some characteristics of antibody-forming cells optimal conditions were determined for enrichment of plaque-forming cells (PFC) in suspensions of rabbit lymph node cells (LNC) by density gradient centrifugation in bovine plasma albumin. The most enriched fractions contained 5 to 15 times their concentration in the original unfractionated cell suspension. There was a correlation between the size distribution of the LNC and their density, the smallest cells appearing in the high density region of the gradient, and the medium and large cells in the low density region.

PFC obtained from rabbits 3 to 4 days after secondary injection of *Shigella paradysenteriae* were all in low density fractions. On days 4 to 5 some PFC appeared among the highest density fractions, with a gradual shift in that direction until, by day 10, all PFC were in high density fractions. The plaques produced by cells of the low density region of the gradient were prevented by treatment of the plates with 2-mercaptoethanol (2-ME), whereas the antibody produced by the high density cells was 2-ME resistant. Mouse spleen cells and LNC did not show such high density PFC at these times.

The antigen-binding capacity of LNC from normal and immunized rabbits was studied with ^{131}I-labeled soluble Shigella antigen. It was found that the antigen-binding profile of LNC from immunized rabbits followed the profile of the PFC, but among cells obtained from normal rabbits, or rabbits immunized with an unrelated antigen, high density cells were found to bind the antigen.

The biosynthetic activity of mouse spleen cells was measured by the incorporation of radioactive amino acids, uridine and thymidine into macromolecules. The density gradient fractions containing the PFC showed greater incorporation of the precursors than the rest of the population.

Fractionation of complex populations of cells, with resulting concentration of subpopulations which differ in some physical property and still retain their normal function, is an effective tool for the study of problems in cellular biology. Many techniques for separating cells have been tested (1). An important method is density gradient centrifugation, in which cells are spun to their equilibrium position in a gradient of bovine plasma albumin (2, 3).

Antibody-producing cells resemble most of the other cells in antibody-producing organs. However, it is generally accepted that the antibody-producing cells are newly synthesized (4–6) and therefore will show a range of stages of differentiation, at least shortly after induction. Recent electron microscopic studies of cells isolated during antibody formation have shown that these vary in certain characteristics, especially in the size and degree of development of the cytoplasmic organelles (7). It is suggested that the changes observed in the relative size of cytoplasm and nucleus of these cells could affect their net

[1] This investigation was supported by United States Public Health Service Research Grant HE04598 from the National Heart and Lung Institute and Grant T-526B of the American Cancer Society.

[2] Present address: Department of Microbiology, Tel Aviv University, Tel Aviv, Israel.

density. Changes in density correlated with synthesis of protein and RNA have, in fact, been found in avian erythrocytes (8). Density gradient centrifugation in bovine plasma albumin (BPA) has also been used for fractionation of various cells where differences in density might be involved (2, 9). Using this technique, Szenberg and Cunningham (3) fractionated peripheral lymphocytes according to their densities and obtained fractions with relative enrichment of small, medium and large lymphocytes, respectively.

In an attempt to correlate the density of cells with their biologic activities, lymph node cells, obtained from normal and immunized rabbits, and spleen cells of mice were fractionated on BPA density gradients, and cell fractions in which cells of various ranges of density were concentrated were studied in terms of cell size, antigen binding, biosynthetic activity and plaque production at various times after injection of antigen.

MATERIALS AND METHODS

Materials and chemicals. Bovine plasma albumin (fraction V) was obtained from the Armour Co., Chicago, Illinois.

Shigella paradysenteriae Z11 were grown in brain heart infusion medium (Difco Laboratories, Detroit, Mich.), centrifuged and washed several times with phosphate-buffered saline (PBS) and killed by exposure to ethyl alcohol at 70%. A sterile 10% stock suspension of Shigella in PBS was used for immunization.

Labeled compounds. ^{14}C-amino acid mixture (uniformly labeled), 0.05 mCi/0.0335 mg, was obtained from New England Nuclear Co., Boston, Mass., and uridine, 5-^{3}H, specific activity 20 Ci/mM, and thymidine-methyl-^{3}H, specific activity 6 Ci/mM, from Schwarz Bio-Research Co., Orangeburg, N. Y.

Immunization. Male mice, C57BL/6, from The Jackson Laboratory, Bar Harbor, Maine, were injected intraperitoneally with 0.2 ml 50% sheep red blood cells (SRBC) washed in PBS, for primary and secondary immunization. Rabbits were injected with 0.5 ml of 50% SRBC in each hind footpad twice, with an interval of 5 to 6 weeks. For immunization with *Shigella paradysenteriae*, 0.2 ml of 1:10 dilution of a 10% stock suspension was injected in each hind footpad as a primary immunization. Secondary injections were of 0.4 ml of 1:5 of the stock suspension, 30 days or more after the first.

Cell preparations. Rabbit popliteal lymph nodes were obtained immediately after sacrifice by air injection into the heart. The fat was trimmed away and the nodes were teased with forceps on stainless steel mesh no. 40, and then no. 80. The cells were centrifuged at 1500 rpm for 10 min at 4°C. Mice were killed by cervical dislocation and their spleens were similarly teased. The cells were washed through the screen with Hanks' medium to disperse most of the large aggregates, and then centrifuged at 1500 rpm for 10 min at 4°C.

Hemolytic plaque assay. The direct hemolytic plaque test was performed according to the method of Jerne and Nordin (10). The indirect hemolytic test for facilitated plaques, presumably due to 7S antibodies, was performed according to Sterzl and Riha (11) and Dresser and Wortis (12).

Anti-Shigella plaques were detected by the use of SRBC which had been incubated at 30% suspension with an equal volume of pyridine extract of Shigella O antigen (13) at a final concentration of 0.25 mg/ml, for 30 min at 37°C. The coated SRBC were washed three times with PBS and incorporated into agarose (L'Industrie Biologique Francaise S. A. Gennevilliers (Seine), France) at a final concentration of 3%, as for the usual plaque test.

Density gradient centrifugation. Preparation of BPA. Bovine plasma albumin was deionized by the procedure described by Leif and Vinograd (2) and gradients were prepared as in the preceding paper (1.106 to 1.060 g/cm^{3}).

Fractionation of separated cells by density gradient centrifugation. Cell suspensions obtained from mouse spleens or rabbit lymph nodes (40 to 70 $\times$ 10^{6}) were mixed into 2.5 ml of the BPA with density of 1.106 g/cm^{3}. A linear gradient was prepared by mixing this BPA-cell mixture with 2.5 ml of BPA of density 1.06 g/cm^{3}. The tube was centrifuged for 30 min at 5000 rpm at 4°C, in an SW25 rotor. Fractions were collected by piercing the base of the tube with an 18-gauge needle. The number of nucleated cells in each fraction was determined after lysis of the erythrocytes present, by diluting the samples with 1.5% acetic acid.

Incorporation of radioactive precursors. Cell

suspensions were preincubated for 10 min at 37°C. The radioactive compound was then added and the suspensions were incubated for an additional hour with tritiated thymidine or uracil, or an additional 10 min with ^{14}C amino acid mixture. At the end of the incubation the cell suspensions were washed twice with cold PBS and three times with 5% cold trichloroacetic acid. The precipitate was dissolved by suspending in 0.5 ml Hyamine 10 × overnight. The samples were then transferred to 10 ml of Bray's scintillation liquid (14) and counted in a Packard Tri-Carb liquid scintillation spectrometer.

Preparation of ^{131}I-labeled antigen. The iodination was carried out by transfer of iodine from a chloroform phase to an aqueous phase containing the protein, according to Cinader and Dubert (15). ^{131}Iodine, obtained from E. R. Squibb & Sons in aqueous solution of NaI and $NaHSO_3$ (0.2%), was used at 5 to 10 mCi for iodination of 100 mg of protein, about 30% of the iodine being incorporated.

RESULTS

Preliminary experiments were done to determine the effects of a number of factors which influence the distribution of cells in BPA density gradient centrifugation.

pH. Lymph node cells (LNC) obtained from rabbits 4 days after secondary immunization with Shigella were fractionated on BPA gradients prepared in salt solution at pH 5.5, 6.0 and 6.8. Higher levels of pH caused a shift in the distribution of the cells on the BPA gradient from higher to lower densities. At pH 5.5, 6.0 and 6.8, the peaks of cell distribution were, respectively, at densities of 1.088, 1.086 and 1.078 g/cm³. (This shift in density could be due to swelling of the cells, which would decrease their average density.) The enrichment factor of plaque-forming cells (PFC) (PFC/10^6 cells) in the richest fraction, relative to the original population, was highest at pH 6.8 (5 to 10 ×), and this was chosen for subsequent experiments.

Osmotic pressure. At pH 6.8, BPA gradients were prepared which were isotonic or 90% of this level, and LNC obtained from rabbits 4 days following immunization with SRBC were fractionated on these gradients. The lower tonicity of BPA solution caused a shift in the density of the LNC to a lower level and a decrease in the enrichment factor of PFC to about one-fourth

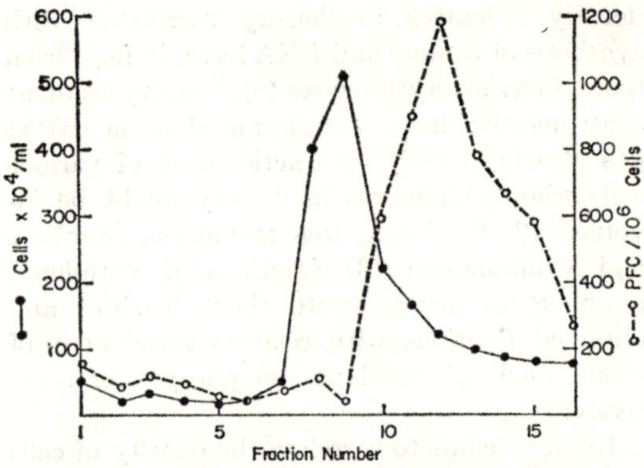

Figure 1. Distribution of plaque-forming cells on bovine plasma albumin density gradient. Lymph node cells were obtained from rabbits 4 days after a secondary injection of Shigella. 40 to 50 × 10^6 cells were applied to BPA density gradient prepared at pH 6.8. Cells were centrifuged 30 min at 5000 rpm. Each fraction was assayed for the number of cells and the number of plaques formed with Shigella-coated SRBC. The low fraction numbers correspond to the high density fractions.

that at isotonicity. BPA gradients were therefore prepared in isotonic solution at pH 6.8. Figure 1 shows a typical distribution of cells and PFC in a suspension obtained from a popliteal lymph node 4 days after a secondary injection of Shigella. The cells are seen to peak rather sharply at the center of the gradient, whereas the peak of PFC was two or three fractions removed, toward the lower density end of the gradient.

Centrifugation to equilibrium. An increase in time and speed of centrifugation from 30 min at 5000 rpm to 120 min at 20,000 rpm did not change the distribution of the cells on the gradients nor did it change the distribution of the PFC. When isolated fractions were recentrifuged in new gradients they appeared at their original density, with no evidence of redistribution of the cells. The conditions of centrifugation used here are thus seen to bring the cells to equilibrium, and the density of the BPA at that position represents the true buoyant density of the cells.

Fractionation of cells from normal rabbits or from rabbits immunized with a variety of soluble or particulate antigens did not show any differences in the distribution profiles of the cells on the BPA gradients.

Exposure of the cells to various concentrations of BPA at 4°C with or without centrifugation, for periods up to 4 hr, had no detectable effect

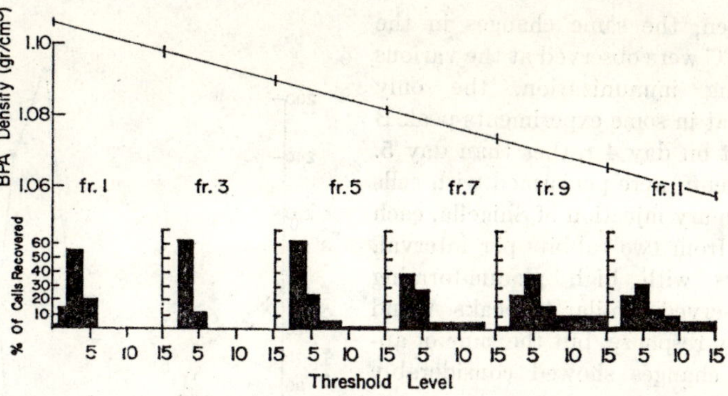

Figure 2. **Size distribution of rabbit lymph node cells on bovine plasma albumin density gradient. Size distribution of the cells given as percentage of the total cells counted in each fraction. Threshold level is in micrograms.**

on the total number of nucleated cells in the suspension or on their plaque-forming capacity.

Size distribution of LNC on BPA gradient. The size distribution of the lymph node cells in each fraction of the gradient was determined by a Coulter counter. The cells in each fraction were counted at threshold settings from 1 to 15 and calculated as percentage of the total cells in the fraction. A relation between the density of the cells and their size could be demonstrated. The higher density fractions consisted mainly of small lymphocytes, while the medium and the large lymphocytes appeared in the fractions of the lower densities (Fig. 2).

Distribution of PFC on bovine plasma albumin density gradients in relation to the time after injection of antigen. The distribution of PFC was examined at various intervals after secondary immunization with Shigella, in order to see whether the antibody-producing cells undergo density changes in the course of differentiation.

Suspensions of rabbit LNC (4 to 7 × 10⁷/ml) were analyzed in BPA gradients. The recovery of cells, as determined by counting in a hemacytometer, was 60% to 100%, and the recovery of PFC was usually between 70% and 100%. Figure 3 shows the density profiles of PFC on days 4, 5, 7 and 10 after secondary immunization with Shigella. It can be seen that the PFC underwent density changes following immunization. In LNC obtained from rabbits 4 days after injection almost all of the PFC were in a single peak, with density in the range of 1.069 to 1.087 g/cm³ (Fig. 3*a*, peak A). On day 5 a separate, smaller peak of PFC appeared, among the high density cells, 1.096 to 1.106 g/cm³ (Fig. 3*b*, peak B).

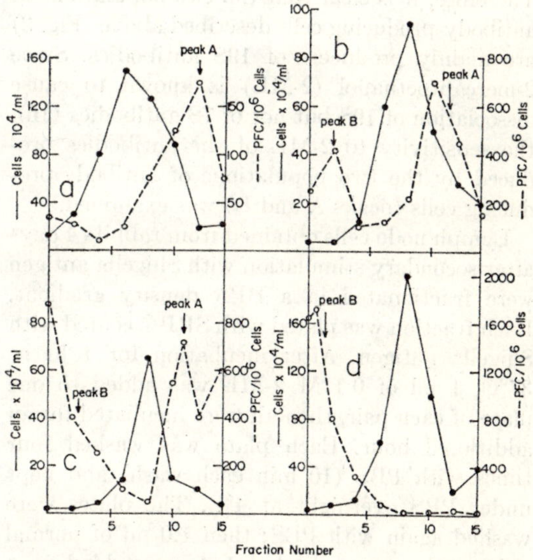

Figure 3. **Distribution of plaque-forming cells from rabbit lymph node cells on bovine plasma albumin density gradient at various days following secondary immunization with Shigella. Lymph node cells were obtained from rabbits 4 days (*a*), 5 days (*b*), 7 days (*c*) and 10 days (*d*) after secondary immunization with Shigella. 40 to 60 × 10⁶ cells were fractionated on BPA density gradient (30 min at 5000 rpm); each fraction was assayed for cell number and direct PFC.**

On day 7 the distribution was quite similar to day 5, but with more of the cells of peak B in the fraction of high density. On day 10 the peak B was similar to that of day 7, and the low density peak, A, had disappeared. When the same experiment was repeated, with Shigella or SRBC as the immunizing antigen, the same changes in the densities of the PFC were observed at the various intervals following immunization, the only variation being that in some experiments peak B became prominent on day 4 rather than day 5.

Similar experiments were performed with cells obtained after primary injection of Shigella, each with cells pooled from two rabbits per interval. Two main peaks with high plaque-forming capacity were observed, similar to peaks A and B of the secondary response, but the time of appearance of the changes showed considerably more variation.

Sensitivity to 2-mercaptoethanol. It is generally accepted that direct hemolytic antibody plaques are produced by cells synthesizing 19S antibody. Therefore, it is clear that the two populations of antibody-producing cells described above (Fig. 3) are mainly producers of 19S antibodies. Since 2-mercaptoethanol (2-ME) is known to cause dissociation of 19S but not of 7S antibodies (16), the sensitivity to 2-ME of the antibodies produced by the two populations of antibody-producing cells (peaks A and B) was examined.

Lymph node cells obtained from rabbits 4 days after secondary stimulation with Shigella antigen were fractionated in a BPA density gradient. Each fraction was plated with SRBC coated with Shigella antigen. After incubation for 1 hr at 37°C, 1 ml of 0.1 M 2-ME was added to one plate of each pair, then all were incubated for an additional hour. Each plate was washed four times with PBS (10 min each wash) and kept under PBS overnight at 4°C. The plates were washed again with PBS; then 1.0 ml of normal guinea pig serum diluted 1:4 was added as a source of complement. After an hour of incubation at 37°C the plaques were counted. The other plates were treated similarly, except for the omission of 2-ME treatment. It can be seen in Figure 4 that the antibodies produced by the cells in the high density and the low density peaks showed a difference in sensitivity to 2-ME. Plaques due to cells in the low density peak failed to appear altogether, but no change was observed in the number of plaques produced by cells of the high density peak.

These experiments indicated the presence in the higher density fractions of the gradient of a cell population producing 2-ME resistant antibody with high hemolytic efficiency.

Distribution of PFC from mouse spleen and lymph node on BPA density gradients. To see

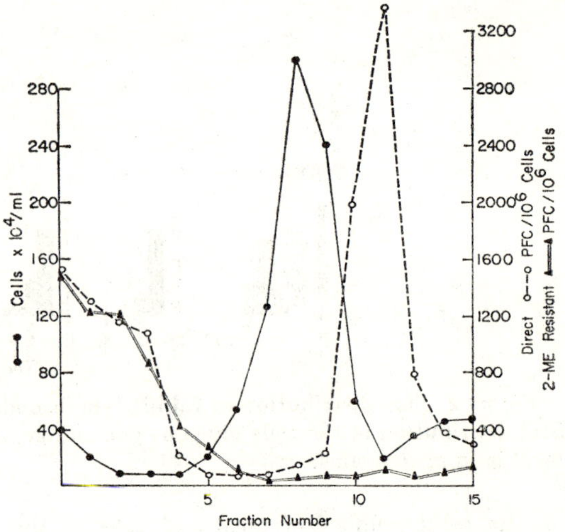

Figure 4. Effect of 2-ME on the distribution profile of plaque-forming cells on bovine plasma albumin density gradient. 40 × 10^6 lymph node cells were obtained from rabbits 4 days after secondary immunization with Shigella and were centrifuged in BPA density gradient for 30 min at 5000 rpm. Fractions were assayed for number of cells and the number of PFC exposed and unexposed to 0.1 M 2-ME.

whether the distribution and changes in density observed in PFC of rabbit lymph nodes were also found in PFC of the mouse, spleen cells were obtained from mice on days 4, 5, 7 and 12, after secondary injection of SRBC. The cells were mixed into BPA gradients, centrifuged for 30 min at 5000 rpm and fractionated. Each fraction was assayed for the number of nucleated cells and the number of direct and facilitated plaques. As can be seen in Figure 5*a* the PFC obtained on day 3 were all found at the low density end of the gradient, as in the rabbit LNC, but no clear changes in the distribution profile of the PFC on the gradient could be demonstrated at the longer intervals following immunization. As seen in Figure 5, during this period of day 3 to 12 the 19S plaques were largely replaced by 7S plaques, but the PFC appeared at the same density, indicating that 7S and 19S antibodies are synthesized by cells with the same density.

Since changes in the density of PFC found in rabbit LNC were not shown by mouse spleen cells, the question arose whether this difference was associated with the difference in species or of the organ from which PFC were obtained. Mice were injected with 0.1 ml of 20% SRBC

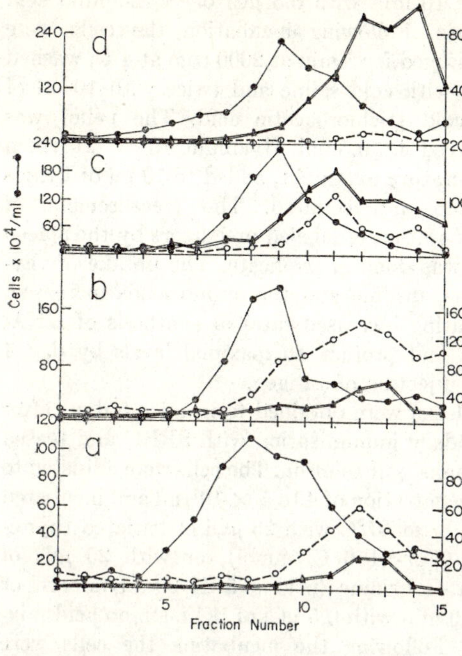

Figure 5. Distribution of plaque-forming cells from mouse spleen cells on bovine plasma albumin density gradients. Spleen cells were obtained from mice 3 days (*a*), 4 days (*b*), 6 days (*c*) and 12 days (*d*) after secondary injection of SRBC. There were at least five mice for each group. 40 to 60 $\times$ 10^6 spleen cells were fractionated on BPA density gradient for 30 min at 5000 rpm. Each fraction was assayed for the number of nucleated cells and number of direct and indirect PFC.

in each of the front footpads, and 1 month later the injection was repeated. At various intervals after the secondary injection the brachial lymph nodes were removed and cells obtained from these nodes were mixed into BPA gradients. When the cells were fractionated, counted and assayed for plaque-forming capacity it was found that all the PFC appeared at the light end of the gradient. No changes in their densities could be observed at various days following immunization, and peaks of the 7S and 19S plaques appeared at the same density, as in the case of the mouse spleen cells. Thus the data indicate a difference between the two species in their cellular response to this antigen.

Antigen uptake by LNC fractionated on BPA density gradients. LNC from normal rabbits and from Shigella-immunized rabbits were exposed *in vivo* and *in vitro* to soluble Shigella antigen labeled with ^{131}I. Exposure of the LNC to the antigen *in vivo* was done by injecting 1.0 mg of iodinated Shigella antigen directly into the left popliteal lymph node. After exposure to the antigen *in vivo* for 30 min, the lymph node was removed, and the cells were teased and washed three times with PBS to remove unbound antigen. The right popliteal lymph node was also removed, teased separately, and exposed *in vitro* to 0.25 mg of the labeled antigen for 15 min at 37°C. The cells were then washed three times with PBS to remove the unbound antigen. Control experiments showed that when the labeled antigen was injected at that dose into one popliteal lymph node *in vivo* no radioactivity could be demonstrated in the contralateral popliteal lymph node 30 min later.

The cells exposed to the antigen *in vivo* or *in vitro* were applied to BPA density gradients, and each fraction was assayed for antigen uptake

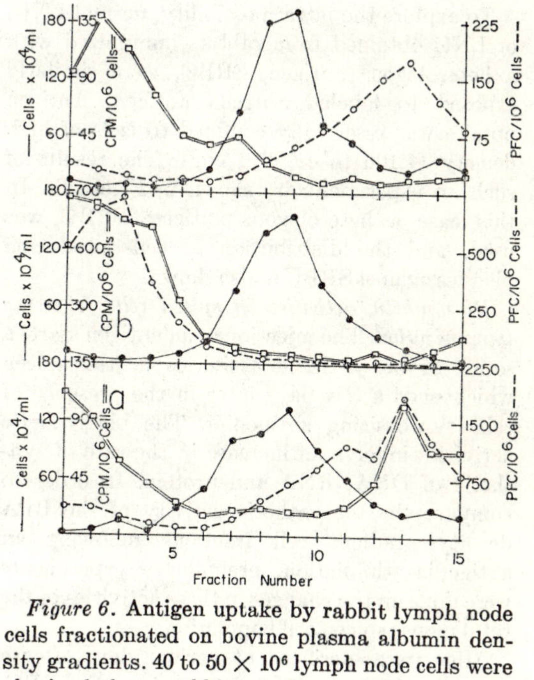

Figure 6. Antigen uptake by rabbit lymph node cells fractionated on bovine plasma albumin density gradients. 40 to 50 $\times$ 10^6 lymph node cells were obtained from rabbits 4 days after secondary immunization with Shigella (*a*), 10 days following immunization with Shigella (*b*) or 4 days following secondary immunization with SRBC (*c*). After fractionation on BPA gradients, each fraction was assayed for number of cells, plaque formation against the appropriate antigen (Shigella or SRBC) and the radioactivity incorporated.

and for plaque-forming capacity of the cells. Antigen uptake by fractionated LNC obtained from rabbits 4 days after injection of Shigella antigen showed two peaks of density of cells binding the antigen: one at the high density end, and the other at low density, corresponding to the peak of PFC. At 10 days, all of the antigen-binding cells were at the high density end of the gradient, as were the PFC. These results were the same whether the exposure to labeled antigen was *in vivo* or *in vitro*.

The presence of a substantial part of the antigen-binding cells of the 4-day LNC in the high density fractions, which included few PFC (Fig. 6*a*), suggested that the LNC could bind antigen by two mechanisms. Antigen could be bound by newly synthesized antibody still on the surface of cells engaged in active synthesis, as indicated by their ability to form plaques, or by receptors on the cell surface of inactive cells, which would account for at least a substantial portion of the binding by the high density cells.

To explore the latter possibility, normal LNC, or LNC obtained from rabbits immunized with a heterologous antigen, SRBC, were similarly exposed to labeled Shigella antigen. Antigen uptake was essentially confined to cells of high density (1.106 to 1.096 g/cm^3). The results of such an experiment are shown in Figure 6*c*. In this case a heterologous antigen, SRBC, was used, and the distribution of cells producing plaques against SRBC is also shown.

Biosynthetic activities in spleen cells following immunization. The injection of an antigen starts a series of biosynthetic activities in the spleen which ends a few days later in the presence of cells synthesizing antibodies. The biosynthetic activities involve an increase in the rate of synthesis of DNA, RNA and protein. In order to compare the biosynthetic activity of the BPA density gradient cell fractions following an antigenic stimulation, preliminary experiments were done on the changes in these activities of the total mouse spleen cell population.

Mice were sacrificed at various days after a secondary intraperitoneal injection of SRBC. The spleen cells were teased immediately in Hanks' basal salt solution (pH 6.8) at room temperature and were adjusted to 15 × 10^6 cells/ml. The cell suspension was incubated in a roller for 1 hr at 37°C with 10 μCi of tritiated thymidine (TdR-^{3}H 6Ci/mmol), or with 25 μCi of tritiated uridine (uridine-5-^{3}H 20Ci/mmol), or for 10 min with 0.5 μCi of ^{14}C L-amino acid mixture. Following incubation the cells were centrifuged for 5 min at 2000 rpm at 4°C, washed twice with cold saline and twice with 10 ml of 5% cold trichloroacetic acid. The pellet was dissolved in 0.5 ml Hyamine 10 × at room temperature overnight, added to 10 ml of Bray's solution and counted. The measurement of incorporation of labeled precursors by the spleen cells was done in triplicate. The uptake of thymidine, uridine and the amino acids increased, indicating increased rates of synthesis of DNA, RNA and protein, to maximal levels by day 4 after injection of antigen.

Spleens were obtained from mice 5 days after secondary immunization with SRBC and teased in Hanks' salt solution. The cells were adjusted to a concentration of 4 to 5 × 10^7/ml and incubated for 1 hr at 37°C with 25 μCi of tritiated thymidine (Tdr-^{3}H 6 Ci/mmol), or with 25 μCi of tritiated uridine (uridine-5-^{3}H 20 Ci/mmol), or for 10 min with 0.5 μCi of ^{14}C L-amino acid mixture. Following the incubation the cells were layered on BPA density gradients and centrifuged for 30 min at 5000 rpm at 4°C. The cells of each fraction were assayed for the radioactivity

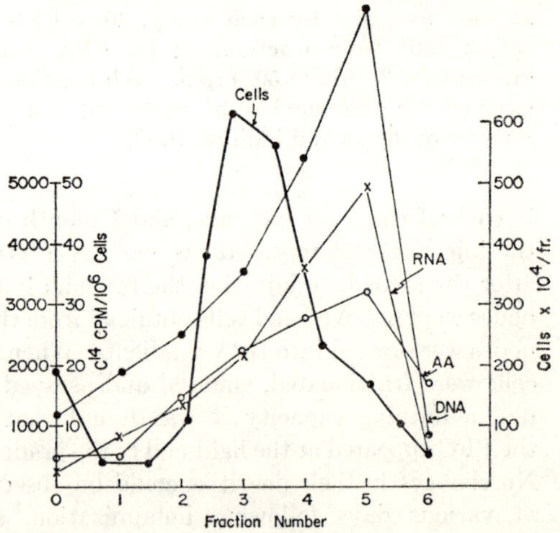

Figure 7. **Biosynthetic activities of spleen cells fractionated on bovine plasma albumin density gradient. Spleen cells were obtained from mice 5 days after secondary injection of SRBC. 40 to 50 × 10^6 cells were exposed to 25 μCi of tritiated thymidine, or to 25 μCi tritiated uridine or to 0.5 μCi of L-amino acid ^{14}C. The cells were fractionated on BPA gradients and each fraction was assayed for the number of cells and radioactivity incorporated.**

incorporated. As can be seen in Figure 7, the cells with the highest rates of incorporation of amino acids, thymidine and uracil were the cells at the light end of the gradient. Cells of this range of density are the ones we have found to be most active in antibody synthesis, as measured by the plaque or the rosette tests.

DISCUSSION

Recent investigations have given evidence of the pleomorphism of antibody-forming cells (7, 17–21). Major differences were observed in the amount and degree of organization of the protein-synthesizing organelles in the cytoplasm of active cells of both the lymphocytic and plasmacytic categories. On the basis of these morphologic data it was expected that gradient density centrifugation would make it possible to concentrate the antibody-producing cells within fractions of the population.

In lymph node cells obtained from rabbits at various days following secondary immunization with Shigella antigen, two peaks of PFC were observed, at the low and at the high density regions of the gradient. A shift was found in the density of the PFC, from the low density on the 4th day to a higher density on the 10th day following immunization. This shift might have been due to a differentiation of one population of cells to a second population producing different types of immunoglobulins. When the antibody produced by the cells at the various days following immunization was tested for its sensitivity to 2-ME, it was found that the low density cell population produced plaques which were 2-ME sensitive, and the high density cells produced plaques which were 2-ME resistant. The latter might be due to a 2-ME resistant IgM, or to IgG, the most active cells, those not requiring facilitation, being detected.

The distribution of PFC after secondary immunization of rabbits suggests that we are dealing with two populations of cells which differ in their density, according to time of appearance following immunization and the nature of the immunoglobulin they synthesize. The assignment of the terms "19S" and "7S" to direct and indirect hemolytic plaques is based on the early appearance and similar kinetics of direct plaques and 19S serum antibody and the somewhat later appearance of indirect plaques and 7S antibody in the serum. There is no reason, however, to exclude the possibility that some direct plaques are due to a class of antibody other than IgM, that can fix complement and cause hemolysis directly, like γ_2 antibody in the mouse (22), or that some facilitated plaques may be formed by IgM antibody, depending on the antibodies in the antiglobulin serum. Plotz *et al.* (23, 24) have demonstrated that sera of mice immunized with SRBC contain two types of IgM anti-SRBC antibody: one type complement-fixing and hemolytic, the other, unable to fix complement or lyse RBC except in the presence of anti-mouse macroglobulin serum.

Changes in size of antibody-forming cells have been demonstrated recently (25). Rosette-forming cells (RFC) in uninjected mice were all small lymphocytes, whereas at 4 days after immunization the majority were large blast-like cells. The predominant RFC after 14 days were once again the small lymphocytes, these attaining a percentage as high as 70 by day 54, and 90 by day 200. Changes in density of antibody-producing cells have been demonstrated as early as 10 to 18 hr after antigenic stimulation (26, 27). Basically, the density of a cell reflects its average chemical composition, a cytoplasmic mass relative to that of the nucleus, which is related to its biochemical activity. We have shown that the low density cells have high biosynthetic activity 4 days after immunization, as indicated by the incorporation of radioactive precursors into macromolecules. Correlation between metabolic activity in the lymphoid organs and titers of serum antibody has been demonstrated in other studies (28–30).

A correlation was also shown here between the size of cells and their density. The large and medium size cells were of lower density, whereas most of the small cells had a higher density. In the mouse, all antibody-forming cells obtained from spleen were among the larger, lower density, cells. In the rabbit, two populations of antibody-forming cells were found in the lymph nodes, one which contains mostly the larger cells and appears early after immunization and the second, among the smaller denser cells, which appears later after immunization. The latter accounted for only a small fraction of the entire antibody-producing population.

The possibility that factors not relevant to the immunologic capacity of the cells might have affected the results was studied, especially the question of whether exposure of the cells to BPA affected their ability to produce plaques. These observations on the effect of BPA were in agreement with data reported by others (31–33).

Immunologic activities of various cell fractions have been measured by the graft-*vs*-host reaction in the chicken (23) and by testing cells for "antigen-sensitivity" and for hemolytic antibody (27, 34). In the latter studies, Haskill found at least 3 to 6 peaks of PFC following fractionation of the cells on BPA density gradient; however, the enrichment factors for PFC from spleen and lymph nodes in the various fractions were no more than two. In the present study only one peak of of cells appeared in the mouse spleen suspension, at the density range of 1.076 to 1.090 g/cm^3, and the PFC appeared at a density range of 1.062 to 1.074 g/cm^3. The enrichment factor of PFC was in the range of 5 to 15.

Various cell types have been suggested as the cells which first interact with the antigen and initiate the immune response. Mitchell and Miller (35) suggested a model in which the initial contact with antigen is made by thymus-derived antigen-sensitive cells. These cells are then thought to induce antibody-forming cells from precursor cells which are derived from the bone marrow. On the other hand, direct interaction between lymphoid cells from normal animals and antigen is suggested by experiments in which lymphoid cells differing in histocompatibility antigens are shown to divide when incubated together *in vivo* (36).

In an approach to this question, antigen-binding cells were identified on BPA gradients by using labeled antigen and measuring the amount of antigen bound to cells obtained from various fractions. When LNC obtained from immunized rabbits were exposed to the antigen either *in vitro* or *in vivo*, and the radioactivity incorporated into each cell fraction was assayed, it was shown that the radioactivity profile followed the profile of plaque-forming cells in the low density region of the gradient. However, when LNC from normal rabbits or from rabbits immunized with a non-related antigen were studied, all antigen-binding cells were found in the high density range.

The binding of antigen by cells from immunized animals is probably due to the binding of antigen by newly synthesized antibody, still bound to the surface of cells actively engaged in antibody synthesis. The antigen binding by the normal cells could be interpreted in several ways. The simplest hypothesis is that this is the interaction of antigen with those cells which could develop into cells producing the homologous antibody. However, binding of antigen by LNC from normal rabbits might also represent a low level of antibody synthesis. In this connection it is interesting to note that as soon as 10 days after immunization the plaque-forming cells have already returned to the high density range, suggesting that the long-lived antibody-synthesizing cells are mainly high density cells.

The binding of Shigella antigen to high density cells of non-immunized rabbits might also be a nonspecific binding which has no relation to the induction of the immune response. However, this explanation would require an additional assumption that the surface structure of some of the high density cells differs from that of the rest of the cells.

REFERENCES

1. Morse, R. K., Institute for Cellular Biology, The University of Connecticut, *11:* 4, 1969.
2. Leif, R. C. and Vinograd, V., Proc. Nat. Acad. Sci., *51:* 520, 1964.
3. Szenberg, A. and Cunningham, A. J., Nature, *217:* 747, 1968.
4. Urso, P. and Makinodan, T., J. Immun., *90:* 897, 1963.
5. Dutton, R. W. and Mishell, R. I., J. Exp. Med., *126:* 443, 1967.
6. Koros, A. M. C., Mazur, J. M. and Mowery, M. J., J. Exp. Med., *128:* 235, 1968.
7. Harris, T. N., Hummeler, K. and Harris, S., J. Exp. Med., *123:* 161, 1966.
8. Kabat, D. and Attardi, G., Biochem. Biophys. Acta, *138:* 382, 1967.
9. Turner, R. W. A., Siminovitch, L., McCulloch, E. A. and Till, J. E., J. Cell. Physiol., *69:* 73, 1967.
10. Jerne, N. K., Nordin, A. and Henry, C., in *Cell Bound Antibodies*, Edited by B. Amos and H. Koprowski, p. 109, The Wistar Institute Press, Philadelphia, 1963.
11. Sterzl, J. and Riha, I., Nature, *208:* 858, 1965.
12. Dresser, D. W. and Wortis, H. H., Nature, *208:* 859, 1965.
13. Goebel, W. F., Binkley, F. and Perlman, E., J. Exp. Med., *81:* 315, 1945.
14. Bray, G. A., Anal. Biochem., *1:* 279, 1960.
15. Cinader, B. and Dubert, J. M., Proc. Roy. Soc. Ser. B., *146:* 18, 1956.
16. Deutsch, H. F. and Morton, J. I., Science, *125:* 600, 1957.
17. Hummeler, K., Harris, T. N., Tomassini, N., Hechtel, M. and Farber, M. B., J. Exp. Med., *124:* 405, 1966.

18. Cunningham, A. J., Smith, J. B. and Mercer, E. H., Immunology, *11:* 515, 1966.
19. Cunningham, A. J., Aust. J. Exp. Biol. Med. Sci., *46:* 141, 1968.
20. Storb, U., Chambers, V., Storb, R. and Weiser, R. S., J. Reticuloendothel. Soc., *5:* 81, 1968.
21. Storb, U., Bauer, W., Storb, R., Fliedner, T. M. and Weiser, R. S., J. Immun., *102:* 1474, 1969.
22. Nussenzweig, V., Green, I., Vassalli, P. and Benacerraf, B., Immunology, *14:* 601, 1968.
23. Plotz, P. H., Talal, N. and Asofsky, R., J. Immun., *100:* 744, 1968.
24. Plotz, P. H., Colten, H. and Talal, N., J. Immun., *100:* 753, 1968.
25. McConnell, I., Munro, A., Gurner, B. W. and Coombs, R. R. A., Int. Arch. Allerg., *35:* 209, 1969.
26. Raidt, D. J., Mishell, R. I. and Dutton, R. W., J. Exp. Med., *128:* 681, 1968.
27. Haskill, J. S., Legge, D. G. and Shortman, K., J. Immun., *102:* 703, 1969.
28. Harris, T. N. and Harris, S., J. Exp. Med., *90:* 169, 1949.
29. Juhasz, H. and Rose, B., Canad. J. Biochem., *41:* 179, 1963.
30. Schoenberg, M. D., Moore, R. D., Stavitsky, A. B. and Gusdon, J. P., J. Cell. Physiol., *71:* 133, 1968.
31. Shortman, K., Aust. J. Exp. Biol. Med. Sci., *46:* 375, 1968.
32. Legge, D. G. and Shortman, K., Brit. J. Haemat., *14:* 323, 1968.
33. Shortman, K. and Szenberg, A., Aust. J. Exp. Biol. Med. Sci., *47:* 1, 1969.
34. Haskill, J. S., J. Exp. Med., *130:* 877, 1969.
35. Mitchell, G. F. and Miller, J. F. A. P., J. Exp. Med., *128:* 821, 1968.
36. Wilson, D. B. and Billingham, R. E., Advances Immun., *7:* 189, 1967.

THE JOURNAL OF IMMUNOLOGY
Copyright © 1970 by The Williams & Wilkins Co.

Vol. 105, No. 6, December 1970
Printed in U.S.A.

PRECURSOR CELLS IN DENSITY FRACTIONS OF LYMPH NODE CELLS: RELATION TO ANTIBODY-PRODUCING CELLS[1]

NEOMI MOAV[2] AND T. N. HARRIS

From The Children's Hospital of Philadelphia and the Department of Pediatrics, University of Pennsylvania, School of Medicine, Philadelphia, Pennsylvania

Received for publication June 22, 1970

Spleen cells of mice were transferred intravenously into x-irradiated syngeneic recipients which were also injected with sheep red blood cells (SRBC). The dose of irradiation was sufficient to prevent active immunization by the SRBC injected. At intervals thereafter, spleens of recipients were teased and the cells plated in agar against SRBC, to determine relative numbers of precursor cells for this immunologic response which had been transferred.

In normal mouse spleen cells fractionated by bovine plasma albumin (BPA) density gradient centrifugation, cells pooled from the higher or the lower density range of fractions yielded equal numbers of plaque-forming cells (PFC) in the recipients' spleens 6 to 8 days later. The same was found in cells obtained from spleens 30 days after primary injection of SRBC. In cells obtained 5 days after secondary injection of SRBC, however, the low density cells contained more precursor cells per million than cells in the high density fractions. In other portions of such spleen cell suspensions, which had been incubated for the production of anti-SRBC rosettes and then fractionated, the high density fraction again contained fewer precursor cells per million than the low density fraction. In this case, the high density fractions also contained the rosette-forming cells (RFC) because these were now included in rosettes. The latter, the high density, rosette-rich, fraction of the rosette preparation produced no more precursor cells than the similar fraction of the original suspension, indicating that the cells currently producing antibody were not a major source of precursor cells.

When cells from spleen, lymph nodes or thoracic duct lymph are transferred together with SRBC to heavily irradiated recipients, an immune response occurs in the recipient, the magnitude of which is related to the number and kind of cells injected and the previous contact with the antigen (1–4). The procedures of Playfair *et al.* (3), and of Kennedy *et al.* (4) give methods for determining the number of cells which are sensitive to the antigen in such an inoculum, but very little is known about the nature of these cells. Morphologic and other evidence have implicated small lymphocytes as the hypothetical "memory cells" (5). This identification does not bear on the questions recently raised in the literature as to whether more than one cell type is originally involved in the immune response (6–9).

In the following experiments the cell transfer technique was used to study the possible role of rosette-forming cells as antibody-forming cells or as precursors of such cells. Spleen cells were fractionated on BPA density gradients and various fractions were transferred into irradiated recipients. The kinetics and the magnitude of the antibody formation in the host were studied. These results were compared with results of experiments in which rosette-rich fractions and rosette-depleted fractions were transferred to irradiated hosts.

MATERIALS AND METHODS

Immunization. C57BL/6 male mice, obtained from The Jackson Laboratory, Bar Harbor, Maine, were injected intraperitoneally with 0.2

[1] This investigation was supported by Public Health Service Research Grant HE-04598 from the National Heart and Lung Institute and Grant T-526B of the American Cancer Society.

[2] Present address: Department of Microbiology, Tel Aviv University, Tel Aviv, Israel.

ml 50% sheep red blood cells (SRBC) for primary and secondary immunization.

Preparation of mouse spleen cells. Mice were killed by cervical dislocation and the spleens were removed. The spleens were teased on a stainless steel (no. 80) mesh screen. The cells were washed through the screen with Eagle's medium supplemented with 10% fetal calf serum (Microbiological Associates, Bethesda, Md.) to disperse most of the large aggregates, then centrifuged at 1500 rpm for 10 min at 4°C.

Antibody assay. Hemagglutinin titration. Sera were tested for anti-SRBC antibodies by agglutination of SRBC. Twofold dilutions of the sera were made in a volume of 0.4 ml, and 0.2 ml of 1% SRBC suspension was added. After 2 hr at room temperature the tubes were examined for hemagglutination.

The rosette test was done as described elsewhere (10).

Hemolytic plaque assay. The direct plaque test was performed according to the method of Jerne *et al.* (11). The indirect (facilitated) hemolytic plaque test was done with the use of anti-mouse IgG (12, 13).

Density gradient centrifugation in bovine plasma albumin was done by the method of Leif and Vinograd (14) as described in a preceding paper (10).

X-irradiation. Recipient mice, 12 weeks old, were exposed, 24 hr prior to cell transfer, to 400 R of x-irradiation, using 200 kv and filters of 1 mm Cu and 0.5 mm Al.

RESULTS

Transfer of spleen cells from SRBC-immunized mice into irradiated and non-irradiated syngeneic mice. Spleen cells were obtained from mice 5 days after secondary injection of SRBC. These were incubated for 1 hr at 37°C with 2% SRBC, and the mixture of cells and SRBC was then injected intraperitoneally at 2×10^7 spleen cells per mouse. The recipients were either non-irradiated or had been exposed to 400 R x-irradiation 24 hr previously. The recipient mice were bled daily following the cell transfer, and their sera were assayed for hemagglutinin.

It can be seen in Figure 1 that in the group of irradiated mice given only SRBC no hemagglutinin titer could be detected, indicating that the dose of 400 R of x-irradiation suppressed the recipients' immune response to this dose of antigen. In irradiated recipient mice which received a mixture of spleen cells and SRBC, the titers rose rapidly. No significant differences in hemagglutinin titers in irradiated or non-irradiated recipients were observed following the cell transfer after the fourth day, when the titers of irradiated recipients had reached those of the non-irradiated.

Transfer of fractionated spleen cells to x-irradi

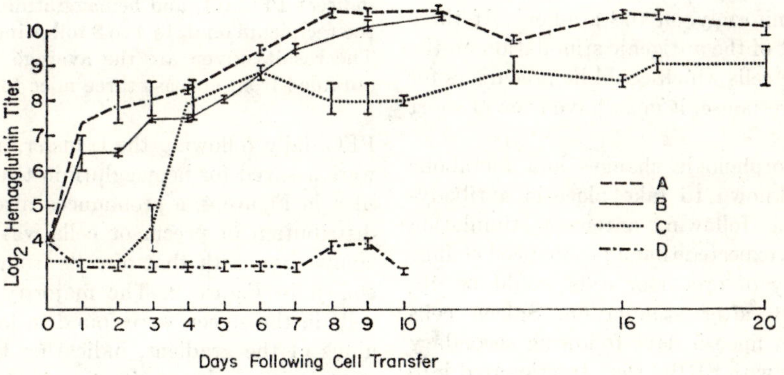

Figure 1. Hemagglutinin titers in x-irradiated and non-irradiated mice following a transfer of spleen cells from SRBC-immunized syngeneic donors. Spleen cells obtained from mice 5 days following secondary immunization with SRBC incubated at a concentration of 4×10^7 cells/ml for 1 hr at 37°C with 2% SRBC. Mixture of cells and SRBC injected intraperitoneally into non-irradiated recipients (*A*), irradiated mice (*B*); SRBC, 0.5 ml of 2%, injected into non-irradiated mice (*C*); heat-killed spleen cells and SRBC injected into irradiated mice (*D*). Recipients bled daily and the sera assayed for hemagglutinins. The values shown are the average agglutinin titers from at least three recipients in each experimental group.

ated mice. Experiments were done to study the effects of transfer of density gradient fractions of suspensions of spleen cells from normal or primed mice to x-irradiated syngeneic mice.

Spleen cells obtained from normal mice were fractionated on BPA density gradients and pooled according to their density to a bottom fraction (1.085–1.106 g/cm^3) and a top fraction (1.06–1.085 g/cm^3). Of each fraction, 10^7 cells were transferred intravenously into x-irradiated mice. Other x-irradiated mice were injected with 10^7 unfractionated spleen cells. Two hours after the cell transfer, the mice were injected intraperitoneally with 0.2 ml of 20% SRBC. The recipients were assayed for direct and indirect PFC and for hemagglutinin titers. As can be seen in Figure 2, there was no observable difference in the number of PFC which subsequently appeared in the spleens of recipients injected with cells of low density (top fractions), or of high density (bottom), or the total cell population. The hemagglutinin titers also showed no difference associated with the density of the cells transferred. These results indicate that the antibody precursor cells were distributed equally throughout the BPA gradients.

In the next group of experiments, the density of antibody precursor cells was examined in animals which had been injected with antigen 30 days prior to cell transfer. The results, shown in Figure 3, were similar to the results obtained with normal cells. The antibody precursor cells were distributed uniformly on the gradient. If there was any effect of the antigenic stimulation on the density of the cells which could be precursors for this immune response, it must have been of short duration.

Because morphologic changes and metabolic changes are known to take place in antibody-forming organs following antigenic stimulation (15, 16) it was expected that a pronounced change in the density of precursor cells would be observed shortly after stimulation. Spleen cells obtained from mice 5 days following secondary immunization with SRBC were fractionated into two fractions on BPA density gradients as described before. Of each fraction, 10^7 cells were injected intravenously into irradiated mice; 2 hr later the recipients were injected intraperitoneally with 0.2 ml of 20% SRBC. Spleens of recipients were assayed for direct and indirect

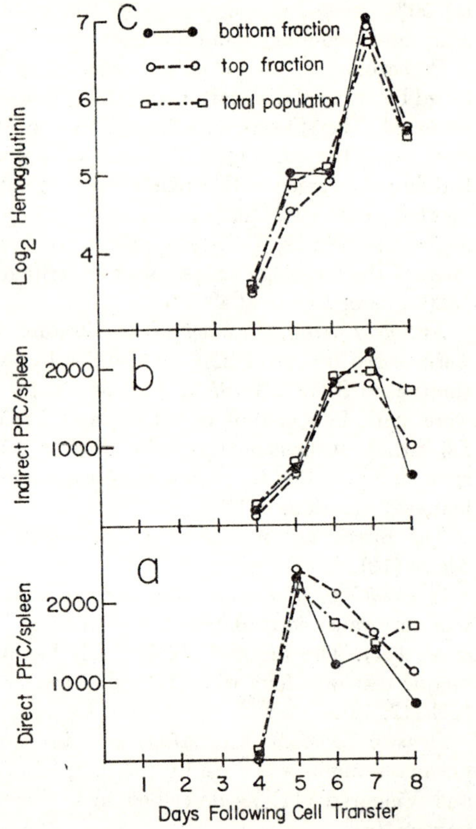

Figure 2. Appearance of antibody and PFC in x-irradiated mice following transfer of fractionated spleen cells from normal mice. Direct PFC (*a*), indirect PFC (*b*), and hemagglutinin titers (*c*), in the recipients on days 4 to 8 following the transfer. The results given are the average of the results obtained from at least three mice for every point.

PFC daily following the transfer, and their sera were assayed for hemagglutinin titers. As can be seen in Figure 4, a pronounced alteration in the distribution of precursor cells was observed, in comparison with that of cells from normal mice shown in Figure 2. The majority of precursor cells in the spleen were found in low-density regions of the gradient, indicating that antigenic stimulation induces significant changes in the density of cells which are the precursors for production of the homologous antibody.

Transfer of rosette-rich fraction and rosette-depleted fraction into irradiated syngeneic mice. Rosette-forming cells are clearly receptor-bearing cells, and the possibility has been raised that

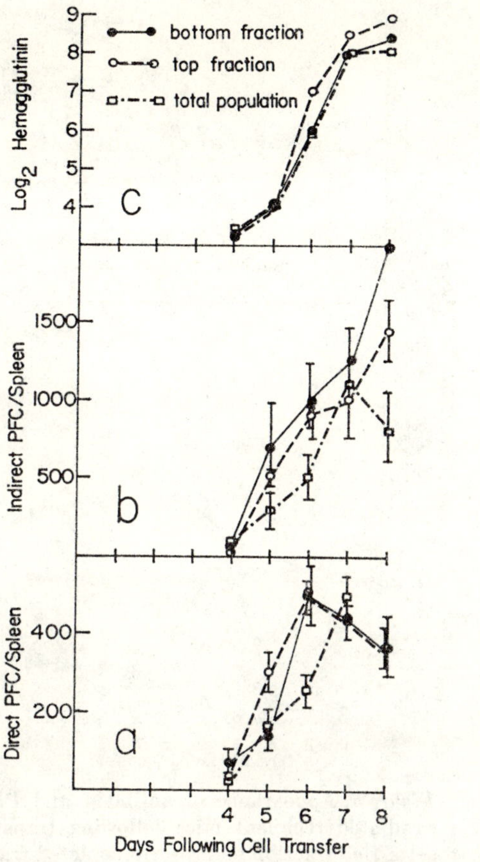

Figure 3. Appearance of antibody and PFC in x-irradiated mice following transfer of fractionated spleen cells obtained from mice 30 days following immunization with SRBC. Spleen cells obtained from 15 mice 30 days following immunization with SRBC, fractionated on BPA density gradient into bottom fraction (density 1.085 to 1.106 g/cm^3) and top fraction (density 1.06 to 1.085 g/cm^3). Of each fraction 10^7 cells per mouse injected intravenously into recipient mice which were exposed to 400 R x-irradiation 24 hr before the transfer (15 to 20 mice per group). Another group of mice was injected with unfractionated cells which were exposed to BPA for 30 min at 4°C. Two hours following cell transfer the recipients were injected with 0.2 ml of 20% SRBC intraperitoneally. On days 4 to 8 following the cell transfer the recipients were assayed for direct PFC (*a*), indirect PFC (*b*) and hemagglutinin titers (*c*). The results given are the average of the results obtained from at least three mice for every point.

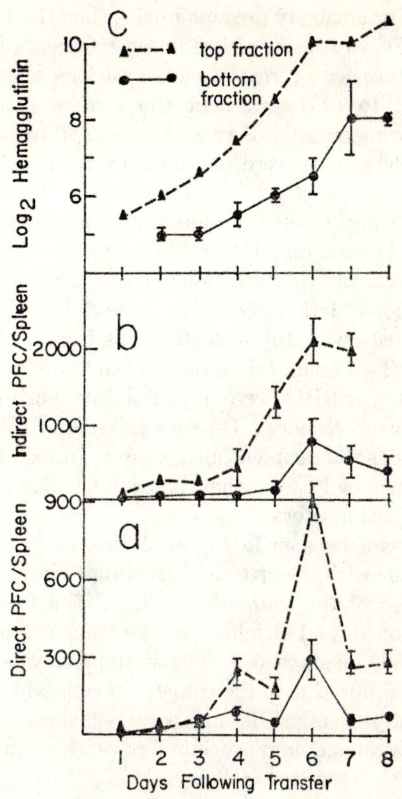

Figure 4. Antibody and splenic PFC in x-irradiated mice following transfer of fractionated spleen cells from mice 5 days after secondary immunization. Direct PFC (*a*), indirect PFC (*b*), hemagglutinin titers (*c*). The results given are the average of the results obtained from at least three mice for every point.

some of the RFC are "memory cells," which on re-exposure to the antigen at the cell surface, are stimulated into division and antibody formation (17).

Experiments were carried out to test directly whether the immunologic memory for production of anti-SRBC antibody is carried largely by RFC or by non-rosette-forming cells. An adoptive transfer system was used to demonstrate immunologic memory. It was postulated that if the RFC are indeed the memory cells then transfer of a fraction in which rosettes have been concentrated should produce a higher number of PFC in recipients' spleens 6 to 8 days following the transfer than rosette-depleted fractions. On the other hand, if the RFC are not the memory cells, or antibody precursor cells, then the number of PFC in spleens of irradiated recipients following transfer of rosette-rich fractions should be equal to or lower than the number obtained following transfer of a rosette-depleted fraction.

Spleen cells were obtained from mice 5 days after secondary immunization with SRBC. Following rosette production, the suspensions were layered on BPA gradients, and fractionated into rosette-rich fractions and rosette-depleted fractions. Irradiated mice were injected intravenously with 10^7 nucleated cells from each fraction. Two hours following the cell transfer 0.2 ml of 20% SRBC were injected intraperitoneally into each recipient. On successive days after cell transfer the recipient mice were examined for the number of PFC in their spleens and for hemagglutination titers.

It can be seen in Figure 5 that recipients injected with rosette-rich fractions showed two phases of the immune response. The first peak was on days 1–3 following the transfer, and the second, on days 6–8. The first peak was in all probability due to the transfer of cells which were already engaged in antibody synthesis in the donor animal, and continued to produce antibody in the recipient following the transfer. The second peak was due to precursor cells which, upon exposure to the antigen, were triggered into division and antibody formation (4). It can be seen that on days 6 to 8 following transfer, hemagglutinin titers in the sera and the number of PFC in the spleens of the recipients which received the rosette-depleted fraction were higher than in the recipients of the rosette-rich fractions. These results argue against the role of rosette-forming cells as memory cells, or as precursor cells for antibody-forming cells.

In order to show that the splenic PFC and the serum antibody observed immediately following the transfer in the irradiated recipient was due to transfer of antibody-forming cells, the following experiment was carried out. Spleen cells were obtained from mice 5 days following secondary immunization with SRBC, and rosette preparations made with these suspensions were fractionated on BPA density gradients. The rosette-rich fractions were injected intraperitoneally into irradiated mice. No attempt was made to eliminate the SRBC in these preparations. The recipients were bled daily following the cell transfer

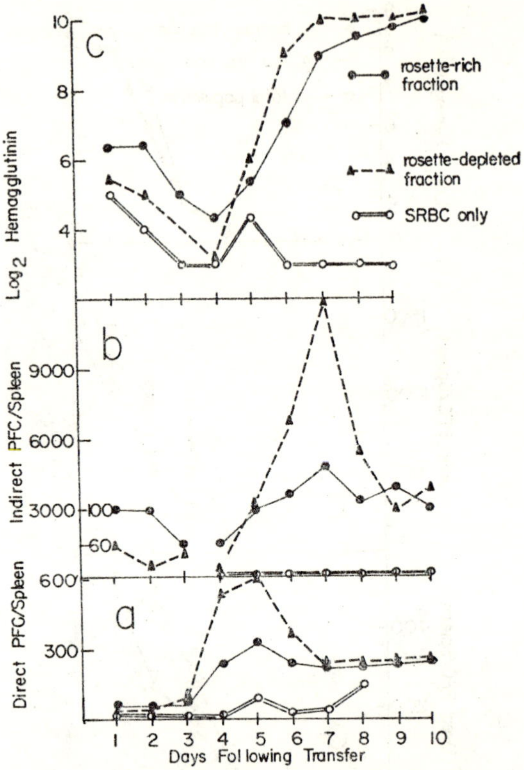

Figure 5. Appearance of antibody and PFC in x-irradiated recipient mice following transfer of rosette-rich fraction and rosette-depleted fraction. Spleen cells obtained from 15 mice 5 days following secondary immunization with SRBC. Rosette preparations layered on BPA density gradients and centrifuged for 30 min at 5000 rpm. Rosette-rich fractions and rosette-depleted fractions pooled from six gradients, and the percentage of the RFC in each fraction determined. (Rosette-rich fraction, 15.4% RFC; rosette-depleted fraction, 0.4% RFC; total population, 1.9% RFC.) Of each fraction, 10^7 cells were injected intravenously into each of 30 mice which had been exposed to 400 R 24 hr before cell transfer. Another group of x-irradiated mice received 10^7 cells per mouse from a rosette preparation which was unfractionated but exposed to BPA for 30 min at 4°C. A control group of mice was injected with 4×10^7 heat-killed cells per mouse. Two hours after the cell transfer all the recipients were injected with 0.2 ml 20% SRBC intraperitoneally. The recipients were assayed daily for direct PFC (*a*) indirect PFC (*b*) and hemagglutinin titers (*c*). The results given are the average of the results obtained from at least three mice for every point.

and their sera assayed for hemagglutinins. It can be seen (Fig. 6) that high hemagglutinin titers could be detected as early as one day following the transfer. No lag period was observed in any of the experiments in which rosette-rich fractions were transferred. The hemagglutinin titers in the recipients were directly proportional to the number of rosettes transferred. These results indicate that the rosette-forming cells are cells engaged in active antibody synthesis in the donor and that they continue to do so following the transfer, in the recipient animal.

Variations in the appearance of the peak of the immune response in the recipients following cell

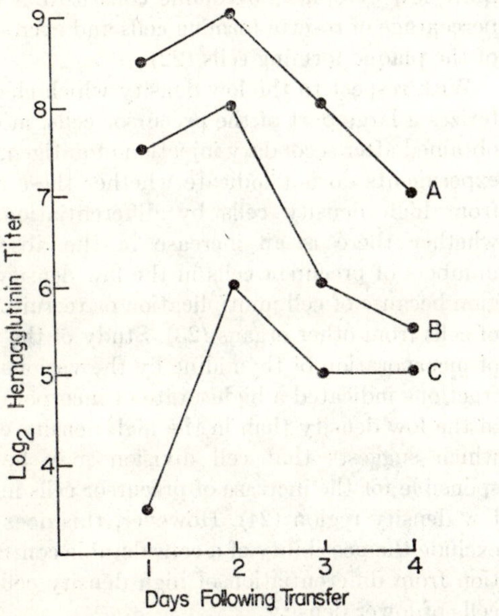

Figure 6. Correlation between hemagglutinin titers in x-irradiated recipients and the number of rosette-forming cells transferred. Spleen cells obtained from mice 5 days following secondary immunization with SRBC. The rosette preparations fractionated on BPA density gradients, and each fraction assayed for the number of cells and of RFC. The fractions most enriched with RFC transferred intraperitoneally into x-irradiated mice. Recipients in group A injected with 2×10^6 cells—35% RFC. Recipients in group B injected with 3×10^6 cells—20% RFC. Recipients in group C injected with 2×10^6 cells—5% RFC. Recipients were bled daily following the cell transfer, and sera were assayed for hemagglutinin titers. The results are the average hemagglutinin titer of 2 to 3 mice for every point.

transfer were observed in different experiments; the peaks were on days 4–6 for the direct PFC, and on days 6–8 for the indirect PFC.

From Figures 4 and 5 it can be seen that the relation between the numbers of PFC in spleens of recipients of rosette-depleted and rosette-rich fractions (Fig. 5, *a*, *b*) of donor cells is similar to that of recipients of low density cells and high density cells (Fig. 4, *a*, *b*), respectively. This indicates that there is no contribution to the PFC in the recipients, on days 4–8 following transfer, by cells which were present in the high density band because they were involved in rosettes, above the immune response elicited by the true high-density cells of the original spleen cell suspension. These results confirm the previous conclusion that the rosette-forming cells are not the precursor cells, nor do they carry the immunologic memory.

DISCUSSION

Since the precursor cells for a given immune response probably represent no more than one in 10^5 cells (18), it is especially useful for studies of precursor cells to have some means of separating total spleen cell suspensions into special subpopulations.

It was suggested by Zaalberg (17) that at least part of the RFC are the cells which carry immunologic memory. Such memory can be defined as the net excess of the secondary over the primary immune response (19, 20). Alternatively, as in this study, assay for memory cells can be made by the "precursor" technique of cell transfer, using a procedure in which the cells are injected intravenously, antigen is supplied by injection into the recipient, and antibody producing cells are sought in the spleens of the recipients roughly 1 week later (3, 4). In the present study the question of the relation of cells currently producing antibody to precursor cells was approached by transferring in this way cells from donors recently injected with antigen, and concentrating the antibody-producing cells in the suspension to be transferred, by rosette formation and density gradient centrifugation. Rosette-rich and rosette-depleted fractions were transferred into irradiated mice and compared in terms of PFC subsequently appearing in the spleens of the recipients. It was considered that if the RFC constitute a major part of the memory cells then the PFC in the mice which were injected with the rosette-rich fraction should be higher than the PFC in recipients which received rosette-depleted fractions.

Our results showed that a greater number of PFC, and a higher serum agglutinin titer, per 10^6 cells transferred, was induced in recipients on days 6–8 by the rosette-depleted fractions than by the rosette-rich fractions. It can be concluded, therefore, that the precursors for antibody-forming cells are, at least largely, cells other than those currently synthesizing antibody. Experiments done by Cunningham (21) demonstrated that transfer of PFC into irradiated mice did not lead to the appearance of antibody-producing cells in the recipients 6–8 days following transfer, while cells depleted of PFC did so. This experiment demonstrates a similarity in the behavior of RFC and PFC upon transfer into x-irradiated recipients.

The contrast between the contribution of the RFC to the precursor population and their activity as current antibody-producing cells was shown in Figure 5, where it was seen that the rosette-rich fraction, when transferred into x-irradiated recipients, elicited the appearance of PFC in the spleen of the host immediately following the transfer, the level of these declining in the first few days after transfer. This early peak was higher than that following the transfer of the rosette-depleted fraction, in contrast to the 6–8 day intervals which reflect the numbers of precursor cells.

The density gradient fractionation of the original suspensions of spleen cells (not rosette preparations) also showed some points of interest. In such suspensions, no difference could be found between the frequency of precursor cells in the upper or lower range of density, indicating a roughly uniform distribution of precursor cells for this immune response throughout the range of densities of such cells. The same was observed in cells obtained 30 days after the most recent injection of the donor animals with antigen, indicating that the metabolic changes attending the active immune response had generally subsided. In cells obtained 5 days after the secondary injection of antigen into the donor, however, there was a distinct increase in the level of precursor cells per million spleen cells in the lower density range, indicating that cells which could act as precursors are involved in some metabolic activity with the attendant increase in cytoplasm to nucleus ratio and, therefore, lower density, although not all of these cells were producing antibody, even by the very sensitive rosette technique. In fact, as was shown in Figure 5, the cells that are currently involved in the antibody synthesis are not a major part of the precursor population for this immune response.

The nature of this higher level of metabolic activity in precursor cells is not clear as yet. The simplest explanation would be that there is merely a quantitative difference between the cytoplasmic development of precursor cells and actively synthesizing cells, but this would not seem likely in view of our observations, by electron microscopy, that lymphocytes with quite low cytoplasmic volume constitute a high percentage of rosette-forming cells and even some of the plaque-forming cells (22).

With respect to the low density which characterizes a large part of the precursor cells, in cells obtained after secondary injection of antigen, our experiments do not indicate whether these arise from high density cells by differentiation, or whether there is an increase in the absolute numbers of precursor cells in the low density region because of cell multiplication or recruitment of cells from other organs (23). Study of the rate of incorporation of thymidine by the various cell fractions indicated a higher rate of incorporation in the low density than in the high density cells, which suggests that cell division may be responsible for the increase of precursor cells in the low density region (24). However, this does not exclude the possibility of a considerable contribution from differentiation of high density cells to cells of lower density.

It has been shown that precursor cells of lower density appear as early as 12 hr following an antigenic stimulation (25). Haskill (26) suggested that these density changes may last up to 60 days following the stimulation. We were not able to detect any differences in number of precursor cells between the high and low density cell fractions 30 days following antigenic stimulation. However, we fractionated the cells into only two main fractions, which might not be sensitive enough to detect minor differences.

The question might be raised whether there is an inconsistency between the demonstration in Figures 2 and 3 of the present paper that cells not actively involved in an immune response yield the same number of precursor cells per million in the upper and lower part of the density range, and

Figure 6 of the preceding paper (24), which shows more antigen uptake per million cells in the highest density fractions than in those of medium and low density. This may seem inconsistent on an assumptional basis of equating antigen uptake with a precursor function. However, even within terms of this assumption, it should be pointed out that in Figure 6 of the preceding paper the fractions of highest density had total cell counts which were quite low, so that an increase in antigen uptake in those fractions might not correspond to a number of precursor cells sufficient to be detectable in comparisons of the upper half and lower half of the range of density, as were examined for precursor activity in the present study.

REFERENCES

1. Harris, S. and Harris, T. N., J. Immun., *74:* 318, 1954.
2. Perkins, E. H., Robinson, M. A. and Makinodan, T., J. Immun., *86:* 533, 1961.
3. Playfair, J. H. L., Papermaster, B. W. and Cole, L. J., Science, *149:* 998, 1965.
4. Kennedy, J. C., Siminovitch, L., Till, J. E. and McColloch, E. A., Proc. Soc. Exp. Biol. Med., *120:* 868, 1965.
5. Gowans, J. L. and Uhr, J. W., J. Exp. Med., *124:* 1017, 1966.
6. Mosier, D. E., J. Exp. Med., *129:* 351, 1969.
7. Miller, J. F. A. P. and Mitchell, G. F., J. Exp. Med., *128:* 801, 1968.
8. Mitchell, G. F. and Miller, J. F. A. P., J. Exp. Med., *128:* 821, 1968.
9. Mitchison, N. A., in *Regulation of the Antibody Response*, Edited by M. Landy and W. Braun, Academic Press, New York, 1969.
10. Moav, N. and Harris, T. N., J. Immun., *105:* 1501, 1970.
11. Jerne, N. K., Nordin, A. and Henry, C., in *Cell Bound Antibodies*, Edited by B. Amos and H. Koprowski, The Wistar Institute Press, Philadelphia, 1963.
12. Sterzl, J. and Riha, I., Nature, *208:* 858, 1965.
13. Dresser, D. W. and Wortis, H. H., Nature, *208:* 859, 1965.
14. Leif, R. C. and Vinograd, V., Proc. Nat. Acad. Sci., *51:* 520, 1964.
15. Harris, T. N. and Harris, S., J. Exp. Med., *90:* 169, 1949.
16. Harris, T. N., Hummeler, K. and Harris, S., J. Exp. Med., *123:* 161, 1966.
17. Zaalberg, O. B., Van der Neul, V. A. and Van Twisk, J. M., J. Immun., *100:* 451, 1968.
18. Nettesheim, P. and Makinodan, T., J. Immun., *94:* 868, 1965.
19. Nossal, G. J. F., Austin, C. M. and Ada, G. L., Immunology, *9:* 333, 1965.
20. Sercarz, E. E. and Byers, V. S., J. Immun., *98:* 836, 1967.
21. Cunningham, A. J., Immunology, *16:* 621, 1969.
22. Gudat, F. G., Harris, T. N., Harris, S. and Hummeler, K., J. Exp. Med., *132:* 448, 1970.
23. Moav, B. and Harris, T. N., J. Immun., *104:* 950, 1970.
24. Moav, N. and Harris, T. N., J. Immun., *105:* 1512, 1970.
25. Raidt, D. J., Mishell, R. I. and Dutton, R. W., J. Exp. Med., *128:* 681, 1968.
26. Haskill, J. S., J. Exp. Med., *130:* 877, 1969.

THE JOURNAL OF IMMUNOLOGY
Vol. 105, No. 6, December 1970

Printed in U.S.A.

CARBONYL IRON: A NEW ADJUVANT FOR EXPERIMENTAL AUTOIMMUNE DISEASES

SEYMOUR LEVINE AND RICHARD SOWINSKI

From the Pathology Department, New York Medical College, Center for Chronic Disease, Bird S. Coler Hospital, Welfare Island, New York, New York

Received for publication June 19, 1970

Carbonyl iron, a form of metallic iron characterized by spherical particles, was a potent adjuvant for production of allergic encephalomyelitis in rats. It was injected intraperitoneally as a saline suspension mixed with an aqueous homogenate of whole neural tissue. Adjuvant activity was also found in kaolin suspensions but not in other forms of metallic iron, iron oxides, iron dextran, or a number of other particulate materials. Carbonyl iron was effective when administered 1 day before or after the antigen but not when given by a different route. Cell suspensions from lymph nodes draining the site of inoculation were capable of transferring the disease passively to unimmunized recipients. The ease of detecting iron and its magnetic qualities should make carbonyl iron a useful material for investigation of adjuvant mechanisms and of cellular immunology.

Mineral oil adjuvants, with or without killed mycobacteria, have been used extensively for the elicitation of cellular (delayed) hypersensitive reactions, including the experimental autoimmune diseases (1). Many microorganisms and a few particulate chemical agents are capable of replacing the mycobacteria of oily adjuvants (2). Particulate adjuvants in aqueous suspension have been employed but little for producing cellular immunity despite a venerable history in the field of humoral immunity (3–5). Aqueous suspensions of bentonite were relatively ineffective for the production of delayed hypersensitive corneal reactions to ovalbumin (6). Aqueous alum, aluminum hydroxide gel, silica, beryllium oxide and killed streptococci did not facilitate production of allergic thyroiditis (7, 8) or encephalomyelitis (9, 10). However, aqueous suspensions of *Bordetella pertussis* have marked adjuvant activity for allergic encephalomyelitis (11) or orchitis (12) and for a cutaneous hypersensitivity reaction (13).

Warren *et al.* reported recently that aqueous suspensions of ferric oxide increased the antibody response to viruses and offered exciting possibilities because of its ferromagnetic properties (14). In the present work, we have used experimental allergic encephalomyelitis (EAE) as a prototype of cellular hypersensitivity. Although ferric oxide has not been effective in our system, striking adjuvant activity has been found in aqueous suspensions of "carbonyl iron," a unique form of metallic iron.

MATERIALS AND METHODS

Rats were obtained from Microbiological Associates, Inc., Bethesda, Md., or bred in our laboratories, and were maintained on Purina Laboratory Chow and water. In most experiments, the antigen was a 10% saline homogenate of previously frozen guinea pig spinal cord. It was thoroughly mixed with an equal volume of a 10% saline suspension of the particulate material under investigation for adjuvant properties. The dose of 2 ml of the mixture contained 100 mg (wet weight) of cord and 100 mg (dry weight) of particulate material. It was injected intraperitoneally without anesthesia. Each experiment included a control group in which saline was substituted for the particulate suspension.

Carbonyl irons were provided by GAF Corporation, Linden, N. J., through the courtesy of T. Tarantino. Asbestos was supplied by C. Berkley and A. M. Langer of Mt. Sinai Hospital, New York. Other particulate agents were obtained commercially and were used without treatment except that bentonite was allowed to settle for 10 min and the supernatant portion was washed with saline by centrifugation (6). The aluminum hydroxide gels were obtained in liquid form and were used without modification in place of the 10% suspension of the dry agents. Amphogel (Wyeth Laboratories, Philadelphia, Pa.) and Alhydrogel (kindly supplied by Superfos Export Co., Copenhagen) are said to contain 4% and 1.3% aluminum oxide as the hydroxide, respectively. Iron dextran (Imferon, Lakeside Laboratories, Milwaukee, Wisc.) was also in a liquid form and is not a particulate agent, but it was included for comparison with other forms of iron; the volume of injection was adjusted to provide a dose of 100 mg elemental iron. No oil was added to any of the agents.

Starting 7 days after injection, the rats were examined daily for signs of EAE: limp tail (1+), weakness of hind limbs (2+), or paralysis (3+). Rats were killed when they became paralyzed, or 18 days after injection. Entire spinal cord and hind brain were fixed in Bouin's solution, embedded in paraffin, sectioned and stained by hematoxylin-eosin or phosphotungstic acid-hematoxylin. Omentum, mediastinal lymph nodes (the main draining nodes of the peritoneal cavity) and spleen were also studied in hematoxylin-eosin stain and in Prussian blue stain for iron. Bouin's fixation should not be used for lymph nodes or spleen that contain carbonyl iron because there may be postmortem gas formation artifacts.

TABLE I

Adjuvant property of particulate agents for EAE in Lewis rats[a]

Agent	EAE, Clinical Signs		
	Incidence[b]	Onset[c]	Severity[d]
Saline controls	19/24	11	1.3
Iron dextran	0/3		0
Aluminum hydroxide (Alhydrogel)	0/4		0
Beryllium oxide, BeO	0/4		0
Crocydolite (asbestos)	0/4		0
Chrysotile (asbestos)	1/4	11	0.3
Starch	2/4	11	0.5
Ferric oxide, Fe_2O_3	3/4	12	1.0
Ferric-ferrous oxide, Fe_3O_4	3/4	13	1.8
Bentonite	2/2	12	2.0
Aluminum hydroxide (Amphogel)	4/4	11	2.3
Kaolin	4/4	10	3.0
Carbonyl iron (SF)	8/8	8	3.0
Carbonyl iron-starch	4/4	8	3.0

[a] Composite results of six experiments each of which included a saline control group.

[b] Numerator, number of rats with clinical signs; denominator, total number of rats.

[c] Average day of onset of clinical signs, rounded to nearest whole number.

[d] Average of highest scores achieved by each rat during course of illness, graded 0, 1+ (limp tail), 2+ (weakness), or 3+ (paralysis).

RESULTS

The particulate agents were tested for adjuvant activity in strains of rats of high and moderate susceptibility to EAE. Lewis rats are highly susceptible and respond to aqueous homogenates of spinal cord tissue *without any adjuvants* (15). In these experiments, although the dose of spinal cord was only half that used in previous reports, all the controls developed histologic lesions and many of them had clinical signs despite the omission of adjuvants. However, signs were usually mild and only occasionally progressed to paralysis. Furthermore, signs did not appear until 9 to 14 days after immunization (Table I). Mixtures of spinal cord antigen with iron oxides or iron dextran gave similar results but beryllium oxide, asbestos and Alhydrogel appeared to inhibit EAE. On the other hand, Amphogel, kaolin and especially carbonyl iron increased the incidence and severity of clinical signs and accelerated their onset. All rats injected with spinal cord antigen and carbonyl iron, for example, had onset of signs after 7 to 9 days and rapidly become paralyzed and moribund. Histologic examination of brain and cord revealed innumerable perivascular collections of mononuclear cells, typical of EAE. In addition, phosphotungstic acid-hematoxylin stains revealed some fibrin, a feature not usually seen in the ordinary form of EAE.

Fischer 344 rats are less susceptible to EAE than are Lewis rats (15). Inoculation of spinal cord antigen without adjuvants produced histologic lesions in some of the controls but none had clinical signs. Most of the added particulate agents, including an iron oxide specimen kindly supplied by Dr. J. Warren, had no adjuvant activity (Table II). Only kaolin and carbonyl iron were active, causing lesions and clinical signs in all the treated rats. The signs were not as early or as severe as in Lewis rats, reflecting the lower susceptibility of the Fischer 344 strain.

A series of carbonyl iron products was tested

in Lewis rats. All were produced by thermal decomposition of iron pentacarbonyl gas. However, they differed in particle size and some had been nitrided, reduced with hydrogen, or surface coated with phosphate or other materials. Their adjuvant potencies varied from none for the L variety to the strong activity already described for the SF powder (Table III).

TABLE II

Adjuvant property of particulate agents for EAE in Fischer 344 rats[a]

Agent	EAE, Clinical Signs		
	Incidence	Onset	Severity
Saline controls	0/12		0
Aleuronate	0/4		0
Alumina, adsorption, 80–200 mesh	0/4		0
Bentonite	0/2		0
Graphite	0/4		0
Sephadex, G-50 fine	0/4		0
Silica gel, 100–200 mesh	0/4		0
Ferric oxide, Fe_2O_3	0/4		0
Iron metal, electrolytic	0/4		0
Kaolin	4/4	12	1.8
Carbonyl iron (SF)	8/8	13	1.4

[a] Composite results of three experiments, each of which included a saline control group.

The possibility that the adjuvant effect of carbonyl iron was due to a soluble contaminant was excluded by the following experiment. Ten milliliters of saline and 5 g carbonyl iron SF were gently mixed in a 37°C water bath for 2 days. The supernatant was obtained and then mixed with the usual spinal cord homogenate and injected. This saline "extract" had no adjuvant effect. In this connection, it is pertinent that an endotoxin contaminant cannot be suspected because endotoxins have no adjuvant activity in our system (16).

Other antigens. Carbonyl iron SF had adjuvant activity when mixed with rat cord as well as with guinea pig cord. However, it had no adjuvant activity with respect to a soluble encephalitogenic basic protein derived from guinea pig myelin, kindly supplied by Dr. Marian Kies. The usual dose of 100 mg iron was incubated 30 min at 37°C with 0.2 mg basic protein. The whole mixture was injected intraperitoneally into each of four Lewis rats. No EAE signs or lesions were produced. On the other hand, the incubation with carbonyl iron had no adverse effect on the basic protein because one-fortieth of this dose, after emulsification in Freund's incomplete adjuvant and injection into the footpads of Lewis rats, caused EAE signs and lesions.

TABLE III

Adjuvant property of various carbonyl irons for EAE in Lewis rats[a]

Carbonyl Iron	Type	Particle Size[b]	EAE, Clinical Signs		
			Incidence	Onset	Severity
		μ			
SF Superfine	Straight	3.7	5/5	9	2.8
SF	Straight	3.8	10/10	8	3.0
Th	Straight	4.6	5/5	9	2.8
E	Straight	5.3	5/5	9	2.6
Phosphated E	Straight, coated	5.3	5/5	9	2.6
Crude E	Straight		4/5	11	1.0
W	Nitrided	4.0	5/5	9	2.4
J	Nitrided	5.3	10/10	9	2.8
GQ4	Reduced, coated	5.9	5/5	11	2.0
L	Reduced	11.3	3/5	15	0.6
Saline controls			5/10	11	0.8

[a] Composite results of two experiments.

[b] Detectable amounts of each of the powders occur in particle sizes that vary from a little less than 1 μ to 9 to 13 μ (and even larger for L powder). Fifty per cent of the weight of the powder is less than the size indicated in this column. These figures were read from particle size distribution analysis curves provided by the manufacturer and do not represent the particular lots provided for this study. However, all but minor differences in particle size could be confirmed by simple microscopic inspection of our samples.

Route, dose and timing. Adjuvant activity was observed only when carbonyl iron was given by the same route as the antigen. No enhancement of EAE was found when the guinea pig cord antigen was given i.p. and the iron was injected i.v. or subcutaneously. Nor was iron in the peritoneal cavity effective when the antigen was injected in the footpads.

Because of rapid settling, it was impossible to be certain that the prescribed 100 mg of carbonyl iron were administered to each rat. Nevertheless, our results were reasonably uniform. In addition, we tested various doses and observed a nearly identical adjuvant effect after only 25 mg as after 100 mg, and the very large dose of 400 mg was almost as effective. Settling of the carbonyl iron was retarded by suspension in 5% soluble starch (17) or 1% gum tragacanth. Injection of the starch-iron mixture gave as good an effect as the iron alone, but gum tragacanth slightly inhibited the adjuvant potency. Carbonyl iron had an adjuvant effect when injected i.p. 1 day before or 1 day after the guinea pig cord antigen.

Passive transfer. Exploitation of a ferromagnetic particulate adjuvant in the field of cellular immunology may depend on the ability to transfer hypersensitivity passively with living cell suspensions. Therefore, Lewis donor rats were immunized with guinea pig cord homogenate and carbonyl iron. Eight days later, when most donors had clinical signs of EAE, they were exsanguinated. Draining lymph nodes, identified by their gray discoloration, included mediastinal, renal, celiac and occasionally lumbar, axillary and posterior abdominal wall nodes. They were harvested, cleaned, minced, sieved, washed in saline three times in the cold, to yield a gray cell suspension. Cells derived from two donors (4.8×10^8 cells in 2 ml saline) were injected into the dorsal penile vein of each of four Lewis rat recipients. The recipients were unimmunized but had been prepared 2 days earlier with a thermal injury of the brain (18). This pretreatment accelerates passive EAE so the recipients were killed 1 day after transfer. Histologic study revealed abundant EAE lesions around the brain injury. This successful passive transfer is a necessary preliminary to future experiments concerned with separation of cell types by magnetic fields.

Morphologic observations. After i.p. injection of carbonyl iron, the omentum and sometimes other peritoneal areas were discolored gray by iron-laden phagocytes. Very frequently, there were sequestered masses of iron up to 0.5 cm in diameter in the omentum, in the pelvis or around the tail of the epididymis, often causing adhesion to the scrotal wall. The retrosternal lymphatics were visibly distended with iron and many anterior mediastinal and upper abdominal nodes were colored by it. Microscopically, the nodes contained many epithelioid cell granulomas, due largely to concomitant absorption of neural tissue. Iron was present in the epithelioid cells as well as in sinusoidal phagocytes and endothelium. The largest amounts were in the subcapsular sinusoids.

Some iron passed through the draining lymph nodes and was observed in liver phagocytes and in large amounts in splenic red pulp. No iron was observed in the central nervous system, even in the presence of EAE lesions. The control rats that had received only the neural tissue inoculum had no iron in the liver and only small amounts in lymph nodes and spleen.

Carbonyl iron L differed from the other types in causing little discoloration of the omentum. Its absorption into lymph nodes was less than the others and its distribution was more restricted. Also, most of it occurred as discrete, relatively large masses rather than small, widely distributed granules. Crude E powder also appeared to be strongly aggregated in the lymph nodes. These features may account for the poor performance of L and crude E as adjuvants. On the other hand, there was abundant absorption of the iron oxides and dextran complex, and moderate absorption of the iron metal powder, so their ineffectiveness will require some other explanation. Absorption into lymph nodes was also demonstrated histologically for aluminum hydroxide gel and kaolin, which possessed adjuvant activity, and for graphite and beryllium oxide, which were inactive in our system.

DISCUSSION

It is of interest to compare carbonyl iron with pertussis vaccine because both are effective adjuvants in aqueous systems. Pertussis vaccine is clearly a more potent agent. It accelerates and intensifies EAE, and also converts it to a hyperacute form characterized by exudation of polymorphonuclear neutrophils and large amounts of fibrin (11). Nevertheless, carbonyl iron has considerable potency, even to the point of inducing some fibrin in the EAE lesions. A conspicuous difference is the requirement that iron and antigen be injected by the same route, while pertussis vaccine is effective when given in remote sites (19, 20) or intravenously (19). Evidence suggests that the active component of pertussis vaccine may be a soluble material, the histamine-sensitizing factor (16). Carbonyl iron is not likely to have any sort of soluble component.

The absence of adjuvant activity in iron dextran, iron oxides, electrolytic iron metal and the L type of carbonyl iron suggests that the SF and other carbonyl irons were not acting merely as sources of iron atoms or ions for chemical interaction with antigen or tissues. Particle size, shape and surface are more likely to be the important factors for adjuvant effect. Carbonyl iron particles are spherical and have to be handled under nitrogen during certain stages of manufacture in order to obviate the danger of oxidation and combustion created by large surface area. All the "straight" (i.e., chemically unaltered) powders except crude E were strong adjuvants without regard for small differences in average particle size or phosphate coating of their surfaces. The lesser activity of the crude E preparation might be related to aggregation of its particles. The increase of nitrogen content from 0.9% to 6% in the "nitrided" powders did not have much effect on adjuvancy. Of the two nitrided powders, the one with the larger average size was slightly more active. The L powder, reduced with hydrogen so that the carbon and nitrogen impurities were very small, had no adjuvant activity. However, the L powder also had the largest average particle size of any carbonyl iron preparation we have tested. Under the microscope the rarity of small particles was immediately evident. The poor performance of this powder was probably due to its meager absorption and restricted distribution in draining nodes. It is not clear whether this, in turn, was due to its chemistry or large particle size. It should be noted that each carbonyl iron had a wide spectrum of particle size, so there was much overlap among them despite differences indicated in Table III. Furthermore, the evaluation of the role of particle size was complicated by aggregation into clumps. Our observations that particles with altered surfaces or different carbon and nitrogen contents had the same or less adjuvant effect as "straight" powders discourage attempts to manipulate chemical composition or surface. Rather, we believe that efforts to design a better carbonyl iron adjuvant should aim at production of SF straight powders of uniform sizes and free of aggregation.

Immunologic adjuvants may augment absorption and dissemination of antigen, protect it from metabolic breakdown, act as a carrier and promote an appropriate cellular reaction (1). Our data on carbonyl iron do not exclude any of these explanations. However, we are impressed by the histology of draining lymph nodes which reveal iron in the epithelioid cell granulomas that probably also contain neural antigen. Perhaps the phagocytosis of iron promotes the entry of neural antigen into macrophages (21) or enhances its processing. It may be instructive to search for some structural or ultrastructural specificity to explain the fact that other forms of iron and other particulates have no adjuvant effect despite their appearance in draining lymph nodes.

It remains to be determined whether carbonyl iron will be a useful adjuvant for delayed hypersensitivity other than autoimmune diseases, or for production of humoral antibodies. However it seems certain to be valuable for investigations of mechanisms of adjuvant action in autoimmune diseases. It is inexpensive and easily prepared as an aqueous suspension. Its absorption can be followed with the unaided eye, quantitated chemically and detected in minute amounts by histochemical stains for iron. It is electron opaque. Its magnetic properties can be used for concentration *in vivo*. Iron, including the carbonyl type, has been used *in vitro* for some time in magnetic procedures for separating macrophages from lymphocytes (17, 22). Experiments of this type should prove even more interesting when the iron has entered the cells *in vivo* and has acted as adjuvant for the immunologic system under study.

ADDENDUM

Recent experiments revealed that 10% latex suspension (2.0-μ uniform spherical particles of polyvinyltoluene, Dow Chemical Co., Indianapolis, Ind.) had strong adjuvant properties when mixed with the usual guinea pig spinal cord antigen. After centrifugation at the commercial suspension, the latex sediment retained full activity and the supernatant had none. No adjuvant activity was found in rat or human red blood cells or in activated charcoal. The mild adjuvant activity reported above for Amphogel could not be confirmed in two additional trials, perhaps because this agent caused bloody ascites on these occasions.

REFERENCES

1. Freund, J., Advances Tuberc. Res., *7:* 130, 1956.
2. Shaw, C-M., Alvord, E. C., Jr., Fahlberg, W. J. and Kies, M. W., J. Immun., *92:* 28, 1964.
3. International Symposium on Adjuvants of Immunity, Utrecht 1966; Symposium Series Immunobiological Standard., vol. 6, Karger, Basel, 1967.
4. Allegranza, A. and Rovescalli, A., Biologica Latina *6 (Suppl. 2):* 24–29, 1953.
5. Malkiel, S. and Hargis, B. J., J. Allerg. *30:* 387, 1959.
6. Wilkinson, P. C., and White, R. G., Immunology, *11:* 229, 1966.
7. Rose, N. R., Kite, J. H., Jr., Doebbler, T. K., Spier, R., Skelton, F. R. and Witebsky, E., Ann. N. Y. Acad. Sci., *124:* 201, 1965.
8. Twarog, F. J., Kenney, E. and Rose, N. R., Proc. Soc. Exp. Biol. Med., *133:* 185, 1970.
9. Lumsden, C. E. and Blight, R., *Proceedings of the Fourth International Congress of Neuropathology*, Edited by H. Jacob, p. 255, Georg Thieme Verlag, Stuttgart, 1962.
10. Lumsden, C. E., Brain, *72:* 198, 1949.
11. Levine, S. and Wenk, E. J., Amer. J. Path., *47:* 61, 1965.
12. Hargis, B. J., Malkiel, S. and Berkelhammer, J., J. Immun., *101:* 374, 1968.
13. Rowley, D. A., Chutkow, J. and Attig, C., J. Exp. Med., *110:* 751, 1959.
14. Warren, J., Kende, M. and Takano, K., J. Immun., *102:* 1300, 1969.
15. Levine, S. and Wenk, E. J., Ann. N. Y. Acad. Sci., *122:* 209, 1965.
16. Levine, S., Wenk, E. J., Devlin, H. B., Pieroni R. E. and Levine, L., J. Immun., *97:* 363, 1966.
17. Levine, S., Science, *123:* 185, 1956.
18. Levine, S. and Hoenig, E. M., J. Immun., *100:* 1310, 1968.
19. Levine, S. and Wenk, E. J., Amer. J. Path., *50:* 465, 1967.
20. Lee, J. M. and Olitsky, P. K., Proc. Soc. Exp. Biol. Med., *89:* 263, 1955.
21. Sbarra, A. J., Shirley, W. and Bardawil, W. A., Nature, *194:* 255, 1962.
22. Gray, J. G. and Russell, P. S., *Histocompatibility Testing*. Edited by H. Balner et al., p. 175. The Williams & Wilkins Co., Baltimore, 1967.

THE JOURNAL OF IMMUNOLOGY
Vol. 105, No. 6, December 1970

ULTRASTRUCTURAL LOCALIZATION OF HORSERADISH PEROXIDASE AND ENDOGENOUS PEROXIDASE ACTIVITY IN GUINEA PIG PERITONEAL MACROPHAGES[1]

RAMZI S. COTRAN[2] AND MORTIMER LITT

From the Harvard Pathology Unit, Mallory Institute of Pathology, and Channing Laboratory and Department of Medical Microbiology, Boston City Hospital, Boston, Massachusetts 02118; and the Departments of Pathology, and Bacteriology and Immunology, Harvard Medical School, Boston, Massachusetts 02115

Received for publication June 19, 1970

Normal guinea pig peritoneal cells were examined for peroxidase activity by the diaminobenzidine ultrastructural histochemical technique before and after exposure to horseradish peroxidase in vitro. Macrophages exhibited endogenous peroxidase activity in the nuclear envelope, endoplasmic reticulum, occasional golgi vesicles and saccules, and rare granules. The majority of granules and phagolysosomes from normal and horse serum-stimulated macrophages were peroxidase negative. When cells were incubated *in vitro* with exogenous horseradish peroxidase, the latter was localized in vesicles and vacuoles; the proportion of macrophages showing the distribution pattern of endogenous activity did not increase. The evidence thus suggests that when exogenous peroxidase is used as antigen, enzymatic activity in the endoplasmic reticulum and nuclear envelope may be attributed to endogenous enzyme. The possible nature and function of endogenous peroxidase-like activity in the peritoneal cells are discussed.

The fate of antigens within macrophages has been the subject of numerous biochemical and morphologic studies (1). Ultrastructural investigations, using electron-dense or radioactive tracers (2–6), have shown that such tracers are taken up by pinocytosis vesicles and vacuoles and are segregated in various intracytoplasmic phagocytic bodies. Recently, the enzyme horseradish peroxidase (HRP) has been used to trace the fate of antigen (7, 8) and to detect the site of appearance of antibody (7, 9, 10). Catanzaro *et al.* (8), using the Graham and Karnovsky diaminobenzidine tetrachloride (DAB) technique (11) to localize HRP ultrastructurally, reported that the enzyme gained access to the endoplasmic reticulum (ER) and perinuclear envelope of guinea pig peritoneal macrophages; these are intracellular sites where antigens previously had not been reported to localize.

[1] This work was supported by Grants HE-08251 from the National Heart Institute and AI-04716 from the National Institute of Allergy and Infectious Diseases.

[2] Recipient of a Career Development Award from the National Heart Institute.

The DAB cytochemical method can detect, in addition to exogenous peroxidase tracers, several enzymes possessing peroxidase activity that are present endogenously in a variety of mammalian cells, including leukocytes (2). Thus, endogenous peroxidase has been demonstrated in lysosomal granules of mature neutrophils (12) and eosinophils (13, 14), and in the ER in immature forms of these cells (12, 13). In both cells, the enzyme empties into phagocytic vacuoles after ingestion of microorganisms (14, 15). The function of peroxidase remains obscure, but in the case of the neutrophil, it may be involved in bactericidal activities (16). To date, there have been no comparable detailed ultrastructural studies on the localization of endogenous peroxidase either in monocytes or macrophages.

The present communication reports on the presence of endogenous peroxidase-like activity in the ER and nuclear envelope of certain guinea pig peritoneal macrophages. It also compares the localization of such endogenous activity with that obtained when the cells are exposed to exogenous HRP *in vitro*: exogenous enzyme is localized in vesicles, vacuoles and phagocytic bodies.

MATERIALS AND METHODS

Collection of macrophages. Peritoneal macrophages were lavaged from normal 275-g female guinea pigs with 15 to 30 ml of physiologic saline or medium 199, Hanks' base, containing 10% calf serum. Saline was used in most experiments in order to exclude the possibility that any exogenous substances were responsible for what was interpreted as "endogenous" activity. Cells from three to five guinea pigs were pooled. Normal peritoneal cells consisted of mononuclear cells (95% to 100%) and eosinophils (0% to 5%) (17). In addition, some of the observations on endogenous peroxidase activity were made during the course of studies on eosinophils (14). In these studies, peritoneal exudate cells were lavaged from guinea pigs which had been immunized by weekly intraperitoneal injections of 0.5 ml of horse serum for 15 to 18 months; the cells were collected 2 days after the last injection of serum, a time at which the population of cells consisted of eosinophils (28% to 66%), macrophages and lymphocytes (34% to 72%), and neutrophils (less than 1%). Some of these cells were also exposed *in vitro* to *Escherichia coli* or zymosan particles, as previously described (14).

Exposure to HRP. Normal peritoneal exudate cells were centrifuged at 750 rpm for 5 min and resuspended in medium 199 containing 0.5 mg/ml of HRP type II (Sigma Chemical Co., St. Louis, Mo.). Exposure was for 30 min at 37°C in a reciprocating shaker at 150 strokes/min. The cells were then washed and fixed for electron microscopy.

Electron microscopy. The procedure used for ultrastructural localization of peroxidase was detailed previously (14). In brief, centrifuged cells were fixed in 2.5% glutaraldehyde in 0.1 M cacodylate for 30 to 40 min, washed in cacodylate buffer, incubated in a solution containing 0.05% DAB, 0.007% to 0.02% H_2O_2, Tris buffer (pH 7.6), for 10 to 60 min at room temperature, washed, fixed in osmium-collidine, and embedded in Epon. Thin sections were cut on an LKB Ultrotome and examined unstained or lightly stained with lead; uranyl acetate was used sparingly, to bring out nuclear detail, as it appeared to mask the peroxidase reaction in the ER.

The specificity of the reaction for peroxidase was assessed by the following procedures: Fixed cells were incubated in DAB medium in the absence of H_2O_2. In order to exclude endogenous production of H_2O_2, 5 mg of beef liver catalase (Sigma Chemical Co.) were added to 10 ml of DAB-Tris buffer (18). 2) Fixed cells were incubated in medium containing DAB + 2% H_2O_2. 3) Fixed cells were incubated in 10^{-1} to 10^{-2} M KCN for 10 min, and then in complete histochemical medium containing 10^{-1} to 10^{-2} M KCN. 4) Cells were boiled in glutaraldehyde for 5 min before incubation in complete medium (18).

RESULTS

Endogenous peroxidase

Ultrastructural localization. Peroxidase activity, identified as a grayish-black reaction product, was present in some peritoneal mononuclear cells in all preparations which were examined. The distribution in cells was fairly characteristic: the perinuclear cisternae, occasional small vesicles in the golgi zones and many of the cisternae of the rough ER were stained (Figs. 1 and 2). Rarely, segments of golgi saccules were stained (Fig. 3). Occasionally, small black vesicles 500 to 700 Å in diameter bound by smooth membranes were seen that did not appear to be within the golgi zone; larger (> 1000 Å), reactive granules were present in some cells (Fig. 1), often in the absence of ER staining (Fig. 4), but such cells were rare. Although the ER staining was ascribed to peroxidase activity (see under controls), it was not established that the reaction product in all reactive granules was specific for peroxidase, since some granules stained even when H_2O_2 was excluded from the incubation medium. The majority of membrane-bounded bodies that contained amorphous gray or dense material (secondary lysosomes) were unstained (Fig. 4).

The cells which contained reaction product had the ultrastructural characteristics of peritoneal macrophages (1): a large indented nucleus, considerable cytoplasmic strands of ER, bands of fibrils, peripheral pseudopods and villi and occasional granules of variable density. They were also capable of phagocytizing *E. coli* (Fig. 5), zymosan particles (14) and HRP. No other consistent distinguishing features were observed between peroxidase-positive and -negative cells, except for the relative paucity of dense bodies in peroxidase-positive cells. Cells which had the typical morphology of lymphocyte gave a negative reaction. Macrophages from animals that had

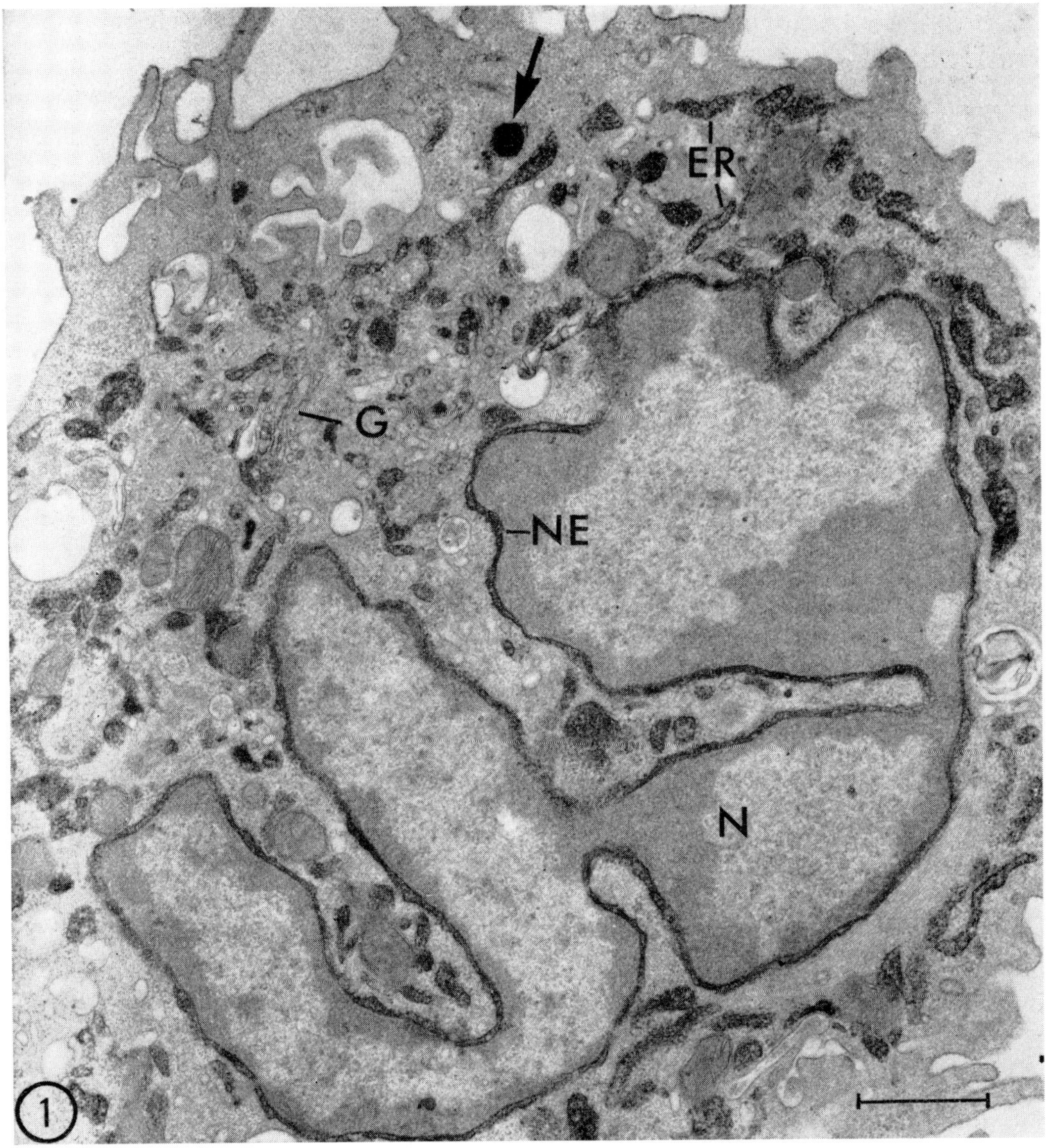

Figure. 1. Saline-lavaged peritoneal macrophage from a normal guinea pig, reacted for peroxidase activity. Note the grayish black reaction product in the nuclear envelope (*NE*), endoplasmic reticulum (*ER*), a granule (*arrow*), and occasional vesicles in the golgi region (*G*). *N*, nucleus (× 18,000). (For this and all other figures, magnifications are approximate.)

received injections of horse serum were more heterogeneous in structure and often contained large phagolysosomes, but the latter were negative for peroxidase, even when the ER was positive. An occasional macrophage contained an erythrocyte or a degenerated eosinophil; these ingested structures showed their own endogenous peroxidase activity.

Technical considerations. The proportion of normal peritoneal macrophages exhibiting a positive reaction as well as the intensity of the reaction were variable and seemed to depend in

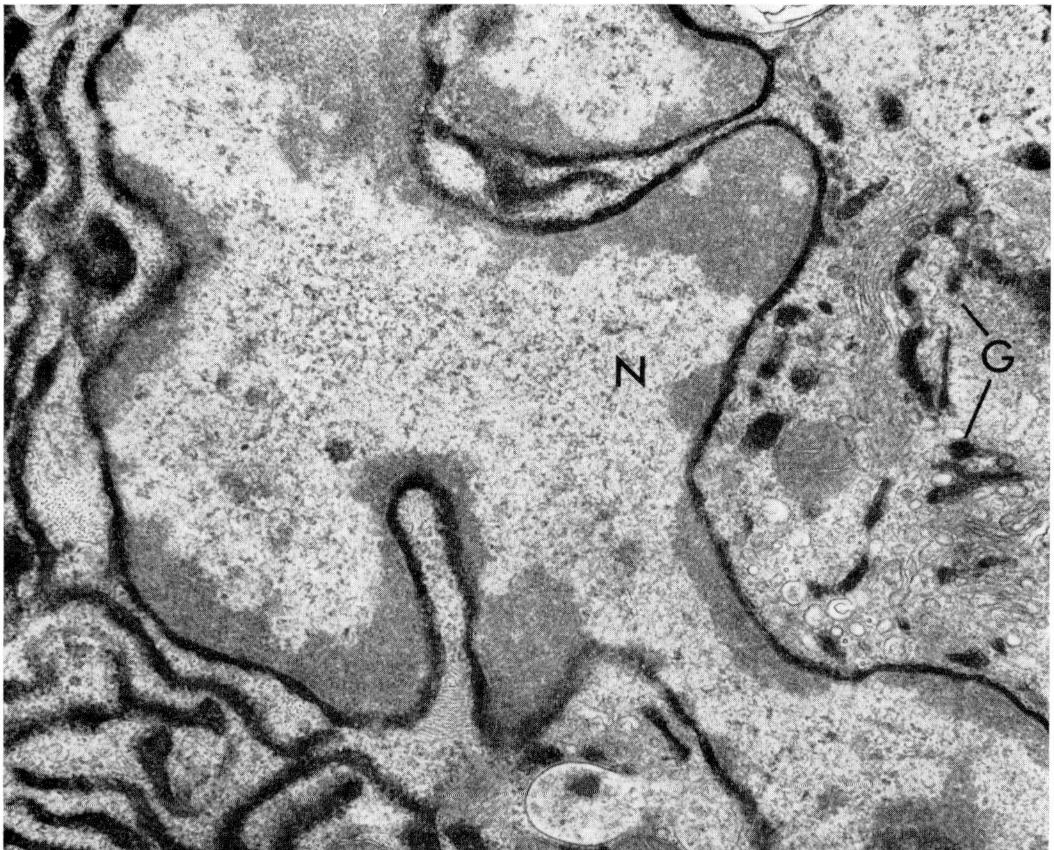

Figure 2. Part of a normal peritoneal macrophage showing heavy labeling of the perinuclear cisternae, and endoplasmic reticulum. *M*, mitochondria; *N*, nucleus; *G*, golgi complex (× 32,000).

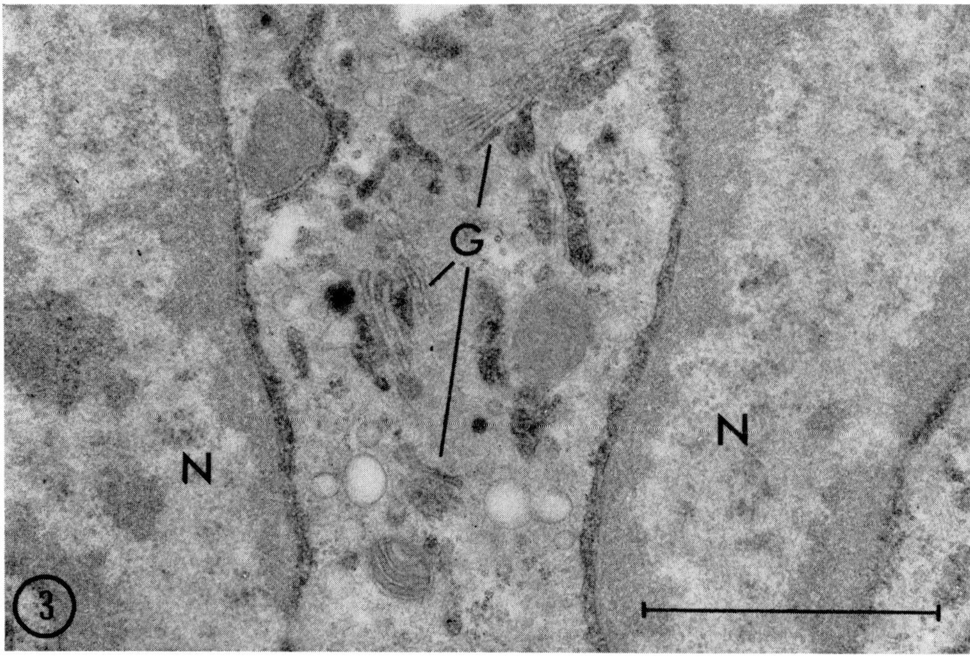

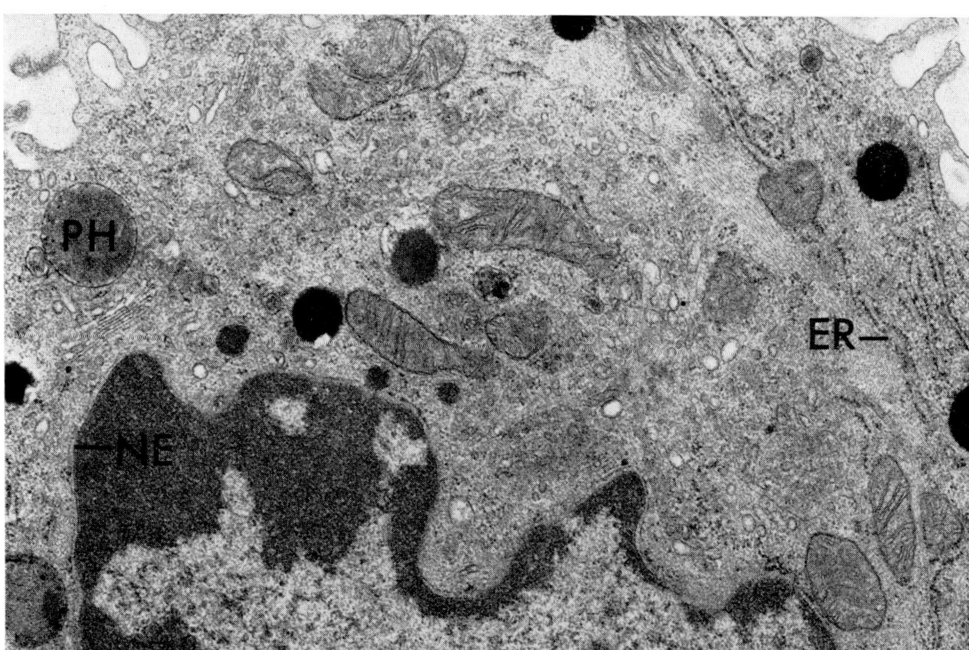

Figure 3. Portion of a peritoneal macrophage from a normal guinea pig. There is staining of the nuclear envelope, and some golgi vesicles and saccules. *N*, nucleus (× 38,000).

Figure 4. Portion of a normal guinea pig peritoneal mononuclear cell. In this cell the endoplasmic reticulum (*ER*) and nuclear envelope (*NE*) are unstained, but there are several large black granules. Note the negatively stained membrane-bounded phagolysosomes (*PH*) (× 22,000).

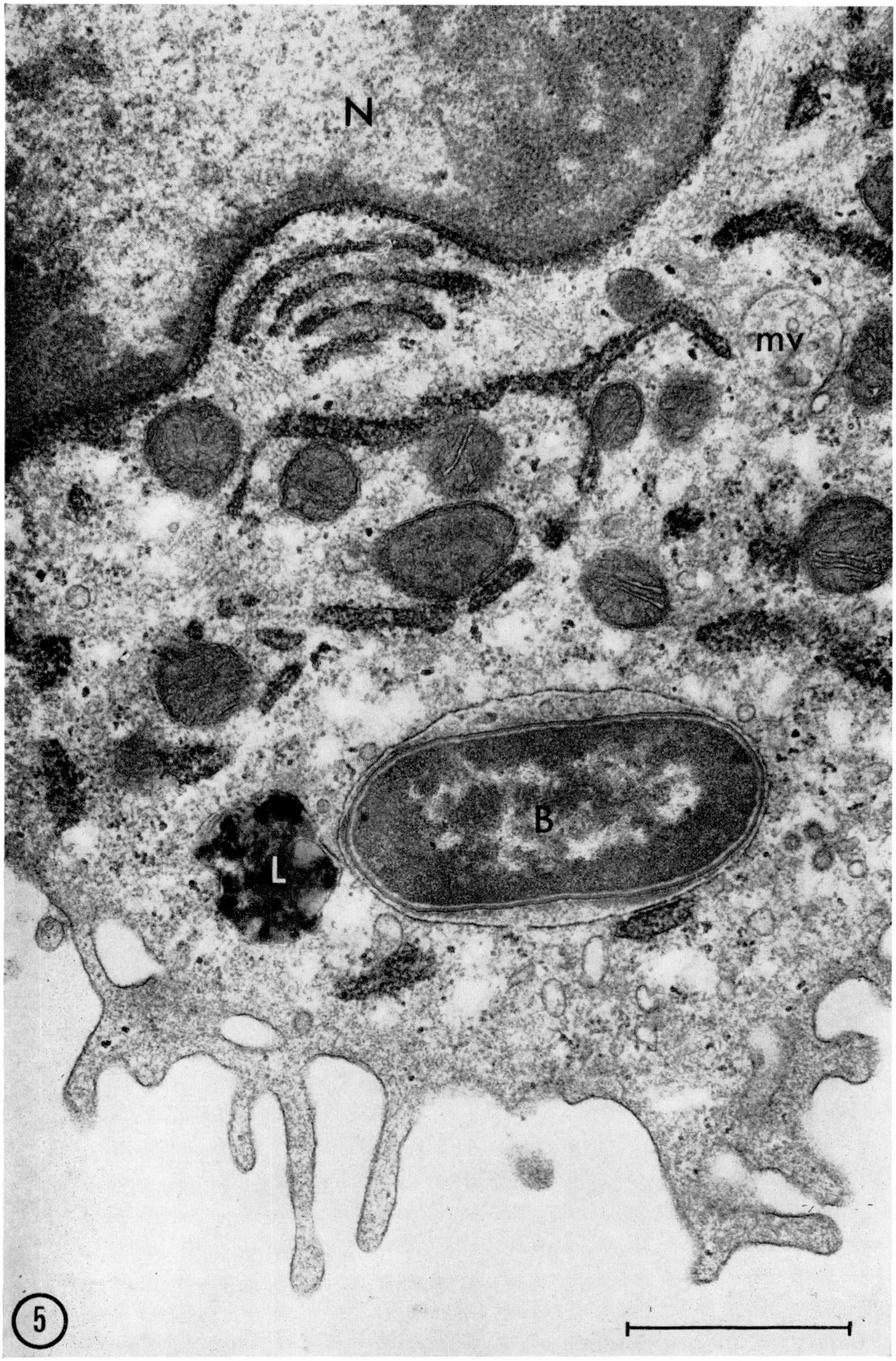

Figure 5. Portion of a peritoneal macrophage from a normal guinea pig which had been incubated with *E. coli* for 30 min. The nuclear envelope and endoplasmic reticulum are stained. *B* is a phagocytized bacterium; note absence of reaction product in the phagocytic vacuole and in the multivesicular body (*MV*). *L* is a lysosome probably filled with lipid material. *N*, nucleus (× 33,000).

part on technical considerations: mainly fixation time and time of incubation in the histochemical medium. In the initial experiments, fixation time was 40 min and incubation time 10 min, these being the optimal conditions for localization of peroxidase in eosinophil granules (14). Under these conditions, 5% to 25% of macrophages were reactive in different experiments (total number of cells counted in each preparation 75 to 200). When the fixation time was 30 min and incubation time 30 min, 20% to 40% of macrophages exhibited positive ER. After fixation for 4 hr and incubation for 30 min, only occasional cells stained and the reaction was weak in most positive cells. In addition, lowering the concentration of H_2O_2 in the incubation medium from 0.02% to 0.007% seemed to enhance the intensity of the reaction. Thus the optimal conditions for the demonstration of macrophage peroxidase appeared to be: 30-min fixation, 0.007% H_2O_2, and 30-min incubation; all subsequent experiments for controlling the specificity of the reaction were carried out under these conditions. In a more recent experiment prolongation of incubation in the histochemical medium to 60 minutes resulted in some ER staining in nearly all macrophages.

The proportion of macrophages with endogenous peroxidase activity did not depend on whether the cells had been obtained from normal or immunized animals or whether they had been exposed to bacteria or zymosan.

Controls. The reaction product in the ER was absent when H_2O_2 was omitted from the incubation medium (Fig. 6), or when the latter contained excess (2%) H_2O_2, or when the cells were boiled before incubation. 10^{-2} M KCN diminished the strength of the reaction, but occasional cells continued to stain; 10^{-1} M KCN inhibited the reaction.

Exogenous peroxidase

Almost all peritoneal macrophages exposed to HRP showed evidence of having taken up the exogenous enzyme. Reaction product was present within surface and intracytoplasmic pinocytosis vesicles, structures suggesting fused vesicles and vacuoles, and a few multivesicular bodies (Figs. 7 and 8). In some cells, there was, in addition, staining that was identical with that described for endogenous peroxidase, i.e., within the perinuclear cisternae, golgi vesicles, and rough ER (Fig. 8, cell 1, and Fig. 9). Endogenous-type staining, was always weaker (less black) than the exogenous-type staining. The proportion of cells showing the endogenous pattern of staining was similar in cells that had been exposed to HRP and in cells which had been fixed immediately after lavage. In an experiment in which the same initial pool of saline-lavaged macrophages was used, approximately the same proportion of cells (25%) exhibited "endogenous" peroxidase irrespective of whether they were 1) exposed to HRP for 30 min, 2) incubated in medium 199 for 30 min, or 3) fixed immediately.

DISCUSSION

Our observations indicate that peroxidase activity is present in the protein-synthesizing apparatus of certain guinea pig peritoneal mononuclear cells. The activity is considered to be endogenous since: 1) it was detected in normal peritoneal cells, fixed immediately after lavage with saline and not exposed to chemicals containing peroxidase, and 2) the pattern of distribution differed significantly from that attributable to uptake of exogenous peroxidase. The latter localization is in vesicles and phagocytic bodies, as amply described previously with other tracers (1, 3–5). The mononuclear cells that exhibited endogenous peroxidase activity were considered to be macrophages since they had the characteristic ultrastructure (1) and, in addition, were phagocytic; virtually all such cells avidly took up HRP (Fig. 8) and many were capable of ingesting *E. coli* and zymosan particles. Whether, however, the peroxidase-positive cells constitute a special type of peritoneal mononuclear cell which is distinct from the peroxidase-negative cells is at present unknown. Typical lymphocytes were negative.

The fate of HRP in guinea pig peritoneal macrophages has been reported recently by Catanzaro *et al.* (8). They found staining in vesicles and vacuoles, the classic locations for phagocytized material, but they also noted staining of the perinuclear cisternae and rough ER, where antigens had not previously been reported to localize. It was suggested that these latter sites might contain that portion of a labeled dose of antigen that has been reported to lie outside the lysosomal fraction (19, 20) and that some type of processing might be occurring there. Only 25% to 30% of the cells they studied

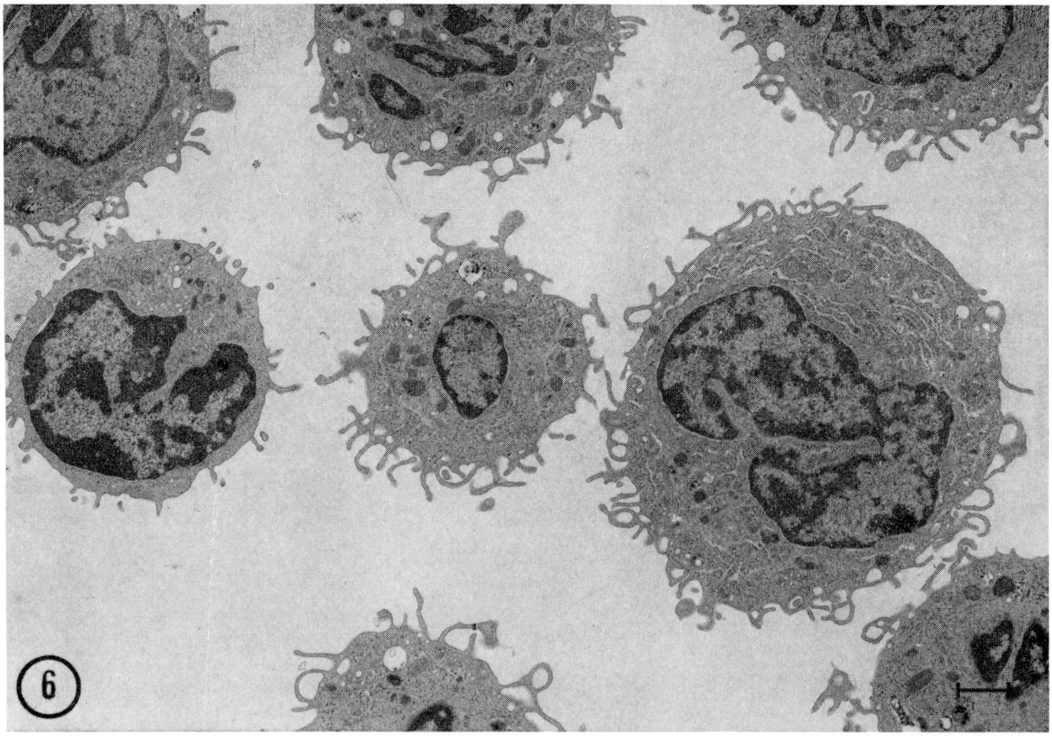

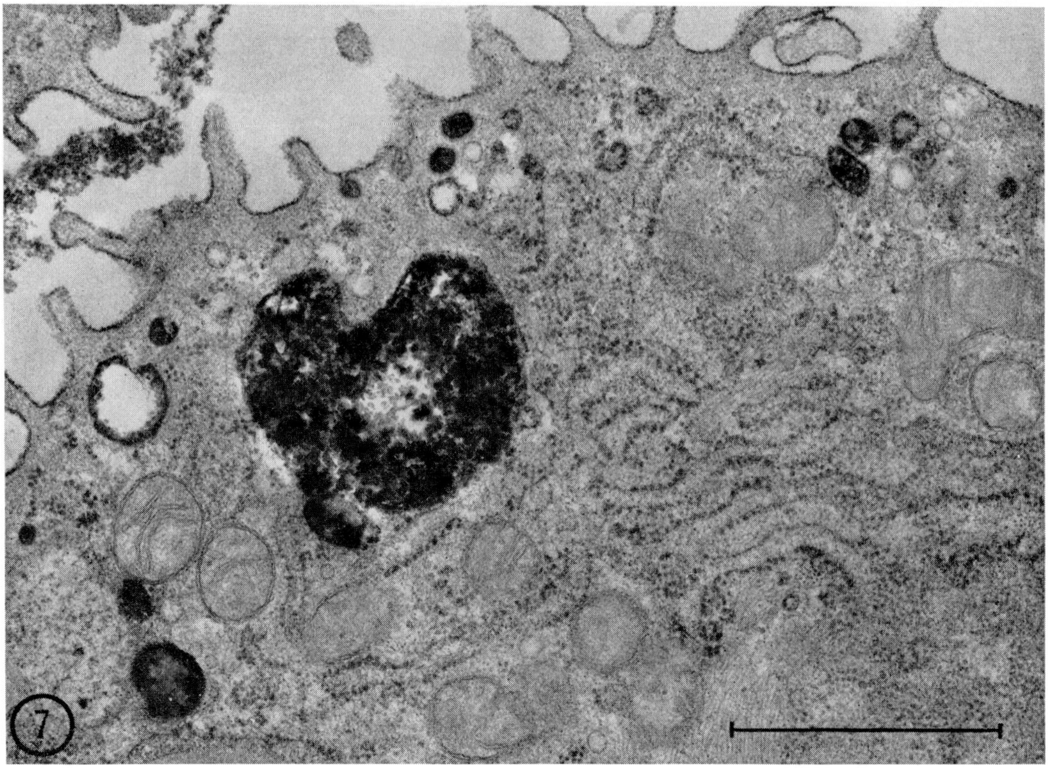

Figure 6. Survey micrograph of several guinea pig mononuclear cells incubated in diaminobenzidine in the absence of hydrogen peroxide. There is no staining for peroxidase in the *ER* in any of the eight cells (× 6,000).

Figure 7. Portion of a normal peritoneal macrophage incubated with horseradish peroxidase for 30 min and reacted for peroxidase. Note the presence of reaction product in surface pinocytosis vesicles, as well as vesicles and vacuoles of various sizes within the cytoplasm (× 35,000).

showed the reaction, and the proportion of positive cells did not increase after more prolonged exposure to HRP. In their experiments, control macrophages which had not been incubated with HRP were negative; thus, all staining in exposed cells was interpreted as exogenous. The discrepancy between our results and those reported by Catanzaro *et al.* may be attributable to 1) sampling or technical differences or 2) the masking in our experiments of exogenous peroxidase at the protein-synthesizing apparatus by the presence of endogenous enzyme. We believe that the latter explanation is less likely since the proportion of cells containing enzyme in the rough ER did not increase after exposure to peroxidase (in our studies), or after prolonged exposure in the studies of Catanzaro *et al.* (8). No other tracer taken up by macrophages has been shown to enter the ER (3–5). Our studies do not rule out this localization, but it will be necessary to differentiate exogenous from endogenous peroxidase (e.g., by autoradiography with labeled peroxidase) in any studies which use this enzyme as a tracer.

The nature of this endogenous enzyme in macrophages bears consideration. The black reaction product is ascribed to enzyme activity since the reaction was abolished by the omission of H_2O_2, excess H_2O_2, and by prior boiling of cells, and was inhibited by cyanide. Histochemical procedures which employ DAB detect (in addition to peroxidase) several substances with peroxidase and oxidase activity, such as catalase (18) and some of the cytochromes (21, 22). For example, mitochondrial staining has been ascribed to cytochrome oxidase (21) and cytochrome c (22). Cytochrome P-450, a hemeprotein that could conceivably oxidize diaminobenzidine, is localized biochemically in the microsomal fraction (23). The possible role of cytochrome P-450 in the staining of the ER peroxidase activity in rat endometrium has been recently discussed in detail by Brokelmann and Fawcett (24). Aminotriazole, an inhibitor of beef liver catalase, gave equivocal inhibition of macrophage peroxidase activity, an observation similar to that obtained with eosinophils (14) and Kupffer cells (25). In any case, the histochemical inhibition methods currently available are too imprecise to allow a definitive identification of the enzyme; and as for macrophages and monocytes, there has not been, to our knowledge, a detailed biochemical analysis of peroxidase content. It is to be emphasized that the vast majority of lysosomal structures seen in both normal and horse serum-stimulated macrophages in this study were negative. The relationships between the peroxidase in ER of peritoneal macrophages and the peroxidase in granules of rare peritoneal cells (Fig. 4) or peripheral blood monocytes (26, 27) remain to be investigated.

It may be that macrophage peroxidase participates in bactericidal functions, as has been suggested for neutrophil peroxidase (16). However, there is no evidence that hydrogen peroxide plays a role in the bactericidal activity of macrophages (1). Whether, alternatively, the enzyme may serve in the metabolic functions of the ER, as recently suggested for endometrial peroxidase (24), is also conjectural. It is noteworthy, however, that virtually identical patterns of localization of endogenous peroxidase activity have been seen in other cell types which are comparable to peritoneal macrophages in many respects: Kupffer cells of the liver (25, 28) and the histiocytes in the lamina propria of rat small intestine (M. A. Venkatachalam, personal communication). In particular, endogenous peroxidase activity is present in a large proportion (up to 40%) of Kupffer cells in apparently normal rats, and as in macrophages, it can be clearly differentiated from exogenous peroxidase uptake in control experiments (25). Finally the present study deals with guinea pig cells, but there may

Figure 8. Portion of two peritoneal macrophages exposed *in vitro* to horseradish peroxidase for 30 min and reacted for peroxidase. Cell 1 exhibits reaction product within vesicles and larger vacuoles (*V*), as well as in the stacks of endoplasmic reticulum (*ER*). Cell 2 shows staining only of vacuoles and vesicles, but there is no staining in the endoplasmic reticulum (× 10,000).

Figure 9. Portion of a normal peritoneal macrophage exposed to horseradish peroxidase for 30 min and showing both exogenous and endogenous patterns of peroxidase activity. The staining of vesicles and vacuoles (*V*) is interpreted as exogenous uptake, and the staining of the nuclear envelope and endoplasmic reticulum (*arrows*) is interpreted as endogenous activity. *N*, nucleus (× 26,000).

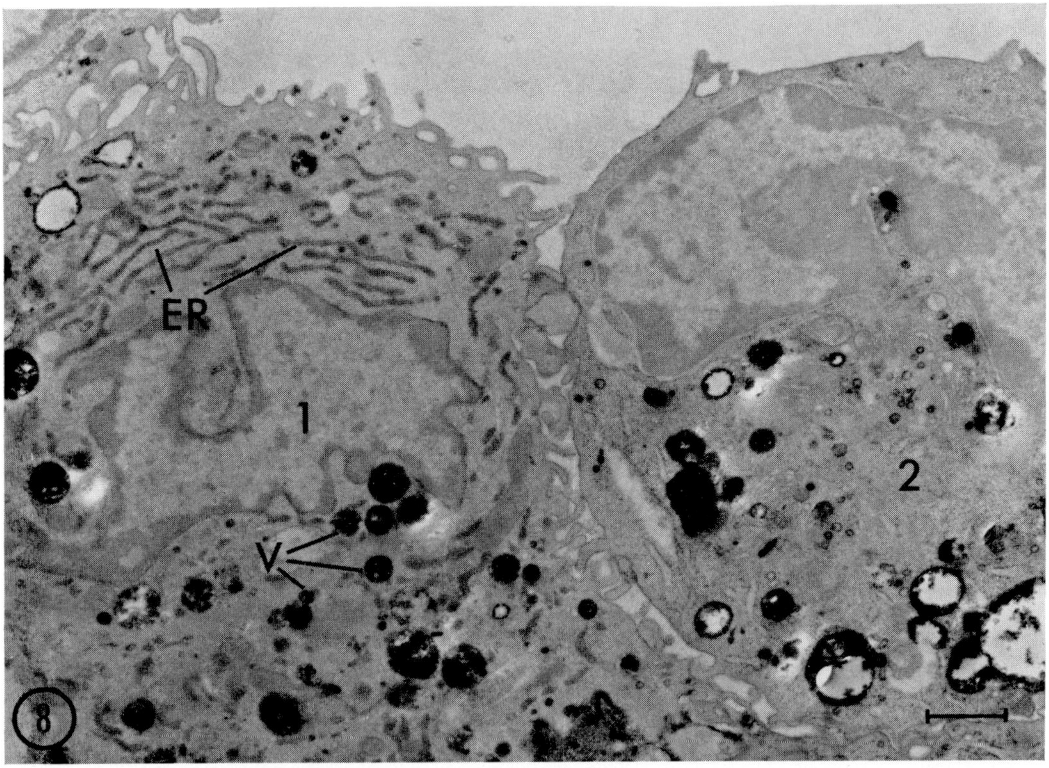
ER
1
2
V
8

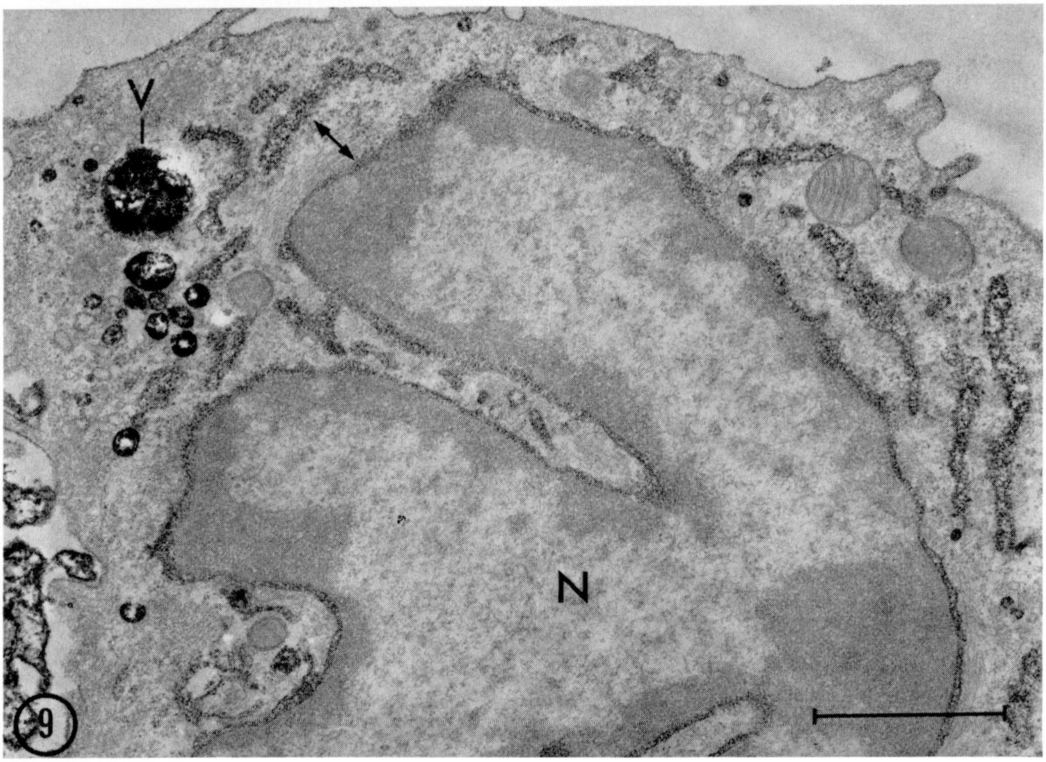
V
N
9

be species differences in peroxidase reactivity of peritoneal macrophages. In a review available since submission of this paper (29) reference is made that peritoneal macrophages of the mouse are peroxidase negative. In the rat, under the technical conditions described in this study, we (Cotran, R. S., Robbins, D and Fahimi, D., in preparation) have found that ER staining is present in a smaller proportion of macrophages than in the guinea pig and is consistently weaker in intensity.

REFERENCES

1. Cohn, Z. A., Advances in Immun., *9:* 163, 1968.
2. Saunders, B. C., Holmes-Siedle, A. G. and Stark, B. P., *Peroxidase,* Butterworth & Co., Ltd., London, 1964.
3. Nossal, G. J. V., Abbot, A. and Mitchel, J., J. Exp. Med., *127:* 263, 1968.
4. Casley-Smith, J. R., J. Micro., *90:* 15, 1969.
5. Cohn, Z. A., Fedorko, M. E., and Hirsch, J. G., J. Exp. Med., *123:* 757, 1966.
6. Wellerniek, H. J. and Coons, A. H., J. Exp. Med., *119:* 685, 1964.
7. Sordat, B., Sordat, M., Sess, M. W., Stoner, R. D. and Cottier, H., J. Exp. Med., *131:* 77, 1970.
8. Catanzaro, P. J., Graham, R. C., and Schwartz H. J., J. Immun., *103:* 618, 1969.
9. Leduc, E. H., Avrameas, S. and Bouteille, M., J. Exp. Med., *127:* 109, 1968.
10. Straus, W., J. Histochem. Cytochem., *18:* 120, 1970.
11. Graham, R. D. and Karnovsky, M. J., J. Histochem. Cytochem., *14:* 291, 1966.
12. Ackerman, G. A., Lab. Invest., *19:* 290, 1968.
13. Bainton, D. F. and Farquhar, M. G., J. Cell Biol., *45:* 54, 1970.
14. Cotran, R. S., and Litt, M., J. Exp. Med., *129:* 1291, 1969.
15. Baehner, R. L., Karnovsky, M. J. and Karnovsky, M. L., J. Clin. Invest., *48:* 187, 1969.
16. Klebanoff, S. F., J. Exp. Med., *126:* 1063, 1967.
17. Litt, M., Blood, *16:* 1318, 1960.
18. Fahimi, H. D., J. Cell. Biol., *43:* 275, 1969.
19. Kolsch, E. and Mitchison, N. A., J. Exp. Med., *128:* 1059, 1968.
20. Unanue, E. R. and Askonas, B. A., J. Exp. Med., *127:* 915, 1968.
21. Seligman, A. M., Karnovsky, M. J., Wasserkrug, H. L., and Hanker, J. S., J. Cell Biol., *38:* 1, 1968.
22. Novikoff, A. B. and Goldfischer, S., J. Histochem. Cytochem., *17:* 675, 1969.
23. Omura, T., Sato, R., Cooper, D. Y., Rosenthal, O. and Estabrook, R. W., Fed. Proc., *24:* 1181, 1965.
24. Brokelmann, J. and Fawcett, D. W., Biol. Reprod., *1:* 59, 1969.
25. Fahimi, H. D., J. Cell Biol., In Press.
26. Kaplow, L. S., Blood, *26:* 215, 1965.
27. Dunn, W. B., Hardin, J. H. and Spicer, S. S., Blood, *32:* 935, 1968.
28. Novikoff, A. B., Biempica, L., Quintana, N., Albola, A. and Dominitz, R., J. Cell Biol., *39:* 100a, 1968.
29. Fedorko, M. E. and Hirsch, J. G., Seminars Hemat., *7:* 109, 1970.

THE JOURNAL OF IMMUNOLOGY
Vol. 105, No. 6, December 1970
Printed in U.S.A.

REACTIVITY OF NORMAL SHARK IMMUNOGLOBULINS WITH NITROPHENYL LIGANDS[1]

GERRIE A. LESLIE[2] AND L. WILLIAM CLEM

From the Department of Microbiology, College of Medicine, University of Florida, Gainesville, Florida

Received for publication May 18, 1970

Normal nurse shark and lemon shark sera contain ~17S and 7S immunoglobulins with anti-dinitrophenyl activity. Specifically purified 17S "anti-DNP" precipitated in gels with DNP-BSA conjugates, bound to DNP-immunoadsorbents (~60%) but did not give detectable binding by equilibrium dialysis. The 7S "anti-DNP" did not precipitate in gels, nor did it bind radiolabeled hapten and only about 25% bound to DNP-immunoadsorbents. Of special interest was the observation that specifically purified 17S "anti-DNP" also agglutinated sheep erythrocytes. However, the agglutination of sheep erythrocytes could not be inhibited with DNP-OH. Whole nurse shark serum contains agglutinins to both sheep and chicken erythrocytes. Experiments showed that this was not due to heteroligating antibodies. The possibility is raised that many of the shark immunoglobulin molecules have a dual function, that is, as antibody and as a carrier for certain hormones or other small molecules.

The use of defined antigenic determinants such as the 2,4-dinitrophenyl group (DNP) greatly facilitates the specific purification and measurements of valences and thermodynamic properties of antibodies. Interest in the phylogenetic development of antibody structure and function prompted a study of the immunogenicity of DNP in various lower vertebrates. The results of that study showed that representatives of practically all classes of the subphylum Vertebrata (exclusive of the Cyclostomes, which were not studied) could synthesize humoral antibodies to DNP (1). Since sharks appeared to be rather poor responders to DNP it was quite surprising to note that, under certain conditions, normal shark sera formed precipitates with DNP-protein conjugates. Therefore, in light of recent reports of anti-DNP activity in normal human (2), and pathologic human (3–5) and mouse (6, 7) sera, it was deemed of interest to further investigate this normal shark "anti-DNP" activity. The results of these studies form the basis of this paper.

[1] This work was supported by Grant GB-8632 from National Science Foundation.

[2] G.A.L. is the recipient of a Research Fellowship Award 1-F02-A144187-01 from the Department of Health, Education, and Welfare, United States Public Health Service.

MATERIALS AND METHODS

Nurse and lemon sharks. Sharks were maintained in tidal sea water at the Lerner Marine Laboratory, Bimini, Bahamas. The sharks were anesthetized with MS-222 (Sandoz Inc., New York, N. Y.) and bled by hemal arch puncture. Sera were collected as described previously (8, 9).

Antigens. The 2,4-dinitrophenylated (DNP) and 2,4,6-trinitrophenylated (TNP) proteins were prepared and analyzed as described by Eisen (10). Arsanylic acid conjugates (11) and acetylated bovine serum albumin (12) were prepared according to published methods. Other antigens and inhibitors used were: bovine serum albumin (BSA) (Armour), bovine γ globulin (Pentex Inc., Kankakee, Ill.), caffeine (Sigma Chemical Co., St. Louis, Mo.) and purine base (Sigma).

Quantitative precipitin analysis. Three-tenths-milliliter volumes of shark serum were mixed with equal volumes of varying concentrations of hapten-conjugated proteins in NaCl-Tris buffer (0.14 M NaCl, 0.01 M Tris-HCl, pH 7.4 and and 0.01 M EDTA), at 37°C for 1 hr followed by 2.5°C for 24 hr. The washed precipitates were then assayed spectrophotometrically for protein content. Corrections were made, when necessary, for absorption contributions by the antigen.

Purification of "anti-DNP." The proteins from the precipitates formed between shark serum and

DNP-BSA were purified similarly to the method of Farah *et al.* (13) as discussed under *Results*.

Equilibrium dialysis. Equilibrium dialysis was performed essentially as described by Eisen (14) using tritiated 2,4-dinitrophenyl-ϵ-amino caproic acid. Lucite cells in which the two compartments were separated by dialysis membrane (cellulose tubing, size 36, Union Carbide, Chicago, Ill.) were employed; the "antibody-side" usually contained 0.3 to 0.4 ml of ~3 mg/ml of immunoglobulin solution and the "hapten-side" contained a similar volume of hapten containing solution (1.59×10^{-6} M-84.4×10^{-6} M). Duplicate 100-μl samples were counted for tritium using 10 ml of BBOT scintillation fluid (Packard Instrument Co., Downer's Grove, Ill.) in a Packard Tri-Carb scintillation spectrometer.

Physicochemical methods. Analytical ultracentrifugation, immunodiffusion, immunoelectrophoresis and radioiodination of proteins were conducted as described previously (15).

Immunoadsorbents. ϵ-DNP-lysine was coupled to Sephadex G-25 by the cyanogen bromide method of Porath *et al.* (16).

DNP-T$_4$ phage neutralization assay. The modified phage and neutralization procedure was exactly as described previously (1).

Hemagglutination. Tube agglutinations were done with 0.5-ml dilutions of serum or purified "anti-DNP" and 0.05 ml of 2% chicken or sheep erythrocytes. To test for the presence of heteroligating antibodies, slide agglutinations were done and the agglutinates were examined under the microscope.

RESULTS

Precipitation of nitrophenyl ligands by normal shark sera. Individual serum samples from all of 15 nurse and 7 of 8 lemon sharks showed visible precipitates by the capillary tube method with 0.4 mg/ml DNP$_{46}$ BSA and TNP$_{28}$ BSA. None of these sera showed visible capillary precipitates with BSA. Similarly, no precipitates were observed with DNP$_{46}$ BSA, TNP$_{28}$ BSA, or BSA by gel diffusion. To test the spectrum of this precipitating activity several concentrations of arsanylic acid-BSA and acetylated BSA were employed. In no case did visible precipitates form with these latter preparations.

The quantitative precipitin curves of two normal nurse shark sera with DNP$_{46}$ BSA are shown in Figure 1. These curves showed no post-zone when high concentrations of DNP$_{46}$ BSA were employed and thus can be viewed as being similar to the curves obtained with macroglobulin antibodies (17, 18). The shark precipitin curves depicted here, however, differed from classic macroglobulin curves in that soluble or free antigen was present in all concentrations used as attested to by the yellow color of the supernatants. Thus, there was no true equivalence zone in this system. Similarly shaped curves with somewhat shallower slopes were obtained with several normal lemon shark sera. These sera also showed the presence of soluble DNP$_{46}$ BSA even at low concentrations of conjugate.

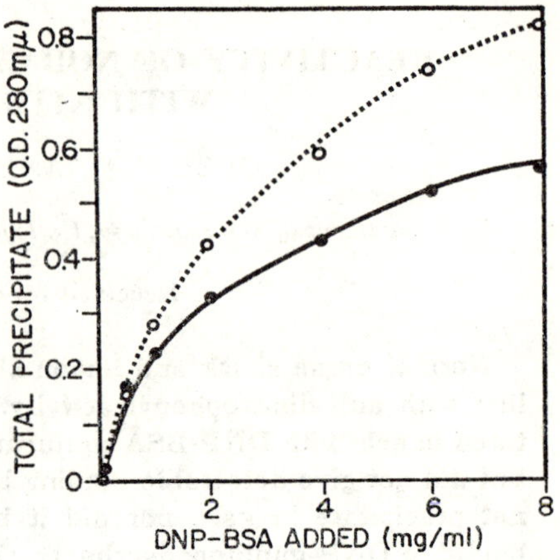

Figure 1. Quantitative precipitin reaction between DNP$_{46}$ BSA and normal nurse shark sera.

Since the precipitation appeared to be specific for nitrophenylated-BSA, an experiment was performed to test the inhibitory effects of 2,4-dinitrophenol, purine base and caffeine on precipitation. The results of this experiment are given in Table I. No inhibition was seen with caffeine or purine and only 67% inhibition was obtained when 100 mM DNP-OH were added into the reaction mixture.

Effect of degree of hapten substitution on precipitin reaction. Bovine γ globulin was conjugated with 52, 30 and 9 mols of DNP/mol of protein and each preparation was tested quantitatively for precipitation with two normal nurse shark sera. Figure 2 shows that a high degree of substitution (> 30 DNP/molecule) is necessary in order to yield significant amounts of precipitate. In fact, one serum gave no precipitate with DNP$_9$BGG. Several additional experiments were performed to test the importance of the concen-

TABLE I

Effect of various inhibitors on the precipitation of DNP_{46}-BSA by normal nurse shark serum[a]

Inhibitor	Inhibitor Conc.	Inhibition[b]
	mM	%
DNP-OH	100	67
	10	4
	1	0
	0.10	0
Purine	20	0
Caffeine	20	0

[a] Two-tenths-milliliter of serum + 0.2 ml of inhibitor were incubated for 1 hr at 37°C, then 0.2 ml DNP_{46}-BSA was added.

[b] Inhibition is expressed as percentage decrease in the amount of protein precipitated when compared with protein precipitated in the absence of the inhibitor.

tration of DNP groups in the precipitin reaction mixture. The addition of 5 to 10 times the amount of DNP_9 BGG did not appreciably increase precipitate formation, indicating that precipitate formation was a function of the density of DNP on the carrier molecule and not a function of the concentration of DNP groups in the reaction mixture. As a control several immune sheep anti-DNP sera were tested by the capillary precipitin method; each immune serum gave considerable visible precipitation with DNP_9BGG.

Purification and characterization of the shark reactive moiety. Washed precipitates formed by normal nurse shark serum and DNP_{46}BSA (5 mg/ml) were extracted at 37°C with 0.1 M DNP-OH in the presence of streptomycin and the supernatants were gel filtered on Sephadex G-200 (Pharmacia Fine Chemicals, Uppsala, Sweden). A representative elution profile is given in Figure 3 and shows both excluded and included protein peaks; the small molecule peak (not shown here) contained DNP-OH. The shark serum precipitate extracted here yielded about 430 μg protein/ml of which ~280 μg/ml were excluded from the G-200 column. In a parallel experiment no DNP-OH was added when the washed precipitate was brought to 37°C with 0.14 M NaCl in 0.015 M Tris-HCl, pH 7.4. The supernatant from this extracted material yielded a profile remarkably similar to that discussed above when subjected to Sephadex G-200 gel filtration. Thus, incubation at 37°C was sufficient to dissociate the precipitates and the DNP-OH was unimportant in this regard.

The excluded peak from the Sephadex G-200 columns depicted above was homogeneous and contained only 17.4S material (5 mg/ml) when examined by analytical ultracentrifugation. Immunoelectrophoresis and Ouchterlony type analysis with rabbit antisera to whole nurse shark serum and immunoglobulin (9) indicated this excluded material to be pure and to be antigenically identical to nurse shark immunoglobulins. It was therefore considered to represent a portion of the nurse shark's 19S immunoglobulin and will be referred to as "19S anti-DNP."

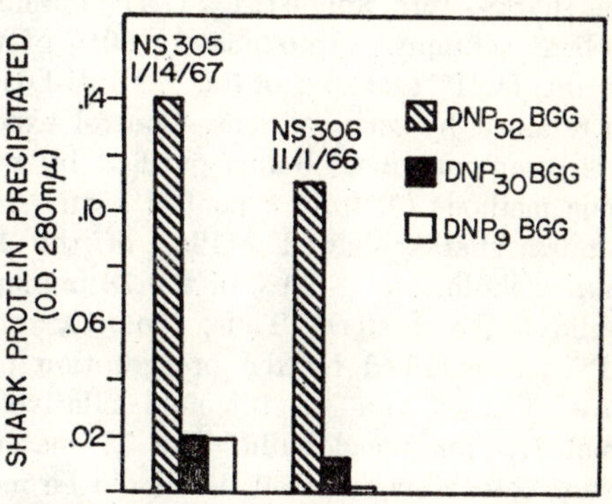

Figure 2. The effect of various DNP concentrations per mol of BGG on the amount of precipitate formed with normal shark sera. Optical densities are corrected for the DNP contributions.

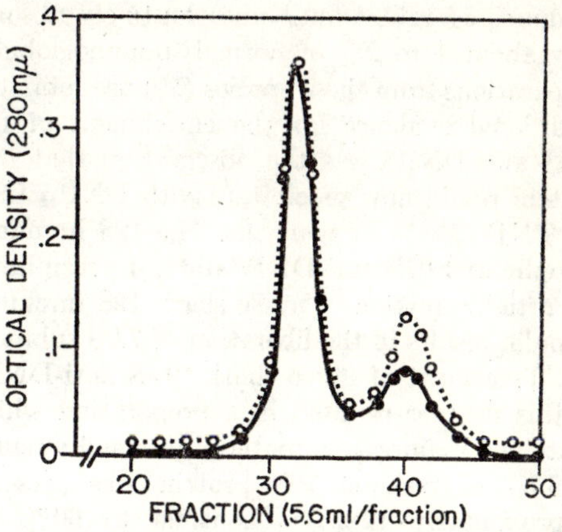

Figure 3. Gel filtration on Sephadex G-200 of washed precipitates formed by normal nurse shark serum and DNP_{46} BSA and extracted with 0.1 M DNP-OH at 37°C (——) and similar precipitates incubated at 37°C in the absence of DNP-OH (-----).

Similar studies on the material included on the Sephadex G-200 column showed it to contain only nurse shark 7S immunoglobulin. This material will be referred to as "7S anti-DNP." Similar results were obtained with three other normal nurse shark sera.

Binding activities of purified reactive shark immunoglobulins. To test the binding of normal nurse shark "19S anti-DNP" and "7S anti-DNP" to the DNP determinant two types of experiments were performed: a) binding to DNP-lysine-Sephadex immunoadsorbent columns, b) equilibrium dialysis. In the first approach 10 to 20 μg of a pool of ^{125}I-labeled "anti-DNP" from three sharks were applied to DNP immunoadsorbent columns. Approximately 60% of the "19S anti-DNP" and 25% of the "7S anti-DNP" were retained by such columns. Control experiments using immunoglobulins purified by nonspecific methods (9) from a pool of serum from five nurse sharks showed ~19% of the 19S immunoglobulin and ~30% of the 7S immunoglobulin to be retained. Thus, the "19S anti-DNP" was enriched by the precipitation procedure at least two- to threefold relative to normal 19S immunoglobulin. The 7S material was not detectably enriched. It should be mentioned that the affinity of shark immunoglobulins for nitrophenol ligands is further substantiated by other experiments employing such DNP-lysine-Sephadex columns. For example, while greater than 70% of specifically purified grouper and rabbit antibodies routinely absorb, only about 1 to 2% of normal immunoglobulin preparations from these species (19) are retained. Additional evidence for the enrichment of the "19S anti-DNP" was the observation that this protein would now precipitate with DNP_{46} BSA (or TNP_{28} BSA) in agar gels. The 19S immunoglobulin and "7S anti-DNP" did not precipitate.

Partial reduction of nurse shark 19S immunoglobulin results in the liberation of 7.2S subunits (9). Treatment of nurse shark "19S anti-DNP" in this manner resulted in a preparation which contained mainly 7.2S material; a small amount (<5%) of residual 19S protein was present. Approximately 12% (in contrast to 60% for the unreduced material) of this preparation was retained by the immunoadsorbent. Similarly, papain digestion of shark 19S immunoglobulin yields 6.4S fragments containing a portion of the H chain and all of the L chain determinants. These fragments are considered to be analogous to $F(ab')_2$ (G. A. Leslie and L. W. Clem, unpublished observation). When nurse shark "19S anti-DNP" was treated with papain, only 2% of the digested material was retained by the immunoadsorbent column.

In an attempt to quantify the binding of nitrophenyl ligands by normal nurse shark "anti-DNP," several equilibrium dialysis experiments employing ^3H-DNP-ϵ-amino caproic acid (1.5×10^{-6} M to 10^{-4} M) were done. Concentrations of shark "19S anti-DNP" and "7S anti-DNP" of about 3 mg protein/ml showed no detectable binding of hapten. Therefore, these data suggest the K_0 of this reaction to be less than 10^4 M^{-1}.

Neutralization of DNP-bacteriophage. One of the most sensitive methods of assaying for antibodies to the DNP group is by the bacteriophage neutralization technique employing DNP-conjugated phage (1, 20). For example, rabbit IgG antibodies to DNP with $K_0 \sim 10^7$ M^{-1} can neutralize 50% of the DNP-T_4 phage in 10 min at concentrations approximating 4×10^{-10} M. Likewise, grouper macroglobulin antibodies to DNP with $K_0 \sim 10^4$ neutralize at concentrations of $\sim 10^{-10}$ M (21). It was, therefore, surprising that nurse shark "19S anti-DNP" and "7S anti-DNP" showed no neutralization of DNP-T_4 at concentrations up to 10^{-6} M. It should be mentioned that specifically induced nurse shark antibodies to DNP can neutralize such phage (1).

Hemagglutination of erythrocytes by normal shark "anti-DNP." Normal nurse sharks have previously been shown to have natural agglutinins for sheep and chicken erythrocytes (9, 22). It was therefore, deemed of interest to determine if the normal "anti-DNP" and the normal hemagglutinins represented the same or different populations of molecules. The hemagglutinating activities for sheep erythrocytes of purified "19S anti-DNP" and "7S anti-DNP" from the sera of two sharks were compared to 19S and 7S immunoglobulins obtained from a pool of serum from five sharks. The results of these studies are given in Table II. Both "19S anti-DNP" preparations caused agglutination at concentrations of ~0.05 to 0.1 mg/ml. This is very similar to the activity of normal 19S immunoglobulin. The "7S anti-DNP" and 7S immunoglobulin activities were at least eight times less efficient than the 19S proteins. In light of the apparent "dual" specificity of the normal shark "19S anti-DNP," inhibition of hemagglutination by DNP-OH was attempted.

TABLE II

Hemagglutination of sheep erythrocytes by nurse shark "anti-DNP"

Shark	Sample	Titer[a]
305	19S "anti-DNP"	0.05
	7S "anti-DNP"	0.40
306	19S "anti-DNP"	0.10
	7S "anti-DNP"	>0.80
Pooled	19S immunoglobulin	0.10
Pooled	7S immunoglobulin	>0.80

[a] Titers are reported as the minimum amount of protein (mg/ml) that is required to give positive agglutination.

No inhibition was detectable at the concentrations of DNP-OH employed, i.e., 10^1 and 10^2 mM. Since these concentrations of hapten are considered sufficient to inhibit the hemagglutination reaction with DNP-erythrocytes and antibodies to DNP (23), the experiments reported here indicate that the natural antibody sites for erythrocytes do not appear to be the same sites involved in the DNP-associated reaction.

Since the data discussed in the previous paragraph are consistent with the presence of heteroligating immunoglobulin molecules in the shark, an attempt to demonstrate heteroligating hemagglutinins was undertaken. Nine normal nurse shark sera were found to have hemagglutinins for both sheep and chicken erythrocytes. The titers ranged from 1:100 to 1:1600 for each cell type. When both types of erythrocytes were added to the serum simultaneously (or in sequential fashion), no mixed agglutination was observed microscopically. That is, the abundant clumps of cells were either all chicken or all sheep, never both. It therefore, seems unlikely that a significant portion of the individual shark immunoglobulin molecules contain sites for both these antigens.

DISCUSSION

A survey of the recent literature makes it clear that "anti-DNP" activity in non-immune sera is not a particularly unusual finding. It has been reported in normal human sera (2), pathologic human sera (3–5), teleost and bufo sera (1) and in some sera from mice bearing plasma cell tumors (6, 7). In those cases in which it has been closely studied, the moiety responsible for the binding is an immunoglobulin. In man, for example, some myeloma proteins of the IgM, IgG and IgA classes have been implicated (5). Stone and Metzger (24) isolated a human Waldenström macroglobulin which by equilibrium dialysis showed a marked homogeneity of binding and a $K_0 = 3.8 \times 10^4\ M^{-1}$. Likewise, the binding curves with several myeloma proteins have indicated homogeneity and K_0's $> 10^5\ M^{-1}$. In contrast, the nurse shark "anti-DNP" proteins isolated herein did not show detectable binding. It therefore seems likely that these shark immunoglobulins are not behaving as typical antibodies to DNP. Recently, immune shark antibodies to DNP have been isolated and shown to have binding constants $> 10^5\ M^{-1}$. These antibodies did not agglutinate erythrocytes, and thus behave in a "typical" antibody-like fashion (25).

The perplexing problem therefore arises as to why some of the shark's normal immunoglobulin reacts with DNP-conjugated proteins. It has been suggested that the structure of DNP is such that it resembles some of the purine bases (26). The fact that all vertebrates at one time or another come in contact with foreign (or their own) nucleic acids may result in the formation of natural antibodies to such compounds. Thus, the normal shark "anti-DNP" may really be only a cross-reacting antibody of low affinity for DNP. While this may be true, it seems that an alternative explanation must be entertained. In sharks and some of the other "lower" vertebrates very little, if any, albumin is present in the serum. In higher animals albumin functions primarily as a carrier protein and helps to maintain the intravascular osmotic pressure, and since ~50% of the shark's serum proteins are immunoglobulins it seems reasonable to suggest that some of the functions of albumin may be assumed by shark immunoglobulins. It is therefore possible that many of shark immunoglobulin molecules may have a dual function, that is, as antibody and as a carrier for certain hormones or other small molecules. The experiments wherein a fairly high concentration of DNP was found per molecule of carrier protein suggest that multiple hydrophobic-hydrophobic interactions are necessary for the observed precipitation. The observation that purified "anti-DNP" agglutinates sheep erythrocytes could thus be explained on the basis of the antibody-functional aspects of these molecules. The failure to inhibit sheep erythrocyte agglutination with DNP-OH is consistent with this suggestion, i.e., the "anti-DNP" and anti-erythrocyte sites may occupy different regions of the shark immunoglobulin molecule. In the event that the two types of binding sites (for DNP and for erythrocytes) of shark 19S immunoglobulin overlap in a manner similar to that discussed by Glazer (27) for the binding of dyes to globular proteins, an intriguing possibility arises. Namely, did antibodies evolve from proteins exhibiting "nonspecific" carrier functions, and if so, does the shark immunoglobulin represent a transitional stage?

REFERENCES

1. Leslie, G. A. and Clem, L. W., J. Immun., *103:* 613, 1969.
2. Brandriss, M. W., Nature, *221:* 960, 1969.
3. Eisen, H. N., Little, J. R., Osterland, C. K. and Simms, E. S., Cold Spring Harbor Symp. Quant. Biol., *32:* 75, 1967.
4. Hannestad, K., Clin. Exp. Immun., *4:* 555, 1969.
5. Terry, W. D., Boyd, M. M., Rea, J. S. and Stein, R., J. Immun., *104:* 256, 1970.
6. Eisen, H. N., Simms, E. S. and Potter, M., Biochemistry, *7:* 4126, 1968.
7. Schubert, D., Jobe, A. and Cohn, M., Nature, *220:* 882, 1968.
8. Clem, L. W. and Small, P. A., J. Exp. Med., *125:* 893, 1967.
9. Clem, L. W., De Boutaud, F. and Sigel, M. M., J. Immun., *99:* 1226, 1967.
10. Eisen, H., Meth. Med. Res., *10:* 94, 1964.
11. Campbell, D. H., Garvey, J. S., Cremer, N. E. and Sussdorf, D. H., in *Methods in Immunology*, p. 79, W. A. Benjamin, Inc., New York, 1964.
12. Fraenkel-Conrat, H., in *Methods in Enzymology*, Edited by S. P. Colowick and N. O. Kaplan, Vol. 4, p. 251, Academic Press, New York, 1957.
13. Farah, F. S., Kern, M. and Eisen, H., J. Exp. Med., *112:* 1195, 1960.
14. Eisen, H. N., Meth. Med. Res., *10:* 106, 1964.
15. Leslie, G. A. and Clem, L. W., J. Exp. Med., *130:* 1337, 1969.
16. Porath, J., Axen, R. and Ernback, S., Nature, *215:* 1491, 1967.
17. Hill, W. C. and Cebra, J. C., Biochemistry, *4:* 2575, 1965.
18. Lindquist, K. and Bauer, D. C., Immunochemistry, *3:* 373, 1966.
19. Clem, L. W., and Small, P. A., J. Exp. Med., *132:* 385, 1970.
20. Mäkelä, O., Immunology, *10:* 81, 1966.
21. Blank, S., Master of Science Thesis, University of Florida, 1970.
22. Sigel, M. M. and Clem, L. W., in *Phylogeny of Immunity*, Edited by R. T. Smith, P. A. Meischer and R. A. Good, p. 190, University of Florida Press, Gainesville, Fla., 1966.
23. Levine, B. B. and Levytska, V., J. Immun., *98:* 648, 1967.
24. Stone, M. J. and Metzger, H., J. Biol. Chem., *243:* 5977, 1968.
25. Voss, E. W., Russell, W. J. and Sigel, M. M., Biochemistry, *8:* 4866, 1969.
26. Eisen, H. N., Michaelides, M. C., Underdown, B. J., Schulenburg, E. P. and Simms, E. S., Fed. Proc., *29:* 78, 1970.
27. Glazer, A. N., Proc. Nat. Acad. Sci., *65:* 1057, 1970.

THE JOURNAL OF IMMUNOLOGY
Vol. 105, No. 6, December 1970

PRODUCTION OF INTERFERON IN PRIMARY CHICK EMBRYONIC CELLS INFECTED WITH *RICKETTSIA MOOSERI*

SEIYA KOHNO, MASAYOSHI KOHASE, HIROKO SAKATA, YUKIKO SHIMIZU, MICHIKO HIKITA AND AKIRA SHISHIDO

From the Department of Measles Virus, National Institutes of Health, Murayamamachi, Kitatama-gun, Tokyo 190-12, Japan

Received for publication January 26, 1970

***Rickettsia mooseri* was found to stimulate the production of a viral inhibitory factor in primary chick embryonic cells. This factor possesses the major properties of interferon. Avian leukosis-free chick cells and chick cells carrying RAV-1 are equally potent producers of rickettsial interferon, suggesting that the interferon production is not mediated by viral factors persisting in the cells. The molecular weight of rickettsial and viral interferon was approximately 35,000.**

Hopps, Kohno, Kohno and Smadel (1) made a preliminary report that interferon is produced by primary chick embryonic (PCE) cells infected with *Rickettsia tsutsugamushi* (Karp strain). The inhibitor possessed properties characteristic of interferon induced by viral infection, including species-specificity and a broad antiviral spectrum. However, further investigations on the mode of its production were greatly hampered by the following difficulties: a) the maximum titer is relatively low (10 to 20 units/2 ml), and b) interferon is produced very late during infection (7 to 10 days) when the cells are apt to detach from the glass surface due to aging and/or overgrowth.

The present communication describes the production of interferon in PCE cells infected with a partially purified, concentrated suspension of *Rickettsia mooseri*. This system permits *in vitro* studies of the production of interferon by these non-viral parasites. Efforts were made to rule out the possibility that interferon production was mediated by a virus latent in the culture. The biologic and biochemical characteristics of the interferon were investigated.

MATERIALS AND METHODS

Rickettsia. The Wilmington strain of *R. mooseri* was used throughout. The rickettsiae were grown in the yolk sacs of embryonated hens' eggs and were partially purified and concentrated by serial treatment with Amberlite XE-64 (potassium) and bovine serum albumin (BSA, Armour fraction V) (2) as illustrated in Figure 1. The concentrated rickettsial suspension always contained more than $10^{7.5}$ egg infecting units/0.25 ml. Normal yolk sac tissue was fractionated only by XE-64 and served as the control inoculum.

Viruses. Vesicular stomatitis (VSV), western equine encephalitis (WEE) and Sindbis viruses were propagated in PCE cells fed with Eagle's medium containing 2% unheated calf serum and antibiotics. Either UV-irradiated (UV-NDV) (3) or pH 2-treated (PH-NDV) (4) Miyadera strain of Newcastle disease virus (NDV) was employed as viral interferon inducer. Rous-associated virus (RAV-1) was furnished by Dr. Yamanouchi of this department.

Cells and media. PCE cells were prepared from 11-day-old embryos as described previously (3). The medium used in preparing rickettsial interferon was either Hanks' balanced salt solution (BSS) or Earle's BSS containing 10% calf serum, 0.5% lactalbumin hydrolysate and 0.1% yeast extract. No antibiotic was incorporated in the medium when rickettsiae were employed. In the preparation of viral interferon, Eagle's medium supplemented with 2% calf serum and antibiotics was used. Cells free of the avian leukosis virus complex were obtained from embryonated eggs purchased from Kimber Farms, California.

Interferon. Interferon was prepared in bottle cultures of PCE cells (7.5 x 5 cm²). One-half milliliter of rickettsial suspension was adsorbed on the cell sheet for 1 hr at 35°C, and subsequently 5 ml of the culture medium was added per bottle without removing the inoculum. After 3 to 5 days at 30°C (in some experiments 35°, 37° and 40°C),

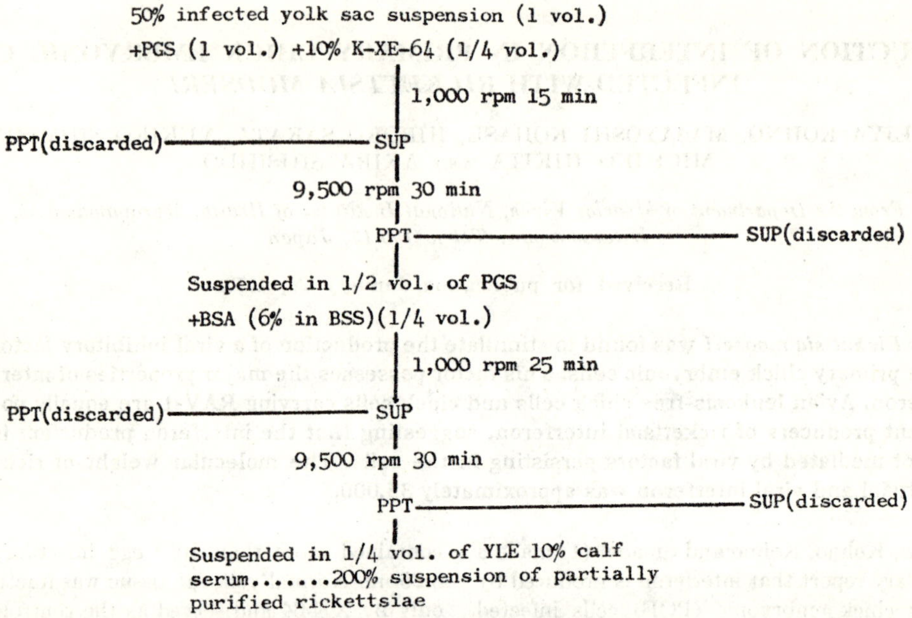

Figure 1. **Partial purification of *Rickettsia mooseri*. PGS: 8.5% sucrose solution containing phosphate buffer (pH 7.0) 10 mM, glutamic acid 47 mM. BSA: Bovine serum albumin (Armour fraction V). YLE: Earle's BSS containing lactalbumin hydrolysate and yeast extract (see Materials and Methods).**

the culture medium was harvested and heated at 60°C for 1 hr to inactivate the rickettsiae. The procedures for preparing viral interferon and for assaying interferon by the VSV plaque-reduction method have been described elsewhere (3).

COFAL test. RAV-1 antigen in third-passage cell homogenate, produced by freezing and thawing five times, was quantitated by the complement fixation procedure (5) using the serum from hamsters bearing tumors induced by the Schmidt-Ruppin strain of Rous sarcoma virus in its 44th passage.

Chromatography. Viral and rickettsial interferons were concentrated either by filtration through a Diaflo membrane (UM-2) or by dialysis against polyvinylpyrrolidone powder at 4°C. The resulting interferon concentrates and the appropriate reference compounds were applied in 0.5-ml amounts to Sephadex G-100 columns (15 x 850 mm) previously equilibrated with BSS, pH 6.9. Using the same solution (BSS, pH 6.9) to elute the compounds from the column, 3-ml fractions were collected. The following reference standards were used: cytochrome C monomer, m.w. 12,900; ovalbumin, m.w. 45,000; and bovine serum albumin, m.w. 67,000.

Infection index. Infected PCE cells were dispersed with the aid of 0.05% trypsin, smeared on a glass slide and stained by the Macchiavello method. One hundred well stained cells were scored microscopically (6) and the infection index was calculated by the following equation:

$$\text{Infection index} = 3 \times H + 2 \times M + S$$

where H (heavily infected) denotes number of cells containing more than 20 rickettsial particles; M (moderately infected), 6 to 20 particles; and S (slightly infected), 1 to 5 particles.

RESULTS

Kinetics of interferon production by rickettsia-infected PCE cells at various incubation temperatures. PCE cells, on the 3rd day of cultivation, were infected with 0.5 ml of undiluted rickettsial suspension/bottle and incubated at 30°, 35°, 37° and 40°C. The rate of accumulation of interferon in the culture medium was then followed. As shown in Figure 2, a steady accumulation of interferon was observed at 30°C. At 35° and 37°C interferon production increased rapidly. A very poor response was seen at 40°C. Based on these observations the incubation temperature of 30°C was selected for most of the experiments reported here. This dependence on temperature seems to-be an unusual feature of *R. mooseri*-induced interferon production, since at 40°C no such suppression of viral interferon production was observed in PCE cells infected with UV-NDV or PH-NDV (Table I).

Growth of R. mooseri at 30°, 35°, 37° and 40°C. The infection index (6) was employed to estimate

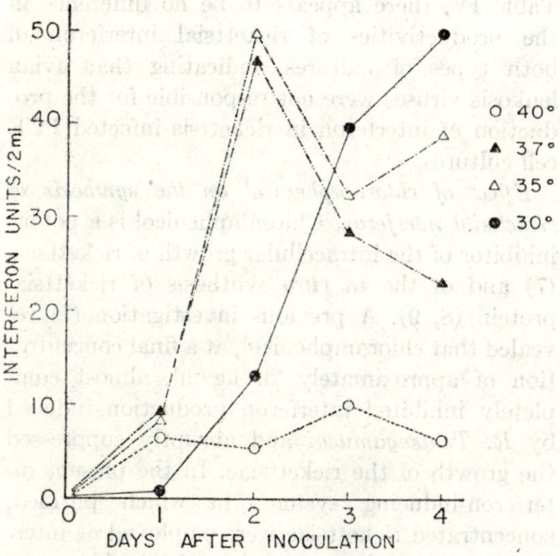

Figure 2. Time course of interferon synthesis by PCE cells infected with *Rickettsia mooseri*.

TABLE I

Effect of temperature on viral interferon production in PCE cells

Incubation Temperature	Interferon Inducer	Interferon Produced (units/2 ml) on Day:		
		1	2	3
°C				
30	UV-NDV[a]	9	40	40
	PH-NDV[b]	14	14	16
35	UV-NDV	80	50	46
	PH-NDV	34	30	28
37	UV-NDV	64	53	50
	PH-NDV	50	43	ND[c]
40	UV-NDV	75	40	43
	PH-NDV	45	38	24

[a] Egg-grown NDV irradiated by about 700 erg/mm² of UV.

[b] Egg-grown NDV treated at pH 2, 30 sec at 4°C.

[c] ND, not done.

TABLE II

Infection indices of R. mooseri in PCE cells at various temperatures

Incubation Temperature	Rickettsial Infection Indices on Day:			
	1	2	3	4
°C				
30	3	60	112	206
35	6	39	130	248
37	29	75	52	44
40	37	31	28	12

TABLE III

Effect of inoculum dilution on rickettsial interferon induction

Dilution of Inoculum	Interferon (Units/2 Ml) Produced on Day:				
	2	3	4	5	6
Undiluted[a]	43	45	53	43	NT[b]
1:10	13	43	140	210	160
1:100	<4	20	46	58	49
1:1,000	<4	<4	<4	<4	<4

[a] 200% yolk sac suspension containing $10^{7.5}$ egg-infecting units/0.25 ml. One-half milliliter was inoculated/bottle.

[b] NT, not tested.

the intracellular growth of this agent. The results of an experiment designed to follow the growth of *R. mooseri* in PCE cells incubated at four different temperatures are listed in Table II. As can be seen, rickettsial growth (or more precisely the intracellular accumulation of rickettsial particles) was also suppressed at 40°C.

Inoculum size. The relationship between the dilution of rickettsial inoculum used and production of interferon is shown in Table III. The most potent activity was usually observed when a 1:10 dilution of the concentrated materials was used. The normal yolk sac fraction (*Materials and Methods*) had no inducing activity at the dilution range tested (undiluted to 1:1,000), indicating that the production of interferon was induced by rickettsial infection and not by contaminating yolk sac materials. Also, in other experiments a UV-irradiated, concentrated rickettsial suspension did not induce cellular interfering activity. Based on these findings, the optimal inoculum size was determined for every preparation of purified rickettsiae prior to its use.

Several basic properties of the interferon induced by rickettsiae. The interferon induced by rickettsial infection was found to be non-dialyzable, stable after incubation at 60°C for 1 hr, stable to overnight pH 2-treatment at 4°C, and not sedimentable at 108,000 × G for 2 hr. From 70 to 80% of the inhibitory activity was lost after trypsinization (0.1% trypsin, 35°C for 1 hr). Interferon-like activity was not demonstrable by plaque reduction of VSV in L cells. In PCE cells, the plaque-forming efficiencies of WEE, VSV and Sindbis viruses were equally suppressed. These properties are very similar to those attributed to interferon induced by viral infections. Therefore, the interferon present in the culture medium of PCE cells infected with *R. mooseri* will hereafter be designated "rickettsial interferon."

Production of rickettsial interferon by PCE cells free of the avian leukosis virus complex. As chick cells are noted for harboring latent avian leukosis viruses, it is possible that the rickettsial interferon was induced by rickettsial enhancement of latent virus multiplication. To test this possibility, leukosis virus-free PCE cell cultures were prepared from Kimber Farms embryos known to be free of the avian leukosis virus complex. These cultures were divided into two groups: one was infected with RAV-1 and passaged three times to boost intracellular RAV-1 particles (intracellular accumulation of RAV-1 was determined by the COFAL test); the other was not infected but similarly passaged three times. As shown in Table IV, there appears to be no difference in the productivities of rickettsial interferon in both types of cultures, indicating that avian leukosis viruses were not responsible for the production of interferon in rickettsia-infected PCE cell cultures.

TABLE IV

Rickettsial interferon synthesis in PCE cells with and without persistent RAV-1 infection

Group	Interferon Produced (Units/2 Ml) on Day:		
	2	3	6
Carrying RAV-1[a]	21	32	21
Control uninfected	18	43	27

[a] COFAL antigen titer against Hm-P-44 serum was 1:64.

Effect of chloramphenicol on the synthesis of rickettsial interferon. Chloramphenicol is a potent inhibitor of the intracellular growth of rickettsiae (7) and of the *in vitro* synthesis of rickettsial protein (8, 9). A previous investigation (7) revealed that chloramphenicol, at a final concentration of approximately 20 μg/ml, almost completely inhibited interferon production induced by *R. Tsutsugamushi* and abruptly suppressed the growth of the rickettsiae. In the present interferon-inducing system, in which purified, concentrated rickettsiae were employed as interferon inducer, the production of interferon was found to be less sensitive to the antibiotic. As shown in Table V, a clear-cut inhibition of interferon production was observed only when the control interferon yield was very low. In most cases where control interferon yields were relatively high (50 to 200 units/2 ml), chloramphenicol up to 400 μg/ml inhibited interferon produc-

TABLE V

Effects of chloramphenicol on interferon synthesis and infection indices in PCE cells infected with Rickettsia mooseri or treated with UV-irradiated NDV

	Interferon Inducer	Chloramphenicol Concentration	Days of Infection		
			1	3	4
		μg/ml			
Infection indices		0	NT[a]	62	40
		100	NT	22	31
		200	NT	9	18
Interferon units (per 2 ml)	Rickettsiae	0	NT	12	4
	Rickettsiae	100	NT	<4	<4
	Rickettsiae	200	NT	<4	<4
	UV-NDV	0	71	NT	NT
	UV-NDV	100	80	NT	NT
	UV-NDV	200	71	NT	NT

[a] NT, not tested.

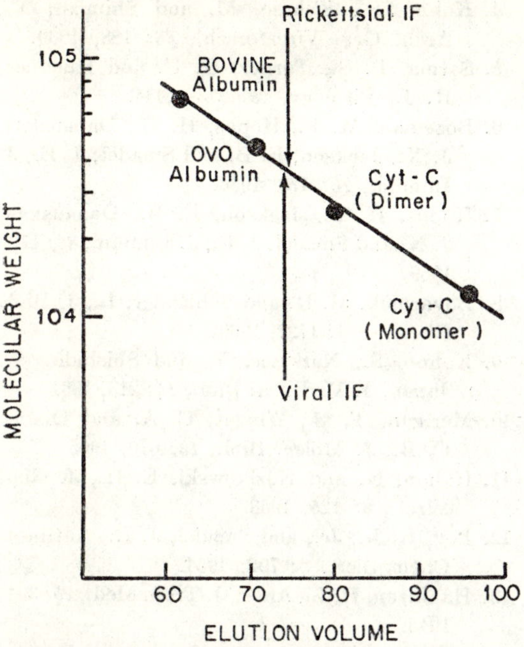

Figure 3. Determination of molecular weights of viral and rickettsial interferons. Elution volume in milliliters.

tion only by 10 to 60%. As seen in Table V, this antibiotic had no effect on viral interferon production. This partial inhibition of interferon yield by chloramphenicol might be related to the use of a large inoculum of rickettsiae, which could have acted as a stimulus for interferon production without intracellular multiplication.

Molecular weights of viral and rickettsial interferon. The molecular species of the interferons produced by rickettsial and viral infections of PCE cells was determined by molecular sieving. The procedure was given in the section on *Materials and Methods*. Figure 3 summarizes the results. Molecules of the standard compounds eluted in linear proportion to the logarithm of their molecular weights, ruling out adsorption to the column. Both interferons eluted in the same fraction. Molecules which eluted in this fraction had an estimated molecular weight of 35,000. This value agrees with the molecular weight of chick cell interferon reported previously (10).

DISCUSSION

The *in vitro* synthesis of rickettsial interferon has been demonstrated in PCE cells infected with *R. tsutsugamushi* (1) and in McCoy cells infected with *Coxiella burneti* (11). The results presented in this communication have also shown that PCE cells infected with partially purified, concentrated *R. mooseri* synthesize an inhibitor exhibiting characteristics of viral interferons.

Time course studies of its accumulation in the culture fluid of infected PCE cells have revealed that the accumulation rate was very rapid compared with that of the PCE cells-*R. tsutsugamushi* system where the peak interferon titer was usually obtained 7 to 10 days after infection. The synthesis of rickettsial interferon was extensively blocked at 40°C, whereas the rate of viral interferon production remained unaffected (Table I). The apparent parallelism between the blockade of rickettsial interferon synthesis at 40°C and the decrease of infection indices of rickettsiae at temperatures above 37°C (Fig. 2, Table II) indicates that the cellular synthesis of rickettsial interferon is dependent on the quantity and stability of the intracellular rickettsial particles. Chloramphenicol, which is highly effective in the treatment of experimental typhus infections (12) and is a potent inhibitor of *in vitro* interferon synthesis induced by *R. tsutsugamushi* (1), only partially suppressed the synthesis of interferon induced by *R. mooseri*.

We also explored the possibility that the production of rickettsial interferon might be mediated by a virus contaminating the embryonated eggs used for the preparation of the parasite seed pools. The rickettsial infection might somehow have had an influence on the growth of the virus contaminant resulting in the stimulation of interferon production. However, a normal yolk sac fraction prepared from uninfected embryonated eggs of the same batch employed for the production of rickettsial seed pools did not stimulate interferon in PCE cells, and this finding ruled out the existence of a virus contaminant in yolk sac tissue. Next, a hypothetical mechanism attributing the stimulation of interferon production by PCE cells to a latent virus, e.g., the avian leukosis virus complex, was examined. This agent could theoretically induce interferon if its multiplication were enhanced by rickettsial infection. As seen in Table IV, cells free of avian leukosis virus were capable of producing interferon when infected with rickettsiae. Furthermore, chronic infection of PCE cells with RAV-1 did not significantly enhance cellular ability to synthesize rickettsial interferon. Taken together, these findings show that interferon production was the direct consequence of rickettsial infection and intracellular accumulation of the parasite.

The fact that we could not discriminate between viral and rickettsial interferons by their molecular weights (Fig. 3) indicated that the cells responded to viral and rickettsial stimuli by producing only one molecular species of interferon. It would be of prime importance, therefore, to determine the component(s) of rickettsiae or substance(s) produced by rickettsial infection (13) which is responsible for the stimulation of interferon production in chick cells.

REFERENCES

1. Hopps, H. E., Kohno, S., Kohno, M. and Smadel, J. E., Bact. Proc., *1:* 115, 1964.
2. Kohno, S., Japan J. Med. Sci. Biol., *12:* 375, 1959.
3. Kohno, S., Kohase, M. and Suganuma, M., Japan. J. Med. Sci. Biol., *21:* 239, 1968.
4. Kohno, S., Kohase, M. and Shimizu, Y., Arch. Ges. Virusforsch., *28:* 188, 1969.
5. Sarma, P. S., Turner, H. C. and Huebner, R. J., Virology, *23:* 313, 1964.
6. Bozeman, M. F., Hopps, H. E., Danauskas, J. X., Jackson, E. B. and Smadel, J. E., J. Immun., *76:* 475, 1956.
7. Hopps, H. E., Jackson, E. B., Danauskas, J. X. and Smadel, J. E., J. Immun., *82:* 172, 1959.
8. Bovarnick, M. R. and Schneider, L., J. Biol. Chem., *235:* 1727, 1960.
9. Kohno, S., Natsume, Y. and Shishido, A., Japan. J. Med. Sci. Biol., *14:* 213, 1961.
10. Merigan, T. C., Winget, C. A. and Dixon, C. B., J. Molec. Biol., *13:* 679, 1965.
11. Hahon, N. and Kozikowski, E. H., J. Gen. Virol., *3:* 125, 1968.
12. Ley, H. L., Jr., and Smadel, J. E., Antibiot. Chemother., *4:* 792, 1954.
13. Hamilton, H. L., Amer. J. Trop. Med., *25:* 391, 1945.

THE JOURNAL OF IMMUNOLOGY
Vol. 105, No. 6, December 1970
Printed in U.S.A

COMMUNICATIONS

Immunoglobulin Elevations in the Serum of Patients with Chronic Bronchitis and Emphysema[1]

GEORGE A. FALK,[2] GREGORY W. SISKIND[3] AND JAMES P. SMITH, JR.

From the Department of Medicine, Cornell University Medical College, New York, New York 10021

Chronic bronchopulmonary infection has been identified as one of the manifestations of hypogammoglobulinemia and has been particularly associated with decreased concentrations of immunoglobulin A (IgA) in both serum and external secretions (1). However, increased rather than decreased serum concentrations of IgA have been found in a small group of adults with chronic bronchitis and emphysema (2).

In order to determine which if either of these reported abnormalities of immunoglobulin concentration is characteristic of adults with chronic bronchitis and emphysema, serum immunoglobulin levels were studied in 49 such patients and compared to levels in normal subjects.

MATERIAL AND METHODS

Serum immunoglobulin levels were determined in 49 patients with chronic bronchitis and emphysema and in 67 normal subjects. Both patients and normal subjects ranged from 41 to 80 years of age (mean age respectively 62.6 and 59.5 years). All patients satisfied the commonly accepted clinical criteria for chronic bronchitis and emphysema (3), which were confirmed by appropriate physiologic measurements. All patients were free of other illnesses known to alter serum immunoglobulin levels. Control subjects were healthy individuals reporting for routine annual physical examinations and found to be free of signs and symptoms of respiratory tract disease. All but three of the patients and all normal subjects were Caucasian. Thirty-seven of the 49 patients (76%) and 45 of the 67 normal subjects (67%) were males.

Serum concentrations of IgG, IgA and IgM were determined by the Mancini method (4) of radial immunodiffusion on commercially available agar plates (Hyland Laboratories, Los Angeles, Calif.). In order to assess the reproducibility of these immunoglobulin determinations, 12 repeated measurements of IgG, IgA and IgM concentrations were performed on a single serum sample. The mean concentration of each immunoglobulin in the test sample and its standard deviation were then used to determine the coefficient of variation, defined as 100 × standard deviation/mean concentration. Coefficients of variation for concentrations of IgG, IgA, and IgM were respectively ±2.1%, ±1.0%, and ±2.4%.

The significance of differences in mean serum immunoglobulin concentrations was evaluated by the Student *t* test. Values of "*t*", confidence limits, correlation coefficients, the statistical significance of correlation coefficients, and linear regression equations were calculated by standard methods (5). Since immunoglobulin concentrations have been said to be distributed in lognormal fashion (6), all statistical analyses were performed upon the logarithms of immunoglobulin concentrations.

RESULTS

Serum concentrations of IgG and IgM in normal adults did not vary with age (Tables I and II). In contrast, the serum concentration of IgA in normal subjects rose with increasing age (Table III). Although there was considerable variation in serum IgA concentrations among individual subjects at any age level, the overall correlation of IgA concentration with age was highly significant.[4]

[1] This work was supported in part by United States Public Health Service Grant AI-00255 and in part by New York Tuberculosis and Health Association Grants 212 and 226.

[2] Edward Livingston Trudeau Fellow of the American Thoracic Society.

[3] Career scientist of the Health Research Council of the City of New York under Investigatorship I-593.

[4] The linear regression of IgA concentration on age in normal subjects fits the equation $y = 0.0100x + 1.81$, where $y = \log_{10}$ IgA concentration (mg/100 ml serum), x = age (years), and the 90% confidence limit on y was ±0.053 at the mean age of 59.5 years. The correlation coefficient of y on x was 0.473 and this correlation was significant at the 99.9% confidence limits.

TABLE I

Serum IgG levels: chronic bronchitis and emphysema patients vs normal subjects

Age	Patients			Normal Subjects		
	No.	Mean IgG	S.E.	No.	Mean IgG	S.E.
		mg/100 ml			*mg/100 ml*	
41-50	6	1090	56.7	22	1110	54.4
51-60	16	1215	61.6	21	1150	53.5
61-70	15	1360	88.7	12	1070	69.1
71-80	12	1360	90.7	12	1130	95.4
Total	49	1280	43.3	67	1120	31.7

A different relationship of immunoglobulin concentrations to age was observed in the patients with chronic bronchitis and emphysema. In these patients, serum concentrations of IgA and IgM remained constant, whereas IgG increased in concentration with increasing age (Tables I to III). Although individual values again showed considerable variation at each age level, the positive correlation of IgG concentration with age was statistically highly significant.[5]

In order to directly compare data obtained in patients and normal subjects, both patients and normal subjects were grouped by decade, and average serum immunoglobulin concentrations were compared at each age level. In the younger patients (ages 41 to 50), the average serum concentration of IgA was 25% higher than in age-matched normal subjects. Although the range of individual IgA concentrations in patients and normal subjects showed considerable overlap, the mean IgA concentrations in these two groups were significantly different ($p < 0.05$).[6] Concentrations of IgG and IGM, in contrast, were similar in 41- to 50-year-old patients and normal subjects.

In the older patients (ages 61 to 80), the average serum concentrations of IgA and IgM were similar to concentrations in normal subjects. The average concentration of IgG, however, was 24% higher in patients than in normal subjects. Again, although the range of individual IgG concentrations in patients and normal subjects overlapped, the mean IgG concentrations in these two groups were significantly different ($p < 0.001$).[7]

Concentrations of IgM did not significantly differ in patients and normal subjects at any age level. At no age were average serum concentrations of IgG, IgA or IgM significantly lower in patients than in normal subjects. Serum concentrations of IgA and IgG were not higher in patients with heart failure secondary to cor pulmonale than in those without heart failure. Chronic hepatic congestion thus did not appear to raise serum immunoglobulin levels as do certain other forms of chronic liver disease (7, 8).

DISCUSSION

The present results confirm the report of Lichtman *et al.* (9) that serum concentrations of IgG and IgM remain constant in normal adults whereas concentrations of IgA rise significantly with increasing age. Present results are also consistent with the finding that patients with recurrent bronchopulmonary infections associated with cystic fibrosis have elevated serum concentrations of both IgG and IgA but normal concentrations of IgM (10). The present observations differ somewhat from those of Biegel and Krumholz (2), who noted increased serum concentrations of IgA but normal concentrations of IgG and IgM in 15

[5] The linear regression of IgG concentration on age in patients fits the equation $y = 0.00316x + 2.90$, where $y = \log_{10}$ IgG concentration (mg/100 ml serum), x = age (years), and the 90% confidence limit on y was ± 0.026 at the mean age of 62.6 years. The correlation coefficient of y on x was 0.294 and this correlation was significant at the 95% confidence limit.

[6] Log mean serum IgA concentration in 41- to 50-year-old patients was 2.47, with 95% confidence limits from 2.37 to 2.57 and a standard error of ± 0.0501. Log mean serum IgA concentration in 41- to 50-year-old normal subjects was 2.32, with 95% confidence limits from 2.21 to 2.43 and a standard error of ± 0.0539. Although the 95% confidence limits in patients and normal subjects overlapped, the mean IgA concentration for each group fell outside the 95% confidence limits of the other, indicating a significant difference in mean IgA concentration in the two groups.

[7] Log mean serum IgG concentration in 61- to 80-year-old patients was 3.17, with 99.9% confidence limits from 3.06 to 3.28 and a standard error of ± 0.031. Log mean serum IgG concentration in 61- to 80-year-old normal subjects was 3.02, with 99.9% confidence limits from 2.94 to 3.11 and a standard error of ± 0.023. The mean serum IgG concentration of each of the two populations under comparison thus fell outside the 99.9% confidence limits of the other, indicating a highly significant difference in the mean serum IgG concentration in patients and normal subjects.

TABLE II

Serum IgM levels: chronic bronchitis and emphysema patients vs normal subjects

Age	Patients			Normal Subjects		
	No.	Mean IgM	S.E.	No.	Mean IgM	S.E.
		mg/100 ml			*mg/100 ml*	
41–50	6	94.2	21.3	22	104	13.2
51–60	16	115	22.1	21	110	15.3
61–70	15	102	11.4	12	95.6	12.3
71–80	12	125	33.9	12	121	21.7
Total	49	111	11.8	67	108	7.84

TABLE III

Serum IgA levels: chronic bronchitis and emphysema patients vs normal subjects

Age	Patients			Normal Subjects		
	No.	Mean IgA	S.E.	No.	Mean IgA	S.E.
		mg/100 ml			*mg/100 ml*	
41–50	6	306	35.7	22	244	31.9
51–60	16	328	48.1	21	266	43.7
61–70	15	342	28.6	12	328	51.3
71–80	12	310	33.1	12	377	37.1
Total	49	325	20.0	67	290	21.1

patients with chronic bronchitis and emphysema. These investigators' patient and control groups were too small to be significantly divided by age, however, and age-related variations in IgA and IgG would not have been apparent.

It is not clear why only IgA levels were significantly elevated in the younger patients whereas only IgG levels were significantly elevated in older patients in the present study. It is of interest, however, that lymphoid cells in the bronchial tree are evenly divided between those containing IgA and IgG whereas far fewer contain IgM (11, 12). It is similarly of interest that IgA- and IgG-producind lymphoid cells in the bronchial tree increase in number in patients with chronic bronchopulmonary disease, whereas the number of IgM-producing lymphoid cells is unchanged (11). The finding of increased serum levels of IgG and IgA in patients with chronic bronchitis and emphysema thus might reflect increased local production of these immunoglobulin classes in the bronchial tree. At present, however, this explanation is entirely speculative.

Acknowledgment. The authors are grateful to Dr. Lawrence Blau for his advice on questions of statistical analysis.

SUMMARY

Serum concentrations of immunoglobulins G, A and M (IgG, IgA and IgM) were measured in 49 patients aged 41 to 80 with severe chronic obstructive pulmonary disease (chronic bronchitis and emphysema) and in 67 normal subjects of similar age and sex distribution. In the normal subjects, concentrations of IgA rose significantly with increasing age whereas concentrations of IgG and IgM remained constant. In contrast, concentrations of IgA and IgM remained constant in the patient group whereas concentrations of IgG rose significantly with increasing age. When patients were compared to normal subjects of comparable age, average serum concentrations of IgA were found to be elevated in the younger patients (ages 41 to 50) whereas average concentrations of IgG were elevated in the older patients (ages 61 to 80). Deficiency in IgG, IgA or IgM was not a feature of chronic bronchitis and emphysema at any age.

REFERENCES

1. South, M. A., Cooper, M. D., Wollheim, F. A. and Good, R. A., Amer. J. Med., *44:* 168, 1968.
2. Biegel, A. A., and Krumholz, R. A., Amer. Rev. Resp. Dis., *97:* 217, 1968.
3. Committee on Diagnostic Standards for Nontuberculous Respiratory Diseases of the American Thoracic Society, Amer. Rev. Resp. Dis., *85:* 762, 1962.
4. Mancini, G., Vaerman, J. P., Carbonara, A. O. and Heremans, J. F., *Protides of the Biologi-*

cal Fluids, Proceedings of the 11th Colloquium, Bruges, 1963, p. 370, Elsevier, New York, 1964.
5. Fisher, R. A. and Yates, F., *Statistical Tables for Biological, Agricultural and Medical Research*, Hafner, New York, 1963.
6. Buckley, C. E., III and Dorsey, F. C., Ann. Int. Med., *72:* 37, 1970.
7. McKelvey, E. M. and Fahey, J. L., J. Clin. Invest., *44:* 1778, 1965.
8. Tomasi, T. B., Jr., *Immunological Diseases*, Ed. by M. Samter, p. 881, Little, Brown and Co., Boston, 1965.
9. Lichtman, M. A., Vaughan, J. H. and Hames, C. G., Arthritis Rheum., *10:* 204, 1967.
10. Schwartz, R. H., Amer. J. Dis. Child., *111:* 408, 1966.
11. Martinez-Tello, F. J., Braun, D. G. and Blanc, W. A., J. Immun., *101:* 989, 1968.
12. Tourville, D. R., Adler, R. H., Bienenstock, J. and Tomasi, T. B., Jr., J. Exp. Med., *129:* 411, 1969.

THE JOURNAL OF IMMUNOLOGY

Vol. 105, No. 6, December 1970
Printed in U.S.A.

Temporal Dissociation of Experimental Allergic Encephalomyelitis Transfer Activity and γ Globulin Staining of Lymphoid Cells from Sensitized Lewis Rats[1]

WALTER P. RICHARDSON[2] AND PHILIP Y. PATERSON

From the Samuel J. Sackett Research Laboratories and Infectious Diseases, Hypersensitivity Section, Department of Medicine, Northwestern University Medical Center, Chicago, Illinois 60611

In attempts to define the cellular factor(s) produced by sensitized lymph node cells (LNC) responsible for development of experimental allergic encephalomyelitis (EAE), LNC were collected from donor Lewis rats 9 days after sensitization and incubated *in vitro* with rabbit anti-whole rat serum or goat anti-rat γ globulin prior to transfer into recipients (1). Transfer of EAE was not inhibited, even though a small proportion of the LNC contained γ globulin as demonstrated by indirect immunofluorescence. Further studies, briefly reported here, revealed that maximum staining for γ globulin occurred in LNC removed 6 days after sensitization, a time when such cell suspensions lack EAE transfer activity (2). We believe this dissociation between γ globulin staining and transfer activity may explain several diverse observations recorded in the EAE literature and may provide new leads to the pathogenesis of this disease.

MATERIALS AND METHODS

The source of the male Lewis rats, their maintenance and the details concerning intracutaneous sensitization to guinea pig spinal cord emulsified in complete Freund's adjuvant, and the method of transfer of EAE using LNC have been previously published (1, 3). The procedures for determining the number of LNC that contained γ globulin, using commercially prepared goat anti-rat γ globulin and rabbit anti-goat γ globulin fluorescein isocyanate, also were previously described (1). LNC suspensions from different donor rats were used for γ globulin staining and for EAE cell transfers. Recipients of LNC were killed after 7 days and sections of the brain and spinal cord from each animal were stained with hematoxylin-eosin to evaluate the incidence of EAE lesions.

RESULTS

As shown in Table I, EAE transfer activity was not demonstrable in day (D) 6 cells, was of low order of activity in D8 cells and appeared to reach maximal activity in D9 or D10 cells. Cells collected 14 days after sensitization had no transfer competence. None of the recipients, including those scored positive for lesions of EAE, developed clinical neurologic signs, in agreement with our previous transfer experience in this rat strain (2). In contrast, γ globulin staining increased abruptly between D3 and D6 and appeared to reach maximal intensity in D6 LNC. The proportion of positive staining cells subsequently decreased through D9 and by D14 was close to the level of staining observed in control rats sensitized to complete adjuvant only.

DISCUSSION AND SUMMARY

The occurrence of peak EAE transfer activity in LNC several days after time of maximum staining for γ globulin suggests that the factor(s) responsible for transfer of EAE lesions is distinct from conventional immunoglobulins. This finding provides a clear explanation for our earlier observation, *viz.*, anti-rat γ globulin serum does not alter EAE transfer activity of D9 LNC (1).

We are aware that we have no evidence as to whether any of the γ globulin demonstrated in LNC represents antibody specifically reactive with nervous tissue. Our findings agree with that of Oldstone and Dixon (unpublished) that antibody reactive with brain is demonstrable in thoracic duct lymph of Lewis rats only between

[1] This work was supported in part by United States Public Health Service Research Grant NB 06262 from the National Institute of Neurologic Diseases and Training Grant AM 05069 from the National Institute of Arthritis and Metabolic Diseases.

[2] Work done during tenure of a United States Public Health Service Predoctoral Traineeship, Training Grant AM 05069.

TABLE I

EAE transfer activity and γ globulin staining of lymph node cells (LNC) collected from Lewis rats following spinal cord-adjuvant sensitization

No. of Days after Sensitization of LNC Donor	EAE Transfer Activity	γ Globulin-Containing Cells (per 1000 LNC)
3		9[a]
6	0/5[b]	106, 129, 148
7		83
8	1/4	54
9	26/39	37, 38, 51
10	3/4	
14	0/3	25
Not sensitized		2, 3
6[c]		20, 20
9[c]		21, 16

[a] Each number represents individual rats studied.

[b] Numerator, number of recipients with lesions of EAE; denominator, number of recipients receiving LNC.

[c] Donors sensitized to water-adjuvant emulsion only.

5 and 7 days after sensitization. At no time could they find such antibody in blood serum.

Based on the results here reported (Table I), it is conceivable that two different immune responses, i.e., antibody production and delayed-type hypersensitivity, account for development of clinical neurologic signs and lesions, respectively—both being essential for occurrence of typical EAE. Under the conditions we employed for LNC transfer of EAE during the past 8 years, occurrence of paralytic signs has been a rare event in recipient Lewis rats receiving D9 LNC. This is true despite the fact that many animals develop severe lesions of EAE throughout the brain and spinal cord. Recent work has shown that phytohemagglutinin injected simultaneously with spinal cord-adjuvant markedly suppresses clinical signs of EAE in Lewis rats but has little, if any, effect on development of lesions of the disease (G. O. Westenfelter, P. Y. Paterson and D. G. Drobish, to be published). Bornstein and Crain (4) have reported a dissociation between serum factors causing synaptic blockade and those causing demyelination when acute phase EAE serum is added to myelinating and electrically active nervous tissue cultures. Pabst and Dupuy (5) have described production of paralytic, often lethal, disease without appreciable histologic changes in guinea pigs injected with plasma derived from donors sensitized to nervous tissue and given lethal doses of x-irradiation. Finally, Brown *et al.* (6) and Tung and Unanue (7) have secured strong evidence that in another well established experimental autoimmune disease, allergic orchitis, both antibody and sensitized lymphoid cells must act in concert in order for the full-blown disease to occur.

REFERENCES

1. Richardson, W. P. and Paterson, P. Y., Clin. Exp. Immun., *6:* 337, 1970.
2. Paterson, P. Y., Advances Immun., *5:* 131, 1966.
3. Paterson, P.Y., J. Exp. Med., *111:* 119, 1960.
4. Bornstein, M. B. and Crain, S. M., J. Neuropath. Exp. Neurol., (abstract), In press.
5. Pabst, H. and Dupuy, J.-M., Fed. Proc., *29:* 22, (abstract), 1970.
6. Brown, P. C., Glyn, L. E. and Holborow, E. J., Immunology, *13:* 307, 1967.
7. Tung, K. S. K. and Unanue, E. R., Fed. Proc., *29:* 287 (abstract), 1970.

THE JOURNAL OF IMMUNOLOGY

Vol. 105, No. 6, December 1970
Printed in U.S.A.

Partial Purification and Characterization of a Dengue Virus Soluble Complement-Fixing Antigen[1]

WALTER E. BRANDT, DUMRONG CHIEWSILP, DONALD L. HARRIS AND PHILIP K. RUSSELL

From the Department of Virus Diseases, Walter Reed Army Institute of Research, Washington, D. C. 20012

Rate-zonal centrifugation of dengue-2 infected mouse brain or cell culture has revealed two hemagglutinins (HA) and a non-hemagglutinating soluble complement-fixing (CF) antigen (1, 2). A rapidly sedimenting HA (RHA) consists of infectious particles measuring 48 to 50 nm in diameter and a slowly sedimenting HA (SHA) contains small doughnut structures measuring 14 nm in diameter. The third antigen was described as a soluble CF antigen (SCF) since it could not be readily removed from suspension by ultracentrifugation. Subsequent studies suggested that SCF is a nonstructural antigen which can be distinguished from the structural polypeptides of the virion by co-electrophoresis in polyacrylamide gels (R. D. Cardiff, W. E. Brandt, T. G. McCloud and P. K. Russell, to be published). SCF was also found to be the only antigen unaffected by exposure to sodium lauryl sulfate (SLS) and 2-mercaptoethanol (2-ME) (3); further, exposure of standard dengue-1 and dengue-2 sucrose-acetone antigens to SLS and 2-ME or 8M urea reduced the level of cross-reactions with other dengue serotypes. This communication describes a method for preparing partially purified SCF and compares some physicochemical properties of SCF with those of RHA and SHA.

MATERIALS AND METHODS

Preparation of crude antigen. Brains were harvested from 30 to 50 litters of moribund suckling mice infected at 2 to 3 days of age with 10^4 suckling mouse (SM) LD_{50} New Guinea "C" dengue-2 virus in the 31st mouse passage. Brains were suspended (20% w/v) in 0.02 M tris(hydroxymethyl)aminomethane (Tris) buffer, pH 8.2, by homogenization in a Sorvall Omnimixer. Suspensions were clarified at 8000 × G for 30 min at 4°C, treated with 2 mg/ml protamine sulfate for 45 min and again clarified at 8000 × G for 30 min.

Characterization of antigens. Rate-zonal centrifugation was carried out in sucrose gradients (5% to 25% in Tris buffer), and equilibrium centrifugation in cesium chloride as previously described (2). Sedimentation coefficients of the antigens were determined by the method of Martin and Ames (4) using as markers 70S ribosomes (courtesy of Dr. A. D. Wolf), 158S type 2 poliovirus, and 4S hemoglobin. $MgCl_2$ (0.01 M) was incorporated into sucrose gradients to prevent dissociation of the ribosomes. Gel filtration was carried out on Sephadex G-100 (Pharmacia) columns measuring 2 x 70 cm. Samples (2 ml) were washed through with 0.02 M phosphate-buffered saline, pH 7.2, and collected in 2-ml fractions. Zone electrophoresis was performed according to Fahey and McLaughlin (5) with equal mixtures of polyvinyl chloride (Geon) and polyvinyl chloride, polyvinyl acetate copolymer (Pevikon). Absorption and elution from aluminum hydroxide gel was done by batch methods. Aluminum hydroxide was prepared according to Sabin (6) and resuspended in 0.005 M phosphate buffer (PB) before mixing it with an equal volume of sample previously dialyzed against 0.005 M PB. Mixtures were shaken for several minutes, then centrifuged at 8000 × G for 10 min. Supernatant fluids were removed for antigen assay and the precipitate was resuspended again in 0.005 M PB. Stepwise increases in molarity of PB were carried out by washing the precipitate twice with each concentration of buffer, the eluted materia being recovered in the supernatant fluid following centrifugation.

Antigen assay. HA was assayed by a micro-

[1] In conducting the research described in this report, the investigators adhered to the "Guide for Laboratory Animal Facilities and Care," as promulgated by the Committee on Revision of the Guide for Laboratory Animal Facilities and Care of the Institute of Laboratory Animal Resources, National Academy of Sciences-National Research Council.

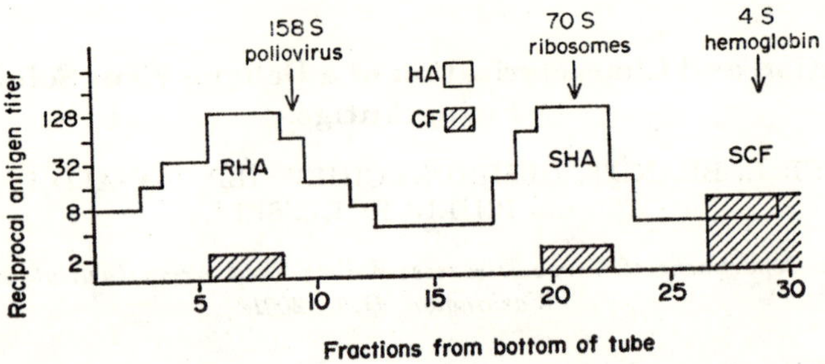

Figure 1. Rate-zonal centrifugation of crude dengue-2 antigen in 5% to 25% sucrose gradients for 3 hr at 63,000 × G. Position of sedimentation markers determined by simultaneous centrifugations with antigen. RHA, rapidly sedimenting hemagglutinin; SHA, slowly sedimenting hemagglutinin; SCF, soluble complement-fixing antigen.

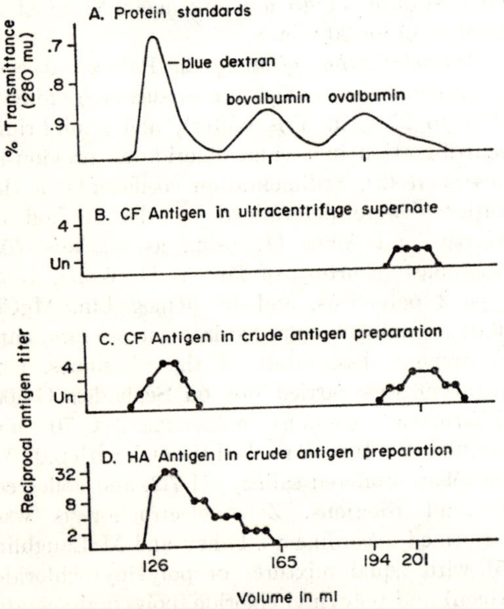

Figure 2. Gel filtration of dengue-2 complement-fixing (CF) and hemagglutinating (HA) antigens through Sephadex G-100.

titer modification of methods reported by Clarke and Casals (7). CF antigen was detected in the presence of excess specific antibody in mouse hyperimmune ascitic fluid (8) by a microtiter modification of the test described by Kent and Fife (9).

RESULTS

Rate-zonal separation of dengue antigens. Separation of the three antigens present in crude antigen suspensions as described above was readily achieved by rate-zonal centrifugation in sucrose gradients (Fig. 1). The sedimentation coefficient of each antigen was calculated from the position of the nearest marker. Ultracentrifugation of crude antigen at 105,000 × G for 2.5 hr prior to sucrose gradient analysis removed all detectable HA leaving only the soluble CF antigen (SCF) in the ultracentrifuge supernatant fluid.

Gel filtration of dengue antigens. Ultracentrifugal supernatant which contained SCF as the only detectable viral antigen was passed through Sephadex G-100 columns (2 x 70 cm) and its elution volume compared with those of ovalbumin and bovalbumin (Fig. 2, *A* and *B*). Application of the formula of Determann (10) (Log M = 5.941 − 0.847 × elution volume/void volume) provided a molecular weight estimate of 39,000 daltons. In contrast to ultracentrifugal supernatant, gel filtration of crude antigen resulted in two peaks of serologic activity: the first peak or void volume contained large particle CF and HA antigens (Fig. 2, *C* and *D*), and the second peak corresponded exactly with the elution of SCF. In other filtration experiments SCF was compared with proteins of known Stokes' radius (11, 12): γ globulin (5.2 nm), bovalbumin (3.5 nm) and hemoglobin in its known dissociated form on Sephadex gels (2.5 nm). A linear relationship was found when the distribution coefficients (11) of each protein were plotted against Stokes' radius (Fig. 3). SCF eluted in the same volume of buffer as the dissociated form of hemoglobin indicating that SCF has a Stokes' radius of 2.5 nm, or a diameter of 5 nm if it is spherical.

Effective separation of SCF from other serologically active viral antigens by Sephadex G-100 encouraged its use for larger scale production of partially purified SCF. CF antigens in either crude antigen or ultracentrifuge supernatant were found to precipitate maximally in the presence of ammonium sulfate at 60% saturation. These precipitates were dissolved in a volume of Tris buffer effecting a 10-fold concentration of original material, clarified at 9000 × G for 15 min, and applied to large Sephadex columns (15- to 20-ml samples on a 5- x 80-cm bed volume). SCF-containing fractions were concentrated 100-fold by nitrogen pressure dialysis over a neutral PM-30 membrane (Amicon Corp., Cambridge, Mass.) to a CF titer of at least 1:256. SCF titers were not affected by exposure to 0.1% SLS and 0.1% 2-ME as previously described (3); however, titers of antigen in the column void volume were reduced 8-fold by the same treatment. Infectivity was reduced from 8.0×10^8 $SMLD_{50}$/ml in the original brain suspension to 1.5×10^2 $SMLD_{50}$/ml in the concentrated SCF preparation. Antisera prepared

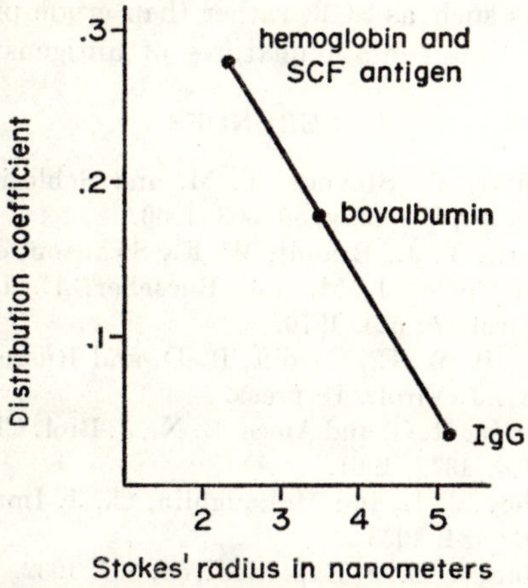

Figure 3. Molecular size of dengue SCF antigen by comparison with distribution coefficients (K_d) of protein standards obtained by Sephadex G-100 filtration and plotted against known Stokes' radii (11, 12). $K_d = (Ve - Vo)/Vi$; Ve = volume of buffer required to elute protein or antigen; Vo = void volume of column; Vi = internal volume of unbound solvent (11).

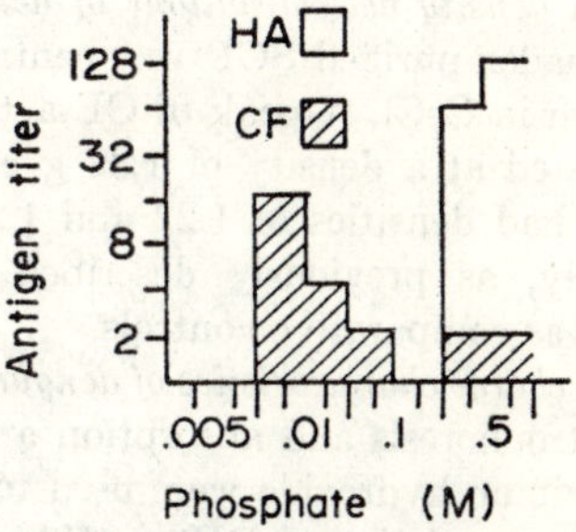

Figure 4. Elution of dengue-2 antigens found in crude antigen preparations from aluminum hydroxide by duplicate washing in increasing molarity of phosphate buffer.

TABLE I

Complement-fixation titers of dengue-2 hyperimmune mouse ascitic fluid when tested against Sephadex-purified soluble complement-fixing antigen (SCF) and crude antigen

Units	Antigen	
	SCF	Crude[a]
1	16[b]	8
2	512	256
4	256	256
8	256	512
16	128	512
32	128	1024

[a] 20% infected suckling mouse brain suspension clarified at 8000 × G.

[b] Reciprocal titer.

TABLE II

Characteristics of dengue-2 antigens propagated in mouse brain and separated by rate-zonal centrifugation in sucrose gradients[a,b]

	RHA	SHA	SCF
Morphology	Virion	"Ring"	Unknown
Diameter (nm)	48	14	5
Sedimentation coefficient	175	70	4
Density (g/cm³)	1.22	1.23	1.32
Electrophoretic mobility	0.20	0.17	0.20
Infectivity	+	−	−
Hemagglutination	+	+	−
Complement-fixation	+	+	+
Stability of CF titer after SLS[c] and 2-ME[c]	−	−	+

[a] Summarized from present work and other investigations (1, 2, 4).

[b] RHA, rapidly sedimenting hemagglutinin; SHA, slowly sedimenting hemagglutinin; SCF, soluble complement-fixing antigen.

[c] SLS, sodium lauryl sulfate; 2-ME, 2-mercaptoethanol.

in mice against SCF fixed complement (CF titer = 1:64) with crude antigen, but did not neutralize the virus. The serologic characteristics of the Sephadex-purified SCF were markedly different from the initial crude antigen (Table I); the highest antibody titers of dengue-2 hyperimmune mouse ascitic fluid were obtained with low concentrations of SCF whereas high concentrations of crude antigen were required to obtain the highest possible antibody titers.

Buoyant density determinations of dengue antigens. Sephadex-purified SCF was centrifuged to equilibrium in CsCl. A peak of CF activity was demonstrated at a density of 1.32 g/cm^3. RHA and SHA had densities of 1.22 and 1.23 g/cm^3, respectively, as previously described (2), and were used as comparative controls.

Relative charge characteristics of dengue antigens. Zone electrophoresis and absorption and elution from aluminum hydroxide were used to compare charge characteristics of RHA, SHA and SCF. RHA and SHA were isolated in sucrose gradients and then applied to the Pevikon-Geon supporting medium for zone electrophoresis. Ultracentrifugal supernatant served as a source of SCF as described above. All three antigens migrated similarly, the electrophoretic mobilities relative to albumin being 0.20, 0.17 and 0.20, respectively, for RHA, SHA and SCF. However, SCF was separated from both hemagglutinins by its early elution from aluminum hydroxide, indicating that it has a smaller total charge. SCF eluted in 0.01 M PB free of hemagglutinins (Fig. 4).

DISCUSSION

The characteristics of dengue-2 antigens determined by present and previous investigations are summarized in Table II. The soluble complement-fixing antigen (SCF) has several properties (size, density and chemical stability) which clearly distinguish it from virions or hemagglutinins. The data presented herein indicate that SCF (39,000 daltons) can be effectively separated from hemagglutinins by Sephadex G-100 filtration. The Sephadex-purified SCF has been shown to produce a single precipitin line in Ouchterlony-type immunodiffusion, and antigenic differences between dengue serotypes were observed (13). It is anticipated that more meaningful analysis of interrelationships among group B arboviruses may be approached by using physically homogeneous antigens such as SCF, rather than crude preparations that contain mixtures of antigens.

REFERENCES

1. Stollar, V., Stevens, T. M. and Schlesinger, R. W., Virology, *30:* 303, 1966.
2. Smith, T. J., Brandt, W. E., Swanson, J. L., McCown, J. M. and Buescher, E. L., J. Virol., *5:* 524, 1970.
3. Brandt, W. E., Cardiff, R. D. and Russell, P. K., J. Virol., In press.
4. Martin, R. G. and Ames, B. N., J. Biol. Chem., *236:* 1372, 1961.
5. Fahey, J. L. and McLaughlin, C., J. Immun., *91:* 484, 1963.
6. Sabin, A. B., J. Exp. Med., *56:* 307, 1932.
7. Clarke, D. H. and Casals, J., Amer. J. Trop. Med. Hyg., *7:* 561, 1958.
8. Brandt, W. E., Buescher, E. L. and Hetrick, F. M., Amer. J. Trop. Med. Hyg., *16:* 339, 1967.
9. Kent, J. F. and Fife, E. H., Jr., Amer. J. Trop. Med. Hyg., *12:* 103, 1963.
10. Determann, H., *Gel Chromatography*, Springer-Verlag, New York, 1969.
11. Ackers, G. K., Biochemistry, *3:* 723, 1964.
12. Siegel, L. M. and Monty, K. J., Biochim. Biophys. Acta, *112:* 346, 1966.
13. Russell, P. K., Chiewsilp, D. and Brandt, W. E., J. Immun., *105:* 838, 1970.

THE JOURNAL OF IMMUNOLOGY
Vol. 105, No. 6, December 1970

The *in Vitro* Effects of Goat Antisera to Rabbit Thymocyte Subcellular Fractions[1]

STEWART SELL,[2] RUTH ANN MASCARI AND PETER J. GOLDBLATT[3]

From the Department of Pathology, University of Pittsburgh, School of Medicine, Pittsburgh, Pennsylvania 15213

Xenogeneic antisera to lymphocytes have been shown to affect immunologically reactive cells *in vitro* and immunologic reactions *in vivo* (1). The importance of the immunosuppressive effects of such antisera has become of interest in programs of organ transplantation. Although the effects of anti-lymphocyte sera are well documented, little is known about the specificity of reactivity of such antisera. In the present study goat antisera to subcellular fractions of rabbit thymus cells were prepared and the *in vitro* effects of such antisera tested.

MATERIALS AND METHODS

Thymus cell suspension. The thymus glands from two 5- to 6-week-old rabbits were carefully dissected and washed free of blood. The glands were sterilely cut into small sections and scraped over stainless steel wire mesh into Eagle's medium. The suspension obtained was then passed through sterile cheese cloth and the cells were washed three times in Eagle's medium.

Subcellular fractions. Subcellular fractions of rabbit thymocytes were prepared in the following manner:

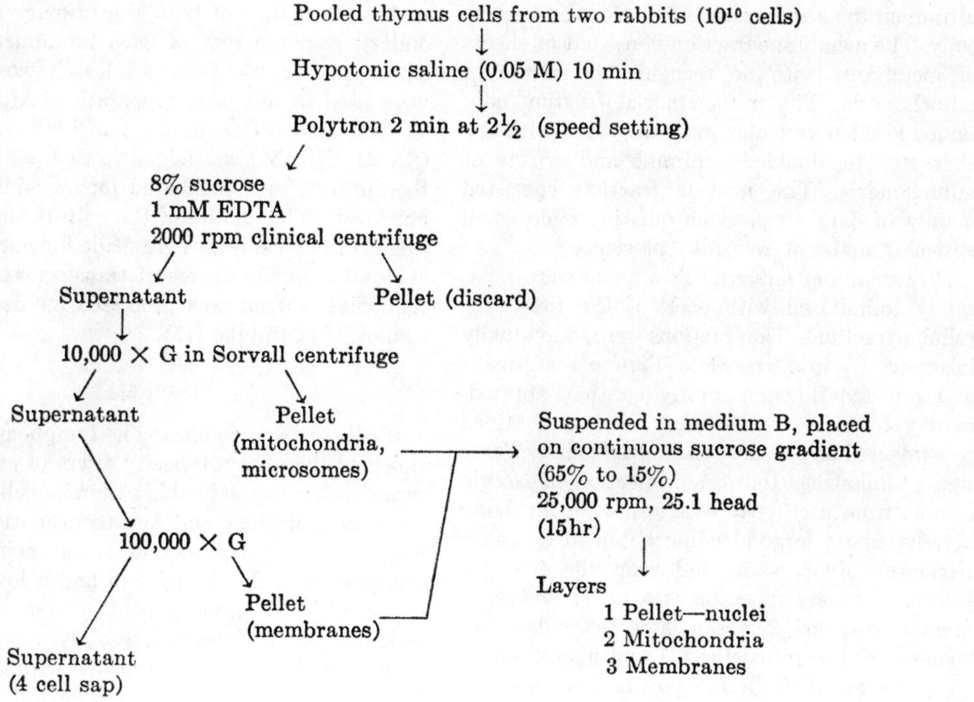

[1] This work was supported by Grant GB-8361 from the National Science Foundation and by Grant AI-07725 from the National Institute of Allergy and Infectious Diseases.

[2] Supported by Research Career Development Award 1-K3-AI-23308 from the National Institutes of Health. Present address: Dept. of Pathology, University of California at San Diego, La Jolla, California 92037.

[3] Present address: Department of Pathology, University of Connecticut Medical School, Farmington, Connecticut 06032.

Other methods for disruption and fractionation of rabbit thymocytes were attempted, but were not as effective as the above. The fractions obtained—nuclei, mitochondria, membrane and cell sap—were each divided into two parts. One part, amounting to approximately one-fifth of each sample, was examined by electron microscopy, and the remainder was used for immunization.

Electron microscopy. Two milliliters of a mixture of three parts Karnovsky's fixative (2) (pH 7.2 to 7.3) and 1 part 4% OsO_4 were added dropwise at 0 to 4°C to a pellet of the portion of the subcellular fraction to be examined. After 30 min at 0 to 4°C the pellet was removed from the tube and minced. The particles were transferred into a vial with 3 ml of fixative and held for 90 min at 0 to 4°C. The fixative was poured off and the particles were dehydrated by passage through ethyl alcohol and embedded in Steiner's Epon Araldite (3). Sections were cut with an ultramicrotome and examined by electron microscopy. The membrane fraction consisted of sheets of membrane with no recognizable cristae of mitochondria. The mitochondrial fraction contained swollen vesicular material, some with the characteristic double membrane and cristae of mitochondria. The nuclear fraction consisted mainly of dark stripped chromatin; some small vesicular material was also present.

Preparation of antisera. Two goats were separately immunized with each of the four subcellular fractions. The fractions were individually incorporated into complete Freund's adjuvant and injected intramuscularly so that approximately one-fifth of the total fraction obtained was injected as one dose in multiple sites. Three weeks following the first injection a serum sample from each goat was tested for antibody activity and a large bleeding obtained (primary response). Four weeks following the first injection a second injection was given and each animal was bled 2 weeks later (secondary response). The cytotoxicity (4) and agglutination (5) titers to rabbit thymocytes and the agglutination of rabbit erythrocytes (6) were tested using modified Takatsy dilution loops (7, 8). The antisera were also tested for reactivity with rabbit serum proteins by double-diffusion-in-agar (9). Since the addition of the whole goat antisera proved to be toxic for the lymphocyte cultures (see below) diethylaminoethyl cellulose (DEAE) chromatography was used to elute IgG fractions from each antiserum (10, 11). IgG was eluted with 0.01 M phosphate buffer, pH 8.0. The IgG fractions were concentrated by evaporation dialysis to approximately 5 mg/ml and sterilized by Seitz filtration. The elution peak obtained under these conditions contained only IgG when tested with polyvalent rabbit anti-whole goat sera. Exclusion chromatography on Sephadex G-200 was performed using Tris-buffered saline, pH 8.0 (12).

Blast transformation. Lymphocyte cultures were carried out as previously described (13, 14). Lymphocyte-rich suspensions were obtained from the peripheral blood of young adult rabbits by gelatin sedimentation, washed with Eagle's medium and cultured as described previously with 3×10^6 lymphocytes in 1.6 ml Eagle's medium enriched with tryptose broth and 0.4 ml normal rabbit serum.

To individual cultures were added 0.2, 0.1, 0.05 and 0.025 ml of the IgG fraction (approximately 5 mg/ml) of both the primary and secondary response sera of each immunized goat. The lymphocytes from at least two rabbits were used to test each preparation. After 44 hr at 37°C in 5% CO_2 in air, 1 μCi ^{3}H thymidine (SA 2.0 Ci/mM) was added to each culture and the cultures were incubated for an additional 4 hr. After 48 hr, 0.5 ml of the culture suspension was taken and smears were made for microscopic evaluation of the degree of transformation. The remaining 1.5 ml was processed for determination of ^{3}HdT uptake (15).

RESULTS

Whole antisera in vitro. The lymphoagglutination and lymphocytotoxicity titers of each antiserum using washed rabbit thymus cell suspensions as indicators and hemagglutination titers using washed rabbit erythrocytes as indicators are given in Table I. All sera had a low preimmunization lymphoagglutinin titer and an insignificant preimmunization lymphocytotoxicity titer. Only the goats injected with the membrane preparation gave a significant primary response when measured by lymphoagglutination, i.e., greater than two tubes increase. All sera to membrane and mitochondria showed a marked lymphoagglutination response after a second immunization, but only one each of the two antisera to nuclei and cell sap gave a significant increase over prebleeding controls. Each

TABLE I

Effect of whole goat antisera on rabbit thymus cells and erythrocytes in vitro

Immunization Antigen	Goat No.	Bleeding Data[a]	Lympho-agglutination[b]	Lympho-cytotoxicity[b]	Hemag-glutination[b]
Membrane	137	5/12/69	2	Neg	8
		6/3/69	5	6	7
		6/24/69	8	10	
Membrane	138	5/12/69	1	Neg	8
		6/3/69	5	6	9
		6/24/69	9	7	
Mitochondria	163	5/12/69	2	Neg	5
		6/3/69	3	4	9
		6/24/69	7	3	
Mitochondria	164	5/12/69	2	Neg	8
		6/3/69	3	4	5
		6/24/69	7	6	
Nucleus	D95	5/12/69	4	Neg	7
		6/3/69	4	3	7
		6/24/69	5	7	
Nucleus	167	5/12/69	2	Neg	8
		6/3/69	4	4	9
		6/24/69	7	9	
Cell Sap	165	5/12/69	3	Neg	7
		6/3/69	5	7	6
		6/24/69	7	9	
Cell Sap	181	5/12/69	3	1	5
		6/3/69	4	5	6
		6/24/69	5	7	

[a] 5/12/69 is bleeding prior to immunization.
[b] Log_2 of serum titer.

serum had a moderate increase in lymphocytotoxicity titer following the first injection, but the titers of the sera of the goats injected with the membrane and cell sap fractions averaged two tubes greater than those injected with the mitochondrial and nuclear fractions. The cytotoxicity titers following the second injection were generally higher than after the first injection except for the sera of the goats injected with mitochondria. All sera active against thymus cells were also active against peripheral blood lymphocytes, although usually two to three tubes less in titer. The secondary response sera from goats injected with membrane, nuclei or cell sap did not differ from each other in lymphocytotoxicity titers. The hemagglutination titers of the preimmunization sera, which averaged 2^7, did not change significantly after immunization and were present in the first elution peak on Sephadex G-200 of all sera tested.

IgG in vitro. Since the whole goat serum was toxic to rabbit lymphocyte cultures even in the absence of complement, the IgG fraction of each antiserum was prepared and tested *in vitro* for the ability to induce lymphocyte transformation (Table II). The IgG fractions contained no hemagglutinating activity (consistent with the observation that all of the hemagglutinating activity of several of the sera used was eluted in the first Sephadex G-200 peak, i.e., presumably in the IgM fraction). The lymphoagglutination activity generally remained after DEAE frac-

TABLE II

Effect of the IgG fraction of goat anti-lymphocyte sera on rabbit thymus cells and peripheral blood lymphocyte cultures

Antigen	Goat	Bleeding Date	Lymphoagglutination[a]	Lymphocytotoxicity[a]	Transformation[b]	
					Degree[c]	R[d]
Membrane	137	6/3	6	7	1+	2.2
		6/24	5	8	Toxic	
Membrane	138	6/3	5	7	1+	2.1
		6/24	4	6	3+	3.2
Mitochondria	163	6/3	3	0	0	0.6
		6/24	4	0	0	0.9
Mitochondria	164	6/3	4	2	0	1.1
		6/24	3	6		2.1
Nucleus	D95	6/3	0	0	0	1.4
		6/24	0	0	0	0.8
Nucleus	167	6/3	6	0	0	1.7
		6/24	5	7	0	1.6
Cell sap	165	6/3	5	5	2+	2.1
		6/24	5	7	3+	3.2
Cell sap	181	6/3	5	0	2+	2.5
		6/24	4	4	Toxic	

[a] Agglutination and cytotoxicity titers with thymus cells (Log_2).

[b] 1.0, 0.5, 0.25 and 0.125 mg IgG of each preparation added to separate cultures.

[c] Because cells in culture are agglutinated the degree of transformation is estimated from 0 to 4.

[d] Ratio of maximum cts/10 min in culture containing ALG to maximum cts/10 min in mean of two control cultures containing normal calf serum. All cultures made with peripheral blood lymphocytes. A result >2 is considered positive.

tionation, but, except for the membrane antisera and one of the cell sap antisera, the cytotoxicity titers of the primary response bleeding were lost. The cytotoxicity activity of the secondary response sera was retained in the IgG of six of the eight sera indicating a shift in the immunoglobulin class of antibody responsible for cytotoxicity. Only the antisera prepared against membrane and cell sap induced consistent transformation of lymphocytes *in vitro*. One of the two secondary response antisera to mitochondria gave a marginal result. There appeared to be little correlation between the lymphoagglutinin and lymphocytotoxicity titers and the ability to induce transformation. Although all transforming antisera contained lymphoagglutinin activity, five antisera with lymphoagglutinin activity did not induce transformation. Six of the seven IgG preparations active in induction of transformation had high lymphocytotoxicity titers but one preparation with a high toxicity titer did not induce transformation. Examination of the smears of cultures treated with nonmitogenic lymphoagglutinin positive sera revealed marked agglutination of the lymphocytes present, but few, if any, blast cells.

DISCUSSION

The properties and effects of various antilymphocytic sera (16) both *in vitro* and *in vivo* have recently been reviewed (1, 17) and have been the subject of a recent symposium (18). Many of the findings are difficult to compare due to a) differences in the source of the lymphocytes used for immunization, b) differences in the species used for production of the ALS, and c) differences in the system used to test the effect of ALS. A basic problem that remains unanswered is that of the immunologic specificity of the ALS. In other words, if an ALS causes suppression of immunologic reactivity, with what lymphocyte antigen or antigens does the ALS react to produce this effect? The purpose of the present project was to prepare antisera to different subcellular fractions of purified lymphocyte preparations and to characterize these antisera by testing *in vitro*.

Subcellular fractions of lymphoid cells are not

obtainable with methods used for other cell types (19–23). The property of the lymphocytes that is important in this regard is the relative scarcity of cytoplasm. Methods generally used to disrupt cells will either not be sufficient to disrupt lymphocytes or if severe, such as freezing and thawing, will result in a preparation that is impossible to fractionate, presumably because of a denaturation of the relatively large amounts of nuclear material present or destruction of fractionable structures (24). However, permitting the cells to swell in hypotonic saline (21) conditions the cells to be disrupted by more gentle techniques (24).

Antisera to the membrane and cell sap fractions were found to be consistently active *in vitro*. Antisera to the nuclear and mitochondrial fractions were not consistently active. Of interest is the lack of lymphocytotoxicity activity in the IgG fraction obtained from the antisera to nuclei and mitochondria in face of the activity present in the whole antisera and the presence of lymphocytotoxicity in the IgG fraction of the anti-membrane sera. It is possible that the immunoglobulin class responsible for the lymphocytotoxic activity may be affected by the antigen used for immunization. However, the number of sera tested was insufficient to rule out differences in the individual animals used as being responsible.

Antisera to lymphocytic subcellular fractions have been studied by others. Lance *et al.* (25) found antisera to mouse thymocyte membrane were best for prolongation of skin allografts. Antiserum to a mitochondrial fraction was also effective but to a lesser extent. Moynihan and Grogan (26) used rabbit antiserum to rat subcellular fractions of thymus-lymph node mixtures and also tested for skin allograft survival. Their antisera were all active in prolonging graft survival. Although an antiserum to the mitochondrial fraction gave the most prolonged survival, each antiserum produced a similar reduction in circulating lymphocytes *in vivo*. Warnatz and Scheiffarth (27) used rabbit antisera to rat lymph node fractions. Antisera to cell sap produced the longest allograft survival and strongest mitogenic effect. Zola *et al.* (24) found rabbit antisera to mouse thymocyte membrane and soluble cell sap fractions most effective in prolonging skin allografts. Anti-nuclear and anti-mitochondrial sera were also active, but to a lesser degree. Although direct comparisons cannot be made, these inconsistent results do not prove but suggest that membrane or cell sap fractions are best for production of effective ALS.

Difficulties in interpretation arise because complete purity of the immunizing fractions cannot be guaranteed. This may account for the appearance of activity in secondary response sera of nuclear and mitochondrial antisera found in the present experiments. By acid elution from thymocytic membrane preparations Lance (28) produced a more purified anti-membrane sera that was effective in prolonging skin allograft survival and was cytotoxic *in vitro*. Antisera to membrane fractions appear to be the most consistently active in the various systems used.

SUMMARY

The *in vitro* activity of goat antisera to rabbit thymus cell subcellular fractions prepared by differential centrifugation was determined by lymphoagglutination, lymphocytotoxicity and lymphocyte transformation. Primary response antisera to membranes and cell sap gave consistently greater effects than primary antisera to nuclei or mitochondria. Secondary response antisera to all fractions were active in lymphocytotoxicity and lymphoagglutination tests. Most of the activity resided in the IgG fraction of the antisera studied. Only anti-membrane and anti-cell sap IgG induced significant lymphocyte transformation. The results indicate that lymphocyte membranes and cell sap may be more effective than nuclei or mitochondria for use as antigens for the production of anti-lymphocytic sera.

REFERENCES

1. Sell, S., Ann. Int. Med., *71:* 177, 1969.
2. Karnovsky, M. J., J. Cell Biol., *27:* 137a, 1965.
3. Mollenhaur, H. H., Stain Technol., *39:* 111, 1964.
4. Mittal, K. K., Mickey, M. R., Singal, D. P. and Terasaki, P. I., Transplantation, *6:* 913, 1968.
5. Gray, J. G., Monaco, A. P., Wood, M. L. and Russell, P. S., J. Immun., *96:* 217, 1966.
6. Sell, S., Proc. Soc. Exp. Biol. Med., *114:* 362, 1963.
7. Takatsy, G., Acta Microbiol. Acad. Sci. Hung., *3:* 191, 1955.
8. Sever, J. L., J. Immun., *88:* 320, 1962.

9. Ouchterlony, O., Prog. Allerg., *5:* 1, 1958.
10. Peterson, E. A., Wyckoff, M. M. and Sober, H. A., Arch. Biochem., *93:* 428, 1961.
11. Sell, S., J. Exp. Med., *120:* 967, 1964.
12. Sell, S., Immunochemistry, *4:* 49, 1967.
13. Sell, S. and Gell, P. G. H., J. Exp. Med., *122:* 423, 1965.
16. Metchnikoff, E., Ann. Inst. Pasteur, *13:* 737, 1899.
17. James, K., Prog. Surg., *7:* 140, 1969.
18. Amos, D. B., Billingham, R. E., Lawrence, H. S. and Russell, P. S. (eds.), *Proceedings of the Conference on Antilymphocyte Serum*, Fed. Proc., *29:* 93, 1970.
19. Emmelot, P. and Benedetti, E. L., *in Carcinogenesis: A Broad Critique*, p. 471, The Williams & Wilkins Company, Baltimore, 1967.
20. Bosmann, H. B., Hagopian, A. and Eylar, E. H., Arch. Biochem., *128:* 51, 1968.
21. Warren, L., Glick, M. C. and Nass, M. K., J. Cell Physiol., *68:* 269, 1966.
22. Perdue, J. F. and Sneider, J., Biochim. Biophys. Acta, *196:* 125, 1970.
23. Rapaport, F. T., Dausset, J., Converse, J. M. and Lawrence, H. S., Transplantation, *3:* 490, 1965.
24. Zola, H., Mosedale, B. and Thomas, D., Transplantation, *9:* 259, 1970.
25. Lance, E. M., Foro, P. H. and Ruskiewicz, M., Immunology, *15:* 571, 1968.
26. Moynihan, P. C. and Grogan, J. B., Surg. Gyn. Obst., *129:* 551, 1969.
27. Warnatz, H. and Scheiffarth, F., Fed. Proc., *29:* 301, 1970.
28. Lance, E. M., J. Exp. Med., *130:* 49, 1969.

THE JOURNAL OF IMMUNOLOGY
Vol. 105, No. 6, December 1970

Cells Involved in the Immune Response. XX. The "All or None" Nature of the Primary Immune Response (19S Antibody) by Individual Antibody-Forming Cells in the Rabbit[1]

MAXWELL RICHTER,[2] YOUSSEF BEHELAK, ROBERT HAASZ AND NABIH I. ABDOU[3]

From the Harry Webster Thorp Laboratories, Division of Immunochemistry and Allergy, McGill University Clinic, Royal Victoria Hospital, Montreal, Quebec, Canada

The cells that synthesize 19S antibodies in the rabbit following primary intravenous immunization have been shown to be localized in the spleen, using the hemolysis in agar (plaque) technique (1). The temporal relationships are such that the 19S antibody-forming cells (AFC) cannot be detected in appreciable numbers before 4 to 5 days after immunization, but they then increase in number markedly within 24 hr. However, what has not been ascertained is whether this explosive increase in the AFC population is due to a) rapid division of these cells, each progeny being immediately capable of synthesizing large quantities of antibody, b) a synchronous phase of rapid antibody formation by non-dividing cells, or c) increasing amounts of antibody being synthesized by the AFC, thus permitting the detection of increasing numbers of non-dividing AFC. The results presented below strongly support but do not discriminate between the first two hypotheses.

METHODS AND MATERIALS

The protocol followed is diagrammatically presented in Figure 1. The animals used were New Zealand White rabbits, weighing 4 to 6 lb. Sheep red blood cells (S-rbc) were obtained as a sterile suspension in Alsever's solution and kept at 4°C until used. The S-rbc were washed twice with medium 199 (Microbiological Associates, Bethesda, Md.), diluted to the appropriate cell concentration in medium 199 and injected intravenously in the marginal ear vein. At the appropriate day following immunization, the rabbits were bled, killed by intravenous administration of Nembutal (50 mg/kg body wt) and the spleens were excised and placed into sterile plastic tubes (Falcon Plastics, Los Angeles, Calif.) containing medium 199. Each spleen was then pressed through a sterile wire mesh (50 mesh) and the cells were collected in medium 199). They were washed three times in medium 199 and made up to the appropriate concentration in medium 199. They were then analyzed for their content of plaque-forming cells (PFC) by the technique of Jerne and Nordin (2) and Ingraham and Bussard (3), as described previously (1). Only direct (PFC) (19S antibodies) were measured. For antigen, S-rbc and S-rbc sensitized *in vitro* with rabbit anti-S-rbc antiserum were used. The antiserum was obtained 2 to 3 weeks following intravenous immunization with S-rbc (three injections of 10^9 S-rbc over a period of 5 days). The hemolytic titer of the antiserum was determined in the conventional manner and is defined as the maximum dilution of the antiserum capable of effecting complete hemolysis of the S-rbc incubated in a water bath at 37°C for 30 min. The antiserum, in a dilution equivalent to 0.5 or 0.25 hemolytic unit/ml, was then incubated with an equal volume of S-rbc for 30 min at 37°C. The sensitized S-rbc were then washed twice with medium 199 and made up to a concentration of 10^9 cells/ml. These cells were used for plating with the spleen cells and for determining the hemolytic titers of the serum samples obtained when the immunized spleen donors were killed.

RESULTS

As can be seen in Table I, the hemolytic titers of the antisera were generally greater when tested with the sensitized S-rbc than they were with the unsensitized S-rbc. However, with the exception of only a few rabbits, the numbers of PFC detected with the sensitized S-rbc did not differ significantly from those detected using unsensitized S-rbc.

[1] This investigation was supported by a grant from the Medical Research Council, Canada.

[2] Medical Research Associate, Medical Research Council, Canada.

[3] Present address: Johnson Pavilion, School of Medicine, University of Pennsylvania, Philadelphia, Pa. 19104.

DISCUSSION

A question that both puzzles and intrigues cellular immunologists is the number of virgin cells that are committed to respond with antibody formation to a specific antigen. It has been demonstrated that the number of cells releasing 19S antibodies at the height of the immune

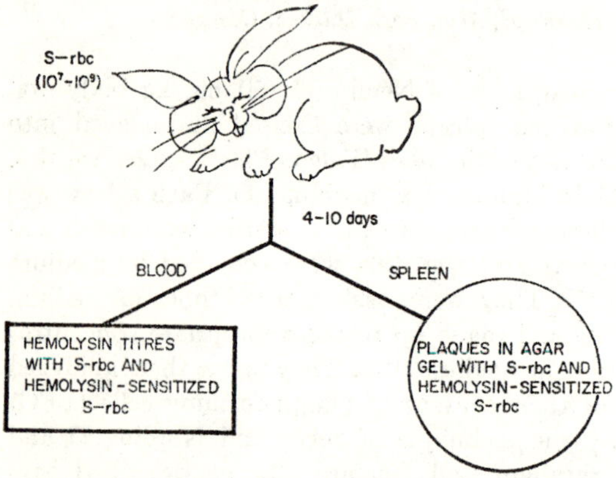

Figure 1. Protocol for demonstrating the "all or none" response of rabbit antibody-forming cells.

response is too large to permit the operation of clonal selection at the AFC level, i.e., in excess of 30,000 PFC/10^6 spleen lymphoid cells (4) if the assumption is made that these AFC had been precommitted in their virgin state and that they are unipotential cells. However, if as has been demonstrated it is the antigen-reactive cell (ARC) that is precommitted (5–7), then it is possible that the AFC is, in fact, an uncommitted or pluripotential cell, unaffected by clonal selection. In other words, any lymphoid cell with the potential of synthesizing antibodies may be triggered by interaction with the native antigen (8) or a processed antigenic determinant (9). If the latter be the case, then the large numbers of PFC observed do not at all contradict clonal selection. It must therefore be determined to what extent the overt AFC may have arisen by division of other antibody-synthesizing AFC or by direct transformation of an immunocompetent uncommitted AFC. Although the increase in number of PFC per 10^6 spleen cells during the initial phase of antibody formation is almost logarithmic, it can nevertheless be attributed to

TABLE I

The hemolytic titers of serum samples and the PFC responses of spleens obtained from rabbits at intervals of time following intravenous immunization with varying doses of S-rbc

Rabbit Injected with	Time Interval between Immunization and Death	Hemolytic Titers with:		Plaque-Forming Cells/10^6 spleen cells plated with:	
		Unsensitized S-rbc	Sensitized S-rbc	Unsensitized S-rbc	Sensitized S-rbc
	days				
10^9 S-rbc	4	20	320	253	250
	4	5	20	8	15
	5	512	1024	110	149
	5	20	256	260	340
	6	20	256	185	300
	6	20	256	195	170
	6	160	10000	167	137
	6	640	10000	205	167
	7			47	52
	7			362	360
	7	128	512	63	68
	7	64	1024	18	8
	10	256	640	25	23
	10	128	128	69	56
	10	256	256	56	40
10^8 S-rbc	5	128	1024	183	250
	6	256	2056	211	230
	6	16	64	9	60
10^7 S-rbc	5	4	32	48	71
	6	2	32	0	0

rapid proliferation of a small number of antibody-forming cells originally present in the cell suspension (10). However, it is possible that AFC do not synthesize antibodies in a synchronous fashion and that some cells are rapid antibody formers and some are slow antibody formers. Only the former cells are detected initially, while the antibody content of the latter cells is still too small to permit their detection. This assumption is especially relevant as the actual sensitivity of the plaque technique to detect the PFC, in terms of antibody molecules released into its microenvironment, is not known. To test this latter hypothesis, spleen cells of immunized rabbits were analyzed for their content of PFC by plating them with either untreated S-rbc or S-rbc already sensitized with a sub-hemolytic concentration of antibodies. These latter cells are much more labile than ordinary S-rbc and hemolyze in the presence of much smaller quantities of hemolytic antibodies. It was therefore not surprising to find that the hemolytic titers of sera of rabbits immunized 5 to 6 days before testing were much higher when tested with presensitized S-rbc than with untreated S-rbc (Table I). However, the number of PFC detected using the sensitized and unsensitized S-rbc was identical, although one might have anticipated an increased number of PFC using the sensitized S-rbc on the assumption that cells just beginning to form antibody would be detected with the presensitized S-rbc but not be detected using normal S-rbc. These results suggest that although rabbits were capable of synthesizing antibodies which could hemolyze the sensitized S-rbc, their PFC were apparently unable to hemolyze sensitized S-rbc to any greater degree than unsensitized S-rbc. The explanation may be that the AFC detected by the plaque assay is either not the same AFC which secretes antibody into the circulation or that the AFC behaves in an "all or none" fashion, that is, it either secretes sufficient quantities of antibody *in vitro* to hemolyze sensitized S-rbc or normal S-rbc equally well, or synthesizes no antibody at all. Since the initial experiments utilized spleen cells of rabbits immunized with a suprathreshold dose of S-rbc (10^9 cells) the results could be explained on the basis that all the potential AFC which could respond to this antigen did so maximally. A smaller dose of antigen was therefore administered (10^7 and 10^8 S-rbc) and the spleens were analyzed 5 and 6 days later. Since a dose of 10^7 S-rbc is, in our hands, a threshold concentration of antigen, it would probably be unreasonable to assume that all potential AFC could be maximally stimulated. Similar results were, however, obtained. Furthermore, it made no apparent difference if the spleen cells were tested 5 days after immunization, at a time when the immune response is just becoming apparent. One might have anticipated that AFC which had just begun to form antibody might have been detected using the sensitized cells, but such was not the case.

A possible criticism of these experiments might be that, although the sera of the immunized rabbits could easily hemolyze the sensitized S-rbc in saline, they may not do so in the presence of agarose, which is used in a concentration of 0.6% in the plaque assay. However, it was observed (not shown in the Table) that the agarose did not interfere with the hemolysis of the sensitized S-rbc in the test tube. It must therefore be concluded that, in the majority of instances, AFC in the spleens of rabbits immunized with S-rbc behave in an "all or none" fashion with respect to 19S antibody production. Although the results support the concept of proliferation of overt committed antibody synthesizing AFC to account for the rapid rise in the number of PFC during the phase of logarithmic rise, they do not completely exclude the possibility of a rapid phase of antibody formation by a non-dividing population of AFC.

The situation with respect to 7S antibody formation was not investigated in this study and must be dealt with separately.

REFERENCES

1. Abdou, N. I. and Richter, M., J. Exp. Med., *129:* 757, 1969.
2. Jerne, N. K. and Nordin, A. A., Science, *140:* 405, 1963.
3. Ingraham, J. S. and Bussard, A., J. Exp. Med., *119:* 667, 1964.
4. Pierce, C. W., J. Exp. Med., *130:* 345, 1969.
5. Richter, M. and Abdou, N. I., J. Exp. Med., *129:* 1261, 1969.
6. Davies, A. J. S., Leuchars, E., Wallis, V., Marchant, R. and Elliot, E. V., Transplantation, *5:* 222, 1967.
7. Abdou, N. I. and Richter, M., Adv. Immun., In press.
8. Richter, M., Proc. Nat. Acad. Sci., *64:* 75, 1969.
9. Abdou, N. I. and Richter, M., J. Immun., *104:* 1009, 1970.
10. Claflin, A. J. and Smithies, D., Science, *157:* 1561, 1967.

THE JOURNAL OF IMMUNOLOGY
Vol. 105, No. 6, December 1970

Printed in U.S.A

C3 in High Molecular Weight Complexes: Separation from Plasma of Nephritic Patients and Normal Subjects by a Method That Avoids *in Vitro* Artifacts

PHILIP W. ASKENASE AND EDWARD J. LEONARD[1]

From the Arthritis and Rheumatism Branch, National Institute of Arthritis and Metabolic Disease, the Laboratory of Kidney and Electrolyte Metabolism, National Heart and Lung Institute, and the Immunochemistry Section, Biology Branch, National Cancer Institute

The demonstration of host γ globulin and complement components in glomeruli of patients with post-streptococcal glomerulonephritis (1–3) or the nephritis associated with systemic lupus erythematosus (2, 4, 5) supports the view that the inflammatory lesions are caused by deposition of circulating complement-fixing soluble antigen-antibody complexes (6). Immune complexes, therefore, might be present in the circulation during active disease and, given sufficient assay sensitivity, should be detectable. When immune complexes activate complement, the third component (C3) becomes bound to the complex and can, therefore, be used as a marker of immune complexes. Since C3 has a molecular weight of about 185,000 (7) and in an immune complex behaves like a much larger molecule, separation of unreacted from complexed C3 on the basis of size is possible by gel filtration on Sephadex G-200.

The proteins of normal whole serum are eluted from Sephadex G-200 in three main peaks. The largest molecules such as lipoproteins or IgM are found in the first peak; IgG and normal C3 are among the globulins found in the second peak; and the bulk of the third peak is made up of serum albumin. The use of Sephadex to separate normal plasma C3 from C3 bound to an immune complex was tested as follows: 0.1 ml of an ovalbumin-anti-ovalbumin soluble complex containing about 1.3 mg of anti-ovalbumin antibody was incubated at 37°C for 50 min with 1.0 ml of whole human serum. Under these conditions human complement is activated by the soluble immune complex and C3 is incorporated into the complex. The serum was chromatographed on G-200 and eluates were tested for C3 by formation of precipitin lines in gel with an antiserum against C3. As expected from previous studies (8), C3 was found not only in its normal second peak location, but also in the first peak. Ovalbumin, characteristically a third peak protein, was also found in the first peak, presumably combined with antibody and C3. No C3 was found in first peak eluates from freshly prepared normal human serum incubated without immune complex.

After establishing the presence of first peak C3 in serum incubated with soluble immune complexes, we chromatographed on Sephadex G-200 samples of plasma from hospitalized patients with active lupus renal disease. The eluted fractions were concentrated by ultrafiltration and tested for formation of precipitin lines in gel with antiserum against human C3. No C3 was detected in the first peak samples from any of the six patients or seven controls. Subsequently we developed a solid phase radioimmunoassay capable of detecting as little as 10 nanograms of C3 (9). With the increased sensitivity of radioimmunoassay, about 0.1% of the total plasma C3 was detected in first peak eluates of even normal subjects. A typical example is shown in Figure 1. Concentration of C3 in eluted fractions is plotted against cumulative eluate volume. The curve with the triangles was obtained by applying 100 μl EDTA plasma to the column. C3 in the first peak is represented by the first four points; the great increase in concentration of the next fraction is the beginning of the second peak C3. The cross-hatched area indicates nanograms of total C3 in the first peak.

A striking increase in the amount of first peak C3 can occur *in vitro*, as illustrated in the upper curve of Figure 1, which shows first peak C3 of heparinized plasma that was incubated at 37°C for 50 min before chromatography The increase in first peak C3 does not occur when heparinized plasma is kept cold, nor does it occur at 37°C with EDTA plasma.

Since EDTA prevented *in vitro* increase in first peak C3, comparison of patient-control pairs was made with EDTA plasma rather than

[1] Please send reprint requests to Dr. Edward J. Leonard, National Institutes of Health, Building 37, Room 2B-15, Bethesda, Maryland 20014.

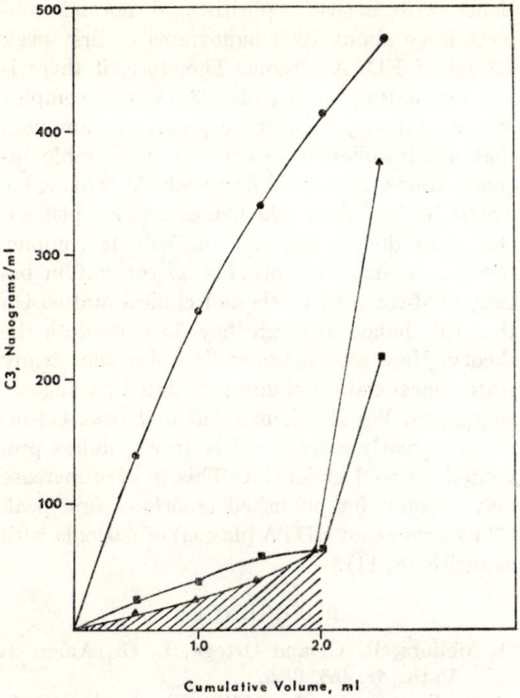

Figure 1. Conditions affecting first peak C3 of normal plasma. All fractions were eluted from Sephadex G-200 Superfine columns at 4°C with EDTA buffer. The concentration of C3 determined by radioimmunoassay for each eluted fraction is plotted against cumulative eluate volume. Only the beginning of the chromatogram is shown, corresponding approximately to the first O.D.$_{280}$ peak of the usual three-peak plasma chromatogram. The first peak was eluted in a volume of 2.5 ml; a volume of 11 ml was required for elution of all the plasma proteins. ▲, plasma containing 0.005 M EDTA chromatographed immediately; ■, plasma containing 0.016 mg heparin/ml, chromatographed immediately; ●, heparinized plasma chromatographed after 50 min at 37°C.

serum. Eight patients with systemic lupus erythematosus (SLE) and two with post-streptococcal nephritis were chosen. All had active renal disease so it could be presumed that the pathogenic mechanism was operating at the time of blood sampling. All were hospitalized and had abnormal urine sediments; four of four had biopsy evidence of glomerular pathology; seven of ten had low hemolytic complement titers. All had elevated erythrocyte sedimentation rates and seven of eight SLE patients had positive LE tests. Each patient was matched with a normal control of the same sex, color and approximate age. Blood from a patient and matched control was drawn and mixed with EDTA to make the final plasma concentration about 0.006 M. Blood plasma was iced within 7 min of the time of venipuncture and within 2 hr 100 µl were applied to a 0.9- x 60-cm column packed with Sephadex G-200 Superfine. In order to compare plasma samples, it was essential to apply precise amounts of plasma to columns with stable chromatographic qualities. Details of column construction sample application and collection methods are available from the authors. Chromatography was done at 4°C. Composition of the eluting buffer was 0.15 M NaCl; 0.005 M potassium phosphate buffer, pH 7.4; 0.006 M EDTA; sodium azide 0.05%. The eluted first peak fractions were assayed by radioimmunoassay. Table I shows that there was no significant difference in the amount of first peak C3 between patients and cotrols.

Further observations on first peak C3 were made when it was noted that the plasma from patient 5 developed a voluminous cryoprecipitate within an hour of cooling. C3 has been detected in cryoprecipitates and it has been suggested that C3 and associated cryoprecipitable protein circulate as a pathogenic immune complex (10). The unanswered question is whether the protein forming the cryoprecipitate circulated *in vivo* as a C3-immune complex or whether the C3 only reacted with the cryoprecipitating protein *in vitro*. Therefore, we chromatographed one sample of plasma from patient 5 at 4°C after the cryopre-

TABLE I

First peak C3 of patients and matched controls

Patient-Control Pair No.	Patient First Peak C3[a]	Control First Peak C3	Patient Minus Control
1	79	112	−33
2	183	98	85
3	110	102	8
5	143	124	19
7	83	98	−15
8	183	105	78
10	133	167	−34
12	200	200	0
15	278	260	18
17	200	217	−17
Mean (S.D.)	159 (62)	148 (59)	11 (35)

[a] Nanograms of first peak C3 after application of 0.01 ml plasma to G-200 column.

cipitate had been removed and another that was kept at 23°C so that a cryoprecipitate never formed. The first peak C3 values of the 4° and 23° samples were 139 and 179 nanograms, respectively, both within the normal range If the components forming the cryoprecipitate existed as a C3 complex before cooling, the first peak C3 of the 23°C sample would have been much more than that of the 0°C sample from which the cryoprecipitate had been removed Since this was not observed, the results provide one example in which the bulk of the cryoprecipitable plasma protein was not combined with C3 *in vivo* before precipitation, since removal of the cryoprotein did not significantly alter the amount of first peak C3.

We have shown that the amount of first peak C3 can increase greatly after blood is drawn, unless prevented by cold or EDTA. It follows that in the analysis of serum rather than EDTA plasma, high values of first peak C3 may be found because of *in vitro* formation during the approximately 40 min required for clotting and processing of human blood. Possible pathways for *in vitro* formation include: 1) formation of γ globulin soluble aggregates and activation of complement, 2) association of C3 with itself or other protein, 3) liberation of antigen from formed elements in the blood and its combination with specific antibody and activation of complement. The last possibility could apply particularly to patients with SLE because of their antibodies to many cellular antigens. Other workers (8, 11) have found first peak C3 in the *serum* of patients with nephritis, using precipitin-in-gel detection methods that are much less sensitive than radioimmunoassay By the precipitin-in-gel method we found no first peak C3 in eluates from EDTA *plasma* of patients and controls. The results with serum (8, 11) may be due to *in vitro* formation of first peak C3.

In conclusion, using quantitative gel filtration chromatography and solid phase radioimmunoassay for measuring C3, we found that both patients with active nephritis and normal subjects have about 1600 nanograms of first peak C3/ml of EDTA plasma. Therefore, if there is any circulating pathogenic C3-immune complex in the patients, it must be present in amounts that are insufficient to cause a measurable increase above the normal first peak C3. This value would be less than 400 nanograms/ml plasma. Our data do not support the soluble complex theory, in that they provide no correlation between C3-complex levels and clinical status. On the other hand, although they do not refute the theory, they set an upper limit for the steady state concentration of any postulated pathogenic complexes. We also found that first peak C3 increases greatly after blood is drawn, unless prevented by cold or EDTA. This *in vitro* increase may account for published reports of first peak C3 in serum (not EDTA plasma) of patients with nephritis (8, 11).

REFERENCES

1. Mellors, R. C. and Ortega, L. G., Amer. J. Path., *32:* 455, 1956.
2. Lachmann, P. J., Müller-Eberhard, H. J., Kunkel, H. G. and Paronetto, F., J. Exp. Med., *115:* 63, 1962.
3. Andres, G. A., Accinni, L., Hsu, K. C., Zabriskie, J. B. and Seegal, B. C., J. Exp. Med., *123:* 399, 1966.
4. Mellors, R. C., Ortega, L. G. and Holman, H. R., J. Exp. Med., *106:* 191, 1957.
5. Svec, K. H., Blair, J. D. and Kaplan, M. H., J. Clin. Invest., *46:* 558, 1967.
6. Dixon, F. J., The Harvey Lectures, *68:* 21, 1962–1963.
7. Müller-Eberhard, H. J., Nilsson, U. and Aronsson, T., J. Exp. Med., *111:* 201, 1960.
8. Soothill, J. F. and Hendrickse, R. G., Lancet, *2:* 629, 1967.
9. Askenase, P. W. and Leonard, E. J., Immunochemistry, *7:* 29, 1969.
10. Stastny, P. and Ziff, M., New England J. Med., *280:* 1376, 1969.
11. tenBensel, R., Cochrane, C. G. and Williams, R. C., Jr., Arthritis Rheum., *11:* 515, 1968.

THE JOURNAL OF IMMUNOLOGY
Copyright © 1970 by The Williams & Wilkins Co.

Vol. 105, No. 6, December 1970
Printed in U.S.A.

Evidence for the Existence of Two Functionally Distinct Types of Cells Which Regulate the Antibody Response to Type III Pneumococcal Polysaccharide

PHILLIP J. BAKER,[1] PHILIP W. STASHAK,[1] DIANA F. AMSBAUGH,[1] BENJAMIN PRESCOTT[2] AND ROLF F. BARTH[3]

From the Laboratory of Microbial Immunity and the Laboratory of Microbiology, National Institute of Allergy and Infectious Diseases, National Institutes of Health, Bethesda, Maryland 20014, and the Department of Pathology and Oncology, University of Kansas Medical Center, Kansas City, Kansas

Previous studies have shown that the antibody response to type III pneumococcal polysaccharide (SSS-III) is exclusively a macroglobulin response in which two types of antibody-producing or plaque-forming cells (direct and indirect PFC) are involved (1). The administration of antilymphocyte serum (ALS) produces a significant increase in the magnitude of the direct—but not the indirect—PFC response (2). In the present work, the results of recent studies on the mechanism by which ALS influences the direct PFC response to SSS-III are described. Evidence is presented that at least two functionally distinct types of cells act in opposition to regulate the response; the ability of ALS to increase the magnitude of the direct PFC response is apparently the result of the inactivation of a thymic-derived cell which normally acts to suppress the antibody response produced following immunization with SSS-III.

MATERIALS AND METHODS

Animals, antigen and immunization procedure. Female BALB/cAnN mice (8 to 10 weeks of age), obtained from the Rodent and Rabbit Production Section of the National Institutes of Health, were immunized with a single intraperitoneal injection of type III pneumococcal polysaccharide (SSS-III). The magnitude of the direct PFC response produced was assessed 5 days after immunization, i.e., at the peak of the response. The immunologic properties of the preparation of SSS-III used have been described (1).

Antilymphocyte serum. The immunologic activity of the burro anti-mouse lymphocyte serum (ALS) used in this work and the manner in which it was prepared have been reported (2, 3). Mice treated with ALS received a single intraperitoneal injection (0.25 ml) at the time of immunization with SSS-III. Such treatment resulted in a 5- to 10-fold increase in the magnitude of the SSS-III specific PFC response to 0.5 μg of SSS-III (2).

Assessment of the direct PFC response. Sheep erythrocytes sensitized with SSS-III by the chromium chloride coupling method (4) were used in an adaptation of the technique of localized hemolysis-in-gel for the detection of SSS-III specific PFC (1, 4). The magnitude of the cellular antibody response obtained was expressed as the number of direct SSS-III specific PFC produced/spleen (1).

TABLE I

Effect of antilymphocyte serum (ALS) on the magnitude of the splenic PFC response produced in mice immunized with various amounts of SSS-III[a]

Immunizing Dose	Treatment	
	SSS-III	SSS-III + ALS
μg		
0.01	630	398
0.05	5,260	8,100
0.10	8,760	23,600
0.50	16,200	162,000
1.00	9,860	313,500
5.00	3,600	
10.00		21,800

[a] Values listed represent the number of SSS-III-specific PFC/spleen produced in response to each immunizing dose. Pooled spleen cell suspensions, obtained from six to eight mice, were used for each determination.

Preparation of spleen, thymus and peripheral white blood cell suspensions. Suspensions of spleen cells and thymus cells from normal untreated

[1] Laboratory of Microbial Immunity, National Institutes of Health.

[2] Laboratory of Microbiology, National Institutes of Health.

[3] University of Kansas Medical Center.

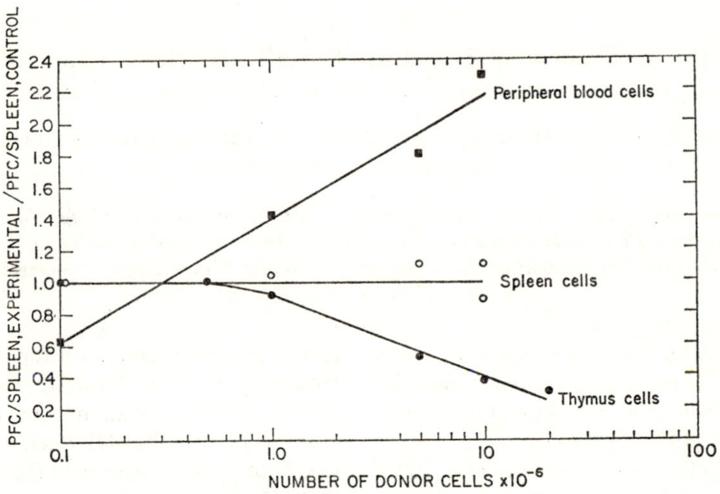

Figure 1. Effect of administering various types of syngeneic lymphoid cells on the magnitude of the SSS-III specific PFC response to 0.5 μg SSS-III in ALS-treated mice. Control group represents the response obtained without transferred syngeneic lymphoid cells.

BALB/c mice were prepared by rubbing the organs over the surface of a stainless steel screen immersed in cold medium 199 (4). Peripheral white blood cell suspensions (PB cells) were obtained as described by Wilson *et al.* (5), with the exception that erythrocytes were sedimented only once. All cell suspensions were washed twice in cold medium 199 and adjusted to an appropriate cell density before use. Known numbers of cells were administered intravenously in a volume of 0.1 to 0.2 ml, 1 day after immunization with SSS-III and treatment with ALS

RESULTS AND DISCUSSION

The data in Table I show that over a 100-fold range of immunizing doses the magnitude of the PFC response to SSS-III in ALS-treated mice was greater than that produced in mice not given ALS. Within a given dose range (0.01 μg to 5 μg of SSS-III), PFC increased linearly with dose; 10-fold increases in immunizing dose resulted in about 5-fold and 25-fold increases in the magnitude of the PFC response elicited in non-ALS-treated and ALS-treated mice, respectively. Maximal numbers of PFC were produced in both groups of mice with different doses of antigen. Also, treatment with ALS resulted in a significant increase in the rate of antibody synthesis by SSS-III specific PFC (to be published). One may conclude from these findings that the immunogenic and the tolerogenic properties of the various doses of SSS-III used for immunization had been increased and decreased, respectively, as a consequence of ALS treatment.

ALS has been shown to suppress the antibody response to other antigens by acting upon antigen-sensitive thymic-derived lymphocytes (6). For this reason, we decided to determine whether the administration of various numbers and types of syngeneic lymphoid cells would alter the PFC response to SSS-III in ALS-treated mice. Such studies revealed that when 10^6 and 10^7 thymus cells were given, the magnitude of the PFC response obtained was reduced by 20% and 70%, respectively (Fig. 1); however, equivalent numbers of PB cells produced a 40% and a 120% *increase* in the response. Similar numbers of spleen cells, as well as thymus cells which had been incubated for 2 hr at 37°C in the presence of ALS, were without effect. These findings indicate that two functionally distinct types of presumably thymic-derived cells, i.e., a suppressor cell and an amplifier cell, act in an opposing manner to regulate the antibody response; treatment with ALS results in the inactivation of a suppressor cell which normally serves to impose some restraints upon the development of the direct PFC response produced following immunization with SSS-III.[4]

[4] The fact that 10^5 PB cells reduced the magnitude of the PFC response suggests that suppressor cells are probably present in larger numbers than amplifier cells in the blood, but the specific activity of amplifier cells may be greater than that of suppressor cells.

Humphrey, Parrott and East (7) reported that the antibody response to SSS-III in neonatally thymectomized mice was just as great—and in some instances even greater—than that obtained in intact mice; data were presented indicating that thymectomy may have removed some restraints upon the capacity of lymphoid cells to synthesize immunoglobulin. More recently, Gershon and Kondo (8) reported that the induction of tolerance to sheep erythrocytes appeared to require the cooperation of thymic-derived cells; they postulated that thymic-derived cells produce not only a substance which facilitates, but also a substance which "shuts off" the antibody response. The present work provides direct support for such a view. It remains to be established whether a) splenic precursor cells can differentiate directly into SSS-III specific PFC in the event that both types of "regulatory" cells are inactivated by ALS, and b) PB cells may not truly represent amplifier cells but simply precursor cells which differentiate to PFC upon stimulation by SSS-III and localization in the spleen. These issues, as well as the significance of the findings presented in this work to the establishment of immunity and tolerance, are being investigated.

SUMMARY

The administration of various types of syngeneic lymphoid cells to mice immunized with type III pneumococcal polysaccharide (SSS-III) and treated with anti-lymphocyte serum (ALS) revealed that at least two functionally distinct types of presumably thymic-derived cells (a suppressor cell and an amplifier cell) act in an opposing manner to regulate the antibody response to SSS-III. The ability of ALS to increase the magnitude of the antibody response to SSS-III is apparently the result of the inactivation of a cell type that normally suppresses the antibody response produced following immunization with SSS-III.

REFERENCES

1. Baker, P. J. and Stashak, P. W., J. Immun., *103:* 1342, 1969.
2. Baker, P. J., Barth, R. F., Stashak, P. W. and Amsbaugh, D. F., J. Immun., *104:* 1313, 1970.
3. Barth, R. F., J. Immun., *103:* 648, 1969.
4. Baker, P. J., Stashak, P. W. and Prescott, B., Appl. Microbiol., *17:* 422, 1969.
5. Wilson, D. B., Silvers, W. K. and Nowell, P. C., J. Exp. Med., *126:* 625, 1967.
6. Martin, W. J. and Miller, J. F. A. P., J. Exp. Med., *128:* 855, 1968.
7. Humphrey, J. H., Parrott, D. M. V. and East, J., Immunology, *7:* 419, 1964.
8. Gershon, R. K. and Kondo, K., Immunology, *18:* 273, 1970.

Statement of Ownership, Management and Circulation required by the Act of October 23, 1962; Section 4369, Title 39, United States Code.

1. *Date of Filing:* October 1, 1970.
2. *Title of Publication:* Journal of Immunology.
3. *Frequency of Issue:* Monthly.
4. *Location of known Office of Publication:* 428 E. Preston St., Baltimore, Md. 21202.
5. *Location of the Headquarters or General Business Offices of Publisher:* 428 E. Preston St., Baltimore, Md. 21202.
6. *Publisher:* The Williams & Wilkins Company, 428 E. Preston St., Baltimore, Md. 21202.

Editor: Dr. Harry M. Rose, Columbia University College of Physicians and Surgeons, New York, N. Y. 10032.

7. *Owners:* (If owned by a corporation, its name and address must be stated and also immediately thereunder the names and addresses of stockholders owning or holding 1 percent or more of total amount of stock. If not owned by a corporation, the names and addresses of the individual owners must be given. If owned by a partnership or other unincorporated firm, its name and address, as well as that of each individual, must be given.) American Association of Immunologists, 9650 Rockville Pike, Bethesda, Md. 20014. No stockholders.
8. *Known bondholders, mortgagees and other security holders owning or holding 1 percent or more of total amount of bonds, mortgages or other securities are:* None.
9. Paragraphs 7 and 8 include, in cases where the stockholder or security holder appears upon the books of the company as trustee or in any other fiduciary relation, the name of the person or corporation for whom such trustee is acting, also the statements in the two paragraphs show the affiant's full knowledge and belief as to the circumstances and conditions under which stockholders and security holders who do not appear upon the books of the company as trustees, hold stock and securities in a capacity other than that of a bona fide owner. Names and addresses of individuals who are stockholders of a corporation which itself is a stockholder or holder of bonds, mortgages or other securities of the publishing corporation have been included in Paragraphs 7 and 8 when the interests of such individuals are equivalent to 1 percent or more of the total amount of the stock or securities of the publishing corporation.

	(a)*	(b)†
10. A. Total No. Copies Printed (Net Press Run)	5502	5456
B. Paid Circulation		
1. To term subscribers by mail, carrier delivery or by other means	4108	4779
2. Sales through agents, news dealers or otherwise	—	—
C. Free Distribution (including samples), by mail, carrier delivery or by other means	58	65
D. Total No. of copies distributed	4166	4844

* Average no. of copies for each issue during preceding 12 months.

† Single issue nearest to filing date.

I certify that the statements made by me above are correct and complete. (Signed) Mary G. MacIsaac Publisher.

THE JOURNAL OF IMMUNOLOGY
Vol. 105, No. 6, December 1970

Printed in U.S.A.

Plaque-Forming Cells of Two Different Origins in Single Hemolytic Foci[1]

D. C. VANN[2] AND P. A. CAMPBELL[3]

From the Department of Experimental Pathology, Scripps Clinic and Research Foundation and Department of Biology, University of California at San Diego, La Jolla, California 92037

When small numbers of spleen cells and heterologous red blood cells as antigens are injected into lethally irradiated mice, regions of hemolytic antibody-forming cell activity—hemolytic foci—can be detected in the spleens of these recipient mice. It has been shown that the number of hemolytic foci in a recipient spleen is directly proportional to the number of cells injected (1, 2), suggesting that each focus represents a single clone of antibody-forming cells, i.e., plaque-forming cells arising from one precursor cell only.

Recent observations indicate, however, that formation of hemolytic foci may depend on interaction between at least two cell types. Claman *et al.* (3) showed that the spleens of irradiated mice injected with sheep red blood cells (SRBC) and either bone marrow or thymus cells did not develop hemolytic foci but that foci were seen when mice were injected with both cell types. It has been suggested that the thymus contains an antigen-reactive cell required for initiation of antibody production (4), that the bone marrow contains precursor cells which are the direct progenitors of antibody-forming cells (5, 6), and that both cells are required to form a responding unit (7, 8). When bone marrow cells are added to inocula containing small numbers of spleen or thoracic duct cells, there is an increase in the plaque-forming cell response, but not in the number of hemolytic foci in the recipient spleens (9, 10). Based on this observation, the experiments presented here ask the question: Can a single hemolytic focus contain plaque-forming cells derived from more than one precursor cell? This question could be answered by using specific antisera to examine the plaque-forming cells from a single hemolytic focus in mice injected with spleen and bone marrow of different isoantigenic types. The presence of plaque-forming cells of both isoantigenic types in a single focus would indicate that at least two precursor cells gave rise to the plaque-forming cells in the focus.

First it was necessary to demonstrate synergism between bone marrow and spleen cells of differing isoantigenic types. We used male BDF_1 mice (C57BL/6 × DBA/2) as recipients and normal spleen cell donors, and male DBA/2 mice as donors of bone marrow cells. Mice were irradiated with 1000 to 1100 R from a ^{60}Co source, and spleen and bone marrow cells were injected intravenously within 6 hr of irradiation. The mice received 0.1 ml 20% SRBC intravenously 1 day after irradiation and intraperitoneally 3 days later. On day 8 the spleens were removed for plaque-forming cell assay by the slide method (11), or hemolytic focus assay by a modification of the Playfair technique as described earlier (12). Each spleen was cut transversely into 10 to 15 slices, then each slice was cut into 3 to 8 pieces, approximately 1 to 2 mm^3 in size. The pieces were carefully placed on a 1% agarose base in a Petri dish so that the orientation of the pieces in the original organ was maintained. The spleen pieces were overlaid with 4 ml of 0.5% agarose containing 0.2 ml 40% SRBC and incubated at 37°C for 90 min. After adding 10% guinea pig complement and incubating for an additional hour at 37°, the hemolytic foci were counted. Zones of hemolysis around adjacent spleen pieces indicated the presence of a single hemolytic focus.

Table I shows the number of plaque-forming cells and hemolytic foci in spleens of mice injected with spleen cells only or with spleen and bone marrow cells. Although the number of plaque-forming cells seen at the two doses of spleen cells tested was increased 5- to 6-fold by the addition of bone marrow cells, the number of

[1] This is Publication 421 from Scripps Clinic and Research Foundation and was supported by United States Public Health Service Grants AI 07007 and AI 08795.

[2] Supported by United States Public Health Service Training Grant GM 683. Present address: Department of Genetics, University of Hawaii, School of Medicine, Honolulu, Hawaii 96822.

[3] Supported by United States Public Health Service Postdoctoral Fellowship AI40639. Present address: Division of Allergy and Clinical Immunology, National Jewish Hospital and Research Center, Denver, Colorado 80206.

TABLE I

Plaque-forming cells and hemolytic foci following SRBC injection into lethally irradiated BDF_1 mice injected with BDF_1 spleen cells ± 10^7 DBA/2 bone marrow cells

No. of Spleen Cells Injected	PFC/Spleen		Foci/Spleen	
	−BM[a]	+BM	−BM	+BM
6×10^5	63 (4)[b]	310 (5)	—[c]	—
8×10^5	—	—	0.56 (23)	0.43 (54)
18×10^5	137 (6)	791 (6)	—	—
None	13 (4)	28 (6)	0 (31)	0.03 (33)

[a] BM = 10^7 bone marrow cells.

[b] Numbers in parentheses indicate number of mice/group.

[c] —, not done.

TABLE II

Percentage plaque-forming cells surviving after incubation with antiserum and complement[a]

Antiserum	Spleen Cell Origin		
	C57BL/6 (H2-b)	DBA/2 (H2-d)	BDF_1 (H2-bd)
Anti H2-b	4	100	7
Anti H2-d	76	2	3

[a] These data are the means from three experiments.

hemolytic foci did not change following bone marrow addition. It was thus shown that in this semi-allogeneic system bone marrow cells and spleen cells can cooperate in the production of plaque-forming cells.

We then examined single hemolytic foci for the presence of plaque-forming cells derived from two precursor cells, using isoantisera to identify the H2 antigens of the plaque-forming cells. These antisera were raised in congenic resistant mice (13). Prior to and during use in these experiments, the antisera were tested against parental and F_1 spleen cells of mice immunized 4 days earlier with 0.1 ml 20% SRBC. Table II shows the percentage of plaque-forming cells surviving antiserum treatment compared with plaque-forming cells detected after incubation in normal mouse serum. As shown in this table, anti-H2-b antiserum inactivated only BDF_1 (H2-bd) and C57BL/6 (H2-b) spleen cells, and anti-H2-d antiserum inactivated only BDF_1 and DBA/2 (H2-d) spleen cells. In the hemolytic focus experiments discussed below, plaque-forming cells arising from the injected BDF_1 spleen cells would be killed by either anti-H2-b antiserum or anti-H2-d antiserum, and plaque-forming cells arising from the injected DBA/2 bone marrow cells would be killed by anti-H2-d antiserum, but would survive treatment with anti-H2-b antiserum.

For these experiments, 8- to 14-week-old irradiated male BDF_1 mice were injected with 8×10^5 BDF_1 spleen cells and 10^7 DBA/2 bone marrow cells followed by SRBC antigen. The spleens were assayed for hemolytic foci on day 8. As shown in Table I, this dose of spleen cells resulted in an average of about 0.5 hemolytic foci/spleen, thus minimizing the chance of two foci overlapping in a single spleen. Each positive focus consisted of only three to six pieces containing 2 to 3 million cells. To confirm that pieces not showing lysis and therefore not detected as hemolytic foci were, in fact, devoid of plaque-forming cell activity, groups of seven to ten such negative pieces were assayed. They never contained more than three plaque-forming cells/seven to ten pieces.

We used the antisera to analyze individual hemolytic foci for the progeny of more than one precursor cell. Hemolytic foci were developed, and the active pieces from a single focus were picked, pooled, and made into a single cell suspension The cells were centrifuged at 1000 rpm for 10 min and resuspended to 0.2 ml in balanced salt solution. Portions of each cell suspension were treated with 25 µl of anti-H2-d antiserum, anti-H2-b antiserum, or normal mouse serum. After incubating the cells for 20 min on ice, 25 µl of normal guinea pig serum were added to the tubes and the cells were incubated for an additional 10 min at 37°. The cell suspensions were then assayed for direct plaque-forming cells by adding the agarose and SRBC mixture directly to the tubes in which the spleen cells and antisera were incubated. Each tube was poured onto one slide and was rinsed by a second addition of

TABLE III

Plaque-forming cells from single hemolytic foci: Percentage survival after treatment with antiserum

Anti-H2-b Antiserum	Anti-H2-d Antiserum	Normal Mouse Serum	Percentage Bone Marrow Type[a]	Percentage Spleen Type[b]
20	0	17	100	0
9	1	14	64	36
14	0	30	47	53
5	0	11	45	55
11	0	25	44	56
14	2	49	29	71
3	0	14	21	79
2	1	12	16	84
18	2	118	15	85
1	1	17	6	94
0	0	26	0	100
0	1	10	0	100

[a] Percentage plaque-forming cells surviving treatment with anti-H2-b antiserum. Bone marrow cells are H2-d.

[b] Total plaque-forming cells seen with normal mouse serum - plaque-forming cells of bone marrow origin.

agarose and SRBC, which was poured onto a second slide. After the slides were incubated at 37° for 1 hr, complement was added and the plaque-forming cells were counted 2 hr later.

In three experiments, a total of 12 usable foci were examined, i.e., those foci containing 10 or more detectable plaque-forming cells in the tubes incubated with normal mouse serum. Table III summarizes the survival of plaque-forming cells after treatment with antiserum or normal mouse serum. Cells surviving treatment with anti-H2-b antiserum were considered to be of DBA/2 bone marrow origin. The percentages of plaque-forming cells of bone marrow and spleen origin are shown in the last two columns. Approximately half of the single hemolytic foci analyzed appeared to contain both bone marrow and spleen derived plaque-forming cells. Random variation in the number of spleen or bone marrow precursors participating in each hemolytic focus could explain the variability in the number of spleen or bone marrow derived plaque-forming cells per focus reported here. Although these data demonstrate that the bone marrow can contribute precursor cells to hemolytic foci initiated by spleen cells, this does not fully explain the enhanced plaque-forming cell response seen when bone marrow cells are added. Nonspecific factors may also contribute to this enhancement. Since a single focus can contain both spleen derived and bone marrow derived plaque-forming cells, a single hemolytic focus need not necessarily represent a clone of antibody-forming cells. Foci in which more than one precursor cell matures may well exist in cell inocula containing spleen cells only, as well as in those containing spleen and bone marrow precursor cells as shown here. These data are compatible with the idea that in the normal immune response, functional units could exist which contain one antigen reactive cell, and several precursors to antibody-forming cells, as suggested by Groves *et al.* (7)

In conclusion, the experiments reported here demonstrate that a single hemolytic focus can contain plaque-forming cells derived from more than one precursor cell

Acknowledgments. We wish to thank Drs. F. J. Dixon and R. W. Dutton for their support, and Mr. Irving Goldman and the Salk Institute for Biological Studies for the use of their cobalt irradiator.

REFERENCES

1. Playfair, J. H. L., Papermaster, B. W. and Cole, L. J., Science, *149:* 998, 1965.
2. Kennedy, J. C., Siminovitch, L., Till, J. E. and McCulloch, E. A., Proc. Soc. Exp. Biol. Med., *120:* 868, 1965.
3. Claman, H. N., Chaperon, E. A. and Triplett, R. F., Proc. Soc. Exp. Biol. Med., *122:* 1167, 1966.
4. Miller, J. F. A. P. and Mitchell, G. F., Nature, *216:* 659, 1967.
5. Talmage, D. W., Radovich, J. and Hemmingsen, H., J. Allerg., *43:* 323, 1969.
6. Cunningham, A. J., Immunology, *17:* 933, 1969.
7. Groves, D. L., Lever, W. E. and Makinodan, T., Nature, *222:* 95, 1969.
8. Shearer, G. M. and Cudkowicz, G., J. Exp. Med., *129:* 935, 1969.
9. Mitchell, G. F. and Miller, J. F. A. P., J. Exp. Med., *128:* 821, 1968.
10. Radovich, J., Hemmingsen, H. and Talmage, D. W., J. Immun., *100:* 756, 1968.
11. Mishell, R. I. and Dutton, R. W., J. Exp. Med., *126:* 423, 1967.
12. Kind, P. and Campbell, P. A., J. Immun., *100:* 55, 1968.
13. Mishell, R. I., Dutton, R. W. and Raidt, D. J., Cell. Immun., In press.

THE JOURNAL OF IMMUNOLOGY
Copyright © 1970 by The Williams & Wilkins Co.

Vol. 105, No. 6, December 1970
Printed in U.S.A.

INDEX

Abdou, Nabih I., 1575
Abramoff, P., 1244
Acid, *see* specific acid
Adachi, Mitsuo, 256
Adenovirus, type 8, relation to canine hepatitis virus, 1036
Adherence, natural and antibody-induced, of phagocytic cells to autologous and heterologous thymocytes, 879
Adler, Frank L., 797
Adler, W. H., 984
Adler, William H., 1453
Agammaglobulinemia, chemical, use of immunoadsorption techniques in preparation of, 1292
Ahmed, Ansaruddin, 431
Aikin, Barbara S., 55
Albumin
  bovine plasma, activities of lymph node cells fractionated on, 1512
  bovine serum
    denatured, aggregates of, titration of antibody against determinants unique for, 797
    effect of antilymphocyte serum on, 108
    response to subsequent injection of, 1231
  pre-albumin activator of prekallikrein, 802
Allen, Jerry L., 193, 1001
Allen, Peter Z., 1253
Allen, Rae, 872
Allotypes
  A14 and A15, typing method for, 1046
  rabbit serum α_2-macroglobulin, allotypes, 856
Allotypic determinants, and antibody specificity, independence of, 653
Ambrose, K. R., 524
Amino acids, synthetic polymers of, immune response against, 704, 710
Amsbaugh, Diana F., 1581
Anaphylaxis
  passive cutaneous, γ globulins and, 1296
  slow-reacting substance of
    capacity of IgE to mediate, 1087
    IgE-mediated release of, 1096
Anderson, N. G., 524
Anderson, Truman O., 146
Anthony, Bascom F., 379
Antibodies, *see also* Immunoglobulins and specific type of antibodies
  action on tissues, 755, 764
  active synthesis of, rosette formation in relation to, 1501
  activity, lymphocytophilic, using Cr-labeled thymocytes, 746
  affinity, and complement fixation, 215
  against determinants unique for aggregated denatured bovine serum albumin, 797
  anti-DNP
    fine specificity of, 306, 314
    of gray snapper, 262
  anti-myelin, humoral, 248
  appearance during viral respiratory infection, changes in IgA and IgG concentrations in nasal secretions prior to, 584
  autoantibodies, *see* Autoantibodies
  bacteriophage-neutralizing, induction by immunogenic RNA, 771, 779
  calcium dependent and independent, 567
  complexes, virus-anti-viral, 829
  cross-reacting, secreted *in vitro*, 704, 710
  formation, γM, appendix and, 791
  -forming cells
    conversion of spleen cells to, by RNA, 541
    IgA, after oral immunization, 1049
    immunoglobulin classes of, 154
    in secondary response, staircase rise in, 642
    primary immune response in, 1575
    stimulation and inhibition of, 442
  fragments, and rabbit lymphocytes, 1400
  hepatitis-associated "Australia," 604
  homocytotropic, production of, 1264
  -induced adherence, of phagocytic cells to autologous and heterologous thymocytes, 879
  modified, teratogenic effectiveness of, 1175
  nasal, to influenza neuraminidase, 620
  natural, in shark, 1344
  of different specificities, frequency of production by single spleen cells, 537
  pepsin digestion of, 1294
  -producing cells, relation to precursor cells in density fractions of lymph node cells, 1522
  production, in x-irradiated hosts, 957
  reagents, fluorescein-conjugated, method for preparing, 1151
  response, *see* Response, antibody
  secretory, specificity of, 1477
  serum, to cellular antigens, 912
  sites, variation in size of, 460
  specificity
    correlation with complement-fixing behavior, 677
    independence of allotypic determinants and, 653
  sulfanilic acid-specific, induction by RNA, 1244
  to foot-and-mouth disease, detection and quantitation by radial immunodiffusion, 557
  to streptococcal M-protein, 379
  to *Vibrio cholerae*, 431

Antigens
-antibody complexes and complement, mechanisms of release of constituents from rabbit platelets by, 476, 490
antigenic competition to thyroid, 1201
antigenic differences between normal and neoplastic cells, 1052
antigenic properties of chemically modified collagen, 1131
antigenic relationships between avian immunoglobulins, 1215
antigenic stimuli, mast cell responses to, 187
antigenically stimulated and unstimulated leukocytes, heterogeneity of blastogenic factors produced by, 1162
Ascaris, hypersensitivity to, 1264
binding and the immune response, 355
brain, 512
cellular, serum antibodies to, 912
complement-fixing, dengue virus soluble, 1565
elution of, by antigen-reactive cells, 259
Epstein-Barr virus-induced, in lymphoid cells, relationship to viral envelop antigens, 793
fetal and tumor immunity, 524
hepatitis-associated "Australia," 604
histocompatibility, 1031
in mixed cell culture, specific stimulation by, 984
immunosuppressants in antigenic competition, 118
in cultures of rabies virus, 291
M and R, of type 43 and serologically related streptococci, 1124
nervous tissue, species-restricted, 512
of heart tissue, 416
phage, in immunogenic RNA, 779
protein, early primary response to, 355
quantitation in experimental immune complex glomerulonephritis, 279
-reactive cells, elution of antigen by, 259
release of virus inhibitor from tuberculin-sensitized peritoneal cells stimulated by, 1068
response of guinea pig lymphocytes to, 204
rheumatic fever, 1031
rheumatoid factors reacting with, 928
soluble
cytotoxic test for, 919
immune response to, 1416
of dengue virus, 838
somatic (O), of *Proteus mirabilis*, heterogeneity of immune response to, 404
-stimulated lymphocytes, activation of normal rabbit macrophage monolayers by supernatants of, 1138
surface, of fibroma virus, 1181
SV40 S, and pregnant hamster serum, 521
viral envelop, relationship of Epstein-Barr virus-induced membrane antigens in lymphoid cells to, 793
Antiglobulin reagents, transformation of peripheral lymphocytes by, 1484
Antilymphocyte serum
correlative assay for, 746
effect on humoral antibody response to *Salmonella typhi* "H" antigen and bovine serum albumin, 108
reticuloendothelial system blockade produced by, 634
Antinuclear factor, presence in hybrids of NZB and A/J mice, 1108
Antisera
monospecific, to C1 esterase, preparation of, 162
tissue, use in production of congenital malformations, 1175
to thymocyte subcellular fractions, 1569
Arginine residues of basic brain protein, effect on encephalitogenic activity, 865
Ascaris antigens, hypersensitivity to, 1264
Askenase, Philip W., 1578
L-Asparaginase, in allergic encephalomyelitis, 256
Augener, Wiprecht, 1024
Austen, K. Frank, 14, 802, 1082, 1087, 1096
Autoantibodies, γG erythrocyte
comparison of *in vivo* complement coating and *in vitro* "Rh" specificity, 221
serologic specificity of, 677
Ayoub, Elia M., 342

Bach, Gerhard L., 146
Bach, Michael K., 746
Bacillus Calmette-Guérin-sensitized rabbits, migratory response of granulomatous alveolar cells from, 227
Bacteriophage
-neutralizing antibody, induction by immunogenic RNA, 771, 779
ϕX174, immune response to, 872
Bakemeier, Richard F., 677
Baker, Phillip J., 1581
Bancroft, Frank C., 396
Barker, Lewellys F., 1040
Barnett, E. V., 824
Barnett, Jack A., 404
Barta, O., 350
Barta, Vera, 350
Barth, Rolf F., 634, 1581
Bazin, H., 1049
Becker, Elmer L., 1057
Behelak, Youssef, 238, 1575
Beinenstock, John, 274
Bell, Clara, 541
Bell, Rosalind, 1271
Benacerraf, Baruj, 306, 314
Benedict, Albert A., 534, 1215

Benjamin, David C., 537, 1231
Bennett, J. Claude, 846
Bentonite immunoadsorbents, in preparation of fluorescein-conjugated antibody reagents, 1151
Berne, Bernard H., 856
Bhattacharjee, A. K., 431
Bing, David H., 1289
Bishop, C. T., 265
Blank, F., 265
Blood group specificity of fresh water catfish, 299
Boose, Dorothy, 426
Borella, L., 786
Borsos, Tibor, 1439
Bovine serum albumin, *see under* Albumin, bovine serum
Bragonier, J. Robert, 1175
Brandriss, Michael W., 1416
Brandt, Walter E., 838, 1565
Brashler, John R., 746
Brent, Robert L., 1175
Brody, Thomas, 126, 139
Brooks, David K., 1427
Bruno, Pauline N., 1124
Buckley, C. E., III, 964
Bullock, Ward E., Jr., 1416
Butler, William T., 584, 1151, 1427, 1432

Campbell, Dan H., 1264
Campbell, P. A., 1584
Capra, J. Donald, 949
Carbohydrate, of IgA myeloma proteins, 1286
Carbonyl iron: a new adjuvant for experimental autoimmune diseases, 1530
Carnegie, Patrick R., 1223
Casey, Francis B., 1294
Ceglowski, Walter S., 442, 1406
Cells, *see also* specific types of cells
  allogeneic spleen, antibody production by host cells in x-irradiated recipients of, 957
  alveolar, granulomatous, migratory response of, from BCG-sensitized rabbits, 227
  antibody-forming
    immunoglobulin classes of, 154
    primary immune response in, 1575
    staircase rise in, in secondary response, 642
    stimulation and inhibition of, 442
  antibody-producing, relation to precursor cells in density fractions of lymph node cells, 1522
  appendix and bone marrow, synergism of, in early antibody response to sheep erythrocytes, 791
  causing graft-*vs*-host disease, separation of, 1168
  cellular heterogeneity in hemolytic foci, 1584
  cellular reactions to streptococcal M protein, 898
  cellular reactivity to tuberculin, 527
  cellular recognition by mouse lymphocytes, *in vitro*, 984
  chemical modification of, inhibition of anti-hapten response by, 1322
  culture
    mixed, specific stimulation by histocompatibility antigens in, 984
    monolayer, cytostasis of, by normal, unstimulated lymphocytes, 7
  hemolysin-forming clusters, ultrastructural analysis of, 1299
  hepatoma, synthesis of C9 by clonal strain of, 396
  host, x-irradiated, antibody production by, 957
  IgA antibody-forming, after oral immunization, 1049
  in immune response, 1575
  lymph node
    fractionated on bovine plasma albumin, 1512
    precursor cells in density fractions of, 1522
    ribonucleic acid synthesis in, 592
    suspensions to KLH, anamnestic response to, 1389
  lymphoblastoid, from hepatitis patients, 1040
  lymphoid
    γ globulin staining of, 1563
    relationship of Epstein-Barr virus-induced membrane antigens in, to viral envelop antigens, 793
    RNA-treated, transfer of delayed hypersensitivity using, 1313
    role in passive transfer with plasma of delayed hypersensitivity, 1111
  -mediated immunity to soluble antigen, detection of, 919
  myeloid stem, differentiation from rosette-forming cells, 719
  normal and neoplastic, antigenic differences, 1052
  "O," human, antibody to, 738
  phagocytic, adherence to heterologous thymocytes, 879
  plaque-forming
    effect of soluble polypeptides on, 710
    γ_1, incorporation of tritiated-thymidine into, during primary immune response, 154
  precursor, in density fractions of lymph node cells, 1522
  proliferation, lymphocyte inhibition of, 48
  radioresistant, and lymphocytes, interaction in PPD-stimulated human leukocyte cultures, 661
  red, heterologous, in mice, immune response to, 118
  regulation of antibody response of type III pneumococcal polysaccharide by, 1581
  required for immunocompetence, 126, 139

rosette-forming
antibody synthesis by, 1501
differentiation from myeloid stem cells, 719
sensitized, and immune serum, interaction, 471
serum antibodies to cellular antigens, 912
spleen
conversion to antibody-forming cells by RNA, 541
single, from hyperimmune rabbits, frequency of producing antibody of two different specificities, 537
SV40 hamster tumor, fetal antigen capable of inducing transplantation immunity against, 524
transformed by SV40, reaction of serum from pregnant hamsters with surface of, 521
tuberculin-sensitized peritoneal, stimulated by antigen, release of virus inhibitor from, 1068
Chiewsilp, Dumrong, 838, 1565
Chiroptera, immune response in, 872
Choriomeningitis, lymphocytic, persistent, 829
Chowdhury, Parimal, 238
Christian, Charles L., 1493
Chuba, Joseph V., 299
Claman, Henry N., 1146
Clark, Connie, 574
Clark, L. G., 567
Clem, L. William, 29, 1547
Clough, John D., 687
Cobra venom, depletion of plasma complement by protein of, 55
Cochrane, Charles G., 55, 1307
Coe, J., 1006
Coggin, J. H., 524
Cohen, J. John, 1146
Collagen, chemically modified, antigenic properties of, 1131
Colten, Harvey R., 1439
Competence, immunologic, selection experiment for, 908
Complement
and conglutinin in piglet serum, 350
C1a fixation and transfer, IgA, IgM and IgG antihapten responses assayed by, 687
C1-binding affinity, effects of IgG and IgM antibody concentration on, 1013
C1 esterase
immunochemical quantitation of, 170
preparation of monospecific antisera to, 162
C1s
immunochemical quantitation of, 162
purified, microheterogeneity of, 162
C2 and C4, immune hemolysis and functional properties of, 1439
C3 in high molecular weight complexes, 1578
C9, synthesis by clonal strain of rat hepatoma cells, 396
-dependent release of platelet constituents, 476, 490
fixation
and antibody affinity, 215
by IgM-RF and immune complexes, 1206
effects of IgG and IgM antibody concentration on C1-binding affinity, 1013
-fixing behavior, correlation of antibody specificity with, 677
guinea pig C2, purification, 327
hamster, consumption by bacterial endotoxin, 268
inhibition by aromatic amidine and guanidine compounds, 1289
plasma, depletion of, by protein of cobra venom, 55
receptor sites, 670
Complexes, immune, soluble, 1493
Conglutinin, and complement in piglet serum, 350
Conway, Thomas P., 70
Cooney, Marion K., 531
Cooperband, S. R., 48
Cortisone, effect on antigenic competition, 118
Cosenza, Humberto, 154
Cotran, Ramzi S., 1536
Couch, Robert B., 584
Cowan, K. M., 557
Crouch, Norman A., 1181
Cruse, J. M., 1072
Cyclophosphamide
effect on antigenic competition, 118
effect on ontogeny of humoral immune response, 614
Cytophilic activity, of human immunoglobulins, 362

Dalessio, Donald J., 248
Damrongsak, Damri, 442
Das, Saroj, 938
David, John R., 1447
Dengue
antigens, 1565
virus, soluble antigens of, 838
Dietrich, Felix M., 118
Diseases, *see* specific diseases
Dixon, Frank J., 279, 829
DNA, single-stranded, in adeno-associated satellite virions, 824
Donahue, Helaine, A., 592
Doria, G., 1049
Dorsey, F. C., 964
Douglas, R. Gordon, Jr., 584
Downie, Jean C., 620
Dray, S., 1313
Dray, Sheldon, 70, 541, 653, 856, 1334
Drusin, Ronald E., 1493
Duff, Ronald, 521

Dukor, Peter, 118
Dupuy, J. M., 1111, 1292

Edelin, Joseph B., 634
Edgington, Thomas S., 248
Edwards, G. E., 719
Egan, Marianne, 704, 710
Ehrlich, G., 755, 764
Ellison, George W., 322
Encephalitis, virus, immunodiffusion of, 1194
Encephalitogen, inhibition of encephalomyelitis by, 322
Encephalitogenic protein, modified, 865
Encephalomyelitis
  allergic, L-asparaginase in, 256
  encephalitogenic peptides, immunogenicity of, 1223
  experimental allergic, transfer activity and γ globulin staining of lymphoid cells, 1563
  inhibition by encephalitogen, 322
Endotoxin
  bacterial, consumption of hamster complement by, 268
  mitogenicity of, 1453
  tolerance, mechanisms of, 1468
Enterotoxin B, staphylococcal, mitogenicity of, 1453
Epstein-Barr virus-induced membrane antigens in lymphoid cells, relationship to viral envelop antigens, 793
Epstein, Robert B., 627
Erythrocytes
  autoantibodies, γG
    comparison of *in vivo* complement coating and *in vitro* "Rh" specificity, 221
    serologic specificity of, 677
  sheep, early antibody response to, 791
Escherichia coli somatic antigen, tolerance to, 1001
Espinosa, Enrique, 416
Esterase
  activatable, of neutrophil, 1057
  C1,
    immunochemical quantitation of, 170
    preparation of monospecific antisera to, 162
Eyster, M. Elaine, 221

Falk, George A., 1559
Fanger, Michael W., 1043, 1484
Fauci, Anthony S., 215
Faulkner, W., 786
Fehr, Kurt, 886, 973
Fibroblasts, intraperitoneal, rejection, 1375
Fibroma virus, surface antigen of, 1181
Field, Charles, 193
Fielder, R. J., 265
Finstad, J., 1278
Finstad, Joanne, 738
Fischbach, Michael, 1146
Foot-and-mouth disease, immunochemical studies, 557
Fox, Eugene N., 898, 1031,
Frank, Michael M., 215, 1175
Friedman, Herman, 193, 442, 1001, 1406
Frommel, D., 1, 1278, 1292
Fudenberg, H. Hugh, 1286

Gaarder, Per Ivar, 928
Galindo, Benito, 227
Gamma globulin, *see under* Globulins
Gasser, David L., 908
Gehle, Warren D., 1036
Gelatin studies, 797
Genetic control of the specificity of anti-DNP antibodies, 306, 314
Gerber, Paul, 793
Gill, Thomas J., III, 14
Gilman-Sachs, Alice, 70
Globulins, *see also* specific type of globulin
  anti-allotypic, antibody fragments of, 1400
  antiglobulin reagents, transformation of peripheral lymphocytes by, 1484
  γ globulins
    and passive cutaneous anaphylaxis, 1296
    bovine, immunologic tolerance to, 370
    bovine, ultracentrifuged, immunosuppressive effect of serum from CBA mice made tolerant by supernatant from, 426
    staining of lymphoid cells, 1563
    γG globulins, interaction with staphylococcal protein A, 1353
  γG, mechanism of heat aggregation of, 1024
  Peromyscus $7s\gamma_1$ and $7s\gamma_2$, 1006
Glomerulonephritis, antigen quantitation in, 279
Glycosyl transferases for mouse IgG, 271
Goldblatt, Peter J., 1569
Goldlust, Marvin B., 396
Goldstein, Gerald, 793
Good, R. A., 1, 1111, 1278, 1292
Good, Robert A., 738
Graft
  intraperitoneal, rejection, 1375
  marrow, effect of pre-transfusion on, 627
  -*vs*-host activity
    hydrocortisone resistance of, 1146
    separation of cells causing, 1168
Grappel, S. F., 265
Green, J. A., 48
Greisman, Sheldon E., 1468
Grey, Howard M., 75, 362, 1024, 1116

Haasz, Robert, 1575
Habeeb, A. F. S. A., 846
Hamilton, L. D., 175
Hammon, W. McD., 1194
Hammond, William S., 1299

Hand, Terry L., 442
Hapten
-altered native product, hypersensitivity induced by, 1416
phosphatidylinositol, immunochemistry of, 502
poly-L-aspartate, variation in size of antibody sites for, during immune response, 460
polysaccharide, streptococcal group A, 342
simple, genetic control of antibody response to, in congenic strains of mice, 98
-specific delayed reactions, 471
Harris, Donald L., 1565
Harris, T. N., 1501, 1512, 1522
Harrison, Bettina Hall, 38
Hart, David A., 1043, 1484
Hatten, Betty A., 872
Heart tissue, human, antigenic analysis of, 416
Heat aggregation of human γG, 1024
Heiner, Douglas C., 238
Helms, Charles M., 1253
Hemagglutination, passive, 797
Hemagglutinin-inhibiting antibodies to influenza, 620
Hemocyanin
keyhole limpet, anamnestic response to, 1389
thymus dependency of immune response to, 1339
Hemolysin-forming cell structures, ultrastructural analysis of, 1299
Hemolysis, immune, and functional properties of C2 and C4, 1439
Henney, Christopher S., 919
Henson, Peter M., 476, 490
Hepatitis
-associated "Australia" antigen and antibodies, 604
patients, lymphoblastoid cells from, 1040
Hepatoma cells, synthesis of C9 by clonal strain of, 396
Herpes-like virus, in continuous lymphoblastoid cell lines from patients with viral hepatitis, 1040
Herscowitz, Herbert B., 771, 779, 1389
Hikita, Michiko, 1553
Hildemann, W. H., 98, 912
Hill, Joseph M., 256
Histamine, immunologic release of, capacity of IgE to mediate, 1087
Hook, William A., 268
Hopps, Hope E., 1040
Howell, J., 1278
Howell, John, 738
Huber, Heinz, 670
Hughes, Stephanie J., 1400
Hurvitz, Arthur I., 949
Hydrocortisone resistance of GvH reactions, 1146
Hypersensitivity
delayed, 471
inhibition of macrophage migration in, 1360
interspecies transfer with RNA, 1334
passive transfer of, 1111
RNA transfer of, 1313
to a soluble antigen, 1447
to insulin and its component polypeptide chains, 574
to *Trichinella spiralis*, 175
induced by hapten-altered native product, 1416
to Ascaris antigens, 1264
Hypogammaglobulinemia, metabolism of γG and γM immunoglobulins in chickens with, 1

Immune complexes, soluble, 1493
Immune reaction, cytotoxic, 755, 764
Immune response, *see* Response, immune
Immunity
and tolerance, interrelationships, 370
cell-mediated, to soluble antigen, detection of, 919
transplantation, against SV40 hamster tumor cells, 524
Immunoadsorbents, bentonite, in preparation of fluorescein-conjugated antibody reagents, 1151
Immunoadsorption techniques, in preparation of chemical agammaglobulinemia, 1292
Immunocompetence, cells required for, 126, 139
identification of, 126
ontogeny of, 139
Immunofluorescence methods of humoral antimyelin antibodies in man, 248
Immunoglobulins, *see also* Globulins
avian, antigenic relationships between, 1215
canine, quantitation of, 698
classes of antibody-forming cells, 154
concentration, human serum, effect of aging on, 964
cross-reacting, abrogation of immunologic unresponsiveness by, 1072
degradation by intracellular proteases, 886
equine, 1253
γA, rabbit colostral, presence of allotypic specificities of three loci on individual molecules of, 70
γE, human, in respiratory fluid, 85
γG erythrocyte autoantibodies, comparison of *in vivo* complement coating and *in vitro* "Rh" specificity, 221
γG, in normal and hypogammaglobulinemic chickens, 1
γM, in normal and hypogammaglobulinemic chickens, 1
human colostral γA, synthesis of, 274
human, cytophilic activity of, 362
IgA
antibody-forming cells after oral immunization, 1049

antihapten responses assayed by C1a fixation and transfer, 687
concentrations in nasal secretions, changes in, 584
in cord sera, immunoassay, 786
isolation, 146
myeloma proteins, carbohydrate content of, 1286
secretory, in human serum, 43
secretory component, identification of 1327
subunit structure of, 75
IgD, physicochemical characterization of, 238
IgE
immunochemical and biologic properties, 1082, 1087, 1096
immunochemical identification of, 1082
molecules, presence on basophilic, leukocytes, 1459
structural studies, 783
IgG
antibody concentration, effects on C1-binding affinity, 1013
antigens of, rheumatoid factors reacting with, 928
antihapten responses assayed by C1a fixation and transfer, 687
anti-IgG, antibody fragments of, 1400
concentrations in nasal secretions, changes in, 584
degradation by lysosomal acid proteases, 973
glycosyl transferases for, 271
IgG2a myeloma protein with anti-dinitrophenyl activity, 812
IgG(T) and antipneumococcal γ_1-component, antigenic interrelationships, 1253
λ-like light chains, unblocked N-terminal sequence of, 534
molecules, presence on basophilic leukocytes, 1459
protein A-myeloma IgG complement-fixing complexes, 944
IgM
antibody concentration, effects on C1-binding affinity, 1013
antihapten responses assayed by C1a fixation and transfer, 687
incorporation of tritriated thymidine into, during primary immune response, 154
maleylated chains of, 846
reductive fragmentation of, 451
-RF, complement fixation by, 1206
in bronchitis and emphysema, 1559
λ chains, subtypes of, 1033
lamprey, 738
structure of, 1278
protein A reactivity with, 1116
serum 19S and 7S IgM of sharks, metabolic properties of, 29
shark, normal, reactivity with nitrophenyl ligands, 1547
Immunosuppression
by leukemia viruses, 1406
with procarbazine, 1271
Implants, tonsillar, in neonatally thymectomized mice, 38
Inchley, Christopher, 362
Influenza
neuraminidase, nasal antibody to, 620
virus, specificity of respiratory secretion antibody against, 1477
Ingram, D. G., 350
Inhibition of guinea pig complement, 1289
Inman, F. P., 451
Insulin, delayed hypersensitivity to, 574
Interferon induced by *Rickettsia mooseri*, 1553
Iron, carbonyl: a new adjuvant for experimental autoimmune diseases, 1530
Ishizaka, Kimishige, 85, 1459
Ishizaka, Teruko, 1459

Jamieson, Crawford W., 7
Jamuar, M. P., 175
Janicki, Bernard W., 527
Jenkins, David E., Jr., 221
Johnson, Armead H., 1427, 1432
Johnson, John S., 215, 698
Joslin, Fenneke G., 1103
Juras, D. S., 1244
Jureziz, R. E., 1313

Kanner, Steven P., 1052
Kantor, Fred S., 471
Kaplan, Allen P., 802
Kaplan, Melvin H., 416
Karakawa, Walter W., 389
Kasakura, Shinpei, 1162
Kataoka, Tateshi, 502
Kenny, George E., 531
Khan, Amanullah, 256
Kibrick, S., 48
Kim, C. W., 175
Klapper, David G., 29
Knight, Katherine L., 856
Kniker, William T., 1036
Kochwa, Shaul, 783
Kohase, Masayoshi, 1553
Kohno, Seiya, 1553
Kong, Yi-Chi M., 370
Koopman, William J., 1096
Koprowski, Hilary, 291
Kronvall, Göran, 1116, 1353
Kubo, Ralph T., 534
Kühn, K., 1131
Kuhns, William J., 299
Kunkel, Henry G., 1103

Kunz, Heinz W., 14
Kyriakos, Michael, 1201

Lance, Eugene M., 108
Lantz, Marjorie A., 1108
Leachman, Robert D., 1427
Lecithin, role as auxiliary lipid, 502
Leddy, John P., 677
Lennette, Edwin H., 604
Lennon, Vanda A., 1223
Leonard, Edward J., 1578
Lerman, S. P., 614
Leskowitz, Sidney, 938
Leslie, Gerrie A., 1215, 1547
Leukemia viruses, immunosuppression by, 1406
Leukocytes
antigenically stimulated and unstimulated, heterogeneity of blastogenic factors produced by, 1162
basophilic, presence of IgE and IgG molecules on, 1459
cultures, interaction of lymphocytes in, 661
migration, inhibition of, 1447
Levi, G., 1049
Levine, Seymour, 1530
Liakopoulou, Athanasia, 512
Liberti, P. A., 567
Lichter, Edward A., 70
Lightfoot, Robert W., Jr., 1493
Linscott, William D., 1013
Linthicum, D. Scott, 912
Lipids, auxiliary, role of lecithin as, 502
Litman, G. W., 1278, 1292
Litman, Gary W., 738
Litt, Mortimer, 1536
Little, J. Russell, 592
Liu, Chi Tan, 797
Liver, role in endotoxin tolerance, 1468
Logan, Leslie C., 1108
LoSpalluto, Joseph, 973
LoSpalluto, Joseph J., 886
Lymph nodes
cells fractionated on bovine plasma albumin, 1512
mouse popliteal, mouse cell responses in, to primary antigenic stimuli, 187
Lymphoblastoid cells, from hepatitis patients, 1040
Lymphocytes
allogeneic, transformation of mouse lymphocytes to, 90
antibody fragments and, 1400
antigen-stimulated, activation of normal rabbit macrophage monolayers by supernatants of, 1138
antilymphocytic serum, correlative assay for, 746
cellular recognition by, 984
fractions, antisera to, 1569
human peripheral
inhibition of target cell proliferation by supernatants from cultures of, 48
receptor sites for complement on, 670
interaction in PPD-stimulated leukocyte cultures, 661
normal, unstimulated, cytostasis of mouse and human monolayer cell cultures by, 7
peripheral
effect of reducing agents on, 1043
transformation by antiglobulin reagents, 1484
proliferative rates of, 734
response to PHA and antigen, 204
tissue distribution of, 730
transformation to allogeneic lymphocytes and phytohemagglutin, 90
tumor reaction, 1052
yellow fever and, 1304
virus replication in, 1304
Lymphocytic choriomeningitis viral infection, 829
Lymphoid cells, *see* Cells, lymphoid
Lysine residues of basic brain protein, effect on encephalitogenic activity, 865

Mach, J. P., 43
MacPherson, Catherine F. C., 512
Macroglobulin
α_2, Mt-3 and Mt-4 allotypes, 856
monoclonal, canine, 949
Macrophages
and lymph node supernatants, 1138
in thymectomized mice, role of, 1339
migration in delayed hypersensitivity, inhibition of, 1360
peritoneal, peroxidase in, 1536
Mage, R. G., 1046
Makinodan, T., 642
Malmgren, Richard A., 634
Mangi, Richard J., 90, 1052
Manski, W., 755, 764
Mardiney, Michael R., Jr., 90, 1052
Marsh, B., 984
Mascari, Ruth A., 1400
Mascari, Ruth Ann, 1569
Mast cells, responses to primary antigenic stimuli, 187
Maurer, Paul H., 567, 704, 710, 1011
Mayer, Manfred M., 327, 396
Mayor, H. D., 824
McDevitt, Hugh O., 1190
McDonald, Hugh C., 389
McFarland, William, 661
McMaster, Philip R. B., 1201
Meigel, W., 1131
Mergenhagen, Stephan E., 268
Messner, Ronald P., 1353

Meyer, Harry M., Jr., 1040
Michael, J. Gabriel, 411
Michlmayr, Gerhard, 670
Miller, Jimmie A., 327
Miller, R. G., 719, 1168
Milstone, Leonard M., 1068
Miniats, O. P., 350
Mishell, Robert I., 1322
Mittal, Kamal K., 1427, 1432
Moav, Neomi, 1501, 1512, 1522
Modabber, Farrokh, 355
Mooney, John J., 1138
Moore, Virginia G., 592
Morris, James E., 451
Mosley, Wiley H., 431
Müller-Eberhard, Hans J., 55
Munoz, J., 574
Murphy, P. Dianne, 460
Murray, Caroline, 411
Myelin, immunogenicity of EAE peptides from basic protein of, 1223
Myeloma
  anti-DNP, biologic properties, 812
  proteins
    carbohydrate content of, 1286
    reverse passive cutaneous anaphylaxis with, 1103
Myocardium, human, acid extracts of, antigens with restricted organ distribution in, 416
Myrvik, Quentin N., 227

Nagaki, K., 162, 170
Naor, David, 1322
Natvig, Jacob B., 928
Neuraminidase-inhibiting antibodies to influenza, 620
Neutrophils
  activatable esterase of, 1057
  interaction with platelets, 490
Newcomb, Richard W., 85
Nigrelli, Ross F., 299
Nisonoff, Alfred, 653, 1043, 1484
Nojima, Shoshichi, 502
Nora, James J., 1427
Nordin, Albert A., 154
Norins, Leslie C., 1108

Ogawa, Makio, 783
Oldstone, Michael B. A., 829
Orange, Robert P., 1082, 1087
Osserman, Elliott F., 1033
Ovary, Zoltan, 812, 1103
Oxford, J. S., 818
Ozer, H., 791

Pachman, Lauren M., 898
Papermaster, Ben W., 139
Paque, Ronald E., 1334
Parish, W. E., 1296
Paterson, Philip Y., 1563
Patterson, Roy, 1327
Paul, William E., 306, 314
Peavy, Duane L., 1453
Peel, L., 1006
Pepsin digestion of mouse antibody, 1294
Peptides, encephalitogenic, immunogenicity of, 1223
Perey, D. Y. E., 1
Perkins, E. H., 642
Peroxidase, in macrophages, 1536
Perper, Robert J., 746
Peterson, Phyllis, 677
Peterson, Raymond D. A., 1031
Phage, *see* Bacteriophage
Phair, John P., 471
Phillips, R. A., 719, 1168
Phillips, S. Michael, 204
Phosphatidylinositol, haptenic activity of, 502
Phospholipids, immunochemical studies of, 502
Phytohemagglutinin
  response of gunea pig lymphocytes to, 204
  transformation of mouse lymphocytes to, 90
Plasma
  complement, depletion of, by protein of cobra venom, 55
  kinin system, proenzymes of, 1307
Platelets
  constituents, complement-dependent release of, 476, 490
  interaction with neutrophils, 490
Pneumococcal polysaccharide, type III, regulation of antibody response to, 1581
Polack, F. M., 755
Pollara, B. W., 1278
Pollara, Bernard, 738
Poly-L-aspartate hapten, variation in size of antibody sites for, during immune response, 460
Polymers
  synthetic, of amino acids, detection of immune response against, 704, 710
  uronic acid, of *Staphylococcus epidermidis*, strain 53, 389
Polypeptides
  antigenicity of, 567, 1011
  chains, insulin and component, delayed hypersensitivity to, 574
  soluble, effect of incorporation into plaque assay medium, 710
  synthetic
    antibody responses to, 1190
    cross-reacting antibody secreted *in vitro* against, 704
Polysaccharide
  haptens, streptococcal group A, 342
  pneumococcal, type III, regulation of antibody response to, 1581

-protein conjugate, immunogenic, 265
Pontz, B., 1131
Potter, C. W., 818
PPD-stimulated leukocyte cultures, interaction of lymphocytes and a radioresistant cell in, 661
Prekallikrein, pre-albumin activator of, 802
Prescott, Benjamin, 1581
Procarbazine, as immunosuppressant, 1271
Proteases
intracellular, degradations of immunoglobulins by, 886
lysosomal acid, degradation of immunoglobulin G by, 973
Proteins
A from *Staphylococcus aureus*, 944
A reactivity with mouse immunoglobulins, 1116
A, staphylococcal, interaction with γG globulin, 1353
antigen, early primary response to, 355
basic, of human myelin, immunogenicity of EAE peptide from, 1223
basic brain, effect of tryptophan, lysine and arginine residues of, on encephalitogenic activity, 865
IgA myeloma, carbohydrate content of, 1286
IgG2a myeloma with anti-dinitrophenyl activity, biologic properties, 812
myeloma, reverse passive cutaneous anaphylaxis with, 1103
of cobra venom, depletion of plasma complement by, 55
streptococcal M-protein, antibody to, 379
Proteus mirabilis, somatic (O) antigens of, heterogeneity of immune response to 404

Rabies virus, antigen in cultures of, 291
Rapp, Fred, 521
Rapp, Herbert J., 1439
Rathbun, W. E., 98
Rawls, William E., 1181
Reactions, *see also* specific type of reaction
delayed, hapten-specific, 471
Reisberg, Margaret A., 1151
Response
anamnestic, to KLH, 1389
antibody
early, to sheep erythrocytes, synergism of appendix and bone marrow cells in, 791
genetic control of, to simple haptens in congenic strains of mice, 98
humoral, to *Salmonella typhi* "H" antigens and bovine serum albumin, effect of heterologous antilymphocyte serum on, 108
in hagfish, 912
initiation by different classes of lymphocytes, 730, 734
lymphocytotoxic, to cardiac allotransplantation, 1427, 1432
to Poly Glu^{52} Lys^{33} Tyr^{15} in the inbred rat strains ACI and F344, 14
to streptococcal M protein, 898
to synthetic polypeptides, 1190
to type III pneumococcal polysaccharide, 1581
chemotactic, activatable esterase of rabbit neutrophil in, 1057
immune
against synthetic polymers of amino acids, detection of, 704, 710
antigen binding and, 355
anti-hapten, inhibition of, 1322
cells involved in, 259, 1575
contribution of IgA antibody-forming cells to, 1049
evolution of, 738, 1278
genetic and cellular factors in, 14
genetic control, 908
humoral, effect of cyclophosphamide on ontogeny of, 614
in Chiroptera, 872
of mice to *Serratia marcescens* LPS or intact bacteria, 193
primary, effects of blockading agent on, 411
primary, incorporation of tritiated thymidine into IgM and γ_1 plaque-forming cells during, 154
to DNP-HSA, 1416
to hemocyanin, thymus dependency of, 1339
to heterologous red cells in mice, 118
to somatic (O) antigens of *Proteus mirabilis*, 404
variation in size of antibody sites for poly-L-aspartate hapten during, 460
primary, early, to protein antigen, 355
secondary, antibody-forming cells in, staircase rise in, 642
Reticuloendothelial system, blockade produced by antilymphocyte serum, 634
Reynolds, Herbert Y., 698
Rheumatic fever antigens, 1031
Rheumatoid factors
and "non a" antigen, 928
-IgM, complement fixation by, 1206
Rhinovirus types 9 and 32, reciprocal neutralizing cross-reaction between, 531
Ribonucleic acid, synthesis, in rabbit lymph node cells, 592
Richardson, Walter P., 1563
Richter, Maxwell, 259, 1575
Rickettsia mooseri, interferon induced by, 1553
Ricks, John, 1327
RNA
antibodies induced by, 1244
immunogenic
induction of bacteriophage-neutralizing antibody by, 771, 779
phage antigen in, 779

Roberts, Audrey N., 187
Roberts, Mary, 1327
Rochelle, Donald G., 1427
Rommel, Fred A., 396
Rose, Bram, 238
Rosenberg, Steven A., 1447
Rosenblum, Irwin Y., 534
Rosette formation, *see* Cells, rosette-forming
Rossen, Roger D., 584, 1151, 1427, 1432
Rowe, D. S., 43
Rubella, Cendehill vaccine strain, immunologic marker for, 818
Rudikoff, Stuart, 1344
Rudolph, Robert H., 627
Russell, Philip K., 838, 1565
Russell, Warren J., 262
Rutstein, J. A., 48

Sado, Toshihiko, 642
Sage, Harvey J., 460
Saha, Anil, 238
Sakata, Hiroko, 1553
Salmonella typhi "H," humoral antibody response to, effect of antilymphocyte serum on, 108
Sambury, Sheldon, 238
Sanford, Jay P., 404
Sather, G. E., 1194
Saunders, George C., 1299
Scales, R. W., 1072
Schechter, Geraldine P., 527, 661
Schenkein, Isaac, 271
Schlumberger, H. Dieter, 291
Schmid, Frank R., 1206
Schmidt, Nathalie J., 604
Schmidt, Willard C., 342
Schrohenloher, Ralph E., 846
Schultz, Karen E., 527
Sell, Stewart, 154, 1400, 1569
Sensitization, passive, mechanisms of, 1459
Sercarz, Eli, 355
Serratia marcescens, immune response of mice to, 193
Serum
  albumin, bovine, *see under* Albumin, bovine serum
  antibodies, to cellular antigens, 912
  antilymphocyte, *see* Antilymphocyte serum
  complement and conglutinin in, 350
  cord, IgA in, immunoassay, 786
  for A14 and A15 allotypes, typing, 1046
  from CBA mice, immunosuppressive effect of, 426
  human
    isolation of IgA from, by immunoabsorption, 146
    secretory IgA in, 43
  immune, and sensitized cells, interaction of, 471
  pregnant hamster, and SV40 S antigen, 521
  sickness, acute, 279
Shalitin, Nurit, 75
Sheagren, John N., 634
Sher, Alan, 75
Shimizu, Yukiko, 1553
Shin, Hyun S., 327
Shishido, Akira, 1553
Siegel, Israel, 879
Sigel, M. Michael, 262, 1344
Siskind, Gregory W., 1559
Sjöquist, J., 944
Small, P. A., Jr., 1477
Small, Parker A., Jr., 29
Smith, James P., Jr., 1559
Smith, James W., 404
Smith, Kendall O., 1036
Smith, R. F., 1006
Smith, R. T., 984
Smith, Richard T., 1453
Smyth, A. Collier, 1360
Smyth, Prudence, 1375
Snyderman, Ralph, 268
Sowinski, Richard, 1530
Spring, Susan B., 653
Stålenheim, G., 944
Staphylococcal enterotoxin B, mitogenicity of, 1453
Staphylococcus aureus
  protein A from, 944
    interaction with γG globulin, 1353
Staphylococcus epidermidis, strain 53, uronic acid polymer of, 389
Streptococcus
  group A, cross-reactions among, 1124
  M protein, cellular and antibody reactions to, 898
  streptococcal M-protein
    antibody to, 379
    vaccines, 1031
Stashak, Philip W., 1581
Stavitsky, Abram B., 1389
Stechschulte, Daniel J., 14, 1082, 1087
Steffen, C., 1131
Stella, M. M., 43
Stelos, Peter, 771, 779
Stevens, David P., 1040
Stewart, P. Brian, 1271
Stjernholm, Rune L., 1304
Storb, Rainer, 627
Storb, U., 957
Straus, Hans, 274
Strejan, Gill, 1264
Strober, Samuel, 730, 734
Strober, Warren, 687
Stroud, R. M., 162, 170
Sulkin, S. Edward, 872
Swanborg, Robert H., 865

Syphilis, serologic test for, false-positive reactions, 1108

Takiguchi, T., 984
Tashjian, Armen H., Jr., 396
Terry, William D., 783
Tesar, Joseph T., 1206
Tevethia, S. S., 1181
Thomas, E. Donnall, 627
Thor, D. E., 1313
Thymidine, tritiated, incorporation into IgM and γ_1 plaque-forming cells during primary immune response, 154
Thymocytes
  autologous and heterologous, adherence of phagocytic cells to, 879
  Cr-labeled, lymphocytophilic antibody activity using, 746
  subcellular fractions, antisera to, 1569
Thymus
  dependency of immune response to hemocyanin, 1339
  fractions, calf, stimulation and inhibition of antibody-forming cells by, 442
  -independent antibody responses, 1190
  role in tolerance, 322
Thyroid, antigenic competition to, 1201
Thyroiditis, allergic, prevention by antigenic competition, 1201
Timpl, R., 1131
Tischendorf, Frank W., 1033
Tischendorf, Margrit M., 1033
Tissue, *see also* specific type of tissue
  action of antibodies on, 755, 764
  antisera, production of congenital malformations using, 1175
  nervous, species-restricted antigen of, isolation and partial characterization of, 512
Tokuda, Sei, 1294
Tolerance
  and immunity, interrelationships, 370
  endotoxin, mechanisms of, 1468
  immunologic, to *Escherichia coli* somatic antigen, 1001
  induction, kinetics of, 938
  role of thymus in, 322
Tomioka, Hisao, 1459
Tompkins, Wayne, A. F., 1181
Tong, James L., 426
Torikai, K., 824
Tosi, S. Landucci, 1046
Toy, Stephen T., 1304
Transferases, glycosyl, for mouse IgG, 271
Transplantation
  cardiac, lymphocytotoxic antibody response to, 1427, 1432
  immunity against SV40 hamster tumor cells, 524
Trichinella spiralis
  delayed hypersensitivity to, 175
Tryptophan residues of basic brain protein, effect on encephalitogenic activity, 865
Tuberculin
  cellular reactivity to, 527
  hypersensitivity and virus inhibition, 1068
Tucker, Ernest S., III, 1307
Tyan, Marvin L., 1190

Uhr, Jonathan W., 271, 362
Unanue, Emil R., 1339
Unresponsiveness, immunologic, to BSA, termination of, 1231
Uronic acid, polymer of *Staphylococcus epidermis*, strain 53, 389

Vann, D. C., 1584
Venom, cobra, depletion of plasma complement by protein of, 55
Vibrio cholerae, antibodies to, 431
Virions, adeno-associated sattelite, single-stranded DNA in, 824
Virus, *see also* specific virus
  canine hepatitis, in man, 1036
  dengue, soluble antigens of, 838
  encephalitis, immunodiffusion of, 1194
  fibroma, surface antigen of, 1181
  influenza, specificity of respiratory secretion antibody against, 1477
  inhibition, tuberculin hypersensitivity and, 1068
  leukemia, immunosuppression by, 1406
  lymphocytic choriomeningitis, persistent, 829
  rabies, antigen in cultures of, 291
  replication, in lymphocytes, 1304
  rubella, Cendehill vaccine strain, immunologic marker for, 818
Voss, Edward W., 1344
Voss, Edward W., Jr., 262

Wagner, G. G., 557
Waksman, B. H., 791
Waksman, Byron H., 322, 1068, 1138
Waldman, R. H., 43, 1477
Waldmann, Thomas A., 584
Wallace, John H., 7
Wang, An-Chuan, 1286
Ward, Peter A., 1057
Warner, Noel L., 812
Weidanz, W. P., 614
Weigle, William O., 537, 1231
Weiser, R. S., 957
Weiss, Leon, 1360, 1375
Wellings, F. M., 1194
Wells, J. Vivian, 1043, 1484
Wheelock, E. Frederick, 1304

Wiger, Donna L., 370
Wigley, F. M., 1477
Wiktor, Tadeusz J., 291
Wiley, Grove G., 1124
Wilks, Ann V., 1223
Williams, Ralph C., Jr., 1116, 1353
Wilson, Curtis B., 279
Wofsy, Leon, 1322
Wolberg, Gerald, 797
Wolff, I., 1131
Woodward, Celeste L., 1468
Wuepper, Kirk D., 1307

Yeaw, Marilyn A., 677
Yoshida, Takeshi 306, 314

Zaccari, June, 687
Ziff, Morris, 886, 973
Zweiman, Burton, 204
Zschocke, Rainer H., 146